MUSIC MASTER
COUNTRY MUSIC CATALOGUE
2nd EDITION

Edited by
Tony Byworth

Waterlow

Music Master is a division of Waterlow Information Services Ltd,
Paulton House, 8 Shepherdess Walk, London N1 7LB

2nd edition published by Music Master 1993.

First edition published March 1991.

Editorial and advertising enquiries: 071 490 0049. Fax: 071 253 1308.

Book trade and record trade enquiries: Music Sales, Newmarket Road, Bury St Edmunds, Suffolk, IP33 3YB. Tel: 0284 702600. Fax: 0284 768301.

Private book orders: Music Master, Bournehall House, Bournehall Road, Bushey, Herts WD2 3YG. Tel: 081 421 8123. Fax: 081 421 8155.

Database typeset by BPCC Whitefriars, Tunbridge Wells.

Printed and bound in Great Britain by BPCC Wheatons Ltd, Exeter, Devon.

Cover artwork and design by IIIIi, London.

Managing Editor: Liz O'Connor. **Product Developement Manager:** Chris Spalding. **Reseacher:** John Wheeler. **Editorial Assistant:** Matthew J Garbutt. **Technical Co-Ordinator:** Jason Philpott. **Editorial Team:** Gary Ford, Anthony Murphy, Jane Scarratt, Paula Worsfold. **Group Product Manager:** Stephen Cave. **Product Manager:** Neil Lewis. **Group Sales Manager:** Brenda Daly. **Sales Executives:** Anna Sperni, Nick Wakefield. **Publishing Director:** Gregor Rankin

ISBN 0 904520 75 7

DPA
DIRECTORY PUBLISHERS ASSOCIATION

© **Waterlow Information Services Ltd.**

MUSIC MASTER
COUNTRY MUSIC CATALOGUE
2ND EDITION

CONTENTS

You'll love this new way to buy music.

MusicLink offers an unrivalled choice of music on both CD or cassette that can be ordered by telephone from the comfort of your home.

Simply call the number below and tell the operator the name of the album, and if possible the catalogue number quoted in this guide. We'll tell you there and then if it is a stock item – or, if not, whether we can obtain it for you.

We will process your order immediately and your music will be rushed to you by first class mail, post free.

MusicLink gives you the convenience of phoning from home – yet you pay only high street prices.

We are not a club. There is absolutely no commitment.

All you need is a credit or debit card – and a love of music.

So call us now.

MusicLink
Simply a better way to buy music.

081 812 0998
Lines open 24 hours a day, 7 days a week.

HOW TO USE THE COUNTRY MUSIC CATALOGUE

Welcome to Music Master's 2nd edition of the Country Music Catalogue.

The **Main Section** contains the majority of the recording information. It is divided into 26 separate chapters from A through to Z. The 'black strip' headings are the key to finding the artist you want, and are listed alphabetically by name. Recordings under each 'black strip' heading are listed in alphabetical order. Where a recording has a sub-title, this appears in brackets after the recording title. Tracks are listed, where available, after the recording title. Format and catalogue numbers are shown in bold on the same line to make them easier to read and are sorted chronologically where appropriate. This is followed by the record label, release date and the distributor. Deleted recordings are marked with a solid black square.

The **Compilation Section** has been re-organised to make searching easier and quicker. Recordings are listed alphabetically by title (shown in upper case) and thereafter the format and layout are as for the Main Section of the catalogue.

There is a **Useful Address Section** at the back of the catalogue which contains information on record companies, dealers, magazines and relevant organisations.

RECORDING TITLE

BLACK STRIP HEADING

Williams, Hank

COUNTRY STORE: HANK WILLIAMS.
Tracks / Lovesick blues / You're gonna change / I just don't like this kind of livin' / Moanin' the blues / Howlin' at the moon / I'll never get out of this world alive / Lost highway / Mind your own business / My bucket's got a hole in it / Why don't you leave me / Cold cold heart / I can't help it / Baby we're really in love / Jambalaya.

FORMAT

CD . . . . **CDCST 50**
MC . . . . **CSTK 50**
Country Store / '88 / BMG
LP . . . . **CST 50**
■ Country Store / '88

CATALOGUE NUMBER

DELETED

GREAT HITS OF HANK WILLIAMS SNR.
Tracks / Hey good lookin' / Lovesick blues / My son calls another man daddy / You win again / Take these chains from my heart / Your cheatin' heart / Jambalaya / I'm so lonesome I could cry / Settin' the woods on fire / Kaw-liga / My bucket's got a hole in it / Cold, cold heart.

TRACK LISTING

CD . . . . **PWK 114**
Pickwick / Jun '89 / Pickwick Records
MC **CN4 2076**
LP . . . . **CN 2076**
Contour / Aug '85 / Pickwick Records

DISTRIBUTOR

RECORD LABEL

I AIN'T GOT NOTHIN' BUT TIME.
Tracks / You're gonna change / My son calls another man daddy / First year blues / Are you building a temple in heaven / No one will ever know / I'm so lonesome I could cry / House without love / When the book of life is read / You better keep it in your mind / Fool about you / Wedding bells / I've just told mama goodbye / If you'll be a baby to me / House of gold / We're getting close to the grave each day / Thy burdens are greater than mine / I just don't like this kind of living / My bucket's got a hole in it / Waltz of the wind / How can you refuse him now.

CD **825 548-2**
■ Polydor / Mar '90
Double LP **825 548-1**
Polydor / Jan '88 / PolyGram

RELEASE DATE

v

INTRODUCTION

The best indication that the first edition of the Music Master Country Music Catalogue was a success is that it completely sold out! Along with that, there was a very positive response from the media, and from letters of praise written by readers. There was also the occasional brickbat! Obviously, the catalogue met a demand from a public wanting more information about country music, and, as far as brickbats are concerned, we've tried to overcome any problems second time around.

When the first edition was being put to bed in January 1991, I made note of country music's popularity in the Introduction. With the publication of the second edition, the situation has changed dramatically. It's appeal has increased so much that Country now rates as the second most popular musical genre in the United States.

Among the facts recently published by the Country Music Association (the US trade organisation) it was revealed that country music album sales have doubled since 1989, with 1992 sales exceeding one billion dollars, and roughly one in every four albums that appeared in the Billboard Top 200 chart was a country music album. At the same time, over 2,600 radio stations were programming Country music, with more than 36% of the population tuning in during 1992. There were two television channels wholly devoted to country music broadcasting - TNN (The Nashville Network), and CMT (Country Music Television). The Top 10 Country acts showed a 40% increase in touring revenue, whilst the Top 10 Pop/Rock acts grossed 32% less. For the country music industry the most important fact of all was that country was winning new fans, with 36.7% of the audience now revealed as young adults (18 - 34), undoubtedly attracted by the proliferation of new, young acts on the scene .

A lot of the responsibility for the success of country music can be firmly laid upon the shoulders of one man, Garth Brooks. In the first edition of the Country Music Catalogue, he was noted as 'the first country music superstar of the 1990's. Two years later, he was the most successful artist in the United States, outselling the likes of Madonna, Michael Jackson and Guns 'n' Roses, and building up a vast business empire all around him.

Then, challenging the Brooks' kingdom, Billy Ray Cyrus made his appearance, and was another Country singer set to be catapulted into pop super stardom. He had one of 1992's biggest selling singles with *Achy Breaky Heart*, which was matched by an album that has scored nine million sales a year since its release. How many rock acts can still do that sort of business?

As country music grew in popularity, so Nashville's industry techniques changed alongside it. Billy Ray Cyrus was a perfect example, with *Achy Breaky Heart* initially being marketed to the dance clubs only, quickly creating the 'Achy Breaky dance craze', and leading to other songs attracting their own steps. In turn, Nashville reacted by meeting the new market demands by making their hits available in a variety of formats. Suddenly there were album versions, extended versions, dance versions and club mixes in abundance, sitting alongside the original single that was promoted on the radio. country music has indeed come a long, long way from it's earliest days, when commercialism meant a one track, mono recording, or even the ground-breaking days of the late 1950's, when country made it's first overtures to the pop audiences with the advent of the 'Nashville sound'.

In Britain, country music's success is somewhat less spectacular. Nevertheless, it retains a popularity that ranges from the dedicated enthusiast who supports the numerous festivals and other annual events alongside regular tours and the local club scene, to those members of the general public who might not admit to 'being a country music fan', but who certainly enjoy the music from the likes of Glen Campbell, Johnny Cash, Crystal Gayle, Anne Murray, Willie Nelson, Dolly Parton, Charley Pride, Kenny Rogers, Billie Jo Spears, Don Williams, Boxcar Willie and Tammy Wynette, as well as home-grown talent such as Daniel O'Donnell.

In recent years, marketing campaigns by the record companies, several in conjunction with the Country Music Association, have resulted in a whole new breed of young country entertainers reaching beyond the normal realms of appreciation, and finding favour with younger, more rock-oriented audiences. Amongst these artists are Clint Black, Suzy Bogguss, Garth Brooks, Mary-Chapin Carpenter, Steve Earle, Nanci Griffith, The Judds, k.d.lang, Lyle Lovett, Ricky Skaggs, George Strait, Randy Travis, Trisha Yearwood and Dwight Yoakam. Britain also saw the launch of CMT-Europe in late 1992, and the likelihood of the first 24-hour Country music radio station becoming more and more of a reality.

But away from the success stories and the superstars, what of the music itself? Perhaps, mainly for the sake of the uninitiated, a brief insight is called for into that multi-layered creature known as country, which represents something different to almost everyone hearing it. To some devotees, country music means old traditions - the sound of guitar, fiddle and banjo, the Grand Ole Opry, and a much-revered cast list that began with Jimmie Rodgers and the Carter Family, and continued with the likes of Roy Acuff and Hank Williams. To others, it is crossing that vast spectrum and enjoying a music that bears a very close relationship to rock, whether through early pioneering groups like The Dillards, The Byrds, Poco and the New Riders Of The Purple Sage, or through more contemporary exponents such as Steve Earle, Joe Ely, Hank Williams Jr., The Kentucky Headhunters, Restless Heart, or The Cactus Brothers.

Both the traditional and the Rock oriented artists share equal credibility, with the music of each providing an equal contribution to the overall country landscape. On one hand, it was the early settlers, in particular the British and Irish, who brought their music to the New World, and created the foundation for what is today known as country music. Rock musicians, however, are simply carrying on a sound that was first created in the 1950s, and known then as rockabilly - a fusion of white man's country music and black man's rhythm and blues. Didn't rock'n'roll breathe its' first breath with Hank WIlliams' Move It On Over in 1947?

Dig deeper still and you'll start finding the regional variations. There is, for example, western swing from Texas and Oklahoma, put on the map by such artists as Bob Wills, Spade Cooley and Milton Brown - and continued through the years by the likes of Hank Thompson, Merle Haggard and Asleep At The Wheel. Western swing also moved into Hollywood during the height of it's popularity in the 1940s, a location that also created its own unique brand of country music, the singing cowboy. The most famous, and most financially successful, was, of course, Gene Autry, but he had a good run for his money from the likes of Roy Rogers, Tex Ritter and Rex Allen. Ironically however, although the singing cowboy was a Hollywood creation (with many of their songs penned by Tin Pan Alley writers), a great number of the original cowboy songs were derived from the folk ballads of the settlers over a century earlier. *Streets Of Laredo*, later popularised by Marty Robbins amongst others, is a prime example.

More country music genres? There is bluegrass music from Kentucky, arguably the only original American country music artform created by 'Hall Of Famer', Bill Monroe, with such artists as the Stanley Brothers, Lester Flatt & Earl Scruggs, the Osbourne Brothers, Hylo Brown, Jimmy Martin and Jim & Jesse later adding to its development. In the 1980s, it gained a fresh new appraisal thanks largely to Ricky Skaggs, an artist who started off in the business as a bluegrass child prodigy. Then there is cajun, a hybrid music that originated from the French settlers in Nova Scotia, who later relocated themselves to Louisiana. Although cajun has never reached prime popularity, there have been a number of acts who have obtained regular chart success including Rusty & Doug Kershaw, Jimmy C Newman, and, most recently, Jo-El Sonnier, whilst artists such as Nathan Abshire, the Balfa Brothers and Clifton Chenier have maintained a regular output of more traditional styled material.

Another traditionalist was Roy Acuff, who, in a recording career that stretched over seven decades, was the genuine, one hundred percent 'real' country singer. Once again, many of his songs had a direct relationship to British and Irish origins, whilst his band, The Smoky Mountain Boys, always favoured the traditional, acoustic instrumental lineup. Hank Snow and Webb Pierce can also be noted as carrying on the grand tradition, though somewhat removed from Acuff's hillbilly culture, whilst artists like Eddy Arnold and Ray Price, both still active recording artists, were among the first to successfully transpose country music into the metropolitan areas, and win the acclaim of brand new audiences.

Keeping up the traditional sound, and at the same time paving the way for the modern age of country music in the post WWII years, was the aforementioned Hank Williams, an incredibly successful singer/songwriter who couldn't read or write music, but who created some 125 compositions, many of which have stood the test of time well, and are now standards in both the country and pop music circles. There is no better testimony than a quick glance at some of the titles ... *I'm So Lonesome I Could Cry, You Win Again, I Can't Help It, Hey Good Lookin', Jambalaya, Your Cheatin' Heart, Kaw-liga* and *Cold, Cold Heart* are just a few of the WIlliams' classics. His whole catalogue is now being reactivated, reassessed and, once again, critically acclaimed as the compact disc breathes new life into those much revered recordings. Besides setting the pace in country music and making vital contributions to the pop world, Williams' music also played a vital role in the creation of rock'n'roll. Ironically, he also became its first casualty, dying at the age of 29, the victim of a drugs, booze and rock'n'roll lifestyle.

Whilst mentioning Hank Williams, the names of Jim Reeves and Patsy Cline should not be overlooked. They are two other artists whose music has not only survived the passing years, but who were also very successful in 'crossing over' to pop audiences. Unlike Williams, these artists were among the early exponents of the Nashville Sound, and won instant favour with the easy listening end of the market, possessing voices and songs that would ensure the regular repackaging and reissuing of their recordings over the years. In the case of Patsy Cline, it meant a return to the UK pop charts two decades after her death. *Crazy*, which was originally a US hit in 1962, made its UK chart debut in 1987, and then returned to enjoy a Top 20 placing four years later! Like WIlliams though, both Patsy Cline and Jim Reeves met with tragically early deaths - both from airplane crashes - in 1963 and 1964 respectively.

The preceeding, brief insight into country music's various realms is by way of an explanation for the entries that appear in this catalogue. The majority of artists' entries will be obvious; others, perhaps less so. As rockabilly was directly born out of country music, various rockabilly artists are included, alongside those more commonly thought of as rock'n'rollers such as Bill Haley and Elvis Presley, whose roots were most certainly in country and gospel music. Another is Pat Boone, and his inclusion here is valid because of his latterday involvement with the genre. A similar situation occurs with his daughter Debbie Boone, who made her debut with the country-pop, multi-million seller *You Light Up My Life* in 1977. The case of Brenda Lee is far more obvious. A singer with country origins, she enjoyed tremendous pop success during the early and mid 1960s, before returning to country music and pursuing that career in earnest during subsequent years. Likewise with Conway Twitty, Carl Perkins, Jerry Lee Lewis and Wanda Jackson, though country boys The Everly Brothers were to enjoy their greatest success in a rock'n'roll environment.

Finally, there are a few other artists whose entries are included purely at the whim of the editor. Frankie Laine, who learnt his trade in popular music's big band era, was never a country singer, but recorded many of western movies' most memorable themes, including *High Noon, Gunfight At The OK Corral* and TV's *Rawhide*. This has secured him placings in various country music compilation albums, and also tagged him as a 'Country singer'. Kay Starr and Margaret Whiting also enjoyed country chart success, whilst folk artists Joan Baez and Buffy Sainte-Marie recorded some outstanding country albums. The list could go on and on, rather, let the Country Music Catalogue be a source of reference which, hopefully, will further add to your listening pleasure.

Whilst the listings are drawn from the vast Music Master database, it is in no way intended to be a fully comprehensive listing of all the country music product available. Nevertheless, it is a very accurate guide to country music recordings released in the British Isles, plus a great deal of the product available via import dealers. Alongside the new product, and thanks largely to compact disc and its generous playing time, the last couple of years have seen a substantial increase in the reissuing of vintage and historic recordings, many of which have not been available for many years. Certainly the leader in this field is Germany's Bear Family Records (distributed in the UK by Rollercoaster), who have presented many artists' complete careers in amazing box sets that combine the music with vastly informative books. On a more modest level, I'm glad to be playing my part as a historian, by seeking out recordings for inclusion in EMI's 'Capitol Country Music Classics' and 'Country Music Masters' series, while Kenwest has turned to many different label sources for its 'History of Country Music' double CD/cassette releases.

The volume of listings has increased considerably during the two years since the publication of the Country Music Catalogue's first edition, as have the number of biographies. This edition contains almost 300 new biographies, with a great deal of attention being given to British and Irish country music artists, generally overlooked in other publications, but who play their own, very relevant role in the country music scene overall. In addition, over 100 existing biographies have been updated or completely rewritten.

In addition to the original biographical material provided by Donald Clarke and Bob MacDonald, I am extremely indebted to Maurice Hope for providing a substantial amount of biographical data and additional listings for the Country Music Catalogue. His efforts have stretched way beyond the call of duty during the past three years.

Tony Byworth

September 1993

x

TONY BYWORTH

London-born Tony Byworth took on the task of editing the Music Master Country Music Catalogue, 2nd Edition, backed with considerable insight and a practical understanding of the music. One of the most active persons on the British Country music scene, he has worked in virtually every area of the industry since his initial involvement with the music in the late 1960s. As a journalist he has contributed country music columns to numerous British and American trade and consumer publications, including Billboard, Music Week, Record Mirror, Sounds and Country Song Roundup. During the period from 1977 to 1983 he edited Britain's longest established country music magazine, Country Music People. Much of his first-hand understanding of the country music scene comes from regular, lengthy visits to Nashville, which he calls a 'second home', and from lasting friendships with artist and industry executives alike.

In addition to his journalistic skills, Tony Byworth has also worked in the music publishing and record company ends of the industry, leading him to create his own unique country music operation comprising publishing, recording, management and public relations services, with offices in London and Nashville. He, along with his PR partner Richard Wootton, has played a vital role in the development of the majority of US country artists' careers in the British Isles during recent years, whilst, internationally, he has set up deals on behalf of Ireland's Daniel O'Donnell in the USA, Australia and South Africa. As the International Director of Eagle Radio, he is disappointed that this company did not win the recent London licence, but pleased nevertheless that there will be a country music radio station in London.

A founding member of the British Country Music Association, and an active committee member of the Country Music Association, Tony Byworth has been recipient of several trade and consumer awards in recognition of his services to country music. In 1990 he was listed by the International Biographical Centre, Cambridge, as one of it's 'Men of Achievement', and two years later, he was made a Fellow of the American Biographical Institute in Raleigh, North Carolina.

MAURICE HOPE

Northumbrian-bred, Hexham-based Maurice Hope became interested in fringe country/folk music in the late 1960s, via Wally Whyton's weekly BBC Radio 2 show 'Country meets Folk', with more serious interest in country occurring around the time that Colin Chandler commenced producing Whyton's 'Country Club' show in 1974.

He served over ten years on local hospital radio (1979 - 1991), and commenced writing for the monthly Country Music Round Up in 1988. He has provided Country music columns for the Gateshead Post, the Hexham Weekly Messenger and Tyneside's rock magazine Paint It Red. Hope also covers local Folk events for Tyne Valley's long-established Hexham Courant.

A

Abshire, Nathan

Nathan Abshire (1913-81) was an accordionist, vocalist and composer of Louisiana Cajun music and one of its seminal influences. Illiterate himself, he translated everyday concerns into memorable songs which placed him among the greatest of the genre. He began playing local functions at the age of eight. His *Pine Grove Blues*, was an important hit. His catchphrase 'Good Times Are Killing Me' was emblazoned on his battered accordion case. (Donald Clarke)

CAJUN LEGEND, A (Best of Nathan Abshire).
Tracks: Not Advised.
LP. **6061**
Swallow (USA) / Oct '86 / Swift / Wellard Dist.
MC . . . . **6061 TC**
Swallow (USA) / '87 / Swift / Wellard Dist.

CAJUN TRADITION, A.
Tracks: Not Advised.
LP. **139**
La Louisiane / '87 / Swift.

CAJUN TRADITION, A-VOL. 2.
Tracks: Not Advised.
LP. **144**
MC . . . . **144 TC**
La Louisiane / '87 / Swift.

CAJUNS VOL 1 (Abshire, Nathan & Balfa Brothers).
Tracks: Acadian two step / Mamou hot step / Ce voulait separe / Le valse de la prison / Johnny ne pas danse / Apres du midi / Mon chapeau / Lacassine special / Les veuves de Basile / Pinegrove blues / J'ai passe devant ta porte / La valise de grand bois.
LP. . . . . **SNTF 643**
Sonet / '73 / Swift / C.M. Distribution / Roots Records / Jazz Music / Sonet Records / Cadillac Music / Projection / Wellard Dist. / Hot Shot.

FRENCH BLUES.
Tracks: Not Advised.
CD . . . . **ARHCD 373**
Arhoolie (USA) / Jun '93 / Pinnacle / Cadillac Music / Swift / Projection / Hot Shot / A.D.A Distribution / Jazz Music.

GOOD TIMES ARE KILLING ME (Abshire, Nathan & Balfa Brothers).
Tracks: Not Advised.
LP. **6023**
MC . . . . **6023 TC**
Swallow (USA) / Feb '79 / Swift / Wellard Dist.
LP. . . . . **SNTF 776**
Sonet / Jul '88 / Swift / C.M. Distribution / Roots Records / Jazz Music / Sonet Records / Cadillac Music / Projection / Wellard Dist. / Hot Shot.

GREAT CAJUN ACCORDIONIST, THE.
Tracks: La valse de meche / La valse de bayou teche / La valse du kaplan / T'en as eu. t'en n'auras plus / La calse de belezaire / Let two step del'acadian / Cher timonde / Allons tuer la tortue / La valse des valses / Le blues francais / La valse de grand basile / Le two-step de chuopique / Pauvre hobo / J'aimerais connaitre / La valse de la porte ouverte / Blues du tac tac / La valse du reveur / Hip et taiau / Jolie blon / Pine grove blues / La valse de choupique / Les flames d'enfer / Le temps est apres finir.
CD . . . . **CDCHD 401**
Ace / Apr '93 / Pinnacle / Hot Shot / Jazz Music / Complete Record Co. Ltd.

NATHAN ABSHIRE & OTHER CAJUN GEMS.
Tracks: Not Advised.
LP. . . . . **ARHOOLIE 5013**
Arhoolie (USA) / May '81 / Pinnacle / Cadillac Music / Swift / Projection / Hot Shot / A.D.A Distribution / Jazz Music.
MC . . . . **C 5013**
Arhoolie (USA) / '88 / Pinnacle / Cadillac Music / Swift / Projection / Hot Shot / A.D.A Distribution / Jazz Music.

NATHAN ABSHIRE & THE PINEGROVE BOYS (Abshire, Nathan & The Pinegrove Boys).
Tracks: Popcorn blues / Chere petite blonde / Jolie catin / Gabriel waltz / Good time two step / Pinegrove stomp / Dans grand bois / La la blues, The / French two step.
LP. . . . . **FLY 535**
Flyright / Jun '86 / Hot Shot / Roots Records / Wellard Dist. / Charly / Swift / Projection.
CD . . . . **FLYCD 19**
Flyright / Mar '90 / Hot Shot / Roots Records / Wellard Dist. / Charly / Swift / Projection.

PINE GROVE BLUES/THE GOOD TIMES ARE KILLING ME.
Tracks: Not Advised.
CD . . . . **CDCHD 329**
Ace / Jul '91 / Pinnacle / Hot Shot / Jazz Music / Complete Record Co. Ltd.

PINEGROVE BLUES.
Tracks: Pinegrove blues / Sur le courteblue / Musicians's life, A / Choupique two step / Off shore blues / La valse de bayou teche / Games people play / Lemonade song / Tramp sur la rue / I don't hurt anymore / Phil's waltz / Service blues / Maison lafayette two step / French blues / La valse de holly beach / Shamrock.
LP. **6014**
MC . . . . **6014 TC**
Swallow (USA) / Feb '79 / Swift / Wellard Dist.
LP. . . . . **CHD 217**
Ace / Nov '87 / Pinnacle / Hot Shot / Jazz Music / Complete Record Co. Ltd.

Acuff, Roy

Roy Acuff was born in 1903, Maynardsville, Tennessee. The singer, fiddler and bandleader remains the grand old man of country music. He first performed on the radio in 1933 and began recording in 1936 for one of the ancestors of today's CBS label, with the legendary producer Art Satherley (who was born in Bristol, England). His biggest hits included *Great Speckled Bird*: the hymn based on Jeremiah 12:9 used the traditional melody known as *I'm Thinking Tonight Of My Blue Eyes* (recorded by the Carter family) and was sung in Southern churches. *Wabash Cannon Ball* was also sung by the Carters; Roy's version sold a million and is one of the most famous country records ever made. His band, the Smokey Mountain Boys, was one of the first to include a dobro or Hawaiian guitar. He formed Acuff-Rose in Nashville in 1942 with Fred Rose, which published all of Hank Williams' songs. A postwar poll of the USA Armed Forces Network saw Acuff beat Frank Sinatra as the soldiers' favourite vocalist. He later formed the Hickory label, and played on *Will The Circle Be Unbroken* in 1973 with the Nitty Gritty Dirt band. Hits include *Wreck On The Highway*, *Fireball Mail*, *Pins and Needles*, *Low And Lonely*. His last chart hit in 1965 was a remake of *Freight Train Blues*. Roy Acuff passed away on November 23, 1992. His reputation as the King of Country Music remained and, although he wasn't a major player on Nashville' changing commercial scene of recent years, he never lost the respect and reverence that such a title implied. He remained the real star of thr Grand Ole Opry, making regular appearances right up until his death and holding court in the No. 1 dressing room where musicians, led by the various members of his band the Smoky Mountain Boys, would informally gather and play together. After the death of his wife Mildred, he even made the Opry his permanent home, living in a house adjoining the Opryhouse. On the occasion of his 80th birthday many of country musics' stars, past and present, assembled to pay tribute to him for a prime time television special and, at Opry's annual birthday celebrations each October, he was always the guest of honour. He continued appearing on the stage of the Grand Ole Opry right up until a month before his death. Then, back in the star dressing room, he would talk with his visitors and well wishers, a pleasurable task that had been part of his lifestyle throughout his 54 years on the Opry. (Tony Byworth)

BEST OF ROY ACUFF, THE.
Tracks: Not Advised.
MC **4XL 9371**
Capitol (Specials) / Dec '88.

ESSENTIAL ROY ACUFF 1936-1949 (Columbia country classics).
Tracks: Great speckle bird / Steel guitar blues / Just to ease my worried mind / Lonesome old river blues / Precious jewel, The / It won't be long (till I'll be leaving) / Wreck on the highway / Fireball mail / Night train to Memphis / Prodigal son, The / Not a word from home / I'll forgive you, but I can't forget you / Freight train blues / Wabash cannon ball / Jole Blon / This world can't stand long / Waltz of the wind / Sinner's death (I'm dying), A / Tennessee waltz / Black mountain rag.
CD **48956**
Columbia (USA) / Sep '92 / Columbia (Imports).

FIREBALL MAIL (Acuff, Roy & Boxcar Willie).
Tracks: Fireball mail / Stage.
■ 7" . . . . **EVB 1002**
Everest (Premier) / Jun '83.

FLY, BIRDIE, FLY (1939 - 41) (Acuff, Roy & His Smokey Mountain Boys).
Tracks: Not Advised.
MC . . . . **CSS 24**
Rounder / '88 / Projection / Roots Records / Swift / C.M. Distribution / Topic Records / Jazz Music / Hot Shot / A.D.A Distribution / Direct Distribution.
LP. . . . . **SS 024**
Rounder / Dec '88 / Projection / Roots Records / Swift / C.M. Distribution / Topic Records / Jazz Music / Hot Shot / A.D.A Distribution / Direct Distribution.

GREAT ROY ACUFF, THE.
Tracks: Sunshine special / Is it love or is it lies / I closed my heart's door / Don't judge your neighbour / Thief upon the tree,The / Rushing around / Sweep around your own back door / I'm planting a rose / Oh those tombs / Swamp lily / Please daddy forgive / Little Moses.
LP. . . . . **HAT 3055**
MC . . . . **HATC 3055**
Stetson / Jan '88 / Crusader Marketing Co. / Swift / Wellard Dist. / Midland Records / C.M. Distribution.

GREATEST HITS, VOL 2.
Tracks: Not Advised.
■ LP. . . . . **K 62029**
Elektra / Jun '80.

GREATEST HITS: ROY ACUFF.
Tracks: Lonesome old river blues / Were you there when they crucified my lord / Tennessee waltz / Waiting for my call to glory / Mule skinner blues (Blue yodel £8) / I saw the light / Fire ball mail / Night train to Memphis / Great speckled bird / If I could hear my mother pray again / Wreck of the highway / Freight train blues / Devil's train, The / It won't be long (Til I'm leaving) washbash cannonball.
CD **983256 2**
Sony Collector's Choice / Aug '93 / Pickwick Records.

GREATEST HITS: ROY ACUFF VOL.1.
Tracks: Wabash cannonball / Blue eyes crying in the rain / Great speckled bird, The / Two different worlds / Wreck on the highway / Jole Blon / Pins and needles / Precious jewel / Fireball mail / Back in the country / Story of the violin / Smokey Mountain memories / Take me home, country roads / End of Memory Lane / Rolling in my sweet baby's arms / That's the man I'm looking for / Precious memories / Will the circle be unbroken / Turn your radio on / I saw the light.
■ Double LP . . . . **K 62023**
Elektra / Feb '79.

KING OF COUNTRY MUSIC.
Tracks: Tied down / What will I do / Is it love or is it lies / Lonesome Joe / Sweep around your back door / Don't say goodbye / Swamp Lily / Sixteen chicken and a tamborine / Rushing around / Whoa mule / Sunshine special / I closed my heart's door / I'm planting a rose / River of crystal / Please daddy forgive / Streamline heartbreaker / Six more days / Thief upon thee tree, The / Don't judge your neighbor / Night spots (Of the town), The / Great speckled bird, The / Lonely mound of clay / Pins and needles (In my heart) / Wabash cannon ball / Great judgement morning, The / Wreck on the highway, The / Precious jewel, The / Night train to Memphis / That's what makes the jukebox play / Little Moses / What do you think about me / Oh those tombs / Come back little pal / Fire ball mail / I'm building a home (In the sky) / Great Titanic, The / Goodbye Mr brown / Mother hold me tight / Crazy worried mind / Along the China coast / It's hard to love / Plant some flowers by my graveside / I wanta to be loved / I like mountain music / Jesus died for me / Thank god / Were you there when they crucified my lord / How beautiful heaven must be / Unclouded day, The / Hold to God's unchanging hand / Lord build me a cabin / Where the soul never dies / Shake my mother's hand for me / Take my hand, Precious Lord / This world is not my home / Where could I go (But to my lord).
CD Set . . . . **BCD 15652**
Bear Family / Mar '93 / Rollercoaster Records / Swift / Direct Distribution.

SONGS OF THE SMOKEY MOUNTAIN (Acuff, Roy & His Smokey Mountain Boys).
Tracks: Not Advised.
LP. . . . . **HAT 3038**
MC . . . . **HATC 3038**
Stetson / Jul '87 / Crusader Marketing Co. / Swift / Wellard Dist. / Midland Records / C.M. Distribution.

STEAMBOAT WHISTLE BLUES.
Tracks: Yes Sir that's my baby / Red lips / Steamboat whistle blues / You've gotta see mama every night / Sad memories / Smokey Mountain rag / Shout on Lulu / Old three room shack, An / Charming Betsy / One old shirt / Automobile of life / Honky tonk mamas.
MC . . . . **SSC 23**
Rounder / '88 / Projection / Roots Records / Swift / C.M. Distribution / Topic Records / Jazz Music / Hot Shot / A.D.A Distribution / Direct Distribution.

LP. . . . . SS 23
Rounder / Dec '88 / Projection / Roots Records / Swift / C.M. Distribution / Topic Records / Jazz Music / Hot Shot / A.D.A Distribution / Direct Distribution.

TWO DIFFERENT WORLDS.
Tracks: Wabash cannonball / Blue eyes crying in the rain / Great speckled bird, The / Two different worlds / Wreck on the highway / Jole blon / Pins and needles / Precious jewel, The / Fireball mail / Back in the country.
LP. . . . . SDLP 028
Sundown / Oct '86 / Terry Blood Dist. / Jazz Music / C.M. Distribution.

Adams, Tom

RIGHT HAND MAN.
Tracks: Bluegrass breakdown / John Hardy / You are my sunshine / Fiddle and the banjo, The / I saw the light / Old rugged cross / Old Joe Clark / Fire ball mail / Polk country breakdown / Little Maggie / Cumberland gap.
CD . . . . CD 0282
MC . . . . MC 0282
Rounder / '90 / Projection / Roots Records / Swift / C.M. Distribution / Topic Records / Jazz Music / Hot Shot / A.D.A Distribution / Direct Distribution.

Adams, Trevor

COUNTRY CLASSICS.
Tracks: Not Advised.
■ LP. . . . . BSS 178
Tank / Jun '79.

I BELIEVE IN COUNTRY MUSIC.
Tracks: Not Advised.
■ LP. . . . . BSS 124
Tank / Jun '79.

Adcock, Eddie

2ND GENERATION, THE (Adcock, Eddie & Martha).
Tracks: Old man / Bound to ride / Make me a pallet on the floor / Eddie's matchbox blues / Wayward wind, The / Foggy lady / Remember me / Sugarfoot rag / High hill, The / Singer, The / Scream theme.
LP. . . . . CMH 6263
MC . . . . CMH 6263 C
CMH (USA) / '89 / C.M. Distribution / Projection.

ACOUSTIC COLLECTION, THE.
Tracks: Good ol' Sallie Gooden (inst) / Where will I shelter my sheep / I'll go steppin' too / Emotions (inst) / Loose talk / Love and wealth / I'd rather die young / Limehouse blues (inst) / (There'll be) peace in the valley for me / No letter in the mail today / I can hear Kentucky calling me / Eddie on the high ground / Gathering flowers from the hillside / Heartaches (inst) / Before I met you / (I'll pawn my) gold watch / Waiting for the sunrise (inst) / Go down yonder Moses / Mom and Dad's waltz / Meet Mister Callaghan (inst) / Next Sunday is my birthday / Where could I go (but to the Lord) / Come in stranger / Freight train (inst).
Double LP . . . . CMH 9039
CMH (USA) / '89 / C.M. Distribution / Projection.

EDDIE ADCOCK & HIS GUITAR.
Tracks: Guitar echoes / Sun fall 1988 / Under the double eagle / Love is blue / Bluegrass boogie / Sunshine / Exodus (Theme from) / Sugarfoot rag / Eddie's love theme / Birth of the blues / Silver blue / Guitar rag / Bump and jump / Strollin'.
LP. . . . . CMH 6265
MC . . . . CMH 6265C
CMH (USA) / '89 / C.M. Distribution / Projection.

Adkins, Hasil

CHICKEN WALK (Adkins, Hasil 'Haze').
Tracks: Shake that thing / Ugly woman / Let's slop tonight / Chicken walk / She's mine / Tell me baby / If you want to be my baby / Big fat mama / Get out of my car / Donnio boogie / Walk and talk with me / I need your head / Roll roll train / I don't want nobody the way I want you.
LP. . . . . BB 2043
Buffalo Bop (Germany) / '88.

HE SAID (Adkins, Hasil 'Haze').
Tracks: She said / My baby loves me / D.P.A. on the moon / Baby rock / Let's make it up / Louise wait for me / I'm in misery / Comin' home to you / We got a date / Reagun blues / Chicken twist / W.P.A / Fast run / You're my baby / Turn my coat tails loose.
LP. . . . . WIK 34
Big Beat / May '85 / Pinnacle / Hot Shot / Jazz Music.

OUT TO HUNCH (Adkins, Hasil 'Haze').
Tracks: Not Advised.
LP. 201
Norton / Oct '87 / Nightshift Distribution.

ROCK 'N' ROLL TONIGHT (Adkins, Hasil 'Haze').
Tracks: I could never be blue / I want some lovin' / Jenny Lou / Let me go / Rock the blues / I don't love you / Rock 'n' roll tonight / Shake with me / Miami kiss / Hunch, The / Duncens / No more hot dogs / Truly ruly / Is that right.
LP. . . . . BB 2044
Buffalo Bop (Germany) / '88.

SHE SAID (Adkins, Hasil 'Haze').
Tracks: She said.
7" 45 126
Bison Bop / Jan '85 / C.M. Distribution / Swift.

WILD MAN, THE (Adkins, Hasil 'Haze').
Tracks: Not Advised.
LP. 203
Norton / Aug '87 / Nightshift Distribution.

Adkins, Wendell

Wendell Adkins was born in Kentucky and raised in Ohio. He was discovered by Willie Nelson but given a real promotional push when associated with the famed Gilley's Club, on the outskirts of Houston, Texas. During the late 1970's he enjoyed a handful of hits on Motown's short-lived country labels Hitsville and MC, but built up British and European popularity through regular tours. (Tony Byworth)

I CAN'T LET YOU BE A MEMORY.
Tracks: Shotgun rider / What'll I do / I can't let you be a memory / Trying to survive loving / Too far gone / Feeling about you, A / Call the breeze / Falling for you / Back in you dreams / Missing the kid / I wish I was single again.
LP. . . . . SDLP 058
MC . . . . SDC 058
Sundown / Apr '88 / Terry Blood Dist. / Jazz Music / C.M. Distribution.

IF THAT AIN'T COUNTRY.
Tracks: Rodeo cowboys / Back to back / Bright morning light / If that ain't country / Lonesome, on'ry and mean / I came here to party / What a way to go / Willie, Waylon and me / Funny how time slips away / Crazy / Night life.
LP. . . . . SDLP 029
Sundown / Aug '86 / Terry Blood Dist. / Jazz Music / C.M. Distribution.
MC . . . . SDC 029
Sundown / May '88 / Terry Blood Dist. / Jazz Music / C.M. Distribution.

Alabama

The most successful vocal group/band in country music history, originally formed when cousins Jeff Cook (lead guitar), Randy Owen (guitar) and Teddy Gentry (bass) joined forces as a semi-professional outfit in Fort Payne, Alabama. First recording for small labels as Wild Country, they changed their name to Alabama in 1977 when on GRT Records. Mark Herndon (drums) joined the group just prior to signing with RCA in 1980 - and began an amazing run of more than two dozen consecutive number one records with "Tennessee River". The group's enjoyed considerable pop chart success, multi-million selling albums and a mass of awards that have included Grammies, ACM's, CMA's, People's Choice, as well as setting a record by being named CMA Entertainer Of The Year for three years running (1982, 1983 and 1984). (Tony Byworth)

ALABAMA.
Tracks: My homes in Alabama / Feels so right / Love in the first degree / Why lady why / Getting over you / I wanna come over / Fantasy / Old flame / Tennessee River / Some other place, some other time / Can't forget about you / Get it while it's hot / Woman back home / See the embers, feel the flame / I'm stoned.
LP. . . . . PL 89247
■ MC . . . . PK 89247
RCA / Mar '84.

CLOSER YOU GET.
Tracks: Closer you get / Lady down on love / She put the sad in all his songs / Red river / What in the name of love / Dixieland delight / Alabama sky / Very special love / Dixie boy / Lovin' man.
■ CD . . . . PD 84663
RCA / Sep '85.

CLOSER YOU GET.
Tracks: Closer you get / Dixieland delight.
7" . . . . RCA 337
RCA / Jun '83 / BMG.

FANTASY.
Tracks: Fantasy / Can't forget about you.
7" . . . . RCA 421
RCA / May '84 / BMG.

FEELS SO RIGHT.
Tracks: Feels so right / Love in the first degree / Burn Georgia burn / Ride the train / Fantasy / Hollywood / Old flame / Woman back home / See the embers feel the flame / I'm stoned.
■ LP. . . . . RCALP 5025
RCA / Aug '81.

FEELS SO RIGHT.
Tracks: Feels so right / See the embers feel the flame.
7" . . . . RCAV 382
7" . . . . RCA 382
RCA / Feb '84 / BMG.

FORTY HOUR WEEK.
Tracks: As right now / If it ain't Dixie / Nobody but me / Forty hour week / Can't keep a good man down / There's no way / Down on longboat key / Lousiana moon / I want to know you before we make love / Fire works.
CD . . . . PD 85339
LP. . . . . PL 85339
■ MC . . . . PK 85339
RCA / Mar '85.

GREATEST HITS: ALABAMA.
Tracks: She and I / Mountain music / Feels so right / Old flame / Tennessee river / Love in the first degree / Forty hour week (for a livin') / Why lady why / Fans, The / My home's in Alabama.
LP. . . . . PL 87170
■ MC . . . . PK 87170
RCA / '86.
■ CD . . . . PD 87170
RCA / '86.
DCC. 07863610405
RCA / Jan '93 / BMG.

JUST US.
Tracks: Tar top / I can't stop / I saw the time / You're my explanation for living / Face to face / I wish it could always be 55 / Old man / If I could just see you now / Falling again.
CD . . . . PD 86495
LP. . . . . PL 86495
■ MC . . . . PK 86495
RCA / Feb '88.

MOUNTAIN MUSIC.
Tracks: Mountain music / Close enough to perfect / Words at twenty paces / Changes comin' on / Green river / Take me down / You turn me on / Never be one / Loving you is killing me / Gonna have a party.
MC . . . . PK 84229
RCA / '84 / BMG.
■ LP. . . . . PL 84229
RCA / '84.
■ CD . . . . PD 84229
RCA / '84.

MY HOME'S IN ALABAMA.
Tracks: My home's in Alabama / Hanging up my travelling shoes / Why lady why / Getting over you / I wanna come over / Tennessee River / Some other place / Can't forget about you / Get it while it's hot / Keep on dreamin'.
■ LP. . . . . PL 13644
RCA / Nov '80.
LP. . . . . NL 89966
■ MC . . . . NK 89966
RCA / Oct '86.

ROLL ON.
Tracks: Roll on (18 wheeler) / Carolina mountain dew / End of the lyin', The / I'm not the way anymore / If your gonna play in Texas (you gotta have a fiddler..) / There's a fire in the night / When we make love / Country side of life / Boy, The / Food on the table.
■ CD . . . . PD 84939
RCA / Dec '84.

TAKE ME DOWN.
Tracks: Take me down / Love in the first degree.
7" . . . . RCA 251
RCA / Jul '82 / BMG.

TENNESSEE RIVER.
Tracks: Tennessee River / Can't forget about you.
■ 7" . . . . PB 2018
RCA / Oct '80.

THERE'S NO WAY.
Tracks: There's no way / All right now.
7" . . . . PB 49991
RCA / Apr '85 / BMG.

TOUCH, THE.
Tracks: Cruisin' / Touch me when we're dancing / Let's hear it for the girl / It's all coming back to me now / I taught her everything she knows / Pony express / You've got the touch / Vacation / True true housewife / Is this how love begins?.
LP. . . . . PL 85649
■ MC . . . . PK 85649
RCA / Nov '86.

Alexander, Larry 'Jinx'

RIVERBOAT MAN.
Tracks: Hey riverboat / Greenville woman / Tadpole Simpson / Sunday morning woman / Mighty fine picker / River song, The / Shady was a lady from Louisville / P-nut song, The / Take things when you can / Johnny Walker.
LP. . . . . FIEND 139
Demon / May '89 / Pinnacle.

Alger, Pat

TRUE LOVE AND OTHER STORIES.
Tracks: True love / Lone star state of mind / Goin' gone / Like a hurricane / This town / Love can be a dangerous thing / I do / She came from Fort Worth / Forever lovin' you / Small town Saturday night / Once in a very blue moon / Blue highway 29.
CD . . . . SHCD 1029
MC . . . . SHMC 1029

A 2 ■ DELETED

Sugarhill(USA) / '91 / Roots Records / Projection / Impetus Records / C.M. Distribution / Jazz Music / Swift / Duncans / A.D.A Distribution.

Allan, Johnnie

Born John Allan Guillot on 10.03.1938 in Rayne, Louisiana. A leading purveyor of cajun's swamp pop idiom, he started his recording career in 1958 with the Krazy Kats, by which time he was accomplished on both rhythm and steel guitar. As a solo act he's recorded for Mercury, Jin and Viking. His greatest success was *Promised land* which was successfully re-released in 1970 and backed with other Louisiana regional hits, such as *South To Louisiana* (a cajun version of Johnny Horton's *North To Alaska*), *Somewhere On Skid Row* and *I'm Missing You* . In 1992 Ace Records compiled his best work also released under the title of *Promised Land* (Maurice Hope)

1959-1960'S (Allan, Johnnie & The Crazy Cats).
Tracks: I'll be waiting / My baby is gone / Tell me do you love me so / Lonely days lonely nights / Rubber dolly / Letter of love / Family rules / Prisoner's song / One more chance / Give me more of your kisses / Crying over you / Please accept my love / You got me whistling / Nobody's darlin' but mine.
LP . . . . KK 792
Krazy Kat / Jan '85 / Hot Shot / C.M. Distribution / Wellard Dist. / Roots Records / Projection / Charly / Jazz Music.

ANOTHER MAN'S WOMAN.
Tracks: Not Advised.
LP . . . . JIN 9015
Jin / Feb '79 / Swift.

CAJUN COUNTRY.
Tracks: Not Advised.
MC . . . . JIN 9022 TC
Jin / '87 / Swift.

DEDICATED TO YOU.
Tracks: Not Advised.
LP . . . . JIN 9006
Jin / Feb '79 / Swift.

GOOD TIMIN' MAN.
Tracks: Not Advised.
LP . . . . FLY 551
Flyright / Feb '87 / Hot Shot / Roots Records / Wellard Dist. / Charly / Swift / Projection.

JOHNNIE ALLAN SINGS.
Tracks: Not Advised.
LP . . . . JIN 9002
Jin / Feb '79 / Swift.

JOHNNIE ALLAN SINGS CAJUN NOW.
Tracks: Not Advised.
LP 6069
MC . . . . 6069 TC
Swallow (USA) / '87 / Swift / Wellard Dist.

JOHNNIE ALLAN'S GREATEST HITS.
Tracks: Not Advised.
LP . . . . JIN 9017
Jin / '79 / Swift.

LOUISIANA SWAMP FOX.
Tracks: Not Advised.
LP . . . . JIN 9019
Jin / '79 / Swift.

PORTRAIT OF JOHNNIE ALLAN.
Tracks: Not Advised.
LP . . . . JIN 9012
Jin / Feb '79 / Swift.

PROMISED LAND.
Tracks: Not Advised.
CD . . . . CDCHD 380
Ace / Jun '92 / Pinnacle / Hot Shot / Jazz Music / Complete Record Co. Ltd.

PROMISED LAND.
Tracks: Promised land / Sweet dreams.
7" . . . . CAJUN 1
Oval / Mar '82 / WEA.

PROMISED LAND (Allan, Johnnie & Peter Fowler).
Tracks: Promised land / One heart one song.
■ 7" . . . . LOT 1
Island / Aug '79.

SOUTH TO LOUISIANA.
Tracks: Promised land / Cajun man / I'll never love again / Let's do it / Talk to me / Convict and the rose, The / South to Louisiana / Just a little bit / This life I live / Whatcha do / Nights of misery / Love me all the way / Do you love me so / Your picture.
LP . . . . JIN 4001
Jin / Feb '79 / Swift.
■ LP . . . . CH 145
Ace / Sep '85.

THANKS FOR THE MEMORIES.
Tracks: Not Advised.
LP . . . . JIN 9026
Jin / Swift.

MC . . . . JIN 9026 TC
Jin / '87 / Swift.

Allanson, Susie

Born in Minneapolis, Minnesota, on March 17 1952, Allanson enjoyed her greatest chart success in the late 1970s, with *We Belong Together* (Warner Bros. 1978) being her highest (No. 2) chart record. Making show business debut in musicals *Hair* and *Jesus Christ Superstar*. She was spotted as a session singer by record producer Ray Ruff, whom she later married (and divorced). (Tony Byworth)

SUSIE.
Tracks: While I was makin' love to you / Something different / Just when I was beginning to like it / You never told me about goodbye / Home again / Step right up / Dance the two step / Michael / That's all I want from you / Just between the two of us / I'm born again.
■ LP . . . . LBG 30335
Liberty / May '81.

Allen Brothers

ALLEN BROTHERS, THE.
Tracks: Not Advised.
LP . . . . OT 115
Old Timey (USA) / '88 / Projection.

CLARA'S BOYS.
Tracks: Not Advised.
LP . . . . ROUNDER 0154
Rounder / '88 / Projection / Roots Records / Swift / C.M. Distribution / Topic Records / Jazz Music / Hot Shot / A.D.A Distribution / Direct Distribution.

SWEET RUMOURS.
Tracks: Not Advised.
LP . . . . ROUNDER 0079
Rounder / '88 / Projection / Roots Records / Swift / C.M. Distribution / Topic Records / Jazz Music / Hot Shot / A.D.A Distribution / Direct Distribution.

Allen, Caz

BETWEEN THE LINES.
Tracks: Between the lines / Southern breed.
7" . . . . CAZ 7802
Hard Hat (USA) / '90.

I ASKED THE MAN IN THE MOON.
Tracks: I asked the man in the moon / Oh, don't look back.
7" 561639
Hard Hat (USA) / '90.

IN - AND - OUT URGE.
Tracks: In - and - out urge / Don't stop.
7" 255408
Hard Hat (USA) / '90.

JEALOUS BEAST.
Tracks: Jealous beast / Shot in the dark.
7" 66804
Hard Hat (USA) / '90.

SKINNY WINNIE.
Tracks: Skinny Winnie / It just ain't so man.
7" 50677
Hard Hat (USA) / '90.

SOMETIMES OUT OF MY MIND.
Tracks: Sometimes out of my mind / Eyes.
7" . . . . CAZ 341-02
Hard Hat (USA) / '90.

TENNESSEE'S ON MY MIND.
Tracks: Tennessee's on my mind / Texas red, white and blue step.
7" . . . . HH 548 553
Hard Hat (USA) / Oct '89.

THERE AIN'T NO BEER IN HEAVEN.
Tracks: There ain't no beer in Heaven / All my love tonite.
7" 5601
Hard Hat (USA) / '90.

Allen, Jules

TEXAS COWBOY, THE.
Tracks: Little Joe the wrangler / Jack O' Diamonds / Po mourner / Somebody but you don't mean me / Day's of 49, The / Home on the range / Texas cowboy, The / Prisoner for life, A / Gal I left behind me, The / Cowtrail to Mexico / Chisholm trail / Long side the Santa Fe Trail / Cowboy's lament, The / Little old sod shanty / Punchin' the dough / Dying cowboy, The.
LP . . . . BF 15502
Bear Family / Jan '83 / Rollercoaster Records / Swift / Direct Distribution.

WHEN I WAS A COWBOY (Allen, Jules & Carl Sprague).
Tracks: Not Advised.
LP . . . . MS 45008
Moonshine / Dec '88 / A.D.A Distribution / Projection / Swift / C.M. Distribution / Impetus Records / Ross Records / Duncans.

Allen, Rex

Rex Allen, was born in 1924 in Arizona; he was one of the few singing cowboys who was a real cowboy, and he was a better actor and singer than most, as well as a good songwriter,publishing over 300 songs. He made many cheap second features for the Republic studio, later had his own TV show; he also narrated documentaries, often for Walt Disney. He had hits in the USA country chart in the '50s and '60s. Rex Allen Jr (born in Chicago in 1947) also became a country star on Warner Brothers, having top ten country chart hits in the USA in the late '70s and becoming a headliner on the Grand Ole Opry.(Donald Clarke)

BONEY KNEED, HAIRY LEGGED COWBOY SONGS.
Tracks: Little Joe / Wrangler, The / Moonshine steer / Fireman cowboy, The / Braggin' / Drunk from Wilcox / Fiddling medley / Tyin' knots in the Devil's tail / Droop ears / Windy Bill / When the work's all done this fall / Streets of Laredo.
LP . . . . BFX 15024
Bear Family / Jul '84 / Rollercoaster Records / Swift / Direct Distribution.

HAWAIIAN COWBOY.
Tracks: Texas tornado / Queen of the rodeo / Teardrops in my heart / Loaded pistol / Arizona waltz / Hawaiian cowboy / Who shot that hole in my sombrero / Wind is my woman / Cowpoke / Cattle call / Chime bells / Tennessee tears / Song of the hills / Slap her down again, Paw / Miranda Doakes / Lord protect my darlin'.
LP P.Disc. . . . . BDP 15192
Bear Family / Apr '86 / Rollercoaster Records / Swift / Direct Distribution.

MISTER COWBOY.
Tracks: Cindy / Sweet Betsy from Pike / Sleep with Moses / Cowboy's dream / Alla en el rancho grande / Softly and tenderly / Lonesome valley / Hoosen Johnny / Curtains of the night / Rarin' to go / Old Joe Clark / On top of old smokey / Feeling bad / Prayer of the frontier doctor.
LP . . . . HAT 3034
MC . . . . HATC 3034
Stetson / Apr '87 / Crusader Marketing Co. / Swift / Wellard Dist. / Midland Records / C.M. Distribution.

UNDER WESTERN SKIES.
Tracks: Trail of the lonesome pine / Nothin' to do / Last round-up, The / Last frontier, The / Rocky mountain lullaby / Ole faithful / Twilight on the trail / Railroad corral / I'm a young cowboy / At the rainbows end / Sky boss / Too-lee Roll-um.
LP . . . . HAT 3001
MC . . . . HATC 3001
Stetson / Nov '85 / Crusader Marketing Co. / Swift / Wellard Dist. / Midland Records / C.M. Distribution.

VOICE OF THE WEST.
Tracks: Tyin' knots in the Devil's tail / Moonshine steer / Fireman cowboy, The / Today I started loving you again / Windy Bill / Little Joe the wrangler / When the works all done this fall / Droop ears / Streets of Laredo / Braggin' drunk from Wilcox / Gone girl / Catfish John / You never did give up on me / Just call me lonesome / Reflex reaction.
CD . . . . BCD 15284
Bear Family / Aug '86 / Rollercoaster Records / Swift / Direct Distribution.

Allen, Terry

AMERASIA - THE SOUNDTRACK.
Tracks: Not Advised.
LP . . . . FETE 4
Fete / Mar '90.

BLOODLINES.
Tracks: Not Advised.
LP . . . . SPIN 114
Spindrift / Nov '85 / C.M. Distribution / Roots Records / Projection.
LP . . . . FETE 3
Fete / Mar '90.

JUAREZ.
Tracks: Not Advised.
■ LP . . . . FETE 1394
Fete / Dec '88.
LP . . . . FETE 1
Fete / Mar '90.

LUBBOCK (ON EVERYTHING).
Tracks: Not Advised.
Double LP . . . . SPD 1007/8
MC . . . . SPDC 1007
Special Delivery / Mar '88 / Revolver-APT / A.D.A Distribution / Topic Records / Direct Distribution / Jazz Music / C.M. Distribution.
■ CD . . . . SPDCD 1007
Special Delivery / Apr '91.

PEDAL STEAL (Allen, Terry & The Panhandle Mystery Band).
Tracks: Not Advised.
CD . . . . FATE 7655266
Fate / Apr '93 / Projection / A.D.A Distribution / Topic Records / Direct Distribution.

SILENT MAJORITY, THE.
Tracks: Blue velvet/we're here now / Jawohl asshole / School's for fools / Telephone call / Farm song / Fuckin' shit ass / Hey buddy / Train / Wet your lips / Tank / Raise a little hell / Guatemala / Big black bush / Rise above.
CD . . . . **FATE 7453266**
Fate / May '93 / Projection / A.D.A Distribution / Topic Records / Direct Distribution.

SMOKIN' THE DUMMY.
Tracks: Heart of California, The / Cocaine cowboy / Whatever happened to Jesus (and Maybeline) / Helena Montana / Texas tears / Cajun roll / Feelin' easy / Night Cafe, The / Roll truck roll / Red bird / Lubbock tornado (I don't know), The.
LP. **FPSS 1002**
Fate / Dec '88 / Projection / A.D.A Distribution / Topic Records / Direct Distribution.
CD . . . . **FRCD 02**
Fate / '92 / Projection / A.D.A Distribution / Topic Records / Direct Distribution.

SMOKIN' THE DUMMY.
Tracks: Smokin' the dummy.
7". . . . . **FETE 2**
Fete / Mar '90.

WHATEVER HAPPENED TO JESUS.
Tracks: Whatever happened to Jesus? / Cajun roll.
7". **FRSS 1001**
Fate / Jun '89 / Projection / A.D.A Distribution / Topic Records / Direct Distribution.

Anderson, Bill

Singer/songwriter/musician, nicknamed 'Whispering Bill', he was born James William Anderson III on Nov 1, 1937, in Columbia, South Carolina. After obtaining a BA degree at University of Georgia, he worked as a sportswriter and DJ before achieving success as a songwriter with hits such as *City Lights, Saginaw Michegan* and *Once A Day*. He began his recording career on Decca in 1958 and has scored over 70 chart entries, as well as duets with Jan Howard and Mary Lou Turner. A member of the Grand Ole Opry since 1961, he has appeared in some movies and, more recently achieved success as a television host. (Tony Byworth)

BEST OF BILL ANDERSON.
Tracks: Still / Happiness / I get the fever / Golden guitar / Quits / Sometimes / Wild weekend / Peanuts and diamonds / Walk out backwards / World of make believe / Don't she look good / Head to tow / Mama sang a song / I still feel the same about you / Po' folks / Liars one, believers zero / For loving you / My life / 8 X 10 / Every time I turn the radio on.
■ **LP**. **MCF 2865**
MCA / Jan '79.

BILL ANDERSON STORY.
Tracks: Bright lights and country music / No one's gonna hurt you anymore / I get the fever / Mama sang a song / I love you drops / Tip of my fingers, The / Po' folks / City lights / Get while the getting's good / 8 x 10 / That's what it's like to be lonesome / For loving you / Still / Easy come - easy go / Once a day / I can do nothing alone / Cincinnati / Golden guitar / Wild weekend / Think I'll go somewhere and cry myself to sleep / Ninety nine / Papa / Happiness / Five little fingers.
Double LP . . . . **IMCA 24001**
MCA (Import) / Mar '86 / Pinnacle / Silver Sounds (CD).

BILLY BOY AND MARY LOU (Anderson, Bill & Mary Lou Turner).
Tracks: Country lay on my mind / I'm way ahead of you / What we're taking here tonight / Just enough to make me want it all / I've been lovin' you too long / Building fires / Children / We made love (but where's the love we made) / Where are you going, Billy boy / Sad ol' shade of grey / Sometimes / Circle in a triangle / Gone at last / Come walk with me / Can we still be friends / That's what made me love you / Without / Charlie, Mary and us / I can't sleep with you / Let me take you away.
LP. . . . . **BDL 4000**
Bulldog Records / Jul '82 / President Records / Jazz Music / Wellard Dist. / TKO Records Ltd.

BRIGHT LIGHTS AND COUNTRY MUSIC (Anderson, Bill & The PO Boys).
Tracks: Bright lights and country music / Wild side of life / Golden guitar / Wine / How the other half lives / Good ole mountain dew / Truck driving man / I'll go down swinging / Stranger's story, The / Sittin' in an all nite cafe / Cocktails / I'm walking the dog.
LP. . . . . **HAT 3005**
MC . . . . **HATC 3005**
Stetson / Nov '85 / Crusader Marketing Co. / Swift / Wellard Dist. / Midland Records / C.M. Distribution.

GOLDEN GREATS: BILL ANDERSON.
Tracks: Mama sang a song / Still / I get the fever / My life / 8 x 10 / Wild weekend / Happy state of mind / But you know I love you / Tip of my fingers, The / For loving you / I love you drops / Five little fingers / Get while the getting's good / Love is a something thing / Bright lights and country music / Three AM.
LP. . . . . **MCM 5017**
■ **MC** . . . . **MCMC 5017**
MCA / Oct '85.

GREATEST HITS: BILL ANDERSON.
Tracks: I get the fever / Tip of my fingers, The / Bright lights and country music / Mama sang a song / Easy come - easy go / Still / I love you drops / 8 x 10 / Po' folks / Five little fingers / Three A.M. / Golden guitar.
■ **LP**. . . . . **IMCA 13**
MCA (Import) / Mar '86.

I LOVE YOU DROPS.
Tracks: I love you drops / Golden guitar.
■ **7"** **05959**
Brunswick / May '66.

LADIES CHOICE.
Tracks: Trust me / One more sexy lady / This is a love song / Remembering the good / Ladies get lonesome too / I can't wait any longer / Kiss you all over / Doubles / Married lady / Stay with me / Three times a lady.
LP. . . . . **BDL 4001**
Bulldog Records / Jul '82 / President Records / Jazz Music / Wellard Dist. / TKO Records Ltd.

MAGIC OF BILL ANDERSON, THE.
Tracks: Not Advised.
CD . . . . **TKOCD 018**
MC . . . . **TKOCS 018**
TKO Records / '92 / TKO Records Ltd / President Records.

MISTER PEEPERS.
Tracks: Mister Peepers / How married are you Mary Ann.
■ **7"** . . . . **BD 21**
Bulldog Records / May '81.

PEANUTS AND DIAMONDS.
Tracks: Peanuts and diamonds / I get the fever / Still.
■ **7"** . . . . **MCA 286**
MCA / Feb '77.

PLACE OUT IN THE COUNTRY, A.
Tracks: Place out in the country, A / Once more / No ordinary memory / Unicorn / Your eyes / Sheet music / Fathers and sons / I wonder where you are tonight / Maybe go down / Mr. Peepers / Family reunion / We may never pass this way again.
LP. . . . . **BDL 1061**
Bulldog Records / Aug '88 / President Records / Jazz Music / Wellard Dist. / TKO Records Ltd.

SLIPPIN' AWAY.
Tracks: Slippin' away / Hush..not a word to Mary.
■ **7"** . . . . **MCA 177**
MCA / Feb '75.

Anderson, Lynn

Born on September 26, 1947, in Grand Forks, North Dakota, the daughter of songwriters Liz and Casey Anderson. She commenced her recording career with Chart Records in 1966 and scored over a dozen hits before moving to Columbia (CBS) where, in 1970 enjoyed a multi million, international success with *Rose Garden*. More hits followed throughout the decade, though the 1980s were proved to be pretty unsuccessful. She is also an expert equestrian whose success began as a teenager when she was named California Horse Show Queen. (Tony Byworth)

20 GOLDEN HITS: LYNN ANDERSON.
Tracks: Not Advised.
CD . . . . **SPEC 85007**
Spectrum (CD) / Dec '88 / M.S.D.

ALL THE KING'S HORSES.
Tracks: All the king's horses / Lyin' eyes / Long long time / If all I have to do is just love you / Rodeo cowboy / Dixieland, you will never die / That's all she wrote / Paradise / Tomorrow / I want to be part of you.
LP. **81217**
CBS / '76 / Sony.

ANGEL IN YOUR ARMS.
Tracks: Angel in your arms / It's your love that keeps me going.
■ **7"** . . . . **CBS 6122**
CBS / Mar '78.

ANGELS IN YOUR ARMS, THE.
Tracks: He ain't you / Desparado / Angel in your arms, The / It's your love that keeps me going / My world begins and ends with you / I love what love is doing to me / We got love / Right time of the night / Will I ever hear those church bells ring.
LP. . . . . **CBS 82294**
CBS / '78 / Sony.

BEST OF LYNN ANDERSON.
Tracks: Not Advised.
LP. . . . . **NE 1196**
MC . . . . **CE 2196**
K-Tel / Oct '82 / I & B Records / C.M. Distribution / Arabesque Ltd. / Mono Distributors (Jersey) Ltd. / Prism Leisure PLC / PolyGram / Ross Records / Prism Leisure PLC.
MC . . . . **GM 0219**
K-Tel Goldmasters / Aug '84 / C.M. Distribution / Arabesque Ltd. / Ross Records / PolyGram.

COLLECTION: LYNN ANDERSON.
Tracks: Not Advised.
LP. . . . . **MA 04484**
Masters (Holland) / '88.
MC . . . . **MAMC 94484**
Masters (Holland) / Dec '88.

COUNTRY GIRL.
Tracks: Not Advised.
LP. . . . . **CBS 31486**
Embassy / Jul '77 / Sony.
CD . . . . **PWK 005**
Pickwick / '88 / Pickwick Records.
MC . . . . **DTO 10099**
Ditto / '88 / Pickwick Records.
MC . . . . **HSC 3401**
Pickwick / '88 / Pickwick Records.

COUNTRY STORE: LYNN ANDERSON.
Tracks: Rose garden / Sweet talking man / Honey come back / For the good times / Sea of heartbreak / I love how you love me / You're my man / Cry / Killing me softly with his song / Top of the world / It's only make believe / Stay there 'til I get there / Snowbird / Even cowgirls get the blues / Love me tonight / Sunday morning coming down / Bedtime story.
CD . . . . **CDCST 25**
MC . . . . **CSTK 25**
Country Store / '88 / BMG.
■ **LP**. . . . . **CST 25**
Country Store / '88.

DREAM ON (Anderson, Lynn & Tam White).
Tracks: Dream on.
7". . . . . **RESL 245**
BBC / Aug '90 / Pinnacle / Bond Street Music.

EVEN COWGIRLS GET THE BLUES.
Tracks: Even cowgirls get the blues / Poor side of town / Shoulder to shoulder / Give you up to get you back / Lonely hearts cafe / Blue baby blue / You thrill me / See through me / Love me tonight / Louisiana 1927.
■ **LP**. . . . . **CBS 84634**
CBS / Feb '81.

GREATEST HITS: LYNN ANDERSON (IMPORT).
Tracks: Not Advised.
LP. . . . . **FUN 9036**
MC . . . . **FUNC 9036**
Fun (Holland) / Oct '88 / Pinnacle.

GREATEST HITS:LYNN ANDERSON.
Tracks: Rose garden / Cry / Can I unlove you / Stay there 'til I get there / That's what loving you has meant to me / Listen to a country song / You're my man / No love at all / Don't say things you don't mean / I'm gonna write a song / Nothing between us.
LP. . . . . **CBS 32771**
■ **MC** **40 32771**
CBS / Mar '86.

HER TOP HITS.
Tracks: Not Advised.
MC **805**
Timeless Treasures / Jul '86 / Terry Blood Dist.

I'VE NEVER LOVED ANYONE MORE.
Tracks: I've never loved anyone more / I'm growing up all over again / Faithless love best the kept secret in Santa Fe / He worshipped me / He turns it into love again / I'm not Lisa / Love had no pride / We've got it all together now / Life's no bed of roses / Good old country song, A.
LP. **80998**
CBS / '75 / Sony.

LISTEN TO A COUNTRY SONG.
Tracks: Listen to a country song / It don't do no good to be a good girl / If you can't be your woman / Fool me / That's what your loving has meant to me / Take me to your world / There's a party going on / Reason to believe / You're everything / Everybody's reaching out for someone.
LP. . . . . **SHM 991**
■ **MC** . . . . **HSC 369**
Hallmark / Apr '79.

LYNN ANDERSON.
Tracks: Rose garden / I still belong to you / Another lonely night / It's only make believe / Your sweet love lifted me / You're my man / Help me make it through the night / I'm gonna write a song / Cry, cry again / I might as well be here alone / Flying machine.
MC Set. . . . . **DTO 10041**
Ditto / '83 / Pickwick Records.

LYNN ANDERSON'S GREATEST HITS.
Tracks: Rose garden / Cry / How can I unlove you / Stay there til I get there / That's what loving you has meant to me / Listen to a country song / You're my man / No love at all / Don't say things you don't mean / I'm gonna write a song / Nothing between us.
CD **4714132**
MC **4714134**
Sony Music / '92 / Sony.

OUTLAW IS JUST A STATE OF MIND.
Tracks: Isn't it always love / I love how you love me / Child with you tonight / This night won't last forever / I am alone / Say you will / Outlaw is just a state of mind / Come as you are / Come running / Sea of heartbreak.
■ **LP**. . . . . **CBS 83611**
CBS / '79.

A 4 ■ DELETED

OUTLAW IS JUST A STATE OF MIND.
Tracks: Outlaw is just a state of mind / Child with you tonight.
■ 7" . . . . CBS 7390
CBS / '79.

ROSE GARDEN.
Tracks: Not Advised.
CD . . . . .WMCD 5655
MC . . . . WMMC 4655
Woodford Music / Jun '92 / Terry Blood Dist. / Midland Records.

ROSE GARDEN.
Tracks: Rose garden / Snow bird.
7" . . . . CBS 5360
CBS / Feb '71 / Sony.
7" . . . . CBS 7069
CBS / Apr '82 / Sony.

ROSE GARDEN.
Tracks: Not Advised.
CD 2604042
MC 2604044
Mainline (2) / Feb '90.

ROSE GARDEN.
Tracks: Not Advised.
LP . . . . CBS 64333
CBS / Apr '71 / Sony.

ROSE GARDEN.
Tracks: Not Advised.
CD .ENT CD 242
MC . . . . ENT MC 13063
Entertainers / Mar '92.

ROSE GARDEN (OLD GOLD).
Tracks: Rose garden / You're my man.
7" . . . . .OG 9397
Old Gold / Mar '90 / Pickwick Records.

WHAT A MAN MY MAN IS.
Tracks: What a man my man is / I honestly love you / Everything's falling in place (for me and you) / Tell me a lie / Someone to finish what you started / E'rybody's don't tell me how the story ends / Walk me to the door / Where is all that love you talked about / I feel like a new man today.
LP 80621
CBS / '74 / Sony.

WRAP YOUR LOVE AROUND YOUR MAN.
Tracks: Wrap your love around your man / Feelings / Let your love flow / Big news in Tennamock, Georgia, The / This country girl is woman wise / You've got me to hold on to / I'll be loving you / I couldn't be lonely (Even if I wanted to) / Sweet talkin' man.
LP 81817
CBS / '76 / Sony.

Anger, Darol

CHIAROSCURO (Anger, Darol & Mike Marshall).
Tracks: Dolphins / Saurian's farewell / Beneath the farewell / Beloved infidel / Placenza / Coming back / Dardanelles / Spring gesture.
LP . . . . .WHA 1043
Windham Hill / Jul '86 / Pinnacle.
■ MC 371043-4
Windham Hill / May '86.
CD . . . . .CDW 1043
Windham Hill / '88 / Pinnacle.

DUO, THE (Anger, Darol & Mike Marshall).
Tracks: Not Advised.
LP . . . . ROUNDER 0168
MC . . . . .ROUNDER 0168C
Rounder / Aug '88 / Projection / Roots Records / Swift / C.M. Distribution / Topic Records / Jazz Music / Hot Shot / A.D.A Distribution / Direct Distribution.

FIDDLISTICS.
Tracks: Not Advised.
LP . . . . .K 8
Kaleidoscope (USA) / Projection / Ross Records / Roots Records / Swift / C.M. Distribution / Topic Records / Duncans.

JAZZ VIOLIN CELEBRATION: RECORDED LIVE.
Tracks: Not Advised.
LP . . . . F 22
MC . . . . C 22
Kaleidoscope (USA) / '88 / Projection / Ross Records / Roots Records / Swift / C.M. Distribution / Topic Records / Duncans.

LIVE AT MONTREUX: DAROL ANGER (Anger, Darol & Barbara Higbie Quintet).
Tracks: Not Advised.
CD . . . . .CDW 1036
LP . . . . .WHA 1036
Windham Hill / Jul '86 / Pinnacle.
CD 371036-2
LP 371036-1
■ MC 371036-4
Windham Hill / May '86.

TIDELINE (Anger, Darol & Barbara Higbie).
Tracks: Tideline / Movie / Above the fog / Keep sleeping / Onyame / True story / Fortunate / Gemini / Gualala / Lifeline.
LP . . . . .WHA 1021
Windham Hill / Jul '86 / Pinnacle.
LP 371021-1
■ MC 371021-4
Windham Hill / May '86.

Appalachian Express

EXPRESS TRACKS.
Tracks: I'm old Kentucky bound / Cabin of love / Have I loved you too late / Express lane / Water's so cold, The / It takes one to know one / Cabin on the mountain / Blue mountain memories / Going home / Two in the morning / When the bees are in the hive / Tiny doll.
LP . . . . .REBEL 1674
MC . . . . .REBELMC 1674
Rebel (1) / '90 / Projection / Backs Distribution.

I'LL MEET YOU IN THE MORNING.
Tracks: Not Advised.
LP . . . . UNKNOWN
Rebel (1) / '88 / Projection / Backs Distribution.

Arceneaux, Fernest

FROM THE HEART OF THE BAYOUS (Arceneaux, Fernest & his Louisiana French band).
Tracks: Mother's love / Last night / It's alright / You don't have to go / I don't want nobody / Mean woman blues / London zydeco / Everyday I have the blues / Chains of love / Reconsider, baby.
LP . . . . JSP 1064
JSP / Jan '84 / '90 / Swift / Wellard Dist. / A.D.A Distribution / Cadillac Music / Jazz Music.

GUMBO SPECIAL (Arceneaux, Fernest & Thunders).
Tracks: Not Advised.
LP . . . . .SCH 104
Schubert / '88

ZYDECO STOMP (Arceneaux, Fernest & Thunders).
Tracks: Not Advised.
CD . . . . .JSP CD 220
LP . . . . JSP 1029
JSP / Oct '88 / Hot Shot / Swift / Wellard Dist. / A.D.A Distribution / Cadillac Music / Jazz Music.

Archers

STAND UP.
Tracks: Only His love / We're all gonna leave here / Fool's paradise / Moments with you / Stand up / Blame it on the one I love / More (so much more) / Livin' in your love / God loves you / Picking up the pieces.
LP . . . . LS 7055
MC . . . . LC 7055
Light / May '82 / Word Records (UK) / Sony.

Ardoin Family

COUPLE OF CAJUNS (Ardoin Family Orchestra & Dewey Balfa).
Tracks: La Cucaracha / Grande mamou / La valse de gros garcon / Valse de meche / La valse fonce / Cher toute toute.
LP . . . . SNTF 873
Sonet / Nov '81 / Swift / C.M. Distribution / Roots Records / Jazz Music / Sonet Records / Cadillac Music / Projection / Wellard Dist. / Hot Shot.

Ardoin, Boisec

LA MUSIQUE CREOLE.
Tracks: Not Advised.
LP . . . . ARHOOLIE 1070
Arhoolie (USA) / '85 / Pinnacle / Cadillac Music / Swift / Projection / Hot Shot / A.D.A Distribution / Jazz Music.
■ MC . . . . .ARHC 1070
Arhoolie (USA) / '90.

Ardoin, Lawrence

AND HIS FRENCH BAND (Ardoin, Lawrence 'Black').
Tracks: Not Advised.
■ MC . . . . .ARHC 1091
Arhoolie (USA) / '90.

Arhelger, Jerry

LONDON LADY.
Tracks: Travellin' on / No heart to go home to / Never lonely again / You don't have very far to go / Moanin' the blues / London lady / I like winning / It's been that kind of night / For all the lonely hearts / Do you wanna / Beside you, beside me / Tell me who / Nashville without Jesus.
LP . . . . SDLP 064

Sundown / Feb '89 / Terry Blood Dist. / Jazz Music / C.M. Distribution.

Armstrong Twins

HILLBILLY MANDOLIN.
Tracks: Not Advised.
LP . . . . OT 118
Old Timey (USA) / May '79 / Projection.

JUST COUNTRY BOYS.
Tracks: Not Advised.
LP . . . . ARHOOLIE 5022
Arhoolie (USA) / May '81 / Pinnacle / Cadillac Music / Swift / Projection / Hot Shot / A.D.A Distribution / Jazz Music.

Armstrong, Billy

BILLY, DON'T SELL YOUR FIDDLE.
Tracks: Fraulein / Truck driving man / San Antonio medley / Kind of love I can't forget, The / Six days on the road / Roly poly / Last letter, The / Take me back to Tulsa / Liberty.
LP . . . . WRS 135
Westwood / '82 / Pinnacle.

MR. FIDDLE.
Tracks: Not Advised.
LP . . . . WRS 104
Westwood / '76 / Pinnacle.

Arnold, Eddy

Born in West Tennessee in 1918, Eddy Arnold became the most successful artist in the history of country music. Arnold's most triumphant year came relatively early in his lengthy career. Having turned professional in 1943, he dominated the fledgling country charts in 1948 with four back-to-back monster hits: I'll Hold You In My Heart, Bouquet Of Roses/Texarkana Baby, Any Time and Just A Little Lovin' (Will Go A Long Long Way). Further No.1s on the Billboard country chart included I Wanna Play House With You (1951) and Cattle Call (1955), amongst others. Arnold's forte was the slow rambling country and western ballad. While his music was perfect for his own market, however, he was unable to sell it in any great quantities to the world outside. Make The World Go Away, became a transatlantic Top 10 hit in the mid-sixties A couple of smaller pop hits followed it up, but Arnold always stuck to the style and the audience he knew best. In 1966 Eddy Arnold was awarded one of the highest accolades in his field, being elected to the Country Music Association Hall of Fame. (Bob McDonald)

20 OF THE BEST: EDDY ARNOLD.
Tracks: Make the world go away / Cattle call / Just call me lonesome / What's he doing in my world / I really don't want to know / I want to go with you / Somebody like me / Lonely again / Turn the world around / Then you can tell me goodbye / I'll hold you in my heart / Bouquet of roses / Anytime / Just a little lovin' / Don't rob another man's castle / I'm throwing rice at the girl I love / There's been a change in me / Kentucky waltz? / I wanna play house with you / Eddy's song.
LP . . . . NL 89316
■ MC . . . . NK 89316
RCA / '82.

ALL-TIME FAVOURITES.
Tracks: Moonlight and roses / Missouri waltz / The (Hush-a-bye, my baby) / I'm gonna lock my heart / You always hurt the one you love / I'm thinking tonight of my blue eyes / It makes no difference now / I'm waiting for ships that never come in / I'm gonna sit right down and write myself a letter / When your hair has turned to silver / Angry / Prisoner's song / Seven years with the wrong woman.
LP . . . . NL 90004
■ MC . . . . NK 90004
RCA / Jan '87.

ANYTIME.
Tracks: Bouquet of roses / That's how much I like you / Rockin' alone in an old rocking chair / I'll hold you in my heart / Anytime / Will the circle be unbroken / It's a sin / Don't rob another man's castle / Molly darling / Heart full of love, A / Texarkane baby / Who at my door is standing.
LP . . . . HAT 3086
Stetson / '88 / Crusader Marketing Co. / Swift / Wellard Dist. / Midland Records / C.M. Distribution.
MC . . . . HATC 3086
Stetson / Jan '89 / Crusader Marketing Co. / Swift / Wellard Dist. / Midland Records / C.M. Distribution.

BEST OF EDDY ARNOLD, THE.
Tracks: Bouquet of roses / Make the world go away / Anytime / I'll hold you in my heart / Last word in lonesome is me, The / What's he doin' in my world / Just a little lovin' (will go a long way) / I really don't want to know / You don't know me / That's how much I love you / Cattle call.
■ LP . . . . LSA 3028
RCA / '75 / BMG.

CATTLE CALL.
Tracks: Streets of Laredo, The / Cool water / Cattle call / Leanin' on the old top rail / Ole faithful / Cowboy's

dream, A / Wayward wind, The / Tumbling tumbleweeds / Cowpoke / Where the mountains meet the sky / Sierra Sue / Carry me back to the lone prairie / I wore a tie today.
■ LP.................................RD 7804
RCA / Apr '71 / BMG.

CATTLE CALL/THEREBY HANGS A TALE.
Tracks: Streets of Laredo, The / Cool water / Cattle call / Leanin' on the old top rail / Ole faithful / Cowboy's dream / Wayward wind, The / Tumbling tumbleweeds / Cowpoke / Where the mountains meet the sky / Sierra Sue / Carry me back to the Lone Prairie / Jim I wore a tie today / Tom Dooley / Nellie sits a waitin' / Tennessee stud / Battle of Little Big Horn, The / Wreck of the old 97, The / Red headed stranger, The / Johnny Reb that's me / Riders in the sky / Boot Hill / Ballad of Davy Crockett, The / Partners / Jesse James.
CD..................................BCD 15441
Bear Family / Apr '90 / Rollercoaster Records / Swift / Direct Distribution.

EDDY.
Tracks: Cowboy / My woman's eyes / Goodnight, Irene / Freedom ain't the same as being free / Remember the good / Put me back into your world / Don't let the good times roll away / I wouldn't be so sad (if we hadn't been so happy) / She's just an old love turned memory / We found it in each other's arms.
■ LP..................................PL 11817
RCA / '78 / BMG.

HERE COME THE RAIN, BABY.
Tracks: Here comes the rain, baby / World I used to know, The.
7".................................RCA 1661
RCA / Apr '71 / BMG.

I WANT TO GO WITH YOU.
Tracks: I want to go with you.
■ 7"...................................1519
RCA / May '66.

IF YOU WERE MINE MARY.
Tracks: If you were mine Mary.
■ 7"...................................1529
RCA / Jul '66.

IT'S OVER.
Tracks: It's over.
■ 7".................................RCA 1712
RCA / Apr '71 / BMG.

MEMORIES ARE MADE OF THIS.
Tracks: Memories are made of this / I wish I had loved you better.
■ 7"...............................MGM 2006
MGM (EMI) / Jan '75.

MISTY BLUE.
Tracks: Misty blue / Calling Mary names.
■ 7".................................RCA 1618
RCA / Aug '71 / BMG.

MY WORLD.
Tracks: What's he doin' in my world / Too many rivers / It comes and goes / Make the world go away / Days gone by, The / I'm letting you go / As usual / I'm walking behind you / If you were mine, Mary / Taking chances / You still got a hold on me.
■ LP.................................RD 7790
RCA / Apr '71 / BMG.

SOMEBODY LIKE ME.
Tracks: Somebody like me / Lay some happiness on me / There's always me / Come by me nice and slowly / You made up for everything / At sunset / Tip of my fingers, The / Love on my mind / I love you drops / Don't laugh at my love / Ev'ry step of the way / It's only love.
■ LP.................................RD 7955
RCA / Apr '70 / BMG.

THEN YOU CAN TELL ME GOODBYE.
Tracks: They don't make love like they used to / What a wonderful world.
■ 7".................................RCA 1780
RCA / Aug '73 / BMG.

THEREBY HANGS A TALE.
Tracks: Tom Dooley / Nellie sits a-waiting / Tennessee stud / Battle of little big horn, The / Wreck of the old '97, The / Red headed stranger, The / Johnny Rec, that's me / Riders in the sky / Boot hill / Ballad of Davey Crockett / Partners / Jesse James.
■ LP.................................RD 27155
RCA / Jun '70 / BMG.

TURN THE WORLD AROUND THE OTHER WAY.
Tracks: Turn the world around the other way / Long ride home, The.
■ 7".................................RCA 1655
RCA / Jun '71 / BMG.

Arnold, Jimmy

RAINBOW RIDE.
Tracks: Not Advised.
MC............................REBELMC 1603
Rebel (1) / '73 / Projection / Backs Distribution.
LP..............................REBEL 1603
Rebel (1) / '75 / Projection / Backs Distribution.

SOUTHERN SOUL.
Tracks: Jesse James / Georgia moon / Rebel soldier, The / Southern comfort / Night they drove old Dixie down, The / Sail away ladies / General Lee / My home's across the blue ridge mountains / Dixon line, The / Bonaparte's retreat / Arkansas soldier / Lorena / Southern soul / Heroes / Sally Ann.
LP.................................REBEL 1621
MC..............................REBELMC 1621
Rebel (1) / '83 / Projection / Backs Distribution.

Arnold, Lloyd

MEMPHIS -- ROCK 'N' ROLL CAPITAL, VOL 7.
Tracks: Red coat, green pants & red suit shoes / Hangout / Dixie doodle / Half my fault / Great speckled bird, The / School days / Cold duck blues / I got the blues / 'Cause I love you / Gonna love my baby / Schooldays, Part 2 / Tennessee twist / Go go go / Sugaree / Don't care blues.
LP.................................WLP 8921
White Label (Germany) / '87 / Pinnacle / Bear Family Records (Germany) / CSA Tell Tapes.

Arthur, Charline

WELCOME TO THE CLUB.
Tracks: Welcome to the club / Burn that candle / What about tomorrow / Honey bun / Kiss the baby goodnight / Just look, don't touch, she's mine / How many would there be / Later on / I heard about you / Anything can happen / Looking at the moon and wishing on a star / I'm having a party all by myself / Leave my man alone / Please darlin' please / Heartbreak ahead / I was wrong / Count your blessings / Real love / Nobody walks in L.A. / How does it fit / Relations / What becomes of love / Way ahead / 10th round.
LP.................................BFX 15234
Bear Family / Jun '86 / Rollercoaster Records / Swift / Direct Distribution.

Ashdown, Doug

WINTER IN AMERICA.
Tracks: Not Advised.
■ MC..............................KTXCR 125
Decca / Nov '77.

WINTER IN AMERICA.
Tracks: Winter in America / Skid row.
■ 7".................................FR 13730
Decca / Apr '78.

Asleep At The Wheel

Western swing group formed by singer/guitarist Ray Benson in Paw Paw, West Virginia, in 1970. Although they've never achieved the greatest commercial success, Asleep At The Wheel has remained in business into a third decade with various personnel changes and Benson always remaining at the helm. Signed to an assortment of labels (UA, Epic, Capitol, MCA, Arista etc), they've scored some 18 chart hits, much critical acclaim and a 1978 Grammy for their rendition of Count Basie's *One O Clock Jump*. (Tony Byworth)

COLLISION COURSE.
Tracks: Not Advised.
LP.................................EST 11726
Capitol / Jul '78 / EMI.

COMIN' RIGHT AT YA'.
Tracks: Take me back to Tulsa / Daddy's advice / Before you stopped loving me / Drivin' nails in my coffin / I'll never get out of this world alive / Space buggy / Cherokee boogie / Hillbilly nut / Your down home is uptown / I'm the fool / I've been everywhere / Sun shines down on me.
LP.................................ED 187
MC................................CED 187
Edsel / May '86 / Pinnacle.

FRAMED.
Tracks: Midnight in Memphis / Lonely Avenue revisited / Slow dancing / Cool as a breeze / You wanna give me a lift / Don't get caught out in the rain / Whatever it takes / Fiddle funk - corn fusion / Up up up / Musical talk.
■ LP.................................IMCA 742
MCA (Import) / Mar '86.

JUMPING AT THE WOODSIDE.
Tracks: Choo choo ch'boogie / You & me instead / Jumpin' at the woodside / Last letter / Don't ask me why (I'm going to Texas) / Kind of love I can't forget, The / I'm gonna be a wheel some day / Our names aren't mentioned (together anymore) / Miss Molly / Bloodshot eyes / Dead man.
LP.................................ED 169
Edsel / Feb '86 / Pinnacle.

MY BABY THINKS SHE'S A TRAIN.
Tracks: My baby thinks she's a train / Ragtime Annie.
■ 7".................................CL 15928
Capitol / Jun '77.

PASTURE PRIME.
Tracks: Across the valley from the Alamo / Switchin' in the kitchen / Write your own song / Cotton-eyed Joe / Baby / Shorty / That chick's too young to fry / Big beaver / This is the way we make a broken heart / Deep water / Natural thing to do, The / Liar's moon / That's your red wagon.
LP.................................FIEND 44
MC..............................FIENDCASS 44
Demon / Apr '85 / Pinnacle.
CD................................FIENDCD 44
Demon / Mar '91 / Pinnacle.

ROUTE 66.
Tracks: Route 66 / Shout wa hey.
■ 7".................................CL 15890
Capitol / Oct '76.

SERVED LIVE.
Tracks: Choo choo ch' boogie / Last meal / God bless the child / Jumpin' at the Woodside / Am I high? / Route 66 / Baby, you've got what it takes / Too many bad habits / Miles and miles of Texas / Will the circle be unbroken.
■ LP.................................EST 11945
Capitol / '79.

TEN.
Tracks: Way down Texas way / Tulsa straight ahead / Coast to coast / House of blue lights / Blowin' like a bandit / I want a new drug / Big foot stomp / Boogie back to Texas / String of pars / Blues stay away from me.
LP.................................4506291
MC.................................4506294
Epic / Jun '87 / Sony.

VERY BEST OF ASLEEP AT THE WHEEL.
Tracks: Cherokee boogie / I'll never get out of this world alive / Space buggy / Letter that Johnny Walker read, The / Let me go home whiskey / Trouble in mind / Runnin' after fools / Miles and miles of Texas / Route 66 / My baby thinks she's a train / Am I high? / Ragtime Annie / Somebody stole his body / When love goes wrong / Louisiana 1927 / Ain't nobody here but us chickens / One o'clock jump.
CD.................................SEECD 81
LP.................................SEE 81
See For Miles / Apr '93 / Pinnacle.

WESTERN STANDARD TIME.
Tracks: Chattanooga choo choo / Don't let go / Hot rod Lincoln / That's what I like about the South / That lucky old sun / Walk on by / San Antonio rose / Roly poly / Sugarfoot rag / Walking the floor over you.
LP.................................4609851
■ MC.................................4609854
Epic / Sep '88.

WHEEL, THE.
Tracks: Not Advised.
LP.................................EST 11620
Capitol / Apr '77 / EMI.

Aston, John

JOHN ASTON.
Tracks: I love Waylon and Willie / Old Lamplighter, The / Cowboys don't ride horses anymore / Crazy.
■ LP.................................BN 111
Birds Nest / '85 / Pinnacle.

YOU TAKE THE BLAME FOR THE ROSES.
Tracks: Not Advised.
LP.................................MMLP 1017
Happy Face / Oct '80 / Swift / Pinnacle.

Atkins, Chet

Born in Tennessee in 1924, Chet Atkins successfully combined careers as musician, producer and executive. Learning to play fiddle and then guitar, he signed to RCA Records in 1946. He established himself as a leading session guitarist, moved to Nashville in 1950 and helped make the town the centre of country music. During the early fifties Atkins was living a double life, he became artists and repertoire assistant to RCA's Steve Sholes while simultaneously commencing a solo recording career. His debut album *Gallopin' Shoes* was the first of numerous strong selling country LP's that dotted his career. In the mid-fifties he played sessions with RCA's new signing Elvis Presley and was soon assigned by the company to supervise Elvis's recording career. In 1960 he became RCA's head of Nashville A & R. As well as steering the careers of many fledgling country singers who were to become major artists, he played on many of their records himself, together with pianist Floyd Cramer. Atkin's guitar and Cramer's piano characterised many country records of the period. By both playing on so many Nashville hits and supervising the artists involved, Atkins became all powerful. He created the Nashville Sound with the familiar pedal steel guitars and the massed strings. The style revolved not only from traditional country, but also from Atkin's interests in jazz and rock. Having been responsible for such a distinctive sound, however, he became less and less interested in progression. The Nashville establishment grew more and more conservative in

■ DELETED

an attempt to preserve their musical trademark and their output became samey. Having gained further promotion within his record company, Atkins was elected to the Country Music Association Hall of Fame in 1973. As guitarist, writer, producer, executive and above all, catalyst, he was the man most responsible for bringing about RCA's dominance of the US country charts. He was an important figure in the careers of Elvis Presley, Jim Reeves, Charley Pride, Jerry Reed and numerous others. As far as UK recognition is concerned, Chet Atkins scored three top 20 albums in the early sixties and also a minor chart single called *Teensville*.

20 OF THE BEST: CHET ATKINS.
Tracks: Yakety axe / Yankee doodle Dixie / Galloping on the guitar / Walkin' on strings / You're just in love / In the mood / Whispering / Summer place, Theme from / Hidden charms / Heartaches / When you wish upon a star / Over the rainbow / Music to watch girls by / Siboney / El relicario / Early dawn (La madrugada) / Steeplechase Lane / Funky junk / Cascade / Black mountain rag.
LP. . . . . NL 89849
■ MC . . . . NK 89849
RCA / Mar '86.

ALONE.
Tracks: Hawaiian slack key / Claw, The / Spanish fandango / Flop-eared mule and other classics / Over the waves / Just as I am / Take five / Smile / Blue finger / Me and Bovvy McGee / Londonderry air / Watkins man, The.
■ LP. . . . . LSA 3187
RCA / '78 / BMG.

ATKINS - TRAVIS TRAVELLING SHOW, THE (Atkins, Chet & Merle Travis).
Tracks: Down South blues / Mutual admiration / Muskrat ramble / If I had you / Cannonball rag / Boogie for Cecil / Is anything better than this / Dance of the golden rod / Who's sorry now / Nine pound hammer / I'll see you in my dreams.
■ LP. . . . . AFL 10479
RCA / '75 / BMG.

BEST OF CHET ATKINS.
Tracks: Not Advised.
LP. . . . . CDS 1217
■ MC . . . . CAM 1217
RCA/Camden / Jul '86.

BEST OF CHET ATKINS (RCA).
Tracks: Teensville / Boo boo stick beat / One mint julep / Jitterbug waltz / Peanut vendor / Django's castle / Blue ocean echo / Yankee doodle Dixie / Swedish rhapsody / Vanessa / Trombone / Malaguena / Meet Mr. Callaghan / Main street breakdown / Country gentleman / Yakety axe.
LP. . . . . INTS 5051
MC . . . . INTK 5051
RCA International / Oct '80 / BMG.

BEST OF CHET ATKINS AND FRIENDS (Atkins, Chet & Friends).
Tracks: Terry on the turnpike / Sail along silv'ry moon / Sweet Georgia Brown / Avalon / Sugarfoot rag / Battle of New Orleans / Do I ever cross your mind / Frog kissin' / Twichy / Fiddlin' around / Poison love / I'll see you in my dreams.
■ LP. . . . . PL 11985
RCA / '79.
LP. . . . . MFP 5766
■ MC . . . . TCMFP 5766
MFP / Sep '86.

BEST OF CHET ATKINS, THE.
Tracks: Jitterbug waltz / Peanut vendor, The / Djanog's castle / Blue ocean echo / Yankee doodle dixie / Swedish rhapsody / Vanessa / trambone / Malaguena / Meet Mister Callaghan / Main street breakdown / Country gentlemen.
■ LP. . . . . RD 7664
RCA / Feb '70 / BMG.

CARIBBEAN GUITAR.
Tracks: Not Advised.
■ LP. . . . . RD 7519
RCA / Feb '63.

CERTIFIED GUITAR PLAYER (Atkins, Chet & Friends).
Tracks: Walk of life / I'll see you in my dreams / Imagine / Dream / Bye bye love / Wake up little Suzie / I keep forgetting / Fire in his eyes / Good-hearted woman / I am a cowboy / Sunrise / I still can't say goodbye / Corinna corinna.
VHS. . . . . E 1303
Excalibur (video) / Jun '90.
VHS. . . . . MMGV 021
MMG Video / Jun '91 / Terry Blood Dist.

CHESTER AND LESTER (Atkins, Chet & Les Paul).
Tracks: It's been a long, long time / Moonglow and theme from Picnic / Caravan / It had to be you / Out of nowhere / Avalon / Birth of the blues / Someday, sweetheart / Deed I do / Lover come back to me.
LP. . . . . LSA 3290
RCA / Jan '77 / BMG.

CHET ATKIN'S GUITAR WORKSHOP.
Tracks: Not Advised.
■ LP. . . . . RD 27214
RCA / Jun '61.

CHET ATKINS AND FRIENDS.
Tracks: Not Advised.

CHET ATKINS PICKS ON THE HITS.
Tracks: Masterpiece, The / After midnight / Song sung blue / An old fashioned love song / Amazing grace / Sweet Caroline / I'd like to teach the world to sing (in perfect harmony) / Vincent / Love theme from "The Godfather" / Me and Julio down by the schoolyard.
■ LP. . . . . LSA 3121
RCA / '75 / BMG.

CHET ATKINS PICKS THE BEST.
Tracks: You'll never walk alone / Lovely weather / Insensatez (how insensitive) / Colonel Bogey / Nuages / Anna (el negro zumbon) / Battle hymn of the Republic / All (theme from "Run for your wife") / El Paso / Tears / I wish I knew / Ay ay ay.
■ LP. . . . . PQ 81261
RCA / '75 / BMG.

COLLECTION, THE.
Tracks: On the road again / Tenderly / Orange blossom special / Rodrigo concerto / Take five / Caravan / Vincent / Mostly Mozart / Storms never last / Limehouse blues / Over the waves / It don't mean a thing (if it ain't got that swing) / Brandenburg / Struttin' / I'll see you in my dreams / Heart of glass / Black and white/ Ragtime Annie/Hot Toddy.
CD 7432114094-21
RCA / Jul '93 / BMG.

EAST TENNESSEE CHRISTMAS.
Tracks: Jingle bell rock / White Christmas / Let it snow, let it snow, let it snow / Winter wonderland / Christmas song, The / I'll be home for Christmas / East Tennessee Christmas / Do you hear what I hear? / Little drummer boy / God rest ye merry gentlemen / Silent night / Away in a manger.
LP. . . . . CBS 25735
MC 40 25735
CBS / Dec '83 / Sony.

FAMOUS COUNTRY MUSIC MAKERS.
Tracks: Yakety axe / Walkin' on strings / Bells of St. Mary's / Corina Corina / Amazing grace / Third man, Theme from / Little bit of blues, A / Dill pickle rag / Country style / Django's castle / Glow worm / Stephen Foster medley / Trombone / Remembering / Prisoner's song / Country gentleman / Oh by jingo, oh by gee / Will the circle be unbroken / Greensleeves / Windy and warm / Arkansas traveller / Squirrelly / Red wing / Twelfth St. Rag / Get on with it / Little Rock getaway / South / When you wish upon a star / Whispering / Halacious / Main street breakdown.
Double LP . . . . DPS 2063
RCA / Mar '76 / BMG.

FIRST NASHVILLE GUITAR QUARTET.
Tracks: Carolina shout / Londonderry air / Love song of Pepe Sanchez / Skirts of Mexico / You needed me / Bound for Boston / Washington post / Someday my prince will come / Rings of grass / Concierto de Aranjuez / Brandenburg.
■ LP. . . . . PL 13302
RCA / Feb '80.

GALLOPIN' GUITAR.
Tracks: Guitar blues / Brown eyes cryin' in the rain / Ain'tcha tired of makin' me blue / I'm gonna get tight / Canned heat / Standing room only / Don't hand me that line / Bug dance / I know my baby loves me / Nashville jump, The / My guitar is my sweetheart / I'm pickin' the blues / Gone, gone, gone / Barnyard shuffle / Save your money / (I may be colour blind but) I know when.. / I've been working on the guitar / Dizzy strings / Money, marbles & chalk / Wednesday night waltz / Guitar waltz / Telling my troubles to my old guitar / Dance of the goldenrod / Gallopin' guitar / Barber shop rag / Centipede boogie / Under the Hickory nut tree / I was bitten by the same bug twice / One more chance / Old buck dance, The / Boogie man boogie / Main street breakdown / Confusin' / Music in my heart / Indian love call / Birth of the blues / Mountain melody / You're always brand new / My crazy heart / Hybrid corn / Jitterbug waltz / One man boogie / Crazy rhythm (instrumental) / Crazy rhythm / Rustic dance / Rainbow / In the mood / Spanish fandango / Midnight / Goodbye blues / Your mean little heart / Sweet bunch of daisies / Blue gypsy / Third man theme, The / One man boogie (take D) / St. Louis blues / Listed knot / Lover come back to me / Stephen Foster medley / Hangover blues / Imagination / Black mountain rag / Guitar polka / Dream train / Meet Mr. Callaghan / Chinatown, my Chinatown / High rockin' swing / Pig leaf rag / Oh by jingo / Hello ma baby / Bells of St. Mary's, The / Country gentlemen / Memphis blues / Alice blue gown / 12th street rag / Peeping Tom / Three o'clock in the morning / Georgia camp meeting / City slicker / Dill pickles rag / Rubber doll rag / Beautiful Ohio (1) / Kentucky derby / Wildwood flower / Guitars on parade / Simple Simon / Rubber doll rag (alternate version) / Get up & go / Pagan love song / Beautiful Ohio (2) / Down hill drag / Avalon / Sunrise serenade / San Antonio rose / Set a spell / Mister Misery / Get up & go (vocal: Red Kirk) / South / Alabama jubilee / Corrine, Corrina / Indiana (back home in Indiana) / Red wing / Frankie & Johnnie / Gay Ranchero, A / Ballin' the Jack / Honeysuckle rose / Darktown strutters ball / Old spinning wheel, The / Silver bells / Under the double eagle / Have you ever been lonely / Caravan / Old man river / Mister Sandman / New Spanish two-step.
CD . . . . BCD 15714
Bear Family / Oct '93 / Rollercoaster Records / Swift / Direct Distribution.

GUITAR COUNTRY.
Tracks: Freight train / Little bit of blues, A / Nine pound hammer / Dobro / Kentucky / Vaya con dios / Winter walkin' / Guitar country / Sugarfoot rag / Gone / Copper kettle / Yes ma'am.
■ LP. . . . . SF 7617
RCA / Apr '70 / BMG.

GUITAR MONSTERS (Atkins, Chet & Les Paul).
Tracks: Limehouse blues / I want to be happy / Over the rainbow / Meditacao / Lazy river / I'm your greatest fan / It don't mean a thing / I surrender dear / Brazil / Give my love to Nell / Hot toddy.
LP. . . . . PL 12786
■ MC . . . . PK 12786
RCA / Aug '78.

GUITAR PICKIN' MAN.
Tracks: Swedish rhapsody / Liza / Tiger rag / In the mood / Mountain melody / Heartaches / Glow worm / Malaguena / Hot mocking bird / Rainbow / I know that you know / Hello bluebird / Siesta / Country style / Show me the way to go home / Goofus / Petite waltz / Gavotte in D / Jitterbug waltz / Tara's theme / Downhill drag / Portuguese washerwoman / Unchained melody / Backwoods / Country gentleman / Summers place, Theme from / Slinky / Jessie / Rhythm guitar / Poor people of Paris, The / Dizzy fingers.
Double LP . . . . CR 062
■ MC Set. . . . . CRT 062
Cambra / '83.

HOMETOWN GUITAR.
Tracks: Big Daddy / Sittin' on top of the world / Huntin' boots / Blue guitar / Cattle call / Back to old smokey mountain / Sweet Georgia Brown / Blue angel / Get on with it / Reed's ramble / Pickin' pot pie / Last thing on my mind, The.
LP. . . . . RD 7986
RCA / Feb '70 / BMG.

LEGENDARY PERFORMER VOL 1, THE.
Tracks: Ain'tcha tired of makin' me blue / I've been working on the guitar / Barber shop rag / Chinatown, my Chinatown / Oh, by jingo, oh by gee (you're the only girl) / Tiger rag / Jitterbug waltz / Little bit of blues, A / How's the world treating you / In the pines (medley) / Michelle: Chet's tune.
LP. . . . . PL 12503
■ MC . . . . PK 12503
RCA / '79.

MAN AND HIS GUITAR, A.
Tracks: Not Advised.
LP. . . . . NL 89160
MC . . . . NK 89160
RCA (Germany) / Jan '85 / BMG.

ME AND CHET (see under Reed, Jerry).

ME AND MY GUITAR.
Tracks: Cascade / West Memphis serenade / Long long ago / All thumbs / Vincent / Me and my guitar / Struttin' / You'd be nice to come home to / David's dance / Song for Anna, A (Chanson pour Anna) / My little waltz.
■ LP. . . . . PL 12405
RCA / '79.

NASHVILLE GOLD.
Tracks: Not Advised.
LP. 26 21233
RCA (Germany) / Oct '84 / BMG.

NECK AND NECK (Atkins, Chet & Mark Knopfler).
Tracks: Poor boy blues / Sweet dreams / There'll be some changes made / Just one time / So soft / Your goodbye / Yakety axe / Tears / Tahitian skys / I'll see you in my dreams / Next time I'm in town, The.
CD 4674352
MC 4674354
CBS / Nov '90 / Sony.
■ LP. 4674351
CBS / Nov '90.
MiniDisc 467435-3
Columbia / Feb '93 / Sony.

OTHER CHET ATKINS, THE.
Tracks: Not Advised.
■ LP. . . . . RD 27194
RCA / Mar '61.

OUR MAN IN NAHSVILLE.
Tracks: Scare crow / Alexander's ragtime band / Melissa / Goodnight Irene / Old double shuffle, The / Down home / Always on Saturday / I'll drown in my tears / Spanish harlem / Streamlined cannon ball / House in New Orleans, A / Little bitty tear, A.
■ LP. . . . . SF 7529
RCA / Apr '71 / BMG.

PICKS ON THE BEATLES.
Tracks: I feel fine / Yesterday / If I fell / Can't buy me love / I'll cry instead / Things we said today / Hard day's night, A / I'll follow the sun / She's a woman / And I love her / Michelle / She loves you.
■ LP. . . . . NL 12002
Star Call / Feb '77.

■ DELETED
A 7

POOR BOY BLUES (Atkins, Chet & Mark Knopfler).
Tracks: Poor boy blues.
7" 6563733
CBS / Nov '90 / Sony.

SAILS.
Tracks: Sails / Why worry / Sometime, someplace / Up in my treehouse / Waltz for the lonely / Laffin' at life / On a roll / My song / Wobegon (the way it used to be).
LP 4505041
MC 4505044
CBS / Jun '87 / Sony.

SOLID GOLD GUITAR.
Tracks: White silver sands / Never on Sunday / Freight train / Wheels / Banana boat song / Tammy / Vaya con dios / Blowin' in the wind / Spanish Harlem / Yesterday / Hard day's night, A / And I love her / Things we said today / Love letters / I love how you love me / Sleepwalk / Calcutta / Exodus / Summers place, Theme from) / Stranger on the shore.
MC . . . . INTK 9008
RCA International / Jun '82 / BMG.

STAY TUNED.
Tracks: Sunrise / Please stay tuned / Quiet eyes / Mouse in the house, A / Some leather and lace / Cricket ballet, The / Cosmic square dance / Boot and the stone, The / Tap room / If I should lose you.
LP . . . . CBS 26265
MC 40 26265
CBS / May '85 / Sony.
■ **CD** . . . . CD 26265
CBS / May '85.
CD 473914-2
MC 473914-4
Columbia / Jun '93 / Sony.

STREET DREAMS (Atkins, Chet C.G.P.).
Tracks: Spat 'n' hats / Crystal in the light, The / Official beach music, The / Street dreams / Stay a little longer (if you'll) / Classical gas / Last farewell, The / Alisha / Homecoming anthem, The / Honolulu blues.
LP . . . . CBS 26855
MC 40 26855
CBS / Jun '86 / Sony.

SUPERPICKERS.
Tracks: Paramaribo / Fiddlin' around / Mr. Bojangles / Beef and biscuits / Sweet dreams / Just another rag / Canadian Pacific / City of New Orleans / Bells of St. Mary's / Are you from the Dixie ('cause I'm from Dixie too).
■ **LP** APL1 0329
RCA / '75 / BMG.

TEENSVILLE.
Tracks: Teensville.
■ **7"** . . . . RCA 1174
RCA / Mar '60.

WORK IT OUT.
Tracks: Warm up medley / Grandfather's clock / Jubilo / Swanee river/Humoresque / Climbing up the golden stairs / Goodnight Irene / Walk me home / Strolling medley / Bicycle built for two / Farewell blues / Bye bye blues / Bouree / Streak / Walk don't run / Chase, The / In the good old summertime / Tara's theme / Cross country medley / Take me home country roads / Jersey bounce / On the street where you live / Physical / Army Air Corp song, The / Harlequin romance.
■ **LP** . . . . CBS 24345
CBS / Jul '83.

YAKETY AXE.
Tracks: Yakety axe / Letter edged in black.
7" . . . . RCA 1464
RCA / '65 / BMG.

Auldridge, Mike

Mike Auldridge is a dobro/guitar/steel guitar picker and alongside Jerry Douglas he features at the top of league of modern - day exponents of the dobro. Auldrige's uncle Ellsworth Cozzens, a steel guitarist with 1920s group The Blue & Gray Troubadours, also recorded with and wrote several hit songs for Jimmie Rodgers. Meanwhile Auldrige's main affections lay in the dobro - which apart from appearing on countless country recordings (Emmylou Harris, Linda Ronstadt, Mary-Chapin Carpenter, Peter Rowan, Hank Williams Jr etc) he has guested on the Country Gents' albums. He's a founder member of Washington DC's much respected modern bluegrass band, the Seldom Scene, a unit that's enjoyed 21 successful years. Auldridge's own solo work has appeared on Takoma, Flying Fish and Sugar hill including a 1989 trio affair *High Time* with Scene members Lou Reid and Michael T.Coleman. (Maurice Hope)

AN OLD DOG.
Tracks: Not Advised.
LP . . . . FLY 0004
Flyright / Feb '79 / Hot Shot / Roots Records / Wellard Dist. / Charly / Swift / Projection.

BLUES AND BLUEGRASS.
Tracks: New Camptown races / Mexican rose / Killing me softly / This ain't grass / 8 more miles to Louisville / Sum of Marcy's blues: Bottom dollar, The / Struttin' the blues / Panhandle country / Summertime / Walk don't run / Everybody slides.
■ **LP** . . . . SNTF 641
Sonet / '78 / Swift / C.M. Distribution / Roots Records / Jazz Music / Sonet Records / Cadillac Music / Projection / Wellard Dist. / Hot Shot.

DOBRO.
Tracks: Hillbilly hula / Tennessee stud / It's over / Pickaway / Rolling fog / Dobro island train 451-2 / Take me / Greensleeves / Silver threads / Rockbottom / Jamboree / House of the rising sun.
LP . . . . SNTF 657
Sonet / '74 / Swift / C.M. Distribution / Roots Records / Jazz Music / Sonet Records / Cadillac Music / Projection / Wellard Dist. / Hot Shot.

EIGHT STRING SWING.
Tracks: Little rock getaway / Redskin rag / Bethesada / Swing scene / Caravan / Almost to Tulsa / Bluegrass boogie / Eight string swing / Brown's baggin' / Pete's place / Crazy red top / Stompin at the Savoy (Features on CD only.).
LP . . . . SH 3725
MC . . . . SH 3725 MC
Sugarhill(USA) / '88 / Roots Records / Projection / Impetus Records / C.M. Distribution / Jazz Music / Swift / Duncans / A.D.A Distribution.
CD . . . . SHCD 3725
Sugarhill(USA) / '92 / Roots Records / Projection / Impetus Records / C.M. Distribution / Jazz Music / Swift / Duncans / A.D.A Distribution.

HIGH TIME (Auldridge, Reid & Coleman).
Tracks: Not Advised.
CD . . . . SH 3776CD
LP . . . . SH 3776
MC . . . . SH 3776C
Sugarhill(USA) / '90 / Roots Records / Projection / Impetus Records / C.M. Distribution / Jazz Music / Swift / Duncans / A.D.A Distribution.

MIKE AULDRIDGE.
Tracks: Not Advised.
■ **LP** . . . . FLY 0003
Flyright / Feb '79.
LP . . . . FF 029
Flying Fish (USA) / Mar '89 / Cadillac Music / Roots Records / Projection / C.M. Distribution / Direct Distribution / Jazz Music / Duncans / A.D.A Distribution.

MIKE AULDRIDGE AND OLD DOG.
Tracks: Not Advised.
LP . . . . FF 054
Flying Fish (USA) / Mar '89 / Cadillac Music / Roots Records / Projection / C.M. Distribution / Direct Distribution / Jazz Music / Duncans / A.D.A Distribution.

SLIDIN' SMOKE (Auldridge, Mike & Jeff Newman).
Tracks: Not Advised.
LP . . . . FF 080
Flying Fish (USA) / Mar '89 / Cadillac Music / Roots Records / Projection / C.M. Distribution / Direct Distribution / Jazz Music / Duncans / A.D.A Distribution.

Austin Lounge Lizards

CREATURES FROM THE BLACK SALOON.
Tracks: Golden triangle, The / Hot tubs of tears / Pflugerville / Car Hank died in, The / Swingin' from your crystal chandeliers / Kool whip / We are in control / Didn't go to college / Saquaro / Keeping up with the Jones' / War between the States / Old, fat and drunk / Chester Woolah / Anahuac.
CD . . . . WM 1000
Watermelon / Jun '93 / Topic Records.

HIGHWAY CAFE OF THE DAMNED.
Tracks: Highway Cafe of the Damned, The / Cornhusker refugee / Industrial strength tranquilizer / Wendell, the uncola man / Acid rain / I'll just have one beer / Dallas, Texas / Ballad of Ronald Reagan / When drunks go bad / Jalapeno Maria / Get a haircut Dad / Chester Nimitz oriental garden waltz.
CD . . . . WM 1001
Watermelon / Jun '93 / Topic Records.

Australia

Short-lived working title, during the early 1980's, for Australian twin brothers, Ted and Tom LeGarde, resident in the USA from 1957. They scored a few minor chart successes as the LeGardes (or LeGarde Twins) and, in the early 1990's, were hosting their own Nashville recorded TV series *Country Down Under* for transmission in Australia. (Tony Byworth)

OLD ENGLAND (FOR MOM).
Tracks: Old England (for Mom) / I love the other woman in my life.
7" . . . . MAGIC 6
Magic (2) / Apr '83.

Autry, Gene

Singer/songwriter/musician/actor, born Orvon Gene Autry on September 29, 1907, in Tioga Springs, Texas. Worked as a cowboy and telegraph operator before joining Fields Brothers Medicine Show as saxophonist, then switched to guitar and started singing. Performed on major radio stations' country shows (KVOO, Tulsa, WLS, Chicago National Barn Dance) before making movie debut in *Old Santa Fe* (1934). Starred in over 90 films and launched his very popular Melody Ranch radio shows on CBS in 1940. Sold over 9 million copies of *Rudolph The Red Nosed Reindeer* and over one million each with *Silver Haired Daddy Of Mine* and *Back In The Saddle Again*. The most famous of all Hollywood's singing cowboys, and one of the wealthiest people in show business, Autry has owned several radio stations, record labels, and California Angels baseball team. He was elected into the Country Music Hall Of Fame in 1969. (Tony Byworth)

20 GOLDEN PIECES: GENE AUTRY.
Tracks: Dixie cannonball / My old Kentucky home / Down in the valley / Cowboy blues / Boy from Texas, a girl from Tennesse, A / West a nest and you, The / Don't bite the hand that's feeding you / Missouri waltz / There's no back door to heaven / Kentucky babe / You're the only good thing / When day is done / You are my sunshine / I hang my head and cry / San Antonio rose / Goodbye little darling / Trouble in mind / Lonely river / You're the only star in my blue heaven / Tweedle-o-twill.
LP . . . . BDL 2013
MC . . . . BDC 2013
Bulldog Records / Jul '82 / President Records / Jazz Music / Wellard Dist. / TKO Records Ltd.

AT HIS VERY BEST.
Tracks: You are my sunshine / Dixie cannonball / My old Kentucky home / Missouri waltz / Kentucky baby / Be honest with me / Tweedle-o-twill / You're the only good thing (that's happened to me) / You belong to my heart / Vaya con dios (May God be with you) / South of the border / Goodbye little darlin', goodbye / When day is done / San Antonio rose / Mexicali rose / In a little Spanish town / There's no back door to heaven / You're the only star (in my blue heaven) / Trouble in mind / Someday (you'll want me to want you) / Silver haired Daddy of mine / Last letter, The / Half as much / Blue Canadian Rockies / There's a gold mine in the sky.
■ **MC** . . . . ZCE 6004
Ember / '78 / TKO Records Ltd / President Records.

BACK IN THE SADDLE AGAIN (22 Cowboy Classics).
Tracks: Back in the saddle again / I hang my head and cry / Tears on my pillow / Be honest with me / Goodbye little darlin' / Lonely river / Tweedle-o-twill / Under fiesta stars / Le me cry on your shoulder / Blue canadian rockies / (I was) just walking out the door / Cowboy's trademark / Can't shake the sands of Texas from my shoes / Last mile home / Dixie Cannonball / Cowboy blues / You're the only good thing / Voice in the choir, A / Angel song, The / New star is shining in heaven, A / Silver spurs / Keep rolling lazy longhorns.
CD . . . . PLATCD 25
MC . . . . PLAC 25
Platinum Music / Jul '89 / Prism Leisure PLC / Ross Records.

BEST OF GENE AUTRY.
Tracks: Not Advised.
MC 16-21
Creole (Everest-Europa) / Jul '84.

FAVOURITES.
Tracks: You are my sunshine / I hang my head & cry / Blues stay away from me / San Antonio rose / Tears on my pillow / Be honest with me / Godbye little darlin', goodbye / Hang your head in shame / Trouble in mind / Lonely river / You're the only star / Tweekle-o-twill.
■ **LP** . . . . CW 145
Ember / '78 / TKO Records Ltd / President Records.

GENE AUTRY.
Tracks: Tumbling tumbleweeds / I'll go riding down that old Texas trail / It makes no difference now / There's a new Moon over my shoulder / Amapola / Ridin' down the canyon / Deep in the heart of Texas / Same old fashioned hoedown / Don't fence me in.
LP . . . . CBS 25016
CBS / Sep '82 / Sony.

GENE AUTRY 50TH ANNIVERSARY.
Tracks: Not Advised.
Double LP . . . . RLP 6022 9001
Republic / Jan '79 / RTM / Pinnacle.

LIVE FROM MADISON SQUARE GARDENS.
Tracks: Down yonder / Anytime / My lazy day / Someday you'll want me to want you / Silver haired daddy of mine / Last letter, The / Let me cry on your shoulder / Half as much / Blue Canadian Rockies / I was just walking out the door / Rounded up in glory / There's a goldmine in the sky.
LP . . . . BDL 1024
MC . . . . BDC 1024
Bulldog Records / Jul '82 / President Records / Jazz Music / Wellard Dist. / TKO Records Ltd.

RUDOLF THE RED NOSED REINDEER.
Tracks: Rudolph the red nosed reindeer / Frosty the snowman.
■ **7"** . . . . CBS 4739
CBS / Dec '76.

SINGS SOUTH OF THE BORDER.
Tracks: El rancho grande / You belong to my heart / In a little Spanish town / My adobe hacienda / Under fiesta stars / Vaya con dios / Gay ranchero, A / It happened in

A 8 ■ DELETED

Monterey / Rancho pillow / Mexicali rose / Serenade of the bells / South of the border.
LP. . . . . **BDL 1021**
Bulldog Records / Jul '82 / President Records / Jazz Music / Wellard Dist. / TKO Records Ltd.
MC . . . . **BCD 1021**
President / Oct '92 / Grapevine Distribution / Target Records / Jazz Music / Taylors.

YELLOW ROSE OF TEXAS, THE.
Tracks: Yellow rose of texas / Cattle ranch house on the old Circle B, The / Louisiana moon / Cowboy's heaven / Kentucky lullaby / Black bottom blues / That ramshackle shack / Back home in the blue ridge mountain / Do right daddy blues / Money ain't no use anyway / That's how I got my start / Bear cat papa blues / Don't do me that way / High steppin' mama / There's a good gal in the mountains / My dreaming of you.
LP P.Disc. . . . . **BDP 15204**
Bear Family / Nov '86 / Rollercoaster Records / Swift / Direct Distribution.

Axton, Hoyt

Hoyt Axton, son of Mae Boren Axton who wrote Elvis' monster hit *Heartbreak Hotel*, is a country singer-songwriter/actor of far-reaching proportions. Hoyt, a larger than life character, was born 25.5.1938 in Commanche, Oklahoma and started out as a folk singer in the Fifties. His creations include *Greenback Dollar*, a hit for The Kingston Trio, followed in the seventies with two biggies for rock group Three Dog Night. Namely *Joy To The World* & *Never Been To Spain*. Others to come from the illustrious pen of Axton include *Boney Fingers*, and *When The Morning Comes* (duet with Linda Ronstadt) which were both found on his 1974 album *Life Machine* album on A&M records. Axton also enjoyed considerable commercial success on his own Jeremiah label, with the likes of *Della & The Dealer* & *Rusty Old Halo* in 1979. Between moves, in 1977, Hoyt recorded one album for MCA, *Snowblind Friend*, where he dueted with leading light, Tanya Tucker on *You Taught Me How To Cry*, Axton's rich voice shining. If he'd concentrated more on recording instead of going into the acting he could have reaped more personal success. His most notable films were *The Black Stallion* & the much lauded *Gremlins*. Axton, by now on his mother's well supported DPI label, put out the album *Spin The Wheel*. His songs meanwhile, have been recorded by the likes of Joan Baez, Glen Campbell, John Denver, Waylon Jennings, Ringo Starr and Tanya Tucker. (Maurice Hope)

20 GREATEST HITS: HOYT AXTON.
Tracks: Not Advised.
LP. . . . . **FUN 9048**
MC . . . . **FUNC 9048**
Fun (Holland) / Oct '88 / Pinnacle.

BONEY FINGERS.
Tracks: Boney fingers / Flash of fire.
■ 7" . . . . **AMS 7338**
A&M / Mar '78.

DELLA AND THE DEALER.
Tracks: Della and the dealer / Gotta keep rollin'.
■ 7" . . . . **YB 0082**
Young Blood / Jun '80.
■ 12" . . . . **YB GOLD 82**
Young Blood / Mar '80.

EVERYBODY'S GOIN' ON THE ROAD.
Tracks: Everybody's goin' on the road / Betty La Rue / Boozers are losers / Politicians / You do not tango / Smile as you go by / Where did the money go / Some people ride / Midnight In Memphis / Ease your pain / Battle of New Orleans / House song.
LP. . . . . **YB LP 120**
Young Blood / Jan '82 / Pinnacle.

EVERYBODY'S GOIN' ON THE ROAD.
Tracks: Everybody's goin' on the road / Battle of New Orleans.
■ 7" . . . . **YB 120**
Young Blood / Nov '81.

FEARLESS.
Tracks: Idol of the band / Evangelina / Flash of the fire / Lay / Jealous man / Paid in advance / An old greyhound / Stone and a feather, A / Gypsy moth / Beyond these walls / Penny whistle song / Devil, The.
LP. . . . . **AMLH 64571**
A&M / '88 / PolyGram.

HOTEL RITZ.
Tracks: Hotel Ritz / Evangelina.
■ 7" . . . . **YB 92**
Young Blood / Jul '80.

I LIGHT THIS CANDLE.
Tracks: I light this candle / You taught me how to cry.
■ 7" . . . . **MCA 321**
MCA / Sep '77.

LESS THAN THE SONG.
Tracks: Sweet misery / Less than the song / Sweet fantasy / Days are short / Mary makes magic / Peacemaker / Nothin' to lose / Oklahoma song / Mexico city, hangover / Hungry man / Somebody turned on the light / Blue prelude.

LP. . . . . **AMLH 64376**
A&M / '88 / PolyGram.

LIFE MACHINE.
Tracks: Maybelline / Life machine / That's alright / Geronimo's cadilac / When the morning comes / Good lookin' child / I dream of highways / Pet parade / Telephone booth / Boney fingers / Billie's theme.
LP. . . . . **SP 3604**
A&M / '74 / PolyGram.

ROAD SONGS.
Tracks: No no song / Boney fingers / In a young girl's mind / Telephone booth / Paid in advance / Lion in the winter / I love to sing / When the morning comes / Lay, lady, lay / Sweet misery / Flash of fire / Less than the song.
■ LP. . . . . **AMLH 64669**
A&M / Jan '78.

RUSTY OLD HALO, A.
Tracks: Rusty old halo / Della and the dealer / Hotel Ritz / So hard to give it all up / Evangelina / Torpedo / Viva Pancho Villa / Wild bull rider / In a young girl's mind / Gotta keep rollin'.
LP. . . . . **YBC 800**
Young Blood / Jul '80 / Pinnacle.
■ LP. . . . . **YBLP 800**
Young Blood / Jul '80.
LP. . . . . **MFP 50520**
■ MC . . . . **TCMFP 50520**
MFP / Aug '81.

SNOWBLIND FRIEND.
Tracks: You're the hangnail in my life / Little white moon / Water for my horses / Funeral of the King / I light this candle / Never been to Spain / You taught me how to cry / Snowblind friend / Poncho and lefty / Seven come / I don't know why I love you.
■ LP. . . . . **IMCA 647**
MCA (Import) / Mar '86.

SOUTHBOUND.
Tracks: I love to sing / Southbound / Lion in the winter / Blind fidler / Pride of man / Greensleeves / No no song / Nashville / Speed trap (Out of state cars) / Roll your own / Whiskey / In a young girl's mind / Sometimes it's easy.
LP. . . . . **AMLH 64510**
A&M / '88 / PolyGram.

WILD BULL RIDER.
Tracks: Wild bull rider / Torpedo.
■ 7" . . . . **YB 101**
Young Blood / Sep '80.

B

Backwoods Band

JES' FINE.
Tracks: Not Advised.
LP . . . . **ROUNDER 0128**
Rounder / '88 / Projection / Roots Records / Swift / C.M. Distribution / Topic Records / Jazz Music / Hot Shot / A.D.A Distribution / Direct Distribution.

Baez, Joan

Born in New York in 1941, Joan Baez moved to Boston with her family after leaving school. She taught herself to sing and play guitar and proceeded to make a striking impact at the first Newport Folk Festival in 1959. She met Bob Dylan, a fellow up-and-coming young folk singer, and their two careers became intertwined. As well as developing a deep personal relationship the two toured together. Baez was heavily influenced by Dylan's style of social and political commentary and she began to incorporate her strongly-held views, mainly against war into her own songs. The album *Joan Baez In Concert* issued in 1962, received enthusiastic cult acceptance. As the Dylan-led folk protest movement grew, Baez's music became accepted by a wider audience. In 1964 *Joan Baez In Concert, Vol 2*, was a strong seller, reaching No 8 in Britain with 19 weeks on the chart. Britain was becoming very responsive to her work and '65 saw her score her first UK hit singles, none of the three doing as well in her native America. The Dylan influence was clearly displayed by the choice of two of the songs *We Shall Overcome* (No 26) and *It's All Over Now, Baby Blue*), (No 22). But the biggest hit of the three was Baez's recording of the Phil Ochs' album track, *There But For Fortune*,which took her into the British Top Ten. Although a competent and supple acoustic guitarist, her main strength was her pure, crystal-clear voice. Her singing was technically superb but, being untrained, had an added passion. It was rewarded by no less than three further Top Ten albums in 1965, making Baez one of the biggest-selling American acts in Britain that year. Back at home the politically-motivated singer was making headlines with her pacifist activities. As well as refusing to pay that portion of her taxes estimated to be spent on arms and warfare she founded California's Institute for the Study of Non-Violence. Having been a regular participant in civil rights and peace demonstrations, she married fellow campaigner David Harris in 1968. Both were embroiled in draft-resistance activities, she being sent to prison for two 10-day terms, he being jailed for three years. In 1971, the year Harris and Baez were divorced, she scored her biggest hit on either side of the Atlantic. *The Night They Drove Old Dixie Down*, was her most commercial single, reaching No 3 in the States and, No 6 in Britain. Though continuing her involvement in politics by becoming an active member of Amnesty International, her music was becoming less political. The *Diamonds And Rust Set*, in 1975 was backed by the Crusaders and saw her moving into jazz-rock - it was a strong seller at home but not in Britain, where record sales since *Dixie*, have eluded her. Never enamoured of the trappings of stardom, Baez has continued to record and tour. (Bob MacDonald)

100 MINUTES OF JOAN BAEZ.
Tracks: Not Advised.
MC . . . . **ZCTON 106**
PRT / Jun '82 / BMG.

ANY DAY NOW.
Tracks: Love minus zero / No limit / You ain't goin' nowhere / Drifter's escape / I pity the poor immigrant / Tears of rage / Sad eyed lady of the Lowlands / Love is just a four letter word / I dreamed I saw St. Augustine / Walls of red wing, The / Dear landlord / One too many mornings / I shall be released / Boots of Spanish leather / Walkin' down the line / Restless farewell.
Double LP . . . . **VSD 79306/7**
Vanguard / Complete Record Co. Ltd.
CD Set . . . . **VCD 79306/7**
MC Set . . . . **CVSD 79306/7**
Start / Sep '89.

BALLAD BOOK VOL 2, THE.
Tracks: Not Advised.
CD . . . . **VFCD 7108**
LP . . . . **VFLP 5108**
MC . . . . **VFTC 6108**
Start / Jun '89.

BALLAD BOOK VOL.1, THE.
Tracks: Not Advised.
CD . . . . **VFCD 7106**
LP . . . . **VFLP 5106**
MC . . . . **VFTC 6106**
Start / May '89.

BAPTISM.
Tracks: Not Advised.
CD . . . . **VFCD 7103**
LP . . . . **VFLP 5103**
MC . . . . **VFTC 6103**
Start / Aug '89.

BEST OF JOAN BAEZ.
Tracks: Diamonds and rust / Prison trilogy (Billy Rose) / Never dreamed you'd leave in summer / Please come to Boston / Sweeter for me / Gracias a la vida / Forever young / Simple twist of fate / Love song to a stranger / Children and all that jazz / Imagine / Night they drove old Dixie down, The.
MC Set . . . . **DTO 10078**
Ditto / Mar '84 / Pickwick Records.
LP . . . . **SHM 3173**
MC . . . . **HSC 3173**
Hallmark / Aug '85 / Pickwick Records.
CD . . . . **PWKS 544**
Pickwick / Sep '89 / Pickwick Records.

BEST OF JOAN BAEZ.
Tracks: Not Advised.
CD . . . . **CDMID 108**
MC . . . . **CMID 108**
A&M / Oct '92 / PolyGram.

BLESSED ARE..
Tracks: Blessed are / Night they drove old Dixie down, The / Salt of the earth / Three horses / Brand new Tennessee waltz / Last lonely and wretched / Lincoln freed me today / Outside the Nashville City Limits / San Francisco Mabel Joy / When time is stolen / Heaven help us all / Angeline / Help me make it through the night / Let it be / Put your hand in the hand / Gabriel / And me / Milanese waltz / Marie Flore / Hitchhikers song, The / 33rd of August, The / Fifteen months.
Double LP . . . . **VSD 6570/1**
Vanguard / Complete Record Co. Ltd.

CONTEMPORARY BALLAD BOOK.
Tracks: North country blues / It ain't me babe / Children of darkness / E'era un ragazzo che come me amaya / Beatles E I Rolling stones / I am a poor way faring stranger / Birmingham Sunday / San Francisco Mabel Joy / Be not too hard / Restless farewell / Rangers command / Long black veil / Hickory wind / Lady came from Baltimore, The / I dreamed I saw St. Augustine / Tramp on the street / Saigon bride / Donna Donna / Song in the blood / Magic wood, The / Babe I'm gonna leave you.
Double LP . . . . **VSD 49**
Vanguard / Nov '74 / Complete Record Co. Ltd.

COUNTRY MUSIC.
Tracks: Take me back to the sweet sunny South / Hickory wind / Will the circle be unbroken / Tramp on the street / Carry it on / Gospel ship / Little Moses / Banks of the Ohio / Engine 143 / Pal of mine / Night they drove old Dixie down / Brand new Tennessee waltz / Outside the Nashville city limits / Ghetto, The / My home's across the Blue Ridge Mountains / Rock salt and nails / Help me make it through the night / Long black veil / I still miss someone / San Francisco Mabel Joy.
Double LP . . . . **VSD 79200**
Vanguard / Complete Record Co. Ltd.
Double LP . . . . **VSD 105**
Vanguard / Oct '79 / Complete Record Co. Ltd.

DIAMONDS AND RUST IN THE BULLRING.
Tracks: Diamonds and rust / No woman no cry / Swing low sweet chariot / El preso numero nuevo / Txoria txori / Gracias a la vida / Ain't gonna let nobody turn me round / Famous blue raincoat / Let it be / Llego con tres heridas / Ellas danzan solas (cueca sola) / No nos moveran.
■ **MC** . . . . **TCVGC 9**
Virgin / Jun '89.
■ **LP** . . . . **VGC 9**
Virgin / Jun '89.
CD . . . . **CDVGC 9**
Virgin / Aug '91 / EMI.
■ **MC** . . . . **OVEDC 370**
Virgin / Aug '91.

EUROPEAN TOUR.
Tracks: Boxer, The / Don't cry for me Argentina / Cracias a la vida / Rose / Donna Donna / Diamonds and rust / Jari ya hamoude / Cambodia / Soyuz druzyei / Here's to you / Blowin' in the wind.
■ **LP** . . . . **PRT 84790**
Portrait / Mar '81.

FAREWELL ANGELINA.
Tracks: Farewell Angelina / Daddy, you've been on my mind / It's all over now / Baby blue / Will you go laddie go / Rangers command / Colours / Satisfied mind, A / River in the pines, The / Pauvre rutebeuf / Sagt mir wo die blumen sind / Hard rain's gonna fall.
CD **139 203**
Accord / Jun '84 / Discovery.

FAREWELL ANGELINA.
Tracks: Farewell Angelina.
■ **7"** . . . . **TF 639**
Fontana / Dec '65.

FIRST TEN YEARS.
Tracks: Ghetto, The / If I were a carpenter / Silver dagger / Love is just a four letter word / There but for fortune / Will the circle be unbroken / John Riley / You ain't goin' nowhere / Mary Hamilton / Carry it on / Manha de carnaval / If I knew.
Double LP . . . . **VSD 6560/1**
Vanguard / Complete Record Co. Ltd.
LP **6635 003**
Vanguard / Apr '71 / Complete Record Co. Ltd.

GREATEST HITS:JOAN BAEZ.
Tracks: Night they drove old Dixie down, The / Help me make it through the night / It's all over now, baby blue / If I were a carpenter / Put your hand in the hand / House of the rising sun / Will the circle be unbroken / Let it be / Farewell Angelina / Sagt mir wo die blumen sind.
■ **CD** **811677-2**
IMS / '84.
■ **CD** . . . . **CDA 3234**
A&M / '84.

HITS GREATEST AND OTHERS.
Tracks: Night they drove old Dixie down, The / Dangling conversation, The / Help me make it through the night / Blessed are / Eleanor Rigby / Let it be / There but for fortune / Brand new Tennessee waltz / I pity the poor immigrant / Love is just a four letter word / Heaven help us all.
LP . . . . **VSD 79332**
Vanguard / '73 / Complete Record Co. Ltd.

HONEST LULLABY.
Tracks: Let your love flow / No woman, no cry / Light a light / She sings at the end of the movie / Before the deluge / Honest lullaby / Michael / For Sasha / For all we know / Free at last.
■ **LP** . . . . **PRT 83474**
Portrait / '79.

I'M BLOWIN' AWAY.
Tracks: I'm blowin' away / Luba the Baroness.
■ **7"** . . . . **PRT 5442**
Portrait / Jul '77.

IT AIN'T ME, BABE.
Tracks: Not Advised.
CD . . . . **CD 66120**
MC . . . . **MC 62120**
Ce De International / May '93 / Taylors.

IT'S ALL OVER NOW BABY BLUE.
Tracks: It's all over now baby blue.
■ **7"** . . . . **TF 604**
Fontana / Sep '65.

JOAN BAEZ.
Tracks: Silver dagger / East Virginia / Ten thousand miles / House of the rising sun / All my trials / Wildwood flower / Donna Donna / John Riley / Rake and the rambling boy / Little Moses / Mary Hamilton / Henry Martin / El preso numero nuevo.
LP . . . . **VSD 79073**
Vanguard / Complete Record Co. Ltd.
■ **LP** . . . . **TFL 6002**
Fontana / Jun '65.

JOAN BAEZ BALLAD BOOK, THE.
Tracks: East Virginia / Henry Martin / All my trials / Old blue / House of rising son / Wagoner's lad / Black is the colour of my true love's hair / Lily of the west / Silkie / House carpenter / Trees they do grow high, The / 10,000 miles / Barbara Allen / Jackaroe / John Riley / Matty Groves / Queen of hearts / Fe-nario / Go way from my window / Railroad boy / Mary Hamilton / Once I had a sweetheart / Silver dagger.
Double LP . . . . **VSD 41-2**
Vanguard / Complete Record Co. Ltd.

JOAN BAEZ IN CONCERT.
Tracks: Not Advised.
LP . . . . **VSD 79112**
Vanguard / Apr '71 / Complete Record Co. Ltd.
Double LP . . . . **VSD 23007/8**
Musidisc / Jun '84 / Revolver-APT / Discovery.

JOAN BAEZ IN CONCERT.
Tracks: Not Advised.
VHS . . . . **OGV 0007**
Old Gold / Oct '90 / Pickwick Records.

JOAN BAEZ IN CONCERT VOL.2.
Tracks: Once I had a sweetheart / Jackaroe / Don't think twice / We shall overcome / Portland Town / Queen of hearts / Manha de carnaval / Te ador / Long black veil / Fennario / Ne belle cardillo / With God on our side / Three fishers / Hush little baby / Battle Hymn of the republic.
LP . . . . **VSD 79113**
Vanguard / Complete Record Co. Ltd.
■ **LP** . . . . **TFL 6033**
Fontana / Jul '64.

JOAN BAEZ ON VANGUARD.
Tracks: Not Advised.
■ **LP** . . . . **SVXL 100**
Vanguard / Jul '69.

JOAN BAEZ VOL. 1.
Tracks: Not Advised.
CD . . . . **VFCD 7101**
Start / Oct '88.

JOAN BAEZ VOL. 2.
Tracks: Not Advised.
CD . . . . **VFCD 7102**
Start / Oct '88.

JOAN BAEZ VOL.5.
Tracks: There but for fortune / Stewball / It ain't me babe / Death of Queen Jane, The / Child No.170 / Bachianas Brasileires No.5 -Aria / Go 'way from my window / I still miss someone / When you hear them cuckoos hollerin' / Birmingham Sunday / So we'll go no more a- roving / O'Cangaceiro / Unquiet grave, The / Child No. 78.
LP . . . . **VSD 79160**
Vanguard / Complete Record Co. Ltd.
■ **LP** . . . . **TFL 6043**
Fontana / May '65.

JOAN BAEZ: IN CONCERT.
Tracks: Not Advised.
VHS . . . . **SVM 807**
Start (Video) / Nov '92 / Sony Video Software.

LIVE EUROPE '83'.
Tracks: Not Advised.
CD **610.586**
LP **206.742**
MC **205 742**
Ariola / Dec '88 / BMG.

LOVE SONGS: JOAN BAEZ.
Tracks: Come all ye fair and tender maidens / No limit / Sweet Sir Galahad / Love is just a four letter word / Wild mountain thyme / Lass from the low country, The / Sad eyed lady of the lowlands / Plaisir d'amour.
Double LP . . . . **VSD 79**
MC . . . . **ZC VSD 79**
Vanguard / Oct '76 / Complete Record Co. Ltd.

NIGHT THEY DROVE OLD DIXIE DOWN.
Tracks: Night they drove old dixie down, The / Brand new Tennessee waltz / Outside the Nashville City limits / Ghetto, The / My home's across the blue ridge mountains / Rock salt and nails / Help me make it through the night / Long black veil / I still miss someone / San Francisco Mabel Joy.
CD . . . . **VFCD 7104**
Start / Sep '88.
LP . . . . **VFLP 5104**
MC . . . . **VFTC 6104**
Start / Aug '89.

NIGHT THEY DROVE OLD DIXIE DOWN.
Tracks: Night they drove old Dixie down, The / There but for fortune.
■ **7"** . . . . **VS 35138**
Vanguard / Oct '71.
7" . . . . **FBS 12**
Flashback / Jan '83.

NIGHT THEY DROVE OLD DIXIE DOWN (OLD GOLD).
Tracks: Night they drove old Dixie down, The / We shall overcome.
7" . . . . **OG 9931**
Old Gold / Jan '90 / Pickwick Records.

NO WOMAN NO CRY.
Tracks: Not Advised.
CD **15 450**
MC **79 450**
Laserlight / Jun '92 / TBD / Taylors.

NOEL.
Tracks: Not Advised.
CD . . . . **VFCD 7107**
Start / Oct '88.
LP . . . . **VFLP 5107**
MC . . . . **VFTC 6107**
Start / Aug '89.

ONE DAY AT A TIME.
Tracks: Sweet Sir Galahad / No expectations / Long black veil / Ghetto, The / Carry it on / Take me back to the sweet sunny south / Seven bridges road / Jolie blonde / Joe Hill / Song for David / One day at a time.
LP . . . . **VSD 79310**
Vanguard / Complete Record Co. Ltd.

PACK UP YOUR SORROWS.
Tracks: Pack up your sorrows.
■ **7"** . . . . **TF 727**
Fontana / Jul '66.

PLAY ME BACKWARDS.
Tracks: Play me backwards / Amsterdam / Isaac and Abraham / Stones in the road / Steal across the border / I'm with you / I'm with you (reprise) / Strange rivers / Through your hands / Dream song,The / Edge of glory.
CD . . . . **CDV 2705**
LP . . . . **V 2705**
MC . . . . **TCV 2705**
Virgin / Aug '92 / EMI.

QUEEN OF HEARTS.
Tracks: Not Advised.
CD . . . . **CD 66107**
MC . . . . **MC 62107**
Ce De International / May '93 / Taylors.

RECENTLY.
Tracks: Brothers in arms / Recently / Asimbonanga / Moon is a harsh mistress, The / James and the gang / Let us break bread together / MLK / Do right woman, do right man / Biko.
CD . . . . **CDVGC 1**
LP . . . . **VGC 1**
■ **MC** . . . . **TCVGC 1**
Goldcastle / May '88.
LP . . . . **OVED 354**
MC . . . . **OVEDC 354**
Goldcastle / Mar '91 / EMI / Projection.

SPEAKING OF DREAMS.
Tracks: China / Warriors of the sun / Carrickfergus / Hand to mouth / Speaking of dreams / El Salvador / Rambler gambler / Whispering bells / Fairfax county / A mi manera (Only on CD and MC.).
■ **MC** . . . . **TCVGC 12**
Goldcastle / '90.
■ **LP** . . . . **VGC 12**
Goldcastle / '90.
CD . . . . **CDVGC 12**
Goldcastle / Aug '91 / EMI / Projection.
■ **MC** . . . . **OVEDC 371**
Goldcastle / Aug '91.

SPOTLIGHT ON JOAN BAEZ.
Tracks: There but for fortune / Lady came from Baltimore, The / Suzanne / Don't think twice / All my trials / We shall overcome / It's all over now baby blue / Farewell Angelina / It ain't me babe / If I were a carpenter / Joe Hill / Long black veil / Love's just a four letter word / Love minus zero / No limit / Blessed are / What have they done to the rain / I shall be released / Sagt Mir wo die blumen sind / Night they drove old Dixie down, The / Eleanor Rigby / Donna Donna / Colours / Let it be / Hush little baby.
Double LP . . . . **SPOT 1008**
MC . . . . **ZCSPT 1008**
PRT / '80 / BMG.

THERE BUT FOR FORTUNE.
Tracks: There but for fortune.
■ **7"** . . . . **TF 587**
Fontana / Jul '65.

THERE BUT FOR FORTUNE (OLD GOLD).
Tracks: There but for fortune / It's all over now baby blue.
7" . . . . **OG 9933**
Old Gold / Jan '90 / Pickwick Records.

VERY EARLY JOAN.
Tracks: Last night I had the strangest dream / Willie Moore / She's a trouble maker / Tears in my eyes / Somebody got lost in a storm / Water is wide, The / Man of constant sorrow / Freight train / Lady Gay / Johnny Cuckoo / Lonesome valley / Riddle song, The / Streets of Laredo / Railroad Bill / My good old man / Little darlin' / In the pines / Pilgrim of sorrow / Where have all the flowers gone / Rambler gambler / Come all ye fair and tender maidens / Hallowed be thy name / Twelve gates to the city / Silver dagger.
Double LP . . . . **VSD 79436**
MC Set . . . . **ZCVS 79436**
Vanguard / Jan '83 / Complete Record Co. Ltd.

WE SHALL OVERCOME.
Tracks: We shall overcome.
■ **7"** . . . . **TF 564**
Fontana / May '65.

WHERE ARE YOU NOW MY SON.
Tracks: Not Advised.
■ **LP** . . . . **AMLS 64390**
A&M / '73.

WHERE HAVE ALL THE FLOWERS GONE.
Tracks: Not Advised.
CD **352136**
MC **252136**
Duchesse (Holland) / Sep '93 / Pinnacle / Taylors.

Bailey Brothers

JUST AS THE SUN WENT DOWN.
Tracks: Not Advised.
LP . . . . **ROUNDER 0056**
Rounder / '88 / Projection / Roots Records / Swift / C.M. Distribution / Topic Records / Jazz Music / Hot Shot / A.D.A Distribution / Direct Distribution.

TAKE ME BACK TO HAPPY VALLEY.
Tracks: Not Advised.
LP . . . . **ROUNDER 0030**
Rounder / '88 / Projection / Roots Records / Swift / C.M. Distribution / Topic Records / Jazz Music / Hot Shot / A.D.A Distribution / Direct Distribution.

Bailey, Deford

Deford Bailey the harmonica player was born in 1899 near Nashville Tennessee. He was slightly handicapped by polio as a child and became the very first musician to play his *Pan American Blues* on the WSM (Nashville) radio show in 1927 which was soon dubbed the Grand Ole Opry. For many years he was the only black who had ever appeared on the show. He got $5 a performance and was sacked in 1941 when the show was beginning to tour and make films. His records included eight sides for Victor in 1928, mostly blues. Deford Bailey may have been the first artist to record in Nashville. (Donald Clarke)

HARMONICA SHOWCASE (Bailey, Deford & D.H. 'Bert' Bilbro).
Tracks: Not Advised.
LP . . . . **MSE 218**
Matchbox / Oct '85 / Roots Records / C.M. Distribution / Projection.

Bailey, Razzy

The country/pop singer, Razzy Bailey was born in 1939 in Alabama. He formed his first band in his teens and spent almost 20 years on the honky-tonk circuit. He was produced by Freddie Weller at ABC Records in 1969, but recorded for several labels and wrote hit songs for others, for example Dicky Lee's *'9,999,999 Tears*, in 1976 before having his own successes on RCA from 1978,and more recently on MCA. (Donald Clarke)

FEELIN' RIGHT.
Tracks: She left love all over me / I've had my limit (of two timing women) / Blaze of glory / Travellin' time / Night life / Bad news look / Everytime you cross my mind (you break my heart) / Sittin' here wishing (I was someplace else) / I loved 'em all / Your momma and daddy sure did something right.
LP . . . . **INTS 5216**
MC . . . . **INTK 5216**
RCA International / '82 / BMG.

MAKIN' FRIENDS.
Tracks: Friend's too far gone and much too close to you / Scratch my back and whisper in my ear / Best kept secret in town, The / Spending my nights with you / Midnight hauler / Blind faith and the naked truth / Anywhere there's a duke box / Old no Homer / Late night honky tonk country song.
LP . . . . **RCALP 5051**
MC . . . . **RCAK 5051**
RCA / Jul '81 / BMG.

RAZZY BAILEY.
Tracks: What time do you have to be back to heaven / If love had a face / Too old to play cowboy / True life country music / There's really nothing to it / What's a little love between friends / Wifey / Is it over / I ain't got no business today / Tonight she's gonna love me / Loving up a storm / I can't get enough of you / Let's go find some country music / I keep coming back / That's the way a cowboy rocks and rolls / 9,999,999 tears.
LP . . . . **PL 43482**
RCA / Apr '81 / BMG.

SHE LEFT LOVE ALL OVER ME.
Tracks: She left love all over me / Blaze of glory.
■ **7"** . . . . **RCA 204**
RCA / Apr '82.

STILL GOING STRONG.
Tracks: Still going strong / Suzie Q / Mona Lisa / Loki / Lover please come back / Let the good times roll / Linda Lu / Pretend / Sunshine / High heel sneakers.
LP . . . . **SDLP 049**
Sundown / Jul '87 / Terry Blood Dist. / Jazz Music / C.M. Distribution.

Baker, Carroll

Born in Bridgewater, Nova Scotia, her recording career kicked off in 1970 on the Gaiety label and was voted Canada's top female country singer 5 years later. Hosted her own CBC-TV series *Sounds Good Country*, she switched to RCA in 1976. Although she's yet to achieve success in U.S.A., she has been seen in Britain on several occasions. (Tony Byworth)

ALL FOR THE LOVE OF A SONG.
Tracks: It's snowing outside / Brand new tears / Time you're the healer / Breaking and entering / Here I am / It's only make believe / Burning up your memory / Still falling in love / This is it / Ev'ry good song is a bad song.
■ **LP** . . . . **RCALP 5012**
RCA / May '81.

B 2

■ DELETED

AT HOME IN THE COUNTRY.
Tracks: Death and taxis / Slowly / Such a true love / You've lost that lovin' feeling / If you only knew / I fall for that feeling / She's in love with the radio / First comes the fire / As long as we both shall live / Dreamin' ain't cheatin'.
LP	. TMT 4333
■ MC	TMK 4333
Tembo / Mar '88.

CARROLL BAKER.
Tracks: You've never been this far before / Hungry fire of love, The / Picture in my mind / One is one too many (and a thousand's not) / Why me / One night of cheatin' (ain't worth reapin') / Tonight with love / Gone, gone, gone (revolving man) / Why I had to pass this way / Like you touched me.
■ LP	PL 10171
RCA / '79.

HEARTBREAK TO HAPPINESS.
Tracks: I found a l-i-e in the middle of believe / I'm an old rock'n'roller (dancin' to a different beat) / Too late for the two of us / You are my everything / Arms that love (hearts that don't) / It always hurts like the first time / Star in momma's eyes, A / You still excite me / I'm taking care of myself / If you can't stand the heat don't light the fi / Anything but hearts.
LP	TMB 109
■ MC	TMBC 109
Tembo / Feb '86.

HOLLYWOOD LOVE.
Tracks: My turn / It wasn't me / Second time around / Fooling my senses / Hollywood love / I know I can / Play your steel guitar for me / God I'm sorry / Tarnished wedding band / Deeper than the eye can see / I'll live in dreams / Just a closer walk with thee / How great Thou Art.
■ LP	PL 43061
RCA / Apr '80.

IF IT WASN'T FOR YOU.
Tracks: If it wasn't for you / Me and Bobby McGhee / Hooked on a feeling / Born winner / We got nothin' / Don't touch me / I'm getting high remembering / Let me be your woman / I'm so lonesome I could cry / Build my life around you.
■ LP	PL 42770
RCA / Feb '79.

IT ALWAYS HURTS LIKE THE FIRST TIME.
Tracks: It always hurts like the first time.
7"	TML 113
Tembo / Mar '86 / PolyGram.

SWEET SENSATION.
Tracks: It's my party / Portrait in the window / I can't stop loving you / Love's golden rule / It's late (and I have to go) / Who's gonna love me when the morning comes / Morning after baby let me down, The / Slow / Sweet sensation / I might as well believe (I'll live forever).
LP	PL 43414
■ MC	PK 43414
RCA / '79.

Baker, Kenny

BAKER'S DOZEN, A
LP	CO 730
Country Records / '78 / Country Records (USA)

DARKNESS ON THE DELTA (Baker, Kenny and Bobby Hicks)
LP	CO 782
MC	CO 782MC
Country Records / '82 / Country Records (USA)

FARMYARD SWING
Tracks: Lost indian /Bean blossom /Chickens under the back porch /Blue mountain waltz /Old Kentucky home /Dailey's reel /Indian creek /Arkansas traveller /Georgianna moon /Smokey mountain /Rag /Farmyard swing /Paddy on the turnpike.
LP	CO 775
MC	CO 775MC
Country Records /'80 /Country Records (USA)

HIGHLIGHTS
Tracks: Tom and Jerry /A and E reel /Rooster dog /Beautiful dreamer /Nova Scotia breakdown /Goldrush, The /Tee totaller's reel /Bobby Van's hornpipe /Call of the shepherd /Last train to Durham /Whispering hope /Tune for Andy.
LP	CO 785
MC	CO 785MC
Country Records / '84 / Country Records (USA)

HIGH COUNTRY (Baker, Kenny and Joe Greene)
LP	CO 714
Country Records /'77 /Country Records (USA)

PLAYS BILL MONROE (Baker, Kenny and Bill Monroe)
LP	CO 761
MC	CO 761MC
Country Records /'80 /Country Records (USA)

PORTRAIT OF A BLUEGRASS FIDDLER
LP	CO 719
MC	CO 719MC
Country Records /'79 /Country Records (USA)

Balfa Brothers

The Balfa Brothers are Cajun musicians who have helped preserve Louisiana music. The Balfa Brotherhood consisted of Dewey, Burkeman, Harry, Rodney and Will, (the latter of the two were killed in a car crash in 1979). They learned old songs from their father, a fiddler, and became accomplished on traditional Cajun instruments: accordion, fiddle, guitar, harmonica, petit fer (triangle) and spoons. They were also influenced by Harry Choates, Leo Soileau and Bob Willis. The Balfa Brothers played and recorded with Nathan Abshire as well as in their own right.However,cajun musicians do not make a good living, no matter how influential; Dewey also ran a furniture business before his death on June 17, 1992. (Donald Clarke)

ARCADIAN MEMORIES.
Tracks: 'Tit galop pour mamou / Drunkars's sorrow waltz / Lacassine special / Indian on a stomp / T'ai petite et t'ai meon / Two step a Hadley / Valse de Balfa / Pealez nous a boure / Two step de l'anse a Paille / Enterre moi pas / La valse de grand bois / T'en as eu mais t'en n'auras plus / Je suis Orphelin / J'ai passe devant ta porte / Madeleine / La danse de Mardi Gras.
LP	CHD 183
Ace / Nov '86 / Pinnacle / Hot Shot / Jazz Music / Complete Record Co. Ltd.
MC	CHDC 183
Ace / Sep '90 / Pinnacle / Hot Shot / Jazz Music / Complete Record Co. Ltd.

CAJUN DAYS.
Tracks: Don't bury me / Drunkard's waltz, The / Think of me once a day / La valse du Charley de Blanc / Old fashioned two-step / Fruge waltz, The / Shoepick two-step / Prison blues / Black bayou two-step / Tit yeux noir / Bayou malle / Midnight special.
LP	SNTF 813
Sonet / Jun '80 / Swift / C.M. Distribution / Roots Records / Jazz Music / Sonet Records / Cadillac Music / Projection / Wellard Dist. / Hot Shot.

CAJUNS VOL. 1 (see under Abshire, Nathan).

J'AI VU LE LOUP, LE RENARD ET LA BELETT.
Tracks: Not Advised.
LP	ROUNDER 6007
MC	ROUNDER 6007C
Rounder / '88 / Projection / Roots Records / Swift / C.M. A.D.A Distribution / Topic Records / Jazz Music / Hot Shot / A.D.A Distribution / Direct Distribution.

LOUISIANA CAJUN MUSIC.
Tracks: Not Advised.
LP	ARHOOLIE 5019
Arhoolie (USA) / May '81 / Pinnacle / Cadillac Music / Swift / Projection / Hot Shot / A.D.A Distribution / Jazz Music.
MC	C 5019
Arhoolie (USA) / '88 / Pinnacle / Cadillac Music / Projection / Hot Shot / A.D.A Distribution / Jazz Music.

MORE TRADITIONAL CAJUN MUSIC.
Tracks: Not Advised.
LP	6019
MC	6019 TC
Swallow (USA) / Swift / Wellard Dist.

NEW YORK CONCERTS PLUS, THE.
Tracks: Not Advised.
CD	CDCHD 338
Ace / Oct '91 / Pinnacle / Hot Shot / Jazz Music / Complete Record Co. Ltd.

NEW YORK CONCERTS, THE.
Tracks: Not Advised.
LP	6037
MC	6037 TC
Swallow (USA) / '87 / Swift / Wellard Dist.

TRADITIONAL CAJUN MUSIC.
Tracks: Not Advised.
LP	6011
MC	6011 TC
Swallow (USA) / Sep '87 / Swift / Wellard Dist.

TRADITIONAL CAJUN MUSIC VOLS. 1 & 2.
Tracks: Drunkard's sorrow waltz / Lacassine special / My true love / La valse de Grand Bois / Family waltz / Newport waltz / Indian on a stomp / T'ai petite et t'ai meon / Two step a Hadley / Valse de Balfa / Pealez nous a boire / Les blues de cajun / 'Tit galop pour mamou / Je suis Orphelin / T'en as eu mais t'en n'auras plus / Two step de l'anse a paille / La danse de Mardi Gras / Je me suis Marilie / Enterre moi pas / Chere joules roses / Chere bassette / J'ai passe devant ta porte / Les flames d'enfer / Madeleine.
CD	CDCHD 955
Ace / Nov '90 / Pinnacle / Hot Shot / Jazz Music / Complete Record Co. Ltd.

Balfa, Dewey

Traditional cajun fiddler/vocalist, son of Charles, a tenant farmer on Bayou Grand Louie, Louisiana. He has played since the age of 12 with his family and then in 1946 as the Balfa Freres or Dewey Balfa and his Musical Brothers. The group had their own radio programme on KSLO, and were the first cajun group to appear at the Newport Folk Festival (1964). They recorded for Swallow, Arhoolie, Sonet and Cezame (French). Dewey was also an occasional member of the Louisiana Aces, during the seventies. Alongside other traditional cajun contemporaries Marc Savoy (accordion player and instrument maker) and D.L. Menard, he recorded the album Underneath The Cajun Oak Tree , and also did some work on Swallow with accordionist Nathan Abshire. Dewey died of cancer on June 17, 1992 but his children and brothers still strive to keep their rich musical heritage alive. (Maurice Hope)
Tracks: Not Advised.

FAIT A LA MAIN (Balfa, Dewey & Friends).
Tracks: Not Advised.
MC	6063 TC
Swallow (USA) / '87 / Swift / Wellard Dist.
LP	6063
Swallow (USA) / Jun '87 / Swift / Wellard Dist.

SOUVENIRS.
Tracks: Not Advised.
LP	6056
Swallow (USA) / Swift / Wellard Dist.
MC	6056 TC
Swallow (USA) / '87 / Swift / Wellard Dist.

SOUVENIRS & FAIT A LA MAIN (Balfa, Dewey & Friends).
Tracks: Not Advised.
CD	CDCHD 328
Ace / Jul '91 / Pinnacle / Hot Shot / Jazz Music / Complete Record Co. Ltd.

Ball, Marcia

Born Marcia Mouton in Orange, Texas in 1950 she had a brief association with Capitol in 1978 resulting in one chart single I'm a Fool to Care. She now lives in Austin where she is one of the city's leading performers releasing her western swing style records on independent labels-.(Tony Byworth)

HOT TAMALE BABY.
Tracks: Not Advised.
LP	REU 1012
Rounder Europa (USA) / Mar '87 / Pinnacle.
CD	CD 3095
LP	ROUNDER 3095
MC	ROUNDER 3095C
Rounder / '88 / Projection / Roots Records / Swift / C.M. Distribution / Topic Records / Jazz Music / Hot Shot / A.D.A Distribution / Direct Distribution.

SOULFUL DRESS.
Tracks: Not Advised.
LP	ROUNDER 3078
MC	ROUNDER 3078C
Rounder / '88 / Projection / Roots Records / Swift / C.M. Distribution / Topic Records / Jazz Music / Hot Shot / A.D.A Distribution / Direct Distribution.

Ball, Tom

BLOODSHOT EYES (Ball, Tom & Kenny Sultan).
Tracks: Not Advised.
LP	FF 386
Flying Fish (USA) / May '88 / Cadillac Music / Roots Records / Projection / C.M. Distribution / Direct Distribution / Jazz Music / Duncans / A.D.A Distribution.
CD	FF 386CD
MC	FF 386C
Flying Fish (USA) / Feb '93 / Cadillac Music / Roots Records / Projection / C.M. Distribution / Direct Distribution / Jazz Music / Duncans / A.D.A Distribution.

GUITAR MUSIC.
Tracks: Not Advised.
LP	KM 185
Kicking Mule / '92 / Roots Records / Swift / Projection / C.M. Distribution / Impetus Records / Ross Records / Duncans.

TOO MUCH FUN (Ball, Tom & Kenny Sultan).
Tracks: Not Advised.
CD	FF 532CD
LP	FF 532
MC	FF 532C
Flying Fish (USA) / '92 / Cadillac Music / Roots Records / Projection / C.M. Distribution / Direct Distribution / Jazz Music / Duncans / A.D.A Distribution.

WHO DRANK MY BEER (Ball, Tom & Kenny Sultan).
Tracks: Not Advised.
LP	KM 176

Kicking Mule / '92 / Roots Records / Swift / Projection / C.M. Distribution / Impetus Records / Ross Records / Duncans.

Ballew, Michael

Texas born Michael served his apprenticeship working the honky tonks of the Lone Star State, before heading out West to California where he eventually recorded for a series of labels, including Liberty, giving him a couple of hits in the early 1980's. A decade later the enterprising Bear Family label released 22 of his finest songs under the title *I Love Texas* . (Tony Byworth)

I LOVE TEXAS.
Tracks: Music is sweet, The / Greatest Texas song, The / Glenda Pearl / Ain't no future / I love Texas / Blue water / Country music / Rodeo cool / Hot spot / Lovin' me / Cheatin' / Take it slow / My family / Your daddy don't live in heaven / Pretending fool / Seminole County Jail / Crazy dreams / Dark side of the dancefloor / As precious as you are / Women love, love out there / Hazelwood Avenue.
CD . . . . **BCD 15669**
Bear Family / Jun '92 / Rollercoaster Records / Swift / Direct Distribution.

Band Of Blacky Ranchette

BAND OF BLACKY RANCHETTE.
Tracks: Not Advised.
LP . . . . **ROSE 62**
New Rose (1) / Jun '85 / Pinnacle.

CODE OF..
Tracks: Code of..
7" . . . . **NEW 62**
New Rose (1) / Pinnacle.

HEARTLAND.
Tracks: Heartland / Moon over Memphis / All done in / Badlands / Roof's on fire / Underground train / Nowhere / Steadfast / One way ticket / Changing heart.
LP . . . . **ZONG 014**
Zippo / Sep '86 / Swift / Pinnacle / RTM / C.M. Distribution.

SAGE ADVICE.
Tracks: Loving cup / Burning desire / Trouble man / Dreamville, New Mexico / Indiosa / Wild dog waltz / Sage advice / Outside an angel's reach (3 6ixes) / Shards of time / Still too far / Blanket of stars / You are my sunshine.
CD . . . . **FIEND CD 181**
LP . . . . **FIEND 181**
Demon / May '90 / Pinnacle.

Bandy, Moe

The honky-tonk country singer was born in 1944 in Meridian, Mississippi. His grandfather had worked on the railroad with Jimmie Rodgers. Moe had a TV series with his own band in San Antonio, Texas; he went solo in 1972 and his national USA country hits began in 1974 with *I Just Started Hatin' Cheatin' Songs Today'*: for a while he specialised in cheatin' songs, including *Honky Tonk Amnesia*, *It Was Always So Easy To Find An Unhappy Woman* and *Doesn't Anybody Make Love At Home Anymore*. Following an appearance with Joe Stampley at Wembley in London they formed a duo; Moe and Joe have had hit albums and singles and have always been popular in the UK. (Donald Clarke)

CHAMP, THE.
Tracks: Champ, The / Cowboy's a kitten at home, The / Wild side of life / Beethoven was before my time / Giver took all she could stand, The / Yesterday once more / I just can't leave those honky tonks alone / She took out the outlaw in me / Like some good ol' boy / Accidentally on purpose tonight.
LP . . . . **CBS 84426**
MC . . . . **.40 84426**
CBS / Aug '80 / Sony.

COUNTRY STORE: MOE BANDY.
Tracks: Champ, The / Yesterday once more / You're gonna lose her / She's not really cheatin' / Wild side of life, The (Only on CD.) / My woman loves the devil out of me (Only on CD.) / Where's the dress / Jambalaya / Still on a roll / Don't sing me no songs about Texas / Your cheatin' heart (Only on CD.) / Hank and Lefty raised my country soul (Only on CD.).
CD . . . . **CDCST 29**
MC . . . . **CSTK 29**
Country Store / '88 / BMG.
■ **LP** . . . . **CST 29**
Country Store / '88.

COWBOY'S AIN'T SUPPOSED TO CRY.
Tracks: Cowboy's ain't supposed to cry / Till I stop needing you.
■ **7"** . . . . **CBS 6425**
CBS / Jun '78.

COWBOYS AIN'T SUPPOSED TO CRY.
Tracks: Cowboy's ain't supposed to cry / She finally rocked you out of my mind / Up to now I wanted everything but you / Misery loves company / Why don't you love me / She just loved the cheatin' out of me / No deal / All I can handle at home / Till I stop needing you / I could never be ashamed of you.
LP . . . . **CBS 82295**
MC . . . . **CBS 82295 MC**
CBS / '77 / Sony.

DEVOTED TO YOUR MEMORY.
Tracks: Let's get over them together / One more port / Devoted to your memory / Don't sing me no songs about Texas / You're gonna lose her like that / Barroom is my battleground tonight / Country side / Someone like you / She's looking good.
■ **LP** . . . . **CBS 25552**
CBS / Nov '83.

FOLLOWING THE FEELING.
Tracks: Following the feeling / Today I almost stopped loving you / Would you mind if I just called you Julie / Mexico winter / Liquor emotion / My woman loves the devil out of me / It's you and me again / I've got your love all over me / If I lay down the bottle / It's better than being alone.
LP . . . . **CBS 84891**
CBS / Apr '81 / Sony.

GOOD OL' BOYS - ALIVE AND WELL, THE (Bandy, Moe & Joe Stampley).
Tracks: Where's the dress / He's back in Texas / Honky tonk money / Wild and crazy guys / We've got our moe-joe workin' / Boy's night out / Daddy's honky tonk / Wildlife sanctuary / Alive and well / Still on a roll.
LP . . . . **CBS 26068**
■ **MC** . . . . **.40 26068**
CBS / Aug '84.

HEY JOE, HEY MOE (Bandy, Moe & Joe Stampley).
Tracks: Honky tonk queen / Girl don't ever get lonely / I'd rather be a pickin' / Drinkin' dancin' / Drunk front / Hey Joe, hey Moe / Country boys / Let's hear it for the workin' man / Get off my case / Two beers away.
■ **LP** . . . . **CBS 84966**
CBS / Jun '81.

I CAN STILL LOVE YOU IN THE SAME OL' WAY.
Tracks: I can still love you in the same ol' way / I took a princess home with me / City boy / One lonely heart lead to another / Early Nancy / I lost her to a Dallas cowboy / What Chicago took from me / Leave the honky tonks alone / Drivin' my love back to you / Monday night cheatin'.
■ **LP** . . . . **CBS 25296**
CBS / Apr '83.

I LOVE COUNTRY.
Tracks: Barroom is my battleground tonight, The / Wound time can't erase, A / Barroom roses / There's nobody home on the range / That's as close to cheatin' as I came / Yippi cry yi / Yesterday once more / Two lonely people / Soft lights and Hard Country Music / Jambalaya / One of a kind / Barstool mountain / It's a cheating situation / Would you mind if I just called you Julie / My woman loves the devil out of me / I cheated me right out of you.
■ **LP** **4504291**
CBS / Mar '87.
■ **MC** **4504294**
CBS / Mar '87.

I'M SORRY FOR YOU, MY FRIEND.
Tracks: I'm sorry for you, my friend / Someone I can forget / Lady came from the country (Of eleven hundred springs), The / So much for you, so much for me / All the beer and friends are gone / Four letter fool, A / High inflation blues / Does fort worth ever cross your mind / She's an angel / She's everbody's woman, I'm nobody's man.
LP . . . . **CBS 82003**
MC . . . . **.40 82003**
CBS / '77 / Sony.

IT'S A CHEATING SITUATION.
Tracks: It's a cheating situation / Barstool mountain / Cheaters never win / Conscience where were you / Try my love on for size / To cheat or not to cheat / She stays in the name of love / It just helps to keep the hurt from hurtin' / When my working girl comes home / They haven't made the drink.
■ **LP** . . . . **CBS 83552**
CBS / '79.

IT'S A CHEATING SITUATION (Bandy, Moe & Janie Frickie).
Tracks: It's a cheating situation / Try my love on for size.
■ **7"** . . . . **CBS 7217**
CBS / Apr '79.

JUST GOOD OL' BOYS (Bandy, Moe & Joe Stampley).
Tracks: Just good ol' boys / Make a little love each day / Tell Ole I ain't here, he better get on home / Honky tonk man / Partner's in rhyme / Holding the bag / Bye bye love / Only the names have been changed / When it comes to cowgirls / Thank goodness it's Friday.
■ **LP** **84012**
CBS / Feb '80.

LIVE FROM BAD BOB'S (Bandy, Moe & Joe Stampley).
Tracks: We've got our moe joe working / Hey joe / Daddy's honky tonk / Holding the bag / Boy's night out / Tell ole i ain't here he better get on home / Where's the dress / Your cheatin' heart / Still on a roll / Just good ol' boys.
LP . . . . **CBS 26364**
CBS / May '85 / Sony.

LOVE IS WHAT LIFE IS ALL ABOUT.
Tracks: Love is what life is all about / Ghost of a chance / I guess I had a real good time last night / Bic flicking baby / For tears to come / Two lonely people / Jambalaya / Mom and dad's waltz / I never miss a day / Yippy cry yi.
■ **LP** . . . . **CBS 83174**
CBS / Feb '79.

MOTEL MATCHES.
Tracks: Motel matches / Woman your love / Beauty lies in the eyes of the beholder / Don't start me cheatin' again / That horse that you can't ride / It took a lot of drinkin' / Lovin' it up / In Mexico / Your memory always finds it's way home / Texas Saturday night.
■ **LP** . . . . **CBS 25927**
CBS / May '84.

ONE OF A KIND.
Tracks: I cheated me right out of you / One of a kind / Gonna honky tonk right out on you / Bitter with the sweet / We start the fire / In the middle of losing you / Tell her it's over / Sweet Kentucky woman / Honky tonk merry go round / Man of means.
■ **LP** . . . . **CBS 84145**
CBS / Apr '80.

SHE'S NOT REALLY CHEATIN' (SHE'S JUST GETTIN' EVEN).
Tracks: She's not really cheatin' / He's taking my place at your place / Can I pick you up / Hank and Lefty raised my country soul / All American dream, The / Only if there is another you / Our love could burn Atlanta down again / Your memory is showing all over me / Angel like you, An / Jesus in a Nashville jail.
LP . . . . **CBS 85868**
CBS / Jul '82 / Sony.

SINGS 20 GREAT SONGS OF THE AMERICAN COWBOY.
Tracks: Home on the range / I'm an old cowhand / Back in the saddle again / Streets of Laredo / Old faithful / Don't fence me in / San Antonio rose / Deep in the heart of Texas / Oklahoma hills / When it's springtime in the rockies / Take me back to Tulsa / Red river valley / Cool water / Sioux City Sue / Tumbling tumbleweeds / Bury me not on the lone prairie / High noon / Good old paint / Strawberry roan, The / Old Chisholm trail, The.
MC . . . . **PLAC 3907**
Platinum Music / Jul '89 / Prism Leisure PLC / Ross Records.
CD . . . . **PLATCD 3907**
Platinum Music / '90 / Prism Leisure PLC / Ross Records.

SOFT LIGHTS AND HARD COUNTRY MUSIC.
Tracks: Soft lights and hard country music / Darling, will you marry me / Paper chains / This haunted house / If she keeps loving me / That's what makes the juke box play / There's nobody home on the range anymore / Are we making love of just making friends / Wound time can't erase, A / Baby and a sowing machine, A.
LP . . . . **CBS 82669 LP**
MC . . . . **CBS 82669**
CBS / '78 / Sony.

TWENTY GREAT SONGS OF THE AMERICAN COWBOY.
Tracks: Springtime in the rockies / Red river valley / Take me back to Tulsa / Bury me not on the lone prairie / Don't fence me in / Tumbling tumbleweeds / San Antonio rose / I'm an old cowhand / Oklahoma hills / Old faithful / Home on the range / Sioux City Sue / Deep in the heart of Texas / Cool water / Good old paint / Back in the saddle again / Streets of Laredo / High noon / Strawberry roan, The / Old Chisholm trail, The.
LP . . . . **WW 5118**
MC . . . . **WW 4 5118**
Warwick / Mar '82 / Sony / Henry Hadaway Organisation / Multiple Sound Distributors.

WHERE'S THE DRESS? (Bandy, Moe & Joe Stampley).
Tracks: Where's the dress / Wild life sanctuary.
7" . . . . **A 4641**
CBS / Aug '84 / Sony.

YOU HAVEN'T HEARD THE LAST OF ME.
Tracks: One man band / I forgot that I don't live here anymore / Sunny side of you, The / Times I tried to love you, The / You can't straddle the fence anymore / Till I'm too old to die young / Ridin' her memory down / Between us / You haven't heard the last of me / Rodeo Song.
LP . . . . **IMCA 5914**
MCA / Mar '87 / BMG.
MC . . . . **IMCAC 5914**
Polygram T.V / Mar '87 / PolyGram.

Banjo Express

OLD TIME COUNTRY MUSIC.
Tracks: Not Advised.
CD . . . . **PV 710 781**
Pierre Verany (France) / '88 / Kingdom Records.

B 4

■ DELETED

Barbary Coast

CLEAN UP.
Tracks: Last ride, The / Rollin' on / Take me home truck / Toe the line / Many roads I ride / Truck driver's blues / Trucker's life, A / God bless the trucker's bike / Rockabilly trucker / Breaker's blues.
LP. . . . . KO 1013
MC . . . . TC KO 1013
Champ / '82 / Champ Records.

COASTLINES.
Tracks: Did it rain / Fool such as I, A / Leave them with a smile / Living on sunshine / Give my love to Rose / If this is just a game / Blowin' away / You only live once in a while / Old five and dimers like me / Long gone.
LP. . . . . KO 1004
Champ / '82 / Champ Records.

FISTFUL OF ROSES.
Tracks: Not Advised.
LP. . . . . BSS 184
Tank / Jun '79.

HEARTS ON FIRE (ROCK MIX).
Tracks: Hearts on fire (rock mix).
7" . . . . BCAJ 001
MDE / Apr '84 / MDE Records.

LONG VEHICLE.
Tracks: Son of a son of a trucker / Ridin' rubber / Move on down the road / Don's cafe / Keep those wheels a rollin' / High rollin' lonesome / Truck stop woman / Queen of the road / Joe's rig road / Reversing song, The / Pedal to the metal.
LP. . . . . KO 1008
MC . . . . TC KO 1008
Champ / '82 / Champ Records.

Bare, Bobby

The country singer-songwriter was born in 1935 in Ohio. He recorded his own song *All American Boy* at his own expense weeks before joining the US Army, sold it for $50 and it became a no.2 pop hit credited to Bill Parsons in 1958. He has subsequently become a legend, his album-orientated career also including many hit singles, and such great songs as the Grammy winning *Detriot City* in 1964. He also helped the careers of such artists as Kris Kristofferson, Waylon Jennings, Ian Tyson, Shel Silverstein, Rodney Crowell and Guy Clark, and has made over 40 albums. (Donald Clarke)

20 OF THE BEST: BOBBY BARE.
Tracks: All American boy / Detroit City / 500 miles away from home / Four strong winds / Millers cave / It's alright shame on me / Streets of Baltimore / Come kiss me love / Charleston railroad tavern / Have I stayed away too long / Piney wood hills / Find out what's happening / You know who / I hate goodbyes / Winner, The / Singing in the kitchen / Daddy what if / Where'd I come from.
MC . . . . INTK 5187
RCA International / Aug '82 / BMG.
■ LP. . . . . INTS 5187
RCA International / Aug '82.
MC . . . . NK 89332
RCA / '84 / BMG.
■ LP. . . . . NL 89332
RCA / '84.

AIN'T GOT NOTHIN' TO LOSE.
Tracks: Ain't got nothin' to lose / Candle in the wind / Old swimmin' hole / Isn't that just like love / Goodnight Irene / Golden memories / I've been rained on too / Cold day in hell / So good to so bad / Praise the lord and send me the money.
LP. 85504
CBS / Jun '88 / Sony.

AS IS.
Tracks: Dollar pool fool / Learning to live again / Call me the breeze / Take me as I am / Let him roll / New cut road / She is gone / Dropping out of sight / Summer wages / White freight liner blues.
■ LP. . . . . CBS 84989
CBS / Aug '81.

BEST OF BOBBY BARE.
Tracks: Detroit city / It's all right / Four strong winds / Miller's cave / I'd fight the world / Times are gettin' hard / All-American boy / Shame on me / 500 miles away from home / Dear waste-basket / He was a friend of mine / When the wind blows (in Chicago).
■ LP. . . . . LSA 3004
RCA / '78 / BMG.
LP. . . . . COLT 2001
MC . . . . COLTK 2001
Nightflite / Aug '87.

BETTER NOT LOOK DOWN.
Tracks: Better not look down / Wait until tomorrow.
7" . . . . EA 217
EMI-America / May '86 / EMI.

BIGGEST HITS OF BOBBY BARE.
Tracks: Tequila Shelia / Till I gain control again / Learning to live again / Let him roll / Greasy grit gravy / Numbers / Take me as I am / Big Dupree / New cut road / Goin' back to Texas / Sleep tight goodnight man / Too many nights alone / Healin' / Food blues / Willie Jones / Dropping out of sight.
■ LP. . . . . CBS 32303
CBS / Apr '83.

BOBBY BARE (I Love Country).
Tracks: Gambler, The / Jogger, The / Last time, The / Numbers / Tequila Sheila / Let him roll / Goin' up's easy, comin' down's harder / Praise the Lord and send the money / Goodnight Irene / I've never gone to bed with an ugly woman / Food blues / Desperados waiting for the train / Three legged man / Finger on the button / Greasy grit gravy / Big dupree / Yard full of rusty cars / Too many nights alone / Childhood hero / February snow / This guitar is for sale / Sing for the song.
LP. . . . . CBS 32095
MC 40 32095
CBS / Nov '81 / Sony.
■ LP. . . . . CBS 54950
CBS / Mar '87.
■ MC 40 54950
CBS / Mar '87.

BOBBY BARE SINGS LULLABYS, LEGENDS & LIES.
Tracks: Lullabys, legends and lies / Paul / Marie Lavaau / Daddy what if / Wonderful soup stones, The / Winner, The / In the hills of Shiloh / She's my ever lovin' machine / Mermaid, The / Rest awhile / Bottomless well / True story / Sure hit songwriters pen / Rosalie's good eat's cafe.
■ LP. AFL1 0290
RCA / '75 / BMG.
CD . . . . BCD 15683
Bear Family / Apr '93 / Rollercoaster Records / Swift / Direct Distribution.

CHARLESTON RAILROAD TAVERN.
Tracks: Charleston railroad tavern / Vicennes.
■ 7" . . . . RCA 1591
RCA / Feb '71 / BMG.

CITY BOY.
Tracks: Fool / Fallen star, A / Hello darlin' / Lonely street / Under it all / Crazy arms / Alabama rose / High and dry / City boy country born / New York City snow / Leaving on a jet plane.
Double LP . . . . CR 5153
■ MC Set . . . . CRT 5153
Cambra / Apr '85.

COUNTRY STORE: BOBBY BARE.
Tracks: Way I feel tonight, The / Gambler, The / Goodnight Irene / If you ain't got nothing / Jogger, The / Till I gain control again / Drinkin' from the bottle / Desperados waiting for the train (Only on CD.) / Call me the breeze (Only on CD.) / Take me as I am or let me go / Tequila Sheila / Too many nights alone / I'm not a candle / Numbers / She is gone / Praise the Lord and send the money / New cut road (Only on CD.) / Some days are diamonds (Only on CD.).
CD . . . . CDCST 28
MC . . . . CSTK 28
Country Store / '88 / BMG.
■ LP. . . . . CST 28
Country Store / '88.

COUNTRY SUPERSTARS (Bare, Bobby & Don Williams).
Tracks: Not Advised.
CD 100 036
Bridge (MCS Bridge) / '86 / Pinnacle.

DETROIT CITY.
Tracks: Not Advised.
LP. 26.21212
RCA (Germany) / Oct '84 / BMG.

DOWN AND DIRTY.
Tracks: Good for nothing blues / Numbers / Some days are diamonds / Tequila Sheila / Rock star's lament / Crazy again / Tecumseh Valley / Blind Willie Harper / Rough on the living / Down to my last come and get me / Qualudes again / Goin' back to Texas / I can't watch the movie anymore.
LP. . . . . CBS 84132
CBS / Mar '80 / Sony.

DRINKIN' FROM THE BOTTLE..
Tracks: Jogger, The / Easy as dreaming / Rodeo queen / Me and Jimmy Rodgers / Three legged man / Diet song / Jennifer Johnson and me / Drinkin' from the bottle / Some place to come when it rains / Stacy Brown got two / Time.
■ LP. 25470
CBS / Dec '83.

DRUNK AND CRAZY.
Tracks: Drunk & crazy / Food blues / World's last truck drivin' man / I can almost see Houston from here / If that ain't love / Rock and roll hotel / Song of the south / Appaloosa rider / Bathroom tissue paper letter / Willie Jones / Gotta get rid of this band / I've never gone to bed with an ugly woman / Desperados waiting for the train.
MC 40 84643
CBS / Dec '80 / Sony.
■ LP. . . . . CBS 84643
CBS / Jan '81.

FAMOUS COUNTRY MUSIC MAKERS.
Tracks: Daddy what if / Sunday mornin' down / You made a believer out of me / Dropkick me Jesus (through the goalposts of life) / Wonderful soup stone, The / Bird named yesterday, A / Vegas / High plains jamboree / They covered up the old swimmin' hole / Woman in every man's life, The / Up against the wall / If you think I'm crazy / Amarillo highway / Great snowman, The / Red-neck hippie / Don't turn out the light / Somebody bought my old home town / Chester / (There was a) tall oak tree / Ride me down easy / Salt Lake City / Marie Laveau / Faster horses / Long black veil / Vince / Old gang's gone, The / Put a little lovin' on me / Little bit later on down the line / Hillbilly hell / Jackson / Back home in Huntsville again / I've got a thing about trains / Last dance at the Texas Moon / One among the three of us / Singer of sad songs / Wilma Lou / Cowboys and daddies / Alimony / Air conditioner song, The.
Double LP . . . . PL 42958
RCA / BMG.

FIND OUT WHAT'S HAPPENING.
Tracks: Find out what's happening / When am I ever gonna settle down / Little bit later on down the line, A / Don't do like I done son.
■ 7" . . . . RCA 1723
RCA / Aug '71 / BMG.
■ 7" . . . . RCA 1690
RCA / Feb '71 / BMG.

HARD TIMES HUNGRYS.
Tracks: Hard times hungrys / Farmer feeds us all, The / Alimony / Two for a dollar / Back home in Huntsville again / Daddy's been around the house too long / Warm and free / Able bodied man / $100,000 in pennies / Bottles and boxes / Truck driver, truck driver / Unemployment line, The.
■ LP. . . . . LSA 3231
RCA / '75 / BMG.

I'VE NEVER GONE TO BED WITH AN UGLY WOMAN.
Tracks: I've never gone to bed with an ugly woman / If that ain't love / Numbers / Bathroom tissue paper letter.
■ 7" . . . . A 1026
CBS / May '81.

LATER ON DOWN THE LINE.
Tracks: Later on down the line.
7" . . . . RC 1723
RCA / '68 / BMG.

LITTLE BIT LATER ON DOWN THE LINE, A.
Tracks: Not Advised.

LULLABYS, LEGENDS AND LIES.
Tracks: Lullabys, legends and lies / Paul / Marie Laveau / Daddy what if / Winner, The / In the hills of Shiloh / She's my ever lovin' machine / Mermaid, The / Rest awhile / Bottomless well / Wonderful soup stone, The / True story / Sure hit songwriters pen / Rosalie's good eats cafe.
LP. . . . . NL 89998
■ MC . . . . NK 89998
RCA / Jan '87.

MERCURY YEARS 1970-72, THE.
Tracks: That's how I got to Memphis / Come sundown / I took a memory to lunch / I'm her hoss if I never win a race / Woman you've been a friend to me / It's freezing in El Paso / Mrs. Jones your daughter cried all night / Don't it make you wanna go home / Mary Ann regrets / Leaving on a jet plane / Fool, The / Waitress in the Main Street cafe, The / Please don't tell me how the story ends / How about you / Help me make it through the night / Rosalie / Dropping out of sight / Where have all the flowers gone / Travelling minstrel man / For the good times / Hello darlin' / Alabama rose / World is weighing heavy on my mind, The / Mama bake a pie (papa kill a chicken) / Coal river / Christian soldier / Don't you ever get tired of hurting me / West Virginia woman / New York City snow / Jesus is the only one that loves us / Loving her was easier / I need some good news bad / Me and Bobby McGee / Million miles to the city, A / Just the other side of nowhere / City boy, country born / Short and sweet / Puppet and the parakeet, The / Great society talking blues / Year that Clayton Delaney died, The / Roses are red / Lonely street / Crazy arms / Jesus Christ, what a man / Fallen star, A / That's alright / Pamela Brown / When I want to love a lady / Love forever / Darby's castle / Lot of soul, A / Just in case / What am I gonna do / When love is gone / Lorena / Don't ask me, ask Marie / Laying here lying in bed / Take some and give some / Sylvia's mother / Footprints in the snow / Lord, let a lie come true / Under it all / Are you sincere / Even the bad times are good / High and dry / She gave her heart to Jethro / Music City, U.S.A.
CD Set . . . . BCD 15417
Bear Family / Dec '87 / Rollercoaster Records / Swift / Direct Distribution.

MORE TUNES FOR TWO (Bare, Bobby & Skeeter Davis).
Tracks: Your husband my wife / Before the sunrise / True love you'll never find, A / I'm so afraid of losing you again / Dream baby / My elusive dreams / Let's make love not war / I got you / Jackson / There was never a time.
LP. . . . . INTS 5055
RCA International / Nov '80 / BMG.

MUSIC CITY USA.
Tracks: Not Advised.
MC 441624-4
Pilz / Dec '92 / BMG.

NUMBERS.
Tracks: Numbers / When hippies get older.
■ 7" . . . . CBS 8245
CBS / Mar '80.

SINGIN' IN THE KITCHEN.
Tracks: Singin' in the kitchen / Monkey and the elephant, The / Lovin' you anyway / Where'd I come from / Ricky ticky song / Giving tree, The / You are / Unicorn, The / Cloudy sky / She thinks I can / Scarlet ribbons / See that bluebird.
■ LP . . . . LSA 3198
RCA / '75 / BMG.

SLEEP TIGHT GOODNIGHT MAN.
Tracks: Sleep tight goodnight man / Hot afternoon.
■ 7" . . . . CBS 7117
CBS / '79.

SLEEPER WHEREVER I FALL.
Tracks: Sleep tight, goodnight man / Hot afternoon / What did it get me / Goin' up's easy, comin' down's harder / Way I feel tonight / Healin' / Love is a cold wind / I'll feel a whole lot better / Last time, The / On a real good night.
■ LP . . . . CBS 83533
CBS / Apr '79.

STREETS OF BALTIMORE, THE.
Tracks: Early mornin' rain / Houston / Saginaw / Michigan / Take me home to Mama / Memphis Tennessee / Streets of Baltimore / That's how I wanted it to be / Vicennes / Cold and lonely city / Changin' my mind / There ain't no fun in this town / Green, green grass of home.
■ LP . . . . RD 7862
RCA / Feb '71 / BMG.

TEQUILA SHEILA.
Tracks: Tequila Sheila / Gotta get rid of this band (Only on 12" single.) / Call me the breeze / Sleep tight, goodnight man (Only on 12" single.)
12" . . . . A 13 1618
■ 7" . . . . A 1618
CBS / Sep '81.

THIS IS BARE.
Tracks: Not Advised.
Double LP 26 28046
RCA (Germany) / Oct '84 / BMG.

TOO MANY NIGHTS ALONE.
Tracks: Too many nights alone / Yard full of rusty cars.
■ 7" . . . . CBS 6319
CBS / Jul '78.

TUNES FOR TWO (Bare, Bobby & Skeeter Davis).
Tracks: Dear John letter, A / Too used to being with you / In the misty moonlight / We'll sing in the sunshine / I don't care / True love / Love you / (We must have been) Out of our minds / Let it be me / Together again / That's all I want from you / Invisible tears.
LP . . . . LSA 3252
RCA / BMG.
■ LP . . . . RD 7711
RCA / Oct '69 / BMG.

Barefoot Jerry

A successor to pioneering Nashville group Area Code 615, this innovative group comprised Nashville session musicians such as Wayne Moss (guitar), Charlie Mccoy (harmonica), Si Edwards (drums) and Russell Hicks (steel guitar) and recorded spasmodically during the period 1971-76. (Tony Byworth)

WATCHING TV.
Tracks: Not Advised.
LP . . . . TAKE 2
Houdini / Jan '80.

YOU CAN'T GET OFF WITH YOUR SHOES ON.
Tracks: You can't get off with your shoes on / Cades Cove.
■ 7" . . . . MNT 3276
Monument / Oct '75.

Barlow, Randy

One-time Dick Clark Caravan Of Stars MC, this Detroit singer enjoyed modest success in the 1970's and early 1980's, with Sweet Melinda being his highest placed single (No. 10: 1979). (Tony Byworth)

ARRIVAL.
Tracks: Not Advised.
■ LP . . . . JULEP 5
Mint / Aug '77.

FALL IN LOVE WITH ME.
Tracks: No sleep tonight / Our honeymoon has never ended / Singing the blues / One more time / One of the great love affairs / Fall in love with me tonight / It should've been me / Burning bridges / Little bird fly home / Slow and easy.
■ LP . . . . SHU 8526
London-American / Mar '79.

NO SLEEP TONIGHT.
Tracks: No sleep tonight / Slow and easy.
■ 7" . . . . HLU 10562
London-American / Sep '78.

Barnes, Kathy

Born in Henderson, Kentucky, she first sang in a duo with brother Larry before working with Gene Autry and signing with his Republic Records. Achieved modest success in mid 1970s, included a couple of rhythm and blues records that made the U.S. soul charts in 1978. (Tony Byworth)

BODY TALKIN'.
Tracks: I'm in it for the love / Paradise island / Something's burning / When I need you / I'm in love with you / Off / Your eyes give you away / Loving arms / After you / It's not the spotlight / You make me feel it again.
■ LP . . . . SHU 8525
London-American / Mar '79.

I'M IN LOVE WITH LOVE.
Tracks: I'm in love with love / Mr.Dreamweaver.
■ 7" . . . . HLU 10560
London-American / Aug '78.

Barnes, Max D.

Born in Hardscratch, Iowa, he has enjoyed far greater success as a songwriter than a singer, with 1989 CMA Song of the Year Chiseled In Stone, (co-written with Vern Gosdin) being among his many successes. (Tony Byworth)

PIECES OF MY LIFE.
Tracks: Not Advised.
LP . . . . NOLA LP 17
No Label / Apr '79 / Fast Forward Distribution.
■ LP . . . . DBWLP 1005
Country Roads Records / Nov '81.

SHE LOVES MY TROUBLES AWAY.
Tracks: She loves my troubles away / Givin' out from givin' in.
■ 7" . . . . CRE 007
Country Roads Records / Aug '81.

Barreta

BARRETA.
Tracks: Not Advised.
LP . . . . BSS 212
Tank / '77.

Barrett, Al Linemen

DEEP WATER.
Tracks: Miles of Texas / Heart, The / Rodeo clown man / Drifter / Faded lover / Pure love / Sweet dreams / Why ask why / Deep water / Desperation.
MC . . . . TC KO 1006
Champ / '82 / Champ Records.

DON'T GET AROUND MUCH ANYMORE.
Tracks: Rollin' with the flow / Do you right tonight / When loves goes wrong / Don't get around much anymore / Harder times / Vincent / I changed everything but my mind / Two dollars in the jukebox.
LP . . . . KO 1012
MC . . . . TC KO 1012
Champ / '82 / Champ Records.

OPEN COUNTRY.
Tracks: Muddy Mississippi line / Take me / I still miss someone / Hawaiian wedding song / Everything a man could ever need / Break my mind / Dear God / I fall to pieces / Truck driving man / Twelfth of never / Last thing on my mind / Crazy / Try a little kindness / Buckaroo.
LP . . . . SFA 026
Sweet Folk All / '81 / Cadillac Music / Projection / C.M. Distribution / Wellard Dist. / Impetus Records.

OPEN COUNTRY - VOL.2.
Tracks: See you in the windshield / Drinking again / Corina Corina / Streets of Laredo / Pop a top / I forget you everyday / Streets of Baltimore / Drinking champagne / Back of my hand / Games people play / Every fool has a rainbow / Where love used to live.
LP . . . . SFA 045
Sweet Folk All / '81 / Cadillac Music / Projection / C.M. Distribution / Wellard Dist. / Impetus Records.

Barrie, J.J.

Canadian J.J. Barrie is a true one-hit wonder in the UK - one chart-topper and nothing else, ever. Following Tammy Wynette's 1975 hits Stand By Your Man and D.I.V.O.R.C.E., Barrie figured that a remake of another Wynette country hit might chart in Britain. He recorded a husky-voiced version of No Charge, a saga of a parent-child discussion containing more sugar than a Tate and Lyle refinery. J.J. Barrie has released numerous singles since his one week of No 1 fame, but none have surfaced in the charts. (Bob MacDonald)

BUENOS DIAS SENORITA.
Tracks: Buenos dias senorita / Borsche boogie.
7" . . . . MON 031
Monarch / '82 / Pinnacle.

CALL MY NAME.
Tracks: Call my name / Why did you have to go and do it / Say goodbye to my life / Lady singer with a country music band / First goodnight, The / Save me / While the feeling's good / Sunday morning blues / Deanna Yates / I don't love you anymore.
LP . . . . PL 25161
MC . . . . PK 25161
RCA / '78 / BMG.

CALL MY NAME.
Tracks: Call my name / Lady singer with a country music band.
■ 7" . . . . PB 5101
RCA / '79.

CHRISTMAS.
Tracks: Christmas / You look like an angel.
■ 7" . . . . PB 5126
RCA / Oct '78.

CHRISTMAS (J.J. BARRIE).
Tracks: Christmas / Sssscrooge xmas.
7" . . . . MON 028
Monarch / '81 / Pinnacle.

ESPECIALLY FOR YOU.
Tracks: Not Advised.
LP . . . . JJB 1
MC . . . . ZCJJB 1
Starblend / '84.

FORTY AND FADING.
Tracks: Not Advised.
LP . . . . MAGIC 10
Magic (2) / '83.

I LOVE YOU.
Tracks: I love you / Late night movies.
■ 7" . . . . PX 259
Power Exchange / May '77.

I'M JUST FALLING IN LOVE AGAIN.
Tracks: I'm just falling in love again / Who told the band to pack.
7" . . . . MON 029
Monarch / '82 / Pinnacle.

IF I COULD ONLY LOVE YOU ONCE MORE.
Tracks: If I could only love you once more / In love with you.
7" . . . . MAGIC 5
Magic (2) / '83.

LOVE 'N' COUNTRY.
Tracks: Not Advised.
LP . . . . MON LP 027
Monarch / '82 / Pinnacle.

MY SON.
Tracks: Why did you have to go and do it.
LP . . . . MAGIC LP 3
MC . . . . MAGIC C 3
Magic (2) / '83.

MY SON.
Tracks: My son / Why did you have to go and do it.
7" . . . . MAGIC 9
Magic (2) / '83.

NO CHARGE.
Tracks: No charge / It's a crying shame.
■ 7" . . . . PX 209
Power Exchange / Apr '76.
■ 7" . . . . CHOP 104
Chopper / Mar '81.
■ 7" . . . . MAGIC 100
Magic (2) / '85.

SINGS SONGS FROM FRAGGLE ROCK.
Tracks: Not Advised.
LP . . . . PIPLP 712
MC . . . . ZCPIP 712
Cherry Lane / '84 / Cherry Lane Productions.

SO LONG BING.
Tracks: So long Bing / How many times.
■ 7" . . . . EMI 2727
EMI / Nov '77.

TOP TEN FOOL.
Tracks: Top ten fool / She don't wanna play house today / Send me no roses / Till you're loving me again.
■ EP . . . . PXE 100
Power Exchange / Feb '77.

WHERE'S THE REASON.
Tracks: Where's the reason / Lucille.
7" . . . . MAGIC 1
Magic (2) / '83.

WHILE THE FEELINGS GOOD.
Tracks: While the feelings good.

YOU CAN'T WIN 'EM ALL.
Tracks: You can't win 'em all / I'll have to say I love you in a song / Where's the reason / I just fall in love again / Walk away from me / Bottle of gin / You look like an angel.
■ LP . . . . PL 25294
RCA / Jul '80.

YOU CAN'T WIN 'EM ALL.
Tracks: You can't win 'em all / It's only a game.
■ 7" .... **MCA 658**
MCA / Nov '80.

YOU CAN'T WIN 'EM ALL (SINGLE) (2).
Tracks: You can't win 'em all / Together.
■ 7" .... **PB 5222**
RCA / Jan '80.

Bashful Brother Oswald

Musician and vocalist, Bashful Brother Oswald was born Ray Beecher Kirby in Sevier County, Tennessee. Lifetime member of Roy Acuff's Smoky Mountain Boys, since it's early beginnings - taking over from Cousin Jody in 1938 - when called the Crazy Tennesseans. A big favourite with Grand Ole Opry, working as straight old-time dobroist, distinctive harmony vocalist, comic, and banjo picking hillibilly. Own recordings include work with fellow Smoky Mountain Boy guitarist Charlie Collins - on Rounder during the 1970s. (Maurice Hope)

BASHFUL BROTHER OSWALD.
Tracks: Not Advised.
LP .... **SLP 192**
MC .... **GT 5192**
Starday (USA) / Apr '87 / Crusader Marketing Co.

BROTHER OSWALD.
Tracks: Not Advised.
LP .... **ROUNDER 0013**
Rounder / '88 / Projection / Roots Records / Swift / C.M. Distribution / Topic Records / Jazz Music / Hot Shot / A.D.A Distribution / Direct Distribution.

DON'T SAY ALOHA.
Tracks: Not Advised.
LP .... **ROUNDER 0080**
MC .... **ROUNDER 0080C**
Rounder / '88 / Projection / Roots Records / Swift / C.M. Distribution / Topic Records / Jazz Music / Hot Shot / A.D.A Distribution / Direct Distribution.

OZ AND CHARLIE (Bashful Brother Oswald & Charlie Collins).
Tracks: Mountain dew / Indian killed the woodcock / Homestead on the farm / Hilo march / Nobody's darling but mine / Stoney point / Black smoke / Oswald's special / Polly wolly doodle / Hills of old Kentucky / Snowflake reel / Mother, the queen of my heart / Loo Loo's nest / What a friend we have in Jesus.
LP .... **ROUNDER 0060**
MC .... **ROUNDER 0060C**
Rounder / '88 / Projection / Roots Records / Swift / C.M. Distribution / Topic Records / Jazz Music / Hot Shot / A.D.A Distribution / Direct Distribution.

THAT'S COUNTRY (Bashful Brother Oswald & Charlie Collins).
Tracks: Not Advised.
LP .... **ROUNDER 0041**
MC .... **ROUNDER 0041C**
Rounder / '88 / Projection / Roots Records / Swift / C.M. Distribution / Topic Records / Jazz Music / Hot Shot / A.D.A Distribution / Direct Distribution.

Battin, Skip

DON'T GO CRAZY.
Tracks: Not Advised.
LP .... **AP 034**
Appaloosa / '83 / Roots Records / C.M. Distribution / Wellard Dist. / Projection / Hot Shot / A.D.A Distribution.

NAVIGATOR.
Tracks: Not Advised.
LP .... **AP 014**
Appaloosa / '82 / Roots Records / C.M. Distribution / Wellard Dist. / Projection / Hot Shot / A.D.A Distribution.

Bayne, Pam

BORDER COUNTRY (Bayne, Pam & Phil).
Tracks: Not Advised.
LP .... **NA 104**
MC .... **NC 104**
Neptune / Apr '78 / Neptune Tapes / A.D.A Distribution.

Beausoleil

Louisiana cajun band, formed in 1976 by Michael Doucet and his brother, David - who like Michael is involved in other ventures . Beausoleil were originally given their chance by Floyd Solieau of Swallow records in 1977. Apart from this their work has appeared on Arhoolie, Rhino, Rounder and in UK on Ace. Michael with his band Cajun Brew also recorded the Rounder albums *Hot Cajun Rhythm 'N' Blues* and *Bayou Cadillac* , where blues slide guitarist/producer Sonny Landreth is in attendance. David is a hightly adept acoustic guitarist and vocalist, playing cajun in a Appalachian finger-style akin to Doc Watson, backed by Beausoliel. He recorded what's said to be the first ever cajun guitar based album *Quand J'Ai Parti* . Doucet and Co. were brought to the attention of wider audience in 1991, when Mary-Chapin Carpenter used them on her Grammy winning hit *Down At The Twist And Shout*, along with some select dates/TV appearances, including appearing with Carpenter and her band at the CMA's 1991 awards show. (Maurice Hope)

ALLONS A LAFAYETTE.
Tracks: Not Advised.
LP .... **ARHOOLIE 5036**
MC .... **C 5036**
Arhoolie (USA) / '88 / Pinnacle / Cadillac Music / Swift / Projection / Hot Shot / A.D.A Distribution / Jazz Music.
CD .... **ARH 308**
Arhoolie (USA) / '92 / Pinnacle / Cadillac Music / Swift / Projection / Hot Shot / A.D.A Distribution / Jazz Music.

ALLONS A LAFAYETTE & MORE.
Tracks: Not Advised.
CD .... **ARHCD 308**
Arhoolie (USA) / Mar '93 / Pinnacle / Cadillac Music / Swift / Projection / Hot Shot / A.D.A Distribution / Jazz Music.

BAYOU BOOGIE.
Tracks: Zydeco gris gris / Fais pas ca / It's you I love / Dimanche apres-midi / Madame Bozo / Kolinda / Maman Rosin Boudreaux / Chez Seychelles / Jongle a moi / Flame will never die, The / La vaise de malchanceaux / Beausoleil boogie.
LP .... **REU 1027**
Rounder Europa (USA) / Aug '87 / Pinnacle.
CD .... **CD 6015**
LP .... **ROUNDER 6015**
MC .... **ROUNDER 6015C**
Rounder / '88 / Projection / Roots Records / Swift / C.M. Distribution / Topic Records / Jazz Music / Hot Shot / A.D.A Distribution / Direct Distribution.

CAJUN CONJA.
Tracks: Not Advised.
CD .... **FIENDCD 704**
Demon / Sep '91 / Pinnacle.

DANSE DE LA VIE.
Tracks: Danse de la vie / Dans le Grand Brouillard / L'ouragon / Dis-moi pas / Jeunes filles de la campagne / Quelle belle vie / R.D. special / Chanson pour Ezra / Menage a trois reels / Zydeco X / Je tombe aux Genoux / Attrape mes larmes / La fille de quatorze ans.
CD **812271221-2**
MC **812271221-4**
Atlantic / Jun '93 / WEA.

HOT CHILI MAMA (Beausoleil & Michael Doucet).
Tracks: Not Advised.
CD .... **ARHCD 5040**
MC .... **C 5040**
Arhoolie (USA) / '88 / Pinnacle / Cadillac Music / Swift / Projection / Hot Shot / A.D.A Distribution / Jazz Music.
LP .... **ARHOOLIE 5040**
Arhoolie (USA) / May '88 / Pinnacle / Cadillac Music / Swift / Projection / Hot Shot / A.D.A Distribution / Jazz Music.

SPIRIT OF CAJUN MUSIC.
Tracks: Not Advised.
LP **6031**
MC .... **6031 TC**
Swallow (USA) / Sep '87 / Swift / Wellard Dist.

THEIR SWALLOW RECORDINGS.
Tracks: J'ai vu le loup / Valse a Beausoleil / Two-step des freres Mathieu / Travallier, c'est trop dur / Potpourri cadjin / He, Mom / Valse des Balfa / Zydeco grigris / Les barres de la prison / Hommage aux freres Balfa / Chanson / Love bridge waltz / Tu peux cognai / Contredanse de mamou / Reel de Dennis McGee / Blues a bebe / Talle du ronces / Blues de morse / Fi fi a Poncho / J'ai fait la tour de grand bois / Je m'endors, je m'endors / La valse de grand bois / Trinquez, trinquez.
CD .... **CDCHD 379**
Ace / Sep '92 / Pinnacle / Hot Shot / Jazz Music / Complete Record Co. Ltd.

ZYDECO GRIS GRIS.
Tracks: Not Advised.
LP **6054**
MC .... **6054 TC**
Swallow (USA) / '87 / Swift / Wellard Dist.

Beckett, Chris

20 COUNTRY AND WESTERN HITS (Beckett, Chris & the Sandpipers).
Tracks: Crying time / Together again / Burning bridges.
LP .... **HRL 106**
Homespun (Ireland) / May '88 / Homespun Records / Ross Records / Wellard Dist.

SHE WEARS MY RING.
Tracks: She wears my ring / Diana.
7" .... **HS 046**
Homespun (Ireland) / Jun '81 / Homespun Records / Ross Records / Wellard Dist.

Begley, Philomena

One of Britain's most successful country singers, hailing from County Tyrone in Ireland. She has regularly recorded and performed in the USA thanks to the support of Porter Wagoner. She celebrated her 25th anniversary in the business in 1990. She has won numerous awards including the BCMA's Top Female Country Singer on four occasions between 1985 and 1989. Her albums sell well her K-Tel Greatest Hits LP went platinum. (Tony Byworth).

BEST OF PHILOMENA BEGLEY.
Tracks: What's wrong with the way that we're doing it now? / Down river road / Truck driving woman / Why me, Lord? / Once around thedance floor / here today, gone tomorrow / Umbrella song / Route 65 to Nashville / One drink is one too many / Blanket on the ground / Tonight I'll throw a party of my own / Mommy and daddy's little girl / Texas in my heart / How great thou art / Light in the window / Village in County Tyrone / I'll be your woman tonight / Queen of the Silver Dollar / Medals for mothers / San Antone rose.
LP .... **RITZLP 0021**
■ MC .... **RITZLC 0021**
Ritz / Mar '84.
MC .... **RITZSC 406**
Ritz / Dec '88 / Pinnacle / Midland Records.

BLANKET ON THE GROUND.
Tracks: Not Advised.
LP .... **TSLP 82**
MC .... **TSC 82**
Topspin (Ireland) / Jan '76 / I & B Records.

COUNTRY QUEEN FOR 30 YEARS.
Tracks: Every second / Look at us / Walkin', talkin', cryin', barely beatin' broken heart / Picture of me (without you), A / Bright lights & country music / Start living again / Bed you made for me, The / Home I'll be / Our wedding day / Just one time / If my heart had windows / Family tree / Last rose of summer / Life is not always a rainbow / Gold & silver days / Bing bang boom.
CD .... **RITZRCD 522**
MC .... **RITZRC 522**
Ritz / Nov '92 / Pinnacle / Midland Records.

COUNTRY SCENES.
Tracks: Not Advised.
LP .... **KLP 110**
K-Tel (Ireland) / '88 / I & B Records / Ross Records / Prism Leisure PLC.

COUNTRY SCOTS 'N' IRISH.
Tracks: Big wheel cannonball / Flower of Scotland / Rose of Mooncoin / Way old friends do, The / Mummy and daddy's little girl / Making love to you is just like eating peanuts / Cliffs of Dooneen / Come by the hills / I'm crying my heart out over you / Mull of Kintyre / That's what your love means to me / Cottage on the hill / Everything I touch turns to sugar / Scotland again.
LP .... **ITV 476**
MC .... **KITV 476**
Scotdisc / Dec '88 / Duncans / Ross Records / Target Records / Conifer Records.

COUNTRY STARS (Begley, Philomena & Ray Lynam).
Tracks: You're the one I can't live without / Papa's wagon / You never were mine / My elusive dreams / Truck driving woman / Door is always open, The / You and me, her and him / What's your mamma's name child / I can't believe that you stopped loving me / Jeannie's afraid of the dark / Gypsy Joe and Me / Here today and gone tomorrow.
LP .... **PHL 409**
Homespun (Ireland) / May '84 / Homespun Records / Ross Records / Wellard Dist.
MC .... **CPHL 409**
Homespun (Ireland) / '88 / Homespun Records / Ross Records / Wellard Dist.

IN HARMONY (Begley, Philomena & Mick Flavin).
Tracks: No love left / Just between you and me / I'm wasting your time you're wasting mine / 'Till a tear becomes a rose / Always, always / We're strangers again / We'll get ahead someday / All you've got to do is dream / Daisy chain / Don't believe me I'm lying / You can't break the chains of love / Let's pretend we're not married tonight / How can I help you forgive me / Somewhere between.
CD .... **RITZCD 0061**
MC .... **RITZLC 0061**
Ritz / Apr '91 / Pinnacle / Midland Records.
MC .... **RITZRC 528**
Ritz / Apr '93 / Pinnacle / Midland Records.

IRISH COUNTRY QUEEN.
Tracks: 41st St. Lonely Hearts Club / Irish eyes / Grandma whistled / Can I sleep in your arms / County Tyrone / Once around the dancefloor / How great thou art / My Mother's home / Medals for mothers / Lonesome end of the line / Tipperary town / Light in the window.
LP .... **TSLP 90**
MC .... **CSLP 90**
Topspin (Ireland) / Jan '77 / I & B Records.
LP .... **RITZLP 0019**
■ MC .... **RITZLC 0019**
Ritz / Apr '84.
MC .... **RITZSC 404**
Ritz / Dec '88 / Pinnacle / Midland Records.

LIVE IN CONCERT.
Tracks: Queen of the Silver Dollar / Truck drivin' woman / Sentimental old you / After all these years / Isle of Innisfree / Pal like mother, A / I'm so afraid of losing you / Route 65 to nashville / Dark island / Hillbilly girl

with the blues / One drink is one too many / I'll be faithful to you / How great thou art / Blanket on the ground.
MC . . . . .RITZRC 502
Ritz / May '91 / Pinnacle / Midland Records.

LIVE IN CONCERT.
Tracks: Queen of the Silver Dollar / Truck drivin' woman / Sentimental old you / After all these years / Isle of Innisfre / Pal like mother, A / I'm so afraid of losing you / Route to Nashville / Dark island / Hillbilly girl with the blues / One drink is one too many / I'll be faithful to you / How great thou art / Blanket on the ground.
VHS. . . . . RITZV 0010
Ritz / May '91 / Pinnacle / Midland Records.

MORE ABOUT LOVE.
Tracks: That's more about love / Grandpa / Mama she's crazy / Standing in line / Another chance / Sailor / Captured by love / It only hurts for a little while / I'll be faithful to you / Memories are made of this / One love at a time / Real men don't make quiche.
LP. . . . . RITZLP 0040
■ MC . . . . RITZSC 040
Ritz / Feb '87.
MC . . . . .RITZSC 424
Ritz / '89 / Pinnacle / Midland Records.

NASHVILLE COUNTRY.
Tracks: Not Advised.
LP. . . . . TSLP 110
Shannon / '78.

OLD CROSS OF ARBOE.
Tracks: Old cross of Arboe.
7". . . . . HIS 18
Homespun (Ireland) / '88 / Homespun Records / Ross Records / Wellard Dist.

ONE LOVE AT A TIME.
Tracks: One love at a time / Real men don't make quiche.
7". . . . . RITZ 171
Ritz / Feb '87 / Pinnacle / Midland Records.

PHILOMENA.
Tracks: Not Advised.
LP. . . . . RITZLP 0018
MC . . . . RITZLC 0018
Ritz / Apr '84 / Pinnacle / Midland Records.

PHILOMENA'S COUNTRY.
Tracks: Triangle song, The / Foolin' around / Faded love / Everything I've always wanted / Okie from Muskogee / God if only I could write your love song / If this is what love's all about / I don't believe I'll fall in love today / One night of cheating / Daydreams about night things / I can't keep my hands off you / Sweet baby Jane.
MC . . . . .RITZSC 403
Ritz / Dec '88 / Pinnacle / Midland Records.

QUEEN OF THE SILVER DOLLAR.
Tracks: Not Advised.
LP. . . . . TSLP 86
Topspin (Ireland) / May '76 / I & B Records.
MC . . . . BTC 305
Ritz / Dec '88 / Pinnacle / Midland Records.

REFLECTIONS.
Tracks: Not Advised.
CD . . . . ONCD 3471
MC . . . . OCE 2471
K-Tel / Jun '90 / I & B Records / C.M. Distribution / Arabesque Ltd. / Mono Distributors (Jersey) Ltd. / Prism Leisure PLC / PolyGram / Ross Records / Prism Leisure PLC.
CD . . . . .KCD 310
MC . . . . KMC 310
K-Tel (Ireland) / Feb '93 / I & B Records / Ross Records / Prism Leisure PLC.

SENTIMENTAL OLD YOU.
Tracks: Sentimental old you.
7". . . . . RITZ 080
Ritz / '88 / Pinnacle / Midland Records.

SILVER ANNIVERSARY ALBUM.
Tracks: Key is in the mailbox, The / Here today and gone tomorrow / Rose of my heart / Behind the footlights / Jeannie's afraid of the dark / Red is the rose / Dark island / Leavin' on your mind / Queen of the silver dollar / Blanket on the ground / Truck drivin' woman / One is one too many / Galway Bay / Old arboe.
LP. . . . . RITZLP 0046
MC . . . . RITZLC 046
Ritz / May '88 / Pinnacle / Midland Records.
CD . . . . .RITZCD 505
MC . . . . .RITZRC 505
Ritz / '90 / Pinnacle / Midland Records.

SIMPLY DIVINE (Begley, Philomena & Ray Lynam).
Tracks: You don't know love / Simply divine / Together alone / Near you / Don't cross over an old love / Making plans / Sweetest of all / I'll never need another you / She sang the melody / As long as we're dreaming / Hold on / Fire of two old flames.
LP. . . . . RITZLP 0028
■ MC . . . . RITZLC 028
Ritz / Apr '85.
MC . . . . .RITZSC 425
Ritz / '89 / Pinnacle / Midland Records.
CD . . . . .RITZSCD 425
Ritz / Apr '93 / Pinnacle / Midland Records.

TOGETHER AGAIN (Begley, Philomena & Ray Lynam).
Tracks: Not Advised.
LP. . . . . BRL 4057
Release (Ireland) / Nov '76.

TRUCK DRIVING WOMAN.
Tracks: Never again / Truck driving woman / I'll be all smiles / I really think I'm crying / How can I face tomorrow / Here today and gone tomorrow / Ramblin' man / Darling are you ever coming home / Philadelphia lawyer / Village in County Tyrone / My little son (England's motorway) / Old Arboe.
MC . . . . CPHL 405
Homespun (Ireland) / May '84 / Homespun Records / Ross Records / Wellard Dist.
LP. . . . . PHL 405
Homespun (Ireland) / May '88 / Homespun Records / Ross Records / Wellard Dist.

TRUCKIN' QUEEN.
Tracks: Big wheel cannonball / Highwayman / In God I trust / Long legged truckdrivers / Ravishing Ruby / Truckin' queen / Route 65 to Nashville / Truck driving mother / Old Ben / Big Mack / Roll on Big Mama.
LP. . . . . TSLP 98
Topspin (Ireland) / Apr '78 / I & B Records.
LP. . . . . RITZLP 0020
■ MC . . . . RITZLC 0020
Ritz / Apr '84.
MC . . . . .RITZSC 405
Ritz / Dec '88 / Pinnacle / Midland Records.

WAY OLD FRIENDS DO.
Tracks: Way old friends do, The / Heart to heart salesman.
7". . . . . RITZ 065
Ritz / Apr '84 / Pinnacle / Midland Records.

YOU'RE IN MY HEART.
Tracks: Sentimental old you / Honky tonkin' / Have I told you lately that I love you / Pull the covers over me / Old flames / Deportees / Way old friends do, The / Ease the fever / One of those days / Jealous heart / Dancin' your memory away / Daddy's side of the bed.
LP. . . . . RITZLP 0026
■ MC . . . . RITZLC 0026
Ritz / Dec '84.
MC . . . . .RITZSC 415
Ritz / Dec '88 / Pinnacle / Midland Records.

Bell, Crawford

ANGELINE.
Tracks: Angeline / Littlest cowboy rides again, The.
7". . . . . HS 040
Homespun (Ireland) / Jan '81 / Homespun Records / Ross Records / Wellard Dist.

ANOTHER TEXAS SONG.
Tracks: (When you're in love) everything's a waltz / Learning to live again / Lullabies, legends and lies / Three / Another Texas song / Stay a little longer / Queen bee / Texas when I die / Some days are diamonds.
LP. . . . . PHL 442
MC . . . . CPHL 442
Homespun (Ireland) / '82 / Homespun Records / Ross Records / Wellard Dist.

BEST OF CRAWFORD BELL.
Tracks: Not Advised.
MC . . . . CPHL 483
Homespun (Ireland) / '89 / Homespun Records / Ross Records / Wellard Dist.

C.B. COUNTRY.
Tracks: Molly darlin' / Mama sang a song / Saginaw, Michigan / Mother country music / Real thing, The / Good morning darling / Mama's waiting / God only knows / Too late / Silver medals and sweet memories / Lightning express.
MC . . . . CPHL 419
Homespun (Ireland) / Nov '79 / Homespun Records / Ross Records / Wellard Dist.
LP. . . . . PHL 419
Homespun (Ireland) / May '88 / Homespun Records / Ross Records / Wellard Dist.

COWBOY SINGER.
Tracks: Union mare and confederate grey / Ozark mountain / Tequila Sheila / Cowboy singer, The / Old flames / Angelina / Hard to be humble / Littlest cowboy rides again, The / Mississippi you're on my mind / Leaving Louisiana in the broad daylight / Evangeline / Mother of a wandering boy.
LP. . . . . PHL 428
MC . . . . CPHL 428
Homespun (Ireland) / '82 / Homespun Records / Ross Records / Wellard Dist.

EVERYTHING'S A WALTZ.
Tracks: Everything's a waltz / She has my heart.
7". . . . . HS 050
Homespun (Ireland) / Sep '81 / Homespun Records / Ross Records / Wellard Dist.

HEAD TO TOE (Bell, Crawford & Steelrail).
Tracks: Head to toe / Connie.
■ 7". . . . . MD 1198
Emerald / Jul '77.

HYMNS AND SONGS FROM THE FAMILY ALBUM.
Tracks: Where the soul never dies / Softly and tenderly / Let the lower lights be burning / Tell mother I'll be there / Angel band / In the garden / Life's railway to Heaven / Jesus tender shepherd / He's the one / Jesus hold my hand / Precious memories / At the end of the day / Another bridge to burn / I dreamed I saw our country on her knees / Peace of mind.
LP. . . . . PHL 466
MC . . . . CPHL 466
Homespun (Ireland) / Dec '83 / Homespun Records / Ross Records / Wellard Dist.

IT'S HARD TO BE HUMBLE (Bell, Crawford & The Dollar Brand).
Tracks: It's hard to be humble / Tequilia Sheila / Last cheater's waltz, The.
■ 7". . . . . HS 037
Homespun (Ireland) / Oct '82.

SIOUX CITY SUE.
Tracks: Sioux city Sue / Down the trail of aching hearts.
7". . . . . HS 062
Homespun (Ireland) / Feb '83 / Homespun Records / Ross Records / Wellard Dist.

STAR SPANGLED BANNER.
Tracks: There's a star spangled banner waving somewhere / Have I stayed away too long / Down the trail of aching hearts / Sioux city Sue / Vaya con dios / Molly darling / Blue moon of Kentucky / Down in the little green valley / Can I sleep in your arms / Lamplighting time in the valley / Sweetheart of the valley / Three little bells.
LP. . . . . PHL 452
MC . . . . CPHL 452
Homespun (Ireland) / Dec '82 / Homespun Records / Ross Records / Wellard Dist.

STAY A LITTLE LONGER.
Tracks: Stay a little longer / Peace of mind.
7". . . . . HS 056
Homespun (Ireland) / Feb '82 / Homespun Records / Ross Records / Wellard Dist.

Bell, Delia

Old style, Texas-born singer who was discovered by Emmylouu Harris and signed to Warner Bros. in 1983. An album, and a couple of chart singles, added up to her moment of commercial glory, after which she drifted back into obscurity. (Tony Byworth)

BLUER THAN MIDNIGHT.
Tracks: Bluer than midnight / God gave you to me / My Kentucky Mountain home / Heartless / I want to be loved / Broken heart, a wedding band, A / Dirt you throw, The / Roses in the snow / Come walk with me / Oklahoma bluegrass blues / My last request / Come back and get these memories.
LP. . . . . CO 768
MC . . . . CO 768 MC
County (USA) / '79 / Projection / Mike's Country Music Room / Swift.

CHEER OF THE HOMEFIRES (Bell, Delia & Bill Grant).
Tracks: Dreaming / Cheer of the home fires, The / Fields of flowers / Wall, The / Where did we go wrong / Heartbreak express / Thinking of the old days / Sad situation / It'll be me / There'll be no teardrops tonight / Shadows of my mind / Don't let me cross over.
LP. . . . . ROUNDER 0187
MC . . . . .ROUNDER 0187C
Rounder / '88 / Projection / Roots Records / Swift / C.M. Distribution / Topic Records / Jazz Music / Hot Shot / A.D.A Distribution / Direct Distribution.

FEW DOLLARS MORE, A (Bell, Delia & Bill Grant).
Tracks: Foggy mountain home / Silver tongue and gold plated lies / Don't worry about me / Love's turned you to stone / Red clay Georgia / Few dollars more, A / I'll get by / Night flyer / Lonely violet / Louisa / Cold hard facts of life, The / Jack and Lucy.
LP. . . . . ROUNDER 0217
Rounder / Jun '86 / Projection / Roots Records / Swift / C.M. Distribution / Topic Records / Jazz Music / Hot Shot / A.D.A Distribution / Direct Distribution.
MC . . . . .ROUNDER 0217C
Rounder / Aug '88 / Projection / Roots Records / Swift / C.M. Distribution / Topic Records / Jazz Music / Hot Shot / A.D.A Distribution / Direct Distribution.

FOLLOWING A FEELING (Bell, Delia & Bill Grant).
Tracks: If I had my life to live over / No one mends a broken heart like you / Following a feeling / They'll soon pay the price / Two lonely hearts / Could this have been the man / Fiddler, The / Beggin' to you / Flame in my heart / Love you've the teacher / River, The / Won't you come and sing for me.
LP. . . . . ROUNDER 0257
MC . . . . .ROUNDER 0257C
Rounder / Aug '88 / Projection / Roots Records / Swift / C.M. Distribution / Topic Records / Jazz Music / Hot Shot / A.D.A Distribution / Direct Distribution.

ROLLIN' (see under Grant, Bill).

B 8 ■ DELETED

Bellamy Brothers

The American vocal duo of David and Howard Bellamy scored an international smash in the early summer of 1976 with the exuberant country rock-flavoured *Let Your Love Flow*. It reached No 1 in America and No 7 in the UK. Their eponymous album reached No 21 on the British album charts, but a similar follow-up single, *Satin Sheets*, failed to crack the Top Forty on either side of the Atlantic. Success then eluded the brothers until 1979, when they topped the US country chart with the cheekily-titled *If I Said You Had A Beautiful Body Would You Hold It Against Me?* It crossed over to No 39 on the American pop chart and then became a surprise British smash, reaching No 3. Since then the Bellamys have concentrated on the country market, but without the same crossover success. (Bob MacDonald)

BEAUTIFUL FRIENDS.
Tracks: Slippin' away / Make me over / Bird dog / My shy Anne / It's just the gypsy in your soul / Let's give love a go / Wild honey / Tumbleweed and Rosalie / Mornin' mockingbird / When the music plays.
■ LP . . . . K 56485
WEA / Jun '78 / WEA.

BEST OF THE BELLAMY BROTHERS, THE.
Tracks: Not Advised.
MC . . . . MCFC 3248
MCA / Mar '85 / BMG.
■ LP . . . . MCF 3248
MCA / Mar '85.
CD . . . . MCLD 19132
MC . . . . MCLC 19132
MCA / Mar '93 / BMG.

BOUND TO EXPLODE.
Tracks: Bound to explode / Can somebody hear me now.
■ 7" . . . . K 16963
WEA / Jun '77.

COUNTRY.
Tracks: Not Advised.
CD 31306
MCA (USA) / Jun '88 / MCA (Imports).

CRAZY FROM THE HEART.
Tracks: Not Advised.
CD . . . . MCAD 42039
MCA (Import) / May '89 / Pinnacle / Silver Sounds (CD).

DANCING COWBOYS.
Tracks: Dancing cowboys / Sugar daddy.
■ 7" . . . . K 17573
Curb / Apr '80.

DO YOU LOVE AS GOOD AS YOU LOOK.
Tracks: Do you love as good as you look / Classic case of the blues.
■ 7" . . . . K 17732
WEA / Dec '80.

GREATEST HITS VOL.1.
Tracks: Let your love flow / If I said you had a beautiful body .. / You ain't just whistlin' Dixie / Sugar daddy / Dancin' cowboys / Lovers live longer / Do you love as good as you look / For all the wrong reasons / Get into reggae cowboy / Redneck girl.
■ CD . . . . CMCAD 31012
MCA / Jul '87.
CD 4686062
MC 4686064
Sony Music / '91 / Sony.

GREATEST HITS: BELLAMY BROTHERS VOL.2.
Tracks: Feeling the feeling / When I'm away from you / Old hippie / I'd lie to you for your love / Too much is not enough / Forget about me / World's greatest lover / I need more of you / Strong weakness / I love her mind.
LP . . . . IMCA 5812
MC . . . . IMCAC 5812
MCA / Jun '87 / BMG.
■ CD . . . . MCAD 5812
MCA / Jun '87.

HOWARD & DAVID.
Tracks: Wheels / Season of the wind / Single man and his wife, The / I'm gonna hurt her on the radio / Feeling the feeling / You're my favourite waste of time / Lie to you for your love / Old hippie / Everybody's somebody's darling / Jeannie Rae.
■ LP . . . . IMCA 5586
MCA (Import) / Mar '86.

I NEED MORE OF YOU.
Tracks: I need more of you / Restless.
7" . . . . MCA 899
MCA / Aug '84 / BMG.

IF I SAID YOU HAD A BEAUTIFUL BODY.
Tracks: If I said you had a beautiful body / Make me over.
■ 7" . . . . K 17405
WEA / Aug '79.

IF I SAID YOU HAD A BEAUTIFUL BODY (OLD GOLD).
Tracks: If I said you had a beautiful body / Let your love flow.

7" . . . . OG 9552
Old Gold / Sep '85 / Pickwick Records.

LET YOUR LOVE FLOW.
Tracks: Satin sheets / Nothin' heavy / Rainy, windy, sunshine / Rodeo Road / Let fantasy live / Highway 2-18 (hang on to your dreams) / Living in the west / I'm the only sane man left alive / Inside of my guitar / Hell cat / Let your love flow.
LP . . . . K 56242
WEA / Jun '76 / WEA.

LET YOUR LOVE FLOW.
Tracks: Let your love flow / Inside of my guitar.
7" . . . . K 16690
WEA / Mar '76 / WEA.

LOVIN' ON.
Tracks: Lovin' on / Ole faithful.
■ 7" . . . . K 17548
Curb / Feb '80.

OLD HIPPIE.
Tracks: Old hippie / Wheels.
7" . . . . MCA 995
MCA / Oct '85 / BMG.

PLAIN AND FANCY.
Tracks: You made me / Tiger Lily lover / Memorabilia / Maybe by then / Cross fire / Misunderstood / If it's so easy / Hard rockin' / Can somebody hear me now.
LP . . . . K 56357
WEA / WEA.

RESTLESS.
Tracks: Forget about me / World's greatest lover / Down to you / We're having some fun now / Rockabilly / Restless / I love it / Diesel cafe / Tragedy / I need more of you.
LP . . . . IMCA 5489
MCA (Import) / Mar '86 / Pinnacle / Silver Sounds (CD).

SATIN SHEETS.
Tracks: Satin sheets.
■ 7" . . . . K 16775
WEA / Aug '76.

SONS OF THE SUN.
Tracks: Lovers live longer / Do you love as good as you look / It's hard to be a cowboy these days / Dancin' romance / Endangered species / Givin' in to love again / Honey, we don't know no one in Nashville / Spiders and snakes / Classic case of the blues / Illusions of love.
LP . . . . K 56872
■ MC 456872
WEA / Nov '80 / WEA.

WET T-SHIRT.
Tracks: Wet T-shirt / Blue ribbons.
■ 7" . . . . K 17487
Curb / '79.

YOU CAN GET CRAZY.
Tracks: Dancin' cowboys / Sugar daddy / Foolin' around / Comin' back for more / I could be makin' love to you / Dead aim.
■ LP . . . . K 56777
WEA / May '80.

Bennett, Pinto

BIG IN WINNEMUCCA (Bennett, Pinto & The Motel Cowboys).
Tracks: Wood and steel / Winnemucca / Bad girl / First door to the wrong / Hard core cowboy / Honky tonk asshole / Two waltzing mice / Dream lover / Wine me up / Ol' blue / Jack Tarr the sailor.
CD . . . . PTCD 003
LP . . . . PTLP 003
MC . . . . PTLC 003
P.T. Music / Sep '88 / ACD Trading Ltd.

CAROLINA MORNIN'S.
Tracks: Carolina mornin's.
7" . . . . PTL 001
P.T. Music / Mar '88 / ACD Trading Ltd.

FAMOUS MOTEL COWBOY SONGS (Bennett, Pinto & The Motel Cowboys).
Tracks: Valuable time / Shelter / Pardner I know / More or less / Moonlight at the oasis / Carolina morning / Only in my dreams / She almost reminds me of you / She wouldn't take nothing / What the hell am I doin' here.
CD . . . . PTCD 001
MC . . . . PTLC 001
P.T. Music / Mar '88 / ACD Trading Ltd.
■ LP . . . . PTLP 001
P.T. Music / Mar '88.

PURE QUILL (Bennett, Pinto & The Motel Cowboys).
Tracks: You cared enough to lie / Livin' and dyin' for love / Peaceful woman / I ain't in it for the money / True lovin' daddy / No sweat / Stranger in the mirror / Prarie blues / Ballad of Hai-Sing / The different ways to sing the blues / Pure quill.
CD . . . . PTCD 007
MC . . . . PTLC 007
P.T. Music / Feb '89 / ACD Trading Ltd.
■ LP . . . . PTLP 007
P.T. Music / Feb '89.

Berg, Matraca

Contemporary singer/songwriter, the daughter of Nashville session musician Icee Berg, she won a grammy nomination with the self-penned *The Last One to Know*, and made her recording debut on RCA. (Tony Byworth)

BABY, WALK ON.
Tracks: Baby, walk on / I got it bad and that ain't good.
■ CD Single . . . . PD 49209
RCA / Apr '91 / BMG.
■ 7" . . . . PB 49209
RCA / Apr '91.

I GOT IT BAD.
Tracks: I got it bad and that ain't good / Appalachian rain / Things you left undone, The (Only on CD single.).
■ 7" . . . . PB 49239
■ CD Single . . . . PD 49240
RCA / Jan '91.

LYING TO THE MOON.
Tracks: Things you left un-done / I got it bad and that ain't good / Lying to the moon / I must have been crazy / You are the storm / Calico plains / Appalachian rain / Alice in the looking glass / Dancin' on the wire (Only on CD).
MC . . . . PK 90532
RCA / Oct '90 / BMG.
■ CD . . . . PD 90532
RCA / Oct '90.
■ LP . . . . PL 90532
RCA / Oct '90.

Berline, Byron

West Coast fiddle player who first came to attention whilst sitting in with The Flying Burrito Brothers in 1971. Had led, and been a member of, numerous groups including Country Gazette and Sundance and has won ACM instrumental awards several times. (Tony Byworth)

B-C-H (Berline, Byron & Dan Crary & John Hickman).
Tracks: Not Advised.
LP . . . . SH 3720
MC . . . . SH 3720 MC
Sugarhill(USA) / '82 / Roots Records / Projection / Impetus Records / C.M. Distribution / Jazz Music / Swift / Duncans / A.D.A Distribution.
MC . . . . SH 3755 MC
Sugarhill(USA) / '89 / Roots Records / Projection / Impetus Records / C.M. Distribution / Jazz Music / Swift / Duncans / A.D.A Distribution.
LP . . . . SH 3755
Sugarhill(USA) / Mar '89 / Roots Records / Projection / Impetus Records / C.M. Distribution / Jazz Music / Swift / Duncans / A.D.A Distribution.

BYRON BERLINE & L.A. FIDDLE BAND.
Tracks: Roanoke / Dixie hoedown / I'll just stay around / All the good times / Jack rabbit / Sitting on top of the world / Red haired boy / Don't put it away / On and on / Brown county breakdown / Uncle pen.
LP . . . . SH 3716
Sugarhill(USA) / '88 / Roots Records / Projection / Impetus Records / C.M. Distribution / Jazz Music / Swift / Duncans / A.D.A Distribution.

DAD'S FAVORITES.
Tracks: Coming down from Denver / New broom / Grey eagle / B & B rag / Redbird / Ragtime Annie / Limerock / Stones rag / Millers reel / Arkansas traveller / Sweet memories waltz / Birmingham fling.
LP . . . . ROUNDER 0100
Rounder / Jan '87 / Projection / Roots Records / Swift / C.M. Distribution / Topic Records / Jazz Music / Hot Shot / A.D.A Distribution / Direct Distribution.
MC . . . . ROUNDER 0100C
Rounder / '88 / Projection / Roots Records / Swift / C.M. Distribution / Topic Records / Jazz Music / Hot Shot / A.D.A Distribution / Direct Distribution.

DOUBLE TROUBLE (Berline, Byron & John Hickman).
Tracks: Not Advised.
LP . . . . SH 3750
MC . . . . SH 3750MC
Sugarhill(USA) / Oct '88 / Roots Records / Projection / Impetus Records / C.M. Distribution / Jazz Music / Swift / Duncans / A.D.A Distribution.

FIDDLER'S DREAM (Berline, Byron & Sundance).
Tracks: Not Advised.
LP . . . . AP 043
Appaloosa / '85 / Roots Records / C.M. Distribution / Wellard Dist. / Projection / Hot Shot / A.D.A Distribution.

NIGHT RUN (Berline, Byron & Dan Crary & John Hickman).
Tracks: Not Advised.
LP . . . . SH 3739
MC . . . . SH 3739 MC
Sugarhill(USA) / Mar '89 / Roots Records / Projection / Impetus Records / C.M. Distribution / Jazz Music / Swift / Duncans / A.D.A Distribution.

NOW THERE ARE FOUR (Berline, Byron & Dan Crary & John Hickman).
Tracks: Big dog / Train of memory / Weary blues from waiting / Moonlight motor inn / They don't play George Jones on MTV / Speak softly you're talking to my heart / Santa Ana / Leave me the way I am / Kodak 1955 / Hallelujah Harry.
CD . . . . SH 3773 CD
LP . . . . SH 3773
MC . . . . SH 3773 MC
Sugarhill(USA) / '90 / Roots Records / Projection / Impetus Records / C.M. Distribution / Jazz Music / Swift / Duncans / A.D.A Distribution.

OUTRAGEOUS.
Tracks: Not Advised.
LP . . . . FF 227
Flying Fish (USA) / Mar '89 / Cadillac Music / Roots Records / Projection / C.M. Distribution / Direct Distribution / Jazz Music / Duncans / A.D.A Distribution.

Berry, Benny

Alabama born Benny Berry was discovered by Northern Ireland's Hawk Records in the late 1980's and subsequently built up a loyal European following via regular releases and visits. (Tony Byworth)

SOME THINGS NEVER CHANGE.
Tracks: Not Advised.
CD . . . . HAWCD 171
MC . . . . HAWC 171
Prism / Apr '91 / Pinnacle / Midland Records.

STANDING HERE ALONE.
Tracks: Love me one more time / I die ten thousand times a day / I'm turning off a memory / Standing here alone / Forever's a long long time / I can't get over you / Pick up the pieces / It's not her memory, it's mine / Give my heart to you / Time enough to say goodbye.
CD . . . . HAW 139
Hawk / Dec '90 / C.M. Distribution.

Best, Tony

BY REQUEST.
Tracks: San Antonio rose / You're my best friend / Words / One day at a time / I don't want to cry / Turn out the light (love me tonight) / Old rugged cross, The / Love or something like it / Legend in my time, A / Today I started loving you again / Crazy / Some broken hearts never mend / Nobody's child / China doll.
LP . . . . KZ 1002 LS
Accordion Record Club / '84 / Accordion Record Club.

DOING WHAT I LIKE DOING.
Tracks: Doing what I like doing / Mansion on the hill / Great El Tigre, The / Let's keep it that way / Some days are diamonds / Angelean / Jimmy Brown song, The / Do what you do do well / Catfish John / Who were you thinking of / Drinking them beers / Smooth sailing.
LP WW1003
Accordion Record Club / '84 / Accordion Record Club.

Big Bob

WE'VE MADE MEMORIES (Big Bob & The Fugitives).
Tracks: I love you forever and forever / Old flames / All my cloudy days are gone / Cold windy city of Chicago / We've made memories / I've news for you / If those lips could only speak / Foolin' around / Ashes of love / Tears on the roses / Perfect strangers / I love the country way of life / Don't you sweet love die / Charleston railroad tavern / Happy anniversary / Pearly shells / On the beach at Waikiki / There's nobody home at the range.
MC . . . . ARDV 002
Ardvene / Jun '87 / Ross Records.

Big Bopper

At 28, the Big Bopper died in the same North Dakota plane crash that also killed touring partners Buddy Holly and Ritchie Valens in February 1959. Born J.P. Richardson in Texas, the Big Bopper became well known as a disc jockey in the early 50's. The draft interrupted his broadcasting career in the middle of the decade but, on his return to radio, he staged a broadcasting marathon - his continuous stretch of 122 hr 8 min broke the existing world record by eight minutes. He turned to songwriting and, unintentionally, singing: his novelty smash Chantilly Lace, released in 1958, reached No 6 in the US and No 12 in the UK and is now regarded as a rock 'n' roll classic. The next 45, The Big Bopper's Wedding, was far less successful, bearing out the music business axiom that a novelty hit is hard to follow up. Towards the end of his life he encouraged a protege, Johnny Preston. Running Bear, Preston's single written and produced by the Big Bopper, went to No 1 on both sides of the Atlantic in 1960, about a year after his death. (Bob MacDonald)

CHANTILLY LACE.
Tracks: Not Advised.
LP 6463 057

MC 7245 057
Mercury / Nov '81 / PolyGram.
LP 832 902-1
Polydor / Jun 88 / PolyGram.

CHANTILLY LACE.
Tracks: Chantilly lace / Monkey song / Old maid.
■ 7" . . . . AMT 1002
Mercury (EMI) / Oct '58.
7" D45 1008
Swift / Mar '83 / Wellard Dist.

Big Tom

Arguably the most successful Irish country music artist of the 1960's and 1970's. Big Tom (McBride) built up a large Irish following on both sides of the Atlantic. His reputation was made even more legendary thanks to the song Big Tom is Still the King which gave Susan McCann her first number one record in Ireland.- (Tony Byworth)

20 GREATEST HITS: BIG TOM.
Tracks: Not Advised.
MC . . . . KMC 55
K-Tel / Dec '88 / I & B Records / C.M. Distribution / Arabesque Ltd. / Mono Distributors (Jersey) Ltd. / Prism Leisure PLC / PolyGram / Ross Records / Prism Leisure PLC.

ALL TIME HITS OF.. (Big Tom & The Mainliners).
Tracks: Gentle mother / Sunset years of life, The / Please mama please / Tears on a bridal bouquet / Old log cabin for sale, An / Bunch of violets blue / Old rustic bridge / Flowers for Mama / I'll settle for old Ireland / Wheels fell off the wagon again, The.
LP . . . . GES 1051
MC . . . . KGEC 1051
Emerald / Oct '81 / I & B Records.

AROUND IRELAND WITH BIG TOM.
Tracks: Not Advised.
LP . . . . DNV 16
WEA (Ireland) / '88 / WEA / C.M. Distribution / Projection / Roots Records.

BLUE WINGS/FOUR COUNTRY ROADS.
Tracks: Not Advised.
MC . . . . DNVC 14
WEA (Ireland) / '88 / WEA / C.M. Distribution / Projection / Roots Records.

CLONES CYCLONE.
Tracks: Clones cyclone.
7" . . . . DMC 1032
I&B / '88 / I & B Records.

I LOVE YOU STILL.
Tracks: I love you still.
7" . . . . DMC 1010
I&B / '88 / I & B Records.

I'LL SETTLE FOR OLD IRELAND.
Tracks: Not Advised.
LP . . . . GES 1102
Emerald / '88 / I & B Records.
CD . . . . SWCD 1006
TC Records / Aug '92 / Midland Records.

KING OF COUNTRY MUSIC, VOLUME 1.
Tracks: Not Advised.
LP . . . . BT 1
WEA (Ireland) / '88 / WEA / C.M. Distribution / Projection / Roots Records.

KING OF COUNTRY MUSIC, VOLUME 2.
Tracks: Not Advised.
LP . . . . BT 2
WEA (Ireland) / '88 / WEA / C.M. Distribution / Projection / Roots Records.

KING OF COUNTRY MUSIC, VOLUME 3.
Tracks: Not Advised.
LP . . . . BT 3
WEA (Ireland) / '88 / WEA / C.M. Distribution / Projection / Roots Records.

KING OF COUNTRY MUSIC, VOLUME 4.
Tracks: Not Advised.
LP . . . . BT 4
WEA (Ireland) / '88 / WEA / C.M. Distribution / Projection / Roots Records.

KING OF COUNTRY MUSIC, VOLUME 5.
Tracks: Not Advised.
LP . . . . BT 5
WEA (Ireland) / '88 / WEA / C.M. Distribution / Projection / Roots Records.

KING OF COUNTRY MUSIC, VOLUME 6.
Tracks: Not Advised.
LP . . . . BT 6
WEA (Ireland) / '88 / WEA / C.M. Distribution / Projection / Roots Records.

LITTLE BIT OF COUNTRY & IRISH (Big Tom & The Mainliners).
Tracks: Isle of Innisfree / Don't be angry / My world's come down / Guess things happen that way / Back in my babys arms / Tears on a bridal bouquet / She's gone / Cold hard facts of life / Before (I met you) / Gentle mother.

CD . . . . KGEC 1076
Emerald / Oct '81 / I & B Records.
LP . . . . .BER 004
MC . . . . KBER 004
Emerald / Nov '84 / I & B Records.

OLD LOVE LETTERS.
Tracks: Old love letters.
7" . . . . DMC 1012
I&B / '88 / I & B Records.

RAMBLING MAN.
Tracks: Rambling man.
7" . . . . UNIC 13
I&B / '88 / I & B Records.

TEARDROPS IN THE SNOW.
Tracks: Not Advised.
LP . . . . DNV 15
WEA (Ireland) / '88 / WEA / C.M. Distribution / Projection / Roots Records.

TUBBERCURRY.
Tracks: Tubbercurry.
7" . . . . DMC 1033
I&B / '88 / I & B Records.

Black Ace

BLACK ACE AND HIS STEEL GUITAR.
Tracks: Not Advised.
LP . . . . ARHOOLIE 1003
Arhoolie (USA) / May '81 / Pinnacle / Cadillac Music / Swift / Projection / Hot Shot / A.D.A Distribution / Jazz Music.

I'M THE BOSS CARD IN YOUR HAND.
Tracks: Not Advised.
CD . . . . ARHCD 374
Arhoolie (USA) / Mar '93 / Pinnacle / Cadillac Music / Swift / Projection / Hot Shot / A.D.A Distribution / Jazz Music.

Black, Bill

Born in Memphis, Tennessee in 1926, Bill Black joined Memphis' Sun label in the fifties as a session bass guitar player. It was with Sun Records that the young Elvis Presley cut his first series of singles in 1954, before being signed by RCA in '56 and turned into a massive star. Black played with Presley in both Sun and RCA days, backing him on the vast majority of his discs between 1955 & 1958. His driving, pulsating bass was perfectly suited to Elvis' powerful singing. From 1959 Bill switched to electric bass and led the successful Bill Black Combo on the local Hi label, the instrumental quintet linking country music with bass-heavy Southern soul sounds of the Stax era. He retired from touring and died of a brain tumour in 1965; the group was still active under his name in the '80s.(Bob MacDonald)

DON'T BE CRUEL (Black, Bill Combo).
Tracks: Don't be cruel.
■ 7" . . . . HLU 9212
London-American / Nov '60.

FIRST YEAR, THE (see under Presley, Elvis).

GOES WEST & PLAYS (Black, Bill Combo).
Tracks: Not Advised.
CD . . . . HIUKCD 124
Demon / Jun '93 / Pinnacle.

GREATEST HITS: BILL BLACK'S COMBO (Black, Bill Combo).
Tracks: Do it rat / Josephine / Rollin' / Hearts of stone / Yogi / White silver sands / Blue tango / Willie / Ole butter milk sky / Royal blue / Don't be cruel / Smokie, part 2 / School days / Sweet little sixteen / Roll over Beethoven / Maybellene / Carol / Little queenie / Brown-eyed handsome man / Nadine / Thirty days / Johnny B. Goode / Reelin' and rockin' / Memphis Tennessee.
CD . . . . HIUKCD 115
Hi! / '91 / Pinnacle / Swift.

LET'S TWIST HER (Black, Bill Combo).
Tracks: Not Advised.
CD . . . . HIUKCD 131
Hi! / Jun '92 / Pinnacle / Swift.

LET'S TWIST HER/THE UNTOUCHABLE SOUND OF.. (Black, Bill Combo).
Tracks: Not Advised.

MEMPHIS ROCK 'N' SOUL PARTY (Black, Bill & Willie Mitchell).
Tracks: Don't be cruel / Honky tonk / Blueberry Hill / Hearts of stone / Movin' / Hey Bo Diddley / Work with me Annie / Twist-her / My girl Josephine / Night train / So what / Do it - rat now / Monkey shine / School days / Memphis, Tennessee / Little queenie / Secret home / Buster Browne / Woodchopper's ball / That driving beat / Everything is gonna be alright / Champion, The / Bad eye / Sugar T / Mercy / Up-hard / 30-60-90 / Who's making love / Come see about me / My babe / I'm a midnight mover / Set free.

■ DELETED

CD . . . . HIUKCD 102
Hi! / Jul '89 / Pinnacle / Swift.

MOVIN' (Black, Bill Combo).
Tracks: Movin' / Honky train.
7" . . . . HLU 9436
London-American / '61.

SOLID AND RAUNCHY AND MOVIN' (Black, Bill Combo).
Tracks: Don't be cruel / Singing the blues / Blueberry hill / I almost lost my mind / Cherry pink / Mona Lisa / Honky Tonk / Tequila / Raunchy / You win again / Bo Diddley / Mack the knife / Movin' / What'd I say? / Hey Bo Diddley / Witchcraft / Work with me Annie / Be bop a lula / My babe / 40 miles of bad road / Ain't that lovin' you baby / Honky train / Walk, The / Torquay.
CD . . . . HIUKCD 112
Hi! / '91 / Pinnacle / Swift.

UNTOUCHABLE SOUND OF BILL BLACK'S COMBO.
Tracks: White silver sands / Smokie part 2 / Movin' / Monkey-shine / Don't be cruel / Little Queenie / Josephine / Willie / Turn on your lovelight / Memphis, Tennessee / Hearts of stone / Twist-her / Honky train / Little Jasper / Do it-rat now / So what.
LP. . . . . HIUKLP 410
Hi! / Pinnacle / Swift.

WHITE SILVER SANDS (Black, Bill Combo).
Tracks: White silver sands.
■ 7" . . . . HLU 9090
London-American / Sep '60.

Black, Bobby

LADIES ON THE STEAMBOAT.
Tracks: Ladies on the steamboat / Monroe's blues / Jerusalem ridge / Star of the county down / Staten Island hornpipe / Nervous breakdown / Limerock / Saratoga blues / Flight to DC / Over the waterfall / Flowers of Edinburgh / Little black moustache.
LP. . . . . RRR 0018
Ridgerunner (USA) / '80 / Mike's Country Music Room / Projection.

Black, Clint

Although he was born in Long Beach, New Jersey in 1962, Clint Black grew up in Houston, Texas - an area rich in country music traditions. By the age of 13 he was playing harmonica and, by 15, guitar. Soon he was working the local clubs where he met with another local musician, Hayden Nicholas, with whom he was to commence a continuing songwriting relationship. Their demos impressed ZZ Top's manager Bill Ham, who secured them a deal with RCA in Nashville. Black debuted on the country scene around the same time as Garth Brooks and, for the first year, the two were frequently (unfairly) compared and mistaken for each other. Black kicked off in the stronger position, though, with his first single *A Better Man*, released in June 1989, going straight to the top of the charts (the first time that a new male artist had achieved this feat in 14 years). His first album, the two million selling *Killing Time*, enjoyed similar success. By the end of 1989 he won the CMA's Horizon award for most successful newcomer and, a few months later, swept the board at the ACM Awards by being named both Male Vocalist and New Male Vocalist and securing single and album accolades. By 1993 Clint Black was established as RCA's top country artist, ensuring his position with high chart offerings such as *Put Yourself In my Shoes*, *We Tell Ourselves* and *Where Are You Now* alongside an array of highly acclaimed album releases. He also cut a duet with his boyhood hero Roy Rogers, *Hold On Partner*, and is married to Hollywood actress Lisa Hartman. (Tony Byworth)

HARD WAY, THE.
Tracks: We tell ourselves / Hard way, The / Something to cry about / Buying time / When my ship comes in / Woman has her way, A / There never was a train (Only on CD.) / Good old days, The / Burn one down / Wake up yesterday.
CD 078636603221
MC 078636603245
RCA Nashville / Jul '92 / BMG.

KILLIN' TIME.
Tracks: Straight from the factory / Nobody's home / You're gonna leave me again / Winding down / Live and learn / Better man, A / Walkin' away / I'll be gone / Killin' time.
CD . . . . PD 90443
RCA / Feb '90 / BMG.
■ LP. . . . . PL 90443
RCA / Feb '90.
■ MC . . . . PK 90443
RCA / Feb '90.
DCC. 07863596685
RCA / Jan '93 / BMG.

NO TIME TO KILL.
Tracks: No time to kill / Thinking again / Good run of bad luck, A / State of mind / Bad goodbye (duet with Wynonna Judd), A / Back to back / Half the man / I'll take Texas / Happiness alone / Tuckered out.
CD 7863662 392
MC 7863662 394
RCA / Jul '93 / BMG.

PUT YOURSELF IN MY SHOES.
Tracks: Put yourself in my shoes / Gulf of Mexico, The / One more payment / Where are you now / Old man, The / This nightlife / Loving blind / Heart like mine, A / Goodnight-loving, The.
CD . . . . PD 90544
RCA / Jan '90 / BMG.
■ LP. . . . . PL 90544
RCA / Jan '90.
■ MC . . . . PK 90544
RCA / Jan '90.

Black, Jeanne

HE'LL HAVE TO STAY.
Tracks: He'll have to stay.
■ 7" . . . . CL 15131
Capitol / Jun '60.

Blackstone, Eddie

LIGHT AND SHADE OF EDDIE BLACKSTONE, THE.
Tracks: After dark / 1643 Pennsylvania Boulevard / Spencer Walker Rose / Dolly McGraw / Never let a dream go by / Blues for a weirdo / You never left me side / Turn back the years / Lay my feet down on the street / Hero of the dreamers.
LP. . . . . PROP 5
T.W. / May '83.

NEVER LET A DREAM GO BY.
Tracks: Never let a dream go by / You never left my side.
■ 7" . . . . HIT 115
T.W. / May '83.

Blake, Nancy

GRAND JUNCTION.
Tracks: Not Advised.
LP. . . . . ROUNDER 0231
MC . . . . .ROUNDER 0231C
Rounder / Aug '88 / Projection / Roots Records / Swift / C.M. Distribution / Topic Records / Jazz Music / Hot Shot / A.D.A Distribution / Direct Distribution.

NATASHA'S WALTZ (see under Blake, Norman).

Blake, Norman

Acoustic musicain and top sessionman, Norman Blake was born 10.3.1938 in Chattanooga, Tennessee. Since the early Sixties, Blake has been a prominent musicain, doing countless sessions - including working on the Nitty Gritty Dirt Band's *Will The Circle Be Unbroken*, with Johnny Cash and on Bob Dylan's famed *Nashville Skyline* . He has toured with June Carter, Kris Kristofferson and Joan Baez, and shared the stage over the years with Vasser Clements, Tut Taylor, Tony Rice, wife Nancy and John Hartford. His recordings include joint releases with Rice, Red Rector, Nancy and the Rising Fawn Ensemble issued on the Takamo, County, Rounder and Flying Fish labels showing his prowess as both picker and vocalist. (Maurice Hope)

BLACKBERRY BLOSSOM.
Tracks: Are you from Dixie? / Right of a man, The / Hornpipe / Highland light, The / Railroad blues / Foggy valley / Lonesome Jenny / Blackberry blossom / D medley / Jerusalem ridge.
■ LP. . . . . FLY 0005
Flyright / Feb '79.
LP. . . . . FF 047
Flying Fish (USA) / Mar '89 / Cadillac Music / Roots Records / Projection / C.M. Distribution / Direct Distribution / Jazz Music / Duncans / A.D.A Distribution.

BLAKE AND RICE (Blake, Norman & Tony Rice).
Tracks: Not Advised.
CD . . . . CD 0233
LP. . . . . ROUNDER 0233
MC . . . . .ROUNDER 0233C
Rounder / Aug '88 / Projection / Roots Records / Swift / C.M. Distribution / Topic Records / Jazz Music / Hot Shot / A.D.A Distribution / Direct Distribution.

BLIND DOG (Blake, Norman & Nancy).
Tracks: Not Advised.
CD . . . . ROUNDERCD 0254
LP. . . . . ROUNDER 0254
MC . . . . .ROUNDERC 0254
Rounder / '90 / Projection / Roots Records / Swift / C.M. Distribution / Topic Records / Jazz Music / Hot Shot / A.D.A Distribution / Direct Distribution.

FIELDS OF NOVEMBER.
Tracks: Not Advised.
LP. . . . . FF 004
Flying Fish (USA) / Mar '89 / Cadillac Music / Roots Records / Projection / C.M. Distribution / Direct Distribution / Jazz Music / Duncans / A.D.A Distribution.

FIELDS OF NOVEMBER/OLD & NEW.
Tracks: Not Advised.
CD . . . . FF 004CD
MC . . . . FF 004C
Flying Fish (USA) / May '93 / Cadillac Music / Roots Records / Projection / C.M. Distribution / Direct Distribution / Jazz Music / Duncans / A.D.A Distribution.

FULL MOON ON THE FARM (Featuring Nancy Blake and James Bryan).
Tracks: Not Advised.
LP. . . . . ROUNDER 0144
MC . . . . .ROUNDER 0144C
Rounder / '88 / Projection / Roots Records / Swift / C.M. Distribution / Topic Records / Jazz Music / Hot Shot / A.D.A Distribution / Direct Distribution.

HOME IN SULPHUR SPRINGS.
Tracks: Not Advised.
LP. . . . . ROUNDER 0012
Rounder / Jan '87 / Projection / Roots Records / Swift / C.M. Distribution / Topic Records / Jazz Music / Hot Shot / A.D.A Distribution / Direct Distribution.
MC . . . . .ROUNDER 0012C
Rounder / '88 / Projection / Roots Records / Swift / C.M. Distribution / Topic Records / Jazz Music / Hot Shot / A.D.A Distribution / Direct Distribution.

JUST GIMME SOMETHIN' I'M USED TO (Blake, Norman & Nancy).
Tracks: Not Advised.
CD . . . . SHCD 6001
MC . . . . SHMC 6001
Shanachie / Apr '92 / A.D.A Distribution / Jazz Music / C.M. Distribution.

LIGHTHOUSE ON THE SHORE.
Tracks: Not Advised.
LP. . . . . ROUNDER 0211
MC . . . . .ROUNDER 0211C
Rounder / Dec '85 / Projection / Roots Records / Swift / C.M. Distribution / Topic Records / Jazz Music / Hot Shot / A.D.A Distribution / Direct Distribution.

NASHVILLE BLUES.
Tracks: Not Advised.
LP. . . . . ROUNDER 0188
Rounder / Sep '84 / Projection / Roots Records / Swift / C.M. Distribution / Topic Records / Jazz Music / Hot Shot / A.D.A Distribution / Direct Distribution.
MC . . . . .ROUNDER 0188C
Rounder / Aug '88 / Projection / Roots Records / Swift / C.M. Distribution / Topic Records / Jazz Music / Hot Shot / A.D.A Distribution / Direct Distribution.

NATASHA'S WALTZ (Blake, Norman & Nancy).
Tracks: Not Advised.
CD . . . . CD 11530
Rounder / '88 / Projection / Roots Records / Swift / C.M. Distribution / Topic Records / Jazz Music / Hot Shot / A.D.A Distribution / Direct Distribution.

NORMAN & NANCY BLAKE COMPACT DISC.
Tracks: Hello stranger / New bicycle hornpipe / Marquis Huntley / Florida rag / Jordon am a hard road to travel / Belize / Elzic's farewell / Lighthouse on the shore / Grand junction / Butterfly weed / President Garfield's hornpipe / In Russia (we have parking lots too) / Wroxall / If I lose I don't care / Chrysanthemum / Lima road jig / Boston boy / Last night's joy / My love is like a red rose / Wildwood flower / Tennessee mountain fox chase.
CD . . . . CD 11505
Rounder / '88 / Projection / Roots Records / Swift / C.M. Distribution / Topic Records / Jazz Music / Hot Shot / A.D.A Distribution / Direct Distribution.

NORMAN BLAKE & JETHRO BURNS (Blake, Norman & Jethro Burns).
Tracks: Not Advised.
LP. . . . . HDS 701
Flying Fish (USA) / '88 / Cadillac Music / Roots Records / Projection / C.M. Distribution / Direct Distribution / Jazz Music / Duncans / A.D.A Distribution.

NORMAN BLAKE & TONY RICE 2 (Blake, Norman & Tony Rice).
Tracks: It's raining here this morning / Lost Indian / Georgie / Father's hall / Two soldiers, The / Blackberry blossom / Eight more miles to Louisville / Lincoln's funeral train (The sad journey to Springfield) / Molly Bloom / D-18 Song (Thank you, Mr. Martin) / Back in yonder's world / Bright days / Salt creek.
MC . . . . ROU 0266
Rounder / '90 / Projection / Roots Records / Swift / C.M. Distribution / Topic Records / Jazz Music / Hot Shot / A.D.A Distribution / Direct Distribution.
CD . . . . CDROU 0266
Rounder / Jul '90 / Projection / Roots Records / Swift / C.M. Distribution / Topic Records / Jazz Music / Hot Shot / A.D.A Distribution / Direct Distribution.

OLD AND NEW.
Tracks: Widow's creek / Bristol in the bottle / Billy Gray / Forked deer / Rubagfre / Cuckoo's nest, The / Witch of the wave / My old home on the mountainside / Miller's reel / Dry grass on the high fields / Harvey's reel / Railroad days, The / Valley head / Sweet heaven / Sally in the garden / Ajimina / Flat rock.
LP. . . . . FF 010

Flying Fish (USA) / Mar '89 / Cadillac Music / Roots Records / Projection / C.M. Distribution / Direct Distribution / Jazz Music / Duncans / A.D.A Distribution.

ORIGINAL UNDERGROUND MUSIC FROM MYSTERIOUS SOUTH (Blake, Norman & Other Mandolin Pickers).
Tracks: Not Advised.
LP. . . . . **ROUNDER 0166**
MC . . . . **ROUNDER 0166C**
Rounder / Aug '88 / Projection / Roots Records / Swift / C.M. Distribution / Topic Records / Jazz Music / Hot Shot / A.D.A Distribution / Direct Distribution.

RISING FAWN STRING ENSEMBLE (Featuring Nancy Blake and James Bryan).
Tracks: Not Advised.
LP. . . . . **ROUNDER 0122**
MC . . . . **ROUNDER 0122C**
Rounder / '88 / Projection / Roots Records / Swift / C.M. Distribution / Topic Records / Jazz Music / Hot Shot / A.D.A Distribution / Direct Distribution.

SLOW TRAIN THROUGH GEORGIA.
Tracks: Not Advised.
CD . . . . **CD 11526**
Rounder / '88 / Projection / Roots Records / Swift / C.M. Distribution / Topic Records / Jazz Music / Hot Shot / A.D.A Distribution / Direct Distribution.

WHISKEY BEFORE BREAKFAST.
Tracks: Hand me down my walking cane / Under the double eagle / Six white horses / Salt river / Old grey mare / Down at Mylow's house / Sleepy eyed Joe / Indian creek / Arkansas traveller / Girl I left in Sunny Tennessee, The / Mistrel boy to war has gone, The / Ash grove, The / Church Street blues / Macon rag / Fiddler's dream / Whiskey before breakfast / Slow train through Georgia.
LP. . . . . **ROUNDER 0063**
MC . . . . **ROUNDER 0063C**
Rounder / '88 / Projection / Roots Records / Swift / C.M. Distribution / Topic Records / Jazz Music / Hot Shot / A.D.A Distribution / Direct Distribution.
CD . . . . **ROUCD 063**
Rounder / Aug '93 / Projection / Roots Records / Swift / C.M. Distribution / Topic Records / Jazz Music / Hot Shot / A.D.A Distribution / Direct Distribution.

Blue Bandanna Country..

COUNTRY BLUES (Blue Bandanna Country Band).
Tracks: Not Advised.
MC . . . . **C 1**
Hard Hat (USA) / Oct '89.

Blue Grass Cardinals

CARDINAL CLASS.
Tracks: Not Advised.
LP. . . . . **SH 3731**
MC . . . . **SH 3731 MC**
Sugarhill(USA) / '82 / Roots Records / Projection / Impetus Records / C.M. Distribution / Jazz Music / Swift / Duncans / A.D.A Distribution.

CARDINAL SOUL.
Tracks: Low and lonely / Nothing can my loving you / With half a heart / Blue is the color of lonesome / I feel good / Gift of love / Don't give up on me / 32 acres / Old man in the park, The / I've had a time / Mountain Laurel.
LP. . . . . **CMH 6235**
MC . . . . **CMHC 6235**
CMH (USA) / C.M. Distribution / Projection.

HOME IS WHERE THE HEART IS.
Tracks: Be good as my little girl / Rebel's last request / I don't believe you've met my baby / Home is where the heart is / Wicked path of sin / Slowly / Five days in heaven / Slowly getting you out of the way / It rained / Tiny broken heart / Colarado / It's mighty dark to travel.
LP. . . . . **SH 3741**
Sugarhill(USA) / Mar '85 / Roots Records / Projection / Impetus Records / C.M. Distribution / Jazz Music / Swift / Duncans / A.D.A Distribution.

LIVIN' IN THE GOOD OLD DAYS.
Tracks: I think we're livin' in the good old days / Knee deep in loving you / Dedication to Lester Flatt / What's good for you (should be alright for me) / Darling is it too late now? / Sweet hour of prayer / On down the line / I wonder where you are tonight / First one to love you, The / Greener pastures / You took all the ramblin' out of me / Uncle Billy play your fiddle for me.
LP. . . . . **CMH 6229**
MC . . . . **CMHC 6229**
CMH (USA) / C.M. Distribution / Projection.

SHINING PATH, THE.
Tracks: Not Advised.
LP. . . . . **SH 3751**
MC . . . . **SH 3751 MC**
Sugarhill(USA) / Mar '89 / Roots Records / Projection / Impetus Records / C.M. Distribution / Jazz Music / Swift / Duncans / A.D.A Distribution.

SUNDAY MORNIN' SINGIN'.
Tracks: Not Advised.
LP. . . . . **CMH 6247**
MC . . . . **CMHC 6247**
CMH (USA) / C.M. Distribution / Projection.

WELCOME TO VIRGINIA.
Tracks: Not Advised.
LP. . . . . **ROUNDER 0097**
MC . . . . **ROUNDER 0097C**
Rounder / '88 / Projection / Roots Records / Swift / C.M. Distribution / Topic Records / Jazz Music / Hot Shot / A.D.A Distribution / Direct Distribution.

WHERE RAINBOWS TOUCH DOWN.
Tracks: Not Advised.
LP. . . . . **CMH 6259**
MC . . . . **CMHC 6259**
CMH (USA) / C.M. Distribution / Projection.

Blue Ridge Rangers

BLUE RIDGE RANGERS.
Tracks: Blue Ridge Mountain blues / Somewhere listening (for my name) / You're the reason / Jambalaya / She thinks I still care / California blues / Workin' on a building / Please help me I'm falling / Have thine own way / I ain't never / Hearts of stone / Today I started loving you again.
■ **LP.** **5C 038 94373**
EMI / Dec '82.
CD . . . . **CDFE 506**
LP. . . . . **FACE 506**
MC . . . . **FACC 506**
Fantasy / Oct '87 / Pinnacle / Target Records / Jazz Music.

Blue Rose

BLUE ROSE.
Tracks: Not Advised.
LP. . . . . **SH 3768**
Sugarhill(USA) / '88 / Roots Records / Projection / Impetus Records / C.M. Distribution / Jazz Music / Swift / Duncans / A.D.A Distribution.

Blue Sky Boys

Brothers Bill and Earl Bolick - both from Hickory, North Carolina - served their apprenticeship working in various local bands before signing with RCA Victor in 1936, when they first used the name Blue Sky Boys. They remained active until 1951, at which time they quit the music scene and pursued other occupations. Their best known song is *The Sunnyside Of Life*, while their distinctive harmonies were to influence such acts as the Everly Brothers, the Louvin Brothers and Jim and Jessie McReynolds. (Tony Byworth)

BLUE SKY BOYS, BILL AND EARL BOLICK.
Tracks: Don't this road look rough and rocky / Green grow the lilacs / Lawson family, The / Tragedy / You could be a millionaire / Curly headed baby / If I could hear my mother pray again / Tramp on the street / Searching for a soldier's grave / Unloved and unclaimed / Let me be your salty dog / My ma in trail / What does the deep sea say / When I take my vacation in heaven.
LP. . . . . **ROUNDER 0052**
Rounder / '88 / Projection / Roots Records / Swift / C.M. Distribution / Topic Records / Jazz Music / Hot Shot / A.D.A Distribution / Direct Distribution.

IN CONCERT 1964.
Tracks: Not Advised.
CD . . . . **CD 11536**
LP. . . . . **ROUNDER 0236**
MC . . . . **ROUNDERC 0236**
Rounder / Projection / Roots Records / Swift / C.M. Distribution / Topic Records / Jazz Music / Hot Shot / A.D.A Distribution / Direct Distribution.

PRESENTING THE BLUE SKY BOYS.
Tracks: Not Advised.
LP. . . . . **JEMF 104**
JEMF (USA) / '88 / Projection.

SUNNY SIDE OF LIFE.
Tracks: Not Advised.
LP. . . . . **ROUNDER 1006**
MC . . . . **ROUNDER 1006C**
Rounder / '88 / Projection / Roots Records / Swift / C.M. Distribution / Topic Records / Jazz Music / Hot Shot / A.D.A Distribution / Direct Distribution.

Bluegrass

A Country music genre representing the earliest traditional style - that of hillbilly string bands, originating in the Appalachian mountains of southeastern USA. Traditional songs (many descended from Elizabethan Engalnd and Scotland) with high-harmony vocals were backed by a basic instrumentation of fiddle, guitar, mandolin, and 5-string banjo. The dobro was added, with a cone of aluminium to mechanically amplify the guitar. The term 'Dobro' derives from the Dopyera Brothers, who invented it. Roy Acuff's classic hits from the mid-30s conveyed the 'high lonesome' bluegrass sound, while Bill Monroe and His Blue Grass Boys who joined the Grand Ole Opry in 1939, added a banjo for rhythm in 1942. Earl Scruggs joined in 1945 with an astonishing banjo technique and North Carolina style that was characterised by improvisation and influenced by jazz. Bill Monroe was influenced by black music, he experimented until he had a fast, intricate mandolin style while others such as Frank Wakefield and John Duffey have moved even closed to jazz. Monroe's music began to be called bluegrass around 1950 but was considered old fashioned. Scruggs made a solo appearance at the first Newport Folk Festival in 1959. Many bluegrass festivals since then have established its popularity. The Dillards moved from Missouri to Los Angeles and continued developing bluegrass, other West Coast bands such as Country Gazette, and the Kentucky Colonels attracted fans from the rock audience of the 1970s. The film *Deliverence*, gave a shot in the arm to bluegrass, yielding the hit single *Duelling Banjos*, played in the movie by Eric Weissberg on banjo and guitarist Steve Mandel. A movement called *Newgrass*, led by the band Newgrass Revival continued to popularise bluegrass.(Donald Clarke)

Bob & Lucille

CANADIAN SWEETEARTS.
Tracks: Not Advised.
LP. . . . . **LP 100**
Ditto (USA) / Oct '87.

Bogguss, Suzy

One of the 1990's leading female country entertainers, Suzy Kay Bogguss was born on December 30, 1956 in Aledo , Illinois. Growing up in a family circle that possessed diverse musical tastes - her father liked country and her mother big bands - she already had plenty of performing experience under her belt by the time she graduated from Illinois State University (with a B.A. degree in metalsmithery). Then, living the adventurous streak that was part of her nature, she spent five years travelling through the USA, Canada and Mexico, booking her own shows, negotiating her own contracts and advertising her own performances. Finally she arrived in Nashville, where she landed a job singing at a rib restaurant while her entry into the music industry came via demo recordings and back-up singing on studio sessions. In 1986, while appearing at Dollywood, the East Tennessee theme park owned by Dolly Parton, her specially recorded road album came to the attention of Capitol Records, which led on to a contract. Suzy's debut chart single was *I Don't Want To Set The World On Fire*, a revival of 1941's big band hit, and her follow-ups included Merle Haggard's *Somewhere Between*, and Patsy Montana's yodelling classic *I Want To Be A Cowboy's Sweetheart*. It wasn't until 1991 that she started moving into the higher regions of the charts with singles such as *Hopelessly Yours*, (a duet with Lee Greenwood), *Someday Ssoon*, and *Aces*. Her third Capitol album *Aces*, earned Suzy Bogguss her first gold disc (500,000 sales) and, in October 1992, she won the CMA's Horizon Award. She made her UK debut at the 1989 Wembley Festival and her first tour in 1993. (Tony Byworth)

ACES.
Tracks: Outbound plane / Aces / Someday soon / Let goodbye hurt like it should / Save yourself / Yellow river road / Part of me / Letting go / Music on the wind / Still hold on.
CD **C2 95847**
MC **C4 95847**
Capitol Nashville / Feb '92 / EMI.

DRIVE SOUTH.
Tracks: Drive south / Outbound train / Letting go (Features on CDS only.).
7" . . . . **CL 691**
CD Single . . . . **CDCL 691**
MC Single . . . . **TCCL 691**
EMI / Jul '93 / EMI.

HEY CINDERELLA.
Tracks: Hey Cinderella / Heartache / Diamonds & tears (On CD single only).
7" . . . . **CL 695**
CD Single . . . . **CDCL 695**
MC Single . . . . **TCCL 695**
EMI / Sep '93 / EMI.

LETTING GO.
Tracks: Letting go / Eat at Joe's / Let goodbye hurt like it should (Available on CD Single only.).
7" . . . . **CL 680**
CD Single . . . . **CDCL 680**
■ **MC Single** . . . . **TCCL 680**
EMI / Feb '93.

SOMETHING UP MY SLEEVE.
Tracks: Diamonds & tears / Just like the weather / Just keep comin' back to you / You never will / You'd be the one / Take it to the limit / Hey Cinderella / Souvenirs / You wouldn't say that to a stranger / Take it like a man / No green eyes / Something up my sleeve.
CD **72438273982**
MC **72438273984**
EMI / '93 / EMI.

B 12 ■ DELETED

VOICES IN THE WIND.
Tracks: Heartache / Drive south / Don't wanna / How come you go to her / Other side of the hill / In the day / Love goes without saying / Eat at Joe's / Lovin' a hurricane / Letting go / Cold day in July.
CD C2 98585
MC C4 98585
Liberty / Oct '92 / EMI.

Bond, Eddie

Associated with both the country and rockabilly scenes, Eddie Bond - who was born in Memphis in 1933 - recorded for a couple of dozen independent labels from 1955 onwards, the only major being Mercury Starday. A frequent visitor to European shores, he's been seen on rock'n'-roll festivals and tours, often appearing with British musician/bandleader Dave Travis, who's produced some of his recordings. (Tony Byworth)

CAUTION.
Tracks: Caution / Call your bluff / Before it's too late let's talk it over / It's wonderful / Another man's shoes / Mississippi dreams / That glass / Was it really that bad / Whatever makes you happy / Before the next teardrop falls / Free.
VHS . . . . MMGV 008
MMG Video / Jan '88 / Terry Blood Dist.

CAUTION EDDIE BOND MUSIC IS..
Tracks: Caution / Traitor / It's wonderful / Another man's shoes / That glass / Whatever makes you happy / Before the next teardrop falls / Somebody that won't lie / Time / Free / Devil is a woman.
LP. . . . . MFLP 057
Magnum Force / Dec '87 / Terry Blood Dist. / Jazz Music / Hot Shot.

EARLY YEARS, THE.
Tracks: Monkey and the baboon, The / Jukejoint Johnny / Cliff Finch train, The / When the jukebox plays / Hey Joe / It's been so long darling / Standing in your window / Blues got me, The / Here comes that train / Someday I'll sober up / Rockin' daddy / You don't miss your water / Boo bop da caa caa / You'll never be a stranger to me / Big boss man / My buckets got a hole in it / I'll step aside / Can't win for losing / Doody do right.
LP. . . . . SJLP 574
Sunjay / Feb '88 / CSA Tell Tapes.

EDDIE BOND (Original Early Recordings).
Tracks: Rockin' daddy / I got a woman / Baby, baby / Hershey bar / Backslidin' / Love, love, love / Double duty lovin' / Talkin' off the wall / Flip flop mama / Slip, slip, slippin' in / Boppin' Bonnie / You're a part of me / They say we're too young / Lovin' you, lovin' you / Love makes a fool / Your eyes.
LP. . . . . WLP 8876
White Label (Germany) / Dec '86 / Pinnacle / Bear Family Records (Germany) / CSA Tell Tapes.

EDDIE BOND SINGS COUNTRY GOSPEL HITS.
Tracks: Not Advised.
LP. 33.1962.01
Starclub / Nov '87 / Swift.

I GOT A WOMAN.
Tracks: Not Advised.
■ EP. . . . . RSREP 2002
Rockstar (1) / May '88 / Swift / C.M. Distribution.

NIGHT TRAIN TO MEMPHIS.
Tracks: Not Advised.
LP. . . . . RLP 002
Rundell / Jun '88 / Swift.

ROCKIN' DADDY.
Tracks: Double duty lovin / Talking off the wall / Love makes a fool (Everyday) / Your eyes / I got a woman / Rockin Daddy / Slip, slip slippin in / Baby, baby , baby (What am I gonna do) / Flip flop Mama / Boppin' Bonnie / You're part of me / King on your throne / They say we're too young / Backslidin / Love, love, love / Lovin you, lovin you / Hershey bar / One step close to you / Show me (Without sax) / Broke my guitar / This old heart of mine / Show me (With sax) / One more memory / I can't quit / My bucket's got a hole in it / Back home in Indiana (Instrumental) / They'll never take her love from me / Day I found you, The / Standing in the window / Back street affair / Our secret rendezvous / I'd just be fool enough / You nearly lost your mind / I thought I heard you call my name / Big boss man / In my solitude / Most of all I want to see Jesus / Where could I go but to the Lord / Satisfied / When they ring those golden bells / If we never meet again / Will I be lost or will I be saved / Just a closer walk with thee / Pass me not, oh gentle saviour / I saw the light / Letter to God / Precious memories / Hallelujah way.
CD Set . . . . BCD 15708
Bear Family / May '93 / Rollercoaster Records / Swift / Direct Distribution.

ROCKIN' DADDY.
Tracks: Rockin' daddy / Big boss man / Can't win for losing / When the jukebox plays / Hey Joe / Monkey and the baboon / Blues got me, The / Standing in your window / Look like a monkey / I'll step aside / Memphis, Tennessee / My bucket's got a hole in it / Winners circle / Jukejoint Johnnie / You'll never be a stranger to me / Boo bop da caa caa / Heart full of heartaches, A / Here comes the train / Someday I'll sober up / Double duty lovin' / Let's make the parting sweet / Tomorrow I'll be gone / One more memory / Country shindig / When the jukebox plays (2) / Raunchy / Cold dark waters / Your eyes / It's been so long darling / Your old standby / This old heart of mine.
CD . . . . STCD 1
Stomper Time / '92 / Magnum Music Group.

ROCKIN' DADDY FROM MEMPHIS VOL.1.
Tracks: Not Advised.
LP. . . . . LP 8206
Rockhouse / Oct '88 / Charly / C.M. Distribution / Nervous Records.

ROCKIN' DADDY FROM MEMPHIS VOL.2.
Tracks: Not Advised.
LP. . . . . LPL 8406
Rockhouse / Sep '84 / Charly / C.M. Distribution / Nervous Records.
LP. . . . . LP 8406
Rockhouse / Oct '88 / Charly / C.M. Distribution / Nervous Records.

Bond, Johnny

Country singer, songwriter and actor, Johnny Bond was was part of the Jimmy Wakely trio in 1937.Bond joined Gene Autry on the West Coast, appeared in Autry's Melody Ranch CBS Broadcasts between 1940-55 and as his guitar-playing sidekick in films with Autry, Tex Ritter, Roy Rogers and Hopalong Cassidy. Johnny Bond also appeared in the feature film; *Duel In The Sun*, in 1945. He had many country hits from 1940 and wrote country classics such as *I Wonder Where You Are Tonight*, *Tomorrow Never Comes*, *I'll Step Aside* and *Your Old Love Letters*. Among his best-known hits were *Hot Rod Lincoln*, which crossed over to the top 30 in the USA in 1960 *Ten Little Bottles*.(Donald Clarke)

BEST OF JOHNNY BOND.
Tracks: Not Advised.
LP. . . . . SLP 954
MC . . . . GT 5954
Starday (USA) / Apr '87 / Crusader Marketing Co.

SINGS THE GREAT SONGS OF THAT WILD WICKED BUT WONDERFUL WEST.
Tracks: Pass, The / Fool's paradise, The / Bully, The / Night noon / At dawn I die / Empty saddles / Conversation with a gun / Sadie was a lady / Wanderers of the wasteland / Long tall shadow, The / Deadwood stage, The / Carry me back to the lone prairie / Dusty skies / Belle starr.
LP. . . . . OFF 9000
Official / '88 / Charly / Cadillac Music / Jazz Music.

Bonnie Lou

TENNESSEE WIG WALK.
Tracks: Tennessee wig walk.
■ 7". . . . . R 3730
Parlophone / Feb '54.

Bonsall, Joe

CAJUN JAMBOREE.
Tracks: Not Advised.
LP. 6008
Swallow (USA) / Feb '82 / Swift / Wellard Dist.

CAJUN JAMBOREE VOL 2.
Tracks: Not Advised.
LP. 6012
Swallow (USA) / Feb '79 / Swift / Wellard Dist.

JOE BONSALL'S GREATEST HITS.
Tracks: Not Advised.
LP. 6049
Swallow (USA) / Swift / Wellard Dist.
MC . . . . 6049 TC
Swallow (USA) / '87 / Swift / Wellard Dist.

Boone Creek

BOONE CREEK.
Tracks: Dixieland / Dark is the night / Walkin' in Jerusalem / Gonna settle down / Drifting too far from the shore / White house blues / Boone Creek / Memory of your smile, The / Intro / Satisfy my mind / Sugar daddy / Ain't nobody gonna miss me.
LP. . . . . SDLP 017
Sundown / May '85 / Terry Blood Dist. / Jazz Music / C.M. Distribution.
LP. . . . . ROUNDER 0081
MC . . . . ROUNDER 0081C
Rounder / '88 / Projection / Roots Records / Swift / C.M. Distribution / Topic Records / Jazz Music / Hot Shot / A.D.A Distribution / Direct Distribution.

ONE WAY TRACK.
Tracks: One way rider / Head over heels / Little community church / Mississippi queen / In the pines / Can't you hear me callin' / No mother or dad / Blue and lonesome / Daniel prayed / Sally Goodun.
LP. . . . . SH 3701
MC . . . . SH 3701 MC
Sugarhill(USA) / Jun '79 / Roots Records / Projection / Impetus Records / C.M. Distribution / Jazz Music / Swift / Duncans / A.D.A Distribution.

Boone Girls

HEAVENLY LOVE.
Tracks: Heavenly love / He lives / My sisters and brothers / Praise the Lord / No I've never / Because I love him / You came softly / No I can't stop / Your love / Fairest Lord Jesus.
LP. . . . . LL 2021
MC . . . . LLC 2021
Lamb & Lion / May '82 / Word Records (UK).

Boone, Debbie

A pop/country singer, born in 1956 in Hackensack, New Jersey. The daughter of Pat Boone, she sang on the Boone family gospel albums. Debbie Boone's first solo single was from the Oscar-winning film *You Light Up My Life*, which won the Song Of The Year Grammy 1977, spent 10 weeks at the top of the USA pop chart ,and reached the top five of the country chart. After that she had country hits, diversified into acting, wrote an autobiography.(Donald Clarke)

CALIFORNIA.
Tracks: California / Hey everybody.
■ 7". . . . . K 17097
WEA / Feb '78.

CHOOSE LIFE.
Tracks: Not Advised.
LP. . . . . LLR 3008
MC . . . . LLC 3008
Lamb & Lion / Jul '85 / Word Records (UK).

FREE TO BE LONELY AGAIN.
Tracks: Free to be lonely again / Love put a song.
■ 7". . . . . K 17682
WEA / Sep '80.

FRIENDS FOR LIFE.
Tracks: Not Advised.
CD . . . . CDO 3011
LP. . . . . R 03011
MC . . . . C 03011
Word (UK) / '89 / Word Records (UK) / Sony.

SURRENDER.
Tracks: Not Advised.
LP. . . . . LLR 3001
MC . . . . LLC 3001
Lamb & Lion / Aug '84 / Word Records (UK).
CD . . . . LLD 3001
Word (UK) / Aug '85 / Word Records (UK) / Sony.

YOU LIGHT UP MY LIFE.
Tracks: You light up my life / Hasta manana.
■ 7". . . . . K 17043
WEA / '79.

Boone, Larry

SWINGING DOORS, SAWDUST FLOORS.
Tracks: I just called to say goodbye / It's our year to see the bluebird / Under a love star moon / Blue collar dollar / I'm not fool enough to fool around / Ten times Texas.
CD 836 710-2
LP. 836 710-1
■ MC 836 710-4
Mercury / Mar '89.

Boone, Pat

Born Charles Eugene Boone in 1934 in Jacksonville, Florida, Pat Boone was the second most successful male artist in USA pop after Elvis Presley in the late '50s. His first single *Two Hearts, Two Kisses* was first of 38 USA top 40 hits 1955-62, including 10 top 10 entries, six at No. 1. His style was distinguished by his clean-cut image; many hits were covers of black artists: Fats Domino's *Ain't That A Shame*, Ivory Joe Hunter's *I Almost Lost My Mind*, most ludicrously Little Richard's *Long Tall Sally*; ballads included *Love Letters In The Sand* and *April Love*, both chart toppers. He made several films; fade from charts was accompanied by business and marriage trouble; he turned to religion, made gospel albums and had country hits.(Donald Clarke)

16 CLASSIC TRACKS: PAT BOONE.
Tracks: April love / Don't forbid me / I almost lost my mind / At my front door / Friendly persuasion / Sugar moon / Moody river / I'll be home / Love letters in the sand / Gospel boogie / Remember you're mine / Ain't that a shame / Main attraction / It's too soon to know / Why baby why? / Speedy Gonzales.
LP. . . . . MCL 1676
MC . . . . MCLC 1676
ABC Records / Apr '82.
■ LP. . . . . MFP 50549
MFP / Mar '82.

20 BEST LOVED GOSPEL SONGS - PAT BOONE.
Tracks: Down from his glory / He touched me / Whispering hope / It's free / Answer, The / I'm coming home / Thank you / Woman at the well / Do Lord / Lord's prayer, The / There's a song in my heart / Face to face / Saved by grace / Man called Billy, A / Yesterday, today and tomorrow / How great thou art / Heaven is my home / Lead the way Lord / My wish my prayer.
LP . . . . SHARON 323
Pilgrim.

20 GOLDEN PIECES: PAT BOONE.
Tracks: Not Advised.
MC . . . . BDC 2053
Bulldog Records / '86 / President Records / Jazz Music / Wellard Dist. / TKO Records Ltd.
LP . . . . BDL 2053
Bulldog Records / Nov '86 / President Records / Jazz Music / Wellard Dist. / TKO Records Ltd.
CD . . . . BDCD 2053
Bulldog Records / May '89 / President Records / Jazz Music / Wellard Dist. / TKO Records Ltd.

20 GREATEST HITS: PAT BOONE.
Tracks: Not Advised.
CD 30CP 26
EMI (Import) / '88.

AIN'T THAT A SHAME?.
Tracks: Ain't that a shame.
■ 7" . . . . HLD 8173
London-American / Nov '55.

ALL FOR THE LOVE OF SUNSHINE.
Tracks: All for the love of sunshine.
■ 7" 2006 257
MGM (Polydor) / Apr '74.

ALL THE HITS.
Tracks: Speedy Gonzales / Ain't that a shame / Love letters in the sand / Johnny Will / April love / I'll be home / Moody river / Don't forbid me / Remember you're mine / I almost lost my mind / Why baby why / Wonderful time up there, A.
LP . . . . TOP 154
MC . . . . KTOP 154
Topline / May '87 / Charly / Swift / Black Sun Records.

ALL-TIME FAVOURITES.
Tracks: Not Advised.
MC . . . . GM 0218
K-Tel Goldmasters / Aug '84 / C.M. Distribution / Arabesque Ltd. / Ross Records / PolyGram.

APRIL LOVE.
Tracks: April love.
■ 7" . . . . HLD 8512
London-American / Dec '57.

APRIL LOVE (OLD GOLD).
Tracks: April love.
■ 7" . . . . OG 9211
Old Gold / Jul '82.

BABY OH BABY.
Tracks: Baby, oh baby / Rose Marie / Baby sonnenschein / Wie eine lady / Ein goldener stern / Komm zu mir wenn du einsam bist / Oh lady / Nein nein valentina / Mary Lou / Wo find ich meine traume / Que pasa contigo / Y te quiero / Recuerdame siempre / Amor al reves / En cualquier lugar / Cartas en la arena / Tu che non hai amato mai / E fuori la pioggia cade / Se tu non fossi qui.
■ LP . . . . BFX 15185
Bear Family / Feb '86.
CD . . . . BCD 15645
Bear Family / Jun '92 / Rollercoaster Records / Swift / Direct Distribution.

BEST OF PAT BOONE.
Tracks: Not Advised.
LP . . . . WW 5089
MC . . . . WW 4 5089
Warwick / Jan '81 / Sony / Henry Hadaway Organisation / Multiple Sound Distributors.

DON'T FORBID ME.
Tracks: Don't forbid me.
■ 7" . . . . HLD 8370
London-American / Feb '57.

FOR A PENNY.
Tracks: For a penny.
■ 7" . . . . HLD 8855
London-American / May '59.

FRIENDLY PERSUASION.
Tracks: Ain't that a shame / I'll be home / I almost lost my mind / Friendly persuasion / No other arms / Gee Whittakers / Love letters in the sand / Spring rain / Don't forbid me / Wonderful time up there, A / Cherie I love you / Moody river / Long tall Sally / Why baby why? / Mona Lisa / It's too soon to know / Are you lonesome tonight / When I fall in love / Speedy Gonzales / Tutti frutti / Johnny will / When the swallows come back to Capistrane / Fools hall of fame / Wang dang tally apple, The / I'll see you in my dreams / Bernadine.
Double LP . . . . CR 042
■ MC Set . . . . CRT 042
Cambra / Apr '85.

FRIENDLY PERSUASION.
Tracks: Friendly persuasion.
■ 7" . . . . HLD 8346
London-American / Dec '56.

FRIENDLY PERSUASION (OLD GOLD).
Tracks: Friendly persuasion.
7" . . . . OG 9210
Old Gold / Jul '82 / Pickwick Records.

GEE BUT IT'S LONELY.
Tracks: Gee but it's lonely.
■ 7" . . . . HLD 8739
London-American / Dec '58.

GOLDEN GREATS.
Tracks: April love / Don't forbid me / I almost lost my mind / At my front door (Crazy little Mama) / Friendly persuasion (Thee I love) / Sugar moon / Moody river / I'll be home / Love letters in the sand / Gospel boogie (Ev'rybody's gonna have a wonderful time up th / Remember your mine / Ain't that a shame / Main attraction, The / It's too soon to know / Why baby why / Speedy Gonzales.
CD . . . . MCLD 19182
MC . . . . MCLC 19182
MCA / Mar '93 / BMG.

GOLDEN GREATS: PAT BOONE.
Tracks: I'll be home / Love letters in the sand / Friendly persuasion / Speedy Gonzales / April love / Don't forbid me / I almost lost my mind / At my front door / Sugar moon / Moody river / Gospel boogie / Remember you're mine / Ain't that a shame / Main attraction / It's too soon to know / Why baby why.
■ LP . . . . MCM 5006
MCA / Jul '85.
■ MC . . . . MCMC 5006
MCA / Jul '85.

GOLDEN HITS: PAT BOONE.
Tracks: Not Advised.
LP . . . . MA 81285
MC . . . . MAMC 981285
Masters (Holland) / '88.

GREAT PRETENDER, THE.
Tracks: Not Advised.
CD . . . . CD 66064
Ce De International / Jul '93 / Taylors.

GREATEST HITS:PAT BOONE.
Tracks: Not Advised.
LP P.Disc. . . . . AR 30043
Astan (USA) / Dec '85.
CD . . . . CD 860701
Card/Grand Prix / Dec '86.
CD 120 105
MCS Look Back / Jul '87.

HIS TOP HITS.
Tracks: Not Advised.
MC 802
Timeless Treasures / Jul '86 / Terry Blood Dist.

HOME.
Tracks: Not Advised.
LP . . . . R 03012
MC . . . . C 03012
Word (UK) / '89 / Word Records (UK) / Sony.

HYMNS WE HAVE LOVED.
Tracks: Not Advised.
■ LP . . . . HAD 2228
London-American / May '60.

HYMNS WE LOVE.
Tracks: Not Advised.
■ LP . . . . HAD 2092
London-American / Jun '60.

I ALMOST LOST MY MIND.
Tracks: I almost lost my mind.
■ 7" . . . . HLD 8303
London-American / Aug '56.

I'LL BE HOME.
Tracks: I'll be home.
■ 7" . . . . HLD 8253
London-American / Apr '56.

I'LL REMEMBER TONIGHT.
Tracks: I'll remember tonight.
■ 7" . . . . HLD 8775
London-American / Jan '59.

I'LL SEE YOU IN MY DREAMS.
Tracks: I'll see you in my dreams.
■ 7" . . . . HLD 9504
London-American / Feb '62.

IF DREAMS COME TRUE.
Tracks: If dreams come true.
■ 7" . . . . HLD 8675
London-American / Aug '58.

JIVIN' PAT.
Tracks: Good rockin' tonight / For my good fortune / Flip flop and fly / Shotgun boogie / Fat man / Tutti frutti / Two hearts / Rock boll weevil / Honey hush / Bingo / Rock around the clock / I'll walk with you / Money honey / Wonderful time up there, A / Ain't nobody here but us chickens.
LP . . . . BFX 15230

Bear Family / Feb '86 / Rollercoaster Records / Swift / Direct Distribution.

JOHNNY WILL.
Tracks: Johnny will.
■ 7" . . . . HLD 9461
London-American / Dec '61.

LONG TALL SALLY.
Tracks: Long tall Sally.
■ 7" . . . . HLD 8291
London-American / Jul '56.

LOVE LETTERS IN THE SAND.
Tracks: Not Advised.
CD . . . . ONCD 5106
K-Tel / Jan '86 / I & B Records / C.M. Distribution / Arabesque Ltd. / Mono Distributors (Jersey) Ltd. / Prism Leisure PLC / PolyGram / Ross Records / Prism Leisure PLC.
CD . . . . ENTCD 238
LP . . . . ENT LP 13030
MC . . . . ENT MC 13030
Entertainers / '88.

LOVE LETTERS IN THE SAND.
Tracks: Love letters in the sand.
■ 7" . . . . HLD 8445
London-American / Aug '57.

LOVE LETTERS IN THE SAND (OLD GOLD).
Tracks: Love lettes in the sand.
■ 7" . . . . OG 9209
Old Gold / Jul '82.

LOVE SONGS: PAT BOONE.
Tracks: Who's sorry now / It's a sin to tell a lie / True in my dreams / True love / Secret love / I'm in the mood for love / I'll see you in my dreams / Deep purple / Ebb tide / Stardust / Send me the pillow that you dream on / Blue moon / Misty / Night and day / Yesterday / He'll have to go / Are you lonesome tonight / Love letters in the sand.
LP . . . . MFP 5758
■ MC . . . . TCMFP 5758
MFP / Aug '86.

MAIN ATTRACTION, THE.
Tracks: Main attraction.
■ 7" . . . . HLD 6920
London-American / Oct '62.

MOODY RIVER.
Tracks: Moody river.
■ 7" . . . . HLD 9350
London-American / Jul '61.

PAT BOONE ORIGINALS.
Tracks: Not Advised.
■ Double LP . . . . ABSD 301
ABC Records / Apr '76.

QUANDO QUANDO QUANDO.
Tracks: Quando, quando, quando.
■ 7" . . . . HLD 9543
London-American / May '62.

REMEMBER YOU'RE MINE.
Tracks: Remember you're mine / There's a goldmine in the sky.
■ 7" . . . . HLD 8479
London-American / Sep '57.

SPEEDY GONZALES.
Tracks: Speedy Gonzales / Johnny will.
■ 7" . . . . HLD 9573
London-American / Jul '62.
■ 7" . . . . MCA 701
MCA / Aug '80.

SPEEDY GONZALES (OLD GOLD).
Tracks: Speedy Gonzales.
7" . . . . OG 9213
Old Gold / Jul '82 / Pickwick Records.

SPEEDY GONZALES (OLD GOLD) (2).
Tracks: Speedy Gonzales / Johnny will / Moody river.
CD Single . . . . OG 6153
Old Gold / Nov '90 / Pickwick Records.

STARDUST.
Tracks: Not Advised.
■ LP . . . . HAD 2127
London-American / Nov '58.

SUGAR MOON.
Tracks: Beach girl / Anastasia / Exodus / Dear John / Welcome new lovers / 500 miles / Blueberry Hill / For a penny / Candy sweet / Sugar moon / Ten lonely guys / Twixt 12 and 20 / At my front door.
■ MC Set . . . . CRT 012
Cambra / May '84.

SUGAR MOON.
Tracks: Sugar moon.
■ 7" . . . . HLD 8640
London-American / Jun '58.

TWIXT TWELVE AND TWENTY.
Tracks: Twixt twelve and twenty.
■ 7" . . . . HLD 8910
London-American / Jul '59.

■ DELETED

UNFORGETTABLE: PAT BOONE (16 Golden Classics).
Tracks: I'll be home / Ain't that a shame / Speedy Gonzales / Yesterday / Exodus / Misty / By the time I get to Phoenix / Who's sorry now / April love / Quando, quando, quando / Johnny will / Friendly persuasion / Love letters in the sand / Wonderful time up there, A / I'll see you in my dreams / Words / Walking the floor over you / At my front door / No other arms.
CD . . . . UNCD 023
LP. . . . . UNLP 023
MC . . . . UNMC 023
Unforgettable / Nov '87 / BMG.

VERY BEST OF PAT BOONE.
Tracks: Love letters in the sand / Speedy Gonzales / April love / I'll be home / Gospel boogie / Johnny will / Sugar moon / Ain't that a shame / Don't forbid me / Remember you're mine / I almost lost my mind / It's too soon to know / Moody river / Main attraction / There's a goldmine in the sky / Friendly persuasion.
CD . . . . PWK 074
Pickwick / Sep '88 / Pickwick Records.
MC . . . . HSC 3279
Hallmark / Jun '89 / Pickwick Records.

WALKING THE FLOOR OVER YOU.
Tracks: Walking the floor over you.
■ 7" . . . . HLD 9138
London-American / Jun '60.

WHAT I BELIEVE.
Tracks: Old rugged cross, The / Softly and tenderly / Onward christian soldiers / Wonderful words of life / How a firm foundation / It was his love / People need the Lord / Let me live / What I believe.
LP. . . . . LLR 3004
MC . . . . LLC 3004
Lamb & Lion / Aug '85 / Word Records (UK).

WHISPERING HOPE.
Tracks: Whispering hope / Mine eyes have seen the glory / Yield not to temptation / I love to tell the story / Have thine own way / Take the name of Jesus with you / He (can turn the tide) / I walked today where Jesus walked / Saviour like a shepherd lead us / It is no secret / How great thou art / Sofly and tenderly / Abide with me / Let the lower lights be burning / Old rugged cross, The / Blessed assurance / Jesus is mine / I believe / What a friend we have in Jesus / God be with you till we meet again / Will the circle be unbroken.
LP. . . . . TWE 6008
MC . . . . TC TWE 6008
Word 20 / May '82 / Sony.

WHITE CHRISTMAS.
Tracks: White Christmas.
■ 7" . . . . HLD 8520
London-American / Dec '57.

WHY BABY WHY.
Tracks: Why baby why.
■ 7" . . . . HLD 8404
London-American / Apr '57.

WITH THE WIND AND THE RAIN IN YOUR HAIR.
Tracks: With the wind and the rain in your hair.
■ 7" . . . . HLD 8824
London-American / Apr '59.

WONDERFUL TIME UP THERE.
Tracks: Wonderful time up there, A / It's too soon to know.
■ 7" . . . . HLD 8574
London-American / Apr '58.

Bowen, Jimmy

JIMMY BOWEN.
Tracks: Not Advised.
LP. . . . . R 25004
Roulette / Nov '87 / EMI.

Bowie, Jim

NEWGRASS.
Tracks: Not Advised.
MC . . . . C 205
Topic / Apr '93 / Roots Records / Jazz Music / C.M. Distribution / Cadillac Music / Direct Distribution / Swift / Topic Records.

Bowler, Belinda

TURNING POINT.
Tracks: I thought I was a child / Millworker / Baby I'm fallin' / Come down in time / How can I keep from singing? / Turning point / Lovin' arms / For Holden / Whitebark / Weakness in me.
LP. . . . . PTLP 006
P.T. Music / Feb '89 / ACD Trading Ltd.

Boxcar Willie

Lecil Travis Martin was born in Texas in 1931. He began semi-pro in early '50s as Marty Martin, was a pilot in the USAF, then adopted a hobo persona and a new name. after tours of Scotland and an appearance at the Wembley Festival in 1979 he finally became a star. His repertoire is based on music of his idols Jimmy Rodgers, Hank Williams and Lefty Frizzell. Boxcar Willie has also written more than 400 songs of his own and made his USA chart debut in 1983 with *Not The Man I Used To Be*. His *King Of The Road* compilation reached number 5 in the UK charts. (Donald Clarke)

20 GREAT HITS.
Tracks: I've got a bad case of feeling sorry for me / Lord made a hobo out of me, The / Blue eyed girl of Berlin / Six pound fish / Fragrance of her perfume, The / Daddy was a railroad man / Day Elvis died, The / Hot box blues / I'm going back to Texas / I can't help it (if I'm still in love with you) / I'm so lonesome I could cry / Lonesome whistle / Waiting for a train / T B blues / Cold windy city of Chicago / Take me home / I wake up every morning with a smile on my face / Trouble / Train medley.
LP. . . . . BRA 1012
MC . . . . BRC 1012
Big R / Sep '81 / Pinnacle.

BEST LOVED FAVOURITES VOL.1.
Tracks: Blue moon of Kentucky / Crazy arms / In the jailhouse now / I won't get over you / Six days on the road / Wings of a dove / Pistol packin' mama / Half as much / Whistle ain't made of gold / Almost persuaded / Louisiana Saturday night.
CD . . . . ND 71946
LP. . . . . NL 71946
MC . . . . NK 71946
RCA / Dec '88 / BMG.

BEST LOVED FAVOURITES VOL.2.
Tracks: This ole house / Good hearted woman / Mom and dad's waltz / I'm thinking tonight of my blue eyes / Fraulein / I'll fly away / Goodnight Irene / Cold cold heart / L.A. lady / Lovesick blues / Don't pretend.
CD . . . . ND 74210
LP. . . . . NL 74210
MC . . . . NK 74210
RCA / May '90 / BMG.

BEST OF BOXCAR WILLIE.
Tracks: Waitin' for a train / From a Rolls to the rails / Lord made a hobo out of me / Take me home / I wake up every morning with a smile / I came so close to calling you last night / I'm so lonesome I could cry / Lonesome whistle / Daddy was a railroad man / Hot box blues / I can't help it / Day Elvis died, The / Hank, you still make me cry / Train medley.
LP. . . . . SHM 3117
Hallmark / '88 / Pickwick Records.
■ MC . . . . HSC 3117
Hallmark / '88.

BOXCAR WILLIE.
Tracks: Songs of songs / Dreary days / Gypsy lady and the hobo / Honey I love you / Cheating wife / Boxcar's my home / My hearts deep in the heart of Texas / Hobo heaven / Big freight train carry me home / Ain't gonna be your day.
LP. . . . . BRA 1001
Big R / Nov '80 / Pinnacle.
LP. . . . . MCF 3309
■ MC . . . . MCFC 3309
MCA / Mar '86.

BOXCAR WILLIE SINGS COUNTRY.
Tracks: I love the sound of a whistle / Train medley / T for Texas / Waiting for a train / Lord made a hobo outta me / Hank Williams medley / Wreck of the old 97 / He stopped lovin' her today / I'm not the man I used to be / Papa's old pocketwatch / Wabash Cannonball / Y'all come.
VHS. . . . . BBCV 4044
BBC Video / '88 / Sony / Gold & Sons / Terry Blood Dist.

COLLECTION: BOXCAR WILLIE.
Tracks: Lost highway / We made memories / S.U.C.K.E.R. / Ain't no record / Tomorrow the sun's gonna shine / Sioux city Sue / Living it up in Washington D.C. / Blue, blue days / Hee haw honey / Booze, broads & bad times / I'm so lonely I could cry / Your tip's on the table, Mable / Tennessee rain / Atomic bum / Rebel soldier / Cattle call / I'm mad / Deprsssin' recession blues / I was kind of in the neighbourhood / Streamline cannonball / Every time your love touches me / Mansion on the hill / Old iron trail, The / Waltz across Texas.
Double LP . . . . CCSLP 159
Castle Collector Series / Jul '87 / BMG / Pinnacle / Castle Communications.
CD . . . . CCSCD 159
MC . . . . CCSMC 159
Castle Collector Series / Feb '93 / BMG / Pinnacle / Castle Communications.

COLLECTION: BOXCAR WILLIE (2).
Tracks: Lost highway / We made memories / S.U.C.K.E.R. / Living it up in Washington D.C. / Blue blue days, blue blue nights / Tennessee rain / Atomic bum / I was kind of in the neighbourhood / Streamline cannon ball.
LP. . . . . SPLP 005
MC . . . . SPLC 005
Spartan / Jan '86.

COUNTRY STORE: BOXCAR WILLIE.
Tracks: Gotta travel on / Wayward wind / If you've got the money, I've got the time / When my blue moon turns to gold again / I love you because / Have I told you lately that I love you / Packy / Jambalaya / Movin' on / Walking the floor above you / Mama tried / Rock Island line / Baby we're really in love / Will the circle be unbroken.
CD . . . . CDCST 26
MC . . . . CSTK 26
Country Store / Nov '88 / BMG.
■ LP. . . . . CST 26
Country Store / Nov '88.

DADDY WAS A RAILROAD MAN.
Tracks: Not Advised.
LP. . . . . BRA 1004
MC . . . . BRC 1004
Big R / Nov '80 / Pinnacle.

FREIGHT TRAIN BLUES.
Tracks: Last train to heaven / Bummin' around / Bad news / Keep on rollin' down the line / Freight train blues / Lonesome blues / We made memories / You got the kind of love that grabs a hold / To my baby I'm a big star all the time / Don't blame me for what happened last night / There's nothing like a good ol' country song / Lefty left us lonely.
LP. . . . . N 23001
Colorado / Apr '85.

GERTRUDE STEIN (Martin, Marty).
Tracks: Not Advised.
MC 0367
Caedmon (USA) / '81 / Gower Publishing.

GOOD HEARTED WOMAN.
Tracks: Good hearted woman / Cold windy city of Chicago.
7" . . . . BRS 01
Big R / Mar '81 / Pinnacle.

GOOD OL' COUNTRY SONGS.
Tracks: Bummin' around / Bad news / That sinking feeling / Keep on rollin' down the line / Freight train blues / Lefty left us lonely / Eagle / Lonesome Joe / Alligator song, The / To my baby I'm a big star all the time / You got the kind of love that grabs a hold.. / We made memories / Dearest darling / Don't blame me for what happened last night / There's nothing like a good ol' country song.
LP. . . . . NE 1168
MC . . . . CE 2168
K-Tel / Apr '82 / I & B Records / C.M. Distribution / Arabesque Ltd. / Mono Distributors (Jersey) Ltd. / Prism Leisure PLC / PolyGram / Ross Records / Prism Leisure PLC.

GREAT TRACKS.
Tracks: Not Advised.
CD 2630042
LP. 2630041
MC 2630044
Big Country / May '88.

GREATEST HITS: BOXCAR WILLIE.
Tracks: Not Advised.
CD 2430025
LP. 2230025
MC 2130025
Big Country / May '88.

KING OF THE ROAD.
Tracks: King of the road / Warbash cannonball / You are my sunshine / Boxcar blues / Don't let the stars get in your eyes / Your cheatin' heart / I saw the light / Wreck of the old '97 / Hank and the hobo / Peace in the valley / Mule train / Hey good lookin' / Kaw-liga / Move it on over / London leaves / Rolling in my sweet baby's arms / Divorce me C.O.D. / Red river valley / Heaven / San Antonio rose.
■ LP. . . . . WW 5084
Warwick / May '80.
LP. . . . . N 23004
Colorado / Apr '85.
MC 43004
Colorado / Dec '85.
CD . . . . PLATCD 23
LP. . . . . PLAT 23
MC . . . . PLAC 23
Platinum Music / Apr '88 / Prism Leisure PLC / Ross Records.

LIVE AT WEMBLEY (Boxcar Willie & Friends).
Tracks: Jambalaya / He'll have to go / You are my sunshine.
CD . . . . PWK 068
Pickwick / Aug '88 / Pickwick Records.

LIVE IN CONCERT.
Tracks: Wreck of the old 97 / Mule train / Cold cold heart.
LP. . . . . SHM 3137
MC . . . . HSC 3137
Hallmark / Apr '84 / Pickwick Records.
CD . . . . PWK 048
Pickwick / Jan '88 / Pickwick Records.

MAN I USED TO BE, THE.
Tracks: Man I used to be, The.
7" . . . . SP 21
Spartan / Apr '85.

MARTY MARTIN SINGS COUNTRY.
Tracks: Boxcar Willie / Mississippi river queen / This kind of man / Change of heart / Picture of you and me / River thru Reno / Living loving angel / Speed limit's thirty / I hope your world don't end / Was it all in fun / You and a fool / Hey doctor man.

■ LP.................... WRS 161
Westwood / Apr '82.

NO MORE TRAINS TO RIDE.
Tracks: Man I used to be, The / Not on the bottom yet / Watching a new love grow / I just gotta go / Luther / Whine whistle / Daddy played over the waves / It ain't no record / Hobo's lament / Mister can you spare a dime / No more trains to ride.
LP...................... N 23002
Colorado / Apr '85.

SINGS HANK WILLIAMS AND JIMMIE RODGERS.
Tracks: Not Advised.
LP...................... BRA 1006
MC...................... BRC 1006
Big R / Nov '80 / Pinnacle.

TAKE ME HOME.
Tracks: Train medley / From a boxcar door / Take me home / Cold windy city of Chicago / Hank, you still make me cry / Country music nightmare / I can't help it (if I'm still in love with you) / I love the sound of a whistle / Blue blue days, blue blue nights / Six pound fish / 'T' for Texas.
LP...................... BRA 1011
MC...................... BRC 1011
Big R / Nov '80 / Pinnacle.
LP...................... N 23003
Colorado / Apr '85.

THEY CALL ME BOXCAR WILLIE (Martin, Marty).
Tracks: Boxcar Willie / Mississippi river queen / Kind of man / Change of heart / Picture of you and me / River thru' Reno / Living, loving angel / Speed limit's thirty, The / I hope your world don't end / Was it all in fun? / You and a fool / Hey doctor man.
LP...................... BDL 1060
Bulldog Records / Aug '88 / President Records / Jazz Music / Wellard Dist. / TKO Records Ltd.

TWO SIDES OF BOXCAR
Tracks: Freightline fever / Truck drivin' man / Phantom 309 / Truck drivin' son of a gun / Six days on the road / Teddy bear / Whiteline fever / Girl on a billboard / How fast them trucks will go / Truckers' prayer / Forty acres / Convoy / Spirit of America / Old Kentucky home / Dixie / Thank you old flag of mine / America / North to Alaska / Play the star spangled banner over me / Battle hymn of the republic / Yankee doodle / Ametrica the beautiful / Battle of New Orleans.
CD...................... CDGRF 151
MC...................... MCGRF 151
Tring Feb '93 / Prism Leusire PLC / Midland Records / Taylors

WATCHING NEW LOVE GROW.
Tracks: Watching new love grow / Luther.
7"...................... SP 129
Spartan / Dec '85.

Boyens, Phyllis

Phyllis Boyens, born in West Virginia. Daughter of Nimrod Workman, a retired coalminer who wrote *Black Lung Blues*. Boyens has been performing/recording since 1975, with the likes of Hazel Dickens, John Prine, Steve Young & Odetta.

I REALLY CARE.
Tracks: Have you ever / Mean papa blues / One night stand / Truck driving man / Last old shovel / Coal tattoo / Here I am / Don't sell daddy no more whiskey / Hewed out of the mountain / To hell with the land / Old fashioned cheatin' / I really care for you.
LP...................... ROUNDER 0162
Rounder / Aug '88 / Projection / Roots Records / Swift / C.M. Distribution / Topic Records / Jazz Music / Hot Shot / A.D.A Distribution / Direct Distribution.

Bradley, Owen

This musician, producer and studio owner was born in 1915 in Tennessee; he became a pioneer of recording in Nashville. For USA Decca (now MCA) he took over A&R production in Nashville, recording Red Foley, Ernest Tubb, Webb Pierce and the Wilburn brothers. Bradley built his famous Quonset Hut in 1955, recorded Buddy Holly there and sold the studio to CBS when he built a new one on 16th Avenue South; now known as Music Row. Here, he produced Brenda Lee, Gene Vincent, Marty Robbins, Kitty Wells and others. With his studio group the Owen Bradley Quintet, he made USA country and pop charts periodically from 1949 to 1958. In 1964 he built Bradley's Barn (burned down in 1980) and worked with Loretta Lynn and Conway Twitty. (Donald Clarke)

BIG GUITAR.
Tracks: Big guitar / Cannonball / Rumble / Ramrod / Tequila / Tricky / Raunchy / Blueberry Hill / Honky Tonk / Five o'clock jump / Hound dog / Stroll, The / Cool daddy / Funky.
■ LP...................... CR 30234
Charly / Jun '84 / Charly.

Brady, Phil

LIVERPOOL SOUNDS.
Tracks: Not Advised.
LP...................... SFA 034
Sweet Folk & Country / Dec '77 / Wellard Dist.

Bray Brothers

PRAIRIE BLUEGRASS (Bray Brothers & Red Cravens).
Tracks: Not Advised.
LP...................... ROUNDER 0053
Rounder / '88 / Projection / Roots Records / Swift / C.M. Distribution / Topic Records / Jazz Music / Hot Shot / A.D.A Distribution / Direct Distribution.

Breakfast Special

BREAKFAST SPECIAL.
Tracks: Not Advised.
LP...................... ROUNDER 3012
Rounder / '88 / Projection / Roots Records / Swift / C.M. Distribution / Topic Records / Jazz Music / Hot Shot / A.D.A Distribution / Direct Distribution.

Breaux, Cleoma

CAJUN CLASSIC.
Tracks: Not Advised.
LP...................... CW 203
Jambalaya / Dec '88 / Charly.

Breedlove, Jimmy

I CAN'T HELP LOVING YOU.
Tracks: I can't help loving you / I saw you.
■ 7"...................... DDS 110
Pye Disco Demand / Jan '75.

JIM BREEDLOVE SINGS ROCK 'N' ROLL HITS.
Tracks: Rock and roll music / Swanee River rock / Whole lotta shakin' goin' on / C.C. rider / Hound dog / My prayer / Long tall Sally / Lonesome road / Killer diller / Great pretender, The / Jailhouse rock / Mother's love, A.
LP...................... OFF 6013
Official / Aug '88 / Charly / Cadillac Music / Jazz Music.
LP...................... BFX 15327
Bear Family / Apr '89 / Rollercoaster Records / Swift / Direct Distribution.

Breen, Ann

Hailing from the Irish Republic, this middle-of-the-road singer released her first album in 1981. By the end of '84 she had released five LPs. She is best known for her recording of *Pal Of My Cradle Days*, a 1982 single that sold in very slow but steady quantities in Britain, gaining a Top 75 placing at one point. Such consistent sales figures suggest major hit potential, which a large record company might have been able to exploit. However, Dublin's Homespun label seemed unable to capitalise. Breen remains a well-known name in the somewhat insular Irish music scene and her regular UK releases reach a small but reliable audience (Bob MacDonald).

AN EVENING WITH.
Tracks: Not Advised.
VHS...................... ABV1
Play / Aug '92 / BMG.

AN EVENING WITH ANN BREEN.
Tracks: Not Advised.
CD...................... DPLAY 1025
MC...................... CPLAY 1025
Play / Sep '90 / BMG.
MC...................... PLAYC 1025
Play / Dec '92 / BMG.

ANN BREEN COLLECTION.
Tracks: Not Advised.

ANN BREEN IN CONCERT.
Tracks: Not Advised.
CD...................... CDPLAY 1034
MC...................... CPLAY 1034
Play / Mar '93 / BMG.

BLUE VIOLETS AND RED ROSES.
Tracks: Blue violets and red roses / Teddy bear.
7"...................... HS 063
Homespun (Ireland) / Feb '83 / Homespun Records / Ross Records / Wellard Dist.

BOY OF MINE.
Tracks: Among my souvenirs / I'm guilty of loving you / Where no one stands alone / Three good reasons / Will you love me tomorrow / Blue violets & red roses / Boy of mine / Teddy bear / Careless hands / By the light of the silvery moon / Carolina moon / Souvenirs.
LP...................... PHL 447
MC...................... CPHL 447
Homespun (Ireland) / Nov '84 / Homespun Records / Ross Records / Wellard Dist.
MC...................... CDHL 447

Homespun (Ireland) / '90 / Homespun Records / Ross Records / Wellard Dist.

BREAKAWAY.
Tracks: Breakaway / Moon behind the hill.
7"...................... HS 094
Homespun (Ireland) / Feb '85 / Homespun Records / Ross Records / Wellard Dist.

BY THE SILVERY LIGHT OF THE MOON.
Tracks: By the silvery light of the moon / Dear little boy of mine.
7"...................... HS 059
Homespun (Ireland) / Sep '82 / Homespun Records / Ross Records / Wellard Dist.

COLLECTION: ANN BREEN.
Tracks: Not Advised.
LP...................... PLAY 1019
MC...................... CPLAY 1019
Play / Nov '86 / BMG.

DIVIDED WE FALL.
Tracks: Divided we fall / Divided we fall (instrumental).
7"...................... PLAY 215
Play / Mar '87 / BMG.

DOMINO.
Tracks: Domino (easy listening mix) / Domino (slap remix).
12"...................... PLAY 210 T
7"...................... PLAY 210
Play / Sep '86 / BMG.

ENTERTAINER, THE.
Tracks: Not Advised.
VHS...................... ABV 2
Play / Mar '93 / BMG.

EVENING WITH ANN BREEN, AN.
Tracks: Not Advised.
VHS...................... ABV 1
Play Video / Nov '91.

GENTLE MOTHER.
Tracks: Gentle mother / Bunch of violets blue.
7"...................... HS 072
Homespun (Ireland) / Oct '83 / Homespun Records / Ross Records / Wellard Dist.

GIVE ME ONE GOOD REASON.
Tracks: Give me one good reason / Tennessee waltz.
7"...................... HS 080
Homespun (Ireland) / May '84 / Homespun Records / Ross Records / Wellard Dist.

HEART YOU BREAK WILL BE YOUR OWN.
Tracks: Heart you break will be your own / Two loves.
■ 7"...................... H 055
Homespun (Ireland) / Feb '82.

HOLD ME IN YOUR ARMS.
Tracks: Hold me in your arms.
7"...................... PLAY 222
Play / '88 / BMG.

I WISH ALL MY BABIES WERE CHILDREN.
Tracks: I wish all my babies were children.
7"...................... PLAY 236
Play / '88 / BMG.

I'LL BE YOUR SWEETHEART.
Tracks: I'll be your sweetheart / In your heart / Have you ever been lonely / Music, music, music, put another nickle in / Don't think love ought to be that way / Spinning wheel / We all have a song in our hearts / Cottage by the Lee / Da doo ron ron / Skye boat song / I just called to say I love you / Carnival is over, The.
LP...................... DHL 705
MC...................... CDHL 705
Homespun (Ireland) / Sep '85 / Homespun Records / Ross Records / Wellard Dist.

IF I HAD MY LIFE TO LIVE OVER.
Tracks: If I had my life to live over / When you & I were young Maggie / Walk right back / I'll be your sweetheart / Will you love me tomorrow / Save the last dance for me / Have you ever been lonely / I just called to say I love you / Who's sorry now / It's a sin to tell a lie / Among my souvenirs / You always hurt the one you love.
LP...................... DHL 714
MC...................... CDHL 714
Homespun (Ireland) / May '87 / Homespun Records / Ross Records / Wellard Dist.

IF THOSE LIPS COULD ONLY SPEAK.
Tracks: If those lips could only speak / Golden Jubilee.
7"...................... PLAY 251
Play / Dec '90 / BMG.

IRISH STYLE.
Tracks: Gentle mother / Noreen Bawn / Two loves / Cottage by the lee / Moon behind the hill / I'll remember you love in my prayers / Spinning wheel / Bunch of violets blue / Too-ra-loo-ra-loo-ra / Old rustic bridge / When you and I were young Maggie / By the light of the silvery moon.
LP...................... PHL 493
MC...................... CPHL 493
Homespun (Ireland) / Jun '87 / Homespun Records / Ross Records / Wellard Dist.
MC...................... CDHL 493
Homespun (Ireland) / '90 / Homespun Records / Ross Records / Wellard Dist.

■ DELETED

IT'S FOR MY DAD.
Tracks: It's for my dad.
CD . . . . DPLAY 1027
MC . . . . CPLAY 1027
Play / Dec '92 / BMG.

LOVE BY LOVE.
Tracks: Love by love.
7" . . . . HS 084
Homespun (Ireland) / Sep '84 / Homespun Records / Ross Records / Wellard Dist.

LOVE IS.
Tracks: Love is.
7" . . . . PLAY 243
Play / Feb '90 / BMG.

MEDALS FOR MOTHERS.
Tracks: Pal of my cradle days / Among my souvenirs / Gentle mother / It's a sin to tell a lie / What a friend we have in mother / Noreen Bawn / Medals for mothers / Two loves / When you & I were young Maggie / If I had my life to live over / Carolina moon / (Dear little) boy of mine.
LP. . . . . PHL 487
MC . . . . CPHL 487
Homespun (Ireland) / Nov '86 / Homespun Records / Ross Records / Wellard Dist.
MC . . . . CDHL 487
Homespun (Ireland) / '90 / Homespun Records / Ross Records / Wellard Dist.

MOONSHINER.
Tracks: Moonshiner.
7" . . . . PLAY 231
Play / '88 / BMG.

MY MOTHER'S PEARLS.
Tracks: My mother's pearls.
7" . . . . PLAY 229
Play / '88 / BMG.

OLD COUNTRY WALTZ, THE.
Tracks: Old country waltz, The.
7" . . . . PLAY 235
Play / '88 / BMG.

PAL OF MY CRADLE DAYS.
Tracks: Those brown eyes / Who's sorry now / Blue Kentucky girl / You needed me / Two loves / What a friend we have in mother / Walk right back / Save the last dance for me / Love is teasin' / Pal of my cradle days / Hey good lookin' / Heart you break will be your own, The.
LP. . . . . PHL 437
MC . . . . CPHL 437
Homespun (Ireland) / Aug '86 / Homespun Records / Ross Records / Wellard Dist.
MC . . . . CDHL 437
Homespun (Ireland) / '90 / Homespun Records / Ross Records / Wellard Dist.

PAL OF MY CRADLE DAYS.
Tracks: Pal of my cradle days / Love is teasin'.
7" . . . . HS 052
Homespun (Ireland) / Mar '86 / Homespun Records / Ross Records / Wellard Dist.

QUE SERA SERA.
Tracks: Que sera sera.
7" . . . . HS 089
Homespun (Ireland) / Oct '84 / Homespun Records / Ross Records / Wellard Dist.

SAVE THE LAST DANCE FOR ME.
Tracks: Save the last dance for me / Rustic bridge.
7" . . . . HS 076
Homespun (Ireland) / Jan '84 / Homespun Records / Ross Records / Wellard Dist.

THIS ALBUM IS JUST FOR YOU.
Tracks: Noreen Bawn / Last thing on my mind / Star, The / Too ra loo ra loo ra / This song is just for you / It's a sin to tell a lie / Whatever will be will be / Only you / Love by love / When I fall in love / It keeps right on a-hurtin' / Medals for mothers.
LP. . . . . DHL 703
MC . . . . CDHL 703
Homespun (Ireland) / Aug '84 / Homespun Records / Ross Records / Wellard Dist.

THOSE BROWN EYES.
Tracks: Those brown eyes / Love is teasin'.
7" . . . . HS 047
Homespun (Ireland) / Jul '81 / Homespun Records / Ross Records / Wellard Dist.

TWO LOVES.
Tracks: Two loves / Heart you break will be your own, The.
7" . . . . HS 055
Homespun (Ireland) / Sep '82 / Homespun Records / Ross Records / Wellard Dist.

WHAT A FRIEND WE HAVE IN MOTHER.
Tracks: What a friend we have in mother / Falling.
7" . . . . HS 053
Homespun (Ireland) / Sep '82 / Homespun Records / Ross Records / Wellard Dist.

WHEN I GROW TOO OLD TO DREAM.
Tracks: Not Advised.
LP. . . . . PLAY 1023
Play / Nov '88 / BMG.
CD . . . . CDPLAY 1023
MC . . . . CPLAY 1023
Play / Dec '92 / BMG.

YOU ALWAYS HURT THE ONE YOU LOVE.
Tracks: You always hurt the one you love / Jambalaya / Moon behind the hill / Bunch of violets blue / Save the last dance for me / If I had my life to live over / Behind the footlights / Old rustic bridge / When you & I were young Maggie / Tennessee waltz / Everybody's somebody's fool / Gentle mother / Maggie.
LP. . . . . DHL 701
MC . . . . CDHL 701
Homespun (Ireland) / May '88 / Homespun Records / Ross Records / Wellard Dist.

YOU ALWAYS HURT THE ONE YOU LOVE.
Tracks: You always hurt the one you love.
7" . . . . HS 069
Homespun (Ireland) / Jun '83 / Homespun Records / Ross Records / Wellard Dist.

Brennan, Walter

OLD RIVERS.
Tracks: Old rivers.
■ 7" . . . . LIB 55436
Liberty / Jun '62.

Brett, Ann

SOMEBODY LOVES YOU (Brett, Ann & Ray).
Tracks: Not Advised.
LP. . . . . SFA 070
Sweet Folk & Country / Nov '76 / Wellard Dist.

THERE'S NO MORE YOU AND ME (Brett, Ann & Ray).
Tracks: There's no more you and me / Lay in your arms.
■ 7" . . . . AR 003
A & R / Jun '83.

Brislin, Kate

OUR TOWN (Stecher, Jody & Kate Brislin).
Tracks: Going to the West / Home / Old country stomp / In between dreams / Showerbread reel/The twisted arm, The / Too late, too late / Bramble and the rose, The / Our town / Twilight is stealing / Curtains of the night / Queen of the Earth and child of the stars / Roving on last winter's night / Henry the true machine / Won't you come and sing for me.
CD . . . . ROUCD 0304
MC . . . . ROUC 0304
Rounder / Jul '93 / Projection / Roots Records / Swift / C.M. Distribution / Topic Records / Jazz Music / Hot Shot / A.D.A Distribution / Direct Distribution.

Britt, Elton

A yodelling country singer (1917-72) whose real name was James Britt Baker was born in Marshall, Arkansas. He recorded with Victor from 1937 and made 672 records over 20 years. His wartime hit *There's A Star Spangled Banner Waving Somewhere*, eventually sold two million, and resulted in Elton Britt being the first country star to visit the White House in 1942. He had duet hits with Rosalie Allen in the late '40s, made B-films, recorded for ABC in the '60s and went back to RCA, having country chart hits as late as 1969. (Donald Clarke).

BEST OF BRITT.
Tracks: There's a star spangled banner waving somewhere / Blue eyes crying in the rain / Mockin' Bird Hill / I almost lost my mind / Roving gambler / It is no secret / Someday you'll want me to want you / Detour / I get the blues when it rains / Candy kisses / I hung my head and cried / Beyond the sunset.
LP. . . . . NL 89995
RCA / Jan '87 / BMG.
■ MC . . . . NK 89995
RCA / Jan '87.

YODEL SONGS.
Tracks: Give me a pinto pal / Chime bells / St. James Avenue / Yodel blues, The / Tennessee yodel polka / St. Louis blues yodel / Maybe I'll cry over you / That's how the yodel was born / Alpine milkman, The / Cannonball yodel / Patent leather boots / Skater's yodel, The.
LP. . . . . HAT 3067
MC . . . . HATC 3067
Stetson / Apr '88 / Crusader Marketing Co. / Swift / Wellard Dist. / Midland Records / C.M. Distribution.

Brooks, Garth

Singer/songwriter/musician, Garth Brooks is the biggest sensation to hit country music in recent times, if not in its entire history. Brooks was by the beginning of the 1990's outselling all other country contenders and, a couple of years later, as he broke down the musical boundaries he had put the likes of Michael Jackson, U2 and Madonna in the shade. Undoubtedly it was the presence of Garth Brooks that built country music into a major force in the early 1990's. Troyal Garth Brooks was born on February 7 1962 in Yukon, Oklahoma. His mother was the former Capitol Records country singer Colleen Carroll, whose greatest claim to fame was as a member of the weekly 'live' radio show, Ozark Mountain Jubilee. A graduate of Oklahoma State University (with an advertising degree), his first visit to Nashville was a sobering, 24 hour stop-over in 1985 during which he realized that the city didn't have his name in lights and nobody was waiting to make him a star. He returned back home and married Sandy Mahl, a girl he'd met whilst working as a club bouncer. Two years after the first visit, Brooks returned to Nashville, secured himself a publishing deal with former ASCAP executive Bob Doyle, who later joined forces with former MTV and RCA publicist Pam Lewis in a co-management capacity. Brooks was then introduced to record producer Allen Reynolds, hitherto best known for his work with Crystal Gayle and Don Williams, and shortly afterwards a deal was struck with the Nashville division of Capitol (subsequently to be known as Liberty Records as a move to establish the division's own identity). Garth Brooks's first single *Much Too Young (To Feel This Damn Old)* was released in February 1989, eventually securing a top 10 slot five months later, by which time his debut album, *Garth Brooks*, was also released. *If Tomorrow Never Comes* was his second single and went to number one, setting the pace for all that followed in its wake. By the end of his first year in the business Brooks had sold around 350,000 albums, though his career suffered as he was constantly in the shadows of another 'hat act' newcomer who started off around the same time as himself, Clint Black. Another year on, though, with his second album *No Fences* going to number one the week after its release and with the sales into the millions, comparisons no longer existed. Two years later Garth Brooks had become the biggest selling artist in the USA. His third album *Ropin' The Wind*, went to No. 1 in the pop charts (as well as, of course, the country charts) as did his 1992 album; *The Chase*. At the same time he's enjoyed an endless stream of top singles that included *The Dance*, *Friends In Low Places*, *The Thunder Rolls*, *What's She Doing Now*, *That Summer* and *We Shall Be Free*. The success of his recordings - together with his much acclaimed, high energy concert performances - have ensured that Garth Brooks has been the recipient of virtually every major award during the past couple of years, including being named twice 'Entertainer of the Year' by both Country Music Association and the Academy of Country Music. As a final assessment of his talents, let the figures speak for themselves. His 1992 TV special *This is Garth Brooks* (filmed at Dallas' Reunion Arena, and later to become a top selling video) attracted 28 million viewers, giving the NBC network its best Friday night audience in over two years. As a concert artist the 195,000 tickets for his three night stand at Dallas' Texas stadium (September 1993) sold out in five hours. The previous record was held by Paul McCartney who had sold 54,000 tickets for a concert at this venue. As a recording artist, just prior to the release of his 1993 album *In Pieces*, he had sold over 32 million albums generating some $400 million in revenue, with *The Chase* becoming the first album in music history to be certified for out-of-the-box sales of 5 million units. The previous record of 4 million was shared by his own Grammy-winning *Roping The Wind* and Michael Jackson's *Dangerous* . (Tony Byworth)

BEYOND THE SEASON.
Tracks: Go tell it on the mountain / God rest ye merry gentleman / Old man's back in town, The / Gift, The / Unto you this night / White Christmas / Friendly beasts, The / Santa looked a lot like daddy / Silent night / Mary's dream / What child is this.
CD . . . . CDP 7987422
Liberty / Sep '92 / EMI.

CHASE, THE.
Tracks: That summer / Somewhere other than the night / Face to face / Every now and then / Mr. Right / Learning to live again / Walkin' after midnight / Dixie chicken / Night rider's lament.
CD . . . . CDESTU 2184
MC . . . . TCESTU 2184
Liberty / Sep '92 / EMI.
■ LP. . . . . ESTU 2184
Liberty / Sep '92.

FRIENDS IN LOW PLACES.
Tracks: Friends in low places / Not counting you / Much too young (to feel this damn old) (CD single only.).
7" . . . . CL 609
■ CD Single . . . . CDCL 609
Capitol Nashville / Feb '91.

GARTH BROOKS.
Tracks: Not counting you / I've got a good thing going / If tomorrow never comes / Everytime that it rains / Alabama clay / Much too young (to feel this damn old) / Cowboy Bill / Nobody gets off in this town / I know one / Dance, The.
LP. 7 908 971
Capitol / Mar '90 / EMI.
■ MC C4 90897
Capitol / Mar '90.

■ DELETED B 17

■ CD . . . . CZ 304
Capitol / Mar '90.

GARTH BROOKS EP.
Tracks: Not Advised.
VHS. . . . . MVR 4900133
PMI / Sep '93 / EMI / Gold & Sons / Terry Blood Dist.

IN PIECES.
Tracks: Standing outside / Night I called the old man out, The / American honky-tonk bar association / One night a day / Kickin' and screamin' / Ain't going down (til the sun comes up) / Red strokes, The / Callin' baton rouge / Night will only know, The / Cowboy song, The / Fire, The.
CD . . . . CDEST 2212
MC . . . . .TCEST 2212
Liberty / Aug '93 / EMI.

NO FENCES.
Tracks: If tomorrow never comes / Not counting you / Much too young (to feel this damn old) / Dance, The / Thunder rolls, The / New way to fly / Two of a kind, workin' on a full house / Victim of the game / Friends in low places / Wild horses / Unanswered prayers / Same old story / Mr. Blue / Wolves.
CD . . . . CDP 795 503 2
CD . . . . CDEST 2136
LP. 795 503 1
LP. . . . . EST 2136
MC 795 503 4
MC . . . . TCEST 2136
Capitol Nashville / Nov '90 / EMI.

ROPIN' THE WIND.
Tracks: Against the grain / Rodeo / What she's doing now / Burning bridges / Papa loved Mama / Shameless / Cold shoulder / We bury the hatchet / In lonesome dove / River, The / Alabama clay / Everytime that it rains / Nobody gets off in this town / Cowboy Bill.
CD . . . . CDESTU 2162
MC . . . . TCESTU 2162
■ LP. . . . . ESTU 2162
Capitol Nashville / Jan '92 / EMI.
Capitol Nashville / Jan '92.

SHAMELESS.
Tracks: Shameless / Dance, The / Rodeo (Only on CD Single.) / Thunder rolls, The (Only on CD Single.).
7" . . . . .CL 646
CD Single . . . . CDCL 646
■ MC Single . . . . TCCL 646
Capitol Nashville / Jan '92.

THIS IS GARTH BROOKS.
Tracks: Not counting you / Rodeo / We bury the hatchet / Two of a kind, workin' on a full house / Thunder rolls, The / River, The / Much too young (to feel this damn old) / What's she doing now / Papa loved Mama / If tomorrow never comes / Shameless / Friends in low places / Dance, The / You may be right / Keep your hands to yourself.
VHS. . . . . MVP 4910303
PMI / Aug '93 / EMI / Gold & Sons / Terry Blood Dist.

WE SHALL BE FREE.
Tracks: We shall be free / River, The / Mr. Blue (On CDs only).
7" . . . . .CL 675
■ CD Single . . . . CDCL 675
Capitol / Oct '92.

WHAT SHE'S DOING NOW.
Tracks: What she's doing now / Shameless / We bury the hatchet (CD single only).
7" . . . . .CL 656
CD Single . . . . CDCL 656
MC Single . . . . TCCL 656
Liberty / Apr '92 / EMI.

Brooks, Karen

I WILL DANCE WITH YOU.
Tracks: Nobody's angel / I'll dance with you / Hard way, The / Have a heart / Last time, The / I do blues / Last one to know, The / Other night, The / Too bad for love / Great divide, The.
■ MC 925277 4
WEA / Jun '85 / WEA.

I WILL DANCE WITH YOU (Brooks, Karen & Johnny Cash).
Tracks: I will dance with you / Too bad for love.
7" . . . . W 8979
WEA / Aug '85 / WEA.

Brother Boys

BROTHERS BOYS.
Tracks: Not Advised.
CD . . . . .NHD 1101
MC . . . . .NH 1101
Zu Zazz / Aug '90 / Hot Shot / A.D.A Distribution / C.M. Distribution.

PLOW.
Tracks: Gonna row my boat / I got over the blues / Kiss the dream girl / Alone with you / Twist you up / Then and only then / Hoping that you're hoping / I see love / Blue guitar / Little box / Darkest day / Satelite shack / What will be in the fields tomorrow.
CD . . . . SH CD 3805
MC . . . . SH MC 3805

Sugarhill(USA) / '92 / Roots Records / Projection / Impetus Records / C.M. Distribution / Jazz Music / Swift / Duncans / A.D.A Distribution.

Brown Family

FAMILIAR FACES, FAMILIAR PLACES.
Tracks: No ones' gonna love me / Millpond / Love is a contact sport / Tag along Joe / Stay with me / Dear hearts and gentle people / Love was on our side / Heaven's just a sin away / Way I love you.
■ LP . . . . PL 42948
RCA / Feb '80.

Brown's Ferry Four

A shifting group of musicians, developed in the 1940's by the Delmore Brothers as an outlet for religious material, with recordings released by King Records. Others appearing in the vocal line-up, from time to time, included Grandpa Jones, Wayne Raney, Merle Travis and Red Foley. (Tony Byworth)

16 GREATEST HITS: BROWN'S FERRY FOUR.
Tracks: Not Advised.
LP. . . . . SLP 3017
MC . . . . GT 53017
Starday (USA) / Apr '87 / Crusader Marketing Co.

Brown, Alison

SIMPLE PLEASURES.
Tracks: Mambo banjo / Leaving cottondale / Fantasy / Daytime TV / Wolf moon / From the coast / Weetabix / Bright and early / Waltzing with Tula / Reedy rooster / Sundaze / Simple pleasures.
CD . . . . .VHD 74959CD
MC . . . . VHD 74959
Vanguard / '91 / Complete Record Co. Ltd.

Brown, Hylo

One of the many bluegrass musicians to follow in the footsteps of Bill Monroe, and one of the very few to enjoy a major label deal (Capitol records: 1954-60). Kentucky's Hylo Brown was born in 1922 and first claimed attention on a variety of radio stations from Ohio north to Chicago. After Capitol he recorded for Starday, and has continued to record over the years. (Tony Byworth)

HYLO BROWN.
Tracks: Flower blooming in the wildwood / When it's lamplighting time in the valley / Old home town / I'll be all smiles tonight / Love and wealth / Gathering flowers from the hillside / Blue eyes darling / Will the angels play their harps for me / Put my little shoes away / Darling Nellie across the sea / Why do you weep dear willow.
LP. . . . . HAT 3077
MC . . . . HATC 3077
Stetson / '88 / Crusader Marketing Co. / Swift / Wellard Dist. / Midland Records / C.M. Distribution.

HYLO BROWN 1954 - 1960 (Brown, Hylo & The Timberliners).
Tracks: Flower blooming in the wildwood / Put my little shoes away / Blue eyed darling / Will the angels play their harps for me / Old home town, The / Love and wealth / I'll be all smiles tonight / Gathering flowers from the hillside / Little Joe / Darling Nellie across the sea / When it's lamp lightin' time in the valley / Why do you weep dear willow / Test of love / Dark as a dungeon / Lost to a stranger / Sweethearts or strangers / In the clay beneath the tomb / Wrong kind of life, The / I'll be broken hearted / Let's stop fooling our hearts / Lovesick and sorrow / Get lost, you wolf! / One sided love affair, A / Only one, The / Prisoner's song / Nobody's darlin' but mine / One way train / Foolish pride / John Henry / There's more pretty girls than one / Stone wall (around my heart) / Shuffle of my feet, The / Your crazy heart / You can't relive the past / I've waited as long as i can / It's all over (but the crying) / Thunder clouds of love / Just any old love / Darlin' how can you forget so soon / Sweethearts and strangers.
CD Set . . . . BCD 15572
Bear Family / Mar '92 / Rollercoaster Records / Swift / Direct Distribution.

HYLO BROWN MEETS THE LONESOME PINE FIDDLERS (Brown, Hylo & Lonesome Pine Fiddlers).
Tracks: Not Advised.
LP. . . . . SLP 220
MC . . . . GT 5220
Starday (USA) / Apr '87 / Crusader Marketing Co.

Brown, Jim Ed

ENEMY, THE.
Tracks: Enemy, The / I just came from there.
■ 7" . . . . RCA 1696
RCA / Aug '70 / BMG.

GREATEST HITS:JIM ED BROWN & HELEN CORNELIUS (Brown, Jim Ed & Helen Cornelius).
Tracks: I don't want to have to marry you / If the world ran out of love tonight / Bedroom, The / Morning comes to early / Born believer / Lying in love with you / You don't bring me flowers / Saying hello, saying I love you, saying goodbye / Fools / Don't bother to knock.
LP . . . . .INTS 5113
MC . . . . .INTK 5113
RCA International / Oct '81 / BMG.

I DON'T WANT TO HAVE TO MARRY YOU (Brown, Jim Ed & Helen Cornelius).
Tracks: I don't want to have to marry you / Have I told you lately that I love you?.
■ 7" . . . . PB 0711
RCA / Jan '77.

JIM ED BROWN & HELEN CORNELIUS (Brown, Jim Ed & Helen Cornelius).
Tracks: I don't want to have to marry you / Love was what we had / I've rode with the best / I'm leaving it all up to you / Saying hello, saying I love you, saying goodbye / My heart cries for you / One man woman, one woman man / Burning bridges / There's always goodbye / Have I told you lately that I love you.
■ LP . . . . PL 12024
RCA / Jan '77.

JUST JIM.
Tracks: You can have her / If you were mine, Mary / Have I stayed away too long / Last laugh, The / Have I told you lately that I love you / How long has it been / What does it take / There goes my everything / Have you ever been lonely / Hold me, thrill me, kiss me / I'd walk a country mile / Pop a top.
■ LP . . . . RD 7952
RCA / Feb '70 / BMG.

SAYING HELLO, SAYING I LOVE YOU, SAYING GOODBYE (Brown, Jim Ed & Helen Cornelius).
Tracks: Saying hello, saying I love you, saying goodbye / My heart cries for you.
■ 7" . . . . PB 0822
RCA / May '77.

Brown, Milton

A founding father of the western swing movement, Texas born Milton Brown (1903 - 35) joined forces with Bob Wills in 1931, as a member of the Wills Fiddle Band, which eventually blossomed into the Light Crust Doughboys, the first western swing band. The association was to be shortlived, with Brown departing to create his own outfit, Milton Brown & The Brownies, while Wills went on to form his Texas Playboys. Who knows the role Milton Brown would have played in the development of western swing had he survived that tragic car crash in 1935. (Tony Byworth)

DANCE-O-RAMA (Brown, Milton & The Brownies).
Tracks: St. Louis blues / Sweet Jenny Lee / Texas hambone blues / Brownie special / Right or wrong / Washington and Lee swing / Beautiful Texas / Little Betty Brown.
LP. . . . . WS 1001
Rambler (USA) / Jul '81 / Roots Records / Projection / Swift / Wellard Dist.

EASY RIDIN' PAPA (Brown, Milton & The Brownies).
Tracks: Down by the O-H-I-O / Easy ridin' papa / Sweet Jenny Lee / Ida sweet as apple cider / Little Betty Brown (Traditional.) / Black and white rag / Brownie special / Wabash blues / Hesitation blues / St. Louis Blues / I've got the blues for my mamy / Texas hambone blues / Beautiful Texas / Right or wrong.
■ LP. . . . . CR 30264
Charly / Mar '87 / Charly.

TAKING OFF (Brown, Milton & The Brownies).
Tracks: Chinatown, my Chinatown / St. Louis blues / In El Rancho Grande / Taking off / If you can't get five take two / Fan it / Little Betty Brown / Some of these days / Sweet Georgia Brown / Texas hambone blues / Washington and Lee swing / My Mary / Goofus / Honky tonk blues / Sweet Jenny Lee / There'll be some changes made.
LP. . . . . STR 804
String / '81 / Projection / Roots Records / A.D.A Distribution / C.M. Distribution / Swift / Ross Records / Duncans.

Brown, T. Graham

Soul/country performer. He has a road band called the Hardtops. Unfortunately his albums on Capitol have met with criticism owing to unsympathetic rock-style production.(Donald Clarke).

BRILLIANT CONVERSATIONALIST.
Tracks: R.F.D 30529 / Save that dress / Talkin' to it / Anything to lose / Power of love, The / Brilliant conversationalist / She couldn't love me anymore / Walk on water / Last resort, The / (Sittin' on) the dock of the bay.
CD . . . . CDP 746 773 2
CD . . . . CDEST 2037
LP. . . . . EST 2037
■ MC . . . . TCEST 2037
Capitol / Sep '87.

BRILLIANT CONVERSATIONALIST.
Tracks: Brilliant conversationalist.
■ 7" . . . . CL 470
Capitol / Sep '87.

BUMPER TO BUMPER.
Tracks: Moonshadow road / You can't make her love you / I'm expecting miracles / If you could only see me now / I'm sending one up for you / I've been loving you too long / Eyes wide open / Bring a change / Blues of the month club / We tote the note / For real (CD only.).
CD CDC1 91780
■ MC C4 91780
Capitol / Jun '90.

I TELL IT LIKE IT USED TO BE.
Tracks: Say when / Don't go to strangers / Rock it, Billy / I tell it like it used to be / I wish that I could hurt that way again / Later train / You're trying to hard / Hell and high water / Don't make a liar out of me / Is there anything that I can do.
■ CD . . . . CDP 7469012
EMI / '87.
LP. . . . . EST 2026
■ MC . . . . TCEST 2026
Capitol / Mar '87.

POWER OF LOVE, THE.
Tracks: Power of love, The / Save that dress / Brilliant conversationalist (Available on 12" format only.).
12" 12CL 494
7" . . . . CL 494
■ CD Single . . . . CDCL 494
Capitol / Jun '88.

ROCK IT BILLY.
Tracks: Rock it, Billy / Later train.
■ 7" . . . . CL 449
Capitol / May '87.

SAY WHEN.
Tracks: Say when / She's mine.
■ 7" . . . . CL 443
Capitol / Feb '87.

TALKIN' TO IT.
Tracks: Talkin' to it.
7" . . . . CL 462
Capitol / Aug '87 / EMI.

Browns

This American vocal trio consisted of Jim Edward Brown and his sisters; Maxine and Bonnie. This family group had sung together since childhood. Hailing from Arkansas, their version of the quasi-religious *The Three Bells*, soared to the US No. 1 position in 1959 and reached No. 6 in the UK. In both the UK and the US, it is the Browns' recording of this gentle, sentimental song that is best remembered. They never had another in Britain but scored two follow-up successes in their native America. *Scarlet Ribbons (For Her Hair)*, peaked at No. 13, and *The Old lamplighter*, reached No. 5 in 1960. During the sixties Jim Ed Brown became a solo country singer, but his sisters drifted into obscurity. (Bob MacDonald).

20 OF THE BEST: BROWNS.
Tracks: I take the chance / I heard the bluebirds sing / Would you care / Beyond the shadow of a doubt / Three bells, The / Scarlet ribbons / Teen ex / Old lamplighter / Ground hog / Blue Christmas / Send me the pillow that you dream on / Oh no / Then I'll stop loving you / Every body's darlin' plus mine / Meadow green / I'd just be fool enough / Coming back to you / I hear it now / Big daddy / I will bring you water.
LP. . . . . NL 89524
■ MC . . . . NK 89524
RCA / Apr '85.

LOOKING BACK TO SEE.
Tracks: Lookin' back to see / Rio De Janeiro / Draggin' main street / You thought, I thought / Itsy witsy bitsy me / Your love is as wild as the west wind / Grass is green, The / Lookin' on / Jungle magic / Set the dawgs on 'em' (Previously unissued track) / I'm your man, I'm your gal (previously unissued track.) / Why am I falling / Do memories haunt me / It's love, I guess (Previously unissued track) / Here today and gone tomorrow / Cool green.
LP. . . . . BFX 15190
Bear Family / Sep '86 / Rollercoaster Records / Swift / Direct Distribution.

ROCKIN ROLLIN.
Tracks: Three bells (Les trois cloches), The / Teen ex / Blue bells ring / This time I would know / Heaven fell last night / Beyond a shadow / Margo (The ninth of may) / You're so much part of me / Bye bye love / Only one way to love you / Buttons and bows / Brighten the corner where you are / Trot, The / Dream on (She'll break your heart) / Oh, no / Tabacco road.

ROCKIN' ROLLIN' BROWNS.
Tracks: Three bells, The / Teen-ex / Blue bells ring / This time I would know / Heaven fell last night / Beyond a shadow / Margo (The ninth of May) (Previously unissued.) / You're so much apart of me / Bye bye love (Previously unissued.) / Only one way to love you / Buttons and bows / Brighten the corner where you are / Dream on (she'll break your heart) / Oh no / Tobacco Road (Previously unissued.).
LP. . . . . BFX 15104
Bear Family / Sep '84 / Rollercoaster Records / Swift / Direct Distribution.

THREE BELLS, THE.
Tracks: Three bells, The.
■ 7" . . . . RCA 1140
RCA / Sep '59.

THREE BELLS, THE (OLD GOLD).
Tracks: Three bells, The / Lion sleeps tonight, The.
7" . . . . OG 9653
Old Gold / Nov '86 / Pickwick Records.

Bruce, Ed

Born 19.12.1940 in Keiser Arkansas, this singer-songwriter/actor started out 1957, recording rockabilly on the legendary Sun label. After three fruitless years he quit music and returned to work at his father's used-car business. Bruce moved to Nashville in 1964, and recorded his debut album *If I Could Come Home* for RCA in 1965. He signed to Monument in 1968 and recorded the album *Shades of Ed Bruce*. His first real break came when he co-wrote, with wife Patsy, *Mamas Don't Let Your Babies Grow Up To Be Cowboys*, a Billboard top twenty single. Later, the song gained a wide audience when Waylon & Willie took it to no.1 in 1978. Other hits penned by Bruce include; *The Man That Turned My Mama On*, *Texas When I Die* (both hits for Tanya Tucker, the latter a no.1), *Restless*, *See The Big Man Cry* and *Working Man's Prayer*. Ed Bruce himself has charted regularly during the eighties, on both MCA and RCA, making no.1 with *You're The Best Break This Heart Ever Had* in 1981. Other hits include: *My First Taste Of Texas*, *The Last Cowboy Song* (with Willie Nelson), *Diane and Girls*, *Women and Ladies*, all good authentic material delivered by Bruce's strong vocals. During the eighties, Bruce appearing regularly on TV in *Bret Maverick* (playing Tom Guthrie and also composing the theme), *The Chisholms* and portrayed *The Tennessean* in the TV advertisement. (Maurice Hope)

BEST OF ED BRUCE.
Tracks: Not Advised.
■ LP. . . . . MCF 3142
MCA / Jul '82.

DIANE.
Tracks: Diane / Last cowboy song, The.
7" . . . . MCA 810
MCA / Apr '83 / BMG.

ED BRUCE.
Tracks: Last thing she said, The / Last cowboy song, The / Red doggin' again / Love ain't something I can do alone / Girls, women and ladies / Neon fool / Blue umbrella / I still wish / Outlaw & the stranger, The.
LP. . . . . IMCA 27068
MCA (Import) / Mar '86 / Pinnacle / Silver Sounds (CD).

GREATEST HITS: ED BRUCE.
Tracks: Last cowboy song, The / Girls, women, and ladies / Everything's a waltz (When you fall in love) / You're the best break this old heart ever had / Love's found you and me / Ever, never lovin' you / My first taste of Texas / You're not leavin' here tonight / If it was easy / After all.
■ LP. . . . . IMCA 5577
MCA (Import) / Mar '86.

I WRITE IT DOWN.
Tracks: My first taste of Texas / Ever, never lovin' you / Somebody's crying / One more shot of "Old back home again" / Songwriter, The (I write it down) / Brett Maverick / Memories can't stand to be alone / Your jukebox could use a few more sad songs / Babe in arms / Mamas don't let your babies grow up to be cowboys.
LP. . . . . MCF 3169
MC . . . . MCFC 3169
MCA / Apr '83 / BMG.
■ LP. . . . . IMCA 893
MCA (Import) / Mar '86.

LAST TRAIN TO CLARKESVILLE.
Tracks: I know better / Why can't I come home / Walker's woods / Ninety seven more to go / I could just go home / By route of New Orleans / Shadows of her mind / Lonesome is me / I'm getting better / Her sweet love and the baby / I'll take you away / Last train to Clarksville / I'd best be leaving you / Tiny golden locket / Ballad of the drummer boy, The / Something else to mess your mind / Puzzles / Memphis morning / Painted girls and wine / Blue bayou.
LP. . . . . INTS 5199
MC . . . . INTK 5199
RCA International / May '82 / BMG.

NIGHT THINGS.
Tracks: Nights / You are a rose / Fools for each other / Down the hall / Quietly / 15 to 43 / Fishin' in the dark / Somebody's somebody new / Memphis roots.
LP. . . . . PL 85808
RCA / Nov '86 / BMG.

ONE TO ONE.
Tracks: When you fall in love / Evil angel / You're the best break this old heart ever had / It just makes me want you more / Hundred dollar lady / Love's found you and me / I take the chance / No regrets / Thirty nine and holding / Easy temptations.
LP. . . . . IMCA 27063
MCA (Import) / Mar '86 / Pinnacle / Silver Sounds (CD).

ROCK BOPPIN' BABY.
Tracks: Rock boppin' baby / More than yesterday / Eight wheel (Previously unissued track) / Ballad of Ringo (Previously un-issued track) / King of fools (Previously un-issued track) / Just being with you (Previously un-issued track) / Alone with a broken heart (Previously un-issued track) / You come to me (Previously un-issued track) / Sweet woman / Doll baby (previously un-issued track) / Flight 303 / Sun gold.
LP. . . . . BFX 15194
Bear Family / Apr '86 / Rollercoaster Records / Swift / Direct Distribution.

TELL 'EM I'VE GONE CRAZY.
Tracks: If I just knew what she said / She never could dance / It's all in your mind / Straight shooter / Devil inside, The / Tell 'em I've gone crazy / Old time's sake / Birds of paradise / Someone who would care / If she just helps me get over you.
LP. . . . . IMCA 5511
MCA (Import) / Mar '86 / Pinnacle / Silver Sounds (CD).

YOU'RE NOT LEAVIN' HERE TONIGHT.
Tracks: You're not leavin' here tonight / It would take a fool / In Mexico / If it was easy / It's the lovers (who give love a bad name) / After all / Lucky arms / You've got her eyes / I think I'm in love / I'll be there to catch you.
LP. . . . . MCF 3172
MC . . . . MCFC 3172
MCA / '83 / BMG.
LP. . . . . IMCA 5416
MCA (Import) / Mar '86 / Pinnacle / Silver Sounds (CD).

Brush Arbor

HERO.
Tracks: Only for the love of the Lord / Come back home / Witness / All I want to be / Hero / Hey there stranger / Running / Trust in the Lord / God is good / St. Peter / Rescue me.
LP. . . . . MYR 1116
MC . . . . MC 1116
Myrrh / May '82 / Word Records (UK) / Sony.

Bryan, James

FIRST OF MAY, THE.
Tracks: Not Advised.
LP. . . . . ROUNDER 0215
Rounder / Jun '86 / Projection / Roots Records / Swift / C.M. Distribution / Topic Records / Jazz Music / Hot Shot / A.D.A Distribution / Direct Distribution.
MC . . . . ROUNDER 0215C
Rounder / Aug '88 / Projection / Roots Records / Swift / C.M. Distribution / Topic Records / Jazz Music / Hot Shot / A.D.A Distribution / Direct Distribution.

LOOKOUT BLUES.
Tracks: Not Advised.
LP. . . . . ROUNDER 0175
MC . . . . ROUNDER 0175C
Rounder / '88 / Projection / Roots Records / Swift / C.M. Distribution / Topic Records / Jazz Music / Hot Shot / A.D.A Distribution / Direct Distribution.

Bryant, Anita

MY LITTLE CORNER OF THE WORLD.
Tracks: My little corner of the world.
■ 7" . . . . HLL 9171
London-American / Oct '60.

MY MIND'S PLAYING TRICKS ON ME AGAIN.
Tracks: My mind's playing tricks on me again / Another year, another love, another heartache.
■ 7" . . . . CBS 202026
CBS / Jan '66.

PAPER ROSES.
Tracks: Paper roses.
■ 7" . . . . HLL 9144
London-American / May '60.

Bryant, Felice

ALL I HAVE TO DO IS DREAM (Bryant, Felice & Boudleaux).
Tracks: All I have to do is dream / Love hurts / Raining in my heart / Yeh bye love / Wake up little Susie.
LP. . . . . DBLP 3
DB / Nov '80 / DB Records.

■ DELETED B 19

Bryant, Jimmy

BRYANT'S BACK IN TOWN.
Tracks: Not Advised.
LP . . . . HAT 3137
MC . . . . HATC 3137
Stetson / Apr '90 / Crusader Marketing Co. / Swift / Wellard Dist. / Midland Records / C.M. Distribution.

COUNTRY CABIN JAZZ.
Tracks: Not Advised.
LP . . . . HAT 3078
Stetson / '88 / Crusader Marketing Co. / Swift / Wellard Dist. / Midland Records / C.M. Distribution.
MC . . . . HATC 3078
Stetson / Dec '88 / Crusader Marketing Co. / Swift / Wellard Dist. / Midland Records / C.M. Distribution.

GUITAR TAKE OFF.
Tracks: Bryant's boogie / Leetle Juan Pedro / T-bone rag / Liberty bell polka / Okie boogie / Pickin' the chicken / Comin' on / Jammin' with Jimmy / Deep water / Stratosphere boogie / Arkansas traveller / Low man on a totem pole / Catfish boogie / Country capers / Old Joe Clark / Gotta give me whatcha got / Whistle stop / Chatterbox / Cotton pickin' / Sleepwalker's lullaby.
LP . . . . SEE 267
See For Miles / Nov '89 / Pinnacle.

TWO GUITARS COUNTRY STYLE (Bryant, Jimmy & Speedy West).
Tracks: Not Advised.
LP . . . . PM 155 083-1
Pathe Marconi (France) / Jun '84 / Thames Distributors Ltd.

Buck, Bobby

TAKE TIME TO CARE (Buck, Bobby, Ian Botham & Poacher).
Tracks: Take time to care (All royalties to leukaemia research.) / Ian,Viv & Me.
7" . . . . BOTH 1
Spartan / Mar '86.

Buckwheat Zydeco

100% FORTIFIED ZYDECO.
Tracks: Not Advised.
LP . . . . BT 1024
Black Top (USA) / Feb '85 / C.M. Distribution / Direct Distribution / Hot Shot / Topic Records.
CD . . . . CD 1024
MC . . . . BT 1024C
Black Top (USA) / '88 / C.M. Distribution / Direct Distribution / Hot Shot / Topic Records.

BUCKWHEAT ZYDECO.
Tracks: Not Advised.
LP . . . . REU 1005
Rounder Europa (USA) / Apr '86 / Pinnacle.

BUCKWHEAT ZYDECO & THE 11'S SONT PARTIS BAND (Buckwheat Zydeco & The 11's Sont Partis Band).
Tracks: Not Advised.
CD . . . . CD 11528
Rounder / '88 / Projection / Roots Records / Swift / C.M. Distribution / Topic Records / Jazz Music / Hot Shot / A.D.A Distribution / Direct Distribution.

BUCKWHEAT ZYDECO LIVE.
Tracks: Not Advised.
VHS 0823683
Polygram Music Video / '91 / PolyGram.

DOWN DALLAS ALLEY.
Tracks: Down Dallas Alley / Why does love got to be so sad / Make a change.
■ **CD Single** . . . . CID 398
Island / Jun '89.

MAKE A CHANGE.
Tracks: Make a change / In and out of my life / These things you do (Only on 12" and CD single.) / Takin' it home (Only on CD single.).
12" 12IS 412
■ **7"** . . . . IS 412
Island / Mar '89.
■ **CD Single** . . . . CID 412
Island / Mar '89.

MARIE MARIE.
Tracks: Marie Marie / Time is tight / Buckwheat's special (Extra track on 12" only).
■ **12"** 12IS 331
Island / Jul '87.
■ **7"** . . . . IS 331
Island / Jul '87.

ON A NIGHT LIKE THIS.
Tracks: On a night like this / Time is tight / Space Zydeco / Hot Tamale baby / People's choice / Ma 'tit fille / Buckwheat's special / Zydeco honky tonk / Marie, Marie.
■ **CD** . . . . CID 9877
Island / Jul '87.
■ **LP** . . . . ILPS 9877
Island / Jul '87.
■ **MC** . . . . ICT 9877
Island / Jul '87.
CD . . . . IMCD 4
Island / '89 / PolyGram.
MC 842 739 4
MC . . . . ICM 2016
Island / '90 / PolyGram.

ON TRACK.
Tracks: Won't you let me go / Cooking with Pierre / Cry to me / Midnight special, The / Everything hurts (tout que'qu' chose fail mal) / There will always be tomorrow / Funky Filly / You lied to me / On track.
CD . . . . CDCUS 13
LP . . . . CUSLP 13
Charisma / Apr '92 / EMI.
■ **MC** . . . . CUSMC 13
Charisma / Apr '92.

TAKING IT HOME.
Tracks: Creole country / These things you do / Make a change / Ooh wow / Taking it home / Down Dallas alley / Drivin' old grey / Why does love got to be so sad / In and out of my life / Creole country part 2.
CD . . . . CID 9917
■ **LP** . . . . ILPS 9917
Island / Jan '89.
■ **MC** . . . . ICT 9917
Island / Jan '89.
MC 842 603 4
Island / '90 / PolyGram.
■ **MC** . . . . ICM 2015
Island / '90.

TAKING IT HOME.
Tracks: There's good rockin' tonight / Taking it home / On a night like this / Let the good times roll / Rock me baby / Ya ya / Why does love got to be so sad / Make a change.
VHS . . . . IVA 016
Island Visual Arts / May '89 / PolyGram / Terry Blood Dist.

TURNING POINT.
Tracks: Not Advised.
LP . . . . ROUNDER 2045
MC . . . . ROUNDER 2045C
Rounder / '88 / Projection / Roots Records / Swift / C.M. Distribution / Topic Records / Jazz Music / Hot Shot / A.D.A Distribution / Direct Distribution.

WAITIN' FOR MY YA-YA.
Tracks: Not Advised.
LP . . . . REU 1055
Rounder / '87 / Projection / Roots Records / Swift / C.M. Distribution / Topic Records / Jazz Music / Hot Shot / A.D.A Distribution / Direct Distribution.
LP . . . . ROUNDER 2051
MC . . . . ROUNDER 2051C
Rounder / '88 / Projection / Roots Records / Swift / C.M. Distribution / Topic Records / Jazz Music / Hot Shot / A.D.A Distribution / Direct Distribution.

WHERE THERE'S SMOKE, THERE'S FIRE.
Tracks: Not Advised.
LP . . . . ILPS 9962
LP 846215-1
MC 846215-4
Island / May '90 / PolyGram.
CD . . . . CID 9962
■ **MC** . . . . ICT 9962
Island / May '90.

WHY DOES LOVE GOT TO BE SO SAD.
Tracks: Why does love got to be so sad / Creole country (part 2) / Drivin' old grey (Only on 12" version.).
12" 12IS 386
■ **7"** . . . . IS 386
Island / Jan '89.
■ **CD Single** . . . . CID 386
Island / Jan '89.

Buffett, Jimmy

Singer - songwriter born 25.12.1946 in Mobile, Alabama. Worked in New Orleans, prior to a two year spell in Nashville (1969-1971). Buffett who holds a BS degree in history and journalism then settled in Key West, Florida - enjoying universal appeal with his innovative creations. Whilst *Margitaville*, in 1977 has been his best selling single backed with among others the Merle Haggard *Come Monday*, Buffett has accumulated his most notable success via strong album sales. *Son Of A Sailor*, *Changes In Latitudes, Changes In Attitudes*, *Songs You Know By Heart*, *Feeding Frenzy* and *Boats, Beaches, Bars & Ballads* all having either achieved gold or platinum status. Buffett's greatest contribution to the development of music has been his ability to be both innovative and bring a smile to the business, his repertoire features such delights as *If The Phone Doesn't Ring, It's Me*, *God Don't Own A Car* and *Cheeseburger In Paradise*. On a mnore serious note, he co-wrote the much-covered *Railroad Lady* with Jerry Jeff Walker and Lefty Frizzell. After having recorded for Barnaby, Dunhill and ABC, Jimmy Buffett founded the Margaritaville label in 1992 with MCA - with Buffet as it's president. He is now concentrating on promoting the label's roster, featuring all girl outfit Evangeline, Iguanas and Buffett himself. His first album on Margaritaville was *Boats, Beaches, Bars, & Ballads*.His work still houses rich, free flowing carribean elements supported by the Coral Reefer Band. Buffett has also released two live albums; *Feeding Frenzy*, (1990) and *You Had To Be There*, (1979).

CHANGES IN LATITUDES/HAVANA DAY DREAMIN'.
Tracks: Changes in latitudes, changes in attitudes / Wonder why we ever go home / Banana republic / Tampico trauma / Lovely sea cruise / Margaritaville / Miss you so badly / Biloxi / Landfall / Woman goin' crazy in Caroline Street / My head hurts / My feet stink and I don't love Jesus / Captain and the kid, The / Big rig / Defying gravity / Havana daydreamin' / Cliches / Something so feminine about a mandolin / Kick it in second wind / This hotel room.
CD . . . . MCAD 5875
MCA / Oct '87 / BMG.

CHANSON POUR LES PETITS ENFANTS.
Tracks: Chanson pour les petits enfants / Boat drinks.
■ **7"** . . . . MCA 540
MCA / Nov '79.

CHEESEBURGER IN PARADISE.
Tracks: Cheeseburger in paradise / African friend.
■ **7"** . . . . ABC 4219
ABC Records / Jun '78.

COCONUT TELEGRAPH.
Tracks: Coconut telegraph / Little Miss Magic.
■ **7"** . . . . MCA 679
MCA / Feb '81.

CREOLA.
Tracks: Creola.
12" . . . . MCAT 1093
7" . . . . MCA 1093
MCA / Oct '86 / BMG.

FINS.
Tracks: Fins / Dreamside.
■ **7"** . . . . MCA 532
MCA / Oct '79.

FLORIDAYS.
Tracks: Creola / I love the now / First look / Meet me in Memphis / Nobody speaks to the captain no more / Floridays / If it all falls down / No plane on Sunday / When the coast is clear / You'll never work in dis bisness again.
CD . . . . MCAD 5730
LP . . . . IMCA 5730
MC . . . . IMCAC 5730
MCA / Feb '87 / BMG.

LAST MANGO IN PARIS.
Tracks: Everybody on the run / Frank and Lola / Perfect partner, The / Please bypass this heart / Gypsies in the palace / Deperation Samba (Halloween in Tijuana) / Last mango in Paris / Jolly mon sing / Beyond the end.
CD . . . . MCAD 5600
MCA / '87 / BMG.

LIVE BY THE BAY.
Tracks: Not Advised.
VHS . . . . VHR 1206
CIC Video / Nov '86 / Sony / Pickwick Records / Terry Blood Dist. / Gold & Sons.

MARGARITAVILLE.
Tracks: Margaritaville / Miss you so badly.
■ **7"** . . . . ABC 4179
ABC Records / Jun '77.

MARGARITAVILLE.
Tracks: Margaritaville / Come Monday.
■ **7"** . . . . MCA 510
MCA / Nov '79.

SONGS YOU KNOW BY HEART (Greatest Hits).
Tracks: Cheeseburger in paradise / He went to Paris / Fins / Son of a son of a sailor / Pirate looks at forty, A / Margaritaville / Come Monday / Changes in latitudes / Why don't we get drunk / Pencil thin moustache / Grapefruit-juicy fruit / Boat drinks / Volcano.
CD . . . . MCAD 5633
MCA / '86 / BMG.

STARS FELL ON ALABAMA.
Tracks: Stars fell on Alabama / Growing older but not up.
■ **7"** . . . . MCA 724
MCA / May '81.

VOLCANO.
Tracks: Volcano / Stranded on a sandbar.
■ **7"** . . . . MCA 562
MCA / Jan '80.

VOLCANO.
Tracks: Not Advised.
■ **LP** . . . . MCG 4006
MCA / Dec '79.

Burgess, Sonny

Gaining prominence at the time that rockabilly entered the music scene, Arkansas born Albert 'Sonny' Burgess started performing country music in 1955. He recorded for Sun Records but enjoyed only regional success, *Ain't Got A Thing* probably being the nearest he came to the national charts. Earning the reputation as a

B 20 ■ DELETED

wild, raunchy performer, he toured with Conway Twitty in 1959. A favourite with UK rock'n'roll enthusiasts, he also recorded for Arbur, TSBS and Razorback among a variety of other labels. (Tony Byworth)

1956 - 1959.
Tracks: We wanna boogie / Red headed woman / Prisoner's song, The / All night long / Life's too short to live / Restless / Ain't got a thing / Daddy blues / Fannie Brown / Ain't gonna do it / You / Hand me down my walking cane / Please listen to me / Gone / My babe / My bucket's got a hole in it / Sweet misery / Whatcha gonna do / Oh mama / Truckin' down the avenue / Feelin' good / So glad you're mine / One night / Always will / Little town baby / You're not mine / Mr. Blues / Find my baby for me / Tomorrow night / Tomorrow never comes / Skinny Ginny / So soon / Mama Loochie (1) / Mama Loochie (2) / Itchy / Thunderbird / Kiss goodnite, A / Sadie's back in town / Smoochin' Jill / My baby loves me / One broken heart.
CD Set . . . . BCD 15525
Bear Family / Jul '91 / Rollercoaster Records / Swift / Direct Distribution.

FLOOD TAPES 1959-62, THE.
Tracks: Flip flop and fly / Dizzy Miss Lizzy / Stones in love with you / K.K.'s boogie / Mellow soul / What ever happened to the girls I knew / City lights / We wanna boogie / Ain't got a thing / Crazy arms / Drinkin' wine spo / Dee o dee / Meet me anywhere / Sea cruise / Little town baby.
LP . . . . SJLP 561
Sunjay / Oct '87 / CSA Tell Tapes.

I NEED A MAN (Burgess, Sonny/Barbara Pittman/Warren Smith/M.Yelvington).
Tracks: Not Advised.
■ LP . . . . CFM 502
Charly / Sep '81.

LEGENDARY SUN PERFORMERS.
Tracks: Red headed woman / Restless / Going home / Ain't got a thing / Find my baby for me / Tomorrow night / You're not the one for me / Thunderbird / We wanna boogie / Feel so good / Y.O.U / My bucket's got a hole in it / All my sins are taken away / Sally Brown / I love you so / Sadie's back in town.
■ LP . . . . CR 30136
Charly / '77 / Charly.

OLD GANG,THE.
Tracks: Not Advised.
■ LP . . . . CRM 2025
Charly / '81 / Charly.

RAW DEAL.
Tracks: Not Advised.
LP . . . . LPL 8601
Rockhouse / Oct '88 / Charly / C.M. Distribution / Nervous Records.

ROCK-A-BILLY (Burgess, Sonny & Larry Donn).
Tracks: Honey bun / Milkcow boogie blues / Blue moon of Kentucky / I forgot to remember to forget / I'm left you're right she's gone / She's gone / Baby, let's play house / Mystery train / That's what I call a baby / She's mine / Brown eyed handsome man / Kentucky home rock / All night stomp / Sunshine rock / Girl next door.
LP . . . . WLP 8817
White Label (Germany) / Apr '87 / Pinnacle / Bear Family Records (Germany) / CSA Tell Tapes.

SONNY BURGESS & THE PACERS (Burgess, Sonny & The Pacers).
Tracks: Don't be that way / Oh Mama / Truckin' down the avenue / All my sins are taken away / My babe / My bucket's got a hole in it / Sweet misery / So glad you're mine / Mr. Blues / Tomorrow night / Feel so good / Find my baby for me / One night.
LP . . . . SUN 1027
Sun / '85 / Charly / Swift.

SONNY BURGESS VOLUME 3.
Tracks: Itchy (Instrumental) / Always will / Little town baby / Changed my mind / Kiss goodnight, A / Sadie's back in town / Thunderbird (Instrumental) / So soon / Smootchin' Jill / Sweet Jenny / Tomorrow never comes / Oochie coochie / You're not the one for me.
LP . . . . SUN 1039
Sun / Oct '86 / Charly / Swift.

SPELLBOUND.
Tracks: Move it on over / Spellbound / I'll be there (if you ever want me) / I'm counting on you / Everybody's movin' again / Rock 'n' roll daddy / Raw deal / Get on the right track baby / Hot mama / Blue highway / Sunrock / Louisiana lady.
LP . . . . WIK 50
Off-Beat (2) / Sep '86 / Pinnacle.

TENNESSEE BORDER.
Tracks: Tennessee border / Enough of you / My heart is aching for you / Flattop joint / As far as I could go / Old, old man / Automatic woman / There's talk in your sleep / Stuck up / I don't dig it.
CD . . . . FIENDCD 720
Edsel / Jun '92 / Pinnacle.

WE WANNA BOOGIE (Burgess, Sonny & The Pacers).
Tracks: We wanna boogie / Red headed woman / Feeling good / Ain't got a thing / Restless / Truckin' down the avenue / Fannie Brown / Going home / Sadie

Brown / My bucket's got a hole in it / Sweet misery / All my sins are taken away / My babe / Tomorrow night / Daddy blues / So glad you're mine / Hoochie coochie man / Find my baby for me / One night / Itchy / Thunderbird / Little town baby / Kiss goodnight, A / Sadie's back in town.
LP . . . . SUN 1022
Sun / '85 / Charly / Swift.
CD . . . . CDCHARLY 92
Charly / '87 / Charly.

Burnette, Dorsey

Making his musical debut as a member of the Johnny Burnette Trio, older brother Dorsey Burnette (1932-79) secured pop success in 1960 with *Tall Oak Tree*, and *Hey Little One*, on Era Records. Throughout the 1970's he scored 15 hits in the country charts, most of them on Capitol Records. His son, Billy Burnette, carries on the musical traditions. (Tony Byworth)

DORSEY BURNETTE.
Tracks: Not Advised.
■ LP . . . . SKYLINE 1990
Skyline / Nov '87.

DORSEY BURNETTE VOL. 1 (Great shakin' fever).
Tracks: Not Advised.
LP 501
Hollywood Rockabilly / Jul '87.

DORSEY BURNETTE VOL. 2 (Keep a knockin').
Tracks: Not Advised.
LP 502
Hollywood Rockabilly / Jul '87.

GREAT SHAKIN' FEVER.
Tracks: Great shakin' fever / Don't let go / Dying ember / Rainin' in my heart / Sad boy / He gave me my hands / Good good lovin' / Full house, A / Feminine touch / It's no sin / Creator, The / Biggest lover in town, The / Buckeye road / That's me without you / No one but him / Cry for your love / Rains came down, The / Country boy in the army, A / Somebody nobody wants / It could've been different / Little child / With all your heart / Look what you've missed / Gypsy magic / I would do anything.
CD . . . . BCD 15545
Bear Family / '93 / Rollercoaster Records / Swift / Direct Distribution.

GREATEST LOVE, THE.
Tracks: Greatest love, The / Thin little, pretty line.
7" . . . . .LBF 15190
Liberty / '69 / EMI.

JIMMY BROWN.
Tracks: Jimmy Brown.
■ 7" . . . . TMG 534
Tamla Motown / '65.

TALL OAK TREE.
Tracks: Not Advised.
LP . . . . EL 102
Era (USA) / Oct '87.

Burnette, Johnny

10TH ANNIVERSARY ALBUM.
Tracks: Not Advised.
LP 2C 068 83099
Liberty (import) / '83 / EMI.

14 DEMO RECORDINGS (Burnette, Johnny & Dorsey).
Tracks: Not Advised.
LP . . . . ROCK 8112
Rockhouse / Apr '90 / Charly / C.M. Distribution / Nervous Records.

20 ROCK'N'ROLL HITS: JOHNNY BURNETTE.
Tracks: You're 16 / Little boy sad / You're the reason / Settin' the woods on fire / Walk on by / Fool, The / Why don't you haul off and love me / Me & the bear / Clown shoes / Cincinnati fireball / Lovesick blues / Finders keepers / Mona Lisa / Fool of the year, The / Just out of reach / Poorest boy in town, The / Moody river / Girl of my best friend / In the chapel in the moonlight / Dreamin'.
LP . . . . IC 064 82751
EMI (Germany) / '83.

ALL BY MYSELF (Burnette, Johnny & R & R Trio).
Tracks: All by myself / Drinkin' wine.
7" . . . . REV 6014
Revival / Jul '82 / EMI.

CLOWN SHOES.
Tracks: Clown shoes.
■ 7" . . . . LIB 55416
Liberty / May '62.

COMPLETE RECORDINGS (Burnette, Johnny & R & R Trio).
Tracks: Rockabilly boogie / Please don't leave me / Rock therapy / Lonesome train (on a lonesome track) / Sweet love on my mind / My love, you're a stranger /

Your baby blue eyes / I love you so / Train kept a rollin' / All by myself / Drinking wine spo dee o dee / Blues stay away from me / Honey hush / Lonesome tears in my eyes / I just found out / Chains of love / Lonesome train on a lonesome track (alt) / I love you so (master) / If you want it enough / Butterfingers / Eager beaver baby / Touch me / Tear it up / Oh baby babe / You're undecided / Midnight train / Shattered dreams.
CD . . . . BCD 15474
Bear Family / '88 / Rollercoaster Records / Swift / Direct Distribution.

DREAMIN'.
Tracks: Dreamin' / Big big world.
■ 7" . . . . HLG 9127
London-American / Sep '60.
■ 7" . . . . UP 36526
United Artists / Sep '79.

GIRLS.
Tracks: Girls.
■ 7" . . . . HLG 9388
London-American / Aug '61.

JOHNNY & DORSEY BURNETTE (Burnette, Johnny & R & R Trio).
Tracks: Not Advised.
LP . . . . LPL 8112
Rockhouse / Nov '82 / Charly / C.M. Distribution / Nervous Records.

JOHNNY BURNETTE ROCK 'N' ROLL TRIO, THE (Burnette, Johnny & R & R Trio).
Tracks: Not Advised.
LP . . . . SS 8001
Solid Smoke (USA) / Apr '79 / C.M. Distribution.

LEGENDARY JOHNNY BURNETTE ROCK 'N' ROLL TRIO (Burnette, Johnny & R & R Trio).
Tracks: Tear it up / You're undecided / Oh baby babe / Midnight train / Shattered dreams / Train kept a rollin' / Blues stay away from me / All by myself / Drinkin' wine spo-dee-o-dee / Chains of love / Honey hush / Lonesome tears in my eyes / I just found out / Please don't leave me / Rock therapy / Rockabilly boogie / Lonesome train (on a lonesome track) / Sweet love on my mind / My love you're a stranger / I love you so / Your baby blue eyes / Touch me / If you want it enough / Butterfingers / Eager beaver baby / On baby babe.
Double LP . . . . CDX 3
■ MC . . . . TCCDX 3
Charly / Jun '84 / Charly.

LITTLE BOY SAD.
Tracks: Little boy sad.
■ 7" . . . . HLG 9315
London-American / Apr '61.

LONESOME TRAIN (Burnette, Johnny & R & R Trio).
Tracks: Lonesome train / Sweet love on my mind.
7" . . . . REV 6011
Revival / Jul '82 / EMI.

PLEASE DON'T LEAVE ME (Burnette, Johnny & R & R Trio).
Tracks: Please don't leave me / Oh baby babe.
7" . . . . REV 6012
Revival / Jul '82 / EMI.

R 'N' R TRIO / TEAR IT UP.
Tracks: Not Advised.
CD .BGOCD 177
Beat Goes On / Jun '93 / Pinnacle.

ROCK 'N' ROLL (Burnette, Johnny & R & R Trio).
Tracks: Not Advised.
■ LP . . . . SKYLINE 1254
Skyline / Nov '87.

ROCK 'N' ROLL MASTERS (Best of Johnny Burnette).
Tracks: Dreamin' / Let me be with you / That's the way I feel / You'll learn to cry / it's my way / Walk on by / It's the after / Little boy sad / You're sixteen / Lover's question, A / Fools like me / Second chance / Girls / Standing on the outside of her door / Gimme gimme lovin' / Clown shoes / Dream lover (CD only.) / Some enchanted evening (CD only.) / Lonesome waters (CD only.) / Kentucky waltz (CD only.).
LP . . . . EMS 1324
■ MC . . . . TCEMS 1324
EMI / Aug '89.
■ CD . . . . CZ 154
Liberty / Aug '89.

ROCK 'N' ROLL TRIO - TEAR IT UP.
Tracks: Train kept a-rollin' / Lonesome train / Oh baby babe / All by myself / Blues stay away from me / Sweet love on my mind / Rock therapy / Please don't leave me / Rockbilly boogie / Drinkin' wine spo-dee-o-dee / Tear it up / You're undecided / If you want it enough / Eager beaver baby / Your baby blue eyes / Butterfingers / Honey hush.
■ LP . . . . ROLI 306
Rollercoaster / Oct '81.

ROCKABILLY BOOGIE (Burnette, Johnny & R & R Trio).
Tracks: Rockabily boogie / Tear it up.
7" . . . . REV 6013
Revival / Jul '82 / EMI.

SINGS COLLECTIBLE HITS (Burnette, Johnny & R & R Trio).
Tracks: Not Advised.
LP . . . . **LSP 1062**
Musketeer / Oct '87 / D.A.D. Records.

TOGETHER AGAIN (Burnette, Johnny & Dorsey).
Tracks: Little ole you / I wanna love my baby / I'm happy / That's the way I feel / Just keep on a-goin' / Baby doll blue eyes / Cincinnati fireball / You're sixteen / Hey stranger / Address unknown / Lovesick blues / Finders keepers / Interview with Johnny Burnette / One-sided love affair.
■ **LP** . . . . **ROLI 308**
Rollercoaster / Oct '81.

TRAIN KEPT A ROLLIN' (Burnette, Johnny & R & R Trio).
Tracks: Train kept a rollin' / Honey hush.
7" . . . . **REV 6010**
Revival / Jul '82 / EMI.

WE'RE HAVING A PARTY (Burnette, Johnny & R & R Trio).
Tracks: Not Advised.
LP . . . . **RSRLP 1017**
Rockstar (1) / Oct '88 / Swift / C.M. Distribution.

YOU'RE SIXTEEN.
Tracks: You're sixteen / Little boy sad.
■ **7"** . . . . **UP 36527**
United Artists / Sep '79.

YOU'RE SIXTEEN.
Tracks: You're sixteen.
■ **7"** . . . . **HLG 9254**
London-American / Jan '61.

YOU'RE SIXTEEN (OLD GOLD).
Tracks: You're sixteen / Dreamin'.
7" . . . . **OG 9987**
Old Gold / '92 / Pickwick Records.

Burns, Jethro

Although generally regarded as a country comedian and one half of the Homer and Jethro duo (see separate entry), Kenneth C. Burns (1920-89) - like his long-time partner, Henry Haynes - was an outstanding musicians. Their skills were first exposed, as members of the Nashville String Band, on a 1970 Chet Atkins album. Burns was an outstanding mandolin player and when Haynes died in 1971, he carried on his career as a musician, frequently touring with Steve Goodman as well as recording several albums. (Tony Byworth)

BACK TO BACK (Burns, Jethro & Tiny Moore).
Tracks: Not Advised.
LP . . . . **F 9**
Kaleidoscope (USA) / Sep '79 / Projection / Ross Records / Roots Records / Swift / C.M. Distribution / Topic Records / Duncans.

JETHRO BURNS.
Tracks: Not Advised.
LP . . . . **FF 042**
Flying Fish (USA) / Mar '89 / Cadillac Music / Roots Records / Projection / C.M. Distribution / Direct Distribution / Jazz Music / Duncans / A.D.A Distribution.

JETHRO LIVE.
Tracks: Not Advised.
LP . . . . **FF 072**
Flying Fish (USA) / Mar '89 / Cadillac Music / Roots Records / Projection / C.M. Distribution / Direct Distribution / Jazz Music / Duncans / A.D.A Distribution.

TEA FOR ONE.
Tracks: Not Advised.
LP . . . . **F 14**
Kaleidoscope (USA) / '88 / Projection / Ross Records / Roots Records / Swift / C.M. Distribution / Topic Records / Duncans.

Burrito Brothers

Latterday evolvement of the famed West Coast country-rock outfit, The Flying Burrito Brothers (see seperate entry). Comprising cajun fiddle player Gib Guilbeau and singer/songwriter John Beland. The duo traded under the shortened name and established themselves in Nashville in 1981 where they set out to win the country music market. They scored a handful of chart successes with *She Belongs To Everyone But Me* being the highest placed at no.16. They disbanded in 1985. (Tony Byworth)

BACK TO THE SWEETHEART OF THE RODEO.
Tracks: Not Advised.
Double LP . . . . **AP 054/55**
MC Set . . . . **AP 054/55C**
Appaloosa / Jul '90 / Roots Records / C.M. Distribution / Wellard Dist. / Projection / Hot Shot / A.D.A Distribution.

ENCORE (LIVE 1990).
Tracks: Dim lights, thick smoke / You ain't going nowhere / Hickory wind / White line fever / Sweet little Colette / Big bayou / Sweet Suzanna / Wild horses / Silverwings / Help wanted / Cannonball rag / When it all comes down to love / Wheels.
CD . . . . **CDSD 069**
MC . . . . **SDC 069**
Sundown / Nov '90 / Terry Blood Dist. / Jazz Music / C.M. Distribution.

WHEELS: TRIBUTE TO CLARENCE WHITE & GRAM PARSONS (Burrito Brothers & CO).
Tracks: Six white horses / Emmy / Bugler / Promised land, The / Freeborn man / Games people play / Detroit City / 500 miles / Four strong winds / Shame on me / Streets of Baltimore / Millers cave / Christine's tune / Wheels.
CD . . . . **APCD 049**
LP . . . . **AP 049**
Appaloosa / '88 / Roots Records / C.M. Distribution / Wellard Dist. / Projection / Hot Shot / A.D.A Distribution.

Burroughs, Chris

WEST OF TEXAS.
Tracks: Not Advised.
CD . . . . **ROSE 203 CD**
LP . . . . **ROSE 203**
New Rose (1) / Jul '90 / Pinnacle.

Bush, Sam

LATE AS USUAL.
Tracks: Not Advised.
LP . . . . **ROUNDER 0195**
Rounder / Jun '85 / Projection / Roots Records / Swift / C.M. Distribution / Topic Records / Jazz Music / Hot Shot / A.D.A Distribution / Direct Distribution.
CD . . . . **CD 0195**
Rounder / '88 / Projection / Roots Records / Swift / C.M. Distribution / Topic Records / Jazz Music / Hot Shot / A.D.A Distribution / Direct Distribution.
MC . . . . **ROUNDER 0195C**
Rounder / Aug '88 / Projection / Roots Records / Swift / C.M. Distribution / Topic Records / Jazz Music / Hot Shot / A.D.A Distribution / Direct Distribution.

TOGETHER AGAIN - FOR THE FIRST TIME (Bush, Sam & Alan Munde).
Tracks: Stymied / Banjalin / Forked deer / Small change / Clear skies / Old widder woman / Cattle in the cane / Counterblast rag / Town and country / Foster's reel / Panhandle country / Howdy in Hickman County / Eleanor Rigby.
LP . . . . **RRR 0007**
Ridgerunner (USA) / '77 / Mike's Country Music Room / Projection.

Byaela, Jane

ON THE EDGE.
Tracks: Child of the sun / On the edge / Childkeeper / Mr Dream Maker / Longer than time / Business of love / Riddles of blue / Running in the rain / Secrets are burning / Jimi's song / After the storm / Angel of dreams / Drifter of the wind / Road of Autumn.
CD . . . . **SDCD 9.00437**
Sawdust / '90.

Byrds

In their heyday this American group consisted of Gene Clark, Michael Clarke, David Crosby, Chris Hillman and Roger McGuinn. The band formed in 1964, its members having individually been involved in America's burgeoning folk movement. Heavily influenced by Bob Dylan, the Byrds decided to record one of his songs as their first single. the song chosen was a recent Dylan album track *Mr Tambourine Man*, which they enlivened to create a catchy pop single. It proved a runaway debut success, surging to No. 1 in both the US and UK. It was also a musical innovation, being the first 'folk-rock' hit. While Dylan was America's most important musical act, the Beatles and the Rolling Stones were leading the field in Britain - the Byrds fused the folk style of Dylan with the melodic pop strength of the Beatles and it was a winner. The band recorded another Dylan album track for the follow-up single; *All I Really Want To Do*, peaking at No. 40 in the USA and at No. 4 in the UK. The next Byrds single was a cover of folk singer Pete Seeger's *Turn! Turn! Turn!*, this Bible-inspired number gave them their second US no. 1 of 1965 but reached only no.26 in the UK. In 1966 The Byrds scored their final American Top 20 single with *Eight Miles High*, one of their best remembered tracks. At the time its success was slightly hindered by its drug connotations - once these were understood by radio stations, the disc received little airplay. That same year Gene Clark departed and the group thus lost one of its three voices that made up its distinctive vocal harmony sound. As hit singles tailed off, the Byrds concentrated on albums, which continued to sell well. They began to experiment with electronic sounds and issued some fine LPs. In late '67 however, arguments about musical direction led to the departure of two more members, Michael Clarke and David Crosby. They were replaced by Kevin Kelley and Gram Parsons (see seperate entry), with whom the Byrds recorded 1968's *Sweetheart Of The Rodeo*, album. This again broke new ground, by being virtually the first country-rock record. It was a major influence on the early Seventies work of such names as the Eagles and Jackson Browne. Shortly after the album's emergence, Hillman and Parsons quit and were replaced by Gene Parsons and Clarence White. The early Seventies brought several more album projects, which were partially successful, plus their final British Top 20 single *Chestnut Mare*. The group folded in 1973 and McGuinn attempted to reform the original quartet. He succeeded for the duration of one reunion album, simply called *Byrds*, but it was not a worthy LP. The trio of McGuinn, Clark & Hillman scored a one-off US Top 40 single *Don't You Write Her Off* in 1979, but failed to follow it up. In the Eighties the various ex-Byrds' careers went through the floor, with some members even finding difficulty getting record contracts. Nonetheless, for all their later troubles, the Byrds had achieved a great deal in the Sixties, virtually inventing both folk-rock and country-rock. (Bob MacDonald).

20 ESSENTIAL TRACKS FROM THE BOXED SET.
Tracks: Mr Tambourine Man / I'll feel a whole lot better / All I really want to do / Turn turn turn / 5-D / Eight miles high / Mr Spaceman / So you want to be a rock 'n' roll star / Have you seen her face / Ladyfriend / My back pages / Goin' back / Ballad of Easy Rider / Jesus is just alright / Chestnut mare / I wanna grow up to be a politician / He was a friend of mine / Paths of victory / From a distance / Love that never dies.
CD **4716652**
MC **4716654**
Sony Music / '93 / Sony.

6 TRACK HITS.
Tracks: Lay lady lay / Turn turn turn / Gon' back / So you want to be a rock'n'roll star / Chestnut mare / All I really want to do.
EP **7SR 5016**
MC **7SC 5016**
Scoop 33 / Aug '83.

ALL I REALLY WANT TO DO.
Tracks: All I really want to do.
■ **7"** . . . . **CBS 201796**
CBS / Aug '65.
■ **7"** . . . . **CBS 3952**
CBS / Feb '76.

BALLAD OF EASY RIDER.
Tracks: Ballad of Easy Rider / Fido / Oil in my lamp / Tulsa coutry blue / Jack Tarr the sailor / Jesus is just alright / It's all over now, baby blue / There must be someone / Gunga Din / Plane wreck at Los Gartos (Deportee) / Armstrong, Aldrin and Collins.
■ **LP** **63795**
CBS / Feb '70.

BYRDS PLAY DYLAN, THE.
Tracks: Mr. Tambourine man / All I really want to do / Chimes of freedom / Spanish Harlem incident / Time they are a changin', The / Lay down your weary tune / My back pages / You ain't goin' nowhere / Nothing was delivered / This wheel's on fire / It's all over now / Baby blue / Lay lady lay / Positively 4th street.
LP . . . . **CBS 31503**
CBS / Jul '77 / Sony.
MC **40 31795**
CBS / Feb '80 / Sony.
■ **LP** . . . . **CBS 31795**
CBS / Feb '80.

BYRDS, THE.
Tracks: Full circle / Sweet Mary / Changing heart / For free / Born to rock 'n' roll / Things will be better / Cowgirl in the sand / Long live the King / Borrowing time / Laughing / See the sky about to rain.
■ **LP** . . . . **SYLA 8754**
Asylum / Apr '73.
■ **LP** . . . . **K 42006**
Asylum / '78.

CHESTNUT MARE.
Tracks: Chestnut mare.
■ **7"** . . . . **CBS 5322**
CBS / Feb '71.

CHESTNUT MARE (OLD GOLD).
Tracks: Chestnut mare.
■ **7"** . . . . **OG 9182**
Old Gold / Jul '82.

COLLECTION: BYRDS.
Tracks: Lady friend / Chestnut mare / Bells of Rhymney / He was a friend of mine / Why / Everybody's been burned / Eight miles high / Girl with no name / Goin' back / So you want to be a rock 'n' roll star / 5D (fifth dimension) / Old John Robertson / Here without you / Wasn't born to follow / Draft morning / It won't be wrong / John Riley / My back pages / Mr. Tambourine man / Turn,turn,turn / Feel a whole lot better / Have you seen her face / All I really want to do / You ain't goin' nowhere.
MC . . . . **CCSMC 151**
Castle Collector Series / Sep '86 / BMG / Pinnacle / Castle Communications.
■ **Double LP** . . . . **CCSLP 151**

B 22

■ DELETED

Castle Collector Series / Sep '86.
CD .... CCSCD 151
Castle Collector Series / '88 / BMG / Pinnacle / Castle Communications.

DR BYRDS & MR HYDE.
Tracks: This wheel's on fire / Old blue / Your gentle way of loving me / Child of the universe / Nashville West / Drug store truck driving man / King Apathy III / Candy / Bad night at the whiskey / Medley: My back pages / B.J. blues / Baby, what do you want me to do.
■ LP 63545
CBS / May '69.
CD .... BGOCD 107
LP .... BGOLP 107
Beat Goes On / Aug '91 / Pinnacle.

EIGHT MILES HIGH.
Tracks: Eight miles high.
■ 7" .... CBS 202067
CBS / May '66.

FIFTH DIMENSION.
Tracks: 5D (fifth dimension) / Wild mountain thyme / Mr. Space-man / I see you / What's happening?! / I come and stand at every door / Eight miles high / Hey Joe / Captain soul / John Riley / 2-4-2 foxtrot (the lear jet song).
■ LP .... BPG 62783
CBS / Oct '66.
LP .... CBS 32284
MC 40 32284
CBS / '84 / Sony.
CD .... BGOCD 106
LP .... BGOLP 106
Beat Goes On / Sep '91 / Pinnacle.

FULL CIRCLE.
Tracks: Full circle / Long live the King.
7" .... AMY 517
Liberty / '69 / EMI.

FULL FLYTE 1965-1970.
Tracks: Mr. Tambourine man / Feel a whole lot better / All I really want to do / Turn turn turn / Chimes of freedom / She don't care about time / Eight miles high / 5D / Mr. Spaceman / So you want to be a rock 'n' roll star / Have you seen her face / Renaissance fair / My back pages / Everybody's been burned / Why / Lady friend / Going back / Wasn't born to follow / Old John Robertson / Artificial energy / You ain't goin' nowhere / Hickory wind / You're still on my mind / Drug store truck driving man / Gunga din.
■ CD .... RVCD 10
Raven / Feb '91.

GOIN' BACK.
Tracks: Goin' back / Change is now.
■ 7" .... CBS 5300
CBS / Jun '77.

GOLDEN HIGHLIGHTS.
Tracks: Not Advised.
LP 54737
MC 40 54737
CBS (import) / Jun '86 / C.M. Distribution / Silva Screen.

GREATEST HITS: BYRDS.
Tracks: Mr. Tambourine man / I'll feel a whole lot better / Bells of Rhymney / Turn turn turn / All I really want to do / Chimes of freedom / Eight miles high / Mr. Space-man / 5D (fifth dimension) / So you want to be a rock 'n' roll star / My back pages.
LP .... CBS 32068
MC 40 32068
CBS / Jan '84 / Sony.
CD .... CD 32068
CBS / Jun '89 / Sony.
CD 4678432
MC 4678434
Columbia / Feb '91 / Sony.
■ LP 4678431
Columbia / Feb '91.
MiniDisc 467843-3
Columbia / Apr '93 / Sony.

HISTORY OF THE BYRDS.
Tracks: Mr. Tambourine man / Turn turn turn / She don't care about time / Wild mountain thyme / Eight miles high / Mr. Spaceman / 5D (fifth dimension) / So you want to be a rock'n'roll star / Time between / My back pages / Lady friend / Goin back / Old John Robertson / Wasn't born to follow / You ain't goin nowhere / Hickory wind / Nashville West / Drug store truck driving man / Gunga din / Jesus is just alright / Ballad of easy rider / Chestnut mare / Yesterday's train / Just the season / Citizen Kane / America's great national pastime / Jamaica (say you will) / Tiffany queen.
■ LP 68242
CBS / May '73.
LP 4601151
■ MC 4601154
CBS / Sep '87.

MR TAMBOURINE MAN (OLD GOLD).
Tracks: Mr. Tambourine man / Turn turn turn.
7" .... OG 9747
Old Gold / Jan '88 / Pickwick Records.

MR TAMBOURINE MAN/TURN TURN TURN/ YOUNGER THAN YESTERDAY.
Tracks: Not Advised.
CD Set 4683382
CBS / '92 / Sony.

MR. TAMBOURINE MAN.
Tracks: Mr. Tambourine man / I'll feel a whole lot better / Spanish Harlem incident / You won't have to cry / Here without you / Bells of Rhymney, The / All I really want to do / I knew I'd want you / It's no use / Don't doubt yourself babe / Chimes of freedom / We'll meet again.
■ LP .... EMB 3107
Embassy / Jan '77 / Sony.

MR.TAMBOURINE MAN.
Tracks: Not Advised.
■ LP .... BPG 62571
CBS / Aug '65.
■ MC 40 31503
CBS / Jul '77.

MR.TAMBOURINE MAN.
Tracks: Mr. Tambourine man.
■ 7" .... CBS 201765
CBS / Jun '65.
■ 7" .... A 4575
CBS / Jul '84.

NEVER BEFORE.
Tracks: Not Advised.
LP .... MH 70318
Re-Flyte / Apr '88.

NOTORIOUS BYRD BROTHERS, THE.
Tracks: Artificial energy / Goin' back / Natural harmony / Draft morning / Wasn't born to follow / Get to you / Change is now / Old John Robertson / Tribal gathering / Dolphins smile / 2001.
■ LP 63169
CBS / May '68.
LP .... ED 262
Edsel / Jun '88 / Pinnacle.
■ CD .... EDCD 262
Edsel / Jun '88.
CD 468014-2
Columbia / Aug '93 / Sony.

ORIGINAL SINGLES-VOL 1, THE.
Tracks: Mr. Tambourine man / I knew I'd want you / All I really want to do / I'll feel a whole lot better / Turn, turn, turn / She don't care about time / Set you free this time / It won't be wrong / Eight miles high / Why / 5D (fifth dimension) / Captain Soul / Mr. Spaceman / What's happening? / So you want to be a rock 'n' roll star / Everybody's been burned.
■ LP .... CBS 31851
CBS / Sep '80.
LP .... CBS 32069
CBS / Nov '81 / Sony.
■ MC 40 32069
CBS / Nov '81.

ORIGINAL SINGLES-VOL 2, THE.
Tracks: My back pages / Renaissance fair / Have you seen her face / Don't make waves / Lady friend / Old John Robertson / Goin' back / Change is now / You ain't goin' nowhere / Artificial energy / I am a pilgrim / Pretty boy Floyd / Bad night at the whiskey / Drug store truck driving man / Lay lady lay / Old blue.
LP .... CBS 32103
CBS / Apr '82 / Sony.
■ MC 40 32103
CBS / Apr '82.

SO YOU WANT TO BE A ROCK'N'ROLL STAR.
Tracks: So you want to be a rock'n'roll star / Everybody's been burned.
■ 7" .... CBS 202559
CBS / Feb '67.

SWEETHEART OF THE RODEO.
Tracks: You ain't goin' nowhere / I am a pilgrim / Christian life, The / You don't miss your water / You're still on my mind / Pretty boy Floyd / Hickory wind / One hundred years from now / Blue Canadian Rockies / Life in prison / Nothing was delivered.
CD .... EDCD 234
Edsel / Jul '87 / Pinnacle.
LP .... ED 234
MC .... CED 234
Edsel / May '87 / Pinnacle.

SWEETHEARTS OF THE RODEO/THE NOTORIOUS BYRD BROTHERS.
Tracks: Not Advised.
LP Set 22040
MC 4022040
Columbia / Sep '77 / Sony.

TURN TURN TURN.
Tracks: Turn Turn Turn / It won't be wrong / Set you free this time / Lay down your weary tune / He was a friend of mine / World turns all around her, The / Satisfied mind / If you're gone / Times they are-a changing / Wait and see / Oh Susannah.
■ LP .... CBS 31526
CBS / Jan '76 / Sony.

TURN, TURN, TURN.
Tracks: Turn, turn, turn / I feel a whole lot better / Mr Tambourine man / Eight miles high.
12" 6565446
7" 6565447
■ CD Single 6565445
CBS / Dec '90.
■ CD Single 6565442
CBS / Dec '90.
■ MC Single 6565444
CBS / Dec '90.

TURN, TURN, TURN (ORIGINAL SINGLE).
Tracks: Turn turn turn.
■ 7" .... CBS 202008
CBS / Nov '65.

ULTIMATE BYRDS, THE.
Tracks: Mr Tambourine man / I'll feel a whole lot better / Chimes of freedom / She has a way / All I really want to do / Spanish harlem incident / Bells of Rhymney, The / It's all over now, baby blue / She don't care about time / Turn, turn, turn (to everything there is a Season) / It won't be wrong / Lay down your weary tune / He was a friend of mind / World turns all around her, The / Day walk (never before), The / Times are a a-changing, The / 5D (Fifth dimension) / I know my rider / Eight miles high / Why / Psychodrama City / I see you / Hey Joe (where you gonna go) / Mr Spaceman / John Riley / Roll over Beethoven / So you want to be a rock 'n' roll star / Have you seen her face / My back pages / Time between / It happens each day / Renaissance Fair / Everybody's been burned / Girl with no name, The / Triad / Lady friend / Old John Robertson / Goin' back / Draft morning / Wasn't born to follow / Dolphin's smile / Reputation / You ain't going nowhere / Christian life, The / I am a pilgrim / Pretty boy Floyd / You don't miss your water / Hickory wind / Nothing was delivered / One hundred years from now / Pretty Polly / Lazy days / This wheel's on fire / Nashville West / Old blue / Drug store truck drivin' man / Bad night at the whiskey / Lay lady lay / Mae Jean goes to Hollywood / Easy rider (Theme from Easy Rider) / Oil in my lamp / Jesus is just alright / Way beyond the sun / Tulsa county / Deportee / Lover of the Bayou / Willin' / Black mountain rag (solider's joy) / Positively 4th Street / Chestnut mare / Just a season / Kathleen's song / Truck stop girl / Just like a woman / Stanley's song / Glory, glory / I trust / I wanna grow up to be a politician / Green apple quick step / Tiffany Queen / Bugler / Lazy waters / Farther along / White's lightning / He was a friend of mine / Paths of victory / From a distance / Love that never dies.
CD Set 4676112
CBS / Dec '90 / Sony.
■ MC Set 4676114
CBS / Dec '90.

UNTITLED.
Tracks: Lover of the Bayou / Positively 4th Street / Nashville West / So you want to be a rock 'n' roll star / Mr. Tamborine man / Mr Spaceman / Eight miles high / Chestnut mare / Truck stop girl / All things / Yesterday's train / Hungry planet / Just a season / Take a whiff / You all look alike / Well come back home.
■ LP 66253
CBS / Nov '70.
CD .... CD 30127
CBS / May '89 / Sony.

YOU AIN'T GOIN' NOWHERE.
Tracks: You ain't goin' nowhere.
■ 7" .... CBS 3411
CBS / Jun '68.

YOUNGER THAN YESTERDAY.
Tracks: So you want to be a rock 'n' roll star / Have you seen her face / C.T.A. / Renaissance fair / Time between / Everybody's been burned / Thoughts and words / Mind gardens / My back pages / Girl with no name / Why.
■ LP .... SBPG 62988
CBS / Apr '67.
CD .... EDCD 227
Edsel / Aug '87 / Pinnacle.
LP .... ED 227
MC .... CED 227
Edsel / May '87 / Pinnacle.
MC 4670454
CBS / Dec '90 / Sony.
CD 468181-2
Columbia / Aug '93 / Sony.

Byrne, Julie

COUNTRY.
Tracks: Not Advised.
MC .... AIM 47
AIM (2) / Feb '83 / Topic Records / Direct Distribution.
MC .... AM 47
VFM Cassettes / '86 / VFM Children's Entertainment Ltd. / Midland Records / Morley Audio Services.

RAMBLIN' ROUND.
Tracks: Route 65 to Nashville / Legend in my time, A / King of country music / I'm easy / I can't stop loving you / It don't worry me / Talk talk / Crazy arms / I'd like to go to Memphis / Ramblin' round / Honey / My babe.
LP .... FHR 079
Folk Heritage / Jul '82 / Terry Blood Dist.

C

Cache Valley Drifters

Californian based folk/acoustic country musicians who appeared on Kate Wolf's *Lines On Paper* album. (Maurice Hope)

CACHE VALLEY DRIFTERS.
Tracks: Deep river / Sweet Mary / Masters / Dixieland lady / Sorrow of saying goodbye, The / Columbus stockade blues / Joanne / Roly poly / Russian river song / Angol from Montgomery / I shot the sheriff.
LP . . . . FF 001
Flying Fish (USA) / Mar '89 / Cadillac Music / Roots Records / Projection / C.M. Distribution / Direct Distribution / Jazz Music / Duncans / A.D.A Distribution.

STEP UP TO BIG PAY.
Tracks: Not Advised.
LP . . . . FF 220
Flying Fish (USA) / Mar '89 / Cadillac Music / Roots Records / Projection / C.M. Distribution / Direct Distribution / Jazz Music / Duncans / A.D.A Distribution.

TOOLS OF THE TRADE.
Tracks: Not Advised.
LP . . . . FF 290
Flying Fish (USA) / Mar '89 / Cadillac Music / Roots Records / Projection / C.M. Distribution / Direct Distribution / Jazz Music / Duncans / A.D.A Distribution.
CD . . . . MOSH 049CD
Earache / Aug '92 / Revolver-APT / Pinnacle.

Cactus Brothers

Described as "Nashville's answer to the Pogues", the Cactus Brothers were created out of the ashes of the 1970's rock band Walk The West, and countrified via the presence of champion dulcimer player David Schnaufer and dobro/steel guitarist Sam Poland. The group achieved a considerable amount of international attention prior to their debut self-titled LP - released by Liberty in May 1993. (Tony Byworth)

CACTUS BROTHERS, THE.
Tracks: Sixteen Tons / Crazy heart / Our love / Devil wind / Sweet old fashioned girl / Blackberry blossom / Price of love, The / Big train / Swimmin' hole / One more night (with you) / Bubba Bubba / Fisher's hornpipe.
CD C2-80473
Liberty / May '93 / EMI.

Cain, Cindi

PLACE WHERE MEMORIES LIVE, A.
Tracks: Not Advised.
■ CD . . . . CDCOT 101
Cottage / Jun '92.

Cajun Aces

DEAF HEIGHTS.
Tracks: Les flames d'enfer / Madame Edourarde / New pinegrove blues / Grand Mamou / Moi et mon cousin / La danse de la limonade / Bosco strip / Bayou pom pom / Colinda / La robe barree / Allons a lafayette / 'Tit galot / Hackberry zydeco.
LP . . . . TP 025
Temple (Scotland) / Jul '87 / Roots Records / Projection / Jazz Music / C.M. Distribution / Duncans / A.D.A Distribution / Direct Distribution / Conifer Records.
MC . . . . CTP 025
Temple (Scotland) / Oct '88 / Roots Records / Projection / Jazz Music / C.M. Distribution / Duncans / A.D.A Distribution / Direct Distribution / Conifer Records.

Cajun Music

A music that's synonymous with Louisiana, though its origins - like country music itself - stretches back to European sources. In the case of cajun music, it's France and its native folk music, though re-located via that nation's colonists settling in Nova Scotia (which they named Acadia, and eventually corrupted to Cajun. From there, during the reign of George II, many of these colonists were deported, a great number settling in south-west Louisiana where their music and language survived. The music that developed in the new surroundings was built on strong folk and fiddle traditions, with the Germans (en route, across the continent, to their new land in Texas) adding the accordian. Further influences were country music from the north east, jazz from New Orleans and Texas dancehall music. Although cajun was first recorded, along with other ethnic styles during the 1920's, the sound initially made a national impact a couple of decades later with Harry Choates' *Jole Blon* , a song that's been covered many times over the years. Although cajun has never gained mass commercial success, it has bred a few commercial artists - the most successful being Rusty and Doug Kershaw, Jimmy C. Newman and, more recently Jo-el Sonnier - while there are a substantial amount of recordings available by more traditional styled artists such as Harry Choates, Balfa Brothers and the group Beausoleil (who gained the national spotlight when accompanying Mary Chaplin-Carpenter on the 1991 award winning hit *Down at the Twist and Shout*). The black musician's presence created a variation of cajun music, named zydeco (see seperate entry).(Tony Byworth)

Cajun Tradition

A LA VEILLE FACON.
Tracks: Not Advised.
LP 6076
MC . . . . 6076 TC
Swallow (USA) / '88 / Swift / Wellard Dist.

Cajun, R

BAYOU RHYTHMS.
Tracks: Jambalaya / Cajun two step / Back door (La porte d'en arriere) / Trouble in mind / Madame Edward / Deportess / Lemonade dance (Le danse de limonade) / Mardi gras / Bayou pom pom / Criminal waltz, The (La valse criminelle) / It's hard to believe / I made a big mistake (J'ai fait un gros erreur).
LP . . . . MOO 4
MC . . . . MOOC 4
Moonraker / Oct '84 / Projection / New Note.

JAMBALAYA (GRAND TEXAS).
Tracks: Jambalaya.
7" . . . . MOOS 1
Moonraker / Sep '84 / Projection / New Note.

NO KNOWN CURE (Cajun, R. & The Zedeco Brothers).
Tracks: Not Advised.
CD . . . . BCAT 03CD
MC . . . . BCAT 03C
Bearcat / Jun '93 / Topic Records / Direct Distribution.

PIG STICKING IN ARCADIA (Cajun, R. & The Zedeco Brothers).
Tracks: Not Advised.
LP . . . . EFNILP 001
MC . . . . LPO 1
Disc Ethnique / Oct '87.

Caledonia

ONE OF THE POOREST PEOPLE.
Tracks: One of the poorest people / All day groover.
■ 7" 2058 839
Polydor / Feb '77.

California

HE'S ALMOST THERE.
Tracks: He's almost there / Three times loser.
7" . . . . RCA 306
RCA / Feb '83 / BMG.

I CAN HEAR MUSIC.
Tracks: I can hear music / Love's supposed to be that way.
■ 7" . . . . RSO 14
RSO / Jul '78.

TRAVELER.
Tracks: Rocker arm reel / Walk in the Irish rain, A / Scissors, paper & stone / My sweet blue-eyed Darlin' / Spurs / Farmers son, A / California traveler / I'll dry every tear that falls / Whiplash / Sasquatch / Uncle Pen / Band of angels.
CD . . . . SHCD 3803
MC . . . . SHMC 3803
Sugarhill(USA) / '92 / Roots Records / Projection / Impetus Records / C.M. Distribution / Jazz Music / Swift / Duncans / A.D.A Distribution.

Cameron, Stuart

HOW DID YOU CHANGE YOUR MIND ?.
Tracks: How did you change your mind ?.
12" . . . . CUFF 1A
Silver Heart / Jul '89 / Silver Heart Records.

Campbell, Ethna

This British singer entered the UK chart with her only hit in the final week of '75. *The Old Rugged Cross*, a traditional gospel song, proved a slow but steady seller -- it peaked at No 33 but spent 11 weeks in the Top Fifty, moving up and down in a seeminly endless yo yo pattern. Campbell went on to release a couple of albums, but little has been heard of her since. (Bob MacDonald)

FOR THE GOOD TIMES.
Tracks: All my trials / Early morning rain / For the good times / From Clare to here / Hallelujah I love him so / I'll be your baby tonight / I'm so lonesome I could cry / Isn't it funny / Love is strange / Loving you / Song of evening / Til tomorrow.
LP 6381 138
Philips / '77 / PolyGram.

OLD RUGGED CROSS, THE.
Tracks: Airport song / Boulder to Birmingham / By the time I get to Phoenix / Going my way / House of gold / How great Thou art / It is no secret / Jeannie's afraid of the dark / Old rugged cross, The / Try to remember / Wedding song, The / Wichita lineman.
LP 6382 115
Philips / Apr '86 / PolyGram.

OLD RUGGED CROSS, THE.
Tracks: Old rugged cross, The.
■ 7" 6006 475
Philips / Dec '75.

PEACE IN THE VALLEY.
Tracks: Not Advised.
LP . . . . ITV 439
MC . . . . KITV 439
Scotdisc / Oct '87 / Duncans / Ross Records / Target Records / Conifer Records.

Campbell, Glen

This American singer, guitarist and multi-instrumentalist is the seventh son of a seventh son and was born into a highly musical family. Already an accomplished musician by the time he left school, he spent the late Fifties and early Sixties building up his reputation in the music business, first in a number of various gigging groups and then as a session musician. His varied instrumental skills won him back-up appearances on many stars' records during the early and mid-Sixties, including Frank Sinatra, Bobby Darin, Nat King Cole, the Mamas and the Papas and the Monkees. He also joined the Beach Boys on tour for a brief period, when leader Brian Wilson's troubled psyche forced him to quit the road. During the era of all these guest appearances, Campbell was simultaneously trying to make it big as a solo artist. He failed dismally in this regard for several years. It was not until 1967, when he began selecting his material himself, that he hit the American Top 40. *By The Time I Get To Pheonix*, a plaintive song penned by Jim Webb, reached No. 26 on the US chart at the end of '67. This helped to establish Webb as a major composer, a status he cemented the following year with the huge success of Richard Harris' *MacArthur Park*. Webb then wrote two smash hits for Campbell - the haunting *Wichita Lineman*, reached No. 3 in the US, followed by the No. 4 success of *Galveston*. They also gave the artist his first two UK hits. Having been a bigger star in America than in Britain up to this point, Campbell scored two hits in 1970 that were much more successful in the UK than the US: *All I Have To Do Is Dream*, a duet remake with Bobbie Gentry of the Everly Brothers classic reached No. 3 in the UK (and would thus prove to be the biggest British single of Campbell's career) and the Jim Webb ballad *Honey Come Back*, peaked at No. 4. Meanwhile back in the States, the singer was selling large quantities of albums and also making a smash movie debut, co-starring with John Wayne in *True Grit*. He ended 1970 by making the Top 10 on both sides of the Atlantic with a cover version of Conway Twitty's late Fifties chart-topper *It's Only Make Believe*. From 1971, hit singles were not as forthcoming. Instead Campbell concentrated on further film success and on US television work. A *Greatest Hits*, set was issued in the autumn of '71, selling particularly well in Britain, where it logged no less than 113 weeks on the chart. He returned to the singles charts in a big way in 1975, when the catchy *Rhinestone Cowboy* gave him his first US No. 1 and reached No. 4 in the UK. This track was typical Campbell - a middle-of-the-road number rooted in country music, but also incorporating elements of rock. Another country/rock flavoured single *Southern Nights* gave him a second American No. 1 in 1977, soon after he had topped the British album chart for six weeks with the TV-advertised *20 Golden Greats* collection. Through this continued acceptance, Glen Campbell had proved himself to be a highly durable star. As the Seventies became the Eighties, he retired from the pop market and concentrated solely on his adult MoR following. he remains active in showbusiness, both in recording and touring terms. (Bob MacDonald).

20 CLASSIC TRACKS: GLEN CAMPBELL.
Tracks: Southern nights / God only knows / If not for you / Amazing grace / Your cheatin' heart / Bonapartes retreat / Both sides now / All the way / Dreams of the everyday housewife / Rhinestone cowboy / Rose garden / Help me make it through the night / Dream baby / MacArthur park / Take these chains from my heart / Bridge over troubled water / You'll never walk alone / Yesterday when I was young / Galveston.
MC . . . . **TCMFP 50532**
MFP / Nov '81 / EMI.
■ **LP** . . . . **MFP 50532**
MFP / Sep '81.

20 GOLDEN PIECES: GLEN CAMPBELL.
Tracks: Dreams of the everyday housewife / If you go away / Twelfth of never / True grit / Homeward bound / Take my hand for a while / Straight life / Elusive butterfly / Where's the playground / Until it's time for you to go / Crying / Words / By the time I get to Phoenix / It's over / Turn around and look at me / Mary in the morning / Gentle on my mind / You're my world / (Sittin' on) the dock of the bay / Impossible dream, The.
LP . . . . **BDL 2031**
Bulldog Records / Oct '82 / President Records / Jazz Music / Wellard Dist. / TKO Records Ltd.
MC . . . . **BDC 2031**
Bulldog Records / '90 / President Records / Jazz Music / Wellard Dist. / TKO Records Ltd.

ALL I HAVE TO DO IS DREAM (Campbell, Glen & Bobbie Gentry).
Tracks: All I have to do is dream / Less of me / Gentle on my mind / Heart to heart talk / My elusive dreams / Let it be me / Little green apples / Mornin' glory / Terrible tangled web / Sunday morning / (It's only your) imagination / Scarborough fair / Canticle.
LP . . . . **MFP 5600**
■ **MC** . . . . **TCMFP 5600**
MFP / Jan '83.

ALL I HAVE TO DO IS DREAM (Campbell, Glen & Bobbie Gentry).
Tracks: All I have to do is dream.
■ **7"** . . . . **CL 15619**
Capitol / Dec '69.

ALL MY TOMORROWS.
Tracks: All my tomorrows.
■ **7"** . . . . **CL 15742**
Capitol / Jan '73.

BASIC.
Tracks: Sing it nice and loud for me Sonny / Stranger in the mirror / Can you fool / I see love / I got no love in me / Love takes you higher / Never tell you no lies / I'm gonna love you / California / Let's all sing a song about it / Grafhaidh me thu.
■ **LP** . . . . **EST 11722**
Capitol / Jan '79.

BOBBIE GENTRY & GLEN CAMPBELL (see under Gentry, Bobbie).

CAN YOU FOOL.
Tracks: Can you fool / Let's all sing a song about it.
■ **7"** . . . . **CL 16036**
Capitol / Jan '79.

COLLECTION: GLEN CAMPBELL (EMBER LABEL).
Tracks: Not Advised.
MC Set . . . . **ZCPP 601**
Ember / Sep '78 / TKO Records Ltd / President Records.

COLLECTION: GLEN CAMPBELL (EMI GERMANY).
Tracks: Not Advised.
LP . . . . **IC 038 81964**
EMI (Germany) / '83.

COLLECTION: GLEN CAMPBELL (KNIGHT LABEL).
Tracks: Not Advised.
CD . . . . **KNCD 13050**
■ **MC** . . . . **KNMC 13050**
Knight / Apr '90.

COMPLETE GLEN CAMPBELL, THE (His 20 Greatest Hits).
Tracks: Southern nights / All I have to do is dream / It's only make believe / Can't help it / Help me make it through the night / Little kindness, A / Bridge over troubled water / Dream baby / Rhinestone cowboy / Gentle on my mind / Wichita lineman / Honey come baby / Everything a man could ever need / Both sides now / Reason to believe / Galveston.
CD . . . . **SMD 979**
LP . . . . **SMR 979**
MC . . . . **SMC 979**
Stylus / Jul '89.

COUNTRY BOY.
Tracks: Country boy (you got your feet in L.A.) / Back in the race / This land is your land / Galveston / Your cheatin' heart / Tennessee home / 12-string special / California / Rhinestone cowboy / Country girl / 500 miles / Gentle on my mind / Arkansas / I'm so lonesome I could cry / True grit / Oklahoma Sunday morning.
MC . . . . **MFP 41 5692 4**
MC . . . . **TCMFP 5692**
MFP / Jan '85 / EMI.
■ **LP** . . . . **MFP 41 5692 1**
MFP / Jan '85.
MC . . . . **MFP 5692**
MFP / '88 / EMI.
MC **4XL 8352**
Capitol (Specials) / Dec '88.
CD . . . . **CD MFP 6034**
MFP / Oct '88 / EMI.

COUNTRY COLLECTION.
Tracks: Not Advised.
CD . . . . **KNCD 13054**
■ **MC** . . . . **KNMC 13054**
Knight / Jul '90.

COUNTRY FAVOURITES.
Tracks: Together again / Truck driving man / My elusive dreams / Your cheatin' heart / She thinks I still care / Manhattan Kansas / I want to be with you always / Help me make it through the night / Gentle on my mind / Burning bridges / Long black limousine / Heart-to-heart talk / I can't help it (if I'm still in love with you) / Rose garden / Bonaparte's retreat / Rhinestone cowboy.
■ **LP** . . . . **EG 2600521**
Capitol / Apr '84.
■ **MC** . . . . **EG 2600524**
Capitol / Apr '84.

DREAM BABY.
Tracks: Dream baby.
■ **7"** . . . . **CL 15674**
Capitol / Mar '71.

EVENING WITH GLEN CAMPBELL, AN.
Tracks: Not Advised.
VHS . . . . **MC 2038**
Music Club Video / Sep '89 / Video Collection / Gold & Sons / Terry Blood Dist.

EVERYTHING A MAN COULD EVER NEED.
Tracks: Everything a man could ever need.
■ **7"** . . . . **CL 15653**
Capitol / Sep '70.

FAVOURITE HYMNS.
Tracks: Not Advised.
CD **701 997 763 4**
■ **LP** . . . . **CAAR 9977**
Power / Nov '89.
■ **MC** . . . . **CAAC 9977**
Power / Nov '89.

GALVESTON.
Tracks: Galveston.
■ **7"** . . . . **EMBS 263**
Ember / May '69.

GENTLE ON MY MIND.
Tracks: Gentle on my mind / It's over / Rose garden / She thinks I still care / Homeward bound / Honey, come back / Last thing on my mind / Cold, cold heart / Southern nights.
MC **4XL-9051**
Capitol (Specials) / '89.

GLEN CAMPBELL.
Tracks: Not Advised.
■ **VHS** . . . . **CMP 6051**
Castle Music Pictures / Oct '91.

GLEN CAMPBELL ALBUM, THE.
Tracks: Not Advised.
■ **LP** . . . . **ST 22493**
Capitol / Dec '70.

GLEN CAMPBELL GOLDEN CD COLLECTION.
Tracks: Not Advised.
CD . . . . **BDCD 3006**
Bulldog Records / May '89 / President Records / Jazz Music / Wellard Dist. / TKO Records Ltd.

GLEN CAMPBELL LIVE.
Tracks: Not Advised.
VHS . . . . **CFV 02162**
Channel 5 / '88 / Channel 5 Video / P.R.O. Video / Gold & Sons.

GLEN CAMPBELL SINGS WITH ANNE MURRAY & BOBBIE GEE.
Tracks: Not Advised.
LP **1A 022 1582701**
MC **1A 222 1582704**
MFP (Holland) / Mar '84 / Pinnacle.

GLEN CAMPBELL STORY, THE.
Tracks: Not Advised.
CD . . . . **NCD 5112**
CD . . . . **ONCD 5112**
K-Tel / Jan '86 / I & B Records / C.M. Distribution / Arabesque Ltd. / Mono Distributors (Jersey) Ltd. / Prism Leisure PLC / PolyGram / Ross Records / Prism Leisure PLC.

GREATEST HITS - LIVE.
Tracks: Rhinestone cowboy / Gentle on my mind / Medley (Wichita Lineman, Galveston & Country Boy) / By the time I get to Phoenix / Dreams of an everyday housewife / Heartache number two / Please come to Boston / It's only make believe / Crying / Blue grass medley / Milk cow blues / Rollin' in my sweet baby's arms / I'm so lonesome I could cry / Southern nights / Amazing grace / Try a little kindness / Mull of Kintyre / In your loving arms again / It's your world girls & boys / Trials & tribulations.
CD . . . . **CDGRF 182**
MC . . . . **MCGRF 182**
Tring / Feb '93 / Prism Leisure PLC / Midland Records / Taylors.

GREATEST HITS: GLEN CAMPBELL.
Tracks: Honey come back / Everything a man could ever need / Galveston / Try a little kindness / Dreams of the everyday housewife / By the time I get to Phoenix / Where's the playground / It's only make believe / Wichita lineman / All I have to do is dream / Dream baby.
MC . . . . **TCATAK 4**
Capitol / Mar '85 / EMI.
■ **LP** . . . . **ATAK 4**
Capitol / Mar '85.
■ **CD** . . . . **CZ 205**
Capitol / Jul '89.

HIGHWAY MAN.
Tracks: Highwayman / Hound dog man / I was just thinking about you / Love song / My prayer / Tennessee home / Don't lose me in the confusion / Cajun caper / Darlin' Darlinka / Fool ya.
■ **LP** . . . . **EST 12008**
Capitol / Dec '79.

HOLLYWOOD SMILES.
Tracks: Hollywood smiles / Hooked on love.
■ **7"** . . . . **CL 16167**
Capitol / Sep '80.

HONEY COME BACK.
Tracks: Honey come back.
■ **7"** . . . . **CL 15638**
Capitol / May '70.

HOUND DOG MAN.
Tracks: Hound dog man / Highwayman.
■ **7"** . . . . **CL 16122**
Capitol / Feb '80.

I'M GONNA LOVE YOU.
Tracks: I'm gonna love you / Love takes you higher.
■ **7"** . . . . **CL 16074**
Capitol / '79.

IF YOU WERE MY LADY (Campbell, Glen & Diane Solomon).
Tracks: If you were my lady / It's one to grow on.
7" . . . . **NRG 008**
Energy / Oct '82 / President Records / TKO Records Ltd.

IT'S JUST A MATTER OF TIME.
Tracks: It's just a matter of time / Wild winds / Cowboy hall of fame / Rag doll / Call home / Do what you gotta do / Cowpoke / Shattered / Sweet sixteen / Gene Autry, my hero.
LP **790 483-1**
■ **MC** **790 483-4**
Atlantic / Jan '86.

IT'S JUST A MATTER OF TIME.
Tracks: It's just a matter of time / Gene Autry, my hero.
7" . . . . **A 9600**
Atlantic / Mar '86 / WEA.

IT'S ONLY MAKE BELIEVE.
Tracks: It's only make believe.
■ **7"** . . . . **CL 15663**
Capitol / Nov '70.

IT'S THE WORLD GONE CRAZY.
Tracks: Why don't we just sleep on it tonight / I don't want to know your name / In cars / It's the world gone crazy / Rollin' / Nothing quite like love / Daisy a day / Any which way you want / It's your world.
■ **LP** . . . . **EST 12124**
Capitol / Apr '81.
■ **MC** . . . . **TC E-ST 12124**
Capitol / Apr '81.

LETTER TO HOME.
Tracks: I'll be faithful to you / Letter to home / Faithless love / Leavin' eyes / Goodnight lady / After the glitter fades / Tennessee / Lady like you / Scene of the crime / American trilogy.
■ **LP** **790 164-1**
Atlantic / Jul '84.

LETTING GO.
Tracks: Letting go / Face to face.
■ **7"** . . . . **CLT 3**
Compleat (USA) / Apr '84.

LIVE: GLEN CAMPBELL.
Tracks: Rhinestone cowboy / Gentle on my mind / Wichita lineman / Galveston / Country boy / By the time I get to Phoenix / Dreams of the everyday housewife / Heartache no.3 / Boston / Trials and tribulations / It's only make-believe / Crying / Blue grass medley / Milk

C 2 ■ DELETED

cow blues / Rollin' in my sweet baby's arms / I'm so lonesome I could cry / Southern nights / Amazing grace / Try a little kindness / In your loving arms again / It's your world / Mull of Kintyre.
■ LP. SB 21444
Capitol / Jan '70.
Double LP . . . . RCALP 9002
RCA / Dec '81 / BMG.
■ MC . . . . RCAK 9002
RCA / Dec '81.
LP. ENL 3619
MC . . . . ENC 3619
EEC Imports / Jan '83.
CD 15 346
MC 79 346
Laserlight / Aug '91 / TBD / Taylors.

LOVE SONGS: GLEN CAMPBELL.
Tracks: Gentle on my mind / Reason to believe / By the time I get to Phoenix / It's only make believe / Honey come back / Country girl / One last time / I'm getting used to the crying / Last thing on my mind / Everything a man could ever need / Dream baby (how long must I dream) / Hey little one / Your cheatin' heart / This is Sarah's song / Let go / God only knows / How high did we go (CD only.) / If this is love (CD only.) / Love is not a game (CD only.) / For my woman's love (CD only.).
CD . . . . CDMFP 5881
MC . . . . TCMFP 5881
MFP / Apr '90 / EMI.

MAGIC OF GLEN CAMPBELL, THE.
Tracks: Not Advised.
CD . . . . TKOCD 001
MC . . . . TKOCS 001
TKO Records / '92 / TKO Records Ltd / President Records.

MARY IN THE MORNING.
Tracks: Mary in the morning / Got to have tenderness.
■ 7" . . . . EMBS 335
Ember / Jan '75.

NO MORE NIGHT.
Tracks: Not Advised.
MC . . . . WST C 9653
Word (UK) / Aug '88 / Word Records (UK) / Sony.
■ LP. . . . . WST R 9653
Word (UK) / Aug '88.
LP. WST 9653
Word (UK) / '89 / Word Records (UK) / Sony.

OLD HOME TOWN.
Tracks: Old home town / I love how you love me / Hang on baby / Blue (my naughty sweetie gives to me / Few good men, A / On the wings of my victory / I was too busy loving you / Ruth / Womans touch, A / Mull of Kintyre.
LP. 9900161
■ MC 790 016-4
Atlantic / '84 / WEA.

RHINESTONE COWBOY.
Tracks: Country boy (You got your feet in L.A.) / Comeback / Count on me / I miss you tonight / My girl / Rhinestone cowboy / I'd build a bridge / Pencils for sale / Marie / We're over.
■ LP. . . . . ESW 11430
Capitol / Oct '75.
■ LP. . . . . GO 2020
Capitol Greenlight Series / Jun '81.
■ MC . . . . TC 2020
Capitol Greenlight Series / Jun '81.

RHINESTONE COWBOY.
Tracks: Rhinestone cowboy / Lovelight.
■ 7" . . . . CL 15824
Capitol / Oct '75.

SOMEBODY LIKE THAT.
Tracks: Somebody like that / Those words / I will be here / Love's old song / One who hung the moon, The / Swimming upstream / Best part of Texas, The / Ain't it just like love / (If I'd only known it was the last time) / Rising above it all.
CD . . . . CDP 7979622
Liberty / Apr '93 / EMI.

SOMETHIN' 'BOUT YOU BABY I LIKE.
Tracks: Somethin' 'bout you baby I like / Through my eyes / That kind / Part time love / Hollywood smiles / If this is love / Hooked on love / Show me you love me / Late night confession / It goes like it goes.
■ LP. . . . . EST 12075
Capitol / Aug '80.

SOUTHERN NIGHTS.
Tracks: Southern nights / This is Sarah's song / For cryin' out loud / God only knows / Sunflower / Guide me / Early morning sun / I'm getting used to the crying / Let go / How high did we go.
■ LP. . . . . EST 11601
Capitol / Apr '77.
MC . . . . TC GO 2008
Capitol Greenlight Series / Jun '81 / EMI.
■ LP. . . . . GO 2008
Capitol Greenlight Series / Jun '81.

SOUTHERN NIGHTS.
Tracks: Southern nights / William Tell overture.
7" . . . . CL 15907
Capitol / Mar '77 / EMI.
■ 7" . . . . CL 375
Capitol / Sep '85.

STILL WITHIN THE SOUND OF MY VOICE.
Tracks: I'm a one woman man / Still within the sound of my voice / Hand that rocks the cradle, The / For sure, for certain, forever, for always / I have you / You are / Arkansas / In my life / Leavin's not the only way to go / I remember you.
CD . . . . DMCF 3394
LP. MCF 3394
MC . . . . MCFC 3394
MCA / Oct '87 / BMG.

SUNFLOWER.
Tracks: Sunflower / This is Sarah's song.
■ 7" . . . . CL 15926
Capitol / May '77.

THAT CHRISTMAS FEELING.
Tracks: Christmas is for children / Old toy trains / Little altar boy / It must be getting close to Christmas / Have yourself a merry little Christmas / Blue Christmas / Christmas song, The / Pretty paper / There's no place like home / I'll be home for Christmas / Christmas day.
LP. MFP 5589
■ MC . . . . TCMFP 5589
MFP / Dec '82.

THEY STILL DANCE TO WALTZES IN ENGLAND.
Tracks: They still dance to waltzes in England / Letter to home.
7" . . . . A 9755
Atlantic / May '84 / WEA.

TOGETHER (Campbell, Glen & Anne Murray).
Tracks: You're easy to love / United we stand / Love story / Ease your pain / Let me be the one / My ecstasy / I say a little prayer / By the time I get to Phoenix / We all pull the load / Canadian sunset / Bring back the love.
LP. MFP 41 5689 1
■ MC . . . . MFP 41 5689 4
MFP / Jan '85.

TRY A LITTLE KINDNESS.
Tracks: Not Advised.
■ LP. . . . . ESW 389
Capitol / May '70.

TRY A LITTLE KINDNESS.
Tracks: Try a little kindness.
■ 7" . . . . CL 15622
Capitol / Feb '70.

TWENTY GOLDEN GREATS.
Tracks: Rhinestone cowboy / Both sides now / By the time I get to Phoenix / Too many mornings / Wichita lineman / One last time / Don't pull your love, then tell me goodbye / Reason to believe / It's only make believe / Honey come back / Give me back that old familiar feeling / Galveston / Dreams of the everyday housewife / Last thing on my mind / Where's the playground / Try a little kindness / Country boy (you got your feet in L.A.) / All I have to do is dream / Amazing Grace.
MC . . . . TCEMTV 2
Capitol / Oct '76 / EMI.
■ LP. . . . . EMTV 2
Capitol / Oct '76.
CD . . . . CDEMTV 2
Capitol / Nov '87 / EMI.
CD . . . . CZ 363
LP. ATAK 159
MC . . . . TCATAK 159
EMI / Oct '90 / EMI.

UNCONDITIONAL LOVE.
Tracks: Unconditional love / We will / Right down to the memories / Livin' in a house full of love / Healing hands of time / Next to you / Somebody's doin' me right / I'm gone this time / Once a day / Light of a clear blue morning.
CD . . . . CDP 790992 2
LP. C2 90992
Capitol Nashville / Jun '91 / EMI.
■ MC C4 90992
Capitol Nashville / Jun '91.

VERY BEST OF GLEN CAMPBELL.
Tracks: Rhinestone cowboy / Wichita lineman / Galveston / By the time I get to Phoenix / Try a little kindness / My little one / Where's the playground / Gentle on my mind / Dreams of the everyday housewife / All I have to do is dream / Dream baby / It's only make believe / Sunflower / Southern nights / Country boy (you got your feet in L.A.).
CD . . . . CDMFP 6023
MFP / Apr '88 / EMI.

WALKIN' IN THE SUN.
Tracks: She's gone, gone, gone / You will not lose / On a good night / If I could only get my hands on you now / Even a blind man can tell when walkin' in the sun / William Tell overture / Woodcarver / Cheatin' is / Tied to the tracks / Somebody's leaving / Jesus on your mind.
LP. C1 93884
Capitol / May '90 / EMI.
CD CD-C1 93884
■ MC C4 93884
Capitol / May '90.

WHEREFORE AND WHY.
Tracks: Wherefore and why / Give me back that old familiar feeling.
7" . . . . CL 15768
Capitol / '73 / Jetstar.

WHY DON'T WE JUST SLEEP ON IT TONIGHT (Campbell, Glen & Tanya Tucker).
Tracks: Why don't we just sleep on it tonight / Daisy a day.
■ 7" . . . . CL 16182
Capitol / Feb '81.

WICHITA LINEMAN.
Tracks: Wichita lineman / True grit / Hound dog man / By the time I get to Phoenix / Country girl / God only knows / Galveston / Let it be me / Your cheatin' heart / Kentucky means paradise / Early morning song / If you could read my mind / Rhinestone cowboy / Gentle on my mind / Until it's time for you to go / Heart to heart / Highwayman / Words / Southern nights / Take these chains from my heart / Part time love / Any which way you can / Too late to worry, too blue to cry.
Double LP . . . . VSOPLP 120
MC . . . . VSOPMC 120
Connoisseur Collection / May '88 / Pinnacle.
CD . . . . VSOPCD 120
Connoisseur Collection / Apr '90 / Pinnacle.

WICHITA LINEMAN.
Tracks: Wichita lineman.
■ 7" . . . . EMBS 261
Ember / Jan '69.

WOMAN'S TOUCH, A.
Tracks: Woman's touch, A.
7" 799 960-7
Atlantic / Oct '82 / WEA.

Campbell, Pat

Hailing from the Irish Republic, this vocalist scored his only British chart record in late 1969 with *The Deal*. The single, on the Major Minor label reached no.31 in the UK. Pat Campbell continued recording into the Seventies but little of note was heard from him or Major Minor. (Bob MacDonald)

DEAL, THE.
Tracks: Deal, The.
■ 7" . . . . MM 648
Major Minor / Nov '69.

JUST A QUIET CONVERSATION.
Tracks: Not Advised.
LP. DRL 2017
Release (Ireland) / Jan '78.

Campbell, Sarah Elizabeth

LITTLE TENDERNESS, A.
Tracks: Mexico / I never meant to fall / Part of a story / Waltz with you / Geraldine and Ruthie Mae / Heartache / Tell me baby / To remember / My heart can't seem to forget / I could use a little tenderness.
CD . . . . K 42
MC . . . . C 42
Kaleidoscope (USA) / Jul '90 / Projection / Ross Records / Roots Records / Swift / C.M. Distribution / Topic Records / Duncans.

Campi, Ray

With his family's move from New York to Austin, Texas in 1944, the young Roy Campi listened to many genres including rhythm'n'blues, country, western swing and big band, all of which were to play a role in his own brand of 'hillbilly boogie'. He formed his first group Ramblin' Ray & The Ramblers and made his record debut on the San Antonio label, TNT. Although he later recorded for Dot, D and other labels, he never achieved any national hits and, in 1964, took up a teaching career. Nevertheless Campi built up a cult reputation, has toured Europe on several occasions and his records are eagerly collected. (Tony Byworth)

BOOZE IT.
Tracks: Booze it.
7" 45 027
Rollin' Rock / Jun '80 / Pinnacle.

CATERPILLAR.
Tracks: Caterpillar.
7" . . . . PFE 003
Rollin' Rock / Jul '81 / Pinnacle.

EAGER BEAVER BOY.
Tracks: Hot dog / All the time / Boogie boogie boo / Rock it / Thought of losing, The / Waffle stompin' mama / Blue ranger / Ballin' keen / Let 'er roll / Dobro daddio from Del Rio / Born to be wild / How low can you feel / Where my sweet baby goes / Tribute to 'You know who' / Eager beaver boy / Pretty mama / One part stops where the other begins / Pinball millionaire / When two ends meet / Good time woman / It ain't me (piano version) / Chug-a-lug / Parts unknown / Wicked wicked woman / Shelby county penal farm / Don't give your heart to a rambler / Play anything / Major label blues.
LP. LP 008
Rollin' Rock / Jun '80 / Pinnacle.
CD . . . . BCD 15501

■ DELETED C 3

Bear Family / Sep '90 / Rollercoaster Records / Swift / Direct Distribution.

EAGER BEAVER BOY.
Tracks: Eager beaver boy.
7" **45 006**
Rollin' Rock / Jun '80 / Pinnacle.

GIVE THAT LOVE TO RAY CAMPI.
Tracks: Not Advised.
LP. . . . . **DLP 1001**
Domino (2).

GONE, GONE, GONE.
Tracks: Not Advised.
LP. . . . . **BRP 2008**
Rollin' Rock / Oct '86 / Pinnacle.
LP. . . . . **ROUNDER 3047**
MC . . . . **ROUNDER 3047C**
Rounder / Aug '88 / Projection / Roots Records / Swift / C.M. Distribution / Topic Records / Jazz Music / Hot Shot / A.D.A Distribution / Direct Distribution.

LIVE AT CANTERBURY HALL.
Tracks: Not Advised.
VHS. . . . . **JE 176**
Jettisoundz / Jun '88 / Terry Blood Dist. / Visionary Communications.

MY BABY LEFT ME.
Tracks: My baby left me.
7" **45 019**
Rollin' Rock / Jun '80 / Pinnacle.

NEWEST WAVE, THE.
Tracks: Newest wave, The / Once is enough.
7" **45 047**
Rollin' Rock / Jun '80 / Pinnacle.
■ 7" . . . . **ROUND 1000**
Rondelet Music / May '81.

NEWEST WAVE, THE (Campi, Ray & His Rockabilly Rebels).
Tracks: Newest wave, The / Lucky to be in love / Rockabilly music / Boo hoo / Cruisin / Once is enough / Will of love, The / I've been around / Sweet woman blues / You nearly lose your mind / Sweet mama baby / Do what you did / She don't belong to me / My heart's on fire / Right back where we started from.
LP. . . . . **ABOUT 1000**
Rondelet Music / Apr '81 / Pinnacle.

ORIGINAL ROCKABILLY ALBUM, THE.
Tracks: Caterpillar / It ain't me / Let go of Louise / Livin' on love / My screamin' screamin' Mimi / Long tall Sally / Johnny's jive / Play it cool / Give that love to me / You can't catch me / I didn't mean to be mean / Crossing, The / Loretta.
LP. . . . . **MFLP 063**
Magnum Force / Jun '88 / Terry Blood Dist. / Jazz Music / Hot Shot.
CD . . . . **CDMF 063**
Magnum Force / Jul '90 / Terry Blood Dist. / Jazz Music / Hot Shot.

PLAY IT COOL (Campi, Ray & His Snappers).
Tracks: Play it cool.
■ EP. . . . . **PFE 003**
Rollercoaster / Sep '81.

RAY CAMPI ROLLIN' ROCK SINGLES COLLECTION 1971-1978, THE.
Tracks: Eager beaver boy / Tore up / If it's all the same to you / Pan American boogie / Sixteen chicks / Baby left me / Li'l bit of heartache, A / Booze it / Wrong wrong wrong / Rockin' at the Ritz / Quit your triflin' / Rattlin' daddy / Wild one.
LP. . . . . **ABOUT 1004**
Rondelet Music / Nov '81 / Pinnacle.

RAY CAMPI WITH FRIENDS IN TEXAS.
Tracks: Guitar rag / Austin waltz / Quit your triflin' / Wee mouse / Blue ranger / Bobbro daddio from Del Rio / Merle's boogie woogie / Drifting Texas sands / Caterpillar / Sweet temptation / How low can you feel / Spanish two step.
LP. . . . . **BFX 15258**
Bear Family / Aug '88 / Rollercoaster Records / Swift / Direct Distribution.

ROCKABILLY LIVES.
Tracks: Not Advised.
LP. . . . . **LP 004**
Rollin' Rock / Jun '80 / Pinnacle.

ROCKABILLY MAN (Campi, Ray & His Rockabilly Rebels).
Tracks: Rockabilly man / Love and lots more love / No way out / Don't come knockin' / Don't let the bad times let you down / Give me a taste / Can't you yodel blues / Hollywood cats / Recipe for love / Soul sisters / Little love lies / Hold that train / It's blowing away.
LP. . . . . **ABOUT 1006**
Rondelet Music / Nov '81 / Pinnacle.

ROCKABILLY REBELLION.
Tracks: Not Advised.
LP. **6902**
Rollin' Rock / Jun '80 / Pinnacle.
LP. . . . . **BRP 2001**
Rollin' Rock / Oct '86 / Pinnacle.

ROCKABILLY ROCKET.
Tracks: Second story man / Don't get pushy / Cravin' / Separate ways / Gonna bid my blues goodbye / How can I get on top / Little young girl / Chew tobacco rag / You don't rock and roll at all / Ruby Ann / I don't know why you still come around / Runnin' after fools / Jimmie skins the blues.
LP. . . . . **LP 013**
Rollin' Rock / Jun '80 / Pinnacle.
LP. . . . . **MFLP 046**
Magnum Force / Nov '87 / Terry Blood Dist. / Jazz Music / Hot Shot.

ROCKIN' AT THE RITZ (Campi, Ray & His Rockabilly Rebels).
Tracks: Rockin' at the Ritz / Quit your trifelin' / How low can you feel / Tor up.
■ EP. . . . . **ROUND 1008**
Rondelet Music / Dec '81.
■ EP. . . . . **RR 101**
Magnum Music / '89 / Conifer Records.

SIXTEEN CHICKS.
Tracks: Sixteen chicks.
7" **45 014**
Rollin' Rock / Jun '80 / Pinnacle.

TAYLOR, TEXAS 1988.
Tracks: Curtain of tears / Haunted hungry heart / Woods are full of them now, The / Dessau waltz / When they operated on papa / Butterball bounce / Wild side of live / That's that / Million tears, A / Honk your horn / Love for sale / Honky tonk women / Bermuda grass waltz.
CD . . . . **BCD 15486**
Bear Family / Nov '89 / Rollercoaster Records / Swift / Direct Distribution.

TEENAGE BOOGIE.
Tracks: Teenage boogie / Rockabilly rebel.
■ 7" . . . . **ADA 15**
Radar / '79.

TORE UP.
Tracks: Tore up.
7" **45 008**
Rollin' Rock / Jun '80 / Pinnacle.

WILDCAT SHAKEOUT (Campi, Ray & His Rockabilly Rebels).
Tracks: Rockabilly rebel / Gone, gone, gone / Wildcat shakeout / Don't turn me down / Honey bop / Sack of love / She will come back to me / Teenage boogie / When a guitar gets the blues / Don't blame it on me / Mister Whizz / Mind your own business / Cat clothes shop / It ain't me.
■ LP. . . . . **RAD 9**
Radar / Apr '79.

Cannon, Noel

YOUR CAROLINA BUDDY.
Tracks: Not Advised.
LP. . . . . **WGR 099**
MC . . . . **CWGR 099**
Ross (1) / Aug '86 / Ross Records / Duncans / Entertainment UK.

Capitol Records

Capitol Records which has been in business for over half a century, was founded in Los Angeles, California in 1942 by songwriter Johnny Mercer, film producer Buddy DeSylva and record store owner Glen Wallichs. Among the first artists to be signed was Tex Ritter, already a successful 'singing cowboy', with many of the early country signings originating from the Hollywood studios, or from the local West Coast music scene. Among other artists during the label's first decade were Merle Travis, Cliffie Stone (who also worked in executive and production capacities with the label), Tex Williams, Jimmy Wakely and Tennessee Ernie Ford. Then during the 1950's and 60's Capitol secured all the artists originating out of the new country hotspot Bakersfield, including Buck Owens and Merle Haggard, while also setting up regular recording sessions (and, in turn, a divisional office) in Nashville. The acclaimed 'Capitol Country Music Classics' series was launched by EMI Records in 1991, and features 50 years of chart recordings and also spotlights particular themes and individual artists. (Tony Byworth)
Tracks: Not Advised.

Carlin, Bob

BANGING AND SAWING.
Tracks: Not Advised.
LP. . . . . **ROUNDER 0197**
Rounder / '85 / Projection / Roots Records / Swift / C.M. Distribution / Topic Records / Jazz Music / Hot Shot / A.D.A Distribution / Direct Distribution.
MC . . . . **ROUNDER 0197C**
Rounder / '88 / Projection / Roots Records / Swift / C.M. Distribution / Topic Records / Jazz Music / Hot Shot / A.D.A Distribution / Direct Distribution.

OLD TIME BANJO.
Tracks: Not Advised.
LP. . . . . **ROUNDER 0132**
Rounder / '88 / Projection / Roots Records / Swift / C.M. Distribution / Topic Records / Jazz Music / Hot Shot / A.D.A Distribution / Direct Distribution.

WHERE DID YOU GET THAT HAT?.
Tracks: Not Advised.
LP. . . . . **ROUNDER 0172**
MC . . . . **ROUNDER 0172C**
Rounder / Aug '88 / Projection / Roots Records / Swift / C.M. Distribution / Topic Records / Jazz Music / Hot Shot / A.D.A Distribution / Direct Distribution.

Carlisle, Cliff

CLIFF CARLISLE VOL.1.
Tracks: Not Advised.
LP. . . . . **OT 103**
Old Timey (USA) / '88 / Projection.

CLIFF CARLISLE VOL.2.
Tracks: Not Advised.
LP. . . . . **OT 104**
Old Timey (USA) / '88 / Projection.

Carlisles

Brothers Cliff and Bill Carlisle, both from Kentucky, were a popular hillbilly group in the 1930's-40's, noted for novelties, blues and risque numbers. Cliff pioneered the use of the dobro, accompanying Jimmie Rodgers on records in 1931; he teamed with Bill but retired in 1947. The brothers re-formed for an album on King in 1958. Bill's solo career included country hits into the mid-'60's. (Donald Clarke)

BUSY BODY BOOGIE.
Tracks: New Liza Jane / Busy body boogie / Money tree / Pickin' peas / Goo goo da da (baby latin meaning daddy) / Female Hercules / Honey love / That little difference / No help wanted / I need a little help / Leave that liar alone / Is that you, Myrtle / I'm rough stuff / Knot hole / Old fashioned love / Too old to cut the mustard.
LP. . . . . **BFX 15172**
Bear Family / '85 / Rollercoaster Records / Swift / Direct Distribution.

Carlson, Ralph

THANKS FOR THE DANCE.
Tracks: Thanks for the dance / Ain't got time / John's / Out of the snow / Southern bells / Somebody's woman / Silence on the line / Lights of Denver / General store of Silas McVie / Looking for someone like you.
■ LP. . . . . **WRS 160**
Westwood / Apr '82.

Carman, Jenks Tex

A native of Kentucky, Jenks Carman (1903-68) was one of the most popular performers on West Coast radio and television in the post WW II years. Yet, inspite of the seriousness of his musical intent, he remains best remembered for his inability to hold notes, his frequently out-of-tune guitar and his speciality numbers. If it weren't for Bear Family, who re-issued his recordings in 1991, this unique character's music probably would never have seen the light of day again. (Tony Byworth)

HILLBILLY HULA.
Tracks: Hillbilly hula / Another good dream gone wrong / Hilo march / Gosh I miss you all the time / Locust hill rag / Caissons go rolling along, The / Samoa stomp / Dixie cannon ball / Sweet luwanna / My lonely heart and I / Indian polka / I'm a poor lonesome fellow / Don't feel sorry for me / My trusting heart / Gonna stay right here / (I've recieved) A penny postcard / Ten thousand miles (Away from home) / I could love you darling / You tell her 'cause I stutter / Blue memories.
CD . . . . **BCD 15574**
Bear Family / Mar '92 / Rollercoaster Records / Swift / Direct Distribution.

Carpenter, Mary-Chapin

Singer - songwriter/vocalist, born 21.2.1958 in Princeton, New Jersey - home base since 1974, Washington DC. Carpenter's rise from being a folk/country circuit act, within six years to becoming CMA's 1992 Top Female Vocalist is on the face of it, almost like something out of a novel. In reality Mary-Chapin served almost ten years plying her trade as a solo act in clubs, coffee houses and other assorted small venues. Signed to Columbia in 1986 (she'd already won many Wammie Awards (Washington Area Music Awards), prior to recording her gig tape - which turned into her debut album *Hometown Girl*. Her potential was underlined in 1989, when she reaped ACM's Top New Female Vocalist Award - her album *State Of The Heart*, garnering hit singles *How Do*, *Something Of A Dreamer* & *Quitting Time*, was a Grammy winner, and she won the award for the best female country vocal performance. Carpenter's biographical themed songs were by now, gaining much acclaim in both rock & country climes. Gold-selling album

Shooting Straight In The Dark, heralded her coming of age. From which, the singles; *You Win Again, Going Out Tonight, Right Nnow* & her cajun (Beausoleil) backed dynamic Grammy winning *Down At The Twist & Shout*. Carpenter's 1993 *Come On, Come On*, again reached gold status and she co-wrote four of the tracks with Nashville hitmaker Don Schiltz. The hit single *I Feel Lucky*, underlied her qualities of obtaining gilt-edged, entertaining, surreal vignettes. Other top 20 cuts *Not Too Much To Ask* (duet with Joe Diffie), and *Passionate Kisses*, & *The Hard Way*. In 1993, Mary-Chapin Carpenter made her first round of UK dates. (Maurice Hope)

COME ON, COME ON.
Tracks: Hard way,The / He thinks he'll keep her / Rhythm of the blues / I feel lucky / Bug,The / Not too much to ask / Passionate kisses / Only a dream / I am a town / Walking through fire / I take my chances / Come on,come on.
CD **4718982**
MC **4718984**
Columbia / Sep '92 / Sony.

HOMETOWN GIRL.
Tracks: Lot like me, A / Other streets & other towns / Hometown girl / Downtown train / Family hands / Road is just a road, A / Come on home / Waltz / Just because / Heroes & heroines.
CD . . . . **.473915-2**
MC . . . . **.473915-4**
Columbia / Jun '93 / Sony.

PASSIONATE KISSES.
Tracks: Passionate kisses / Downtown train / Bug quittin' time, The (On CDS only.).
CD Single . . . . **.658996 5**
MC Single . . . . **.658996 4**
Columbia / Feb '93 / Sony.

SHOOTING STRAIGHT IN THE DARK.
Tracks: Going out tonight / Right now / More things change, The / When she's gone / Middle ground / Can't take love for granted / Down at the twist and shout / When Halley came to Jackson / What you didn't say / You win again / Moon and St Christopher, The.
CD **4674682**
LP **4674681**
MC **4674684**
Columbia / Oct '91 / Sony.

STATE OF THE HEART.
Tracks: How do / Something of a dreamer / Never had it so good / Read my lips / This shirt / Quittin' time / Down in Mary's land / Goodbye again / Too tired / Slow country dance / It don't bring you.
CD **4666912**
MC **4666914**
CBS / Apr '90 / Sony.
■ **LP** **4666911**
CBS / Apr '90.

Carrasco, Joe 'King'

BANDIDO ROCK (Carrasco, Joe 'King' Y Las Coronas).
Tracks: Not Advised.
CD . . . . **CD 9012**
LP . . . . **ROUNDER 9012**
MC . . . . **.ROUNDER 9012C**
Rounder / '88 / Projection / Roots Records / Swift / C.M. Distribution / Topic Records / Jazz Music / Hot Shot / A.D.A Distribution / Direct Distribution.

BORDER TOWN (Carrasco, Joe 'King' & The Crowns).
Tracks: Escondido / Hola coca cola / Who bought the guns / Are you Amigo / Put me in jail / Mr. Bogota / Walk it like you talk it / Current events (are making me tense) / Cucaracha taco / Baby let's go to Mexico / Vamos a bailar / Tamale baby.
LP . . . . **ROSE 40**
New Rose (1) / Nov '84 / Pinnacle.
LP . . . . **WIK 26**
MC . . . . **.WIKC 26**
Big Beat / Oct '84 / Pinnacle / Hot Shot / Jazz Music.
CD . . . . **.ROSE 40CD**
New Rose (1) / '88 / Pinnacle.

BUENA (Carrasco, Joe 'King' & The Crowns).
Tracks: Buena / Tuff enuff.
■ **7"** . . . . **BUY 88**
Stiff / Sep '80.

DON'T LET A WOMAN.
Tracks: Don't let a woman / That's the love.
7" . . . . **NEW 59**
New Rose (1) / Pinnacle.
■ **7"** . . . . **MCA 803**
MCA / Nov '82.

EL MOLINO.
Tracks: Jalapeno con big red / Mexcal Road / Black cloud / Tell me / I'm a fool to care / Rock esta noche / Funky butt / Every woman / Please Mr. Sandman / Just a mile away.
LP . . . . **WIK 11**
Big Beat / Sep '79 / Pinnacle / Hot Shot / Jazz Music.

JOE 'KING' CARRASCO (Carrasco, Joe 'King' & The Crowns).
Tracks: Buena / Betty's world / I get my kicks on you / One more time / Don't bug me baby / Nervoused out / Caca de vaca / Susan friendly / Party doll / Federals / Wild 14 / Let's get pretty.
■ **LP** . . . . **SEEZ 28**
Stiff / Sep '80.

JOE KING CARRASCO & THE CROWNS (Carrasco, Joe 'King' & The Crowns).
Tracks: Not Advised.
LP . . . . **HNBL 1308**
Hannibal / Revolver-APT.

LAS CORONAS BANDIDO ROCK.
Tracks: Not Advised.
LP . . . . **ROSE 116**
New Rose (1) / Jun '87 / Pinnacle.

MANANA.
Tracks: Manana.
7" . . . . **NEW 44**
New Rose (1) / Pinnacle.

PARTY SAFARI.
Tracks: Not Advised.
LP . . . . **HNBL 3301**
Hannibal / May '89 / Revolver-APT.

SYNAPSE GAP (Mundo total) (Carrasco, Joe 'King' & The Crowns).
Tracks: Imitation class / Person-person / Don't let a woman make a fool out of you / Where we at? / Senor Lover / I wanna get that feel again / Bad rap / Front me some love / Rip it up, shake it up, go go / That's the love / Man overboard.
LP . . . . **MCF 3143**
■ **MC** . . . . **MCFC 3143**
MCA / Jun '82.

TALES FROM THE CRYPT.
Tracks: Not Advised.
MC . . . . **A 128**
Reach Out International / Aug '84 / Reach Out Int. Records / Windsong International Ltd.

VIVA SAN ANTONE.
Tracks: Viva San Antone.
12" . . . . **NEW 58**
New Rose (1) / Pinnacle.

Carroll, Johnny

BLACK LEATHER REBEL (Carroll, Johnny & The Caps).
Tracks: Black leather rebel / Be bop a lula.
■ **7"** . . . . **RRC 2002**
Rollercoaster / '79.

CRAZY HOT ROCK.
Tracks: You two timed me two times too often / Crazy crazy lovin' / Trying to get to you / Rock 'n' roll Ruby / Hot rock.
■ **LP** . . . . **CR 30241**
Charly / Jul '85 / Charly.

JOHNNY CARROLL.
Tracks: Not Advised.
■ **LP** . . . . **SKYLINE 1515**
Skyline / Nov '87.

RATTLE MY BONES.
Tracks: Rattle my bones / Screamin' demon heatwave.
7" . . . . **SEV 1029**
Seville / Jul '83 / President Records / Swift.

ROCK 'N' ROLL RARITIES.
Tracks: Rockin' Maybelle / Sugar baby / Crazy crazy lovin' / Wild wild women / Lonesome / Love me baby / Cut out / Trudy / Run come see / Hearts of stone / Why cry / Love is a merry go round / Stingy thing / Crazy little mama / Sexy ways / Cry.
LP . . . . **SJLP 581**
Magnum Force / '89 / Terry Blood Dist. / Jazz Music / Hot Shot.

SCREAMIN' DEMON HEATWAVE.
Tracks: Screamin' demon heatwave / Ooby dooby / Sarah Lee / Rockabilly daddy / Don't that road look rough and rocky / Feel so bad / Hang up my rock 'n' roll shoes / Rattle my bones / Fujiyama mama / Don't tear me up / Maybe / Blue Levi jeans / Shove it on home / Baby let's play house.
LP . . . . **SEL 7**
Seville / Jul '83 / President Records / Swift.

SHADES OF VINCENT (Carroll, Johnny & Judy Lindsey).
Tracks: Rock road blues / I gotta baby / Git it / Dance to the bop / Wear my ring / Lotta lovin' / Maybe / Swing, The / Dance at Billy Bob's / Honey don't / Baby let's play house / I've had it / Savin' my love / I want you to be my baby / What I'd say / Hurt so good / Love me up.
■ **LP** . . . . **CR 30249**
Charly / '86.

TEXABILLY.
Tracks: Li'l bit of your time, A / Is it easy to be easy / Judy Judy Judy / Does your mama know / My bucket's got a hole in it / Sixteen tons rockabilly / Who's to say / People in Texas like to dance / Two timin' / Whatcha gonna do / Why doncha quit that teasin' lonesome boy.
LP . . . . **LP 014**
Rollin' Rock / Jun '80 / Pinnacle.
LP . . . . **MFLP 054**
Magnum Force / Sep '87 / Terry Blood Dist. / Jazz Music / Hot Shot.

Carson, Des

WALTZ ACROSS TEXAS.
Tracks: Waltz across Texas / Cup of conversation.
■ **7"** . . . . **HS 039**
Homespun (Ireland) / Oct '80.

Carson, Fiddlin' John

OLD HEN CACKLED., THE.
Tracks: Not Advised.
LP . . . . **ROUNDER 1003**
Rounder / '88 / Projection / Roots Records / Swift / C.M. Distribution / Topic Records / Jazz Music / Hot Shot / A.D.A Distribution / Direct Distribution.

Carson, Joe

IN MEMORIAM.
Tracks: Not Advised.
LP . . . . **PM 1550761**
Pathe Marconi (France) / Jun '84 / Thames Distributors Ltd.

Carson, Martha

EXPLODES.
Tracks: Music drives me crazy, especially rock'n'roll / Dixieland roll / Let the light shine down on me / OK amen / Now stop / Git on board, li'l chilun / Saints and chariot / Let's talk about that old time religion / Just whistle or call / Rocka my soul / This ole house / I'm gonna walk and talk with the Lord / All these things / Satisfied / Be not disencouraged / Get that golden key.
LP . . . . **BFX 15215**
Bear Family / Sep '86 / Rollercoaster Records / Swift / Direct Distribution.

SATISFIED.
Tracks: Not Advised.
LP . . . . **HAT 3109**
MC . . . . **HATC 3109**
Stetson / Aug '89 / Crusader Marketing Co. / Swift / Wellard Dist. / Midland Records / C.M. Distribution.

Carter Family

Vocal and instrumental trio of great influence on American music: A.P. Carter (1891-1960) sang bass, collected and published songs; his wife Sara (1899-1979) sang lead; Maybelle (1909-78) was Sara's cousin, married to A.P.'s brother Ezra, and sang harmony. Both women played guitar and autoharp. They were first recorded in 1927 by Ralph Peer in Bristol, Tennessee, the same week he also discovered Jimmie Rodgers. Rodgers and the Carter Family between them pratically invented country music. Rodgers combining vaudeville, yodelling and blues, while the Carters brought the folk influence of mountain songs plus their unique harmony singing, Sara's mastery of the autoharp and Maybelle's guitar playing. Maybelle Carter's method of playing the melody on the bass strings and rhythm on the treble became known as the Carter style. The trio made about 250 sides, their songs still recorded decades later by the Weavers, Joan Baez, Flatt & Scruggs, Roy Acuff, Emmylou Harris and many others. Maybelle was a regular on the Grand Old Opry 1950-67, sang with daughters Anita, Helen and June, who was married to Carl Smith (daughter Carlene Carter), then Johnny Cash. (Donald Clarke)

20 OF THE BEST: CARTER FAMILY.
Tracks: Keep on the sunny side / Little darling pal of mine / John Hardy / Wildwood flower / Sweet fern / My Clinch Mountain home / I'm thinking of my blue eyes / Lula wall / Foggy mountain top / Jimmy Brown the newsboy / Carters' blues / Wabash cannonball / Diamonds in the rough / Kitty waltz / Cannonball / Worried man blues / Lonesome valley / Lonesome pine special / Church in the wildwood, The / I never will marry.
LP . . . . **NL 89369**
■ **MC** . . . . **NK 89369**
RCA / Mar '84.

CARTER FAMILY ALBUM.
Tracks: Not Advised.
LP . . . . **HAT 3103**
MC . . . . **HATC 3103**
Stetson / Mar '89 / Crusader Marketing Co. / Swift / Wellard Dist. / Midland Records / C.M. Distribution.

CARTER FAMILY ON BORDER RADIO.
Tracks: Not Advised.
LP . . . . **JEMF 101**
JEMF (USA) / '88 / Projection.

COLLECTION OF FAVOURITES BY.., A.
Tracks: Not Advised.
LP . . . . **HAT 3022**
MC . . . . **HATC 3022**

Stetson / Oct '86 / Crusader Marketing Co. / Swift / Wellard Dist. / Midland Records / C.M. Distribution.

FAMOUS COUNTRY MUSIC MAKERS.
Tracks: River of Jordan / I have no one to love me (but the sailor of the deep blue se / Lover's farewell / When the springtime comes again / I have an aged Mother / No more the moon shines on Lorena / I'm on my way to Canaan's land / Where shall I be / My old cottage home / Sunshine in the shadows / Let the church roll on / Amber tresses / Sun of the soul / If one won't another will / On the Sea of Galilee / Poor orphaned child / On a hill lone & grey / Away out on the old Saint Sabbath / Darling daisies / East Virginia blues / Lover's return / Hello Central, give me Heaven / I'm working on a building / There'll be joy, joy, joy / There's no hiding place down here / In the valley of the Shenendoah / Something got hold of me / Waves on the sea / Rambling boy.
■ LP. . . . . DPM 20465
RCA / '75 / BMG.

JUST A FEW MORE (The Carter Family Volume 3).
Tracks: Charlie and Nellie / You're nothing to me / Little Joe / Reckless motorman, The / You denied your love / Lonesome for you / I'll never forsake you / Waves of the sea / Rambling boy / Little red shoes / Climbing Zions Hill / Longing for home / Beyond the river / Titanic, The / Will my mother know me there / Little Moses.
MC 60-913
Folktracks Cassettes / '80 / C.M. Distribution / Roots Records.

LITTLE LOG CABIN, THE (The Carter Family Volume 1).
Tracks: Single girl / Pal of mine / Sunny side / John Hardy / River of Jordan / Wildwood flower / No-one to love me / Sweet fern / Clinch me home / Thinking tonite of my blue eyes / Lulu walls / Blue-eyed boy / Engine / Western hobo / Carter's blues / Wabash cannonball / Lover's farewell / When the Springtime comes again / When the world's on fire / Worried man blues / I can't feel at home / Green fields of Virginia / Picture on the wall / Amber tresses / I never loved but one.
MC 90-911
Folktracks Cassettes / '80 / C.M. Distribution / Roots Records.

SPIRIT OF LOVE, THE (The Carter Family Volume 2).
Tracks: I never will marry / All smiles tonite / Happy or lonesome / One little word / Darling daises / East Virginia blues / Lover's return / Hello Central / You've been fooling me, baby / March winds / Joy, joy, joy / Are you tired of me darling / My heart's tonite in Texas / Mountains of Tennessee / I'll be home some day / Faded coat of blue / Sailor boy / When silver threads are gold again / Bonnie blue eyes / My honey Lou / Where the silvery Colorado / My native home / Jealous hearted me / Hello stranger / Never let the devil get the upper hand / Little girl that played / Farewell Nellie.
MC 90-912
Folktracks Cassettes / '80 / C.M. Distribution / Roots Records.

WILDWOOD FLOWER.
Tracks: Not Advised.
LP. . . . . MERH 128
MC . . . . . MERHC 128
Mercury / PolyGram.

Carter Sisters

MAYBELLE, ANITA, JUNE & HELEN.
Tracks: I like my lovin' overtime / Like all get out / Unfit mother / You're right but I wish you were wrong / You flopped when you got me alone / Jukebox blues / We've got things to do / Don Juan / Heartless romance / Faithless Johnny Lee / There'll be no teardrops tonight / Keep it a secret / Cool, cold, colder / Love, oh, crazy love / Time's a wastin' / He went slippin' around.
■ LP. . . . . BFX 15080
Bear Family / '86.

Carter, Anita

Anita Carter, one of Mother Maybelle and Ezra Carter's three daughters (alongside June and Helen), born 31.3.1934 in Maces Springs, Virginia. Performed on XERA radio in Del Rio, Texas with her mother at a very young age. Later worked on Richmond, Virginia's WRNL station, with Sara Carter, husband A.P and their children Janette and Joe.After disbanding in 1943, she reformed with Maybelle and her sisters and joined the Grand Ole Opry in 1948. Set out on a solo career in 1950,and gained her first success singing on Hank's Snow's *Bluebird Island*, in 1951. Other duet hits were to be with Waylon Jennings (*I Got You*, 1968) and Johnny Darrell (*The Coming Of The Roads*, 1969). Her own recordings on RCA, Jamie and Mercury met with only limited success, yet her pure, aching soprano has honourably graced albums by; Johnny Cash , Merle Haggard, Maybelle Carter and the Carter Sisters. That's besides her regular session work on vocals and bass guitar in the 1960's & 1970's. Most recent work includes the 1988 album on Phonogram *Wildwood Flower*, where June's daughter Carlene Carter joins the sisters. Along with her sisters Anita she has been an essential cog for many years as part of Johnny Cash's roadshow - both in lending him vocal support and as part of the Carter's slot where they air Original Carter Family songs.

FOLK SONGS OLD AND NEW.
Tracks: Love's ring of fire / All my trials / Sour grapes / Fair and tender ladies / My love / Voice of the Bayous / Fly pretty swallow / Johnny I hardly knew you / Satan's child / Few short years ago, A (Previously unissued) / Kentuckian song, The (Previously unissued) / Brian running back / As the sparrow goes.
■ LP. . . . . BFX 15004
Bear Family / Sep '84.

RING OF FIRE.
Tracks: Ring of fire / Fair and tender ladies / Satan's child / Fly pretty swallow / As the sparrow goes / All my trials / Voice of the bayou / Sour grapes / Johnny, I hardly knew you / My love / Kentuckian song, The / Five short years ago, A / No my love, no farewell / Running back / Take me home / John, John, John / John Hardy / I never will marry / In the highways / Bury me beneath the willow / Beautiful isle o'er the sea / Wildwood flower, The.
CD . . . . . BCD 15434
Bear Family / '88 / Rollercoaster Records / Swift / Direct Distribution.

Carter, Carlene

Born Rebecca Carlene Smith on 26.09.1955, daughter of June Carter and Carl Smith. She gained her inital introduction to country music as a member of the Carter Family. Her solo work has covered both country and rock. Nick Lowe, her husband of the time, produced her albums *Blue Nun*, and *Musical Shapes*, where the backing musicians included Dave Edmunds and Graham Parker's Rumour. *Do It In A Heartbeat*, and *Baby Ride Easy*, both made modest indents in the American country charts - the latter a duet with Dave Edmunds. Carter's composition, *Easy From Now*, was covered by Emmylou Harris, who also featured it on her 1978 album *Quarter Moon In A Ten Cent Town*. Her 1983 release *C'Est Si Bon*, was the last from Carlene Carter for seven years. In the meantime, she featured as a actress in the 1985 London musical *Pump Boys And Dinettes*, gaining critical acclaim for her part. In mid to late 1980s she was to return to the Carter Family, now minus mother Maybelle (1909-1978), recording on Anita, Helen and June Carter's 1988 Mercury album *Wildwood Flower*. Carlene's work on the many old standards being mostly noteworthy. After a barren period, Carter was to return with her 1990 album *I Fell In Love*, doing enough to rekindle much interest in her career. It's title track allowed Carter the luxury of a top 3 single slot, backed with *Come On Back*. Better still was to follow when the breezy talent released *Little Love Letters* in 1993 on WEA's Giant label. This included the hit single *Every Little Thing*. Carter had found more success in country, from her two albums of the 1990s than all her other efforts combined, serving notice that she was well capable of carving out a successful career in country music. (Maurice Hope)

BABY RIDE EASY.
Tracks: Baby ride easy / Too bad about Sandy.
■ 7" . . . . . XX 8
F-Beat / Sep '80.

BLUE NUN.
Tracks: Love is a 4 letter verb / That boy / 300 pounds of hongry / Tougher stuff / I need a hit / Rockababy / Me and my .38 / Do me lover / Home run hitter / Billy / Born to move / Think dirty.
LP. . . . . XXLP 12
■ MC . . . . . XXC 12
F-Beat / '84.

C'EST C BON.
Tracks: Meant it for a minute / Heart to heart / Third time charm / Heart's in traction / I'm the kinda sugar daddy likes / Love like a glove / Cool reaction / Don't give my heart a break / That boy / One way ticket / Patient love.
MC 40 25523
Epic / Aug '83 / Sony.
■ LP. . . . . EPC 25523
Epic / Aug '83.

CARLENE CARTER.
Tracks: Not Advised.
■ LP. . . . . K 56502
WEA / Jun '78 / WEA.

DO IT IN A HEARTBEAT.
Tracks: Do it in a heartbeat / Swapmeat rag.
■ 7" . . . . . K 17597
WEA / Apr '80.

DO ME LOVER.
Tracks: Do me lover / If the shoe fits.
■ 7" . . . . . XX 16
F-Beat / Sep '81.

HEART TO HEART.
Tracks: Heart to heart / One way ticket.
12" . . . . . TA 3470
■ 7" . . . . . A 3470
Epic / Oct '83.

I FELL IN LOVE.
Tracks: I fell in love / Come on back / Sweetest thing, The / My dixie darlin' / Goodnight Dallas / One love / Leaving side, The / Guardian angel / Me and the wildwood rose / You are the one / Easy from now on.
CD 7599261392
LP. 7599261391
MC 7599261394
Reprise / May '91 / WEA.

LOVE IS GONE.
Tracks: Love is gone / Smoke dreams.
■ 7" . . . . . K 17220
WEA / Aug '78.

LOVE LIKE A GLOVE.
Tracks: Love like a glove / I'm the kinda sugar daddy likes.
■ 7" . . . . . A 3542
Epic / Jul '83.

MUSICAL SHAPES.
Tracks: Cry / Madness / Baby ride easy / Bandit of love / I'm so cool / Appalachian eyes / Ring of fire / Too bad about Sandy / Foggy mountain top / That very first kiss / To drunk (to remember) / Too proud.
■ LP. . . . . XXLP 3
F-Beat / Aug '80.

MUSICAL SHAPES/BLUE NUN (2 albums on 1 CD).
Tracks: Not Advised.
CD . . . . . FIENDCD 703
Demon / Sep '91 / Pinnacle.

NEVER TOGETHER.
Tracks: Never together / Who needs words.
■ 7" . . . . . K 17144
WEA / Apr '78.

OH HOW HAPPY.
Tracks: Oh how happy / Billy.
■ 7" . . . . . XX 18
F-Beat / Oct '81.

OPEN FIRE.
Tracks: Not Advised.
■ VHS. . . . . HEN 2195
Hendring Video / Feb '90.

RING OF FIRE.
Tracks: Ring of fire / That very first kiss.
■ 7" . . . . . XX 6
F-Beat / Jun '80.

Carter, Lisa

COUNTRY ROADS.
Tracks: Not Advised.
CD . . . . . SOV 017CD
MC . . . . . SOV 017TC
Sovereign Music / Jan '93 / Terry Blood Dist. / ACD Trading Ltd. / Taylors.

DOCTOR'S ORDERS.
Tracks: Doctor's orders / Good medicine (instrumental).
12" . . . . . 12 NHS 1
■ 7" . . . . . NHS 1
EMI / Jul '88.

Carter, Mother Maybelle

MOTHER MAYBELLE CARTER.
Tracks: Dialogue / Good old mountain dew / Still / Arkansas traveller / Waterloo / Black mountain rag / Jimmy Rogers and train / Wabash Cannonball / Rocky top / Release me / Hey liberty / Chinese breakdown / Bells of St. Mary's / World need a melody, The / Never on Sunday / Tennessee waltz / Red wing.
Double LP . . . . . KG 32436
Columbia (EMI) / '73 / EMI.

Carter, Wilf

Born in 1904 in Nova Scotia, Wilf Carter was Canada's first country star, adopting the name 'Montana Slim' on his USA debut in 1937. He wrote more than 500 songs, including *Swiss Mountain Lullaby* and *(There's a) Bluebird On Your Windowsill*, a hit for Doris Day around 1950. He recorded for Starday in the '60's and retired in 1980. (Donald Clarke)

DYNAMITE TRAIL - THE DECCA YEARS, 1954-58.
Tracks: One golden curl / My mountain high yodel song / I'm gonna tear down the mailbox / Maple leaf waltz / There's a tree on every road / I bought a rock for a rocky mountain gal / Shoo shoo sh'lala / Sunshine bird, The / Kissing on the sly / Alpine milkman, The / Dynamite trail / Strawberry road / Ragged but right / There's a padlock on your heart / Yodelin' song, The / On a little two acre farm / Strawberry road (2) / My little lady / Silver bell yodel / Away out on the mountain / Blind boy's prayer, The / X's from down in Texas / Let a little sunshine in your heart / There's a bluebird on your windowsill / My French Canadian girl / Sick, sober and sorry / Sinner's prayer, A / My prairie rose / Yodeling my babies to sleep / Born to lose.

CD Set . . . . **BCD 15507**
Bear Family / Jul '90 / Rollercoaster Records / Swift / Direct Distribution.

MONTANA SLIM.
Tracks: Not Advised.
LP . . . . **SLP 300**
MC . . . . **GT 5300**
Starday (USA) / Apr '87 / Crusader Marketing Co.

REMINISCIN' WITH.
Tracks: Not Advised.
LP . . . . **HAT 3085**
Stetson / '88 / Crusader Marketing Co. / Swift / Wellard Dist. / Midland Records / C.M. Distribution.
MC . . . . **HATC 3085**
Stetson / Jan '89 / Crusader Marketing Co. / Swift / Wellard Dist. / Midland Records / C.M. Distribution.

Cartwright, Lionel

LIONEL CARTWRIGHT.
Tracks: Not Advised.
CD . . . . **MCAD 42276**
LP . . . . **MCA 42276**
MC . . . . **MCAC 42276**
MCA / Jun '89 / BMG.

Cash, Johnny

This American singer, guitarist and songwriter was born in Kingsland, Arkansas in 1932. After a spell in the US Air Force, he had a short-lived job as an electrical salesman, before joining Sun Records in Memphis in 1955. That label, owned by Sam Phillips, signed Elvis Presley at around the same time as Cash. The first record by Cash called *Cry, Cry, Cry*, made the Top 10 of the US country charts. In '56 he crossed over to the pop chart, reaching No. 17 with *I Walk The Line*. Further Top 30 pop hits followed in 1958 with *Ballad Of A Teenage Queen*, *Guess Things Happen That Way* and *The Ways Of A Woman In Love*. All featured his distinctive, deep, doomy voice. In late '58 he switched to Columbia records a move that suggested further success. In the event however, Cash's career went into decline for several years; this slack period, which lasted throughout the early mid-Sixties, was interrupted only by 1963's *Ring Of Fire*. This song was co-written by country singer June Carter, a member of the famous Carter country music family, his future wife. One of the main reasons for Cash's long-lasting mediocre era was his serious drug addiction, a condition that he eventually overcame with June's help. A revitalised Johnny Cash bounced back bigger than ever in 1968, when he took the unprecedented step of recording a live concert at California's Folsom Prison. The resulting album was a monster success, remaining on the US album charts for over two years. It was also the artist's first major chart record in the UK, reaching No. 8 and staying on the survey for exactly a year. Indeed, so successful was the idea that Cash did exactly the same thing in 1969. *Johnny Cash At San Quentin*, was another smash LP on both sides of the Atlantic. In Britain it reached No. 2 and logged no less than 114 weeks on the listings. The album yielded the single *A Boy Named Sue*, penned by Shel Silverstein. It reached No. 2 in the States, Cash's only American Top 10 pop hit and No. 4 in Britain, his first Top 20 single in the latter country. No longer was he just a country star - he was given his own US networked TV show and became an international showbusiness phenomenon. In 1972 he achieved a second British Top 10 single with *A Thing Called Love*, a gospel-inflected record on which he was backed by the Evangel Temple Choir. Since then he has concentrated less on recording, with only 1976's amusing *One Piece At A Time* returning him to the pop charts. He developed a substantial acting career, appearing both in movies and on television. By the early Eighties two interesting family developments had taken place; his stepdaughter Carlene Carter married Nick Lowe, thereby establishing an intriguing link between an American country music legend and a British rock star; and his daughter Rosanne Cash became a leading figure on the US country charts. In recent years, Johnny Cash has also guested on Emmylou Harris LPs, and in 1981 recorded *Survivors*, with Carl Perkins - the first time the pair had worked together for over 20 years. In 1985, Carl Perkins, Jerry Lee Lewis and Johnny Cash together with Roy Orbison who took the place of Elvis Presley, reformed the Million Dollar Quartet. The resulting *Class of '55* album featured guest spots from Dave Edmunds, John Fogerty, the Judds and Rick Nelson (his last session). Another project, The Highwayman (see seperate entry) which features Johnny Cash, Waylon Jennings, Willie Nelson and Kris Kristofferson has produced a couple of very successful albums and yielded a number one country single. With 58 top 40 country hits in 25 years, Johnny Cash is one of the leading figures in the Country music world.(Bob MacDonald)

..WITH HIS HOT AND BLUE GUITAR.
Tracks: Rock Island line / I heard that lonesome whistle blow / Country boy / If the good Lord's willing and the creeks don't rise / Cry cry cry / Remember me / I'm so doggone lonesome / I was there when it happened / I walk the line / Wreck of the old '97 / Folsom Prison blues / Doin my time.
■ **LP** . . . . **CRM 2013**
Charly / Feb '81 / Charly.

18 GOLDEN HITS.
Tracks: Not Advised.
LP . . . . **MA 91183**
Masters (Holland) / '88.
CD . . . . **SPEC 85008**
Spectrum (CD) / Dec '88 / M.S.D.
MC . . . . **MAMC 91191183**
Masters (Holland) / Dec '88.

1958-1986 THE CBS YEARS.
Tracks: Oh, what a dream / I still miss someone / Pickin' time / Don't take your guns to town / Five feet high and rising / Seasons of my heart / Legend of John Henty's hammer / Ring of fire / Ballad of Ira Hayes, The / Orange Blossom special / Folsom Prison blues / San Quentin / Boy named Sue, A / Sunday morning coming down / Man in black / One piece at a time / Riders in the sky / Without love / Baron, The / Highway patrolman.
LP **4504661**
■ **MC** **4504664**
CBS / Apr '87.
CD **4504662**
CBS / May '87 / Sony.

20 FOOT TAPPIN' GREATS (Itchy Feet).
Tracks: Folsom Prison blues / I walk the line / Ring of fire / Forty shades of green / I still miss someone / There ain't no good chain gang / Busted / 25 minutes to go / Orange blossom special / It ain't me babe / Boy named Sue, A / San Quentin / Don't take your guns to town / One on the right is on the left, The / Jackson / Hey porter / Daddy sang bass / I got stripes / Thing called love, A / One piece at a time.
MC **40 10009**
CBS / Aug '78 / Sony.
■ **LP** . . . . **CBS 10009**
CBS / Aug '78.

20 GREATEST HITS: JOHNNY CASH.
Tracks: Not Advised.
CD **290 13 001**
Starr / '88 / PolyGram.

6 TRACK HITS.
Tracks: Boy named Sue, A / I walk the line / Ring of fire / If I were a carpenter / Folsom Prison blues / What is truth?.
EP **7SR 5015**
MC **7SC 5015**
Scoop 33 / Sep '83.

ADVENTURES OF JOHNNY CASH.
Tracks: I've been to Georgia on a fast train / John's / Fair weather friends / Paradise / We must believe in magic / Only love / Good old American guest / I'll cross over Jordan / Sing a song / Ain't gonna hobo no more.
■ **LP** . . . . **CBS 85881**
CBS / Dec '82.

ANY OLD WIND THAT BLOWS.
Tracks: Any old wind that blows / Kentucky straight / Loving gift, The (With June Carter) / Good earth, The / Best friend / Oney / Too little, too late / If I had a hammer (With June Carter) / Country trash / Welcome back Jesus.
LP . . . . **S 65431**
CBS / '73 / Sony.

AT FOLSOM PRISON.
Tracks: Folsom Prison blues / Dark as a dungeon / I still miss someone / Cocaine blues / Twenty five minutes to go / Orange blossom special / Long black veil / Send a picture of mother / Wall, The / Dirty old egg-sucking dog / Flushed from the bathroom of your heart / Jackson / Give my love to Rose / I got stripes / Green green grass of home / Greystone Chapel.
LP . . . . **CBS 63308**
MC **40 63308**
CBS / '87 / Sony.

BALLAD OF A TEENAGE QUEEN.
Tracks: Not Advised.
LP . . . . **XELLP 111**
MC . . . . **XELMC 111**
Exel / Jul '88 / Henry Hadaway Organisation / EMI.

BARON.
Tracks: Baron / Mobile Bay / Magnolia blossoms / Hard way, The / Ceiling, four walls and a floor / Hey train / Reverend Mr. Black / Blues keep gettin' bluer / Chattanooga city limit sign / Thanks to you / Greatest love affair.
■ **LP** . . . . **CBS 84990**
CBS / Aug '81.

BARON.
Tracks: Baron / I will dance with you.
■ **7"** . . . . **A 1155**
CBS / May '81.

BELIEVE IN HIM.
Tracks: Believe in Him / Another wide river to cross / God ain't no stained glass window / Over there / Old rugged cross, The / My children walk in truth / You're drifting away / Belshazar / Half a mile a day / One of these days I'm gonna sit down and talk to Paul.
■ **LP** . . . . **WST R 9678**
Word (UK) / Sep '86.
■ **MC** . . . . **WST C 9678**
Word (UK) / Sep '86.
MC . . . . **TC MFP 5840**
MFP / Sep '88 / EMI.
■ **LP** . . . . **MFP 5840**
MFP / Sep '88.

BELIEVER SINGS THE TRUTH.
Tracks: Wings in the morning / Gospel boogie / Over the next hill / He's alive / I've got Jesus in my soul / When He comes / I was there when it happened / I'm a newborn man / There are strange things happening everyday / Children go where I send thee / I'm just an old chunk of coal / Lay me down in Dixie / Don't take everybody for your friend / You'll get yours, I'll get mine / Oh come, angel band / This train is bound for glory / I'm gonna try to be that way / What on earth / That's enough / Greatest cowboy of them all, The.
■ **LP** . . . . **CBS 84123**
CBS / Apr '80.

BEST OF JOHNNY CASH.
Tracks: Not Advised.
■ **LP** . . . . **CBS 10000**
CBS / Oct '76.
MC **16-23**
Creole (Everest-Europa) / Jul '84.

BEST OF THE SUN YEARS 1955-1961.
Tracks: Not Advised.
CD . . . . **MCCD 082**
Music Club / Sep '92 / Gold & Sons / Terry Blood Dist. / Video Collection.

BIG LIGHT, THE.
Tracks: Big light, The / Sixteen tons.
■ **7"** . . . . **MER 263**
Mercury / May '88.

BIGGEST HITS.
Tracks: Don't take your guns to town / Ring of fire / Understand your man / One on the right is on the left, The / Rosanna's going wild / Folsom Prison blues / Baddy sand bass / Boy named Sue, A / Sunday morning coming down / Flesh and blood / Thing called love, A / One piece at a time / There ain't no good chain gang / Riders in the sky / Baron, The.
MC **40 32304**
CBS / Mar '83 / Sony.
■ **LP** . . . . **CBS 32304**
CBS / Mar '83.
CD . . . . **CD 32304**
CBS / Jun '91 / Sony.

BITTER TEARS (Ballads of The American Indian).
Tracks: Big foot / As long as the grass shall grow / Apache tears / Custer / Talking leaves, The / Ballad of Ira Hayes, The / Drums / White girl / Old Apache squaw / Vanishing race, The / Intro.
LP . . . . **BPG 62463**
CBS / '64 / Sony.
LP . . . . **BFX 15127**
Bear Family / Jul '84 / Rollercoaster Records / Swift / Direct Distribution.

BLISTERED.
Tracks: Blistered / See Ruby fall.
7" . . . . **CBS 4638**
CBS / '69 / Sony.

BOOM CHICKA BOOM.
Tracks: Backstage pass / Farmer's almanac / Family bible / I love you, I love you / Monteagle Mountain / Cat's in the cradle / Don't go near the water / Harley / Hidden shame / That's one you owe me.
CD **8421552**
LP **8421551**
MC **8421554**
Mercury / Feb '90 / PolyGram.

BORN TO LOSE.
Tracks: I walk the line / Ballad of a teenage queen / Big river / Wreck of the old 97 / Guess things happen that way / Born to lose / Give my love to Rose / Folsom prison blues / Rock Island line / Luther played the boogie / Straight A's in love / Get rhythm / Next in line / You're the nearest thing to heaven.
CD . . . . **CDINS 5007**
LP . . . . **INS 5007**
MC . . . . **TCINS 5007**
Instant (2) / Jul '89 / Charly.

BOY NAMED SUE.
Tracks: Boy named Sue, A / Green green grass of home / Still in town / Peace in the valley / When papa played the dobro / Tall men / After taxes / Pick the wild wood flowers / Praise the Lord and pass the soup / Old Shep / Keep on the sunny side / Time changes everything / Second honeymoon / Diamonds in the rough / Whirl and the suck, The / San Quentin.
LP **31827**
MC **40 31827**
CBS / '84 / Sony.

BOY NAMED SUE.
Tracks: Boy named Sue, A.
■ **7"** . . . . **CBS 4460**
CBS / Sep '69.
7" . . . . **CBS 1152**
CBS / Apr '82 / Sony.

BOY NAMED SUE, A (OLD GOLD).
Tracks: Boy named Sue, A / San Quentin.
7" . . . . OG 9180
Old Gold / Jul '82 / Pickwick Records.

CHICKEN IN BLACK.
Tracks: Chicken in black / Duck a l'orange.
■ 7" . . . . A 4723
CBS / Nov '84.

CHRISTMAS SPIRIT, THE.
Tracks: Christmas spirit, The / I heard the bells on Christmas day / Blue Christmas / Gifts they gave, The / Here was a man / Christmas as I knew it / Silent night / Little drummer boy / Ringing the bells for Jim / We are the shepherds / Who kept the sheep / Ballad of the harp weaver, The.
■ LP 4604611
CBS Cameo / Dec '87.
■ MC 4604614
CBS Cameo / Dec '87.

CLASSIC CASH.
Tracks: Get rhythm / Long black veil / I still miss someone / Blue train / Five feet high and rising / Don't take your guns to town / Guess things happen that way / I walk the line / Ballad of Ira Hayes, The / Folsom Prison blues / Tennessee flat top box / Thing called love, A / Cry cry cry / Sunday morning coming down / Peace in the valley / Home of the blues / I got stripes / Ring of fire / Ways of a woman in love, The / Supper time.
CD 834 526-2
Mercury / Mar '89 / PolyGram.
LP 834 526-1
■ MC 834 526-4
Mercury / Mar '89.

COLLECTION: JOHNNY CASH.
Tracks: Wide open road / Cry cry cry / Folsom Prison blues / So doggone lonesome / Mean eyed cat / New Mexico / I walk the line / I love you because / Straight A's in love / Home of the blues / Rock Island line / Country boy / Doin' my time / Big river / Ballad of a teenage queen / Oh lonesome me / You're the nearest thing to heaven / Always alone / You win again / Hey good lookin' / Blue train / Katy too / Fools hall of fame / Ways of a woman in love, The / Down the street to 301.
■ Double LP . . . . CCSLP 146
Castle Collector Series / '86.
CD . . . . CCSCD 146
MC . . . . CCSMC 146
Castle Collector Series / Feb '93 / BMG / Pinnacle / Castle Communications.

COLLECTION: JOHNNY CASH VOL 3.
Tracks: Seasons of my heart / I feel better all over / I couldn't keep from crying / Time changes everything / I'd just be fool enough / Transfusion blues / Why do you punish me / I'm so lonesome I could cry / Just one more / Honky tonk gal / Drink to me / Man on the hill / Hank and Joe and me / Clementine / Great speckled bird, The / Austin prison / I want to go home / Caretaker / Old Apache squaw / Don't step on mother's roses / My grandfather's clock / It could be you.
■ Double LP . . . . PDA 062
Pickwick / '79.

COME ALONG AND RIDE THIS TRAIN.
Tracks: Come along and ride this train / Loading coal / Slow rider / Lumberjack / Dorraine of ponchartrain / Going to Memphis / When papa played the dobro / Boss Jack / Old Doc Brown / Legend of John Henry's hammer, The / Tell him I'm gone / Another man done gone / Shifting whispering sand, The / Casey Jones / Nine pound hammer / Chain gang / Busted / Waiting for a train / Roughneck / Pick a bale of cotton / Cotton pickin' hands / Hiawatha's vision / Road to Kaintuck, The / Hammer and nails / Shifting whispering sands, (part 1) / Ballad of boot hill, The / I ride an old paint / Hardin' wouldn't run / Mr. Garfield / Streets of Laredo, The / Johnny Reb / Letter from home / Bury me not on the lone prairie / Mean as hell / Sam Hall / 25 minutes to go / Blizzard, The / Sweet Betsy from Pike / Green grow the lilacs / Rodeo hand / Stampede / Shifting whispering sands (part 2) / Remember the Alamo / Reflections / Big foot / As long as the grass shall grow / Apache tears / Custer / Talking leaves, The / Ballard of Ira Hayes, The / Drums / White girl / Old apache squaw / Vanishing race, The / Paul Revere / Road to Kaintuck / Battle of New Orleans, The / Lorena / Gettysbury address, The / Big battle, The / Come and take a trip in my airship / These are my people / From the sea to shining sea / Whirl and the suck, The / Call daddy from the mine / Frozen four hundred pound to middin' cotton picker / Walls of a prison, the / Masterpiece, The / You and Tennesse / She came from the mountains / Another song to sing / Flint arrowhead, The / Cisco Clifton's fillin' station / Shrimpin' sailin' / From sea to shining sea / Hit the road and go / If it wasn't for the Wabash river / Lady / After the ball / No earthly good / Wednesday car, A / My cowboy's last ride.
CD Set . . . . BCD 15563
Bear Family / May '91 / Rollercoaster Records / Swift / Direct Distribution.

COUNTRY BOOGIE.
Tracks: Wreck of the old 97 / Get rhythm / Luther played the boogie / Two timin' woman / Next in line / Belshazar / Hey porter / I heard that lonesome whistle blow / Train of love / Sugartime / Don't make me go / There you go / Boy named Sue, A / Jackson / Daughter of the railroad man / Go on blues / Mamas baby / So do I / Folsom prison blues (live) / In a young girls mind / One piece at a time / How did you get away from me / Rodeo hand / Walkin' the blues.
Double LP . . . . VSOPLP 121
MC . . . . VSOPMC 121
Connoisseur Collection / Jul '88 / Pinnacle.
CD . . . . VSOPCD 121
Connoisseur Collection / Apr '90 / Pinnacle.

COUNTRY BOY.
Tracks: I walk the line / Wide open road / Cry cry cry / Hey porter / Folsom Prison blues / Get rhythm / Luther played the boogie / There you go / Train of love / Straight A's in love / Give my love to Rose / Goodnight Irene / Rock Island line / Country boy / If the Lord's willing / Big river / Ballad of a teenage queen / Come in stranger / Guess things happen that way / Life goes on / Blue train / Katy too / Ways of a woman in love, The / Thanks a lot.
CD . . . . CDCHARLY 18
Charly / Apr '86 / Charly.

COUNTRY STORE: JOHNNY CASH.
Tracks: Thing called love, A / Long black veil / Jackson / Ring of fire / Don't take your guns to town / One piece at a time / Boy named Sue, A / Folsom Prison blues / Busted / Daddy sang bass / Let there be country / What is truth / Johnny 99 / Greatest love affair / Ghost riders in the sky (Only on CD.) / Song of the patriot (Only on CD.) / Gambler, The (Only on CD.) / It'll be her (Only on CD.).
CD . . . . CDCST 11
MC . . . . CSTK 11
Country Store / '88 / BMG.
■ LP . . . . CST 11
Country Store / '88.

COWBOYS, THE (Cash, Johnny & Marty Robbins).
Tracks: Dont' take your guns to town / Big iron / Twenty five minutes to go / Hangin' tree, The / Cottonwood tree, The / Long black veil / Bury me not on the lone prairie / Cool water / Riders in the sky / Red river valley / Old Doc Brown / Meet me tonight in Laredo / Bonanza / Take me back to the prairie / Ira Hayes / Running gun / Ballad of Boot Hill / Mr. Garfield / El Paso / Billy the Kid / Streets of Laredo / Five brothers / Last gunfighter ballad, The / Shifting, whispering sands / Saddle tramp / Remember the Alamo / Sweet Betsy from Pike / Little Joe the wrangler / Give my love to Rose / Stampede.
Double LP . . . . RTL 2070A/B
MC Set 4CRTL 2070A/B
Ronco / Mar '82.

DADDY SANG BASS.
Tracks: Daddy sang bass / Water into wine.
7" . . . . CBS 3878
CBS / '68 / Sony.

DESTINATION VICTORIA STATION.
Tracks: Not Advised.
■ LP . . . . BFX 15021
Bear Family / '85.

DIAMOND IN THE ROUGH, A.
Tracks: Jesus / Preacher said "Jesus said" (With Billy Graham) / That's enough / Miracle man, The / I never met a man like you before / Look for me / I talk to Jesus every day / Peace in the valley / Pie in the sky / Supper time / Far banks of Jordan / Matthew 24 (is knocking at the door) / Diamonds in the rough / I'm just an old chunk of coal.
LP . . . . WST 9629
MC . . . . WC 9629
Word (UK) / May '85 / Word Records (UK) / Sony.

ESSENTIAL JOHNNY CASH 1955-1983, THE (Columbia Country Classics).
Tracks: Hey porter / Cry, cry, cry / Folsom Prison blues / Luther played the boogie / Get rhythm / I walk the line / Home of the blues / Give my love to Rose / Rock Island line / Doin' my time / Big river / Ballad of a teenage queen / Guess things happen that way / Ways of a woman in love, The / Thanks a lot / Oh, what a dream / What do I care / All over again / I still miss someone / I'd just be fool enough (to Fall) / Walking the blues / Frankie's man Johnny / Tennessee flat top box / Sing it pretty Sue / Pickin' time / Five feet high and rising / Old account, The / (There'll be) Peace in the valley (for me) / Were you there (when they crucified my lord).
CD 47992
Columbia (USA) / Sep '92 / Columbia (Imports).

EVERYBODY LOVES A NUT.
Tracks: Not Advised.
■ LP . . . . BPG 62717
CBS / Jul '66.

FIRST YEARS, THE.
Tracks: Folsom Prison blues / I can't help it / You win again / Mean eyed cat / My treasure / Hey porter / Straight A's in love / Two timin' woman / Oh lonesome me / Sugartime.
LP . . . . ALEB 2303
MC . . . . ZCALB 2303
Allegiance / Apr '84.

FOLSOM PRISON BLUES.
Tracks: If the good Lord's willing / I was there when it happened / Down the street to 301 / Blue train / Don't make me go / I could never be ashamed of you / There you go / Thanks a lot / I couldn't keep from crying / Just about time / Straight A's in love / I just thought you'd like to know / You're the nearest thing to heaven / Rock Island line / Cold cold heart / Folsom Prison blues / Hey good lookin' / Ways of a woman in love, The.
LP . . . . SHLP 126
MC . . . . SHTC 126
Castle Showcase / Apr '86 / Arabesque Ltd.
MC 511444.6
Magnum Music / Nov '88 / Conifer Records.

FOLSOM PRISON BLUES.
Tracks: Folsom prison blues / Folk singer, The.
7" . . . . CBS 3549
CBS / '68 / Sony.

FROM SEA TO SHINING SEA.
Tracks: Not Advised.
■ LP . . . . CBS 62972
CBS / May '68.

GET RHYTHM.
Tracks: Get rhythm.
■ 7" . . . . MER 286
Mercury.

GET RHYTHM (Cash, Johnny & The Tennessee Two).
Tracks: Get rhythm / Mean eyed cat / You win again / Country boy / Two timin' woman / Oh lonesome me / Luther's boogie / Doin' my time / New Mexico / Belshazah / Sugartime.
LP 6467014
Sun / Aug '91 / Charly / Swift.

GONE GIRL.
Tracks: Gone girl / I will rock'n'roll with you / Diplomat / No expectations / It comes and goes / It'll be her / Gambler, The / Cajun born / You and me / Song for the life.
■ LP . . . . CBS 83323
CBS / Apr '79.

GRAFFITI COLLECTION.
Tracks: Not Advised.
CD . . . . GRCD 02
MC . . . . GRMC 02
Graffiti Collection / Aug '90 / Terry Blood Dist.

GREAT COUNTRY LOVE SONGS.
Tracks: Not Advised.
CD . . . . PWK 014
Pickwick / '88 / Pickwick Records.

GREAT JOHNNY CASH, THE (BRAVO LABEL).
Tracks: Not Advised.
■ MC . . . . BRC 2501
Bravo / Feb '80.

GREAT JOHNNY CASH, THE (DITTO).
Tracks: Not Advised.
MC Set . . . . DTO 10249
Ditto / Sep '86 / Pickwick Records.

GREAT SONGS OF JOHNNY CASH.
Tracks: I walk the line / Rock Island line / Folsom Prison line / Born to lose / Remember me / Wreck of the old '97 / Ballad of a teenage queen / I heard that lonesome whistle blow / Home of the blues.
LP . . . . F 50004
MC . . . . MF 950004
IMS / Oct '82 / PolyGram.
LP 20086
LP P.Disc. . . . . PD 50004
MC 40086
Astan (USA) / Nov '84.

GREATEST HITS: JOHNNY CASH.
Tracks: Not Advised.
CD . . . . WMCD 5661
MC . . . . WMMC 4661
Woodford Music / Aug '92 / Terry Blood Dist. / Midland Records.

GREATEST HITS: JOHNNY CASH VOL. 1.
Tracks: Jackson / I walk the line / Ballad of Ira Hayes, The / Orange blossom special / One on the right is on the left, The / Ring of fire / It ain't me babe / Understand your man / Rebel - Johnny Yuma, The / Five feet high and rising / Don't take your guns to town.
■ LP . . . . CBS 63062
CBS / Oct '69.
LP . . . . CBS 32565
CBS / Feb '85 / Sony.
CD 9021252
Pickwick / Jul '89 / Pickwick Records.
MC 9021254
Pickwick / Jul '92 / Pickwick Records.

GREATEST HITS: JOHNNY CASH VOL. 2 (A Johnny Cash portrait).
Tracks: Boy named Sue, A / Hey porter / Guess things happen that way / Blistered / Big river / Long legged guitar pickin' man / Folsom Prison blues / Sunday morning coming down / If I were a carpenter / Frankie's man Johnny / Daddy sang bass.
LP 64506
■ MC 4064506
CBS / '78 / Sony.
■ LP . . . . CBS 32766
CBS / Mar '86.
■ MC 40 32766
CBS / Mar '86.

HELLO I'M JOHNNY CASH.
Tracks: Not Advised.
■ LP . . . . CBS 63796
CBS / Mar '70.

HEROES (Cash, Johnny & Waylon Jennings).
Tracks: Folks out on the road / I'm never gonna roam again / American by birth / Field of diamonds / Heroes / Even cowgirls get the blues / Love is the way / Ballad of forty dollars / I'll always love you - in my own crazy way / One too many mornings.
LP . . . . CBS 26922
CBS / Jun '86 / Sony.
■ MC 40 26922
CBS / Jun '86.

HOME OF THE BLUES.
Tracks: Port of lonely hearts / My treasure / So doggone lonesome / Goodbye little darling / I love you because / Next in line / Don't make me go / Home of the blues / Belshazar / Leave that junk alone / Story of a broken heart, The / You win again / I could never be ashamed of you / It's just about time / I just thought you might like to know / I forgot to remember to forget.
CD . . . . TOP CD 521
Topline / May '87 / Charly / Swift / Black Sun Records.

I LOVE COUNTRY.
Tracks: Ghost riders in the sky / Highway patrolman / Who's Gene Autry / Baron / Boy named Sue, A / Diplomat / No charge / To beat the devil / Gambler, The / Rev.Mr. Black / Ballad of Ira Hayes, The.
■ LP . . . . SHM 739
Hallmark / Nov '71.
CD . . . . PCD 813
Pickwick / Apr '86 / Pickwick Records.
LP . . . . CBS 54938
CBS / Mar '87 / Sony.
■ MC 40 54938
CBS / Mar '87.

I WALK THE LINE.
Tracks: I walk the line / Ballad of a teenage queen / Big river / Wreck of the old 97 / Guess things happen that way / Born to lose / Give my love to Rose / Rock Island line / Luther played the boogie / Straight A's in love / Get rhythm / You win again / Hey good lookin' / Cold cold heart / Sugartime / I heard that lonesome whistle blow / Goodnight Irene / Folsom Prison blues / I forgot to remember to forget / Oh lonesome me.
CD . . . . OR 0020
Music Collection International / Aug '87 / Terry Blood Dist. / Jazz Music.

I WALK THE LINE.
Tracks: Not Advised.
■ CD 500 063
Intertape / Jul '87.

I WALK THE LINE.
Tracks: Not Advised.
LP . . . . SM 3988
MC . . . . MC 3988
Joker (USA) / '88 / C.M. Distribution / Jazz Horizons / Jazz Music.

I WALK THE LINE.
Tracks: Not Advised.
CD . . . . CTS 55406
MC . . . . CTS 45406
Country Stars / Jan '92.

I WALK THE LINE.
Tracks: Not Advised.
LP . . . . BGP 62371
CBS / '64 / Sony.

I WALK THE LINE.
Tracks: Not Advised.
LP . . . . TOP 129
MC . . . . KTOP 129
Topline / '86 / Charly / Swift / Black Sun Records.

I WALK THE LINE.
Tracks: Not Advised.
CD . . . . U 4065
Spectrum (1) / Jun '88 / PolyGram.

I WALK THE LINE.
Tracks: Not Advised.
CD . . . . OCN 2032WD
LP . . . . OCN 2032WL
MC . . . . OCN 2032WK
Ocean (2) / Jun '89.

I WALK THE LINE (OCEAN LABEL).
Tracks: Not Advised.

I WILL ROCK 'N' ROLL WITH YOU.
Tracks: I will rock 'n' roll with you.
■ 7" . . . . CBS 7153
CBS / '79.

I'M SO LONESOME I COULD CRY.
Tracks: I'm so lonesome I could cry / Cottonfields / My shoes keep walking back to you / I feel better all over / I still miss someone / I want to go home / One more ride / Delia's gone / Pickin' time / Suppertime.
■ LP . . . . SHM 3027
Hallmark / Apr '80.
■ MC . . . . HSC 3027
Hallmark / Apr '80.

IN SAN QUENTIN.
Tracks: Not Advised.
VHS . . . . VA 16872
Vestron Music Video / Oct '87 / Sony / Gold & Sons / Terry Blood Dist.

INSIDE A SWEDISH PRISON.
Tracks: Orleans parish prison / Jacob green / Me and Bobby McGee / Prisoner's song / Invertebrate, The / That silver haired daddy of mine / City jail of a prisoner / Looking back in anger / Nobody cared / Help me make it through the night / I saw a man.
LP . . . . BFX 15092
Bear Family / Oct '82 / Rollercoaster Records / Swift / Direct Distribution.

IS COMING TO TOWN.
Tracks: Big light, The / Ballad of Barbara, The / I'd rather have you / Let him roll / Night Hank Williams came to town, The / Sixteen tons / Letters from home / W.Lee O'Daniel and the Light Crust Dough Boys / Heavy metal (don't mean rock and roll to me) / My ship will sail.
CD 832 031 2
LP . . . . MERH 108
■ MC . . . . MERHC 108
Mercury / Jun '87.

IT AIN'T ME, BABE.
Tracks: It ain't me babe.
■ 7" . . . . CBS 201760
CBS / Jun '65.

ITCHY FEET - 20 FOOT-TAPPIN' GREATS.
Tracks: Folsom prison blues / I walk the line / Ring of fire / Forty shades of green / I still miss someone / There ain't no good chain gang / Busted / 25 minutes to go / Orange blossom special / It ain't me babe / Boy named Sue, A / San Quentin / Don't take your guns to town / One on the right is on the left / Jackson / Hey, porter / Daddy sang bass / I got stripes / Thing called love, A / One piece at a time.
CD 4681162
MC 4681164
Columbia / Mar '91 / Sony.

JOHNNY 99.
Tracks: Highway patrolman / That's the truth / God bless Robert E.Lee / New cut road / Johnny 99 / Ballad of the ark / Joshua gone Barbados / Girl from the canyon / Brand new dance / I'm ragged but I'm right.
■ LP . . . . CBS 25471
CBS / Dec '83.

JOHNNY 99.
Tracks: Johnny 99 / Brand new dance.
■ 7" . . . . A 3804
CBS / Oct '83.

JOHNNY AND JUNE (Cash, Johnny, June Carter & Anita Carter).
Tracks: (I'm proud) the baby is mine / Cotton pickin' hands / Thunderball (Previously unissued) / One too many mornings (Previously unissued) / Wer kennt wer weg (I walk the line) / Smiling Bill McCall / In Virginia / Close the door lightly (Previously unissued) / Adios aloha (Previously unissued) / Ain't you ashamed (Previously unissued) / That's what it's like to be lonesome (Previously unissued) / How did you get away from me (Previously unissued).
LP . . . . BFX 15030
Bear Family / Sep '84 / Rollercoaster Records / Swift / Direct Distribution.

JOHNNY CASH.
Tracks: Wanted man / Wreck of the old 97 / I walk the line / Darling companion / Starkville City jail / San Quentin / Boy named Sue, A / Peace in the valley / Folsom Prison blues.
CD 9825862
Pickwick/Sony Collectors Choice / Jul '91 / Pickwick Records.

JOHNNY CASH (BELLAPHON LABEL) (Original Golden Hits Vol 1).
Tracks: Not Advised.
CD 288 07 002
Bellaphon / Nov '86 / New Note.

JOHNNY CASH (EMBASSY LABEL).
Tracks: I walk the line / Streets of Laredo / Don't take your guns to town / Five feet high and rising / I promise you / I'm gonna try to be that way / Don't think twice / It's alright / Hey porter / Give my love to Rose / Big river / I still miss someone / All God's children ain't free.
LP . . . . CBS 31495
Embassy / Jul '77 / Sony.
■ MC 40 31495
Embassy / Jul '77.

JOHNNY CASH (HAMMER LABEL).
Tracks: Not Advised.
■ LP . . . . HMB 7001
Hammer / Dec '79.

JOHNNY CASH AT SAN QUENTIN.
Tracks: Wanted man / Wreck of old 97 / I walk the line / Darling companion / Starkville city jail / San Quentin / Boy named Sue, A / Peace in the valley / Folsom prison blues.
■ LP 63629
CBS / Aug '69.
■ LP . . . . CBS 32209
CBS / May '84.
■ MC 40 32209
CBS / May '84.
MC 40 63629
CBS / '85 / Sony.
■ LP . . . . CBS 63629
CBS / '85.

JOHNNY CASH COLLECTION (DEJA VU LABEL) (20 Country Greats).
Tracks: Wreck of the old '97 / Ballad of a teenage queen / I heard that lonesome whistle blow / Rock island line / Goodbye little darling / Train of love / Down the street to 301 / Give my love to Rose / Come in, stranger / Get rhythm / Folsom Prison blues / I walk the line / Hey porter / Guess things happen that way / Ways of a woman in love, The / There you go / Big river / Sugartime / Blue train / Doin' my time.
LP . . . . DVLP 2103
MC . . . . DVMC 2103
Deja Vu / Dec '87 / Jazz Music / Music Collection International.

JOHNNY CASH COLLECTION (PICKWICK).
Tracks: Folsom Prison blues / Country boy / Doin' my time / Cold cold heart / Sugar time / Wide open road / I walk the line / There you go / Rock Island line / Wreck of the old '97 / Cry cry cry / Big river / I can't help it / Don't make me go / Hey porter / New Mexico / Mean eyed cat / You win again / Life goes on / I could never be ashamed of you.
■ MC Set . . . . PDC 005
Pickwick / Dec '79.
■ MC Set . . . . PDC 033
Pickwick / Jul '80.
MC Set . . . . DTOL 10001
Ditto / Jul '82 / Pickwick Records.

JOHNNY CASH RECORDINGS (1954 - 1957).
Tracks: Cry cry cry / Luther played the boogie / Folsom Prison blues / So doggone lonesome / Mean eyed cat / Wide open road / Two timin' woman / There you go / I walk the line / Country boy / Train of love / Get rhythm / Hey, porter / Belshazar / If the good Lord's willing / Wreck of the old '97 / You tell me / Oh lonesome me / Big river / Doin' my time / Rock Island line / Don't make me go / Home of the blues / Straight A's in love / Come in stranger / Blue train / Next in line / Hey good lookin' / Life goes on / Katy too / Thanks a lot.
■ CD . . . . CDCHARLY 146
Charly / Oct '88 / Charly.

JOHNNY CASH SHOW.
Tracks: Not Advised.
■ LP . . . . CBS 64089
CBS / Dec '70.

JOHNNY CASH'S TOP HITS (Cash, Johnny & The Tennessee Two).
Tracks: Cry cry cry / Luther played the boogie / Folsom Prison blues / So doggone lonesome / Mean eyed cat / Wide open road / Two timin' woman / There you go / I walk the line / Country boy / Train of love / Get rhythm / Hey, porter!.
LP . . . . SUN 1015
Sun / Aug '88 / Charly / Swift.

LADY.
Tracks: Kate / Oney / Any ole wind that blows / Lady came from Baltimore, The / Ragged old flag / My old Kentucky home / Sold out of flag poles / Last gunfighter ballad, The / Lady / After the ball / I would like to see you again / Gone girl / I will rock and roll with you / Ghost riders in the sky.
LP . . . . PMP 1004
MC . . . . PMPK 1004
Premier (Sony) / Feb '87 / Sony / Pinnacle.

LADY.
Tracks: Lady / Hit the road and go.
■ 7" . . . . CBS 5564
CBS / Aug '77.

LADY CAME FROM BALTIMORE.
Tracks: Lady came from Baltimore / Lonesome to the bone.
■ 7" . . . . CBS 2900
CBS / Jan '75.

LAST GUNFIGHTER BALLAD, THE.
Tracks: Not Advised.
MC 40 81566
CBS / Feb '77 / Sony.

LIL' BIT OF GOLD: JOHNNY CASH.
Tracks: I walk the line / Folsom Prison blues / Guess things happen that way / Ballad of a teenage queen.
■ CD Single . . . . R 373002
Rhino (USA) / May '88 / WEA.

LIVE IN LONDON: JOHNNY CASH.
Tracks: Ring of fire / Fulsom Prison blues / Forty shades of green / Baron / If I were a carpenter / Jackson / I walk the line / Don't take your guns to town / Big river / Riders in the sky / Will the circle be unbroken / Orange blossom special.
VHS . . . . BBCV 4043
BBC Video / '87 / Sony / Gold & Sons / Terry Blood Dist.

LOOK AT THEM BEANS.
Tracks: Texas 1947 / What have you got planned tonight, Diana / Look at them beans / No charge / I hardly ever sing beer drinking songs / Down the road I go / I never met a man like you before / All around cowboy / Gone / Down at drippin' springs.

■ DELETED C 9

LP. 81012
CBS / '75 / Sony.

MAN IN BLACK.

Tracks: Not Advised.
■ **LP.** . . . . **CBS 64331**
CBS / Sep '71.

MAN IN BLACK VOL.1, THE.

Tracks: Wide open road / You're my baby / My treasure x2 / Hey porter / Folsom Prison blues / Wide open road (2) / My two timin' woman / Hey porter (2) / Cry cry cry / Port of lonely hearts / I couldn't keep from crying / New Mexico / Folsom Prison blues (2) / So doggone lonesome / Mean eyed cat / Luther played the boogie / Rock 'n' roll Ruby / I walk the line / Brakeman's blues / Get rhythm / Get rhythm (2) / I walk the line (2) / Train of love x2 / There you go / One more ride / I love you because / Goodbye little darling / I love you because (2) / Straight A's in love / Don't make me go / Next in line / Don't make me go x2 / Home of the blues / Give my love to Rose / Give my love to Rose (2) / Home of the blues (2) / Rock Island line / Wreck of the old 97 / Belshazar / Country boy / Leave that junk alone / Doin' my time / If the good Lord's willing / I heard that lonesome whistle blow / I was there when it happened / Remember me / Big river / Ballad of a teenage queen / Goodnight Irene / Ballad of a teenage queen (2) / Come in stranger / Guess things happen that way / Come in stranger (2) / Sugartime / Born to lose / You're the nearest thing to heaven / Sugartime (2) / Story of a broken heart / Always alone / Always alone (2) / Story of a broken heart (false starts) / You tell me / Life goes on / You win again / I could never be ashamed of you / Hey good lookin' / I can't help it / Cold, cold heart / Blue train / Katy too / Ways of a woman in love, The / Fools hall of fame / Ways of a woman in love, The (2) / Thanks a lot / It's just about time / I forgot to remember to forget / I just thought you'd like to know / It's just about time (2) / Down the street to 301 / Oh what a dream / I'll remember you / Drink to me / What do I care / Suppertime / It was Jesus / Oh, what a dream (2) / I'll remember you (2) / Mama's baby / Troubador, The / Run softly blue river / All over again / That's all over / Frankie's man / Johnnie / Fools hall of fame (2) / Walkin' the blues / Lead me father / That's enough / I still miss someone / Pickin' time / Don't take your guns to town / I'd rather die young / Shepherd of my heart, The / Cold shoulder.
CD Set . . . . **BCD 15517**
Bear Family / Sep '90 / Rollercoaster Records / Swift / Direct Distribution.

MAN IN BLACK VOL.2, THE (1959-1962).

Tracks: Snow in his hair / I saw a man / Lead me gently home / Are all the children in / Swing low, sweet chariot / I call him / Old account, The / He'll be a friend / These things shall pass / It could be you / God will / Great speckled bird, The / Were you there / He'll understand and say well done / God has my fortune laid away / When I've learned / I got shoes / Let the lower lights be burning / If we never meet again / When I take my vacation in heaven / When he reached down his hand for me / Taller than trees / I won't have to cross Jordan alone / My god is real / These hands / Peace in the valley / Day in the Grand Canyon, A / I'll remember you / I got stripes / You dreamer you / Five feet high and rising / Rebel Johnny Yuma , The / Lorena / Second honeymoon / Fable of Willie Brown, The / Smiling Bill McCall / Johnny Yuma theme / Man on the hill, The / Hank and Joe and me / Caretaker, The / Clementine / I want to go home / Old Apache squaw / Don't step on mother's roses / My grandfather's clock / I couldn't keep from crying / My shoes keep walking back to you / I will miss you when you go / I feel better all over / Bandana / Wabash blues / Viel zu spat / Woistzuhause, mama / Heartbeat / Hello again / Tall man / Girl in Saskatoon / Locomotive man / Losing kind, The / Five minutes to live / Forty shades of green / Big battle, The / Blues for two / Jeri and Nina's melody / Why do you punish me / Just one more / Seasons of my heart / Honky tonk girl / I'm so lonesome I could cry / Time changes everything / I'd just be fool enough / Transfusion blues / Lovin' locomotive man / Mr. Lonesome / Folsom Prison blues / I walk the line (Take 6-slow, take 9-fast.) / Hey porter / I forgot more than you'll ever know about her / There's a mother always waiting / Tennessee flat top box / Sing it pretty Sue / Little at a time, A / So do I / Bonanza / Shamrock doesn't grow in California / I'm free from the chain gang now / Delia's gone / Lost on the desert / Accidentally on purpose / You remember me / In the jailhouse now / Let me down easy / In them cottonfields back home / You won't have to go far / No one will ever know / Danger zone, The / I'll be all smiles tonight / Send a picture of mother / Hardin wouldn't run / Blue bandana / So doggone lonesome / Johnny Reb.
CD Set . . . . **BCD 15562**
Bear Family / Aug '91 / Rollercoaster Records / Swift / Direct Distribution.

MAN, THE WORLD, HIS MUSIC, THE.

Tracks: Born to lose / Story of a broken heart / Two timin' woman / Goodbye little darling / Port of lonely hearts / I forgot to remember to forget / Goodnight Irene / My treasure / I heard that lonesome whistle blow / Mean eyed cat / New Mexico / Sugartime / Life goes on / Wreck of the old 97 / Belshazah / You're my baby / Fools hall of fame / Blue train / Country boy / Wide open road / I just thought you'd like to know / Down the street to 301.
LP. **6641008**
Sun / '65 / Charly / Swift.

MORE OF OLD GOLDEN THROAT.

Tracks: Bottom of a mountain / You beat all I ever saw / Put the sugar to bed / Girl from Saskatoon / Time and time again / Honky tonk gal / Locomotive man / Second honeymoon / I'll remember you / Lorena / Roll call / Blues for two / Jerry and Nina's melody / Bandana / Wabash blues.
LP. . . . . **BFX 15073**
Bear Family / Sep '82 / Rollercoaster Records / Swift / Direct Distribution.

MYSTERY OF LIFE, THE.

Tracks: Mystery of life, The / Greatest cowboy of them all, The / I'm an easy rider / Hey porter / Beans for breakfast / Goin' by the book / Wanted man / I'll go somewhere and sing my somgs again / Hobo song, The / Angel and the badman.
CD **8480512**
LP. **8480511**
MC **8480514**
Mercury / Feb '91 / PolyGram.

MYSTERY OF LIFE, THE.

Tracks: Mystery of Life, The.
7" . . . . **MER 340**
■ **CD Single** . . . . **MERCD 340**
Mercury / Feb '91.

NIGHT HANK WILLIAMS CAME TO TOWN, THE.

Tracks: Night Hank Williams came to town, The.
7" . . . . **MER 225**
Mercury / Aug '87 / PolyGram.

OLD GOLDEN THROAT (BEAR FAMILY).

Tracks: I got stripes / Certain kinda hurtin', A / Little at a time, A / All over again / Still in town / Smiling Bill McCall / Wind changes, The / Sons of Katie Elder, The / Dark as a dungeon / Tennessee flat top box / Matador, The / Send a picture of mother / You dreamer you / Red Velvet.
LP. . . . . **BFX 15072**
Bear Family / Sep '82 / Rollercoaster Records / Swift / Direct Distribution.

OLD GOLDEN THROAT (CHARLY & CBS).

Tracks: Big river / Luther's boogie / You are my baby / Folsom Prison blues / Hey porter / Next in line / Oh lonesome me / Belshazar / Get rhythm / Rock Island line / Country boy / Train of love / I walk the line / Katy too / Ballad of a teenage queen / Mean eyed cat.
■ **LP.** . . . . **CBS 63316**
CBS / Jul '68.
■ **LP.** . . . . **CR 30005**
Charly / Oct '75 / Charly.

ONE PIECE AT A TIME.

Tracks: Let there be country / One piece at a time / In a young girl's mind / Mountain lady / Michigan city howdy do / Sold out of flagpoles / Committed to Parkview / Daughter of the railroad man / Love has lost again / Go on blues.
■ **LP.** . . . . **CBS 81416**
CBS / Jul '76.
MC . . . . **HSC 3179**
Hallmark / Sep '85 / Pickwick Records.
■ **LP.** . . . . **SHM 3179**
Hallmark / Sep '85.

ONE PIECE AT A TIME.

Tracks: One piece at a time.
■ **7"** . . . . **CBS 4087**
CBS / Jul '76.

ORIGINAL GOLDEN HITS, VOL. 1 (Cash, Johnny & The Tennessee Two).

Tracks: Folosom Prison blues / Hey porter / So doggone lonesome / There you go / Next in line / Cry cry cry / I walk the line / Don't make me go / Train of love / Home of the blues / Get rhythm.
LP. **6467001**
Sun / Aug '91 / Charly / Swift.

ORIGINAL GOLDEN HITS, VOL. 2 (Cash, Johnny & The Tennessee Two).

Tracks: Ballard of a teen-age queen / Come in stranger / Ways of a woman in love / You're the nearest thing to heaven / I just thought you'd like to know / Give my love to Rose / Guess things happen that way / Just about time / Luther's boogie / Thanks a lot / Big river.
LP. **6467007**
Sun / '69 / Charly / Swift.

ORIGINAL HITS.

Tracks: Not Advised.
CD **2430712**
LP. **2230712**
MC **2130712**
Big Country / May '88.

ORIGINAL JOHNNY CASH, THE.

Tracks: Don't make me go / Next in line / Home of the blues / Give my love to Rose / Guess things happen that way / Come in stranger / Ways of a woman in love, The / You're the nearest thing to heaven / I just thought you'd like to know / It's just about time / You tell me / Goodbye little darling / Story of a broken heart, The / Down the street to 301 / Blue train / Born to lose.
LP. . . . . **CR 30113**
■ **MC** . . . . **TCCR 30113**
Charly / Sep '86 / Charly.

PORTRAIT IN MUSIC, A.

Tracks: Just about time / Straight A's in love / I just thought you'd like to know / You're the nearest thing to heaven / Rock Island line / Cold cold heart / Folsom Prison blues / Hey good lookin' / I love you because / Big river / Ballad of a teenage queen / Goodbye little darling / I could never be ashamed of you / Next in line / Port of lonely hearts / Sugar-time / There you go / Two timin' woman.
LP. . . . . **CBR 1015**
MC . . . . **KCBR 1015**
Premier (Sony) / May '85 / Sony / Pinnacle.

RAGGED OLD FLAG.

Tracks: Ragged old flag / Don't go near the water / All I do is drive / Southern comfort / King of the hill / Pie in the sky / Lonesome to the bone / While I've got it in mind / Good morning friend / I'm a worried man / Please don't let me out / What on earth (Will you do for heaven's sake).
LP. **80113**
CBS / '74 / Sony.

RAINBOW.

Tracks: I'm leaving now / Here comes that rainbow again / They're all the same to me / Easy street / Have you ever seen the rain / You beat all I ever saw / Unwed fathers / Love me like you used to / Casey's last ride / Borderline.
LP. . . . . **CBS 26689**
■ **MC** . . . . **.40 26689**
CBS / Dec '85.

RAMBLER, THE.

Tracks: Not Advised.
MC . . . . **.40 82156**
CBS / Aug '77 / Sony.

REPLAY ON JOHNNY CASH.

Tracks: Not Advised.
LP. . . . . **FEDB 5015**
MC . . . . **FEDC 5015**
Sierra / Nov '88.

RIDERS IN THE SKY.

Tracks: Riders in the sky / I'm gonna sit on my porch.
■ **7"** . . . . **CBS 7852**
CBS / Oct '79.

RIDING THE RAILS.

Tracks: Not Advised.
MC Set . . . . **.40 88153**
CBS / '79 / Sony.

RIDING THE RAILS.

Tracks: Not Advised.
■ **VHS** . . . . **HEN 2286**
Hendring Video / Nov '90.

RING OF FIRE.

Tracks: Ring of fire / I'd still be there / What do I care / I still miss someone / Forty shades of green / Were you there / Rebel / Johnny Yuma / Bonanza / Big battle, The / Remember the Alamo / Tennessee flat top box / Peace in the valley.
LP. . . . . **SHM 988**
■ **MC** . . . . **HSC 367**
Hallmark / Apr '79.

ROCK ISLAND LINE.

Tracks: Belshazar / If the good Lord's willing / Wreck of the old '97 / You tell me / Oh lonesome me / Big river / Doin' my time / Rock Island line / Home of the blues / Straight A's in love / Come in stranger / Blue train / Next in line / Hey good lookin' / Life goes on / Katy too.
LP. . . . . **SUN 1047**
Sun / Sep '88 / Charly / Swift.

ROCKABILLY BLUES.

Tracks: Cold lonesome morning / Without love / W.O.-M.A.N. / Cowboy who started the fight, The / Twentieth century is almost over, The / Rockabilly blues (Texas 1955) / Last time, The / She's a go-er / It ain't nothing new babe / One way rider.
LP. . . . . **CBS 84607**
CBS / Dec '80 / Sony.
■ **MC** . . . . **.40 84607**
CBS / Dec '80.

SILVER.

Tracks: L and N don't stop here anymore, The / Lonesome to the bone / Bull rider / I'll say it's true / Riders in the sky / Cocaine blues / Muddy Waters / West Canterbury subdivision blues / Lately I been leanin' toward the blues / I'm gonna sit on the porch & pick on my old ..
LP. . . . . **CBS 83757**
CBS / Sep '79 / Sony.
■ **MC** . . . . **.40 83757**
CBS / Sep '79.

SINGS THE BALLADS OF THE TRUE WEST.

Tracks: Hiawatha's vision / Road to Kaintuck, the / Shifting whispering sands, The / Ballad of Boot Hill, The / I ride an old paint / Hardin' wouldn't run / Mr. Garfield / Streets of Laredo, The / Johnny Reb / Letter from home, A.
LP. . . . . **BPG 62538**
CBS / '65 / Sony.

SINGS THE BALLADS OF THE TRUE WEST, VOL. 2.

Tracks: Bury me not on the Lone Prairie / Mean as hell / Sam Hall / 25 minutes to go / Blizzard, The / Sweet

C 10 ■ DELETED

Betsy from Pike / Green grow the lilacs / Stampede / Shifting whispering sands, The / Reflections.
LP. . . . . BPG 62591
CBS / '66 / Sony.

STAR PORTRAIT: JOHNNY CASH.
Tracks: Boy named Sue, A / Orange blossom special / Wildwood flower / Understand your man / Daddy sang bass / Wreck of the old '97 / Ring of fire / Bonanza / In them old cottonfields back home / If I were a carpenter / Long black veil / Forty shades of green / Folsom Prison blues / Long-legged guitar pickin' man / Five feet high and rising / Big river / Don't take your guns to town / Sunday morning coming down / I walk the line / Wabash cannon ball / Tennessee flat-top box / What is truth / Man in black / Singin' in Vietnam talkin' blues.
■ Double LP . . . . CBS 67201
CBS / Oct '72.
■ MC 4067201
CBS / '78 / Sony.

STILL IN TOWN.
Tracks: Stil in town / Matador, The.
7" . . . . AAG 173
CBS / '63 / Sony.

STORY SONGS OF THE TRAINS AND RIVERS (Cash, Johnny & The Tennessee Two).
Tracks: Hey porter / Train of love / Blue train / I heard that lonesome whistle blow / Port of lonely hearts / Wreck of the old 97 / Rock Island line / Big river / Wide open road / Down the street to 301 / Life goes on.
LP. 6467012
Sun / '69 / Charly / Swift.

SUN SOUNDS SPECIAL.
Tracks: Cry cry cry / I'm so doggone lonesome / There you go / I heard that lonesome whistle blow / Doin' my time / If the good Lord's willing / Wide open road / Two timin' woman / Cold cold heart / Hey good lookin' / I could never be ashamed of you / Always alone / Thanks a lot / I forgot to remember to forget / New Mexico / I couldn't keep from crying.
■ LP. . . . . CR 30153
Charly / '78 / Charly.

SUN YEARS, THE.
Tracks: Wide open road / You're my baby / Folsom Prison blues / Two timin' woman / Goodnight Irene / Port of lonely hearts / My treasure / Cry cry cry / Hey porter / Luther played the boogie / So doggone lonesome / Mean-eyed cat / I couldn't keep from crying / New Mexico / Rock 'n' roll Ruby / Get rhythm / I walk the line / Train of love / There you go / One more ride / Goodbye little darling / I love you because / Straight A's in love / Don't make me go / Next in line / Give my love to Rose / Home of the blues / Wreck of the old '97 / Rock Island line / Belshazar / Leave that junk alone / Country boy / Doin' my time / If the good Lord's willing / I heard that lonesome whistle blow / Remember me / I was there when it happened / Come in stranger / Big river / Ballad of a teenage queen / Oh lonesome me / Guess things happen that way / You're the nearest thing to Heaven / Sugartime / Born to lose / Always alone / Story of a broken heart, The / You tell me / Life goes on / You win again / I could never be ashamed of you / Cold cold heart / Hey good lookin' / I can't help it / Blue train / Katy too / Ways of a woman in love, The / Thanks a lot / It's just about time / I just thought you'd like to know / I forgot to remember to forget / Down the street to 301.
LP Set . . . . SUN BOX 103
Sun / '84 / Charly / Swift.

SURVIVORS, THE (Cash, Johnny/Jerry Lee Lewis/Carl Perkins).
Tracks: Get rhythm / I forgot to remember to forget / Goin' down the road feeling bad / That silver-haired daddy of mine / Matchbox / I'll fly away / Whole lotta shakin' goin' on / Rockin' my life away / Blue suede shoes / There will be peace in the valley for me / Will the circle be unbroken? / I saw the light.
LP. . . . . CBS 85609
MC 40 85609
CBS / May '82 / Sony.
LP. . . . . SHM 3180
■ MC . . . . HSC 3180
Hallmark / Sep '85.

TALL MAN.
Tracks: Tall man / Foolish questions (Previously unissued) / Pick a bale of cotton / I tremble for you (Previously unissued) / Besser so, Jenny Joe / My old faded rose (Previously unissued) / Kleine Rosmarie / Rodeo hand (Previously unissued) / Sound of laughter, The (Previously unissued) / Hammer and nails / Engine 143 / On the line.
LP. . . . . BFX 15033
Bear Family / Sep '84 / Rollercoaster Records / Swift / Direct Distribution.

THERE AIN'T NO GOOD CHAIN GANG (Cash, Johnny & Waylon Jennings).
Tracks: There ain't no good chain gang / I wish I was crazy again.
■ 7" . . . . CBS 6401
CBS / Jun '78.

THING CALLED LOVE, A.
Tracks: Kate / Melva's wine / Thing called love / I promise you / Papa was a good man / Tear stained letter / Mississippi sand / Daddy / Arkansas lovin' man / Miracle man.
■ LP. . . . . CBS 64898
CBS / May '72.
LP. . . . . CBS 32698
CBS / Dec '85 / Sony.

THING CALLED LOVE, A.
Tracks: Thing called love, A.
■ 7" . . . . CBS 7797
CBS / Jul '72.

THING CALLED LOVE, A (OLD GOLD).
Tracks: Thing called love, A / One piece at a time.
■ 7" . . . . OG 9177
Old Gold / Jul '82.

UNISSUED JOHNNY CASH, THE.
Tracks: Mama's baby / Fool's hall of fame / Walking the blues / Cold shoulder / Viel zu spat / Wo ist zu hause, mama / Fable of Willie Brown, The / Losing kind of love / So do I / Shamrock doesn't grow in California / Danger zone / I'll be all smiles tonight.
LP. . . . . BFX 15016
Bear Family / Sep '84 / Rollercoaster Records / Swift / Direct Distribution.

UP THROUGH THE YEARS '1955 - 1957'.
Tracks: Cry cry cry / Hey Porter / Folsom Prison blues / Luther played the boogie / So doggone lonesome / I walk the line / Get rhythm / Train of love / There you go / Goodbye little darling / I love you because / Straight A's in love / Next in line / Don't make me go / Home of the blues / Give my love to Rose / Rock Island line / Wreck of the old '97 / Ballad of a teenage queen / Big river / Guess things happen that way / Come in stranger / You're the nearest thing to heaven / Blue train.
CD . . . . BCD 15247
Bear Family / Nov '86 / Rollercoaster Records / Swift / Direct Distribution.

VERY BEST OF JOHNNY CASH.
Tracks: What is truth / All over again / I'm so lonesome I could cry / Understand your man / Daddy sang bass / Busted / Let there be country / Ghost riders in the sky / Thing called love, A / It ain't me babe / Don't take your guns to town / Wreck of the old '97 / Ring of fire / If I were a carpenter / Green green grass of home / Folsom Prison blues.
LP. . . . . SHM 3146
MC . . . . HSC 3146
Hallmark / Jul '84 / Pickwick Records.

WATER FROM THE WELLS OF HOME (Cash, Johnny & Friends).
Tracks: As long as I live / Ballad of a teenage queen / Last of the drifters / Where did we go right / Call me the breeze / That ole wheel / Sweeter than the flowers / Ballad of Robb MacDunn / New moon over Jamaica.
■ MC 834778-4
Mercury / Oct '88.
■ LP. 834778-1
Mercury / Oct '88.
■ CD 834778-2
Mercury / Oct '88.

WELCOME FRIEND.
Tracks: Man in black / No earthly good / Papa was a good man / Song to Mamma, A / That silver haired Daddy of mine / Daddy / Daddy sang bass / Good earth, The / Good morning friend / Best friend / Thing called love, A / Jesus was a carpenter / Were you there? / God shine / Welcome back Jesus / Great speckled bird, The.
LP. . . . . WRD 3008
MC . . . . TCWR 3008
Word (UK) / May '85 / Word Records (UK) / Sony.

WHAT IS TRUTH?.
Tracks: What is truth?.
■ 7" . . . . CBS 4934
CBS / May '70.

WORLD OF JOHNNY CASH, THE.
Tracks: I still miss someone / Pickin' time / My shoes keep walking back to you / I want ot go home / I feel better all over / I'm so lonesome I could cry / Supper time in them old cottonfields back home / Delia's gone / One more ride / Accidentally on purpose / In the jailhouse now / I forgot more than you'll ever know / Casy Jones / Frankie's man Johnny / Legend of John Henry's hammer, The / When Papa played the dobro / Busted / Sing it pretty, Sue / Waiting for a train.
■ LP. . . . . CBS 66237
CBS / Aug '70.
MC 40 66237
CBS / '74 / Sony.

Cash, Rosanne

Born in 1955 in Memphis, Tennessee, this successful pop/country singer is one of four daughters from Johnny Cash's first marriage. She worked for CBS records in London, studied drama and signed to Arista Records in Germany in 1977, then switched to American CBS. Her album *Right Or Wrong*, in 1979 included a hit duet with Bobby Bare on *No Memories Hangin' Round*. She married singer/songwriter Rodney Crowell that year and he produced her second album *Seven Year Ache*, in 1981. This including two number one country singles, *My Baby Thinks She's A Train*, and the album's title track. *Somewhere In The Stars*, in 1982 was followed by the biographical concept album *Rhythm And Romance*, in 1985. *King's Record Shop* was recorded in 1987 and was named after a shop in Louisville, Kentucky. (Donald Clarke)

AIN'T NO MONEY.
Tracks: Ain't no money / Feeling.
■ 7" . . . . ARO 286
Ariola / Sep '82.

I DON'T KNOW WHY.
Tracks: I don't know why / You don't want me / What you gonna do about it.
7" . . . . A 6808
CBS / Feb '86 / Sony.

I LOVE COUNTRY.
Tracks: Not Advised.
LP. 4510041
■ MC 4510044
CBS / '88.

INTERIORS.
Tracks: On the inside / Dance with the tiger / On the surface / Real woman / This world / What we really want / Mirror image / Land of nightmares / I want a cure / Paralyzed.
CD 4673312
LP. 4673311
MC 4673314
CBS / Nov '90 / Sony.

KING'S RECORD SHOP.
Tracks: Rosie strikes back / Way we make a broken heart, The / If you change your mind / Real me, The / Somewhere sometime / Runaway train / Tennessee flat top box / I don't have to crawl / Green, yellow and red / Why don't you quit leaving me alone.
LP. 4509161
■ MC 4509164
CBS / Aug '87.

RETROSPECTIVE 1979-1989.
Tracks: Seven year ache / Hold on / I don't want to spoil the party / My baby think's he's a train / Tennessee flat top box / My baby thinks he's a train / I don't wanna spoil the party / Blue moon with heartache / No memories hangin' around / Black and white.
LP. 4633281
■ MC 4633284
CBS / Mar '89 / Sony.
■ CD 4633282
CBS / Mar '89.
CD 463328-2
MC 463328-4
Columbia / Jun '93 / Sony.

RETROSPECTIVE 1979-89.
Tracks: Seven year ache / Hold on / Blue moon with heartache / No memories hangin' around / I don't know why you don't want me / I wonder / Never be you / Way we make a broken heart, The / Tennessee flat top box / Black & white.

RHYTHM AND ROMANCE.
Tracks: Hold on / I don't know why you don't want me / Never be you / Second to no one / Halfway house / Pink bedroom / Never alone / My old man / Never gonna hurt / Closing time.
LP. . . . . CBS 26366
■ MC 40 26366
CBS / Mar '86.

RIGHT OR WRONG.
Tracks: Right or wrong / Take me, take me / Man smart, woman smarter / This has happened before / Anybody's darlin' (anything but me) / No memories hangin' round / Couldn't do nothin' right / Seeing's believing / Big river / Not a second time.
LP. . . . . ARL 5059
MC . . . . ARLC 5059
Ariola / '80 / BMG.

SEVEN YEAR ACHE.
Tracks: Seven year ache / Raining.
■ 7" . . . . ARO 263
Ariola / Jul '81.

SOMEWHERE IN THE STARS.
Tracks: Ain't no money / Down on love / I wonder / Oh yes I can / Looking for a corner / It hasn't happened yet / That's how I got to Memphis / Third rate romance / I look for love / Somewhere in the stars.
■ LP. 204 848
Chrysalis / '83.

TAKE ME, TAKE ME.
Tracks: Take me, take me / Big river.
■ 7" . . . . ARO 239
Ariola / Jul '80.

WHEEL, THE.
Tracks: Wheel, The / Seventh avenue / Change partners / Sleeping in Paris / You won't let me in / From the ashes / Truth about you, The / Tears falling down / Roses in the fire / Fire of the newly alive / If there's a God on my side.
CD 472977 2
MC 472977 4
Columbia / May '93 / Sony.

Cash, Tommy

25TH ANNIVERSARY ALBUM.
Tracks: Not Advised.

■ CD . . . . CDCOT 103
Cottage / Jun '92.

Cassady, Linda

CB WIDOW.
Tracks: CB widow / Do you still want what's left of me.
7" . . . . AMGO 006
Amigo / Nov '81 / C.M. Distribution / Wellard Dist. /
Cadillac Music / C.M. Distribution.

DUSTY RAVEN.
Tracks: Dusty raven.
7" . . . . AMGO 001
Amigo / Nov '81 / C.M. Distribution / Wellard Dist. /
Cadillac Music / C.M. Distribution.

INTRODUCING LINDA CASSADY.
Tracks: Not Advised.
LP . . . . AMOLP 002
Amigo / Nov '81 / C.M. Distribution / Wellard Dist. /
Cadillac Music / C.M. Distribution.

Castille, Hadley J.

**GOING BACK TO LOUISIANA (Castille, Had-
ley J. & the Cajun Grass Band).**
Tracks: Not Advised.
LP 6057
Swallow (USA) / Swift / Wellard Dist.
MC . . . . 6057 TC
N/A / '87.

Central Park Sheiks

HONEYSUCKLE ROSE.
Tracks: Not Advised.
LP . . . . FF 026
Flying Fish (USA) / Mar '89 / Cadillac Music / Roots
Records / Projection / C.M. Distribution / Direct Distri-
bution / Jazz Music / Duncans / A.D.A Distribution.

Chalker, Bryan

CROSS TRACKIN'.
Tracks: Not Advised.
■ LP . . . . GES 5013
Emerald / '78.

EARLY DAYS.
Tracks: Not Advised.
LP . . . . SFA 020
Sweet Folk & Country / Nov '76 / Wellard Dist.

**I CAN'T READ THE THOUGHTS IN YOUR
MIND.**
Tracks: I can't read the thoughts in your mind / Smokin'
talkin' blues.
7" . . . . AR 004
Acuff-Rose / Aug '83.

SIMPLE GIFTS.
Tracks: Simple gifts / Wayward wind.
■ 7" . . . . .MD 1211
Emerald / Nov '78.

SONGS AND BALLADS.
Tracks: Going from cotton fields / Molly darling / Great
Titanic, The / Give me your love / When I swim the
Golden river / Rosewood casket / Wreck on the high-
way / Long black veil / Mary on the wild moore /
Legend of the Irish rebel / Ballad of the blue tail fly /
Blue Ridge Mountain blues.
LP . . . . SFA 025
Sweet Folk All / May '81 / Cadillac Music / Projection /
C.M. Distribution / Wellard Dist. / Impetus Records.

Chalker, Curly

NASHVILLE SUNDOWN.
Tracks: Not Advised.
■ LP . . . . SNTF 694
Sonet / Apr '85.
LP . . . . GNPS 2099
GNP Crescendo / '88 / Swift / Silva Screen / Flexitron
Ltd.

Chapman, Marshall

Born in Spartanburg, North Carolina in 1949, a
female singer, songwriter and guitarist in
country rock whose work falls between stools in
the marketplace. She recorded for Epic, which
dropped her for lack of sales; some of her songs
were too grown up for country radio. Jessi
Colter, Tompall Glaser, Crystal Gayle and
others covered her songs; she recorded for
Rounder in 1981 and released a strong country
boogie set on her own Tall Girl records in 1987.
(Donald Clarke)

TAKE IT ON HOME.
Tracks: Not Advised.
LP . . . . ROUNDER 3069
MC . . . . .ROUNDER 3069C
Rounder / Aug '88 / Projection / Roots Records / Swift /
C.M. Distribution / Topic Records / Jazz Music / Hot
Shot / A.D.A Distribution / Direct Distribution.

Charles, Ray

This American singer, pianist, arranger and
songwriter is one of the most important artists
in the post-war history of black music. Born Ray
Charles Robinson in Georgia in 1932, he was
blinded at the age of six and rendered an orphan while in his early teens. After moving to
Seattle, Washington, he spent the early 50's
playing in a trio which based its style heavily on
that of Nat King Cole. It was about this time that
he dropped his surname, in order to avoid confusion with star boxer Sugar Ray Robinson.
During the mid to late 50's Charles developed
his own highly distinctive style, fusing rhythm
and blues, gospel and jazz, and helping to
create soul music, a genre that exploded into
fashion in the 60's. Charles' first American Top
Forty hit was 1957's Swanee River Rock, which
reached No 34. His big breakthrough was 1959's
self-penned What'd I Say?, a frantic call-and-
response single. Charles' next milestone record
was a 1960 rendition of a 1930 Hoagy Carmi-
chael number: Georgia On My Mind, a tribute to
Ray's own birthplace, which gave him his first US
No 1 and his first UK hit. A second American
chart-topper came in '61 with another classic,
the highly catchy Hit The Road, Jack, a No 6 hit
in Britain. All these achievements, though, were
dwarfed by the red-hot Ray Charles' 1962 exploits. I Can't Stop Loving You, a country ballad
written by fellow hitmaker Don Gibson, was
reworked by Charles and became his biggest-
ever single on both sides of the Atlantic and his
only single to go to No 1 in both America and
Britain. It was featured on his seminal, highly
influential LP Modern Sounds In Country And
Western Music, which further enhanced his status as a bridge between white country music
and black R & B style. Its success inspired a
Volume 2 follow-up the following year. By the
mid-60's he had chalked up two more transatlantic Top Ten singles - You Don't Know Me
and Take These Chains From My Heart - plus
another three US Top Tenners with You Are My
Sunshine, Busted and Cryin' Time. By this time
he had lost the raw edge that had been so much
a part of his earlier work and was concentrating
on ballads. His late 70's and early 80's recordings did not break new ground but were nonetheless competent restatements of his eclectic
approach that, 20 years earlier, had opened up
new possibilities for countless future stars. (Bob
MacDonald)

**14 ORIGINAL GREATEST HITS:RAY
CHARLES.**
Tracks: Not Advised.
LP . . . . .K 5011
King (USA) / Mar '88 / Charly.

16 GREATEST HITS.
Tracks: What'd I say / Busted / Here we go again / I
can't stop loving you / That lucky old sun / Let's go get
stoned / Hide nor hair / Georgia on my mind / Unchain
my heart / I got a woman / Hit the road Jack / Eleanor
Rigby / Don't set me free / America the beautiful.
CD 264823 2
MC 264823 4
Mainline (2) / Jan '90.

16 ORIGINAL HITS: RAY CHARLES.
Tracks: Not Advised.
MC . . . . .MC 1631
Timeless Treasures / Sep '87 / Terry Blood Dist.

1950.
Tracks: Not Advised.
LP 522 011
Vogue / '84 / BMG.

20 GOLDEN PIECES: RAY CHARLES.
Tracks: Alone in the city / Can anyone ask for more? /
Rockin' chair blues / Let's have a ball / How long how
long blues / Sentimental blues, A / You always miss the
water (when the well runs dry) / I've had my fun / Sitting
on top of the world / Ain't that fine? / Don't put all your
dreams in one basket / Ray Charles blues / Honey
honey / She's on the ball / Baby won't you please come
home? / If I give you my love / This love of mine / Can't
you see me, darling? / Someday / I'm going down to the
river.
LP . . . . BDL 2012
Bulldog Records / Jul '82 / President Records / Jazz
Music / Wellard Dist. / TKO Records Ltd.

20 GREATEST HITS: RAY CHARLES.
Tracks: Not Advised.
LP . . . . B 90108
MC . . . . MB 990108
Masters (Holland) / Jan '87.

25TH ANNIVERSARY IN SHOW BUSINESS.
Tracks: Not Advised.
■ LP . . . . K 60014
Atlantic / '87 / WEA.

AIN'T IT SO.
Tracks: Some enchanted evening / Blues in the night /
Just because / What'll I do / One of these days / Love
me or set me free / Drift away / Love me tonight.
■ LP . . . . SHL 8537
London / '79.

ALONE IN THE CITY.
Tracks: Not Advised.
CD . . . . RMB 75009
MC . . . . RMB 45009
Remember / Jan '92 / Midland Records / Taylors.

BEST OF RAY CHARLES, THE.
Tracks: Not Advised.
CD .756781368-2
WEA / Mar '93 / WEA.

BLUES IS MY MIDDLE NAME.
Tracks: Not Advised.
CD . . . . ONN 37
Object Enterprises / May '89 / Gold & Sons / Terry
Blood Dist. / Midland Records.

BROTHER RAY.
Tracks: Compared to what / Anyway you want to / Don't
you love me anymore / Poor man's song / Now that
we've found each other / Ophelia / I can't change it /
Questions.
■ LP . . . . SH 8546
London / Jan '81.

BUSTED.
Tracks: Busted.
■ 7" . . . . POP 1221
H.M.V. / Oct '63.

BUSTED.
Tracks: Not Advised.
CD . . . . TL 1325
Traditional Line / Sep '92 / Charly.

C.C. RIDER.
Tracks: C.C. Rider / I wonder who's kissing her now /
Going down slow / Lovin' the girls / Kiss me baby / All
alone again / Sitting on top of the world / Tell me baby /
Baby let me hold your hand / Hey now / All to myself
alone / Walkin' and talkin'.
LP . . . . CBR 1018
MC . . . . KCBR 1018
Premier (Sony) / Jun '85 / Sony / Pinnacle.

CAN'T STOP LOVING YOU.
Tracks: Not Advised.
LP . . . . PLP 22
MC . . . . PMC 22
Platinum (W.Germany) / Oct '85.

CLASSIC YEARS, THE.
Tracks: Not Advised.
CD . . . . ESBCD 144
Essential / Jul '91 / BMG / Castle Communications /
Total.

COLLECTABLES, THE.
Tracks: Not Advised.
CD . . . . NCD 5149
K-Tel / '89 / I & B Records / C.M. Distribution /
Arabesque Ltd. / Mono Distributors (Jersey) Ltd. /
Prism Leisure PLC / PolyGram / Ross Records / Prism
Leisure PLC.

COLLECTION: RAY CHARLES (2).
Tracks: Yesterday / Your cheatin' heart / Georgia on my
mind / I can't stop loving you / Busted / Together again
/ Take these chains from my heart / Crying time / Half
as much / Here we go again / Born to lose / Eleanor
Rigby / You don't know me / Hit the road Jack / I gotta
woman (live) / What'd I say (live).
CD . . . . RCLD 101
LP . . . . RCLP 101
MC . . . . RCLC 101
Arcade / Mar '90 / Sony.

COLLECTION: RAY CHARLES (2) (CASTLE).
Tracks: Not Advised.
CD . . . . CCSCD 328
Castle Collector Series / Apr '92 / BMG / Pinnacle /
Castle Communications.

**COLLECTION: RAY CHARLES (20 GOLDEN
GREATS).**
Tracks: Georgia on my mind / What'd I say / Sitting on
top of the world / Ain't that fine / Can't you see darling /
Sentimental blues, A / If I give you my love / She's on
the ball / Ray Charles blues / How long / Come rain or
come shine / Alone in the city / Someday / This love of
mine / I'm going down to the river / You always miss
the water (when the well runs dry) / Baby won't you
please come home / Don't put all your dreams in one
basket / I've had my fun / Let's have a ball.
LP . . . . DVLP 2005
MC . . . . DVMC 2005
Deja Vu / Aug '85 / Jazz Music / Music Collection
International.
CD . . . . DVCD 2005
Deja Vu / Sep '87 / Jazz Music / Music Collection
International.

**COLLECTION: RAY CHARLES (CASTLE
COLLECTOR).**
Tracks: Not Advised.
CD . . . . CCSCD 241
Double LP . . . . CCSLP 241
MC . . . . CCSMC 241
Castle Collector Series / Mar '90 / BMG / Pinnacle /
Castle Communications.

■ DELETED

COLLECTION: RAY CHARLES (STAR JAZZ USA).
Tracks: Not Advised.
LP . . . . . SJAZZ 1
MC . . . . . SJAZZC 1
Star Jazz (USA) / Apr '86 / Charly.

COLLECTION: RAY CHARLES (THE LOVE SONGS).
Tracks: I wonder who's kissing her now / Here am I / Oh baby / I used to be so happy / Honey honey / Ego song, The / Hey now / Late in the evening blues / I live only for you / St. Pete's blues / I'm glad for your sake / I'm just a lonely boy / All night long / See see rider / All to myself alone / Blues is my middle name.
CD . . . . . DVCD 2123
Deja Vu / Jul '88 / Jazz Music / Music Collection International.
LP . . . . . DVLP 2123
MC . . . . . DVMC 2123
Deja Vu / Jun '88 / Jazz Music / Music Collection International.

COME LIVE WITH ME.
Tracks: Not Advised.
LP . . . . . SHU 8467
London-American / '74.

COMPARED TO WHAT.
Tracks: Compared to what / Now that found each other.
■ **7"** . . . . . HL 10579
London-American / Feb '81.

COUNTRY SIDE OF RAY CHARLES.
Tracks: Not Advised.
LP . . . . . ADAH 447
MC . . . . . ADAHC 447
Arcade Music Gala / Apr '86.

CRYIN' TIME.
Tracks: Cryin' time.
■ **7"** . . . . . POP 1502
H.M.V. / Feb '66.

DO I EVER CROSS YOUR MIND?.
Tracks: I had it all / Do I ever cross your mind / Woman sensuous woman / Then I'll be over you / Lay around and love on you / Love of my life / They call it love / If I were you / Workin' man's woman / I was on Georgia time.
LP . . . . . CBS 25764
■ **MC** 40 25764
CBS / Jul '84.

DON'T SET ME FREE.
Tracks: Don't set me free.
■ **7"** . . . . . POP 1133
H.M.V. / Mar '63.

EARLY YEARS.
Tracks: Not Advised.
LP . . . . . ZET 707
Zeta / '88 / Discovery.

ELEANOR RIGBY.
Tracks: Eleanor Rigby.
■ **7"** . . . . . SS 2120
Stateside / Jul '68.

EVERYTHING.
Tracks: Kiss me baby / Sitting on top of the world / I'm gonna drown myself / All alone again / Lovin' the girls / I will not let you go / I'm glad for your sake / Walkin' and talkin'.
LP . . . . . MAN 5029
Manhattan Records / Sep '80 / EMI.

FANTASTIC RAY CHARLES, THE.
Tracks: Going down slow / Blues is my middle name / If I give you my love / Can't you see, darling? / Goin' away blues / Sitting on top of the world / Late in the evening blues / Here am I / Ray's blues / I'm just a lonely boy / St. Pete blues / Easy ridin' gal / See see rider / I wonder who's kissing her now / I'm going down to the river / I'm glad for your sake / Ego song, The / I used to be so happy / Hey now / What have I done? / All night long / All to myself alone / Oh baby / I live only for you.
Double LP . . . . . ALB 103
Musidisc / Mar '85 / Revolver-APT / Discovery.

FRIENDSHIP.
Tracks: Two old cats like us / This old heart of mine / We didn't see a thing / Who cares / Rock and roll shoes / Friendship / It ain't gonna worry my mind / Little hotel room / Crazy old soldier / Seven Spanish angels.
■ **LP** . . . . . CBS 26060
CBS / Oct '84.
■ **MC** 40 26060
CBS / Oct '84.
CD 9825942
Pickwick/Sony Collectors Choice / Oct '91 / Pickwick Records.

GENIUS + SOUL = JAZZ.
Tracks: From the heart / I've got news for you / Moanin' / Let's go / One mint julep / I'm gonna move to the outskirts of town / Stompin' room / Mister C / Strike up the band / Birth of the blues / Alabamy bound / Basin Street blues / New York's my home.
CD . . . . . ESSCD 009
LP . . . . . ESSLP 009
Essential / Aug '89 / BMG / Castle Communications / Total.
■ **MC** . . . . . ESSMC 009
Essential / Aug '89.
CD JZ-CD310
Suisa / Feb '91 / Jazz Music / Terry Blood Dist.
CD . . . . . CLACD 339
Castle / Aug '93 / BMG.

GENIUS OF RAY CHARLES, THE.
Tracks: Not Advised.
CD 756781338-2
Atlantic / Jun '93 / WEA.

GENIUS, THE.
Tracks: Sitting on top of the world / Kiss my baby / I'm gonna drown myself / All alone again / I had my fun / Snow is falling / Blues is my middle name / Oh baby / C.C. rider / Hey now / Tell me baby / Going down slowly / Walkin' and talkin' / I'm glad for your sake / Baby let me hold your hand / All to myself alone.
CD . . . . . XELCD 106
LP . . . . . XELLP 106
MC . . . . . XELMC 106
Exel / Mar '88 / Henry Hadaway Organisation / EMI.

GEORGIA ON MY MIND.
Tracks: Not Advised.
LP . . . . . SM 3926
Joker (USA) / '88 / C.M. Distribution / Jazz Horizons / Jazz Music.

GEORGIA ON MY MIND.
Tracks: Georgia on my mind.
■ **7"** . . . . . POP 792
H.M.V. / Dec '60.

GEORGIA TIME.
Tracks: I had it all / Do I ever cross your mind / Workin' mans woman / I was on Georgia time / Two old cats like us / This ole heart / Friendship / This page on my mind / Slip away / Love is worth the pain / Rock and roll shoes / Stranger in my hometown / Let's call the whole thing off / Save the bones for Henry Jones / Nothing like a hundred miles / I wish I'd never loved you at all.
CD . . . . . PWKS 4169
MC . . . . . PWKMC 4169
Pickwick / Sep '93 / Pickwick Records.

GOIN' DOWN SLOW.
Tracks: Going down slow / Alone in the city / Now she's gone / Rockin' chair blues / Can anyone ask for more / Let's have a ball / This love of mine / Can't see you darling? / If I give you my love.
LP . . . . . MTM 002
Meteor / Jun '84 / Terry Blood Dist. / Jazz Music.

GOLD COLLECTION, THE.
Tracks: Not Advised.
CD D2CD05
MC D2MC05
Recording Arts / Dec '92 / Terry Blood Dist.

GREAT HITS.
Tracks: Going down slow / All night long / I'm givin' up / Guitar blues / Talkin' 'bout you / I found my baby there / I'm wonderin' and wonderin' / By myself / Snowfall.
LP . . . . . PHX 1013
Phoenix (2) / '82 / Gamut Distribution.

GREAT RAY CHARLES, THE.
Tracks: Not Advised.
CD 756781731-2
Atlantic / Jun '93 / WEA.

GREATEST COUNTRY AND WESTERN HITS.
Tracks: Your cheating heart / Hey good lookin' / Take these chains from my heart / Don't tell me your troubles / I can't stop loving you / Just a little lovin' / It makes no difference now / You don't know me / You are my sunshine / Someday (you'll want me to want you) / I love you so much it hurts / Careless love / Oh, lonesome me / Midnight / No letter today / Crying time / Together again / Don't let her know / I'll never stand in your way (Only on CD.) / Hang your head in shame (Only on CD.).
CD . . . . . NEXCD 100
LP . . . . . NEXLP 100
Sequel / Dec '89 / Castle Communications / BMG / Hot Shot.
■ **MC** . . . . . NEXMC 100
Sequel / Dec '89.

GREATEST HITS: RAY CHARLES.
Tracks: Not Advised.
■ **LP** . . . . . CLP 1626
H.M.V. / Jul '63.

GREATEST HITS: RAY CHARLES, VOL. 2.
Tracks: Not Advised.
■ **LP** . . . . . SSL 10241
Stateside / Oct '68.

HEART TO HEART - 20 HOT HITS.
Tracks: Not Advised.
■ **LP** . . . . . RAY TV 1
London / Jul '80.

HERE AM I.
Tracks: Easy riding gal / Tapeworld / Ray's blues / Here am I / Blow my baby back home / Blues is my middle name.
LP . . . . . B 10106
MC MB9 10106
Barclay (France) / Apr '83.

HERE WE GO AGAIN.
Tracks: Here we go again / Someone ought to write a book about it.
■ **7"** . . . . . POP 1595
H.M.V. / Jul '67.

HIT THE ROAD JACK.
Tracks: Not Advised.
LP . . . . . PLP 21
MC . . . . . PMC 21
Platinum (W.Germany) / Oct '85.

HIT THE ROAD JACK.
Tracks: Hit the road Jack / Georgia on my mind.
7" . . . . . RACH 1
Arcade / May '90 / Sony.

HIT THE ROAD JACK.
Tracks: Hit the road Jack.
■ **7"** . . . . . POP 935
H.M.V. / Oct '61.

HITS OF A GENIUS.
Tracks: Not Advised.
CD 99009
LP 39009
MC 69009
Commander / May '88.

HOPELESSLY.
Tracks: Hopelessly / I chose to sing the blues.
■ **7"** . . . . . POP 1551
H.M.V. / '66.

I CAN SEE CLEARLY NOW.
Tracks: I can see clearly now / Let it be.
■ **7"** . . . . . HL 10554
London / Aug '80.

I CAN'T STOP LOVING YOU.
Tracks: Hit the road Jack / Hallelujah I love her so / Mess around / Let's go get stoned / Don't let the sun catch you cryin' / What'd I say / Georgia on my mind / I got a woman / Drown in my own tears / Night time is the right time / Eleanor Rigby / I can't stop loving you.
LP . . . . . SSP 3075
Pickwick / Sep '80 / Pickwick Records.
LP 24004
Colorado / '88.

I CAN'T STOP LOVING YOU.
Tracks: I can't stop loving you.
■ **7"** . . . . . POP 1034
H.M.V. / Jun '62.

I CHOSE TO SING THE BLUES (Charles, Ray Band).
Tracks: I chose to sing the blues.

I DON'T NEED NO DOCTOR.
Tracks: I don't need no doctor / Please say you're fooling.
■ **7"** . . . . . POP 1566
H.M.V. / Dec '66.

I WISH YOU WERE HERE TONIGHT.
Tracks: 3/4 time / I wish you were here tonight / Ain't your memory got no pride at all? / Born to love me / I don't want no stranger sleepin' in my bed / Let your love flow / You feel good all over / String bean / You've got the longest leaving act in town / Shakin' your head.
LP . . . . . CBS 25065
CBS / Mar '83 / Sony.
■ **MC** 40 25065
CBS / Mar '83.
CD 9022892
Collector's Choice / Apr '90 / Silver Sounds (CD).

I WISH YOU WERE HERE TONIGHT.
Tracks: I wish you were here tonight / You feel good all over.
7" . . . . . A 3407
CBS / May '83 / Sony.

I WONDER WHO'S KISSING HER NOW?.
Tracks: I wonder who's kissing her now / She's on the ball / Baby won't you please come home.
7" . . . . . CYZ 7 119
Charly / '87 / Charly.
12" . . . . . CYZ 119
Charly / Feb '87 / Charly.

IF I GIVE YOU MY LOVE.
Tracks: Alone in the city / Can anyone ask for more / Rockin' chair blues / Let's have a ball / If I give you my love / Can't see you darling? / This love of mine / Sentimental blues, A / Now she's gone / Going down slow.
LP . . . . . F 50014
MC . . . . . MF 950014
IMS / Oct '82 / PolyGram.
CD . . . . . PD 50014
IMS / May '88 / PolyGram.

JAMMIN' THE BLUES.
Tracks: Not Advised.
LP 20078
MC 40078
Astan (USA) / Nov '84.

JUST BETWEEN US.
Tracks: Nothing like a hundred miles / I wish I'd never loved you at all / Too hard to love you / Now I don't believe that anymore / Let's call the whole thing off /

Stranger in my own hometown / Over the top / I'd walk a little more for you / If that's what'cha want / Save the bones for Henry Jones.
CD 4611832
LP 4611831
MC 4611834
CBS / Sep '88 / Sony.

KING OF THE BLUES.
Tracks: Not Advised.
MC . . . . AMP 011
Ampro / Sep '81.

LEGEND LIVES.
Tracks: Not Advised.
■ CD . . . . ADEHCD 780
Arcade / May '88.

LIVE.
Tracks: Not Advised.
CD .756781732-2
Atlantic / Jun '93 / WEA.

LIVE : RAY CHARLES.
Tracks: Not Advised.
■ Double LP 2-503
Atlantic / Nov '87 / WEA.

MAKIN' WHOOPEE.
Tracks: Makin' whoopee.
■ 7" . . . . POP 1383
H.M.V. / Jan '65.

MODERN SOUNDS IN COUNTRY AND WESTERN MUSIC VOL.1.
Tracks: Not Advised.
■ LP . . . . CLP 1580
H.M.V. / Jul '62.

MODERN SOUNDS IN COUNTRY AND WESTERN MUSIC VOL.2.
Tracks: Not Advised.
■ LP . . . . CLP 1613
H.M.V. / Feb '63.

MY WORLD.
Tracks: My world / Song for you, A / None of us are free / So help me God / Let me take over / One drop of love / If I could / Love has a mind of its own / I'll be there / Still crazy after all theses years.
CD .759926735-2
MC .759926735-4
WEA / Mar '93 / WEA.

NO ONE TO CRY TO.
Tracks: No one to cry to.
■ 7" . . . . POP 1333
H.M.V. / Sep '64.

OH LORD I'M ON MY WAY.
Tracks: Oh Lord I'm on my way / Oh Bess, oh where's my Bess?
■ 7" . . . . HLU 10541
London-American / Oct '76.

PAGES OF MY MIND, THE.
Tracks: Pages of my mind, The / Slip away / Anybody with the blues / Class reunion / Caught a touch of your love / Little bit of heaven, A / Dixie moon / Over and over (again) / Beaucoup love / Love is worth the pain.
LP. . . . . CBS 26856
MC 40 26856
CBS / Aug '86 / Sony.

RAY CHARLES.
Tracks: Not Advised.
MC . . . . SSC 3075
Pickwick / Sep '80 / Pickwick Records.
MC . . . . ZCGAS 729
Audio Fidelity(USA) / Oct '84 / Stage One Records.
CD .ENT CD 203
LP. . . . . ENT 13005
Entertainers / Sep '87.
LP. ENT LP 13005
MC . . . . ENT MC 13005
Entertainers / '88.
LP. . . . . BID 8011
Bellaphon / Jul '88 / New Note.

RAY CHARLES (DOUBLE CASSETTE).
Tracks: Not Advised.
MC Set . . . . DTO 10202
Ditto / '88 / Pickwick Records.

RAY CHARLES (JOKER (USA)).
Tracks: Not Advised.
LP. . . . . .SM 3712
Joker (USA) / '88 / C.M. Distribution / Jazz Music.

RAY CHARLES AND BETTY CARTER (Charles, Ray & Betty Carter).
Tracks: Every time we say goodbye / You and I / Goodbye, we'll be together again / People will say we're in love / Cocktails for two / Side by side / Baby it's cold outside / Together / For all we know / It takes two to tango / Alone together / Just you and me / But on the other hand baby / I never see Maggie alone / I like to hear it sometimes.
■ CD . . . . ESSCD 012
Essential / Dec '89.
LP. . . . . ESSLP 012
MC . . . . ESSMC 012
Essential / Nov '89 / BMG / Castle Communications / Total.

RAY CHARLES BLUES.
Tracks: Not Advised.
LP 20079
MC 40079
Astan (USA) / Nov '84.

RAY CHARLES COLLECTION.
Tracks: Yesterday / Your cheatin' heart / I can't stop loving you / Eleanor Rigby / Hit the road Jack.
CD . . . . .RCLD 101
MC . . . . .RLCL 101
Westmoor / Aug '92.

RAY CHARLES IN L.A.
Tracks: Not Advised.
CD . . . . TL 1313
Traditional Line / Sep '92 / Charly.

RAY CHARLES STORY, THE.
Tracks: Baby won't you please come home / Ego song, The / You always miss the water (when the well runs dry) / St. Pete's blues / I live only for you / What have I done / C.C. rider / I've had my fun / Honey honey / Here am I / I wonder who's kissing her now / Ray Charles blues / She's on the ball / If I give you my love / I'm going down to the river / Let's have a ball / Hey now / Sitting on top of the world / Sentimental blues, A / I used to be so happy / Ain't that fine / All to myself alone / Georgia on my mind / What'd I say / Come rain or come shine.
CD Set . . . . .DVRECD 02
MC Set . . . . .DVREMC 02
Deja Vu / May '89 / Jazz Music / Music Collection International.

RAY CHARLES VOL.2.
Tracks: Alone in the city / Can anyone ask for more / Rockin' chair blues / Let's have a ball / If I give you my love / Can't see you darling? / This love of mine / Sentimental blues, A / Now she's gone / Going down slow.
LP. . . . . .SM 3729
Joker (USA) / Apr '81 / C.M. Distribution / Jazz Horizons / Jazz Music.

RAY OF HOPE.
Tracks: See see rider / I wonder who's kissing her now / Hey now / Tell me baby / Kiss me baby / I'm gonna drown myself / Winter scene / Lovin' the girls.
LP. . . . . MAN 5020
Manhattan Records / Aug '80 / EMI.

RIGHT TIME, THE.
Tracks: Leave my woman alone / My Bonnie / That's enough / Drown in my own tears / Fool for you, A / Hallelujah I love her so / This little girl of mine / Mary Ann / I got a woman / Yes indeed / Swanee River rock / Lonely avenue / I had a dream / Early in the morning / Right time, The / I'm movin' on / What kind of man are you (Extra track on CD only) / I want to know (Extra track on CD only) / What'd I say (part 1) (Extra track on the CD only) / What'd I say (part 2) (Extra track on the CD only) / Jumpin' in the mornin'.
CD 241 119-2
■ LP 241 119-1
Atlantic / Jul '87 / WEA.
■ MC 241 119-4
Atlantic / Jul '87.

ROCK + SOUL = GENIUS.
Tracks: Not Advised.
CD .JMY 1009-2
JMY / Aug '91 / Harmonia Mundi (UK).

ROCKIN' WITH RAY.
Tracks: Not Advised.
LP. . . . . .SM 3871
Joker (USA) / '88 / C.M. Distribution / Jazz Horizons / Jazz Music.

SEVEN SPANISH ANGELS.
Tracks: Seven spanish angels / Who cares.
■ 7" . . . . .A 4991
CBS / May '85.

SHAKE YOUR TAIL FEATHER.
Tracks: Shake your tail feather / Minnie the moocher.
■ 7" . . . . .K 11615
Atlantic / Oct '80.

SIMPLY RAY.
Tracks: All to myself alone / Going down slow / Baby let me hold your hand / I won't let you go / Sitting on top of the world / By myself / Winter scene / Lovin' the girls.
LP. . . . . MAN 5019
Manhattan Records / May '80 / EMI.

SOUL MEETING (Charles, Ray & Milt Jackson).
Tracks: Hallelujah I love her so / Blue genius / X-ray blues / Soul meeting / Love on my mind / Bags of blues.
■ LP . . . . K 50234
Atlantic / Jul '76 / WEA.
CD 756781951-2
Atlantic / Mar '93 / WEA.

SPIRIT OF CHRISTMAS, THE.
Tracks: What child is this / Little drummer boy / Santa Claus is coming to town / This time of the year / Rudolph the red nosed reindeer / That spirit of Christmas / All I want for Christmas / Christmas in my heart / Winter wonderland / Christmas time.
■ LP . . . . CBS 26562
CBS / Dec '85.

■ MC 40 26562
CBS / Dec '85.

STAR COLLECTION.
Tracks: I got a woman / Let the good times roll / Ray, The / Loosing hand / Mess around / Mary Ann / This little girl of mine / Undecided / Alexanders ragtime band / Don't let the sun catch you crying.
LP. . . . . K 20015
■ MC K4 20015
Atlantic / '88 / WEA.

TAKE THESE CHAINS FROM MY HEART.
Tracks: Take these chains from my heart.
■ 7" . . . . POP 1161
H.M.V. / May '63.

TELL THE TRUTH.
Tracks: Mess around / It should've been me / Losing hand / Greenbacks / I got a woman / This little girl of mine / Hallelujah / I love her so / Drown in my own tears / Leave my woman alone / Lonely Avenue / That's enough / Talkin' 'bout you / You be my baby / Right time, The / Tell the truth / What'd I say?.
LP. . . . . CRB 1071
■ MC . . . . TCCRB 1071
Charly R&B / Mar '84.

THIS LOVE OF MINE.
Tracks: Kiss me baby / Baby let me hold your hand / C.C. rider / I wonder who's kissing her now / I'm going down to the river / They're crazy about me / Going down slow / Sentimental blues, A / Can anyone ask for more / Rockin' chair blues / If I give you my love / This love of mine.
LP. . . . . .TOP 126
MC . . . . .KTOP 126
Topline / '86 / Charly / Swift / Black Sun Records.
CD . . . . TOP CD 512
Topline / Apr '87 / Charly / Swift / Black Sun Records.

TOGETHER AGAIN.
Tracks: Together again.
■ 7" . . . . POP 1519
H.M.V. / Apr '66.

TRUE TO LIFE.
Tracks: Not Advised.
LP. . . . . SHU 8509
London-American / Jan '78.

WHAT IS LIFE?.
Tracks: Going to the river / Steppin' out baby / Dear heart / Glow worm / Take some and leave some / All alone / I'll do anything but work / My mama told me / I'm yours for the asking / Blow my baby back home / Too late to change / What is life?.
LP. . . . . B 90112
MC MB9 90112
Barclay (France) / Apr '83.

WHAT'D I SAY.
Tracks: Not Advised.
CD 15 091
MC 79 540
Laserlight / Aug '91 / TBD / Taylors.

YESTERDAY.
Tracks: Yesterday.
■ 7" . . . . SS 2071
Stateside / Dec '67.

YOU DON'T KNOW ME.
Tracks: You don't know me.
■ 7" . . . . POP 1064
H.M.V. / Sep '62.

YOUR CHEATIN' HEART.
Tracks: Your cheatin' heart.
■ 7" . . . . POP 1099
H.M.V. / Dec '62.

Chase, Carol

THIS MUST BE MY SHIP.
Tracks: This must be my ship / It always takes a fool to fool around.
■ 7" .CWS 1001
Casablanca / Feb '80.

Chatwell, J.R.

JAMMIN' WITH JR.
Tracks: Never slept a wink last night / Little coquette / Jammin' with JR / Ragged but right / Right or wrong / Pipedreams / Corina Corina / Pipeliner's blues / John the baptist / You can count on me / Worried over you.
LP. . . . . SDLP 063
Sundown / '88 / Terry Blood Dist. / Jazz Music / C.M. Distribution.

Chenier, Clifton

Influenced by everybody from Amade Ardoin to Lowell Fulson, the accordionist and vocalist Clifton Chenier (1925-87) was one of the most celebrated artists in the USA southwest's genre of Zydeco, the French Creole-speaking black community's variant of Cajun music. It is a foot tapping good time music that just won't quit; Chenier described it as 'simply the French two-

■ DELETED

step with new hinges so she can swing'. (Donald Clarke)

60 MINUTES WITH THE KING OF ZYDECO.
Tracks: Not Advised.
CD . . . . ARCD 301
Arhoolie (USA) / '88 / Pinnacle / Cadillac Music / Swift / Projection / Hot Shot / A.D.A Distribution / Jazz Music.

BAYOU BLUES.
Tracks: Boppin' the rock / Things I did for you, The / Yesterday / Clifton's squeeze box / I'm on my way (part 1) / Eh, petite fille / All night long / Opelousas hop / I'm on my way (part 2) / Think it over / Zydeco stomp / Cat's dreaming, The.
LP. . . . . SNTF 5012
Sonet / Swift / C.M. Distribution / Roots Records / Jazz Music / Sonet Records / Cadillac Music / Projection / Wellard Dist. / Hot Shot.

BAYOU SOUL.
Tracks: Not Advised.
LP. 1002
Maison de Soul(USA) / Mar '79 / Swift.

BLACK SNAKE BLUES (October 10, 1967).
Tracks: Not Advised.
MC . . . . C 1038
Arhoolie (USA) / May '81 / Pinnacle / Cadillac Music / Swift / Projection / Hot Shot / A.D.A Distribution / Jazz Music.
LP. ARHOOLIE 1038
Arhoolie (USA) / '84 / Pinnacle / Cadillac Music / Swift / Projection / Hot Shot / A.D.A Distribution / Jazz Music.

BOGALUSA BOOGIE (Zydeco accordion dance music).
Tracks: Not Advised.
LP. . . . . F 1076
Arhoolie (USA) / Jul '87 / Pinnacle / Cadillac Music / Swift / Projection / Hot Shot / A.D.A Distribution / Jazz Music.
MC . . . . C 1076
Arhoolie (USA) / '88 / Pinnacle / Cadillac Music / Swift / Projection / Hot Shot / A.D.A Distribution / Jazz Music.
CD . . . . ARH 347
Arhoolie (USA) / '92 / Pinnacle / Cadillac Music / Swift / Projection / Hot Shot / A.D.A Distribution / Jazz Music.
CD . . . . ARHCD 347
Arhoolie (USA) / Mar '93 / Pinnacle / Cadillac Music / Swift / Projection / Hot Shot / A.D.A Distribution / Jazz Music.

BON TON ROULET.
Tracks: Not Advised.
LP. ARHOOLIE 1031
Arhoolie (USA) / May '81 / Pinnacle / Cadillac Music / Swift / Projection / Hot Shot / A.D.A Distribution / Jazz Music.
MC . . . . C 1031
Arhoolie (USA) / '88 / Pinnacle / Cadillac Music / Swift / Projection / Hot Shot / A.D.A Distribution / Jazz Music.
CD . . . . ARH 345
Arhoolie (USA) / '92 / Pinnacle / Cadillac Music / Swift / Projection / Hot Shot / A.D.A Distribution / Jazz Music.

BON TON ROULET & MORE.
Tracks: Not Advised.
CD . . . . ARHCD 345
Arhoolie (USA) / Mar '93 / Pinnacle / Cadillac Music / Swift / Projection / Hot Shot / A.D.A Distribution / Jazz Music.

BOOGIE'N'ZYDECO.
Tracks: Shake it don't break it / Oh my Lucille / Choo choo ch' boogie / Nonc helaire / You can't sit down / Road runner / You used to call me / Je me fu pas mal.
LP. . . . . SNTF 801
Sonet / Jan '80 / Swift / C.M. Distribution / Roots Records / Jazz Music / Sonet Records / Cadillac Music / Projection / Wellard Dist. / Hot Shot.
LP. 1003
MC 1003TC
Maison de Soul(USA) / '87 / Swift.
CD . . . . SNTCD 801
Sonet / Oct '90 / Swift / C.M. Distribution / Roots Records / Jazz Music / Sonet Records / Cadillac Music / Projection / Wellard Dist. / Hot Shot.

CAJUN SWAMP.
Tracks: Not Advised.
LP. . . . . TOM 2-7002
Tomato (USA) / Mar '79 / Revolver-APT.
CD 2696062
Tomato (USA) / May '88 / Revolver-APT.

CAJUN SWAMP MUSIC LIVE.
Tracks: Not Advised.
CD 269 621 2
Tomato (USA) / Mar '90 / Revolver-APT.

CLASSIC CLIFTON.
Tracks: Not Advised.
LP. ARHOOLIE 1082
Arhoolie (USA) / '84 / Pinnacle / Cadillac Music / Swift / Projection / Hot Shot / A.D.A Distribution / Jazz Music.
MC . . . . C 1082
Arhoolie (USA) / '88 / Pinnacle / Cadillac Music / Swift / Projection / Hot Shot / A.D.A Distribution / Jazz Music.

CLIFTON CHENIER & HIS RED HOT LOUISIANA BAND.
Tracks: Not Advised.
LP. ARHOOLIE 1078
Arhoolie (USA) / '84 / Pinnacle / Cadillac Music / Swift / Projection / Hot Shot / A.D.A Distribution / Jazz Music.

CLIFTON CHENIER AND ROCKIN' DOPSIE (Chenier, Clifton & Rod Bernard).
Tracks: Night and day / Everybody calls me crazy / If ever I get lucky / Rockin' accordian / It happened so fast / Goodbye baby / Worried life blues / Hey ma ma / Blues / Run here to me baby / Woman, I don't want your troubles / Things I used to do / Ma Negresse / She's my little girl / Rockin' with Dopsie.
CD . . . . FLYCD 17
Flyright / Mar '90 / Hot Shot / Roots Records / Wellard Dist. / Charly / Swift / Projection.

CLIFTON CHENIER SINGS THE BLUES (Home Cookin' & Prophesy sides from 1969).
Tracks: Not Advised.
LP. ARHOOLIE 1097
Arhoolie (USA) / Feb '88 / Pinnacle / Cadillac Music / Swift / Projection / Hot Shot / A.D.A Distribution / Jazz Music.

COUNTRY BOY NOW (Grammy award winner 1984).
Tracks: Not Advised.
LP. 1012
Maison de Soul(USA) / Swift.
MC . . . . 1012 TC
Maison de Soul(USA) / '87 / Swift.

FRENCHIN' THE BOOGIE.
Tracks: Caldonia / Laissez le bon temps roulez / Tu peux cogner mais tu peux pas rentrer (Keep-a-knock-in'..) (Full Translation: Keep-a-knockin' but you can't come in.) / Blues de la vache a lait, Le (Milkcow blues) / Moi, j'ai une petite femme (I got a woman) / Tous les jours mon coeur est blue / Je veux faire l'amour a toi (I just wanna make love to you) / Choo choo ch' boogie / La valse de Paris / Shake, rattle and roll / Going down slow (in Paris) / Aye, aye mama / Don't you lie to me.
LP. 80608
Barclay (France) / Nov '79.

HOT PEPPER.
Tracks: Not Advised.
VHS. . . . . KJ 066
Kay Jazz (video) / '88 / Gold & Sons / Cadillac Music.

HOT ROD (Chenier, Clifton & His Red Hot Louisiana Band).
Tracks: I feel all right / Got my eyes on you / It's a shame / Zydeco express / You're still the king to me / Before it's too late / Harmonica zydeco / Your time to cry / Hot rod / Old fashioned party / Jole blon / Just the beginning.
CD 8282402
London / Mar '91 / PolyGram.
■ LP. 8282401
London / Mar '91.
■ MC 8282404
London / Mar '91.

I'M HERE (Chenier, Clifton & His Red Hot Louisiana Band).
Tracks: Not Advised.
LP. . . . . SNTF 882
Sonet / May '82 / Swift / C.M. Distribution / Roots Records / Jazz Music / Sonet Records / Cadillac Music / Projection / Wellard Dist. / Hot Shot.
CD . . . . SNTCD 882
Sonet / Jun '88 / Swift / C.M. Distribution / Roots Records / Jazz Music / Sonet Records / Cadillac Music / Projection / Wellard Dist. / Hot Shot.

KING OF THE BAYOUS.
Tracks: Not Advised.
LP. ARHOOLIE 1052
Arhoolie (USA) / May '81 / Pinnacle / Cadillac Music / Swift / Projection / Hot Shot / A.D.A Distribution / Jazz Music.
CD . . . . ARHCD 339
MC . . . . C 1052
Arhoolie (USA) / '88 / Pinnacle / Cadillac Music / Swift / Projection / Hot Shot / A.D.A Distribution / Jazz Music.

KING OF ZYDECO.
Tracks: My baby she's gone to stay / Driftin' blues / Tutti frutti / Love me or leave me / Old time waltz / Zydeco boogie / What'd I Say / Moon is rising blues / Zydeco jazz / Zydeco is back again / Mama told papa / Tired of being alone.
MC . . . . C 1086
Arhoolie (USA) / '88 / Pinnacle / Cadillac Music / Swift / Projection / Hot Shot / A.D.A Distribution / Jazz Music.
LP. ARHOOLIE 1086
Arhoolie (USA) / Dec '88 / Pinnacle / Cadillac Music / Swift / Projection / Hot Shot / A.D.A Distribution / Jazz Music.
■ LP. . . . . CHD 234
Ace / Mar '88.
CD . . . . CDCH 234
Ace / Feb '91 / Pinnacle / Hot Shot / Jazz Music / Complete Record Co. Ltd.
CD . . . . ARH 301
Arhoolie (USA) / '92 / Pinnacle / Cadillac Music / Swift / Projection / Hot Shot / A.D.A Distribution / Jazz Music.

KING OF ZYDECO.
Tracks: Not Advised.
VHS. . . . . ARV 401
Arhoolie (USA) / '88 / Pinnacle / Cadillac Music / Swift / Projection / Hot Shot / A.D.A Distribution / Jazz Music.

KING OF ZYDECO LIVE AT MONTREUX.
Tracks: Not Advised.
CD . . . . ARHCD 355
Arhoolie (USA) / Mar '93 / Pinnacle / Cadillac Music / Swift / Projection / Hot Shot / A.D.A Distribution / Jazz Music.

LET ME IN YOUR HEART (Chenier, Clifton & His Red Hot Louisiana Band).
Tracks: Not Advised.
LP. . . . . F 1098
Arhoolie (USA) / Dec '88 / Pinnacle / Cadillac Music / Swift / Projection / Hot Shot / A.D.A Distribution / Jazz Music.

LIVE AT A FRENCH DANCE.
Tracks: Not Advised.
LP. ARHOOLIE 1059
Arhoolie (USA) / May '81 / Pinnacle / Cadillac Music / Swift / Projection / Hot Shot / A.D.A Distribution / Jazz Music.
MC . . . . C 1059
Arhoolie (USA) / '88 / Pinnacle / Cadillac Music / Swift / Projection / Hot Shot / A.D.A Distribution / Jazz Music.

LIVE AT MONTREUX: CLIFTON CHENIER.
Tracks: Tu est si jolie / No salt in your snap beans / You're just fussing too much / Pinetop's boogie woogie / Marcher plancher / Here little girl / Release me / Jambalaya / I'm a hog for you / Louisiana two step / When you going to sing for me / Who who who / You promised me love / Black girl / Money / Hush hush / Calinda / Duo (encore).
■ Double LP . . . . CDX 2
Charly / Apr '84 / Charly.

LIVE AT St. MARK'S.
Tracks: Not Advised.
CD . . . . ARH 313
Arhoolie (USA) / '92 / Pinnacle / Cadillac Music / Swift / Projection / Hot Shot / A.D.A Distribution / Jazz Music.
CD . . . . ARHCD 313
Arhoolie (USA) / Mar '93 / Pinnacle / Cadillac Music / Swift / Projection / Hot Shot / A.D.A Distribution / Jazz Music.

LIVE AT THE SAN FRANCISCO BLUES FESTIVAL.
Tracks: Not Advised.
LP. ARHOOLIE 1093
Arhoolie (USA) / Aug '85 / Pinnacle / Cadillac Music / Swift / Projection / Hot Shot / A.D.A Distribution / Jazz Music.
MC . . . . C 1093
Arhoolie (USA) / '88 / Pinnacle / Cadillac Music / Swift / Projection / Hot Shot / A.D.A Distribution / Jazz Music.

LOUISIANA BLUES & ZYDECO.
Tracks: Not Advised.
CD . . . . ARH 329
Arhoolie (USA) / '92 / Pinnacle / Cadillac Music / Swift / Projection / Hot Shot / A.D.A Distribution / Jazz Music.

LOUISIANA BLUES AND ZYDECO.
Tracks: Not Advised.
LP. ARHOOLIE 1024
Arhoolie (USA) / Apr '81 / Pinnacle / Cadillac Music / Swift / Projection / Hot Shot / A.D.A Distribution / Jazz Music.
MC . . . . C 1024
Arhoolie (USA) / '88 / Pinnacle / Cadillac Music / Swift / Projection / Hot Shot / A.D.A Distribution / Jazz Music.
CD . . . . ARHCD 329
Arhoolie (USA) / Mar '93 / Pinnacle / Cadillac Music / Swift / Projection / Hot Shot / A.D.A Distribution / Jazz Music.

MY BABY DON'T WEAR NO SHOES.
Tracks: Not Advised.
CD . . . . ARHCD 1098
Arhoolie (USA) / '88 / Pinnacle / Cadillac Music / Swift / Projection / Hot Shot / A.D.A Distribution / Jazz Music.

NEW ORLEANS.
Tracks: Boogie Lousiana / Cotton picker blues / J'aime pain de mais / Pousse cafe waltz / Hello Rosa-Lee / Jusque parce que je t'aime / Boogie in Orleans / Rumblin' on the bayou / I'm gonna take you home tonite / Mon vieux buggy / Crying my heart out to you / Tous les jours / Mardi gras boogie.
CD . . . . GNPD 2119
MC GNP5 2119
GNP Crescendo / Jun '92 / Swift / Silva Screen / Flexitron Ltd.

ON TOUR.
Tracks: Not Advised.
CD 157722
Blues Collection / Feb '93 / Discovery.

OUT WEST.
Tracks: Not Advised.
LP. ARHOOLIE 1072
Arhoolie (USA) / '81 / Pinnacle / Cadillac Music / Swift / Projection / Hot Shot / A.D.A Distribution / Jazz Music.
MC . . . . C 1072
Arhoolie (USA) / '88 / Pinnacle / Cadillac Music / Swift / Projection / Hot Shot / A.D.A Distribution / Jazz Music.
CD . . . . ARHCD 350
Arhoolie (USA) / Mar '93 / Pinnacle / Cadillac Music / Swift / Projection / Hot Shot / A.D.A Distribution / Jazz Music.

RED HOT LOUISIANA BAND.
Tracks: Not Advised.
LP . . . . **ARHOOLIE 1098**
Arhoolie (USA) / '81 / Pinnacle / Cadillac Music / Swift / Projection / Hot Shot / A.D.A Distribution / Jazz Music.
MC . . . . **C 1098**
Arhoolie (USA) / '88 / Pinnacle / Cadillac Music / Swift / Projection / Hot Shot / A.D.A Distribution / Jazz Music.

ZYDECO BLUES AND BOOGIE.
Tracks: Not Advised.
CD . . . . **CDCHD 389**
Ace / May '92 / Pinnacle / Hot Shot / Jazz Music / Complete Record Co. Ltd.

ZYDECO LEGEND.
Tracks: Not Advised.
CD . . . . **MDSCD 105**
Maison de Soul(USA) / May '89 / Swift.

Chevis, Wilfred

FOOT STOMPIN' ZYDECO (Chevis, Wilfred & the Texas Zydeco Band).
Tracks: Not Advised.
LP **1013**
Maison de Soul(USA) / Swift.
MC . . . . **1013 TC**
Maison de Soul(USA) / '87 / Swift.

Chiavola, Kathy

LABOR OF LOVE.
Tracks: Well all right / Woman in love, A / Man after my own heart, A / Cry cry darlin' / Traveling at night / Passing of the train, The / Fool such as I, A / Lost dog blues / Labor of love / Twinkle, twinkle little star / Distant melody / Faithless love.
CD . . . . **RBR 1002**
MC . . . . **RBR 1002MC**
Ragged But Right / '93.

Chicken Chokers

SHOOT YOUR RADIO.
Tracks: Not Advised.
LP . . . . **ROUNDER 0241**
MC . . . . **ROUNDER 0241C**
Rounder / Aug '88 / Projection / Roots Records / Swift / C.M. Distribution / Topic Records / Jazz Music / Hot Shot / A.D.A Distribution / Direct Distribution.

Childre, Lew

OLD TIME GET TOGETHER.
Tracks: Not Advised.
LP . . . . **SLP 153**
MC . . . . **GT 5153**
Starday (USA) / Apr '87 / Crusader Marketing Co.

Choates, Harry

Arguably cajun music's first star, Louisiana born fiddler Choates put the music on the map during the 1940's with its first hit record, a reworking of an old folk song *Jole Blon* . Among his original material was *Poor Hobo*, *Struttin' around*, and *Poor Arthur Waltz* . Very little is known about Choates apart from his reputation as a heavy drinker, and the sobering up process that followed his arrest in 1951 (for wife and child desertion) was reputedly too much for his system, quickly leading onto his death at the age of 28 years. (Tony Byworth)

FIDDLE KING OF CAJUN SWING.
Tracks: Not Advised.
LP . . . . **ARHOOLIE 5027**
MC . . . . **ARHC 5027**
Arhoolie (USA) / '88 / Pinnacle / Cadillac Music / Swift / Projection / Hot Shot / A.D.A Distribution / Jazz Music.

FIDDLE KING OF CAJUN SWING, THE.
Tracks: Not Advised.
CD . . . . **ARHCD 380**
Ace / Jun '93 / Pinnacle / Hot Shot / Jazz Music / Complete Record Co. Ltd.

FIVE TIMES LOSER.
Tracks: Louisiana boogie / She's sweet sweet / Old cow blues / My pretty brunette / Big mamou / What's the use / Five time loser / Je passa durvan ta port / Cat'n around / Big woods.
LP . . . . **KK 7453**
Krazy Kat / Aug '90 / Hot Shot / C.M. Distribution / Wellard Dist. / Roots Records / Projection / Charly / Jazz Music.

JOLE BLON.
Tracks: Not Advised.
LP **7000**
D/D (US) / Mar '79.

TRIBUTE TO..
Tracks: Not Advised.
LP . . . . **FLY 572**
Flyright / Oct '86 / Hot Shot / Roots Records / Wellard Dist. / Charly / Swift / Projection.

Chokers & Flies

OLD TIME MUSIC.
Tracks: Not Advised.
LP . . . . **ROUNDER 0213**
Rounder / Sep '85 / Projection / Roots Records / Swift / C.M. Distribution / Topic Records / Jazz Music / Hot Shot / A.D.A Distribution / Direct Distribution.
MC . . . . **ROUNDER 0213C**
Rounder / Aug '88 / Projection / Roots Records / Swift / C.M. Distribution / Topic Records / Jazz Music / Hot Shot / A.D.A Distribution / Direct Distribution.

Clark, Gene

AMERICAN DREAMER 1964-1974.
Tracks: Not Advised.
CD . . . . **RVCD 21**
Raven / Feb '93 / Revolver-APT / A.D.A Distribution / New Note / Jazz Music / Topic Records.

GENE CLARK & THE GOSDIN BROTHERS (Clark, Gene & The Gosdin Brothers).
Tracks: Echoes / Think I'm gonna feel better / Tried so hard / Is yours is mine / Keep on pushing / I found you / So you say you lost your baby / Elevator operator / Same one, The / Couldn't believe her / Needing someone.
CD . . . . **ED CD 263**
LP . . . . **ED 263**
Edsel / Apr '88 / Pinnacle.

NO OTHER.
Tracks: Life's greatest fool / Silver raven / No other / Strength of strings / From a silver phial / Some misunderstanding / True one, The / Lady of the North.
LP . . . . **ED 299**
Edsel / '88 / Pinnacle.
LP **K53 005**
Asylum / '88 / WEA.

NO OTHER.
Tracks: No other / True one.
■ **7"** . . . . **AYM 536**
Asylum / Jan '75.

ROADMASTER.
Tracks: She's the kind of girl / One in a hundred / Here tonight / Full circle song / In a misty morning / Rough and rocky / Roadmaster / I really don't want to know / I remember the railroad / She don't care about the time / Shooting star.
LP . . . . **ED 198**
Edsel / '88 / Pinnacle.
CD . . . . **ED CD 198**
Edsel / Jun '90 / Pinnacle.

SILHOUETTED IN LIGHT (Clark, Gene & Carla Olsen).
Tracks: Your fire burning / Number one is to survive / Love wins again / Fair and tender ladies / Photograph / Set you free this time / Last thing on my mind / Gypsy rider / Train leaves here this morning / Almost Saturday night / Del Gato / I'll feel a whole lot better / She don't care about time / Speed of the sound of loneliness / Will the circle be unbroken.
CD . . . . **FIENDCD 710**
MC . . . . **FIENDCASS 710**
Demon / Feb '92 / Pinnacle.

SO REBELLIOUS A LOVER (Clark, Gene & Carla Olsen).
Tracks: Drifter, The / Gypsy rider / Every angel in heaven / Del gato / Deportees / Fair and tender ladies / Almost Saturday night / I'm your toy / Why did you leave me / Don't it make you wanna go home / Are we still making love.
LP . . . . **FIEND 89**
Demon / Apr '87 / Pinnacle.
CD . . . . **FIENDCD 89**
Demon / Aug '87 / Pinnacle.

TWO SIDES TO EVERY STORY.
Tracks: Home run king / Lonely Saturday / In the pines / Kansas City Southern / Give my love to Marie / Sister moon / Marylou / Hear the wind / Past address / Silent crusade.
LP **2394 176**
Polydor / Mar '77 / PolyGram.

Clark, Guy

Singer - songwriter born 06.11.1941 in Rockport, Texas. Clark is one of the finest merchants to ply the trade from America's Lone Star state. Clark was raised in Monahans, Texas - from which period he's regularly drawn much of his material, especially stories learnt from his grandfather. His earliest stabs at music were folk orientated, playing coffee houses and small bars, some solo, others as part of a trio featuring Kay Oslin (now K.T. Oslin). Clark, on moving to Nashville, secured a publishing deal and his debut 1975 RCA album *Old No.1* was hailed as an all-time classic. It included such songs as: *L.A. Freeway* , *She Ain't Goin Nowhere*, *Texas - 1947*, *Desperados Waiting For A Train*, and *Let It Roll* - all of which have been covered in recent years. Clark's album *Texas Cookin'* issued in 1976, with it's cast of thousands,again found favour with the critics - sales though were only modest. Johnny Cash used *The Last Gunfighter Ballad*, as the title track of his album, charting with the single. In 1978, Guy Clark signed to Warner and his *Guy Clark* LP included *Foolish For Each Other*, which was a chart hit and added to the rapidly growing list of his songs covered by top acts. Clark by now was becoming more and more aware that it was to be with songwriting that he was to make his mark. Subsequent albums *Gulf Coast Of Texas* (1981) and *Better Days* (1983), both produced by Rodney Crowell, were to establish him as a master of the craft. The former contained *Heartbroke*, (Ricky Skaggs No.1 in 1981), *She's crazy for leaving*, (No.1 for it's co-writer Rodney Crowell in 1989) and *New Cut Road* (Bobby Bare top 20 hit in 1982). Clark himself charted in 1983 with the top 40 cut *Homegrown Tomatoes*, and John Conlee in 1986 took his finely crafted *The Carpenter*, into the country top ten. Clark has also written for Vince Gill (*Oklahoma Borderline*), Foster and Lloyd (*Fair Shake*), and Steve Wariner (*Baby I'm Your's*). After *Better Days*, it was six years before he was back recording, the resulting album *Old Friends*, was recorded on 8 track and released on Sugar Hill in 1989. Clark as usual was to draw on his friends Crowell, Emmylou Harris and new musician - songwriter Verlon Thompson to contribute. His covers of Ely's *The Indian Cowboy*, and Van Zandt's *To Live Is To Fly*, are most noteworthy. The title track, alongside *Immigrant Eyes*, has already been covered by others. After signing to Elektra's Asylum American Explorer series, Guy Clark released *Boats To Build*, in 1992. (Maurice Hope)

BEST OF GUY CLARK.
Tracks: Rita Ballou / L.A. freeway / She ain't going nowhere / That old feeling / Texas, 1947 / Desperados waiting for the train / Instant coffee blues / Nickel for the fiddler, A / Texas cookin' / Anyhow I love you / Virginia's real / Broken hearted people / Black haired boy / Last gunfighter ballad, The / Let him roll / Like a coat from the cold.
LP . . . . **INTS 5196**
MC . . . . **INTK 5196**
RCA International / May '82 / BMG.

BETTER DAYS.
Tracks: Not Advised.
■ **LP** **238801**
WEA / Aug '90 / WEA.

BOATS TO BUILD.
Tracks: Baton Rouge / Picasso's mandolin / How'd you get this number / Boats to build / Too much / Ramblin' Jack & Mahan / I don't love you much do I / Jack of all trades / Madonna w/Child ca. 1969 / Must be my baby.
CD **7559 61442-2**
MC **7559 61442-4**
Asylum / '93 / WEA.

GOOD LOVE AFTER BAD.
Tracks: Good love after bad / Old friends / Watermelon dream (Only on CD single.).
■ **7"** . . . . **MUM 11**
Mother / May '89.
■ **CD Single** . . . . **MUMCD 11**
Mother / May '89.

GUY CLARK.
Tracks: Fool on the roof / Roots for each other / Shade of all greens / Voila, an American dream / One paper kid / In the jailhouse now / Comfort and crazy / Don't you take it too bad / Houston kid / Fool on the roof blues.
■ **LP** . . . . **K 56565**
WEA / May '78 / WEA.

OLD FRIENDS (MOTHER LABEL).
Tracks: Old friends / Hands / I'm all through throwin' good love / Immigrant eyes / Heavy metal (don't mean rock & roll to me) / Come from the heart / Indian cowboy, The / To live is to fly / Watermelon days / Doctor Good Doctor.
LP . . . . **MUM 893**
Mother / Mar '89 / PolyGram.
CD . . . . **MUMCD 893**
■ **MC** . . . . **MUMC 893**
Mother / Mar '89.

OLD FRIENDS (SUGARHILL USA).
Tracks: Not Advised.
LP . . . . **SH 1025**
Sugarhill(USA) / '88 / Roots Records / Projection / Impetus Records / C.M. Distribution / Jazz Music / Swift / Duncans / A.D.A Distribution.

OLD NUMBER ONE.
Tracks: Rita Ballou / L.A. freeway / She ain't goin' nowhere / Nickel for the fiddler, A / That old time feeling / Texas - 1947 / Desperados waiting for the train / Like a coat from the cold / Instant coffee blues / Let him roll.
■ **LP** **APL1 1303**
RCA / '79.
■ **LP** . . . . **ED 285**
Edsel / May '88.
CD . . . . **EDCD 285**
Edsel / Jul '90 / Pinnacle.

SOUTH EAST OF TEXAS, THE.
Tracks: Not Advised.
■ **LP** . . . . **BSK 3381**
WEA / Aug '90 / WEA.

C 16 ■ DELETED

TEXAS COOKIN'.
Tracks: Texas cookin' / Anyhow, I love you / Virginia's real / It's about time / Good to love you lady / Broken hearted people / Black haired boy / Me I'm feelin' the same / Ballad of Laverne and Captain Flint / Last gunfighter ballad, The.
LP........................... ED 287
Edsel / Jun '88 / Pinnacle.
CD..........................EDCD 287
Edsel / Jul '90 / Pinnacle.

Clark, Roy

Born in 1933 in Virginia, the country singer, guitarist and comedian had hits in the USA country chart from 1963, but was bigger as a concert artist: he was the highest paid country star in 1969-74 and was named 'Comedian of the year' 1970-72 and 'Entertainer of the year' in 1973 by the Country Music Association. He played Cousin Roy on the *Beverly Hillbillies* and was co-host of *Hee-Haw*. He also recorded with banjoist Duck Trent and bluesman (actually an all-rounder) Clarence 'Gatemouth' Brown. (Donald Clarke)

20 GOLDEN PIECES: ROY CLARK.
Tracks: Then she's a lover / Unchained melody / Me and Bobby Magee / For once in my life / All the way / I still miss someone / Make the world go away / Days of sand and shovels, The / Simple thing as love, A / September song / You don't have very far to go / Come live with me / Daddy don't you walk so fast / Somewhere between love and tomorrow / Most beautiful girl, The / Why me / I really don't want to know / I'll paint you a song / Kiss an angel good morning / Onward christian soldiers (good old time religion).
LP........................... BDL 2038
Bulldog Records / Feb '84 / President Records / Jazz Music / Wellard Dist. / TKO Records Ltd.
MC........................... BDC 2038
Bulldog Records / '90 / President Records / Jazz Music / Wellard Dist. / TKO Records Ltd.

BEST OF ROY CLARK.
Tracks: Simple thing as love, A / Then she's a lover / Do you believe this town / September song / I never picked cotton / Tips of my fingers, The / Yesterday when I was in love / Right or left at Oak street / Love is just a state of mind / Thank God and greyhounds / Malaguena.
LP........................IMCA 27015
MCA (Import) / Mar '86 / Pinnacle / Silver Sounds (CD).

LIVE IN CONCERT.
Tracks: Rocky top / Riders in the sky / If I had to do it all over again / Somewhere my love / Duellin' banjos / Back up and push / Think summer / Malaguena.
■ LP........................... MCL 1657
MCA / Feb '82.

ROY CLARK IN CONCERT.
Tracks: Not Advised.
■ LP........................... ABCL 5268
ABC Records / Apr '79.

YESTERDAY WHEN I WAS YOUNG.
Tracks: Yesterday when I was young / Somewhere my love.
■ 7"........................... ABC 4213
ABC Records / Apr '78.

YOU'RE GONNA LOVE YOURSELF IN THE MORNING.
Tracks: You're gonna love yourself in the morning / Brand new day.
■ 7"........................... EMBS 339
Ember / Feb '75.

Clark, Sanford

In terms of chart records, Tulsa, Oklahoma born Sanford Clark was virtually a one hit wonder - but a very distinctive one hit at that, *The Fool*, in 1956. His entrance into the music business came when he was living in Phoenix, Arizona where he met Lee Hazelwood who took Clark's demo recordings to Randy Wood at Dot Records. Nearly 40 years later his recordings (and several unissued items) have been revived by Bear Family. (Tony Byworth)

FOOL, THE.
Tracks: Fool, The / Man who made an angel cry, The / Love charms / Cheat / Lonesome for a letter / Ooh baby / Darling dear / Modern romance / Travellin' man / Swanee river rock / Lou be doo / Usta be my baby / Nine pound hammer / Glory of love / Don't care / Usta be my baby (2).
■ LP........................... CH 83
Ace / Nov '83.
CD........................... BCD 15549
Bear Family / Jun '92 / Rollercoaster Records / Swift / Direct Distribution.

ROCKIN' ROLLIN' VOL.1.
Tracks: Modern romance / That's the way I feel / Man who made an angel cry, The / Ooo baby / Cross-eyed alley cat, A / Till my baby comes back / Lou be doo / Travellin' man / Lonesome for a letter / Fool, The / Love charms / Every minute of the day / Ain't nobody here but us chickens / Don't care / Cheat / Usta be my baby / Nine pound hammer / Swanee river rock.

LP........................... BFX 15198
Bear Family / Apr '86 / Rollercoaster Records / Swift / Direct Distribution.

ROCKIN' ROLLIN' VOL.2.
Tracks: Darling dear / Don't cry / Why did I choose you / Come what may / Fool's blues, A / Juice / Guitar man / Run boy run / I can't help it / Son of a gun / New kind of fool / Sing 'em some blues / Bad luck / Go on home / Pledging my love / Still as the night / My jealousy / Promise me baby / Glory of love.
LP........................... BFX 15199
Bear Family / Apr '86 / Rollercoaster Records / Swift / Direct Distribution.

SHADES.
Tracks: Better go home (throw that blade away) / Pledging my love / Girl on Death Row, The / Step aside / (They call me) Country / Shades / Fool, The / Climbin' the walls / Once upon a time / It's nothing to me / Where's the door / Big lie, The / Calling all hearts / Black Jack county chain / Big, big day tomorrow / Bad case of you / Wind will blow (demo) / Streets of San Francisco / Oh Julie / Kung Fu U / Mother Texas (you've been a mother to me) / Taste of you, A / Movin' on / Wind will blow / Feathers / Now I know I'm not in Kansas / Nine pound hammer.
CD........................... BCD 15731
Bear Family / Jul '93 / Rollercoaster Records / Swift / Direct Distribution.

THEY CALL ME COUNTRY.
Tracks: Big, big day tomorrow / Big lie, The / Black Jack county chain / Calling all hearts / Climbin' the walls / Fool, The / It's nothing to me / Look out floor / Shades / They call me country.
■ MC........................... ZCEB 131
Ember / Dec '78 / TKO Records Ltd / President Records.

Clarke, Terry

BUDDY'S ON THE FLATLAND ROAD.
Tracks: Buddy's on the flatland road.
■ CD Single........................... M 1001
Minidoka / '90 / ACD Trading Ltd.

CALL UP A HURRICANE.
Tracks: Rock the baby / New Camelot, The / Stars of Austin, The / Blow wind blow / Wish you were here / Tennessee wind / Why don't you take me / Blue hills / Arizona girls / Valley of the blue eyes / Buddy's waitin; on the Flatland road / Warbirds.
LP........................... MILP 001
MC........................... MILC 001
Minidoka / '90 / ACD Trading Ltd.
CD........................... MICD 001
Minidoka / Jan '91 / ACD Trading Ltd.

LET'S WORSHIP.
Tracks: Let's worship / Dear Lord / I am yours / You're all my life / These are the gates / You're my Lord God / Give thanks / Moses' song / I am gonna sing his praises / God you're so good.
CD........................... ARD 003
MC........................... ARC 003
Asaph / Apr '92 / Word Records (UK).

LIVING WORSHIP.
Tracks: Throne of grace / Jesus look down / Thank you Jesus / Free us / Nobody like you / Fill me / Just keep it / Psalm 151 / Hear the hallelujahs ring / I remember.
CD........................... ARD 001
MC........................... ARC 001
Asaph / Apr '92 / Word Records (UK).

RHYTHM OIL (Clarke, Terry/Michael Messer/Jesse Taylor).
Tracks: Not Advised.
CD........................... MICD 006
Minidoka / Oct '93 / ACD Trading Ltd.

SHELLEY RIVER, THE.
Tracks: Irish rockabilly blues / Leaving of Sligo, The / Sea song / Edge of Shamrock City, The / Last summer at Cloonacool / This town's too small / Raining all over the world / Johnny's on the road (from the north country) / American lipstick / Detroit to Dingle / Shelley river, The / Dream of time / Sligo honeymoon 1946 / Song of the streets.
MC........................... MILC 005
Minidoka / Jul '92 / ACD Trading Ltd.

SHELLY RIVER, THE.
Tracks: Not Advised.
CD........................... MICD 005
MC........................... MILC005
Minidoka / Nov '91 / ACD Trading Ltd.

Clawson, Cynthia

HYMN SINGER.
Tracks: Not Advised.
CD........................... DAYCD 4162
LP........................... DAY R 4162
MC........................... DAY C 4162
Dayspring / '88 / Word Records (UK) / Sony.

Clay, Joe

DUCKTAIL.
Tracks: Ducktail / Did you mean jelly bean (what you said cabbage head) / Crackerjack / Goodbye goodbye /

Sixteen chicks / Slipping out and sneaking in / Doggone it / Get on the right track baby / You look good to me.
LP........................... BFX 15224
Bear Family / Aug '86 / Rollercoaster Records / Swift / Direct Distribution.
CD........................... BCD 15516
Bear Family / Jul '90 / Rollercoaster Records / Swift / Direct Distribution.

Clayton, Lee

Born in Russellville, Alabama but raised in Oak Ridge, Tennessee. Lee Clayton moved to Nashville in the early 1970's following military service in the Air Force. Pre-empting the outlaw scene by several years, he provided Waylon Jennings with *Ladies Love Outlaws*, in 1972 while launching his own recording career on Capitol. He never achieved any chart singles and, during the 1980's, took on additional artistic talents of novelist and playwrite. Apparently Bono, of U2, cites Clayton as his only country influence. (Tony Byworth)

ANOTHER NIGHT.
Tracks: Not Advised.
CD........................... PRLD 700812
LP........................... PRL 70081
MC........................... PRLC 70084
Provogue / Nov '89 / Pinnacle.

BORDER AFFAIR.
Tracks: Silver stallion / If you can touch her at all / Back home in Tennessee / Border affair / Old number nine / Like a diamond / My woman my love / Tequila is addictive / My true love / Rainbow in the sky.
LP........................... EST 11751
Capitol / Apr '78 / EMI.

DREAM GOES ON.
Tracks: What's a mother gonna do / Industry / Won't you give me one more chance / Draggin' them chains / Where is the justice / Whatcha gonna do / Oh how lucky I am / Dream goes on, The.
■ LP........................... EST 12139
Capitol / May '81.

DREAM GOES ON.
Tracks: Dream goes on / Saturday night special.
■ 7"........................... CL 16195
Capitol / May '81.

I LOVE YOU.
Tracks: I love you / Wind and rain.
■ 7"........................... CL 16108
Capitol / Jan '80.

NAKED CHILD.
Tracks: Saturday night special / I ride alone / 10,000 years / Sexual moon / Wind and rain / I love you / Jaded virgin / Little cocaine / If I can do it.
■ LP........................... EST 11942
Capitol / '79.

OH HOW LUCKY I AM.
Tracks: Oh how lucky I am / Won't you give me one more chance.
■ 7"........................... CL 16193
Capitol / Apr '81.

SILVER STALLION.
Tracks: Silver stallion / Border affair.
■ 7"........................... CL 15982
Capitol / May '78.

TEQUILA IS ADDICTIVE.
Tracks: Tequila is addictive / 10, 000 years / Sexual moon.
7"........................... PRS 10167
■ CD Single........................... PRM 20167
Provogue / Sep '90 / Pinnacle.

Clayton, Paul

BLUEGRASS SESSION, 1952, A (see under Clifton, Bill).

DAYS OF MOBY DICK.
Tracks: Not Advised.
LP........................... TLP 1005
Tradition / Nov '74 / Roots Records / Projection / C.M. Distribution.

Clement, Jack

Cowboy Jack Clement as he's often, affectionately called, is a genial, walking history of country/rockabilly music - a man who's been at it since 1952 and one of life's true characters. Producer/music publisher/recording studio owner/singer -songwriter, Clement is an accomplished man in many fields, and a versatile musician, playing guitar, dobro and mandolin. Born in Memphis on 5.4.1931, before moving to Washington DC in early 1950's, he worked with The Stoneman Family, Roy Clark and Buzz Busby and the Banjo Boys. Prior to starting his association with Sun Records (1956 -1959) he was with the Dixie Ramblers. At Sun, Clement produced Cash's recordings (and others) penning him the hit songs *Ballad Of A Teenage*

Queen, and *Guess Things Happend That Way*. Some 35 years on, Clement can still be found working the controls. Since his days at Sun Records Clement has had his own labels Fernwood and JMI, where he shaped Don Williams' career in 1972. He's already been largely responsible for doing likewise for Charley Pride, producing his albums, and supplying him such hits as *I Know One*, and *Let The Chips Fall*. Other songs that Jack Clement wrote for others include; *Miller's Cave*, (Hank Snow/Bobby Bare), *Gone Girl*, (Johnny Cash) and *Gone, On The Other Hand*, (Tompall & Glaser Bros). Acts that Clement has produced include Louis Armstrong, Waylon Jennings, and Jerry Lee Lewis. He also produced the film *Dear Dead Delilah*. (Maurice Hope)

ALL I WANT TO DO IN LIFE.
Tracks: Gone girl / Roving gambler / We must believe in magic / Good hearted woman / When I dream / All I want to do in life / It'll be her / There she goes / Queen Bee / You ask me to.
■ **LP.** . . . . **K 52126**
Elektra / Apr '79.

Clements, Vassar

The veteran bluegrass fiddler, born in 1928 in South Carolina. Vassar Clements has been at the centre of the 'Newgrass' movement, and has proved that good players can make it together no matter where they come from. He played with Bill Monroe on the Grand Ole Opry in 1949 and recorded with him the next year. He's played and sessioned with Jim & Jesse, Faron Young, Emmylou Harris, Linda Ronstadt, Charlie Daniels, Paul McCartney, the Boston Pops, the Grateful Dead, the Nitty Gritty Dirt Band and many others including the not-quite-traditional Earl Scruggs Revue. The *Hillbilly Jazz*, LP on Flying Fish included David Bromberg. Clements has also recorded for Rounder, and plays in the group Old And In The Way on the USA Sugar Hill label, with Jerry Garcia and David Grisman. He made a duet album in Nashville in 1985 with Stephane Grappelli. (Donald Clarke)

BLUEGRASS SESSION, THE.
Tracks: Reno shuffle / Vasillee II / It's mighty dark / Nine pound hammer / Stompin' grazz / Six more miles / Scuffin' / White house blues / Swingin' low / Rocky top / Silly Millie.
■ **LP.** . . . . **SNTF 748**
Sonet / '78.
LP. . . . . **FF 038**
Flying Fish (USA) / Mar '89 / Cadillac Music / Roots Records / Projection / C.M. Distribution / Direct Distribution / Jazz Music / Duncans / A.D.A Distribution.

CLEMENTS, HARTFORD & HOLLAND (Clements, Vassar/John Hartford/Dave Holland).
Tracks: Not Advised.
LP. . . . . **ROUNDER 0207**
Rounder / Jul '85 / Projection / Roots Records / Swift / C.M. Distribution / Topic Records / Jazz Music / Hot Shot / A.D.A Distribution / Direct Distribution.
MC . . . . **ROUNDER 0207C**
Rounder / Aug '88 / Projection / Roots Records / Swift / C.M. Distribution / Topic Records / Jazz Music / Hot Shot / A.D.A Distribution / Direct Distribution.

CROSSING THE CATSKILLS.
Tracks: Not Advised.
LP. . . . . **ROUNDER 0016**
Rounder / Jan '87 / Projection / Roots Records / Swift / C.M. Distribution / Topic Records / Jazz Music / Hot Shot / A.D.A Distribution / Direct Distribution.
MC . . . . **ROUNDER 0016C**
Rounder / '88 / Projection / Roots Records / Swift / C.M. Distribution / Topic Records / Jazz Music / Hot Shot / A.D.A Distribution / Direct Distribution.

GRASS ROUTES.
Tracks: Beats me / Westport Drive / Come on home / Florida blues / Other end, The / Rain, rain, rain / Rambling / Rounder blues / Fiddlin' will / Non stop / Flame of love / Turkey in the straw.
MC . . . . **ROU 0287**
Rounder / '91 / Projection / Roots Records / Swift / C.M. Distribution / Topic Records / Jazz Music / Hot Shot / A.D.A Distribution / Direct Distribution.
CD . . . . **CDROU 0287**
Rounder / Feb '92 / Projection / Roots Records / Swift / C.M. Distribution / Topic Records / Jazz Music / Hot Shot / A.D.A Distribution / Direct Distribution.

HILLBILLY JAZZ RIDES AGAIN.
Tracks: Hillbilly jazz / Don't hop don't skip / Airmail special / Say goodbye to the blues / Swing street / Woodsheddin' / Be a little discreet / Your mind is on vacation / Caravan / How can I go on without you / Triple stop boogie / Take a break.
LP. . . . . **FF 385**
Flying Fish (USA) / Feb '87 / Cadillac Music / Roots Records / Projection / C.M. Distribution / Direct Distribution / Jazz Music / Duncans / A.D.A Distribution.
CD . . . . **FF 385CD**
MC . . . . **FF 385C**
Flying Fish (USA) / May '93 / Cadillac Music / Roots Records / Projection / C.M. Distribution / Direct Distribution / Jazz Music / Duncans / A.D.A Distribution.

NASHVILLE JAM (Clements, Vassar/Doug Jernigan/J. McReynolds).
Tracks: Not Advised.
LP. . . . . **FF 073**
Flying Fish (USA) / May '79 / Cadillac Music / Roots Records / Projection / C.M. Distribution / Direct Distribution / Jazz Music / Duncans / A.D.A Distribution.

VASSAR (Clement, Vassar Band).
Tracks: Not Advised.
LP. . . . . **FF 232**
Flying Fish (USA) / Dec '88 / Cadillac Music / Roots Records / Projection / C.M. Distribution / Direct Distribution / Jazz Music / Duncans / A.D.A Distribution.

Clifton, Bill

Born William Marburg in Riverdale, Maryland on 05.04.1931. Vocalist, guitarist, fiddler/autoharp exponent, Bill Clifton did much to ensure that the hard worked, traditional aspect of the music would continue. Clifton's dedication brought him to England in 1963 (until 1967), playing the folk circuit (where he hosted the weekly BBC show Cellar Full Of Folk). He'd already recorded an entire album of Carter Family songs on Starday in 1961. He began playing during the 40's, and sang with friend folk revival stalwart Paul Clayton - before forming his own band, the Dixie Mountain Boys, in 1954. Worked as both adviser and organiser of festival's, including the Newport Folk Festival, where acoustic country, folk and bluegrass acts have appeared regularly. Clifton was also responsible for opening the way for bluegrass acts to come over to England - 1975's Monroe debut just one instance. In 1955 he financed his own songbook *150 Old - Time Folk and Gospel Songs*, the aspiring traditional folk singer's essential handbook. Apart from solo work all over Europe, New Zealand (where he lived for a spell during the 70's - forming the Hamilton County Band), and Japan, he toured the States and Europe alongside Red Rector (they'd previously recorded the *Another Happy Day* in 1975), and Don Stover in 1978. He's still organising bluegrass/folk festivals and generally sharing his love/knowledge of old time music. (Maurice Hope)

ARE YOU FROM DIXIE? (see under Rector, Red).

BEATLE CRAZY.
Tracks: Beatle crazy / Little girl dressed in blue (Original Decca recording) / Keep that wheel a turning (Original Decca recording.) / Jug of punch / Baby lie easy / Green to grey.
LP P.Disc. . . . . **BFP 15121**
Bear Family / Oct '83 / Rollercoaster Records / Swift / Direct Distribution.

BLUE RIDGE MOUNTAIN BLUEGRASS (Clifton, Bill & The Dixie Mountain Boys).
Tracks: Little whitewashed chimney / Mary dear / Pal of yesterday / Cedar grove / Livin' the right life now / Another broken heart / Girl I left in sunny Tennessee, The / Corey / Are you alone? / Lonely heart blues / You go to your church / Dixie Mountain express / Dixie darling / Blue Ridge Mountain blues.
LP. . . . . **WRS 047**
Westwood / '82 / Pinnacle.

BLUEGRASS SESSION, 1952 (A) (Clifton, Bill & Paul Clayton).
Tracks: John Henry / Watermelon on the vine / Roll on the ground (1) / Pleasant and delightful / Fox, The / John Hardy / East Virginia blues / Jealous lover / Beautiful Mabel Clare / Bury me beneath the willow / Poor boy / Roll on the ground (2).
LP. . . . . **BF 15001**
Bear Family / Sep '84 / Rollercoaster Records / Swift / Direct Distribution.

EARLY YEARS 1957-1958, THE.
Tracks: Girl I left in Tennessee, The / Dixie darlin' / You don't need to think about me .. / I'll be there Mary dear / Paddy on the turnpike / I'll wander back someday / Darlin' Corey / When you kneel at my mother's grave / Blue ridge mountain blues / Are you alone / Springhill disaster / I'm living the right life now / Lonely heart blues / Cedar Grove / You go to your church / Walking in my sleep / Pal of yesterday / Just another broken heart / Little white washed chimney.
CD . . . . **CD 1021**
Rounder / '92 / Projection / Roots Records / Swift / C.M. Distribution / Topic Records / Jazz Music / Hot Shot / A.D.A Distribution / Direct Distribution.

GOING BACK TO DIXIE.
Tracks: Going back to Dixie / Your mother still prays for you, Jack / Moonshiner / Just a smile / Lonely little cabin / Dream of the miner's child / Ground hog hunt / Engine 23 / Jim Hartfield's son / Saturday night / Lonesome for you / Lazy courtship / Across the shining river / Roll the cotton down / Take me back / Lonesome field / Little green valley / When I lay my burden down / At my window / Gonna lay down my old guitar / Where the willow gently sways / When I'm with you / My nights are lonely / I'm gonna blow out the lamp in the window / Louis Collins / I'll be satisfied / Old Reuben / My Cindy girl / Dixie ramble / Big Bill / Bringing Mary home / Mother, where is your daughter tonight? / Prisoner's dream / Sweet fern / Forsaken love / Sales tax to the woman.
■ **Double LP** . . . . **BFD 15000**
Bear Family / Sep '84.

MOUNTAIN FOLK SONGS.
Tracks: Not Advised.
LP. . . . . **SLP 111**
MC . . . . **GT 5111**
Starday (USA) / Apr '87 / Crusader Marketing Co.

Cline, Charlie

COUNTRY DOBRO.
Tracks: Not Advised.
LP. . . . . **AD 2001**
Adelphi (1) / May '81 / Jetstar.

MORE DOBRO (Cline, Charlie with the Marakesh Express).
Tracks: Not Advised.
LP. . . . . **AD 2008**
Adelphi (1) / May '81 / Jetstar.

Cline, Patsy

Born Virginia Patterson Hensley in Winchester, Virginia on 08.09.1932. Patsy Cline was to enjoy only a short career - due to her death in a plane crash on 05.03.1963, near Patterson, Tennessee, when returning from a benefit show with fellow Opry acts Cowboy Copas, Hawkshaw Hawkins and her manager Randy Hughes. Thirty years later, Patsy Cline's music still figures strongly in the country music market place. Her slow rise to fame coming via her appearance on the Arthur Godfrey CBS Talent Show in 1956. Patsy Cline appeared regularly on Connie B Gay's *Town & Country Jamboree*, a TV show that originally started out in radio format. Her debut single *A Church, A Courtroom, And Then Goodbye* was issued on Decca's Coral label in 1955. Patsy Cline then signed to Four Star Recordings, with whom she was to be contracted until 1960. During this time Cline enjoyed limited success - apart from *Walking After Midnight*, a No. 2 hit in 1957. That year also saw her winning Billboard Magazine's "Most Promising Country and Western Artist". However, it wasn't until 1961 that she really broke through. As her most rewarding spell unfolded, legendary record producer Owen Bradley was to prove an influential figure, helping to guide her career at new label, Decca. Patsy gained major success with Hank Cochran/Harlan Howard's 1961 chart topper *I Fall To Pieces*, and her version of Willie Nelson's *Crazy*, was a No. 2 hit. This record is reputedly No. 2 on the all-time juke box play list, the song alone has been an inspiration to countless aspiring talents both country and pop. Following hits were to include *She's Got You*, (No. 1 in 1962), the top ten single *Leaving On Your Mind*, and the posthumous 1963 singles *Sweet Dreams*, and *Faded Love*. Patsy, apart from becoming the first female act to cross over into the pop charts also achieved the distinction of playing Las Vegas during the entire month of December in 1962, an indication that her career was progressively becoming more pop orientated, whilst still retaining sufficient country content to appeal to her faithful. Patsy Cline was posthumously elected to the Country Music Hall Of Fame in 1975, the ultimate honour in country music. RCA and MCA records in 1980, through modern electronic technology, blended the voices of Patsy and Jim Reeves together. Among the resulting songs was *Have You Ever Been Lonely*, issued as a single in 1981 which reached No. 5 on the country charts. Her music continues to be re-packaged by the likes of Arcade, Columbia, the Country Music Foundation, MCA, Magnum Music, Pickwick and Prism Leisure. (Maurice Hope)

12 GREATEST HITS: PATSY CLINE.
Tracks: Walking after midnight / Sweet dreams / Crazy / I fall to pieces / So wrong / Strange / Back in baby's arms / She's got you / Faded love / Why can't he be you / You're stronger than me / Leavin' on your mind.
■ **CD** . . . . **DMCL 1875**
MCA / Jul '88.

20 CLASSIC TRACKS.
Tracks: If I could stay asleep / Heart you break may be your own, The / Try again / Three cigarettes in an ashtray / If I could see the world / Cry not for me / Yes I understand / Dear God / I'm blue again / Love me, love me honey do / Stop look and listen / Don't ever leave me / You'll know, The / Come on in (and make yourself at home) / Pick me up on your way down / Turn the cards slowly / I cried all the way to the altar / Honky tonk merry go round / I'm moving along / Gotta lot of rhythm in my soul.
CD . . . . **CDSM 005**
MC . . . . **SMTC 005**
Starburst / '87 / Terry Blood Dist. / Jazz Music.
LP. . . . . **SMT 005**
Starburst / '88 / Terry Blood Dist. / Jazz Music.

20 GOLDEN GREATS: PATSY CLINE.
Tracks: Not Advised.
LP. **20066**

C 18 ■ DELETED

MC 40066
Astan (USA) / Nov '84.

20 GOLDEN HITS: PATSY CLINE.
Tracks: Not Advised.
LP ..... MA 41285
MC ..... MAMC 941285
Masters (Holland) / '88.

20 GOLDEN PIECES: PATSY CLINE.
Tracks: I don't wanta / Let the teardrops fall / I've loved and lost again / Fingertips / I can't forget / Just out of reach / Hungry for love / If I could only stay asleep / Today, tomorrow and forever / I love you honey / Never no more / Walking after midnight / Pick me up on your way down / Honky tonk merry go round / I cried all the way to the altar / Too many secrets / Three cigarettes in an ashtray / In care of the blues / Stop the world / I can see an angel.
LP ..... BDL 2003
MC ..... BDC 2003
Bulldog Records / Jul '82 / President Records / Jazz Music / Wellard Dist. / TKO Records Ltd.

20 GREATEST HITS: PATSY CLINE.
Tracks: Stop the world / Walking after midnight / I can see an angel / Three cigarettes in an ashtray.
LP ..... FUN 9019
MC ..... FUNC 9019
Fun (Holland) / Sep '88 / Pinnacle.

ALWAYS.
Tracks: Always / Love letters in the sand / Crazy arms / Bill Bailey won't you please come home / Have you ever been lonely / You made me love you / I can see an angel / That's my desire / Your cheatin' heart / That's how a heartache begins / I love you so much it hurts / Half as much / You belong to me.
LP ..... SHM 3219
Hallmark / Oct '87 / Pickwick Records.
CD ..... PWKS 502
MC ..... HSC 3219
Pickwick / Sep '93 / Pickwick Records.

BACK IN BABY'S ARMS.
Tracks: Back in baby's arms / Sweet dreams.
7" 05888
Brunswick / '63.

BEST OF PATSY CLINE.
Tracks: Walking after midnight / I fall to pieces / Crazy / Who can I count on / She's got you / Strange / When I get thru with you / Imagine that / Someone / Heartaches / Sweet dreams / Faded love / When you need a laugh / He called me baby / Anytime.
LP ..... SHM 3192
Hallmark / Sep '86 / Pickwick Records.
CD ..... WMCD 5656
MC ..... WMMC 4656
Woodford Music / Jun '92 / Terry Blood Dist. / Midland Records.
CD ..... PWKS 524
MC ..... HSC 3192
Pickwick / Sep '93 / Pickwick Records.

CLASSIC PATSY CLINE.
Tracks: Not Advised.
CD 6 6450072
MC 6 6450074
BMG / Dec '92 / BMG.

COUNTRY MUSIC HALL OF FAME, THE.
Tracks: Walking after midnight / I fall to pieces / Crazy / Who can I count on / She's got you / Strange / When I get thru with you / Imagine that / So wrong / Heartaches / Leavin' on your mind / Sweet dreams / Faded love / When you need a laugh / He called me baby / Anytime.
■ LP ..... CDLM 8077
Coral / '79.
LP ..... MCL 1739
MC ..... MCLC 1739
MCA / '83 / BMG.

CRAZY.
Tracks: Crazy / Walking after midnight.
7" ..... MCA 1137
MCA / Mar '87 / BMG.

CRAZY.
Tracks: Crazy / Sweet dreams.
7" ..... MCA 1465
CD Single ..... DMCAT 1465
■ MC Single ..... MCAC 1465
MCA / Nov '90.

CRAZY DREAMS.
Tracks: Hidin' out / Turn the cards slowly / Church, a courtroom and then goodbye, A / Honky tonk merry go round / I love you honey / Come on in (and make yourself at home) / I cried all the way to the altar / Stop, look and listen / I've loved and lost again / Dear God / He will do for you (what he's done for me) / Walkin' after midnight / Heart you break may be your own, The / Pick me up on your way down / Poor man's (or a rich man's gold), A / Today, tomorrow and forever / Fingertips / Stranger in my arms, A / Don't ever leave me again / Try again / Too many secrets / Then you'll know / Three cigarettes (in an ashtray) / That wonderful someone / (Write me) in care of the blues / Hungry for love / I can't forget / I don't wanta / Ain't no wheels on this ship / Stop the world (and let me off) / Walking dream / Cry not for me / If I could see the world / Just out of reach / I can see an angel / Let the teardrops fall / Never no more / If I could only stay asleep / I'm moving along / I'm blue again / Love love, love me honey do / Yes I understand / Gotta lot of rhythm in my soul / Life's railway to heaven / Just a closer walk with thee / Lovesick blues / How can I face tomorrow / There he goes / Crazy dreams.
LP Set ..... SDBS 001
Sundown / Oct '89 / Terry Blood Dist. / Jazz Music / C.M. Distribution.
CD Set ..... CDSD 3.001
MC Set ..... SDC 3.001
Sundown / Jul '90 / Terry Blood Dist. / Jazz Music / C.M. Distribution.

DEFINITIVE PATSY CLINE, THE.
Tracks: Not Advised.
CD ..... ARC 94992
MC ..... ARC 94994
Arc / Sep '92 / ARC Music Distribution Ltd / Projection / Koch International.

DREAMING.
Tracks: Sweet dreams / I fall to pieces / Crazy / Heartaches / Tra le la le la triangle / Have you ever been lonely? / Faded love / Your cheatin' heart / She's got you / Walking after midnight / San Antonio rose / Three cigarettes in an ashtray / When I need a laugh / Always.
LP ..... PLAT 303
MC ..... PLAC 303
Platinum Music / Apr '88 / Prism Leisure PLC / Ross Records.
CD ..... PLATCD 303
Platinum Music / Dec '88 / Prism Leisure PLC / Ross Records.

ESSENTIAL COLLECTION, THE.
Tracks: Not Advised.
CD Set ..... MCAD 410421
MC Set ..... MCAC 410421
MCA / Nov '91 / BMG.

FOREVER & ALWAYS.
Tracks: Walkin' after midnight / Stranger in my arms, A / Poor man's roses, A / Dear God / Then you'll know / Fingerprints / Stop the world / Walkin' dream / Hidin' out / (If I could see the world through) The eyes of a child.
CD 472864-2
MC 472864-4
Epic / Jun '93 / Sony.

GOLDEN GREATS: PATSY CLINE.
Tracks: I fall to pieces / She's got you / Crazy / Walkin' after midnight / Sweet dreams / Who can I count on / Strange / When I get thru with you / Imagine that / So wrong / Heartaches / Leavin' on your mind / Faded love / When you need a laugh / He called me baby / Anything.
■ LP ..... MCM 5008
MCA / Jul '85.
■ MC ..... MCMC 5008
MCA / Jul '85.
■ CD ..... DMCM 5008
MCA / Sep '91.
CD ..... MCLD 19038
■ MC ..... MCLC 19038
MCA / Apr '92.

GREATEST HITS: PATSY CLINE & JIM REEVES (Cline, Patsy & Jim Reeves).
Tracks: Have you ever been lonely? / Welcome to my world / He'll have to go / Crazy / Sweet dreams / Four walls / Am I losing you? / Golden memories and silver tears / I fall to pieces / She's got you.
LP ..... RCALP 3057
MC ..... RCAK 3057
RCA / Mar '82 / BMG.
LP ..... NL 85152
■ MC ..... NK 85152
RCA / '87.

HAVE YOU EVER BEEN LONELY?.
Tracks: Not Advised.
LP ..... MCF 2725
MCA / '75 / BMG.

HEARTACHES.
Tracks: Heartaches.
■ 7" 05878
Brunswick / Nov '62.

HONKY TONK MERRY GO ROUND.
Tracks: Not Advised.
CD ..... ONN 42
Object Enterprises / May '89 / Gold & Sons / Terry Blood Dist. / Midland Records.

I FALL TO PIECES.
Tracks: I fall to pieces.
7" ..... MCS 1512
CD Single ..... MCSTD 1512
■ MC Single ..... MCSC 1512
MCA / Feb '91.

LEGENDARY PATSY CLINE, THE.
Tracks: Walking after midnight / Just out of reach / I've loved and lost again / Fingerprints / I can't forget / Hungry for love / If I could only stay asleep / I love you honey / Never no more / Pick me up on your way down / Honky tonk merry go round / I cried all the way to the altar / Three cigarettes in an ashtray / Stop the world and let me off.
■ LP ..... MFP 50460
MFP / Feb '80.

LIVE AT THE OPRY.
Tracks: Church, a courtroom, and then goodbye / I've loved and lost again / Walkin' after midnight / Lovesick blues / How can I face tomorrow? / Loose talk / Crazy dreams / There he goes / Lovin' in vain / I fall to pieces / She's got you / Crazy.
■ CD ..... DMCL 1891
MCA / Aug '89.
MC ..... MCLC 19111
MCA / Dec '92 / BMG.

LOT OF RHYTHM IN MY SOUL.
Tracks: Not Advised.
■ CD ..... PCD 841
Pickwick / Oct '86.

LOVE SONGS.
Tracks: Not Advised.
CD ..... CDMFP 5957
MC ..... TCMFP 5957
MFP / Jan '92 / EMI.

MAGIC OF PATSY CLINE, THE.
Tracks: Not Advised.
CD ..... TKOCD 003
MC ..... TKOCS 003
TKO Records / '92 / TKO Records Ltd / President Records.

OFF THE RECORD WITH..
Tracks: I love you honey / Never no more / Walking after midnight / I don't wanna / Let the teardrops fall / I've loved and lost again / Fingerprints / I can't forget / Just out of reach / Hungry for love / Don't ever leave me / Then you'll know / If I could see the world / I'm moving along / Gotta lot of rhythm in my soul / Stop, look and listen / Love me, love me, honey do / I'm blue again / Dear god / Yes, I understand.
Double LP ..... FEDD 1007
MC Set ..... CFEDD 1007
Sierra / Aug '87.

ORIGINAL HITS.
Tracks: Not Advised.
LP 35006
MC 65006
Grand Canyon / May '88.

PATSY CLINE.
Tracks: Just a closer walk with thee / Never no more / Ain't no wheels on this ship / He'll do for now / Honky tonk merry go round / Poor man's roses, A / Pick me up / Turn the cards slowly / Dear God / I love you honey / I can't forget you / Crazy dreams.
MC ..... ZCGAS 711
Audio Fidelity(USA) / Oct '84 / Stage One Records.

PATSY CLINE COLLECTION, THE.
Tracks: I'm walking the dog / It wasn't god who made honky tonk angels / Turn the cards slowly / Church, a courtroom, and then goodbye, A / Honky tonk merry go round / I love you, honey / Come on in (and make yourself at home) / I don't wanta / Stop, look and listen / I've loved and lost again / Yes, I know why / For rent / Walkin' after midnight / Heart you break my be your own, The / Pick me up on your way down / Poor man's roses (Or a rich man's gold), A / Today, tomorrow and forever / Don't ever leave me again / Try again / Too many secrets / Then you'll know / Three cigarettes in an ashtry / That wonderful someone / In car of the blues / Hungry for love / I can't forget / If I could see the world (Through the eyes of a child) / Just out of reach / I can see an angel / Let the teardrops fall / Never no more / If only I could stay asleep / I'm moving along / I'm blue again / Love, love, love me honey do / Yes, I understand / Got a lot of rhythm in my soul / Life's railway to heaven / Just a closer walk with thee / Lovesick blues / How can I face tomorrow / There he goes / Crazy dreams / When your house is not a home / Stupid cupid / Loose talk / I fall to pieces / Shoes / Lovin' in vain / Side by side / True love / San Antonio rose / Wayward wind, The / Crazy / Who can I count on / Seven lonely days / I love you so much it hurts / Foolin' around / Have you ever been lonely (Have you ever been blue) / South of the border (Down Mexico way) / Strange / You're stronger than me / Bill Bailey, won't you please come home / She's got you / You made me love you (I didn't want to do it) / You belong to me / Heartaches / Your cheatin' heart / That's my desire / Half as much / Lonely street / Anytime / You were only fooling (While I was falling in love) / I can't help it (If I'm still in love with you) / When I get through with you (You'll love me too) / Imagine that / So wrong / Why can't he be you / Your kinda love / When you need a laugh / Leavin' on your mind / Back in baby's arms / Tra le la le la triangle / That's how a heartache begins / Tennessee waltz / Faded love / Someday (you'll want me to want you) / Love letters in the sand / Blue moon of Kentucky / Sweet dreams (Of you) / Always / Does your heart beat for me / He called me baby / Crazy arms / You took him off my hands / I'll sail my ship alone / eust a closer walk with thee.
CD Set MCAD4 10421
MC Set MCAC4 10421
MCA / '92 / BMG.

PATSY CLINE SHOWCASE.
Tracks: I fall to pieces / Foolin' round / Wavering wind, The / South of the border / I love you so much it hurts / Seven lonely days / Crazy / San Antonio rose / True love / Walking after midnight / Poor mans roses, A.
LP ..... HAT 3036
MC ..... HATC 3036
Stetson / Apr '87 / Crusader Marketing Co. / Swift / Wellard Dist. / Midland Records / C.M. Distribution.

PATSY CLINE STORY.
Tracks: Heartaches / She's got you / Walking after midnight / Strange / Leavin' on your mind / South of the border / Foolin' round / I fall to pieces / Poor man's roses, A / Tra le la le la triangle / True love / Imagine that / Back in baby's arms / Crazy / You're stronger than me / Seven lonely days / Sweet dreams / Your cheatin' heart / San Antonio rose / Why can't he be you / Wayward way, The / So wrong / I love you so much it hurts / You belong to me.
■ **Double LP** . . . . **IMCA 24038**
MCA (Import) / Mar '86.

PORTRAIT OF PATSY CLINE, A.
Tracks: Who can I count on / You took him off my hands / Your kinda love / Does your heart beat for me / Faded love / I'll sail my ship alone / When you need a laugh / Crazy arms / Always / When I'm through with you (you'll love me too) / Blue moon of Kentucky / Someday you'll want me to want you.
■ **LP** . . . . **IMCA 224**
MCA (Import) / Mar '86.

QUEEN OF COUNTRY.
Tracks: Just a closer walk with thee / Never no more / Ain't no wheels on this ship / He'll do for now / Honky tonk merry go round / Poor man's roses, A / Gotta lot of rhythm in my soul / I've loved and lost again / Lovesick blues / Cry not for me / Stranger in my arms, A / In care of the blues / Just out of reach / Three cigarettes in an ashtray / Heart you break may be your own, The / That wonderful someone / I cried all the way to the altar / Church, a courtroom, then goodbye, A / Pick me up (on your way down) / Turn the cards slowly / Dear God / I love you honey / I can't forget you / Crazy dreams.
MC Set . . . . **DTO 10006**
Ditto / Jul '82 / Pickwick Records.
MC Set . . . . **DTOL 10006**
Ditto / Feb '90 / Pickwick Records.

REAL PATSY CLINE, THE.
Tracks: Seven lonely nights / Sweet dreams / Walkin' after midnight / C'mon in / I fall to pieces / Crazy / She's got you / Love sick blues / How can I face tomorrow.
VHS . . . . **PLATV 301**
Platinum Music / Jul '89 / Prism Leisure PLC / Ross Records.

REMEMBERING (Cline, Patsy & Jim Reeves).
Tracks: Fall to pieces / So wrong / Misty moonlight / Back in baby's arms / Missing you / Walking after midnight / Blizzard / Why can't he be you / Distant drums / Leavin' on your mind (Patsy).
■ **MC** . . . . **IMCAC 1467**
MCA (Import) / Mar '86.
■ **LP** . . . . **IMCA 1467**
MCA (Import) / Mar '86.

REMEMBERING PATSY.
Tracks: Walkin after midnight / I've loved and lost again / Strange / Imagine that / San antonio rose / Faded love / Lovesick blues / I fall to pieces / So wrong / Crazy / Sweet dreams.
VHS . . . . **PLATV 313**
Prism / Mar '93 / Pinnacle / Midland Records.

REPLAY ON PATSY CLINE.
Tracks: Not Advised.
LP . . . . **FEDB 5033**
MC . . . . **CFEDB 5033**
Sierra / Apr '86.

SHE'S GOT YOU.
Tracks: She's got you.
■ **7"** **05866**
Brunswick / Apr '62.

SONGWRITER'S TRIBUTE.
Tracks: Lovin' in vain / Crazy / I love you so much it hurts / You're stronger than me / Imagine that / So wrong / When you need a laugh / Your kinda love / That's how a heartache begins / He called me baby / You took him off my hands.
■ **LP** . . . . **IMCA 25019**
MCA / Mar '87.
■ **MC** . . . . **IMCAC 25019**
MCA / Mar '87.

SWEET DREAMS WITH..
Tracks: Not Advised.
CD . . . . **ENTCD 267**
Entertainers / Oct '87.
LP . . . . **ENT LP 13018**
MC . . . . **ENT MC 13018**
Entertainers / '88.

TOO MANY SECRETS.
Tracks: Walking after midnight / I've loved and lost again / I love you honey / Fingerprints / Never no more / Hiding out / Walking dream / Let the teardrops fall / Just out of reach / Ain't no wheels on this ship / I can't forget / Too many secrets / In care of the blues / Hungry for love / I don't wanna / If I could see the world / Stop the world / I can see an angel / Today tomorrow and forever / Life's railway to heaven.
CD . . . . **CDSM 013**
LP . . . . **SMT 013**
Starburst / Feb '88 / Terry Blood Dist. / Jazz Music.
MC . . . . **SMTC 013**
Starburst / Nov '88 / Terry Blood Dist. / Jazz Music.

TRIBUTE TO PATSY CLINE, A.
Tracks: Leavin' on your mind / Tra le la le la triangle / Imagine that / Back in baby's arms / You're stronger than me / Sweet dreams / Why can't he be you / So wrong / When I get thru with you / Lovin' in vain / Who can I count on / Crazy.
LP . . . . **HAT 3008**
MC . . . . **HATC 3008**
Stetson / Feb '86 / Crusader Marketing Co. / Swift / Wellard Dist. / Midland Records / C.M. Distribution.

UNFORGETTABLE.
Tracks: Not Advised.
CD . . . . **PWK 017**
Pickwick / '91 / Pickwick Records.

WALKIN AFTER MIDNIGHT (28 Country Classics).
Tracks: Walkin' after midnight / I've loved and lost again / Poor man's roses (or a rich man's gold), A / Turn the cards slowly / I cried all the way to the alter / Pick me up (on your way down) / Stranger in my arms, A / Honky tonk merry-go round / Church a courtroom and then goodbye, A / Three cigarettes in an ashtray / Never no more / Dear God / Lovesick blues / If I could stay asleep / Just out of reach / Then you'll know / I love honey / Fingerprints / There he goes he'll do for you (what he's done for me) / I can't forget you / Today, tomorrow and forever / Crazy dreams / I can see an angel / If I could see the world.
CD . . . . **PLATCD 27**
MC . . . . **PLAC 27**
Platinum Music / Jul '89 / Prism Leisure PLC / Ross Records.

WALKIN AFTER MIDNIGHT (2).
Tracks: Not Advised.
CD . . . . **CTS 55404**
MC . . . . **CTS 45404**
Country Stars / Jan '92.

WALKIN' AFTER MIDNIGHT.
Tracks: Not Advised.
CD **550 0542**
MC **550 0544**
Spectrum (1) / May '93 / PolyGram.

WALKING AFTER MIDNIGHT.
Tracks: Walkin' after midnight / I've loved & lost again / I can't forget / Just out of reach / I'm hungry for love / I can see an angel / Walking dream / If I could see the world / Hidin' out / Too many secrets.
LP . . . . **CW 134**
■ **MC** . . . . **ZCEB 134**
Ember / Dec '78 / TKO Records Ltd / President Records.
CD . . . . **CDCD 1066**
Charly / Mar '93 / Charly.

Cline, Tammy

A singer from Yorkshire who worked in a factory, sang in a pub with a local band, the Falcons. Tammy Cline later formed her own Southern Comfort Band. She's made several appearances at Wembley, was named Best British Female Country Vocalist each year 1980-84, and represented the UK at the International Fan Fair Show in Nashville in 1980 and the International Country & Western Music Association Awards Gala in Galveston, Texas in 1984. (Donald Clarke)

I WISH I'D WROTE THAT SONG.
Tracks: I wish I'd wrote that song.
7" . . . . **PT 519**
President / Sep '83 / Grapevine Distribution / Target Records / Jazz Music / Taylors.

LOVE IS A PUZZLE.
Tracks: Love is a puzzle / My heart strings along.
■ **7"** . . . . **A 2076**
CBS / Mar '82.

SINGS THE COUNTRY GREATS WITH THE SOUTHERN COMFORT BAND.
Tracks: Here you come again / Help me make it through the night / Rose garden / Hurt / Harper Valley PTA / Carolina Moon / Stand by your man / Don't it make my brown eyes blue / Coalminers daughter / Love letters / Sweet dreams / I fell in love again last night.
MC . . . . **TC-MFP 5787**
MFP / Mar '87 / EMI.
■ **LP** . . . . **MFP 5787**
MFP / Mar '87.

TAMMY CLINE & THE SOUTHERN COMFORT BAND (Cline, Tammy & The Southern Comfort Band).
Tracks: He's a rounder / Crazy / Street talk / Yesterday just passed my way again / Take good care of my baby / Last cheater's waltz, The / My baby thinks he's a train / You've got a friend / Single girl / Miss the Mississippi / Way we make a broken heart, The / I wish I'd wrote that song.
LP . . . . **PRCV 114**
President / Sep '83 / Grapevine Distribution / Target Records / Jazz Music / Taylors.

TAMMY CLINE'S COUNTRY GOSPEL ALBUM.
Tracks: Our God reigns / One day at a time / It is no secret / I saw the light / I believe / Old rugged cross, The / It's good to be home / This little light of mine / He is my everything / Heaven's gonna be a blast / Softly and tenderly / How great Thou art.
LP . . . . **WRD R 3032**
■ **MC** . . . . **WRD C 3032**
Word (UK) / Mar '87.

Clower, Jerry

Born in 1926 in Mississippi, Jerry Clower worked for 18 years for a chemical factory selling fertilizer. To help sales he began spinning yarns and ended up Country Comedian of the Year every year from 1974-82. *Jerry Clower From Yazoo City, Mississippi Talkin'*, was released on MCA in 1974 and was followed by several more big hits. (Donald Clarke)

JERRY CLOWER'S GREATEST HITS.
Tracks: Not Advised.
LP . . . . **IMCA 37247**
MCA (Import) / Mar '86 / Pinnacle / Silver Sounds (CD).

RUNAWAY TRACK.
Tracks: Trucker and the lady, The / Marcell, The truck driver / Feudin's stars / Pulpit committee, The / Peanuts / John Dunn / Preacher's water, The / Mean brothers, The / Grassers, The / How to tell time / Runaway truck / Baptizing, The / Negativism / Procto / Sonny and rambo / Terrance meeting / Positive attitude, A / Clowerisms / Coon huntin' on TV / Shake it off.
LP . . . . **IMCA 5773**
MC . . . . **IMCAC 5773**
MCA / Apr '87 / BMG.

Coates, Ann

PLEASE DON'T CUT THE ROSES.
Tracks: Not Advised.
LP . . . . **WRS 129**
Westwood / '78 / Pinnacle.

Cochran, Charles

HAUNTED HEART.
Tracks: Not Advised.
LP . . . . **AP 177**
Audiophile (USA) / Aug '88 / Jazz Music / Swift.

Cochran, Jackie Lee

BOP TOWN.
Tracks: Bop town / Mystery train.
7" **45 002**
Rollin' Rock / Jun '80 / Pinnacle.

FIDDLE FIT MAN.
Tracks: Fiddle fit man / Out across the tracks / Trouble is her name / Why don't I leave you alone / Rock and roll blues / Wasting love / Bayou Joe / She's mine all mine / Peace of mind / Greasy dollar bill / Rock'n'roll refrain / Billy is a rocker.
LP . . . . **WIK 44**
Off-Beat (2) / Nov '85 / Pinnacle.

JACK THE CAT.
Tracks: Not Advised.
LP . . . . **BLK 7701**
Hydra / Dec '87 / Swift.

ROCKABILLY LEGEND.
Tracks: Rockabilly legend / Gal's wicked, The / They oughta call you Miss Heartbreak / Lovin' I crave, The / Walkin', cryin' blues / Lulu / Dance doll / Ain't gonna let it happen / Boogie woogie man gonna getcha / Memories / I love you a thousand ways / She rocks me.
LP . . . . **LP 010**
Rollin' Rock / Jun '80 / Pinnacle.
LP . . . . **MFLP 045**
Magnum Force / Nov '86 / Terry Blood Dist. / Jazz Music / Hot Shot.

SWAMP FOX.
Tracks: Not Advised.
LP . . . . **LP 005**
Rollin' Rock / Jun '80 / Pinnacle.

Coe, David Allan

Born in 1939 in Akron, Ohio, the flamboyant country singer, after almost 20 years in and out of reform schools and prisons, became one of the members of the 'Outlaw' movement in country music. Released from Ohio State Correctional Facilty in 1967, he went to Nashville, signed with Shelby Singleton and recorded in a heavy blues style. Coe began a new career as *The Mysterious Rhinestone Cowboy*, after signing with CBS in 1974 and made a breakthrough as a writer. *Would You Lay With Me In A Field Of Stone*, was a hit for Tanya Tucker in 1975 and *Take This Job And Shove It*, for Johnny Paycheck in 1977. His own albums sold well and there were a few hit singles: *You Didn't Even Call Me By My Name*, and *Willie, Waylon & Me*. *The Ride*, concerning a ghostly meeting with Hank Williams was a country number one in 1983. Highly thought of by Willie Nelson, Waylon Jennings and Kris Kristofferson, his work is more rewarding for some fans than of most hitmakers. (Donald Clarke)

CASTLE IN THE SAND.
Tracks: Cheap thrills / Son of a rebel son / Fool inside of me / Castle in the sand / Gotta serve somebody /

Ride / I can't let you be a memory / Missin' the kid / Don't be a stranger / For lovers only.
■ LP. CBS 25346
CBS / Jul '83.

D.A.C.
Tracks: Looking in the mirror / Lyin' comes so easy to your lips / Last time she'll leave me this time, The / I gave up (on trying to get over you) / Voices / She loved the leavin' out of me / I'll never regret loving you / It's a sad situation / Those low down blues / Whisky, whisky (take my mind).
LP. CBS 85880
MC .40 85880
CBS / Jan '83 / Sony.

DAVID ALLAN COE (I love country).
Tracks: Would you lay with me (in a field of stone) / This bottle / Please come to Boston / Divers do it deeper / Stand by your man / Take it easy rider / Ride / Willie, Waylon and me.
LP. CBS 54945
■ MC .40 54945
CBS / Mar '87.

FOR THE RECORD - THE FIRST 10 YEARS.
Tracks: You never even called me by my name / Please come to Boston / Jody like a melody / Longhaired redneck / If that ain't country / Tennessee whisky / Now I lay me down to cheat / What made you change your mind / Ride, The / Mona Lisa's lost her smile.
MC .40 88655
CBS / Mar '85 / Sony.
■ LP. CBS 88655
CBS / Mar '85.

HELLO IN THERE.
Tracks: Crazy old soldier / Out of your mind / Mister, don't speak bad about my music / Drinkin' to forget / Gotta travel on / He will break your heart / For lovers only / Hello in there / Someone special / I ain't gonna let you go again.
■ LP. CBS 25722
CBS / Dec '83.

JUST DIVORCED.
Tracks: Mona Lisa's lost her smile / Sweet Angeline / He's taking it hard / For lovers only / Thief in my bedroom / Just divorced / It's great to be single again / Blue grass morning / I wanna know I'm goin' home / For your precious love.
■ LP. CBS 26012
CBS / Aug '84.

LONGHAIRED REDNECK/ RIDES AGAIN.
Tracks: Longhaired redneck / When she's got me (Where she wants me) / Revenge / Texas lullaby / living on the run / Family reunion / Rock and roll holiday / Free born rambling man / Spotlight / Dakota the dancing bear, Part 2 / Willie, Waylon & Me / House we've been calling home, The / Young Dallas cowboy / Sense of humour, A / Pumkin certer barn dance, The / Willie, Waylon and Me (Reprise) / Lately I've been thinking too much lately / Laid back and wasted / Under Rachel's wings / Greener than the grass we laid on / If that ain't country.
CD . . . . BCD 15707
Bear Family / Mar '93 / Rollercoaster Records / Swift / Direct Distribution.

MATTER OF LIFE AND DEATH, A.
Tracks: Ten commandments of love / Jody like a melody / Tanya Montana / If only your eyes could lie / Need a little time off for bad behaviour / Southern star / Actions speak louder than words / Child of God / Wild Irish rose / It's a matter of life and death.
LP. 4504791
MC 4504794
CBS / Apr '87 / Sony.
■ CD 4504792
CBS / Apr '87.

MYSTERIOUS RHINESTONE COWBOY, THE/ ONCE UPON A RHYME.
Tracks: Sad country song, A / Crazy Mary / River / 33rd of August, The / Bossier city / Atlanta song / Old men tell me / Desperados waiting for the train / I still sing the old songs / Old grey goose is dead, The / Would you lay with me (In a field of stone) / Jody like a melody / Loneliness in Ruby's eyes / Would you be my lady / Sweet vibrations / Another pretty country song / Piece of wood and steel / Fraulein / Shine it on / You never called me by my name.
CD . . . . BCD 15706
Rollercoaster / Mar '93 / Rollercoaster Records / Swift.

TEXAS MOON.
Tracks: Got you on my mind / These days / Satisfied mind, A / Why you been gone so long / Why me, Mary Magdeline / Fuzzy was an outlaw / That old time feeling / Ride me down easy / Give my love to Rose.
■ LP. CRL 5006
Charly / Nov '77 / Charly.

UNCHAINED.
Tracks: Not Advised.
LP. CBS 26742
MC .40 26742
CBS / Sep '86 / Sony.

Colder, Ben

The alter-ego of country singer/western actor Shep Wooley, A hillbilly character whose forte was recording country comedy, much of his material being parodies of contemporary hit titles. Colder made his first chart appearance in 1962 with *Don't Go Near The Eskimos*, and still remains a part of the Wooley stage routines. (Tony Byworth)

GOLDEN HITS: BEN COLDER.
Tracks: Not Advised.
LP. GT 0051
Gusto (USA) / Oct '79.

Cole, B.J.

PIE IN THE SKY.
Tracks: Pie in the sky / Remington ride.
■ 7" . . . . UP 36423
United Artists / Jul '78.

TRANSPARENT MUSIC.
Tracks: Not Advised.
CD . . . . HNCD 1325
LP. HNDL 1325
MC . . . . HNBC 1325
Hannibal / May '89 / Revolver-APT.

Coleman, Albert

JUST HOOKED ON COUNTRY (Coleman, Albert Atlanta Pops).
Tracks: Just hooked on country / Just hooked on country (pt 2).
■ 7" . . . . EPCA 2597
Epic / Sep '82.

Coll, Brian

A native of Omagh, County Tyrone, Brian Coll has been one of the stalwarts of the Irish country music scene for over three decades. Having gained his first break as lead vocalist in the 1960's showband the Polka Dots, Coll formed his own band, the Buckaroos, in 1968. Among his many hit singles, both *These Are My Mountains*, and *Home Town On The Foyle*, enjoyed long runs on the Irish pop charts. (Tony Byworth)

BEST OF BRIAN COLL.
Tracks: Sweet Mary & the miles between / Picture on the wall / Hello darlin / I'll be glad / These are my mountains / Your old love letters / China doll / When my blue moon turns to gold again / Second fiddle / Silver haired Daddy of mine / They'll never take her love from me / Farmer, The.
MC . . . . CPHL 477
Homespun (Ireland) / Dec '84 / Homespun Records / Ross Records / Wellard Dist.
LP. PHL 477
Homespun (Ireland) / '88 / Homespun Records / Ross Records / Wellard Dist.

COUNTRY CALLING.
Tracks: Home town on the Foyle / Picture on the wall / She's mine / Tonight I'll throw a party / China doll / These are my mountains / Farmer, The / Time changes everything / Little bit slow to catch on / Fool's castle / Mail call / Second fiddle.
LP. PHL 412
MC . . . . CPHL 412
Homespun (Ireland) / '82 / Homespun Records / Ross Records / Wellard Dist.

COVER MAMAS FLOWERS.
Tracks: Not Advised.
LP. HPE 603
Harp (Ireland) / May '80 / C.M. Distribution.

OLD LOVES NEVER DIE.
Tracks: Not Advised.
LP. HM 031
Harmac (Ireland) / '89 / I & B Records / Prism Leisure PLC.

SILVER HAIRED DADDY OF MINE.
Tracks: That silver haired daddy of mine / Remember me / Lonesome heart, A / From heart to heart / Not once but 100 times / Hello darlin / Your old love letters / They'll never take her love from me / Tell me / Doors of love / Sweet Mary and the miles between.
LP. PHL 420
MC . . . . CPHL 420
Homespun (Ireland) / '82 / Homespun Records / Ross Records / Wellard Dist.

THESE ARE MY MOUNTAINS.
Tracks: Not Advised.
LP. HPE 636
Harp (Ireland) / Jul '81 / C.M. Distribution.

TOWN I LOVE SO WELL.
Tracks: Town I love so well / Hometown on the Foyle.
7" . . . . HIS 6
Homespun (Ireland) / '88 / Homespun Records / Ross Records / Wellard Dist.

Collins Kids

Lorrie and Larry Collins were a country-pop vocal duo. They signed to Columbia (CBS/USA) in 1955 and made some classic rockabilly singles. They were influential and seen on TV country shows including the Grande Ole Opry, but never made any charts. They split in 1965 when Lorrie married. Larry became a writer - he co-wrote *Delta Dawn*, an early '70s hit for Tanya Tucker & Helen Reddy - and a producer and publisher. (Donald Clarke)

COLLINS KIDS 1959-60.
Tracks: Not Advised.
LP. RFD 9002
Country Routes / Sep '90 / Jazz Music / Hot Shot.

HOP, SKIP AND JUMP.
Tracks: Go away don't bother me / Rock and roll polka / Move a little closer / My first love / Hush money / I wish / Cuckoo rock, The / Beetle bug bop / I'm in my teens / Rockaway rock, The / They're still in love / Make him behave / Hop, skip and jump / Shortnin' bread rock / Just because / Hoy hoy / Hot rod / Heartbeat / Mama worries / Party / Walking the floor over you / Missouri waltz / You are my sunshine / Soda poppin' around / Young heart / Ain't you ever / What'cha gonna do now / Waitin' and watchin' / Home of the blues / Lonesome road / Early American / Rockin' gypsy, The / Bye, bye / Hurricane / Mercy / Rock boppin' baby / Whistle bait / Sweet talk / Spur of the moment / Rebel, The / Johnny Yuma / There'll be some changes made / Fire ball mail, The / T-bone / What about tomorrow / Get along home Cindy / You've been gone too long / One step down / There stands the one / Wild and wicked love / Hey mama boom-a-lacka / More than a friend / Pied piper poodle, The / Blues in the night / Another man done gone / Sugar plum / Kinda like love / Are you certain / That's your affair.
CD Set . . . . BCD 15537
Bear Family / Aug '91 / Rollercoaster Records / Swift / Direct Distribution.

INTRODUCING LARRY AND LORRIE.
Tracks: Hoy hoy / Rock boppin' baby / Just because / Hop skip and jump / Hurricane / Shortnin' bread rock / Whistle bait / Mercy / Soda poppin' around / Walking the floor over you / Hot rod / Party.
■ LP. EPC 25334
Epic / Apr '83.

ROCKIN' ROLLIN' COLLINS KIDS.
Tracks: Cuckoo rock, The (Previously unissued.) / Beetle bug hop / Rockaway rock, The / They're still in love / Make him behave / Go away, don't bother me / Hush money / I wish (Previously unissued.) / Rock & roll polka / Shortnin' bread rock (Previously unissued.) / Just because / Hoy hoy / Hot rod (Previously unissued.) / Soda poppin' rock (2nd recording) (Previously unissued.) / Mercy / Sweet talk.
LP. BFX 15074
Bear Family / Sep '84 / Rollercoaster Records / Swift / Direct Distribution.

ROCKIN' ROLLIN' COLLINS KIDS VOL.2.
Tracks: Whistle bait / Party / In my teens / Rock boppin' baby / Mama worries / Heartbeat / My first love / Young heart / Hop skip and jump / Soda Poppin around (1st recording) (Previously unissued.) / Walking the floor over you / Missouri Waltz / You are my sunshine / There'll be some changes made (Previously unissued.) / Lonesome road (Previously unissued.) / Cuckoo rock, The / Beetle bug hop / Rockaway road, The / They're still in love / Make him behave / Go away don't bother me / I wish / Rock and roll polka / Shortnin' bread rock / Just because / Hoy hoy / Jones progress / Hot rod / Soda poppin' around / Mercy / Sweet talk.
LP. BFX 15108
Bear Family / Oct '83 / Rollercoaster Records / Swift / Direct Distribution.

TELEVISION PARTY.
Tracks: Not Advised.
LP. TV 5758
T.V. (Holland) / Jul '88 / Pinnacle.

Collins, Earl

BLUEGRASS CARDINALS.
Tracks: Not Advised.
LP. SBR 4205
Sierra Briar (USA) / Mar '79 / Mike's Country Music Room.

THAT'S EARL.
Tracks: Not Advised.
LP. SBR 4204
Sierra Briar (USA) / Apr '79 / Mike's Country Music Room.

Collins, Larry

ROCKIN' ROLLIN' (Collins, Larry & Joe Maphis).
Tracks: Hurricane / Early American / Rockin' gypsy / Bye bye Joe Maphis / Flying fingers / Rock and roll / Tennessee two step / Fire on the strings / You've been gone too long (Previously unissued.) / One step down / Hey mama boom a lacka / Wild and wicked love / What about tomorrow / Pied piper poodle (Previously unissued.) / T-Bone / Rebel - Johnny Yuma, The.
LP. BFX 15106
Bear Family / Oct '83 / Rollercoaster Records / Swift / Direct Distribution.

Collins, Tommy

Tommy Collins, born Leonard Raymond Sipes on September 28 1930 in Oklahoma City, was one of the founding figures of the Bakersfield sound, which gained worldwide recognition via Buck Owens and, later Merle Haggard. A one-time DJ, Collins settled in California after military service in the US Marines and began his recording career on the minor Morgan Records. He signed with Capitol in 1953, where he scored high chart placings with novelty titles like *You Better Not Do That, Whatcha Gonna Do Now*, and *It Tickles*. He has appeared in Britain on several occasions and is the subject of Merle Haggard's song *Leonard*. Tommy Collins recording career is documented on the Bear Family compilation which features all his work on the Morgan, Capitol and Columbia labels between 1951 and 1968. (Tony Byworth)

COWBOYS GET LUCKY SOME OF THE TIME.
Tracks: Carolyn / Loud mouthed talking oldmobile, A / Goodbye comes hard to me / Man who picked the wildwood flower, The / Those old love letters from you / I'm tracing your tracks across Texas / All Robyns can sing / I can outkiss him (With one lip tied behind me) / Love won't come between us anymore / Conversion of Ronnie Jones. The / My son call another man Daddy.
LP . . . . **GW 105**
Greenwood / '80 / EMI.

LEONARD.
Tracks: Campus boogie / Too beautiful to cry / Smooth sailin' / Fool's gold / You gotta have a license / Let me love you / There'll be no other / I love you more and more each day / Boob-i-lak / You better not do that / I always get a souvenir / High on a hilltop / Untied / Whatcha gonna do now / Love-a-me, s'il vous plait / You're for me / I'll be gone / Wait a little longer / Let down / It tickles / It's nobodys fault but yours / I guess I'm crazy / You oughta see pickles now / Those old love letters from you / I wish I had died in my cradle / I'll never, never let you go / I'll always speak well of you / What kind of sweetheart are you / No love have I / All of the monkey's ain't in the zoo / That's the way love is / How do I say goodbye / Man we all ought to know, A / Are you ready to go / Think it over boys / I think of you yet / Upon this rock / Feet of the traveler / Don't you love me anymore / Retirement in heaven / What have you done / Love is born, A / I'm nobody's fool but yours / O Mary don't you weep / Did you let your light shine / In the shadow of the cross / When I survey the wonderous cross / Who at my door is standing / My saviour's love / Where could we go but to the lord / What a friend we have in Jesus / Each step of the way / Softly and tenderly / That'a why I love him / Jesus keep me near the cross / Amazing grace / Old rugged cross, The / Heart's don't break / You belong in my arms / Hundred years from now, A / Little June / My last chance with you / Sidewalks of New York / Last letter, The / Oklahoma hills / Great speckled bird, The / Broken engagement / Wreck of the old 97 / I'm just here to get my baby out of jail / Have I told you lately that I love you / It makes no differenc now / Let's live a little / I'll keep on loving you / I over looked an orchid / I wonder if you feel the way I do / Juicy fruit / Black cat / We kissed again with tears / Keep dreaming / Don't let me stand in his footsteps / Summer's almost gone / Take me back to the good old days / Oh what a dream / Let her go / When did right become wrong / If I could just go back / I got mine / You'd better be nice / I can do that / I got mine (Live) / Shindig in the barn / Million miles, A / Good goody gumdrop / Clock on the wall, The / Bee that gets the honey, The / It's a big jump / It's a pretty good ol' world after all / Take me back to the good old days (With chorus) / Oh what a dream (Without chorus) / Klipps kloppa / If you can't bite, don't growl / Man gotta do what a man gotta go, A / Man machine / Girl on sugar pie lane, The / Poor, broke, mixed up mess of a heart / Be serious Ann / Fool's castle, The / Little time for a little love, A / I'm not getting anywhere with you / Two sides of life / You're everything to me / Big dummy / There's no girl in my life anymore / Skinny / I'm not lookin for an angel / Don't wipe the tears that you cry / Birmingham / Put me irons, lock me up (Throw away the key) / Sam hill / It's to much like lonesome / Wine take me away / High on a hill top / General delivery U.S.A. / Roll, truck, roll / If that's the fashion / Piedras negras / Laura (What's he got that I ain't got) / Branded man / Cincinnati, Ohio / Break my mind / I made a prison band / Best thing I've done in my life, The / Woman you have been told / Sunny side of life / He's gonna have to catch me first.
CD Set . . . . **BCD 15577**
Bear Family / Jan '93 / Rollercoaster Records / Swift / Direct Distribution.

THIS IS TOMMY COLLINS.
Tracks: You better not do that / I always get a souvenir / United / How do I say goodbye / I'll be gone / It tickles / You gotta have a licence / High on a hilltop / Boob-i-lak / Smooth sailing / Love a me s'il vous plait / What'cha gonna do now.
LP . . . . **PM 1550771**
Pathe Marconi (France) / Jun '84 / Thames Distributors Ltd.
LP . . . . **HAT 3071**
MC . . . . **HATC 3071**
Stetson / Aug '88 / Crusader Marketing Co. / Swift / Wellard Dist. / Midland Records / C.M. Distribution.

WORDS AND MUSIC COUNTRY STYLE.
Tracks: All of the monkeys ain't in the zoo / How do I say goodbye / Love a me s'il vous plait / Those old love letters from you / Man we all ought to know, A / Feet of the traveller, The / Smooth sailing / I'll always speak well of you / Think it over boys / I think of you yet / Are you ready to go / Upon this rock.
LP . . . . **HAT 3050**
MC . . . . **HATC 3050**
Stetson / Oct '87 / Crusader Marketing Co. / Swift / Wellard Dist. / Midland Records / C.M. Distribution.

Colm & Sundowners

COUNTRY IS MY STYLE.
Tracks: It's time to pay the fiddler / Hello darlin / Stop the world / If we don't make it home before the sunrise / Hell blues and down the road I go / You're still the only one I'll ever love / Everybody's reaching out for someone / Ghost of Jim Bob Wilson / Some broken hearts never mend / I wouldn't want to live if you didn't love me / Cowboy / You're the only good thing that's happened to me / Southern comfort / You're my best friend.
LP . . . . **PHL 403**
MC . . . . **CPHL 403**
Homespun (Ireland) / '82 / Homespun Records / Ross Records / Wellard Dist.

DEAR LITTLE IRELAND.
Tracks: Wild Irish rose / Galway Bay / Irish eyes.
MC . . . . **CHRL 131**
Homespun (Ireland) / '88 / Homespun Records / Ross Records / Wellard Dist.
LP . . . . **HRL 131**
Homespun (Ireland) / May '88 / Homespun Records / Ross Records / Wellard Dist.

Colorado

All male five piece Scottish group which came into existence in the late 1970's and quickly developed as one of the most popular touring, country music outfits on the local scene. Annual awards - including BCMA and IMCA accolades - come Colorado's way with great regularity. A number of their albums were recorded in Nashville. The lead singer, Geordie Jack, also hosts a weekly country music show on BBC Radio Highland in 1990. With patriotic aplomb, the group changed its name from Colorado to Caledonia.
Tracks: Not Advised.

CALIFORNIA DREAMIN'.
Tracks: California dreamin' / Space lady love.
■ **7"** . . . . **PIN 67**
Pinnacle / Oct '78.

EXCLUSIVE.
Tracks: Crazy celtic music / You two timed me one time too many / Will the circle be unbroken / Making friends / Little bit crazy / Leavin' eyes / Dary Farrow / Free to be / I won't take less than your love / Dark Island.
LP . . . . **TT 107**
MC . . . . **CTT 107**
Trimtop / Jun '88 / Ross Records.

STILL BURNING.
Tracks: Something to say / Stories we could tell / After the night has gone / I've tried to write a love song / Savin' the best for last / We're still burnin' / He'll never be a superstar / Back to the country / Good for nothin' guitar pickin' man / Whisky man.
LP . . . . **TT 104**
MC . . . . **CTT 104**
Trimtop / Jan '87 / Ross Records.

Colorado

BOOGIE GRASS SATURDAY NIGHT.
Tracks: Boogie grass Saturday night / Love is like an echo.
7" . . . . **BRS 05**
Big R / Aug '81 / Pinnacle.

GREEN FIELDS OF FRANCE PARTS 1 & 2.
Tracks: Green fields of France (part 1) / Green fields of France (part 2).
7" . . . . **BRS 09**
Big R / May '82 / Pinnacle.

SINGS COUNTRY MUSIC.
Tracks: Not Advised.
LP . . . . **BRA 1008**
MC . . . . **BRC 1008**
Big R / Nov '80 / Pinnacle.

TENNESSEE INSPIRATION.
Tracks: Not Advised.
LP . . . . **BRA 1014**
MC . . . . **BRC 1014**
Big R / Oct '81 / Pinnacle.

TENNESSEE WHISKY AND TEXAS WOMAN.
Tracks: Tennessee whisky and Texas woman / Thrill of the chase.
7" . . . . **BRS 07**
Big R / Dec '81 / Pinnacle.

Colter, Jessi

Jessi Colter was born in 1947 in Phoenix, Arizona. She wrote under the name Miriam Eddy and had songs recorded by Eddy Arnold, Dottie West, Don Gibson and others. She changed her name to Jessi Colter because her great, great uncle was a member of Jesse James' gang. She signed to RCA in 1966 and Capitol ten years later. She appeared on the classic album *The Outlaws*, on RCA in 1976 with Waylon Jennings, Willie Nelson and Tompall Glaser, the first country album to sell more than a million copies. Later, Colter returned to RCA. She is married to Waylon Jennings, tours with him, and still records sporadically. (Donald Clarke)

COUNTRY STAR IS BORN, A.
Tracks: Too many rivers / Cry softly / I ain't the one / It's not easy / He called me baby / Why you been gone so long / If she's where you like livin' / Healing hands of time / That's the chance I'll have to take / Don't let him go / It's all over now.
LP . . . . **INTS 5072**
RCA International / Apr '81 / BMG.
MC . . . . **INTK 5072**
RCA International / Feb '81 / BMG.

I'M NOT LISA.
Tracks: I'm not Lisa / For the first time.
■ **7"** . . . . **CL 15823**
Capitol / Jul '75.

Commander Cody

George Frayne took the name 'Commander Cody' from the 1940's serial hero, and formed a group called the Lost Planet Airmen while at the University of Michigan. They enjoyed only minimal success in the charts with their hit version of Charlie Ryan's 1960 hit *Hot Rod Lincoln*. His live shows are characterised by a stage act with a unique blend of country, boogie-woogie, cajun and truck-driving songs. (Tony Byworth)

BAR ROOM CLASSICS.
Tracks: Not Advised.
CD . . . . **AIM 1024CD**
MC . . . . **AIM 1024C**
AIM (2) / Sep '93 / Topic Records / Direct Distribution.

CODY RETURNS FROM OUTER SPACE (Commander Cody & His Lost Planet Airmen).
Tracks: Minnie the moocher / It's gonna be one of those nights / I been to Georgia on a fast train / Lightning bar blues / Tina Louise / Shadow knows, The / Roll your own / Southbound / Don't let go / Boogie man boogie, The / Hawaii blues / House of blue lights / Four or five times / That's what I like about the South / Gypsy fiddle.
LP . . . . **ED 202**
Edsel / Mar '87 / Pinnacle.

COMMANDER CODY.
Tracks: Southbound / California okie / Willing / Boogie man boogie, The / Hawaii blues / House of blue lights / Keep on lovin' her / Devil and me / Four or five times / That's what I like about the South.
LP . . . . **K 56108**
WEA / WEA.

HOT LICKS, COLD STEEL AND TRUCKERS' FAVOURITES.
Tracks: Not Advised.
CD **31186**
MCA (USA) / Jun '88 / MCA (Imports).

LET'S ROCK.
Tracks: Let's rock / Rockin' over China / Midnight on the strand / Do you mind? / Angel got married / Truckstop at the end of the world / One more ride / Your cash ain't nothin' but trash / Rockabilly funeral / Transfusion / Home of rock 'n' roll.
LP . . . . **SPD 1001**
Special Delivery / Aug '87 / Revolver-APT / A.D.A Distribution / Topic Records / Direct Distribution / Jazz Music / C.M. Distribution.
MC . . . . **SPDC 1001**
Special Delivery / May '87 / Revolver-APT / A.D.A Distribution / Topic Records / Direct Distribution / Jazz Music / C.M. Distribution.
LP **BP-2086**
Blind Pig (USA) / '88 / Topic Records / Projection / Swift / C.M. Distribution / Roots Records / Direct Distribution / Impetus Records / Hot Shot.
CD . . . . **LICD 9.00277**
Line / '90 / C.M. Distribution / Grapevine Distribution.

LOSE IT TONIGHT (Commander Cody Band).
Tracks: Lose it tonight / Two triple cheese / Either he's wrong / All tore up / Get your love / Go to hell / Sea wolf / Working girls / Jukebox jury / Who's got the rock / Roll the dice / Buddy's cafe.
CD . . . . **LICD 9.00054**
Line / Dec '88 / C.M. Distribution / Grapevine Distribution.

SEVEN ELEVEN.
Tracks: Seven eleven / Snooze you lose.
■ **7"** . . . . **ARIST 148**
Arista / Nov '77.

SLEAZY ROADSIDE STONES.
Tracks: Not Advised.
CD . . . . **CCRCD 106**
Relix / Apr '93 / Projection.

C 22
■ DELETED

TALES FROM THE OZONE.
Tracks: Minnie the moocher / It's gonna be one of those nights / Connie / I been to Georgia on a fast train / Honky tonk music / Lightning bar blues / Paid in advance / Cajun baby / Tina Louise / Shadow knows, The / Roll your own / Gypsy fiddle.
LP. . . . . K 56158
WEA / WEA.

VERY BEST OF COMMANDER CODY AND HIS LOST PLANET (Commander Cody & His Lost Planet Airmen).
Tracks: Back to Tennessee / Wine do yer stuff / Seeds and stems (again) / Daddy's gonna treat you right / Family Bible / Lost in the ozone / Hot rod Lincoln / Beat me daddy, eight to the bar / Truckstop rock / Truck drivin' man / It should've been me / Watch my .38 / Everybody's doing it now / Rock that boogie / Smoke, smoke, smoke / Honeysuckle honey / Sunset on the sage (live) / Cryin' time (live).
LP. . . . . SEE 64
See For Miles / Apr '86 / Pinnacle.
CD . . . . SEECD 64
See For Miles / Aug '91 / Pinnacle

WE'VE GOT A LIVE ONE HERE (Commander Cody & His Lost Planet Airmen).
Tracks: One of those nights / Semi truck / Smoke, smoke, smoke / Big mamou / San Antonio rose / 18 wheels / Mama hated diesels / Lookin' at the world through a windshield / My window faces the south / Milkcow blues / It should've been me / Back to Tennessee / Seeds and stems / Rock that boogie / Riot in cell block 9 / Don't let go / Too much fun / Hot rod Lincoln / Lost in the ozone.
Double LP . . . . K 66043
WEA / WEA.

Compton, Mike

CLIMBING THE WALLS (Compton, Mike & David Grier).
Tracks: Climbing the walls / Honky tonk swing / Waters street waltz / Black mountain rag / Bye bye blue / Going up Caney / Huffy / Over the waterfall / Flop eared mule / New five cents, The / Paul's blues / Fun's all over, The.
CD . . . . CDROU 0280
MC . . . . ROU 0280
Rounder / '91 / Projection / Roots Records / Swift / C.M. Distribution / Topic Records / Jazz Music / Hot Shot / A.D.A Distribution / Direct Distribution.

Comstock, Bobby

TENNESSEE WALTZ.
Tracks: Not Advised.
LP. . . . . MOHAWK 124
Not Advised / Jul '88.

Conlee, John

A soulful country singer, born in 1946 and raised on a tobacco farm. His first number one country hit *Rose Colored Glasses*, in 1978 was followed by many more hits. He struck a combination of adult subject matter and a ballad style for country music fans who now live mostly in the suburbs. His hits were on ABC, then MCA and CBS since 1986. (Donald Clarke)

GOT MY HEART SET ON YOU.
Tracks: You've got a right / Got my heart set on you.
7" 6502757
CBS / Nov '86 / Sony.

ROSE COLOURED GLASSES.
Tracks: Rose coloured glasses / I'll be easy.
■ 7" . . . . ABC 4243
ABC Records / '79.

Conley, Earl Thomas

Singer-songwriter, possessing a strong ballad voice ideally suited to modern country presentations. Conley was born on 17.10.1941 in Portsmouth, Ohio into a working class family. Conley himself has worked at various jobs to supplement his musical ambitions. Played a while in Huntsville, Alabama during early 70s following a spell in the army, where the country music bug struck. Moved to Nashville and had the good fortune to have some covers of his songs recorded by Mel Street . Conley signed to GRT in 1975, obtaining minor singles success before moving to Warner Bros, still recording as Earl Conley. The Earl Thomas Conley title came into effect with his second single *Middle-Age Madness* to avoid confusion with similarly named acts John Conlee and Con Hunley. Conley's career blossomed in 1980 after moving to the indie Sunbird label. His debut album *Blue Pearl*, included a No.1 single in *Fire & Smoke*. A move to RCA soon ensued, and an album of the same title was issued. Conley's sometimes smokey blues/country vocals proving a winner time and time again for RCA. During the space of only eight years he acquired an amazing 17 No.1 singles, including; *Somewhere Between Right And Wrong*, *Holding Her And Loving You*, *Love Don't Care (Who's Heart It Breaks)*, and *I Can't Win For Losin' You*. Edging further into pop/country environs, Conley dueted with Anita Pointer for *Too Many Times*, a No.2 success. Other duet partners for Conley have been Gus Hardin on *We Believe In Happy Endings* - the 1988 chart-topper, *What She Is (Is A Woman In Love)*, and *What I'd Say* . In 1989 Conley's *Love Out Loud*, registered as Conley's sixteenth successive No.1 Country singles, a records equalled by Sonny James and bettered only by Alabama. Conley lost some time performing in 1989 due to a throat problem but charted again in 1991 with the top ten singles *Brotherly Love*, (a duet with late Keith Whitley) and *Shadow Of A Doubt*. Since which time Earl Thomas Conley's chart action has been limited. (Maurice Hope)

CAROL.
Tracks: Carol / Too far from the heart of it all.
■ 7" . . . . PB 49505
RCA / Nov '88.

GREATEST HITS: EARL THOMAS CONLEY.
Tracks: Nobody falls like a fool / Holding her and loving you / Somewhere between right and wrong / Angel in disguise / Fire and smoke / Once in a blue moon / I have loved you girl-but not like this before / Don't make it easy for me / Your love's on the line / Silent treatment / Heavenly bodies / Too many times (Duet with Anita Pointer.) / That was a close one / I need a good woman bad / Love don't care (whose heart it breaks) / Too hot to handle.
CD . . . . ND 90314
■ LP. . . . . NL 90314
RCA / Apr '89.
■ MC . . . . NK 90314
RCA / Apr '89.

HEART OF IT ALL, THE.
Tracks: What she is (is a woman in love) / Love out loud / What I'd say / You must not be drinking enough / Carol / No chance, no dance / I love the way he left you / Finally Friday / We believe in happy endings / Too far from the heart of it all.
CD . . . . PD 86824
LP. . . . . PL 86824
■ MC . . . . PK 86824
RCA / Oct '88.

WHAT SHE IS (IS A WOMAN IN LOVE).
Tracks: What she is (is a woman in love) / No chance (no dance).
■ 7" . . . . PB 49537
RCA / Jul '88.

Conlon, Bill

Bill Conlon was born Portaferry, Co. Down, N.Ireland and is one of that elite band of country singers from this side of the Atlantic to not only have enjoyed substantial airplay on regional country programmes, but also on the national network. In 1989, his album, *Woman Your Love*, on the Etude label caused BBC Radio 2's Ken Bruce to tip the artist as a 'Future success story'. Conlan first gained attention from country audiences with his self-produced album *Undecided*, and has furthered his reputation with fine stage sets supported by his band Emerald. (Tony Byworth)

I DON'T HAVE FAR TO FALL.
Tracks: I don't have far to fall / Please please.
7" . . . . ET 4
Etude / Feb '90 / Total / BMG.

WITH YOU IN MIND.
Tracks: Lucille / I know one / Cowboys don't get lucky all the time / I don't have far to fall / Please please (tell me that you..) / Chair, The / Carmen / Not counting you / She's holding her own now / That ain't like your memory / Let's start forever / Streets of Bakersfield.
MC . . . . ETCAS 189
Total / Feb '90 / Total / BMG.
■ CD . . . . ETCD 189
Total / Feb '90.
■ MC . . . . ETMC 189
Total / Apr '91.

WOMAN YOUR LOVE.
Tracks: Got no reason now for going home / Woman your love / Bunch of thyme / Living on these back streets / Rose of Clare / Mother's love's a blessing, A / Old loves never die / You took off my hands / Gentle mother / Old rustic bridge / Angeline.
LP. . . . . ETLP 188
■ MC . . . . ETCAS 188
Etude / Sep '88.

Connie & Babe

BACKWOODS BLUEGRASS (Connie & Babe & The Backwoods Boys).
Tracks: Not Advised.
LP. . . . . ROUNDER 0043
Rounder / '88 / Projection / Roots Records / Swift / C.M. Distribution / Topic Records / Jazz Music / Hot Shot / A.D.A Distribution / Direct Distribution.

BASIC BLUEGRASS (Connie & Babe & The Backwoods Boys).
Tracks: Not Advised.
LP. . . . . ROUNDER 0042
Rounder / '88 / Projection / Roots Records / Swift / C.M. Distribution / Topic Records / Jazz Music / Hot Shot / A.D.A Distribution / Direct Distribution.

Conway, Lee

LOVE STILL MAKES THE WORLD GO ROUND.
Tracks: Not Advised.
■ LP. . . . . GES 5005
Emerald / Jun '78.

Cooley, Spade

A Western Swing fiddler, singer and bandleader who got his nickname from playing cards. Spade Cooley was born in Oklahoma in 1910 and filled ballrooms on the West Coast during the war. His *Shame On You*, was a number one country hit in 1945 and featured a vocal by Tex Williams. His big band style fell on hard times and he was imprisoned for life in 1961 for killing his wife. Cooley was let out to play a benefit in 1969 but he died of a heart attack. (Donald Clarke)

ROMPIN', STOMPIN', SINGIN', SWINGIN' (Cooley, Spade & Tex Williams).
Tracks: Bronco buster's ball / Shame on you / Sinful / Shrimp boats / Miracle waltz / What did ya mean (when you said I love you) / Don't call me, I'll call you / Sweet little boogalie / Only polickin' / All aboard for Oklahoma / Big chief boogie / Hillbilly fever / You can't get Texas out of me / Wagon wheels / Last round-up, The / Like someone in love / Isn't it romantic / Something wonderful / I'm comin', Virginia / Cheek to cheek.
LP. . . . . BFX 15110
Bear Family / Jun '83 / Rollercoaster Records / Swift / Direct Distribution.

SWINGING THE DEVIL'S DREAM.
Tracks: Chew tobacco rag / Horse hair boogie / Down yonder / Hitsitty hotsitty / Rhumba boogie, The / Crazy cause I love you / Carmen's boogie / Nashville special / Y'hear / You clobbered me / Break up down / Swinging the devil's dream / Anita / One sweet letter from you / Cowboy waltz / Down by the pecos / Y'ready.
■ LP. . . . . CR 30239
Charly / '84.

Coolidge, Rita

This American singer was born in Nashville, the capital of country music and has always incorporated a country flavour in her records, although veering further towards easy listening as her career has progressed. Her father was a Baptist minister, and she sang in religious choirs from early childhood. Her professional career began to take off as the Sixties gave way to the Seventies - she toured the States with Delaney & Bonnie & Friends and then with Joe Cocker and Leon Russell as part of the Mad Dogs and Englishmen Show, both semi-legendary tours that helped to spread Coolidge's name in the music business. She achived moderate sales with a series of albums during the early and mid-Seventies, and also recorded with singer/songwriter Kris Kristofferson, whom she married in 1973. Coolidge's real breakthrough album was 1977's *Anytime Anywhere*, this was a big seller on both sides of the Atlantic, and yielded the international hit single *We're All Alone*, a Boz Scaggs ballad that reached No.7 in the US and No.6 in the UK. The LP also contained *Higher And Higher*, a remake of a Jackie Wilson oldie that she took to No.2 in the US, four places higher than the original, and *Words*, a Bee Gees song that gave Coolidge a British Top 30 hit. Although apparently established as a major star, her career quickly went off the rails. She never had another major hit single, and subsequent albums failed to live up to the success of *Anytime Anywhere*. However, her smooth and pleasant voice assured her of a steady living in the music business, even without hit records. She achieved a chart comeback of sorts with *All Time High*, the theme song from the 1983 James Bond movie *Octopussy*. Although this single was not a major pop hit, it enjoyed an extended run at the top of the US AOR charts. Rita Coolidge has had 13 hit albums and 15 Billboard hits between 1969 and 1983 including duets with Kris Kristofferson and Glen Campbell. She tours incessantly and she was one third of *Trio*, in 1987 with Dolly Parton and Emmylou Harris, an album that was in the USA country chart for over 80 weeks. (Bob MacDonald)

ALL TIME HIGH.
Tracks: All time high / Octopussy.
■ 7" . . . . AM 007
A&M / Jun '83.

ALL TIME HIGH.
Tracks: Not Advised.
CD 550 0792

MC .... .550 0794
Spectrum (1) / May '93 / PolyGram.

ANYTIME..ANYWHERE.
Tracks: Your love keeps lifting me higher and higher / Way you do the things you do, The / We're all alone / I feel the burden (being lifted off my shoulders) / I don't want to talk about it / Words / Good times / Who's to bless and who's to blame / Southern lady / Hungry years.
■ LP.................... AMLH 64616
■ MC.................... CAM 64616
A&M / May '78.

BREAKAWAY (Coolidge, Rita & Kris Kristofferson).
Tracks: Lover please / We must've been out of our minds / Dakota (the dancing bear) / What'cha gonna do / Things I might've been, The / Slow down / Rain / Sweet Susannah / I've got to have you / I'd rather be sorry / Crippled crow.
MC.................... .40 32775
CBS / Mar '86 / Sony.
■ LP.................... CBS 32775
CBS / Mar '86.

CLASSICS: RITA COOLIDGE.
Tracks: Not Advised.
■ CD.................... CDA 2504
A&M.

CLOSER YOU GET.
Tracks: Closer you get / Take it home.
■ 7".................... AMS 8162
A&M / Sep '81.

FOOL THAT I AM.
Tracks: Fool that I am / Can she keep you satisfied.
■ 7".................... AMS 8103
A&M / Jan '81.

FULL MOON (Coolidge, Rita & Kris Kristofferson).
Tracks: Hard to be friends / It's all over / I never had it so good / From the bottle to the good / Take time to love / Tennessee blues / Part of your life / I'm down (but I keep falling) / I heard the bluebirds sing / After the fact / Loving arms / Song I'd like to sing.
■ LP.................... AMLH 64403
A&M / '73.

GREATEST HITS.
Tracks: Not Advised.
CD.................... CDMID 109
MC.................... CMID 109
A&M / Oct '92 / PolyGram.

HEARTBREAK RADIO.
Tracks: Walk on in / One more heartache / Closer you get / Wishin' and hopin' / Heartbreak radio / Man and woman / I did my part / Hold on / Basic lady / Stranger to me now / Take it home.
■ LP.................... AMLK 63727
A&M / Sep '81.

HIGHER AND HIGHER.
Tracks: Higher and higher / I don't want to talk about it.
■ 7".................... AMS 7315
A&M / Oct '77.

I'D RATHER LEAVE WHILE I'M IN LOVE.
Tracks: I'd rather leave while I'm in love / Can she keep you satisfied.
■ 7".................... AMS 7480
A&M / May '81.

INSIDE THE FIRE.
Tracks: Hit me on the loveside / Do you believe in love / I can't afford that feeling anymore / Games / Wishing star / I'm comin' home / Love from Tokyo / Something said love / Survivor / Love is muddy water.
LP.................... AMA 5003
A&M / Sep '89 / PolyGram.

LADY'S NOT FOR SALE, THE.
Tracks: Donut man / Inside of me / Fever / Bird on the wire / My crew / I'll be your baby tonight / Woman left lonely, A / Shiskey whiskey / Everybody loves a winner / Lady's not for sale, The.
■ LP.................... MFP 50500
MFP / Mar '81.
LP.................... SPR 8568
MC.................... SPC 8568
Spot / Sep '85.

LET'S GO DANCIN'.
Tracks: Let's go dancing / Keep the candle burning.
■ 7".................... AMS 8119
A&M / Mar '81.

LOVE ME AGAIN.
Tracks: Not Advised.
■ LP.................... AMLH 64699
A&M / Jul '78.

LOVE ME AGAIN.
Tracks: Love me again / Jealous kind, The.
■ 7".................... AMS 7405
A&M / Dec '78.

NEVER LET YOU GO.
Tracks: You do it / Fools in love / Do you really want to hurt me / You ought to be with me / We've got tonite / I'll never let you go / Stop wasting your time / Tempted / Only you / All time high.

■ LP.................... AMLX 64914
A&M / Oct '83.

ONLY YOU.
Tracks: Only you / Shadow in the night.
■ 7".................... AM 141
A&M / Sep '83.

SATISFIED.
Tracks: One fine day / Fool in me / Trust it all to somebody / Let's go dancing / Pain of love / I'd rather leave while I'm in love / Sweet emotion / Crime of passion / Can she keep you satisfied.
■ LP.................... AMLH 64781
A&M / Nov '79.

SLOW DANCER.
Tracks: Slow dancer / He's so fine.
■ 7".................... AMS 7362
A&M / Jun '78.

STAR.
Tracks: Star / Keep the candle burning.
■ 7".................... AMS 7222
A&M / Apr '76.

STAR PORTRAITS: RITA COOLIDGE.
Tracks: Not Advised.
VHS.................... GEMV 5010
Gemini Vision / Nov '92 / Sony.

VERY BEST OF RITA COOLIDGE, THE (Greatest hits).
Tracks: We're all alone / I'd rather leave while I'm in love / Higher and higher / One fine day / Only you know and I know / Bye, bye love / Fever / Am I blue? / Slow dancer / Way you do the things you do, The / Let's go dancing / Keep the candle burning / I don't want to talk about it / Fool that I am / Mean to you.
CD.................... CDA 3238
■ MC.................... CAM 68520
A&M / '88.
■ LP.................... AMLH 68520
A&M / '88.

WE'RE ALL ALONE.
Tracks: Higher and higher / Way you do the things you do, The / We're all alone / I feel the burden (being lifted off my shoulders) / I don't want to talk about it / Words / Good times / Who's to bless and who's to blame / Southern lady / Hungry years.
LP.................... SHM 3140
MC.................... HSC 3140
Hallmark / May '84 / Pickwick Records.

WE'RE ALL ALONE.
Tracks: We're all alone / Who's to bless and who's to blame.
■ 7".................... AMS 7295
A&M / Jun '77.

WE'RE ALL ALONE (OLD GOLD).
Tracks: We're all alone / Words.
7".................... OG 9812
Old Gold / Oct '88 / Pickwick Records.

WORDS.
Tracks: Words / Who's to bless and who's to blame.
■ 7".................... AMS 7330
A&M / Feb '78.

YOU.
Tracks: You / Only you know that I know.
■ 7".................... AMS 7375
A&M / Aug '78.

Cooper, Wilma Lee & Stoney

Husband and wife duo who were stars of 1950's/1960's. Wilma Lee Leary was born on 07.02.1921 in Valley Head, West Virginia. She sang, played banjo, guitar and piano in the Leary family band during the 1930's /early 1940's and recording some sides for the Library Of Congress. Dale T.'Stoney' Cooper (16.10.1918 - 23.03.1977) from Harman, West Virginia (vocals/fiddle) joined The Leary Family band on leaving school. In 1947, Wilma and Stoney married and set out together playing Virginia's WWVA Wheeling Jamboree 1947-1957, complete with their own band the Blue Chasers (later the Clinch Mountain-Clan), which included the dobroists Bill Carver and Josh Graves. The Coopers recorded for the indie label Rich-R-Tone, Columbia and Fred Rose's Hickory label in the late 50's/60's and Decca. They enjoyed four top ten hits with *Come Walk With Me*, *Big Midnight Special*, *There's A Big Wheel*, and *Wreck On The Highway*. The live act was complemented by a strong selection of gospel favourites including *Tramp On The Street*, *Matthew 24*, and their theme tune *The West Virginia Polka*. Soulful-voiced traditionalist Wilma Lee has, since Stoney's death kept the road show going. (Maurice Hope)

CARTER FAMILY'S GREATEST HITS (Lee, Wilma & Stoney Cooper).
Tracks: Not Advised.
LP.................... SLP 980
MC.................... GT 5980
Starday (USA) / Apr '87 / Crusader Marketing Co.

DAISY A DAY (Cooper, Wilma Lee & Stoney).
Tracks: Daisy a day / Tomorrow I'll be gone / Pretty Polly / Uncle pen / Shackles and chains / I'm tying the leaves / Peggy Lou / I closed my hearts / Ain't gonna work tomorrow / I couldn't believe it was true / No one now / As long as I live.
LP.................... REBEL 1625
Rebel (1) / '75 / Projection / Backs Distribution.

EARLY RECORDINGS (Lee, Wilma & Stoney Cooper).
Tracks: West Virginia polka / All on account of you / No one now / Can you forget / Thirty pieces of silver / On the banks of the old river / Sunny side of the mountain / I cried again / Walking my lord up Calgary Hill / You tried to ruin my name / White rose, The / I'm taking my audition.
LP.................... CCS 103
County (USA) / '81 / Projection / Mike's Country Music Room / Swift.

WHITE ROSE (Cooper, Wilma Lee & Stoney).
Tracks: Not Advised.
LP.................... REBEL 2623
MC.................... REBELMC 1623
Rebel (1) / '75 / Projection / Backs Distribution.

WILMA LEE & STONEY COOPER (Lee, Wilma & Stoney Cooper).
Tracks: Not Advised.
LP.................... ROUNDER 0066
Rounder / '88 / Projection / Roots Records / Jazz Music / Hot Shot / A.D.A Distribution / Direct Distribution.

WILMA LEE COOPER (Cooper, Wilma Lee & Stoney).
Tracks: You tried to ruin my name / Forsaken love / Curly headed baby / Far beyond the starry sky / Sinful to flirt / What'll do with baby - o / Still there's a spark of love / Nobody's darling but mine / Bury me beneath the willow / Who's gonna shoe your pretty little feet / Cowards over Pearl Harbour.
LP.................... ROUNDER 0143
Rounder / '88 / Projection / Roots Records / Swift / C.M. Distribution / Topic Records / Jazz Music / Hot Shot / A.D.A Distribution / Direct Distribution.

Copas, Cowboy

Born on July 15, 1921 in Muskogee, Oklahoma, Lloyd 'Cowboy' Copas first gained national re-cognition on Cincinatti's Midwest Hayride radio show, before moving on to Nashville's Grand Ole Opry. A backbone artist of the post-war years, he was one of the most successful country acts on King Records before securing his first (and only) number one with *Alabam* on Starday in 1960. Three years later (on March 5, 1963) he died in that tragic plane crash that also took the lives of Patsy Cline, Hawkshaw Hawkins and manager Randy Hughes. (Tony Byworth - August 1993)

16 GREATEST HITS: COWBOY COPAS.
Tracks: Not Advised.
MC.................... GT 53012
Starday (USA) / Apr '87 / Crusader Marketing Co.
LP.................... SD 3012
Starday (USA) / Mar '88 / Crusader Marketing Co.

BEST OF THE COWBOY COPAS.
Tracks: Not Advised.
LP.................... SLP 958
Starday (USA) / Jan '80 / Crusader Marketing Co.

BEYOND THE SUNSET.
Tracks: Beyond the sunset / Cowboy's deck of cards / Cowboy's meditation / God put a rainbow in the clouds / Legend of the robin's red breast / Man upstairs' family reunion, The / Picture from life's other side, A / Shake a hand / What will my answer be / Who at my door is standing / Wreck on the highway, The.
■ MC.................... ZCEB 118
Ember / '78 / TKO Records Ltd / President Records.

MISTER COUNTRY MUSIC.
Tracks: Sal / Thousand miles of ocean, A / Soft rain / Penny for your thoughts, A / You are the one / How do you talk to a baby / Black eyed Susan Brown / Seven seas from you / Louision / There'll come a time some-day / First things first / I dreamed of a Hillbilly heaven.
LP.................... OFF 9001
Official / '88 / Charly / Cadillac Music / Jazz Music.

NOT FORGOTTEN (Copas, Cowboy & Patsy Cline/Hawkshaw Hawkins).
Tracks: Not Advised.
LP.................... SLP 346
MC.................... GT 5346
Starday (USA) / Apr '87 / Crusader Marketing Co.

OPRY STAR SPOTLIGHT ON COWBOY COPAS.
Tracks: Sixteen fathoms / Now that you're gone / Sweet lips / Mental cruelty / Wings of a dove / Flat top pickin' / Rebel, The / Johnny Yuma / That's all I can remember / Loose talk / Sleepy eyed John / Twenty fourth hour, The / Satisfied mind, A.

LP. . . . . OFF 9003
Official / '88 / Charly / Cadillac Music / Jazz Music.

TRAGIC TALES OF LOVE & LIFE.
Tracks: Not Advised.
CD . . . . KCD 00714
King / Feb '93 / New Note / Koch International.

Cordle, Larry

LARRY CORDLE, LARRY DUNCAN & LONE-SOME STANDARD TIME (Cordle, Larry & Larry Duncan).
Tracks: Lonesome standard time / Delta queen / You can't do wrong and get by / Fields of home, The / Lower on the hog / Castellion springs / Down the road to gloryland / Kentucky king / Little Cecil / Old river rock / Highway 40 blues / Lonesome dove / You can't take it with you when you go.
CD . . . . .SH CD 3802
MC . . . . SH MC 3802
Sugarhill(USA) / '92 / Roots Records / Projection / Impetus Records / C.M. Distribution / Jazz Music / Swift / Duncans / A.D.A. Distribution.

Cormier, Clarence

HEE HAW BREAKDOWN.
Tracks: Hee haw breakdown / Cajun waltz.
7" 1004
Swallow (USA) / Dec '82 / Swift / Wellard Dist.

Cornelius, Helen

HELEN CORNELIUS.
Tracks: Don't bother to knock / Mama he's crazy / Love is too close to be too far away / Time of my life, The / He thinks hearts were made to break / Give me one more chance / You don't bring me flowers / I don't want to have to marry you / Old friends / God bless the U.S.A.
LP. .IMCA 39034
MC . . . . IMCAC 39034
MCA / Mar '87 / BMG.

I DON'T WANNA HAVE TO MARRY YOU (see under Brown, Jim Ed).

Cotton Mill Boys

AS IS.
Tracks: Not Advised.
LP. . . . . UNKNOWN
Square Deal / Sep '87 / Ross Records.

BEST OF THE COTTON MILL BOYS VOL.1.
Tracks: Not Advised.
LP. . . . . .HPE 627
MC . . . . .HPC 627
Harp (Ireland) / Jul '80 / C.M. Distribution.

GOLD WATCH AND CHAIN.
Tracks: Gold watch and chain / Devil went.
7" . . . . HS 067
Homespun (Ireland) / May '83 / Homespun Records / Ross Records / Wellard Dist.

ORANGE BLOSSOM SPECIAL.
Tracks: Not Advised.
MC . . . . HACS 7058
Hawk / Mar '77 / C.M. Distribution.

Country All Stars

JAZZ FROM THE HILLS.
Tracks: Stompin' at the Savoy / Tennessee rag / Do something / Indiana march / Sweet Georgia Brown / Midnight train / In a little spanish town / My little girl / Lady in red, The / Marie / It goes like this / What's the reason (I'm not pleasing you) / When it's darkness on the delta / Vacation train, The / Fiddle patch / Fiddle sticks.
LP. BFX 15350
Bear Family / Jun '89 / Rollercoaster Records / Swift / Direct Distribution.

Country Billy

MIDNIGHT RIDER.
Tracks: Midnight rider / Six days on the road / Tequila Sheila / Sella and the dealer / Coward of the county / Tulsa time / Louisianna woman.
12" . . . . YB 12124
■ EP . . . . YB 124
Young Blood / Dec '81.

Country Breeze

ALWAYS.
Tracks: When God comes and gathers his jewels / When my blue moon turns to gold again / Together again / Always / Let the rest of the world go by / Tennessee waltz / Country roads / Love me tender / If you need a friend / Making plans / Could I have this dance / Rockin' alone in an old rocking chair / Say it again / Through the eyes of a child.
LP. .KMLP 308

Igus / Oct '81 / C.M. Distribution / Ross Records / Duncans.

BEAUTIFUL THINGS.
Tracks: One day at a time / You and me / Boil them cabbage down / White rose of Athens, The / Run to the door / Old Scotia's drum / Beautiful things / Wrong road again / Glad to be back home again / Sweetest gift, The / I wanna see Nashville / Spinning wheel.
LP. . . . . NA 119
MC . . . . NC 119
Neptune / Jul '80 / Neptune Tapes / A.D.A. Distribution.

CENTRE SOUND OF COUNTRY BREEZE, THE.
Tracks: Not Advised.
LP. NEVLP 141
Nevis / May '79.

COUNTRY BREEZE.
Tracks: Do what you do do well / Dear John / Crying time / Ain't love good.
LP. . . . . LILP 5071
■ MC LIC5 5071
Lismor / Jul '77.

Country Code

SHELLEY'S WINTER LOVE.
Tracks: Just out of reach / Someday you'll call my name / No one will ever know (how much I love you).
LP. . . . . .HRL 122
Homespun (Ireland) / May '88 / Homespun Records / Ross Records / Wellard Dist.

Country Gazette

A bluegrass group formed in 1971 by the remaining members of the Flying Burrito Brothers: Herb Pederson on banjo, Byron Berline on fiddle, Kenny Wertz on guitar, Roger Bush on bass. Very popular in Europe, with successful tours. Together all their session credits would take up a whole page. (Donald Clarke)

AMERICA'S BLUEGRASS BAND.
LP. . . . . FF 295
Flying Fish (USA) / Mar '89 / Cadillac Music / Roots Records / Projection / C.M. Distribution / Direct Distribution / Jazz Music / Duncans / A.D.A. Distribution.

AMERICAN AND CLEAN.
Tracks: Not Advised.
LP. . . . . FF 253
Flying Fish (USA) / Mar '89 / Cadillac Music / Roots Records / Projection / C.M. Distribution / Direct Distribution / Jazz Music / Duncans / A.D.A. Distribution.

BLUEGRASS TONIGHT.
Tracks: Not Advised.
LP. . . . . FF 383
MC . . . . FF 383C
Flying Fish (USA) / '80 / Cadillac Music / Roots Records / Projection / C.M. Distribution / Direct Distribution / Jazz Music / Duncans / A.D.A. Distribution.

BLUEGRASS TONIGHT VOL.2.
Tracks: Not Advised.
LP. . . . . FF 384
Flying Fish (USA) / '88 / Cadillac Music / Roots Records / Projection / C.M. Distribution / Direct Distribution / Jazz Music / Duncans / A.D.A. Distribution.

FROM THE BEGINNING.
Tracks: Keep on pushing / Sounds of goodbye / Huckleberry hornpipe / My Oklahoma / Hot burrito breakdown / Aggravation / Forget me not / Fallen eagle, The / Lonesome blues / Deputy Dalton / Down the road / Tried so hard / Snowball / Lost indian.
LP. .SLS 50414
Sunset (Liberty) / Apr '78 / EMI.

HELLO OPERATOR.
Tracks: Not Advised.
CD . . . . FF 112CD
MC . . . . FF 112C
Flying Fish (USA) / Jul '92 / Cadillac Music / Roots Records / Projection / C.M. Distribution / Direct Distribution / Jazz Music / Duncans / A.D.A. Distribution.

OUT TO LUNCH.
Tracks: Still feeling blue / Sure didn't take him long / Out to lunch / Melody for baby / Sing a sad song / Sunny side of the mountain / Down down down / Why you been gone so long / Forked deer / Time left to wander / Last thing on my mind / Uncle Cloony played the banjo / Blue light.
LP. . . . . FF 027
Flying Fish (USA) / Mar '89 / Cadillac Music / Roots Records / Projection / C.M. Distribution / Direct Distribution / Jazz Music / Duncans / A.D.A. Distribution.

STRICTLY INSTRUMENTAL.
Tracks: Not Advised.
LP. . . . . FF 446
Flying Fish (USA) / Jul '89 / Cadillac Music / Roots Records / Projection / C.M. Distribution / Direct Distribution / Jazz Music / Duncans / A.D.A. Distribution.

Country Gentlemen

Bluegrass vocal, instrumental group founded on July 4, 1957 by Louisiana-born vocalist/guitarist Charlie Waller and John Duffey, mandolin/tenor vocals. Later joined by banjoist Eddie Adcock and in 1959 by bassist Tom Gray, this formed the Country Gents strongest line up, spanning some 10 years. Their material was to encompass bluegrass and sixties folk, Duffy and Gray were latear to become founder members of the Seldom Scene. Other to feature in the aggregation were to include Ricky Skaggs, Jerry Douglas, Bill Emerson, Doyle Lawson, Bill Yates and Keith Littlea. The Country Gentlemen recorded for Starday, Vanguard, Rebel and Sugar Hill, where in 1989 the original members, supplemented by dobroist Mike Auldrige, released their *Classic Country Gents Reunion.* (Maurice Hope)

25 YEARS (25 SONGS).
Tracks: Not Advised.
CD . . . . REBELCD 1102
Double LP . . . . REBEL 2202
MC . . . . .REBELMC 2202
Rebel (1) / '89 / Projection / Backs Distribution.

AWARD WINNING, THE.
Tracks: Not Advised.
CD . . . . REBEL 1506
Rebel (1) / '75 / Projection / Backs Distribution.

BLUEGRASS AT CARNEGIE HALL.
Tracks: Not Advised.
LP. . . . . GT 0102
Gusto (USA) / Mar '88.

BRINGING MARY HOME.
Tracks: Not Advised.
LP. REBEL 1478
Rebel (1) / '75 / Projection / Backs Distribution.

CALLING MY CHILDREN HOME.
Tracks: Not Advised.
LP. REBEL 1574
Rebel (1) / '75 / Projection / Backs Distribution.

COUNTRY GENTLEMEN FEAT. RICKY SKAGGS ON FIDDLE.
Tracks: Travelling kind / Souvenirs / Leaves that are green, The / Irish Spring / Home in Louisiana / City of New Orleans / House of the rising sun / Catfish John / Heartaches / One morning in May / Bringing Mary home / Welcome to New York.
CD . . . . VMD 73123
LP. . . . . VMLP 73123
MC . . . . VMMC 73123
Vanguard / Jun '90 / Complete Record Co. Ltd.

COUNTRY SONGS OLD AND NEW.
Tracks: Not Advised.
CD . . . . SFCD 40004
LP. SF 40004
MC . . . . SFC 40004
Smithsonian Folkways / '89 / A.D.A Distribution / Topic Records / Direct Distribution / C.M. Distribution.

GOOD AS GOLD.
Tracks: Not Advised.
LP. . . . . SH 3734
MC . . . . ZCSH 3734
Sugarhill(USA) / Mar '88 / Roots Records / Projection / Impetus Records / C.M. Distribution / Jazz Music / Swift / Duncans / A.D.A. Distribution.

JOE'S LAST TRAIN.
Tracks: Not Advised.
LP. REBEL 1559
Rebel (1) / '75 / Projection / Backs Distribution.

LIVE IN JAPAN.
Tracks: Not Advised.
CD . . . . REBELCD 1104
Rebel (1) / '75 / Projection / Backs Distribution.

ONE WIDE RIVER.
Tracks: Not Advised.
LP. REBEL 1497
Rebel (1) / '75 / Projection / Backs Distribution.

RETURN ENGAGEMENT.
Tracks: Not Advised.
LP. REBEL 1663
Rebel (1) / '75 / Projection / Backs Distribution.

RIVER BOTTOM.
Tracks: Not Advised.
LP. . . . . SH 3723
MC . . . . ZCSH 3723
Sugarhill(USA) / '88 / Roots Records / Projection / Impetus Records / C.M. Distribution / Jazz Music / Swift / Duncans / A.D.A. Distribution.

SIT DOWN YOUNG STRANGER.
Tracks: Come sit down by the river / Meet me on the other side / Love and wealth / Likes of you, The / You're always the one / Darby's Castle / Sit down young stranger / It's just like Heaven / For the first time / South Elm Street / Blue Ridge Mountains turning green / Lonely dancer.
LP. . . . . SH 3712
MC . . . . ZCSH 3712

Sugarhill(USA) / '88 / Roots Records / Projection / Impetus Records / C.M. Distribution / Jazz Music / Swift / Duncans / A.D.A Distribution.

SOUND OFF.
Tracks: Not Advised.
LP. . . . . **REBEL 1501**
Rebel (1) / '75 / Projection / Backs Distribution.

YESTERDAY AND TODAY VOL.1.
Tracks: Not Advised.
LP. . . . . **SAVE 030**
Fundamental / Jun '87 / Plastic Head.

YESTERDAY AND TODAY VOL.2.
Tracks: Not Advised.
LP. . . . . **SAVE 031**
Fundamental / Sep '87 / Plastic Head.

Country Jays

SILVER MEDALS AND SWEET MEMORIES.
Tracks: What goes on when the sun goes down / When the roses bloom again / Green grass / Triangle song, The / Mama I'm not the boy I used to be / Running bear / Big wheel cannonball / Lord made a hobo out of me, The / I saw the light / Silver medals and sweet memories / Cover mama's flowers / Apache / If your lonesome at your table / Take me back to yesterday once more.
LP. . . . . **BGC 325**
■ **MC** . . . . **KBGC 325**
Country House / Feb '83.

Country Music

Country music's roots came from many quarters, the cowboys in the bunkhouse, or out under the stars, railroad workers, cotton pickers, travelling medicine shows and the roaming drifters all made the great contributions. Men would gather after the weeks work, go to the nearest residence of any size, with barn dances providing ideal opportunities for any musician to show their skills, while others would pass away the hours entertaining their fellow workers with some ol' hand-me-down, fiddle, guitar or banjo. Settlers from the British Isles and Ireland didn't just take with them a pocketful of dreams, they also shipped over a great many tunes with the Celts particularly productive. Those tiny rural communities throughout the South Eastern states of America proved to be a real hotbed for aspiring musicians. The earliest recordings were made in New York (1922) on (Victor), with the likes of fiddle player Erik Robertson. These were soon followed in 1927 by the historic recordings of The Carter Family and Jimmie Rodgers (The Singing Breakman). Other artists of the era to leave lasting marks include Gid Tanner and The Skillet Lickers (who's musical influences stretch beyond country's boundries), J.E. Mainer, Vernon Dalhart (who's 1924 version of *The Wreck Of Old '97*, and *The Prisoner's Song*, sold over six million copies) and The Stoneman Family, to mention but a few. Arguably, The Carters Family and Jimmie Rodgers opened more doors than anyone. The Carter Family's folky mountain ballads even today feature most prominently in many bluegrass musician's repertoire. While Rodgers vocal styling has been influenced in the careers of Lefty Frizzell and Merle Haggard for example. Another major factor in the development of the music is radio coverage, with the then WSM Barn Dance (1925) at the hub of the action. Two years latter George D. Hay christened it The Grand Ole Opry and an institution was born. On a Saturday evening families would huddle around the family radio to hear their favourites during the coming years, with stars like Roy Acuff, Bill Monroe, Ernest Tubb, Kitty Wells, Eddy Arnold, The Louvin Brothers, Lefty Frizzell and Hank Williams. Country music's advance into the sixties heralded the introduction of rhinestone suits, extensive everlasting tours and TV coverage. Acts at the centre of the boom included Buck Owens, Johnny Cash, Tammy Wynette, Loretta Lynn, Merle Haggard and Marty Robbins. Sadly two other acts at the heart of it all, Jim Reeves and Patsy Cline were victims of tragic plane crashes. During the second half of the seventies country music went through it's bleakest period (*Urban Cowboy* etc) and many feared the direction it was taking. At this point the "outlaw" cliche was born, pioneered by the likes of Waylon Jennings, Willie Nelson, Jerry Jeff Walker (who helped put Texas on the map) and Tompall Glaser, giving country music some much needed fire and identity. The dawning of the eighties saw the welcome emergence of Ricky Skaggs and George Strait who in their separate ways gave country music back its roots, the former showing his bluegrass upbringing while Straits leaned towards Western-swing. Other notable contributions came from Emmylou Harris, John Conlee, Vern Gosdin, Reba McEntire, Gene Watson and The Judds. Country music's future looks to be in the most capable hands, fronted by promising acts like Clint Black, Garth Brooks, Dwight Yoakam, Susy Bogguss, Patty Loveless, Alan Jackson and Vince Gill along with established names Kathy Mattea, Ricky Skaggs, Randy Travis and George Strait. (Maurice Hope).

Country Sailor

HEARTACHES ARE KNOCKING.
Tracks: Not Advised.
LP. . . . . **SRTZ 78/105**
SRT / Sep '78 / Pinnacle / Projection.

Country Shack

PORTRAIT, A.
Tracks: How can I / Lonely street / All I want is you / Just out of reach / Sunset on the sage / Shall we meet / Good-hearted woman / Milwaukee here I come / What I've got in mind / Back home again / Fill my cup, Lord / Ain't that a shame / Sweet folk and country.
LP. . . . . **SFA 056**
Sweet Folk All / May '81 / Cadillac Music / Projection / C.M. Distribution / Wellard Dist. / Impetus Records.

WHICH WAY IS GONE?.
Tracks: If you want me / I'll do anything / Special kind of man, A / Help me make it through the night / Wine in the cellar / Your good girl's gonna go bad / I'll be there / Come on home / Namedropper / Never miss a real good thing / Silver threads and golden needles / Which way is gone.
LP. . . . . **SFA 076**
Sweet Folk All / May '81 / Cadillac Music / Projection / C.M. Distribution / Wellard Dist. / Impetus Records.

Cowboy Jazz

SWING BOOGIE.
Tracks: Not Advised.
LP. . . . . **ROUNDER 0173**
MC . . . . **ROUNDER 0173C**
Rounder / '88 / Projection / Roots Records / Swift / C.M. Distribution / Topic Records / Jazz Music / Hot Shot / A.D.A Distribution / Direct Distribution.

THAT'S WHAT WE ALL LIKE ABOUT THE WEST.
Tracks: Not Advised.
LP. . . . . **ROUNDER 0149**
MC . . . . **ROUNDER 0149C**
Rounder / '88 / Projection / Roots Records / Swift / C.M. Distribution / Topic Records / Jazz Music / Hot Shot / A.D.A Distribution / Direct Distribution.

Cox Family

EVERYBODY'S REACHING OUT FOR SOMEONE.
Tracks: Standing by the bedside of a neighbour / Look me up by the ocean door / Everybody's reaching out for someone / Little whitewashed chimney / Cry baby cry / I've got that old feeling / But I do / Why not confess / Pardon me / My favorite memory / When God dips his pen of love in my heart / Backroads.
CD . . . . **CDROU 0297**
MC . . . . **ROU 0297**
Rounder / May '93 / Projection / Roots Records / Swift / C.M. Distribution / Topic Records / Jazz Music / Hot Shot / A.D.A Distribution / Direct Distribution.

Craddock, Billy Crash

Born in 1939 in Greensboro, North Carolina, this country-rock singer got his nickname from his hobby of stock-car racing. He had a minor hit on CBS in 1959 and made an impression in Australia, leading some to believe he was Australian. He left USA/Columbia (he wanted to sing country, they wanted him for rock'n'roll pop), returned to his home town, worked day jobs and sang weekends. After 10 years he signed to the Cartwheel label in Nashville; his first record *Knock Three Times* was a country top 3 in 1971. He switched to ABC for over 30 hits, then to Capitol in 1978. (Donald Clarke).

BEST OF BILLY CRASH CRADDOCK.
Tracks: Rub it in / Broken down in tiny pieces / You better move on / First time / Sweet magnolia blossom / Easy as pie / Still thinkin' bout you / Ain't nothing shakin' / Don't be angry / Slippin' and slidin' / Knock three times / Dream lover / I'm gonna knock on your wall / Walk softly / I love the blues / Ruby baby / Tear fell, A / Till the water stops runnin' / Afraid i'll want to love her one more time / You rubbed it in all wrong.
Double LP **IMCA2 4165**
MCA (Import) / Mar '86 / Pinnacle / Silver Sounds (CD).

BILLY 'CRASH' CRADDOCK.
Tracks: I cheated on a good woman's love / Jailhouse rock / Roll in my sweet baby's arms / Rock and roll madness / You're the girl / I've been too long lonely baby / Not a day gone by / Blue eyes crying in the rain / Say you'll stay until tomorrow / We never made it to Chicago.
LP. . . . . **EST 11758**
Capitol / May '78 / EMI.

BOOM BOOM BABY.
Tracks: Not Advised.

CRASH CRADDOCK.
Tracks: Not Advised.
LP. . . . . **IMCA 39054**
MCA (Import) / Mar '86 / Pinnacle / Silver Sounds (CD).

GREATEST HITS: BILLY CRASH CRADDOCK.
Tracks: Not Advised.
MC . . . . **CORONET 1707**
Coronet / Nov '87 / Cassette Developments.
LP. . . . . **CR 721**
Colonial / Oct '87.

I CHEATED ON A GOOD WOMANS LOVE.
Tracks: I cheated on a good womans love / Not a day goes by.
■ **7"** . . . . **CL 15971**
Capitol / Mar '78.

RUBY RASH.
Tracks: Ruby Rash / Walk when love walks.
■ **7"** . . . . **ABC 4031**
Anchor (1) / Jan '75.

WELL DON'T YOU KNOW.
Tracks: Sweet pie / School day dreams / Lulu Lee / Ah, poor little baby / I miss you so much / Blabbermouth / Am I to be the one / Sweetie Pie / Well don't you know / Boom boom baby / Don't destroy me / (What makes you) Treat me like you do / I want that / Since she turned seventeen / All I want is you / Letter of love / One last kiss / Is it true or false / Is it true or is it false / Report card of love / Heavenly love / Goodtime Billy.
CD . . . . **BCD 15610**
Bear Family / Jun '92 / Rollercoaster Records / Swift / Direct Distribution.

Craftsmen

YOUR COUNTRY AND IRISH REQUESTS.
Tracks: Gypsy woman / Hannigan's hooley / Old bog road.
MC . . . . **CHRL 135**
Homespun (Ireland) / '88 / Homespun Records / Ross Records / Wellard Dist.
LP. . . . . **HRL 135**
Homespun (Ireland) / May '88 / Homespun Records / Ross Records / Wellard Dist.

Cramer, Floyd

This American pianist, born in Louisiana, began playing keyboards while a young child. After leaving school, he spent the early Fifties accompanying many stars on the *Louisiana hayride* radio programme. In 1955 he moved to Nashville and, from that time onwards, his career was guided by Chet Atkins, the prime mover in RCA Victor Records' Nashville division. Atkins teamed Cramer with the newly signed Elvis Presley. The association worked extremely well, and Cramer thus played piano on all of Elvis' historic early hits. This fact alone would have assured Floyd of an important place in musical history; but he went on to help create the distinctive 'Nashville sound' that was to become the trademark of virtually all country and western records - his simple but brilliantly infectious keyboard style, which relied on the treble end of the board to provide the rhythm, was closely imitated by hundreds of others. In addition to backing Presley, Jim Reeves and a host of others, Cramer enjoyed a brief but highly successful career as a solo chart star. This began with *Last date*, an acclaimed single that perfectly encapsulated his influential style. This entered the American charts in late 1960, becoming the first of four US Top 40 hits (all of which were instrumentals); it climbed to No.2 and stayed there for four weeks. His 1961 follow-up *On the rebound*, another self-penned single went to No.4 in the US and hit No.1 in the UK, becoming the artist's only major British hit. The next disc was *San Antonio Rose*, which reached No.8 on the American listings. Cramer continued to work as a Nashville session man through the Sixties and Seventies, and also released a large number of LP's in his own right, most of which were insubstantial restatements of his familiar style. (Bob MacDonald, 6th Feb 1985)A country pianist, born in 1933 in Shreveport, Louisiana. He was a Nashville session player for RCA from 1955, playing on hits by the Browns, Jim Reeves, Elvis Presley (*Heartbreak Hotel*), many others. He described his distinctive piano style as 'whole-tone slur' or 'slip note'. His own hits included *Last Date*, a USA number two in 1960, and *On The Rebound*, a number four in 1961, both his own compositions. He's made more than 24 albums. (Donald Clarke).

20 OF THE BEST: FLOYD CRAMER.
Tracks: On the rebound / Java / Flip flop and bop / Lovesick blues / Corn crib symphony / Dream baby / Honky tonk (part 2) / Maple leaf rag / Sugarfoot rag / Boogie, boogie, boogie / What'd i say / Boogie woogie / Proud Mary / In crowd, The / Work song / Himmo a la Alegria / My melody of love / Games people play / Smile / Last date.
LP. . . . . **NL 89850**
■ **MC** . . . . **NK 89850**
RCA / Mar '86.

C 26 ■ DELETED

BEST OF FLOYD CRAMER.
Tracks: Let's go / Impossible dream, The / Yesterday / Look of love, The / Java / You are the sunshine of my life / Do you know the way to San Jose / Proud Mary / Sunny / Valley of the dolls, Theme from / Strangers in the night / This guy's in love with you / Man and a woman, A / Goin' out of my head / Can't take my eyes off you.
LP **107 4066**
MC **770 4066**
RCA (Brazil) / Jan '84.

BEST OF FLOYD CRAMER (1980).
Tracks: Last date / Tricky / Lovesick blues / Unchained melody / Satan's doll / San Antonio rose / On the rebound / Your last goodbye / Java / Swing low / Young years, The / Flip flop and bop.
LP . . . . **INTS 5008**
MC . . . . **INTK 5008**
RCA International / Apr '80 / BMG.

DALLAS.
Tracks: Dallas (Dallas dreams), Theme from / Incredible Hulk, Theme from / Taxi, Theme from / All in the Family / Waltons - theme / Little house on the prairie / Young and the restless, Theme from / M.A.S.H., Theme from / Laverne and Shirley (Theme) / Knots Landing.
■ **LP** . . . . **PL 13618**
RCA / Oct '80.
LP . . . . **INTS 5155**
MC . . . . **INTK 5155**
RCA International / Sep '81 / BMG.

DALLAS.
Tracks: Dallas / Knots Landing.
■ **7"** . . . . **JR 1**
RCA / Jun '80.

FLOYD CRAMER PLAYS MACARTHUR PARK.
Tracks: MAcArthur park / Autumn of my life / Our winter love / For lovers' sake / Turn around look at me / Sleep safe and warm / Do you know the way to San Jose / Odd couple, The / Impossible dream, The / Don't give up / This guy's in love with you.
■ **LP** . . . . **SF 8004**
RCA / Aug '70 / BMG.

HOT PEPPER.
Tracks: Hot pepper.
■ **7"** . . . . **RCA 1301**
RCA / Aug '62.

LAST DATE.
Tracks: Last date / San Antonio rose.
■ **7"** . . . . **PB 9379**
RCA / Apr '79.

ON THE REBOUND.
Tracks: On the rebound / Boogie woogie.
■ **7"** . . . . **RCA 1231**
RCA / Apr '61.
7" . . . . **GOLD 513**
RCA Golden Grooves / Jul '81 / BMG.

SAN ANTONIO ROSE.
Tracks: San Antonio rose.
■ **7"** . . . . **RCA 1241**
RCA / Jul '61.

Crampsey, Shaunie

MORNING SUN AND MEMORIES.
Tracks: Morning sun and memories / I wish it would rain.
CD Single . . . . **RITZCD 249**
Ritz / Oct '92 / Pinnacle / Midland Records.

Crary, Dan

Master - flatpicker and , founder member of the Bluegrass Alliance, formed at the back-end of the 1960s, with such stalwarts as Ebo Walker (later of New Grass revival) and Wayne Stewart. Apart from his own instrumental albums, his 1970 album *Bluegrass guitar* on American Heritage (reissued on Sugar Hill in 1992) was the first album of flat-picked fiddle tunes played on the guitar. He's also been involved in projects with banjoist John Hickman and fiddler Byrom Berline - who in 1990 with Crary helped form Traveler, augumented with Steve Spurgin on bass and John Morre on mandolin. *California* , their 1992 debut album on Sugar Hill, helped gain them IBMA's Instrumental Group Of The Year Award in 1993. (Maurice Hope)
Tracks: Not Advised.

GUITAR.
Tracks: Cotton patch rag / Stanley Brothers medley / Sweet laree / Memories of Mozart / Green in the blue medley, The / Tom and Jerry / Bill Monroe medley.
LP . . . . **SH 3730**
Sugarhill(USA) / Mar '89 / Roots Records / Projection / Impetus Records / C.M. Distribution / Jazz Music / Swift / Duncans / A.D.A Distribution.

LADY'S FANCY.
Tracks: Huckleberry hornpipe / Lime rock / If the devil dreamed about playing flamenco / With a flatpick / Jenny's waltz / Sally goon'n / Julie's reel / Dill pickle rag / Pretty little indian / Grey eagle / Lady's fancy.
LP . . . . **ROUNDER 0099**
MC . . . . **ROUNDER 0099C**
Rounder / '88 / Projection / Roots Records / Swift / C.M. Distribution / Topic Records / Jazz Music / Hot Shot / A.D.A Distribution / Direct Distribution.

SWEET SOUTHERN GIRL.
Tracks: Sweet southern girl / Blackbird, The / Devil played the fiddle, The / Jesse James was an outlaw / Stories we could tell / Butcher boy / Foggy mountain special / Big river / Lovin' her was easier / Don't mess around with Jim / Sally Ann / Mama said yeah / Cajun train.
LP . . . . **SH 3707**
MC . . . . **ZCSH 3707**
Sugarhill(USA) / '79 / Roots Records / Projection / Impetus Records / C.M. Distribution / Jazz Music / Swift / Duncans / A.D.A Distribution.

TAKE A STEP OVER.
Tracks: Bugle call rag / Take a step over / Great tunes/ Dumb names medley / Raleigh and special / Come hither / Willow, the wandering gypsy / Hot canary / Traditional suite in "E" medley / Lord build me a cabin.
CD . . . . **SHCD 3770**
LP . . . . **SHLP 3770**
MC . . . . **SHMC 3770**
Sugarhill / Jan '89 / Hot Shot / A.D.A Distribution / C.M. Distribution.

THUNDERATION.
Tracks: Banderilla / Depoe Bay / West O' the moon / Amsterdance / Songs of Makoraka-o / Thunderation / Lady's fantasy / Lime rock / Andante in steel / Denouement.
CD . . . . **SHCD 1135**
MC . . . . **SH 1135**
Sugarhill(USA) / '91 / Roots Records / Projection / Impetus Records / C.M. Distribution / Jazz Music / Swift / Duncans / A.D.A Distribution.

Cravens, Red

419 WEST MAIN (Cravens, Red & Bray Brothers).
Tracks: Not Advised.
LP . . . . **ROUNDER 0015**
Rounder / '88 / Projection / Roots Records / Swift / C.M. Distribution / Topic Records / Jazz Music / Hot Shot / A.D.A Distribution / Direct Distribution.

Craver, Mike

FISHING FOR AMOUR.
Tracks: Not Advised.
LP . . . . **FF 330**
Flying Fish (USA) / Mar '89 / Cadillac Music / Roots Records / Projection / C.M. Distribution / Direct Distribution / Jazz Music / Duncans / A.D.A Distribution.

Creed, Kyle

KYLE CREED WITH BOBBY PATTERSON & THE CAMP CREEK (Creed, Kyle/Bobby Patterson/Camp Creek Boys).
Tracks: Dance all night / Roustabout / Red wing / Old country church / John Hardy / Weeping willow / Pig in the pen / Cacklin' hen, The / Lost indian / Sunny side of the mountain / Sweet sunny South / Coleman ridge / Backstep / Soldier's joy / I don't love nobody.
LP . . . . **LED 2053**
Leader / '73 / Roots Records / Projection / Duncans / C.M. Distribution / Ross Records.

Creedence Clearwater..

This American rock band comprised brothers John and Tom Fogerty, Doug 'Cosmo' Clifford and Stu Cook. Creedence Clearwater Revival were one of the most successful groups in American rock history. Though their reign was comparatively brief - three golden years in 1969, 1970 and 1971 - they sold huge quantities of records and were one of the most exciting acts in the world. The group were formed at the end of the Fifties when three of the four were still in their early teens, and the same four members remained together under a variety of titles and styles until evolving into Creedence Clearwater Revival in 1967. The new name heralded the start of the sound that would make the group famous - an energetic, tightly played blend of rock'n'roll and R & B. The California quartet made it big in the autumn of 1968, when *Suzie Q.* hit No.11 on the US singles chart, sixteen places higher than the 1957 original by Dale Hawkins. In early '69 they achieved the first of three consecutive No.2 singles in the States, with John Fogerty's song *Proud Mary*. From that time onwards it was clear that John was totally dominant in the group, and the vast majority of their future output was penned by him; he was also the vocalist and lead guitarist. *Proud Mary* was an instant classic and was followed by the equally superlative *Bad moon rising*, which reached No.2 in the States and No.1 in Britain. Strangely, they never hit the top slot in their native country but picked up three more US No.2 singles, in the shape of *Green river*, the double A sided *Travelin' band/Who'll stop the rain* and *Lookin' out my back door*. CCR's consistent success with singles was somewhat out of step with the philosophy of many rock groups of their era, who preferred to concentrate on albums; but it was a fitting state of affairs, because Creedence's music was unusual for its time, being far closer to basic rock'n'roll than the psychedelic groups, the jazz-rock combos or the heavy metal bands. And yet CCR also sold LPs in massive quantities - some half a dozen of their albums passed the million-selling mark in quick succession. The best album by this prolific outfit was *Cosmo's factory*, a 1970 release that enjoyed an extended run at the top of the US album charts, and shot straight into the charts at No.1 in the UK. Personal differences within the band led to Creedence's termination. After the departure of Tom Fogerty, the three remaining members released one final album, 1972's *Mardi gras*. John Fogerty took less creative control over this project, with the result that it disgraced itself by peaking at No.12 in the States, failing to chart at all in Britain, and being ridiculed by reviewers. By the end of '72, the group were defunct. Little success greeted the various subsequent careers of Clifford, Cook and Tom Fogerty. John Fogerty launched a solo career under a false group name, the Blue Ridge Rangers, and scored a US Top 20 single with Hank Williams' song *Jambalaya (on the bayou)*; but even he found the going tough, and retired from recording in the mid-Seventies. Successful cover versions of his material have included Ike & Tina Turner's *Proud Mary* (No.4 in US in 1971) and Status Quo *Rockin' all over the world* (No.3 in UK in 1977). After almost a decade away from the limelight the solo John Fogerty made a dramatic return to the American charts in 1985, reaching the Top 10 with the album *Centerfield* and achieving a big US single with a typically straightforward and uncluttered number, *The old man down the road*. (Bob MacDonald).

10 CD COLLECTION (Creedence Clearwater Revival).
Tracks: I put a spell on you / Working man, The / Susie Q / 99 1/2 won't do / Get down woman / Porterville / Gloomy / Walk on the water / Born on the bayou / Bootleg / Graveyard train / Good golly miss molly / Penthouse pauper / Proud Mary / Keep on chooglin' / Green river / Commotion / Tombstone shadow / Wrote a song for everyone / Bad Moon Rising / Lodi / Cross tie walker / Sinister purpose / Night time is the right time / Down on the corner / It came out of the sky / Cotton fields / Poorboy shuffle / Feelin' blue / Don't look now / Midnight special / Side O' the road / Effigy / Ramble tamble / Before you accuse me / Travellin' band / Ooby dooby / Lookin' out my back door / Run through the jungle / Up around the bend / My baby left me / Who'll stop the rain / I heard it through the grapevine / Long as I can see the light / Pagan baby / Sailor's lament / Chameleon / Have you ever seen the rain / (Wish I could) Hideaway / Born to move / Hey tonight / It's just a thought / Molina / (Theme from) Rude awakening / Lookin' for a reason / Hello Mary Lou / Cross-tie Walker / Take it like a friend / Need someone to hold / Tearin' up the country / Someday never comes / What are you gonna do / Sail away / Door to door / Sweet Hitch-Hiker / Born on the bayou (live) / Green river (live) / Susie Q (live) / It came out of the sky (live) / Travellin' Band (live) / Fortunate son (live) / Commotion (live) / Lodi (live) / Bad moon rising (live) / Proud Mary (live) / Up around the bend (live) / Hey tonight (live) / Keep on chooglin' (live).
CD Set . . . . **FCDCCR 10**
Fantasy / Oct '92 / Pinnacle / Target Records / Jazz Music.

BAD MOON RISING (Creedence Clearwater Revival).
Tracks: Bad moon rising / If you don't know me by now / More today than yesterday.
7" **6580047**
CD Single **6580042**
■ **MC Single** **6580044**
Epic / Apr '92.

BAD MOON RISING (Creedence Clearwater Revival).
Tracks: Bad moon rising / Have you ever seen the rain / Keep on chooglin'.
■ **7"** . . . . **LBF 15230**
Liberty / Aug '69.
7" . . . . **GOLD 530**
Fantasy / Oct '81 / Pinnacle / Target Records / Jazz Music.
12" . . . . **NS 124**
■ **12"** . . . . **NST 124**
Fantasy / Jun '88.

BAD MOON RISING (OLD GOLD) (Creedence Clearwater Revival).
Tracks: Long as I can see the light / Bad moon rising.
7" . . . . **OG 9569**
Old Gold / Sep '85 / Pickwick Records.

BAYOU COUNTRY (Creedence Clearwater Revival).
Tracks: Born on the bayou / Bootleg / Graveyard train / Good golly Miss Molly / Penthouse pauper / Proud Mary / Keep on chooglin'.
■ **LP** . . . . **LBS 83261**
Liberty / May '70.
LP . . . . **FASLP 5003**
MC . . . . **FASK 5003**

■ DELETED C 27

Fantasy / Jul '84 / Pinnacle / Target Records / Jazz Music.
CD . . . . CDFE 502
LP. . . . . FACE 502
MC . . . . FACC 502
Fantasy / Aug '87 / Pinnacle / Target Records / Jazz Music.

BEST OF CREEDENCE CLEARWATER REVIVAL VOL.1 (Creedence Clearwater Revival).
Tracks: Proud Mary / Down on the corner / Bad moon rising / Green river / Long as I can see the light / Travellin' band / Midnight special, The / Have you ever seen the rain / Born on the Bayou / Susie Q.
MC . . . . FACC 509
Fantasy / Aug '88 / Pinnacle / Target Records / Jazz Music.
LP. . . . . FACE 509
Fantasy / Jul '88 / Pinnacle / Target Records / Jazz Music.
LP. . . . . FAX 509
Fantasy / Jun '88 / Pinnacle / Target Records / Jazz Music.

BEST OF CREEDENCE CLEARWATER REVIVAL VOL.2 (Creedence Clearwater Revival).
Tracks: Hey tonight / Run through the jungle / Fortunate son / Bootleg / Lookin' out my back door / Molina / Who'll stop the rain / Sweet hitchhiker / Good golly Miss Molly / Don't look now / I put a spell on you / Porterville / Up around the bend / Lodi.
LP. . . . . FACE 510
MC . . . . FACC 510
Fantasy / Aug '88 / Pinnacle / Target Records / Jazz Music.

CHRONICLE (20 Greatest hits) (Creedence Clearwater Revival).
Tracks: Susie Q / I put a spell on you / Proud Mary / Bad moon rising / Lodi / Green river / Commotion / Down on the corner / Fortunate son / Travellin' band / Who'll stop the rain / Up around the bend / Run through the jungle / Lookin' out my back door / Long as I can see the light / I heard it through the grapevine / Have you ever seen the rain / Hey tonight / Sweet hitchhiker / Some day never comes.
Double LP 1081115
MC Set 1681115
Fantasy (import) / Apr '86 / Pinnacle.
CD . . . . CDCCR 2
Fantasy / Jun '87 / Pinnacle / Target Records / Jazz Music.
■ CD 8217422
Polydor / Jun '87.

CHRONICLE VOL.2 (Creedence Clearwater Revival).
Tracks: Walk on the water / Susie Q (part 2) / Born on the Bayou / Good golly Miss Molly / Tombstone shadow / Wrote a song for everyone / Night time is the right time / Cottonfields / It came out of the sky / Don't look now (it ain't you or me) / Midnight special, The / Before you accuse me / My baby left me / Pagan baby / (I wish I could) hideaway / It's just a thought / Molina / Born to move / Lookin' for a reason / Hello Mary Lou.
CD . . . . CDCCR 3
Fantasy / Jun '87 / Pinnacle / Target Records / Jazz Music.

COMPLETE HITS ALBUM VOL.1 (Creedence Clearwater Revival).
Tracks: Not Advised.
■ CD 01279161
Arcade / May '88.

COMPLETE HITS ALBUM VOL.2 (Creedence Clearwater Revival).
Tracks: Not Advised.
■ CD 01279261
Arcade / May '88.

CONCERT, THE (Creedence Clearwater Revival).
Tracks: Born on the bayou / Green river / Tombstone shadow / Don't look now / Travellin' band / Who'll stop the rain / Bad moon rising / Proud Mary / Fortunate son / Commotion / Midnight special, The / Night time (is the right time) / Down on the corner / Keep on chooglin'.
LP. . . . . MPF 4501
MC . . . . MPF 54501
Fantasy / Feb '81 / Pinnacle / Target Records / Jazz Music.
CD . . . . CDFE 511
MC . . . . FACC 511
Fantasy / Jul '89 / Pinnacle / Target Records / Jazz Music.
■ LP. . . . . FACE 511
Fantasy / Jul '89.

COSMO'S FACTORY (Creedence Clearwater Revival).
Tracks: Ramble tamble / Before you accuse me / Lookin' out my back door / Run through the jungle / Up around the bend / My baby left me / Who'll stop the rain / I heard it through the grapevine / Long as I can see the light / Travellin' band / Ooby dooby.
■ LP. . . . . LBS 83388
Liberty / Sep '70.
LP. 5C 062 91666
EMI (Holland) / '83.
LP. . . . . FASLP 5006
MC . . . . FASK 5006
Fantasy / Jul '84 / Pinnacle / Target Records / Jazz Music.
CD . . . . CDFE 505
LP. . . . . FACE 505
MC . . . . FACC 505
Fantasy / Aug '87 / Pinnacle / Target Records / Jazz Music.

CREEDENCE CLEARWATER REVIVAL (Creedence Clearwater Revival).
Tracks: I put a spell on you / Working man / Suzie Q / Ninety-nine-and-a-half (won't do) / Get down, woman / Porterville / Gloomy / Walk on the water.
LP. . . . . FASLP 5002
MC . . . . FASK 5002
Fantasy / Jul '84 / Pinnacle / Target Records / Jazz Music.
CD . . . . CDFE 501
LP. . . . . FACE 501
MC . . . . FACC 501
Fantasy / Jul '87 / Pinnacle / Target Records / Jazz Music.

CREEDENCE CLEARWATER REVIVAL HITS ALBUM (Creedence Clearwater Revival).
Tracks: Bad moon rising / Travellin' band / Up around the bend / Long as I can see the light / Who'll stop the rain? / Lodi / Commotion / Fortunate son / Born on the corner / Green river / Have you ever seen the rain? / Sweet hitchhiker / Lookin' out my back door / Hey tonight / I heard it through the grapevine / Good golly Miss Molly / Suzie Q.
LP. . . . . MPF 4500
MC . . . . MPF 54500
Fantasy / Mar '82 / Pinnacle / Target Records / Jazz Music.

CREEDENCE COLLECTION, THE (Creedence Clearwater Revival).
Tracks: Suzie Q / I put a spell on you / Proud Mary / Born on the bayou / Bootleg / Good golly Miss Molly / Keep on chooglin' / Bad moon rising / Lady / Green river / Commotion / Cottonfields / Down on the corner / Fortunate son / Travellin' band / Who'll stop the rain? / Up around the bend / Run through the jungle / Lookin' out my back door / Long as I can see the light / I heard it through the grapevine / Have you ever seen the rain? / Hey tonight / Sweet hitchhiker.
Double LP . . . . IMDP 3
MC . . . . IMDK 3
Impression / Oct '85 / Pinnacle.

CREEDENCE COUNTRY (Creedence Clearwater Revival).
Tracks: Lookin' for a reason / Don't look now / Lodi / My baby left me / Hello Mary Lou / Ramble tamble / Cotton fields / Before you accuse me / Wrote a song for everyone / Ooby dooby / Cross-tie Walker / Lookin' out my back door.
CD . . . . CDFE 518
Fantasy / Sep '92 / Pinnacle / Target Records / Jazz Music.

CREEDENCE GOLD (Creedence Clearwater Revival).
Tracks: Proud Mary / Down on the corner / Bad moon rising / I heard it through the grapevine / Midnight special, The / Have you ever seen the rain / Born on the Bayou / Suzie Q.
CD . . . . CDFE 515
Fantasy / Aug '91 / Pinnacle / Target Records / Jazz Music.

DOWN ON THE CORNER (Creedence Clearwater Revival).
Tracks: Down on the corner.
■ 7" . . . . LBF 15283
Liberty / Feb '70.

GOLD (Creedence Clearwater Revival).
Tracks: Not Advised.
LP. 1A 022 58089
EMI (Holland) / '83.

GREATEST HITS: CREEDENCE CLEARWATER REVIVAL (Creedence Clearwater Revival).
Tracks: Bad moon rising / Travelin' band / Up around the bend / Long as I can see the light / Who'll stop the rain / Lodi / Commotion / Fortunate son / Run through the jungle / I put a spell on you / Proud Mary / Down on the corner / Green river / Have you ever seen the rain / Sweet hitch-hiker / Lookin' out my back door / Hey tonight / I heard it through the grapevine / Someday never comes / Susie Q.
■ LP. . . . . FT 558
Fantasy / Jun '79.

GREEN RIVER (Creedence Clearwater Revival).
Tracks: Bad moon rising / Cross-tie walker / Sinister purpose / Night time is the right time / Green River / Commotion / Tombstone Shadow / Wrote a song for everyone / Lodi.
■ LP. . . . . LBS 83273
Liberty / Jan '70.
LP. . . . . FASLP 5004
MC . . . . FASK 5004
Fantasy / Jul '84 / Pinnacle / Target Records / Jazz Music.
LP. . . . . FACE 503
MC . . . . FACC 503
Fantasy / Aug '87 / Pinnacle / Target Records / Jazz Music.
CD . . . . CDFE 503
Fantasy / '88 / Pinnacle / Target Records / Jazz Music.

GREEN RIVER (Creedence Clearwater Revival).
Tracks: Green river.
■ 7" . . . . LBF 15250
Liberty / Nov '69.

HAVE YOU EVER SEEN THE RAIN (Creedence Clearwater Revival).
Tracks: Have you ever seen the rain.
■ 7" . . . . LBF 15440
Liberty / Mar '71.

HEY TONIGHT (Creedence Clearwater Revival).
Tracks: Not Advised.
CD 825 174-2
Fantasy / '88 / Pinnacle / Target Records / Jazz Music.

I HEARD IT THROUGH THE GRAPEVINE (Creedence Clearwater Revival).
Tracks: I heard it through the grapevine / Rockin' all over the world.
■ 7" . . . . FTC 128
Fantasy / Mar '76.
■ 7" . . . . FTC 178
Fantasy / Jun '79.

LIVE IN EUROPE (Creedence Clearwater Revival).
Tracks: Born on the bayou / It came out of the sky / Fortunate son / Lodi / Proud Mary / Hey tonight / Green River / Suzie Q / Travelin' band / Commotion / Bad moon rising / Up around the bend / Keep on chooglin'.
CD . . . . CDFE 514
LP. . . . . FACE 514
MC . . . . FACC 514
Fantasy / Feb '90 / Pinnacle / Target Records / Jazz Music.

LONG AS I CAN SEE THE LIGHT (Creedence Clearwater Revival).
Tracks: Long as I can see the light.
■ 7" . . . . LBF 15384
Liberty / Sep '70.

MARDI GRAS (Creedence Clearwater Revival).
Tracks: Looking for a reason / Take it like a friend / Need someone to hold / Tearin' up the country / Some day never comes / What are you gonna do? / Sail away / Hello Mary Lou / Door to door / Sweet hitchhiker.
LP. . . . . FASLP 5008
■ MC . . . . FASK 5008
Fantasy / Jul '84.
CD . . . . CDFE 513
LP. . . . . FACE 513
Fantasy / Aug '89 / Pinnacle / Target Records / Jazz Music.
MC . . . . FACC 513
Fantasy / Feb '90 / Pinnacle / Target Records / Jazz Music.

MORE CREEDENCE GOLD (Creedence Clearwater Revival).
Tracks: Hey tonight / Run through the jungle / Fortunate son / Bootleg / Lookin' out my back door / Molina / Who'll stop the rain / Sweet hitch-hiker / Good golly Miss Molly / I put a spell on you / Don't look now / Lodi / Porterville / Up around the bend.
CD . . . . CDFE 516
Fantasy / Aug '91 / Pinnacle / Target Records / Jazz Music.

MUSIC FOR THE MILLIONS (Creedence Clearwater Revival).
Tracks: Proud Mary / Down on the corner / Bad moon rising / I heard it through the grapevine / Midnight special / Have you ever seen the rain? / Born on the bayou / Suzie Q.
LP. 817870 1
MC 817870 4
Polydor (Holland) / Jul '84 / Pinnacle.

PENDULUM (Creedence Clearwater Revival).
Tracks: Pagan baby / I wish I could hide away / It's just a thought / Rude awakening number two / Sailor's lament / Chameleon / Born to move / Hey tonight / Molina / Have you ever seen the rain?.
■ LP. . . . . LBG 83400
Liberty / Jan '71.
LP. . . . . FASLP 5007
MC . . . . FASK 5007
Fantasy / Jul '84 / Pinnacle / Target Records / Jazz Music.
CD . . . . CDFE 512
LP. . . . . FACE 512
Fantasy / Aug '89 / Pinnacle / Target Records / Jazz Music.
MC . . . . FACC 512
Fantasy / Feb '90 / Pinnacle / Target Records / Jazz Music.

PROUD MARY (Creedence Clearwater Revival).
Tracks: Proud Mary.
■ 7" . . . . LBF 15223
Liberty / May '69.
7" . . . . GOLD 521

C 28

■ DELETED

Fantasy / Aug '81 / Pinnacle / Target Records / Jazz Music.

PROUD MARY (OLD GOLD) (Creedence Clearwater Revival).
Tracks: Proud Mary / Travelling band.
7" . . . . OG 9570
Old Gold / Sep '85 / Pickwick Records.

SINGLES 1968-72 (Creedence Clearwater Revival).
Tracks: Suzie Q / I put a spell on you / Proud Mary / Bad moon rising / Green river / Down on the corner / Who'll stop the rain? / Up around the bend / Long as I can see the light / Have you ever seen the rain? / Sweet hitchhiker / Some day never comes.
LP. 5C 038 62427
EMI (Holland) / '83.

SWEET HITCH-HIKER (Creedence Clearwater Revival).
Tracks: Sweet hitch-hiker.
■ 7" . . . . UP 35261
United Artists / Jul '71.

TRAVELLIN' BAND (Creedence Clearwater Revival).
Tracks: Travellin' band.
■ 7" . . . . LBF 15310
Liberty / Apr '70.

UP AROUND THE BEND (Creedence Clearwater Revival).
Tracks: Up around the bend.
■ 7" . . . . LBF 15354
Liberty / Jun '70.

VERY BEST OF CREEDENCE CLEARWATER REVIVAL (The Greatest Hits) (Creedence Clearwater Revival).
Tracks: Not Advised.
CD Set . . . . ZYX 700622
ZYX / Jul '92.

WHO'LL STOP THE RAIN? (Creedence Clearwater Revival).
Tracks: Who'll stop the rain? / Proud Mary / Hey tonight.
■ 7" . . . . FTC 154
Fantasy / Oct '78.

WILLY AND THE POORBOYS (Creedence Clearwater Revival).
Tracks: Down on the corner / It came out of the sky / Cottonfields / Poor boy shuffle / Feeling blue / Fortunate son / Don't look now / Midnight special, The / Side of the road / Effigy.
■ LP. . . . . LBS 83338
Liberty / Mar '70.
LP. . . . . FASLP 5005
MC . . . . FASK 5005
Fantasy / Jul '84 / Pinnacle / Target Records / Jazz Music.
■ CD . . . . FCD 6138397
Fantasy (import) / Nov '86.
CD . . . . CDFE 504
LP. . . . . FACE 504
MC . . . . FACC 504
Fantasy / Aug '87 / Pinnacle / Target Records / Jazz Music.

Crickets

At the time of their greatest success, this American group consisted of Jerry Allison, Buddy Holly, Joe Mauldin and Niki Sullivan. Buddy Holly ran twin careers, with some of his records being released solely under his name, and others being credited to the Crickets. The two most important members of the Crickets, Holly and Allison, began playing together as schoolfriends, with the former on vocals and guitar and the latter on drums. They formed a professional partnership in 1955 and then decided to form a group called the Crickets. By '57, the line-up of Holly, Allison, Mauldin and Sullivan had been established. A complicated chain of events led them to Norman Petty, a New Mexico studio owner and bandleader. *That'll be the day*, penned by Holly, Allison and Petty and produced by the later, became their first and biggest smash hit, reaching No.1 in both the US and UK in late '57. This perfect pop record, which was infectiously catchy and imaginatively performed, was followed by a series of hits of equal quality: *Oh boy*, *Maybe baby* and *Think it over* gave the Crickets success on both sides of the Atlantic. The group also played on early solo hits by Holly, including the big hit *Peggy Sue*. Holly and the three other Crickets split in 1958, but the singer continued using the group name with newly recruited musicians. Holly was killed in a tragic plane crash in Feb 1959 along with the Big Bopper and Richie Valens at the age of 22, and passed into legendary status. Having split from Holly mere months before his death, the old Crickets continued to function but with the numerous personnel variations. The constant nucleus of the group was Allison and vocalist/guitarist Sonny Curtis. They never achieved a hit record in the States but, in Britain, they enjoyed seven hit singles between 1959 and 1964, benefiting from a perennial Buddy Holly fervour in the UK - the Holly legacy commanded, and still commands, greater respect in Britain than in America, and the Crickets received a spin-off acceptance from this. Their biggest early Sixties single was 1962's *Don't ever change*, a Gerry Goffin/Carole King song that took them to No.5 on the UK chart. This period also saw the group touring Britain and recording with *Bobby Vee meets the Crickets* which stayed on the listing for six months; *Just for fun*, an Extended Play record by the two acts, topped the UK EP charts in May 1963. The Beatles revolution finally put paid to the Crickets' career, and they officially broke up in 1965. Attempts to revive the band in the Seventies, with musical assistance from some respected British players, met with little interest from the public. (Bob MacDonald).

BACK HOME IN TENNESSEE EP.
Tracks: Blackmail / I can't hold it / We helped each other out / Back home in Tennessee.
■ EP. . . . . RCEP 111
Rollercoaster / May '90 / Rollercoaster Records / Swift.

COMPLETE CRICKETS.
Tracks: After it's over / Smooth guy / More than I can say / Baby my heart / So you're in love / Someone, someone / Great balls of fire / Sweet love / Time will tell / Just this once / I fought the law / When you ask about love / Doncha know / Peggy Sue got married / Rockin' pneumonia / Deborah / Ting a ling / Love's made a fool of you / Why did you leave me?.
■ LP. . . . . CR 30226
Charly / Feb '84.

CRUISE IN IT.
Tracks: Cruise in it / Rock around with Ollie Vee.
7" . . . . RRC 2001
Rollercoaster / Jul '79 / Rollercoaster Records / Swift.

DON'T EVER CHANGE.
Tracks: Don't ever change.
■ 7" . . . . LIB 55441
Liberty / Jun '62.

DON'T TRY TO CHANGE ME.
Tracks: Don't try to change me.
■ 7" . . . . LIB 10092
Liberty / Jun '63.

FILE 1961 - 1965.
Tracks: He's old enough to know better / I'm feeling better / I'm not a bad guy / Parisian girl / My little girl / Don't try to change me / Lost and alone / April Avenue / Don't say you love me / You can't be in between / Right or wrong / Money / Fool never learns, A / From me to you / California sun / All over you / I pledge my love to you / Now hear this / We gotta get together / Everybody's got a little problem.
LP. . . . . SEE 79
See For Miles / Feb '87 / Pinnacle.
CD . . . . SEECD 79
See For Miles / Feb '90 / Pinnacle.

IN STYLE WITH THE CRICKETS.
Tracks: Not Advised.
■ LP. . . . . LVA 9142
Coral / Mar '61.

LA BAMBA (THEY CALL HER).
Tracks: La bamba.
■ 7" . . . . LIB 55696
Liberty / Jul '64.

LIBERTY YEARS, THE: CRICKETS.
Tracks: He's old enough to know better / I'm feeling better / Don't ever change / I'm not a bad guy / Parisian girl / I believe in you / Little Hollywood girl / Break it easy / My little girl / Teardrops fall like rain / Looking all over town / Pretty blue eyes / Love is strange / Lost and alone / Don't try to change me / Surfin' special / April Avenue / Don't breathe a word / Don't say you love me / Right or wrong / You can't be inbetween / Playboy / Lonely Avenue / Fool never learns, A / (They call her) La Bamba / All over you / I thing I've caught the blues / We gotta get together / Everybody's got a little problem / Now hear this / Thoughtless.
■ CD . . . . CZ 420
EMI / Apr '91.

LOVE'S MADE A FOOL OF YOU.
Tracks: Love's made a fool of you.
■ 7" . . . . Q 72365
Coral / Apr '59.

MAYBE BABY.
Tracks: Maybe baby.
■ 7" . . . . Q 72307
Coral / Mar '58.
■ 7" . . . . Q 72483
Coral / '65.

MAYBE BABY (OLD GOLD).
Tracks: Maybe baby / Tell me how.
7" . . . . OG 9224
Old Gold / Jul '82 / Pickwick Records.

MILLION DOLLAR MOVIE.
Tracks: Million dollar movie / Million miles apart, A / Rock and roll.
■ EP. . . . . RCEP 101
Rollercoaster / Mar '80 / Rollercoaster Records / Swift.

MORE THAN I CAN SAY.
Tracks: More than I can say / Baby my heart.
■ 7" . . . . Q 72395
Coral / May '60.

MY LITTLE GIRL.
Tracks: My little girl.
■ 7" . . . . LIB 10067
Liberty / Jan '63.

MY LOVE IS BIGGER THAN A CADILLAC.
Tracks: Not Advised.
■ VHS. . . . . HEN 2241
Hendring Video / Sep '90.

OH BOY.
Tracks: Oh boy.
■ 7" . . . . Q 72298
Coral / Dec '57.

OH BOY (OLD GOLD).
Tracks: Oh boy / Not fade away.
7" . . . . OG 9223
Old Gold / Jul '82 / Pickwick Records.

RAVIN' ON - FROM CALIFORNIA TO CLOVIS.
Tracks: Not Advised.
CD . . . . RSRCD 002
Rockstar (1) / Apr '92 / Swift / C.M. Distribution.

ROCK 'N' ROLL MASTERS (Best of The Crickets).
Tracks: My little girl / Teardrops fall like rain / Lost and alone / Little Hollywood girl / What'd I say / Right or wrong / Blue Monday / La bamba / Lonely Avenue / Don't ever change / Willie and the hand jive / I think I've caught the blues / Summertime blues / Love is strange / I'm not a bad guy / Now hear this / Thoughtless (CD only.) / Slippin' and slidin' (CD only.) / Someday (CD only.) / I believe in you (CD only.).
CD . . . . CDP 791 757 2
CD . . . . CZ 155
Liberty / Aug '89 / EMI.
■ LP. . . . . EMS 1318
Liberty / Aug '89.
■ MC . . . . TCEMS 1318
Liberty / Aug '89.

SOMETHING OLD, SOMETHING NEW.
Tracks: Not Advised.
LP. . . . . PM 1550781
Pathe Marconi (France) / Jun '84 / Thames Distributors Ltd.

STILL IN STYLE - THE CRICKETS.
Tracks: Someone, someone / Love's made a fool of you / I fought the law / Sweet love, A / Time will tell / When you ask about love / Deborah / Why did you leave / Just this once / Ting a ling / Great balls of fire / Rockin' pneumonia and the boogie woogie flu / Smooth guy / After it's over / So you're in love / Baby my heart / More than I can say / Don't cha know / Peggy Sue got married.

T-SHIRT.
Tracks: T-shirt / Holly would / Forever in mind (12" only).
12" . . . . TSH T1
7" . . . . TSH 1
■ CD Single . . . . CD TSH 1
CBS / Sep '88.

T-SHIRT.
Tracks: Your m-m-memory is t-t-torturing me / Rockin' socks / Weekend, The / Holly would / T-Shirt / Forever in mind / Cruise in it / Tree piece / Don't tell me that you can't come out tonight / That's all she wrote.
CD 4628762
LP. 4628761
■ MC 4628764
CBS / Oct '88.

THAT'LL BE THE DAY.
Tracks: That'll be the day.
■ 7" . . . . Q 72279
Vogue Coral / Sep '57.

THAT'LL BE THE DAY (OLD GOLD).
Tracks: That'll be the day / I'm looking for someone to love.
7" . . . . OG 9208
Old Gold / Mar '90 / Pickwick Records.

THINK IT OVER.
Tracks: Think it over.
■ 7" . . . . Q 72329
Coral / Jul '58.

THREE PIECE.
Tracks: Not Advised.
■ LP. . . . . ROLL 2014
Rollercoaster / Mar '88.

WHEN YOU ASK ABOUT LOVE.
Tracks: When you ask about love.
■ 7" . . . . Q 72382
Coral / Jan '60.

YOUR M-M-MEMORY.
Tracks: Your m-m-memory is t-t-torturing me / Three piece / Weekend, The / Forever in mind.
■ 7" . . . . RRC 2007
Rollercoaster / Apr '88.

■ DELETED

C 29

Critchlow, Slim

COWBOY SONGS.
Tracks: Not Advised.
LP. . . . . **ARHOOLIE 5007**
Arhoolie (USA) / May '81 / Pinnacle / Cadillac Music / Swift / Projection / Hot Shot / A.D.A Distribution / Jazz Music.

Crook Brothers

OPRY OLD TIMERS (Crook Brothers with Sam & Kirk McGee).
Tracks: Not Advised.
LP. . . . . **SLP 182**
MC . . . . **GT 5182**
Starday (USA) / Apr '87 / Crusader Marketing Co.

Cross, Mike

BORN IN THE COUNTRY.
Tracks: Not Advised.
LP. . . . . **SH 1002**
Sugarhill(USA) / Mar '89 / Roots Records / Projection / Impetus Records / C.M. Distribution / Jazz Music / Swift / Duncans / A.D.A Distribution.

BOUNTY HUNTER, THE.
Tracks: Not Advised.
LP. . . . . **SH 1003**
Sugarhill(USA) / Mar '89 / Roots Records / Projection / Impetus Records / C.M. Distribution / Jazz Music / Swift / Duncans / A.D.A Distribution.

CAROLINA SKY.
Tracks: Not Advised.
LP. . . . . **SH 1006**
Sugarhill(USA) / Mar '89 / Roots Records / Projection / Impetus Records / C.M. Distribution / Jazz Music / Swift / Duncans / A.D.A Distribution.

CHILD PRODIGY.
Tracks: Not Advised.
LP. . . . . **SH 1001**
Sugarhill(USA) / Mar '89 / Roots Records / Projection / Impetus Records / C.M. Distribution / Jazz Music / Swift / Duncans / A.D.A Distribution.

LIVE AND KICKIN'.
Tracks: Not Advised.
LP. . . . . **SH 1005**
Sugarhill(USA) / Mar '89 / Roots Records / Projection / Impetus Records / C.M. Distribution / Jazz Music / Swift / Duncans / A.D.A Distribution.

ROCK 'N RYE.
Tracks: Not Advised.
LP. . . . . **SH 1004**
Sugarhill(USA) / Mar '89 / Roots Records / Projection / Impetus Records / C.M. Distribution / Jazz Music / Swift / Duncans / A.D.A Distribution.

SOLO AT MIDNIGHT.
Tracks: Not Advised.
LP. . . . . **SH 1007**
Sugarhill(USA) / Mar '89 / Roots Records / Projection / Impetus Records / C.M. Distribution / Jazz Music / Swift / Duncans / A.D.A Distribution.

Crow, Alvin

WELCOME TO TEXAS.
Tracks: Not Advised.
LP. . . . . **TRP 851**
TRP / Feb '89 / Roots Records / Swift / Charly / ACD Trading Ltd.

Crowe, J.D.

Born in Lexington, Kentucky. From an early age he pursued a career in bluegrass music, after seeing Flatt & Scruggs perform at 'The Kentucky Barndance'. Since then he's become reknown for his hard driving banjo pickin' and has formed The New South. (Maurice Hope).

BLACKJACK.
Tracks: Born to be with you / Sin City / Somehow tonight / Ramblin' boy / Black Jack / Bouquet in heaven / I'll stay around / Please search your heart / Portrait of the blues / There'll be no blind ones there / So afraid of losing you again.
LP. . . . . **SDLP 046**
Sundown / Jun '87 / Terry Blood Dist. / Jazz Music / C.M. Distribution.
LP. . . . . **REB 1583**
MC . . . . **REBMC 1583**
Rebel (1) / Jun '87 / Projection / Backs Distribution.

BLUEGRASS HOLIDAY.
Tracks: Little girl in Tennessee / Down where the river bends / Philadelphia lawyer / Will you be satisfied that way / Train 45 / You go to your church / Helen / Before I met you / Orange blossom special / Dark hollow / She's just a cute little thing / Little Bessie.
LP. . . . . **REB 1598**
Rebel (1) / '82 / Projection / Backs Distribution.

J.D. CROWE AND THE NEW SOUTH (Crowe, J.D. & The New South).
Tracks: Old home place / Some old day / Rock salt and nails / Sally Goodin / Ten degrees / Nashville blues / You are what I am / Summer wages / I'm walkin' / Home sweet home revisited / Cryin' Holly.
CD . . . . **CD 0044**
LP. . . . . **ROUNDER 0044**
MC . . . . **ROUNDER 0044C**
Rounder / '88 / Projection / Roots Records / Swift / C.M. Distribution / Topic Records / Jazz Music / Hot Shot / A.D.A Distribution / Direct Distribution.

LIVE IN JAPAN (Crowe, J.D. & The New South).
Tracks: Not Advised.
LP. . . . . **ROUNDER 0159**
MC . . . . **ROUNDER 0159C**
Rounder / '88 / Projection / Roots Records / Swift / C.M. Distribution / Topic Records / Jazz Music / Hot Shot / A.D.A Distribution / Direct Distribution.

MODEL CHURCH, THE.
Tracks: I'll talk it all over with him / It's me again Lord / I shall be at home with Jesus / Journeys End / Model Church, The / Going up / Let the spirit descend / Look For Me / Are you lost in sin / No Mother or Dad / Oh heaven.
LP. . . . . **SDLP 038**
Sundown / Jan '87 / Terry Blood Dist. / Jazz Music / C.M. Distribution.
LP. . . . . **REB 1585**
Rebel (1) / Jan '87 / Projection / Backs Distribution.

MY HOME AIN'T IN THE HALL OF FAME (Crowe, J.D. & The New South).
Tracks: Not Advised.
LP. . . . . **ROUNDER 0103**
MC . . . . **ROUNDER 0103C**
Rounder / '88 / Projection / Roots Records / Swift / C.M. Distribution / Topic Records / Jazz Music / Hot Shot / A.D.A Distribution / Direct Distribution.

SOMEWHERE BETWEEN (Crowe, J.D. & The New South).
Tracks: I never go around mirrors / I would have loved you all night long / Another town / Dance with me Molly / Long black limosine / To be loved by a woman / Girl from the canyon / Where are all the girls I used to chat with / Somewhere between / Family tree.
LP. . . . . **ROUNDER 0153**
MC . . . . **ROUNDER 0153C**
Rounder / '88 / Projection / Roots Records / Swift / C.M. Distribution / Topic Records / Jazz Music / Hot Shot / A.D.A Distribution / Direct Distribution.

STRAIGHT AHEAD.
Tracks: Not Advised.
CD . . . . **CD 0202**
Rounder / Jun '87 / Projection / Roots Records / Swift / C.M. Distribution / Topic Records / Jazz Music / Hot Shot / A.D.A Distribution / Direct Distribution.
LP. . . . . **ROUNDER 0202**
MC . . . . **ROUNDER 0202C**
Rounder / Aug '88 / Projection / Roots Records / Swift / C.M. Distribution / Topic Records / Jazz Music / Hot Shot / A.D.A Distribution / Direct Distribution.

YOU CAN SHARE (Crowe, J.D. & The New South).
Tracks: You can share my blanket / As tears go by / Hesitating / Too long / Hurtin' when you go, The / Ten miles from Natchex / Did she mention my name / Are you sad tonight / I don't know you / Hickory wind / Gypsy woman.
LP. . . . . **ROUNDER 0096**
MC . . . . **ROUNDER 0096C**
Rounder / '88 / Projection / Roots Records / Swift / C.M. Distribution / Topic Records / Jazz Music / Hot Shot / A.D.A Distribution / Direct Distribution.

Crowell, Rodney

Singer - songwriter possessing contemporary ambitions, born on 07.08.1950 in Houston, Texas. Has the distinction of his 1988 self-produced Columbia album *Diamonds and dirt* spawning no fewer than a record five straight country No.1 singles *It's such a small world* (with wife Rosanne),*After all this time* , *I couldn't leave you if I could* , *She's crazy for leaving* , with only Harlan Howard's oldie *Above and beyond* not featuring Crowell's own pen (it had previously been a No.3 hit for Buck Owens in 1960). It was with Howard that Crowell wrote highway 101's 1987 debut No.1 *Somewhere tonight* . Having been brought up on country music (his father having played the Texas bars himself), Crowell's own early ventures were to include a spell with The Arbitrators in 1965, playing with his father and doing the circuit of folk clubs, before advancing to Nashville in 1972 and working as a staff writer for Jerry Reed. He joined Emmmylou Harris' Hot Band in 1975, before he set out on a solo career in 1977. Recorded three, critically acclaimed albums for Warner Brothers. Crowell, a very deep artistically rooted talent, was only to make the top thirty once with *Stars on the water* (1981), whilst in comparison he found it easy to supply others with country No.1's - Crystal Gayle *Till I gain control again* , The Oak Ridge Boys *Leavin' Louisiana in the broad daylight*, Waylon Jennings *I ain't livin' long like this* and the NGDB *Long hard road (The sharecroppers dream)* . His wealth of material also gained their way on to numerous albums, including those from Emmylou Harris and his then wife Rosanne Cash who was just one of the acts he's produced (their professional partnership going as far as sharing the same band - Crowell's Dixie Pearls). Others to benefit from his skills were to include Bobby Bare's 1981 release *As is* (one of his finest), fellow Texas Guy Clark's *South coast of Texas* and *Better days* in 1981 and 1983 respectively, alongside new contemporary singer - songwriter Jim Lauderdale. After his recording career peaked with *Diamonds and dirt* his following work has been something of an anti-climax, with *Keys to the highway* (1989) and *Life is messy* (1992) both containing some very personal traumas, although the former did spawn top ten hits *Many a long and lonesome highway* and *My past is present* , with friend and former Hot Band colleague Tony Brown as usual co-producing. (Maurice Hope)

AIN'T LIVING LONG LIKE THIS.
Tracks: Elvira / Fool such as I, A / Leaving Louisiana in the broad daylight / Voila, An American dream / I ain't living long like this / Baby, better start turning 'em down / Song for the life / I thought I heard you calling my name/California Earthquake.
LP. . . . . **K 56564**
WEA / WEA.

BEST OF RODNEY CROWELL.
Tracks: Not Advised.
CD . . . . **K 9259652**
■ **LP.** . . . . **K 9259651**
WEA / Aug '89 / WEA.
■ **MC** . . . . **K 9259654**
WEA / Aug '89.

DIAMONDS AND DIRT.
Tracks: Crazy baby / I couldn't leave you if I tried / She's crazy for leaving / After all this time / I know you're married / Above and beyond / It's such a small world / I didn't know I could lose you / Brand new rag / Last waltz, The.
CD **4608732**
CBS / Apr '89 / Sony.
LP. **4608731**
■ **MC** **4608734**
CBS / Apr '89.

HERE COMES THE 80'S.
Tracks: Here comes the 80's / Blues in the daytime.
■ **7"** . . . . **K 17596**
WEA / May '80.

I COULDN'T LEAVE YOU IF I TRIED.
Tracks: I couldn't leave you if I tried.
■ **7"** **6549357**
CBS / Apr '89.

IT'S SUCH A SMALL WORLD.
Tracks: It's such a small world / Crazy baby.
7" **6548177**
CBS / May '89 / Sony.

KEYS TO THE HIGHWAY, THE.
Tracks: My past is present / If looks could kill / Soul searchin' / Many a long and lonesome highway / We gotta go on meeting like this / Faith is mine, The / Tell me the truth / Don't let your feet slow you down / Now that we're alone / Things I wish I'd said / I guess we've been together for too long / You've been on my mind.
LP. **4660021**
MC **4660024**
CBS / Jan '90 / Sony.
■ **CD** **4660022**
CBS / Jan '90.

LIFE IS MESSY.
Tracks: It's not for me to judge / What kind of love / Lovin' all night / Life is messy / I hardly know how to be myself / It don't get better than this / Alone but no / Let's make trouble / Answer is yes, The / Maybe next time.
CD **4718682**
MC **4718684**
Columbia / Aug '92 / Sony.

RODNEY CROWELL.
Tracks: Stars on the water / Just wanta dance / She ain't going nowhere / Don't need no other now / Shame on the moon / Only two hearts / Victim or a fool / All you've got to do / Till I gain control again / Old pipeliner.
LP. . . . . **K 56934**
■ **MC** **K4 56934**
WEA / '88 / WEA.

RODNEY CROWELL COLLECTION, THE.
Tracks: Not Advised.
CD . . . . **.925965-2**
■ **MC** . . . . **.925965-4**
WEA / Oct '89 / WEA.

SHAME ON THE MOON.
Tracks: Shame on the moon.
7" . . . . **K 17919**
WEA / Mar '82 / WEA.

STARS ON THE WATER.
Tracks: Stars on the water / Ain't no money.
■ **7"** . . . . **K 17858**
WEA / Jan '82.

Culpepper County

AT HOME: CULPEPPER COUNTY.
Tracks: Not Advised.
LP. . . . . .SFA 051
Sweet Folk All / May '77 / Cadillac Music / Projection /
C.M. Distribution / Wellard Dist. / Impetus Records.

YOUR REQUEST OUR PLEASURE.
Tracks: Not Advised.
LP. . . . . .BUFFL 2003
Buffalo (UK) / M.I.S.Records.

Curless, Dick

A deep voiced, truck driving singer, born in
Maine in 1932. He won Arthur Godfrey's Talent
Scout TV competition in 1957; the truck driving
song *A tombstone every mile* made the USA
country top 5 in 1965 and was followed by more
hits. He was with Buck Owens' All American
Show in 1969-71 but preferred living and working in the Northeast.(Donald Clarke).

20 GREAT TRUCK HITS: DICK CURLESS.
Tracks: Big wheel cannonball / Drag 'em off the inter-
state, sock it to 'em J.P.blues / Hard, hard travelling
man / Goin' down the road feeling bad / Truck stop /
Jukebox man / Drop some silver in the juke box /
Leaving it all behind / Coastline Charlie / 6 days on the
road / Tombstone every mile / Golden girl / Old ramblin
Alabama me / Woman, don't try to sing my song / Hot
springs / Carter days / Born on country music / Homing
pigeon / Chick inspector / Pinch o' powder, A.
LP. 7C 062 85894
EMI (Sweden) / '83.

IT'S JUST A MATTER OF TIME.
Tracks: Not Advised.
LP. . . . . HAT 3139
MC. . . . . HATC 3139
Stetson / Apr '90 / Crusader Marketing Co. / Swift /
Wellard Dist. / Midland Records / C.M. Distribution.

LONG, LONESOME ROAD.
Tracks: Not Advised.
LP. . . . . HAT 3102
MC. . . . . HATC 3102
Stetson / Mar '89 / Crusader Marketing Co. / Swift /
Wellard Dist. / Midland Records / C.M. Distribution.

WELCOME TO MY WORLD.
Tracks: Not Advised.
CD . . . . .RRCD 007
Rocade / Aug '93 / Topic Records / Direct Distribution.

Curtis, Mac

BLUE JEAN HEART.
Tracks: Not Advised.
CD . . . . CDCHARLY 164
Charly / Feb '91 / Charly.

GOOD ROCKIN' TOMORROW.
Tracks: Not Advised.
LP. . . . . .LP 007
Rollin' Rock / Jun '80 / Pinnacle.

GRANDADDY'S ROCKIN'.
Tracks: Not Advised.
LP. . . . . KAY 5046
Kay / Nov '87.

GRANDADDY'S ROCKIN'.
Tracks: Grandaddy's rockin'.
7". 45 016
Rollin' Rock / Jun '80 / Pinnacle.

HOT ROCK BOOGIE.
Tracks: Hot rock boogie.
7". . . . . .HR 45 001
Hot Rock / Jun '80 / Hot Rock Records.

HOW COME IT.
Tracks: How come it.
7". 45 018
Rollin' Rock / Apr '80 / Pinnacle.

HOW LOW DO YOU FEEL?.
Tracks: How low do you feel ?.
7". 45 046
Rollin' Rock / Jun '80 / Pinnacle.

PISTOL PACKIN' MAMA.
Tracks: Pistol packin' mama.
7". 45 043
Rollin' Rock / Jun '80 / Pinnacle.

ROCK ME.
Tracks: Side thang / That's how much I love you / Turn
away from me / Making it right / Real good itch / She
knows all the good ways to be bad / Suntan girl / You
can't take the boogie woogie outta me / Good love
sweet love / Don't you love me / Rock me.
LP. . . . . .LP 016
Rollin' Rock / Jun '80 / Pinnacle.
LP. . . . . MFLP 047
Magnum Force / Nov '87 / Terry Blood Dist. / Jazz
Music / Hot Shot.

ROCK ME (Curtis, Mac & Johnny Carrou).
Tracks: Rock me.
7". 45 026
Rollin' Rock / Jun '80 / Pinnacle.

ROCKIN' MOTHER.
Tracks: Ducktail / Grandaddy's rockin' you / You've
oughta see Gramma rock / How long will it take / If I
had me a woman / Good rockin' tomorrow / Rockin'
mother / How come it / Slip slip slippin' in / Johnny
Carroll rock / Turn away from me / That ain't nothin' but
time / Crazy crazy lovin' / Hungry Hill.
LP. . . . . RAD 22
Radar / May '79.

RUFFABILLY.
Tracks: Not Advised.
LP. . . . . .LP 002
Rollin' Rock / Jun '80 / Pinnacle.

Curtis, Sonny

Singer/ songwriter/ musician, a native of Meadow, Texas, he gained his initial experience in
the early 1950's as a member of *The Three
Tunes* (with Buddy Holly and Don Quess) before
joining Slim Whitman's band as a guitarist. He
has regularly recorded over the years, though
wasn't to enjoy chart success until 1969 when
My Way Of Life gave him his first Top 50 entry.
His greatest success, however, has come as a
songwriter and is one of the selected band of
composers to belong to the *Millionaires Club*
with *Walk Right Back, More Than I Can Say, The
Straight Life* and *I Fought The Law* each ac-
counting for over 50,000 hours of airplay. More
recently he's been achieving success with
country songs, with the late Keith Whitley's version of *No Stranger To The Rain* being named
as CMA 1989 single of the year. Sonny Curtis
also tours Britain on a regular basis (Tony
Byworth).

I THINK I'M IN LOVE.
Tracks: I think I'm in love / There's a whole lot less to
me.
■ 7". S1
Songworks / Jun '85.

MORE THAN I CAN SAY.
Tracks: More than I can say / When Amarillo blows.
7" . . . . RITZ 229
Ritz / Apr '91 / Pinnacle / Midland Records.

NO STRANGER TO THE RAIN.
Tracks: I'm no stranger to the rain / Hello Mary Lou /
You are the lesson I never learned / When Amarillo
blows / Back when has been lover / I saved my last
name for you / Bad case of love / Think it over / That'll
be the day / More than I can say / Well alright / Rock
around with Ollie Vee / Midnight shift.
CD . . . . RITZCD 0055
LP. RITZLP 0055
MC. RITZLC 0055
Ritz / Sep '90 / Pinnacle / Midland Records.
CD .RITZCD 509
MC. .RITZRC 509
Ritz / '91 / Pinnacle / Midland Records.

NOW I'VE GOT A HEART OF GOLD.
Tracks: Now I've got a heart of gold / Why did you say 'I
do'' to me.
■ 7". S2
Songworks / Oct '85.

SPECTRUM.
Tracks: Not Advised.
LP. COLT 2003
Nightflite / Aug '87.

Cyrus, Billy Ray

The biggest selling country single of 1992 was
Billy Ray Cyrus' *Achy breaky heart* , while the
biggest selling album of the year was the same
artist's *Some gave all* whose sales, by August
1993, was around the nine million mark and still
holding a Top 50 pop chart position. Born on
August 25, 1961, in Flatwoods, Kentucky, Billy
Ray Cyrus' first ambitions lay towards a base
ball career but he decided upon country music
in the early 1980's when he bought a guitar,
formed a band (Sly Dog) and headed out to Los
Angeles where he remained for two years without anything happening for him. Nashville eventually provided him the break when he came to
the attention of Jack McFadden, the managerial
power behind Buck Owens, a songwriter Buddy
Cannon who recommended the artist to Harold
Shedd at Mercury Records. *Achy breaky heart*
was his first single and was given an original
marketing approach by being launched towards
the country music dance clubs (with the *Achy
Breaky* dance steps), and a video given heavy
rotation on Nashville's TNN and CMT television
networks. Cyrus' second album, *It won't be the
last* , was released in July 1993 and went
straight to the top of the charts, only time will
tell whether it will repeat the success of *Some
Gave all* . (Tony Byworth)

ACHY BREAKY HEART.
Tracks: Achy breaky heart / I'm so miserable / Wher'm I
gonna live (Only available on CD Single).
7". . . . . MER 373
CD Single . . . . MERCD 373
MC Single . . . . MERMC 373
Mercury / Jun '92 / PolyGram.

IT WON'T BE THE LAST.
Tracks: Not Advised.
CD 51475824-2
MC. 51475824-4
Mercury / Jul '93 / PolyGram.

LIVE ON TOUR.
Tracks: Should I stay or should I go / These boots are
made for walkin' / She's not cryin' anymore / Wher'm I
gonna live / Someday, somewhere, somehow /
Could've been me / I'm so miserable / Never thought I'd
fall in love with you / Ain't no goodbye / Some gave all /
Only time will tell / It won't be the last / Achy breaky
heart / Star spangled banner.
VHS. 85954-3
Polygram Music Video / '93 / PolyGram.

SOME GAVE ALL.
Tracks: Could've been me / Achy breaky heart / She's
not cryin' anymore / Wher'm I gonna live / These boots
are made for walkin' / Someday, somewhere, somehow
/ Never thought I'd fall in love with you / Ain't no good
goodbye / I'm so miserable / Some gave all.
CD 510635-2
Mercury / Mar '92 / PolyGram.
DCC. 510 635-5
Mercury / Jan '93 / PolyGram.

THESE BOOTS ARE MADE FOR WALKING.
Tracks: These boots are made for walking / Ain't no
good goodbye / Could've been me (On CDs only) / Achy
breaky heart (On CDs only).
7". . . . . MER 384
Mercury / Nov '92 / PolyGram.
CD Single . . . . .MERCD 384
■ MC Single . . . . MERMC 384
Mercury / Nov '92.

Future Titles from Music Master   MUSIC MASTER

The Official Music Master Jazz Catalogue, 2nd Edition. £14.95 Published January 1994

The second edition of this highly acclaimed catalogue includes new and expanded entries for many historical and contemporary Jazz and Blues artists. All Biographies have been fully updated. 1000 pages (approximately).

To order:

Please send payment (cheques made payable to Music Master) plus postage as follows:
UK: add £1.75, Europe: add £4.00 per catalogue, Outside Europe: add £12.00 per catalogue. All books are sent registered delivery in the UK and by Airmail elsewhere.

Music Master, Paulton House, 8 Shepherdess Walk, London, N1 7LB.
Tel: +44-(0)71-490-0049, Fax: +44-(0)71-253-1308.

D

Daigle, Paul

CAJUN EXPERIENCE (Daigle, Paul with Robert Elkins & Michael Doucet).
Tracks: Not Advised.
LP 6058
Swallow (USA) / Swift / Wellard Dist.
MC . . . . 6058 TC
Swallow (USA) / '87 / Swift / Wellard Dist.

CAJUN GOLD (Daigle, Paul/ Robert Elkins/ Cajun Gold).
Tracks: Not Advised.
LP 6060
Swallow (USA) / Swift / Wellard Dist.
MC . . . . 6060 TC
Swallow (USA) / '87 / Swift / Wellard Dist.

COEUR FAROUCHE (Daigle, Paul/ Robert Elkins/ Cajun Gold).
Tracks: Not Advised.
LP 6077
MC . . . . 6077 TC
Swallow (USA) / '88 / Swift / Wellard Dist.

LA LUMIERE DANS TON CHASSIS (Daigle, Paul/ Robert Elkins/ Cajun Gold).
Tracks: Not Advised.
LP 6068
Swallow (USA) / Aug '87 / Swift / Wellard Dist.

Dallas, Rex

REX DALLAS SINGS.
Tracks: Fireside yodel / Roaming yodeller, The / Dutch girl yodel / My Swiss miss yodel / Yodel and smile / Happy free yodel / Yodelling Erich / Mexican yodel / Hear the yodeller / My Lancashire yodelling lass / Yodeller's dream girl / Cuckoo yodel / My yodelling lady / Australian yodel / Prairie yodel / Mississippi yodel / Gypsy yodel.
LP . . . . WRS 123
Westwood / '82 / Pinnacle.

Dallas, T.R.

HARD TO BE HUMBLE.
Tracks: Not Advised.
LP . . . . CMRLP 1004
Release (Ireland) / May '81.

IN CONCERT.
Tracks: Not Advised.
LP . . . . FRC 001
BI / '88 / Jetstar.

SOLID GOLD.
Tracks: Not Advised.
LP . . . . CMRLP 1015
MC . . . . CMCS 1015
CMR/Failte / '88 / I & B Records.

T.R. DALLAS.
Tracks: Not Advised.
Double LP . . . . CMCSB 001
CMR/Failte / '88 / I & B Records.

WHO SHOT J.R. EWING.
Tracks: Who shot J.R. Ewing / Oil bubble.
■ 7" . . . . YB 90
Young Blood / Jun '80.

Dalton, Lacy J

Country/rock singer and songwriter, born in 1948. She began as a folk/protest singer in the late '60's; moved to the West Coast in the early '70's and was lead singer with a psychedelic band, Office using the name Jill Corston; a demo reached Billy Sherrill in Nashville in 1979 and she signed to CBS. Her gravelly bluesy voice and self-penned songs won a big following.Can't Run Away From Your Heart in 1985 was followed by Highway Diner, including Can't See Me Without You written by Jonathan Cain of Heart; the album is described as populist rock like that of Bruce Springsteen. (Donald Clarke).

BLUE EYED BLUES.
Tracks: That's good, that's bad / Gotta serve somebody / I'll love them whatever they are / Hillbilly girl with the blues / 16th Avenue / My old yellow car / Love gone cold / Have I got a heart for you / It's a dirty job / Blue eyed blues.
LP 4508711
■ MC 4508714
CBS / Jun '87.

CAN'T RUN AWAY FROM YOUR HEART.
Tracks: You can't run away from your heart / Too late to stop lovin' you now / Don't fall in love with me / Over you / Perfectly crazy / If that ain't love / Night has a heart of its own, The / Silver eagle / Adios and run / Slow movin' outlaw.
LP . . . . CBS 26452
MC 40 26452
CBS / Aug '85 / Sony.

FEEDIN' THE FIRE.
Tracks: Feedin' the fire / Golden memories.
■ 7" . . . . .A 1468
CBS / Jul '81.

HARD TIMES.
Tracks: Hard times / Hillbilly girl with the blues / China doll / Old soldier / Ain't nobody who could do it like my daddy could / You can't fool love / Wide eyed and willing / Girls from Santa Cruz, The / Whisper / Me 'n' you.
MC 40 32769
■ LP . . . . CBS 32769
CBS / Apr '86.

HARD TIMES.
Tracks: Hard times / Old soldier.
■ 7" . . . . CBS 9322
CBS / Nov '80.

HIGHWAY DINER.
Tracks: Working class man / 12:05 / Changing all the time / Taking it all in stride / Can't see me without you / This ol' town / Up with the wind / Boomtown / Gone again / Closing time.
LP . . . . CBS 57042
CBS / Aug '86 / Sony.
■ MC 40 57042
CBS / Aug '86.

I LOVE COUNTRY.
Tracks: Dream baby / That's good, that's bad (with George Jones) / Slow down / Crazy blue eyes / Takin' it easy / Whisper / Wild turkey / 16th Avenue / Tennessee waltz / My old yellow car.
■ MC 4504244
CBS / Mar '87.
■ LP 4504241
CBS / Mar '87.

TAKIN' IT EASY.
Tracks: Takin' it easy / Everybody makes mistakes / Where were you when I needed you / Come to me / Comes a time / Wild turkey / Golden memories / Let me in the fast lane / Feedin' the fire / Somebody killed Dewey Jones' daughter.
■ LP . . . . CBS 85048
CBS / Oct '81.

Dalton, Mike

COUNTRY SIDE OF MIKE DALTON.
Tracks: Not Advised.
LP . . . . BSS 216
Tank / Dec '77.

Damron, Dick

LOST IN THE MUSIC.
Tracks: Minstrel, The / Whiskey Jack / My good woman (that ain't right) / It ain't easy goin' home / When Satan spins the bottle / Lost in the music / California friends / Only way to say goodbye, The / Woman / Sweet lady.
LP . . . . PL 42490
MC . . . . PK 42490
RCA / Jun '78 / BMG.

NORTHWEST REBELLION (Damron, Dick & Roy Warhurst).
Tracks: Not Advised.
LP . . . . WRS 102
Westwood / Nov '76 / Pinnacle.

SOLDIER OF FORTUNE.
Tracks: Not Advised.
LP . . . . WRS 099
Westwood / Nov '76 / Pinnacle.

THOUSAND SONGS OF GLORY, A.
Tracks: Not Advised.
LP . . . . WRS 119
Westwood / May '78 / Pinnacle.

Daniels, Charlie

This American singer, violinist and guitarist, born in North Carolina in 1937, was in his mid-Thirties when he achieved his big US breakthrough in 1973, and had been playing professionally for over fifteen years up to that point. The late Sixties and early Seventies were spent largely on session work, notably for Bob Dylan and Ringo Starr. Daniels' first solo album was released in 1970. Success came in 1973 with the US Top 10 success of Uneasy Rider, a novelty single released in answer to the Easy Rider movie and its spin off crazes. With the acceptance of this hit and of 1975's Top 30 single The South's Gonna Do It, he was benefitting from a mini-boom in Southern rock during the early to mid-Seventies, a period that also gave national US success to such acts as the Allman Brothers Band, Wet Willie and the Marshall Tucker Band. Daniels' pair of hits generated great demand on the concert circuit, to which his brand of tongue in cheek country rock was ideally suited. His plump, rounded, bearded physique helped to make him a charismatic and appealing figure. During the mid-Seventies, the Charlie Daniels Band instituted a yearly get-together of Southern combos known as the "Volunteer Jam"; these festivals were captured on a series of live albums. The Daniels Band enjoyed their biggest US - and only UK - hit in 1979 with The Devil Went Down To Georgia, a novelty story single that described a fiddle-playing contest between the devil and a Georgia citizen; the devil lost. Silly though the record may have been, it provided a perfect vehicle for Daniels' violin playing and his personality, and reached No 3 in America and No 14 in Britain. The eighties brought him occasional US hits, and showed his right-wing political views coming to the fore on 1980's In America (No 11) and 1982's Still In Saigon (No 22), singles which suited the mood of the new Reagan-ruled America. (Bob MacDonald)

AMERICA, I BELIEVE IN YOU.
Tracks: All night long / Troubles on my mind / Tennessee two step / Girl next door, The / America, I believe in you / Oh Juanita / Sweet little country girl / Alley cat / What you gonna do about me / San Miguel.
CD . . . . CDP 7804772
Liberty / May '93 / EMI.

BELIEVE THE KID (Daniels, Charlie Band).
Tracks: Believe the kid / Slow song.
■ 7" . . . . EPC 5012
Epic / Apr '77.

DECADE OF HITS (Daniels, Charlie Band).
Tracks: Devil went down to Georgia / South's gonna do it again / Stroker's theme / Uneasy rider / Let it roll / In America / Still in Saigon / Long haired country boy / Legend of Wooley swamp / Everytime I see him.
■ LP . . . . EPC 15587
Epic / Sep '83.

DEVIL WENT DOWN TO GEORGIA (OLD GOLD) (Daniels, Charlie Band).
Tracks: Devil went down to Georgia / Jitterbuggin'.
7" . . . . OG 9743
Old Gold / Jan '88 / Pickwick Records.

DEVIL WENT DOWN TO GEORGIA, THE (Daniels, Charlie Band).
Tracks: Devil went down to Georgia, The / Jitterbuggin'.
■ 7" . . . . EPC 7737
Epic / Sep '79.

FIRE ON THE MOUNTAIN (Daniels, Charlie Band).
Tracks: Cabello Diablo / Long haired country boy / Trudy / Georgia / Feeling free / South's gonna do it / New York City / Kingsize rosewood bed / No place to go / Orange blossom special.
■ LP . . . . CBS 31830
CBS / Jul '80.

FULL MOON (Daniels, Charlie Band).
Tracks: Legend of Wooley swamp / Carolina / Lonesome boy from Dixie / No potion for the pain / El toreador / South Sea song / Dance gypsy dance / Money / In America.
■ LP . . . . EPC 84461
Epic / Nov '80.
CD . . . . EK 365 71
Epic (import) / '88 / Pinnacle.

HIGH LONESOME.
Tracks: Billy the Kid / Carolina / High lonesome / Running with the crowd / Right now Tennessee blues / Roll Mississippi / Slow song / Tennessee / Turned my head around.
■ LP . . . . EPC 81666
CBS / '78 / Sony.

■ DELETED

JITTERBUG (Daniels, Charlie Band).
Tracks: Jitterbug / Blue star.
■ 7" . . . . EPC 8056
Epic / Nov '79.

LEGEND OF WOOLEY SWAMP (Daniels, Charlie Band).
Tracks: Legend of Wooley swamp / Money.
■ 7" . . . . EPC 9019
Epic / Oct '80.

ME AND THE BOYS (Daniels, Charlie Band).
Tracks: Me and 4he boys / Still hurtin' me / Talking to the moon / Class of 63 / American farmer / M.I.A. / American rock 'n' roll / Ever changing lady / Louisiana fai dodo / Drinkin' my baby goodbye.
LP. . . . . EPC 26700
Epic / Jan '86 / Sony.
■ MC 40 26700
Epic / Jan '86.

MILLION MILE REFLECTIONS (Daniels, Charlie Band).
Tracks: Passing lane / Blue star / Jitterbug / Behind your eyes / Reflections / Devil went down to Georgia / Mississippi / Blind man / Rainbow ride.
■ LP. . . . . EPC 83446
Epic / Nov '79.

NIGHT RIDER (Daniels, Charlie Band).
Tracks: Texas / Willie Jones / Franklin Limestone / Evil / Everything is kinda alright / Funky funky / Birmingham blues / Damn good cowboy / Tomorrow's gonna be another day.
LP. . . . . KSLP 7009
Kama Sutra.

POWDER KEG (Daniels, Charlie Band).
Tracks: Not Advised.
LP. 4600341
MC 4600344
Epic / Sep '87 / Sony.

SADDLE TRAMP (Daniels, Charlie Band).
Tracks: Dixie on my mind / Saddle tramp / Sweet Louisiana / Wichita Jail / Cumberland mountain number 9 / It's my life / Sweetwater Texas.
■ LP. . . . . EPC 81335
CBS / '78 / Sony.

SIMPLE MAN (Daniels, Charlie Band).
Tracks: What this world needs is a few more rednecks / Was it 26 / Oh Atlanta / Midnight wind / Saturday night down South / Play me some fiddle / Simple man / Old rock 'n' roller / Mister DJ / It's my life.
CD 4664952
LP. 4664951
MC 4664954
Epic / Mar '90 / Sony.

SOUTH'S GONNA DO IT (Daniels, Charlie Band).
Tracks: South's gonna do it / New York City, king size rosewood bed.
■ 7" . . . . KSS 704
Kama Sutra / Apr '75.

STILL HURTIN' ME (Daniels, Charlie Band).
Tracks: Still hurtin' me / Runnin' with that crowd.
■ 7" .A 6706
Epic / Nov '85.

STILL IN SAIGON (Daniels, Charlie Band).
Tracks: Still in Saigon / Blowing along with the wind.
■ 7" . . . . EPCA 2246
Epic / Jun '82.

UNEASY RIDER (Daniels, Charlie Band).
Tracks: Uneasy rider / Midnight lady.
■ 7" . . . . EPC 8337
Epic / Apr '80.

VOLUNTEER JAM VI (Daniels, Charlie Band).
Tracks: Rich kids / New Orleans ladies / Night they drove old Dixie down / Same old story / Funky junky / Amazing grace / Will the circle be unbroken / Keep on smilin' / So long / Down home blues / Carol / Do the funky chicken / Lady luck.
■ Double LP . . . . EPC 22107
Epic / Sep '80.

WINDOWS (Daniels, Charlie Band).
Tracks: Still in action / Ain't no ramblers anymore / Lady in red / We had it all one time / Partyin' gal / Ragin' cajun / Makes you want to go home / Blowing along with the wind / Nashville moon / Universal hand.
LP. . . . . EPC 85443
Epic / May '82 / Sony.

Daniels, Roly

Born in Jabulpur, India, Roly Daniels toured the UK with Johnny Burnette in the 1960's, before settling down in Ireland, fronting the successful Nevada Show Band and achieving a No. 2 single in the Irish pop charts with a cover of Conway Twitty's *Hello darlin'*. He has recorded for Release and Emerald records (the latter steering the artist more towards the pop music field), and represented Ireland on the International Show at the 1984 Fan Fair in Nashville.

In 1992 he proceeded to make his country comeback with the self-financed album *Ol' what's his name* , and a series of much praised appearances, including the 1993 Morecambe Festival where (reportedly) he stole the show. (Tony Byworth)

ALMOST SOMEONE.
Tracks: Almost someone / Your eyes.
■ 7" . . . . CHEW 40
Mint / Oct '80.

BECAUSE I LOVE YOU.
Tracks: Because I love you / Wind beneath my wings.
■ 7" . . . . .CHEW 107
Mint / Sep '86.

BEST OF ROLY DANIELS.
Tracks: Not Advised.
LP. . . . . .HPE 646
Harp (Ireland) / Oct '81 / C.M. Distribution.

CLASSIC LOVE SONGS.
Tracks: Not Advised.
Double LP . . . . HM 036D
Harmac (Ireland) / '89 / I & B Records / Prism Leisure PLC.

HE STOPPED LOVIN' HER TODAY.
Tracks: (When you've lost) your golden glitter / He stopped loving her today.
■ 7" . . . . CHEW 90
Mint / Apr '84.

HELLO DARLIN'.
Tracks: Hello darlin' / Happy anniversary.
7" . . . . HS 081
Homespun (Ireland) / Jun '84 / Homespun Records / Ross Records / Wellard Dist.
■ 7" . . . . CHEW 95
Mint / Sep '84.

I CAN FLY HIGHER.
Tracks: Wind beneath my wings / She's gonna win your heart / Part of me / Hey Lord it's me / More of you / Touch me / Only a lonely heart knows / If all the magic is gone / I'm the one who's breaking up / Seven Spanish angels / Let's leave the lights on tonight / Womans touch, A.
LP. . . . . MINT 14
Mint / Dec '85 / RTM / Pinnacle.
MC . . . . KMINT 14
Mint / Nov '87 / RTM / Pinnacle.

I FEEL LIKE LOVING YOU AGAIN.
Tracks: I feel like loving you again.
■ 7" . . . . CHEW 60
Mint / Feb '82.

I WILL LOVE YOU ALL MY LIFE.
Tracks: I will love you all my life / I don't wanna lose you.
■ 7" . . . . CHEW 86
Mint / Nov '83.

I WISH YOU LOVE.
Tracks: Sometimes when we touch / Someone I ain't / I will love you all my life / You've lost that lovin' feeling / Hello Darlin' / Rest your love on me / Stand by me / What's forever for? / I will always love you / Together again / He stopped loving her today / Happy the clown.
LP. . . . . MINT 12
MC . . . . KMINT 12
Mint / Apr '84 / RTM / Pinnacle.

IT'S ALL IN THE GAME.
Tracks: It's all in the game / Sometimes when we touch.
■ 7" . . . . .CHEW 114
Mint / Jul '87.

LAST CHEATER'S WALTZ.
Tracks: Do you wanna go to Heaven? / I feel like loving you again / Lying blue eyes / In memory of a memory / Foolish feelings / Girls, women, and ladies / Last cheater's waltz, The / She can't say that anymore / I don't wanna lose you / One in a million / Tennessee waltz / No one but you.
LP. . . . . JULEP 26
MC . . . . KJULEP 26
Mint / Nov '87 / RTM / Pinnacle.

LAST CHEATER'S WALTZ.
Tracks: Last cheater's waltz, The / No one but you.
■ 7" . . . . CHEW 52
Mint / Oct '81.

LET'S FALL IN LOVE.
Tracks: Ain't no California / If you've got ten minutes-lets fall in love / Friend, lover, wife / Almost someone / Your eyes / Normal crazy person / Do you ever fool around / Mr. Jones / Heart on fire / Devil went down to Georgia, The / I'm comin' home mama / Sweet love.
LP. . . . . .BER 002
MC . . . . KBER 002
Emerald / Nov '84 / I & B Records.

LET'S LEAVE THE LIGHTS ON TONIGHT.
Tracks: Let's leave the lights on tonight.
■ 7" . . . . .CHEW 104
Mint / Apr '86.

LIKE STRANGERS (Daniels, Roly & Ann Williamson).
Tracks: Like strangers / I'll get over you / No one but you.

■ 7" . . . . CHEW 74
Mint / Feb '83.

LOVE DON'T COME ANY BETTER THAN THIS.
Tracks: Love don't come any better than this / Wonderful tonight.
■ 7" . . . . .CHEW 116
Mint / Apr '88.

OL' WHAT'S HIS NAME.
Tracks: Spanish night is over, The / Blue ridge mountain girl / Come home to Belfast town / Somebody lied / Rambling Rose / Making believe / Old time waltz / Nobody's darling (But mine) / Island in the sun / Country medley / Hangin' on / Ol' what's his name / Closer walk with thee / Just as long as you love me.
CD . . . . SD 120
MC . . . . SC 120
Star / '92 / RTM / Pinnacle.

PART OF ME.
Tracks: Part of me / Seven spanish angels.
■ 7" . . . . .CHEW 100
Mint / Nov '87.

ROLY DANIELS' GREATEST HITS.
Tracks: Last cheater's waltz, The / Wind beneath my wings / I will love you all my life / Mr. Jones / She can't say that anymore / He stopped loving her today / Hello darlin' / Do you wanna go to heaven / Seven Spanish angels / Part of me / Hearts on fire / Sometimes when we touch / Love don't come any better than this / If all the magic is gone.
CD . . . . .ERTVCD 4
LP. . . . . ERTV 4
MC . . . . ERTVC 4
Emerald / Nov '88 / I & B Records.

SOMEONE I AIN'T.
Tracks: Someone I ain't.
■ 7" . . . . CHEW 92
Mint / Apr '84.

Dardis, Paul

BYE BYE LOVE (EVERLY BROTHERS HITS).
Tracks: Not Advised.
MC . . . . .VCA 110
VFM Cassettes / May '81 / VFM Children's Entertainment Ltd. / Midland Records / Morley Audio Services.

Darrell, Johnny

The manager of the Holiday Inn in Nashville, born in 1940 in Alabama, got into music and had country hits in the late '60's, often giving exposure to good songs which later became bigger hits for others. He also made duets with Anita Carter. (Donald Clarke).

GREATEST HITS: JOHNNY DARRELL.
Tracks: Not Advised.
LP. . . . . .GT 0048
Gusto (USA) / Oct '79.

Dave & Sugar

Very successful vocal trio of the mid 70's, created by former Stamps Quartet singer Dave Rowlands who joined forces with Vicki Hackman and Jackie Frantz. They worked initially on the road with Charley Pride (booked by Pride's company Chadron, in Dallas) and made their first impression in the charts with *Queen of the silver dollar*. Their second single, *The door is always open* , went straight to number one. Several changes occured in the group's line-up during the remainder of the decade and, in 1982, after a dozen and a half hits, Rowland went solo but was to achieve only minimal success. (Tony Byworth)

DAVE AND SUGAR.
Tracks: I'm gonna love you / Door is always open, The / Can't help but wonder / Whole lotta things to sing about, A / Queen of the silver dollar / I've been so wrong for so long / Fools / Late nite country lovin' music / I'm leavin' the leavin' to you / Queen of my heart.
■ LP. . . . . .RS 1079
RCA / '79.

DAVE AND SUGAR (2).
Tracks: How 'bout us / Two broken hearts / Got my heart set on you / No secret anymore / My angel baby / Signal for help / Feel good with me / Take it from the heart / Don't walk away / Queen of the silver dollar.
LP. . . . . .IMCA 39050
MCA (Import) / Mar '86 / Pinnacle / Silver Sounds (CD).

DON'T THROW IT AWAY.
Tracks: Don't throw it away / Queen of my heart.
■ 7" . . . . PB 0876
RCA / Mar '77.

DOOR IS ALWAYS OPEN, THE.
Tracks: Door is always open, The / Late night country lovin' music.
■ 7" . . . . .RCA 2743
RCA / Oct '76.

■ DELETED

GOTTA QUIT LOOKIN' AT YOU BABY.
Tracks: Gotta quit lookin' at you baby / We are the one.
■ 7"........................... PB 1251
RCA / '79.

GREATEST HITS: DAVE AND SUGAR.
Tracks: It's a heartache / Queen of the silver dollar / Tear time / Golden tears / Door is always open, The / Don't throw it all away / Gotta quit lookin at you baby / Baby take your coat off / I'm knee deep in loving you / My world begins and ends with you / Can't help but wonder.
LP............................. INTS 5112
MC............................. INTK 5112
RCA International / May '82 / BMG.

I'M KNEE DEEP IN LOVING YOU.
Tracks: I'm knee deep in loving you / Livin' at the end of the rainbow.
■ 7"........................... PB 1141
RCA / '79.

NEW YORK WINE & TENNESSEE SHINE.
Tracks: New York wine and Tennessee shine / You / Make believe it's your first time / Things to do / Changing / Delta queen / It ain't easy lovin' me / Learning to feel love again / Just a whole lotta love / Love song.
■ LP........................... PL 13623
RCA / Oct '80.

STAY WITH ME/GOLDEN TEARS.
Tracks: Stay with me / Golden tears / What I feel is you / Take a ride on a river boat / Why did you have to be so good / I thought you'd never ask / Don't stop now / That's how much I love you / My world begins and ends with you / Remember me.
■ LP........................... PL 13360
RCA / Feb '80.

TEAR TIME.
Tracks: Tear time / It's a heartache / Gotta quit lookin' at you baby / We are the one / Tie me to your heart again / How can I stop my lovin' you / Somebody wake me / Nothing makes me feel as good as a love song / Baby take your coat off / Easy to love.
MC............................. PK 12861
■ Mini LP...................... PL 12861
RCA / '79.

THAT'S THE WAY LOVE SHOULD BE.
Tracks: That's the way love should be / Don't throw it all away / Got leavin' on her mind / We've got everything / I'm knee deep in loving you / I love to be loved by you / Feel like a little love / It's a beautiful morning with you / I ain't leavin' Dallas 'til the fire goes out / Livin' at the end of the rainbow.
LP............................. PL 12477
■ MC........................... PK 12477
RCA / '79.

Davidson, Dianne

AIN'T GONNA BE TREATED THIS WAY.
Tracks: Ain't gonna be treated this way.
■ 7".......................... .6146 021
Janus / Mar '73.

Davies, Gail

The daughter of a Louisiana Hayride musician, Oklahoma born Gail Davies was brought up in country music surroundings, though she initially attempted a jazz career (when married to a jazz musician). Her song Bucket to the South, a 1978 hit for Ava Barber, opened up the doorways for her debut album, Gail Davies, released on the short-lived Lifesong Records. Subsequently she's had albums out on Warner Bros., RCA and Capitol, and enjoyed the freedom of producing them herself. While at RCA she also put together the all-girl group Wild Choir, which only had minimal success during its short time in existence. (Tony Byworth)

GAIL DAVIES.
Tracks: No love have I / What can I say? / Are you teasing me? / Bucket to the south / Soft spoken man / Someone's looking for someone like me / Need your lovin' / It's no wonder I'm still blue.
LP............................. KZ 35504
■ MC........................... KZ 35504C
Lifesong / '78.

GAME, THE.
Tracks: Blue heartache / Game, The / Good lovin' man / Careless love / Love is living around us / Sorry that you're leavin' / Never seen a man like you / Drown in the flood / Like strangers / When I had you in my arms.
■ LP........................... BSK 3395
WEA / '80.

GIVIN' HERSELF AWAY.
Tracks: Givin' herself away / It's amazing what a little love can do.
■ 7".......................... K 17916
WEA / Apr '82.

I'LL BE THERE.
Tracks: I'll be there / It's a lovely world / Mama's gonna give you sweet things / Kentucky / Honky tonk waltz / Farewell song / Object of my affection / Get that feelin' inside / I'm hungry, I'm tired / Grandma's song / No one to welcome me home.

LP............................. BSK 3509
WEA / '80.
■ LP........................... K 56981
WEA / '82.

JAGGED EDGE OF A BROKEN HEART.
Tracks: Jagged edge of a broken heart / Lion in the winter.
7"............................ .RCA 481
RCA / Apr '85 / BMG.

OTHER SIDE OF LOVE, THE.
Tracks: I'm a little bit lonely / Happy ever after / Holdin' out for you / Someone like me / Love that could last, A / With a boy like you / Remember / I need my baby back / Other side of love / One more night with you.
LP............................. 94105
Capitol (import) / '89 / Pinnacle / EMI.

PRETTY WORDS.
Tracks: Waiting here for you / I don't know why / Hearts in the wind / I've had enough / Somewhere tonight / Pretty words / It's just a matter of time / I'm ready to fall in love again / Meet me halfway / I will rise and shine again.
CD............................. MCAD 42274
LP............................. MCA 42274
MC............................. MCAC 42274
MCA / Jun '89 / BMG.

WHAT CAN I SAY.
Tracks: Boys like you / Following you around / On a real good night / Hallelujah / I love him so / What can I say / You're a hard dog (to keep under the porch) / It's you alone / If you can lie a little bit / Boy in you is showing, The / Setting me up.
LP............................. 23972-1
■ MC........................... 23972-4
Warner Bros.(USA) / '83.

WHERE IS A WOMAN TO GO?.
Tracks: Lion in the winter / Diffferent train of thought / Where is a woman to go / Jagged edge of a broken heart / Not a day goes by / Trouble with love / Breakaway / Nothing can hurt me now / Lovin' me too / Unwed fathers.
LP............................. PL 81587
MC............................. PK 81587
RCA / Apr '85 / BMG.

Davis, Link

1948-1963.
Tracks: Not Advised.
CD............................. CD 06
Krazy Kat / Jul '93 / Hot Shot / C.M. Distribution / Wellard Dist. / Roots Records / Projection / Charly / Jazz Music.

BIG MAMOU.
Tracks: Big mamou / Pretty little dedon / Mamou waltz / Hey, garcon / Lonely heart / Time will tell / Gumbo ya-ya (everybody talks at once) / Falling for you / Crawfish crawl, The / You're little but you're cute / Mama say no / Every time I pass your door / You show up missing / Cajun love / Kajalena / Va t'cacher (go hide yourself).
LP............................. ED 279
Edsel / Oct '89 / Pinnacle.
CD............................. EDCD 279
Edsel / Mar '92 / Pinnacle.

LINK DAVIS 1948-63.
Tracks: Not Advised.
CD............................. KKCD 06
Krazy Kat / Apr '91 / Hot Shot / C.M. Distribution / Wellard Dist. / Roots Records / Projection / Charly / Jazz Music.

SLIPPING AND SLIDING SOMETIMES.
Tracks: Slipping and sliding sometimes / Allons a lafayette.
■ 7".......................... NS 52
Ace / Jul '79.

Davis, Mac

This American singer-songwriter, born in Lubbock, Texas, began playing rock 'n' roll in the late Fifties. During the Sixties he worked as an executive in the record and music publishing industries, while refining his songwriting techniques. His big breakthrough came in 1969, when Elvis Presley recorded his song In The Ghetto and took it to the Top 3 on both sides of the Atlantic - this hit had an added significance because, in both the US and UK, it gave Elvis his biggest single for four years, and marked a career resurgence for the King after half a dozen years in the wasteland of forgettable films. Hence, In The Ghetto led to numerous other artists recording Davis' material. During 1969-71, other hit Davis songs included, in America, Daddy's Little Man (O C Smith) and Watching Scotty Grow (Bobby Goldsboro) and, in both America and Britain, Don't Cry Daddy (Elvis again) and Something's Burning (Kenny Rogers & the First Edition). All were in a country music vein but with a mild hint of Southern Rock; and all were sentimental while managing to stay just this side of schmaltzy.This success led to Davis resuming his performing career and, in 1972, he landed his first - and biggest - US hit as an artist. Baby Don't Get Hooked On Me reached No 1 in the States and hit No 29 in

Britain. This single showed that, as a performer, Davis was including a trace of humour into his act in order to offset the sentimentality. The mid-Seventies saw him enjoy three US Top 20 singles in quick succession with One Hell Of A Woman, Stop And Smell The Roses and Rock 'N' Roll (I Gave You The Best Years Of My Life), the latter a UK hit for Kevin Johnson. He then faded into the background, to the undoubted delight of 'Rolling Stone' magazine whose "Rolling Stone Record Guide" gave every Mac Davis album a zero star rating! However, he bounced back briefly in late 1980 with the delightful It's Hard To Be Humble, a comedy song recorded live. This single fared notably well in Britain, where it peaked at No 27 but logged an impressive total of 15 weeks on the Top 75.(Bob MacDonald)

20 GOLDEN SONGS.
Tracks: Not Advised.
LP............................. 20112
MC............................. 40112
Astan (USA) / Nov '84.

BABY DON'T GET HOOKED ON ME.
Tracks: Baby don't get hooked on me.
■ 7".......................... CBS 8250
CBS / Nov '72.

CAROLINE'S STILL IN GEORGIA.
Tracks: Caroline's still in Georgia / Most of all.
7"............................ .CAN 1019
Casablanca / Apr '84.

IT'S HARD TO BE HUMBLE.
Tracks: It's hard to be humble / Greatest gift of all / Let's keep it that way / It was time / Gravel on the ground / Tequila Sheila / I will always love you / Why don't we sleep on it / I wanta make up with you / I know you're out there somewhere.
■ LP........................... NBLP 7207
Casablanca / Feb '81.

IT'S HARD TO BE HUMBLE.
Tracks: It's hard to be humble.
■ 7".......................... .CAN 210
Casablanca / Nov '80.

ME AND FAT BOY.
Tracks: Me and fat boy / Hooked on music.
■ 7".......................... .CAN 1002
Casablanca / May '81.

MIDNIGHT CRAZY.
Tracks: Midnight crazy / Dammit girl / I've got the hots for you / You're my bestest friend / Comfortable / Tell me your fantasies / You are so lovely / Kiss it and make it better / Something burning / Float away.
LP............................. .6480 057
MC............................. .7190 057
Casablanca / Nov '81.

ONE HELL OF A WOMAN.
Tracks: One hell of a woman / Poor man's gold.
■ 7".......................... CBS 2398
CBS / Jun '74.

SOFT TALK.
Tracks: Caroline's still in Georgia / Good news bad / Patch of blue / Most of all / Soft talk / Springtime in Dixie / Nickel dreams / Put a bar in my car / Deep down / I've got a dream.
LP............................. CANL 9
MC............................. CANLC 9
Casablanca / Apr '84.

TEQUILA SHEILA.
Tracks: Tequila Sheila / It was time.
■ 7".......................... .CAN 219
Casablanca / Jan '81.

TEXAS IN MY REAR VIEW MIRROR.
Tracks: Texas in my rear view mirror / Hooked on music / Remember when / Me 'n' fat boy / Hot Texas night / Sad songs / Hello Hollywood / Rodeo clown / Secrets / In the eyes of my people.
■ LP........................... NBLP 7239
Casablanca / May '81.

THUNDER IN THE AFTERNOON.
Tracks: Thunder in the afternoon / Plastic saddle.
■ 7".......................... CBS 5157
CBS / Jun '77.

THUNDER IN THE AFTERNOON.
Tracks: Thunder in the afternoon (let it rain) / Picking up the pieces of my life / Morning side, The / Plastic saddle / Do it (with someone you love) / Please be gentle / Jennifer Johnson and me / Where did the good times go / Play me a lttle travelling music / When I dream.
■ LP........................... 81562
CBS / '78 / Sony.

TILL I MADE IT WITH YOU.
Tracks: I never made love (till I made it with you) / Too big for words / Shake, Ruby, shake / Rainy day lovin' / Regrets / Special place in heaven, A / Save that dress / I think I'm gonna rain / I feel the country callin' me / Sexy young girl.
■ LP........................... IMCA 5590
MCA (Import) / Mar '86.

YOU'RE MY BESTEST FRIEND.
Tracks: You're my bestest friend / Midnight crazy.
■ 7" . . . . CAN 1007
Casablanca / Feb '82.

Davis, Paul

Singer - songwriter/producer, born 21.4.1948 in Meridan, Mississippi, recording for Bang (1970's) and Capitol (1980's) breaking with *Ride em cowboy* in 1975 from the album of the same name. had some moderate success on America's top 100 charts with *I go crazy* and *Sweet life* before making himself a career in Nashville, initially as a songwriter, creating such No 1 hits as *Bop* (Dan Seals - it earned him the CMA Single of The Year Award in 1986), and *Meet me in Montana* (Seals - Marie Osmond). In 1986 he got in at the recording end when *You're still new to me* , a duet with Osmond, went No 1. subsequent chart topper have come in the form of *Just another love* for Tanya Tucker - also 1986. Davis kept up his association with the Texas belle, and alongside RCA's Paul Overstreet, collaborated with Tucker on the Don Schiltz - Overstreet *I won't take less than your love* , a 1988 No.1 hit. Tucker, who'd also had seen *Love me like you used to do* (1987) to No.2 was to keep the run going into the 90's. repeating the feat with *Down to my last teardrop* . (Maurice Hope)

65 LOVE AFFAIR.
Tracks: 65 love affair / We're still together.
■ 7" . . . . ARIST 469
Arista / '82.

COOL NIGHT.
Tracks: Cool night / You came to me / One more time for the lonely / Nathan Jones / Oriental eyes / 65 love affair / Somebody's gettin to you / Love or let me be lonely / What you got to say about love? / We're still together.
LP. . . . . SPART 1187
Arista / Mar '82 / BMG.

COOL NIGHT.
Tracks: Cool night / One more time for the lonely.
■ 7" . . . . ARIST 449
Arista / '82.

I GO CRAZY.
Tracks: I go crazy / Reggae kind of way.
■ 7" . . . . BANG 11
Bang / Jan '78.

PAUL DAVIS.
Tracks: Can't get back to Alabama / Keep our love alive / Little bit of soap, A / Medicine woman / Midnight woman / Mississippi river / One night lovers / Ride'em cowboy / Superstar / Teach me how to rock and roll / Thank you shoes / Thinkin' of you / You're not just a rose.
LP. . . . . SHOT 002
Phonogram / Jul '78 / PolyGram.

SONG OF CHANTER (Davis, Paul & Brian Vallelly).
Tracks: Not Advised.
LP. . . . . SOLP 1028
Outlet / Jul '76 / Projection / Duncans / C.M. Distribution / Ross Records / Topic Records / Direct Distribution / Midland Records.

THINKING OF YOU.
Tracks: Thinking of you / Medicine woman.
■ 7" . . . . BANG 006
Bang / Mar '77.

Davis, Skeeter

This American singer, born Mary Frances Penik in Kentucky, came to fame in 1953 as 50% of the Davis Sisters, who scored a smash hit on the US country and western charts that year with *I Forget More Than You'll Ever Know*. However, later in that same year, Bee Jay Davis, her singing partner, was killed in a car accident on the way home from a show. This led to Skeeter giving up performing for several years, until persuaded back into the limelight in the late Fifties by Nashville's two leading music executives, Chet Atkins and Steve Sholes. In 1960 she hit the country charts and the US pop Top 40 with *(I Can't Help You) I'm Falling Too*, an answer to Hank Locklin's *Please Help Me, I'm Falling*, which had been a Top Tenner earlier in the year. Davis repeated the 'answer' formula in early '61 with *My Last Date (With You)*, a vocal version of Floyd Cramer's instrumental smash *Last Date*.Davis achieved her biggest hit in 1963. *The End Of The World*, a charmingly angst-ridden love song, took her to No 2 on the US pop chart; in Britain the single reached No 18 and logged 13 weeks on the Top 50, thus becoming her only UK hit. *I Can't Stay Mad At You* provided her with a second US pop smash later in '63, reaching No 7 on the Billboard Hot 100. The Beatles revolution soon spelt the end of her pop success, however, and she relied thereafter on the country charts for success. Her records were standard products of the Nashville studios. But she upset the Nashville establishment in 1974 when she used the Grand Ole Opry, country music's most famous forum, to give vent to her views about the city's police; this led to Davis being banned from performing at the venue. (Bob MacDonald).

20 OF THE BEST: SKEETER DAVIS.
Tracks: I forgot more than you'll ever know / Set me free / Homebreaker / Am I that easy to forget? / (I can't help you) I'm falling too / My last date (with you) / Hand you're holding now, The / Optimistic / Where I ought to be / End of the world / I can't stay mad at you / I'm saving my love / Gonna get along without you now / He says the same things to me / Dear John letter, A / Fuel to the flame / What does it take to keep a man like you / There's a fool born every minute / I'm a lover (not a fighter) / Bus fare to Kentucky.
■ LP. . . . . NL 89522
RCA International / Apr '85.
■ MC . . . . NK 89522
RCA / Apr '85.

BEST OF SKEETER DAVIS.
Tracks: End of the world / I can't help you (I'm falling too) / I will / Something precious / Now I lay me down too sleep / Gonna get along without you now / He says the same things to me / I can't stay mad at you / I forgot more than you'll ever know / My last date (with you) / Am I that easy to forget.
■ LP. . . . . LSA 3153
RCA / '79.
■ LP. . . . . INTS 5011
RCA International / Jul '80.
LP. . . . . NL 89319
MC . . . . NK 89319
RCA / '84 / BMG.
LP. . . . . CDS 1218
■ MC . . . . CAM 1218
RCA/Camden / Jul '86.

BEST OF SKEETER DAVIS VOL. 2.
Tracks: What does it take (to keep a man like you satisfied) / Set him free / One tin soldier / Fuel to the flame / Love takes a lot of time / I'm a lover (not a fighter) / Bridge over troubled water / Sunglasses / Let me get close to you / Bus fare to Kentucky / There's a fool born every minute.
■ LP. APL1 0190
RCA / '75 / BMG.

BRING IT ON HOME.
Tracks: One tin soldier / Bring it on home / Never ending song of love / He loved me too little / Take me home, country roads / Loving him was easier (than anything I'll ever do again) / All I ever wanted was love / Just as soon as I get over loving you / Reason to believe / Night they drove old Dixie down.
■ LP. . . . . LSA 3102
RCA / '75 / BMG.

CLOUDY, WITH OCCASIONAL TEARS.
Tracks: I will follow him / Why, why, why / I'm saving my love / I will / Moonlight promises / Can't get used to losing you / Don't let it happen to us / Cloudy, with occasional tears / You, you, you / They listened while you said goodbye / It was only a heart / Somebody loves you.
■ LP. . . . . RD 7604
RCA / Feb '70 / BMG.

END OF THE WORLD.
Tracks: End of the world / Silver threads and golden needles / Mine is a lonely life / Once upon a time / Why I'm walkin' / Don't let me cross over / My colouring book / Where nobody wants me (I want to go) / Keep your hands off my baby / Something precious / Longing to hold you again / He called my baby.
LP. . . . . NL 90001
■ MC . . . . NK 90001
RCA / Jan '87.

END OF THE WORLD.
Tracks: End of the world / I can't stay mad at you.
■ 7" . . . . RCA 1328
RCA / Mar '63.
■ 7" . . . . GOLD 507
RCA Golden Grooves / Jul '81.

END OF THE WORLD (OLD GOLD).
Tracks: End of the world / Make the world go away.
7" . . . . OG 9619
Old Gold / Oct '86 / Pickwick Records.

END OF THE WORLD, THE.
Tracks: End of the world, The / Silver threads and golden needles / Mine is a lonely life / Once upon a time / Why I'm walkin' / Don't let me cross over / My colouring book / Where nobody knows me / Keep your hands off my baby / Something precious / Longing to hold you again / He called me baby.
LP. . . . . RD 7563
RCA / Mar '70 / BMG.

HILLBILLY SINGER, THE.
Tracks: Hillbilly song, A / Colour of the blues / You done me wrong / Making believe / Try Jesus / Crazy arms / My shoes keep walking back to you / It wasn't God who made honky tonk angels / Half a mind / How long has it been.
■ LP. . . . . LSA 3151
RCA / '75 / BMG.

HOMEBREAKER.
Tracks: End of the world / Gonna get along without you now / What does it take (to win your love) / Goin' down the road feeling bad / I forgot more than you'll ever know / Set him free / Homebreaker / My last date with you / Am I that easy to forget / I can't help you (I'm falling too) / I can't believe it's over.
LP. . . . . TOP 152
MC . . . . KTOP 152
Topline / Dec '86 / Charly / Swift / Black Sun Records.

LET ME GET CLOSE TO YOU.
Tracks: Now I lay me down to sleep / Gonna get along without ya now / Didn't I / My sweet loving man / I can't stay mad at you / My happiness / Let me get close to you / Another you / Ladder of success / He says the same things to me / Ask me / Easy to love.
■ LP. . . . . RD 7676
RCA / Mar '70 / BMG.

LOVE TAKES A LOT OF MY TIME.
Tracks: Love takes a lot of my time / I can't seem to say goodbye / Fire & rain / Mama your big girls about to cry / You've got a friend / Hello darlin' / If you could read my mind / He wakes me with a kiss each morning / You call this love (I call it hate) / Amazing grace.
■ LP. . . . . LSA 3054
RCA / '75 / BMG.

MORE TUNES FOR TWO (see under Bare, Bobby & Skeeter Davis).

SHE SINGS THEY PLAY (Davis, Skeeter & NRBQ).
Tracks: Things to you / Everybody wants a cowboy / I can't stop loving you now / Heart to heart / Ain't nice to talk like that / Everybody's clown / Some day my prince will come / How many tears / You don't know what you got till you lose it / Roses on my shoulder / Temporarily out of order / May you never be alone.
MC . . . . ROUNDER 3092C
Rounder / '85 / Projection / Roots Records / Swift / C.M. Distribution / Topic Records / Jazz Music / Hot Shot / A.D.A Distribution / Direct Distribution.
LP. . . . . ROUNDER 3092
Rounder / Dec '85 / Projection / Roots Records / Swift / C.M. Distribution / Topic Records / Jazz Music / Hot Shot / A.D.A Distribution / Direct Distribution.
LP. . . . . FIEND 81
Demon / Nov '86 / Pinnacle.
CD . . . . CD 3092
Rounder / '88 / Projection / Roots Records / Swift / C.M. Distribution / Topic Records / Jazz Music / Hot Shot / A.D.A Distribution / Direct Distribution.

SINGS BUDDY HOLLY.
Tracks: Early in the morning / Well..alright / True love ways / It doesn't matter anymore / Heartbeat / Think it over / Maybe baby / That'll be the day / Its so easy / I'm looking for someone to love / Oh boy / Raining in my heart.
■ LP. . . . . DT 33002
Detour / Apr '83.

TUNES FOR TWO (see under Bare, Bobby).

YOU'VE GOT A FRIEND.
Tracks: Hello darlin' / Daddy sang bass / Angel of the morning / My colouring book / Place in the country / Son of a preacher man / If you could read my mind / I'm so lonesome I could cry / I can't seem to say goodbye / Today I started loving you again / He wakes me with a kiss.
MC . . . . CAM 485
RCA / Apr '80 / BMG.
LP. . . . . CDS 1173
RCA/Camden / Feb '80 / BMG / Arabesque Ltd.

Day, Jimmy

One of the world's finest steel guitarists ("the only one no-one has been able to copy" commented fellow musician Speedy West), Alabama born Day has worked with many legends of the business - including Hank Williams, Jim Reeves, Willie Nelson, Leftyy Frizzell, Ray Price and Elvis Presley - as well as being a much sought after session musician and artist in his own right. He co-founded the Sho-Bud (steel guitar) Co., with Shot Jackson, has won numerous awards and was inducted into the Steel Guitar Hall of Fame in 1982. The Bear Family cd comprises two highly collectable early 1960's albums *Golden steel guitar hits* and *Steel and strings* . (Tony Byworth)

STEEL & STRINGS (Golden Steel Guitar Hits).
Tracks: Panhandle rag / Roadside rag / Texas playboy rag / Remington ride / Coconut grove / Boot hill drag / Bud's bounce / B. Bowman's hop / Georgia steel guitar / Steelin' the blues / Indian love call / Please help me I'm falling / I love you because / Am I that easy to forget / Fallen star, A / She thinks I still care / Makin' believe / I love you so much it hurts / Wild side of life / Release me / Funny how time slips away / I can't stop loving you / I fall to pieces.
CD . . . . BCD 15583
Bear Family / Apr '92 / Rollercoaster Records / Swift / Direct Distribution.

Dean, Billy

Born 2.4.1962 in Quincy, near Tallahasee, Florida, a singer - songwriter, boasting a musical background of singing in barbershop quartets

D 4

■ DELETED

and playing in the hotel lounges along the Gulf Coast before he'd reached 16. Son of a singer/mechanic, Dean, a star athlete, looked at stage set to be heading towards making a career in basketball. He turned to music, winning a regional Wrangler County competition and reaching the Nashville finals. Signed to Capitol, his debut album *Young Man* in 1990 starting him along the road to success. He has steadily built himself a following-charting regulary with his smooth country ballads. *If There Hadn't Been You* from the *Billy Dean* gold selling album making country's top five in 1992 later to be joined by *Billy The Kid*, which in turn is shored up with such singles as *Only The Wind*. Mid - 1993 his third album *Fire In The Dark* with the top ten release *Tryin To Hide A Fire In The Dark* continuing the run. (Maurice Hope)

BILLY DEAN.
Tracks: I miss Billy the Kid / Simple things / Hammer down / Only the wind / Small favors / I shoulda listened / You don't count the cost / Gone but not forgotten / If there hadn't been you / Intro (daddy's will) / Daddy's will.
CD Set . . . . **CDP 796 728 2**
■ MC **C4 96728**
Capitol Nashville / Feb '92.

LOVE SELLER.
Tracks: Love seller / Let's go home.
■ 7" **7N 45370**
Pye / Jun '74.

Dean, Jimmy

Enormously popular country singer in the '60's, born in 1928 in Texas; also a TV host and actor. First minor hit with the Wildcats was *Bummin' Around* in 1953 on Four Star; he pioneered country music on TV, reaching network status in 1960: he signed with CBS and had collosal hit *Big Bad John* in 1961: number one in both country and pop charts and won a Grammy. He retired in the mid '70's to sell sausages. (Donald Clarke)

BIG BAD JOHN.
Tracks: Steelman / Big bad John.
■ 7" . . . . **PB 1187**
Philips / Oct '61.

BIG BAD JOHN.
Tracks: Big bad John / I won't go huntin' with you Jake / Smoke, smoke, smoke that cigarette / Dear Ivan / To a sleeping beauty / Cajun Queen, The / P.T. 109 / Walk on boy / Little bitty big John / Steel man / Little black book / Please pass the biscuits / Gonna raise a ruckus tonight / Day that changed the world, A / Gotta travel on / Sixteen tons / Oklahoma Bill / Night train to Memphis / Make the waterwheel roll / Lonesome road / Grasshopper MacClean / Old Pappy's new banjo / You're nobody 'til somebody loves you / Cajun Joe / Nobody / Kentucky means paradise.
CD . . . . **BCD 15723**
Bear Family / Jul '93 / Rollercoaster Records / Swift / Direct Distribution.

BIG BAD JOHN (OLD GOLD).
Tracks: Big bad John / Steel man.
7" . . . . **OG 9399**
Old Gold / Jan '87 / Pickwick Records.

GREATEST HITS: JIMMY DEAN.
Tracks: Big bad John / Cajun Queen, The / Harvest of sunshine / Little black book / Steel men / First thing every morning (and the last thing at night), The / Sam hill / P.T. 109 / To a sleeping beauty / Farmer and the Lord, The / I won't go huntin' With you Jake (But I'll go chasin' wimmin).
CD . . . . **.983000 2**
Sony Collector's Choice / Aug '93 / Pickwick Records.

HIS TOP HITS.
Tracks: Not Advised.
MC . . . . **.804**
Timeless Treasures / Jul '86 / Terry Blood Dist.

LITTLE BLACK BOOK.
Tracks: Little black book.
■ 7" . . . . **AAG 122**
CBS / Nov '62.

Dee, Jeannie

INTRODUCING JEANNIE.
Tracks: Your good girl's gonna go bad / You and me / I fall to pieces / Peaceful easy feeling / Standing tall / What I've got in mind / Blue eyes crying in the rain / How many lovers / Crazy arms / Fight and scratch / Stand by your man.
LP . . . . **STON 8405**
MC . . . . **CSTON 8405**
Sylvantone / Aug '84 / Sylvantone Records.

NO LIFE WITHOUT LOVE.
Tracks: No life without love (mixes).
12" . . . . **PERF 004T**
CD Single . . . . **PERF 004CD**
Perfecto (London) / Sep '93 / Revolver-APT.

Delmore Brothers

A county blues and boogie duo popular in '30's and '40s, their biggest record success on King 1940-51. Alton (1908-64) and Rabon Delmore (1916-52) were from Alabama, and Alton's guitar was particularly influential in the country boogie genre which was one of the predecessors of rock'n'roll. He also wrote more than 1000 songs, including *Blues Stay Away From Me, Beautiful Brown Eyes, Freight Train Boogie, Brown's Ferry Blues*, etc. (Donald Clarke)

BEST OF THE DELMORE BROTHERS.
Tracks: Not Advised.
LP . . . . **SLP 962**
MC . . . . **GT 5962**
Starday (USA) / Apr '87 / Crusader Marketing Co.

FREIGHT TRAIN BOOGIE.
Tracks: Blues stay away from me / Freight train boogie / Trouble ain't nothin' but the blues / Boogie woogie baby / Rounder's blues / Mobile boogie / Used car blues / Pan American blues / Pan American boogie / Field hand man / Brown's ferry blues / Peach tree street boogie / Blues you never lose / Steamboat boogie / Muddy water / Sand mountain blues / Hillbilly boogie / You can't do wrong and get by / Kentucky Mountain / Weary day / Take it to the Captain.
CD . . . . **CDCHD 455**
Ace / Aug '93 / Pinnacle / Hot Shot / Jazz Music / Complete Record Co. Ltd.

WHEN THEY LET THE HAMMER DOWN (Delmore Brothers & Wayne Raney).
Tracks: Red ball to nather / Jack and Jill boogie / Lost John boogie / Beale street boogie / Peach Tree Street boogie / Boogie woogie baby / When they let the hammer down / Barnyard boogie / Hillbilly boogie / Freight train boogie / Down home boogie / Stop that boogie / Del Rio boogie / Pan American boogie / Real hot boogie / Used car blues.
LP . . . . **BFX 15167**
Bear Family / Nov '84 / Rollercoaster Records / Swift / Direct Distribution.

DeMent, Iris

Female folk/sountry singer - songwriter, born into a musical family (youngest of 14 children) on a small farm in Paragould, Arkansas - later moving to California. Her father had played fiddle around the state, during her younger days - whilst later, along with her mother, sang at church. Meanwhile The DeMent Sisters were formed, allowing Iris a platform to perform. Iris' first attempt at breaking into the music business came during the mid - 80s when she moved to Nashville as a writer. While it didn't turn out too grand, she got to record singing harmony alongside Barry Tashian and irish singers Delores Keane & Mary Black on Emmylou's 1988 *Brand new dance* album. DeMents highly acclaimed acoustic folk/country Philo album of 1992 *Infamous Angel* showed both her pure, clear vocal talents and ablility to write fine autobiographical songs - where Jim Rooney produces and Harris makes a guest appearance. This brought her to the attention of Warner Brothers, who signed her to their Los Angeles division in early 1993 and since re - released her debut Philo album. She made her UK debut in May of that year at London's Bloomsbury theatre. (Maurice Hope)

INFAMOUS ANGEL.
Tracks: Let the mystery be / These hills / Hotter than mojave in my heart / When love was young / Our town / Fifty miles of elbow room / Infamous angel / Sweet forgivness / After you've gone / Mama's opry / Higher ground.
CD . . . . **PH 1138CD**
MC . . . . **PH 1138C**
Philo (USA) / '92 / Roots Records / Projection / Topic Records / Direct Distribution / Ross Records / C.M. Distribution / Impetus Records.
CD . . . . **.936245238-2**
MC . . . . **.936245238-4**
Warner Bros. / May '93 / WEA.

OUR TOWN.
Tracks: Our town / Heart's highway / God may forgive you (but I won't) (On CD single only).
7" . . . . **WO 194**
CD Single . . . . **WO 194 CD**
MC Single . . . . **WO 194 C**
WEA / Aug '93 / WEA.

Dempsey, Little Jimmy

GOLDEN GUITAR.
Tracks: Not Advised.
MC Set . . . . **DTO 10243**
Ditto / '88 / Pickwick Records.

GUITAR MUSIC.
Tracks: Not Advised.
CD . . . . **CNCD 5937**
MC . . . . **CNMC 4937**
Corner Music / Jun '92 / Terry Blood Dist.

Denver, Jeannie

LIVE - SPUR AND SADDLE.
Tracks: Not Advised.
LP . . . . **WRS 105**
Westwood / Nov '76 / Pinnacle.

QUEEN OF THE SILVER DOLLAR.
Tracks: Not Advised.
LP . . . . **WRS 094**
Westwood / '76 / Pinnacle.

WITH LOVE.
Tracks: Cash on the barrelhead / I don't wanna cry / Dolly's drive / With love / Standing room only / Jacob and Marcie / That's what friends are for / Devoted to you / Some of Shelly's blues / Mississippi, you're on my mind / One more day away / Country baptizing
LP . . . . **WRS 128**
Westwood / '82 / Pinnacle.

YORKSHIRE ROSE.
Tracks: Not Advised.
LP . . . . **WRS 056**
Westwood / '76 / Pinnacle.

Denver, John

This American singer, songwriter and guitarist, born John Deutschendorf in New Mexico, was brought up in an Air Force family, and therefore spent his childhood and youth moving round the States from one school to another. His father held three world records in military aviation, but John's similar aspirations were thwarted when the USAF rejected him on grounds of shortsightedness. He took up folk singing, changed his name to Denver (inspired by the Colorado city), moved to Los Angeles and, from 1964 onwards, joined the Chad Mitchell Trio, a folk music threesome. After four years with the band, they split up and Denver was faced with a large debt. It was not too long, however, before he was able to pay this - in December 1969, his song *Leavin' On A Jet Plane* gave famous folk trio Peter Paul and Mary their first ever US No 1; it was also their biggest British hit, reaching No 2 in 1970. Suddenly, Denver's name began to attract major attention and his debut album, 1969's *Rhymes And Reasons*, started to sell. 1971 brought him his first US smash as a performer: *Take Me Home, Country Roads* hit No 2, and was a typical example of his songwriting style - evoking rural America, expressing his love for natural beauty, sentimental but not twee, melodic, halfway between folk and country, and eminently remake-able. Olivia Newton-John took the song into the British Top 20 in 1973, the same year that Denver's premature *Greatest Hits* album was issued in the States - though this compilation LP contained only four US Top 40 hits, it was an excellent showcase of his talent and proved to be the marketing masterstroke that cemented his American popularity. From '74 onwards, it was plain sailing for the bespectacled all-American boy. Denver chalked up four US No 1 singles during 1974-5. These included *Sunshine On My Shoulders, Thank God I'm A Country Boy* and *I'm Sorry*; but the biggest was *Annie's Song*. Dedicated to his wife, *Annie's Song* was both a perfect love tribute and a perfect expression of the singer's country-loving, ecology-conscious views and emotions. It was also No 1 in Britain and, amazingly, remains his only UK Top 40 single despite high album sales in Britain. Denver's highest charting LP in the UK was 1976's *Live In London*, which hit No 2. In the late Seventies, record sales dropped off on both sides of the Atlantic. Denver concentrated more on live work, made his movie debut with George Burns in 1977's *Oh God*, and settled into the comfortable and complacent niche of being an all-round showbusiness personality. (Bob MacDonald)

AERIE.
Tracks: Starwood in Aspen / Everyday / Casey's last ride / City of New Orleans / Friends with you / Sixty second song for a bank with the phrase / May we help you today? / Spanish pipe dream / All of my memories / She won't let me fly away / Readjustment blues / Eagle and the hawk, The / Tools.
■ LP . . . . **SF 8252**
RCA / '79.

ANNIE'S SONG.
Tracks: Annie's song / Cool and green and shady eclipse.
■ 7" . . . . **APBO 0295**
RCA / Aug '74.

ANNIE'S SONG (OLD GOLD).
Tracks: Annie's song / Take me home country roads.
7" . . . . **OG 9633**
Old Gold / Nov '86 / Pickwick Records.

AUTOGRAPH.
Tracks: Dancing with the mountains / Mountain song / How mountain girls can love / Song for the life / Ballad of St. Anne's reel / In my heart / Wrangell mountain song / Whale bones and crosses / American child / You say that the battle is over / Autograph.

■ LP. . . . . PL 13449
RCA / Apr '80.

BACK HOME AGAIN.
Tracks: Back home again / On the road / Grandma's feather bed / Matthew / Thank God I'm a country boy / Music is you, The / Annie's song / It's up to you / Cool and green and shady eclipse / Sweet surrender / This old guitar.
LP. APL1 0548
■ MC APK1 0548
RCA / Sep '74.
MC . . . . NK 85193
RCA / Nov '84 / BMG.
■ LP. . . . . NL 85193
RCA / Nov '84.
CD . . . . ND 85193
RCA / Oct '87 / BMG.

BEST OF JOHN DENVER.
Tracks: Take me home, country roads / Follow me / Starwood in Aspen / For baby (for Bobbie) / Rhymes and reasons / Leaving on a jet plane / Eagle and the hawk, The / Sunshine on my shoulders / Goodbye again / Poems, prayers and promises / Rocky mountain high.
LP. APL1 0374
■ MC APK1 0374
RCA / Mar '74.

BEST OF JOHN DENVER VOL.2.
Tracks: Annie's song / Welcome to my morning (farewell Andromeda) / Fly away / Like a sad song / Looking for space / Baby you look good to me tonight / Grandma's feather bed / I'd rather be a cowboy / I'm sorry / My sweet lady / Calypso / This old guitar.
LP. . . . . PL 42120
■ MC . . . . PK 42120
RCA / Mar '77.
LP. . . . . RCALP 3019
MC . . . . RCAK 3019
RCA / Sep '81 / BMG.

COLLECTION: JOHN DENVER.
Tracks: Annie's song / Take me home country roads / Rocky mountain high / Starwood in Aspen / Follow me / I'd rather be a cowboy / Rhymes and reasons / Perhaps love (With Placido Domingo.) / Calypso / Country love / Leaving on a jet plane / Thank God I'm a country boy / Dancing with the mountains / Baby you look good to me tonight / Wild Montana skies / Love again (With Sylvie Vartan.).
MC . . . . STAC 2253
Telstar/Ronco / Dec '84 / BMG.
■ LP. . . . . STAR 2253
Telstar/Ronco / Dec '84.

DIFFERENT DIRECTIONS.
Tracks: Not Advised.
CD 887425
MC 895425
Concord / Oct '91 / New Note.

DON'T CLOSE YOUR EYES.
Tracks: Don't close your eyes / Wild heart looking for home.
7" . . . . PB 49961
RCA / Apr '86 / BMG.

DOWNHILL STUFF.
Tracks: Downhill stuff / Life is so good.
■ 7" . . . . PB 1479
RCA / Mar '79.

DREAMLAND EXPRESS.
Tracks: Dreamland express / Claudette / Gimme your love / Got my heart set on you / Harder they fall / Don't close your eyes tonight / Wild heart looking for home / Desired / Trail of tears / African sunrise.
CD . . . . PD 85458
LP. . . . . PL 85458
■ MC . . . . PK 85458
RCA / '87.

EARTH SONGS.
Tracks: Windsong / Rocky mountain suite (Cold nights in Canada) / Rocky mountain high / Sunshine on my shoulders / Eagle and the hawk, The / Eclipse / Flower that shattered the stone, The / Raven's child / Children of the universe / To the wild country / American child / Calypso / Islands / Earth day every day (celebrate).
CD . . . . MCCD 035
MC . . . . MCTC 035
Music Club / Sep '91 / Gold & Sons / Terry Blood Dist. / Video Collection.

EVENING WITH JOHN DENVER, AN.
Tracks: Music is you, The / Farewell Andromeda / Mother Nature's son / Summer / Today / Saturday night / Mathew / Rocky mountain suite / Sweet surrender / Grandma's feather bed / Annie's song / Eagle and the hawk, The / My sweet lady / Annie's other song / Boy from the country / Rhymes and reasons / Forest lawn / Pickin' the sun down / Thank God I'm country boy / Take me home, country roads / Poems, prayers and promises / Rocky mountain high / This old guitar.
Double LP . . . . LSA 3211-12
■ MC . . . . DPTK 5014
RCA / '79.

FAREWELL ANDROMEDA.
Tracks: I'd rather be a cowboy / Berkeley woman / Please daddy / Angel from Montgomery / River of love / Rocky mountain suite / Whisky basin blues / Sweet misery / Zachary and Jennifer / We don't live here no more / Farewell Andromeda.
■ LP. . . . . SF 8369
RCA / '79.
■ LP. . . . . NL 85195
RCA / Nov '84.
■ MC . . . . NK 85195
RCA / Nov '84.
CD . . . . ND 85195
RCA / Feb '89 / BMG.

FLOWER THAT SHATTERED THE STONE, THE.
Tracks: Flower that shattered the stone, The / Thanks to you / Postcard from Paris / High, wide and handsome / Eagles and horses / Little further north, A / Raven's child / Ancient rhymes / Gift you are, The / I watch you sleeping / Stonehaven sunset / Flower that shattered the stone, The (reprise).
CD 884900
MC 895599
Windstar / Feb '92 / New Note.

FOR YOU.
Tracks: For you / Alaska and me.
■ 7" . . . . PB 49497
RCA / Nov '88.

GREATEST HITS, VOLUME 2.
Tracks: Annie's song / Perhaps love / Fly away / Like a sad song / Looking for space / Thank God I'm a cowboy / Granma's feather bed / Back home again / I'm sorry / My sweet lady / Calypso / This old guitar.
CD 74321 15480-2
MC 74321 15480-4
RCA / Oct '93 / BMG.

GREATEST HITS: JOHN DENVER.
Tracks: Take me home country roads / Follow me / Starwood in Aspen / For baby (for Bobbie) / Rhymes and reasons / Leaving on a jet plane / Eagle and the hawk, The / Sunshine on my shoulders / Goodbye again / Poems, prayers and promises / Rocky mountain high.
LP. . . . . PL 80374
■ MC . . . . PK 80374
RCA / '84.
■ CD . . . . PD 80374
RCA / Oct '84.
CD . . . . ND 90523
MC . . . . NK 90523
RCA / Nov '90 / BMG.

GREATEST HITS: JOHN DENVER VOL.2.
Tracks: Annie's song / Perhaps love (With Placido Domingo.) / Fly away (With Olivia Newton John.) / Like a sad song / Looking for space / Thank God I'm a country boy / Grandma's feather bed / Back home again / I'm sorry / My sweet lady / Calypso / This old guitar.
■ LP. . . . . RCALP 3106
RCA / Dec '82.
LP. . . . . PL 82195
RCA / '84 / BMG.
■ CD . . . . PD 89566
RCA / '84.
■ MC . . . . PK 82195
RCA / '84.

GREATEST HITS: JOHN DENVER VOL.3.
Tracks: Dancing with the mountains / Wild Montana skies / I want to live / Gold and beyond / Autograph / How can I leave you again? / Some days are diamonds / Shanghai breezes / Seasons of the heart / Perhaps love / Love again.
CD . . . . PD 85313
RCA / BMG.
MC . . . . PK 85313
RCA / Mar '85 / BMG.
■ LP. . . . . PL 85313
RCA / Mar '85.

HIGHER GROUND.
Tracks: Alaska and me / Higher ground / Whispering Jesse / Never a doubt / Deal with the ladies / Sing Australia / Country girl in Paris, A / For you / All this joy / Falling leaves / Bread and roses / Homegrown tomatoes.
LP. . . . . PL 90240
RCA / Nov '88 / BMG.
CD . . . . PD 90240
MC . . . . PK 90240
RCA / Oct '88 / BMG.

HOLD ME TIGHTLY.
Tracks: Hold me tightly / Flight.
7" . . . . RCA 374
RCA / Oct '83 / BMG.

HOW CAN I LEAVE YOU AGAIN.
Tracks: How can I leave you again / To the wild country.
■ 7" . . . . PB 1036
RCA / '79.

I WANT TO LIVE.
Tracks: How can I leave you / Tradewinds / Bet on the blues / It amazes me / To the wild country / Ripplin' waters / Thirsty boots / Dearest Esmerelda / Singing skies and dancing waters / I want to live / Druthers.
LP. . . . . PL 12521
■ MC . . . . PK 12521
RCA / Feb '78.

IT'S ABOUT TIME.
Tracks: Hold on tight / Thought of you, The / Somethin' about / On the wings of a dream / Fight (the higher we fly) / Falling out of love / I remember romance / Wild Montana skies / World game / It's about time.
■ LP. . . . . RCALP 6087
RCA / Oct '83.
■ CD . . . . PD 84740
RCA / Apr '84.
LP. . . . . PL 84740
■ MC . . . . PK 84740
RCA / Nov '84.

JOHN DENVER.
Tracks: Downhill stuff / Sweet Melinda / What's on your mind / Joseph and Joe / Life is so good / Berkeley woman / Johnny B. Goode / You're so beautiful / Southwind / Garden song / Songs of..
■ LP. . . . . PL 13075
RCA / Apr '79.

LIVE IN LONDON: JOHN DENVER.
Tracks: Starwood in Aspen / Sunshine on my shoulders / Back home again / Grandma's feather bed / Pickin' the sun down / Thank God I'm a country boy / Eagle and the hawk, The / Spirit / Calypso / Amsterdam / Annie's song / Take me home country roads / Leaving on a jet plane.
LP. . . . . RS 1050
■ MC . . . . PK 11725
RCA / May '76.
■ MC . . . . PK 89225
RCA / '84.
■ LP. . . . . PL 89255
RCA / '85.

LOVE AGAIN (Denver, John & Sylvia Vartan).
Tracks: Love again / It's about time.
■ 7" . . . . RCA 450
RCA / Oct '84.

ONE WORLD.
Tracks: Along for the ride / I can't escape / One world / It's a possibilty / Love is the master / Love again / Let us begin / Flying for me / I remember you / Hey there lonely heart / True love takes time.
■ CD . . . . PD 85811
RCA / '86.
MC . . . . PK 85811
RCA / Aug '86 / BMG.
■ LP. . . . . PL 85811
RCA / Aug '86.

PEACE CAROL (Denver, John & Muppets).
Tracks: Peace carol / We wish you a merry Christmas / Deck the halls.
■ 7" . . . . PB 9463
RCA / Dec '79.

PERHAPS LOVE (see under Domingo, Placido).

POEMS, PRAYERS AND PROMISES.
Tracks: Poems, prayers and promises / Let it be / My sweet lady / Wooden Indian / Junk / Gospel changes / Take me home, country roads / I guess he'd rather be in Colorado / Sunshine on my shoulders / Around and around / Fire and rain / Box, The.
LP. . . . . SF 8219
■ MC . . . . PK 11647
RCA / Jun '73.
MC . . . . NK 85189
RCA / Nov '84 / BMG.
■ LP. . . . . NL 85189
RCA / Nov '84.

RHYMES AND REASONS.
Tracks: Love of the common people / Catch another butterfly / Daydream / Ballad of Spiro Agnew / Circus / When I'm sixty-four / Ballad of Richard Nixon, The / Rhymes and reasons / Yellow cat / Leaving on a jet plane / My heart / My old man / I wish I knew how it would feel to be free / Today is the first day of the rest of my life.
LP. . . . . SF 8348
■ MC . . . . PK 11658
RCA / Jun '73.

ROCKY MOUNTAIN CHRISTMAS.
Tracks: Aspenglow / Christmas song, The / Rudolph the red nosed reindeer / Silver bells / Please, daddy don't get drunk this Christmas / Christmas for cowboys / Away in a manger / What child is this? / Coventry carol / Oh holy night / Silent night, holy night / Baby just like you, A.
LP. APL1 1201
■ MC . . . . PK 11696
RCA / '79.

ROCKY MOUNTAIN HIGH.
Tracks: Rocky mountain high / Mother nature's son / Paradise / For baby (for Bobbie) / Darcy Farrow / Prisoners / Goodbye again / Season suite.
LP. . . . . SF 8308
■ MC . . . . PK 11649
RCA / '79.
■ LP. . . . . NL 85190
RCA / Nov '84.
■ MC . . . . NK 85190
RCA / Nov '84.
■ CD . . . . ND 85190
RCA / Oct '88.

SEASONS OF THE HEART.
Tracks: Seasons of the heart / Opposite tables / Relatively speaking / Dreams / Nothing but a breeze / What one man can do / Shanghai breezes / Islands / Heart to heart / Perhaps love / Children of the Universe.
■ LP. . . . . RCALP 6032
RCA / Sep '82.

D 6 ■ DELETED

CD . . . . PD 84256
LP . . . . PL 84256
■ MC . . . . PK 84256
RCA / '84.

SHANGHAI BREEZES.
Tracks: Shanghai breezes / What one man can do.
■ 7" .RCA 218
RCA / Nov '82.

SOME DAYS ARE DIAMONDS.
Tracks: Some days are diamonds / Gravel on the ground / San Francisco Mabel Joy / Sleepin' alone / Easy on Easy Street / Cowboy and the lady, The / Country love / Till you opened my eyes / Wild flowers in a mason jar / Boy from the country.
■ LP . . . . RCALP 5034
RCA / Aug '81.
LP . . . . PL 84055
■ MC . . . . PK 84055
RCA / '84.

SPIRIT.
Tracks: Come and let me look in your eyes / Eli's song / Wrangle mountain song / Hitchhiker / In the grand way / Polka dots and moonbeams / It makes me giggle / Baby you look good to me tonight / Like a sad song / San Antonio rose / Pegasus / Wings that fly us home.
LP APL1 1694
■ MC . . . . PK 11731
RCA / Sep '76.
MC . . . . NK 85194
RCA / Nov '84 / BMG.
■ LP . . . . NL 85194
RCA / Nov '84.

SWEET SURRENDER.
Tracks: Sweet surrender / Summer.
■ 7" . . . . RCA 2509
RCA / Jan '75.

TAKE ME TO TOMORROW.
Tracks: Take me to tomorrow / Isabel / Follow me / Forest lawn / Aspenglow / Amsterdam / Anthem - revelation / Sticky summer weather / Carolina on my mind / Jimmy Newman / Molly.
■ LP . . . . SF 8354
RCA / '79.

WELCOME TO MY MORNING.
Tracks: Welcome to my morning / This old guitar.
■ 7" . . . . PB 9046
RCA / Mar '77.

WHOSE GARDEN WAS THIS?.
Tracks: Tremble if you must / Sail away home / Night they drove old Dixie down, The / Mr. Bojangles / I wish I could have been there (Woodstock) / Whose garden was this / Game is over, The / Eleanor Rigby / Old folks / Jingle bells.
■ LP . . . . SF 8355
RCA / '79.

WINDSONG.
Tracks: Windsong / Cowboy's delight / Spirit / Looking for space / Shipmates and Cheyenne / Late nite radio / Love is everywhere / Two shots / I'm sorry / Fly away / Calypso / Song of Wyoming / Amor Jibaro / First of May / Windmills of your mind / By the time I get to Phoenix / Miss Otis regrets / Little red rooster / She's a woman / Lady Madonna / Rain / Hey Jude.
LP APL1 1183
■ MC . . . . PK 11693
RCA / Oct '75.
■ LP . . . . NL 85191
RCA / Nov '84.
■ MC . . . . NK 85191
RCA / Nov '84.
■ CD . . . . ND 85191
RCA / Jun '88.

Denver, Karl

This British singer and guitarist enjoyed four UK Top 10 hits in a twelve-month period during 1961-2. Denver's name was consistently in the Top 40 until 1964, but the hits became smaller as the Beatles revolution got underway. His style was pseudo-country and western, at a time when British record buyers were largely unaware of authentic country music and the Dylan-led folk boom had not yet exploded into the charts. On many of his singles, Denver yodelled away in the manner of Slim Whitman. Denver's first two Top Tenners were *Marcheta* and *Mexicali Rose* - both were ballads and both hit No 8. Then came his biggest success, which was the only one which was slightly out of keeping with his usual formula. *Wimoweh* was a Zulu chant that had first been popularised in the American Top 20 in 1952 by Pete Seeger's group, the Weavers. The Tokens took the song to the US No 1 slot at Christmas 1961 under the title *The Lion Sleeps Tonight*, which inspired Denver to rapidly record his own version; he reached No 4 on the UK chart, while the Tokens peaked at No 11. The evergreen song was a US smash in 1972 for Robert John, and a UK No 1 in '82 for Tight Fit. Denver followed his rendition with a fourth and final Top 10 single *Never Goodbye*. Subsequent singles included two more UK Top 20 hits - *A Little Love A Little Kiss* and a rendition of Bill Anderson's American hit *Still* - plus a No 32 version of *Indian Love Call*,

the singer's most unashamed bow to Slim Whitman. Denver's final chart single *Love Me With All Your Heart* peaked at No 37 in the summer of '64. He should also be given credit for a big selling EP with 1962's *By A Sleepy Lagoon* plus a long run on the LP charts in the same year with his debut album, *Wimoweh* (Bob MacDonald)

BLUE WEEKEND.
Tracks: Blue weekend.
■ 7" . . . . F 11505
Decca / Sep '62.

CAN YOU FORGIVE ME.
Tracks: Can you forgive me.
■ 7" . . . . F 11608
Decca / Mar '63.

GREATEST HITS: KARL DENVER.
Tracks: Not Advised.
MC .ASK 776
Autograph / Apr '85.

INDIAN LOVE CALL.
Tracks: Indian love call.
■ 7" . . . . F 11674
Decca / Jun '63.

JUST LOVING YOU.
Tracks: From a Jack to a King / Garden party / I can't stop loving you / San Fernando / King of the road / Just loving you / Song for Maria / Walk on by / Won't give up / Runaway / Voices of the Highlands / Little bitty tear / Travelling light / Answer to everything, The / Story of my life.
CD . . . . PZA 004CD
MC . . . . PZA 004MC
Plaza / Oct '93 / Pinnacle.

LITTLE LOVE A LITTLE KISS, A.
Tracks: Little love, a little kiss, A.
■ 7" . . . . F 11470
Decca / Jun '62.

LOVE ME WITH ALL YOUR HEART.
Tracks: Love me with all your heart.
■ 7" . . . . F 11905
Decca / Jun '64.

MARCHETA.
Tracks: Marcheta.
■ 7" . . . . F 11360
Decca / Jun '61.

MEXICALI ROSE.
Tracks: Mexicali rose.
■ 7" . . . . F 11395
Decca / Oct '61.

MY WORLD OF BLUE.
Tracks: My world of blue.
■ 7" . . . . F 11828
Decca / Mar '64.

NEVER GOODBYE.
Tracks: Never goodbye.
■ 7" . . . . F 11431
Decca / Feb '62.

NEVER GOODBYE - HIS VERY BEST.
Tracks: Wimoweh / Still / Marcheta / Toodle-um-day / 8 x 10 / If I had my way / Blue weekend / I can't help it / Mexicali rose / Love me with all of your heart / Can you forgive me / Indian lovecall / My world of blue / O'brian the brave engineer / My mother's eyes / Never goodbye.
LP . . . . PWKM 4096P
MC . . . . PWKMC 4096P
Pickwick / Feb '92 / Pickwick Records.

STILL.
Tracks: Still.
■ 7" . . . . F 11720
Decca / Aug '63.

VERY BEST OF KARL DENVER.
Tracks: Not Advised.
■ LP . . . . TAB 90
Decca / Feb '86.

VOICES OF THE HIGHLANDS.
Tracks: Voices of the highlands / Kaya.
12" . . . . PZA 064T
7" . . . . PZA 064
Plaza / Nov '90 / Pinnacle.

WIMOWEH.
Tracks: Not Advised.
■ LP . . . . ACL 1098
Ace Of Clubs / Nov '61.

WIMOWEH.
Tracks: Wimoweh / Gypsy Davey.
■ 7" . . . . F 11420
Decca / '82.

WIMOWEH (OLD GOLD).
Tracks: Wimoweh / Never goodbye.
7" .OG 9535
Old Gold / '85 / Pickwick Records.

WON'T GIVE UP.
Tracks: Won't give up / Just loving you / Answer to everything, The / San Fernando.

CD Single . . . . PZA 074CD
Plaza / Sep '93 / Pinnacle.

Derek, John

HEY DUKE (Derek, John's Country Fever).
Tracks: Hey Duke / Gee ain't it funny.
■ 7" . . . . AMGO 005
Amigo / Jan '81.

WITH A LITTLE HELP FROM MY FRIENDS.
Tracks: Not Advised.
LP . . . . WRS 098
Westwood / Nov '76 / Pinnacle.

Derksen, Arnie

MY DANCIN' SHOES.
Tracks: Crazy me / Blue streets / Let the whole world know / She wanna rock / I'd like to be alone / My dancin' shoes / K4WO / Party was over, The / There stands the glass / I'm with you.
LP . . . . BF 15362
Bear Family / Apr '89 / Rollercoaster Records / Swift / Direct Distribution.

Derry, Pat

FISTFUL OF COUNTRY.
Tracks: Kentucky in the morning / Is anybody going to San Antone? / Crystal chandeliers / Kiss an angel good morning / Some broken hearts never mend / Hello blues and down the road I go / Turn out the lights (love me tonight) / Take these chains from my heart / You win again / Wedding bells / I still miss someone / I'm gonna be a country boy again / Blizzard / I dreamed about mama last night / Sing me back home / Today I started loving you again / Swinging doors / Welcome to my world / Have I told you lately that I love you / I won't forget you / This world is not my home / Beautiful life / Me & Jesus / There goes my everything / Wanted man / I got stripes / San Quentin.
LP . . . . PHL 430
MC . . . . CPHL 430
Homespun (Ireland) / '82 / Homespun Records / Ross Records / Wellard Dist.

GHOST RIDERS IN THE SKY.
Tracks: Frankie and Johnny / Little box of pine in the 7:29, The / Life to go / Sunday morning coming down / Alamo, The / Silver target / Old dogs, children and watermelon wine / Drunkards child / Country hall of fame / Precious memories / Ghost riders in the sky / Don't step on mother's roses.
LP . . . . PHL 458
MC . . . . CPHL 458
Homespun (Ireland) / May '83 / Homespun Records / Ross Records / Wellard Dist.

Devine, Mike

AFTER ALL THESE YEARS.
Tracks: Cramen / Maggie / Rose of ol' Pawnee / Country hall of fame / Funny face / Can I say it's new / Down river road / Massacre of Glencoe / Older than the violin, The / She taught me how to yodel.
MC . . . . .HHC 001
Hairy Haggis / Aug '88 / Ross Records.

PART OF ME, A.
Tracks: Long stemmed Rosie / Rocky top / Bonnie Shetland Isle / In the middle of nowhere / Baby is gone / Send me the pillow / Part of me, A / Never been this far before / Filipino rose / They wont' let you rock n roll at the Palamino / I'm a lonesome figure / Born for loving you / Wedding bells / My bonnie Maureen / Follow me / Wings of a dove.
LP . . . . WGR 012
Ross (1) / Sep '81 / Ross Records / Duncans / Entertainment UK.
MC . . . . CWGR 012
Ross (1) / Oct '92 / Ross Records / Duncans / Entertainment UK.

Devine, Sydney

This British singer, born in Cleland, near Glasgow, entered showbusiness in 1955. He spent the next twenty years building a reputation, primarily in Scotland, as a live performer. Initially a rock 'n' roll imitator, Devine later made country and western his primary style. He did not begin his recording career until the mid-Seventies, and it was this move that substantially increased his following, after two decades in the second division he cracked the UK National charts in 1976 with *Doubly Devine*, which reached No 14 on the LP listings. Later that year, *Devine Time* entered the chart but peaked at No 49. Further album chart success was not forthcoming, but *Doubly Devine* had done its job - the LP had won Devine major concert bookings and, during the late Seventies and Eighties, he was able to make a good living from his predictable but competently executed repertoire. This included country and MOR standards such as *I Can't Stop Loving You* and *Lovesick Blues*, combined with less well known numbers such as *Favourite Memory Of Mine* and *Room Full Of Roses*. He continues to appeal to a mainly female audience, and women sometimes occupy 90% of the seats at his shows. Outside Scotland, the singer's popularity strongholds are East Anglia, Liverpool and Newcastle. Devine's only UK chart single occurred in April 1978. *Scotland Forever* was released to capitalise on the fervour surrounding the Scottish football squad's participation in the World Cup. Unfortunately for Devine, another artist had the same idea - in the week that *Scotland Forever* peaked at No 48, Andy Cameron reached No 6 with the enthusiastically amateurish *Ally's Tartan Army*. *Scotland Forever* was re-issued in time for the 1982 World Cup. (Bob MacDonald).

25TH ANNIVERSARY ALBUM: SYDNEY DEVINE.
Tracks: Three steps to heaven / Love is just a game / Crazy / Let me be there / It's too soon to know / She's my woman / Crystal chandeliers / My friend / Blanket on the ground / I don't wanna cry / I'm afraid to go back home / I really don't want to know / There goes my everything / Don't forget to remember / I believe.
LP . . . . **.6382 152**
MC . . . . **.7252 707**
Philips / Apr '80 / PolyGram.

50 COUNTRY WINNERS.
Tracks: Country roads / Early morning rain / Gentle on my mind / Hello Mary Lou / Oh lonesome me / Sea of heartbreak / Lonesome number one / Blue, blue day / Four walls / He'll have to go / You're free to go / Sweet dreams / Send me the pillow that you dream on / Satin sheets / Wild side of life / This song is just for you / Blackboard of my heart / Married by the Bible / Crying time / Together again / I can't stop loving you / Take these chains from my heart / Dear God / Where could I go but to the Lord / House of gold / You'll never walk alone / Blanket on the ground / Old flames / Blowing in the wind / Sing me / Tiny bubbles / Early shells / Stand beside me / Gypsy woman / You're my best friend / 'Till the rivers all run dry / Please help me, I'm falling / Fraulein / I fall to pieces / It keeps right on a-hurtin' / Eighteen yellow roses / Ramblin' rose / Red roses for a blue lady / Irene / Lucille / Amanda / Lovesick blues / Singing the blues / Knee deep in the blues / Long gone lonesome blues.
CD Set . . . . **PLATCD 18**
Double LP . . . . **.PLAT 18**
MC Set . . . . **.PLAC 18**
Platinum Music / Oct '87 / Prism Leisure PLC / Ross Records.

ALMOST PERSUADED.
Tracks: Almost persuaded / Do you remember / Funny way of laughing / Here in my heart / I wonder if I ever said goodbye / It's only make-believe / Last thing on my mind, The / Lay down beside me / Lucille / She called me baby / Till the rivers all run dry / Together again / Travelling light / With one exception.
LP . . . . **.6308 291**
MC . . . . **.7108 172**
Philips / Sep '78 / PolyGram.

ALWAYS AND FOREVER.
Tracks: Molly darling / Distant drums / Daisy a day / Mockin' Bird Hill / When you were sweet sixteen / There stands the glass / Sweet bunch of daisies / Born to love me / More and more / Let the heartaches begin / Remember you're mine / Always on your mind words / What do you want to make those eyes.. / Anytime (You're feeling lonely).
LP . . . . **ITV 430**
MC . . . . **KITV 430**
Scotdisc / Dec '87 / Duncans / Ross Records / Target Records / Conifer Records.

BY REQUEST.
Tracks: Pearly shells / Mansion on the hill / Some days are diamonds / If I were a blackbird / We're gonna go fishin' / Hawaiian wedding song / Heartaches by the number / Release me / Bigger leirinmore / You win again / Flyin' South.
LP . . . . **BGC 352**
MC . . . . **.KBGC 352**
Country House / Dec '83 / Duncans / BGS Productions Ltd.

COUNTRY.
Tracks: Lovesick blues / I can't stop loving you / Fraulein / Blackboard of my heart / Bye bye, love / It keeps right on a-hurtin' / May the bird of paradise fly up your nose / Help me make it through the night / Donna / She wears my ring / You're sixteen / You'll never miss a woman.
LP . . . . **GES 1093**
MC . . . . **KGEC 1093**
Emerald / '87 / I & B Records.

CRYING TIME.
Tracks: Crying time / Broken engagement / My son calls another man daddy / Long black limousine / Two little orphans / Eighteen yellow roses / Old Shep / Letter edged in black / Nobody's child / I ain't crying, mister / Gentle mother / Come home, rolling stone.
LP . . . . **GES 1111**
MC . . . . **KGEC 1111**
Emerald / Oct '81 / I & B Records.
MC . . . . **4 HOM 007**
Homeland / Mar '88 / Midland Records / Music Collection International.
CD . . . . **2 HOM 007**
Homeland / Sep '88 / Midland Records / Music Collection International.

DAISY A DAY.
Tracks: Daisy a day / Molly darling.
7" . . . . **ITV 7S 441**
Scotdisc / Sep '87 / Duncans / Ross Records / Target Records / Conifer Records.

DEVINE TIME.
Tracks: After sweet memories / Bonny Mary / Come on home / Dream lover / Grand tour, A / Green, green grass of home / Half as much / Happy whistler, The / Hello Mary Lou / High noon / I recall a gypsy woman / Just out of reach / Last kiss, The / Rags to riches / Roses are red / We will make love.
MC . . . . **.7299 405**
Philips / Nov '76 / PolyGram.
■ **LP** . . . . **.6308 283**
Philips / Nov '76.

DOUBLE DEVINE.
Tracks: Answer to everything, The / Are you lonesome tonight / Be careful of stones that you throw / Break my mind / Butterfly / Fabulous / Five little fingers / Goodnight Irene / Honey come back / I don't wanna play house / I fall to pieces / I never loved no-one but you / Knee deep in the blues / Legend in my time / Lightning express, The / Make the world go away / My heart cried for you / Picture of you / Please help me I'm falling / Rockin' alone / Sea of heartbreak / Stand beside me / Stop / Wedding bells.
■ **LP** . . . . **.6625 019**
Philips / Apr '76.

ENCORES.
Tracks: Nobody's child / Singing the blues / Down the trail of aching hearts / Tiny bubbles / Church, a courtroom and then goodbye, A / China doll / Have a drink on me / Mockin' Bird Hill / Am I that easy to forget / Forty shades of green / There's nothing there / Jealous heart / Things / When Mexico gave up the rumba.
LP . . . . **.BER 014**
Emerald / Jan '86 / I & B Records.
MC . . . . **KBER 014**
Emerald / Nov '87 / I & B Records.

FAVOURITE MEMORIES OF MINE.
Tracks: I'm back / Favourite memory of mine / Till the rivers all run dry / With one exception / Long black veil / Love me tender / Last kiss, The / Pretty woman / Merry-go-round world / Travelling light / Almost persuaded / She called.
LP . . . . **BGC 336**
MC . . . . **.KBGC 336**
Country House / Sep '83 / Duncans / BGS Productions Ltd.

FAVOURITE MEMORY OF MINE.
Tracks: Almost persuaded / Favourite memory of mine.
7" . . . . **.BGC 7S 356**
Country House / Dec '83 / Duncans / BGS Productions Ltd.

FROM SCOTLAND WITH LOVE.
Tracks: Scotland we love you / Silver threads / Mother I love you / Careless love / Suvla bay / My ain folk / Maggie / Old rustic bridge / Scotty boy / Wild mountain thyme / Born again / Red red rose / From Scotland with love / Scotland for me.
LP . . . . **ITV 373**
MC . . . . **KITV 373**
Scotdisc / Sep '84 / Duncans / Ross Records / Target Records / Conifer Records.

GREATEST HITS: SYDNEY DEVINE.
Tracks: Lovesick blues / Send me the pillow that you dream on / Rose Marie / Two little orphans / May the bird of paradise fly up your nose / Take these chains from my heart / Crying time / It keeps right on a-hurtin' / Corina Corina / Room full of roses / Ain't that a shame / Blueberry Hill / I ain't crying, mister.
LP . . . . **GES 1183**
MC . . . . **KGEC 1183**
Emerald / Oct '81 / I & B Records.

GREEN GRASS OF HOME, THE.
Tracks: Not Advised.
CD . . . . **.CDITV 530**
MC . . . . **KITV 530**
Scotdisc / Dec '90 / Duncans / Ross Records / Target Records / Conifer Records.

HEARTACHES.
Tracks: Hurt / He'll have to go / Dear John / I can't help it / I'd rather die young / Teddy Bear / You're free to go / When I leave the world behind / Oh lonesome me / Party's over / She's not you / Guilty one / Free to be lonely again / Blue eyes crying in the rain / Nothing in the world's too good for you / I'm here to get my baby out of jail.
MC . . . . **.7150 051**
Philips / Feb '81 / PolyGram.
■ **LP** . . . . **.6359 051**
Philips / Mar '81.

HOW GREAT THOU ART.
Tracks: How great Thou art.
7" . . . . **IMP EP 2**
Time / Mar '82 / Jetstar / Pinnacle.

LIKE STRANGERS.
Tracks: Like strangers.
■ **7"** . . . . **CHEW 71**
Mint / Oct '82.

LIVE FROM THE CITY HALL, GLASGOW.
Tracks: Wolverton Mountain / Send me the pillow that you dream on / My truly, truly fair / Song sung blue / Room full of roses / When you and I were young, Maggie.
■ **LP** . . . . **SHM 958**
Hallmark / Apr '78.

MY WORLD OF MUSIC.
Tracks: Bed of roses / Bluest heartache of the year / Burning bridges / Dreaming / Can't help falling in love / That's all right / Wonder of you / Favourite memory of mine / Forget me not / Here in love / Hickory Holler's tramp / It's a sin to tell a lie / John B / Long black veil / Love letters / Lucy, ain't your loser looking good / Me and Bobby McGee / My world is filled with music / Other people's sad songs / Save the last dance for me / Spanish / Till you can make it on your own / Tips of my fingers / Valentine partner / What made Milwaukee famous / You needed me / You're my world.
■ **Double LP** **6641930**
Philips / '79.

PEARLY SHELLS.
Tracks: Pearly shells.
7" . . . . **.BGC 7S 360**
Country House / Nov '83 / Duncans / BGS Productions Ltd.

PRIDE OF BONNY SCOTLAND.
Tracks: Pride of bonny Scotland / John B.
■ **7"** . . . . **SCOT 2**
Philips / Nov '78.

SCOTLAND FOREVER.
Tracks: Scotland forever.
■ **7"** . . . . **SCOT 1**
Philips / Apr '78.
7" . . . . **IMP EP 1**
Time / Mar '82 / Jetstar / Pinnacle.

SCOTLAND WE LOVE YOU.
Tracks: Scotland we love you.
7" . . . . **ITV 7S 378**
Scotdisc / Sep '84 / Duncans / Ross Records / Target Records / Conifer Records.

SYD'S SING-SONG COUNTRY ALBUM.
Tracks: Country roads / Early morning rain / Gentle on my mind / Hello Mary Lou / Gypsy woman / You're my best friend / 'Till the rivers all run dry / Four walls / He'll have to go / You're free to go / Tiny bubbles / Pearly shells / Stand beside me / Sweet dreams / Send me the pillow that you dream on / Satin sheets / Eighteen yellow roses / Room full of roses / Ramblin' rose / Red roses for a blue lady / Dear God / Where could I go but to the Lord / House of gold / You'll never walk alone / Oh lonesome me / Sea of heartbreak / Lonesome / Blue blue day / Blanket on the ground / Old flames / Blowing in the wind / Sing me / Irene / Lucille / Amanda / Please help me, I'm falling / Fraulein / I fall to pieces / It keeps right on a-hurtin' / Lovesick blues / Singing the blues / Knee deep in the blues / Long gone lonesome blues / Wild side of life / This song is just for you / Blackboard of my heart / Married by the Bible / Crying time / Together again / I can't stop loving you / Take these chains from my heart.
LP . . . . **BGC 398**
MC . . . . **.KBGC 398**
Country House / Dec '86 / Duncans / BGS Productions Ltd.

SYDNEY DEVINE COLLECTION, THE.
Tracks: Love is a good thing / Tear fell / Ain't that a shame / Blueberry Hill / Corrine Corrina / Spread it around / No one will ever know / Laura / Take these chains from my heart / Kelly / Rose Marie / From a jack to a king / Walk on by / Wolverton Mountain / Woman sensuous woman / Send me the pillow you dream on / Road to Dundee / My truly truly fair / Only you / Married man blues / Song sung blue / Railroad burn / Teddy bear / All shook up / Room full of roses / When you and I were young Maggie blues / One night / It's now or never / Everything is beautiful.
Double LP . . . . **.PDA 060**
Pickwick / Jul '79 / Pickwick Records.
MC Set . . . . **.PDC 060**
Pickwick / Jul '80 / Pickwick Records.

SYDNEY DEVINE COUNTRY VOL.1.
Tracks: Not Advised.
VHS . . . . **VITV 524**
Scotdisc / Dec '90 / Duncans / Ross Records / Target Records / Conifer Records.

SYDNEY DEVINE SINGS YOUR FAVOURITE COUNTRY SONGS.
Tracks: This song is just for you / Ten guitars / Tennessee waltz / Only the heartaches / Married by the Bible, divorced by the law / Do what you do do well / Wild side of life / Act naturally / When you and I were young Maggie / Your cheatin' heart / I love you because / Little arrows.
MC . . . . **.KBER 012**
Emerald / Aug '85 / I & B Records.
LP . . . . **.BER 012**
Emerald / May '85 / I & B Records.

SYDNEY DEVINE'S SING-SONG COUNTRY.
Tracks: Sydney Devine's sing-song country.
7" . . . . **.GBH 7S 406**
August (USA) / Nov '85.

D 8

■ DELETED

TAKE MY HAND, PRECIOUS LORD.
Tracks: Old rugged cross, The / Peace in the valley / Midnight special (I'd like to see Jesus) / What a friend we have in Jesus / Only believe / Take my hand, precious Lord / Precious memories / We call on Him / Family Bible / It is no secret / Who am I? / Only if you praise the Lord.
LP . . . . **GES 1220**
Emerald / May '82 / I & B Records.
MC . . . . **KGEC 1220**
Emerald / Nov '87 / I & B Records.

VERY BEST OF SYDNEY DEVINE.
Tracks: I can't stop loving you / Laura / Road to Dundee, The / Fraulein / My son calls another man daddy / From a jack to a king / Eighteen yellow roses / She wears my ring / Nobody's child / My truly, truly fair / Kelly / When you and I were young, Maggie.
LP . . . . **GES 1142**
Emerald / Oct '81 / I & B Records.
MC . . . . **KGEC 1142**
Emerald / Nov '87 / I & B Records.

WAY UP IN CLACHLAN.
Tracks: Way up in Clachlan / Moxicali Rose.
7" **ITV7 S531**
Scotdisc / Nov '90 / Duncans / Ross Records / Target Records / Conifer Records.

Dexter, Al

Coming to prominence in the latter stages of World War II, Texas born Dexter (1902-84: real name Albert Poindexter) achieved overnight success with *Pistol packin' Man* on Okeh Records in 1944. His other No. 1's include *Rosalita* and *Too late to worry, too blue to cry* , and he spent the later stages of his life running a club in Dallas. (Tony Byworth)

SINGS AND PLAYS HIS GREATEST HITS.
Tracks: Not Advised.
LP . . . . **HAT 3101**
MC . . . . **HATC 3101**
Stetson / Mar '89 / Crusader Marketing Co. / Swift / Wellard Dist. / Midland Records / C.M. Distribution.

Dexter, Ray

SOUND SHOW.
Tracks: Not Advised.
LP . . . . **SFA 042**
Sweet Folk All / Nov '76 / Cadillac Music / Projection / C.M. Distribution / Wellard Dist. / Impetus Records.

UP COUNTRY.
Tracks: Not Advised.
MC . . . . **AM 6**
AIM (2) / Feb '83 / Topic Records / Direct Distribution.

Dey, Charley

COUNTRY DAYS.
Tracks: Daddy Frank / Gypsy woman / Country boy / When the roses bloom again / Crystal chandeliers / Queen of the silver dollar / Coat of many colours / Country roads / Anna Marie / You're my best friend / We sure danced / Kelly.
MC . . . . **CWGR 001**
Ross (1) / Oct '91 / Ross Records / Duncans / Entertainment UK.

TIME ON MY HANDS.
Tracks: Bed of roses / Saginaw Michigan / Green fields of France.
MC . . . . **CWGR 090**
Ross (1) / May '86 / Ross Records / Duncans / Entertainment UK.

Diamond Brothers

SILVER MEDALS AND SWEET MEMORIES.
Tracks: Some I wrote / Movies / Silver medals and sweet memories / Bed of roses / Do you remember these / Flowers on the wall / Class of '57, The / I'll go to my grave loving you / Susan when she tried / Whatever happened to Randolph Scott?.
■ **LP** . . . . **GES 5018**
Emerald / Dec '79.

Diamond Rio

Formerly known as the Tennessee River Boys, Diamond Rio, fronted by lead vocalist/songwriter Marty Roe were to make history in 1991, when they became the first ever group to make No. 1 with its debut single. Since which time the Marty Roe (lead vocals/guitarist - nephew of the Osbourne Brothers) led six-piece outfit have built on the success of *Meet in the middle* , with hit singles *Mirror mirror* , *Mama don't forget to pray for me* , *Norma Jean Riley* (No. 2), *Nowhere bound* and *Oh me, oh my, sweet baby* being spawned from the top selling albums *Diamond Rio* and *Close to the edge* . They were voted Top Vocal Group in 1992, by both the ACM and CMA. (Maurice Hope)

CLOSE TO THE EDGE.
Tracks: Oh me, oh my, sweet baby / In a week or two / It does get better than this / Sawmill road / Calling all hearts (Come back home) / This Romeo ain't got Julie yet / I was meant to be with you / Old weakness (Coming on strong) / Demons and angels / Nothing in this world / Close to the edge.
CD **7822 18656-2**
Arista / Oct '93 / BMG.

Dickens, Hazel

BY THE SWEAT OF MY BROW.
Tracks: Beyond the river bend / Only the lonely / By the sweat of my brow / Scars from an old love / Old and in the way / Ballad of Ira Hayes, The / Go away with me / Mama's hands / Your greedy heart / Little Lenaldo / Here today and gone tomorrow.
LP . . . . **ROUNDER 0200**
MC . . . . **ROUNDER 0200C**
Rounder / '88 / Projection / Roots Records / Swift / C.M. Distribution / Topic Records / Jazz Music / Hot Shot / A.D.A Distribution / Direct Distribution.

FEW OLD MEMORIES, A.
Tracks: Not Advised.
CD . . . . **CD 11529**
Rounder / '88 / Projection / Roots Records / Swift / C.M. Distribution / Topic Records / Jazz Music / Hot Shot / A.D.A Distribution / Direct Distribution.

HARD HITTING SONGS FOR HARD HITTING PEOPLE.
Tracks: Busted / Aragon mill / Old calloused hands / Scraps from your table / Out among the stars / Tomorrow's already lost / Lonesome pine special / Lost patterns / Beautiful hills of Galilee / Rocking chair blues / They'll never keep us down.
LP . . . . **ROUNDER 0126**
MC . . . . **ROUNDER 0126C**
Rounder / '88 / Projection / Roots Records / Swift / C.M. Distribution / Topic Records / Jazz Music / Hot Shot / A.D.A Distribution / Direct Distribution.

HAZEL & ALICE (see under Dickens, Hazel).

HAZEL DICKENS AND ALICE GERRARD (Dickens, Hazel & Alice Gerrard).
Tracks: When I loved you / Working girl blues / Mama's gonna stay / Montana cowboy / Mean papa blues / Nice like that / Mary Johnson / Ramblin' woman / Beaufort county jail / Banjo pickin' girl / James Alley blues / True life blues.
LP . . . . **ROUNDER 0027**
MC . . . . **ROUNDER 0027C**
LP . . . . **ROUNDER 0054**
MC . . . . **ROUNDER 0054C**
Rounder / '88 / Projection / Roots Records / Swift / C.M. Distribution / Topic Records / Jazz Music / Hot Shot / A.D.A Distribution / Direct Distribution.

IT'S HARD TO TELL THE SINGER FROM THE SONG.
Tracks: Not Advised.
LP . . . . **ROUNDER 0226**
MC . . . . **ROUNDER 0226C**
Rounder / Aug '88 / Projection / Roots Records / Swift / C.M. Distribution / Topic Records / Jazz Music / Hot Shot / A.D.A Distribution / Direct Distribution.

Dickens, Little Jimmy

Born 19/12/1925, Bolt, West Virginia. Known as "Tater", this country music stalwart still works the Grand Old Opry, including much wit into his act. His biggest hit came with *May The Bird Of Paradise Fly Up Your Nose* (1965), others include his 1949 debut success *Take An Old Cold Tater (and wait)*, *Hillbilly Fever*, *Out Beyond The Barn* and *Sleeping At The Foot Of The Bed*. They were all released on Columbia for whom he recorded until 1967, followed by spells with Decca and United Artists. Member of Grand Ole Opry since 1948, elected to the Country Hall of Fame in 1982. Since his early beginnings as "Jimmy The Kid" back in the forties. Dickens has possibly clocked up more miles than any country act. Rounder recently released some of his Columbia sessions taken from the mid-fifties. (Maurice Hope)

BEST OF THE BEST OF JIMMY DICKENS.
Tracks: Not Advised.
LP . . . . **GT 0041**
Gusto (USA) / Mar '88.

I GOT A HOLE IN MY POCKET.
Tracks: Not Advised.
LP . . . . **REV 3007**
Revival / Aug '88 / EMI.

STRAIGHT FROM THE HEART (1949-1955).
Tracks: Sea of broken dreams / Wedding bell waltz / I've just got to see you once more / Rose from a bride's bouquet / Be careful of stones that you throw / That little old country church house / Teardrops (fell like teardrops) / Out of business / My heart's bouquet / Lovin' lies / Ribbon and a rose, A / Bring your broken heart to me.
LP . . . . **SS 26**
MC . . . . **SSC 26**
Rounder / '89 / Projection / Roots Records / Swift / C.M. Distribution / Topic Records / Jazz Music / Hot Shot / A.D.A Distribution / Direct Distribution.

Dillard & Clark

AIN'T IT GOOD TO BE FREE?.
Tracks: Ain't it good to be free / Bo Diddley put the rock in rock 'n' roll.
7" . . . . **NEW 42**
New Rose (1) / Aug '84 / Pinnacle.

FANTASTIC EXPEDITION OF DILLARD & CLARK.
Tracks: Out on the side / She darked the sun / Don't come rollin' / Train leaves here this morning / Radio song, The / Git it on brother (git in line brother) / In the plan / Something's wrong / Why not your baby / Lyin' down the middle / Don't be cruel.
LP . . . . **ED 192**
Edsel / '86 / Pinnacle.
CD . . . . **EDCD 192**
Edsel / Jun '90 / Pinnacle.

THROUGH THE MORNING, THROUGH THE NIGHT.
Tracks: No longer a sweetheart of mine / Through the morning, through the night / Rocky top / So sad / Corner street bar / I bowed my head and cried holy / Kansas City Southern / Four walls / Polly / Roll in my sweet baby's arms / Don't let me down.
LP . . . . **ED 195**
Edsel / Jul '86 / Pinnacle.
CD . . . . **EDCD 195**
Edsel / Feb '91 / Pinnacle.

Dillard, Doug

HEARTBREAK HOTEL (Dillard, Doug Band).
Tracks: Not Advised.
LP . . . . **FF 477**
Flying Fish (USA) / Jul '89 / Cadillac Music / Roots Records / Projection / C.M. Distribution / Direct Distribution / Jazz Music / Duncans / A.D.A Distribution.

HEAVEN.
Tracks: Stars in my crown / Lord's last supper, The / Heaven / Cast your bread upon the water / Let the light shine down on me / Daniel prayed / Turn your radio / God's record book of life / St.Peter / Singin' all day.
LP . . . . **FF 086**
Flying Fish (USA) / Mar '89 / Cadillac Music / Roots Records / Projection / C.M. Distribution / Direct Distribution / Jazz Music / Duncans / A.D.A Distribution.

JACK RABBIT.
Tracks: Hamilton country breakdown / Salty dog blues / Teardrops in my eyes / Ocean of diamonds / Byron's barn / Rolling in my sweet baby's arms / I'll just stay around / Jack Rabbit / Last old shovel / Hickory holler.
LP . . . . **SDLP 018**
Sundown / Mar '86 / Terry Blood Dist. / Jazz Music / C.M. Distribution.
LP . . . . **FF 208**
Flying Fish (USA) / Mar '89 / Cadillac Music / Roots Records / Projection / C.M. Distribution / Direct Distribution / Jazz Music / Duncans / A.D.A Distribution.

WHAT'S THAT?.
Tracks: Not Advised.
LP . . . . **FF 377**
Flying Fish (USA) / Dec '88 / Cadillac Music / Roots Records / Projection / C.M. Distribution / Direct Distribution / Jazz Music / Duncans / A.D.A Distribution.

Dillard, Rodney

LET THE ROUGH SIDE DRAG.
Tracks: Not Advised.
CD . . . . **FF 537CD**
MC . . . . **FF 537C**
Flying Fish (USA) / Jul '92 / Cadillac Music / Roots Records / Projection / C.M. Distribution / Direct Distribution / Jazz Music / Duncans / A.D.A Distribution.

SILVER DOLLAR CITY.
Tracks: Not Advised.
LP . . . . **FF 369**
Flying Fish (USA) / Apr '86 / Cadillac Music / Roots Records / Projection / C.M. Distribution / Direct Distribution / Jazz Music / Duncans / A.D.A Distribution.

SILVER DOLLAR CITY.
Tracks: Silver dollar city.
12" . . . . **CHS 12501**
Champagne / Jan '86.

Dillard-Hartford-Dillard

DILLARD-HARTFORD-DILLARD.
Tracks: Not Advised.
LP . . . . **SNTF 730**
Sonet / Jul '77 / Swift / C.M. Distribution / Roots Records / Jazz Music / Sonet Records / Cadillac Music / Projection / Wellard Dist. / Hot Shot.

GLITTERGLASS FROM THE NASHWOOD HOLLYVILLE STRING.
Tracks: Don't come rollin' / Cross the border line / Two hits and the joint turned brown / Don't lead me on / Bear creek hop / No end of love / Biggest whatever /

Lost in the world / High Dad in the morning / California is nicer than you / Artificial limitations / Get no better.
LP. . . . . .FF 036
Flying Fish (USA) / Mar '89 / Cadillac Music / Roots Records / Projection / C.M. Distribution / Direct Distribution / Jazz Music / Duncans / A.D.A Distribution.

PERMANENT WAVE.
Tracks: Break it to me gently / That'll be the day / Same thing (makes you laugh, makes you cry) / Yakety yak / Something's wrong / Boogie on reggae woman / Country boy rock'n'roll / No beer in heaven.
LP. . . . . .FF 233
Flying Fish (USA) / Mar '89 / Cadillac Music / Roots Records / Projection / C.M. Distribution / Direct Distribution / Jazz Music / Duncans / A.D.A Distribution.

Dillards

Bluegrass/country-rock musicians Douglas Flint Dillard (born in 1937) and Rodney Adean Dillard (born in 1942) were both born in East St Louis, Illinois but grew up across the river in Salem, Missouri, playing guitar and banjo. They made a single in St Louis that got local airplay and made their first album for Elektra in 1963. They played the dimwitted Darlin family on an Andy Griffith TV show, also showcasing the music; they upset purists with amplifiers at the Newport Folk Festival in 1964 and added drummer Paul York in 1968. Doug left that year, replaced by Herb Pederson, who soon left to form Country Gazette; with personnel changes the group carried on playing festivals and recording, while Doug toured with the Byrds, formed the Dillard and Clark Expedition with Gene Clark, and sessioned, his film soundtrack work, including Bonnie & Clyde; he organised the Doug Dillard Band for several albums on Chicago's Flying Fish label. As interest in folk-roots grew the original band, still led by Rodney, turned up on Flying Fish as well. Both Dillards appeared in *The Rose* in 1979 and in the group Dillard-Hartford-Dillard (with John Hartford from St Louis days on fiddle). Rodney's *At Silver Dollar City* came out in 1986. Flying fingers, fine ballads and comedy never failed; they were sending up Joan Baez before it was Fashionable. (Donald Clarke).

COUNTRY TRACKS.
Tracks: Copperfields / Little Pete / Duelin' banjo / Old home place / Close the door lightly / Doug's tune / Yesterday / Woman turn around / Banjo in the hollow / Brother John / She sang hymns out of tune / I'll fly away / Reason to believe / Lonesome Indian / Hey boys / Nobody knows / Binding the strings / Single saddle / Dooley hickory hollow / I've just seen a face / Ebo walker / Sundown / Rainmaker.
LP. . . . . .K 52035
Elektra / WEA.

DECADE WALTZ.
Tracks: Not Advised.
LP. . . . . .FF 082
Flying Fish (USA) / May '79 / Cadillac Music / Roots Records / Projection / C.M. Distribution / Direct Distribution / Jazz Music / Duncans / A.D.A Distribution.

DILLARDS VS THE INCREDIBLE L.A. TIME MACHINE.
Tracks: Gunman's code / Poet, The / Do, Magnolia, do / Annabelle Lee / Softly / Ding dong howdy / Jayne / In one ear / Old Cane press / Let the music flow.
LP. . . . . .SNTF 743
Sonet / '77 / Swift / C.M. Distribution / Roots Records / Jazz Music / Sonet Records / Cadillac Music / Projection / Wellard Dist. / Hot Shot.
LP. . . . . .FF 040
Flying Fish (USA) / Mar '89 / Cadillac Music / Roots Records / Projection / C.M. Distribution / Direct Distribution / Jazz Music / Duncans / A.D.A Distribution.

HOMECOMING AND FAMILY REUNION.
Tracks: Not Advised.
LP. . . . . .FF 215
Flying Fish (USA) / Mar '89 / Cadillac Music / Roots Records / Projection / C.M. Distribution / Direct Distribution / Jazz Music / Duncans / A.D.A Distribution.

I'LL FLY AWAY.
Tracks: I'll fly away / Nobody knows / Hey boys / Biggest whatever / Single saddle / I've just seen a face / Bending the strings / Pictures / Ebo walker / She sang hymns out of tune / Rainmaker / Old man at the mill / Touch her if you can / Woman turn around / Yesterday / Copperfields / West Montana Hanna / Close the door lightly.
LP. . . . . .ED 246
Edsel / Feb '88 / Pinnacle.

LET IT FLY.
Tracks: Darlin' boys / Close the door lightly / Old train / Big ship / Missing you / Out on a limb / Ozark nights / Tears won't dry in the rain / Livin' in the house / One too many mornings / Let it fly / Wizard of song.
MC . . . . .VHD 79460MC
Vanguard / '91 / Complete Record Co. Ltd.
CD . . . . .VHD 79460
Vanguard / Jul '91 / Complete Record Co. Ltd.

MOUNTAIN ROCK.
Tracks: Caney Creek / Don't you cry / Reason to believe / Big bayou / Walkin' in Jerusalem / I've just seen a face / High sierra / Never see my home again / Somebody touched me / Fields have turned brown, The / Orange blossom special (13 minutes).
CD 8.26534
Teldec (Germany) / Sep '88 / Pinnacle / Swift.
CD 15 295
MC 79 169
Laserlight / Aug '91 / TBD / Taylors.

NIGHT IN THE OZARKS, A.
Tracks: Not Advised.
VHS. . . . . .HEN 2334
Hendring Video / Jun '91 / BMG / Terry Blood Dist.

THERE IS A TIME.
Tracks: Not Advised.
CD . . . . .VCD 13132
Start / Oct '92.

Dillon, Dean

One of country music's new breed of Nashville's hitmakers is also scratching himself a niche as a performer in his own right. Dillon born 26.3.1955 in Lake City, Tennessee has already penned countless hits - his first big break coming soon after moving to Nashville, where he secured a slot on the Opryland's USA theme park. Next came a publishing deal and, in 1979 Jim Ed Brown & Helen Cornelius took *Lyin' in love with you* to number 2 on the country charts. Texan George Strait has especially found Dillon's songwriting most beneficial apart from Dean supplying him with his initial hit *Unwound* in 1981 there's been an amazing string of chart toppers since. Dillon has written *The chair* , *Nobody in her right mind would have left her* , *I ain't cool to be crazy about you* , *Ocean front property* , *Famous last words of a fool* , *I've come to expect it from you* & *If I know me* . He's also penned such good songs as *Tennessee whiskey* (George Jones), *Leave them boys alone* (Hank Williams Jr) & *What's new with you* (Con Hunley). Dillon's own recording career has seen him first on RCA - both solo (batch of singles) & with honky-tonk singer Gary Stewart. Solo hits were to feature top 30 singles *I'm into the bottle (To get you out of my mind)* , *Nobody in his right mind* - whilst with Gary Stewart he enjoyed three chart entries (1982 - 1983), *Brotherly love* the title track of their 1982 album being the highest (No 41). Beset with personal problems during the mid-eighties including a growing drink problem, Dillon's career was put on hold until his short - lived sojourn with Capitol, where he recorded two albums 1988'2 *Slick nickel* , where he made limited chart progress with his own *The new never wore off my baby* & *Hey heart* & a re-make of pop hit *I go to pieces* . Capitol released *I've learned to live again* , whilst it kept him in the market place. Moved to Atlantic records in 1991, debuting for the label with Out of your ever lovin' mind spawning such chart material as *Holed up in some honky tonk* and backed with his 1993 releases *Hot, country and single* the title track giving him a minor hit. (Maurice Hope)

SLICK NICKEL.
Tracks: Hey heart / New never wore off my sweet baby, The / When the feelin's right / I go to pieces / Hard time for lovers / Appalachia got to have you feelin' in my bones / You sure got this ol' redneck feelin' blue / Still got a crush on you / Station to station / Father, Son and Holy Ghost.
CD 748 920 2
LP. C1 48920
LP. 748 920 1
MC 748 920 4
■ MC C4 48920
Capitol / May '89.

Dinning Sisters

DINNING SISTERS-VOL.2.
Tracks: Lolita Lopaz / My adobe hacienda / Do you love me? / I wonder who's kissing her now / Iggedy song, The / Last thing I want is your pity, The / Bride and groom polka, The / I get blue when it rains / Years and years ago / Fun and fancy free / Melancholy / Wave to me my lady / If I had to live my life over / Oh Monah.
■ MC . . . . .TCEMS 1144
Capitol / Jan '86.
■ LP. . . . . .EMS 1144
Capitol / Jan '86.

Dixie & Allen

COTTAGE IN THE COUNTRY.
Tracks: Cottage in the country / Before I'm over.
7" . . . . .SR 001
Snap Shot / Aug '88.

Doherty, Al

SEEING THE COUNTRY.
Tracks: Yonder comes a sucker / Alright / Just someone I used to know / Snowbird / Lorna Faye / You cheated me / Welcome to my world / I'm so afraid of losing you again / Shutters and boards / Wildwood flower / Our hearts belong together / Railroad bum / I was raised on country sunshine.
LP. . . . . .FHR 062
Folk Heritage / Jul '82 / Terry Blood Dist.

Dolan's Acoustic Rangers

ACOUSTIC RANGERS.
Tracks: Nite hawkin' the dawn / Rhythm rider / Lost cargo / Tree moon and tide / So hard to be soft / Borrow love and go / Waters of life / Playin' to win / First kiss, The / Corina, Corina / Wish I was your river.
CD . . . . .SDCD 9.00453
Sawdust / '90.

Don & Annie

QUEEN OF THE SILVER DOLLAR.
Tracks: Not Advised.
MC . . . . .BBM 139
Bibi (Budget Cassettes) / Jan '83.

Donegan, Lonnie

This British singer, guitarist and banjoist, born in Glasgow, was christened Anthony Donegan but adopted the name Lonnie in 1952, in deference to Lonnie Johnson, the noted American blues artist whom he idolised. Donegan began playing the guitar as a 15 year old during the mid-Forties; by this time, his family was based in London. Between 1949 and 1951, he did his National Service in the Army where, during his spare time, he took up banjo and also drums. Soon after discharge, he joined Ken Colyer's Jazz Band; in 1954 the entire combo, including Lonnie, deserted their leader and became the Chris Barber Band. With Donegan on guitar and banjo, they became a regular fixture at Humphrey Lyttelton's club in London's Oxford Street. The Chris Barber Band included in their act a skiffle interlude, which gave Lonnie a chance to espouse his favourite music.*Rock Island Line*, an LP track recorded in 1954 featuring Donegan (guitar), Barber (string bass) and Beryl Bryden (washboard), was later issued as a single and jumped into the UK Top 10 in early '56. Even more surprisingly, it became a similar success in the US (then a rare feat for a British act), peaking at No 8 on both sides of the Atlantic. The success of this record prompted Donegan to quit Barber and begin a full-time solo career. Donegan never looked back. He quickly became Britain's 'King of Skiffle', popularising this intriguing offshoot of jazz. The main attractions of skiffle were its sheer straight-forwardness and the cheapness of the necessary instruments - washboards, tea chests and broom handles were used by numerous improvised groups up and down the UK, either as additions to or substitutes for the guitar/banjo/bass/drums line-up. This UK boom, which happened at the same time as the arrival of rock 'n' roll, found favour with rock, folk and jazz fans. Prior to the 1958 arrival of Cliff Richard, Donegan was Britain's top homegrown act. Even after that, the hits kept on coming until late 1962. During his seven year chart life, Donegan chalked up no less than 30 UK hits; even as late as 1985, the "Guinness Book Of British Hit Singles" still ranked him as Britain's 4th biggest domestic chart act of all time, despite his 23 year absence. In 1957 he managed two consecutive UK No 1 hits, with the traditional *Cumberland Gap* and the double A sided smash *Gamblin' Man* (adapted from a Woody Guthrie number)/*Putting On The Style* (a traditional song). His status as a leading folk music expert was exemplified by his inspired choice of material, which included adaptations of songs by Leadbelly (*Rock Island Line* and *Bring A Little Water, Sylvie*), Woody Guthrie, the Carter Family and Jimmie Driftwood. His third UK No 1 single, 1960's *My Old Man's A Dustman*, confirmed that he was moving into the world of music hall comedy and showbiz variety; also in this category was *Does Your Chewing Gum Lose Its Flavour (On The Bed Post Overnight)*, his only American Top 5 hit. The arrival of Beatlemania immediately knocked Donegan's chart career on the head; but his TV and concert appearances kept the star of skiffle, who had inspired so many young UK musicians, in steady money. (Bob MacDonald).

BATTLE OF NEW ORLEANS.
Tracks: Battle of New Orleans.
■ 7" 7N 15206
Pye / Jun '59.

BATTLE OF NEW ORLEANS (RE-RELEASE).
Tracks: Battle of New Orleans / Puttin' on the style.
■ 7" 7N 45548
Pye / Jan '76.

BEST OF LONNIE DONEGAN (KAZ).
Tracks: Not Advised.
CD . . . . .KAZCD 21
MC Set . . . . .KAZMC 21
Kaz / Jul '92 / BMG.

BEST OF LONNIE DONEGAN, THE.
Tracks: Not Advised.
CD . . . . .PWK 076
Pickwick / Jan '89 / Pickwick Records.

BRING A LITTLE WATER SYLVIE.
Tracks: Bring a little water Sylvie / Dead or alive.
■ 7" . . . . N 15071
Pye Nixa / Sep '56.

COLLECTION: LONNIE DONEGAN.
Tracks: Rock Island line / Lost John / Nobody's child / Bring a little water Sylvie / Frankie and Johnny / Cumberland gap / Mule skinner blues / Putting on the style / My Dixie darling / Ham 'n' eggs / Grand Coulee dam / Times are getting hard boys / Long summer day / Does your chewing gum lose it's flavour / Whoa buck / Battle of New Orleans / Fancy talking tinker / Miss Otis regrets / Talking guitar blues / My old man's a dustman / Have a drink on me / Keep on the sunny side / Pick a bale of cotton / This train.
Double LP . . . . CCSLP 223
Castle Collector Series / Sep '89 / BMG / Pinnacle / Castle Communications.
CD . . . . CCSCD 223
MC . . . . CCSMC 223
Castle Collector Series / Feb '93 / BMG / Pinnacle / Castle Communications.

COMANCHEROS, THE.
Tracks: Comancheros, The.
■ 7" 7N 15410
Pye / Jan '62.

CUMBERLAND GAP.
Tracks: Cumberland gap.
■ 7" . . . . N 15087
Pye Nixa / Apr '57.

CUMBERLAND GAP (OLD GOLD).
Tracks: Cumberland gap / Don't you rock me daddy o / Bring a little water Sylvie / Lost John.
12" . . . . OG 7705
Old Gold / Jul '90 / Pickwick Records.

DOES YOUR CHEWING GUM LOSE ITS FLAVOUR..
Tracks: Does your chewing gum lose its flavour (On the bed post overnight.).
■ 7" 7N 15181
Pye / Feb '59.

DON'T YOU ROCK ME DADDY-O.
Tracks: Don't you rock me daddy-o.
■ 7" . . . . N 15080
Pye Nixa / Jan '57.

EP COLLECTION VOLUME TWO, THE.
Tracks: Midnight special / Worried man blues / Railroad Bill / Ballad of Jesse James, The / Mule-skinner blues / On a monday / Bewildered / It is no secret / Corrine, Corrina / Nobody understands me / No hiding place / Lorelei / Party's over, The / New burying ground / When the sun goes down / Stackalee / Ol' Riley / Old Hannah / Glory / Kevin Barry / My laggan love / Junko partner / Sorry, but I'm gonna have to pass / Pick a bale of cotton / Losing by a hair.
CD . . . . SEECD 382
See For Miles / Oct '93 / Pinnacle.

EP COLLECTION, THE: LONNIE DONEGAN.
Tracks: Lost John / Stewball / Railroad Bill / Ballad of Jesse James, The / Little water, Sylvie, A / Dead or alive / Don't you rock me daddy-o / Cumberland Gap / Puttin' on the style / Gamblin' man / My dixie darling / Jack O'Diamonds / Grand Coulee Dam / Sally, don't you grieve / Betty, Betty, Betty / Tom Dooley / Does your chewing gum lose it's flavour / Fort Worth jail / Battle of New Orleans, The / Sal's got a sugar lip / My old man's a dustman / I wanna go home / Have a drink on me / Michael (row the boat) / Lumbered.
CD . . . . SEECD 346
MC . . . . SEEK 346
See For Miles / May '92 / Pinnacle.

FORT WORTH JAIL.
Tracks: Fort Worth jail.
■ 7" 7N 15198
Pye / Jun '59.

GAMBLIN' MAN.
Tracks: Gamblin' man / Putting on the style.
■ 7" . . . . N 15093
Pye Nixa / Jun '57.

GAMBLIN' MAN (OLD GOLD).
Tracks: Gamblin' man / Puttin' on the style.
■ 7" . . . . OG 9131
Old Gold / Jul '82.

GOLDEN AGE OF LONNIE DONEGAN VOL.1.
Tracks: Not Advised.
■ LP . . . . GGL 0135
Golden Guinea / Sep '62.

GOLDEN AGE OF LONNIE DONEGAN VOL.2.
Tracks: Not Advised.
■ LP . . . . GGL 0170
Golden Guinea / Feb '63.

GOLDEN HOUR OF GOLDEN HITS.
Tracks: Not Advised.
MC . . . . ZCGH 514
PRT / '74 / BMG.

GOLDEN HOUR OF GOLDEN HITS, VOL 2.
Tracks: Mule skinner blues / Pick a bale of cotton / Times are getting hard boys / Sal's got a sugar lip / My dixie darling / Ham 'n' eggs / Lively / Stewball / Fort Worth Jail / Dead or alive / I'm just a rolling stone / Aunt Rhody / Rock o' my soul / Golden vanity / Corina Corina / Seven golden daffodils / Lumbered / Very good year, A.
LP . . . . GH 565
Golden Hour / '73 / Midland Records.

GOLDEN HOUR OF LONNIE DONEGAN, A.
Tracks: Not Advised.
CD . . . . KGHCD 129
■ **LP** . . . . KGHMC 129
Knight / Sep '90.

GRAND COULEE DAM.
Tracks: Grand Coulee dam.
■ 7" . . . . N 15129
Pye Nixa / Apr '58.

GREATEST HITS: LONNIE DONEGAN.
Tracks: Not Advised.
MC Set . . . . DTO 10048
Ditto / Mar '83 / Pickwick Records.

GREATEST HITS: LONNIE DONEGAN (BRAVO LABEL).
Tracks: Not Advised.
■ **MC** . . . . BRC 2530
Bravo / Feb '80.

HAVE A DRINK ON ME.
Tracks: Have a drink on me.
■ 7" 7N 15354
Pye / May '61.

HIT SINGLES COLLECTION, THE.
Tracks: Rock Island line / Stewball / Lost John / Railroad Bill / Old Riley / Bring a little water, Sylvie / Dead or alive / Don't you rock me daddy-o / Cumberland Gap / Gamblin' man / Putting on the style / My dixie darling / Jack o' diamonds / Grand Coulee dam / Sally don't you grieve / Betty, Betty, Betty / Lonesome traveller / Tom Dooley / Does your chewing gum lose its flavour? / Fort Worth Jail / Battle of New Orleans / Sal's got a sugar lip / San Miguel / My old man's a dustman / I wanna go home / Lorelei / Lively / Virgin Mary / Have a drink on me / Michael row the boat ashore / Lumbered / Comancheros, The / Party's over, The / Pick a bale of cotton / Lonnie's skiffle party (Parts 1 & 2).
Double LP . . . . PYL 7003
MC Set . . . . PYM 7003
PRT / Oct '87 / BMG.
CD Set . . . . PYC 7003
PRT / Sep '87 / BMG.

I WANNA GO HOME.
Tracks: I wanna go home.
■ 7" 7N 15267
Pye / May '60.

JACK O' DIAMONDS.
Tracks: Jack o' diamonds.
■ 7" . . . . N 15116
Pye Nixa / Dec '57.

JUBILEE CONCERT.
Tracks: Ace in the hole / Isle of Capri / Going home / Shine / Jenny's ball / One sweet letter from you / Hush-a-bye / Bugle call march / Ice cream / John Henry / Take this hammer / Railroad Bill / Tom Dooley / New burying ground / Grand Coulee dam / New York town / Miss Otis regrets / Does your chewing gum lose its flavour? / One night of love / Rock Island line / Gloryland / Corina Corina / Goodnight Irene.
LP . . . . ICSD 2001
Cube / Dec '81.
MC . . . . ZCICSD 2001
Dakota / Dec '81.

LIVELY.
Tracks: Lively.
■ 7" 7N 15312
Pye / Nov '60.

LONESOME TRAVELLER.
Tracks: Lonesome traveller.
■ 7" . . . . N 15158
Pye Nixa / Sep '58.

LONNIE DONEGAN.
Tracks: Not Advised.
CD . . . . CDMFP 5917
MC . . . . TCMFP 5917
MFP / '91 / EMI.

LONNIE DONEGAN FILE, THE.
Tracks: Not Advised.
MC . . . . ZCFLD 011
PRT / Nov '77 / BMG.

LONNIE DONEGAN SHOWCASE.
Tracks: Wabash cannonball / How long how long blues / Nobody's child / I shall not be moved / I'm Alabamy bound / I'm a ramblin' man / Wreck of the old '97 / Frankie and Johnny.
■ **Mini LP** . . . . NPT 19012
Pye / Dec '56.

LONNIE'S SKIFFLE PARTY.
Tracks: Lonnie's skiffle party.
■ 7" . . . . N 15165
Pye Nixa / Nov '58.

LORELEI.
Tracks: Lorelei.
■ 7" 7N 15275
Pye / Aug '60.

LOST JOHN.
Tracks: Lost John / Stewball.
■ 7" . . . . N 15036
Pye Nixa / Apr '56.

MICHAEL ROW THE BOAT.
Tracks: Michael row the boat / Lumbered.
■ 7" 7N 15371
Pye / Aug '61.

MORE THAN 'PYE IN THE SKY.
Tracks: Rock Island line / John Henry / Nobody's child / Wabash cannonball / Hard time blues / You don't know my mind / Midnight special / Precious Lord lead me on / Passing stranger, The / On a christmas day / Take my hand, precious Lord / When the sun goes down / New buryin' ground / Worried man blues / Harmonica blues / Ballad of Jesse James, The / Ol' Riley / Railroad Bill / Lost John / Stewball / Stackalee / Bring a little water, Sylvie / Dead or alive / Frankie & Johnnie / How long, how long blues / I'm a ramblin' man / I'm Alabammy bound / Wreck of the old 97 / Nodody's child / I shall not be moved / Don't you rock me Daddy-o / Cumberland Gap / Love is strange / Theme from film "Light Fingers" / Gamblin' man / Puttin' on the style / My Dixie darling / I'm just a rolling stone / Jack O'Diamonds / Grand Coulee Dam, The / Hard travellin' / Ham 'n' eggs / Nobody loves like an Irishman / Sally don't you grieve / Ain't you glad you got religion / Lonesome traveller / Light from the lighthouse / I've got rocks in my bed / I've got rocks in my bed (alt.) / Long summer day / Sunshine of his love, The / Times are getting hard boys / Ain't no more cane on the Brazos / Lazy John / Betty, Betty, Betty / Whoa Buck (whoa back, Buck) / Shorty George / Baby don't you know that's love / Lonnie with Alan Freeman / Lonnie's skiffle party / Lonnie's skiffle party (part 2) / Darling Corey / Bewildered (so bewildered) / It is no secret / My Lagan love / Rock o' my soul / Aunt Rhody (the old grey goose) / Tom Dooley / Does your chewing gum lose it's flavour on the bedpost overn / Kevin Barry / My only son was killed in Dublin / Chesapeake Bay / Ace in the hole / Fortworth Jail / Battle of New Orleans / Sal's got a sugar lip / Just a closer walk with thee / Ice cream / Fancy talking tinker / Gloryland / Goldrush is over, The / House of the rising sun, The / Miss Otis regrets / Take this hammer / San Miguel / Jimmie Brown the newsboy / John Hardy / John Hardy (alt.) / Mr. Froggy / You pass me by / Talking guitar blues (American version) / Talking guitar blues (British version) / Golden vanity, The / My old man's a dustman / I wanna go home / I wanna go home (alt.) / Corrine, Corrina / In all my wildest dreams / Beyond the sunset / Nobody understands me / Junco partner / Lorelei / Wreck of the John B. / Sorry, but I'm gonna have to pass / Lively / Black cat (crossed my path today) / Banana split for my baby / Leave my woman alone / (Bury me) beneath the willow / When I was young / Virgin Mary / Just a-wearying for you / Ramblin' round / Have a drink on me / Seven daffodils (seven golden daffodils) / Keep on the sunny side / Tiger rag / Michael, row the boat (mono) / Lumbered / Michael, row the boat (stereo) / Red berets / Comancheros, The / Party's over / Over the rainbow / I'll never fall in love again / (It was) a very good year / I'll never smile again / I'll never fall in love again (alt.) / His eye is on the sparrow / Nobody knows the kind of trouble I've seen / Steal away / Good news, chariot's a-comin' / Born in Bethlehem / Joshua fit de battle of Jericho / New burying ground / No hiding place / Noah found grace in the eyes of the Lord / Sing Hallelujah / This train / We shall walk through the valley / Pick a bale of cotton / Market song, The / Tit bits / Losing by a hair / Trumpet sounds / Rise up / I've got a girl so fine / It's a long road to travel / Lemon tree / 500 miles away from home / Cajun Joe (the bully of the bayou) / Fisherman's luck / Louisiana man / Interstate 40 / Bad news / There's a big wheel / Diamonds of dew / Nothing to gain / Lovey told me goodbye / Beans in my ears / Get out of my life / Blistered / Bound for Zion / Where in this world are we going / Doctor's daughter, The / Reverend Mr. Black / Farewell (fare-thee-well) / Wedding bells / Won't you tell me / My sweet Marie / After taxes / I'm gonna be a bachelor / She was a T-bone talking woman / World cup Willie / Ding ding / Leaving blues / Aunt Maggie's remedy / Over in the new buryin' ground / Leavin' blues / Bury my body / Diggin' my potatoes / When I move to the sky / On a Monday / (In the evening) when the sun goes down / Old Hannah (go down old Hannah) / Muleskinner blues / Precious memories / Brother Moses smote the water / Ella speed / Glory (false start) / Black girl / Glory.
CD . . . . BCD 15700
Bear Family / Oct '93 / Rollercoaster Records / Swift / Direct Distribution.

MY DIXIE DARLING.
Tracks: My dixie darling.
■ 7" . . . . N 15108
Pye Nixa / Oct '57.

MY OLD MAN'S A DUSTMAN.
Tracks: My old man's a dustman.
■ 7" 7N 15256
Pye / Mar '60.

MY OLD MAN'S A DUSTMAN.
Tracks: My old man's a dustman / Does your chewing gum lose its flavour.
■ 7" .... FBS 10
Flashback / May '79.

ORIGINALS.
Tracks: Not Advised.
CD .... SEECD 331
See For Miles / Sep '91 / Pinnacle.

PARTY'S OVER,THE.
Tracks: Party's over, The.
■ 7" 7N 15424
Pye / Apr '62.

PICK A BALE OF COTTON.
Tracks: Pick a bale of cotton.
■ 7" 7N 15455
Pye / Aug '62.

PUTTIN' ON THE STYLE.
Tracks: Rock Island line / Have a drink on me / Ham 'n' eggs / I wanna go home / Diggin' my potatoes / Nobody's child / Putting on the style / Frankie and Johnny / Drop down baby / Lost John.
LP .... CHR 1158
Chrysalis / Feb '78 / EMI.
MC .... ZCHR 1158
Chrysalis / '79 / EMI.

PUTTING ON THE STYLE.
Tracks: Not Advised.
CD Set .... NXTCD 233
BMG / Nov '92 / BMG.

RARE AND UNISSUED GEMS.
Tracks: Cajun Joe / Louisiana moon / There's a big wheel / Fisherman's luck / Lovey told me goodbye / Bad news / Nothing to gain / Five hundred miles / Tiger rag / Keep on the sunny side / Red beret / Kevin Barry / Comancheros, The / Just a-wearyin' for you / Ding ding / Leaving blues.
LP .... BFX 15170
Bear Family / Jun '85 / Rollercoaster Records / Swift / Direct Distribution.

ROCK ISLAND LINE.
Tracks: My old man's a dustman / Pick a bale of cotton / Bring a little water Sylvie / Cumberland Gap / Michael row the boat ashore / Rock Island line / It takes a worried man / Don't you rock me daddy-o / Does your chewing gum lose its flavour? / Putting on the style / Battle of New Orleans / Have a drink on me.
LP .... FBLP 8071
MC .... ZCFBL 8071
Flashback / Oct '85.

ROCK ISLAND LINE.
Tracks: Rock Island line / John Henry.
7" .... F 10647
Decca / '55 / PolyGram.

ROCK ISLAND LINE (OLD GOLD).
Tracks: Rock Island line / Last train to San Fernando.
7" .... OG 9902
Old Gold / '89 / Pickwick Records.

SAL'S GOT A SUGAR LIP.
Tracks: Sal's got a sugar lip.
■ 7" 7N 15223
Pye / Sep '59.

SALLY DON'T YOU GRIEVE.
Tracks: Sally don't you grieve / Betty Betty Betty.
■ 7" .... N 15148
Pye Nixa / Jul '58.

SAN MIGUEL.
Tracks: San Miguel.
■ 7" 7N 15237
Pye / Dec '59.

SKIFFLE SESSION.
Tracks: Railroad Bill / Stockalee / Ballad of Jesse James / Ol' Riley.
■ EP. .... NJE 1017
Pye / Jul '56.

TOM DOOLEY.
Tracks: Tom Dooley.
■ 7" 7N 15172
Pye / Nov '58.

VIRGIN MARY.
Tracks: Virgin Mary.
■ 7" 7N 15315
Pye / Dec '60.

Donnelly, Philip

TOWN AND COUNTRY.
Tracks: Ballad of Robin Wintersmith / Donegal / From Clare to here / Speed of the sound of loneliness / Home is wherever you are / Cajun rock'n'roll stanza / I just kissed a devil last night / Abandoned love / No 1 / Tequila is addictive.
LP .... DUB 1
MC .... DUBC 1
Dublin / Jan '89 / C.M. Distribution.

Doolittle Band

WHO WERE YOU THINKIN' OF.
Tracks: Who were you thinkin' of / Arizona highways.
■ 7" .... CBS 9323
CBS / Jan '81.

Dore, Charlie

This British singer and guitarist worked as a session vocalist during the latter half of the Seventies. In 1979 she launched a solo career with the LP *Where to Now*. Receiving strong assistance from musician and producer Alan Tarney (who co-produced the album with Bruce Welch), it contained an unadventurous but catchy batch of country-flavoured pop songs. Amongst them was *Pilot of the Airwaves*, a ditty about a radio listener asking her friendly DJ for a request. This was issued as a single but, despite predictably heavy airplay, it peaked at No.66 on the UK chart in November '79. Dore, definitely a female artist in spite of her Christian name, never returned to the British charts. But in the Spring of 1980, a re-edited and remixed version of *Pilot of the Airwaves* cruised to No.13 on the American listings. Surprisingly, this was her only Stateside success too. After switching from Island to Chrysalis in 1981, she released a second album *Listen*, but this fell on deaf ears. She nosedived into obscurity, which was surprising in view of the fact that some observers had initially believed that this artist possessed considerable commercial potential in the pop and country markets.(Bob MacDonald).

FEAR OF FLYING.
Tracks: Fear of flying / Sweetheart.
■ 7" .... WIP 6476
Island / Jun '79.

LISTEN.
Tracks: Listen (I just want you) / Do me a favour / You should hear / Falling / Don't say no / Wise to the lines / I'm over here / Like they do it in America / Sister revenge / Didn't I tell you.
LP .... CHR 1325
MC .... ZCHR 1325
Chrysalis / Aug '81 / EMI.

LISTEN.
Tracks: Listen / Falling.
■ 7" .... CHS 2536
Chrysalis / Aug '81.

PILOT OF THE AIRWAVES.
Tracks: Pilot of the airwaves.
■ 7" .... WIP 6526
Island / Nov '79.

WHERE TO NOW?.
Tracks: Where to now? / Fear of flying.

WHERE TO NOW?.
Tracks: Pilot of the airwaves / Falling / Sad old world / Where to now? / Sleepless / Fear of flying / Wise owl / Hula valley / Pickin' apples o-sweetheart.
■ LP .... ILPS 9559
Island / Dec '79.

YOU SHOULD HEAR.
Tracks: You should hear / Like they do it in America.
■ 7" .... CHS 2557
Chrysalis / Sep '81.

Dorman, Harold

Dorman can be considered one of the more obscure artists of the Sun era. Since the mid 50's he has been well known in the Memphis music scene and well respected for his songwriting by his fellow musicians. Dorman penned songs are still recorded even by today's superstars like Charley Pride and *Mountain of love* achieved top 20 success for Dorman in the 1960's. The 1926 Mississippi born Dorman arrived in Memphis in the mid 50's.He had grown up with Hank Williams' music. When Roland Janes and Billy Riley tried to build up their new Rita label in Memphis Dorman was one of the first artists they recorded. They remembered Dorman from their own Sun times. 'I knew Harold was a great songwriter', recalled Roland Janes, and I couldn't understand why someone didn't pick on him. When we decided to form a record label he was one of the first people we wanted to record. He turned out to be one of the greatest singers from this part of the country.'

MOUNTAIN OF LOVE.
Tracks: Mountain of love / I'll come running / Sounds like big trouble / Remember me / Is she willing to forget / Do you want to go steady / Mister tears / Love will find a way / Mountain of love (undubbed version) / Moving up to love / Moved to Kansas / Let there be love / Diamond rings / Soda pop baby / Lonely nights / Sweet sweet love (Medley).
LP .... BFX 15262
Bear Family / Apr '88 / Rollercoaster Records / Swift / Direct Distribution.

Doss, Tommy

OF THE SONS OF THE PIONEERS.
Tracks: Call, The / So much to remember / If you would only be mine / I invented the word / Memory, The / Trouble in mind / Rosa / King of the fools / Sing a sad song / I care no more / Every fool has a rainbow.
LP .... BFX 15225
Bear Family / Jun '87 / Rollercoaster Records / Swift / Direct Distribution.

Dottsy

SWEETEST THING, THE.
Tracks: I'll be your San Antonio rose / If only I had the words (To tell you) / We still love songs here (In Texas) / There is a place / Lying in my arms / Sweetest thing (I've ever known), The / Good love is like a good song, A / Storms never last / Follow me / Just remember who your friends are.
LP .... LSA 3276
RCA / '76 / BMG.

TRYIN' TO SATISFY YOU.
Tracks: Tryin' to satisfy you / Play born to lose again / Everybody's reaching out for someone / Send me the pillow you dream on / It should have been easy / So hard living without you / Here in love / Love is a two way street / Just had you on my mind / If you say it's so / Slip away.
MC .... PLK 42811
RCA / '79 / BMG.
■ LP .... PL 42811
RCA / '79.

Doucet, Camey

CAJUN GOOD TIME MUSIC.
Tracks: Not Advised.
LP 6034
Swallow (USA) / Swift / Wellard Dist.
MC .... 6034 TC
Swallow (USA) / '87 / Swift / Wellard Dist.

CAJUN GOODIES.
Tracks: Not Advised.
LP 6028
MC .... 6028 TC
Swallow (USA) / Feb '79 / Swift / Wellard Dist.

CAMEY DOUCET ET MUSIQUE.
Tracks: Not Advised.
LP 6024
MC .... 6024 TC
Swallow (USA) / Feb '79 / Swift / Wellard Dist.

Doucet, David

QUAND J'AI PARTI.
Tracks: T'en as eu / Balfa waltz / Zydeco sont pas sales / J'ai passe / Bee la manche / Ton papa / French blues (Je m'endors) / J'etais au bal / Les bons temps rouler / Pacquent d'epingles / Coulee rodair / J'ai fait la tour / La valse des cajuns.
CD .... CD 6040
MC .... MC 6040
Rounder / '91 / Projection / Roots Records / Swift / C.M. Distribution / Topic Records / Jazz Music / Hot Shot / A.D.A Distribution / Direct Distribution.

Doucet, Michael

BEAU SOLO.
Tracks: Not Advised.
CD .... ARHCD 321
Arhoolie (USA) / '92 / Pinnacle / Cadillac Music / Swift / Projection / Hot Shot / A.D.A Distribution / Jazz Music.

CAJUN EXPERIENCE (see under Daigle, Paul).

CHRISTMAS BAYOU.
Tracks: We three kings of Orient are / It came upon a midnight clear / Il est ne / Vive le vent / Deck the halls / Little drummer boy / O holy night / Bonne Annee / God rest ye merry gentlemen / Christmas bayou / Please come home for Christmas / Trinquez trinquez / Auld lang syne.
MC .... 6064 TC
Swallow (USA) / '87 / Swift / Wellard Dist.
LP 6064
Swallow (USA) / Jun '87 / Swift / Wellard Dist.

DIT BEAUSOLEIL.
Tracks: Not Advised.
LP .... ARHOOLIE 5025
Arhoolie (USA) / '88 / Pinnacle / Cadillac Music / Swift / Projection / Hot Shot / A.D.A Distribution / Jazz Music.
■ MC .... ARHC 5025
Arhoolie (USA) / '88.

GREAT CAJUN (Doucet, Michael & Cajun Brew).
Tracks: Not Advised.
CD .... CDROU 6017
Rounder / Apr '93 / Projection / Roots Records / Swift / C.M. Distribution / Topic Records / Jazz Music / Hot Shot / A.D.A Distribution / Direct Distribution.

■ DELETED

HOT CAJUN RHYTHM AND BLUES (Doucet, Michael & Cajun Brew).
Tracks: Wooly bully / Bayou pom pom / Un autre soir ennuyant / Hey good lookin' / Last Wednesday night / Louie Louie / Woman or a man / Pauline / Zydeco boogaloo / Like a real cajun / J'ai passe devant ta porte / Do you want to dance.
LP. . . . . **SPD 1013**
Special Delivery / May '88 / Revolver-APT / A.D.A Distribution / Topic Records / Direct Distribution / Jazz Music / C.M. Distribution.
■ CD . . . . **SPDCD 1013**
Special Delivery / Aug '89.

MICHAEL DOUCET & CAJUN BREW (Doucet, Michael & Cajun Brew).
Tracks: Not Advised.
LP. . . . . **ROUNDER 6017**
MC . . . .**ROUNDER 6017C**
Rounder / '88 / Projection / Roots Records / Swift / C.M. Distribution / Topic Records / Jazz Music / Hot Shot / A.D.A Distribution / Direct Distribution.
CD . . . .**CDROU 607**
Rounder / May '93 / Projection / Roots Records / Swift / C.M. Distribution / Topic Records / Jazz Music / Hot Shot / A.D.A Distribution / Direct Distribution.

PARLEZ NOUS A BOIRE (Doucet, Michael & Beausoleil).
Tracks: Not Advised.
LP. . . . . **ARHOOLIE 5034**
MC . . . .**C 5034**
Arhoolie (USA) / Mar '85 / Pinnacle / Cadillac Music / Swift / Projection / Hot Shot / A.D.A Distribution / Jazz Music.
CD . . . .**ARHCD 322**
Arhoolie (USA) / Mar '93 / Pinnacle / Cadillac Music / Swift / Projection / Hot Shot / A.D.A Distribution / Jazz Music.

Douglas, Jerry

Dobro master, sessionman/solo performer - recording act, born Ohio in 1956. While still at high school Douglas took a keen interest in music, taking after his father, a guitarist in local bluegrass unit. Upon seeing Josh Graves & Brother Oswald perform on a Flatt & Scruggs show, he relinquished his desires to play guitar like his father, instead he converted his Silverstone guitar for use with a slide. He joined the Country Gents in 1973, later to play with J.D. Crowe & The New South, Ricky Skaggs (Boone Creek) & David Grisman. Douglas recorded albums *Under the wire* , *Changing channels* & *Plant early* - his busy studio session work schedule also found him playing on numerous quality bluegrass, country & acoustic albums. Douglas in 1992, augmented by guest vocalists Tim O'-Brien, The Brother Boys, Maura O'Connell & Alison Krauss released *Slide rule* on Sugar Hill (the highly acclaimed venture recipient of bluegrass. Top Recording Event Of The Year Award). Amongst most recent projects, he has recorded with Joan Baez, his artistry continuing to take the dobro to new and higher echelons. (Maurice Hope)

EVERYTHING'S GONNA WORK OUT FINE.
Tracks: Not Advised.
CD . . . .**ROUNDER 11535**
Rounder / '89 / Projection / Roots Records / Swift / C.M. Distribution / Topic Records / Jazz Music / Hot Shot / A.D.A Distribution / Direct Distribution.

FLUXEDO.
Tracks: Not Advised.
LP. . . . . **ROUNDER 0112**
MC . . . .**ROUNDER 0112C**
Rounder / '88 / Projection / Roots Records / Swift / C.M. Distribution / Topic Records / Jazz Music / Hot Shot / A.D.A Distribution / Direct Distribution.

FLUXOLOGY.
Tracks: Fluxology / Bill Cheatham / Say a little prayer / C-biscuit / Randy Lynn rag / Wheel hoss / Red Bud rag / Alabama / Dixie hoedown / Blues for Vickie.
LP. . . . . **ROUNDER 0093**
Rounder / May '79 / Projection / Roots Records / Swift / C.M. Distribution / Topic Records / Jazz Music / Hot Shot / A.D.A Distribution / Direct Distribution.
MC . . . .**ROUNDER 0093C**
Rounder / '88 / Projection / Roots Records / Swift / C.M. Distribution / Topic Records / Jazz Music / Hot Shot / A.D.A Distribution / Direct Distribution.

SLIDE RULE.
Tracks: Ride the wild turkey / Pearlie Mae / When papa played the dobro / We hide & seek / Shoulder to shoulder / Uncle Sam / It's a beautiful life / I don't believe you've met my baby / Rain on Oliviatown / Hey Joe / New day medley, A / Shenendoah breakdown.
CD . . . . **SHCD 3797**
Sugarhill(USA) / '92 / Roots Records / Projection / Impetus Records / C.M. Distribution / Jazz Music / Swift / Duncans / A.D.A Distribution.

UNDER THE WIRE.
Tracks: T.O.B. / Dhaka rock / Time gone by / Monroe's hornpipe / Before the blues / Trip to Kilkerrin / Grant's corner / Redhill / Two friends / New day, A.
LP. . . . . **IMCA 5675**
MC . . . . **IMCAC 5675**
MCA / Jun '86 / BMG.
CD . . . . **MCAD 5675**
MCA / Apr '87 / BMG.

Down County Boys

BETTER TIMES A' COMING.
Tracks: Not Advised.
LP. . . . . **BSS 168**
Tank / Dec '77.

Downliners Sect

COUNTRY SECT, THE.
Tracks: If I could just go back / Rocks in my bed / Ballad of the hounds / Little play soldiers / Hard travellin' / Wait for the light to shine / I got mine / Waiting in heaven / Above & beyond / Bad storm coming / Midnight special / Wolverton mountain.
■ LP. . . . . **CR 30137**
Charly / Nov '77 / Charly.

CROSS SECTION.
Tracks: Little Egypt / One ugly child / Our little rendezvous / Sect appeal / Baby what's on your mind / Cops and robbers / Blood hound / Ballad of the hounds / Rocks in my bed / I got mine / Bad storm coming / I want my baby back again / Now she's dead / Everything I've got to give / Comin' home baby / Why don't you smile now / Outside.
LP. . . . . **LIK 10**
Decal / May '87 / Charly / Swift.

I CAN'T GET AWAY FROM YOU (see under Crane, Don).

ROCK SECTS IN, THE.
Tracks: Hang on Sloopy / Fortune teller / Hey hey hey hey / Everything I've got to give / Outside / I'm hooked on you / Comin' home baby / Why don't you smile now / Don't lie to me / May the bird of paradise fly / Up to your nose / He was a square / I'm looking for a woman / Rock sects in again / Brand new cadillac.
LP. . . . . **CR 30140**
Charly / Charly.

SECT, THE.
Tracks: Not Advised.
■ LP. . . . . **CR 30122**
Charly / Apr '77 / Charly.

Doyle, Danny

BORN A RAMBLIN' MAN.
Tracks: Not Advised.
LP. . . . . **SOLO 7009**
Solo / Jan '76 / Black Sun Records.

DAISY A DAY, A.
Tracks: Not Advised.
LP. . . . .**HPE 638**
Harp (Ireland) / Jul '81 / C.M. Distribution.

DANNY DOYLE VOL.1.
Tracks: Not Advised.
LP. . . . . **MBR 001**
Music Box (Ireland) / Jul '76.

DANNY DOYLE VOL.2.
Tracks: Not Advised.
LP. . . . . **MBR 002**
Music Box (Ireland) / Jul '76.

GRAND OLE IRISH OPREY.
Tracks: Not Advised.
LP. . . . . **BRL 4038**
Release (Ireland).

SUSAN.
Tracks: Susan / For what it's worth.
■ 7" . . . . **GY 162**
Galaxy (1) / Dec '79.

TWENTY YEARS A GROWING.
Tracks: Not Advised.
LP. . . . . **TA 3020**
Tara (Ireland) / Mar '89 / Pinnacle / C.M. Distribution / A.D.A Distribution / Topic Records / Direct Distribution / Conifer Records / Jazz Music.

VERY SPECIAL LOVE SONG, A.
Tracks: Not Advised.
LP. . . . . **BRL 4052**
Release (Ireland) / Nov '76.

WEST'S AWAKE, THE.
Tracks: Not Advised.
LP. . . . .**MBLP 003**
MC . . . . **MBC 003**
Music Box (Ireland) / Mar '77.

Dr. Hook

The most successful line-up of this American band was Rik Elswit, William Francis, Jance Garfat, Bob Henke, Dennis Locorriere, Ray Sawyer and John Walters. Originally known as Dr. Hook & The Medicine Show, they shortened the name when they switched labels from CBS to Capitol in 1975. The band were formed in New Jersey in 1969, the two key figures in their early career were manager/producer, Ron Haffkine, and Shel Silverstein who was their songwriter, responsible for the whole of the band's first two albums and hit singles. The breakthrough hit for Dr. Hook was the single, *Sylvia's Mother*, which reached no.5 in America and no.2 in Britain. The following year, they reached no.6 in the US with the comedy song *Cover Of Rolling Stone*. However, by 1974, Dr. Hook suffered a series of setbacks. The band were on the brink of financial ruin and they were transferred to a different record label. Around this time they released their aptly titled LP *Bankrupt*. The band's determination paid off and in 1976, a revival of Sam Cooke's *Only Sixteen*, reached the US top 10. In the UK the risque *A Little Bit More* spent five weeks at no.2 in the singles chart. It was as a live attraction however, that Dr. Hook were at their most entertaining. Lead vocalists Locorriere and Sawyer provided the funniest double act in pop music. In 1979, *When you're in love with a beautiful woman* reached no.1 in the UK and the 1980 hit *Sexy Eyes* reached no.4. In the early 1980's Sawyer left to pursue a solo country career. The group survived a few more hitless years but disbanded in 1985. (Bob MacDonald)

BABY MAKES HER BLUE JEANS TALK.
Tracks: Baby makes her blue jeans talk / Turn-on.
■ 7" . . . . **MER 93**
Mercury / Feb '82.

BALLAD OF LUCY JORDAN.
Tracks: Sylvia's mother / Hey, Lady Godiva / Four years older than me / Makin' it natural / Last mornin' / (Freakin' at) The freaker's ball / If I'd only come & gone / Carry me, Carrie / Queen of the silver dollar / Cover of 'Rolling Stone', The / Penicillin Penny / Life ain't easy / Monterey Jack / Roland the roadie & Gertrude the groupie / Wonderful soup stone, The / Ballad of Lucy Jordan, The.
LP. **80787**
■ MC **4087087**
CBS / '78 / Sony.
■ LP. . . . . **CBS 32087**
CBS / Dec '81.

BELLY UP.
Tracks: Acapulco goldie / Penicilin Penny / Life ain't easy / When Lily was Queen / Monterey Jack / You ain't got the right / Put a little bit on me / Ballad of .. / Roland the roadie & Gertrude the groupie / Come on in / Wonderful soup stone, The.
■ LP. **65560**
Cupido Disque / '78 / Total / BMG.

BEST OF DOCTOR HOOK.
Tracks: I can't touch the sun / Things I didn't say / Carry me Carrie / When she cries / Kiss it away / Sing me a rainbow / Life ain't easy / Sylvia's mother / Last mornin' / Turn on the world / Ballad of Lucy Jordan / Hey Lady Godiva / Four years older than me / Makin' it natural / Freakers ball / Roland the roadie and Gertrude the groupie / Queen of the Silver Dollar / Cover of the Rolling Stone / Penicillin Penny / Monterey Jack / If I'd only come and gone / Wonderful soup stone.
■ Double LP . . . . **CBS 22102**
CBS / Jun '82.

BETTER LOVE NEXT TIME.
Tracks: Better love next time / Mountain Mary.
■ 7" . . . . **CL 16112**
Capitol / Jan '80.

COLLECTION: DOCTOR HOOK.
Tracks: Not Advised.
LP. . . . . **IC 038 85 156**
EMI (Germany) / '83.

COMPLETELY HOOKED - THE BEST OF DR. HOOK.
Tracks: Sylvia's mother / Cover of the 'Rolling Stone' / Everybody's makin' it big but me / You make my pants want to get up and dance / Sleeping late / Only sixteen / Walk right in / Millionaire, The / More like the movies / When you're in love with a beautiful woman / Sexy eyes / If not you / Little bit more, A / Sharing the night together / I don't want to be alone tonight / Better love next time / In over my head / Years from now / Sweetest of all / Couple more years, A.
CD . . . .**CDESTV 2**
LP. . . . . **ESTV 2**
MC . . . . **TCESTV 2**
Capitol / May '92 / EMI.

COMPLETELY HOOKED - THE BEST OF DR. HOOK.
Tracks: Sylvia's mother / Cover of the 'Rolling Stone' / Millionaire, The / Little bit more, A / If not you / Making love and music / Sleeping late / I don't want to be alone tonight / Sharing the night together / When you're in love with a beautiful woman / You make my pants want to get up and dance / Storms never last / Sexy eyes / Years from now.
VHS. . . . . **MVP 4910083**
PMI / Jun '92 / EMI / Gold & Sons / Terry Blood Dist.

COUNTRY STORE: DOCTOR HOOK VOL 2.
Tracks: Sylvia's mother / Sing me a rainbow / Carry me Carrie / Penicillin Penny / Marie Laveux / Cover of the Rolling Stone / Kiss it away / When she cries / Turn on the world / Queen of the silver dollar.
CD . . . . **CDCST 41**
MC . . . . **CSTK 41**

■ DELETED D 13

Country Store / '88 / BMG.
■ LP. . . . . CST 41
Country Store / '88.

DOCTOR HOOK.
Tracks: Sylvia's mother / Marie Laveaux / Sing me a rainbow / Hey, Lady Godiva / Four years older than me / Kiss it away / Makin' it natural / I call that true love / When she cries / Judy / Mama, I'll sing one song for you.
■ LP. 64754
CBS / '78 / Sony.

DR. HOOK'S GREATEST HITS.
Tracks: Sylvia's mother / Cover of the Rolling Stone / Everybody's making it big but me / You make my pants want to get up and dance / Sleeping late / Only sixteen / Walk right in / Millionaire / More like the movies / When you're in love with a beautiful woman / Sexy eyes / If not you / Little bit more, A / Sharing the night together / I don't want to be alone tonight / Better love next time / In over my head / Years from now.
LP. . . . . EST 26037
■ MC . . . . . TCEST 26037
Capitol / Nov '80.

GIRLS CAN GET IT.
Tracks: Girls can get it / Body talking / Hold me like you never had me / Boy talk / Lady sundown / Baby makes her blue jeans talk / Let me drink from your well / When you're 18 / Crazy Rosie / Fire in the night / Devil's daughter / SOS for love.
LP. 822 693 1
MC 822 693 4
Karussell Gold / Aug '85.

GIRLS CAN GET IT.
Tracks: Girls can get it / Doing it.
■ 7" . . . . . MER 51
Mercury / Nov '80.

GREATEST HITS (AND MORE): DOCTOR HOOK.
Tracks: Sylvia's mother / Cover of the Rolling Stone / Only sixteen / Little bit more, A / Walk right in / Make love and music / I couldn't believe / Couple more years, A / Sharing the night together / When you're in love with a beautiful woman / Better love next time / Sexy eyes / Years from now / Radio, The / Sweetest of all.
CD . . . . . CDP 746 620 2
Capitol / May '87 / EMI.

HEARTS LIKE YOURS AND MINE.
Tracks: Hearts like yours and mine / Sex drive.
■ 7" . . . . . MER 84
Mercury / Sep '81.

I DON'T WANT TO BE ALONE TONIGHT.
Tracks: I don't want to be alone tonight / You make my pants want to get up and dance.
■ 7" . . . . . CL 16013
Capitol / Sep '78.
■ 7" . . . . . CL 16198
Capitol / May '81.

IF NOT YOU.
Tracks: If not you.
■ 7" . . . . . CL 15885
Capitol / Oct '76.

LITTLE BIT MORE, A.
Tracks: Little bit more, A / When you're in love with a beautiful woman / More like the movies / Radio, The / Up on the mountain / If not you / Jungle to the zoo / Bad eye Bill / What about you / I need the high / Couple more years, A.
■ LP. . . . . EST 23795
Capitol / Oct '75.
LP. . . . . FA 41 3106 1
MC . . . . . FA 41 3106 4
Fame / Sep '84 / EMI.

LITTLE BIT MORE, A.
Tracks: Little bit more, A.
■ 7" . . . . . CL 15871
Capitol / May '76.

LITTLE BIT MORE, A (SINGLE).
Tracks: Little bit more, A / Sylvia's mother / If not you (12" & CD single only).
12" 12EMCT 6
7" . . . . . EMCT 6
CD Single . . . . . CDEMT 6
■ MC Single . . . . . TCEMT 6
Capitol / May '92.

LIVE IN THE U.K.
Tracks: You make my pants want to get up and dance / Sexy eyes / Cover of the Rolling Stone / Carry me Carrie / I got stoned and I missed it / When you're in love with a beautiful woman / Ooh-poo-pah-doo / Sylvia's mother.
■ LP. . . . . EST 26706
Capitol / Nov '81.
LP. . . . . MFP 41 5691 1
■ MC . . . . . MFP 41 5691 4
MFP / Jan '85.

LOVE SONGS (16 Original Greats).
Tracks: When you're in love with a beautiful women / Only sixteen / Sharing the night together / Sexy eyes / More like the movies / Years from now / Everybody's making it big but me / Sylvia's msother / Little bit more, A / Walk right in / Better love next time / You make me pants want to get up and dance / If not you / Sweetest of all / Bubbling up / Cover of the rolling stone.
LP. . . . . PLAT 3902
Platinum Music / '88 / Prism Leisure PLC / Ross Records.
MC . . . . . PLAC 3902
Platinum Music / Dec '88 / Prism Leisure PLC / Ross Records.

LOVELINE.
Tracks: Loveline / Chained to your memory.
7" . . . . . MER 104
Mercury / May '82 / PolyGram.

MAKIN' LOVE AND MUSIC.
Tracks: Makin' love and music / Laying too low too long / What a way to go / Sleeping late / Walk right in / Who dat / Let the loose end drag / I'm a lamb / I wanna make the women tremble / Sexy eyes.
MC . . . . . TC EST 11632
Capitol / Oct '77 / EMI.
■ LP. . . . . EST 11632
Capitol / Oct '77.

MAKIN' LOVE AND MUSIC.
Tracks: Makin' love and music / I wanna make the women tremble.
■ 7" . . . . . CL 15958
Capitol / Jan '78.

MAKING LOVE AND MUSIC - THE 1976-79 RECORDINGS.
Tracks: When you're in love with a beautiful woman / Little bit more, A / If not you / Up on the mountain / Bad eye Bill / Who dat / Let the loose end drag / I'm a lamb / Making love and music / Radio, The / Everybody loves me / Oh Jesse / Jungle in the zoo / More like the movies / I don't feel much like smilin' / Mountain Mary / Leviate / Dooley Jones / Sexy energy / Love monster.
CD . . . . . CDMFP 5979
MC . . . . . TCMFP 5979
MFP / Apr '93 / EMI.

MORE LIKE THE MOVIES.
Tracks: More like the movies.
■ 7" . . . . . CL 15967
Capitol / Mar '78.

PLAYERS IN THE DARK.
Tracks: Baby makes her blue jeans talk / Turn on / Lady sundown / I can't say no to her / Loveline / Pity the fool / Chained to your memory / Devil's daughter / Hearts like yours and mine / Fire in the night.
CD 800 054-2
Mercury / PolyGram.
LP. . . . . MERS 002
Mercury / May '82 / PolyGram.

PLEASURE AND PAIN.
Tracks: Sharing the night together / Sweetest of all / Storms never last / I don't want to be alone tonight / Knowing she is there / Clyde / When you're in love with a beautiful woman / Dooley Jones / I gave her comfort / You make my pants want to get up and dance.
■ LP. . . . . EAST 11859
Capitol / Oct '79.
LP. . . . . ATAK 3
MC . . . . . TCATAK 3
Capitol / '85 / EMI.

RADIO, THE.
Tracks: Radio, The / Only sixteen / Makin' love and music.
■ 7" . . . . . CL 15992
Capitol / Jun '78.

RINGS.
Tracks: Rings / Crazy Rosie.
■ 7" . . . . . MER 124
Mercury / Nov '82.

RISING.
Tracks: Girls can get it / Body talking / That didn't hurt too bad / Blown away / SOS for love / Doin' it / Before the tears / Hold me like you never had me / Do you right tonight / 99 and me.
■ LP. 6302 076
Mercury / Nov '80.

RISING/PLAYERS IN THE DARK.
Tracks: Girls can get it / Body talking / That didn't hurt too bad / Blown away / SOS for love / Doing it / Before the tears / Hold me like you never had me / Do you right tonight / 99 and me / Baby makes her blue jeans talk / Turn on, The / Lady Sundown / I can't say no to her / Loveline / Pity the fool / Chained to your memory / Devil's daughter / Hearts like yours and mine / Fire in the night.
Double LP 8326111
Mercury / May '88 / PolyGram.

S.O.S. FOR LOVE.
Tracks: S.O.S. for love / 99 and me.
■ 7" . . . . . MER 58
Mercury / Jan '81.

SEXY EYES.
Tracks: Sexy eyes / Help me Mama / When you're in love with a beautiful woman.
■ 7" . . . . . CL 16127
Capitol / Mar '80.

SHARING THE NIGHT TOGETHER.
Tracks: Not Advised.
MC 4XL 9042
Capitol (Specials) / Dec '88.

SHARING THE NIGHT TOGETHER.
Tracks: Sharing the night together / Dooley Jones.
■ 7" . . . . . CL 16171
Capitol / Nov '80.

SLEEPIN' LATE.
Tracks: Sleepin' late / Who dat.
■ 7" . . . . . CL 15943
Capitol / Aug '77.

SLOPPY SECONDS.
Tracks: Freaker's ball / If I'd only come & gone / Carry me, Carrie / Things I didn't say, The / Get my rocks off / Last mornin' / I can't touch the sun / Queen of the silver dollar / Turn on the world / Stayin' song / Cover of 'Rolling Stone', The.
■ LP. 65132
CBS / '78 / Sony.

SOMETIMES YOU WIN.
Tracks: Better love next time / In over my head / Sexy eyes / Oh Jesse / Years from now / I don't feel much like smilin' / When you're in love with a beautiful woman / What do you want / Love monster / Mountain Mary / Help me mama.
■ LP. . . . . EST 12018
Capitol / Nov '79.
LP. . . . . FA 3012
■ MC . . . . . TCFA 3012
Fame / May '82.

SYLVIA'S MOTHER.
Tracks: I can't touch the sun / Things I didn't say, The / Carry me, Carrie / When she cries / Kiss it away / Sing me a rainbow / Life ain't easy / Sylvia's mother / Last mornin' / Turn on the world.
LP. . . . . CBS 32082
CBS / Nov '81 / Sony.
■ MC 40 32082
CBS / Nov '81.
LP. . . . . SHM 3136
MC . . . . . HSC 3136
Hallmark / Apr '84 / Pickwick Records.
CD 902120-2
Pickwick / Jul '89 / Pickwick Records.
MC 9021204
Pickwick / Jul '92 / Pickwick Records.

SYLVIA'S MOTHER.
Tracks: Sylvia's mother.
■ 7" . . . . . CBS 7929
CBS / Jun '72.

SYLVIA'S MOTHER (2).
Tracks: Queen of the silver dollar / Put a little bit on me / Get my rocks off / Cover of the Rolling Stone / Sing me a rainbow / Sylvia's mother / Lady Godiva / Turn on the world / Life ain't easy / I can't touch the sun / Carry me Carrie / Ballad of Lucy Jordan.
CD . . . . . PWKS 4046
Pickwick / Apr '91 / Pickwick Records.

SYLVIA'S MOTHER (OLD GOLD).
Tracks: Sylvia's mother / Ballad of Lucy Jordan.
7" . . . . . OG 9309
Old Gold / Apr '83 / Pickwick Records.

TAKE THE BAIT.
Tracks: Not Advised.
CD 550 0552
MC 550 0554
Spectrum (1) / May '93 / PolyGram.

VOICE OF DR. HOOK, THE (see under Crane, Don).

WALK RIGHT IN.
Tracks: Walk right in / Sexy energy.
■ 7" . . . . . CL 15924
Capitol / May '77.

WHEN YOU'RE IN LOVE WITH A BEAUTIFUL WOMAN.
Tracks: When you're in love with a beautiful woman / Sexy eyes / Dr. Hook medley.
7" G45 23
EMI Golden 45's / May '84 / EMI.
7" . . . . . EMCT 4
CD Single . . . . . CDEMCT 4
MC Single . . . . . TCEMCT 4
EMI / Oct '91 / EMI.

WHEN YOU'RE IN LOVE WITH A BEAUTIFUL WOMAN.
Tracks: When you're in love with a beautiful woman / Clyde.
■ 7" . . . . . CL 16039
Capitol / Feb '79.

WHEN YOU'RE IN LOVE WITH A BEAUTIFUL WOMAN.
Tracks: When you're in love with a beautiful woman / Sexy eyes / Dr. Hook medley.

WHEN YOU'RE IN LOVE WITH A BEAUTIFUL WOMAN (OLD GOLD).
Tracks: When you're in love with a beautiful woman / Little bit more, A.

D 14 ■ DELETED

■ 7" . . . . .OG 9714
Old Gold / Apr '87.

YEARS FROM NOW.
Tracks: Years from now / I don't feel much like smilin'.
■ 7" . . . . CL 16154
Capitol / Aug '80.

Drake, Pete

Steel guitarist, publisher, producer and label boss (1933-88). One of Nashville's most accomplished sidemen, he had hit albums of his own, and formed First Generation Records in 1977 and made a series of albums by veterans including Ernest Tubb. (Donald Clarke)

PETE DRAKE SHOW, THE.
Tracks: Not Advised.
LP . . . . STOP 1001
Stop / Jun '76 / C.M. Distribution.

STEEL AWAY.
Tracks: Not Advised.
LP . . . . CGS 8502
Canaan / Word Records (UK) / Sony.

Draper, Rusty

A USA pop/country singer and actor. He had a series of hits 1953-60 including No Help Wanted and Gambler's Guitar; his Muleskinner Blues reached the UK chart in 1960. He had country chart hits in the '60's. He toured in plays and acted on TV in 77 Sunset Strip, Rawhide, Laramie etc. (Donald Clarke)

COUNTRY AND WESTERN.
Tracks: Not Advised.
MC 7581 701
Phonogram / Oct '75 / PolyGram.

COUNTRY AND WESTERN BONANZA.
Tracks: Not Advised.
MC . . . . CMP 7025
Philips / Oct '75 / PolyGram.

HIS TOP HITS.
Tracks: Not Advised.
MC 825
Timeless Treasures / Sep '87 / Terry Blood Dist.

MULE SKINNER BLUES.
Tracks: Mule skinner blues.
■ 7" . . . . AMT 1101
Mercury (EMI) / Aug '60.

SEVEN COME ELEVEN.
Tracks: Seven come eleven / Two hearts, two kisses.
7" . . . . PRM 901
Pinner / Jul '84.

YOU CAN'T BE TRUE DEAR.
Tracks: You can't be true dear / Folsom prison blues.
■ 7" . . . . HLU 9989
London-American / Sep '65.

Dreadful Snakes

SNAKES ALIVE.
Tracks: Not Advised.
LP . . . . ROUNDER 0177
Rounder / Apr '84 / Projection / Roots Records / Swift / C.M. Distribution / Topic Records / Jazz Music / Hot Shot / A.D.A Distribution / Direct Distribution.
MC . . . . ROUNDER 0177C
Rounder / Aug '88 / Projection / Roots Records / Swift / C.M. Distribution / Topic Records / Jazz Music / Hot Shot / A.D.A Distribution / Direct Distribution.

Driftwood, Jimmie

James Morris, born in Arkansas in 1917, was a high school teacher and song collector who sang, played guitar and mouth bow. His albums on RCA included Battle of New Orleans, subsequently a huge hit for Johnny Horton and Tennessee Stud, a hit for Eddy Arnold. He performed for teachers conventions, on TV and at Carnegie Hall and won Grammies. Of all his albums to be re-issued Billy Yank and Johnny Reb is spoiled by its 'countrypolitan' production, the honesty his presentation sullied with an incessant snare drum and a slick Nashville chorus. (Donald Clarke)

AMERICANA.
Tracks: Unfortunate man / Fair Rosamund's bower / Soldier's joy / Country boy / I'm too young to marry / Pretty Mary / Sailor man / Zelma Lee / Rattlesnake song / Old Joe Clark / Tennesse stud / Razorback steak / First covered wagon / Maid of Argenta, The / Bunker Hill / Song of the cowboys / Peter Francisco / Four little girls in Boston / Slack your rope / Run Johnny run / Arkansas traveller / Damn Yankee lad / Chalamette / Battle of New Orleans, The / Land where the bluegrass grows, The / Widders of Bowling green, The / Get along

boys / Sweet Betsy from pike / Shoot the buffalo / Song of the pioneer / I'm leavin' on the wagon train / Jordan am a hard to travel / Marshall of Silver City, The / Wilderness road, The / Pony express, The / Mooshatonio / Shanty in the holler, The / Big river man / Big John Davy / On top of Pikes peak / Fi di diddle um-a-dazey / Song of creation, The / Battle of San Juan hill, The / Banjer pickin' man / Tucumcari / St. Brendan's Isle / He had a long chain on / Big Hoss / Sal's got a sugar lip / Ox driving song / General Custer / What was your name in the States / Billy the Kid / Jesse James / Billy Yank & Johnny Reb / Won't you come along & go / Rock of Chickamauga / How do you like the army / Git along little yearlings / Oh Florie / I'm a poor rebel soldier / My black bird has gone / Goodbye Reb, you all come / On top of Shiloh's hill / When I swim the Golden River / Giant of the thunderhead, The / Shang-hied / Santy Anny O-Roe / Bullies Row / Land of the Amazon, The / What could I do / Driftwood at sea / In a cotton shirt & a pair of dungarees / Davy Jones (Song of a dead soldier) / Sailor, sailor marry me / Diver boy, The / Ship that never returned, The / Sailing away on the ocean / John Paul Jones / Bear flew over the ocean, The.
CD Set . . . . BCD 15465
Bear Family / Apr '02 / Rollercoaster Records / Swift / Direct Distribution.

SONGS OF BILLIE YANK AND JOHNNY REB.
Tracks: Won't you come along and go / Billy Yank and Johnny Reb / How do you like the army? / On top of Shiloh's Hill / I'm a pome rebel soldier / Giant on the thunderhead, The / Rock of Chickamauga / My blackbird has gone / Oh Florie / When I swim the golden river / Git along little yearlings / Goodbye Reb, you'all come.
LP . . . . NL 89994
■ MC . . . . NK 89994
RCA / Jan '87.

Drusky, Roy

Country pop singer/songwriter born in 1930 in Atlanta. He had recorded for Starday and CBS and written hits for others (Faron Young's Alone with You was a number one) and finally had his own hits on MCA and Mercury after 1960. On Capitol from 1974 he had no more hit singles, but recorded highly praised albums. The title song of Anymore was a 1960 hit for Teresa Brewer. (Donald Clarke)

ALL MY HARD TIMES.
Tracks: All my hard times.
■ 7" 6052 188
Mercury / Jan '73.

ANYMORE.
Tracks: Anymore / Burning bridges / He had it on his mind / I'd rather loan you out / Almost can't / I wonder where you are tonight / I've got some / Three hearts in a tangle / Another / Alone with you / Before I lose my mind / Swing wide your gate of love.
LP . . . . HAT 3033
MC . . . . HATC 3033
Stetson / Apr '87 / Crusader Marketing Co. / Swift / Wellard Dist. / Midland Records / C.M. Distribution.

COUNTRY CLASSICS FROM..
Tracks: Anymore / Fraulein / Jody and the kid / My grass is green / New lips / Rainbows and roses / Such a fool / Where the blue and lonely go / White lightnin' express / Woman, woman / You'd better sit down kids.
LP 6336 261
Philips / Oct '77 / PolyGram.

COUNTRY ROSE.
Tracks: Not Advised.
LP . . . . N 23005
MC 43005
Colorado / Dec '85.

NIGHT FLYING.
Tracks: Not Advised.
LP . . . . BRA 1013
MC . . . . BRC 1013
Big R / Oct '81 / Pinnacle.

NIGHT FLYING.
Tracks: Night flying / Daddy's little cowboy.
7" . . . . BRS 04
Big R / Aug '81 / Pinnacle.

ROY.
Tracks: Not Advised.
LP . . . . BRA 1009
Big R / Feb '81 / Pinnacle.

Dry Cane

WITH COUNTRY IN MIND.
Tracks: Not Advised.
LP . . . . BGC 295
Country House / Dec '81 / Duncans / BGS Productions Ltd.
■ MC . . . . KBGC 295
Country House / Dec '81.

Dudley, Dave

Country singer born in Wisconsin in 1920, famous for truck driving songs. He had worked in

music for 20 years before he recorded Six Days on the Road in 1961, which didn't get released until 1963: it became a top pop and country hit and launched hundreds of truck driving songs. He signed to Mercury and had many hits, later recording for other labels including Sun, where he made a duet album with Charlie Douglas, the truckdrivers favourite DJ. (Donald Clarke).

20 GREAT TRUCK HITS: DAVE DUDLEY.
Tracks: Six days on the road / Counterfeit cowboy / Rollin' on your track / Me and ole C.B. / Wave at 'em Billy Boy / I have been known not to go home / One more plane / Fireball rolled a seven / Let me dream / Denimus & diamonds / Texas Ruby / Rollin' rig / 1776 / Big stuff / Truckin' dad / Rooster Hill / Been around the Horn / Sentimental journey / My sunny overgrown country town / Sugarland USA.
LP 7C 062 82631
EMI (Sweden) / '83.

COLLECTION: DAVE DUDLEY.
Tracks: Not Advised.
LP . . . . IC 028 64521
EMI (Germany) / '83.

COUNTRY BEST.
Tracks: John Henry, No 2 / I'm goin' home / I'm single again / Waterin' hole, The / Roving gambler / Now and then / Yellow rose of Texas / Charlie's shoes / Soldier's spouse lament / Six days on the road / Lookin' south / Place in the sun, A.
LP . . . . BDL 1062
Bulldog Records / Aug '88 / President Records / Jazz Music / Wellard Dist. / TKO Records Ltd.

HERE HE IS.
Tracks: Not Advised.
■ CD 11040
Delta (1) / '86.

ON THE ROAD.
Tracks: Not Advised.
MC 0660 324
IMS / Apr '81 / PolyGram.

SIX DAYS ON THE ROAD.
Tracks: Not Advised.
MC 4XLL 9039
Capitol (Specials) / Dec '88.

TRUCK DRIVIN' SON OF A GUN.
Tracks: D.J. Memphis Joe / I got lost / Jack-knife / Just a few more miles / Operation X / Quittin' time / Speed traps, weigh stations and detour signs / Sugarland USA / Truck driver's waltz / Truck drivin' son of a gun / Two six packs away / Wreck of the old slow binder.
LP 6336 254
Philips / Sep '77 / PolyGram.

TRUCK SONGS.
Tracks: Wreck of the old slow binder / Two six packs away / I got lost / Truck drivin' son of a gun / Jack knife / Sugarland USA / Truck driver's waltz / Speed traps, weigh stations and detour signs.
LP 9279 147
MC 7259 147
Mercury (Import) / Mar '84.

Duff, Mary

Born in Lobin Town, County Meath. Mary Duff is one of the most successful new breed of female singers on the Irish scene, possessing a voice that well surpasses country music boundaries, as winessed by her much radio programmed Homeland in 1992. She first gained attention by touring with tour attraction Daniel O'donnell and, in 1989, beat all competition in the annual EuroMasters presentation, opening up the doorways for a series of prime European events. One of the highlights of her career was supporting Garth Brooks at his sell-out London debut concert in February 1991. (Tony Byworth)

AMAZING GRACE.
Tracks: Amazing grace / White rose of Athens, The / Beautiful Meath / Sally gardens.
EP . . . . RITZ 191
MC Single . . . . .RITZC 191
Ritz / Oct '88 / Pinnacle / Midland Records.

AN EVENING WITH MARY DUFF.
Tracks: Come on in / Goin' gone / Your one & only / Silver & gold / Mama was a working man / Cliffs or Dooneen, The / Just loving you / Homeland / Medley (Sweet dreams; Faded love; Walking after midnight; I fall to pieces; A poor mans roses; Crazy) / Picture of me without you, A / I'll fly away / Sunshine & rain / Power of love, The / I quit / Goin' home.
VHS . . . . RITZV 0014
Ritz / Jan '93 / Pinnacle / Midland Records.

DADDY'S HANDS.
Tracks: Daddy's hands / Spancil Hill.
7" . . . . RITZ 179
Ritz / Oct '87 / Pinnacle / Midland Records.

DEAR GOD.
Tracks: Dear God / Love someone like me.
7" . . . . RITZ 184
Ritz / Apr '88 / Pinnacle / Midland Records.

GOIN' GONE.
Tracks: Goin' gone.
7" . . . . **RITZ 198**
Ritz / Apr '89 / Pinnacle / Midland Records.

HOMELAND.
Tracks: Homeland / Down by the Sally gardens.
7" . . . . **RITZ 242**
CD Single . . . . **RITZCD 242**
MC Single . . . . **RITZ C 242**
Ritz / Oct '92 / Pinnacle / Midland Records.

LIVE IN CONCERT.
Tracks: Come on in / There won't be any patches in heaven / Beautiful heath / Forever and ever amen / From a distance / Daddy's hands / Maggie / Me and Bobby Magee / Yellow roses / Chicken every Sunday / White rose of Athens / Golden jubilee / Amazing grace / Jambalaya.
VHS . . . . **RITZV 0009**
Ritz / '90 / Pinnacle / Midland Records.

LOVE SOMEONE LIKE ME.
Tracks: Love someone like me / She's got you / Are you teasing me / Crazy / Forever and ever amen / It's not over (if I'm not over you) / Daddy's hands / Pick me up (on your way down) / Dear God / Chicken every Sunday / There won't be any patches in heaven / Do me with love.
CD . . . . **RITZCD 106**
Ritz / Apr '88 / Pinnacle / Midland Records.
LP . . . . **RITZLP 0044**
MC . . . . **RITZLC 0044**
Ritz / Mar '88 / Pinnacle / Midland Records.
CD . . . . **RITZCD 503**
MC . . . . **RITZRC 503**
Ritz / '91 / Pinnacle / Midland Records.

SILVER AND GOLD.
Tracks: Your one and only / Picture of me (without you), A / Walk the way the wind blows / Deep watr / Silver and gold / Mama was a working man / Sunshine and rain / Homeland / One you slip around with / Where would that leave me / I'll be your San Antone rose / Fields of Athenry, The / Beautiful meath / Down by the Sally gardens.
CD . . . . **RITZCD 0066**
MC . . . . **RITZLC 0066**
Ritz / May '92 / Pinnacle / Midland Records.

WINNING WAYS.
Tracks: Goin' gone / Yellow roses / Eighteen wheels and a dozen roses / Can I sleep in your arms / Once a day / Does Fort Worth ever cross your mind / One bird on a wing / Just out of reach / Heartaches by the number / I'm not that lonely yet / Come on in / Maggie.
CD . . . . **RITZCD 112**
MC . . . . **RITZC 051**
Ritz / Mar '90 / Pinnacle / Midland Records.
CD . . . . **RITZCD 506**
MC . . . . **RITZRC 506**
Ritz / '91 / Pinnacle / Midland Records.

YELLOW ROSES.
Tracks: Yellow roses / Come on in.
7" . . . . **RITZ 208**
Ritz / Mar '90 / Pinnacle / Midland Records.

Duffy Brothers

HILLBILLY COUNTRY.
Tracks: Not Advised.
MC . . . . **VCA 047**
VFM Cassettes / Aug '78 / VFM Children's Entertainment Ltd. / Midland Records / Morley Audio Services.

IF I NEEDED YOU.
Tracks: If I needed you / Banjo boogie.
7" . . . . **DBW 021**
Marina / Dec '82.

NASSINGTON FLYER (Duffy Brothers & Ron Ryan).
Tracks: Not Advised.
LP . . . . **BUFF L-2001**
Buffalo (UK) / Mar '79 / M.I.S.Records.

WILD OVER US.
Tracks: Uncle Pen / Handsome Molly / Bucking mule / Black mountain rag / I wonder if you're lonesome too / I'll be going to Heaven sometime / Can't tell the boys from the girls / Cedar Hill / I'm crying my heart out over you / Wild over me / You've been fooling me baby / This weary heart / Will the circle be unbroken?.
LP . . . . **FHR 074**
Folk Heritage / Jul '82 / Terry Blood Dist.

Duncan, Carey

ALL I HAVE TO DO IS DREAM.
Tracks: All I have to do is dream.
7" . . . . **DBS 7**
Decibel / Jul '81.

I'M YOUR WOMAN.
Tracks: I'm your woman.
7" . . . . **DBS 3**
DB / Nov '80 / DB Records.

NOBODY'S CHILD.
Tracks: Nobody's child / They call it CB.
7" . . . . **BB 001**
Double B / Apr '82.

RAGSY.
Tracks: Ragsy.
■ **7"** . . . . **MAM 180**
M.A.M / Oct '78.

RAINING IN MY HEART.
Tracks: Raining in my heart.
7" . . . . **RITZ 070**
Ritz / Jun '84 / Pinnacle / Midland Records.

TURNING AWAY.
Tracks: Turning away / It's her you're thinking of.
7" . . . . **RITZ 094**
Ritz / Jan '85 / Pinnacle / Midland Records.

Duncan, Johnny

This American singer and guitarist, born in Tennessee, enjoyed brief British fame in 1957 while remaining unknown in his home country. His first important musical experience occurred in his early teens when he sang in a gospel quartet. He started playing guitar at the age of 16 (1947) and soon joined Bill Monroe's Blue Grass Boys, Monroe being a noted country/blues fusionist. Duncan was drafted into the US Army and, in 1953, was posted in Britain; later that year he married a British girl. He then decided to settle in the UK after his discharge. In 1956 his musical career received a boost, when he replaced the fast-rising star Lonnie Donegan as skiffle singer in the Chris Barber Band; with *Rock Island Line* becoming a transatlantic Top 10 hit, Donegan was in the process of spearheading the UK's skiffle boom. Because of his nationality and his experience in bluegrass music, Duncan's style was more authentic than Donegan's, and he therefore attracted a credibility tag. By the start of 1957, Duncan felt confident enough to leave Barber and form his own combo, Johnny Duncan & The Blue Grass Boys. Later that year, Duncan and his group achieved their first and only major UK hit - *Last Train to San Fernando*, an evocative and enjoyable single, was a no.2 smash. However, the two follow-up singles, *Blue Blue Heartaches* and *Footprints in the Snow*, both peaked at no.27, and subsequent attempts failed to make the British charts. They continued to be a successful live group for a while, but Duncan was fading into obscurity by the end of the 50's. (Bob MacDonald).

BLUE BLUE HEARTACHES (Duncan, Johnny & The Blue Grass Boys).
Tracks: Blue blue heartaches.
■ **7"** . . . . **DB 3996**
Columbia (EMI) / Oct '57.

FOOTPRINTS IN THE SNOW (Duncan, Johnny & The Blue Grass Boys).
Tracks: Footprints in the snow.
■ **7"** . . . . **DB 4029**
Columbia (EMI) / Nov '57.

LAST TRAIN TO SAN FERNANDO (Duncan, Johnny & The Blue Grass Boys).
Tracks: Last train to San Fernando / Itching for my baby / Geisha girl / Jig along home / Railroad, steamboat, river and canal / I heard the bluebirds sing / Git along home Cindy / Raise a ruckus tonight / Rockabilly baby / Detour / Which way did he go / Blue, blue heartaches / Footprints in the snow / My little baby / Yellow moon / Pan American / I'm movin' on / Dang me.
LP . . . . **BFX 15169**
Bear Family / '86 / Rollercoaster Records / Swift / Direct Distribution.

LAST TRAIN TO SAN FERNANDO (Duncan, Johnny & The Blue Grass Boys).
Tracks: Last train to San Fernando.
■ **7"** . . . . **DB 3959**
Columbia (EMI) / Jul '57.

WORLD OF COUNTRY MUSIC VOL 2 (Duncan, Johnny & The Blue Grass Boys).
Tracks: Mustang prang / Life can be beautiful / Hello heartache / If it feels good, do it / Wild side of life / Just for what I am / Salty dog blues / Just a little lovin' / Footprints in the snow / Blue, blue heartaches / Someone to give my love to / Hey good lookin' / I can't help it / Jambalaya / Smoke, smoke, smoke / Tom Dooley / Last train to San Fernando / Mustang prang (revisited).
LP . . . . **SPA 295**
Decca / '73 / PolyGram.

Duncan, Johnny

Born in Dublin, Texas, he moved to Nashville in 1964 and worked as a DJ before establishing himself as a recording artist. A cousin of England Dan Seals and Jimmy Seals, his chart successes total around the the 40 mark with the biggest being *Thinkin' of a rendezvous* , *It couldn't have been any better* and *She can put her shoes under my bed (anytime)* . It was Duncan's recordings that first gave recognition to the talents of session singer Janie Fricke, who became a hit artist in her own right. (Tony Byworth)

COME A LITTLE BIT CLOSER.
Tracks: Come a little bit closer (with Janie Fricke) / Star-studded nights / Cheatin' in the key of 'C' / Jukebox Cinderella / Red, red wine / Song in the night, A / Cowboy and the lady, The / Lonliness (can break a good man down) / Last night made my day / Use my love.
■ **LP** **82571**
CBS / '78 / Sony.

GREATEST HITS: JOHNNY DUNCAN.
Tracks: Stranger / Sweet country woman / Atlanta Georgia stray / She can put her shoes under my bed / Come a little bit closer / Song in the night / It couldn't have been any better / Jo and the cowboy / Thinkin' of a rendezvous / Scarlet water.
■ **LP** . . . . **CBS 83486**
CBS / Apr '79.

IT COULDN'T HAVE BEEN ANY BETTER.
Tracks: It couldn't have been any better / Denver woman.
■ **7"** . . . . **CBS 5184**
CBS / Jun '77.

JOHNNY DUNCAN.
Tracks: Thinkin' of a rendezvous / Ain't you something else / Maybe I just crossed your mind / Atlanta Georgia stray / Damn it all / It couldn't have been any better / Love should be easy / Charley is my name / Third rate romance / Denver woman.
■ **LP** **82021**
CBS / '78 / Sony.

NICE 'N' EASY (Duncan, Johnny & Janie Fricke).
Tracks: He's out of my life / Nice 'n' easy / There's nothing stronger than our love / Baby / Loving arms / Come a little bit closer / It couldn't have been any better / Atlanta Georgia stray / Thinkin' of a rendezvous / Stranger.
■ **LP** . . . . **CBS 85111**
CBS / Sep '81.

Duncan, Stuart

STUART DUNCAN.
Tracks: Bushy fork of John Creek/Mason's apron / G Forces / Thai clips / Passing, The / Miles to go / Lee highway blues / Lonely moon / Whistlin' Rufus / Summer of my dreams, The / My dixie home / Two o'clock in the morning.
CD . . . . **ROUCD 0263**
MC . . . . **ROU 0263**
Rounder / '92 / Projection / Roots Records / Swift / C.M. Distribution / Topic Records / Jazz Music / Hot Shot / A.D.A Distribution / Direct Distribution.

Dunn, Holly

Born 22.8.1957 San Antonio, Texas - singer songwriter, started out in 1975, singing lead & playing drums/guitar for the Freedom Folk Singers. Moved to Nashville in 1979, became staff writer (teaming up with her brother Chris Walters) for CBS & MTM, for whom she'd later record (1985 - 1988). Early covers coming from Louise Mandrell and The Whites (*Daddy's Hands*). Meanwhile she scored in her ownright top ten hits with *A Face In The Crowd* (with Michael Martin Murphy), no 2 position with *Love Someone Like Me, That's what love does to me.* Signed to Warner Bros in 1988, after MTM had folded - her debut no 1 *Are You Ever Gonna Love Me* (1989) from her well recieved album *The Blue Rose Of Texas*, joined in 1990 by *You Really Had Me Goin.* Since which time this expansive talent's work has met with only limited success, Her 1992 Warner Bros album *Getting It Dunn* whilst once again displaying her fine songwriting prowess, once again failed to spawn the anticipated hits. Dunn's remake of Mel Tillis' *No love have I* going the same way as *Golden Years*all failing to score hits. For the moment she's left without a major label. (Maurice Hope)

BLUE ROSE OF TEXAS, THE.
Tracks: Are you ever gonna love me? / Most of all, Why? / No one takes the train anymore / Sometime today / If I'd never loved you / You're still keeping me up at night / Thunder and lightnin' / Blue rose of Texas, The / There goes my heart again / There's no heart so strong.
■ **CD** . . . . **K 9259392**
WEA / Jul '89 / WEA.
LP . . . . **K 9259391**
■ **MC** . . . . **K 9259394**
WEA / Jul '89.

GETTING IT DUNN.
Tracks: Not Advised.
CD **7599269492**
WEA / Sep '92 / WEA.

Durkin, Kathy

MEMORIES.
Tracks: Not Advised.
Double LP . . . . **HM 032D**
Harmac (Ireland) / '89 / I & B Records / Prism Leisure PLC.

D 16

■ DELETED

MOONLIGHT REFLECTIONS.
Tracks: Midnight to moonlight / Tie that binds, The / Clock in the tower, The / Love makes the world go round / Mama's angels / Rose, The / Anger and tears / Flight of Earls / Water is wide, The / Way back home, The / Boulder to Birmingham / As I leave behind Neidin / Jones on the jukebox / Blue Kentucky girl / Jigs / Save the last dance for me.
LP. . . . . HM 056
Harmac (Ireland) / Apr '90 / I & B Records / Prism Leisure PLC.

Dusty, Slim

This Australian singer achieved a one-off British smash in 1959. *A Pub with No Beer*, one of the year's most unexpected hits, reached no.3 and spent 15 weeks in the UK charts. The record did not manage to crack the American Top 40, and subsequent releases returned him to the obscurity of the then insular Australian music scene. (Bob Macdonald).

AUSTRALIA IS HIS NAME.
Tracks: Not Advised.
MC . . . . PH 1119C

Philo (USA) / '88 / Roots Records / Projection / Topic Records / Direct Distribution / Ross Records / C.M. Distribution / Impetus Records.
LP. . . . . PH 1119
Philo (USA) / Jun '88 / Roots Records / Projection / Topic Records / Direct Distribution / Ross Records / C.M. Distribution / Impetus Records.

DUNCAN.
Tracks: Duncan (part 1) / Duncan (part 2).
■ 7″. . . . . EMI 5141
EMI / Feb '81.

PUB WITH NO BEER (ORIGINAL).
Tracks: Pub with no beer, A.
■ 7″. . . . . .DB 4212
Columbia (EMI) / Jan '59.

E

Eagles

At the time of their greatest success, this American band consisted of Don Felder, Glenn Frey, Don Henley, Randy Meisner and Joe Walsh. The Eagles were formed in 1971 by Frey, Henley, Meisner and guitarist Bernie Leadon. Meisner had also been a member of Poco, and Leadon had played with the Flying Burrito Brothers. The new group flew from their Californian base to London to record their self-titled debut album, which was released in 1972. With its laid-back country rock sound, it became a major success in the States, yielding three US Top 30 singles *Take it easy* (written by Frey and singer/songwriter Jackson Browne), *Witchy woman* and *Peaceful easy feeling*. The Eagles' second album, 1973's *Desperado*, did not produce any major hit singles, but consolidated their position as one of America's most important new bands of the seventies; the title track, a touching ballad, was later covered by the Carpenters and other acts. A fifth Eagle, Felder, joined the group for 1974's *On the border* album. From 1975 onwards, the Eagles could do no wrong. Their blend of vocal harmonies, ace musicianship and well-crafted melodic songs (emanating mainly from Frey & Henley) made them America's favourite purveyors of the Los Angeles soft rock sound. In that year, they enjoyed two US no.1 singles; the ballad *Best of my love* and *One of these nights* and a no.2 hit with *Lyin' eyes*. '75 also brought the group their first significant inroads into the UK market. In 1976 Leadon, overburdened by the pressure of the Eagles' growing international superstardom, was replaced by the acclaimed guitar wizard Joe Walsh. This was a somewhat unexpected move for Walsh, who had already made his name as a member of the James Gang and also a solo performer. His style was heavier than the rest of the Eagles, but the two sounds complemented each other superbly. The *Hotel California* LP was a worldwide smash; the title track was a US no.1 and their only UK Top 10 single; and they also topped the American charts with another track, *New kid in town*. The Eagles' sixth and final studio LP *The long run* was not issued until 1979, by which time Meisner had quit and had been replaced by another ex-Poco player, Timothy Schmit. Like *Hotel California*, *The long run* enjoyed a long run at the top of the US album charts, but it was not as good as its predecessor. After 1980's live album, the Eagles drifted apart, although no official split was announced. Henley & Frey, the only two perennial members, both went on to achieve solo successes. (Bob Macdonald)

BEST OF MY LOVE.
Tracks: Best of my love / Midnight flyer.
■ 7" . . . . AYM 538
Asylum / Jan '75.

BEST OF THE EAGLES.
Tracks: Tequila sunrise / Lyin' eyes / Take it to the limit / Hotel California / Life in the fast lane / Heartache tonight / Long run, The / Take it easy / Peaceful easy feeling / Desperado / Best of my love / One of these nights / New kid in town.
CD 960 342-2
Asylum / Jun '85 / WEA.
LP . . . . EKT 5
MC . . . . EKT 5 C
Elektra / May '85 / WEA.

DESPERADO.
Tracks: Doolin Dalton / 21 / Out of control / Tequila sunrise / Desperado / Certain kind of fool / Outlaw man / Saturday night / Bitter Creek.
LP . . . . K 53008
MC K4 53008
Asylum / Jun '76 / WEA.
CD 288 07 004
Bellaphon / '86 / New Note.
CD . . . . K 253008
Asylum / '89 / WEA.

DESPERADO.
Tracks: Desperado.
■ 7" . . . . SYLL 9011
Asylum / Jul '75.

DESPERADO/ONE OF THESE NIGHTS.
Tracks: Doolin Dalton / Twenty one / Out of control / Tequila sunrise / Desperado / Certain kind of fool / Doolin Dalton (instrumental) / Outlaw man / Saturday night / Bitter creek / Desperado (reprise) / One of these nights / Too many hands / Hollywood waltz / Journey of the sorcerer / Lyin' eyes / Take it to the limit / Visions / After the thrill is gone / I wish you peace.
MC K4 62033
Asylum / '83 / WEA.

EAGLES.
Tracks: Take it easy / Witchy woman / Chug all night / Most of us are sad / Nightingale / Train leaves here this morning / Take the devil / Earlybird / Peaceful easy feeling / Trying / Doolin Dalton / Twenty one / Out of control / Tequila sunrise / Desperado / Certain kind of fool / Outlaw man / Saturday night / Bitter creek.
MC K4 53009
Asylum / Jun '76 / WEA.
■ LP . . . . K 53009
Asylum / Jun '76.
CD 253 009-2
Asylum / Feb '87 / WEA.
CD . . . . K 253009
WEA / '89 / WEA.

EAGLES LIVE.
Tracks: Hotel California / Heartache tonight / I can't tell you why / Long run, The / New kid in town / Life's been good / Seven bridges road / Wasted time / Take it to the limit / Doolin Dalton / Desperado / Saturday night / All night long / Life in the fast lane / Take it easy.
MC K4 62032
Asylum / Nov '80 / WEA.
■ LP . . . . K 62032
Asylum / Nov '80.

GREATEST HITS: EAGLES VOL.2.
Tracks: Heartache tonight / I can't tell you why / Seven bridges road / Victim of love / Sad cafe, The / Life in the fast lane / I can't tell you why / New kid in town / Long run, The / After the thrill is gone.
LP 9602051
■ MC 9602054
Asylum / Dec '82.
CD 9602052
Asylum / Oct '82 / WEA.

GREATEST HITS: THE EAGLES.
Tracks: Not Advised.

HEARTACHE TONIGHT.
Tracks: Heartache tonight.
■ 7" . . . . K 12394
Asylum / Oct '79.

HOTEL CALIFORNIA.
Tracks: Hotel California / New kid in town / Life in the fast lane / Wasted time / Wasted time (reprise) / Pretty maids all in a row / Try and love again / Last resort, The / Victim of love.
LP . . . . K 53051
MC K4 53051
Asylum / Jan '77 / WEA.
CD 253 051
Asylum / May '87 / WEA.

HOTEL CALIFORNIA.
Tracks: Hotel California / Pretty maids all in a row.
■ 7" . . . . K 13079
Elektra / Jul '81.
12" . . . . EKR 10T
■ 7" . . . . EKR 10
Elektra / Sep '88.

HOTEL CALIFORNIA (OLD GOLD).
Tracks: Hotel California / Desperado.
7" . . . . OG 9511
Old Gold / Sep '85 / Pickwick Records.

HOTEL CALIFORNIA/LONG RUN, THE.
Tracks: Hotel California / New kid in town / Life in the fast lane / Wasted time / Wasted time (reprise) / Victim of love / Pretty maids all in a row / Try and love again / Last resort, The / Long run, The / I can't tell you why / In the city / Disco strangler, The / King of Hollywood / Heartache tonight / Those shoes / Teenage jail / Greeks don't want no freaks, The / Sad cafe, The.
MC Set 9602754
Asylum / '84 / WEA.

LIFE IN THE FAST LANE.
Tracks: Life in the fast lane / Last resort, The.
■ 7" . . . . K 13085
Asylum / Jul '77.

LONG RUN, THE.
Tracks: Long run, The / I can't tell you why / In the city / Disco strangler, The / King of Hollywood / Heartache tonight / Those shoes / Teenage jail / Greeks don't want no freaks, The / Sad cafe, The.
LP . . . . K 52181
MC K4 52181
Asylum / Sep '79 / WEA.
CD 252 181
Asylum / '86 / WEA.

LONG RUN, THE.
Tracks: Long run, The / Disco strangler.
■ 7" . . . . K 12404
Elektra / Dec '79.

LYIN' EYES.
Tracks: Lyin' eyes / Too many hands.
■ 7" . . . . AYM 548
Asylum / Nov '75.
■ 7" . . . . K 13025
Asylum / Oct '77.

LYIN' EYES (OLD GOLD).
Tracks: Lyin' eyes / One of these nights.
7" . . . . OG 9526
Old Gold / Sep '85 / Pickwick Records.

NEW KID IN TOWN.
Tracks: New kid in town / Victim of love.
■ 7" . . . . K 13069
Asylum / Jan '77.

ON THE BORDER.
Tracks: Already gone / You never cry like a lover / Midnight flyer / My man / On the border / James Dean / 01 55 / Is it true / Good day in hell / Best of my love.
■ LP . . . . SYL 9016
Asylum / Apr '74.
CD 243 005
LP . . . . K 43005
MC K4 43005
Asylum / Jun '76 / WEA.

ONE OF THESE NIGHTS.
Tracks: One of these nights / Too many hands / Hollywood waltz / Journey of the sorcerer / Lyin' eyes / Take it to the limit / Visions / After the thrill is gone / I wish you peace.
■ LP . . . . SYLA 8759
Asylum / Jul '75.
LP . . . . K 53014
MC K4 53014
Asylum / Jun '76 / WEA.
CD K253014
Asylum / '89 / WEA.

ONE OF THESE NIGHTS.
Tracks: One of these nights.
■ 7" . . . . AYM 543
Asylum / Aug '75.

PLEASE COME HOME FOR CHRISTMAS.
Tracks: Please come home for Christmas / Funky New Year.
■ 7" . . . . K 13145
Asylum / Dec '78.

SAD CAFE.
Tracks: Sad Cafe / Those shoes.
■ 7" . . . . K 12440
Asylum / May '80.

TAKE IT EASY.
Tracks: Take it easy / Witchy woman.
■ 7" . . . . K 13044
WEA / '79.

TAKE IT TO THE LIMIT.
Tracks: Take it to the limit / Seven bridges road.
■ 7" . . . . K 13029
Asylum / Mar '76.
7" . . . . K 12504
Elektra / Feb '81 / WEA.

TAKE IT TO THE LIMIT (OLD GOLD).
Tracks: Take it to the limit / Best of my love.
7" . . . . OG 9510
Old Gold / Sep '85 / Pickwick Records.

THEIR GREATEST HITS 1971-1975.
Tracks: Take it easy / Witchy woman / Lyin' eyes / Already gone / Desperado / One of these nights / Tequila sunrise / Take it to the limit / Peaceful easy feeling / Best of my love.
MC K4 53017
Asylum / Feb '76 / WEA.
■ LP . . . . K 53017
Asylum / Feb '76.
CD 253 017-2
Asylum / May '87 / WEA.

TRYING TO GET TO YOU.
Tracks: What a crazy feeling / Trying to get to you / Don't you wanna be mine / Such a fool / I told myself / Do you need me (like I need you) / Please, please / Just right / I stole a rose.
LP . . . . BF 15232
Bear Family / '89 / Rollercoaster Records / Swift / Direct Distribution.

Eanes, Jim

BLUEGRASS BALLADS.
Tracks: Where the cool water flows / Orchids of love / Just for you / Legend of the girl / On the cliff / If I had my time to live over / Sally's the girl for me / I'll pretend it's raining / Rose garden waltz / Sleeping where the

---

■ DELETED

E 1

roses grow / Baby blue eyes / All the good times are past and gone / Kentucky bluegrass angels.
LP. . . . . REBEL 1643
MC . . . . REBEL 1643C
Rebel (1) / '86 / Projection / Backs Distribution.

LET HIM LEAD YOU.
Tracks: Welcome in / Crown of thorns / Jesus is my guiding light / Mother taught me how to pray / In his arms I'm not afraid / Coming of the Lord / Little house of prayer / Old Satan / Let him lead you / Candle song / When they ring those golden bells / Take me home blessed Jesus.
LP. . . . . REBEL 1673
Rebel (1) / '90 / Projection / Backs Distribution.

REMINISCING.
Tracks: Not Advised.
LP. . . . . REBEL 1653
MC . . . . REBEL 1653C
Rebel (1) / '88 / Projection / Backs Distribution.

Earle, Steve

Born 17.01.1955 in Fort Monroe, Virginia, raised near Schertz in San Antonio, Texas. Came to the fore during the late 1980's new country boom, although he'd been writing songs in Nashville for ten years or more since moving there in 1974. Worked for various publishing companies, becoming a manager of one, and did some demo work to complement his writing. His initial recording contract came in 1983 with Epic - *Nothin' but you* being his debut chart single. Moved to MCA in 1986, after the album *Cadillac* was made for Epic but not released until 1987 under the title *Early tracks* . His folk country ballad *Devil's right hand* gained a number of covers. On the singles charts he charted with *Hillbilly highway* , top ten track *Guitar town* (it's parent album, apart from topping the country charts, is considered one of the finest albums to come out of the country era) and *Goodbye's all we've got left* . Earle, with his band The Dukes, was from then on to veer away from country, venturing into the heavier country rock regions. More hits were to include *Sweet little '66* , and *Six days on the road* , featured in the film "Planes, Trains and Automobiles". His 1988 album *Copperhead Road* found him in the company of the Pogues, who joined him on the hit single *Johnny come lately* . The follow-up album *The hard way* made it to No. 22 in the UK pop charts. Despite his wild rugged image, he's also toured the UK as an acoustic act. (Maurice Hope)

BACK TO THE WALL.
Tracks: Back to the wall.
12" . . . . MCAT 1319
■ 7" . . . . MCA 1319
MCA / Feb '89.
■ CD Single . . . . DMCAT 1319
MCA / Feb '89.

BBC RADIO 1 IN CONCERT.
Tracks: Not Advised.
CD . . . . WINCD 020
MC . . . . WINMC 020
Windsong / Jun '92 / Pinnacle.

COPPERHEAD ROAD.
Tracks: Copperhead Road / Snake oil / Back to the wall / Devil's right hand / Johnny come lately / Even when I'm blue / You belong to me / Waiting on you / Once you love / Nothing but a child.
■ LP. . . . . MCF 3426
MCA / Oct '88.
CD . . . . DMCF 3426
■ MC . . . . MCFC 3426
MCA / Oct '88.
LP. . . . . UNID 7280
UNI / Jan '89 / Jazz Horizons.
CD . . . . MCLD 19213
MCA / Sep '93 / BMG.

COPPERHEAD ROAD.
Tracks: Copperhead road.
12" . . . . MCAT 1280
MCA / Oct '88 / BMG.
■ CD Single . . . . DMCA 1280
N/A / Oct '88.
■ 7" . . . . MCA 1280
MCA / Oct '88.

EARLY TRACKS.
Tracks: Nothin' but you / If you need a fool / Continental railway blues / Open up your door / Breakdown lane / Squeeze me in / Annie, is tonight the night / My baby worships me / Cadillac / Devil's right hand.
LP. 4508731
MC 4508734
Epic / Jul '87 / Sony.
CD 9825972
Pickwick/Sony Collectors Choice / Jul '91 / Pickwick Records.

EXIT O.
Tracks: Nowhere road / Sweet little '66 / No. 29 / Angry young man / San Antonio girl / Rain came down, The / I ain't ever satisfied / Week of living dangerously, The / I love you too much / It's all up to you.
MC . . . . MCFC 3379
MCA / Apr '87 / BMG.
■ CD . . . . DMCF 3379
MCA / Apr '87.
■ LP. . . . . MCF 3379
MCA / Apr '87.
CD . . . . DMCL 1904
■ MC . . . . MCLC 1904
MCA / Aug '90.

FEARLESS HEART.
Tracks: Fearless heart / Little rock 'n' roller.
12" . . . . MCAT 1141
7" . . . . MCA 1141
MCA / Mar '87 / BMG.

GUITAR TOWN.
Tracks: Guitar town / Goodbye's all we've got left / Hillbilly highway / Good ol' boy (getting tough) / My old friend the blues / Someday / Think it over / Fearless heart / Little rock 'n' roller / Down the road.
■ LP. . . . . MCF 3335
MCA / Aug '86.
■ MC . . . . MCFC 3335
MCA / Aug '86.
■ CD . . . . DMCF 3335
MCA / Apr '87.
CD . . . . DMCL 1888
■ MC . . . . MCLC 1888
MCA / Jan '90.
CD . . . . MCLD 19008
■ MC . . . . MCLC 19008
MCA / Apr '92.

HARD WAY, THE (Earle, Steve & the Dukes).
Tracks: Other kind, The / Promise you anything / Esmerelda / Hopeless romantics / This highway / Billy Austin / Justice in Ontario / Have mercy on me / When the people find out / Country girl / Regular guy / West Nashville.
CD . . . . DMCG 6095
MCA / Jun '90 / BMG.
■ LP. . . . . MCG 6095
MCA / Jun '90.
■ MC . . . . MCGC 6095
MCA / Jun '90.

I AIN'T NEVER SATISFIED.
Tracks: I ain't never satisfied / Nowhere Road.
12" . . . . MCAS 1162
7" . . . . MCA 1162
MCA / May '87 / BMG.

JOHNNY COME LATELY.
Tracks: Johnny come lately / Nothing but a child / Nebraska (live) (Only on 12".) / Nothing but a child (album version) (Only on 12".).
■ CD Single . . . . DMCA 1301
MCA / Dec '88.
12" . . . . MCAT 1301
■ 7" . . . . MCA 1301
MCA / Nov '88.

JUSTICE IN ONTARIO (Earle, Steve & the Dukes).
Tracks: Justice in Ontario.
12" . . . . MCAT 1441
7" . . . . MCA 1441
■ CD Single . . . . DMCAT 1441
MCA / Sep '90 / BMG.

OTHER KIND (BACK OUT ON THE ROAD AGAIN), THE.
Tracks: Other kind (back out on the road again), The.
12" . . . . MCAT 1426
7" . . . . MCA 1426
CD Single . . . . DMCAT 1426
■ CD Single . . . . DMCAX 1426
MCA / May '90 / BMG.

RAIN CAME DOWN, THE.
Tracks: Rain came down, The / I love you too much / Guitar town / No. 29.
7" . . . . MCA 1209
MCA / Oct '87 / BMG.

SHUT UP AND DIE LIKE AN AVIATOR.
Tracks: Not Advised.
CD . . . . MCAD 10315
MC . . . . MCAC 10315
MCA / Aug '91 / BMG.
■ LP. . . . . MCA 10315
MCA / Aug '91.

SOMEDAY.
Tracks: Someday / Guitar town / Good ol' boy (live) / Goodbye's all we've got left (Available on 12" version only.).
7" . . . . MCA 1083
MCA / Oct '86 / BMG.
12" . . . . MCAS 1123
7" . . . . MCA 1123
MCA / Feb '87 / BMG.

WE AIN'T EVER SATISFIED (Earle, Steve & the Dukes).
Tracks: Guitar town / Someday / Fearless heart / My old friend the blues / Good ol' boy (gettin' tough) / Rain came down, The / I ain't ever satisfied / Copperhead road / Devil's right hand / Johnny come lately / Other kind Billy Austin, The.
CD . . . . MCAD 10570
MC . . . . MCAC 10570
MCA / Jul '92 / BMG.
■ LP. . . . . MCA 10570
MCA / Jul '92.

Earls, Jack

LET'S BOP.
Tracks: Let's bop / Slow down / My gal Mayann / Sign on the dotted line / Crawdad hole / They can't keep me from you / Hey Slim / Take me to that place / Fool for loving you, A / Hey Jim / When I dream / If you don't mind.
LP. . . . . BFX 15273
Bear Family / May '90 / Rollercoaster Records / Swift / Direct Distribution.

Eastwood, Clint

MAKE MY DAY (see under Sheppard, T.G.).

Echo Valley Boys

HILLBILLY ROCK.
Tracks: Wash machine boogie / Breaking hearts / Dark hollow / Born with the blues.
■ EP. . . . . RCEP 106
Rollercoaster / Feb '88 / Rollercoaster Records / Swift.

WASH MACHINE BOOGIE.
Tracks: Wash machine boogie.
■ 7" . . . . RRC 2003
Rollercoaster / Jul '79.

Edmunds, Dave

Singer/songwriter/lead guitarist/producer, born 15.04.1944 in Cardiff. Formed his band Love Sculpture in 1967 and had a 1968 hit with *Sabre Dance* . Scored a No. 1 pop hit in the U with *I Hear You Knocking* in 1971. During the 1970's he was to enjoy steady chart action as he mixed rockabilly, country remakes and pop tunes including *I Knew The Bride* , *Girl's Talk* , *Queen Of Hearts* - the first cover of Frank DeVito's composition, and a spirited remake of *Singing The Blues* . With the Stray Cats, Edmunds found chart action with *The Race Is On* taken from David Essex's sixties movie, "Stardust" , where Edmunds figures in the band. His work especially during the early 1980's, with his band Rockpile, showed distinct influences of the Everly's and rockabilly, allowing his music to take on a country feel not unlike that of Sun acts such as Carl Perkins. He has produced such acts as Brinsley Schwartz, Shakin' Stevens and the Stray Cats. He is one of the finest ever rock lead guitarists to come out of the UK. (Maurice Hope)

A.1 ON THE JUKEBOX.
Tracks: A.1 on the jukebox / It's my own business.
■ 7" . . . . SSK 19417
Swansong / '79.

ALMOST SATURDAY NIGHT.
Tracks: Almost Saturday night.
■ 7" . . . . SSK 19424
Swansong / Mar '81.

BABY I LOVE YOU.
Tracks: Baby I love you / Born to be with you.
■ 7" . . . . ROC 1
Rockfield / Jan '73.
7" . . . . GOLD 548
RCA Golden Grooves / May '82 / BMG.

BABY I LOVE YOU.
Tracks: Baby I love you / Da doo ron ron / Born to be with you / Shot of rhythm and blues.
■ EP. . . . . PE 5243
RCA / Jul '80.

BEST OF DAVE EDMUNDS.
Tracks: Deborah / Girls talk / I knew the bride / A1 on the jukebox / Race is on, The / I hear you knocking / Almost saturday night / Sabre dance / Queen of hearts / Crawling from the wreckage / Here comes the weekend / Trouble boys / Ju ju man / Singing the blues / Born to be with you.
LP. . . . . SSK 59413
MC SK4 59413
Swansong / Nov '81 / WEA.

BLUE MONDAY.
Tracks: Blue Monday / I'll get along.
7" . . . . RZ 2037
Regal Zonophone / '71 / EMI.

BORN TO BE WITH YOU.
Tracks: Born to be with you.
■ 7" . . . . ROC 2
Rockfield / Jun '73.

BORN TO BE WITH YOU (OLD GOLD).
Tracks: Born to be with you / Baby I love you.
7" . . . . OG 9833
Old Gold / Nov '88 / Pickwick Records.

CLASSIC TRACKS 1968-1972 (Edmunds, Dave & Love Sculpture).
Tracks: I hear you knocking / You can't catch me / In the land of the few / Farandole / Summertime / Blues helping / Stumble, The / Down down down / Seagull / Sabre dance / Outlaw blues / Promised land.
■ LP. . . . . OU 2047

E 2 ■ DELETED

One-Up / Sep '74.
LP. . . . . FA 413 138 1
MC . . . . FA 413 138 4
Fame / Mar '86 / EMI.

CLOSER TO THE FLAME.
Tracks: King of love / Don't talk to me / Every time I see her / Closer to the flame / Stockholm / Fallin' through a hole / Never take the place of you / I got your number / Sincerely / Test of love.
CD . . . . CDEST 2113
Capitol / Mar '90 / EMI.
LP. . . . . EST 2113
■ MC . . . . TCEST 2113
Capitol / Mar '90.
CD . . . . CZ 144
LP. ATAK 172
MC . . . . TCATAK 172
Capitol / Mar '91 / EMI.

COMPLETE EARLY EDMUNDS, THE.
Tracks: Morning dew / It's a wonder / Brand new woman / Stumble, The / 3 o'clock blues / I believe to my soul / So unkind / Summertime / On the road again / Don't answer the door / Wang-dang-doodle / Come back baby / Shake your hips / Blues helping / In the land of the few / Seagull / Nobody's talking / Farandole / You can't catch me / Mars / Sabre dance (single version) / Sabre dance / Why / People people / Think of love / Down down down / I hear you knocking / Hell of a pain / It ain't easy / Promised land, The / Dance dance dance / (I am) a lover not a fighter / Egg or the hen / Sweet little 'n' roller / Outlaw blues / Black Bill / Country roll / I'm comin' home / Blue Monday / I'll get along.
CD Set . . . . CDEM 1406
EMI / Jul '91 / EMI.
■ MC Set . . . . TCEM 1406
EMI / Jul '91.

CRAWLING FROM THE WRECKAGE.
Tracks: Crawling from the wreckage / As lovers do.
7" . . . . SSK 19420
Swansong / Nov '79 / WEA.

D.E.7.
Tracks: From small things, big things come / Me and the boys / Bail you out / Generation rumber / Other guy's girls / Warmed over kisses / Deep in the heart of Texas / Louisiana man / Paula meet Jeanne / Oe more night / Dear dad.
MC . . . . TCART 1184
Arista / '82 / BMG.
■ LP. . . . . SPART 1184
Arista / '82.
LP. . . . . FA 4130901
MC . . . . TCFA 41 30904
Fame / Mar '84 / EMI.

DAVE EDMUNDS - LOVE SCULPTURE YEARS (Vol.1) (Edmunds, Dave & Love Sculpture).
Tracks: In the land of the few / Seagull / Nobody's talking / Why (how-now) / You can't catch me / Sabre dance / People, people / Brand new woman / River to another day / Think of love / Farandole.
LP. . . . . EMS 1127
MC . . . . TCEMS 1127
EMI / Feb '87 / EMI.

DEBORAH.
Tracks: Deborah / What looks best on you.
■ 7" . . . . SSK 19413
Swansong / Sep '78.

EARLY EDMUNDS, THE.
Tracks: Not Advised.
■ CD . . . . CDP 7467122
Capitol.

EARLY WORKS 1968/72.
Tracks: Sabre dance / Think of love / River to another day / Brand new woman / Farandole / You can't catch me / In the land of the few / Stumble / Wang dang doodle / I believe to my soul / So unkind / On the road again / Shake your hips / Blues helping / Down down down / I hear you knocking / Hell of a pain / It ain't easy / Promised land / Black Bill / I'm coming home / Egg or the hen / Sweet little 'n' roller / Outlaw blues / Blue Monday / I'll get along.
Double LP . . . . 2 C 15099546/7
EMI (France) / '83 / EMI.

FROM SMALL THINGS.
Tracks: From small things / Your true love.
■ 7" . . . . ARIST 478
Arista / '82.

GET IT.
Tracks: Get out of Denver / I knew the bride / Back to schooldays / Here comes the weekend / Worn out suits, brand new pockets / Where or when / Ju ju man / Get it / Let's talk about us / Hey good lookin' / What did I do last night / Little darlin' / My baby left me.
LP. . . . . SSK 59404
Swansong / '88 / WEA.

GIRLS TALK.
Tracks: Girls talk / Bad is bad.
■ 7" . . . . SSK 19418
Swansong / Jun '79.

HIGH SCHOOL NIGHTS.
Tracks: High school nights / Porky's revenge.
. . . . A 6277
CBS / Jul '85 / Sony.

I AIN'T NEVER.
Tracks: I ain't never / Some other guy.
■ 7" . . . . ROC 6
Rockfield / Jan '75.

I HEAR YOU KNOCKING.
Tracks: I hear you knocking.
■ 7" . . . . MAM 1
M.A.M. / Nov '70.

I HEAR YOU KNOCKING.
Tracks: I hear you knocking / Black Bill.
■ 7" . . . . BLU 2010
Blue Print / Apr '80.
■ 7" G45 4
EMI Golden 45's / Mar '84.

I HEAR YOU KNOCKING (OLD GOLD).
Tracks: I hear you knocking / She's about a mover / Sabre dance.
. . . . OG 9711
Old Gold / Apr '87 / Pickwick Records.

I HEAR YOU ROCKIN'.
Tracks: I hear you knocking / Down down down / Hell of a pain / It ain't easy / Country roll / Dance, dance, dance / Lover not a fighter / Egg or the hen / Sweet little rock 'n' roller / Outlaw blues / Blue Monday / Black Bill / I'll get along / Promised land / Sabre dance.
LP. 208228
Arista / Jun '87 / BMG.
■ CD 258228
Arista / Jun '87.
■ MC 408228
Arista / Jun '87.

I KNEW THE BRIDE.
Tracks: Back to schooldays / I knew the bride.
■ 7" . . . . SSK 19411
Swansong / Jun '77.

INFORMATION.
Tracks: Slipping away / Don't you double / I want you bad / Wait / Watch on my wrist, The / Shape I'm in, The / Information / Feel so right / What have I got to do to win / Don't call me tonight / Have a heart.
LP. 205348
■ MC 405348
Arista / '83.

INFORMATION.
Tracks: Information / What have I got to do to win.
12" . . . . ARIST 12532
■ 7" . . . . ARIST 532
Arista / May '83.

KING OF LOVE.
Tracks: King of love / Stay with me tonight / Every time I see her (Not on 7").
10" 203 783 8
10" 10CL 568
12" 203 783 6
12" 12CL 568
7" 203 783 7
7" . . . . CL 568
CD Single 203 783 2
■ CD Single . . . . CDCL 568
Capitol / Mar '90.
7" . . . . CLX 568
■ 7" 203 881 7
Capitol / May '90.

ME AND THE BOYS.
Tracks: Me and the boys / Queen of hearts.
■ 7" . . . . ARIST 471
Arista / '82.

ORIGINAL ROCKPILE, THE (Volume II).
Tracks: I hear you knocking / Down down down / Hell of a pain / It ain't easy / Country roll / Dance, dance, dance / Lover not a fighter / Egg or the hen / Sweet little rock 'n' roller / Outlaw blues / Blue Monday / Black Bill / I'll get along / Promised land / I'm comin' home / Sabre dance.
LP. . . . . EMS 1126
Harvest / Aug '87 / EMI.
■ MC . . . . TCEMS 1126
Harvest / Aug '87.

QUEEN OF HEARTS.
Tracks: Queen of hearts.
■ 7" . . . . SSK 19419
Swansong / Nov '79.

RACE IS ON, THE (Edmunds, Dave & The Stray Cats).
Tracks: Race is on, The / I'm gonna start living again if it kills me.
■ 7" . . . . SSK 19425
Swansong / Jun '81.

REPEAT WHEN NECESSARY.
Tracks: Girls talk / Crawling from the wreckage / Black lagoon / Sweet little Lisa / Dynamite / Queen of hearts / Home in my hand / Goodbye Mr. Good Guy / Take me for a little while / We were both wrong / Bad is bad.
LP. . . . . SSK 59409
MC SK4 59409
Swansong / '88 / WEA.

RIFF RAFF.
Tracks: Something about you / Breaking out / Busted loose / Far away / Rules of the game / Steel claw / S.O.S. / Hang on / How could I be so wrong / Can't get away.
LP. 206396
Arista / Nov '84 / BMG.

ROCKPILE.
Tracks: Down down down / I hear you knocking / Sweet little rock 'n' roller.
LP. . . . . 5 C 038 93282
EMI (France) / Apr '83 / EMI.

SINGING THE BLUES.
Tracks: Singing the blues / Boys talk.
■ 7" . . . . SSK 19422
Swansong / Feb '80.

SINGLES A'S & B'S (Edmunds, Dave & Love Sculpture).
Tracks: I hear you knocking / Blue Monday / Down down down / Brand new woman / Black Bill / Wang dang doodle / Morning dew / Seagull / People, people / Sabre dance / Stumble, The / In the land of the few / It's a wonder / River to another day / It ain't easy / I'll get along / Country roll / I'm coming home / Think of love / Farandole.
LP. . . . . SHAM 2032
■ MC . . . . TCSHSM 2032
Harvest / Aug '80 / EMI.
CD . . . . SEECD 282
LP. . . . . SEE 282
See For Miles / '89 / Pinnacle.

SLIPPING AWAY.
Tracks: Slipping away / Don't call me tonight.
12" . . . . ARIST 12522
7" . . . . ARIST 522
Arista / Mar '83 / BMG.

SOMETHING ABOUT YOU.
Tracks: Something about you / Can't get enough.
12" . . . . ARIST 12562
7" . . . . ARIST 562
Arista / Jul '84 / BMG.

STEEL CORE.
Tracks: Steel core / How could I be so wrong.
■ 7" . . . . ARIST 583
Arista / Oct '84.

SUBTLE AS A FLYING MALLET.
Tracks: Baby I love you / Leave my woman alone / Maybe da doo ron ron / Let it be me / No money down / Shot of rhythm and blues, A / Billy the Kid / Born to be with you / She's my baby / I ain't never / Let it rock.
LP. . . . . PL 25129
■ MC . . . . PK 25129
RCA / '79.
LP. . . . . INTS 5131
MC . . . . INTK 5131
RCA International / Sep '81 / BMG.

TELEVISION.
Tracks: Television / Never been in love.
■ 7" . . . . SSK 19414
Swansong / Dec '78.

TRACKS ON WAX 4.
Tracks: Trouble boys / Never been in love / Not a woman, not a child / Television / What looks best on you / Readers wives / Deborah / Thread your needle / A1 on the jukebox / It's my own business / Heart of the city.
LP. . . . . SSK 59407
MC SK4 59407
Swansong / '88 / WEA.

TWANGIN'..
Tracks: Something happens / It's been so long / Singing the blues / I'm gonna start living again if it kills me / Almost Saturday night / Cheap talk, patter and jive / You'll never get me up / I'm only human / Race is on, The / Baby let's play house.
■ LP. . . . . SSK 59411
■ MC SK4 59411
Swansong / May '81.

WARMED OVER KISSES.
Tracks: Warmed over kisses.
■ 7" . . . . ARIST 439
Arista / '82.

WHERE OR WHEN.
Tracks: Where or when / New York's a lonely town.
■ 7" . . . . SSK 19409
Swansong / Oct '76.

Edwards, Bill

COUNTRY SOUNDS.
Tracks: Not Advised.
LP. . . . . LKLP 6581
Look / '88 / C.M. Distribution.

Edwards, Stoney

JUST FOR OLD TIMES SAKE.
Tracks: Just for old times sake / You're the one I sing my love songs to / I miss you / That old river / They all come down / Lately I've been leanin' towards the blues

/ After all / Me and you / I can't find a way to say goodbye / Dixie sundown.
CD . . . . RBRCD 1000
Ragged But Right / Jul '91.

Edwards, Terry

MARTY ROBBINS SONGBOOK.
Tracks: Big iron / Cool water / Devil woman / Streets of Laredo / El Paso / Singing the blues / Story of my life.
MC . . . . AIM 112
AIM (2) / Sep '83 / Topic Records / Direct Distribution.

SLIM WHITMAN SONGBOOK (VOL.2), THE.
Tracks: Tell me / Tumbling tumbleweeds / We stood at the altar / Love sick blues / Mockin' Bird Hill.
MC . . . . AIM 116
AIM (2) / Sep '83 / Topic Records / Direct Distribution.

Elkin, Greta

MARRIED AND THE FREE, THE.
Tracks: Not Advised.
LP. . . . . RBA 1001
Rainbow (Ireland) / '88.

MOCKIN' BIRD, THE.
Tracks: Not Advised.
LP. . . . . RBA 132
Rainbow (Ireland) / '88.

Elliott, Jack

Born Elliott Charles Adnopez in 1931, a folksinger, songwriter and guitarist, aka Ramblin' Jack, the singing cowboy from Brooklyn. He ran away from home (a 45,000-acre ranch in the middle of Flatbush) to join the rodeo, soon met Woody Guthrie and toured with him until Woody said that Jack 'sound more like me than I do'. he spent the mid-'50's in Europe, acquiring a large following which had never been able to hear Guthrie; he played with Derroll Adams in London ,and was a considerable influence on UK music. He also toured with the Weavers, recorded with Johnny Cash and Tom Rush; like Arlo Guthrie he is major link between a bygone age and today's folk scene. (Donald Clarke).

HARD TRAVELLIN' (Songs by Woody Guthrie & others).
Tracks: Hard travelin' / Grand Coulee Dam / New York Town / Tom Joad / Howdido / Dust bowl blues / This land is your land / Pretty Boy Floyd / Philadelphia lawyer / Talking Columbia blues / Dust storm disaster / Riding in my car / 1913 massacre / So long (it's been good to know yuh) / Sadie Brown / East Virginia blues / I belong to glasgow / Cuckoo, The / Roll in my sweet baby's arms / South coast / San Francisco Bay blues / Last letter, The / Candy man / Tramp on the street / Railroad Bill.
CD . . . . CDWIK 952
Big Beat / Aug '90 / Pinnacle / Hot Shot / Jazz Music.

JACK ELLIOTT OF BIRTLEY.
Tracks: Not Advised.
LP. . . . . LEA 4001
Leader / '81 / Roots Records / Projection / Duncans / C.M. Distribution / Ross Records.

KEROUAC'S LAST DREAM.
Tracks: Not Advised.
LP. . . . . FF 4005
Folk Freak / '88 / Roots Records / Projection / Duncans / C.M. Distribution / Impetus Records / Ross Records.

MULESKINNER.
Tracks: San Francisco bay blues / Ol' Riley / Boll weevil / Bed bug blues / New York town / Old blue / Grey goose / Mule skinner blues / East Texas talking blues / Cocaine / Dink's song / Black baby / Salt dog.
LP. 12T 106
Topic / '81 / Roots Records / Jazz Music / C.M. Distribution / Cadillac Music / Direct Distribution / Swift / Topic Records.

ROLL ON BUDDY.
Tracks: Rich and rambling boy / Buffalo skinners / I wish I was a rock / It's hard ain't it hard / All around the water tank / Mother's not dead / East Virginia blues / Old bachelor, The / Danville girl / State of Arkansas / Death of Mr.Garfield / Roll on Buddy.
LP. 12T 105
Topic / '81 / Roots Records / Jazz Music / C.M. Distribution / Cadillac Music / Direct Distribution / Swift / Topic Records.

TALKING DUST BOWL.
Tracks: Pretty boy Floyd / Roll in my sweet baby's arms / Tom joad / Riding in my car / Grand Coulee dam / East Virginia blues / South coast / Tramp on the street / Cuckoo, The / Talking dustbowl blues / New York Town / So long (it's been good to know you) / Railroad Bill / Talking Columbia blues / Last letter, The / This land is your land.
LP. . . . . WIK 86
Big Beat / May '89 / Pinnacle / Hot Shot / Jazz Music.

TALKING WOODY GUTHRIE.
Tracks: Talking Columbia blues / Pretty Boy Floyd / Ludlow massacre / Talking miner blues / Hard travellin' / So long, it's been good to know you / Talking dustbowl blues / 1913 / Massacre / Rambling blues / Talking sailor blues.
LP. 12T 93
Topic / '81 / Roots Records / Jazz Music / C.M. Distribution / Cadillac Music / Direct Distribution / Swift / Topic Records.

Ellis, Red

FIRST FALL OF SNOW.
Tracks: Not Advised.
LP. . . . . OHCS 322
Old Homestead (USA) / Oct '87 / Swift.

Elmo & Patsy

GRANDMA GOT RUN OVER BY A REINDEER.
Tracks: Grandma got run over by a reindeer / Christmas.
7" . . . . BUY 99
Stiff / '80 / WEA.

Ely, Joe

Born 09.02.1947, in Amarillo, Texas raised in Lubbock. Spent his early years hanging around the music venues in Austin. Joinded Butch Hancock and Jimmie Dale Gilmoreto form the acoustic band the Flatlanders. Headed off to Nashville, in 1972 where they recorded their only album *More of a legend than a band* (Which apart from some B-track issues, remained unavailable until 1980 when Charly released it in the UK). After it's non-appearance Ely moved to New York for a spell, playing in it's subways and Greeenwich Village before joining up with the travelling circus. Looked after the Arabian horses and camels and it is from this experience his song *The indian cowboy* hails. In 1974 it was back to Texas, where he formed a band that was to include local acts Jesse Taylor and Lloyd Maines. Ely's signing to MCA came in 1977, where his brand of hard-biting Texas country/rock found early critical acclaim. His albums were decorated with songs from thr prolific Hancock and gained a positive start with *Joe Ely* (1977) and *Honky tonk masquerade* (1978). He then moved towards a rock audience. The British group The Clash became attached to the Ely's forceful brand of music to the extent that he was to go on tour with them, as support act. During the interim period, his releases were to become somewhat sporadic MCA issuing *Live shots* and *Hi-res* in 1984. An on- off relationship with MCA was to ensue before Ely and his band resurfaced on the indie Hoghtone label. The west coast label released his *Lord of the highway* and *Dig all night long* albums, the former held over from his MCA days. Ely's best work though was, still from the old days - as displayed on Sunstorm 1988 compilation *Milkshakes and malts*), made up entirely of songs written by Butch Hancock. Ely's chart record, prior to the 1990's was down to one brief encounter in 1978 (*All my love*) although his fortunes then looked brighter. Now back with MCA, Ely had his Texas show taped for the *Live at the liberty lunch* release and in 1992 released *Love and danger* - his most accepted country album since late 1970's. He also appeared as one of the Buzzin cousins on John Mellencamp's *Falling from grace* soundtrack album with the single *Sweet Suzzane* making the charts. Radio play lists have never seen favour with Ely's work - yet video may well do. (Maurice Hope)

BOXCARS.
Tracks: Boxcars / Honky tonk masquerade.
■ 7" . . . . MCA 368
MCA / May '78.

DALLAS.
Tracks: Dallas / Hard livin'.
■ 7" . . . . MCA 729
MCA / Jun '81.

DIG ALL NIGHT.
Tracks: Settle for love / For your love / My eyes got lucky / Maybe she'll find me / Drivin' man / Dig all night / Grandfather blues / Jazz street / Rich man, poor boy / Behind the bamboo shade.
CD . . . . FIENDCD 130
LP. . . . . FIEND 130
Demon / Oct '88 / Pinnacle.

DOWN ON THE DRAG.
Tracks: Fools fall in love / B.B.Q. and foam / Standin' at the big hotel / Crazy lemon / Crawdad train / In another world / She leaves you where you are / Down on the drag / Time for travelin' Maria.
■ LP. . . . . MCG 3532
MCA / May '79.

DOWN ON THE DRAG.
Tracks: Down on the drag / In another world.
■ 7" . . . . MCA 421
MCA / '79.

FINGERNAILS.
Tracks: Fingernails / Suckin' a big bottle of gin / Standin' at the Big Hotel.
■ EP. . . . . MCA 579
MCA / Feb '78.

GAMBLER'S BRIDE.
Tracks: Gambler's bride / Tennessee's not the state I'm in.
■ 7" . . . . MCA 324
MCA / Sep '77.

HI-RES.
Tracks: What's shakin' tonight / Cool rockin' Loretta / Madame Wo / Dream camera / Letter to Laredo / She's gotta get the gettin' / Lipstick in the night / Imagine Houston / Dame tu mano / Locked in a boxcar with the queen of Spain.
LP. . . . . MCF 3214
MC . . . . MCFC 3214
MCA / Apr '84 / BMG.

JOE ELY.
Tracks: I had my hopes up high / Mardi Gras waltz / She never spoke Spanish to me / Gambler's bride / Suckin' a big bottle of gin / Tennessee's not the State I'm in / If you were a bluebird / Treat me like a Saturday night / All my love / Johnny blues.
LP. . . . . MCF 2808
MC . . . . MCF 2808MC
MCA / '77 / BMG.
LP. . . . . MCL 1604
MC . . . . MCLC 1604
MCA / Aug '81 / BMG.
■ CD . . . . MCAD 10219
MCA / Sep '91.
CD . . . . MCLD 19071
MCA / Oct '92 / BMG.

LIVE AT LIBERTY LUNCH.
Tracks: Me and Billy the kid / Are you listening Lucky? / Grandfather blues / B.B.Q. and foam / Row of dominoes / Dallas / Where is my love / She gotta get the gettin' / Drivin' to the poorhouse / Cool rockin' Loretta / Musta notta gotta lotta / Letter to L.A. / If you were a bluebird.
■ CD . . . . DMCG 6113
MCA / Nov '90.
■ LP. . . . . MCG 6113
MCA / Nov '90.
■ MC . . . . MCGC 6113
MCA / Nov '90.

LIVESHOTS.
Tracks: Not Advised.
■ LP. . . . . MCF 3064
MCA / May '80.

LORD OF THE HIGHWAY.
Tracks: Lord of the highway / (Don't put a) lock on my heart / Me and Billy The Kid / Letter to L.A. / No rope, Daisy-o / Thinks she's French / Everybody got hammered / Are you listening Lucky ? / Row of dominoes / Silver City.
CD . . . . FIENDCD 101
LP. . . . . FIEND 101
Demon / Sep '87 / Pinnacle.

LOVE & DANGER.
Tracks: Sleepless in love / Pins and needles / Love is the beating of hearts / Slow you down / Road goes on forever, The / Settle for love / Highways and heartaches / Whenever kindness fails / She collected / Every night about this time.
CD . . . . MCAD 10584
MC . . . . MCAC 10584
MCA / Sep '92 / BMG.

MILKSHAKES AND MALTS.
Tracks: She never spoke Spanish to me / Boxcars / West Texas waltz / Down on the drag / Suckin' a big bottle of gin / Tennessee is not the State I'm in / If you were a bluebird / Jericho (your walls must come tumbling down) / Fools fall in love / Standin' at the big hotel / In another world / I keep wishing for you / Road hawg.
LP. . . . . SSAD 05
Sunstorm / Nov '88 / Greyhound Records / Probe Plus Records / Projection / Roots Records / Charly.

MUSTA NOTTA GOTTA LOTTA.
Tracks: Musta notta gotta lotta / Dallas / Wishin' for you / Hold on / Rock me my baby / I keep gettin' paid the same / Good rockin' tonight / Hard livin' / Road hawg / Dam of my heart / Bet me.
■ LP. . . . . MCF 3099
MCA / May '81.

MUSTA NOTTA GOTTA LOTTA.
Tracks: Musta notta gotta lotta / Wishin' for you.
■ 7" . . . . MCA 688
MCA / Apr '81.

ROW OF DOMINOES.
Tracks: Row of dominoes.
7" . . . . MCA 1453
■ CD Single . . . . DMCAT 1453
MCA / Oct '90 / BMG.

WHATEVER HAPPENED TO MARIA.
Tracks: Not Advised.
CD . . . . SAD 007
LP. . . . . SSAD 007
Heartland (1) / Feb '91 / Revolver-APT.

Ely, Pat

COUNTRY TRACKING.
Tracks: Good old days / Blue eyes crying in the rain / Red necks, white socks and blue ribbon beer / Waiting

for a train / In the middle of nowhere / Johnny Cash medley / Pinto the wonder horse is dead / You're gonna wonder about me / They're all going home but one / I took a memory to lunch / You remember me / Soft lights and hard country music.
LP. . . . . PHL 411
MC . . . . CPHL 411
Homespun (Ireland) / '82 / Homespun Records / Ross Records / Wellard Dist.

MY DONEGAL SHORE.
Tracks: Newport town / Nancy Miles / Galtee mountain boy / Galway shawl / Rose of Castlerea / Boys from County Armagh / Old rustic bridge / Shanagolden / Boys from County Mayo / My lovely Rose of Clare / My Donegal shore / Town I loved so well, The.
LP. . . . . DOLS 2013
MC . . . . DOCS 2013
Dolphin (Ireland) / Jun '88 / C.M. Distribution / I & B Records / Midland Records.

MY FAVOURITE IRISH SONGS.
Tracks: Rose of Mooncoin / Pretty little girl from Omagh.
MC . . . . CHRL 136
Homespun (Ireland) / '88 / Homespun Records / Ross Records / Wellard Dist.
LP. . . . . HRL 136
Homespun (Ireland) / May '88 / Homespun Records / Ross Records / Wellard Dist.

Emery, Jon

HILLYBILLY ROCK'N'ROLL.
Tracks: Hillbilly rock'n'roll / Brown boots / Bring back love / Delmore trilogy / Delmore blues / Fast freight train / Endless river / Hillbilly jukebox / Beer thirty / Dutchess / Strangers in the dark / Long train home / Rockin' Rhonda.
LP. . . . . BFX 15208
Bear Family / '88 / Rollercoaster Records / Swift / Direct Distribution.

Emmons, Buddy

Steel guitarist born in 1937 in Indiana; a Nashville session musician and designer of steel guitars. He toured with Little Jimmy Dickens, Ernest Tubb and Ray Price; he played bass for Roger Miller and sessioned widely, returning to Nashville in 1973, where he sessions, makes his own albums and makes and promotes his own guitars. Winner of Guitar Player magazine poll in 1978, ACM Steel Player five times. (Donald Clarke).
Tracks: Not Advised.

BUDDY EMMONS SINGS BOB WILLS.
Tracks: Deep in the heart of Texas / Bottle baby boogie / Boot heel drag / Deep water / I need you / New road under my wheels / Roley poley / If no news is good news / Four, five times / Twinkle, twinkle little star / Time changes everything / End of the line.
■ LP. . . . . SNTF 706
Sonet / '76.
LP. . . . . SDLP 033
Sundown / Jun '86 / Terry Blood Dist. / Jazz Music / C.M. Distribution.

MINORS ALOUD.
Tracks: Scrapple from the apple / Compared to what.
■ LP. . . . . SNTF 799
Sonet / '79.
LP. . . . . FF 088
Flying Fish (USA) / May '79 / Cadillac Music / Roots Records / Projection / C.M. Distribution / Direct Distribution / Jazz Music / Duncans / A.D.A Distribution.

STEEL GUITAR.
Tracks: Indian killed the woodcock / Sugar foot rag / Wild mountain thyme / Orange blossom special / Nothing was delivered / Rose in Spanish Harlem / Top heavy / Canon in D major.
LP. . . . . SNTF 708
Sonet / '76 / Swift / C.M. Distribution / Roots Records / Jazz Music / Sonet Records / Cadillac Music / Projection / Wellard Dist. / Hot Shot.
LP. . . . . FF 007
Flying Fish (USA) / Mar '89 / Cadillac Music / Roots Records / Projection / C.M. Distribution / Direct Distribution / Jazz Music / Duncans / A.D.A Distribution.

Endsley, Melvin

I LIKE YOUR KIND OF LOVE.
Tracks: I like your kind of love / Is it true / I got a feeling / Keep a lovin' me, baby / Let's fall out of love / Just want to be wanted / I ain't gettin' nowhere with you / Hungry eyes / Loving on my mind / Lonely all over again / There's bound to be / Gettin' used to the blues / Bringin' the blues to my door / I'd just be fool enough.
LP. . . . . BFX 15275
Bear Family / Dec '87 / Rollercoaster Records / Swift / Direct Distribution.
CD . . . . BCD 15595
Bear Family / May '93 / Rollercoaster Records / Swift / Direct Distribution.

Erwin, Randy

COWBOY RHYTHM.
Tracks: Cowboy rhythm / Long gone lonesome blues / Bring it on down to my house / Cowboy night herd song / In the jailhouse now.
LP. . . . . HLD 006
Heartland (1) / Feb '88 / Revolver-APT.

TILL THE COWS COME HOME.
Tracks: Not Advised.
LP. . . . . HLDM 001
Heartland (1) / Jun '87 / Revolver-APT.

Evans, Dave

BLUEGRASS MEMORIES.
Tracks: Not Advised.
LP. . . . . REBEL 1630
MC . . . . REBELMC 1630
Rebel (1) / '75 / Projection / Backs Distribution.

CLOSE TO HOME (Evans, Dave & River Bend).
Tracks: Another night / I'll just pretend / Second handed flowers / Last public hanging in West Virginia, The / Salt Creek / Rovin' gambler / Wild Bill Jones / Meet me by the moonlight / I just got wise / Home sweet home / Why don't you tell me so / Father's table grace.
LP. . . . . REBEL 1639
Rebel (1) / '85 / Projection / Backs Distribution.

FEW MORE SEASONS, A.
Tracks: Not Advised.
LP. . . . . REBEL 1608
MC . . . . REBELMC 1608
Rebel (1) / '75 / Projection / Backs Distribution.

GOIN' ROUND THIS WORLD.
Tracks: Not Advised.
LP. . . . . REBEL 1602
Rebel (1) / '75 / Projection / Backs Distribution.

POOR RAMBLER.
Tracks: Not Advised.
LP. . . . . REBEL 1616
Rebel (1) / '75 / Projection / Backs Distribution.

SAD PIG DANCE.
Tracks: Stagefright / Chaplinesque / Train and the river, The / Veronica / Captain / Knuckles and buster / Mole's moan / Gentle man / Sad pig dance / Raining cats and dogs / Braziliana / Sun and moon / Steppenwolf / Morocco John / Sneaky.
■ LP. . . . . SNKF 107
Kicking Mule / '80.
LP. . . . . KM 120
Kicking Mule / Mar '89 / Roots Records / Swift / Projection / C.M. Distribution / Impetus Records / Ross Records / Duncans.

TAKE A BITE OUT OF LIFE.
Tracks: Keep me from the cold / Whistling milkman / Illustrated man / You and me / Insanity rag / Every bad dog / Take a bit out of life / Willie me / You're wrong / Sunday is beautiful / Tear away / Lucky me / I'm all right.
■ LP. . . . . SNKF 122
Kicking Mule / Jan '78.
LP. . . . . KM 134
Kicking Mule / Mar '89 / Roots Records / Swift / Projection / C.M. Distribution / Impetus Records / Ross Records / Duncans.

Everette, Leon

LEON EVERETTE'S GREATEST HITS.
Tracks: Giving up easy / Don't feel like the lone ranger / I love that woman (like the devil loves sin) / I don't want to lose / Over / If I keep on going crazy / Hurricane / Midnight rodeo / Don't be angry / Just give me what you think is fair / Soul searching / Shadows of my mind / My lady loves me (just as I am) / Lady she's right / I could'a had you / Shot in the dark.
LP. . . . . NL 90010
■ MC . . . . NK 90010
RCA / Jan '87.

OVER.
Tracks: Over / Don't feel like the Lone Ranger.
■ 7" . . . . RCA 187
RCA / Mar '82.

THIS IS LEON EVERETTE.
Tracks: If I keep on going crazy / Over / I love that woman / It's not supposed to be that way / This moment of love / Giving up easy / I don't want to lose / Champagne dreams / Shadows of my mind / Don't feel like the Lone Ranger / Hurricane / Make me stop loving her / Betty Ruth / Don't be angry / Feelin's right / Midnight rodeo / Let me apologise / Think it over / Running on love / If you're serious about cheating.
LP. . . . . INTS 5211
RCA International / Jul '82 / BMG.

Everhart, Bob

COUNTRY.
Tracks: Not Advised.
LP. . . . . WRS 162
Westwood / Nov '81 / Pinnacle.

Everly Brothers

Don & Phil Everly, born in Kentucky, are one of America's most successful duos of all time. Their immaculate vocal harmonies and twin guitar sound made them one of the most distinctive musical forces of the late 1950's and early 1960's. The brothers were born into a country music environment - their parents were successful musicians with their own local radio show, it wasn't long before the two children joined the family act. By the time they had recorded their first single in 1957, the Everly Brothers were experienced musicians. They teamed up with ace Nashville guitarist Chet Atkins and songwriter Boudleaux Bryant. Bryant wrote many of their early hits, often in conjunction with his wife Felice. Their first hit *Bye Bye Love*, reached no.2 in the US and no.6 in the UK, while the follow up *Wake Up Little Susie*, became their first US no.1 and secured a no.2 slot in the UK. The Everly Brothers two biggest hits were *All I Have To Do Is Dream*, and *Cathy's Clown*, both of which spent five weeks at no.1 in the States and seven weeks at no.1 in the UK. In the US, they also hit the top slot with *Bird Dog*. In the UK they had further no.1 singles with *Walk Right Back*, and *Temptation*. The key to the Everly Brothers success was the shrewdness of their musical direction. They steered a pure pop course, inclining towards country music and of course, the girls screamed. However from 1962 onwards, except for a no.2 hit in 1965 with *Price Of Love*, the career of the Everly Brothers began to decline. Beatlemania, conscription into the marines and differences between the group, their arrangers, their musicians and eventually between the brothers themselves contributed to this decline. After an on-stage row and final split in 1973, the Everly Brothers began to pursue their solo careers. The brothers reformed in 1983 and remain very popular, especially in the UK.

('TIL) I KISSED YOU.
Tracks: ('Til) I kissed you.
■ 7" . . . . HLA 8934
London-American / Sep '59.

('TIL) I KISSED YOU (OLD GOLD) (1).
Tracks: ('Til) I kissed you / Oh what a feeling.
■ 7" . . . . OG 9065
Old Gold / Jul '82.

('TIL) I KISSED YOU (OLD GOLD) (2).
Tracks: ('Til) I kissed you / Bird dog.
7" . . . . OG 9734
Old Gold / Nov '87 / Pickwick Records.

20 GOLDEN LOVE SONGS: EVERLY BROTHERS.
Tracks: Not Advised.
CD . . . . SPEC 85016
Spectrum (CD) / Jul '86 / M.S.D.
LP. . . . . MA 5785
Masters (Holland) / '88.
MC . . . . MAMC 95785
Masters (Holland) / Dec '88.

20 GREATEST HITS: EVERLY BROTHERS.
Tracks: Not Advised.
CD . . . . SPEC 85010
Spectrum (CD) / Jul '86 / M.S.D.
LP. . . . . MA 3785
Masters (Holland) / '88.
MC . . . . MAMC 93785
Masters (Holland) / Dec '88.

6 TRACK HITS: EVERLY BROTHERS.
Tracks: All I have to do is dream / Wake up little Susie / Bye bye love / Bird dog / Problems / Till I kissed you.
EP. 7SR 5000
MC 7SC 5000
Scoop 33 / Sep '83.

ALBUM FLASH.
Tracks: Not Advised.
BETA 041 061 4
VHS. 041 061 2
Polygram Music Video / Oct '84 / PolyGram.

ALL I HAVE TO DO IS DREAM.
Tracks: All I have to do is dream / Claudette.
■ 7" . . . . HLA 8618
London-American / May '58.

ALL I HAVE TO DO IS DREAM.
Tracks: All I have to do is dream / Cathy's clown.
■ 7" . . . . K 16562
WEA / Jun '75.

ALL I HAVE TO DO IS DREAM (OLD GOLD).
Tracks: All I have to do is dream / Bye bye love (Only on CD single.) / Wake up little Susie (Only on CD single.).
7" . . . . OG 9062
Old Gold / '88 / Pickwick Records.
CD Single . . . . OG 6111
Old Gold / Feb '89 / Pickwick Records.

ALL THEY HAD TO DO WAS DREAM.
Tracks: Not Advised.
LP. . . . . RNLP 214
Rhino (USA) / Jan '86 / WEA.

AMANDA RUTH.
Tracks: Amanda Ruth / Born yesterday.
■ 7" . . . . **MER 206**
Mercury / Nov '85.

BEAT AND SOUL.
Tracks: Love is strange / Money / What am I living for / High heel sneakers / C.C. rider / Lonely avenue / Man with money / People get ready / My babe / Walking the dog / I almost lost my mind / Girl can't help it, The.
LP. . . . . **ROLI 319**
Rollercoaster / Dec '85 / Rollercoaster Records / Swift.

BEST OF THE EVERLY BROTHERS (CREOLE).
Tracks: Not Advised.
MC **16-24**
Creole (Everest-Europa) / Jul '84.

BEST OF THE EVERLY BROTHERS (WB).
Tracks: Not Advised.
LP. . . . . **.923994 1**
MC . . . . **.923994 4**
WEA / Nov '83 / WEA.

BIRD DOG.
Tracks: Bird dog.
■ 7" . . . . **HLA 8685**
London-American / Sep '58.

BIRD DOG.
Tracks: Bird dog / Devoted to you.
■ 7" . . . . **LIG 9018**
Lightning / Apr '79.

BORN YESTERDAY.
Tracks: Amanda Ruth / I know love / Born yesterday / These shoes / Arms of Mary / That uncertain feeling / Thinking 'bout you / Why worry / Abandoned love / Don't say goodnight / Always drive a Cadillac / You send me.
LP. . . . . **MERH 80**
MC . . . . **MERHC 80**
Mercury / Nov '85 / PolyGram.
■ CD **826 142-2**
Mercury / Nov '85.

BOTH SIDES OF AN EVENING.
Tracks: My mammy / Muskrat / My gal Sal / My grandfather's clock / Bully of the town / Chloe / Mention my name in Sheboygan / Hi lili hi lo / Wayward wind / Don't blame me / Now is the hour / Little old lady / When I grow too old to dream / Love is where you find it.
LP. . . . . **ROLI 315**
Rollercoaster / May '85 / Rollercoaster Records / Swift.

BROTHER JUKE BOX.
Tracks: Brother juke box / Never like this.
7" . . . . **SDS 001**
Sundown / Nov '85 / Terry Blood Dist. / Jazz Music / C.M. Distribution.

BYE BYE LOVE.
Tracks: Not Advised.
LP. . . . . **ENT LP 13025**
Entertainers / Nov '87.
CD . . . . **.ENT CD 207**
Entertainers / Sep '87.
MC . . . . **ENT MC 13025**
Entertainers / '88.

BYE BYE LOVE.
Tracks: Bye bye love.
■ 7" . . . . **HLA 8440**
London-American / Jul '57.

BYE BYE LOVE (OLD GOLD).
Tracks: Bye bye love / I wonder if I care as much.
7" . . . . **.OG 9060**
Old Gold / Jul '82 / Pickwick Records.

CADENCE CLASSICS (20 greatest hits).
Tracks: Not Advised.
CD . . . . **RNCD 5258**
Rhino (USA) / '86 / WEA.

CATHY'S CLOWN.
Tracks: Crying in the rain / Lucille / Cathy's clown / Don't blame me / Walk right back / That's old fashioned / So sad / Temptation / Ebony eyes / I'm not angry / Muskrat / How can I meet her?.
■ LP. . . . . **.SHM 3030**
Pickwick / Jun '80.

CATHY'S CLOWN.
Tracks: Cathy's clown / Temptation.
■ 7" . . . . **K 16002**
WEA / Jul '81.

CATHY'S CLOWN.
Tracks: Cathy's clown.
■ 7" . . . . **WB 1**
WEA / Sep '60.

CATHY'S CLOWN (OLD GOLD).
Tracks: Cathy's clown.
7" . . . . **.OG 9069**
Old Gold / Jul '82 / Pickwick Records.

CLASSIC EVERLY BROTHERS (1955-60).
Tracks: Keep a lovin' me / Suns keeps shining, A / If here love isn't true / That's the life I have to live / I wonder if I care as much / Bye bye love / Should we tell him / Wake up little Susie / Hey doll baby / Maybe tomorrow / Brand new heartache / Keep a knockin' / Leave my woman alone / Rip it up / This little girl of mine / Be bop a lula / All I have to do is dream / Claudette / Devoted to you / Bird dog / Problems / Love of my life / Take a message to Mary / Poor Jenny (one o'clock version) / Poor Jenny (ten o'clock version) / Oh true love / Till I kissed you / Oh, what a feeling / Let it be me / Since you broke my heart / Like strangers / When will I be loved / Roving gambler / Who's gonna shoe your pretty little feet / Rocking alone (In an old rocking chair) / Put my little shoes away / Down in the willow garden / Long time gone / Lightnin' express / That silver haired daddy of mine / Barbara Allen / Oh, so many years / I'm here to get my baby out of jail / Kentucky.
CD Set . . . . **BCD 15618**
Bear Family / Feb '92 / Rollercoaster Records / Swift / Direct Distribution.

COLLECTION: EVERLY BROTHERS.
Tracks: Problems / When will I be loved / This little girl of mine / Be bop a lula / Leave my woman alone / Roving gambler / Lightning express / Rockin' alone in an old rockin' chair / Like strangers / Wake up little Susie / Devoted to you / Bird dog / Rip it up / Brand new heartache / Should we tell him / Keep a knockin' / Put my little shoes away / Kentucky / Long time gone / Down in the willow garden / Take a message to Mary / Maybe tomorrow / Since you broke my heart / Let it be me.
■ Double LP . . . . **CCSLP 139**
Castle Collector Series / May '86.
■ MC . . . . **.CCSMC 139**
Castle Collector Series / May '86.
CD . . . . **CCSCD 139**
Castle Collector Series / '88 / BMG / Pinnacle / Castle Communications.

CRYING IN THE RAIN.
Tracks: Crying in the rain.
■ 7" . . . . **.WB 56**
WEA / Jan '62.

DATE WITH THE EVERLY BROTHERS, A.
Tracks: Made to love / That's just too much / Stick with me baby / Baby what you want me to do / Sigh cry almost die / Always it's you / Love hurts / Lucille / So how come / Donna Donna / Change of heart, A / Cathy's clown.
LP. . . . . **ROLI 314**
Rollercoaster / May '85 / Rollercoaster Records / Swift.

DEVOTED TO YOU.
Tracks: Devoted to you.
12" . . . . **IMST 1**
7" . . . . **IMS 1**
Impression / Nov '83 / Pinnacle.

DON'T WORRY BABY (Everly Brothers & Beach Boys).
Tracks: Don't worry baby / Born yesterday / Wings of a nightingale.
■ 7" . . . . **MER 280**
Mercury / Apr '89.
■ CD Single . . . . **.MERCD 280**
Mercury / Apr '89.

DREAMING.
Tracks: Not Advised.
CD . . . . **.550 0562**
MC . . . . **.550 0564**
Spectrum (1) / May '93 / PolyGram.

EB 84/BORN YESTERDAY.
Tracks: On the wings of a nightingale / Danger danger / Story of me / I'm takin' my time / First in line / Lay, lady, lay / Following the sun / You make it seem so easy / More than I can handle / Asleep / Amanda Ruth / I know love / Born yesterday / These shoes / Arms of Mary / Uncertain feeling / Thinkin' 'bout you / Why worry? / Abandoned love / Don't say goodnight / Always drive a Cadillac / You send me.
Double LP **8321731**
Mercury / May '88 / PolyGram.

EBONY EYES.
Tracks: Ebony eyes / Wake up little Susie.
■ 7" . . . . **K 16709**
WEA / '79.

EVERLY BROTHERS (Nashville, Tennessee, November 1955).
Tracks: Keep a' lovin' me / Sun keeps shining, The / If her love isn't true / That's the life I have to live.
■ EP. . . . . **BFE 15075**
Bear Family / Sep '81 / Rollercoaster Records / Swift / Direct Distribution.

EVERLY BROTHERS.
Tracks: Not Advised.
CD **8224312**
Mercury / Dec '84 / PolyGram.
LP. . . . . **RNLP 211**
Rhino (USA) / Jan '86 / WEA.
LP. **1 A022 58092**
MC **1 A222 58092**
EMI (Holland) / '88.
DCC. . . . . **DCC 8015**
MiniDisc . . . . **MDISC 801**
Disky Communications Ltd / Apr '93 / Swift / Terry Blood Dist.

EVERLY BROTHERS AND THE FABULOUS STYLE OF..
Tracks: This little girl of mine / Maybe tomorrow / Bye bye love / Brand new heartache / Keep a knockin' / Be bop a lula / Poor Jenny / Rip it up / I wonder if I care as much / Wake up little Susie / Leave my woman alone / Should we tell him / Hey doll baby / Claudette / Like strangers / Since you broke my heart / Let it be me / Oh what a feeling / Take a message to Mary / Devoted to you / When will I be loved / Bird dog / 'Til I kissed you / Problems / Love of my life / Poor Jenny (2nd version) / All I have to do is dream.
CD . . . . **.CDCH 932**
Ace / Apr '90 / Pinnacle / Hot Shot / Jazz Music / Complete Record Co. Ltd.

EVERLY BROTHERS REUNION CONCERT.
Tracks: Walk right back / Claudette / Bird dog / Bye bye love / Wake up little Susie / All I have to do is dream / Cathy's clown / Lucille.
CD **824 136 2**
Mercury / May '86 / PolyGram.

EVERLY BROTHERS REUNION CONCERT.
Tracks: All I have to do is dream / Be bop a lula / Walk right back / Cathy's clown / When will I be loved / Bye bye love / Wake up a little Susie / Let it be me / Bird dog.
■ VHS. . . . . **SMV 10331**
MGM/UA (Video) / '88.
■ VHS. . . . . **.CMP 6022**
Castle Music Pictures / Nov '90.

EVERLY BROTHERS SHOW.
Tracks: Mama tried / Kentucky / Bowling green / Till I kissed you / Wake up little Susie / Cathy's clown / Bird dog / Mabellene / Lord of the manor / I wonder if I care as much / Love is strange / Let it be me / Give peace a chance / Rock and roll music / End, The / Aquarius / If I were a carpenter / Price of love, The / Thrill is gone, The / Games people play / Baby what you want me to do / All I have to do is dream / Walk right back / Suzie Q / Hey Jude.
Double LP . . . . **K 66003**
WEA / '88 / WEA.

EVERLY BROTHERS SING GREAT COUNTRY HITS.
Tracks: Oh lonesome me / Born to lose / Just one time / Send me the pillow that you dream on / Release me / Please help me, I'm falling / I walk the line / Lonely street / Silver threads and golden needles / I'm so lonesome I could cry / Sweet dreams / This is the last song I'm ever going to sing.
LP. . . . . **ROLI 320**
Rollercoaster / Dec '85 / Rollercoaster Records / Swift.

EVERLY BROTHERS, THE (MERCURY).
Tracks: On the wings of a nightingale / Danger danger / Story of me / I'm taking my time / First in line / Lay lady lay / Following the sun / You make it seem so easy / More than I can handle / Asleep.
LP. . . . . **MERH 44**
MC . . . . **MERHC 44**
Mercury / Oct '84 / PolyGram.
■ CD **822 431-2**
Mercury / Oct '84.
LP. . . . . **PRICE 110**
Mercury / Jun '87 / PolyGram.
■ MC . . . . **PRIMC 110**
Mercury / Jun '87.

EVERLY BROTHERS, THE (WARNER BROS).
Tracks: Gone gone gone / So how come (no one loves me) / Always its you / Silver threads and golden needles / That'll be the day / All I have to do is dream / Made to love / That's just too much / Memories are made of this / Oh boy / Change of heart, A / Ain't that loving you baby.
LP. . . . . **K 26010**
MC **K4 26101**
WEA / Aug '88 / WEA.

FABULOUS EVERLY BROTHERS, THE.
Tracks: Bye bye love / Wake up little Susie / All I have to do is dream / Bird dog / Problems / ('Til) I kissed you / Let it be me / When will I be loved / Take a message to Mary / Claudette / Poor Jenny / Devoted to you.
CD . . . . **.CDFAB 006**
MC . . . . **.FABC 006**
Ace / Sep '91 / Pinnacle / Hot Shot / Jazz Music / Complete Record Co. Ltd.

FABULOUS STYLE OF THE EVERLY BROTHERS.
Tracks: Not Advised.
■ LP. . . . . **.HAA 2266**
London-American / Oct '60.
LP. . . . . **.RNLP 213**
Rhino (USA) / Jan '86 / WEA.

FERRIS WHEEL.
Tracks: Ferris wheel.
■ 7" . . . . **WB 135**
WEA / Jul '64.

FERRIS WHEEL.
Tracks: Ferris wheel / Walk right back.
■ 7" . . . . **K 16613**
WEA / Oct '75.

GIRL SANG THE BLUES, THE.
Tracks: Girl sang the blues, The.
■ 7" . . . . WB 109
WEA / Oct '63.

GOLDEN HITS: EVERLY BROTHERS.
Tracks: That's old fashioned (that's the way love should be) / How can I meet her? / Crying in the rain / I'm not angry / Don't blame me / Ebony eyes / Cathy's clown / Walk right back / Lucille / So sad to watch good love go bad / Muskrat / Temptation.
LP. . . . . K 46005
WEA / '87 / WEA.
CD 927159 2
MC K4 46005
WEA / '89 / WEA.

GOLDEN YEARS OF THE EVERLY BROTHERS.
Tracks: Walk right back / Crying in the rain / Wake up little Susie / Love hurts / Claudette / (Til) I kissed you / Love is strange / Ebony eyes / Temptation / Let it be me / Don't blame me / Cathy's clown / All I have to do is dream / Lucille / So sad (To watch good love go bad) / Bird dog / When will I be loved / No one can make my sunshine smile / Ferris wheel / Price of love / Muskrat / Problems / How can I meet her / Bye Bye love.
CD 954831992-2
MC 954831992-4
Warner Bros. / May '93 / WEA.

GONE GONE GONE.
Tracks: Lonely island / Facts of life / Ain't that loving you baby / Love is all I need / Torture / Drop out, The / Radio and TV / Honolulu / It's been a long dry spell / Ferris wheel / Gone gone gone.
LP. . . . . ROLI 316
Rollercoaster / May '85 / Rollercoaster Records / Swift.

GONE GONE GONE.
Tracks: Gone gone gone.
■ 7" . . . . WB 146
WEA / Dec '64.

GREATEST HITS: EVERLY BROTHERS (2) (NEON).
Tracks: Not Advised.
CD . . . . NCD 833 300 7
Neon / '88 / Pinnacle / Neon Records.

GREATEST HITS: EVERLY BROTHERS (ASTAN).
Tracks: Not Advised.
LP P.Disc. . . . . AR 30046
Astan (USA) / Dec '85.

GREATEST HITS: EVERLY BROTHERS (DITTO).
Tracks: All I have to do is dream / Wake up little Susie / When will I be loved? / Be bop a lula.
MC Set. . . . . DTO 10054
Ditto / Mar '83 / Pickwick Records.

GREATEST HITS: EVERLY BROTHERS (PICKWICK).
Tracks: Bye bye love / I wonder if I care as much / Wake up little Suzie / Maybe tomorrow / This little girl of mine / Should we tell him / All I have to do is dream / Claudette / Bird dog / Devoted to you / Problems / Love of my life / Take a message to Mary / Poor Jenny / Till I kissed you / Oh what a feeling / Let it be me / Since you broke my heart / When will I be loved / Be bop a lula / Like strangers / Brand new heartache / I'm here to get my baby out of jail / Lightning express.
■ Double LP . . . . .PDA 063
Pickwick / '79.

GREATEST HITS: EVERLY BROTHERS VOL 1.
Tracks: Not Advised.
LP. . . . . .SHM 3161
MC . . . . .HSC 3161
Hallmark / Feb '85 / Pickwick Records.

GREATEST HITS: EVERLY BROTHERS VOL 2.
Tracks: Take a message to Mary / Poor Jenny / Till I kissed you / Oh what a feeling / Let it be me / I'm here to get my baby out of jail / When will I be loved? / Be bop a lula / Like strangers / Brand new heartache / Since you broke my heart / Lightning express.
LP. . . . . .SHM 3168
Hallmark / May '85 / Pickwick Records.
MC . . . . .HSC 3168
Pickwick / May '85 / Pickwick Records.

GREATEST RECORDINGS.
Tracks: Wake up little Susie / Problems / Take a message to Mary / I wonder if I care as much / Poor Jenny / Love of my life / Bird dog / Like strangers / Hey doll baby / Leave my woman alone / Till I kissed you / Claudette / Should we tell him / All I have to do is dream / Rip it up / When will I be loved / Bye bye love / Let it be me.
LP. . . . . .CHA 194
MC . . . . .CHC 194
Ace / Nov '86 / Pinnacle / Hot Shot / Jazz Music / Complete Record Co. Ltd.
CD . . . . .CDCH 903
Ace / '88 / Pinnacle / Hot Shot / Jazz Music / Complete Record Co. Ltd.

HOW CAN I MEET HER.
Tracks: How can I meet her.
■ 7" . . . . WB 67
WEA / May '62.

I'LL NEVER GET OVER YOU.
Tracks: I'll never get over you.
■ 7" . . . . .WB 5639
WEA / Aug '65.

IN GERMANY AND ITALY.
Tracks: Not Advised.
LP. . . . . LSP 1056
Musketeer / Jan '87 / D.A.D. Records.

IN OUR IMAGE.
Tracks: Leave my girl alone / Chained to a memory / I'll never get over you / Doll house is empty, The / Glitter and gold / Power of love, The / Price of love, The / It's all over / I used to love you / Lovely Kravezit / June is as cold as December / It only cost a dime.
LP. . . . . ROLI 318
Rollercoaster / May '85 / Rollercoaster Records / Swift.

IN THE STUDIO.
Tracks: Leave my woman alone / Hey doll baby / I wonder if I care as much / Wake up little Susie / Maybe tomorrow / All I have to do is dream / Like strangers / Poor Jenny / Oh true love / Till I kissed you / Love of my life / When will I be loved / Should we tell him / Kentucky.
LP. . . . . CH 159
Ace / Nov '85 / Pinnacle / Hot Shot / Jazz Music / Complete Record Co. Ltd.

INSTANT PARTY.
Tracks: Jezebel / Oh mein papa / Step it up and go / True love / Bye bye blackbird / Trouble in mind / Love makes the world go round / Long lost John / Autumn leaves / Party's over, The / Ground hawg / When it's night time in Italy.
■ LP. . . . . WM 4061
WEA / Jul '62.
LP. . . . . ROLI 321
Rollercoaster / Oct '86 / Rollercoaster Records / Swift.

IT'S BEEN NICE.
Tracks: It's been nice.
■ 7" . . . . WB 99
WEA / Jun '63.

IT'S EVERLY TIME.
Tracks: So sad / Just in case / Memories are made of this / That's what you do to me / Sleepless nights / What kind of girl are you / Oh true love / Carol Jane / Some sweet day / Nashville blues / You thrill me / I want you to know.
■ LP. . . . . WM 4006
WEA / Jul '60.
LP. . . . . ROLI 313
Rollercoaster / May '85 / Rollercoaster Records / Swift.

IT'S MY TIME.
Tracks: It's my time.
■ 7" . . . . .WB 7192
WEA / May '68.

LET IT BE ME.
Tracks: Let it be me / Since you broke my heart.
■ 7" . . . . HLA 9039
London-American / Feb '60.

LET IT BE ME (OLD GOLD).
Tracks: Let it be me.
■ 7" . . . . .OG 9066
Old Gold / Jul '82.

LIKE STRANGERS.
Tracks: Like strangers / Should we tell him.
■ 7" . . . . HLA 9250
London-American / Dec '60.

LIKE STRANGERS (OLD GOLD).
Tracks: Like strangers.
■ 7" . . . . .OG 9068
Old Gold / Jul '82.

LIL' BIT OF GOLD: THE EVERLY BROTHERS.
Tracks: Wake up little Susie / Bird dog / Let it be me / All I have to do is dream.
■ CD Single . . . . R 373008
Rhino (USA) / May '88 / WEA.

LIVING LEGENDS.
Tracks: Not Advised.
■ LP. . . . . WW 5027
Warwick / Apr '77.

LOVE HURTS.
Tracks: All I have to do is dream / Till I kissed you / So sad / Let it be me / Problems / Love of my life / No one can make my sunshine smile / Devoted to you / Take a message to Mary / When will I be loved? / Love hurts / Walk right back / Memories are made of this / Like strangers / Brand new heartache / Since you broke my heart / Love is strange / Crying in the rain / Donna Donna / Cathy's clown.
LP. . . . . .NE 1197
MC . . . . .CE 2197
K-Tel / Dec '84 / I & B Records / C.M. Distribution / Arabesque Ltd. / Mono Distributors (Jersey) Ltd. / Prism Leisure PLC / PolyGram / Ross Records / Prism Leisure PLC.

LOVE IS STRANGE.
Tracks: Love is strange.
■ 7" . . . . .WB 5649
WEA / Oct '65.

LUCILLE.
Tracks: Lucille / So sad (to watch good love go bad).
■ 7" . . . . WB 19
WEA / Sep '60.

MUSKRAT.
Tracks: Muskrat / Don't blame me.
■ 7" . . . . WB 50
WEA / Oct '61.

NEW ALBUM, THE.
Tracks: Silent treatment / Dancing on my feet / Gran Mamou / Burma shave / Nancy's minuet / He's got my sympathy / Little Hollywood girl / Omaha / Empty boxes / I can't say goodbye to you / Nothing matters but you / When snowflakes fall in the summer / I'll see your light / Why not?.
■ LP. . . . . K 56415
WEA / Oct '77 / WEA.

NICE GUYS.
Tracks: Trouble / What about me / Eden to Cainin / Chains / Meet me in the bottom / In the good old days / Nice guys / Stained glass morning / Dancing on my feet / Mr. Soul / Don't you even try / Kiss your man goodbye.
LP. . . . . MFLP 1.028
Magnum Force / Sep '84 / Terry Blood Dist. / Jazz Music / Hot Shot.
MC . . . . MFC 1.028
Magnum Force / '86 / Terry Blood Dist. / Jazz Music / Hot Shot.
CD . . . . .CDMF 1.028
Magnum Force / Nov '88 / Terry Blood Dist. / Jazz Music / Hot Shot.

NO ONE CAN MAKE MY SUNSHINE SMILE.
Tracks: No one can make my sunshine smile.
■ 7" . . . . WB 79
WEA / Oct '62.

ON THE WINGS OF A NIGHTINGALE.
Tracks: On the wings of a nightingale / Asleep.
7" . . . . MER 170
Mercury / Sep '84 / PolyGram.

ORIGINAL GREATEST HITS.
Tracks: Not Advised.
■ LP. 66255
WEA / Sep '70.

ORIGINAL HITS 57-60.
Tracks: Not Advised.

PASS THE CHICKEN AND LISTEN.
Tracks: Lay it down / Husbands and wives / Woman don't you try to tie me down / Sweet memories / Ladies love outlaws / Not fade away / Watchin' it go / Paradise / Somebody nobody knows / Good hearted woman / Nickel for the fiddler, A / Rocky top.
CD . . . . .EDCD 319
LP. . . . . ED 319
Demon / '91 / Pinnacle.

PERFECT HARMONY.
Tracks: Bye bye love / I wonder if I care / Wake up little Susie / This little girl of mine / All I have to do is dream / Claudette / Bird dog / Problems / Devoted to you / Take a message to Mary / Poor Jenny / ('Til) I kissed you / Let it be me / Like strangers / When will I be loved / Cathy's clown / Always its you / So sad (to watch good love go bad) / Lucille / Don't blame me / Walk right back / Ebony eyes / Temptation / Stick with me baby / Muskrat / That's old fashioned (that's the way love) / How can I meet her? / Don't ask me to be friends / True love (from High Society) / Crying in the rain / No one can make my sunshine smile / (So it was - so it is) So it will always be / Girl sang the blues, The / Gone, gone, gone / Ferris wheel / That'll be the day / Price of love, The / I'll never get over you / Love is strange / Love hurts / Dancing in the street / Bowling green / It's my time / Oh boy / Air that I breathe, The / Sweet grass county Montana / God bless older ladies / Snowflake bombadier / Yesterday just passed my way again / Since you broke my heart / Love at last sight / Brother juke box / On the wings of a nightingale / Lay lady lay / Why worry / Born yesterday / Arms of Mary / Ride the wind / Don't worry baby.
■ MC Set. . . . . EVYMC 47004
Knight / Nov '90.
CD Set . . . . EVYCD 47004
■ LP Set . . . . EVYLP 47004
Knight / Nov '90.
CD Set . . . . NXTCD 245
Sequel / May '93 / Castle Communications / BMG / Hot Shot.

POOR JENNY.
Tracks: Poor Jenny.
■ 7" . . . . HLA 8863
London-American / May '59.

POOR JENNY (OLD GOLD).
Tracks: Poor Jenny / Take a message to Mary.
■ 7" . . . . .OG 9064
Old Gold / Jul '82.

POWER OF LOVE.
Tracks: Power of love / Leave my girl alone.
■ 7" . . . . WB 5747
WEA / Mar '66.

PRICE OF LOVE, THE.
Tracks: Price of love, The / Crying in the rain.
■ 7" . . . . WB 161
WEA / May '65.

PRICE OF LOVE, THE (OLD GOLD).
Tracks: Price of love.
■ 7" . . . . OG 9072
Old Gold / Jul '82.

PROBLEMS.
Tracks: Problems.
■ 7" . . . . HLA 8781
London-American / Jan '59.

PROBLEMS (OLD GOLD).
Tracks: Problems / Love of my life.
■ 7" . . . . OG 9063
Old Gold / Jul '82.

PROFILE: EVERLY BROTHERS.
Tracks: Not Advised.
LP. 6.24003
MC CL4 24003
Teldec (1) / Jun '81 / Pinnacle / C.M. Distribution / Swift.

PURE HARMONY.
Tracks: Bye bye love / Like strangers / Oh what a feeling / Bird dog / I wonder if I care as much / Take a message to Mary / All I have to do is dream / Wake up little Susie / Devoted to you / Maybe tomorrow / Love of my life / Till I kissed you / Since you broke my heart / Let it be me.
■ LP. . . . . CH 118
Ace / Oct '84.

REUNION ALBUM.
Tracks: Not Advised.
Double LP . . . . IMDP 1
MC . . . . IMDK 1
Impression / Oct '84 / Pinnacle.

RIP IT UP.
Tracks: Rip it up / Leave my woman alone / Hey doll baby / Brand new heartache / Problems / Be bop a lula / Poor Jenny / This little girl of mine / Claudette / Should we tell him? / When will I be loved? / Keep a knockin'.
LP. . . . . CH 64
Ace / Feb '83 / Pinnacle / Hot Shot / Jazz Music / Complete Record Co. Ltd.

RIP IT UP/PURE HARMONY.
Tracks: Rip it up / Leave my woman alone / Hey doll baby / Brand new heartache / Problems / Be bop a lula / Poor Jenny / This little girl of mine / Claudette / Should we tell him / When will I be loved / Keep a knockin' / Bye bye love / Like strangers / Oh what a feeling / Bird dog / I wonder if I care as much / Take a message to Mary / All I have to do is dream / Wake up little Susie / Devoted to you / Maybe tomorrow / Love of my life / (Til) I kissed you / Since you broke my heart / Let it be me.
MC Set . . . . CHC 804
Ace / '89 / Pinnacle / Hot Shot / Jazz Music / Complete Record Co. Ltd.

ROCK 'N' ROLL FOREVER.
Tracks: Wake up little Susie / Bird dog / Good golly Miss Molly / Oh Boy / Donna Donna / Lucille / Gone gone gone / Walk right back / Bye bye love / That'll be the day / Slippin' and slidin' / Price of love, the.
LP. . . . . K 26063
MC K4 26063
WEA / WEA.

ROCK 'N' ROLL ODYSSEY.
Tracks: Cathy's clown / Bye bye love / Wake up little Susie / All I have to do is dream / Walk right back / Bird dog.
■ VHS. . . . . SMV 10366
MGM/UA (Video) / Oct '84.
■ VHS. . . . . CMP 6021
Castle Music Pictures / Nov '90.

ROCK 'N' SOUL.
Tracks: That'll be the day / So fine / Maybellene / Dancing in the street / Kansas City / I got a woman / Love hurts / Slippin' and slidin' / Suzie Q / Hound dog / I'm gonna move to the outskirts of town / Lonely weekends.
LP. . . . . ROLI 317
Rollercoaster / May '85 / Rollercoaster Records / Swift.

ROCKING IN HARMONY.
Tracks: Wake up little Susie / Devoted to you / This little girl of mine / Like strangers / Roving gambler / Leave my woman alone / Bird dog / Long time gone / Problems / When will I be loved / I'm here to get my baby out of jail / Be bop a Lula.
LP. . . . . GEM 002
Crown / Feb '86 / Pinnacle / Nervous Records.
■ MC . . . . GEMC 002
Crown / Feb '86.

ROOTS (EDSEL).
Tracks: Intro: The Everly family / Mama tried / Less of me / T for Texas / I wonder if I care as much / Ventura Boulevard / Shady grove / Illinois / Living too close to the ground / You done me wrong / Turn around / Sing me back home / Montage: The Everly family / Kentucky.
LP. . . . . ED 203
Edsel / '87 / Pinnacle.

ROOTS (ROLLERCOASTER).
Tracks: Mama tried / Less of me / T for Texas / I wonder if I care as much / Ventura Boulevard / Shady grove / Illinois / Living too close to the ground / You done me wrong / Turn around / Sing me back home.
LP. . . . . ROLI 322
Rollercoaster / Oct '86 / Rollercoaster Records / Swift.

SINGLES SET.
Tracks: Not Advised.
LP Set . . . . SET 1
Old Gold / Jul '80 / Pickwick Records.

SO IT WILL ALWAYS BE.
Tracks: So it will always be.
■ 7" . . . . WB 94
WEA / Mar '63.

SO MANY YEARS.
Tracks: Not Advised.
CD 260 471 2
LP. 260 471 1
MC 260 471 4
Mainline (2) / Feb '90.

SO SAD.
Tracks: So sad / Lucille.
■ 7" . . . . OG 9070
Old Gold / Jul '82.

SOME HEARTS.
Tracks: Some hearts / Ride the wind / Can't get over it / Brown eyes / Julianne / Don't worry baby / Be my love again / Angel of the darkness / Three bands of steel / Any single solitary heart.
LP. 832 520 1
Mercury / Apr '89 / PolyGram.
■ CD 832 520 2
Mercury / Apr '89.
■ MC 832 520 4
Mercury / Apr '89.

SONGS OUR DADDY TAUGHT US.
Tracks: Roving gambler / Down in the willow garden / Long time gone / Lightning express / That silver haired daddy of mine / Who's gonna shoe your pretty little feet? / Barbara Allen / Oh so many years / I'm here to get my baby out of jail / Rockin' alone in an old rockin' chair / Kentucky / Put my little shoes away.
■ LP. . . . . CH 75
Ace / Aug '83.
CD . . . . CDCHM 75
Ace / Nov '90 / Pinnacle / Hot Shot / Jazz Music / Complete Record Co. Ltd.

STORIES WE COULD TELL.
Tracks: All I really want to do / Breakdown / Green River / Mandolin wind / Up in Mabel's room / Del Rio Dan / Ridin' high / Christmas eve can kill you / Three-armed, poker-playin' river rat / I'm tired of singing my song in Las Vegas / Brand new Tennessee waltz, the / Stories we could tell.
■ LP. . . . . MPK 223
RCA / '75 / BMG.

STORY OF ME.
Tracks: Story of me.
7" . . . . ER 185
Mercury / Nov '84 / PolyGram.

SUSIE Q.
Tracks: Love with your heart / How can I meet her / Nothing but the best / Sheik of Araby, The / To show I love you / Susie Q / Am abend auf der heide / Sag su wiedersehen / When snowflakes fall in the summer / Little Hollywood girl / He's got my sympathy / Silent treatment, The.
LP. . . . . MFLP 052
MC . . . . MFC 052
Magnum Force / Jun '87 / Terry Blood Dist. / Jazz Music / Hot Shot.
CD . . . . CDMF 052
Magnum Force / Jun '88 / Terry Blood Dist. / Jazz Music / Hot Shot.

SWEET MEMORIES.
Tracks: Not Advised.
CD 295 728
Ariola Express / Sep '92.

TAKE A MESSAGE TO MARY.
Tracks: Take a message to Mary.

TEMPTATION.
Tracks: Temptation.
■ 7" . . . . WB 42
WEA / Jun '61.

THAT'LL BE THE DAY.
Tracks: That'll be the day.
■ 7" . . . . WB 158
WEA / May '65.

TWO YANKS IN ENGLAND.
Tracks: Somebody help me / So lonely / Kiss your man goodbye / Signs that will never change / Like everytime before / Pretty flamingo / I've been wrong before / Have you ever loved somebody / Collector, The / Don't run and hide / Fifi the flea / Hard, hard year.

LP. . . . . ED 297
Edsel / '88 / Pinnacle.

VERY BEST OF THE EVERLY BROTHERS (FUN (HOLLAND)).
Tracks: Not Advised.
CD . . . . FUNCD 9024
LP. . . . . FUN 9024
MC . . . . FUNC 9024
Fun (Holland) / Oct '88 / Pinnacle.

VERY BEST OF THE EVERLY BROTHERS (HALLMARK).
Tracks: Not Advised.
CD . . . . PWKS 515
Pickwick / Oct '88 / Pickwick Records.
LP. . . . . SHM 3246
MC . . . . HSC 3246
Hallmark / Oct '88 / Pickwick Records.

VERY BEST OF THE EVERLY BROTHERS VOL.2.
Tracks: Cathy's clown / Price of love, The / Muskrat / Temptation / Love is strange / So sad (to watch good love go bad) / So it will always be / Cryin' in the rain / Walk right back / Lucille / Ebony eyes / No one can make my sunshine smile / How can I meet her / Don't blame me / Gone gone gone / Ferris wheel.
CD . . . . PWKS 4028
MC . . . . PWKMC 4028
Pickwick / Oct '90 / Pickwick Records.

VERY BEST OF THE EVERLY BROTHERS, THE (WARNER BROS.).
Tracks: Bye bye love / ('Til) I kissed you / Wake up little Susie / Crying in the rain / Walk right back / Cathy's clown / Bird dog / All I have to do is dream / Devoted to you / Lucille / So sad to watch good love go bad / Ebony eyes.
LP. . . . . K 46008
MC K4 46008
WEA / '74 / WEA.
CD 9271612
WEA / '89 / WEA.

WAKE UP LITTLE SUSIE.
Tracks: Wake up little Susie / Maybe tomorrow.
■ 7" . . . . HLA 8498
London-American / Nov '57.

WAKE UP LITTLE SUSIE (OLD GOLD).
Tracks: Wake up little Susie.
■ 7" . . . . OG 9061
Old Gold / Jul '82.

WALK RIGHT BACK.
Tracks: Walk right back.
■ 7" . . . . WB 33
WEA / Feb '61.

WALK RIGHT BACK (OLD GOLD).
Tracks: Walk right back / Ebony eyes.
7" . . . . OG 9071
Old Gold / Mar '90 / Pickwick Records.

WALK RIGHT BACK WITH THE EVERLYS.
Tracks: Walk right back / Crying in the rain / Wake up little Susie / Love hurts / Till I kissed you / Love is strange / How can I meet her? / Temptation / Don't blame me / Cathy's clown / So sad to watch good love go bad / Bird dog / No one can make my sunshine smile / Ferris wheel / Price of love, The / Muskrat / Ebony eyes / Bye bye love.
LP. . . . . K 56168
MC K4 56168
WEA / Oct '75 / WEA.
■ CD K2 56168
WEA / Jan '87 / WEA.

WARNER BROS. YEARS VOL.1, THE.
Tracks: It's been nice / No one can make my sunshine smile / Nancy's minuet / I'm afraid / Girl who sang the blues / Don't forget to cry / Ring around my Rosie / Don't ask me to be friends / So it always will be / Whatever happened to Judy / Love her / Hello Amy / You're the one I love / You're my girl.
LP. . . . . CH 272
Ace / May '89 / Pinnacle / Hot Shot / Jazz Music / Complete Record Co. Ltd.

WARNER BROTHERS YEARS VOL. 2, THE.
Tracks: Lord of the manor / My little yellow bird / Cuckoo bird / I'm on my way home again / Carolina in my mind / Yves / Human race / Give me a sweetheart / Don't let the whole world know / Follow me / Love of the common people / You're just what I was looking for today / It's my time / Milk train.
■ LP. . . . . CH 281
Ace / Oct '89.

WHEN WILL I BE LOVED?.
Tracks: When will I be loved / Be bop a lula.
■ 7" . . . . HLA 9157
London-American / Jul '60.

WHEN WILL I BE LOVED? (OLD GOLD).
Tracks: When will I be loved?.
■ 7" . . . . OG 9067
Old Gold / Jul '82.

YOU'RE JUST WHAT I WAS LOOKING FOR.
Tracks: You're just what I was looking for.
7" . . . . BONUS 1
Revival / Jul '82 / EMI.

E 8 ■ DELETED

Everly, Don

BROTHER JUKE BOX.
Tracks: Love at last sight / So sad to watch good love go bad / Letting go / Since you broke my heart / Never like this / Deep water / Yesterday just passed my way again / Oh I'd like to go away / Oh what a feeling / Turn the memories loose again / Brother juke box.
LP.........................SDLP 002
Sundown / '83 / Terry Blood Dist. / Jazz Music / C.M. Distribution.
CD.........................CDSD 002
MC.........................SDC 002
Sundown / May '88 / Terry Blood Dist. / Jazz Music / C.M. Distribution.

BROTHER JUKE BOX.
Tracks: Brother juke box / Oh what a feeling.
■ 7".........................DJS 10846
DJM / Mar '78.

LET'S PUT OUR HEARTS TOGETHER.
Tracks: Let's put our hearts together / So sad
■ 7".........................POSP 315
Polydor / Aug '81.

SO SAD.
Tracks: So sad / Love a last sight.
■ 7".........................DJS 10760
DJM / Mar '77.

Everly, Phil

AIR THAT I BREATHE, THE.
Tracks: Air that I breathe, The.
■ 7".........................RCA 2409
RCA / Sep '73.

DARE TO DREAM AGAIN.
Tracks: Dare to dream again / Lonely day, lonely night.
■ 7".........................EPC 9575
Epic / Mar '81.

LONDON SESSIONS, THE.
Tracks: Not Advised.
CD.........................NEXCD 164
Sequel / Apr '91 / Castle Communications / BMG / Hot Shot.

LOUISE.
Tracks: Louise / Sweet Suzanne / She means nothing to me / Man and a woman, A / Who's gonna keep me warm / One way love / Sweet pretender / Better than now / Oh baby oh / God bless older ladies / Never gonna dream again / I'll mend your broken heart / When I'm dead and gone.
LP.........................MFLP 053
MC.........................MFC 053
Magnum Force / Aug '87 / Terry Blood Dist. / Jazz Music / Hot Shot.
CD.........................CDMF 053
Magnum Force / Jan '88 / Terry Blood Dist. / Jazz Music / Hot Shot.

LOUISE.
Tracks: Louise / Sweet Suzanne.
■ 7".........................CL 266
Capitol / Nov '82.

OH BABY OH.
Tracks: Oh baby oh / God bless older ladies.
■ 7".........................CL 294
Capitol / Jun '83.

PHIL EVERLY.
Tracks: She means nothing to me (Featuring Cliff Richard with Phil Everly) / I'll mend your broken heart (Featuring Cliff Richard with Phil Everly) / God bless older ladies / Sweet pretender / Never gonna dream again / Better than now / Woman and a man / Louise / When I'm dead and gone / Sweet Suzanne / Oh baby oh (you're the star).
LP.........................EST 27670
MC.........................TC EST 27670
Capitol / Apr '83 / EMI.
CD.........................BGOCD 199
Beat Goes On / Oct '93 / Pinnacle.

SHE MEANS NOTHING TO ME (Everly, Phil & Cliff Richard).
Tracks: She means nothing to me / Man and woman.
■ 7".........................CL 276
Capitol / Jan '83.

STAR SPANGLED SPRINGER.
Tracks: SF 8370 / Air that I breathe, The / Sweet grass county / God bless older ladies (for they made rock'n'-roll) / It pleases me to please you / Lady Anne / Red, white & blue / Our song / Poisonberry pie / La divorce / Snowflake bombardier.
■ LP.........................SF 8370
RCA / '75 / BMG.

SWEET PRETENDER.
Tracks: Sweet pretender / Better than now.
■ 7".........................CL 285
Capitol / Apr '83.

Ewing, Skip

WILL TO LOVE, THE.
Tracks: Will to love, The / Please don't leave me now / If a man could live on love alone / Karen / Door, The / It wasn't his child / It's you again / Age doesn't matter at all / Ain't that the way it always ends / She's makin' plans.
CD.........................MCAD 42301
LP.........................MCA 42301
MCA / Nov '89 / BMG.

Exile

Lexington, Kentucky based country/pop group, formed in 1963,as the then Exiles. Toured with Dick Clark's Caravan of Stars in 1965. After trying their luck with Columbia and RCA's Wooden Nickel label they enjoyed some long awaited reaction from the pop audience in 1978, with Kiss you all over on Warners giving them a US No.1, whilst peaking at No.6 in the UK (RAK). Founder member J.P.Pennington and Sonny Lemair wrote the bulk of their material. Others to cover songs from Exile members were to include Alabama (their 1983 No.1 The closer you get being a J.P. - Mark Gray creation) , Bill Anderson, Sheena Easton, Janie Fricke, Terri Gibbs, Mark Gray, Juice Newton, Dave and Sugar, and Kenny Rogers. In 1983, now signed to Epic, Exile embarked on a rich run of success in the country field. With Les Taylor assisting Pennington on vocals, a number of hits and nominations were to come their way. The band members were, Steve Goetzman (drums), Marlon Hargis (keyboards replaced in 1985 by Lee Carroll) , Lemaire (bass/vocals) and J.P. and Taylor on guitars. The group's track record, bettered only by Texas' Alabama. They scored ten chart topping singles in the next five years. At a time when country music was struggling to find it's identity, their debut top 30 single High cost of living broke the ice. Woke up in love , I don't want to be a memory , Give me one more and Crazy for your love were to race to the top by 1984. Their uptempo, rocking country spawning more winners in the form of She's a miracle , Hang on to your heart , I could get used to you , (1985) , It'll be me , She's too good to be true , and I can't get close enough (1986). By 1988 the main vocalists, J.P. and Les Taylor had set out on solo careers, and their run had been broken, only Just one kiss making country's top ten that year. After four albums, Epic pulled the plug - in 1990 the band were to join Nashville's fledgling label, Arista. In 1990 Yet from the band's debut album Still standing , made the top slot - with new band members Paul Martin and Mark Jones. (Maurice Hope)

ALL THERE IS.
Tracks: How could this go wrong / All there is / Too proud to cry / Part of me that needs you most / Destiny / Being in love with you is easy / Let's do it again / Come on over.
■ LP.........................SRAK 535
RAK / '79.

EXILE.
Tracks: Take me to the river / Woke up in love / Red dancing shoes / We've still got love / I just came back to break my heart again / This could be the start of something good / After all these years / High cost of leaving / I don't want to be a memory / Here I go again.
LP.........................EPC 25809
Epic / Sep '84 / Sony.
■ MC.........................40 25809
Epic / Sep '84.

GIVE ME ONE MORE CHANCE.
Tracks: Give me one more chance / Ain't that a pity.
■ 7".........................A 5022
Epic / Jan '85 / Sony.

GREATEST HITS: EXILE.
Tracks: Woke up in love / I don't want to be a memory / Give me one more chance / She's a miracle / Hang on to your heart / Girl can't help it, The / I could get used to you / Crazy for your love / Super love / Kiss you all over.
■ LP.........................EPC 57089
Epic / Sep '86 / Sony.
■ MC.........................40 57089
Epic / Sep '86.

HANG ON TO YOUR HEART.
Tracks: Promises promises / I could get used to you / Hang on to your heart / She likes lovin' / Music / I got love (super duper love) / It'll be me / Practice makes perfect / She's too good to be true / Proud to be her man.
LP.........................EPC 26617
■ MC.........................40 26617
Epic / Mar '86.

HANG ON TO YOUR HEART.
Tracks: Hang on to your heart / She likes lovin'.
■ 7".........................A 6532
Epic / Dec '85 / Sony.

HEART AND SOUL.
Tracks: Heart and soul / Your love is everything.
12".........................12RAK 333
■ 7".........................RAK 333
RAK / Jul '81.

HOW COULD THIS GO WRONG.
Tracks: How could this go wrong / Being in love with you is easy.
■ 7".........................RAK 293
RAK / May '79.

I COULD GET USED TO YOU.
Tracks: I could get used to you.
■ 7".........................7149
Epic / Apr '86 / Sony.

I LOVE COUNTRY.
Tracks: Super love / I could get used to you / Hang on to your heart / It'll be me / Proud to be her man / Woke up in love / I don't want to be a memory / Red dancing shoes / Here I go again / Give me one more chance / She's a miracle / Crazy for your love / Comin' apart at the seams / You make it easy / Take me to the river / Kiss you all over / Dancing the night away / Ain't no sunshine / If you ever change your mind / It's like we never said goodbye / Blue side, The / Little bit of rain, A / Love crazy love / Tennessee / Half the way / Lean on me / You never gave up on me / Crying in the rain / Woman in me, The / Same old story / Livin' in these troubled times / Miss the Mississippi and you.
LP.........................4510071
■ MC.........................4510074
Epic / Mar '88.

KISS YOU ALL OVER.
Tracks: Kiss you all over / There's been a change.
■ 7".........................RAK 279
RAK / Aug '78.

NEVER GONNA STOP.
Tracks: Never gonna stop / One step at a time.
■ 7".........................RAK 287
RAK / Nov '78.

SHE'S A MIRACLE.
Tracks: She's a miracle / I've never seen anything.
■ 7".........................A 6454
Epic / Aug '85.

SHE'S TOO GOOD TO BE TRUE.
Tracks: She's too good to be true / Promises promises.
■ 7".........................6513147
Epic / Dec '87.

WOKE UP IN LOVE.
Tracks: Woke up in love.
■ 7".........................A 4404
Epic / Jun '84 / Sony.

YOU THRILL ME.
Tracks: You thrill me / Don't do it.
■ 7".........................RAK 273
RAK / Mar '78.

ALSO PUBLISHED BY MUSIC MASTER:

The Official Music Master CD Catalogue, 14th Edition. £14.95
Published October 1993

The 14th Edition of Music Master's best selling CD Catalogue is our most comprehensive listing of recordings released on CD in the UK. This fully revised and updated publication supplies track listings, catalogue numbers, label and distributor details as well as release and deletion dates. It is a must for all CD fans and those who want to find favourite recordings or complete collections. 1,114 pages.

*Lists CD discographies for over 15,000 popular music artists.
*Contains information on over 55,000 CD released recordings.

Labels' and Distributors' Directory 11th Edition

The Who's Who of Labels and Distributors! Fully revised and updated to include full contact details for every UK label and distributor known at the time of going to press. Cross reference sections make it even easier to find out who distributes which label.
£29.95

Tracks Catalogue 4th Edition

Who Recorded Which Track? The Tracks catalogue identifies 750,000 track names, the artists who recorded them and the albums/singles on which they appear. 1480 pages.
£24.95

Directory of Popular Music - compiled and edited by Leslie Lowe

Who wrote that song? This catalogue identifies the composer, publisher and recording artist for over 9,000 of the most popular songs this century. 554 pages.
£14.95

Price Guide for Record Collectors 2nd Edition

This catalogue prices 42,000 collectable LPs, EPs, Singles and Picture Discs. It includes a full colour section of photographs of collectable covers and extensive notes from the editor Nick Hamlyn. 792 pages.
£12.95

To order:

Please send payment (cheques made payable to Music Master) plus postage as follows:
UK: add £1.75,   Europe: add £4.00 per catalogue,   Outside Europe: add £12.00 per catalogue. All books are sent registered delivery in the UK and by Airmail elsewhere.

Music Master, Paulton House, 8 Shepherdess Walk, London, N1 7LB.
Tel: +44-(0)71-490-0049,   Fax: +44-(0)71-253-1308.

F

Fairchild, Barbara

Country singer and songwriter born in 1950 in Arkansas. Her songs were recorded by Loretta Lynn, Lynn Anderson, Conway Twitty; her own hits began in 1970 and she has made many fans in the UK since 1979. (Donald Clarke).

ANSWER GAME, THE (Fairchild, Barbara & Billy Walker).
Tracks: Bye, bye, love / If we take our time / Somewhere between leaving and gone / Answer game, The / Let me be the one / You've still got it baby / Deep purple / Broken trust / Over my head in love with you / Love's slipping through our fingers.
LP . . . . INTS 5124
■ MC . . . . INTK 5124
RCA International / '82.

ANSWER GAME, THE (Fairchild, Barbara & Billy Walker).
Tracks: Answer game, The / Bye bye love.
■ 7" . . . . .RCA 188
RCA / '82.

FREE AND EASY.
Tracks: She can't give it away / For all the right reasons / Other side of the morning, The / Sing the blues / Bluebirds / When the morning comes / Someone loves him / Love me like you never will again / This haunted house / Good side of tomorrow / Painted faces.
■ LP 82272
CBS / '78 / Sony.

GREATEST HITS: BARBARA FAIRCHILD.
Tracks: Teddy Bear song / You've lost that loving feeling / Cheatin' is / Kid stuff / Love is a gentle thing / Mississippi / Let me love you once before you go / Standing in your line / Let's love while we can / Too far gone.
■ LP 82675
CBS / '78 / Sony.

JUST OUT RIDING AROUND.
Tracks: Just out riding around / You burned me so bad.
■ 7" . . . . .CL 411
Capitol / Jun '86.

LET ME LOVE YOU ONCE BEFORE YOU GO.
Tracks: Let me love you once before you go / Standing in your line.
■ 7" . . . . CBS 6322
CBS / May '78.

MISSISSIPPI.
Tracks: Mississippi / Let me love you once before you go / Under your spell again / You are always there / Touch my heart / Cheatin' is / Music of love, The / Did it rain? / What you left my memory / Let Jesse rob this train.
■ LP . . . . CBS 82020
CBS / '77.

Family Brown

FAVOURITES.
Tracks: You're the light / Lovin' fool / I'm available / Family love / Stay with me / Amazing grace / Juke box lover / Love was on our side / Heaven's just a sin away / Feeling's too strong / How great thou art / Poor mans crown.
■ LP . . . . PL 10360
RCA / Jul '80.

I'M GONNA GETCHA.
Tracks: I'm gonna getcha.
12" . . . . .VIBE 4T
Buzz Int. / Apr '84 / Pinnacle.

NOTHING REALLY CHANGES.
Tracks: Sing a family song / Coat of many colours / Family circle / Nothing really changes / Momma was a fighter / Careless hands / But its cheating / It's really love this time / Ribbon of gold / One day at a time / Another broken hearted melody / Antique / Sing a song of love / Old rugged cross.
■ LP . . . . RCALP 5021
RCA / Jun '81.

Fargo, Donna

Country singer, born in 1949 in North Carolina. She taught high school, sang in clubs in LA, met and married record producer Stan Silver; she reached number one on the country chart in 1972 with her own song: *Happiest girl in the whole USA* won a Grammy for Song Of The Year, ACM song, Album and Female Vocalist Of

The Year. She was stricken with multiple sclerosis in 1979, but fought against it and carried on. (Donald Clarke).

DO I LOVE YOU.
Tracks: Do I love you / Dee dee.
■ 7" . . . . K 17141
WEA / Mar '78.

QUEENS OF COUNTRY (see under Parton, Dolly).

SHAME ON ME.
Tracks: Shame on me / Ragamuffin man / Loving you / Happy together / Do I love you / Gone at last / That was yesterday / Dee dee / Time / Kirksville, Missouri / Race is on, The.
LP . . . . K 56442
WEA / WEA.

THAT WAS YESTERDAY.
Tracks: That was yesterday / Cricket song.
■ 7" . . . . K 16960
WEA / Jun '77.

YOU CAN'T BE A BEACON.
Tracks: You can't be a beacon / Just a friend of mine.
■ 7" . . . . .DOT 147
Dot / Jun '74.

Farr, Richard

FARR COUNTRY.
Tracks: Let the rest of the World go by / Della and the dealer / Tonight / Bottle let me down, The / It's four in the morning / Lucille / My way of life / Walk on by / Buck's polka / Guilty / How can I write on paper what I feel in my heart / Your my best friend / Send me the pillow that you dream on / Take these chains from my heart / Jealous heart / Someday you'll want me to want you.
LP . . . . KLP 25
MC . . . . ZCKLP 25
Igus / Apr '81 / C.M. Distribution / Ross Records / Duncans.

Farrell & Farrell

MANIFESTO.
Tracks: Not Advised.
■ LP . . . . .SR R 2074
Solid Rock / '81.

Fats, Happy

CAJUN & COUNTRY SONGS (Fats, Happy & Alex Broussard).
Tracks: Not Advised.
LP 6005
Swallow (USA) / Feb '79 / Swift / Wellard Dist.

FAIS DO DO BREAKDOWN (see under Sonnier, Lee).

Feathers, Charlie

A singer, guitarist and songwriter born in 1932 in Mississippi, a legendary rockabilly who never made the big time. He went to Memphis at 18, hung around at Sun and first recorded for subsidiary Flip, then on Meteor, King, Kay, Walmay and Philips between 1956-59 in country and rockabilly styles. Charlie Feathers gained much respect and status but few actual sales. His single *Rollin' Rock* secured him a date at London's Rainbow Theatre in 1977, recorded by EMI's Harvest label. (Donald Clarke).

ALL TORE UP.
Tracks: Bottle to the baby / I can't hardly stand it / One hand loose / Everybody's lovin' my baby / Dinky John / South of Chicago / Corina, Corina / Defrost your heart / Running around / I've been deceived / Wild of side, The / Don't you know / Where's she at tonight.
LP . . . . .Z 2008
Zu Zazz / '88 / Hot Shot / A.D.A Distribution / C.M. Distribution.

CHARLIE FEATHERS.
Tracks: Man in love, A / When you come around / Pardon me mister / Fraulein / Defrost your heart / Mean woman blues / (I don't care)If tomorrow never comes / Cootzie coo / We can't seem to remember to forget / Long time ago, A / Seasons of my heart / Uh huh honey / Oklahoma hills.
CD 7559611472
MC 7559611474
WEA / Jul '91 / WEA.

GONE GONE GONE.
Tracks: Peepin' eyes / I've been deceived / Defrost your heart / Wedding gown of white / We're getting closer to being apart / Bottle to the baby / One hand loose / Can't hardly stand it / Everybody's loving my baby / Too much alike / When you come around / When you decide / Nobody's woman / Man in love, The / I forgot to remember to forget / Uh huh honey / Mound of clay / Tongue tied Jill / Gone gone gone / Two to choose / Send me the pillow that you dream on / Folsom Prison blues.
CD . . . . CDCHARLY 278
Charly / Sep '91 / Charly.

GOOD ROCKIN TONITE.
Tracks: Not Advised.
CD . . . . .EDCD 355
Demon / Sep '92 / Pinnacle.

GOOD ROCKIN' TONIGHT/LIVE IN MEMPHIS, TENNESSEE.
Tracks: Not Advised.

HONKY TONK MAN.
Tracks: Not Advised.
CD . . . . ROSE 144CD
LP . . . . ROSE 144
New Rose (1) / Jun '88 / Pinnacle.

JUNGLE FEVER.
Tracks: Not Advised.
LP . . . . KAY 5045
Kay / Nov '87.

LEGENDARY 1956 DEMO SESSION, THE.
Tracks: Bottle to the baby / So ashamed / Frankie and Johnny / Honky tonk kind / Frankie and Johnny (take 5) / So ashamed (take 4) / Honky tonk kind (take 4 and false starts) / Bottle to the baby (take 2).
LP . . . . ZZ 1001
Zu Zazz / Oct '86 / Hot Shot / A.D.A Distribution / C.M. Distribution.

LIVING LEGEND, THE.
Tracks: Not Advised.
LP . . . . .REDITA 107
Redita (Holland) / Oct '88 / Swift.

NEW JUNGLE FEVER.
Tracks: Not Advised.
LP . . . . ROSE 117
New Rose (1) / Jun '87 / Pinnacle.

ROCK-A-BILLY.
Tracks: Not Advised.
CD . . . . ZCD 2011
Zu Zazz / May '91 / Hot Shot / A.D.A Distribution / C.M. Distribution.

ROCKABILLY'S MAIN MAN.
Tracks: Peepin' eyes / I've been deceived / Defrost your heart / Wedding gown of white / Mad at you / I forgot to remember to forget / Uh huh honey / Mound of clay / Send me the pillow that you dream on / Tongue tied Jill / Gone gone gone / Two to choose.
LP . . . . CR 30161
Charly / Charly.

THAT CERTAIN FEMALE.
Tracks: That certain female.
7" 45 025
Rollin' Rock / Jun '80 / Swift.

THAT ROCKABILLY CAT.
Tracks: Gone gone gone / Tongue tied-Jill / Wild side of life / Do you know / Rock me / Wide river / Crazy heart / Uh huh honey / Cold dark night / Rain / Mama oh Mama / Cherry wine / They'll be three / I'm movin on.
CD . . . . .EDCD 348
Edsel / Jun '92 / Pinnacle.

WILD WILD PARTY.
Tracks: Not Advised.
LP . . . . RSRLP 1014
Rockstar / Dec '87 / Swift / C.M. Distribution.

Felts, Narvel

Narvel the Marvel, born in 1938 in Missouri; a singer in rock'n'roll, then country with unique dramatic falsetto vocal style. He had a rock'n'roll hit with *Honey love* in 1959 (banned due to risque lyrics); his biggest hit was *Reconsider baby* in 1975, number one in both pop and country charts. (Donald Clarke).

MEMPHIS DAYS.
Tracks: Night creature / Your true love / Blue darlin' / What you're doing to me / Sad and blue / She's in your heart to stay / Return / Welcome home / Love is gone / Tear down the wall / Four seasons of life, The / Come what may / Lola did a dance / Lovelight man / Mr.

Pawnshop broker / Tongue tied Jill / All that heaven sent / I had a girl / Slippin' and slidin' / Larry and Joellen / You were mine / Get on the right track, baby / Sweet, sweet loving / Mountain of love / Private detective / One man at a table.
CD . . . . BCD 15515
Bear Family / Oct '90 / Rollercoaster Records / Swift / Direct Distribution.

NARVEL FELTS STORY.
Tracks: Not Advised.
■ **LP.** . . . . SKYLINE 1880
Skyline / Nov '87.

RADIO ROCKABILLIES (Felts, Narvel & Jerry Mercer).
Tracks: Not Advised.
LP. . . . . RSRLP 1016
Rockstar (1) / Jun '88 / Swift / C.M. Distribution.

TEEN'S WAY, A (Felts, Narvel & The Rockets).
Tracks: I'm headin' home / Foolish thoughts / Cry, baby, cry / Vada Lou / Little girl step this way / Rocket ride / Why don't you love me / Remember me / Come back baby / Fool in Paradise, A / Lonely river / Kiss me baby / Your touch / Your first broken heart / Teen's way, A / Dream world / Lonesome feeling.
LP. . . . . BFX 15242
Bear Family / May '87 / Rollercoaster Records / Swift / Direct Distribution.

THIS TIME.
Tracks: This time / Since I met you baby / Butterfly / You're out of my reach / Chased by the dawn / No one will ever know / Endless love / Little bit of soap, A / Sound of the wind / All in the game / I'd trade all of my tomorrows / Greatest gift, The / I had to cry / Dee Dee / 86 Miles.
CD . . . . HIUKCD 123
Demon / Sep '92 / Pinnacle.

Fender, Freddy

A Tex-Mex, country and rockabilly singer and songwriter, born Baldemar Huerta in 1937 in Texas. He spoke only Spanish until he was a teenager, and worked picking vegetables and cotton. He began playing Texas honky tonks '56-9 and made records for many small labels, rockabilly titles and songs in Spanish, including an early version of his best known song *Wasted days and wasted nights*, which reached the Cash Box Top 100. But then he was arrested and spent three years in prison for possession of marijuana. He worked clubs in New Orleans in the later '60's; finally an update of *Before the next teardrop falls* performed in English and Spanish led to a big pop and country hit in 1975, CMA Single Of The Year, and he was ACM Top New Male Vocalist, followed by further pop country hits in the '70's. (Donald Clarke).

20 GREATEST HITS.
Tracks: Before the next teardrop falls / Wasted days and wasted nights / You'll lose a good thing / Almost persuaded / She's about a mover / Lovin' cajun style / Man can cry, A / Crazy baby / I'm leaving it (all) up to you / Rains came, The / Wild side of life / Silver wings / Enter my heart / What I'd say / Sweet summer day / Mathilda / Running back / Going out with the tide / Baby I want to love you / Girl who waits on tables.
LP. 20017
MC 40017
Astan (USA) / Nov '84.
CD 2630012
LP. 2630011
MC 2630014
Big Country / Sep '89.

BEFORE THE NEXT TEARDROP FALLS.
Tracks: Before the next teardrop falls / Mathilda / Loving cajun style / What'd I say / Sweet Summer day / Silver wings / Running back / Enter my heart / Going out with the tide / Baby I want to love you.
LP. . . . . SDLP 1020
Sundown / Mar '85 / Terry Blood Dist. / Jazz Music / C.M. Distribution.

BEFORE THE NEXT TEARDROP FALLS (2).
Tracks: Coming home soon / Just because / Mean woman blues / Something on your mind / Only one / Since I met you baby / Before the next teardrop falls / Wasted days and wasted nights / La Bamba / Ooh poo pah doo / Rains came, The / Wild side of life.
LP. . . . . TOP 170
MC . . . . KTOP 170
Topline / Apr '87 / Charly / Swift / Black Sun Records.

BEFORE THE NEXT TEARDROP FALLS (OLD GOLD).
Tracks: Before the next teardrop falls / Wasted days and wasted nights.
■ **7"** . . . . OG 9217
Old Gold / Jul '82.

BEST OF FREDDY FENDER.
Tracks: Before the next teardrop falls / Wasted days and wasted nights / I can't put my arms / Wild side of life / Vaya con dios / Livin' it down / I love my Rancho Grande / We'll take our last walk tonight / Sugar coated love / Rains came, The / Matilda, Matilda / Don't do it darling / If you don't love me (why don't you just leave me alone) / You'll lose a thing / 50's medley.
LP. . . . . MCL 1809
■ **MC** . . . . MCLC 1809
MCA / Apr '85.

CANCIONES DE MI BARRIO.
Tracks: Not Advised.
CD . . . . ARHCD 366
Arhoolie (USA) / Sep '93 / Pinnacle / Cadillac Music / Swift / Projection / Hot Shot / A.D.A Distribution / Jazz Music.

COUNTRY STORE: FREDDY FENDER.
Tracks: Not Advised.
CD . . . . CDCST 47
MC . . . . CSTK 47
Country Store / Oct '89 / BMG.

CRAZY BABY.
Tracks: Crazy baby / Wasted days and wasted nights / What's I say / Something on your mind / Loving cajun / Style / Mean woman / La bamba / Get out of my life woman / Only one / Coming home soon / Before the next teardrop falls / Since I met you baby / Wild side of life / Rains came, The / Mathilda / You'll loose a good thing / Just because / Black shirt / You made a fool / Coming 'round the mountain.
LP. . . . . SMT 012
MC . . . . SMTC 012
Starburst / Sep '87 / Terry Blood Dist. / Jazz Music.

EARLY YEARS 1959-1963.
Tracks: I'm gonna leave / Wasted days & wasted nights / Mean woman / Crazy baby / Wild side of life / You're something else for me / Going out with the tide / San Antonio rock / Louisiana blues / Since I met you baby / Little mama / You told me you loved me / I can't remember when I didn't love you / Only one / Find somebody new / Roobie doobie.
LP. . . . . KK 7437
Krazy Kat / May '86 / Hot Shot / C.M. Distribution / Wellard Dist. / Roots Records / Projection / Charly / Jazz Music.

LIVIN' IT DOWN.
Tracks: Livin' it down / Take her a message I'm lonely.
■ **7"** . . . . ABC 4155
ABC Records / Dec '76.

WASTED DAYS & WASTED NIGHTS.
Tracks: Wasted days & wasted nights / Rains came, The / You'll lose a good thing / Almost persuaded / I'm leaving it up to you / Man can cry, A / Wild side of life / She's about a mover / Crazy baby / Girl who waits on tables, The / Before the next teardrop falls / Lovin' cajun style / But I do / Sweet summer days / Silver wings / Running back / Enter my heart / Going out with the tide / Baby I want to love you / Just because.
CD . . . . CDGRF 072
Tring / Feb '93 / Prism Leisure PLC / Midland Records / Taylors.

File

2 LEFT FEET.
Tracks: Not Advised.
CD . . . . FF 507CD
LP. . . . . FF 507
MC . . . . FF 507C
Flying Fish (USA) / '92 / Cadillac Music / Roots Records / Projection / C.M. Distribution / Direct Distribution / Jazz Music / Duncans / A.D.A Distribution.

CAJUN DANCE BAND.
Tracks: Not Advised.
LP. . . . . FF 418
Flying Fish (USA) / '88 / Cadillac Music / Roots Records / Projection / C.M. Distribution / Direct Distribution / Jazz Music / Duncans / A.D.A Distribution.

Films

ANY WHICH WAY YOU CAN (Original Soundtrack) (Various Artists).
Tracks: Beers to you / Any which way you can / You're the reason God made Oklahoma / Whiskey heaven / One too many women in your life / Cow Patti / Acapulco / Anyway you want me / Cotton eyed Clint / Orangutan hall of fame / Too loose / Good guys and the bad guys.
■ **LP.** . . . . K 56884
WEA / Feb '81.
LP. . . . . HS 3499
Silva Screen / Jan '89 / Silva Screen / Conifer Records / Total / BMG.

BANJO MAN (Original Soundtrack) (Various Artists).
Tracks: Lonesome Ruben / Battle of New Orleans / You ain't goin' nowhere / Freight train boogie / T for Texas / Roll over Beethoven / Me and Bobby McGee / Mr. Tambourine man / Black mountain rag / Night they drove old dixie down, The / Diggy liggy lo / Blowin' in the wind / Foggy mountain breakdown / Billy Fehr.
LP. . . . . SRK 6026
Sire / Feb '79 / WEA.

BELIZAIRE - THE CAJUN (Film Soundtrack) (Doucet, Michael & Beausoleil).
Tracks: Not Advised.
LP. . . . . ARHOOLIE 5038
MC . . . . ARHC 5038
Arhoolie (USA) / Aug '87 / Pinnacle / Cadillac Music / Swift / Projection / Hot Shot / A.D.A Distribution / Jazz Music.

BEST LITTLE WHOREHOUSE IN TEXAS (Original Soundtrack) (Various Artists).
Tracks: Not Advised.
CD . . . . MCAD 31007
LP. . . . . MCA 37218
MC . . . . MCAC 37218
MCA / Jan '89 / BMG.

COAL MINER'S DAUGHTER (1980 Film Soundtrack) (Various Artists).
Tracks: Titanic, The / Blue moon of Kentucky / There he goes / I'm a honky tonk girl / Amazing grace / Walking after midnight / Crazy / I fall to pieces / Sweet dreams / Back in my baby's arms / One's on the way / You ain't woman enough / You're lookin' at country / Coal miner's daughter.
LP. . . . . MCF 3068
MC . . . . MCFC 3068
MCA / Apr '81 / BMG.
■ **LP.** . . . . MCL 1847
MCA / Mar '87.
■ **MC** . . . . MCLC 1847
MCA / Mar '87.

CONVOY (Film Soundtrack) (Various Artists).
Tracks: Convoy / Lucille / Don't it make my brown eyes blue? / Cowboys don't get lucky all the time / I cheated on a good woman's love / Okie from Muskogee / Southern nights / Keep on the sunny side / Blanket on the ground / Walk right back.
■ **LP.** . . . . EST 24590
Capitol / Oct '78.
LP. . . . . ICK 064 85597
Conifer / '83 / Conifer Records / Jazz Music.

DELIVERANCE (Original Soundtrack) (Various Artists).
Tracks: Duelling banjos (fuedin' banjos) / Little Maggie / Shuckin' the corn / Pony express / Old Joe Clark / Eight more miles to Louisville / Farewell blues / Earl's breakdown / End of a dream / Buffalo gals / Reuben's train / Riding the waves / Fire on the mountain / Eighth of January / Bugle call rag / Hard ain't it hard / Mountain dew / Rawhide.
MC . . . . K 446214
WEA / Nov '81 / WEA.
CD . . . . K 246214
WEA / Dec '87 / WEA.

DREAM ON - WRECK ON THE HIGHWAY (TV Soundtrack) (Various Artists).
Tracks: Not Advised.
CD . . . . BBCCD 769
BBC / Jul '90 / Pinnacle / Bond Street Music.
■ **LP.** . . . . REB 769
BBC / Jul '90.

ELECTRIC HORSEMAN, THE (Film Soundtrack) (Various Artists).
Tracks: Midnight rider / My heroes have always been cowboys / Mamas don't let your babies grow up to be. / Hands on the wheel / Electro-phantasma / Rising star / Electric horseman / Tumbleweed morning / Disco magic / Freedom / Epilogue.
LP. 70177
MC 40 70177
CBS / Apr '80 / Sony.
CD . . . . CK 36327
CBS (import) / Jan '89 / C.M. Distribution / Silva Screen.
LP. . . . . JS 36327
MC . . . . JST 36327
Silva Screen / Jan '89 / Silva Screen / Conifer Records / Total / BMG.

EVERY WHICH WAY BUT LOOSE (Film Soundtrack) (Various Artists).
Tracks: Every which way but loose / Send me down to Tucson / I seek the night / Coca cola cowboy / Monkey see, monkey do / Salty dog blues (instrumental) / I'll wake you up when I get home / Red eye special / Eastwood's alley walk / Behind closed doors / I can't say no to a truck drivin' man / Under the double eagle (instrumental) / Bikers theme (instrumental) / Don't say you don't love me no more / Six pack to go, A / Overture (instrumental).
LP. . . . . K 52119
Elektra / Feb '79 / WEA.

FASTEST GUITAR ALIVE, THE (1966 Film Soundtrack) (Various Artists).
Tracks: Not Advised.
LP. . . . . MCA 1437
MCA / Jan '89 / BMG.
■ **MC** . . . . MCAC 1437
MCA / Jan '89.

FASTEST GUITAR ALIVE/YOUR CHEATIN' HEART (Film Soundtracks) (Various Artists).
Tracks: Whirlwind (Fastest Guitar Alive.) / Medicine man (Fastest Guitar Alive.) / River (Fastest Guitar Alive.) / Fastest guitar alive, The (Fastest Guitar Alive.) / Rollin' on (Fastest Guitar Alive.) / Pistolero (Fastest Guitar Alive.) / Good time party (Fastest Guitar Alive.) / Heading South (Fastest Guitar Alive.) / Best friend (Fastest Guitar Alive.) / There won't be many coming home (Fastest Guitar Alive.) / Your cheatin' heart (Your Cheatin' Heart.) / Hey good lookin' (Your Cheatin' Heart.) / I saw light (Your Cheatin' Heart.) / Jambalaya (Your Cheatin' Heart.) / Ramblin' man (Your Cheatin' Heart.) / I'm so lonesome I could cry (Your Cheatin' Heart.) / Cold cold heart (Your Cheatin' Heart.) / Kaw-liga (Your Cheatin' Heart.) / I couldn't help it (Your

F 2

■ DELETED

Cheatin' Heart.) / Long gone lonesome blue (Your Cheatin' Heart.) / You win again (Your Cheatin' Heart.).
LP . . . . **LPMGM 18**
■ **MC** . . . . **TCMGM 18**
MGM (EMI) / Apr '90.
■ **CD** . . . . **CDMGM 18**
MGM (EMI) / Apr '90.

GOSPEL ROAD, THE (Film Soundtrack) (Cash, Johnny).
Tracks: Not Advised.
Double LP . . . . **CBS 68253**
CBS / '73 / Sony.

GREAT BALLS OF FIRE (Film Soundtrack) (Various Artists).
Tracks: Great balls of fire / High school confidential / I'm on fire / Whole lotta shakin' goin' on / Breathless / Crazy arms / Wild one / That lucky old sun / Great balls of fire (Original) / Big legged woman / Route 88 / Whole lotta shakin' going on.
CD **839 516 2**
MC **839 516 4**
Polydor / Nov '89 / PolyGram.
■ **LP** **839 516 1**
Polydor / Nov '89.

HONKY TONK MAN (Original Soundtrack) (Various Artists).
Tracks: Not Advised.
LP **23739.1**
Silva Screen / Jan '89 / Silva Screen / Conifer Records / Total / BMG.

J'AI ETE AU BAL (Cajun & Zydeco Music Of Louisiana Vol.1) (Various Artists).
Tracks: Not Advised.
CD . . . . **ARHCD 331**
Arhoolie (USA) / '88 / Pinnacle / Cadillac Music / Swift / Projection / Hot Shot / A.D.A Distribution / Jazz Music.

J'AI ETE AU BAL VOL.2 (Cajun & Zydeco Music of Louisiana Vol.2) (Various Artists).
Tracks: Not Advised.
CD . . . . **ARHCD 332**
Arhoolie (USA) / '88 / Pinnacle / Cadillac Music / Swift / Projection / Hot Shot / A.D.A Distribution / Jazz Music.

JAMBOREE (Various Artists).
Tracks: Not Advised.
MC . . . . **AIM 74**
Aim (2) / Feb '83 / Topic Records / Direct Distribution.

MY RIFLE, MY PONY & ME (Various Artists).
Tracks: My rifle, my pony & me / Legend of Shenandoah, The / Montana/The searchers/Wagons west/Song of the wagonmaster / Nevada Smith / Ballad of the Alamo/ The hanging tree / Ballad of Palladin / Sons of Katie Elder, The/The rebel Johnny Yuma / Rawhide/ Gunfight at the O.K. Corral / Ballad of Davy Crockett / Rio Bravo / I'm a runaway / Bonanza / North to Alaska / High noon / And the moon grew brighter / Pecos Bill / Yellow rose of Texas, The/Roll on Texas moon/Don't fence me / Cowboy.
CD . . . . **BCD 15625**
Rollercoaster / Mar '93 / Rollercoaster Records / Swift.

ONCE UPON A TIME IN THE WEST (Morricone, Ennio).
Tracks: Once upon a time in the west / As a judgement / Farewell to Cheyenne / Transgression, The / First tavern, The / Second tavern, The / Man with a harmonica / Dimly lit room, A / Bad orchestra / Man / Jill's America / Death rattle / Finale.
LP . . . . **PL 31387**
■ **MC** . . . . **PK 31387**
RCA / '79.
LP . . . . **NL 70032**
MC . . . . **NK 70032**
RCA / Oct '83 / BMG.
■ **CD** . . . . **ND 71704**
RCA / Jun '88.
CD **4736.2**
Silva Screen / Feb '90 / Silva Screen / Conifer Records / Total / BMG.

ONE FROM THE HEART (Film Soundtrack) (Waits, Tom & Crystal Gayle).
Tracks: Opening montage / Tom's piano / Once upon a town / Wages of love, The / Is there any way out of this dream? / Presents / Picking up after you / Old boy friends / Broken bicycles / I beg your pardon / Little boy blue / Instrumental montage / Tango, The / Circus girl / You can't unring a bell / This one's from the heart / Take me home.
LP . . . . **CBS 70215**
CBS / Feb '83 / Sony.
MC . . . . **.40 70215**
CBS / Jan '89 / Sony.
CD **4676092**
MC **4676094**
CBS / Dec '90 / Sony.
■ **LP** **4676091**
CBS / Dec '90.

OUTLAW BLUES (Film Soundtrack) (Various Artists).
Tracks: Everybody's goin' on the road / Jailbirds don't fly / I dream of highways / Outlaw on the run / Beyond these walls / Outlaw blues / Outlaw blues love theme / Water for my horses / Whisper in a velvet night / Little more holy.
LP . . . . **EST 11691**
Capitol / Nov '77 / EMI.

PLACES IN THE HEART (Film Soundtrack) (Various Artists).
Tracks: Not Advised.
LP . . . . **A 269**
SPI Milan (France) / Apr '85 / Silva Screen / PolyGram.
LP . . . . **.STV 81229**
MC . . . . **CTV 81229**
Varese Sarabande Records(USA) / Jan '89 / Silva Screen / Pinnacle.

PURE COUNTRY (Original Soundtrack Recording) (Strait, George).
Tracks: Heartland / Baby your baby / I cross my heart / When did you stop loving me / She lays it all on the line / Overnight male / Last in love / Thoughts of a fool / King of broken hearts, The / Where the sidewalk ends / Heartland (Main title sequence) (Feat. George Strait Jr.).
CD . . . . **MCD 10651**
MC . . . . **MCC 10651**
MCA / Apr '93 / BMG.

SMOKEY AND THE BANDIT (Original Soundtrack) (Various Artists).
Tracks: Not Advised.
LP . . . . **.MCA 1673**
MC . . . . **MCAC 1673**
Silva Screen / Jan '89 / Silva Screen / Conifer Records / Total / BMG.

SMOKEY AND THE BANDIT 2 (Various Artists).
Tracks: Not Advised.
LP . . . . **MCA 37161**
Silva Screen / Jan '89 / Silva Screen / Conifer Records / Total / BMG.

SWEET DREAMS (Life And Times Of Patsy Cline) (Cline, Patsy).
Tracks: San Antonio rose / Seven lonely days / Your cheatin' heart / Lovesick blues / Walking after midnight / Foolin' around / Half as much / I fall to pieces / Crazy / Blue moon of Kentucky / She's got you / Sweet dreams.
CD . . . . **MCAD 6149**
MC . . . . **MCGC 6003**
MCA / Feb '86 / BMG.
■ **LP** . . . . **.MCG 6003**
MCA / Feb '86.

TENDER MERCIES (Film Soundtrack) (Various Artists).
Tracks: Not Advised.
■ **LP** . . . . **LBG 7511471**
Liberty / Aug '83.

URBAN COWBOY (Film Soundtrack) (Various Artists).
Tracks: Hi lo Texas / All night long / Times like these / Nine tonight / Stand by me / Here comes the hurt again / Orange blossom special / Hoedown / Could I have this dance / Cherokee fiddle / Lookin' for love / Lyin' eyes / Look what you've done to me / Don't it make you want to dance / Darlin' / Hearts against the wind / Devil went down to Georgia / Love the world away / Falling in love for the night.
LP . . . . **K 99101**
■ **MC** **K4 99101**
Asylum / Jul '80.

WILD WEST (Original Soundtrack Recording) (Various Artists).
Tracks: Nowhere road / I ain't never satisfied / River / Fearless heart / No. 29 / Love wore a halo / Anyone can be somebody's fool / Akhan naz akhan / Wild west / Guitars & cadillacs.
CD . . . . **COOKCD 056**
MC . . . . **COOKC 056**
Cooking Vinyl / May '93 / Revolver-APT.

Fink. Cathy

CATHY FINK & DUCK DONALD (Fink, Cathy & Duck Donald).
Tracks: Not Advised.
LP . . . . **FF 053**
Flying Fish (USA) / Mar '89 / Cadillac Music / Roots Records / Projection / C.M. Distribution / Direct Distribution / Jazz Music / Duncans / A.D.A Distribution.

CATHY FINK & MARCY MARXER (Fink, Cathy & Marcy Marxer).
Tracks: Last night I dreamed / Love's last chance / Frieght train blues / My prairie home / I've endured / Early / I'm not alone anymore / Names / Walkin'n in the glory / Are you tired of me / Tune medley (Available on CD only) / Crawdad song (from the Crackle Sisters), The (Available on CD only).
CD . . . . **SHCD 3775**
LP . . . . **SHLP 3775**
MC . . . . **SHMC 3775**
Sugarhill(USA) / '89 / Roots Records / Projection / Impetus Records / C.M. Distribution / Jazz Music / Swift / Duncans / A.D.A Distribution.

DOGGONE MY TIME.
Tracks: Where the west begins / I'm so lonesome I could cry / Cuckoo, The / Sara McCutcheon / Cat's got the measles, The / Coal mining woman / Monkey medley / Midnight prayerlight / No tell motel, The / When it's darkness on the delta / Cottonpatch rag / Coming home / Little Billy Wilson / Shenandoah Falls / My old Kentucky home.

CD . . . . **SHCD 3783**
LP . . . . **SH 3783**
MC . . . . **SH 3783C**
Sugarhill(USA) / '90 / Roots Records / Projection / Impetus Records / C.M. Distribution / Jazz Music / Swift / Duncans / A.D.A Distribution.

GRANDMA SLID DOWN THE MOUNTAIN.
Tracks: Not Advised.
LP **8010**
I.R.S (Illegal) / Jul '84 / EMI.
LP . . . . **ROUNDER 8010**
Rounder / Jan '85 / Projection / Roots Records / Swift / C.M. Distribution / Topic Records / Jazz Music / Hot Shot / A.D.A Distribution / Direct Distribution.
MC . . . . **ROUNDER 8010C**
Rounder / Aug '88 / Projection / Roots Records / Swift / C.M. Distribution / Topic Records / Jazz Music / Hot Shot / A.D.A Distribution / Direct Distribution.
CD . . . . **CD 8010**
Rounder / Oct '88 / Projection / Roots Records / Swift / C.M. Distribution / Topic Records / Jazz Music / Hot Shot / A.D.A Distribution / Direct Distribution.

LEADING ROLE.
Tracks: Not Advised.
LP . . . . **ROUNDER 0223**
Rounder / Jun '86 / Projection / Roots Records / Swift / C.M. Distribution / Topic Records / Jazz Music / Hot Shot / A.D.A Distribution / Direct Distribution.
MC . . . . **ROUNDER 0223C**
Rounder / Aug '88 / Projection / Roots Records / Swift / C.M. Distribution / Topic Records / Jazz Music / Hot Shot / A.D.A Distribution / Direct Distribution.

WHEN THE RAIN COMES DOWN.
Tracks: Not Advised.
CD . . . . **CD 8013**
LP . . . . **ROUNDER 8013**
MC . . . . **.ROUNDER 8013C**
Rounder / '88 / Projection / Roots Records / Swift / C.M. Distribution / Topic Records / Jazz Music / Hot Shot / A.D.A Distribution / Direct Distribution.

Firewater

BRAND NEW VINTAGE.
Tracks: Crazy / Almost Saturday night / Sea of heartbreak / Lonely road cafe / Whisky drinking man / Driving my life away.
LP . . . . **SDLP 031**
Sundown / Apr '86 / Terry Blood Dist. / Jazz Music / C.M. Distribution.
MC . . . . **SDC 031**
Sundown / May '88 / Terry Blood Dist. / Jazz Music / C.M. Distribution.

CRAZY.
Tracks: Crazy / Saving up my nights.
7" . . . . **SDS 003**
Sundown / Apr '86 / Terry Blood Dist. / Jazz Music / C.M. Distribution.

Fisher. Sonny

PINK AND BLACK.
Tracks: Pink and black / Sneaky Pete.
■ **7"** . . . . **NS 54**
Ace / Jul '79.

SHAKE THAT THING.
Tracks: Shake that thing / Mathilda / Birthday party / If you leave me tonight I'll cry.
■ **EP** . . . . **SW 60**
Ace / Aug '80.

TEXAS ROCKABILLY.
Tracks: Rockin' daddy / Hold me baby / Sneaky Pete / Rockin' and rollin' / Pink and black / I can't lose / Hey mama / Little red wagon.
■ **LP** . . . . **CH 14**
Ace / Mar '79.

TEXAS ROCKABILLY TEAR UP.
Tracks: Driving my life away / Sweet sixteen / You're right / Raining in my heart / Truckstop baby / Shake it around / I'm flying in / Rockabilly tonight / I miss you Elvis / On the road again.
■ **LP** . . . . **MFM 005**
Magnum Force / Jul '82.

Fjellgaard. Gary

HEART OF A DREAM.
Tracks: Not Advised.
CD . . . . **SVCD 9211**
LP . . . . **SVLP 9211**
MC . . . . **SVMC 9411**
Savannah / Oct '89 / Sony / ACD Trading Ltd.

NO TIME TO LOSE.
Tracks: Not Advised.
LP . . . . **SVLP 9203**
MC . . . . **SVMC 9403**
Savannah / '90 / Sony / ACD Trading Ltd.

Flacke. Ray

UNTITLED ISLAND.
Tracks: Squeeze the weazel / Untitled island / Wring that neck / Devoted to the dog / Main Street breakdown

/ Bandits on Bordbon / South Downs gallop / Raison d'etre / Going on after the theatre / Blarneystoned / New land shining.
CD . . . . **INCD 901149**
Line / Mar '92 / C.M. Distribution / Grapevine Distribution.

Flatlanders

Shortlived Texas unit (1970 - 1973), comprising singer-songwriter luminaries Butch Hancock, Jimmie Dale Gilmore and Joe Ely, accompanied at various stages by Steve Wesson (who played musical saw), Tommy Hancock, Tony Pearson and Sly Rice. During their old time related acoustic country venture, the Flatlanders dates included regular Texas baroom venues such as the Armadillo Beer Gardens in Austin and at Kerville's first folk festival. March 1972 found them recording in Shelby Singleton's Nashville studios - due to no Texas offers forthcoming. Eventually released an B-track on the Plantation label which the UK's 17-track Charly records released of 1980 (CD-1989) gave it it's only full coverage although Rounder came near in 1990 when using the apt sub-title *More a legend than a band*. On the split in 1973, when they took up their own personal directions, Ely headed for Nashville, broke through into the contemporary country scene (thanks greatly to Hancock's songs), went rock and then back again to the fold in 1992. Hancock kept writing and singing his songs recording his own Rainlight label and in 1993 Sugar Hill, who put put the compilation *Own the way over here* (Maurice Hope).

MORE A LEGEND THAN A BAND.
Tracks: Dallas / Tonight I'm gonna go downtown / You've never seen me cry / She had everything / Rose from the mountain / One day at a time / Jole Blon / Down in my hometown / Bhagavan decreed / Heart you left behind, The / Keeper of the mountain / Stars in my life / One more road.
CD . . . . **SSCD 34**
LP . . . . **SS 34**
MC . . . . **SSC 34**
Rounder / '90 / Projection / Roots Records / Swift / C.M. Distribution / Topic Records / Jazz Music / Hot Shot / A.D.A Distribution / Direct Distribution.

ONE MORE ROAD.
Tracks: You've never seen me cry / Dallas / Tonight I think I'm gonna go downtown / She had everything / Bhagavan decreed / Rose from the mountain / Down in my hometown / One road more / Waitin' for a train / Hello stranger / One day at a time / Stars in my life / Not so long ago / I know you / Heart you left behind, The / Jole Blon / Keeper of the mountain.
CD . . . . **CDCHARLY 192**
LP . . . . **CRM 2038**
Charly / Oct '89 / Charly.

Flatt, Lester

Legendary bluegrass guitarist/vocalist/songwriter born Lester Raymond Flatt, 19.06.1914 Overton County, Tennessee (died 11.05.1979). Flatt, alongside Bill Monroe and his partner Earl Scruggs made invaluable contributions to the evolving/popularising of bluegrass music. Prior to meeting up with Scruggs in 1945 (as members of Bill Monroe's bluegrass boys) Flatt played with the Harmonizers, and in the 1943 Charlie Monroe's band The Kentucky Partners (mandolin/tenor vocals). In 1944 joined Bill Monroe's Bluegrass Boys, staying their until 1948, when Scruggs and Flatt broke away on their own - forming The Foggy Mountain Boys with Mac Wiseman. He worked on WCYB, Bristol, through until 1949, recorded for Mercury up until 1950 - rated by many, as their best output. Toured during early 1950s with Ernest Tubb, Lefty Frizzell and the likes, clinched their own radio slot in 1953 on WSM. Flatt and Scrugg's 15 minute sponsored *Marth white flour biscuit time* , became a long running affair - the 5.45 am show, originally done live. Flatt's runs on his Martin D - 28 guitar has been copied many times through the years, his easy manner and warm baritone vocals were to endear him to live audiences. Columbia's recording act joined the Grand Ole Opry in 1955, Flatt and Scruggs with their own individual styles also had the added visual aspect of their show - as each member would be constantly weaving with amazing dexterity to the single mic, leaving an indelible mark on their audience that often included folk festivals and university/college dates. As the sixties wore on their bluegrass roots became the subject of much experimenting and garnered material from the folk revival (a live album at Carnegie Hall), which brought about the duo's break-up in 1969. Earl and his young sons were all for developing his music towards more popular themes. Lester meanwhile felt they'd already strayed too far away from bluegrass music's traditional values. Lester formed Nashville Grass after the split with musicians Paul Warren, Curly Seckler, Clarence 'Tater' Tate and during his final days, a then budding talent called Marty Stuart. (Maurice Hope)

20 GREATEST HITS: FLATT LESTER (Flatt, Lester & Earl Scruggs).
Tracks: Not Advised.
CD . . . . **CD 1031**
Gusto (USA) / '88.

BEFORE YOU GO.
Tracks: It's not too late / Have you come to say goodbye / Before you go / Haskel stomp, The / Love's come over me / Country living / Never ending song of love / I'm gonna get my picture took.
■ **LP** **APL1 0325**
RCA / '75 / BMG.

BLUE RIDGE CABIN HOME (Flatt, Lester & Earl Scruggs).
Tracks: Blue ridge cabin home / Don't let your deal go down / Some old day / I'll never shed another tear / I'll take the blame / Six white horses / Hundred years from now / On my mind / Shuckin' the corn / Let those brown eyes smile at me / No mother in this world / I won't be hanging around.
LP . . . . **CCS 102**
LP . . . . **P 14370**
County (USA) / '78 / Projection / Mike's Country Music Room / Swift.

DON'T GET ABOVE YOUR RAISIN' (Flatt, Lester & Earl Scruggs).
Tracks: Not Advised.
MC . . . . **SSC 08**
Rounder / '88 / Projection / Roots Records / Swift / C.M. Distribution / Topic Records / Jazz Music / Hot Shot / A.D.A Distribution / Direct Distribution.
LP . . . . **SS 08**
Rounder / Dec '88 / Projection / Roots Records / Swift / C.M. Distribution / Topic Records / Jazz Music / Hot Shot / A.D.A Distribution / Direct Distribution.

FANTASTIC PICKIN' (Flatt, Lester & Nashville Grass).
Tracks: Roanoke / Cannon ball blues / When it's lamplighting time in the valley / Two in the morning / Old spinning wheel / Peacock rag / Drive time / In the garden / Nashville wagoner / When I saw sweet Nellie home / Fiddlin' cricket / Last waltz, The.
LP . . . . **CMH 6232**
N/A.

FLATT AND SCRUGGS (Flatt, Lester & Earl Scruggs).
Tracks: I'll go stepping too / Dear old Dixie / No doubt about it / You put me on my feet / Before I met you / Foggy mountain special / Till the end of the world rolls round / What's good for you / Who knows right from wrong / Cabin in the hills.
■ **LP** . . . . **CBS 25018**
CBS / Oct '82.

FOGGY MOUNTAIN BREAKDOWN (Flatt, Lester & Earl Scruggs).
Tracks: Foggy mountain breakdown.
■ **7"** . . . . **CBS 3038**
CBS / Nov '65.

FOGGY MOUNTAIN BREAKDOWN (Flatt, Lester & Earl Scruggs).
Tracks: Bouquet in heaven / Cora is gone / Doin' my time / Foggy mountain breakdown / I'll be going to heaven sometime / My cabin in Caroline / My little girl in Tennessee / No mother or dad / Pike county breakdown / Roll in my sweet baby's arms / Take me in the lifeboat / Why don't you tell me so.
LP **6336 255**
Philips / Jan '76 / PolyGram.

GOLDEN ERA, THE (Flatt, Lester & Earl Scruggs).
Tracks: Flint Hill special / Your love is like a flower / I'm waiting to hear you call me darling / I'm head over heels in love with you / I'm working on a road (To Glory Land) / Till the end of the world rolls 'round / Jimmie Brown the newsboy / Earl's breakdown / Someone took my place with you / I'm gonna sleep with one eye open / Dim lights, thick smoke (And loud, loud music) / Don't this road look rough and rocky / Randy lynn rag / Old home town, The / Brother I'm getting ready to go.
MC . . . . **SSC 05**
Rounder / '88 / Projection / Roots Records / Swift / C.M. Distribution / Topic Records / Jazz Music / Hot Shot / A.D.A Distribution / Direct Distribution.
LP . . . . **SS 05**
Rounder / Dec '88 / Projection / Roots Records / Swift / C.M. Distribution / Topic Records / Jazz Music / Hot Shot / A.D.A Distribution / Direct Distribution.
CD . . . . **SSCD 05**
Rounder / '92 / Projection / Roots Records / Swift / C.M. Distribution / Topic Records / Jazz Music / Hot Shot / A.D.A Distribution / Direct Distribution.

GOLDEN HITS (Flatt, Lester & Earl Scruggs).
Tracks: Not Advised.
LP . . . . **PO 297**
Gusto (USA) / Mar '88.

GOLDEN YEARS, THE (Flatt, Lester & Earl Scruggs).
Tracks: Not Advised.
LP . . . . **CCS 101**
County (USA) / '78 / Projection / Mike's Country Music Room / Swift.

HEAVEN'S BLUEGRASS BAND (Flatt, Lester & Nashville Grass).
Tracks: Dixie flyer / Home without love is just a house / Great big woman / Night Daddy passed away, The / You know you caused it all by telling lies / House of bottles and cans, The / Heaven's bluegrass band / Ten years of heartaches / Love me Lorena / Gone with the delta queen / I'm gonna sit down beside my Jesus.
■ **LP** . . . . **CMH 6207**
CMH (USA) / '76.

LESTER AND MAC (Flatt, Lester & Mac Wiseman).
Tracks: You're the best of all the leading / Homestead on the farm / Now that you have me / Will you be loving another man / Sweetheart you done me wrong / Your love is like a flower / Bluebirds singing for me, The / Jimmy Brown the newsboy / I'll never love another.
LP . . . . **HAT 3065**
MC . . . . **HATC 3065**
Stetson / Jun '88 / Crusader Marketing Co. / Swift / Wellard Dist. / Midland Records / C.M. Distribution.

LESTER FLATT'S BLUEGRASS FESTIVAL (Flatt, Lester & Nashville Grass).
Tracks: Why did you wander / Columbus stockade blues / Down the road / Jimmie Brown the newsboy / Before I met you / Backin' to Birmingham / Martha White theme / Roll in sweet baby's arms / She's my little Georgia rose / Tennessee mountain home / Panhandle county / When I stop dreaming / Georgia cotton / Ugly girl, The / I don't love nobody / I know what it means to be lonesome / We'll meet again, sweetheart / Joshua / Little Lewis wildwood flower / Dim lights, thick smoke / Goin' up Cripple Creek / Til the end of the world rolls round / Randy Lynn rag / Hot corn, cold corn / Get in line, brother / Will the circle be unbroken.
Double LP . . . . **CMH 9009**
CMH (USA) / '77 / C.M. Distribution / Projection.

LESTER RAYMOND FLATT.
Tracks: Come back darling / Wreck of old '97 / Some old day / Listen to my mockingbird / When it's time for the whippoorwill to sing / Down the road / I won't care / It was only the wind / My cabin in Caroline / Sleep with one eye open / Foggy mountain chimes / That old book of mine.
LP . . . . **FF 015**
Flying Fish (USA) / Mar '89 / Cadillac Music / Roots Records / Projection / C.M. Distribution / Direct Distribution / Jazz Music / Duncans / A.D.A Distribution.

LIVE AT THE BLUEGRASS FESTIVAL.
Tracks: Foggy mountain breakdown(Instrumental) / Lost all my money / Homestead on the farm / Rawhide(Instrumental) / Wabash cannonball / Orange blossom special (instrumental) / Nine pound hammer / Flint hill special (instrumental) / Get in line brother / Blue moon of Kentucky / Will you be loving another man / Little cabin on the hill / Salty dog blues / Dig a hole in the meadow / Cumberland gap.
LP . . . . **NL 84071**
■ **MC** . . . . **NK 84071**
RCA / Mar '86.

LIVE BROADCAST (Flatt, Lester & Earl Scruggs).
Tracks: Not Advised.
LP . . . . **SH 2104**
Sandy Hook (USA) / Dec '86 / Pinnacle.

LIVING LEGEND, A (Flatt, Lester & Nashville Grass).
Tracks: I don't care anymore / It's too late now / Shuckin' the corn / Legend of the Johnson mountain boys / Please don't wake me / Good times are past and gone / Don't drink that mash and talk that trash / Why don't you tell me so / Gonna have myself a ball / Ballad of Jed Clampett / Why did you wander / Regina / I'll be the life of Riley / Foggy mountain special / We can't be darlings anymore / I still miss someone / Black eyed Susan Brown / If I wander back tonight / Bummin' and old freight train / Thinking about you.
■ **Double LP** . . . . **CMH 9002**
CMH (USA) / '76.

MERCURY SESSIONS VOL. 1 (Flatt, Lester & Earl Scruggs).
Tracks: Not Advised.
CD . . . . **SSCD 18**
Rounder / Dec '87 / Projection / Roots Records / Swift / C.M. Distribution / Topic Records / Jazz Music / Hot Shot / A.D.A Distribution / Direct Distribution.
MC . . . . **SSC 18**
Rounder / '88 / Projection / Roots Records / Swift / C.M. Distribution / Topic Records / Jazz Music / Hot Shot / A.D.A Distribution / Direct Distribution.
LP . . . . **SS 18**
Rounder / Dec '88 / Projection / Roots Records / Swift / C.M. Distribution / Topic Records / Jazz Music / Hot Shot / A.D.A Distribution / Direct Distribution.

MERCURY SESSIONS VOL. 2 (Flatt, Lester & Earl Scruggs).
Tracks: My little girl in Tennessee / Will the roses bloom / I'll never shed another tear / Bouquet in heaven / Cabin in Caroline / I'll never love another / God loves his children / Pain in my heart / Baby blue eyes / Doing my time / Preaching, praying, singing / Why don't they tell me so / Foggy mountain breakdown / I'm going to make heaven my home.
CD . . . . **CD 2056**
CD . . . . **SSCD 19**

F 4 ■ DELETED

Rounder / Dec '87 / Projection / Roots Records / Swift / C.M. Distribution / Topic Records / Jazz Music / Hot Shot / A.D.A Distribution / Direct Distribution.
MC . . . . SSC 19
Rounder / '88 / Projection / Roots Records / Swift / C.M. Distribution / Topic Records / Jazz Music / Hot Shot / A.D.A Distribution / Direct Distribution.
LP . . . . SS 19
Rounder / Dec '88 / Projection / Roots Records / Swift / C.M. Distribution / Topic Records / Jazz Music / Hot Shot / A.D.A Distribution / Direct Distribution.

PICKIN' TIME (Flatt, Lester & Nashville Grass).
Tracks: Uncle Billy play your fiddle for me / Pickin' time / Cabin on the hill / Bluegrass shuffle / Goin' up on black mountain / I love you until I am dizzy / We don't care what Mama allow / If you ain't tried it don't knock it / On my mind / I'll be all smiles tonight / Auction sale / Little brown church.
■ LP . . . . CMH 6226
CMH (USA) / '79.

YOU CAN FEEL IT IN YOUR SOUL (Flatt, Lester & Earl Scruggs).
Tracks: Not Advised.
LP . . . . CCS 111
MC . . . . CCS 111MC
County (USA) / '88 / Projection / Mike's Country Music Room / Swift.

Flavin. Mick

One of the most highly praised, traditional styled country singers to emerge on the Irish scene in recent years. Mick Flavin was born in Co.Longford in 1950, and turned professional in the mid 1980's. He has made several recordings in his homeland and has recently signed to Ritz in the UK. (Tony Byworth)

I'M GONNA MAKE IT AFTER ALL.
Tracks: Not Advised.
Double LP . . . . HM 026D
Harmac (Ireland) / '89 / I & B Records / Prism Leisure PLC.

IN CONCERT.
Tracks: Break her heart or mine / Rarest flowers, The / Old side of town, The / Jennifer Johnson & me / County of Mayo / Streets of Bakersfield / Travellin' light / Cold grey ashes / Carrickfergus / Wild flowers / Girl from Wexford Town / Medley (Westmeath batchelor; Dan O'hara; Jolly tinker; Irish washer woman) / Lover with from me / Working woman / Medley: (Kiss an angel good morning; Anybody going to San Antone) / Crystal chandeliers / Home to donegal / Going home again.
MC . . . . RITZSC 426
Ritz / Jun '93 / Pinnacle / Midland Records.

IN HARMONY (see under Begley, Philomena).

INTRODUCING MICK FLAVIN.
Tracks: Dream of me / Who will I be lovin' / Leaving on her mind / Precious jewel / Come back today / Tipperary, so far away / Gone gone gone / After the fire is gone / Never was a fool / Little bitty heart.
LP . . . . IHLP 09
MC . . . . IHMC 09
Irish Music Heritage / Apr '88.

JENNIFER JOHNSON AND ME.
Tracks: Jennifer Johnson and me / You'll be home.
7" . . . . RITZ 200
MC Single . . . . RITZC 200
Ritz / May '89 / Pinnacle / Midland Records.

LIGHTS OF HOME, THE.
Tracks: Someday you'll love me / I see an angel every day / On the wings of love / It started all over again / For a minute there / One of these days (I want to be in your nights) / I never loved you more / Little things in life, The / Lights of home, The / Connemara rose / Keeper of my heart, The / You done me wrong / Old home in Mayo / Table in the corner, The / Little mountain church mouse, The / Longford on my mind.
CD . . . . RITZRCD 533
MC . . . . RITZRC 533
Ritz / Aug '93 / Pinnacle / Midland Records.

MICK FLAVIN IN CONCERT.
Tracks: Brfeak her heart or mine / Rarest flowers, The / Old side of town, The / Jennifer Johnson and me / County of Mayo, The / Streets of Bakersfield / Travellin' light / Cold grey ashes / Carrickfergus (inst.) / Wild flowers / Girl from Wexford, The / Westmeath bachelor / Dan O'Hara / Jolly tinker / Irish washer woman / Never take her love away from me / Working woman / Kiss an angel good morning / Anybody going to San Antone / Crystal chandeliers / Home to Donegal / Going home again.
MC . . . . RITZRC 501
Ritz / '91 / Pinnacle / Midland Records.

MICK FLAVIN IN CONCERT.
Tracks: Break her heart or mine / Rarest flowers / Old side of town / Jennifer Johnson and me / County of Mayo, The / Streets of Bakersfield / Travellin' light / Cold grey ashes / Carrickfergus (instrumental) / Wild flowers / Girl from Wexford Town / Never take her love away from me / Working woman / Home to Donegal / Going home again.
VHS . . . . RITZV 0003
Ritz / '90 / Pinnacle / Midland Records.

OLD SCHOOL YARD, THE.
Tracks: Old school yard / Wine flowed freely, The.
MC Single . . . . RITZC 235
Ritz / Sep '91 / Pinnacle / Midland Records.
■ 7" . . . . RITZ 235
Ritz / Sep '91.

RAREST FLOWERS, THE.
Tracks: Rarest flowers, The / Ten thousand miles away.
7" . . . . RITZ 207
Ritz / Mar '90 / Pinnacle / Midland Records.

SHE'S MY ROSE.
Tracks: She's my rose / Hills of Tyrone, The.
CD Single . . . . RITZCD 245
Ritz / Oct '92 / Pinnacle / Midland Records.

SWEET MEMORY.
Tracks: If you're gonna do me wrong (do it right) / Gonna have love / What she don't know won't hurt her / Way down deep / I took a memory to lunch / Old school yard, The / She's my rose / Haven't you heard / Wine flowed freely, The / Lady Jane / Hills of Tyrone, The / All I can be (is a sweet memory).
CD . . . . RITZRCD 517
MC . . . . RITZRC 517
Ritz / Jun '92 / Pinnacle / Midland Records.

TRAVELLIN' LIGHT.
Tracks: Jennifer Johnson and me / Blue blue day / Hard times lovin' can bring / Where have all the lovers gone / Home to Donegal / Old side of town, The / Roads and other reasons / Travellin' light / There is no other way / Rarest flowers, The.
CD . . . . RITZCD 0053
MC . . . . RITZLC 0053
Ritz / Apr '90 / Pinnacle / Midland Records.
CD . . . . RITZCD 507
MC . . . . RITZRC 507
Ritz / '91 / Pinnacle / Midland Records.

TRAVELLIN' LIGHT.
Tracks: Travellin' light.
7" . . . . RITZ 214
Ritz / Jul '90 / Pinnacle / Midland Records.

YOU'RE ONLY YOUNG ONCE.
Tracks: Not Advised.
Double LP . . . . HM 044D
Harmac (Ireland) / '89 / I & B Records / Prism Leisure PLC.

Fleck. Bela

Innovative banjoist, formerly with the New Grass Revival (joining during the mid-1980's) and Spectrum - recording with the former on Sugar Hill and Capitol, and with Spectrum on Rounder. On the solo front, he's recorded a string of albums for Rounder - often as not supported by such close friends as Sam Bush, Jerry Douglas and Mark O'Connor. More recently Fleck, with his band the Flecktones, has been producing an intense jazzy toned new age acoustic music, as on, his second WEA release *Flight Of The Cosmic Hippo* (1991). (Maurice Hope)

CROSSING THE TRACKS.
Tracks: Not Advised.
LP . . . . ROUNDER 0121
MC . . . . ROUNDER 0121C
Rounder / '88 / Projection / Roots Records / Swift / C.M. Distribution / Topic Records / Jazz Music / Hot Shot / A.D.A Distribution / Direct Distribution.

DAYBREAK.
Tracks: Not Advised.
CD . . . . CD 11518
Rounder / '88 / Projection / Roots Records / Swift / C.M. Distribution / Topic Records / Jazz Music / Hot Shot / A.D.A Distribution / Direct Distribution.

DEVIATION (Fleck, Bela & The New Grass Revival).
Tracks: Not Advised.
MC . . . . ROUNDER 0196C
Rounder / Aug '88 / Projection / Roots Records / Swift / C.M. Distribution / Topic Records / Jazz Music / Hot Shot / A.D.A Distribution / Direct Distribution.
LP . . . . ROUNDER 0196
Rounder / Oct '88 / Projection / Roots Records / Swift / C.M. Distribution / Topic Records / Jazz Music / Hot Shot / A.D.A Distribution / Direct Distribution.

DOUBLE TIME.
Tracks: Not Advised.
LP . . . . ROUNDER 0181
MC . . . . ROUNDER 0181C
Rounder / '88 / Projection / Roots Records / Swift / C.M. Distribution / Topic Records / Jazz Music / Hot Shot / A.D.A Distribution / Direct Distribution.

DRIVE.
Tracks: Whitewater / Slipstream / Up and around the bend / Natchez trace / See rock city / Legend, The / Lights of home, The / Down in the swamp / Sanctuary / Open road, The.
CD . . . . CD 0255
LP . . . . ROUNDER 0255
MC . . . . ROUNDER 0255C
Rounder / Aug '88 / Projection / Roots Records / Swift / C.M. Distribution / Topic Records / Jazz Music / Hot Shot / A.D.A Distribution / Direct Distribution.

FLIGHT OF THE COSMIC HIPPO.
Tracks: Blu-bop / Flying saucer dudes / Turtle rock / Flight of the cosmic hippo / Star spangled banner, The / Star of the county down / Jekyll and hyde / Star of county down / Jekyll and Hyde (and Ted and Alice) / Michelle / Hole in the wall / Flight of the comsic hippo (reprise).
CD 7599265622
MC 7599265624
WEA / Nov '91 / WEA.

INROADS.
Tracks: Tonino / Somerset / Cecata / Four wheel drive / Ireland / Perplexed / Old country, The / Hudson's bay / Close to home.
LP . . . . ROUNDER 0219
MC . . . . ROUNDER 0219C
Rounder / Aug '88 / Projection / Roots Records / Swift / C.M. Distribution / Topic Records / Jazz Music / Hot Shot / A.D.A Distribution / Direct Distribution.
CD . . . . ROU 0219CD
MC . . . . ROU 0219C
Rounder / May '93 / Projection / Roots Records / Swift / C.M. Distribution / Topic Records / Jazz Music / Hot Shot / A.D.A Distribution / Direct Distribution.

NATURAL BRIDGE.
Tracks: Punch drunk / Flexibility / Dawg's due / Daybreak / Bitter gap / October winds / Crossfire / Applebutter / Old hickory waltz / Rock road / Natural bridge suite.
LP . . . . ROUNDER 0146
MC . . . . ROUNDER 0146C
Rounder / '88 / Projection / Roots Records / Swift / C.M. Distribution / Topic Records / Jazz Music / Hot Shot / A.D.A Distribution / Direct Distribution.

PLACES.
Tracks: Not Advised.
CD . . . . CD 11522
Rounder / '88 / Projection / Roots Records / Swift / C.M. Distribution / Topic Records / Jazz Music / Hot Shot / A.D.A Distribution / Direct Distribution.

Flores. Rosie

CRYING OVER YOU.
Tracks: Crying over you / Midnight to moonlight.
7" . . . . W 8250
WEA / Jul '88 / WEA.

ROSIE FLORES.
Tracks: Crying over you / Lovin' in vain / Heart beats to a different drum / Somebody loses, somebody wins / Turn around / Midnight to moonlight / God may forgive you (but I won't) / Blue side of town / Heartbreak train / I gotta know.
CD . . . . K 925626 2
WEA / Mar '88 / WEA.
LP . . . . K 925626 1
■ MC . . . . K 925626 4
WEA / Mar '88.

Flying Burrito Brothers

The Flying Burrito Brothers were formed in 1968 by ex-Byrds; Gram Parsons and Chris Hillman, together with Chris Ethridge, Sneaky Pete and Jon Corneal. The band were among the first groups to bring country music to the West Coast audiences. The new country rock genre led to the creation of the Eagles, Country Gazette, Flying Burrito Revue etc. Personnel changed rapidly and has included Bernie Leadon, Byron Berlin and Gib Guibeau. By the late 1970's the band was down to a duo and the name had been shortened to the Burrito Brothers (see seperate entry) who were now primarily a country act. The Flying Burrito Brothers resurfaced briefly for a concert and an LP in 1986. (Tony Byworth)

ALMOST SATURDAY NIGHT.
Tracks: Almost Saturday night / Jukebox kind of night.
7" . . . . MCA 868
MCA / Jan '84 / BMG.

BURRITO DELUXE.
Tracks: Lazy days / Image of me, The / High fashion queen / If you gotta go, go now / Man in the fog / Farther along / Older guys / Cody, Cody / God's own singer / Down in the churchyard.
LP . . . . ED 194
Edsel / Jul '86 / Pinnacle.
CD . . . . EDCD 194
Edsel / Jun '90 / Pinnacle.

COLLECTION.
Tracks: Not Advised.
CD . . . . CCSCD 366
MC . . . . CCSMC 366
Castle / Mar '93 / BMG.

DIM LIGHTS, THICK SMOKE AND LOUD MUSIC.
Tracks: Train song / Close up the honky tonks / Sing me back home / Tonight the bottle let me down / Your angel steps out of heaven / Crazy arms / Together again / Honky tonk women / Green green grass of

■ DELETED

F 5

home / Bony Moronie / To love somebody / Break my mind / Dim lights, thick smoke and loud music.
CD . . . . .EDCD 197
Edsel / Mar '87 / Pinnacle.
■ LP. . . . . ED 197
Edsel / Mar '87.
LP. . . . . ED 197
Demon / Jun '93 / Pinnacle.

FROM ANOTHER TIME.
Tracks: Diggi diggi li / Wheels / Dim lights, thick smoke / Faded love / Devil in disguise / Building fires / Bon soir blues / White line fever / Sin City / She thinks I still care / Why baby why / Close up the honky tonks.
CD . . . . .CDSD 072
MC . . . . .SDC 072
Sundown / Apr '91 / Terry Blood Dist. / Jazz Music / C.M. Distribution.
■ LP. . . . . CDLP 072
Sundown / Apr '91.

GILDED PALACE OF SIN, THE.
Tracks: Christine's tune / Sin city / Do right woman, do right man / Dark end of the street / My uncle / Wheels / Juanita / Hot burrito no.1 / Hot burrito no.2 / Do you know how it feels / Hippie boy.
LP. . . . . ED 191
MC . . . . .CED 191
Edsel / Jul '86 / Pinnacle.
CD . . . . .EDCD 191
Edsel / '88 / Pinnacle.

HOLLYWOOD NIGHTS 79-82.
Tracks: She belongs to everyone but me / Somewhere tonight / Baby, how'd we ever get this way / Too much honky tonkin' / My abandoned heart / She's a friend of mine / Louisiana / Why must the ending always be so sad / That's when you know it's over / She's a hell of a deal / Another shade of grey / Damned if I'll be lonely tonight / If something should come between us / Run to the night / Coast to coast / Closer to you / True love never runs dry / Tell me it ain't so.
CD . . . . .CDSD 067
LP. . . . . .SDLP 067
Sundown / May '90 / Terry Blood Dist. / Jazz Music / C.M. Distribution.

LAST OF THE RED HOT BURRITOS.
Tracks: Devil in disguise / Six days on the road / My uncle / Dixie breakdwon / Don't let your deal go down / Orange blossom special / Ain't that a lot of love / High fashion Queen / Don't fight it / Hot burrito no.2 / Losing game.
LP. . . . . AMLS 64343
A&M / PolyGram.
CD . . . . .CDA 4343
A&M / Apr '89 / PolyGram.

LIVE FROM TOKYO.
Tracks: Big bayou / White line fever / Dim lights, thick smoke / There'll be no teardrops tonight / Rollin' in my sweet baby's arms / Hot burrito no.2 / Colorado / Rocky top / Six days on the road / Truck drivin' man.
CD . . . . .CDSD 025
Sundown / '86 / Terry Blood Dist. / Jazz Music / C.M. Distribution.
LP. . . . . .SDLP 025
Sundown / Jan '86 / Terry Blood Dist. / Jazz Music / C.M. Distribution.

SLEEPLESS NIGHTS.
Tracks: Not Advised.
■ LP. . . . . AMLH 64578
A&M / Jun '76.

SOUTHERN TRACKS.
Tracks: Crazy horses / Born for honky tonkin' / Armed and dangerous / Shelly's little girl / Thunder road / Matchbox / She's your lover now / Love minus zero / They want to hang a bad boy / My believing heart / Christine's tune / My bucket's got a hole in it.
CD . . . . VD 103
Dixie Frog / Sep '90 / Discovery.

Fogerty, John

Singer - songwriter/musician and founder member, alongside brother Tom Fogerty (d 06.09.1990) guitar, Stu Cook keyboards/vocals, Doug Clifford drums, of Creedance Clearwater Revival. Fogerty himself was born 28.5.1945 in Berkeley, California. Prior to CCR they'd played at high school in El Cerrito, Califonia before, in 1959, recording as the Blue Velvets on the Orchestra label and as the Golliwogs for Fantasy in 1964, where they welded an enduring association - their work being repackaged many times. John Fogerty's self penned material featuring their pop hits *Bad moon rising* , *Lodi* (both covered by Emmylou Harris), *Up around the bend* and *Green River* would have been accepted by country audiences today. Their music, forever high on energy , has nevertheless encouraged listeners to explore it's connecting avenues, Consequently their country chart success is limited to the 1980 top fifty effort *Cottonfields* . Under the banner of the Blue Ridge Rangers Fogerty recorded a solo album, on Fantasy in 1973. Charting with old perennial *Jambalaya*, his career lost ground during the 70/80s, although he did gain attention from the country media in 1985 upon release of Warner Bros album *Centerfield* - Fogerty both responsible for playing all the instruments and all the vocals. (Maurice Hope)

ALMOST SATURDAY NIGHT.
Tracks: Almost Saturday night / Sea cruise.
■ 7". . . . . .FTC 120
Fantasy / Feb '76.

BLUE RIDGE RANGERS.
Tracks: Not Advised.
LP. 1061150
Fantasy / Aug '86 / Pinnacle / Target Records / Jazz Music.

CENTERFIELD.
Tracks: Old man down the road, The / Rock and roll girls / Big train / I saw it on T.V. / Mr. Greed / Searchlight / Centerfield / I can't help myself / Zanz kant danz.
■ CD 925203 4
WEA / Feb '85 / WEA.
■ LP. 925203 1
WEA / Feb '85.
■ MC 925203 2
WEA / Feb '85.

EYE OF THE ZOMBIE.
Tracks: Eye of the zombie / Goin' back home / Headlines / Knockin' on your door / Change in the weather / Wasn't that a woman / Violence is golden / Soda pop / Sail away.
CD 925449 2
LP. 925449 1
MC 925449 4
WEA / Oct '86 / WEA.

EYE OF THE ZOMBIE.
Tracks: Eye of the zombie.
12" . . . . W 8657T
■ 7". . . . . W 8657
WEA / Oct '86.

JOHN FOGERTY.
Tracks: Rockin' all over the world / You rascal you / Wall, The / Travellin' high / Lonely teardrops / Almost Saturday night / Where the river flows / Sea cruise / Dream song / Flying away / Comin' down the road / Ricochet.
CD . . . . .CDFE 507
LP. . . . . .FACE 507
MC . . . . .FACC 507
Fantasy / Sep '87 / Pinnacle / Target Records / Jazz Music.

OLD MAN DOWN THE ROAD.
Tracks: Old man down the road / Big train from Memphis.
■ 7". . . . . W 9100
WEA / Feb '85.

ROCK AND ROLL GIRLS.
Tracks: Rock and roll girls / Centerfield.
■ 7". . . . . W 9053
WEA / Apr '85.

YOU GOT THE MAGIC.
Tracks: You got the magic / Evil thing.
■ 7". . . . . .FTC 133
Fantasy / May '76.

Foley, Red

Country singer, guitarist, harmonica player, songwriter and entertainer (1910-68): his smooth baritone and stage personality won many fans outside the country charts. He appeared on the WLS National Barn Dance in Chicago in 1932 and became one of the first country singers to have network radio show (co-star was comic Red Skelton); he went to Hollywood in the '40's. One of his first hits was the wartime *Smoke on the water.* He was famous for *Old Shep*, with which Elvis Presley won an amateur contest. Hits like *Chattanoogie shoe shine boy* in 1950 (number one in both country and pop charts) made him one of the biggest country attractions of all time. (Donald Clarke).

COMPANY'S COMING.
Tracks: Not Advised.
LP. . . . . .HAT 3122
Stetson / '89 / Crusader Marketing Co. / Swift / Wellard Dist. / Midland Records / C.M. Distribution.

RED AND ERNIE (Foley, Red & Ernest Tubb).
Tracks: Tennessee border (no.2) / Goodnight Irene / Hillbilly fever (no.2) / Don't be ashamed of your age / It's a mileage that's slowin' us down / Double datin' / No help wanted (No.2) / Too old to cut the mustard / Kentucky waltz / I'm in love with Molly / Strange little girl / You're a real good friend.
LP. . . . . .HAT 3000
MC . . . . .HATC 3000
Stetson / Nov '85 / Crusader Marketing Co. / Swift / Wellard Dist. / Midland Records / C.M. Distribution.

RED FOLEY SHOW, THE.
Tracks: Not Advised.
LP. . . . . .HAT 3016
MC . . . . .HATC 3016
Stetson / Sep '86 / Crusader Marketing Co. / Swift / Wellard Dist. / Midland Records / C.M. Distribution.

RED FOLEY STORY, THE.
Tracks: Chattanooga shoeshine boy / Blues in my heart / Salty dog rag / Old Shep / Tennessee Saturday night / Hominy grits / Tennessee polka / Hearts of stone / Nobody / Tennessee Border / M-i-s-s-i-s-s-i-p-p-i / Steal away / Old pappy's new banjo / Peace in the valley / Satisfied mind, A / I'll be a sunbeam / My God is real / Beyond the sunset / Should you go first / Take my hand, precious Lord / Just a closer walk with thee / God walks these hills with me / Jesus loves me / He'll understand and say well done.
Double LP IMCA2 4053
MCA (Import) / Mar '86 / Pinnacle / Silver Sounds (CD).

TENNESSEE SATURDAY NIGHT.
Tracks: Tennessee Saturday night / Plantation boogie / Hot dog rag / Hillbilly fever / Freight train boogie / Pinball boogie / Milkbucket boogie / Hoot owl boogie / Hobo boogie / Night train to Memphis / Shake a hand / Hearts of stone / Crawdad song / Rockin' 'n' reeling crazy little guitar man / Sugarfoot rag / Hot rod race / Kentucky fox chase.
LP. . . . . .CR 30230
Charly / Feb '84 / Charly.

Fontenot, Allen

CAJUN HONKY TONK SONGS.
Tracks: Not Advised.
LP. 11012
MC . . . . 11012 TC
Great Southern (USA) / '87 / Swift.

Fontenot, Canray

CANRAY FONTENOT & CARRIER BROS. (Fontenot, Canray & Carrier Bros.).
Tracks: Not Advised.
LP. . . . . ARHOOLIE 5031
Arhoolie (USA) / '88 / Pinnacle / Cadillac Music / Swift / Projection / Hot Shot / A.D.A Distribution / Jazz Music.

LOUISIANA HOT SAUCE CREOLE STYLE.
Tracks: Not Advised.
CD . . . . .ARHCD 381
Arhoolie (USA) / Mar '93 / Pinnacle / Cadillac Music / Swift / Projection / Hot Shot / A.D.A Distribution / Jazz Music.

Ford, Gerry

Irish born, Scotland based Gerry Ford has been recording country albums since 1977 - a total of 11, with 8 recorded in Nashville using top sessionmen. Ford regularly tours the UK and Europe, and has made 15 appearances at the Grand Ole Opry. As well as an artist, Ford is also a DJ on BBC Radio Scotland's Country Corner. (Tony Byworth)

ALL OVER AGAIN.
Tracks: If I had to do it all over again / After all these years / Till it snows in Mexico / They call him boxcar / There I go dreaming again / I always get it right / Till I'm too old to die young / True true love never dies / I never once stopped loving you / Jesus, I need to talk to you / Dim the lights and pour wine / Your love.
LP. . . . . .TT 108
MC . . . . .CTT 108
Trimtop / May '88 / Ross Records.

BETTER MAN.
Tracks: On second thought / If tomorow never comes / Somebody up there / What God has joined together / It don't hurt to dream / Fourteen minutes old / Better man, A / It's our anniversary / Lonely farmer's daughter / Alone / Don't play faded love.
CD . . . . .CDTT 117
LP. . . . . .TT 117
MC . . . . .CTT 117
Trimtop / Mar '91 / Ross Records.

CAN I COUNT ON YOU.
Tracks: Cottage in the country / Can I count on you / Twice the speed of love / Whispering Bill / Tell me again / Where are you / If you want to find love / Heckel & Jeckel / All the time / (If it weren't for country music) I'd go crazy / After the storm / Look at us.
CD . . . . .CDDT 118
MC . . . . .CTT 118
Trimtop / '93 / Ross Records.

FAMILY BIBLE.
Tracks: Family bible / Who will sing for me / Lord I'd forgotten / One of these days / Someone is looking for someone like you / He took your place / What God has joined together / Jesus I need to talk to you / Just a closer walk with thee / 'Til I'm too old to die young / Gone away.
MC . . . . .CTT 116
Trimtop / '91 / Ross Records.

FAMILY BIBLE.
Tracks: Family bible / She thinks I still care.
■ 7". . . . . .MD 1209
Emerald / Sep '78.

LET'S HEAR IT FOR THE WORKING MAN.
Tracks: Let's hear it for the working man / Goodbye / I'll be there (if you ever want me) / Roads and other reasons / Storms never last / I wish that I had loved you

F 6

■ DELETED

better / Slippin' away / I came so close to calling you last night / Drink it down lady / I'm getting better / Sweet dreams / Freedom highway.
MC . . . . BRC 1016
Big R / Jan '82 / Pinnacle.
■ LP. . . . . BRA 1016
Big R / Jan '82.

LORD I'D FORGOTTEN.
Tracks: Lord I'd forgotten / Easy.
7" . . . . BRS 03
Big R / Jun '81 / Pinnacle.

MEMORY MACHINE.
Tracks: Memory machine / There goes my everything / Teddy bear song, The / Daisy a day / Rainbows and roses / I love love songs / Lonesome medley / I will love you all my life / Everything's a waltz / I wouldn't change you if I could / Make the world go away / Daddy's farm.
MC . . . . CTT 102
Trimtop / '85 / Ross Records.

ON THE ROAD.
Tracks: On the road to loving me again / Teardrop on a rose / I want you back again / It wasn't me who said I owned a goldmine / Ruby, don't take your love to town / Blue eyes crying in the rain / She loves my troubles away / Lord I'd forgotten / One of these days / Great mail robbery, The / Heartache following me, A / Easy.
LP. . . . . BRA 1010
MC . . . . BRC 1010
Big R / Mar '81 / Pinnacle.

SIXTEEN COUNTRY FAVOURITES.
Tracks: Thank God for the radio / Heartache following me, A / Storm's never last / Let's hear it for the working man / Blue eyes crying in the rain / Daddy's farm / I wouldn't change you if I could / Daisy a day / Rainbows and roses / Amazing love / I'll never need another you / Teardrop on a rose, A / I don't care / I came so close to calling you last night / On the road to loving me again / Sweet dreams.
CD . . . . CDTT 113
Trimtop / '90 / Ross Records.

SOMEONE TO GIVE MY LOVE TO.
Tracks: Someone to give my love to / While.
■ 7" . . . . MD 1201
Emerald / Mar '78.

STRANGEST THINGS HAVE HAPPENED.
Tracks: I wish that I could fall in love today / Forgiving you was easy / Even cowgirls get the blues / You make me feel like a man / Slowly but surely / I have you / Stranger things have happened / Storms of life, The / Anger and tears / Excuse me (I think I've got a heartache) / Life turned her that way / Carmen.
MC . . . . CTT 110
Trimtop / '87 / Ross Records.

THANK GOD FOR RADIO.
Tracks: Thank God for radio / I don't care / What is love? / Are you teasing me? / Who will sing for me / Let the rest of the world go by / I'll never need another you / Amazing love / Got no reason now for going home / This working mans got you / Have you ever been lonely / Someone is looking for someone like you.
LP. . . . . TT 103
MC . . . . CTT 103
Trimtop / Jan '86 / Ross Records.

Ford, Tennessee Ernie

Ernest Jennings Ford was born in Bristol, Tennessee in 1919. After a spell in the US Air Force he became a singer in a local Pasadena quartet. In 1948 he was heard on the radio by a Capitol Records executive and signed up. The following year, he achieved success on the US country charts with *Mule Train*. In 1950, Ford's *Shotgun Boogie*, reached no.1. His next release was *I'll Never Be Free*, a duet with Kay Starr that reached no.4. In the mid 1950's, Ford began to set his sights beyond the world of country music. Three major pop hits followed: *Give Me Your Word, The Ballad Of Davy Crockett* and *Sixteen Tons*. The latter occupied the no.1 position in the US for 8 weeks and 4 weeks in the UK. Ford had his own TV show from 1956 to 1961, during this period his pop career declined but he concentrated more on religious recordings. He always closed his show with a hymn and his 1956 LP *Hymns* became Capitol's best selling album of all time. Ford recorded approximately 20 religious albums and by the early 1970's was in semi-retirement. (Bob MacDonald)

BALLAD OF DAVY CROCKETT.
Tracks: Ballad of Davy Crockett, The.
■ 7" . . . . CL 14506
Capitol / Jan '56.

CAPITOL COLLECTORS SERIES: TENNESSEE ERNIE FORD.
Tracks: Tennessee border No. 1 / Country junction / Smokey Mountain boogie / Mule train / Anticipation blues / Cry of the wild goose / I'll never be free / Ain't nobody's business / Shot gun boogie / Tailor made woman / I'm a bad man / Strange little girl, The / Mister and Mississippi / Kissin' bug boogie / Blackberry boogie / Hog-tied over you / I don't know / Hey Mr. Cotton picker / Celebration / Catfish boogie / Honeymoon's over, The / River of no return / Ballad of Davy Crockett, The / His hands / Sixteen tons / Nine pound hammer / That's all / In the middle of an island / Hicktown.
■ MC C4 95291
Capitol / Aug '91.
CD . . . . CZ 418
Capitol / Jun '91 / EMI.

CAPITOL COUNTRY MUSIC CLASSICS.
Tracks: Sixteen tons / Stack-O-Lee / Philadelphia lawyer / Ocean of tears / Give me your word / Sweet temptation / Barbara Allen / Streamlined cannonball / Mule train / Kentucky waltz / Hey good lookin' / Release me / Bright lights and blonde haired women / This must be the place / First born / Shotgun boogie / You don't have to be a baby to cry / Ballad of Davy Crockett / I really don't want to know / Born to lose / You're my sugar / I gotta have my baby back / Rovin' gambler / Colorado county morning / Baby / This land is your land / Just a little talk with Jesus / Old rugged cross, The.
CD . . . . CDEMS 1442
Capitol Nashville / Feb '92 / EMI.
■ MC . . . . TCEMS 1442
Capitol Nashville / Feb '92.

COUNTRY COLLECTION.
Tracks: Not Advised.
CD . . . . KNCD 13056
■ MC . . . . KNMC 13056
Knight / Jul '90.

EARLY STOMPIN' SIDES.
Tracks: Not Advised.
■ EP. . . . . MSEP 10.001
Muleskinner / Feb '88.

FARMYARD BOOGIE (Ford, Tennessee Ernie & Friends).
Tracks: Hey Mr. Cotton Picker / Tennessee local / Celebratin' / I'm hog tied over you / Ain't gonna let it happen no more / Rock city boogie / I'll never be free / Stack o lee / Milk 'em in the morning / Kiss me big / Tailor made woman / Ain't nobody's business / Everybody's got a girl but me / Snowshoe Thompson / Anticipation blues / Feed 'em in the morning blues / Kissin' bug boogie / Don't start courtin' in a hot rod / My hobby / False hearted girl.
CD . . . . SEECD 262
LP. . . . . SEE 262
See For Miles / May '89 / Pinnacle.

FORD FAVOURITES.
Tracks: Watermelon song, The / One suit / Have you seen her / Call me darling / That's all / Sixteen tons / River of no return / You don't have to be a baby to cry / First born / Give me your word.
MC . . . . HATC 3051
Stetson / Dec '87 / Crusader Marketing Co. / Swift / Wellard Dist. / Midland Records / C.M. Distribution.
LP. . . . . HAT 3051
Stetson / Oct '87 / Crusader Marketing Co. / Swift / Wellard Dist. / Midland Records / C.M. Distribution.

GIVE ME YOUR WORD.
Tracks: Give me your word.
■ 7" . . . . CL 14005
Capitol / Jan '55.

HE TOUCHED ME.
Tracks: Glory to His name / He'll understand and say "Well done" / I will sing of my Redeemer / Am I a soldier of the Cross? / Since Jesus came into my heart / He touched me / Almighty Father, strong to save / We're marching to Zion / He leadeth me / Evening prayer, An.
LP. . . . . WST 9579
MC . . . . WC 9579
Word (UK) / May '82 / Word Records (UK) / Sony.

OL' ROCKIN' ERN.
Tracks: Milk 'em in the morning blues / Catfish boogie / Anticipation blues / Country junction / Shotgun boogie / She's my baby / Blackberry boogie / Kiss me big / Ain't nobody's business / Smokey mountain boogie / I ain't gonna let it happen no more / Lord's lariat, The.
LP. . . . . HAT 3040
MC . . . . HATC 3040
Stetson / Jul '87 / Crusader Marketing Co. / Swift / Wellard Dist. / Midland Records / C.M. Distribution.

PRECIOUS MOMENTS.
Tracks: Not Advised.
CD . . . . CDP 746 621-2
Capitol / EMI.

SIXTEEN TONS.
Tracks: Milk 'em in the morning blues / Country junction / Smoky mountain boogie / Anticipation blues / Mule train / Cry of the wild goose / My hobby / Feed 'em in the morning blues / Shot gun boogie / Tailor-made woman / You're my sugar / Rock City boogie / Kissin' bug boogie / Hey good lookin' / Hambone / Everybody's got a girl but me / Snow shoe Thompson / Blackberry boogie / Hey Mr. Cotton Picker / Kiss me big / Catfish boogie / Ballad of Davy Crockett, The / Sixteen tons / Rovin' gambler / Black eyed Susan Brown.
MC 1A220 1583344
EMI (Holland) / '88.
LP. . . . . HAT 3118
MC . . . . HATC 3118
Stetson / Sep '89 / Crusader Marketing Co. / Swift / Wellard Dist. / Midland Records / C.M. Distribution.
CD . . . . BCD 15487
Bear Family / Feb '90 / Rollercoaster Records / Swift / Direct Distribution.

SIXTEEN TONS.
Tracks: Sixteen tons / Zambesi.
■ 7" . . . . CL 14500
Capitol / Jan '56.

SUNDAY'S STILL A SPECIAL DAY.
Tracks: Turn your radio on / Holy holy holy / Name of Jesus, The / Holy Holy / Reach out to Jesus / Put your hand in the hand / Jesus I come / May I introduce you to a friend / I've found a friend / Goodnight and good morning / Sunday's still a special day / Break thou the bread of life / Come, ye thankful people, come / My tribute / Crown him with many crowns / Face to face / Won't be long / When I reach that city / Saved by grace / I wish we'd all been ready.
LP. . . . . WRD 3009
MC . . . . TCWR 3009
Word (UK) / May '85 / Word Records (UK) / Sony.

SWEET HOUR OF PRAYER.
Tracks: Not Advised.
MC 4XL 9169
Capitol (Specials) / Dec '88.

SWING WIDE YOUR GOLDEN GATE (Ford, Tennessee Ernie & The Jordanaires).
Tracks: Swing wide your golden gate / How big is God? / Just a little while / Mansion over the hilltop / I like the old time way / What would you give in exchange? / Bring back the springtime / Unclouded day, The / Room at the cross / One day at a time.
LP. . . . . WST 9588
MC . . . . WC 9588
Word (UK) / May '82 / Word Records (UK) / Sony.

TELL ME THE OLD, OLD STORY.
Tracks: Tell me the old, old story / Send the light / When we all get to Heaven / Let others see Jesus in you / Stand up for Jesus / Only believe / Yield not to temptation / Are you washed in the blood? / Standing on the promises / Revive us again.
LP. . . . . WST 9598
MC . . . . WC 9598
Word (UK) / May '82 / Word Records (UK) / Sony.

THERE'S A SONG IN MY HEART.
Tracks: I'll fly away / His hands / I'll be a friend to Jesus / If I could hear my mother pray again / Ol' wooded brook, The / Leavin' on my mind / Operator (give me Jesus on the line) / Jesus paid it all / Handshakes and smiles / He knows what I need / Amazing grace.
LP. . . . . WST 9622
MC . . . . WC 9622
Word (UK) / May '82 / Word Records (UK) / Sony.

VERY BEST OF TENNESSEE ERNIE FORD.
Tracks: Sixteen tons / Kentucky waltz / Blackberry boogie / River of no return / Milk 'em in the morning blues / Bright lights and blonde haired women / Tennessee local / Ballad of Davy Crockett, The / Shot gun boogie / Give me your word / Feed 'em in the morning blues / Stack-o-lee / Anticipation blues / You don't have to be a baby to cry / Mule train / Old rugged cross, The.
■ LP. . . . . MFP 5611
MFP / Apr '83.

Forrester Sisters

ALL I NEED.
Tracks: Not Advised.
CD . . . . K 9257792
LP. . . . . K 9257791
■ MC . . . . K 9257794
WEA / Apr '89 / WEA.

PERFUME, RIBBONS, AND PEARLS.
Tracks: 100% chance of blue / Heartache headed my way / Back into my arms again / Somebody's breakin' a heart / That's easy for you to say / Blame it on the moon / Lonely alone / Heartless night / You were the one / Drawn to the fire.
LP. . . . . K 925411 1
■ MC . . . . K 925411 4
WEA / Apr '87 / WEA.

SINCERELY.
Tracks: Not Advised.
■ CD 925746 2
WEA / Sep '88 / WEA.
LP. 925746 1
■ MC 925746 4
WEA / Sep '88.

YOU AGAIN.
Tracks: That's what your love does to me / (I'd choose) you again / Before you / Too many rivers / My mothers eyes / Sooner or later / I can't lose what I never had / Lyin' in his arms again / Down the road / Wrap me up.
CD 925571 2
LP. 925571 1
■ MC 925571 4
WEA / Sep '87 / WEA.

Foster & Lloyd

VERSION OF TRUTH.
Tracks: Is it love? / I wishdaida run into you / Side of the road / Lonesome run / Workin' on me / Version of the truth / Leavin' in your eyes / It's a done deal / All said and done / Whoa.
CD . . . . PD 90487
LP. . . . . PL 90487

MC . . . . PK 90487
RCA / May '90 / BMG.

Foster, Jerry

DON'T LET GO.

Tracks: Don't let go / Memories to cling to.
■ 7" . . . . SON 2237
Sonet / Dec '81.

FOOL FOR YOU MAMA.

Tracks: Fool for you mama / Put it on me strong.
7" . . . . RANS 72
Range (1).

Francis, Connie

This American singer, born Concetta Franconero in New Jersey, showed leanings towards showbusiness from early childhood. By the age of 17 (1955), she had written and produced a school musical, made numerous US national television appearances and signed a recording contract. Her first taste of disc success came with *Majesty Of Love*, a 1957 duet with Marvin Rainwater.After a few solo flops, Francis stormed to stardom in the spring of 1958 with *Who's Sorry Now*, a revival of a 1923 love ballad. This reached No 4 in the US, and went to No 1 for 6 weeks in the UK (coincidentally, dethroning Rainwater's *Whole Lotta Woman*). Later in '58, she achieved another six week UK chart topper with the double A sided single *Carolina Moon/Stupid Cupid*. The latter song, written by Neil Sedaka and Howard Greenfield, contrasted sharply with *Who's Sorry Now* - she tackled romantic, smoochy ballads and bouncy novelty rockers with equal verve, and these two strands were to typify her whole recording career. The attractive Connie possessed a powerful and pleasant, though not fantastic voice. What she lacked in musical refinement, she made up for in energy and choice of material.During the late Fifties and early Sixties, in the gap between the rock 'n' roll explosion and the arrival of the Beatles. Francis was one of the biggest pop stars on both sides of the Atlantic and certainly the world's top female singer. Her American No 1 singles included *Everybody's Somebody's Fool* (1960), *My Heart Has A Mind Of Its Own* (1960), *Don't Break The Heart That Loves You* (1962). *My Happiness* (1959), *Lipstick On Your Collar* (1959), *Mama* (1960), *Where The Boys Are* (1961), *Together* (1961) and *Vacation* (1962) all reached the Top 10 in both the US and the UK. Several of Connie's hits were remakes of standards from the Twenties, Thirties and Forties.Francis was not such hot property in the cinema - she made her big screen debut in the 1961 movie *Where The Boys Are*, but later admitted that she was no actress. From 1963 onwards, Francis gradually faded from the British and American charts, making way for the new era of Sixties pop talent. The singer directed her talents to MOR, cabaret and nightclub audiences around the world, and skilfully made records in a variety of different languages.A series of traumas dogged Connie's personal life during the Seventies. In 1974, shortly after suffering a miscarriage, she was raped She consequently had a nervous breakdown, became a recluse and underwent a two year course of psychiatric treatment. In 1978, while courageously attempting a showbiz comeback, the singer had $50,000 worth of jewelry stolen from a London hotel room. During the early Eighties, she continued to perform and make personal appearances, particularly in the States.A TV advertised collection of the singer's *20 All Time Greats* reached No 1 on the British LP chart in 1977).

24 GREATEST HITS.

Tracks: Where the boys are / If I didn't care / Hurt / Vacation / Are you lonesome tonight / Together among my souvenirs / Everybody's somebody's fool / Old time rock 'n' roll / My heart has a mind of its own / Cryin' time / My happiness / Lipstick on your collar / Who's sorry now / Stupid cupid / Misty blue / Torn between two lovers / Breakin' in a brand new broken heart / Many tears ago / Don't break the heart that loves you / Cry / Frankie / Second hand love / Something stupid.
CD . . . . PLATCD 3910
MC . . . . PLAC 3910
Prism / Nov '90 / Pinnacle / Midland Records.

AMONG MY SOUVENIRS.

Tracks: My happiness / Stupid Cupid / Let's have a party / Valentino / Among my souvenirs / Who's sorry now? / Plenty good lovin' / Mama / Carolina moon / Lipstick on your collar / Everybody's somebody's fool / My heart has a mind of its own.
LP. 825 799-1
MC 825 799-4
Karussell Gold / Aug '85.
MC . . . . STAC 2393
Telstar/Ronco / Oct '89 / BMG.
■ LP. . . . . STAR 2393
Telstar/Ronco / Oct '89.
■ CD . . . . TCD 2393
Telstar/Ronco / Oct '89.

AMONG MY SOUVENIRS.

Tracks: Among my souvenirs.
■ 7" . . . . MGM 1046
MGM (EMI) / Dec '59.

BABY'S FIRST CHRISTMAS.

Tracks: Baby's first christmas.
■ 7" . . . . MGM 1145
MGM (EMI) / Dec '61.

BEST OF, THE.

Tracks: Not Advised.
CD . . . . CD 66061
MC . . . . MC 62061
Ce De International / Jul '93 / Taylors.

BREAKIN' IN A BRAND NEW BROKEN HEART.

Tracks: Breakin' in a brand new broken heart.
■ 7" . . . . MGM 1136
MGM (EMI) / Jun '61.

BURNING BRIDGES.

Tracks: Burning bridges / Let's go where the good times go.
■ 7" 2066881
Polydor / Feb '78.

CAROLINA MOON.

Tracks: Carolina moon / Stupid cupid.
■ 7" . . . . MGM 985
MGM (EMI) / Aug '58.

COLLECTION: CONNIE FRANCIS.

Tracks: Not Advised.
CD . . . . CCSCD 325
MC . . . . CCSMC 325
Castle Collector Series / Feb '92 / BMG / Pinnacle / Castle Communications.

CONNIE FRANCIS.

Tracks: Delilah / Les bicyclettes de Belsize / Don't say a word / Kiss me goodbye / Three good reasons / Mr. Love / It's not unusual / Last waltz, The / What's wrong with my world / Lifetime of love / What the world needs now / Promises, promises / Do you know the way to San Jose / Trains & boats & planes / Make it easy on yourself / Alfie / This girl's in love with you / I say a little prayer / Wanting things / Walk on by / Magic moments / Blue on blue / Don't make me over.
■ Double LP 2675180
Polydor / '79.

CONNIE FRANCIS & HANK WILLIAMS JR. SING GREAT COUNTRY HITS.

Tracks: Send me the pillow that you dream on / Wolverton mountain / Please help me / I'm falling / Singing the blues / Walk on by / If you've got the money, I've got the time / Mule skinner blues / Making believe / Blue blue day / No letter today / Bye bye love / Wabash cannonball.
LP. 2354 038
MC 3140 115
Polydor / Jan '77 / PolyGram.

CONNIE FRANCIS & PETER KRAUS - VOL.1 (Francis, Connie & Peter Kraus).

Tracks: Oh I like it (Previously unissued) / Schreib mire eine (Send a picture postcard) / Mission bell / Das haben die madchen gern / Susi sagt es gabi / Honeymoon / Keine nacht kann ich schlafen / Par le monde (Honey moon) / Gondola d'amore / Oh so wunderbar (wunderbar wie du) / Columbino / Alright, okay you win / Ich denk an dich (I think of you.) / Doll doll dolly / Ich komm' nie mehr von dir los (Many tears ago.) / Comme un tigre.
LP. . . . . BFX 15061
Bear Family / Sep '84 / Rollercoaster Records / Swift / Direct Distribution.

CONNIE FRANCIS & PETER KRAUS - VOL.2 (Francis, Connie & Peter Kraus).

Tracks: Darlin' meine liebe / Twenty four hours (Ich denk an dich) / Mondschein und liebe (Sweet love) / Everybody else but me / Sag mir was du denkst / Je pense a toi / Ein rendezvous mit dir / C'est toi la plus belle / Niemand / Wenn ich traume (Where the boys are) / Alle jungen leute / Das ist zuviel (too many rules) / Immer und uberall / Immer wenn's am schonsten ist / Weine nicht um mich / Ein boy fur mich (kiss 'n' twist).
LP. . . . . BFX 15062
Bear Family / Sep '84 / Rollercoaster Records / Swift / Direct Distribution.

CONNIE FRANCIS IN DEUTSCHLAND (The Complete German, Dutch & Swedish Connie).

Tracks: Not Advised.
LP Set . . . . BFX 15305-9
Bear Family / Dec '88 / Rollercoaster Records / Swift / Direct Distribution.

CONNIE'S GREATEST HITS.

Tracks: Someone else's boy / Who's sorry now / Stupid cupid / Plenty good lovin' / My happiness / Lipstick on your collar / Many tears ago / My heart has a mind of its own / Everybody's somebody's fool / Among my souvenirs / Let's have a party / Looking for love / Don't break the heart that loves you / Mr. Twister / Frankie / Robot man.
LP. 831 994 1
MC 831 994 4
Polydor (Germany) / Oct '87 / PolyGram.
CD 931 994 2
Mercury / May '88 / PolyGram.

CONNIE'S GREATEST HITS (MGM).

Tracks: Not Advised.
■ LP. . . . . MGM C 831
MGM (EMI) / Mar '60.

COUNTRY STORE: CONNIE FRANCIS.

Tracks: Your cheatin' heart / Oh lonesome me / She'll have to go / I don't hurt anymore / Bye bye love / I walk the line / I don't wanna play house / I can't stop loving you / There'll be no teardrops tonight / Please help me, I'm falling / Heartaches by the number / How's the world treating you / I'm movin' on / (I'd be a) legend in my own time.
CD . . . . .CDCST 56
MC . . . . .CSTK 56
Country Store / '88 / BMG.
■ LP. . . . . CST 56
Country Store / '88.

DON'T BREAK THE HEART THAT LOVES YOU.

Tracks: Don't break the heart that loves you.
■ 7" . . . . MGM 1157
MGM (EMI) / Apr '62.

EVERYBODY'S SOMEBODY'S FOOL.

Tracks: Everybody's somebody's fool.
■ 7" . . . . MGM 1086
MGM (EMI) / Aug '60.

GREATEST HITS: CONNIE FRANCIS VOLS.1 & 2.

Tracks: Who's sorry now / Stupid cupid / Plenty good lovin' / My happiness / Lipstick on your collar / Many tears ago / My heart has a mind of its own / Everybody's somebody's fool / Among my souvenirs / Carolina moon / Mama / Where the boys are / Frankie / Vacation / If I didn't care / Together / I'm sorry I made you cry / When the boy in your arms / Teddy / If my pillow could talk / Fallin' / You're gonna miss me / Valentino / Happy days and lonely nights / Secondhand love / Drownin' my sorrows / He's my dreamboat / My child / Don't break the heart that loves you / Jealous heart / Robot man.
MC Set 327 130 5
Polydor / Jul '82 / PolyGram.
■ Double LP 262 403 8
Polydor / Jul '82.

I'LL GET BY.

Tracks: I'll get by / Fallin'.
■ 7" . . . . MGM 993
MGM (EMI) / Nov '58.

I'M GONNA BE WARM THIS WINTER.

Tracks: I'm gonna be warm this winter.
■ 7" . . . . MGM 1185
MGM (EMI) / Dec '62.

I'M ME AGAIN - SILVER ANNIVERSARY ALBUM.

Tracks: I'm me again / Milk and honey / Lincoln street chapel / No sun today / What good are tears / Comme ci comme ca / Where the boys are / Don't break the heart that loves you / My happiness / I don't want to walk without you / White cliffs of Dover, The / Cry.
■ LP. 2315426
Polydor / Jun '81.

I'M SORRY I MADE YOU CRY.

Tracks: I'm sorry I made you cry.
■ 7" . . . . MGM 982
MGM (EMI) / Jun '58.

ICH GEB'NE PARTY HEUT'NACHT.

Tracks: Ich geb'ne party heut'nacht (Let's have a party.) / Weekend boy / Ich war / Gerne verliebt (Looking for love) / Komm zu mir, Joe / Nino / Meinen sunny Krieg ich nie mehr wielder / Jedes boot hat seinen hafen / Abschiedsmelodie / Oh blieb bei mir (Previously unissued.) / Denk nicht an die and're / Sternenmelodie / Keine liebe ohne tranen / Jeder traum ist einmal ausgetraumt / Traumboot / Mein herz ruft nach dir (My heart cries for you) / Blauer wind (Previously unissued.).
LP. . . . . BFX 15137
Bear Family / Jul '84 / Rollercoaster Records / Swift / Direct Distribution.

JEALOUS HEART.

Tracks: Jealous heart.
■ 7" . . . . MGM 1293
MGM (EMI) / Jan '66.

LEGEND IN HER TIME - THE COUNTRY HITS.

Tracks: Not Advised.
CD 8477512
MC 8477514
Polydor / Jun '91 / PolyGram.

LEGEND LIVE, THE.

Tracks: I don't want to walk without you / I'm ready to take a chance again / Maybe this time / Stupid cupid / Lipstick on your collar / Robot man / Everybody's somebody's fool / Vacation / Among my souvenirs / Don't break the heart that loves you / Carolina moon / My happiness / Together / Who's sorry now / Where the boys are / Mama / Born free / Malaguena / Hava nagila / Exodus / Over the rainbow / Trolley song / You made me love you / If I never sing another.
VHS. . . . . PLATV 305

F 8

■ DELETED

Prism Video / Nov '90 / Terry Blood Dist. / Gold & Sons / Prism Leisure PLC.

LIPSTICK ON YOUR COLLAR.
Tracks: Lipstick on your collar.
7" . . . . **MGM 1018**
MGM (EMI) / Jul '59 / EMI.

LIPSTICK ON YOUR COLLAR (OLD GOLD).
Tracks: Lipstick on your collar / Frankie.
7" . . . . **OG 9444**
Old Gold / Jul '84 / Pickwick Records.

LOVE SONGS.
Tracks: Not Advised.
CD **5500862**
MC **5500864**
Spectrum (1) / Oct '93 / PolyGram.

LOVE SONGS: CONNIE FRANCIS.
Tracks: Who's sorry now / Carolina Moon / Jealous heart / He thinks I still care / Fallin' / I don't hurt anymore / Bye bye love / When the boy in your arms / My heart has a mind of its own / Half as much / Make it easy on yourself / Walk on by / Oh lonesome me / Among my souvenirs.
CD . . . . **PWKS 540**
LP. . . . . **CN 2098**
MC **CN4 2098**
Pickwick / Sep '89 / Pickwick Records.

LOVE'N'COUNTRY.
Tracks: My happiness / This girl's in love with you / I'm sorry I made you cry / What's wrong with my world / I'm a fool to care / Please help me, I'm falling / Many tears ago / I can't stop loving you / You always hurt the one you love / Look of love, The / If I didn't care / Breaking in a brand new broken heart / If you ever change your mind / Send me the pillow that you dream on / Everybody's somebody's fool / My heart cries for you.
LP. . . . . **CN 2081**
MC **CN4 2081**
Contour / Sep '86 / Pickwick Records.
CD . . . . **PWK 113**
Pickwick / Jun '89 / Pickwick Records.

MAMA.
Tracks: Mama / Robot man.
■ 7" . . . . **MGM 1076**
MGM (EMI) / May '60.

MANY TEARS AGO.
Tracks: Many tears ago.
■ 7" . . . . **MGM 1111**
MGM (EMI) / Mar '61.

MY CHILD.
Tracks: My child.
■ 7" . . . . **MGM 1271**
MGM (EMI) / Jun '65.

MY HAPPINESS.
Tracks: My happiness.
■ 7" . . . . **MGM 1001**
MGM (EMI) / May '59.

MY HEART HAS A MIND OF IT'S OWN.
Tracks: My heart has a mind of it's own.
■ 7" . . . . **MGM 1100**
MGM (EMI) / Nov '60.

MY MOTHER'S EYES.
Tracks: My mother's eyes / Lovin' man.
■ 7" . . . . **UP 36463**
United Artists / Oct '78.

MY SOUVENIRS.
Tracks: Not Advised.
LP. . . . . **ADAH 437**
MC . . . . **ADAHC 437**
Arcade Music Gala / Apr '86.

PLENTY GOOD LOVIN'.
Tracks: Plenty good lovin'.
■ 7" . . . . **MGM 1036**
MGM (EMI) / Sep '59.

PORTRAIT OF A SONG STYLIST.
Tracks: Come rain or come shine / All by myself / Song is ended, The / Moon river / Mack the knife / Love is a many splendoured thing / True love / All the way / Second time around / Lili Marlene / Milord / Am I blue / La vie en rose / Take me to your heart again / Fascination.
CD . . . . **HARCD 108**
LP. . . . . **HARLP 108**
MC . . . . **HARMC 108**
Masterpiece / Apr '89 / BMG.

ROCK 'N' ROLL MILLION SELLERS.
Tracks: Heartbreak hotel / Tweedle dee / I almost lost my mind / I hear you knocking / Just a dream / Don't be cruel / Lipstick on your collar / Sincerely / Ain't that a shame / Silhouette / I'm walking / It's only make believe.
■ LP. . . . . **MGM C 804**
MGM (EMI) / Mar '60.
LP. . . . . **LSP 1061**
Musketeer / Oct '87 / D.A.D. Records.
LP. **831 995-1**
MC **831 995-4**
Polydor (Germany) / Oct '87 / PolyGram.
CD **831 995-2**
Polydor (Germany) / May '88 / PolyGram.

SING GREAT COUNTRY FAVORITES (Francis, Connie & Hank Williams Jr).
Tracks: Bye bye love / Send me the pillow you dream on / Wolverton mountain / No letter today / Please help me I'm falling / Singing the blues / Walk on by / If you've got the money, I've got the time / Mule skinner blues / Making believe / Blue blue day / No letter today (alt) / Wabash cannonball / Mule skinner blues (alt).
CD . . . . **BCD 15737**
Bear Family / Aug '93 / Rollercoaster Records / Swift / Direct Distribution.

SINGLES COLLECTION :CONNIE FRANCIS, THE.
Tracks: Lipstick on your collar / Everybody's somebody's fool / I'm sorry I made you cry / I'm gonna be warm this winter / Together / V-A-C-A-T-I-O-N / I'll get by / Frankie / Many tears ago / Mama/Robot man / Fallin / Among my souvenirs / In the valley of love / Who's sorry now / Stupid cupid/Carolina moon / Breakin' in a brand new broken heart / Plenty good lovin' / Baby's first Christmas / You always hurt the one you love / Don't break the heart that loves you / My happiness / Valentino / Where the boys are/Baby Roo / My heart has a mind of its own / Senza fine / Jealous heart / My child.
CD **519 131-2**
LP. **519 131-1**
MC **519 131-4**
Polygram T.V / Apr '93 / PolyGram.

SINGS GREAT COUNTRY HITS.
Tracks: I walk the line / I really don't want to know / I'm movin' on / He thinks I still care / I can't stop loving you / Oh, lonesome me / She'll have to go / Heartaches by the number / Your cheatin' heart / Bye bye, love / Tennessee waltz / Singing the blues / Half as much / Cold, cold heart / Hearts of stone / I'm a fool to care.
MC . . . . **SPEMC 62**
MGM (Polydor) / Mar '84.
■ LP. . . . . **SPELP 62**
MGM (Polydor) / Mar '84.

STUPID CUPID.
Tracks: Stupid cupid / Carolina moon.
7" . . . . **OG 9442**
Old Gold / Jul '84 / Pickwick Records.

TOGETHER.
Tracks: Together.
■ 7" . . . . **MGM 1138**
MGM (EMI) / Jun '61.

TWENTY ALL-TIME GREATS.
Tracks: Who's sorry now? / Stupid Cupid / My happiness / Everybody's somebody's fool / Carolina moon / Plenty good lovin' / Where the boys are / Robot man / When the boy in your arms / Mama / Lipstick on your collar / Among my souvenirs / Many tears ago / Breaking in a brand new broken heart / Vacation / Together / Jealous heart / You always hurt the one you love / My heart has a mind of its own / My child.
MC **317 729 0**
Polydor / Jun '77 / PolyGram.
■ LP. **239 129 0**
Polydor / Jun '77.

UNFORGETTABLE MEMORIES.
Tracks: Not Advised.
CD **66125**
MC **62125**
Ce De International / Sep '93 / Taylors.

V.A.C.A.T.I.O.N.
Tracks: V.A.C.A.T.I.O.N.
■ 7" . . . . **MGM 1165**
MGM (EMI) / Aug '62.

V.A.C.A.T.I.O.N. (RE-RELEASE).
Tracks: V.A.C.A.T.I.O.N. / My heart has a mind of its own.
■ 7" **2066 824**
Polydor / Jun '77.

VALENTINO.
Tracks: Valentino.
■ 7" . . . . **MGM 1060**
MGM (EMI) / Mar '60.

VERY BEST OF CONNIE FRANCIS.
Tracks: Who's sorry now? / Stupid Cupid / Carolina moon / Mama / My happiness / Lipstick on your collar / Everybody's somebody's fool / Among my souvenirs / Many tears ago / Lili Marlene / La Bamba.
Double LP **2670 168**
Polydor / Jan '83 / PolyGram.
CD **827 569-2**
Polydor / '87 / PolyGram.

VERY BEST OF VOL II.
Tracks: Not Advised.
CD **831 699-2**
Polydor / May '88 / PolyGram.

WHERE THE BOYS ARE.
Tracks: Where the boys are / Baby roo.
■ 7" . . . . **MGM 1121**
MGM (EMI) / Mar '61.

WHERE THE BOYS ARE.
Tracks: Where the boys are / A-bi-ni-bi.
■ 7" . . . . **UP 36430**
United Artists / Jul '78.

WHITE SOX, PINK LIPSTICK & STUPID CUPID.
Tracks: Didn't I love you enough / Freddy / (Oh please) Make him jealous / Goody goodbye / Are you satisfied / My treasure / My first real love / Believe in me / Forgetting / Send for my baby / I never had a sweetheart / Little blue wren / Everyone needs someone / My sailor boy / No other one / I leaned on a man / Faded orchid / Eighteen / My sisters clothes / Majesty of love, The / You my darlin' you / Who's sorry now / You were only fooling (while I was falling..) / I'm beginning to see the light / Rudolph the red nosed reindeer / Wheel of fortune, The / How can I make you believe in me / You belong to me / Daddy's little girl / I'm sorry I made you cry / I cried for you / You always hurt the one you love / I'll get by / Lock up your heart / Heartaches / I'm nobody's baby / My melancholy baby / I miss you so / It's the talk of the town / If I had you / How deep is the ocean / Carolina moon / Stupid Cupid / Happy days & lonely nights / Fallin' / You're my everything / My happiness / Don't speak of love / Love eyes / Never before / In the valley of love / Time after time / Blame it on my youth / How did he look / That's all / Toward the end of the day / I really don't want to know / No-one to cry to / If I didn't care / If you love me tonight / If you love me tonight (Take 6) / Come rain or come shine / All by myself / Hold me, thrill me, kiss me / Song is ended (but the melody lingers on), The / There will never be another you / Melancholy serenade / Rock-a-bye your baby with a Dixie melody / Hallelujah, I love him so / My thanks to you / Bells of St. Mary's, The / Good luck, good health, God bless you / Garden in the rain, A / Try a little tenderness / Goodnight sweetheart / Cruising down the river / I'll close my eyes (British version) / I'll close my eyes (American version) / Very thought of you, The / These foolish things (remind me of you) / Tree in the meadow, A / Gypsy, The / Now is the hour / You're gonna miss me / Frankie / Lipstick on your collar / Oh, Frankie / I almost lost my mind / I'm walkin' / Just a dream / Heartbreak hotel / I hear you knockin' / Tweedle dee / Ain't that a shame / It's only make believe / Sincerely / Don't be cruel / Bye bye love / Earth angel / Hearts of stone / Silhouettes / Plenty good lovin' / Singin' the blues / My special angel / Tennessee waltz / Let me go lover / Young love / Half as much / Anytime / Your cheatin' heart / Cold, cold heart / (There'll be) Peace in the valley / Too young / Temptation / You made me love you / Prisoner of love / Young at heart / It's not for me to say / Thinking of you / That's my desire / Because of you / Where the blue of the night / April love / Cry / God bless America / Among my souvenirs / Snapdragon / No one / Tiger & the mouse, The / Forgetting (take 10) / Lock up your heart (slow version) / My melancholy baby (take 2) / No one (take 2) / Tiger & the mouse, The (take 4).
CD . . . . **BCD 15616**
Bear Family / Jul '93 / Rollercoaster Records / Swift / Direct Distribution.

WHO'S SORRY NOW.
Tracks: Who's sorry now.
■ 7" . . . . **MGM 975**
MGM (EMI) / Apr '58.

WHO'S SORRY NOW.
Tracks: Who's sorry now / Lipstick on your collar.
■ 7" **206 6839**
Polydor / Aug '77.

WHO'S SORRY NOW (OLD GOLD).
Tracks: Who's sorry now / Mama.
7" . . . . **OG 9443**
Old Gold / Mar '90 / Pickwick Records.

YOU ALWAYS HURT THE ONE YOU LOVE.
Tracks: You always hurt the one you love.
■ 7" . . . . **MGM 998**
MGM (EMI) / Dec '58.

Franklin, Rex

COUNTRY WORLD OF..
Tracks: Not Advised.
MC . . . . **SPVP 171C**
Viking (New Zealand) / Apr '80 / Harmonia Mundi (UK) / Discovery.

Frickie, Janie

Born 19.12.1947, in South Whitney, Indiana - raised on a small farm. After taking a Bachelor Of Arts Degree in Elementry Education at the University of Indiana, Fricke (as her name was spelt then) started out on a career as a demo singer, working out of Dallas, Memphis and Los Angeles. She was signed to the William Tanner Agency and would work 6 hours a day - earning up to $100,000 a year, recording jingles, coupled with some back-up work. After moving to Nashville, she joined the Lea Jane Singers, and also worked with the Halladay Singers and the Nashville Edition (by doing which, Frickie became one of the most sought after backing vocalists around - figuring on a mass of hits by John Conlee, Elvis, Crystal Gayle, Vern Gosdin, Barbara Mandrell, Conway Twitty and John Duncan). Due to these many successful collaborations she reluctantly took on a solo career. Riding on the back of such previous vocal tie-ups, *Jo and the cowboy* produced her 1977 Columbia debut single *What you're doing tonight* , which just failed to make the top twenty. *Come a little bit closer* with the aforementioned Duncan went to the top 5, a feat bettered in 1978, when Charlie Rich's *On my knees* topped the charts, and almost equalled in 1979 with Moe Bandy's *It's a cheatin' situation* . Frickie's rise on the solo front (under the guidance of famed record producer Billy Sherril) gained impetus as the 1980s dawned. *Down to my last broken heart* just missed out on the No.1 slot in 1980. Other hits were to include *I'll need someone to hold me (When I cry)* , *Do me with love* (1981), rounded off in 1982 with *Don't worry 'bout me baby* allowing her a debut No. 1. Frickie, at the height of her popularity, also took the CMA's Female Vocalist Award that October. Her run of singles (and albums) was unabated with her first and only chart topping album *Black and White* releasing no fewer than three chart topping singles, *If it ain't easy* , *He's a heartache* and *Tell me a lie* (Judy Rodman, later to record for MTM, a friend from her Memphis days lending harmony support on all three). Stretching well into the mid - 1980s, Frickie's popularity held, the subsequent chart toppers being *Let's stop talkin' about it* , *You're heart's not in it* , and with Merle Haggard *A place to fall apart* (1984) an finally in 1986, *Always have, always will* . As the 1980s drew to a close it found Frickie making her most country commited albums for some while - *Saddle in the wind* (1987) and *Labour of love* (1989). Her success gradually became less profitable and more infrequent, with her days at Columbia ending in 1990 as a result.(Maurice Hope)

AFTER MIDNIGHT.
Tracks: Are you satisfied / I hurt / I don't like being lonely / Teach me how to forget / If I didn't care / Baby you're gone / My eternal flame / Nobody ever loved me so good / From time to time / I won't be easy.
LP. **4504861**
■ **MC** **4504864**
CBS / May '87.

ALWAYS HAS ALWAYS WILL.
Tracks: Don't put it past my heart / Always has always will.
7" **6502737**
CBS / Nov '86 / Sony.

BELIEVE IN YOU.
Tracks: Believe in you / Weekend friend.
■ **7"** . . . . **CBS 6975**
CBS / Jan '79.

BLACK AND WHITE.
Tracks: Till I can't take it anymore / He's breathing down my neck / Take me like a vacation / Nothing left to say / Comin' apart at the seams / Always have always will / Don't put it past my heart / When a woman cries / He's making a long short story / I'd take you back again.
LP. . . . . **CBS 57022**
CBS / Aug '86 / Sony.
■ **MC** . . . . **.40 57022**
CBS / Aug '86.

BLUE SKY SHINING.
Tracks: Blue sky shining / It's raining too.
■ **7"** . . . . **A 1146**
CBS / Jun '81.

COUNTRY STORE: JANIE FRICKE.
Tracks: Please help me, I'm falling / Loving arms / Blue sky shining / Got my mojo working / Tell me a lie / Do me with love / Your hearts not in it / It ain't easy bein' easy (Only on CD.) / Don't worry 'bout me baby (Only on CD.) / If you could see me now / Lonely people / But love me / Come a little bit closer / Cry / Enough of each other / Homeward bound / When I fall in love (Only on CD.) / Till I can't take it anymore (Only on CD.).
CD . . . . **CDCST 13**
MC . . . . **CSTK 13**
Country Store / '88 / BMG.
■ **LP.** . . . . **CST 13**
Country Store / '88.

DO ME WITH LOVE.
Tracks: Do me with love / Heart.
■ **7"** . . . . **A 1731**
CBS / Oct '81.

ENOUGH OF EACH OTHER.
Tracks: Enough of each other / Down to my last broken heart.
■ **7"** . . . . **CBS 9396**
CBS / Jan '81.

FIRST WORD IN MEMORY.
Tracks: Talkin' through / First word in memory is me / One way ticket / First time out of the rain / Love like ours / Your heart's not in it / In between the heartache / Another man like that / Without each other / Take it from the top.
LP. . . . . **CBS 26101**
CBS / Nov '84 / Sony.

FROM THE HEART.
Tracks: But love me / Fallin' for you / My world begins and ends with you / Cool September / When I fall in love / Pass me by / Gonna love ya / Some fools don't ever learn / One piece at time / This ain't Tennessee and he ain't you.
■ **LP.** . . . . **CBS 84130**
CBS / Apr '80.

I'LL NEED SOMEONE TO HOLD ME WHEN I CRY.
Tracks: I'll need someone to hold me when I cry / Enough of each other / Going through the motions / Pride / Down to my last broken heart / Cry / Every time a teardrop falls / It's raining too / I just can't fool my heart / Blue sky shining.
■ **LP.** **84729**
CBS / Mar '81.

IT AIN'T EASY.
Tracks: He's a heartache / Who better than an angel / It ain't easy bein' easy / Too hard on my heart / Little more love / Love have mercy / Tell me a lie / You don't know love / Heart to heart talk / Tryin' to fool a fool.
■ **LP.** . . . . **CBS 85983**
CBS / Dec '82.

IT'S A CHEATING SITUATION (see under Bandy, Moe).

JANIE FRICKE: I LOVE COUNTRY.
Tracks: Please help me, I'm falling / He's a heartache / Walking a broken heart / Pride / But love me / Homeward bound / Cry / Do me with love / Always / She's single again.
■ **LP.** **54948**
CBS / Mar '87.
■ **MC** . . . . **.40 54948**
CBS / Mar '87.

LABOR OF LOVE.
Tracks: Love is one of those words / Give 'em my number / What are you doing here with me / Last thing that I didn't do, The / Walking on the moon / Feeling is believing / I can't help the way I don't feel / No ordinary memory / One of those things / My old friend the blues.
CD **4657912**
CBS / Aug '89 / Sony.
LP. **4657911**
■ **MC** **4657914**
CBS / Aug '89.

LOVE LIES.
Tracks: If the fall don't get you / Have I got a heart / How do you fall out of love / Love lies / Tell me a lie / Let's stop talkin' about it / Lonely people / Walkin' a broken heart / I've had all the love I can stand / Where's the fire.
■ **LP.** . . . . **CBS 25551**
CBS / Dec '83.

LOVE NOTES.
Tracks: I'll love away your troubles for awhile / Somewhere to come when it rains / River blue / Let's try again / Let me love you good-bye / Love is worth it all / You're the one I love / Playin' hard to get / Stirrin' up feelin's / Got my mojo working.
LP. . . . . **CBS 83543**
CBS / Jun '79 / Sony.
LP. . . . . **CBS 32768**
■ **MC** . . . . **.40 32768**
CBS / Mar '86.

SADDLE THE WIND.
Tracks: Sugar moon / I'll walk before I'll crawl / Heart / I'm not that good at goodbye / Don't touch me / Where does love go / If I were only her tonight / Healing hands of time / Crazy dreams / Saddle the wind.
LP. **4651281**
■ **MC** **4651284**
CBS / Apr '89.

SINGER OF SONGS.
Tracks: I loved you all the way / We could have been the closest of friends / You changed my life in a moment / No one's ever gonna love you / I believe in you / Please help me, I'm falling / What're you doing tonight / Week-end friend / Baby it's you / I think I'm fallin' in love.
■ **LP.** . . . . **CBS 83154**
CBS / Jan '79.
■ **LP.** . . . . **CBS 32078**
CBS / Dec '81.

SLEEPING WITH YOUR MEMORY.
Tracks: Do me with love / Homeward bound / Love me / Don't worry 'bout me baby / Sleeping with your memory / Heart / Always / If you could see me now / There's no future in the past / Midnight words.
■ **LP.** . . . . **CBS 85309**
CBS / Dec '81.

TELL ME A LIE.
Tracks: Tell me a lie / Love have mercy.
7" . . . . **A 3848**
CBS / Mar '84 / Sony.

VERY BEST OF JANIE FRICKE, THE.
Tracks: Not Advised.
LP. . . . . **CBS 26671**
CBS / Sep '86 / Sony.
MC . . . . **.40 26671**
Epic / Sep '86 / Sony.

Frizzell, David

I'M GONNA HIRE A WINO TO DECORATE..
Tracks: I'm gonna hire a wino to decorate..
7" . . . . **K 15002**
WEA / Sep '82 / WEA.

Frizzell, Lefty

William Orville Frizzell (1928-75) from Corsicana, Texas, was one of the great and influential honky-tonk singers. His nickname came from a short boxing career; he began singing on Texas radio in the late '30's and his demo of *If you've got money, I've got the time* led to a CBS contract in 1950 and became a No. 2 country hit; he continued with ten more top 10 country hits in two years. His move to the West Coast led to a fall off in his hits, a move back to Nashville and he returned to the charts strongly in the mid-'60's. Deeply influenced by Jimmie Rodgers, his distinctive, drawling vocal style in turn influenced John Anderson, Willie Nelson, Merle Haggard and indeed a whole generation of country stars. One of the most influential singers of the 1950's, Lefty was certainly worthy of a retrospective tribute - and he received it with Bear Family's 1984 14-lp boxset, *His life, his music* which covered his entire recording career. But it was nothing compared the set that the same company issued 8 years later. Titled *Life's like poetry* , this set contained 12 cd's with the additional material including his first known recordings prior to his Columbia and ABC work, more demos from the 1950's and 60's and his transcription radio shows on behalf of the U.S. military services. In all, a total of 80 new items (in addition to the 239 songs previously issued, which at the time had included 50 previously unreleased recordings), adding up to a running time of well over two and a half hours. Richard Weize, Bear Family's founder and owner, modestly commented "we just didn't know that this material existed when we finished the LP set". *Life's like poetry* is probably the finest retrospective ever given an artist, country or otherwise. (Tony Byworth)

20 GOLDEN HITS OF LEFTY FRIZZELL.
Tracks: Not Advised.
MC Set . . . . **GTV 15595**
Gusto (USA) / Mar '88.

HIS LIFE HIS MUSIC.
Tracks: I love you a thousand ways / If you've got the money, I've got the time / Shine, shave shower (It's Saturday) / Cold feet / Don't think it ain't been fun dear / When payday comes around / My baby's just like money / Look what thoughts will do / You want everything but me / I want to be with you always / Give me more, more more (Of your kisses) / How long will it take (To stop loving you) / Always late (With your kisses) / Mom and Dad's waltz / You can go on your way now / Treasure untold / Blue yodel, no.6 / Travelin' blues / My old pal / Blue yodel no.2 / Lullaby yodel / Brakeman's blues / My rough and rowdy ways / Love you (Though I know you're no good) / It's just you (I could love always) / You're here, so everything's alright (Darlin) / I've got reasons to hate you / I love you though I know you're no good / Don't stay away (Till love grows cold) / It's just you I could love always / If you can spare the time (I won't miss the M/A king without / Forever and always / I know you're lonesome (While waiting for me) / Lost love blues / That's me without you / I won't be good for nothin' / If I lose you (I'll lose my world) / I'm an old, old man (Tryin' to live while I cry) / You're just mine (only in my dreams) / I'll try / Bring your sweet self back to me (Honey baby) / Time changes things / All of me loves all of you / California blues (Blue yodel, No 4) / Never no mo'blues / We crucified our Jesus / When it comes to measuring love / Sleep, baby sleep / Lonely and blue (I'm) / Before you go, make sure you know / Two friends of mine (In love) / Hopeless love / Then I'll come back to you / Tragic letter, The / Two hearts broken now / You can always count on me / I've been away 'way to long / Run'em off / Darkest moment is just before the light, The / You're too late / My little her and him / I love you mostly / You're there, I'm here / Let it be so / Mama / Making believe / Moonlight, Darling and you / I'll sit alone and cry / Forest fire (Is in your heart), A / Sweet lies / Your tomorrows will never come / It gets late so early / I'm lost between right and wrong / Promises (Promises, promises) / My love and baby's gone / Today is that tomorrow (I dreamed of yesterday) / First to have a second chance / These hands / You can't divorce my heart / Treat her right / Heart's highway / I'm a boy left alone / Just can't live that fast anymore / Waltz of the angels, The / Lullaby waltz / Glad I found you / Now that you are gone / From an angel to a devil / Lover by appointment / Sick, sober and sorry / No one to talk to (But the blues) / Is it only that you're lonely / Mailman bring me no more blues / You've still git it / Tell me dear / To stop loving you (Means cry) / Torch within my heart, The / Time out for the blues / Why should I be lonely / Signed sealed and delivered / Nobody knows but me / Silence / Release me / You're humbuggin' me / She's gone / Cigarettes and coffee blues / I need your love / My buckets got a hole in it / If you've got the money I've got the time / Sin will be the chaser / If you're every lonely Darling / Knock again, true love / Long black veil, The / One had been to another / Father than my eyes can see / My blues will pass / Ballad of the blue and grey / That's all I can remember / So what, let it rain / What you gonna do Leroy / I feel sorry for me / Heaven's plan / Looking for you / Stranger / Few steps, A / Forbidden lovers / Just passing through / That reminds me of me / Don't let her see me cry / Through the eyes of a fool / James River / Preview of coming attractions / Lonley heart / What good did you get (Out of breaking my heart) / When it rains the blues / I'm not the man I'm supposed to be / Saginaw Michigan / There is no food in this house / Rider, The / Nester, The / I was coming home to

F 10

■ DELETED

you / Hello to him (Goodbye to me) / I can tell / Make that one for the road a cup of coffee / Gator hollow / It costs is much to die / She's gone gone gone / Running into memories of you / Confused / How far down can I go / It's bad (When it's thataway) / I don't trust you anymore / Little unfair, A / Woman, let me sing you a song / Preperations to be blue / Love, looks good on you / Writing on the wall / I just couldn't see the forest (For the trees) / Everything keeps coming back (But you) / Heart (Don't love her anymore) / You don't have to be presesnt to win / Song from a lonely heart, A / You gotta be puttin' me on / Get this stranger out of me / Money tree / Hobo's pride / When the rooster leaves the yard / Anything you can spare / Only way to fly / Prayer on your lips is like freedom in your ,life, A / Little old winedrinker me / Almost persuaded / Have you ever been untrue / You've got the money / When the grass grows green again / Marriage bit, The / Wasted way of life / Keep them flowers watered while I'm gone / An article from life / Honky tonk hill / My baby is a tramp / She brought love sweet love / Watermelon time in Georgia / I must be getting over you / Out of you / Three cheers for the good guys / Honky tonk stardust cowboy / What am I gonna do / You, babe / Down by the railroad track / Let me give her the flowers / If I had half the sense of a fool was born with / Somebody's words / Lucky arms / True love needs to be in touch / My house is your honky tonk / I buy the wine / If she just helps me get over you / Falling / Railroad lady / I can't get over you to save my life / I never go around mirrors / That's the way love goes / She found the key / I wondaer who's building the bridge / My wishing room / I'm gonna hang out my mind today / Sittin' and thinkin' / I'm not that good at goodbye / Yesterday just passed my way again / Life's like poetry / Bridges to burn / Just can't live that fast (Anymore) / Honey Baby, you were wrong / Please be mine, Dear blue eyes / I'm yours, if you want me / I'll be a bachelor till I die / Yesterday's mail / Stay all night, stay a little longer / Somebody's pushing.
■ **LP Set** . . . . BFX 15100/15
Bear Family / Nov '84.

HONKY TONKIN'.
Tracks: Not Advised.
LP . . . . FLY 596
Flyright / Oct '86 / Hot Shot / Roots Records / Wellard Dist. / Charly / Swift / Projection.

LEFTY FRIZZELL.
Tracks: I love you a thousand ways / Cold feet / I want to be with you always / Mama / I'm an old, old man trying to love while I can / Forever / Heart's highway / King without a queen / No one to talk to.
■ **LP** . . . . CBS 25017
CBS / Oct '82.

LEFTY FRIZZELL GOES TO NASHVILLE.
Tracks: It's lonely and blue / It's got so late so early / Lost love blues / Sweet lies / Two broken hearts now / Tragic letter, The / Lullaby waltz / How far down can I go / Stranger / Little ole wine drinker me / Get this stranger out of me / Hello to him (goodbye to me) / Almost persuaded.
LP . . . . SS 16
Rounder / Dec '88 / Projection / Roots Records / Swift / C.M. Distribution / Topic Records / Jazz Music / Hot Shot / A.D.A Distribution / Direct Distribution.

LEGENDARY LAST SESSIONS, THE.
Tracks: I can't get over you to save my life / I never go around mirrors / If I had half the sense (A fool was born with) / Somebody's words / Lucky arms / That's the way love goes / If she just helps me get over you / I buy the wine / Let me give her the flowers / Railroad lady / Lites's like poetry / She's found the key / Falling / I'm not that good at goodbye / My house is your honky tonk / Yesterday just passed my way again / Sittin' and thinkin' / My wishing room / I love you a thousand ways.
Double LP IMCA2 4161
MCA (Import) / Mar '86 / Pinnacle / Silver Sounds (CD).

LIFE'S LIKE POETRY.
Tracks: I love you a thousand ways / If you've got the money, I've got the time / Shine, shave, shower (It's Saturday) / Cold feet / Don't think it ain't been fun dear / When payday comes around / My baby's just like money / Look what thoughts will do / You want everything but me / I want to be with you always / Give me more more more (of your kisses) / How long will it take (to stop loving you) / Always late (with your kisses) / Mom and dad's waltz / You can go on your way now / Treasure untold / Blue yodel / Travellin' blues / My old pal / Lullaby yodel / Breakman's blues / My rough and rowdy ways / I love you (Though you're no good) / It's just you (I could love always) / (Darling now) you're here so everything's alright / I've got reasons to hate you / Don't stay away (Till love grows cold) / If you can spare the time (I won't miss the money) / King without a Queen, A / Forever (and always) / I know you're lonesome (while waiting for me) / Lost love blues / That's me without you / Send her here to be mine / I won't be good for nothin' / If I loose you (I'll loose my world) / I'm an old old man (Tryin' to love while I can / You're just mine (Only in my dreams) / I'll try / (Honey, baby, hurry) Bring your sweet self back / Time changes things / All of me loves all of you / California blues / Never no' mo' blues / We crucified our Jesus / When it comes to measuring love / Sleep baby sleep / (I'm) Lonely and blue / Before you go, make sure you know / Two friends of mine in love / Hopeless love / Then I'll come back to you / Tragic letter (The letter that you left), The / You can always count on me / I've been away way too long / Run 'em off / Darkest moment (Just before the light of

da / You're too late / My little her and him / I love you mostly / You're there, I'm ere / Let it be so / Mama / Making believe / Moonlight, Darling and you / I'll sit alone and cry / Forest fire (Is in your heart), A / Sweet lies / Your tomorrows will never come / It gets late so early / I'm lost between right and wrong / Promises (promises, promises) / My love and baby's gone / Today is that tomorrow (I dreamed of yesterday) / First to have a second chance / These hands / You can't divorce my heart / Treat her right / Heart's highway / I'm a boy left alone / Just can't live that fast (anymore) / Waltz of the angels, The / Lullaby waltz / Glad I found you / Now that you are gone / From an angel to a devil / Lover by appointment / Sick, sober and sorry / No one to talk to (but the blues) / Is it only that you're lonely / Mailman bring me more blues / You've still got it / Tell me dear / To stop loving you (means cry) / Torch within my heart, The / Time out for the blues / If you've got the money I've got the time / (Darling) let's turn backthe years) / You win again / Why should I be lonely / Signed, sealed and delivered / Nobody knows but me / If you're ever lonely darling / Silence / Release me / Our love's no bluff / You're humbugging me / She's gone / Cigarettes and coffee blues / I need your love / My bucket's got a hole in it / 3In will be the chaser for the wine / Knock again, true love / Long black veil, The / One has been to another / Farther than my eyes can see / My blues will pass / Ballad of the blue and grey / That's all I can remember / So what, let it rain / What you gonna do, Leroy? / I feel sorry for me / Heaven's plan / Looking for you / Stranger / Few steps away, A / Forbidden lovers / Just passing through / That reminds me of me / Don't let her see me cry / Through the eyes of a fool / James river / Preview of coming attractions / Lonely heart / What good did you get (out of breaking my heart) / When it rains the blues / I'm not the man I'm supposed to be / Saginaw Michigan / There's no food in this house / Rider, The / Nester, The / I was coming home to you / Hello to him (goodbye to me) / I can tell / Make that one for the road a cup of coffee / (Gator hollow / It costs too much to die / She's gone, gone, gone / Confused / How far down can I go / It's bad (when it's that way) / I don't trust you anymore / Little unfair, A / Woman let me sing you a song / Preparations to be blue / Love looks good on you / It's hard to please you / You don't want me to get well / Writing on the wall / I just couldn't see the forest (for the trees) / I'm not guilty / It couldn't happen to a nicer guy / Everything keeps coming back (but you) / Heart (don't love her anymore) / You don't have to be present to win / My feet are getting cold / Is there anything I can do / Old gang's gone, The / Song from a lonely heart, A / You gotta me puttin' me on / There in the mirror / Get this stranger out of me / Money tree / Hobo's pride / When the rooster leaves the yard / Anthing you can spare / Only way to fly (Laughing version) / Prayer on your lips is like freedon in your hands / Little old winedrinker me / Word or two to Mary, A / Almost persuaded / Have you ever been untrue / I'll remember you / Wasted way of live / Blind street singer / Honky tonk hill / My baby is a tramp / She brought love sweet love / Watermelon time in Georgia / I must be getting over you / Out of you / It's raining all over the world / There's something lonley in this house / Three cheers for the good guys / An article from life / Honky tonk hill (without overdub) / Honky tonk stardust cowboy / What am I gonna do / You babe / This just ain't a good day for leavin' / Down by the railroad track / Let me give her the flowers / If I had half the sense (A fool was born with) / Somebody's words / Lucky arms / True love needs to be in touch / My house is your honky tonk / I buy the wine / If she just helps me to get over you / Falling / I never go around mirrors (I've got heartache to hide) / That's the way love goes / She found the key / I wonder who's building the bridge / My wishing room / I'm gonna hang out my mind today / Sittin' and thinkin' / I'm not that good at goodbye / Yesterday just passed my way again / I'll never cry over you / My confession / I hope you're not lonely when I'm gone / My baby and my wife / It's all over now / Worried mind / Maiden's prayer / I'm wasting my life away / You nearly lose your mind / If you've got the money / Just can't live that fast anymore (1) / Just can't live that fast anymore (2) / Honey baby / Please me mine, dear blue eyes / I'm yours it you want me / I'll be a bachelor / Yesterday's mail / Shine, shave and shower / I want to be with you / Always / Ida red boogie / Always late / Theme and If you've got the money / Make the one for the road a cup of coffee / Darling let's turn back the years / Things / Woodchopper's ball (instrumental) / Stay all night / Somebody's pushing / Mona Lisa / Sunday down in Tenessee / I'll make it up to you / Too much love / My abandoned heart / Wait till I'm asleep / Not this time / Why didn't you tell me our love was wrong / Forever and always / Please don't stay away so long (1) / Please don't stay away so long (2) / You have never known to be wrong / Reason why my heart's in misery, The / Just little things like that / I love you so / Fool's advice, A / When me and my baby go steppin' out (1) / When me and my baby go steppin' out (2) / Brakeman's blues.
CD Set . . . . BCD 15550
Bear Family / Feb '92 / Rollercoaster Records / Swift / Direct Distribution.

TREASURES UNTOLD.
Tracks: Shine shave shower (it's Saturday) / It's just you / How long will it take (to stop loving you) / Run 'em off / Now that you are gone / If you can spare the time / Look what thoughts will do / My baby's just like money / Time changes everything / Waltz of the winds / Then I'll come back to you / Treasure untold.
LP . . . . SS 11

Rounder / Dec '88 / Projection / Roots Records / Swift / C.M. Distribution / Topic Records / Jazz Music / Hot Shot / A.D.A Distribution / Direct Distribution.

Froggatt. Raymond

Arguably one of the most well known, and most awarded of the British country entertainers, Birmingham born (on November 13, 1941) Raymond Froggatt started out as a pop singer and writer and enjoyed his biggest success when Dave Clark Five scored a Top 10 hit with his *Red balloon* in 1968. He enjoyed another substantial hit when Cliff Richard recorded *Big ship* the following year. In the mid-1970's he made the move to country music, establishing his reputation with the Nashville recorded album *Southern fried frog*, produced by Larry Butler. In 1983 he achieved a near hit in the British charts with the much programmed *Don't let me cry again* , and virtually monopolizes the Most Popular Male Singer category in all the annual UK country award polls. He's also one of the very few musicians to have been given the Freedom of the City of Birmingham. (Tony Byworth)

DON'T LET ME CRY AGAIN.
Tracks: Don't let me cry again / Magic carpet.
7" . . . . ESM 405
Astra / May '83 / Astra Records.

JETTIN'.
Tracks: Don't let me cry again / Jettin'.
7" . . . . RPC 004
Lots More Music / Nov '86.

ME AND MY IDEAS.
Tracks: Me and my ideas / Luci Mae.
■ 7" . . . . JET 119
Jet / Sep '78.

STAY WITH ME.
Tracks: I will stay with you / Sometimes people get hurt / Festival of fools / Goodbye in a letter / Naz, The / Bandman / High as Georgia pines / It's only the memories / Fools rush in / Smile and a song, A.
LP . . . . DSM 002
Merco / Jan '81 / M.S.D.

TRY TO GET YOU INTO MY LIFE (Froggatt, Raymond Band).
Tracks: Try to get you into my life / This could last all night.
■ 7" . . . . JET 749
Jet / Jan '75.

WHY.
Tracks: Not Advised.
LP . . . . MMLP 1032
Happy Face / '84 / Swift / Pinnacle.

Front Porch String Band

FRONT PORCH STRING BAND.
Tracks: If you're ever in Oklahoma / Heart against the winds / Living in our country world / Come unto me / Girl I love, The / Singer, The / Go my way / Hills of Alabama / Back to my love / Grant's mill / Wabash cannonball.
LP . . . . REBEL 1624
MC . . . . REBEL 1624C
Rebel (1) / '81 / Projection / Backs Distribution.

Front Range

NEW FRONTIER, THE.
Tracks: Waiting for the real thing / Chains of darkness / Down in Caroline / Without you / Why don't you leave me baby / Lonesome night / When I still needed you / So far away / Burning the breakfast / Shady river / Building on the rock / Happy after all.
CD . . . . SHCD 3801
Sugarhill(USA) / '92 / Roots Records / Projection / Impetus Records / C.M. Distribution / Jazz Music / Swift / Duncans / A.D.A Distribution.

Furtado, Tony

SWAMPED.
Tracks: John Henry / Swamped / Glory at the meeting house / Old homestead waltz / Daddio / Crossing at the Severn / Celtic medley / Broken pledge, The / Golden eagle hornpipe / Blues for Alice / Salutations.
CD . . . . CD 0277
LP . . . . ROUNDER 0277
MC . . . . ROUNDER 0277C
Rounder / '90 / Projection / Roots Records / Swift / C.M. Distribution / Topic Records / Jazz Music / Hot Shot / A.D.A Distribution / Direct Distribution.

WITHIN REACH.
Tracks: Ralph Trischka / St. John's fire / I will / Waiting for Guiteau/President Garfield's Hornpipe / Queen Anne's lace / Sao Miguel / Julia Dealaney/The Drunken landlady / Drake's bay / Magpie on the gallows / Duskus.
CD . . . . CDROU 0290
MC . . . . ROU 0290
Rounder / '92 / Projection / Roots Records / Swift / C.M. Distribution / Topic Records / Jazz Music / Hot Shot / A.D.A Distribution / Direct Distribution.

Fuzzy Mountain String..

FUZZY MOUNTAIN STRING BAND (Fuzzy Mountain String Band).
Tracks: Not Advised.
LP . . . . ROUNDER 0010

Rounder / '88 / Projection / Roots Records / Swift / C.M. Distribution / Topic Records / Jazz Music / Hot Shot / A.D.A Distribution / Direct Distribution.

SUMMER OAKS AND PORCH (Fuzzy Mountain String Band).
Tracks: Not Advised.

LP . . . . ROUNDER 0035
Rounder / '88 / Projection / Roots Records / Swift / C.M. Distribution / Topic Records / Jazz Music / Hot Shot / A.D.A Distribution / Direct Distribution.

G

Gadney, Reg

FAVOURITE COUNTRY LOVE SONGS.
Tracks: Not Advised.
MC . . . . BBM 113
Bibi (Budget Cassettes) / Jan '82.

Gadsden, T

COUNTRY MUSIC (Gadsden, T & F Kinck-Peterson).
Tracks: Smokin' steel guitar / Slim's waltz / Along the border / Together 1 - song / Together 2 - instrumental / Rockabilly boogie 1 - song / Rockabilly boogie 2 - instrumental / Sally Goodin - traditional / Three am blues / Tex's swing / Rainbows 1 / Rainbows 2 - remix (no strings) / If only 1 - song / If only 1 - instrumental / Love is 1 / Love is 2 - remix (no strings) / Autumn waltz / Key west / Southern express / I'll be gone 1 - song / I'll be gone 1 - instrumental.
CD . . . . DWCD 0054
De Wolfe / '89 / De Wolfe Records.

Gaither, Bill

One of the foremost contributors to the country-gospel scene. From Alexandria, Indiana, former school teacher, Bill Gaither together with his wife and brother formed a trio that released its first album in 1964. Shortly afterwards, Gaither's brother was replaced by Gary McSpadden. By the early 1980's, the trio had recorded 22 albums, sold over 3 million records, won two Grammys and ten Dove awards. The band have attracted over half a million people to their annual concert appearances. Bill Gaither also owns a recording studio, booking agency and music publishing company. (Tony Byworth)

20 BEST-LOVED GOSPEL SONGS: BILL GAITHER (Gaither, Bill Trio).
Tracks: He touched me / Get all excited / Rejoice, you're a child of the King / My faith still holds / Thank God for the promise of spring / Longer I serve Him, The / It's no wonder / I came to praise the Lord / Plenty of room in the family / Blessed Jesus / I could never out-love the Lord / God gave the song / That's what Jesus means to me / Walk on the water / Resurrection morn / Contented / Waters are troubled, The / All my hopes / I believe what the Bible says / I believe it.
LP . . . . PC 321
Pilgrim.

BLESS THE LORD WHO REIGNS IN BEAUTY.
Tracks: Perfect heart, A / Lord is my light, The / I have decided / Sanctus / Majesty / Yes / Right place, right time / God hath provided a Lamb / Resurrection / I then shall live.
LP . . . . WST 9617
MC . . . . WC 9617
Word (UK) / May '82 / Word Records (UK) / Sony.

ESPECIALLY FOR CHILDREN (Gaither, Bill Trio).
Tracks: Hello / I've got a friend / I wonder how it felt / God can / You're something special / Sing with us / Jesus loves the little children / I'd like to teach the world to sing / Only a boy named David / Shadrach, Meshach and Abednego / All night, all day / Safe am I / God is watching over you / This little light of mine / God thought of everything / That's him / Sunday school song parade / Everybody ought to go to Sunday school / Heavenly sunshine / Be careful, little hands, what you do / Happy day express, The / I have the joy / A-B-C-D-E-F-G / For God so loved the world / Oh how I love Jesus / Into my heart.
LP . . . . PC 779
Pilgrim.

HE TOUCHED ME (Gaither, Bill Trio).
Tracks: He touched me / I will serve Thee / Longer I serve Him, The / Broken pieces / All my hopes / I believe it / He was there every time / One of those days / It's no wonder / Now I have everything / I believe what the Bible says.
LP . . . . PC 737
Pilgrim.

LEROY'S BUDDY 1935-41.
Tracks: Not Advised.
■ LP . . . . PY 1804
Magpie / Sep '87.
LP . . . . DLP 508
Document / '89 / Revolver-APT / Hot Shot / Jazz Music / SRD.

Gaither. Bill

LEROY'S BUDDY 1936-39.
Tracks: Pins & needles / Curbstone blues / Too many women / Gravel in my bed / I just keep on worryin' / Another big leg woman.
MC . . . . NEO 852
Neovox / Apr '90 / Wellard Dist.

LIVE ACROSS AMERICA (Gaither, Bill Trio).
Tracks: Praise for the Lord / Feeling at home in the presence of the Lord / Let's just praise the Lord / This is the time I must sing / Something beautiful / I just feel that something good is about to happen / Difference is in me, The / Tell it to a few close friends / We are persuaded / Things I must tell the children / Because He lives / Praise you / Precious Jesus / I am loved / Your first day in Heaven / Rejoice, you're a child of the King / Plenty of room in the family / Family of God, The / He touched me / Old rugged cross made the difference, The / I believe in a hill called Mount Calvary / Get all excited / Church triumphant, The / It is finished.
LP . . . . WSX 9605
MC . . . . WC 9605
Word (UK) / May '82 / Word Records (UK) / Sony.

VERY BEST OF THE VERY BEST (Gaither, Bill Trio).
Tracks: I am loved / There's something about that name / Joy comes in the morning / Plenty of room in the family / Family of God, The / Church triumphant, The / God gave the song / He touched me / I am a promise / I will serve thee / Jesus is Lord / King is coming.
LP . . . . WST 9592
MC . . . . WC 9592
Word (UK) / May '82 / Word Records (UK) / Sony.

WE ARE PERSUADED (Gaither, Bill Trio).
Tracks: We are persuaded / Praise you / I do believe / My father's angels / Seek and you shall find / Because He lives / All the time / Heavens declare the glory of God, The / Two prayers / I will go on.
LP . . . . WST 9599
MC . . . . WC 9599
Word (UK) / May '82 / Word Records (UK) / Sony.

Garland, Hank

Guitarist sessionman, born Walter Louis (Hank) Garland near Spartanburg, South Carolina in 1930 and playing on many hit recordings of the fifties. Looked set for life, until he injured his hand in a automobile accident in 1961, by which time Garland had registered much respect and acclaim and had been featured on the recordings by Ernest Tubb and Red Foley (*Sugarfoot rag*) and worked on stage backing Eddy Arnold. Garland is also a kingpin session guitarist figuring alongside Chet Atkins, Grady Martin and Harold Bradley.He appeared on such hits as Jim Reeves *He'll have to go* , Don Gibson's *Sea of heartbreak* , Patsy Cline's *I fall to pieces* and many more. He toured with Elvis in 1961, including Presley's famed Hawaiian date. Garland acquired himself quite a reputation as a jazz musician,and recorded a solo album on Columbia *Winds from a new direction* following his country boogie album for Decca. (Maurice Hope)

GUITAR GENIUS (Garland, Hank/Grady Martin/Les Paul).
Tracks: E string rag / Guitar shuffle / I'm movin' on / Hillbilly express / Third man, Theme from / Low down Billy / Doll dance / Slewfoot rag / Blue skies / Guitar boogie / Steel guitar rag / Dark eyes / Sioux city Sue / Hot lips / Pork chop stomp / Diesel smoke, dangerous curves.
■ LP . . . . CR 30243
Charly / Jul '85 / Charly.

HANK GARLAND AND HIS SUGAR FOOTERS.
Tracks: Sugarfoot rag / Third man theme, The / Flying eagle polka / Sugarfoot boogie / Hillbilly express / Seventh and union / Lowdown Billy / Sentimental journey / Doll dance / Chic, No. 1 / Chic, No. 2 / E string rag / Guitar shuffle / I'm movin' on / This cold war with you / I'll never slip around again / Some other world / I'm crying.
CD . . . . BCD 15551
Bear Family / Apr '92 / Rollercoaster Records / Swift / Direct Distribution.

Garrett, Pat

JUMPIN' JOHN.
Tracks: Jumpin' John / Sexy ole lady.
■ 7" . . . . POSP 481
Polydor / Jul '82.

Gatlin, Larry

Singer/songwriter/musician, Larry Wayne Gatlin was born on May 28th 1948 in Seminole, Texas. Brought up on gospel music, he grew up performing with his two brothers and sister as the Gatlins. His break came when Dottie West recorded a couple of his songs in 1971 and offered him a writer's contract, resulting in his songs being recorded by Elvis Presley, Tom Jones and Glen Campbell. Later, Kris Kristofferson recorded his *Why Me*, in 1975. His first album, *The Pilgrim*, was released in 1974. Also that year, Gatlin's first single *Delta Dirt*, went top 5. Two years later, he won a grammy for *Broken Lady*. To date he's secured over 40 hit singles. Gatlin works in the company of his brothers, Steve & Rudy, billed in concert and on record as the Larry Gatlin & The Gatlin Brothers. The band have been members of the Grand Ole Opry since 1976. (Tony Byworth)

ALL THE GOLD IN CALIFORNIA.
Tracks: All the gold in California / How much is a man supposed to take.
■ 7" . . . . CBS 8247
CBS / Mar '80.

ANYTHING BUT LEAVIN'.
Tracks: Anything but leavin' / Kiss it all goodbye.
■ 7" . . . . MNT 6217
Monument / Mar '78.

BROKEN LADY.
Tracks: Broken lady / Heart.
■ 7" . . . . MNT 5142
Monument / Sep '78.

BROKEN LADY.
Tracks: Broken lady / Trying to matter / Odetotheroad / Maggie Lou's massage parlour blues / He's a star / Silence of the mornin' / Dealt a losin' hand / Fagan's Chapel / Heart is quicker than the eye, The / Statues without hearts.
■ LP . . . . MNT 82004
CBS / '78 / Sony.

DELTA DIRT.
Tracks: Delta dirt / Those also love.
■ 7" . . . . MNT 3487
Monument / Aug '75.

GREATEST HITS: GATLIN BROTHERS.
Tracks: Not Advised.
MC . . . . SPC 8576
Spot / Apr '86.

GREATEST HITS: LARRY GATLIN.
Tracks: Broken lady / Night time magic / Sweet Becky Walker / I just wish you were someone I love / Delta duet / I don't wanna cry / Do it again tonight / Bigger they are, harder they fall / Statues without hearts / Heart / Love is just a game.
■ LP . . . . MNT 83665
Monument / Oct '79.
■ LP . . . . CBS 32129
CBS / May '82.

HELP YOURSELF (Gatlin, Larry & The Gatlin Brothers Band).
Tracks: Take me to your lovin' place / It don't get no better than this / Must be all the same to you / Until she said goodbye / I still don't love you anymore / Help yourself to me / Wind is bound to change / Straight to my heart / Daytime heroes / Songwriter's trilogy.
LP . . . . CBS 84730
MC 40 84730
CBS / Jan '81 / Sony.

LARRY GATLIN (I love country).
Tracks: All the gold in California / Denver / Houston / Indian Summer / Sure feels like love / Midnight choir / We're number one / Nothing but your love matters / Almost called her baby.
■ MC 4504274
CBS / Mar '87.
■ LP 4504271
CBS / Mar '87.

LARRY GATLIN AND THE GATLIN BROTHERS.
Tracks: Not Advised.
CD . . . . UVLD 78003
LP . . . . UVL 78003
MCA (Import) / Nov '89 / Pinnacle / Silver Sounds (CD).

LOVE IS JUST A GAME.
Tracks: Love is just a game / Tomorrow / Anything but leavin' / If practice makes perfect / Everytime a plane flies over our house / I wish you were someone I love / Kiss it all goodbye / I don't wanna cry / It's love at last / Steps / Alleluia.
LP . . . . MNT 82382

■ DELETED

■ MC . . . . MNT 4082382
CBS / '78 / Sony.

NIGHT TIME MAGIC.
Tracks: Night time magic / It's love at last.
■ 7" . . . . MNT 6921
Monument / Jan '79.

OH BROTHER.
Tracks: Do it again tonight / I've done enough dyin' today / L.A., you're a killer / I've got you / Standin' by me / Night time magic / You happened to me / Nothin' you could do / Cold day in hell / Everything I know about cheatin'.
LP. MNT 82984
■ MC . . . . MNT 4082984
CBS / '78 / Sony.

PURE 'N' SIMPLE (Gatlin, Larry/Gatlin Bros. Band/Roy Orbison/Barry Gibb).
Tracks: Not Advised.
CD . . . . UVLD 42277
LP. UVL 42277
MC . . . . UVLC 42277
MCA / Jun '89 / BMG.

SMILE (Gatlin, Larry & The Gatlin Brothers).
Tracks: Runaway go home / One on one / Say / I saved your place / Everytime freedom changes hands / Can't stay away from her fire / Get me into this love, Lord. / I'd throw it all away / Nothing but your love matters / Indian Summer.
LP. CBS 26621
■ MC 40 26621
CBS / Jan '86.

STRAIGHT AHEAD (Gatlin, Larry & The Gatlin Brothers Band).
Tracks: All the gold in California / Piece by piece / Way I did before / Can't cry anymore / Gypsy flower child / We're number one / Taking somebody with me when I fall / How much is man supposed to take / Hold me closer / Midnight choir.
LP. CBS 84057
MC 40 84057
CBS / Jan '80 / Sony.

SURE FEELS LIKE LOVE (Gatlin, Larry/Gatlin Bros. Band/Roy Orbison/Barry Gibb).
Tracks: Sure feels like love / Almost called her baby / Anything but leavin' / What a wonderful way to die / Easy on the eye / Luau / Only been wounded / Whole wide world stood still / Somethin' like each other's arms / Home is where the healin' is.
■ LP. CBS 85982
CBS / Dec '82.

Gayle, Crystal

Born Brenda Gail Webb, on 9.1.1951 in Paintsville, Kentucky younger sister of Loretta Lynn, who gave Brenda her stage name. This was taken from a shop sign (Krystal's) which was the name of a Nashville fast food chain. Crystal started touring when only 16, becoming part of the Loretta Lynn roadshow. Began persuing a solo career on the Decca label, making her chart debut in 1970, her single *(I've cried) the blues right out of my eyes* rising to top 30 slot. Real success soon followed after Crystal's signing to United Artists in 1974, where for the next five years, she was to enjoy her most successful chart run, along with many awards coming her way. She has proved a most popular visitor to the UK, appearing on TV and live, headlining the Wembley festival in 1979 and 1991. Chart toppers for the exceptionally long-haired beauty (her black hair eventually reaching floor level) were to feature such blockbusters as 1977's *Don't it make my brown eyes blue* (also her best hot 100 placing - peaking at No 2 and being a Grammy winner), and 1978's *Talking in your sleep* , guaranteeing her world - wide fame. Others to reach the mark include in 1976 debut affair *I'll get over you* and the 1978 tracks *Ready for the times to get better* and *Why have you left the one you left me for* . That year also saw her winning the ACM and CMA's female vocalist of the year award. Coming to Columbia in 1979 (the same year which saw her become the first country act to perform in China), Gayle kept her roll going. By this time her music had taken on a even stronger pop feel (unlike sister Loretta, Crystal had never considered herself primarily as a country act - more M.O.R. country based), her bluesy tones topping the charts twice in 1980 with *It's like you never said goodbye* and *If you ever change your mind* . She enjoyed a short association with the smaller Elektra label in 1982, having a No 1 duet success with Eddie Rabbitt on *You and I* . Gayle followed this with another solo No 1, her version of Rodney Crowell's much acclaimed and well covered *Til I gain control again* being the first of four successive chart topper for her. Now working under the Warner Brothers umbrella (who had taken over Elektra) she reeled off *Our love is on the faultline* and *What about you* that year. Crystal's Vegas - styled act stood firm throughout the eighties before making way for the new country traditional movement. Songs to garner her more top slot positions were to include *The sound of goodbye* , and *Turning away* (1983 and 1984), while in 1986 she revisited the No 1 slot twice with Johnnie Ray's 1951 pop hit *Cry* and the album title track *Straight to the heart* doing the business, these subsequent cuts complementing a No 1 duet *Making up for lost time* (*The Dallas lovers song*) from the Dallas TV soap series theme in 1985 - with country singer & TV actor Gary Morris. Morris and Gayle also made a M.O.R. album together, from which were three chart singles, including *Another world* (another TV theme song) , which made country's top five in 1987. With Tom Waits she also wrote the soundtrack for Francis Ford Coppola's acclaimed movie *One from the heart* . In 1990 Gayle made another label change - returning to Capitol Liberty where she was to record another two albums with her former producer, the influential Allen Reynolds guiding her through *Ain't gonna worry* , spawning minor hit single *Never ever song of love* . Showing more country roots was to be the follow up album *Three good reasons* . Whilst the hit cupboard was bare, Crystal has no need to worry. With her Crystal Store gift stores, many charitable obligations and a family along with 100 odd shows a year, she's still got a busy schedule. She's still recording with irish owned label Ritz putting out her album *Best always* with covers of old country standards *Break my mind* , *Crazy* and *I fall to pieces* alongside remakes of Crystal's hits making up the 1993 affair. The album was released to complement her first full UK tour in 15 years. (Maurice Hope)

20 LOVE SONGS.
Tracks: Hello I love you / Cry me a river / Dreaming my dreams with you / Someday soon / I'll do it all over again / I wanna come back to you / Somebody loves you / It's alright with me / Coming closer / Don't it make my brown eyes blue? / When I dream / I'll get over you / Heart mender / Funny / I still miss someone / Talking in your sleep / Right in the palm of your hand / Beyond you / Going down is slow / Woman's heart, (is a handy place to be) (CD only.).
■ LP. LBR 1044
Liberty / Apr '82.
MC . . . . TCMFP 4156294
MFP / Sep '83 / EMI.
■ LP. MFP 4156291
MFP / Sep '83.
CD . . . . CDMFP 5629
MFP / Apr '91 / EMI.

6 TRACK HITS.
Tracks: If you ever change your mind / Blue side, The / Ain't no sunshine / Lovin' in these troubled times / Dancing the night away / I just can't leave your love alone.
EP. 7SR 5048
MC 7SC 5048
Scoop 33 / Aug '84.

AIN'T GONNA WORRY.
Tracks: Everybody's reaching out for someone / It ain't gonna worry my mind / Just an old love / Just like the blues / Whenever it comes to you / Never ending song of love / Once in a very blue moon / More than love / What he's doing now / Faithless love.
■ CD C2 94301
Capitol / Sep '90.
■ MC C4 94301
Capitol / Sep '90.

ALWAYS.
Tracks: Always.
CD Single . . . . RITZCD 259
MC Single . . . . RITZC 259
Ritz / May '93 / Pinnacle / Midland Records.

BABY WHAT ABOUT YOU.
Tracks: Baby what about you / Till I gain control again.
12" . . . . E 9880T
7" . . . . E 9880
Elektra / Apr '83 / WEA.

BEST ALWAYS.
Tracks: Ready for the times to get better / Crazy / For the good times / Silver threads and golden needles / When I dream / Talkin' in your sleep / Oh Lonesome me / I fall to pieces / Beyond you / Don't it make my brown eyes blue / Break my mind.
CD . . . . RITZRCD 530
MC . . . . RITZRC 530
Ritz / Jun '93 / Pinnacle / Midland Records.

BEST OF CRYSTAL GAYLE.
Tracks: Cry / Turning away / Baby what about you / Straight to the heart / Till I gain control again / Only love can save me now / Long and lasting love, A / Our love is on the faultline / I don't wanna lose your love / Sound of goodbye, The.
LP. K 925622 1
■ MC . . . . K 925622 4
WEA / Oct '87.
■ CD 925622 2
WEA / Jul '88.

BLUE SIDE.
Tracks: Blue side / Little bit of the rain.
■ 7" . . . . CBS 8076
CBS / Jan '80.

CAGE THE SONGBIRD.
Tracks: Sound of goodbye, The / I don't wanna lose your love / Me against the night / Cage the songbird / Turning away / Come back / Victim of a fool / You made a fool of me / On our way to love / Take me home.
■ LP. 923958 1
WEA / Oct '83.
■ MC 923958 4
WEA / Oct '83.

CLASSIC CRYSTAL.
Tracks: Somebody loves you / Don't it make my brown eyes blue / Ready for the times to get better / You never miss a real good thing (until he says / When I dream / I'll do it all over again / I'll get over you / Wrong road again / Talking in your sleep / Why have you left the one you left me for.
■ CD . . . . CDP 746 549 2
EMI / Mar '87.

COLLECTION: CRYSTAL GAYLE (CBS).
Tracks: Half the way / Ready for the times to get better / Other side of me, The / Hollywood / Blues side, The / Crying in the rain / Why have you left the one you left me for? / Livin' in these troubled times / Don't go, my love / Don't it make my brown eyes blue / Talking in your sleep / Woman in me, The / If you ever change your mind / Keepin' power / Same old story, same old song / Love, crazy love / Miss the Mississippi and you / Dancing the night away / Too many lovers / What a little moonlight can do.
LP. CBS 25169
MC 40 25169
CBS / Dec '82 / Sony.

COLLECTION: CRYSTAL GAYLE (KNIGHT).
Tracks: Not Advised.
CD . . . . KNCD 13052
■ MC . . . . KNMC 13052
Knight / Apr '90.

COUNTRY GIRL.
Tracks: Why have you left the one you left me for? / Wrong road again / When I dream / They come out at night / Wayward wind / You never miss a real good thing ('til he says goodbye) / Forgettin' 'bout you / I'll do it all over again / Someday soon / Ready for the times to get better / I still miss someone / Sweet baby on my mind / Somebody loves you / We should be together / River road / This is my year for Mexico.
MC . . . . TCMFP 5693
MC . . . . MFP 41 5693 4
MFP / Jan '85 / EMI.
■ LP. MFP 41 5693 1
MFP / Jan '85.
CD . . . . CDMFP 6037
MFP / Nov '88 / EMI.

COUNTRY STORE: CRYSTAL GAYLE VOL.2.
Tracks: Keepin' power / Same old story, same old song / Crying in the rain / It's like we never said goodbye / Livin' in these troubled times / Blue side, The / Other side of me, The / Too many lovers / What a little moonlight can do / Love crazy love / Half the way / You never gave up on me / Lean on me / Take it easy / Miss the Mississippi and you / Woman in me, The / If you ever change your mind.
CD . . . . CDCST 40
MC . . . . CSTK 40
Country Store / '88 / BMG.
■ LP. CST 40
Country Store / '88.

CRY.
Tracks: Crazy in the heart / Cry.
■ 7" . . . . W 8689
WEA / Nov '86.

CRYSTAL.
Tracks: I'll do it all over again / On my soul / Ready for the times to get better / Come home Daddy / One more time / You never miss a real good thing / Right in the palm of your hand / Forgettin' 'bout you / Let's do it right / I'm not so far away.
■ LP. GO 2009
Liberty / May '81.

CRYSTAL CHRISTMAS.
Tracks: White Christmas / Oh holy night / Winter wonderland / I'll be home for Christmas / Have yourself a merry little christmas / Rudolph the red nosed reindeer / Little drummer boy / Christmas songs, The / Jingle bells / Silver bells / Silent night.
■ LP. 925508 1
WEA / Nov '86.

CRYSTAL GAYLE.
Tracks: Wrong road again / Woman's heart / Hands / When I dream / Beyond you / Loving you so long now / Gonna lay me down beside my memories / You / This is my year for Mexico / Counterfeit love.
■ LP. LBR 1014
United Artists / Jun '80.

CRYSTAL GAYLE (CAPITOL).
Tracks: Not Advised.
MC 4XL 9019
Capitol (Specials) / Dec '88.

CRYSTAL GAYLE IN CONCERT.
Tracks: Don't it make my brown eyes blue / Talkin' in your sleep.
VHS. VC 4003
Video Collection / May '87 / Gold & Sons / Video Collection / Terry Blood Dist.
VHS. MV 048
Mastervision / Nov '87 / Mastervision Dist.
VHS. MC 2011
Music Club Video / Apr '89 / Video Collection / Gold & Sons / Terry Blood Dist.

■ DELETED

VHS. . . . . .ODY 703
Odyssey Video / Sep '91 / Pinnacle.

DON'T IT MAKE MY BROWN EYES BLUE?.
Tracks: Don't it make my brown eyes blue / All I wanna do in life.
7" . . . . UP 36307
United Artists / Oct '77 / EMI.

DON'T IT MAKE MY BROWN EYES BLUE?.
Tracks: Don't it make my brown eyes blue? / Talking in your sleep.
■ 7" G45 18
EMI Golden 45's / May '84.

EMI COUNTRY MASTERS.
Tracks: Somebody loves you / High time / I'll get over you / Woman's heart (Is a handy place to be), A / Restless / You / Wrong road again / Beyond you / Hands / Counterfeit love (I know you've got it) / This is my year for Mexico / Dreaming my dreams with you / One more time (Karneval) / Oh my soul / Come home Daddy / You never miss a real good thing (Til he says goodbye) / I'll do it all over again / It's alright with me / Going down slow / Make a dream come true / Funny / We must believe in magic / Cry me a river / Wayward wind / Why have you left the one you left me for / Don't it make my brown eyes blue / Ready for the times to get better / Someday soon / I still miss someone / Talking in your sleep / Green door / Paintin' this old town blue / All I wanna do in life / When I dream / Time will prove I'm right / Your kisses will / Your old cold shoulder / Too deep for tears / We should be together / River road / I wanna come back to you / Heart mender / Everybody's reaching out for someone / Just an old love / Never ending song of love / Once in a very blue moon / Trouble with me (Is you) / Love to, can't do / 99% Of the time / Faithless love.
CD . . . . CDEM 1499
MC . . . . TCEM 1499
EMI / May '93 / EMI.

EVERYTHING I OWN.
Tracks: Everything I own / Easier said than done.
7" . . . . E 9909
Elektra / Dec '82 / WEA.
12" . . . . E 9909T
Elektra / Jan '83 / WEA.

FAVOURITES.
Tracks: Don't treat me like a stranger / I wanna come back to you / Right in the palm of your hand / You / Wayward wind / River Road / Heart mender / All I wanna do in life / Come home daddy / What I've been needing.
■ CD . . . . CDP 746 582 2
EMI-America / Jan '88.

HALF THE WAY.
Tracks: Half the way / Room for one more.
■ 7" . . . . CBS 7859
CBS / Sep '79.
■ 7" . . . . .A 1024
CBS / Mar '81.

HOLLYWOOD/TENNESSEE.
Tracks: Keepin' power / Woman in me / Ain't no sunshine / You never gave up on me / Hollywood / Lovin' in these troubled times / Love crazy love / Lean on me / Crying in the rain / Tennessee.
■ LP. . . . . CBS 85171
CBS / Nov '81.

I LOVE COUNTRY.
Tracks: Not Advised.
■ LP. 4510001
CBS / '88.

I'VE CRIED THE BLUE RIGHT OUT OF MY EYES.
Tracks: Not Advised.
■ LP. . . . . MFP 50398
MFP / Dec '79.

I'VE CRIED THE BLUES RIGHT OUT OF MY EYES.
Tracks: I've cried (The blues right out of my eyes) / Sparklin' look of love / Too far / Everybody ouhta cry / Mama it's different this time / Touching me again / Clock on the wall / Show me how / M.R.S. Degree / I hope you're havin' a better time than me.
LP. . . . . CDL 8059
MCA / '78 / BMG.

IF YOU EVER CHANGE YOUR MIND.
Tracks: If you ever change your mind / I just can't leave your love alone.
■ 7" . . . . CBS 9058
CBS / Oct '80.

IN CONCERT.
Tracks: Not Advised.
VHS. . . . . MMGV 059
Magnum / Jul '93 / Hot Shot / Swift / Cadillac Music / Arabesque Ltd. / Roots Records.

LIVIN' IN THESE TROUBLED TIMES.
Tracks: Livin' in these troubled times / Tennessee.
■ 7" . . . . .A 1680
CBS / Feb '82.

LOVE SONGS: CRYSTAL GAYLE.
Tracks: Other side of me, The / I just can't leave your love alone / What a little moonlight can do / It's like we never said goodbye / You've almost got me believin' / Help yourselves to each other / If you ever change your mind / Miss the Mississippi and you / Don't go, my love / Too many lovers / Half the way / Blue side, The.
LP. . . . . SHM 3125
■ MC . . . . HSC 3125
Hallmark / Apr '83.
CD . . . . PWKS 521
Pickwick / '88 / Pickwick Records.

LOVE, CRAZY LOVE.
Tracks: Love, crazy love / Tennessee.
■ 7" . . . . .A 1681
CBS / Oct '81.

MISS THE MISSISSIPPI.
Tracks: Half the way / Other side for one more,The / Room for one more, honey / Don't go my love / Dancing the night away / It's like we never said goodbye / Blue side, The / Little bit of rain, A / Danger zone / Miss the Mississippi and you.
■ LP. . . . . CBS 86102
CBS / Nov '79.
LP. . . . . CBS 32767
■ MC 40 32767
CBS / Mar '86.

MOST BEAUTIFUL SONGS OF CRYSTAL GALE, THE.
Tracks: Not Advised.
LP. 022 58165
MC 222 58165
MFP (Holland) / Jan '86 / Pinnacle.

NOBODY WANTS TO BE ALONE.
Tracks: Long and lasting love, A / Tonight, tonight / Nobody wants to be alone / Love does that to fools / Coming to the dance / You were there for me / Touch and go / Someone like you / New way to say I love you, A / God bless the child.
■ MC 925154 4
WEA / May '85 / WEA.
■ LP. 925154 1
WEA / May '85.

NOBODY'S ANGEL.
Tracks: Nobody's angel / Prove me wrong / Tennessee nights / When love is new / Hopeless romantic / Love found me / Heat / After the best / Love may find out.
■ CD 925706 2
WEA / Aug '88 / WEA.
LP. 925706 1
■ MC 925706 4
WEA / Aug '88.

READY FOR THE TIMES TO GET BETTER.
Tracks: Ready for the times to get better / Beyond you.
■ 7" . . . . UP 36362
United Artists / Mar '78.

SINGLES ALBUM: CRYSTAL GAYLE.
Tracks: Somebody loves you / Wrong road again / I'll get over you / High time / Ready for the times to get better / You never miss a real good thing (till he says goodbye) / River road / Don't it make my brown eyes blue / When I dream / Talking in your sleep / Why have you left the one you left me for / All I wanna do in life / We should be together / Too deep for tears.
LP. . . . . ATAK 1
MC . . . . TCATAK 1
Liberty / Jan '80 / EMI.
MC . . . . TCK 30287
United Artists / Jan '80 / EMI.
■ LP. . . . . UAG 30287
United Artists / Jan '80.
CD . . . . CZ 204
Liberty / Jul '89 / EMI.

SOMEBODY LOVES YOU.
Tracks: Before I'm fool enough / I'll get over you / Sweet baby on my mind / I want to lose me in you / High time / Wrong road again / Somebody loves you / What you've done for me / Coming closer / Dreaming my dreams with you / What I've been needin' / They come out at night.
■ LP. . . . . .GO 2023
Liberty / Jun '81.

STRAIGHT TO THE HEART.
Tracks: Straight to the heart / Cry / Take this heart / Little bit closer, A / Do I have to say goodbye / Deep down / Crazy in the heart / Only love can save me now / Nobody should have to love this way / Lonely girl.
■ MC 925405 1
WEA / Oct '86 / WEA.
■ CD 925405 2
WEA / Mar '87 / WEA.

TALKING IN YOUR SLEEP.
Tracks: Don't it make my brown eyes blue / All I wanna do in life / Paintin' this old town blue / I want to lose me in you / Your old cold shoulder / Green door / When I dream / It's alright with me / Before I'm fool enough / Gonna lay me down beside my memories / Your kisses will / One more time / Lay back lover / You / Let's do it right / Restless / Too deep for tears / Too good to throw away / Loving you so long now / Talking in your sleep.
■ LP. . . . . EMS 1289
EMI / Apr '88.
■ MC . . . . TCEMS 1289
EMI / Apr '88.

TALKING IN YOUR SLEEP.
Tracks: Talking in your sleep.
7" . . . . UP 36422
United Artists / Jun '78 / EMI.

THESE DAYS.
Tracks: Too many lovers / If you ever change your mind / Ain't no love in the heart of the city / Same old story / Help yourselves to each other / Take it easy / I just can't leave your love alone / You've almost got me believin' / Lover man / What a little moonlight can do.
■ LP. . . . . CBS 84529
CBS / Nov '80.

TOO DEEP FOR TEARS.
Tracks: Too deep for tears / Your old cold shoulder.
■ 7" . . . . UP 607
United Artists / Feb '80.

TRUE LOVE.
Tracks: Our love is on the faultline / Deeper in the fire / Till I gain control again / Baby what about you? / You bring out the lover in me / Take me to the dance / True love / Everything I own / Let your feelings show / Easier said than done / He is beautiful to me.
MC . . . . E 02224
Elektra / Dec '82 / WEA.
■ LP. . . . . .E 0222
Elektra / Dec '82.

WE MUST BELIEVE IN MAGIC.
Tracks: Don't it make my brown eyes blue / I wanna come back to you / River road / It's alright with me / Going down slow / All I wanna do in life / Make a dream come true / Green door / We must believe in magic.
■ CD . . . . CDP 748 380 2
Capitol.
MC . . . . TCK 30108
United Artists / Aug '77 / EMI.
■ LP. . . . . UAG 30108
United Artists / Jan '78.
■ LP. . . . . .GO 2016
Liberty / Jun '81.

WE SHOULD BE TOGETHER.
Tracks: We should be together / Time will prove that I'm right.
■ LP. . . . . UAG 30256
United Artists / Nov '79.

WHEN I DREAM.
Tracks: When I dream / Someday soon.
■ 7" . . . . UP 36503
United Artists / '79.

WHEN I DREAM.
Tracks: Why have you left the one you left me for / Heart mender / Hello I love you / Talking in your sleep / Paintin' this old town blue / When I dream / Don't treat me like a stranger / Too good to through away / Cry me a river / Wayward wind / Someday soon / Still miss someone.
LP. . . . . UAG 30169
■ MC . . . . TCK 30169
United Artists / '78 / EMI.

WHY HAVE YOU LEFT THE ONE YOU LEFT ME FOR.
Tracks: Why have you left the one you left me for / Cry me a river.
■ 7" . . . . UP 36494
United Artists / Feb '79.

WOMAN IN ME, THE.
Tracks: Not Advised.
LP. . . . . .SHM 3166
■ MC . . . . HSC 3166
Hallmark / Mar '85.

YOU NEVER MISS A GOOD THING.
Tracks: You never miss a good thing / Forgettin' 'bout you.
■ 7" . . . . UP 36225
United Artists / Mar '77.

Gentry, Bobbie

This American singer, songwriter, guitarist and dancer was born in Chickasaw County, Mississippi of Portuguese descent. Her real name was Roberta Streeter but she was inspired to change her surname by the movie "Ruby Gentry". Having dabbled in music and acting during childhood, Bobbie studied music and philosophy in Los Angeles before taking up a job as a Las Vegas nightclub dancer. Suddenly, in August 1967, the 23-year-old Gentry stormed into the US Top 40 - two weeks after entering that list, she was no. 1 with *Ode to Billy Joe* and stayed there for a further four weeks. This sombre folk/country single, which could hardly have been further removed from the music of Las Vegas, was stunning in the sparseness of its arrangement, the terseness of its melody and the moroseness of its message - Billy Joe MacAllister takes a suicide jump off the Tallahatchie Bridge, but the neighbours keep on living their lives as if nothing has happened. *Ode to Billy Joe* was Gentry's first record - her voice was accompanied by her own guitar, six violins and two cellos, and the song took barely 15 minutes of studio time to record. *Ode to Billy Joe* peaked at no. 13 in Britain, but she obtained a UK no. 1 two years later with Burt Bacharach and Hal David's *I'll never fall in love again*, a song taken from the Broadway musical *Promises Promises*. Soon afterwards, at the beginning of 1970, she duetted with Glen Campbell on a cover version of the Everly Brothers' classic

All I have to do is dream - this reached no. 3 in Britain and no. 27 in the States. She also reached no. 31 in the States with the self-penned *Fancy* and no. 40 in the UK with *Raindrops keep fallin' on my head*. After writing and recording *Ode to Billy Joe* and other songs such as *Mississippi delta* and *Chickasaw county child*, Bobbie Gentry was hailed as a great new singer-songwriter. But as the above history shows, she was quickly whisked away into the showbiz world of TV specials and MOR cover versions, her own songwriting skills being virtually abandoned. She had left her heart in Vegas not Chickasaw, a fact confirmed by her marriage to Las Vegas magnate Bill Hurrah. (Bob MacDonald).

BEST OF BOBBIE GENTRY.
Tracks: I'll never fall in love again / Mississippi delta / Raindrops keep falling on my head / Son of a preacher man.
LP. . . . . **048 CRY 81802**
EMI (Germany) / Aug '83.

BOBBIE GENTRY & GLEN CAMPBELL (Gentry, Bobbie & Glen Campbell).
Tracks: Not Advised.
■ **LP.** . . . . **ST 2928**
Capitol / Feb '70.

I'LL NEVER FALL IN LOVE AGAIN.
Tracks: I'll never fall in love again.
■ **7"** . . . . **CL 15606**
Capitol / Aug '69.

ODE TO BILLY JOE.
Tracks: Ode to Billy Joe.
■ **7"** . . . . **CL 15511**
Capitol / Sep '67.

RAINDROPS KEEP FALLIN' ON MY HEAD.
Tracks: Raindrops keep falling on my head.
■ **7"** . . . . **CL 15626**
Capitol / Dec '69.

TOUCH 'EM WITH LOVE.
Tracks: Not Advised.
■ **LP.** . . . . **EST 155**
Capitol / Oct '69.

Germino, Mark

CAUGHT IN THE ACT OF BEING OURSELVES.
Tracks: Caught in the act of being ourselves.
■ **12"** . . . . **PT 43020**
RCA / Aug '89.
■ **CD Single** . . . . **PD 43020**
RCA / Aug '89.
■ **7"** . . . . **PB 49369**
RCA / Jul '89.

CAUGHT IN THE ACT OF BEING OURSELVES.
Tracks: From the Brooklyn Bridge / Third coast rag / Propaganda requiem in A minor / Rex Bob Lowenstein / Intermission at the Belcourt Twin / Backstreet Mozart / Teasin' me do / Diamonds are out, rubies are in / Caught in the act of being ourselves.
■ **MC** . . . . **PK 86608**
RCA / Apr '89.
■ **CD** . . . . **PD 86608**
RCA / Jan '89.
LP. . . . . **PL 86608**
RCA / Nov '90 / BMG.

LONDON MOON AND BARNYARD REMEDIES.
Tracks: Political / Oriental drag / Barnyard (rhapsody in brown) / God ain't no stained glass window / Sally Baker's (low tar) dream / Broken man's lament / We got away / Immigrant shuffle.
CD . . . . **PD 85852**
LP. . . . . **PL 85852**
■ **MC** . . . . **PK 85852**
RCA / Jan '87.
CD . . . . **ND 90446**
LP. . . . . **NL 90446**
MC . . . . **NK 90446**
RCA / Feb '90 / BMG.

POLITICAL.
Tracks: Political / Oriental drag / Broken mans' lament (Extra track on 12" version only).
12" . . . . **PT 41108**
■ **7"** . . . . **PB 41107**
RCA / Mar '87.

RADARTOWN (Germino, Mark & The Sluggers).
Tracks: Radartown / Let freedom ring (Vol. 4, 5, and 6) / Leroy and Bo's totalitarian showdown / Unionville / Economics (of the rat and snake) / She's a mystery / Pandora's boxcar blues / Exalted rose / Burning the firehouse down / Serenade of Red Cross / Rex Bob Lowenstein.
CD . . . . **PD 90550**
RCA / Jun '91 / BMG.
■ **MC** . . . . **PK 90550**
RCA / Jun '91.

REX ROB LOWENSTEIN.
Tracks: Rex Rob Lowenstein / Teasing we do.
■ **7"** . . . . **PB 42769**
RCA / Apr '89.
■ **12"** . . . . **PT 42770**
RCA / May '89.
■ **7"** . . . . **PB 49165**
RCA / Sep '91.

Gibb, Steve

DON'T BLAME IT ON LOVE.
Tracks: Don't blame it on love / She believes in me.
■ **7"** . . . . **EPC 7781**
Epic / Aug '79.

SHE BELIEVES IN ME.
Tracks: She believes in me / Cynthia.
■ **7"** . . . . **EPC 7287**
Epic / Apr '79.

Gibbs, Terri

I'M A LADY.
Tracks: Not Advised.
■ **LP.** . . . . **MCF 3132**
MCA / Apr '82.

SOMEBODY'S KNOCKIN'.
Tracks: Somebody's knockin' / Magic time.
■ **7"** . . . . **MCA 685**
MCA / Mar '81.

TURN AROUND.
Tracks: Not Advised.
LP. . . . . **CAA R 0014**
■ **MC** . . . . **CAA C 0014**
Power.

Gibson, Don

Singer - songwriter/guitarist born Donald Eugene Gibson on 3.4.1928 in Shelby, North Carolina. After working on Knoxville's WNOX Barn Dance radio series upon leaving school Gibson in 1956, made country's top ten - his own *Sweet dreams* on MGM setting his career in motion. Signed to Acuff-Rose as a writer, Roy Orbison was to cover many of his songs. Like the Big 'O' he too has enjoyed a lasting cross-over appeal. Gibson's blues tones, reflecting much about his own state of mind/troubles, were to become his hallmark. In an attempt to overcome his problem during the sixties he became addicted to tranquillisers. His career, as fruitful as it's been, has undoubtedly suffered - well illustrated by the fact he never topped the charts during the entire 60's. Fame came early for the RCA hitmaker with *Oh lonesome me* and *Blue blue day* had both making No.1 in 1958, alongside other top ten 50's hits *I can't stop lovin' you* (coincidently written by Gibson on the very same day as *Oh lonesome me* , which itself alone has picked up no fewer than four million radio plays on US radio), *Look who's blue* , *Who cares* and *Don't tell me your troubles* . Even then he did amass three runners-up hits with *Just one time* (1960) and a year later *Sea of heartbreak* and *Lonesome number one* , backed with *I can mend your broken heart* and an early Mickey Newbury song *Funny, familiar, forgotten feelings* (1966). Signed with Wesley Rose's Hickory label in 1969, going to No. 1 with *Woman (sensuous woman)* in 1972, and later hits were to include *Touch the morning* , *One day at a time* and *Bring back your love to me* . On the songwriting front, apart from doing most of his own, he also supplied such classics as *(I'd be) A legend in my time)* (1974 No.1 for Ronnie Milsap), *Sweet dreams* (Patsy Cline, Roy Orbison and Ray Charles respective pop hits), *Too soon to know* and *I can't stop loving you* , to name but a few. Gibson, as with many in country music, especially during the 60's/70's , did soem duet recordings, pairing with Dottie West and having hits with *Rings of gold* , *There's a story (Goin' round)* Whilst on RCA and Sue Thompson at Hickory (1971-1976) clocking up a tidy sum of mid-table chart singles. The end of the 70's found Gibson having brief stays at MCA and then Warner Bros without much success. (Maurice Hope)

15 GREAT HITS.
Tracks: Not Advised.
LP. . . . . **CL 42838**
MC . . . . **CK 42838**
RCA (Germany) / Oct '84 / BMG.

20 OF THE BEST: DON GIBSON.
Tracks: Oh lonesome me / I can't stop loving you / Blue blue day / Gonna give myself a party / Look who's blue / Who cared for me / Lonesome old house / Don't tell me your troubles / Just one time / Far far away / Sweet dreams / (I'd be a) legend in my own time / What about me / Sea of heartbreak / Lonesome number one / I can mend your broken heart / Watch you're going / Yes I'm hurting / I think it's best to forget me / Same old trouble, The.
LP. . . . . **INTS 5184**
RCA International / Aug '82 / BMG.
LP. . . . . **NL 89089**
RCA / Aug '82 / BMG.
MC . . . . **INTK 5184**
RCA International / Aug '82 / BMG.
■ **MC** . . . . **NK 89089**
RCA / Aug '82.

ALL MY LOVE.
Tracks: All my love / No doubt about it.
■ **7"** . . . . **RCA 1626**
RCA / Jan '70 / BMG.

ASHES OF LOVE.
Tracks: Ashes of love / Good morning, dear.
■ **7"** . . . . **RCA 1680**
RCA / Sep '70 / BMG.

COLLECTION: DON GIBSON.
Tracks: Oh lonesome me / Snap your fingers / Just one time / Take these chains from my heart / Sweet dreams / Release me / Blue blue day / Funny, familiar forgotten feelings / Kaw-liga / There goes my everything / Touch the morning / Too soon to know / Cold cold heart / I'm all wrapped up in you / You've still got a place in my heart / Sweet sensuous sensation / Why you been gone so long / I can't stop loving you / Lonesome number one / You win again / Mansion on the hill / (I'd be a) legend in my own time / Yesterday just passed my way again / Fan the flame feed the fire.
■ **Double LP** . . . . **CCSLP 158**
Castle Collector Series / Jul '87.
■ **MC** . . . . **CCSMC 158**
Castle Collector Series / Jul '87.
CD . . . . **CCSCD 158**
Castle Collector Series / Feb '93 / BMG / Pinnacle / Castle Communications.

COUNTRY NUMBER ONE.
Tracks: Not Advised.
MC . . . . **WW 4 5079**
Warwick / Feb '80 / Sony / Henry Hadaway Organisation / Multiple Sound Distributors.

DON GIBSON & LOS INDIOS TABAJARAS (Gibson, Don & Los Indios Tabajaras).
Tracks: I can't tell my heart that / Cryin' heart blues / My adobe hacienda / Address unknown / That's how it goes / When will this end / So how come (no one loves me) / What about me / I couldn't care less / Same old trouble, The / Hurting inside / Fireball mail / Above and beyond / Camptown races.
LP. . . . . **BFX 15193**
Bear Family / Aug '86 / Rollercoaster Records / Swift / Direct Distribution.

DON GIBSON THE SINGER, THE SONGWRITER (1949-1960).
Tracks: I lost my love / Why am I so lonely? / Automatic mamma / Cloudy skies / I love no one but you / Carolina breakdown / Roses are red / Wiggle wag / Dark future / Just let me love you / Blue million tears, A / Red lips, white lies and blue hours / Sample kisses / No shoulder to cry on / Let me stay in your arms / We're stepping out tonight / Waitin' down the road / Walkin' in the moonlight / I just love the way you tell a lie / You cast me out (forevermore) / Symptoms of love / Selfish with your kisses / Ice cold heart / Many times I've waited / Road of life alone, The / Run boy / Sweet dreams / I must forget you / Taller than trees / Satisfied / Wait for the light to shine / Cannan's land / (Prayer is the key to heaven)faith unlocks the door / Evening prayer / Lord I'm coming home / Climbing up the mountain / Where no one stands alone / Known only to him / My God is real / That lonesome valley / Who cares (for me) / When will this ever end / Sweet sweet girl / Stranger to me, A / Won't cha come bact to me / Stranger to me, A (2) / As much / Who cares (for me) (2) / I wish it had been a dream / Ages and ages ago / Even tho' / Didn't work out did it? / It's my way / Almost / Do you think / Foggy river / Midnight / Lonesome old house / Ah-ha / It happens everytime / I ain't gonna waste my time / I ain't a-studyin' you baby / I'm gonna fool everybody / I believed in you / What a fool I was for you / You're the only one for me / I love you still / Everything turns out for the best / I can't leave / Sittin' here cryin' / Too soon to know / Pretty rainbow / Blue blue day / Tell it like it is / Oh lonesome me / I can't stop loving you / It has to be / Give myself a party / Look who's blue / Bad bad day / Take me as I am / Heartbreak Avenue / We could / If you don't know it / Blues in my heart / Give myself a party (2) / Don't tell me your troubles / I couldn't care less / Don't tell me your troubles (2) / Heartbreak Avenue (2) / Big hearted me / Maybe tomorrow / Everybody but me / I'm movin' on / Just one time / I may never get to heaven / Lonely Street / On the banks of the Old Ponchartrain / Why don't you love me / If I can stay away / Never love again / Streets of Laredo, The / My love for you / My hands are tied / It only hurts for a little while / (I'd be) a legend in my time / Far far away / Foolish me / My tears don't show / World is waiting for the sunrise, The / What about me / Next voice you hear, The / Hurtin' inside / Time hurts (as well as it heals) / What's the reason I'm not pleasing you / Sweet dreams (2) / Same street, The.
CD Set . . . . **BCD 15475**
Bear Family / Jan '92 / Rollercoaster Records / Swift / Direct Distribution.

EARLY DAYS, THE.
Tracks: Automatic mama / Why am I so lonely / I lost my love / Cloudy skies / Dark future / Blue miliion tears, A / Just let me love you / Roses are red / Red lips white lies and blue hours / I love no one but you / Caroline breakdown / Wigglewag.
LP. . . . . **BFX 15196**
Bear Family / Aug '86 / Rollercoaster Records / Swift / Direct Distribution.

■ DELETED

FAMOUS COUNTRY MUSIC MAKERS.
Tracks: Oh lonesome me / I can't stop loving you / Blue blue day / Give myself a party / Look who's blue / Who cares (for me) / Lonesome old house / Don't tell me your troubles / I'm movin' Juston / One time / Far, far away / Sweet dreams / What about me / Sea of heartbreak / Lonesome number one / I can mend your broken heart / Head over heels in love with you / Anything new gets old (except my love for you) / Again / Watch where you're going / Born loser / (Yes) I'm hurting / Funny familiar, forgotten feelings / All my love / It's a long long way to Georgia / Solitary / I will always / There's a story (goin 'round).
■ **Double LP** . . . . **PL 42002**
RCA / '79.

GOD WALKS THESE HILLS.
Tracks: God walks these hills with me / You dont' knock / If I can help somebody / Do you know my Jesus / Then I met the master / Old ship of Zion / Hide me, rock of ages / Where else would I want to be / He's everywhere / When they ring the golden bells for you and me / Be ready / I'd rather have Jesus.
■ **LP** . . . . **RD 7641**
RCA / Mar '71 / BMG.

I WROTE A SONG.
Tracks: I can't stop loving you / Don't tell me your troubles / Legend in my time, A / Blue, blue day / Oh such a stranger / Love has come my way / Oh, lonesome me / Lonesome number one / Just one time / After the heartache / Give myself a party / Anything new gets old.
■ **LP** . . . . **SF 7576**
RCA / Feb '70 / BMG.

KING OF COUNTRY SOUL, THE.
Tracks: Ashes of love / Faded love / They'll never taker her love from me / Headin' down the wrong highway / Maiden's prayer / Thing called sadness, A / What now my love / You've still got a place in my heart / Everlovin' never, changing mind / Good morning dear / I just said goodbye to my dreams / What locks the door.
■ **LP** . . . . **RD 7985**
RCA / May '70 / BMG.

LEGEND IN HIS OWN TIME.
Tracks: Give myself a party / I can't stop loving you / Oh lonesome me / I let her get lonely / Just one time / Don't tell me your troubles / I think it's best (to forget me) / Sea of heartbreak / Same old trouble, The / Lonesome number one / I can mend your broken heart / Blue dream / It's a sin / Baby we're really in love / Sweet dreams / Hurting inside / Far far away / World is waiting for the sunrise, The / What about me? / What's the reason I'm not pleasing you? / Big hearted me / (I'd be a) legend in my own time / Foolish me / My tears don't show / Next voice you hear, The / Again / Time hurts (as well as it heals) / Maybe tomorrow.
Double LP . . . . **CR 063**
■ **MC Set** . . . . **CRT 063**
Cambra / Apr '85.

LEGEND IN MY TIME, A.
Tracks: Sittin' here cryin' / Blue blue day / Oh lonesome me / I can't stop loving you / Look who's blue / If you don't know it / Bad bad day / Sweet sweet girl / Give myself a party / Who cares / Didn't work out did it / Lonesome old house / Don't tell me your troubles / I couldn't care less / Just one time / Legend in my time, A / Far far away / Sweet dreams / Sea of heartbreak / I sat back and let it happen / Lonesome number one / I can mend your broken heart / If you knew me / If you don't know the sorrow / Think of me / I'm crying inside.
CD . . . . **BCD 15401**
Bear Family / Nov '87 / Rollercoaster Records / Swift / Direct Distribution.

LONESOME NUMBER ONE.
Tracks: Lonesome number one.
■ **7"** . . . . **RCA 1272**
RCA / Feb '62.

MORE COUNTRY SOUL.
Tracks: Low and lonely / Someday you'll call my name / Funny familiar forgotten feelings / It's a long, long way to Georgia / Half a man / Someday / Forget me / She's looking good / I walk alone / You can't pick a rose in December / Don't rob another man's castle / I'm so lonesome I could cry.
■ **LP** . . . . **SF 8005**
RCA / Dec '70 / BMG.

OH HOW LOVE CHANGES (Gibson, Don & Sue Thompson).
Tracks: Oh how love changes / Sweet and tender times.
■ **7"** . . . . **HLE 10504**
London / Aug '75.

ROCKIN' ROLLIN' GIBSON VOL.1.
Tracks: Pretty rainbow (Previously unissued.) / Sittin' here cryin' / I love you still / I can't leave / Tell it like it is (1st recording) (Previously unissued.) / Oh lonesome me / Blue blue day / If you don't know it / Even tho' / Didn't work out, did it / Sea of heartbreak / Who cares? (Previously unissued.) / Sweet sweet girl (Previously unissued.) / Don't tell me your troubles (Previously unissued.) / Far far away / I sat back and let it happen (Previously unissued.).
LP . . . . **BFX 15089**
Bear Family / Sep '84 / Rollercoaster Records / Swift / Direct Distribution.

ROCKIN' ROLLIN' GIBSON VOL.2.
Tracks: Just one time / Lonesome old house / Who cares / Sweet sweet girl / Won't cha come back to me / I know the score (Previously unissued.) / Tell it like it is (2nd recording) (Previously unissued.) / Look who's blue / Don't tell me your troubles / Everybody but me / Cute little girls / Why don't you love me / Let's fall out of love (Previously unissued.) / Lonesome number one / I'm movin' on / Bad, bad day.
LP . . . . **BFX 15097**
Bear Family / Sep '84 / Rollercoaster Records / Swift / Direct Distribution.

SEA OF HEARTBREAK.
Tracks: Please help me, I'm falling (Hank Locklin) / Sea of heartbreak.
■ **7"** . . . . **RCA 1243**
RCA / Aug '61.

SINGER SONGWRITER 1961 - 1966.
Tracks: Sweet dreams / I think it's best (To forget me) / That's how it goes / Sea of heartbreak / No one will ever know / Born to lose / Beautiful dreamer / Camptown races / Fireball mail / Last letter, The / White silver sands / Driftwood on the river / Lonesome road / Above and beyond / I sat back and let it happen / I know the score / Same old trouble, the / So how come (no one loves me) / Lonesome number one / Let's fall out of love (Tonight) / I let her get lonely / I can mend your broken heart / For a little while / It makes no difference now / Settin' the woods on fire / Baby we're really in love / I love you so much it hurts / It's a sin / I'm sorry for you my friend / This cold war with you / Where is your heart tonight / Blue dream / How's the world treating you / May you never be alone / We live in two different worlds / Old ship of zion / Then I met the master / I'd rather have Jesus / Be ready / Can't see myself / For old time sake / It was worth it all / Head over heels in love with you / I can't stop loving you / (I'd be) A legend in my time / Give myself a party / Oh lonesome me / Don't tell me your troubles / Love has come my way / Blue blue days / Just one time / Oh such a stranger / After the heartache / Anything new gets old (Except my love for you) / God walks these hills / Do you know my Jesus / Hide me rock of ages / Where else would I want to be / If I can help somebody / He's everywhere / You don't knock / When they ring the golden bells / There she goes (Let her go) / If you knew me / If you don't know the sorrow / Mixed up love / There she goes / Think of me / Cause' I believe in you / Then I'll be free / (All for the sake of) A love that can't be / Waltz of regret / When your house is not a home / Watch where you're going / You're going away / Again / Too much hurt / Born loser, A / Wound time can't erase, A / Around the town / I'm crying inside / Dark as a dungeon / Right away / Lovin' lies / All the world is lonely now / Worried mind / There's a big wheel / Take these chains from my heart / Singing the blues / With your love on my mind / Adress unknown / My adobe hacienda / Lonely street / Cryin' heart blues / I can't tell my heart that / (Yes) I'm hurting / My whole world is hurt / You can't laugh (At a fool) / My tomorrows (They don't come easy) / Don't you ever get tired (Of hurting me) / Once a day / My friends are gonna be strangers / Vaya con dios / Just call me lonesome / With love on my mind / Stranger to me, A / Maria Elena / Blues in my mind / Making believe / Somebody loves you darlin' / I'd just be fool enough / Lost highway / Let's fall out of love / I thought I heard you calling my name / Don't touch me / How do you tell someone / Just out of reach / When I stop dreaming / Cute little girls.
CD Set . . . . **BCD 15664**
Bear Family / May '93 / Rollercoaster Records / Swift / Direct Distribution.

SINGS COUNTRY FAVOURITES.
Tracks: Green green grass of home / There goes my everything / Release me / I heard that lonesome whistle blow / Cold cold heart / Kaw-liga / She even woke me up to say goodbye / Sea of heartbreak / My elusive dreams / You win again / I love you because / Window shopping / (I'd be) a legend in my time / Too soon to know / Take these chains from my heart / Lonesome number one / Sweet dreams / I can't stop loving you / Oh, lonesome me / Funny, familiar, forgotten feelings.
CD . . . . **PWK 4049**
MC . . . . **PWKMC 4049**
Pickwick / Feb '91 / Pickwick Records.
LP . . . . **PWKS 4049**
Pickwick / Jun '91 / Pickwick Records.

STARTING ALL OVER AGAIN.
Tracks: Starting all over again / I'd rather die young.
■ **7"** . . . . **DJS 10848**
DJM / Mar '78.

SWEET SENSUOUS SENSATION.
Tracks: Sweet sensuous sensation / Stranger to me.
■ **7"** . . . . **K 17624**
WEA / Jun '80.

THAT GIBSON BOY.
Tracks: Even tho' / It's my way / Midnight / As much / Do you think / Didn't work out, did it? / Won't cha' come back to me / I wish it had been a dream / Ages and ages ago / Almost / It has to be / Foggy river.
LP . . . . **NL 90002**
■ **MC** . . . . **NK 90002**
RCA / Jan '87.

YOU WIN AGAIN.
Tracks: I heard that lonesome whistle blow / You win again / Cold cold heart / Mansion on the hill / Take these chains from my heart / Kaw-liga / Window shopping / My heart would know / Crazy heart / On the banks of the old pontchartrain.
LP . . . . **SDLP 023**
Sundown / Aug '85 / Terry Blood Dist. / Jazz Music / C.M. Distribution.
MC . . . . **SDC 023**
Sundown / May '88 / Terry Blood Dist. / Jazz Music / C.M. Distribution.

Giddens, Jerry

LIVIN' AIN'T EASY.
Tracks: Remember Reuben Salazar / Train, The / Livin' ain't easy / Captured live / Inspiration / Whispering wires / Lost angels / St. Mary's gate / Diana / Satisfy tomorrow / Words / I was coming for you.
CD . . . . **SDCD 9.00701**
Sawdust / '90.

Gill, Vince

Born Vincent Grant Gill on April 4, 1957, in Norman, Oklahoma. He is an artist highly regarded by his Nashville colleagues. He had learnt to play guitar by the age of 10 and five years later, was leading his own high school band. While in the school he also worked with Mountain Smoke and, after graduation, went on the road with Boone Creek and Byron Berline's Sundance though it was his three year association with Pure Prairie League, beginning in 1979, that was to first bring his name to wider attention. He then joined Rodney Crowell's band the Cherry Bombs, prior to signing to MCA. He scored modest success with the singles *Victim of life's circumstances* and *Turn me loose* (both 1984), though it was enough to impress the CMA who named him Top New Male Vocalist. Following the move to MCA in 1989 Gill's chart status improved immediately with his single *When I call your name* voted CMA's 1990 Single of the Year. With the arrival of the 1990's Gill's success increased substantially, scoring high chart placings with singles such as *Pocket full of gold* , *Look at us* and *I still believe in you* , with the industry showing it's support by naming him winner of a series of top awards, including the CMA's Male Vocalist of the Year for two consecutive years, 1991 - 1992, as well as the 1992 Song of the Year for *Look at us* which he co-wrote with Max D. Barnes. And it's certain that his success is going to continue through the decade (Tony Byworth)

DON'T LET OUR LOVE START SLIPPIN' AWAY.
Tracks: Don't let our love start slippin' away.
CD Single . . . . **MCSTD 1768**
■ **MC Single** . . . . **MCSC 1768**
MCA / Apr '93.

I STILL BELIEVE IN YOU.
Tracks: Don't let our love start slippin' away / No future in the past / Nothin' like a woman / Tryin' to get over you / Say hello / One more last chance / Under these conditions / Pretty words / Love never broke anyone's heart / I still believe in you.
CD . . . . **MCD 10630**
MC . . . . **MCC 10630**
MCA / Sep '92 / BMG.
DCC . . . . **MCAX 10630**
MCA / Apr '93 / BMG.

POCKET FULL OF GOLD.
Tracks: I quit / Look at us / Take your memory with you / Pocket full of gold / Strings that tie you down, The / Liza Jane / If I didn't have you in my world / Little left over, A / What's a man to do / Sparkle.
CD . . . . **MCAD 10140**
LP . . . . **MCA 10140**
MC . . . . **MCAC 10140**
MCA / May '92 / BMG.

POCKETFUL OF GOLD.
Tracks: Not Advised.
CD Single . . . . **MCAX 10140**
MCA / Dec '92 / BMG.

TURN ME LOOSE.
Tracks: Turn me loose / Victim of life's circumstances.
7" . . . . **PB 49993**
RCA / Mar '85 / BMG.

VINCE GILL.
Tracks: Victim of life's circumstances / Turn me loose / Oh Carolina / Savannah (Do you ever think of me) / Colder than the winter / Waitin' for you love / Lucy Dee / Oklahoma borderline / True love / Ain't it always that way / She don't know.
LP . . . . **PL 89567**
■ **MC** . . . . **PK 89567**
RCA / Apr '85.

WHEN I CALL YOUR NAME.
Tracks: Never alone / Sight for sore eyes / Oh girl / Oklahoma swing / When I call your name / Ridin' the rodeo / Never knew lonely / We won't dance / We could have been / Rita Ballou.
CD . . . . **MCAD 42321**
LP . . . . **MCA 42321**
MCA (Import) / Mar '90 / Pinnacle / Silver Sounds (CD).

Gilley, Mickey

A rockabilly, later a honky-tonk singer born in 1938 in Louisiana; a piano playing cousin of Jerry Lee Lewis and for many years under his shadow. He played at a Houston club through the '60's, had his own Astro record label in 1964 and had a minor hit on Paula in 1968; then suddenly four number one country hits in a row in 1974-5 on Playboy; he switched to Epic in 1979 and had well over 40 hits through to 1984, most of them in the country top 10 and 17 at No. 1. He was a co-owner of Gilley's 1971-89 (when it closed); Gilley and 'the largest honky-tonk in the world' were featured in the film *Urban cowboy* in 1980. (Donald Clarke).

20 GOLDEN SONGS.
Tracks: Not Advised.
LP. 20113
MC 40113
Astan (USA) / Nov '84.

DOWN THE LINE.
Tracks: Not Advised.
■ LP. . . . . CR 30192
Charly / Jan '81 / Charly.

FROM PASADENA WITH LOVE.
Tracks: Still care about you / Keepin' on / That's how it's got to be / I miss you so / Just out of reach / Grapevine / Fraulein / No greater love / Boy who didn't pass / I ain't going home.
LP. . . . . SDLP 1016
MC . . . . SDC 1016
Sundown / Jun '85 / Terry Blood Dist. / Jazz Music / C.M. Distribution.

I LOVE COUNTRY.
Tracks: Headache tomorrow or a headache tonight / Power of positive drinking, The / City lights / Lonely nights / Lawdy Miss Clawdy / Stand by me / True love ways / Talk to me / Tears of the lonely.
MC . . . . ZCGAS 713
Audio Fidelity(USA) / Oct '84 / Stage One Records.
■ MC 4504324
CBS / Mar '87.
■ LP. 4504321
CBS / Mar '87.

MICKEY AT GILLEY'S.
Tracks: Not Advised.
LP. . . . . CMLF 1012
Checkmate / Apr '78.

PUT YOUR DREAMS AWAY.
Tracks: Talk to me / Don't you be foolin' with a fool / I really don't want to know / If I can't hold her on the outside / Put your dreams away / Honky tonkin' / Rocky road to romance.
■ LP. . . . . EPC 85851
Epic / '83.

ROCKIN' ROLLIN' PIANO.
Tracks: Not Advised.
LP. . . . . MINOR 1006
Minor / Nov '87 / Impetus Records / Charly / New Note.

STAND BY ME.
Tracks: Stand by me / Here comes the hurt again.
■ 7". . . . . K 79181
WEA / Oct '80.

THAT HEART BELONGS TO ME.
Tracks: I'm to blame / Night after night / Susie Q / I'll make it all up to you / Breathless / Is it wrong / Lonely wine / Forgive / My babe / Turn around look at me / She's still got a hold on you / Running out of reasons / World of our own / That heart belongs to me / I'm gonna put my love in the want ads / Without you / It's just a matter of making up my mind / New way to live, A / There's no one like you / You can count me missing / Still care about you / Grapevine / That's how it's gotta be / Boy who didn't pass, The / Fraulein / I miss you so / Just out of reach / Keepin' on / Watching the way.
CD . . . . CDGRF 074
Tring / Feb '93 / Prism Leisure PLC / Midland Records / Taylors.

THAT'S ALL THAT MATTERS TO ME.
Tracks: That's all that matters to me / Blues don't care who's got 'em / More I turn the bottle up / Jukebox argument / Million dollar memories / Blame lies with me / True love ways / Lyin' again / So easy to begin / Headache tomorrow or a headache tonight.
LP. . . . . EPC 84391
Epic / Dec '80 / Sony.

TOO GOOD TO STOP NOW.
Tracks: Too good to stop now / Make it like the first time / Shoulder to cry on / When she runs out of fools / Right side of the wrong bed / Everything i own / Reminders / You can lie to me tonight / I'm the one mama warned you about / Quittin' time.
MC 40 26070
Epic / Oct '84 / Sony.
■ LP. . . . . EPC 26070
Epic / Oct '84.

YOU DON'T KNOW ME.
Tracks: You don't know me / Jukebox argument.
■ 7". . . . . EPCA 1567
Epic / Oct '81.

Gilmore, Jimmie Dale

Singer - songwriter, born 1945 in Tulia, (near Lubbock where he was raised) Texas. He's played music for 25 years, working solo during late 60s, prior to brief spell 1971-73 with the Flatlander's. Left Texas and the recording scene (but continued playing) in 1974, moving to Denver, Colorado, to live in a guru-led spiritual community. Gilmore returned to Texas in 1980, making two albums for the Hightone indie label *Fair and square* and *Jimmie Dale Gilmore* . His West Texas blend of songs *Dallas* , *Treat me like a Saturday night* and *Tonight I think I'm gonna go down town* fitting into the cultural western beat slot. Made a live recording, *Two roads*, in Sydney with fellow Texan Butch Hancock in Feb 1990 from their Australian tour. 1991 saw him debut on the Elektra/Nonesuch outlet, featuring on it's specialist American Explorer series with *After awhile* . His latest career step, sees him signing an extended contract with the outlet connected to Elektra's main body. (Maurice Hope)

SPINNING AROUND THE SUN.
Tracks: Where are you going / Santa fe thief / So I'll run / I'm so lonesome I could cry / Mobile line (France blues) / Nothing of the kind / Just a wave, reunion / I'm gonna love you / Another colorado / Thinking about you.
MC 7559615024
Elektra / '93 / WEA.
CD 7559615022
Elektra / Sep '93 / WEA.

Gimble, Johnny

One of country music's most respected instrumentalists, fiddle player Johnny Gimble was born in Texas, and began playing local gigs at the age of 12. Trained as a hairdresser, he gained vital musical experience while playing with the famed Bob Wills & Texas Playboys, before beginning a lengthy career as one of the most sought after session musicians. Johnny Gimble has also recorded several albums and played gigs in his own right. He has also won many awards including the CMA Instrumentalist Of The Year four times. (Tony Byworth)

HONKY TONK HITS.
Tracks: Not Advised.
CD . . . . .CD 9038
Double LP .CMH 9038
MC . . . . .CMHC 9038
CMH (USA) / Feb '89 / C.M. Distribution / Projection.

ON THE ROAD AGAIN (see under Nelson, Willie).

STILL SWINGIN' (Gimble, Johnny & The Texas Swing Pioneers).
Tracks: Not Advised.
LP. . . . . .CMH 9020
MC . . . . CMHC 9020
CMH (USA) / Feb '89 / C.M. Distribution / Projection.

TEXAS FIDDLE COLLECTION, THE.
Tracks: Not Advised.
LP. . . . . .CMH 9027
MC . . . . CMHC 9027
CMH (USA) / C.M. Distribution / Projection.

Ginger, Debbie

DOLLY PARTON'S GREATEST HITS.
Tracks: Not Advised.
MC . . . . BBM 115
Bibi (Budget Cassettes) / Jan '82.

Glaser, Jim

Tenor with the now defunct Tompall & The Glaser Brothers. Glaser was born in 1936 in Spalding, Nebraska. As a solo artist he has had a chequered career. Glaser enjoyed modest success on RCA, MGM & MCA during the 1960's and 70's and had hit the big time during the mid 1980's, however, this period was shortlived. He scored a chart topper with *You're Gettin' To Be Me Again*, in 1984. (Tony Byworth)

COUNTRY STORE: JIM GLASER.
Tracks: Love of my woman, The / You were gone before you said goodbye / Past the point of no return / It's not easy / Merry go round / Tough act to follow / Early morning love / I'll be your fool tonight / In another minute / If I don't love you / Those days.
MC . . . . .CSTK 16
Country Store / '88 / BMG.
■ CD . . . . .CDCST 16
Country Store / '88.
■ LP. . . . . CST 16
Country Store / '88.

MAN IN THE MIRROR.
Tracks: When you're not a lady / You're gettin' to me again / You got me running / Pretend / Woman, woman / I'd love to see you again / Close friends / If I could only dance with you / Let me down easy / Stand by the road / Man in the mirror.
LP. . . . . RANGE 7003
Range (1).
■ LP. . . . . IMCA 5636
MCA (Import) / Mar '86.

PAST THE POINT OF NO RETURN.
Tracks: Merry-go-round / Those days / Tough act to follow / Love of my woman, The / Early morning love / You were gone before you said goodbye / I'll be your fool tonight / Past the point of no return / In another minute / It's not easy / If I don't love you.
■ LP. . . . . IMCA 5612
MCA (Import) / Mar '86.

WHO WERE YOU THINKING OF.
Tracks: Who were you thinking of.
■ 7". . . . . CHEW 32
Mint / '79.

WOMAN WOMAN.
Tracks: Woman woman / I'd love to see you again.
7". . . . . RANS 73
Range (1) / Apr '84.

Glaser, Tompall

The Glaser brothers, Thomas Paul, Chuck and Jim, all came from Nebraska and separately and together have been a force to reckon with in country music as singers and songwriters. Their Glaser Sound Studios were designed by Chuck in 1969 and became a hangout for Willie Nelson, Waylon Jennings and others. It was a Glaser employee who coined the term 'outlaw' to describe the iconoclastic country music scene that was so influential. They had backed Marty Robbins on his massive hit *El Paso* in 1959; lead singer Tompall wrote for Robbins, Jimmy Dean, Bobby Bare; Jim wrote hits for Skeeter Davis, Warner Mack and Gary Puckett; Chuck was credited with discovering John Hartford and co-produced his classic *Gentle on my mind*, also writing such hits as *Where has all the love gone* for Hank Snow. Chuck had a minor hit in the USA country chart in 1974, then suffered a massive stroke and wasn't supposed to walk or talk again, but rejoined the brothers by 1979. Jim has had over 20 solo hits 1968-86, Tompall had 8 in the '70's; the Brothers had 15 hits 1966-73, split up, reunited in 1979, had half a dozen more hits and split again in '82. (Donald Clarke).

COUNTRY STORE: TOMPALL GLASER (Glaser, Tompall & the Glaser Brothers).
Tracks: Gentle on my mind / We live in two different worlds / When it goes, it's gone girl / Good hearted woman / Time changes everything / Broken down momma / I can't remember / Wild side of life / Faded love / Hunger, The / Take the singer with the song / If I'd only come and gone / Charlie / Lay down beside me.
CD . . . . CDCST 27
MC . . . . .CSTK 27
Country Store / '88 / BMG.
■ LP. . . . . CST 27
Country Store / '88.

NIGHTS ON THE BORDERLINE.
Tracks: Night on the border / Mamma don't let you big boy play outside / I cried a mile (for every inch I laughed) / Put another log on the fire / Up where we belong / I don't care anymore / Auction, The / Lovely Lucy / Streets of Baltimore / Till the right one comes along.
LP. . . . . .IMCA 39051
MCA (Import) / Mar '86 / Pinnacle / Silver Sounds (CD).
MC . . . . .IMCAC 39051
MCA / Mar '87 / BMG.

OUTLAW, THE.
Tracks: It never crossed my mind / Bad times, The / What are we doing with our lives / How I love them old songs / On second thought / Drinking them beers / My mother was a lady / Duncan and Brady / Easy on my mind / Wonder of it all, The / You can have her / Release me / Tennessee blues / Come back Shane / It'll be her / It ain't fair medley / Sweethearts or strangers / Late nite show / I just want to hear the music / Storms never last.
CD . . . . BCD 15605
Bear Family / Jun '92 / Rollercoaster Records / Swift / Direct Distribution.

ROGUE, THE.
Tracks: Rogue, The / Tears on my pillow / Forever and ever / Shackles and chains / My pretty quadron / Lean on me / I'll hold you in my heart / True love / Open arms / I love you so much it hurts / Chattanooga shoe shine boy / You can't borrow back any time / Like an old country song / Sad country songs / What a town / Don't think you're too good for country music / Unwanted outlaw / Man you think you see, The / When I dream / Burn, Georgia burn / Billy Tyler / Carry me on.
CD . . . . BCD 15596
Bear Family / Apr '92 / Rollercoaster Records / Swift / Direct Distribution.

Glenn, John

ALONE WITH YOU.
Tracks: Not Advised.

G 6

■ DELETED

MC . . . . .TAC 117
Topspin (Ireland) / '88 / I & B Records.

BACK AGAIN (Glenn, John & Mainliners).
Tracks: Not Advised.
LP. . . . . MYLP 5003
Misty / Jun '76.

BEST OF JOHN GLENN.
Tracks: Blue Ridge mountain turning green / Boys from County Armagh / Keep on the sunny side / Sunny side of the mountain / Your my best friend / Turn out the light (love me tonight) / Annabelle Lee / Call me darling / Say you're gone / Let's turn back the years / Couple more years, A / Little country town in Ireland / Before this day ends / Town of Galway.
LP. . . . . .PHL 451
MC . . . . .CPHL 451
Homespun (Ireland) / Jul '82 / Homespun Records / Ross Records / Wellard Dist.

BOYS OF THE COUNTY ARMAGH (Glenn, John & Marge).
Tracks: Boys of the County Armagh / Irish eyes.
7" . . . . .HIS 11
Homespun (Ireland) / '88 / Homespun Records / Ross Records / Wellard Dist.

COUNTRY STAR (Glenn, John & Mainliners).
Tracks: Keep on the sunny side / Ghost story / Bob Wills is still the king / Rainbow at midnight / Lone Lyville / Say your gone / Can you hear the Robin sing / Lets turn back the years / Boys from County Armagh / This is my year for Mexico / Can I sleep in your arms / Call me darling / Don't wait until the last minute to pray / I keep looking for tomorrow.
LP. . . . . .PHL 432
MC . . . . .CPHL 432
Homespun (Ireland) / '82 / Homespun Records / Ross Records / Wellard Dist.

LITTLE COUNTRY TOWN IN IRELAND (Glenn, John & Mainliners).
Tracks: Little country town in Ireland / Somebody to love / Old mud cabin on the hill / September in Miami / Last date / Love me like I love you / Couple more years, A / Queen of our town / Feeling better / Velvet wallpaper / House without love / Before this day ends / Colour of the blues / That's why I am walking / Gone away / Barney McShane / IOU.
LP. . . . . .PHL 433
MC . . . . .CPHL 433
Homespun (Ireland) / '82 / Homespun Records / Ross Records / Wellard Dist.

MAKE MINE COUNTRY STYLE (Glenn, John & Mainliners).
Tracks: There's a bluebird singing / She's in love with a rodeo man / Half as much / Leona / Streets of San Francisco / Arkensaw river / Ghost of Jim Bob Wilson / I need someone to hold me when I cry / Deep deep down / Farewell to Galway / All over again / I never had a thing that ain't been used.
LP. . . . . .PHL 435
MC . . . . .CPHL 435
Homespun (Ireland) / '82 / Homespun Records / Ross Records / Wellard Dist.

SUNNYSIDE OF THE MOUNTAIN (Glenn, John & Mainliners).
Tracks: Sunny side of the mountain / Turn out the light (love me tonight) / Who will I be lovin' / Drink up and go home / Annabelle Lee / Blue Ridge Mountain turning green / Picture from lifes other side, A / Sunset & Vine / You're my best friend / More than words can tell / I think it's time she learned / Bury me beneath the willow / Noreen bawn / Sweet Charlotte Ann.
LP. . . . . .PHL 431
MC . . . . .CPHL 431
Homespun (Ireland) / '82 / Homespun Records / Ross Records / Wellard Dist.

Golbey, Brian

Along with his long-time partner banjoist Pete Stanley, Golbey has been a stalwart of the British old time scene since the Sixties. Golbey, a fine vocalist/fiddler/guitarist and illustrator of country music's origins, Struck up his partnership with Stanley back in October 1967 - their initial venture lasting until 1971. Golbey has appeared on such US shows as Ernest Tubb's Midnight Jamboree and WSM's Early Morning Show, Apart from his work with the band Cajun Moon, Golbey has also worked with American artists Mac Wiseman and Patsy Montana. He reformed his association with Stanley in 1977. Ever popular in clubs and at bluegrass festivals, his 1983 album (with Nick Strutt) *Last train south* on Waterfront defines his all-round talent. He is someone who's seen country music clubs in the UK blossom as the folk clubs had before them, his old time music traversing between the two. (Maurice Hope)

COUNTRY MUSIC STORY.
Tracks: Not Advised.
MC . . . . .AMP 023
Ampro / Sep '81.

LAST TRAIN SOUTH (Golbey, Brian & Nick Strutt).
Tracks: Days of the railroad / I'm bound to ride a boxcar / Rancho grande / Faded love / Yellow rose of Texas / Last train south / Texas when I die / Jimmie's Texas blues / Last cowboy, The / South of the border / Black smoke.
LP. . . . . .WF 011
Waterfront / Mar '86 / SRD / Jazz Music / A.D.A Distribution / C.M. Distribution.

WHEN THE DEALINGS DONE (Golbey, Brian & Pete Stanley).
Tracks: Not Advised.
LP. . . . . .WF 002
Waterfront / Mar '84 / SRD / Jazz Music / A.D.A Distribution / C.M. Distribution.

Golden, William Lee

AMERICAN VAGABOND.
Tracks: Not Advised.
CD 31075
MCA (USA) / Jun '88 / MCA (Imports).

Goldsboro, Bobby

This American singer, songwriter and guitarist, born in Florida, celebrated his 21st birthday in 1962 by becoming a guitarist with Roy Orbison's group. Having moved with his family to Alabama during childhood, where he studied at high school and university, he gained initial experience in a student combo before joining Orbison. While with Roy, Bobby developed his songwriting skills and made a tentative solo bid with the single *Molly*, which became a minor US hit. His solo performing career began in earnest in early 1964, when the self-penned *See the funny little clown* surged to no. 9 on the American chart. A year later, came his next big hit, *Little things*, which reached the US no. 13 position; it was a no. 5 hit in Britain for Dave Berry, who recorded an opportunistic cover version. Goldsboro's first UK hit as a performer was also his biggest ever success on both sides of the Atlantic - *Honey*, a swirling death disc written by Bobby Russell, was no. 1 in America for 5 weeks in 1968 and reached no. 2 in Britain. Many listeners found the record mawkish, while others thought it poignant and moving. Amazingly, it became a UK no.2 hit all over again as a 1975 re-issue, by which time the artist had chalked up various other successes - *Watching Scotty grow* (written by Mac Davis) was a US no. 11 hit in 1971; Goldsboro's own 1973 song *Summer (the first time)* was the ultimate in romantic narratives, and reached no. 21 in the US and no. 9 in the UK; and *Hello summertime*, which started life as a TV Coke ad, was a 1974 Top 20 success in Britain. Goldsboro's style contained elements of country, pop and easy listening, and he was able to give full vent to these on his own syndicated US TV series. By the mid-seventies, the twee side of his musical character was winning the upper hand and he was getting acquainted with Las Vegas. (Bob Macdonald)

BEST OF BOBBY GOLDSBORO.
Tracks: Honey / Little things / Summer (the first time) / Hello summertime.
LP. 1A 222 58138
MC . . . . .TC 1A 222 58138
MFP (Holland) / Apr '83 / Pinnacle.

GOLDEN HITS.
Tracks: Not Advised.
MC 4XLL 9171
Capitol (Specials) / Dec '88.

GREATEST HITS: BOBBY GOLDSBORO (2).
Tracks: Honey / With pen in hand / Mississippi delta queen / See the funny little clown / Voodoo woman / Autumn of my life / Watchin' Scotty grow / Little things / Hello summertime / Broomstick cowboy / Butterfly for Bucky / Summer (the first time).
■ LP. . . . . .SLS 50421
Sunset (Liberty) / Oct '78.

GREATEST HITS: BOBBY GOLDSBORO (PREMIER).
Tracks: Honey / Straight life / With pen in hand / Muddy Mississippi line / Blue Autumn / Little things / Summer (the first time) / Watchin' Scotty grow / See the funny little clown / Broomstick cowboy / It's too late / Autumn of my life / Hello summertime / I'm a drifter.
LP. . . . . .PMP 1008
MC . . . . .PMPK 1008
Premier (Sony) / Feb '88 / Sony / Pinnacle.

HELLO SUMMERTIME.
Tracks: Hello summertime.
■ 7" . . . . .UP 35705
United Artists / Aug '74.

HONEY.
Tracks: Honey / Danny.
■ 7" . . . . .UP 2215
United Artists / Apr '68.
■ 7" . . . . .UP 35633
United Artists / Feb '74.

HONEY.
Tracks: Not Advised.
MC 495898
Ariola / Dec '92 / BMG.

HONEY (OLD GOLD).
Tracks: Honey / Summer (the first time) / Hello summertime.
7" . . . . .OG 9993
Old Gold / '92 / Pickwick Records.
CD Single . . . . .OG 6171
Old Gold / Jun '92 / Pickwick Records.

HONEY - THE BEST OF BOBBY GOLSBORO.
Tracks: See the funny little clown / Hello loser / Whenever he holds you / My Japanese boy, I love you / I don't know you anymore / Little things / Voodoo woman / It breaks my heart / If you wait for love / If you've got a heart / Broomstick cowboy / It's too late / It hurts me / Blue Autumn / Honey / Autumn of my life / Straight life, The / Glad she's a woman / I'm a drifter / Can you feel it / Watching Scotty grow / Brand new kind of love / Summer (the first time).
CD . . . . .CZ 478
EMI / Oct '91 / EMI.
CD 295898
RCA / Jul '93 / BMG.

I WROTE A SONG.
Tracks: I wrote a song / All the woman I've wanted.
■ 7" . . . . .UP 36005
United Artists / Aug '75.

SUMMER (THE FIRST TIME).
Tracks: Summer (the first time) / Marlena / He's part of us / L and N don't stop here anymore, The / Brand new kind of love / Sing me a smile / Mississippi delta queen / I can see clearly now / She / Killing me softly with her song / Spread my wings and fly / If'n I was God (from the film Tom Sawyer) / Summer(The first time).
LP. . . . . .SLS 50405
Sunset (Liberty) / Sep '77 / EMI.

SUMMER (THE FIRST TIME).
Tracks: Summer (the first time) / Childhood (1949).
7" . . . . .UP 35558
United Artists / Jun '73 / EMI.

TOO MANY PEOPLE.
Tracks: Too many people / It's too late / She chased me.
■ 7" . . . . .UP 36495
United Artists / Feb '79.

VERY BEST OF BOBBY GOLDSBORO, THE.
Tracks: Honey / Straight life / With pen in hand / Muddy Mississippi line / Blue Autumn / Little things / Summer (the first time) / Watchin' scotty grow / See the funny little clown / Cowboy and the lady, The / Broomstick cowboy / It's too late / Autumn of my life / Hello summertime / I'm a drifter / Love divine / Payin' for the good times / Street dancin'.
CD C5CD-534
MC C5K-534
C5 / Dec '89 / Pinnacle.
LP. C5-534
C5 / May '89 / Pinnacle.

Good Ol' Persons

ANYWHERE THE WIND BLOWS.
Tracks: Anywhere the wind blows / Wildflowers / Danny J, The / Dreaming in three quarter time / Waterbound / Hamsters in the pantry / Suffer the consequences / Walkin' the floor over you / Waking up alone / La arboleda / Think about me.
CD . . . . .K 38
LP. . . . . .F 38
MC . . . . .C 38
Kaleidoscope (USA) / Mar '90 / Projection / Ross Records / Roots Records / Swift / C.M. Distribution / Topic Records / Duncans.

I CAN'T STAND TO RAMBLE.
Tracks: I can't stand to ramble / Kissing comes easy / Broken tie / Itzbin reel / You don't miss your water / I will arise / Get up and go to work / In dreams / I'm satisfied with you / Not this time / China camp Ellie / Open your heart.
LP. . . . . .F 17
Kaleidoscope (USA) / Feb '85 / Projection / Ross Records / Roots Records / Swift / C.M. Distribution / Topic Records / Duncans.

OLD-TIME BLUEGRASS MUSIC.
Tracks: Not Advised.
LP. . . . . .BAY 208
Bay / Jul '88 / Projection.

PART OF A STORY.
Tracks: Broken hearted lover / Easy substitute / My my my / I don't hurt anymore / It's gonna rain / You're a flower / Crossing the Cumberlands / It seems there's nothing I can do / This young boy / Part of a story.
LP. . . . . .F 26
MC . . . . .C 26
Kaleidoscope (USA) / Mar '89 / Projection / Ross Records / Roots Records / Swift / C.M. Distribution / Topic Records / Duncans.

Goodacre, Tony

One of the busiest artists on the UK country music scene, Tony Goodacre (born February 3, 1938, in Leeds) matches an active touring schedule with an impressive array of albums released over the years. Beginning his musical career as founding member of the Tigers Skiffle Group in 1957, it wasn't until the early 1970's that he turned fully professional, working with steel guitarist Arthur Layfield and creating the band Goodacre Country. His prolific output of albums began in 1974 with *Roaming round in Nashville* though it took another four years before Goodacre recorded his first Nashville album, *Mr. Country Music* . A great supporter of home grown material, he has always tried to feature a selection of British songs in each of his albums, giving many local writers their first chance to have a song cut. He has also proved himself to be an astute businessman, having launched his own record label (Sylvantone, a joint venture with his wife Sylvia) in 1980, leading onto a management/booking operation and most recently, video releases. Goodacre's also built up a loyal following in Australia, where he's toured on several occasions. (Tony Byworth)

25TH ANNIVERSARY: TONY GOODACRE.
Tracks: Everyday love / Love me tender / Blue Hawaii / California cottonfields / Through the eyes of love / I'd love to lay down / Why me lord / Another long day / Desert blues / Mr. Ting-a-ling..pick me up on the way / Wait a moment, Wendy / Honey girl / Worried man blues (medley) / Midnight special (medley) / Cottonfields / Freight train / Wabash cannonball / Putting on the style / Rock Island line.
LP. . . . . **STON 8108**
MC . . . . **CSTON 8108**
Sylvantone / '84 / Sylvantone Records.

GRANDMA'S FEATHER BED.
Tracks: Grandma's feather bed / Idaho / Out and free / Streets of London / When a woman leaves home / Morning past the night before, The / Jimmie the kid / That's you and me / Kelly's wife / Old shep / All that glitters / Key, The / Nashville rail.
LP. . . . . **SBOL 4021**
MC . . . . **COB 4021**
Outlet / '84 / Projection / Duncans / C.M. Distribution / Ross Records / Topic Records / Direct Distribution / Midland Records.

GUERNSEY, I'LL KEEP COMING BACK TO YOU.
Tracks: Guernsey, I'll keep coming back to you / Sarnia cherie.
7" . . . . **HS 078**
Homespun (Ireland) / May '84 / Homespun Records / Ross Records / Wellard Dist.

LIVIN' ON LOVIN'.
Tracks: Livin' on lovin' / No such place as heaven / Face in the crowd / When we first fell in love / Three bells, The / With this ring / Raise the flag / Love is just like fishing / Best we're gonna get, The / Song of the river / South will rise again, The / Edinburgh song / Life turned her that way / Bird on the wing / How many lovers / Ballad of a young woman / My music city friends / Part of me, A / Something special / I need you / Love's a losing game / Mr Country music.
CD . . . . **CDSTON 9204**
Sylvantone / Sep '92 / Sylvantone Records.

MR COUNTRY MUSIC.
Tracks: My music city friends / Do you know you are my sunshine / Old rugged cross, The / Susan Flowers / My elusive dreams / Mr. Country music..bird on the wing / Blue eyes crying in the rain / Merry go round of love / China doll / My little son / Dear old sunny south by the sea.
LP. . . . . **SBOL 4029**
MC . . . . **COB 4029**
Outlet / '84 / Projection / Duncans / C.M. Distribution / Ross Records / Topic Records / Direct Distribution / Midland Records.

RECORDED LIVE IN ILKLEY.
Tracks: Country music in my soul / Red river valley / Mermaid, The / Back home again / Great El Tigre, The / Triad / I love you because / One day at a time / Railroad bum / Lord made a hobo out of me, The / Slowly / What's wrong with the way that we're doing it now / Forty shades of green / Letter edged in black / Travelling blues / Tenessee border / Rose of San Antone (instrumental).
LP. . . . . **STON 8003**
MC . . . . **CSTON 8003**
Sylvantone / '84 / Sylvantone Records.

RED ROSES.
Tracks: Red roses for a blue lady / Walking the floor / Funny face / Sail away / There'll never be anyone else but you / Country boy / Lucy ain't your loser looking good / Before I met you / Annie's song / Saginaw Michigan / If heaven ain't a lot like Dixie / Roses in the winter / Old flame.
LP. . . . . **STON 8301**
MC . . . . **CSTON 8301**
Sylvantone / '84 / Sylvantone Records.

RED ROSES FOR A BLUE LADY (EP).
Tracks: Red roses for a blue lady / Remember you're mine / It's almost tomorrow / I wonder who's kissing her now.
■ **EP.** . . . . **HS 068**
Homespun (Ireland) / Jun '83.

ROAMIN' ROUND IN NASHVILLE.
Tracks: Canadian Pacific / Peach picking time in Georgia / Welcome to my world / Country hall of fame / Abilene / Golden rocket / There goes my everything / I wonder where you are tonight / Jody and the kid / Satin sheets / Year that Clayton Delaney died, The / Why should I be so lonely / Don't it make you wanna go home / Your cheatin' heart.
LP. . . . . **SBOL 4019**
MC . . . . **COB 4019**
Outlet / '84 / Projection / Duncans / C.M. Distribution / Ross Records / Topic Records / Direct Distribution / Midland Records.

SYLVANTONE SHOWCASE, THE (Goodacre, Tony/Jeannie Dee/Stu Page/Remuda/Geoff Ashford).
Tracks: Don't play me no love songs / Your leaving song / Me or the bottle / Rags to riches / We belong together / Country picker / You'll be home / Radio nights / My name is Billy / One of a kind / Love made a fool / Falling apart at the seams / Artist, The / Texas music.
LP. . . . . **STON 8504**
MC . . . . **CSTON 8504**
Sylvantone / Jul '85 / Sylvantone Records.

THANKS TO THE HANKS.
Tracks: Thanks to the Hanks / And thanks to George Hamilton VI / Wild side of life / From here to there to you / Pan American / Rockin' rollin' ocean / My front door is open / Fool such as I, A / We're gonna go fishing / Blackboard of my heart / Teardrops on a rose / Last ride, The / Send me the pillow that you dream on / Standing on the outside / This song is just for you / I don't hurt anymore / Blues come around, The.
LP. . . . . **SBOL 4024**
MC . . . . **COB 4024**
Outlet / '84 / Projection / Duncans / C.M. Distribution / Ross Records / Topic Records / Direct Distribution / Midland Records.

TONY GOODACRE COLLECTION, THE.
Tracks: Nashville marathon / It's almost tomorrow / Girl I used to know, A / Workin' my way through a heartache / Have I told you lately that I loved you / Down in Waikiki / I wonder who's kissing her now / Man in the sky / Woman's touch, A / No tomorrow for yesterdays dreams / Place in the choir / Mockin' Bird Hill / You've made my life complete / Country music is my life / Ain't got nothing to wear.
LP. . . . . **STON 8607**
N/A / Jan '86.
MC . . . . **CSTON 8607**
Sylvantone / Jan '86 / Sylvantone Records.

WRITTEN IN BRITAIN.
Tracks: Written in Britain / Let me be there / Call of the wild / Last farewell, The / Let's live the good life again / Turn me round / Mississippi fireball.. ten guitars / Ballad of a young woman / World of our own, A / Come back to me / Yesterday / You do love me don't you.
LP. . . . . **SBOL 4027**
MC . . . . **COB 4027**
Sylvantone / '84 / Sylvantone Records.

YOU'VE MADE MY LIFE COMPLETE.
Tracks: You've made my life complete / Burn Atlanta down / Railway bridge at Crewe, The / I love you in an old fashion way / High on your love / Bingo Bill..country music is my life / It's not the end of the world / Load of bread, A (a jug of wine) / Only way to say goodbye, The / International ambassador country music / Show me a sign.
LP. . . . . **SBOL 4043**
MC . . . . **COB 4043**
Outlet / '84 / Projection / Duncans / C.M. Distribution / Ross Records / Topic Records / Direct Distribution / Midland Records.

Goodman, Steve

Born 25.07.1948, in Chicago, outstanding singer-songwriter, died of leukemia on 20.09.1984. In his early days in Chicago, apart from playing the clubs, Goodman paid the rent with money obtained from his commercial jingles, for products such as Maybelline's Blushing Eye Shadow. On the recording front Goodman duets with John Prine on the latter's US Oh, boy! /UK This way up *Live* album, having his own work released on Buddah (debut in 1971), Elektra/ Asylum and Red pyjamas label. Best known for his writing of the 1984 Grammy winning *City of New Orleans* which was a No. 1 hit for Willie Nelson that year. Arlo Guthrie previously had top twenty pop success with it in 1972. Nelson and Guthrie apart, Sammi Smith also saw country's topfifty with the song in 1973, and Judy Collins and Jerry Reed are among others to have recorded it. David Allan Coe's version of Goodman's 'spoof' *You never called me by my name* , was said by Coe (tongue in cheek) to be the perfect country song, registering him a top ten in 1975. A concert in Goodman's honour took place st the Pacific Amphitheatre in Costa Mesa, California on Nov 3, 1984 and featured 54 star acts. In 1986 Red pajamas, Goodman's final label, released *Tribute to Steve Goodman - Recorded live at the Arie Crown Theatre* , with Prine, John Hartford, the Nitty Gritty Dirt Band and Michael Smith among those involved. (Maurice Hope)

BANANA REPUBLIC.
Tracks: Banana republic / Spoon river.
■ **7"** . . . . **K 13067**
Asylum / Dec '76.

BLUE UMBRELLA.
Tracks: Blue umbrella / Jessie's jig.
■ **7"** . . . . **AYM 551**
Asylum / Nov '75.

SAY IT IN PRIVATE.
Tracks: I'm attracted to you / You're the girl I love / Video tape / There's a girl in the heart of Maryland / Two lovers / Is it true what they say about Dixie / Weary blues from waitin' / Daley's gone / My old man / Twentieth century is almost over, The.
LP. . . . . **K 53067**
Asylum / WEA.

SOMEBODY ELSE'S TROUBLES.
Tracks: Dutchman, The / Six hours ahead of the sun / Song for David / Chicken Gordon blues / Somebody elses troubles / Loving of the game, The / I ain't heard you play no blues / Don't do me any favours anymore / Vegetable song, The (The barnyard dance) / Lincoln Park pirates / Ballad of Penny Evans, The / Election year rag.
CD . . . . **NEMCD 607**
Sequel / Feb '91 / Castle Communications / BMG / Hot Shot.

SOMETIMES LOVE FORGETS (Goodman, Steve & Phoebe Snow).
Tracks: Sometimes love forgets.
■ **7"** . . . . **K 12509**
Elektra / Mar '81.

STEVE GOODMAN.
Tracks: I don't know where I'm going / Rainbow road / Donald and Lydia / You never even call me by my name / Mind your own business / Eight ball blues / City of New Orleans / Turnpike Tom / Yellow coat / So fine / Jazzman / Would you like to learn to dance.
CD . . . . **NEMCD 606**
Sequel / Feb '91 / Castle Communications / BMG / Hot Shot.

WORDS WE CAN DANCE TO.
Tracks: Roving cowboy / Tossin' and turnin' unemployed / Between the lines / Old fashioned / Can't go back / Banana republic / Death of a salesman / That's what friends are for / Story of love.
LP. . . . . **K 53038**
Asylum / WEA.

Gordon, Joe

CROOKIT BAWBEE (Gordon, Joe & Sally Logan).
Tracks: Ballad of the slippy stone, The / Mother's love's a blessing, A / Old rustic bridge / My wee laddie / Two loves / Dumbarton's drums / Crooked bawbee / Spinning wheel / Auld meal mill, The / Road and the miles to Dundee, The / If you will marry me / Granny's heilan' hame.
LP. . . . . **KLP 51**
MC . . . . **ZCKLP 51**
Klub / Oct '85 / C.M. Distribution / Ross Records / Duncans / A.D.A Distribution.

END OF A PERFECT DAY, THE (Gordon, Joe & Sally Logan).
Tracks: Loves old sweet song / Beautiful Isle of somewhere / Old rugged cross, The / Until it's time for you to go / Memories / Heaven's just a sin away / Garden, The / You needed me / Mother of mine / Everybody wants to go to heaven / You're free to go / Keep on the sunny side.
LP. . . . . **KLP 33**
MC . . . . **ZCKLP 33**
Klub / Oct '82 / C.M. Distribution / Ross Records / Duncans / A.D.A Distribution.

FAVOURITES (Gordon, Joe & Sally Logan).
Tracks: Somebody else is taking my place / Silver threads among the gold / In the gloaming / My prayer / Will you always call me sweetheart / Words / Anniversary waltz / It's only a hole in the wall / If I had my way / If I could only make you care / Poor blind boy / Daddy's little girl.
LP. . . . . **KLP 27**
MC . . . . **ZCKLP 27**
Klub / May '81 / C.M. Distribution / Ross Records / Duncans / A.D.A Distribution.

GORDON FAMILY, THE (Gordon, Joe & Sally Logan).
Tracks: Rose of Allandale, The / Craigieburn woods / Band boys / Holy City, The / Wee toon clerk, The / Faraway land, The / Jig selection / Dark lochnagar / Medley of reels / Hunting tower / Bonnio gallows / Charness waltz, The / My ain folk / Dantesque / Darvol dam, The.
CD . . . . **CDGR 142**
MC . . . . **CWGR 142**
Ross (1) / Oct '92 / Ross Records / Duncans / Entertainment UK.

G 8

■ DELETED

JOE GORDON & SALLY LOGAN (Gordon, Joe & Sally Logan).
Tracks: Snowbird / Sunshine of your smile, The / Valley where the Leven flows, The / Silver threads among the gold / Ooor ain fireside / Don't ever leave me / Love is a beautiful song / We'd better bide a wee / Granny Fraser's flitting / House with the spire, The / Dreaming of home / Auld Scots sangs, The / I adore thee.
■ LP . . . . LILP 5032
Lismor / '75.

JOE GORDON & SCOTT LA FARO (Gordon, Joe & Scott La Faro).
Tracks: Not Advised.
CD . . . . FSCD 1030
Fresh Sounds / Jan '93 / Charly / Cadillac Music / Jazz Music.

LOOKIN' GOOD.
Tracks: Not Advised.
LP 1007 597
Contemporary (Import) / Apr '82.

MOONLIGHT AND ROSES.
Tracks: Moonlight & roses.
7" . . . . ODS 5
Coda / Jun '84 / Roots Records / Pinnacle / C.M. Distribution / Zodiac Records.

MOONLIGHT AND ROSES (Gordon, Joe & Sally Logan).
Tracks: Moonlight and roses / Whispering hope / My happiness / Old fashioned mother of mine / Island of dreams / When I leave the world behind / September song / My heart cries for you / Beautiful dreamer / Let the rest of the world go by / To him we're all the same / When you were sweet sixteen.
LP . . . . NA 106
MC . . . . NC 106
Neptune / Jun '78 / Neptune Tapes / A.D.A Distribution.

TOGETHER (Gordon, Joe & Sally Logan).
Tracks: Where has all the love gone / I can wait until forever / Faraway land / Just out of reach / Why did you make me care / If I will marry me / Songs my mother used to sing / Bonnie Aberdeen / It is no secret / Dark Lochnagar / Bright shining light o' the moon, The / Ribbon of darkness.
MC . . . . LICS 5053
Lismor / '76 / Duncans / Roots Records / Conifer Records / C.M. Distribution / Ross Records / A.D.A Distribution / Topic Records / Direct Distribution / Lismor Records.
LP . . . . LILP 5053
Lismor / Nov '76 / Duncans / Roots Records / Conifer Records / C.M. Distribution / Ross Records / A.D.A Distribution / Topic Records / Direct Distribution / Lismor Records.

Gosdin, Vern

Singer - songwriter, born 5.8.1934 in Woodland, Alabama, into a musical family - part of the Gosdin family radio show, in Birmingham, Alabama. In 1960 he moved to California. With younger brother Rex and Chris Hillman formed the Golden State Boys. Had little success, although he did some recordings with Rex for Together and Capitol including a *Gene Clark with the Gosdin Brothers* album. Vern then returned to Birmingham, working at a glass company for 6 years. In 1976 he was back again, recording remake of the Gosdin's *Hangin on* in Nashville for Elektra, the record paving the way for *Yesterday's gone* , *Till the end* (on the album of which he had Emmylou Harris and Janis Frickie assisting on harmony vocals), and *Never my love* all top ten singles. Moved to Ovation in 1981, just as they were about to fold, signed breifly to AMI (1982) before enjoying four years success with Compleat Records, including the top five cuts If you're gonna do me wrong (Do it right) , *Way down deep* and his label debut No.1 *I can tell by the way you dance* (1984), by which time Gosdin was showing potential as a rival to George Jones as country music's finest ballad singer. In 1987 Gosdin moved to Columbia, just as the hits dried up. The move saw Vern's career gain another upturn with the top selling album *Chiseled in stone* and the No.1 single *Set em' up Joe* making 1988 a most memorable year, overspilling into 1989. The man they call 'The Voice' along with his co-writer Max D.Barnes, collected CMA's song of the year for *Chiseled in stone* . On 1991 *Is it raining in your house* was to be added to his list of top ten singles. Veteran Columbia act Gosdin has once again defied the odds, making traditional albums *Out of the heart* (1991) and *Nickels and dimes and love* (1993) for a major label when being the wrong side of 50 (and then some). (Maurice Hope)

I CAN TELL BY THE WAY YOU DANCE.
Tracks: I can tell by the way you dance / You're gonna love me tonight / My heart's in good hands.
■ 7" . . . . CLT 5
Compleat (USA) / Aug '84.

THERE IS A SEASON.
Tracks: Turn, turn, turn / to everything there is a season) / Love me right to the end / How can I believe you (when you'll be leaving me)? / Slow-healing heart / I can tell by the way you dance / What would your

memories do? / Slow-burning memory / Dead from the heart on down / Stone-cold heart / I've got a heart full of you.
LP . . . . CLTLP 352
■ MC . . . . ZCCLT 352
Compleat (USA) / Sep '84.

Grace, Brendan

BOTTLER THE ALUMINIUM ALBUM.
Tracks: Not Advised.
LP . . . . STAR 2325
WEA (Ireland) / '88 / WEA / C.M. Distribution / Projection / Roots Records.

FATHER OF THE BRIDE.
Tracks: Father of the bride.
7" . . . . RITZ 077
Ritz / Oct '84 / Pinnacle / Midland Records.

HUMOURS OF IRELAND.
Tracks: Humours of Ireland / Song for Mira.
7" . . . . BO 21
Bottler / Mar '83.

Grand, Johnny

PARADE OF BROKEN HEARTS.
Tracks: Parade of broken hearts / Casey's last ride / Cookie and Lila / Lookin' out my back door / Sweet memories / Everybody wants to be somebody / Wanna be a star / Today I started loving you again / Let me be there / Hello heartache / We're all goin' nowhere / Teach your children.
■ LP . . . . LILP 5066
Lismor / Apr '77.

Grandpa Jones

Singer/banjoist, he was born Louis Marshall Jones on October 20th 1913 in Niagra, Kentucky. Jones won a talent contest at the age of 16 and built a loyal following by playing old time banjo. By the late 1930's, he was led the group, Granpa Jones & The Grandchildren. Jones has also performed as a member of Brown's Ferry Four, alongside Merle Haggard and the Delmore Brothers. After his military service he joined Nashville's Grand Ole Opry in 1946 and has been a regular member ever since. Jones has also appeared on the long running TV series, Hee Haw since 1969. He was elected to the Country Music Hall Of Fame in 1978. (Tony Byworth)

FAMILY ALBUM.
Tracks: Old mountain dew / Muleskinner blues / Banks of the Ohio / Cannon ball blues / Falling leaves / Pig in the pen / Nellie Bly / The flowers of Edinburgh / There'll come a time / Autoharp concerto / Blind girl, The / My pretty quadroon / I gave my love a cherry / Billy Richardson's last ride / 10th of November / Clear in the kitchen / Red haired boy / Autoharp trilogy / Let him go, God bless him / Down home waltz / Who will sing for me / Ramona's choice / Over the waterfall / Johnson boys, The.
Double LP . . . . .CMH 9015
CMH (USA) / '79 / C.M. Distribution / Projection.

GRANDPA JONES STORY.
Tracks: Sweet dreams of Kentucky / My Carolina sunshine girl / Jesse James / Raising here this morning / Eight more miles to Louisville / Tragic romance / Kentucky / Old rattler / Mountain Laurel / I'm on my way back home / Sweeping through the gates / There's a hand that's a waiting / Old camp meeting time / Closer to God than ever before / I'll meet you in the morning / You'll make our shack a mansion / Dark as a dungeon / I'm on my way somewhere / Rosalee / Gone home.
Double LP . . . . .CMH 9007
■ MC .CMHC 9007
CMH (USA) / '76.

Grant, Bill

BILL GRANT AND DELIA BELL (Grant, Bill & Della Bell).
Tracks: Not Advised.
LP . . . . REB 1593
Rebel (1) / Projection / Backs Distribution.

CHEER OF THE HOMEFIRES (see under Bell, Della).

FEW DOLLARS MORE, A (see under Bell, Della).

FOLLOWING A FEELING (see under Bell, Della).

ROLLIN' (Grant, Bill & Della Bell).
Tracks: Rollin' / No one else / Only you / Take my hand and tell me / Bluest girl in town, The / Goin' to see my Jesus / Girl at the crossroads bar, The / Moods of a fool, The / Rock pile, The / Stone walls and steel bars / Memories in the fall / I am the man, Thomas.
LP . . . . REB 1604
Rebel (1) / '81 / Projection / Backs Distribution.

Grant, Manson

AWARD WINNERS (Grant, Manson & The Dynamos Showband).
Tracks: Heartaches by the number / I won't go huntin' with you Jake / Weatherman, The / Legend in my time, A.
LP . . . . WGRTV 2
Ross (1) / Dec '86 / Ross Records / Duncans / Entertainment UK.
MC . . . . CWGRTV 2
Ross (1) / Oct '92 / Ross Records / Duncans / Entertainment UK.

COUNTRY STARS (Grant, Manson & The Dynamos Showband).
Tracks: Thibodeaux and his cajun band / Kingdom I call home, A / Love, love / Shutters and boards / I believe in marriage / Changing partners / Your old standby / Alone with you / When you and I were young Maggie / Little band of gold / (Lying here with) Linda on my mind / Katy Daly / Slieve na mon / Be my guest.
LP . . . . WGR 038
Ross (1) / Sep '82 / Ross Records / Duncans / Entertainment UK.
MC . . . . CWGR 038
Ross (1) / Oct '92 / Ross Records / Duncans / Entertainment UK.

COUNTRYWIDE REQUESTS (Grant, Manson & The Dynamos Showband).
Tracks: Not Advised.
LP . . . . WGR 070
MC . . . . CWGR 070
Ross (1) / Nov '84 / Ross Records / Duncans / Entertainment UK.

HAPPY HEART (Grant, Manson & The Dynamos Showband).
Tracks: Not Advised.
LP . . . . WGR 085
MC . . . . CWGR 085
Ross (1) / Nov '85 / Ross Records / Duncans / Entertainment UK.

I WON'T GO HUNTIN' WITH YOU JAKE (Grant, Manson & The Dynamos Showband).
Tracks: I won't go huntin' with you Jake / What can I tell the folks?.
7" . . . . SWGR 011
Ross (1) / Dec '85 / Ross Records / Duncans / Entertainment UK.

MANSON GRANT & THE DYNAMOS SHOWBAND (Grant, Manson & The Dynamos Showband).
Tracks: Not Advised.
LP . . . . WGR 007
MC . . . . CWGR 007
Ross (1) / Sep '80 / Ross Records / Duncans / Entertainment UK.

ON THE COUNTRY TRAIL.
Tracks: Not Advised.
LP . . . . WGR 065
MC . . . . CWGR 065
Ross (1) / Nov '83 / Ross Records / Duncans / Entertainment UK.

PICTURES FROM THE PAST (Grant, Manson & The Dynamos Showband).
Tracks: Pictures from the past / Bricklayer's song.
7" . . . . SWGR 010
Ross (1) / Dec '84 / Ross Records / Duncans / Entertainment UK.

SING ANOTHER SONG (Grant, Manson & The Dynamos Showband).
Tracks: Not Advised.
LP . . . . WGR 019
MC . . . . CWGR 019
Ross (1) / Nov '81 / Ross Records / Duncans / Entertainment UK.

Grass Roots

GRASS ROOTS VOLUME 1.
Tracks: Not Advised.
LP . . . . LALP 009
La / Dec '90 / Revolver-APT.

Grassroots

14 GREATEST HITS.
Tracks: Not Advised.
■ CD . . . . CD 1004
Gusto (USA) / '88.

LET'S LIVE FOR TODAY.
Tracks: Let's live for today / Depressed feeling.
■ 7" . . . . TN 25422
Pye International / Jun '67.

SONGS OF OTHER TIMES (see under Sloan, P.F.).

Graves, Josh

DAD THE DOBRO MAN (Graves, Josh & Billy Troy).
Tracks: Don't let the stars get in your eyes / Cory belle / In the jailhouse now / Elareeb / She's loving me blind / Doin' my time / Come walk with me / Dad the dobro man / All for the love of a girl / Coal field march / Harvest of my heart / California blues.
LP......................CMH 6264
MC......................CMH 6264C
CMH (USA) / '89 / C.M. Distribution / Projection.

KING OF THE DOBRO.
Tracks: Not Advised.
LP......................CMH 6252
CMH (USA) / '79 / C.M. Distribution / Projection.

SING AWAY THE PAIN.
Tracks: I'm gonna sing away the pain tonight / Movin' South / Calico gypsy / Evelina / Good time Charlie's got the blues / Lay down Sally / Brand new Carroll County blues / I still get funny when it rains / Easy money / Easin' down the turnpike / Crazy mama / Uncle Josh plays 'lectrified dobro.
LP......................CMH 6233
■ MC......................CMH 6233C
CMH (USA) / '79.

SWEET SUNNY SOUTH (Graves, Josh/ Bobby Smith & Boys From Shiloh).
Tracks: Dixieland for me / Jennifer waltz / Take me back to the sweet sunny South / Juarez / Head over heels in love with you / Crossin' the rockies / Mississippi flood / On my mind / Trouble in mind / Starlight waltz / Pleasant valley.
LP......................CMH 6209
■ MC......................CMH 6209C
CMH (USA) / '76.

Gray, Dobie

This American singer was born Leonard Victor Ainsworth in Brookshire, Texas, and was one of eight children of sharecropping parents. He travelled to California in the early sixties as a young man in search of a musical career. After impressing Sonny Bono Gray first cracked the Billboard Hot 100 with 1963's *Look at me*. His big breakthrough came in early '65, when his pulsating dance single *The "In" crowd* which reached no. 13 in the US and no. 25 in the UK. Later that year, it became a bigger American hit for pianist Ramsey Lewis; in 1974 it was a British hit for Bryan Ferry. Dobie Gray failed to consolidate upon the success of *The "In" crowd*. For the next eight years, apart from a brief spell in an insignificant group called Pollution, he dropped out of recording: he spent his time studying law at a Los Angeles college and pursuing a stage career, including a two-year period in *Hair*. Gray suddenly returned to chart action in 1973 with a song written and produced by the appropriately named Mentor Williams. *Drift away* combined Dobie's soulful voice with a country-rock arrangement; thus, a memorable song was given an unusual, relaxing and distinctive feel. *Drift away* was a million-selling no. 5 pop hit in the States and became a classic; in Britain, where glitter pop and heavy rock were the order of the day, the single was a complete flop. The *Drift away* and *Loving arms* albums were hailed by the critics in America. Britain, which ignored them, did manage to give Gray a minor hit single in autumn 1975 with *Out on the floor*(an all-time Northern Soul classic) plus a turntable hit in 1979 with the infectious disco cash-in *You can do it*. But apart from these, the spasmodic Gray has drifted away from the charts on both sides of the Atlantic - he has never really known in which direction to channel his musical talents. (Bob Macdonald).

DRIFT AWAY.
Tracks: Drift away.
7".......................MCA 146
MCA / Jul '74 / BMG.
7".......................MCA 1154
MCA / Jun '87 / BMG.

DRIFT AWAY.
Tracks: Not Advised.
■ CD......................CDCOT 106
Cottage / Jun '92.

DRIFT AWAY (OLD GOLD).
Tracks: Drift away / Why can't we live together.
7".......................OG 9428
Old Gold / Jul '84 / Pickwick Records.

IN CROWD, THE.
Tracks: In crowd, The / Be a man.
■ 7".......................HL 9953
London-American / Feb '65.
■ 7".......................F 13918
Decca / Mar '82.

LONDON BOYS (see under Sloan, P.F.).

OUT ON THE FLOOR.
Tracks: Out on the floor / Funky funky feeling.
■ 7".......................BM 107
Black Magic (soul) / Sep '75.

■ 7" P.Disc................UKBURN 2 P
Inferno (1) / Feb '83.
12"......................12 UKBURN 2
7".......................UKBURN 2
Inferno (1) / Oct '83 / Inferno Records / Pinnacle.

SINGS FOR 'IN' CROWDERS THAT GO 'GO-GO'.
Tracks: The 'in' crowd / Blue ribbons (for her curls) / Monkey jerk / Walk with love / Look at me / Be a man / No room to cry / Out on the floor / See you at the 'go-go' / Mr Engineer / In Hollywood / Broken in two / That's how you treat a cheater / Feeling in my heart.
LP......................KENT 071
Kent / Aug '87 / Pinnacle.

SPENDING TIME MAKING LOVE AND GO-ING CRAZY.
Tracks: Spending time making love and going crazy / In crowd, The.
■ 7".......................INF 115
Infinity / Aug '79.

WATCH OUT FOR LUCY.
Tracks: Watch out for Lucy / Turning on you.
■ 7".......................MCA 171
MCA / Jan '75.

WHAT A LADY.
Tracks: What a lady / If love must go.
■ 7".......................2089 017
Capricorn / Apr '76.

WHO'S LOVIN' YOU.
Tracks: Who's lovin' you / I can see clearly now.
■ 7".......................INF 105
Infinity / '79.

Gray, Mark

FEELING INSIDE,THE.
Tracks: Please be love / She will / You're the reason / Born to be a music man / Strong heart dance with me / Back when love was enough / I need you again / Walking after midnight / That feeling inside.
LP......................CBS 26694
MC......................40 26694
CBS / Mar '86 / Sony.

MAGIC.
Tracks: It ain't real if it ain't you / Wounded hearts / Whatever happened to the good old days / Lean on me / Till her heartbreak is over / Left side of the bed / Sun don't shine on the same folks all the time / If all the magic's gone / Till you and your lover are lovers again / Fire from a friend.
■ LP......................CBS 25838
CBS / Oct '84.

THIS OL' PIANO.
Tracks: Diamond in the dust / Twenty years ago / You're gonna be the last love / This ol' piano / I guess you must have touched me just right / Smooth sailing / Dixie girl / Lonely people / It's got to be you / Sometimes when we touch.
LP......................CBS 26149
CBS / Apr '85 / Sony.

Green, Lloyd

Steel guitarist, Lloyd Green was born on October 4th in 1937, in Mobile, Alabama. Following graduation from the University of Mississippi in 1956, he moved to Nashville and worked with Faron Young's band before establishing himself as one of Nashville's most successful session musicians during the 1960's and 1970's. Green has enjoyed modest chart success and has attracted a following as a live attraction. Sadly his style has lost popularity in recent years. (Tony Byworth)

GREEN VELVET.
Tracks: Rainbows and roses / Heartbreak Tennessee / Motel time again / Seven days of crying (makes one weak) / Almost persuaded / Green velvet / Touch my heart / Show me the way to the circus / Cave, The / Bridge washed out, The.
LP......................PRCV 112
President / Oct '82 / Grapevine Distribution / Target Records / Jazz Music / Taylors.

LLOYDS OF NASHVILLE.
Tracks: Not Advised.
LP......................RRL 8013
Release (Ireland) / May '81,

STAINLESS STEEL.
Tracks: Edgewater beach / Desperado / Kiss the moonlight / My love / Stainless steel / Little bit more, A / Twilight dew / Feelings / You and me.
LP......................NSPL 28249
Pye International / Apr '78.

STEEL RIDES.
Tracks: Sally G / Coconut Grove / Steelin' away / Canadian sunset / Spirit of '49 / San Antonio rose / I can help / Crying time / Seaside / Phase phive / Lutetia.
LP......................MNT 81245
Monument / Apr '76 / Sony.

STEELIN' FEELIN'S.
Tracks: Not Advised.
LP......................CMLF 1010
Checkmate / Apr '78.

STEELS THE HITS.
Tracks: Misty moonlight / Ruby (don't take your love to town) / My elusive dream / Crazy arms / Too much of you / There goes my everything / Take these chains from my heart / Moody river / No another time / Moon river / Feelings / My love / Little bit more, A / You & me / Amie / Desperado / Kiss the moonlight / Edgewater beach / Stainless steel.
CD......................PLATCD 33
MC......................PLAC 33
Platinum Music / Jul '92 / Prism Leisure PLC / Ross Records.

SWEET CHEEKS.
Tracks: Sweet cheeks / Green strings / Skillet lickin' / Drifter's polka / Funny bunny / Red eye / Pickin' pot pie / Lovin' machine, The / Pedal pattle / Little darlin'.
LP......................PRCV 103
President / May '88 / Grapevine Distribution / Target Records / Jazz Music / Taylors.

TEN SHADES OF GREEN.
Tracks: Not Advised.
LP......................CMLF 1001
Checkmate / Apr '77.

Greenbriar Boys

BEST OF THE GREENBRIAR BOYS (Greenbriar Boys featuring John Herald).
Tracks: Not Advised.
LP......................VLP 79317
MC......................VMC 79317
Vanguard / '72 / Complete Record Co. Ltd.
CD......................VMD 79317
Vanguard / '89 / Complete Record Co. Ltd.

Greene, Jack

Born 7.1.1930, in Maryville, Tennessee - member of Grand Ole Opry since 1967, the 'Jolly Giant' has enjoyed almost twenty years of the singles chart action. Recorded for Decca, MCA , Firstline and EMH, starting out in country music as a frummer/vocalist with The Cherokee Trio during the mid 40's. Subsequent career moves were to feature spells with the Rhythm Ranch Boys in the early 50's and the Peachtree Cowboys during the mid-50's. Also worked as a member of Ernest Tubb's Texas Troubadours (1962-1967). During 1966, whilst still connnected to Rubb, Greene established himself, and his band of Jolly Greene Giants (changed to the Renegades via the Jolly Giants, due to the Green Giant Food Co's rights to such a title, and instantly made a mark. Signed to Decca, Greene enjoyd a No.1 with *There goes my everything* (Dallas Frazier) in late 1966, getting him off to a flyer. As as result of it's success, Greenne collected four awards at the 1976 Awards Male Vocalist, Song, Single and Album Of The Year.No.1 hits to carry him to 1969 include *All the time* , *Until my dreams come true* and *Statue of a fool* / By this time Jeanie Seeley, his ex-singing partner whilst with Ernest Tubb, had joined his outfit and they made some recordings together with *Wish I didn't have to miss you* making it to No.2. After a decade touring together they dissolved the association - although not before making the fine album *Live at the Grand Ole Opry* , a 1978 recording. Greene later recorded for the Front Line and Step One labels. (Maurice Hope)

GREATEST HITS: JACK GREENE.
Tracks: Not Advised.
LP......................GT 0096
Gusto (USA) / Mar '88.

GREATEST HITS: JACK GREENE & JEAN-NIE SEELY (Greene, Jack & Jeannie Seely).
Tracks: Not Advised.
LP......................GT 0092
Gusto (USA) / Mar '88.

Greene, Lorne

RINGO.
Tracks: Ringo.
■ 7".......................RCA 1428
RCA / Dec '64.

Greene, Richard

DUETS.
Tracks: Not Advised.
LP......................ROUNDER 0075
Rounder / '88 / Projection / Roots Records / Swift / C.M. Distribution / Topic Records / Jazz Music / Hot Shot / A.D.A Distribution / Direct Distribution.

RAMBLIN'.
Tracks: Not Advised.
LP......................ROUNDER 0110
MC......................ROUNDER 0110C

■ DELETED

Rounder / '88 / Projection / Roots Records / Swift / C.M. Distribution / Topic Records / Jazz Music / Hot Shot / A.D.A Distribution / Direct Distribution.

Greenwood, Lee

This American country singer released his debut album *Inside and out* in 1982. The following year, he issued the LP *Somebody's gonna love you*. These platters showed that, when given the right song, Greenwood's powerful and evocative voice could really deliver the goods. One of these songs was *The wind beneath my wings*, a memorable ballad that gave him a sizeable entry on the US country charts plus his first UK chart entry - the single reached the UK no. 49 position in the summer of 1984. By the mid 80's, Greenwood was a substantial star in the American country and MoR markets; his 1985 *Greatest hits* collection logged more thaa half a year on Billboard's Country Albums List. (Bob Macdonald)

CHRISTMAS TO CHRISTMAS.
Tracks: Christmas to Christmas.
7" . . . . **MCA 1021**
MCA / Nov '85 / BMG.

FOOL'S GOLD.
Tracks: Fool's gold / Worth it for the ride.
■ 7" . . . . **LEE 2**
MCA / Jan '85.

GREATEST HITS: LEE GREENWOOD.
Tracks: Fool's gold / Somebody's gonna love you / It turns me inside out / She's lying / Dixie road / Ain't no trick (It takes magic) / Ring on her finger, time on her hands / I.O.U. / Going, going, gone. / God bless the U.S.A.
■ LP. . . . . **IMCA 5582**
MCA (Import) / Mar '86.

I.O.U.
Tracks: I.O.U. / Going, going, gone.
■ 7" . . . . **MCA 844**
MCA / Oct '83.

LOVE WILL FIND IT'S WAY TO YOU.
Tracks: Love will find it's way to you / Look what we made (when we made love) / Silver saxophone / Gonna leave the light on / Heartbreak radio / Just another somebody's body / Didn't we / Mornin' ride / From now on / Little red caboose.
MC . . . . **IMCAC 5770**
MCA / Mar '87 / BMG.
■ LP. . . . . **IMCA 5770**
MCA / Mar '87.
CD . . . . **MCAD 5770**
MCA / Oct '87 / BMG.

SOMEBODY'S GONNA LOVE YOU.
Tracks: I.O.U. / Somebody's gonna love you / Going, going, gone / Call it what you want to (It's still love) / Barely holding on / Love won't let us say goodbye / Ladies love / Wind beneath my wings / Think about the good times / Someone who remembers.
MC . . . . **MCFC 3186**
MCA / Feb '84 / BMG.
■ LP. . . . . **MCF 3186**
MCA / Feb '84.
CD . . . . **MCAD 5403**
MCA / Jan '86 / BMG.

SOMEBODY'S GONNA LOVE YOU.
Tracks: Somebody's gonna love you / Another you.
■ 7" . . . . **MCA 825**
MCA / Jul '83.

STREAMLINE.
Tracks: Streamline / Lonely people / I don't mind the thorns (If you're the rose) / Hearts aren't meant to break (They're meant to love) / Little at a time, A / Breakin' even / Don't underestimate my love for you / Same old song / Will to love,The / Leave my heart the way you found it.
■ LP. . . . . **IMCA 5622**
MCA / Mar '86.
■ CD . . . . **MCAD 5622**
MCA / Mar '86.

WIND BENEATH MY WINGS.
Tracks: Wind beneath my wings / Barely holding on.
■ 7" . . . . **MCA 877**
MCA / May '84.

WIND BENEATH MY WINGS, THE.
Tracks: You've got a good love comin' / I found love in time / I don't want to wake you / Love me like I'm leavin' tonight / Worth it for the ride / Wind beneath my wings / Two heart serenade / I.O.U. / Fools' gold / Even love can't save us now.
LP. . . . . **MCF 3228**
■ MC . . . . **MCFC 3228**
MCA / Jul '84.

YOU'VE GOT A GOOD FRIEND COMIN'.
Tracks: You've got a good love comin' / Love in time / I don't want to wake you / Love me like I'm leaving tonight / Worth it for the ride / Two heart serenade / Fool's gold / Lean, mean, lovin' machine / Even love can't save us now / God bless the U.S.A.
LP. . . . . **MCA 5488**
MCA (USA) / Jan '84 / MCA (Imports).

Greer, John

Making his recording debut in 1971, John Greer is one of Northern Ireland's most prolific artists with 17 albums to his credit. He's recorded twice in Nashville and, while there, appeared twice on the Grand Ole Opry and Ralph Emery's high rating *Nashville now* TV show. *Roses for Mama* was a substantial hit for him in 1980, and the duets that he recorded with American Jennifer O' Brien resulted in BCMA "Single of the year" awards in 1988-1989. In addition to his performing activities Greer has been presenting country music on radio for 16 years and currently has a show on Belfast's Downtown radio. (Tony Byworth)

BEST OF JOHN GREER VOL 1.
Tracks: All I have to offer you is me / Crystal chandeliers / Jack to a king / Don't let me cross over / I threw away the rose / Sing me back home / Swingin' doors / Streets of Baltimore / Letter edged in black / Fraulein / Broken engagement / Mama tried / Silver haired daddy of mine / Teardrop on a rose.
LP. . . . . **HRL 147**
MC . . . . **CHRL 147**
Homespun (Ireland) / May '88 / Homespun Records / Ross Records / Wellard Dist.

COUNTRY HALL OF FAME.
Tracks: Help me make it through the night / I threw away the rose / So afraid of losing you / Fraulien / Letter edged in black / Did she mention my name / Country hall of fame / Almost persuaded / Streets of Baltimore / She's mine / Fugitive, The / Me and Bobby McGee.
MC . . . . **CT 121**
Outlet / '73 / Projection / Duncans / C.M. Distribution / Ross Records / Topic Records / Direct Distribution / Midland Records.

COUNTRY REQUESTS.
Tracks: You're my best friend / Among the Wicklow hills / Truck drivin' man / Sing me back home / Silver sandals / Broken engagement / Day the blizzard hit our town, The / Country music has gone to town / Able bodied man / Soldier's last letter / Two little orphans / Swingin' doors / Five little fingers / Once again.
LP. . . . . **HRL 123**
Homespun (Ireland) / Nov '76 / Homespun Records / Ross Records / Wellard Dist.

COUNTRY SIDE OF JOHN GREER.
Tracks: Mamma tried / Blue side of lonesome / Today I started lovin' you again / Suny side of my life, The / Teardrop on a rose / Farmer's daughter, The / Jambalaya / Good old country music / Cover mama's flowers / Santa and the kids / Silver haired daddy of mine / Pass me by / Crystal chandeliers / Try it, you'll like it.
LP. . . . . **STOL 126**
MC . . . . **CT 126**
Outlet / Sep '75 / Projection / Duncans / C.M. Distribution / Ross Records / Topic Records / Direct Distribution / Midland Records.

HITS OF JOHN GREER.
Tracks: Teddy bear / Dust on the bible / Love's gonna live here again / Singin' on a Sunday / If teardrops were pennies / Good old country music / Marriage CB way (Romance on the airwaves) / Coat of many colours / Silver sandals / Truck drivin' man / Keep it country / Roses for Mama.
LP. . . . . **PHL 438**
MC . . . . **CPHL 438**
Homespun (Ireland) / '82 / Homespun Records / Ross Records / Wellard Dist.

IRISH SONGS, COUNTRY STYLE.
Tracks: Boys from County Armagh / Let us sing of dear old Ireland / Little country town in Ireland / Forty shades of green / Any Tipperary town / Green green grass of home / Isle of Innisfree / Gentle mother / Galway bay / Danny boy / Irish eyes / I'll settle for old Ireland.
LP. . . . . **PHL 426**
MC . . . . **CPHL 426**
Homespun (Ireland) / '82 / Homespun Records / Ross Records / Wellard Dist.

JOHN GREER'S COUNTRY & WESTERN HITS.
Tracks: Two loves / All I have to offer you is me / Jack to a king / Lonely music / Most of the time / Coat of many colours / When two worlds collide / 21 years / Pub with no beer / Don't let me cross over / Jeannie Norman / If teardrops were pennies / Crown of thorns / Rocking alone in an old rocking chair.
LP. . . . . **CHRL 109**
Homespun (Ireland) / '75 / Homespun Records / Ross Records / Wellard Dist.

KEEP IT COUNTRY.
Tracks: Keep it country / Hank William's guitar / Branded man / So much for me so much for you / Don't squeeze my Sharmon / I'll tell you where to go / Hear the family sing / Red rose from blue side of town / Okie from Muskogee / She just loved the cheatin' out of me / Love gonna live here again / Holding things together.
LP. . . . . **PHL 402**
MC . . . . **CPHL 402**
Homespun (Ireland) / '82 / Homespun Records / Ross Records / Wellard Dist.

MY MOTHER PRAYED FOR ME.
Tracks: Jesus take a hold / If Jesus came to your house / Family who prays shall never part, The / Great speckled bird, The / What a friend we have in Jesus / Wait a little longer dear Jesus / I saw the light / When you get to heaven / If I were alone with God / Flowers, the sunset, the trees, The / On the wings of a dove / Take time out for Jesus / I'm using my buble for a roadmap / My mother prayed for me.
LP. . . . . **HRL 144**
MC . . . . **CHRL 144**
Homespun (Ireland) / May '88 / Homespun Records / Ross Records / Wellard Dist.

OLD COUNTRY CHURCH.
Tracks: Old country church / It is no secret / Church in the wildwood, The / Family bible / Mother went a walkin' / This world is not my home / Trouble in Amen Corner / Kneel down and pray / When the roll is called up yonder / Good folks in my life, The / When God comes and gathers his jewels / Old rugged cross, The / Lay your mighty hand on me / Dust on the bible.
LP. . . . . **HRL 126**
Homespun (Ireland) / Feb '78 / Homespun Records / Ross Records / Wellard Dist.

R&B IN NEW YORK CITY.
Tracks: Woman is a five letter word / Tell me so / Got you on my mind / Let me hold you / You played on my piano / Lonesome and blue / I need you / I'll never let you go / I'm the fat man / Beginning to miss you / Rhythm in the breeze / Drinkin' fool / Getting mighty lonesome for you / Too long / Come back Maybeline / Night crawlin'.
LP. . . . . **OFF 6026**
Official / Charly / Cadillac Music / Jazz Music.

ROSES FOR MAMA.
Tracks: What's wrong with the way that we're doing it now / Roots of my raising / Shindig in the barn / Nothing sure looked good on you / Each season changes you / My daddy's eyes / Roses for Mama / That's what makes a country sing / Honky tonk blues / D.J cried, The / We sure danced us some good'uns / I gotta thing about trains.
LP. . . . . **PHL 423**
MC . . . . **CPHL 423**
Homespun (Ireland) / '82 / Homespun Records / Ross Records / Wellard Dist.

ROSES FOR MAMA.
Tracks: Roses for mama / D.J. cried.
7" . . . . **HS 038**
Homespun (Ireland) / Nov '83 / Homespun Records / Ross Records / Wellard Dist.

SINGIN' ON A SUNDAY.
Tracks: Whispering hope / Help me understand / Hear the family sing / Supper time / Precious memories / Shall we gather at the river? / No earthly God / Singin' on a Sunday / That's where I learned to pray / Childhood memories / In the sweet bye and bye.
LP. . . . . **PHL 424**
MC . . . . **CPHL 424**
Homespun (Ireland) / '82 / Homespun Records / Ross Records / Wellard Dist.

SINGS COUNTRY.
Tracks: Two loves / From a jack to a king / Pub with no beer.
LP. . . . . **HRL 109**
Homespun (Ireland) / May '88 / Homespun Records / Ross Records / Wellard Dist.

SOMEWHERE BETWEEN.
Tracks: New patches / Somewhere between / Reasons / I still believe in waltzes / Old time sake / You sure make cheatin' seem easy / One I'm holding now / God must be a cowboy at heart / Promise, The / Forget me not.
LP. . . . . **HAW 091**
Hawk / '90 / C.M. Distribution.

TEDDY BEAR.
Tracks: Teddy bear.
7" . . . . **HS 042**
Homespun (Ireland) / Feb '81 / Homespun Records / Ross Records / Wellard Dist.

THAT'S COUNTRY.
Tracks: That's only / Charlie's angel / I made the prison band / My last day / Mom & dad waltz / Rooftop lullaby / Sing me a song papa / Sundown in Nashville / Last country song, The.
LP. . . . . **RBA 1002**
Rainbow (Ireland) / '88.

WHAT A FRIEND WE HAVE IN JESUS.
Tracks: What a friend we have in Jesus / Just a little longer please, Jesus / On the wings of a dove / Family who prays shall never part, The / Kneel down and pray / Shall we gather at the river? / Whispering hope / In the sweet bye and bye / It is no secret / Old rugged cross, The / Church in the wildwood, The / When the roll is called up yonder.
LP. . . . . **PHL 459**
MC . . . . **CPHL 459**
Homespun (Ireland) / Dec '82 / Homespun Records / Ross Records / Wellard Dist.

■ DELETED

Gribbin, Tom

Florida based singer/songwriter Tom Gribbin gave up a successful attorney's practice in favour of music. Based in St. Petersburg, he and his band the Saltwater Cowboys built up a loyal following in Britain before his career was curtailed by a drug bust. His first album *Saltwater convoy* featured members of Jimmy Buffett's and Don Williams' band. Back on the scene in late 1992, Gribbin is continuing his songwriting ambitions while operating (with his friend, former manager, Bob Shoemaker) a successful string of comedy clubs, Coconuts, throughout the Sunshine State and other regions of the USA and West Indies. (Tony Byworth)

GUNS OF BRIXTON (Gribbin, Tom & The Saltwater Cowboys).
Tracks: Guns of Brixton / Honky tonk blues.
■ 7" . . . . **CRE 002**
Country Roads Records / Jun '81.

SON OF LIGHTNING.
Tracks: Train to Dixie / Waymore's blues / Saltwater gypsy / Champagne ladies / Son of lightning / Guns of Brixton / Honky tonk blues / Johnny deepwater / Big rig / To be your man.
■ LP. . . . . **CRLP 1001**
Country Roads Records / Nov '81.

USEPPA ISLAND RENDEVOUS (Gribbin, Tom & The Saltwater Band).
Tracks: My images come / Gospel rock / Sad cafe / Time will tell / Out of my hands / Rich in the blues / Love you too / Fisherman's prayer / What am I supposed to do / Salty dog cracker man.
LP. . . . . **RANGE 7002**
Range (1) / May '84.

Grier, David

CLIMBING THE WALLS (see under Compton, Mike).

FREEWHEELING.
Tracks: Wheeling / Shadowbrook / Old hotel rag, The / Angeline the baker / Bluegrass itch / Alabama jubilee / Blue midnite star, A / Roanoke / If I knew her name / Gold rush / Fog rolling over the Glen / New soldier's joy, The.
MC . . . . **ROU 0250**
Rounder / '88 / Projection / Roots Records / Swift / C.M. Distribution / Topic Records / Jazz Music / Hot Shot / A.D.A Distribution / Direct Distribution.
LP. . . . . **ROUNDER 0250**
Rounder / Aug '88 / Projection / Roots Records / Swift / C.M. Distribution / Topic Records / Jazz Music / Hot Shot / A.D.A Distribution / Direct Distribution.
CD . . . . **CDROU 0250**
Rounder / '91 / Projection / Roots Records / Swift / C.M. Distribution / Topic Records / Jazz Music / Hot Shot / A.D.A Distribution / Direct Distribution.

Griffith, Nanci

Texas - born (06.07.1953) 'folkabilly' singer-songwriter, and guitarist figuring strongly in both the eighties' new country boom and Texas' own surge of singer-songwriters, and helping prise open doors and gain the art it's deserved recognition. Griffith, as yet, has to establish her true standing in the country music business - something that could well soon be rectified. her mini-novel songs first came to light in 1978 with her album *There's a light beyond these woods* on the F.B Deal outlet (then her former husband Eric Taylor's Featherbed label- which was the label on which 1988's *Poet in the window* debuted) prior to making their way onto MCA's catalogue via Philo records. In the early days Griffith at 14 could be found, accompanied by her parents, singing in Austin's honky tonks, followed on the late 60s / 70s with appearances at Kerrville's Folk Festival, coffee houses and dancehalls. She also spent some time teaching kindergarten .Griffith's vocal style, was musch influenced by that of folk singer Carolyn Hester and the simple songwriting themes of Loretta Lynn. Became a star of the state's folk circuit, drawing a new young audience singing in a fragile-pure voice and gaining more than just favourable comparisons against the best of the genre. Songs very much associated with Griffith, include her definitive rendering of New York writer Julie Gold's *From a distance* and own her songs *Love at the five and dime* (a hit for Kathy Mattea). Among her songwriting collaborations there's *Outbound plane* (Tom Russell) charting for Suzy Bogguss. Griffith's own chart record meanwhile is disappointing, with Pat Alger's *Lone star state of mind* , Harlan Howard's *Never mind* and Roger Brown's *I knew love* remarkably enjoying only relatively short chart careers. Griffith's style developed much while at Philo, surrounded by fine acoustic musicians like Mark O'Connor, Roy Huskey Jr. Lloyd Green and Dublin's electric lead guitarist Phil Donnelly as well as co-producer Jim Rooney. *Once in a very blue moon* and Grammy's 1986 Best Folk Album *Last of the true believers* , setting it up for MCA to sign her (with her band the Blue Moon Orchestra) in 1987. Waif-like Nanci, dressed in school girl dresses and bobby socks, found herself a ready made audience in Ireland and England. Since initial sell-out venues in Dublin (where she's influenced both it's artists and record buying public), she'a been a regular touring visitor to the UK. Backed by her band the Blue Moon Orchestra with lifetime member, keyboard player James Hooker and the likes of Donnelly, Fran Breen, Frank Christian and Lee Satterfield making up the compliment. Griffith appeared solo at the Peterborough Country Festival (1986) and has also performed at Cambridge Folk Festivals. A steady flow of albums ensued at MCA, which were progressively becoming more artistic affairs - *Storms* (selling around 400,00 copies) and *Late night grande* , both recorded away from Nashville (Los Angeles and Berkshire respectively) taking her in a new direction. In the midst of which we had her plaintive 1988 *One fair Summer evening* live album, recorded at Anderson's Fair, in Houston, Texas. In 1993, Griffith's music was to take another about turn returning to her folk/country acoustic roots when she recorded *Other voices, other rooms* . The accolade winning release (promoted via her extensive European tour during that spring) a fitting tribute to the songwiters (who've been largely responsible for introducing her to the art) (songs featured, including *Speed of the sound of loneliness* , *Do Re Me* , *Boots of spanish leather* and *10 Degrees and getting colder*). Apart from guest slots from Guy Clrk, Bob Dylan, Iris DeMent, Emmylou Harris, and John Prine it has also found Griffith renewing her association with producer/early mentor Jim Rooney. Griffith, who also recorded a cover of the Elvis' hit *Wooden Heart* on an extended CD single, has also made an appearance with the Chieftains on the Irish unit's 1991 RCA album/ video *An Irish Evening, Live at the Grand Opera House Belfast* besides her early three 'live' slots on the Kerrville Folk Festival tapes during the period 1978-1982. (Maurice Hope)

COLD HEARTS.
Tracks: Cold hearts, closed minds / Ford econoline / Lonestar state of mind.
■ EP. . . . . **MCA 1221**
MCA / Nov '87 / BMG.

FROM A DISTANCE.
Tracks: From a distance / Sing one for sister.
7" . . . . **MCA 1169**
MCA / Jul '87 / BMG.
■ CD Single . . . . **DMCA 1282**
MCA / Sep '88 / BMG.
■ 7" . . . . **MCA 1282**
MCA / Sep '88.

FROM CLARE TO HERE.
Tracks: From Clare to here.
CD Single . . . . **MCSTD 1771**
■ MC Single . . . . **MCSC 1771**
MCA / Apr '93.

HEAVEN.
Tracks: Heaven.
12" . . . . **MCST 1596**
7" . . . . **MCS 1596**
■ CD Single . . . . **MCSTD 1596**
MCA / Nov '91.

I KNEW LOVE.
Tracks: I knew love / Never mind / Lone star state of mind.
12" . . . . **MCAT 1240**
7" . . . . **MCA 1240**
MCA / Apr '88 / BMG.

IT'S A HARD LIFE.
Tracks: It's a hard life.
12" . . . . **MCAT 1358**
7" . . . . **MCA 1358**
■ CD Single . . . . **DMCAT 1358**
MCA / Jul '89.

LAST OF THE TRUE BELIEVERS.
Tracks: Last of the true believers, The / Love at the five and dime / St. Olav's gate / More than a whisper / Banks of the old Pontchartrain / Looking for the time / Goin' gone / One of these days / Love's found a shoulder / Fly by night / Wing and the wheel.
CD . . . . **CDPH 1109**
Philo (USA) / Dec '86 / Roots Records / Projection / Topic Records / Direct Distribution / Ross Records / C.M. Distribution / Impetus Records.
LP. . . . . **PH 1109**
MC . . . . **CPH 1109**
Philo (USA) / '88 / Roots Records / Projection / Topic Records / Direct Distribution / Ross Records / C.M. Distribution / Impetus Records.
CD . . . . **REUCD 1013**
LP. . . . . **REU 1013**
MC . . . . **REUC 1013**
Rounder Europa (USA) / Jun '88 / Pinnacle.

LATE NIGHT GRANDE HOTEL.
Tracks: Not Advised.
CD . . . . **MCAD 10304**
MCA / Aug '91 / BMG.
■ LP. . . . . **MCA 10304**
MCA / Aug '91.
■ MC . . . . **MCAC 10304**
MCA / Aug '91.

LATE NIGHT GRANDE HOTEL.
Tracks: Late night Grande Hotel.
12" . . . . **MCST 1566**
7" . . . . **MCS 1566**
■ CD Single . . . . **MCSTD 1566**
MCA / Aug '91.
■ MC Single . . . . **MCSC 1566**
MCA / Oct '91.

LITTLE LOVE AFFAIRS.
Tracks: Not Advised.
■ LP. . . . . **MCF 3413**
MCA / Aug '90.
CD . . . . **DMCF 3413**
■ MC . . . . **MCFC 3413**
MCA / Aug '90.
CD . . . . **MCLD 19211**
MC . . . . **MCLC 19211**
MCA / Aug '93 / BMG.

LONE STAR STATE OF MIND.
Tracks: Lone star state of mind / Cold hearts, closed minds / From a distance / Beacon Street / Nickel dreams / Sing one for sister / Ford econoline / Trouble in the fields / Love in a memory / Let it shine on me / There's a light beyond these woods.
LP. . . . . **MCF 3364**
■ MC . . . . **MCFC 3364**
MCA / Apr '87.
CD . . . . **MCAD 5927**
MCA / Jul '87 / BMG.
CD . . . . **MCLD 19176**
MCA / Oct '92 / BMG.

ONCE IN A VERY BLUE MOON.
Tracks: Ghost in the music / Love is a hard waltz / Roseville fair / Mary and Omie / Friend out in the madness / I'm not drivin' these wheels / Ballad of Robin Winter-Smith / Daddy said / Once in a very blue moon / Year down in New Orleans / Spin on a red brick floor.
MC . . . . **PH 1096C**
Philo (USA) / Dec '85 / Roots Records / Projection / Topic Records / Direct Distribution / Ross Records / C.M. Distribution / Impetus Records.
CD . . . . **CDPH 1096**
Philo (USA) / Dec '86 / Roots Records / Projection / Topic Records / Direct Distribution / Ross Records / C.M. Distribution / Impetus Records.
LP. . . . . **PH 1096**
Philo (USA) / Dec '87 / Roots Records / Projection / Topic Records / Direct Distribution / Ross Records / C.M. Distribution / Impetus Records.
■ LP. . . . . **MCG 6054**
MCA / Jul '89.
■ CD . . . . **DMCG 6054**
MCA / Jul '89.
■ MC . . . . **MCGC 6054**
MCA / Jul '89.
CD . . . . **MCLD 19039**
MCA / Apr '92 / BMG.
■ MC . . . . **MCLC 19039**
MCA / Apr '92.

ONE FAIR SUMMER EVENING.
Tracks: Once in a very blue moon / Looking for the time / Deadwood, South Dakota / More than a whisper / Wing and the wheel / Spin on a red brick floor / Roseville fair / Workin' in corners.
CD . . . . **DMCF 3435**
MC . . . . **MCFC 3435**
MCA / Nov '88 / BMG.
■ LP. . . . . **MCF 3435**
MCA / Nov '88.

ONE FAIR SUMMER EVENING.
Tracks: Once in a very blue moon / More than a whisper / Love at the Five & Dime / Looking for the time (working girl) / Deadwood, South Dakota / Workin' in corners / Daddy said / From a distance / I would bring you Ireland / Spin on a red brick floor / There's a light beyond these woods (Mary Margaret).
VHS. . . . . **MCV 9003**
MCA / Jun '90 / BMG.

OTHER VOICES, OTHER ROOMS.
Tracks: Across the great divide / Woman of the phoenix / Tecumseh valley / Three fights up / Boots of spanish leather / Speed of the sound of loneliness / From Clare to here / I can't help but wonder where I'm bound / Do re mi / This old town / Comin' down in the rain / Ten degrees and getting colder / Morning song to Sally / Night rider's lament / Are you tired of me darling / Turn around / Wimoweh.
CD . . . . **MCD 10796**
MC . . . . **MCC 10796**
MCA / Mar '93 / BMG.

OUTBOUND PLANE.
Tracks: Outbound plane / So long ago / Trouble in the fields.
12" . . . . **MCAT 1230**
7" . . . . **MCA 1230**
MCA / Feb '88 / BMG.

POET IN MY WINDOW.
Tracks: Not Advised.
CD . . . . **DMCL 1911**
■ MC . . . . **MCLC 1911**
MCA / Oct '91.

SPEED OF SOUND.
Tracks: Speed of sound.
CD Single . . . . **MCSTD 1743**
■ MC Single . . . . **MCSC 1743**
MCA / Mar '93.

G 12

■ DELETED

STORMS.
Tracks: Not Advised.
CD . . . . **DMCG 6066**
MC . . . . **MCGC 6066**
MCA / Sep '89 / BMG.
■ LP . . . . **MCG 6066**
MCA / Sep '89.

THERE'S A LIGHT BEYOND THESE WOODS.
Tracks: Michael's song / West Texas sun / Dollar matinee / Alabama soft spoken blues / Song for remembered heroes / There's a light beyond these woods / Montana backroads.
CD . . . . **PH 1097CD**
MC . . . . **PH 1097C**
Philo (USA) / '87 / Roots Records / Projection / Topic Records / Direct Distribution / Ross Records / C.M. Distribution / Impetus Records.
LP . . . . **PH 1097**
Philo (USA) / Aug '87 / Roots Records / Projection / Topic Records / Direct Distribution / Ross Records / C.M. Distribution / Impetus Records.
■ CD . . . . **DMCG 6052**
MCA / Jul '89.
■ LP . . . . **MCG 6052**
MCA / Jul '89.
■ MC . . . . **MCGC 6052**
MCA / Jul '89.
■ CD . . . . **DMCL 1910**
MCA / Aug '90.
MC . . . . **MCLC 19112**
MCA / Oct '92 / BMG.

YOU MADE THIS LOVE A TEARDROP.
Tracks: You made this love a teardrop.
12" . . . . **MCAT 1379**
7" . . . . **MCA 1379**
■ CD Single . . . . **DMCAT 1379**
MCA / Nov '89 / BMG.

Grisman, David

David played in the Even Dozen Jug Band with Maria Muldaur and John Sebastian, then formed rock band Earth Opera in Boston with Peter Rowan (Grisman played saxophone). In 1973, neo-bluegrass group Old And In The Way comprised Grisman, Rowan and Jerry Garcia, sometimes also with fiddler Vassar Clements. Grisman and Rowan formed Muleskinner with fiddler Richard Greene, Grisman and Greene formed the Great American Music Band with Taj Mahal on bass. He formed his own quintet in 1977, tired of labels, he calls it 'dawg music'. (Donald Clarke).

ACOUSTIC CHRISTMAS.
Tracks: Not Advised.
CD . . . . **CD 0190**
LP . . . . **ROUNDER 0190**
MC . . . . **ROUNDER 0190C**
Rounder / '88 / Projection / Roots Records / Swift / C.M. Distribution / Topic Records / Jazz Music / Hot Shot / A.D.A Distribution / Direct Distribution.

DAVID GRISMAN QUINTET.
Tracks: Not Advised.
CD . . . . **K 5**
LP . . . . **F 5**
MC . . . . **C 5**
Kaleidoscope (USA) / Sep '79 / Projection / Ross Records / Roots Records / Swift / C.M. Distribution / Topic Records / Duncans.

DAVID GRISMAN ROUNDER ALBUM.
Tracks: Hello / Sawing on the strings / Waiting on Vasser / I ain't broke but I'm badly bent / Op 38 / Hold to God's unchanging hand / Boston boy / Cheyenne / Til the end of the world rolls around / You'll find her name written there / On and on / Bob's Brewin / So long.
CD . . . . **CD 0069**
LP . . . . **ROUNDER 0069**
MC . . . . **ROUNDER 0069C**
Rounder / '88 / Projection / Roots Records / Swift / C.M. Distribution / Topic Records / Jazz Music / Hot Shot / A.D.A Distribution / Direct Distribution.

EARLY DAWG.
Tracks: Not Advised.
LP . . . . **SH 3713**
MC . . . . **ZCSH 3713**
Sugarhill(USA) / '88 / Roots Records / Projection / Impetus Records / C.M. Distribution / Jazz Music / Swift / Duncans / A.D.A Distribution.

HERE TODAY (Grisman, David & Various Artists).
Tracks: I'll love nobody but you / Once more / Foggy mountain chimes / Children are cryin', The / Hot corn / Cold corn / Lonesome river / My walking shoes / Love and wealth / Billy in the lowground / Making plans / Sweet little Miss blue eyes / Going up home to live in green pastures.
LP . . . . **ROUNDER 0169**
MC . . . . **ROUNDER 0169C**
Rounder / Aug '88 / Projection / Roots Records / Swift / C.M. Distribution / Topic Records / Jazz Music / Hot Shot / A.D.A Distribution / Direct Distribution.
CD . . . . **ROU 0169CD**
MC . . . . **ROU 0169C**
Rounder / Aug '93 / Projection / Roots Records / Swift / C.M. Distribution / Topic Records / Jazz Music / Hot Shot / A.D.A Distribution / Direct Distribution.

HOME IS WHERE THE HEART IS.
Tracks: True life blues / Down in the willow garden / My long journey home / Little Willie / Highway of sorrow / Sophronie / My aching heart / Close by / Feast here tonight / Leavin' home / Little cabin home on the hill / I'm comin' back / But I don't know when / Salty Dawg blues / If I lose / Sad and lonesome day / My little Georgia rose / Foggy mountain top / I'm my own grandpa / Pretty Polly / Home is where the heart is / Nine pound hammer / Memories of mother and day / Teardrops in my eyes / House of gold.
CD Set . . . . **CD 0251/2**
Double LP . . . . **ROUNDER 0251/2**
MC Set . . . . **ROUND 0251/2**
Rounder / Aug '88 / Projection / Roots Records / Swift / C.M. Distribution / Topic Records / Jazz Music / Hot Shot / A.D.A Distribution / Direct Distribution.

HOT DAWG.
Tracks: Not Advised.
CD . . . . **UDCD 505**
Mobile Fidelity Sound Lab(USA) / Apr '89.

OLD AND IN THE WAY (see under Compton, Mike).

Guilbeau, Gib

TOE TAPPIN' MUSIC.
Tracks: Not Advised.
LP . . . . **SHILOH 4085**
Shiloh / May '79.

Guitar, Bonnie

Virtually unknown in the European marketplace, Bonnie Guitar (born Bonnie Buckingham in Seattle, Washington) first hit national attention in 1957 with her self-penned hit *Dark moon* . Originally a session guitarist, she combined a career as an artist and record executive, the latter including the founding of Dolton Records (and the discovery of the pop band the Fleetwoods) and working in an A&R capacity at Dot and ABC-Paramount. She made a slight comeback in the late 1980's. (Tony Byworth)

DARK MOON.
Tracks: Mister fire eyes / Dark moon / Open the door / Half your heart / If you see my heart dancing / Johnny Vagabond / Making believe / Down where the tradewinds blow / Letter from Jenny / There's a new moon over my shoulder / Moonlight and shadows / Carolina moon / By the light of the silvery moon / Shine on harvest moon / Moon is low, The / Get out and under the moon / Moonlight on the Colorado / Moonlight and roses / It's only a paper moon / Prairie moon / Roll along Kentucky moon / Love is over / Love is done / Stand there mountain / I found you out / Love by the jukebox light / Big Mike / Very precious love, A / If you'll be the teacher.
CD Set . . . . **BCD 15531**
Bear Family / Feb '92 / Rollercoaster Records / Swift / Direct Distribution.

Gunter, Arthur

BLACK AND BLUES.
Tracks: Not Advised.
LP . . . . **LP 8017**
Excello (USA) / Dec '87 / Swift.

Guthrie, Jack

The cousin of the legendary Woody, the recording career of Jack Guthrie (1915-48) was brief and success modest, scoring only three chart placings in the mid 40's, *Oklahoma hills* (cowritten with his famous relation), *I'm brandin' my darlin' with my heart* and *Oakie boogie* . With encouragement to go to Nashville, and become part of its developing country scene, by Ernest Tubb, tuberculosis tragically cut short his life. After being neglected for many years, the majority of Guthrie's recordings for Capitol (including some unissued items) have now resurfaced on a 29 track Bear Family compact disc. (Tony Byworth)

JACK GUTHRIE & HIS GREATEST SONGS.
Tracks: Not Advised.
LP . . . . **HAT 3095**
MC . . . . **HATC 3095**
Stetson / Feb '89 / Crusader Marketing Co. / Swift / Wellard Dist. / Midland Records / C.M. Distribution.

OKLAHOMA HILLS.
Tracks: Oklahoma hills / When the cactus is in bloom / Next to the soil / Shame on you / I'm branding my darlin' / With my heart / Careless darlin' / Oakie boogie / In the shadows of my heart / For Oklahoma / I'm yearning / No need to knock on my door / Shut that gate / I'm tellin' you / Chained to a memory / Look out for the crossing / Dallas darlin' / Colorado blues / Welcome home stranger / I still love you as I did in yesterday / Oklahoma's calling / Clouds rain trouble down, The / Answer to moonlight 'moonlight and skies' / Please, oh please / I loved you once but I can't trust you now / Out of sight / I'm building a stairway to heaven / Ida Red / I told you once / San Antonio Rose / You laughed and I cried.
CD . . . . **BCD 15580**
Bear Family / Nov '91 / Rollercoaster Records / Swift / Direct Distribution.

Guthrie, Woody

Woodrow Wilson Guthrie was born into a pioneer family; his sister was killed in a coal-oil stove explosion, his father failed in a property business, and his mother was committed to a mental institution. He left high school at 16, and hit the road with a harmonica in his pocket. He worked with his cousin Jack Guthrie, a well-known radio country singer, and by 1935 was already writing songs which would total about 1000, including classics *Pastures of plenty, This land is your land, So long, it's been good to know ya* (a top ten hit in 1951 by the Weavers), and many more. He often put new words to old tunes, but as a true folk artist opposed restrictions of copyright laws on his own songs as well as others. He sang on the radio, recorded 'Dust bowl ballads' for Alan Lomax's Library of Congress archive, and was commissioned by the Bonneville Power Administration to write songs, making recordings recently rediscovered and released in the Columbia River Collecton in Topic. He inspired Pete Seeger, Jack Elliott and later Bob Dylan. He formed the Almanac Singers in 1941 with Lee Hays, Seeger and others, worked briefly with the Headline Singers (Leadbelly, Sonny Terry, Brownie McGhee), and wrote his autobiography 'Bound For Glory' in 1943, the year he joined the merchant marine with Cisco Houston. They collected musical instruments, sang in north Africa, Sicily and the UK, surviving torpedo attacks. Folk music was a childrens' genre after the war in the US as Seeger's career was seriously hampered by illegal blacklisting and other folkies put their heads down. It is not too much to say that Woody's spirit - and recording of hundreds of songs for the Folkways label - saved America's folk soul until a new generation could kick over the traces, beginning with the Newport folk festivals in the late 1950s. From the mid-1950s, however, he was seriously ill with Huntington's Chorea, an inherited wasting disease which finally killed him, just as his son Arlo's career took off. (Donald Clarke)

COLUMBIA RIVER COLLECTION.
Tracks: Not Advised.
CD . . . . **CD 1036**
LP . . . . **ROUNDER 1036**
MC . . . . **ROUNDER 1036C**
Rounder / Aug '88 / Projection / Roots Records / Swift / C.M. Distribution / Topic Records / Jazz Music / Hot Shot / A.D.A Distribution / Direct Distribution.
CD . . . . **TSCD 1448**
LP **12T 1448**
Topic / Jan '88 / Roots Records / Jazz Music / C.M. Distribution / Cadillac Music / Direct Distribution / Swift / Topic Records.

DUST BOWL BALLADS.
Tracks: Not Advised.
CD . . . . **CD 1040**
LP . . . . **ROUNDER 1040**
Rounder / '88 / Projection / Roots Records / Swift / C.M. Distribution / Topic Records / Jazz Music / Hot Shot / A.D.A Distribution / Direct Distribution.
LP . . . . **FH 5212**
Folkways (USA) / '88 / Projection / Swift / C.M. Distribution / Hot Shot / Jazz Music.
MC . . . . **ROUNDER 1040C**
Rounder / '88 / Projection / Roots Records / Swift / C.M. Distribution / Topic Records / Jazz Music / Hot Shot / A.D.A Distribution / Direct Distribution.

LEGENDARY PERFORMER, A.
Tracks: Great dust storm, The / I ain't got no home / Talking dust bowl blues / Vigilante man / Dust can't kill me / Dust pneumonia blues / Pretty boy Floyd / Blowin' down this road / Tom Joad (part 1) / Tom Joad (part 2) / Dust bowl refugee / Do re mi / Dust bowl blues / Dusty old dust (so long it's been good to know).
LP . . . . **PL 12099**
■ MC . . . . **PK 12099**
RCA / '79.

LIBRARY OF CONGRESS RECORDINGS VOL. 1.
Tracks: Not Advised.
CD . . . . **CD 1041**
LP . . . . **ROUNDER 1041**
MC . . . . **ROUNDER 1041C**
Rounder / '88 / Projection / Roots Records / Swift / C.M. Distribution / Topic Records / Jazz Music / Hot Shot / A.D.A Distribution / Direct Distribution.

LIBRARY OF CONGRESS RECORDINGS VOL.2.
Tracks: Not Advised.
CD . . . . **CD 1042**
LP . . . . **ROUNDER 1042**
MC . . . . **ROUNDER 1042C**
Rounder / '88 / Projection / Roots Records / Swift / C.M. Distribution / Topic Records / Jazz Music / Hot Shot / A.D.A Distribution / Direct Distribution.

LIBRARY OF CONGRESS RECORDINGS VOL.3.
Tracks: Not Advised.
CD . . . . .CD 1043
LP . . . . ROUNDER 1043
MC . . . . .ROUNDER 1043C
Rounder / '88 / Projection / Roots Records / Swift / C.M. Distribution / Topic Records / Jazz Music / Hot Shot / A.D.A Distribution / Direct Distribution.

POOR BOY.
Tracks: Baltimore to Washington / Little black train / Who's going to shoe your pretty feet / Slip knot / Poor boy / Mean talking blues / Stepstone / Bed on the floor / Little darlin' / Miner's song / Train blues / Danville girl no.2 / Ride old paint.
LP . . . . .TRS 113
Transatlantic / Oct '81 / Roots Records / C.M. Distribution.

SONGS FROM BOUND TO GLORY.
Tracks: Gypsy Davey / Jesus Christ / Pastures of plenty / Columbus Georgia stockade / So long (It's been good to know you) / Howidido / Pretty boy Floyd / Hard travellin' / Better world / This land is your land.
■ LP . . . . K 56535
WEA / Jun '77 / WEA.

STRUGGLE.
Tracks: Struggle blues / Dollar down, A / Get along little doggies / Hang knot / Waiting at the gate / Dying miner, The / Union burying ground / Lost John / Buffalo / Pretty boy Floyd / Ludlow massacre / 1913 massacre.
LP . . . . FA 2485
Folkways (USA) / '88 / Projection / Swift / C.M. Distribution / Hot Shot / Jazz Music.
LP . . . . SPD 1034
Special Delivery / Aug '90 / Revolver-APT / A.D.A Distribution / Topic Records / Direct Distribution / Jazz Music / C.M. Distribution.
CD . . . . SPDCD 1034

■ MC . . . . SPDC 1034
Special Delivery / Aug '90.

THIS LAND IS YOUR LAND.
Tracks: Not Advised.
LP . . . . .FTS 31001
Folkways (USA) / '88 / Projection / Swift / C.M. Distribution / Hot Shot / Jazz Music.

VERY BEST OF WOODY GUTHRIE, THE.
Tracks: This land is your land / Pastures of plenty / Pretty boy Floyd / Take a whiff on me / Do re mi / Put my little shoes away / Hard travelin' / Jesus Christ / Whoopee ti yi yo, get along little doggies / Grand coulee dam / Picture from life's other side, A / Talkin' hard luck blues / Philadelphia lawyer / I ain't got no home / Wreck of the old '97, The / Keep your skillet good and greasy / Dust pneumonia blues / Going down that road feeling bad / Goodnight little arlo (Goodnight little darlin') / So long it's been good to know you.
CD . . . . MCCD 067
MC .MCTC 067
Music Club / Jun '92 / Gold & Sons / Terry Blood Dist. / Video Collection.

VISION SHARED: A TRIBUTE TO WOODY GUTHRIE.
Tracks: Not Advised.
■ VHS 49006 2
CMV Enterprises (video) / Oct '89.

WOODY GUTHRIE.
Tracks: More perty gals / Gypsy Davey / Pretty boy Floyd / Poor boy / Hey Lolly Lolly / Lonesome day / Rangers command / Ain't gonna be treated this way / Buffalo skinners / Hard, ain't it hard / Worried man blues.

LP . . . . CW 129
Pye / '79.

WOODY GUTHRIE COLLECTION (20 golden greats).
Tracks: House of the rising sun / John Henry / More pretty girls than one / Danville girl no.2 / Hard travellin' / Poor boy / Baltimore to Washington / Bed on the floor / Dig my life away / Buffalo skinners / Hard, ain't it hard? / Gypsy Davey / Little darlin' / I ride an old paint / Bury me beneath the willow / Sourwood Mountain / Oregon trail, The / Boll weevil blues / Mean talking blues.
LP . . . . DVLP 2128
MC . . . . DVMC 2128
Deja Vu / Jun '88 / Jazz Music / Music Collection International.

WOODY GUTHRIE SINGS FOLK SONGS VOL.2 (Guthrie, Woody/Cisco Houston/ Sonny Terry).
Tracks: Not Advised.
LP . . . . FA 2484
Folkways (USA) / '88 / Projection / Swift / C.M. Distribution / Hot Shot / Jazz Music.

WOODY GUTHRIE SINGS FOLKSONGS OF LEADBELLY.
Tracks: Not Advised.
LP . . . . FA 2483
Folkways (USA) / '88 / Projection / Swift / C.M. Distribution / Hot Shot / Jazz Music.

WOODY GUTHRIE VOL. 1.
Tracks: Not Advised.
LP . . . . .SM 3960
MC . . . . .MC 3960
Joker (USA) / '88 / C.M. Distribution / Jazz Horizons / Jazz Music.

H

Hackberry Ramblers

FIRST RECORDINGS 1935-48.
Tracks: Not Advised.
MC . . . . .C 0127
Folklyric (USA) / '88 / Topic Records / Direct Distribution / Cadillac Music / Projection / C.M. Distribution / Hot Shot / A.D.A Distribution.

JOLIE BLONDE.
Tracks: Not Advised.
CD . . . . .ARHCD 399
Arhoolie (USA) / Sep '93 / Pinnacle / Cadillac Music / Swift / Projection / Hot Shot / A.D.A Distribution / Jazz Music.

LOUISIANA CAJUN MUSIC.
Tracks: Not Advised.
LP. . . . . ARHOOLIE 5003
Arhoolie (USA) / May '81 / Pinnacle / Cadillac Music / Swift / Projection / Hot Shot / A.D.A Distribution / Jazz Music.
MC . . . . .ARHC 5003
Arhoolie (USA) / '88 / Pinnacle / Cadillac Music / Swift / Projection / Hot Shot / A.D.A Distribution / Jazz Music.

Haggard, Merle

Country singer, songwriter, guitarist and fiddler born in 1937 in Bakersfield, California. His family had migrated from Oklahoma in 1934. Merle ran away from home in 1951 and drifted until sent to San Quentin in 1958 for burglary, paroled in 1960 to become 'the poet of the ordinary man'. He had hit duets with Bonnie Owens, Buck's ex-wife; they were married 1965-75. Later he married Leona Williams and recorded a duet with her. His own style leaned heavily on that of Lefty Frizzell at first, no bad role model. He also recorded a tribute to Bob Wills called *The best damn fiddle player in the world*. He has had over 60 solo hits in the USA country chart, over half at number one, his own compositions including *The fugitive, Branded man, Mama tried, Hungry eyes, Workin' man blues* and *Okie from Muskogee* in 1966-69. His albums often sound like collections of short juke box singles, which is essentially what they are, but country fans love them; the formula is perfected now so that a 1989 release was described as a sort of new age country music. (Donald Clarke).

25TH ANNIVERSARY ALBUM: MERLE HAGGARD.
Tracks: Please Mr. DJ / I wonder what she'll think / Life's like poetry / Holding things together / I've done it all / Home is where a kid grows up / Girl turned ripe, The / Irma Jackson / White man singing the blues / Love and honor / I'm gonna break every heart I can / Farmer's daughter, The / Wine take me away / I wonder where I'll find you at tonight / Someone told my story / After loving you / Working man can't get nowhere today, A / I can't hold myself in line / Way it was in '51, The / Silver wings.
■ **CD** . . . . CZ 149
EMI / Jan '89.
■ **LP**. . . . . EMS 1313
EMI / Jan '89.
■ **MC** . . . . TCEMS 1313
EMI / Jan '89.

5.01 BLUES.
Tracks: Broken friend / Someday we'll know / Sea of hearbreak / If you want to be my woman / Somewhere down the line / Losin' in Las Vegas / Wouldn't that be something / Better love next time / Thousand lies ago, A / 5.01 blues.
CD 4651842
Epic / Jul '89 / Sony.
LP. 4651841
■ **MC** 4651844
Epic / Jul '89.

ALL NIGHT LONG.
Tracks: All night long / Honky tonk / Night-time man / I'm a white boy / Holding things together / Uncle Lem / Farmer's daughter / Man's got to give up a lot, A / I've done it all / Goodbye lefty / If you've got time (to say goodbye) / September in Miami / Bar in Bakersfield, A.
CD D2-77410
Curb / '91 / BMG.

AMBER WAVES OF GRAIN.
Tracks: Amber waves of grain / Tulare dust / Mama tried the farmer's daughter / Okie from Muskogee / I wish things were simple / Working man's blues / Always late with your kisses / American waltz.
LP. . . . . EPC 26811
■ **MC** 40 26811
Epic / May '86.

BACK TO THE BAR ROOMS.
Tracks: Misery and gin / Back to the bar rooms again / Make-up and faded blue jeans / Ever changing woman / Easy come easy go / I don't want to sober up tonight / Can't break the habit / Out paths may never cross / I don't have any more love songs / Leonard / I think I'll just stay here and drink.
LP. . . . . .MCA 5139
LP. . . . . .MCF 3089
MC . . . . .MCA 5139MC
MCA / '80 / BMG.

BEST OF MERLE HAGGARD, THE.
Tracks: Not Advised.
LP. 1A 220 1583354
EMI (Holland) / '88.

BIG CITY.
Tracks: Big city / My favourite memory / Good old American guest / I think I'm gonna live forever / This song is mine / Stop the world / Are the good times really over / You don't have very far to go / I always get lucky with you / Texas fiddle song.
■ **LP**. . . . . EPC 85303
Epic / Dec '81.

BRANDED MAN.
Tracks: My friends are gonna be strangers / Swinging doors / Bottle let me down, The / I'm a lonesome fugitive / I threw away the rose / Branded man / Sing me back home / Legend of Bonnie and Clyde, The / Mama tried / I take a lot of pride in what I am / Hungry eyes / Working man blues / Okie from Muskogee / Street singer / Jesus take a hold / I can't be myself / Sidewalks of Chicago / Soldier's last letter / Someday we'll look back / Here comes the freedom train.
LP. . . . . .EG 2605291
■ **MC** . . . . .EG 2605294
Capitol / Apr '85.

CAPITOL COLLECTORS SERIES: MERLE HAGGARD.
Tracks: Swinging doors / Bottle let me down, The / I'm a lonesome fugitive / Sing me back home / I take a lot of pride in what I am / Hungry eyes / Workin' man blues / Okie from Muskogee / Fightin' side of me, The / Soldier's last letter / Daddy Frank / I wonder if they ever think of me / Emptiest arms in the world, The / Things aren't funny anymore / Old man from the mountain.
CD . . . . CZ 301
Capitol / Apr '90 / EMI.

CAPITOL COUNTRY CLASSICS.
Tracks: Fightin' side of me, The / Daddy Frank / Carolyn / Grandma Harp / It's not love but it's not bad / I wonder if they ever think of me / Everybody had the blues / If we can make it through December / Things aren't funny anymore / Old man from the mountain / Kentucky gambler / Always wanting you / Movin' on / It's all in the movies / Roots of my raising / Cherokee maiden.
■ **MC** . . . . .TCCAPS 1034
Capitol / Jan '80.
■ **LP**. . . . . CAPS 1034
Capitol / Jan '80.

CHILL FACTOR.
Tracks: Chill factor / Twinkle, twinkle lucky star / Man from another time / We never touch at all / You babe / Thanking the good Lord / After dark / 1929 / Thirty again / I don't have any love around / More than this old heart can take.
LP. 4607831
■ **MC** 4607834
Epic / Mar '88.

COUNTRY LEGEND.
Tracks: Twinkle twinkle lucky star / If you want to be my woman / Workin' man blues / Always late / T.B. blues / Fulsom prison blues / Footlights / Big city / Mama tried / Brain Cloudy blues / Milk cow blues / Begging to you / Bottle let me down, The / What am I gonna do (With the rest of my life) / Ida Red / San Antonio rose / Corrina Corrina / Take me back to Tulsa / Faded love / Maiden's prayer, A (instrumental) / Fiddle breakdown (Instrumental) / Right or wrong / Ramblin' fever / That's the way love goes / Today I started loving you again / Okie from Muskogee / Fightin' side of me, The.
CD . . . . PLATCD 358
MC . . . . .PLAC 358
Platinum Music / May '91 / Prism Leisure PLC / Ross Records.

COUNTRY LEGENDS LIVE.
Tracks: Twinkle, twinkle lucky star / If you want to be my woman / Workin' man blues / Always late / T.B. blues / Fulsom Prison blues / Footlights / Big city / Mama tried / Milk cow blues medley / Begging to you / Bottle let me down, The / What am I gonna do (with the rest of my life) / Ida Red / San Antonio rose / Corina corina / Take me back to Tulsa / Faded love / Maidens prayer (Instrumental) / Fiddle breakdown (Instrumental) / Right or wrong / Ramblin' fever / That's the way love goes / Today I started loving you again / Okie from Muskogee / Fightin' side of me, The.
VHS. . . . . PLATV 358
Platinum Music / Mar '90 / Prism Leisure PLC / Ross Records.

COUNTRY STORE: MERLE HAGGARD.
Tracks: There, I've said it again / Poncho and Lefty / I think I'm gonna live forever / Are the good times really over / That's the way love goes / Still water runs the deepest / Silver eagle / Yesterday's wine / Big city / You take me for granted / For all I know / I'm gonna plant me a bed of roses / Going where the lonely go / Natural high / Old flames (Only on CD.) / To all the girls I've loved before (Only on CD.) / Stop the world (Only on CD.) / Okie from Muskogee (Only on CD.).
CD . . . . .CDCST 15
MC . . . . .CSTK 15
Country Store / '88 / BMG.
■ **LP**. . . . . CST 15
Country Store / Nov '88.

EPIC COLLECTION (RECORDED LIVE).
Tracks: Honky tonk night time man / Old man of the mountain, The / Holding things together / Sing a sad song / Every fool has a rainbow / Blue yodel no. 2 (My lovin' gal Lucille) / Trouble in mind / Things aren't funny anymore / Strangers / I always get lucky with you / Working man blues.
LP. . . . . EPC 25806
Epic / Jan '84 / Sony.
■ **MC** 40 25806
Epic / Jan '84.

FAMILY BIBLE, THE.
Tracks: Not Advised.
MC 4XL 9290
Capitol (Specials) / Dec '88.

FIGHTIN' SIDE OF ME, THE.
Tracks: Hammin' it up / I take a lot of pride in what I am / Corrine Corrina / Every fool has a rainbow / T.B. blues / When did right become wrong / Philadelphia lawyer / Stealin' corn / Harold's super service / Today I started loving you again / Okie from Muskogee / Fightin' side of me, The / Closing announcements and theme.
LP. . . . . .EST 451
Capitol / '70 / EMI.

FRIEND OF CALIFORNIA, A.
Tracks: Not Advised.
LP. 26876
MC 40 26876
CBS / Sep '86 / Sony.

GOING WHERE THE LONELY GO.
Tracks: Going where the lonely go / Why am I drinkin / If I left it up to you / I won't give up my train / Someday you're gonna need your friends again / Shopping for dresses / You take me for granted / Half a man / For all I know / Nobody's darlin but mine.
LP. . . . . EPC 25024
Epic / Dec '82 / Sony.

GREAT MERLE HAGGARD SINGS, THE.
Tracks: Lovesick blues / My heart would know / Roots of my raising, The / Amazing grace / Way it was in '51, The / On the sea shores of old Mexico / Working man blues / Movin' on / (My friends are going to be) Strangers / Waiting for a train / Tulare dust / Legend of Bonnie and Clyde / Run 'em off / Seeker, The.
LP. . . . . MFP 50392
MFP / '89 / EMI.

GREATEST HITS:MERLE HAGGARD.
Tracks: I think I'll just stay here and drink / I'm always on a mountain when I fall / Red bandana / Way I am, The / It's been a great afternoon / Ramblin' fever / Misery and gin / My own kind of hat / If were not back in love by Monday / Rainbow stew.
■ **LP**. . . . . IMCA 5386
MCA (Import) / Mar '86.

HEART TO HEART (Haggard, Merle & Leona Williams).
Tracks: Heart to heart / Let's pretend we're married tonight / You can't break the chains of love / Waltz across Texas / We're strangers again / Waitin' on the good life to come / Don't ever let your lover sleep alone / It's cold in California / I'll never be free / Sally let your bangs hang down.
LP. . . . . .MERL 29
MC . . . . .MERLC 29
Mercury / Aug '83 / PolyGram.

I LOVE DIXIE BLUES.
Tracks: Hammin' it up / Everybody's had the blues / Big bad Bill (is sweet William now) / I forget you every day / I ain't got nobody / Carolyn / Champagne / Lovesick blues / Emptiest arms in the world / Nobody knows I'm hurtin' / Way down yonder in New Orleans / Okie from Muskogee / I wonder if they ever think of me / Finale.
LP. . . . . .EST 11200
Capitol / '73 / EMI.

■ DELETED

H 1

I'M A LONESOME FUGITIVE (Haggard, Merle With A Stranger).
Tracks: I'm a lonesome fugitive / All of me belongs to you / House of memories / Life in prison / Whatever happened to me / Drink up and be somebody / Someone told my story / If you want to be my woman / Mary's mine / Skid Row / My rough and rowdy ways / Mixed up mess of a heart.
LP. . . . . SEE 49
See For Miles / Sep '86 / Pinnacle.
MC . . . . .SEEK 49
See For Miles / '87 / Pinnacle.

I'M ALWAYS ON A MOUNTAIN WHEN I FALL.
Tracks: I'm always on a mountain when I fall / It's been a great afternoon / Love me when you can / There won't be another now / Don't you ever get tired (of hurting me) / Life of a rodeo cowboy / There ain't no good chain gang / Dream, The / Immigrant, The / Mama I've to go to Memphis.
LP. . . . . MCF 2848
MC . . . . MCF 2848MC
MCA / '78 / BMG.

I'M ALWAYS ON A MOUNTAIN WHEN I FALL.
Tracks: I'm always on a mountain when I fall / Life of a rodeo cowboy.
■ 7" . . . . MCA 358
MCA / Mar '78.

IF WE'RE NOT BACK IN LOVE BY MONDAY.
Tracks: If we're not back in love by monday / I think it's gone forever.
■ 7" . . . . MCA 303
MCA / Jun '77.

IT'S ALL IN THE GAME.
Tracks: Let's chase each other around the room / Place to fall apart / It's all in the game / Lonely little hotel room / I never go home anymore / All I want to do is sing my song / Natural high / Thank heaven for little girls / To all the girls I've loved before / You nearly lose your mind.
■ LP. . . . . EPC 26071
Epic / Sep '84.

IT'S ALL IN THE MOVIES.
Tracks: It's all in the movies / Nothing's worse than comes / After loving you / Stingeree / I know an ending when it comes / This is the song we sing / Living with the shades pulled down / Hag's Dixie blues / Let's stop pretending / Cotton patch blues / Seeker, The.
LP. . . . . ST 11483
Capitol / '77 / EMI.

IT'S BEEN A GREAT AFTERNOON.
Tracks: It's been a great afternoon / Love me when you can.
■ 7" . . . . MCA 388
MCA / Sep '78.

JUST BETWEEN THE TWO OF US (see under Owens, Bonnie).

KERN RIVER.
Tracks: Kern River / Old flames / There, I've said it again / You don't love me anymore / Natural high / Big butter and egg man / Ridin' high / There's somebody else on your mind / I wonder where I'll find you at tonight / There won't be another now / Old watermill.
■ MC 40 26432
Epic / May '85.

LAND OF MANY CHURCHES, THE (Haggard, Merle & Carter Family).
Tracks: Not Advised.
Double LP . . . . HAT 3097/8
MC Set. HATC 3097/8
Stetson / Feb '89 / Crusader Marketing Co. / Swift / Wellard Dist. / Midland Records / C.M. Distribution.

LEGEND OF BONNIE AND CLYDE, THE.
Tracks: Not Advised.
LP. . . . . HAT 3075
Stetson / '88 / Crusader Marketing Co. / Swift / Wellard Dist. / Midland Records / C.M. Distribution.
MC . . . . HATC 3075
Stetson / Dec '88 / Crusader Marketing Co. / Swift / Wellard Dist. / Midland Records / C.M. Distribution.

LEGENDARY, THE.
Tracks: Not Advised.
MC 4XL 8354
Capitol (Specials) / Dec '88.

LET'S CHASE EACH OTHER AROUND THE ROOM.
Tracks: Let's chase each other around the room / You nearly lose your mind.
■ 7" . . . . A 4964
Epic / Dec '84.

MERLE HAGGARD (I love country).
Tracks: Place to fall apart, A / Someday when things are good / Stop the world / Big city / Kern River / Reasons to quit / Natural high / Yesterday's wine / My favourite memory.
LP. . . . . CBS 54944
CBS / Sep '86 / Sony.
LP. . . . . EPC 54944
Epic / Mar '87 / Sony.
■ MC 40 54944
Epic / Mar '87.

MERLE HAGGARD COLLECTION, THE.
Tracks: Cherokee maiden / Roots of my raising / It's all in the movies / Movin' on / Always wanting you / Kentucky gambler / Old man from the mountain / Things aren't funny anymore / If we make it through December / Everybody's had the blues / I wonder if they ever think of me / It's not love (but it's not bad) / Grandma Harp / Carolyn.
CD . . . . KNCD 13058
■ MC . . . . KNMC 13058
Knight / Feb '91.

MERLE HAGGARD SINGS COUNTRY FAVOURITES.
Tracks: She thinks I still care / Mom and dad's waltz / Making believe / Moanin' the blues / Lovesick blues / Blues stay away from me / You've still got a place in my heart / Right or wrong / Mule skinner blues / Green green grass of home / Folsom Prison blues / Walking the floor over you / Son of Hickory Holler's tramp, The / Long black limousine / San Antonio rose / Take me back to Tulsa / Waiting for a train / This cold war / Little ole wine drinker me / Today I started loving you again.
■ LP. . . . . EMS 1253
EMI / May '87.
■ MC . . . . TCEMS 1253
EMI / May '87.

MERLE HAGGARD: COLLECTORS SERIES.
Tracks: Swinging doors / Bottle let me down, The / I'm a lonesome fugitive / Sing me back home / I take a lot of pride in what I am / Hungry eyes / Workin' man blues / Okie from Muskogee / Fightin' side of me / Soldier's last letter / Daddy Frank (The guitar man) / I wonder if they ever think of me / Emptiest arms in the world, The / Things aren't funny anymore / Old man from the mountain / Always wanting you / Movin' on / Roots of my raising, The / Here comes the freedom train / Cherokee maiden.
CD . . . . CDP 7931912
Capitol (USA) / Sep '90 / Capitol (Imports).

MY FAREWELL TO ELVIS.
Tracks: From Graceland to the promised land / In the ghetto / Don't be cruel / Jailhouse rock / Love me tender / That's all right / Heartbreak Hotel / Blue Christmas / Blue suede shoes / Are you lonesome tonight / Merle's farewell to Elvis.
LP. . . . . MCF 2818
MCA / '77 / BMG.
LP. . . . . IMCA 924
MCA (Import) / Mar '86 / Pinnacle / Silver Sounds (CD).

NATURAL HIGH.
Tracks: Natural high / I never go home anymore.
■ 7" . . . . A 6440
Epic / Aug '85.

OKIE FROM MUSKOGEE - LIVE.
Tracks: Opening introduction and theme / Mama tried / No hard times / Silver wings / Swinging doors / I'm a lonesome fugative / Sing me back home / Branded man / In the arms of love / Workin' man blues / Introduction to "Hobo Bill" / Hobo Bill's last ride / Billy overcame his size / If I had left it up to you / White line fever / Blue rock / Okie from Muskogee.
LP. . . . . ST 384
Capitol / '80 / EMI.

PONCHO AND LEFTY.
Tracks: Poncho and Lefty / It's my last day / My Mary / Half a man / No reason to quit / Still water runs the deepest / M 4 life's been a pleasure / All the soft places to fall / Opportunity to cry.
LP. . . . . EPC 85754
■ MC 40 85754
Epic / Feb '83.

PRESENTS HIS 30TH ALBUM.
Tracks: Old man from the mountain / Things aren't funny anymore / White man singin' the blues / Travelin' / Girl who made me laugh, The / Honky tonk night time man / Holding things together / (The seashores of) Old Mexico / Don't give up on me / King without a queen / It don't bother me.
LP. . . . . ST 11331
Capitol / '74 / EMI.

PRIDE IN WHAT I AM (Haggard, Merle & the Strangers).
Tracks: I take a lot of pride in what I am / Who'll buy the wine / Day the rains came, The / It meant goodbye to me when you said hello to him / I can't hold myself in line / I'm bringin' home good news / Keep me from cryin' today / I just want to look at you one more time / Somewhere on skid row / I'm free / California blues / I think we're livin' in the good old days.
LP. . . . . SKAO 168
Capitol / '80 / EMI.

RAINBOW STEW.
Tracks: Misery and gin / I think I'll just stay here and drink / Back to the bar rooms again / Our paths may never cross / Running kind, The / I'm a lonesome fugitive / Rainbow stew / Blue yodel no. 9 (Standing on the corner) / Dealing with the devil / Fiddle breakdown / Sing me back home.
■ LP. . . . . MCF 3131
MCA / Apr '82.
MC . . . . MCFC 3131
MCA / Mar '82 / BMG.

RAMBLIN' FEVER.
Tracks: Ramblin' fever / When my blue moon turns to gold again / Ghost story / Set me free / Love somebody to death / If we're not back in love by Monday / I think it's gone forever / Ain't your memory got no pride at all / My love for you / Last letter, The.
LP. . . . . MCA 2267
MC . . . . MCF 2805MC
MCA / '77 / BMG.

ROOTS OF MY RAISING.
Tracks: Roots of my raising / Cherokee maiden.
■ 7" . . . . CL 15910
Capitol / Feb '77.

SALUTES THE GREATS.
Tracks: Way it was in '51, The / Moanin' the blues / My heart would know / Lovesick blues / I saw the light / San Antonio rose / Take me back to Tulsa / Brain cloudy blues / Right or wrong / Stay a little longer / Mule skinner blues / My rough and rowdy ways / Waitin' for a train / Peach picking time down in Georgia / Train whistle blues / Mom and dad's waltz / It meant goodbye to me when you said hello to him / I'm an old old man (tryin' to live while I can) / I never go around mirrors / Goodbye lefty.
Double LP . . . . SLB 8137
Capitol / '80 / EMI.

SAME TRAIN, A DIFFERENT TIME.
Tracks: California blues / Waiting for a train / Train whistle blues / Why should I be lonely / Blue yodel No. 6 / Miss the Mississippi and you / Mule skinner blues / Frankie and Johnny / Hobo Bill's last ride / Travelin' blues / Peach picking time down in Georgia / No hard times / Down the old road to home / Jimmie Rodger's last blue yodel.
LP. . . . . ST 21377
Capitol / '69 / EMI.

SERVING 190 PROOF.
Tracks: Footlights / Got lonely too early this morning / Heaven was a drink of wine / Driftwood / I can't get away / Red bandana / My own kind of hat / I must have done something bad / I didn't mean to love you / Sing a family song / Roses in winter.
■ LP. . . . . MCF 3002
MCA / '79.
LP. . . . . MCL 1608
■ MC . . . . MCLC 1608
MCA / Aug '81.

SING ME BACK HOME.
Tracks: Sing me back home / I'm a lonesome fugitive / Where does the good times go / Green green grass of home.
MC 4XL 9028
Capitol (Specials) / Dec '88.

SOMEDAY WE'LL LOOK BACK.
Tracks: Someday we'll look back / Train of life / One sweet hello / One row at a time / Big time Annie's Square / I'd rather be gone / California cottonfields / Carolyn / Tulare dust / Huntsville / Only trouble with me, The.
LP. . . . . EST 835
Capitol / '71 / EMI.

SONGS FOR THE MAMA THAT TRIED.
Tracks: When God comes and gathers his jewels / Supper time / He walks with me / Softly and tenderly / Why me / Where no one stands alone / One day at a time / What a friend we have in Jesus / Swing low sweet chariot / Old rugged cross, The / Keep on the sunny side.
■ LP. . . . . IMCA 5250
MCA (Import) / Mar '86.

SONGWRITER.
Tracks: Footlights / It's been a great afternoon / My own kind of hat / Life's just not the way it used to be / I think I'll just stay here and drink / Ramblin' fever / Make up and faded blue jeans / Red bandana / From Graceland to the promise land / Rainbow stew.
■ LP. . . . . IMCA 5698
MCA (Import) / Mar '86.

STRANGERS.
Tracks: Not Advised.
LP. . . . . HAT 3133
MC . . . . HATC 3133
Stetson / Mar '90 / Crusader Marketing Co. / Swift / Wellard Dist. / Midland Records / C.M. Distribution.

SWINGING DOORS.
Tracks: Swinging doors / If I could be him / Longer you wait, The / I'll look over you / I can't stand me / Girl turned ripe, The / Bottle let me down, The / No more you and me / Someone else you've known / High on a hilltop / This town ain't big enough for the both of us / Shade tree.
■ LP. . . . . SEE 68
See For Miles / Jun '86.

TASTE OF YESTERDAY'S WINE, A (Haggard, Merle & George Jones).
Tracks: Yesterday's wine / After I sing all my songs / I think I've found a way (to life without you) / Brothers / Mobile Bay / C.C. Waterback / Silver Eagle must've been drunk / I haven't found her yet / No show Jones.
LP. . . . . EPC 25012
MC 40 25012
Epic / Oct '82 / Sony.
LP. . . . . SHM 3177

H 2 ■ DELETED

■ MC . . . . HSC 3177
Hallmark / Sep '85.

THAT'S THE WAY LOVE GOES.
Tracks: What am I gonna do / Bed of roses / Someday when things are good / That's the way love goes / Carryin' fire / Don't seem like we've been together all our lives / If you hated me / Love will find you / Last boat of the day / I think I'll stay.
■ LP. . . . . EPC 25573
Epic / Nov '83.

TO ALL THE GIRLS I'VE LOVED BEFORE.
Tracks: My favourite memory / Reasons to quit / You take me for granted / That's the way love goes / Are all good times really over / Big city / Poncho and Lefty / What am I gonna do / Old flames / Going where the lonely go / Let's chase each other around the room / Natural high / Place to fall apart, A / To all the girls I've loved before / It's all in the game / Stop the world.
LP. . . . . PMP 1003
MC . . . . PMPK 1003
Premier (Sony) / Feb '87 / Sony / Pinnacle.

TRIBUTE TO THE BEST DAMN FIDDLE PLAYER IN THE WORLD (My salute to Bob Willis).
Tracks: Brown skinned gal / Right or wrong / Brain cloudy blues / Stay a little longer / Misery / Time changes everything / San Antonio rose / I knew the moment I lost you / Roly poly / Old fashioned love / Corrine Corrina / Take me back to Tulsa.
LP. . . . . ST 638
Capitol / '71 / EMI.

VERY BEST OF MERLE HAGGARD.
Tracks: Everybody's had the blues / If we make it through December / It's not love (but it's not bad) / Old man of the mountain, The / Carolyn / It's all in the movies / Movin' on / Fighting side of me, The / Mama tried / Okie from Muskogee / Working man blues / I wonder if they ever think of me / Things aren't funny anymore / Roots of my raising / Always wanting you.
■ CD . . . . BU 4
EMI / Mar '88.

WALKING THE LINE (Haggard, Merle, George Jones, Willie Nelson).
Tracks: I gotta get drunk / No show Jones / Pancho & Lefty / Yesterday's wine / Half a man / Big butter and egg man / Heaven or hell / Midnight rider / Are the good times really over / Drunk can't be a man, A.
LP. 4505761
■ MC 4505764
Epic / Jul '87.

WORKING MAN CAN'T GET NOWHERE TODAY.
Tracks: Working man can't get nowhere today / Blues stay away from me.
■ 7" . . . . CL 15973
Capitol / Mar '78.

Hague, Mel

MEL HAGUE LIVE.
Tracks: Ruby don't take your love to town / Please don't bury me / Everything big in Texas / Good hearted woman / Dreaming my dreams / Boy named Sue, A / I wore out my knees loving you / You're the only good thing / Fifteen beers ago / Give my love to Rose / Old Joe / Another night's done and gone / Little ole wine drinker me.
LP. . . . . LKLP 6364
Look / Jan '80 / C.M. Distribution.

MERRY GO ROUND.
Tracks: Not Advised.
LP. . . . . LKLP 6558
Look / '88 / C.M. Distribution.

OLD GRAVEL BOOTS.
Tracks: Door is always open, The / Running close behind you / Please remind me / I think I'm being taken for a ride / Couple more years, A / I'm gonna be a truck / Long haired country boy / If I needed you / I read it in rolling stone / Groover, The / Nothing to say.
LP. . . . . LKLP 6270
Look / Nov '79 / C.M. Distribution.

WINNER, THE.
Tracks: Not Advised.
LP. . . . . LKLP 6023
Look / '88 / C.M. Distribution.

Haland, Bjoro

MY NASHVILLE ALBUM.
Tracks: Catfish John / Storms never last / Nickels and dimes / If I can't have all of you / Just call me lonesome / Arizona whiz, The / Some day my day will come / I'll go somewhere and sing my song again / What can I do to get me back on your mind / I've already loved you in my mind / Am I that easy to forget.
LP. . . . . KLP 26
MC . . . . ZCKLP 26
Igus / Apr '81 / C.M. Distribution / Ross Records / Duncans.

TO MY FRIENDS.
Tracks: Kissed by the rain and warmed by the sun / Little miracle, A / Please change your mind / Little ole dime / Forget me not / Am I losing you / Country is / Blue eyes crying in the rain / Some broken hearts never mend / Love or something like it / Talking walls, The / One day at a time.
MC . . . . ZCKLP 20
Klub / Sep '80 / C.M. Distribution / Ross Records / Duncans / A.D.A Distribution.
■ LP. . . . . KLP 20
Klub / Sep '80.

Haley, Bill

When *Rock around the clock* hit no. 1 on the American charts in the summer of 1955 (and in Britain in November of that year), most historians say it was the start of the rock'n'roll era and the beginning of the whole pop music revolution. *Rock around the clock* by Bill Haley & The Comets was one of the biggest-selling singles in history, returning to the record charts on repeated occasions and clocking up an eventual worldwide total in excess of 20 million copies. Not bad, considering that Haley only recorded the song as a favour to his manager, who had co-written and published it a couple of years earlier without success. Bill Haley was born in Detroit in 1925, and moved to Pennsylvania at the age of four. He grew up with C&W and hillbilly music, and turned professional during the early forties. Haley spent the rest of the decade playing in those styles with various small-time bands. In the early fifties, he took the bold decision to record some black rhythm and blues songs and adapt them for the white market - these included, most notably, *Rocket 88* and *Rock the joint*. This fusion of white C&W with black R&B became known as rock'n'roll - Haley was one of the forced to do it, and the first to succeed with it. In 1953 Bill Haley & his Comets (as they had just been christened) reached the US national charts with Bill's own compilation *Crazy man crazy*. During 1954-5 he recorded songs from a variety of sources, and when *Shake rattle and roll*, *Dim dim the lights* and *Mambo rock* began appearing in national Top 20's on both sides of the Atlantic alongside names like Doris Day and Frankie Laine, the music business smelt the whiff of a new musical revolution. This was confirmed by the arrival of *Rock around the clock*, which had actually been recorded in April 1954 but did not make its impact till the second half of 1955. Its elevation to legendary status was fuelled by its use as the theme for the seminal '55 youth movie *Blackboard jungle*. During the remainder of 55 and 56, Haley's Comets chalked up a prolific string of hits, often featuring the word "rock" somewhere in the title. They were especially popular in Britain, where *Rock around the clock*, *Rock a-beatin' boogie*, *See you later alligator*, *The saints rock'n'roll*, *Rockin' through the rye*, *Razzle dazzle*, *Rip it up* and *Rudy's rock* combined to give Haley a golden 1956 and, according to the Guinness book of Hit Singles, the best year for any act in UK chart history. When Bill arrived in Britain in February 1957, he was given an overwhelming reception. Paradoxically, the tour also helped to kill his short career stone dead - fans suddenly realised that he was a somewhat podgy married man in his early 30's. British youngsters quickly followed the leads of their American counterparts by crowning the frenetic 22-year-old Elvis Presley as king of rock'n'roll. During the 60's and 70's Haley remained an active international touring performer, although these tours were latterly interrupted by sporadic periods of semi-retirement. Successful re-issued of *Rock around the clock* also helped keep him in the public eye. Another European tour was being planned when Haley died of a heart attack in February 1981 in Harlingen, Texas; he was 55, and had recently celebrated the 25th anniversary of *Rock around the clock*.(Bob MacDonald).

16 GREATEST HITS: BILL HALEY (Haley, Bill & The Comets).
Tracks: Rock around the clock / See you later alligator / Shake, rattle and roll / Razzle dazzle / Saints rock 'n' roll / Skinny Minnie / Rock-a-beatin' boogie / Rip it up / Rudy's rock / Jenny jenny / Kansas City / Rock the joint / Yakety sax / Johnny B. Goode / Whole lotta shakin' goin' on / What'd I say.
CD . . . . CD 39
Bescol / May '87.

20 GOLDEN PIECES: BILL HALEY (Haley, Bill & The Comets).
Tracks: Saints rock 'n' roll / Razzle dazzle / Blue comet blues / Skokiaan / Shake, rattle and roll / ABC boogie / See you later alligator / Rip it up / Caravana a go-go / Whole lotta shakin' goin' on / How many? / Land of a thousand dances / Skinny Minnie / Harlem nocturne / Justine / Seventh son / Mohair Sam / New Orleans / High heel sneakers / Rock around the clock.
LP. . . . . BDL 2002
Bulldog Records / Jul '82 / President Records / Jazz Music / Wellard Dist. / TKO Records Ltd.

20 GREATEST HITS: BILL HALEY & HIS COMETS (Haley, Bill & The Comets).
Tracks: Rock around the clock / See you later alligator / Shake, rattle and roll / Johnny B. Goode / Lucille / Razzle dazzle / A.B.C. / Helena / This is goodbye, goodbye / I've got news for you / Rip it up.
LP. . . . . FUN 9013
MC . . . . FUNC 9013
Fun (Holland) / Sep '88 / Pinnacle.
CD 26 42 142
MC 26 42144
Point (2) / '92 / Sound Solutions.

20 GREATEST HITS: BILL HALEY & THE COMETS (Haley, Bill & The Comets).
Tracks: Rock around the clock / Shake, rattle and roll / Kansas City / Razzle dazzle / Guitar boogie / Rip it up / See you later alligator.
CD 2636742
LP. 2636741
MC 2636744
Black Tulip / '88.

6 TRACK HITS (Haley, Bill & The Comets).
Tracks: Whole lotta shakin' goin' on / Rock around the clock / Shake, rattle and roll / Kansas City / Me and Bobby McGee / Rip it up.
EP. 7SR 5012
MC 7SC 5012
Scoop 33 / Aug '83.

BEST OF BILL HALEY (Haley, Bill & The Comets).
Tracks: Not Advised.
MC 16-5
Creole / Jul '84 / Terry Blood Dist.

BEST OF BILL HALEY ON STAGE, THE.
Tracks: Not Advised.
CD . . . . VG 651 600 072
Vogue / '88 / BMG.

BIGGEST HITS (Haley, Bill & The Comets).
Tracks: Not Advised.
MC . . . . ZCSNB 9945
Speciality (USA) / '74 / Swift / C.M. Distribution.

BILL HALEY & HIS COMETS (Haley, Bill & The Comets).
Tracks: Not Advised.
MC . . . . ZCGAS 747
Audio Fidelity(USA) / Oct '84 / Stage One Records.

BILL HALEY & HIS COMETS (Haley, Bill & The Comets).
Tracks: Rock around the clock / Fool such as I, A / I got a woman / Goofin' around / Miss you / Rockin' rollin' rover / Calling all comets / Don't knock the rock / Shake, rattle and roll / Forty cups of coffee / Dinah / ABC boogie / Tonights the night / Razzle dazzle / Birth of the boogie / R-O-C-K / Rip it up / Dim, dim, the lights / Two hundred dogs / Mary Mary Lou / Burn that candle / Thirteen women / Vive la rock and roll / Rockin' through the rye / It's a sin / Billy Goat / Blue comet blues / Hot dog buddy buddy / Move it on over / See you later alligator.
■ MC Set . . . . CRT 015
Cambra / '83.

BILL HALEY & THE COMETS (Haley, Bill & The Comets).
Tracks: Rock around the clock / Skinny Minnie / Ling-ting-tong / See you later alligator / Whole lotta shakin' goin' on / Rudy's rock / Caravan / Rock the joint / Johnny B. Goode / Lucille / Kansas City / Shake, rattle and roll / Flip flop and fly / Malaguena / New Orleans / What'd I say / Razzle dazzle / Rip it up / Rock-a-beatin' boogie / Saints rock 'n' roll.
CD . . . . PCD 838
Pickwick / '88 / Pickwick Records.

BILL HALEY AND THE COMETS.
Tracks: Not Advised.
CD . . . . PWK 023
Pickwick / '91 / Pickwick Records.
CD . . . . ENT CD 283
Entertainers / Mar '92.

BILL HALEY GOLDEN CD COLLECTION, THE (Haley, Bill & The Comets).
Tracks: Rock around the clock / Saints rock and roll / Razzle dazzle / Blue comet blues / Skokiaan / Shake rattle and roll / ABC boogie / See you later alligator / Rip it up / Caravan / Whole lotta shakin' goin' on / How many / Land of a thousand dances / Skinny Minnie / Harlem nocturne / Justine / Seventh son, The / Mohair Sam / New Orleans / Hi-heel sneakers / Hambone / California sun.
CD . . . . BDCD 2002
Bulldog Records / Nov '89 / President Records / Jazz Music / Wellard Dist. / TKO Records Ltd.

BILL HALEY RARITIES.
Tracks: Not Advised.
LP. . . . . A 98100
Ambassador / Nov '87 / Wellard Dist.

BOOGIE WITH BILL (Haley, Bill & The Comets).
Tracks: See you later alligator / ABC boogie / Altar of love / Don't mess around with my love / Helena / I've got news for you / Rock around the clock / Panic / Wobble, The / This is goodbye / Train of sin / Skokiaan.
LP. . . . . TOP 114
MC . . . . KTOP 114
Topline / Jan '85 / Charly / Swift / Black Sun Records.

COLLECTION: BILL HALEY (20 rock 'n' roll greats).
Tracks: Rock around the clock / Shake, rattle and roll / Mambo rock / Rockin' rollin' rover / Teenager's mother

■ DELETED H 3

/ Razzle dazzle / Don't knock the rock / Saints rock 'n' roll / Rip it up / Hot dog Buddy Buddy / ABC boogie / R-O-C-K / Forty cups of coffee / Rockin' through the rye / See you later alligator / You hit the wrong note, billy goat / Rock-a-beatin' boogie / Burn that candle / Rudy's rock / Thirteen women.
LP. . . . . DVLP 2069
MC . . . . DVMC 2069
Deja Vu / Jul '86 / Jazz Music / Music Collection International.

CRAZY MAN CRAZY (Haley, Bill & The Comets).
Tracks: Crazy man crazy / Lawdy Miss Clawdy.
■ 7" . . . . SON 2043
Sonet / Jun '74.

DON'T KNOCK THE ROCK (Haley, Bill & The Comets).
Tracks: Don't knock the rock.
■ 7" 05640
Brunswick / Feb '57.

ELVIS PRESLEY WITH BILL HALEY (see under Presley, Elvis).

EVERYONE CAN ROCK 'N' ROLL (Haley, Bill & The Comets).
Tracks: Everyone can rock 'n' roll.
7" . . . . SON 2194
Sonet / Feb '81 / Swift / C.M. Distribution / Roots Records / Jazz Music / Sonet Records / Cadillac Music / Projection / Wellard Dist. / Hot Shot.

EVERYONE CAN ROCK 'N' ROLL (Haley, Bill & The Comets).
Tracks: Hail, hail rock'n'roll / Jim Dandy / That's how I got to Memphis / Juke box cannonball / Let the good times roll again / God bless rock 'n' roll / Everyone can rock'n'roll / Battle of New Orleans / I need the music / Heartaches by the number / Tweedle Dee / So right tonight.
■ LP. . . . . SNTF 808
Sonet / Dec '79.

FROM THE ORIGINAL MASTER TAPES (Haley, Bill & The Comets).
Tracks: Rock around the clock / Thirteen women / Shake, rattle and roll / ABC boogie / Happy baby / Dim, dim the lights / Birth of the boogie / Mambo rock / Two hound dogs / Razzle dazzle / R-O-C-K / Saints rock 'n' roll / Burn that candle / See you later alligator / Paper boy, The / Rudy's rock / Hot dog buddy buddy / Rip it up / Don't knock the rock / Rock-a-beatin' boogie.
CD . . . . DIDX 202
MCA / Sep '85 / BMG.
CD . . . . MCAD 5539
MCA / '91 / BMG.

GOD BLESS ROCK AND ROLL (Haley, Bill & The Comets).
Tracks: God bless rock 'n' roll.
7" . . . . SON 2202
Sonet / Feb '82 / Swift / C.M. Distribution / Roots Records / Jazz Music / Sonet Records / Cadillac Music / Projection / Wellard Dist. / Hot Shot.

GOLDEN COUNTRY ORIGINS.
Tracks: Yodel your blues away / Rovin' eyes / Rose of my heart / Yodeller's lullaby / Candy and women / Foolish question / Covered wagon rolled right along, The / Wreck on the highway / Behind the eight ball / My mom heard me crying / Within this broken heart of mine / Cotton haired gal.
■ LP. . . . . ROL 1300
Rollercoaster.

GOLDEN GREATS: BILL HALEY.
Tracks: Rock around the clock / Shake, rattle and roll / See you later alligator / Rock-a-beatin' boogie / Rip it up / Forty cups of coffee / Two hound dogs / Rudy's rock / Thirteen women / Saints rock 'n' roll / Don't knock the rock / Mambo rock / Corina Corina / Calling all Comets / Skinny Minnie / Rockin' through the rye / ABC boogie / Razzle dazzle / R-O-C-K / Burn that candle.
■ LP. . . . . MCM 5004
MCA / Jul '85.
■ MC . . . . MCMC 5004
MCA / Jul '85.

GOLDEN HITS (Haley, Bill & The Comets).
Tracks: Rock around the clock / Burn that candle / Forty cups of coffee / Two hound dogs / Rudy's rock / Shake, rattle and roll / Rip it up / Rock-a-beatin' boogie / Thirteen women / Saints rock 'n' roll / See you later alligator / Don't knock the rock / Mambo rock / Corina Corina / Calling all Comets / Skinny Minnie / Rockin' through the rye / ABC boogie / Razzle Dazzle / R-O-C-K.
LP. . . . . MCL 1778
MC . . . . MCLC 1778
MCA / Feb '84 / BMG.

GOLDEN HITS/ROCK AROUND THE CLOCK.
Tracks: Rock around the clock / Shake, rattle and roll / ABC boogie / You hit the wrong note Billy goat / Thirteen women / Tonight's the night / Razzle dazzle / Two hound dogs / Dim dim the lights / Happy baby / Birth of the boogie / Rockin' rollin' rover / Mambo rock / Hide and seek / Rock-a-beatin' boogie / Burn that candle / Forty cups of coffee / Rudy's rock / Rip it up / Saints rock 'n' roll / See you later alligator / Don't knock the rock.
■ MC Set . . . . MCA 2 118
MCA (Twinpax Cassettes) / Sep '84.

GREATEST HITS: BILL HALEY (Haley, Bill & The Comets).
Tracks: Not Advised.
■ CD 120 104
MCS Look Back / '87.

GREATEST HITS: BILL HALEY & THE COMETS (Haley, Bill & The Comets).
Tracks: Rock around the clock / Burn the candle / Forty cups of coffee / Two hound dogs / Rudy's rock / Shake, rattle and roll / Rip it up / Rock-a-beatin' boogie / Thirteen women / Saints rock 'n' roll / See you later alligator / Don't knock the rock / Mambo rock / Corina, Corina / Calling all comets / Skinny Minnie / Rockin' through the rye / ABC boogie / Razzle dazzle / R-O-C-K.
CD . . . . DMCA 110
MCA / Feb '85 / BMG.

GREATEST HITS: BILL HALEY & THE COMETS (Haley, Bill & The Comets).
Tracks: Rock this joint tonite / Rock-a-beatin' boogie / Skinny Minnie / Razzle dazzle / Rudy's rock / See you later alligator / When the saints go marching in / Framed / Shake, rattle and roll / Rip it up / Crazy man crazy / Rock around the clock.
LP. 2459 413
MC 3192 626
Polydor (Italy) / '84 / PolyGram.

HAIL HAIL ROCK AND ROLL (Haley, Bill & The Comets).
Tracks: Hail, hail rock'n'roll.
7" . . . . SON 2188
Sonet / Feb '81 / Swift / C.M. Distribution / Roots Records / Jazz Music / Sonet Records / Cadillac Music / Projection / Wellard Dist. / Hot Shot.

HALEY'S GOLDEN MEDLEY (Haley, Bill & The Comets).
Tracks: Haley's golden medley.
■ 7" . . . . MCA 694
MCA / Apr '81.

HIER BIN ICH- HIER BLEIB ICH.. UND ABENDS IN DI (see under Films).

HILLBILLY HALEY.
Tracks: Within this broken heart of mine / Wreck on the highway / Behind the eight ball / Life of the party / I should write a song about you / My mom heard me crying / My dream / Red river valley / Yodeller's lullaby / Yodel your blues away / This is the thanks I get / Cold cold heart / Boquet of roses / All I need is some more loving / Covered wagon rolled right along, The / Rose of my heart / Cotton haired gal / Candy and women / Rovin' eyes / Foolish questions.
LP. . . . . ROLL 2007
Rollercoaster / Nov '84 / Rollercoaster Records / Swift.

JUST ROCK AND ROLL.
Tracks: I'm walking / High heel sneakers / Blue suede shoes / Tossin' and turnin' / Flip, flop and fly / Whole lotta shakin' goin' on / C.C. rider / Lawdy Miss Clawdy / Bring it on home to me / Personality / Crazy man crazy / Rock and roll music.
LP. . . . . SNTF 645
Sonet / '73 / Swift / C.M. Distribution / Roots Records / Jazz Music / Sonet Records / Cadillac Music / Projection / Wellard Dist. / Hot Shot.

KING OF ROCK 'N' ROLL, THE (Haley, Bill & The Comets).
Tracks: Not Advised.
CD 288 07 005
Bellaphon / '86 / New Note.

LIVE IN SWEDEN (Haley, Bill & The Comets).
Tracks: Not Advised.
MC . . . . ZCSND 9989
Speciality (USA) / '74 / Swift / C.M. Distribution.

MAMBO ROCK (Haley, Bill & The Comets).
Tracks: Mambo rock.
■ 7" 05405
Brunswick / Apr '55.

MR ROCK 'N' ROLL.
Tracks: Not Advised.
CD . . . . CDCD 1080
Charly / Apr '93 / Charly.

MR. ROCKIN' ROLLIN' (Essential Bill Haley, The) (Haley, Bill & The Comets).
Tracks: Rock around the clock / Thirteen women / Shake, rattle and roll / ABC boogie / Mambo rock / Razzle dazzle / R-O-C-K / Rock-a-beatin' boogie / Saints rock 'n' roll / Burn that candle / See you later alligator / Rudy's rock / Hot dog buddy buddy / Rockin' through the rye / Teenager's mother / Rip it up / Don't knock the rock / Forty cups of coffee / You hit the wrong note Billy goat / Rockin' rollin' rover / Beak "speaks", The / Move it one over / Rock the joint / Skinny Minnie / Lean Jean / Joey's song / Whoa Mabel / Ooh look-a-there, ain't she pretty / Skokiaan / Green door / Yeah, she's evil / How many?.
Double LP . . . . CDX 5
■ MC . . . . TCCDX 5
Charly / '84 / Charly.

ORIGINAL HITS 1954-57 (Haley, Bill & The Comets).
Tracks: Rock around the clock / Rock the joint / Saints rock 'n' roll / Mambo rock / Rockin' rollin' rover / Don't knock the rock / Calling all Comets / Rockin' through the rye / Choo choo ch' boogie / Razzle dazzle / Rudy's rock / Hot dog buddy buddy / Rocking little tune / R-O-C-K.
LP. . . . . SHM 3207
MC . . . . HSC 3207
Hallmark / Mar '87 / Pickwick Records.
CD . . . . PWKS 575
Pickwick / Mar '90 / Pickwick Records.

R-O-C-K (Haley, Bill & The Comets).
Tracks: Ooh, look-a-there ain't she pretty? / Dim dim the lights / Burn that candle / R-O-C-K / I got a woman / Farewell, so long, goodbye / ABC boogie / I'll be true / Dance with a dolly / Mohair Sam.
LP. . . . . SNTF 710
Sonet / Oct '76 / Swift / C.M. Distribution / Roots Records / Jazz Music / Sonet Records / Cadillac Music / Projection / Wellard Dist. / Hot Shot.

R-O-C-K (Haley, Bill & The Comets).
Tracks: R-O-C-K / Piccadilly rock / Saints rock 'n' roll / Caledonia.
■ 12" . . . . MCEP 2
MCA / '78.

RAZZLE DAZZLE (Haley, Bill & The Comets).
Tracks: Razzle dazzle.
■ 7" 05453
Brunswick / Aug '56.

REAL ROCK DRIVE (Haley, Bill & The Comets).
Tracks: Real rock drive / Live it up / Dance with a dolly / Rockin' chair on the moon.
■ EP. . . . . RCEP 102
Rollercoaster / Jan '80.

RIP IT UP (Haley, Bill & The Comets).
Tracks: Rip it up.
■ 7" 05615
Brunswick / Nov '56.

RIP IT UP, ROCK'N'ROLL (Haley, Bill & The Comets).
Tracks: Rock around the clock / Saints rock'n'roll / You hit the wrong note billy goat / Goofin' around / Thirteen women (and only one man in town) / Caldonia / Shake, rattle and roll / Choo choo ch' boogie / Burn that candle / Happy baby / Hook, line and sinker / Rock Lomond / See you later alligator / Mambo rock / Dim, dim the lights / Lean Jean / Tonight's the night / Calling all Comets / Rip it up / Hide and seek / Mary Lou / Teenage mothers / Move it on over / Vive la rock'n'roll.
CD . . . . VSOPCD 116
Double LP . . . . VSOPLP 116
MC . . . . VSOPMC 116
Connoisseur Collection / '88 / Pinnacle.

ROCK 'N' ROLL GREATS (Haley, Bill & The Comets).
Tracks: Shake, rattle and roll / Rock around the clock / Mambo rock / Rock-a-beatin' boogie / Don't knock the rock / Hot dog Buddy Buddy / Rock the joint / Saints rock 'n' roll / See you later alligator / Rockin' through the rye / Razzle dazzle / Rip it up / Skinny Minnie / Lean Jean / Thirteen women / Choo choo ch' boogie.
■ LP. . . . . MFP 5807
MFP / Oct '87.
■ MC . . . . TCMFP 5807
MFP / Oct '87.

ROCK 'N' ROLL SCRAPBOOK.
Tracks: Not Advised.
CD . . . . NEMCD 600
Sequel / Apr '90 / Castle Communications / BMG / Hot Shot.

ROCK 'N' ROLL STAGE SHOW (Haley, Bill & The Comets).
Tracks: Calling all Comets / Rockin' through the rye / Rocking little tune / Hide and seek / Hey then, there now / Goofin' around / Hook, line and sinker / Rudy's rock / Choo choo ch' boogie / Blue Comet blues / Hot dog Buddy Buddy / Tonight's the night.
■ LP. . . . . LAT 8139
Brunswick / '56.
■ LP. . . . . CR 30221
Charly / Aug '83 / Charly.

ROCK A BEATIN BOOGIE (OLD GOLD) (Haley, Bill & The Comets).
Tracks: Rock a beatin boogie / Razzle dazzle / Burn that candle / Dim dim the lights.
12" . . . . OG 7702
Old Gold / Jul '90 / Pickwick Records.

ROCK AND ROLL (Haley, Bill & The Comets).
Tracks: Not Advised.
LP. . . . . GNPS 2077
MC GNP5 2077
GNP Crescendo / '88 / Swift / Silva Screen / Flexitron Ltd.

H 4 ■ DELETED

ROCK AROUND THE CLOCK.
Tracks: Rock around the clock / Shake, rattle and roll / Saints rock 'n' roll / Love letters in the sand / Rock the joint / Flip flop and fly / Ling-ting-tong / Skinny Minnie / See you later alligator / Rock-a-beatin' boogie / Johnny B. Goode.
■ **LP.** . . . . **AH 13**
Ace Of Hearts / May '68.
■ **LP.** . . . . **MCL 1617**
MCA / Oct '81.
MC . . . . **ORC 006**
Orchid Music / Feb '82 / Pinnacle.
LP. . . . . **SPR 8502**
MC . . . . **SPC 8502**
Spot / Feb '83.
LP. . . . . **AR 30049**
Astan (USA) / Dec '85.
CD **15 098**
MC **79 546**
Laserlight / Aug '91 / TBD / Taylors.

ROCK AROUND THE CLOCK (Haley, Bill & The Comets).
Tracks: Rock around the clock.
■ **7"** **05317**
Brunswick / Jan '55.
■ **7"** . . . . **MU 1013**
MCA / '68.
7" . . . . **MCA 128**
MCA / Feb '81 / BMG.

ROCK AROUND THE CLOCK (Haley, Bill & The Comets).
Tracks: See you later alligator / Rock-beatin' boogie / Shake, rattle and roll / Johnny B. Goode / Skinny Minnie.
CD **100406.9**
MC **511548.5**
Europa / Jul '88.

ROCK AROUND THE CLOCK (JOKER) (Haley, Bill & The Comets).
Tracks: Not Advised.
LP. . . . . **SM 3869**
Joker (USA) / '88 / C.M. Distribution / Jazz Horizons / Jazz Music.

ROCK AROUND THE CLOCK (OLD GOLD) (Haley, Bill & The Comets).
Tracks: Rock around the clock / Thirteen women.
7" . . . . **OG 9220**
Old Gold / '92 / Pickwick Records.

ROCK AROUND THE CLOCK/SEE YOU LATER ALLIGATOR.
Tracks: Not Advised.
LP. . . . . **BHEP 0001**
Sonet / Mar '90 / Swift / C.M. Distribution / Roots Records / Jazz Music / Sonet Records / Cadillac Music / Projection / Wellard Dist. / Hot Shot.

ROCK AROUND THE COUNTRY (Haley, Bill & The Comets).
Tracks: Not Advised.
LP. . . . . **GNPS 2097**
GNP Crescendo / '88 / Swift / Silva Screen / Flexitron Ltd.

ROCK THE JOINT (Haley, Bill & The Comets).
Tracks: Rocket 88 / Tearstains on my heart / Green tree boogie / Jukebox cannonball / Sundown boogie / Icy heart / Rock the joint / Dance with a dolly / Rockin' chair on the moon / Stop beatin' around the mulberry bush / Real rock drive / Crazy man crazy / What cha' gonna do / Pat-a-cake / Fractured / Live it up / Farewell, so long, goodbye / I'll be true / Ten little Indians / Chattanooga choo choo / Straight jacket / Yes indeed.
■ **LP.** . . . . **ROLL 2002**
Rollercoaster / '79.
LP. . . . . **ROLL 2009**
Rollercoaster / Jun '85 / Rollercoaster Records / Swift.
CD . . . . **RCCD 3001**
Rollercoaster / Aug '90 / Rollercoaster Records / Swift.

ROCK THE JOINT (Haley, Bill & The Comets).
Tracks: Rock the joint / Fractured.
7" . . . . **RRC 2004**
Rollercoaster / Sep '80 / Rollercoaster Records / Swift.

ROCK THE JOINT (SINGLE - ORIGINAL RELEASE) (Haley, Bill & The Comets).
Tracks: Rock the joint.
■ **7"** . . . . **HLF 8371**
London-American / Feb '57.

ROCK-A-BEATIN' BOOGIE (Haley, Bill & The Comets).
Tracks: Rock-a-beatin' boogie.
■ **7"** **05509**
Brunswick / Dec '55.

ROCKET 88 (Haley, Bill & The Saddlemen).
Tracks: Rocket 88.
7" . . . . **TU 103**
Thumbs Up / Feb '81.

ROCKIN' ROLLIN HALEY.
Tracks: Rock around the clock / Thirteen women / Shake, rattle and roll / A.B.C. Boogie / Happy baby / Dim, dim the lights / Birth of the boogie / Mambo rock / Two hound dogs / Razzle dazzle / R O C K-Rock a beatin' boogie / See you later, Alligator / Saints rock and roll / Bum that candle / Paper boy, The / Goofin around / Rudy's rock / Hide and seek / Hey then, there now / Tonight's the night / Hook, line and sinker / Blue comet blues / Calling all comets / Choo choo ch'boogie / Rocking little tune / Hot dog buddy buddy / Rockin through the rye / Teenagers mother / Rip it up / Don't rock the knock / Forty cups of coffee / Miss you / You hit the wrong note Billy Goat / Rockin ' rollin' rover / Please don't talk about me when I'm gone / You can't stop me from dreaming / I'm gonna sit right down and write myself a letter / Rock Lomond / Is it true what they say about Dixie / Carolina in the morning / Dipsy doodle, The / Ain't misbehavin' / Beak speaks, The / Moon over Miami / One sweet letter from you / I'll be with you in appleblossom time / Somebody else is taking my place / How many / Move it on over / Rock the joint / Me rock a hula / Rockin' Rita / Jamaica D.J. / Picadilly rock / Pretty Alouette / Rockin' rollin' schnitzlebank / Rockin' Matilda / Vive la rock'n roll / It's a sin / Mary, Mary Lou / El rocko / Come rock with me / Oriental rock / Woodenshoe rock / Walkin' beat, The / Skinny Minnie / Sway with me / Lean Jean / Don't nobody move / Joey's song / Chiquita Linda / Dinah / Ida, sweet as applecider / Whoa Mabel / Marie, Eloise, Corrine, Corrina / B.B. Betty / Sweet Sue, just you / Charmaine / Dragon rock / A C Rock / Catwalk, The / I got a woman / Fool such as I, A / By by me / Where did you go last night / Caldonia / Shaky / Ooh, look a there, ain't she pretty / Summer souvenir / Puerto rican peddler / Music, music, music / Skokiaan / Drowsy waters / Two shadows / In a little Spanish town / Strictly instrumental / Mack the knife / Green door, The / Yeah she's evil / Complete American decca recordings.
LP. . . . . **BFX 15068**
Bear Family / Jan '83 / Rollercoaster Records / Swift / Direct Distribution.

ROCKIN' ROLLIN' BILL HALEY (Haley, Bill & The Comets).
Tracks: Rock around the clock / Thirteen women / Shake, rattle and roll / ABC boogie / Happy baby / Dim dim the lights / Birth of the boogie / Mambo rock / Two hound dogs / Razzle dazzle / R-O-C-K / Rock-a-beatin' boogie / Saints rock 'n' roll / Burn that candle / See you later alligator / Paper boy, The / Goofin' around / Rudy's rock / Hide and seek / Hey then, there now / Tonight's the night / Hook, line and sinker / Blue Comet blues / Calling all Comets / Choo choo ch' boogie / Rocking little tune / Hot dog Buddy Buddy / Rockin' through the rye / Teenager's mother / Rip it up / Don't knock the rock / Forty cups of coffee / Miss you / You hit the wrong note, billy goat / Rockin' rollin' rover / Please don't talk about me when I'm gone / You can't stop me from dreaming / I'm gonna sit right down and write myself a letter / Rock Lomond / Is it true what they say about Dixie? / Carolina in the morning / Dipsy doodle, The / Ain't misbehavin' / Beak "speaks", The / Moon over Miami / One sweet letter from you / I'll be with you in apple blossom time / Somebody else is taking my place / How many? / Move it on over / Rock the joint / Me rock a hula / Rockin' Rita / Jamaica D.J. / Piccadilly rock / Pretty alouette / Rockin' rollin' schnitzlebank / Rockin' Matilda / Vive la rock 'n' roll / It's a sin / Mary Mary-Lou / El rocko / Come rock with me / Oriental rock / Woodenshoe rock / Walkin' beat, The / Skinny Minnie / Sway with me / Lean Jean / Don't nobody move / Joey's song / Chiquita Linda / Dinah / Ida, sweet as apple cider / Whoa Mabel! / Marie / Eloise / Corina, Corina / B.B. Betty / Sweet Sue / Charmaine / Dragon rock / ABC rock / Catwalk, The / I got a woman / Fool such as I, A / By by me / Where did you stay last night? / Caldonia / Shaky / Ooh, look-a-there, ain't she pretty? / Summer souvenir / Puerto Rican peddlar / Music, music, music / Skokiaan / Drowsy waters / Two shadows / In a little Spanish town / Strictly instrumental / Mack the knife / Green door / Yeah, she's evil.
LP Set . . . . **BFX 15068/5**
Bear Family / Sep '84 / Rollercoaster Records / Swift / Direct Distribution.

ROCKIN' ROLLIN' HALEY (Haley, Bill & The Comets).
Tracks: Rock around the clock / Thirteen women / Shake, rattle and roll / A.B.C. boogie / Happy baby / Dim, dim, the lights / Birth of the boogie / Mambo rock / Two hound dogs / Razzle dazzle / R.O.C.K. / Rock a beatin' boogie / Saints rock 'n' roll, The / Burn that candle / See you later, alligator / Paper boy, The / Goofin' around / Rudy's rock / Hide and seek / Hey then, there now / Tonight's the night / Hook, line and sinker / Blue comet blues / Calling all comets / Choo choo ch' boogie / Rocking little tune, A / Hot dog buddy buddy / Rockin' through the rye / Teenager's mother / Rip it up / Don't knock the rock / Forty cups of coffee / Miss you / You hit the wrong note billy goat / Rockin' rollin' rover / Please don't talk about me when I'm gone / You can't stop me from dreaming / I'm gonna sit right down and write myself.. / Rock Lomond / Is it true what they say about Dixie / Carolina in the morning / Dipsy doodle, The / Ain't misbehavin' / Beak speaks, The / Moon over Miami / One sweet letter from you / I'll be with you in Appleblossom time / Somebody else is taking my place / How many / Move it on over / Rock the joint / Me rock a hula / Rockin' Rita / Jamaica D.J. / Piccadilly rock / Pretty alouette / Rockin' rollin' schnitzlebank / Rockin' Matilda / Vive la rock 'n' roll / It's a sin / Mary, Mary Lou / El rocko / Come rock with me / Oriental rock / Woodenshoe rock / Walkin' beat, The / Skinny Minnie / Sway with me / Lean Jean / Don't nobody move / Joey's song / Chiquita Linda / Dinah / Ida, sweet as apple cider / Whoa Mabel / Marie / Eloise / Corina, Corina / BB. Betty / Sweet Sue, just you / Charmaine / Dragon rock / A.C. rock / Catwalk, The / I got a woman / Fool such as I, A / By by me / Where did you go last night / Caldonia / Shaky / Ooh, look a there, ain't she pretty / Summer souvenir / Puerto Rican peddler / Music, music, music / Skokiaan / Drowsy waters / Two shadows / In a little Spanish town / Strictly instrumental / Mack The Knife / Green door / Yeah, she's evil.
CD Set . . . . **BCD 15506**
Bear Family / Oct '90 / Rollercoaster Records / Swift / Direct Distribution.

ROCKIN' THROUGH THE RYE (Haley, Bill & The Comets).
Tracks: Rockin' through the rye.
■ **7"** **05582**
Brunswick / Aug '56.

RUDY'S ROCK (Haley, Bill & The Comets).
Tracks: Rudy's rock.
■ **7"** **05616**
Brunswick / Nov '56.

RUDY'S ROCK (Haley, Bill & The Comets).
Tracks: Rudy's rock.
7" . . . . **REV 6016**
Revival / Jul '82 / EMI.

SAINTS ROCK 'N' ROLL, THE (Haley, Bill & The Comets).
Tracks: Saints rock 'n' roll.
■ **7"** **05565**
Brunswick / May '56.

SCRAPBOOK (Haley, Bill & The Comets).
Tracks: Rock the joint / Rock-a-beatin' boogie / Skinny Minnie / Razzle dazzle / Rudy's rock / See you later alligator / Saints rock 'n' roll / Framed / Shake, rattle and roll / Rip it up / Crazy man crazy / Rock around the clock.
LP. **252261-1**
■ **MC** **252261-4**
Buddah / Jul '85.

SEE YOU LATER ALLIGATOR (Haley, Bill & The Comets).
Tracks: Not Advised.
CD **301374**
MC **301372**
Accord / Dec '89 / Discovery.

SEE YOU LATER ALLIGATOR (Haley, Bill & The Comets).
Tracks: See you later alligator / Rudy's rock.
■ **7"** . . . . **MCA 142**
MCA / Jun '74.

SEE YOU LATER ALLIGATOR (Haley, Bill & The Comets).
Tracks: See you later alligator.
■ **7"** **05530**
Brunswick / Mar '56.

SEE YOU LATER ALLIGATOR (OLD GOLD) (Haley, Bill & The Comets).
Tracks: See you later alligator / Shake, rattle and roll.
7" . . . . **OG 9221**
Old Gold / Jul '82 / Pickwick Records.

SHAKE, RATTLE AND ROLL (Haley, Bill & The Comets).
Tracks: Shake, rattle and roll.
■ **7"** **05338**
Brunswick / Dec '54.

TRIBUTE TO BILL HALEY (Haley, Bill & The Comets).
Tracks: Shake, rattle and roll / See you later alligator / Mambo rock / Burn that candle / Birth of the boogie / Rock Lomond / Rock-a-beatin' boogie / Beat speaks, The / Hot dog buddy buddy / R-O-C-K / Dim dim the lights / Saints rock 'n' roll / Razzle dazzle / Rockin' through the rye / Rip it up / Teenager's mother / Rudy's rock / Billy goat / Rock the joint / Skinny Minnie / Forty cups of coffee / Lean Jean / Don't knock the rock / Rock around the clock.
LP. . . . . **MCL 1770**
MC . . . . **MCLC 1770**
MCA / '83 / BMG.

TWISTIN' KNIGHTS AT THE ROUND TABLE (Haley, Bill & The Comets).
Tracks: Lullaby of Birdland twist / Twist Marie / One two three twist / Down by the riverside twist / Queen of the twisters / Caravan twist / I want a little girl / Whistlin' and walkin' twist / Florida twist / Eight more miles to Louisville.
LP. . . . . **N 5012**
PRT International / May '81.

VERY BEST OF BILL HALEY & THE COMETS (Haley, Bill & The Comets).
Tracks: Rock around the clock / Shake, rattle and roll / See you later alligator / Saints rock and roll, The / Rock-a-beatin' boogie / Rockin' thru the Rye / Rip it up / Don't knock the rock / Mambo rock / Rudy's rock / Razzle dazzle / Skinny minnie / R.O.C.K. / Thirteen women / ABC boogie / Birth of the boogie / Forty cups of coffee / Two hound dogs / Burn that candle / Calling all comets.
CD . . . . **MCCD 068**
MC . . . . **MCTC 068**
Music Club / Jun '92 / Gold & Sons / Terry Blood Dist. / Video Collection.

WHY DO I CRY OVER YOU ?.
Tracks: Why do I cry over you?.
■ 7" . . . . RZ 137
Rollercoaster / '79.

Hall, Ben

COUNTRY WAYS AND ROCKIN' DAYS (Hall, Ben & The Ramblers With Weldon Myrick).
Tracks: Blue days - Black nights / Even tho' / Hanging around / Crying on my shoulder / Make believe / Sleepless nights / Gunfighter's fame / Late hours / Don't ask me why / I'd give anything / All from loving you / Rose of Monterey / Drifting along with the wind / Driftwood on the river / Stormy skies / Season for love / Only 17 / That's the way dreams go / I don't wanna go home / You're here in my mind / Weeping willow / Before you begin / Johnny Law / Hiding alone / So close / Won't you be mine / I'll never be the same / I'll still be hanging around.
CD . . . . RCCD 3004
Rollercoaster / Oct '93 / Rollercoaster Records / Swift.

Hall, Roy

BOOGIE ROCKABILLY.
Tracks: Not Advised.
LP. . . . . R&C 1008
Rock & Country / Oct '88 / Swift.

DIGGIN' THE BOOGIE.
Tracks: Whole lotta shakin' goin' on / All by myself / Christine / Don't stop now / See you later alligator / Blue suede shoes / Diggin' the boogie / You ruined my blue suede shoes / Offbeat boogie / Move on / Luscious / Three alley cats / My girl & his girl.
■ LP. . . . . CR 30227
Charly / Feb '84 / Charly.

HANK 'N THE HOUND.
Tracks: Not Advised.
LP. . . . . R&C 1014
Rock & Country / Oct '88 / Swift.

Hamilton, George IV

Country singer born in North Carolina in 1937. He began with Top 40 pop hits 1957-8 including *A rose and a baby Ruth* (chocolate bar), song written by John D Loudermilk (also from NC). He joined the Grand Ole Opry in 1959, was signed to RCA by Chet Atkins in 1961 and became the International Ambassador of Country Music, more popular all over the world than at home: he was the first USA country star to have his own summer season at a British seaside resort. (Donald Clarke).

16 GREAT PERFORMANCES.
Tracks: Not Advised.
LP. . . . . ABCL 5178
ABC Records / Apr '76.

20 OF THE BEST: GEORGE HAMILTON IV.
Tracks: Three steps to the phone / To you and yours / If you don't know I ain't gonna tell you / Abilene / Fort Worth / Truck drivin' man / Walking the floor over you / Write me a picture / Steel rail blues / Early morning rain / Urge for going / Break my mind / Little world girl / Back to Denver / Canadian Pacific / Blue train / She's a little bit country / Back where it's at / Anyway / West Texas highway.
MC . . . . NK 89371
RCA / Mar '84 / BMG.
■ LP. . . . . NL 89371
RCA / Mar '84.

ABILENE.
Tracks: Abilene / Oh so many years.
7" . . . . RCA 1784
RCA / '68 / BMG.

AMERICAN COUNTRY GOTHIC.
Tracks: If I never see midnight again / My hometown / This is our love / Little country county fairs / Farmer's dream ploughed under / Never mind / I will be your friend / More about love / Heaven knows / Back up grinnin' again / Carolina sky / I believe in you.
CD . . . . CDRR 304
MC . . . . MCRR 304
Request / Jan '90 / Conifer Records / Jazz Music.

BACK HOME AT THE OPRY.
Tracks: Headed for the country / Streets of gold / Winterwood / Blue jeans, ice cream and Saturday shows / Follow me / Bad romancer / Crystal chandeliers / Sleeping through goodbye / It's almost tomorrow / Leaving London.
LP. . . . . PL 10192
■ MC . . . . PK 10192
RCA / '79.

BEST OF GEORGE HAMILTON IV.
Tracks: Abilene / Fort Worth / Break my mind / Rose and a baby Ruth / Before this day ends / Why don't they understand? / Early morning rain / Steel rail blues / Take my hand for a while / Urge for going / Three steps to the phone / Blue train.
LP. . . . . LSA 3005
RCA / '74 / BMG.
■ MC . . . . MPK 213
RCA / '74.

BEST OF GEORGE HAMILTON IV VOL 2.
Tracks: Canadian Pacific / Dirty old man / Blue train / Suzanne / Ten degrees and getting colder / Anyway / She's a little bit country / Streets of London / Countryfied / Let's get together / West Texas highway / Second cup of coffee / Back where it's at / Country music in my soul.
■ LP. LFL1 7504
RCA / '79.

BLUEGRASS GOSPEL.
Tracks: I'm using my bible for a road map / Old time religion / When it's prayer meetin' time in the hollow / I shall not be moved / Father's table grace / Will the circle be unbroken / Shake my mother's hand for me / O come angel band / Where did all the good folks go? / Build me a cabin in glory / Precious memories / Gathering flowers for the master's bouquet.
LP. . . . . LL 2012
MC . . . . LLC 2012
Lamb & Lion / May '82 / Word Records (UK).

CANADIAN PACIFIC.
Tracks: Canadian Pacific / I'm gonna be a country boy again / Shake the dust / Together alone / Steel rail blues / Both sides now / Sisters of mercy / Early morning rain / My Nova Scotia home / Summer wages / Long thin dawn / Home from the forest.
LP. . . . . SF 8062
■ MC . . . . PK 11622
RCA / Apr '71.
■ LP. . . . . CDS 1220
RCA/Camden / Sep '86.
MC . . . . CAM 1220
RCA/Camden / '88 / BMG / Arabesque Ltd.

COUNTRY CHRISTMAS, A.
Tracks: I wonder as I wander / C.H.R.I.S.T.M.A.S. / Christmas in the trenches / See amid the winter's snow / Friendly beast, The / Joy to the world / Little Grave, The / Silent night / Away in a manger / Natividad / Morning star / In the bleak midwinter.
■ MC . . . . WST C 9707
Word (UK) / Nov '89.
CD . . . . WSTCD 9707
Word (UK) / Sep '93 / Word Records (UK) / Sony.

COUNTRY CLASSICS (Hamilton, George IV & George Hamilton V).
Tracks: Abilene / I can't stop loving you / Distant drums / Wayward wind / My truly, truly fair / Raining in my heart / It doesn't matter anymore / American trilogy, An / Sixteen tons / Canadian pacific / Release me / Welcome to my world / Last thing on my mind, The / I walk the line / Try a little kindness / Green green grass of home.
CD . . . . CD MFP 5933
MC . . . . TC MFP 5933
MFP / Feb '92 / EMI.

COUNTRY STORE: GEORGE HAMILTON IV.
Tracks: Not Advised.
LP. . . . . CST 30
MC . . . . CSTK 30
Country Store / Aug '86 / BMG.

CUTTING ACROSS THE COUNTRY.
Tracks: Williams Lake stampede / Dirty old man / Follow me / Crystal chandeliers / Fiddlers green / Abilene / Bad news / Peter Amberlay / Way of a country girl / Into the mountains / Cape Breton / Lullaby / Break my mind / Shores of P.E.I. / Canadian Pacific.
LP. . . . . PL 18106
RCA / Feb '81 / BMG.

ENGLAND.
Tracks: England.
7" . . . . MRE 001
MRE / Sep '82.

FAMOUS COUNTRY MUSIC MAKERS-COAST TO COAST.
Tracks: I don't believe I'll fall in love today / Big big love / Slightly used / Under your spell again / You better not do that / Keep those cards and letters coming in / Above and beyond / Long black limousine / Isle of Newfoundland / My Nova Scotia home / Prince Edward Island is heaven to me / Take me back to old New Brunswick / Ghost of Bras D'or / Squid jigging around / Atlantic lullaby / Apple blossom time in Annapolis Valley / Thanks a lot / You nearly lose your mind / Driftwood on the river / Half a mind / I will miss you when you go / Walking the floor over you / Rainbow at midnight / Soldier's last letter / It's been so long darling / Fortunes in memories / Letters have no arms / Let's say goodbye / Farewell to Nova Scotia / Foolin' around / Excuse me (I think I've got a heartache) / Together again / Under the influence of love.
Double LP . . . . DPS 2043
RCA / '79 / BMG.

FEEL LIKE A MILLION.
Tracks: Feel like a million / Take this heart.
■ 7" . . . . ANC 1052
Anchor (1) / Jun '78.

FOREVER YOUNG.
Tracks: Forever young / Rangement blues.
■ 7" . . . . MCA 526
MCA / Sep '79.

FOREVER YOUNG.
Tracks: Not Advised.
■ LP. . . . . MCF 3016
MCA / Oct '79.

GEORGE HAMILTON IV.
Tracks: Till I gain control again / Can't remember, can't forget / Early morning rain / I will love you all my life / Break my mind / Good ole boys like me / Cornbread, beans and sweet potato pie / Canadian Pacific / Dirty old man / Suzanne / 10 degrees and getting colder / Anyway / She's a little bit country / Streets of London / Countryfied / Let's get together / West Texas highway / Back where it's at / Country music in my soul.
LP. . . . . MFP 5785
■ MC . . . . TCMFP 5785
MFP / Mar '87.

GEORGE HAMILTON IV.
Tracks: Abilene / Forever young / You're the best thing / Till I gain control again / Can't remember, can't forget / Early morning train / I will love you all my life / Break my mind / Good ole boys like me / Cornbread beans and sweet potato pie.
LP. . . . . MCF 3314
■ MC . . . . MCFC 3314
MCA / Mar '86.

GIVE THANKS.
Tracks: Little town / In the bleak mid winter / Sweet little Jesus boy / Mary what ya gonna name that pretty baby / Joseph / God rest ye merry gentlemen / Unto us a child is born / Can it be true?.
■ LP. . . . . WST R 9697
Word (UK) / Nov '88.
■ MC . . . . WST C 9697
Word (UK) / Nov '88.

HITS OF GEORGE HAMILTON IV.
Tracks: Travellin' light / Ten degrees and getting colder / Urge for going / Second cup of coffee / Back to Denver / Anyway / Alberta bound / Take my hand for a while / Truck driving man / Everything is beautiful / Claim on me / Carolina in my mind / She's a little bit country / Write me a picture / West Texas highway / It's my time.
LP. . . . . PL 42335
■ MC . . . . PK 42335
RCA / '79.

HOMEGROWN (Hamilton, George IV & George Hamilton V).
Tracks: Not Advised.
CD . . . . LRCD 10225
LP. . . . . LR 10225
Lamon International / Jun '91.

HYMNS COUNTRY STYLE.
Tracks: What a friend / I'd rather have Jesus / It is no secret / How great Thou art / Rock of ages / Old rugged cross, The / Blessed assurance / Abide with me / Lord's my shepherd, (The).
LP. . . . . WST 9656
MC . . . . WC 9656
Word (UK) / Apr '85 / Word Records (UK) / Sony.

I KNOW WHERE I'M GOING.
Tracks: I know where i'm going.
■ 7" . . . . POP 505
H.M.V. / Jul '58.

MUSIC MAN'S DREAMS.
Tracks: It must be love / Man I used to be, The / Would you still be mine / Double or nothing / Till I gain control again / Are the good times really over / Music man's dream / Growing on me would you still be mine / Keeper of the moon / Back around to me / Water is wide / Life I love / 'Til I gain control again.
LP. . . . . RANGE 7004
Range (1) / '84.

NATIVIDAD.
Tracks: Natividad / I love music.
7" . . . . DSM 7003
Mervyn Conn Presents / Dec '80.

ONE DAY AT A TIME.
Tracks: One day at a time / I shall not be moved / Forever young / Shadow of the cross, The / Someone is looking for someone like you / Where did the good folks go / Some day my prince will come / You were the finger of God / Feel like a million / Old time religion / Mose rankin' / I'm using my bible for a road map.
LP. . . . . WST 9618
MC . . . . WC 9618
Word (UK) / May '85 / Word Records (UK) / Sony.

REFLECTIONS.
Tracks: Not Advised.
■ LP. . . . . WH 5008
Lotus / Feb '79.

SING ME A SAD SONG.
Tracks: Not Advised.
LP. . . . . HAT 3124
Stetson / '89 / Crusader Marketing Co. / Swift / Wellard Dist. / Midland Records / C.M. Distribution.

SONGS FOR A WINTER'S NIGHT.
Tracks: Song for a winter's night / Mull of Kintyre / When we are gone (I will love you) / When I dream / I believe in you / Castles in the air / Lucille / Bunch of thyme / Me and the elephant / England / Only love / Way old friends do, The / Waitin' for the sun to shine / Teach your children / Four strong winds / Blue eyes crying in the rain.
LP. . . . . RTL 20-82
MC 4CRTL 2082
Ronco / Oct '82.

H 6 ■ DELETED

WAY OLD FRIENDS DO.
Tracks: Way old friends do / Songs for a winter's night.
7" . . . . MRE 002
Mervyn Conn Presents / Dec '82.

WHY DON'T THEY UNDERSTAND.
Tracks: Why don't they understand.
■ 7" . . . . .POP 429
H.M.V. / Mar '58.

WILD MOUNTAIN THYME.
Tracks: Wild mountain thyme / I'll be here in the morning.
■ 7" . . . . MCA 558
MCA / Feb '80.

Hamilton, Joe E.

BEST OF JOE E. HAMILTON.
Tracks: Not Advised.
LP. . . . . .HRL 218
MC . . . . .CHRL 218
Homespun (Ireland) / '88 / Homespun Records / Ross Records / Wellard Dist.

COUNTRY.
Tracks: Not Advised.
LP. . . . . .HRL 162
MC . . . . .CHRL 162
Homespun (Ireland) / May '88 / Homespun Records / Ross Records / Wellard Dist.

DO WHAT YOU DO DO WELL.
Tracks: Do what you do do well / China doll / Love thee dearest / Silver threads among the gold / If my world should end tomorrow / Sweet sweet Judy / From the candy store on the corner / From here to there to you / She wears my ring / Golden needles / Danny boy.
LP. . . . . .PHL 441
MC . . . . .CPHL 441
Homespun (Ireland) / '82 / Homespun Records / Ross Records / Wellard Dist.

MOCKIN' BIRD HILL.
Tracks: Mockin' Bird Hill / Mother of mine / Born again / Grandma's rocking chair / I love you more and more every day / Love is all / It take people like you to make people like me / American trilogy / I'll love you for ever and ever / Shame lovin' shame / Wasn't it a party? / If I had my life to live over.
LP. . . . . ARAL 1012
MC . . . . CARAL 1012
Ara (Ireland) / Jul '83.

SING ME A GOOD OLD COUNTRY SONG.
Tracks: Back home again / Sing me a good old country song / When it's Springtime in the Rockies / Why me Lord / Garden of love / Wedding song, The / Pretty brown eyes / I am a fool / Rhinestone cowboy / Village in County Tyrone / Devil woman / Four strong winds.
LP. . . . . .PHL 410
MC . . . . .CPHL 410
Homespun (Ireland) / '82 / Homespun Records / Ross Records / Wellard Dist.

Hancock, Butch

Hancock was born in July 1945 in Lubbock, Texas and is one of the most prolific singer/songwriters to emerge from the state. Rough edged vocals and strong evocative story telling ballads are a feature of his music. The Texan has released 9 LP's on his Rainlight label. The Demon label has packaged a selection of his songs on their *Own & Own* release. Another sample of his songwriting talent is covered on fellow Texan, Joe Ely's *Milkshakes & Malts* on Sunstorm (1989). Every song on this album is written by Butch Hancock. Hancock has also appeared on albums by Emmylou Harris and Jimmie Dale Gilmore. The latter with which he played 5 dates in London in 1990 - not repeating a song during the sequence! Some of Hancock's finest work was with the Flatlanders in the early 1970's which produced some old time West Texas style music and also featured Gilmore and Ely. (Maurice Hope)

DIAMOND HILL.
Tracks: Golden hearted ways / You can take me for one / Neon wind / Diamond Hill / Corona Del Mar / Ghost of Give and Take Avenue, The / Some folks call it style / Her lover of the hour / Wheels of fortune.
LP. . . . . .RLT 777
Rainlight / '80.

ON THE WAY OVER HERE.
Tracks: Talkin' about this Panama Canal / Only born / Smokin' in the rain / Corona del mar / Like the light at dawn / Gift horse of mercy / Neon wind / Perfection in the mud / Only makes me love you more / Already gone / Away from the mountain.
CD . . . . SH 1038CD
MC . . . . SH 1038C
Sugarhill(USA) / May '93 / Roots Records / Projection / Impetus Records / C.M. Distribution / Jazz Music / Swift / Duncans / A.D.A Distribution.

OWN AND OWN.
Tracks: Dry land farm / Wind's dominion, The / Diamond hill / 1981: A spare odyssey / Fire water / West Texas waltz / Horseflies / If you were a bluebird / Own and own / Leo and Leona (Not available on CD) / Fools fall in love / Split and slide (Not available on CD) / Yellow rose / Like a kiss on the mouth / Ghost of Give and Take Avenue, The / Tell me what you want to know / Just a storm / Just tell me that / When will you hold me again?.
CD . . . . FIENDCD 150
Double LP . . . . .DFIEND 150
Demon / Oct '89 / Pinnacle.

TWO ROADS (Hancock, Butch & Jimmie Dale Gilmour).
Tracks: Hello stranger / Rambling man / Her lover of the hour / Tonight I think I'm gonna go downtown / Two roads / Wheels of fortune / One more road / Blue yodel No.9 / Down by the banks of the Guadalupe / Dallas / Already gone / Special treatment / Howlin at midnight / Firewater (seeks it's own level) / West Texas waltz.
CD . . . . CDV 2649
■ MC . . . . TCV 2649
Virgin / Oct '90 / EMI.
■ LP. . . . . .V 2649
Virgin / Oct '90.

WEST TEXAS WALTZES AND DUST BLOWN TRACTOR TUNES.
Tracks: Dry land farm / Where the West wind has blown / You've never seen me cry / I wish I was only workin' / Dirt road song / West Texas waltz.
LP. . . . . RLT 14
Rainlight / '78.

WINDS DOMINION, THE.
Tracks: Sea's deadog catch / Capture, rapture and the rapture / Wind's dominion, The / Long road to Asia minor / Split and slide / Smokin' in the rain / Fighting for my life / Personal rendition of the blues / Dominoes / Once followed by the wind / Wild horses chase the wind / Own and own / Mario y Maria (cryin' statues) / Eternal triangles / Only born / Gift horse of mercy.
Double LP . . . . RLT 1644
Rainlight / '79.

YELLA ROSE (Hancock, Butch & Marce Lacouture).
Tracks: Perfection in the mud / Yella rose / Like a kiss on the mouth / Ain't no mercy on the highway / Only makes me love ya more / So I'll run / Two roads / Sharp cutting wings / Tell me what you know.
LP. . . . . RLP 13711
Rainlight / '85.

Happy Traum Band

AMERICAN STRANGER.
Tracks: Not Advised.
LP. . . . . SNKF 142
Kicking Mule / Jan '78 / Roots Records / Swift / Projection / C.M. Distribution / Impetus Records / Ross Records / Duncans.

BRIGHT MORNING STARS.
Tracks: Not Advised.
LP. . . . . WF 005
Waterfront / Mar '84 / SRD / Jazz Music / A.D.A Distribution / C.M. Distribution.
LP. . . . . .GR 0703
Greenhays (USA) / '92 / Roots Records / Projection / Duncans / Ross Records / Jazz Music.

FRIENDS AND NEIGHBOURS.
Tracks: Not Advised.
LP. . . . . FF 4015
Folk Freak / '88 / Roots Records / Projection / Duncans / C.M. Distribution / Impetus Records / Ross Records.

HARD TIMES IN THE COUNTRY (Traum, Happy & Art).
Tracks: Not Advised.
LP. . . . . ROUNDER 3007
Rounder / May '77 / Projection / Roots Records / Swift / C.M. Distribution / Topic Records / Jazz Music / Hot Shot / A.D.A Distribution / Direct Distribution.

RELAX YOUR MIND.
Tracks: Relax your mind / Gypsy Davey / Worried blues / John Henry / Peggy Gordon / When first unto this country / Poor Howard / Fair and tender ladies / Boat up the river / Willie Moore / Weave room blues / Eighth of January / When I was a cowboy.
LP. . . . . SNKF 111
Kicking Mule / '74 / Roots Records / Swift / Projection / C.M. Distribution / Impetus Records / Ross Records / Duncans.

Harrell, Bill

BALLADS AND BLUEGRASS (Harrell, Bill & Virginians).
Tracks: Not Advised.
LP. . . . . .AD 2013
Adelphi (1) / May '81 / Jetstar.

BLUE VIRGINIA BLUE.
Tracks: Blue Virginia blues / Sonny boy / Fire on the North Ridge / Mary on the wild moor / God must be a cowboy at heart / God put a rainbow in the clouds / Letter at home / Kentucky is just a smile away / Bare foot Nellie / I haven't seen Mama in years / Wreck of old 97 / Muddy little shoes.
LP. . . . . REBEL 1650
Rebel (1) / '86 / Projection / Backs Distribution.

DO YOU REMEMBER.
Tracks: Not Advised.
LP. . . . . REBEL 1640
MC . . . . .REBEL 1640C
Rebel (1) / '83 / Projection / Backs Distribution.

SONG FOR EVERYONE, A.
Tracks: Not Advised.
LP. . . . . REBEL 1655
MC . . . . .REBEL 1655C
Rebel (1) / '85 / Projection / Backs Distribution.

WALKING IN THE EARLY MORNING DEW.
Tracks: Not Advised.
LP. . . . . REBEL 1620
MC . . . . .REBEL 1620C
Rebel (1) / '83 / Projection / Backs Distribution.

Harris, Emmylou

Alabama born (Birmingham 2.4.1947) Emmylou Harris has arguably done more for the advancement of country music than any other, from her days singing harmony with country rock pioneer Gram Parsons to her work with her present band , The Nashville Ramblers. Harris's started out in the music business back in the late 60s , her vocals very much of the Baez mould - her pure, clear soprano with sometimes a falling off on the final enuciation possessing indelible qualities. Harris' early solo recordings garner much from the country rock sphere - yet unlike some of her country contemporaries, she's never found herself being submerged in the smooth, precision - moulded, unidentifiable pop-country idiom (Crystal Gayle, Barbara Mandrell, Lynn Anderson, etc). During her folk days, Harris made the forgettable *Gliding Bird* (1969) on the Jubilee label. She tried her luck in Nashville, working as a cocktail waitress to make ends meet, soon returning to her parents in Maryland. She was spotted by the Flying Burritos Chris Hillman and from there struck out with Gram Parsons, who invited her to sing on his forthcoming debut solo album *G.P.* (1972). On the subsequent tour to promote the release, Emmylou was to go as a member of Parsons' band The Fallen Angels. Harris and Parsons when thrown together held that ever so rare chemistry, as if it was just meant to be a natural progression. Harris' short education came to an abrupt end, when after recording the *Grevious Angel* , Parsons was to die from an overdose of drugs and drink (18.9.1973). Emmylou was now left on her own, her mentor no longer around-although she was to draw inspiration from their short-lived association. An electric blend of the Louvins and Parsons' own country rock creations, and some of her personal preference were to adorn Harris albums for some considerable time. Harris' solo recording career took shape in 1975, when she formed the now legendary Hot Band. Two hot albums ensued *Pieces of the sky* (1975) and *Elite hotel* (1976) - both finding great acclaim in both rock and country quarters. In 1976, she made her UK debut, since when she has established a most rewarding on-going relationship with her European audience. Harris, a headliner on a number of Wembley Country Music Festival Bills, was the first genuine country act to attract a sizeable younger element to the music. On the country singles front, it was her remakes of the standards *Together again* , *Sweet dreams* (both 1976) and *Two more bottles of wine* (1978) that were to go all the way. It was Harris' fine articulate culturing of the various genres (rock, country and bluegrass/acoustic music) on her albums that was showing her to be an incredible innovative talent. Such affairs as *Quarter moon in a ten cent town* , her traditionally directed *Blue Kentucky girl* , *Roses in the snow* (with Ricky Skaggs playing a prominent roll) and *Cimarron* (1981) , featuring the single *Born to run* (Paul Kennerley's song at No.3).She also sang on Bob Dylan's critically acclaimed *Desire* LP. Harris' stage act was captured on record in 1982, the album *Last date* a product of some Californian dates. *(lost our love) on our last date* , a vocal version of Floyd Crammers's instrumental classic. *Last date* allowing Emmylou her only No.1 solo single success of the 80s. Harris seperated from Brian Ahern, her producer husband, moving back to Nashville where she was to settle down. Harris had started the decade alongside her idol George Jones (it was his version that inspired her to record *Beneath still waters* , a 1980 No.1) as the CMA's top performers in their respective categories . Among Harris' other great contributions to country music has been the musicians who have passed through her famed Hot Band (James Burton, Emory Gordy, Glen D Hardin, Bernie Leadon, John Ware). From the wellspring there's been Ricky Skaggs and Rodney Crowell, who've gone on and made it at the highest level. That's not to mention such musicians as England's own Albert Lee and Barry Tashian, who've recorded worthy albums in their own right. Emmylou continued to search out new avenues and approaches for her projects. One such occasion was her 1985 release *The ballad of Sally Rose* , a concept album penned by herself and Paul Kennerley, who also wrote *The legend of Jesse James* in 1980 which had Emmylou, Cash, Waylon and Charlie Daniels playing the leading roles . Kennerley had previously made his mark via his excellent concept American Civil war double album *White mansions* in 1978. A forerunner to her Nash Ramblers days, was to be found when in 1987 the acoustic *Angle band* album emerged. Even though Harris had always kept a steady tour schedule and recording career going, she also found time during the last 18 years to sing harmony and duet on hundreds of albums, many on lesser (to some) projects for example helping out such aspiring talents as Ricky Skaggs on his 1979 Sugar Hill album *Sweet temptation* , Delia Bell (who she had Warners sign in 1980), Carl Jackson and John Starling's grammy winner *Spring training* (with her band The Nash Ramblers consisting of trusty souls Sam Bush, Roy Huskey Jr, Al Perkins, Atamanuik and new boy Randall Stewart) and Iris DeMent, a then unknown singer-songwriter, debuting on Philo (1992). Harris' dedication towards the old traditional themes also found her contributing to the Columbia audio/video release Folkways:A vision shared *A tribute to Woody Guthrie and Leadbelly* . In 1991, alongside Ireland's Mary Black and Delores Keane she formed a trio when working on the Irish-American project *Bringing it all back home* . Among those with whom she has gained commercial successes on the country charts are Earl Thomas Conley, John Denver, The Desert Rose Band, Charlie Louvin, Roy Orbison, Buck Owens and Don Williams, besides being featured alongside Bob Dylan, The Band and Guy Clark on other album cuts. (For her trio work, see Dolly Parton, who wrote Harris' 1977 top 3 single *To Daddy*). Emmylou did in fact duet with Linda Ronstadt on *Sweetest gift* , charting in 1976. Harris' in later years has found chart action becoming more and more infrequent - only 1988s *Heartbreak hill* obtaining a top ten slot. On the album front her standard hasn't wavered as country music's most artistically creative female act - *"Bluebird"* ,*Brand new dance* and *Live at the Ryman* (also on video, 1992) a historic live recording in country music's Mother Church, the old Ryman Auditorium, home of the Grand Ole Opry from 1926 to 1974. It's fitting that Emmylou, who had been for some years an industrious working president of the Country Music Foundation, should terminate her 18 year association with Warner/Reprise with a recording of this stature. 1993 found her on Asylum Records where, with it's American Explorer Series, it's a label more suited to acoustic based material. (Maurice Hope)

13.
Tracks: Mystery train / You're free to go / Sweetheart of the pines / Just someone in the know / My father's house / Lacassine special / Today I started loving you again / When I was yours / I had my heart set on you / Your long journey.
LP. . . . . **K 925352 1**
MC . . . . **K 925352 4**
WEA / Apr '87 / WEA.

ANGEL BAND.
Tracks: Where could I go but to the Lord / Angel band / If I be lifted up / Precious moments / Bright morning stars / When he calls / We shall rise / Drifting too far / Who will sing for me / Someday my ship will sail / Other side of life, The / When they ring those golden bells.
CD . . . . **.925585-2**
Warner Bros.(USA) / Sep '87 / Warner Bros. (Imports).

AT THE RYMAN.
Tracks: Guitar town / Half as much / Cattle call / Guess things happen that way / Hard times / Mansion on the hill / Scotland / Montana cowgirl / Like strangers / Lodi / Calling my children home / If I could be there / Walls of time / Get up John / It's a hard life where you go/ Abraham, Martin and John / Smoke along the track.
CD . . . . **.759926662**
LP. . . . . **.759926661**
MC . . . . **.759926664**
Reprise / Feb '92 / WEA.

BAD MOON RISING.
Tracks: Bad moon rising / I don't have to crawl.
■ **7"** . . . . **K 17804**
WEA / Jun '81.

BALLAD OF SALLY ROSE.
Tracks: Ballad of Sally Rose, The / Rhythm guitar / I think I love him / You are my flower heart to heart / Woman walk the line / Bad news / Timberline / Long tall Sally Rose / White line / Diamond in my crown / Sweetheart of the Rodeo, The / K-S-O-S (Instrumental medly) / Ring of fire / Wildwood flower / Six days on the road / Sweet chariot.
■ **MC** . . . . **.925205 4**
WEA / Feb '85 / WEA.
■ **LP.** . . . . **.925205 1**
WEA / Feb '85.

BLUE BIRD.
Tracks: Heaven only knows / You've been on my mind / Icy blue heart / Love is / No regrets / Lonely street / Heartbreak hill / I still miss someone / River for him, A / If you were a bluebird.
MC . . . . **.K 9257764**
WEA / Feb '89 / WEA.

BLUE KENTUCKY GIRL.
Tracks: Sister's coming home / Beneath still waters / Rough and rocky / Hickory wind / Save the last dance for me / Sorrow in the wind / They'll never take his love from me / Every time you leave / Blue Kentucky girl / Even cowgirls get the blues.
■ **MC** **K4 56627**
WEA / Jun '79 / WEA.
■ **LP.** . . . . **K 56627**
WEA / Jun '79.

BLUEBIRD.
Tracks: Heaven only knows / You've been on my mind / Icy blue heart / Love is / No regrets / Lonely street / Heartbreak hill / I still miss someone / River for him, A / If you were a bluebird.
CD . . . . **K 925776 2**
MC . . . . **K 925776 4**
Reprise / Feb '89 / WEA.
■ **LP.** . . . . **K 925776 1**
Reprise / Feb '89.

BORN TO RUN.
Tracks: Born to run / Ashes by now.
■ **7"** . . . . **K 17896**
WEA / Feb '82.

BRAND NEW DANCE.
Tracks: Wheels of love / In his world / Easy for you to stay / Better off without you / Brand new dance / Tougher than the rest / Sweet dreams of you / Rollin' and ramblin' / Never be anyone else but you / Red red rose.
CD **75992630924**
WEA / Nov '87 / WEA.
CD **7599263092**
WEA / Oct '90 / WEA.
LP. . . . . **WX 396**
MC . . . . **WX 396C**
Reprise / Oct '90 / WEA.

CHRISTMAS ALBUM, THE (Light of the stable).
Tracks: Away in a manger / Golden cradles / First Noel, The / Oh little town of Bethlehem / Christmas time's a coming / Silent night / Beautiful star / Little drummer boy / Angel eyes / Light of the stable.
LP. . . . . **K 56757**
MC **K4 56757**
WEA / Nov '79 / WEA.

CIMARRON.
Tracks: Rose of Cimarron / Spanish is the loving tongue / If I needed you / Another lonesome morning / Last cheater's waltz, The / Born to run / Price you pay, The / Son of a rotten gambler / Tennessee waltz / Tennessee rose.
■ **LP.** . . . . **.K 569 55**
WEA / '84 / WEA.

DUETS (Harris, Emmylou & Various).
Tracks: Price I pay, The / Love hurts / Thing about you / That lovin' feelin' again / We believe in happy endings / Star of Bethlehem / All fall down / Wild Montana skies / Green pastures / Gulf Coast highway / If I needed you / Evangeline.
CD **7599257912**
LP. **7599257911**
MC **7599257914**
WEA / Aug '90 / WEA.

ELITE HOTEL.
Tracks: Amarillo / Together again / Feeling single / Seeing double / Sin city / One of these days / Till I gain control again / Here, there and everywhere / Ooh Las Vegas / Sweet dreams / Jambalaya / Satan's jewelled crown / Wheels.
LP. . . . . **K 54060**
Reprise (USA) / Jan '76 / WEA / Pinnacle.
■ **MC** **K4 54060**
Reprise (USA) / Jan '76.
CD . . . . **K 254060**
Reprise / '88 / WEA.
LP. . . . . **ED 306**
Edsel / Apr '89 / Pinnacle.

EVANGELINE.
Tracks: Don't have to crawl / How high the moon / Spanish Johnny / Bad moon rising / Evangeline / Hot burrito / Millworker / Oh Atlanta / Mister Sandman / Ashes by now.
■ **LP.** . . . . **K 56880**
WEA / Feb '81.

FIRST NOEL.
Tracks: First Noel, The / Silent night.
■ **7"** . . . . **K 17528**
Automatic / Nov '79.

HER BEST SONGS.
Tracks: Not Advised.
■ **LP.** . . . . **NE 1058**
K-Tel / Mar '80.

HERE THERE AND EVERYWHERE.
Tracks: Here, there and everywhere.
■ **7"** . . . . **K 14415**
Reprise / Mar '76.

I AIN'T LIVING LONG LIKE THIS.
Tracks: I ain't living long like this / One paper kid.
■ **7"** . . . . **K 17133**
WEA / Apr '78.

LAST DATE.
Tracks: I'm movin' on / It's not love (but it's not bad) / So sad (to watch good love go bad) / Grievous angel / Restless / Racing in the streets / Long may you run / We'll sweep out the ashes in the morning / Juanita / Devil in disguise / Lost his love on our last date / Buckaroo / Love's gonna live here (medley).
LP. **9237401**
■ **MC** **9237404**
WEA / '84 / WEA.

LEGENDARY 'GLIDING BIRD' ALBUM, THE.
Tracks: I'll be your baby tonight / Fugue for the fox / I saw the light / Clocks / Black gypsy / Gliding bird / Everybody's talkin' / Bobbie's gone / I'll never fall in love again / Waltz of the magic man.
LP. . . . . **PKL 5577**
MC . . . . **ZCPKL 5577**
PRT Special / Apr '79.

LIGHT OF THE STABLE.
Tracks: Light of the stable / Bluebird wine.
■ **7"** . . . . **K 14410**
Reprise / Jan '76.

LUXURY LINER.
Tracks: Luxury liner / Poncho and Lefty / Making believe / You're supposed to be feeling good / I'll be your San Antone Rose / (You never can tell) C'est la vie / When I stop dreaming / Hello stranger / She / Tulsa queen.
LP. . . . . **K 56334**
WEA / WEA.
■ **MC** **K4 66106**
WEA / Oct '82 / WEA.
■ **CD** . . . . **K 456 334**
WEA / '84 / WEA.
CD . . . . **.927338 2**
WEA / Jun '89 / WEA.

MR. SANDMAN.
Tracks: Mr. Sandman / Ashes by now.
7" . . . . **K 17758**
WEA / Feb '81 / WEA.

NASHVILLE COUNTRY DUETS (Harris, Emmylou & Carl Jackson).
Tracks: Not Advised.
CD . . . . **.CDMF 088**
Magnum / Jun '93 / Hot Shot / Swift / Cadillac Music / Arabesque Ltd. / Roots Records.

ON THE RADIO.
Tracks: On the radio / Good news.
7" . . . . **W 9364**
WEA / May '84 / WEA.

PIECES IN THE SKY.
Tracks: Bluebird wine / Too far gone / If I could only win your love / Boulder to Birmingham / Before believing / Bottle let me down, The / Sleepless nights / Coat of many colours / For no one / Queen of the silver dollar.
LP. . . . . **K 54037**
Reprise / WEA.
■ **MC** . . . . **K 454037**
Reprise / '84 / WEA.

PROFILE.
Tracks: One of these days / Sweet dreams / To Daddy / (You never can tell) C'est la vie / Making believe / Easy from now on / Together again / If I could only win your love / Too far gone / Two more bottles of wine / Boulder to Birmingham / Hello stranger.
CD . . . . **.256570**
WEA / Jun '84 / WEA.

PROFILE: EMMYLOU HARRIS.
Tracks: One of these days / Sweet dreams / To daddy / C'est la vie / Making believe / Easy from now on / Together again / If I could only win your love / Too far gone / Two more bottles of wine / Boulder to Birmingham / Hello stranger / You never can tell.
■ **MC** **K4 56570**
WEA / '83 / WEA.
■ **LP.** . . . . **K 56570**
WEA / '83.

QUARTER MOON IN A TEN CENT TOWN.
Tracks: Easy from now on / Two more bottles of wine / To Daddy / My songbird / Leaving Louisiana in the broad daylight / Defying / Gravity / I ain't living long like this / One paper kid / Green rolling hills / Burn that candle.
LP. . . . . **K 56443**
WEA / WEA.
■ **MC** . . . . **K 456 443**
WEA / '84 / WEA.
CD . . . . **.927345 2**
WEA / Jun '89 / WEA.

ROSES IN THE SNOW.
Tracks: Roses in the snow / Wayfaring stranger / Boxer, The / Green pastures / Darkest hour is just before the dawn, The / I'll go stepping too / You're learning / Jordan / Miss the Mississippi / Gold watch and chain.
■ **LP.** . . . . **K 56796**
WEA / Jun '80.

THAT LOVIN' YOU FEELIN' AGAIN.
Tracks: That lovin' you feelin' again / Lola.
■ **7"** . . . . **K 17649**
WEA / Oct '80.

H 8 ■ DELETED

TO DADDY.
Tracks: To daddy / Tulsa queen.
■ 7" . . . . K 17095
WEA / Feb '78.

TO KNOW HIM IS TO LOVE HIM (see under Parton, Dolly).

TRIO (see under Parton, Dolly).

WHITE SHOES.
Tracks: Drivin' wheel / Pledging my love / In my dreams / White shoes / On the radio / It's only rock 'n' roll / Diamonds are a girl's best friend / Good news / Baby, better start turning 'em down / Like an old fashioned waltz.
LP . . . . K 923961 1
■ MC . . . . K 923961 4
WEA / Oct '83.
■ CD . . . . K 923961 2
WEA / Jan '84 / WEA.

YOU NEVER CAN TELL.
Tracks: You never can tell / Boulder to Birmingham / Hello stranger (On K 16888 only).
■ 7" . . . . K 16888
WEA / Feb '77.
■ 7" . . . . K 17580
WEA / Mar '80.

Hart, Freddie

Singer/songwriter/musician, born on December 21st, 1933 in Lockapoka, Alabama. Hart begun his recording career on Capitol in 1953, but it took a return to the label 17 years later, after spells with Columbia and Kapp, before he achieved any significant chart success. His chart topper, *Easy Loving*, was named CMA Song Of The Year in 1971. This and *My Hang Up Is You*, were two of the most successful songs of the decade. Unfortunately, the success was short lived and Hart has virtually disappeared from sight in recent years. (Tony Byworth)

EASY LOVING.
Tracks: Easy loving / Our love (is our castle).
■ 7" . . . . CL 15972
Capitol / Mar '78.

MY LADY.
Tracks: Only woman in the world / Wasn't it easy baby / Look a here / Give a little you to me / My lady loves / My lady / Hangin' on a heartstring / Guilty / More than a bedroom thing / Toe to toe.
■ LP . . . . EST 11911
Capitol / '79.

YOU TURN ON THE MAN IN ME.
Tracks: You turn on the man in me / Why lovers turn to strangers.
■ 7" . . . . CL 15909
Capitol / Mar '77.

Hartford, John

The multi-instrumetalist , singer and songwriter was born in 1937 in New York, and raised in St. Louis, Missouri, where he played folk and country music in bars. He went to Nashville as a session musician in 1966 and signed as a writer with the Glaser Brothers; his *Gentle on my mind* won a Grammy in 1966 and was recorded by over 300 artists: John's record on RCA made the country chart while Glen Campbell had the pop hit. John works solo, accompanying his singing with banjo, fiddle, guitar and percussion effects from an electrified board on which he dances; he uses his own songs and those drawn from traditional country music. (Donald Clarke).

ALL IN THE NAME OF LOVE.
Tracks: All in the name of love / Cuckoo's nest, The / In Sara's eyes / Gentle on my mind / Boogie / Six o'clock train and a girl with green eyes / Don't cry and your tears / Ten chord blues / Dancing in the bathtub / Deck hand's waltz / Also love you for your mind.
LP . . . . FF 044
Flying Fish (USA) / Mar '89 / Cadillac Music / Roots Records / Projection / C.M. Distribution / Direct Distribution / Jazz Music / Duncans / A.D.A Distribution.

ANNUAL WALTZ.
Tracks: Annual waltz.
7" . . . . MCA 1147
MCA / May '87 / BMG.

ANNUAL WALTZ (Hartford, John & The Hartford String Band).
Tracks: All in my love for you / Ohio river rag / Annual waltz / Gone gone gone / Love wrote this song / Pennington bend / Learning to smile all over again / Here's to your dreams / Short life of trouble / Living in the Mississippi valley.
LP . . . . MCF 3366
■ MC . . . . MCFC 3366
MCA / Apr '87.

CATALOGUE.
Tracks: Not Advised.
LP . . . . FF 259
Flying Fish (USA) / Mar '89 / Cadillac Music / Roots Records / Projection / C.M. Distribution / Direct Distribution / Jazz Music / Duncans / A.D.A Distribution.

DOWN ON THE RIVER.
Tracks: Here I am again in love / Bring your clothes back home / Wish I had our time again / All I got is gone away / Delta queen waltz / Old time river man / Men all want to be hobos / Right in the middle of falling for you / There'll never be another you / Little boy / General Jackson.
CD . . . . FF 70514
LP . . . . FF 514
MC . . . . FF 514C
Flying Fish (USA) / '88 / Cadillac Music / Roots Records / Projection / C.M. Distribution / Direct Distribution / Jazz Music / Duncans / A.D.A Distribution.

GUM TREE CANOE.
Tracks: I'm still here / Way down the river road / Gum tree canoe / Your long journey / Jug Harris / Piece of my heart / Take me back to Mississippi / River home / Lorena / Wrong road again / No expectations.
LP . . . . SDLP 030
Sundown / Apr '87 / Terry Blood Dist. / Jazz Music / C.M. Distribution.
LP . . . . FF 289
Flying Fish (USA) / Mar '89 / Cadillac Music / Roots Records / Projection / C.M. Distribution / Direct Distribution / Jazz Music / Duncans / A.D.A Distribution.

MARK TWANG.
Tracks: Skippin' in the Mississippi dew / Long hot summer days / Let him go on Mama / Don't leave your records in the sun / Tater Tate & Allen Mundy / Julia Belle Swain, The / Little cabin home on the hill Waugh Waugh / Austin minor sympathy / Lowest pair, The / Tryin' to do something to get your attention.
LP . . . . FF 020
MC . . . . FF 020C
Flying Fish (USA) / Mar '89 / Cadillac Music / Roots Records / Projection / C.M. Distribution / Direct Distribution / Jazz Music / Duncans / A.D.A Distribution.
CD . . . . FF 70020
Flying Fish (USA) / Oct '89 / Cadillac Music / Roots Records / Projection / C.M. Distribution / Direct Distribution / Jazz Music / Duncans / A.D.A Distribution.

ME OH MY, HOW TIME DOES FLY.
Tracks: Not Advised.
CD . . . . FF 440CD
LP . . . . FF 440
MC . . . . FF 440C
Flying Fish (USA) / Jan '89 / Cadillac Music / Roots Records / Projection / C.M. Distribution / Direct Distribution / Jazz Music / Duncans / A.D.A Distribution.

MYSTERY BELOW.
Tracks: Not Advised.
LP . . . . FF 063
Flying Fish (USA) / Mar '89 / Cadillac Music / Roots Records / Projection / C.M. Distribution / Direct Distribution / Jazz Music / Duncans / A.D.A Distribution.

NOBODY KNOWS WHAT YOU DO.
Tracks: You don't have to do that / Don't want to be forgotten / In tall buildings / John McLaughlin / Granny wont'cha smoke some marijuana / False hearted tenor waltz, The / Joseph's dream / Down / Golden globe award, The / Sly feel / Somewhere my love / We'll meet again sweetheart / Nobody knows what to do.
LP . . . . FF 028
Flying Fish (USA) / Mar '89 / Cadillac Music / Roots Records / Projection / C.M. Distribution / Direct Distribution / Jazz Music / Duncans / A.D.A Distribution.

SLEEPIN' ON THE CUMBERLAND.
Tracks: Not Advised.
LP . . . . FF 095
MC . . . . FF 095C
Flying Fish (USA) / '79 / Cadillac Music / Roots Records / Projection / C.M. Distribution / Direct Distribution / Jazz Music / Duncans / A.D.A Distribution.

YOU AND ME AT HOME.
Tracks: Not Advised.
LP . . . . FF 228
Flying Fish (USA) / Mar '89 / Cadillac Music / Roots Records / Projection / C.M. Distribution / Direct Distribution / Jazz Music / Duncans / A.D.A Distribution.

Hawkes, Chip

ELEANOR RIGBY.
Tracks: Eleanor Rigby / Save your pity.
■ 7" . . . . PB 5033
RCA / Jun '77.

FRIEND OF A FRIEND.
Tracks: Friend of a friend / Times are changing.
■ 7" 2005027
Chelsea Collection / Jun '75.

ONE MORE DUSTY ROAD.
Tracks: One more dusty road / She couldn't figure my reason.
■ 7" . . . . PB 5002
RCA / Jan '77.

Hawkins, Hawkshaw

Country singer and songwriter (1921-63) who had several big hits on King 1948-51 including *I wasted a nickel* and *Slow poke*. He came back with a number 15 country hit *Soldier's joy* in 1959, then his only number one, *Lonesome 7-7203* in 1963, just as he was killed in the same plane crash that killed Patsy Cline. He was married to Jean Shepard. (Donald Clarke).

..SINGS.
Tracks: Not Advised.
LP . . . . HAT 3111
MC . . . . HATC 3111
Stetson / Sep '89 / Crusader Marketing Co. / Swift / Wellard Dist. / Midland Records / C.M. Distribution.

16 GREATEST HITS: HAWKSHAW HAWKINS.
Tracks: Not Advised.
LP . . . . SLP 3013
MC . . . . GT 53013
Starday (USA) / Apr '87 / Crusader Marketing Co.

HAWK 1953-1961.
Tracks: I'll trade yours for mine / Heap of lovin', A / Mark round your finger / Long way / When you say yes / I'll take a chance with you / I'll never close my heart to you / Why don't you leave this town / Rebound / One white rose / I wanna be hugged to death by you / Why didn't I hear from you / Flashing lights / Waitin' for my baby / Ko ko mo / Ling ting tong / Pedro Gonzales Tennessee Lopez / How could anything so pretty / Car hoppin' mama / Love you steal, The / Oh how I cried / Borrowing / If it ain't on the menu / I gotta have you / Standing at the end of the world / I've got it again / Sunny side of the mountain / You just stood there / Dark moon / I'll get even with you / Guilty of dreaming / Are you happy / She was here / Freedom / It's easier said than done / Sensation / Ring on your finger / It would be a doggone lie / My fate is in your hands / I'll be gone / Best of company, The / Action / You can't find happiness that way / I don't apologise for loving you / With this pen / Thank you for thinking of me / Twenty miles from shore / Big ole heartache / Big red benson / Soldier's joy / Patanio / Alaska Lil and Texas Bill / Darkness on the face of the earth / Put a nickel in the jukebox / I can't seem to say goodbye / No love for me / You know me much too well / My story / Love I have for you, The / Your conscience.
CD Set . . . . BCD 15539
Bear Family / Aug '91 / Rollercoaster Records / Swift / Direct Distribution.

HAWKSHAW HAWKINS (Vol. 1).
Tracks: Slow poke / Sunny side of the mountain / I'm kissing your picture counting tears / If I ever get rich mom / Rattlesnakin' daddy / I am slowly dying of a broken heart / I suppose / I can't tell my broken heart a lie / Picking sweethearts / Barbara Allen / I love the way you say goodnight / Got you on my mind / Would you like to have a broken heart / Teardrops from my eyes / Somebody lied / I hope you're crying too.
LP . . . . SING 587
Sing / '88 / Charly / Cadillac Music.

HAWKSHAW HAWKINS.
Tracks: Not Advised.
CD . . . . KCD 587
King / Apr '93 / New Note / Koch International.

Hawkins, Ronnie

Much loved pioneer of rockabilly, born in 1935 in Arkansas. He auditioned unsuccessfully for Sun in Memphis; floundering in the USA he went to Toronto, where he later ran a club, the Hawk's Nest; the edition of the Hawks he recruited there later became The Band (which is why The Band were all Canadians except Levon Helm, from Arkansas). He never had many hits of his own, but appeared in The Band's movie and 3-disc set *Last waltz* as an honoured guest. (Donald Clarke).

40 DAYS.
Tracks: 40 days / Who do you love?.
■ 7" 7N 25763
Pye International / Jan '78.

BEST OF RONNIE HAWKINS & THE HAWKS (Hawkins, Ronnie & The Hawks).
Tracks: Thirty days / Forty days / Mary Lou / Wild little Willy / Oh sugar (CD only.) / One of these days / Dizzy Miss Lizzy (CD only.) / Odessa / Sick and tired / Baby Jean / Come love (CD only.) / Hey bob a lou (CD only.) / Ruby baby / Bo Diddley / Clara / I feel good / Who do you love / What'cha gonna do (when the creek runs dry).
■ MC . . . . TCROU 5009
Roulette (EMI) / Aug '90.
■ CD . . . . CDROU 5009
Roulette (EMI) / Aug '90.

HAWK IN CONCERT, THE.
Tracks: Crazy music / Matchbox / Forty days / What'cha gonna do / Dizzy Miss Lizzy / Bo Diddley / Ruby baby / Wild little Willie / Whole lotta shakin' goin' on / I got my Mojo working / Johnny B Goode / Roll over Beethoven / Weight, The / Crazy music (reprise).
VHS . . . . MMGV 003
MMG Video / '88 / Terry Blood Dist.

HAWK, THE.
Tracks: Matchbox / Dizzy Miss Lizzy / That's alright mama / Odessa / Wild little Willie / Who do you love? /

Bo Diddley / Ruby baby / Johnny B. Goode / Down the line / Marylou / Forty days.
LP. . . . . **UAG 30283**
United Artists / Jan '80 / EMI.
LP. . . . . **MFLP 026**
Magnum Force / Apr '84 / Terry Blood Dist. / Jazz Music / Hot Shot.
MC . . . . **MFC 026**
Magnum Force / '86 / Terry Blood Dist. / Jazz Music / Hot Shot.

HELLO AGAIN, MARY LOU (Hawkins, Ronnie & The Hawks).
Tracks: Not Advised.
CD . . . . **PRD 70242**
LP. . . . . **PRL 70241**
Provogue / Feb '91 / Pinnacle.

ROCKIN'.
Tracks: Forty days / Wild little Willie / Whatcha gonna do (when the creek runs dry)? / Dizzy Miss Lizzy / Odessa / My gal is red hot / One of these days / Ruby baby / Marylou / Honey don't / Bo Diddley / Sick and tired / Suzie Q / Matchbox / Baby Jean / There's a screw loose / I feel good / Kansas City / Who do you love? / Southern love.
LP. . . . . **NSPL 28238**
Pye International / Jan '78.

RONNIE HAWKINS SINGS THE SONGS OF HANK WILLIAMS.
Tracks: Cold cold heart / Hey good lookin' / Your cheatin' heart / Weary blues from waitin' / There'll be no teardrops tonight / Nobody's lonesome for me / Ramblin' man / I'm so lonesome I could cry / You win again / I can't help it (if I'm still in love with you) / Lonesome whistle / Jambalaya.
LP. . . . . **N 5017**
MC . . . . **ZCN 5017**
PRT / Jul '83 / BMG.

THIS COUNTRY'S ROCKIN' (Hawkins, Ronnie & The Band).
Tracks: Not Advised.
VHS. . . . . **MMGV 056**
MMG Video / Feb '93 / Terry Blood Dist.

Hayes, Billy

BALLAD OF DAVY CROCKETT.
Tracks: Ballad of Davy Crockett, The.
■ **7"** . . . . **HLA 8220**
London-American / Jan '56.

Head, Roy

Rock'n'roll based country singer, born in 1943 in Texas. He signed with Sceptor in 1964 but had his first hit on the oscure Back Beat label the next year with *Treat her right*, a national Top. 3. He made the Hot 100 a few more times, then stuck with the country market, where he had 24 hit singles on nine different labels between 1974-85. (Donald Clarke).

MY BABE (Head, Roy & The Traits).
Tracks: My babe / Pain.
■ **7"** . . . . **VP 9269**
Vocalion / Apr '66.

ONE NIGHT.
Tracks: One night / Deep Elem blues.
■ **7"** . . . . **ABC 4151**
ABC Records / Oct '76.

ROY HEAD & THE TRAITS (Head, Roy & The Traits).
Tracks: Not Advised.
LP. . . . . **TNT 101**
TNT / Nov '87 / Jetstar.

TREAT HER RIGHT.
Tracks: Treat her right / One more time / Get back / Just a little bit / Feeling's gone, The / Operator / Get out of my life woman / Bring it to Jerome / Three o'clock blues / Who do you love? / Boogie chillun / High Sheriff.
■ **LP.** . . . . **BFX 15307**
Bear Family / Aug '88.

TREAT HER RIGHT.
Tracks: Treat her right.
■ **7"** . . . . **VP 9248**
Vocalion / Nov '65.

WIGGLIN' AND GIGGLIN'.
Tracks: Wigglin' and gigglin' / Driving wheel.
■ **7"** . . . . **VP 9274**
Vocalion / Jun '66.

Heap, Jimmy

RELEASE ME (Heap, Jimmy & The Melody Mastg).
Tracks: Release me / Love in the valley / Just to be with you / (I wanna go where you go) then I'll be happy / Heartbreaker / You're in love with you / Just for tonight / Girl with a past / Lifetime of shame / You don't kiss me 'cause you love me / One that I won, The / Ethyl in my gas tank (no gal in my arms) / My first love affair / Love can move mountains / Conscience / I'm guilty / This song is just for you / You oughta know / I told you so / Butternut / Long John / Mingling / Heap of boogie / You're nothin' but a nothin' / That's all I want from you / I'll follow the crowd / It takes a heap of lovin' / Cry cry darling / You didn't have time / Let's do it just once / This night won't last forever.
CD . . . . **BCD 15617**
Bear Family / Apr '92 / Rollercoaster Records / Swift / Direct Distribution.

Helms, Bobby

A country-pop star, born in Bloomington, Indiana in 1933, became teen TV star there (his father had a TV show), appeared on Grand Ole Opry at 17, signed with USA Decca (now MCA) in 1956 and had a huge international hit with *Fraulein*. He had country hits off and on through the '70s. (Donald Clarke).

FRAULEIN (His Decca recordings).
Tracks: Tennessee rock 'n' roll / I need to know how / I don't owe you nothing / Sowin' teardrops / (Got a) heartsick feeling / Far away heart / Just a little lonesome (1) / (Now and then) there's a fool such as I / I'm leaving now (long gone daddy) / Tonight's thenight / Jingle bell rock / Captain Santa Claus / No other baby / Standing at the end of my world / My shoes keep walking back to you / New river train / Hundred hearts, A / Hurry baby / Sad eyed baby / Someone was already there / To my sorrow / Lonely River Rhine (2) / Then came you / Just between old sweethearts / I can't take it like you can / My greatest weakness / Yesterday's champagne (1) / One deep love / Once in a lifetime / Fraulein / Most of the time / My special angel / just a little lonesome (2) / Magic song, The / Sugar moon / Schoolboy crush / If I only knew / Love my lady / Plaything / Jacqueline / Living in the shadows of the past / Forget about him / I guess I'll miss the prom / Miss memory / Soon it can be told / Fool and the angel, The / Someone for everyone / Yesterday's champagne (2) / Lonely River Rhine (1) / How can you divide a little child / Borrowed dreams / You're no longer mine / My lucky day / Let me be the one / Guess we thought the world would end / Teach me.
CD Set . . . . **BCD 15594**
Bear Family / Mar '92 / Rollercoaster Records / Swift / Direct Distribution.

JACQUELINE.
Tracks: Jacqueline.
■ **7"** **05748**
Brunswick / Aug '58.

MY SPECIAL ANGEL.
Tracks: Apartment No.9 / Touch my heart / Expressing my love / All I need is you / Things I remember most / I can see it all / I can't promise you won't get lonely / I wouldn't take the world for you / Just between you and me / I know one / Fraulein / My special angel.
LP. . . . . **PRCV 102**
President / May '88 / Grapevine Distribution / Target Records / Jazz Music / Taylors.

MY SPECIAL ANGEL.
Tracks: My special angel.
■ **7"** **05721**
Brunswick / Nov '57.

NO OTHER BABY.
Tracks: No other baby.
■ **7"** **05730**
Brunswick / Feb '58.

TENNESSEE ROCK'N'ROLL (Helms, Bobby & Roy Hall).
Tracks: Tenessee rock'n'roll / See you later alligator.
■ **7"** . . . . **MCA 298**
MCA / May '77.

Henderson, Kelvin

Bristol born and based Kelvin Henderson is another of those U.K. artists able to show that the U.K. scene does possess original talent and presentation, but his failure to breakthrough comes from lack of support (or belief) from the industry. First gaining reputation in Europe, and recording two albums for Polydor in Sweden, he returned home and released a series of albums that clearly defined his talent and direction. These included *Black magic gun* , *Slow movin' outlaw* and *Still on a roll* . These days, in addition to his own concerts, he runs a booking agency, puts together tours by U.S. artists like Sonny Curtis and Joey Davis and hosts a very popular country show for BBC Southwest titled *My style of country* . (Tony Byworth)

DOOR IS ALWAYS OPEN, THE.
Tracks: Door is always open, The.
7" . . . . **BUFF 1001**
Buffalo (UK) / Mar '79 / M.I.S.Records.

FROM A JACK TO A KING.
Tracks: From a Jack to a King / Gotta keep movin'.
■ **7"** . . . . **CRE 003**
Country Roads Records / Jun '81.

HEADLITES.
Tracks: Goodbye Marie / Scarlet woman / Dolly McGraw / Headlites / Never comin' back / Hero of the dreamers / From a jack to a king / Gotta keep movin' / Hello in there / 1643 Pennsylvania Boulevard / Truckstop lover / Hesitation blues.
■ **LP.** . . . . **CRLP 1003**
Country Roads Records / Nov '81.

I FEEL LIKE HANK WILLIAMS TONIGHT..
Tracks: I feel like Hank Williams tonight / Hard hearted / Whiskey eyes.
CD Single . . . . **RIV 91004**
Riviera (1) / Sep '92 / Pinnacle.

SUNDAY SCHOOL TO BROADWAY.
Tracks: Sunday school to Broadway / Big wheel.
■ **7"** . . . . **CHOP 2**
Chopper / '79.

Henriques, Basil

SOUNDS OF SUNSET.
Tracks: Not Advised.
LP. . . . . **TA 1003**
Tara (Ireland) / Oct '88 / Pinnacle / C.M. Distribution / A.D.A Distribution / Topic Records / Direct Distribution / Conifer Records / Jazz Music.

Hickman, John

B-C-H (see under Berline, Byron).

DON'T MEAN MAYBE.
Tracks: Don't mean maybe / Salt river / Turkey knob / Birmingham fling / Sweet Dixie / Sally Goodin / Train 405 / Banjo signal / Ghost dance / Pike county breakdown / Goin' to town / Dixie breakdown.
LP. . . . . **ROUNDER 0101**
MC . . . . **ROUNDER 0101C**
Rounder / '88 / Projection / Roots Records / Swift / C.M. Distribution / Topic Records / Jazz Music / Hot Shot / A.D.A Distribution / Direct Distribution.

DOUBLE TROUBLE (see under Berline, Byron).

NIGHT RUN (see under Berline, Byron).

NOW THERE ARE FOUR (see under Berline, Byron).

Hickory Lake

EASY COME EASY GO.
Tracks: Wurlitzer prize / Who were you thinking of / Looking for a feeling / That's not what life's for / Easy come easy go / Amelia Earhart's last flight / Coca cola cowboy / There's no more you and me / Lucy ain't your loser looking good / I don't wanna cry.
LP. . . . . **KO 1010**
MC . . . . **TC KO 1010**
Champ / '82 / Champ Records.

Hickory Wind

CROSSING DEVIL'S BRIDGE.
Tracks: Not Advised.
LP. . . . . **FF 074**
Flying Fish (USA) / May '79 / Cadillac Music / Roots Records / Projection / C.M. Distribution / Direct Distribution / Jazz Music / Duncans / A.D.A Distribution.

FRESH PRODUCE.
Tracks: Not Advised.
LP. . . . . **FF 018**
Flying Fish (USA) / Mar '89 / Cadillac Music / Roots Records / Projection / C.M. Distribution / Direct Distribution / Jazz Music / Duncans / A.D.A Distribution.

WEDNESDAY NIGHT WALTZ, AT THE.
Tracks: Not Advised.
LP. . . . . **AD 2002**
Adelphi (1) / May '81 / Jetstar.

Hicks, Bob

DARKNESS ON THE DELTA (see under Baker, Kenny).

TEXAS CRAPSHOOTER (Hicks, Bob & Friends).
Tracks: Panhandle rag / Goodbye Liza Jane / Maiden's prayer / Cherokee swing / Texas crapshooter / Big beaver / Scotland / Big man / East Tennessee blue / Cheyenne / Paddy on the turnpike.
LP. . . . . **CO 772**
County (USA) / May '79 / Projection / Mike's Country Music Room / Swift.

Higgins, Bertie

American singer and songwriter Higgins came to fame in 1982 with *Key Largo*, a gentle ballad inspired by the Humphrey Bogart film of the same name. The single was a sleeper smash, entering the US Hot One Hundred in November 1981, reaching the Top Forty the following January and attaining its No 8 peak in April. In Britain *Key Largo* could only peak at No 60. It

H 10 ■ DELETED

seemed that Higgins had a Bogart fixation, for his debut album -- which reached No 38 in America -- included a similar-sounding song called *Casablanca*. But not even the Americans really wanted to know about Higgins' second LP, another laid-back selection of ballads which began and ended with *As Time Goes By*. Somehow "Play it again, Bertie" just didn't sound right.. (Bob MacDonald).

CASABLANCA.
Tracks: Casablanca / She's gone to live on the mountain.
■ 7" . . . . **EPCA 2673**
Epic / Aug '82.

KEY LARGO.
Tracks: Just another day in paradise / Casablanca / Candle dancer / Key Largo / Port of call / White line fever / Heart is the hunter, The / She's gone to live on the mountains / Down at the blue moon / Tropics, The.
LP. **EPC 85595**
MC . . . . **.40 85595**
Epic / Jun '82 / Sony.

KEY LARGO.
Tracks: Key Largo / White line fever.
■ 7" . . . . **EPCA 2168**
Epic / Jun '82.

PIRATES AND POETS.
Tracks: Pirates and poets / When you fall in love (like I fell in love with you) / Leah / Under a blue moon / Tokyo Joe / Beneath the island light / Only yesterday / Marianna / Pleasure pier / Never looking back / As time goes by.
LP. **EPC 25327**
MC . . . . **.40 25327**
Epic / Aug '83 / Sony.

High Country

LAST TRAIN TO GLORY.
Tracks: Not Advised.
LP. **PC 447**
Pilgrim / '79.

ON THE ROAD.
Tracks: Not Advised.
LP. **SHILOH 4089**
Shiloh / Sep '79.

Highwayman

Occasional recording and touring quartet comprising country superstars Johnny Cash, Waylon Jennings, Kris Kristofferson and Willie Nelson. They first joined forces on the single *Highwaymen* in 1985 and its number one success ensured a top 20 placing for the follow-up *Desperados waiting for a train* , leading on to a million selling album and brisk tour business. The group made their U.K. debut in 1991. (Tony Byworth)

HIGHWAYMAN (Cash/Nelson/Jennings/Kristofferson).
Tracks: Highwayman / Last cowboy song, The / Jim, I wore a tie today / Big river / Committed to Parkview / Desperados waiting for the train / Deportees (Plane wreck at Los Gatos) / Welfare line / Against the wind / Twentieth century is almost over, The.
LP. **CBS 26466**
CBS / Jun '85 / Sony.
CD . . . . **CD 26466**
MC . . . . **.40 26466**
Columbia / Apr '92 / Sony.

HIGHWAYMAN 2 (Cash/Nelson/Jennings/Kristofferson).
Tracks: Silver stallion / Born and raised in black and white / Two stories wide / We're all in your corner / American remains / Anthem '84 / Angels love bad men / Songs that make a difference / Living legend / Texas.
CD **4666522**
MC **4666524**
CBS / Apr '90 / Sony.
■ LP. **4666521**
CBS / Apr '90.

HIGHWAYMAN RIDE AGAIN (Cash/Nelson/Jennings/Kristofferson).
Tracks: Twentieth century is almost over, The / How do you feel about foolin' around / Heroes / Down to her socks / Blackjack country chains / They're all the same to me / Whiter shade of pale, A / Last cowboy song, The / Ballad of forty dollars / Pilgrim, The / Casey's last ride / Under the gun / Eye of the storm / Why baby why.
■ LP. **4504311**
CBS / Mar '87.
■ MC **4504314**
CBS / Mar '87.

Highwoods String Band

DANCE ALL NIGHT.
Tracks: Not Advised.
LP. **ROUNDER 0045**
Rounder / '88 / Projection / Roots Records / Swift / C.M. Distribution / Topic Records / Jazz Music / Hot Shot / A.D.A Distribution / Direct Distribution.

FIRE ON THE MOUNTAIN.
Tracks: Not Advised.
LP. **ROUNDER 0023**
Rounder / '88 / Projection / Roots Records / Swift / C.M. Distribution / Topic Records / Jazz Music / Hot Shot / A.D.A Distribution / Direct Distribution.

NO. 3 SPECIAL.
Tracks: Not Advised.
LP. **ROUNDER 0074**
Rounder / '88 / Projection / Roots Records / Swift / C.M. Distribution / Topic Records / Jazz Music / Hot Shot / A.D.A Distribution / Direct Distribution.

Hill, Tommy

GET READY BABY.
Tracks: Ain't nothing like loving / In the middle of the morning (1) / Can't help / Life begins at 4 o'clock / Oh get ready, Baby (1) / Love words / Do me a favor / Have a little faith in me / O get ready baby (2) / In the middle of the morning (2).
CD . . . . **BCD 15709**
Bear Family / Mar '93 / Rollercoaster Records / Swift / Direct Distribution.

Hillbilly

Just as the sound of country has changed over the years, so has the name of the music. Today's multi-billion dollar industry is a far cry from the humble beginnings in the 1920's, back when it was known as 'hillbilly' - a term that had been in existence since the beginning of the century as a description for Southern backwoods inhabitants. The person most responsible for putting 'hillbilly' in the musical vocabulary was Ralph Peer, the most famous of all the field talent scouts whose greatest discoveries were Jimmie Rodgers and the Carter Family, and most certainly applied to other artists of the era like the first real star of the Grand Ole Opry, Roy Acuff. It was the music's increasing commercial popularity, bringing respectability to its artists (alongside the development of other closely related genres, like western swing and Hollywood's Singing Cowboys), that tolled the final death knoll for the term, revealing that there was nothing cheap or inferior about this area of music. The record companies were pressured, in the late 1940's, to replace the word 'hillbilly' with 'country', with the campaign being spearheaded by Eddie Kirk and Cliffie Stone (at Capitol Records) and, Red Foley and Ernest Tubb (at Decca). These artists, and others, did not resent the word, or feel that it was degrading, but believed that other people reacted adversely to it. A major goal was achieved in June 1949 when Billboard magazine changed the name of its 'folk' popularity charts (which had included 'race' music) to 'Country and Western'. (Tony Byworth)

Hillman, Chris

Hillman's rich pedigree in music, goes back to when, as a teenager, he played alongside Rex-Vern Gosdin and Don Parmerly in the Hillmen (formerly the Golden State Boys). Performing bluegrass/folk material, their recordings are found on a Sugar Hill album. Likewise his solo efforts *Morning sky* and *Desert rose* , of 1982-1984 respectively, can also be found on the label. Since his teenage ventures, including playing in the usual high school band (Scottsville Squirrel Barkers with Bernie Leadon and Kenny Wertz) San Diego, California born 4.12.1944 Hillman progressed to the formation of the Byrds, sojourn that lasted from 1964 -1968. It was long enough to help steer through arguably their finest years with pop hits *Mr.Tambourine Man* , *Chestnut mare* and *Turn, turn, turn* - climaxing with the brief Gram Parsons era and ground breaking country rock album *Sweetheart of the rodeo*. Mandolinist, bass guitarist/vocalist Hillman was to experiment for the next few years with a host of formations: The Flying Burrito Bros (1968 - 1971) penning tunes with Parsons, formed Manassas with Stephen Stills and Al Perkins, then in 1973 he helped form Souther-Hillman-Furay followed by contemporary unit McGuinn, Clark and Hillman in 1979. After something of a quiet spell, his subsequent short - lived bluegrass inspired solo career helped re-establish him when, in 1986 he took the Desert Rose Band onto the road it's regular members being Herb Pedersen and John Jorgenson. Hillman's inventive style, coupled with a new traditional edge was well suited for the country music's upsurge - with their self-titled debut album on Curb spawning the top ten hit *Love reunited* , supported with *One step forward* , *He's back* and *I'm blue* , reaching the slots 2 and 1 respectively. Since then they've had further chart successes with *Summer wind* (No.2), *I still believe in you* (No.1) alongside hits *Hello trouble* , *Start it all over* and *In Another lifetime* , they also recorded *The price we pay* with Emmylou Harris. Now signed with MCA/Curb with US albums *Running* , *Pages of life* and *True love* to their name, from which the 1993 compilation *Traditional* was culled, following on from the best of *A dozen roses* . It seems,that with the departure of John Jorgensen their careers are now at the crossroads. (Maurice Hope)

CLEAR SAILING.
Tracks: Nothing gets through / Fallen favourite / Quits / Hot dusty roads / Heartbreaker / Playing the fool / Lucky in love / Rollin' and tumblin' / Ain't that peculiar / Clear sailing.
LP. **K 53060**
Asylum / WEA.

DESERT ROSE.
Tracks: Why you been gone so long / Somebody's back in town / Wall around your heart / Rough and rowdy ways / Desert rose / Running the roadblocks / I can't keep you in love with me / Treasure of love / Ashes of love / Turn your radio on.
LP. **SH 3743**
MC . . . . **SH 3743C**
Sugarhill(USA) / '84 / Roots Records / Projection / Impetus Records / C.M. Distribution / Jazz Music / Swift / Duncans / A.D.A Distribution.
■ LP. **SPIN 113**
Spindrift / Nov '84.
LP. **SDLP 060**
Sundown / Mar '88 / Terry Blood Dist. / Jazz Music / C.M. Distribution.
■ MC . . . . **.SDC 060**
Sundown / Nov '88.

MEAN STREETS (Hillman, Chris & Roger McGuinn).
Tracks: Mean streets / Entertainment / Soul shoes / Between you and me / Angel / Love me tonight / King for a night / Secret side of you / Ain't no money / Turn your radio on.
■ LP. **EA-ST 12108**
Capitol / '81.

MORNING SKY.
Tracks: Tomorrow is a long time / Taker, The / Here today and gone tomorrow / Morning sky / Ripple / Good time Charlie's got the blues / Don't let your sweet love die / Mexico / It's happening to you / Hickory wind.
LP. **SH 3729**
MC . . . . **SH 3729C**
Sugarhill(USA) / '81 / Roots Records / Projection / Impetus Records / C.M. Distribution / Jazz Music / Swift / Duncans / A.D.A Distribution.
LP. **SDLP 053**
Sundown / Nov '87 / Terry Blood Dist. / Jazz Music / C.M. Distribution.
■ MC . . . . **.SDC 053**
Sundown / May '88.

Hillmen

HILLMEN, THE.
Tracks: Not Advised.
LP. **SH 3719**
Sugarhill(USA) / '88 / Roots Records / Projection / Impetus Records / C.M. Distribution / Jazz Music / Swift / Duncans / A.D.A Distribution.

Hillsiders

DAY IN THE COUNTRY, A.
Tracks: Not Advised.
LP. **.LP 004**
LP / '79 / Pinnacle.

DRIVER GET ME HOME ON TIME.
Tracks: Driver get me home on time.
7" . . . . **.LPS 006**
LP / '80 / Pinnacle.

HILLSIDERS, THE.
Tracks: Driver get me home on time / I'll never need you again / Yesterday's lovers / Harpin on / Sail away / I never slept a wink last night / Sleepy eyed Sam / She was my only one / Last dollar / World to him is kind, The / Hold on to me / Let me be the one.
LP. **.LP 005**
LP / '81 / Pinnacle.

LEAVING OF LIVERPOOL, THE.
Tracks: Leaving of Liverpool, the / One time and one time only / I will miss you when you go / One more mile / Don't waste your time / (I'm a) travelling man / Doesn't anybody know my name / Coming home / If you really want me to, I'll go / Road, The / Old memories never die / Someday, someone, somewhere.
■ LP. **RD 8002**
RCA / May '70 / BMG.

SHE WAS MY ONLY ONE.
Tracks: She was my only one / Last dollar.
7" . . . . **LPS 007**
LP / '81 / Pinnacle.

Hinojosa, Tish

AQUELLA NOCHE.
Tracks: Tu que puedas, vuelvete / Cumbia, pola y mas / Manos, hueso y sangre / Reloj / La llorona / Azul cristal / Aquells noche / Historia de un amor / Una noche mas / Carlos dominguez / Samba san pedro / Malaguena salerosa / Estrellita.
CD . . . . **MRCD 156**
MC . . . . **MRMC 156**

Munich / '91 / C.M. Distribution / Swift / Cadillac Music / A.D.A Distribution / Hot Shot / Topic Records / Direct Distribution / New Note.

CULTURE SWING.
Tracks: By the Rio Grande / Something in the rain / Bandera de Sol/Flag in the sun / Every word / Louisiana road song / Corazon viajero (wandering heart) / Drifter's wind / Window, The / In the real West / Chanate el vaquero (Chanate the cowboy) / San Antonio Romeo / Closer still.
CD . . . . **MRCD 165**
Munich / '92 / C.M. Distribution / Swift / Cadillac Music / A.D.A Distribution / Hot Shot / Topic Records / Direct Distribution / New Note.

MEMORABILIA NAVIDENA.
Tracks: Abolito (little Christmas tree) / Milagro / Building / A la nantia nana / Arbolita (in English) / Cada nino/Every child / Everything you wish / Memorabilia (Honky tonker's christmas).
CD . . . . **WMCD 1006**
Watermelon / Jun '93 / Topic Records.

TAOS TO TENNESSEE.
Tracks: Midnight moonlight / Prairie song / According to my heart / Taos to Tennessee / River / Amanecer / Please be with me / Crazy wind and flashing yellows / Highway calls, The / Who showed you the way to my heart / Let me remember / Always.
CD . . . . **MRCD 164**
MC . . . . **MRMC 164**
Munich / '92 / C.M. Distribution / Swift / Cadillac Music / A.D.A Distribution / Hot Shot / Topic Records / Direct Distribution / New Note.

Hoffpauir, Sleepy

SLEEPY HOFFPAUIR FIDDLES TRADITIONAL CAJUN MUSIC.
Tracks: Not Advised.
LP. **6027**
Swallow (USA) / Feb '79 / Swift / Wellard Dist.

Hofner, Adolph

SOUTH TEXAS SWING.
Tracks: Not Advised.
LP. . . . . **ARHOOLIE 5020**
Arhoolie (USA) / May '81 / Pinnacle / Cadillac Music / Swift / Projection / Hot Shot / A.D.A Distribution / Jazz Music.

Hogan, John

One of the hot acts of Ireland's 1990s country scene, County Westmeath native John Hogan launched his career by financing his first single *Brown eyes* , in 1988, out of his family's mortgage money. The record, which displayed his fine country styling, created enough attention for him to gather musicians around him, land a spot on Gay Byrne's top rating Late Late Show and finally lead to a deal with the Ritz Records. Another dream was fulfilled in January 1993 when he travelled to Nashville and recorded an album with former RCA producer Ronny Light, released later in the year with the (appropriate) title *The Nashville album*. (Tony Byworth)

AN IRISH HARVEST DAY.
Tracks: An Irish harvest day / I'll buy her roses.
CD . . . . **RITZCD 248**
MC . . . . **RITZ 248**
Ritz / Sep '92 / Pinnacle / Midland Records.

BACK HOME AGAIN.
Tracks: Back home again.
CD Single . . . . **RITZCD 260**
MC Single . . . . **RITZC 260**
Ritz / Jun '93 / Pinnacle / Midland Records.

BEST OF JOHN HOGAN, THE.
Tracks: Not Advised.
CD . . . . **KCD 348**
MC . . . . **KMC 348**
K-Tel (Ireland) / Feb '93 / I & B Records / Ross Records / Prism Leisure PLC.

EVENING WITH JOHN HOGAN, AN.
Tracks: Cottage in the country / Irish eyes / Send me the pillow that you dream on / Fraulein / Please help me I'm falling / Any Tipperary town / Brown eyes / Stranger in our house, A / My feelings for you / Red river valley / Amazing grace / Calypso / Three leafed shamrock / Moon light in mayo / Little by little / Turn back the years / Thank God I'm a country boy.
MC . . . . **PLAC 332**
Platinum Music / Oct '90 / Prism Leisure PLC / Ross Records.

EVENING WITH JOHN HOGAN, AN.
Tracks: Cottage in the country / Irish eyes / Hank Locklin medley / Any Tipperary town / Brown eyes / Stranger in our house, A / My feelings for you / Red River Valley / Amazing grace / Calypso / Three leafed shamrock / Moonlight in Mayo / Little by little / Turn back the years / Thank god I'm a country boy.
VHS. . . . . **PLATV 332**
Prism Video / Sep '90 / Terry Blood Dist. / Gold & Sons / Prism Leisure PLC.

HUMBLE MAN.
Tracks: Don't fight the feeling / Still got a crush on you / Walkin' in the sun / She's more to be pitied / Picture, The / Wreck of the old No.9 / China doll / Let it be you / Humble man / I'll be gone / Something's wrong / Down by the river / Follow me / Please don't forget me.
CD . . . . **RITZCD 0062**
MC . . . . **RITZLC 0062**
Ritz / Nov '91 / Pinnacle / Midland Records.
MC . . . . **RITZRC 529**
Ritz / Apr '93 / Pinnacle / Midland Records.

LET ME BE THE FIRST TO KNOW.
Tracks: Still got a crush on you / When it's lamp lightin' time in the valley / Down to the river / Let me be the first to know.
MC Single . . . . **RITZC 222**
Ritz / Jun '90 / Pinnacle / Midland Records.

MY FEELINGS FOR YOU.
Tracks: Not Advised.
LP. . . . . **KLP 270**
K-Tel (Ireland) / '88 / I & B Records / Ross Records / Prism Leisure PLC.
MC . . . . **KMC 270**
K-Tel (Ireland) / Dec '88 / I & B Records / Ross Records / Prism Leisure PLC.
CD . . . . **ONCD 3466**
MC . . . . **OCE 2466**
K-Tel / Jul '90 / I & B Records / C.M. Distribution / Arabesque Ltd. / Mono Distributors (Jersey) Ltd. / Prism Leisure PLC / PolyGram / Ross Records / Prism Leisure PLC.

NASHVILLE ALBUM.
Tracks: 'Til the mountains disappear / Walk through this world with me / Baby I'm lovin' you now / Morning sun and memories / I'll give my heart to you / Stepping stone / Back home again / Far away heart / I can't help it if I'm still in love with you / You can't take it with you when you go / Blue moon of Kentucky / Battle hymn of love / My guitar / Fallen angel.
CD . . . . **RITZRCD 531**
MC . . . . **RITZRC 531**
Ritz / Aug '93 / Pinnacle / Midland Records.

TURN BACK THE YEARS.
Tracks: Not Advised.
CD . . . . **KCD 305**
MC . . . . **KMC 305**
Prism / '90 / Pinnacle / Midland Records.

Hogshead

ROCKIN IN THE COUNTRY.
Tracks: I slap the bass boogie / Big Willy and Ramona / Bright morning light / Lola's lightnin' / Plain clothes / I feed the hogs / Alligator bait / Rockabilly queen / Eastbound and down / Bop on back to Memphis.
LP. . . . . **ROLL 2003**
Rollercoaster / Sep '84 / Rollercoaster Records / Swift.

Holland, Jerry

JERRY HOLLAND.
Tracks: Not Advised.
LP. . . . . **ROUNDER 7008**
Rounder / '88 / Projection / Roots Records / Swift / C.M. Distribution / Topic Records / Jazz Music / Hot Shot / A.D.A Distribution / Direct Distribution.

Hollow, Critton

GREAT DREAMS.
Tracks: Not Advised.
LP. . . . . **FF 468**
Flying Fish (USA) / Jul '89 / Cadillac Music / Roots Records / Projection / C.M. Distribution / Direct Distribution / Jazz Music / Duncans / A.D.A Distribution.

Hollowell, Terri

JUST STAY WITH ME.
Tracks: Just stay with me / Say what I feel tonight.
7" . . . . **AMGO 004**
Amigo / Jan '81 / C.M. Distribution / Wellard Dist. / Cadillac Music / C.M. Distribution.

JUST YOU AND ME.
Tracks: We've got it all together / I wrote this song for you / Was that really love that we made / Texas sunrise & me / Ain't got no time to fall in love / Hurry home cowboy / May I / It's too soon to say goodbye / One more singer in Nashville / Sharing / Big Mama Johns / Strawberry fields forever.
■ LP. . . . . **RKLP 5004**
RK / Apr '80.

Holly, Buddy

This American singer, songwriter and guitarist was one of the all-time greats of rock 'n' roll and pop music. Born Charles Hardin Holley (the 'e' of his surname was later dropped) in Lubbock, Texas in September 1936, Buddy took up singing and guitar-playing at school. He played regularly with his drumming schoolfriend Jerry Allison, and the pair formed a professional partnership in 1957 and formed a group called the Crickets. In that year, the combo released the final version of a song Holly had been offering to various unenthusiastic record labels for several months-*That'll Be The Day* proved to be worth waiting for, eventually reaching No.1 on both the US and UK. *That'll Be The Day* was a bright , uplifting record; it made stars of the Crickets and especially leader Buddy Holly. For complicated contractual reasons, subsequent disc were separated into Buddy Holly releases and Crickets releases although the same musicians performed on the records. By the end of 1958, Holly & the Crickets had achieved success with *Peggy Sue, Oh Boy!, Listen To Me, Maybe Baby, Rave On, Think It Over and Early In The Morning* most of these were bigger in Britain than in America. The singer parted company with his group during 1958, but he continued using the old group name with some newly recurted Crickets (including the future country music superstar Waylon Jennings). In February 1959, while travelling on a private plane from concert venue in Iowa to another in North Dakota, the 22 year old Holly was killed as the small aircraft crashed into a frozen cornfield during a heavy snowstorm. The accident also claimed the lives of two other rock 'n' roll stars The Big Bopper and Ritchie Valens, as well as that of the pilot. At the time of his tragically early death, Buddy was suffering a lull of his career fortunes. It is highly probable that this lull would only have been temporary, judging by the unreleased records and unfinished demos that were posthumously embellished by producer Norman Petty and unleashed onto the marketplace. The first posthumous record was Paul Anka's song *It Doesn't Matter Anymore* , which reached No.1 in Britain and No.13 in the States. Numerous other tracks appeared over the next few years, achieving considerable commercial success in the UK. Although Buddy Holly is revered by American pop historians, it is in Britain that his status has become truly legendary. Adam Faith closely imitated his distinctive vocal hiccup, the Hollies named themselves after him and countless artists recorded remakes of his hits. It could be argued that Buddy Holly was the first pop star, as opposed to rock 'n' roll star - i.e. the first to combine the raw energy of rock'n'roll with a fine melodic sensibiity - and Paul McCartney has always been particularly keen to acknowledge the debt that the Beatles owed to him. McCartney purchased the publishing rights to Buddy Holly's catalogue in 1976, organised a 'Buddy Holly week' in September of that year the 40th Anniversary of the artists' birth; this became an annual event. A TV - advertised "20 Golden Greats" collection topped the British LP chart in 1978. Interest in Holly has since increased further with the massive success of Buddy-The Musical in London's West End and the release of another successful TV advertised compilation. (Bob McDonald).

20 GOLDEN GREATS: BUDDY HOLLY (Holly, Buddy & The Crickets).
Tracks: That'll be the day / Peggy Sue / Words of love / Everyday / Not fade away / Oh boy / Maybe baby / Listen to me / Heartbeat / Think it over / It doesn't matter anymore / It's so easy / Well all right / Rave on / Raining in my heart / True love ways / Peggy Sue got married / Bo Diddley / Brown eyed handsome man / Wishing.
■ LP. . . . . **MCTV 1**
Coral / '79.
CD . . . . **DMCTV 1**
MC . . . . **MCTVC 1**
MCA / Aug '93 / BMG.

20 LOVE SONGS.
Tracks: True love ways / Everyday / Listen to me / You've got love / Learning the game / Send me some lovin' / Love is strange / That's what they say / Because I love you / Raining in my heart / Heartbeat / Moondreams / Take your time / Dearest / Look at me / You're the one / Wishing / It doesn't matter anymore / What to do / Words of love.
LP. . . . . **MFP 5570**
■ MC . . . . **TCMFP 5570**
MFP / Sep '82.

23 ALL TIME GREATEST HITS.
Tracks: Not Advised.
LP. **20125**
MC **40125**
Astan (USA) / Nov '84.

BABY I DON'T CARE.
Tracks: Baby I don't care / Valley of tears.
■ 7" . . . . **Q 72432**
Coral / Jul '61.

BEST OF BUDDY HOLLY.
Tracks: That'll be the day / Peggy Sue / Oh boy.
CD **128 503**
Card/Grand Prix / '86.
LP. . . . . **SHM 3199**
Hallmark / Sep '86 / Pickwick Records.
CD . . . . **PCD 888**
Pickwick / Aug '88 / Pickwick Records.
CD . . . . **PWKS 595**
MC . . . . **HSC 3199**
Pickwick / Sep '93 / Pickwick Records.

BO DIDDLEY.
Tracks: Bo Diddley.
■ 7" . . . . Q 72463
Coral / Jun '63.

BROWN EYED HANDSOME MAN.
Tracks: Brown eyed handsome man.
■ 7" . . . . Q 72459
Coral / Mar '63.

BROWN EYED HANDSOME MAN.
Tracks: Brown eyed handsome man / Bo Diddley.
7" . . . . BH 10
MCA / Aug '85 / BMG.

BUDDY HOLLY.
Tracks: Early in the morning / Now we're one / It's so easy / Lonesome tears / Heartbeat / Well all right / Love's made a fool of you / Wishing / Reminiscing / It doesn't matter anymore / Come back baby / True love ways / That's my desire / Moondreams / Raining in my heart / Valley of tears / Baby let's play house / I'm gonna love you too / Peggy Sue / Look at me / Listen to me / Rave on / Ready Teddy / Empty cup / Everyday / It's too late / Mailman bring me no more blues / Words of love / Think it over / Baby I don't care / Fools paradise / Little baby.
MC . . . . SSC 3070
Pickwick / Sep '80 / Pickwick Records.
■ LP. SSP 3070
Pickwick / Sep '80.
■ MC Set . . . . CRT 008
Cambra / '83.
■ LP. MCL 1752
MCA / Nov '86.
■ MC . . . . MCLC 1752
MCA / Nov '86.
■ CD . . . . DMCL 1752
MCA / Dec '88.

BUDDY HOLLY & THE CRICKETS (Holly, Buddy & The Crickets).
Tracks: Raining in my heart / Baby won't you come out tonight / Modern Don Juan / Mailman bring me no more blues / Love's made a fool of you / You've got love / Girl on my mind / That'll be the day (Nashville recording) / Blue days, black nights / Midnight shift / I'm gonna love you too / Don't come back knockin' / Fool's paradise / Empty cup / Rock around the Ollie Vee (version 1) / Think it over / It's not my fault / I guess I was just a fool / I'm gonna set my foot down / Rockabye rock / Because I love you / You're the one / Ready Teddy / Send me some lovin / Lonesome tears / Rock around the Ollie Vee (version 2) / Reminiscing / When you ask about love / Baby my heart (Without Holly).
■ Double LP . . . . CR 123
Cambra / Sep '86.

BUDDY HOLLY (CAMBRA).
Tracks: Not Advised.

BUDDY HOLLY (SEQUEL).
Tracks: I'm gonna love you too / Peggy Sue / Look at me / Listen to me / Valley of tears / Ready Teddy / Everyday / Mailman bring me no more blues / Words of love / Baby I don't care / Rave on / Little baby.
CD . . . . NEMCD 630
Sequel / Sep '92 / Castle Communications / BMG / Hot Shot.

BUDDY HOLLY ROCKS.
Tracks: Gotta get you near me / Down the line / Baby let's play house / I guess I was just a fool / Rip it up / Brown eyed handsome man / Holly hop / Midnight shift / Blue days, black nights / Love me / Don't come back knockin' / I'm changing all those changes / Ting a ling / Modern Don Juan / Rock around with Ollie Vee / That'll be the day / I'm looking for someone to love / Not fade away / Oh boy / Peggy Sue / I'm gonna love you too / Rock me my baby / Tell me how / Rave on / Baby I don't care / Think it over / Love's made a fool of you / It's so easy / Early in the morning / Maybe baby / It doesn't matter anymore.
■ Double LP . . . . CDX 8
Charly / May '85.

BUDDY HOLLY SHOWCASE.
Tracks: Not Advised.
■ LP. LVA 9222
Coral / Jun '64.

BUDDY HOLLY STORY - VOL. 1.
Tracks: Not Advised.
■ LP. LVA 9105
Coral / May '59.
LP. MA 191185
MC . . . . MAMC 9191185
Masters (Holland) / '88.

BUDDY HOLLY STORY - VOL. 2.
Tracks: Not Advised.
■ LP. LVA 9127
Coral / Oct '60.
LP. MA 201185
MC . . . . MAMC 9201185
Masters (Holland) / '88.

BUDDY HOLLY STORY, THE.
Tracks: Gotta get you near me blues / Soft place in my heart / Door to my heart / Flower of my heart / Baby it's love / Memories / Queen of the ballroom / I gambled my heart / You and I are through? / Gone / Have you ever been lonely? / Down the line / Blue suede shoes / Shake rattle and roll / Ain't got no home / Holly bop / Baby let's play house / I'm gonna set my foot down / Baby, won't you come out tonight / Changing all those changes / Rock a bye rock / It's not my fault / I guess I was just a fool / Love me / Don't come back knockin' / Midnight shift / Blue days, black nights / Rock around with Ollie Vee / I'm changing all those changes / That'll be the day / Girl on my mind / Ting a ling / Because I love you / Modern Don Juan / You are my one desire / I'm lookin' for someone to love / Last night / Maybe baby / Words of love / Peggy Sue / Everyday / Mailman bring me no more blues / Tell me how / Send me some lovin' / Little baby / Take your time / Rave on / You've got love / Valley of tears / Rock me baby / Baby I don't care / It's too late / Empty cup / Look at me / Think it over / Fool's paradise / Early in the morning / Now we're one / Lonesome tears / Heartbeat / It's so easy / Well .. all right / Love's made a fool of you / Wishing / Reminiscing / Come back baby / That's my desire / True love ways / Moondreams / Raining in my heart / It doesn't matter anymore / Peggy Sue got married / Crying, waiting, hoping / Learning the game / That makes it tough / What to do / That's what they say / Wait 'til the sun shines, Nellie / Uum oh yeah / Smokey Joe's cafe / Slippin' and slidin' / Love is strange / Dearest / You're the one / Real wild child / Oh you beautiful doll / Jole Blon / When sin stops / Stay close to me / Don't cha know.
■ LP Set . . . . CDMSP 807
MCA / May '79.

CHIRPING CRICKETS, THE (Holly, Buddy & The Crickets).
Tracks: Oh boy / Not fade away / You've got love / Maybe baby / Its' too late / Tell me how / That'll be the day / I'm looking for someone to love / Empty cup / Send me some lovin' / Last night / Rock me my baby.
■ LP. MCL 1753
MCA / Nov '86.
■ MC . . . . MCLC 1753
MCA / Nov '86.
CD 31182
MCA (USA) / Jun '88 / MCA (Imports).
■ CD . . . . DMCL 1753
MCA / Jan '91.

COLLECTION: BUDDY HOLLY.
Tracks: Think it over / That'll be the day / True love ways / Words of love / Rock me baby / I'm gonna love you too / Ready Teddy / Love's made a fool of you / Blue days, black nights / Maybe baby / I'm looking for someone to love / Send me some lovin' / Reminiscing / Listen to me / Well, all right / Oh boy / Wishing / Not fade away / Heartbeat / Moondreams / Raining in my heart / Don't come back knockin'. / Peggy Sue.
Double LP . . . . CCSLP 172
■ MC . . . . CCSMC 172
Castle Collector Series / '88.

COMPLETE BUDDY HOLLY, THE.
Tracks: Not Advised.
CD Set . . . . DCDSP 807
MCA / Sep '89 / BMG.
■ MC Set . . . . CDSPC 807
MCA / Sep '89.
■ LP Set . . . . CDSP 807
MCA / Nov '90.

EARLY IN THE MORNING.
Tracks: Early in the morning.
■ 7" . . . . Q 72333
Coral / Aug '58.

FOR THE FIRST TIME.
Tracks: Not Advised.
MC . . . . MCLC 19185
BMG / Nov '92 / BMG.

FOR THE FIRST TIME ANYWHERE.
Tracks: Rockabye rock / Maybe baby / I'm gonna set my foot down / Because I love you / Changing all those changes / That's my desire / Baby won't you come out tonight? / It's not my fault / Brown eyed handsome man / Bo Diddley.
MC . . . . MCMC 1002
Coral / Mar '83.
■ LP. MCM 1002
Coral / Mar '83.
CD . . . . CMCAD 31048
MCA / Sep '87 / BMG.
■ MC . . . . DMCL 1712
MCA / '91.
CD . . . . MCLD 19185
MCA / Jan '93 / BMG.

FROM THE ORIGINAL MASTER TAPES.
Tracks: That'll be the day / Oh boy / Not fade away / Tell me how / Maybe baby / Everyday / Rock around with Ollie Vee / It's so easy / I'm looking for someone to love / Peggy Sue / I'm gonna love you too / Words of love / Rave on / Well all right / Listen to me / Think it over / Heartbeat / Reminiscing / It doesn't matter anymore / True love ways.
CD . . . . DIDX 203
MCA / Sep '85 / BMG.

GIANT.
Tracks: Not Advised.
■ LP. MUPS 371
MCA / Apr '69.
■ LP. MCL 1825
MCA / '87.
■ MC . . . . MCLC 1825
MCA / '87.
CD . . . . CLACD 307
Castle / Nov '92 / BMG.

GOLDEN GREATS.
Tracks: Not Advised.
■ CD . . . . DMCM 5003
MCA / Sep '91.

GOLDEN GREATS: BUDDY HOLLY.
Tracks: Peggy Sue / That'll be the day / Listen to me / Everyday / Oh boy / Not fade away / Raining in my heart / Brown eyed handsome man / Maybe baby / Rave on / Think it over / It's so easy / It doesn't matter anymore / True love ways / Peggy Sue got married / Bo Diddley.
■ LP. MCM 5003
MCA / Jul '85.
■ MC . . . . MCMC 5003
MCA / Jul '85.
CD . . . . DMCTV 5003
MCA / Mar '89 / BMG.
CD . . . . MCLD 19046
■ MC . . . . MCLC 19046
MCA / Apr '92.

GOOD ROCKIN' TONIGHT.
Tracks: Good rockin' tonight / Rip it up / Ain't got no home / Holly hop.
■ EP. RCEP 104
Rollercoaster / Oct '87 / Rollercoaster Records / Swift.

GREAT BUDDY HOLLY, THE.
Tracks: Not Advised.
CD 31037
MCA (USA) / Jun '88 / MCA (Imports).

GREATEST HITS/LOVE SONGS.
Tracks: That'll be the day / Listen to me / Everyday / Oh boy / Not fade away / Raining in my heart / Maybe baby / Rave on / Think it over / It's so easy / It doesn't matter anymore / True love ways / Peggy Sue got married / You've got love / Learning the game / Send me some lovin' / Love is strange / That's what they say / Because I love you / Heartbeat / Moondreams / Take your time / Dearest / Look at me / Wishing / What to do / Words of love / You're the one.
■ MC Set . . . . MCA 2 117
MCA (Twinpax Cassettes) / Sep '84.

GREATEST HITS: BUDDY HOLLY.
Tracks: Peggy Sue / That'll be the day / Listen to me / Everyday / Oh boy / Not fade away / Raining in my heart / Maybe baby / Rave on / Think it over / It's so easy / It doesn't matter anymore / True love ways / Peggy Sue got married.
■ LP. AH 148
Ace Of Hearts / Jul '67.
■ LP. CP 8
Coral / Aug '71.
■ LP. CDLM 8007
Coral / Jul '75.
CD . . . . DMCA 109
MCA / Aug '81 / BMG.
LP. MCL 1618
MC . . . . MCLC 1618
Coral / Aug '81.

GREATEST HITS: BUDDY HOLLY (IMPORT).
Tracks: Not Advised.
LP. FUN 9043
MC . . . . FUNC 9043
Fun (Holland) / Oct '88 / Pinnacle.

HEARTBEAT.
Tracks: Heartbeat.
■ 7" . . . . Q 72346
Coral / Jan '59.
■ 7" . . . . Q 72392
Coral / Apr '60.

HIS UNDUBBED VERSIONS.
Tracks: Not Advised.
LP. NORVAJAK 1-963
Norvajak / Aug '88.

HOLLY IN THE HILLS.
Tracks: Not Advised.
■ LP. LVA 9227
Coral / Jun '65.

IT DOESN'T MATTER ANYMORE.
Tracks: It doesn't matter anymore / Raining in my heart.
■ 7" . . . . Q 72360
Coral / Feb '59.
■ 7" . . . . BH 7
MCA / Aug '85.

IT DOESN'T MATTER ANYMORE (OLD GOLD).
Tracks: It doesn't matter anymore / Raining in my heart.
■ 7" . . . . OG 9325
Old Gold / Apr '83.

LEARNING THE GAME.
Tracks: Learning the game.
■ 7" . . . . Q 72411
Coral / Oct '60.

LEGEND (From the original master tapes).
Tracks: That'll be the day / I'm looking for someone to love / Not fade away / Oh boy / Maybe baby / Tell me how / Think it over / It's so easy / Peggy Sue / Words of love / Everyday / I'm gonna love you too / Listen to me / Rave on / Well all right / Heartbeat / Early in the morning / Rock around with Ollie Vee / Midnight shift / Love's made a fool of you / Wishing / Reminiscing / Baby I don't care / Brown eyed handsome man / Bo

Diddley / It doesn't matter anymore / Moon dreams / True love ways / Raining in my heart / Learning the game / What to do / Peggy Sue got married / Love is strange.
Double LP . . . . .MCLD 606
■ **MC Set** . . . . .MCLDC 606
Coral / Mar '82.
Double LP . . . . .MCMD 7003
■ **MC Set** . . . . .MCMDC 7003
MCA / '88.
■ **CD** . . . . .DMCMD 7003
MCA / Feb '89.

LEGEND, THE.
Tracks: That'll be the day / Peggy Sue / Listen to me / Because I love you / Slippin' and slidin' / Send me some lovin' / Rave on / Heartbeat / Blue days, black nights / Moondreams / Look at me / Blue suede shoes / It doesn't matter anymore / Midnight shift / You are my one desire / Girl on my mind / Empty cup / (Um oh yeah) dearest / Oh boy / Learning the game / Love is strange / Take your time / Words of love / True love ways.
Double LP . . . . VSOPLP 114
MC . . . . VSOPMC 114
Connoisseur Collection / '88 / Pinnacle.

LEGENDARY BUDDY HOLLY, THE.
Tracks: Listen to me / Words of love / You've got to love / Learning the game / Not fade away / What to do / Early in the morning / Wishing / Love's made a fool of you / Love is strange / Baby I don't care / Midnight shift / Reminiscing / Valley of tears.
LP . . . . .SHM 3221
MC . . . . HSC 3221
Hallmark / Oct '87 / Pickwick Records.
CD . . . . .PWKS 523
Pickwick / Feb '89 / Pickwick Records.

LISTEN TO ME.
Tracks: Listen to me.
■ **7"** . . . . Q 72288
Coral / Mar '58.
■ **7"** . . . . Q 72449
Coral / Mar '62.

LOVE SONGS.
Tracks: Not Advised.
CD . . . . DMCL 1717
■ **MC** . . . . MCLC 1717
MCA / Sep '91.
CD . . . . MCLD 19047
■ **MC** . . . . MCLC 19047
MCA / Apr '92.

LOVE'S MADE A FOOL OF YOU.
Tracks: Love's made a fool of you.
■ **7"** . . . . Q 72475
Coral / Sep '64.

MAYBE BABY.
Tracks: Maybe baby.
7" . . . . .BH 4
MCA / Sep '84 / BMG.

MIDNIGHT SHIFT.
Tracks: Midnight shift.
■ **7"** 05800
Brunswick / Jul '59.

MOONDREAMS.
Tracks: Moondreams / Because I love you / I guess I was just a fool / Girl on my mind / I'm gonna love you too / You and I are through / Come back baby / You're the one / I gambled my heart / You are my one desire / Door to my heart / Crying, waiting, hoping / Now we're one / Love me / Soft place in my heart / Have you ever been lonely?.
CD . . . . .PWKS 560
LP . . . . .SHM 3294
MC . . . . HSC 3294
Pickwick / Mar '90 / Pickwick Records.

NASHVILLE SESSIONS.
Tracks: You are my one desire / Blue days, black nights / Modern Don Juan / Rock around with Ollie Vee / Midnight shift / Don't come back knockin / Girl on my mind / Love me / Ting a ling / That'll be the day / I'm changing all those changes.
■ **LP** . . . . .MCL 1754
MCA / Nov '86.
■ **MC** . . . . MCLC 1754
MCA / Nov '86.

OH BOY.
Tracks: Oh boy / Not fade away.
7" . . . . .BH 3
MCA / Aug '85 / BMG.
10" . . . . .MCAV 1368
7" . . . . .MCA 1368
■ **CD Single** . . . . DMCAT 1368
MCA / Sep '89 / BMG.

ONVERGETELIJKE HITS.
Tracks: Peggy sue / Everyday / Rave on / Brown eyed handsome man / It doesn't matter anymore.
LP 1A 222-58135
MFP (Holland) / Apr '83 / Pinnacle.

ORIGINAL VOICES OF THE CRICKETS.
Tracks: Not Advised.
CD . . . . .CDMF 088
Magnum Music / May '93 / Conifer Records.

PEGGY SUE.
Tracks: Peggy Sue / Everyday.
■ **7"** . . . . Q 72293
Coral / Dec '57.

PEGGY SUE.
Tracks: Peggy Sue.
■ **7"** . . . . .BH 2
MCA / Aug '85.

PEGGY SUE (OLD GOLD).
Tracks: Peggy Sue / Everyday.
7" . . . . .OG 9222
Old Gold / Jul '82 / Pickwick Records.

PEGGY SUE (OLD GOLD) (2).
Tracks: Peggy Sue / Everyday / Rave on.
CD Single . . . . .OG 6154
Old Gold / Nov '90 / Pickwick Records.

PEGGY SUE GOT MARRIED.
Tracks: Peggy Sue got married.
■ **7"** . . . . Q 72376
Coral / Sep '59.

PEGGY SUE/RAVE ON.
Tracks: Peggy Sue.
■ **7"** . . . . .MU 1012
MCA / Apr '68.

RAVE ON.
Tracks: Rave on / Ready Teddy.
■ **7"** . . . . Q 72325
Coral / Jun '58.

RAVE ON.
Tracks: Rave on.
■ **7"** . . . . .BH 5
MCA / Jul '85.

RAVE ON (OLD GOLD).
Tracks: Rave on / True love ways.
7" . . . . .OG 9319
Old Gold / Apr '83 / Pickwick Records.

REAL BUDDY HOLLY STORY, THE.
Tracks: Peggy Sue / That'll be the day / Well alright / Oh boy / It doesn't matter anymore / Maybe baby.
VHS . . . . MVNS 99 1126 2
PMI / Sep '86 / EMI / Gold & Sons / Terry Blood Dist.
■ **BETA** . . . . MXN 99 1126 4
PMI / Sep '86.
■ **VHS** . . . . MVN 99 1126 2
PMI / Sep '86.

REMINISCING.
Tracks: Reminiscing / Slippin' and slidin' / Bo Diddley / Wait till the sun shines Nellie / Baby won't you come out tonight / Brown eyed handsome man / Because I love you / It's not my fault / I'm gonna set my foot down / Changing all those changes / Rock-a-bye-rock.
■ **LP** . . . . LVA 9212
Coral / Apr '63.
■ **LP** . . . . MCL 1826
MCA / Feb '89.
■ **MC** . . . . MCLC 1826
MCA / Feb '89.
CD . . . . CLACD 308
Castle Classics / Aug '92 / BMG / Castle Communications.

REMINISCING.
Tracks: Reminiscing.
■ **7"** . . . . .BH 9
MCA / Aug '85.

REMINISCING.
Tracks: Reminiscing / Baby I don't care.
■ **7"** . . . . Q 72455
Coral / Sep '62.

ROCK 'N' ROLL GREATS.
Tracks: That'll be the day / Peggy Sue / Listen to me / Oh boy / Rave on / Early in the morning / Maybe baby / Think it over / Heartbeat / Not fade away / It's so easy / Words of love / Everyday / I'm gonna love you too.
LP . . . . MFP 5806
MC . . . . TC-MFP 5806
MFP / Oct '87 / EMI.

ROCK AROUND WITH BUDDY HOLLY.
Tracks: Modern Don Juan / Midnight shift / That'll be the day / Raining in my heart / Girl on my mind / Empty cup / I guess I was just a fool / Think it over / You're the one / Ready Teddy / Lonesome tears / Baby won't you come out tonight?.
■ **MC Set** . . . . CRT 123
Cambra / Oct '86.

ROCK ON WITH BUDDY HOLLY.
Tracks: Not Advised.
■ **LP** . . . . MFP 50490
MFP / Oct '80.

SHOWCASE.
Tracks: Not Advised.
■ **LP** . . . . MCL 1824
MCA / Feb '89.
■ **MC** . . . . MCLC 1824
MCA / Feb '89.

SHOWCASE.
Tracks: Not Advised.
CD . . . . CLACD 306
Castle / Mar '93 / BMG.

SOMETHING SPECIAL FROM BUDDY HOLLY.
Tracks: Good rockin' tonight / Rip it up / Blue monday / Honky tonk / Blue suede shoes / Shake, rattle and roll / Ain't got no home / Holly hop / Brown eyed handsome man / Bo Diddley / Gone (take 1) / Gone (take 2) / Have you ever been lonely (take 1) / Have you ever been lonely (take 2) / Have you ever been lonely (take 3).
■ **LP** . . . . ROLL 2013
Rollercoaster / Sep '86.

SPECIAL COLLECTION, A.
Tracks: Listen to me / Words of love / You've got love / Learnin' the game / Not fade away / What to do / Early in the morning / Wishing / Love's made a fool of you / Love is strange / (You're so square) Baby I don't care / Midnight shift / Reminiscing / Valley of tears / That'll be the day / Maybe baby / Peggy Sue got married / Rave on / True love ways / Bo Diddley / Oh boy! / Peggy Sue / Everyday / Think it over / Brown eyed handsome man / Heartbeat / Raining in my heart / It doesn't matter any more / Moondreams / Because I love you / I guess I was a fool for you / Girl on my mind / I'm gonna love you too / You and I are through / Come back baby / You're the one / I gambled my heart / You are my one desire / Door to my heart / Crying, waiting, hoping / Now we're one / Love me / Soft place in my heart / Have you ever been lonely.
CD . . . . BOXD 26
MC . . . . BOXC 26
Pickwick / Oct '92 / Pickwick Records.

THAT'LL BE THE DAY.
Tracks: That'll be the day / I'm looking for someone to love / It doesn't matter anymore / Raining in my heart.
12" . . . . TTHAT 1
MCA / Aug '86 / BMG.
■ **7"** . . . . THAT 1
MCA / Aug '86.

THAT'LL BE THE DAY.
Tracks: Not Advised.
■ **LP** . . . . .AH 3
Ace Of Hearts / Oct '61.
CD . . . . CLACD 309
Castle Classics / Aug '92 / BMG / Castle Communications.

THAT'LL BE THE DAY.
Tracks: That'll be the day / Rock me my baby.
■ **7"** . . . . .BH 1
MCA / Sep '85.

THAT'LL BE THE DAY (BOXED SET).
Tracks: That'll be the day / It doesn't matter anymore / Bo Diddley / I'm looking for someone to love / Raining in my heart / Rock me baby / Peggy Sue / Everyday / Oh boy / Not fade away / May be baby / Tell me how / Rave on / Ready Teddy / Think it over / It's so easy / True love ways / Word of love / Reminiscing / Baby I don't care / Brown eyed handsome man.
■ **7" Set** . . . . BHB 1
MCA / Aug '85 / BMG.

THAT'LL BE THE DAY (OLD GOLD) (Holly, Buddy & The Crickets).
Tracks: That'll be the day / Oh boy / Maybe baby.
CD Single . . . . .OG 6147
Old Gold / May '89 / Pickwick Records.

THINK IT OVER.
Tracks: Think it over / It's so easy.
7" . . . . .BH 6
MCA / Aug '85 / BMG.

TRUE LOVE WAYS.
Tracks: True love ways / Words my love.
■ **7"** . . . . .BH 8
MCA / Sep '85.

TRUE LOVE WAYS.
Tracks: True love ways / Raining in my heart.
■ **7"** . . . . MCA 252
MCA / Sep '81.
■ **12"** . . . . MCAT 1302
MCA / Dec '88.
7" . . . . .MCA 1302
■ **CD Single** . . . . DMCA 1302
MCA / Nov '88.

TRUE LOVE WAYS.
Tracks: Raining in my heart / Peggy Sue / That'll be the day / Oh boy / Everyday / True love ways / It doesn't matter anymore / Learning the game / I'm gonna love you too / Ready Teddy / Wishing / Well..alright / Midnight shift / Love's made a fool of you / Reminiscing.
LP . . . . PLAT 307
MC . . . . PLAC 307
Platinum Music / Apr '88 / Prism Leisure PLC / Ross Records.
CD . . . . TCD 2339
Telstar/Ronco / Feb '89 / BMG.
LP . . . . STAR 2339
■ **MC** . . . . STAC 2339
Telstar/Ronco / Feb '89.

H 14

■ DELETED

TRUE LOVE WAYS.
Tracks: Not Advised.
■ 7" . . . . Q 72397
Coral / May '60.

UNFORGETTABLE, THE.
Tracks: Not Advised.
LP P.Disc. . . . . AR 30068
Exclusive Picture Discs / Nov '87.

VERY BEST OF BUDDY HOLLY.
Tracks: Not Advised.
■ CD 01266061
Arcade / May '88.

WHAT TO DO.
Tracks: What to do.
■ 7" . . . . Q 72419
Coral / Jan '61.
■ 7" . . . . Q 72469
Coral / Dec '63.

WISHING.
Tracks: Wishing / Love's made a fool of you.
■ 7" . . . . Q 72466
Coral / Sep '63.
■ 7" . . . . MCA 344
MCA / Jan '78.

WORDS OF LOVE - 28 CLASSIC SONGS (Holly, Buddy & The Crickets).
Tracks: Words of love / That'll be the day / Peggy Sue / Think it over / True love ways / What to do / Crying, waiting, hoping / Well..all right / Love's made a fool of you / Peggy Sue got married / Valley of tears / Wishing / Raining in my heart / Oh, boy! / Rave on / Brown eyed handsome man / Bo Diddley / It's so easy / It doesn't matter anymore / Maybe baby / Early in the morning / Love is strange / Listen to me / I'm gonna love you too / Learning the game / Baby, I don't care / Heartbeat / Everyday.
CD 514487-2
LP. 514487-1
MC 514487-4
Polygram T.V / Feb '93 / PolyGram.

YOU'VE GOT LOVE.
Tracks: You've got love.
■ 7" . . . . Q 72472
Coral / May '64.

Holm, Dallas

AGAINST THE WIND.
Tracks: Not Advised.
VHS. . . . . .MV 5033
Word (UK) / Jan '89 / Word Records (UK) / Sony.

CHANGE THE WORLD (Holm, Dallas & Praise).
Tracks: Not Advised.
LP. . . . . .DAY R 4138
MC . . . . .DAY C 4138
Dayspring / Jun '86 / Word Records (UK) / Sony.

Holy Modal Rounders

Folk-country band formed early '60's in NYC by vocalists Peter Stampfel on banjo and fiddle, with guitarist Steve Weber. Stampfel knew an uncountable number of songs: their 'progressive old timey' or 'acid folk' found an audience that never goes away. After many permutations of the original group, Peter Stampfel & the Bottle Caps on Rounder in the 80's have won awards in the USA indie industry. (Donald Clarke).

ALLEGED IN THEIR OWN TIME.
Tracks: Not Advised.
LP. . . . . ROUNDER 3004
Rounder / '88 / Projection / Roots Records / Swift / C.M. Distribution / Topic Records / Jazz Music / Hot Shot / A.D.A Distribution / Direct Distribution.

HOLY MODAL ROUNDERS.
Tracks: Blues in the bottle / Cuckoo, the / Long John / Hey hey baby / Mr. Bass man / Better things for you / Hop high ladies / Give the fiddler a dram / Euphoria / Hesitation blues / Reuben's train / Moving day / Same old man / Bound to lose.
LP. . . . . WIK 75
Big Beat / May '88 / Pinnacle / Hot Shot / Jazz Music.

HOLY MODAL ROUNDERS 2.
Tracks: Flop eared mule / Black eyed Susan Brown / Sail away ladies / Clinch mountain backstep / Fishin' blues / Statesboro blues / Juko partner / Mole in the ground / Hot corn, cold corn / Down the old plant road / Chevrolet 6 / Crowley waltz / Bully of the town.
LP. . . . . WIK 79
Big Beat / Oct '88 / Pinnacle / Hot Shot / Jazz Music.

LAST ROUND.
Tracks: Not Advised.
LP. . . . . .AD 1030
Adelphi (1) / May '81 / Jetstar.

Homer & Jethro

Homer (Henry D. Haynes, 1918-71) and Jethro (Kenneth C. Burns, 1923-89) were noted Nashville session musicians - Jethro was one of the best mandolinists in the business - but were more famous as a country comedy team. Successful in radio, they split up during WW II, Homer serving in Europe and Jethro in the Pacific ('I was the unsung hero. They wouldn't let me sing'). They regrouped and signed to RCA in '48. Their dead pan send ups of country and pop songs backed up by solid musicianship often made the pop charts; Jethro later toured for 11 years with singer-songwriter Steve Goodman. (Donald Clarke).

ASSAULT THE ROCK AND ROLL ERA.
Tracks: Houn' dawg / Hart Brake motel / Two tone shoes / Rock boogie / At the flop / Screen door / Hernando's hideaway / Middle-aged teenager / Little arrows / She loves you / I want to hold your hand / No hair Sam / Winchester Cathedral / Ballad of Davy Crockett, The / Yaller rose of Texas, you all / Battle of Kookamonga, The.
LP. . . . . BFX 15281
Bear Family / Jan '89 / Rollercoaster Records / Swift / Direct Distribution.

BAREFOOT BALLARDS.
Tracks: Cigarettes, whisky and wild, wild women / West Virginny Hills, The / Sweet fern / I'll go chasin' women / Frozen logger, The / Ground hog / Keep them icy cold fingers off of me / Boll weevil No.2 / High geared daddy / Dig me a grave in Missouri / Tennessee, Tennessee / Down where the watermelons grow.
LP. . . . . HAT 3068
MC . . . . HATC 3068
Stetson / Apr '88 / Crusader Marketing Co. / Swift / Wellard Dist. / Midland Records / C.M. Distribution.

Horton, Johnny

This American singer, guitarist and songwriter was initially dubbed 'the singing fisherman' because of his original career. He spent the Fifties working his way up the country and western ladder via such shows as *Louisiana hayride*, and eventually establishing himself on the US country charts with a series of rock-influenced singles like *Honky tonk hardwood floor* and *Honky tonk man*. Horton suddenly surged to major pop stardom in 1959 with *Battle of New Orleans*, which logged six weeks on top of the American Hot 100. It was the biggest novelty hit of that year. The tune originally dated from 1815, and was composed in celebration of the victory of Andrew Jackson's men against the British forces of Commander Pakenham at New Orleans during the final battle of a bloody war. Lyrics were written by Jimmy Driftwood in 1955. One would have thought that Horton's *Battle of New Orleans* might have caused some transatlantic offence, by cockily crowing about past conflicts during the modern era of Anglo-American harmony but the song reached No.2 on the British chart, in a cover version by UK singer Lonnie Donegan Johnny's rendition had to be content with a UK No.16 placing. In 1960 Horton achieved two further big hits in America with more examples of the then fashionable 'saga song' genre. He reached No.3 with *Sink the Bismark* (inspired by the movie of the same name) and No.4 with the theme from the John Wayne film *North to Alaska* was climbing the US chart, Johnny Horton was killed in a car crash in November 1960 at the age of 33. It is said that during the last few weeks of his life, he had premonitions of his own death and consequently cancelled potentially risky activities such as aeroplane flights. At the time of his death, Horton's LP material was showing signs of veering towards a more conventional country style; had he lived, he might have been a major C&W artist for several years more. (Bob MacDonald)

1956 - 1960.
Tracks: I'm a one woman / Honky tonky man / I'm ready if you're willing / I got a hole in my pirogue / Take me like I am / Sugar coated baby / I don't like I did / Hooray for that little difference / I'm coming home / Over loving you / She knows why / Honky tonk mind (the woman I need) / Tell me baby I love her / Goodbye lonesome, hello baby doll / I'll do it everytime / You're my baby / Let's take the long way home / Lover's rock / Honky tonk hardwood floor / Wild one, The / Everytime i'm kissing you / Hot in the sugarcrane field / Lonesome and heartbroken / Seven come eleven / Can't forget you, I / Wise to the ways of a woman / Out in New Mexico / Tetched in the head / Just walk a little closer / Don't use my heart for a stepping stone / Love you baby, I / Counterfeit love / Mister moonlight / All grown up / Got the bull by the horns / When it's springtime in Alaska / Whispering pines / Battle of New Orleans, The / All for the love of a girl (CD 2) / Lost highway / Sam Magee / Cherokee Boogie / Golden Rocket / Joe's been a gittin' there / First train headin' south, The / Sal's got a sugarlip / Words / Johnny reb / Ole slew foot / They shined up rudolph's nose / Electrified donkey, The / Same old tale crow told me, The / Sink the bishmarck / Ole slew foot (CD 3) / Miss Marcy / Sleepy eyed john / Mansion you stole, The / They'll never take her love from me / Sinking of the Reuben James, The / Jim Bridger / Battle of bull run, The / Snow shoe thompson / John paul jones / Comanche (the brave horse) / Young abe lincoln / O'leary's cow / Johnny freedom / Go north / North to alaska / Just don't like this kind of livin', I / Rock is / Land line / Hank and joe and me / Sleeping at the foot of the bed, A / Old blind barnabas / Evil hearted me / Hot in the sugarcane field / You don't move me anymore baby / Gosh darn wheel, The / Broken hearted gypsy / Church by the side of the road, The / Vanishing race, The / Broken hearted gypsy (CD 4) / That boy got the habit / Hot in the sugarcane field (CD 4) / You don't move me anymore baby (CD 4) / Church by the side of the road (CD 4) / Just don't like that kind of livin', I / Take it like a man / Hank and joe and me (CD 4) / Old blind baranbas (CD 4) / Empty bed blues / Rock Island line / Shake, rattle and roll / A / Sleeping at the foot of the bed (CD 4) / Old dan tucker / Gosh darn wheel (CD 4) / From memphis to mobile / Back up train / Schottische in texas / My heart stopped, trembled and died / Alley gir ways / How you gonna make it / Witch walking baby / Down that river road / Big wheels rollin' / Got a slow leak in my heart, I / What will i do without you / Janey / Streets of dodge / Give me back my picture & you can keep the frame.
CD Set . . . . BCD 15470
Bear Family / May '91 / Rollercoaster Records / Swift / Direct Distribution.

BATTLE OF NEW ORLEANS.
Tracks: Battle of New Orleans.
7" . . . . PB 932
Philips / May '59 / PolyGram.

BATTLE OF NEW ORLEANS (OLD GOLD) (Horton, Johnny & Stonewall Jackson).
Tracks: Battle of New Orleans / Waterloo.
■ 7" . . . . .OG 9074
Old Gold / Nov '80.

EARLY YEARS, THE.
Tracks: Smokey Joe's barbecue / Devilish love light / Candy Jones / Bawlin' Baby / It's a long rocky road / Plaid and calico / Done rovin' / On the banks of the beautiful Nile / Mean, mean son of gun / Happy millionaire / My home in Shelby County / Coal smoke, valve oil and steam / Talk gobbler, talk / Rhythm in my baby's walk / Birds 'n' butterflies / Shadows on the old bayou / Go and wash those dirty feet / Words / Betty Lorraine / Somebody's rockin' my broken heart / Honky tonk Jelly Roll blues / Love and tell / I wish heartaches were strangers / Confusion / Two eyed Sunday pants / Down that river road / Egg money / Confusion (2) / First train headin' South / Somebody rockin' my broken heart (solo) / Honk tonk Jelly Roll blues (demo recordings 1) / Won't you love me, love, love me / Why did it happen to me / You, you, you / Broken hearted gypsy / All for the love of a girl / My heart stopped, trembled and died / I'm a fishin' man / Where do you think you would stand / Devil made a masterpiece, The / Because I'm a jealous man / I'm the one that breaks in two / Train with the rhumba beat, The / Cause you're the one for me / None of you but all of me / Dark haired beauty from Cuba / Tennessee Jive / S.S. Lureline / I won't get dreamy eyed / Two red lips and warm red wine / I won't forget / Mansion you stole, The / Rest of your life, The / (I wished for an angel but) the devil sent me you / Shadows on the old bayou (demo recordings 1) / Somebody's rockin' my broken heart(demo rec 1) / Talk gobbler talk (demo recordings 1) / Smokey Joe's barbeque (demo recordings 1) / This won't be the first time / Child's side of life / Another women wears my wedding ring / Move down the line / Hey, sweet sweet thing / No true love / Big wheels rollin' / Journey with no end / There'll never be another Mary / Devil made a masterpeice, The (mercury rec.) / Back to my back street / You don't move me baby, anymore / Ha ha and moonface / Ridin' the sunshine special / Where are you / The train with the rhumba beat (mercury rec.) / Broken hearted gypsy (mercury recordings) / Meant so little to you / You cry in the door of your mansion / Coal smoke, valve oil and steam (dot overdubs) / Devlish lovelight / Mean, mean son of gun (dot overdubs) / Talk gobbler talk (dot overdubs) / Shadows on the old bayou (dot overdubs) / In my home in Shelby County (dot overdubs) / Go and wash those dirty feet (dot overdubs) / Smokey Joe's barbeque (dot overdubs) / Done rovin (briar overdubs) / It's a long rocky road (briar overdubs) / Smokey Joe's barbeque (brair overdubs) / Mean, mean, sun of gun (briar overdubs) / Devilish lovelight / Coal smoke, valve oil & steam (briar overdubs) / Words (briar overdubs) / Shadows on the old bayou (briar overdubs) / On the banks of the beautiful Nile (briar) / In my home in Shelby County (briar overdubs) / Go and wash those dirty feet (briar overdubs) / Talk, gobbler talk (briar overdubs) / You, you, you (mecury recordings) / All for the love of a girl(mercury recordings).
LP Set . . . . BFX 15289
Bear Family / May '91 / Rollercoaster Records / Swift / Direct Distribution.

JOHNNY HORTON.
Tracks: Not Advised.
MC . . . . ZCGAS 754
Audio Fidelity(USA) / Oct '84 / Stage One Records.

MORE SPECIALS.
Tracks: Plaid to Calico / Coal, smoke, valveoil and steam / Devilish love light / Done rovin' / Mean, mean, mean son of a gun / Gobbler, the houn' dog / Shadows on the old Bayou / In my home in Shelby county / Go and wash your dirty feet / Smokey Joe's barbeque / Long rocky road / Words.
LP. . . . . HAT 3030
MC . . . . HATC 3030

■ DELETED H 15

Stetson / Apr '87 / Crusader Marketing Co. / Swift / Wellard Dist. / Midland Records / C.M. Distribution.

NORTH TO ALASKA.
Tracks: North to Alaska.
■ 7" . . . . **PB 1062**
Philips / Dec '60.

ROCKIN' ROLLIN' JOHNNY HORTON.
Tracks: Sal's got a sugar lip (rock'n'roll version) (Previously unissued) / Honky tonk hardwood floor / Honky tonk man / I'm coming home / Tell my baby I love her / Woman I need, The (Honky tonk mind) / First train heading South, The / Lover's rock / All grown up / Electrified donkey, The / Sugar coated baby / Let's take the long way home / Ole slew - foot / Sleepy eyed John / Wild one / I'm ready if you're willing.
LP. . . . . **BFX 15069**
Bear Family / Sep '84 / Rollercoaster Records / Swift / Direct Distribution.
CD . . . . **BCD 15543**
Bear Family / Oct '90 / Rollercoaster Records / Swift / Direct Distribution.

ROCKIN' ROLLIN' VOL.2.
Tracks: Tennessee jive / SS Lureline / First train headin' South / No true love / You, you, you / I won't forget / Move down the line / You don't move me baby / Hey sweet sweet thing / Devil made a masterpiece / Ridin' the sunshine special / Train with the rhumba beat.
LP. . . . . **BFX 15248**
Bear Family / '88 / Rollercoaster Records / Swift / Direct Distribution.

Horton, Stephen Wayne

STEPHEN WAYNE HORTON.
Tracks: Roll over / Tennessee plates / Oh Susan / Got a lot of livin' to do / Only crying / Moonlighting / Endless sleep / That woman / Nothin' shakin' / Gone gone gone.
CD **CDC1 91983**
LP. **C1 91983**
■ MC **C4 91983**
Capitol / Nov '89.

Hot Rize

Tim O'Brien (lead vocals/acoustic guitar/mandolin/fiddle), Nick Forster (lead - harmony vocals/bass), Charles Sawtelle (guitar), Pete Wernick (banjo). Colorado based bluegrass group who secured much acclaim during their ten years, headlining many festivals, as well as collecting awards, one for their version of Tim's "Walk the way the wind blows". This obtained pole position on the "Gassometer" radio survey in 1986, as did "Untold Stories" in 1987, while the album took the best bluegrass album award the following year. Peter Wernick (Dr. Banjo) himself has also made solo releases. Finally alter-egos "Red Knuckles & The Trailblazers" won themselves a regular slot on Hot Rize's live shows with their humorous renditions of Hank Williams, Lefty Frizzell, Bob Wills and other jukebox hits from that era.

BLASTS FROM THE PAST (Red Knuckles Trailblazers).
Tracks: Not Advised.
CD . . . . **SH 3767CD**
LP. . . . . **SH 3767**
MC . . . . **SH 3767C**
Sugarhill(USA) / '88 / Roots Records / Projection / Impetus Records / C.M. Distribution / Jazz Music / Swift / Duncans / A.D.A Distribution.

HOT RIZE/ RED KNUCKLES AND THE TRAILBLAZERS.
Tracks: Travellin' blues / Honky tonk man / Slade's theme / Dixie cannonball / I know my baby loves me / Trailblazers theme / Always late / Honky tonk song / Kansas city star / Waldo's discount donuts / Boot heel drag / Window up above, The / You're gonna change or I'm gonna leave / Long gone John from bowling green / Let me love you one more time / Goin' across the sea / My little darlin' / I've been all around this world / I'm gonna sleep with one eye open / Martha White theme / Sally Goodin / Your light leads me on / Sugarfoot rag, The / Intro of Red Knuckles & The Trailblazers / Texas hambone blues / Wendell's fly swatters / Oh, Mona / Rank strangers / Shady grove.
CD . . . . **FF 70107**
Flying Fish (USA) / '89 / Cadillac Music / Roots Records / Projection / C.M. Distribution / Direct Distribution / Jazz Music / Duncans / A.D.A Distribution.

IN CONCERT: HOT RIZE.
Tracks: Not Advised.
LP. . . . . **FF 315**
Flying Fish (USA) / Mar '89 / Cadillac Music / Roots Records / Projection / C.M. Distribution / Direct Distribution / Jazz Music / Duncans / A.D.A Distribution.

PRESENTS RED KNUCKLES TRAILBLAZERS (Red Knuckles Trailblazers).
Tracks: Travellin' blues / Honky tonk man / Slade's theme / Dixie cannonball / I know my baby loves me / Trailblazer theme / Always late / Honky tonk song / Kansas City song / Waldo's discount donuts / Boot heel drag / Window up above, The / You're gonna change or I'm gonna leave / Long gone John from Bowling Green.
LP. . . . . **FF 279**
Flying Fish (USA) / Dec '88 / Cadillac Music / Roots Records / Projection / C.M. Distribution / Direct Distribution / Jazz Music / Duncans / A.D.A Distribution.

RADIO BOOGIE.
Tracks: Not Advised.
LP. . . . . **FF 231**
Flying Fish (USA) / Mar '89 / Cadillac Music / Roots Records / Projection / C.M. Distribution / Direct Distribution / Jazz Music / Duncans / A.D.A Distribution.

TAKE IT HOME.
Tracks: Colleen Malone / Rocky road blues / Voice in the wind, A / Bending blades / Gone fishing / Think of what you've done / Climb the ladder / Money to burn / Bravest cowboy, The / Lamplighting time in the valley / Where the wild river rolls / Old rounder, The / Tenderly calling (Home, come on home).
CD . . . . **SH 3784CD**
LP. . . . . **SH 3784**
MC . . . . **SH 3784C**
Sugarhill(USA) / '90 / Roots Records / Projection / Impetus Records / C.M. Distribution / Jazz Music / Swift / Duncans / A.D.A Distribution.

TRADITIONAL TIES.
Tracks: Not Advised.
LP. . . . . **SH 3748**
Sugarhill(USA) / May '86 / Roots Records / Projection / Impetus Records / C.M. Distribution / Jazz Music / Swift / Duncans / A.D.A Distribution.
CD . . . . **SH CD 3748**
Sugarhill(USA) / Mar '89 / Roots Records / Projection / Impetus Records / C.M. Distribution / Jazz Music / Swift / Duncans / A.D.A Distribution.

UNTOLD STORIES.
Tracks: Are you tired of me, darling / Untold stories / Just like you / Country blues / Bluegrass / Won't you come and sing for me / Life's too short / You don't have to move the mountain / Shadows in my room / Don't make me believe / Wild ride / Late in the day.
CD . . . . **SH 3756CD**
LP. . . . . **SH 3756**
MC . . . . **SH 3756C**
Sugarhill(USA) / Mar '89 / Roots Records / Projection / Impetus Records / C.M. Distribution / Jazz Music / Swift / Duncans / A.D.A Distribution.

House, James

JAMES HOUSE.
Tracks: Not Advised.
CD . . . . **MCAD 42279**
LP. . . . . **MCA 42279**
MC . . . . **MCAC 42279**
MCA / Jun '89 / BMG.
CD . . . . **DMCG 6077**
■ LP. . . . . **MCG 6077**
MCA / Nov '89.
■ MC . . . . **MCGC 6077**
MCA / Nov '89.

Houston, David

Country singer born in 1938 in Louisiana, a big star of the '60's with 17 top 10 country hits in the USA, many of which crossed to the pop chart. He also sang duets with Barbara Mandrell and Tammy Wynette. He continued with less spectacular success through the '70's. (Donald Clarke).

BEST OF DAVID HOUSTON.
Tracks: Not Advised.
LP. . . . . **LWLP 101**
First Base / Mar '85.

MY WOMAN'S GOOD TO ME.
Tracks: My woman's good to me / Almost persuaded.
7" . . . . **LWS 001**
First Base / Mar '85.

Howard, Clint

BALLAD OF FINLEY PRESTON (Howard, Clint & Fred Price).
Tracks: Not Advised.
LP. . . . . **ROUNDER 0009**
Rounder / '88 / Projection / Roots Records / Swift / C.M. Distribution / Topic Records / Jazz Music / Hot Shot / A.D.A Distribution / Direct Distribution.

Howard, Harlan

Harlan Howard is one of country music's greatest songwriters, and his career stretches over four decades. Born on September 8th 1928, in Lexington, Kentucky, his success began when he struck a publishing deal with Tex Ritter and Johnny Bond. Howard has written hits for: Guy Mitchell, Charlie Walker, Buck Owens, Ricky Van Shelton, George Strait, The Judds and Nanci Griffith. His success is toasted by Nashville with an annual Harlan Howard bash. (Tony Byworth)

SINGS HARLAN HOWARD.
Tracks: Not Advised.
LP. . . . . **HAT 3130**
MC . . . . **HATC 3130**
Stetson / Mar '90 / Crusader Marketing Co. / Swift / Wellard Dist. / Midland Records / C.M. Distribution.

Howard, Jan

Country singer born in 1932 in Missouri, once married to top country songwriter Harlan Howard. She had hits of her own in the '60's and continued popular, including duets with Bill Anderson, as well as touring with Johnny Cash and Tammy Wynette. (Donald Clarke).

JAN HOWARD-THE DOT SERIES.
Tracks: When we tried / Ozark mountain jubilee / There's no way / I don't think I've got another love / Wind beneath my wings / Evil on your mind / When I see love / Dixie road / I spent all my love on you / Money don't make a man a lover.
LP. . . . . **IMCA 39030**
MC . . . . **IMCAC 39030**
MCA / Mar '87 / BMG.

Howland, Chris

FRAULEIN.
Tracks: Fraulein / Blonder stern / Venus / Kleines madchen aus Berlin / Das hab'ich in Paris gerlent / Patricia / Verboten / Mama / Susie darlin' / Rain falls on ev'rybody / Ja ja wunderbar / Yes, okay alright / Hundert schone frau'n / Die mutter ist immer dabei / Hammerchen polka.
LP. . . . . **BFX 15116**
Bear Family / Mar '84 / Rollercoaster Records / Swift / Direct Distribution.

Hudd, Bryan

BASICALLY COUNTRY.
Tracks: Not Advised.
LP. . . . . **BSS 360**
Tank / '88.

Hudson Country Players

INSTRUMENTAL COUNTRY.
Tracks: Me and Bobby McGee / She called me baby / Blue bayou / Woman to woman / I'm having your baby / Ruby don't take your love to town / She's got you / Together again / Everytime you touch me I get high / Four walls / Happiest girl in the whole USA / Almost persuaded / Loving her was easier / Jolene / Desperado / Jamestown ferry / My love.
LP. . . . . **SHLP 147**
Castle Showcase / Oct '86 / Arabesque Ltd.
MC . . . . **SHTC 147**
Castle Showcase / '88 / Arabesque Ltd.

Hudson, Jack

SUNDAY MORNING COMING DOWN.
Tracks: Annie's going to sing her song / Teach your children / Fire and rain / Sunday morning, coming down / Four and twenty / Mr. Bojangles / Carolina in my mind / Sweet baby James / Child's song / Yellow cat / Damn you world for turning / Me and Bobby McGee.
LP. . . . . **FHR 017 S**
Folk Heritage / Jul '82 / Terry Blood Dist.

Husky, Ferlin

Pop-country singer and comedy star born in 1927 in Missouri, first known as Terry Preston, then in a comic persona as Simon Crum as well as his real name. Duets in 1953 with Jean Shepard included *A Dear John letter*, No. 1 in the USA country chart, and mercilessly sent up by Stan Freberg. He often crossed over to the pop chart, for example with *Since you're gone* in 1957 (which he'd first recorded in '52 as Preston). He had almost 50 hits in the USA country chart through 1975. (Donald Clarke).

BOP CAT BOP.
Tracks: Not Advised.
LP. . . . . **DEMAND 0040**
Demand / Oct '87.

CAPITOL COLLECTORS SERIES: FERLIN HUSKY.
Tracks: Feel better all over / I'll baby sit with you / Gone / Fallen star, A / My reason for living / Draggin' the river / Wings of a dove / Waltz you saved for me, The / Somebody save me / I know it was you / Timber, I'm falling / I could sing all night / I hear Little Rock calling / Once / You pushed me too far / Just for you / That's why I love you so much / Every step of the way / Heavenly sunshine / Sweet misery.
CD . . . . **CDP 791 629 2**
CD . . . . **CZ 230**
Capitol / Sep '89 / EMI.

FAVOURITES OF..
Tracks: Not Advised.
LP. . . . . **SLP 3018**
MC . . . . **GT 53018**
Starday (USA) / Apr '87 / Crusader Marketing Co.

FERLIN HUSKY-THE DOT SERIES.
Tracks: Sugar moon / Snap your fingers / When love comes home tonight / Once in a blue moon / There ain't

H 16 ■ DELETED

enough whiskey in Tennessee / Gone / Wings of a dove / Sweet misery / Waltz you saved for me, The / Backyard, The.
LP...................IMCA 39077
MC..................IMCAC 39077
MCA / Mar '87 / BMG.

GREATEST HITS OF FERLIN HUSKY.
Tracks: Not Advised.
MC.....................4XL 9385
Capitol (Specials) / Dec '88.

SIX DAYS ON THE ROAD.
Tracks: Not Advised.
CD.....................PWK 012
Pickwick / '88 / Pickwick Records.

SONGS OF THE HEART AND HOME.
Tracks: Not Advised.
LP......................HAT 3115
MC.....................HATC 3115
Stetson / Sep '89 / Crusader Marketing Co. / Swift / Wellard Dist. / Midland Records / C.M. Distribution.

WALKIN' AND HUMMIN'.
Tracks: Walkin' & hummin' / I'm so lonesome I could cry / I could never be ashamed of you / I can't help it / Undesired / May you never be alone / My shadow / I lost my love today / Alone and forsaken / There'll be no teardrops tonight / Living in a trance / Why should we try anymore.
LP......................HAT 3053
MC.....................HATC 3053
Stetson / Dec '87 / Crusader Marketing Co. / Swift / Wellard Dist. / Midland Records / C.M. Distribution.

Ian & Sylvia

Ian Tyson (25/9/33) and Sylvia Tyson (19/9/40) were born in Canada. They both play guitar and sing with Sylvia adding autoharp. They first met in 1959 when both were part-time musicians playing in local Toronto folk-clubs. In the early '60's they settled in New York and began playing the club and campus folk circuit, before releasing their debut album in 1962. The duo were married in 1964, and their second album (released in 1964) contained Ian Tyson's well known song *Four strong winds*. By the late Sixties, their work had become more clearly influenced by country & western and for a short time they toured and recorded with a Country & Western band called 'Great Speckled Bird'. Both Ian & Sylvia also recorded solo albums: Ian in 1975 cut *Ol' eon* (A&M) and *One jump ahead of the devil* in 1979 (Boot), while Sylvia released *Woman's world* (Capitol) in 1975. (Ian Wilkins)

GREATEST HITS.
Tracks: Early morning rain / Tomorrow is a long time / Little beggar man / Mighty Quinn, The / Nancy Whisky / Catfish blues / Come in stranger / French girl, The / Renegade, The / Mary Anne / You were on my mind / Four strong winds / Short grass / Southern comfort / Someday soon / Ella Speed / Circle game / 90 x 90 / Curly Wren, The / Un Canadien errant / Lonely girls / Spanish is a loving tongue / This wheel's on fire.
CD . . . . VNP 7401
LP . . . . VNP 5401
MC . . . . VNP 6401
Start / Jun '89.
CD . . . . VCD 5
LP . . . . VSD 5
MC . . . . VCV 5
Vanguard / Jan '90 / Complete Record Co. Ltd.

Idaho

PALMS E.P.
Tracks: Not Advised.
7" . . . . HREC 2
CD Single . . . . HRECD 2
Quigley / Jun '93 / RTM / Pinnacle.

YEAR AFTER YEAR.
Tracks: Not Advised.
CD . . . . QUIGD 4
LP . . . . QUIGL 4
Quigley / Sep '93 / RTM / Pinnacle.

Ifield, Frank

This British singer was born in Coventry, brought up in Australia and became a major UK star in the early Sixties. He began his career at the age of 15, and spent the fifties building a substantial career on Aussie television and radio. Because Australia was a showbusiness backwater in those days, he followed the example of Rolf Harris and decided to travel to the UK to advance his career. Teaming with Columbia Records' key producer Norrie Paramor he started promisingly enough with the 1960 no.22 hit *Lucky Devil*. But for the next two years, Ifield's luck collapsed.The turning point came in mid-1962, when Ifield and Paramor chose to record a 1942 song called *I remember you*. Making maximum use of his distinctive falsetto sound, which often broke into a yodel, Frank's rendition stormed to the UK no.1 slot and stayed there for seven weeks. This disc introduced millions of record buyers to Ifield's style and the sub Slim Whitman yodel thus became his trademark. *I Remember You* reached no.5 in the States, a notable achievement in pre-Beatle days.Realising that they were onto a good thing, the singer and his producer continued to raid the vaults and scored a lucrative run of UK hits with revivals of ancient songs, many of which had been previously recorded by country and western artists. Ifield's approximation of country music brought him further British chart-toppers with *Lovesick Blues* (No.1 for five weeks in early '63), *Wayward Wind*, (three weeks in early '63) and *Confessin'*- (two weeks in July '63). He was the first British born act to reach the UK no.1 position with three consecutive singles and he also hit big with *Nobody's darlin' but Mine* (No.4 in '63) and *Don't Blame Me* (No.8 in '64).Ifield also achieved a No 1 success on the British EP charts in 1963 and enjoyed several big selling albums. However, he could not hold out against the unstoppable Liverpool pop revolution for very long and his chart career tailed off during the mid-sixties. He maintained a steady income via the well-trodden cabaret circuit, but suffered a severe embarrassment in 1976 when he attempted a pop comeback through the medium of the Eurovision Song Contest - despite being the best-known of the dozen acts taking part in the UK's *Song For Europe* heats, he finished bottom of the pile! (Bob Macdonald).

20 GOLDEN GREATS: FRANK IFIELD.
Tracks: I remember you / Confessin' (that I love you) / Don't blame me / You came along (from out of nowhere) / Nobody's darlin' but mine / Call her your sweetheart / I should care / Lucky devil / Summer is over / Please / Lovesick blues / Wayward wind / Mule train / Wolverton mountain / Gonna find me a bluebird / Paradise / She taught me how to yodel / Angry at the big oak tree / No one will ever know / Waltzing Matilda.
LP . . . . NE 1136
MC . . . . CE 1136
K-Tel / Nov '81 / I & B Records / C.M. Distribution / Arabesque Ltd. / Mono Distributors (Jersey) Ltd. / Prism Leisure PLC / PolyGram / Ross Records / Prism Leisure PLC.
LP . . . . PLAT 12
MC . . . . PLAC 12
Platinum Music / Mar '86 / Prism Leisure PLC / Ross Records.

ANGRY AT THE BIG OAK TREE.
Tracks: Angry at the big oak tree.
7" . . . . DB 7263
Columbia (EMI) / Mar '64.

BLUE SKIES.
Tracks: Not Advised.
LP 5SSX 1588
Columbia (EMI) / Mar '64.

BORN FREE.
Tracks: Not Advised.
LP 33SX 1462
Columbia (EMI) / Sep '63.

CALL HER YOUR SWEETHEART.
Tracks: Call her your sweetheart.
7" . . . . DB 8078
Columbia (EMI) / Nov '66.

CONFESSIN'.
Tracks: Confessin' (that I love you).
7" . . . . DB 7062
Columbia (EMI) / Jun '63.

CRAWLING BACK.
Tracks: Crawling back / So sad.
7" 7P 229
PRT / Jan '82 / BMG.

DON'T BLAME ME.
Tracks: Don't blame me.
7" . . . . DB 7184
Columbia (EMI) / Jan '64.

EP COLLECTION, THE: FRANK IFIELD.
Tracks: Not Advised.
CD . . . . SEECD 312
LP . . . . SEE 312
MC . . . . SEEK 312
See For Miles / Feb '91 / Pinnacle.

GOLDEN HITS: FRANK IFIELD.
Tracks: Not Advised.
Double LP . . . . MFP 1017
MC Set . . . . TCMFP 1017
MFP / Apr '81.

GOTTA GET A DATE.
Tracks: Gotta get a date.
7" . . . . DB 4496
Columbia (EMI) / Jul '60.

GREATEST HITS: FRANK IFIELD.
Tracks: Not Advised.
LP 33SX 1633
Columbia (EMI) / Dec '64.

HIS GREATEST HITS.
Tracks: I remember you / Gotta get a date / She taught me how to yodel / Go tell it on the mountain / I'm confessin' / Mule train / Wolverton mountain / Angry at the big oak tree / Wayward wind / Funny how time slips away / Riders in the sky / Scarlet ribbons / Lovesick blues / Nobody's darlin' but mine / Lucky devil / Summer is over / I should care / Call her your sweetheart / Paradise / No one will ever know / Happy go lucky me / Waltzing Matilda / Young love / Cool water / Don't blame me.
MC . . . . HR 8117
MC . . . . HR 4181174
Hour Of Pleasure / May '86 / EMI.

I REMEMBER YOU.
Tracks: Not Advised.
MC . . . . VCA 067

VFM Cassettes / '78 / VFM Children's Entertainment Ltd. / Midland Records / Morley Audio Services.
LP 1A 220 1583224
EMI (Holland) / '88.

I REMEMBER YOU.
Tracks: I remember you.
7" . . . . DB 4856
Columbia (EMI) / Jun '62.

I REMEMBER YOU (OLD GOLD).
Tracks: I remember you.
7" . . . . OG 9043
Old Gold / Jul '82

I SHOULD CARE.
Tracks: I should care.
7" . . . . DB 7319
Columbia (EMI) / Jun '64.

I'LL REMEMBER YOU.
Tracks: Not Advised.
LP 33SX 1467
Columbia (EMI) / Feb '63.

JOANNE.
Tracks: Joanne.
7" . . . . SRL 1109
Spark (3) / Jun '74.

LOVESICK BLUES.
Tracks: Lovesick blues.
7" . . . . DB 4913
Columbia (EMI) / Sep '62.

LUCKY DEVIL.
Tracks: Lucky devil.
7" . . . . DB 4399
Columbia (EMI) / Jan '60.

MULE TRAIN.
Tracks: Mule train.
7" . . . . DB 7131
Columbia (EMI) / Sep '63.

NO ONE WILL EVER KNOW.
Tracks: No one will ever know.
7" . . . . DB 7940
Columbia (EMI) / May '66.

NOBODY'S DARLING BUT MINE.
Tracks: Nobody's darlin' but mine.
7" . . . . DB 7007
Columbia (EMI) / Mar '63.

PARADISE.
Tracks: Paradise.
7" . . . . DB 7655
Columbia (EMI) / Jul '65.

PORTRAIT OF FRANK IFIELD.
Tracks: Crawling back / Let's take the long way round the world / She cheats on me / Touch the morning / Crowd, The / Crystal (I can see through you) / (After sweet memories) Play born to lose again / Why don't we leave together / So sad (To watch good love go bad) / Yesterday just passed my way again.
LP . . . . N 146
MC . . . . ZCN 146
PRT / Jan '83 / BMG.

REST OF THE EMI YEARS: FRANK IFIELD.
Tracks: Lucky devil / I remember you / She taught me how to yodel / Lovesick blues / Confessin' (that I love you) / Just one more chance / Nobody's darlin' but mine / Wayward wind, The / My blue heaven / Say it isn't so / Don't blame me / You came a long way from St. Louis / Summer is over / Once a jolly swagman (From film: Up Jumped A Swagman) / Botany Bay (From film: Up Jumped A Swagman) / Paradise / Wild rover (From film: Up Jumped A Swagman) / Call her your sweetheart / No one will ever know / Give me your word.
CD . . . . CDEMS 1402
EMI / May '91 / EMI.
MC . . . . TCEMS 1402
EMI / May '91.

SOMEONE TO GIVE MY LOVE TO.
Tracks: Not Advised.
LP . . . . SRLP 111
Spark (3) / '74.

SUMMER IS OVER.
Tracks: Summer is over.
7" . . . . DB 7355
Columbia (EMI) / Sep '64.

TOUCH THE MORNING.
Tracks: Touch the morning / Yesterday just passed my way again.
7" 7P 265
PRT / Mar '83 / BMG.

WAYWARD WIND.
Tracks: Wayward wind / I'm confessin'.
■ 7" . . . . DB 4960
Columbia (EMI) / Jan '63.
■ 7" . . . . POP 2014
H.M.V. / Nov '80.

YODELING SONG, THE (Ifield, Frank & The Backroom Boys).
Tracks: Yodeling song, The / I remember you / Lovesick blues (Only on MC and CD single) / She taught me how to yodel (Only on MC and CD single).
12" 12YODEL 1
7" 7YODEL 1
CD Single . . . . YODELCD 1
■ MC Single . . . . YODELTC 1
EMI / Dec '91.

Indians

DANCE ON.
Tracks: Not Advised.
LP . . . . HALPX 170
MC . . . . HACS 7070
Hawk / Jan '78 / C.M. Distribution.

INDIAN COUNTRY.
Tracks: Not Advised.
LP . . . . HALPX 101
Hawk / '74 / C.M. Distribution.

INDIAN RESERVATION.
Tracks: Not Advised.
LP . . . . HALPX 109
Hawk / '74 / C.M. Distribution.

MAGNIFICENT SEVEN.
Tracks: Not Advised.
LP . . . . HALPX 141
Hawk / Jun '75 / C.M. Distribution.

WE'RE JUST INDIANS.
Tracks: Not Advised.
LP . . . . HALPX 154
Hawk / Sep '76 / C.M. Distribution.

Iona & Andy

ACROSS THE MOUNTAIN.
Tracks: Everything but love / Part of your world / Remembering / Going gone / Even now / I'm a country girl / Across the mountain / Back on my mind again / Eyes of a child / You can take the wings off me / Heading West / Daddy's hands.
LP . . . . BGE LP 1003
MC . . . . BGE C 1003
Barge / Oct '87 / Jay-Cee Music.

GOING GONE.
Tracks: Going gone (re-mix) / Lion in the winter.
7" . . . . BGE 7 1004
Barge / '88 / Jay-Cee Music.

Ives, Burl

Ives, Burl This American singer and actor began his career in folk music during the Thirties, trekking round the States as a solo performer. During the late Forties and Fifties he did much to increase public awareness of folk and had a considerable influence on several of the genre's later artists.In 1962 Ives suddenly achieved a run of hit singles on the pop charts. *A Little Bitty Tear* reached No.9 on both sides of the Atlantic. *Funny Way of Laughin'* got to No.10 in the US and No.29 in UK, *Call Me Mr. In-Between* reached No.19 in the US and *Mary Ann regrets* peaked at No.39 in the US.Ives deep voice graced many novelty and children's records during his career and he later concentrated on religious material. (Bob Macdonald).

ANIMAL FOLK.
Tracks: Not Advised.
■ LP . . . . DQ 1191
Castle Music (USA) / May '74.

BEST, THE.
Tracks: Not Advised.
LP . . . . ENT 13020
Entertainers / Sep '87.

BLUE TAIL FLY.
Tracks: Blue tail fly / I know an old lady / Mr. Frog.
■ 7" . . . . MCA 258
MCA / Oct '76.

BRAND NEW ALBUM.
Tracks: Not Advised.
■ LP 2382094
Polydor / '79.

BRIGHT AND BEAUTIFUL.
Tracks: Brighten the corner where you are / Sailing home / Throw out the life line / Showers of blessing / Amazing grace / Rescue the perishing / Softly and tenderly / Power in the blood / All of my burdens rolling away / Stand up stand up for Jesus / Count your blessings / All things bright and beautiful / Lillie of the valley / What a friend we have in Jesus / Bringing in the sheaves / When we all get to Heaven / Shall we gather at the river? / In the sweet bye and bye / Praise God from whom all blessing flow / God be with you till we meet again.
LP . . . . TWE 6001
MC . . . . TC TWE 6001
Word 20 / May '85 / Sony.

BURL IVES.
Tracks: Not Advised.
LP . . . . ENT LP 13020
MC . . . . ENT MC 13020
Entertainers / '88.

CHILDREN'S FAVOURITES 1.
Tracks: Blue tail fly.
■ 7" . . . . MCP 6
MCA / Dec '78.

CHIM CHIM CHEREE.
Tracks: Not Advised.
■ LP . . . . DQ 1200
Castle Music (USA) / May '74.

CHRISTMAS AT THE WHITE HOUSE.
Tracks: Not Advised.
LP . . . . TC 1415
Caedmon (USA) / May '79 / Gower Publishing.

FAITH AND JOY.
Tracks: Not Advised.
LP . . . . SAC 5069
Sacred / May '74 / Word Records (UK).

FUNNY WAY OF LAUGHING.
Tracks: Funny way of laughing.
■ 7" 05868
Brunswick / May '62.

HOLLY JOLLY CHRISTMAS, A.
Tracks: Holly jolly Christmas, A / Snow for Johnny.
■ 7" 05947
Brunswick / Nov '65.

JUNIOR CHOICE.
Tracks: I know an old lady / Molly Malone / Horace the horse / Whistling rabbit / Polly wolly doodle / Davy Crockett / What kind of animal are you / Blue tail fly / Three jolly huntsmen / Squirrel / Riddle song / Mr. Froggie / Monkey and the elephant / Man on the flying trapeze, The.
■ LP . . . . MFP 50446
MFP / Nov '79.

LITTLE BITTY TEAR, A.
Tracks: Little bitty tear, A.
■ 7" 05863
Brunswick / Jan '62.

LITTLE BITTY TEAR, A.
Tracks: Little bitty tear, A / Long black veil, The / Shang-hied / Almighty dollar bill, The / Forty hour week / Delia / Oh, my side / Lenora, let your hair hang down / Mocking bird hill / I walk the line / Drink to me only with thine eyes / Mama don't want no peas, no rice / Empty saddles / Oregan trail, The / Home on the range / When the bloom is on the sage / My adobe hacienda / Cowboy's dream / Mexicali rose / Last round-up, The / Oh bury me not on the lone prairie / Jingle, jangle, jingle / Cool water / Tumbling tumbleweeds / Royal telephone / Holding hands for Joe / Sixteen fathoms down / What you gonna do Leroy / Brooklyn bridge / Poor little Jimmy / Thumbin' Johnny Brown / Funny way of laughin' / That's all I can remember / Ninety nine / Call me Mr. In-between / I ain't comin' home tonight / How do you fall out of love / In foggy old London / Mother wouldn't do that / Bring them in / Let the lower lights be burning / Beulah land / Standing on the promises / Fairest Lord Jesus / We're marching to Zion / Sunshine in my soul / Blessed assurance / Leaning on the everlasting arms / Where the leads me / Will there be any stars / When they ring those golden bells / Same old hurt, The / Wishin' she was here (instead of me) / Busted / Poor boy in a rich man's town / Mary Ann regrets / Billy Bayou / Moon is high, The / Green turtle / Bury the bottle with me / Blizzard, The / It comes & goes / I'm the boss / Same old hurt (remake), The / Curry road / Deepening snow, The / She didn't let the ink dry on the paper / Late movie, The / Home James / Man about town / She called me baby / My chicken run away to the bush / Baby come home to me / Roses & orchids / Lynching party / Hundred twenty miles from nowhere, A / Two car garage / I found my best friend in the dog pound / I'll hit it with a stick / Saskatoon, Saskatchewan / Some folks / I'll walk away smiling / There goes another pal of mine / This is your day / This is all I ask / Lower forty / Four initials on a tree / Someone hangin' round you all the time / Beautiful

Annabelle Lee / Hobo jungle / Strong as a mountain / Can't you hear me / Cherry blossom song / What I want (I can never have) / Can angels fly over the Rockies / Legend of the T, The / Kentucky turkey buzzard / Funny little show, The / Hard luck & misery / Pearly shells / What little tears are made of / Short on love / Who done it / Two of the usual / Tell me / Among my souvenirs / Gater hollow / I ain't missing nobody / Catfish Bill / Time to bum again / Born for trouble / Unemployment check / Atlantic coastal line / Don't let love die / How deep is the ocean / Okeechobee ocean / My melancholy baby / Jealous / My gal Sal / By the light of the silvery moon / For me & my gal / Red sails in the sunset / Make believe / Oh how I miss you tonight / You know you belong to somebody else / Down in the Okefenokee / (I hear you) Call my name / Mister Make-up man / River boy / Drifting & dreaming / Beyond the reef / My Isle of golden dreams / Now is the hour / Sweet Leilani / Moon of Manakoora / Song of the Islands / Keep your eyes on the hands / Hawaiian bells / Little brown girl / On the beach of Waikiki / Aloha Oe / Thirty thousand feet over Denver / Betsy the cow.
CD . . . . BCD 15667
Bear Family / Jul '93 / Rollercoaster Records / Swift / Direct Distribution.

LITTLE WHITE DUCK.
Tracks: Little white duck, The / Little engine that could, The / Mr. Froggie went a-courtin' / Doughnut song, The / Two little owls / Fooba wooba John / Grey goose, The / Whale, The / Buckeye Jim / Sow took the measles, The / Goat, The / Mr. Rabbit / Tailor & the mouse, The / Mother Goose songs.
■ LP . . . . CBS 31525
Embassy / Jul '77 / Sony.

LOVE AND JOY.
Tracks: King's business, The / Jesus loves the little children / Will there be any stars in my crown / Love lifted me / King Herod and the cock / Friendly beasts, The / Cradle hymn / In the temple / Old rugged cross, The / I can, I will, I do believe / How I love Jesus / When Jesus was a boy / Joy unspeakable / Who made this world / We thank thee / Our helpers / Oh be careful / Life's railway to heaven / Unclouded day, The / Haven of rest.
LP . . . . TWE 6006
MC . . . . TC TWE 6006
Word 20 / Jun '84 / Sony.

RETURN OF THE WAYFARING STRANGER.
Tracks: John Henry / Billy the kid / Fare thee wall / O honey / May Lindy Lou / Mule train / Worried man blues, The / Green country bachelor / Lilly Munroe / Old blue / Ballanderie / Lord Randall / Riders in the sky / Wayfaring stranger / Woolie boogie bee.
LP . . . . BPG 62080
CBS / '80 / Sony.

SHALL WE GATHER AT THE RIVER.
Tracks: Not Advised.
LP . . . . SAC 5073
Sacred / Mar '78 / Word Records (UK).

SONGS I SANG IN SUNDAY SCHOOL.
Tracks: Not Advised.
LP . . . . SAC 5072
Sacred / May '74 / Word Records (UK).

STEPPING IN THE LIGHT.
Tracks: Not Advised.
LP . . . . TWE 6017
MC . . . . TC TWE 6017
Word 20 / Jun '84 / Sony.

TALENTED MAN, THE.
Tracks: Comin' after Jenny / Galisteo / Snowbird / Real roses / Roll up some inspiration / Another day, another year / Raindrops keep falling on my head / One more time Billy Brown / Tied down here at home.
LP . . . . BDL 1027
Bulldog Records / Jul '82 / President Records / Jazz Music / Wellard Dist. / TKO Records Ltd.

TIMES THEY ARE A CHANGIN'.
Tracks: I'll be your baby tonight / By the time I get to Phoenix / Gentle on my mind / Little green apples / Don't think twice, it's all right / One too many mornings / Maria / If I were a carpenter / Homeward bound / Folk singer / Times they are a changin'.
■ LP . . . . CBS 31717
CBS / '79.

VERY BEST OF BURL IVES.
Tracks: Not Advised.
CD . . . . SOW 708
Sound Waves / Jul '93 / Taylors.
CD . . . . SOWCD 0708
MC . . . . SOW 908
Sound Waves / May '93 / Taylors.

■ DELETED

J

J.D. & Dallas

KEEP IT COUNTRY.
Tracks: Queen of the silver dollar / Just out of reach / I fall to pieces / Blanket on the ground / Why me Lord / Blackboard of my heart / Please help me I'm fallin' / Cheating heart / This song' just for you / Tiny bubbles / Crystal chandeliers / Wild side of life / Deadwood stage / Black hills of Dakota, The / Secret love / I wasn't there / Tonight I'll throw a party / Let the rest of the world go by / Texas / American trilogy.
LP . . . . KLP 29
Igus / Oct '81 / C.M. Distribution / Ross Records / Duncans.

Jackson, Alan

Alan Jackson was born in Alabama and exploded onto the country scene during 1990 with top 3 singles, *Here In The Real World*, *Wanted* and *Chasing Rainbows*. Jackson is a gifted singer/songwriter who keeps his approach to country music simple and traditional. (Maurice Hope)

HERE IN THE REAL WORLD.
Tracks: Ace of hearts / Blue blooded woman / Chasin' that neon rainbow / I'd love you all over again / Home / Here in the real world / Wanted / She don't get the blues / Dog river blues / Short sweet ride.
CD 260817
MC 410817
Arista / Jul '90 / BMG.
■ LP 210817
Arista / Jul '90.

HERE IN THE REAL WORLD.
Tracks: Here in the real world.
7" 113481
■ CD Single 663481
Arista / Jul '90 / BMG.

LOT ABOUT LIVIN', A (And A Little 'Bout Love).
Tracks: Chattanoochee / She's got the rhythm (And I got the blues) / Tonight I climbed the wall / I don't need the booze (To get a buzz on) / (Who says) You can't have it all / Up to my ears in tears / Tropical depression / She likes it too / If it ain't one thing (It's you) / Mercury blues.
CD 782218711-2
Arista / '92 / BMG.

Jackson, Carl

Carl Jackson was born in 1953, in Louisville, Mississippi. He is a multi-instrumentalist who started out during the 1970's as one of Glen Campbell's session men. Jackson's early career has seen him recording for Prize, later reissued on Sugar Hill and touring as part of the Jim & Jesse Show. His first major releases on Capitol was the 1973 LP *Banjo Player*, and in 1978 he recorded *Old Friends*, which was a tribute to bluegrass legend Bill Monroe. His next releases *Banjo Man: A Tribute To Earl Scruggs* and *Song Of The South* were released on the fast developing bluegrass outlet Sugarhill Records. (Maurice Hope)

BANJO HITS.
Tracks: Not Advised.
LP . . . . SH 3737
Sugarhill(USA) / Mar '89 / Roots Records / Projection / Impetus Records / C.M. Distribution / Jazz Music / Swift / Duncans / A.D.A Distribution.

BANJO MAN: TRIBUTE TO EARL SCUGGS.
Tracks: Earl's breakdown / John Henry / Grey eagle / You are my flower / Home sweet home / Careless love / Keep on the sunny side / Little darling pal of mine / Reuben / Ground speed / Banjo man.
LP . . . . SH 3715
MC . . . . SH 3715C
Sugarhill(USA) / '88 / Roots Records / Projection / Impetus Records / C.M. Distribution / Jazz Music / Swift / Duncans / A.D.A Distribution.

SONG OF THE SOUTH.
Tracks: Love and wealth / Jerusalem ridge / Lay down my old guitar / Baby you're all mine tonight / Erase the miles / Jesse and me / Lonesome river, The / Stoney creek / Song of the South.
LP . . . . SH 3728
MC . . . . SH 3728C
Sugarhill(USA) / Oct '88 / Roots Records / Projection / Impetus Records / C.M. Distribution / Jazz Music / Swift / Duncans / A.D.A Distribution.

Jackson, Marvin

OZARK ROCKABILLY.
Tracks: Fifty-six V8 Ford / When you rock 'n' roll / Down the rolley rink / He's just a cool man, cool / Keep a shakin' / Jay bird / Debbie Gail / My baby likes to go / Rainstorm / Rock 'n' roll baby / Always-late Johnny / I only know my baby's gone / Rockin' and rollin' / Pretty, pretty Loretta / Alone and so blue / Peek-a-boo / Gee whiz Liz.
LP . . . . WLP 8883
White Label (Germany) / Apr '85 / Pinnacle / Bear Family Records (Germany) / CSA Tell Tapoo.

Jackson, Stonewall

This American country singer and guitarist is named after the Confederate general Stonewall Jackson. The vocalist was born in Georgia and raised in North Carolina, but based his career in Tennessee's burgeoning country and western mecca Nashville. In 1959 Jackson came to fame by John D.Loudermilk; it reached No.4 in the US and No.24 in the UK.Stonewall then disappeared, as far as pop audiences were concerned. But *Waterloo* had established his reputation in Nashville forever and he became one of the country genre's everlasting institutions. His style changed little but then it didn't really need to. (Bob Macdonald)

I CAN'T SING A LOVE SONG.
Tracks: I can't sing a love song / My favourite sin.
■ 7" . . . . PT 486
President / Oct '80.

MY FAVOURITE SIN.
Tracks: My favourite sin / I can't sing a love song / Point of no return, The / Have your next affair with me / Spirit of St Louis / Alcohol of fame / Things that lovers do / We're the kind of people (that make the jukebox play) / Don't you say nothin' at all / Jesus took the outlaw out of me.
LP . . . . PRCV 101
President / May '88 / Grapevine Distribution / Target Records / Jazz Music / Taylors.

STONEWALL JACKSON.
Tracks: Not Advised.
MC . . . . ZCGAS 752
Audio Fidelity(USA) / Oct '84 / Stage One Records.

UP AGAINST THE WALL.
Tracks: Old chunk of coal / Let the sun shine on the people / Mary don't you weep / Help stamp out loneliness / Promises and hearts / Life to go / BJ the DJ / Wound time can't erase, A / Ole show - boat / Muddy water.
LP . . . . ALEB 2300
MC . . . . ZCALB 2300
Allegiance / Apr '84.

WATERLOO.
Tracks: Waterloo.
■ 7" . . . . PB 941
Philips / Jul '59.

Jackson, Wanda

This American singer was one of the few women to have a crack at the rock 'n' roll market during the late Fifties and early Sixties. In those days, the raucousness and raw energy of rock was an almost exclusively male domain; the small number of successful girl singers were usually heard on middle of the road ballads, lightweight pop novelties or country and western songs. Jackson, who hailed from Oklahoma, had a country background but her interest in the 'rock' part of rockabilly led to her achieving a Top 40 hit on both sides of the Atlantic in 1960 with *Let's Have a Party*. The frantic *Mean, Mean Man* gave Wanda a second UK Top 40 single in early 1961. In late 1961 Jackson scored two further American Top 40 singles, *Right or Wrong* and *In The Middle of a Heartache* which saw her veering back towards country. The experiment has been bold and brash while it lasted. In the early Seventies Jackson began a prolific fusion of country and gospel. (Bob Macdonald)

16 ROCK'N'ROLL HITS.
Tracks: Not Advised.
CD . . . . CD 66088
Ce De International / Jul '93 / Taylors.

2 SIDES OF WANDA.

Tracks: Not Advised.
LP 2C 068 86305
Capitol (import) / '83 / Pinnacle / EMI.

BEST OF WANDA JACKSON.
Tracks: Not Advised.
LP 1A 022 58072
EMI (Holland) / '83.
MC 1A 222 58072
EMI (Holland) / '88.

CAPITOL COUNTRY CLASSICS.
Tracks: Right or wrong / In the middle of a heartache / If I cried every time you hurt me / Violet and the rose / Box it came in / Because it's you / Tears will be the chaser for your wine / Both sides of the line / Girl don't have to drink to have fun / My baby walked out on me / My big iron skillet / Two separate bar stools / Woman lives for love / Fancy satin pillows / Back then / I already know.
■ LP . . . . CAPS 1033
Capitol / Feb '80.

CLOSER TO JESUS.
Tracks: Where I'm going / World didn't give it to me, The / Carpenter's son / Grandma sang off key / He was there all the time / Closer to Jesus / Learning to lean / I came to praise the Lord / I just feel that something good is about to happen / Get all excited / Walkin' in the spirit / He's been through it too.
LP . . . . WST 9580
MC . . . . WC 9580
Word (UK) / May '82 / Word Records (UK) / Sony.

COUNTRY GOSPEL.
Tracks: I love you, Jesus / I saw the light / Jesus cares for me / Turn your radio on / I'd rather have Jesus / All in all / I know / Why me, Lord? / Special kind of man, A / Farther along / Let go..let Jesus.
LP . . . . WST 9515
MC . . . . WC 9515
Word (UK) / May '82 / Word Records (UK) / Sony.

EARLY WANDA JACKSON.
Tracks: If you don't somebody else will / You don't have my love / I'd rather have a broken heart / You'd be the first one to know / If you knew what I know / Lovin' country style / Heart you could have had, The / Right to love, The / It's the same old world (wherever you go) / Tears at the Grand Ole Opry / Don't do the things he'd do / Nobody's darlin' but mine / I cried again / Wasted / You won't forget about me.
LP . . . . BFX 15109
Bear Family / Mar '84 / Rollercoaster Records / Swift / Direct Distribution.

GREATEST HITS:WANDA JACKSON.
Tracks: Not Advised.
CD 120 103
MCS Look Back / Jul '87.

HER GREATEST COUNTRY HITS.
Tracks: Stand by your man / Leave my baby alone / Wrong kind of girl / My big iron skillet / Hello darlin' / Break my mind / Two separate bar stools / Please help me, I'm falling / Your good girl's gonna go bad / Right or wrong / One minute past eternity / Silver threads and golden needles / Tuck away my lonesome blues / Jealous heart / Blue model No 6 / Try a little kindness / Love of the common people / Walk through this world with me / Oh lonesome me / Today I started loving you again / Reuben James / Great speckled bird, The / It's such a pretty world today / Both sides of the line / Tips of my fingers, The / More you see me less, The / I'm a believer / Wabash cannonball.
Double LP 5C 134 53025/26
EMI (Holland) / '83.

LET'S HAVE A PARTY.
Tracks: Let's have a party / Rock your baby / Mean mean man / There's a party going on / Fujiyama mama / Honey bop / Rip it up / Man we had a party / Hot dog that made him mad / You bug me bad / Who shot Sam / Tongue tied / Sparklin' brown eyes / Lost weekend / Brown eyed handsome man / Honey don't / It doesn't matter anymore / Whole lotta shakin' goin' on / Long tall Sally / Money honey / Searchin' / Hard headed woman / Slippin' and slidin' / Riot in cell block 9 / I gotta know / Baby loves him / Let me explain / Savin' my love / Just a queen for a day / Cool love / Bye bye baby / Right or wrong.
Double LP . . . . CDX 11
■ MC . . . . TCCDX 11
Charly / May '87 / Charly.

LET'S HAVE A PARTY.
Tracks: Let's have a party.
■ 7" . . . . CL 15147
Capitol / Sep '60.

■ **DELETED**

J 1

LOVIN' COUNTRY STYLE.
Tracks: Not Advised.
LP. . . . . **HAT 3021**
MC . . . . **HATC 3021**
Stetson / Oct '86 / Crusader Marketing Co. / Swift / Wellard Dist. / Midland Records / C.M. Distribution.

MEAN MEAN MAN.
Tracks: Mean mean man.
■ **7"** . . . . **CL 15176**
Capitol / Jan '61.

MY KIND OF GOSPEL.
Tracks: If Jesus changed your heart / Glory train / Jesus is the best thing that ever.. / Help, help me Jesus / Life's journey / Jesus loves cowgirls / I've never been this homesick before / Jesus gave it to me / Thank you lord for loving me / It's your decision.
LP. . . . . **SDLP 026**
Sundown / Aug '86 / Terry Blood Dist. / Jazz Music / C.M. Distribution.
MC . . . . **SDC 026**
Sundown / May '88 / Terry Blood Dist. / Jazz Music / C.M. Distribution.

MY TESTIMONY.
Tracks: Show me the way to Calvary / Holy Ghost baptiser / Walking on the water / I go to the rock / He's still working on me / Hey devil / Come morning / Let me touch Him / Jesus, I believe what You said / My testimony.
LP. . . . . **WST 9619**
MC . . . . **WC 9619**
Word (UK) / May '82 / Word Records (UK) / Sony.

NOW I HAVE EVERYTHING.
Tracks: Don't ever let go of my hand / Let this be my attitude / Heaven's gonna be a blast / When the saints go marching in / Oh how I love Jesus / Jesus put a yodel in my soul / Now I have everything / Pick me up, Lord / Jesus, I love you / Some call him Jesus / Let's just praise the Lord / Pass me not, O gentle Saviour.
LP. . . . . **MYR 1021**
MC . . . . **MC 1021**
Myrrh / May '82 / Word Records (UK) / Sony.

RAVE ON.
Tracks: Let's have a party / Breathless / Right or wrong / Stupid cupid / What in the world's come over you / I fall to pieces / Raining in my heart / Sweet dreams / Sweet nothin's / Oh boy / Rave on.
LP. . . . . **TOP 166**
MC . . . . **KTOP 166**
Topline / Feb '87 / Charly / Swift / Black Sun Records.

RIGHT OR WRONG.
Tracks: Not Advised.
LP. **2C 068 85314**
Capitol (import) / '83 / Pinnacle / EMI.

RIGHT OR WRONG 1954-1962.
Tracks: If you knew what I know / Lovin' country style / Heart, The / You could have had / Right to love, The / You can't have my love / If you don't, somebody else will / You'd be the first one to know / It's the same world (Wherever you go) / Tears at the Grand Old Opre / Don't do the things he'd do / Nobody's darlin' but mine / Wasted / I cried again / I'd rather have a broken heart / You won't forget about me / Step by step / Half as good a girl / I gotta know / Cryin' thru the night / Baby loves him / Honey bop / Silver threads and golden needles / Hot Dog, That made him mad / Did you miss me / Cool love / Let me explain / Don'a Wan'a / No wedding bells for Joe / Fujiyama Mama / Just quwwn for a day / Making believe / Just call me lonesome / Happy, happy birthday / Let me go, lover / (Let's have a) Party / Day dreaming / Heartbreak ahead / Here we are again / I wanna waltz / I can't make my dreams understand / Moner Honey / Long tall Sally / Sinful heart / Mean mean man / Rock your baby / Date with Jerry, A / (Every time they play) our song / You've turned to a stranger / Reaching / I'd rather have you / Savin' my love / You're the one for me / In the middle of a heartache / Please call today / My destiny / Wrong kind of girl, The / Kansas City / Fallin' / Sparkling brown eyes / Hard headed woman / Baby, baby, bye bye / It doesn't matter anymore / Lonely weekends / Tweedle dee / Riot in cell block £9 / Little charm bracelet / Right or wrong / Funnel of love / Tongue tied / There's a party going on / Lost weekend / Man we had a party / Why I'm walkin / I may never get to heaven / Stupid cupid / Brown eyed handsome man / I cried again, / Last letter, the / Who shot Sam / Slippin' and slidin' / My baby left me / So soon / Window up above, The / Sticks and stones / I don't wanta go / In the middle of a heartache, / Little bitty tear, A / I'd be ashamed / Seven lonely days / Don't ask me why / I need you now / This should go on forever / Is it wrong / We could / You don't know, Baby / Before I lose my mind / Tip of my fingers, The / Let me talk to you / (Let's stop) Kickin' our hearts around / Between the window and the phone / If I cried every time you hurt me / I misunderstood / Let my love walk in / To tell you the triuth / Greatest acctor, The / You bug me bad / One teardrop at a time / Funny how time slips away / These empty arms / But I was lying / We haven't a moment to lose / How important can it be / I may never get to heaven, / Things I might have been, The / Little things mean a lot / Have you ever been lonely / Please love me forever / Since I met you baby / May you never be alone / Sympathy / Whirlpool / Pledging my love / What am I living for.
CD Set . . . . **BCD 15629**
Bear Family / Mar '93 / Rollercoaster Records / Swift / Direct Distribution.

ROCKABILLY FEVER.
Tracks: Rockabilly fever / Stupid cupid / Rock 'n' roll away your blues / Sweet nothins' / It's only make believe / Oh boy / Rockabilly hound dog / Breathless / Sad love songs / Rave on / Meet me in Stockholm / Ain't it the gospel.
LP. . . . . **MFLP 037**
Magnum Force / Aug '85 / Terry Blood Dist. / Jazz Music / Hot Shot.
MC . . . . **MFC 037**
Magnum Force / Nov '88 / Terry Blood Dist. / Jazz Music / Hot Shot.

ROCKIN' WITH WANDA.
Tracks: Hot dog / That made him mad / Baby loves him / Mean, mean man / You've turned to a stranger / Don'a wan'a / I gotta know / Yakety yak / Let's have a party / Rock your baby / Fujiyama Mama / You're the one for me / Did you miss me? / Cool love / Honey boy / Whole lotta shakin' goin' on / Savin' my love.
■ **LP.** . . . . **CAPS 1007**
Capitol / Jul '77.
MC **2C 068 82098**
EMI (France) / '83 / EMI.

SANTA DOMINGO (Her German Recordings).
Tracks: Not Advised.
CD . . . . **BCD 15582**
Bear Family / Apr '92 / Rollercoaster Records / Swift / Direct Distribution.

THERE'S A PARTY.
Tracks: Not Advised.
LP. **2C 068 85315**
Capitol (import) / '83 / Pinnacle / EMI.

WANDA JACKSON.
Tracks: Not Advised.
LP. **2C 068 85111**
Capitol (import) / '83 / Pinnacle / EMI.

WANDA JACKSON: CAPITOL COUNTRY MUSIC CLASSICS.
Tracks: I gotta know / Silver threads and golden needles / Cool love / Don'a wan'a / Fujiyama Mama / Making believe / Let's have a party / Long tall Sally / Mean, mean man / Tweedle dee / Little charm bracelet / Right or wrong / There's a party goin' on / I may never get to heaven / Slippin' and slidin' / In the middle of a heartache / This should go on forever / (Let's stop) Kicking our hearts around / Between the window and the phone / If I cried every time you hurt me / Slippin' / Violet and the rose, The / Box it came in, The / Blue Yodel No. 6 / Because it's you / Tears will be a chaser for your wine / Both sides of the line / Girl don't have to drink to have fun, A / My big iron skillet / Woman lives for love, A / Fancy satin pillows.
CD . . . . **CDEMS 1485**
MC . . . . **TCEMS 1485**
Capitol / Apr '93 / EMI.

WONDERFUL WANDA.
Tracks: In the middle of a heartache / Seven lonely boys / If I cried every time you hurt me / Is it wrong / Don't asky me why / Let my love walk in / Little bitty tear, A / I need you now / I don't wanta go / We could / You don't know baby / I'd be ashamed.
MC . . . . **JAS C304**
Jasmine / Feb '88 / Wellard Dist. / Swift / Swift / Scott Butler Distribution / Jazz Music.
LP. . . . . **JAS 304**
Jasmine / Jan '88 / Wellard Dist. / Swift / Swift / Scott Butler Distribution / Jazz Music.

Jambalaya

BUGGY FULL OF CAJUN MUSIC.
Tracks: Not Advised.
LP. **6035**
Swallow (USA) / Swift / Wellard Dist.

LE NOUVEL ESPRIT DE LA MUSIQUE CADIEN.
Tracks: Not Advised.
LP. **6075**
MC . . . . **6075 TC**
Swallow (USA) / '88 / Swift / Wellard Dist.

James, Sonny

Sonny James (nicknamed The Southern Gentleman) was born in Hackleburg, Arkansas in 1929 and had his own radio show in Birmingham, Alabama by the time he reached his teens. His first single charted in 1953 and he was still enjoying country hits in the US in 1983.

ALWAYS DANCING.
Tracks: Me and my girl / Pennsylvania 6 5000 / You forgot to remember / Always (I'll be loving you) / I'll get by / Story of a starry night / My kind of girl / Swingin' safari, A / Dream / Just the way you look tonight / I know him so well / Air that I breathe, The / Music to cha-cha by / Stripper, The / Secret love / Star trek.
LP. . . . . **SUS 509**
Sounds Ultimate / May '85 / Savoy Records / Sounds Ultimate Records.

CAPITOL COLLECTORS SERIES: SONNY JAMES (Southern Gentleman).
Tracks: Young love / First date, first kiss, first love / Minute you're gone, The / Baltimore / Ask Marie / You're the only world I know / True love's a blessing / Take good care of her / Room in your heart / Need you / I'll never find anothyer you / Heaven says hello / Only the lonely / Since I met you baby (Recorded live at the Houston Astrodome.) / It's just a matter of time / My love.
■ **CD** . . . . **CZ 302**
Capitol / Apr '90.

CAT CAME BACK, THE.
Tracks: Cat came back, The.
■ **7"** . . . . **CL 14635**
Capitol / Nov '56.

DANCE TO MY MUSIC.
Tracks: Dance to my music / Crazy rhythm / Why do I love you / I'll never love this way again / Old funky rolls / Sentimental journey / Let's twist again / Five foot two, eyes of blue / Manana / Diamonds are a girl's best friend / Mambo jambo / Make it soon / Every breath you take / I could be so good for you / Oh lady be good / High noon / I will survive.
LP. . . . . **SUD 2000**
Sounds Ultimate / Sep '83 / Savoy Records / Sounds Ultimate Records.

SONNY.
Tracks: Near you / Fool such as I, A / Heartaches / Ages and ages ago / I'll never get over you / Secret love / Beg your pardon / Just out of reach / How's the world treating you / I forgot more than you'll ever know / Almost.
LP. . . . . **HAT 3070**
MC . . . . **HATC 3070**
Stetson / Aug '88 / Crusader Marketing Co. / Swift / Wellard Dist. / Midland Records / C.M. Distribution.

SONNY JAMES COLLECTION, THE.
Tracks: It's just a matter of time / Since I met you baby / World of our own, A / Endlessly / Only the lonely / That's why I love you like I do / Running bear / Take good care of her / Born to be with you / Here comes my honey again / Bright lights big city / Don't keep me hanging on / My love / Empty arms.
CD . . . . **KNCD 13057**
■ **MC** . . . . **KNMC 13057**
Knight / Feb '91.

YOUNG LOVE.
Tracks: Young love.
■ **7"** . . . . **CL 14683**
Capitol / Feb '57.

James, Tina

SAN ANTONIO STROLL.
Tracks: San Antonio stroll / Love is a rose.
■ **7"** . . . . **CHEW 47**
Mint / Feb '81.

Janot, Johnny

EXPOSE YOURSELF TO CAJUN MUSIC.
Tracks: Not Advised.
LP. **6050**
Swallow (USA) / Swift / Wellard Dist.
MC . . . . **6050 TC**
Swallow (USA) / '87 / Swift / Wellard Dist.

KING OF LOUISIANA ROCKABILLY.
Tracks: Not Advised.
LP. . . . . **FLY 531**
Flyright / '88 / Hot Shot / Roots Records / Wellard Dist. / Charly / Swift / Projection.

Javis, Jimmie

BARNYARD STOMP.
Tracks: Barnyard stomp / Doggone that train / Down at the old country church / Wampus Kitty Mama / Market house blues / Alimony blues / Midnight blues / Get on board, Aunt Susan / Shotgun wedding / Keyhole in the door / Bear cat mama from Horner's corners / She's a hum-dinger / She's a hum-dinger (part 2) / Out of town blues / Pea-picking papa / Woman's blues, A.
LP. . . . . **BFX 15285**
Bear Family / Apr '88 / Rollercoaster Records / Swift / Direct Distribution.

ROCKIN' BLUES.
Tracks: There's evil in ye children, gather round / Red nightgown blues / Davis salty dog / Saturday night stroll / Sewing machine blues / Easy rider blues / Davis' last day blues (1982 blues) / High behind blues / Rockin' blues (Previously unissued.) / Home town blues / Tom cat and pussy blues / Organ grinder blues / Penitentiary blues / She left a runnin' like a sewing machine / Lonely hobo / Arabella blues.
LP. . . . . **BFX 15125**
Bear Family / Apr '84 / Rollercoaster Records / Swift / Direct Distribution.

YOU ARE MY SUNSHINE.
Tracks: Not Advised.
LP. . . . . **HAT 3121**
Stetson / '89 / Crusader Marketing Co. / Swift / Wellard Dist. / Midland Records / C.M. Distribution.

J 2
■ DELETED

Jaye, Jerry

Born Jerald Jaye Hateley on 19.10.1937 in Manilla, Arkansas - rock'n'roll/country vocalist/guitarist. His debut recording *My Girl Josephine* was made in Memphis and issued on his own Connie label (1966), titled *Hello Josephine* . It was re-released in 1967 on Hi Records with its original title *My Girl Josephine* reaching No. 29 on Billboard pop charts. He had material released on Mega and Columbia during the 1970's, the latter sojourn restricted to *It's All In The Game* - a No. 53 country single (1975). Blending country, hillbilly and rock'n'roll, he returned to Hi Records where he recorded the album *Honky Tonk Women Love Redneck Men* - the title track supplying him with a top 40 success in 1976. (Maurice Hope)

MY GIRL JOSEPHINE.
Tracks: My girl Josephine / Long black veil / In the middle of nowhere / Got my mojo working / Pipeliner blues / I'm in love again / Sugar bee / I washed my hands in muddy water / Honky tonk women love redneck men / Standing room only / Drinking my way back home / When morning comes to Memphis / Hot and still heating / Let your love flow / Forty days.
CD . . . . **HIUKCD 122**
Hi! / Feb '92 / Pinnacle / Swift.

Jenkins, Snuffy

CAROLINA BLUEGRASS.
Tracks: Not Advised.
LP. . . . . **ARHOOLIE 5011**
Arhoolie (USA) / May '81 / Pinnacle / Cadillac Music / Swift / Projection / Hot Shot / A.D.A Distribution / Jazz Music.

Jennings, Frank

Jennings formed his band Syndicate in 1970, originally as Country Syndicate in 1970. Their initial boost came when they won the ITV Opportunity Knocks Songwriters contest. They enjoyed much success in 1978 with the One - Up album release *Heaven's Just A Woman's Love* and, as the Frank Jennings Syndicate, *Me And My Guitar* with which they found pop recognition. They gained inclusion on EMI's 1979 gold-selling compilation album of cross-over country product *Country Life* , alongside such acts as Olivia Newton-John, Dr. Hook and Merle Haggard. Since then they have many times been recipients of Europe's top awards - with solid album sales coming on Columbia and One - Up. (Maurice Hope)

EVERYBODY NEEDS A RAINBOW.
Tracks: Everybody needs a rainbow / Walk away little girl.
■ **7"** . . . . **EMI 2812**
EMI / Jun '78.

IT'S SO EASY TELLING LIES (Jennings, Frank Syndicate).
Tracks: It's so easy telling lies / Reason why.
■ **7"** . . . . **EMI 2642**
EMI / Jun '77.

LOVE IS THE ANSWER (Jennings, Frank Syndicate).
Tracks: Love is the answer / Forever darling.
■ **7"** . . . . **EMI 2598**
EMI / Mar '77.

LOVE LETTERS IN THE SAND.
Tracks: Love letters in the sand / I believe in you.
■ **7"** . . . . **DB 9067**
Columbia (EMI) / Jul '79.

ME AND MY GUITAR (Jennings, Frank Syndicate).
Tracks: Me and my guitar / Devil came between us / Bed of roses / How great thou art / When you finally realise you're on your own / Everybody needs a rainbow / Thibodeaux and his Cajun band / Here I am in Nashville / Sunshine and flowers / Southbound / Go away little girl / I believe in you.
MC . . . . **TC-SCX 6608**
Columbia (EMI) / Apr '79 / EMI.
■ **LP.** . . . . **SCX 6608**
Columbia (EMI) / Apr '79.

ME AND MY GUITAR (Jennings, Frank Syndicate).
Tracks: Me and my guitar / When you finally realise you're on your own.
■ **7"** . . . . **EMI 2746**
EMI International / Jan '78.

ROSE OF EL PASO.
Tracks: Rose of El Paso / Perfect stranger / I don't want to hear another she's leaving song / Love is a two way street / Memories to burn / Colinda / When you finally realise you're on your own / Carmen / Till the water stops runnin' / Ave Maria Morales.
LP. . . . . **GRALP 11**
MC . . . . **GRTC 11**
Grasmere / Jul '86 / Target Records / Savoy Records.

SILENT NIGHT (Jennings, Frank Syndicate).
Tracks: Silent night.
■ **7"** . . . . **EMI 2716**
EMI / Nov '77.

Jennings, Waylon

Waylon Jennings is one of country music's legends. He was born on 15th June 1937 in Littlefield, Texas. In 1958, his family moved to Lubbock, Texas, where Jennings worked as a DJ on Radio KLL. Shortly afterwards, he had recorded *Jole Blon* in Norman Petty's studio and was playing in Buddy Holly's band, The Crickets. He was not on the plane that crashed killing Buddy Holly, Jennings had given his seat to the Big Bopper, who also died. He formed the Waylors when he moved to Phoenix, and played 6 nights a week at JD's club between 1961 and 1965. Although A&M released some of Jennings's singles in 1963, it wasn't until he signed for RCA in 1965 that his career took off. Wayland's sparsely delivered folk/country saw him charting regularly throughout the 1960's. He moved to Nashville, and during the 1970's he introduced a cutting edge to his music. His strong vocals supplemented by that now familiar rolling guitar. Jennings's albums *Ladies Love Outlaws* and *Honky Tonk Heroes*, were very successful. In 1974, Jennings reached the top spot with his singles; *This Time, I'm A Ramblin' Man*, and *Are You Sure Hank Done It This Way/Bob Wills Is Still The King*. In 1975, he was voted CMA's male vocalist of the year. In 1976, he and wife Jessi Colter were voted CMA,s duo and song of the year for their *Suspicious Minds*. The couple, together with Willie Nelson and Tompall Glaser recorded country's greatest selling album, *Outlaw*. At this point Waylon could do little wrong, another batch of no.1 singles took him into the 1980's at the forefront of country music. Waylon's voice has also used on the narration of the smash TV series, The Dukes Of Hazzard. Around this time he also recorded albums with Johnny Cash and Willie Nelson. These three, together with Kris Kristofferson produced the multi million selling *Highwayman* & *Highwayman 2*, in 1989. Despite ill health, he also appeared alongside his wife at the Wembley International Music Festival. In 1990, he released his debut album for Epic, *The Eagle*. (Maurice Hope)

20 GOLDEN HITS: WILLIE & WAYLON (see under Nelson, Willie).

20 OUTLAW REUNION HITS (Jennings, Waylon & Willie Nelson).
Tracks: Not Advised.
LP. **20020**
MC **40020**
Astan (USA) / Nov '84.

AMANDA.
Tracks: Amanda / Lonesome only and mean.
■ **7"** . . . . **PB 1596**
RCA / Aug '79.

AMERICA.
Tracks: Not Advised.
■ **VHS.** . . . . **COL 1009**
Castle Collector Series / Apr '92.

ARE YOU READY FOR THE COUNTRY.
Tracks: Are you ready for the country / Them old love songs / So good woman / Jack a diamonds / Can't you see / MacArthur Park (revisisted) / I'll go back to her / Couple more years, A / Old friend / Precious memories.
■ **LP.** . . . . **RS 1067**
RCA / '79.

BEST OF WAYLON JENNINGS, THE.
Tracks: Love of the common people / Days of sand and shovels, The / MacArthur Park / Delia's gone / Walk on out of my mind / Anita, you're dreaming / Only daddy that'll walk the line / Just to satisfy you / I got you / Something's wrong in California / Ruby, don't take your love to town / Brown eyed handsome man / Singer of sad songs.
■ **LP.** . . . . **LSA 3000**
RCA / '79.

BLACK ON BLACK.
Tracks: Women do you know how to carry on / Honky tonk blues / Just to satisfy you / We made it as lovers / Shine / Folsom Prison blues / Gonna write a letter / May I borrow some sugar from you / Song for the life / Get naked with me.
MC . . . . **RCAK 3072**
RCA / May '82 / BMG.
■ **LP.** . . . . **RCALP 3072**
RCA / May '82.

BURNING MEMORIES.
Tracks: Sally was a good old girl / Crying / Burning memories / It's so easy / White lightning / Abilene / Dream baby / Loves gonna live here / Big Mamou / Don't think twice.
LP. . . . . **SHLP 107**
MC . . . . **SHTC 107**
Castle Showcase / Apr '86 / Arabesque Ltd.

COLLECTION: WAYLON JENNINGS (VOL. 1).
Tracks: Back in the saddle again / Maria / I'm looking over a four leaf clover / Misty blue / There goes my everything / Sweet mental revenge / Do you ever think of me / Chicken reel / Does your heart beat for me / Sally was a good old girl / Crying / Burning memories / It's so easy / White lightning / Abilene / Dream baby / Love's gonna live here / Big mamou / Don't think twice.
Double LP . . . . **CCSLP 110**
MC . . . . **CCSMC 110**
Castle Collector Series / Nov '85 / BMG / Pinnacle / Castle Communications.

COLLECTION: WAYLON JENNINGS (VOL.2).
Tracks: Ruby, don't take your love to town / If I were a carpenter / Lucille / Entertainer, The / Turn the page / MacArthur park / Folsom Prison blues / Angel eyes / Ladies love outlaws / Honky tonk heroes / Waltz me to Heaven / Looking for Suzanne / Conversation / Shine / America / I'm a ramblin' man / I've always been crazy / Luckenbach, Texas / Come with me / I ain't living long like this / Never been to Spain / Delta dawn / Mental revenge / It's only rock 'n' roll.
■ **Double LP** . . . . **CCSLP 203**
Castle Collector Series / Nov '88.
CD . . . . **CCSCD 203**
MC . . . . **CCSMC 203**
Castle Collector Series / Feb '93 / BMG / Pinnacle / Castle Communications.

COUNTRY STORE: WAYLON JENNINGS.
Tracks: Not Advised.
LP. . . . . **CST 23**
MC . . . . **CSTK 23**
Country Store / Aug '86 / BMG.

COUNTRY STORE: WAYLON JENNINGS AND WILLIE NELSON (Jennings, Waylon & Willie Nelson).
Tracks: Just to satisfy you / Why baby why / No love at all / Year 2003 minus 25, The / Would you lay with me (in a field of stone)? / Slow rollin' low / I can get off on you / Old friends / Why do I have to choose / Homeward bound / Mamas don't let your babies grow up to be cowboys / Blackjack country chains / Till I gain control again / Take it to the limit / Pick up the tempo / Don't cuss the fiddle / Wurlitzer prize / We had it all.
CD . . . . **CDCST 42**
MC . . . . **CSTK 42**
Country Store / '88 / BMG.
■ **LP.** . . . . **CST 42**
Country Store / '88.

DIAMOND SERIES: WAYLON JENNINGS.
Tracks: MacArthur Park / Cindy Oh Cindy / Games people play / Today I started loving you again / Folsom Prison blues / You've got to hide your love away / Love of the common people / Ruby, don't take your love to town / Only daddy that'll walk the line / Such a waste of love / Kentucky woman / No regrets / Honky tonk women / If I were a carpenter / Lonely weekends / Just to satisfy you.
■ **CD** . . . . **CD 90114**
Diamond Series / Apr '88.

DON'T THINK TWICE IT'S ALRIGHT.
Tracks: Don't think twice it's alright / Sally was a good old girl / Big mamou / Burning memories / Jole blon / Lorena / When sin stops love begins / Crying / Money / It's so easy / Whit lightning / Love's gonna live here / Abilene / Dream baby.
LP. . . . . **MFP 50517**
■ **MC** . . . . **TCMFP 50517**
MFP / Jun '81.

DREAMING MY DREAMS.
Tracks: Are you sure Hank done it this way? / Waymore's blues / I recall a gypsy woman / High time (you quit your lowdown ways) / I've been a long time leaving (but I'll be) / Let's all help the cowboys (sing the blues) / Door is always open, The / Let's turn back the years / She's looking good / Dreaming my dreams with you / Bob Wills is still the king.
■ **LP.** . . . . **LSA 3247**
RCA / '79.

DUKES OF HAZZARD.
Tracks: Dukes of Hazzard / Chips Corniche.
7" . . . . **GOLD 550**
RCA Golden Grooves / May '82 / BMG.

EAGLE, THE.
Tracks: Workin' cheap / What bothers me most / Eagle, The / Her man / Wrong / Where corn don't grow / Reno and me / Too close to call / Waking up with you / Old church hymns and nursery rhymes.
CD **4672602**
LP. **4672601**
■ **MC** **4672604**
Epic / Oct '90.

EARLY YEARS.
Tracks: Not Advised.
■ **LP.** . . . . **CDL 8501**
MCA / Dec '79.

FILES: VOL 1.
Tracks: I wonder just where I went wrong / Another bridge to burn / Now everybody knows / Down came the world / I'm a man of constant sorrow / Dream baby / Rime will tell the story / Stop the world / Dark side of fame, The / That's the chance I'll have to take / Cindy of

New Orleans / What's left of me / Look into my teardrops / Anita, you're dreaming / What makes a man wander / What makes a man wander (stereo mix).
LP. . . . . **BFX 15151**
Bear Family / Feb '85 / Rollercoaster Records / Swift / Direct Distribution.

FILES: VOL 10.
Tracks: Games people play / It's all over now / Thirty third of August, The / I'm gonna leave (while I still love you) / Grey eyes you know / I may never pass this way again / Lila / Willie and Laura Mac Jones / I ain't the one / Singer of sad songs / Let me stay a while / Sunday morning coming down / (I'd be a) legend in my own time / It's sure been fun (Previously unissued.) / Where love has died / Yellow haired woman.
LP. . . . . **BFX 15160**
Bear Family / '86 / Rollercoaster Records / Swift / Direct Distribution.

FILES: VOL 11.
Tracks: This time tomorrow / Life goes on / Six white horses / Pickin' white gold / Donna on my mind / Honky tonk women / Time between bottles of wine / Ragged but right / If I were a carpenter / Must you throw dirt in my face / She comes running / No regrets / Rock, salt and nails / Sick and tired / It ain't easy (Previously unissued.) / Woman, you need a man (Previously unissued.).
LP. . . . . **BFX 15161**
Bear Family / '86 / Rollercoaster Records / Swift / Direct Distribution.

FILES: VOL 12.
Tracks: Marriage on the rocks (Previously unissued.) / To beat the devil / Mississippi woman / Shadow of the gallows / Big D / Gone to Denver / Taker, The / Bridge over troubled water / What about you (Previously unissued.) / Thanks / You'll look for me / Tomorrow night in Baltimore / One of my bad habits / Suspicious minds / I knew that you'd be leavin' / Don't let the sun set on you.
LP. . . . . **BFX 15162**
Bear Family / '86 / Rollercoaster Records / Swift / Direct Distribution.

FILES: VOL 13.
Tracks: Loving her was easier / Mobile blues (Previously unissued.) / Mama, I'll sing one song for you (Previously unissued.) / Casey's last ride / Love in the hot afternoon (Previously unissued.) / I've got eyes for you / Under your spell again / Atlanta's burning (Previously unissued.) / Ghost of General Lee (Previously unissued.) / Some kind of fool (Previously unissued.) / I think it's time she learned / Same old lover man / Low down freedom / Unsatisfied / It should be easier now / Crazy arms.
LP. . . . . **BFX 15163**
Bear Family / Dec '85 / Rollercoaster Records / Swift / Direct Distribution.

FILES: VOL 14.
Tracks: Do no good woman / Sweet dream woman / Revelation / Big big love (Previously unissued.) / Ladies love outlaws / Sure didn't take him long / Nothin' worth takin' or leavin' (Previously unissued.) / Lay it down / Sandy sends her best / Come early morning (Previously unissued.) / You can have her / My God and I (Previously unissued.) / Frisco depot / Me and Bobby McGee / Black rose.
LP. . . . . **BFX 15164**
Bear Family / Dec '85 / Rollercoaster Records / Swift / Direct Distribution.

FILES: VOL 15.
Tracks: Pretend I never happened / Delta dawn / Never been to Spain / Laid back country picker (Previously unissued.) / Good time Charlie's got the blues / San Francisco Mabel Joy / Lonesome, on'ry and mean / Freedom to stay / Lisa's only seven (Previously unissued.) / Last one to leave Seattle, The (Previously unissued.) / About that woman (Previously unissued.).
LP. . . . . **BFX 15165**
Bear Family / Dec '85 / Rollercoaster Records / Swift / Direct Distribution.

FILES: VOL 2.
Tracks: I don't mind / Just for you / Baby don't be looking in my mind / Time to bum again / Falling for you / If you really want me to, I'll go / That's what you get for loving me / But that's alright / Doesn't anybody know my name / Taos New Mexico / You're gonna wonder about me / Norwegian wood / I tremble for you / Leavin' town / Beautiful Annabel Lee / Woman let me sing you a song.
LP. . . . . **BFX 15152**
Bear Family / Feb '85 / Rollercoaster Records / Swift / Direct Distribution.

FILES: VOL 3.
Tracks: In this very same room / She called me baby / Everglades, The / Sunset and Vine / She's gone gone gone / Heartaches by the number / Busted / Tiger by the tail / Heartaches for a dime / Foolin' around / Nashville bum / Tennessee / Nashville rebel / Silver ribbons / Green river / I'm a long way from home.
LP. . . . . **BFX 15153**
Bear Family / Feb '85 / Rollercoaster Records / Swift / Direct Distribution.

FILES: VOL 4.
Tracks: Hoodlum / Lang's theme / Lang's mansion / Spanish penthouse / Rush Street blues / You beat all I ever saw / Ruby don't take your love to town / Born to love you / Money cannot make the man / Yes Virginia / If the shoe fits / Young Widow Brown / John's back in town / Down came the world / Mental revenge / Road, The.
LP. . . . . **BFX 15154**
Bear Family / Mar '85 / Rollercoaster Records / Swift / Direct Distribution.

FILES: VOL 5.
Tracks: Woman don't you ever laugh at me / California sunshine / Love of the common people / You've got to hide your love away / Two streaks of steel / Destiny's child / Shutting out the light / Don't waste your time / Chet's tune / It's all over now / Lock, stock and teardrops / I fall in love too easily / She loves me / Let me talk to you / Long gone / Chokin' kind, The.
LP. . . . . **BFX 15155**
Bear Family / Mar '85 / Rollercoaster Records / Swift / Direct Distribution.

FILES: VOL 6.
Tracks: Just across the way / Listen, they're playing my song / Yes Virginia / Gentle on my mind / Crowd, The / Sorrow breaks a good man down / Wave goodbye to me / Right before my eyes / Looking at a heart that needs a home / Hangin' on / Walk on out of my mind / Julie / How long have you been there / I'm doing this for you / I've been needing someone like you / Straighten my mind.
LP. . . . . **BFX 15156**
Bear Family / May '85 / Rollercoaster Records / Swift / Direct Distribution.

FILES: VOL 7.
Tracks: Christina / You love the ground I walk on / All of me belongs to you / No one's gonna miss me / Rings of gold / How much rain can one man stand / Mt Ramona / New York City R.F.D. / You'll think of me / I got you / Such a waste of love / Only daddy that'll walk the line / Your love / Kentucky woman / See you around (on your way down) / Too far gone.
LP. . . . . **BFX 15157**
Bear Family / May '85 / Rollercoaster Records / Swift / Direct Distribution.

FILES: VOL 8.
Tracks: Poor old ugly Gladys Jones / Weakness of a man / Folsom Prison blues / Today I started loving you again / If you were mine to lose / Six strings away / Cedartown, Georgia / I lost me / Brown eyed handsome man / Alone / Something's wrong in California / Days of sand and shovels, The / Just to satisfy you / For the kids / Farewell party / Sing the blues to daddy.
LP. . . . . **BFX 15158**
Bear Family / May '85 / Rollercoaster Records / Swift / Direct Distribution.

FILES: VOL 9.
Tracks: Change of mind / Change of mind (different mix) (Previously unissued.) / Lonely weekends / Don't play the game / House song, The / Delia's gone / World of our own, A / Come stay with me / Mac Arthur Park / Long way back home / These new changing times / Cindy Oh Cindy / Mary Ann regrets / But you know I love you / Drivin' nails in the wall / Let me tell you my mind.
LP. . . . . **BFX 15159**
Bear Family / Dec '85 / Rollercoaster Records / Swift / Direct Distribution.

FOLK - COUNTRY.
Tracks: Another bridge to burn / Stop the world / Cindy of New Orleans / Look into my teardrops / Down came the world / I don't mind / Just for you / Now everybody knows / That's the chance I'll have to take / What makes a man wander / I'm a man of constant sorrow / What's left of me.
LP. . . . . **NL 90005**
■ **MC** . . . . **NK 90005**
RCA / Jan '87.

GOOD OL' BOYS.
Tracks: Good ol' boys / Storms never last.
■ **7"** . . . . **PB 9561**
RCA / Jan '81.

GREATEST HITS: WAYLON JENNINGS.
Tracks: Lonesome, on'ry and mean / Ladies love outlaws / I've always been crazy / I'm a ramblin' man / Only daddy that'll walk the line / Amanda / Honky tonk heroes / Mamas don't let your babies grow up to be cowboys / Good hearted woman / Luckenbach, Texas / Texas / Are you sure Hank done it this way.
■ **LP.** . . . . **PL 13378**
RCA / Feb '80.
CD . . . . **PD 83378**
■ **LP.** . . . . **PL 83378**
RCA / Sep '84.
■ **MC** . . . . **PK 83378**
RCA / Sep '84.
CD . . . . **ND 90304**
LP. . . . . **NL 90304**
RCA / '90 / BMG.
■ **MC** . . . . **NK 90304**
RCA / '90.

GREATEST HITS: WAYLON JENNINGS VOL.2.
Tracks: Looking for Suzanne / Conversation / Waltz me to Heaven / Dukes of Hazzard / Don't you think this outlaw bit's done got out of hand / I ain't living long like this / Come with me / America / Shine / Women do know how to carry on.
■ **CD** . . . . **PD 85325**
RCA / Feb '85.
LP. . . . . **PL 85325**
■ **MC** . . . . **PK 85325**
RCA / Feb '85.

HANGIN' TOUGH.
Tracks: Baker Street / I can't help the way I don't feel / Rose in Paradise / Crying even don't come close / Chevy van / Falling out / Deep in the west / Between fathers and sons / Crown Prince, The / Defying gravity (Executioner's song).
CD . . . . **DMCF 3360**
MCA / Apr '87 / BMG.
LP. . . . . **MCF 3360**
MC . . . . **MCFC 3360**
MCA / Mar '87 / BMG.

HEROES (see under Cash, Johnny).

HIGHWAYMAN (see under Highwayman).

HITS OF WAYLON JENNINGS, THE.
Tracks: Are you sure Hank done it this way? / Dreaming my dreams with you / I'm a ramblin' man / We had it all / This time / You can have her / Rainy day woman / Good hearted woman / Let's all help the cowboys (sing the blues) / Sweet dream woman / You ask me to / Pretend I never happened / Bob Wills is still the king.
LP. . . . . **PL 42211**
■ **MC** . . . . **PK 4211**
RCA / '79.

HONKY TONK HEROES.
Tracks: Honky tonk heroes / Old five and dimers (like me) / Willy the wandering gypsy and me / Low down freedom / Omaha / You ask me to / Ride me down easy / Ain't no God in Mexico / Black rose / We had it all.
■ **LP.** **AFL1 0240**
RCA / '79.

IN THE BEGINNING.
Tracks: Sally was a good old girl / Big mamou / Don't think twice / It's all right / It's so easy / Love's gonna live here / White lightning / Crying / Burning memories / Dream baby / Abilene / Jole blon / Money (that's what I want) / Lorena / When sin stops.
LP. . . . . **BDL 1052**
MC . . . . **BDC 1052**
Bulldog Records / Nov '83 / President Records / Jazz Music / Wellard Dist. / TKO Records Ltd.

JUST TO SATISFY YOU (Jennings, Waylon & Willie Nelson).
Tracks: Just to satisfy you / Get naked with me.
7" . . . . **RCA 224**
RCA / May '82 / BMG.
7" . . . . **RCA 366**
RCA / Oct '83 / BMG.

LADIES LOVE OUTLAWS.
Tracks: Ladies love outlaws / Never been to Spain / Sure didn't take him long / Crazy arms / Revelation / Delta dawn / Frisco depot / Thanis / I think it's time she learned / Under your spell again.
■ **LP.** . . . . **LSA 3142**
RCA / '79.

LEATHER AND LACE (Jennings, Waylon & Jessi Colter).
Tracks: You never can tell / Rainy seasons / I'll be alright / Wild side of life / Pastels and harmonies / I believe you can / What's happened to blue eyes / Storms never last / I ain't the one / You're not my same sweet baby.
■ **LP.** . . . . **RCALP 5017**
RCA / Jun '81.

LEAVIN' TOWN.
Tracks: Leavin' town / Time to bum again / If you really want me to I'll go / Baby, don't be looking in my mind / That's alright / Time will tell the story / You're gonna wonder about me / For lovin' me / Anita, you're dreaming / Doesn't anybody know my name / Falling for you / I wonder just where I went wrong.
LP. . . . . **NL 89469**
■ **MC** . . . . **NK 89469**
RCA / Mar '86.

LOST OUTLAW PERFORMANCE, THE.
Tracks: Are you ready for the country / Lonesome, on'ry and me / Waymore's blues / Amanda / Long time ago, A / Jack of diamonds / Tonight the bottle let me down / This time / Just because you ask me to / I've always been crazy / Don't you think this outlaw bit's done got out of hand / Good hearted women / Luckenbach, Texas / Honky tonk heroes / Are you sure Hank done it this way.
VHS. . . . . **PLATV 309**
Prism Video / '91 / Terry Blood Dist. / Gold & Sons / Prism Leisure PLC.

LUCKENBACH, TEXAS.
Tracks: Luckenbach, Texas / Belle of the ball.
■ **7"** . . . . **PB 0924**
RCA / Jul '77.

MAGIC OF WAYLON JENNINGS, THE.
Tracks: Sally was a good girl / Big mamou / Don't think twice it's alright / It's so easy / Love's gonna live here / White lightning / Crying / Burning memories / Dream baby / Abilene / Jole blon / Money (that's what I want) / Lorena / When sin stops.
CD . . . . **TKOCD 024**
MC . . . . **TKOCS 024**
TKO Records / Apr '92 / TKO Records Ltd / President Records.

J 4 ■ DELETED

MAMA'S DON'T LET YOUR BABIES GROW UP TO BE COWBOYS.
Tracks: Mama's don't let your babies grow up to be . / I can get off on you.
■ 7" .... PB 1198
RCA / '79.

MOST WANTED NASHVILLE REBEL.
Tracks: I'm a ramblin' man / Amanda / Can't you see / Lucille / That's alright / My baby left me / Gold dust woman / Rainy day woman / Luckenbach, Texas / Well all right / It's so easy / Maybe baby / Peggy Sue / Never been to Spain / Lonesome / On'ry and mean / Only daddy that'll walk the line.
LP. .... CL 43169
MC .... CK 43169
RCA(Special Imports Service) / Aug '84 / BMG.

MUSIC MAN.
Tracks: Clyde / It's alright / Dukes of Hazzard / Nashville wimmin / Do it again / Sweet music man / Storms never last / He went to Paris / What about you / Waltz across Texas.
■ LP. .... PL 13602
RCA / Jul '80.

NADINE.
Tracks: Nadine / Buddy Holly medley.
■ 7" .... PB 9367
RCA / '79.

NEVER COULD TOE THE MARK.
Tracks: Not Advised.
LP. .... PL 85017
■ MC .... PK 85017
RCA / Aug '84.

NEW CLASSIC WAYLON.
Tracks: Not Advised.
CD .... MCAD 42287
LP. .... MCA 42287
MC .... MCAC 42287
MCA / Jun '89 / BMG.

OL' WAYLON.
Tracks: Luckenbach, Texas (back to the basics of love) / If you see me getting smaller (With Larry Keith & Steve Pippin.) / Lucille / Sweet Caroline / I think I'm gonna kill myself / Belle of the ball / That's alright / My baby left me / Till I gain control again / Brand new goodbye song / Satin sheets (With Jessi Colter & Toni Wine) / This is getting funny (But there ain't nobody laughing).
LP. .... PL 12317
■ MC .... MK 12317
RCA / Jun '77.
■ CD .... PD 82317
RCA / Aug '85.

OLD FRIENDS (see under Nelson, Willie).

ONLY THE GREATEST.
Tracks: Not Advised.
■ LP. .... SF 8003
RCA / Jan '70 / BMG.

OUTLAWS' REUNION (see under Nelson, Willie).

OUTLAWS' REUNION, VOL.2 (see under Nelson, Willie).

OUTLAWS, THE (Jennings, Waylon & Willie Nelson).
Tracks: Not Advised.
CD .... CTS 55407
MC .... CTS 45407
Country Stars / Jan '92.

RAVE ON.
Tracks: River boy / Twelfth of never / Race is on, The / Just to satisfy you / Kisses sweeter than wine / Unchained melody / I don't believe you / Four strong winds / Love denied.
LP. .... BFX 15029
Bear Family / Sep '84 / Rollercoaster Records / Swift / Direct Distribution.

RENEGADE OUTLAW LEGEND.
Tracks: Honky tonk heroes / This time / Good hearted woman / Storms never last / Luckenbach, Texas / Dreaming my dreams / Are you sure / Hank done it this way / Amanda / Eagle, The.
VHS. .... PLATV 306
Prism / Apr '91 / Pinnacle / Midland Records.

REPLAY ON WAYLON JENNINGS.
Tracks: Not Advised.
LP. .... FEDB 5030
MC .... CFEDB 5030
Sierra / May '86.

SINGER OF SAD SONGS.
Tracks: Singer of sad songs / Sick and tired / Time between bottles of wine / Must you throw dirt in my face / No regrets / Ragged but right / Honky tonk women / She comes running / If I were a carpenter / Donna on my mind / Rock salt and nails.
LP. .... INTS 5020
MC .... INTK 5020
RCA International / Apr '80 / BMG.

SINGS BUDDY HOLLY (see under Davis, Skeeter).

TAKER, THE.
Tracks: Anita you're dreaming / That's what you get for loving me / Too far gone / Today I started loving you again / Gentle on my mind / Tonight the bottle let me down (end s1) / Ruby, don't take your love to town / Loving her was easier / Sunday morning coming down / For the kids / Taker, (The) / (I'd be a) legend in my own time.
LP. .... CBR 1038
MC .... KCBR 1038
Premier (Sony) / '84 / Sony / Pinnacle.

THEY CALL ME THE NASHVILLE REBEL.
Tracks: If you really want me to, I'll go / In this very same room / Nashville rebel / Born to love you / Down came the world / California sunshine / Chokin' kind, The / Hangin' on / Weakness in a man / Kentucky woman / Six strings away / Today I started loving again / Lonely weekends / Cedartown Georgia / Let me stay a while / Taker / Tomorrow night in Baltimore / Casey's last ride / I've got eyes for you / Unsatisfied.
■ LP. .... INTS 5097
RCA International / Mar '82.

THIS TIME.
Tracks: This time / Louisiana woman / Pick up the tempo / Slow rollin' low / Heaven or hell / It's not supposed to be that way / Slow movin' outlaw / Mona / Walkin' / If you could touch her at all.
LP. AFL1 0539
RCA / Apr '74 / BMG.

TURN THE PAGE.
Tracks: Not Advised.
LP. .... PL 85428
■ MC .... PK 85428
RCA / Aug '85.

WANTED (Jennings, Waylon & Willie Nelson).
Tracks: My heroes have always been cowboys / Honky tonk heroes / I'm looking for blue eyes / You mean to say / Suspicious minds / Good-hearted woman / Heaven or Hell / Me and Paul / Yesterday's wine / T for Texas / Put another log on the fire.
LP. .... RS 1048
RCA / Apr '76 / BMG.
■ MC .... PK 11724
RCA / Apr '76.

WAYLON.
Tracks: It's only rock 'n' roll / Living legends (a dyin' breed) / Breakin' down / Let her do the walkin' / Mental revenge / Lucille / Angel eyes / No middle ground / Lover's legalities.
LP. .... RCALP 6078
MC .... RCAK 6078
RCA / May '83 / BMG.

WAYLON AND COMPANY.
Tracks: Hold on I'm coming / Leave them boys alone / Spanish Johnny / Just to satisfy you / So you want to be a cowboy singer / I may be used / Sight for sore eyes / I'll find it where I can / Conversation / Mason Dixon lines.
LP. .... PL 84826
MC .... PK 84826
RCA / Nov '83 / BMG.
■ CD .... PD 84826
RCA / Dec '84.

WAYLON AND WILLIE (Jennings, Waylon & Willie Nelson).
Tracks: Mamas don't let your babies grow up to be cowboys / Year 2003 minus 25,The / Pick up the tempo / If you can touch her at all / Looking for a feeling / It's not supposed to be that way / I can get off on you / Don't cuss the fiddle / Gold dust woman / Couple more years, A / Wurlitzer prize / Mr. Shuck'n'jive / Roman candles / (Sittin' on) the dock of the bay / Year that Clayton Delaney died, The / Lady in the harbour / May I borrow some sugar from you / Last cowboy song, The / Heroes / Teddy bear song / Write your own songs / Old mother's locket trick,The.
LP. .... PL 12686
■ MC .... PK 12686
RCA / '79.
■ CD .... PD 84455
RCA / Dec '84.
■ LP. .... NL 85134
RCA / Mar '86.
■ MC .... NK 85134
RCA / Mar '86.
CD .... ND 85134
RCA / Nov '90 / BMG.

WAYLON LIVE.
Tracks: T for Texas / Rainy day woman / Me and Paul / Last letter, The / I'm a ramblin' man / Bob Wills is still the king / Pick up th tempo / House of the rising sun / Me and Bobby McGee / This time.
LP. .... PL 11108
■ MC .... PK 11108
RCA / '79.

WAYLON MUSIC.
Tracks: I wonder just where I went wrong / Look into my teardrops / Doesn't anybody know my name / Norwegian wood / Woman / Let me sing you a song / Young widow Brown / Green river / Mental revenge / You've got to hide your love away / Destiny's child / It's all over now / Crowd, The / Julie / No one's gonna miss me / Sing the blues to daddy / Let me tell you my mind / 33rd of August, The / Lila / Life goes on / Shadow of the gallows / Don't let the sun set on you / Tulsa / Loving her was easier / It should be easier now / Sweet dream woman / Nothin' worth takin' or leavin' / Pretend I never happened / Freedom to stay / San Francisco Mabel Joy / Got a lot going for me / All around cowboy / Nadine / I never said it was easy.
Double LP .... PL 43166
RCA / Oct '80 / BMG.

WAYLON THE RAMBLIN' MAN.
Tracks: I'm a ramblin' man / Rainy day woman / Cloudy days / Midnight rider / Standing in that Oklahoma sunshine / Hunger, The / I can't keep my hands off you / Memories of you and I / It'll be her / Amanda.
■ LP. .... LSA 3196
RCA / '79.

WHITE LIGHTNING.
Tracks: Not Advised.
CD .... CDCD 1111
Charly / Jul '93 / Charly.

WILL THE WOLF SURVIVE.
Tracks: Will the wolf survive / They ain't got em' all / Working without a net / Where does love go / Dog won't hunt, The / What you'll do when I'm gone / Suddenly single / Shadow of your distant friend,The / I've got me a woman / Devil's right hand.
LP. .... MCF 3308
MC .... MCFC 3308
MCA / Mar '86 / BMG.
CD .... MCAD 5688
MCA / '88 / BMG.

Jernigan, Doug

BLUEGRASS JAM (see under Clements, Vassar).

DOUG & BUCKY (Jernigan, Doug & Bucky Pizzarelli).
Tracks: Not Advised.
LP. .... FF 043
Flying Fish (USA) / Mar '89 / Cadillac Music / Roots Records / Projection / C.M. Distribution / Direct Distribution / Jazz Music / Duncans / A.D.A Distribution.

ROADSIDE RAG.
Tracks: Not Advised.
LP. .... FF 024
Flying Fish (USA) / Mar '89 / Cadillac Music / Roots Records / Projection / C.M. Distribution / Direct Distribution / Jazz Music / Duncans / A.D.A Distribution.

Jess & The Gingerbread

COUNTRY ROOTS.
Tracks: Not Advised.
LP. .... BSS 130
Tank / Dec '77.

UNTIL IT'S TIME.
Tracks: Not Advised.
LP. .... BSS 180
Tank / Dec '77.

Jim & Jesse

Jim & Jesse are a bluegrass act from Coeburn, Virginia. Brothers, Jim and Jesse have been regulars on the Grand Ole Opry since 1964. They made their radio debut in 1947 and signed to Capitol in 1955. However, their most productive spell was with Epic. Jim & Jesse & The Virginia Boys were to score a series of top 40 singles. These included *Cotton Mill Man*, *Diesel On My Tail*, and *Freight Train*. In 1982, they teamed up with Charlie Louvin for a hit single. They have released around 50 bluegrass albums on the labels; Old Dominion, MSR, Columbia, CMH and Cannan. (Maurice Hope)

CLASSIC RECORDINGS (1952-1955).
Tracks: I'll wash your love from my heart / Just wondering why / Are you missing me / I will always be waiting for you / Virginia waltz / Are you lost in sin / Look for me (I'll be there) / Purple heart / Air mail special / My little honeysuckle rose / Waiting for a message / Too many tears / My darling's in heaven / Two arms to hold me / Is it true? / Memory of you, A / I'll wear the banner / My garden of love / Tears of regret / I'll see you tonight (in my dreams).
CD .... BCD 15635
Bear Family / Apr '92 / Rollercoaster Records / Swift / Direct Distribution.

EPIC BLUEGRASS HITS,THE.
Tracks: Nine pound hammer / Are you missing me / It's a long, long way to the top of the world / Cotton mill man / She left me standing on the mountain / Take my ring from your finger / Don't say goodbye if you love me / Drifting and dreaming of you / Why not confess / I wish you knew.
LP. .... SS 20
Rounder / Dec '85 / Projection / Roots Records / Swift / C.M. Distribution / Topic Records / Jazz Music / Hot Shot / A.D.A Distribution / Direct Distribution.
MC .... SSC 20

■ DELETED

Rounder / '88 / Projection / Roots Records / Swift / C.M. Distribution / Topic Records / Jazz Music / Hot Shot / A.D.A Distribution / Direct Distribution.

HANDFUL OF GOOD SEEDS, A (Jim & Jesse & the Virginia Boys).
Tracks: Family who prays shall never part, The / Born again / How great thou art / On the wings of a snow white dove / Truth on the mountain / Family Bible / Little white church, The / Jesus is the key to the kingdom / Two thousand years ago / River of Jordan / Walking my Lord up Calvary's hill / Matthew twenty four.
LP. . . . . CGS 8512
MC . . . . . WC 8512
Canaan / May '82 / Word Records (UK) / Sony.

IN THE TRADITION (Jim & Jesse & the Virginia Boys).
Tracks: Not Advised.
CD . . . . . CD 0234
LP. . . . . ROUNDER 0234
MC . . . . . ROUNDER 0234C
Rounder / Aug '88 / Projection / Roots Records / Swift / C.M. Distribution / Topic Records / Jazz Music / Hot Shot / A.D.A Distribution / Direct Distribution.

JIM & JESSE STORY.
Tracks: Not Advised.
LP. . . . . CMH 9022
CMH (USA) / '88 / C.M. Distribution / Projection.

JIM & JESSE TODAY.
Tracks: Not Advised.
LP. . . . . CMH 6250
CMH (USA) / '88 / C.M. Distribution / Projection.

Jimenez, Flaco

One of the leading contributors to the Tex-Mex sound, Flaco Jimenez grew up amidst musical surroundings,his father Santiago being an accomplished accordianist and RCA recording artist. The younger Jimenez enjoyed regional success before gaining national, and international, attention via recordings in the company of such as Bob Dylan, Doug Sahm and Ry Cooder during the 1970's. A decade or so later he moved closer to country music audiences as a member of the quartet the Texas Tornados, which re-united him with Sahm as well as Augie Meyers and Fredie Fender. (Tony Byworth)

ACCORDION STRIKES BACK.
Tracks: Not Advised.
LP. . . . . WF 037
MC . . . . . WF 037C
Waterfront / Oct '87 / SRD / Jazz Music / A.D.A Distribution / C.M. Distribution.

ARIBA EL NORTE.
Tracks: Not Advised.
CD . . . . . CDZS 92
LP. . . . . ZS 92
Zensor (Germany) / Mar '90 / New Note / A.D.A Distribution / Direct Distribution / Topic Records / C.M. Distribution.

AT THE MILKY WAY.
Tracks: Not Advised.
MC . . . . . PF 0101
Waterfront / Jul '88 / SRD / Jazz Music / A.D.A Distribution / C.M. Distribution.

AY TE DEJO EN SAN ANTONIO.
Tracks: Not Advised.
LP. . . . . ARHOOLIE 3021
Arhoolie (USA) / '86 / Pinnacle / Cadillac Music / Swift / Projection / Hot Shot / A.D.A Distribution / Jazz Music.
MC . . . . . C 3021
Arhoolie (USA) / '88 / Pinnacle / Cadillac Music / Swift / Projection / Hot Shot / A.D.A Distribution / Jazz Music.
CD . . . . . ARHCD 318
Arhoolie (USA) / Mar '93 / Pinnacle / Cadillac Music / Swift / Projection / Hot Shot / A.D.A Distribution / Jazz Music.

EL SONIDO DE SAN ANTONIO.
Tracks: Not Advised.
LP. . . . . ARHOOLIE 3014
Arhoolie (USA) / May '81 / Pinnacle / Cadillac Music / Swift / Projection / Hot Shot / A.D.A Distribution / Jazz Music.
MC . . . . . C 3014
Arhoolie (USA) / '88 / Pinnacle / Cadillac Music / Swift / Projection / Hot Shot / A.D.A Distribution / Jazz Music.
CD . . . . . ARH 318
Arhoolie (USA) / '92 / Pinnacle / Cadillac Music / Swift / Projection / Hot Shot / A.D.A Distribution / Jazz Music.

ENTRE HUMO Y BOTELLAS.
Tracks: Not Advised.
LP. . . . . MUNICH 141
Munich / Jun '89 / C.M. Distribution / Swift / Cadillac Music / A.D.A Distribution / Hot Shot / Topic Records / Direct Distribution / New Note.

FLACO JIMENEZ & HIS CONJUNTO.
Tracks: Not Advised.
LP. . . . . ARHOOLIE 3007
Arhoolie (USA) / May '81 / Pinnacle / Cadillac Music / Swift / Projection / Hot Shot / A.D.A Distribution / Jazz Music.

FLACO'S AMIGOS.
Tracks: La tumba sera el final / Did I tell you / Jennette / Te quiero mas / Mi primer amor / Free Mexican air force / Lucerito / Espero tu regreso / Poquita fe / Feria polka / Para toda la vida / I'm gonna love you like there is no tomorrow / Yo quisiera saber / Atotonilco.
CD . . . . . ARHCD 3027
LP. . . . . ARHOOLIE 3027
MC . . . . . C 3027
Arhoolie (USA) / '88 / Pinnacle / Cadillac Music / Swift / Projection / Hot Shot / A.D.A Distribution / Jazz Music.
CD . . . . . COOKCD 017
MC . . . . . COOKC 017
Cooking Vinyl / Oct '88 / Revolver-APT.
■ LP. . . . . COOK 017
Cooking Vinyl / Oct '88.

OPEN UP YOUR HEART.
Tracks: Open up your heart / Riding high in Texas.
7" . . . . . WFS 10
Waterfront / Apr '85 / SRD / Jazz Music / A.D.A Distribution / C.M. Distribution.

PARTNERS.
Tracks: Change partners / Marina / Carmelita / El puente roto / Accross the borderline / Me esta matando / Girl from Texas, The / West Texas waltz / Las golondrinas / Eres un encanto / Don't worry baby.
CD 7599268222
MC 7599268224
WEA / Aug '92 / WEA.

SAN ANTONIO SOUND, THE (Jimenez, Flaco Y Su Conjunto).
Tracks: Not Advised.
MC . . . . . WF 019C
Waterfront / '85 / SRD / Jazz Music / A.D.A Distribution / C.M. Distribution.
LP. . . . . WF 019
Waterfront / Apr '85 / SRD / Jazz Music / A.D.A Distribution / C.M. Distribution.

SON OF SANTIAGO.
Tracks: Son of Santiago.
12" . . . . . WFT 15
Waterfront / Oct '85 / SRD / Jazz Music / A.D.A Distribution / C.M. Distribution.

TEX MEX BREAKDOWN (Jimenez, Flaco Y Su Conjunto).
Tracks: Open your heart / Mexican Joe / Cielito lindo / La bamba / La moiadita / El Rancho Grande / El pantalon blue / San Antonio rose / Polish polka / For the good times.
LP. . . . . SNTF 895
Sonet / Jul '87 / Swift / C.M. Distribution / Roots Records / Jazz Music / Sonet Records / Cadillac Music / Projection / Wellard Dist. / Hot Shot.

UN MOJADA SIN LICENCIA.
Tracks: Not Advised.
CD . . . . . ARHCD 396
Ace / Jun '93 / Pinnacle / Hot Shot / Jazz Music / Complete Record Co. Ltd.

VIVA SEGUIN.
Tracks: Viva sequin / La botellita / Hasta la vista / Los amores del flaco / Mi duice amor / Horalia / Arriba el norte / Polka town / La piedrera / Viajando en polka marianela / Adios muchachos.
LP. . . . . FMSL 2003
Rogue / Jun '86 / Roots Records / Projection / C.M. Distribution / Jazz Music / A.D.A Distribution / Swift / Sterns Records.

Jimenez, Santiago

EL MERO MERO (Jimenez, Santiago Jnr).
Tracks: Not Advised.
LP. . . . . ARHOOLIE 3016
MC . . . . . C 3016
Arhoolie (USA) / '88 / Pinnacle / Cadillac Music / Swift / Projection / Hot Shot / A.D.A Distribution / Jazz Music.
CD . . . . . ARH 317
Arhoolie (USA) / '92 / Pinnacle / Cadillac Music / Swift / Projection / Hot Shot / A.D.A Distribution / Jazz Music.

SANTIAGO JIMENEZ WITH FLACO JIMENEZ.
Tracks: Not Advised.
LP. . . . . ARHOOLIE 3013
Arhoolie (USA) / May '81 / Pinnacle / Cadillac Music / Swift / Projection / Hot Shot / A.D.A Distribution / Jazz Music.
MC . . . . . C 3013
Arhoolie (USA) / '88 / Pinnacle / Cadillac Music / Swift / Projection / Hot Shot / A.D.A Distribution / Jazz Music.

STRIKES AGAIN (Jimenez, Santiago Jnr).
Tracks: Not Advised.
LP. . . . . ARHOOLIE 3020
Arhoolie (USA) / Mar '85 / Pinnacle / Cadillac Music / Swift / Projection / Hot Shot / A.D.A Distribution / Jazz Music.

TRADICION Y FAMILIA (Jimenez, Santiago Jnr).
Tracks: Not Advised.
LP. . . . . SPD 1025
Special Delivery / Feb '90 / Revolver-APT / A.D.A Distribution / Topic Records / Direct Distribution / Jazz Music / C.M. Distribution.
CD . . . . . SPDCD 1025
■ MC . . . . . SPDC 1025
Special Delivery / Feb '90.

Johnnie & Jack

First known as the Dixie Early Birds on Nashville radio station WSIX, Johnnie Wright (b. 1914) and Jack Anglin (1916-1963) went simply by their christian names when they formed their band the Tennessee Mountain Boys in 1940. It took them another decade to make their chart debut with *Poison love* (1951), which paved the way for regular hits throughout the 1950's. Kitty Wells, who married Anglin, was a member of their show and was thinking about retiring when her own star began to shine. After Anglin's death, in a car crash en route to a memorial service for Patsy Cline, Wright continued his career working with his wife and family. Johnnie and Jack's recordings have been overlooked in recent years - until Bear Family issued its 6 CD, 180 song box-set covering the duo's complete recording career, beginning with Apollo and King Records, and continuing on RCA. (Tony Byworth)

JOHNNIE AND JACK AND THE TENNESSEE MOUNTAIN BOYS (Johnnie & Jack & The Tennessee Mountain Boys).
Tracks: Lord, watch over my Daddy / There's no housing shortage in heaven / Love in the first degree / Too many blues / This is the end / Paper boy / Sing Tom Kitty / Jole Blon / I'll be listening / This world can't stand long / Old country church, The / I heard my name on the radio / Turn your radio on / He will set your fields on fire / What about you / For old times sake / Just when I need you / She went with a smile / Trials & tribulations / Buried alive / I heard my saviour call / Pray together & we'll stay together / Shout / You better get down on your knees & pray / Too much sinning / Jesus hits like an atom bomb / Too far from God / Jesus remembered me / Poison love / Lonesome / I'm gonna love you one more time / Smile on my lips, A / Take my ring from your finger / I can't tell my heart that / Cryin' heat blues / Let your conscience be your guide / Hummingbird / How can I believe in you / You tried to ruin my name / Ashes of love / Three ways of knowing / When you want a little loving / You can't fool God / Precious memories / Shake my mothers hand for me / When the saviour reached down for me / Slow poison / But I love you just the same / Just for tonight / Don't show off / Heart trouble / Two timing blues / I've gone & done it again / Don't let the stars get in your eyes / Only one I ever loved I lost, The / Borrowed diamonds / Private property / S.O.S. / Called from Potter's field / I'll live with God (to die no more) / Angel's rock me to sleep / Eastern gate, The / Hank Williams will live forever / South in New Orleans / You're my downfall / Winner of your heart, The / Don't say goodbye if you love me / Pig latin song, The / Love trap / Cheated out of love / From the manger to the cross / I'm ready to go / God put a rainbow in the cloud / Don't give away your bible / Crazy worried mind / Love's a pleasure not a habit in Mexico / You've got me in your power / Dynamite kisses / I loved you better than you knew / Pickup date / I get so lonely / You're just what the doctor ordered / I ain't got time / All the time / Goodnight sweetheart, goodnight / Honey, I need you / Kiss crazy baby / Beware of it / Sincerely / Carry on / No one dear but you / We live in two different worlds / So lovely baby / Look out / Don't waste your tears / Weary moments / Dream when you're lonely / Tom cat's kittens / Feet of clay / I want to be loved / You can't divorce my heart / Baby, it's in the making / I wonder why you say goodbye / Love, love, love / What's the reason I'm not pleasing you / Love fever / Live & let live / When my blue moon turns to gold again / Why not confess / Banana boat song, The / Mister Clock / Love me now / If tears would bring you back / That's why I'm leavin' / Oh boy, I love her / Baby I need you / Nothing but sweet lies / Move it on over / No one will ever know / I don't mean to cry / I wonder where you are tonight / Slowly / Wedding bells / I never can come back to you / You are my sunshine / Stop the world (& let me off) / Camel walk stroll / I've seen this movie before / Yeah / Leave our moon alone / Lonely island pearl / That's the way the cookie crumbles / Just when I needed you / With a smile on my lips / What do you know about heartaches / I wonder if you know / It's just the idea / Sailor man / Wild & wicked world / Sweetie pie / Happy, lucky love / Just like you / Dreams come true / She loves me no more / Country music has gone to town / Talkin' eyes / Lonesome night blues / Love problems / I'm always by myself when I'm alone / Smiles & tears / Uncle John's bongos / Let my heart be broken / Sweet baby / The moon is high & so am I / Thirty six, twenty two, thirty six / What do you think of her now / Bye bye love / Foolin' around / Waterloo / Little bitty tear, A / I overlooked an orchid / You'll never get a better chance than this.
CD Set . . . . . BCD 15553
Bear Family / Jun '92 / Rollercoaster Records / Swift / Direct Distribution.

TENNESSEE MOUNTAIN BOYS.
Tracks: When my blue moon turns to gold again / Slowly / Dream when you're lonely / I never can come back to you / I wonder where you are tonight / Sweet lies / You are my sunshine / Love fever / I wonder when you said goodbye / Wedding bells / I don't mean to cry.
LP. . . . . HAT 3087
MC . . . . . HATC 3087
Stetson / '88 / Crusader Marketing Co. / Swift / Wellard Dist. / Midland Records / C.M. Distribution.

Johnson Mountain Boys

Washington - based, traditional bluegrass group, formed in 1979 by Dudley O'Connell (guitar/lead vocals), Eddie Stubbs (fiddle/vocals), Richard Underwood (banjo/vocals) and David McLaughlin (mandolin/vocals). O'Connell and Stubbs had also worked as a duo since around 1975. They recorded eight albums for Rounder, amongst which was *At the old schoolhouse* their farewell concert in Lucketts, Virginia on 20.02.1988. By then Tony Adams and Marshall Wilbourn (both since became members of the Lynn Morris Band, bassist Wilbourn being married to Morris) joined at the expense of Underwood. Due to demand from fans and fellow musicians alike they reformed on a part-time basis in May 1989 after a brief break. Since then they've gradually got back to playing more festivals and have re-affirmed their position as leading exponents of bluegrass. On their comeback, Earl Yager took over on bass, a result of Wilbourn's departure - Adams too was back in the fold. An album, *Blue diamond* , was released in 1993 showing them to be back at their best. (Maurice Hope)

AT THE OLD SCHOOLHOUSE (Live Farewell Album).
Tracks: Intro / Black mountain blues / Let the whole world talk / Long journey home / Bluest man in town / John Henry / Steel driving man, The / Weathered gray stone / Unwanted love / Ricestrow / Waltz across Texas / Five speed / Dream of a miner's child / Georgia stomp / Sweetest gift / I've found a hiding place / With body and soul / Orange blossom special / Get down on your knees and pray / Going to Georgia / Now just suppose / Don't you call my name / Do you call that religion / Daniel prayed / Wake up Susan.
LP . . . . **ROUNDER 00260**
MC . . . . **ROUNDER 00260C**
Rounder / Projection / Roots Records / Swift / C.M. Distribution / Topic Records / Jazz Music / Hot Shot / A.D.A Distribution / Direct Distribution.

BLUE DIAMOND.
Tracks: Duncan & Brady (He's been gone so long) / My better days / It don't bring you back to me / Christine Leroy / See God's ark movin' / Blue diamond mines / Teardrops like raindrops / Our last goodbye / Future remains, The / You done me wrong / Roll on blues / There goes my love / Only a hobo / Harbor of love.
CD . . . . **CDROU 0293**
Rounder / Apr '93 / Projection / Roots Records / Swift / C.M. Distribution / Topic Records / Jazz Music / Hot Shot / A.D.A Distribution / Direct Distribution.
MC . . . . **ROU 0293C**
Rounder / May '93 / Projection / Roots Records / Swift / C.M. Distribution / Topic Records / Jazz Music / Hot Shot / A.D.A Distribution / Direct Distribution.

FAVOURITES.
Tracks: Not Advised.
CD . . . . **CD 11509**
Rounder / '88 / Projection / Roots Records / Swift / C.M. Distribution / Topic Records / Jazz Music / Hot Shot / A.D.A Distribution / Direct Distribution.

JOHNSON MOUNTAIN BOYS.
Tracks: Not Advised.
LP . . . . **ROUNDER 0135**
MC . . . . **ROUNDER 0135C**
Rounder / '88 / Projection / Roots Records / Swift / C.M. Distribution / Topic Records / Jazz Music / Hot Shot / A.D.A Distribution / Direct Distribution.

LET THE WHOLE WORLD TALK.
Tracks: Let the whole world talk / Maury river blues / Memories cover everything I own / He said if I be lifted up / Goodbye to the blues / Virginia waltz / Maybe you will change your mind / Memories that we shared / Sweeter love than yours, A / I'll never know / Shouting in the air / Beneath the old Southern skies.
LP . . . . **REU 1017**
Rounder Europa (USA) / Jun '87 / Pinnacle.
CD . . . . **CD 0225**
Rounder / '88 / Projection / Roots Records / Swift / C.M. Distribution / Topic Records / Jazz Music / Hot Shot / A.D.A Distribution / Direct Distribution.
LP . . . . **ROUNDER 0225**
MC . . . . **ROUNDER 0225C**
Rounder / Aug '88 / Projection / Roots Records / Swift / C.M. Distribution / Topic Records / Jazz Music / Hot Shot / A.D.A Distribution / Direct Distribution.

LIVE AT THE BIRCHMERE.
Tracks: Not Advised.
LP . . . . **ROUNDER 0191**
Rounder / Jul '84 / Projection / Roots Records / Swift / C.M. Distribution / Topic Records / Jazz Music / Hot Shot / A.D.A Distribution / Direct Distribution.
MC . . . . **ROUNDER 0191C**
Rounder / Aug '88 / Projection / Roots Records / Swift / C.M. Distribution / Topic Records / Jazz Music / Hot Shot / A.D.A Distribution / Direct Distribution.

REQUESTS.
Tracks: Not Advised.
CD . . . . **CD 0246**
LP . . . . **ROUNDER 0246**
MC . . . . **ROUNDER 0246C**
Rounder / Aug '88 / Projection / Roots Records / Swift / C.M. Distribution / Topic Records / Jazz Music / Hot Shot / A.D.A Distribution / Direct Distribution.

WALLS OF TIME.
Tracks: Not Advised.
LP . . . . **ROUNDER 0160**
MC . . . . **ROUNDER 0160C**
Rounder / '88 / Projection / Roots Records / Swift / C.M. Distribution / Topic Records / Jazz Music / Hot Shot / A.D.A Distribution / Direct Distribution.

WE'LL STILL SING ON.
Tracks: Not Advised.
LP . . . . **ROUNDER 0205**
Rounder / Dec '85 / Projection / Roots Records / Swift / C.M. Distribution / Topic Records / Jazz Music / Hot Shot / A.D.A Distribution / Direct Distribution.
MC . . . . **ROUNDER 0205C**
Rounder / Aug '88 / Projection / Roots Records / Swift / C.M. Distribution / Topic Records / Jazz Music / Hot Shot / A.D.A Distribution / Direct Distribution.

WORKING CLOSE.
Tracks: Tomorrow I'll be gone / Misery loves company / I'm still to blame / You loved died like the rose / Call his name / Five speed / Waves on the sea, The / Don't throw your life away / Say you'll take me back / Day has passed, The / Granite hill / Are you afraid to die.
LP . . . . **ROUNDER 0185**
MC . . . . **ROUNDER 0185C**
Rounder / '88 / Projection / Roots Records / Swift / C.M. Distribution / Topic Records / Jazz Music / Hot Shot / A.D.A Distribution / Direct Distribution.

Johnson, Daniel

ARTISTIC VICES.
Tracks: Not Advised.
LP . . . . **SDE 9237**
Shimmy Disc / Mar '92 / Revolver-APT.

HI, HOW ARE YOU?.
Tracks: Not Advised.
LP . . . . **FU 4**
Furthur / Apr '88 / RTM / Pinnacle.
LP . . . . **HMS 117**
Homestead / Oct '88 / SRD.
MC . . . . **HMS 117C**
Homestead / Sep '88 / SRD.

Johnson, Michael

Michael Johnson was born in 1945 in Denver, Colorado. A singer/songwriter, he was a former member, along with John Denver, of The Chad Mitchell Trio in 1968. Johnson's compositions have seen him top the country charts with *Give Me Wings*, and *The Moon Is Over My Shoulder*. He has hade further top ten successes in the late 1980's and apart from RCA, Johnson has recorded for Atlantic and EMI. (Maurice Hope)

ALBUM.
Tracks: Sailing without a sail / Foolish / Dancin' tonight / Two in love / Ridin' in the sky / Bluer than blue / Almost like being in love / 25 words or less / Gypsy woman / When you come home.
■ **LP** . . . . **AMS 2002**
A&M / '79.

ALMOST LIKE BEING IN LOVE.
Tracks: Almost like being in love / Ridin' in the sky.
■ **7"** . . . . **AM 504**
EMI-America / '78.

BLUER THAN BLUE.
Tracks: Bluer than blue / Two in love.
■ **7"** . . . . **AM 501**
EMI-America / May '78.

DIALOGUE.
Tracks: Not Advised.
■ **LP** . . . . **AML 3006**
A&M / Dec '79.

LIFE'S A BITCH.
Tracks: Roller coaster run / True love / Oh Rosalee / Give me wings / Jacques Costeau / Empty heart / That's what your love does to me / Hangin' on / Life's a bitch / Crying shame / Magic time / That's that / Samson and Delilah / Moon is still over her shoulder / Gotta learn to love without you / Some people's lives.
LP . . . . **PL 90312**
RCA / Mar '89 / BMG.
■ **MC** . . . . **PK 90312**
RCA / Mar '89.
■ **CD** . . . . **PD 90312**
RCA / Mar '89.

THAT'S THAT.
Tracks: Rollercoaster run (up too slow, down too fast) / I will whisper your name / Crying shame / It must be you (Duet with Juice Newton.) / That's that / Oh Rosalee / Too soon to tell / Diamond dreams / Some people's lives.
■ **MC** . . . . **PK 86715**
RCA / Mar '88.
■ **LP** . . . . **PL 86715**
RCA / Mar '88.

Jolene

JOLENE WITH PART TWO.
Tracks: Not Advised.
MC . . . . **NC 108**
Neptune / Aug '78 / Neptune Tapes / A.D.A Distribution.
LP . . . . **NA 108**
Neptune / Jan '79 / Neptune Tapes / A.D.A Distribution.
■ **LP** . . . . **BGC 299**
Country House / '81.

TOGETHER AGAIN.
Tracks: Daydreams about night things / Pure love / Four strong winds / Clap your hands / Together again / Love is a rose / In my hour of darkness / Silver threads and golden needles / Statues without hearts / 57 chevrolet / Keeps right on a hurtin' / Blue eyes crying in the rain / I saw the light.
LP . . . . **BGC 252**
Country House / Aug '80 / Duncans / BGS Productions Ltd.
■ **MC** . . . . **KBGC 252**
Country House / Aug '80.

Jones, Al

AL JONES (Jones, Al/Frank Necessary/ Spruce Mountain Boys).
Tracks: Not Advised.
LP . . . . **ROUNDER 0050**
Rounder / '88 / Projection / Roots Records / Swift / C.M. Distribution / Topic Records / Jazz Music / Hot Shot / A.D.A Distribution / Direct Distribution.

Jones, David Lynn

HARD TIME ON EASY STREET.
Tracks: Bonnie Jean / High ridin' heroes / Home of my heart / Rogue, The / No easy way out / Living in the promised land / Tonight in America / Valley of a thousand years / Hard time on Easy Street / See how far we've come.
LP **832 518-1**
Mercury / Oct '87 / PolyGram.
CD **832 518-2**
■ **MC** **832 518-4**
Mercury / Oct '87.

Jones, George

George Glenn Jones was born September 12, 1931 in Saratoga, Texas and has, through the years, influenced a host of performers with his undiluted honky-tonk brand of country which has brought endless praise from fellow country talents. Jones' unequalled gut-stirring vocals extract every trace of feeling from even the most ordinary song. When only 11, Jones (the youngest of 8) did some singing and played his first chords at the local church, where his mother played piano. George had already been the proud owner of that treasured first guitar since he was nine. Looking for work, his hard-drinking father took the family to Beaumont, Texas, where on the streets George would sing the songs of Grand Ole Opry favourites Roy Acuff and Bill Monroe. Following high school, Jones did some clubs with his band and hosted a radio programme, before joining the Marines at the time of the Korean war . On discharge, he played some rockabilly under the pseudonyms of Thumper Jones and Hank Smith, before meeting Pappy Daily and signing to Starday in 1953. He gained his first chart success in 1955 with *Why baby why* , reaching No. 4 on Billboard - at this time George's vocals were still heavily influenced by Hank Williams. In 1956 he appeared on Louisiana Hayride, while the following year saw Starday merging with Mercury Records. Two years later, Jones had his first country No. 1, singing *White lightning* (written by 'Big Bopper' J.P. Richardson). Since this time George has had eight other country chart toppers including two more with Mercury, *Tender years (1961) and She thinks I still care* (1962). Billboard and Cashbox magazine voted George Number One Male Vocalist in 1962 and 1963. In 1963 he teamed up with southern lady Melba Montgomery - immediately reaching number 3 on Billboard with *We must have been out of our minds* , followed by six lesser chart entries (1963 - 1967), on United Artists and Musicor. Previously, George had gained two chart successes with Margie Singleton (Mercury) and in 1957 *Yearning* with Jeanette Hicks on Starday. The next chapter in Jones' career saw him once again working with Pappy Daily and joining Musicor in 1965, with whom he charted regularly. Surprisingly, *Walk through this world with me* was the only No. 1, though *When the green grass grows over me* , *I'll share my world with you* and *Good year for the roses* (1970) were near misses. He also had a moderate success dueting with Brenda Carter on *Milwaukee, here I come* . George again changed labels in 1972, joining producer Billy Sherrill at Epic - the same label as his third wife Tammy Wynette (married 1969 - 1975). After the late sixties, he became more reliant on drink and then drugs. His often stormy marriage was followed by hell-bent self-destruction, despite which Jones gained many accolades. He was voted CMA's Best Male Vocalist in both 1980 and 1981. Rolling Stone had previously given their seal of approval back in 1976, giving him the best country male vocalist award. During the early seventies George and Tammy could do no wrong - on record. As a duet they registered three number ones between 1971 and 1976 *We're gonna hold on* , *Golden ring* and *Near you* . *Two storey house* was a near miss in 1980. George Jones' best work lays with his Epic recordings led by chart toppers *The Grand Tour* , *The Door* (both 1974) and award winning *He stopped loving her today* which was CMA's song of the year in 1980 and 1981 - a unique feat. Jones' surreal deliveries of hard luck barroom ballads also gained him admirers from the pop field, James Taylor accompanied Jones on *Bartender blues* (1978), while Linda Ronstadt, Elvis Costello, Dr. Hook, Willie Nelson and Johnny Paycheck appeared on his 1979 *My very special guests* release. This was recorded when Jones was at his lowest ebb, around this time he was tagged 'No show Jones' for not turning up for dates. The drink/drug habit eventually resulted in him being admitted to hosptal for a few weeks in Birmingham, Alabama. Other acts who've charted with Jones during the eighties include Ray Charles, Johnny Paycheck, Shelby Lynne, Merle Haggard (*Yesterday's wine* was a No. 1), Lacy J. Dalton and Brenda Lee (the latter's effort coming from his 1984 album *Lady's choice* on Epic). George's early eighties hits include such chart toppers as *Still doin' time* and *I always get lucky* , along with a host of other worthy contenders *Tennessee whiskey* , *Same ole me* and *Who's gonna fill their shoes* being among them. Jones affectionately known as 'The Possum', may no longer be collecting number one singles in the way he used to, but the likes of Garth Brooks, Emmylou Harris and Ricky Scaggs still cite George as country's greatest singer around. That's not to mention Randy Travis who at the back end of 1990 made the upper reaches of Billboard's singles charts with*A few good ole boys* on Warner Brothers. On September 30, 1992, George Jones received country music's greatest honour, induction into Nashville's Country Music Hall of Fame, an event which brought a standing ovation from the capacity audience attending the 26th annual CMA Awards at Nashville's Grand Ole Opry House. A couple of weeks later his latest single entered the charts, a star-studded recording which included Clint Black, Garth Brooks, Vince Gill, Alan Jackson, Pam Tillis and Travis Tritt in the chorus line-up. The appropriate title *I don't need your rockin' chair* , provided another confirmation that he remains an active force on the 1990's country scene. Seven months later he made a precise reference to age when, receiving the Pioneer Award at the Academy of Country Music presentations in Los Angeles, he reminded the radio DJ's not to overlook the oldtimers in the business while playing the youngsters "We're not dead yet" he reminded them. (Tony Byworth)

15 GOLDEN CLASSICS VOL.1.
Tracks: Not Advised.
LP. 20032
MC 40032
Astan (USA) / Nov '84.

15 GOLDEN CLASSICS VOL.2.
Tracks: Not Advised.
LP. 20033
MC 40033
Astan (USA) / Nov '84.

16 GREATEST HITS: GEORGE JONES.
Tracks: Not Advised.
LP. . . . . SLP 3021
Starday (USA) / Apr '87 / Crusader Marketing Co.
MC . . . . GT 53021
Gusto (USA) / Apr '87.
■ **CD** . . . . CD 1012
Gusto (USA) / '88.

20 FAVOURITES OF GEORGE JONES.
Tracks: She thinks I still care / Race is on, The / Little bitty tear, A / Running bear.
■ **LP.** . . . . LBR 1009
Liberty / Jan '80.

20 GOLDEN PIECES: GEORGE JONES.
Tracks: Good year for the roses, A / Developing my pictures / Tender tears / Say it's not you / From here to the door / If my heart had windows / Favourite lies / Accidentally on purpose / Where grass won't grow / Sweet dreams / Things have gone to pieces / White lightning / 4-0-33 / Take me / I'm a people / I'm wasting good paper / Old brush arbors / Love bug / Walk through this world with me / Race is on, The.
LP. . . . . BDL 2035
MC . . . . BDC 2035
Bulldog Records / Feb '86 / President Records / Jazz Music / Wellard Dist. / TKO Records Ltd.

ALL-TIME GREATEST HITS.
Tracks: Race is on, The / My favourite lies / Tender years / Window up above / She thinks I still care / White lightnin' / Walk through this world with me / She's mine / I'll share my world with you / Why, baby, why.
LP. 31567
■ **MC** 4031567
CBS / '78 / Sony.

ANNIVERSARY.
Tracks: We can make it / Loving you could never be better / Bartender blues / Picture of me / What my woman can't do / Nothing ever hurt me / Once you've had the best / Grand time / Same ol' me.
■ **Double LP** . . . . EPC 22142
Epic / '83.

BEST OF SACRED MUSIC.
Tracks: Not Advised.
LP. . . . . GT 0135
Gusto (USA) / Mar '88.

BLUE MOON OF KENTUCKY.
Tracks: I get lonely in a hurry / Love's gonna live here / Holiday for love / Imitation of love / Beggar to a king / What's money / She's lonesome again / Brown to blue / We could / Making the rounds / Lovin' lies / Same sweet girl / Please be my love / Blue moon of Kentucky / Yes I know why / Precious jewel / Matthew twenty four / Beacon in the night / I heard you crying in your sleep / In the shadow of a lie.
■ **LP.** . . . . EMS 1251
Liberty / Nov '87.
■ **MC** . . . . TCEMS 1251
Liberty / Nov '87.

BLUEGRASS HOOTENNANY (Jones, George & Melba Montgomery).
Tracks: Not Advised.
LP. . . . . HAT 3096
MC . . . . HATC 3096
Stetson / Feb '89 / Crusader Marketing Co. / Swift / Wellard Dist. / Midland Records / C.M. Distribution.

BURN THE HONKY TONK DOWN.
Tracks: Burn the honky-tonk down / Developing my pictures / Feeling single - seeing double / Where grass won't grow / Your angel steps out of heaven / I cried myself awake / Milwaukie here I come / Beneath still waters / I'll follow you (up our cloud) / Good year for the roses, A / Small time labouring man / Selfishness man, The / Wandering soul.
LP. . . . . SS 15
Rounder / Dec '88 / Projection / Roots Records / Swift / C.M. Distribution / Topic Records / Jazz Music / Hot Shot / A.D.A Distribution / Direct Distribution.

COLD COLD HEART.
Tracks: You comb her hair / Jonesy / Once a day / World's worst loser / Old brush arbors / Yes, I know why / Jambalaya / Liberty / Cold, cold heart / Just don't like this kind of livin'.
LP. . . . . ALEB 2304
MC . . . . ZCALB 2304
Allegiance / Apr '84.

COLLECTION: GEORGE JONES.
Tracks: Not Advised.
CD . . . . KNCD 13051
■ **MC** . . . . KNMC 13051
Knight / Apr '90.

COUNTRY STARS (see under Wynette, Tammy).

COUNTRY STARS LIVE (see under Wynette, Tammy).

COUNTRY STORE: GEORGE JONES.
Tracks: Yesterday's wine / Almost persuaded / Even the bad times (are good) / Burning bridges / Why baby why / Roll over Beethoven / Hallelujah, I love you so / We can make it / Bartender blues / Wine coloured roses (Only on CD.) / Who's gonna fill their shoes (Only on CD.) / Radio lover (Only on CD.) / He stopped loving her today (Only on CD.) / Size seven round (made of gold) / Proud Mary / Shine on / She thinks I still care / Some day my day will come.
CD . . . . CDCST 12
MC . . . . CSTK 12
Country Store / Nov '88 / BMG.
■ **LP.** . . . . CST 12
Country Store / Nov '88.

COUNTRY STORE: GEORGE JONES & TAMMY WYNETTE (Jones, George & Tammy Wynette).
Tracks: We're not the jet set / Take me / Ceremony, The / Golden ring / Two storey house / We're gonna hold on / We loved it anyway / Pair of old sneakers, A / God's gonna getcha (for that) / Near you / When I stop dreaming / Crying time / Never ending song of love / We could / Did you ever / World needs a melody, The / My elusive dreams / After the fire is gone.
CD . . . . CDCST 45
MC . . . . CSTK 45
Country Store / '88 / BMG.
■ **LP.** . . . . CST 45
Country Store / '88.

CROWN PRINCE OF COUNTRY MUSIC, THE.
Tracks: One is a lonely number / Maybe little baby / Run boy / One woman man / Settle down / Heartbroken me / Rain, rain / Frozen heart / I've got five dollars and it's Saturday night / Cause I love you / You're in my heart / You all goodnight.
LP. . . . . OFF 9002
Official / '88 / Charly / Cadillac Music / Jazz Music.

DON'T STOP THE MUSIC.
Tracks: Into my arms again / Who shot Sam / You gotta be my baby / Mr Fool / Time lock / Candy hearts / What'cha gonna do / Vitamins l-o-v-e / Don't stop the music / Accidentally on purpose / All I want to do / Giveaway girl / Cup of loneliness / Wanderin' soul, A / My sweet Imogene / Likes of you, The / What am I worth / Boogie woogie Mexican boy / I'm with the wrong one / With half a heart / Ship of love / Honky tonk downstairs.
CD . . . . CDCH 912
Ace / Jun '87 / Pinnacle / Hot Shot / Jazz Music / Complete Record Co. Ltd.

DOUBLE TROUBLE (Jones, George & Johnny Paycheck).
Tracks: When you're ugly like us / Along came Jones / Proud Mary / You can have her / Smack dab in the middle / Mabellene / Roll over Beethoven / Kansas City / Tutti frutti / You better move on.
■ **LP.** . . . . EPC 84458
Epic / Sep '80.

EMI COUNTRY MASTERS.
Tracks: She thinks I still care / Sometimes you just can't win / Ragged but right / Color of the blues / We must have been out of our minds / Open pit mine / Girl I used to know, A / Precious jewel, The / Lovin' lies / Running bear / Big fool of the year / Give my love to rose / Beggar to a King / Wait a little longer, please Jesus / Not what I had in mind / I saw me / Take me as I am (Or let me go) / You comb hair / Ain't it funny what a fool will do / Wings of a dove / Seasons of my heart / Little bitty tear, A / My tears are overdue / What's in our heart / Your heart turned left (And I was on the right) / Race is on, The / Something I dreamed / It scares me half to death / Rose from a bride's bouquet, A / Where does a tear come from / Please be my love / Gold and silver / Warm red wine, The / We could / Love's gonna live here / Multiply the heartaches / Don't let the stars get in your eyes / Least of all / Rolling in my sweet baby's arms / Book of memories / I'm gonna change everything / I've been known to cry / Wrong number / She's mine / What's money / I'm just blue enough (To do most anything) / Let's invite them over / Where did the sunshine go / World's worst loser / Peace in the valley.
CD Set . . . . CDEM 1502
MC Set . . . . TCEM 1502
EMI / Aug '93 / EMI.

FRIENDS IN HIGH PLACES.
Tracks: Few ole country boys, A / All fall down / Fiddle and guitar band / All that we've got left / Love's gonna live here / If I could bottle this up / I've been there / You can't do wrong and get by / It hurts as much in Texas (as it did in Tennessee) / Travellers prayer.
CD 4680992
MC 4680994
Epic / Apr '91 / Sony.

GEORGE JONES.
Tracks: Not Advised.
CD . . . . ONN 40
Object Enterprises / May '89 / Gold & Sons / Terry Blood Dist. / Midland Records.

GEORGE JONES (AUDIO FIDELITY LABEL).
Tracks: Not Advised.
MC . . . . ZCGAS 717
Audio Fidelity(USA) / Sep '84 / Stage One Records.

GEORGE JONES (DITTO).
Tracks: Not Advised.
MC Set . . . . DTO 10088
Ditto / '88 / Pickwick Records.

GEORGE JONES AND LADIES (I Love Country) (Jones, George & Ladies).
Tracks: All fall down / Hallelujah, I love you so / Golden ring / All I want to do in life / We sure make good love / Daisy chain / That's good, that's bad / Here we are / Two storey house / Pair of old sneakers, A / If you can touch her at all / I've turned you to stone / Size seven round (made of gold) / Our love was ahead of its time (With Deborah Allen.) / Slow burning fire, A / Best friends.
LP. 4504231
■ **MC** 4504234
Epic / Mar '87.

GEORGE JONES SALUTES HANK WILLIAMS & BOB WILLS.
Tracks: Wedding bells / I just like this kind of living / You win again / I could never be ashamed of you / You're gonna change / House without love / Your cheatin' heart / They'll never take her love from me / Mansion on the hill / Take these chains from my heart / Bubbles in my beer / Faded love / Roly poly / Trouble in mind / Take me back to Tulsa / Warm red wine / Time changes everything / Worried mind / Silver dew on the bluegrass tonight / San Antonio rose / Last night I heard you crying in your sleep / Lonesome whistle / Steel guitar rag / Big beaver.
LP. . . . . EMS 1169
■ **MC** . . . . TCEMS 1169
Liberty / Mar '86.
■ **MC** . . . . TCEMS 1441
Liberty / Apr '92.
CD . . . . CDEMS 1441
Liberty / Mar '92 / EMI.

GOLDEN HITS.
Tracks: Not Advised.
LP. . . . . GT 0080
Gusto (USA) / Mar '88.

GOLDEN MEMORIES.
Tracks: Not Advised.
LP. . . . . MA 10185
Masters (Holland) / '88.
MC . . . . MAMC 910185
Masters (Holland) / Dec '88.

J 8 ■ DELETED

GOLDEN RING (Jones, George & Tammy Wynette).
Tracks: Golden ring / Even the bad times are good / Near you / Cryin' time / I've seen better days / Did you ever / Tattletale eyes / I'll be there if you ever want me / If you don't, somebody else will / Keep the change.
LP . . . . **EPC 81568**
■ **MC** . . . . **EPC 4081568**
CBS / '78 / Sony.

GOOD OL' BOY.
Tracks: World's worst loser / Once a day / Back in baby's arms again / You comb her hair / I can't change overnight / When I wake up from dreaming / Least of all / She's just a girl I used to know / It's funny what a fool will do / Hearts in my dreams.
LP . . . . **SDLP 1.009**
Sundown / Sep '84 / Terry Blood Dist. / Jazz Music / C.M. Distribution.
MC . . . . **SDC 1.009**
Sundown / May '88 / Terry Blood Dist. / Jazz Music / C.M. Distribution.

GOOD YEAR FOR THE ROSES, A (CASTLE).
Tracks: Where the grass won't grow / I'm a people / 4-0-33 / Things have gone to pieces / From here to the door / My favourite lies / Take me / White lightning / Tender years / Walk through this world with me / Say it's not you / Good year for the roses, A / Race is on, The / Developing my pictures / Old brush arbors.
LP . . . . **SHLP 146**
MC . . . . **SHTC 146**
Castle Showcase / '86 / Arabesque Ltd.

GOOD YEAR FOR THE ROSES, A (PREMIER).
Tracks: Apartment No.9 / Swinging doors / Am I that easy to forget? / Okie from Muskogee / Day in the life of a fool, A / Rollin' in my sweet baby's arms / All I have to offer you is me / There goes my everything / Good year for the roses, A / She thinks I still care / Talk back tremblin' lips / Hello darlin' / Almost persuaded / I can't stop loving you / Walk through this world with me.
LP . . . . **CBR 1041**
MC . . . . **KCBR 1041**
Premier (Sony) / May '84 / Sony / Pinnacle.

GOOD YEAR FOR THE ROSES, A (TOPLINE).
Tracks: Good year for the roses, A / If my heart had windows / I'll share my world with you / I'm wasting good paper / Say it's not you / Accidentally on purpose / Love bug / Where grass won't grow / 4033 / Things have gone to pieces / My favourite lies / From here to the door.
LP . . . . **TOP 177**
MC . . . . **KTOP 177**
Topline / Aug '87 / Charly / Swift / Black Sun Records.

GREAT SONGS OF LEON PAYNE.
Tracks: Not Advised.
LP . . . . **GT 0136**
Gusto (USA) / Mar '88.

GREATEST HITS: GEORGE JONES.
Tracks: Not Advised.
CD **2630222**
MC **2630224**
Big Country / May '88.

GREATEST HITS: GEORGE JONES AND TAMMY WYNETTE (Jones, George & Tammy Wynette).
Tracks: Golden ring / We're gonna hold on / We loved it away / Take me / Near you / Southern California / God's gonna getcha (for that) / We're not the Jet set / Let's build a world together / Ceremony, The.
MC . . . . **.40 82035**
Epic / Dec '77 / Sony.
■ **LP** . . . . **EPC 82035**
CBS / '78 / Sony.

HE STOPPED LOVING HER.
Tracks: Grand tour, The / Door, The / We can't make it / Loving you could never be better / Picture of me / These days (I barely get by) / Battle, The / Bartender blues / He stopped loving her today / I'm not ready yet / If drinkin' don't kill me (her memory will) / Still doin' time / Nothing ever hurt (Half as bad) / Once you've had the best / Shine on / Her name is.
LP . . . . **PMP 1002**
MC . . . . **PMPK 1002**
Premier (Sony) / Feb '87 / Sony / Pinnacle.

HEARTACHES AND HANGOVERS.
Tracks: I threw away the rose / Blue side of lonesome / Do what you think's best / Unfaithful one / Say it's not you / Lonely street / Things have gone to pieces / From here to the door / Heartaches and hangovers / My favourite lies / Man that you once knew.
MC . . . . **SSC 17**
Rounder / '88 / Projection / Roots Records / Swift / C.M. Distribution / Topic Records / Jazz Music / Hot Shot / A.D.A Distribution / Direct Distribution.
LP . . . . **SS 17**
Rounder / Dec '88 / Projection / Roots Records / Swift / C.M. Distribution / Topic Records / Jazz Music / Hot Shot / A.D.A Distribution / Direct Distribution.

HOMECOMING IN HEAVEN.
Tracks: Not Advised.
LP . . . . **HAT 3104**
MC . . . . **HATC 3104**
Stetson / Mar '89 / Crusader Marketing Co. / Swift / Wellard Dist. / Midland Records / C.M. Distribution.

I AM WHAT I AM.
Tracks: He stopped loving her today / I've aged twenty five years in five / Brother to the blues / If drikin' don't kill me / His lovin' her is gettin' in my way / I'm not ready yet / I'm the one she missed him with today / Good hearted woman / Hard act to follow / Bone dry.
LP . . . . **EPC 84627**
Epic / Apr '81 / Sony.

I LOVE COUNTRY.
Tracks: Why baby why / Tender years / Window up above / White lightning / Race is on, The / She thinks I still care / Her name is / I'm ragged but right / He stopped loving her today / Still doin' time / Shine on (Shine all your sweet love on me) / Radio lover / I always get lucky with you / Tennessee whisky / If drinkin' don't kill me (her memory will) / She's my rock.
■ **LP** . . . . **CBS 54941**
CBS / Sep '86.
LP . . . . **EPC 54941**
Epic / Mar '87 / Sony.
■ **MC** . . . . **.40 54941**
Epic / Mar '87.

JONES COUNTRY.
Tracks: Radio lover / Dream on / Hello trouble / Burning bridges / Wino the clown / You must have walked across my mind / I'd rather die young / Girl at the end of the bar, The / One of these days / Famous last words.
LP . . . . **EPC 25733**
MC . . . . **.40 25733**
Epic / Nov '83 / Sony.

KING & QUEEN OF COUNTRY MUSIC (see under Wynette, Tammy).

KING OF COUNTRY MUSIC.
Tracks: She thinks I still care / Girl I used to know, A / Sometimes you just can't win / We must have been out of our minds / I saw me / You comb her hair / What's in our heart / Your heart turned left (and I was on the right) / Where does a little tear come from? / World's worst loser / Big fool of the year / Open pity mine / Not what I had in mind / Let's invite them over / My tears are overdue / Something I dreamed / Multiply the heartaches / Race is on, The / Least of all / Wrong number.
■ **MC** . . . . **TC SLS 2600421**
Liberty / Apr '84.
■ **LP** . . . . **SLS 2600 421**
Liberty / Apr '84.

LADIES CHOICE.
Tracks: She's my rock / Hallelujah i love you so / All i want to do in life / We sure make good love / Daisy chain / All fall down / Size seven round / Our love was ahead of its time / Slow burning fire / Best friends.
LP . . . . **EPC 26233**
Epic / Mar '85 / Sony.
■ **MC** . . . . **.40 26233**
Epic / Mar '85.

LIVE AT DANCETOWN USA.
Tracks: White lightning / Something I dreamed / Aching breaking heart / Window up above / Bony Moronie / She thinks I still care / Ragged but right / Poor man's riches / Jole blon / Where does a little tear come from / Big Harlan Taylor / She's lonesome again / Race is on.
■ **LP** . . . . **CH 156**
Ace / Nov '85.
CD . . . . **CDCHM 156**
Ace / May '92 / Pinnacle / Hot Shot / Jazz Music / Complete Record Co. Ltd.

LONE STAR LEGEND, THE.
Tracks: All I want to do / Give away girl / Flame in my heart / Hearts in my dreams / Into my arms again / Cup of loneliness / Still hurtin' / Let him know / With half a heart / Someone sweet to love / I've been known to cry / Holiday for love / Vitamins l-o-v-e / Your old standby / Mr. Fool / Last town I painted, The / Don't lie to me.
LP . . . . **CH 139**
MC . . . . **CHC 139**
Ace / Apr '85 / Pinnacle / Hot Shot / Jazz Music / Complete Record Co. Ltd.

MY FAVOURITES OF HANK WILLIAMS.
Tracks: Not Advised.
LP . . . . **HAT 3136**
MC . . . . **HATC 3136**
Stetson / Apr '90 / Crusader Marketing Co. / Swift / Wellard Dist. / Midland Records / C.M. Distribution.

MY VERY SPECIAL GUESTS.
Tracks: Night life (With Waylon Jennings) / Bartender's blues (With James Taylor) / Here we are (With Emmylou Harris) / I've turned you to stone (With Linda Ronstadt) / It sure was good (With Tammy Wynette) / I gotta get drunk (With Willie Nelson) / Proud Mary (With Johnny Paycheck) / Stranger in the house (With Elvis Costello) / I still hold her body (but I think I've lost her mind) (With Dennis and Ray of Dr.Hook) / Will the circle be unbroken (With Pop and Mavis Staples).
LP . . . . **EPC 83163**
Epic / May '79 / Sony.
■ **LP** . . . . **CBS 32773**
CBS / Mar '86.
■ **MC** . . . . **.40 32773**
Epic / Mar '86.

ONE WOMAN MAN.
Tracks: I'm a one woman man / My baby's gone / Don't you ever get tired (of hurting me) / Burning bridges / Ya ba da ba do (so are you) / Radio lover / Place in the country, A / Just out of reach / Writing on the wall / Pretty little lady from Beaumont Texas.
LP **4651861**
■ **MC** **4651864**
Epic / May '89.

PARTY PICKIN' (Jones, George & Melba Montgomery).
Tracks: Not Advised.
LP . . . . **GT 0134**
Gusto (USA) / Mar '88.

RACE IS ON.
Tracks: Race is on / Don't let the stars get in your eyes / I'll never let go of you / She's mine / Three's a crowd / They'll never take her love from me / Your heart turned left / Ain't it funny what a fool will do / It scares me half to death / World's worse loser / Time changes everything / Take me as I am.
■ **LP** . . . . **SLS 50428**
Sunset (Liberty) / '79.
MC **4XLL 9031**
Capitol (Specials) / Dec '88.

REPLAY ON GEORGE JONES.
Tracks: Not Advised.
LP . . . . **FEDB 5017**
MC . . . . **FEDC 5017**
Sierra / Dec '88.

SAME OLE ME.
Tracks: He stopped loving her today / Bartender's blues / Race is on, The / She thinks I still care / White lightning / Why baby why / Some day my day will come / I always get lucky with you.
VHS . . . . **PLATV 302**
Prism Video / '91 / Terry Blood Dist. / Gold & Sons / Prism Leisure PLC.

SHINE ON.
Tracks: Shine on / She hung the moon / I'd rather have what we had / Tennessee whiskey / Almost persuaded / I always get lucky with you / Mem'ryville / I should've called / Show's almost over / Ol' George stopped drinkin' today.
■ **LP** . . . . **EPC 25400**
Epic / Jun '83.

STILL THE SAME OLE ME.
Tracks: Still doin' time / Couldn't love have picked a better place to die? / I won't need you anymore / Together alone / Daddy come home / You can't get the hell out of Texas / Good ones and bad ones / Girl, you sure know how to say goodbye / Some day my day will come / Same ole me.
LP . . . . **EPC 84949**
MC . . . . **.40 84949**
Epic / Jan '82 / Sony.

STRANGER IN THE HOUSE (Jones, George & Elvis Costello).
Tracks: Stranger in the house / Drunk can't be a man.
■ **7"** . . . . **EPC 8560**
Epic / May '80.

STRANGERS, LOVERS AND FRIENDS.
Tracks: Not Advised.
MC Set . . . . **DTO 10265**
Ditto / May '87 / Pickwick Records.

TASTE OF YESTERDAY'S WINE, A (see under Haggard, Merle).

TENDER YEARS.
Tracks: Not Advised.
MC . . . . **CTS 45405**
Country Stars.
CD . . . . **CTS 55405**
Country Stars / Jan '92.

TEXAS TORNADO.
Tracks: White lightning / You gotta be my baby / What am I worth / Don't stop the music / Play it cool man / I'm gonna burn your playhouse down / Into my arms again / Let him know / Giveaway girl / All I want to do / My fool / Vitamins l-o-v-e.
LP . . . . **GEM 006**
Crown / Feb '86 / Pinnacle / Nervous Records.
■ **MC** . . . . **GEMC 006**
Crown / Feb '86.

TOGETHER AGAIN (Jones, George & Tammy Wynette).
Tracks: Pair of old sneakers / Right in the wrong direction / I just started livin' today / Love in the meantime / We could / Two story house / If we don't make it, it's not my fault / We'll talk about it later / Night spell.
LP . . . . **EPC 84626**
MC . . . . **.40 84626**
Epic / Jan '81 / Sony.

TOO WILD TOO LONG.
Tracks: I'm a survivor / Real McCoy, The / Too wild too long / One hell of a song / Old man no one loves, The / Bird, The / I'm a long gone daddy / New patches / Moments of brilliance / U.S.A. today, The.
CD **2460805**
Epic / May '88 / Sony.
LP **4608051**

■ DELETED

J 9

■ MC 4608054
Epic / May '88.

WALKING THE LINE (see under Haggard, Merle).

WAYS OF THE WORLD.
Tracks: Don't you ever get tired of hurting me / Open pity mind / On the banks of the old pontchartrain / House without love is not a home, A / Ways of the world / Please don't let that woman get me / Yes I know why / Jonesy / Old brush arbors / Liberty / Jambalaya / Cold cold heart / Ragged but right / Tarnished angel / Your tender years / Wedding bells / Things have gone to pieces / World of forgotten people / From now on all of my friends are gonna be strangers / I can't escape from you.
LP. . . . . .SMT 008
MC . . . . .SMTC 008
Starburst / Jul '87 / Terry Blood Dist. / Jazz Music.

WHITE LIGHTNING.
Tracks: White lightning / What am I worth / Taggin' along / Boogie woogie Mexican boy / You gotta be my baby / Revenooer man / Who shot Sam / Play it cool man / My sweet Imogene / How come it / I'm gonna burn your playhouse down / Don't stop the music / Rock it / Maybe little baby.
■ LP. . . . . 10 CH 13
Ace / Sep '79.
■ MC . . . . .CHC 117
Ace / Nov '84.
■ LP. . . . . CH 117
Ace / Nov '84.

WHO'S GONNA FILL THEIR SHOES.
Tracks: Not Advised.
LP. 26696
CBS (import) / Sep '86 / C.M. Distribution / Silva Screen.

WINE COLOURED ROSES.
Tracks: Wine coloured roses / I turn to you / Right left hand, The / Don't leave without taking your silver / Very best of me, The / Hopelessly yours / You never looked that good when you were mine (With Patti Page.) / If only your eyes could lie / Ol' Frank / These old eyes have seen it all.
LP. . . . . EPC 57040
Epic / Nov '86 / Sony.
■ MC 40 57040
Epic / Nov '86.

YOU OUGHT TO BE HERE WITH ME.
Tracks: Hell stays open (all night long) / You oughta be here with me / Somebody always paints the wall / I sleep just like a baby / Someone that you used to know / I want to grow old with you / Cold day in December, A / Six foot deep, six foot down / If the world don't end tomorrow / Ol' Red.
CD 4674702
LP. 4674701
■ MC 4674704
Epic / Nov '90.

YOU'VE STILL GOT A PLACE IN MY HEART.
Tracks: You've still got a place in my heart / From strangers, to lovers, to friends / Second time around / Come sundown / Even the bad times are good / I'm ragged but right / Courtin' in the rain / Loveshine / Your lying blue eyes / Learning to do without me.
■ LP. . . . . EPC 26072
Epic / Sep '84.

Jones, Thumper

ROCK IT.
Tracks: Rock it / How come it.
■ 7" . . . . NS 49
Ace / Feb '79.

Jordanaires

SING ELVIS' GOSPEL FAVOURITES.
Tracks: Didn't it rain / Peace in the valley / Joshua fit de battle of Jerico / Search me lord / Dig a little deeper / You better run / Let us break bread together / Wonderful time up there, A / How great thou art / I'm a rollin' / Dip your fingers in some water / Roll jordan roll / One of these mornings / Onward christian soldiers.
LP. . . . . .MFLP 033
Magnum Force / Jan '86 / Terry Blood Dist. / Jazz Music / Hot Shot.

SING ELVIS'S FAVOURITE SPIRITUALS.
Tracks: Not Advised.
LP. . . . . LP 8505
Rockhouse / Sep '85 / Charly / C.M. Distribution / Nervous Records.

Jory, Sarah

Although she rightly holds a place as one of Britain's new breed of young, contemporary country entertainers, Newark based Sarah Jory is nevertheless a veteran of the business. She began playing steel guitar when she was five years old, and making her stage debut a year later. By the age of nine she was playing gigs with her own band, her father Arthur acting as manager, and two years later made her American debut at the annual Steel Guitar Convention in St. Louis, Missouri. Soon she had top American steelies like Lloyd Green, Buddy Emmons and Jimmy Crawford not only singing her praises, but playing on stage with her and, over the years, involved in a series of independently produced albums. Realizing the limitations of being purely a steel guitarist, Sarah developed her vocal skills and, combined with her talents as a multi-instrumentalist, has become an all-round entertainer with highly energetic stage routines. She's now building up mass audiences following appearances on several top TV shows, as well as concerts with such as Mungo Jerry, Eric Clapton and Glen Campbell, yet continues to maintain her appeal with the country fraternity as witnessed by regular awards (BCMA, CMRU etc.) coming her way. She signed with Ritz Records in 1991, and the label is not only producing her new recordings but also releasing some of her earlier work in compilation form. (Tony Byworth)

20 CLASSIC SONGS.
Tracks: Walk the way the wind blows / Somewhere between / I'll leave this world loving you / Just out of reach / Why me lord / Beyond the point of no return / Let me be there / Dear God / Always have, always will / How great thou art / Jones on the jukebox / Before I'm over you / Just because I'm a woman / Faded love / It is no secret (What god can do) / No time at all / Funny face / Yesterday just passed my way again / Beneath still waters / Old rugged cross, The.
CD . . . . .SCD 429
Ritz / Oct '93 / Pinnacle / Midland Records.

20 CLASSIC SONGS (THE EARLY YEARS).
Tracks: Walk the way the wind blows / Somewhere between / I'll leave this world loving you / Just out of reach / Why me Lord / Beyond the point of no return / Let me be there / Dear God / Always have, always will / How great thou art / Jones on the jukebox / Before I'm over you / Just because I'm a woman / Faded love / It is no secret (What God can do) / No time at all / Funny face / Yesterday just passed my way again / Beneath still waters / Old rugged cross, The.
CD . . . . .RITZSCD 429
MC . . . . .RITZSC 429
Ritz / Apr '93 / Pinnacle / Midland Records.

20 STEEL GUITAR FAVOURITES.
Tracks: (Instrumental) Sticky fingers / Deep in the heart of Texas / Orange blossom special / Jealous heart / Under the boardwalk / Careless hands / Steel line / Way to survive, A / San Antonio stroll / She believes in me / Oklahoma stomp / Highway 40 blues / Rose coloured glasses / Blue jade / Cold, cold heart / Three of us, The / In the garden / City lights / Once upon a time in the West / Remington ride.
CD . . . . .RITZSCD 428
MC . . . . .RITZSC 428
Ritz / Apr '93 / Pinnacle / Midland Records.

NEVER HAD IT SO GOOD.
Tracks: Never had it so good / Orange blossom special.
CD Single . . . . CD 247
Ritz / Jun '92 / Pinnacle / Midland Records.

NEW HORIZONS.
Tracks: Never had it so good / Look at us / Take your memory with you / Strings that tie you down, The / Darlin' / Wind beneath my wings / Orange blossom special / Mississippi / How do / Til' each tear becomes a rose / You'llnever get to heaven / Take a love off my mind / Heartaches by the number / Sarah's dream.
CD . . . . .RITZCD 0067
MC . . . . .RITZLC 0067
Ritz / May '92 / Pinnacle / Midland Records.

NEW RISING STAR.
Tracks: Ashes of love / Jones on the jukebox / Dear God / I'll leave this world loving you / Cotton eyed Joe/ Sugar foot rag / How great thou art / I tell it like it used to be / Rock it Billy / Walk softly on this heart of mine / Sticky fingers / She believes in me / Tennessee flat top box / Wind beneath my wings.
VHS. . . . . RITZV 0015
Ritz / Jan '93 / Pinnacle / Midland Records.

STEEL GUITAR FAVOURITES (INSTRUMENTAL).
Tracks: Sticky fingers / Deep in the heart of Texas / Orange blossom special / Jealous heart / Under the boardwalk / Careless hands / Steel line / Way to survive, A / San Antonio stroll / She believes in me / Oklahoma stomp / Highway 40 blues / Rose coloured glasses / Blue jade / Cold cold heart / Three of us, The / In the garden / City lights / Once upon a time in the west / Remington ride.
CD . . . . .SCD 428
Ritz / Oct '93 / Pinnacle / Midland Records.

Joyce, Gina

COUNTRY 'N' IRISH FORGET-ME-NOTS.
Tracks: Old rustic bridge / You're as welcome as the flowers in May / Mother's love's a blessing, A / Rose of Allandale / Apple blossom county / Will the angels play their harps for me / Medals for mothers / Mother dear of mine / Sweet forget me nots / Gentle mother / Mountains of Mourne / Two little orphans / Golden jubilee / Losing you.
LP. . . . . GES 1239
MC . . . . KGEC 1239
Emerald / Jun '88 / I & B Records.

Judd, Wynonna

Since commencing her solo career in 1991, Wynonna dropped her surname but continued building on the tremendous success she had first enjoyed with her mother Naomi, as part of the award winning duo the Judds (see separate entry). Her first album, simply titled *Wynonna* , sold a million copies in six days and quickly crossed over into the pop market, and her 1993 release *Tell me why* witnessed similar success. She has scored several number one singles with such as *She is his only need* , *I saw the light* and *No-one else on earth* , as well as cutting a duet with touring partner Clint Black *A bad goodbye* . (Tony Byworth)

WYONNA.
Tracks: What it takes / She is his only need / I saw the light / My strongest weakness / When I reach the place I'm goin' / No one else on Earth / It's never easy to say goodbye / Little bit of love (goes a long long way), A / All of that love from here / Live with Jesus.
CD 4716712
Curb / May '92 / BMG.
■ MC 4716714
Curb / May '92.
MiniDisc 471671-3
Curb / Feb '93 / BMG.

Judds

Mother and daughter team, The Judds, provide the real Cinderella story of the 1980's, becoming the most successful duo of the decade. They moved to Nashville in 1979, appeared on Ralph Emery's early morning TV show and were signed by RCA. Their first single, *Had A Dream*, reached the top 20 and was followed by, *Man He's Crazy*, which topped the charts. This set the pattern for virtually all their subsequent singles releases. The Judds have achieved gold and platinum album sales and a staggering collection of awards. These include three Grammys and winning the CMA vocal group/duo award for 6 consecutive years. (Tony Byworth)

CHRISTMAS TIME WITH THE JUDDS.
Tracks: Winter wonderland / Beautiful star of Bethlehem / Who is this babe / Santa Claus is coming to town / Silver bells / What child is this / Away in a manger / Oh holy night / Silent night.
LP. . . . . PL 86422
■ MC . . . . PK 86422
RCA / Nov '87.

DON'T BE CRUEL.
Tracks: Don't be cruel / Sweetest gift, The.
7" . . . . PB 49763
RCA / Jan '87 / BMG.

GIVE A LITTLE LOVE.
Tracks: Turn it loose / Old pictures / Cow cow boogie / Maybe your baby's got the blues / I know where I'm going / Why don't you believe me / Sweetest gift, The / Give a little love to me / Had a dream (for the heart) / John Deere tractor / Isn't he a strange one / Blue Nun Cafe / Change of heart / Don't be cruel / I'm falling in love tonight.
■ CD . . . . PD 90011
RCA / '87.
MC . . . . PK 90011
RCA / Jan '87 / BMG.
■ LP. . . . . PL 90011
RCA / Jan '87.

GREATEST HITS: JUDDS.
Tracks: Why not me / Mama he's crazy / Grandpa / Don't be cruel / Rockin' with the rhythm of the rain / Give a little love / I know where I'm going.
MC . . . . PK 90243
RCA / Sep '88 / BMG.
■ LP. . . . . PL 90243
RCA / Sep '88.
■ CD . . . . PD 90243
RCA / Sep '88.

HAVE MERCY.
Tracks: Have mercy / Mama he's crazy.
12" . . . . ZT 49472
Curb / Jan '89 / BMG.
■ 7" . . . . ZB 49471
Curb / Jan '89.

I'M FALLING IN LOVE TONIGHT.
Tracks: I'm falling in love tonight.
■ 7" . . . . PB 49717
RCA / Apr '87.

LOVE CAN BUILD A BRIDGE.
Tracks: This country's rockin' / Calling in the wind / In my dreams / Rompin' stompin' blues / Love can build a bridge / Born to be blue / One hundred and two / John Deere tractor / Talk about love / Are the roses not blooming.
CD . . . . PD 90531
RCA / Sep '90 / BMG.
■ MC . . . . PK 90531
RCA / Sep '90.
■ LP. . . . . PL 90531
RCA / Sep '90.

J 10 ■ DELETED

MAMA HE'S CRAZY.

Tracks: Mama he's crazy / John Deere tractor.
- 7" .... RCA 480
RCA / May '85.
7" .... PB 49917
RCA / Oct '85 / BMG.

RIVER OF TIME.

Tracks: One man woman / Young love / Not my baby / Let me tell you about life / Sleepless night / Water of love / River of time / Cadillac red / Guardian angels / Do I dare (Only on CD.).
MC .... ZK 74127

RCA / Jul '89 / BMG.
- LP .... ZL 74127
RCA / Jul '89.
- CD .... ZD 74127
RCA / Jul '89.

ROCKIN' WITH THE RHYTHM.

Tracks: Have mercy / Grandpa (tell me 'bout the good old days) / Working in a coalmine / If I were you / Rockin' with the rhythm of the rain / Tears for you / Cry myself to sleep / River roll on / I wish she wouldn't treat you that way / Dream chaser.
- LP .... PL 87042
RCA / Apr '86.

- MC .... PK 87042
RCA / Apr '86.

WHY NOT ME.

Tracks: Mr. Pain / Drops of water / Sleeping heart / My baby's gone / Bye bye baby blues / Girl's night out / Love is alive / Endless sleep / Mama he's crazy.
LP .... PL 85319
MC .... PK 85319
RCA / Mar '85 / BMG.
- LP .... NL 90315
CD .... ND 90315
- MC .... NK 90315
RCA / Sep '89.

You'll love this new way to buy music.

MusicLink offers an unrivalled choice of music on both CD or cassette that can be ordered by telephone from the comfort of your home.

Simply call the number below and tell the operator the name of the album, and if possible the catalogue number quoted in this guide. We'll tell you there and then if it is a stock item – or, if not, whether we can obtain it for you.

We will process your order immediately and your music will be rushed to you by first class mail, post free.

MusicLink gives you the convenience of phoning from home – yet you pay only high street prices.

We are not a club. There is absolutely no commitment.

All you need is a credit or debit card – and a love of music.

So call us now.

Music**Link**
Simply a better way to buy music.

081 812 0998
Lines open 24 hours a day, 7 days a week.

K

Kahn, Si

DOING MY JOB.
Tracks: Not Advised.
LP . . . . FF 221
Flying Fish (USA) / Mar '89 / Cadillac Music / Roots Records / Projection / C.M. Distribution / Direct Distribution / Jazz Music / Duncans / A.D.A Distribution.

HOME.
Tracks: Not Advised.
LP . . . . FF 207
Flying Fish (USA) / Mar '89 / Cadillac Music / Roots Records / Projection / C.M. Distribution / Direct Distribution / Jazz Music / Duncans / A.D.A Distribution.

I HAVE SEEN FREEDOM.
Tracks: Not Advised.
CD . . . . FF 70578
MC . . . . FF 90578
Flying Fish (USA) / Jul '92 / Cadillac Music / Roots Records / Projection / C.M. Distribution / Direct Distribution / Jazz Music / Duncans / A.D.A Distribution.

I'LL BE THERE.
Tracks: Not Advised.
CD . . . . FF 70509
LP . . . . FF 509
Flying Fish (USA) / Oct '89 / Cadillac Music / Roots Records / Projection / C.M. Distribution / Direct Distribution / Jazz Music / Duncans / A.D.A Distribution.

UNFINISHED PORTRAITS.
Tracks: Not Advised.
LP . . . . FF 312
Flying Fish (USA) / Mar '89 / Cadillac Music / Roots Records / Projection / C.M. Distribution / Direct Distribution / Jazz Music / Duncans / A.D.A Distribution.

Karen

BETWEEN ME AND YOU.
Tracks: Not Advised.
MC . . . . CJW 017
Beechwood (Scotland) / Nov '91 / Ross Records / Duncans.
CD . . . . JJCD 1017
Beechwood (Scotland) / Jan '92 / Ross Records / Duncans.

EVERYBODY'S REACHING OUT.
Tracks: Everybody's reaching out / Loving on borrowed time / Bed of roses / Beggin' to you / Snowbird / Give me another chance / Lonesome / Bright lights and country / Apartment No.9 / I wonder where you are / Blanket on the ground.
MC . . . . CWGR 11
Ross (1) / Jun '88 / Ross Records / Duncans / Entertainment UK.

JUST FOR WHAT I AM.
Tracks: Just for what I am / Good hearted woman / Keeping up appearances / I'm gonna change everything / I walk the line / Ring around my rosie / Heartaches by the number / Almost persuaded / Your own man / Oh lonesome me / Once a day / What I've got in mind / While I was making love to you.
MC . . . . CJW 012
Beechwood (Scotland) / Jan '87 / Ross Records / Duncans.
MC . . . . CWGR TV 12
Ross (1) / Oct '92 / Ross Records / Duncans / Entertainment UK.

Kearney, Kevin

FROM A JACK TO A KING.
Tracks: Not Advised.
MC . . . . MB LP 1040
Music Box (Ireland) / '88.

Kearney, Ramsey

TENNESSEE ROCK.
Tracks: Not Advised.
LP . . . . SJLP 591
Sunjay / Sep '90 / CSA Tell Tapes.

Keen, Robert Earl

Singer-songwriter born 11.1.1956 in Houston, Texas, raised in Bandero (west of San Antone), reared on bluegrass/folk music. Quality songs emerged from his hand, including his The front porch song (co-penned with Lyle Lovett) Sing one for sister covered by Nanci Griffith, The road goes on forever & Whenever kindness fails - both appeared on Joe Ely's 1992 Love & danger MCA album, whilst Kelly Willis also delved into Keen's songbook - giving his Steve Earls co-penned Sincerely (Too late to turn back now) an outing. Others who've collaborated with Keen include Peter Rowan, Lynn Anderson & Lisa Silver. It was Steve Earle who pursuaded Keen to head for Nashville in 1985 - where after two fruitless years he returned to Texas, promoting his 1984 debut Workshop Records album No kinda dancer financed with borrowed money, which was later to be released on Philo/Rounder. His follow-up was The live album (which was originally on Rounder Records - who pulled out at the last minute) on Sugar Hill (1988), recorded at the Sons of Hermann Hall, Dallas with Johnathan Yudkin, Roy Huskey Jr, and produced by Jim Rooney. Keen's growing reputation was enhanced even further in 1989, through his West textures release (UK Special Delivery/Topic), setting him up there alongside his Texas comtemporaries Clark, Van Zant, Lovett, Hancock & Griffith. It took until 1993 for him to make the follow - up A bigger piece of the sky (with him for the first time disregarding the JR extention to his name), again with the Sugar Hill release licenced by Topic for UK marketing. Irish singer Maura O'Connell by now something of a regular contributor to Nashville albums was among the musicians featured on an album produced by Garry Velletri, where Marty Stuart, Velletri & Tommy Spurlock all shine. Keen's songs whilst mainly of auto - biographical origins (Here in Arkansas , Corpus Christ Bay , Daddy had a Buick & Crazy cowboy dream do enjoy some broadening of boundaries, but he's carrying on the Texas tradition as the home of the trade. (Maurice Hope)

BIGGER PIECE OF SKY, A.
Tracks: So I can take my rest / Whenever kindness fail / Amarillo highway / Night right for love / Jesse with the long hair.Blow you away / Here in Arkansas / Daddy had a buick / Corpus Christie / Crazy cowboy dream / Paint the town beige.
CD . . . . SH CD-1037
MC SH-MC-1037
Sugarhill(USA) / '93 / Roots Records / Projection / Impetus Records / C.M. Distribution / Jazz Music / Swift / Duncans / A.D.A Distribution.
CD . . . . SPDCD 1048
MC . . . . SPDC 1048
Special Delivery / May. '93 / Revolver-APT / A.D.A Distribution / Topic Records / Direct Distribution / Jazz Music / C.M. Distribution.

LIVE ALBUM, THE.
Tracks: I wanna know / Torch song, The / Goin' down in style / If I were King / Copenhagen / I would change my life / Stewball / I'll go on downtown / Bluegrass widow, The / Who'll be lookin' out for me.
CD . . . . SHCD 1024
LP . . . . SH 1024
MC . . . . ZCSH 1024
Sugarhill(USA) / '88 / Roots Records / Projection / Impetus Records / C.M. Distribution / Jazz Music / Swift / Duncans / A.D.A Distribution.

NO KINDA DANCER.
Tracks: No kinda dancer / Front porch song, The / Between hello and goodbye / Swervin' in my lane / Christabel / Willie / Young lovers waltz / Death of tail Fitzsimmons / Rolling by / Armadillo jackal, The / Lu Ann / Coldest day of Winter, The.
LP . . . . PH 1108
MC . . . . PH 1108C
Philo (USA) / '88 / Roots Records / Projection / Topic Records / Direct Distribution / Ross Records / C.M. Distribution / Impetus Records.
CD . . . . SDCD 9.00815
Sawdust / '90.

WEST TEXTURES.
Tracks: Leavin' Tennessee / Maria / Sing one for sister / Road goes on forever / Sonora's death row / Don't turn out the light / Five pound bass, The / It's the little things / Jennifer Johnson and me / Mariano / Love's a word I never throw around.
LP . . . . SPD 1032
Special Delivery / Feb '90 / Revolver-APT / A.D.A Distribution / Topic Records / Direct Distribution / Jazz Music / C.M. Distribution.
CD . . . . SPDCD 1032
■ MC . . . . SPDC 1032
Special Delivery / Feb '90.

Keith, Bill

BANJOISTICS.
Tracks: Not Advised.
LP . . . . ROUNDER 0148
MC .ROUNDER 0148C
Rounder / '88 / Projection / Roots Records / Swift / C.M. Distribution / Topic Records / Jazz Music / Hot Shot / A.D.A Distribution / Direct Distribution.

BEATING AROUND THE BUSH.
Tracks: Not Advised.
CD . . . . GLCD 2107
CD . . . . CSIF 2107
Green Linnet (UK) / Feb '93 / A.D.A Distribution.

BILL KEITH & JIM COLLIER (Keith, Bill & Jim Rooney).
Tracks: Not Advised.
LP 883020
Hexagone / Sep '79 / Roots Records / Projection / Discovery.

COLLECTION: BILL KEITH & JIMMY ROONEY (Keith, Bill & Jim Rooney).
Tracks: Crazy creek / Done laid around / So lonesome I could cry / Jordu / Detour / Pickin' on the country strings / Gone girl / Tragic romance / Sugarfoot rag / I'll stay around / Darling Corey is one / Interest on the loan / Out of joint / Auld lang syne.
LP . . . . WF 004
Waterfront / Mar '84 / SRD / Jazz Music / A.D.A Distribution / C.M. Distribution.

SOMETHING AULD, SOMETHING NEWGRASS, BORROWED ..
Tracks: Not Advised.
LP . . . . ROUNDER 0084
Rounder / Jan '87 / Projection / Roots Records / Swift / C.M. Distribution / Topic Records / Jazz Music / Hot Shot / A.D.A Distribution / Direct Distribution.
MC .ROUNDER 0084C
Rounder / '88 / Projection / Roots Records / Swift / C.M. Distribution / Topic Records / Jazz Music / Hot Shot / A.D.A Distribution / Direct Distribution.

Kelly, Jerri

WALK ME 'CROSS THE RIVER.
Tracks: Walk me 'cross the river / All that shines is gold.
■ 7" . . . . .CAR 251
Carrere / Jan '82.

Kelly, Jo Ann

JO ANN KELLY.
Tracks: Not Advised.
LP . . . . .OPEN 001
Open / Jun '88 / Cadillac Music.

JUST RESTLESS (Jo Ann Kelly Band).
Tracks: Not Advised.
LP . . . . AP 028
Appaloosa / Roots Records / C.M. Distribution / Wellard Dist. / Projection / Hot Shot / A.D.A Distribution.

RETROSPECT 1964-72.
Tracks: Black rat swing / Walking blues / Ain't seen no whiskey / Boyfriend blues / Try me one more time / Long black hair / Buddy Brown's eyes / New Milkcow blues / Hard time killin' floor blues / Shave 'em dry / I feel so good / When I lay my burden down / Just like I treat her / I look down the road and I wonder.
CD . . . . CSAPCD 101
LP . . . . CSAPLP 101
MC . . . . CSAPMC 101
Connoisseur Collection / Jun '90 / Pinnacle.

STANDING AT THE BURYING GROUND (see under Cochran, Eddie).

Kelly, Sandy

Hailing from Co.Sligo, Kelly was brought up in a show-business environment.After representing her country in the Eurovision Song Contest, she set out her career as a country artist in 1985. With her 7 piece band, she became a leading attraction. In 1989, she achieved a hit with Patsy Cline's Crazy, recorded with Johnny Cash and appeared at Nashville's Grand Ole Opry.

CRAZY.
Tracks: Crazy / Now there's you.
7" . . . . .KTS 018
K-Tel / Dec '89 / I & B Records / C.M. Distribution / Arabesque Ltd. / Mono Distributors (Jersey) Ltd. / Prism Leisure PLC / PolyGram / Ross Records / Prism Leisure PLC.

EVENING WITH SANDY KELLY.
Tracks: Why'd you come here lookin' like that / Good timing woman / I will always love you / Irish medley / Crazy / Do me with love / Back in baby's arms / Reasons / Ford econoline / Ring of fire / Happiness of having you / San Antonio rose / Sweet dreams / Wind beneath my wings, The.
VHS. PLATV 333

Prism Video / Sep '90 / Terry Blood Dist. / Gold & Sons / Prism Leisure PLC.

EVENING WITH SANDY KELLY, AN.
Tracks: Why'd you come here lookin' like that / Good timing woman / I will always love you / Town I love so well, The / Rare ould times / Fields of Athenry, The / Crazy / Do me with love / Back in baby's arms / Reasons / Ford econoline / Ring of fire / Happiness of having you / San Antonio rose / Sweet dreams / Wind beneath my wings, The.
MC . . . . **PLAC 333**
Platinum Music / Oct '90 / Prism Leisure PLC / Ross Records.

I NEED TO BE IN LOVE.
Tracks: Not Advised.
CD . . . . **ONCD 3465**
MC . . . . **OCE 2465**
K-Tel / Jun '90 / I & B Records / C.M. Distribution / Arabesque Ltd. / Mono Distributors (Jersey) Ltd. / Prism Leisure PLC / PolyGram / Ross Records / Prism Leisure PLC.

VOICE OF SANDY KELLY, THE SONGS OF PATSY CLINE.
Tracks: Sweet dreams / Blue moon of Kentucky / Just out of reach / Always / Your cheatin' heart / Have you ever been lonely / Faded love / Walkin' after midnight / I fall to pieces / She's got you / San Antone rose / Crazy.
VHS . . . . **KV 005**
K-Tel (Ireland) / Dec '91 / I & B Records / Ross Records / Prism Leisure PLC.

Kendalls

A father and daughter who shot to fame on the short lived Ovation label. From, St. Loius, Missouri, their first recordings came out on Stop & Dot. After signing to Ovation in 1977, Jeanne's powerful penetrating vocals were soon to make quite an impact on the country music scene. Their second single, *Heaven's Just A Sin Away*, reached the top of the chart. It won the CMA song of the year award and the Kendalls won a grammy as best vocal duo. A number of big hits followed but after much switching of labels, the hits began to dry up. (Maurice Hope)

16 GREATEST HITS.
Tracks: Not Advised.
■ **CD** . . . . **CD 1005**
Gusto (USA) / '88.

BEST COUNTRY DUO 1978.
Tracks: Not Advised.
LP . . . . **GT 0001**
Gusto (USA) / Jul '79.

FIRE AT FIRST SIGHT.
Tracks: Fire at first sight / Central standard time / If you get that close / I'll take you / Party line / Too late / I'm dreaming again / He can't make your kind of love / Little doll / You can't fool love.
MC . . . . **MCAC 5724**
MCA / Mar '87 / BMG.
■ **LP** . . . . **IMCA 5724**
MCA / Mar '87.

HEART OF THE MATTER.
Tracks: You'd make an angel wanna cheat / Put it off until tomorrow / Gone away / Everlasting love / I'll be hurtin' either way / Heart of the matter / I'm already blue / I take the chance / I don't drink from the river / I don't do like that no more.
■ **LP** . . . . **OV 1446**
Ovation / Apr '80.

JUST LIKE REAL PEOPLE.
Tracks: I had a lovely time / Mandolin man / Love seeds / Falling in love / Just like real people / Love is a hurting thing / Never my love / I'm coming down lonely / If you don't want the fire / Another dream just came true.
■ **LP** . . . . **OV 1739**
Ovation / Apr '80.

MAKING BELIEVE.
Tracks: Making believe / I'm a pushover.
■ **7"** **2059026**
Polydor / Jun '78.

MOVIN' TRAIN.
Tracks: Precious love / I'll be faithful to you / Movin' train / Dark end of the street / Say the word / Thank God for radio / I'd dance every dance with you / My baby's gone / Flaming eyes / Wildflower.
LP **8127 791**
Mercury (USA) / Dec '83 / Pinnacle.

THANK GOD FOR THE RADIO.
Tracks: Thank God for radio / Flaming eyes.
■ **7"** . . . . **GULS 79**
Gull / Jun '85.

YOU MAKE AN ANGEL WANT TO CHEAT.
Tracks: You make an angel want to cheat / Mandolin man.
■ **7"** . . . . **OV 1202**
Ovation / Apr '80.

Kennedy Rose

HAI KU.
Tracks: Hai ku / Only chain, The / Faithful / Western fires / Who's gonna hold you / Nightline / Love like this / After your arms / Variation on a theme in D minor / Love is the healer / Born to give my love / Leavin' line.
LP . . . . **EIRSA 1030**
MC . . . . **EIRSAC 1030**
I.R.S (Illegal) / Jun '90 / EMI.

LOVE LIKE THIS.
Tracks: Love like this.
12" . . . . **12 EIRS 137**
7" . . . . **EIRS 137**
I.R.S (Illegal) / Jun '90 / EMI.

Kennedy, Hal

BEST OF HAL KENNEDY.
Tracks: Pity the man / Remind me dear Lord / Keep your mighty hand on me / Family bible / Don't take my cross away / Who am I? / Answer's on the way, The / Same road, The / Breaking of the day / God's old clock / Full up, no vacancy / Old rugged cross, The / Prisoner of love / It'll all be over but the shouting / Sorry, I never knew you / Pilgrims have gone, The.
LP . . . . **CGS 8511**
MC . . . . **WC 8511**
Canaan / May '82 / Word Records (UK) / Sony.

Kennerley, Paul

FEELS SO RIGHT.
Tracks: Feels so right / Been your fool too long.
■ **7"** . . . . **AMS 8185**
A&M / Nov '81.

JEALOUS LOVE.
Tracks: Jealous love / Death of me.
■ **7"** . . . . **AMS 8132**
A&M / May '81.

TAKE THAT WOMAN AWAY.
Tracks: Take that woman away / How long.
■ **7"** . . . . **AMS 8221**
A&M / Jun '82.

Kentucky Colonels

Famous for it's inclusion of the late guitarist Clarence White (born 07.06.1944, died 14.07.1973) who was killed whilst loading his van after a gig. Rock/country/bluegrass musician Clarence and his older and younger brothers Roland (mandolin) and Eric Jnr (tenor banjo) and sister Joanne were of French Canadian ancestry, with the original family name of Leblanc. They started out playing with their multi-talented father Eric and their uncles, playing at the Grand Ole Opry, Richmond's Old Dominion Barndances and Chicago's WLS station. The younger Whites set out in 1955 as the Country Boys, and were winners of Pasadena's KXLA talent contest. In California, Joe and Rose Maphis gained them slots on the Town Hall Party. Clarence's guitar prowess, with him utilizing his flat pick and middle fingers on his right hand, allowed him to develop a style totally of his own. By 1962 Billy Ray Latham, Leroy Mack and Roger Bush had joined Roland and Clarence, and they adopted the name of the Kentucky Colonels, debuting with *New sounds of Bluegrass America* and in 1964 their highly acclaimed all-instumental album *Appalachian Swing* (Rounder). Clarence's music embraced by both the country-rock fraternity and the college campuses alike. He also tackled various other ventures, including becoming a session musician for such acts as Ricky Nelson, the Everly Brothers, Gene Parsons (he also paired with him and cajun fiddler Gib Guilbeau in 1968 formed band Nashville West), Linda Ronstadt, Gene Clark, the Flying Burritos & the Byrds - of whom he was also a member at the back - end of the 1960s. (Maurice Hope)

1966: KENTUCKY COLONELS.
Tracks: Not Advised.
LP . . . . **SHILOH 4084**
Shiloh / May '79.

APPALACHIAN SWING.
Tracks: Clinch mountain backstep / Nine pound hammer / Listen to the mocking bird / Wild Bill Jones / Billy in the low ground / Lee Highway blues / I am a pilgrim / Prisoner's song, The / Sally Godin / Faded love / John Henry / Flat fork.
MC . . . . **ROUSS 31MC**
Rounder / '93 / Projection / Roots Records / Swift / C.M. Distribution / Topic Records / Jazz Music / Hot Shot / A.D.A Distribution / Direct Distribution.
CD . . . . **ROUSS 31CD**
Rounder / Aug '93 / Projection / Roots Records / Swift / C.M. Distribution / Topic Records / Jazz Music / Hot Shot / A.D.A Distribution / Direct Distribution.

FEATURING CLARENCE WHITE.
Tracks: Not Advised.
LP . . . . **ROUNDER 0098**
MC . . . . **ROUNDER 0098C**
Rounder / '88 / Projection / Roots Records / Swift / C.M. Distribution / Topic Records / Jazz Music / Hot Shot / A.D.A Distribution / Direct Distribution.

NEW SOUND OF BLUEGRASS AMERICA, THE.
Tracks: Not Advised.
LP . . . . **BRIAR M109**
Sierra Briar (USA) / Apr '79 / Mike's Country Music Room.

ON STAGE.
Tracks: John Hardy / Used to be / Shackles and chains / Durham's bull / Mountain dew / I might take you back again / Bluegrass breakdown / Flop eared mule / I wonder how the old folks at home / Over in the gloryland / Reno ride / Ocean of diamonds / Bending the strings.
LP . . . . **ROUNDER 0199**
Rounder / Jul '84 / Projection / Roots Records / Swift / C.M. Distribution / Topic Records / Jazz Music / Hot Shot / A.D.A Distribution / Direct Distribution.
LP . . . . **SDLP 050**
Sundown / '88 / Terry Blood Dist. / Jazz Music / C.M. Distribution.
MC . . . . **ROUNDER 0199C**
Rounder / Aug '88 / Projection / Roots Records / Swift / C.M. Distribution / Topic Records / Jazz Music / Hot Shot / A.D.A Distribution / Direct Distribution.

Kentucky County

BACK HOME AGAIN.
Tracks: Not Advised.
LP . . . . **BUFF L-2004**
Buffalo (UK) / Mar '79 / M.I.S.Records.

Kentucky Headhunters

The Kentucky Headhunters comprised; Ricky Lee Phelps, Doug Phelps, Greg Martin, Richard Young & Fred Young. Described as Frank Zappa meets Bill Monroe, this country-rock outfit had been in business for many years and had been turned down by every label in Nashville. Finally, Mercury decided to take the risk and the Kentucky Headhunters first single, *Walk Softly On This Heart Of Mine*, reached the top 30. The follow-up, *Dumas Walker*, hit the top 20, whilst their debut album, *Pickin' On Nashville*, sold over a million copies. At the 1990 CMA awards, the band won the album and vocal group awards. (Tony Byworth)

ELECTRIC BARNYARD.
Tracks: It's chitlin' time / Ballad of Davy Crockett, The / Only Daddy that'll walk the line / With body and soul / Diane / 16 and single / Wishin' well / Spirit in the sky / Always makin' love / Love bug crawl / Big Mexican dinner / Kickin' them blues around / Take me back.
CD **8480542**
LP **8480541**
MC **8480544**
Mercury / Apr '91 / PolyGram.

PICKIN' ON NASHVILLE.
Tracks: Walk softly on this heart of mine / Rag top / Smooth / Oh lonesome me / Dumas walker / Rock'n'roll angel / Skip a rope / My daddy was a milkman.
CD **838 744 2**
LP **838 744 1**
MC **838 744 4**
Phonogram / Mar '90 / PolyGram.

RAVE ON.
Tracks: Not Advised.
CD . . . . **.512568-2**
MC . . . . **.512568-4**
Vertigo / Jun '93 / PolyGram.

Kershaw, Doug

Doug Kershaw was born on 24th January 1936 in Tiel Ridge, Louisiana. This cajun fiddle/vocalist, formed a group with his brother, Rusty and recorded for Feature in 1953. Their first chart entry was *So Lovely Baby*, on the Hickory label. Surprisingly, they only made the top ten once with, *Louisiana Man* in 1961. Doug kershaw turned solo in 1964, recording mainly for Warners, but gaining only minor success. He charted in 1988 with *Cajun Baby*, in a duet with Hank Williams Jr. Doug Kershaw has also appeared in the films, Zachariah, Medicine Ball Caravan and Days Of Heaven. (Maurice Hope)

HOT DIGGITY DOUG.
Tracks: Cajun baby / Louisiana / Jambalaya / I wanna hold you / Calling Baton Rouge / My toot toot / Boogie queen / Just like you / Louisiana man / Mansion in Spain / Cajun stripper / Fiddlin' man.
CD . . . . **CDSD 066**
LP . . . . **SDLP 066**
Sundown / Oct '89 / Terry Blood Dist. / Jazz Music / C.M. Distribution.

Kershaw, Rusty

CAJUN COUNTRY ROCKERS 3 (Kershaw, Rusty & Doug).

Tracks: Sweet sweet girl / Cheated too / Cajun Joe / So lovely baby / Diggy liggy lo / Louisiana man / Mey Mae / Sweet thing tell me that you love me / It's too late / Hey sherriff / Why don't you love me.
LP . . . . **BFX 15036**
Bear Family / Sep '84 / Rollercoaster Records / Swift / Direct Distribution.

JAY MILLER SESSIONS VOL. 22 (Kershaw, Rusty & Doug).
Tracks: Not Advised.
LP . . . . **FLY 571**
Flyright / Oct '86 / Hot Shot / Roots Records / Wellard Dist. / Charly / Swift / Projection.

LOUISIANA MAN (Kershaw, Rusty & Doug).
Tracks: Louisiana man / Diggy liggy lo / Cheated too / Cajun Joe / We'll do it anyway / Jole blon / So lovely baby / Look around / Mister love / Going down the road / Never love again / Kaw-liga.
LP . . . . **SDLP 022**
Sundown / Jul '85 / Terry Blood Dist. / Jazz Music / C.M. Distribution.
CD . . . . **CDSD 022**
Sundown / Mar '92 / Terry Blood Dist. / Jazz Music / C.M. Distribution.

MORE CAJUN COUNTRY ROCK (Kershaw, Rusty & Doug).
Tracks: Look around (take a look at me) / Can I be dreaming / Your crazy crazy heart / I'm gonna gonna gonna see my baby (Previously unissued.) / Mister love / Hey, you there / Money / You'll see / I never had the blues / Love me to pieces / Kaw-liga / Never love again / (Our own) Jole Blon / Make me realize / I'll understand / We'll do it anyway.
LP . . . . **BFX 15143**
Bear Family / Nov '84 / Rollercoaster Records / Swift / Direct Distribution.

RUSTY, DOUG, WILEY & FRIENDS (Kershaw, Rusty & Doug/Wiley Barkdull).
Tracks: Not Advised.
LP . . . . **FLY 619**
Flyright / '89 / Hot Shot / Roots Records / Wellard Dist. / Charly / Swift / Projection.

Kessinger, Clark

CLARK KESSINGER.
Tracks: Not Advised.
LP . . . . **ROUNDER 0004**
Rounder / '88 / Projection / Roots Records / Swift / C.M. Distribution / Topic Records / Jazz Music / Hot Shot / A.D.A Distribution / Direct Distribution.

Ketchum, Hal

Singer/songwriter born in 1952, near Greenwich, New York. After high school, he moved around the country working with his chosen trade, carpentry. Playing part-time in R&B bands down in Florida, then a spell back in Saratoga Springs - before moving to his now adopted home Texas. He learnt his trade whilst playing the folk circuit in the San Antonio region, becoming a regular at Kerrville's Folk Festival - winning its songwriting contest in 1986. His debut solo album *Threadbare Alibis* was released in 1989 on the German Line label, available only on cassette on the Watermelon label. Soon after he secured a writing deal with the Forerunner Music Group, a record deal with MCA Curb followed. Ketchum's 1991 debut million selling album *Past The Point Of Rescue* (the title track written by Ireland's Mick Hanly) featured Pat Alger's *Small Town Saturday Night* a No. 2 hit single, backed-up with the top three title track and top twenty tracks *Five O'Clock World* and *I Know Where Love Lives* . His 1992 album *Sure Love* and *Hearts Are Gonna Roll* peaking at No's 3 & 2 respectively. (Maurice Hope)

PAST THE POINT OF RESCUE.
Tracks: Small town Saturday night / I know where love lies / Old soldiers / Somebody's love / Past the point of rescue / Five o'clock world / I miss my Mary / Don't strike a match (To the book of love) / Long day comin' / She found the place.
CD **D2 774550**
Curb / Jan '92 / BMG.

THREADBARE ALIBIS.
Tracks: Twenty years / Someplace far away / Sawmill song / Bobbie's song / Better left unsaid / Morning side of dawn / Belgian team, The / Black burning air / Came down to ride / Naomi.
CD . . . . **SDCD 9.00749**
Sawdust / '90.

Kilgore, Merle

Songwriter/guitarist. Born Wyatt Merle Kilgore on 08.09.1934 in Chickasha, Oklahoma, raised in Shreveport, Louisiana. Secured a job at 16 as DJ on KENT Shreveport, played the Louisiana Hayride and Grand Ole' Opry during the 1950's and penned hits for others including *More and more* for Webb Pierce, *Wolverton Mountain* for Claude King, *Johnny Reb* for Johnny Horton and *Ring of fire* (penned with June Carter) for Johnny Cash. His recordings can be found on Imperial, Starday, Columbia, Elektra and Warner Brothers. *Dear Mama* and *Love has made you beautiful* his most notable chart entries. Spent some twenty years as the opening act and manager to Hank Williams Jr. Appeared in the films *Country comes to Broadway* , *Nevada Smith* and *Five card stud.* (Maurice Hope)

TEENAGER'S HOLIDAY.
Tracks: Ride Jesse ride / Hang doll / Everybody's needs a little lovin' / Ernie / Start all over again / Tom Dooley Jr. / More and more / It can't rain all the time / Seein' double, feelin' single / What makes me love you / Funny feelin' / Now that you are leavin' / That's when my blues began / Teenager's holiday / Please, please, please / I feel guilty / Trying to find (someone like you) / Goodbye / 42 in Chicago / Wicked city / I'll take Ginger and run away / Girl named Liz, A / Ain't nothin' but a man / Somethin' goin' on that I can't see / There's no food in this house / Lover's hell / Back street affair / Trouble at the tower / Love bug, The / I'll shake your hand.
CD . . . . **BCD 15544**
Bear Family / May '91 / Rollercoaster Records / Swift / Direct Distribution.

King, Bev

MARTY ROBBINS SCRAPBOOK (King, Bev & Joe Knight).
Tracks: Castle in the sky, A / Begging to you / I'll go on alone / Love me / I couldn't keep from (crying) / Sing me something sentimental / Don't worry / At the end of a long lonely day / It's your world / Hands you're holding now, The / Singing the blues / Pretty words.
LP . . . . **BFX 15217**
Bear Family / Nov '85 / Rollercoaster Records / Swift / Direct Distribution.

King, Charlie

FOOD, PHONE, GAS & LODGING.
Tracks: Not Advised.
CD . . . . **FF 536CD**
MC . . . . **FF 536C**
Flying Fish (USA) / '92 / Cadillac Music / Roots Records / Projection / C.M. Distribution / Direct Distribution / Jazz Music / Duncans / A.D.A Distribution.

MY HEART KEEPS SNEAKIN' UP ON MY HEAD.
Tracks: Not Advised.
LP . . . . **FF 349**
Flying Fish (USA) / Mar '89 / Cadillac Music / Roots Records / Projection / C.M. Distribution / Direct Distribution / Jazz Music / Duncans / A.D.A Distribution.

STEPPIN' OUT.
Tracks: Not Advised.
LP . . . . **FF 492**
Flying Fish (USA) / Feb '89 / Cadillac Music / Roots Records / Projection / C.M. Distribution / Direct Distribution / Jazz Music / Duncans / A.D.A Distribution.

King, Claude

CLAUDE KING'S BEST.
Tracks: Not Advised.
LP . . . . **GT 0066**
Gusto (USA) / '80.

King, Eileen

COUNTRY FLAVOUR, THE.
Tracks: Silver threads and golden needles / Texas in my heart / Charlie Brown / Travelling home / Johnny / Jesus hears / You'll never miss the water / Hello trouble / You're driving me out of my mind / You ain't woman enough / Connemara cradle song / What's the bottle done to my baby.
LP . . . . **PHL 408**
MC . . . . **CPHL 408**
Homespun (Ireland) / '82 / Homespun Records / Ross Records / Wellard Dist.

COUNTRY GIFTS.
Tracks: Not Advised.
MC . . . . **TSC 100**
Topspin (Ireland) / '88 / I & B Records.

FROM NASHVILLE.
Tracks: Not Advised.
MC . . . . **TSC 124**
Topspin (Ireland) / '88 / I & B Records.

King, John

KING'S COUNTRY.
Tracks: Not Advised.
MC . . . . **CDR 006**
Donside / Mar '88 / Ross Records.

PORTRAIT: JOHN KING.
Tracks: True life country music / She's a go'er / I'll leave this world loving you / Time after time / Bridge that just won't burn / Coming home to you / No one will ever know / Jesus loves cowboys the same / How sure I am / Lay down beside me / That's all that matters / Neon lights.
LP . . . . **JULEP 25**
Mint / May '82 / RTM / Pinnacle.

TRUE LIFE COUNTRY MUSIC.
Tracks: True life country music / How sure I am.
■ **7"** . . . . **CHEW 79**
Mint / Apr '83.

King, Pee Wee

Born Julius Frank Kuczynski, 18.02.1914 in Abrams, Wisconsin - raised in Milwaukee. Bandleader - playing fiddle and accordian. After a year with the Log Cabin Boys (1935-1936) he formed his own band, the Golden West Cowboys, playing on Knoxville WNOX as regulars on Lowell Blanchard's Mid Day Merry-Go-Round. During 1941-1942, with Minnie Pearl, toured extensively as the Grand Ole Opry's Hillbilly Camel Caravan, entertaining the troops - playing bases, hospitals and the like . King, a member of the Opry from 1937 through to 1947, left to take on his own ten year TV series - Wave Louisiana. It was in 1948 that his impressive run of songs was to emerge including *Tennessee Waltz* (a two time hit for King in 1948 and 1951). King, in six short years was to release such hits as *Tennessee Polka* , *Bonaparte's retreat* and *Slow poke* (No. 1) all featuring his original band. From 1952 it was simply Pee Wee King And His Band, still featuring Redd Stewart on lead vocals, as he scored further top ten success with *Silver and Gold* , *Busybody* , *Changing partners* and *Bimbo*. Good as his work was, it's since ben overshadowed by many covers - a compliment in itself. Jim Reeves (*Bimbo*), Glen Campbell (*Bonaparte's retreat*), Hawshaw Hawkins (*Slow Poke*), Patti Page (*Tennessee Waltz*) and Red Foley (*Tennessee polka*) all having success with his songs, many penned with Stewart. Page's 1951 hit *Tennessee Waltz* made the top slot on the pop charts and No. 2 in the country charts - the much covered song had already seen country's top ten via Roy Acuff and Cowboy Compas. By May 1951 it had sold 4,800,000 copies (grossing the writers/publishers Acuff - Rose $330,000). Lacy J. Dalton added to it's revenue in 1980, when her single version made country's top twenty. After finishing his TV contract, King spent four years working with comedienne Minnie Pearl (1959-1963), and had five more years on the road before retiring in 1968. He was elected to the Country Music Hall Of Fame in 1974. (Maurice Hope)

BALLROOM KING.
Tracks: Catty town / Plantation boogie / I don't mind / Blue suede shoes / Steel rag guitar / Railroad boogie / Rootie tootie / Half a dozen boogie / Ballroom baby / Ten gallon boogie / Hoot scoot / Chew tobacco rag / Forty nine women / Indian giver / Bull fiddle boogie / Tweedle dee.
LP **DT33-001**
Detour / Dec '82 / Swift / Jazz Music / Pinnacle.

BEST OF PEE WEE KING (King, Pee Wee & Redd Stewart).
Tracks: Not Advised.
LP . . . . **SLP 965**
MC . . . . **GT 5965**
Starday (USA) / Apr '87 / Crusader Marketing Co.

HOG WILD TOO.
Tracks: Not Advised.
LP . . . . **Z 2017**
Zu Zazz / Aug '90 / Hot Shot / A.D.A Distribution / C.M. Distribution.

ROMPIN', STOMPIN', SINGIN', SWINGIN'.
Tracks: Birmingham bounce / Ghost and honest Joe, The / Say good morning, Nellie / Goin' back to L.A. (Previously unissued.) / Tennessee central number nine / Texas Toni Lee / Keep them icy cold fingers off of me / Lonesome steel guitar (Previously unissued.) / Quit honkin' that horn / New York to New Orleans / I hear you knocking / Oh Monah / Mop rag boogie / Jukebox blues / Flying home / Slow bike.
LP . . . . **BFX 15101**
Bear Family / Sep '84 / Rollercoaster Records / Swift / Direct Distribution.

King, Sid

BACK DOOR MAN.
Tracks: Back door man / I'd rather hear Willie.
7" . . . . **HR 45 006**
Hot Rock / Sep '80 / Hot Rock Records.

GONNA SHAKE THIS SHACK TONIGHT (King, Sid & The Five Strings).
Tracks: Good rockin' baby / Put something in the pot boy / Drinking spoli oli / When my baby left me / Gonna shake this shack tonight / It's true, I'm blue / Crazy little heart / Mama, I want you / I like it / But I don't care / Warmed over kisses (Previously unissued) / What have ya got to lose / I've got the blues / Ooby dooby / Booger red / Twenty one (Previously unissued) / Sag, drag and fall / Blue suede shoes / Let 'er roll / Purr, kitty, purr.
LP . . . . **BFX 15048**
Bear Family / Sep '84 / Rollercoaster Records / Swift / Direct Distribution.
CD . . . . **BCD 15535**
Bear Family / Mar '92 / Rollercoaster Records / Swift / Direct Distribution.

■ DELETED K 3

LET'S GET LOOSE.
Tracks: House of blue lights / One more time / If you really want me to I'll go / Share what you got with me / Back door man / Boogie woogie country girl / Let's get loose / Decoy baker / Don't get above your raising / It hurts me so (To see love go) / Rockabilly music / Drinkin' wine spoil oil.
LP . . . . **LP 8701**
Rockhouse / Jul '87 / Charly / C.M. Distribution / Nervous Records.

ROCKIN' ON THE RADIO (King, Sid & The Five Strings).
Tracks: Rock the joint / Little Willie boogie / If tears could cry / In the jailhouse now / Slowly / Who put the turtle in Myrtle's girdle / That's alright / Five string hoedown / Rock my soul / Maybellene / Wildwood flower / There she goes / Making believe / Flip flop and fly.
LP . . . . **ROLL 2006**
Rollercoaster / Sep '84 / Rollercoaster Records / Swift.

Kirwan, Dominic

Hailing from Omagh, County Tyrone, he started out as a traditional Irish dancer but switched to singing, with major breaks coming in 1988 when he won two major talent contests. Signing with Ritz Records in 1989, Kirwan first began getting mass exposure when he toured with Charley Pride in autumn 1990. Since then he's been seen in concert with another popular American attraction, Tammy Wynette, though he's now drawing the crowds in his own right thanks to his high energy, cabaret styled performances. Many have tipped him as 'heir apparent' to the Daniel O'Donnell kingdom. (Tony Byworth)

AN EVENING WITH DOMINIC KIRWAN.
Tracks: Life is what you make it / Hello Marylou / Only couple on the floor, The / Someone had to teach you / My Irish rose / Absent friends / My own Donegal / Oh pretty woman / Let it be me / Can't help falling in love with you / Hoots mon / Medley (Amarillo; Beautiful sunday; Clap ypur hands; Knock three times; Amarillo) / Will you go lassie/Wild mountain thyme / Love without end, Amen / I'll leave this world loving you / Medley (2) (Cryin' time; Together again; I can't stop loving you; Take these chains from my heart) / Picture of you, A / I'd be a legend in my time / Medley (3) (If you're Irish come into the parlour; Hannigans hooley; courtin' in the kitchen) / Peter's reel / Golden jubilee / It's a great day for the Irish / Through the eyes of an Irishman / Bless this house.
VHS . . . . **RITZV 0013**
Ritz / Feb '93 / Pinnacle / Midland Records.

DON'T LET ME CRY AGAIN.
Tracks: Don't let me cry again / Through the eyes of an Irish man / Life is what you make it (Not available on 7" format.) / Absent friends (Not available on 7" format.).
7" . . . . **RITZ 256P**
CD Single . . . . **RITZCD 256**
MC Single . . . . **RITZC 256**
Ritz / Feb '93 / Pinnacle / Midland Records.

EVERGREEN.
Tracks: Hold me just one more time / Only couple on the floor, The / My happiness / Picture of you, A / If you're ever in my arms again / I really don't want to know / Evergreen / Absent friends / Release me / One bouquet of roses / Way love's supposed to be, The / Hello Mary Lou / Bless this house.
CD . . . . **CD 0065**
MC . . . . **LC 0065**
Ritz / Nov '91 / Pinnacle / Midland Records.

GREEN FIELDS OF IRELAND.
Tracks: Not Advised.
MC . . . . **MB LP 1037**
Music Box (Ireland) / '88.

GREEN HILLS ARE ROLLING STILL, THE.
Tracks: Green hills are rolling still, The / Golden dreams / More than yesterday (Only on cassette single.) / Little cabin boy, The (Only on cassette single.).
7" . . . . **RITZ 199**
Ritz / Apr '89 / Pinnacle / Midland Records.
MC Single . . . . **RITZC 199**
Ritz / May '89 / Pinnacle / Midland Records.

I'LL LEAVE THE WORLD LOVING YOU.
Tracks: I'll leave the world loving you / Achin' breaking heart.
7" . . . . **RITZ 111**
Ritz / May '90 / Pinnacle / Midland Records.

LIVE IN CONCERT.
Tracks: Please help me I'm falling / Heartaches by the number / My beautiful wife / Oh lonesome me / Hand that rocks the cradle, The / Have you ever been lonely? / There's always me / St. Theresa of the roses / Irish medley / Flower of Scotland / Say you'll stay until tomorrow / If you should come back today / Almost persuaded / Noreen Bawn.
VHS . . . . **RITZV 0007**
Ritz / Nov '90 / Pinnacle / Midland Records.

LOVE WITHOUT END.
Tracks: Like father, like son / Almost persuaded / Love letters in the sand / Straight and narrow / Just for old times sake / Stranger things have happened / Say you'll stay until tomorrow / When the girl in your arms / Love without end, amen / There's always me / Hand that rocks the cradle, The / Fool's pardon / Life is what you make it / Noreen Bawn.
CD . . . . **RITZCD 0060**
MC . . . . **RITZLC 0060**
Ritz / Nov '90 / Pinnacle / Midland Records.
CD . . . . **RITZRCD 527**
MC . . . . **RITZRC 527**
Ritz / Apr '93 / Pinnacle / Midland Records.

ONLY COUPLE ON THE FLOOR, THE.
Tracks: Only couple on the floor, The / There's always me / St Teresa of the roses.
CD Single . . . . **RITZCD 243**
Ritz / Oct '92 / Pinnacle / Midland Records.

TRY A LITTLE KINDNESS.
Tracks: Oh lonesome me / I'll leave this world loving you / Achin' breaking heart / Before the next teardrop falls / Try a little kindness / More than yesterday / My beautiful wife / Sea of heartbreak / Heaven knows / Heartaches by the number / Careless hands / Golden dreams / Paper roses / St. Theresa of the roses.
CD . . . . **CD 111**
MC . . . . **LC 0050**
Ritz / Mar '90 / Pinnacle / Midland Records.
CD . . . . **RITZCD 504**
MC . . . . **RITZRC 504**
Ritz / '91 / Pinnacle / Midland Records.

Knoblock, Fred

KILLIN' TIME (Knoblock, Fred & Susan Anton).
Tracks: Killin' time / Love is no friend to a fool.
■ **7"** . . . . **K 11646**
Scotti Bros (USA) / Mar '81.

WHY NOT ME.
Tracks: Why not me / Can I get a wish.
■ **7"** . . . . **K 11556**
Atlantic / Sep '80.

Knox, Buddy

This American singer, songwriter, guitarist and harmonica player was born Wayne Knox in a place called Happy in Texas. Before committing himself to a full time musical career, he studied accountancy and business administration with a view to joining an oil company. While at West Texas State University, he met two other musically inclined students, Jimmy Bowen and Don Lanier. They formed a group named The Rhythm Orchids in 1955. Eventually recruiting a fourth member, Dave Allred, they reached the US No.14 position in early 1957 with their single *I'm Stickin' With You*. Even more importantly, while *I'm Stickin' With You* was on the Top 20, Knox launched his solo career with an American No.1 smash *Party Doll*. Both hits were written by Knox and Bowen; according to 'The Billboard Book of Number One Hits, Buddy thus became the first artist of the rock era to write his own US No.1 song. A tamer version by Steve Lawrence simulataneously climbed climbed to No.5. Knox's own rendition was categorised into a new mini-genre dubbed 'Tex-Mex' music - this tag was derived from the neighbouring states of Texas and New Mexico. The latter contained producer Norman Petty's studios, which became the recording home of the young Buddy Holly after he had been impressed with the sound achieved on Buddy Knox's *Party Doll*.Knox's musical roots were country and western and hillbilly but he played authentic rock'n'roll, so his music perfectly fitted the term 'rockabilly'. He had several follow-up hits to *Party Doll*, the biggest being *Hula Love* which reached the US No.9 placing. But after 1958, he never returned to the American Top 40 save for a 1961 appearance with *Lovey Dovey*. As the sixties progressed, he moved into convential country music with only moderate success. He settled in Canada during the Seventies and has continued to work as a touring performer ever since.In Britain *Party Doll* had to be content with a No.29 placing. Buddy's only other UK chart entry was *She's Gone*, which struggled to No.45 in August 1962. (Bob Macdonald).

BEST OF BUDDY KNOX.
Tracks: Party doll / Rock your little baby to sleep / Teasable, pleasable you / Storm clouds / Somebody touched me / Lovey dovey / That's why I cry / Hula love / Devil woman / Ling-ting-tong / I think I'm gonna kill myself / Cause I'm in love / Swingin' daddy / C'mon baby / All for you (CD only.) / Girl with the golden hair, The (CD only.) / She's gone (CD only.) / Whenever I'm lonely (CD only.).
CD . . . . **CDP 894 885 2**
CD . . . . **CDROU 5008**
Roulette (EMI) / Aug '90 / EMI.
■ **MC** . . . . **TCROU 5008**
Roulette (EMI) / Aug '90.

BUDDY KNOX.
Tracks: Not Advised.
LP . . . . **BB 575**
Teen / Aug '87.

GREATEST HITS: BUDDY KNOX.
Tracks: Party doll / Rock house / Maybellene / Storm clouds / Devil woman / Somebody touched me / Hula love / Rock your little baby to sleep / Lovey Dovey / Ling-ting-tong / I think I'm gonna kill myself / I washed my hands in muddy water / Travellin'.
LP . . . . **LP 8501**
Rockhouse / Mar '85 / Charly / C.M. Distribution / Nervous Records.
LP . . . . **TOP 142**
MC . . . . **KTOP 142**
Topline / Apr '86 / Charly / Swift / Black Sun Records.

HARMONY IN YOU AND ME IS GONE.
Tracks: Harmony in you and me is gone / Sweet summer winds.
■ **7"** . . . . **RWS 5001**
Redwood (USA) / May '77.

LIBERTY TAKES.
Tracks: Three eyed man / All by myself / Open your lovin' arms / She's gone / Now there's only me / Dear Abby / Three way love affair / Shadoroom / Tomorrow is a comin' / Hitch hike back to Georgia / Thanks a lot / Good lovin / All time loser / Lovey dovey / I got you / Ling-ting-tong.
■ **LP** . . . . **CR 30260**
Charly / Oct '86 / Charly.

PARTY DOLL.
Tracks: Party Doll / Rockhouse / Mabellene / Mary Lou / Rock your little baby to sleep / Hula love / Devil woman / Rockabilly walk / Rock around the clock / I'm in love with you / Swingin' Daddy / C'mon baby / Somebody touched me / That's why I cry / I think I'm gonna kill myself / Whenever I'm lonely / All for you / Long lonely nights / Storm clouds / Girl with the golden hair, The.
LP . . . . **NSPL 28243**
Pye International / Feb '78.

PARTY DOLL.
Tracks: Party doll.
■ **7"** . . . . **DB 3914**
Columbia (EMI) / May '57.

PARTY DOLL (SINGLE) (2).
Tracks: Party doll / Somebody touched me / Don't make me cry.
■ **7"** **7N 25765**
Pye International / Feb '78.

PARTY DOLL AND OTHER HITS.
Tracks: Not Advised.
MC **4XLL 9177**
Capitol (Specials) / Dec '88.

SHE'S GONE.
Tracks: She's gone.
■ **7"** . . . . **LIB 55473**
Liberty / Aug '62.

SWEET COUNTRY MUSIC.
Tracks: Not Advised.
LP . . . . **RSRMP 4001**
Rockstar (1) / Aug '87 / Swift / C.M. Distribution.

TEXAS ROCKABILLY MAN.
Tracks: Lotta lovin' / Ooby dooby / I'm looking for someone to love / Blue levi jeans / Going to Hollywood / Knock kneed Nellie from Knoxville / Hole in the ground / Bip bop boom / Little bitty baby / Ham bone / Nebraska sunrise / Honky tonk man / Back to New Orleans / Kokomo Island / Restless / Too much fun.
LP . . . . **RSRLP 1012**
Rockstar (1) / Apr '87 / Swift / C.M. Distribution.

TRAVELLIN' LIGHT.
Tracks: Not Advised.
LP . . . . **RLP 004**
Rundell / Oct '88 / Swift.

Koloc, Bonnie

WITH YOU ON MY SIDE.
Tracks: Not Advised.
LP . . . . **FF 437**
Flying Fish (USA) / '88 / Cadillac Music / Roots Records / Projection / C.M. Distribution / Direct Distribution / Jazz Music / Duncans / A.D.A Distribution.

Kosek, Kenny

HASTY LONESOME (Kosek, Kenny & Matt Glaser).
Tracks: Not Advised.
LP . . . . **ROUNDER 0127**
Rounder / '88 / Projection / Roots Records / Swift / C.M. Distribution / Topic Records / Jazz Music / Hot Shot / A.D.A Distribution / Direct Distribution.

Krauss, Alison

Illinois born Alison Krauss has been winning awards in America's midwest for her fiddle prowess since 1983. While not yet in her teens, with her band Union Station Alison was soon gaining the reputation as a hot property, winning Louisville's Kentucky Fried Chicken Festival Band contest in 1986. *Too Late To Cry* was her debut release at the tender age of 15.

EVERYTIME YOU SAY GOODBYE.
Tracks: Everytime you say goodbye / Another night / Last love letter / Cluck old hen / Who can blame you / It work this time / Heartstrings / I don't know why / Cloudy

K 4 ■ DELETED

days / New fool / Shield of faith / Lose again / Another day, another dollar / Jesus help me stand.

CD	ROUCD 0285
MC	ROUMC 0285

Rounder / '92 / Projection / Roots Records / Swift / C.M. Distribution / Topic Records / Jazz Music / Hot Shot / A.D.A Distribution / Direct Distribution.

I'VE GOT THAT OLD FEELING.
Tracks: I've got that old feeling / Dark skies / Wish I still had you / Endless highway / Winter of a broken heart / It's over / Will you be leaving / Steel rails / Tonight I'll be lonely too / One good reason / That makes two of us / Longest highway.

CD	CD 0275
LP	ROUNDER 0275
MC	ROUNDER 0275C

Rounder / '90 / Projection / Roots Records / Swift / C.M. Distribution / Topic Records / Jazz Music / Hot Shot / A.D.A Distribution / Direct Distribution.

TOO LATE TO CRY (Krauss, Alison & Various Artists).
Tracks: Too late to cry / Foolish heart / Song for life / Dusty Miller / If I give my heart / In your eyes / Don't follow me / Gentle river / On the borderline / Forgotten pictures / Sleep on.

CD	CD 0235
LP	ROUNDER 0235
MC	ROUNDER 0235C

Rounder / Aug '88 / Projection / Roots Records / Swift / C.M. Distribution / Topic Records / Jazz Music / Hot Shot / A.D.A Distribution / Direct Distribution.

TWO HIGHWAYS (Krauss, Alison & Union Station).
Tracks: Two highways / I'm alone again / Wild Bill Jones / Beaumont rag / Heaven's bright shore / Love you in vain / Here comes goodbye / As lovely as you / Windy City rag / Lord don't you forsake me / Teardrops will kiss the morning dew / Midnight rider.

CD	CD 0257

Rounder / '89 / Projection / Roots Records / Swift / C.M. Distribution / Topic Records / Jazz Music / Hot Shot / A.D.A Distribution / Direct Distribution.

Kristofferson. Kris

Extraodinarily, Kristofferson's only foray in to the UK charts as a performer was with 1978's *Natural act* LP, a joint album with wife Rita Coolidge which peaked at a measly no.35 position. None of his solo records have ever charted in the UK. However, the three pronged singing/songwriting/acting career of the Texas born Kristofferson has ensured that all British observers will have been exposed to his work at some stage. Amongst his best known songs are *Me and Bobby McGee* (a posthumous US no.1 for Janis Joplin in 1971), *Help me make it through the night* (a UK hit for Gladys Knight & The Pips in 1972, and again for reggae star John Holt in 1975, and *For the good times* (another much covered standard, a UK smash for Perry Como in 1973). Kris married Rita Coolidge in 1973 and the two vocalists appeared together in the 1974 movie "Pat Garratt and Billy The Kid". This launched Kristofferson on a healthy acting career, which included notable roles with Barbara Streisand (*A star is born*, whose soundtrack LP was a international smash in 1977) and Jane Fonda (*Rollover*). He entered a bad patch in the late seventies, with the break up of his marriage and some alcohol difficulties. He got himself together again in the eighties and, in 1985, teamed up with fellow country stars Waylon Jennings, Willie Nelson and Johnny Cash for the *Highwayman* album. (Bob Macdonald)

BORDER LORD.
Tracks: Josie / Burden of freedom / Stagger Mountain tragedy / Border Lord / Somebody nobody knows / Little girl lost / Smokey put the sweat on me / When she's wrong / Gettin' by / High and strange / Kiss the world goodbye.

LP	MNT 64963
■ MC	MNT 4064963

CBS / '78 / Sony.

BREAKAWAY (Kristofferson, Kris & Rita Coolidge).
Tracks: Lover please / Sweet Susannah / Dakota / What'cha gonna do / Things I might have been, The / Slow down / Rain / We must have been out of our minds / I've got to have you.

CD	26 10 692
MC	26 10 694

Dillion / '92 / Sound Solutions.

COUNTRY STORE: KRIS KRISTOFFERSON.
Tracks: Loving her was easier / Why me / Kiss the world goodbye / Jody and the kid / Lover please / Out of mind, out of sight / Jesus was a capricorn / Me and Bobby McGee / Help me make it through the night / I'd

rather be sorry / Who's to bless, and who's to blame / Here comes that rainbow again / Breakdown (a long way from home) (Only on CD.) / Taker, The (Only on CD.) / Pilgrim, The (chapter 33) (Only on CD.) / Nobody wins (Only on CD.).

CD	CDCST 5
MC	CSTK 5

Country Store / '88 / BMG.

■ LP	CST 5

Country Store / '88.

EASTER ISLAND.
Tracks: Risky bizness / How do you feel (about foolin' around) / Forever in your love / Sabre and the rose, The / Spooky lady's revenge / Easter Island / Bigger the fool (the harder the fool), The / Lay me down (and love the world away) / Fighter, The / Living legend.

LP	MNT 86056
■ MC	MNT 4086056

CBS / '78 / Sony.

FULL MOON (Kristofferson, Kris & Rita Coolidge).
Tracks: Not Advised.

HELP ME MAKE IT THROUGH THE NIGHT.
Tracks: Help me make it through the night / Year 2000 minus 25, The / If it's all the same to you / Easy come on / Stallion / Rocket to stardom / For the good times / Stranger / Who's to bless and who's to blame / Don't cuss the fiddle / Silver (the hunger).

LP	31839
MC	40 31839

CBS / '84 / Sony.

JESUS WAS A CAPRICORN.
Tracks: Jesus was a capricorn / Nobody wins / It sure was (love) / Sugar man / Help me / Jesse Younger / Give it time to be tender / Out of mind, out of sight / Enough for you / Why me.

LP	MNT 65391
■ MC	MNT 4065391

CBS / '78 / Sony.

CD	26 10 632
MC	26 10 634

Dillion / '92 / Sound Solutions.

LEGENDARY YEARS, THE.
Tracks: Me and Bobby McGee / Josie / Lover please / Jesus was a Capricorn / Magdalena / Living legend / Help me make it (through the night) / Smokey put the sweat on me / Why me? / Silver tongued devil / When she's wrong / I my smoke too much / Easter Island / It's never gonna be the same again / Golden Idol, The / I'd rather be sorry / Bigger the fool, The / Shake hands with the Devil / Nobody loves anybody anymore / Broken freedom song / Here comes that rainbow again / Epitaph(black and blue).

LP	KKVSOPCD 141
Double LP	KKVSOPLP 141
■ MC	KKVSOPMC 141

Connoisseur Collection / Apr '90 / Pinnacle.

LOVER PLEASE (Kristofferson, Kris & Rita Coolidge).
Tracks: Lover please / Slow down.

■ 7"	MNT 3046

Monument / Apr '75.

■ 7"	MNT 6474

Monument / Jun '78.

ME AND BOBBY MCGEE.
Tracks: Blame it on the stones / To beat the devil / Me and Bobby McGee / Best of all possible worlds, The / Help me make it through the night / Law is for protection, The / Of the people.

LP	MNT 64631
■ MC	MNT 4064631

CBS / '78 / Sony.

CD	26 10 662
MC	26 10 664

Dillion / '92 / Sound Solutions.

NATURAL ACT (Kristofferson, Kris & Rita Coolidge).
Tracks: Blue as I do / Not everyone knows / I fought the law / Number one / You're gonna love yourself (in the morning) / Loving her was easier / Back in my baby's arms / Please don't tell me how the story ends / Hoola hoop / Love don't live here anymore / Silver mantis.

LP	AMLH 64690

A&M / May '78.

LP	AMID 118
MC	CMID 118

A&M / Mar '82.

LP	SHM 3184
MC	HSC 3184

Hallmark / Feb '86 / Pickwick Records.

RAIN (Kristofferson, Kris & Rita Coolidge).
Tracks: Rain / What'cha gonna do.

■ 7"	MNT 2871

Monument / Jan '75.

REPOSSESSED.
Tracks: Anthem '84 / Heart, The / This old road / Love is the way / Mean old man / Shipwrecked in the eighties / They killed him / What about me / El gavilan (The hawk) / El coyote.

CD	830 460-2
LP	MERH 103
■ MC	MERHC 103

Mercury / Mar '87.

LP	830 460-1
■ MC	830 460-4

Mercury / Mar '87.

SHAKE HANDS WITH THE DEVIL.
Tracks: Shake hands with the devil / Prove it to you one more time again / Whiskey whiskey / Lucky in love / Seadream / Killer barracuda / Some sundown / Michoacan / Once more with feeling / Fallen angels.

■ LP	MNT 83793

Monument / Oct '79.

SILVER TONGUED DEVIL AND I, THE.
Tracks: Silver tongued devil and I, The / Jody and the kid / Billy Dee / Good christian soldier / Breakdown / Loving her was easier / Taker, The / When I loved her / Pilgrim-chapter, The / Epitaph.

CD	26 10 672
MC	26 10 674

Dillion / '92 / Sound Solutions.

SILVER-TONGUED DEVIL AND I, THE.
Tracks: Silver-tongued Devil & I, The / Jody and the Kid / Billy Dee / Good Christian soldier / Breakdown (a long way from home) / Loving her was easier (than anything I'll ever do again) / Taker, The / When I loved her / Pilgrim, The / Chapter 33 / Epitaph (black & blue).

LP	MNT 64636
■ MC	MNT 4064636

CBS / '78 / Sony.

SONGS OF KRISTOFFERSON.
Tracks: Silver tongued devil and I, The / Loving her was easier / Me and Bobby McGee / Help me make it through the night / For the good times / Sunday morning coming down / You show me yours and I'll show you mine / Pilgrim, The / Chapter 33 / Hang in hopper / Stranger / I got a life of my own / Why me / Who's to bless and who's to blame.

LP	MNT 32106

Monument / Nov '82 / Sony.

■ MC	40 32106

Monument / Nov '82.

CD	26 10 652
MC	26 10 654

Dillion / '92 / Sound Solutions.

SPOOKY LADY'S SIDESHOW.
Tracks: Same old song / Broken freedom song / Shandy (the perfect disguise) / Star-spangled bummer (whores die hard) / Lights of Magdala, The / I may smoke too much / One for the Monday / Late again (gettin' over you) / Stairway to the bottom / Rescue Mission / Smile at me again / Rock'n'roll time.

■ LP	MNT 69074

CBS / '78 / Sony.

SURREAL THING.
Tracks: You show me yours (and I'll show you mine) / Killing time / Prisoner, The / Eddie the eunuch / It's never gonna be the same again / I got a lie of my own / Stranger I love, The / Golden Idol, The / Bad love story / If you don't like Hank Williams.

LP	MNT 81496
■ MC	MNT 4081496

CBS / '78 / Sony.

THIRD WORLD WARRIOR.
Tracks: Eagle and the bear, The / Third world warrior / Aquila del norte / Hero, The / Don't let the bastards (get you down) / Love of money / Third world war / Jesse Jackson / Mal Sacate / Sandinista.

CD	834 629 2
LP	834 629 1
■ MC	834 629 4

Mercury / Jan '90.

TO THE BONE.
Tracks: Magdalena / Star crossed / Blessing in disguise / Devil to pay / Daddy's song / Snakebite / Nobody loves anybody anymore / Maybe you heard / Last time, The / I'll take any chance I can with you.

LP	MNT 84818

Monument / Apr '81.

WATCH CLOSELY NOW.
Tracks: Watch closely now / Crippled crow.

■ 7"	CBS 5336

CBS / Jun '77.

L

La Beef, Sleepy

Although he's only enjoyed the slightest of chart successes (two minor country entries: *Every day* in 1968 and *Blackland farmer* in 1971), Arkansas born Sleepy La Beef played a substantial role in the revival of rockabilly music during the 1970's. Possessing a highly distinctive baritone voice, this 6'6" entertainer made his movie debut as the Swamp Monster in the 1968 production "The Exotic Ones". He has visited the U.K. on several occasions, appearing at both country and rock'n'roll events. (Tony Byworth)

AIN'T GOT NO HOME.
Tracks: Not Advised.
LP . . . . **LPL 8312**
Rockhouse / Sep '83 / Charly / C.M. Distribution / Nervous Records.

BEEFY ROCKABILLY.
Tracks: Good rockin boogie / Blue moon of Kentucky / Send me some lovin / Corina Corina / Matchbox / Party doll / Baby lets play house / Too much monkey business / Roll over Beethoven / Polk salad Annie.
■ **LP** . . . . **CR 30145**
Charly / '74 / Charly.

DOWNHOME ROCKABILLY.
Tracks: Honky tonk hardwood floor / Tore up / Flyin' saucers rock 'n' roll / Red hot / I'm ready if you're willing / I'm a one woman man / Shot-gun boogie / Rock 'n' roll Ruby / Big boss man / Boogie woogie / Country girl / Mystery train / Something on your mind / Jack and Jill boogie / Blues stay away from me.
LP . . . . **CR 30172**
Charly / Charly.

EARLY RARE & ROCKIN' SIDES.
Tracks: Not Advised.
■ **LP** . . . . **CR 30181**
Charly / Feb '80 / Charly.

ELECTRICITY.
Tracks: Not Advised.
LP . . . . **ROUNDER 3070**
MC . . . . **ROUNDER 3070C**
Rounder / '88 / Projection / Roots Records / Swift / C.M. Distribution / Topic Records / Jazz Music / Hot Shot / A.D.A Distribution / Direct Distribution.

IT AIN'T WHAT YOU EAT.
Tracks: I got it / Roosters are crowing, The / Lost highway / I'm ready / Satisfied / Breaking up home / Wonderful time up there, A / Shake a hand / If I ever had a good thing / Let's talk about us / I don't believe you've met my baby / Walking slowly / Tutti frutti / All the time / Lonely / I walk the line / All alone / I'm through / Bell hop blues / I'm a hobo / I can't find the doorknob / Gee whiz.
LP . . . . **ROUNDER 3052**
MC . . . . **ROUNDER 3052C**
Rounder / Aug '88 / Projection / Roots Records / Swift / C.M. Distribution / Topic Records / Jazz Music / Hot Shot / A.D.A Distribution / Direct Distribution.
LP . . . . **SNTF 843**
Sonet / Jun '88 / Swift / C.M. Distribution / Roots Records / Jazz Music / Sonet Records / Cadillac Music / Projection / Wellard Dist. / Hot Shot.

NOTHIN' BUT THE TRUTH.
Tracks: Tore up over you / How do you talk to a baby / Milk cow blues / Just pickin' / Gunslinger / Ring of fire / Boogie at the Wayside Lounge / Worried man blues / Lets talk about us / My toot toot / Jambalaya / Whole lot of shakin'.
LP . . . . **ROUNDER 3072**
MC . . . . **ROUNDER 3072C**
Rounder / Aug '88 / Projection / Roots Records / Swift / C.M. Distribution / Topic Records / Jazz Music / Hot Shot / A.D.A Distribution / Direct Distribution.
CD . . . . **CD 3072**
Rounder / Jul '91 / Projection / Roots Records / Swift / C.M. Distribution / Topic Records / Jazz Music / Hot Shot / A.D.A Distribution / Direct Distribution.

ROCKABILLY GIANT, THE.
Tracks: Not Advised.
LP . . . . **LP 8005**
Rockhouse / Oct '88 / Charly / C.M. Distribution / Nervous Records.

ROCKABILLY HEAVYWEIGHT.
Tracks: Sick & tired / Mind your own business / Lonesome for a letter / Detour / Shame shame shame / Smoking cigarettes and drinking coffee / Cut across shorty / I'm feeling sorry / Honky tonk man / My sweet love ain't around / If you don't love me somebody else will / Milk cow blues / Ride, ride, ride / Are you teasing me? / La boeufs cajun boogie / Go ahead on baby.
■ **LP** . . . . **CRL 5017**
Charly / '80 / Charly.

SLEEPY LA BEEF & FRIENDS (La Beef, Sleepy & Friends).
Tracks: All the time / Lonely / I walk the line / All alone / I'm through / Bell hop blues / I'm a hobo / I can't find the doorknob / Sadie / Gee whiz.
■ **LP** . . . . **CH 16**
Ace / '79.

Ladoux, Chris

RODEO'S SINGING BRONCO RIDER.
Tracks: Not Advised.
LP . . . . **WRS 143**
Westwood / Jun '79 / Pinnacle.

Ladybirds

LADYBIRD COUNTRY.
Tracks: Tracks of my tears / Good 'n' country / Good time Charlie's got the blues / It's a heartache / That'll be the day / Blue eyes crying in the rain / Here, there and everywhere / I'd buy you Chattanooga / Silver threads and golden needles / Don't it make my brown eyes blue / Half as much / Do you hear my heart beat.
■ **LP** . . . . **MOR 517**
Decca / Mar '79.

LaFarge, Peter

Best known for his powerful composition *Ballad of Ira Hayes* , made a hit by Indian rights campaigner Johnny Cash, Peter LaFarge (1931-64) is a figure of historic reference being the first native American (of Pima Indian descent) to win acclaim within music circles. At the same time he denounced social injustice and took up the cause of his fellow Indians. Much decorated during the Korean War, he gained his reputation during the late '50s/early '60s by first playing the coffeehouse circuit before moving on to festivals and concerts. The enterprising Bear Family Records brought fresh attention on him, in 1992, by re-packaging his original Folkways albums in 2 CD's. (Tony Byworth)

ON THE WARPATH/AS LONG AS THE GRASS SHALL GROW.
Tracks: Look again to the wind / Senecas, The / Damn redskins / Tecumseh / Take back your atom bomb / Vision of a past warrior / Coyote / My little brother / Alaska / Custer trail of tears / Hey, Mr. President / Touriste, The / Last words / Ballad of Ira Hayes / Johnny half breed / Radioactive Eskimo / Crimson parson, The / Move over, grap a 'holt / Gather round / If I could not be an Indian / Drums / White girl / I'm an Indian, I'm an alien / Stampede / Please come back, Abe-War Whoop Father.
CD . . . . **BCD 15626**
Bear Family / Jun '92 / Rollercoaster Records / Swift / Direct Distribution.

SONGS OF THE COWBOYS/IRON MOUNTAIN SONGS.
Tracks: Whoopee ti yi yo / Chisom Trail / Sirey peaks / Lavendar cowboy / I've got no use for the women / I ride old paint / Cowboys lament / Yavipii Pete / When the works all done this fall / Cowboys dream / Black walkin', The / John Strawberry Roan / Rodeo hand, The / Cattle calls / Stumbling / Pop Reed / Pony called Nell / Marijuana blues / Snow bird blues / Hungry blues / Avril blues / Santa Fe / Alaska 49th State / Iron mountain / Falling stars / Abraham Lincoln / Cisco Houston.
CD . . . . **BCD 15627**
Bear Family / Jun '92 / Rollercoaster Records / Swift / Direct Distribution.

Lafayette

ALLIGATOR MAN (Lafayette & Jimmy C. Newman).
Tracks: Alligator man.
■ **7"** . . . . **CS 1024**
Charly / Apr '77.

Laine, Frankie

This American singer epitomised the type of big balladeer that dominated the recording scene during the late Forties and early Fifties, in the era prior to rock'n'roll. He was born Frank LoVecchio in Chicago in 1913. His stab at a show-business career looked decidedly shaky until at the age of 24, he replaced the up and coming Perry Como as a vocalist with The Freddie Carlone Band and spent several years touring the Midwest with them. He then became a resident singer with a New York radio station and, after the end of the Second World War, moved to Hollywood where he was supposedly discovered performing in a nightclub by Hoagy Carmichael.Laine came to fame in 1947 with his US Top 10 rendition of a sixteen year old song called *That's My Desire*. It opened the floodgates for a string of smashes over the next few years, including *Shine*, *When You're Smiling*, the highly original *Mule Train*, *That Lucky Old Sun*, *Cry Of The Wild Goose*, *Jezebel*, Frankie Laine quickly made history on the UK's fledgling listings by logging 18 weeks at No.1 with his quasi religious 1953 single *I Believe*. Although *I Believe* was never at the top spot for more than nine weeks at a stretch - beaten by David Whitfield's *Cara Mia* in 1954 and Slim Whitman's *Rose Marie* in 1955 - its aggregate total of 18 weeks at No.1 has never been approached by any other single in all subsequent UK chart history. By the end of 1953 he had chalked up two further British chart-toppers with *Hey Joe* and *Answer Me*, giving him a staggering tally of 27 weeks at No.1 during that calendar year.Laine continued his UK success in 1954 with a further six Top Tenners, plus three more in 1955. His fourth British No.1 hit was achieved in 1956 with *A Woman In Love*. 1957 brought him his final two American Top 10 singles, *Moonlight Gambler* and *Love Is A Golden Ring*. His last British Top Tenner was 1959's *Rawhide*.As it gradually became clear that rock'n'roll and pop music was here to stay, the ageing Frankie became an anachronism. His dramatic delivery of big ballads had made him one of the best middle of the road vocalists of his era but, by the end of the Fifties, he realised that he could not compete effectively with pop singers less than half his age! He remained an active performer, making an American Top 40 comeback in the late Sixties. (Bob MacDonald)

1947: FRANKIE LAINE (Laine, Frankie with Carl Fischer & Orchestra).
Tracks: Not Advised.
LP . . . . **HSR 198**
Hindsight / Mar '84 / Charly.
LP . . . . **HSR 216**
Hindsight / '88 / Charly.

20 GREAT TRACKS (Laine, Frankie & Friends).
Tracks: Not Advised.
CD . . . . **PRCDSP 301**
MC . . . . **PRCASSP 301**
Prestige / Aug '93 / Total / BMG.

20 OF HIS BEST.
Tracks: Rawhide / Moonlight gambler / I believe / Hummingbird / Don't fence me in / Strange lady in town / Rose, Rose I love you / There must be a reason / Answer me / Jezebel / High noon / Mule train / Jealousy / Sixteen tons / Cool water / Wheel of fortune / Rain, rain, rain / Woman in love / Granada / Cry of the wild goose.
CD . . . . **OR 0021**
Music Collection International / Aug '87 / Terry Blood Dist. / Jazz Music.

21 GREATEST HITS.
Tracks: Woman in love, A / Jealousy / High noon / On the sunny side of the street / Cool water / Kids last fight, The / You gave me a mountain / Rawhide / Moonlight gambler / Two loves have I / Jezebel / That's my desire / Cry of the wild goose / I believe / We'll be together / That lucky old sun / Shine / Your cheatin' heart / Memories / Swamp girl / Mule train.
LP . . . . **SPWM 4**
MC . . . . **CSWM 4**
Westmoor / May '89.

ALL OF ME.
Tracks: Old fashioned love / All of me / Coquette / That's my desire / Georgia on my mind / Rosetta / Hold me / Singing the blues / I wish you were jealous of me / You can depend on me.
LP . . . . **BDL 1035**
MC . . . . **AJKL 1035**
Bulldog Records / Mar '82 / President Records / Jazz Music / Wellard Dist. / TKO Records Ltd.

ALL TIME HITS.
Tracks: High noon / I believe / Answer me / Granada / Jealousy / Rain, rain, rain / Cool water / Strange lady in town / Hummingbird / Sixteen tons / Woman in love, A / Moonlight gambler / Cry of the wild goose / Mule train / Jezebel / Wheel of fortune / Rose, Rose I love you / Rawhide / Don't fence me in (CD only) / There must be a reason (CD only).
CD . . . . **CDMFP 5907**
MC . . . . **TCMFP 5907**
MFP / Apr '91 / EMI.

AMERICAN LEGEND.
Tracks: Not Advised.
MC 40 31599
CBS / Feb '78 / Sony.

ANSWER ME.
Tracks: Answer me / Jezebel.
■ 7" . . . . PB 196
Philips / Oct '53.
7" . . . . BD 24
Bulldog Records / Apr '82 / President Records / Jazz
Music / Wellard Dist. / TKO Records Ltd.

BEST OF FRANKIE LAINE.
Tracks: I believe / Mule train / Jezebel / High noon /
Answer me.
LP 1A 222-58228
MC 1A 022 58228
MFP (Holland) / Apr '83 / Pinnacle.
MC 16-16
Creole (Everest-Europa) / Jul '84.

BLOWING WILD.
Tracks: Blowing wild.
■ 7" . . . . PB 207
Philips / Jan '54.

COOL WATER.
Tracks: Cool water.
■ 7" . . . . PB 465
Philips / Jun '55.

COUNTRY STORE: FRANKIE LAINE.
Tracks: Rawhide / Hanging tree, The / Your cheatin'
heart / Cry of the wild goose / Call of the wind / Mule
train / Sixteen tons / Bowie knife / On the trail / Cool
water / Wanted man / 3.10 to Yuma, The / North to
Alaska / Gunfight at the OK Corral / Along the Navajo
trail / City boy / High noon / Tumbling tumbleweeds.
CD . . . . .CDCST 43
MC . . . . .CSTK 43
Country Store / '88 / BMG.
■ LP . . . . CST 43
Country Store / '88.

FRANKIE LAINE.
Tracks: Not Advised.
MC Set . . . . DTO 10272
Ditto / '88 / Pickwick Records.

FRANKIE LAINE.
Tracks: High noon / Jezebel / Answer me / Cool water /
Blowing wild / That lucky old sun / That's my desire /
Granada / Your cheatin' heart / Jealousy.
LP . . . . SPR 8538
MC . . . . SPC 8538
Spot / Aug '83.
LP 022 58228
MC 222 58228
MFP (Holland) / '86 / Pinnacle.

FRANKIE LAINE SINGS WESTERN.
Tracks: Not Advised.
■ CD 4650512
CBS / '89.

GIRL IN THE WOOD.
Tracks: Girl in the wood.
■ 7" . . . . DB 2907
Columbia (EMI) / Mar '53.

GOIN' LIKE WILDFIRE (Laine, Frankie & Jo
Stafford).
Tracks: Pretty eyed baby / That's the one for me / That's
good, that's bad / In the cool, cool, cool of the night /
Cambella / Hey good lookin' / Hambone / Let's have a
party / Settin' the woods on fire / Piece a puddin' /
Christmas roses / Chow willy / Bushel and a peck, A /
Floatin' down to cotton town / Way down yonder in New
Orleans / Basin Street blues / High society / Back
where I belong.
CD . . . . BCD 15620
Bear Family / Mar '92 / Rollercoaster Records / Swift /
Direct Distribution.

GOLDEN GREATS: FRANKIE LAINE.
Tracks: Memories in gold / Jealousy / High noon / On
the sunny side of the street / That's my desire / Cool
water / Woman in love / Georgia on my mind / Moonlight gambler / Jezebel / Mule train / I believe / Your
cheatin' heart / That lucky old sun / Shine / We'll be
together again.
LP 2486 263
MC 3196 093
Polydor / May '83 / PolyGram.

GOLDEN MEMORIES.
Tracks: Not Advised.
■ LP 2371 472
Polydor / Nov '74.

GOLDEN YEARS, THE.
Tracks: That's my desire / Mule train / All of me / By the
river Sainte Marie / Cry of the wild goose / I'm in the
mood for love / That lucky old sun / Mam'selle / Kiss
me again / Georgia on my mind / On the sunny side of
the street / S.H.I.N.E.
LP . . . . TIME 12
■ MC . . . . TIMEC 12
Philips (Timeless) / Nov '84.

GOOD EVENING FRIENDS (Laine, Frankie &
Johnny Ray).
Tracks: Good evening friends / Up above my head.
■ 7" . . . . PB 708
Philips / Oct '57.

GRANADA.
Tracks: Granada.
■ 7" . . . . PB 242
Philips / Mar '54.

GREATEST HITS.
Tracks: Not Advised.
CD . . . . CDGFR 044
MC . . . . MCGFR 044
IMD / Jun '92 / BMG.

GREATEST HITS: FRANKIE LAINE.
Tracks: Rawhide / Moonlight gambler / I believe /
Hummingbird / Don't fence me in / Strange lady in town
/ Red rose I love you / There must be a reason / Answer
me / Jezebel / High noon / Mule train / Jealousy /
Sixteen tons / Cool water / Wheel of fortune / Rain rain
rain / Woman in love, A / Granada / Cry of the wild
goose.
CD . . . . .U 4022
Spectrum (1) / Jun '88 / PolyGram.
CD . . . . CDGRF 044
Tring / Feb '93 / Prism Leisure PLC / Midland Records /
Taylors.

GUNSLINGER.
Tracks: Gunslinger.
■ 7" . . . . PB 1135
Philips / May '61.

HAWKEYE.
Tracks: Hawkeye.
■ 7" . . . . PB 519
Philips / Nov '55.

HELL BENT FOR LEATHER.
Tracks: Not Advised.
■ LP . . . . BBL 7468
Philips / Jun '61.

HELL HATH NO FURY.
Tracks: Hell hath no fury.
■ 7" . . . . PB 585
Philips / May '56.

HEY JOE.
Tracks: Hey Joe.
■ 7" . . . . PB 172
Philips / Oct '53.

HIGH NOON.
Tracks: High noon.
■ 7" . . . . DB 3113
Columbia (EMI) / Nov '52.

HIGH NOON.
Tracks: High noon / Cool water.
7" . . . . CBS 1156
CBS / Apr '82 / Sony.

HIGH NOON (OLD GOLD).
Tracks: High noon / Cool water.
■ 7" . . . . .OG 9082
Old Gold / Nov '80.

HIS GREATEST HITS.
Tracks: I believe / Moonlight gambler / Jealousy / Rain,
rain, rain / Sixteen tons / Cry of the wild goose /
Granada / Don't fence me in / Rose, Rose I love you /
Answer me / Woman in love / Wheel of fortune /
Rawhide / Still runs cool water / Strange lady in town /
Mule train / Hummingbird / Jezebel / There must be a
reason / High noon.
LP . . . . WW 2014
MC . . . . WW 20144
Warwick Reflections / Jun '86 / Sony.

HUMMINGBIRD.
Tracks: Hummingbird.
■ 7" . . . . PB 498
Philips / Nov '55.

I BELIEVE.
Tracks: I believe.
■ 7" . . . . PB 117
Philips / Apr '53.

IN THE BEGINNING.
Tracks: In the beginning.
■ 7" . . . . PB 404
Philips / Mar '55.

KID'S LAST FIGHT, THE.
Tracks: Kid's last fight, The.
■ 7" . . . . PB 258
Philips / Apr '54.

LOVE IS A GOLDEN RING.
Tracks: Love is a golden ring.
■ 7" . . . . PB 676
Philips / Apr '57.

MEMORIES IN GOLD (20 great hits).
Tracks: Memories in gold / Jealousy / High noon / On
the sunny side of the street / Mule train / Cool water /
Kid's last fight, The / Woman in love, A / Georgia on my
mind / Moonlight gambler / You gave me a mountain /
Jezebel / That's my desire / Cry of the wild goose / I

believe / Your cheatin' heart / Rawhide / That lucky old
sun / Shine / We'll be together again.
LP . . . . PREC 5004
MC . . . . ZPREC 5004
Prestige (BBC) / Mar '90 / Pinnacle.
CD . . . . CDPC 5004
Prestige (BBC) / Mar '92 / Pinnacle.

MOONLIGHT GAMBLER.
Tracks: Moonlight gambler.
■ 7" . . . . PB 638
Philips / Mar '57.

MY FAVOURITES.
Tracks: Not Advised.
LP . . . . .ADAH 448
MC . . . . ADAHC 448
Arcade Music Gala / Apr '86.

MY FRIEND.
Tracks: My friend.
■ 7" . . . . PB 316
Philips / Jul '54.

ON THE TRAIL.
Tracks: High noon / Cool water / 3:10 to Yuma, The /
Gunfight at the O.K. Corral / Wanted man / Bowie knife
/ Mule train / Hanging tree, The / Along the Navajo trail
/ City boy / Cry of the wild goose / Rawhide / Gunsl-
inger / Green leaves of Summer / On the trail / North to
Alaska / Call of the wild / Tumbling tumbleweeds /
Ghostriders in the sky / Prairie bell / Lonely man.
CD . . . . BCD 15480
Bear Family / Aug '90 / Rollercoaster Records / Swift /
Direct Distribution.

ON THE TRAIL AGAIN.
Tracks: Strange lady in town / Ramblin' man / Rawhide
/ Champion, the wonderhorse / Black gold / Where the
wind blows / I let her go / Drill ye tarriers / El diablo /
Ride through the night / Ghostriders in the sky / Beyond
the blue horizon / Swamp girl / Song of the open road /
My journey's end / Wagon wheels / 3-10 to Yuma / Cool
water / Gunfight at O.K. Corral / High noon / New
frontier, The / Deuces wild / Moonlight gambler / Wheel
of fortune / Dead man's hand / Hard way, The / Wayfar-
ing stranger, The / Roving gambler, The / El diablo (2).
CD . . . . BCD 15632
Bear Family / Jun '92 / Rollercoaster Records / Swift /
Direct Distribution.

PORTRAIT OF A SONG STYLIST.
Tracks: Blue moon / Side by side / Body and soul / Too
marvellous for words / Try a little tenderness / Cottage
of sale, A / Answer me / I get along without you very
well / I cover the waterfront / Woman in love / We just
couldn't say goodbye / Lover come back to me / I'm
gonna live 'til I die / September in the rain / Second
honeymoon / Touch of your lips, The / On the road to
Mandalay.
CD . . . . HARCD 102
LP . . . . HARLP 102
MC . . . . .HARMC 102
Masterpiece / Apr '89 / BMG.

RAIN, RAIN, RAIN.
Tracks: Rain, rain, rain.
■ 7" . . . . PB 311
Philips / Oct '54.

RAWHIDE.
Tracks: Rawhide / Mule train / Moonlight gambler / I
believe / Don't fence me in / Strange lady in town /
Rose, Rose I love you / There must be a reason /
Answer me / Jezebel / High noon / Jealousy / Sixteen
tons / Cool water / Wheel of fortune / Rain, rain, rain /
Granada / Cry of the wild goose.
LP . . . . SHLP 148
MC . . . . SHTC 148
Castle Showcase / Sep '86 / Arabesque Ltd.
CD . . . . 30252 AAD
CRC (USA) / Oct '89.

RAWHIDE.
Tracks: Rawhide.
■ 7" . . . . PB 965
Philips / Nov '59.

RAWHIDE (OLD GOLD).
Tracks: Rawhide / Mule train.
■ 7" . . . . .OG 9665
Old Gold / Jan '87 / Pickwick Records.

SEND IN THE CLOWNS.
Tracks: Send in the clowns / Hey hey Jesus.
■ 7" 2058982
Polydor / Feb '78.

SIXTEEN EVERGREENS.
Tracks: Not Advised.
LP . . . . .SM 3957
MC . . . . .MC 3957
Joker (USA) / '88 / C.M. Distribution / Jazz Horizons /
Jazz Music.

SIXTEEN TONS.
Tracks: Sixteen tons.
■ 7" . . . . PB 539
Philips / Jan '56.

SOMETHIN' OLD, SOMETHIN' NEW.
Tracks: Not Advised.
CD . . . . PRCDSP 300
MC . . . . PRCASSP 300
Prestige (Total) / Jun '92 / BMG.

SONGBOOK.
Tracks: Not Advised.
LP Set . . . . ALBUM 53
MC Set . . . . CASSETTE 53
World Records / '81 / EMI.

STRANGE LADY IN TOWN.
Tracks: Strange lady in town.
■ 7" . . . . PB 478
Philips / Jul '55.

TELL ME A STORY (Laine, Frankie & Jimmy Boyd).
Tracks: Tell me a story.
■ 7" . . . . PB 126
Philips / May '53.

THERE MUST BE A REASON.
Tracks: There must be a reason.
■ 7" . . . . PB 306
Philips / Oct '54.

UNCOLLECTED, THE.
Tracks: Not Advised.
LP. . . . . .HUK 198
Hindsight / Apr '86 / Charly.

VERY BEST OF FRANKIE LAINE, THE.
Tracks: Rawhide / Moonlight gambler / High noon / Mule train / Jezebel / I believe.
■ LP. . . . . PR 5032
Warwick / Sep '77.
CD . . . . FUNCD 9057
LP. . . . . FUN 9057
MC . . . . FUNC 9057
Fun (Holland) / Sep '88 / Pinnacle.

VERY BEST OF FRANKIE LAINE, THE.
Tracks: I believe / Hey Joe / Answer me / Woman in love, A / Where the wind blows / Blowing / Cool water / Kids, The / Cry of the wild goose / Tell me a story / Strange lady in town / Rawhide / High noon / Hawkeye / Sugarbush / Rain rain rain.
CD . . . . PWKS 4167
MC . . . . PWKMC 4167
Pickwick / Sep '93 / Pickwick Records.

WHERE THE WIND BLOWS.
Tracks: Where the wind blows.
■ 7" . . . . PB 167
Philips / Sep '53.

WOMAN IN LOVE (OLD GOLD).
Tracks: Woman in love / Jezebel.
7" . . . . OG 9079
Old Gold / Jul '82 / Pickwick Records.

WOMAN IN LOVE, A.
Tracks: Woman in love.
■ 7" . . . . PB 617
Philips / Sep '56.

WORLD OF FRANKIE LAINE, THE.
Tracks: Not Advised.
MC .4CRTL 2071
Ronco / Mar '82.

Laird. Skee

LOVELY LADY WITH A LOVELY VOICE.
Tracks: Not Advised.
MC . . . . .NEVC 131
Nevis / Jan '80.

SKEE LAIRD SINGS COOL COUNTRY.
Tracks: Not Advised.
LP. . . . . NEVLP 131
Nevis / Apr '79.

Lamb. Barbara

FIDDLE FATALE.
Tracks: Sally Gooden / Panhandle rag / A good woman's love / Paddy on the turnpike/gone again / Montana glide / Herman's hornpipe / So what / Foster's reel / Old French reel / I'll never be free / Katy Hill / Princess Angeline / Ducks on the Millpond (ducks with bongas).
CD . . . . SH 3810CD
MC . . . . SH 3810C
Sugarhill(USA) / May '93 / Roots Records / Projection / Impetus Records / C.M. Distribution / Jazz Music / Swift / Duncans / A.D.A Distribution.

Landreneau. Adam

CAJUN SOLE (Landreneau, Adam & Cyp).
Tracks: Not Advised.
LP. 8001
Swallow (USA) / '88 / Swift / Wellard Dist.

Landsborough. Charlie

Although born in Wrexham, Charlie Landsborough has spent most of his life living on Merseyside where his musical activities are supplemented by a full-time career as a teacher. He's best known as a songwriter and has achieved success with cuts of his songs by such as George Hamilton IV (*Heaven knows*) and Foster & Allen (*I will love you all my life* , a 1983 U.K.

chart hit). It was the duo's Tony Allen who helped put together Landsborough's album *Songs from the heart* , a collection of songs that added to his nationwide visibility as a touring singer/songwriter. (Tony Byworth)

I WILL LOVE YOU ALL MY LIFE.
Tracks: I will love you all my life / Listen Louise.
7" . . . . PF 3008
Pastafont / Feb '83 / Pastafont Music.

SONGS FROM THE HEART.
Tracks: I dreamed I was in heaven / Sill blue / things that my ears can do / Walking on my memories / Song of my heart / All over but crying / One more time / You and me / Constantly / I cried / You're not the only one / Fireside dreaming / Summer country skies / Close your eyes / lily of the valley / still blue.
CD . . . . .RITZRCD 521
MC .RITZRC 521
Ritz / Jun '92 / Pinnacle / Midland Records.

THANK YOU LORD.
Tracks: Thank you lord / Down to earth.
7" . . . . PF 3007
Pastafont / Nov '82 / Pastafont Music.

Lane. Christy

ASK ME TO DANCE.
Tracks: Ask me to dance / Once or twice / I will / Eyes of misty blue / I knew the reason / Sexy eyes / One day at a time / Maybe i'm thinkin' / First time in a long time / Danny boy.
■ LP . . . . UAG 30293
United Artists / May '80.

LET ME DOWN EASY.
Tracks: Let me down easy / By the way.
■ 7" 7N 25791
Pye International / Aug '78.

SIMPLE LITTLE WORDS.
Tracks: Not Advised.
■ LP . . . . UAG 30277
United Artists / Dec '79.

SLIPPIN' UP, SLIPPIN' AROUND.
Tracks: Slippin' up, slippin' around / He's back in town.
■ 7" . . . . UP 611
United Artists / Feb '80.

Lang. k.d.

Born Karen Dawn Lang, this artist came to prominence with the onset of the 'new country' movement. She was greatly influenced by the music of Patsy Cline and her backing group, formed in 1983 were known as The Reclines. A year later she released her debut LP *A Truly Western Experience* after which she was signed by Sire who released the follow-up *Angel With A Lariat*. By this time she was attracting a good deal of press but was viewed with some suspicion by elements of the country fraternity. After scoring her first U.S. hit with her *Cryin'* duet with Roy Orbison she overcame this prejudice with the release of the *Shadowland* LP. This album featured a number of highly credible guest artists including Kitty Wells, Loretta Lynn and the Jordanaires. She consolidated this success with the release of 1989's *Absolute Torch and Twang* which won a Grammy award. Since then she has broadened her appeal into the mainstream singer-songwriter field with the release of her well-received *Ingenue* LP. To underline this she was the winner of the 1993 MTV award for the top video by a female artist for *Constant Craving*. (James Bowen)

ABSOLUTE TORCH AND TWANG (Lang, k.d. & The Reclines).
Tracks: Luck in my eyes / Trail of broken hearts / Didn't I / Full moon full of love / Big big love / Walkin' in and out of your arms / Three days / Big boned gal / Wallflower waltz / Pullin' back the reins / It's me / Nowhere to stand.
CD 9258772
CD . . . . WX 259 CD
LP. . . . . WX 259
MC . . . . WX 259 C
Sire / May '89 / WEA.

ANGEL WITH A LARIAT (Lang, k.d. & The Reclines).
Tracks: Turn me around / High time for detour / Diet of strange places / Got the bull by the horns / Watch your step polka / Rose garden / Tune into my wave / Angel with a lariat.
LP. 925441 1
Sire / Aug '88 / WEA.
■ MC .925441 4
Sire / Aug '88.

CONSTANT CRAVING.
Tracks: Constant craving.
12" . . . . W 0100T
7" . . . . W 0100
CD Single . . . . .W 0100CD
MC Single . . . . .W 0100C
Sire / May '92 / WEA.

CONSTANT CRAVING.
Tracks: Constant craving / Miss Chateline / Constant craving (live) (On W 0157CDX only) / Wash me clean (On W 0157CD).
7" . . . . W 0157
CD Single . . . . .W 0157CDX
CD Single . . . . .W 0157CD
MC Single . . . . .W 0157C
WEA / Feb '93 / WEA.

HARVEST OF SEVEN YEARS.
Tracks: Not Advised.
VHS. 7599382343
Warner Music Video / May '92 / WEA.

INGENUE.
Tracks: Save me / Mind of love, The / Miss Chatelaine / Wash me clean / So it shall be / Still thrives this love / Seasons of hollow soul / Outside myself / Tear of love's recall / Constant craving.
CD 7599268402
LP. 7599268401
MC 7599268404
Sire / Mar '92 / WEA.

MIND OF LOVE, THE.
Tracks: Mind of love, The / Three cigarettes in an ashtray / Mind of Love, The (Live) (On CDS2 only).
7" . . . . W 0107
CD Single . . . . .W 0170CD2
CD Single . . . . .W 0107CD
MC Single . . . . .W 0107C
WEA / Apr '93 / WEA.

MISS CHATELAINE.
Tracks: Miss Chatelaine.
7" . . . . W 0181
CD Single . . . . .W 0181CDX
MC Single . . . . .W 0181C
Sire / Jun '93 / WEA.

OUR DAY WILL COME.
Tracks: Our day will come / Three cigarettes in an ashtray / Johnny get angry (Available on 12" only).
12" . . . . W 7697T
■ 7" . . . . W 7697
WEA / Nov '88.

RIDIN' THE RAILS (Lang, k.d. & Take 6).
Tracks: Ridin' the rails / Mr. Fix It.
7" . . . . W 9535
WEA / Oct '90 / WEA.

SHADOWLAND (The Owen Bradley Sessions) (Lang, k.d. & The Reclines).
Tracks: Western stars / Lock, stock and teardrops / Sugar moon / I wish I didn't love you so / Once again around the dance floor / Black coffee / Shadowland / Don't let the stars get in your eyes / Tears don't care who cry them / I'm down to my last cigarette / Your busy being blue / Honky tonk angel's medley.
MC . . . . WX 171 C
WEA / '88 / WEA.
CD .925724 2
■ LP. WX 171
WEA / Apr '88 / WEA.

SUGAR MOON.
Tracks: Sugar moon / Honky tonk medley (On 12" only) / I'm down to my last cigarette (On 12" only).
12" . . . . W 7841T
7" . . . . W 7841
WEA / Jun '88 / WEA.

Lange. Don

LIVE : DON LANGE.
Tracks: Not Advised.
LP. . . . . .FF 222
Flying Fish (USA) / Mar '89 / Cadillac Music / Roots Records / Projection / C.M. Distribution / Direct Distribution / Jazz Music / Duncans / A.D.A Distribution.

NATURAL BORN HEATHEN.
Tracks: Not Advised.
LP. . . . . .FF 060
Flying Fish (USA) / Mar '89 / Cadillac Music / Roots Records / Projection / C.M. Distribution / Direct Distribution / Jazz Music / Duncans / A.D.A Distribution.

Lariat. Lash

BITTER TEARS (Lariat, Lash & The Long Riders).
Tracks: Bitter tears / Railroad steamboat / Oh baby / Long gone lonesome blues / Red blue jeans / I feel like yellin'.
■ EP . . . . NED 10
Big Beat / Mar '85.

DOLE QUEUE BLUES (Lariat, Lash & The Long Riders).
Tracks: Dole queue blues / Goodbye and good luck.
12" .NST 108
■ 7" . . . . NS 108
Big Beat / Nov '85.

Larsen, Brett

SILVER WINGS (Larsen, Brett & Country Line).

Tracks: Not Advised.
LP. . . . . BSS 322
Tank / '88.

Larson, Nicolette

Born 17.07.1952 in Helena, Montana, raised in Kansas City. Studied at university in Missouri, prior to moving out to California in 1974, where she worked with the Nocturnes. An oft-used session singer, she has featured on albums by Hoyt Axton, Emmylou Harris, Linda Ronstadt, Gary Stewart, Neil Young and Van Halen, besides touring with Axton in 1975 -1976 and Commander Cody (lead vocalist) straight after. As a recording act in her own right, she's seen action on both the pop and country charts with Warner Bros *Lotta Love* (1978) and *That's How I Know Love Is Right* (1986) respectively, making the top ten position. She had an extended run on the country charts while on MCA, during the mid-eighties - her albums *Nicolette* , *Radio Land* and *Rose Of My Heart* being favourable West Coast flavoured country collections. (Maurice Hope)

BACK IN MY ARMS.
Tracks: Back in my arms / Trouble.
■ 7" . . . . K 17550
WEA / Jan '80.

FOOL ME AGAIN.
Tracks: Fool me again / Arthur's theme.
7" . . . . K 17892
WEA / Mar '82 / WEA.

IN THE NICK OF TIME.
Tracks: Dancin' Jones / In the nick of time / Let me go love / Rio De Janeiro blue / Breaking too many hearts / Back in my arms again / Fallen / Daddy / Isn't it always love / Trouble.
■ LP. . . . . K 56750
WEA / Jan '80 / WEA.

LOTTA LOVE.
Tracks: Lotta love / Angel rejoiced last night.
■ 7" . . . . K 17303
WEA / Feb '79.

NICOLETTE.
Tracks: Lotta love / Rhumba girl / You send me / Can't get away from you / Mexican divorce / Baby, don't you do it / Give a little / Angels / Rejoiced / French waltz / Come early mornin' last in love.
■ LP. . . . . K 56569
WEA / '78 / WEA.

RADIOLAND.
Tracks: Radioland / Ooo-eee / How can we go on / When you come around / Tears, tears and more tears / Straight from the heart / Been gone too long / Fool for love / Long distance love.
■ LP. . . . . K 56878
WEA / Jan '81 / WEA.

RADIOLAND.
Tracks: Radioland / How can we go on.
■ 7" . . . . K 17752
WEA / Feb '81.

SAY WHEN.
Tracks: Not Advised.
LP. . . . . MCF 3266
MC . . . . MCFC 3266
MCA / Apr '85 / BMG.

YOU CAN'T SAY YOU DON'T LOVE ME ANYMORE.
Tracks: You can't say you don't love me anymore / Blow on chilly wind.
7" . . . . MCA 956
MCA / Apr '85 / BMG.
■ 12" . . . . MCAT 956
MCA / May '85.

Lasalle, Denise

COME TO BED.
Tracks: Come to bed / I was not the best woman.
12" . . . . MAL 12 009
■ 7" . . . . MAL 009
Malaco / May '83.
12" . . . . TA 6513
■ 7" . . . . A 6513
Epic / Aug '85.

HITTIN' WHERE IT HURTS.
Tracks: Not Advised.
LP. . . . . MAL 7447
MC . . . . MALC 7447
Malaco / Mar '89 / C.M. Distribution / Charly / Pinnacle.
CD . . . . MALCD 7447
Malaco / Mar '93 / C.M. Distribution / Charly / Pinnacle.

HOLDING HANDS WITH THE BLUES.
Tracks: Not Advised.
LP. . . . . MALP 013
Malaco / '88 / C.M. Distribution / Charly / Pinnacle.

IT'S LYING TIME AGAIN.
Tracks: Not Advised.
LP. . . . . MAL 7441
MC . . . . MALC 7441
Malaco / Mar '89 / C.M. Distribution / Charly / Pinnacle.

LADY IN THE STREET, A.
Tracks: Not Advised.
LP. . . . . MAL 7412
MC . . . . MALC 7412
Malaco / May '83 / C.M. Distribution / Charly / Pinnacle.

LET THE FOUR WINDS BLOW.
Tracks: Let the four winds blow.
12" . . . . MAL 12 030
■ 7" . . . . MAL 030
Malaco / Feb '86.

LOVE ME RIGHT.
Tracks: Not Advised.
CD . . . . MALCD 7464
Malaco / Mar '93 / C.M. Distribution / Charly / Pinnacle.

LOVE TALKIN'.
Tracks: Not Advised.
LP. . . . . MAL 7422
Malaco / '88 / C.M. Distribution / Charly / Pinnacle.
MC . . . . MALC 7422
Malaco / Mar '89 / C.M. Distribution / Charly / Pinnacle.

MY TOOT TOOT.
Tracks: Talkin' in your sleep / Someone else is steppin' in / Nobody loves me like you do / Give me yo' most strongest whisky / Love is a five letter word / Lady in the street, A / Love talkin' / Get what you can get / Linger a little longer / Keeps me runnin' back / Too many lovers / My toot toot / Come to bed.
LP. . . . . EPC 26603
Epic / Aug '85 / Sony.
■ MC 40 26603
Epic / Aug '85.

MY TOOT TOOT.
Tracks: My toot toot / Give me yo' most strongest whisky.
12" . . . . TX 6334
■ 7" . . . . A 6334
Epic / Jun '85.

ON THE LOOSE.
Tracks: Man size job, A / What it takes to get a good woman / Harper Valley PTA / What am I doing wrong / Breaking up somebody's home / There ain't enough hate around (to make me turn around) / Your man and your best friend / Lean on me / Making a good thing better / I'm over you / I'm satisfied.
CD . . . . CDSEW 005
LP. . . . . SEW 005
MC . . . . SEWC 005
Westbound / Jul '89 / Pinnacle.

RAIN AND FIRE.
Tracks: It be's that way sometimes / I'm sho gonna mess with yo man / What's goin' on in my house / Look what can happen to you.. (Look what can happen to you (if you get caught messin' with my tu tu)) / Shame shame shame / Dip, bam, thank you maam / Learnin' how to cheat on you / Rain and fire / It takes you all night / Is he lovin' someone else tonight.
LP. . . . . MAL 7434
Malaco / '88 / C.M. Distribution / Charly / Pinnacle.
MC . . . . MALC 7434
Malaco / Mar '89 / C.M. Distribution / Charly / Pinnacle.

RIGHT PLACE, RIGHT TIME.
Tracks: Not Advised.
LP. . . . . MAL 7417
Malaco / '88 / C.M. Distribution / Charly / Pinnacle.
MC . . . . MALC 7417
Malaco / Mar '89 / C.M. Distribution / Charly / Pinnacle.

RIGHT PLACE, RIGHT TIME (Lasalle, Denise & Latimore).
Tracks: Right place, right time / Come to bed / Let's straighten it out.
12" . . . . MAL 12 022
■ 7" . . . . MAL 022
Malaco / Jun '84.

STILL TRAPPED.
Tracks: Not Advised.
CD . . . . MALCD 7454
Malaco / Mar '93 / C.M. Distribution / Charly / Pinnacle.

TRAPPED BY A THING CALLED LOVE.
Tracks: Trapped by a thing called love / Now run and tell that / Heartbreaker of the year / Good goody getter / Catch me if you can / Hung up, strung out / Do me right / Deeper I go (the better it gets), The / You'll lose a good thing keep it coming / It's too late.
CD . . . . CDSEW 018
LP. . . . . SEW 018
MC . . . . SEWC 018
Westbound / Jan '90 / Pinnacle.

TRAPPED BY A THING CALLED LOVE/ON THE LOOSE.
Tracks: Man sized job, A / What it takes to get a good woman / Harper Valley P.T.A. / What am I doing wrong / Breaking up somebody's home / There ain't enough hate around / Your man and your best friend / Lean on me / Making a good thing better / I'm over you / I'm satisfied / Trapped by a thing called love / Now run and tell that / Heartbreaker of the year / Goody goody getter / Catch me if you can / Hung up, strung up / Do me right / Deeper I go (better it gets), The / You'll lose a good thing / Keeping it coming / It's too late.
CD Set . . . . CDSEWD 018
Westbound / Feb '92 / Pinnacle.

WHEN WE'RE MAKING LOVE.
Tracks: When we're making love.
12" . . . . DEBTX 3143
Debut (1) / Nov '92 / Pinnacle.

Last Roundup

TWISTER.
Tracks: Not Advised.
LP. . . . . ROUNDER 9006
Rounder / Dec '87 / Projection / Roots Records / Swift / C.M. Distribution / Topic Records / Jazz Music / Hot Shot / A.D.A Distribution / Direct Distribution.
MC . . . . ROUNDER 9006C
Rounder / Aug '88 / Projection / Roots Records / Swift / C.M. Distribution / Topic Records / Jazz Music / Hot Shot / A.D.A Distribution / Direct Distribution.

Lauer, Martin

ICH WILL MORGEN SCHON IN TEXAS SEIN.
Tracks: Ich will morgen schon in Texas sein / Heut' am Missouri morgen bei dir / Mississippi melodie / Smoky / Das ist die gross strasse / Heidelberg / Tabak und rum / Das alte haus von rocky docky / Lass mich gehn' Madeleine / Ich gab' mein herz / Ich kenn' die welt / Rosen und kusse / Rosen und dornen / Beat unde rote rosen / Oh serenader / Eine trane sagt mir die wahrheit.
LP. . . . . BFX 15324
Bear Family / Mar '88 / Rollercoaster Records / Swift / Direct Distribution.

TAXI NACH TEXAS.
Tracks: Sacramento / Die letzte rose der prairie / Wenn ich ein cowboy war / Jim und Joe / Am lagerfeuer / Sein bestes pferd / Taxi nach Texas / John Brown's baby / Silver dollar / Roll 'em over / Die blauen berge / Pierde und sattel / King John / Cowboy lady / Smoky / Wenn die sonne scheint in Texas.
LP. . . . . BFX 15205
Bear Family / Sep '86 / Rollercoaster Records / Swift / Direct Distribution.
CD . . . . BCD 15485
Bear Family / '88 / Rollercoaster Records / Swift / Direct Distribution.

Lawson, Doyle

Bluegrass vocalist/musician, born in East Tennessee, formed his present group Quicksilver in 1979, after having worked with Jimmy Martin (banjo - 1963), J.D.Crowe's New South (mandolin - 1966) and Country Cents (tenor vocalist - 1971). Since forming Quicksilver the multi-talented and much-respected Lawson has become Sugar Hill's most recorded act, blending blue grass with a capella gospel. Gospel music is very mush an integral part of their work, with their 1981 album *Rock My Soul* a best seller in the field. Lawson, along with Quicksilver, have in recent times hosted their own annual Family Style Festival in Denton, North Carolina. (Maurice Hope)

BEYOND THE SHADOWS (Lawson, Doyle & Quicksilver).
Tracks: Not Advised.
LP. . . . . SH 3753
MC . . . . SH 3753C
Sugarhill(USA) / Mar '89 / Roots Records / Projection / Impetus Records / C.M. Distribution / Jazz Music / Swift / Duncans / A.D.A Distribution.

DOYLE LAWSON & QUICKSILVER (Lawson, Doyle & Quicksilver).
Tracks: Not Advised.
LP. . . . . SH 3708
MC . . . . SH 3708C
Sugarhill(USA) / '80 / Roots Records / Projection / Impetus Records / C.M. Distribution / Jazz Music / Swift / Duncans / A.D.A Distribution.

HEAVEN'S JOY AWAITS (Lawson, Doyle & Quicksilver).
Tracks: Not Advised.
CD . . . . SH 3760CD
LP. . . . . SH 3760
MC . . . . SH 3760C
Sugarhill(USA) / Dec '87 / Roots Records / Projection / Impetus Records / C.M. Distribution / Jazz Music / Swift / Duncans / A.D.A Distribution.

HEAVENLY TREASURES (Lawson, Doyle & Quicksilver).
Tracks: Not Advised.
LP. . . . . SH 3735
MC . . . . SH 3735C
Sugarhill(USA) / Mar '89 / Roots Records / Projection / Impetus Records / C.M. Distribution / Jazz Music / Swift / Duncans / A.D.A Distribution.

HYMN TIME IN THE COUNTRY (Lawson, Doyle & Quicksilver).
Tracks: Not Advised.
LP. . . . . SH 3765
MC . . . . SH 3765C

Sugarhill(USA) / Mar '89 / Roots Records / Projection / Impetus Records / C.M. Distribution / Jazz Music / Swift / Duncans / A.D.A Distribution.

I HEARD THE ANGELS SINGING (Lawson, Doyle & Quicksilver).
Tracks: Holy city, The / Stormy weather / Little mountain church house / In the shelter of his arms / I heard the angels singing / He's my guide / Little white church, The / City where's comes no strife / Rock of ages, hide thou me / I won't have far to cross Jordan alone / That new Jerusalem / That home far away.
CD . . . . **SH 3774CD**
LP . . . . **SH 3774**
MC . . . . **SH 3774C**
Sugarhill(USA) / '89 / Roots Records / Projection / Impetus Records / C.M. Distribution / Jazz Music / Swift / Duncans / A.D.A Distribution.

I'LL WANDER BACK SOMEDAY (Lawson, Doyle & Quicksilver).
Tracks: Not Advised.
CD . . . . **SH 3769CD**
LP . . . . **SH 3769**
MC . . . . **SH 3769C**
Sugarhill(USA) / '88 / Roots Records / Projection / Impetus Records / C.M. Distribution / Jazz Music / Swift / Duncans / A.D.A Distribution.

MY HEART IS YOURS (Lawson, Doyle & Quicksilver).
Tracks: All in my love for you / Still got a crush on you / Move to the top of the mountain / I don't care / My heart is yours / Dreaming of you / Look for me and I'll be there / Date with an angel / Now there's you / Between us / I'm satisfied with you / We were made for each other.
CD . . . . **SH 3782CD**
LP . . . . **SH 3782**
MC . . . . **SH 3782C**
Sugarhill(USA) / '90 / Roots Records / Projection / Impetus Records / C.M. Distribution / Jazz Music / Swift / Duncans / A.D.A Distribution.

NEWS IS OUT, THE (Lawson, Doyle & Quicksilver).
Tracks: Sweetheart you done me wrong / This dream I'm in / I've heard these words before / Vision of Jesus, A / Up on the blue ridge / I'll be true / Grass that I'm playing is really blue, The / Have I loved you too late / Let the best man win / She's walking through my memory / Wonderful, beautiful place.
LP . . . . **SH 3757**
MC . . . . **SH 3757C**
Sugarhill(USA) / Mar '89 / Roots Records / Projection / Impetus Records / C.M. Distribution / Jazz Music / Swift / Duncans / A.D.A Distribution.

ONCE AND FOR ALWAYS (Lawson, Doyle & Quicksilver).
Tracks: Blue road, The / Once and for always / Lover of the Lord, A / Speak softly, you're talking to my heart / Old timer's waltz / Come back to me in my dreams / Carolina in my dreams / Stone cold heart / Julie Ann (come on home) / You only have to say you've changed your mind / When the sun of my life goes down.
LP . . . . **SH 3744**
MC . . . . **SH 3744C**
Sugarhill(USA) / Mar '89 / Roots Records / Projection / Impetus Records / C.M. Distribution / Jazz Music / Swift / Duncans / A.D.A Distribution.

QUICKSILVER RIDES AGAIN (Lawson, Doyle & Quicksilver).
Tracks: Misery river / Georgia girl / Till all the rivers run dry / Rocking on the waves / Yellow river / Poet with wings / Kentucky song / Calm the storm / I'll be around somewhere / Mountain girl / Lonesome river, The.
MC . . . . **SH 3727C**
Sugarhill(USA) / '82 / Roots Records / Projection / Impetus Records / C.M. Distribution / Jazz Music / Swift / Duncans / A.D.A Distribution.
LP . . . . **SH 3727**
Sugarhill(USA) / Mar '89 / Roots Records / Projection / Impetus Records / C.M. Distribution / Jazz Music / Swift / Duncans / A.D.A Distribution.

ROCK MY SOUL (Lawson, Doyle & Quicksilver).
Tracks: Not Advised.
LP . . . . **SH 3717**
Sugarhill(USA) / '88 / Roots Records / Projection / Impetus Records / C.M. Distribution / Jazz Music / Swift / Duncans / A.D.A Distribution.

TENNESSEE DREAM.
Tracks: Not Advised.
LP . . . . **CO 766**
County (USA) / '89 / Projection / Mike's Country Music Room / Swift.

Ledford String Band

LEDFORD STRING BAND.
Tracks: Not Advised.
LP . . . . **ROUNDER 0008**
Rounder / '88 / Projection / Roots Records / Swift / C.M. Distribution / Topic Records / Jazz Music / Hot Shot / A.D.A Distribution / Direct Distribution.

LeDoux, Chris

Real life cowboy, spending years combining ranching & working the rodeos - both as a bronco buster & casual singer. In fact he spent 15 years riding rodeos. Early (spanning some years in fact) days found him financing his own, prolific recordings - and quite a profitable thing he had going too. His own American Cowboy Songs Inc releases (around twenty in total) yielding sales, marketed through Western Merchandising, in excess of 4 million - a real family concern with his father Al as his manager. During his 18 year career, all have since been made available on American Liberty - alongside his work since signing to the label. Chris' initial material was rcorded back home in Sheridan, Wyoming, later to move to Salt Lake City Studio and he has toured extensively with his road band, the Western Underground, blending together what he describes as cowboy folk, western soul, rock 'n' roll & sagebrush blues. Megastar Garth Brooks is just one of his admirers in the business so much so that it prompted him to mention his music in his song *much too young (to feel this damn old)* . Brooks also duets with LeDoux, on his 1992 top twenty (12) hit *Whatcha gonna do with a cowboy* the title track also being the title track of LeDoux's debut Liberty recordings - whilst the single *Cadillac ranch* also emulated the feat. LeDoux's album, the first to have the luxury of record company promotion gained a top slot. Liberty have added to his catalogue the 1993 album *Under this old hat*. He could be termed as a young 18 year overnight success, whose career is now really beginning. (Maurice Hope)

COWBOYS AIN'T EASY TO LOVE.
Tracks: Not Advised.
LP . . . . **CLD 79**
Chris LeDoux / '88 / Bear Family Records (Germany).

HE RIDES THE WILD HORSES.
Tracks: Not Advised.
LP . . . . **CLD 84**
Chris LeDoux / '88 / Bear Family Records (Germany).

LIFE AS A RODEO MAN.
Tracks: Not Advised.
LP . . . . **CLD 76**
Chris LeDoux / '88 / Bear Family Records (Germany).

OLD COWBOY CLASSICS.
Tracks: Not Advised.
LP . . . . **CLD 87**
Chris LeDoux / '88 / Bear Family Records (Germany).

OLD COWBOY HEROES.
Tracks: Not Advised.
LP . . . . **CLD 83**
Chris LeDoux / '88 / Bear Family Records (Germany).

PAINT ME BACK HOME IN WYOMING.
Tracks: Not Advised.
LP . . . . **CLD 80**
Chris LeDoux / '88 / Bear Family Records (Germany).

RODEO SONGS OLD AND NEW.
Tracks: Not Advised.
LP . . . . **CLD 73**
Chris LeDoux / '88 / Bear Family Records (Germany).

SING ME A SONG MR. RODEO MAN.
Tracks: Not Advised.
LP . . . . **CLD 78**
Chris LeDoux / '88 / Bear Family Records (Germany).

SONGBOOK OF THE AMERICAN WEST.
Tracks: Not Advised.
LP . . . . **CLD 77**
Chris LeDoux / '88 / Bear Family Records (Germany).

SONGS OF LIVING FREE.
Tracks: Not Advised.
LP . . . . **CLD 75**
Chris LeDoux / '88 / Bear Family Records (Germany).

SONGS OF RODEO & COUNTRY.
Tracks: Not Advised.
LP . . . . **CLD 74**
Chris LeDoux / '88 / Bear Family Records (Germany).

SONGS OF RODEO LIFE.
Tracks: Not Advised.
LP . . . . **CLD 72**
Chris LeDoux / '88 / Bear Family Records (Germany).

SOUNDS OF THE WESTERN COUNTRY.
Tracks: Not Advised.
LP . . . . **CLD 82**
Chris LeDoux / '88 / Bear Family Records (Germany).

THIRTY DOLLAR COWBOY.
Tracks: Not Advised.
LP . . . . **CLD 88**
Chris LeDoux / '88 / Bear Family Records (Germany).

UNDER THIS OLD HAT.
Tracks: Under this old hat / Get back on that pony / Every time I roll the dice / Strugglin' blues / Cowboys like a little rock and roll / She's tough / Soft place to fall / For your love / Wild and wooly / Powder river home / Cadillac ranch.
CD **C2 80892**
Capitol / Aug '93 / EMI.

WATCHA GONNA DO WITH A COWBOY.
Tracks: Call of the wild / You just can't see him from the road / Little long haired outlaw / Making ends meet / Whatcha gonna do with a cowboy / Hooked on an eight second ride / I'm ready if you're willing / Look at you girl / Cadillac ranch / Western skies.
■ **CD** . . . . **CDP 7988182**
Liberty / Sep '92.

WESTERN TUNESMITH.
Tracks: Not Advised.
LP . . . . **CLD 81**
Chris LeDoux / '88 / Bear Family Records (Germany).

Lee, Albert

Born 21.12.1943 in Leominster, Hertfordshire, lead guitarist/session musician/recording act. Played with Chris Farlowe during the mid-1960's, before spells with Country Fever and the well received Hands Head & Feet at the end of the 1960's and into the early 1970's. Joined Emmylou Harris' famed Hot Band in 1976, replacing James Burton - and played on a host of her albums debuting on *Luxury Liner* . His own debut solo album *Hiding* featured the above band members. Skaggs was later to record one of the songs from it, Lee's own *Country Boy* . Using it as an album title track and, taking the single with its dynamic 'lead solo' to No. 1 in 1985. It no doubt, had a bearing on Skaggs being the recipient of the CMA's Entertainer Of The Year that Autumn. Lee's keenly sort after expertise, has seen him appearing on chart topping material from Rosanne Cash, Emmylou Harris & her Trio Venture and more from Skaggs. Before moving on to play with Jackson Browne, Joe Cocker, Eric Clapton and the Everly Bros. He worked between times on the road, usually accompanied by Hogan's Heroes - steel player in Gerry Hogan's band. Lee's mastery of the electric guitar is surpassed by few. (Maurice Hope)

ALBERT LEE.
Tracks: Sweet little Lisa / Radio girl / Your boys / So sad to watch good love go bad / Rock 'n' roll man / Real wild child / On the boulevard / Pink bedroom / Best I can / One way rider.
■ **LP** . . . . **SPELP 29**
Polydor / Aug '83.

BLACK CLAW AND COUNTRY FEVER.
Tracks: Not Advised.
CD . . . . **LICD 901057**
Line / Oct '91 / C.M. Distribution / Grapevine Distribution.

COUNTRY BOY.
Tracks: Country boy / Ain't living long like this.
■ **7"** . . . . **AMS 7443**
A&M / '79.

COUNTRY GUITAR MAN.
Tracks: Jack of all trades / Meal ticket / I won't let you down / Soft word Sunday morning / One woman / Just another ambush / Stripes / Another useless day.
LP . . . . **SDLP 037**
Sundown / Nov '86 / Terry Blood Dist. / Jazz Music / C.M. Distribution.
■ **MC** . . . . **SDC 037**
Sundown / Nov '86.
CD . . . . **CDSD 037**
Sundown / Apr '88 / Terry Blood Dist. / Jazz Music / C.M. Distribution.

GAGGED BUT NOT BOUND.
Tracks: Flowers of Edinburgh / Don't let go / Midnight special / Tiger rag / Forty miles of bad road / Fun ranch boogie / Walking after midnight / Schon Rosemarin / Country gentleman / Monte Nido.
CD . . . . **MCAD 42063**
■ **LP** . . . . **IMCA 42063**
MCA / Mar '88.
■ **MC** . . . . **IMCAC 42063**
MCA / Mar '88.

HIDING.
Tracks: Country boy / Billy Tyler / Are you wasting my time / Now and then it's gonna rain / O a real good night / Setting me up / Ain't living long like this / Hiding / Hotel love / Come up and see me anytime.
LP . . . . **AMLH 64750**
A&M / Apr '86 / PolyGram.
■ **MC** . . . . **CAM 64750**
A&M / Apr '86.
CD . . . . **CDMID 121**
A&M / Oct '92 / PolyGram.

HUNT THEM.
Tracks: Hunt them / Have you heard the news.
■ **7"** . . . . **AMS 8108**
A&M / Feb '81.

ON THE BOULEVARD.
Tracks: On the boulevard / Your boys.
■ **7"** . . . . **POSP 504**
Polydor / Sep '82.

■ DELETED L 5

RADIO GIRLS.
Tracks: Radio girls / Your boys.
■ 7".......................................POSP 434
Polydor / Jun '82.

SETTING ME UP.
Tracks: Setting me up / Hotel love.
■ 7".......................................AMS 7467
A&M / Aug '79.

SPEECHLESS.
Tracks: T-Bird to Vegas / Bullish boogie / Arkansas traveller / Romany rye / Erin / Seventeenth summer / Salt creek / Cannonball.
CD.......................................MCAD 5693
MCA / Feb '87 / BMG.
LP..IMCA 5693
MC.......................................IMCAC 5693
MCA / Jul '87 / BMG.

Lee, Brenda

Lee, Brenda This American singer was born Brenda Mae Tarpley in Atlanta, Georgia in December 1944. She was a child prodigy, starting to sing almost before she could speak. Brenda was just six years old when she won a local talent contest. By the age of eight, she had become a regular performer on Atlanta radio and television programmes. By the time Brenda made her first record in Nashville in July 1956, she had appeared on many of America's leading network TV shows, including those hosted by Perry Como, Steve Allen and Ed Sullivan. Lee's early records were not successful, but a 1959 season in Paris sparked off much interest in showbusiness circles and comparisons with Judy Garland were invoked. The disc that made her a major star was *Sweet Nothin's* a rock'n'roll belter that cruised to No.4 on both sides of the Atlantic in early 1960. It was followed by the ballad *I'm Sorry* which reached No.1 in America and No.12 in Britain. These two hits clearly demonstrated that a versatile and exciting young performer had been discovered. By the time she celebrated her 16th birthday, *Little Miss Dynamite*, as she was dubbed, had chalked up her second US No.1 smash with *I Want To Be Wanted*.Between 1960 and 1964 Brenda achieved a formidable string of Top 20 singles in both the US and UK. In terms of energy and verve, she was like a junior Connie Francis; but whereas Francis tended to veer close to middle of the road material, Lee was nearer to country and rock'n'roll.After the pop hits dried up in the mid-sixties, Lee returned to her country and western roots. She has remained active in that market ever since, scoring the occasional big hit on the American country charts and continuing to tour. She appeared at the 1985 Country Music Festival in Wembley, London. (Bob Macdonald).

16 CLASSIC TRACKS: BRENDA LEE.
Tracks: Sweet nothin's / Speak to me pretty / Dum dum / I wonder / Losing you / Christmas will be just another lonely day / Is it true / All alone am I / Let's jump the broomstick / Here comes that feeling / As usual / It started all over again / Emotions / Sweet impossible you / Rockin' around the Christmas tree / I'm sorry.
■ MC.....................................TCMFP 50548
MFP / Feb '82.
■ LP......................................MFP 50548
MFP / Mar '82.

25TH ANNIVERSARY.
Tracks: Not Advised.
Double LP................................MCLD 609
MCA / Jan '84 / BMG.

ALL ALONE AM I.
Tracks: Not Advised.
■ LP......................................LAT 8530
Brunswick / Apr '63.
CD.......................................CD 66071
Ce De International / Jul '93 / Taylors.

ALL ALONE AM I.
Tracks: All alone am I.
■ 7"......................................05882
Brunswick / Jan '63.

ALL THE WAY.
Tracks: Not Advised.
■ LP......................................LAT 8383
Brunswick / Nov '62.

AS USUAL.
Tracks: As usual.
■ 7"......................................05899
Brunswick / Jan '64.

BEST OF BRENDA LEE.
Tracks: Sweet nothin's / I'm sorry / Emotions / Dum dum / Fool number one / You always hurt the one you love / Will you love me tomorrow / When i fall in love / I'll be seeing you / Speak to me pretty / Here comes that feeling / It started all over again / My colouring book / Someday you'll want me to want you / End of the world / All alone am i / Losing you / I wonder / My whole world / Sweet impossible you / As usual / Is it true / Think / Love letters / Too many rivers / Make the

world go away / Crying time / Sweet dreams / Yesterday / Always on my mind / For the good times / Feelings.
Double LP................................LETV 1
■ MC.....................................LETC 1
MCA / May '86.

BEST OF BRENDA LEE (2).
Tracks: Not Advised.
LP.......................................1A 022 58249
MC.......................................1A 222 58249
EMI (Holland) / '88.

BREAK IT TO ME GENTLY.
Tracks: Break it to me gently.
■ 7"......................................05864
Brunswick / Feb '62.

BRENDA - THAT'S ALL.
Tracks: Not Advised.
■ LP......................................LAT 8516
Brunswick / Feb '63.

BRENDA LEE.
Tracks: Wiedersehn ist wunderschon / Kansas City / Ohne dich / Drei rote rosen bluh'n / Ich will immer auf dich warten / No my boy / Geh am gluck nicht vorbei / Am strand von Hawaii / Darling bye bye / In meinen traumen / Wo und wann fangt die liebe an / Darling was ist los mit dir / La premiere fool / Pourqui jamais moi / Sono sciocca / Nulla di me.
CD.......................................BCD 15644
Bear Family / Jun '92 / Rollercoaster Records / Swift / Direct Distribution.

BRENDA LEE.
Tracks: Not Advised.
VHS......................................TVE 1042
Telstar Video / May '92 / BMG.

BRENDA LEE - LIVE.
Tracks: Not Advised.
VHS......................................V 9096
MSD / Jun '88 / Multiple Sound Distributors / Gold & Sons.

BRENDA'S BEST.
Tracks: Not Advised.
LP P.Disc................................AR 30084
Exclusive Picture Discs / Nov '87.
CD.......................................CD 66043
Ce De International / '89 / Taylors.
CD.......................................CD 99043
MC.......................................WSC 92043
World Star Collection / Sep '93 / Taylors.

BYE BYE BLUES.
Tracks: Not Advised.
■ LP......................................LAT 8649
Brunswick / Jul '66.

CHRISTMAS WILL BE JUST ANOTHER LONELY DAY.
Tracks: Christmas will be just another lonely day.
■ 7"......................................05921
Brunswick / Dec '64.

DUM DUM.
Tracks: Dum dum.
■ 7"......................................05854
Brunswick / Jul '61.

EMOTIONS.
Tracks: Emotions.
■ 7"......................................05847
Brunswick / Apr '61.

EVEN BETTER.
Tracks: Not Advised.
■ LP......................................MCF 3054
MCA / May '80.

FOOL NUMBER ONE.
Tracks: Fool number one.
■ 7"......................................05860
Brunswick / Nov '61.

GOLDEN DECADE, THE.
Tracks: Jambalaya / Bigelow 6200 / Some people / Your cheatin' heart / Doodlebug rag / One step at a time / Dynamite / Ain't that love? / One teenager to another / Rock a bye baby blues / Rock the bop / Ring-a-my-phone / Little Jonah / Rockin' around the Christmas tree / Let's jump the broomstick / Stroll, The / Sweet nothin's / Weep no more / I'm sorry / Wee rivers / Coming on strong.
■ Double LP..............................CDX 6
Charly / Jan '85.

GREATEST HITS.
Tracks: Coming on strong / Silver threads and golden needles / Johnny one time / You're the one that I want / You don't have to say you love me / Jambalaya / Is it true / My whole world is falling down / Sweet nothings / End of the world, The / All alone am I / How much love / All you gotta do / You mamma don't dance / I'm sorry / When you're smiling / You ought to be in pictures / Put on a happy face / Smile / Baby face / Soul to soul / Old landmarks / Some glad morning / Operator / Up above my head / Saved / Dum dum / Fool number one / Too mnay rivers.
CD.......................................PLATCD 362
MC.......................................PLAC 362
Prism / '91 / Pinnacle / Midland Records.

HERE COMES THAT FEELING.
Tracks: Here comes that feeling.
■ 7"......................................05871
Brunswick / Jun '62.

HERE COMES THAT FEELING (OLD GOLD).
Tracks: Here comes that feeling.
7".......................................OG 9172
Old Gold / Jul '82.

I WANT TO BE WANTED.
Tracks: I want to be wanted.
■ 7"......................................05839
Brunswick / Oct '60.

I WONDER.
Tracks: I wonder.
■ 7"......................................05891
Brunswick / Jul '63.

I'M SORRY.
Tracks: I'm sorry.
■ 7"......................................05833
Brunswick / Jun '60.

I'M SORRY (OLD GOLD).
Tracks: Im sorry / Alone am I.
7".......................................OG 9163
Old Gold / Jul '82 / Pickwick Records.

IS IT TRUE.
Tracks: Is it true.
■ 7"......................................05915
Brunswick / Sep '64.

IT STARTED ALL OVER AGAIN.
Tracks: It started all over again.
■ 7"......................................05876
Brunswick / Sep '62.

IT'S ANOTHER WEEKEND.
Tracks: It's another weekend / Lumberjacks had a lady.
■ 7"......................................MCA 276
MCA / Feb '77.

L.A. SESSIONS.
Tracks: Oklahoma superstar / Taking what I can get / I let you let me down again / Ruby's lounge / When our love began / Mary's going out of her mine / Your favourite worn-out nightmare's comin home / One more time / Saved / Lumberjacks had a lady / It's another weekend.
■ LP......................................MCF 2783
MCA / Feb '77.

LET'S JUMP THE BROOMSTICK.
Tracks: Let's jump the broomstick.
■ 7"......................................05823
Brunswick / Jan '61.

LET'S JUMP THE BROOMSTICK.
Tracks: Not Advised.
■ EP......................................MCEP 4
MCA / Sep '78.

LITTLE MISS DYNAMITE.
Tracks: Not Advised.
■ 7"......................................WW 5083
Warwick / Nov '80.

LOSING YOU.
Tracks: Losing you.
■ 7"......................................05886
Brunswick / Mar '63.

LOVE SONGS: BRENDA LEE.
Tracks: No one / I'll be seeing you / My colouring book / Who can I turn to / Softly as I leave you / Crying time / Can't help falling in love / Feelings / Something / Masquerade / Killing me softly with his song / My way.
LP.......................................MCL 1793
MC.......................................MCLC 1793
MCA / Sep '86 / BMG.

RIDE RIDE RIDE.
Tracks: Ride ride ride / Lonely people do foolish things.
■ 7"......................................05970
Brunswick / Feb '67.

ROCKIN' AROUND THE CHRISTMAS TREE.
Tracks: Rockin' around the Christmas tree / Bill Bailey won't you please come home.
■ 7"......................................05880
Brunswick / Nov '62.
■ 7"......................................MCA 556
MCA / Nov '80.

RUSTY BELLS.
Tracks: Rusty bells / If you don't.
■ 7"......................................05943
Brunswick / Oct '65.

SPEAK TO ME PRETTY.
Tracks: Speak to me pretty / Here comes that feeling.
■ 7"......................................05867
Brunswick / Apr '62.
■ 7"......................................MCA 700
MCA / Aug '80.

SWEET IMPOSSIBLE YOU.
Tracks: Sweet impossible you.
■ 7"......................................05896
Brunswick / Oct '63.

SWEET NOTHIN'S.
Tracks: Sweet nothin's.
■ 7" 05819
Brunswick / Mar '60.

SWEET NOTHIN'S (OLD GOLD).
Tracks: Sweet nothin's / Let's jump to the broomsticks.
7" . . . . OG 9162
Old Gold / Jul '82 / Pickwick Records.

THANKS A LOT.
Tracks: Thanks a lot.
■ 7" 05927
Brunswick / Feb '65.

THINK.
Tracks: Think.
■ 7" 05903
Brunswick / Apr '64.

TOO LITTLE TIME.
Tracks: Too little time / Time and time again.
■ 7" 05957
Brunswick / May '66.

TOO MANY RIVERS.
Tracks: Too many rivers.
■ 7" 05936
Brunswick / Jul '65.

VERY BEST OF BRENDA LEE, VOL.1.
Tracks: Sweet nothin's / Emotions / Fool number one / Will you love me tomorrow / I'll be seeing you / Here comes that feeling / My colouring book / End of the world / I'm so sorry / Dum dum / You always hurt the one you love / When I fall in love / Speak to me pretty / It started all over again / Someday you'll want me to want you / All alone am I.
■ CD . . . . DMCL 1713
MCA / Jan '90.

VERY BEST OF BRENDA LEE, VOL.2.
Tracks: Not Advised.
■ CD . . . . DMCL 1714
MCA / Jan '90.

WHERE'S THE MELODY.
Tracks: Where's the melody / Born to be by your side.
■ 7" 05976
Brunswick / '67.

WIEDERSEHN IST WUNDERSCHON.
Tracks: Wiedersehn ist wunderschon / Ohne dich / Drei rote / Ich will immer auf dich warten / No my boy / Darling bye bye / Geh' nicht am gliuck vorbei / Am strand von Hawaii / Kansas City / Darling was ist los mit dir / In meinen traumen / Wo und wann fangt die liebe an / Pourquoi jamais (In French) / La premier fool (In French) / Nulla di me (In Italian) / Sono Sciocca (In Italian).
LP . . . . BFX 15186
Bear Family / Feb '86 / Rollercoaster Records / Swift / Direct Distribution.

WINNING HAND, THE (see under Parton, Dolly).

Lee, David H.

ME.
Tracks: Not Advised.
LP . . . . BSS 316
Tank / Sep '79.

Lee, Dickie

9,999,999 TEARS.
Tracks: 9,999,999 tears / I will never get over you.
■ 7" . . . . PB 0764
RCA / Jan '77.

Lee, Johnny

Born John Lee Ham on 03.07.1946 in Texas City and raised on a dairy farm in Alta Loma, Texas. After playing in rock bands as a trumpet player, (his own Road Runners amongst them during the sixties), Lee changed his allegiances to country music during the early 1970s. Played in Michey Gilley's band from 1974, debuting on the charts as a solo act with Sometimes (1975) a solitary success with ABC/DOT. He then found the charts with GRT, the hits to feature Red sails in the sunset and Country party . From the 1980 film "Urban Cowboy" came the million selling country/pop hit Lookin' for love (on the Full Moon label), Lee's debut No. 1. Lee was to become a resident at Gilley's nightclub in Pasadena and he later opened his own night spot six miles away. To prove he was no "one-hit wonder", Lee was to build upon his success - scoring regularly and impressively right up to 1985. His follow-up single One in a million also topped the charts, and was his one and only effort for Asylum records. Picking up with the Full Moon label, Lee embarked on a successful run, taking him into the mid-eighties with hits that included the top 5 tracks Pickin' up strangers , Prisoner of hope and another chart topper, Bet your heart on me . All were re-leased in 1981, the year he gaines ACM's Male

Vocalist Award. The top ten hit Cherokee fiddler (1982) with Michael Martin Murphy and Charlie Daniels is one of his most popular numbers, alongside the 1983 hits Sounds like love and Hey bartender . In 1984 Lee moved to Warner Bros, where he teamed up with little known vocalist Lane Brody on Yellow rose , the theme song from a short-lived TV series going to number one. A feat he was to repeat once more, only this time as a solo act with You could have heard a heart break . Lee was beset with personal troubles and difficulties with his stormy marriage to actress Charlene Tilton (Lucy in Dallas) over, his career was about to slide. Only Rollin' lonely , Save the last and They never had to get over you scoring any success. His days on Warners subsequently ended in 1986. (Maurice Hope)

JOHNNY LEE.
Tracks: Not Advised.
MC . . . . ZCGAS 712
Audio Fidelity(USA) / Oct '84 / Stage One Records.

JOHNNY LEE & WILLIE NELSON (see under Nelson, Willie).

LOOKING FOR LOVE (Lee, Johnny & The Eagles).
Tracks: Looking for love / Lyin' eyes.
■ 7" . . . . K 79153
Asylum / Aug '80.

Lee, Leapy

Lee, Leapy This British singer and actor was born Lee Graham in Eastbourne, Sussex in 1942. He got involved in amateur dramatics at school and, after leaving school at the age of 15, quickly developed a promising acting career at the London Palladium, The Prince's Theatre and on the television programme 'State Your Case'. However, his showbusiness life did not quite blossom in the intended manner. Leapy Lee's only subsequent significant contribution to the entertainment world was his 1968 single Little Arrows - this highly commercial pop offering reached No.2 in Britain and logged 21 weeks on the UK charts; it peaked at No.16 in the States. Little Arrows was the first big break for the successful songwriting team of Albert Hammond & Mike Hazelwood; it was produced by Gordon Mills, who was more famous for managing Tom Jones and Engelbert Humperdinck. Leapy Lee achieved one smaller UK hit - Good Morning which reached No.29 in early 1970 - before fading into obscurity. (Bob Macdonald).

EVERY ROAD LEADS BACK TO YOU.
Tracks: Every road leads back to you / Honey, go drift away.
■ 7" . . . . BELL 1419
Bell / Apr '75.

GOOD MORNING.
Tracks: Good morning.
■ 7" . . . . MK 5021
MCA / Dec '69.

KING OF THE WHOLE WIDE WORLD.
Tracks: King of the whole wide world / Shake hands.
■ 7" . . . . F 12369
Decca / Mar '66.

LITTLE ARROWS.
Tracks: Little arrows.
■ 7" . . . . MU 1028
MCA / Aug '68.
■ 7" . . . . MCA 704
MCA / Aug '80.

LITTLE ARROWS (OLD GOLD).
Tracks: Little arrows.
■ 7" . . . . OG 9169
Old Gold / Jul '82.

MAN ON THE FLYING TRAPEZE, THE.
Tracks: Man on the flying trapeze, The / My mixed up mind.
■ 7" . . . . CBS 202550
CBS / Feb '67.

OUR SWEET PRECIOUS LOVE.
Tracks: Our sweet precious love / New York city.
■ 7" . . . . BELL 1475
Bell / Apr '76.

Legg, Adrian

FRETMELT.
Tracks: Not Advised.
LP . . . . SPIN 115
Spindrift / Mar '85 / C.M. Distribution / Roots Records / Projection.

GUITARS AND OTHER CATHEDRALS.
Tracks: Thump the clouds / Cajun interlude / Irish girl, The / Midwest Sunday / Guitars and other cathedrals / Montreux ramble / Tracy's big moment / Divorcee's waltz / Tune for Derrol / Nail talk / Reckless love / Pass the valium (with knobs on) / Dying embers.
CD . . . . CDP 790 700 2

■ CD . . . . CDMMC 1014
MMC / Aug '88.
■ LP . . . . LPMMC 1014
MMC / Aug '88.
■ MC . . . . TCMMC 1014
MMC / Aug '88.

LOST FOR WORDS.
Tracks: Not Advised.
LP . . . . SPIN 127
Spindrift / Aug '86 / C.M. Distribution / Roots Records / Projection.

MRS CROWE'S BLUES WALTZ.
Tracks: Kinvarra's child / Frank the part-time clown / Mrs Crowe's Blues waltz / Gebrauchmusik II / Brooklyn blossom / Sour grapes / Norah Handley's waltz / Kiss-curl / Lunch-time at Rosie's / Paddy goes to Nashville / Green ballet II / Last track.
CD . . . . CDRR 9085 2
Relativity (USA) / Mar '93 / Pinnacle.

REQUIEM FOR A HICK.
Tracks: Not Advised.
LP . . . . WRS 125
Westwood / Oct '77 / Pinnacle.

TECHNOPICKER.
Tracks: Not Advised.
LP . . . . SPIN 201
Spindrift / Oct '83 / C.M. Distribution / Roots Records / Projection.

Leigh, Richard

CALL ME BUTTERFINGERS.
Tracks: Call me butterfingers / Pillow kissing.
■ 7" . . . . UP 36425
United Artists / Jul '78.

I'VE COME A LONG WAY.
Tracks: I've come a long way / Let's do it right.
■ 7" . . . . UP 630
United Artists / Jul '80.

RICHARD LEIGH.
Tracks: Right from the start / Too good to throw away / Maybe tomorrow / I've come a long way / Let's do it right / If it's so easy / That's what I got for loving you / Years from now / Our love will never die / In the arms of a pretty gal.
■ LP . . . . UAG 30307
United Artists / Aug '80.

RIGHT FROM THE START.
Tracks: Right from the start / Let's do it right.
■ 7" . . . . UP 638
United Artists / Jan '81.

LeJeune, Eddie

Cajun accordionist/vocalist born in Ardoin Cove, near Laccassine, Louisiana in 1951 - son of the legendary Iry Lejeune. His work, a dedication to the preservation of cajun music's heritage, includes Rounder's (Hannibal in UK) Cajun Soul (1988) with D.L.Mennard, rhythm guitar and Ken Smith, fiddle accompanying him. In 1991, Eddie Lejeune And The Morse Playboys was issued. His work has been popularised through recent tours of the UK, where a resurgence of the music is taking place. (Maurice Hope - August 1993)

CAJUN SOUL.
Tracks: Not Advised.
CD . . . . CD 6013
LP . . . . ROUNDER 6013
MC . . . . ROUNDER 6013C
Rounder / '88 / Projection / Roots Records / Swift / C.M. Distribution / Topic Records / Jazz Music / Hot Shot / A.D.A Distribution / Direct Distribution.
CD . . . . HNCD 1353
LP . . . . HNBL 1353
MC . . . . HNBC 1353
Hannibal / Feb '90 / Revolver-APT.

IT'S IN THE BLOOD.
Tracks: Le l'ai rencontree / Duralde waltz / Boire mon whiskey / Happy hop, The / Valse criminelle / Madeleine / Les conseils j'ai ecoutes / Je seras la apres t'espere / J'ai quitte ma famille dans les miseres / Teche / Fille a 'n oncle Hilaire / Reve du saoulard / Donnez moi la / J'aimerais tu viens me chercher.
CD . . . . HNCD 1364
LP . . . . HNBL 1364
MC . . . . HNBC 1364
Hannibal / Jul '91 / Revolver-APT.

Leon

BEST OF LEON.
Tracks: Not Advised.
MC . . . . CPHL 484
Homespun (Ireland) / '88 / Homespun Records / Ross Records / Wellard Dist.

COUNTRY.
Tracks: Slow / Nobody's baby but mine / Satan's jewelled crown / Sweet baby Jane / Love is a rose / Mama, let me shelter in your sweet loving arms / You made my life complete / It's a heartache / Rose has to die, A /

Daytime friends / God bless the children / It only hurts for a little while.
LP. . . . . PHL 404
MC . . . . CPHL 404
Homespun (Ireland) / '82 / Homespun Records / Ross Records / Wellard Dist.

COWGIRL AND THE DANDY.
Tracks: World needs a melody, The / Blue bayou / Rose, The / Mandolin man / Only momma, The / You needed me / Love is a word / Cowgirl and the Dandy / Stand by me, Jesus / I have a dream / Soft-spoken man / Are you teasing me?.
LP. . . . . PHL 416
MC . . . . CPHL 416
Homespun (Ireland) / '82 / Homespun Records / Ross Records / Wellard Dist.

GREAT COUNTRY SINGER COUNTRY LOVE.
Tracks: One day at a time / To daddy / I'm gonna be a country girl again / Sunday school to Broadway / Walking piece of Heaven / Medals for mothers / Single girl / Mississippi / Heaven's just a sin away / Lonely hearts club / When I stop dreaming / River road.
LP. . . . . PHL 401
MC . . . . CPHL 401
Homespun (Ireland) / '82 / Homespun Records / Ross Records / Wellard Dist.

JEALOUS HEART.
Tracks: Bye bye love / Your cheatin' heart / Amazing grace / When will I be loved / Stand by your man / Daddy's little girl / Can I have this dance / Please help me, I'm falling / Doesn't matter anymore / Crazy / Golden ring / Jealous heart.
LP. . . . . PHL 443
MC . . . . CPHL 443
Homespun (Ireland) / Jul '82 / Homespun Records / Ross Records / Wellard Dist.

JEALOUS HEART (Leon & Johnnie Johnston).
Tracks: Jealous heart / Please help me.
7" . . . . HS 066
Homespun (Ireland) / Apr '83 / Homespun Records / Ross Records / Wellard Dist.

JEALOUS HEART (Leon & Johnnie Johnston).
Tracks: Jealous heart / Amazing grace.
7" . . . . HS 058
Homespun (Ireland) / Feb '83 / Homespun Records / Ross Records / Wellard Dist.

SATAN'S JEWELLED CROWN.
Tracks: Satan's jewelled crown / God bless the children.
■ 7" . . . . HS 029
Homespun (Ireland) / Nov '79.

WORLD NEEDS A MELODY, THE.
Tracks: World needs a melody, The / Love is a word.
■ 7" . . . . HS 036
Homespun (Ireland) / Oct '80.

YOU MADE MY LIFE COMPLETE.
Tracks: You made my life complete / Nobody's darling but mine.
7" . . . . HS 033
Homespun (Ireland) / May '80 / Homespun Records / Ross Records / Wellard Dist.

Lewis Family

16 GREATEST HITS: LEWIS FAMILY.
Tracks: Not Advised.
LP. . . . . SLP 3019
MC . . . . GT 53019
Starday (USA) / Apr '87 / Crusader Marketing Co.

Lewis, Bobby

TOSSIN' AND TURNIN'.
Tracks: What a walk / Cry no more / Lonely teardrops / Let me be the one you love / Turn over a new leaf / Tossin' and turnin' / Yes, oh yes, it did / Are you ready / Boom-a-chick-chick / Oh yes I love you / Head over heels / One track mind.
CD BLCD9.00323
Line / Mar '89 / C.M. Distribution / Grapevine Distribution.

Lewis, Hugh X

GOODWILL AMBASSADOR.
Tracks: What can I do to make you love me / Once before I die / Have your next affair with me / Ballad of baby brother / Things that lovers do / My favourite sin / One night only / I'm thinkin of you thinking of him / God is making house calls / When love is the victim / Beginning tomorrow / Love don't hide from me / Meanest mother in the world / If it wasn't for the kids.
LP. . . . . PRCV 106
President / Dec '80 / Grapevine Distribution / Target Records / Jazz Music / Taylors.

LOOKING IN THE FUTURE.
Tracks: Looking in the future / Too late.
■ 7" . . . . HLR 10032
London-American / Mar '66.

Lewis, Jerry Lee

Lewis, Jerry Lee This American singer and pianist was one of the greatest of the original Fifties rock'n'rollers. He was born in Ferriday, Louisiana in 1935 and began his career in the mid Fifties; in 1956 he joined Sam Phillips' seminal Memphis based label, Sun Records, where the similarly youthful Elvis Presley had recently launched his recording career. Lewis' first single *Crazy Arms* was issued in that same year. It flopped but the singing pianist soon gained valuable experience by touring and recording with Carl Perkins, Johnny Cash and other lesser stars. Piano was a rock'n'roll instrument in those days - guitars were not totally dominant and Jerry Lee decided that it could be used not just as a musical medium but as a dynamic stage prop. He began to develop a wild live act in which he would leap from his seated position on the piano stool, kick the chair away and play his keyboards standing up; his playing postures became more and more ludicrous and outrageous. His act was later borrowed and developed by Elton John.The four crucial singles of Lewis' career were released in a 12 month period from mid 1957 to mid 1958. These were the four hits that made him famous in the first place and then secured his legendary status for all time. *Whole Lotta Shakin' Goin' On* (No.3 in US, No.8 in UK) and *High School Confidential* (No.21 in US, No.12 in UK) overflowed with energy and raw riotous rebellion. Both voice and piano were employed in an exuberantly intense and overtly sexual manner. Though his music was rooted in country and western, a genre to which he would later return, Jerry Lee was the ultimate rock'n'roll performer to many people. After this brief but golden period, Lewis' musical career was overshadowed by the uncertainties of his personal life; this state of affairs has continued ever since. In the summer of '58 he attracted a wave of adverse publicity because the press disapproved of the fact that his third wife was in fact his thirteen year old cousin. Occasional musical highlights, such as his 1961 UK Top 10 version of Ray Charles *What'd I Say*, were accompanied by frequent stories of his heavy drinking, verbal abuse towards fellow musicians, and family tragedies. He attracted a reputation as one of the most unpleasant and obnoxious characters in the entertainment business; but he had much to contend with - his elder brother had been killed by a drunken driver at an early age and Jerry Lee lost two sons in accidents Against this unhappy backdrop, Lewis returned to his country roots during the late Sixties and early Seventies and became a major force on the US country charts. Singles like *What's Made Milwaukee Famous (has made a loser of me), There Must Be More To Love Than This, She Even Woke Me Up To Say Goodbye* and a remake of the Big Bopper's *Chantilly Lace* were perfect vehicles for his increasingly emotional and reflective voice. Lewis continued recording and performing throughout th Seventies and into the Eighties but his personal life did not become any happier. He teetered on the brink of death in 1981 on account of a drink related stomach illness. In 1985 two further bouts of ill health sent the 50 year old star back into hospital. He has since recovered and toured the U.K. and been the subject of a biopic starring Dennis Quaid in the title role.(Bob McDonald).

18 ORIGINAL SUN HITS.
Tracks: Not Advised.
CD . . . . RNCD 5255
Rhino (USA) / '86 / WEA.

20 GREATEST HITS: JERRY LEE LEWIS.
Tracks: Not Advised.
LP. . . . . MA 71184
Masters (Holland) / '88.
MC . . . . MAMC 971184
Masters (Holland) / Dec '88.
LP. 28011
MC 48011
Black Tulip / May '88.

20 SUPER HITS: JERRY LEE LEWIS.
Tracks: Not Advised.
CD 290 13 002
Bellaphon / Jan '86 / New Note.

6 TRACK HITS.
Tracks: Great balls of fire / Breathless / Whole lotta shakin' goin' on / High school confidential / Good golly Miss Molly / What'd I say.
EP. 7SR 5014
MC 7SC 5014
Scoop 33 / Sep '83.

AT THE STAR CLUB, HAMBURG.
Tracks: I got a woman / High school confidential / Money / Matchbox / What'd I say? / Great balls of fire / Good golly Miss Molly / Lewis boogie / Hound dog / Long tall Sally / Whole lotta shakin' goin' on.
LP. 9279 460
Mercury (USA) / Oct '83 / Pinnacle.

BABY BABY BYE BYE.
Tracks: Baby baby bye bye.
■ 7" . . . . HLS 9131
London-American / Jun '60.

BENNIE B.
Tracks: Bennie B. / Baby baby bye bye / Down the line / I'm feeling sorry.
■ EP. . . . . BDE 17
Bulldog (USA) / Feb '80.

BEST OF JERRY LEE LEWIS.
Tracks: Not Advised.
CD . . . . ENTCD 253
Entertainers / Jul '88.
MC . . . . ENT MC 13043
Entertainers / Mar '92.

BEST OF JERRY LEE LEWIS (MUSIC CLUB).
Tracks: Not Advised.
CD . . . . MCCD 081
Music Club / Sep '92 / Gold & Sons / Terry Blood Dist. / Video Collection.

BEST OF THE COUNTRY MUSIC HALL FAME HITS.
Tracks: I wonder where you are tonight / I'm so lonesome I could cry / Jambalaya / Four walls / Heartaches by the number / Born to lose / Oh lonesome me / You've still got a place in my heart / I love you because / Jackson / I can't stop loving you / Fraulein / He'll have to go / Why don't you love me / It makes no difference now / Pick me up on your way down / One has my name / I get the blues when it rains / Cold cold heart / Sweet thang.
LP. 6463 085
Mercury / Apr '81 / PolyGram.

BREATHLESS.
Tracks: Breathless / High school confidential.
12" . . . . CYZ 110
Charly / Nov '83 / Charly.

BREATHLESS (2).
Tracks: Breathless.
■ 7" . . . . HLS 8592
London-American / Apr '58.

CARL PERKINS AND JERRY LEE LEWIS LIVE (see under Perkins, Carl).

CHANTILLY LACE.
Tracks: Chantilly lace.
■ 7" 6052 141
Mercury / May '72.

CLASSIC JERRY LEE LEWIS, THE.
Tracks: Whole lotta shakin' goin' on / Great balls of fire / Ubangi stomp / Down the line / Breathless / High school confidential / Jailhouse rock / Don't be cruel / Johnny B. Goode / Little Queenie / What'd I say / Sweet little sixteen / Hang up my rock 'n' roll shoes.
CD . . . . OCN 2021WD
LP. . . . . OCN 2021WL
MC . . . . OCN 2021WK
Ocean (2) / Apr '89.

COLLECTION : JERRY LEE LEWIS.
Tracks: Be bop a lula / Dixie (instrumental) / Goodnight Irene / Great balls of fire / High school confidential / Lewis boogie / Matchbox / Money / Sixty minute man / Ubangi stomp / Whol lotta shakin' goin' on / Wine drinkin' spo-dee-o-dee / C.C. rider / Good golly Miss Molly / Good rockin' tonight / Hang up my rock 'n' roll shoes / Johnny B. Goode / Long gone lonesome blues / Mean woman blues / Pumpin' piano rock / Sweet little sixteen / What'd I say / Will the circle be unbroken / Let the good times roll.
LP Set . . . . CCSLP 143
MC . . . . CCSMC 143
Castle Collector Series / Jul '86 / BMG / Pinnacle / Castle Communications.
CD . . . . CCSCD 143
Castle Collector Series / Dec '90 / BMG / Pinnacle / Castle Communications.

COLLECTION: JERRY LEE LEWIS (20 Rock 'n' roll greats).
Tracks: Whole lotta shakin' goin' on / Great balls of fire / It'll be me / Lovin' up a storm / High heel sneakers / Roll over, Beethoven / I got a woman / Good golly Miss Molly / I believe in you / Hound dog / Long tall Sally / Johnny B. Goode / Flip flop and fly / Maybellene / What'd I say / Money / Lewis boogie / High school confidential / Breathless / Matchbox.
LP. . . . . DVLP 2070
MC . . . . DVMC 2070
Deja Vu / Jul '86 / Jazz Music / Music Collection International.

COLLECTION: JERRY LEE LEWIS.
Tracks: Not Advised.
Double LP . . . . PDA 007
Pickwick / Mar '86 / Pickwick Records.

COMPLETE LONDON SESSION VOL.1.
Tracks: Drinkin' wine spo-dee-o-dee / Music to the man. / Baby what you want me to do? / Bad moon rising / Sea cruise / I can't get no satisfaction / Jukebox / No headstone on my grave / Big boss man / Pledging my love / Dungaree Doll / Memphis Tennessee / I can't give you anything but love Baby.
LP. . . . . BFX 15240

L 8 ■ DELETED

Bear Family / Aug '86 / Rollercoaster Records / Swift / Direct Distribution.

COMPLETE LONDON SESSION VOL.2.
Tracks: Be bop a lula / Trouble in mind / Johnny B. Goode / High school confidential / Early morning rain / Singing the blues / Goldmine in the sky / Whole lotta shakin' goin' on / Sixty minute Man / Down the line / What'd I say / Rock and roll medley.
LP. . . . . **BFX 15241**
Bear Family / Aug '86 / Rollercoaster Records / Swift / Direct Distribution.

COMPLETE PALOMINO CLUB RECORDINGS.
Tracks: Not Advised.
CD Set **2696742**
Tomato (USA) / Oct '91 / Revolver-APT.

COMPLETE SUN RECORDINGS (8-CD Box set).
Tracks: Crazy arms / End of the road / You're the only star in my blue heaven / Born to lose / Silver threads among the gold / I'm throwing rice / I love you so much it hurts / Deep Elem blues / Goodnight Irene / Goodnight Irene (undubbed master) / Honey hush / Crawdad song / Dixie / Marines' hymn, The / That lucky old sun / Hand me down my walking cane / You're the only star in my blue heaven (unissued/Lewis boogi / I love you because / I can't help it / Cold, cold heart / Shame on you / I'll keep on loving you / You are my sunshine / Tomorrow night / Sixty minute man / It all depends (who'll buy the wine) / I don't love nobody / Whole lotta shakin' goin' on / It'll be me (alt.) / It'll be me (alt.2) / Whole lotta shakin' goin' on (master) / False start & It'll be me / It'll be me (single master) / Ole pal of yesterday / You win again / Love letters in the sand / Little green valley (unissued) / Lewis boogie (master) / Pumpin' piano rock / It'll be me (lp master) / All night long / Old time religion / When the saints go marchin' in (undubbed master) / My Carolina sunshine girl / Long gone lonesome blues / Drinkin' wine spo dee o dee / Singing the blues / (snatch of) Keep your hands off it & Rocki / Matchbox (undubbed master) / Matchbox / Ubangi stomp / Rock'n'roll ruby / So long I'm gone / Ooby dooby / I forgot to remember to forget (unissued) / You win again (undubbed master) / I'm feeling sorry (4 takes) / Mean woman blues / Turn around / Great balls of fire (movie cut) / (chatter) & Great balls of fire / Why should I cry over you / Religious discussion / Great balls of fire (master) / You win again (overdubbed master) / Down the line (unissued) / Down the line (false start) / I'm sorry I'm not sorry / Down the line (master) / Sexy ways (false start) / Cool, cool ways (sexy ways) / Milkshake madamoiselle / Breathless (unissued) / Milkshake madamoiselle (false starts) / Breathless (master) / High school confidential (false start) / High school confidential (unissued) / High school confidential / Put me down (unissued) / Good rockin' tonight / Pink pedal pushers / Jailhouse rock / Hound dog / Don't be cruel / Someday / Jambalaya / Friday nights / Big legged woman / Hello, hello baby / Frankie & Johnny / Your cheatin' heart / Lovesick blues / Goodnight Irene (overdubbed master) / When the saints go marchin' in (overdubbed master) / Matchbox (overdubbed master) / Put me down / Fools like me (undubbed master) / Carrying on (sexy ways) / Crazy heart (false start) / High school confidential (master) / Slippin' around / I'll see you in my dreams / Real wild child / Let the good times roll / Fools like me (overdubbed master) / Settin' the woods on fire (unissued) / Memory of you / Come what may / Break up / Crazy heart / Live & let live / I'll make it all up to you (false start) / Johnny B. Goode / Settin' the woods on fire (false start) / Return of Jerry Lee / Break up (unissued) / I'll make it all up to you (unissued) / Break up (master) / I'll make it all up to you / I'll sail my ship alone / It hurt me so (chatter) / You're the only star in my blue heaven (unissued) / It hurt me so / Lovin' up a storm (unissued) / Big blon' baby / Lovin' up a storm / Sick & tired / Shanty town (just a shanty in old) / Release me / I could never be ashamed of you (false start) / Near you (takes 1&2) / I could never be ashamed of you / Hillbilly fever / My blue heaven / Let's talk about us (false start) / Little Quennie / Home / Will the circle be unbroken / Ballad of Billie Joe / Sail away / Am I to be the one (false starts) / Night train to Memphis / I'm the guilty one / Let's talk about us / Wild side of life (stereo), The / Charming Billy (stereo) / Bonnie (stereo) / Mexicali rose (slow) / Mexicali rose (fast) / Gettin' in the mood / In the mood / I get the blues when it rains / Don't drop it / Great speckled bird / Bonnie B. / Baby, baby bye bye / I can't help it (unissued & false starts) / Old black Joe / As long as I live (unissued) / As long as I live / What'd I say / Keep your hands off it (birthday cake) / Hang up my rock'n'roll shoes / John Henry (master slightly extended) / What'd I say (stereo) / C.C. Rider (stereo) / When my blue moon turns to gold again (unissued) / Lewis workout (stereo) / When my blue moon turns to gold again (stereo) / When I get paid (stereo) / Love made a fool of me (stereo) / No more than I get (stereo) / Livin', lovin' wreck / Cold, cold heart (stereo) / I forgot to remember to forget (stereo) / It won't happen with me (stereo) / I love you because (stereo) / Save the last dance for me (stereo) / Hello Josephine (my girl Josephine) (stereo) / High powered woman (stereo) / My blue heaven 1 (stereo) / My blue heaven 2 (stereo) / Sweet little sixteen (stereo & unissued) / Ramblin' rose (master extended) / Money (stereo) / Rockin' the boat of love (stereo) / Ramblin' rose / I've been twistin' / Whole lotta twistin' goin' on (stereo) / I've been twistin' (stereo) / I know what it means / Sweet little sixteen (stereo) / My girl Josephine (stereo) / Set my mind at ease (stereo) / Waiting for a train 1 (stereo) / Waiting for a train 2 (stereo) / How's my ex treating you (stereo & unissued) / Good rockin' tonight (stereo) / Be bop a lula (stereo) / My girl Josephine (stereo & unissued) / How's my ex treating you / Good golly Miss Molly (unissued) / I can't trust me (master) / My pretty quadroon (stereo) / Waiting for a train (unissued) / Teenage letter (stereo) / Seasons of my heart (stereo) / Your lovin' ways (stereo) / Just who is to blame (stereo) / Just who is to blame (unissued) / Hong Kong blues (unissued) / Love on Broadway (stereo) / One minute past eternity (stereo) / Invitation to your party (false start & unissued) / Invitation to your party (stereo) / I can't seem to say good bye (stereo) / Carry me back to old Virginia (unissued) / Carry me back to old Virginia (stereo).
CD Set . . . . **BCD 15420**
Bear Family / Aug '89 / Rollercoaster Records / Swift / Direct Distribution.

COUNTRY SOUND OF, THE.
Tracks: Not Advised.
CD . . . . **PWK 015**
Pickwick / '88 / Pickwick Records.

COUNTRY STORE: JERRY LEE LEWIS.
Tracks: I'm so lonesome I could cry / Heartaches by the number / Jambalaya / Cold cold heart / Sweet thang / Oh, lonesome me / You win again / Your cheatin' heart / I love you because / Jackson / You've still got a place in my heart / Pick me up on your way down / He'll have to go / I can't stop loving you.
MC . . . . **CSTK 39**
Country Store / Apr '87 / BMG.
■ **LP.** . . . . **CST 39**
Country Store / Apr '87.
CD . . . . **CDCST 39**
Country Store / '88 / BMG.

DON'T DROP IT.
Tracks: Not Advised.
LP. . . . . **Z 2004**
Zu Zazz / '89 / Hot Shot / A.D.A Distribution / C.M. Distribution.

DON'T LET IT GO.
Tracks: Don't let it go / I wish I was 18 again.
■ **7"** . . . . **K 12351**
Elektra / '79.

DUETS (Lewis, Jerry Lee & Friends).
Tracks: Save the last dance for me / Sweet little sixteen / I love you / Because / C.C. rider / Am I to be the one? / Cold, cold heart / Hello Josephine / It won't happen with me / What'd I say? / Good golly Miss Molly.
■ **LP.** . . . . **SUNLP 1002**
Sun / '80.

EP COLLECTION, THE: JERRY LEE LEWIS.
Tracks: Not Advised.
CD . . . . **SEECD 307**
LP. . . . . **SEE 307**
MC . . . . **SEEK 307**
See For Miles / Dec '90 / Pinnacle.

ESSENTIAL JERRY LEE LEWIS, THE (20 original Rock 'n' Roll hits).
Tracks: Down the line / Let the good times roll / Jambalaya / High school confidential / Jailhouse rock / Lewis boogie / Hound dog / What'd I say / Lovin' up a storm / Wild one / Great balls of fire / Singing the blues / Little Queenie / Mean woman blues / Sixty minute man / Lovesick blues / Breathless / It'll be me / Whole lotta shakin' goin' on / Don't be cruel.
LP. . . . . **CRM 2001**
Charly / Charly.
MC . . . . **TCCRM 2001**
Charly R&B / Nov '86 / Charly.

ESSENTIAL ONE AND ONLY, THE.
Tracks: Not Advised.
MC . . . . **MODEMC 1043**
Trax / Oct '89 / BMG.
■ **CD** . . . . **MODCD 1043**
Trax / Oct '89.
■ **LP.** . . . . **MODEM 1043**
Filmtrax / Oct '89.

EVERYDAY I HAVE TO CRY SOME.
Tracks: Everyday i have to cry some / Who will the next fool be.
■ **7"** . . . . **K 12399**
Elektra / Jan '80.

FERRIDAY FIREBALL.
Tracks: Lewis boogie / It'll be me / High school confidential / Whole lotta shakin' goin' on / Good rockin' tonight / Big legged woman / Great balls of fire / Drinkin' wine spo-dee-o-dee / Matchbox / You win again / Will the circle be unbroken / That lucky old sun / Crazy arms / Break up / Memory of you / Johnny B. Goode / Little Queenie / Milkshake mademoiselle / Big blon' baby / Breathless / Mean woman blues / Down the line / When the saints go marching in / End of the road / What'd I say.
CD . . . . **CDCHARLY 1**
Charly / Mar '86 / Charly.

FROM LONDON TO HAMBURG.
Tracks: Not Advised.
LP. . . . . **SUNSTAR 003**
Sunstar / Oct '87.

GOLDEN HITS.
Tracks: Break-up / Breathless / Crazy arms / Down the line / End of the road / Fools like me / Great balls of fire / High school confidential / I'll make it all up to you / Whole lotta shakin' goin' on / You win again / Your cheatin' heart.
LP. **6336 245**
Philips / Sep '78 / PolyGram.

GOOD GOLLY MISS MOLLY.
Tracks: Not Advised.
■ **MC** . . . . **BRC 2504**
Bravo / Feb '80.

GOOD GOLLY MISS MOLLY.
Tracks: Good golly Miss Molly.
■ **7"** . . . . **HLU 8560**
London-American / Feb '58.
■ **7"** . . . . **HLS 9688**
London-American / Mar '63.

GOOD ROCKIN' TONIGHT.
Tracks: Good rockin' tonight / John Henry / Rockin' the boat of love / Big blon' baby / Big legged woman / My blue heaven / Wild one / Livin' lovin' wreck / Frankie and Johnny / Jambalaya / Cold cold heart / Sail away / C.C. rider / Hang up my rock 'n' roll shoes / All night long / I'll make it all up to you / Don't be cruel / Lovin' up a storm / Slippin' around / Crazy arms / Break up / High powered woman / Rock 'n' roll baby / Teenage letter.
MC Set . . . . **DTOL 10248**
Ditto / Sep '86 / Pickwick Records.

GOOD ROCKIN' TONIGHT.
Tracks: Drinkin' win spo-dee-o-dee / I could never be ashamed of you / Pink pedal pushers / Old black Joe / Johnny B. Goode / Honey hush / Big legged woman / Good rockin' tonight / Be bop a lula / Waiting for a train / Let's talk about us / Hand me down my walking cane / Matchbox / Setting the woods on fire / Bonnie B / Deep elem blues.
LP. . . . . **SUNLP 1003**
Sun / '80 / Charly / Swift.

GRAFFITI COLLECTION.
Tracks: Not Advised.
CD . . . . **GRCD 15**
MC . . . . **GRMC 15**
Graffiti Collection / Aug '90 / Terry Blood Dist.

GREAT BALLS OF FIRE.
Tracks: Great balls of fire / Breathless / Sweet little sixteen / Big blon' baby / It'll be me / Crazy arms / Your cheatin' heart / Good golly Miss Molly / What'd I say / Whole lotta shakin' goin' on / High school confidential / Little Queenie / You win again / That lucky old sun / Frankie and Johnny / Big legged woman / Let the good times roll / Release me / Lovin' up a storm / Wild one.
CD . . . . **PWKS 562**
LP. . . . . **SHM 3296**
MC . . . . **HSC 3296**
Pickwick / Dec '89 / Pickwick Records.

GREAT BALLS OF FIRE.
Tracks: Great balls of fire / High school confidential / Breathless / Whole lotta shakin' goin' on.
■ **CD Single** . . . . **CDS 2**
Charly / Feb '89 / Charly.

GREAT BALLS OF FIRE.
Tracks: Great balls of fire.
■ **7"** . . . . **HLS 8529**
London-American / Dec '57.

GREAT BALLS OF FIRE.
Tracks: I'm feeling sorry / You're the only star in my blue heaven / I'll keep on loving you / Cool cool ways / Milkshake Mademoiselle / Mean woman blues / Great balls of fire / Turn around / Rock 'n' roll baby / Ubangi stomp / Jambalaya / Down the line / Breathless.
LP. . . . . **SUNLP 1043**
Charly / Jun '82 / Charly.

GREAT BALLS OF FIRE.
Tracks: Not Advised.
CD . . . . **U 46064**
Spectrum (1) / Jun '88 / PolyGram.

GREAT BALLS OF FIRE.
Tracks: Rock 'n' roll Ruby / Ubangi stomp / Jambalaya / Down the line / Breathless / Lovin' up a storm / Don't be cruel / Great balls of fire / Mean woman blues / Cool cool ways.
LP. . . . . **CFM 516**
Charly / Jun '82 / Charly.

GREAT BALLS OF FIRE.
Tracks: Great balls of fire / Breathless.
12" . . . . **PZ 57**
7" . . . . **PO 57**
Polydor / Sep '89 / PolyGram.

GREAT BALLS OF FIRE (CHARLY).
Tracks: Whole lotta shakin' goin' on / It'll be me / Lewis boogie / Drinkin' wine spo-dee-o-dee / Rock 'n' roll Ruby / Matchbox / Ubangi stomp / Great balls of fire / You win again / Mean woman blues / Milkshake mademoiselle / Breathless / Down the line / Good rockin' tonight / Jambalaya / High school confidential / Pink pedal pushers / Don't be cruel / Johnny B. Goode / Break-up / Big blon' baby / Lovin' up a storm / Little queenie / In the mood / What'd I say / Sweet little sixteen / Good golly Miss Molly / Be bop a lula / Teenage letter / Carry me back to old Virginia.
CD . . . . **CD CHARLY 185**
Double LP . . . . **CDX 44**
MC . . . . **TCCDX 44**
Charly / Jul '89 / Charly.

GREAT BALLS OF FIRE (OLD GOLD).
Tracks: Great balls of fire / Whole lotta shakin' goin' on / What'd I say.
7" . . . . OG 9110
Old Gold / Jul '82 / Pickwick Records.
CD Single . . . . OG 6115
Old Gold / Feb '89 / Pickwick Records.

GREATEST HITS, VOL 2: JERRY LEE LEWIS.
Tracks: Not Advised.
CD . . . . PWK 025
Pickwick / '91 / Pickwick Records.

GREATEST HITS: JERRY LEE LEWIS.
Tracks: Not Advised.
LP. 28012
MC 48012
Black Tulip / May '88.

GREATEST HITS: JERRY LEE LEWIS VOL.1.
Tracks: Not Advised.
CD . . . . PCD 814
Pickwick / Apr '86 / Pickwick Records.

GREATEST HITS: JERRY LEE LEWIS VOL.2.
Tracks: Not Advised.
CD . . . . PCD 840
Pickwick / Oct '86 / Pickwick Records.

GREATEST LIVE SHOWS ON EARTH, THE.
Tracks: Jenny Jenny / Who will the next fool be / Memphis Tennessee / Hound dog / Mean woman blues / Hi heel sneakers / No particular place to go / Together again / Long tall Sally / Whole lotta shakin' goin' on / Little queenie / How's my ex treating you / Johnnie B. Goode / Green, green grass of home / What'd I say (part 2) / You win again / I'll sail my ship alone / Crying' time / Money / Roll over Beethoven.
CD . . . . BCD 15608
Bear Family / Nov '91 / Rollercoaster Records / Swift / Direct Distribution.

HEARTBREAK.
Tracks: What made Milwaukee famous / Careless hands / Who will the next fool be / Touching home / More to love than this / Cold cold heart / You win again / Your cheatin' heart / I can't stop lovin' you / Another place, another time / 39 and holding / She even woke me up / I wished I was 18 again / Who is going to play this ole piano.
CD 598 0067 29
Tomato (USA) / Aug '93 / Revolver-APT.

HELLO JOSEPHINE.
Tracks: Hello Josephine / What'd I say.
■ 7" . . . . CYS 1047
Charly / Mar '79.

HIGH SCHOOL CONFIDENTIAL.
Tracks: High school confidential.
■ 7" . . . . HLS 8780
London-American / Jan '59.

HONKY TONK ROCK'N'ROLL PIANO MAN.
Tracks: My fingers do the talking / Why you been gone so long / Daughters of Dixie / Teenage Queen / I'm lookin' over a four leaf clover / I am what I am / Better not look down / Only you (and you alone) / Honky tonk rock 'n' roll piano man / Circumstantial evidence / I'm lookin' under a skirt / Rock 'n' roll money / Forever forgiving (alternative take no.1) / Why you been gone so long (alt. take no.3) / Get out your big roll daddy.
CD . . . . CDCH 332
Ace / Oct '91 / Pinnacle / Hot Shot / Jazz Music / Complete Record Co. Ltd.

I AM WHAT I AM.
Tracks: Whole lotta shakin' goin' on / Great balls of fire / Big legged woman / Breathless / High school confidential / I'm throwing rice (at the girl I love) / Crazy arms / That lucky ole sun / What'd I say / Sweet little sixteen / Johnny B. Goode / Wild one (real wild child) / Jailhouse rock / Be bop a lula.
CD . . . . CDINS 5008
LP. . . . . INS 5008
MC . . . . TCINS 5008
Instant (2) / Aug '89 / Charly.

I AM WHAT I AM.
Tracks: Not Advised.
VHS. . . . . VIDJAM 21
Charly Video / Jan '90 / Charly / Terry Blood Dist.

I AM WHAT I AM.
Tracks: I am what I am / Only you (and you alone) / Get out your big roll Daddy / Have I got a song for you / Careless hands / Candy kisses / I'm looking over a four leaf clover / Send me the pillow that you dream on / Honky tonk heart / That was the way it was then.
LP. . . . . MCF 3227
MC . . . . MCFC 3227
MCA / Jul '84 / BMG.
LP. . . . . MCL 1810
MC . . . . MCLC 1810
MCA / May '85 / BMG.

I KNOW WHAT IT MEANS.
Tracks: I know what it means / Carry me back to old Virginia.
■ 7" . . . . HLS 9980
London-American / '65.

I'M A ROCKER.
Tracks: Big blon' baby / Boogie woogie country man / Chantilly lace / Don't be cruel / Down the line / Drinkin' wine spo-dee-o-dee / Flip flop and fly / Hi-heel sneakers / I betcha gonna like it / I got a woman / I'm on fire / I'm walkin' / Memphis beat / Sexy ways / Turn on your lovelight / Whole lotta shakin' goin' on.
LP. 6338 602
Philips / Sep '79 / PolyGram.

JERRY LEE LEWIS.
Tracks: Not Advised.
CD . . . . OR 0033
Music Collection International / Aug '87 / Terry Blood Dist. / Jazz Music.

JERRY LEE LEWIS.
Tracks: Not Advised.
VHS. 634050
Fox Video / Oct '89.

JERRY LEE LEWIS.
Tracks: Long tall Sally / Johnny B. Goode / Breathless / Herman the hermit / High heel sneakers / Hound dog / Roll over Beethoven / Maybelline / Flip, flop & fly / I believe in you.
■ LP. . . . . HMB 7002
Hammer / Dec '79.

JERRY LEE LEWIS.
Tracks: Not Advised.
■ LP. . . . . CR 30002
Charly / Oct '75 / Charly.

JERRY LEE LEWIS.
Tracks: Not Advised.
LP Set . . . . CR 100
■ MC Set. . . . . CRT 100
Cambra / Feb '85.

JERRY LEE LEWIS.
Tracks: Great balls of fire / High school confidential / Goodnight Irene / You are my sunshine / Mean woman blues / Hound dog / Lovesick blues / Your cheatin' heart / Johnny B. Goode / Wild side of life / Save the last dance for me / My girl Josephine / Wild one / Singing the blues.
LP. 6463 042
MC 7145 042
Mercury / Nov '81 / PolyGram.

JERRY LEE LEWIS (2).
Tracks: Good golly Miss Molly / Breathless / Frankie and Johnny / Let the good times roll / Move down the line / It'll be me / Sweet little sixteen / Be bop a lula / Matchbox / What'd I say / Hound dog / Jailhouse rock / Crazy arms / Mean woman blues / Little Queenie / Singin' the blues / Night train to Memphis / Money / Great balls of fire / Swiss boogie / Whole lotta shakin' goin' on / High school confidential / Pumpin' piano rock / Johnny B Goode.
MC Set. . . . . DTO 10005
Ditto / Jul '82 / Pickwick Records.
MC Set. . . . . DTOL 10005
Ditto / Feb '90 / Pickwick Records.

JERRY LEE LEWIS (ELEKTRA).
Tracks: Don't let go / Rita May / Every day I have to cry / I like it like that / Number one lovin' man / Rockin' my life away / Who will the next fool be (you've got) / Personality / I wish I was eighteen / Again / Rocking little angel.
■ LP. . . . . K 52132
Elektra / '77.

JERRY LEE LEWIS EP.
Tracks: Lewis boogie / High school confidential / Little queenie / Break-up.
■ EP. . . . . CEP 105
Charly / Feb '77.

JERRY LEE LEWIS SHOW, THE.
Tracks: Whole lotta shakin' goin' on / When you wore a tulip / Bad motorcycle / Autumn leaves / Higher and higher / Lonely teardrops / Things that matter most to me / Strangers in the night / Once more with feeling / Another place, another time / What made Milwaukee famous / One minute past eternity / Honey don't / Mean woman blues / Blue suede shoes / I'll follow him / Daddy sang bass / I'll fly away / Down the old sawdust trail / This land.
VHS. . . . . MMGV 030
MMG Video / '91 / Terry Blood Dist.

JERRY LEE LEWIS VOL.2.
Tracks: Not Advised.
■ LP. . . . . HA 2440
London-American / Jun '62.

JERRY LEE'S GREATEST.
Tracks: Not Advised.
■ LP. . . . . CRM 2008
Charly / Feb '81 / Charly.

KEEP YOUR HANDS OFF OF IT.
Tracks: Not Advised.
LP. . . . . Z 2003
Zu Zazz / Nov '87 / Hot Shot / A.D.A Distribution / C.M. Distribution.

KICKIN' UP A STORM.
Tracks: Who will buy the wine / Frankie and Johnny (Trad. arr. Jerry Lee Lewis.) / Home / Little Queenie / Friday night / Big blon' baby / Lovin' up a storm / Hillbilly fever / I could never be ashamed of you / It all depends (who will buy the wine) / I'll sail my ship alone / Bonnie B. / As long as I live / Night train to Memphis / Mexicali Rose / In the mood.
LP. . . . . SUN 1045
Sun / Feb '87 / Charly / Swift.

KILLER 1963-1968, THE.
Tracks: Whole lotta shakin' goin' on / Crazy arms / Great balls of fire / High school confidential / I'll make it all up to you / Break up / Down the line / Hit the road, Jack (1) / End of the road / Your cheatin' heart / Wedding bells / Just because / Breathless / He took it like a man / Drinkin' wine spo dee o dee / Johnny B. Goode / hallelujah, I love her so / You went back on your word / Pen and paper / Hole he said he did for me, The / You win again / Fools like me / Hit the road Jack (2) / I'm on fire (1) / I'm on fire (2) / She was my baby (He was my friend) / Bread and butter man / I bet you're gonna like it / Got you on my mind / Mathilda, Corrine, Corina / Sexy ways / Wild side of life, The / Mean woman blues / Money / Matchbox / What'd I say, parts 1 & 2 / Good golly Miss Molly / Lewis boogie / You cheatin' heart / Hound dog / Long tall Sally / Jenny, Jenny / Who will the next fool be / Memphis, Tennessee / Hi heel sneakers / No particular place to go / Together again / Flip, flop and fly / Don't let go / Mabellene / Roll over Beethoven / Just in time / I believe in you / Herman, The hermit / Baby hold me close / Skid row / This must be the place / Rockin pneumonia and the boogie woogie flu / Four seasons of my heart / Big boss man / Too young / Danny boy / City lights / Funny how times slips away / North to Alaska / Walk right in / Wolverton mountain / King of the road / Detroit city / Ring of fire / Baby (You've got what it takes) / Green green grass of home / Sticks and stones / What a heck of a mess / Lincoln limousine / Rockin' Jerry Lee / Memphis beat (1) / Urge, The / Whenever you're ready / She thinks I still care / Memphis beat (2, take 1) / Memphis beat (2, take 2) / Twenty four hours a day / Swinging doors / Little queenie / How's my ex treating you / What'd I say / I'll sail my ship alone / Cryin' time / If I had it all to do over / Just dropped in / It's hang up baby / Holdin' on / Hey baby / Dream baby / Treat her right / Turn on her lovelight / Shotgun man / All the good is gone / Another place another time / Walking the floor over you / I'm a lonesome fugitive / Break my mind / Play me a song I can cry to / Before the next teardrop falls / All night long / We live in two different worlds now / What's made Milwaukee famous / On the back row / Slipping around / She still comes around / Today I started loving you again / Louisiana man / There stands the glass / I can't have a merry Christmas , Mary / I can't get over you / Listen they're playing my song / Echoes / Release me / Let's talk about us / To make love sweeter for you.
LP Set . . . . BFX 15210/10
Bear Family / Sep '86 / Rollercoaster Records / Swift / Direct Distribution.

KILLER 1963-1968, VOL. 1.
Tracks: Not Advised.
CD 836 935 2
LP. 836 935 1
■ MC 836 935 4
Mercury / Nov '89.

KILLER 1969-1972, THE.
Tracks: Not Advised.
LP Set . . . . BFX 15228/11
Bear Family / Dec '86 / Rollercoaster Records / Swift / Direct Distribution.

KILLER 1969-1972, VOL. 2.
Tracks: Not Advised.
LP. 836 938 1
Mercury / Nov '89 / PolyGram.
CD 836 938 2
■ MC 836 938 4
Mercury / Nov '89.

KILLER 1973-1977, THE (12 unit box set).
Tracks: Drinkin' wine spo-dee-o-dee / Music to the man / Baby what do you want me to do / Bad moon rising / Sea cruise / (I can't get no) Satisfaction / Jukebox / No headstone on my grave / Big boss man / Pledging my love / Dungaree doll / Memphis Tennessee / I can't give you anything but love, Baby / Be bop a lula / Trouble in mind / Johnny B Goode / High school confidential (Instrumental) / Early morning rain / Singing the blues / Goldmine in the sky / Whole lotta shakin' goin on / Dixty minute man / Sown the line / What'd I say / Rock and roll medley / Jack Daniels (Old number 7) / Why me Lord / Ride me down easy / Cold cold morning light / Alcohol of fame, the / Tomorrow's taking my baby away / Mama's hands / What my woman can't do / Tell tale signs / Morning after baby let me down, The / I think I need to pray / Hate goodbyes / Wher would I be / My cricket and me / Falling to the bottom / Gods were angry with me, The / Sometimes a memory aint' enough / Bluer words / Meat man / When a man loves a woman / Hold on I'm coming / Just a little bit / Born to be a loser / Haunted house, The / Blueberry hill / Revolutionary man, The / Big blue diamond / That old bourbon street church / All over hell and half of Georgia / Take your time / Haunted house (extended version) / I sure miss those good old times / Margie / Raining in my heart / Hold on I'm coming (Alternate version) / Cry / Honey hush / Silver thread among the gold / Big blue diamonds / Sure miss those good old times (Duet) / Silver threads among the gold / Hold on I'm comign (Fast) / Hold on I'm coming (Slow) / He can't fill my shoes / I'm left you're right, she's gone / Keep me from blowing away / Honky tonk wine / Room full of roses / Picture from life's other side, A / I've forgot more about you, than he'll / Until the day forever ends / Boogie woogie country man / I can still hear the music in the restroom / Speak a little louder to us Jesus / Jesus is on the main line / Remember me (I'm the one who loves you) / Shake, rattle and roll / Love inflation / I

L 10 ■ DELETED

don't want to be lonely tonight / Forever forgiving / Little peace and harmony, A / No one knows me / When I take my vacation in heaven / I'm still jealous of you / You ought ot see my mind / Don't boogie woogie (When you say your.) / Thanks for nothing / Red hot memories (Ice cold beers) / I was sorta wonderin' / Jerry's place / That kind of fool / Your cheatin' heart / Crawdad song / House of blue lights, The / Goodnight Irene / Damn good country song (1), A / Damn good country song (2), A / Lord, what's left for me to do / Great balls of fire / One rose left in my heart, The / I'm knee deep in loving you / I can help (1) / I can help (2) / Slippin' and slidin' / From a Jack to a king (1) / From a Jack to a king (2) / After the fool you've made of me / Closest thing to you, The / I can't keep my hands off you / Wedding bells / Fifties, The / No one will ever know / Only love can get you in my door / Old country church, The / Harbour lights / Jerry Lee's rock and roll revival show / Let's put it all back together again / Country memories / As long as we live / Jealous heart / (You'd think by now) I'd be over you / Come on in / Who's sorry now / Let's say goodbye like we said hello / Georgia on my mind / What's so good about goodbye / Tennessee saturday night / Ivory tears / Middle age crazy / Last letter, The / Last cheater's waltz, The / Let's live a little / I hate you / Before the night is over / Sittin' and thinkin' / Blue suede shoes / Lucille / Corrine, Corrina / Don't let the stars get in your eyes / Sweet little sixteen / Life's railway to heaven / You call everybody darling / Wild an wooly ways / I find it where I can / Lord I've tried everything but you / You're all too ugly tonight / Arkansas seesaw / Pee Wee's place.
LP Set . . . . **BFX 15229/12**
Bear Family / Mar '87 / Rollercoaster Records / Swift / Direct Distribution.

KILLER 1973-1977, VOL. 3.
Tracks: Not Advised.
LP **836 941 1**
Mercury / Nov '89 / PolyGram.
CD **836 941 2**
■ **MC** **836 941 4**
Mercury / Nov '89.

KILLER COUNTRY.
Tracks: Folsom Prison blues / I'll do it all again / Jukebox junky / Too weak to fight / Late night lovin' man / Change places with me / Let me on / Thirty nine and holding / Mama, this one's for you / Over the rainbow.
■ **LP** . . . . **K 52246**
Elektra / Jun '81.
LP . . . . **ED 250**
Edsel / Jul '87 / Pinnacle.

KILLER PERFORMANCE, THE.
Tracks: Not Advised.
BETA . . . . **VVD 053B**
Virgin Vision / Dec '84 / Gold & Sons / Terry Blood Dist.
VHS . . . . **VVD 053**
Virgin Vision / Sep '91 / Gold & Sons / Terry Blood Dist.

KILLER ROCKS ON, THE.
Tracks: Don't be cruel / You can have her / Games people play / You don't miss the water / Me and Bobby McGee / Shotgun man / Chantilly lace / Walk a mile in my shoes / C.C. rider / Lonely weekends / Turn on your love light / I'm walking.
LP **2872 119**
MC **3472 119**
Karussell (Germany) / Oct '82.

KILLER STRIKES, THE.
Tracks: Whole lotta shakin' goin' on / You win again / Break up / I'll make it all up to you / What'd I say / Sweet little sixteen / Breathless / High school confidential / It'll be me / Milkshake mademoiselle / Lovin' up a storm / I'll sail my ship alone.
LP . . . . **TOP 105**
MC . . . . **KTOP 105**
Topline / Nov '84 / Charly / Swift / Black Sun Records.

KILLER, THE - LIVE! (Lewis, Jerry Lee & An All-Star Band).
Tracks: Don't let me be lonely tonight / You win again / I got a woman / I am what I am / What'd I say / Chantilly lace / High school confidential / Rockin' my life away / Johnny B. Goode / Whole lotta shakin' goin' on / Great balls of fire / Good golly Miss Molly / Tutti frutti / High heel sneakers / Wild one.
VHS . . . . **TVE 1031**
Telstar Video / Feb '91 / BMG.

KILLERS BIRTHDAY CAKE.
Tracks: My blue heaven / Let's talk about us / Break up / You can't help it / Your cheatin' heart / Hound dog / Birthday cake (hands off it) / You win again / Goodnight Irene / Great speckled bird, The / Don't drop it / Old black Joe / Bonnie B / Ballad of Billy Joe.
LP . . . . **SUNLP 1051**
Sun / Nov '89 / Charly / Swift.

KILLERS RHYTHM AND BLUES.
Tracks: John Henry / Hang up my rock 'n' roll shoes / When my blue moon turns to gold again / Billy boy / My girl Josephine / High powered woman / Hello hello baby / Matchbox / See see rider / Good rockin' tonight / Sweet little sixteen / Feeling good / Big legged woman.
LP . . . . **SUNLP 1053**
Sun / Nov '89 / Charly / Swift.

LIL' BIT OF GOLD: JERRY LEE LEWIS.
Tracks: Whole lotta shakin' goin' on / High school confidential / End of the road / What'd I say.
■ **CD Single** . . . . **R 373012**
Rhino (USA) / May '88 / WEA.

LIVE AT THE STAR CLUB, HAMBURG.
Tracks: Mean woman blues / High school confidential / Money / Matchbox / What'd I say / Great balls of fire / Good golly Miss Molly / Lewis boogie / Your cheatin' heart / Hound dog / Long tall Sally / Whole lotta shakin' goin' on / Down the line.
LP . . . . **TIME 06**
Philips (Timeless) / Sep '84 / PolyGram.
■ **MC** . . . . **TIMEC 06**
Philips (Timeless) / Sep '84.
CD . . . . **BCD 15467**
Bear Family / Jul '89 / Rollercoaster Records / Swift / Direct Distribution.

LIVE AT THE VAPORS CLUB.
Tracks: Don't put no headstone on my grave / Chantilly lace / I'll find it where I can / Drinkin' wine spodee-o-dee / Sweet little sixteen / Boogie woogie country man / Me and Bobby McGhee / Rockin' my life away / Whole lot of shakin' going on / You can have her / Hey good lookin' / Will the circle be unbroken.
CD . . . . **CDCH 326**
Ace / May '91 / Pinnacle / Hot Shot / Jazz Music / Complete Record Co. Ltd.

LIVE IN BERLIN, 1977 (The Killer's 20th Anniversary Show).
Tracks: Not Advised.
LP **20JLL 1977**
JLL / Nov '87.

LIVE IN GEORGIA, VOL 1.
Tracks: Not Advised.
LP . . . . **SUNSTAR 004**
Sunstar / Oct '87.

LIVE IN GEORGIA, VOL 2.
Tracks: Not Advised.
LP . . . . **SUNSTAR 005**
Sunstar / Oct '87.

LIVE IN ITALY.
Tracks: Roll in my sweet baby's arms / High school confidential / Me and Bobby McGee / Jackson / There must be more to love than this / Great balls of fire / What'd I say / Jerry Lee's rock'n'roll revival show / I am what I am / Whole lotta shakin' goin' on / You win again / Mona Lisa / One of those things we all go through / Hang up my rock 'n' roll shoes.
CD . . . . **CDMF 071**
LP . . . . **MFLP 071**
Magnum Force / Jun '89 / Terry Blood Dist. / Jazz Music / Hot Shot.

LIVE VIDEO: JERRY LEE LEWIS (see under Perkins, Carl).

LONG TALL SALLY.
Tracks: Long tall Sally / Jenny Jenny.
7" . . . . **MF 1105**
Mercury / '65 / PolyGram.

LOVIN' UP A STORM.
Tracks: Lovin' up a storm.
■ **7"** . . . . **HLS 8840**
London-American / May '59.

MILESTONES.
Tracks: Not Advised.
LP . . . . **RNDA 1449**
Rhino (USA) / Jan '86 / WEA.

MOTIVE SERIES.
Tracks: Movin' on down the line / Lonely weekends / You don't miss your water / Chantilly lace / Whole lotta shakin' goin' on / What'd I say / High school confidential / Baby what you want me to do / Bad moon rising / Sea cruise / Pledging my love / Don't be cruel.
LP **6463 097**
MC **7145 097**
Mercury / May '82 / PolyGram.

MY FINGERS DO THE TALKING.
Tracks: Not Advised.
■ **LP** . . . . **MCF 3162**
MCA / May '83.

MY FINGERS DO THE TALKING.
Tracks: My fingers do the talking forever / Forever forgiving.
7" . . . . **MCA 808**
MCA / Feb '83 / BMG.

NUGGETS VOL 1.
Tracks: Sweet little sixteen / Hello Josephine / I've been twistin' / It won't happen with me / Ramblin' Rose / When I get paid / Love made a fool of me / I get the blues when it rains / In the mood / Ubangi stomp / It'll be me / Put me down / I'm feelin' sorry / Ballad of Billy Joe / Baby baby bye bye.
■ **LP** . . . . **CR 30121**
Charly / Mar '77 / Charly.

NUGGETS VOL 2.
Tracks: Crazy arms / Hillbilly music / Turn around / Night train to Memphis / My blue Heaven / It hurt me so / I can't help it / When the saints go marching in / Whole lot o' twistin' goin' on / I'll sail my ship alone / Friday nights / Just who is to blame / I just can't trust me in your arms any more / Hello hello baby / High powered woman / Crawdad hole.
■ **LP** . . . . **CR 30129**
Charly / Dec '77 / Charly.

OLD BLACK JOE.
Tracks: Old black Joe / Return of Jerry Lee.
■ **7"** . . . . **CS 1023**
Charly / Mar '77.

ORIGINAL JERRY LEE LEWIS, THE.
Tracks: Crazy arms / End of the road / It'll be me / Whole lotta shakin' goin' on / You win again / Great balls of fire / Down the line / Breathless / High school confidential / Fools like me / Breakup / I'll make it all up to you / Lovin' up a storm / Big blon' baby / Livin' lovin' wreck / What'd I say.
■ **LP** . . . . **CR 30111**
Charly / Oct '76 / Charly.
MC . . . . **TCCR 30111**
Charly / Sep '86 / Charly.

OUTTAKES.
Tracks: Not Advised.
LP . . . . **SUNSTAR 002**
Sunstar / Jul '88.

PRETTY MUCH COUNTRY.
Tracks: Honky tonk heaven / She never said goodbye / That was the way it was then / Candy kisses / I am what I am / Come as you were / She sang amazing grace / Have I got a song for you / Daughters of Dixie / Send me the pillow that you dream on / She sure makes leavin' look easy / My fingers do the talkin' / Honky tonk heart / Careless hands / Honky tonk rock'n'roll piano man / Forever forgiving.
CD . . . . **CDCH 348**
Ace / Feb '92 / Pinnacle / Hot Shot / Jazz Music / Complete Record Co. Ltd.

PUMPIN' PIANO CAT, THE.
Tracks: Born to lose / My Carolina sunshine girl / Long gone lonesome blues / Crazy arms / Silver threads among the gold / You're the only star in my blue heaven / End of the road / My old pal of yesterday / Little green valley / It'll be me / All night long / Pumpin piano rock / Sixty minute man / Lewis boogie / You are my sunshine / Ole pal of yesterday / Hand me down my walking cane / When the saints go marching in / I'm feeling sorry / If the world keeps on turning / Shame on you / I don't love nobody.
■ **LP** . . . . **CFM 514**
Charly / Jun '82.
LP . . . . **SUN 1041**
Sun / Jul '86 / Charly / Swift.

RARE AND ROCKIN'.
Tracks: It won't happen with me / Teenage letter / Pink pedal pushers / Hillbilly music / Deep elm blues / You win again / I'm feeling sorry / I'm the guilty one / It hurt me so / I love you because / Cold, cold heart / Whole lotta shakin' goin' on / In the mood / Great balls of fire / I forgot to remember to forget / Turn around / It all depends (who will buy the wine) / It'll be me (slow version) / It'll be me (fast version) / Sixty minute man / Lovin' up a storm / Rockin' with red (she knows how to rock me) / Honey hush / Hound dog / Hang up my rock 'n' roll shoes.
CD . . . . **CDCHARLY 70**
Charly / Apr '87 / Charly.

RARE JERRY LEE LEWIS, VOL 1.
Tracks: Not Advised.
■ **LP** . . . . **CR 30006**
Charly / Jul '88 / Charly.

RARE JERRY LEE LEWIS, VOL 2.
Tracks: Not Advised.
■ **LP** . . . . **CR 30007**
Charly / Oct '75 / Charly.

ROCKET.
Tracks: Meat man / Jailhouse rock / House of blue lights / Rock'n'roll funeral / Don't touch me / Changing mountains / Beautiful dreamer / I'm alone because I love you / Lucille / Seventeen / Mathilda / Wake up little Susie.
CD . . . . **CDINS 5023**
LP . . . . **INS 5023**
MC . . . . **TCINS 5023**
Instant (2) / Feb '90 / Charly.

ROCKIN'.
Tracks: Not Advised.
LP . . . . **MULE 201**
Mule / Oct '87 / SRD.

ROCKIN' ALL NIGHT LONG.
Tracks: Not Advised.
CD . . . . **QSCD 6001**
MC . . . . **QSMC 6001**
Quality (Charly) / Oct '91 / Charly.

ROCKIN' MY LIFE AWAY.
Tracks: Rockin' my life away / Rita May.
■ **7"** . . . . **K 12374**
Elektra / '79.

ROCKIN' MY LIFE AWAY.
Tracks: Not Advised.
CD . . . . **.269661-2**
LP . . . . **.269661-1**
MC . . . . **.269661-4**
Tomato (USA) / Apr '90 / Revolver-APT.

ROCKIN' WITH JERRY LEE LEWIS.
Tracks: Brown-eyed handsome man / Corine, Corina / Great balls of fire / High school confidential / Hi-heel sneakers / Jenny, Jenny / Johnny B. Goode / Mabellene

/ Memphis / Roll over Beethoven / Sticks and stones / Whole lotta shakin' goin' on.
LP. 6336 300
Philips / Sep '79 / PolyGram.
LP. . . . . KILLER 7005
Killer (USA) / Jul '88 / Pinnacle.

ROCKING JERRY LEE.
Tracks: Rocking Jerry Lee / Goodtime Charlie's got the blues.
■ 7". . . . . K 12432
Elektra / Mar '80.

ROLL OVER BEETHOVEN.
Tracks: Not Advised.
CD 15 100
Laserlight / Aug '91 / TBD / Taylors.

SESSION, THE.
Tracks: Johnny B. Goode / Trouble in mind / Early morning rain / No headstone on my grave / Pledging my love / Memphis / Drinkin' wine spo-dee-o-dee / Music to the man / Bad moon rising / Sea cruise / Sixty minute man / Movin' on down the line / What'd I say.
CD 822 751-2
Mercury / May '85 / PolyGram.

SOUTHERN ROOTS.
Tracks: Big blue diamond / Blueberry hill / Born to be a loser / Haunted house, The / Hold on I'm coming / Just a little bit / Meat man / Revolutionary man, The / That old Bourbon Street Church / When a man loves a woman.
LP. 6338 452
Philips / Sep '80 / PolyGram.

STORY OF ROCK 'N' ROLL.
Tracks: High School confidential / I'm on fire / Don't be cruel / Great balls of fire / Night has a thousand eyes, The / Breathless / Deep elem / Hound dog / I believe in you / This could be the start of something / Mystery train / Whole lotta shakin' / I got a woman / Jailhouse rock.
VHS. 791 096
BMG Video / Jun '93 / BMG.

SUN YEARS, THE (8 CD SET).
Tracks: Not Advised.
CD Set . . . . . CDSUNBOX 1
Sun / Sep '89 / Charly / Swift.

SUN YEARS, THE (LP SET).
Tracks: Born to lose / Goodnight irene / I love you because / Pumpin' piano rock / Long gone lonesome blues / Ubangi stomp / Ooby dooby / Milkshake mademoiselle / Breathless / Good rockin' tonight / Frankie and johnny / I'll see you in my dreams / Come what may / Settin' the woods on fire / It hurts me so.
LP Set . . . . . SUN BOX 102
Sun / '84 / Charly / Swift.

SURVIVORS, THE (see under Cash, Johnny).

SWEET LITTLE SIXTEEN.
Tracks: Sweet little sixteen.
■ 7". . . . . HLS 9584
London-American / Sep '62.

THAT BREATHLESS CAT.
Tracks: Ragtime doodle / Meat man / Lovin' up a storm / Ubangi stomp / Rock 'n' roll ruby / Piano doodle / House of the blue lights / My life would make a damn good country song / Beautiful dreamer / Autumn leaves / Pilot baby / Room full of roses / Keep a knockin' / Silver threads among the gold / Alabama jubilee / Lazy river / Mama, this song's for you / Breathless / Whole lotta shakin' goin' on.
CD . . . . . STCD 2
Stomper Time / Feb '93 / Magnum Music Group.

THIRTIETH ANNIVERSARY.
Tracks: Not Advised.
■ CD 830 207-2
Philips / Feb '87.

TRIO PLUS.
Tracks: Be bop a lula / On my knees / Dixie fried / Gentle as a lamb / Money / Breakup / Matchbox / Good rockin' tonight / Gone gone gone / Sittin' and thinkin'.
LP. . . . . SUN 1004
Sun / May '80 / Charly / Swift.

UP THROUGH THE YEARS 1956-63.
Tracks: End of the road / Crazy arms / It'll be me / Whole lotta shakin' goin' on / You win again / Mean woman blues / Great balls of fire / Down the line / Breathless / Don't be cruel / Put me down / Break up / I'll make it up to you / I'll sail my ship alone / Lovin' up a storm / Big blon' baby / Night train to Memphis / Little Queenie / John Henry / Livin, lovin, wreck / What'd I say / Cold cold heart / Sweet little sixteen / Carry me back to old Virginia.
CD . . . . . BCD 15408
Bear Family / Dec '87 / Rollercoaster Records / Swift / Direct Distribution.

VERY BEST OF JERRY LEE LEWIS.
Tracks: Not Advised.
LP. HO-3
Philips / Aug '87 / PolyGram.

WHEN TWO WORLDS COLLIDE.
Tracks: Rockin' Jerry Lee / Who will buy the wine / Love game / Alabama jubilee / Goodtime charlie's got the blues / When two worlds collide / Good news travels fast / I only want a buddy not a sweetheart / Honky tonk stuff / Toot toot tootsie.
LP. . . . . K 52213
Elektra / Apr '80 / WEA.

WHOLE LOTTA SHAKIN' GOIN' ON.
Tracks: Whole lotta shakin' goin' on / Golden rocket.
■ 7". . . . . CYS 1042
Charly / Sep '78.

WHOLE LOTTA SHAKIN' GOIN' ON.
Tracks: Whole lotta shakin' goin' on.
■ 7". . . . . HLS 8457
London-American / Sep '57.

WHOLE LOTTA SHAKIN' GOIN' ON (CHARLY).
Tracks: Lewis Boogie / Singing the blues / Honey hush / Whole lotta shakin' goin' on / Pink pedal pushers / Drinkin' wine spo-dee-o-dee / It'll be me / All night long / Pumping piano rock / Sixty minute man.
■ LP. . . . . CFM 515
Charly / Jun '82.

WHOLE LOTTA SHAKIN' GOIN' ON (SUN).
Tracks: You are my sunshine / Shame on you / I don't know anybody / Whole lotta shakin' goin' on / Drinkin' wine spo-dee-o-dee / When the saints go marching in / I'll be me / Deep elem blues no.2 / Singing the blues / Honey hush / Lewis boogie / You win again / Hand me down my walking cane / Old time religion / Crawdad song.
LP. . . . . SUN 1042
Sun / Jul '86 / Charly / Swift.

WILD ONE AT HIGH SCHOOL HOP THE.
Tracks: Friday night / Big blon' baby / Put me down / Let the good times roll / High school confidential / Break up / Ooby dooby / Hound dog / Jailhouse rock / Wild one.
■ LP. . . . . CFM 517
Charly / Mar '84 / Charly.

WILD ONE, THE.
Tracks: Don't be cruel / Good rockin' tonight / Pink pedal pushers / Ooby dooby / Hound dog / Jailhouse rock / Real wild child / I forgot to remember to forget / Break up / Put me down / Milkshake Mademoiselle / Carrying on (sexy ways) / Let the good times roll / High school confidential.
LP. . . . . SUN 1044
Sun / Aug '86 / Charly / Swift.

Lewis, Laurie

LOVE CHOOSES YOU.
Tracks: Old friend / Hills of home / Point of no return / I don't know why / I'd be lost without you / When the nightbird sings / Women of Ireland / Ryestraw / Light, The / Texas bluebonnets / Love chooses you.
CD . . . . . FF 70487
LP. . . . . FF 487
Flying Fish (USA) / Oct '89 / Cadillac Music / Roots Records / Projection / C.M. Distribution / Direct Distribution / Jazz Music / Duncans / A.D.A Distribution.

RESTLESS RAMBLING HEART.
Tracks: Bowling green / Cowgirl's song, The / Restless rambling heart / Cry cry darlin' / Stealin' / Chickens / Magpie's lament, The / Here we go again / Green fields / Hold to a dream / I'm gonna be the wind.
LP. . . . . FF 406
Flying Fish (USA) / May '88 / Cadillac Music / Roots Records / Projection / C.M. Distribution / Direct Distribution / Jazz Music / Duncans / A.D.A Distribution.

SINGIN' BY TROUBLES.. (Lewis, Laurie & Grant Street).
Tracks: Not Advised.
CD . . . . . FF 515CD
LP. . . . . FF 515
MC . . . . . FF 515C
Flying Fish (USA) / '92 / Cadillac Music / Roots Records / Projection / C.M. Distribution / Direct Distribution / Jazz Music / Duncans / A.D.A Distribution.

SINGING MY TROUBLES AWAY.
Tracks: Not Advised.
CD . . . . . FF 70515
Flying Fish (USA) / '90 / Cadillac Music / Roots Records / Projection / C.M. Distribution / Direct Distribution / Jazz Music / Duncans / A.D.A Distribution.

TOGETHER (Lewis, Laurie & Kathy Kallick).
Tracks: Going up the mountain / Just like the rain / Is the blue moon still shining / Don't you see the train / Hideaway / Touch of the master's hand, The / Lost John / Maverick / That dawn the day you left me / Count your blessing / Little Annie / Don't leave your little girl all alone / Gonna lay down my old guitar.
CD . . . . . KCD 44
MC . . . . . K 44
Kaleidoscope / '91 / A.D.A Distribution / Discovery.

TRUE STORIES.
Tracks: Not Advised.
CD . . . . . ROU 300CD
MC . . . . . ROU 300C
Rounder / Sep '93 / Projection / Roots Records / Swift / C.M. Distribution / Topic Records / Jazz Music / Hot Shot / A.D.A Distribution / Direct Distribution.

Liberties

DISTRACTED.
Tracks: Lonely night / Feat for a King / Strong heart / From rags to riches / So much joy / Straight down the highway / This city's in love / Clouds just burst on you, The / All my doubts / I've hurt enough / Colour of my car / Man in the moon, The.
CD . . . . . CCD 1787
LP. . . . . CHR 1787
■ MC . . . . . ZCHR 1787
Chrysalis / Aug '90.

LONELY TONIGHT.
Tracks: Lonely tonight.
12" . . . . . CHS 123555
7". . . . . CHS 3555
CD Single . . . . . CHSCD 3555
■ MC Single . . . . . CHSMC 3555
Chrysalis / Jul '90.

Light Crust Doughboys

LIVE 1936.
Tracks: Not Advised.
LP. . . . . CW 207
Jambalaya / Mar '90 / Charly.

Lightfoot, Gordon

Guitarist/singer-songwriter, born 17.11.1938 in Orilla, Ontario, Canada, whose songs have ably lent themselves to country and his native folk genre. Among those songs that have graced the country market have been the song he wrote for sixties folk trio Peter, Paul and Mary *Early Morning Rain* (a 1966 hit for George Hamilton IV) and *Ribbon Of Darkness*, a number 1 for Marty Robbins in 1965 . It's been readily covered, as is the case with many of his songs- Connie Smith also garnering a minor hit in 1979. Others from his inexhaustible songbook include *Ten Degress And Gettin' Colder* for Joan Baez, J.D Crowe's New South and more recently Nanci Griffith, his work also being a great favourite for the such acoustic acts as Tony Rice. Own pop/folk country flavoured fare has featured such lasting material as *Sundown* , his highest country placing (No.12 in 1974), whilst making it on the pop charts Lightfoot scored with *If I Could Read Your Mind* , *Carefree Highway* and his true story - ballad *The Wreck Of The Edmund Fitzgerald* . Since his 1970s spotlight years with songs *Cotton Jenny* and *Day light Katy* among his most requested songs, his work had been found on United Artists - following prolific sojourns on Reprises/Warner Brothers. Most recently, his material has been reissued on back catalogue labels BGO and Bear Family. (Maurice Hope)

ADIOS ADIOS.
Tracks: Adios adios / Is my baby blue tonight.
■ 7". . . . . PT 138
President / Jun '67.

BABY STEP BACK.
Tracks: Baby step back / Thank you for the promises.
■ 7". . . . . K 17945
WEA / May '82.

BEST OF GORDON LIGHTFOOT.
Tracks: Early morning rain / Wreck of the Edmund Fitzgerald, The / Carefree highway / Minstrel of / Rainy day people / Sundown / Summer side of life / Cold on the shoulder / Endless wire / If you could read my mind / Canadian railroad trilogy / If there's a reason / Cotton Jenny / Song for the winters night / Daylight Katy / Old Dan's records / Me and Bobby McGee / Circle is small, The.
MC K4 56915
WEA / May '81 / WEA.
■ LP. . . . . K 56915
WEA / May '81.

CIRCLE IS SMALL, THE.
Tracks: Circle is small, The / Sweet Guinevere.
■ 7". . . . . K 17132
WEA / Apr '78.

COLD ON THE SHOULDER.
Tracks: Bend in the water / Rainy day / People / Cold on the shoulder / Soul is the rock / Bells of the evening / Rainbow trout / Tree to weak to stand, A / All the lovely ladies / Fine as fine can be / Cherokee bend / Now and then / Slide on over.
LP. . . . . K 54033
Reprise (USA) / Mar '75 / WEA / Pinnacle.

DAYLIGHT KATY.
Tracks: Daylight Katy / Hangdog hotel room.
■ 7". . . . . K 17214
WEA / Aug '78.

DID SHE MENTION MY NAME/BACK HERE ON EARTH PLUS SPIN, SPIN.
Tracks: Did she mention my name / Wherefor and why / Last time I saw her, The / Black day in July / May I / Magnificent outpourings / Does your mother know / Mountains and Maryann, The / Pussywillows, Cattails / I want to hear from you / Something very special / Boss man / Long way back home / Unsettled ways / Long thin dawn / Bitter green / Circle is small, The / Marie

Christine / Cold hands from New York / Affair on 8th Avenue / Don't beat me down / Gypsy, The / If I could / Spin, spin (New Yok remake version).
CD . . . . BGOCD 167
Beat Goes On / Mar '93 / Pinnacle.

DON QUIXOTE.
Tracks: Don Quixote / Christian Island / Alberta bound / Looking at the rain / Ordinary man / Brave mountaineers / Ode to big blue / Second cup of coffee / Beautiful / On Susan's floor / Patriot's dream, The.
■ LP. K 44166
Reprise / May '72.

DON QUIXOTE/SUMMER SIDE OF LIFE (Two Originals of).
Tracks: Don Quixote / Christian island / Alberta bound / Looking at the rain / Ordinary man / Brave mountaineers / Ode to big blue / Second cup of coffee / Beautiful / On Susan's floor / Patriot's dream, The / 10 degrees and getting colder / Miguel / Go my way / Summer side of life / Cotton Jenny / Talking in your sleep / Nous vivons ensemble / Same old lover man / Redwood hill / Love and maple syrup / Cabaret.
■ Double LP . . . . K 64022
Reprise / '75 / WEA.

DREAM STREET ROSE.
Tracks: Sea of tranquility / Ghosts of Cape Horn / Dream street rose / On the high seas / Whisper my name / If you need me / Hey you / Make way for the lady / Mister rock of ages / Auctioneer, The.
LP. K 56802
■ MC K4 56802
WEA / Jun '80 / WEA.

DREAM STREET ROSE.
Tracks: Dream Street rose / Make way for the lady.
■ 7" . . . . K 17637
WEA / Jun '80.

EARLY LIGHTFOOT/SUNDAY CONCERT.
Tracks: Rich man's spiritual / Long river / Way I feel, The / For lovin' me / First time, The / Changes / Early morning rain / Steel rail blues / Sixteen miles (To Seven lakes) / I'm not sayin' / Pride of man / Ribbon of darkness / Oh, Linda / Peaceful waters / In a windowpane / Lost children, The / Leaves of grass / Medley: I'm not sayin'; Ribbon of darkness / Apology / Bitter green / Ballad of the Yarmouth Castle / Softly / Boss man / Pussy willows, Cat-tails / Canadian road trilogy.
CD . . . . BGOCD 166
Beat Goes On / Apr '93 / Pinnacle.

EARLY MORNING RAIN.
Tracks: Not Advised.
MC 4XLL 9041
Capitol (Specials) / Dec '88.

EAST OF MIDNIGHT.
Tracks: Stay loose / Morning glory / East of midnight / Lesson in love / Anything for love / Let it ride / Ecstacy made easy / You just gotta be / Passing ship, A / I'll tag along.
LP. 925482 1
■ MC 925482 4
WEA / Oct '86 / WEA.

ENDLESS WIRE.
Tracks: Daylight Katy / Sweet Guinevere / Hangdog hotel room / If there's a reason / Endless wire / Dreamland / Songs the minstrel sang / Sometimes I don't mind / If children had wings / Circle is small, The.
LP. K 56444
■ MC K4 56444
WEA / Feb '78 / WEA.

GORD'S GOLD.
Tracks: If it should please you / Endless wire / Hangdog hotel room / I'm not supposed to care / High and dry / Wreck of the Edmund Fitzgerald, The / Pony man, The / Make way for the lady / Race among the ruins / Christian island / All the lovely ladies / Alberta bound.
■ CD . . . . K 925784 2
WEA / '88 / WEA.
LP. K 925784 1
■ MC . . . . K 925784 4
WEA / '88.

GORD'S GOLD (2).
Tracks: Not Advised.
■ Double LP . . . . K 64033
Reprise / Jan '91 / WEA.

IF YOU COULD READ MY MIND.
Tracks: If you could read my mind / Sundown / Minstrel of the dawn / Me and Bobby McGee / Approaching lavender Saturday clothes / Cobweb and dust / Poor little Allison / Sit down young stranger / Baby it's alright / Your love's return / Pony man, The.
LP. K 44091
Reprise (USA) / '74 / WEA / Pinnacle.

IF YOU COULD READ MY MIND.
Tracks: If you could read my mind.
■ 7" . . . . RS 20974
Reprise / Jun '71.

IF YOU COULD READ MY MIND (OLD GOLD).
Tracks: If you could read my mind.
7" . . . . OG 9572
Old Gold / Apr '86 / Pickwick Records.

LIGHTFOOT.
Tracks: If you got it / Softly / Crossroads / Minor ballad, A / Go-go round / Rosanna / Home from the forest / I'll be alright / Song for a winter's night / Canadian railroad trilogy / Way I feel, The / Rich man's spiritual / Long river / For lovin' me / First time / Changes / Early morning rain / Steel rail blues / Sixteen miles / I'm not sayin' / Pride of man / Ribbon of darkness / Oh Linda / Peaceful waters.
CD . . . . BCD 15576
Bear Family / Apr '92 / Rollercoaster Records / Swift / Direct Distribution.

OLD DANS RECORDS.
Tracks: Farewell to Annabel / That same old obsession / Old Dan's records / Lazy mornin' / You are what I am / Can't depend on love / My pony won't go / It's worth believing / Mother of a miner's child / Hi way songs.
LP. K 44219
Reprise / WEA.

SALUTE.
Tracks: Salute / Gotta get away / Whispers of the north / Someone to believe in / Romance / Knotty pine / Biscuit city / Without you / Tattoo / Broken dreams.

SHADOWS.
Tracks: 14 karat gold / In my fashion / Shadows / Blackberry wine / Heaven help the devil / Thank you for the promises / Baby step back / All I'm after / Triangle / I'll do anything / She's not the same.
■ LP. K 56970
WEA / Feb '82 / WEA.
■ MC K4 56970
WEA / Feb '82.

SUMMER SIDE OF LIFE.
Tracks: 10 degrees and getting colder / Miguel go my way / Summer side of life / Cotton Jenny / Talking in your sleep / Nous vivons ensemble / Same old lover man / Redwood hill / Love maple syrup / Cabaret.
LP. K 44132
Reprise / WEA.

SUMMERTIME DREAM.
Tracks: Race among the ruins / Wreck of the Edmund Fitzgerald, The / I'm not supposed to care / I'd do it again / Never too close / Protocol / House you live in , The / Summertime dream / Spanish moss / Too many clues in this room.
LP. K 54067
MC K4 54067
Reprise (USA) / Jun '76 / WEA / Pinnacle.

SUNDAY CONCERT PLUS EXTRA STUDIO CUTS.
Tracks: In a windowpane / Lost children, The / Leaves of grass / I'm not sayin & ribbon of darkness / Apology / Bitter green / Ballad of Yarmouth Castle / Softly / Boss man / Pussy willows, cat-tails / Canadian railroad trilogy / Just like Tom Thumb's blues / Movin' (1) / I'll be alright / Spin, spin (Nashville version, Tk 8) / Movin' (2).
CD . . . . BCD 15691
Rollercoaster / Mar '93 / Rollercoaster Records / Swift.

SUNDOWN.
Tracks: Somewhere USA / High and dry / Seven Island suite / Circle of steel / Is there anyone home / Watchman's gone, The / Sundown / Carefree highway / List, The / Too late for pryin'.
■ LP. K 44258
WEA / Jun '74.

SUNDOWN.
Tracks: Sundown.
■ 7" . . . . K 14327
Sundown / Aug '74.

WRECK OF THE EDMUND FITZGERALD, THE.
Tracks: Wreck of the Edmund Fitzgerald, The.
■ 7" . . . . K 14451
Reprise / Jan '77.

Lilly Brothers

BLUEGRASS BREAKDOWN.
Tracks: Not Advised.
■ LP. SS 01
Rounder / Dec '88.

COUNTRY SONGS.
Tracks: Not Advised.
LP. SS 02
Rounder / Dec '88 / Projection / Roots Records / Swift / C.M. Distribution / Topic Records / Jazz Music / Hot Shot / A.D.A Distribution / Direct Distribution.

Lillywhite, Derek

BANJO REMINISCENCES.
Tracks: Not Advised.
LP. ROUNDER 0095
Rounder / '88 / Projection / Roots Records / Swift / C.M. Distribution / Topic Records / Jazz Music / Hot Shot / A.D.A Distribution / Direct Distribution.

Linde, Dennis

TRAPPED IN THE SUBURBS.
Tracks: Trapped in the suburbs / Burn away my blues.
■ 7" . . . . K 12166
Elektra / Jan '75.

UNDER THE EYE.
Tracks: Under the eye / Lookin' at Ruby.
■ 7" . . . . MNT 6365
Monument / Jun '78.

Lingo, Laurie

CONVOY G.B. (Lingo, Laurie & The Dipsticks).
Tracks: Convoy G.B.
■ 7" . . . . STAT 23
State / Apr '76.

LIVE AT THE BLUE BOAR (Lingo, Laurie & The Dipsticks).
Tracks: Live at the Blue Boar / Good King Wenceslas.
■ 7" . . . . STAT 35
State / Dec '76.

Lipari, Bo

THAT OLD SONG AND DANCE (Lipari, Bo & Jim Winner).
Tracks: Not Advised.
■ LP. BF 15025
Bear Family / '85.

Lipscomb, Mance

MANCE LIPSCOMB.
Tracks: Not Advised.
MC . . . . C 205
Arhoolie (USA) / '88 / Pinnacle / Cadillac Music / Swift / Projection / Hot Shot / A.D.A Distribution / Jazz Music.

MANCE LIPSCOMB VOL 4.
Tracks: Not Advised.
LP. ARHOOLIE 1033
Arhoolie (USA) / May '81 / Pinnacle / Cadillac Music / Swift / Projection / Hot Shot / A.D.A Distribution / Jazz Music.

MANCE LIPSCOMB VOL. 2.
Tracks: Not Advised.
LP. C 5521
Collectors Issue / '88.

MANCE LIPSCOMB, VOL. 3.
Tracks: Not Advised.
LP. F 1026
Arhoolie (USA) / '88 / Pinnacle / Cadillac Music / Swift / Projection / Hot Shot / A.D.A Distribution / Jazz Music.

MANCE LIPSCOMB, VOL. 5.
Tracks: Not Advised.
LP. F 1049
Arhoolie (USA) / '88 / Pinnacle / Cadillac Music / Swift / Projection / Hot Shot / A.D.A Distribution / Jazz Music.

MANCE LIPSCOMB, VOL. 6.
Tracks: Not Advised.
LP. F 1069
Arhoolie (USA) / '88 / Pinnacle / Cadillac Music / Swift / Projection / Hot Shot / A.D.A Distribution / Jazz Music.

TEXAS BLUES.
Tracks: Not Advised.
LP. ARHOOLIE 1049
Arhoolie (USA) / May '81 / Pinnacle / Cadillac Music / Swift / Projection / Hot Shot / A.D.A Distribution / Jazz Music.

TEXAS SONGSTER.
Tracks: Not Advised.
LP. ARHOOLIE 1001
Arhoolie (USA) / May '81 / Pinnacle / Cadillac Music / Swift / Projection / Hot Shot / A.D.A Distribution / Jazz Music.
CD . . . . ARH 305
Arhoolie (USA) / '92 / Pinnacle / Cadillac Music / Swift / Projection / Hot Shot / A.D.A Distribution / Jazz Music.
CD . . . . ARHCD 306
Arhoolie (USA) / Mar '93 / Pinnacle / Cadillac Music / Swift / Projection / Hot Shot / A.D.A Distribution / Jazz Music.

TEXAS SONGSTER VOL 2.
Tracks: Not Advised.
LP. ARHOOLIE 1023
Arhoolie (USA) / May '81 / Pinnacle / Cadillac Music / Swift / Projection / Hot Shot / A.D.A Distribution / Jazz Music.

TEXAS SONGSTER VOL 3.
Tracks: Not Advised.
LP. ARHOOLIE 1026
Arhoolie (USA) / May '81 / Pinnacle / Cadillac Music / Swift / Projection / Hot Shot / A.D.A Distribution / Jazz Music.

TEXAS SONGSTER VOL 6.
Tracks: Not Advised.
LP. ARHOOLIE 1069
Arhoolie (USA) / May '81 / Pinnacle / Cadillac Music / Swift / Projection / Hot Shot / A.D.A Distribution / Jazz Music.

■ DELETED L 13

YOU GOT TO REAP WHAT YOU SOW.
Tracks: Not Advised.
CD . . . . **ARHCD 398**
Arhoolie (USA) / Sep '93 / Pinnacle / Cadillac Music / Swift / Projection / Hot Shot / A.D.A Distribution / Jazz Music.

YOU'LL NEVER FIND ANOTHER.
Tracks: Not Advised.
LP . . . . **ARHOOLIE 1077**
Arhoolie (USA) / May '81 / Pinnacle / Cadillac Music / Swift / Projection / Hot Shot / A.D.A Distribution / Jazz Music.

Little Ginny

A stalwart of the British country scene, Kingston-upon-Thames born Ginnette Brown (first known as Little Ginny when she played the country music clubs as a youngster), began her career at the age of 15 as a front vocalist with the famous Ivy Benson All Girl Band. Twice voted "U.K. Country Female Vocalist, she's worked with such famed entertainers as Marty Robbins, Charley Pride, Roy Castle, Frank Ifield and Olivia Newton-John as well as being seen on a number of TV specials both in Britain and Europe. In recent years Ginny - who has also taken her brand of country music to the Nashville recording studios and the Grand Ole Opry - has further broadened her talents to the theatrical stage by touring with Joe Brown and Tammy Cline in *Pump boys and Dinettes* , Hazel O'Connor in *Sing out sister* and Charlie Drake in the pantomime *Jack and the beanstalk* . In the 1980's she teamed with Tammy Cline to create Two Hearts. (Tony Byworth)

CHASING THE WIND.
Tracks: Chasing the wind.
7" . . . . **PF 3004**
Pastafont / Jul '82 / Pastafont Music.

COMING ON NICELY.
Tracks: Not Advised.
LP . . . . **SRT 2L003**
SRT / Mar '79 / Pinnacle / Projection.

MY DIXIE DARLING.
Tracks: My dixie darling / No time at all / Kiss and say goodbye / Dixie chicken / Whisky get me gone / I'm an old cowhand / Miss the Mississippi / Elvira / Too good to throw away / Crystal chandeliers / Girls in love.
LP . . . . **PFL 3003**
Pastafont / Jun '82 / Pastafont Music.

MY DIXIE DARLING.
Tracks: My Dixie darling / Whisky get me gone.
■ **7"** . . . . **PF 3002**
Pastafont / Nov '81.

Locklin, Hank

Born Lawrence Hankins Locklin in Florida in 1918, this singer, guitarist and songwriter inherited a love of music from his parents. By the time he reached his teens he was playing and singing at school parties and local contests. Although he toured regularly from the age of 20 he didn't begin his recording career until the 50's. His 1953 single, *Let Me Be The One*, was a promising success on 4-Star Records but two years later he made a wise move by signing to RCA Victor and teaming up with the company's seminal Nashville producer/executive/guitarist Chet Atkins. Locklin proceeded to carve out a long career in country-and-western music, highlighted by two notable crossover successes: *Please Help Me, I'm Falling* reached No 8 in the States and No 9 in Britain in 1960 and his own song, *Send Me The Pillow You Dream On* was a big country hit for himself and a US Top Forty pop success for Johnny Tillotson (1962) and Dean Martin (1965). In Britain Locklin achieved a No 18 hit at the end of '62 with *We're Gonna Go Fishin'* and a No 28 in the summer of '66 with *I Feel A Cry Coming On*. (Bob MacDonald).

20 OF THE BEST: HANK LOCKLIN.
Tracks: Please help me, I'm falling / Send me the pillow that you dream on / It's a little more like Heaven / Geisha girl / One step ahead of my past / From here to there to you / You're the reason / Happy birthday to me / Happy journey / We're gonna go fishing / Flyin' south / Wooden soldier / Followed closely by my teardrops / Forty-nine, fifty-one / Girls get prettier (every day) / Country hall of fame / Love song for you / Where the blue of the night / Galway Bay / Forty shades of green.
■ **LP** . . . . **INTS 5209**
RCA International / Nov '82.
LP . . . . **NL 89331**
■ **MC** . . . . **NK 89331**
RCA / '84.

ALL KINDS OF EVERYTHING.
Tracks: Not Advised.
LP . . . . **TSLP 112**
MC . . . . **TSC 112**
Topspin (Ireland) / Jul '79 / I & B Records.

BEST OF HANK LOCKLIN', THE.
Tracks: Please help me, I'm falling / I was coming home to you / Danny boy / Happy journey / Fraulein / Flying South / Send me the pillow you dream on / Geisha girl / From here to there to you / It's a little more like heaven / Old bog road, The / Let me be the one.
■ **LP** . . . . **LSA 3099**
RCA / '79.

COUNTRY HALL OF FAME.
Tracks: High noon / Four walls / Country hall of fame, The / I'll hold you in my heart / Walking the floor over you / Lovesick blues / Night train the Memphis / Signed sealed and delivered / No one will ever know / Blue yodel 'T' for Texas / When I stop dreaming / (There'll be) peace in the valley.
MC . . . . **TSC 102**
Topspin (Ireland) / '88 / I & B Records.
■ **LP** . . . . **RD 7967**
RCA / Oct '88 / BMG.

COUNTRY HALL OF FAME, THE.
Tracks: Country hall of fame, The / Evergreen.
■ **7"** . . . . **RCA 1641**
RCA / Jul '70 / BMG.

ENCORES.
Tracks: Come share the sunshine with me / Could you / I could call you darling / No-one is sweeter than you / Paper face / Pin ball millionaire / Song of the whispering leaves / Stumpy Joe / Tell me you love me / To whom it may concern / Who do you think you're foolin' / Year of time, A.
■ **MC** . . . . **ZCEB 122**
Ember / Dec '78 / TKO Records Ltd / President Records.

EVERLASTING LOVE.
Tracks: Everlasting love / I'm slowly going out of your mind.
■ **7"** . . . . **RCA 1729**
RCA / Jan '70 / BMG.

FAMOUS COUNTRY MUSIC MAKERS.
Tracks: Please help me, I'm falling / Blue side of lonesome / Why don't you haul off and love me / Just call me darling / Night train to Memphis / Jonas P. Jones / There'll be peace in the valley (for me) / Foreign love / Country hall of fame / Geisha girl / I forgot to live today / Bless her heart .. I love her / We're gonna go fishing / Where the blue of the night / It's a little more like heaven / I like a woman / Forty shades of green / Foreign car / Sweet memories / My heart needs a friend / Flying South / Softly / Who can I count on / Jambalaya / I love you because / Bonaparte's retreat / Goodbye dear old Ryman / Only a fool / Silver dew on the blue grass tonight / I'm blue / She's as close as I can get to loving you / Behind by back.
Double LP . . . . **DPS 2060**
RCA / Sep '75 / BMG.

FOREIGN LOVE.
Tracks: Not Advised.
LP . . . . **HAT 3082**
Stetson / '88 / Crusader Marketing Co. / Swift / Wellard Dist. / Midland Records / C.M. Distribution.
MC . . . . **HATC 3082**
Stetson / Feb '89 / Crusader Marketing Co. / Swift / Wellard Dist. / Midland Records / C.M. Distribution.

FROM HERE TO THERE TO YOU.
Tracks: Please help me, I'm falling / Geisha girl / Happy birthday to me / Happy journey / Send me the pillow that you dream on / It's a little more like Heaven / Flyin' South / From here to there to you / I was coming home to you / We're gonna go fishing.
LP . . . . **BDL 1033**
MC . . . . **BDC 1033**
Bulldog Records / Jul '85 / President Records / Jazz Music / Wellard Dist. / TKO Records Ltd.

FROM HERE TO THERE TO YOU.
Tracks: From here to there to you.
■ **7"** . . . . **RCA 1273**
RCA / Feb '62.

GOLDEN HITS OF HANK LOCKLIN, THE.
Tracks: Please help me I'm falling / Geisha girl / Happy birthday to me / Happy journey / Send me the pillow you dream on / These arms you push away / Let me be the one / It's a little more like heaven / Flying south / From here to there to you / I was coming home to you / We're gonna go fishin'.
LP . . . . **CW 147**
■ **MC** . . . . **ZCEB 147**
Ember / Dec '78 / TKO Records Ltd / President Records.

HANK LOCKLIN.
Tracks: Not Advised.
MC Set . . . . **DTO 10216**
Ditto / '88 / Pickwick Records.

HANK LOCKLIN SINGS HANK WILLIAMS.
Tracks: Cold, cold heart / Why don't you love me / May you never be alone / Hey good lookin' / Your cheatin' heart / Mansion on the hill / There'll be no teardrops tonight / I can't help it / You win again / Long gone lone some blues / I'm so lonesome I could cry.
LP . . . . **RD 7692**
RCA / Mar '70 / BMG.

HASTA LEUGO.
Tracks: Hasta luego / Whishing on a star.
■ **7"** . . . . **RCA 1610**
RCA / Jan '70 / BMG.

I FEEL A CRY COMING ON.
Tracks: I feel a cry coming on.
■ **7"** . . . . **RCA 1510**
RCA / May '66.

IRISH SONGS - COUNTRY STYLE.
Tracks: Old bag road, The / Too-r-loo-ra-ral / Danny Dear / If only we had old Ireland over here / I'll take you home again / Kathleen / My wild Irish rose / Danny boy / When Irish eyes are smiling / Little bit of heaven, A / Galway bay.
■ **LP** . . . . **RD 7623**
RCA / Jun '70 / BMG.

IRISH SONGS COUNTRY STYLE.
Tracks: Old bog road / Too-ra-loo-ra-loo-ra / Danny dear / If we only had old Ireland over here / I'll take you home again, Kathleen / My wild Irish rose / Danny boy / When Irish eyes are smiling / Little bit of Heaven, A / Galway Bay / Kevin Barry / Forty shades of green.
■ **LP** . . . . **LSA 3079**
RCA / '79.
■ **LP** . . . . **NL 89470**
RCA / Nov '84.
■ **MC** . . . . **NK 89470**
RCA / Nov '84.
■ **CD** . . . . **ND 89470**
RCA / May '90.

LAST THING ON MY MIND, THE.
Tracks: Last thing on my mind, The / Best part of loving you, The.
■ **7"** . . . . **RCA 1548**
RCA / Nov '70 / BMG.

LOVE SONG FOR YOU.
Tracks: Love song for you / Little geisha girl.
■ **7"** . . . . **RCA 1678**
RCA / Oct '70 / BMG.

MAGIC OF HANK LOCKLIN, THE.
Tracks: Please help me I'm falling / Geisha girl / Happy birthday to me / Happy journey / Send me the pillow that you dream on / Let me be the one / It's a little more like heaven / Flying South / From here to there to you / I was coming home to you / We're gonna go fishin' / Queen of hearts / Mysteries of life / I'm lonely darling / Come share the sunshine with me / Year of time, A / To whom it may concern / Tell me you love me / Who you think you're foolin' / I could call you darling.
CD . . . . **TKOCD 025**
MC . . . . **TKOCS 025**
TKO Records / May '92 / TKO Records Ltd / President Records.

MR.COUNTRY.
Tracks: Same sweet girl / Tho' I lost / Mysteries of life, The / Empty bottle, empty heart / Stumpy Joe / No one is sweeter than you / I always lose / Rio Grande waltz / I could call you darling / Year of time, A / It's hard to say I love you / Who will it be? / Place and the time, The / Queen of Hearts.
LP . . . . **SPR 8505**
MC . . . . **SPC 8505**
Spot / Feb '83.

MY LOVE SONG FOR YOU.
Tracks: Tender side of me, The / Before the next teardrop falls / Danny boy / Toujours moi / Longing to hold you again / Loving arms / I'm slowly going out of your mind / Minute you're gone, The / You've still got a place in my heart / Love song for you / I came so close to living alone / Lovin' you.
■ **LP** . . . . **RD 7996**
RCA / Nov '70 / BMG.

ONCE OVER LIGHTLY.
Tracks: Send me the pillow you dream on / Same sweet girl, The / Fraulein / Flying South / I walk the line / I don't hurt anymore / Tennessee border / Wild side of life, The / Loose talk / Before I'm over you / Geisha girl / Fool No. 1 / Please help me, I'm falling / Backstreet affair / Shame on you / My shoes keep walking back to you / I'll be there / Together again / Act naturally / From here to there to you / Let me be the one / Faith and truth / This song is just for you / No one is sweeter than you.
■ **LP** . . . . **RD 7774**
RCA / Jan '70 / BMG.
■ **LP** . . . . **LSA 3041**
RCA / '79.

PLEASE HELP ME I'M FALLING.
Tracks: Please help me, I'm falling / Geisha girl / Send me the pillow that you dream on / Its a little more like heaven / Let me be the one / Happy Birthday to me / Happy journey / Down on my knees / Night life queen / Day time love affair / There never was a time / Baby I need you.
■ **LP** . . . . **RD 27201**
RCA / Oct '70 / BMG.
MC **40068**
Astan (USA) / Nov '84.
LP **20068**
Astan (USA) / Dec '85.

PLEASE HELP ME I'M FALLING.
Tracks: Please help me, I'm falling.
■ **7"** . . . . **RCA 1188**
RCA / Aug '60.

PLEASE HELP ME I'M FALLING (2).
Tracks: Not Advised.
LP . . . . **TOP 132**
Topline / '86 / Charly / Swift / Black Sun Records.

L 14 ■ DELETED

PLEASE HELP ME I'M FALLING (OLD GOLD).
Tracks: Please help me I'm falling / Sea of heartbreak.
7"..........................OG 9621
Old Gold / Oct '86 / Pickwick Records.

PLESE HELP ME, I'M FALLING.
Tracks: Not Advised.

SEND ME THE PILLOW YOU DREAM ON.
Tracks: Maiden's prayer / Bonaparte's retreat / I'll go on alone / Forgive me / Are you teasing me / Silver dew on the blue grass tonight / Send me the pillow you dream on / Blue side of lonesome / Almost persuaded / Singing the blues / Who can I count on / Last thing on my mind, The.
■ LP..........................RD 7905
RCA / Nov '70 / BMG.

UPPER ROOM, THE.
Tracks: Upper room, The / It is love.
7"..........................RCA 1575
RCA / Nov '70 / BMG.

WE'RE GONNA GO FISHIN'.
Tracks: We're gonna go fishing / Please help me, I'm falling.
■ 7"..........................RCA 1305
RCA / Nov '62.
7"..........................GOLD 537
RCA Golden Grooves / Oct '81 / BMG.

YOU'RE THE REASON.
Tracks: You're the reason / Happy birthday to me.
■ 7"..........................RCA 1252
RCA / Nov '70 / BMG.

Locorriere. Dennis

VOICE OF DR. HOOK, THE (Live on Stage in Oxford).
Tracks: Not Advised.
VHS..........................SHPCMV 01
Silver Heart Television / Jun '92 / ACD Trading Ltd.

Lomax, Alan

MURDERERS HOME AND BLUES IN THE MISSISSIPPI NIGHT.
Tracks: Road song / No more my Lord / Katy left Memphis / Old Alabama / Black woman / Jumpin' lady / Whoa back / Prettiest train / Old dollar mamie / It makes a long time man feel bad / Rosie / Leave camp roller / Early in the morning / Tangle eyes blues / Stackerlee / Prison blues / Sometimes I wonder / Bye bye baby / Blues in the Mississippi night.
LP..........................VJD 515
Vogue Jazz (France) / Jun '83.

ROVING GAMBLER, THE.
Tracks: Bound to follow the long horn cows / Lord Lovel / Rich old lady / Long summer days / Ain't no more can on the brazia / All the pretty little horses / Billy Barlow / Wild rippling water / Rattlesnake / Sam Bass / Dying cowboy / Goo-a-mighty drag / Go away Edie / Black Betty / My little John Henry.
MC..........................60-904
Folktracks Cassettes / '81 / C.M. Distribution / Roots Records.

TEXAS FOLK SONGS.
Tracks: Rambling gambler / I'm bound to follow the longhorn cows / Lord Lovel / Rich old lady, The / Long summer days / Ain't no more cane / All the pretty little horses / Billy Barlow / Wild rippling water, The / Rattlesnake / Sam Bass / Dying cowboy, The / God almighty drag / Eradie / Black Betty / My little John Henry.
LP..........................ARN 33690
MC..........................ARN 433690
Arion / May '88 / Discovery.

Lonesome Pine Fiddlers

14 MOUNTAIN SONGS.
Tracks: Not Advised.
LP..........................SLP 155
MC..........................GT 5155
Starday (USA) / Apr '87 / Crusader Marketing Co.

WINDY MOUNTAIN.
Tracks: Pain in my heart / Lonesome sad and blue / Don't forget me / Will I meet Mother in Heaven / You broke your promise / I'm left alone / Nobody cares (not even you) / Twenty one years / My brown eyed darling / You left me to cry / That's why you left me so blue / I'll never make you blue / Honky tonk blues / You're so good / I'll never change my mind / Dirty dishes blues / Lonesome pine breakdown / Five string rag / Baby you're cheatin' / I'm feeling for you (but I can't reach you) / Some kinda sorry / Windy mountain / No curb service / New set of blues, A / There's just one you.
CD..........................ECD 501
Rollercoaster / Apr '92 / Rollercoaster Records / Swift.

Lonesome Strangers

LONESOME PINE.
Tracks: Not Advised.
LP..........................SPD 1012

LONESOME STRANGERS, THE.
Tracks: Just can't cry no more / Don't back down / Daddy's gone gray / Just walk away / We used to fuss / Clementine / Lay down my old guitar / Goodbye lonesome / Oh my train / Don't you run away from me.
LP..........................SPD 1023
MC..........................SPDC 1023
Special Delivery / Apr '89 / Revolver-APT / A.D.A Distribution / Topic Records / Direct Distribution / Jazz Music / C.M. Distribution.
■ CD..........................SPDCD 1023
Special Delivery / Aug '89.

Lord. Bobby

EVERYBODY IS ROCKIN'.
Tracks: Not Advised.
LP..........................REV 3006
Revival / Aug '88 / EMI.

Lore & The Legends

Born in Ramona, California, Lore Cayote Orion created his brand of country out of his Texas-Spanish heritage, Mariachi music and the songs of Hank Williams, coming up with a sound that he once described as "authentic 1980's rock'n'roll". A multi-talented individual, he's achieved success in such diverse fields as graphic art, cartoons (including work for Rolling Stone), songwriting (That's what made me love you was a top 10 duet for Bill Anderson and Mary Lou Turner), writing children's books and, of course, performing. He was a founding member of short-lived MCA group Bandera in the early 1980's and, later in the decade, started building up a following in the U.K. via concert appearances. In the 1990's he's concentrated upon songwriting and developing a much in-demand business designing western wear items. (Tony Byworth)

ONE STEP AHEAD OF THE LAW.
Tracks: Plains of Madalene / Just across the river / El Bandito / Yankees in Houston / Taffeta memories / Saying goodbye to the West / One step ahead of the law / Silver spurs / Cowboy arms hotel / Pearly gates / Sometimes it's hard to be a cowboy / Hairtrigger colts 44.
LP..........................COLT 2002
Nightflite / Aug '87.

Los Angeles Zydeco Band

T-LOU.
Tracks: Not Advised.
LP..........................1014
Maison de Soul(USA) / Swift.
MC..........................1014 TC
Maison de Soul(USA) / '87 / Swift.

Lost & Found

ENDLESS HIGHWAY.
Tracks: Not Advised.
LP..........................REBEL 1607
Rebel (1) / '78 / Projection / Backs Distribution.

HYMN TIME.
Tracks: Mount up with wings / When was the last time / I'm going to make heaven my home / Boat of love / Sing an old fashioned song / When the saints go marching in / Raging storm / Shall we gather at the river / You're drifting away / Peace in the valley / What a friend we have in Jesus / Give me flowers while I'm living.
LP..........................REBEL 1668
Rebel (1) / '90 / Projection / Backs Distribution.

LOST AND FOUND.
Tracks: Forever lasting plastic words / Everybody's here / There would be no doubt / Don't fall down / Zig zag blues / Let me be / Realize / Stroke blues / I'm so hip to pain / Living eyes.
LP..........................LIK 23
Decal / Mar '88 / Charly / Swift.

NEW DAY.
Tracks: Not Advised.
LP..........................REBEL 1678
Rebel (1) / '78 / Projection / Backs Distribution.

SUN'S GONNA SHINE.
Tracks: Not Advised.
LP..........................REBEL 1638
Rebel (1) / '78 / Projection / Backs Distribution.

Loudermilk, John D.

Gifted singer - songwriter (born 31.3.1934 in Durham, North Carolina) provider of hits for many artists - country/pop profiting from his work during the late 50s and into the sixties. Able to lace his tunes with genuine wit, teenage love trials/tribulations and Erskine Caldwell-type vignettes, readily grasping aspects of rural, southern life. Loudermilk, a former sign painter and TV presenter, was an RCA recording artist (country hits including Bad News, Blue Train and That Ain't All) during the sixties, and crafted up an almost endless supply of hit songs, initiated with his ground breaking 1956 4 million seller A Rose For Baby Ruth (a pop hit for George Hamilton IV - the writer himself on National Guard duty at the time). Among the remaining list (reading like a Who's Who), Sittin' In The Balcony , Tabacco Road , Waterloo , Abilene , Take Back Trembling Lips , Ebony Eyes , Sad Moves, Norman and It's My Time songs that have defied categories, with people like Eddie Cochran, Dolly Parton, The Nashville Teens, Barbara Mandrell, Sue Thompson, Jefferson Airplane, The Everly Bros, The Box Tops and Boston Pops recording them. His songwriting feats are only matched by those of Felice and Boudleaux Bryant such is his diverse repertoire. Additionally, this popular folk oriented act has served on various Nashville's Songwriting Association boards and The CMA. (Maurice Hope)

BLUE TRAIN - 1961/1962.
Tracks: Blue train / Mister Jones / Language of love / Jimmie's song / Angela Jones / Bully of the beach, The / Rhythm and blues / What would you take for me? / Great snowman, The / Everybody knows / Google eye / Darling Jane / Song of the lonely teen / All of this for Sally / Road hog / He's just a scientist (that's all) / Rocks of Reno, The / Big daddy / Callin' Dr Casey / You just reap what you sow / Little wind-up doll, The / Two strangers in love / Th'wife / Bad news / Run on home baby brother / Oh how sad.
CD..........................BCD 15421
Bear Family / Jun '89 / Rollercoaster Records / Swift / Direct Distribution.

IT'S MY TIME.
Tracks: It's my time / No playing in the snow today / Little grave, The / I'm looking for a world / What is it? / Bubble, please break / Ma Baker's little acre / Mary's no longer mine / To hell with love / Talkin' silver cloud blues / Joey stays with me / I can't hold of the Cherokee reservation / Jones', The / You're the guilty one / Where have they gone / Little bird / Brown girl, The / Givin' you all my love / I chose you / Honey / That ain't all / Interstate forty / Do you / Tobacco Road.
CD..........................BCD 15422
Bear Family / Jun '89 / Rollercoaster Records / Swift / Direct Distribution.

LANGUAGE OF LOVE.
Tracks: Language of love.
■ 7"..........................RCA 1269
RCA / Jan '62.

SIDEWALKS.
Tracks: Sidewalks / Odd folks of Okracoke, The.
■ 7"..........................RCA 1761
RCA / Nov '70 / BMG.

TWELVE SIDES OF LOUDERMILK.
Tracks: All of this for Sally / Angela Jones / Big daddy / Bully of the beach, The / He's just a scientist (that's all) / Rhythm and bluesy / Tobacco Road / Everybody knows / Goggle eye / This little bird / Road hog / Oh how sad.
LP..........................NL 89993
■ MC..........................NK 89333
RCA / Jan '87.

Louisiana Honeydrippers

BAYOU BLUEGRASS.
Tracks: Not Advised.
LP..........................ARHOOLIE 5010
Arhoolie (USA) / May '81 / Pinnacle / Cadillac Music / Swift / Projection / Hot Shot / A.D.A Distribution / Jazz Music.

Louisiana Playboys

CAJUN TOOT TOOT MUSIC.
Tracks: Lucille / Lacassine special / I don't care / Canton two step / Zydeco et pas sale / Steel guitar rag / Sugar bee / Musicians waltz / Think about me baby / Wagonwheel special / Hathaway one step.
LP..........................JSP 1098
JSP / Oct '85 / Hot Shot / Swift / Wellard Dist. / A.D.A Distribution / Cadillac Music / Jazz Music.

SATURDAY NIGHT SPECIAL.
Tracks: Lafayette / Why don't we do it in the road / Cajun blues / Saturday night special / Maggie Thatcher, won't you give me a hand / Louisiana playboy's theme / Memphis / Jole blon / Mathilda / Te petite and te meon / Accordion waltz.
LP..........................JSP 1080
JSP / '88 / Hot Shot / Swift / Wellard Dist. / A.D.A Distribution / Cadillac Music / Jazz Music.
CD..........................JSPCD 225
JSP / Apr '89 / Hot Shot / Swift / Wellard Dist. / A.D.A Distribution / Cadillac Music / Jazz Music.

Louvin Brothers

A quintessential country music duo, Lonnie Ira (1924-65) and Charlie Elzer (b. 1927) Louvin - both from Rainesville, Alabama - scored only a dozen chart entries but secured their reputation on fine musicianship and songwriting (virtually everything they recorded) alongside impeccable harmonies. Their biggest successes were *When I stop dreaming* , *I don't believe you've met my baby* , *Hopin' that you're hoping* , *You're running wild*, *Cash on the barrelhead* and *My baby's gone* , and it's the rediscovery of these recordings by the likes of Gram Parsons and Emmylou Harris that has led to the Louvins gaining a fresh, much deserved reappraisal. Such attention has also meant the re-issuing of the Louvin Brothers' recordings, which range from the modest *Capitol Country Music Classics* collection, presenting a worthy 28 tracks on one cd, to the duo's complete 220 song catalogue (around 10 hours running time) issued by Bear Family in a mammoth 8 cd box-set that comes complete with a well detailed 52 page, LP sized booklet written by historian Charles Wolfe. The latter traces the Louvin's story from their rural Alabama background, and working with the local group Foggy Mountain Boys (before Flatt & Scruggs used the name), their association with Fred Rose and the Acuff-Rose music publishing company, the Grand Ole Opry and their songs that began with the initial (one) recording for Apollo, through two sides for Decca and a dozen for MGM before finally establishing themselves on Capitol - an association that commenced on September 30, 1952 and continued up until September 12, 1963, the final session after which Charlie and Ira split up. The parting of the ways, which was threatened on several earlier occasions, finally came about due to the brothers' irreconcilable differences and contrasting personalities. Less than two years later Ira died in a car crash. Charlie Louvin enjoyed a successful solo career, amd membership of the Grand Ole Opry, which has continued into the 1990's. (Tony Byworth)

BEST OF THE EARLY LOUVIN BROTHERS.
Tracks: Not Advised.
LP . . . . **REBEL 852**
MC . . . . **REBEL 852C**
Rebel (1) / '85 / Projection / Backs Distribution.

CAPITOL COUNTRY MUSIC CLASSICS.
Tracks: Broadminded / Family who prays (Shall never part), The / When I stop dreaming / Alabama / I don't believe you've met my baby / Hoping that you're hoping / Kentucky / Katie dear / Knoxville girl / Don't laugh / You're running wild / Cash on the barrel head / Plenty of everything but you / Little light of mine, The / Tennessee waltz / Are you teasing me / My baby's gone / If I could only win your love / Satan is real / Christian life, The / Blues stay away from me / I love you best of all / How's the world treating you / Great atomic power, The / Must you throw dirt in my face / Stuck up blues / Thank God for my Christian home / What would you give me in exchange for my soul.
CD . . . . **CDEMS 1492**
Capitol / Apr '93 / EMI.

CLOSE HARMONY.
Tracks: Alabama Alabama / Seven year blues / My love song for you / "Get acquainted" waltz, The / Weapon of prayer, The / They've got the church outnumbered / Do you live what you preach / You'll be rewarded over there / I'll live with God (to die no more) / Rove of white / Great atomic power, The / Insured beyond the grave / Gospel way, The / Sons & daughters of God, The / Broadminded / Family who prays, The / I know what you're talking about / Let us travel, travel on / I love God's way of living / Born again / Preach the gospel / From mother's arms to Korea / If we forget God / Satan & the Saint / Satan lied to me / God bless her ('cause she's my mother) / Last chance to pray / No one to sing for me / Swing low sweet chariot / Nearer my God to thee / Make him a soldier / I can't say no / Just rehearsing / Love thy neighbour as thyself / Where will you build / Pray for me / When I stop dreaming / Pitfall / Alabama / Memories & tears / Don't laugh / I don't laugh you've met my baby / Childish love / In the middle of nowhere / Hoping that you're hoping / First one to love you, The / I cried after you left / That's all he's asking of me / I'll be all smiles tonight / In the pines / What is home without love / Mary of the wild moor / Knoxville girl / Kentucky / Katie dear / My brother's will / Take the news to mother / Let her go, God bless her / Tiny broken heart, A / Plenty of everything but you / Cash on the barrelhead / You're running wild / New partner waltz / I won't have to cross Jordan alone / Praying / Wait a little longer please Jesus / This little light of mine / Steal away & pray / There's no excuse / Are you washed in the blood / Lord, I'm coming home / Thankful / Take me back into your heart / Here today & gone tomorrow / We could / Tennessee waltz / Too late / Are you teasing me / Nobody's darling but mine / Don't let your sweet love die / I wonder where you are tonight / Why not confess / Making believe / Have I stayed away too long / Call me / I wish you knew / Dog sled / When I loved you / My baby's gone / She didn't even know I was gone / My baby came back / Are you wasting my time / My curly headed baby / Lorene / I wish it had been a dream / While you're cheatin' on me / If I could only win your love / You're learning / Blue from now on / Today / My heart was trampled on the street / Send me the pillow you dream on / On my way to the show / Red hen hop / She'll get lonesome / I wonder if you know / Blue / Angels rejoiced last night, The / Dying from home & lost / Satan's jewelled crown / River of Jordan, The / I'm ready to go home / Kneeling drunkards plea, The / Satan is real / Christian life, The / Are you afraid to die / He can be found / There's is a higher power / Drunkard's doom, The / I see a bridge / Just suppose / Stagger, The / Nellie moved to town / What a change one day / Ruby's song / Last old shovel, The / Midnight special / Brown's ferry blues / Southern moon / Sand mountain blues / Nashville blues / Blues stay away from me / When it's time for the whippoorwill to sing / Put me on the train to Carolina / Freight train blues / Lonesome blues / Gonna lay down my old guitar / It's Christmas time / Santa's big parade / Love is a lonely street / If you love me stay away / I ain't gonna work tomorrow / I love you best of all / I can't keep you in love with me / Scared of the blues / I have found the way / He set me free / Kneel at the cross / Leaning on the everlasting arms / O why not tonight / You can't find the Lord too soon / Keep your eyes on Jesus / Almost persuaded / I feel better now / O who shall be able to stand / If today was the day / You'll meet him in the clowds / You'll meet him in the clouds (alt. take) / Away in the manger / Friendly beasts, The / Hark the herald angels sing / Good christian men rejoice / While shepherds watched their flocks / First noel, The / It came upon a midnight clear / O come all ye faithfull / O little town of Bethlehem / Silent night / Deck the halls / Joy to the world / It hurts me more the second time around / How's the world treating you / Every time you leave / Time goes slow / I died for the red, white & blue / Searching for a soldiers grave / At mail call today / Soldier's last letter, A / There's a star spangled banner waving somewhere / There's a grave in the wave of the ocean / Mother I thankyou for the bible you gave me / Seaman's girl, A / Robe of white / Weapon of prayer / Broken engagement / First time in life / There's no easy way / Love turned to hate / Must you throw dirt in my face / Great speckled bird, The / Wabash cannonball / Lonely mound of clay / Wreck on the highway / Wait for the light to shine / Low & lonely / We live in two different worlds / Precious jewel, The / Great judgement morning, The / Branded wherever I go / Not a word from home / Stuck up blues / Don't let them take the bible out of our school / I'm glad that I'm not him / Message to your heart, A / Thank God for my christian home / I'll never die / Price on the bottle / I've known a lady / He included me / Keep watching the sky / Now Lord, what can I do for you / Way up on a mountain / Gonna shake hands with mother over there / He was waiting at the altar / Oh Lord, my God / What would you take in exchange for my soul.
CD Set . . . . **BCD 15561**
Bear Family / Jun '92 / Rollercoaster Records / Swift / Direct Distribution.

IRA & CHARLIE.
Tracks: Don't let your sweet love die / We could / Tennessee waltz / Are you teasing me? / Too late / Here today and gone tomorrow / I wonder where you are tonight / Have I stayed away too long / Nobody's darlin' but mine / Why not confess / Making believe / Take me back into your heart.
LP . . . . **HAT 3057**
MC . . . . **HATC 3057**
Stetson / Jan '88 / Crusader Marketing Co. / Swift / Wellard Dist. / Midland Records / C.M. Distribution.

LIVE AT THE NEW RIVER RANCH.
Tracks: Born again / When I stop dreaming / Comedy / In the jailhouse / Family who prays shall never part, The / Is that you Myrtle / God bless her / I don't believe you've met my baby / Childish love / Just rehearsaing / Where one stands alone / Guitar inst. / There's a hole in the bottom of the sea / Listen to the mockingbird.
LP . . . . **CCLP 0105**
Copper Creek / '89.

LOUVIN BROTHERS, THE (1).
Tracks: Not Advised.
MC . . . . **SSC 07**
Rounder / '88 / Projection / Roots Records / Swift / C.M. Distribution / Topic Records / Jazz Music / Hot Shot / A.D.A Distribution / Direct Distribution.
LP . . . . **SS 07**
Rounder / Dec '88 / Projection / Roots Records / Swift / C.M. Distribution / Topic Records / Jazz Music / Hot Shot / A.D.A Distribution / Direct Distribution.

LOUVIN BROTHERS, THE (2).
Tracks: When I stop dreaming / I don't believe you've met my baby / Hoping that you're hoping / You're running wild / Cash on the barrelhead / My baby's gone / Knoxville girl / I love you best of all / How's the world treating you / Must you throw dirt in my face / If I could only win your love / Blues stay away from me / Nashville blues / Brown's ferry blues / Gonna lay down my old guitar / My baby came back.
LP . . . . **SDLP 044**
Sundown / '87 / Terry Blood Dist. / Jazz Music / C.M. Distribution.
■ **MC** . . . . **SDC 44**
Sundown / '89.

MY BABY'S GONE.
Tracks: Not Advised.
LP . . . . **HAT 3028**
MC . . . . **HATC 3028**
Stetson / Oct '86 / Crusader Marketing Co. / Swift / Wellard Dist. / Midland Records / C.M. Distribution.

MY CHRISTIAN HOME.
Tracks: Not Advised.
LP . . . . **SLP 5041**
MC . . . . **GT 55041**
Starday (USA) / Apr '87 / Crusader Marketing Co.

NEARER MY GOD TO THEE.
Tracks: Are you washed in the blood / Wait a little longer, please Jesus / I won't have to cross Jordan alone / This little light of mine / Thankful / Last chance to pray / Nearer my God to thee / I can't say no / There's no excuse / Praying / Lord, I'm coming home / I steal away and pray.
LP . . . . **HAT 3081**
MC . . . . **HATC 3081**
Stetson / '88 / Crusader Marketing Co. / Swift / Wellard Dist. / Midland Records / C.M. Distribution.
LP . . . . **RL 304**
Roots (Germany) / Oct '88 / Swift / C.M. Distribution.

RADIO FAVOURITES 1951-57.
Tracks: Not Advised.
MC . . . . **CMFC 009**
Country Music Foundation / Jan '93 / Topic Records / Direct Distribution.
CD . . . . **CMFCD 009**
Country Music Foundation / Jul '93 / Topic Records / Direct Distribution.

RUNNING WILD.
Tracks: Not Advised.
CD . . . . **CDSD 044**
Sundown / Jul '92 / Terry Blood Dist. / Jazz Music / C.M. Distribution.

SATAN IS REAL.
Tracks: Not Advised.
LP . . . . **HAT 3117**
MC . . . . **HATC 3117**
Stetson / Sep '89 / Crusader Marketing Co. / Swift / Wellard Dist. / Midland Records / C.M. Distribution.

SING THEIR HEARTS OUT.
Tracks: If you love me, stay away / Curly headed baby / Nellie moved to town / Stagger, The / Ruby's song / Love is a lonely street / You're learning / Childish love / Call me / What a change / New partner waltz / It hurts me more the second time around / Broken engagement / I can't keep you / Love turned to hate / I'm glad that I'm not him / Give this message to your heart / Everytime you leave / Time goes so slow / I ain't gonna work tomorrow.
LP . . . . **SEE 250**
See For Miles / Feb '89 / Pinnacle.

SONGS THAT TELL A STORY.
Tracks: Theme / Kneel at the cross / I have found the way / Weapon of prayer / I'll never go back / What a friend we have in mother / Jesus is whispering now / Family that prays, The / Robe of white / Let us travel on / Sinner you'd better get ready / Shut in at Christmas / Shut in prayer.
LP . . . . **ROUNDER 1030**
MC . . . . **ROUNDER 1030C**
Rounder / '88 / Projection / Roots Records / Swift / C.M. Distribution / Topic Records / Jazz Music / Hot Shot / A.D.A Distribution / Direct Distribution.
LP . . . . **SDLP 061**
Sundown / Sep '88 / Terry Blood Dist. / Jazz Music / C.M. Distribution.

TRAGIC SONGS OF LIFE.
Tracks: Kentucky / I'll be all smiles tonight / Let her go God bless her / What is home without love / Tiny broken heart, A / In the pines / Alabama / Katy dear / My brother's will / Knoxville girl / Take the news to mother / Mary of the wild moor.
LP . . . . **HAT 3043**
MC . . . . **HATC 3043**
Stetson / Sep '87 / Crusader Marketing Co. / Swift / Wellard Dist. / Midland Records / C.M. Distribution.
LP . . . . **SS 12**
MC . . . . **CSS 12**
Rounder / '88 / Projection / Roots Records / Swift / C.M. Distribution / Topic Records / Jazz Music / Hot Shot / A.D.A Distribution / Direct Distribution.

Louvin, Charlie

50 YEARS OF MAKIN' MUSIC.
Tracks: Not Advised.
■ **CD** . . . . **CDCOT 104**
Cottage / Jun '92.

CHARLIE LOUVIN.
Tracks: Who's gonna love me now? / Store up love / Warm, warm woman / Fancy place to cry, A / She's just an old love turned memory / When love is gone / Apartment No.9 / Wherever you are / Can I have what's left? / Nobody cares.
LP . . . . **PRCV 104**
President / '86 / Grapevine Distribution / Target Records / Jazz Music / Taylors.

I FORGOT TO CRY.
Tracks: Not Advised.
LP . . . . **HAT 3134**
MC . . . . **HATC 3134**
Stetson / Mar '90 / Crusader Marketing Co. / Swift / Wellard Dist. / Midland Records / C.M. Distribution.

Loveless, Patty

Patricia Ramey was born on the 4th of January 1957 in Pikesville, Kentucky. She was spotted performing with her brother on Nashville's Music Row in 1972 by the Wilburn Brothers, Doyle and Teddy. Patty was invited to become a member of their show in order to replace departing singer Loretta Lynn who was embarking on a solo career. After marrying Wilburn Brothers drummer, Terry Lovelace and moving to North Carolina, she played a host of small venues, embracing country and rock genres

L 16 ■ DELETED

between 1973 and 1985. Patty moved to Nashville, following the break up of her marriage, and signed to MCA. After charting with a few singles, Patty Loveless's powerful vocals began to gain many admirers. However, the album *Patty Loveless*, made only a fleeting appearance on the Billboard chart. Following more top ten hits, *If My Heart Had Windows*, *A Little Bit Of Love*, *Blue Side Of Love*, and the success of her third album, *Honky Tonk Angel*, the early promise was at last being fulfilled. The album produced two further chart topping singles and the title track of her MCA album, *On Down The Line* has added to Patty's list of top ten successes. (Maurice Hope)

GREATEST HITS.
Tracks: If my heart had windows / Blue side of town / Don't toss us away / Timber I'm falling in love / Lonely side of love, The / Chains / On down the line / I'm that kind of girl / Hurt me bad (In a real good way) / Jealous bone.
CD . . . . MCAD 10653
MCA (USA) / Sep '93 / MCA (Imports).

HONKY TONK ANGEL.
Tracks: Not Advised.
CD . . . . MCAD 42223
LP. . . . . MCA 42223
MC . . . . MCAC 42223
MCA / Jun '89 / BMG.

I DID.
Tracks: I did / Lonely days lonely nights.
7" . . . . MCA 1158
MCA / Jul '87 / BMG.

IF MY HEART HAD WINDOWS.
Tracks: So good to be in love / Working man's hands / You saved me / If my heart had windows / Little bit of love, A / I can't get you off my mind / Baby's gone blues / Little on the lonely side, A / Fly away / Once upon a lifetime.
CD . . . . MCAD 42092
LP. . . . . IMCA 42092
MC . . . . IMCAC 42092
MCA / Apr '88 / BMG.

ON DOWN THE LINE.
Tracks: Overtime / Night's too long, The / Blue memories / Some morning soon / You can't run away from your heart / On down the line / I've got to stop loving you (and start living) / Looking in the eyes of love / I'm that kind of girl / Feelings of love.
CD . . . . MCAD 6401
LP. . . . . MCA 6401
MC . . . . MCAC 6401
MCA / Jul '90 / BMG.

ONLY WHAT I FEEL.
Tracks: You will / How about you / Nothin' but the wheel / Love builds the bridges (pride builds the walls) / Me man in the moon / Blame it on your heart / You don't know how lucky you are / All I need (is not to need you) / What's a broken heart / How can I help you say goodbye.
LP. 473088 4
MC 473088 2
Epic / Aug '93 / Sony.

PATTY LOVELESS.
Tracks: Lonely days, lonely nights / I did / You are everything / Blue is not a word / Slow healing heart / After all / Wicked ways / Half over you / Some blue moons ago / Sounds of Loneliness.
LP. . . . . MCF 3359
MC . . . . MCFC 3359
MCA / Mar '87 / BMG.
CD . . . . MCAD 5915
MCA (Import) / May '89 / Pinnacle / Silver Sounds (CD).

Lovett, Lyle

He was born 1/11/1957 in Klein, Texas, Lyles broad musical style is influenced by country, jazz & blues, and rock. He attended the Texas A & M University in Houston, where he coupled studying with playing at local bars. Lovett is a great admirer of fellow Texan Guy Clarke, and Jerry Jeff Walker,and gained from them the inspiration he needed to create his own material. The self titled MCA album (1986) best illustrates his influences. Not surprisingly he was hanging out with the likes of Robert Earl Keen Jr; (his co-writer on *This old porch* and Darden Smith, and had supported Nanci Griffith. This LP featured his top twenty hits *Cowboy man*, *God will*, *Farther down the lin*. Lovett's quirky dress sense and poetic work has gained him a strong youthful following, although his subsequent MCA releases *Pontiac* and the jazz based *Lyle Lovett and his large band* did little to enhance his country standing. In 1993 Lyle had a whirlwind romance with actress Julia Roberts and married her. (Maurice Hope)

COWBOY MAN.
Tracks: Cowboy man / God will / Farther down the line / This old porch / Why I don't know / If I weren't the man you wanted / You can't resist it / Waltzing fool / Acceptable level of ecstasy, An (The wedding song) / Closing time.
■ LP. . . . . MCF 3361
MCA / Mar '87.
CD . . . . DMCF 3361
■ MC . . . . MCFC 3361
MCA / Mar '87.

COWBOY MAN.
Tracks: Cowboy man.
7" . . . . MCA 1222
MCA / Nov '87 / BMG.

HERE I AM.
Tracks: Not Advised.
MiniDisc 468980-3
Curb / Feb '93 / BMG.

JOSHUA JUDGES RUTH.
Tracks: Not Advised.
CD . . . . MCAD 10475
MC . . . . MCAC 10475
MCA / Mar '92 / BMG.
■ LP. . . . . MCA 10475
MCA / Mar '92.

LYLE LOVETT.
Tracks: Not Advised.
MC . . . . MCLC 19134
BMG / Nov '92 / BMG.

LYLE LOVETT AND HIS LARGE BAND.
Tracks: Here I am / I know you know / I married her just because she looks / Once is enough / Stand by your man / Crying shame / What do you do / Nobody knows me / Which way does that old pony run / If you were to wake up.
CD . . . . DMCG 6037
MC . . . . MCGC 6037
MCA / Feb '89 / BMG.
■ LP. . . . . MCG 6037
MCA / Feb '89.

PONTIAC.
Tracks: If I had a boat / I loved you yesterday / L.A. country / M-O-N-E-Y / Simple song / She's hot to go / Give back my heart / Walk through the bottomland / She's no lady / Black and blue / Pontiac.
CD . . . . DMFC 3389
MCA / Apr '88 / BMG.
■ LP. . . . . MCF 3389
MCA / Feb '88.
■ MC . . . . MCFC 3389
MCA / Feb '88.

SHE'S NO LADY.
Tracks: She's no lady / Pontiac / You can't resist it'.
12" . . . . MCAT 1254
7" . . . . MCA 1254
MCA / May '88 / BMG.

STAND BY YOUR MAN.
Tracks: Stand by your man.
7" . . . . MCA 1322
■ CD Single . . . . DMCAT 1322
MCA / Mar '89.

WALK THROUGH THE BOTTOMLAND.
Tracks: Walk through the bottomland (Featuring Emmylou Harris.) / Simple song / This old porch (Extra track on 12".).
12" . . . . MCAT 1234
7" . . . . MCA 1234
MCA / Feb '88 / BMG.

YOU CAN'T RESIST IT.
Tracks: You can't resist it.
7" . . . . MCA 1165
MCA / Jul '87 / BMG.
7" . . . . MCA 1355
MCA / Jul '89 / BMG.
■ CD Single . . . . DMCAT 1355
MCA / Jul '89.

Lucas, "Lazy" Bill

LAZY BILL LUCAS.
Tracks: Not Advised.
LP. . . . . PH 1007
Philo (USA) / '88 / Roots Records / Projection / Topic Records / Direct Distribution / Ross Records / C.M. Distribution / Impetus Records.

Luman, Bob

This American singer and guitarist was born in Nacogdoches, Texas, and became a rockabilly vocalist in the late Fifties. Despite a series of great records, all his early rock releases failed. He did, nonetheless, win an appearance in the film *Carnival Rock*. In late 1960 he suddenly became famous with *Let's think about living*, a rousing message-filled pop single which reached the top 10 on both sides of the Atlantic; it was written by Boudleaux Bryant, source of many of The Everly Brothers hits. During the rest of the sixties and seventies, Luman returned to the style that had always been at the root of his music - country and western. In view of the optimistic tone of his most famous disc, it was ironic that he should die an early death; he passed away in December 1978 at the age of 40, after a moderately successful country career. (Bob Macdonald)

BOB LUMAN ROCKS.
Tracks: Let's think about living / My baby walks all over me / Class of 59 / Buttercup / Dreamy doll / You win again / Great snowman, The / Meet Mr.Mud / Hey Joe / Louisiana man / Fool / Private eye / Why why bye bye / You've got everything.
■ LP. . . . . DJM 22057
DJM / Jan '77.

CARNIVAL ROCK.
Tracks: Try me / Everbody's talkin' / Precious / I know my baby cares / Svengali / Chain of love / Lover's prayer / Carnival rock (This is the night) / Carnival rock (instrumental) / All night long / Saving it for you / Yes dear, there's a Virginia / So happy for you / Something special / Almost persuaded / Night without end / Love stay away from me.
LP. . . . . BFX 15345
Bear Family / Nov '88 / Rollercoaster Records / Swift / Direct Distribution.

GREAT SNOWMAN, THE.
Tracks: Great snowman, The.
■ 7" . . . . WB 37
WEA / May '61.

LET'S THINK ABOUT LIVING.
Tracks: Still loving you / Oh lonesome me / Hey Joe / Bad bad day / Louisiana man / Interstate forty / I love you because / Go on home boy / Great snowman, The / Jealous heart / You win again / Let's think about living.
■ LP. . . . . WM 4025
WEA / Jan '61.
LP. . . . . SDLP 1013
Sundown / Aug '84 / Terry Blood Dist. / Jazz Music / C.M. Distribution.
MC . . . . SDC 1013
Sundown / '89 / Terry Blood Dist. / Jazz Music / C.M. Distribution.

LET'S THINK ABOUT LIVING.
Tracks: Let's think about living.
■ 7" . . . . WB 18
WEA / Jun '60.
7" . . . . SDS 002
Sundown / Apr '85 / Terry Blood Dist. / Jazz Music / C.M. Distribution.

LORETTA.
Tracks: Loretta / It's a sin / If you don't love me / Love worked a miracle / Poor boy blues / Sentimental / You're welcome / Running scared / Freedom of living / Tears from out of nowhere / It's all over / Best years of my wife, The / Bigger man than I / Too hot to dance / I like your kind of love / Hardly anymore.
CD . . . . CDSD 068
LP. . . . . SDLP 068
Sundown / Nov '89 / Terry Blood Dist. / Jazz Music / C.M. Distribution.

MORE OF THAT ROCKER.
Tracks: Let's think about living / Boom boom boom yippy yi ya (Previously unissued) / Envy / Hey Joe / You've got everything / Love creator (Previously unissued) / Louisiana man / Fool, The / My baby walks all over me / Old friends / Big river rose / Throwing kisses / Great snowman, The / Pig latin song / Oh lonesome me / Bad bad day.
LP. . . . . BFX 15039
Bear Family / Sep '84 / Rollercoaster Records / Swift / Direct Distribution.

MORE ROCK-A-BILLY ROCK (Luman, Bob & Friends).
Tracks: That's alright / Hello baby / In the deep dark jungle / Let 'er go / Meaner than an alligator / Sorry I'll never let you go / Run run run / So wild / Lover lover / That cat / Crazy about you baby / Grinding / Big boy rock / Saturday jump.
LP. . . . . WLP 8828
White Label (Germany) / Feb '87 / Pinnacle / Bear Family Records (Germany) / CSA Tell Tapes.

ROCKER, THE.
Tracks: Loretta (Previously unissued) / I love you because / Private eye / Everytime the world goes round / Buttercup / Boston rocker / Why why bye bye / Meet Mister Mud / Class of 59 / You're like a stranger in my arms (Previously unissued) / Dreamy doll / You've turned down the lights / You're everything / Belonging to you / I love you so much it hurts / Rocks of Reno, The.
LP. . . . . BFX 15037
Bear Family / Sep '84 / Rollercoaster Records / Swift / Direct Distribution.

STILL ROCKIN'.
Tracks: Lonely road* (Previously unissued.) / I'm gonna write a song about you / (Empty walls) A lonely room / Freedom of living / Run on home, baby brother / Fire engine red / (I can't get you) Off my mind / Interstate forty / File, The / Old George Dickel / Go on home boy / Five miles from home / Come on and sing / You can't take the country from the boy / Jealous heart* / You win again*.
LP. . . . . BFX 15140
Bear Family / Nov '84 / Rollercoaster Records / Swift / Direct Distribution.

STRANGER THAN FICTION.
Tracks: Stranger than fiction.
7" 45 028
Rollin' Rock / Jun '80 / Pinnacle.

THAT'S ALRIGHT.
Tracks: That's alright.
7" 45 034
Rollin' Rock / Jun '80 / Pinnacle.

TRY ME.
Tracks: Not Advised.
LP. . . . . RSRLP 1015
Rockstar (1) / Jan '87 / Swift / C.M. Distribution.

WHY WHY BYE BYE.
Tracks: Why why bye bye.
■ 7" . . . . WB 28
WEA / Dec '60.

WILD-EYED WOMAN.
Tracks: Red cadillac and a black moustache (Over-dubbed chorus.) / Whenever you're ready / Black days, blue nights / Your love (Over-dubbed electric guitar.) / Wild-eyed woman / Your love (1st recording) / Amarillo blues / Red hot / All night long / Your love (undubbed 2nd recording) / Make up your mind / In the deep dark jungle / That's alright / Hello baby / Stranger than fiction / You're the cause of it all / Let her go.
LP. . . . . BFX 15268
Bear Family / Nov '88 / Rollercoaster Records / Swift / Direct Distribution.

Lumpkin, Gary

MISSISSIPPI MEMORY (Lumpkin, Gary & Connie Lee Stich).
Tracks: Let's hate ourselves in the morning / There ain't no me (if there ain't no you) / Love letters in the sand / San Antonio days / Yodelin' blues / Building a bridge / I only want to love you forever / Mississippi memory / Heaven on a back porch / Old faithful / I can count on you / Life's railroad to heaven.
CD . . . . RBRCD 1001
MC . . . . RBRCS 1001
Ragged But Right / Aug '92.

Lundy, Emmett W.

FIDDLE TUNES FROM GRAYSON COUNTY, VIRGINIA.
Tracks: Fisher's hornpipe / Flatwoods / Evening star waltz / Sugar hill / Highlander's farewell / Sheep shell corn by the rattle of his horn / Piney woods gal / Chapel Hill march / Forky deer / Molly put the kettle on / Waves on the ocean / Deaf woman's courtship / Duck on the millpond / Lost gal / Bonapartes retreat / Susanna gal / Wild goose chase / Cleveland's march / Belle of Lexington.
LP. . . . . STR 802
String / '81 / Projection / Roots Records / A.D.A Distribution / C.M. Distribution / Swift / Ross Records / Duncans.

Lundy, Ted

LOVE SICK AND SORROW (Lundy, Ted/Bob Paisley/Southern Mountain Boys).
Tracks: Not Advised.
LP. . . . . ROUNDER 0107
Rounder / Mar '79 / Projection / Roots Records / Swift / C.M. Distribution / Topic Records / Jazz Music / Hot Shot / A.D.A Distribution / Direct Distribution.

SLIPPIN' AWAY.
Tracks: Not Advised.
LP. . . . . ROUNDER 0055
Rounder / '88 / Projection / Roots Records / Swift / C.M. Distribution / Topic Records / Jazz Music / Hot Shot / A.D.A Distribution / Direct Distribution.

Lynam, Ray

Ray Lynam was born in Mote, Co.Westmeath, and began singing professionally in 1970. He built his career on the sound of country music and achieved his earliest chart success in Ireland with, Sweet Rosie Jones, and There Ought To Be A Law. He further developed his reputation by teaming up with top favourite Philomena Begley for occassional recordings and concerts. An artist who's never been afraid to experiment, Lynam has won much critical acclaim for setting new standards within Irish country music, although his recordings have not always been commercially successful. (Tony Byworth)

20 SHOTS OF COUNTRY.
Tracks: Not Advised.
LP. . . . . CBRL 4069
Outlet / '88 / Projection / Duncans / C.M. Distribution / Ross Records / Topic Records / Direct Distribution / Midland Records.

BACK IN LOVE BY MONDAY.
Tracks: Back in love by Monday / Time / Hold her in your hand / Moon is still over her shoulder, The / Speak softly / Fewer threads than these / Rose in paradise / Maybe this time / Beautiful woman.
LP. . . . . RITZLP 0047
MC . . . . RITZLC 0047
Ritz / Aug '88 / Pinnacle / Midland Records.

BACK IN LOVE BY MONDAY.
Tracks: Back in love by Monday.
7" . . . . RITZ 189
Ritz / Jun '88 / Pinnacle / Midland Records.

BEAUTIFUL WOMAN.
Tracks: Beautiful woman / Maybe this time.
7" . . . . RITZ 190
Ritz / Oct '88 / Pinnacle / Midland Records.

BRAND NEW MR ME.
Tracks: Not Advised.
LP. . . . . HPE 634
Harp (Ireland) / Jul '81 / C.M. Distribution.

COUNTRY FAVOURITES (Lynam, Ray & The Hillbillies).
Tracks: Not Advised.
MC . . . . CBRL 4086
Release (Ireland) / May '77.

COUNTRY STARS (see under Begley, Philomena).

FIRE OF TWO OLD FLAMES.
Tracks: Fire of two old flames.
7" . . . . RITZ 114
Ritz / '88 / Pinnacle / Midland Records.

GYPSY JOE AND ME.
Tracks: Not Advised.
LP. . . . . HPE 602
Harp (Ireland) / C.M. Distribution.

MONA LISA.
Tracks: Mona Lisa lost her smile / Road to Dundee, The / Too late / From now on / Winter time / Devil inside, The / To be lovers / You put the blue in me / He stopped loving her today / Blue grass medley / I heard the bluebirds sing / Nancy Myles.
LP. . . . . RITZLP 0033
MC . . . . RITZLC 0033
Ritz / Jun '86 / Pinnacle / Midland Records.

MONA LISA LOST HER SMILE.
Tracks: Mona Lisa lost her smile / Winter time.
7" . . . . RITZ 093
Ritz / Aug '86 / Pinnacle / Midland Records.

SHADES OF RAY LYNAM.
Tracks: Not Advised.
LP. . . . . RITZSP 414
MC . . . . RITZSC 414
Ritz / Apr '86 / Pinnacle / Midland Records.

SHE SANG THE MELODY (Lynam, Ray & Philomena Begley).
Tracks: She sang the melody / Hold on.
7" . . . . RITZ 099
Ritz / May '85 / Pinnacle / Midland Records.

TO BE LOVERS.
Tracks: To be lovers / Winter time.
7" . . . . RITZ 145
Ritz / Mar '86 / Pinnacle / Midland Records.

VERY BEST OF RAY LYNAM, THE.
Tracks: If we're not back in love by Monday / What a lie / He stopped loving her today / You put the blue in me / You win again / Gambler, The / Moon is still over her shoulder / Beautiful woman / To be lovers / Mona Lisa has lost her smile / Girls women and ladies / Hold her in your hand / Speak softly (you're talking to my heart) / I'll never get over you / Rainy days stormy nights / I don't want to see another town.
CD . . . . RITZCD 513
MC . . . . RITZC 513
Ritz / Dec '91 / Pinnacle / Midland Records.

WE GO TOGETHER AGAIN (Lynam, Ray & Philomena Begley).
Tracks: Not Advised.
LP. . . . . SOLP 1010
MC . . . . SOCAS 1010
Sonus / Mar '84.

WHAT A LIE.
Tracks: What a lie / I don't want to see another town.
7" . . . . RITZ 013
Ritz / Apr '82 / Pinnacle / Midland Records.

Lynch, Claire

BREAKIN' IT.
Tracks: Listen to a country song / Breakin' it / Old by and by / I'll never grow tired of you / I can't get you off my mind / Somebody loves you / Once in a lifetime / All the way to Texas / Livin' in the name of love / Heart made of stone / Feelings of love.
LP. . . . . AMB 004
Ambush (Belgium) / '83 / Ambush Records (Belgium).

Lynn, Loretta

Loretta Lynn is often regarded as country music's first female superstar. Born Loretta Webb in 1935 in Kentucky her success story was a rags-to-riches tale immortalised in Coalminer's Daughter with Sissy Spacek in the starring role of the hit film. She married Oliver Lynn when she was 13. Her first record was Honky Tonk Girl which was released on the Zero label and became a best seller in 1960. This impressed The Wilburn Brothers who then took charge of Lynn's career and secured her a deal with Decca. She was a top attraction at The Grand

Ole Opry which she was invited to join in 1962. She built up close friendships with Ernest Tubb and Patsy Cline. Her first Decca single Success was a top ten success. In the mid 60's she scored a series of number one singles including the classic Don't Come Home A Drinkin' (With Lovin' On Your Mind) released in 1966. She wrote the majority of her own hits and several also reached the pop charts. In total she has had more than 60 chart singles not counting the several duets. Among her many other awards she has been named CMA Female Vocalist and Entertainer Of The Year. In 1988 recieved country's finest honour by being elected into The Country Music Hall Of Fame. (Tony Byworth).

20 GREATEST HITS: LORETTA LYNN.
Tracks: Blue Kentucky girl / Don't come home a drinkin' / Your squaw is on the warpath / You're looking at country / Rated X / Pill, The / Hey Loretta / Out of my head and back in my bed / She's got you / I've got a picture of us on my mind / You ain't woman enough to take my man / Fist city / Coal miner's daughter / One's on the way / They don't make 'em like my daddy / Love is the foundation / When the tingle becomes a chill / Somebody somewhere don't know what / We've come a long way baby / I lie.
CD . . . . MCAD 5943
MCA (Import) / May '89 / Pinnacle / Silver Sounds (CD).

BEST OF CONWAY AND LORETTA (see under Twitty, Conway).

COAL MINERS DAUGHTER.
Tracks: Not Advised.
LP. . . . . IMCA 37236
MCA (Import) / Mar '86 / Pinnacle / Silver Sounds (CD).

COAL MINERS DAUGHTER.
Tracks: Honky tonk girl / Coal miner's daughter / Hey Loretta / Don't come home a drinkin' / One's on the way / You're lookin' at country / Fist City / You ain't woman enough.
VHS. . . . . PLATV 311
Prism Video / '91 / Terry Blood Dist. / Gold & Sons / Prism Leisure PLC.

COUNTRY PARTNERS (Lynn, Loretta & Conway Twitty).
Tracks: As soon as I hang up the phone / Don't mess up a good thing / Love's not where love should be / Two lonely people / I changed my way / Country bumpkin / Spiders and snakes / I'm getting tired of losing you / Sweet things I remember about you / It all falls down / Lifetime before, A.
■ LP. . . . . IMCA 836
MCA (Import) / Mar '86.

COUNTRY STORE: LORETTA LYNN.
Tracks: Coal miners daughter / Letter, The / Faded love / Don't come home a drinkin' / Other woman, The / Put your hand in the hand / Behind closed doors / While he's making love / Delta dawn / Hey Loretta / As soon as I hang up the phone / Take me home country roads / Heart don't do this to me / Woman of the world.
CD . . . . CDCST 19
LP. . . . . CST 19
MC . . . . CSTK 19
Country Store / Dec '88 / BMG.

DYNAMIC DUO (Lynn, Loretta & Conway Twitty).
Tracks: I don't love you enough / You're much too close / Hey good lookin' / We can try it one more time.
LP. . . . . MFP 5599
■ MC . . . . TCMFP 5599
MFP / Jan '83.

GOLDEN GREATS: LORETTA LYNN.
Tracks: Before I'm over you / Wine women and song / Happy birthday / Blue Kentucky girl / You ain't woman enough / Don't come home a drinkin' / Fist city / Woman of the world / Coalminer's daughter / One's on the way / Love is the foundation / Hey Loretta / Trouble in paradise / Somebody, somewhere / She's got you / Out of my head and back in my bed.
■ LP. . . . . MCM 5028
MCA / Feb '86.
CD . . . . DMCM 5028
■ MC . . . . MCMC 5028
MCA / Feb '86.
CD . . . . MCLD 19040
■ MC . . . . MCLC 19040
MCA / Apr '92.

GREAT COUNTRY HITS.
Tracks: Minute you're gone, The / I still miss someone / You're the only good thing (that's happened to me) / End of the world / Oh lonesome me / Send me the pillow that you dream on / I won't forget you / Race is on, The / Jealous heart / I really don't want to know / There goes my everything / Your cheatin' heart / I don't wanna play house / Satisfied mind, A / Stand by your man / Snowbird / Rose garden / Me and Bobby McGee / Help me make it through the night / Paper house / Behind closed doors / Satin sheets / I fall to pieces / Sweet dreams / Crazy / Wrong road again / Rhinestone cowboy / Another somebody done somebody wrong song.
Double LP . . . . MCLD 615
■ MC Set . . . . MCLDC 615
MCA / May '85.

GREATEST HITS.
Tracks: Hey, Loretta / You're looking at country / Let your love flow / We've come along way, Baby / Spring fever / Your squaw is on the warpath / Fist city / I fall to pieces / Walking after midnight / Crazy / Back in baby's arms / She's got you / Me and Bobby McGee / Somebody, somewhere (don't know what he's missing tonight) / Out of my head and back in my bed / Coal miner's daugher / They don't make 'em like my daddy / One's on the way / Pill, The / Y'all come / You ain't woman enough.
CD . . . . PLATCD 363
MC . . . . PLAC 363
Prism / '91 / Pinnacle / Midland Records.

GREATEST HITS: LORETTA LYNN.
Tracks: Not Advised.
CD 31234
MCA (USA) / Jun '88 / MCA (Imports).

I REMEMBER PATSY.
Tracks: She's got you / Walking after midnight / Why can't he be here / Faded love / I fall to pieces / Crazy / Sweet dreams / Back in baby's arms / Leavin' on your mind / I remember Patsy.
■ LP . . . . IMCA 1621
MCA (Import) / Mar '86.

JUST A WOMAN.
Tracks: Stop the clock / Heart don't do this to me / Wouldn't it be great / When I'm in love all alone / I can't say it on the radio / I'll think of something / Adam's rib / Take me in your arms (and hold me) / Just a woman / One man band.
■ LP . . . . IMCA 5613
MCA (Import) / Mar '86.

LORETTA LYNN.
Tracks: Not Advised.
CD 31235
MCA (USA) / Jun '88 / MCA (Imports).

LORETTA LYNN.
Tracks: Not Advised.
VHS . . . . TVE 1041
Telstar Video / May '92 / BMG.

LORETTA LYNN LIVE.
Tracks: Not Advised.
VHS . . . . V 9094
MSD / Jun '88 / Multiple Sound Distributors / Gold & Sons.

LORETTA LYNN STORY, THE.
Tracks: Honky tonk angels / Success / One's on the way / You ain't woman enough / Your squaw is on the warpath / Fist city / Don't come home a drinkin' / You're lookin' at country / Walking after midnight / Crazy / I fall to pieces.
■ LP . . . . MFP 50518
MFP / Jun '81.

NEVER ENDING SONG OF LOVE (Lynn, Loretta & Conway Twitty).
Tracks: Not Advised.
■ LP . . . . MFP 50474
MFP / May '80.

OUT OF MY HEAD AND BACK IN MY BED.
Tracks: Out of my head and back in my bed / Old rooster.
■ 7" . . . . MCA 356
MCA / Mar '78.

SINGS.
Tracks: Not Advised.
LP . . . . HAT 3023
MC . . . . HATC 3023
Stetson / Oct '86 / Crusader Marketing Co. / Swift / Wellard Dist. / Midland Records / C.M. Distribution.

SINGS COUNTRY.
Tracks: Stand by your man / Snowbird / Minute you're gone, The / Rose garden / Crazy / Paper roses / You're the only good thing (That's happened to me) / Me and Bobby McGee / Send me the pillow (That you dream on) / Behind closed doors / I won't forget you / Race is on, The / (Hey won't you play) (Full title: (Hey won't you play) Another somebody done somebody wrong so) / Help me make it through the night.
LP . . . . MFP 41 5742 1
■ MC . . . . MFP 41 5742 4
MFP / Feb '86.

SOMEBODY SOMEWHERE.
Tracks: Somebody somewhere / You're lookin' at country / I wanna be free.
■ 7" . . . . MCA 283
MCA / Mar '77.

VERY BEST OF CONWAY & LORETTA,THE (Lynn, Loretta & Conway Twitty).
Tracks: Not Advised.
LP . . . . IMCA 37237
MCA (Import) / Mar '86 / Pinnacle / Silver Sounds (CD).

VERY BEST OF LORETTA LYNN.
Tracks: Coal miner's daughter / You're looking at country / Blue Kentucky girl / Wine, women and song / She's got you / One's on the way / Happy birthday / Before I'm over you / Out of my head and back in my bed / Woman of the world / Trouble in paradise / Hey Loretta / You ain't woman enough / Fist city / Somebody, somewhere / Don't come a drinkin' (with ..).
LP . . . . PLAT 308
MC . . . . PLAC 308
Platinum Music / Apr '88 / Prism Leisure PLC / Ross Records.
CD . . . . PLATCD 308
Platinum Music / Dec '88 / Prism Leisure PLC / Ross Records.

WE'VE COME A LONG WAY, BABY.
Tracks: We've come a long way, baby / Easy street / Lady that lived here before / Lullabies to a memory / I can't feel you anymore / True love needs to keep in touch / My conscience goes to sleep / No love left inside of me / Between the preacher and the lawyer / Standing at our bedroom door.
■ LP . . . . MCF 2881
MCA / '79.

YOU'RE LOOKING AT COUNTRY.
Tracks: You're looking at country / Coal miner's daughter.
■ 7" . . . . MCA 691
MCA / Mar '81.

GARTH BROOKS
America's biggest selling artist

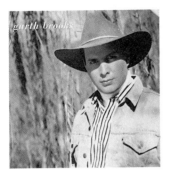

Garth Brooks

No Fences

Ropin' The Wind

The Chase

Beyond The Season

This is Garth Brooks (video)

In Pieces

Plate 1

VINTAGE COUNTRY
Historic Recordings and Reissues

Capitol Country Music Classics: 1940s

The Essential Roy Acuff 1936-1949

Bill Monroe: Mule Skinner Blues

Tex Ritter: Collectors Series

Davis Sisters: Memories

Bob Wills: Tiffany Transcriptions

Cliffie Stone's Radio Transcriptions

Hank Williams 40 Greatest Hits

Plate 2

VINTAGE COUNTRY
Historic Recordings and Reissues

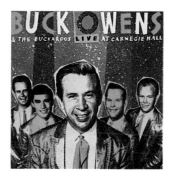

Buck Owens: Live At Carnegie Hall

Merle Travis: Folk Songs Of The Hills

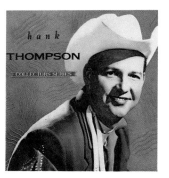

Hank Thompson: Collectors Series

Nitty Gritty Dirt Band: Will The Circle Be Unbroken

George Jones: Salutes Wills & Williams

The Essential Ray Price 1951 - 1962

Louvin Brothers: Capitol Country Classics

History Of Country Music The Fifties

Plate 3

ROCKIN' COUNTRY
Rockabilly & Country Rock

Byrds: Sweetheart Of The Rodeo

Jerry Lee Lewis: Greatest Live Shows On Earth

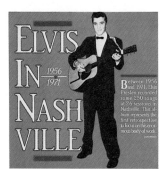

Elvis Presley: Elvis In Nashville

Capitol Country Classics: Rockabilly

Linda Ronstadt: Greatest Hits

Steve Earle: Guitar Town

Restless Heart: Fast Movin' Train

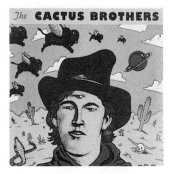

The Cactus Brothers

Plate 4

TOURING ATTRACTIONS
America's Popular Exports

Don Williams: True Love

Bobby Bare: Lullabys, Legends And Lies

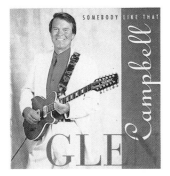

Glen Campbell: Somebody Like That

Billie Jo Spears: Unmistakably

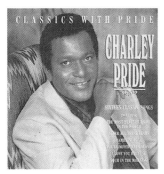

Charley Pride: Classics With Pride

The Essential Johnny Cash 1955 - 1983

George Hamilton IV: A Country Christmas

Tammy Wynette: Anniversary

Plate 5

LONG TIME FAVOURTIES
Popular Artists Over The Years

Willie Nelson: Liberty Recordings 1962-1964

Loretta Lynn: The Very Best Of...

Jim Reeves: Live At The Opry

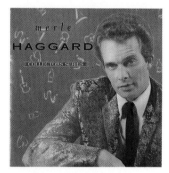

Merle Haggard: Collectors Series

Tanya Tucker: Hits

Anne Murray: Special Collection

Kenny Rogers

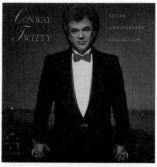

Conway Twitty: Silver Anniversary Collection

Plate 6

LONG TIME FAVOURITES
Popular Artists Over The Years

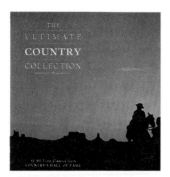

Various: Ultimate Country Collection

Ronnie Milsap: Greatest Hits

Dolly Parton: Slow Dancing With The Moon

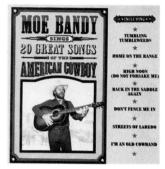

Moe Bandy: Sings Songs Of The American Cowboy

Tom T. Hall: Ballad Of Forty Dollars

Patsy Cline: Dreaming

Crystal Gayle: 50 Original Tracks

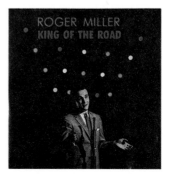

Roger Miller: King Of The Road

Plate 7

HOMEGROWN
UK and Irish Artists

Hank Wangford: Hard Shoulder to Cry On

Tony Goodacre: Livin' On Lovin'

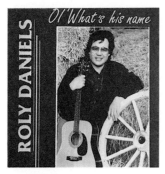

Roly Daniels: Ol' What's His Name

Philomena Begley: Country Queen

Sarah Jory: 20 Steel Guitar Favourites

John Hogan: The Nashville Album

Charlie Landsborough: Songs From The Heart

Southern Exposure: Small Town

Plate 8

HOMEGROWN
UK and Irish Artists

Kelvin Henderson: I Feel Like ...

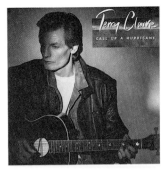

Terry Clark: Call Up A Hurricane

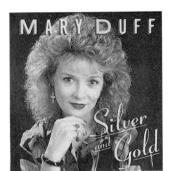

Mary Duff: Silver & Gold

Dominic Kirwan: Evergreen

Mick Flavin: The Lights Of Home

Susan McCann: Memories

Wes McGhee: Neon & Dust

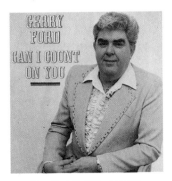

Gerry Ford: Can I Count On You

Plate 9

COUNTRY MUSICIANS
Artists In Their Own Right

Mark O'Connor: The New Nashville Cats

David Schnaufer: Dulcimer Sessions

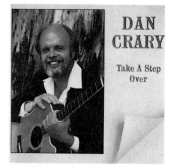

Dan Crary: Take A Step Over

Bela Fleck: Inroads

Jimmy Day: Steel And Strings

Jerry Douglas: Slide Rule

Stuart Duncan

Norman Blake & Tony Rice 2

Plate 10

CUTTING EDGE
Fringe Areas Of Country Music

John Prine: The Missing Years

k.d.lang: Shadowland

Iris DeMent: Infamous Angel

Guy Clark: Boats To Build

Lyle Lovett

Emmylou Harris: Angel Band

Nanci Griffith: Lone Star State Of MInd

Dwight Yoakam: If There Was A Way

Plate 11

SOUNDS OF THE '80S
Artists Of The Past Decade

George Strait: Greatest Hits

Kathy Mattea: Walk The Way The Wind Blows

Highwaymen: Highwayman 2

Keith Whitley: Don't Close Your Eyes

Lee Greenwood: You've Got A Good Love Comin'

Rosanne Cash: Retrospect 1979-1989

Sweethearts Of The Rodeo

Rodney Crowell: Keys To The Highway

Plate 12

SOUNDS OF THE '80S
Artists Of The Past Decade

Soundtrack: Urban Cowboy

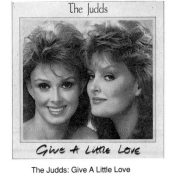

The Judds: Give A Little Love

Ricky Skaggs: Comin' Home To Stay

Alabama

Reba McEntire: Reba

Randy Travis: Old 8 x 10

Hank Williams Jr: Five-O

K.T. Oslin: 80's Ladies

Plate 13

CONTEMPORARY TIMES
Country Acts Of The '90S

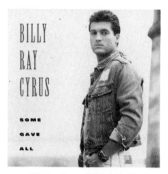

Billy Ray Cyrus: Some Gave All

Hal Ketchum: Past The Point Of Rescue

Mary-Chapin Carpenter: Come On Come On

Clint Black: No Time To Kill

Kentucky Headhunters: Electric Barnyard

Patty Loveless: Greatest Hits

Travis Tritt: Country Club

Collin Raye: All I Can Be

Plate 14

CONTEMPORARY TIMES
Country Acts Of The '90S

Alan Jackson: A Lot About Livin'

Ricky Van Shelton: Wild-Eyed Dream

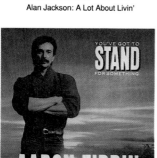

Aaron Tippin: You've Got To Stand For Something

Trisha Yearwood: Hearts In Armor

Suzy Bogguss: Something Up My Sleeve

Radney Foster: Del Rio, TX 1959

Vince Gill: I Still Believe In You

Brooks & Dunn: Brand New Man

Plate 15

DANIEL O'DONNELL
U.K.'s Biggest Selling Country Artist

I Need You

Don't Forget To Remeber

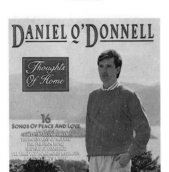

Thoughts Of Home

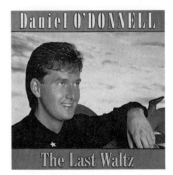

The Last Waltz

The Very Best Of Daniel O'Donnell

Follow Your Dream

An Evening With Daniel O'Donnell (video)

Plate 16

M

M'Carver, Kimberly

Kimberly M'Carver, born Mesquite, Texas, is another in the long line of singer-songwriters from the Lone Star state. Husband Dennis M'Carver plays acoustic guitar on her first release. Also featured Stuart Duncan, Jeff White (of Union Station), Jerry Douglas, Roy Husky Jr.

BREATHE THE MOONLIGHT.
Tracks: Silver wheeled pony / Whistle down the wind / Oryin' wolf / Borrowed time / Only in my dreams / Jose's lullaby / Springtime friends / My way back home to you / Carnival man / Serious doubt / Texas home.
CD . . . . CDPH 1129
LP . . . . PH 1129
MC . . . . PH 1129C
Philo (USA) / '90 / Roots Records / Projection / Topic Records / Direct Distribution / Ross Records / C.M. Distribution / Impetus Records.

McAuliffe, Leon

Steel guitarist/performer/recording artist born William Leon McAuliffe on 03.01.1917 in Houston, Texas (died - 20.08.1988 in Tulsa). Started out with Jim Lewis, before joining W O'Daniels the Light Crust Doughboys when only 16 alongside Tommy Duncan, Wills' long-time vocalist, Leon joined Bob Wills' western swing band the Texas Playboys in 1935. During his seven year stay Will's famous catch-phrase "Take it away, Leon" came about due to his dexterity on steel guitar. McAuliffe's own tunes feature *Steel guitar rag* , *Pan handle rag* (the Columbia release charting at No. 6 in 1949) and *Blue bonnet* . Such was his prowess that he helped popularise the instrument and was one of the pioneers of the steel guitar. After a spell in the forces (1942-1946), he formed his own band the Cimarron Boys and followd in the 1960's with the forming of his Cimarron record label, charting around the top twenty mark with *Cozy inn* and *Faded love* . McAuliffe appeared in ten westerns, and came out of retirement in 1973 - playing and singing Will's *Last session* double album on United Artists, featuring Merle Haggard. He played regularly with the reformed Texas Playboys, and his own recordings are to be found on Capitol, Stoneway and Pine Mountain. (Maurice Hope)

COZY INN.
Tracks: Not Advised.
LP . . . . ABC 394
ABC Records / Sep '87.

EVERYBODY DANCE, EVERYBODY SWING.
Tracks: Not Advised.
LP . . . . HAT 3108
MC . . . . HATC 3108
Stetson / Aug '89 / Crusader Marketing Co. / Swift / Wellard Dist. / Midland Records / C.M. Distribution.

MEMBERS 1 (McAuliffe, Leon & Bob Wills' Texas Playboys).
Tracks: Not Advised.
LP . . . . CW 205
Jambalaya / Aug '89 / Charly.

MEMBERS 2 (McAuliffe, Leon & Bob Wills' Texas Playboys).
Tracks: Not Advised.
LP . . . . CW 206
Jambalaya / Aug '89 / Charly.

McBride, Frankie

This Irish singer and entertainer has been an institution in the showbusiness of Ireland since the sixties. During the latter part of that decade, he chalked up a pair of UK chart entries. *Five little fingers* , a cover version of a 1964 US country and western hit written and originally recorded by Bill Anderson, reached No. 19 and logged 15 weeks of the British top 50 in 1967; the McBride rendition was produced by Tommy Scott, who was fresh from his success with the Dubliners' *Seven drunken nights* . The *Frankie McBride* album reached No 29 on the UK LP list in early 1968. (Bob MacDonald).

COULD I HAVE THIS DANCE.
Tracks: Could i have this dance / Laura (what's he got that i ain't got) / I'm that easy to forget / Till the end / Help me / Acapulco / Just beyond the moon / Rock 'n' roll (I gave you the best years) / I'm being good / Let's build a love together / If you love me / Play another slow song.
LP . . . . JULEP 27

MC . . . . KJULEP 27
Mint / Nov '87 / RTM / Pinnacle.

COULD I HAVE THIS DANCE.
Tracks: Could i have this dance / Gentle to your senses.
■ 7" . . . . CHEW 41
Mint / Jun '82.

FIVE LITTLE FINGERS.
Tracks: Burning bridges / Forty shades of green / I really don't want to know / If I kiss you (will you go away) / Long black limousine / Do you mind if you leave me sleeping / Wanting you / How are things in Glocca morra? / Remember me / I don't love you anymore / Five little fingers / Don't make me go.
LP . . . . GES 1097
MC . . . . KGEC 1097
Emerald / Oct '81 / I & B Records.

FIVE LITTLE FINGERS.
Tracks: Five little fingers (single).
7" . . . . MD 1081
Emerald / Jun '67 / I & B Records.

FRANKIE MCBRIDE.
Tracks: Not Advised.
■ LP . . . . SLD 28
Emerald / Feb '68.

HOW ARE THINGS IN GLOCCA MORRA.
Tracks: How are things in Glocca morra.
■ 7" . . . . MD 1116
Emerald / Jan '69.

I'M BEING GOOD.
Tracks: I'm being good / Laura.
■ 7" . . . . CHEW 56
Mint / Nov '81.

JUST BEYOND THE MOON.
Tracks: Just beyond the moon / Let's build a love together.
■ 7" . . . . CHEW 61
Mint / Feb '82.

VERY BEST OF FRANKIE MCBRIDE, THE.
Tracks: Laura / Five little fingers / Acapulco / If I kiss you (will you go away) / Burning bridges / Teach me to dance / Four in the morning / Give a lonely heart a home / Got another mountain to climb.
MC . . . . MCLP 1008
Music City / Jul '87 / Ross Records.

WHY ME LORD.
Tracks: Not Advised.
MC . . . . MB LP 1020
Music Box (Ireland) / '88.

McCaffrey. Frank

Born in Westport, County Mayo, Frank McCaffrey kept up his family's musical traditions by joining his first band, the Beat Minstrels, while still at school. His initial break came when he joined the Country Folk, which boasted Margo as it's lead singer but also gave him some vocal opportunities. From there he created his own group, Band of Gold. An artist with an easy listening style, he earned plenty of airplay (and just missed the U.K. pop charts) with the single *It's our anniversary* . (Tony Byworth)

CANDLELIGHT AND WINE.
Tracks: Candlelight and wine / I'll take you home again Kathleen.
7" . . . . RITZ 167
Ritz / Jan '87 / Pinnacle / Midland Records.

I'LL TAKE YOU HOME AGAIN KATHLEEN.
Tracks: I'll take you home again Kathleen / Road by the river / If we only had old Ireland / Gypsy, The / Little grey home in the west / Moonlight in Mayo / More than yesterday / Jody & the kid / Candlelight & wine / Ring your mother wore, The / Love is a game / Daisy a day, A.
MC . . . . RITZSC 422
Ritz / Jun '93 / Pinnacle / Midland Records.

I'LL TAKE YOU HOME AGAIN KATHLEEN & OTHER...
Tracks: I'll take you home again Kathleen / Road by the river / If we only had old Ireland over here / Gypsy, The / Little grey home in the West / Moonlight in Mayo / More than yesterday / Jody and the kid / Candlelight and wine / Ring your mother wore / Love is a game / Daisy a day.
LP . . . . RITZLP 0037
■ MC . . . . RITZLC 0037
Ritz / Jan '87.

JEALOUS HEART.
Tracks: Not Advised.
LP . . . . BRL 4096
Release (Ireland) / Jun '78.

MY WILD IRISH ROSE.
Tracks: Not Advised.
LP . . . . HRL 222
Homespun (Ireland) / '88 / Homespun Records / Ross Records / Wellard Dist.

PLACE IN MY HEART, A.
Tracks: Clock in the tower, The / Place in my heart, A / Day the world stood still, The / Drive safely darling / I'd rather be sorry / Annie's story / Blackboard of my heart, The / All alone in New York City / It's our anniversary / Give a lonely heart a home / Rose, The / Always Mayo.
CD . . . . RITZCD 512
MC . . . . RITZC 512
Ritz / '91 / Pinnacle / Midland Records.

PLACE IN MY HEART, A (EP).
Tracks: Place in my heart, A / I'd rather be sorry / Blackboard of my heart / Clock in the tower, The.
EP . . . . RITZ 188
MC Single . . . . RITZC 188
Ritz / Jun '88 / Pinnacle / Midland Records.

PLACE IN MY HOME.
Tracks: Clock in the tower, The / Place in my heart, A / Day the world stood still, The / Drive safely darling / I'd rather be sorry / Annie's story / Blackboard of my heart / All alone in New York City / It's our anniversary / Give a lonely heart a home / Rose, The / Always Mayo.
CD . . . . RITZCD 110
LP . . . . RITZLC 0049
Ritz / Nov '89 / Pinnacle / Midland Records.

RING YOUR MOTHER WORE, THE.
Tracks: Ring your mother wore / Jody and the kid.
7" . . . . RITZ 119
Ritz / Nov '85 / Pinnacle / Midland Records.

RING YOUR MOTHER WORE, THE.
Tracks: Ring your mother wore.
7" . . . . RITZ 141
Ritz / '88 / Pinnacle / Midland Records.

TODAY.
Tracks: Today / Things I wish I'd said / Silver medals and sweet memories / I wish it was me / You make me feel like a man / Forever lovers / In dreams / Wedding song, The / Broken wings / Lady from Glenfarn / Memories of Mayo / Sarah's smile.
CD . . . . RITZCD 0063
MC . . . . RITZLC 0063
Ritz / Apr '91 / Pinnacle / Midland Records.

VERY BEST OF FRANK MCCAFFREY.
Tracks: It's our anniversary / Blackboard of my heart, The / I'll take you home again Kathleen / Ring your mother wore, The / Silver medals & sweet memories / Little grey home in the west / I wish it was me / Daisy a day, A / Place in my heart, A / Memories of Mayo / More than yesterday / If we only had old Ireland / Clock in the tower, The / Give a lonely heart a home / Moonlight in Mayo / My lady from Glenfarne / Things I wish I'd said / Broken wings / Day the world stood still, The / Wedding song, The.
CD . . . . RITZCD 532
MC . . . . RITZRC 532
Ritz / Apr '93 / Pinnacle / Midland Records.

McCall, C.W.

Born William Fries, on 15.11.1928 in Audubon, Iowa. As the Citizen's Band radio craze swept across the US (and beyond), primarily through its truckers, McCall came up with *Convoy* , and will always be associated with the character C.W. McCall, created by Fries for a TV advertising campaign, when working for the Mezt Bread Company. Fries thereafter transformed himself into C.W. McCall, scoring with a dozen hit singles of narration-type fare, with *Old Home Filler-Up An' Keep On A-Truckin' Cafe* setting it in motion. The seven million seller *Convoy* topped both country and pop charts in 1975, and was later picked up by Sam Pekinpah for a movie starring Kris Kristofferson. At this time he left MGM, moving over to Polydor and making strong indentations in the charts with *There won't be no more country music (there won't be no more rock 'n' roll)* , *Crispy Critters* and the 1978 No. 2 single *Roses for mama* , supplementing such earlier fare as *Classified* , *Wolf Creek Pass* and *Black Bear Road* . Such was the C.B. craze that within weeks of *Convoy's* success, Cledus Maggard and The Citizen's Band also made No. 1 via *The White Knight* . Since then, the story-telling singer has done little recording, moving to Colorado in 1982, and getting into politics, gaining election as mayor of Olathe. (Maurice Hope)

BLACK BEAR ROAD.
Tracks: Black bear road / Silverton, The / Lewis and Clark / Oregon trail / Ghost town / Convoy / Long lonesome road / Green river / Write me a song / Mountains of my mind.
LP. 2315 354
MC 3110 354
Polydor / Jan '77 / PolyGram.

CLASSIFIED.
Tracks: Classified / Green river.
■ 7" 2066 668
Polydor / Apr '76.

CONVOY.
Tracks: Convoy.
■ 7" 2066 560
MGM (Polydor) / Feb '76.

CONVOY (OLD GOLD).
Tracks: Convoy.
■ 7" . . . . .OG 9452
Old Gold / Jul '84.

ROUND THE WORLD WITH RUBBER DUCK.
Tracks: Round the world with Rubber Duck / Night rider.
■ 7" 2066 760
Polydor / Jan '77.

WILDERNESS.
Tracks: Wilderness / Jackson hole / Riverside slide / Crispy critters / Roy / Little brown sparrow and me, The / There won't be no country music / Telluride breakdown / Four wheel cowboy / Silver Iodide blues / Columbine / Aurora borealis.
LP. 2391 225
MC 3177 225
Polydor / Jan '77 / PolyGram.

McCall, Cash

NO MORE DOGGIN'.
Tracks: Not Advised.
LP. . . . . .LR 42.058
L&R / '88 / New Note.

McCann, Susan

Born Patricia Susan Mary Heaney on February 26, 1949 in Forkhill, County Amagh. She has developed as one of Ireland's most popular country entertainers who, at the end of 1990, was making a concentrated effort at breaking into the UK crossover market following much airplay on a revival of *Blue velvet* and the releaes of her *Country love affair* album and video. Susan, who made the initial breakthrough in 1976 with a tribute single to an Irish legend *Big Tom is still King* , has firmly secured her country status not only by recording some 26 albums (many in Nashville, working with Porter Wagoner) but also by appearing at many major events, including multiple slots at the Grand Ole Opry and the Wembley Festival. She has toured with such US stars as Charley Pride, won the 1982 Euro Masters, represented Ireland in the 1987 International Show at Fan Fair and, the following year became the first non-American to appear at Dolly Parton's East Tennessee theme park, Dollywood. Her success has been underlined by her being the recipient of numerous awards. (Tony Byworth)

18 VERY BEST.
Tracks: Not Advised.
LP. . . . . .TSC 209
Topspin (Ireland) / '88 / I & B Records.

20 COUNTRY CLASSICS.
Tracks: Not Advised.
MC . . . . .MB LP 1034
Music Box (Ireland) / '88.

AT HOME IN IRELAND.
Tracks: Johnny, lovely Johnny / Eileen McManus / Curragh of Kildare, The / Once upon a time / Nightingale / Blossom will flower, The / Rose of Clare / Where the river Shannon flows / Isle of Innisfree / If those lips could only speak / Noreen Bawn / Rose of Tralee, The.
LP. . . . . .DHL 706
MC . . . . .CDHL 706
Homespun (Ireland) / Nov '85 / Homespun Records / Ross Records / Wellard Dist.

BACK TO ME.
Tracks: Not Advised.
LP. . . . . .KLP 180
K-Tel (Ireland) / '88 / I & B Records / Ross Records / Prism Leisure PLC.
■ MC . . . . .KMC 180B
K-Tel (Ireland) / '88.

BEST OF 20 HITS.
Tracks: Not Advised.
LP. . . . . .KLP 105
K-Tel (Ireland) / '88 / I & B Records / Ross Records / Prism Leisure PLC.
MC . . . . .KMC 105
K-Tel (Ireland) / Dec '88 / I & B Records / Ross Records / Prism Leisure PLC.

BEST OF SUSAN MCCANN.
Tracks: Someone is looking for someone like you / Heaven help the working girl / Rockabilly can rock / Love is supposed to be / Coat of many colours / Even cowgirls get the blues / I want your loving arms around me / Late late show, The / Seeing is believing / While I was making love to you / Blue Kentucky girl / Nothing like a rainy night / Lie to Linda / Hi-fi to cry by / Blue ribbon beer drinking song / Down to my last broken heart / '57 Chevrolet / I feel sorry for anyone who isn't me tonight / What I've got in mind / River road.
LP. . . . . .NE 1205
MC . . . . .CE 2205
K-Tel / Apr '83 / I & B Records / C.M. Distribution / Arabesque Ltd. / Mono Distributors (Jersey) Ltd. / Prism Leisure PLC / PolyGram / Ross Records / Prism Leisure PLC.
LP. . . . . .TSLP 205
Topspin (Ireland) / Apr '85 / I & B Records.
MC . . . . .TSC 205
Topspin (Ireland) / May '88 / I & B Records.

BEST OF THE SIXTIES.
Tracks: Daydream believer / My boy lollipop / Downtown / Bobby's girl / Come what may / Walkin' back to happiness / Lipstick on your collar / Saturday night at the movies / Stupid Cupid / Calendar guy / Another Saturday night / Mr. Tambourine man.
MC . . . . .MCLP 1005
Music City / Jul '87 / Ross Records.

BLUE VELVET.
Tracks: Blue velvet / Two broken hearts.
7" . . . . .PLA 07
Platinum Music / Sep '90 / Prism Leisure PLC / Ross Records.

BROKEN SPEED OF THE SOUND OF LONELINESS (McCann, Susan & Storytellers).
Tracks: Broken speed of the sound of loneliness.
CD Single . . . . .PLA 777D
MC Single . . . . .PLA 777C
Prism / Feb '92 / Pinnacle / Midland Records.

CHART HITS.
Tracks: Flashback / He's a heartache / Single girl / I feel love comin' on / It's you, it's you, it's you / Song for Gloria / Tennessee mountain home / I wouldn't change you if I could / True love ways / I hope you're having better luck / Broken lady / Let me go to Texas.
MC . . . . .MC 1
Fame (Ireland) / May '88.

COUNTRY LOVE AFFAIR.
Tracks: Never ending love affair / Johnny lovely Johnny / Blue velvet / Forever and ever amen / Little ole wine drinker me / Travellin' light / Let the rest of the world go by / Two broken hearts / Someone is looking for someone like you / Irish eyes / Boy in your arms / Wind in the willows / Mother's love is a blessing, A / Patches in heaven / How great thou art / When the sun says goodbye to the mountain.
CD . . . . .IHCD 482
MC . . . . .IHMC 482
Prism / Nov '90 / Pinnacle / Midland Records.

COUNTRY LOVE AFFAIR.
Tracks: Never ending love affair / Johnny lovely Johnny / Someone is looking for someone like you / Boy in your arms / Patches in heaven / Coat of many colours / Let the rest of the world go by / Wind in the willows / Sound of music medley / Travellin' light / Irish eyes / Forever and ever amen / Blue velvet / Little ole wine drinker me / How great thou art / When the sun says goodbye to the mountains.
VHS. . . . . .PLATV 308
Prism Video / Nov '90 / Terry Blood Dist. / Gold & Sons / Prism Leisure PLC.

DIAMONDS AND DREAMS.
Tracks: Love me one more time / When I hear the music / Have you ever been lonely / String of diamonds / Always / You're never too old to love / He never will be mine / Lovin' you / I vow to thee my country / Yellow roses / Sonny's dream / Broken speed of the sound of the loneliness / Rose of my heart / Hillbilly girl with the blues / Everything is beautiful / Give me more time.
CD . . . . .IHCD 591
MC . . . . .IHMC 591
Prism / Oct '91 / Pinnacle / Midland Records.

DOWN RIVER ROAD.
Tracks: 57 Chevrolet / Mama say a prayer / Baby nothing's wrong with me / It don't take much to make me cry / That little boy of mine / Hi-fi to cry by / Down river road / Most precious than ever / Awareness of nothing / Daddy come and get me / My blue tears / Good ole country music.
MC . . . . .TSC 118
Topspin (Ireland) / May '88 / I & B Records.

GOOD 'N' COUNTRY.
Tracks: Other side of the morning / Take me back / Lie to Linda / Sparkling look of love / I don't want to wear diamonds / Your old handy man / Seeing is believing / I'm just not that good at goodbye / Under cover lovers / Isle of Ireland / Nickels & dimes / All the love I have I give to you.
MC . . . . .TSC 122
Topspin (Ireland) / May '88 / I & B Records.

IN NASHVILLE.
Tracks: Someone is looking for someone like you / Slipping around again / Someone just like you / All day sucker / He's everything I wanted you to be / Just like you / Little girl gone / Dream, The / Life turned him that way / She's out there dancing alone / Love is supposed to be / Blue Kentucky girl.
LP. . . . . .SSC 501
Topspin (Ireland) / May '88 / I & B Records.

IRELAND'S FIRST LADY OF COUNTRY MUSIC.
Tracks: Thank God I'm a country girl / Mothers love is a blessing / Old Dungarvan oak / Give me more time / Someone is looking for someone like you / Making love to you / Country roads / All day sucker / Marino waltz / Cooley's reel, high reel / By the light of the silvery moon / Shine on harvest moon / Singing in the rain / Daisy bell / Good old Summertime, The / In the shade of the old apple tree / When you're smiling / Pack up your troubles / I got the sun in the morning / Anything you can do I can do better / There's no business like show business / Town I love so well, The / Walking back to happiness / I only wanna be with you / Bobby's girl / My Bob lollipop / It's you, it's you, it's you.
VHS. . . . . .PLATV 303
Prism Video / '91 / Terry Blood Dist. / Gold & Sons / Prism Leisure PLC.

ISLE OF IRELAND.
Tracks: Travelling people / Village of Astee, The / Green willow / 5,000 miles from Sligo / Big Tom is still the king / Heaven around Galway Bay / Cottage on the Old Dungannon Road / Where is my Nora / Rose of Allandale / Isle of Ireland / Limerick you're a lady / Christmas time in Innisfree.
LP. . . . . .TSLP 206
MC . . . . .TSC 206
Topspin (Ireland) / Jun '85 / I & B Records.

JOHNNY LOVELY JOHNNY.
Tracks: Johnny lovely Johnny / Where the river Shannon flows.
7" . . . . .HS 106
Homespun (Ireland) / May '86 / Homespun Records / Ross Records / Wellard Dist.

MEMORIES.
Tracks: Softly Softly / String Of Diamonds (Medley) / What Ever Happened To Old fashioned Love / Irish Memories (Medley) / Dreaming Of A Little Island / Help Me make It Thru the Night / Bus To L.A. / Penny Arcade / If The Whole World Stopped Loving / Once A Day / Love Has Joined Us Together / Since Johnny Went Away / Darlin' / Angels, Roses And Rain.
CD . . . . .IHCD 592
MC . . . . .IHMC 592
VHS. . . . . .PLATV 312
Irish Music Heritage / Nov '92.

MERRY CHRISTMAS.
Tracks: It's gonna be one happy Christmas / Pretty papers / Santa looks a lot like daddy / We must be having one / Christmas time in Innisfree / White Christmas / Santa & the kids / Angel and the stranger, The / Let's celebrate this Christmas / Lonely Christmas / Please daddy / Silent night.
MC . . . . .TSC 114
Topspin (Ireland) / Dec '85 / I & B Records.

PAPA'S WAGON.
Tracks: I can feel the leaving coming on / Patches in heaven / It's a no no / If you want me / Time can't erase / Big Tom is still the king / Papa's wagon / Dreamin' my dreams / Tabernacle Tom / I don't believe you've met my baby / Gentle on my mind / Country music in my soul.
MC . . . . .MBLP 1017
Music Box (Ireland) / '88.
MC . . . . .TSC 94
Topspin (Ireland) / May '88 / I & B Records.

SENTIMENTAL JOURNEY.
Tracks: Not Advised.
LP. . . . . .KLP 120
K-Tel (Ireland) / '88 / I & B Records / Ross Records / Prism Leisure PLC.

SINCERELY YOURS.
Tracks: Dirty cheezy jeans / When the rain disappears / I feel sorry for anyone who isn't me tonight / Blue ribbon beer drinking song / Hard loved lady and the guitar player from Tennessee, The / Nothing like a rainy night / Down to my last broken heart / Does your mama know what you're doing / Chuck the chuck wagon (Duet with Porter Wagoner) / They won't let you rock and roll no more at the Palomino / Rainy days & stormy nights / Wishful thinking.
LP. . . . . .SSC 507
Topspin (Ireland) / May '88 / I & B Records.

SINGS COUNTRY.
Tracks: Feeling single seeing double / Galway Bay / Adios, farewell, goodbye / I don't want to play house / Did you ever hear the robin sing / What I've got in mind / Keep on the sunny side / Wrong road again / Coat of many colours / Where is my Nora / Old fashioned song / Wild side of life.
MC . . . . .MBLP 1016
Music Box (Ireland) / '88.
MC . . . . .TSC 92
Topspin (Ireland) / May '88 / I & B Records.

SOMETIMES WHEN WE TOUCH (McCann, Susan & Ronan Collins).
Tracks: Islands in the stream / Everything is beautiful / All I have to do is dream / Nobody loves me like you do / Welcome home / Little bit of love, A / Just to satisfy you / Have you ever been lonely / Sometimes when we touch / Rose of my heart / I just want to stay here and love you / Somebody done somebody wrong.
MC . . . . **MCLP 1003**
Music City / Jul '87 / Ross Records.

SONGS JUST FOR YOU.
Tracks: Could it be I don't belong here anymore / Have I told you lately that I love you / This song is just for you / There goes my everything / Could I have this dance / Baby blue / Paper roses / Jealous heart / Country roads / Remember you're mine / Buried treasure / Part of me.
LP . . . . **DHL 713**
MC . . . . **CDHL 713**
Homespun (Ireland) / Dec '86 / Homespun Records / Ross Records / Wellard Dist.

SONNY'S DREAM (McCann, Susan & Brendan Quinn).
Tracks: Not Advised.
MC . . . . **MB LP 1019**
Music Box (Ireland) / '88.

SOUND OF MUSIC, THE.
Tracks: Not Advised.
LP . . . . **MC 2**
Topspin (Ireland) / '88 / I & B Records.

STORYBOOK COUNTRY.
Tracks: Blue jean country queen / Last one to touch me, The / Even cowgirls get the blues / Late late show, The / Heaven help the working girl / You're driving me out of my mind / I don't blame my papa / They'll never ever take his love from me / Hands / Conscience keep an eye on me tonight / It's no wonder I'm still blue / I want you loving arms around me.
LP . . . . **SSLP 503**
MC . . . . **SSC 503**
Topspin (Ireland) / May '81 / I & B Records.

STRING OF DIAMONDS.
Tracks: String of diamonds.
7" . . . . **PLA 077**
CD Single . . . . **PLA 077D**
MC Single . . . . **PLA 077C**
Prism / Sep '91 / Pinnacle / Midland Records.

TOWN I LOVE SO WELL, THE.
Tracks: Dublin in my tears / Old Dungarvan Oak / Sarah Jane / Dan O'Hara / Town I loved so well, The / Galway races / What price is peace / If I came back home / Wild colonial boy / Lakes of Coolfin / Irish rover, The.
MC . . . . **MBMC 1032**
Music Box (Ireland) / '88.
LP . . . . **MBLP 1032**
Music Box (Ireland) / Aug '88.

TRIBUTE TO BUCK OWENS (Live at the Grand).
Tracks: Buckaroo / I'll love you for ever and ever / Act naturally / Foolin' around / Love's gonna live here again / Gonna roll out the red carpet / Second fiddle / Lay it on the line / Crying time / We split the blanket down the middle / Above and beyond / There never was a fool / Excuse me (I think I've got a heartache) / Together again / She don't deserve you any more / I've got a tiger by the tail / It takes people like you to make people like me / Buck's polka.
LP . . . . **HOTV 1**
MC . . . . **CHOTV 1**
Homespun (Ireland) / Dec '85 / Homespun Records / Ross Records / Wellard Dist.

TWENTY COUNTRY CLASSICS.
Tracks: Not Advised.
LP . . . . **HM 028**
Harmac (Ireland) / '89 / I & B Records / Prism Leisure PLC.

WHEN THE SUN SAYS GOODBYE TO THE MOUNTAINS.
Tracks: Bus to L.A. / Nickels & dimes / Once a day / Down river road / They'll never take his love from me / Someone is looking for someone like you / When the sun says goodbye to the mountains / It's you, it's you, its you / Single girl / Last one to touch me, The / Sing me an old fashioned song / '57 Chevrolet.
LP . . . . **TSLP 207**
MC . . . . **TSC 207**
Topspin (Ireland) / Jul '85 / I & B Records.

WHEN THE SUN SAYS GOODBYE TO THE MOUNTAINS(SINGL.
Tracks: When the sun says goodbye to the mountains / Rose of Tralee.
7" . . . . **HS 103**
Homespun (Ireland) / Nov '85 / Homespun Records / Ross Records / Wellard Dist.

YOU GAVE ME LOVE.
Tracks: Not Advised.
LP . . . . **WST R 9699**
MC . . . . **WST C 9699**
Word (UK) / Jan '89 / Word Records (UK) / Sony.

McCarters

The McCarters are made up of sisters Jennifer, Lisa and Teresa from Serville, a small town in Tennessee's Smokey Mountains. Their down home sibling vocals are best demonstrated on their debut album *The Gift* on Warner Bros. From the album the girls enjoyed top five singles with their first two releases *Timeless and true love* and the title track, both in 1988. Also from the debut album they reached the top 30 with *I give you music* . For the girls second album they changed thir name to Jennifer McCarter and the McCarters, *Better be home soon* didn't build on the initial effort, reflected with *Up and gone* the only major chart success and *Quit while I'm behind* only gaining moderate success. (Maurice Hope)

GIFT, THE.
Tracks: I give you music / Timeless and true love / I know love / Quiet desperation / Flower in the desert / Whoro would that leave me / Loving you / Letter from home.
■ **CD** **925737 2**
WEA / Nov '88 / WEA.
■ **MC** **925737 4**
WEA / Sep '88 / WEA.
■ **LP** **925737 1**
WEA / Sep '88.

McCaslin & Ringer

BRAMBLE AND THE ROSE.
Tracks: Not Advised.
LP . . . . **PH 1055**
MC . . . . **PH 1055C**
Philo (USA) / '88 / Roots Records / Projection / Topic Records / Direct Distribution / Ross Records / C.M. Distribution / Impetus Records.

SUNNY CALIFORNIA.
Tracks: Not Advised.
LP . . . . **PH 1099**
MC . . . . **PH 1099C**
Philo (USA) / '88 / Roots Records / Projection / Topic Records / Direct Distribution / Ross Records / C.M. Distribution / Impetus Records.

McCaslin, Mary

Guitarist/singer-songwriter with a passion for ballads associated with the old West. Something of a female Marty Robbins, gaining a respected niche in the folk/country field.

BEST OF MARY MCCASLIN.
Tracks: Things we said today / Northfield / Wayward wind / Prairie in the sky / San Berardino waltz / Dealers, The / Ghost riders in the sky / Cole Younger / Living without you / Circle of friends / Blackbird / Bramble and the rose, The / Last cannonball / Way out west / My world is empty without you / Young Westertly / Back to Salinas / Old friends.
CD . . . . **PHCD 1149**
MC . . . . **PH 1149**
Philo (USA) / '92 / Roots Records / Projection / Topic Records / Direct Distribution / Ross Records / C.M. Distribution / Impetus Records.

LIFE AND TIME, A.
Tracks: Northfield / You keep me hangin' on / Tender love and care / Fair and tender ladies / Band of Jesse James, The / Some of Shelley's blues / Life and time, A / Pinto pony / Farewell Lone Ranger / Santana song.
MC . . . . **FF 203C**
Flying Fish (USA) / '81 / Cadillac Music / Roots Records / Projection / C.M. Distribution / Direct Distribution / Jazz Music / Duncans / A.D.A Distribution.
LP . . . . **FF 203**
Flying Fish (USA) / Mar '89 / Cadillac Music / Roots Records / Projection / C.M. Distribution / Direct Distribution / Jazz Music / Duncans / A.D.A Distribution.

OLD FRIENDS.
Tracks: Things we said today / Oklahoma hills / Wendigo / Way out there / Pinball wizard / My world is empty without you babe / Wayward wind / Blackbird / Don't fence me in / Old friends.
LP . . . . **PHILO 1046**
Philo (USA) / May '79 / Roots Records / Projection / Topic Records / Direct Distribution / Ross Records / C.M. Distribution / Impetus Records.
MC . . . . **PH 1046C**
Philo (USA) / '88 / Roots Records / Projection / Topic Records / Direct Distribution / Ross Records / C.M. Distribution / Impetus Records.

PRAIRIE IN THE SKY.
Tracks: Pass me by / Priscilla Drive / Ballad of Weaverville, The / Back to Silas / Ghost riders in the sky / Last cannonball / It's my time / Cornerstone cowboy / Prairie in the sky / Cole Younger / Dealers, The / My love.
LP . . . . **PH 1024**
MC . . . . **PH 1024MC**
Philo (USA) / '75 / Roots Records / Projection / Topic Records / Direct Distribution / Ross Records / C.M. Distribution / Impetus Records.

WAY OUT WEST.
Tracks: (Waiting) music strings / Oh Hollywood / Waiting / Let it be me / Living without you / Way out West / (Down the road) down the road / San Bernardino waltz / Circle of friends / Ballad of a wanted man / Northfield / Young Westley.
LP . . . . **PHILO 1011**
Philo (USA) / May '79 / Roots Records / Projection / Topic Records / Direct Distribution / Ross Records / C.M. Distribution / Impetus Records.
MC . . . . **PH 1011C**
Philo (USA) / '88 / Roots Records / Projection / Topic Records / Direct Distribution / Ross Records / C.M. Distribution / Impetus Records.

McCauley, Johnny

OUR KIND OF COUNTRY.
Tracks: Not Advised.
MC . . . . **CMC 004**
Celtic Music / '88 / C.M. Distribution / Roots Records / Projection.

McCauley, Max

20 GOLDEN YODELS.
Tracks: Blue velvet band / Blue yodel no. 6 / Shearer's jamboree / Swiss moonlight lullaby / Lovesick blues / Ding dong bells / Yellow rose of Texas / Sunny south by the sea / Blue eyes crying in the rain / She taught me how to yodel / Down by the singing waterfall / I'll bet you my heart I love you.
■ **LP** . . . . **GES 1203**
Emerald / Jul '79.

McClain, Charly

Born Charlotte Denise McClain, on 26.03.1956 in Jackson, Tennessee. Apart from recording a bunch of albums on Epic, she's also an accredited actress - having appeared on Hart To Hart, Fantasy Island and Chips. McClain's early career found her working on the Mid - South Jamboree (1973 - 1975), before heading to Nashville - with help from Ray Pillow and the group Shylo's producer Larry Rogers. Her debut album *Here's Charly McClain* on Epic in 1977, yielded three modest hits, from which point, the fine voiced singer's career steadily gained impetus - with top ten hits *That's What You Do To Me* and *Men* by early 1980. Also from 1980 came McClain's debut No. 1 single launching a run of six top ten consecutive hits, with *Surround Me With Love* , *Sleepin' With The Radio On* , *The Very Best Is You* , *Dancing Your Memory Away* and *With You* - all scoring by 1982. Her country/pop flavoured work gained two No. 1's in 1983, *Radio Heart* and *Paradise Tonight* with Mickey Gilley - they all went top 5 with a remake of the Roy Orbison hit *Candy Man* in 1984. McClain, no stranger to duets, had already scored with Jimmy Rodriguez in 1979 (*I Hate The Way You Love It*). With her solo career on the wane, she teamed up in 1985 with actor/husband Wayne Massey, a former star of One Life To Live, making country's top ten with *With Just One Look In Your Eyes* and *You Are My Music, You Are My Song* . In 1989, McClain moved to Mercury, where attempts to relaunch her career were fruitless. (Maurice Hope)

CHARLY MCLAIN (I Love Country).
Tracks: Sentimental ol' you / Fly into love / Dancing your memory away / With just one look in your eyes / Women get lonely / With you / Everyday love / Radio heart / Who's cheating who / Band of gold / Some hearts get all the breaks / You are my music, you are my song / When it's down to me and you / Someone just like you / Sleepin' with the radio on / Paradise tonight.
LP **4504251**
MC **4504254**
CBS / Mar '87 / Sony.

ONLY THE LONELY KNOW.
Tracks: Only the lonely know / Who's cheating who.
■ **7"** . . . . **EPCA 2606**
Epic / Jul '82.

WHO'S CHEATIN' WHO.
Tracks: Who's cheating who / Love scenes.
7" . . . . **EPC A 1087**
Epic / Apr '81 / Sony.

WOMEN GET LONELY.
Tracks: When a love ain't right / Keep on loving you / Who's cheatin' who / That's what you do to me / Make believe it's your first time / I've been alone too long / Competition / Only the lonely know / Stuck right in the middle of your love / Women get lonely / You're a part of me / Men / Lay down / Let me be your baby / Sweet and East, soft and slow / Sleeping with the radio on.
■ **LP** . . . . **EPC 85778**
Epic / Sep '82.

McClintock, Harry

HALLELUJAH I'M A BUM.
Tracks: Not Advised.
LP . . . . **ROUNDER 1009**
Rounder / '88 / Projection / Roots Records / Swift / C.M. Distribution / Topic Records / Jazz Music / Hot Shot / A.D.A Distribution / Direct Distribution.

McClinton, Delbert

Born in Lubbock, Texas on 04.11.1940, McClinton has proved his worth many times over as a singer-songwriter/harmonica player (as featured on Bruce Channel's 1962 hit *Hey Baby* , touring with him in States and UK on same bill as the Beatles) who's music covers R&B, country, rock & pop. McLinton's recordings appearing on ABC (mid - 70s), with *Victim Of Life's Circumstances* (the song well-covered in the country field - top 40 hit for Vince Gill in 1984), *Genuine Cowhide* & *Love Rustler*, Capricorn, Capitol, Alligator & his present label, Curb - who've released the R&B/Texas blues controlled albums *I'm with You* & *Never Been Rocked Enough* albums. The 90s auger well for this enduring talent - writer of Emmylou Harris' 1978 no 1 *Two More Bottles Of Wine* his latest albeit rare excursion in to the country charts coming in mid - 1993 when a duet with Tanya Tucker *Tell Me About It* made country's top twenty. (Maurice Hope)

FEELIN' ALRIGHT.
Tracks: Not Advised.
LP **20030**
MC **40030**
Astan (USA) / Nov '84.

GIVING IT UP FOR YOUR LOVE.
Tracks: Giving it up for your love / My sweet baby.
■ 7" . . . . **CL 16180**
Capitol / Jan '81.

I'M WITH YOU.
Tracks: That's the way I feel / My baby's lovin' / Go on / Got you on my mind / Crazy 'bout you / I'm with you / Who's foolin' who / Real thing, The / My love is burnin'.
■ CD **4689012**
Sony Music / Aug '91.

JEALOUS KIND.
Tracks: Shotgun rider / I can't quit you / Giving it up for your love / Jealous kind, The / Going back to Lousiana / Baby Ruth / Bright side of the road / Take me to the river / Shaky ground / My sweet baby.
■ LP . . . . **EST 12115**
Capitol / Mar '81.

LIVE FROM AUSTIN.
Tracks: Not Advised.
LP . . . . **AL 4773**
MC . . . . **AC 4773**
Alligator / Aug '90 / Topic Records / Direct Distribution / C.M. Distribution / A.D.A Distribution.
CD . . . . **ALCD 4773**
Alligator / May '93 / Topic Records / Direct Distribution / C.M. Distribution / A.D.A Distribution.

LIVE FROM AUSTIN.
Tracks: Not Advised.

NEVER BEEN ROCKED ENOUGH.
Tracks: Every time I roll the dice / I used to worry / Miss you fever / Why me? / Have a little faith in me / Never been rocked enough / Blues as blues can get, The / Can I change my mind / Cease and desist / Stir it up / Good man, good woman.
CD **4717092**
LP **4717091**
MC **4717094**
Curb / Aug '92 / BMG.
MiniDisc **471709-3**
Curb / Feb '93 / BMG.

SHOTGUN RIDER.
Tracks: Shotgun rider / Baby Ruth.
■ 7" . . . . **CL 16191**
Capitol / Apr '81.

McCloud, Barry

LADY RODEO RIDER.
Tracks: Lady rodeo rider / Lovers rock.
7" . . . . **MSR 19901**
Not Advised / Apr '90.

McComb, Carol

LOVE CAN TAKE YOU HOME AGAIN (McComb, Carol & Friends).
Tracks: Not Advised.
LP . . . . **BAY 302**
Bay / Jul '88 / Projection.

TEARS INTO LAUGHTER.
Tracks: Indaho sky / Forgive and forget / Faded dresden blue / Tears into laughter / Little more love, A / Queen of sorrow / Hazel's song / Next to my skin / Through thick and thin / Ice on the fire / Bird in the wood.
CD . . . . **K 41**
MC . . . . **C 41**
Kaleidoscope (USA) / Mar '90 / Projection / Ross Records / Roots Records / Swift / C.M. Distribution / Topic Records / Duncans.

McCormick, Gayle

IT'S A CRYING SHAME.
Tracks: It's a crying shame / Rescue me.
■ 7" . . . . **ABC 4222**
ABC Records / Jul '78.

McCoury Brothers

MCCOURY BROTHERS.
Tracks: Not Advised.
LP . . . . **ROUNDER 0230**
MC . . . . **ROUNDER 0230C**
Rounder / Aug '88 / Projection / Roots Records / Swift / C.M. Distribution / Topic Records / Jazz Music / Hot Shot / A.D.A Distribution / Direct Distribution.

McCoury, Del

Traditional bluegrass musicain/vocalist/recording artist - born Delano Floyd McCoury in 1941 in Bakersville, Mitchell County, N.Carolina near the Tennessee border (raised in Pennsylvania). Del has been ploughing the bluegrass trail since leaving high school in 1956, playing with Keith Daniels and the Blue Ridge Rangers, promptly followed by spells with Jack Cooke and Bill Monroe - a member of Monroe's Bluegrass Boys for 12 months (1962 - 63), singing lead and playing guitar (switching from his usual banjo - for Bill Keith held that slot). Had a spell with West Coast unit, The Golden State Boys, did some recordings on Rebel, with Bill Baker, Bill Keith and Del's brother Jerry as the Shady Valley Boys. Formed his own band, The Dixie Pals, in 1967, Since which time they've recorded on Rebel, the Japanese Trio label (a live album taken from one of their concerts whilst touring there i 1979), Renovah, Leather and now Rounder - where he's done three albums as the Del McCoury Band. In 1988 he also did a recording with brother Jerry (bass) - *The McCoury brothers* . Apart from McCoury holding the position for the last three years as the IBMA's Male Vocalist Award, his band, featuring his sons, Robbie and Ronnie, regularly figures among the nominations. They are regular visitors to Europe, playing Edale's festival in 1993. (Maurice Hope)

BEST OF DEL MCCOURY.
Tracks: Not Advised.
LP **1610**
MC **1610C**
Rebel (1) / '89 / Projection / Backs Distribution.

BLUE SIDE OF TOWN, THE.
Tracks: Beauty of my dreams / Queen Anne's Lace / If you need a fool / Old memories mean nothing to me / Try me one more time / Before the fire comes down / Blue side of town, The / Seasons in my heart / That's alright mama / Make room for the blues / High on the mountain / I believe.
CD . . . . **CD 0292**
Rounder / '92 / Projection / Roots Records / Swift / C.M. Distribution / Topic Records / Jazz Music / Hot Shot / A.D.A Distribution / Direct Distribution.

BLUEGRASS BAND.
Tracks: Not Advised.
LP . . . . **ARHOOLIE 5006**
Arhoolie (USA) / May '81 / Pinnacle / Cadillac Music / Swift / Projection / Hot Shot / A.D.A Distribution / Jazz Music.

DEL MCCOURY.
Tracks: Not Advised.
LP . . . . **ROUNDER 0245**
Rounder / '89 / Projection / Roots Records / Swift / C.M. Distribution / Topic Records / Jazz Music / Hot Shot / A.D.A Distribution / Direct Distribution.

HIGH ON A MOUNTAIN (McCoury, Del & The Dixie Pals).
Tracks: Not Advised.
LP . . . . **ROUNDER 0019**
MC . . . . **ROU 0019C**
Rounder / '88 / Projection / Roots Records / Swift / C.M. Distribution / Topic Records / Jazz Music / Hot Shot / A.D.A Distribution / Direct Distribution.

SAWMILL.
Tracks: Not Advised.
LP **1636**
MC **1636C**
Rebel (1) / '89 / Projection / Backs Distribution.

TAKE ME TO THE MOUNTAINS.
Tracks: Not Advised.
LP **1622**
MC **1622C**
Rebel (1) / '89 / Projection / Backs Distribution.

McCoy, Charlie

McCoy is a multi-instrumentalist, being proficient on piano, organ, bass, trumpet, sax, marimba, vibraphone and harmonica. He's made his name playing countless sessions, featuring on records by performers as diverse as Joan Baez, Perry Como, Bob Dylan, Elvis, Buffy Sainte Marie and Ringo Starr. Mccoy was born on 28.03.1941 in Oak Hill, West Virginia, and took to music whilst only 8 years of age, buying his first harmonica for fifty cents - from an ad in a comic book. McCoy's instrumental tune *Stone Fox Chase* (from his days with Area Code 61 in 1969) gained him an unexpected audience when 1970's BBC 2 programme the Old Grey Whistle adopted it as their signature theme. Apart from his solo act/band he also spent time as a member of Barefoot Jerry during the mid-70's. Making the charts in 1974 with *Boogie Woogie* as a solo instrumentalist, he scored quite regularly through the 1970's - *I Started Loving You Again* , *Orange Blossom Special* and *Release Me* all gaining favourable placings. In 1977 he made the first of a handful of vocal appearances when *Fair And Tender Ladies* made country's top thirty. He also found fleeting success with vocalist Laney Smallwood (who, like Charlie has featured at Wembley's Country Music Festival - McCoy being almost a regular during it's later years). Most recently seen touring with the United Steels of Europe, and after a lengthy recording sojourn with Monument, he's now with Step One Records, where ace steelie Buddy Emmons, Ray Price, Faron Young and Floyd Crammer now also reside. (Maurice Hope)

1928-36 (McCoy, Charlie & Walter Vincson).
Tracks: Not Advised.
LP . . . . **BD 612**
Earl Archives / Jan '85 / Jazz Music.

APPALACHIAN FEVER.
Tracks: Fair and tender / Ladies / Midnight flyer / Ramblin' music man / West Virginia mountain melody / Cripple creek / Red haired boy / Drifting lovers / Ruby / In the pines / Carolina morning / Appalachian fever.
■ LP . . . . **MNT 83516**
Monument / '79.

BOOGIE WOOGIE (Nashville Hit Man).
Tracks: Not Advised.
LP . . . . **MNT 80115**
Monument / Jun '88 / Sony.

GREATEST HITS: CHARLIE MCCOY.
Tracks: Not Advised.
CD **4658622**
Monument / Aug '90 / Sony.

NASHVILLE SOUND.
Tracks: Not Advised.
LP . . . . **MNT 81117**
Monument / Jun '88 / Sony.

SILVER THREADS AND GOLDEN NEEDLES.
Tracks: Silver threads and golden needles / I just can't stand to see you cry.
■ 7" . . . . **MNT 2380**
Monument / Jul '74.

STONE FOX CHASE.
Tracks: Stone fox chase / I honestly love you.
■ 7" . . . . **MNT 5103**
Monument / Mar '77.

YOUR VALVES NEED GRINDING (1929-36).
Tracks: Not Advised.
LP . . . . **BD 602**
Earl Archives / '89 / Jazz Music.

McCurdy, Ed

LAST NIGHT I HAD THE STRANGEST DREAM.
Tracks: Last night I had the strangest dream / Mrs. McGraw / Spanish is the loving tongue / Streets of Laredo / Chisholm trail, The / Whoopie ti yi yo / Jolly old Rogers / Ballynore / Good old mountain dew / Nightingale, The / Poor boy / Venezuela / Acres of clams / Drill ye tarriers drill / Blow the candle out / Midnight special.
LP . . . . **BF 15009**
Bear Family / '86 / Rollercoaster Records / Swift / Direct Distribution.

McDaniel, Mel

Born 06.09.1942 in Checotah, Oklahoma payed his dues working the clubs in Oklahoma, Arkansas, Tulsa, Kansas and Anchorage in Alaska (1970 - 1972), where he'd be doing night gigs - consisting of one six hour set. Moved to Nashville in 1973, working as a staff writer/demo singer for Combine Music, his previous stay had seen him pumping gas to earn his way. Had to wait until 1984 for his first No. 1 *Baby's Got Her Blue Jeans On* . Foot-tapping top ten country hits include *Louisiana Saturday Night* , *Right In The palm of my hand* (1981), *Take Me To The Country* and *Big Ole Brew* (1982). Joined the Grand Ole Opry in 1986. He was to be a regular in the charts - scoring with *Let It Roll (Let It Rock)* , *Stand Up* , *Shoe String* , *Stand On It* and in 1988 *Right Good Feel Real Song* . By this time his music had gradually become more upbeat and hard driving and his Capitol albums *Countrified* , *Mello* and *Naturally Country* were some of the best country products of the period. McDaniel, progressed from his rockabilly roots (to which he paid tribute in 1989 when recording his Capitol album *Rock-A-Billy Boy*), to become one of the most traditional of country music's mainstream acts during the late 1970's / early 80's. It's rather ironic that he was to lose out

M 4
■ DELETED

when new country broke in 1986, Travis, Yoakham and Co stealing his thunder. Now signed to Mae Axton's DPI label, an album *Country Pride* was issued in 1991. (Maurice Hope)

GREATEST HITS: MEL MCDANIEL.
Tracks: Louisiana Saturday night / Anger and tears / Stand up / Hello daddy, good morning darling / Let it roll (let it rock) / Baby's got her blue jeans on / Ol' man river / Love is everywhere / Big ole brew / Do you want to say goodbye.
CD . . . . **CDP 746 867 2**
■ **CD** . . . . **BU 3**
EMI / Mar '88.

McDevitt, Chas

This British guitarist and singer symbolised the class of '57. The American rock 'n' roll explosion had just taken Britain by storm but, apart from the brief rock sounds of Tommy Steele and Tony Crombie, the UK had no real rock 'n' roll stars of it's own until the arrival of Cliff Richard in late 1958. The void was filled by the Lonnie Donegan - led boom in skiffle, an intriguing genre that stemmed from the first UK trad-jazz scene of the early Fifties. Skiffle was, by its very nature, amateurish - all that was needed was a rudimentary guitar, a washboard and a tea chest, plus a basic knowledge of folk and jazz music. Apart from the legions of amateur enthusiasts up and down Britain, there were only four successful professional skiffle acts: Donegan, Johnny Duncan, the Vipers and the Chas McDevitt Skiffle Group. The latter had just one significant hit - *Freight train*, an adaptation of an American folk standard, reached No.5 and logged 18 weeks on the British chart. The follow-up *Greenback dollar* peaked at No.28 in June of that year, Nancy Whiskey quit in September. *Freight train* managed to reach No.40 in the States, an impressive showing for a UK act in those days. McDevitt opened a Freight train coffee bar in London, and installed a jukebox which contained a selection of obscure rock and rhythm and blues discs. The future Shadows star Hank Marvin often visited the bar, and was said to have been inspired by the records he heard. (Bob MacDonald).

FREIGHT TRAIN (McDevitt, Chas & Nancy Whisky).
Tracks: Freight train.
■ **7"** . . . . **CB 1352**
Oriole / Apr '57.

FREIGHT TRAIN (OLD GOLD).
Tracks: Freight train / Greenback dollar.
7" . . . . **OG 9052**
Old Gold / Jul '82 / Pickwick Records.

GREEN BACK DOLLAR (McDevitt, Chas & Nancy Whisky).
Tracks: Greenback dollar.
■ **7"** . . . . **CB 1371**
Oriole / Jun '57.

NANCY & CHAS E.P. (McDevitt, Chas & Nancy Whisky).
Tracks: Every day of the week / I saw the light / Ballad of the Titanic / Greenback dollar / Freight train.
EP . . . . **RCEP 113**
Rollercoaster / Aug '93 / Rollercoaster Records / Swift.

TAKES YA BACK DON'T IT.
Tracks: Bloodshot eyes / Thirty days / Peggy Sue / La bamba / What a crazy world we're livin' in / Freight train / Walk right in / Cottonfields / San Francisco bay / Rock Island line / Tom Dooley / Wabash cannonball.
LP . . . . **JOYS 263**
MC . . . . **TC JOY S 263**
Joy / Jun '76 / President Records / Jazz Music / Wellard Dist.

McDonald, Country Joe

ANIMAL TRACKS.
Tracks: Not Advised.
LP . . . . **FEEL 1**
Animus / Aug '83 / SRD.

BEST OF COUNTRY JOE MCDONALD.
Tracks: Fish cheer & I feel like I'm fixing to die rag, The / Roll on Columbia (based on Goodnight Irene) / Here I go again / Janis / Tricky Dicky / Hold on it's coming / Twins, The / Jean Desprez / Entertainment is my business / Travelling / Love machine / Not so sweet Martha Lorraine / Coulene Anne / Tonight I'm singin just for you / It's finally over.
LP . . . . **GH 865**
Golden Hour / Apr '77 / Midland Records.
MC . . . . **ZCGH 865**
PRT / Apr '77 / BMG.

BLOOD ON THE ICE.
Tracks: Blood on the ice.
7" . . . . **TOUCH 1**
Animus / Sep '83 / SRD.

CHILD'S PLAY.
Tracks: Not Advised.
LP . . . . **RAG 1018**
Rag Baby / Feb '89 / Pinnacle / Roots Records / Charly.

CLASSICS.
Tracks: Not Advised.
CD . . . . **CDWIK 108**
Big Beat / Jul '92 / Pinnacle / Hot Shot / Jazz Music.

COLLECTED COUNTRY JOE & THE FISH, THE.
Tracks: Not Advised.
CD . . . . **VCD 111**
Pickwick / Jun '91 / Pickwick Records.

COLLECTORS ITEMS (First Three EP's, The) (Country Joe & the Fish).
Tracks: I feel like I'm fixin' to die rag (take 1) / I feel like I'm fixin' to die rag (take 2) / Superbird / (Thing called) love / Bass strings / Section 43 / Fire in the city / Johnny's gone in the war / Kiss my ass / Tricky dicky / Free some day.
LP . . . . **RAG 1000**
Rag Baby / Jul '81 / Pinnacle / Roots Records / Charly.
LP . . . . **NEW 87**
New World / Mar '87 / Harmonia Mundi (UK).
CD . . . . **RBCD 901201**
Line / Jun '92 / C.M. Distribution / Grapevine Distribution.

ELECTRIC MUSIC FOR THE MIND AND BODY (Country Joe & the Fish).
Tracks: Flying high / Not so sweet Martha Lorraine / Death sound blues / Porpoise mouth / Section 43 / Super bird / Sad and lonely times / Love / Bass strings / Masked marauder, The / Grace.
LP . . . . **VSD 79244**
Vanguard / Complete Record Co. Ltd.
CD . . . . **VMCD 7301**
LP . . . . **VMLP 5301**
MC . . . . **VMTC 6301**
Start / Mar '89.

FIRST THREE EP'S (Country Joe & the Fish).
Tracks: I feel like I'm fixin' to die rag / Super bird / Thing called love / Bass strings / Section 43 / Fire in the city / Johnny's gone to war / Kiss my ass / Tricky dicky / Free some day.
LP . . . . **LIK 8**
Decal / Apr '87 / Charly / Swift.
CD . . . . **NEXCD 228**
Sequel / Nov '92 / Castle Communications / BMG / Hot Shot.

I FEEL LIKE I'M FIXIN' TO DIE (Country Joe & the Fish).
Tracks: Fish cheer and I feel like I'm fixin' to die rag / Who am I? / Pat's song / Rock coast blues / Magoo / Though dream / Thursday / Eastern jam / Colors for Susan.
LP . . . . **VSD 79266**
Vanguard / Complete Record Co. Ltd.
CD . . . . **VMCD 7306**
LP . . . . **VMLP 5306**
MC . . . . **VMTC 6306**
Start / Jul '89.

INTO THE FRAY.
Tracks: Kiss my ass / Quiet days in clichy / Sexist pig / Here I go again / Breakfast for two / Love is a fire / Picks and lasers / Coyote / Hold on it's coming / Entertainment is my business / Holy roller / Not so sweet Martha Lorraine / janis / Get it all together / Ring of fire.
Double LP . . . . **RAG 2001**
Rag Baby / Feb '89 / Pinnacle / Roots Records / Charly.
CD . . . . **RBCD 9.00603**
Rag Baby / '90 / Pinnacle / Roots Records / Charly.

LA DI DA.
Tracks: La di da / Ring of fire.
■ **7"** . . . . **FTC 143**
Fantasy / Sep '77.

LEISURE SUITE.
Tracks: Private parts / Take time out / Sure cure for the blues / La di da / Hard work and no play / Reaching for the stars / Bo wop oh.
■ **LP** . . . . **FT 565**
Fantasy / May '80.
CD . . . . **RBCD 9.00317**
Rag Baby / '90 / Pinnacle / Roots Records / Charly.

LIFE AND TIMES OF HAIGHT ASHBURY TO WOODSTOCK, THE (Country Joe & the Fish).
Tracks: I feel like I'm fixin' to die rag / Bass strings / Flying high / Porpoise mouth / Untitled protest, An / Who am I? / Superbird (tricky Dicky) / Not so sweet Martha Lorraine / Marijuana / Rock and soul music / Garage / Waltzing in the moonlight / Death sound blues / Janis / Sing, sing, sing / Crystal blues / Masked marauder, The / Love machine / "Fish" cheer, The.
LP . . . . **VSD 27**
Vanguard / Nov '83 / Complete Record Co. Ltd.

ON MY OWN.
Tracks: Not Advised.
LP . . . . **RAG 1012**
Rag Baby / Sep '81 / Pinnacle / Roots Records / Charly.
LP . . . . **INT 147 406**
Rag Baby / '88 / Pinnacle / Roots Records / Charly.

PEACE ON EARTH.
Tracks: Live in peace / Sunshine / Let it rain / You can get it if you really want / War hero / Girl next door, The / Darlin' Dan (the rocket man) / Pledging my love / Garden of Eden / Space lovin' / Peace on earth.
CD **RBCD9.00068**
Line / Feb '89 / C.M. Distribution / Grapevine Distribution.

SUPERSTITIOUS BLUES.
Tracks: Standing at the crossroads / Eunecita / Superstitious blues / Tranquility / Starship ride / Cocaine (rock) / Blues for breakfast / Clara Barton / Blues for Michael.
CD . . . . **RBCD 9.00942**
Rag Baby / '90 / Pinnacle / Roots Records / Charly.

THINKING OF WOODY GUTHRIE.
Tracks: Pastures of plenty / Talkin' dust bowl blues / Blowing down that dusty road / So long it's been good to know yuh / Tom Joad / Sinking of Reuben James / Roll on Columbia / Pretty boy Floyd / When the curfew blows / This land is your land.
CD . . . . **CDVMD 6546**
MC . . . . **MCCV 6546**
Start / Sep '89.

VIETNAM EXPERIENCE.
Tracks: I feel like I'm fixin' to die rag / Foreign policy blues / Agent orange song / Girl next door, The / Kiss my ass / Secret agent / Vietnam veteran still alive / Vietnam never again / Mourning blues / Welcome home / Vietnam requiem pt. 1 and 2.
CD . . . . **LICD 9.00418**
Line / Jun '89 / C.M. Distribution / Grapevine Distribution.

McDonald, Skeets

Born Enos William McDonald on 01.10.1915 in Greenway, Arkansas (died 31.03.1968). After playing the clubs of Michigan, he moved to the West Coast in 1946. Savouring it's heady days of the 1950's-1960's and appearing on Cliffie Stone's Saturday Night Town Hall Party in Compton, broadcasting on KFL radio and, KTTV - TV. Enjoyed lasting recognition through his 1952 Capitol released country No. 1 *Don't Let The Stars Get In Your Eyes* . Later made a top ten placing with *Call Me Mr. Brown* (1963), whilst signed to Columbia. (Maurice Hope)

DON'T LET THE STARS GET IN YOUR EYES.
Tracks: Don't let the stars get in your eyes / Looking at the moon and wishing on a star / I am music / I've got to win your love again / I need your love / But I do / Be my life's companion / Heartbreaking one / All American boy / What a lonesome life it's been / I'll make believe / I can't hold a memory in my arms / Bless your little ol'heart (You're mine) / Big family trouble / Love that hurts me so,The / Today I'm movin' out.
LP . . . . **BFX 15195**
Bear Family / May '86 / Rollercoaster Records / Swift / Direct Distribution.

GOING STEADY WITH THE BLUES.
Tracks: Not Advised.
LP **2C 068 86307**
Capitol (import) / '83 / Pinnacle / EMI.
LP . . . . **HAT 3138**
MC . . . . **HATC 3138**
Stetson / Apr '90 / Crusader Marketing Co. / Swift / Wellard Dist. / Midland Records / C.M. Distribution.

ROCKIN' ROLLIN'.
Tracks: You oughta see grandma rock / Heart breaking mama / I love you mama mia / Fingertips / Keep her off your mind / What am I doing here? / I love you ,I love you / You gotta be my baby / Look who's crying now / You better not go / Let's spend some time with me / Let me know / Smoke comes out of my chimney (just the same) / I can't stand it any longer / Echo of your footsteps, The.
LP . . . . **BFX 15191**
Bear Family / May '86 / Rollercoaster Records / Swift / Direct Distribution.

WEST COAST ROCKABILLIES (see under Cochran, Eddie).

McDowell, Ronnie

Born Fountain Head, Tennessee, raised in Portland, Tennessee. First recorded in 1977 with his tribute to Elvis, *The King is gone* , a scorpion pop and country hit, charting in the top 13 of both. Since then this former commercial sign painter has run up a string of country hits - many delivered in a stance similar to Elvis, a link that was underlined in 1979, when McDowell sang on the soundtrack of Kurt Russell's film "Elvis". During his two year spell on Scorpion he reached the top 5 slot with *I love you, I love you, I love you* . His early years on Epic were steady until 1980 - from which point he was to set out on a run of 14 consecutive high flyers. Only *I just cut myself* a No. 11 shot in 1982, failed to make the top 10. Among those which did were *Wandering eyes* his debut chart topper *Older woman* (1981), *Step back* (1982), *Personally* , *You're gonna ruin my bad reputation* (a big No. 1 in 1983), *You made a wanted man of me* (1983), *In a New York minute* and *Love talks* (1985), his last hit for Epic. In 1986 McDowell signed to MCA, immediately scoring with *All tied up* . His next best effort came in 1987 when

Conway Twitty joined him on *It's only make believe* , Twitty having previously enjoyed a No. 1 pop hit with the song in 1958. (Maurice Hope - August 1993)

ALL TIED UP IN LOVE.
Tracks: All tied up / Baby me baby / I love the way you say goodnight / Let me teach you how to slow dance / Sugar baby pop / When you hurt I hurt / My heart belongs to Shirley / When God made you / Lovin' that crazy feelin' / Whooplah.
MC . . . . **IMCAC 5725**
MCA / Mar '87 / BMG.
■ **LP** . . . . **IMCA 5725**
MCA / Mar '87.

KING IS GONE, THE.
Tracks: King is gone, The / Walking through Georgia in the rain.
■ **7"** **7N 25752**
Pye International / Sep '77.

McEntire, Reba

Born 28.3.1954 in Chockie, Oklahoma. Reba began singing with her brother Pake and her sister Susie as the Singin McEntires at rodeos, where she also competed as a horseback barrel rider. The trio first recorded on the Boss label in 1972, but it was after singing the National Anthem at the National Rodeo Final in Oklahoma City, in 1974 that she was discovered by Red Steagall and subsequently signed to Mercury. Her first success was *I don't want no one night stand* from her self-titled debut album in 1976. In 1979 her rendition of *Sweet Dreams* broke into the top 20 and two years later *(You lift me) Up to heaven* was a top ten hit. Reba notched her first No. 1 in 1982. Other hits include *Can't even get the blues* , *You're the first time* and *I thought about leaving* . In 1984 she moved to MCA and released the album *My kind of country* . For her efforts she has received the CMA's Female Vocalist of the Year award on a staggering four consecutive occasions and also claimed the Entertainer of the Year award in 1986 (the first female act to do so since Barbara Mandrell five years earlier). She made her Grand Ole Opry debut back in 1977 and was made a member in 1985 since which her career has continued to be extremely successful with chart toppers such as *One promise too late* and *The last one to know* (both 1987). (Maurice Hope)

BEHIND THE SCENE.
Tracks: Love isn't love / Is it really love / Reasons / Nickel dreams / One good reason / You really better love me after this / There ain't no future in this / Why do we want (what we know we can't have) / I sacrificed more than you'll ever lose / Pins and needles.
LP **8127 811**
Mercury (USA) / Dec '83 / Pinnacle.

CATHY'S CLOWN.
Tracks: Cathy's clown.
7" . . . . **MCA 1336**
■ **CD Single** . . . . **DMCAT 1336**
MCA / Apr '89.

COUNTRY STORE: REBA MCENTIRE.
Tracks: I can see forever in your eyes / Ol' man river / Sweet dreams / Can't even get the blues / You're the first time I've thought / Only you (and you alone) / That makes two of us / Today all over again / (You lift me up) to Heaven / Poor man's roses / Who? / Gonna love ya / Tears on my pillow / I'm not that lonely yet.
CD . . . . **CDCST 32**
MC . . . . **CSTK 32**
Country Store / Nov '88 / BMG.
■ **LP** . . . . **CST 32**
Country Store / Nov '88.

FOR MY BROKEN HEART.
Tracks: Not Advised.
CD . . . . **MCAD 10400**
MC . . . . **MCAC 10400**
MCA / Oct '91 / BMG.
DCC . . . . **MCAX 10400**
MCA / Dec '92 / BMG.

GREATEST HITS: REBA MCENTIRE.
Tracks: Just a little love / He broke your memory last night / How blue / Somebody should leave / Have I got a deal for you / Only in my mind / Whoever's in New England / Little rock / What am I gonna do about you / One promise too late.
■ **CD** . . . . **DMCG 6026**
MCA / May '87.
LP . . . . **MCG 6026**
■ **MC** . . . . **MCGC 6026**
MCA / May '87.
MC . . . . **MCLC 19177**
MCA / Jan '93 / BMG.
CD . . . . **MCLD 19177**
MCA / Mar '93 / BMG.

IT'S YOUR CALL.
Tracks: It's your call / Straight from you / Take it back / Baby's gone blues / Heart won't lie, The / One last good hand / He wants to get married / For herself / Will he ever go away / Lighter shade of blue.
CD . . . . **MCD 10673**
MC . . . . **MCC 10673**
MCA / Jan '93 / BMG.

LAST ONE TO KNOW, THE.
Tracks: Last one to know, The / Girl who has everything, The / Just across the Rio Grande / I don't want to mention any names / Someone else / What you gonna do about me / I don't want to be alone / Stairs, The / Love will find it's way to you / I've still got the love we made.
MC . . . . **MCFC 3401**
MCA / Oct '87 / BMG.
■ **CD** . . . . **DMCF 3401**
MCA / Oct '87.
■ **LP** . . . . **MCF 3401**
MCA / Oct '87.

REBA.
Tracks: So so so long / New fool at the game / Silly me / Do right by me / Wish I were only lonely / Sunday kind of love / You're the one I dream about / Respect / I know how he feels / Everytime you touch her.
■ **CD** . . . . **DMCG 6040**
MCA / Mar '89.
■ **LP** . . . . **MCG 6040**
MCA / Mar '89.
■ **MC** . . . . **MCGC 6040**
MCA / Mar '89.

REBA NELL MCENTIRE.
Tracks: I've never stopped dreaming of you / Hold on / I know I'll have a better day tomorrow / Don't say goodnight, say good morning / Muddy Mississippi / It's another silent night / Empty arms / Love is never easy / Waitin' for the sun to shine / Good friends.
LP **822 455 1**
MC **822 455 4**
Mercury (USA) / Sep '86 / Pinnacle.

UNLIMITED.
Tracks: Not Advised.
LP . . . . **SRM 14047**
Mercury (USA) / Mar '83 / Pinnacle.

WHAT AM I GONNA DO ABOUT YOU.
Tracks: Why not tonight / What am I gonna do about you / Lookin' for a new love story / Take me back / My mind is on you / Let the music lift you up / I heard her cryin' / No such thing / One promise too late / Till it snows in Mexico.
LP . . . . **MCF 3346**
■ **MC** . . . . **MCFC 3346**
MCA / Nov '86.

WHAT AM I GONNA DO ABOUT YOU.
Tracks: What am I gonna do about you / One promise too late.
7" . . . . **MCA 1136**
MCA / Mar '87 / BMG.

WHOEVER'S IN NEW ENGLAND.
Tracks: Can't stop now / You can take the wings off me / Whoever's in New England / I'll believe it when I feel it / I've seen better days / Little Rock / If you only knew / One thin dime / Don't touch me there / To make the same mistake again.
■ **LP** . . . . **IMCA 5691**
MCA (Import) / Mar '86.
CD . . . . **MCAD 5691**
MCA / Feb '87 / BMG.

McEvoy, Gloria

GOLDEN DUETS (McEvoy, Gloria & Johnny).
Tracks: Not Advised.
LP . . . . **HPE 612**
Harp (Ireland) / May '80 / C.M. Distribution.

McEvoy, Johnny

A native of Bannagher, County Offaly, Johnny McEvoy has been a stalwart of the Irish music scene for over a quarter of a century, having made his impression in the charts with *Mursheen Durkin* in 1966. He's equally well known in the U.K., has toured the USA and Canada on several occasions and hosted the RTE television series *My Ireland*. These days he takes things a little easier and mainly plays the cabaret circuit. (Tony Byworth)

20 GREATEST HITS: JOHNNY MCEVOY.
Tracks: Mursheen Durkin / Those brown eyes / Life of the rover / Long before your time / Three score and ten / Come to the bower / Cliffs of Dooneen / Sliabh na mban / Town I loved so well, The / Daniel O'Connell and his steam engine / Boston burglar / Spancil Hill / Where my Eileen is waiting / Old bog road / Gypsy, The / Nora / Sullivan's John / Rambles of spring / Bound for Botany Bay / Carrickfergus.
LP . . . . **HALP TV 1**
MC . . . . **HACS TV 1**
Hawk / Jun '88 / C.M. Distribution.

20 IRISH REQUESTS.
Tracks: Rose of Allendale / Old rustic bridge / Bunclody / Sam Hall / Wind in the willows / Mountains of Mourne / Bard of Armagh, The / Leaves in the wind / Three flowers / Molly darlin' / And the band played Waltzing Matilda / Ramblin' boy / Slieve Gallion braes / Crick-lewood / Come up the stairs, Molly O / James Connolly / Dan O'Hara / Four strong winds / All I have to offer you is me / Carnlough Bay.
MC . . . . **HATVC 3**
Dolphin (Ireland) / Jun '88 / C.M. Distribution / I & B Records / Midland Records.

20 MORE HITS.
Tracks: Spanish lady / Matt Hyland / Rose of Moray / Fiddlers green / She moved through the fair / Snowy breasted pearl, The / Mary of the curling hair / Whistling gypsy / Hills of Greymore / Avondale / Wild colonial boy / Black velvet band / Sammy's Bar / Flower of sweet Strabane / Alice Ben Bolt / Dawning of the day / Galway shawl / Danny boy / Rosaleen, sweet Rosaleen / Green hills of Kerry.
LP . . . . **HALP TV 2**
MC . . . . **HACS TV 2**
Hawk / Jun '88 / C.M. Distribution.

BEST OF JOHNNY MCEVOY.
Tracks: Not Advised.
LP . . . . **HSLP 005**
Heritage / Jun '76 / Swift / Roots Records / Wellard Dist. / Topic Records / Hot Shot / Jazz Music / Direct Distribution.

CHRISTMAS DREAMS.
Tracks: Not Advised.
LP . . . . **HALP 157**
Hawk / Dec '76 / C.M. Distribution.

COUNTRY FAVOURITES.
Tracks: Not Advised.
MC Set . . . . **DBXC 004**
Dolphin (Ireland) / Jun '88 / C.M. Distribution / I & B Records / Midland Records.

GOLDEN HOUR - JOHNNY MCEVOY.
Tracks: Not Advised.
LP . . . . **GH 570**
Golden Hour / '88 / Midland Records.

GREATEST HITS: JOHNNY MCEVOY, VOLUME 1.
Tracks: Not Advised.
MC . . . . **ARANC 017**
Dolphin (Ireland) / '88 / C.M. Distribution / I & B Records / Midland Records.

I'LL SPEND A TIME WITH YOU.
Tracks: Not Advised.
LP . . . . **HALP 174**
Hawk / Aug '78 / C.M. Distribution.

JOHNNY MCEVOY.
Tracks: Not Advised.
LP . . . . **HALPX 112**
Hawk / '74 / C.M. Distribution.
MC . . . . **RTE 72**
Lunar (Ireland) / '89 / I & B Records / A.D.A Distribution.

JOHNNY MCEVOY GOES COUNTRY.
Tracks: Not Advised.
LP . . . . **HPE 621**
Harp (Ireland) / Jul '80 / C.M. Distribution.

JOHNNY MCEVOY SINGS FOR YOU.
Tracks: Not Advised.

LEAVES IN THE WIND.
Tracks: Not Advised.
LP . . . . **HALPX 164**
Hawk / Jun '77 / C.M. Distribution.

LONG BEFORE YOUR TIME.
Tracks: Not Advised.
LP . . . . **HALP 150**
Hawk / Sep '76 / C.M. Distribution.

LONGWAY FROM THE SUN.
Tracks: Longway from the sun.
7" . . . . **PLAY 257**
Play / Nov '91 / BMG.

MY FAVOURITE IRISH SONGS.
Tracks: Not Advised.
LP . . . . **HPE 640**
Harp (Ireland) / Jul '81 / C.M. Distribution.

ORIGINAL JOHNNY MCEVOY, THE.
Tracks: Not Advised.
MC . . . . **CPLAY 1028**
Play / Dec '92 / BMG.
■ **CD** . . . . **DPLAY 1028**
Play / Dec '92.

SINCE MAGGIE WENT AWAY.
Tracks: Not Advised.
LP . . . . **MCF 3274**
■ **MC** . . . . **MCFC 3274**
MCA / Sep '85.

SINCE MAGGIE WENT AWAY.
Tracks: Since Maggie went away / Losing game.
■ **7"** . . . . **MCA 953**
MCA / May '85.

SINGS COUNTRY.
Tracks: Not Advised.
LP . . . . **HALP 115**
Hawk / '74 / C.M. Distribution.

SINGS FOR YOU.
Tracks: Not Advised.
LP . . . . **PLAY 1021**
Play / Apr '88 / BMG.

M 6 ■ DELETED

■ MC . . . . CPLAY 1021
Play / Dec '92.

SONGS OF IRELAND.
Tracks: Home boys home / Red is the rose / Black velvet band / Maggie / Good ship Kangaroo / Wild mountain thyme / I wish I had someone to love me / Town of ballybay, The / Molly,my Irish Molly / Rare ould times / Streets of New York,The / Travelling people / Shores of America / Bunch of thyme / Irish soldier laddie / Song for Ireland, A.
. . . . MCF 3327
■ MC . . . . MCFC 3327
MCA / Jul '86.

SOUNDS LIKE MCEVOY.
Tracks: Not Advised.
LP . . . . HALPX 117
Hawk / '74 / C.M. Distribution.

STATEN ISLAND.
Tracks: Staten Island.
7" . . . . PLAY 226
Play / '88 / BMG.

WHEN WE DANCED TO AN OLD FAS-HIONED TUNE.
Tracks: When we danced to an old fashioned tune.
7" . . . . PLAY 233
Play / '88 / BMG.

WHERE MY EILEEN IS WAITING.
Tracks: Not Advised.
LP . . . . HALP 143
Hawk / Aug '75 / C.M. Distribution.

YOU SELDOM COME TO SEE ME ANYMORE.
Tracks: You seldom come to see me anymore.
7" . . . . PLAY 216
Play / '88 / BMG.

McFarland, Billy

BEYOND THE SUNSET.
Tracks: Each step of the way / How great thou art / Pastors on vacation.
LP . . . . HRL 140
Homespun (Ireland) / May '88 / Homespun Records / Ross Records / Wellard Dist.

COUNTRY SONGS AND SAD TALES.
Tracks: Hill above the city / House without love is not a home / She gave her heart to Jethro / Wedding bells / Brown to blue / Funeral / Jennifer Johnson / Mansion on the hill / Be careful of stones that you throw / City lights / Waltz of the angels / Deck of cards.
LP . . . . HRL 183
Homespun (Ireland) / Oct '80 / Homespun Records / Ross Records / Wellard Dist.
MC . . . . CHRL 183
Homespun (Ireland) / '82 / Homespun Records / Ross Records / Wellard Dist.

DOWN THE TRAIL OF ACHING HEARTS.
Tracks: Not Advised.
LP . . . . STOL 127
Outlet / Jul '76 / Projection / Duncans / C.M. Distribution / Ross Records / Topic Records / Direct Distribution / Midland Records.

GOD'S LITTLE CORNER.
Tracks: God's little corner / She wears my ring.
7" . . . . SRT 92S3375
Ream / Nov '92 / C.M. Distribution / Ross Records / Duncans.

JENNIFER JOHNSON.
Tracks: Jennifer Johnson / Little Rosa.
7" . . . . HS 041
Homespun (Ireland) / Feb '81 / Homespun Records / Ross Records / Wellard Dist.

LITTLE ROSA (Country monologues).
Tracks: Golden guitar / Don't forget me little darlin' / Old Doc Brown / Pappa sing me a song / Royal telephone / Boot Hill / Mother went a walkin' / 99 years / Old rugged cross / Drunken driver / Little Rosa / Mama sang a song.
MC . . . . CHRL 189
Homespun (Ireland) / '88 / Homespun Records / Ross Records / Wellard Dist.

OLDER THE VIOLIN THE SWEETER THE MUSIC, THE.
Tracks: Older the violin the sweeter the music, The / Santa Lucia.
7" . . . . NRC 02
Ream / Mar '92 / C.M. Distribution / Ross Records / Duncans.

RATHLIN ISLAND.
Tracks: Rathlin island / Mama sang a song.
7" . . . . HS 057
Homespun (Ireland) / Apr '82 / Homespun Records / Ross Records / Wellard Dist.

WHEN THE HARVEST MOON IS SHINING.
Tracks: When the harvest moon is shining / Beautiful dreamer.
7" . . . . HS 074
Homespun (Ireland) / Mar '84 / Homespun Records / Ross Records / Wellard Dist.

McGee, Sam

COUNTRY GUITAR.
Tracks: Not Advised.
LP . . . . ARHOOLIE 5012
Arhoolie (USA) / May '81 / Pinnacle / Cadillac Music / Swift / Projection / Hot Shot / A.D.A Distribution / Jazz Music.

McGhee, Wes

Much acclaimed and under-rated, London based singer/songwriter, who has spent some 20 years in the business. He initially fronted up one of the original pub-rock bands (named, simply, McGhee) before moving on to display his own very distinctive country-rock stylings on the independently produced album *Long nights and banjo music* , released on his own Terrapin Records. Over the years McGhee has maintained his output of highly original albums while spending a lot of his time in Austin, Texas, a place where creative country talent is encouraged. He recently signed a Nashville publishing deal. (Tony Byworth)

AIRMAIL.
Tracks: Not Advised.
LP . . . . TRP 8062
TRP / Feb '81 / Roots Records / Swift / Charly / ACD Trading Ltd.

I'LL BE THINKING OF YOU.
Tracks: I'll be thinking of you.
7" . . . . TRPS 861
TRP / '88 / Roots Records / Swift / Charly / ACD Trading Ltd.

IT'S NO USE BEIN' A FAST DRAW.
Tracks: It's no use bein' a fast draw / How do we get there from here.
■ 7" . . . . CRE 006
Country Roads Records / Aug '81.

LANDING LIGHTS.
Tracks: Not Advised.
LP . . . . TRP 843
TRP / Jan '85 / Roots Records / Swift / Charly / ACD Trading Ltd.

LONG NIGHTS AND BANJO MUSIC.
Tracks: Not Advised.
LP . . . . TRP 7861
TRP / Feb '81 / Roots Records / Swift / Charly / ACD Trading Ltd.

MEZCAL ROAD.
Tracks: Mezcal road.
■ 7" . . . . TRPS 184
TRP / Feb '85.

NEON AND DUST.
Tracks: Whiskey is my driver / Texas £1 / How do we get there from here / Texas fever / Too high to sing the blues / Boys in the band (taught the girl how t'boogie) / Heat of the highway / (They used to say) Train time / Neon and dust / Soy extranjero / I'll be thinking of you / Devil from Del Rio / Monterrey / Cheaters' own blues / Funny where the time goes / No angel on my wing / Loud dirty fast and loose / Half forgotten tunes.
CD . . . . MICD 004
MC . . . . MILC 004
Minidoka / Dec '90 / ACD Trading Ltd.

THANKS FOR THE CHICKEN.
Tracks: Not Advised.
LP . . . . TRP 852
TRP / Aug '85 / Roots Records / Swift / Charly / ACD Trading Ltd.
CD . . . . MICD 007
Minidoka / Oct '93 / ACD Trading Ltd.

WHISKY IS MY DRIVER.
Tracks: Whisky is my driver.
■ 7" . . . . TRP 8171S
Terrapin Records / Feb '82.

ZACATECAS.
Tracks: Not Advised.
LP . . . . TRP 286
TRP / Oct '86 / Roots Records / Swift / Charly / ACD Trading Ltd.

McGuinn, Roger

AMERICAN GIRL.
Tracks: American girl / Russian Hill.
■ 7" . . . . CBS 5231
CBS / May '77.

BACK FROM RIO.
Tracks: Someone to love / Car phone / You bowed down / Suddenly blue / Trees are all dead / King of the hill / Without your love / Time has come, The / Your love is a gold mine / If we never meet again.
■ CD 261348
Arista / Feb '91.
LP 211348
■ MC 411348
Arista / Feb '91.
CD 261 348
Arista / Feb '93 / BMG.

BORN TO ROCK AND ROLL.
Tracks: I'm so restless / My new woman / Draggin' / Water is wide, The / Same old sound / Bag full of money / Gate of horn / Peace on you / Love of the bayou / Stone (the Lord loves a rolling stone) / Lisa / Jolly Roger / Friend / Dreamland / Dixie highway / American girl / Up to me / Russian hill / Born to rock and roll.
CD 4712692
MC 4712694
Legacy (Columbia) / Mar '92 / Sony.

DON'T YOU WRITE HER OFF (McGuinn, Roger & Gene Clark & Chris Hillman).
Tracks: Don't you write her off / Sad boy.
■ 7" . . . . CL 16077
Capitol / Apr '79.

KING OF THE HILL.
Tracks: King of the hill / Your love is a goldmine / Time has come, The (Only on 12" single).
7" 113993
■ CD Single 663993
Arista / Feb '91

LONG, LONG TIME (McGuinn, Roger & Gene Clark & Chris Hillman).
Tracks: Long, long time / Little mama / Don't you write her off / Surrender to me / Backstage pass / Stopping traffic / Feeling higher / Sad boy / Release me girl / Bye bye baby.
■ LP . . . . EST 11910
Capitol / Mar '79.

MCGUINN, CLARK AND HILLMAN (McGuinn, Roger & Gene Clark & Chris Hillman).
Tracks: Long long time / Little mama / Don't you write her off / Surrender to me / Backstage pass / Stopping traffic / Feelin' higher / Sad boy / Release me girl / Bye bye, baby.
CD . . . . CZ 458
Capitol / Aug '91 / EMI.
■ CD . . . . CDP 7963552
Capitol / Oct '91.

RETURN FLIGHT VOL.2 (McGuinn, Roger & Gene Clark & Chris Hillman).
Tracks: Little mama / Stopping traffic / Feelin' higher / Release me girl / Bye bye, baby / One more chance / Won't let you down / Street talk / Deeper in / Painted fire / Mean streets / Entertainment / Soul shoes / Love me tonight / Secret side of you, A / Ain't no money / Making movies.
CD . . . . EDCD 373
Demon / Jun '93 / Pinnacle.

RETURN FLYTE (McGuinn & Clark).
Tracks: Not Advised.
CD . . . . EDCD 358
Demon / Dec '92 / Pinnacle.

ROGER MCGUINN.
Tracks: I'm so restless / My new woman / Lost my drivin' wheel / Draggin' / Time cube / Bag full of money / Hanoi Hannah / Stone / Heave away / M'Linda / Water is wide, The.
LP . . . . ED 281
Edsel / Jun '88 / Pinnacle.
CD . . . . EDCD 281
Edsel / Feb '91 / Pinnacle.

SURRENDER TO ME (McGuinn, Roger & Gene Clark & Chris Hillman).
Tracks: Surrender to me / Bye bye baby.
■ 7" . . . . CL 16065
Capitol / Feb '79.

THUNDERBYRD.
Tracks: Not Advised.
LP 81883
CBS / '87 / Sony.

Mack, Warner

PRINCE OF COUNTRY BLUES.
Tracks: Is it wrong / Dragging the river / Don't wake me, I'm dreaming / Bridge is washed out, The / Love hungry / Talking to the wall / I'll still be missing you / How long will it take / Sittin' in an all nite cafe / Drifting apart.
LP . . . . SDLP 056
Sundown / Jun '88 / Terry Blood Dist. / Jazz Music / C.M. Distribution.

McLain, Tommy

McLain was part of the esoteric music scene centred round the swamplands of southern Louisiana, known as swamp pop or Cajun. Because this vibrant genre evolved in virtual isolation in one particular region, it has never become part of the pop mainstream apart from the occasional crossover hit. One such hit was *Sweet Dreams*, McLain's Cajun cover version of the well-known Don Gibson song. The McLain single reached No 15 on the US national chart in the summer of 1966 and peaked at No 49 in the UK. This one-off pop success for McLain was produced by Floyd Soileau, the swamps' leading record executive. (Bob MacDonald).

BEFORE I GROW TOO OLD.
Tracks: Before I grow too old / Sweet dreams.
7" . . . . OVAL 1004
Oval / May '82 / WEA.

BEST OF TOMMY MCLAIN.
Tracks: Not Advised.
LP . . . . JIN 9016
MC . . . . JIN 9016 TC
Jin / Feb '79 / Swift.

SWEET DREAMS.
Tracks: Sweet dreams / Before I grow too old / Think it over / Barefootin' / I can't take it no more / Try to find another man / When a man loves a woman / After loving you / Tribute to Fats Domino, A / Going home / Poor me / Going to the river / Just because / I'd be a legend in my time / Together again / I thought I'd never fall in love again / So sad (to watch good love go bad) / Sticks and stones / Mu heart remembers.
CD . . . . CDCH 285
LP . . . . CH 285
MC . . . . CHC 285
Ace / Jan '90 / Pinnacle / Hot Shot / Jazz Music / Complete Record Co. Ltd.

SWEET DREAMS.
Tracks: Sweet dreams / Think it over.
7" . . . . OVAL 1012
Oval / Aug '76 / WEA.

SWEET DREAMS.
Tracks: Sweet dreams.
■ 7" . . . . HL 10065
London-American / Sep '66.

TOMMY MCLAIN.
Tracks: Not Advised.
LP . . . . JIN 9009
MC . . . . JIN 9009 TC
Jin / Feb '79 / Swift.

McLaughlin, Pat

PAT MCLAUGHLIN.
Tracks: In the mood / Lynda / Real thing, The / Wrong number / No problem / Heartbeat from havin' fun / Is that my heart breakin' / Prisoner of your love / You done me wrong / Moment of weakness / Without a melody.
CD . . . . CDEST 2061
CD . . . . CDP 748 033 2
LP . . . . EST 2061
■ MC . . . . TCEST 2061
Capitol / Sep '88.

WIND IT ON UP.
Tracks: Not Advised.
LP . . . . AP 021
Appaloosa / Jun '88 / Roots Records / C.M. Distribution / Wellard Dist. / Projection / Hot Shot / A.D.A Distribution.

MacLean & MacLean

DOLLI PARTEN'S TITS.
Tracks: Dolli Parten's tits.
7" . . . . PUP 1
Safari / May '81 / Pinnacle.

TAKING THE 'O' OUT OF COUNTRY.
Tracks: Not Advised.
LP . . . . DOG 1
MC . . . . CORG 1
Singing Dog / Jul '81.

McNeely, Larry

POWER PLAY (McNeely, Larry Band).
Tracks: Not Advised.
LP . . . . FF 218
Flying Fish (USA) / Mar '89 / Cadillac Music / Roots Records / Projection / C.M. Distribution / Direct Distribution / Jazz Music / Duncans / A.D.A Distribution.

RHAPSODY FOR BANJO.
Tracks: Not Advised.
LP . . . . FF 025
Flying Fish (USA) / Mar '89 / Cadillac Music / Roots Records / Projection / C.M. Distribution / Direct Distribution / Jazz Music / Duncans / A.D.A Distribution.

Macon, Uncle Dave

This singer/songwriter and banjoist, nicknamed the Dixie Dewdrop, was born on October 7, 1870 in Smart Station, Tennessee. He built up a considerable reputation as an entertainer in Tennessee and surrounding areas before being invited to perform on the newly launched Grand Ole Opry in 1926. He quickly became the show's first star, appearing solo, with his son or with the group the Fruit Jar Drinkers. He remained an Opry member right up until his death at the age of 82 on March 22, 1952. (Tony Byworth)

AT HOME - IN 1950.
Tracks: Cumberland Mountain deer race / Rabbit in the pea patch / Bully of the town / Mountain dew / Old maid's love song / Rock of ages / Keep my skillet good and greasy / Death of John Henry / That's where my money goes / Long John Green / Lady in the car / Cotton-eyed Joe / Something's sure to tickle me / Chewing gum / All in down and out blues / Hungry hash house / Who mule / No one to welcome me home / Banjo solo / Jenny put the kettle on / Kissing in the sly.
LP . . . . BFX 15214
Bear Family / May '87 / Rollercoaster Records / Swift / Direct Distribution.

LAUGH YOUR BLUES AWAY.
Tracks: Not Advised.
LP . . . . ROUNDER 1028
Rounder / '88 / Projection / Roots Records / Swift / C.M. Distribution / Topic Records / Jazz Music / Hot Shot / A.D.A Distribution / Direct Distribution.

OVER THE MOUNTAIN (1935-38 vol. 2).
Tracks: Not Advised.
LP . . . . OHCS 183
Old Homestead (USA) / Oct '87 / Swift.

WAIT TILL THE CLOUDS.
Tracks: Not Advised.
LP . . . . HLP 8006
Historical (USA) / Aug '90 / Wellard Dist.

McPeak Brothers

MCPEAK BROTHERS, THE.
Tracks: Not Advised.
LP . . . . SAVE 034
Fundamental / Oct '87 / Plastic Head.

McQuaig, Scott

SCOTT MCQUAIG.
Tracks: Not Advised.
CD . . . . UVLD 76000
LP . . . . UVL 76000
MC . . . . UVLC 76000
MCA / '89 / BMG.

Maddox Bros.

FAMILY FOLKS (Maddox Bros. & Rose).
Tracks: Tall man / I'll go stepping too / One two three four Anyplace Road / Did you ever come home (Previously unissued.) / I wonder if I can lose the blues this way / Marry me again / Burrito Joe / I'm a little red Caboose / Coquita of Laredo / On Mexico's beautiful shores / I'll make sweet love to you / Kiss me quick and go / Little Willie waltz / Let this be the last time / Wish you would / Beautiful bouquet, A / Paul Bunyan love / I gotta go get my baby / Let me love you / I've four big brothers (to look after me) / Old black choo choo / Ugly and slouchy / Death of rock and roll, The / Stop whistlin' wolf / Love is strange / Short life of it's troubles, A / Empty mansions / Looky there over there / You won't believe this / I'll find her / No help wanted.
LP . . . . BFX 15083
Bear Family / Sep '84 / Rollercoaster Records / Swift / Direct Distribution.

MADDOX BROS & ROSE ON THE AIR VOL.1 (1940 & 1945).
Tracks: Not Advised.
LP . . . . ARHOOLIE 5028
Arhoolie (USA) / '88 / Pinnacle / Cadillac Music / Swift / Projection / Hot Shot / A.D.A Distribution / Jazz Music.

MADDOX BROS & ROSE ON THE AIR VOL.2 (Maddox Bros. & Rose).
Tracks: Not Advised.
LP . . . . ARHOOLIE 5033
Arhoolie (USA) / Feb '86 / Pinnacle / Cadillac Music / Swift / Projection / Hot Shot / A.D.A Distribution / Jazz Music.

MADDOX BROTHERS & ROSE VOL.1 (1946-1951) (Maddox Bros. & Rose).
Tracks: Not Advised.
LP . . . . ARHOOLIE 5016
Arhoolie (USA) / May '81 / Pinnacle / Cadillac Music / Swift / Projection / Hot Shot / A.D.A Distribution / Jazz Music.
MC . . . . C 209
Arhoolie (USA) / '88 / Pinnacle / Cadillac Music / Swift / Projection / Hot Shot / A.D.A Distribution / Jazz Music.

MADDOX BROTHERS & ROSE VOL.2 (1946-1951) (Maddox Bros. & Rose).
Tracks: Not Advised.
LP . . . . ARHOOLIE 5017
Arhoolie (USA) / May '81 / Pinnacle / Cadillac Music / Swift / Projection / Hot Shot / A.D.A Distribution / Jazz Music.
MC . . . . C 222
Arhoolie (USA) / '88 / Pinnacle / Cadillac Music / Swift / Projection / Hot Shot / A.D.A Distribution / Jazz Music.

ROCKIN' ROLLIN' (Maddox Bros. & Rose).
Tracks: Paul Bunyan love / I gotta go get my baby / Let me love you / No more time / I've got four big brothers (to look after me) / My black choo choo / Ugly and slouchy / Death of rock and roll, The / Stop whistlin' wolf / Love is strange / Short life of its troubles, A (Previously unissued.) / Empty mansions / Looky there, over there / You won't believe this / I'll find her / No help wanted / Payl Bunyan Lovel / I gotta get my baby.
LP . . . . BFX 15076

Bear Family / Sep '84 / Rollercoaster Records / Swift / Direct Distribution.

STANDARD SACRED SONGS (Maddox Bros. & Rose).
Tracks: Not Advised.
CD . . . . KCD 000669
King / Dec '92 / New Note / Koch International.

Madigan, Gerry

TAKE ME BACK TO TULSA.
Tracks: Take me back to Tulsa.
7" . . . . HS 086
Homespun (Ireland) / Sep '84 / Homespun Records / Ross Records / Wellard Dist.

Maggie & Tennessee..

MAGGIE & TENNESSEE EXPRESS (Maggie & Tennessee Express).
Tracks: Will you love me tomorrow / Last train to Memphis / Teddy bear song / Little peace, A / Bonnie Shetland / Rhythm of the rain / Don't forget to remember me / Born to be with you / Tennessee Express / Seasons of your love / I'll get over you / Foolin' around / Amanda / Single girl / Language of love.
MC . . . . CMP 021
X Press / Mar '88 / Ross Records.

Mainer, J.E.

GOOD OLE MOUNTAIN MUSIC (Mainer, J.E. & Mountaineers).
Tracks: Not Advised.
LP . . . . KLP 666
MC . . . . GT 5666
King (USA) / Apr '87 / Charly.

J.E. MAINER & HIS MOUNTAINEERS.
Tracks: Not Advised.
LP . . . . ARHOOLIE 5002
Arhoolie (USA) / May '81 / Pinnacle / Cadillac Music / Swift / Projection / Hot Shot / A.D.A Distribution / Jazz Music.

J.E. MAINERS MOUNTAINEERS (Mainer, J.E. & Mountaineers).
Tracks: Not Advised.
LP . . . . OT 106
Old Timey (USA) / '88 / Projection.

J.E. MAINERS MOUNTAINEERS VOL.2 (Mainer, J.E. & Mountaineers).
Tracks: Not Advised.
LP . . . . OT 107
Old Timey (USA) / '88 / Projection.

Maines Brothers

AMARILLO HIGHWAY.
Tracks: Amarillo highway / Ain't nobody lonely / Honky tonk blues / Love is a gamble / Kay / Dreams of Destree / Farm Road 40 / Time for one more song / Shelley's winter love / Home in Louisiana / Dream spinner / If I don't love you / I like your music / That's alright mama.
■ LP . . . . CRLP 1000
Country Roads Records / Nov '81.

AMARILLO HIGHWAY.
Tracks: Amarillo highway / That's alright mama.
■ 7" . . . . CRE 004
Country Roads Records / Aug '81.

Malchak, Tim

DIFFERENT CIRCLES.
Tracks: Not like this / Different circles / I've been there / I owe it all to you / Sweet Virginia / I wish you had a heart / I always leave my heart at home / That's no way to love / On a good night / American man.
CD . . . . UVLD 76002
LP . . . . UVL 76002
MC . . . . UVLC 76002
MCA / '89 / BMG.

Mallett, David

FOR A LIFETIME.
Tracks: For a lifetime / Sweet Tennessee / My old man / Some peace will come / Night on the town / Hometown girls / This city life / Lost in a memory of you / Light at the end of the tunnel / Summer of my dreams.
CD . . . . FF 70497
LP . . . . FF 497
MC . . . . FF 497C
Flying Fish (USA) / Jul '89 / Cadillac Music / Roots Records / Projection / C.M. Distribution / Direct Distribution / Jazz Music / Duncans / A.D.A Distribution.

OPEN DOORS AND WINDOWS.
Tracks: Not Advised.
LP . . . . FF 291
MC . . . . FF 291C
Flying Fish (USA) / Mar '89 / Cadillac Music / Roots Records / Projection / C.M. Distribution / Direct Distribution / Jazz Music / Duncans / A.D.A Distribution.

VITAL SIGNS.
Tracks: Not Advised.
LP . . . . FF 373
MC . . . . FF 373C
Flying Fish (USA) / Mar '89 / Cadillac Music / Roots Records / Projection / C.M. Distribution / Direct Distribution / Jazz Music / Duncans / A.D.A Distribution.

Mandrell, Barbara

She was born on December 25, 1948 in Houston, Texas and is now truly a show-business veteran, having started her career very young, as a part of the Mandrell Family Band. By the age of 11 she was playing steel guitar in Las Vegas nightspots and two years later, having mastered the piano, bass, saxaphone, banjo and guitar, she was touring with Johnny Cash. In the mid 60's she entertained troops in Vietnam, appeared on virtually all the TV shows and made her recording debut. By 1969 she had been signed to CBS/Columbia and scored her first chart success with a version of Otis Redding's pop hit *I've been loving you too long* but the partnership was not a particularly fruitful one. It wasn't until her move to ABC/Dot Records that her career really took off. *Standing room only* gave her an instant top 5 hit in 1975 and within a couple of years she'd hit top spot with records like *Sleeping single in a double bed* and *(If loving you is wrong) I don't want to be right* . At the same time her fast-paced Las Vegas styled shows were grossing top receipts at the box office and landed her a TV series of her own. After collecting numerous awards throughout the 70's she made history by receiving the prestigious Entertainer of the Year award on two consecutive occasions (1980 and 81) and gave country music a new anthem *I was country when country wasn't cool* . In 1984 she and her children narrowly escaped death in a car accident, resulting in lengthy hospitalization and recuperation. She has continued to have hit records but her career sadly hasn't recaptured the momentum of a decade ago.(Tony Byworth)

BARBARA MANDRELL LIVE.
Tracks: Not Advised.
■ LP . . . . MCF 3124
MCA / Dec '81.

CLEAN CUT.
Tracks: Not Advised.
LP . . . . MCF 3218
MCA / Apr '84 / BMG.
■ MC . . . . MCFC 3218
MCA / Apr '84.

COUNTRY STORE: BARBARA MANDRELL.
Tracks: Not Advised.
CD . . . . .CDCST 36
MC . . . . .CSTK 36
Country Store / '88 / BMG.
■ LP . . . . CST 36
Country Store / '88.

DARLIN'.
Tracks: Darlin' / Tears.
■ 7" . . . . MCA 584
MCA / Apr '80.

GET TO THE HEART.
Tracks: I'm a believer / Fast lanes and country roads / I'd fall in love tonight / Don't look in my eyes / Angel in your arms / For your love / If they grew tired of my music / You only you / Survivors / When you get to the heart.
■ LP . . . . IMCA 5619
MCA (Import) / Mar '86.

GREENWOOD & MANDRELL (see under Greenwood, Lee).

I FEEL THE HURT COMING ON.
Tracks: I feel the hurt coming on / Higher and higher.
■ 7" . . . . MCA 765
MCA / Mar '82.

IF LOVING YOU IS WRONG.
Tracks: If loving you is wrong / Sleeping single in a double bed.
■ 7" . . . . MCA 753
MCA / Oct '81.

IF LOVING YOU IS WRONG (1ST ISSUE).
Tracks: If loving you is wrong / I feel the hurt coming on.
■ 7" . . . . ABC 4255
ABC Records / '79.

IN BLACK AND WHITE.
Tracks: Not Advised.
■ LP . . . . MCF 3140
MCA / Aug '82.

LOOKING BACK.
Tracks: Not Advised.
LP . . . . CBS 32127
CBS / May '82 / Sony.

MIDNIGHT ANGEL.
Tracks: From Saturday night to Sunday quiet / Partners / Better off by myself / Fool's gold / It's a beautiful

morning with you / Pillow pleasure / Midnight angel / I count you / I never said I love you / Slippin' around again / Married but not to each other.
■ LP . . . . ABCL 5206
ABC Records / Jan '77.

MOODS.
Tracks: Not Advised.
■ LP . . . . MCF 3011
MCA / '79.

OPERATOR LONG DISTANCE PLEASE.
Tracks: Operator long distance please / You're not supposed to be here.
■ 7" . . . . MCA 784
MCA / Jul '82.

SURE FEELS GOOD.
Tracks: You keep me hangin' on / Child support / Angels love bad men / One of us is always leaving / Sunshine street / I'm glad I married you / Sure feels good / Just to satisfy you / You can't get there from here / It all came true / Hangin' on / If it don't come easy / Love me like you used to / I won't take less than your love / I wonder what he's doing tonight / I'll Tennessee you in / Alien / Temporarily blue / If I didn't love you / Heartbreaker / Hope you find what you're loving for.
CD . . . . CDAML 3122
CD . . . . CDP 746 956 2
■ MC . . . . TCAML 3122
EMI-America / Aug '87.
■ LP . . . . AML 3122
EMI-America / Jul '87.

WOMAN TO WOMAN.
Tracks: Woman to woman / Let the rain out.
■ 7" . . . . ABC 4215
ABC Records / Apr '78.

Mandrell, Louise

LOUISE MANDRELL.
Tracks: Not Advised.
LP . . . . EPC 32130
MC 40 32130
Epic / Apr '82 / Sony.

Manifold, Keith

Another of the 1970's Great Hopes for the U.K. country scene, Matlock's Keith Manifold appeared on the threshold of success when, first, he appeared on television's 'Opportunity Knocks' (he didn't win but was a popular runner-up to Lena Zavaroni) and, second, signed a deal with DJM Records with promise of exposure in the USA. An album, *Inheritance* , was released, but the record company quickly dropped its' interest in country music (both American and British). This entertaining singer, who also yodels, carried on regardless and built up an entertainment agency to compliment his own activities. (Tony Byworth)

DANNY BOY.
Tracks: Not Advised.
LP . . . . WRS 096
Westwood / Nov '76 / Pinnacle.

REMEMBERING.
Tracks: Not Advised.
LP . . . . WRS 139
Westwood / '82 / Pinnacle.

SHE CAN'T BE.
Tracks: She can't be / Be careful of stones that you throw.
■ 7" . . . . DJS 10757
DJM / Mar '77.

TIME.
Tracks: Not Advised.
■ LP . . . . FER 020
Future Earth / Mar '84.

Mann, Carl

Rockabilly singer/pianist, born 24.08.1942 in Huntington, Tennessee. Recorded for Jaxon label in 1957 and had a No. 25 pop hit in 1959 with *Mona Lisa* on Phillips International (a subsidiary of Sun Records). Toured with Carl Perkins between 1962 and 1964, prior to starting his spell in the American Forces in 1964. He was out of music between 1967 and 1974, by which time he had a drink problem. Scraped into the country chart in 1976 with *Twilight Time* , a remake of the Platters' song, and one of five singles he recorded for ABC/Dot. (Maurice Hope)

GONNA ROCK'N'ROLL TONIGHT.
Tracks: Till I waltz again with you / Gonna rock'n'roll tonight / Why do I keep telling lies to me / Look at that moon / Paradise / I'm left you're right she's gone / No one to talk to / Red sails in the sunset / I'm coming home / South of the border / Mountain dew / Rockin love / If I could change you / Pretend / You win again / Mona Lisa.
■ LP . . . . CRL 5008
Charly / '78 / Charly.

IN ROCKABILLY COUNTRY.
Tracks: Not Advised.
■ LP . . . . CR 30205
Charly / Apr '81 / Charly.

LEGENDARY SUN PERFORMERS.
Tracks: Mona Lisa / Rockin' love / Pretend / Kansas City / I'm coming home / Walkin' and thinkin' / If I ever needed love / Don't let the stars get in your eyes / Ain't got no home / Look at the moon / Baby I don't care / I'm bluer than anyone can be / Mexicala rose / Tbangi stomp / Walking the dog.
■ LP . . . . CR 30130
Charly / '77 / Charly.

LIKE MANN.
Tracks: Not Advised.
■ LP . . . . CRM 2006
Charly / Feb '81 / Charly.

MONA LISA.
Tracks: Gonna rock & roll tonight / Rockin' love / Mona Lisa (master) / Foolish one / Rockin' love (master) / Pretend / I can't forget you (master) / Some enchanted evening (master) / I'm coming home / South of the border (master) / Ain't got no home / If I ever needed you / Island of love / Walkin' & thinkin' / Baby I don't care / I'm bluer than anyone can be / Wayward wind, The (single version) / Born to be bad / If I could change you / When I grow too old to dream / Mountain dew / Mona Lisa (alt.) / Look at that moon / Rockin' love (alt.) / Too young / Take these chains from my heart / I can't forget you (undubbed) / South of the border (alt.) / Kansas city / Today is Christmas / Wayward wind, The (alt.) / Crazy fool / Blueberry Hill / I'll always love you darlin' / Ain't you got no lovin' for me / Then I turned & walked slowly away / Serenade of the bells / It really doesn't matter now / Sentimental journey / Born to be bad (undubbed) / I love you, I adore you / Are you teasing me / Stop the world & let me get off / I don't care / I'm walking the dog / Ubangi stomp / Don't let the stars get in your eyes / Long black veil / Canadian sunset / Even tho' / Chinatown, my Chinatown / Because of you / 'Til the end of forever / Mexicali rose / Hey doll baby / Vanished / Down to my last forgive you / Blue river / Yesterday is gone / Burnin' holes in the eyes of Abraham Lincoln / German town / She was young / Paying for the crimes / Met her in Alaska / Funny way of gettin' over someone else / When the leaves turn brown / Everyday grows sweet with the wine / More to life / Going to church with mama / It really matters / Toast to a fool / I'm married friend / My favorite bunch of roses / Ballad of Johnny Clyde, The / Cheatin' time / Keep feeding her the wine / Let's turn back the pages / If I ever love again / Make a man want to / Neon lights / I'm just about out of my mind / It's not the coffee that's keeping me awake / No easy way to say goodbye / Back lovin' / Annie over time / I've got feelings too / Twilight time / 18 yellow roses / Belly rubbin' country soul / Tennemonk, Georgia / She loves to love for the feeling / Love died a long time ago / Darling of Atlanta / Country was the song / Second guessing / One last goodbye / On the back streets of Dallas / Tripping on teardrops / I love you too much.
CD . . . . BCD 15713
Bear Family / Aug '93 / Rollercoaster Records / Swift / Direct Distribution.

MONA LISA ROCKER, THE.
Tracks: Not Advised.
■ LP 33.8022
Charly / Oct '88 / Charly.

ROCKIN' LOVE.
Tracks: Mona Lisa / Foolish one / Rockin' love / Pretend / Baby I don't care / I'm bluer than anyone can be / Some enchanted evening / South of the border / Kansas City / Ain't got no more / I'm coming home / If I ever needed love / Walkin' and thinkin' / Walking the dog / Stop the world / Mexicali rose / Look at the moon / Take these chains from my heart / When I grow too old to dream / Mountain dew / Too young / Because of you / Ain't you got no lovin' for me.
CD . . . . CDCHARLY 93
Charly / Aug '87 / Charly.

ROCKING MANN, THE.
Tracks: Mona Lisa / Foolish one / Pretend / Rockin' love / Some enchanted evening / I can't forget / South of the border / I'm coming home / Baby I don't care / Vanished / Wayward wind / Born to be bad / I ain't got no home / If I could change you / Mountain dew / When I grow too old to dream / I'm bluer than anyone can be / Walkin' and thinkin' / If I ever needed love / Island of love / Stop the world / Don't let the stars get in your eyes / Look at that moon / Too young / Because of you / Ain't you got no lovin' for me? / Kansas City / Blueberry Hill / Walking the dog / Ubangi stomp / Mona Lisa (reprise).
■ Double LP . . . . CDX 17
Charly / Jun '87 / Charly.

TILL I WALTZ AGAIN WITH YOU.
Tracks: Till I waltz again with you / Paradise.
■ 7" . . . . CYS 1038
Charly / Aug '78.

Mann, Charles

WALK OF LIFE.
Tracks: Walk of life / Borderline / She's about a mover / Hearts of stone / Slowdown / Mama mama / Red red wine / Don't tell me, tell my heart / My life is a lonely

one / I'm just a wondering / Hey baby / She's my kind of girl / You're no longer mine.
CD . . . . GUMBOCD 002
Gumbo / Dec '89.
MC . . . . GUMBOC 002
Gumbo / Jan '90.
■ LP. . . . . GUMBO 002
Gumbo / Jan '90.

WALK OF LIFE.
Tracks: Walk of life / My life is a lonely one / All that's left for me is right.
12" . . . . STEW 1T
7" . . . . STEW 1
Gumbo / Dec '89.
■ CD Single . . . . STEW 1CD
Gumbo / Jan '90.

Maphis, Joe

Guitarist/recording artist/songwriter - born Otis W 'Joe' Maphis on 12.05.1921 in Virginia (died 27.06.1986), known as 'King Of The Strings'. After an initial start in his native Virginia - he played with his father's Railsplinter's Band at 11 years of age. Later he featured while still in his teens in the Lazy K Ranch Boys Band and then Sunshine Sue And Her Rangers. Maphis' crowd-pleasing guitar playing, with his unique ability to play fiddle lead runs on the guitar, coupled with the vocals of his wife Rose Lee (born 29.12.1922 in Baltimore, Maryland) made up the duo Joe and Rose Lee Maphis. Moved out to California in 1951, where he became part of the thriving West Coast scene, helping to form the nucleus for Cliffie Stone's Hometown Jamboree and the Town Hall Party, alongside such acts as Merle Travis, Tex Ritter and Lefty Frizzell. Maphis' amazing picking, apart from being found on his many albums - including Columbia, Chart, Starday and, during his later years, CMH Two. With fellow guitar great Merle Travis alongside, he recorded *Dim lights, Thick Smoke (And Loud, Loud Music)* with Rose Lee and Son, Dale, it's title track being Maphis' most famous creation, although only once has it made the charts - Vern Gosdin's cover reaching the top 20 in 1985. Barbara Mandrell obtained her first break aged 12 which she played the Town Hall Party, on the recommendations of Maphis and Chet Atkins, after seeing her play steel guitar at the annual Chicago convention in 1960. (Maurice Hope)

BOOGIE WOOGIE FLAT TOP GUITAR PICK-IN' MAN.
Tracks: Boogie woogie flat top guitar pickin' man / Fiddle pickin' / Joe Maphis blues / Devil's dream / Old fiddler Joe / Somewhere between / Don't you cry Melinda / Sweet Georgia Brown / Your sweet, sweet lips / Six by five.
■ LP. . . . . CMH 6239
CMH (USA) / '79.

DIM LIGHTS, THICK SMOKE.
Tracks: Dim lights, thick smoke / Mother Maybelle / Eighteen wheels / Down at the front of the mountain / Town Hall rag / Carter county / My baby's doin' alright / Hilltop pickin' / Rocky mountain special / Yodeling bird / You ain't got the sense you were born with / Snowflakes.
■ LP. . . . . CMH 6224
CMH (USA) / '79.

JOE MAPHIS & ROSE LEE WITH THE BLUE RIDGE MOUNTAIN BOYS (Maphis, Joe & Joe Lee).
Tracks: Flowers on the sunny side / Why do you weep, dear willow / There'll come a time / Maple on the hill / Teardrops falling in the snow / Put my little shoes away / Lonesome train / Little rosewood casket, The / Whisky is the devil in liquid form / Speak to me little darlin' / Little mother of the hills / Picture on the wall.
LP. . . . . HAT 3048
MC . . . . HATC 3048
Stetson / Sep '87 / Crusader Marketing Co. / Swift / Wellard Dist. / Midland Records / C.M. Distribution.

Marcotte, Marion

CAJUN FRENCH HUMOR.
Tracks: Not Advised.
LP. 6018
Swallow (USA) / '88 / Swift / Wellard Dist.

FAVORITE CAJUN TALES.
Tracks: Not Advised.
LP. 6004
MC . . . . 6004 TC
Swallow (USA) / '88 / Swift / Wellard Dist.

Margo

One of the top names of the Irish country music scene during the 1970's, Margo is equally well known these days as the sister of the top country/easy listening attraction of the 1990's, Daniel O'Donnell. Hailing from Kincasslagh, County Donegal, she began her career as a member of a local group, the Keynotes, quickly attaining chart success with *Bonny Irish boy* and *Road by the river*. From there she moved on to form her own band Country Folk and established her own brand of "Country'n'Irish", resulting in recognition from around the world and concerts in such prestigious venues as Carnegie Hall, New York and the Royal Albert Hall in London. In 1990 she recorded a duet single with her famous brother, *Two's company* . (Tony Byworth)

18 IRISH SONGS.
Tracks: If we only had old Ireland over here / Old Claddagh ring / Golden jubilee / Cottage by the Lee / Road by the river / Donegal Danny / Cliffs of Dooneen / Boys of Killybegs / Gra mo chroi / Boys from County Mayo / Irish eyes / I'll settle for old Ireland / Slievenamon / Three leaf shamrock / Girl from Donegal / Shades of green / Boys from County Armagh / Any Tipperary town.
LP. . . . . ARAM 2005
MC . . . . CARAM 2005
Ara (Ireland) / Aug '82.

ALL TIME HITS.
Tracks: Irish eyes / Gra mo chroi / Cliffs of Dooneen / Dear God / Through the eyes of a child / Galway Bay / Road by the river / Destination Donegal / Road and miles to Dundee / Shamrock from Glenore / Banks of Mulroy Bay / Girl from Donegal.
LP. . . . . ARAL 1011
Ara (Ireland) / Oct '79.
MC . . . . TC/ARAL 1011
Homespun (Ireland) / '88 / Homespun Records / Ross Records / Wellard Dist.

AT HOME IN IRELAND.
Tracks: Dear old Killarney / Irish rover, The / If we only had old Ireland over here.
LP. . . . . ARAL 1004
Homespun (Ireland) / May '88 / Homespun Records / Ross Records / Wellard Dist.

BOYS FROM COUNTY MAYO.
Tracks: Boys from County Mayo.
7" . . . . HIS 1
Homespun (Ireland) / '88 / Homespun Records / Ross Records / Wellard Dist.

COALMINERS DAUGHTER.
Tracks: Coalminers daughter / Mass rock in the glen.
7" . . . . HS 045
Homespun (Ireland) / Apr '81 / Homespun Records / Ross Records / Wellard Dist.

COUNTRY GIRL.
Tracks: There has to be an end to it someday / Coat of many colours / To Chicago with love / You ain't woman enough / Our last night together (soldier's farewell) / Tomorrow never comes / Lovely Stornoway / I thought I heard you calling my name / Baby's back again / Yodel I love you / It rains the same in Missouri / Memories from the past.
LP. . . . . PHL 422
MC . . . . CPHL 422
Homespun (Ireland) / May '82 / Homespun Records / Ross Records / Wellard Dist.

COUNTRY LOVIN'.
Tracks: Be nice to everybody / Crazy dreams / Hello darlin'.
MC . . . . TC/ARAL 1002
Homespun (Ireland) / '88 / Homespun Records / Ross Records / Wellard Dist.
LP. . . . . ARAL 1002
Homespun (Ireland) / May '88 / Homespun Records / Ross Records / Wellard Dist.

COUNTRY STYLE.
Tracks: I love you drops / Billy Christian / Ribbon of darkness / Once a day / I don't love you anymore / Family bible / Lonely hearts club / Don't read the letter / Gathering flowers for the master's bouquet / Eight more miles to Louisville / Why / Mama say a prayer.
LP. . . . . ARAL 1010
Ara (Ireland) / Oct '79.
MC . . . . TC/ARAL 1010
Homespun (Ireland) / '88 / Homespun Records / Ross Records / Wellard Dist.

DESTINATION DONEGAL.
Tracks: Not Advised.
LP. . . . . ARAM 2004
Outlet / '88 / Projection / Duncans / C.M. Distribution / Ross Records / Topic Records / Direct Distribution / Midland Records.

FROM MARGO WITH LOVE.
Tracks: Roving Galway Bay / San Antonio rose / Hills of Glenswilly.
MC . . . . TC/ARAL 1001
Homespun (Ireland) / '88 / Homespun Records / Ross Records / Wellard Dist.
LP. . . . . ARAL 1001
Homespun (Ireland) / May '88 / Homespun Records / Ross Records / Wellard Dist.

GALWAY BAY.
Tracks: Not Advised.
LP. . . . . ARAL 1009
Outlet / '88 / Projection / Duncans / C.M. Distribution / Ross Records / Topic Records / Direct Distribution / Midland Records.

GIRL FROM DONEGAL.
Tracks: Donegal / Goodbye Johnny dear / Sprig of Irish heather, A / Old rustic bridge / Village in County Tyrone / Noreen Bawn / Isle of Innisfree / Tipperary, so far away / Old flames / Rose of Mooncoin / Doonaree / Green white and gold / Isle of Ireland / My gentle daddy / Green hills of Sligo.
LP. . . . . IHLP 03
MC . . . . IHMC 03
Irish Music Heritage / Oct '87.

GOLDEN JUBILEE.
Tracks: Golden jubilee.
7" . . . . HIS 2
Homespun (Ireland) / '88 / Homespun Records / Ross Records / Wellard Dist.

GREATEST HITS: MARGO (Volume 1).
Tracks: Not Advised.
LP. . . . . ARAL 1005
Homespun (Ireland) / May '88 / Homespun Records / Ross Records / Wellard Dist.

GREATEST HITS: MARGO VOL.2.
Tracks: Not Advised.
LP. . . . . ARAM 2002
MC . . . . TC ARAM 2002
Ara (Ireland) / May '78.

I LONG TO SEE OLD IRELAND FREE ONCE MORE.
Tracks: Not Advised.
LP. . . . . CSDBL 519
Outlet / '88 / Projection / Duncans / C.M. Distribution / Ross Records / Topic Records / Direct Distribution / Midland Records.

IF WE ONLY HAD OLD IRELAND OVER HERE.
Tracks: If we only had old Ireland over here.
7" . . . . HIS 15
Homespun (Ireland) / '88 / Homespun Records / Ross Records / Wellard Dist.

IRELAND MUST BE HEAVEN.
Tracks: Not Advised.
LP. . . . . SMLP 9002
MC . . . . ROLP 1001
EMI (Ireland) / '88 / EMI (Ireland) Records / Roots Records / C.M. Distribution.

IRELAND ON MY MIND.
Tracks: I would like to see you again / Poverty / Tribute to Packie Bonner / Tipperary far away / Born in Ireland / Consider the children / Little town on the Shannon / Man from the glen, The / Rented room / Little white house / Ireland on my mind / How far is heaven.
CD . . . . RITZRCD 516
MC . . . . RITZRC 516
Ritz / Apr '92 / Pinnacle / Midland Records.

IRISH COLLEEN.
Tracks: Not Advised.
MC . . . . BTC 304
Ritz / Dec '88 / Pinnacle / Midland Records.

IRISH REQUESTS.
Tracks: Boys from the County Armagh / Forty shades of green / Cottage by the Lee / Cutting the corn in Cresslough today / Spinning wheel / I'll settle for old Ireland / Donegal Danny / Little sweetheart / Faithful sailor boy / Slievenamon / Shores of Amerikay / Come my little son.
LP. . . . . ARAM 2003
MC . . . . CARAM 2003
Ara (Ireland) / Jul '79.

MARGO'S FAVOURITES.
Tracks: Not Advised.
LP. . . . . HPE 622
MC . . . . HPC 622
Harp (Ireland) / Jul '80 / C.M. Distribution.

NEW TOMORROW, A.
Tracks: New tomorrow, A / All I have for you mum.
7" . . . . IRS 010
I&B / Jul '89 / I & B Records.

NOW.
Tracks: Violet and the rose, The / Country music / Plains of sweet Kildare / Home is where you're happy / Signed, sealed, delivered, I'm yours / Sweethearts in Heaven / Two's company / These are the colours / Forty miles to Donegal / Little more like Heaven, A / Shanagolden / You'll never miss the water.
LP. . . . . RITZLP 0045
■ MC . . . . RITZLC 0045
Ritz / Aug '88.
MC . . . . RITZSC 421
Ritz / '91 / Pinnacle / Midland Records.

TOAST FROM AN IRISH COLLEEN.
Tracks: Thank you for the roses / Bunch of thyme / Little Isle of Green / Toast from an Irish Colleen, A / James Connolly.
LP. . . . . RRL 8018
MC . . . . CRRL 8018
Stoic (Ireland) / Mar '84 / C.M. Distribution.

TOAST TO CLADDAGH, A.
Tracks: Not Advised.
LP. . . . . ARAM 2001
MC . . . . TC ARAM 2001
Ara (Ireland) / Jan '78.

TRIP TO IRELAND.
Tracks: Three leaf shamrock / Shanagolden / Old house / Old Claddagh ring / Cliffs of Dooneen / Mass rock in the glen / Galway Bay / If we only had old Ireland over

M 10 ■ DELETED

here / Boys of Killybegs / Boys from County Mayo / West of the old River Shannon.
LP. . . . . PHL 436
MC . . . . . CPHL 436
Homespun (Ireland) / May '82 / Homespun Records / Ross Records / Wellard Dist.

Marlettes

BOTH SIDES OF THE MARLETTES.
Tracks: Daddy Frank / We can't go on / Country roads / Why don't you spend the night / There never was a time / Together / Kelty clippie / Mountain thyme / Massacre of Glencoe / Bonnie Galloway / Bonnie Scotland / Granny's heilan' hame.
LP. . . . . BGC 312
MC . . . . . KBGC 312
Country House / Jun '82 / Duncans / BGS Productions Ltd.

MASSACRE OF GLENCOE.
Tracks: Not Advised.
MC . . . . . KITV 392
Scotdisc / Oct '89 / Duncans / Ross Records / Target Records / Conifer Records.

MORNING IN THE COUNTRY.
Tracks: Grandma's feather bed / Somebody loves you / Your good girl's gonna go bad / Morning / Happiest girl in the whole USA / Sing me an old fashioned song / Keep on singing / We'll get ahead someday / Let me be / I washed my face in the morning dew / Kiss an angel good morning / Race is on, The.
LP. . . . . NA 102
MC . . . . . NC 102
Neptune / Jan '78 / Neptune Tapes / A.D.A Distribution.

PURE LOVE.
Tracks: Pure love / Some days are diamonds / Tennessee / Islands in the stream / Let it shine / I wish you joy / Liberty / Silver darlin' / Willawhit / Come by the hills / Scotland again / Loch Lomond.
LP. . . . . ITV 370
MC . . . . . KITV 370
Scotdisc / Sep '84 / Duncans / Ross Records / Target Records / Conifer Records.

SONGS OF SCOTLAND.
Tracks: Fiery cross, The / Sing me a song medley / Tobermory bay / Dark island / Mull of Kintyre/Amazing grace / Nut brown maiden / Rose of Allandale / Rowan tree / Wee room underneath, The / Stair, The / Skye boat song / Old rugged cross, The / Roses of Prince Charlie / Way old friends do, The / Pride of bonnie Scotland, The / People all over the world.
MC . . . . . KITV 457
Scotdisc / Dec '88 / Duncans / Ross Records / Target Records / Conifer Records.

TENNESSEE MOUNTAIN HOME.
Tracks: Tennessee mountain home / Blanket on the ground / Every road leads back to you / Silver threads and golden needles / Allentown jail / Farewell party / Sweet surrender / I wish you joy / Wolverton mountain / Did you ever / I won't go huntin' with you, Jake / I'm going to parcel up my broken heart.
■ LP. . . . . LILP 5068
Lismor / Nov '76.

Martin, Asa

DOCTOR GINGER BLUE.
Tracks: Not Advised.
LP. . . . . ROUNDER 0034
Rounder / '88 / Projection / Roots Records / Swift / C.M. Distribution / Topic Records / Jazz Music / Hot Shot / A.D.A Distribution / Direct Distribution.

Martin, Benny

FIDDLE COLLECTION, THE.
Tracks: Muleskinner blues / Sweet bunch of daisies / Alabama jubilee / Home sweet home / Little footprints in the snow / Georgia moon / Back up and push / Flint Hill special / Blue moon of Kentucky / Bile the cabbage down / Salty dog / Fiddler's dream / Dueling fiddles / Somewhere my love / Black mountain rag / Under the double eagle / How will I explain about you / Beautiful dream / Foggy mountain breakdown / Ragtime Annie / Fire on the mountain / Bury beneath the willow / Cotton-eyed Joe / Sunnyside of the mountain / Night train to Memphis.
■ Double LP . . . . . CMH 9006
CMH (USA) / '76.

TENNESSEE JUBILEE.
Tracks: Lester, Bill and Earl / Sunny side of the mountain / Windows in my mind / Will someone be lonesome too / Someone took my place with you / Six white horses / Bonaparte's retreat / Smell good on Sunday / That's a good enough reason / Pig in the pen / If I had my life to live over / Ice cold love / One drink is too many / Crag rock pass.
LP. . . . . SNTF 703
Sonet / Oct '76 / Swift / C.M. Distribution / Roots Records / Jazz Music / Sonet Records / Cadillac Music / Projection / Wellard Dist. / Hot Shot.
LP. . . . . FF 012
Flying Fish (USA) / Mar '89 / Cadillac Music / Roots Records / Projection / C.M. Distribution / Direct Distribution / Jazz Music / Duncans / A.D.A Distribution.

TURKEY IN THE GRASS (Martin, Benny & His Electric Turkeys).
Tracks: Turkey in the grass / I love you a thousand ways / Freight train blues / Dixie on my mind / Wash 'n' wear conscience / Poison love / Oh baby mine / Gentle on my mind / Who's gonna hold you when I'm gone / Mockingbird Hill / Always late / I can hear the hallelujahs in the air.
■ LP. . . . . CMH 6218
CMH (USA) / '78.

Martin, Janis

COMPLETE RCA JANIS MARTIN.
Tracks: Drugstore rock n roll / Bang bang / My boy Elvis / Blues keep calling / One more year to go / Will you, Willyum / Love and kisses / Billy boy my Billy boy / I'll never be free / Love me love / Just squeeze me / I don't hurt anymore / Ooby dooby / Let's elope baby / Love me to pieces / All right baby / Half loved / Please be my love / William / Barefoot baby / Two long years / Crackerjack / My confession.
■ Double LP . . . . . PL 43153
RCA / Aug '80.

ELVIS PRESLEY & JANIS MARTIN (see under Presley, Elvis).

FEMALE ELVIS, THE.
Tracks: Drugstore rock 'n roll / Will you Willyum / Love and kisses / My boy Elvis / Crackerjack / Bang bang / Ooby dooby / Barefoot baby / Good love / Little bit / Two long years / All right baby / Billy boy my Billy boy / Let's elope baby / Love me love / Love me to pieces / William / Here today and gone tomorrow / Teen street / Hard times ahead / Cry guitar / Just squeeze me / One more year to go / Blues keep calling / Please be my love / I don't hurt anymore / Half loved / My confession / I'll never be free.
CD . . . . . BCD 15406
Bear Family / Jul '87 / Rollercoaster Records / Swift / Direct Distribution.

MY BOY ELVIS.
Tracks: My boy Elvis / Crackerjack / Love me love / Good love.
■ EP. . . . . PE 9494
RCA / Jul '80.

THAT ROCKIN' GAL ROCKS ON.
Tracks: Love and kisses / Love me love (Previously unissued) / Two long years / All right / Billy boy my Billy boy / Let's elope baby / Please be my love / One more year to go / Here today and gone tomorrow / Teen street / Hard times ahead / Cry guitar / I don't hurt anymore / Half loved / My confession / I'll never be free.
LP. . . . . BFX 15046
Bear Family / Sep '84 / Rollercoaster Records / Swift / Direct Distribution.

THAT ROCKIN' GAL SINGS MY BOY ELVIS.
Tracks: Just squeeze me / Crackerjack / Good love drugstore rock 'n' roll / Bang bang / Will you Willyum? / Blues keep calling (Previously unissued) / My boy Elvis / Love me to pieces / Barefoot baby / Little bit / William (Previously unissued) / Love me, love (Previously unissued).
LP. . . . . BFX 15032
Bear Family / Sep '84 / Rollercoaster Records / Swift / Direct Distribution.

Martin, Jimmy

Traditional bluegrass musician/band leader, born 1927 1927, on farm near Sneedville, Tennessee. Former member of Bill Monroe's Bluegrass Boys (1949 -'54), lead vocalist/guitar one of many to move up through the ranks via Monroe. Martin has interspersed his time during the early Fifties between recording/playing with the Osbourne Bros (Kitty, King and RCA) and forming his own band the Sunny Mountain Boys, using such acts as J.D Crowe, Bill Emerson, Allen Munde and Louis Johnson (who once made an album with Hank Williams JR). Worked out of Detroit before moving to the Louisiana Hayride. Recorded numerous albums for MCA, alongside some mixed quality Gusto recordings - his famed songs include *Sophronie* and *Sunnyside Of the Mountain* which he did and more on the NGDB's *Will The Circle Be Broken* triple album. Martin, who's contribution to bluegrass music has sometimes been overlooked, has also recorded with Ralph Stanley. (Maurice Hope)

GREATEST BLUEGRASS HITS.
Tracks: Not Advised.
LP. . . . . GT 0003
Gusto (USA) / Mar '88.

SING.
Tracks: Widow maker / I'll never take no for an answer / There's more pretty girls than one / My walking shoes / Ocean of diamonds / Old man's drunk again / Six days on the road / I'm thinking tonight of / Hey lonesome / Truck driving man / Truck driver's queen / In foggy old London.
LP. . . . . HAT 3062
MC . . . . . HATC 3062
Stetson / Jun '88 / Crusader Marketing Co. / Swift / Wellard Dist. / Midland Records / C.M. Distribution.

WILL THE CIRCLE BE UNBROKEN.
Tracks: Not Advised.
LP. . . . . GT 0059
Gusto (USA) / '80.

YOU DON'T KNOW MY MIND.
Tracks: Not Advised.
CD . . . . . CDROU 5521
Rounder / Dec '90 / Projection / Roots Records / Swift / C.M. Distribution / Topic Records / Jazz Music / Hot Shot / A.D.A Distribution / Direct Distribution.

Martin, Lou

RECENT WORK.
Tracks: Not Advised.
LP. . . . . ROUNDER 0214
MC . . . . . ROUNDER 0214C
Rounder / Aug '88 / Projection / Roots Records / Swift / C.M. Distribution / Topic Records / Jazz Music / Hot Shot / A.D.A Distribution / Direct Distribution.

Martindale, Wink

Martindale started his career as a DJ in Memphis while studying for a degree in speech and drama. His deep resonant voice made him a natural for radio, and he eventually moved on to TV with his own show 'Teenage dance party' as well as being the host of game shows. His radio narration of *The Elvis Presley story* series was heard around the world. To the record industry, Wink Martindale will always be known as the man who popularised the religious recital *Deck of cards* . This spoken monologue had originally been a hit for it's writer T. Texas Tyler in 1948. Martindale's 1959 version reached No. 7 on the American pop chart.

DECK OF CARDS.
Tracks: Deck of cards.
■ 7". . . . . HLD 8962
London-American / Dec '59.
■ 7". . . . . DOT 109
Dot (USA) / Oct '73.

DECK OF CARDS (OLD GOLD) (Martindale, Wink & Lee Marvin).
Tracks: Deck of cards / Wand'rin star.
7". . . . . OG 9170
Old Gold / Jul '82 / Pickwick Records.

Martinez, Narciso

FATHER OF TEX MEX (Conjunto, 1948-60).
Tracks: Not Advised.
LP. . . . . FL 9055
Folklyric (USA) / '88 / Topic Records / Direct Distribution / Cadillac Music / Projection / C.M. Distribution / Hot Shot / A.D.A Distribution.
CD . . . . . ARHCD 361
Arhoolie (USA) / Jun '93 / Pinnacle / Cadillac Music / Swift / Projection / Hot Shot / A.D.A Distribution / Jazz Music.

Masters

MASTERS, THE.
Tracks: Josh away / Rambling gambling rag / Night runner / Crying heart waltz / Tyler's tuition / Thomas Jefferson's breakdown / My Louisiana / Waggin' the dog / Ball river / Deep sea cruise / Rocky ford / Kelly Lynn waltz / Whisky chitto / Roadside breakdown.
CD . . . . . CMH 6266
CMH (USA) / '90 / C.M. Distribution / Projection.

Matchbox

Just like another rock'n'roll revivalist, Shakin' Stevens, this British band had to toil away in clubs and halls throughout the Seventies before breaking into the UK national charts at the beginning of the Eighties. Matchbox first charted in November 1979, beating Shaky by a few months; but they were not able to sustain their fame for as long as him. Strictly speaking, Matchbox played rockabilly (the hillbilly rock that emerged from the Southern United States in the Fifties) rather than pure rock'n'roll. This fact was announced by the band's first hit single *Rockabilly rebel*, which reached the UK No.18 position; it was written by lead guitarist Steve Bloomfield. It was followed by *Buzz buzz a diddle it* (no.22) and *Midnite dynamos* (No.14). The group then achieved their only British Top Tenner with *When you ask about love*, a slick revival of a small Crickets hit (post Buddy Holly - No.27 in 1960). At Christmas 1980 the band scored a No.15 placing with a tasteful revamp of the Judy Garland evergreen *Over the rainbow*. Just as Matchbox seemed to be riding high, their success declined during 1981. As they watched Shaky and the Stray Cats shoot up the charts, their own singles failed to penetrate the UK Top 40. These disappointments included another Crickets cover, *Love's made a fool of you* Matchbox's final UK chart entry, the self-penned *One more Saturday night*, peaked at

No.63 in 1982. Subsequent releases failed to chart. (Bob MacDonald).

ANGELS ON SUNDAY.
Tracks: Angels on Sunday / City women.
■ 7" . . . . MAG 196
Magnet / Sep '81.

BLACK SLACKS.
Tracks: Black slacks / Mad rush.
■ 7" . . . . MAG 152
Magnet / Jul '79.

BUZZ BUZZ A DIDDLE IT.
Tracks: Buzz buzz a diddle it / Everybody needs a little love.
■ 7" . . . . MAG 157
Magnet / Jan '80.

CROSSED LINE.
Tracks: One more Saturday night / I ain't taking no prisoners / Crossed line / Mad, bad and dangerous / I want out / Rollin' on / Riding the night / Gatecrashing / Hot loving / Dreamers sometimes do / Mean 'n' evil / Ain't much fun.
LP. . . . . MAGL 5052
MC . . . . ZCMAG 5052
Magnet / Jul '83 / WEA.

FLYING COLOURS.
Tracks: Love's made a fool of you / Heartaches by the number / Angels on Sunday / Lonestar dreamer / Bonaparte's retreat / Whiplash / Babe's in the wood / Don't let the stars get in your eyes / You're the one / 24 hours / Wish that I had never / Arabella's on her way.
LP. . . . . MAGL 5042
MC . . . . ZCMAG 5042
Magnet / Sep '81 / WEA.

GOING DOWN TOWN.
Tracks: Get up and get out / Going down town / Stealing hearts / Nothing to do but rock'n'roll all day / She's hot / Can't get over you / Roller skating Sally / Flip flop floosie / Shooting gallery / Think you took my loving and run / Hot love / This is where I'm getting off.
LP. . . . . MFLP 038
MC . . . . MFC 038
Magnum Force / Oct '85 / Terry Blood Dist. / Jazz Music / Hot Shot.
LP. . . . . SJLP 570
Sunjay / Dec '87 / CSA Tell Tapes.

I WANT OUT.
Tracks: I want out / Heaven can wait.
7" . . . . MAG 238
Magnet / Jan '83 / WEA.

LOVE'S MADE A FOOL OF YOU.
Tracks: Love's made a fool of you / Springheel Jack.
■ 7" . . . . MAG 194
Magnet / Aug '81.

MATCHBOX.
Tracks: Rockabilly rebel / Buzz buzz a diddle it / Seventeen / Tell me how / Hurricane / Everybody needs a little love / Rockin' at the Ritz / Hi-fly woman / Love is going out of fashion / Poor boy / Lord Mr. Ford / Black slacks.
MC . . . . TCMAGL 5031
Magnet / Sep '79 / WEA.
■ LP. . . . . MAG 5031
Magnet / Feb '80.

MIDNITE DYNAMOS.
Tracks: Midnite dynamos / Shocked'n'shattered / C'mon let's go / Marie Marie / Southern boys / Back row Romeo / Green chicks / Lolita / When you ask about love / Jellyroll / We were in Boston / Stranded in Nevada.
■ LP. . . . . MAG 5036
Magnet / Oct '80.
LP. . . . . MAGL 5036
■ MC . . . . ZCMAG 5036
Magnet / '83.

MIDNITE DYNAMOS.
Tracks: Midnite dynamos / Love is going out of fashion.
■ 7" . . . . MAG 169
Magnet / May '80.

ONE MORE SATURDAY NIGHT.
Tracks: One more Saturday night / Rollin' on.
■ 7" . . . . MAG 223
Magnet / May '82.

OVER THE RAINBOW.
Tracks: Over the rainbow / You belong to me.
■ 7" . . . . MAG 192
Magnet / Nov '80.

PLEASE DON'T TOUCH.
Tracks: Please don't touch / All the boys love my baby.
■ 7" . . . . CYS 1074
Charly / Apr '81.

RIDERS IN THE SKY.
Tracks: Matchbox / All the boys (love my baby) / Washmachine boogie / Only wanna rock / In the mood / Crying heart / Let's go crazy / Race with the devil / Three alley cats / Please don't touch / Undeclared / Baby let's play house / Teenage boogie / It's only make believe / Make like a rock and roll / Steelabilly / It don't take but a few minutes / (Ghost) Riders in the sky.
■ LP. . . . . CR 30157
Charly / '78 / Charly.

RIDING THE NIGHT.
Tracks: Riding the night / Mad, bad and dangerous.
■ 7" . . . . MAG 231
Magnet / Jan '82.

ROCK AND ROLL BAND.
Tracks: Rock and roll band / Born to rock and roll.
■ 7" . . . . DNS 1104
Dawn / Feb '75.

ROCK ROLLIN' BOOGIE.
Tracks: Rock rollin' boogie / Troublesome bay.
■ 7" . . . . RAW 9
Raw / Mar '78.

ROCKABILLY REBEL.
Tracks: Rockabilly rebel.
■ 7" . . . . MAG 155
Magnet / Nov '79.

ROCKABILLY REBEL.
Tracks: Not Advised.
CD 4509 91882
MC 4509 91884
Pickwick / Jan '93 / Pickwick Records.

SETTIN' THE WOODS ON FIRE.
Tracks: Not Advised.
LP. . . . . WIK 80
Chiswick Records / Apr '79 / Pinnacle.

THOSE ROCKBILLY REBELS.
Tracks: Not Advised.
LP. . . . . MFP 5627
■ MC . . . . TCMFP 5627
MFP / Nov '83.

WHEN YOU ASK ABOUT LOVE.
Tracks: When you ask about love / You've made a fool of me.
■ 7" . . . . MAG 191
Magnet / Sep '80.

Matsu, Tokyo

COUNTRY LADY FROM JAPAN.
Tracks: Not Advised.
LP. . . . . CMLF 1031
Checkmate / Apr '78.

Mattea, Kathy

Singer/songwriter born on June 21, 1959 in Cross Lane, West Virginia. Kathy Mattea played in the bluegrass group Pennsboro while attending West Virginia University. She first came to Nashville when she was 19 years old and made her entrance into the business by singing demos while holding down a job as a tour guide at the Country Music Hall of Fame. Her first two years with Mercury Records (1983-85) produced poor chart results and, reportedly, she was about to be dropped when *Love at the Five and Dime* became a top 3 hit. A year later she began a run of number ones with *Goin' gone* and with the award winning *18 wheels and a dozen roses* .She was named CMA's vocalist of the Year in 1989 and 1990, while her husband, Jon Reznor, co-penned the CMA's 1990 Song of the Year, *Where've you been* , which was another chart-topper for the songstress. (Tony Byworth - January 1991)

ASKING US TO DANCE.
Tracks: Asking us to dance / What could have been / From a distance (Only on CD Single).
7" . . . . MER 343
■ CD Single . . . . MERCD 343
Mercury / May '91.

COME FROM THE HEART.
Tracks: Come from the heart.
7" . . . . MER 294
Mercury / Dec '89 / PolyGram.

EIGHTEEN WHEELS AND A DOZEN ROSES.
Tracks: Eighteen wheels and a dozen roses / Goin' gone.
■ 7" . . . . MER 268
Mercury / Jun '88.

GOIN' GONE.
Tracks: Goin' gone / Every love.
■ 7" . . . . MER 260
Mercury / Mar '88.

LONESOME STANDARD TIME.
Tracks: Lonesome standard time / Lonely at the bottom / Standing knee deep in a river (Dying of thirst) / Forgive and forget / Last night I dreamed of loving you / Listen to the radio / Slow boat / 33, 45, 78 (Record time) / Amarillo / Seeds.
DCC. 512 567-5
Mercury / Jan '93 / PolyGram.

TIME PASSES BY.
Tracks: Time passes by / Whole lotta holes / What could have been / Asking us to dance / Summer of my dreams / Harley / Quarter moon / I wear your love / Few good things remain, A / Ready for the storm / From a distance.
CD 8469752
MC 8469754
Mercury / Jun '91 / PolyGram.
■ LP. 8469751
Mercury / Jun '91.

UNTASTED HONEY.
Tracks: Not Advised.
LP. 832 793-1
MC 832 793-4
Mercury / Feb '88 / PolyGram.
■ CD 832 793-2
Mercury / Feb '88.

UNTOLD STORIES (A Collection of Hits).
Tracks: Train of memories / Eighteen wheels and a dozen roses / Goin' gone / Love at the five & dime / Come from the heart / She came from Fort Worth / Walk the way the wind blows / Where've you been / Life as we knew it / Burnin' old memories / Battle hymn of the Republic / Few good things remain, A / Untold stories.
LP. 846 877-1
MC 846 877-4
Mercury / Feb '91 / PolyGram.
■ CD 846 877-2
Mercury / Feb '91.

WALK THE WAY THE WIND BLOWS.
Tracks: Walk the way the wind blows / Train of memories / Reason to live / Evenin' / Leaving West Virginia / Love at the five and dime / You plant my fields / Back up grinnin' again / You're the power / Song for the life.
LP. . . . . MERH 104
■ MC . . . . MERHC 104
Mercury / Apr '87.
CD 830 405-2
LP. 830 405-1
■ MC 830 405-4
Mercury / May '87.

WHERE HAVE YOU BEEN?.
Tracks: Eighteen wheels and a dozen roses / Where have you been?.
7" . . . . MER 338
■ CD Single . . . . MERCD 338
Mercury / Feb '91.

WILLOW IN THE WIND.
Tracks: Come from the heart / Burnin' old memories / True North / Willow in the wind / I'll take care of you / Here's hopin' / She came from Fort Worth / Hills of Alabama / Love chooses you / Where've you been.
CD 836 950-2
LP. 836 950-1
■ MC 836 950-4
Mercury / May '89.

Matthews Southern Comfort

At the time of their No.1 smash, this British band consisted of singer/songwriter/guitarist Ian Matthews plus Carl Barnwell, Ray Duffy, Mark Griffiths, Gordon Huntley and Andy Leigh. In 1967 Ian Matthews was a founder member of the highly influential folk group Fairport Convention. He quit in 1969 over musical differences. *Matthews' Southern Comfort* began life as the title of his first solo album, issued in January 1970. Partly written and produced by pop svengalis Ken Howard & Alan Blaikley, the Lp received sufficient critical acclaim to warrant the formation of a band bearing its title. The prolific group released two more albums before the end of 1970, *Second spring* and *Later that same year*. Working in a soft, country-rock vein, these established MSC as the UK's first West Coast type band. To crown 1970, Matthews' Southern Comfort achieved a sudden UK No.1 single in the autumn of that year with *Woodstock*, a cover version of Joni Mitchell's tribute to the legendary 1969 rock festival. The single reached No.23 in America, where Crosby, Stills, Nash & Young had already scored a hit with their hard rock rendition of the same song. In the event, MSC were a short-lived wonder. The restless Matthews broke away from the band at the end of 1970 to pursue a solo career. Barnwell led the remainder of the group, simply known as Southern Comfort, through three unsuccessful albums; the combo died a natural death in late 1972. Apart from a brief 1972 period with an unsuccessful band called Plainsong, Matthews' solo career lasted throughout the Seventies and into the Eighties. With his soft and pleasant tenor voice, he became better known for his interpretations of other people's songs than for his own compositions. Generally recording in a folk-rock manner, he was an underrated cult figure whose only taste of solo commercial success was an American Top 20 single in 1979 with *Shake it*. His limited success was probably due to his temperamental personality, which resulted in frequent changes of record company, management and backing musicians. (Bob MacDonald)

BEST OF MATTHEWS SOUTHERN COMFORT.
Tracks: Not Advised.
■ LP. . . . . MCL 1644
MCA / Feb '82.

LATER THAT SAME YEAR.
Tracks: Not Advised.
LP. . . . . MCF 2686
MCA / '74 / BMG.

M 12 ■ DELETED

MATTHEWS SOUTHERN COMFORT MEET SOUTHERN COMFORT.
Tracks: Woodstock / Something in the way she moves / Blood red roses / And when she smiles (she makes the sun shine) / I've lost you / Once in a lifetime / Brand new Tennessee waltz / To love / I sure like your smile / Wedding song (there is love) / I need help / April lady / I wanna be your mama again / Something said / Dreadful ballad of Willie Hurricane / Belle.
LP . . . . SEE 85
MC . . . . TCSEE 85
See For Miles / Mar '87 / Pinnacle.

SECOND SPRING.
Tracks: Not Advised.
■ LP . . . . UNLS 112
UNI / Jul '70.

WOODSTOCK.
Tracks: Woodstock.
■ 7" . . . . UNS 526
MCA / '70.

WOODSTOCK.
Tracks: Woodstock.
■ 7" . . . . MCA 708
MCA / '80.
12" 2574585
7" 2574567
■ CD Single 2574542
MCA / Aug '89 / BMG.

WOODSTOCK (OLD GOLD).
Tracks: Woodstock / Joy to the world.
7" . . . . OG 9795
Old Gold / Jun '88 / Pickwick Records.

Matthews, Ian

BRIDE 1945.
Tracks: Bride 1945 / Sing me back home.
■ 7" . . . . MOON 53
Mooncrest / Mar '77.

CRYING IN THE NIGHT.
Tracks: Crying in the night / Live.
■ 7" . . . . ROCS 218
Rockburgh / Feb '80.

DIRTY WORK.
Tracks: Dirty work / Wailing goodbye.
■ 7" . . . . K 12150
Elektra / Apr '74.

DISCREET REPEAT.
Tracks: Lonely hunter / Knowing the game / Ol' 35 / Thru' my eyes / Darkness, darkness / I don't want to talk about it / Da doo ron ron / Wailing goodbye, A / Bride 1945 / Just one look / Keep on sailing / Tribute to Hank Williams / For the second time / Biloxi / Carefully taught / One day without you / Reno Nevada / Met her on a plane / Midnight on the water / Seven Bridges Road.
CD . . . . LICD 900 560
Line / Jan '89 / C.M. Distribution / Grapevine Distribution.

GIMME AN INCH GIRL.
Tracks: Gimme an inch girl / Stealin' home.
7" . . . . ROCS 207
Rockburgh / '79.

GO FOR BROKE.
Tracks: Not Advised.
■ LP 81316
CBS / '78 / Sony.

HIT AND RUN.
Tracks: Not Advised.
LP . . . . CBS 81930
CBS / May '77 / Sony.

I DON'T WANNA TALK ABOUT IT.
Tracks: I don't wanna talk about it / Keep on sailing.
■ 7" . . . . K 12197
Elektra / Jan '76.

IF YOU SAW THRO/TIGERS WILL..
Tracks: Not Advised.
CD 5141672
MC 5141674
Phonogram / Jan '93 / PolyGram.

JOURNEYS FROM GOSPEL OAK.
Tracks: Things you gave me / Tribute to Hank Williams / Met her on a plane / Do right woman / Knowing the game / Polly / Mobile blue / Bride 1945 / Franklin Avenue / Sing me back home.
LP . . . . CREST 18
Mooncrest / Aug '74 / Pinnacle / Jazz Music / Projection / A.D.A Distribution / Total / BMG.
■ LP . . . . BD 3009
Boulevard / Dec '79.
CD . . . . LICD 9.00133
Line / '90 / C.M. Distribution / Grapevine Distribution.
CD . . . . CREST CD 004
MC . . . . CREST MC 004
Mooncrest / Mar '91 / Pinnacle / Jazz Music / Projection / A.D.A Distribution / Total / BMG.
■ LP . . . . CREST 004
Mooncrest / Mar '91.

MET HER ON A PLANE.
Tracks: Met her on a plane / Knowing the game.
■ 7" . . . . MOON 27
Mooncrest / Jun '74.

PURE AND CROOKED.
Tracks: Like dominoes / Mercy Street / Hardly innocent mind, A / Rains of '62 / New shirt / Bridge of Cherokee / Busby's babes / Say no more / Perfect timing / Out of my range / This town's no lady.
■ LP . . . . VGC 15
■ MC . . . . TCVGC 15
Goldcastle / Sep '90.
■ CD . . . . CDVGC 15
Goldcastle / Sep '90.

SHE MAY CALL YOU UP TONIGHT.
Tracks: She may call you up tonight / See me.
■ 7" 205 925 5
Rockburgh / Jun '80.

SHOOK.
Tracks: Not Advised.
CD . . . . LICD 900014
Line / '89 / C.M. Distribution / Grapevine Distribution.

SIAMESE FRIENDS.
Tracks: You don't see me / Survival / Heatwave / Home somewhere / Crying in the night / Baby she's on the street / Hearts on the line / Anna / Lies / Runaway.
■ LP . . . . ROC 107
Rockburgh / Nov '79.
CD . . . . LICD 9.00150
Line / '90 / C.M. Distribution / Grapevine Distribution.

SPOT OF INTERFERENCE.
Tracks: I lauter need yfn th 20ru r/ Sh Enthisyocal liyona ubsostight Why am I? / No time at all / For the lonely hunter / See me / Civilization / What do I do?.
■ LP 2383 582
Rockburgh / Aug '80.
LP . . . . SDLP 034
Sundown / Jun '86 / Terry Blood Dist. / Jazz Music / C.M. Distribution.

STEALIN' HOME/SIAMESE FRIENDS.
Tracks: Not Advised.
CD Set . . . . LICD 921193
Line / Mar '92 / C.M. Distribution / Grapevine Distribution.

WALKING A CHANGING LINE.
Tracks: Dream sequence / Standing still / Except for a tear / Following every finger / Alive alone / On Squirrel Hill / Shadows break / This fabrication / Lovers by rote / Only a motion.
LP 37 1070 1
■ MC 37 1070 4
■ CD 37 1070 2
Windham Hill / Apr '88.

Maxwells

COUNTRY STYLE.
Tracks: Not Advised.
LP . . . . SRTZ 77379
SRT / Oct '77 / Pinnacle / Projection.

Mayne, Lynda

MY FAVOURITE 14 COUNTRY SONGS.
Tracks: Rose garden / Tennessee waltz / Crazy dreams / Tear fell, A / I fall to pieces / Just out of reach.
MC . . . . CPHL 445
Homespun (Ireland) / May '88 / Homespun Records / Ross Records / Wellard Dist.

Meal Ticket

British country-rock band of the mid 1970's, the brainchild of Steve Simpson (a stalwart of the U.K. country scene and one-time member of Ronnie Lanes' Slim Chance band). Other original members were Jack Brand, Willy Finlayson, Rick Jones, Ray Flacke and Chris Hunt. After two albums, Three times a day and Take away, the band split up, with Flacke departing to Nashville and establishing himself as one of the town's top guitarists. (Tony Byworth)

CODE OF THE ROAD.
Tracks: Not Advised.
LP . . . . INS 3008
EMI International / Jun '77.

KEEPIN' THE FAITH.
Tracks: Not Advised.
LP . . . . MACH 9
Razor / Aug '87 / Grapevine Distribution.

OUT OF THE BLUE.
Tracks: Out of the blue / Day job.
■ 7" . . . . INT 533
EMI International / May '77.

SHAPE I'M IN.
Tracks: Shape I'm in / Why in the world.
■ 7" . . . . GO 342
Logo / '79.

SIMPLE.
Tracks: Simple / Funy farm / Son of the creature from the black lagoon / Boogie farm.
■ 7" . . . . GOD 330
Logo / Nov '78.

TAKE AWAY.
Tracks: Why in the world / Down on my knees after Memphis / Lucy / Lone star motel / Shape I'm in / Blame / Simple / Bonnie Lee's dinette / At the funny farm / Get on board.
■ LP . . . . LOGO 1008
Logo / Apr '79.

THREE TIMES A DAY.
Tracks: Not Advised.
LP . . . . INS 3010
EMI International / Nov '77.

YESTERDAY'S MUSIC.
Tracks: Yesterday's music / Man from Mexico.
■ 7" . . . . INT 539
EMI International / Sep '77.

Medicine Bow

SINCE YOU'VE BEEN GONE.
Tracks: Since you've been gone.
7" . . . . SINCE 1
Bark / Apr '89 / EMI.

Menard, D.L

French/English guitarist/vocalist born Doris (D.L.) Mennard in 1932, in Erath, Louisiana, and ofter refered to as cajun's Hank Williams - such is his vocal styling. The cajun rhythm machine is another tag attributed to Menard who started out on the road as a part -time musician while only 16. member (1952-1971) of the Louisiana Aces, founded by accordionist Elias Badeaux in 1950 - since to make his mark as a solo perfomrmer. Toured the far east with Ricky Skaggs and The Whites in the early 80's - who also appear on his country/cajun rounder album Cajun saturday night . Best known song being his 1962 creation The back door, his second single - a hit for the Badeaux and the Louisiana Aces of whom he was a member at the time. Menard who also has Swallow , Arhoolie and other Rounder recordings to his name is supported on occasions by fiddler Ken Smith, accordionists Eddie Lejeune and Blackie Forestier and is an experienced carpenter, who for years, at his home in Erath has had a chair factory. (Maurice Hope)

BACK DOOR, THE.
Tracks: Not Advised.
LP 6038
Swallow (USA) / Swift / Wellard Dist.
MC . . . . 6038 TC
Swallow (USA) / '87 / Swift / Wellard Dist.

CAJUN SATURDAY NIGHT.
Tracks: Cajun Saturday night / Why should we try anymore / This little girl / Wedding bells / Judge did not believe my story, The / Green oak tree / Letters have no arms / House of gold / Bachelor's life, The / Banks of the old Pontchartrain / My son calls another man Daddy / Long gone lonesome blues.
LP . . . . ROUNDER 0198
Rounder / Jan '85 / Projection / Roots Records / Swift / C.M. Distribution / Topic Records / Jazz Music / Hot Shot / A.D.A Distribution / Direct Distribution.
LP . . . . FIEND 64
Demon / Feb '86 / Pinnacle.
MC . . . . ROUNDER 0198C
Rounder / Aug '88 / Projection / Roots Records / Swift / C.M. Distribution / Topic Records / Jazz Music / Hot Shot / A.D.A Distribution / Direct Distribution.

D.L. MENARD (Menard, D.L. & Louisiana Aces).
Tracks: Not Advised.

D.L. MENARD AND THE LOUISIANA ACES (Menard, D.L. & Louisiana Aces).
Tracks: Not Advised.
LP . . . . ROUNDER 6003
Rounder / '88 / Projection / Roots Records / Swift / C.M. Distribution / Topic Records / Jazz Music / Hot Shot / A.D.A Distribution / Direct Distribution.

NO MATTER WHERE YOU AT, THERE YOU ARE.
Tracks: Not Advised.
CD . . . . CD 6021
LP . . . . ROUNDER 6021
MC . . . . ROUNDER 6021C
Rounder / '88 / Projection / Roots Records / Swift / C.M. Distribution / Topic Records / Jazz Music / Hot Shot / A.D.A Distribution / Direct Distribution.
CD . . . . HNCD 1352
LP . . . . HNBL 1352
MC . . . . HNBC 1352
Hannibal / Feb '90 / Revolver-APT.

SWALLOW RECORDINGS, THE (Menard, D.L. & Austin Pitre).
Tracks: Louisiana aces special / Back door, The / I can't forget you / She didn't know I was married / Bachelor's

■ DELETED

M 13

life / Valse de Jolly Rodgers / Miller's cave / Water pump, The / It's too late you're divorced / Riches of a musician / Vail and the crown, The / I can live a better life / Rebecca Ann / Two step de bayou teche / Opelousas waltz / Two step a tante adele / Rainbow waltz / Rene's special / Grand mamou blues / Flumes d'enfer / Chinaball blues / Le pauvre hobo / Pretty rosie cheeks / Don't shake my tree / La valse d'amour / Jungle club waltz / J'ai coiner a ta porte / Chataigner waltz.
CD . . . . **CDCHD 327**
Ace / Jul '91 / Pinnacle / Hot Shot / Jazz Music / Complete Record Co. Ltd.

Merle & Roy

REQUESTS.
Tracks: Not Advised.
LP . . . . **RMBR 8713**
Mynod Mawr / Sep '87.

UNTIL WE MEET AGAIN...
Tracks: Let your love flow / Always on my mind / It keeps right on a-hurtin' / Somewhere my love / You keep me hangin' on / Just a closer walk with thee / Don't forget to remember / When your old wedding ring was new / Harbour lights / I can't stop loving you / Sunshine of your smile, The / Forty shades of green / In the chapel in the moonlight / Home is where you're happy / May the road rise to meet you.
LP . . . . **GRALP 31**
MC . . . . **GRTC 31**
Grasmere / Aug '88 / Target Records / Savoy Records.

Merrell, Ray

BIG COUNTRY.
Tracks: Riders in the sky / One day at a time / Movin' on down to Nashville / I recall a gypsy woman / I love you because / He'll have to go / I won't forget you / Snowbird / Take me home country roads / Lucille / I believe / Make the world go away / High noon / Big John Wayne / Old rugged cross, The.
LP . . . . **PRX 18**
MC . . . . **TC PRX 18**
President / Dec '80 / Grapevine Distribution / Target Records / Jazz Music / Taylors.

BIG JOHN WAYNE.
Tracks: Big John Wayne / Movin' on down.
7" . . . . **PT 493**
President / Apr '81 / Grapevine Distribution / Target Records / Jazz Music / Taylors.

BINGO COWBOYS.
Tracks: Bingo cowboys / Seeds.
7" . . . . **PT 508**
President / Sep '82 / Grapevine Distribution / Target Records / Jazz Music / Taylors.

CITY GIRL.
Tracks: City girl / Ghost of love.
■ **7"** . . . . **PT 473**
President / May '78.

DISCO COUNTRY STYLE.
Tracks: City girl / Freight train / Green green grass of home / Two little pieces of heaven / Red chimneys / Distant drums / My prayer / Send me the pillow that you dream on / How lucky you are / Ghost of love / Morning has broken / Jezebel.
LP . . . . **PRX 6**
President / Apr '84 / Grapevine Distribution / Target Records / Jazz Music / Taylors.

I WILL LOVE YOU.
Tracks: I will love you / Little white lies.
7" . . . . **RM 005**
Satril / Dec '83 / Henry Hadaway Organisation.

SEEDS OF LOVE.
Tracks: My mother's eyes / Door is still open, The / Every step I made / Seed / Bingo cowboys / Crystal chandeliers / You're my best friend / Touch my heart / Sixteen tons / Apartment No.9 / Love me tender.
LP . . . . **PRX 20**
President / Feb '82 / Grapevine Distribution / Target Records / Jazz Music / Taylors.

TEARS OF JOY.
Tracks: Tears of joy.
■ **7"** . . . . **BOY 22**
Jay Boy / '70.

Merrill, Buddy

25 GREAT HITS.
Tracks: Not Advised.
Double LP . . . . **GNPS 2-5038**
GNP Crescendo / '88 / Swift / Silva Screen / Flexitron Ltd.

BEST OF BUDDY MERRILL.
Tracks: Not Advised.
LP . . . . **GNPS 5030**
MC **GNP5 5030**
GNP Crescendo / '88 / Swift / Silva Screen / Flexitron Ltd.

BEYOND THE REEF HAWAIIAN.
Tracks: Not Advised.
LP . . . . **GNPS 5034**
GNP Crescendo / '88 / Swift / Silva Screen / Flexitron Ltd.

STEEL GUITAR COUNTRY.
Tracks: Not Advised.
LP . . . . **GNPS 5036**
GNP Crescendo / '88 / Swift / Silva Screen / Flexitron Ltd.

SWEET SEPTEMBER.
Tracks: Sweet September / Sherk, The.
■ **7"** . . . . **VN 9261**
Vocalion / '65.

Messer, Michael

DIVING DUCK.
Tracks: Write me a few short lines / Hum hum dinger from Dingersville / Milk cow blues / Secret to a long life, The / Minnetonka stomp / Wild Canadian swan / If you were the river / Hula girl / Rollin' and tumblin' / Shouldn't do that / Brownsville blues / Death letter.
CD . . . . **MICD 002**
Minidoka / Jun '88 / ACD Trading Ltd.
MC . . . . **PTLC 002**
P.T. Music / Jun '88 / ACD Trading Ltd.
■ **LP** . . . . **PTLP 002**
P.T. Music / Jun '88.

HUMMINGBIRD.
Tracks: Hummingbird.
■ **CD Single** . . . . **M 1002**
Minidoka / '90 / ACD Trading Ltd.

SLIDEDANCE (Messer, Michael Band).
Tracks: Lone wolf, The / Hummingbird / What life brings / Hilo / Cherry blossom Hawaiian agency / Rolling in my sweet baby's arms / Dead sea scrolls / Doghouse / Savannah le mar / Sweetheart darling / Mannish boy.
CD . . . . **MICD 003**
MC . . . . **MILC 003**
Minidoka / Jan '91 / ACD Trading Ltd.

Meyers, Augie

AUGIE'S BACK.
Tracks: Not Advised.
LP . . . . **SNTF 955**
Sonet / Mar '86 / Swift / C.M. Distribution / Roots Records / Jazz Music / Sonet Records / Cadillac Music / Projection / Wellard Dist. / Hot Shot.

AUGUST IN NEW YORK.
Tracks: Baby of mine / Before I grow too old / Don't turn away / Looking for the money / Cruisin' (on a Saturday night) / I'm not someone you want / All my life / Missing you / Sugar blue / Money / To nothing at all.
LP . . . . **SNTF 910**
Sonet / Mar '84 / Swift / C.M. Distribution / Roots Records / Jazz Music / Sonet Records / Cadillac Music / Projection / Wellard Dist. / Hot Shot.

FINALLY IN LIGHTS (Meyers, Augie & Doug Shams).
Tracks: Release me / Deep in the heart of Texas / Cryin' out loud / It's alright / My friend / Sky high / Deed to Texas / Miller's cave / Don't let me / Baby, baby.
LP . . . . **SNTF 803**
Sonet / Nov '79 / Swift / C.M. Distribution / Roots Records / Jazz Music / Sonet Records / Cadillac Music / Projection / Wellard Dist. / Hot Shot.

I'M NOT SOMEONE YOU WANT.
Tracks: I'm not someone you want / Money.
7" . . . . **SON 2264**
Sonet / Apr '84 / Swift / C.M. Distribution / Roots Records / Jazz Music / Sonet Records / Cadillac Music / Projection / Wellard Dist. / Hot Shot.

JUST YOU AND ME.
Tracks: Just you and me / Sitting up all night.
7" . . . . **SON 2242**
Sonet / May '82 / Swift / C.M. Distribution / Roots Records / Jazz Music / Sonet Records / Cadillac Music / Projection / Wellard Dist. / Hot Shot.

SAN ANTONIO SATURDAY NIGHT.
Tracks: Not Advised.
LP . . . . **SNTF 933**
Sonet / Jan '86 / Swift / C.M. Distribution / Roots Records / Jazz Music / Sonet Records / Cadillac Music / Projection / Wellard Dist. / Hot Shot.

STILL GROWING.
Tracks: Not Advised.
LP . . . . **SNTF 883**
Sonet / May '82 / Swift / C.M. Distribution / Roots Records / Jazz Music / Sonet Records / Cadillac Music / Projection / Wellard Dist. / Hot Shot.

YOU'RE ON MY MIND.
Tracks: You're on my mind / Peace of mind.
7" . . . . **SON 2301**
Sonet / Apr '86 / Swift / C.M. Distribution / Roots Records / Jazz Music / Sonet Records / Cadillac Music / Projection / Wellard Dist. / Hot Shot.

Midnite Ramblers

ALWAYS LEAVING.
Tracks: I've got a yearning / Back home again / Put another log on the fire / Drift away / Crazy arms / City of New Orleans / Unmitigated gall / Good time Charlie's got the blues / Too many bridges / Someone to give my love to / Ram jig / Kentucky gambler / Always leaving.
LP . . . . **FHR 097**
Folk Heritage / Jul '82 / Terry Blood Dist.

MIDNITE RAMBLERS, THE.
Tracks: Love of the common people / Streets of Baltimore / Teach your children / Anne / Midnite breakdown / Send tomorrow to the moon / Ride me down easy / Ruby / Cotton Jenny / Shelly's winter love / Kentucky woman / Sundown.
LP . . . . **FHR 064**
Folk Heritage / Jul '82 / Terry Blood Dist.

ONE NIGHT STAND.
Tracks: Redwood hill / Little green apples / Divorce / Good old days / What's your mamma's name child / Shutters and boards / Omaha / Mrs. Jones your daughter cried all night / What made Milwaukee famous / Yakety axe / Sunday morning coming down / One night stand.
LP . . . . **FHR 076**
Folk Heritage / Jul '82 / Terry Blood Dist.

Miki & Griff

The husband and wife team of Barbara and Emyr Griffith met while members of the George Mitchell Choir and were married in 1950. They were, of course, better known as Miki and Griff, and developed into one of the U.K's most beloved country/easy listening acts, having first become aware of country music via the recordings of the Everly Brothers and the Louvin Brothers. They secured a deal with Pye Records thanks to Lonnie Donegan, enjoyed a run of chart successes - *Hold back tomorrow* , *Rockin' alone (in an old rockin' chair)* , *Little bitty tear* and *I wanna stay here* - and were regularly seen on TV variety shows during the 1960's. They furthered their connections with country music by visiting Nashville in 1964, receiving a standing ovation when they appeared at the Grand Ole Opry, and by the early 1970's were gaining the appreciation of British country music fans. Over the subsequent years they toured with several American acts and worked the country venues, as well as maintaining a regular schedule of album releases. Since Miki's death in 1981, Griff no longer performs but still puts his entertaining skills to fine use as a hospital visitor. (Tony Byworth)

AT HOME WITH MIKI AND GRIFF.
Tracks: Born to be with you / Please Mr. Conductor / Way old friends do, The / Old rugged cross, The / My grandfather's clock / Loves old sweet song / He stopped loving her today / Nobody's child / Please help me, I'm falling / Wino the clown / Love lifted me / Who's your friend / Your cheatin' heart / Lonely in a crowd.
LP . . . . **ITV 425**
MC . . . . **KITV 425**
Scotdisc / Aug '87 / Duncans / Ross Records / Target Records / Conifer Records.

BEST OF MIKI AND GRIFF.
Tracks: Walk through this world / You're my best friend / Country roads / These hands / I have to say I love you in a song / You lay so easy on my mind / Even the bad times are good / Baptism of Jesse Taylor, The / Streets of London / Shelly's winter love / Before the day is done / One day at a time / For the good times / I thought I'd drop by (and pick up the pieces) / Annie's song / When I stop dreaming / Crying time / Top of the world / Let it be me / Making believe / God was here / Tell me my lying eyes were wrong / Blowin' in the wind.
LP . . . . **COMP 8**
MC . . . . **ZCCOM 8**
PRT / Jun '83 / BMG.

BOWLING GREEN.
Tracks: Bowling green / Lean on me.
■ **7"** **7N 46123**
Pye / Nov '78.

COUNTRY.
Tracks: Bowling green / Please don't tell me how the story ends / I thought I'd drop by (and pick up the pieces) / When I need you / God was here (but I think he left early) / I'd rather be sorry / When I stop dreaming / Highway leading nowhere, The / Making believe / Sad songs and waltzes / Nothing but silence / Some broken hearts never mend / Lean on me (if you're ever gonna fall).
LP . . . . **NSPL 18588**
■ **MC** . . . . **ZCP 18588**
Pye / '78.

COUNTRY IS.
Tracks: Country is / For the good times / Baptism of Jesse Taylor, The / Never grow old / You lay so easy on my mind / Pass me by / I will care for you love / World needs a melody, The / Shelly's winter love / Before this day is done / Autumn leaves / Family bible / We're not getting old (we're getting better).
LP . . . . **PKL 5522**
Pye Special / Feb '75.

ETCHINGS.
Tracks: Not Advised.
LP . . . . **NSPL 18533**
Pye / Oct '77.

GOLDEN HOUR OF MIKI AND GRIFF.
Tracks: Rockin' alone (in an old rocking chair) / We should be together / It's my way / Amazing Grace / Worst is yet to come, The / All for the love of a girl / I

M 14

■ DELETED

don't know / We could / Never be anyone else but you / Po' folks / Someday you'll call my name / Mad, mad world / Crying time / Everybody but me / Waltz of the angels / I never will marry / Changing partners / When I was young / I've just told Mama goodbye / Satisfied mind, A / These hands / Pretty country / Be careful of the stones you throw / Storybook children.
LP. . . . . GH 573
Golden Hour / Midland Records.
■ MC . . . . ZCGH 631
Golden Hour / '78 / Midland Records.

HOLD BACK TOMORROW.
Tracks: Hold back tomorrow.
■ 7" 7N 15213
Pye / Oct '59.

I WANNA STAY HERE.
Tracks: I wanna stay here.
■ 7" 7N 15555
Pye / Aug '63.

LITTLE BITTY TEAR.
Tracks: Little bitty tear, A.
■ 7" 7N 15412
Pye / Feb '62.

LITTLE BITTY TEAR.
Tracks: Not Advised.
CD . . . . SSLCD 203
MC . . . . SSLMC 203
Savanna / Jan '93 / Crusader Marketing Co. / Prism Leisure PLC / Duncans.

MIKI & GRIFF.
Tracks: Not Advised.
CD . . . . MATCD 259
MC . . . . MATMC 259
Castle / Apr '93 / BMG.

ROCKIN' ALONE.
Tracks: Rockin' alone.
■ 7" 7N 15296
Pye / Oct '60.

THIS IS MIKI, THIS IS GRIFF.
Tracks: We've got it all together now / I recall a gypsy woman / Sunshine on my shoulder / I wouldn't want to live / If teardrops were pennies / Over the rainbow / Let your love flow / Blowin' in the wind / Master's bouquet / Don't it make you wanna go home / Don't you believe / Take me home country roads / Sentimental journey.
■ LP. . . . . PKL 5547
Pye / '78.

WORLD NEEDS A MELODY.
Tracks: World needs a melody / Before this day is done.
■ 7" 7N 45438
Pye / Feb '75.

Miles, Luke 'Long Gone'

COUNTRY BOY.
Tracks: Not Advised.
■ LP. . . . . CG 709-05
Sundown (Import) / Oct '82.
LP. . . . . SG 709-05
Sundown (Import) / Dec '88 / Making Waves.

Miller, Frankie

HEY WHERE YA GOIN'.
Tracks: I don't know why I love you / Day by day / It's not big thing to me / What have I ever done (Previously unissued.) / My wedding song to you / You're crying on my shoulder again / Hey where ya goin' / Paid in full / You don't show me much / Paint powder and perfume / You'll never be true / What you do from now on.
LP. . . . . BFX 15082
Bear Family / Sep '84 / Rollercoaster Records / Swift / Direct Distribution.

Miller, Jay

JAY MILLER STUDIO BAND 1961-63.
Tracks: Not Advised.
LP. . . . . FLY 608
Flyright / Jul '85 / Hot Shot / Roots Records / Wellard Dist. / Charly / Swift / Projection.

Miller, Jody

HOME OF THE BRAVE.
Tracks: Home of the brave.
■ 7" . . . . CL 15415
Capitol / Oct '65.

Miller, Mary

ON THE ROAD (Miller, Mary & Saratoga Freeway).
Tracks: Not Advised.
LP. . . . . LKLP 6556
Look / '88 / C.M. Distribution.

Miller, Ned

This American singer, songwriter and guitarist was born in Raines, Utah in 1925. After periods as a US marine and as a pipefitter, he enjoyed success in 1957 as writer of *Dark Moon*. This song was simultaneously in the American Top 10 for both Bonnie Guitar and Gale Storm; in Britain, it was successfully covered by Tony Brent.In that same year Miller decided to record his own version of another of his songs, *From A Jack To A King*. This single was initially a flop, but it suddenly became a big hit when re-issued in 1963: it reached No. 6 in the States and zoomed to No. 2 in Britain.Working in a country bop vein, Miller chalked up success as a singer and more often as a songwriter on the US C&W charts during the late Fifties and the Sixties. Amongst his better known compositions were *Invisible Tears*, *Southbound* and *Do What You Do Well*; the latter gave him a UK No. 48 hit in 1965.(Bob MacDonald).

DO WHAT YOU DO DO WELL.
Tracks: Do what you do do well.
■ 7" . . . . HL 9937
London-American / Feb '65.

FROM A JACK TO A KING.
Tracks: From a jack to a king / Parade of broken hearts.
■ 7" . . . . HL 9648
London-American / Feb '63.
■ 7" . . . . F 13910
Decca / Mar '82.

FROM A JACK TO A KING.
Tracks: From a jack to a king / Parade of broken hearts / Turn around / Lights in the street / Old mother nature and old father time / Rollin' o' rollin' stone / One among the many / Man behind the gun, The / Another fool like me / Magic moon / Sunday morning tears / Big love / Old restless ocean / Invisible tears / Do what you do do well / Dusty guitar / Just before dawn / Go on back you fool / Dark moon / Cold grey bars / My heart waits at the door / Big lie, The / Heart without a heartache / Billy Carino / Cry of the wild goose / Long shadow / Mona Lisa / Stage coach / You belong to my heart / King of fools / Girl across the table.
CD . . . . BCD 15496
Bear Family / Feb '91 / Rollercoaster Records / Swift / Direct Distribution.

FROM A JACK TO A KING (OLD GOLD).
Tracks: From a jack to a king / Do what you do do well.
■ 7" . . . . OG 9340
Old Gold / Oct '83.

Miller, Roger

Roger Miller was a true original, a singer whose voice was refreshingly different and a songwriter whose work was to ring the changes in Nashville's country music circles. His great success helped open up the doorways for the likes of Kris Kristofferson, Chris Gantry and John Hartford, all waiting for their songs to be heard. Equally important, he possessed a great sense of humour that was reflected in his writing, stage routines and life generally. He was born in Fort Worth, Texas on January 2, 1936 and grew up in Erick, Oklahoma, with Hank Williams being the influence for him to seek out a country music career. After his discharge from the Army, Miller headed for Nashville, where he stayed the first night at the Andrew Jackson Hotel and, reputedly, asked for the job of bellhop the next day. At the same time he started putting his songs around town. Ray Price was the first artist to record a Miller original *Invitation to the blues*, in 1958, and found him a job in his band, as did Faron Young later. The next artists to enjoy success with one of his songs were Jim Reeves (*Billy Bayou*) and Ernest Tubb (*Half a mind*) . As a recording artist Miller achieved a top 10 hit with *When two worlds collide* on RCA in 1961, but three years later - on Smash Records - he cast all songwriting logic aside and staggered both the country and pop music circles with such offerings as *Chug-a-lug* , *Dang me* and *King of the road* . The results were not only several million sales but 11 Grammy awards in two years (1964-65). (To date only Michael Jackson has beaten Miller's record with more awards in one year). Sadly these were Roger Miller's true glory days in chart terms, though he moved on to successes in other fields. Working in the wider world of showbiz he provided the soundtracks for the comic western *Waterhole 3* (1967) and Disney's *Robin Hood* (1973) and, in 1982, created the Broadway musical *Big River* , based on Mark Twain's *Adventures of Huckleberry Finn* . Miller described the show as the biggest piece of work he'd ever attempted, and it went on to win seven Tony Awards. The original cast album, on MCA, was the first of its kind ever to be recorded in Nashville. Roger Miller, who died on October 25, 1992, described himself as a sort of 'Jekyll and Hammerstein'. He's credited for writing more than 800 songs and was elected into the Nashville Songwriters Hall of Fame in 1973. He was truly one of a kind. (Tony Byworth)

BEST OF ROGER MILLER.
Tracks: By the time I get to Phoenix / Chug-a-lug / Dang me / Do-wacka-do / Engine engine No.9 / England swings / Green green grass of home / Kansas City star / King of the road / Little green apples / One dyin' and a-buryin' / You can't roller skate in a buffalo herd.
LP. 6336 229
Philips / Jan '78 / PolyGram.

COUNTRY COLLECTION, THE.
Tracks: Not Advised.
CD . . . . CDCST 51
MC . . . . CSTK 51
Country Store / Oct '89 / BMG.

ENGINE ENGINE NO.9.
Tracks: Engine no.9.
■ 7" . . . . BF 1416
Philips / Jun '65.

ENGLAND SWINGS.
Tracks: England swings.
■ 7" . . . . BF 1456
Philips / Dec '65.

KANSAS CITY STAR.
Tracks: Kansas City star.
■ 7" . . . . BF 1437
Philips / Oct '65.

KING OF THE ROAD.
Tracks: You're part of me / Fair Swiss maiden / Every which a way / It happened just that way / I get up early in the morning / I catch myself crying / I'll be somewhere / Little green apples / I know who it is (and I'm gonna tell on him) / But I love you more / If you want me too / Burma shave / You don't want my love / Sorry Willie / You can't do me that way / When two worlds collide / Lock, stop and teardrops / Trouble on the turnpike / Hey little star / Footprints in the snow / Hitchhiker / Dang me / King of the road / Chug-a-lug / Engine no.9 / Kansas City star / England swings / Do-wacka-do / One dyin' and a buryin'.
CD . . . . BCD 15477
Bear Family / Feb '90 / Rollercoaster Records / Swift / Direct Distribution.

KING OF THE ROAD.
Tracks: King of the road / England swings / Little green apples.
■ 7" . . . . BF 1397
Philips / Mar '65.

KING OF THE ROAD.
Tracks: Not Advised.
CD 15478
MC 79478
Laserlight / Jun '93 / TBD / Taylors.

KING OF THE ROAD (2).
Tracks: Not Advised.
CD . . . . WMCD 5658
MC . . . . WMMC 4658
Woodford Music / Jul '92 / Terry Blood Dist. / Midland Records.

KING OF THE ROAD (OLD GOLD).
Tracks: King of the road / Little green apples.
7" . . . . OG 9480
Old Gold / Jan '85 / Pickwick Records.

LITTLE GREEN APPLES.
Tracks: Not Advised.
■ LP. . . . . CN 2013
Contour / Jan '76.

LITTLE GREEN APPLES.
Tracks: Little green apples.
■ 7" . . . . MF 1021
Mercury / Mar '68.

LITTLE GREEN APPLES (RE-RELEASE).
Tracks: Little green apples / England swings / King of the road / Jody and the kid.
■ 7" 6198019
Philips / Jul '77.

MAKING A NAME FOR MYSELF.
Tracks: Hat / If I ever fall in love / Ringing up Rosie / Freedom / Hey would you hold it down / It's a miracle that you're mine / Pleasing the crowd / Disco man / Old friends / Opera ain't over till the fat lady sings.
■ LP. . . . . T 592
20th Century / Feb '80.

MOTIVE SERIES.
Tracks: Not Advised.
LP. 6463 059
MC 7145 059
Mercury / Dec '81 / PolyGram.

OFF THE WALL.
Tracks: Oklahoma woman / There's nobody like you / Baby me, baby / Dark side of the woman / Stephen Foster / Some people make it / I've gotten used to the cryin' / Roll away / Ain't gonna work no more / Na-nominee.
LP. . . . . FL 12337
Windsong / Jan '78 / Pinnacle.

OLD FRIENDS (Miller Roger & Willie Nelson).
Tracks: Not Advised.
LP. . . . . CBS 32195
MC 40 32195
CBS / Nov '82 / Sony.

OUR LOVE.
Tracks: Our love / Yester waltz.
■ 7" . . . . CBS 2904
CBS / Jan '75.

ROGER MILLER.
Tracks: River in the rain / Hand for the hog / Leavin's not the only way to go / Guv'ment / You oughta be here with me / Some hearts get all the breaks / Arkansas / Indian giver / Days of our wives / Muddy water.
MC . . . . **IMCAC 5722**
MCA / Mar '87 / BMG.
■ LP . . . . **IMCA 5722**
MCA / Mar '87.

ROGER MILLER'S GREATEST HITS.
Tracks: Not Advised.
LP . . . . **CDS 2073**
RCA/Camden / Mar '85 / BMG / Arabesque Ltd.
MC . . . . **CAM 2073**
RCA / Mar '85 / BMG.

SPOTLIGHT ON ROGER MILLER.
Tracks: As long as there's a shadow / Ballad of Waterhole 3, The / Best of all possible worlds, The / Boeing boeing 707 / Darby's castle / England swings / Got two again / Heartbreak hotel / Hey good lookin' / Husbands and wives / I ain't comin' home tonight / I'm gonna teach my heart to bend / I've been a long time leavin' / In the summertime / It takes all kinds to make a world / Jody and the kid / King of the road / Little green apples / Lou's got the flu / Me and Bobby McGee / Million years or so, A / My uncle used to love me but she died / Nothing can stop my love / Swiss Cottage place / That's the way it's always been / Tom Green County Fair, The / Walkin' in the sunshine / When two worlds collide.
LP **6619 029**
Philips / Sep '78 / PolyGram.

Million Dollar Quartet

COMPLETE MILLION DOLLAR QUARTET.
Tracks: You belong to my heart / When God dips his love in my heart / Just a little walk with Jesus / Walk that lonesome valley / I shall not be moved / Peace in the valley / Down by the riverside / I'm in the crowd but oh so alone / Farther along / Blessed Jesus hold my hand / As we travel along the Jericho road / I just can't make it by myself / Little cabin on the hill / Summertime has passed and gone / I hear a sweet voice calling / Sweetheart you done me wrong / Keeper of the key / Crazy arms / Don't forbid me / Brown eyed handsome man / Out of sight out of mind / Brown eyed handsome man (take 2) / Don't be cruel / Don't be cruel (take 2) / Paralysed / Don't be cruel (take 3) / There's no place like home / When the saints go marching in / Softly and tenderly / Is it so strange / That's when the heartaches begin / Brown eyed handsome man (take 3) / Rip it up / I'm gonna bid my blues goodbye / Crazy arms (take 2) / That's my desire / End of the road / Jerry's boogie / You're the only star in my blue heaven / Elvis, farewell.
CD . . . . **CDCHARLY 102**
Double LP . . . . **CDX 20**
MC . . . . **TCCDX 20**
Charly / Jan '88 / Charly.

MILLION DOLLAR QUARTET.
Tracks: Peace in the valley / Just a little walk with Jesus / Walk that lonesome valley / Down by the riverside / I shall not be moved / I'm with the in crowd but oh so alone / Farther along / Blessed Jesus hold my hand / As we travel along the Jericho road / I just can't make it by myself / Little cabin on the hill / Summertime has passed and gone / I hear a sweet voice calling / And now sweetheart / You've done me wrong / Keeper of the key / Crazy arms / Don't forbid me.
LP . . . . **SUN 1006**
MC . . . . **CFK 1019**
Sun / Sep '81 / Charly / Swift.
CD . . . . **CDCHARLY 65**
Charly / Feb '87 / Charly.

Mills, Betty Lou

20 BEST LOVED GOSPEL SONGS - BETTY LOU MILLS.
Tracks: Not Advised.
LP . . . . **PC 320**
Pilgrim / '87.

COUNTRYSTYLE.
Tracks: Not Advised.
LP . . . . **PC 824**
Pilgrim / '87.

Mills, Mick

MUSIC.
Tracks: Not Advised.
LP . . . . **WRS 084**
Westwood / May '77 / Pinnacle.

Milsap, Ronnie

Born in Robinsville, North Carolina, and raised by his grandparents until he was five, Ronnie Milsap began taking chances early. He was kicked out of music class at the Governor Morehead School for the Blind in Raleigh for playing rock'n'roll instead of classical music. After attending Young-Harris Junior College near Atlanta, Georgia for two years, he turned down a scholarship to Emory University School of Law in favor of playing music for a living. For a while, that chance didn't look as if it was going to pan out. For the next few years, success seemed always to be just around the corner. In 1965, Ronnie was living in Atlanta, working as a sideman and playing sessions when two significant events occurred: he married Joyce, and he signed to New York based Scepter Records as an R&B artist. His first Scepter single *Never had it so good* was a top five R&B hit. Nonetheless, although Ronnie continued to record for Scepter throughout the '60's, he never had another big record, and by the end of the decade, he had formed his own band and moved to Memphis, where his was the house band at T.J.'s club. The most notable thing that happened to Milsap in Memphis was that he caught the attention of Elvis Presley, who asked Ronnie to play at his private New Year's Eve party and to do some session work for him - the most famous of the Milsap/Presley sessions was for Elvis's *Kentucky rain*. Still Ronnie didn't feel that he could ensure a secure future for his family - for by then he and Joyce had a son, Todd - by continuing his career in Memphis. Bedeviled by management problems and without a record label, the Milsap family moved to Nashville, Tennessee in 1972. Ronnie Milsap's first Nashville job was playing four shows a night at the rooftop club of Roger Miller's King of the Road Hotel, and those shows became legendary in Nashville. There were lines at the elevators every night, and everybody who was anybody in Nashville flocked to see the blind guy at the King of the Road. By the year's end, however, 'that blind guy' had a recording contract with RCA and everybody knew his name. Ronnie Milsap's first RCA single *Altogether now (let's fall apart)* sold a hundred thousand copies. From there on, there was no looking back; it became a rare occurrence for a Ronnie Milsap single or album not to be a hit, beginning with his first number one single *Pure love*. First, Ronnie established himself solidly in the country music field, and rapidly acquired a loyal legion of fans with hits like *Daydreams about night things* and *(I'm a) stand by my woman man*. He won his first CMA award for Best Male Vocalist only a year after signing with RCA. The hits and the awards kept coming, the Milsap style kept developing and in 1977, he had his first big crossover pop hit with the Archie Jordan composition *It was almost like a song*. After that it became almost routine for a Milsap hit to find itself on pop adult contemporary and country radio. In 1980, there was *Smokey mountain rain* and in 1981, it was *There's no gettin' over me*. In 1982, there were *Any day now* (Billboard Adult Contemporary Song Of The Year), *He got you* and *Inside*.

20-20 VISION.
Tracks: 20-20 vision / Lovers, friends and strangers / Not that I care / Lovesick blues / You snap your fingers / Looking out my window through the pain / What goes on when the sun goes down / You've still got a place in my heart / I got home just in time to say goodbye / (I'm a) stand by my woman man.
■ LP . . . . **LSA 3278**
RCA / '79.

GET IT UP.
Tracks: Get it up / Hi-heel sneakers.
12" . . . . **PC 1683**
■ 7" . . . . **PB 1683**
RCA / Oct '79.

GREATEST HITS: RONNIE MILSAP.
Tracks: Smokey mountain rain / Legend in my time, A / Pure love / Stand by my woman man / I hate you / It was almost like a song / Let's take the long way round the world / Daydreams about night things / Let my love be your pillow / Please don't tell me how the story ends / Back on my mind again / What a difference you've made in my life.
■ MC . . . . **PK 13772**
RCA / Jan '81 / BMG.
■ LP . . . . **PL 13772**
RCA / Jan '81.

GREATEST HITS: RONNIE MILSAP VOL.2.
Tracks: Not Advised.
LP . . . . **PL 85425**
■ MC . . . . **PK 85425**
RCA / '86.

HITS OF RONNIE MILSAP, THE.
Tracks: (I'd be) a legend in my time / What goes on when the sun goes down / Pure love / Daydreams about night things / Honky tonk women / Country cookin' / Please don't tell me how the story ends / (After sweet memories) Play born to lose / 20-20 vision / (I'm a) Stand by my woman man / Remember to remind me (I'm leaving) / That girl who waits on tables / Too late to worry, too blue to cry / Four walls.
LP . . . . **PL 42429**
■ MC . . . . **PK 42429**
RCA / '79.

I WOULDN'T HAVE MISSED IT FOR THE WORLD.
Tracks: I wouldn't have missed it for the world / It happens every time.
■ 7" . . . . **RCA 168**
RCA / Nov '81.

I'D BE A LEGEND IN MY TIME.
Tracks: I'd be a legend in my time / Please don't tell me how the story ends.
■ 7" . . . . **RCA 501**
RCA / Jan '75.

IMAGES.
Tracks: Nobody likes sad songs / Keep the night away / I really don't want to know / Just because it feels good / You don't look for love / Hi heel sneakers / In no time at all / Delta queen / All good things don't have to end / Get it up.
■ LP . . . . **PL 13346**
RCA / '79.

INSIDE.
Tracks: Inside / Carolina dreams / Wrong end of the rainbow / I love New Orleans music / He got you / Hate the lies, love the liar / Who's counting / You took her off my hands / It's just a room / Any day now.
LP . . . . **RCALP 3095**
MC . . . . **RCAK 3095**
RCA / Sep '82 / BMG.
■ CD . . . . **PD 84311**
RCA / Sep '82.

IT WAS ALMOST LIKE A SONG.
Tracks: What a difference you've made in my life / No one will ever know / It was almost like a song / Selfish / Long distance memory / Here in love / Future's not what it used to be, The / It don't hurt to dream / Crystal fallin' rain / Lovin' kind.
■ LP . . . . **PL 12439**
RCA / '79.

IT WAS ALMOST LIKE A SONG.
Tracks: It was almost like a song / It don't hurt to dream.
■ 7" . . . . **PB 0976**
RCA / '79.

KEYED UP.
Tracks: Stranger in my house / Show her / Don't your memory ever sleep at night / Watch out for the other guy / I'm just a redneck at heart / Don't you know how much I love you / Feelings change / Like children I have known / Is it over / We're here to love.
LP . . . . **RCALP 6077**
MC . . . . **RCAK 6077**
RCA / May '83 / BMG.

LEGEND IN MY TIME, A.
Tracks: Busiest memory in town / Too late to worry, too blue to cry / (I'd be) a legend in my time / Biggest lie, The / Country cookin' / She came here for the change / I'll leave this world loving you / I'm still not over you / I honestly love you / Clap your hands.
LP . . . . **LSA 3209**
RCA / '79 / BMG.

LOST IN THE FIFTIES TONIGHT.
Tracks: Lost in the fifties tonight / In love / Old fashioned girl like you / I heard it through the grapevine / Don't take it tonight / How do I turn you on? / Happy, happy birthday baby / Nashville moon / I only remember the good times / Money.
LP . . . . **PL 81794**
MC . . . . **PK 81794**
RCA / Apr '86 / BMG.

LOST IN THE FIFTIES TONIGHT.
Tracks: Lost in the 50's tonight / I might have said.
■ 7" . . . . **PB 49931**
RCA / Sep '85.

MILSAP MAGIC.
Tracks: Why don't you spend the night / She thinks I still care / My heart / Silent night / It's a beautiful thing / Misery loves company / I let myself believe / If you don't want me / What's one more time / Still in love with you.
■ LP . . . . **PL 13563**
RCA / Jul '80.

MR MAILMAN.
Tracks: Nothing's as good as it used to be / Only one woman / Denver / Kentucky woman / I saw pity in the face of a friend / Ain't no soul / If you go away / When it comes to my baby.
LP . . . . **PHX 1002**
Phoenix (2) / Jul '81 / Gamut Distribution.

MY HEART.
Tracks: My heart / Silent night.
■ 7" . . . . **PB 1952**
RCA / Jun '80.

NIGHT THINGS.
Tracks: (After sweet memories) Play born to lose again / Who'll turn out the lights (in your world) / Daydreams about night things / I'm no good at goodbyes / Just in case / Remember to remind me (I'm leaving) / Borrowed angel / Love takes a long time to die / (Lying here with) Linda on my mind / I'll be there (if you ever want me).
■ LP . . . . **LSA 3261**
RCA / '79.

NO GETTIN' OVER ME.
Tracks: No gettin' over me / I live my whole life at night.
■ 7" . . . . **RCA 136**
RCA / '82.

NOBODY LIKES SAD SONGS.
Tracks: Nobody likes sad songs / Just because it feels good.
■ 7" . . . . **PB 1553**
RCA / Apr '79.

M 16
■ DELETED

ONE MORE TRY FOR LOVE.
Tracks: One more try for love / She loves my car / Still losing you / Suburbia / Prisoner of the highway / She's always in love / I might have said / I guess I just missed you / I'll take care of you / Night by night.
LP. . . . . PL 85016
MC . . . . PK 85016
RCA / Jul '84 / BMG.

ONLY ONE LOVE IN MY LIFE.
Tracks: Let's take the long way around the world / Back on my mind again / Only one love in my life / I'm not trying to forget / No relief in sight / Once I get over you / Santa Barbara / Too soon to know / Yesterday's lovers never make good friends / I've got the music in me.
LP. . . . . PL 12780
■ MC . . . . PK 12780
RCA / '79.

ONLY ONE LOVE IN MY LIFE.
Tracks: Only one love in my life / Back in my life again.
■ 7". . . . . PB 1270
RCA / '78.

OUT WHERE THE BRIGHT LIGHTS ARE GLOWING.
Tracks: Out where the bright lights are glowing / Four walls / Pride goes before a fall / I'm beginning to forget you / He'll have to go / I'm getting better / Am I losing you / I won't forget you / I guess I'm crazy / When two worlds collide / Missing you / Dear friend.
LP. . . . . RCALP 5022
MC . . . . RCAK 5022
RCA / Jun '81 / BMG.

RONNIE MILSAP.
Tracks: Not Advised.
MC . . . . ZCGAS 756
Audio Fidelity(USA) / Oct '84 / Stage One Records.

RONNIE MILSAP LIVE.
Tracks: Pure love / I hate you (medley) / Welcome / I'm a stand by my woman man (medley) / Busy makin' plans / Kaw-liga / Country cookin' / I can almost see Houston from here / After sweet memories play born to lose again / Daydreams about night things (medley) / Let my love be your pillow / (I'd be) a legend in my time / Honky tonk women.
■ LP. . . . . PL 12043
RCA / '79.

SHE LOVES MY CAR.
Tracks: She loves my car / Prisoner of the highway.
12" . . . . RCAT 436
■ 7". . . . . RCA 436
RCA / Oct '84.

SMOKY MOUNTAIN RAIN.
Tracks: Smoky mountain rain / Crystal fallin' rain.
■ 7". . . . . RCA 41
RCA / Mar '81.

SPINNING WHEEL.
Tracks: Do what you gotta do / Didn't we / House of the rising sun / Spinning wheel / Only one woman / Let's go get stoned / I can't stop crying.
LP. . . . . SDLP 1.041
Sundown / Apr '87 / Terry Blood Dist. / Jazz Music / C.M. Distribution.

STRANGER IN MY HOUSE.
Tracks: Stranger in my house.
7". . . . . RCA 338
RCA / May '83 / BMG.

THERE GOES MY HEART.
Tracks: Not Advised.
MC . . . . ORC 010
Orchid Music / Feb '82 / Pinnacle.

WHAT A DIFFERENCE YOU'VE MADE IN MY LIFE.
Tracks: What a difference you've made in my life / Selfish.
■ 7". . . . . PB 1146
RCA / Mar '78.

Minting Sisters

STRIKE COUNTRY.
Tracks: Listen to a country song / Soupstone, The / Rocky top / Paper roses / Streets of London / I'll get over you / All I ever need is you / Operator / Let's get together / Ozark mountain lullaby / Somebody loves you.
LP. . . . . BGC 274
MC . . . . KGBC 274
Country House / Jun '81 / Duncans / BGS Productions Ltd.

Mirror, Danny

I REMEMBER ELVIS PRESLEY (King is dead, The).
Tracks: I remember Elvis Presley.
■ 7". . . . . SON 2121
Sonet / Sep '77.

I REMEMBER ELVIS PRESLEY.
Tracks: Don't believe it / Vaya con dios / Freedom forever / When I see you / I remember you / I'm gonna love you / I remember Elvis Presley / I believe in the man in the sky / Why should I tell you this story / We wish you.
LP. . . . . SNTF 751
■ MC . . . . ZCSN 751
Sonet / '78 / Swift / C.M. Distribution / Roots Records / Jazz Music / Sonet Records / Cadillac Music / Projection / Wellard Dist. / Hot Shot.

SUSPICION (Elvis Medley) (Mirror, Danny & Jordanaires).
Tracks: Suspicion.
7" . . . . MIR 123
Albion / Nov '81.

Mitchell, Marty

YOU ARE THE SUNSHINE OF MY LIFE.
Tracks: You are the sunshine of my life / Yester-me, yester-you, yesterday.
■ 7" . . . . MC 7001
MC / Aug '78.

Mizell, Hank

This American singer and guitarist's story was one of the oddest in rock history. When the rock 'n' roll explosion happened in the mid-Fifties, he was, like numerous other youngsters of the era, inspired to have a go at playing the music himself. He formed a local band and became a proficient amateur. He and his friends wrote some songs, one of which was called *Jungle Rock*. They recorded this number in a garage, which was the standard alternative for those rockers who could not afford to book a studio. The record was made and forgotten, Hank Mizell did not become a star, and he continued living an ordinary life.Suddenly in 1976, *Jungle Rock* was unearthed by Charly Records, a UK label with an enthusiastic penchant for re-discovering and re-issuing old rock 'n' roll material. For some inexplicable reason, this particular single zoomed onto the British chart and climbed to No. 3. No-one had ever heard of Hank Mizell, and the sound quality was pretty primitive - but the strength of the song and the untainted enthusiasm of the performance won through. Its success neatly coincided with an organised march on the BBC by rock 'n' roll fanatics, who cited the national UK acceptance of the Mizell single as evidence that a specialist programme was required; their demonstration proved successful.Mizell knew nothing about the success of *Jungle Rock* until it was high on the chart. It took several weeks to track down this most obscure of hit performers; but when he was finally located in the United States, he came over to Britain for a publicity visit, and also recorded an album.(Bob MacDonald).

I'M READY (Mizell, Hank & his Country Rockers).
Tracks: I'm ready.
7" . . . . JB 501
Juke Box (Re-issue) / Jul '85.

JUNGLE ROCK.
Tracks: Jungle rock / Burning eyes.
■ MC . . . . ZCCH 5000
Charly / '79.

JUNGLE ROCK.
Tracks: Jungle rock / Red Cadillac and a black moustache.
■ 7". . . . . CYS 1040
Charly / Sep '78.

JUNGLE ROCK.
Tracks: Jungle rock.
7" . . . . CS 1005
Charly / Mar '76 / Charly.

JUNGLE ROCK.
Tracks: Jungle rock / Ain't got a thing / Ready Freddy / Higher / Easy money / Rakin' and scrapin' / Singing in the jungle / Sweetie Pie / Kangaroo rock / Animal rock'n'roll / Ubangi stomp / Flatfoot stomp.
■ LP. . . . . CRL 5000
Charly / '78 / Charly.

JUNGLE ROCK (OLD GOLD).
Tracks: Jungle rock / Burning eyes.
7" . . . . OG 9115
Old Gold / Jul '82 / Pickwick Records.

Moffatt, Hugh

Singer - songwriter Moffatt was born in Fort Worth, Texas on 10.11.1948, payed his early dues as a folk singer in Austin. Moved to Nashville in 1973, recording for Mercury - having a No 95 hit with his version of the Don Schlitz song *The gambler* . Has crafted such hits as *Old flames (Can't hold a candle to you)* (with his former wife Pebe Serbert). A career song for Joe Sun (No 14 in 1978) - whilst it gave Dolly Parton a No.1 in 1980, it has seen numerous covers-including Ireland's Foster & Allen. Other songs coming from Hugh's studious pen are *Wild turkey* (a 1981 top 5 double - sided hit for Lacy J Dalton) *Words at twenty paces* (Alabama) *Praises the lord and send me out the money* (Bobby Bare), *Rose of my heart* (Whitstein Brothers) whilst John Starling featured Hugh's *Carolina Star* & *Slow movin' freight train* on his acclaimed 1982 Sugar Hill album *Waitin' on a southern train* . On the recording front, Moffatt's seen two solo releases on Philo *Lovin' you* - 1987, *Troubadour* 1989, on which Hugh's glossary is well represented, the writer's low-key vocals, warmly covering such fare as *Rose of my heart* , *The old songs* , *Last night I dreamed of loving you* . His 1992 *Dance me outside* duet album with sister Katy, sees him covering standards *We'll sweep out the ashes in the morning* , *I don't believe you've met my baby* & *Dark end of the street* to complement his own work.., with ace acoustic musicians Stuart Duncan, Tim O'-Brien & Buddy Emmons in attendance. His 1993 release *Live & alone* was a live set recorded in Switzerland in 1989. (Maurice Hope)

DANCE ME OUTSIDE (Moffatt, Hugh & Katy).
Tracks: It's been decided / We'll sweep out the ashes in the morning / On the borderline / I don't believe you've met my baby / Dance me outside / Right over me / La Luna / Making new / Walking on the moon / Dark end of the street.
CD . . . . PH 1144CD
MC . . . . PH 1144C
Philo (USA) / '92 / Roots Records / Projection / Topic Records / Direct Distribution / Ross Records / C.M. Distribution / Impetus Records.

LOVING YOU.
Tracks: When you held me in your arms / Mama Rita / Old flames can't hold a candle to you / Words at twenty paces / Slow moving freight train / No stranger to the blues / Loving you / Tomorrow is a long time / Carolina star / Jack and Lucy / Roll with weather.
LP. . . . . PH 1111
Philo (USA) / Dec '87 / Roots Records / Projection / Topic Records / Direct Distribution / Ross Records / C.M. Distribution / Impetus Records.
CD . . . . PH 1111CD
MC . . . . PH 1111C
Philo (USA) / '88 / Roots Records / Projection / Topic Records / Direct Distribution / Ross Records / C.M. Distribution / Impetus Records.

TROUBADOUR.
Tracks: Way love is, The / Rose of my heart / I'll leave the rest to you / Somewhere in Kansas / How could I love her so much / Roses, love and promises / Hard times come again no more / Praise the Lord and send me the money / Devil took the rest, The / Old songs, The / For Mary.
CD . . . . CDPH 1127
LP. . . . . PH 1127
MC . . . . PH 1127C
Philo (USA) / '89 / Roots Records / Projection / Topic Records / Direct Distribution / Ross Records / C.M. Distribution / Impetus Records.
CD . . . . BD 500CD
LP. . . . . BD 500
MC . . . . BD 500MC
Breakdown / Feb '90.

Moffatt, Katy

Texas - born (Fort Worth) Moffatt, as a singer - songwriter and younger sister of hit songwriter/ singer Hugh Moffatt, welds rich elements of country, folk & rock into her gutsy bluesy styled work. Started out in Texas, before moving to Denver, Colorado in 1979 which became her longtime base, playing various venues - by which time Moffatt had two contemporary country albums to her name *Katy* & *Kissing in the California sun* (1976 & 1979 respectively). Through the years, Katy's played support for a huge array of talent - from the 1970's with J.D.Souther, to John Stewart & Michael Martin Murphy to Don Williams & the Everly Bros. Had some singles out on the Dallas - based Permian record label during late Seventies, three charting in the lower regions including *This ain't Tennessee and he ain't you* . Did some acting roles-featuring in the movies *Billy Jack* & *Hard country* , singing harmony support with Tanya Tucker, Hoyt Axton & Lynn Anderson to Michael Martin Murphy. Moffatt's *Love and only love* gained admission onto the 1986 album *A town somewhere south of Bakersfield* , starring alongside Yoakam, Billy Swan & Albert Lee. Fiery - haired Moffatt, after going through a fallow spell on the recording front, had the good fortune to hook up with the Stellar singer - songwriter Tom Russell, who with Moffatt penned the much covered *Walkin' on the moon* . Since then they've done some twenty collaborations- including *The greatest show on earth* the title track of her 1993 story-filled album on RTM, on which apart from *Dance me outside* , also the title track of Hugh & Katy's Rounder album, they're responsible for six more songs. Used Russell's erstwhile band, featuring Hank Bones, Fats Kaplin & Andrew Hardin (the sole musician Moffatt accepted on her acoustic Swiss recording *Walking on the moon*). Amidst her country releases, Moffatt also had a 1989 contemporary release out on the now defunct Heartland Records (later taken up by Rounder) *Child bride* , aflow with west coast rock influences, via it's musicians Greg Leisz, Dave Alvin (ex-Blasters) & producer/guitarist Steve Berlin (Los Lobos). Alongside the title track Moffatt gives good account on Hank Williams' hit *Settin' the woods on fire* & Billy Burnette's *Blow out the candle* . Has toured around the UK's club circuit & Wembley Country Music Festival - during the event's twilight years. (Maurice Hope)

CHILD BRIDE.
Tracks: Child bride / In a moment / Lonely avenue / Look out it must be love / Playin' fool / We ran / You better move on / Anna / Settin' the woods on fire.
CD . . . . **HLDCD 009**
LP. . . . . **HLD 009**
MC . . . . **HLD 009C**
Heartland (1) / Sep '89 / Revolver-APT.
CD . . . . **PH 1133CD**
LP. . . . . **CPH 1133**
MC . . . . **PH 1133MC**
Philo (USA) / '90 / Roots Records / Projection / Topic Records / Direct Distribution / Ross Records / C.M. Distribution / Impetus Records.

GREATEST SHOW ON EARTH.
Tracks: Not Advised.
CD . . . . **RTMCD 50**
MC . . . . **RTMC 50**
Round Tower / Feb '93 / Pinnacle / A.D.A Distribution / ACD Trading Ltd. / Topic Records / Direct Distribution / BMG.

WALKIN' ON THE MOON.
Tracks: Walkin' on the moon / I'm sorry darlin' / If anything comes to mind / Papacita (Mama Rita) / Mr. Banker / Borderline / Fire in your eyes / I'll take the blame / Hard time on Easy street / I know the difference now.
CD . . . . **CDPH 1128**
LP. . . . . **PH 1128**
MC . . . . **PH 1128C**
Philo (USA) / '89 / Roots Records / Projection / Topic Records / Direct Distribution / Ross Records / C.M. Distribution / Impetus Records.

Monroe, Bill

Born 13.9.1911 in Rosine, Kentucky. Bill Monroe was raised on a farm, the youngest of eight children, he learnt to play mandolin and guitar by the age of 10, playing in the family band at local dances. He moved to Louisiana with his brothers, Charlie and Birch, to work on an oil refinery during the day, by night the brothers played dance halls and parties and later toured with Chicago WLS station Barn Dance. After Birch dropped out, Bill and Charlie carried on as the Monroe Brothers, but the partnership was shortlived - they split due to artistic differences. By this time Bill's high lonesome sound was beginning to take shape, after a spell in Arkansas, Bill moved to Georgia and formed the first Bluegrass Boys line-up. That same year (1939) saw Bill signed to the Grand Ole Opry where he debuted with *Mule skinner blues*. He signed with Columbia in 1945 where he was joined by Earl Scruggs and Lester Flatt for three glorious years. Songs in their repertoire included *Blue moon of Kentucky* , *I hear a sweet voice calling* and *I'm going back to old Kentucky* . He left for Decca after Columbia signed the Stanley Brothers (another bluegrass act), with his main man now being Jimmy Martin. The 50's proved to be his most fruitful period with compositions like *Uncle Pen* , *Roanoke* , *Scotland* (in recognition of the birthplace of many of his mandolin tunes), *My little Georgia rose* and *Walking in Jerusalem* being among his best work. Bill's only top 5 singles *Kentucky waltz* and *Footprints in the snow* had come already in 1946, but his legacy continued with Elvis recording *Blue moon of Kentucky* as one of his first cuts for Sun. His influence can also be seen in the work of Ricky Scaggs and Peter Rowan (who played with Monroe for a time in the 70's). Monroe was elected into the Country Music Hall of Fame in 1970 and continued to play many festivals in the following years. (Maurice Hope)

87.
Tracks: Not Advised.
CD **31310**
MCA (USA) / Jun '88 / MCA (Imports).

BEST OF BILL MONROE.
Tracks: Gold rush / Blue moon of Kentucky / Close by / Memories of mother and dad / Is the blue moon still shining / Kentucky mandolin / I'm going back to old Kentucky / Footprints in the snow / Little girl and the dreadful snake / Highway of sorrow / Uncle Pen / Let me rest at the end of the day / Blue grass twist / It's mighty dark to travel / Roane country prison / Pretty fair maiden in the garden / First whippoorwill / I live in the past / Come back to me in my dreams / Put my little shoes away.
Double LP **IMCA2 4090**
MCA / Mar '86 / BMG.

BLUE GRASS RAMBLES (Monroe, Bill & His Blue Grass Boys).
Tracks: Not Advised.
LP. . . . . **HAT 3014**
MC . . . . **HATC 3014**
Stetson / Apr '86 / Crusader Marketing Co. / Swift / Wellard Dist. / Midland Records / C.M. Distribution.

BLUE MOON OF KENTUCKY.
Tracks: Not Advised.

BLUE RIDGE MOUNTAIN BLUES.
Tracks: Blue ridge mountain blues / John Hardy.
■ 7" **05960**
Brunswick / May '66.

BLUEGRASS 1950-58 (Vols 1, 2, 3 & 4).
Tracks: Blue grass ramble / New muleskinner blues / My little Georgia rose / Memories of you / I'm on my way to the old home / Alabama waltz / I'm blue, I'm lonesome / I'll meet you in the church Sunday morning / Boat of love / Old fiddler, The / Uncle Pen / When the golden leaves begin to fall / Lord protect my soul / River of death / Letter from my darling / On the old Kentucky shore / Rawhide / Poison love / Kentucky waltz / Prisoner's song / Swing low sweet chariot / Angels rock me to sleep / Brakeman's blues / When the cactus is in bloom / Sailors plea / My Carolina sunshine girl / Ben Dewberry's final run / Peach pickin' time in Georgia / Those gamblers blues / Highway of sorrow / Rotation blues / Lonesome truck driver's blues / Sugar coated love / You're drifting away / Cabin of love / Get down on your knees and pray / Christmas time's a coming / First whippoorwill, The / In the pines / Footprints in the snow / Walking in Jerusalem / Memories of Mother and Dad / Little girl and the dreadful snake / Country waltz / Don't put it off till tomorrow / My dying bed / Mighty pretty waltz, A / Pike County breakdown / Wishing waltz / I hope you have learned / Get up John / Sittin' alone in the moonlight / Plant some flowers by my grave / Changing partners / Y'all come / On and on / I believed in you darling / New John Henry blues / White House blues / Happy on my way / I'm working on a building / Voice from on high, A / He will set your fields on fire / Close by / Blue moon of Kentucky / Wheel hoss / Cheyenne / You'll find her name written there / Roanoake / Wait a little longer, please Jesus / Let the light shine down on me / Used to be / Tall timbers / Brown County breakdown / Fallen star, A / Four walls / Good woman's love, A / Cry cry darlin' / I'm sitting on top of the world / Out in the cold world / Roane Country prison / Goodbye old pal / In despair / Molly and tenbrooks / Come back to me in my dreams / Sally Joe / Brand new shoes / Lonesome road / I saw the light / Lord build me a cabin / Lord lead me on / Precious jewel / I'll meet you in the morning / Life's railway to heaven / I've found a hiding place / Jesus hold my hand / I am a pilgrim / Wayfaring stranger / Beautiful life / House of gold / Panhandle country / Scotland / Gotta travel on / No one but my darlin' / Big mon / Monroe's hornpipe.
CD Set . . . . **BCD 15423**
Bear Family / Jul '89 / Rollercoaster Records / Swift / Direct Distribution.

BLUEGRASS 1959-1969.
Tracks: When the phone rang / Tomorrow I'll be gone / Dark as the night, blue as the day / Stoney lonesome / Lonesome wind blues / Thinking about you / Come go with me / Sold down the river / Linda Lou / You live in a world all your own / Little Joe / Put my rubber doll away / Seven year blues / Time changes everything / Lonesome road blues / Big river / Flowers of love / It's mighty dark to travel / Bluegrass / Little Maggie / I'm going back to old Kentucky / Toy heart / Shady grove / Nine pound hammer / Live and let live / Danny boy / Cottonfields / Journey's end / John Hardy / Bugle call rag / Old Joe Clark / There was nothing we could do / I was left on the street / Cheap love affair / When the bees are in the hive / Big ball in Brooklyn / Columbus / Stockade blues / Blue Ridge mountain blues / How will I explain about you / Foggy river / Old country Baptising / I found the way / This world is not my home / Way down deep in my soul / Drifting too far from the shore / Going home / On the Jericho road / We'll understand it better / Somebody touched me / Careless love / I'm so lonesome I could cry / Jimmie Brown, the newsboy / Pass me not / Gloryland, way, The / Farther along / Big Sandy river / Baker's breakdown / Darling Corey / Cindy / Master builder / Let me rest at the end of the day / Salt Creek / Devil's dream / Sailor's hornpipe / Were you there / Pike county breakdown / Shenandoah breakdown / Santa Claus / I'll meet you in church Sunday morning / Mary at the home place / Highway of sorrow / One of God's sheep / Roll on, Buddy, roll on / Legend of the Blue Ridge mountains / Last old dollar / Bill's dream / Louisville breakdown / Never again / Just over in the Gloryland / Fire on the mountain / Long black veil, The / I live in the past / There's an old old house / When my blue moon turns to gold again / I wonder where you are tonight / Turkey in the straw / Pretty fair maiden in the garden / Log cabin in the lane / Paddy in the turnpike / That's all right / It makes no difference now / Dusty Miller / Midnight on the stormy deep / All the good times are past and gone / Soldier's joy / Blue night / Grey eagle / Gold rush / Sally Goodin' / Virginia darlin' / Is the blue moon still shining? / Train 45 / Kentucky mandolin / I want to go with you / Crossing the Cumberlands / Walls of time / I haven't seen Mary in years / Fireball male / Dead march, The / Cripple creek / What about you / With body and soul / Methodist preacher / Walk softly on my heart / Tall pines / Candy gal / Going up Caney / Lee wedding' tune, The / Bonnie / Sweet Mary and miles between.
CD Set . . . . **BCD 15529**
Bear Family / Feb '91 / Rollercoaster Records / Swift / Direct Distribution.

CLASSIC BLUEGRASS INSTRUMENTALS.
Tracks: Not Advised.
LP. . . . . **REB 850**
MC . . . . **REB 850C**
Rebel (1) / '90 / Projection / Backs Distribution.

CLASSIC BLUEGRASS RECORDINGS VOL.1.
Tracks: True life blues / Travelling this lonesome road / Kentucky waltz / I'm travelling on and on / Bluegrass special / Mother's only sleeping / Can't you hear me callin' / How will I explain about you / Old cross road, The / Goodbye old pal / Alone about daybreak / Little community church.
LP. . . . . **CCS 104**
MC . . . . **CCS 104MC**
County (USA) / '81 / Projection / Mike's Country Music Room / Swift.

CLASSIC BLUEGRASS RECORDINGS VOL.2 (Monroe, Bill & Flatt & Scruggs).
Tracks: Not Advised.
LP. . . . . **CCS 105**
MC . . . . **CCS 105MC**
County (USA) / '81 / Projection / Mike's Country Music Room / Swift.

COUNTRY MUSIC HALL OF FAME.
Tracks: Mule skinner blues / Kentucky waltz / Get up John / You'll find her name written there / Blue Moon of Kentucky / Put my little shoes on / Rocky road blues / Girl in the blue velvet band / Summertime is past and gone / Footprints in the snow / Gold rush.
■ LP. . . . . **CDL 8505**
MCA / May '80.
LP. . . . . **IMCA 140**
MCA (Import) / Mar '86 / Pinnacle / Silver Sounds (CD).

FATHER OF BLUE GRASS MUSIC.
Tracks: Six white horses / Dog house blues / Tennessee blues / No letter in the mail today / Blue yodel no. 7 (Anniversary blue yodel) / Orange blossom special / Mule skinner blues / Katy Hill / I wonder if you feel the way I do / Honky tonk swing / In the pines / Back up.
LP. . . . . **NL 90008**
MC . . . . **NK 90008**
RCA / Jan '87 / BMG.

HIGH, LONESOME SOUND OF BILL MONROE.
Tracks: My little Georgia rose / Letter from my darling / Memories of mother and dad / Highway of sorrow / On the old Kentucky shores / On and on / My dying bed / Memories of you / Whitehouse blues / Sugar coated love / I'm blue, I'm lonesome / When the golden leaves begin to fall.
■ LP. . . . . **IMCA 110**
MCA (Import) / Mar '86.

IN THE PINES.
Tracks: Not Advised.
LP. . . . . **REB 853**
MC . . . . **REB 853C**
Rebel (1) / '90 / Projection / Backs Distribution.

KNEE-DEEP IN BLUEGRASS (Monroe, Bill & His Blue Grass Boys).
Tracks: Cry cry darlin' / Roane country prison / Goodbye old pal / Out in the cold world / Good women's love / Come back to me in my dreams / Lonesome road to travel / I'm sitting on top of the world / Sally Joe / Brand new shoes / Molly and Ten Brooks.
LP. . . . . **HAT 3002**
MC . . . . **HATC 3002**
Stetson / Nov '85 / Crusader Marketing Co. / Swift / Wellard Dist. / Midland Records / C.M. Distribution.

MULE SKINNER BLUES.
Tracks: Mule skinner blues / No letter in the mail / Cryin' holy unto my Lord / Six white horses / Dog house blues / I wonder if you feel the way I do / Katy Hill / Tennessee blues / Shake my mother's hand for me / Were you there / Blue yodel No 7 / Coupon song, The / Orange blossom special / Honky tonk swing / In the pines / Back up and push.
CD . . . . **RCA 2494**
RCA (USA) / Aug '92 / RCA (Imports).

ORANGE BLOSSOM SPECIAL.
Tracks: Not Advised.
LP. **20018**
MC **40018**
Astan (USA) / Nov '84.

STARS OF THE BLUEGRASS HALL OF FAME.
Tracks: I'm on my way back to the old home / Can't you hear me callin' / Lord, protect my soul / Golden west / Travellin' this lonesome road / I'm going back to old Kentucky / I hear a sweet voice calling / Remember the cross / True life blues / Let the gates swing wide.
■ LP. . . . . **IMCA 5825**
MCA / Mar '86.

Montana, Lee

ON THE RUN.
Tracks: Not Advised.
LP. . . . . **SFA 060**
Sweet Folk & Country / Nov '76 / Wellard Dist.

YOU'RE ON MY MIND (WITH TIME ON MY HANDS).
Tracks: It's a hard life / Amanda / Big iron / That was before I met you / Thing called love, A / Just out of reach / In the shelter of your eyes / Canadian Pacific / I don't want the money / Streets of Baltimore / Partners / Time on my hands.
LP. . . . . **SFA 090**

M 18

■ DELETED

Sweet Folk All / May '81 / Cadillac Music / Projection / C.M. Distribution / Wellard Dist. / Impetus Records.

Moody Brothers

First coming to the attention of British audiences in the mid 1980's as the accompanying band to their long-time North Carolina friend and associate George Hamilton IV, the Moody Brothers have subsequently picked up a firm following in their own right through regular tours and album releases. Hailing from Charlotte, the group comprises brothers Carlton, David and Trent and, besides entertaining, they're well experienced in industry matters running the family's successful recording and music publishing operation. In 1984 they received a Grammy nomination with their version of the Texas dance tune *Cotton eyed Joe* . In the early 1990's David quit to look after business enterprises while his two brothers took up a long-term residency at Paris' EuroDisney resort. (Tony Byworth)

CARLTON MOODY & THE MOODY BROTHERS.
Tracks: Shame on me / I tried at first not to / You turned the light on / Aunt Bea's breakdown / I'll know you're gonna cheat on me / You / You left the water running / Dreaming / Showboat gambler / Little country county fair / Start with the talking / Drive over the mountain.
CD . . . . **LR 10157**
Sundown / Dec '87 / Terry Blood Dist. / Jazz Music / C.M. Distribution.
LP. . . . . **SDLP 042**
Sundown / Jul '87 / Terry Blood Dist. / Jazz Music / C.M. Distribution.
MC . . . . **SDC 042**
Sundown / '89 / Terry Blood Dist. / Jazz Music / C.M. Distribution.

COTTON EYED JOE.
Tracks: Midnight flyer / My mind's already home / Let me dance with you / Redneck girl / It's my turn to sing with ol' Willie / Southern railroad / Brown eyed girl / When she tells you goodbye / Line dancing / Our love / Cotton-eyed Joe.
LP. . . . . **SDLP 032**
Sundown / Feb '86 / Terry Blood Dist. / Jazz Music / C.M. Distribution.
MC . . . . **SDC 032**
Sundown / May '88 / Terry Blood Dist. / Jazz Music / C.M. Distribution.
CD . . . . **LRCD 10116-2**
Sundown / '89 / Terry Blood Dist. / Jazz Music / C.M. Distribution.

Moody, George

I'M IN LOVE WITH A MEMORY.
Tracks: I'm in love with a memory / Michelle.
7" . . . . **DBW 022**
Marina / Dec '82.

Moore & Napier

BEST OF MOORE & NAPIER.
Tracks: Not Advised.
LP. . . . . **SLP 963**
MC . . . . **GT 5963**
Starday (USA) / Apr '87 / Crusader Marketing Co.

LONESOME TRUCK DRIVERS.
Tracks: Not Advised.
LP. . . . . **KLP 936**
MC . . . . **GT 5936**
King (USA) / Apr '87 / Charly.

Moore, Bob

MEXICO.
Tracks: Mexico / Hot spot / Cologne / Ooh la la Paloma / Fireball mail / Blue tango / Auf wiedersehen, Marlene / El picador / South of the border / Hooten trumpet / My adobe hacienda / Mexicali rose / Nuevo laredo / Mexican wedding / Vaya con dios.
LP. . . . . **BFX 15288**
Bear Family / Apr '89 / Rollercoaster Records / Swift / Direct Distribution.

Moore, Charlie

ORIGINAL REBEL SOLDIER, THE.
Tracks: Rebel soldier / Lonesome road blues / Convict and the rose, The / Best female actress of the year / Chubby's lonesome blues / Philadelphia lawyer / Six white horses / Little blossom / Cacklin' hen, The / Don't let your sweet love die / Put my little shoes away.
LP. . . . . **REBEL 1662**
MC . . . . **REBELMC 1662**
Rebel (1) / '89 / Projection / Backs Distribution.

Moore, Merrill E.

20 GOLDEN PIECES: MERRILL E. MOORE.
Tracks: Buttermilk baby / Ten, ten, a.m. / Cow cow boogie / Sweet Jenny Lee / Five foot two, eyes of blue / It's a one-way door / Down the road apiece / Gotta gimme whatcha got / Nola boogie / King Porter stomp / Yes, indeed / She's gone / Snatchin' and grabbin' / Cooing to the wrong pigeon / House of blue lights / Rock rockola / Fly right boogie / Corina Corina / Hard top race / Bartender's blues.
LP. . . . . **BDL 2011**
Bulldog Records / Jul '82 / President Records / Jazz Music / Wellard Dist. / TKO Records Ltd.

BOOGIE MY BLUES AWAY.
Tracks: Rock rock ola / House of blue lights / Big bug boogie / Saddle boogie / Corina, Corina / Red light / Bartender's blues / Hard top race / Nola boogie / Bell bottom boogie / Doggie house boogie / Sweet Jenny Lee / Fly right boogie / It's a one-way door / Snatchin' and grabbin' / I think I love you too / Ten ten am / Yes indeed / Five foot two eyes of blue / Cow cow boogie / Boogie my blues away / Rock Island line / King Porter stomp / Cooing to the wrong pigeon / She's gone / Down the road a piece / Gotta gimme what'cha got / Nursery rhyme blues / Buttermilk baby / Barrel house Bessie / Tuck me to sleep in my old Kentucky home / Music music music / Sun Valley walk / Lazy river / Back home again in Indiana / South / Shanty in old shanty town / Sweet Georgia Brown / Nobody's sweetheart / Jumpin' at the woodside / Somebody stole my gal / Moore blues / Sentimental journey.
CD Set . . . . **BCD 15505**
Bear Family / Sep '90 / Rollercoaster Records / Swift / Direct Distribution.

RED LIGHT.
Tracks: Red light / House of blue lights.
7" . . . . **BD 20**
President / Jan '80 / Grapevine Distribution / Target Records / Jazz Music / Taylors.

Moore, Scotty

FIRST YEAR, THE (see under Presley, Elvis).

GUITAR THAT CHANGED THE WORLD.
Tracks: Hound dog / Loving you / Honey honey / My baby left me / Heartbreak hotel / That's alright / Milk cow blues / Don't / Mystery train / Don't be cruel / Love me tender / Mean woman blues.
■ **LP.** . . . . **EPC 32306**
Epic / May '83.

Moore, Tiny

TINY MOORE'S MUSIC.
Tracks: Not Advised.
LP. . . . . **F 12**
Kaleidoscope (USA) / '88 / Projection / Ross Records / Roots Records / Swift / C.M. Distribution / Topic Records / Duncans.

Morgan, George

Singer/songwriter born on June 28, 1925 in Waverley, Tennessee and raised in Barbeton, Ohio. He first caught the public's attention via appearances on the Wheeling Jamboree, which led on to a contract with Columbia Records and an immediate million seller with *Candy kisses* , his first release, in 1949. Unfortunately he was never able to repeat this success although he scored another 20 chart placings with the label up until the mid-60's. He then continued on several independent outlets up until he died of a heart attack in 1975. He was the father of Lorrie Morgan. (Tony Byworth)

BEST OF GEORGE MORGAN.
Tracks: Not Advised.
LP. . . . . **SLP 957**
MC . . . . **GT 5957**
Starday (USA) / Apr '87 / Crusader Marketing Co.

Morgan, Lorrie

Born Loretta Lynn Morgan on June 27, 1960 in Nashville, Tennessee, the daughter of successful recording artist and Grand Ole Opry star George Morgan. Country music made an immediate impression and, by the age of 13, she had made her own Opry debut, receiving a standing ovation for her rendition of *Paper roses* . She launched her recording career on Hickory Records with *Two people I love* and also recorded for MCA and 4 Star before her career really took off on RCA with *Trainwreck of emotion* in 1988. She was married to the late Keith Whitley and, in 1990, won the CMA Vocal Event award for their performance on *'Til a tear becomes a rose* . (Tony Byworth)

LEAVE THE LIGHT ON.
Tracks: Trainwreck of emotion / Out of your shoes / I'll take the memories / Far side of the bed / Dear me / Five minutes / He talks to me / It's too late (to love me now) / Gonna leave the light on / Eight days a week (CD only.) / If I didn't love you (CD only.).
■ **LP.** . . . . **PL 90392**
RCA / Oct '89.
■ **MC** . . . . **PK 90392**
RCA / Oct '89.
■ **CD** . . . . **PD 90392**
RCA / Oct '89.

SOMETHING IN RED.
Tracks: Autumn's not that cold / We both walk / Something in red / Except for Monday / Picture of me (without you) / Tears on my pillow / In tears / Best woman wins / Hand over your heart / Faithfully.
LP. . . . . **PL 90560**
RCA / Jun '91 / BMG.
■ **CD** . . . . **PD 90560**
RCA / Jun '91.
■ **MC** . . . . **PK 90560**
RCA / Jun '91.

Morris, Gary

Born on December 7, 1948 in Fort Worth, Texas, he gained initial experience singing with his twin sister Carrie and, later, had his own band Breakaway in Colorado. He initially recorded for MCA but it wasn't until producer Norro Wilson secured him a deal with Warners that his career took off in 1980 with *Sweet red wine* . Since then he's had a couple of dozen chart successes including the original version of *Wind beneath my wings* and some duets with Crystal Gayle. A singer with considerable vocal ability, he's appeared in a Broadway production of the opera *La Boheme* (opposite Linda Ronstadt) and was seen in a dramatic role in the TV series *The Cosby's*. (Tony Byworth)

SECOND HAND HEART.
Tracks: Love she found in me, The / Velvet chains / Runaway heart / Sweet red wine / Headed for a headache / West Texas highway and me / Roll back the rug and dance / Baby bye bye / Wind beneath my wings / Mama you can't give me no whippin' / Why lady why / Lasso the moon / 100% chance of rain / Second hand heart.
LP. . . . . **.925392 1**
■ **MC** . . . . **.925392 4**
WEA / Mar '86.

SECOND HAND HEART.
Tracks: Second hand heart.
7" . . . . **W 8781**
WEA / Feb '86 / WEA.

TRY GETTING OVER YOU.
Tracks: Try getting over you / Back in her arms again.
■ **7"** . . . . **W 8720**
WEA / Mar '86.

Morris, Leon

HONKY TONK BLUEGRASS (Morris, Leon & Buzz Busby).
Tracks: Not Advised.
LP. . . . . **ROUNDER 0031**
Rounder / '88 / Projection / Roots Records / Swift / C.M. Distribution / Topic Records / Jazz Music / Hot Shot / A.D.A Distribution / Direct Distribution.

Morris, Lynn

Female vocalist/banjoist, born in Lamesa, Texas in 1948 - leader of the Lynn Morris Band. Twice winner of the National Banjo Championship at Winfield, Kansas. Played in the Denver based three-piece bluegrass band City Limits (1972 - 1978), followed by two USA tours of the Far East as part of a country act, before opting for bluegrass in 1982, joining Pennsylvania's Whetstone Run, where she met her present husband, Marshall Wilborn (ex-Jimmy Martin & The Johnson Mountain Boys). Member of Lynn Morris Band (formed 1988) as bassist, vocalist and songwriter, alongside Chris Jones (ex - Whetston Run, Weary Hearts) on guitar vocals and Tim McLaughlin on mandolin. So far there are two albums out on Rounder both being quality blends of country & bluegrass. (Maurice Hope)

BRAMBLE AND THE ROSE (Morris, Lynn Band).
Tracks: Blue skies and teardrops / Coat of many colors / Engineers don't wave from the trains anymore, The / Why tell me why / Love grows cold / Bramble and the rose, The / I'll pretend it's raining / Hey porter / New patches / My younger days / Red line too Shady Grove / Heartstrings.
MC . . . . **ROU 0288**
Rounder / '92 / Projection / Roots Records / Swift / C.M. Distribution / Topic Records / Jazz Music / Hot Shot / A.D.A Distribution / Direct Distribution.
CD . . . . **CDROU 0288**
Rounder / Feb '92 / Projection / Roots Records / Swift / C.M. Distribution / Topic Records / Jazz Music / Hot Shot / A.D.A Distribution / Direct Distribution.

LYNN MORRIS BAND (Morris, Lynn Band).
Tracks: My heart skips a beat / You'll get no more me / Adams county breakdown / Black pony / Come early morning / Help me climb that mountain / Kisses don't die / Handy man / What was I supposed to do / If lonely was the wind / Don't tell me stories / Valley of peace.
CD . . . . **ROUNDER 0276CD**
LP. . . . . **ROUNDER 0276**
MC . . . . **ROUNDER 0276C**
Rounder / '90 / Projection / Roots Records / Swift / C.M. Distribution / Topic Records / Jazz Music / Hot Shot / A.D.A Distribution / Direct Distribution.

Morrissey, Bill

BILL MORRISSEY.
Tracks: Not Advised.
LP. . . . . PHILO 1105
Philo (USA) / Apr '86 / Roots Records / Projection / Topic Records / Direct Distribution / Ross Records / C.M. Distribution / Impetus Records.
MC . . . . PHILO 1105C
Philo (USA) / '88 / Roots Records / Projection / Topic Records / Direct Distribution / Ross Records / C.M. Distribution / Impetus Records.

FRIEND OF MINE (Morrissey, Bill & Greg Brown).
Tracks: Not Advised.
CD . . . . PH 1151CD
MC . . . . PH 1151C
Philo (USA) / May '93 / Roots Records / Projection / Topic Records / Direct Distribution / Ross Records / C.M. Distribution / Impetus Records.

NORTH.
Tracks: Not Advised.
LP. . . . . PH 1106
MC . . . . PH 1106C
Philo (USA) / '88 / Roots Records / Projection / Topic Records / Direct Distribution / Ross Records / C.M. Distribution / Impetus Records.

Morrissey, Louise

Born into a musical family in County Tipperary, she first worked with her brothers as the Morrisseys in a local youth club, before achieving success on an Irish presentation of Hughie Green's Opportunity Knocks. They enjoyed more than a decade of success until, in 1988, several changes happened and the outfit gained a new identity as Louise Morrissey and her Band. The new outfits' second single, *The night Daniel O'Donnell came to town* (a variation on the Johnny Cash song *The night Hank Williams came to town*), was a great success that well and truly put Louise in the spotlight. (Tony Byworth)

HE THINKS I STILL CARE.
Tracks: He thinks I still care / If you were gone / Slievenamon.
7" . . . . RITZ 206
Ritz / Mar '90 / Pinnacle / Midland Records.

HILLS OF KILLENAULE, THE.
Tracks: Hills of Killenaule.
7" . . . . CMR 84
I&B / '88 / I & B Records.

LOUISE.
Tracks: Not Advised.
LP. . . . . CMLP 1034
CMR/Failte / '88 / I & B Records.

MEMORIES OF HOME.
Tracks: I couldn't leave you if I tried / Let the rest of the world go by / In an Irish country home / Rose of Allendale, The / Cottage in the country / Bright silvery light of the moon / Hills of Killinaule / Tennessee waltz / Night Daniel O'Donnell came to town / Old rustic bridge, The / Flying home to Aherlow / Part of me / Slievenamon / Amazing grace.
VHS. . . . . RITZV 0005
Ritz / Nov '90 / Pinnacle / Midland Records.

WHEN I WAS YOURS.
Tracks: I couldn't leave you if I tried / He thinks I still care / Old flames / Blue eyes crying in the rain / Oh what a love / I still love you / Night Daniel O'Donnell came to town, The / When I was yours / Tipperary on my mind / Rose of Allendale / Hills of Killinaule / Green willow / Slieveenamon / Roses and violets / Amazing grace.
CD . . . . RITZCD 0054
MC . . . . RITZLC 0054
Ritz / Nov '90 / Pinnacle / Midland Records.
CD . . . . RITZCD 508
MC . . . . RITZC 508
Ritz / '91 / Pinnacle / Midland Records.

WHEN I WAS YOURS.
Tracks: When I was yours.
7" . . . . RITZ 215
Ritz / Jul '90 / Pinnacle / Midland Records.

Mourant, Norman

IT'S HARD TO LIVE ON DREAMS.
Tracks: I'll never leave my woman's love / Sunday morning coming down / I know you've never been this far before / Pass the glass / If we're not back in love by Monday / It's hard to live on dreams / More like the movies / Night coach out of Dallas / Diana / All in the movies / Two less lonely people / My love for you.
LP. . . . . FHR 100
Folk Heritage / Jul '82 / Terry Blood Dist.

Mud Acres

MUSIC AMONG FRIENDS.
Tracks: Not Advised.
LP. . . . . ROUNDER 3001
Rounder / '88 / Projection / Roots Records / Swift / C.M. Distribution / Topic Records / Jazz Music / Hot Shot / A.D.A Distribution / Direct Distribution.

Muldoon Brothers

BACK O' THE BARN.
Tracks: Not Advised.
CD . . . . FLACD 101
MC . . . . FLAMC 101
BMG / Nov '92 / BMG.

CIGAREETS IN WHISKEY.
Tracks: Cigareets in whiskey.
■ 7" . . . . FLA 501
Flair / Nov '92.

Muleskinner

MULESKINNER.
Tracks: Mule skinner blues / Footprints in the snow / Dark hollow / Whitehouse blues / Opus 57 in G minor / Runways of the moon / Roanoake / Rain and snow / Soldier's joy / Blue mule.
LP. . . . . ED 219
Edsel / Mar '87 / Pinnacle.

Mullican, Moon

Born Aubrey Mullican, 27.03.1929 near Corrigan, Texas (died 01.01.1967), pianist - lauded as the 'king of hillbilly' piano players through his two-finger right hand efforts, complemented with his enthusiastic vocal deliveries. Played in the Blue Ridge Playboys and with Cliff Bruner and the Texas Wanderers (1940) prior to forming his own band in 1946 and touring the south west. Along with such acts as the Delmores he did much to popularise boogie woogie blues country during the 1940's - 1950's. His own work took in shades of cajun drawn from his time in Lafayette, Louisiana. Among his hits, mainly coming at the backend of the 1940's, were *New pretty blonde (jole blonde)* , *Jole Blon's sister* and *Sweeter than the flowers* . During 1950 he registered a chart topper with *I'll sail my ship alone* (a second million seller for him, following the example of *New pretty blonde*) and two top five efforts in *Goodnight Irene* and *Mona Lisa* . He was to only manage two more on King - *Cherokee boogie* (1951) and *Ragged but right* some ten years later with Starday. (Maurice Hope)

GREATEST HITS:MOON MULLICAN.
Tracks: Not Advised.
LP. . . . . SLP 398
MC . . . . GT 5398
Starday (USA) / Apr '87 / Crusader Marketing Co.

HIS ALL TIME GREATEST HITS.
Tracks: I'll sail my ship alone / Honolulu rock-a-roll-a / Leaves mustn't fall, The / Mona Lisa / Sugar beet / New Jole Blon / Sweeter than the flowers / Pipeliner's blues / I was sorta wonderin' / Cherokee boogie / You don't have to be a baby to cry / Foggy river.
LP. . . . . SING 555
Sing / '88 / Charly / Cadillac Music.
CD . . . . KCD 555
King / Mar '90 / New Note / Koch International.

MOON'S ROCK.
Tracks: Moon's rock / Jenny Lee / Pipeliner blues / Sweet rockin' music / That's me / Cush cush ky yay / Writin' on the wall, The / Wedding of the bugs, The / Nobody knows but my pillow / My love / I'm waiting for ships that never come in / You don't have to be a baby to cry / I'll sail my ship alone / I was sort a wonderin' / Every which a way / I don't know why (I just do) / Sweeter that the flowers / Leaves mustn't fall, The / Anything that's part of you / Early morning blues / My baby's gone / Colinda / Make friends / Cajun coffee song, The / Quarter mile rows / Just to be with you / I'll pour the wine / Fools like me / Big big city / Mr. Tears / She once lived here / This glass I hold.
CD . . . . BCD 15607
Bear Family / Apr '92 / Rollercoaster Records / Swift / Direct Distribution.

MOONSHINE JAMBOREE.
Tracks: Hey Mr Cotton Picker / Leaving you with a worried mind / What's the matter with the mill / Pipeliner blues / Triflin' woman blues / Nine tenths of the Tennessee River / Cherokee boogie / All I need is you / I'll sail my ship alone / Good deal Lucille / Moonshine blues / Rocket to the moon / Downstream / i done it / Goodnight Irene / Rheumatism boogie / Well oh well / Don't ever take my picture down / Lonesome hearted blues, The / It's a sin to love you like I do / I'm gonna move home and bye and bye / I left my heart in Texas / I'll take your hat right off my rack.
CD . . . . CDCHD 458
Ace / Sep '93 / Pinnacle / Hot Shot / Jazz Music / Complete Record Co. Ltd.

OLD TEXAN, THE.
Tracks: Not Advised.
CD . . . . KCD 628
King / Mar '90 / New Note / Koch International.

SEVEN NIGHTS TO ROCK.
Tracks: Not Advised.
LP. . . . . WESTERN 2001
Western (USA) / Feb '89.

SINGS HIS ALL TIME HITS.
Tracks: Not Advised.
CD . . . . KCD 00555
King / Feb '93 / New Note / Koch International.

SWEET ROCKIN' MUSIC.
Tracks: Jenny Lee / That's me / Sweet rockin' music / Moon's rock / Cush cush ky-yay / Writing on the wall / Wedding of the bugs / Big big city / Pipeliner's blues / I was sorta wonderin' / Early morning blues / Sweeter than flowers / Leaves mustn't fall, The / My baby's gone / Every which a way / I'm waiting for ships that never come in.
■ LP. . . . . CR 30231
Charly / Feb '84 / Charly.

Munde, Alan

FESTIVAL FAVOURITES REVISITED.
Tracks: Not Advised.
CD . . . . CDROU 0311
Rounder / Apr '93 / Projection / Roots Records / Swift / C.M. Distribution / Topic Records / Jazz Music / Hot Shot / A.D.A Distribution / Direct Distribution.
MC . . . . ROU 0311C
Rounder / May '93 / Projection / Roots Records / Swift / C.M. Distribution / Topic Records / Jazz Music / Hot Shot / A.D.A Distribution / Direct Distribution.

Murphey, Michael

FLOWING FREE FOREVER.
Tracks: Flowing free forever / North wind and a new moon, A / Cherokee fiddle / See how all the horses come dancing / Yellow house / Changing woman / High country caravan (aka Song for Stephen Stills) / Running wide open / Our Lady of Santa Fe / Wandering minstrel, The.
■ LP. . . . . EPC 81713
CBS / '78 / Sony.

MICHAEL MARTIN MURPHEY.
Tracks: Still taking chances / Two-step is easy / What's forever for / Take it like a man / First taste of freedom / Love affairs / Ring of truth / Interlude / Crystal / Lost river / Hearts in the right place.
■ LP. . . . . LBG 30356
Liberty / Feb '83.

RENEGADE.
Tracks: Renegade / Mansion on the hill.
■ 7" . . . . EPC 3978
Epic / Feb '76.

WHAT'S FOREVER FOR?.
Tracks: What's forever for? / Crystal.
■ 7" . . . . UP 656
United Artists / Sep '82.

Murphy Gospel Group

BUILD ME A CABIN IN THE CORNER OF GLORYLAND.
Tracks: Family who prays shall never part, The / I've found a friend in Jesus / Build me a cabin in the corner of Gloryland / Speak my Lord / Take me back to the old fashioned meeting / Living where the healing waters flow / We'll understand it better bye and bye / This train I'm riding / Precious memories / I'm using my Bible for a roadmap / Take your burden to the Lord.
■ LP. . . . . POL 831
Praise (USA) / Sep '80.

Murray, Anne

This Canadian singer was born in Springhill, Nova Scotia, and worked as a qualified physical education teacher for a year before entering the music business professionally in the mid-sixties. She started out as a regular Canadian TV show *Sing along jubilee*. Its musical director Brian Ahern persuaded her to try her hand at recording. He became her studio producer, and her first album *This was my way* was released on the small Arc label. She then went to Toronto to sign with Capitol Records, with whom she has remained ever since. Murray's first album for Capitol spawned *Snowbird*, the single that made her famous in 1970. *Snowbird* reached No.8 on the American pop chart, and was also a sizeable country hit; it was the first ever record by a Canadian female artist to sell a million copies in the US. Ever since then, she has continued to work in a pleasant middle-of-the-road vein, incorporating tinges of country and folk into her style. Her American Top 20 singles include Kenny Loggins' *Danny's song* (No.7 in 1973), *Love song* (No.12 in 1974) and a cover version of the Beatles *You won't see me* (No.8 in 1974). After a break in the middle of the Seventies to start a family, she returned in 1978 with her biggest hit, the slow building US No.1 ballad *You needed me*. During 1979-80 the singer chalked up three US Top 20 hits which all peaked at No.12: *I just fall in love again, Broken*

M 20 ■ DELETED

hearted me and a revival of the Monkee's *Daydream believer*. During the early Eighties, she scaled down her concentration on ballads in favour of a more uptempo approach; her chart success, in terms of both singles and albums, suffered markedly as a result. Throughout her career, Murray has often been criticised for submerging her deep, potentially intense voice in a lukewarm sea of middle-of-the-road blandness. She has chosen her material from a wide variety of sources, including many remakes of Beatles oldies and other standards. Never in the top league of easy listening performers, she has nonetheless been highly successful. In Britain, only *Snowbird* and *You needed me* reached the Top 40. She finally achieved UK Top 20 status in 1981 with a TV advertised *Very best of* album. (Bob MacDonald).

ANOTHER SLEEPLESS NIGHT.
Tracks: Another sleepless night / It should have been easy.
■ 7" . . . . .CL 209
Capitol / Jul '81.

BOTH SIDES NOW.
Tracks: It's all over / For baby / Last thing on my mind / Both sides now / Paths of victory / All the time / Some birds / Buffalo in the park.
LP 20023
MC 40023
Astan (USA) / Nov '84.
LP . . . . SHLP 123
MC . . . . SHTC 123
Castle Showcase / Apr '86 / Arabesque Ltd.
LP . . . . MTM 028
Meteor / Dec '87 / Terry Blood Dist. / Jazz Music.

CHRISTMAS WISHES.
Tracks: Winter wonderland / Silver bells / Little drummer boy / I'll be home for Christmas / Christmas wishes / Joy to the world / Away in a manger / O holy night / Go tell it on the mountain / Silent night.
■ CD . . . . CDP 746 319 2
Capitol / Dec '86.

COULD I HAVE THIS DANCE.
Tracks: Could I have this dance.
■ 7" . . . . CL 16175
Capitol / Nov '80.

COUNTRY HITS.
Tracks: Cotton Jenny / He still thinks I care / Son of a rotten gambler / Walk right back / Lucky me / Blessed are the believers / It's all I can do / Another sleepless night / Hey baby / Somebody's always saying goodbye / Little good news, A / Just another woman in love / Nobody loves me like you do / Time don't run out on me / I don't think I'm ready for you.
■ CD . . . . CDP 746 487 2
Capitol / Apr '87.

DAYDREAM BELIEVER.
Tracks: Daydream believer / Do you think of me?
■ 7" . . . . CL 16123
Capitol / Apr '80.

DESTINY.
Tracks: Destiny.
■ 7" . . . . CL 15734
Capitol / Oct '72.

FAVOURITES.
Tracks: Not Advised.
MC 4XL 9180
Capitol (Specials) / Dec '88.

HARMONY.
Tracks: Are you still in love with me / Great divide, The / Tonight (I want to be in love) / Perfect strangers / Give me your love / It happens all the time / Harmony / Natural love / Without you.
■ MC . . . . .TCEST 2035
Capitol / Aug '87.
■ CD . . . . CDEST 2035
Capitol / Jun '87.
■ LP . . . . EST 2035
Capitol / Jun '89.

HEART OVER MIND.
Tracks: Once you've had it / Time don't run out on me / I don't think I'm ready for you (Film 'Stick.) / Let your heart do the talking / You haven't heard the last of me / Nobody loves me like you do (With Dave Loggins.) / I should know by now / Love you out of your mind / Take good care of my heart / Our love.
LP . . . . EJ 2402241
Capitol / Dec '84 / EMI.
■ CD . . . . CDP 746 059 2
Capitol / Jul '85.

HEY BABY.
Tracks: Hey baby / Song for the Mira.
■ 7" . . . . .CL 262
Capitol / Aug '82.

HIGHLY PRIZED POSSESSION.
Tracks: Highly prized possession / Uproar.
■ 7" . . . . CL 15806
Capitol / Jan '75.

I JUST FALL IN LOVE AGAIN.
Tracks: I just fall in love again.
■ 7" . . . . CL 16069
Capitol / Apr '80.

I'LL ALWAYS LOVE YOU.
Tracks: I'll always love you / You've got me to hold on to / Stranger at my door / Good old song / Why don't you stick around / Broken hearted me / Easy love / Daydream believer / Wintery feeling / Lovers knot.
■ LP . . . . .EST 12012
Capitol / Dec '79.

IRISH SONGS BY ANNE MURRAY.
Tracks: Not Advised.

LITTLE GOOD NEWS.
Tracks: That's not the way / I'm not afraid anymore / More we try / Little good news, A / Come on love / Come to me / Sentimental favourite / Just another woman in love / When i can't have you / Heart stealer.
■ LP EST7123011
Capitol / Dec '83.

LITTLE GOOD NEWS.
Tracks: Little good news, A / I'm not afraid anymore.
■ 7" . . . . .CL 309
Capitol / Oct '83.

LUCKY ME.
Tracks: Lucky me / You set my dreams to music.
■ 7" . . . . CL 16144
Capitol / May '80.

NEW KIND OF FEELING.
Tracks: Shadows in the moonlight / You've got what it takes / I just fall in love again / Take this heart / Yucatan cafe / You needed me / For no reason at all / Rainin' in my heart / That's why I love you / He's not you / Heaven is here.
■ LP . . . . .EST 11849
Capitol / Apr '79.

NOBODY LOVES ME LIKE YOU DO (Murray, Anne & Dave Loggins).
Tracks: Nobody loves me like you do.
■ 7" . . . . .CL 340
Capitol / Oct '84.

NOW AND FOREVER.
Tracks: Now and forever (you and me) / I don't wanna spend another night without you.
■ 7" . . . . .CL 391
Capitol / Mar '86.

SHADOWS IN THE MOONLIGHT.
Tracks: Shadows in the moonlight / Yucatan cafe.
■ 7" . . . . CL 16091
Capitol / '79.

SNOWBIRD.
Tracks: Snowbird / Fire and rain / Break my mind / Just bidin' my time / Put your hand in the hand / Running / Musical friends / Get together / I'll be your baby tonight.
■ LP . . . . FA 3013
Fame / May '82.
■ MC . . . . TCFA 3013
Fame / May '82.
LP . . . . MFP 41 5738 1
■ MC . . . . MFP 41 5738 4
MFP / Feb '86.

SNOWBIRD.
Tracks: Snowbird.
■ 7" . . . . CL 15654
Capitol / Oct '70.

SOMEBODY'S WAITING.
Tracks: Lucky me / You set my dreams to music / What's forever for / Do you think of me / French waltz / Daydream believer / I'm just happy to dance with you / Moon over Brooklyn / Nevertheless / Beginning to feel like home / Somebody's waiting.
MC . . . . TC EST 1206 4
Capitol / May '80 / EMI.

SOMETHING TO TALK ABOUT.
Tracks: Now and forever (you and me) / Who's leaving who / My life's a dance / Call us fools / On and on / Heartaches / Reach for me / When you're gone / You never know / Gotcha.
LP . . . . EST 2002
■ MC . . . . .TCEST 2002
Capitol / Apr '86.

SONGMAKERS ALMANAC (Murray, Anne & Graham Johnson).
Tracks: Not Advised.
LP . . . . A 66176
Hyperion / Nov '86 / Gamut Distribution / Complete Record Co. Ltd.

SONGS OF THE HEART.
Tracks: You needed me / Hold me tight / That's why I love you / I just fall in love again / You've got me to hold on to / Broken hearted me / Falling in love (falling apart) / I'm happy just to dance with you / Take good care of my heart / More we try, The / You haven't heard the last of me / Heart stealer / Let your heart do the talking / Once you've had it / Lovers chain.
■ CD . . . . CDP 746 488 2
Capitol / Nov '87.

SPECIAL COLLECTION.
Tracks: Snowbird / Destiny / Danny's song / Love song, A / You won't see me / He thinks I still care / You needed me / I just fall in love again / Shadows in the moonlight / Broken hearted me / Daydream believer / Time don't run out on me / Just another woman in love / Now and forever (you and me) / I'd fall in love tonight / If I ever fall in love again / Little good news, A / When I fall / Another sleepless night / Blessed are the believers / Nobody loves me like you do.
CD . . . . CDEST 2112
MC . . . . .TCEST 2112
Capitol / Feb '90 / EMI.
■ LP . . . . EST 2112
Capitol / Feb '90.

TALK IT OVER IN THE MORNING.
Tracks: Not Advised.
LP 022 58168
MC 222 58168
MFP (Holland) / Jan '86 / Pinnacle.
LP 1A 022 58168
MC 1A 222 58168
EMI (Holland) / '88.

TOGETHER (see under Campbell, Glen).

VERY BEST OF ANNE MURRAY.
Tracks: Snowbird / Danny's song / Love song / I just fall in love again / You won't see me / Shadows in the moonlight / Another sleepless night / Where do you go when you dream? / You needed me / Broken hearted me / Daydream believer / Could I have this dance? / I'm happy just to dance with you / Tennessee waltz / Cotton Jenny / Destiny.
■ LP . . . . EMTV 31
Capitol / Sep '81.
■ MC .TCEMTV 31
Capitol / Sep '81.
■ CD . . . . CDP 746 949 2
Capitol / '87.

WALK RIGHT BACK.
Tracks: Walk right back / Just to feel this love from you.
■ 7" . . . . CL 15974
Capitol / Mar '78.

WHERE DO YOU GO WHEN YOU DREAM.
Tracks: Blessed are the believers / It should have been easy / If a heart must be broken / Bitter they are / It's all I can do / We don't have to hold out / Another sleepless night / Where do you go when you dream / Call me with the news / Only love.
■ LP . . . . .EST 12144
Capitol / May '81.

WHERE DO YOU GO WHEN YOU DREAM.
Tracks: Where do you go when you dream / Only dream.
■ 7" . . . . CL 16192
Capitol / Mar '81.

YOU NEEDED ME.
Tracks: You needed me / I still wish the very best for you.
■ 7" . . . . CL 16011
Capitol / Sep '78.

Nadine

JAGGED EDGE OF A BROKEN HEART (Nadine & Nebraska Falls).
Tracks: Jagged edge of a broken heart.
12" . . . . .CUFF 1F
Silver Heart / Jul '89 / Silver Heart Records.

Nash, Cody

LONG RIDE HOME.
Tracks: Please be kind / From the bottle to bottom / Long ride home / Papa / Grass won't grow / Oklahoma city / Please look over me / Irma Jackson / Nashville queen / Keeping each other satisfied / Circle of tears / Don't think I'll ever love again.
LP. . . . . .FHR 081
Folk Heritage / Jul '82 / Terry Blood Dist.

Nash, Terry

TERRY NASH COUNTRY.
Tracks: Six days on the road / Deepening snow, The / Time on my hands / Wheels fell off the wagon / Let me give her the flowers / Walkin' on the other side of Heaven / Hello darlin' / Kiss an angel good morning / I didn't jump the fence / Way it was in '51, The / If my world should end tomorrow / Fighting side of me, The.
LP. . . . . .BGC 269
MC . . . . .KBGC 269
Country House / Jun '81 / Duncans / BGS Productions Ltd.

Nashville All-Stars..

AFTER THE RIOT IN NEWPORT (Nashville All-Stars Country Band).
Tracks: Relaxin' / Nashville to Newport / Opus de funk / Wonderful / 'Round midnight / Frankie and Johnny / Riot-chorus.
CD . . . . BCD 15447
Bear Family / Jun '89 / Rollercoaster Records / Swift / Direct Distribution.

BEAUTIFUL COUNTRY MUSIC: VOL 1 (Nashville All-Stars Country Band).
Tracks: Not Advised.
MC . . . . BBM 110
Bibi (Budget Cassettes) / Jan '82.

BEAUTIFUL COUNTRY MUSIC: VOL 2 (Nashville All-Stars Country Band).
Tracks: Not Advised.
MC . . . . BBM 111
Bibi (Budget Cassettes) / Jan '82.

Nashville Bluegrass Band

Bluegrass group, officially formed in 1985 as a four man unit - after having played informal sessions in Nashville since the 1970's. It's founder members being Pat Enright (guitar vocals), Alan O'Bryant (banjo/vocals/songwriter - his songs covered by Vern Gosdin, Emmylou Harris, Peter Rowan - with *Memories of you* featured on the Harris - Parton - Rondstadt *Trio* album), Mark Hembree (bass), and Mike Compton (mandolin). Toured extensively, taking in China, South America and Europe - playing England's Edale bluegrass festival in 1990 - during which time they'd recorded three albums, for Rounder Records. Stuart Duncan, the mandolin/ fiddle player joined the group in 1986 Other changes saw Roland White replacing Compton in the winter of 1988, while Gene Libbea took Hambree's slot shortly after the founder members had recorded *New Moon Rising* with Peter Rowan. Since joining NBB they've done two outstanding albums - The *Boys Are Back In Town* , the Jerry Douglas produced *Home Of The Blues* (where America's oldest a cappella group The Fairfield Four guest) and *Waiting For The Hard Times To Go* . Their superb musicianship garnered much acclaim. They are also winners of the IBMA's Entertainer and Best Group awards - alongside a string of Grammy nominations. (Maurice Hope)

BOYS ARE BACK IN TOWN, THE.
Tracks: Get a transfer to home / Long time gone / Big river / Hard times / Connie and Buster / Don't let our love die / I'm rollin' through this unfriendly world / Rock bottom blues / Diamonds and pearls / Ghost of Eli Renfro, The / Weary blues from waitin' / Big cow in Carlisle / Dark as the night, blue as the day / Boys are back in town.
CD . . . . SH 3778CD

LP. . . . . SH 3778
MC . . . . SH 3778C
Sugarhill(USA) / '90 / Roots Records / Projection / Impetus Records / C.M. Distribution / Jazz Music / Swift / Duncans / A.D.A Distribution.

IDLE TIME.
Tracks: Idle time / Old devil's dream / Two wings / I closed my heart's door / All I want is you / Angeline the baker / Little Magpie / Last night I dreamed of loving you / No one but my darling / My Lord heard Jerusalem when she moaned / Old timey risin' damp / Train carryin' Jimmie Rodgers home.
CD .CD 0232
LP. . . . . ROUNDER 0232
MC . . . . .ROUNDER 0232C
Rounder / Aug '88 / Projection / Roots Records / Swift / C.M. Distribution / Topic Records / Jazz Music / Hot Shot / A.D.A Distribution / Direct Distribution.

MY NATIVE HOME.
Tracks: Not Advised.
LP. . . . . ROUNDER 0212
Rounder / Sep '85 / Projection / Roots Records / Swift / C.M. Distribution / Topic Records / Jazz Music / Hot Shot / A.D.A Distribution / Direct Distribution.
MC . . . . .ROUNDER 0212C
Rounder / Aug '88 / Projection / Roots Records / Swift / C.M. Distribution / Topic Records / Jazz Music / Hot Shot / A.D.A Distribution / Direct Distribution.
CD . . . . ROUCD 0212
Rounder / Jul '93 / Projection / Roots Records / Swift / C.M. Distribution / Topic Records / Jazz Music / Hot Shot / A.D.A Distribution / Direct Distribution.

ORIGINAL BLUEGRASS BAND, THE.
Tracks: Heavy traffic ahead / I'm going back to old Kentucky / Little cabin on the hill / Bluegrass breakdown / Sweetheart you done me wrong / Molly and Tenbrooks / Toy heart / My Rose of old Kentucky / Wicked path of sin / Summertime is past and gone / When you are lonely / Will you be loving another man.
MC . . . . SSC 06
Rounder / '88 / Projection / Roots Records / Swift / C.M. Distribution / Topic Records / Jazz Music / Hot Shot / A.D.A Distribution / Direct Distribution.
LP. . . . . SS 06
Rounder / Dec '88 / Projection / Roots Records / Swift / C.M. Distribution / Topic Records / Jazz Music / Hot Shot / A.D.A Distribution / Direct Distribution.

TO BE HIS CHILD.
Tracks: Not Advised.
CD .CD 0242
LP. . . . . ROUNDER 0242
MC . . . . .ROUNDER 0242C
Rounder / Aug '88 / Projection / Roots Records / Swift / C.M. Distribution / Topic Records / Jazz Music / Hot Shot / A.D.A Distribution / Direct Distribution.

WAITIN' FOR THE HARD TIMES TO GO.
Tracks: Back trackin' / Waitin' for the hard times to go / Kansas City railroad line / Open pit mine / Train of yesterday / Father I stretch my hand to thee / When I get where I'm goin' / Waltzin's for dreamers / I ain't goin' down / We decided to make Jesus our choice / On again off again / Soppin' the gravy.
CD . . . . SH 3809CD
MC . . . . SH 3809C
Sugarhill(USA) / May '93 / Roots Records / Projection / Impetus Records / C.M. Distribution / Jazz Music / Swift / Duncans / A.D.A Distribution.

Nashville Cats

ALL-TIME COUNTRY AND WESTERN HITS: VOL 3.
Tracks: Not Advised.
MC . . . . BBM 137
Bibi (Budget Cassettes) / Jan '83.

COWBOYS AND CLOWNS.
Tracks: Not Advised.
MC . . . . BBM 112
Bibi (Budget Cassettes) / Jan '82.

Nashville Superpickers

LIVE FROM AUSTIN CITY LIMITS.
Tracks: Canadian sunset / Rollin' in my sweet baby's arms / Fiddlin' around / Long tall Texan / New road under my wheels / Sweet dreams / Shadow of your smile / What a friend we have in Jesus / Orange blossom special.
LP. . . . . .FF 097
Flying Fish (USA) / Mar '89 / Cadillac Music / Roots Records / Projection / C.M. Distribution / Direct Distribution / Jazz Music / Duncans / A.D.A Distribution.

SUPERPICKIN'.
Tracks: Just a little bit of you / Honky tonk blues / Tennessee waltz / Li'l Red Riding Hood / Move it on

---

over / Short on love / She's a yum yum / Howlin' at the moon / Talk back tremblin' lips / Twelfth of never.
LP. . . . . SDLP 021
Sundown / Mar '85 / Terry Blood Dist. / Jazz Music / C.M. Distribution.

Naylor, Jerry

FOR OLD TIME SAKE.
Tracks: For old time sake.
7" . . . . W 723
West Records / '86.

RAVE ON.
Tracks: Rave on / Lady, would you like to dance.
■ 7" .MC 7002
MC / May '78.

Neely, Bill

BLACKLAND FARM BOY.
Tracks: Not Advised.
LP. . . . . ARHOOLIE 5014
Arhoolie (USA) / May '81 / Pinnacle / Cadillac Music / Swift / Projection / Hot Shot / A.D.A Distribution / Jazz Music.

Neilson, Chris

LADY FROM VIRGINIA.
Tracks: Not Advised.
LP. MWSL5 508
Music World / Jan '77.

Nelson, Jackie

BOY WITH A FUTURE.
Tracks: Midnight in heaven / Boy with a future.
7" .GBH 7S 421
August (USA) / Oct '86.

DEAREST MOTHER MINE.
Tracks: Dearest mother mine.
7" .BGC 7S 361
Country House / Sep '84 / Duncans / BGS Productions Ltd.

FOOL SUCH AS I, A.
Tracks: Fool such as I, A / Legend in my time, A.
■ 7" . . . . CHEW 50
Mint / Jun '81.

LET THERE BE PEACE.
Tracks: Let there be peace / Holy City, The.
7" .ITV 7S 458
Scotdisc / Aug '88 / Duncans / Ross Records / Target Records / Conifer Records.

TILL WE MEET AGAIN.
Tracks: I'll be with you in apple blossom time / Two little orphans / Because he lives / When I grow too old to dream / Bringing Mary home / Aloha-oe / Beautiful lady / I overlooked an orchard / Man of calvary / Answer to everything, The / Sad songs / Home along the highway / Walking talking dolly.
LP. JULEP 29
Mint / Nov '87 / RTM / Pinnacle.
LP. . . . . KJULEP 29
Emerald / Nov '87 / I & B Records.

WALKING TALKING DOLLY.
Tracks: Silent night / Walking talking dolly.
■ 7" . . . . CHEW 44
Mint / Nov '81.

WITH LOVE.
Tracks: Dearest mother mine / Sail away / Please don't go / Love is all / Every step of the way / Guilty / Penny arcade / Old lamplighter / If these lips could only speak / Isle of innisfree / If I only had time / Mansion over the hilltop.
LP. . . . . BGC 355
Country House / Sep '84 / Duncans / BGS Productions Ltd.
MC .KBGC 355
N/A / Sep '84.

Nelson, Rick

20 ROCK'N'ROLL HITS: RICKY NELSON.
Tracks: Not Advised.
LP. . . . . IC 064 82749
EMI (Germany) / '83.

ALBUM SEVEN BY RICK.
Tracks: Not Advised.
LP. 1A 058 61357
Pathe Marconi (France) / '88 / Thames Distributors Ltd.

ALL MY BEST.
Tracks: Travellin' man / Hello Mary lou / Poor little fool / Stood up / You are the only one / It's late / You know what I mean / Young world / Lonesome town / I got a feeling / Just a little too much / Believe what you say / It's up to you / Waitin' in school / Never be anyone elese but you / Don't leave me this way / Fools rush in / Teenage idol / I'm walkin' / Mighty good / Sweeter than you / Garden party.
CD . . . . SLCD 801
LP. . . . . SL 801
Silver Line / '88.
MC . . . . MCSL 801
Silver Line / Dec '88.
CD . . . . U 4048
Spectrum (1) / Jun '88 / PolyGram.
CD . . . . CDMF 081
Magnum Force / Mar '92 / Terry Blood Dist. / Jazz Music / Hot Shot.

BELIEVE WHAT YOU SAY.
Tracks: Believe what you say / Do the best you can.
■ 7" . . . . CL 16188
Capitol / Mar '81.

BEST OF RICK NELSON VOL. 1 (Legendary Masters Series).
Tracks: Be-bop baby / Have I told you lately that I love you? / Stood up / Waitin' in school / Believe what you say / My bucket's got a hole in it / Poor little fool / Lonesome town / I got a feeling / Never be anyone else but you / It's late / Just a little too much / Sweeter than you / I wanna be loved / Mighty good / Young emotions / Right by my side / I'm not afraid / Yes sir, that's my baby / Milk cow blues.
CD . . . . CDP 792 771 2
EMI-America / Jul '90 / EMI.

BEST OF RICK NELSON VOL. 2 (Legendary Masters Series).
Tracks: You are the only one / Travelin' man / Hello Mary Lou / Wonder like you, A / Everlovin' / Young world / Summertime / Teenage idol / I've got my eyes on you (and I like what I see) / It's up to you / I need you / That's all / I'm in love again / If you can't rock me / Old enough to love / Long vacation, A / There's not a minute / Today's teardrops / Congratulations / Lucky star / My one desire / You'll never know what you're missing / Tryin' to get to you / One of these mornings / It's all in the game / If you can't rock me (version 2) / More songs by Ricky (Album radio spots).
CD . . . . CZ 417
EMI / Mar '91 / EMI.

BEST OF RICKY NELSON (Hello Mary Lou, Goodbye Heart).
Tracks: Hello Mary Lou (goodbye heart) / Never be anyone else but you / Be bop baby / Stood up / I got a feeling / Someday / Poor little fool / Waitin' in school / It's late / Lonesome town / Sweeter than you / Have I told you lately that I love you / You are the only one / Mighty good / Yes sir that's my baby / Just a little too much / Everlovin' / Young world / It's up to you / Travelin' man / If you can't rock me / Young emotions / Today's teardrops / Wonder like you, A.
CD . . . . CDEMC 3603
Liberty / Aug '91 / EMI.
■ LP. . . . . EMC 3603
Liberty / Aug '91.
■ MC . . . . TCEMC 3603
Liberty / Aug '91.

BEST OF RICKY NELSON.
Tracks: Believe what you say / Poor little fool / It's late / Yes sir thats my baby / Just a little too much / Poor loser / Today's teardrops / Hello Mary Lou / Lonesome two / Sweeter than you / Everlovin' travelin' man / It's up to you / Teenage idol / Someday / Be bop baby / Stood up / Waitin' in school / My bucket's got a hole in it / Never be anyone else but you.
LP. . . . . EG 2607581
MC . . . . EG 2607584
Liberty / Oct '85 / EMI.
CD . . . . CDMFP 6025
CD . . . . CDB 746 588 2
MFP / Apr '88 / EMI.
CD . . . . CDP 790 317 2
CD . . . . CZ 112
Liberty / Jul '88 / EMI.

COLLECTION: RICKY NELSON (Live).
Tracks: Stood up / Waitin' in school / I got a feeling / Travellin' man / Hello Mary Lou / Garden party / You know what I mean / That's alright mama / Believe what you say / Milk cow blues boogie / Never be anyone else but you / Fools rush in / It's up to you / Poor little fool / It's late / Honky tonk women / My bucket's got a hole in it / Boppin' the blues / Lonesome town.
CD . . . . CCSCD 211
MC . . . . CCSMC 211
Castle Collector Series / Mar '89 / BMG / Pinnacle / Castle Communications.
■ Double LP . . . . CCSLP 211
Castle Collector Series / Mar '89.

COMES OF AGE (Nelson, Rick with The Stone Canyon Band).
Tracks: Rock and roll lady / Flower opens gently by, A / Life / Last time around / The / We've got a long way to go / Anytime / Down the Bayou country / Sweet Mary / Let it bring you along / Try (try to fall in love) / Someone to love / Wild nights in Tulsa / I don't want to be lonely tonight / California / Feel so fine / Gypsy pilot.
■ LP. . . . . SEE 217
See For Miles / Nov '87.

COUNTRY FEVER, BRIGHT LIGHTS AND COUNTRY MUSIC.
Tracks: Salty dog / Truck drivin' man / You just can't quit / Louisiana man / Welcome to my world / Kentucky means paradise / Here I am / Bright lights and country music / Hello walls / No vacancy / I'm a fool to care / Congratulations / Night train to Memphis / Take a city bride / Funny how time slips away / Bridge washed out, The / Alone / Big Chief Buffalo Nickel / Mystery train / Things you gave to me / Take these chains from my heart / Lonesome whistle blow (I heard that) / Walkin' down the line / You win again.
LP. . . . . SEE 84
See For Miles / Mar '87 / Pinnacle.
MC . . . . SEEK 84
See For Miles / Sep '87 / Pinnacle.

EVERLOVIN'.
Tracks: Everlovin'.
■ 7" . . . . HLP 9440
London-American / Nov '61.

FOOLS RUSH IN.
Tracks: Fools rush in.
■ 7" 05895
Brunswick / Oct '63.

FOR YOU.
Tracks: For you.
■ 7" 05900
Brunswick / Jan '64.

GARDEN PARTY (Nelson, Rick with The Stone Canyon Band).
Tracks: Let it bring you along / Garden party / So long Mama / I wanna be with you / Are you really real / I'm talking about you / Nightime lady / Flower opens gently by, A / Don't let your goodbye stand / Palace guard.
CD . . . . BGOCD 38
LP. . . . . BGOLP 38
Beat Goes On / Oct '88 / Pinnacle.

GARDEN PARTY.
Tracks: Garden party.
■ 7" . . . . MU 1165
MCA / Oct '72.

GOLDEN GREATS: RICK NELSON.
Tracks: Garden party / Fools rush in / Gypsy woman / She belongs to me / Mystery train / Since I don't have you / Take these chains from my heart / Legend in my time / A / For you / Very thought of you, The / String along / I got a woman / Reason to believe / It doesn't matter anymore / I think it's gonna rain today / Funny how time slips away.
■ LP. . . . . MCM 5027
MCA / Feb '86.
■ MC . . . . MCMC 5027
MCA / Feb '86.

GRAFFITI COLLECTION.
Tracks: Not Advised.
CD . . . . GRCD 07
MC . . . . GRMC 07
Graffiti Collection / Aug '90 / Terry Blood Dist.

GREATEST HITS VOL.1.
Tracks: Not Advised.
VHS. . . . . MMGC 001
Magnum Music / Oct '92 / Conifer Records.

GREATEST HITS VOL.2.
Tracks: Not Advised.
VHS. . . . . MMGV 052
Magnum Music / Oct '92 / Conifer Records.

GREATEST HITS: RICKY NELSON.
Tracks: Not Advised.
LP. . . . . RNLP 215
LP P.Disc. . . . . RNDF 259
Rhino (USA) / Jan '86 / WEA.

HELLO MARY LOU.
Tracks: Hello Mary Lou.
■ 7" . . . . HLP 9347
London-American / Jun '61.

HELLO MARY LOU.
Tracks: Hello Mary Lou.
7" . . . . UP 36522
United Artists / Oct '80 / EMI.
■ 7" G45 31
EMI Golden 45's / Jul '84.
CD Single . . . . CDEMCT 2
MC Single . . . . TCEMCT 2
Liberty / Aug '91 / EMI.
■ 7" . . . . EMCT 2
Liberty / Aug '91.

HEY PRETTY BABY.
Tracks: Not Advised.
LP. . . . . RSRLP 1010
Rockstar (1) / Oct '88 / Swift / C.M. Distribution.

I WANNA BE LOVED.
Tracks: I wanna be loved.
■ 7" . . . . HLP 9021
London-American / Jan '60.

IN CONCERT (From Chicago to LA).
Tracks: Stod up / Waitin' in school / I got a feeling / Travellin' man / Hello Mary Lou / Garden party / You know what I mean / That's alright mama / Believe what you say / Milk cow blues boogie / Never be anyone else but you / Fools rush in / It's up to you / Poor little fool / It's late / Honky tonk woman / My bucket's got a hole in it / Boppin' the blues / Lonesome town.
CD . . . . CDMF 083
Magnum Force / Jan '92 / Terry Blood Dist. / Jazz Music / Hot Shot.

INTAKES.
Tracks: You can't dance / One by one / I wanna move with you / It's another day / Wings / Five minutes more / Change your mind / Something you can't buy / Gimme a little sign / Stay young.
LP. . . . . EPC 81802
Epic / Nov '77 / Sony.
■ MC . . . . EPC 4082089
CBS / '78 / Sony.

IT'S LATE.
Tracks: It's late / Never be anyone else but you.
■ 7" . . . . HLP 8817
London-American / Apr '59.

IT'S UP TO YOU.
Tracks: It's up to you.
■ 7" . . . . HLP 9648
London-American / Jan '63.

JUST A LITTLE TOO MUCH.
Tracks: Just a little too much / Waitin' in school.
■ 7" . . . . UP 633
United Artists / Sep '80.

JUST FOR YOU.
Tracks: Believe what you say / It's up to you / Waitin' in school / Never be anyone else but you / Don't leave me this way / I'm walking / Fools rush in / Teenage idol / Mighty good / Sweeter than you / Garden party / Travellin' man / Hello Mary Lou / Poor little fool / Stood up / You are the only one / It's late / You know what I mean / Young world / Lonesome town / I got a feeling / Just a little too much.
CD . . . . 30232 AAD
CRC (USA) / Oct '89.

LIVE.
Tracks: Not Advised.
CD 15 178
MC 79 052
Laserlight / Aug '91 / TBD / Taylors.

LIVE AT THE ALADDIN.
Tracks: Garden party / Poor little fool / My buckets got a hole in it / Last time around / Milkcow blues / She belongs to me / Lonesome town / Travelling man / Hello Marylou / It's late / Merry Christmas baby / Mystery train.
CD . . . . CDMF 078
MC . . . . MFC 078
Magnum Force / Feb '91 / Terry Blood Dist. / Jazz Music / Hot Shot.

LIVE AT THE UNIVERSAL AMPHITHEATRE.
Tracks: Stood up / Waitin' in school / Lonesome town / It's up to you / I got a feeling / Travellin' man / Hello Mary Lou / Garden party / You know what I mean / Never be anyone else but you / That's alright mama / Poor little fool / Believe what you say / It;s late / Rave on.
VHS. . . . . MMGV 034
MMG Video / Jan '92 / Terry Blood Dist.

LIVE IN CHICAGO.
Tracks: Not Advised.
VHS. . . . . MMGV 053
Magnum Music / Nov '92 / Conifer Records.

MIGHTY GOD.
Tracks: Not Advised.
CD . . . . CD 66129
Ce De International / Jul '93 / Taylors.

MORE SONGS BY RICKY.
Tracks: I'm not afraid / Baby won't you please come home / Here I go again / I'd climb the highest mountain / Make believe / Ain't nothin' but love / When your lover has gone / Proving my love / Hey pretty baby / Time after time / I'm all through with you / Again.
LP. 1A 058 61356
EMI (Holland) / Sep '86.

OZZIE & HARRIET SHOWS, THE VOL. 1.
Tracks: Not Advised.
VHS. . . . . MMGV 051
MMG Video / May '92 / Terry Blood Dist.

PLAYING TO WIN.
Tracks: Almost Saturday night / Believe what you say / Little Miss American dream / Loser babe is you / Back to schooldays / It hasn't happened yet / Call it what you want / I can't take it no more / Don't look at me / Do the best you can.
■ LP. . . . . EST 12109
Capitol / '81.

POOR LITTLE FOOL.
Tracks: Poor little fool.
■ 7" . . . . HLP 8670
London-American / Aug '58.

RICK NELSON IN CONCERT.
Tracks: Not Advised.
CD . . . . MMGV 034
Magnum Music / Jan '93 / Conifer Records.

RICKY.
Tracks: Not Advised.
LP **2C 068 99106**
Liberty (import) / '83 / EMI.

RICKY IS 21.
Tracks: Not Advised.
LP **2C 068 60542**
EMI (France) / '83 / EMI.

RICKY NELSON.
Tracks: Not Advised.
LP **2C 068 99107**
Liberty (import) / '83 / EMI.

RICKY NELSON SINGS RARE TRACKS.
Tracks: Not Advised.
LP . . . . **UF 4086**
United Factories / Oct '87.

RICKY SINGS AGAIN.
Tracks: Not Advised.
LP **2C 068 60543**
EMI (France) / '83 / EMI.

ROCKIN' ROCK.
Tracks: Not Advised.
LP . . . . **MCA 414049**
MCA / Sep '79 / BMG.

ROCKIN' WITH RICKY.
Tracks: Mighty good / Milk cow blues / If you can't rock me / Bebop baby / There's good rockin' tonight / It's late / Waitin' in school / Shirley Lee / There goes my baby / Boppin' the blues / I got a feeling / My babe / Stood up / Down the line / Almost Saturday night / Believe what you say / Little Miss American dream / Loser babe, is you, The / Back to schooldays / It hasn't happened yet / Call it what you want / I can't take it no more / Don't look at me / Do the best you can.
■ **LP** . . . . **CH 85**
Ace / Jan '84.

SINGLES ALBUM (1958-1963), THE.
Tracks: Bebop baby / Have I told you lately that I love you? / Stood up / Waiting in school / Believe what you say / Poor little fool / Lonesome town / Someday / Never be anyone else but you / It's late / Just a little too much / Sweeter than you / Young emotions / Hello Mary Lou / Travellin' man / Everlovin' / Wonder like you, A / It's a young world / Teenage idol / It's up to you.
LP . . . . **UAK 30246**
United Artists / Dec '79 / EMI.
LP . . . . **FA 3045**
MC . . . . **TCFA 3045**
Fame / Nov '82 / EMI.

SINGS SONGS FOR YOU.
Tracks: Not Advised.
■ **CD** . . . . **DMCL 1907**
MCA / Aug '90.

SOMEDAY.
Tracks: Someday / I got a feeling.
■ **7"** . . . . **HLP 8732**
London-American / Nov '58.

SONGS BY RICKY.
Tracks: Not Advised.
LP **2C 068 61358**
EMI (France) / '83 / EMI.

STOOD UP.
Tracks: Stood up.
■ **7"** . . . . **HLP 8542**
London-American / Feb '58.

STRING ALONG WITH RICK.
Tracks: String along / Just relax / I'm a fool / Stop, look and listen / Mean old world / Since I don't have you / You don't know me / Blue moon of Kentucky / Louisiana man / Night train to Memphis / Take a broken heart / Your kind of lovin' / Mystery train / Take a city bride / Helpless / Fire-breathing dragon.
■ **LP** . . . . **CR 30238**
Charly / Jul '84 / Charly.

SWEETER THAN YOU.
Tracks: Sweeter than you / Just a little too much.
■ **7"** . . . . **HLP 8927**
London-American / Sep '59.

TEENAGE IDOL.
Tracks: Teenage idol.
■ **7"** . . . . **HLP 9583**
London-American / Aug '62.

TEENAGE IDOL, A.
Tracks: Not Advised.
CD . . . . **CD 99009**
MC . . . . **WSC 92009**
World Star Collection / Sep '93 / Taylors.

YOUNG EMOTIONS.
Tracks: Young emotions.
■ **7"** . . . . **HLP 9121**
London-American / Aug '60.

YOUNG WORLD.
Tracks: Young world.
■ **7"** . . . . **HLP 9524**
London-American / Mar '62.

Nelson, Tracy

Born 27.12.1947 in Madison, Wisconsin. Singer-songwriter/session vocalist Nelson, after playing in folk and sixties R & B bands (including the Fabulous Limitations and San Francisco's Mother Earth), started paddling her own canoe. Recorded for Atlantic, Flying Fish, Adelphi - and has also featured on numerous recordings as a back-up singer, including the Amazing Rhythm Aces, Guy Clark, Nitty Gritty Dirt Band, Willie Nelson (their duet of *After the fire is gone* a top 20 single in 1974) and Townes Van Zandt being some of those who've utilized one of the most distinctive blues coloured voices around. (Maurice Hope)

COME SEE ABOUT ME.
Tracks: Not Advised.
LP . . . . **FF 209**
Flying Fish (USA) / Mar '89 / Cadillac Music / Roots Records / Projection / C.M. Distribution / Direct Distribution / Jazz Music / Duncans / A.D.A Distribution.

DOIN' IT MY WAY.
Tracks: Not Advised.
LP . . . . **AD 4119**
Adelphi (1) / '81 / Jetstar.

HOMEMADE SONGS.
Tracks: Not Advised.
LP . . . . **FF 052**
Flying Fish (USA) / Mar '89 / Cadillac Music / Roots Records / Projection / C.M. Distribution / Direct Distribution / Jazz Music / Duncans / A.D.A Distribution.

IN THE HERE & NOW.
Tracks: Not Advised.
CD . . . . **ROUCD 3123**
Rounder / Jun '93 / Projection / Roots Records / Swift / C.M. Distribution / Topic Records / Jazz Music / Hot Shot / A.D.A Distribution / Direct Distribution.

Nelson, Willie

Born Abbott, Texas on 30.04.1933, a singer-songwriter who gained extraordinary fame during a ten year period spanning 1975-1985, only to fall into the hands of the receivers when failing to pay his tax returns to the IRS in 1990, owing $16.7 million, some of which went back to the Outlaw period of 1975-1978. He offset some of the debt when he sold the Willie Nelson Music Company for $2.7 million, a dispute that's since been settled to some extent through the selling of the 'IRS tapes' and *Who'll buy my memories* a double cassette which sold via mail order. From the meagre makings of a club singer and DJ in Waco, Texas back in the 50 /60s (he was in the airforce during the Korea War), Nelson made it the hard way, and has gone through three marriages and spent, lost or given away millions of dollars, some lavished on his huge entourage, some by way of the exorbitant wages he pays to his Roadband/crew (it's members over the years featuring Paul English, Grady Martin, Jody Payne, Bee Spears, Mickey Raphael and sister Bobbie), and always living for today because tomorrow may never happen. Nelson's strategy has seen him amass a catalogue of releases second to none. Nelson's small town upbringing had him singing alongside his older sister Bobbie while she played piano. He still has a love for both the old pop standards and gospel music, as has been illustrated many times during his career. Willie's slight stature, dressed casual with his long plaited, red hair tied back, and singing just a little behind the beat, accentuating a distinctive vocal style and fronting an old beat up gut-string guitar, has been a familiar sight for two decades. Musically Nelson's influences, like most Texans, boast a colourful cross-section, harbouring native swing/jazz and blues intonations. Some of his standards go back over thirty years. He moved to Nashville in 1960, where he was soon reeling off hit songs including *Funny* (1961), *Hello Walls* (Faron Young) and *Crazy* (Patsy Cline), by which time the likes of *Family album* and *Night life* had already been conceived. *Pretty paper* was another to hail from this period. Willie's rise to fame as a recording artist didn't take real shape until 1975, although the now Texan - based (since 1970) singer had been plugging away for years, recording mainly for RCA under producer Chet Atkins, before a spell on Atlantic, from where the upturn first took shape, seemingly unbeknown to the label chiefs, who closed their Nashville office whilst Willie was with them. His career-making move came through his recording of Fred Roses's *Blue eyes in the rain* , giving him his first No. 1 country single. He'd only once before made the top ten, and you have to go back to 1963, when the debut charting single *Touch me* on Liberty made the No. 7 slot. From this point Nelson was made. His popularity also wasn't to be confined to the making of records. As a festival organiser there was his Dripping Springs, Texas Annual Picnic an event since 1972, where old friends, both of the contemporary mould and traditional school get to share the same stage. Another Nelson brainchild being Farm Aid, 1993's event being the sixth charity bash for America's displaced farmers. Films that have seen Willie play the lead role include the westerns 'Barbarosa' with Gary Busey, 'Red headed stranger' with Katherine Ross, 'The Electric Horseman' with Robert Redford with the sountrack album released of the same name - featuring the chart topping *My heroes have always been cowboys* and 'Honey-suckle rose' with Dyan Cannon (it's soundtrack spawning *On the road again* , yet another No. 1). In 1978 *Stardust* was released and Willie came up with the ingenious idea (and an idea which took it's appeal to saturation point with middle-class America) to record an album of old pop classics. It included songs which he grew-up on such as *Blue skies* and *Georgia on my mind* both No. 1 singles. As the album was to stay on Billboard's country charts for the next ten years. In the mid to late '70s he put all the frustrating days at RCA and Atlantic behind him. These were what many recall, with no little affection, as country music's 'Outlaw' years. Waylon , Willie, Tompall, Kristofferson and hell-raiser Jerry Jeff Walker were at the heart of the movement, all seeming to be stretching country music's parameters away from the stereotyped Nashville establishment. RCA cleverly put together the *Outlaws* album in 1976, featuring tracks from Tompall, Jessie Colter (Waylon's wife), Waylon and Willie (including their No. 1 hit duet *Good hearted woman* which was the CMA's Single of the year, and also gave them CMA's Duo of the year). It was an outstanding commercial success, becoming the first album out of Nashville to Platinum by selling one million units. The CMA also voted him "Entertainer Of The Year", whilst in 1982 he was recipient of the CMA's Single and Album Of the Year with *Always on my mind.* Nelson's duet albums are a catalogue on their own - although he still found time to pay tribute to the legendary Lefty Frizzell. Willie's Columbia album of 1977 *To Lefty From Willie* featured the No. 1 single *If you've got the money I've got the time* , and was one of two tribute releases, the other being *Willie Nelson Sings Kristofferson* (1979). Willie proved that you no longer had to work out of Music City. By way of his massive cult following Willie Nelson opened the doors for many acts to follow him out of Texas, a state with a great country tradition ranging from swing king Bob Wills to the Texas troubadour himself Ernest Tubb. As the eighties beckoned, Willie (voted CMA's Entertainer Of The Year in 1979) was to be found recording with just about everyone from the old days, including both those with and without recording contracts (Willie never forgot how it was when he too had struggled) including, Roger Miller, Webb Pierce, Ray Prince, Hank Snow and Faron Young. He had met many of these guys at the likes of Tootsie's Lounge bar as a hungry songwriter back in the early sixties. Nelson who owns his own golf course (apart from being a keen golfer he's also quite an avid jogger) and recording studio, at Pedernales, Texas (where he recorded his 1983 concept album about reincarnation *Tougher than leather*). He also had some acts issue releases on his Lonestar label during the late '70s, including Steve Fromholtz, funnyman Don Bowman and Geezinslaw Bros among them. In the mid-eighties, as part of his film career Willie became a member of the Highwaymen - a foursome that included such durable talents as Johnny Cash, Waylon Jennings and Kris Kristofferson. Jimmy Webb's title track creation gave them a No. 1 single in 1985, since which time they've recorded a sequel *Highwaymen 2* and had a video of their live show made whilst touring the States, Canada and Europe in 1993. This was one of Willie's busiest periods on the road, which was to include over 100 shows in Branson. Nelson's own, distinct styling, with that habit of singing behind the beat, also took Steve Goodman's timeless *City of New Orleans* to No. 1 in 1984, a feat likewise achieved by *Forgiving you was easy* . The following were all No. 1 combinations; *Just to satisfy you* (with Waylon Jennings - with whom he recorded four albums, including their 1978 *Waylon and Willie*), *Pancho and Lefty* (with Merle Haggards - they also to record two fine albums *Pancho and Lefty* and *Shores of old Mexico* in 1982 and 1987 respectively and due to their single success they couped the CMA's Duo Award in 1983), *Seven Spanish Angels* (with Ray Charles - his only country No. 1 hit - the song coming from Ray's 1984 CBS album *Friendship*), *To all the girls I;'ve loved before* (1984, with Julio Iglesias - who surprisingly also collected CMA's Duo Award that year with Willie) and *Heartbreak Hotel* (with Leon Russell). Once when hospitalised Nelson, who was inducted into Nashville's Songwriter's Hall Of Fame in 1973, was reported to be still busy writing new material. Nelson, even with his 60th birthday having passed, is still out there showing them all how it's done - both on stage (where his playing of his battered gut-string guitar borders on the hypnotic) and in the recording studio. His Don Was produced 1993 release *On the borderline* , with it's all-star line-up including Paul Simon, Sinead O'Connor and Bonnie Raitt suitably underlined the fact. (Maurice Hope)

18 GOLDEN HITS (Nelson, Willie & Waylon Jennings).
Tracks: Not Advised.
LP. . . . . MA 11141183
Masters (Holland) / '88.

18 GREAT SONGS.
Tracks: Not Advised.
LP. . . . . DELP 308
■ MC . . . . . ZCELP 308
Design / May '84.

20 GOLDEN CLASSICS: WILLIE NELSON.
Tracks: Not Advised.
LP. 20021
MC 40021
Astan (USA) / Nov '84.
CD 2430513
Big Country / Sep '87.
CD 2630512
Big Country / Sep '89.

20 GOLDEN HITS: WILLIE & WAYLON (Nelson, Willie & Waylon Jennings).
Tracks: Not Advised.
CD . . . . . SPEC 85003
Spectrum (CD) / Dec '88 / M.S.D.

20 GOLDEN HITS: WILLIE NELSON.
Tracks: Not Advised.
CD . . . . . SPEC 85002
Spectrum (CD) / Oct '86 / M.S.D.
LP. . . . . MA 11121183
MC . . . . . MAMC 911121183
Masters (Holland) / '88.

20 OF THE BEST: WILLIE NELSON.
Tracks: Funny how time slips away / Night life / My own peculiar way / Hello walls / Mr. Record man / To make a long story short (she's gone) / Good times / She's still gone / Little things / Pretty paper / Bloody Mary morning / What can you do to me now? / December day / Yesterday's wine / Me and Paul / Good-hearted woman / She's not for you / It should be easier now / Phases and stages / Circles, cycles and scenes.
■ LP. . . . . INTS 5208
RCA International / Sep '82.
■ LP. . . . . NL 89137
RCA International / '84.
■ MC . . . . . NK 89137
RCA International / '84.
CD . . . . . ND 89137
RCA / Mar '91 / BMG.

20 OUTLAW REUNION HITS (see under Jennings, Waylon).

ACROSS THE BORDERLINE.
Tracks: American tune / Getting over you / Most unoriginal sin, The / Don't give up / Heartland / Across the borderline / Graceland / Farther down the line / Valentine / What was it you wanted / I love the life I live / If I were the man you wanted / She's not for you / Still is still moving tom me.
CD 472942 2
MC 472942 4
Columbia / May '93 / Sony.

ACROSS THE TRACKS: BEST OF WILLIE NELSON.
Tracks: Not Advised.
■ CD . . . . . TCD 2317
Telstar/Ronco / Dec '88.

ALWAYS ON MY MIND.
Tracks: Always on my mind / Blue eyes crying in the rain / Do right woman, do right man / Whiter shade of pale / Let it be / Staring each other down / Bridge over troubled water / Old fords and natural stone / Permanantly lonely / Last thing I needed first thing this morning / Party's over.
LP. . . . . CBS 85685
■ MC 40 85685
CBS / Apr '82.
CD 35DP 28
CBS / '88 / Sony.
■ CD . . . . . CD 85685
CBS / '88.

ALWAYS ON MY MIND.
Tracks: Always on my mind / Let it be me / Unchained melody / What a wonderful.
7" . . . . . A 4455
CBS / May '84 / Sony.
7" 6558697
CD Single 6558692
■ MC Single 6558694
CBS / Apr '90.

ALWAYS ON MY MIND.
Tracks: Always on my mind.
7" . . . . . A 2511
CBS / May '84 / Sony.

ALWAYS ON MY MIND (OLD GOLD).
Tracks: Always on my mind / Blue eyes crying in the rain.
7" . . . . . OG 9755
Old Gold / Jan '88 / Pickwick Records.

ANGEL EYES.
Tracks: Not Advised.
CD 35DP 150
CBS (import) / '88 / C.M. Distribution / Silva Screen.

BEAUTIFUL TEXAS 1936-1986.
Tracks: Dallas / San Antonio / Streets of Laredo / Who put all my ex's in Texas / Hill country theme / Waltz across Texas / San Antonio rose / Travis letter / Remember the Alamo / Texas in my soul / There's a little bit of everything in Texas / Beautiful Texas / San Antonio rose (2) / Home in San Antone.
LP. . . . . BFX 15256
Bear Family / Nov '86 / Rollercoaster Records / Swift / Direct Distribution.

BEST OF WILLIE NELSON, THE.
Tracks: Will you remember mine / Some other time / I hope so / Is there something on your mind / Broken promises / Blame it on the times / Face of a fighter / Shelter of my arms / End of understanding / Home is where you're happy / And so will you my love / Waiting time / No tomorrow in sight / Everything but you / Happiness lives next door / Right from wrong / Go away / I'll stay around.
■ CD . . . . . CDP 748 398 2
Capitol.
LP. . . . . IC 064 82878
EMI (Germany) / '83.
CD . . . . . OR 0028
Music Collection International / Aug '87 / Terry Blood Dist. / Jazz Music.
MC 4XLL 9391
Capitol (Specials) / Dec '88.
LP. . . . . TCS 2317
MC . . . . . STAC 2317
Telstar/Ronco / '89 / BMG.
■ LP. . . . . STAR 2317
Telstar/Ronco / '89.

BEST OF WILLIE NELSON, THE.
Tracks: Not Advised.
VHS. . . . . VA 30100
Vestron Music Video / Sep '90 / Sony / Gold & Sons / Terry Blood Dist.

BLUE EYES CRYING IN THE RAIN.
Tracks: Blue eyes crying in the rain / Bandera.
■ 7" . . . . . CBS 3675
CBS / Jan '76.

BLUE SKIES.
Tracks: Blue eyes crying in the rain / Georgia on my mind / All of me / Lucky old sun / Whiskey rover / Always / Moonlight in Vermont / On the sunny side of the street / For the good times / Amazing grace / Stardust / Blue skies / My heroes have always been cowboys / Help me make it through the night / On the road again / Tenderly / Summertime / Unchained melody / Funny how time slips away / Red headed stranger.
MC 40 10025
CBS / Sep '81 / Sony.
■ LP. . . . . CBS 10025
CBS / Sep '81.

BLUE SKIES.
Tracks: Blue skies / Moonlight in Vermont.
■ 7" . . . . . CBS 6744
CBS / Oct '78.

BLUE SKIES (SINGLE).
Tracks: Blue skies / Funny how time slips away.
■ 7" . . . . . A 1248
CBS / May '81.

CITY OF NEW ORLEANS.
Tracks: City of New Orleans / Just out of reach / Good time Charlie's got the blues / Why are you picking on me? / She's out of my life / Cry / Please come to Boston / It turns me inside out / Wind beneath my wings / Until it's time for you to go.
LP. . . . . CBS 26135
■ MC 40 26135
CBS / Nov '84.

CITY OF NEW ORLEANS.
Tracks: City of New Orleans.
7" . . . . . A 4707
CBS / Jan '85 / Sony.

CLASSIC WILLIE NELSON.
Tracks: Funny how time slips away / Hello walls / Wake me when it's over / Crazy / Touch me / Half a man / Darkness of the face of the earth / Mr. Record man / Country Willie / There'll be no teardrops tonight / Right or wrong / Night life / Seasons of my heart / Columbus stockade blues.
■ LP. . . . . SLS 50430
Sunset (Liberty) / '79.
LP. . . . . MFP 5602
■ MC . . . . . TCMFP 5602
MFP / Jan '83.

COLLECTION: WILLIE NELSON.
Tracks: On the road again / To all the girls I've loved before / Whiter shade of pale, A / They all went to Mexico / Golden earrings / Always on my mind / City of New Orleans / Seven Spanish angels / Georgia on my mind / Highwayman / Over the rainbow / Let it be me.
CD 4609302
LP. 4609301
MC 4609304
CBS / Mar '88 / Sony.
CD . . . . . NCD 5156
K-Tel / Feb '89 / I & B Records / C.M. Distribution / Arabesque Ltd. / Mono Distributors (Jersey) Ltd. / Prism Leisure PLC / PolyGram / Ross Records / Prism Leisure PLC.

COLLECTION: WILLIE NELSON (2).
Tracks: Blue eyes crying in the rain / Red headed stranger / Crazy / Stormy weather / Blue skies / Homeward bound / Nightlife / Crazy arms / Old friends / Take it to the limit / Trouble in mind / Trouble maker / Healing hands of time / Will the circle be unbroken / Bridge over troubled water / Poncho and Lefty / On the road again / Time of the preacher / Take this job and shove it / Faded love.
■ Double LP . . . . . CCSLP 178
Castle Collector Series / May '88.
CD . . . . . CCSCD 178
MC . . . . . CCSMC 178
Castle Collector Series / Feb '93 / BMG / Pinnacle / Castle Communications.

COMPLETE LIBERTY RECORDINGS 1962-1964 (45 Original Tracks).
Tracks: Roly poly / Lonely little mansion / Am I blue / Willingly / Second fiddle / Let me talk to you / Our chain of love / How long is forever / Things that might have been, The / Way you see me, The / There's gonna be love at my house tonight / You dream about me / You took my happy away / Is this my destiny / Hello walls / River boy / Darkness on the face of the Earth / Mr. Record man / I'll walk alone / Take me as I am (Or let me go) / There goes a man / Funny how time slips away / Country Willie / Crazy / (Blue must be) The colour of the blues / Wake me when it's over / Right or wrong / Last letter, The / Night life / Part where I cry, The / Undo the right / Home Motel / Seasons of my heart / Opportunity to cry / Three days / Where my house lives / Columbus Stockade blues / Half a man / One step beyond / Take my word / Feed it memory / There'll be no teardrops tonight / Tomorrow night / I hope so / Touch me.
CD Set . . . . . CDEM 1505
MC Set . . . . . TCEM 1505
EMI / Aug '93 / EMI.

COUNTRY FAVOURITES.
Tracks: Columbus stockade blues / Seasons of my heart / I'd trade all of my tomorrows (for just one yesterday) / My window faces the south / Go on home / Fraulein / San Antonio rose / I love hyou because / Don't you ever get tired (of hurting me) / Home in San Antone / Heartaches by the number / Making believe.
LP. . . . . NL 90006
■ MC . . . . . NK 90006
RCA / Jan '87.

COUNTRY SONGS (I love country).
Tracks: Me and Bobby McGee / Songwriter / Till I gain control again / Would you lay with me (in a field of stone) / Angel flying too close to the ground / Please come to Boston / Pretend I never happened / Good time Charlie's got the blues / Heart of gold / Railroad lady / Wind beneath my wings / When I dream / We had it all / That's the way love goes / She's not for you / Old five and dimers like me.
■ MC 4510084
CBS / Mar '88.

COUNTRY STORE: WAYLON JENNINGS AND WILLIE NELSON (see under Jennings, Waylon).

COUNTRY STORE: WILLIE NELSON.
Tracks: Not Advised.
LP. . . . . CST 22
MC . . . . . CSTK 22
Country Store / Aug '86 / BMG.

COUNTRY WILLIE.
Tracks: Country Willie / River boy / Darkness on the face of the Earth / Mr. Record man / Night life / I'll walk alone / Take me as I am (or let me go) / Tomorrow night / Take my word / Home motel / Blue must be the colour of the blues / Feed it a memory / Three days / One step beyond / Undo the right / Right or wrong / Columbus stockade blues / Part where I cry, The / Where my house lives / There goes a man.
■ LP. . . . . EMS 1252
Capitol / Nov '87.
■ MC . . . . . TCEMS 1252
Capitol / Nov '87.

CRY.
Tracks: Cry / Why don't you stop picking on me.
7" . . . . . A 4830
CBS / Oct '84 / Sony.

DIAMOND SERIES: WILLIE NELSON.
Tracks: Born to lose / What now my love? / Teach me to forget / Have I told you lately that I love you? / San Antonio rose / I love you because / Don't you ever get tired of hurting me? / Heartaches by the number / My own peculiar way / I walk alone / It will come to pass / Suffer in silence / To make a long story short (she's gone) / Party's over, The / Crazy arms / Both sides now.
■ CD . . . . . CD 90116
Diamond Series / Apr '88.

DON'T GIVE UP.
Tracks: Don't give up (Duet with Sinead O'Connor) / Still is still moving to me / Valentine (On CD single only).
CD Single 659350 2
MC Single 659350 4
Columbia / Jun '93 / Sony.

N 4

■ DELETED

FAMILY BIBLE.
Tracks: Not Advised.
LP. . . . . **IMCA 37167**
MCA / Mar '86 / BMG.

FAMOUS COUNTRY MUSIC MAKERS.
Tracks: Mr. Record Man / It could be said that way / Night life / I gotta get drunk / My own peculiar way / Family bible / One step beyond / Hello walls / Me and Paul / Little things / Wabash cannon ball / Wonderful future / Wake me up when it's over / End of understanding / Who do I know in Dallas? / Funny how time slips away / Suffer in silence / Mountain dew / Moment isn't very long / Healing hands of time / Pretty paper / Darkness on the face of the earth / Yesterday's wine / Sweet memories / One day at a time / Ages / There's a little bit of everything in Texas / Party's over, The.
■ **Double LP** . . . . **DPS 2062**
RCA Red Seal / '79.

FORGIVING YOU WAS EASY.
Tracks: Forgiving you was easy / You wouldn't cross the street.
■ **7"** . . . . **A 6511**
CBS / Aug '85.

GEORGIA ON MY MIND.
Tracks: Stardust / Blue skies / All of me / Unchained melody / September song / On the sunny side of the street / Moonlight in Vermont / Don't get around much anymore / Someone to watch over me.
MC . . . . **HSC 3159**
Hallmark / Sep '84 / Pickwick Records.
■ **LP.** . . . . **SHM 3159**
Hallmark / Sep '84.

GEORGIA ON MY MIND.
Tracks: Georgia on my mind / On the sunny side of the street.
■ **7"** . . . . **CBS 6452**
CBS / Jun '78.

GREAT WILLIE NELSON, THE.
Tracks: Not Advised.
CD . . . . **CDSR 016**
MC . . . . **TCSR 016**
Telstar/Ronco / Jun '93 / BMG.

GREAT, THE.
Tracks: Not Advised.
CD . . . . **PWK 020**
Pickwick / '88 / Pickwick Records.

GREATEST HITS: WILLIE NELSON.
Tracks: Railroad lady / Heartaches of a fool / Blue eyes crying in the rain / Whisky river / Good-hearted woman / Georgia on my mind / If you've got the money, I've got the time / Look what thoughts will do / Uncloudy day / Mamas don't let your babies grow up to be cowboys / My heroes have always been cowboys / Help me make it through the night / Angel flying too close to the ground / I'd have to be crazy / Faded love / On the road again / Heartbreak hotel / If you could touch her at all / Till I gain control again / Stay a little longer.
MC Set **40 88567**
CBS / Jan '82 / Sony.
■ **Double LP** . . . . **CBS 88567**
CBS / Jan '82.

HALF NELSON.
Tracks: Pancho & Lefty / Slow movin' outlaw / Are there any more real cowboys / I told a lie to my heart / Texas on a Saturday night / Seven Spanish angels / To all the girls I've loved before / They all went to Mexico / Honky tonk women / Half a man.
LP. . . . . **CBS 26596**
CBS / Oct '85 / Sony.
■ **MC** **40 26596**
CBS / Oct '85.

HEARTACHES.
Tracks: Not Advised.
CD . . . . **CDSGP 052**
Prestige / Apr '93 / Total / BMG.

HELP ME MAKE IT THROUGH THE NIGHT.
Tracks: Help me make it through the night / I love you because / Heartaches by the number / Both sides now / Have I told you lately that I love you / I'm so lonesome I could cry / Bring me sunshine / What now my love / Born to lose / Everybody's talkin' / Fire and rain / Funny how time slips away / Yesterday / Pretty paper.
MC . . . . **NK 89475**
RCA / Nov '84 / BMG.
■ **LP.** . . . . **NL 89475**
RCA / Nov '84.

HIGHWAYMAN (see under Highwayman).

HIS 28 GREATEST HITS.
Tracks: Not Advised.
CD . . . . **ENT CD 257**
Entertainers / Mar '92.

HISTORIC RE-ISSUE.
Tracks: Not Advised.
CD **100 027 2**
Bridge (MCS Bridge) / Oct '86 / Pinnacle.

HOME IS WHERE YOU'RE HAPPY.
Tracks: Building heartaches / Slow down / Old world / Healing hands of time / And so will you my love / Things to remember / One step beyond / If you can't undo the right undo the wrong / Home is where you're happy / Moment isn't very long, A / Some other time / Blame it on the times / Shelter of my arms / End of an understanding / Will you remember mine / Everything but you / I hope so.
LP. . . . . **SHLP 111**
MC . . . . **SHTC 111**
Castle Showcase / Apr '86 / Arabesque Ltd.
CD . . . . **SHCD 111**
Castle Showcase / Apr '90 / Arabesque Ltd.

HONDO'S SONG.
Tracks: Hondo's song / I'd have to be crazy.
■ **7"** . . . . **YB 122**
Young Blood / Dec '81.

HONEYSUCKLE ROSE (Original soundtrack).
Tracks: On the road again / Pick up the tempo / Heaven or hell / Fiddlin' around / Blue eyes crying in the rain / Working man blues / Jumpin' cotton eyed Joe / Whiskey river / Bloody Mary morning / Loving you was easier than anything / I don't do windows / Coming back to Texas / If you want me to love you I will / It's not supposed to be that way / You show me yours and I'll show you mine / If you could touch her at all / Angel flying too close to the ground / I guess I've come to live here in your eyes / Angel eyes / So you think you're a cowboy / Make the world go away / Two sides to every story / Song for you / Uncloudy day.
■ **Double LP** . . . . **CBS 22080**
CBS / Nov '80.

HORSE CALLED MUSIC.
Tracks: Nothing I can do about it now / Highway, The / I never cared for you / If I were a painting / Spirit / There you are / If my world didn't have you / Horse called music, A / Is the better part over.
LP. **4654381**
MC **4654384**
CBS / Jul '89 / Sony.
■ **CD** **4654382**
CBS / Jul '89.

IS THERE SOMETHING ON YOUR MIND.
Tracks: Ghost, The / Lets pretend / I'm gonna lose a lot of teardrops / Wastin' time / Go away / No tomorrow in sight / New way to cry, A / Broken promises / I let my mind wander / December days / I can't find the time / I didn't sleep a wink / You wouldn't cross the street to say goodbye / Suffering in silence / I feel sorry for him / You'll always have someone / I just don't understand / Building heartaches / Pages / Is there something on your mind / Face of a fighter / I hope so / Everything but you / Moment isn't very long, A / Some other time / Shelter of my arms / Blame it on the times / End of an understanding / One step beyond.
CD . . . . **CDGRF 032**
MC . . . . **MCGRF 032**
Tring / Feb '93 / Prism Leisure PLC / Midland Records / Taylors.

ISLAND IN THE SEA.
Tracks: Island in the sea / Wake me when it's over / Little things / Last thing on my mind / There is no easy way (but there is a way) / Nobody there but me / Cold November wind / Women who love too much / All in the name of love / Sky train.
LP. **4510401**
MC **4510404**
CBS / Aug '87 / Sony.

JAMMIN' WITH JR (see under Chatwell, J.R.).

JUST TO SATISFY YOU (see under Jennings, Waylon).

KING OF THE OUTLAWS.
Tracks: Not Advised.
CD . . . . **CDCD 1088**
MC . . . . **CDMC 1088**
Charly / Jun '93 / Charly.

LEGEND BEGINS, THE.
Tracks: Some other time / I hope so / Will you remember mine? / Is there something on your mind? / Everything but you / Moment isn't very long, A / Blame it on the times / Face of a fighter / Shelter of my arms / End of understanding.
LP. . . . . **ALEB 2302**
MC . . . . **ZCALB 2302**
Allegiance / Apr '84.
CD . . . . **CDMF 086**
Magnum / Nov '92 / Hot Shot / Swift / Cadillac Music / Arabesque Ltd. / Roots Records.

LET IT BE ME.
Tracks: Let it be me / Permanently lonely.
■ **7"** . . . . **A 2742**
CBS / Sep '82.

LONGHORN JAMBOUREE, THE (Nelson, Willie & Friends).
Tracks: What a way to live / Misery mansion / Rainy day blues / Night life / Man with the blues / Storm was in my heart, The / West Virginia man / Mississippi woman / What'd I say / Save the last dance for me / Honey don't / Blue suede shoes.
■ **LP.** . . . . **CR 30120**
Charly / Jan '77 / Charly.

LOVE SONGS: WILLIE NELSON.
Tracks: To all the girls I've loved before / Blue skies / Let it be me / Tenderly / Harbour lights / Mona Lisa / To each his own / Over the rainbow / Seven Spanish angels / Georgia on my mind / Bridge over troubled water / Without a song / Unchained melody / That lucky old sun / In my mother's eyes / Always on my mind.
CD **4501902**
CBS / May '87 / Sony.
CD **4674512**
MC **4674514**
CBS / Oct '90 / Sony.

LOVE SONGS: WILLIE NELSON (ARENA).
Tracks: Moment Isn't very long, A / Some other time / Blame it on the times / Shelter of my arms / End of understanding / Will you remember mine / Everything but you / I hope so / Face of a fighter / Is there something on your mind / Follow me around / Any old arms won't do / I just don't understand / You'll always have someone / I feel sorry for him / Suffering in silence / You wouldn't cross the street / I didn't sleep a wink.
LP. . . . . **ARA 1009**
MC . . . . **ARAC 1009**
Arena / Feb '87.

MY HEROES HAVE ALWAYS BEEN COWBOYS.
Tracks: My heroes have always been cowboys / Rising stars.
■ **7"** . . . . **CBS 8316**
CBS / Mar '80.

MY LIFE.
Tracks: Not Advised.
VHS. . . . . **PLATV 315**
Prism / Mar '93 / Pinnacle / Midland Records.

NIGHT LIFE.
Tracks: Today I started loving you again / Everybody's talkin' / I'm so lonesome I could cry / One day at a time / Sunday morning coming down / Party's over / Night life / Couple more years / Fire and rain / If you can touch her at all / It's not supposed to be that way / Funny how time slips away.
CD . . . . **KCBR 1039**
■ **LP.** . . . . **CBR 1039**
Premier (Sony) / Apr '84.
LP. . . . . **PMP 1015**
MC . . . . **PMPK 1015**
Premier (Sony) / Feb '88 / Sony / Pinnacle.

NIGHTLIFE.
Tracks: Not Advised.
CD **15 485**
MC **79 485**
Laserlight / Jan '93 / TBD / Taylors.

OFF THE RECORD WITH WILLIE NELSON.
Tracks: Some other time / I hope so / Will you remember mine / Is there something on your mind / Everything but you / Moment isn't very long, A / Blame it on the times / Face of a fighter / Shelter of my arms / End of understanding / I'm going to lose a lot of teardrops / Waiting time / No tomorropw in sight / New way to cry, A / Both ends of the candle / Broken promises / Happiness lives next door / Right from wrong / Go away / I'll stay around.
Double LP . . . . **FEDD 1008**
MC Set . . . . **CFEDD 1008**
Sierra / Aug '87.

OLD FRIENDS (Nelson, Willie & Waylon Jennings).
Tracks: We had it all / Why do I have to choose / Blackjack country chains / Till I gain control again / Why baby why / Old friends / Take it to the limit / Would you lay down with me (In a field of stone) / No love at all / Homeward bound.
LP. . . . . **SHM 3212**
MC . . . . **HSC 3212**
Hallmark / Jul '87 / Pickwick Records.
CD . . . . **PWKS 4041**
Pickwick / Feb '91 / Pickwick Records.

OLD TIME RELIGION (Nelson, Willie & Bobby Nelson).
Tracks: Not Advised.
CD **12 114**
MC **72 114**
Laserlight / May '93 / TBD / Taylors.

ON THE ROAD AGAIN (Nelson, Willie & Johnny Lee).
Tracks: On the road again / Jumpin' cotton eyed Joe.
■ **7"** . . . . **A 1632**
CBS / Oct '81.

ONE FOR THE ROAD (Nelson, Willie & Leon Russell).
Tracks: Detour / I saw the light / Heartbreak Hotel / Let the rest of the world go by / Trouble in mind / Don't fence me in / Wild side of life / Ridin' down the Canyon / Sioux City Sue / You are my sunshine / Danny boy / Always / Summertime / Because of you / Am I blue / Tenderly / Far away places / That lucky old sun / Stormy weather / One for my baby.
■ **Double LP** . . . . **CBS 88461**
CBS / '79.

ONE STEP BEYOND.
Tracks: I let my mind wander / December days / I can't find the time / I didn't sleep a wink / You wouldn't cross the street / Suffering in silence / I feel sorry for him / You'll always have someone / I just don't understand / Pages / Any old arms won't do / Slow down old world / Healing hands of time / And so will you my love /

Things to remember / One step beyond / Undo the wrong / Home is where you're happy / Why are you picking on me / I hope so.
CD . . . . CDSM 011
Starburst / Nov '87 / Terry Blood Dist. / Jazz Music.
LP. . . . . SMT 011
Starburst / '88 / Terry Blood Dist. / Jazz Music.

OUTLAW REUNION (Nelson, Willie & Waylon Jennings).
Tracks: Crying / Ghost, The / Sally was a good old girl / Let's pretend / Abilene / I'm gonna lose a lot of teardrops / It's so easy / Wasting time / Love's gonna live here / Go away / Don't think twice / No tomorrow in sight / Dream baby / New way to cry, A / Lorena / Broken promises / Burning memories / I let my mind wander / White lightning / A moment isn't very long / Big Mamou / I can't find the time / Money / I feel sorry for him.
MC Set. . . . . TTMC 030
Tring / Jun '92 / Prism Leisure PLC / Midland Records / Taylors.
CD . . . . CDGRF 058
MC . . . . MCGRF 058
Tring / Jun '93 / Prism Leisure PLC / Midland Records / Taylors.

OUTLAWS (Nelson, Willie & Allan Coe).
Tracks: What a way to live / Misery mansion / Rainy day blues / Night life / Man with the blues / Storm has just begun, The / Got you on my mind / These days / Mississippi woman / Why you been gone so long / Mary Magdelene / West Virginia man.
LP. . . . . TOP 133
MC . . . . KTOP 133
Topline / '86 / Charly / Swift / Black Sun Records.

OUTLAWS' REUNION (Nelson, Willie & Waylon Jennings).
Tracks: Crying / Sally was a good old girl / Abilene / It's so easy / Love's gonna live here / Don't think twice / Building heartaches / Mean old greyhound / Is there something on your mind? / Face of a fighter.
LP. . . . . SDLP 1005
Sundown / Sep '83 / Terry Blood Dist. / Jazz Music / C.M. Distribution.

OUTLAWS' REUNION, VOL.2 (Nelson, Willie & Waylon Jennings).
Tracks: I hope so / Dream baby / Lorena / Everything but you / Burning memories / Moment isn't very long, A / White lightnin' / Big Mamou / Some other time.
LP. . . . . SDLP 1007
Sundown / Apr '84 / Terry Blood Dist. / Jazz Music / C.M. Distribution.
MC . . . . SDC 1007
Sundown / '87 / Terry Blood Dist. / Jazz Music / C.M. Distribution.

OUTLAWS, THE (see under Jennings, Waylon).

POCHO AND LEFTY (see under Haggard, Merle).

PORTRAIT IN MUSIC, A.
Tracks: Face of a fighter / End of understanding / Some other time / Moment isn't very long, A / Blame it on the times / I hope so / Everything but you / Is there something on your mind? / Will you remember mine? / I'm building heartaches / Slow down old world / Healing hands of time / And so will you, my love / Things to remember / One step beyond / If you can't undo the wrong / Home is where you're happy / Why are you picking on me?.
LP. . . . . CBR 1016
MC . . . . KCBR 1016
Premier (Sony) / Jun '85 / Sony / Pinnacle.

PRETTY PAPER.
Tracks: Pretty paper / White Christmas / Winter wonderland / Rudolph the red-nosed reindeer / Jingle bells / Here comes Santa Claus / Blue Christmas / Santa Claus is coming to town / Frosty the Snowman / Silent night, holy night / O little town of Bethlehem / Christmas blues.
■ LP. . . . . CBS 83878
CBS / Dec '82.

PROMISED LAND (Nelson, Willie & Allan Coe).
Tracks: Living in the promised land / I'm not trying to forget you / Here in my heart / I've got the craziest feeling / No place but Texas / You're only in my arms (to cry on my shoulder) / Pass it on / Do you ever think of me / Old fashioned love / Basin street blues / Bach minuet in G.
LP. . . . . CBS 26852
MC 40 26852
CBS / Apr '86 / Sony.

RED HEADED STRANGER.
Tracks: Time of the preacher / I couldn't believe it was true / Blue rock Montana / Blue eyes crying in the rain / Red headed stranger / Just as I am / Denver / O'er the waves / Down yonder / Can I sleep in your arms / Remember me when the candlelights are gleaming / Hands on the wheel / Bandera.
■ LP. 69200
CBS / '78 / Sony.
CD 902123-2
Pickwick / Jul '89 / Pickwick Records.

REPLAY ON WILLIE NELSON.
Tracks: Not Advised.
LP. . . . . FEDB 5007
MC . . . . FEDC 5007
Sierra / Dec '88.

SAN ANTONIO ROSE (Nelson, Willie & Ray Price).
Tracks: San Antonio rose / I'll be there / I fall to pieces / Crazy arms / Release me / Don't you ever get tired / This cold war with you / Funny how time slips away / Night life / Deep water / Faded love.
■ LP. . . . . CBS 84358
CBS / Sep '80.

SHOTGUN WILLIE.
Tracks: Not Advised.
CD 756781426-2
WEA / Mar '93 / WEA.

SLOW DOWN OLD WORLD.
Tracks: Any old arms won't do / Slow down old world / Healing hands of time / And so will you, my love / Things to remember / One step beyond / If you can't undo the wrong / Home is where you're happy / Why are you picking on me?.
LP. . . . . SDLP 1006
Sundown / Apr '84 / Terry Blood Dist. / Jazz Music / C.M. Distribution.
MC . . . . SDC 1006
Sundown / '87 / Terry Blood Dist. / Jazz Music / C.M. Distribution.

SONG FOR YOU, A.
Tracks: Song for you, A / Just as I am / For the good times / Amazing grace / Stormy weather / Blue eyes crying in the rain / Help me make it through the night / Thanks again / One for my baby / Loving her was easier / Moonlight in Vermont / That lucky old sun / Do right woman, do right man / Always on my mind / Whiter shade of pale, A / Let it be me / Staring each other down / Bridge over troubled water / Old fords and a natural stone / Permanently lonely / Last thing I needed first thing this morning / Party's over, The.
LP. . . . . SHM 3127
MC . . . . HSC 3127
Hallmark / Aug '83 / Pickwick Records.
CD . . . . PWKS 578
Pickwick / May '90 / Pickwick Records.

SOUND IN YOUR MIND.
Tracks: That lucky old sun / If you've got the money I've got the time / Penny for your thoughts / Healing hands of time / Thanks again / I'd have to be crazy / Amazing grace / Sound in your mind / Funny how time slips away / Crazy / Night life.
■ LP. . . . . CBS 31838
CBS / Jul '80.
MC 40 22144
CBS / Feb '83 / Sony.
CD 983260 2
MC 983260 4
Sony Collector's Choice / Aug '93 / Pickwick Records.

STARDUST.
Tracks: Stardust / Georgia on my mind / Blue skies / All of me / Unchained melody / September song / On the sunny side of the street / Moonlight in Vermont / Don't get around much anymore / Someone to watch over me.
■ MC 82710
CBS / '78 / Sony.
■ MC 40 82710
CBS / Jun '78.
CD 35DP 120
Import (label unknown) / '88.

STARDUST.
Tracks: Stardust / Funny how time slips away.
■ 7" . . . . A 1083
CBS / Mar '81.

TAKE IT TO THE LIMIT (Nelson, Willie & Waylon Jennings).
Tracks: No love at all / Why do I have to choose / Why baby why / We had it all / Take it to the limit / Homeward bound / Blackjack country chains / Till I gain control again / Old friends / Would you lay with me.
LP. . . . . CBS 25351
MC 40 25351
CBS / Sep '83 / Sony.

TEXAS IN MY SOUL.
Tracks: Dallas / San Antonio / Streets of Laredo / Who put all my ex's in Texas / Hill country theme, The / Waltz across Texas / Travis letter / Remember the Alamo / Texas in my soul / There's a little bit of everything in Texas / Beautiful Texas.
■ LP. . . . . RD 7997
RCA / Sep '71 / BMG.

THERE'LL BE NO MORE TEARDROPS TONIGHT.
Tracks: There'll be no more teardrops tonight / Blue must be the colour of the blues.
■ 7" . . . . UP 36493
United Artists / '79.

THERE'LL BE NO MORE TEARDROPS TONIGHT.
Tracks: River boy / I'll walk alone / Take me as I am or let me go / Tomorrow night / Am I blue? / Take my word / Home motel / Blue must be the colour of the blues / There'll be no more teardrops tonight / Feed a memory.
LP. . . . . UAS 30215
United Artists / Mar '79 / EMI.

THEY ALL WENT TO MEXICO (Nelson, Willie & Carlos Santana).
Tracks: They all went to Mexico / Mudbone.
7" . . . . A 3359
CBS / May '83 / Sony.

THINGS TO REMEMBER.
Tracks: Not Advised.
CD . . . . CTS 55401
MC . . . . CTS 45401
Country Stars / Jan '92.

TO ALL THE GIRLS I'VE LOVED BEFORE (Nelson, Willie & Julio Iglesias).
Tracks: To all the girls I've loved before.
7" . . . . A 4252
CBS / Mar '84 / Sony.

TOUCH ME.
Tracks: Touch me / Half a man / You took my happy away / Willingly / How long is forever? / Is this my destiny? / There's gonna be love in my house tonight / Way you see me, The / Let me talk to you / Things I might have been, The / Roly poly / Second fiddle / Lonely little mansion / Opportunity to cry / Cabin of love / I hope so / You dream about me / Last letter, The / There'll be no more teardrops tonight / Funny how time slips away.
LP. . . . . ED 2606831
■ MC . . . . ED 2606834
Capitol / Aug '85.

TOUGHER THAN LEATHER.
Tracks: My love for the rose / Changing skies / Tougher than leather / Little old fashioned karma / Somewhere in Texas / Beer barrel polka / Summer of roses / Convict and the rose, The / I am the forest / Nobody slides / My friend.
■ LP. . . . . CBS 25063
CBS / Jun '83.

TROUBLEMAKER.
Tracks: Uncloudy day / When the roll is called up yonder / Whispering hope / There is a fountain / Will the circle be unbroken / Trouble maker / In the garden / Where the soul never dies / Sweet by and by / Shall we gather? / Precious memories.
LP. . . . . CBS 32770
■ MC 40 32770
CBS / Mar '86.

UNCHAINED MELODY.
Tracks: Unchained melody / On the sunny side of the street.
7" . . . . A 3408
CBS / May '83 / Sony.

WALKING THE LINE (see under Haggard, Merle).

WAYLON AND WILLIE (see under Jennings, Waylon).

WHAT A WONDERFUL WORLD.
Tracks: Spanish eyes / Moon river / Some enchanted evening / What a wonderful world / South of the border / Ole buttermilk sky / Song from Moulin Rouge / To each his own / Twilight time / Accentuate the positive.
■ LP. 4625141
CBS / Oct '88.
CD 4625142
■ MC 4625144
CBS / Oct '88.

WILD AND WILLIE.
Tracks: I'm going to lose a lot of teardrops / Waiting time / No tomorrow in sight / New way to cry, A / Both ends of the candle / Broken promises / Happiness lives next door / Right from wrong / Go away / I'll stay around.
LP. . . . . ALEB 2309
MC . . . . ZCALB 309
Allegiance / Apr '84.

WILLIE NELSON.
Tracks: Not Advised.
MC Set . . . . DTO 10087
Ditto / '88 / Pickwick Records.

WILLIE NELSON.
Tracks: No tomorrow in sight / New way to cry, A / I'll stay around / Broken promises / Lets pretend / Take it to the limit / Angel eyes / I'm movin' on / Faded love / Old friends / Jim, I wore a tie today / I gotta get drunk / Reasons to quit / Seven Spanish angels / Loving her was easier / Show me yours (and I'll show you mine) / They all went to Mexico / Hello walls / There stands the glass / Heartbreak hotel.
MC . . . . ZCGAS 757
Audio Fidelity / Oct '84 / Telstar/Ronco.
CD 100 027
Bridge (MCS Bridge) / '86 / Pinnacle.
LP. . . . . CBS 54946
CBS / Mar '87 / Sony.
■ MC 40 54946
CBS / Mar '87.
CD . . . . ONN 39
Object Enterprises / May '89 / Gold & Sons / Terry Blood Dist. / Midland Records.

WILLIE NELSON & JOHNNY LEE (Nelson, Willie & Johnny Lee).
Tracks: Not Advised.
LP . . . 20022
MC . . . 40022
Astan (USA) / Nov '84.

WILLIE NELSON AND FAMILY IN CONCERT.
Tracks: Whiskey river / Stay a little longer / Funny how time slips away / Crazy / Night life / If you've got the money, I've got the time / Mama's don't let your babies grow up to be cowboys / I can get off on you / If you could touch her at all / Good hearted woman / Red headed stranger medley / Just as I am / Under the double eagle / Till I gain control again / Bloody Mary morning / I'm a memory / Mr. Record man / Hello walls / One day at a time / Will the circle be unbroken / Amazing grace / Take this job and shove it / Uncloudy day / Only daddy that'll walk the line / Song for you / Roll in my sweet baby's arms / Georgia on my mind / I gotta get drunk.
■ **Double LP** . . . CBS 88333
CBS / Apr '79.

WILLIE NELSON AND FAMILY IN CONCERT (Nelson, Willie & Family).
Tracks: Not Advised.
VHS . . . 662350
Fox Video / '88.

WILLIE NELSON SINGS KRISTOFFERSON.
Tracks: Me and Bobby McGee / Help me make it through the night / Pilgrim chapter 33, The / Why me / For the good times / You show me yours (and I'll show you mine) / Loving her was easier / Sunday mornin' comin' down / Please don't tell me how the story ends.
CD . . . 9827262
Pickwick/Sony Collectors Choice / Apr '92 / Pickwick Records.

WILLIE NELSON'S GREATEST HITS.
Tracks: Railroad lady / Heartaches of a fool / Blue eyes crying in the rain / Whiskey river / Good hearted woman, A / Georgia on my mind / If you've got the money I've got the time / Look what thoughts will do / Uncloudy day / Mammas / Don't let your babies grow up to be cowboys / My heroes have always been cowboys / Help me make it through the night / Angel flying too close to the ground / I'd have to be crazy / Faded love / On the road again / Heartbreak hotel / If you could touch her at all / Till I gain control again / Stay a little longer.
CD . . . 4714122
MC . . . 4714124
Sony Music / '92 / Sony.

WINNING HAND, THE (see under Parton, Dolly).

WITHOUT A SONG.
Tracks: Without a song / Once in a while / Autumn leaves / I can't begin to tell you / Harbour lights / Golden earrings / To each his own / As time goes by / Dreamer's holiday.
LP . . . CBS 25736
CBS / Mar '85 / Sony.
■ **MC** . . . 40 25736
CBS / Mar '85.
CD . . . 35DP 107
CBS / '88 / Sony.

WORLD OF WILLIE NELSON, THE.
Tracks: Will you remember mine / Some other time / I hope so / Is there something on your mind / Broken promises / Blame it on the times / Face of a fighter / Shelter of my arms / End of understanding / Home is where you're happy / And so will you my love / Waiting time / Everything but you / Happiness lives next door / No tomorrow in sight / Right from wrong / Go away / I'll stay around.
LP . . . WW 2004
MC . . . WW 20044
Warwick Reflections / Jun '86 / Sony.

YESTERDAY'S WINE.
Tracks: Where's the show? / Let me be a man / In God's eyes / Family Bible / It's not for me to understand / These are difficult times / Remember the good times / Summer of roses / December day / Yesterday's wine / Me and Paul / Going home.
LP . . . INTS 5014
MC . . . INTK 5014
RCA International / Apr '80 / BMG.

Nerney, Declan

IF I WERE IN YOUR SHOES.
Tracks: If I were in your shoes.
CD Single . . . RITZCD 258
MC Single . . . RITZC 258
Ritz / Jun '93 / Pinnacle / Midland Records.

PHOTOGRAPHS AND MEMORIES.
Tracks: Walkin' on new grass / Crazy dreams / Kelly's mountain dew / World of our own, A / Those green hills are rolling still / Never again will I knock on your door / North to Alaska / My native town Drumish / I found my girl in the good U.S.A. / Just call me lonesome from now on / When we were sweet sixteen / Old man trouble / Among the Wicklow Hills / Picture of my world.
VHS . . . RITZV 0011
Ritz / '90 / Pinnacle / Midland Records.

WALKIN' ON NEW GRASS.
Tracks: Walkin' on new grass / Among the Wicklow hills / I found my girl in the USA / Give an Irish girl to me / North to Alaska / Just call me lonesome from now on / Stand at your window / Crazy dreams / Tipperary on my mind / Never again will I knock on your door / I still miss someone / I'd rather love and lose you / World of our own, A / Molly Bawn.
CD . . . CD 0059
MC . . . LC 0059
Ritz / '90 / Pinnacle / Midland Records.
CD . . . RITZRCD 526
MC . . . RITZRC 526
Ritz / Apr '93 / Pinnacle / Midland Records.

Nesmith, Michael

Country-rock singer-songwriter , founder member of sixties pop group the Monkees. Left the group in 1969 to carve out a solo career - just when the West Coast country-rock movement was breaking. Born Michael Robert Nesmith in Houston, Texas on 30.12.1942, he grew up in Dallas and was later to play the folk clubs of San Antonio. Following a stint in the Air Force he played in Michael Murphy's Wildfire than in a folk group called The Survivors. He recorded solo for the Colpix label under the name of Michael Blessing. Nesmith was a great contributor to the country rock genre - his fine songwriting being much admired. His writing gained more commercial acceptance than his own, often unclassified recordings. His best known probably being *Some of Shelley's blues* (NGDB and Linda Ronstadt - also registering, modestly on the country charts for Texas band the Maine Brothers (1985)). Linda Ronstadt while still with the Stone Poneys in 1967 enjoyed her first chart success with Nesmith's *Different drum* a US No.13 pop hit. After issuing his 1968 instrumental album *The whitcha tain whistle sings* on Dot records and breaking away from the Monkees, he formed his First and Second National Band. His subsequent albums have been *Magnetic south* , *Loose salute* and *Navada fighter* on RCA. In the line-up were Illinois - born West Coast based session Steel guitarist Orville J 'Red' Rhodes (together they also recorded *And the hits just keep on comin'*) as he cut six albums in double quick time on the label. Set up his own Countryside label (under Elektra), with Steve Fromholtz and Linda Hargrove both recording for it. Sadly the latter's work wasn't released, due to Elektra withdrawing it's support as a result of a personnel change. He formed the Pacific Arts Corporation during mid - 70's, a record label, and later video label - winner of video's first Grammy 1982. It's early subjects including a video for Nesmith's *Rio* (1977), top 30 pop hit in UK - *Joanne* (1970) being his best US pop Success. Much of his work's been made available since in CD format on Awareness. (Maurice Hope)

AND THE HITS JUST KEEP ON COMING (Nesmith, Michael & Countryside Band).
Tracks: Not Advised.
■ **LP** . . . ILPS 9439
Island / Feb '77.
CD . . . AWCD 1027
Awareness / Nov '91 / Total / BMG / A.D.A Distribution.

BEST OF MIKE NESMITH.
Tracks: Silver moon / Different drum / Harmony constant / Two different roads / Mama Nantucket / Bonaparte's retreat / Some of Shelly's blues / Rainmaker / Listen to the band / Grand ennui / Nevada fighter / Conversations / Joanne / I've just begun to care.
LP . . . RS 1064
RCA / Aug '76 / BMG.

ELEPHANT PARTS.
Tracks: Not Advised.
VHS . . . AWV 101
Awareness Video / Apr '92.

FROM A RADIO ENGINE.
Tracks: Not Advised.
CD . . . AWCD 1029
Awareness / Mar '92 / Total / BMG / A.D.A Distribution.

INFINITE RIDER.
Tracks: Not Advised.
CD . . . AWCD 1031
Awareness / Mar '92 / Total / BMG / A.D.A Distribution.

LOOSE SALUTE (Nesmith, Michael & The First National Band).
Tracks: Silver moon / I fall to pieces / Thanx for the ride / Dedicated friend / Conversations / Tengo amore / Listen to the band / Bye, bye, bye / Lady of the valley / Hello lady.
CD . . . AWCD 1024
MC . . . AWT 1024
Awareness / Mar '91 / Total / BMG / A.D.A Distribution.

MAGNETIC SOUTH (Nesmith, Michael & The First National Band).
Tracks: Calico girlfriend / Nine times blue / Little red rider / Crippled lion, The / Joanne / First national rag / Mama Nantucket / Keys to the car / Hollywood / One rose / Beyond the blue horizon.
CD . . . AWCD 1023
MC . . . AWT 1023
Awareness / Mar '91 / Total / BMG / A.D.A Distribution.

NAVAJO TRAIL.
Tracks: Navajo trail / Love's first kiss.
■ **7"** . . . WIP 6398
Island / Jul '77.

NEVADA FIGHTER (Nesmith, Michael & The First National Band).
Tracks: Grand ennui / Propinquity (I've begun to care) / Here I am / Only bound / Nevada fighter / Texas morning / Tumbling tumbleweed / I looked away / Rainmaker / Rene.
CD . . . AWCD 1025
MC . . . AWT 1025
Awareness / Mar '91 / Total / BMG / A.D.A Distribution.

NEWER STUFF, THE.
Tracks: Not Advised.
CD . . . AWCD 1014
Awareness / Apr '89 / Total / BMG / A.D.A Distribution.
LP . . . AWL 1014
■ **MC** . . . AWT 1014
Awareness / Apr '89 / Total / BMG / A.D.A Distribution.

OLDER STUFF, THE.
Tracks: Not Advised.
CD . . . AWCD 1032
Awareness / Mar '92 / Total / BMG / A.D.A Distribution.

PRETTY MUCH YOUR STANDARD RANCH STASH (Nesmith, Michael & Countryside Band).
Tracks: Not Advised.
■ **LP** . . . ILPS 9440
Island / Feb '77.
CD . . . AWCD 1028
Awareness / Sep '91 / Total / BMG / A.D.A Distribution.

PRISON, THE.
Tracks: Not Advised.
CD . . . AWCD 1020
MC . . . AWT 1020
Awareness / Dec '90 / Total / BMG / A.D.A Distribution.
LP . . . AWL 1020
Awareness / '92 / Total / BMG / A.D.A Distribution.

RIO.
Tracks: Rio / Life the unsuspecting captive.
■ **7"** . . . WIP 6373
Island / Mar '77.
7" . . . AWP 014
Awareness / Apr '89 / Total / BMG / A.D.A Distribution.

TANTAMOUNT TO TREASON.
Tracks: Not Advised.
CD . . . AWCD 1026
Awareness / Sep '91 / Total / BMG / A.D.A Distribution.

New Grass Revival

Modern 'new age' bluegrass quartet. Their debut album was on Flying Fish in 1972, when lifetime member and multi-instrumentalist Sam Bush, banjoist Courtney Johnson, guitarist dobroist Curtis Burch and bass player Ebbo Walker (replaced by vocalist John Cowan in 1972) joined forces, playing support to Leon Russell - with whom they made an album in 1981. Since then they have recorded regularly, particularly for Flying Fish, and Sugar Hill during the mid-eighties. Burch and Johnson having by then moved on, they were replaced by banjo virtuoso Bela Fleck and guitarist/songwriter Pat Flynn (in time to figure on Sugar Hill's deferred 1989 *Live* album - recorded in Toulouse five years before), and gaining major distribution in 1987 when signing to Capitol - with two albums forthcoming before disbanding in 1991. Singles action has been confined to four relatively small hits , with only *Unconditional Love* and *Can't Stop Now* making country's top fifty. In 1988 they took part in the Nitty Gritty Dirt Band's *Circle 2* album, playing on the charting *Don't You Hear Jerusalem Moan* . Sam Bush, has since joined Emmylou Harris' Nash Ramblers. (Maurice Hope)

BARREN COUNTRY.
Tracks: Not Advised.
LP . . . FF 083
Flying Fish (USA) / May '79 / Cadillac Music / Roots Records / Projection / C.M. Distribution / Direct Distribution / Jazz Music / Duncans / A.D.A Distribution.

CAN'T STOP NOW.
Tracks: Can't stop now / Unconditional love.
■ **7"** . . . CL 499
Capitol / Jun '88.

COMMONWEALTH.
Tracks: Not Advised.
LP . . . FF 254
Flying Fish (USA) / Mar '89 / Cadillac Music / Roots Records / Projection / C.M. Distribution / Direct Distribution / Jazz Music / Duncans / A.D.A Distribution.

FLY THROUGH THE COUNTRY.
Tracks: Not Advised.
■ **LP** . . . FLY 0001
Flyright / Feb '79.
LP . . . FF 016

Flying Fish (USA) / Mar '89 / Cadillac Music / Roots Records / Projection / C.M. Distribution / Direct Distribution / Jazz Music / Duncans / A.D.A Distribution.

FRIDAY NIGHT IN AMERICA.
Tracks: Friday night in America / You plant your fields / Let's make a baby king / Do what you gotta do / Let me be your man / Lila / Callin' Baton Rouge / Whatever way the wind blows / Big foot / Angel eyes / I'm down.
CD . . . . CDP 790 739-2
CD . . . . CZ 224
LP. C1 90739
■ MC C4 90739
Capitol / Aug '89.

HOLD ON TO A DREAM.
Tracks: Hold on to a dream / One way street / Can't stop now / I'll take tomorrow / Before the heartache rolls in / Looking past you / How about you / Metric lips / I can talk to you / Unconditional love.
CD . . . . CDEST 2063
CD . . . . CDP 746 962 2
LP. . . . . EST 2063
■ MC . . . . .TCEST 2063
Capitol / Jun '88.

NEW GRASS REVIVAL.
Tracks: What you do to me / Love someone like me / Lonely rider / Sweet release / How many hearts / In the middle of the night / Saw you runnin' / Ain't that peculiar / Seven by seven.
LP. . . . . AML 3116
■ MC . . . . TCAML 3116
EMI-America / Apr '87.

ON THE BOULEVARD.
Tracks: Not Advised.
LP. . . . . SH 3745
Sugarhill(USA) / Mar '85 / Roots Records / Projection / Impetus Records / C.M. Distribution / Jazz Music / Swift / Duncans / A.D.A Distribution.

STORM IS OVER, THE.
Tracks: Not Advised.
LP. . . . . FLY 0002
Flyright / Feb '79 / Hot Shot / Roots Records / Wellard Dist. / Charly / Swift / Projection.

TOO LATE TO TURN BACK NOW.
Tracks: White freight liner blues / Good woman's love, A / One more love song / Walk in Jerusalem / Watermelon man / Reach / Sapporo.
■ LP. . . . . SNTF 722
Sonet / Aug '78 / Swift / C.M. Distribution / Roots Records / Jazz Music / Sonet Records / Cadillac Music / Projection / Wellard Dist. / Hot Shot.
LP. . . . . FF 050
Flying Fish (USA) / Mar '89 / Cadillac Music / Roots Records / Projection / C.M. Distribution / Direct Distribution / Jazz Music / Duncans / A.D.A Distribution.

WHEN THE STORM IS OVER.
Tracks: Not Advised.
■ LP. . . . . FF 032
Flying Fish (USA) / Mar '89.
CD . . . . FF 032CD
Flying Fish (USA) / Jul '92 / Cadillac Music / Roots Records / Projection / C.M. Distribution / Direct Distribution / Jazz Music / Duncans / A.D.A Distribution.

New Lost City Ramblers

20TH ANNIVERSARY CONCERT.
Tracks: Old Joe Clark / Hot corn, cold corn / Barbara Allen / Freight train / Wreck of the old '97 / C & NW railroad blues / Did you ever see the devil / Keep on the sunny side / Soldier and the lady, The / Cold bottom strut / La cassine special / Give the fiddler a dram / Well may the world go / Medley.
LP. . . . . FF 090
Flying Fish (USA) / Feb '87 / Cadillac Music / Roots Records / Projection / C.M. Distribution / Direct Distribution / Jazz Music / Duncans / A.D.A Distribution.

EARLY YEARS, 1958-62, THE.
Tracks: Colored aristocracy / Hopalong Peter / Don't let your deal go down / When first into this country / Sales tax on the women / Rabbit chase / Leaving home / How can a poor man stand such times and live / Franklyn D. Roosevelt's back again / I truly understand you love another man / Old fish song, The / Battleship of Maine, The / No depression in heaven / Dallas rag / Bill Morgan and his gal / Fly around my pretty little Miss / Lady from Carlisle, The / Brown's ferry blues / My long journey home / Talking hard luck / Teetotals, The / Sal got a meatskin / Railroad blues / On some foggy mountain top / My sweet farm girl / Crow black chicken.
CD . . . . SFCD 40036
MC . . . . SFMC 40036
Smithsonian Folkways / '91 / A.D.A Distribution / Topic Records / Direct Distribution / C.M. Distribution.

NEW LOST CITY RAMBLERS VOL.11 (1963-1973).
Tracks: John Brown's dream / Riding on that train / Titanic, The / Don't get trouble in your mind / Cowboy waltz / Shut up in the mines of coal creek / Private John Q / Old Johnny Brooker won't do / I've always been a rambler / Automobile trip through Alabama / Who killed poor Robin / My wife died on Saturday night / Little satchel / Black bottom strut / Cat's got the measles / Dog's got the whooping cough, The / Dear Okie / Smoketowe strut / Little girl and dreamful snake, The / Fishing creek blues / '31 depression blues / Black Jack daisy / Victory rag / Little carpenter, The / On our turpentine farm / Parlez - nous a' boire / Valse du bambaoucheur / Old Joe bone.
CD . . . . SFCD 440040
Smithsonian Folkways / '92 / A.D.A Distribution / Topic Records / Direct Distribution / C.M. Distribution.

OUT STANDING IN THE FIELD.
Tracks: Not Advised.
CD . . . . SF 40040CD
Smithsonian Folkways / Aug '93 / A.D.A Distribution / Topic Records / Direct Distribution / C.M. Distribution.

TWENTY YEARS.
Tracks: Not Advised.
LP. . . . . FF 102
Flying Fish (USA) / May '79 / Cadillac Music / Roots Records / Projection / C.M. Distribution / Direct Distribution / Jazz Music / Duncans / A.D.A Distribution.

New Mississippi Sheiks

NEW MISSISSIPPI SHEIKS AND SAM CHATMON.
Tracks: Not Advised.
LP. . . . . ROUNDER 2004
Rounder / '88 / Projection / Roots Records / Swift / C.M. Distribution / Topic Records / Jazz Music / Hot Shot / A.D.A Distribution / Direct Distribution.

New Ovation

COUNTRY FAVOURITES.
Tracks: Open up your heart / If I said you had a beautiful body / Snow white dove / You're my best friend / Try a little kindness / Good luck charm / Having daydreams / Do you know you are my sunshine / Please help me, I'm falling / If you're not happy / Happy family / Mr. Music Man.
LP. . . . . NA 117
MC . . . . NC 117
Neptune / Jul '80 / Neptune Tapes / A.D.A Distribution.

NEW OVATION.
Tracks: Not Advised.
LP. . . . . NA 110
MC . . . . NC 110
Neptune / Jan '79 / Neptune Tapes / A.D.A Distribution.

New Riders Of The Purple....

Late 1960's San Francisco - formed country - rock band, a splinter group from psychedelic cult rock band the Grateful Dead. Utilized the talents of comtemporary acts Skip Battin (ex - Byrds), the Dead's Mickey Hart, Phil Lesh and Jefferson Starship's Spencer Dryden. Enjoyed a healthy following with their brand of music through the mid-seventies - yet unable to attain any chart action whilst with Columbia or MCA. (Maurice Hope)

ADVENTURES OF PANAMA RED, THE (New Riders Of The Purple Sage).
Tracks: Panama red / It's alright with me / Lonesome L.A. cowboy / Important exportin' man / One too many stories / Kick in the head / You should have seen me runnin' / Teardrops in my eye / L.A. lady / Thank the day / Cement, clay and gloss.
■ LP. 65687
CBS / '78 / Sony.
CD . . . . BGOCD 26
Beat Goes On / Jan '88 / Pinnacle.

BEST OF NEW RIDERS OF THE PURPLE SAGE (New Riders Of The Purple Sage).
Tracks: I don't know you / Glendale train / Hello Mary Lou (Goodbye heart) / Louisiana lady / Kick in the head / Panama Red / Last lonely eagle / You angel you / I don't need no doctor / Henry.
■ LP. 81742
CBS / '78 / Sony.

LOVE HAS STRANGE WAYS (New Riders Of The Purple Sage).
Tracks: Love has strange ways / Red hot woman and ice cold beer.
■ 7" . . . . MCA 299
MCA / May '77.

MARIN COUNTY LINE (New Riders Of The Purple Sage).
Tracks: Till I met you / Llywelyn / Knights and queens / Green eyes a flashing / Oh what a night / Good woman likes to drink with the boys / Turkeys in a straw / Jasper / Echoes / Twenty good men / Little Miss Bad / Take a red.
LP. . . . . MCF 2820
MCA / Feb '78 / BMG.

NEW RIDERS OF THE PURPLE SAGE (New Riders Of The Purple Sage).
Tracks: I don't know you / Whatcha gonna do / Portland woman / Henry / Dirty business / Glendale train / Garden of Eden / All I ever wanted / Last lonely eagle / Louisiana lady.
LP. . . . . ED 265
Edsel / Feb '88 / Pinnacle.
CD . . . . EDCD 265
Edsel / Jul '88 / Pinnacle.

Newbury, Mickey

Born Milton S, Newbury on May 19, 1940 in Houston, Texas. Newbury began writing songs in high school and sang tenor in a harmony quartet. He moved to Nashville in 1965 after a spell in the USAF, where he began to take his writing seriously and subsequently earned himself a contract with Acuff-Rose. He slept in the back of his car for a few months until he eventually had songs recorded by Eddy Arnold and Don Gibson,(*Here comes the rain baby* and *Funny, familiar, forgotten feelings* respectively). He was signed to RCA for two albums *Harlequin melodies* and *Sings his own* both included many songs which defy categorisation but often ended up on the pop charts (e.g. *Just dropped in* by Kenny Rogers). In 1969 he moved to Mercury Records where he recorded such classics as *She even woke me up to tell me she was leaving* , *San Francisco Mabel Joy* and *I don't think much about her no more* . He then moved again, this time to Elektra, where he continued to gain large critical praise but little sales but he did have a top 30 pop hit with *An American trilogy* in 1971, based on three Civil War songs which was also recorded by Elvis Presley live in Las Vegas in 1972. He still continued to provide hits for Waylon Jennings, Marie Osmond and many others but great stardom eluded him. (Donald Clarke)

'FRISCO MABEL JOY.
Tracks: American trilogy / How many times (must the piper be paid) / Future's not what it used to be, The / Mobile blue / Frisco depot / You're not my same sweet baby / Remember the good / Swiss Cottage place / How I love them old songs.
■ LP. 74107
Elektra (Import) / '71.

AFTER ALL THESE YEARS.
Tracks: Sailor, The / Song of sorrow / Let's say goodbye one more time / That was the way it was then / Country boy Saturday night / Truly blue / Just as long as that someone is you / Over the mountain / Catchers in the rye / I still love you (after all these years).
LP. . . . . SRM 1-4024
Mercury (USA) / '81 / Pinnacle.

AMERICAN TRILOGY, AN.
Tracks: American trilogy, An / San Francisco Mabeljoy.
■ 7" . . . . K 12047
Elektra / Jul '72.

HEAVEN HELP THE CHILD.
Tracks: Heaven help the child / Good morning dear / Sunshine / Sweet memories / Why you been gone so long / Cortelia Clark / Song for Susan / San Francisco Mabel Joy.
■ LP. 75055
Elektra (Import) / '73.

HIS EYE IS ON THE SPARROW.
Tracks: Juble Lee's revival / Westphalia Texas waltz / Wish I was / His eye is on the sparrow / Dragon and the mouse, The / Gone to Alabama / It don't matter anymore / I don't know what they wanted me to say / Saint Cecilia / Juble Lee's revival shout.
LP. . . . . HA 44011
■ MC . . . . HA 44011C
Hickory / '78.

I CAME TO HEAR THE MUSIC.
Tracks: I came to hear the music / Breeze lullaby / You only live once (in a while) / Yesterday's gone if you see her / Dizzy Lizzy / If I could be / Organized noise / Love look at us now / Baby's not home / I an I ain't two.
■ LP. 7E 1007
Elektra (Import) / '74.

IN A NEW AGE.
Tracks: Cortelia Clark / I wish I was a willow tree / Sailor, The / Frisco depot / Poison red berries / Lovers / San Francisco Mabel Joy / American trilogy / All my trials.
LP. . . . . AB 101
Airborne / '88.

LIVE AT MONTEZUMA HALL/LOOKS LIKE RAIN.
Tracks: How I love them old songs / Heaven help the child / Earthquake / Cortelia Clark / I came to hear the music / San Francisco Mabel Joy / Bugger red rap / Bugger red blues / How many times (must the piper be paid) / American trilogy / Please send me someone to love / She even woke me up to say goodbye / Write a song / Angeline / I don't think about her no more / T-total Tommy / 33rd of August, The / When the baby in my lady gets the blues / Looks like baby's gone.
■ Double LP . . . . E 2007
Elektra (Import) / '73.

SAILOR, THE.
Tracks: Blue sky shinin' / Let's have a party / There's a part of her holding on somehow / Weed is a weed, A / Let it go / Looking for the sunshine / Darlin' take care of yourself / Long gone / Night you wrote that song.
■ LP. 9311-44017
Hickory / '79.

SWEET MEMORIES.
Tracks: American trilogy / Good morning, dear / If you ever get to Houston / She even woke me up to say Goodbye / Dizzy Lizzy / Sweet memories / Remember

N 8 ■ DELETED

the good / Sunshine / Future's not what it used to be, The / How I love them old songs.
■ LP. . . . . IMCA 945
MCA (Import) / Mar '86.

Newman, Bob

HANGOVER BOOGIE.
Tracks: Hangover boogie / Sweet orchard vine / Rover, rover / Haulin' freight / Sand boogie / Doodle bug / Practice what you preach / Around the corner / Quarantined love / Leftover hash / Chic a choo freight / Lonesome' truck driver's blues / Baby take me home with you / I'm gonna give you a dose of your own medicine / Phfft you were gone / It hurts me / Turtle dovin / Tonight's the night / Lonesome sailor's dream.
LP. . . . . BFX 15168
Bear Family / Nov '84 / Rollercoaster Records / Swift / Direct Distribution.

Newman, Jimmy C.

Born 27.8.1927 in Big Mamou, Louisiana, Jimmy C. Newman and his exciting Cajun Band, have warmed the hearts of many with their music over the years. None more so than the Wembley Country Festival audience of 1980, who experienced his awesome debut. He was made a member of the Grand Ole Opry in 1956, and had his first hit in 1954 with *Cry, cry darling* , on Dot. He had previously been a member of the Shreveport Louisiana Hayride. His biggest hit, reaching No. 2, was *A fallen star* was released again by Dot, the following year Newman moved to MGM where he stayed until 1960 until he moved again, this time to Decca. Perhaps his most famous songs were *The happy cajun* , *Thibodeaux and his Cajun Band* , *Louisiana Saturday night* and of course *Alligator man* . (Maurice Hope)

ALLIGATOR MAN.
Tracks: Alligator man / Big Mamou / Jole blon / Louisiana man / Hollow log / Pretty Texas girl / Good deal Lucille / Bayou talk / Blues stay away from me / D.J. for a day / Everybody's dying for love / Crazy old heart / Just one more night / Finally / Jungles of the world / Temples of Joy / Conflict / Primitivisation / Keep the children alive / Intentions / Realization / Molecatcher, The / Five gallon jar, The / Mr. Lane's maggot / Green ship, The / Other folks' children / Indian lass, The / Pay me my money down / Balance a straw / Dixie's dog / Treadmill song, The / Bungereye / Bonnie Kate of Aberdeen / Lord Carmarthen's march / Wassailing song, The / Gee whoa, Dobbin / Jack the horse courser / Bonnie bunch of roses, The / Haul away the bowline / Bobbing Joan / Ballad of knocking Nelly, The.
■ LP. . . . . CR 30240
Charly / Jan '84 / Charly.

BOP A HULA/DIGGY LIGGY LO.
Tracks: You didn't have to go / Cry cry darlin' / Can I be right / Your true and faithful one / What will I do / I'll always love you darling / Once again / Let me stay in your arms / Night time is cry time / Diggy liggy lo / You don't want me to know / Do you feel like I feel about you / Daydreamin' / Dream why do you hurt me so / Crying for a pastime / Angel have mercy / Blue darlin' / Let me stay in your arms (version 2) / I thought I'd never fall in love again / God was so good / Let's stay together / What will I do (unissued) / I've got you on my mind / Seasons of my heart / Come back to me / I wanta tell all the world / Yesterday's dreams / Let the whole world talk / Honky tonk tears / Last night / No use to cry / Way you're living is breaking my heart, The / What a fool I was to fall for you / Fallen star, A / I can't go on this way / Need me (unissued) / Sweet kind of love, A / Need me / Cry cry darling / You're the idol of my dreams / Step aside shallow water / Bop a hula / Carry on / With tears in my eyes.
CD Set . . . . BCD 15469
Bear Family / Sep '90 / Rollercoaster Records / Swift / Direct Distribution.

CAJUN AND COUNTRY TOO.
Tracks: Not Advised.
LP. 6052
Swallow (USA) / Swift / Wellard Dist.
MC . . . . 6052 TC
Swallow (USA) / '87 / Swift / Wellard Dist.

CAJUN COUNTRY.
Tracks: Sugar bee / Allons a lafayette / Cajun man can, A / Sweet Suzannah / Alligator man / Diggy liggy lo / Louisiana Saturday night / Jole blon / Cry cry darlin' / Big Mamou / Hippy ti yo / Grand chenier.
LP. . . . . INTS 5186
RCA International / Jan '82 / BMG.
LP. . . . . TOP 131
MC . . . . KTOP 131
Topline / '86 / Charly / Swift / Black Sun Records.
LP. . . . . NL 70438
■ MC . . . . NK 70438
RCA / '87.

CAJUN COUNTRY CLASSICS.
Tracks: Alligator man / Thibodeaux & his cajun band / Jambalaya / Jole Blon / Boo-dan / Diggy liggy lo / Big Mamou / Louisiana Saturday night / Cajun man can, A / Big Bayou / Colinda / Basile Waltz / Daydreaming / Lache pas la Patate / Happy Cajun, The / Sugar bee.
■ LP. . . . . CR 30208
Charly / Nov '81.

MC . . . . TCCR 30208
Charly / Sep '86 / Charly.

FOLK SONGS OF THE BAYOU COUNTRY.
Tracks: Not Advised.
LP. . . . . HAT 3013
Stetson / Apr '86 / Crusader Marketing Co. / Swift / Wellard Dist. / Midland Records / C.M. Distribution.

HAPPY CAJUN THE.
Tracks: Not Advised.
LP. . . . . CR 30177
Charly / Mar '80 / Charly.

JIMMY C. NEWMAN AND CAJUN COUNTRY (Newman, Jimmy C. & Cajun Country).
Tracks: Cochon de lait / Tawna woo woo / Cajun born / Louisiana, the key to my soul / Ragin' cajun (scattin' cajun) / Good ole boys from Louisiana / Laughin' my way back to Lafayette / My toot toot.
LP. . . . . IMCA 39047
MCA (Import) / Mar '86 / Pinnacle / Silver Sounds (CD).

JIMMY NEWMAN.
Tracks: Everybody's dying for love / Big mamou / Sail along silv'ry moon / Good deal lucille / Alligator man / I'll hold you in my heart / My happiness / Blue darlin' / Guess I fooled everybody / Finally / You're the only star / Give me heaven.
LP. . . . . HAT 3060
MC . . . . HATC 3060
Stetson / Jun '88 / Crusader Marketing Co. / Swift / Wellard Dist. / Midland Records / C.M. Distribution.

JIMMY NEWMAN & AL TERRY (see under Terry, Al).

LACHE PAS LA PATATE.
Tracks: Not Advised.
LP. 140
La Louisiane / '87 / Swift.

LOUISIANA SATURDAY NIGHT.
Tracks: Diggy liggy lo / Happy Cajun, The / More happy Cajun, The / Sugar bee / Jambalaya / Alligator man / Louisiana Saturday night / Hippy ti yo / Jole Blon / Thibodeaux and his Cajun band / Boo-dan / Corina Corina / Allons a lafayette / Big bayou / Sweet Suzannah / Big Texas / Cajun man can, A / Big mamou / Colinda / Daydreaming / Lache pas la patate / Basile Waltz / Grand chenier.
CD . . . . CDCHARLY 71
Charly / Apr '87 / Charly.

PROGRESSIVE CC.
Tracks: Alligator man / Boo-dan / Big Mamou / Thibodeaux & his cajun band / Louisiana man / Jambalaya / Diggy liggy lo / Jole blon / Louisiana Saturday night.
LP. . . . . CRL 5005
Charly / Nov '77 / Charly.

WILD 'N' CAJUN.
Tracks: Oh Louisiana / Daddy's in his pirouge / French song / Scattin' Cajun / Sugar cane / Mississippi River / Louisiana woman / Cajun fais do do / Cajun love / Bizzy bayou / That's all you gotta know / Colinda.
LP. . . . . PL 70437
■ MC . . . . PK 70437
RCA / Sep '84.

Newton, Juice

Born in Virginia, singer and guitarist Newton began releasing albums in 1975 under the billing Juice Newton & The Silver Spur. By the end of the 70's the outfit had issued five albums containing a blend of country, rock and pop, but Newton lacked the quality and gusto of an artist like Emmylou Harris. Newton dropped the group billing and her career turned around in 1981 with the release of the LP *Juice*. She now went for an overtly commercial country-pop approach which fitted in perfectly with the country genre's move away from its roots and into the mainstream, a phenomenon which was taking place in the wake of the movie Urban Cowboy. The *Juice* album yielded two million-selling US Top Five singles, both remakes: *Angel Of The Morning* had been recorded in 1968 by Merrilee Rush & The Turnabouts and P.P. Arnold, and *Queen Of Hearts* had been a British hit for Dave Edmunds. *Juice* reached No 20 on the Billboard album chart as did Newton's '82 set *Quiet Lies*, which spawned the US No 7 single, the ultra-catchy *Love's Been A Little Hard On Me*. All in all she enjoyed seven American Top Forty singles from 1981-83. Country music was elbowed out of the pop charts during the mid-80's but the singer was well able to compete on the specialist country listings and hit No 1 on the Billboard country singles chart in February '86 with *Hurt*. One of the flaws of Newton's style was that her voice, while pleasant, lacked conviction: she often sounded more like a session singer with a job to do than a creative artist seeking to make her personal mark. Her only UK chart entry was *Angel Of The Morning*, which peaked at No 43 in 1981. (Bob MacDonald).

ANGEL OF THE MORNING.
Tracks: Angel of the morning / Headin' for a heartache.
■ 7". . . . . CL 16189
Capitol / May '81.

CAN'T WAIT ALL NIGHT.
Tracks: Little love, A / One that gets you / Can't wait all night / Restless heart / Easy way out / Let's dance / He's gone / You don't know me / Eye of the hurricane / Waiting for the sun.
CD . . . . PD 84995
LP. . . . . PL 84995
MC . . . . PK 84995
RCA / Oct '84 / BMG.

CAN'T WAIT ALL NIGHT.
Tracks: Can't wait all night.
7". . . . . RCA 441
RCA / Sep '84 / BMG.

COLLECTION: JUICE NEWTON.
Tracks: Not Advised.
LP. . . . . IC 038 85420
EMI (Germany) / Jan '83.

COME TO ME (Newton, Juice & Silver Spur).
Tracks: Come to me / Low down and lonesome / Back down to lonely / Crying too long / Wouldn't mind the rain / Good luck, baby Jane / Save a heart / Fire down below / Good woman at home / You've been around.
LP. . . . . FA 3025
■ MC . . . . TCFA 3025
Fame / May '82.

DIRTY LOOKS.
Tracks: Dirty looks / Twenty years ago.
■ 7". . . . . CL 311
Capitol / Nov '83.

GREATEST HITS: JUICE NEWTON.
Tracks: Not Advised.
■ CD . . . . CDP 7464892
EMI.

HEART OF THE NIGHT.
Tracks: Heart of the night / Love sail away.
■ 7". . . . . CL 278
Capitol / Feb '83.

HEY BABY.
Tracks: Hey baby / Good luck Baby Jane.
■ 7". . . . . CL 16022
Capitol / Oct '78.

JUICE.
Tracks: Angel of the morning / Shot full of love / Ride 'em cowboy / Queen of hearts / River of love / All I have to do is dream / Headin' for a heartache / Country comfort / Texas heartache / Sweetest thing.
■ MC . . . . TC EST 12136
Capitol / Jun '81.
■ LP. . . . . EST 12136
Capitol / May '81.

LOVE'S BEEN A LITTLE BIT HARD ON ME.
Tracks: Love's been a bit hard on me / Ever true.
■ 7". . . . . CL 248
Capitol / May '82.

QUEEN OF HEARTS.
Tracks: Queen of hearts / River of love.
■ 7". . . . . CL 204
Capitol / Jun '81.

QUIET LIES.
Tracks: Heart of the night / Love's been a little bit hard on me / Break it to me gently / Love sail away / I'm dancing as fast as I can / I'm gonna be strong / Trail of tears / Adios my corazon / Falling in love / Ever true.
■ LP. . . . . EST 12210
Capitol / Jul '82.

SWEETEST THING.
Tracks: Sweetest thing / Shot full of love.
■ 7". . . . . CL 217
Capitol / Feb '82.

WELL KEPT SECRET.
Tracks: So many ways / Close enough / I'll never love again / So easy / Love like yours, A / Hey baby / Tell me, baby, goodbye / No reason / It's not impossible / If there could be.
LP. . . . . EST 11811
Capitol / Jan '78 / EMI.

Newton-John, Olivia

Grew up in Australia, formed schoolgirl vocal quartet; solo, she won talent contest sponsored by Johnny O'Keefe (the Australian 'Elvis') with return to UK as prize. Worked there with Australian Pat O'Carroll as Pat and Olivia before Carroll's work permit ran out, then joined Tomorrow, Monkee creator Don Kirshner's manufactured two boy/two girl vocal group, went solo when planned TV series fell through. Sugary version of Bob Dylan's *If Not for You* reached no. 7 UK/25 USA; country flavoured pop hits in UK helped by connection with prod./fiance Shadows guitarist Bruce Welsh, which led to showcase on Cliff Richard TV spots: *Banks Of The Ohio*, George Harrison's *What Is Life*, John Denver's *Take Me Home Country Roads* all hits '71-3. Surprise breakthrough in USA with *Let Me Be There* '73, MCA LP of same title (which incl. six tracks from two-year-old LP on Universal), coming after Eurovision flop with strident *Long*

■ DELETED N 9

Live Love, led to swift relocation westward; when the hit won a grammy for Best Country Vocalist success seemed assured (though '76 CMA award as Best Female Vocalist led to resignations). Split with Welsh personally/professionally led to his former associate (in Marvin Wlesh and Farrar) taking over as producer. Of four top 5 hits in USA '74-5 incl. two at no. 1 only one charted in UK; big hit USA albums incl. *If You Love Me, Let Me Know, Have You Never Been Mellow, Clearly Love, Come On Over, Don't Stop Believin', Making A Good Thing Better, Greatest Hits* set all '75-7 on MCA. She raunched-up her image playing leather clad role in 'Grease' '78 and scored big hits both solo and with John Travolta, singles plus soundtrack LP; *Totally Hot* '78 was another hit album; soundtrack *Xanadu* '80 with then-fashionable Electric Light Orchestra was a hit LP with three hit singles (incl. duet *Suddenly* with Richard), although the film flopped; then she slid further into raunch, pushing aerobic sex in *Physical* '81 (no. 1 title single; no. 5 with *Make A Move On Me*). *Heart Attack* was a no. 3 single '82, incl. in *Greatest Hits Vol II*; soundtrack 'Two Of A Kind' incl. four tracks by her (*Twist Of Fate* a top 5 hit). By '85 she had posed half topless with riding crop in Helmut Newton photo for sleeve of *Soul Kiss*: title track reached top 20, album top 20 LP chart placing in USA since '77: time for another change of image for the charismatic warbler with the unremarkable voice.(Donald Clarke).

BACK TO BASICS (The Essential Collection 1971-1992).
Tracks: If not for you / Banks of the Ohio / What is life / Take me home country roads / I honestly love you / Have you never been mellow / Sam / You're the one that I want / Hopelessly devoted to you / Summer nights / Little more love, A / Xanadu / Magic / Suddenly / Physical / Rumour, The / Not gonna be the one / I need love / I want to be wanted / Deeper than a river.
CD 5126412
MC 5126414
Mercury / Jul '92 / PolyGram.
■ LP. 5126411
Mercury / Jul '92.

BANKS OF THE OHIO.
Tracks: Banks of the Ohio.
■ 7" 7N 25568
Pye International / Oct '71.

CLEARLY LOVE.
Tracks: Not Advised.
CD 31111
MCA (USA) / Jun '88 / MCA (Imports).

COME ON OVER.
Tracks: Jolene / Pony ride / Come on over / It'll be me / Greensleeves / Blue eyes crying in the rain / Don't throw it all away / Who are you now / Smile for me / Small talk and pride / Wrap me in your arms / Long and winding road, The.
LP. . . . . EMC 3124
■ MC . . . . . TCEMC 3124
EMI / May '76.
CD 31082
MCA (USA) / Jun '88 / MCA (Imports).

COME ON OVER.
Tracks: Come on over / Small talk and pride.
■ 7" . . . . . EMI 2466
EMI / May '76.

DEEPER THAN THE NIGHT.
Tracks: Deeper than the night / Please don't keep me waiting.
■ 7" . . . . . EMI 2954
EMI / Jun '79.

DON'T STOP BELIEVIN'.
Tracks: Don't stop believin' / Thousand conversations, A / Compassionate man / New born babe / Hey Mr. Dream maker / Every face tells a story / Sam / Love you hold the key / I'll bet you a kangaroo / Last time you loved, The.
■ LP. . . . . EMC 3162
EMI / Nov '76.

DOWN UNDER.
Tracks: Not Advised.
VHS. . . . . CFV 02572
Channel 5 / Mar '89 / Channel 5 Video / P.R.O. Video / Gold & Sons.

EARLY OLIVIA.
Tracks: If not for you / Love song / What is life / Everything I own / Air that I breathe, The / Me and Bobby McGee / Music makes my day / Long live love / Banks of the Ohio / Take me home country roads / Help me make it through the night / If you love me (let me know) / Have you never been mellow / Please Mr., please (CD only.) / Let me be there (CD only.) / I honestly love you (CD only.).
CD . . . . . CZ 160
CD . . . . . CDP 792 019 2
EMI / Mar '89 / EMI.
■ LP. . . . . EMS 1322
EMI / Mar '89.
■ MC . . . . . TCEMS 1322
EMI / Mar '89.

EMI COUNTRY MASTERS.
Tracks: Love song / Banks of the Ohio / Me and Bobby McGhee / If not for you / Help me make it through the night / If you could read my mind / In a station / Where are you going to my love / Lullaby / No regrets / If I gotta leave / Would you follow me / If / It's so hard to say goodbye / Winterwood / What is life / Changes / Everything I own / I'm a small and lonely light / Just a little too much / Living in harmony / Why don't you write me / Angel of the morning / Mary Skeffington / If we only have love / My old man's got a gun / Maybe then I'll think of you / Amoureuse / Take me home country roads / I love you, I honestly love you / Music makes my day / Heartbreaker / Leaving / You ain't got the right / Feeling best / Rosewater / Being on the losing end / If we try / Let me be there / Country girl / Loving you ain't easy / Have love will travel / Hands across the sea / Please Mr. please / Air that I breathe, The / Loving arms / If you love me (Let me know) / Have you ever been mellow.
CD Set . . . . . CDEM 1503
MC Set . . . . . TCEM 1503
EMI / Aug '93 / EMI.

EVERY FACE TELLS A STORY.
Tracks: Every face tells a story / Love you hold the key.
■ 7" . . . . . EMI 2574
EMI / Jan '77.

FIRST IMPRESSIONS.
Tracks: If not for you / Banks of the Ohio / Love song / Winterwood / Everything I own / What is life / Take me home country roads / Amoureuse / Let me be there / Changes / Music makes my day / If you love me (let me know).
LP. . . . . MFP 41 5740 1
■ MC . . . . . MFP 41 5740 4
MFP / Feb '86.

GREATEST HITS: OLIVIA NEWTON-JOHN.
Tracks: Physical / Tied up / Heart attack / Make a move on me / You're the one that I want / What is life / Xanadu / Summer nights / Landslide / Take me home country roads / Little more love, A / Magic / Suddenly / Changes / Hopelessly devoted to you / Sam / If not for you / Banks of the Ohio / Rosewater / I honestly love you.
LP. . . . . EMA 785
■ MC . . . . . TCEMA 785
EMI.
MC . . . . . TV EMTV 36
EMI / Oct '82 / EMI.
■ LP. . . . . EMTV 36
EMI / Oct '82.
CD . . . . . CDP 746 019 2
EMI / '88 / EMI.

HAVE YOU NEVER BEEN MELLOW.
Tracks: Not Advised.
■ LP. . . . . EMC 3069
EMI / Apr '75.

HEART ATTACK.
Tracks: Heart attack.
■ 7" . . . . . EMI 5347
EMI / Oct '82.

HOPELESSLY DEVOTED TO YOU.
Tracks: Hopelessly devoted to you / Love is a many splendoured thing.
■ 7" . . . . . RSO 17
RSO / Nov '78.

I HONESTLY LOVE YOU.
Tracks: I honestly love you / Physical.
■ 7" . . . . . EMI 2216
EMI / Oct '74.
12" 12EMI 5360
7" . . . . . EMI 5360
EMI / Jan '83 / EMI.

I NEED LOVE.
Tracks: I need love / Warm and tender (Not on 12") / Physical (CD single only) / Sam (CD single only).
12" . . . . . MERX 370
7" . . . . . MER 370
CD Single . . . . . MERCD 370
■ MC Single . . . . . MERMC 370
Mercury / Jun '92.

IF NOT FOR YOU.
Tracks: If not for you.
■ 7" 7N 25543
Pye International / Mar '71.

IF YOU LOVE ME (LET ME KNOW).
Tracks: If you love me (let me know) / Brotherly love.
■ 7" . . . . . EMI 2180
EMI / Jun '74.

IF YOU LOVE ME LET ME KNOW.
Tracks: Not Advised.
CD 31018
MCA (USA) / Jun '88 / MCA (Imports).

LANDSLIDE.
Tracks: Landslide / Falling.
■ 7" . . . . . EMI 5257
EMI / Jan '82.

LET ME BE THERE.
Tracks: Not Advised.
CD 31017
MCA (USA) / Jun '88 / MCA (Imports).

LITTLE MORE LOVE, A.
Tracks: Little more love, A / Borrowed time.
■ 7" . . . . . EMI 2879
EMI / Dec '78.

LIVE: OLIVIA NEWTON-JOHN.
Tracks: Not Advised.
VHS. . . . . CFV 00522
Channel 5 / Jun '86 / Channel 5 Video / P.R.O. Video / Gold & Sons.

LONG LIVE LOVE.
Tracks: Not Advised.
■ LP. . . . . EMC 3028
EMI / Jun '74.

LONG LIVE LOVE.
Tracks: Long live love.
■ 7" 7N 25638
Pye International / Mar '74.

LOVE SONGS: OLIVIA NEWTON JOHN.
Tracks: Please Mr., please / Have you never been mellow / If / Angel of the morning / Behind that locked door (CD only.) / God only knows / Love song / No regrets / If you could read my mind / Little more love, A / I honestly love you / Amoureuse / Where are we going to (CD only.) / Lullaby / I will touch you (CD only.) / Winterwood / If we only have love / Changes.
CD . . . . . CDB 790 722 2
CD . . . . . CD MFP 6042
MC . . . . . TCMFP 5839
MFP / Sep '88 / EMI.
■ LP. . . . . MFP 5839
MFP / Sep '88.

MAGIC.
Tracks: Magic / Whenever you're away from me.
■ 7" . . . . . JET 196
Jet / Aug '80.

MAKE A MOVE ON ME.
Tracks: Make a move on me / Strangers touch.
■ 7" . . . . . EMI 5291
EMI / Apr '82.

MAKING A GOOD THING BETTER.
Tracks: Making a good thing better / Slow dancing / Ring of fire / Coolin' down / Don't cry for me Argentina / Sad songs / You won't see me cry / So easy to begin / I think I'll say goodbye / Don't ask a friend.
■ LP. . . . . EMC 3192
EMI / Aug '77.
■ LP. . . . . FA 3006
Fame / Jun '82.

MAKING A GOOD THING BETTER.
Tracks: Making a good thing better / I think I'll say goodbye.
■ 7" . . . . . EMI 2680
EMI / Sep '77.

MUSIC MAKES MY DAY.
Tracks: Not Advised.
■ LP. . . . . NSPL 28186
Pye / Mar '74.

PHYSICAL.
Tracks: Landslide / Strangers touch / Make a move on me / Falling / Love make me strong / Physical / Silvery rain / Carried away / Recovery / Promise / Dolphin song.
■ LP. . . . . EMC 3386
EMI / Nov '81.

PHYSICAL.
Tracks: Promise, The (dolphin song) / Physical.
7" . . . . . EMI 5234
EMI / '81 / EMI.

PHYSICAL.
Tracks: Not Advised.
■ BETA . . . . . MXP 99 1015 4
PMI / Oct '84.
■ VHS. . . . . MVP 99 1015 2
PMI / Oct '84.

PLEASE MR. PLEASE.
Tracks: Please Mr. Please / Don't cry for me Argentina.
■ 7" . . . . . EMI 2723
EMI / Jun '78.

RUMOUR, THE.
Tracks: Rumour, The / Can't we talk it over in bed / Get out / Walk through the fire / Love and let live / It's not heaven / Big and strong / Tutta la vita.
CD 834957-2
LP. 834957-1
MC 834957-4
Mercury / Oct '88 / PolyGram.

RUMOUR, THE.
Tracks: Rumour, The / Winter angel.
■ CD Single . . . . . MERCD 272
Mercury / Sep '88 / PolyGram.
■ 12" . . . . . MERX 272
Mercury / Sep '88.
■ 7" . . . . . MER 272
Mercury / Sep '88.

SAM.
Tracks: Sam / Changes.
■ 7" . . . . . EMI 2616
EMI / Jun '77.

N 10 ■ DELETED

SOUL KISS.
Tracks: Toughen up / Soul kiss / Queen of the publication / Emotional tangle / Culture shock / Moth to a flame / Overnight observation / You were great, how was I? / Driving music / Right moment, The / Electric (Only on CD and cassette.).
LP. . . . . MERH 77
MC . . . . MERHC 77
Mercury / Feb '86 / PolyGram.
■ CD 826 169-2
Mercury / Feb '86.
CD 31083
MCA (USA) / Jun '88 / MCA (Imports).

SOUL KISS.
Tracks: Soul kiss / Electric.
12" . . . . MERX 210
7" . . . . MER 210
Mercury / Feb '86 / PolyGram.

SOUL KISS.
Tracks: Not Advised.
VHS. SPC 00052
Spectrum (1) / Oct '89 / PolyGram.

SUDDENLY (Newton-John, Olivia & Cliff Richard).
Tracks: Suddenly / You made me love you.
■ 7" . . . . JET 7002
Jet / Oct '80.

TAKE A CHANCE (Newton-John, Olivia & John Travolta).
Tracks: Take a chance / Silvery rain.
■ 7" . . . . EMI 5452
EMI / Feb '84.

TAKE ME HOME COUNTRY ROADS.
Tracks: Take me home country roads.
■ 7" 7N 25599
Pye International / Jan '73.

TIED UP.
Tracks: Tied up / Silvery rain.
7" . . . . EMI 5375
EMI / Mar '83 / EMI.

TILL YOU SAY YOU'LL BE MINE.
Tracks: Till you say you'll be mine / For ever.
■ 7" . . . . F 12396
Decca / May '66.

TOTALLY HOT.
Tracks: Please don't keep me waiting / Dancing round and round / Talk to me / Deeper than the night / Borrowed time / Little more love, A / Never enough / Totally hot / Boats against the current / Gimme some lovin'.
LP. . . . . EMA 789
MC . . . . TC EMA 789
EMI / Jan '78 / EMI.

TOTALLY HOT.
Tracks: Totally hot / Talk to me.
■ 12" . . . . EMI 2923
EMI / Apr '79.

TWIST OF FATE.
Tracks: Twist of fate / Jolene.
7" . . . . EMI 5438
EMI / Oct '83 / EMI.

VIDEO EP: OLIVIA NEWTON JOHN.
Tracks: Desperate times (Living in) / Shakin' you / Take a chance / Twist of fate.
BETA . . . . MXS 99 0007 4
PMI / Jan '84 / EMI / Gold & Sons / Terry Blood Dist.
■ VHS. . . . . MVS 99 0007 2
PMI / Jan '84.
VHS. . . . . PM 0007
Video Collection / May '87 / Gold & Sons / Video Collection / Terry Blood Dist.

WARM AND TENDER.
Tracks: Jenny Rebecca / Rocking (nativity) / Way you look tonight, The / German lullaby / You'll never walk alone / Sleep my princess / Flower, The / Twinkle twinkle little star / Warm and tender / Rock a bye baby / Somewhere over the rainbow / Twelfth of never / All the pretty little horses / When you wish upon a star / Reach out.
■ MC 842 145 4
Mercury / Dec '89.
■ CD 842 145 2
Mercury / Dec '89.
■ LP. 842 145 1
Mercury / Dec '89.

WHAT IS LIFE.
Tracks: What is life.
■ 7" 7N 25575
Pye International / Mar '72.

XANADU (Newton-John, Olivia & ELO).
Tracks: Xanadu / Fool country.
■ 7" . . . . JET 185
Jet / Jun '80.

Nielsen, Chris

LET ME DOWN EASY.
Tracks: Not Advised.
■ LP. . . . . GES 5001
Emerald / Jun '78.

Nita, Rita & Ruby

ROCK LOVE.
Tracks: Rock love / Lovey lips / Leroy / Not anymore / Jimmy Unknown / Pledging my love / Last night in my dreams / Whose baby are you? / Give me love / Baby you're the one / I just won't care anymore / Losin' my baby again / You came to the prom alone / No sweet love ain't around / But I love you just the same / My man true to me / At the old town hall / Borrowed diamonds / Hi de ank tum.
LP. . . . . BFX 15176
Bear Family / Nov '85 / Rollercoaster Records / Swift / Direct Distribution.

Nitty Gritty Dirt Band

Formed in 1966 by Jeff Hanna, Jimmie Fadden, Ralph Barr, Leslie Thompson, John McEuen and Bruce Kunkel (replaced by Chris Darrow in 1968), the N.G.D.B. blended jugband, blues, boogie, traditional and folk into their music, soon capturing a young audience, their first successes included *Some of Shelly's blues* , *House at Pooh Corner* and *Mr. Bojangles* (a million seller) all in 1971. During the early 70's thay put together the biggest album project of all time, the epic *Will the circle be unbroken* , which featured a star-studded line-up including collaborations with Doc Watson, Roy Acuff, Merle Travis and Earl Scruggs, was an attempt to break down the barriers of mistrust between traditional country artists and the younger 'hippy' generation. However after this tour de force they returned to their former more eclectic approach with less inspiring end results. It wasn't until the early eighties that they truly did themselves justice and returned to the country charts regularly, which coincided with their move to Warner Bros. Their first album for their new label *Plain Dirt fashion* , which showed a blend of solid country spiced with an inventive contemporary feel, also yielded the bands first country No. 1 *Long hard road (Sharecroppers dream)* . They followed this success with a series of fine albums before signing with MCA and releasing *Will the circle be unbroken 2* on which the band re-affirmed the potential shown on the first collection. This time they were helped by stars like Emmylou Harris, Chet Atkins, Johnny Cash, Ricky Scaggs, Roger McGuinn and Chris Hillman; who's contributions have deservedly earned the follow-up a response which echoed the plaudits accorded the first triumph. (Merle Lynne)

20 YEARS OF DIRT.
Tracks: Not Advised.
LP. 925382 1
■ MC 925382 4
WEA / Aug '87 / WEA.

ALL I HAVE TO DO IS DREAM.
Tracks: All I have to do is dream / Raleigh - Durham reel.
■ 7" . . . . UP 35875
United Artists / Aug '75.

ALL THE GOOD TIMES.
Tracks: Sixteen tracks / Fish song / Jambalaya / Down in Texas / Creepin' round your back door / Daisy / Slim Carter / Hoping to say / Baltimore / Jamaica, say you will / Do you feel it to / Civil war trilogy / Diggy liggy lo.
CD . . . . BGOCD 93
LP. . . . . .BGOLP 93
Beat Goes On / Dec '90 / Pinnacle.

AMERICAN DREAM, AN.
Tracks: Not Advised.
■ LP. . . . . UAG 30271
United Artists / Nov '79.

AMERICAN DREAM, AN.
Tracks: American dream.
■ 7" . . . . UP 609
United Artists / Oct '79.

BEST OF NITTY GRITTY DIRT BAND.
Tracks: Not Advised.
CD . . . . CDP 746 591 2
EMI / Apr '88 / EMI.
CD . . . . BU 15
EMI / Mar '88 / EMI.

BEST OF NITTY GRITTY DIRT BAND VOL 2.
Tracks: Cadillac ranch / I've been looking / Oh what a love / Working man / I love only you / Fishin' in the dark / Baby's got a hold on me / Face on the cutting room floor / Down that road tonight / Home again.
CD . . . . K 925830 2
LP. . . . . K 925830 1
MC . . . . K 925830 4
Atlantic / Feb '89 / WEA.

BEST OF THE REST.
Tracks: Not Advised.
■ LP. . . . . .MCG 6106
MCA / Sep '90.
■ CD .DMCG 6106
MCA / Sep '90.
■ MC .MCGC 6106
MCA / Sep '90.

COUNTRY STORE: NITTY GRITTY DIRT BAND.
Tracks: Battle of New Orleans / All I have to do is dream / Bayou jubilee / Rave on / Mr. Bojangles / Honky tonkin' / House of poor corner / Some of Shelly's blues / Moon just turned blue, The / Make a little magic / American dream / Hey good lookin' / Slim Carter / Diggy liggy lo.
LP. . . . . CST 33
MC . . . . .CSTK 33
Country Store / Apr '87 / BMG.

DIRT, SILVER AND GOLD.
Tracks: Buy for me the rain / Melissa / Collegiana / Mournin' blues / Willie the weeper / Uncle Charlie's interview / Mr. Bojangles / Some of Shelly's blues / Cure, The / House at Pooh corner / Randy Lynn rag / Opus 36 / Clementi / Living without you / Sixteen tracks / Fish song / Creepin' round your back door / Honky tonkin' / Togary mountain / Soldiers joy / Rippling waters / You are my flower / Battle of New Orleans / All I have to do is dream / Rocky top / Gavotte no.2 / Jamaica lady / Mother Earth (provides for me) / Falling down slow / Bowlegs / Doc's guitar / Bayou jubilee / Dally was a goodun' / Cosmic cowboy / Wine or lose / Woody Woodpecker / Visiting an old friend / Will the circle be unbroken / Foggy mountain breakdown.
LP Set . . . . UAT 9802
United Artists / EMI.

EARLY DIRT 1967-70.
Tracks: Buy for me the rain / Euphoria / Holding / Song for Julia / Dismal swamp / It's raining here in Long Beach / Shadow dream song / Truly right / Tide of love / Collegiana / Mournin' blues / These days / Some of Shelly's blues / Rave on / Mr. Bojangles / House at Pooh Corner / Living without you.
LP. . . . . LIK 3
Decal / Jun '86 / Charly / Swift.

GOLD FROM DIRT.
Tracks: Mr. Bojangles / Some of Shelley's blues / Jamaica say you will / Battle of New Orleans / All I have to do is dream.
■ LP. . . . . UAG 30275
United Artists / Apr '80.

JEALOUSY.
Tracks: Jealousy / Too close for comfort / Fire in the sky / Love is the last thing / Crossfire / Circular man / Catch the next dream / So you run / Forget it / Easy slow.
LP. . . . . LBG 30345
Liberty / May '82 / EMI.

LET'S GO.
Tracks: Heartaches in heartaches / Special look / Shot full of love / Never together / Goodbye eyes / Maryann / Too many heartaches in paradise / Don't get sand in it / Let's go / Dance little Jean.
■ LP. . . . . LBG 400 184 1
Liberty / Jan '84.

MAKE A LITTLE MAGIC.
Tracks: Make a little magic / Badlands / High school yearbook / Leigh Anne riding alone / Anxious heart / Do it (party lights) / Harmony / Too good to be true / Mullen's farewell to America.
LP. . . . . UAG 30308
United Artists / Mar '81 / EMI.

MAKE A LITTLE MAGIC.
Tracks: Make a little magic / Ja's moon.
■ 7" . . . . UP 631
United Artists / Sep '80.

NITTY GRITTY DIRT BAND, THE.
Tracks: Not Advised.
MC 4XLL 9182
Capitol (Specials) / Dec '88.

SOME OF SHELLEY'S BLUES.
Tracks: Some of Shelley's blues / Honky tonkin'.
7" . . . . UP 35499
United Artists / '70 / EMI.

STARS AND STRIPES FOREVER.
Tracks: Jambalaya / Dirt band interview / Cosmic cowboy Part 1 / Aluminium record award / Fish song / Mr. Bojangles / Vassar Clements interview / Listen to the mockingbird / Sheik of araby, The / Resign yourself to me / Dixie hoedown / Cripple creek / Mountain whippoorwill, The / Honky tonkin' / House at Pooh corner / Buy for me the rain / Oh boy / Teardrops in my eyes / Glocoat blues / Stars and stripes forever / Battle of New Orleans / It came from the 50's / My true story / Diggy diggy lo.
CD . . . . BGOCD 128
Beat Goes On / Jul '90 / Pinnacle.

TONITE.
Tracks: Not Advised.
BETA . . . . MXP 99 1034 4
PMI / Jun '86 / EMI / Gold & Sons / Terry Blood Dist.
■ VHS. . . . . MVP 99 1034 2
PMI / Jun '86.
VHS. . . . . HEN 2173
Hendring Video / Mar '89 / BMG / Terry Blood Dist.

UNCLE CHARLIE AND HIS DOG TEDDY.
Tracks: Some of Shelly's blues / Rave on / Living without you / Uncle Charlie / Mr. Bojangles / Clinch

mountain / Back step / Propinquity / Cure, The / Opus 36 / Clementi / Chicken reel / Travellin' mood / Billy in the low / Swanee river / Randy Lynn rag / Santa Rosa / Prodigal's return / Yukon railroad / House at Pooh Corner.
LP . . . . .BGOLP 22
Beat Goes On / '89 / Pinnacle.
CD . . . . BGOCD 22
Beat Goes On / Apr '90 / Pinnacle.

WILL THE CIRCLE BE UNBROKEN (Music Forms A New Circle) (Nitty Gritty Dirt Band & Various Artists).

Tracks: Grand Ole Opry song / Keep on the sunny side / Nashville blues / You are my flower / Precious jewel, The / Dark as a dungeon / Tennessee stud / Black mountain rag / Wreck on the highway, The / End of the world / I saw the light / Sunny side of the mountain / Nine pound hammer / Losin' you (might be the best thing yet) / Honky tonkin' / You don't know my mind / My walkin' shoes / Lonesome fiddle blues / Cannonball rag / Avalanche / Flint Hill special / Togary mountain / Earl's breakdown / Orange blossom special / Wabash cannonball / Lost highway / Doc Watson & Merle Travis: First meeting / Way downtown / Down yonder / Pins and needles (in my heart) / Honky tonk blues / Sailin' on to Hawaii / I'm thinking tonight of my blue eyes / I am a pilgrim / Wildwood flower / Soldier's joy / Will the circle be unbroken / Both sides now.
LP Set 1867063
Capitol / Dec '72 / EMI.
CD Set . . . . CDP 746 589 1/2
MC 1867099
EMI / '88 / EMI.

WILL THE CIRCLE BE UNBROKEN VOL.II.

Tracks: Life's railway to heaven / Grandpa was a carpenter / When t' get my rewards / Don't you hear Jerusalem moan / Little mountain church house / And so it goes / Mary danced with soldiers / Riding alone / I'm sitting on top of the world / Lovin' on the side / Lost river / Bayou jubilee / Blueberry Hill / Turn of the century / One step over the line / You ain't going nowhere / Valley road, The / Will the circle be unbroken / Amazing grace.
■ CD . . . . DMCFD 9001
MCA / May '89.
■ Double LP . . . . MCFD 9001
MCA / May '89.
■ MC Set . . . . MCFDC 9001
MCA / May '89.

WORKIN' BAND.

Tracks: Not Advised.
CD 925722 2
LP 925722 1
■ MC 925722 4
WEA / Sep '88 / WEA.

Noack, Eddie

EDDIE NOACK.

Tracks: Take it away Lucky / Wind me up / Left over lovin' / Don't trade / Don't worry 'bout me baby / When the bright lights grow dim / It ain' much but it's a home / You done got me / Worm has turned / For you I weep / What's the matter Joe / Think of her now / If it ain't on the menu / Fair today cold tomorrow.
■ LP . . . . CH 21
Chiswick Records / Jun '80.

GENTLEMEN PREFER BLONDES.

Tracks: Scarecrow / Wanderin' oakie / Dust on the river / Walk em off / Man on the wall / Too weak to go / Firewater luke / Price of love.
LP . . . . .CHD 149
Ace / Oct '85 / Pinnacle / Hot Shot / Jazz Music / Complete Record Co. Ltd.

Norman, Chris

BREAK THE ICE.

Tracks: Break the ice / Hearts on fire / Night has turned cold, The / One last kiss / Angie don't you love me? /

Back again / Sarah / One way love affair / Livin' in a fantasy / These arms of mine / Got me in the palm of your hand / Woman in love.
CD . . . . PTCD 009
LP . . . . PTLP 009
MC . . . . PTLC 009
P.T. Music / '89 / ACD Trading Ltd.

JEALOUS HEART.

Tracks: Not Advised.
CD . . . . .DICECD 001
MC . . . . DICEC 001
Dice music / Jun '93 / Koch International.

JEALOUS HEART.

Tracks: Not Advised.
CD Single . . . . .DICE 7CD01
MC Single . . . . .CASSDICE 01
Dice music / Jun '93 / Koch International.

LOVE IS A BATTLEFIELD.

Tracks: Love is a battlefield / Comes the night.
7" . . . . .RCA 386
RCA / Jan '84 / BMG.

MIDNIGHT LADY.

Tracks: Midnight lady / Woman.
12" . . . . ARIST 12670
7" . . . . ARIST 670
Arista / Aug '86 / BMG.

MY GIRL AND ME.

Tracks: My girl and me / Comes the night.
7" . . . . .RCA 427
RCA / Aug '84 / BMG.

STUMBLIN' IN (see under Quatro, Suzi).

Normansell, Amanda

CRAZY.

Tracks: Crazy / It might as well rain until September / Let me try again / Love letters / Sweet nothings / Smile / Heartaches / Dream a little dream / Sweet dreams of you / Hello again / Talking in your sleep / Laughter in the rain / Before the next teardrop falls / Country roads / All alone am I / End of the world / Will you still love me tomorrow / You light up my life.
CD . . . . TCD 2614
LP . . . . STAR 2614
■ MC . . . . STAC 2614
Telstar/Ronco / Nov '92.

Notting Hillbillies

Formed in 1989 the band consists of Brendan Croker, Guy Fletcher, Steve Philips and Mark Knopfler. Croker hails from Leeds and fronts the Five O'Clock Shadows, who recently appeared on the Johnny Cash tribute album *Til things get brighter* playing on all tracks. Guy Fletcher, has both toured and recorded with co-Hillbillies player Knopfler's main concern, Dire Straits. While Steve Philips is a highly accomplished blues guitarist who's career started by playing rock'n'roll in the early sixties. Knopfler himself is undoubtedly one of the world's best guitar pickers, he recently recorded an album *Neck and neck* with one of the all-time greats, Chet Atkins, which was released on CBS. (Maurice Hope)

FEEL LIKE GOING HOME.

Tracks: Feel like going home / Lonesome wind blues / One way gal (Available on 12" and CD single only).
12" . . . . .NHB 212
7" . . . . NHB 2
CD Single . . . . NHBCD 2
MC Single . . . . NHBMC 2
Vertigo / Apr '90 / PolyGram.

MISSING..PRESUMED HAVING A GOOD TIME.

Tracks: Not Advised.
CD 842 671 2
LP 842 671 1
MC 842 671 4
Vertigo / Mar '90 / PolyGram.

NOTTING HILLBILLIES: MISSING.

Tracks: Not Advised.
VHS. . . . . CFV 10672
Channel 5 / May '90 / Channel 5 Video / P.R.O. Video / Gold & Sons.

WILL YOU MISS ME.

Tracks: Will you miss me / That's where I belong / Lonesome wind blues (Only on 12" & CD single.).
MC Single . . . . .NHBMC 3
Vertigo / Jun '90 / PolyGram.
12" . . . . .NHB 312
7" . . . . .NHB 3
■ CD Single . . . . NHBCD 3
Vertigo / Jun '90.

YOUR OWN SWEET WAY.

Tracks: Your own sweet way / Bewildered / That's where I belong.
12" . . . . .NHB 112
■ 7" . . . . .NHB 1
Vertigo / Feb '90.
■ CD Single . . . . NHBCD 1
Vertigo / Feb '90.
■ MC Single . . . . NHBMC 1
Vertigo / Feb '90.

Nunn, Gary P

Born in Austin, Texas. A gritty singer-songwriter/musician, and founder member of Jerry Jeff Walker's famed Lost Gonzo Band (1972-1977), their debut release being the live recording *Viva Terlingua* , done in Luckenback. Prior to going on the road full-time with Jerry Jeff, Nunn and the band had worked part-time with Michael Martin Murphy. In 1977 they were to persue a short-lived career themselves - making two albums on MCA. As a writer, his songs include *The Last Thing I Needed The First Thing This Morning* for Willie Nelson and *London Home-Sick Blues* (Home With The Armadillo) for David Allan Coe - the song used by the Texas TV show Austin City Limits as it's theme song. Nunn recorded his 1985 live album *Home With The Armadillo* on Guacamole Records in Austin. His former boss Jerry jeff, amongst other songs of Nunn's, has covered *I Couldn't Do Nothin' Right* which featured on Walker's MCA *It's A Good Night For Singing* album, a collaboration with Karen Brooks, his ex-wife, who is a vocalist/recording act in her own right. (Maurice Hope)

BORDER STATES.

Tracks: What I like about Texas / I taught her everything she knows / Too many nights in a roadhouse / Money's no good, The / Lesson to be learned from love / Think I'll go to Mexico / Town and county taverns / Old fashion love / Alamogordo / Old home place, The.
LP . . . . DFG 8414
Dixie Frog / Nov '88 / Discovery.
CD . . . . SDCD 9.00576
Sawdust / '90.

Nutter, Mayf

GOIN' SKINNY DIPPIN'.

Tracks: Not Advised.
LP . . . . GNPS 2104
GNP Crescendo / '88 / Swift / Silva Screen / Flexitron Ltd.

Oak Ridge Boys

Although their personnel have changed over the years the Boys' roots stretch back to just after WW II, when they existed as the Country Cut-Ups and were based in Oak Ridge, Tennessee. They turned professional in 1961 as the Oak Ridge Quartet, led by Smitty Gatlin. The recent era of the Oak Ridge Boys really began in 1964 when William Lee Golden joined, quickly followed by Duane Allen of the Southernaires Quartet. The group stayed with playing their original gospel music until the early 70's, when, after moving to MCA the band made a concerted effort to change their musical direction and move into country music. It was a highly successful operation and their first single *Y'all come back saloon* picked up immediate airplay and hit the top 3, while the third release *I'll be true to you* went straight to the top, as well as crossing over to the pop chart. By 1981 they were encamped in both markets as *Elvira* became a million seller. Their success continued throughout the decade, scoring another two dozen high scoring chart entries as well as collecting a stack of awards including CMS Song of the Year and Vocal Group accolades. (Tony Byworth)

20 COUNTRY GOSPEL CLASSICS.
Tracks: Not Advised.
LP 20025
MC 40025
Astan (USA) / Nov '84.

AMERICAN DREAMS.
Tracks: Not Advised
CD . . . . MCAD 42311
LP . . . . MCA 42311
MCA / '89 / BMG.

AMERICAN MADE.
Tracks: Not Advised.
LP . . . . IMCA 5350
MCA (Import) / Mar '86 / Pinnacle / Silver Sounds (CD).
CD 31126
MCA (USA) / Jun '88 / MCA (Imports).

BOBBIE SUE.
Tracks: Not Advised.
■ LP . . . . MCF 3129
MCA / Aug '82.

BOBBIE SUE.
Tracks: Bobbie Sue / I wish you were here.
■ 7" . . . . MCA 773
MCA / May '82.

BREAK MY MIND.
Tracks: Break my mind / Ain't no cure for rock and roll.
■ 7" . . . . MCA 876
MCA / Feb '84.

DELIVER.
Tracks: Ozark mountain jubilee / When you get to the heart / Alice in Wonderland / Ain't no cure for rock and roll / In the pines / I guess it never hurts to hurt sometimes / Through my eyes / Break my mind / Still holding on / Down deep inside.
LP . . . . MCF 3210
■ MC . . . . MCFC 3210
MCA / Mar '84.
CD 31125
MCA (USA) / Jun '88 / MCA (Imports).

EASY.
Tracks: Easy / Old time blue-grass band, An.
■ 7" . . . . ABC 4195
ABC Records / Feb '78.

ELVIRA.
Tracks: Elvira / Woman like you.
■ 7" . . . . MCA 727
MCA / Jun '81.

FANCY FREE.
Tracks: Not Advised.
LP . . . . MCG 4017
MCA / Jul '81 / BMG.

FANCY FREE.
Tracks: Fancy free / How long has it been.
■ 7" . . . . MCA 747
MCA / Oct '81.

GLORY TRAIN.
Tracks: Time has made a change in me / Farther along / Someday / Day of rejoicing / Lead me to Calvary / River of life / You'll never walk alone / One of these mornings / When I lay my burden down / At the roll call.
LP . . . . SDLP 1014
Sundown / Dec '84 / Terry Blood Dist. / Jazz Music / C.M. Distribution.

GREATEST HITS: OAK RIDGE BOYS, VOL.1.
Tracks: You're the one / I'll be true to you / Trying to love two women / Crying again / Dream on / Leaving Louisiana in the broad daylight / Heart of mine / Come on in / Sail away / Y'all come back saloon / Elvira / Ozark mountain jubilee / Love song / Fancy free / Everyday / Beautiful you / Thank God for kids / American made / Make my life with you / I guess it never hurts to hurt sometimes.
■ CD . . . . MCAD 5496
MCA / '86.
■ LP . . . . IMCA 5496
MCA (Import) / Mar '86.

HEARTBEAT.
Tracks: Not Advised.
CD . . . . MCAD 42036
MCA (Import) / May '89 / Pinnacle / Silver Sounds (CD).

I GUESS IT NEVER HURTS TO HURT SOMETIMES.
Tracks: I guess it never hurts to hurt sometimes / Through my eyes.
7" . . . . MCA 879
MCA / Mar '84 / BMG.

I'LL BE TRUE TO YOU.
Tracks: I'll be true to you / Fancy free.
■ 7" . . . . MCA 764
MCA / Mar '82.

KEEP WALKING.
Tracks: Not Advised.
LP . . . . MA 30685
Masters (Holland) / '88.
MC . . . . MAMC 930685
Masters (Holland) / Dec '88.

OAK RIDGE BOYS HAVE ARRIVED, THE.
Tracks: Not Advised.
CD 31114
MCA (USA) / Jun '88 / MCA (Imports).

ROOM SERVICE.
Tracks: Not Advised.
CD 31113
MCA (USA) / Jun '88 / MCA (Imports).

SEASONS.
Tracks: Seasons / What are you doing in my dream / Don't break the code / Juliet / You made a rock of a rolling stone / Take a step (yesterday waltz) / What you do to me / Everybody wins / Bedtime (on CD only) / Hiding place (on CD only).
LP . . . . MCF 3307
■ MC . . . . MCFC 3307
MCA / Mar '86.
LP . . . . MCF 3307
MCA / Feb '87 / BMG.
CD . . . . MCAD 5714
CD 31124
MCA (USA) / Jun '88 / MCA (Imports).

SENSATIONAL.
Tracks: Not Advised.
LP . . . . SLP 356
MC . . . . GT 5356
Starday (USA) / Apr '87 / Crusader Marketing Co.

STEP ON OUT.
Tracks: Not Advised.
LP . . . . MCF 3271
■ MC . . . . MCFC 3271
MCA / May '85.

THANK GOD FOR KIDS.
Tracks: Thank God for kids.
7" . . . . MCA 929
MCA / Nov '84 / BMG.

TOGETHER.
Tracks: Not Advised.
LP . . . . MCF 3063
MCA / May '80 / BMG.
CD 31112
MCA (USA) / Jun '88 / MCA (Imports).

WHERE THE FAST LANE ENDS.
Tracks: Love has a mind of its own / Is there any way for us to say goodbye / Where the fast lane ends / It takes a little rain to make love grow / Looking for love / Little late to say goodbye, A / Rainbow at midnight / This crazy love / Little love can go a long, long way, A / Whatever it takes.
LP . . . . IMCA 5945
MC . . . . IMCAC 5945
MCA / Apr '87 / BMG.

XMAS IS PAINTING THE TOWN.
Tracks: Xmas is painting the town / Thank God for kids.
■ 7" . . . . MCA 796
MCA / Nov '82.

Y'ALL COME BACK SALOON.
Tracks: Not Advised.
LP . . . . ABCL 5241
ABC Records / '78.
CD 31084
MCA (USA) / Jun '88 / MCA (Imports).

YOU'LL NEVER WALK ALONE.
Tracks: I know / Wonderful saviour / Without God / Old country church / I'll wake up on the other side / Dear Jesus, abide with me / Christian way, The / Hide thou me / I asked the lord / Farther along / Day of rejoicing / Lead me to Calvary / River of life / You'll never walk alone / One of these mornings / When I lay my burden down / At the roll call / Time has made a change in me.
LP . . . . SHLP 143
MC . . . . SHLC 143
Castle Showcase / Apr '86 / Arabesque Ltd.

O'Brien, Michael

One of the newer singers on the Irish scene, County Clare's Michael O'Brien came into the public limelight with *The veil of white lace*. It was a big enough hit for him to quit nursing and take up music professionally. A couple of years later he was appearing before 100,000 at the 1987 London Irish Festival and, in 1990, recording his first video in Dublin. (Tony Byworth)

ACTION MAN.
Tracks: Action man / Seven quid a week.
7" . . . . ZILCH 17
Zilch / Apr '82 / Zilch Records.

BEST OF MICHAEL O'BRIEN.
Tracks: My beautiful green fields / Love at first sight / Ave Maria Moralis / My own native land / My own perculiar way / Foolin' around / Gene Autry is my hero / You never do wrong / Veil of white lace / Walking talking dolly, The / Country I belong to you / Bed of roses / Shores of Lake MacNean / Happy times / Same old fool I used to be, The / Tears of the bridal bouquet / Birthplace Donegal / Veil of white lace (part 2).
CD . . . . IHCD 11
MC . . . . IHMC 11
Prism / '91 / Pinnacle / Midland Records.
CD . . . . KCD 311
MC . . . . KMC 311
K-Tel (Ireland) / Feb '93 / I & B Records / Ross Records / Prism Leisure PLC.

CLIFFS OF MOHER, THE.
Tracks: Not Advised.
LP . . . . FALP 003
MC . . . . FACS 003
CMR/Failte / '88 / I & B Records.

DREAMS OF IRELAND.
Tracks: Not Advised.
LP . . . . WS 039
MC . . . . WS 039 C
Western Songs / Mar '86 / Western Songs Records.

EVENING WITH MICHAEL O'BRIEN, AN.
Tracks: Be my guest / Let the four winds blow / Let's twist again / My beautiful green fields / Old Dungarvan oak, The / Above and beyond / Veil of white lace, The / Lonely nights in London / My lovely rose of Clare / Clock in the tower, The / Mac Namara's band / Battering ram, The / Bould O'Donoghue / Irish washerwoman, The / If you're irish / May morning dew, The / Four country roads / Blue eyes crying in the rain / Love at the first sight / Bed of roses / When you get to heaven / It take people like you / Old love letters.
MC . . . . PLAC 331
Platinum Music / Oct '90 / Prism Leisure PLC / Ross Records.

EVENING WITH MICHAEL O'BRIEN, AN.
Tracks: Be my guest medley / My beautiful green fields / Old Dungarvan oak, The / Above and beyond / Veil of white lace, The / Lonely nights in London / My lovely rose of Clare / Clock in the tower, The / Irish medley / May morning dew, The / Four country roads / Blue eyes crying in the rain / Love at first sight / Bed of roses / When you get to heaven / It takes people like you / Love letters.
VHS. . . . . PLATV 331
Prism Video / Sep '90 / Terry Blood Dist. / Gold & Sons / Prism Leisure PLC.

MADE IN GERMANY.
Tracks: Made in Germany / Queen likes pop.
LP . . . . BUY 58
Stiff / Dec '79.

ONE MORE TIME.
Tracks: Not Advised.
LP . . . . FALP 004
MC . . . . FACS 004
CMR/Failte / '88 / I & B Records.

SOMETHING FOR EVERYONE.
Tracks: Not Advised.
LP. . . . . **KLP 245**
K-Tel / '89 / I & B Records / C.M. Distribution / Arabesque Ltd. / Mono Distributors (Jersey) Ltd. / Prism Leisure PLC / PolyGram / Ross Records / Prism Leisure PLC.

VEIL OF WHITE LACE.
Tracks: Veil of white lace.
7" . . . . **FACS 1001**
I&B / '88 / I & B Records.

WAITING FOR YOU.
Tracks: Not Advised.
LP. . . . . **KLP 275**
K-Tel / '89 / I & B Records / C.M. Distribution / Arabesque Ltd. / Mono Distributors (Jersey) Ltd. / Prism Leisure PLC / PolyGram / Ross Records / Prism Leisure PLC.

ZYLOPHONE JET.
Tracks: Zylophone jet.
7" . . . . **ZILCH 14**
Zilch / Nov '81 / Zilch Records.

O'Brien, Tim

Born Wheeling, West Virginia. From an early age played and sang a diverse selection of music. O'Brien is also a noted songwriter, to date he's seen country act Kathy Mattea gain considerable success with "Walk The Way The Wind Blows" and "Untold Stories". Both of which have been recorded by the bluegrass group Hot Rize, with whom he was lead vocalist/mandolin/guitar and fiddle player during the entire 80's. On his departure (1990) to RCA Records the band disbanded. Their music can be found on both Flying Fish and Sugar Hill, along with the band's alter-egos Red Knuckles & The Trailblazers. Tim's outstanding vocals and adept musicial prowess should see him gain wider acclaim in the coming years.

HARD YEAR BLUES.
Tracks: Not Advised.
LP. . . . . **FF 319**
Flying Fish (USA) / Mar '89 / Cadillac Music / Roots Records / Projection / C.M. Distribution / Direct Distribution / Jazz Music / Duncans / A.D.A Distribution.

ODD MAN IN.
Tracks: Fell in love (& I can't get out) / One way street / Circles around you / Handsome Molly / Lonely at the bottom, too / Like I used to do / Lone tree standing / Love on hold / Flora, lily of the west / Hold to a dream / That's what I like about you / Every tear has a reason why / Hungry eyes / Romance is a slow dance.
CD . . . . **SHCD 3790**
MC . . . . **SH 3790**
Sugarhill(USA) / '91 / Roots Records / Projection / Impetus Records / C.M. Distribution / Jazz Music / Swift / Duncans / A.D.A Distribution.

OH BOY OH BOY (O'Brien, Tim & The O'Boys).
Tracks: Church steeple / When I paint my masterpiece / Heartbreak game / Time to learn / Perfect place to hide / Run mountain / Good woman bad / Few are chosen / Shadows to light / Farmer's cused wife / Johnny don't get drunk/Rye straw / He had a log chain on.
CD . . . . **SH 3808CD**
MC . . . . **SH 3808C**
Sugarhill(USA) / May '93 / Roots Records / Projection / Impetus Records / C.M. Distribution / Jazz Music / Swift / Duncans / A.D.A Distribution.

REMEMBER ME (O'Brien, Tim & Mollie).
Tracks: Looking for the stone / If I had my way / Floods of south Dakota / Shut de do / Stagger lee / Remember me / Somebody the blues / Do right to me baby / That's the way to treat your woman / Motherless children / Pilgrim of sorrow / Hush while the little ones sleep / Out in the country.
CD . . . . **SH CD 3804**
MC . . . . **SH MC 3804**
Sugarhill(USA) / '92 / Roots Records / Projection / Impetus Records / C.M. Distribution / Jazz Music / Swift / Duncans / A.D.A Distribution.

TAKE ME BACK (O'Brien, Tim & Mollie).
Tracks: Leave that liar alone / Sweet sunny South / I loved you a thousand ways / Just someone I used to know / Down to the valley to pray / Wave the ocean, wave the sea / Your long journey / When the roses bloom in Dixieland / Unwed fathers / Nobody's fault but mine / Papa's on the housetop / Dream of the miner's child / Christ was born in Bethlehem.
CD . . . . **SH 3766CD**
LP. . . . . **SH 3766**
MC . . . . **SH 3766C**
Sugarhill(USA) / Mar '89 / Roots Records / Projection / Impetus Records / C.M. Distribution / Jazz Music / Swift / Duncans / A.D.A Distribution.

O'Connell, Maura

JUST IN TIME.
Tracks: Scholar, The / If you love me / Feet of a dancer / Isle of Malachy, The / New Orleans / Water is wide, The / Leaving Neidin / Crazy dreams / Loves old sweet song / Another morning / I will / Just in time.
LP. **831 184-1**
MC **8311844**
Polydor / Jan '87 / PolyGram.
CD . . . . **RGCD 10**
Raglan (Ireland) / '88 / I & B Records.
LP. . . . . **PH 1124**
Philo (USA) / '88 / Roots Records / Projection / Topic Records / Direct Distribution / Ross Records / C.M. Distribution / Impetus Records.
LP. . . . . **RGLP 10**
Raglan (Ireland) / '88 / I & B Records.
MC . . . . **PH 1124C**
Philo (USA) / '88 / Roots Records / Projection / Topic Records / Direct Distribution / Ross Records / C.M. Distribution / Impetus Records.
CD . . . . **CDPH 1124**
Philo (USA) / '90 / Roots Records / Projection / Topic Records / Direct Distribution / Ross Records / C.M. Distribution / Impetus Records.

MAURA O'CONNELL.
Tracks: Not Advised.
LP. . . . . **BLB 5007**
Polydor / '88 / PolyGram.

WESTERN HIGHWAY.
Tracks: Trouble in the fields / Cast a long shadow / Summerfly / Bed for the night / Isn't it always love / Helpless heart / Can't stop the girl / Just like the blues / Only a fool / Western highway / You'll never know.
CD . . . . **RGCD 9**
LP. . . . . **RGLP 9**
MC . . . . **RGMC 9**
Raglan (Ireland) / Feb '88 / I & B Records.

O'Connor, Mark

Born 04.08.1962 in Seattle, Washington fiddle/mandolin genius-accomplished flat-picker (champion in all categories). A much in demand session musician, playing on around 500 albums, alongside which are his one-off releases on Rounder, Country Music Foundation & Warner Brothers, his present label, where he recorded the 1991 album The New Nashville Cats, featuring Carl Perkins *Restless* , where stunning performances from Skaggs, Gill, Steve Wariner & O'Connor unfold, and which tilted the vote the way of The New Nashville Cats at the CMA's Awards - securing 1991's Vocal Event Of The Year. O'Connor's inspired playing (CMA's Musicians Of The Year in 1991 - 1992), draws on elements of jazz, country, new age acoustic, and old time traditional folk from his youth - influences ranging from his mentor, Texas fiddle master Benny Thomasson to Kenny Baker to Stephane Grapppelli who he toured with in 1979, playing guitar. At only 12 he cut the Rounder album *National junior champion* , the first of a handful for the label. O'Connor's fiddle contest exploits meanwhile are on Country Music Foundation records *The championship years* (1977-1984). Has toured with the likes of Dan Crary, David Grisman (as part of his quintet), Doc Watson & Peter Rowan, (where alongside Jerry Douglas he featured at the 1987 Wembley Country Music Festival). Sam Bush, Jerry Douglas & O'Connor (during the late 80s) became known as Nashville Mafia, such was their huge involvment in the making of Nashville's top innovative albums. On stage he's also figured alongside Nanci Griffith - prior to her MCA signing, recording her Austin City Limits TV special. In 1992 O'Connor made a welcome one night appearance at Edale's annual Bluegrass Festival , as part of his selective UK solo debut venture. (Maurice Hope)

CHAMPIONSHIP YEARS '75-'84, THE.
Tracks: Grey eagle / Clarinet polka / Dusty Miller / I don't love nobody / Wednesday night waltz / Herman's rag / Sally Goodwin / Sally Johnson / Yellow rose waltz / Tom & Jerry / Billy in the lowground / Herman's rag (2) / Allentown polka / Brilliancy / Black & white rag / Tom & Jerry (2) / Clarinet polka (2) / Dill pickle rag / Grey eagle (2) / Leather britches / Don't let the deal go down / Golden eagle hornpipe / I don't love nobody (2) / Brilliancy (2) / Tug boat / Grey eagle (3) / Beaumont rag / Hell among the yearlings / Bill Cheatum / Sally Goodwin (2) / Herman's rag (3) / Choctaw / Westphalia waltz / Black & white rag (2) / Herman's hornpipe / Dill pickle rag (2) / Sally Ann / Clarinet polka (3) / Arkansas traveller / Jesse polka.
CD . . . . **CMFCD 015**
MC . . . . **CMFC 015**
Country Music Foundation / Jan '93 / Topic Records / Direct Distribution.

FALSE DAWN.
Tracks: Not Advised.
LP. . . . . **ROUNDER 0165**
MC . . . . **ROUNDER 0165C**
Rounder / Aug '88 / Projection / Roots Records / Swift / C.M. Distribution / Topic Records / Jazz Music / Hot Shot / A.D.A Distribution / Direct Distribution.

MARK O'CONNOR.
Tracks: Not Advised.
LP. . . . . **ROUNDER 0046**
MC . . . . **ROUNDER 0046C**
Rounder / '88 / Projection / Roots Records / Swift / C.M. Distribution / Topic Records / Jazz Music / Hot Shot / A.D.A Distribution / Direct Distribution.

MARKOLOGY.
Tracks: Dixie breakdown / Markology / Kit's waltz / Fluid drive / Blackberry blossom / Pickin' the wind / Banks of the Ohio / Berserkeley / On top of the world.
LP. . . . . **ROUNDER 0090**
MC . . . . **ROUNDER 0090C**
Rounder / '88 / Projection / Roots Records / Swift / C.M. Distribution / Topic Records / Jazz Music / Hot Shot / A.D.A Distribution / Direct Distribution.
CD . . . . **ROU 009CD**
Rounder / Aug '93 / Projection / Roots Records / Swift / C.M. Distribution / Topic Records / Jazz Music / Hot Shot / A.D.A Distribution / Direct Distribution.

NEW NASHVILLE CATS, THE.
Tracks: Bowtie / Restless / Nashville shuffle boogie / Pick it apart / Traveller's ridge / Granny White special / Cat in the bag / Ballad of Sally Anne, The / Swang / Dance of the ol' swamp rat / Bowl of bula, A / Limerock / Sweet Suzanne / Orange blossom special / Now it belongs to you.
CD **7599265092**
MC **7599265094**
Warner Bros. / Jun '92 / WEA.

ON THE RAMPAGE.
Tracks: Not Advised.
LP. . . . . **ROUNDER 0118**
MC . . . . **ROUNDER 0118C**
Rounder / '88 / Projection / Roots Records / Swift / C.M. Distribution / Topic Records / Jazz Music / Hot Shot / A.D.A Distribution / Direct Distribution.

PICKIN' IN THE WIND.
Tracks: Pickin' in the wind / Midnight on the water / Tom and Jerry / Cotton patch rag / Tammy's waltz / Lonesome fiddle blues / Daybreak in Dixie / Mark's waltz / Grey eagle / Dixie hoedown / Goodbye waltz / Herman's rag / Faded love / Dixie breakdown.
LP. . . . . **ROUNDER 0068**
MC . . . . **ROUNDER 0068C**
Rounder / '88 / Projection / Roots Records / Swift / C.M. Distribution / Topic Records / Jazz Music / Hot Shot / A.D.A Distribution / Direct Distribution.

RETROSPECTIVE.
Tracks: Not Advised.
CD . . . . **CD 11507**
Rounder / '88 / Projection / Roots Records / Swift / C.M. Distribution / Topic Records / Jazz Music / Hot Shot / A.D.A Distribution / Direct Distribution.

SOPPIN' THE GRAVY.
Tracks: Soppin' the gravy / Misty moonlight waltz / College hornpipe / Calgery polka / Morning star waltz / Tennessee Wagoner / Yellow rose waltz / Medley (Speed the plow/The maid behind the bar (Judy's reel)/ Atottler's reel) / Jesse polka / Dawn waltz, The / Wild fiddler's rag / Over the rainbow.
LP. . . . . **ROUNDER 0137**
MC . . . . **ROUNDER 0137C**
Rounder / '88 / Projection / Roots Records / Swift / C.M. Distribution / Topic Records / Jazz Music / Hot Shot / A.D.A Distribution / Direct Distribution.
CD . . . . **CDROU 0137**
Rounder / '92 / Projection / Roots Records / Swift / C.M. Distribution / Topic Records / Jazz Music / Hot Shot / A.D.A Distribution / Direct Distribution.

O'Day, Molly

MOLLY O'DAY AND THE CUMBERLAND MOUNTAIN FOLKS.
Tracks: Tramp on the street, The / When God comes and gathers his jewels / Black sheep returned to the fold, The / Put my rubber doll away / Drunken driver, The / Tear stained letter / Lonely mound of clay / Six more miles / Singing waterfall / At the first fall of snow / Matthew twenty four / I don't care if tomorrow never comes / Hero's death, A / I'll never see sunshine again / Too late, too late / Why do you weep dear willow / Don't forget the family prayer / I heard my mother weeping / Mother's gone but not forgotten / Evening train, The / This is the end / Fifteen years ago / Teardrops falling in the snow / With you on my mind / If you see my saviour / Heaven's radio / When my time comes to go / Don't sell Daddy anymore whiskey / Higher in my prayers / Travelling the highway home / It's different now / When the angels rolled the stone away / It's all coming true / When we see our Redeemer's face.
CD . . . . **BCD 15565**
Bear Family / Jun '92 / Rollercoaster Records / Swift / Direct Distribution.

O'Donnell, Daniel

Now well established as the most successful country/easy listening entertainer in the British Isles, Daniel O'Donnell (born December 12, 1961 in Kincasslagh, County Donegal) had, by mid 1993, sold around 2 million albums and 600,000 videos. Most of these sales occurred during the preceding three years. He also proved himself one of the hottest box office attractions in the business, touring the U.K. twice a year. Virtually all of his concerts are sold out, many of them at the time the tickets come on sale. A quiet, unassuming entertainer possessing considerable charm, success runs in the O'Donnell family as he is the brother of another top Irish entertainer, Margo. In fact she gave him his first break as a guitarist in her

O 2 ■ DELETED

band, "though I couldn't play a note" he later admitted. He split to go his own way in April 1983, and financed his own single *Donegal shore* , but found the going tough and was seriously considering emigrating when Ritz Records entered the picture. It was the catalyst that his career needed and, with defined marketing and promotion plans, the word about this artist started spreading, first on the Irish circuit and then over to country and easy listening audiences. The U.K. Country charts were first to list his albums (by January 1991 all seven album releases were in the top 20), then the national pop and video charts. 1992 was a particularly amazing year, with Daniel enjoying his first ever top 20 chart single, the Roger Cook-John Prine song *I just want to dance with you* and his *Follow your dream* video entering the pop video charts at No. 1, holding several heavyweights of the pop and rock scene from the top spot. He folowed up with more chart singles, *The three bells* , *The love in your eyes* and *Whatever happened to old fashioned love* . O'Donnell has also made inroads into the international market. In the USA, he made his initial efforts in Nashville, making several radio, television and stage appearances (including the International Show at the 1988 Fan Fair and the Grand Ole Opry), and followed on by recording his *Last Waltz* album with producer Allen Reynolds, whose credits include chart records by such as Don Williams, Crystal Gayle and the biggest star of them all, Garth Brooks. He's also undertaken several American concert tours and in May 1991, notched up another achievement by selling out New York's Carnegie Hall. A couple of years later he made his Australian tour debut, following top 10 Pop Chart success there with his *Very best of Daniel O'Donnell* collection. (Tony Byworth)

BOY FROM DONEGAL, THE.
Tracks: Donegal shore / Old rustic bridge / Galway bay / Forty shades of green / My side of the road / 5,000 miles from Sligo / Old bog road / Slievenamon / Noreen Bawn / Ballyhoe.
LP . . . . **IHLP 04**
MC . . . . **IHMC 04**
Irish Music Heritage / Oct '87.
CD . . . . **IHCD 04**
Irish Music Heritage / Oct '89.

DANIEL O'DONNELL: LIVE IN CONCERT.
Tracks: Stand beside me / Our house is a home / Veil of white lace / Pretty little girl from Omargh / My Donegal shore / I wonder where you are tonight / Don't forget to remember / Old rugged cross, The / Irish rover, The / Wooden heart / Take good care of her / Roses are red / Danny boy.
VHS . . . . **RITZV 0001**
Ritz / Dec '88 / Pinnacle / Midland Records.

DATE WITH DANIEL, A.
Tracks: I just wanna dance with you / What ever happened to old fashioned love / Somewhere between / Follow you dream / You're the reason / Love in your eyes, The / Minute your gone, The / Little things, The / My Irish country home / Isle of Innisfree / I need you / Never ending song of love / Wedding song, The / My Donegal shore / Stand beside me / Old rugged cross, The / How great thou art / Pretty little girl from Omagh / My shoes keep walking back to you / Rose of Tralee / Our house is a home / Mountains of Mourne, The / Roses are red/Moonlight and roses.
CD . . . . **BCD 702**
MC . . . . **BLC 702**
Ritz / Oct '93 / Pinnacle / Midland Records.

DON'T FORGET TO REMEMBER.
Tracks: I don't care / Old loves never die / I wonder where you are tonight / Don't be angry / Roses are red / Before I'm over you / Take good care of her / Pretty little girl from Omagh / Green willow / Don't let me cross over / Good old days / Pat Murphy's meadow / I just can't make it on my own.
CD . . . . **RITZCD 105**
Ritz / Dec '87 / Pinnacle / Midland Records.
LP . . . . **RITZLP 0043**
MC . . . . **RITZLC 043**
Ritz / Sep '87 / Pinnacle / Midland Records.

DON'T FORGET TO REMEMBER.
Tracks: Don't forget to remember.
7" . . . . **RITZ 180**
Ritz / Oct '87 / Pinnacle / Midland Records.

EVENING WITH DANIEL O'DONNELL, AN.
Tracks: I need you / Stand beside me / Geisha girl / Paper roses medley / London leaves / Galway Bay / Last waltz of the evening / Summertime in Ireland / We could / Second fiddle / Road and miles to Dundee, The / Westmeath bachelor / Old Dungarvon oak, The / My shoes keep walking back to you / Medals for mothers / Memory number one / Home sweet home / Heaven with you / Wooden heart / Danny Boy / Talk back trembling lips / Band instrumentals / Take good care of you / Roses are red / Irish medley / Buck Owens medley / Our house is a home / Finale.
VHS . . . . **RITZV 0008**
Ritz / Nov '90 / Pinnacle / Midland Records.

FAR FAR FROM HOME.
Tracks: Far far from home / My shoes keep walking back to you / Home is where the heart is / Shutters and boards.
MC Single . . . . **RITZC 197**
Ritz / '88 / Pinnacle / Midland Records.

FAVOURITES.
Tracks: Bed of roses / Excuse me / Geisha girl / Home sweet home / Home is where the heart is / Forever you'll be mine / Streets of Baltimore, The / Bringin' Mary home / Banks of my own lovely Lee, The / Green hills of Sligo.
CD . . . . **RITZCD 0052**
LP . . . . **RITZLP 0052**
MC . . . . **RITZLC 0052**
Ritz / Apr '90 / Pinnacle / Midland Records.

FOLLOW YOUR DREAM.
Tracks: I Need You (Intro) / Stand Beside Me / Eileen / Pretty Little Girl From Omagh / Destination Donegal / Medley (1) / Medley (2) / The Wedding Song (Ave Maria) / Irish Country Home / Ramblin' Rose / I Just Want To Dance With You / Medley (3) / Medley (4) / White River Stomp / Our House Is A Home / Never Ending Song Of Love / Rockin' Alone / Standing Room Only / Welcome Home / The Love In Your Eyes / You Send Me Your Love / Turkey In The Straw / I Need You / Medley (5) / Reprise / How Great Thou Art.
CD . . . . **RITZBCD 701**
LP . . . . **RITZBLP 701**
MC . . . . **RITZBLC 701**
Ritz / Nov '92 / Pinnacle / Midland Records.

FOLLOW YOUR DREAM.
Tracks: I need you / Stand beside me / Eileen / Pretty little girl from Omagh / Destination Donegal / Medley (Paper roses; Not until the next time; Cryin' time) / Medley (2) (A country boy like me; Home sweet home; Summertime in Ireland) / Wedding song (Ave Maria), The / Irish country home / Ramblin' rose / I just want to dance with you / Medley (3) (Jailhouse rock; Hound dog; Blue suede shoes) / Medley (4) (That's alright Mama; Love me tender; Are you lonesome tonight; Don't be cruel) / White river stomp / Our house is a home / Never ending song of love / Rockin' alone / Standing room only / Welcome home / Love in your eyes, The / You send me your love / Turkey in the straw / Medley (5) (It's a long way to Tipperary; Pack up your troubles; If you're Irish..; The black thorn stick; Kennedy's fancy) / Reprise (Stand beside me; The mockin' bird) / How great thou art.
VHS . . . . **RITZBV 701**
Ritz / Nov '92 / Pinnacle / Midland Records.

FROM THE HEART.
Tracks: Minute you're gone, The / Mary from Dungloe / Wasting my time / Things / It doesn't matter anymore / Bye bye love / Kelly / Old rugged cross, The / Act naturally / Honey / Wooden heart / It keeps right on a-hurtin' / My bonnie Maureen / I know that you know / Old Dungarvan oak / Danny boy.
CD . . . . **TCD 2327**
MC . . . . **STAC 2327**
Telstar/Ronco / Oct '88 / BMG.
■ **LP** . . . . **STAR 2327**
Telstar/Ronco / Oct '88.
CD . . . . **RITZCD 0068**
MC . . . . **RITZLC 0068**
Ritz / Oct '92 / Pinnacle / Midland Records.

I JUST WANT TO DANCE WITH YOU.
Tracks: I just want to dance with you / Rockin' alone / My Irish country home.
7" . . . . **RITZ 250 P**
CD Single . . . . **RITZ CD 250**
MC Single . . . . **RITZ C 250**
Ritz / Sep '92 / Pinnacle / Midland Records.

I NEED YOU.
Tracks: Sing an old Irish song / I need you / From a jack to a king / Lovely rose of Clare / Stand beside me / Irish eyes / Dear old Galway town / Three leaf shamrock / Veil of white lace / Kickin' each others hearts around / Medals for mothers / Wedding bells / Snowflake / Your friendly Irish way / Lough Melvin's rocky shore / I love you because.
LP . . . . **RITZLP 0038**
MC . . . . **RITZLC 0038**
Ritz / Nov '86 / Pinnacle / Midland Records.
CD . . . . **RITZCD 104**
Ritz / Jun '87 / Pinnacle / Midland Records.
MC . . . . **HMC 17**
Harmac (Ireland) / '88 / I & B Records / Prism Leisure PLC.

I NEED YOU.
Tracks: I need you / Your friendly irish way.
7" . . . . **RITZ 169**
Ritz / Jan '87 / Pinnacle / Midland Records.

IRISH FAVOURITES.
Tracks: Not Advised.
MC . . . . **SMAC 9011**
Crashed (Ireland) / '88 / I & B Records / EMI (Ireland) Records.

LAST WALTZ OF THE EVENING.
Tracks: Last waltz of the evening / You know I still love you.
7" . . . . **RITZ 216**
Ritz / Sep '90 / Pinnacle / Midland Records.
MC Single . . . . **RITZC 216**
Ritz / Jun '93 / Pinnacle / Midland Records.

LAST WALTZ, THE.
Tracks: Here I am in love again / We could / Last waltz of the evening / When only the sky was blue / Heaven with you / You know I still love you / Talk back trembling lips / Shelter of your eyes, The / When we get together / Ring of gold / Fool such as I, A / Memory number one / Look both ways / Little patch of blue / Marianne (Only on CD.).
CD . . . . **RITZCD 0058**
LP . . . . **RITZLP 0058**
MC . . . . **RITZLC 0058**
Ritz / Oct '90 / Pinnacle / Midland Records.

LETTER FROM THE POSTMAN'S BAG.
Tracks: Letter from the postman's bag / Loved one's goodbye, A.
7" . . . . **RITZ 233**
MC Single . . . . **RITZ C233**
Ritz / Jun '91 / Pinnacle / Midland Records.

LOVE IN YOUR EYES, THE.
Tracks: Love in your eyes, The / Ramblin' Rose / Old photograph, The / Little things.
7" . . . . **RITZ 257P**
CD Single . . . . **RITZCD 257**
MC Single . . . . **RITZC 257**
Ritz / Apr '93 / Pinnacle / Midland Records.

MARIANNE.
Tracks: Marianne / Country boy like me, A.
MC Single . . . . **RITZC 228**
Ritz / Apr '91 / Pinnacle / Midland Records.
■ **7"** . . . . **RITZ 228**
Ritz / Apr '91.

MUSICAL TOUR OF IRLELAND, A.
Tracks: My shoes keep walking back to you / Forty shades of green / Dublin in the rare old times / Far far from home / I'll take you home again Kathleen / Moonlight and roses / Send me the pillow you dream on / Isle of Innisfree, The / Rose of tralee, The / Donegal shore.
VHS . . . . **TVE 1007**
Telstar Video / '89 / BMG.

MY SHOES KEEP WALKING BACK TO YOU.
Tracks: My shoes keep walking back to you.
7" . . . . **RITZ 197**
Ritz / Apr '89 / Pinnacle / Midland Records.

SUMMERTIME IN IRELAND.
Tracks: Take good care of her / I wonder where you are tonight / Summertime in Ireland / My side of the road.
MC Single . . . . **RITZC 150**
Ritz / Jul '87 / Pinnacle / Midland Records.
■ **7"** . . . . **RITZ 150**
Ritz / Jul '87.

T.V. SHOW FAVOURITES.
Tracks: I don't care / Lovely rose of Clare / Geisha girl / Take good care of her / From a Jack to a King / I wonder where you are tonight / Dear old Galway town / History of country music (medley) / Sing me an old Irish song / I need you / Bed of roses / Elvis medley / Home is where the heart is / Walk right back / Life to go / Lough Melvin's rocky shore / Stand beside me.
VHS . . . . **RITZV 0002**
Ritz / Apr '90 / Pinnacle / Midland Records.

THOUGHTS OF HOME.
Tracks: My shoes keep walking back to you / Mountains of Mourne, The / London leaves / Blue eyes crying in the rain / Old days remembered / Send me the pillow you dream on / Moonlight and roses / Little piece of Heaven, A / Far far from home / Isle of Innisfree / My heart skips / I know one / I'll take you home again Kathleen / Second fiddle / My favourite memory / Forty shades of green.
CD . . . . **TCD 2372**
MC . . . . **STAC 2372**
Telstar/Ronco / Oct '89 / BMG.
■ **LP** . . . . **STAR 2372**
Telstar/Ronco / Oct '89.

THOUGHTS OF HOME.
Tracks: My shoes keep walking back to you / Forty shades of green / Our house is a home / Dublin in the rare old times / Mountains of Mourne, The / Far far from home / I'll take you home again Kathleen / Moonlight and roses / Mary from Dungloe / Send me the pillow you cry on / Isle of Innisfree / Rose of Tralee / Donegal shore.
VHS . . . . **TVE 1007**
Telstar Video / Nov '89 / BMG.
VHS . . . . **RITZV 0016**
Ritz / Jan '93 / Pinnacle / Midland Records.

THREE BELLS.
Tracks: Not Advised.

THREE BELLS, THE.
Tracks: Three bells, The / Silent night / Old Christmas card, An (Not on 7".).
7" . . . . **RITZ 239**
CD Single . . . . **RITZCD 239**
MC Single . . . . **RITZC 239**
Ritz / Dec '91 / Pinnacle / Midland Records.

TWO SIDES OF DANIEL O'DONNELL, THE.
Tracks: Green glens of Antrim / Blue hills of Breffni / Any Tipperary town / Latchyco, The / Home town on the Foyle / These are my mountains / My Donegal shore / Crying my heart out over you / My old pal / Our house is a home / Your old love letters / 21 years / Highway 40 blues / I wouldn't change you if I could.
LP . . . . **RITZLP 0031**
■ **MC** . . . . **RITZLC 0031**
Ritz / Nov '85.
■ **CD** . . . . **RITZCD 107**
Ritz / Aug '88.
CD . . . . **RITZCD 500**

MC . . . . RITZRC 500
Ritz / '91 / Pinnacle / Midland Records.

TWO'S COMPANY (O'Donnell, Daniel & Margo).
Tracks: Two's company / Home sweet home / Violet and the rose, The / Streets of Baltimore.
MC Single . . . . RITZC 185
Ritz / Apr '88 / Pinnacle / Midland Records.
■ **7"** . . . . RITZ 185
Ritz / Apr '88.

VEIL OF WHITE LACE, A.
Tracks: Veil of white lace / Your friendly Irish way.
7" . . . . RITZ 155
Ritz / Oct '86 / Pinnacle / Midland Records.

VERY BEST OF DANIEL O'DONNELL, THE.
Tracks: I need you / Never ending song of love / Don't forget to remember / Country boy like me, A / She's no angel / Stand beside me / Eileen / Pretty little girl from Omagh / Danny boy / Wedding song, The / My Donegal shore / Letter from the postman's bag / Three bells, The / Our house is a home / Loved ones goodbye, A / Home is where the heart is / Old rugged cross, The / You send me your love / Take good care of her / Standing room only.
CD . . . . RITZBCD 700
LP. . . . . RITZBLP 700
MC . . . . RITZBLC 700
Ritz / Oct '91 / Pinnacle / Midland Records.

WHATEVER HAPPENED TO OLD FASHIONED LOVE.
Tracks: Whatever happened to old fashioned love.
7" . . . . RITZ 262
CD Single . . . . RITZCD 262
MC Single . . . . RITZC 262
Ritz / Jul '93 / Pinnacle / Midland Records.

YOUR OLD LOVE LETTERS.
Tracks: Your old love letters.
7" . . . . RITZ 132
Ritz / '88 / Pinnacle / Midland Records.

O'Kanes

Singer-songwriting duo formed in 1986, consisting of Jamie O'Hara, born in Toledo, Ohio, and Kieran Kane born in Queens, New York. Kane played bluegrass with his brother Richard before moving to Boston, followed by work in LA, opening shows for Steve Miller and Country Joe McDonald. On moving to Nashville in the late 70's Kane met O'Hara, who was also signed to Tree publishing. He released solo material for Elektra in the early 80's and just made the top 20 with *You're the best* and *It's who you love* . Meanwhile O'Hara, who'd written *Grandpa (tell me 'bout the good 'ol days)* for the Judds, along with many other songs, joined the talented mandolin picker Kane in doing sessions at the songwriter's haven the Bluebird Cafe, Nashville. Much acclaim greeted their self-titled debut album, which provided the pair with four top 10 singles starting with *Oh Darlin'* and included the number 1 *Daddies grow up too* . They followed this up with their second album *Tired of runnin'* which spawned two top ten singles *One true love* and *Blue love* . Sadly after this the hits were all too infrequent and smaller, with *Imagine that* being their third and final album. (Maurice Hope)

IMAGINE THAT.
Tracks: Not Advised.
CD 4663462
LP. 4663461
MC 4663464
CBS / Mar '90 / Sony.

O'KANES, THE.
Tracks: Oh darlin' (why don't you care for me no more) / Just loving you / Daddies need to grow up too / Can't stop my heart from loving you / Bluegrass blues / Oh lonesome you / When we're gone' long gone / That's alright mama / Gonna walk that line / When I found you.
■ **MC** 4500694
CBS / Mar '87.
■ **LP.** 4500691
CBS / Mar '87.
CD 4500692
CBS / May '87 / Sony.

OH DARLING.
Tracks: Oh darling / When I found you.
7" 6507777
CBS / Apr '87 / Sony.

TIRED OF THE RUNNIN'.
Tracks: One true love / All because of you / If I could be there / Blue love / Rocky road / Highway 55 / Tired of the runnin' / In my heart / I'm lonely / Isn't that so.
LP. 4608311
■ **MC** 4608314
CBS / Mar '88.

Olivier, Jim

CAJUN MUSIC FOR EVERYONE.
Tracks: Not Advised.
LP. 6042
MC . . . . 6042 TC
Swallow (USA) / '87 / Swift / Wellard Dist.

I LOVE CAJUN MUSIC.
Tracks: Not Advised.
LP. 6039
MC . . . . 6039 TC
Swallow (USA) / '87 / Swift / Wellard Dist.

LE MUSIQUE DE JIM OLIVIER.
Tracks: Not Advised.
LP. 6059
MC . . . . 6059 TC
Swallow (USA) / '87 / Swift / Wellard Dist.

LET'S KEEP IT CAJUN.
Tracks: Not Advised.
LP. 6048
Swallow (USA) / Swift / Wellard Dist.
MC . . . . 6048 TC
Swallow (USA) / '87 / Swift / Wellard Dist.

SINGS THE CAJUN WAY.
Tracks: Not Advised.
LP. 6044
Swallow (USA) / Swift / Wellard Dist.
MC . . . . 6044 TC
Swallow (USA) / '87 / Swift / Wellard Dist.

Orbison, Roy

Born and raised in Texas, singer/guitarist/songwriter Orbison was interested in music from early childhood and formed his first group, the Wink Westerners, at the age of 13. His first recording session took place at Norman Petty's studio in Clovis, New Mexico, in 1955, and the following year he became part of Sam Phillips' Sun Records, the legendary Memphis label that launched the careers of Elvis Presley, Johnny Cash, Jerry Lee Lewis and Carl Perkins. The Sun period gave him his first US Hot Hundred entry with Ooby Dooby. Phillips pushed Orbison in a rock 'n' roll direction but because his voice was not suited to this his later Sun singles were unsuccessful: he preferred to record in a ballad style. Orbison's first taste of major success came in 1958 when the Everly Brothers recorded his song *Claudette* (dedicated to his wife) and placed it on the flipside of their classic *All I Have To Do Is Dream*. Orbison then signed with Monument Records and after a couple of hiccups began a string of hit records in 1960. The first was the classic *Only The Lonely* which reached No 2 in the States and No 1 in Britain. During the first five years of the 60's the Big O, as he became known was rarely off the charts on both sides of the Atlantic. Writing either alone or with a co-writer (Joe Melson or Bill Dees), his biggest successes included *Blue Angel, Crying, In Dreams, Falling and Blue Bayou*. Combining the emotional openness of country music with the infectious melodies of the best pop songs, Orbison managed to convey tear-jerking, lovelost numbers without resort to cloying sentimentality. He was virtually motionless on stage but his expressive voice always carried the day. Even the brighter, uptempo songs were infused with emotion. During his career Orbison enjoyed two American No 1 singles, *Running Scared* (1961) and *Oh Pretty Woman* (1964, another song inspired by *Claudette*). He was even more popular in Britain, where he won high praise from and toured with the Beatles. Between August '63 and November '64 his *It's Over* and *Oh Pretty Woman* were the only American records to reach No 1 on the British charts. The sheer strength of his talent withstood the UK explosion in an impressive fashion while the careers of many of his US peers were blown sky high. Orbison's singing and songwriting styles clearly reflected the influence of country pop star Don Gibson and in recognition of this he issued in 1966 Gibson's *Too Soon To Know*, which reached No 3 in Britain, plus a Gibson-penned LP. But that year was marred by the death in a motorcycle accident of his wife, *Claudette*: two years later his personal tragedy was compounded by the death of two of his sons in a house fire. He remarried in 1969. Having first entered the British singles charts in 1960, Orbison neatly ended his UK singles chart career by falling of the final listing of 1969. This "tidiness" was maintained when he attempted a UK come-back in 1985 -- *Wild Hearts*, a single released on Trevor Horn's fashionable ZTT label, missed the UK Top Seventy-Five singles chart by peaking at No 76.. In the meantime he had reached No 1 on the British album chart in January '76 with the TV-advertised compilation *The Best Of Roy Orbison*. During the late 70's and early 80's he embarked on a fresh career on the US country scene, enjoying a substantial duet success with Emmylou Harris on 1980's *That Loving You Feeling*. His oldies lived on: *Blue Bayou* was a US No 3 for Linda Ronstadt in '77; *Crying* was given a stunning new treatment by Don McLean, who took it to No 1 in Britain in 1980 and No 5 in the States in '81; and Van Halen reached No 12 in America the following year with a rock remake of *Oh Pretty Woman*. Roy Orbison died from a heart attack in December 1988. (Bob MacDonald)

(SAY) YOU'RE MY GIRL.
Tracks: (Say) you're my girl.
■ **7"** . . . . HLU 9978
London-American / Jul '65.

..AT ROCK HOUSE.
Tracks: Not Advised.
LP. . . . . CRM 2007
Charly / Feb '81 / Charly.

ALL TIME GREATEST HITS.
Tracks: Only the lonely / Leah / In dreams / Uptown / It's over / Crying / Dream baby / Blue angel / Working for the man / Candy man / Running scared / Falling / Claudette / Ooby dooby / I'm hurting / Mean woman blues / Lana / Blue bayou / Oh pretty woman.
CD . . . . SLCD 805
LP. . . . . SL 805
Skyline / '88 / Swift.
MC . . . . MCSL 805
Skyline / Dec '88 / Swift.
MiniDisc 67290-3
Monument / Feb '93 / Sony.

ALL-TIME GREATEST HITS.
Tracks: Only the lonely (know the way I feel) / Leah / In dreams / Uptown / It's over / Crying / Dream baby / Blue angel / Working for the man / Candy man / Running scared / Falling / Love hurts / I'm hurtin' / Mean woman blues / Pretty paper / Crowd, The.
■ **Double LP** . . . . MNT 67290
Monument / '73.
CD . . . . CD 67290
Monument / Jan '89 / Sony.

ALMOST EIGHTEEN.
Tracks: Almost eighteen / Jolie / Sweet and innocent / Bug, The (Previously unissued) / Paper boy (Previously unissued) / Seems to me.
■ **EP.** . . . . BFE 15019
Bear Family / Sep '82 / Rollercoaster Records / Swift / Direct Distribution.

BALLADS.
Tracks: You got it / Too soon to know / She's a mystery to me / Crawling back / In dreams / Love so beautiful, A / Running scared / Blue bayou / Actress, The / I'm hurtin' / Good night / Only the lonely / California blue / It's over / Evergreen / Crying / Falling / Leah / Love hurts / Blue angel / Penny arcade / Oh pretty woman.
■ **CD** . . . . TCD 2441
Telstar/Ronco / Oct '90.
■ **LP.** . . . . STAR 2441
Telstar/Ronco / Oct '90.
■ **MC** . . . . STAC 2441
Telstar/Ronco / Oct '90.

BEST LOVED STANDARDS.
Tracks: I can't stop loving you / Distant drums / No one will ever know / Beautiful dreamer / Great pretender, The / Let the good times roll / Bye bye love / Dream / (I'd be a) legend in my own time / All I have to do is dream / Cry / What'd I say.
CD 463 419 2
MC 463 419 4
Monument / Apr '89 / Sony.
■ **LP.** 463 419 1
Monument / Apr '89.

BEST OF ROY ORBISON.
Tracks: Not Advised.
■ **Double LP** . . . . ADEP 19
Arcade / Nov '75.

BIG O COUNTRY.
Tracks: Kaw-liga / You win again / I can't help it (if I'm still in love with you) / I'm so lonesome I could cry / Your cheatin' heart / I heard you crying in your sleep / (I'd be a) legend in my own time / Hey good lookin' / Your cold cold heart / Mansion on the hill / There'll be no teardrops tonight / I can't stop loving you / Too soon to know / Jambalaya.
LP. . . . . TAB 72
■ **MC** . . . . KTBC 72
Decca / Aug '83.

BIG O, THE.
Tracks: Rock house / It's too late / You're gonna cry / Ooby dooby / You're my baby / Mean little mamma / Fool's hall of fame / Cause of it all, The / True love goodbye / Lovestruck / Clown, The / One more time / Problem child / Chicken hearted / I like love / Domino.
MC . . . . CFK 1018
Sun / Jan '82 / Charly / Swift.
LP. . . . . CR 30008
Charly / Oct '85 / Charly.
CD . . . . CDCD 1051
Charly / Mar '93 / Charly.

BIG O, THE.
Tracks: Not Advised.
CD . . . . PWK 107
MC . . . . HSC 3264
Pickwick / May '89 / Pickwick Records.

BIG O, THE (MAGNUM FORCE).
Tracks: Go go go / I never knew / It's too late / Chicken hearted / Devil doll / Domino / Ooby dooby / Trying to get to you / You're gonna cry / You're my baby.
LP. . . . . MFM 024
Magnum Force / Jun '86 / Terry Blood Dist. / Jazz Music / Hot Shot.

O 4

■ DELETED

BLACK & WHITE NIGHT (Orbison, Roy & Friends).
Tracks: Oh pretty woman / Only the lonely / In dreams / Dream baby (how long must I dream) / Leah / Move on down the line / Crying / Mean woman blues / Running scared / Blue bayou / Candy man / Uptown / Ooby dooby / Comedians, The / (All I can do is) Dream of you / It's over.
LP . . . . **V 2601**
■ **MC** . . . . **TCV 2601**
Virgin / Nov '89.
CD . . . . **CDV 2601**
MC . . . . **OVEDC 369**
Virgin / Aug '91 / EMI.

BLACK AND WHITE NIGHT (Orbison, Roy & Friends).
Tracks: Only the lonely / Running scared / In dreams / Crying / Oh pretty woman.
VHS . . . . **VVD 308**
Virgin Vision / Jun '88 / Gold & Sons / Terry Blood Dist.

BLUE ANGEL.
Tracks: Blue angel.
■ **7"** . . . . **HLU 9207**
London-American / Oct '60.

BLUE BAYOU.
Tracks: Blue bayou / Mean woman blues.
■ **7"** . . . . **HLU 9777**
London-American / Sep '63.

BLUE BAYOU.
Tracks: Not Advised.
CD . . . . **TL 001316**
Traditional Line / Oct '92 / Charly.

BORNE ON THE WIND.
Tracks: Borne on the wind.
■ **7"** . . . . **HLU 9845**
London-American / Feb '64.

BREAKIN' UP IS BREAKIN' MY HEART.
Tracks: Breakin' up is breakin' my heart / Wait.
■ **7"** . . . . **HL 10015**
London-American / Jan '66.

CALIFORNIA BLUE.
Tracks: California blue / Blue bayou (live) / Leah (live) (Only on 12" and CD single.) / In dreams (live) (Only on CD single.).
■ **12"** . . . . **VST 1193**
Virgin / Jul '89.
■ **7"** . . . . **VS 1193**
Virgin / Jul '89.
■ **CD Single** . . . . **VSCD 1193**
Virgin / Jul '89.

CLASSIC ROY ORBISON, THE.
Tracks: Ooby dooby / Trying to get to you / Go go go / This kind of love / You're gonna cry / You're my baby / Rock house / Claudette / Domino / Sweet and easy to love / Devil doll / Chicken hearted / I like love / It's too late / Mean little mama.
CD . . . . **OCN 2017WD**
LP . . . . **OCN 2017WL**
MC . . . . **OCN 2017WK**
Ocean (2) / Apr '89.

CLASSIC ROY ORBISON, THE (DECCA).
Tracks: Not Advised.
■ **LP** . . . . **HAU 8297**
London-American / Sep '66.

COLLECTION, THE.
Tracks: Not Advised.

COLLECTION: ROY ORBISON.
Tracks: Trying to get to you / Ooby dooby / Go go go / You're my baby / Domino / Sweet and easy to love / Devil doll / Cause of it all, The / Fools hall of fame / True love goodbye / Chicken hearted / I like love / Mean little mama / Problem child / This kind of love / It's too late / I never knew / You're gonna cry / One more time (Demo) / Lovestruck (Demo) / Clown / Claudette.
■ **Double LP** . . . . **CCSLP 147**
Castle Collector Series / Sep '86.
CD . . . . **CCSCD 147**
Castle Collector Series / Feb '93 / BMG / Pinnacle / Castle Communications.
■ **MC** . . . . **CCSMC 147**
Castle Collector Series / Feb '93.

CRAWLING BACK.
Tracks: Crawling back / If you can't say something nice.
■ **7"** . . . . **HLU 10000**
London-American / Nov '65.

CROWD, THE.
Tracks: Crowd, The.
■ **7"** . . . . **HLU 9561**
London-American / Jun '62.

CROWD, THE (OLD GOLD).
Tracks: Crowd, The / Lana.
7" . . . . **OG 9888**
Old Gold / Feb '89 / Pickwick Records.

CRY SOFTLY LONELY ONE.
Tracks: Cry softly lonely one / Pistolero.
■ **7"** . . . . **HLU 10143**
London-American / Jun '67.

CRYING.
Tracks: Not Advised.
■ **LP** . . . . **HAU 2437**
London-American / Jun '63.

CRYING.
Tracks: Crying.
■ **7"** . . . . **HLU 9405**
London-American / Sep '61.

CRYING (Orbison, Roy & KD Lang).
Tracks: Crying / Falling / Oh pretty woman (Only on CD single) / She's a mystery to me (Only on CD single).
CD Single . . . . **VUSCX 63**
CD Single . . . . **VUSCD 63**
MC Single . . . . **VUSC 63**
Virgin America / Aug '92 / EMI.
■ **7"** . . . . **VUS 63**
Virgin America / Aug '92.

DANCIN' WITH ROY ORBISON.
Tracks: Not Advised.
LP . . . . **SP 243**
Point (1) / Jan '88 / Gamut Distribution.

DREAM BABY.
Tracks: Dream baby.
■ **7"** . . . . **HLU 9511**
London-American / Mar '62.

DREAM BABY (OLD GOLD).
Tracks: Dream baby / Pretty paper.
7" . . . . **OG 9885**
Old Gold / Feb '89 / Pickwick Records.

DREAMING WITH ROY ORBISON.
Tracks: Not Advised.
LP . . . . **SP 250**
Point (1) / Jan '88 / Gamut Distribution.

EARLY YEARS, THE.
Tracks: Domino / Ooby dooby / Claudette / Devil doll / Rockhouse / Problem child / Chicken hearted / Mean little mama / Love struck / Cause of it all, The / Clown, The / You're gonna cry / Fools hall of fame / This kind of love.
CD . . . . **CDINS 5010**
LP . . . . **INS 5010**
MC . . . . **TCINS 5010**
Instant (2) / Sep '89 / Charly.

EASY WAY OUT.
Tracks: Easy way out / Tears.
■ **7"** . . . . **K 13153**
Asylum / '79.

EXCITING SOUND OF ROY ORBISON.
Tracks: This kind of love / Devil doll / You're my baby / Trying to get to you / It's too late / Rock house / You're gonna try / I never knew / Sweet and easy / Mean little mama / Ooby dooby / Problem child.
LP . . . . **NR 5013**
Ember / '64 / TKO Records Ltd / President Records.

FALLING.
Tracks: Falling.
■ **7"** . . . . **HLU 9727**
London-American / May '63.

FOCUS ON ROY ORBISON.
Tracks: Twinkletoes / Harlem woman / Lonesome number one / I fought the law / Sugar man / Run, baby, run / Remember the good / Run the engines up high / Shy away / Sweet dreams / Beaujolais / I can't stop loving you / I'm the man on Susie's mind / Memories / Memphis, Tennessee / Take care of your woman / Claudette / Heartache / Land of a thousand dances / Crawling back / Cry softly, lonely one / Cheyenne / Blue blue day / Penny arcade.
■ **Double LP** . . . . **FOS U15/16**
Decca / Jul '76.

FREIGHTLINER FAVOURTIES.
Tracks: Not Advised.
MC . . . . **MC 1240191**
Prism / Aug '92 / Pinnacle / Midland Records.

GO GO GO.
Tracks: Go go go / Ooby dooby / Trying to get to you / You're my baby / Rock house / Domino / Devil doll / Sweet and easy to love / Cause of it all, The / Mean little mama / You're gonna cry / Problem child / True love goodbye / Fools hall of fame / I like love / Chicken hearted / It's too late / This kind of love / I never knew / You tell me / I give up / Lovestruck / Clown, The / Claudette.
CD . . . . **CDCHARLY 27**
Charly / Oct '86 / Charly.

GOLDEN DAYS.
Tracks: Oh, pretty woman / Running scared / Falling / Love hurts / Mean woman blues / I can't stop loving you / Crowd, The / Blue bayou / Borne on the wind / Lana / Only the lonely (know the way I feel) / It's over / Crying / Pretty paper / All I have to do is dream / Dream baby (how long must I dream) / Blue angel / Working for the man / Candy man / In dreams.
LP . . . . **MNT 10026**
MC **40 10026**
Monument / Aug '81 / Sony.
CD **4715552**
MC **4715554**
Monument / Apr '92 / Sony.

GOLDEN DECADE 1960-69, THE.
Tracks: Only the lonely / Bye bye love / I;m hurtin / Love hurts / Here comes that song again / Double date / (I'd be) a legend in my time / Uptown / I can't stop loving you / Candyman / Darkness / Today's teardrops / Twenty two days / Cry / Blue angel / Running scared / Lana / Party heart / Dance / Crying / Dream baby / Beautiful dreamer / Crowd, The / Leah / Love star / Workin' for the man / Distant drums / Mama (german version) / Falling / In dreams / Blue bayou / She wears my ring / How are things in paradise / (They call you) Gigolette / Almost / San Fernando (german version) / Mean woman blues / Pretty paper / Borne on the wind / It's over / Oh pretty woman / Let the good times roll / (Say) your'e my girl / Yes / Goodnight Claudette / Breakin' up is breakin' my heart / Ride away / Crawling back / Communication breakdown / There won't be many coming home / Too soon to know / Twinkle toes / So good / Cry softly lonely one / Lonesome number one / Walk on / Heartache / My friend / Penny arcade.
CD . . . . **NXTCD 246**
Sequel / May '93 / Castle Communications / BMG / Hot Shot.

GOLDEN DECADE BOX SET (1960-1970).
Tracks: Not Advised.
■ **LP Set** . . . . **ROYLP 47002**
Knight / Jul '90.
■ **MC Set** . . . . **ROYMC 47002**
Knight / Jul '90.
■ **CD Set** . . . . **ROYCD 47002**
Knight / Jul '90.

GOODNIGHT.
Tracks: Goodnight.
■ **7"** . . . . **HLU 9951**
London-American / Feb '65.

GREATEST HITS.
Tracks: Only the lonely / Leah / In dreams / Uptown / It's over / Crying / Dream baby / Blue angel / Working for the man / Candy man / Running scared / Falling / Love hurts / Shahadaroba / Oh pretty woman.
CD **26 10 832**
MC **26 10 834**
Dillion / '92 / Sound Solutions.

GREATEST HITS: ROY ORBISON.
Tracks: Crowd, The / Love star / Crying / Evergreen / Running scared / Mama / Candy man / Only the lonely / Dream baby / Blue angel / Uptown / I'm hurtin'.
■ **LP** . . . . **SMO 5007**
Monument / Sep '67.
LP **64 663**
Monument / '74 / Sony.

HEARTACHE.
Tracks: Heartache.
■ **7"** . . . . **HLU 10222**
London-American / Sep '68.

HEARTBREAK RADIO.
Tracks: Heartbreak radio / Crying (Duet featuring K.D. Lang.) / In dreams / You got it / Dream baby / Blue angel / Claudette / Lana.
7" . . . . **VUS 68**
CD Single . . . . **VUSCX 68**
CD Single . . . . **VUSCD 68**
■ **MC Single** . . . . **VUSC 68**
Virgin America / Oct '92.

HITS 1, THE.
Tracks: Only the lonely (know the way I feel) / Candy man / You're my girl / Working for the man / Bye bye love / In dreams / Dream baby (how long must I dream) / Crowd, The / Great pretender, The / Blue Avenue / Party heart / Blue bayou.
CD . . . . **PWKS 576**
LP . . . . **SHM 3303**
MC . . . . **HSC 3303**
Pickwick / Mar '90 / Pickwick Records.

HITS 2, THE.
Tracks: Running scared / Blue angel / Mean woman blues / Loneliness / Lana / Pretty paper / It's over / Love hurts / I'm hurtin' / Dream / House without windows / Goodnight.
CD . . . . **PWKS 582**
LP . . . . **SHM 3305**
MC . . . . **HSC 3305**
Pickwick / May '90 / Pickwick Records.

HITS 3, THE.
Tracks: Oh pretty woman / My prayer / She wears my ring / All I have to do is dream / Uptown / Born on the wind / Crying / Distant drums / Leah / Raindrops / Here comes that song again / Falling.
CD . . . . **PWKS 4024**
MC . . . . **PWKMC 4024**
Pickwick / Oct '90 / Pickwick Records.

I DROVE ALL NIGHT.
Tracks: I drove all night.
CD Single . . . . **MCST 1652**
MCA / Jun '92 / BMG.
7" . . . . **MCS 1652**
■ **MC Single** . . . . **MCSC 1652**
MCA / Jun '92.

I'M STILL IN LOVE WITH YOU.
Tracks: Pledging my love / Rainbow love / Heartache / Still / Circle / All I need is time / Spanish nights / It's lonely / Crying time / Hung up on you / Sweet Mamma blue.

■ DELETED O 5

■ CD 838 433 2
Mercury / Aug.'89.

IN DEUTSCHLAND.
Tracks: San Fernando / Mama.
12" . . . . BFM 15352
Bear Family / Apr '89 / Rollercoaster Records / Swift /
Direct Distribution.

IN DREAMS.
Tracks: In dreams / Lonely wine / Shahdaroba / No-one
will ever know / Sunset / House without windows /
Dream / Blue bayou / (They call you) Gigolette / All I
have to do is dream / Beautiful dreamer / My prayer.
■ LP . . . . HAU 8108
London-American / Nov '63.

IN DREAMS.
Tracks: In dreams.
■ 7" . . . . HLU 9676
London-American / Feb '63.
■ 7" . . . . ROY 1
Virgin / May '87.

IN DREAMS (The Greatest Hits).
Tracks: Only the lonely / Leah / In dreams / Uptown /
It's over / Crying / Dream baby / Blue angel / Working
for the man / Running scared / Falling /
I'm hurtin' / Claudette / Oh pretty woman / Mean
woman blues / Ooby dooby / Lana / Blue bayou.
CD . . . . VGDCD 3514
Virgin / Apr '87 / EMI.
LP Set . . . . VGD 3514
MC . . . . VGDC 3514
Virgin / Jun '87 / EMI.

IN DREAMS (OLD GOLD).
Tracks: In dreams / Falling.
7" . . . . OG 9883
Old Gold / Feb '89 / Pickwick Records.

IT'S OVER.
Tracks: It's over.
■ 7" . . . . HLU 9882
London-American / Apr '64.

IT'S OVER (OLD GOLD).
Tracks: It's over / Blue bayou.
7" . . . . OG 9879
Old Gold / Feb '89 / Pickwick Records.

KING OF HEARTS.
Tracks: You're the one / Heartbreak radio / We'll take
the night / Crying (Duet with K D Lang) / After the love
has gone / Love in time / I drove all night / Wild hearts
run out of time / Coming home / Careless heart (Origi-
nal demo).
CD . . . . CDVUS 58
LP . . . . VUSLP 58
MC . . . . VUSMC 58
Virgin America / Nov '92 / EMI.

LAMINAR FLOW.
Tracks: Easy way out / Love is a cold wind / Lay it down
/ I care / We're into something good / Movin' / Poor
baby / Warm spot hot / Tears / Friday night / Hound dog
man.
■ LP . . . . K 53092
Asylum / '77.

LANA.
Tracks: Lana / House without windows.
■ 7" . . . . HL 10051
London-American / Jun '66.

LEGEND IN HIS TIME.
Tracks: Lonesome number one / Oh such a stranger /
Legend in my time, A / I'm a Southern man / Belinda /
Under suspicion / No chain at all / Can't wait / I'm
hurting / Same street, The / Blue blue day / Too soon to
know / I don't really want you / Old love song / Born to
love you / Big hearted me / What about me.
CD . . . . CDMF 079
Magnum Force / '91 / Terry Blood Dist. / Jazz Music /
Hot Shot.

LEGEND, THE.
Tracks: Too soon to know / (Yes) I'm hurting / Loner,
The / Breaking up is breaking my heart / What about
me / Far far away / Big hearted me / Blue blue day /
Sweet dreams / Oh such a stranger / Maybe / Lone-
some number one / Why hurt the one who loves you /
Crawling back / Same street, The / (I'd be a) legend in
my time.
CD . . . . PWK 111
MC . . . . HSC 3266
Pickwick / May '89 / Pickwick Records.
CD . . . . PWK 4036P
MC . . . . PWKMC 4036P
Pickwick / Feb '91 / Pickwick Records.

LEGENDARY ROY ORBISON, THE.
Tracks: It's over / Only the lonely / Goodnight / Lana /
Crowd, The / All I have to do is dream / Crying / Dream
baby / Mean woman blues / Oh pretty woman / Love
hurts / My prayer / Falling / Blue angel / In dreams /
Blue bayou / Great pretender, The / Pretty paper.
MC . . . . STAC 2330
Telstar/Ronco / Oct '88 / BMG.
■ LP . . . . STAR 2330
Telstar/Ronco / Oct '88.
■ CD . . . . TCD 2330
Telstar/Ronco / Oct '88.

LEGENDARY ROY ORBISON, THE (2).
Tracks: Not Advised.
LP . . . . XELLP 112
MC . . . . XELMC 112
Exel / Jul '88 / Henry Hadaway Organisation / EMI.

LIVE IN CONCERT.
Tracks: Only the lonely / Running scared / Dream baby
/ Mean woman blues / It's over / What'd I say / Oh
pretty woman / Goodnight.
VHS . . . . MC 2000
Music Club Video / Jun '89 / Video Collection / Gold &
Sons / Terry Blood Dist.

LONELY AND BLUE.
Tracks: Not Advised.
■ LP . . . . HAU 2342
London-American / Jun '63.

LOVE SONGS.
Tracks: Born to love me / Sentimental / Evergreen /
Mama / Indian wedding / Yo te amo Maria / Sleepy
hollow / Love star / Born on the wind / Our love song /
Goodnight / You're my girl.
CD 26 10 842
MC 26 10 844
Dillion / '92 / Sound Solutions.

MAGIC OF ROY ORBISON, THE.
Tracks: Chicken hearted / Domino / Go go go / Trying to
get to you / You're my baby / Devil doll / I never knew /
It's too late / You're gonna cry.
MC . . . . VENUMC 6
Venus / Feb '89 / Henry Hadaway Organisation.

MY FRIEND.
Tracks: My friend.
■ 7" . . . . HL 10261
London-American / Apr '69.

MYSTERY GIRL.
Tracks: You got it / Real world / Dream you / Love so
beautiful, A / California blue / She's a mystery to me /
Comedians, The / Windsurfer / Careless heart.
LP . . . . V 2576
■ MC . . . . TCV 2576
Virgin / Dec '88.
CD . . . . CDV 2576
LP . . . . OVED 399
MC . . . . OVEDC 399
Virgin / Apr '92 / EMI.

OH PRETTY WOMAN.
Tracks: Not Advised.
CD . . . . ENT CD 293
Entertainers / Mar '92.

OH PRETTY WOMAN.
Tracks: Oh pretty woman (LP version) (Only on 12"
single) / Claudette / Oh pretty woman (edit).
12" . . . . VST 1224
■ 7" . . . . VS 1224
Virgin / Nov '89.
■ CD Single . . . . VSCD 1224
Virgin / Nov '89.

OH PRETTY WOMAN.
Tracks: Not Advised.
■ LP . . . . HAU 8207
London-American / Dec '64.

OH PRETTY WOMAN (OLD GOLD).
Tracks: Oh pretty woman / Mean woman blues.
7" . . . . OG 9881
Old Gold / Feb '89 / Pickwick Records.

OH PRETTY WOMAN (SINGLE) (2).
Tracks: Oh pretty woman.
■ 7" . . . . HLU 9919
London-American / Sep '64.

ONLY THE LONELY.
Tracks: Not Advised.
LP P.Disc. . . . . AR 30041
Astan (USA) / Dec '85.

ONLY THE LONELY.
Tracks: Only the lonely.
■ 7" . . . . HLU 9149
London-American / Jul '60.

ONLY THE LONELY (2).
Tracks: Crying / Dream baby / Candy man / Running
scared / Oh pretty woman / Lana / Blue bayou / Ooby
dooby.
CD 290 953
MC 490 953
Ariola Express / Jun '92 / BMG Distribution Operations.

ONLY THE LONELY (OLD GOLD).
Tracks: Only the lonely / Blue angel.
7" . . . . OG 9870
Old Gold / Feb '89 / Pickwick Records.

ONLY THE LONELY - GREATEST HITS.
Tracks: Only the lonely / In dreams / Crying / Dream
baby / Working for the man / Candy man / Running
scared / I'm hurtin' / Oh pretty woman / Ooby dooby /
Lana / Blue bayou.
CD . . . . VVIPD 122
MC . . . . VVIPC 122
Pickwick / Nov '92 / Pickwick Records.

ORBISON WAY, THE.
Tracks: Not Advised.
■ LP . . . . HAU 8279
London-American / Feb '66.

ORBISONGS.
Tracks: Not Advised.
■ LP . . . . SMO 5004
London-American / Jul '67.

OTHER SIDE OF, THE.
Tracks: Not Advised.
LP . . . . LSP 1063
Musketeer / Oct '87 / D.A.D. Records.

OUR LOVE SONG.
Tracks: Born to love me / (I get so) Sentimental /
Evergreen / Mama / Indian wedding / Yo te amo maria /
Sleepy hollow / Love star / Borne on the wind / Old love
song / Goodnight / (Say) you're my girl.
LP . . . . MNT 4634171
MC 463 417 4
Monument / Apr '89 / Sony.
■ CD 463 417 2
Monument / Apr '89.

PENNY ARCADE.
Tracks: Penny arcade.
■ 7" . . . . HL 10285
London-American / Sep '69.

PRETTY PAPER.
Tracks: Pretty paper.
■ 7" . . . . HLU 9930
London-American / Nov '64.

PROBLEM CHILD.
Tracks: Problem child / This kind of love / I never knew
/ It's too late / You're gonna cry / Chicken hearted /
Trying to get to you / Problem child (2) / It's too late (2) /
Mean little mama / This kind of love (2) / Claudette.
LP . . . . Z 2006
Zu Zazz / May '88 / Hot Shot / A.D.A Distribution / C.M.
Distribution.

RARE ORBISON COLLECTION.
Tracks: Actress, The / Paper boy / With the bug /
Today's teardrops / Here comes that song again / Only
with you / Pretty one / No chain at all / Blues in my
mind / Drifting away / Wings of glory / Belinda.
■ CD 463 418 2
Monument / Apr '89.
LP 463 418 1
■ MC 463 418 4
Monument / Apr '89.
CD 9825982
Pickwick/Sony Collectors Choice / Jul '91 / Pickwick
Records.

RARE RECORDINGS, THE.
Tracks: Actress, The / Paper boy / With the bug /
Today's teardrops / Here comes that song again / Only
with you / Pretty one / No chain at all / Blues in my
mind / Drifting away / Wings of glory.
CD 26 10 852
MC 26 10 854
Dillion / '92 / Sound Solutions.

RCA SESSIONS, THE (Orbison, Roy &
Sonny James).
Tracks: Almost eighteen / Bug, The / I'll never tell /
Jolie / Paper boy / Sweet and innocent / Seems to me /
Apache / Magnetism / Young love / Lana / Legend of
the brown mountain light / Listen to my heart / Hey little
ducky / Innocent angel / Broken wings / Day's not over
yet, The / Dance her by me (one more time) / Time's
running backwards for me.
CD . . . . BCD 15407
Bear Family / Jul '87 / Rollercoaster Records / Swift /
Direct Distribution.

RIDE AWAY.
Tracks: Ride away / Wondering.
■ 7" . . . . HLU 9986
London-American / Sep '65.

ROY ORBISON.
Tracks: Domino / Ooby dooby / Go go go (down the
line) / Rockhouse / You're my baby / Trying to get to
you / Cause of it all, The / I was a fool / Problem child /
You're gonna cry / Mean little mama / This kind of love
/ I like love / Chicken hearted.
LP . . . . SUNLP 1050
Sun / Jan '90 / Charly / Swift.

ROY ORBISON.
Tracks: Pretty woman / Only the lonely / Crying / Candy
man / Leah / Blue bayou / I'm hurtin' / Love hurts /
Uptown / Blue angel / Devil doll / Mean woman blues /
It's over / It's too late / Working for the man / Running
scared.
CD . . . . BSP 530
BS Production / Oct '91.

ROY ORBISON - VOL 2.
Tracks: Party heart / How are things in paradise /
Darkness / Yes / Double date / Mama / San Fernando /
Zig zag / Tired old country song / Mother / Boogie baby
/ Indian Summer.
CD 9825992
Pickwick/Sony Collectors Choice / Jul '91 / Pickwick
Records.

ROY ORBISON BOX SET.
Tracks: Not Advised.
CD . . . . **BOXD 23**
MC **BOXC23**
Pickwick / Sep '92 / Pickwick Records.

ROY ORBISON EP.
Tracks: Ooby dooby / It's too late / Rock house / Domino.
■ **EP** . . . . **CEP 111**
Charly / Feb '77.

ROY ORBISON: VINTAGE INTERVIEW PIC DISC.
Tracks: Not Advised.
LP P.Disc . . . . **VBAK 3002**
Baktabak / Jun '89 / Arabesque Ltd.

RUNNING SCARED.
Tracks: Running scared.
■ **7"** . . . . **HLU 9342**
London-American / May '61.

RUNNING SCARED (OLD GOLD).
Tracks: Running scared / Crying.
7" . . . . **OG 9872**
Old Gold / Feb '89 / Pickwick Records.

SHE.
Tracks: She / Here comes the rain baby.
7" . . . . **HLU 10159**
London-American / '67.

SHE'S A MYSTERY TO ME.
Tracks: She's a mystery to me / Crying / Dream baby (12" only).
■ **3" CD** . . . . **VSCD 1173**
Virgin / Feb '89.
■ **12"** . . . . **VST 1173**
Virgin / Mar '89.
■ **7"** . . . . **VS 1173**
Virgin / Mar '89.

SINGLES COLLECTION, THE.
Tracks: Not Advised.
■ **LP** **839 234 1**
Polydor / May '89.
CD **839 234 2**
■ **MC** **839 234 4**
Polydor / May '89.

SO GOOD.
Tracks: So good / Memories.
■ **7"** . . . . **HLU 10113**
London-American / Feb '67.
■ **7"** . . . . **HL 10113**
London-American / Feb '67.

SOUTHERN MAN.
Tracks: Southern man / Born to love me.
■ **7"** . . . . **MNT 4797**
Monument / Jan '77.

SUN YEARS, THE.
Tracks: Ooby dooby / Trying to get to you / Go go go / You're my baby / Rock house / Domino / Sweet and easy / Devil doll / Cause of it all, The / Fools' hall of fame / True love goodbye / Chicken hearted / I like love / Mean little mama / Problem child / I was a fool / This kind of love / It's too late / I never knew / You're gonna cry / You tell me / I give up / One more time / Lovestruck / Clown, The / Claudette / Jenny / Find my baby for me.
Double LP . . . . **CDX 4**
Charly / Jul '84 / Charly.
CD . . . . **BCD 15461**
Bear Family / Apr '89 / Rollercoaster Records / Swift / Direct Distribution.

THERE IS ONLY ONE ROY ORBISON.
Tracks: Not Advised.
■ **LP** . . . . **HAU 8252**
London-American / Sep '65.

THERE WON'T BE MANY COMING HOME.
Tracks: There won't be many coming home.
■ **7"** . . . . **HL 10096**
London-American / Dec '66.

TOO SOON TO KNOW.
Tracks: Too soon to know.
■ **7"** . . . . **HLU 10067**
London-American / Sep '66.

TWENTY CLASSIC HITS.
Tracks: Not Advised.
LP . . . . **MA 221185**
MC . . . . **MAMC 9221185**
Masters (Holland) / '88.

TWINKLE TOES.
Tracks: Twinkle toes / Where is tomorrow.
■ **7"** . . . . **HLU 10034**
London-American / Apr '66.

WALK ON.
Tracks: Walk on.
■ **7"** . . . . **HLU 10206**
London-American / Jul '68.

WILD HEARTS.
Tracks: Wild hearts / Time.
7" . . . . **ZTAS 9**
■ **7" Set** . . . . **DZTAS 9**
ZTT / Jun '85 / WEA.
■ **12"** . . . . **12 ZTAS 9**
ZTT / Jun '85.

WORKIN' FOR THE MAN.
Tracks: Working for the man.
■ **7"** . . . . **HLU 9607**
London-American / Nov '62.

YOU GOT IT.
Tracks: You got it / Only one, The / Crying out (Available on 12" format only.).
■ **12"** . . . . **VST 1166**
Virgin / Dec '88.
■ **7"** . . . . **VS 1166**
Virgin / Dec '88.
■ **3" CD** . . . . **VSCD 1166**
Virgin / Jan '89.

Orion

Orrville, Alabama born Jimmy Ellis (1945), came to prominence in 1979. When as the mysterious masked Elvis impersonator suitably recorded for Shelby Singleton's Sun label, with a total of ten singles surfacing in & around the 60 - 70 mark during his five year career behind the mask. Ellis' vocals being so like Elvis (to the point of confusion), can be found anoymously joining Jerry Lee Lewis 1978 Sun album *Duets - Jerry Lee Lewis & Friends* . Lewis making the top 30 with *Save the last dance with me* & just sneaking in the top 100 with *Cold, cold heart* .

INSANE IN ANOTHER WORLD.
Tracks: Insane in another world.
7" . . . . **LM 002**
Lost Moment / Jul '84 / RTM / Pinnacle.

MEN FROM WHITEHALL, THE.
Tracks: Men from Whitehall, The.
7" . . . . **CAT 1**
County Cat / Jan '85 / M.I.S.Records.

REBORN.
Tracks: Not Advised.
LP . . . . **CRL 5020**
Charly / Apr '80 / Charly.

SOME THINK HE MIGHT BE KING ELVIS.
Tracks: That's all right / Blue moon of Kentucky / Rockabilly rebel / See you later, Alligator / Susie Q / I'm gonna be a wheel someday / Rockin' little angel / Crazy little thing called love / Long tall Sally / Memphis sun / Peggy Sue / Matchbox / There's no easy way / Baby please say yes / Born / If I can't have you / Ain't no good / Some you win, some you lose / Look me up (and lay it one me) / Old Mexico / Rainbow maker / Anybody out there / Midnight rendevous / Maybe tomorrow / She hates to be wrong / What now my love / Me and Bobby McGee.
CD . . . . **BCD 15548**
Bear Family / May '91 / Rollercoaster Records / Swift / Direct Distribution.

Osbourne Brothers

Brothers Sonny (born 29.10.1937 - banjo/tenor vocals) and Bobby (born 7.12.1931 mandolin/vocals) hail from the coal mining town of Hyden, Kentucky. Highly innovative exponents of bluegrass music, members of Grand Ole Opry since 1964, voted CMA Vocal Group Of The Year in, Music City News' Bluegrass Group Of The Year, 1971 -1979. Both together and individually played/recorded with Jimmy Martin, Bill Monroe (Sonny at the age of 15) and Red Allen during the Fifties. The Osbournes own career took off in 1958, when MGM released their single with Red Allen. *Once More* went to No.13 on the country charts. Hits to follow appeared on Decca, between 1966 and 1973, and featured such numbers as *Ruby Are You Mad At Me, Tennessee Hound Dog* and Bouldleaux Bryant's *Rocky Top* (Released On Christmas Day 1967) leading the way. Bluegrass chart success had almost dried up by this time, with them scoring only minor hits on MCA and the Californian CMH label *Shackles And Chains, From Rocky Top To Muddy Bottom* was a double album of songs entirely penned by Felice and Boudleaux Bryant during late 1970s. Recent work can be found on Sugar Hill and CMH *Once More Vols.1 & 2* (where they reprise their best known material) and *Hillibilly Fever* respectively. (Maurice Hope)

BLUEGRASS COLLECTION.
Tracks: Kentucky waltz / Pain in my heart / Blue ridge cabin home / When are you lonely / Some old day / I hear a sweet voice calling / Cabin in Caroline / It's a long, long way to the top of the world / Sunny side of the mountain / Head over heel / Don't that road look rough and rocky / I'm going back to old Kentucky / Your sweet love is like a flower / Sweethearts again / Little cabin home on the hill / No mother or Dad / Toy heart / Rank strangers / Vision of mother, A / Lonesome day / My rose of old Kentucky / This heart of mine can never say goodbye / Thinking about you / White dove.
Double LP . . . . **CMH 9011**
MC . . . . **CMH 9011C**
CMH (USA) / '78 / C.M. Distribution / Projection.

BLUEGRASS CONCERTO.
Tracks: Bluegrass concerto / Tina Rene waltz / Bandy's 109 / Shawnee / I'll fly away / Homecoming, The / Jesse James / Bobby Van Waltz / Black mountain drive / Sure-fire / Uncloudy day, The.
LP . . . . **CMH 6231**
CMH (USA) / '79 / C.M. Distribution / Projection.

BOBBY & HIS MANDOLIN.
Tracks: Not Advised.
LP . . . . **CMH 6260**
CMH (USA) / '80 / C.M. Distribution / Projection.

ESSENTIAL BLUEGRASS ALBUM, THE (Osborne Brothers & Mac Wiseman).
Tracks: Midnight flyer / Shackles and chains / Bluebirds are singing for me / Family bible / Don't let your sweet love die / I wonder how the old folks are at home / Little white church, The / It's goodbye and so long to you / Four walls around me / Mother Maybelle / I'll still write your name in the sand / Poison love / Take me back to Renfro Valley / Shenandoah waltz / Mountain fever / Are you coming back to me / I'm a stranger here / You're the girl of my dreams / Pins and needles in my heart / I've always wanted to sing in Renfro Valley / Travellin' this lonesome road / Tis sweet to be remembered
Double LP . . . . **CMH 9016**
MC . . . . **CMH 9016C**
CMH (USA) / '78 / C.M. Distribution / Projection.

FROM ROCKY TOP TO MUDDY BOTTOM (The songs of Boudleaux & Felice Bryant).
Tracks: Rocky top / Georgia mules and county boys / Don't ever tell me you love me / Hey Joe / All I ever have to do is dream / Packing up your heart / Tell it to your old Grandpa / Little boy / Banjo's going home / Georgia piney woods / Just another dream / I can't see the rainbow / Take me as I am / Tennessee hound dog / Where did the sunshine / Country boy / Love hurts / Fortune, fortune / Muddy bottom.
Double LP . . . . **CMH 9008**
MC . . . . **CMH 9008C**
CMH (USA) / '77 / C.M. Distribution / Projection.

HILLBILLY FEVER.
Tracks: Hillbilly fever / Cincinatti Ohio / Last letter, The / Fourteen carat gold / Old flames can't hold a candle to you / Prisoner's song, The / You are my flower / Out behind the barn / Paper Rosie / Breaking in a brand new pair of shoes / Working man blues / First fall of snow, The / Tragic romance / Orange blossom special.
CD . . . . **CMHCD 6269**
MC . . . . **CMH 6269**
CMH (USA) / '91 / C.M. Distribution / Projection.

I CAN HEAR KENTUCKY CALLING ME.
Tracks: Not Advised.
LP . . . . **CMH 6244**
CMH (USA) / '80 / C.M. Distribution / Projection.

MODERN SOUNDS OF BLUE GRASS MUSIC, THE.
Tracks: Kind of woman I got, The / Hard times / Walking the floor over you / Roll muddy water / One tear / Lonesome feeling / One kiss away from you / Memories / Someone before me / Let's say goodbye / World of forgotten people / I'm leaving.
LP . . . . **HAT 3063**
MC . . . . **HATC 3063**
Stetson / Jun '88 / Crusader Marketing Co. / Swift / Wellard Dist. / Midland Records / C.M. Distribution.

NUMBER ONE.
Tracks: Leavin's heavy on my mind / Say old man (can you play the mandolin) / Guide me home my Georgia moon / Memories never die / Each season changes you / Rueben / Last time, The / Bent, broken and blue / Fair and tender ladies / Hobo on a freight train to heaven / Rutland's reel.
■ **LP** . . . . **CMH 6206**
CMH (USA) / '76.

ONCE MORE VOL.1.
Tracks: Not Advised.
LP . . . . **SH 3754**
Sugarhill(USA) / Mar '89 / Roots Records / Projection / Impetus Records / C.M. Distribution / Jazz Music / Swift / Duncans / A.D.A Distribution.

ONCE MORE VOL.2 (Favorite memories).
Tracks: Not Advised.
LP . . . . **SH 3758**
Sugarhill(USA) / Dec '87 / Roots Records / Projection / Impetus Records / C.M. Distribution / Jazz Music / Swift / Duncans / A.D.A Distribution.

OSBOURNE BROTHERS & RED ALLEN (Osborne Brothers & Red Allen).
Tracks: Not Advised.
LP . . . . **SS 03**
Rounder / Dec '88 / Projection / Roots Records / Swift / C.M. Distribution / Topic Records / Jazz Music / Hot Shot / A.D.A Distribution / Direct Distribution.
LP . . . . **HAT 3129**
Stetson / '89 / Crusader Marketing Co. / Swift / Wellard Dist. / Midland Records / C.M. Distribution.

OSBOURNE BROTHERS, THE.
Tracks: Not Advised.
MC . . . . **SSC 04**
Rounder / '88 / Projection / Roots Records / Swift / C.M. Distribution / Topic Records / Jazz Music / Hot Shot / A.D.A Distribution / Direct Distribution.

LP. . . . . SS 04
Rounder / Dec '88 / Projection / Roots Records / Swift / C.M. Distribution / Topic Records / Jazz Music / Hot Shot / A.D.A Distribution / Direct Distribution.

SINGING, SHOUTING PRAISES.
Tracks: Jesus cares what happens / Medals for Mother / Saviour, Lord and guide / Are you so afraid to speak our Saviour's name / What a friend we have in Jesus / Old brush arbors / Still waters / Where no-one stands alone / Nearer my God to thee / Singing, shooting praises / Hide me rock of ages.
MC . . . . SH 3674C
Sugarhill(USA) / '88 / Roots Records / Projection / Impetus Records / C.M. Distribution / Jazz Music / Swift / Duncans / A.D.A Distribution.
LP. . . . . SH 3764
Sugarhill(USA) / Mar '89 / Roots Records / Projection / Impetus Records / C.M. Distribution / Jazz Music / Swift / Duncans / A.D.A Distribution.

SOME THINGS I WANT TO SING ABOUT.
Tracks: How much does it cost to ride this train / February in my heart / Always you / So doggone lonesome / Somehow tonight / Rosie Bokay / Wreck of the old 97 / If you're gonna do me wrong, do it right / Some things I want to sing about / Harvest of my heart / Too long / Can't you hear that whistle blow.
LP. . . . . SH 3740
MC . . . . SH 3740MC
Sugarhill(USA) / Mar '85 / Roots Records / Projection / Impetus Records / C.M. Distribution / Jazz Music / Swift / Duncans / A.D.A Distribution.

VOICES IN BLUEGRASS.
Tracks: Take this hammer / Cottonfields / Me and my old banjo / Pathway of teardrops / Kentucky / Bluegrass express / This heart of mine / Cuckoo bird / Don't ever look at me / Charlie Cotton / Bugle on the banjo / Salty dog blues.
LP. . . . . HAT 3003
MC . . . . HATC 3003
Stetson / Nov '85 / Crusader Marketing Co. / Swift / Wellard Dist. / Midland Records / C.M. Distribution.

Oslin, K.T.

Singer-songwriter born in Crossitt, Arkansas but raised in Alabama and Texas. Oslin's success hasn't come easy, she majored in drama and made her first shot in the music business in the early 60's in a folk trio with David Jones and Guy Clark (who also achieved success a little later). During the following years she appeared in many musical productions on stage, TV commercials in New York and all the time trying to secure herself a deal in Nashville. In 1981 she entered the country charts with *Clean your own tables* on Elektra, but it wasn't until she moved to Nashville four years later that she began to make any real headway. When success came with *80's Ladies* on RCA, it wasn't restricted to country music surroundings. She's subsequently hit the number one spot regularly with songs such as *Do ya* and *I'll always come back* and also crossed over into the pop charts. *80's Ladies* set a record for female debut albums in country music by entering the charts at No. 15 as well as being the first woman since Anne Murray to go Gold. For these achievements Oslin has been awarded three Grammies and also named CMA's Top Female Vocalist. (Tony Byworth)

EIGHTIES LADIES.
Tracks: Wall of tears / I'll always come back / Younger men / Eighties ladies / Do ya' / Two hearts / Doctor Doctor / Lonely but only for you / Old pictures.
CD . . . . PD 85924
LP. . . . . PL 85924
RCA / Apr '88 / BMG.
■ MC . . . . PK 85924
RCA / Apr '88.

EIGHTIES LADIES.
Tracks: Eighties ladies / Two hearts.
■ 7" . . . . PB 49545
RCA / Jun '88.

LOVE IN A SMALL TOWN.
Tracks: Come next Monday / Oo-wee / Mary and Willie / Love is strange / Momma was a dancer / New way home / Cornell Crawford / Still on my mind / You call everybody darling.
■ LP. . . . . PL 90545
RCA / Feb '91.
■ MC . . . . PK 90545
RCA / Feb '91.
■ CD . . . . PD 90545
RCA / Feb '91.

THIS WOMAN.
Tracks: This woman / Money / Round the clock lovin' / Where is a woman to go / Hold me / Hey Bobby / She don't talk like us no more (CD only) / Jealous (CD only) / Didn't expect it to go down this way / Truly blue (CD only).
■ LP. . . . . PL 88369
RCA / Oct '88.
CD . . . . PD 88369
■ MC . . . . PK 88369
RCA / Oct '88.

WALL OF TEARS.
Tracks: Wall of tears / Doctor Doctor.
■ 7" . . . . PB 49559
RCA / Apr '88.

YOUNGER MEN.
Tracks: Younger men / I'll always come back.
■ 7" . . . . PB 49531
RCA / Jul '88.

Osmond Brothers

After the Osmond hysteria of the 1970's faded away, the various members of the family pursued their own individual careers. The older brothers - Alan (b. June 22, 1949), Wayne (b. August 28,1951), Merrill (b. April 30, 1953) and Jay (b. March 2, 1955) - moved into country music and scored a dozen modest hits during the period 1982-1986 on the Elektra, Warner Bros. and EMI America labels. The quartet eventually became a trio as Jay departed, but all were reunited a decade later as they moved home from Utah and set up home and theatre in Branson, Missouri, where they're once again drawing the crowds. (Tony Byworth)

I THINK ABOUT YOUR LOVIN'.
Tracks: I think about your lovin' / One way rider.
7" . . . . RANS 74
Range (1) / Mar '85.

TODAY.
Tracks: I think about your lovin' / It's like falling in love (over and over) / Never ending song of love / Take this heart / Ease the fever / Your leaving was the last thing on my mind / Blue all over you / She's ready for someone to love her / If every man had a woman like you / What do the lonely do / We work hard (to make love easy) / Where does an angel go when she cries / She's back in town again / One way rider.
LP. . . . . RANGE 7005
Range (1) / Mar '85.
MC . . . . SDC 5118
Silver Dollar / Nov '88.
MC . . . . .RANGE 67005
Range (1) / May '90.

Osmond, Marie

Born Olive Marie Osmond on October 13, 1959 in Ogden, Utah a member of one of the most famous families in the world. She began performing with her brothers when she was 14 and released her first record *Paper Roses* in 1973. It went straight to the top of the country charts as well as going top 5 in the pop charts. Although subsequent records also gained country placings (including a couple of duets with brother Donny), it wasn't until the early 80's that she concentrated on the country market - and a deal with Capitol put her back at the top, with *Meet me in Montana* (a duet with Dan Seals) setting the pace. (Tony Byworth)

ALL IN LOVE.
Tracks: I'm in love and he's in Dallas / Raining tears / My hometown boy / Baby's blue eyes / Lonely as the night is long / 99% of the time / Somebody else's moon / Sweet life / All in love / Without a trace.
CD . . . . CDEST 2068
■ CD . . . . CDP 748 968 2
Capitol / Aug '88.
LP. . . . . EST 2068
■ MC . . . . .TCEST 2068
Capitol / Aug '88.

GET ME TO HEAVEN.
Tracks: Get me to heaven / L.A. song.
■ 7" . . . . POSP 147
Polydor / Apr '80.

I ONLY WANTED YOU.
Tracks: Cry just a little / I only wanted you / You're still new to me / Making magic / I know the feeling / Your love carries me away / We're gonna need a love song / New love / More than dancing / Everybody's crazy 'bout me baby.
LP. . . . . EST 2020
■ MC . . . . .TCEST 2020
Capitol / Oct '86.
■ CD . . . . CDP 746 348 2
Capitol / Feb '87.

PAPER ROSES.
Tracks: Not Advised.
■ LP. 2315 262
MGM (Polydor) / Feb '74.

PAPER ROSES.
Tracks: Paper roses.
■ 7" 2006 315
MGM (Polydor) / Nov '73.

THERE'S NO STOPPING YOUR HEART.
Tracks: There's no stopping your heart / Needing a night like this / Read my lips / Best of you, The / I'll be faithful to you / Meet me in Montana / That old devil moon / Love will find it's way to you / Until I fall in love again / Blue sky / Shining.
■ LP. . . . . EST 2000
Capitol.
■ MC . . . . .TCEST 2000
Capitol / Feb '86.

THERE'S NO STOPPING YOUR HEART.
Tracks: There's no stopping your heart / Love will find it's way to you.
■ 7" . . . . .CL 390
Capitol / Mar '86.

THIS IS THE WAY THAT I FEEL.
Tracks: This is the way that I feel / Play the music loud.
■ 7" 2066 793
Polydor / Jun '77.

Outlaws

DREAM OF THE WEST.
Tracks: Dream of the west / Outlaws, The / Husky team / Rodeo / Smoke signals / Ambush / Barbecue / Spring is near / Indian brave / Homeward bound / Western sunset / Tune for short cowboys.
CD . . . . BGOCD 118
LP. . . . . BGOLP 118
Beat Goes On / Sep '91 / Pinnacle.

Overstreet, Paul

Born 17.3.1955 in Mississippi, one of country music's most prolific songwriters. Featured among the impressive line-up of hit songs he's either penned or co-written are *Diggin' up bones* , *Deeper than than the holler* and *I won't take less than your love* which was a number one for the trio Tanya Tucker, Paul Davis and Overstreet in 1987. He also won CMA's Song of the Year award in 1986 for his collaboration with Don Schlitz *On the other hand* . Paul's own recording career wirh RCA started back in 1983 with his self-titled album flopping and a single *Beautiful baby* only reaching No. 76. Next came his short association with Thom Schuyler and J. Fred Knoblock, making the top spot with *Baby's got a new baby* under the shortened banner S-K-O, (It was their second single on MTM Records). Overstreet then left to concentrate on his solo career, his first single *Love helps those* made top 5, but MTM folded. He then released an album *Sowin' love* on RCA which yielded a fine run of singles all four making the top 5. Moving into 1991 Overstreet continued this roll with *Daddy comes around* edging into Billboards top 10. (Tony Byworth)

SOWIN' LOVE.
Tracks: Love helps those / All the fun / Call the preacher / Richest man on Earth / Sowin' love / Love never sleeps / Dig another well / Seein' my father in me / What God has joined together / Homemaker / 'Neath the light of your love (Only on CD.).
■ MC . . . . PK 90354
RCA / Jul '89.
■ LP. . . . . PL 90354
RCA / Jul '89.
■ CD . . . . PD 90354
RCA / Jul '89.
CD . . . . PD 89717
LP. . . . . PL 89717
MC . . . . PK 89717
RCA / May '89 / BMG.

Overstreet, Tommy

Born 10.9.1937 in Oklahoma City.. Overstreet worked on Houston TV during the 60's under the name Tommy Dean from Abilene, moving to Nashville in 1967 to become the manager of Dot Records - soon followed by his own recording contract. His first big hit came in 1971 with *Gwen (Congratulations)* making Billboards top 5, swiftly followed by *I don't know you anymore* and *Ann (don't go runnin')* amongst others. Overstreet was to chart most regularly throughout the 70's, carried on to a lesser degree into the mid-80's, first on Dot with subsequent moves to Elektra, AMI and indie labels Gervasi and Silver D. (Maurice Hope)

HERE COMES THAT GIRL.
Tracks: Here comes that girl / I'll give up.
■ 7" . . . . ABC 4150
ABC Records / Oct '76.

IF I MISS YOU AGAIN.
Tracks: I f I miss you again / Welcome to my world of love.
■ 7" . . . . .EMBS 341
Ember / Feb '75.

SOLID GOLD HITS.
Tracks: Heaven is my woman's love / Gwen / Jeannie Marie, you were a lady / If I miss you again tonight / Send me no roses / I'll never break these chains / Ann, don't go runnin' / That's when my woman begins / Dream maker / Heart of Dixie.
LP. . . . . BDL 1063
Bulldog Records / Aug '88 / President Records / Jazz Music / Wellard Dist. / TKO Records Ltd.

TOMMY OVERSTREET SINGS OF LOVE & THINGS.
Tracks: (Jeannie Marie) You were a lady / Carolyn / Laura (what's he got that I ain't got) / Goodbye Rosie /

O 8

■ DELETED

Sundown Mary / Ruby (don't take your love to town) / Help me make it through the night / Gwen (congratulations) / Smile at me sweet Nancy / Ann (don't go runnin') / Sweet Caroline / Polk salad Annie / If / Put your hand in the hand.
■ LP. . . . . NR 5081
Ember / '78 / TKO Records Ltd / President Records.

Owens, Bonnie

JUST BETWEEN THE TWO OF US (Owens, Bonnie & Merle Haggard).
Tracks: Just between the two of us / House without love is not a home, A / Slowly but surely / Our hearts are holding / I wanta live again / Forever and ever / I'll take a chance / Stranger in my arms / Too used to being with you / So much for me, so much for you / Wait a little longer, please Jesus.
LP. . . . . HAT 3073
MC . . . . HATC 3073
Stetson / Aug '88 / Crusader Marketing Co. / Swift / Wellard Dist. / Midland Records / C.M. Distribution.

Owens, Buck

12 GREAT NUMBER 1 COUNTRY HITS.
Tracks: Not Advised.
■ LP. . . . . MFP 50357
MFP / Mar '78.

ACT NATURALLY.
Tracks: Tijuana lady / Gonna have love / Out there chasing rainbows / I was there / Act naturally / Playboy / Rock hard love / Crying time / Brooklyn Bridge / Take me back again.
CD . . . . CZ 276
CD . . . . CDEST 2119
Capitol / Feb '90 / EMI.
■ CD . . . . CDP 792 893 2
Capitol / Feb '90.
■ LP. . . . . EST 2119
Capitol / Feb '90.
MC 792 893 4
■ MC . . . . .TCEST 2119
Capitol / Feb '90.

BLUE LOVE.
Tracks: House down the block, The / You're fer me / Down on the corner of love / Blue love / It don't show on me / Pease don't take her from me / Three dimension love / Why don't mommy stay with daddy and me / When I hold you / Country girl / I will love you always / Right after the dance / I'm gonna blow / Higher and higher and higher.
LP. . . . . SDLP 055
Sundown / Dec '87 / Terry Blood Dist. / Jazz Music / C.M. Distribution.

BLUE LOVE.
Tracks: Not Advised.
CD . . . . .CDSD 055
Sundown / Jan '93 / Terry Blood Dist. / Jazz Music / C.M. Distribution.

BUCK OWENS.
Tracks: Not Advised.
MC . . . . .ZCGAS 755
Audio Fidelity(USA) / Oct '84 / Stage One Records.

COUNTRY MAN NO. 1.
Tracks: Above and beyond / Down on the corner of love / Excuse me (I think I've got a heartache) / Foolin' around / House down the block, The / It don't show on me / Loose talk / Right after the dance / Sweethearts in heaven / There goes my love / Under the influence of love.
■ MC . . . . .ZCEB 126
Ember / '78 / TKO Records Ltd / President Records.

HOT DOG.
Tracks: Don't let her know / A-11 / Summertime blues / Memphis / Hot dog / Put a quarter in the jukebox / Under your spell again / Second fiddle / Sweethearts in heaven / Keys in the mailbox, The.
■ CD . . . . CDEST 2082
Capitol / Jan '89.
■ LP. . . . . EST 2082
Capitol / Jan '89.
■ MC . . . . TC EST 2082
Capitol / Jan '89.

HOT DOG.
Tracks: Hot dog.
■ 7" P.Disc . . . . PEP 8017
P.E.P. / Jul '88 / Pinnacle.

IT'S POP.
Tracks: It's pop / American girl, The.
■ 7" . . . . HLU 10006
London-American / '65.

LIVE AT CARNEGIE HALL 1966 (Owens, Buck & The Buckaroos).
Tracks: Act naturally / Together again / Love's gonna live here / Medley (I don't care; My heart skips a beat; Gonna have love) / Medley (2) (In the palm of her hand; Cryin' time; Don't let her know; Only you) / Waitin' in your welfare line / Buckaroo / Streets of Laredo, The / I've got a tiger by the tail / Fun'n'games (With Don & Doyle) / Twist & shout / Medley (3) (Under your spell again; Above & beyond; Excuse me; Foolin' around; Truck drivin' man).
CD . . . . .CMFCD 012
Country Music Foundation / Jan '93 / Topic Records / Direct Distribution.

LIVE AT CARNEGIE HALL: BUCK OWENS (Owens, Buck & The Buckaroos).
Tracks: Act naturally / Together again / Love's gonna live here / Medley: In the palm of your hand, Cryin time (Don't let her know, Only you (Can break my heart)) / Medley: I don't care (Just as long as you love me) (My heart skips a beat, Gonna have love) / Waitin' in your welfare line / Buckaroo / Street of Laredo, The / I've got a tiger by the tail / Fun 'n' games with Don & Doyle / Twist and shout / Medley: Under your spell again, Above and beyond (Excuse me (I think I've got a heartache), Foolin' around, Hello trouble, Truck drivin' man).
CD . . . . .CMF 012D
Country Music Foundation / '88 / Topic Records / Direct Distribution.

Oxford, Vernon

Traditional styled singer and fiddle player (of which his father was champion) born 8.6.1941 near Rogers, Arkansas. Had a spell on RCA (1965 - 1968), found himself tagged as 'too country' for American radio. Oxford's nasal vocal style, akin to Hank Williams, is pure country to the core - in keeping with others acts of the time, Stoney Edwards & Stonewall Jackson. After being dropped by RCA, he did some single releases on the Stop label. Cult-like status transpired for Oxford in Europe. His 1973, 17 - day tour of the UK resulted in his fans petitioning RCA to re-sign him, which they duly did, Oxford gaining single/cult success with his *Redneck* (The Redneck National Anthem). Later he became very much involved in gospel - a contrast to his days as a young hellraiser. Visited the UK regulary during 70's and early 80's, popular performer at the annual Wembley Country Music Festival (and it's lesser known gospel shows). In 1989, Vernon was the subject of a religious BBC TV documentary filmed In Northern Ireland *Power In The Blood* , the soundtrack released on BBC records. His most recent work, can be found on Rounder. (Maurice Hope)

20 OF THE BEST: VERNON OXFORD.
Tracks: Redneck / Clean your own tables / Shadows of my mind / Watermelon time in Georgia / This woman is mine / Old folks home, The / Woman, let me sing you a song / Forgetfulness for ale / Fields of flowers / Touch of God's hand / Good old-fashioned Saturday night honky-tonk barroom brawl,A / Redneck roots / Only the shadows know (Wot, even Hank? (sorry)) / Your wanting for me is gone / Baby sister / I've got to get Peter off my mind / Stone by stone / Little sister (throw your red shoes away) / Let's take a cold shower / She's always there.
LP. . . . . NL 89373
■ MC . . . . NK 89373
RCA / Mar '84.

BETTER WAY OF LIFE, A.
Tracks: Lord, I've tried everything but you / Dust on the bible / Sweeter than the flowers / Uncloudy day / House of gold / Wings of a dove / O come, angel band / Better way of life, A / Family bible / Mother's not dead / Where the soul never dies.
■ LP. . . . . JULEP 24
Mint / Mar '82.
LP. . . . . SDLP 035
Sundown / Dec '87 / Terry Blood Dist. / Jazz Music / C.M. Distribution.
LP. . . . . ROUNDER 0138
MC . . . . .ROUNDER 0138C
Rounder / '88 / Projection / Roots Records / Swift / C.M. Distribution / Topic Records / Jazz Music / Hot Shot / A.D.A Distribution / Direct Distribution.
MC . . . . .SDC 035
Sundown / Nov '88 / Terry Blood Dist. / Jazz Music / C.M. Distribution.

BY PUBLIC DEMAND.
Tracks: How high does the cotton grow, Mama / I've got to get Peter off your mind / We came awfully close to sin / Love and Pearl and me / She's always there / I wish you would leave me alone / Woman, you've got a hold of me / Soft and warm / We sure danced us some good'ns / Anymore.
■ LP. . . . . LSA 3222
RCA / '78 / BMG.

FAMOUS COUNTRY MUSIC MAKERS.
Tracks: Watermelon time in Georgia / Babies, stop your crying / Treat yourself right / This woman is mine / Mansion on the hill / Old folks home, The / Honky tonk girls / Woman, let me sing you a song / Nashville woman / Blues come in, The / You win again / Forgetfulness for sale / Stone by stone / Baby sister / Wedding bells / Don't let a little thing like this (stand in your way) / Field of flowers / Move to town in the Fall / Hide / Touch of God's hand / Behind every good man there's a woman / Little sister throw your red shoes away / Roll, big wheels, roll / Let's take a cold shower / Goin' home / That's the way I talk / Come back and see us.
■ LP. . . . . DPS 2045
RCA / '78 / BMG.

HIS AND HERS.
Tracks: Not Advised.
LP. . . . . ROUNDER 0123
MC . . . . .ROUNDER 0123C
Rounder / '88 / Projection / Roots Records / Swift / C.M. Distribution / Topic Records / Jazz Music / Hot Shot / A.D.A Distribution / Direct Distribution.

I JUST WANT TO BE A COUNTRY SINGER.
Tracks: Redneck (the Redneck national anthem) / Leave me alone with your blues / Wait a little longer, please Jesus / Clean your own tables / Your wanting me is gone / Country singer, A / Don't be late / Shadows of my mind / One more night to spare / Giving the pill.
■ LP. . . . . LSA 3281
RCA / '78 / BMG.

I LOVE TO SING.
Tracks: I love to sing / Walkin' my blues away / If kisses could talk / Gonna ease my worried mind / No-one is listening / Turn the record over / I think living is sweet / Blanket of stars / Great stoneface, The / Rainy day / (I just want) somebody to love me / Let your love shine.
LP. . . . . BFX 15050
Bear Family / '86 / Rollercoaster Records / Swift / Direct Distribution.

IF I HAD MY WIFE TO LOVE OVER.
Tracks: Not Advised.
LP. . . . . ROUNDER 0091
Rounder / May '79 / Projection / Roots Records / Swift / C.M. Distribution / Topic Records / Jazz Music / Hot Shot / A.D.A Distribution / Direct Distribution.

KEEPIN' IT COUNTRY.
Tracks: You're the reason / Baby sister / Busiest memory in town / Honky tonk troubles / Bringing Mary home / Early morning rain / I feel chained / Sad situation / Long black veil / Outlaws again / Last letter, The.
LP. . . . . SDLP 019
Sundown / Apr '85 / Terry Blood Dist. / Jazz Music / C.M. Distribution.
LP. . . . . ROUNDER 0156
MC . . . . .ROUNDER 0156C
Rounder / '88 / Projection / Roots Records / Swift / C.M. Distribution / Topic Records / Jazz Music / Hot Shot / A.D.A Distribution / Direct Distribution.
MC . . . . .SDC 019
Sundown / May '88 / Terry Blood Dist. / Jazz Music / C.M. Distribution.

POWER IN THE BLOOD.
Tracks: Intercessary prayer / Where the roses never fade / At calvary / What a friend I have in Jesus / Daughter of the wine / Redneck / Be careful of stones that you throw / Power in the blood / Lord I've tried everything but you / I'll fly away / Little sister throw your red shoes away / Saviour saviour / They'll never take her love from me / Go home.
CD . . . . .BBCCD 729
LP. . . . . .REN 729
■ MC . . . . .ZCN 729
BBC / Feb '89.

REDNECK (REDNECK NATIONAL ANTHEM).
Tracks: Redneck (Redneck national anthem) / Leave me alone with the blues.
■ 7" . . . . .RCA 2742
RCA / Oct '76.

TRIBUTE TO HANK WILLIAMS, A.
Tracks: Not Advised.
LP. . . . . SKYL 7002
Meteor / Mar '78 / Terry Blood Dist. / Jazz Music.

Ozark Mountain Daredevils

HEART OF THE COUNTRY.
Tracks: Not Advised.
LP. . . . . DFG 8409
Dixie Frog / Nov '88 / Discovery.

MODERN HISTORY.
Tracks: Everywhere she goes / Love is calling / I'm still dreaming / Turn it up / True love / Lonely knight / Over again / Heating up / River, The / Heart of the country / Wild the days.
CD . . . . .CDRR 303
LP. . . . . RR 303
MC . . . . MCRR 303
Request / Jan '90 / Conifer Records / Jazz Music.

OZARK MOUNTAIN DAREDEVILS.
Tracks: Take you tonight / Jump at the chance / Sailin' around the world / Lovin' you / Tuff luck / Oh darlin' / Empty cup / Rosalie / Runnin' out / Fools gold.
■ LP. . . . . CBS 84193
CBS / Jun '80.

P

Pacheco, Tom

Pacheco is a much-travelled singer-songwriter. First recordings for the classically trained, wordy songwriter (with influences ranging from sixties icon Bob Dylan to Tom T. Hall and Woody Guthrie) came in the mid 1970's on RCA, *Swallowed up in the great American heartland* followed by *Pacheco and Alexander* and Columbia album *The Outsider*, where critical acclaim and a cult-like status were to be his greatest rewards. He had a spell dabbling in rock 'n' roll during the late seventies, Jefferson Starship recording his song *All fly away*. He's done his fair share of roaming, spending time living in Nashville, Woodstock, California and Austin, Texas before settling in Dublin - where in 1989 he had the contemporary *Eagle in the rain* recorded in Ireland and released on Ringsend Road Records, soon followed by two more on the country's Round Tower Music label *Sunflowers and scarecrows* (1991) and the country-styled *Tales from the Red Lake* (recorded in Nashville). He also figures extensively on Josie Kuhn's RTM *Paradise* album. Celinda Pink, who along with Kuhn sings harmony on Pacheco's album, is carving out her own career on Nashville's Step One indie label. Another RTM act Norwegian Steiner Albrigtsen has also utilized Pacheco's involved songs - putting them to good effect on his label debut album *Bound to wander*. (Maurice Hope)

BIG STORM COMIN' (Pacheco, Tom & Steinar Albrigtsten).
Tracks: Not Advised.
CD . . . . RTMCD 53
MC . . . . RTMMC 53
Round Tower / Jun '93 / Pinnacle / A.D.A Distribution / ACD Trading Ltd. / Topic Records / Direct Distribution / BMG.

EAGLE IN THE RAIN.
Tracks: Not Advised.
CD . . . . TPCD 1
LP . . . . TPLP 1
MC . . . . TPMC 1
Ring Send / Apr '90 / I & B Records / Roots Records.

JESUS IN A LEATHER JACKET.
Tracks: Jesus in a leather jacket.
7" . . . . TPS 1
Round Tower / May '90 / Pinnacle / A.D.A Distribution / ACD Trading Ltd. / Topic Records / Direct Distribution / BMG.

ROBERT AND RAMONA.
Tracks: Robert and Ramona.
7" . . . . RTMS 17
Round Tower / Aug '90 / Pinnacle / A.D.A Distribution / ACD Trading Ltd. / Topic Records / Direct Distribution / BMG.

SUNFLOWERS AND SCARECROWS.
Tracks: Not Advised.
CD . . . . RTMCD 30
LP . . . . .RTMLP 30
MC . . . . RTMMC 30
Round Tower / Apr '91 / Pinnacle / A.D.A Distribution / ACD Trading Ltd. / Topic Records / Direct Distribution / BMG.

SWEET LUCILLE.
Tracks: Sweet Lucille / Strange Gods / Midnite waters of the Rio Grande / Jesus in a leather jacket.
■ CD Single . . . . .RTMCDS 38
Round Tower / Aug '91 / Pinnacle / A.D.A Distribution / ACD Trading Ltd. / Topic Records / Direct Distribution / BMG.

Page, Patti

Patti Page was born Clara Ann Fowler, in 1927 in Oklahoma; she sang with the Benny Goodman combo on Chicago radio in 1947; her distinctive vocal colour and good diction made her a natural star of the era of pop singers. She had more than 70 hits between 1948-62 on the Mercury label, with many top tens during 1950-4. She will always be associated with Pee Wee King's *Tennesse Waltz*, number one in the USA for 13 weeks in 1950. (Donald Clarke)

BEST OF PATTI PAGE.
Tracks: Tennessee waltz / I went to your wedding / Cross over the bridge / Allegheny moon / Mockin' Bird Hill / Old Cape Cod / Detour / With my eyes wide open, I'm dreaming / Changing partners / Mr. & Mississippi / How much is that doggie in the window? / Rock of ages.
MC 16-22
Creole (Everest-Europa) / Jul '84.

HOW MUCH IS THAT DOGGIE IN THE WINDOW.
Tracks: How much is that doggie in the window.
. . . . CB 1156
Oriole / Mar '53.

HOW MUCH IS THAT DOGGIE IN THE WINDOW (OLD GOLD).
Tracks: How much is that doggie in the window / Tennessee waltz.
7" . . . . OG 9482
Old Gold / Jan '85 / Pickwick Records.

PATTI PAGE WITH LOU STEIN'S MUSIC (1949).
Tracks: Not Advised.
LP . . . . HSR 223
Hindsight / '88 / Charly.

Page, Stu

Born 12.05.1954 in Leeds, Yorkshire spent much of the 1970's touring the States as an travelling guitar player. Played in various American bands, before returning home. Voted best newcomer by the BCMA in 1985 he gained the ultimate award of Band Of The Year on 1990, something this powerhouse act has has hung onto since (The band being Terry Clayton, Andy Whelan, Nigel Bromley and Page). To date they've appeared alongside such American performers as Bobby Bare, The Glasers, Billie Jo Spears, Albert Lee and The Desert Rose Band.

ARE YOU STILL IN LOVE WITH ME (Page, Stu & Restless Wheels).
Tracks: Are you still in love with me / Motor radio.
7" . . . . BGE 7 1005
Barge / '88 / Jay-Cee Music.

HONEYSUCKLE DREAMING (Page, Stu & Remuda).
Tracks: Not Advised.
MC . . . . CSTON 8604
Sylvantone / Jul '86 / Sylvantone Records.

STU PAGE (Page, Stu & Restless Wheels).
Tracks: Restless wheels / I got drove to it / Just another country / Slave to the wheel / Drift away / Are you still in love with me / He made the whole world sing.
CD . . . . BGE CD 1006
Barge / '88 / Jay-Cee Music.
LP . . . . BGE LP 1006
■ MC . . . . .BGE C 1006
Barge / '88.

SYLVANTONE SHOWCASE, THE (see under Goodacre, Tony).

Paisley, Bob

BOB PAISLEY AND THE SOUTHERN GRASS (Paisley, Bob & The Southern Grass).
Tracks: Not Advised.
LP . . . . ROUNDER 0142
MC .ROUNDER 0142C
Rounder / '88 / Projection / Roots Records / Swift / C.M. Distribution / Topic Records / Jazz Music / Hot Shot / A.D.A Distribution / Direct Distribution.

LOVE SICK AND SORROW (see under Lundy, Ted).

Palmer, Joe

JUST ONE MORE CHANCE.
Tracks: Just one more chance / Carrickfergus.
7" . . . . ET 1
Etude / Mar '88 / Total / BMG.

PLACE IN YOUR HEART (ISLAND) (Palmer, Joe & Joe Giltrap).
Tracks: Cliffs of Dooneen / Galway boy / Boys from the County Armagh / Bally James Duff / Rose of Tralee / Gurragh of Kildare / Rose of Mooncoin / Isle of Innisfree / Mountains of Mourne / Connemara cradle song / Blackwater side / Mary from Dunloe / In Dublin's fair city / Carrickfergus / Bunclody / Limerick you're a lady.
LP . . . . ETLP 1001
MC . . . . ETCS 1001
Etude / Feb '88 / Total / BMG.

Panic Brothers

IN THE RED.
Tracks: Bivouac / No news / I made a mess of a dirty weekend / Repo man / Almost as blue as Hank Williams / In debt / Later than you think / I'm broke in everything but my heart / Late night picture show / I've forgotten what it is that I was drinking to forget.
LP . . . . SPD 1003
Special Delivery / Jun '87 / Revolver-APT / A.D.A Distribution / Topic Records / Direct Distribution / Jazz Music / C.M. Distribution.

Parker, Wesley

FUGITIVE FROM BROKEN DREAMS.
Tracks: Fugitive from broken dreams.
7" . . . . SRT 5K9 571
Garden Isle / Jan '86 / Maingrove Enterprises / Garden Isle Records.

GOOD TIME TONIGHT.
Tracks: Good time tonight / Baby it's you / Her heart got in the way / Family of man / What love can do / Love must know hard times / Love song / All the things America should be / Valley song / I only wanna be your friend.
LP . . . . PRCV 113
President / Apr '83 / Grapevine Distribution / Target Records / Jazz Music / Taylors.

I'LL TAKE YOU THERE AGAIN.
Tracks: Not Advised.
LP . . . . GIR 506 15
Garden Isle / Jan '86 / Maingrove Enterprises / Garden Isle Records.

MONTANA SKIES.
Tracks: Montana skies.
7" 5KS 451
Garden Isle / Jun '85 / Maingrove Enterprises / Garden Isle Records.

SUSQUEHANNA RIVER VALLEY SONG.
Tracks: Susquehanna river valley song / Her heart got in the way.
7" . . . . PT 515
President / Apr '83 / Grapevine Distribution / Target Records / Jazz Music / Taylors.

WHITE LINES NORTH.
Tracks: White lines north.
7" . . . . .AKS 333
Garden Isle / Mar '85 / Maingrove Enterprises / Garden Isle Records.

Parmerley, David

I KNOW A GOOD THING.
Tracks: I know a good thing when I feel it / Grandpa's radio / Have you come to say goodbye / She keeps hanging on / Soemone took my place with you / Morristown / Excuse me / Down home / Someone on her mind / Sometimes silence says it all / Live and let live / From cotton to satin (Features on CD only).
CD . . . . SHCD 3777
LP . . . . SHLP 3777
MC . . . . SHMC 3777
Sugarhill(USA) / '89 / Roots Records / Projection / Impetus Records / C.M. Distribution / Jazz Music / Swift / Duncans / A.D.A Distribution.

Parnell, Lee Roy

LOVE WITHOUT MERCY.
Tracks: What kind of fool do you think I am / Back in my arms again / Rock, The / Ain't no short way home / Love without mercy / Road scholar / Night after night / Done deal / Tender moment / Roller coaster.
CD 782218684-2
Arista / Oct '93 / BMG.

Parsons, Bill

ALL AMERICAN BOY.
Tracks: All American boy.
■ 7" . . . . HL 8798
London-American / Apr '59.

Parsons, Gene

GENE PARSONS.
Tracks: Not Advised.
LP . . . . SRS 8703
Sierra Briar (USA) / May '79 / Mike's Country Music Room.

Parsons, Gram

Gram Parsons was born Cecil Ingram Connor on 5 November 1946, in Winterhaven, Florida; he died on 19 September 1973 in a motel room near the Joshua Tree National Monument in California, one of his favourite spots. The singer, songwriter, guitarist, keyboardist and bandleader invented the genre of country rock as we know it today, bequeathing it to his friend Emmylou Harris, who took it to the heights of commercial and artistic success that Parsons did not have in his lifetime. His mother's family were wealthy, while his father was a guitarist/ songwriter and ranch hand called Bull Dog Connor, who committed suicide when Gram was 13, his mother married a man named Parsons and died of alcoholism on the day Gram graduated from high school. He sang in a folk group with Kent Lavoie; his first pro-group was the Shilos (tracks later issued as *The Early Years* 1963-65 on Sierra); he formed the International Submarine Band in Cambridge, Massachusetts to make *Cosmic American Music*: album *Safe At Home* was produced in 1967 by Lee Hazlewood. Parsons joined the Byrds and helped them to make history as the first rock band to play the Grand Ole Opry, and inspired and played on their arguably their most important album, *Sweetheart Of The Rodeo* in 1968. With ex-Byrd Chris Hillman he formed the Flying Burrito Brothers, his LPs with them their finest moments: *The Gilded Palace Of Sin* and *Burrito Deluxe* in 1969-70; their later issues *Close Up The Honky Tonks* (1974) and *Sleepless Nights* (1976) also included Parsons' material. He influenced the songwriting of Mick Jagger and Keith Richards (*Dead Flowers*, *Wild Horses*; he sang backup on *Sweet Virginia* in 1972). Parson's own album *GP* in 1973 featured duets with Emmylou, as well as James Burton on guitar, Glen D. Hardin on piano, bassist Rik Grech. He was recording another album with Harris when he died. He had expressed a wish to be cremated and his ashes strewn at Cap Rock, the nearby natural monument; his road manager Phil Kaufman stole the body from a railway platform and carried out these wishes (they were fined $750; it wasn't against the law to steal a corpse). *The Return of the Grievous Angel* and *Gram Parsons and The Fallen Angels Live 1973* were released postumously. Tributes to Parsons included Harris's *Boulder To Birmingham* (on her album *Pieces Of The Sky* 1975), Bernie Leadon's *My Men* (on the Eagles album *On The Border* 1974), Richie Furay's *Crazy Eyes* (title track of 1973 *Poco* LP). Elvis Costello wrote the sleeve note for *The Best of Gram Parsons* (1982) and included Parsons songs in his *Almost Blue* album. (Donald Clarke)

EARLY YEARS 1963-65, THE.
Tracks: Not Advised.
LP . . . . **SRS 8702**
Sierra Briar (USA) / Feb '84 / Mike's Country Music Room.

EARLY YEARS THE.
Tracks: I may be right / Big country / Zah's blues / Mary don't you weep / Bells of Rhymney / Goin' away / Don't you want to go / They shall go down / On my journey home / Surfin' Anny / Oh didn't they crucify my Lord.
LP . . . . **SDLP 1010**
MC . . . . **SDC 1010**
Sundown / May '84 / Terry Blood Dist. / Jazz Music / C.M. Distribution.

G.P.
Tracks: Still feeling blue / We'll sweep out the ashes in the morning / Song for you, A / Streets of Baltimore / That's all it took / New soft shoes, The / Kiss the children / Cry one more time / How much I've lied / Big mouth blues / She.
LP . . . . **K 44228**
Reprise (USA) / Apr '76 / WEA / Pinnacle.

G.P./GRIEVOUS ANGEL.
Tracks: Not Advised.
■ **CD Set** **726 08 2**
WEA / '89 / WEA.

GRAM PARSONS.
Tracks: We'll sweep out the ashes in the morning / Hearts on fire / Kiss the children / That's all it took / Love hurts / In my hour of darkness / Return of the grievous angel / Still feeling blue / $1000 wedding / Las Vegas / New soft shoos / How much I've lied / Cash on the barrelhead / Hickory wind.
LP . . . . **SHILOH 4088**
Shiloh / May '79.
LP . . . . **K 57008**
■ **MC** **K4 57008**
WEA / Jun '82 / WEA.

GRIEVOUS ANGEL.
Tracks: Love hurts / Las Vegas / In my hour of darkness / Return of the grievous angel / Hearts on fire / I can't dance / Brass buttons / 1, 000 dollar wedding.
■ **LP** . . . . **K 54018**
Reprise (USA) / Jun '74.

LIVE: GRAM PARSONS (Parsons, Gram & Emmylou Harris).
Tracks: We'll sweep out the ashes in the morning / Big mouth blues / New soft shoe / Streets of Baltimore / Cry one more time / California cottonfields / Love hurts / Country baptizing / Drug store truck driving man / That's all it took / Six days on the road.
LP **625 106**
Repertoire (Germany) / Apr '82 / Pinnacle.
LP . . . . **SDLP 003**
Sundown / Nov '83 / Terry Blood Dist. / Jazz Music / C.M. Distribution.
LP . . . . **GP 1973**
Sierra Briar (USA) / Feb '84 / Mike's Country Music Room.
CD . . . . **CDSD 003**
MC . . . . **SDC 003**
Sundown / '89 / Terry Blood Dist. / Jazz Music / C.M. Distribution.

LUXURY LINER.
Tracks: Not Advised.
LP . . . . **SHILOH 4086**
Shiloh / Mar '79.

MELODIES.
Tracks: My kingdom for a car / Melodies from a bird in flight / Mama papa / Won't last long / Hot burrito no.1 / No fire here tonight / Pastime / Little jewels / Why you been gone so long.
LP . . . . **SDLP 008**
MC . . . . **SDC 008**
Sundown / May '84 / Terry Blood Dist. / Jazz Music / C.M. Distribution.

SAFE AT HOME (Parsons, Gram International Submarine Band).
Tracks: Blue eyes / I must have been somebody else / You've known a satisfied mind / Folsom Prison blues / That's all right / Millers cave / I still miss someone / Luxury liner / Strong boy / Do you know how it feels to be lonesome?.
LP . . . . **STATLP 26**
Statik / Sep '85 / Pinnacle.
CD . . . . **CDSD 071**
MC . . . . **SDC 071**
Sundown / Jan '91 / Terry Blood Dist. / Jazz Music / C.M. Distribution.

SNEAKY PETE KLENIOW.
Tracks: Not Advised.
LP . . . . **SHILOH 4087**
Shiloh / Mar '79.

WARM EVENINGS, PALE MORNINGS AND BOTTLED BLUES 1963-1973.
Tracks: Zah's blues / Blue eyes / Strong boy / Truck driving man / Hot Burrito £1 / Christine's tune (Devil in disguise) / Sin city / Dark end of the street, The / Wild horses / She / New soft shoe, The / We'll sweep out the ashes in the morning / Brass buttons / Return of the grievous angel / Drug store truck driving man / Brand new heartache / Love hurts.
CD . . . . **RVCD 24**
Raven / Jun '92 / Revolver-APT / A.D.A Distribution / New Note / Jazz Music / Topic Records.

WITH EMMYLOU HARRIS (Parsons, Gram & Fallen Angels).
Tracks: Not Advised.
■ **EP** . . . . **GP/EP 104**
Sierra Briar (USA) / Feb '83 / Mike's Country Music Room.

Parton, Dolly

Famed singer - songwriter, actress/entertainer Dolly Rebecca Parton was born (19.1.1946) in the rural confines of Sevier County. Tennessee - fourth in a family of 12 . From humble beginnings, Dolly has climbed many peaks and been rewarded much gold during the past 25 years - everythings she's tried her hand at has been successful, recording career, showbiz - hosting own TV series, film star, etc. Radio/TV dates coming at a tender age of 10, when appearing on Cas Walker's Knoxville Shows (1956-1959), making recording debut in 1959 on Louisiana's small Gold band label - making Grand Ole Opry debut same year. Following graduation in 1964, Dolly set out to fulfil her dream to be a country star, packing the essentials, complete with some songs she'd written with her uncle Bill (Owens). Dolly's first big break came in 1967 when sequined, top country act Porter Wagoner was in need of someone to replace female act Norma Jean for his TV show. Bubbly blonde Dolly fitted the bill perfectly - in the meantime she was registering her chart debut single, on Monument, self - penned *Dumb blonde* setting her chart exploits into gear. During her early days on RCA (1968-1986) Parton would often revisit in song her rural childhood days *Coat of many colours*, recollecting the people, depicting in the Smokies in it's tiny log cabin homes. In 1969 Parton joined the Grand Ole Opry, by which time she'd become a regular with Porter Wagoner on the charts - *Last thing on my mind* (1967) leading the way for another dozen top ten hits (*We'll get ahead someday* , *Just some one I used to know* & the 1976 No.1, *Please don't stop lovin' me*) carrying them through 'til 1976, many albums/shows later when Dolly set out in earnest on a solo career. Running parallel with her successful duet partnership, Dolly herself had been reeling in hits by the score & albums at a similar rate. With debut No.1 *Joshua* (1970) followed by such songs as*Jolene* , *I will always love you* , *Love is like a butterfly* & *The bargain store*, Dolly was showing herself to be a most capable writer of lovesongs nicely complementing her autobiographical fare. Parton's career took another change in 1976/77 when her recordings took on a more country pop edge - soon she was to be promoted in a slick martketing fashion, utilizing her glamourous attributes. *All I can do* , followed by the self explanatory titled *New Harvest, first gathering* were leading the way, for what was to be a transitional period for Dolly & country music in general. Dolly was a major attaction on TV and in Las Vegas clubs - she could name her price. It came as little surprise when in 1978 she reaped CMA's Entertainer Of The Year Award..she'd previously (1975-1976) walked away with Female Vocalist Of The Year Award. By the time the 70s were over, Parton had scored no fewer than eight No.1s - *Here you come again* , *Old flames* & *9 to 5* , (comedy film soundtrack, Dolly starring alongside Lily Tomlin, & Jane Fonda) amongst them. Parton's film career was to extend to three more top scores - *The best little whorehouse in Texas* , based on an old bordello The Chicken Ranch in La Grange, Texas (1982) with Burt Reynolds co-starring. Next came *Rhinestone* with her singing co-star, Sylvester Stallone - Dolly writing all the soundtrack material, Larry Weiss' title cut excepted. Again it proved an allround success at the box office & *Tennessee homesick blues* making No.1 in the country charts. Another soundtrack cut, her record breaking *I will always love you* , from her previous film in 1982, which had already topped the charts some eight years prior, became the first song ever to give an artist two No.1s. Dolly's singing partner for a fruitful two year spell (1983-1982) yielded another cross-over No.1, backed - up with country chart topper *Real world* . They also got together to do a Christmas TV special/album *Once upon a Christmas* in 1985 - aside from tour dates. During the mid - eighties Dolly's career & life was to have it's ups (opened her theme park Dollywood) and downs, (due to a heavy work load her health suffered). On the bright side, she was still making the charts 1987 signalled the release of the long - waited *Trio* album. The winning formula, boasted four top ten hits (& much adulation), chart topper *To know him is to love him* opening the way..the wait proving worth it Emmylou, Linda Ronstadt & Dolly doing themselves proud . The CMA's, 1988 Album Of The Year, Dolly by now had left RCA after almost 20 years - signing to Columbia in 1987. Dolly's opener for Columbia *Rainbow* was severely criticised, backed with matching sales - this was straight after her $44 million TV series flop for ABC. Ricky Skaggs was recruited as producer for her next album *White limousine* , rewarding them with *What'd you come in here lookin' like* & *Yellow roses* both 1989 No.1 singles. Follow - up album *Eagle when she flies* found her dueting with Ricky Van Shelton on *Rockin' years* , narrowly missing the top slot. Film work, shooting *Straight talk* & recording the sound track were priorities in 1992, Dolly's highest single a modest top 20 slot with *Silver & gold*. Moving into 1993, Whitney Houston was making top slot on the UK pop charts with her *I will always love you* (a record 13 weeks) & Dolly was once again concentrating on country music. Columbia releasing in the spring her guest supported *Slow dancing with the moon* , her debut video/single *Romeo* a top thirty hit featuring Billy Ray Cyrus, Tucker, Carpenter & Mattea. Another 'Trio' album also being scheduled, her partners Loretta Lynn & Tammy Wynette. (Maurice Hope)

9 TO 5.
Tracks: 9 to 5 / Sing for the common man.
■ **7"** . . . . **RCA 25**
RCA / Feb '81.
■ **CD Single** . . . . **PD 49447**
RCA / Jun '89.

9 TO 5 AND ODD JOBS.
Tracks: 9 to 5 / Hush-a-bye hard times / House of the rising sun / Deportees (Plane wreck at Los Gatos) / Sing for the common man / Working girl / Detroit City / But you know I love you / Dark as a dungeon / Poor folks town.
LP . . . . **PL 13852**
RCA / Apr '81 / BMG.
LP . . . . **RCALP 3047**
MC . . . . **RCAK 3047**
RCA / Sep '81 / BMG.
■ **CD** . . . . **ND 84830**
RCA / Apr '88.

ALL I CAN DO.
Tracks: All I can do / Fire that keeps you warm / When the sun goes down tomorrow / I'm a drifter / Falling out of love with me / Shattered image / Boulder to Birmingham / Preacher Tom / Life's like poetry / Hey, lucky lady.
LP . . . . **RS 1068**
■ **MC** . . . . **PK 11737**
RCA / '79.

ANTHOLOGY - DOLLY PARTON.
Tracks: Jolene / Old flames / Two doors down / My blue ridge mountain boy / Save the last dance for me / Put it off until tomorrow / Something fishy / I've lived my life / Coat of many colours / Daddy come and get me / My Tennessee mountain home / 9 to 5 / In the good old days / Joshua / But you know I love you / Daddy won't be home anymore / Happy happy birthday baby / Dumb blonde / Company you keep, The / Too lonely too long / Down from Dover / Love is like a butterfly.
CD . . . . **VSOPCD 165**

P 2 ■ DELETED

MC . . . . VSOPMC 165
Connoisseur Collection / Jul '91 / Pinnacle.

BABY I'M BURNING.
Tracks: Baby I'm burning / I wanna fall in love.
■ 7" . . . . PD 11425
RCA / Jan '79.

BARGAIN STORE.
Tracks: Bargain store / Kentucky gambler / When I'm gone / Only hand you'll need to hold, The / On my mind again / I want to be what you need / Love to remember / You'll always be special to me / He would know / I'll never forget.
LP. . . . . LSA 3217
■ MC . . . . PK 10950
RCA / '79.

BEST OF DOLLY PARTON.
Tracks: Mule skinner blues / Down from Dover / My Blue Ridge Mountain boy / In the good old days / Gypsy, Joe and me / In the ghetto / Just because I'm a woman / Daddy come and get me / How great Thou art / Just the way I am.
■ LP. . . . . LSA 3101
RCA / '79.

BEST OF DOLLY PARTON VOL2.
Tracks: Jolene / Travelling man / Lonely comin' down / Bargain store / Touch your woman / I will always love you / Love is like a butterfly / Coat of many colours / My Tennessee mountain home / When I sing for him.
LP. . . . . LSA 3236
■ MC . . . . MPK 245
RCA / '79.
■ LP. . . . . NL 85146
RCA / '86.
■ MC . . . . NK 85146
RCA / '86.

BEST OF PORTER WAGONER AND DOLLY PARTON, THE (Parton, Dolly & Porter Wagoner).
Tracks: Just someone I used to know / Daddy was an old time preacher man / Tomorrow is forever / Jeannie's afraid of the dark / Last thing on my mind / Pain of loving you, The / Better move it on home / Holding on to nothin' / Run that by me one more time / We'll get ahead someday.
LP. . . . . LSA 3046
■ MC . . . . PK 42008
RCA / '79.

BOTH SIDES.
Tracks: Not Advised.
■ LP. . . . . WH 5006
Lotus / Nov '78.

BURLAP AND SATIN.
Tracks: Ooo-eee / Send me the pillow you dream on / Jealous heart / Gamble either way / Appalachian memories / I really don't want to know / Potential new boyfriend / Cowboy's ways / One of those days / Calm on the water.
■ LP. . . . . RCALP 6080
RCA / Sep '83.
LP. . . . . PL 84691
■ MC . . . . PK 84691
RCA / Jan '84.

CHRISTMAS WITHOUT YOU (Parton, Dolly & Kenny Rogers).
Tracks: Christmas without you / White Christmas.
7" . . . . RCA 465
RCA / Nov '84 / BMG.

COLLECTION, THE.
Tracks: Not Advised.
CD . . . . CCSCD 353
MC . . . . CCSMC 353
BMG / Nov '92 / BMG.

COLLECTION, THE.
Tracks: Save the last dance for me / I walk the line / Turn, turn, turn (to everything there is a season) / Downtown / We had it all / She don't love you (like I love you) / We'll sing in the sunshine / I can't help myself (sugar pie,honey bunch) / Elusive butterfly / Great pretender, The / Harper Valley PTA / D.I.V.O.R.C.E. / I will always love you / Jolene / 9 to 5 / Here you come again.
CD 74321 13987-25
RCA / Jul '93 / BMG.

COUNTRY GIRL.
Tracks: Jolene / My Tennessee mountain home / Bargain store, The / Love is like a butterfly / Just the two of us / I will always love you / Touch your woman / Seeker, The / Travelling man / Daddy come and get me / My blue tears / Coat of many colours / Joshua / Washday blues / Mule skinner blues (Blue yodel No. 8) / Coming for to carry me home / Afraid to love again (CD only.) / I wash my face in the morning dew (CD only.).
CD . . . . CDMFP 5914
MC . . . . TCMFP 5914
MFP / Apr '91 / EMI.

DIAMOND SERIES: DOLLY PARTON.
Tracks: Jolene / I will always love you / Lonely comin' down / It's my time / Harper Valley PTA / Mama say a prayer / D.I.V.O.R.C.E. / We used to / Bobby's arms / Seeker, The / Hold me / Here you come again / Loving you / Sweet music man / I really got the feeling / Baby I'm burning.
■ CD . . . . CD 90108
Diamond Series / Apr '88.

DOLLY.
Tracks: We used to / Love I used to call mine, The / My heart started breaking / Most of all why / Bobby's arms / Seeker, The / Hold me / Because I love you / Only the memory remains / I'll remember you as mine.
LP. . . . . LSA 3260
■ MC . . . . MPK 250
RCA / '79.

DOLLY PARTON.
Tracks: Down on music row / Letter, The / I remember / Doctor Roberts F. Thomas / Daddy's working boots / All I can do / Hey lucky lady / In the good old days / Wrong direction home, The / Better part of life, The / Back home / Old black kettle.
■ LP. . . . . CDS 1164
RCA/Camden / Apr '78.
LP. . . . . CDS 1208
■ MC . . . . CAM 1208
RCA/Camden / Mar '82.

DOLLY PARTON - FAVOURITES.
Tracks: Not Advised.
CD . . . . PWKS 4116
MC . . . . PWKMC 4116
Pickwick / Sep '92 / Pickwick Records.

DOLLY PARTON COLLECTION, THE (MONUMENT VERSION).
Tracks: Dumb blonde / Your ole handy man / I don't want to throw rice / Put it off until tomorrow / I wasted my tears / Something fishy / Fuel to the flame / Giving and the taking, The / I'm in no condition / Company you keep, The / I've lived my life / Little things / Why why why / I wound easy / I don't want you around me anymore / Hillbilly Willy / This boy has been hurt / Daddy won't be home anymore / As long as I love / Habit I can't break, A / I'm not worth the tears / I don't trust me around you / I couldn't wait forever / Too lonely too long.
Double LP . . . . MNT 22105
MC Set. 40 22105
Monument / May '82 / Sony.

DOLLY PARTON COLLECTION, THE (PICKWICK).
Tracks: D.I.V.O.R.C.E. / Love and learn / Big wind / Mule skinner blues / Daddy / She never met a man / I wish I felt this way at home / Love isn't free / Only way out, The / Try being lonely / You're gonna be sorry / We had all the good things going / Mine / Don't let trouble make up your mind / More than their share / Little bird / Mama say a prayer / In the ghetto / Chas / But you loved me then.
Double LP . . . . PDA 053
Pickwick / Apr '79 / Pickwick Records.
MC Set. . . . . PDC 053
Pickwick / Dec '79 / Pickwick Records.

DOLLY PARTON IN LONDON.
Tracks: Not Advised.
VHS. . . . . RVT 20230
RCA/Columbia (video) / '88 / BMG / Gold & Sons / Terry Blood Dist. / Sony.

DOLLY PARTON STORY, THE.
Tracks: Fuel to the flame / I don't want you around me anymore / As long as I love / Giving and the taking, The / I'm in no condition / I couldn't wait forever / I've lived my life / Something fishy / Dumb blonde / I would easy / I don't want to throw rice / Why why why / Too lonely too long / Daddy won't be home anymore / This boy has been hurt / Hillbilly Willy.
LP. . . . . CBS 31582
Embassy / Sep '77 / Sony.
■ MC 4031582
CBS / '78 / Sony.

DOLLY, DOLLY, DOLLY.
Tracks: Starting over again / Same old fool / Old flames can't hold a candle to you / You're the only one I ever needed / Say goodnight / Fool for your love / Even a fool would let go / Sweet agony / I know you when / Packin' it up.
■ LP. . . . . PL 13546
RCA / Jul '80.

EAGLE WHEN SHE FLIES.
Tracks: If you need me / Rockin' years / Country road / Silver and gold / Eagle when she flies / Best woman wins / What a heartache / Runaway feelin' / Dreams do come true / Family / Wildest dreams.
CD 4678542
MC 4678544
Columbia / May '91 / Sony.
■ LP. 4678541
Columbia / May '91.

EVERYTHING IS BEAUTIFUL (Parton, Dolly/ Willie Nelson/Kris Kristofferson).
Tracks: Everything is beautiful / Here comes that rainbow again.
■ 7" . . . . MNT A 2983
Monument / Dec '82.

GREAT BALLS OF FIRE.
Tracks: Star of the show / Down / You're the only one / Help / Do you think that time stands still / Sweet summer lovin' / Great balls of fire / Almost in love / It's not my affair anymore / Sandy's song.
■ LP. . . . . PL 13361
RCA / '79.

GREAT DOLLY PARTON VOL.1, THE.
Tracks: D.I.V.O.R.C.E. / Love and learn / Big wind / Mule skinner blues / Daddy / She never met a man she didn't like / I wish I felt this way at home / Love isn't free / Only way out, The / Try being lonely / You're gonna be sorry / We all had a good thing going.
LP. . . . . CDS 1171
RCA/Camden / Apr '79 / BMG / Arabesque Ltd.

GREAT DOLLY PARTON VOL.2, THE.
Tracks: I'm doing this for your sake / Mama say a prayer / When possession get too strong / In the ghetto / But you loved me then / Carroll County accident / Don't let it trouble your mind / More than their share.
MC . . . . CAM 489
RCA/Camden / Apr '80 / BMG / Arabesque Ltd.
LP. . . . . CDS 1184
RCA/Camden / Feb '80 / BMG / Arabesque Ltd.

GREAT PRETENDER, THE.
Tracks: Save the last dance for me / I walk the line / Turn, turn, turn (to everything there is a season) / Downtown / We had it all / She don't love you (like I love you) / We'll sing in the sunshine / I can't help myself / Elusive butterfly / Great pretender, The.
LP. . . . . PL 84940
■ MC . . . . PK 84940
RCA / Aug '84.
■ CD . . . . PD 84940
RCA / Sep '84.

GREATEST HITS: DOLLY PARTON.
Tracks: 9 To 5 / But you know I love you / Heartbreak express / Old flames can't hold a candle to you / Applejack / Me and little Andy / Here you come again / Hard candy Christmas / Two doors down / It's all wrong but it's all right / Don't I ever cross your mind / I will always love you.
■ LP. . . . . RCALP 6058
RCA / Dec '82.
CD . . . . PD 84422
LP. . . . . PL 84422
■ MC . . . . PK 84422
RCA / Mar '84.
CD . . . . ND 90596
MC . . . . NK 90596
RCA / Apr '92 / BMG.

GREATEST HITS: DOLLY PARTON (2).
Tracks: Here you come again / Think about love / Baby I'm burning / Love is like a butterfly / Save the last dance for me / Heartbreaker / But you know I love you / 9 to 5 / Islands in the stream (duet with Kenny Rogers) / Don't call it love / Old flames can't hold a candle to you / Bargain store / Real love (duet with Kenny Rogers) / Potential new boyfriend / Jolene / I will always love you (from Best Little Whorehouse in Texas) / I really got the feeling (MC & CD only) / Starting over again (MC & CD only) / We had it all (CD only) / You're the only one (CD only).
CD . . . . PD 90407
MC . . . . PK 90407
RCA / Dec '89 / BMG.
■ LP. . . . . PL 90407
RCA / Dec '89.

HEARTBREAK EXPRESS.
Tracks: Heartbreak express / Single woman / My blue ridge mountain / Boy / As much as always / Do I ever cross your mind / Act like a fool / Prime of our love / Hollywood potters.
■ LP. . . . . RCALP 3076
RCA / Sep '82.
LP. . . . . PL 84289
■ MC . . . . PK 84289
RCA / Jan '84.

HEARTBREAKER.
Tracks: I really got the feeling / It's too late to love me now / We're through forever ('til tomorrow) / Sure thing / What am I gonna do with you gone / Baby, I'm burning / Nickels and dimes / Man / Heartbreaker.
LP. . . . . PL 12797
■ MC . . . . PK 12797
RCA / '79.

HEARTBREAKER.
Tracks: Heartbreaker / Baby I'm burnin' / Here you come again / Two doors down.
■ 12" . . . . PC 9401
RCA / Nov '79.

HERE YOU COME AGAIN.
Tracks: Here you come again / Baby, come out tonight / It's all wrong, but it's all right / Me and little Andy / Lovin' you / Cowgirl and the dandy / Two doors down / God's colouring book / As soon as I touched him / Sweet music man.
LP. . . . . PL 12544
■ MC . . . . PK 12544
RCA / '79.

HERE YOU COME AGAIN.
Tracks: Here you come again / Potential new boyfriend / Love is like a butterfly.
■ 7" . . . . RCA 395
RCA / Apr '84.

HERE YOU COME AGAIN.
Tracks: Here you come again / Little Andy.
■ 7" . . . . PB 9182
RCA / '79.

HITS OF DOLLY PARTON.
Tracks: Jolene / My Tennessee mountain home / Touch your woman / Seeker, The / Travelling man / Daddy come and get me / My blue tears / Coat of many colours / Bargain store / Joshua / Love is like a butterfly / Washday blues / We used to / Mule skinner blues / I will always love you / Coming for to carry me home.

LP	PL 42192
■ MC	PK 42192

RCA / '79.

LP	PL 89090
■ MC	PK 89090

RCA / Jan '84.

HOME FOR CHRISTMAS.
Tracks: First noel / Santa Claus is comin' to town / I'll be home for Christmas / Rudolph the red-nosed reindeer / Go tell it on the mountain / Little drummer boy, The / We three kings / Jingle bells / O little town of bethlehem / Joy to the world.

CD	4674672

Columbia / Dec '91 / Sony.

■ MC	4674674

Columbia / Dec '91.

I KNOW YOU BY HEART (Parton, Dolly & Smokey Robinson).
Tracks: I know you by heart / Could I have your autograph / Make love work.

12"	DOLLY T1
7"	DOLLY 1
■ 7"	DOLLY Q1

CBS / Mar '88.

I WILL ALWAYS LOVE YOU.
Tracks: I will always love you / Do I ever.

■ 7"	RCA 270

RCA / Nov '82.

I WILL ALWAYS LOVE YOU (OLD GOLD).
Tracks: I will always love you / Love is like a butterfly.

7"	OG 9667

Old Gold / Jan '87 / Pickwick Records.

IN THE GOOD OLD DAYS (When times were bad).
Tracks: Don't let it trouble your mind / He's a go getter / In the good old days / It's my time / Harper Valley PTA / Little bird / Mine / Carroll County accident, The / Fresh out of forgiveness / Mama say a prayer / Always the first time / D.I.V.O.R.C.E.

LP	NL 90007
■ MC	NK 90007

RCA / Jan '87.

JOLENE.
Tracks: Jolene / When someone wants to leave / River of happiness / Early morning breeze / Highlight of my life / I will always love you / Randy / Living on memories of you / Lonely comin' down / It must be you.

LP	AFL1 0473
■ MC	PK 10473

RCA / '79.

JOLENE.
Tracks: Jolene / Love is like a butterfly / Coat of many colours.

7"	RCA 2675

RCA / Apr '76 / BMG.

JOLENE (OLD GOLD).
Tracks: Bargain store / Jolene.

7"	OG 9603

Old Gold / Mar '90 / Pickwick Records.

JUST BECAUSE I'M A WOMAN.
Tracks: You're gonna be sorry / I felt this way at home / False eye lashes / I'll oil wells love you / Only way out (is to walk over me), The / Little bit slow to catch on / Bridge, The / Love and learn / I'm running out of love / Just because I'm a woman / Baby sister / Try being lonely.

LP	NL 89853
■ MC	NK 89853

RCA / Mar '86.

JUST THE TWO OF US (Parton, Dolly & Porter Wagoner).
Tracks: Closer by the hour / I washed my face in the morning dew / Jeannie's afraid of the dark / Holding on to nothin' / Slip away today / Dark end of the Street / Just the two of us / Afraid to love again / We'll get ahead someday / Somewhere between / Party, The / I can.

■ LP	LSA 3023

RCA / '79.

LOVE ALBUM, THE.
Tracks: You are / Heartbreaker / Bargain store / I will always love you / Love is like a butterfly / Coat of many colours / Islands in the stream / Here you come again / Send me the pillow (that you dream on) / It's all wrong but it's all right / Jolene / One of those days.

CD	ND 90307
LP	NL 90307
MC	NK 90307

RCA / Feb '89 / BMG.

LOVE ALBUM, THE VOL.2.
Tracks: We used to / You're the only one / But you know I love you / We had it all / Sweet music man / My girl (my love) / Almost in love / Sandy's song / I really don't

want to know / Sweet summer lovin' / Love I used to call mine, The / Starting over again.

CD	ND 90455
MC	NK 90455

RCA / Nov '90 / BMG.

LOVE IS LIKE A BUTTERFLY.
Tracks: Love is like a butterfly / In the ghetto / We had all the good things going / Daddy / Mama say a prayer / My Tennessee mountain home / Chicken every Sunday / I wish I felt this way at home / Joshua / Don't let it trouble your mind / Carroll County accident, The / Mule skinner blues.

LP	LSA 3195
■ MC	PK 10712

RCA / '79.

LP	CDS 1202
MC	CAM 1202

RCA/Camden / Apr '81 / BMG / Arabesque Ltd.

LOVE IS LIKE A BUTTERFLY (M.F.P.).
Tracks: Love is like a butterfly / If I cross your mind / My eyes can only see you / Take me back / Blackie, Kentucky / Gettin' happy / You're the one that taught me how to swing / Highway headin' South / Once upon a memory / Sacred memories.

LP	MFP 5774
■ MC	TCMFP 5774

MFP / Sep '86.

MAGIC MOMENTS WITH DOLLY PARTON.
Tracks: Mule skinner blues (blue yodel No. 8) / Down from Dover / My blue ridge mountain boy / In the good old days / Gypsy Joe and me / In the ghetto / Just because I'm a woman / Daddy come and get me / How great Thou Art / Just the way I am / Jolene / Travelling man / Lonely comin' down / Bargain store / Touch your woman / I will always love you / Love is like a butterfly / Coat of many colours / My Tennessee mountain home / When I sing for him / We used to / Seeker, The / You are / Here you come again.

■ MC	NK 89620

RCA / May '85.

MAKING PLANS (Parton, Dolly & Porter Wagoner).
Tracks: Making plans / If you go I'll follow you / Hide me away / Someone just like you / Little David's harp / Beneath the sweet magnolia tree / Touching memories / Daddy did his best / If you say I can.

■ LP	PL 13700

RCA / Oct '80.

ME AND LITTLE ANDY.
Tracks: Me and little Andy / Cowgirl and the dandy.

■ 7"	PB 9526

RCA / Apr '80.

MY TENNESSEE MOUNTAIN HOME.
Tracks: Letter, The / I remember / Old black kettle / Daddy's working boots / Doctor Robert F. Thomas / In the good old days / My Tennessee mountain home / Wrong direction home, The / Back home / Better part of life, The / Down on music row.

■ LP	LSA 3178

RCA / '79.

NEW HARVEST - NEW GATHERING.
Tracks: Light of a clear blue morning / Applejack / My girl / Holdin' on to you / You are / How does it feel / Where beauty lives in memory / (Your love has lifted me) Higher and higher / Getting in my way / There.

LP	PL 12188
■ MC	PK 12188

RCA / '79.

ONCE UPON A CHRISTMAS (Parton, Dolly & Kenny Rogers).
Tracks: I believe in Santa Claus / Sleighride / Winter wonderland / Christmas without you / Christmas song, The / Christmas to remember / With bells on / Silent night / Greatest gift of all / White Christmas / Once upon a Christmas.

LP	PL 85307
■ MC	PK 85307

RCA / Dec '84.

MC	NK 90615

RCA / Nov '92 / BMG.

■ CD	ND 90615

RCA / Nov '92.

POTENTIAL NEW BOYFRIEND.
Tracks: Potential new boyfriend / One of those days.

7"	RCA 335

RCA / May '83 / BMG.

QUEENS OF COUNTRY (Parton, Dolly & Donna Fargo).
Tracks: Honky tonk angels / Making believe / Letter to heaven / Release me / Little blossom / Two little orphans / Daddy / Sticks and stones / All that's keeping me alive / Wishful thinking.

LP	SDLP 1001
MC	ZCSD 1001

Sundown / Jul '83 / Terry Blood Dist. / Jazz Music / C.M. Distribution.

RAINBOW.
Tracks: River unbroken, The / I know you by heart (Duet with Smokey Robinson) / Dump the dude / Red hot screaming love / Make love work / Everyday hero / Two lovers / Could I have your autograph / Savin' it for you / More than I can say.

MC	4604514

CBS / Apr '88 / Sony.

■ LP	4604511

CBS / Apr '88.

■ CD	4604512

CBS / Apr '88.

REAL LOVE.
Tracks: Think about love / Tie our love / We got too much / It's such a heartache / Don't call it love / Real love / I can't be true / I hope you're never happy / Once in every blue moon / Come back to me.

LP	PL 85414
■ MC	PK 85414

RCA / Mar '85.

■ CD	PD 85414

RCA / Mar '86.

REAL LOVE (Parton, Dolly & Kenny Rogers).
Tracks: Not Advised.

VHS	RVT 20795

RCA/Columbia (video) / '88 / BMG / Gold & Sons / Terry Blood Dist. / Sony.

RHINESTONE (Film Soundtrack).
Tracks: Not Advised.

LP	BL 85032
■ MC	BK 85032

RCA / Aug '84 / BMG.

RIVER UNBROKEN, THE.
Tracks: River unbroken, The / More than I can say.

12"	6512026
■ 7"	6512027

CBS / Jan '88.

SAVE THE LAST DANCE FOR ME.
Tracks: Save the last dance for me / Potential new boyfriend / Love is like a butterfly / Bargain store / I can't help myself / Jolene / Here you come again / Seeker, The / Baby I'm burning / Two doors down / Downtown / 9 to 5.

LP	CDS 1225
■ MC	CAM 1225

RCA/Camden / Jul '87.

SAVE THE LAST DANCE FOR ME.
Tracks: Save the last dance for me / Elusive butterfly.

7"	RCA 391

RCA / Jan '84 / BMG.

SLOW DANCING WITH THE MOON.
Tracks: Full circle / Romeo / (You got me over) A heartache tonight / What will baby be / More where that came from / Put a little love in your heart / Why can't we / I'll make your bed / Whenever forever comes / Cross my heart / Slow dancing with the moon / High & mighty.

CD	472944 2
MC	472944 4

Columbia / Mar '93 / Sony.

STARTING OVER AGAIN.
Tracks: Starting over again / Sweet agony.

■ 7"	PB 1926

RCA / Jun '80.

THINK ABOUT LOVE.
Tracks: Think about love / I can't be true.

7"	PB 49995

RCA / Apr '85 / BMG.

THIS IS DOLLY PARTON.
Tracks: Coat of many colours / But you loved me then / It's my time / Do you hear robins sing / Second best / I will always love you / More than their share / Here I am / My kind of man / Before you make up your mind / D-I-V-O-R-C-E / Gypsy Joe & me / Pleasant as May / The monkey's tale / Love with me / He's a go getter / Mine / Baby sister / Little at a time, A / If I lose my mind / False eye lashes / Love you're so beautiful tonight / Little bit slow to catch on / Mama say a prayer / Will he be waiting.

LP	DHY 80007
■ MC	DHYK 0007

RCA / '78 / BMG.

TO KNOW HIM IS TO LOVE HIM (Parton, Dolly/Linda Ronstadt/Emmylou Harris).
Tracks: To know him is to love him.

■ 7"	W 8492

WEA / '86.

TRIO, THE (Parton, Dolly/Linda Ronstadt/Emmylou Harris).
Tracks: Pain of loving you / Making plans / To know him is to love him / Hobo's meditation / Wilflowers / Telling me lies / My dear companion / Those memories of you / I've had enough / Rosewood casket.

CD	K 925491 2
LP	K 925491 1
MC	WX 99C
MC	K 925491 4

WEA / Mar '87 / WEA.

TWO DOORS DOWN.
Tracks: Two doors down / It's all wrong, but it's all right.

■ 7"	PB 1240

RCA / '79.

TWO OF A KIND (Parton, Dolly & Porter Wagoner).
Tracks: Pain of loving you, The / Possum holler / Is it real / Flame, The / Fighting kind, The / Two of a kind /

■ DELETED

All I need is you / Curse of the wild weed flower / Today, tomorrow and forever / There'll be love (with Porter Wagoner).
LP. . . . . LSA 3044
■ MC . . . . MPK 189
RCA / '78 / BMG.

VERY BEST OF DOLLY PARTON, THE.
Tracks: Down from Dover / Joshua / Coat of many colours / Heartbreaker / Jolene / I will always love you / Love is like a butterfly / Bargain store / Seeker, The / We used to / You are / All I can do / Shattered image / Me and little Andy / My Tennessee mountain home / Touch your woman / Two doors down / Here you come again / Baby, I'm burning / Lonely comin' down.
■ LP. . . . . RCALP 5052
RCA / Aug '81.
LP. . . . . PL 89007
MC . . . . PK 89007
RCA / '84 / BMG.

WE FOUND IT (Parton, Dolly & Porter Wagoner).
Tracks: Love City / Between us / We found it / Satan's river / I've been married (just as long as you have) / I am always waiting / Sweet Rachel Ann / That's when love will mean the most / Love have mercy on us / How close they must be (with Porter Wagoner).
LP. . . . . LSA 3171
RCA / '78 / BMG.

WHITE LIMOZEEN.
Tracks: Time for me to fly / Why'd you come in here / Slow healing heart / Wait 'til I get you home / Moon, the stars and me, The / Yellow roses / Lookin' like that / What is it my love / Take me back to the country / He's alive.
LP. 4651351
CBS / Jul '89 / Sony.
CD 4651352
■ MC 4651354
CBS / Jul '89.

WHY'D YOU COME IN HERE LOOKING LIKE THAT.
Tracks: Why'd you come in here looking like that / Wait till I get you home / River unbroken, The (Available on CD only) / Make love work (on CD 5" only.).
7" . . . . DOLLY 2
■ CD Single . . . . DOLLY C2
CBS / Jun '89.

WINNING HAND, THE (Parton, Dolly/Kris Kristofferson/Willie Nelson/Brenda Lee).
Tracks: You're gonna love someone (in the morning) / Ping pong / You'll always have someone / Here comes that rainbow again / Bigger the fool, The / Help me make it through the night / Happy happy birthday baby / You left a long time ago / To make a long story short (she's gone) / Everything is beautiful.
Double LP . . . . MNT 88611
Monument / Jan '83 / Sony.
■ MC Set 40 88611
Monument / Jan '83.

WORLD OF DOLLY PARTON, THE.
Tracks: Dumb blonde / Your ole handy man / I don't want to throw rice / Put it off until tomorrow / I wasted my tears / Something fishy / Fuel to the flame / Giving and the taking, The / I'm in no condition / Company you keep, The / I've lived my life / Little things, The / Why, why, why / I wound easy / I don't want you around me anymore / Hillbilly Willy / This boy has been hurt / Daddy won't be home anymore / As long as I love / Habit I can't break, A / I'm not worth the tears / I don't trust me around you / I couldn't wait forever / Too lonely too long.
■ LP. . . . . MNT 22021
CBS / '78 / Sony.

YOU ARE.
Tracks: You are / Applejack / Down from Dover / Shattered image / Me and little Andy / All I can do / Jeannie's afraid of the dark / We used to / Boulder to Birmingham / Just because I'm a woman / Joshua / Lonely comin' down.
LP. . . . . INTS 5044
MC . . . . INTK 5044
RCA International / Oct '80 / BMG.

YOU ARE.
Tracks: You are / Applejack.
■ 7" . . . . PB 9059
RCA / Mar '77.

YOU'RE THE ONLY ONE.
Tracks: You're the only one / Down.
■ 7" . . . . PB 1577
RCA / '79.

Parton, Stella

One of 11 siblings of country superstar Dolly Parton, Stella was born in Sevier County, Tennessee, in 1949. She made her radio debut with Dolly in 1955, later achieving her own smaller success. She sang in local clubs in '66 before going to Nashville in '72. Her own song, Ode to Olivia, was a 1975 defence of Olivia Newton-John, who had won CMA awards amid protests that she wasn't country. She recorded for Country, Soul & Blues label, had country hits in '75-'76, switched to Elektra and hit the US Top Twenty and the British Top Forty with Danger Of

A Stranger, written by Shel Silverstein. More hits followed in the late 70's and she then worked in television and theatre and recorded for the Town House label in California. (Donald Clarke).

COUNTRY SWEET.
Tracks: Easy to love / Charlie's baby / Little bitty tear, A / If you're a dream / I'm not that good at goodbye / Standard lie number one / Danger of a stranger, The / I've got to have you for mine / It's the little things / More the change, The.
LP. . . . . K 52060
Elektra / Jan '78 / WEA.

DANGER OF A STRANGER, THE.
Tracks: Danger of a stranger, The / More the change.
■ 7" . . . . K 12272
Elektra / Oct '77.

I WANT TO HOLD YOU..
Tracks: Not Advised.
■ LP. . . . . JULEP 1
Mint / Oct '76.

LOVE IS A WORD.
Tracks: Love is a word / Lie to Linda.
■ 7" . . . . K 12300
Elektra / May '78.

LOVE YA.
Tracks: I cried for the lady / Long lost love / Room at the top of the stairs, The / Someone / Little inconvenient / Steady as the rain / I want to hold you in my dreams, tonight / Honey come home / Rest of the way / Stormy weather.
■ LP. . . . . K 52136
Elektra / '77.

STEADY AS THE RAIN.
Tracks: Steady as the rain / Little inconvenient.
■ 7" . . . . K 12363
Elektra / '79.

STELLA PARTON.
Tracks: Four little letters / Undercover lovers / Late late late late show, The / Love is a word / There's a rumour going round / Haven't you heard / Lie to Linda / Wishing well / Fade my blues away / Down to earth.
■ LP. . . . . K 52069
Elektra / May '78 / WEA.

STORMY WEATHER.
Tracks: Stormy weather / Lie to Linda.
■ 7" . . . . K 12332
Elektra / Jan '79.

Patches

DON'T THINK TWICE.
Tracks: Don't think twice / Where does the good times go? / Gambler, The / This time of the year / Four strong winds / Looking for love / City of New Orleans / Dream / Sleepin' alone / Tobermory Bay / Me and you and a dog named Boo.
LP. . . . . BGC 322
MC . . . . KBGC 322
Country House / Feb '83 / Duncans / BGS Productions Ltd.

Patton, Wayland

Singer - songwriter/vocalist/record producer Wayland Patton was born in Weatherford, Texas 28.05.1958. Started out singing in churches - took to playing guitar when in 6th grade. Around late 70's playing in a bluegrass band out of Oklahoma . Had some songs srecorded by Ricky Skaggs - going on to write for his Welk publishing company, along with such talents as Larry Cordle, Peter Rowan, Carl Jackson & Jim Rushing. Became a member of Skaggs' 1986 ACM award - winning band playing rhythm guitar/singing harmonies, for 18 months. Before coming off the road to concentrate on his own solo career, writing and doing session work singing backup harmonies and appearing on albums by Garth Brooks, Emmylou Harris, Kathy Mattea, Tanya Tucker & Daniel O'Donnell among many others. Hits to his credit include Skaggs' no 2 hit Something In My Heart , Dwight Yoakam's Turn It On, Turn It Up, Turn Me Loose . Toured UK twice, as support to Don Williams in 1991 & Crystal Gayle in 1993. Own recording debut Gulf Stream Dreamin', came out in 1991 on Capitol - Kathy Chiavola who appears on the album had her own debut recording on Ragged But Right Labor Of Love produced by Patton. (Maurice Hope)

GULF STREAM DREAMIN'.
Tracks: Gulf stream dreamin' / Fellow travellers / Rockin' the boat / Eight years down the road / Rock my chair / One horse town / We should only have time for love / Hoka hey / Evangelina / Knowin' when to leave the past behind.
CD . . . . CDP 793 872 2
■ MC C4 93872
Capitol Nashville / Aug '91.

Paul, Les

Les Paul was born Lester Polfus in Waukesha, Wisconsin in 1915; he has done more for the electric guitar than anyone else except Charlie Christian, with whom he was sometimes compared. He began playing on the radio in Wisconsin, then Chicago; he played country music as Hot Rod Red and Rhubarb Red; formed a jazz-oriented Les Paul Trio in 1936 and led it for nearly a decade (a few tracks now on Guitar Genius on Charly). He also recorded with Bing Crosby and the Andrews Sisters on the American Decca label; by the time he toured with Jazz At The Philharmonic in the late '40s he was building his own guitars; he took the first solid-body electric guitar to Gibson in 1946, and the Les Paul model became one of the most famous guitars in the world. Lover/Brazil '48 was a two-sided hit on Capitol, overdubbed until it sounded like six guitars; he broke his right elbow in a car crash and had it reset at an angle so he could still play; the instrumental hits continued through 1953, including Nola (a piano novelty from 1919) with Paul playing both electric and Spanish guitars. Meanwhile he met country singer Mary Ford (born Colleen Summers in 1928, they married in 1949, seperated in 1963 and she died in 1977). Les Paul and Mary Ford were among the biggest hitmakers of the early '50s in the USA; 28 hits 1950-57 three at no. 2, How High the Moon and Vaya Con Dios at no.1, the latter for 11 weeks in 1953. Les Paul's Capitol recordings used technology that was ahead of its time, most recorded in his own studio using an 8-track desk of his design, both his guitar and her voice overdubbed, and they stand up very well today. He retired to his work bench except for the album in 1968, but became active again in the mid-'70s, performing and promoting his guitars for Gibson; he moved full circle back to country picking, recording with his old friend Chet Atkins, winning a Grammy for Chester And Lester in 1977, followed by Guitar Monsters '78. He was featured in a TV documentary, The Wizard of Waukesha, in 1980. (Donald Clarke).

16 ORIGINAL HITS (Paul, Les & Mary Ford).
Tracks: Not Advised.
MC . . . . MC 1630
Timeless Treasures / Nov '87 / Terry Blood Dist.

ALL TIME GREATEST HITS (Paul, Les & Mary Ford).
Tracks: How high the moon / Jazz me blues / I'm sitting on top of the world / Nola / Bye bye blues / Chicken reel / Jealous / Lover / Little Rock getaway / I'm forever blowing bubbles / Goofus / St. Louis blues / La Rosita / World is waiting for the sunrise, The / Carioca / Vaya con Dios / Johnny is the boy for me / Walkin' and whistlin' blues / Tiger rag / Lady of Spain / Mockin' Bird Hill / Whispering / Tico tico / Meet Mr Callaghan / Mr. Sandman / Tennessee waltz / I'm a fool to care / 12th Street rag / Falling in love with love / Best things in life are free, The.
■ LP. 5C 134 53027/28
EMI (Holland) / Jan '83.

ALL-TIME HITS (Paul, Les & Mary Ford).
Tracks: Not Advised.
MC 4XL 9101
Capitol (Specials) / Dec '88.

CAPITOL YEARS, THE: LES PAUL AND MARY FORD (Best of) (Paul, Les & Mary Ford).
Tracks: Whispering / World is waiting for the sunrise, The / Lover / Mockin' Bird Hill / Nola / That old feeling / Little Rock getaway / Bye bye blues / Twelfth St. rag / I'm sitting on top of the world / Chicken reel / How high the moon / Walkin' and whistlin' blues / How deep is the ocean / Tico tico / Vaya con dios.
CD . . . . CDP 791 299 2
MC . . . . TCEMS 1309
Capitol / Jan '89 / EMI.
■ LP. . . . . EMS 1309
Capitol / Jan '89.

FEEDBACK (1944-1945) (Paul, Les & His Trio).
Tracks: Not Advised.
LP. . . . . CLP 67
Circle (USA) / Dec '86 / Jazz Music / Swift / Wellard Dist.

HE CHANGED THE MUSIC (Paul, Les & Various Artists).
Tracks: How high the moon / Echo tribute / Back pain boogie / Deep in the blues / It happens / Everyday / I have the blues / Georgia on my mind / God bless the child / Am I blue? / Over the rainbow / It's been a long time / I really don't want to know / Blue suede shoes / Lover.
VHS. . . . . E 1307
Excalibur (video) / Jun '90.
VHS. . . . . MMGV 023
MMG Video / Apr '91 / Terry Blood Dist.

HE CHANGED THE MUSIC (Paul, Les & Various Artists).
Tracks: Not Advised.
CD . . . . MM GV 023
MMG Video / Jan '93 / Terry Blood Dist.

HOW HIGH THE MOON (Paul, Les & Mary Ford).
Tracks: How high the moon / Vaya con Dios.
10" 10CL 282
■ 7" . . . . .CL 282
Capitol / Feb '83.

LEGEND AND THE LEGACY, THE.
Tracks: Lover / Brazil / Hip Billy boogie / What is thing called love / Caravan / Nola / Cryin' / Dry my tears / Goofus / Tennessee waltz / Little rock getaway / Mockin' bird hill / Chicken reel / How high the moon / Walkin' and whistlin' blues / Josephine / I wish I'd never seen sunshine / In the good old summertime / Three little words / Jazz me blues / Just one more chance / Whispering / World is waiting for the sunrise, The / Jingle bells / Tiger rag / Radio show 1-11 / Radio spots 1-7 / Carioca, The / I'm confessing (that I love you) / Smoke rings / Meet Mister Callahan / Take me in your arms and hold me / Lady of Spain / My baby's coming home / Bye bye blues / Deep in the blues / St Louis Blues / Mammy's boogie / I'm sitting on top of the world / Sleep / Vaya con dios / Johnny (Is this boy for me) / Kangroo, The / Don'cha hear them blues / I really don't want to know / South / I'm a fool to care / Auctioneer / Whither thou goest / Mandolina / Mister Sandman / Song in blue / Radio shows 2-9 / Radio spots 8 and 9 / Someday sweetheart / No letter today / On the sunny side of the street / Just one of those things / Twelfth Street rag / Lies / Nuevo laredo / Best things in life are free, The / Moritat / Some of these days / I'm moving on / Farewell (for just awhile) / Hummingbird / Amukiriki (the lord willing) / Magic melody / Alabamy bound / Say the words I love to hear / Send me some money / Cimarron (roll on) / San Antonio rose / Cinco robles (Five Oaks) / I don't want you no more / Fire / Night of the fourth / Goodnight my someone / Radio show 3-11 / Radio spots 1-12 / Dialogue and in the mood / Sentimental journey / I ain't got nobody / Jungle town / Doing the town / Scarlet ribbons / Hawaiian war chant / Everytime I look at you / Sing to me gypsy / Dancing with Ginger / Yearning / To fall in love / I'm still in love with you / Tonight's the night / Honolulu rack-a-rolla / Jumpin' at the Zadicoe / Ro ro Robinson / I love you oh so much / Back home in Indiana / Hey, so long baby, so long, I'm so lonely / Russian Gypsy / Jazz on the reservation / Green champaign / Dark eyes / Cookin' / Hoosier hustle, The / Marie's waltz.
■ CD Set . . . . CDS 7976542
Capitol / Nov '91.

LES PAUL AND MARY FORD (EMI) (Paul, Les & Mary Ford).
Tracks: Mississippi blues / Carry me on / Je t'aime la vie / La ballade du chien loup.
LP. 1A 022 58099
MC 1A 222 58099
EMI (Holland) / '88.

LES PAUL AND MARY FORD (ENTERTAINERS) (Paul, Les & Mary Ford).
Tracks: Three little words / I can't give you anything but love / Vaya con Dios / Just one more chance / Carioca / In the good old Summertime / Moon of Manakoora, The / Lover / How high the moon / I'm confessin' / Bye bye blues / Whispering / Lonesome road / Don'cha hear them bells / How deep is the ocean / World is waiting for the sunrise, The.
LP. . . . . ENT LP 13014
Entertainers / Sep '87.
MC . . . . ENT MC 13014
Entertainers / '88.

NEW SOUND VOLUME II, THE (Paul, Les & Mary Ford).
Tracks: In the good old summertime / Three little words / Lonesome road / Chicken reel / I'm confessin' / Carioca / I can't give you anything but love / Just one more chance / I'm forever blowing bubbles / Moon of Manakoora / Don'cha hear them bells / La rosita.
■ MC . . . . TCEMS 1138
Capitol / Dec '85.
■ LP. . . . . EMS 1138
Capitol / Dec '85.

VAYA CON DIOS (Paul, Les & Mary Ford).
Tracks: Vaya con dios.
■ 7" . . . . CL 13943
Capitol / Nov '53.

VERY BEST OF LES PAUL AND MARY FORD (Paul, Les & Mary Ford).
Tracks: How high the moon / I'm sitting on top of the world / I'm forever blowing bubbles / Nola / Bye bye blues / Chicken reel / Jealous / Lover / Little rock getaway / Goofus / Jazz me blues / St. Louis blues / La Rosita / World is waiting for the sunrise, The / Carioca / Vaya Con Dios.
LP. . . . . MFP 5604
■ MC . . . . TCMFP 5604
MFP / Apr '83.

WORLD IS WAITING FOR THE SUNRISE, THE (Paul, Les & Mary Ford).
Tracks: Not Advised.
CD 15 436
MC 79 436
Laserlight / Jan '93 / TBD / Taylors.

Paulas Country

WELCOME TO PAULA'S COUNTRY.
Tracks: Not Advised.
LP. . . . . BSS 206
Tank / '88.

Paycheck, Johnny

Paycheck was born Donald Lytle in Greenfield, Ohio in 1941. The country singer/songwriter with the abrasive voice had hits in the mid-60s, faded because of his alcohol problem, was lured back to Nashville by producer Billy Sherrill in the mid-70s and was bigger than ever. He provided Tammy Wynette with her first hit (*Apartment No.9*); his own best-known hit was with David Allen Coe's song *Take This Job And Shove It* in 1978. (Donald Clarke).

16 GREATEST HITS.
Tracks: Not Advised.
CD . . . . CD 1008
Gusto (USA) / '88.

APARTMENT NO 9.
Tracks: Apartment No.9 / My baby don't love me anymore / Just between you and me / Yesterday, today and tomorrow / Here we go again / He's in a hurry (to get home to my wife) / Handcuffed to love / Big town baby / Understanding makes love / Fools' hall of fame / Tell me your troubles (I'll tell you mine) / Make me one more memory.
■ LP. . . . . PRC 100
President / Aug '80.
LP. . . . . PRCV 100
President / '86 / Grapevine Distribution / Target Records / Jazz Music / Taylors.

ARMED AND CRAZY.
Tracks: Friend, lover, wife / Armed and crazy / Mainline / Thanks to the cat-house / Leave it to me / Me and the IRS / Let's have a hand for the little lady / Just makin' love don't make it love / Look what the dog drug in / Outlaw's prayer.
■ LP. . . . . EPC 83499
Epic / Apr '79.

BACK ON THE JOB.
Tracks: Not Advised.
LP. 20031
MC 40031
Astan (USA) / Nov '84.

BIGGEST HITS.
Tracks: She's all I got / Someone to give my love to / Love is a good thing / Something about you I love / Mr. Love maker / Song and dance man / My part of forever / Outlaws prayer / Take this job & shove it / Slide off your satin sheets / I'm the only hell / Me & the I.R.S. / Friend, lover, wife / Cocaine train / Drinkin' and drivin' / For a minute there.
LP. . . . . EPC 32305
MC 40 32305
Epic / Mar '83 / Sony.

EVERYBODY'S GOT A FAMILY, MEET MINE.
Tracks: Cocaine train / Ragged old truck / Drinkin' and drivin' / Who was that man that beat me so / Billy Bardo / Fifteen beers / Low class reunion / I never met a girl I didn't like / Save your heart for me / Roll in my sweet baby's arms.
■ LP. . . . . EPC 84112
Epic / Apr '80.

GOLDEN CLASSICS.
Tracks: Not Advised.
LP. . . . . GT 0098
Gusto (USA) / Mar '88.

GREATEST HITS: JOHNNY PAYCHECK.
Tracks: Take this job & shove it / Slide off your satin sheet / Somebody loves me / Motel time again / In memory of memory / Mr. Lovemaker / A-11 / She's all I got / For a minute there / Only hell my mama ever raised, The / Loving you beats all I ever seen / Song & dance man / Keep on lovin' me / Jukebox Charlie / Something about you I love / Someone to give my love to / Green, green grass of home / Don't monkey with another monkey's monkey / Heaven's almost as big as Texas / Close all the Honky Tonks / Almost persuaded / Release me / All the time / Crazy arms / Heartaches by the number / Apartment £ 9.
CD . . . . CDGRF 070
Tring / Feb '93 / Prism Leisure PLC / Midland Records / Taylors.

HONKY TONK AND SLOW MUSIC.
Tracks: Honky tonk and slow music / Nowhere to run / I feel like crying / I'm remembering / Coming home to my heart / Make me one more memory / I'm a coward / Keeping up with the Joneses / I don't know when that will be / Johnsons of Turkey Ridge, The.
LP. . . . . SDLP 1047
MC . . . . SDC 1047
Sundown / May '88 / Terry Blood Dist. / Jazz Music / C.M. Distribution.

I DON'T NEED TO KNOW THAT RIGHT NOW.
Tracks: Happy hour / I've had mine / Georgia in a jug / She's all I got / Song and dance man / I don't need to know that right now / Take this job and shove it / Slide off your satin sheets / Somebody loves me / Jeannie in a bottle.
LP. . . . . ALEB 2301
MC . . . . ZCALB 2301
Allegiance / Apr '84.

JOHNNY PAYCHECK.
Tracks: Not Advised.
MC . . . . ZCGAS 753
Audio Fidelity(USA) / Oct '84 / Stage One Records.

JUKEBOX CHARLIE.
Tracks: Jukebox Charlie / I never had the one I wanted / Everything you touch turns to hurt / Wildfire / Talk to my children mama / If I'm gonna sink / Help me Hank, I'm fallin' / California dreams / Billy Jack Washburn / Lovin machine, The / There's no easy way to die / It's for sure I can't go on / My worst is the best I can give / These things I'm not.
■ LP. . . . . PRCV 109
President / May '81.

MR. HAG TOLD MY STORY.
Tracks: Turnin' off a memory / I've got a yearning / Carolyn / I'll leave the bottle on the bar / All night lady / I can't hold myself in line / Yesterday's news just hit home today / You don't have very far to go / No more you and me / Someone told my story.
■ LP. . . . . EPC 84847
Epic / Jun '81.

SURVIVOR.
Tracks: Not Advised.
CD . . . . VD 102
Dixie Frog / Sep '90 / Discovery.

TAKE THIS JOB & SHOVE IT.
Tracks: Take this job & shove it / Colorado cool aid.
■ 7" . . . . EPC 6171
Epic / Mar '78.

TAKE THIS JOB AND SHOVE IT.
Tracks: Take this job and shove it / From cotton to satin (from Birmingham to Manhattan) / Spirits of St. Louis, The / 4 'F' blues, The / Barstool mountain / Georgia in a jug / Fool strikes again, The / Man from Bowling Green, The / When I had a home to go to / Colorado cool-aid.
LP. . . . . EPC 82857
■ MC . . . . EPC 4082857
CBS / '78 / Sony.
CD 15 483
MC 79 483
Laserlight / May '93 / TBD / Taylors.

Peace In The Valley

PEACE IN THE VALLEY (22 Religious Favourites).
Tracks: Not Advised.
LP. . . . . RTL 2043
MC . . . . RTLC 2043
Ronco / Nov '79.

Pedersen, Herb

Musician (banjo)/vocalist born, 27.4.1944 in Berkeley, California.. a much travelled musician, having played with everyone from Linda Ronstadt to Flatt & Scruggs to the Desert Rose Band (member since 1986). Whilst he's renowned for his marvellous work on banjo, he happens to be one of the finest harmony singers around - an often used session musician. Apart from his own Sugar Hill solo album, *Lonesome Feelings* a modern bluegrass persuasion, his artistry is well featured on Hillman's Sugar Hill solo albums *Morning Sky* & *Desert Rose*, John Starling's *Long Time Gone*. Alongside Dan Fogelberg's well received 1985 Epic album *High Country Snow* & mandolin virtuoso Dave Grisman's release *Home Where The Heart Is* - as well as his work on Emmylou Harris' early Reprise albums. (Maurice Hope)

LONESOME FEELING.
Tracks: Last thing on my mind / Childish love / Fields have turned brown, The / Homecoming, The / Easy ride / Lonesome feeling / Willow garden / It's worth believing / Even the worst of us / Your love is like a flower.
LP. . . . . SH 3738
MC . . . . SH 3738C
Sugarhill(USA) / May '84 / Roots Records / Projection / Impetus Records / C.M. Distribution / Jazz Music / Swift / Duncans / A.D.A Distribution.

Penny, Hank

A devotee of Bob Wills and Milton Brown, Alabama born Hank Penny (1918-92), formed his western swing band, the Radio Cowboys in the late 1930's and was first heard on the Birmingham radio stations WAPI and WKBC. Among his musicians in those early days was steel guitarist Noel Boggs and fiddle player Boudleaux Bryant, later to become (with wife Felice) Nashville's most successful songwriting team. In 1939 Penny recorded *Won't you ride in my little red wagon* , later to become his signature tune, for ARC. In 1945 he moved to Hollywood and secured a residency at Riverside Rancho, as well as appearing in several Western movies with Charles Starrett. At the end of the decade he founded the Palamino Club in Los Angeles. Once married to Hickory artist Sue Thompson, Penny's hits included *Steel guitar stomp* , *Get yourself a redhead* and *Bloodshot eyes*. In addition to his successful (though much underated) music career, Penny also worked as a comedian during the 1950's. (Tony Byworth)

ROMPIN', STOMPIN', SINGIN', SWINGIN'.
Tracks: Catch em' young, treat 'em rough, tell 'em nothin' / What she's got is mine / White shotguns / I like molasses / I want my rib / Hold the phone / No muss, no fuss, no bother / Taxes, taxes / You're bound to look like a monkey / Won't ride you in) my little red wagon / Hadacillin boogie / Fan it / You can't pull the wool over my eyes / That's my weakness now / Mink on her back, The / You played on my piano.
LP. . . . . **BFX 15102**
Bear Family / Sep '84 / Rollercoaster Records / Swift / Direct Distribution.

TOBACCO STATE SWING (Penny, Hank & His Radio Cowboys).
Tracks: Back up a little bit / Tobacco state swing / Mama's getting younger / Lonesome train blues / Hot time mama / Hawaiian honeymoon / Rose's sister / Won't you ride in my little red wagon / Cowboy's swing / Sweet talkin mama / Hesitation blues / All night and all day long / Oh yes take another guess / Blue ridge blues.
LP. . . . . **RAMBLER 100**
Rambler (USA) / Jul '81 / Roots Records / Projection / Swift / Wellard Dist.

Peppers, Nancy

FIRST NIGHT.
Tracks: First night.
7". . . . . **MSSR 2**
Soundsrite / Nov '85 / TBD.

I BELIEVE.
Tracks: I believe / Where did we go wrong.
■ **7".** . . . . **NBP 1**
Fresh (USA) / Jan '82.

JESUS WILL OUTSHINE THEM ALL.
Tracks: Jesus will outshine them all / I never go around mirrors.
■ **7".** . . . . **BP 353**
Liberty / Apr '80.

LEAVING FOR BETTER TIMES.
Tracks: Leaving for better times / You win again.
■ **7".** . . . . **UP 36426**
United Artists / Aug '78.

Perkins, Carl

The name of this American singer, songwriter and guitarist is indelibly associated in everybody's minds with *Blue Suede Shoes*. Perkins wrote and recorded the original version of this rock'n'roll classic in 1956, soon after joining Sam Phillips' Sun label in Memphis. It logged four weeks at No. 2 on the American charts and reached No.10 in Britain. However, the song was quickly covered by Elvis Presley who made the song his own thus tending to overshadow Perkins. A series of personal problems prevented Perkins from building on the success of *Blue Suede Shoes*, and it remained his only pop hit. He subsequently went back to his country roots, and spent much of his time touring with Johnny Cash. During the late Seventies and early Eighties, Carl was a regular live performer in his own right.(Bob MacDonald)

20 GOLDEN PIECES: CARL PERKINS.
Tracks: I don't like what I'm seeing in you / Rise and shine / Hallelujah special / This ole house / Blue suede shoes / All mama's children / Country soul / When you are 21 / Sundays are fundays / Redneck / Every road / Don't get off getting it on / Standing in the need of love / I don't want to fall in love / Sweeter than candy / I want you back / We did it in '54 / Hurt put on by you, The / That's right / Dixie fried.
LP. . . . . **BDL 2034**
Bulldog Records / Nov '83 / President Records / Jazz Music / Wellard Dist. / TKO Records Ltd.

BEST OF AND THE REST OF, THE.
Tracks: Rock around the clock / That's alright mama / Kawliga / Tutti frutti / Yes it's me and I'm in love again / Blue suede shoes / Be bop a lula / Maybelline / Whole lotta shakin' / Hang up my rock 'n' roll shoes / Shake rattle and roll.
CD . . . . **CDAR 1025**
MC . . . . **ARLC 1025**
Action Replay / Mar '91 / Total / BMG.

BLUE SUEDE SHOES.
Tracks: Blue suede shoes / Honey don't / Everybody's trying to be my baby / Boppin' the blues / Wrong yo yo / Cat clothes / Let the juke box keep on playing / Dixie bop / Gone gone gone / You can't make love to somebody / Tennessee / Sure to fall.
LP. . . . . **SUN 1014**
Sun / Sep '88 / Charly / Swift.
MC . . . . **ENT MC 13065**
Entertainers / Mar '92.

BLUE SUEDE SHOES.
Tracks: Blue suede shoes / That's all right / Rock on around the world.
■ **7".** . . . . **CYS 1014**
Charly / Aug '78.
■ **7".** . . . . **UP 36365**
United Artists / Mar '78.
■ **CD Single** . . . . **CDS 9**
Charly / Feb '89 / Charly.

BLUE SUEDE SHOES.
Tracks: Blue suede shoes.
■ **7".** . . . . **HLU 8271**
London-American / May '56.

BLUE SUEDE SHOES (OLD GOLD).
Tracks: Blue suede shoes.
7". . . . . **OG 9737**
Old Gold / Nov '87 / Pickwick Records.

BOPPIN' THE BLUES.
Tracks: Blue suede shoes / I'm sorry, I'm not sorry / Let the juke box keep on playing / All Mama's children / Honey don't / Dixie fried / Boppin' the blues / Your true love / That's alright / Matchbox / Lend me your comb / Gone gone gone.
LP. . . . . **TOP 107**
MC . . . . **KTOP 107**
Topline / Nov '84 / Charly / Swift / Black Sun Records.

BORN TO ROCK.
Tracks: Not Advised.
CD . . . . **UVLD 76001**
LP. . . . . **UVL 76001**
MC . . . . **UVLC 76001**
MCA / Jun '89 / BMG.

CARL PERKINS.
Tracks: Matchbox / If I had 'a known / Green green grass of home / Texas woman / Signs / Blue suede shoes / Honey don't / I'm walking / Suzie Q / Memphis / Maybellene / Slippin' and slidin' / Be bop a lula / Roll over Beethoven / Hound dog / Whole lotta shakin' goin' on / Lucille / Jailhouse rock / All shook up / That's alright mama / Bird dog / Rock Island line.
LP. . . . . **MCF 3315**
■ **MC** . . . . **MCFC 3315**
MCA / Mar '86.
CD . . . . **OR 0027**
Music Collection International / Aug '87 / Terry Blood Dist. / Jazz Music.

CARL PERKINS (CAMBRA).
Tracks: Not Advised.
Double LP . . . . **CR 101**
MC Set . . . . **CRT 101**
Cambra / '88.

CARL PERKINS (DITTO).
Tracks: Not Advised.
MC Set . . . . **DTO 10089**
Ditto / '88 / Pickwick Records.

CARL PERKINS AND JERRY LEE LEWIS LIVE (Perkins, Carl & Jerry Lee Lewis).
Tracks: That's all right momma / Elvis we love you, the whole world misses you / Blue suede shoes / Rockabilly fever / Over the rainbow / High school hop / 39 and holding / Great balls of fire / Whole lotta shakin' goin' on / Chantilly lace / Lucille / Matchbox.
VHS. . . . . **BBCV 4045**
BBC Video / '87 / Sony / Gold & Sons / Terry Blood Dist.

CARL PERKINS EP.
Tracks: Put your cat clothes on / Right string but the wrong yo-yo / Tennessee / Honey don't.
■ **EP.** . . . . **CEP 120**
Charly / '78.

CARL PERKINS EP.
Tracks: Boppin' the blues / Dixie fried / Sure to fall / Movie Magg.
■ **EP.** . . . . **CEP 106**
Charly / Feb '77.

CARL PERKINS ROCK'N'ROLL PARTY, THE.
Tracks: Not Advised.
LP. . . . . **WW 5139**
MC . . . . **WW 45139**
Warwick / Nov '84 / Sony / Henry Hadaway Organisation / Multiple Sound Distributors.

CLASSIC CARL PERKINS (5 CD box set).
Tracks: Honky tonk babe (gal) / Movie Magg / Honky tonk gal / Run around / Turn around / Let the jukebox keep on playing / What you doin' when you're cryin' / You can't make love to somebody / Gone, gone, gone / Dixie bop / Perkin's wiggle / Blue suede shoes (take 1) / Blue suede shoes (take 2) / Blue suede shoes (take 3) / Honey don't (take 1) / Honey don't (take 2) / Honey don't (take 3) / Tennessee / Sure to fall / All mama's children / Everybody's trying to be my baby / Boppin' the blues / Put your cat clothes on / Only you / Right string, wrong yo yo / All mama's children (false start) / Dixie fried / Dixie fried (false start) / I'm sorry I'm not sorry / That don't move me / Lonely street / Drink up & go home / Pink pedal pushers / Way you're living is breaking my heart, The / Take back my love / Somebody tell me / Instrumental number 1 / Instrumental number 2 / Red wing / Down by the riverside / Her love rubbed off / Caldonia / You can do no wrong / Sweethearts or strangers / Be honest with me / Your true love / Matchbox / Your true love (original tempo) / Keeper of the key / Roll over Beethoven / Try my heart out / That's right / Forever yours / Y.O.U. / I care / Lend me your comb / Look at the moon / Glad all over / Tutti frutti / Whole lotta shakin' goin' on / That's alright / Where the Rio de Rosa flows / Shake, rattle & roll / Long tall Sally / I got a woman / Hey good lookin' / Sittin' on top of the world / Good rockin' tonight / Jive after five / Rockin' record hop / Just tonight I'd call / Ready Teddy / Jenny, Jenny / You were there / Because you're mine / Pop, let me have the car / Levi jacket & a longtail shirt / When the moon comes over the mountain / Sister twister / Hambone / This life I live / Please say you'll be mine / Honey, cause I love you / I don't see me in your eyes anymore / Highway of love / Pointed toe shoes / One-way ticket to lonliness / Drifter, The / Too much for a man to understand / LOVEVILLE / Big bad blues / Say when / Lonely heart / Love I'll never win, A / Let my baby be / Monkey shine / Mama of my song / One of these days / I wouldn't have you / Help me find my baby / After sundown / For a little while / Just for you / When the right time comes along / Fool I used to be, The / Forget me (next time around) / Hollywood city / I've just got back from there / Unhappy girls / Someday, somewhere someone waits for me / Anyway the wind blows.
CD Set . . . . **BCD 15494**
Bear Family / Feb '90 / Rollercoaster Records / Swift / Direct Distribution.

CLASSIC CARL PERKINS, THE.
Tracks: Not Advised.
CD . . . . **OCN 2036WD**
LP. . . . . **OCN 2036WL**
MC . . . . **OCN 2036WK**
Ocean (£) / Jun '89.

COUNTRY BOY'S DREAM (The Dollie Masters).
Tracks: Country boy's dream / If I could come back / Star of the show, The / Poor boy blues / Detroit city / Dream on little dreamer / Stateside / Sweet misery / Unmitigated gall / Shine shine shine / Without you / You can take the boy out of the.. / Almost love / Old fashioned singalong / Old number one / My old hometown / Back to Tennessee / It's you / I'll go wrong again / Dear Abby / Lake country, cotton country / All you need to know / Quite like you / Just as long (pop) / Just as long (country) / Baby I'm hung on you / Tom & Mary Jane / Mama & Daddy / Valda.
CD . . . . **BCD 15593**
Bear Family / Apr '92 / Rollercoaster Records / Swift / Direct Distribution.

COUNTRY STORE: CARL PERKINS.
Tracks: Ruby don't take your love to town / Love sweet love / Just as long / (Let's get) dixie fried / Lord I sinned again last night / Help me dream / Sing my song / You tore my Heaven all to Hell / One more loser going home / Never look back / Honky tonk song / Going to Memphis / Sunday dinner / Big bad blues.
CD . . . . **CDCST 53**
MC . . . . **CSTK 53**
Country Store / '88 / BMG.
■ **LP.** . . . . **CST 53**
Country Store / '88.

DANCE ALBUM.
Tracks: Blue suede shoes / Movie magg / Sure to fall / Gone gone gone / Honey don't / Only you / All mama's children / Tennessee / Wrong yo yo / Everybody's trying to be my baby / Matchbox / Your true love / Boppin' the blues.
■ **LP.** . . . . **CRM 2012**
Charly / Jul '81 / Charly.
CD . . . . **TOP CD 503**
Topline / Apr '87 / Charly / Swift / Black Sun Records.

DISCIPLINE IN BLUE SUEDE SHOES.
Tracks: Not Advised.
LP. **20090**
MC **40090**
Astan (USA) / Nov '84.

DIXIE FRIED.
Tracks: Honey don't / Boppin' the blues / Blue suede shoes / Put your cat clothes on / Dixie fried / Matchbox / Pink pedal pushers / Thats right / I'm sorry I'm not sorry / Roll over Beethoven / Glad all over / Right string baby but the wrong yoyo / Everybody's trying to be my baby / Gone gone gone / Lend me your comb / All mama's children / Sweet hearts or strangers / Your true love / Movie Magg / Tennessee / Sure to gall / Honky tonk gal / Turn around / Let the juke box keep on playing.
CD . . . . **CDCHARLY 2**
Charly / Mar '86 / Charly.

EP EXPRESS.
Tracks: Ep express / Big band blues.
■ **7".** . . . . **ELV 15**
Mercury / Sep '77.

EVERY ROAD.
Tracks: Not Advised.
LP. . . . . **SM 3995**
MC . . . . **MC 3995**
Joker (USA) / '88 / C.M. Distribution / Jazz Horizons / Jazz Music.

FRIENDS FAMILY & LEGENDS.
Tracks: Not Advised.
CD . . . . **CDMF 084**
DRG (USA) / Jan '93 / New Note / Silva Screen.

GOIN' BACK TO MEMPHIS.
Tracks: Twenty one / Georgia court room / Hallelujah special / Sweeter than candy / I don't want to fall in love / Hurt put on by you, The / Rise and shine / Take me back / Sing a song / I want you back again.
LP. . . . . **MFLP 1042**
Magnum Force / Feb '86 / Terry Blood Dist. / Jazz Music / Hot Shot.

■ DELETED

GOING BACK TO MEMPHIS (Vol. 2).
Tracks: Not Advised.
LP.............................. SM 3996
Joker (USA) / '88 / C.M. Distribution / Jazz Horizons / Jazz Music.

GREATEST HITS OF CARL PERKINS.
Tracks: Blue suede shoes / Matchbox / Mean woman blues / Turn around / Folsom Prison blues / Daddy sang bass / Boppin' the blues / Honey don't / That's right / Your true love / Restless / Long tall Sally.
■ LP.............................. 31527
CBS / '78 / Sony.

HEART AND SOUL OF CARL PERKINS, THE.
Tracks: I don't want to fall in love / Hurt put on by you, The / I want you back again / Country soul / Redneck / I dont like what I'm seeing in you / We did it in '54 / Don't get off getting it on / 21 / Standing in the need of love.
LP.......................... ALEB 2308
MC.......................... ZCALB 2308
Allegiance / Apr '84.

HONKY TONK GAL.
Tracks: Not Advised.
LP.............................. SS 27
Rounder / Apr '89 / Projection / Roots Records / Swift / C.M. Distribution / Topic Records / Jazz Music / Hot Shot / A.D.A Distribution / Direct Distribution.

LEGENDARY, THE.
Tracks: Born to boogie / I can feel it / Don't get off gettin' it on / Take me back / Redneck / Hurt put on by you, The / Sweeter than candy / Boppin' the blues / We did in '54 / Mama / Standing in the need of love / What am I living for / '21' / Country soul / Georgia court room / I didn't want to fall in love again.
CD.............................. PWK 4037
MC.......................... PWKMC 4037
Pickwick / Feb '91 / Pickwick Records.

LIL' BIT OF GOLD: CARL PERKINS.
Tracks: Blue suede shoes / Honey don't / Everybody's trying to be my baby / Matchbox.
■ CD Single .... R 373015
Rhino (USA) / May '88 / WEA.

LONG TALL SALLY.
Tracks: Jive after five / Tutti frutti / Whole lotta shakin' goin' on / Hey, good lookin' / Pop, let me have the car / Sittin' on top of world / Pink pedal pushers / Long tall Sally / That's all right / Where the Rio de Rosa flows / Levi jacket (and a long tail shirt) / Honey, cause I love you / Pointed toe shoes / Anyway the wind blows / Hambone / Restless.
LP.............................. 31454
■ MC.......................... 4031454
CBS / '78 / Sony.

MAN AND THE LEGEND, THE.
Tracks: Blue suede shoes / Honey don't / I'm walking / Matchbox / Suzie Q / Memphis / Maybellene / Slippin' and slidin' / Be bop a lula / Roll over Beethoven / Hound dog / Whole lotta shakin' goin' on / Lucille / Jailhouse rock / All shook up / That's alright mama / Bird dog / Rock Island line / Singing the blues / Got my mojo working.
LP.............................. MFLP 2039
Magnum Force / Oct '86 / Terry Blood Dist. / Jazz Music / Hot Shot.

MR COUNTRY ROCK.
Tracks: Not Advised.
LP.......................... DEMAND 0015
Demand / Oct '87.

MUSTANG WINE.
Tracks: Mustang wine / Whole world misses you, The.
■ 7".............................. JET 117
Jet / Sep '78.

OL'BLUE SUEDES IS BACK.
Tracks: Not Advised.
■ LP.......................... UATV 30146
Jet / Apr '78.

ORIGINAL CARL PERKINS, THE.
Tracks: Movie Magg / Turn around / Let the juke box keep on playing / Gone gone gone / Blue suede shoes / Honey don't / Boppin' the blues / All mama's children / I'm sorry I'm not sorry / Dixie fried / Matchbox / You true love / Forever yours / That's right / Glad all over / Lend me your comb.
■ LP.............................. CR 30110
Charly / Feb '78 / Charly.

PUT YOUR CAT CLOTHES ON.
Tracks: Sweethearts or strangers / You can do no wrong / Caldonia / Roll over Beethoven / Matchbox / Put your cat clothes on / Her love rubbed off / Pink pedal pushers / That's right / Look at that moon / Glad all over / Lend me your comb / Your true love.
LP.............................. SUN 1046
Sun / Aug '88 / Charly / Swift.

ROCK AND ROLL & COUNTRY SOUL.
Tracks: Didn't the 50's rock / Country soul / I don't like what I'm seeing in you.
EP.............................. MFEP 013
Magnum Force / Terry Blood Dist. / Jazz Music / Hot Shot.

ROCKABILLY SESSION.
Tracks: Not Advised.
VHS.............................. VVD 113

P 8

Virgin Vision / May '86 / Gold & Sons / Terry Blood Dist.
BETA.......................... VVD 133 B
VHS.......................... VVD 133
Virgin Vision / '88 / Gold & Sons / Terry Blood Dist.

ROCKIN' GUITARMAN.
Tracks: Blue suede shoes / Roll over Beethoven / Sweethearts and strangers / Perkins wiggle / Honky tonk gal / You can do no wrong / What do you want when you're crying? / Boppin' the blues / Caldonia / Lonely street / I care / Y.O.U. / Glad all over / Honey don't / Dixie fried / Her love rubbed off.
■ LP.............................. CR 30003
Charly / Feb '78 / Charly.

ROCKIN' THE HOUSE DOWN.
Tracks: Not Advised.
Double LP.................... NETV 1002
MC Set .... NETVC 1002
Network (Rounder) / Nov '85 / Sony.

SUN YEARS, THE.
Tracks: Honky tonk gal / Movie Magg (2 takes) / Turn around (2 takes) / You can't make love to somebody / Gone gone gone / Let the juke box keep on playing / What ya doin' when you're cryin' / Drink up and go home / Blue suede shoes (3 takes) / Honey don't (2 takes) / Sure to fall / Tennessee / Perkins wiggle / Boppin' the blues (2 takes) / All mama's children / Everybody's trying to be my baby (plus Carl Perkins in Richmond - radio plug) / Somebody tell me (plus Carl Perkins in Memphis - radio plug) / Dixie fried / I'm sorry I'm not sorry / Sweethearts or strangers / Keeper of the key / Be honest with me / That don't move me / Lonely street / Pink pedal pushers (2 takes) / Matchbox (2 takes) / Your true love (2 takes) / Caldonia / Her love rubbed off / You can do no wrong / Roll over Beethoven / Put your cat clothes on (2 takes) / That's right (2 takes) / Forever yours / I care / Y.O.U. / Look at that moon / Lend me your comb (2 takes) / Glad all over / Right string baby but the wrong yo / Honky tonk babe.
LP Set .... SUN BOX 101
Sun / '82 / Charly / Swift.
CD Set .... SUN BOX 2
Sun / Feb '90 / Charly / Swift.

SWEETER THAN CANDY.
Tracks: Not Advised.
LP.............................. 20092
MC.............................. 40092
Astan (USA) / Nov '84.

TENNESSEE BOP.
Tracks: Blue suede shoes / Honky tonk gal / Glad all over / Perkins wiggle / Honey don't / Matchbox / Put your cat clothes on / Everybody's trying to be my baby / Lend me your comb / Dixie fried / Boppin' the blues / Tennessee / Gone gone gone / All mama's children.
CD.......................... CDINS 5019
LP.............................. INS 5019
MC.......................... TCINS 5019
Instant (2) / Feb '90 / Charly.

THAT ROCKIN' GUITAR MAN.
Tracks: Born to boogie / Daddy sang bass / Redneck / Standing in the need of love / Mama / We did it in '54 / Disciple in blue suede shoes / I can feel it / What am I living for / Don't get off getting it on.
LP.............................. MFLP 1024
Magnum Force / '88 / Terry Blood Dist. / Jazz Music / Hot Shot.

THIS COUNTRY'S ROCKIN'.
Tracks: Not Advised.
VHS.......................... MMGV 055
MMG Video / Jan '93 / Terry Blood Dist.

TURN AROUND.
Tracks: Not Advised.
■ LP.............................. CP 2003
Culture Press / Sep '85.

TURNAROUND.
Tracks: Turnaround / Blue suede shoes / Lovesick blues / Miss misunderstood.
■ 7".............................. JET 182
Jet / Nov '80.

UP COUNTRY VOL.2.
Tracks: Not Advised.
CD.......................... SOV 021CD
MC.......................... SOV 021MC
Sovereign Music / Sep '93 / Terry Blood Dist. / ACD Trading Ltd. / Taylors.

UP THROUGH THE YEARS '1954-1957'.
Tracks: Honky tonk gal / Movie magg / Turn around / Gone gone gone / Let the juke box keep on playing / You can't make love to somebody / Blue suede shoes / Honey don't / Tennessee / Boppin' the blues / All mama's children / Everybody's trying to be my baby / Dixie fried / I'm sorry I'm not sorry / You can do no wrong / Matchbox / Your true love / Put your cat clothes on / Only you / Pink pedal pushers / That's right / Lend me your comb / Glad all over / Right string baby but the wrong yoyo.
CD.......................... BCD 15246
Bear Family / Nov '86 / Rollercoaster Records / Swift / Direct Distribution.

GONNA ROCK MY BABY TONIGHT.
Tracks: Gonna rock my baby tonight.

■ 7".............................. DT 4502
Detour / Feb '81.

TENNESSEE SATURDAY NIGHT (Perkins, Luther & Tooting Frootles).
Tracks: Tennessee Saturday night / Million dollar quartet.
■ 7".............................. 101
Magic (1) / Aug '80.

ANITA AND TIM (Perras, Anita & Tim Taylor).
Tracks: Not Advised.
MC.......................... SVMC 9401
Savannah / '90 / Sony / ACD Trading Ltd.

TOUCH MY HEART.
Tracks: Not Advised.
LP.......................... UNKNOWN
Savannah / Oct '89 / Sony / ACD Trading Ltd.

Canadian - born (4-11-.60) Peterson promised much during the mid - seventies, only to lose out on making the expected inpression of America's country market. Despite two fine albums on Capitol, her debut 1977 release Colleen (a Lee Hazlewood production) included songs from Bob McDill, Willy P. Bennett, Gail Davies and herself. Souvenirs in '76 being this highly popular Canadian T.V. entertainer's only Billboard entry. Latest work on the Canadian Boot label. (Maurice Hope)

BASIC FACTS.
Tracks: Weather the storm / Let's try / I had it all / Gently lay down / Mr. Conductor / Basic fact of love / 1942 / What a fool I'd be / Love scares me / Ghost of Maggie's sailor.
LP.......................... BSR 33-66
Bookshop (USA) / '88.

COLLEEN.
Tracks: Dynamite rock'n'roll band / Go thru the motions / Beginning to feel like home / Delaney / Stealing away / Bucket to the south / You make it look so easy / Startin' out clean / Closest thing to you, The / Dim lights / Thick smoke and loud loud music.
■ LP.......................... ST 11714
Capitol (import) / '77.

I GO TO PIECES.
Tracks: I go to pieces / Going going gone.
■ 7".......................... CL 16035
Capitol / Jan '79.

TAKIN' MY BOOTS OFF.
Tracks: I go to pieces / Angelina / Last time I saw you / Need your lovin' / Going going gone / Run to her / Maybe it's love / One horse town / Booze the blues away.
LP.......................... EST 11835
Capitol / Jan '79 / EMI.

This American singer had a handful of hits in the late 50's and early 60's, including Corrina Corrina (No 9 in US, No 41 in UK) which was produced by the up-and-coming Phil Spector. Peterson himself never meet much in Britain, but two of his numbers became No 1 hits in the UK for other artists: the sick death ditty Tell Laura I Love Her was recorded by Welshman Ricky Valance in 1960 and the big ballad The Wonder Of Love was a British chart-topper for Elvis Presley in 1970. (Bob MacDonald)

ALL HIS HITS.
Tracks: Corina Corina / I'm gone / Doggone it / I'm tired / Shirley Purly / Is it wrong / Promises / Patricia / Fever / Tell Laura I love her / Tell Tommy I miss him / Give us your blessing / Wonder of you, The / Missing you / We're old enough to cry / Teenage heartache / Come and get it / Be my girl.
LP.......................... BFX 15245
Bear Family / Jul '87 / Rollercoaster Records / Swift / Direct Distribution.

ANSWER ME.
Tracks: Answer me.
■ 7".......................... RCA 1175
RCA / Mar '60.

CORRINE CORRINA.
Tracks: Corina, Corina.
■ 7".......................... HLX 9246
London-American / Jan '61.

WONDER OF YOU, THE.
Tracks: Wonder of you, The.
■ 7".......................... RCA 1131
RCA / Sep '59.

■ DELETED

Petitjean, Dave

CAJUN CAPERS.
Tracks: Not Advised.
LP. 5004
Kom-a-Day (USA) / Swift.
MC . . . . . 5004 TC
Kom-a-Day (USA) / '87 / Swift.

CAJUN HUMOR.
Tracks: Not Advised.
LP. 5002
Kom-a-Day (USA) / Swift.
MC . . . . . 5002 TC
Kom-a-Day (USA) / '87 / Swift.

HUMOR FROM CAJUN COUNTRY.
Tracks: Not Advised.
LP. 5003
Kom-a-Day (USA) / Swift.
MC . . . . . 5003 TC
Kom-a-Day (USA) / '87 / Swift.

MY FANS.
Tracks: Not Advised.
LP. 5001
MC . . . . . 5001 TC
Kom-a-Day (USA) / '88 / Swift.

REAL AND FUNNY CAJUN, A.
Tracks: Not Advised.
LP. 5005
Kom-a-Day (USA) / Swift.
MC . . . . . 5005 TC
Kom-a-Day (USA) / '87 / Swift.

Pfeifer, Diane

DIANE PFEIFER.
Tracks: Free to be lonely again / Second hand heart / Just when I needed a love song / Wishful drinkin' / Sing you to sleep / Roses ain't red / Blue from your little white lies / I believe in fairy tales too / Do you mind (if I fall in love with you) / Oh no not love again.
■ LP. . . . . EST 12046
Capitol / Nov '80.

JUST WHEN I NEEDED A LOVE SONG.
Tracks: Just when I needed a love song / Wishful drinkin'.
■ 7". . . . . CL 16169
Capitol / Oct '80.

Phillips, Steve

BEST OF STEVE PHILLIPS.
Tracks: Not Advised.
LP. . . . . BRAVE 5
Unamerican Activities / Nov '88 / SRD / Hot Shot.

STEEL RAIL BLUES.
Tracks: Not Advised.
CD . . . . . BRAVE 9 CD
LP. . . . . BRAVE 9
MC . . . . . BRAVE 9 C
Unamerican Activities / Dec '89 / SRD / Hot Shot.

Phillips, Utah

ALL USED UP AND A SCRAP BOOK.
Tracks: Not Advised.
LP. . . . . PH 1050
Philo (USA) / Sep '79 / Roots Records / Projection / Topic Records / Direct Distribution / Ross Records / C.M. Distribution / Impetus Records.

EL CAPITAN.
Tracks: Telling takes me home, The / Goodnight - loving trail, The / Old Delores / John D.Lee / Dog canyon / Star of bannock, The / Sitting by the old coral / Johnny Thurman / Scofield mine disaster / Rock me to sleep / I've got a home out in Utah / Jesse's corrido / Enola gay / Larimer Street / Pig hollow / Yuba city / She'll never be mine / Sweet briar, The.
LP. . . . . PHILO 1016
Philo (USA) / May '79 / Roots Records / Projection / Topic Records / Direct Distribution / Ross Records / C.M. Distribution / Impetus Records.

GOOD THOUGH.
Tracks: Not Advised.
LP. . . . . PHILO 1004
Philo (USA) / Sep '79 / Roots Records / Projection / Topic Records / Direct Distribution / Ross Records / C.M. Distribution / Impetus Records.
MC . . . . . PH 1004C
Philo (USA) / '88 / Roots Records / Projection / Topic Records / Direct Distribution / Ross Records / C.M. Distribution / Impetus Records.

WE HAVE FED YOU ALL A THOUSAND YEARS.
Tracks: Boss, The / We have fed you all a thousand years / Sheep and goats / Timberbeast's lament, The / Dump the bosses off your back / Lumberjack's prayer, The / Mr. Block / Preacher and the slave, The / Popular wobbly, The / Casey Jones - the union scab / Where the fraser river flows / Bread and roses / Joe Hill / Union burying ground / Two bums, The / Hallelujah / I'm a bum / Solidarity forever / There's power in a union.
CD . . . . . PHCD 1076
MC . . . . . PHC 1076
Philo (USA) / May '93 / Roots Records / Projection / Topic Records / Direct Distribution / Ross Records / C.M. Distribution / Impetus Records.

WE HAVE FED YOU ALL THESE YEARS.
Tracks: Not Advised.
LP. . . . . PH 1076
Philo (USA) / Apr '85 / Roots Records / Projection / Topic Records / Direct Distribution / Ross Records / C.M. Distribution / Impetus Records.
MC . . . . . PH 1076C
Philo (USA) / Oct '88 / Roots Records / Projection / Topic Records / Direct Distribution / Ross Records / C.M. Distribution / Impetus Records.

Pickens, Slim

FIDDLIN' FOOL, THE.
Tracks: I'm a ladies' man / Uncle Harvey's plane / Up cat pole cat / I won't go huntin' with you Jake / Cousin Pauline / I couldn't spoll **** / Boil them cabbage down / Hoot and holler bar and grill / Fifteen beers ago / Stutterin' bum / Kansas City star / Make me a star.
LP. . . . . WRS 086
Westwood / '82 / Pinnacle.

Pierce, Webb

One of the finest honky-tonk singers of the 1950s. He was born in Louisiana, on 8th August, 1926. Throughout his career he promoted the image of a simple country boy made good. After a spell in the late 1940s with Four Star Records, he was signed in 1951 to Decca. He fast became a star, with songs such as *Wondering* and *There Stands the Glass* (1953). Pierce joined the Grand Ole Opry in 1954, the same year that he produced *Slowly*. This was soon a country No. 1 and featured the then novel pedal-steel guitar, played by Budd Isaacs. *More and More* also topped the country charts in 1954, and was followed in 1955 by ,In the Jailhouse Now, Love, Love, Love and *I Don't Care*. In 1956 he joined Red Sovine for *Little Rosa*; he had a rock'n'roll inflected hit with *Teenage Boogie*, and was often voted No. 1 Country Male Vocalist. Pierce's records continued to reach the charts during the late 1950s and early 1960s, and he produced many strong-selling albums. He left Decca in 1977 and signed to Plantation, recording two volumes of Greatest Hits. By the late 1960s he was touring less often, content to let the fans come to him. Country music lost one of its legendary figures with the death of the flamboyant Pierce on February 24, 1991. He was a singer, songwriter and businessman who will be more remembered for his gaudy rhinestone stage outfits, guitar-shaped swimming pool and silver dollar studded automobiles than for his very impressive array of successful recordings. He was a country artist of the grand honky-tonk tradition, a singer with a high nasal voice and tight-throat delivery who dominated the country music charts throughout the 1950's. A recent researching of the Billboard Country Music Charts reveals that he still rates No. 7 in the all-time top 200 listings with 97 chart entries, 50 of them achieving top 10 status and 13 reaching No. 1. Sadly his hardcore country vocals went out of fashion as the smooth 1960's Nashville sound developed and, by the following decade, Pierce had virtually disappeared from the scene. Webb Pierce was equally successful as a songwriter, penning many of his hit titles, and doubling up as the song publisher. He co-founded Cedarwood Music (with Jim Denny, the manager of the Grand Ole Opry) in the mid-fifties, which was the first music publishing company to be situated on Nashville's Music Row area and quickly established itself as a multi-million dollar business operation. Among his other business interests were the ownerships of a record label and radio stations. He also appeared in the films *Buffalo guns* , *Music City USA* and *Road to Nashville* . The lack of Webb Pierce recordings available in recent years has been rectified by the Bear Family release *The wandering boy* . Containing 4 cd's, and a fully detailed booklet, this set contains 113 tracks covering the artists Decca period 1951 - 1958. (Tony Byworth)

CROSS COUNTRY.
Tracks: Heartaches by the number / You are my life / Cry cry darlin' / Waterloo / Free of the blues / I'm letting you go / Take time / Someday you'll call my name / All my love / Crazy wild desire / I'm falling in love with you / I close my eyes.
LP. . . . . HAT 3004
Stetson / Nov '85 / Crusader Marketing Co. / Swift / Wellard Dist. / Midland Records / C.M. Distribution.
MC . . . . . HATC 3004
Stetson / Nov '86 / Crusader Marketing Co. / Swift / Wellard Dist. / Midland Records / C.M. Distribution.

GOLDEN HITS, VOLS. 1 & 2.
Tracks: Back street affair / Cowtown / Don't do it darling / Fool, fool, fool / Honky tonk song / I ain't never / I don't care / I'm tired / I'm walking the dog / In the jailhouse now / Memory No. 1 / More and more / Slowly / Sparkling brown eyes / That's me without you / There stands the glass / Tupelo County jail / Walking the streets / Why baby why / Wondering.
LP Set 6625 034
Philips / Sep '77 / PolyGram.

GREAT SONGS OF WEBB PIERCE, THE.
Tracks: I'm walking the dog / Slowly / It's been so long / There stands the glass / Even tho' / I'm gonna fall out of love with you / I'm in the jailhouse now / Wondering / You can't be true / I'm not in love with you.
LP. . . . . BDL 1026
Bulldog Records / Jul '82 / President Records / Jazz Music / Wellard Dist. / TKO Records Ltd.

HAYRIDE BOOGIE (1950-51).
Tracks: California blues / Shuffle on down / In the jailhouse / I saw your face in the moon / Sitting on top of the world / Hayride boogie / Last waltz, The / Drifting Texas sand.
LP. . . . . KK 7456
Krazy Kat / Apr '91 / Hot Shot / C.M. Distribution / Wellard Dist. / Roots Records / Projection / Charly / Jazz Music.

I AIN'T NEVER.
Tracks: I ain't never / Teenage boogie / Sittin' alone / Bye bye love / In the jailhouse now / Honky tonk song / After the boy gets the girl / New panhandle rag / California blues / You scared the love light out of me / I'm walking the dog / More and more / I'm gonna see my baby tonight / Sparkling brown eyes / Sneakin' all around / Why baby why.
■ LP. . . . . CR 30235
Charly / Jul '84 / Charly.

ONE AND ONLY WEBB PIERCE, THE.
Tracks: Not Advised.
CD . . . . . KCD 00648
King / Feb '93 / New Note / Koch International.

WEBB!.
Tracks: Not Advised.
LP. . . . . HAT 3019
MC . . . . . HATC 3019
Stetson / Sep '86 / Crusader Marketing Co. / Swift / Wellard Dist. / Midland Records / C.M. Distribution.

WONDERING BOY, THE.
Tracks: Not Advised.
LP. . . . . HAT 3119
Stetson / '89 / Crusader Marketing Co. / Swift / Wellard Dist. / Midland Records / C.M. Distribution.

WONDERING BOY, THE 1951-1958.
Tracks: Drifting Texas sand / If crying would make you care / California blues / You scared the love right out of me / New silver bells / Wondering / You know I'm still in love with you / I'm gonna see my baby / That heart belongs to me / I just can't be true / So used to loving you / I haven't got the heart / I'll always take care of you / Backstreet affair / I'm only wishin' / Slowly / Last waltz, The / Bow thy head / Country church / I'll go on alone / That's me without you / Broken engagement / We'll find a way / It's been so long / Don't throw your life away / Too late to worry now / There stands the glass / There's a better home / Mother call my name in prayer / I'm walking the dog / You just can't be true / Slowly (2) / Broken engagement (2) / Slowly (3) / Even tho' / Sparkling brown eyes / Bugle call from Heaven / Thank you dear Lord / Kneel at the cross / Leaning on the everlasting arms / You're not mine anymore / I'm gonna fall out of love with you / Your good for nothing heart / Just imagination / I love you dear / More and more / I found someone that's true / Waltz you saved for me / One day later / In the jailhouse now / Sneakin' all around / I don't care / Just how long / Why baby why / Yes I know why / I found a true love / 'Cause I love you / Little Rosa / Let forgiveness in / Any old time / You make love to everyone / Teenage boogie / I'm really glad you hurt me / Teenage boogie (2) / Oh, so many years / One week later / When I'm with you / Can I find it in your heart / Crying over you / I'm tired / It's my way / Someday / Honky tonk song / I care no more / Bye bye love / Missing you / Let forgiveness in (2) / Who wouldn't love you / New panhandle rag / I know it was you / Don't do it darlin' / Holiday for love / How long / New raunchy, The / I'll get by somehow / English sweetheart / Down Panama way / Foreign love / You'll come back / New love affair, A / Falling back to me / Sittin' alone / I'm letting you go / Tupelo County jail / Waiting a lifetime / True love never dies / I think of you / I won't be cryin' anymore / I owe it to my heart / Violet and the rose, The / After the boy gets the girl / You make me live again / Crazy arms / Pick me up on your way down / Life to go / My shoes keep walking back to you.
CD Set . . . . . BCD 15522
Bear Family / Sep '90 / Rollercoaster Records / Swift / Direct Distribution.

Pillow, Ray

ONE TOO MANY MEMORIES.
Tracks: One too many memories / Livin' in the sunshine of your love / How do I hide from a memory / Wasted again / Please don't leave me / Days of you and me, The / You're one memory I'd like to make again / How much can love take / Julie loved Boston more than me / We're together again.
LP. . . . . ALEB 2307
MC . . . . . ZCALB 2307
Allegiance / Apr '84.

Pinnacle Boys

PINNACLE BOYS, THE.
Tracks: Not Advised.
LP . . . . ROUNDER 0049
Rounder / '88 / Projection / Roots Records / Swift / C.M.
Distribution / Topic Records / Jazz Music / Hot Shot /
A.D.A Distribution / Direct Distribution.

Pittman, Barbara

I NEED A MAN.
Tracks: I need a man / No matter who's to blame / I'm
getting better all the time / Two young fools in love /
Everlasting love / Cold cold heart / Handsome man /
Eleventh commandment, The / Just one day / Senti-
mental fool / Voice of a fool / I'm getting better all the
time (2) / Sentimental fool (2) / Love is a stranger / Take
my sympathy / I forgot to remember to forget / Senti-
mental fool (3) / I'll never let you go.
LP . . . . BFX 15359
Bear Family / Jul '89 / Rollercoaster Records / Swift /
Direct Distribution.

TEXAS BOOGIE.
Tracks: Diggin' the boogie / You're undecided / Ever-
lasting love / I'm getting better all the time / Money
honey / Right behind you baby / Honey hush / Trying to
get to you / Big boss man / I need a man / Long tall
Sally / Rockin' daddy.
LP . . . . MFLP 050
Magnum Force / Jun '87 / Terry Blood Dist. / Jazz
Music / Hot Shot.

TEXAS BOOGIE (Live in Houston).
Tracks: Diggin' the boogie / You're undecided / Ever-
lasting love / I'm getting better all the time / Money
honey / Right behind you baby / Honey hush / Trying to
get to you / Big boss man / I need a man / Long tall
Sally / Rockin' daddy.
VHS . . . . MMGV 004
MMG Video / Feb '88 / Terry Blood Dist.

Plainsong

DARK SIDE OF THE ROOM.
Tracks: Not Advised.
CD . . . . LICD 901247
Line / Dec '92 / C.M. Distribution / Grapevine
Distribution.

IN SEARCH OF AMELIA EARHART.
Tracks: For the second time / Yo yo man / Louise / Call
the tune / Diesel on my tail / Amelia Earhart's last flight
/ I'll fly away / True story of Amelia Earhart / Even the
guiding light / Side roads / Raider.
LP . . . . K 42120
Elektra / WEA.

ON AIR.
Tracks: Not Advised.
CD . . . . BOJCD 005
Band Of Joy / Nov '92 / Grapevine Distribution.

Playboys

INVITATION TO DEATH.
Tracks: Not Advised.
LP . . . . F 3008
Fury / Aug '89 / RTM / Pinnacle.

LIVE: PLAYBOYS.
Tracks: Not Advised.
LP . . . . BSS 170
Tank / Jun '79.

MADE IN THE COUNTRY.
Tracks: Not Advised.
LP . . . . BSS 118
Tank / Jun '79.

Poacher

Warrington (Lancashire) - based band, rising to
fame during the late 1970s after winning ATV's
'New Faces' TV talent show in 1977. Their debut
single (released on Gene Autrey's Republic label) Darling featured life - time member Tim
Flaherty on lead vocals, and made No. 86 on
America's country charts in 1978. Since then
they've become a firm favourite around the UK
club & festival circuit, appearing on the main
stage at Wembley (more than once), along with
a 1978 visit to Tulsa, Oklahoma. Songs from
their repertoire include You're no angel , One
faded photograph and My uncle - the song that
won them first place in the aforementioned New
Faces show. (Maurice Hope)

DARLING.
Tracks: Darling / So afraid.
■ 7" . . . . RK 1009
RK / Aug '78.

ENGLAND FOREVER.
Tracks: England forever / Buttermarket.
■ 7" . . . . RK 1029
RK / Mar '80.

ONE FADED PHOTOGRAPH.
Tracks: One faded photograph / Bandido.
■ 7" . . . . RK 1016
RK / Feb '79.

ONE MORE FOOL.
Tracks: One more fool / Heartaches and promises.
■ 7" . . . . RK 1014
RK / Sep '78.

POACHER.
Tracks: Not Advised.
■ LP . . . . RKLP 5002
RK / Sep '78.

SUZY LOVES YOU NO MORE.
Tracks: Suzy loves you no more.
7" . . . . RITZ 054
Ritz / Nov '83 / Pinnacle / Midland Records.

YOU ARE NO ANGEL.
Tracks: You are no angel / Look up to me.
7" . . . . RITZ 030
Ritz / Nov '82 / Pinnacle / Midland Records.
7" . . . . RITZ 139
Ritz / Mar '86 / Pinnacle / Midland Records.

Poco

Poco was a country rock band formed in 1968 by
Buffalo Springfield alumni Richie Furay and Jim
Messina. They recruited steel guitarist Rusty
Young, who played on the last Springfield LP,
and he recommended drummer George Gran-
tham and bass player Randy Meisner, from
Colorado groups. The band was first called
Pogo, after a comic strip, but its creator sued.
They auditioned for Apple, then Epic. After their
first album Pickin' Up The Pieces in '69, Meisner
quit to join Rick Nelson and was replaced by
Tim Schmit. Messina left after Poco and the live
album Deliverin' The Goods (70-'71), to be replaced by ex-Illinois Speed Press singer-guitarist
Paul Cotton. This was the most creative line-up,
with both Cotton and Furay being prolific songwriters. But Furay left after From The Inside
('71) and A Good Feelin' To Know and Crazy
Eyes ('71-'73) to join ill-fated supergroup
Souther Hillman Furay. Young's steel guitar
helped replace Furay's voice in the vocal blend
and with more changes they kept selling in the
new, lucrative West Coast rock market. Legend
in '78, was their top seller in America but earlier
albums stayed the course as they descended
into Eagles-style FM radio music. They broke up
in 1982. Furay rejoined for a reunion album in
1984 on Atlantic, but it didn't sell. (Donald
Clarke)

CALL IT LOVE.
Tracks: Call it love / Lovin' you every minute / Who else
(CD single & 12" only).
■ 12" . . . . PT 49340
RCA / Oct '89.
■ 7" . . . . PB 49339
RCA / Oct '89.
■ CD Single . . . . PD 49340
RCA / Oct '89.

CANTAMOS.
Tracks: Sagebrush serenade / Susannah / High and dry
/ Western Waterloo / One horse blue / Bitter blue /
Another time around / Whatever happened to your
smile / All the ways.
■ LP . . . . EPC 80595
CBS / '78 / Sony.

CRAZY EYES.
Tracks: Blue water / Fool's gold / Here we go again /
Brass buttons / Right along, A / Crazy eyes / Magnolia /
Let's dance tonight.
■ LP . . . . EPC 65631
CBS / '78 / Sony.

DELIVERIN'.
Tracks: I guess you made it / C'mon / Kind woman /
Medley 1 (Hard luck; Child's claim to fame; Pickin' up
the pieces) / You'd better think twice / Man like me, A /
Medley 2 (Just in case it happens; Yes indeed; Grand
junction; Consequently so long) / Hear that music.
■ LP . . . . EPC 64204
CBS / '78 / Sony.

FROM THE INSIDE.
Tracks: Hoe down / Bad weather / What am I gonna do /
You are the one / Railroad days / From the inside / Do
you feel it too / Ol' forgiver / What if I should say I love
you / Just for me and you.
LP 64 543
Epic / '74 / Sony.

GHOST TOWN.
Tracks: Ghost town / How will you feel tonight / Shoot
for the moon / Cry no more / Midnight rodeo / Break of
hearts / Love's so cruel / Special care / When hearts
collide / High sierra.
■ LP . . . . K 50902
Atlantic / Nov '82.

GOOD FEELIN' TO KNOW, A.
Tracks: And settlin' down / Ride the country / I can see
everything / Go and say goodbye / Keeper of the fire /
Early times / Good feelin' to know, A / Restrain / Sweet
lovin'.

■ LP . . . . EPC 65126
CBS / '78 / Sony.

HEART OF THE NIGHT.
Tracks: Heart of the night / Last goodbye.
■ 7" . . . . MCA 509
MCA / Aug '79.

INDIAN SUMMER.
Tracks: Indian Summer / Find out in time.
■ 7" . . . . ABC 4178
ABC Records / Jun '77.

LEGACY.
Tracks: When it all began / Call it love / Nature of love,
The / What do people know / Nothin' to hide (Only on
cassette and CD.) / Look within / Rough edges / Who
else / Lovin' you every minute / If it wasn't for you /
Follow your dreams.
CD . . . . PD 90395
LP . . . . PL 90395
■ MC . . . . PK 90395
RCA / Nov '89.

LEGEND.
Tracks: Boomerang / Spellbound / Barbados / Little
darlin' / Crazy love / Love comes, love goes / Heart of
the night / Last goodbye / Legend.
MC . . . . CAB 5264
ABC Records / '78.
■ LP . . . . ABCL 5264
ABC Records / Jan '79.
■ CD . . . . DMCL 1879
MCA / Jun '88.
CD . . . . MCLD 19143
MC . . . . MCLC 19143
MCA / Jan '93 / BMG.

LIVE.
Tracks: Medley (Blue water; Fool's gold; Rocky moun-
tain breakdown) / Bad weather / Ride the country /
Angel / High and dry / Restrain / Good feelin' to know,
A.
■ LP . . . . EPC 80705
CBS / '78 / Sony.

PICKING UP THE PIECES.
Tracks: Foreword / What a day / Nobody's fool / Calico
lady / First love / Make me a smile / Short changed /
Pickin' up the pieces / Grand junction / Oh yeah / Just
in case it happens / Tomorrow / Consequently.
■ LP . . . . XED 161
Edsel / Feb '86 / Pinnacle.

ROSE OF CIMARRON.
Tracks: Stealaway / Just like me / Rose of Cimarron /
Company's coming / Slow poke / Too many nights too
long / When you come around / Starin' at the sky / All
alone together / Tulsa turnaround.
■ LP . . . . MCL 1638
MCA / Feb '82.
CD . . . . DMCL 1638
■ MC . . . . MCLC 1638
MCA / Feb '82.
CD . . . . MCLD 19015
■ MC . . . . MCLC 19015
MCA / Apr '92.

ROSE OF CIMARRON.
Tracks: Rose of Cimarron / Legend.
■ 7" . . . . MCA 589
MCA / May '80.

SEVEN.
Tracks: Drivin' wheel / Rocky mountain breakdown /
Just call my name / Skatin' / Faith in the families /
Krikkit's song / Angel / You've got your reasons.
■ LP . . . . EPC 80082
CBS / '78 / Sony.

SONGS OF RICHIE FURAY.
Tracks: Good feelin' to know / Hurry up / Don't let it
pass by / What if I should say I love you / Pickin' up the
pieces / Crazy eyes / Settin' down / C'mon / What am I
gonna do.
LP . . . . CBS 31781
MC 40 31781
CBS / Mar '80 / Sony.

UNDER THE GUN.
Tracks: Under the gun / Reputation.
■ 7" . . . . MCA 635
MCA / Aug '80.

VERY BEST OF POCO.
Tracks: You better think twice / Just for me and you /
Bad weather / Fool's gold / Good feelin' to know, A /
Another time around / Faith in the families / Medley
(Just in case it happens; Yes indeed; Grand junction;
Consequently so long) / Railroad days / Sweet lovin' /
Rocky mountain breakdown / Here we go again / C'mon
/ Right along, A / Man like me, A / And settlin' down /
Skatin' / Pickin' up the pieces.
LP . . . . EPC 88135
■ MC . . . . EPC 4088135
CBS / '78 / Sony.

Poole, Charlie

CHARLIE POOLE 1926-1930.
Tracks: Not Advised.
LP . . . . HLP 8005
Historical (USA) / Aug '90 / Wellard Dist.

Poor Man, Rich Man

POOR MAN, RICH MAN.
Tracks: Not Advised.
LP . . . . ROUNDER 1026
Rounder / Aug '88 / Projection / Roots Records / Swift /
C.M. Distribution / Topic Records / Jazz Music / Hot
Shot / A.D.A Distribution / Direct Distribution.

Poovey, Groovey Joe

LIFE'S AMBITION.
Tracks: Life's ambition.
7" 45 030
Rollin' Rock / Jun '80 / Pinnacle.

TWO SIDES, THE.
Tracks: Move around / Careful baby / Ten long fingers /
Thrill of love, The / Livin' alone / You may seek / I
dreamed about the blues / My life's ambition / Ole
Louella / Jamaica Jill / Silence baby / Two young
hearts / It's a lonely night / What have I got to lose'/.
LP . . . . SJLP 562
Sunjay / Oct '87 / USA Tell Tapes.

YESTERDAY AND TODAY.
Tracks: Ten long fingers / Sweet Louella / Careful baby
/ Move around / Part time hero / My life's ambition /
Silence baby / Nursery rock / Don't blame it on me /
Baby let's rock / Little Miss Linda / Cold margarita, A /
Last stroke of midnight / Dream, dream baby / To get
from there to here / Lost in the shuffle / All dressed up
for the blues / Boogie woogie weekend.
LP . . . . DJLP 2054
Dee-Jay Jamboree / May '86 / C.M. Distribution.
LP . . . . BB 2054
Buffalo Bop (Germany) / '88.

YOU ARE MY SUNSHINE.
Tracks: You are my sunshine / Lightning 'cross the sky.
■ 7" . . . . PT 497
President / Nov '81.

Posey, Sandy

Born 18.06.1947 in Jaspar, Alabama - raised in
West Memphis, Arkansas - session singer
during the early 1960's in Nashville and Memphis. had a pop/country career going in the mid-
sixties, ahieving pop hits in both US & UK
charts. her MGM singles hit Born a woman
(1966) and Single girl (1967), both charting at
No.12 in the US and the latter an all-time UK
best for her. Retired, briefly in 1968, returning in
1970 as a country singer/back-up singer on the
Nashville network-her gentle voice finding most
success with Bring him home safely (1971) and
Born to be with you (1978). Recordings for Columbia, Monument, Warner Bros and Audiograph. (Maurice Hope)

**BEST OF SANDY POSEY & SKEETER DAVIS
(Posey, Sandy & Skeeter Davis).**
Tracks: Not Advised.
LP . . . . GT 0005
Gusto (USA) / Mar '88.

**BEST OF SANDY POSEY & SKEETER DA-
VIS, VOL 2 (Posey, Sandy & Skeeter Davis).**
Tracks: Not Advised.
CD . . . . BTBCD 002
MC . . . . BTB 002
Sound Waves / Jul '93 / Taylors.

BORN A WOMAN.
Tracks: Not Advised.
■ LP . . . . MGM CS 8035
MGM (EMI) / Mar '67.

BORN A WOMAN.
Tracks: Born a woman.
■ 7" . . . . MGM 1321
MGM (EMI) / Sep '66.

SINGLE GIRL (OLD GOLD).
Tracks: Single girl / Born a woman.
7" . . . . OG 9584
Old Gold / Mar '86 / Pickwick Records.

SINGLE GIRL (RE-ISSUES).
Tracks: Single girl.
■ 7" . . . . MGM 1330
MGM (EMI) / Jan '67.
■ 7" 2006 533
MGM (Polydor) / Sep '75.

VERY BEST OF SANDY POSEY.
Tracks: Single girl, The / I take it back / What a woman
in love won't do / Just out of reach / It's all in the game /
Hey mister / Don't touch me / I've been loving you too
long / Born a woman / Sunglasses / Twelfth of never,
The / Satin pillows / Arms full of sin / Here comes my
baby back again / Blue is my best color / Are you never
coming home.
LP 2353 087
MC 3110 220
Polydor / Aug '84 / PolyGram.
■ MC . . . . SPEMC 60
MGM (Polydor) / Mar '84.
■ LP . . . . SPELP 60
MGM (Polydor) / Mar '84.
CD . . . . SOW 705

Sound Waves / Jul '93 / Taylors.
CD . . . . SOWCD 0705
MC . . . . SOW 905
Sound Waves / May '93 / Taylors.

WHAT A WOMAN IN LOVE WON'T DO.
Tracks: What a woman in love won't do.
■ 7" . . . . MGM 1335
MGM (EMI) / Apr '67.

Powell, Patsy

**FOR THE GOOD TIMES (Powell, Patsy &
The Goodtimers).**
Tracks: Not Advised.
LP . . . . FHR 066
Folk Heritage / Jul '82 / Terry Blood Dist.

THANK YOU FOR LOVING ME.
Tracks: Not Advised.
LP . . . . FHR 073
Folk Heritage / Jul '82 / Terry Blood Dist.

**THAT'S WHAT THE WORLD NEEDS (Powell,
Patsy & The Goodtimers).**
Tracks: Not Advised.
LP . . . . FHR 099
Folk Heritage / Jul '82 / Terry Blood Dist.

Pozo Seco Singers

Pop - folk Texas trio formed in 1964, consisting
of Susan Taylor, Lofton Kline and Don Williamson. They found modest top 40 successes in the
US pop charts with Columbia releases I can
make it without you and Look what you've done
(in 1965 and 1966). In all they recorded three
albums blending contemporary folk and pop,
resulting, during their five year stint with the
label, in a modest number of chart singles,
including the 1966 hit Time . On Kline's departure in 1969, when Columbia terminated their
contract, Taylor and Williamson continued as a
duo, recording an unissued album for Certon,
although some unfruitful singles emerged. After
a short break from the scene having returned to
Texas to work for his father-in-law in his furniture business, Williams was back in Nashville in
1972 writing some songs at Susan Taylor's request for her forthcoming album. (Maurice
Hope)

BEST OF THE POZO SECO SINGERS.
Tracks: It's all right / I can make it with you / Time /
Proper Mrs. Brown, The / If I were a carpenter /
Renegade, The / Guantanamera / Look what you've
done / Morning dew / Louisiana man / Spanish Harlem
Incident / Green, green grass of home / I believed it all
/ Keep on keeping on / I'll be gone / Good morning
today.
LP 31455
■ MC 4031455
CBS / '78 / Sony.

**POZO SECO SINGERS (Pozo Seco Singers
featuring Don Williams).**
Tracks: Take my hand for a while / There's never never
a time / Where do I go from here / On her way to be a
woman / Follow me back to Louisville / Spend some
time with me / There's always something there to
remind me / Ruby Tuesday / Storybook children /
Coming apart / Tears'.
■ CD . . . . PCD 812
Pickwick / '86.
LP . . . . SHM 3021
MC . . . . HSC 3021
Hallmark / '88 / Pickwick Records.

Preacher Jack

3000 BARROOMS LATER.
Tracks: Not Advised.
LP . . . . ROUNDER 3077
MC . . . . ROUNDER 3077C
Rounder / '88 / Projection / Roots Records / Swift / C.M.
Distribution / Topic Records / Jazz Music / Hot Shot /
A.D.A Distribution / Direct Distribution.
CD 8207672
Deram / Jan '89 / PolyGram.

BREAK UP.
Tracks: Break up / Preacher's boogie woogie.
■ 7" . . . . SON 2210
Sonet / Jun '80.

ROCK 'N' ROLL PREACHER.
Tracks: Going to the river / Preacher's boogie woogie /
Almost persuaded / Who will buy the wine / Can't
believe you wanna leave / All for the love of a girl /
Lovin' up a storm / Singing waterfall / Say you'll stay
until tomorrow / All by myself.
LP . . . . SNTF 836
Sonet / Jun '80 / Swift / C.M. Distribution / Roots
Records / Jazz Music / Sonet Records / Cadillac Music
/ Projection / Wellard Dist. / Hot Shot.
LP . . . . ROUNDER 3033
MC . . . . ROUNDER 3033C

Rounder / Aug '88 / Projection / Roots Records / Swift /
C.M. Distribution / Topic Records / Jazz Music / Hot
Shot / A.D.A Distribution / Direct Distribution.

Presley, Elvis

This American singer, guitarist and actor is
referred to all over the world as the King of
Rock'n'Roll, or simply the King. Although Bill
Haley was the first artist to reach No.1 in America and Britain with a rock'n'roll record and
although many rock historians would claim that
Chuck Berry was a greater and more influential
artist than Elvis, nothing had quite the same
impact upon popular music or youth culture as
the Presley explosion of 1956.He was born in
Tupelo, Mississippi in 1935 and made his first
public singing appearance in a State Fair talent
contest at the age of 10. He moved with his
family to Memphis, Tennessee at the age of 13.
Elvis' first record was cut in 1953 at Sun Studios, an important Memphis musical haven
owned by Sam Phillips - that first disc was an
acetate which he recorded for four dollars as a
gift to his mother. Presley began recording professionally for the Sun label in 1954.To most
rock'n'roll purists, the discs that were made for
Sam Phillips in 1954-55 were Elvis Presley's
finest work. That's Alright Mama, Mystery Train,
Blue Moon of Kentucky and I Forgot to Remember to Forget were exhilarating examples
of an innovative talent - here was a white lad
who sang like a black rhythm and blues vocalist
and yet also understood country and western.
These early records featured the vital accompa-
niment of guitarist Scotty Moore and string bassist Bill Black.In the wake of Haley's spectacular success with Rock Around The Clock, the
potential of the younger and better looking
Presley was obvious. He was bought from Sun
by the big RCA corporation and turned into a
giant international superstar almost immediately. By the end of 1956 Elvis had reached No.1
in America with Heartbreak Hotel, I Want You, I
Need You, I Love You, Don't Be Cruel, Hound
Dog and Love Me Tender. He had also collected
four Top 10 hits in Britain and starred in his first
movie Love Me Tender. Presley's music revolu-
tionised the charts and effectively ended the
recording careers of many conventional middle
of the road crooners; his highly suggestive
stage gyrations were so outrageous to older TV
viewers that the famous 'Ed Sullivan Show'
insisted that the young superstar be screened
from the waist up. Presley's music and image
emphasised the generation gap that was opening up during the mid-Fifties, adored by millions
of girls and idolised for his toughness by millions of young men, but spurned by millions of
parents.The Presley phenomenon continued
apace on both sides of the Atlantic during 1957
and, thanks to RCA's clever catalogue exploi-
tation, the hits kept coming during his Army
years from 1958 till 1960. When his military
service ended, he embarked upon a string of
records that appealed to audiences across a
broad age spectrum - in the gap between the
rock'n'roll revolution of the mid Fifties and the
forthcoming Beatles explosion, Elvis supplied
safe but worthy smashes like It's Now or Never,
Are You Lonesome Tonight, Can't Help Falling
In Love and Good Luck Charm.Unfortunately,
the obsession of manager Colonel Tom Parker
with money proved to be the source of Elvis'
musical downfall during the Sixties. Most of the
decade was totally wasted on an endless
stream of dreadful movies containing throwaw-
ay songs. It was a tribute to the Presley legend
that most of these substandard offerings managed to reach the Top 40 on both sides of the
Atlantic, but few cracked the Top 10. The trashy
films finally stopped in the late Sixties, where-
upon Elvis returned to musical and commercial
form with smash hits like In The Ghetto, Suspicious Minds and The Wonder of You.The re-
surgance was short lived, however, and the
Seventies yielded only sporadic greats such as
Burning Love and Promised Land. Presley grew
increasingly overweight, unpredictable and de-
pendent on drugs. The bad habits and un-
healthy living that plagued him in his later years
have subsequently been the subject of numerous sensational books and analyses, but the
tragedy of the 42 year old Presley's death in
August 1977 cannot take away his importance to
rock music. (Bob Macdonald)

'56 - IN THE BEGINNING.
Tracks: Not Advised.
VHS . . . . VVD 238
Virgin Vision / Nov '87 / Gold & Sons / Terry Blood Dist.
VHS 0837883
4 Front / '91 / PolyGram Video.

'56 SESSIONS VOL.1, THE.
Tracks: I got a woman / Heartbreak hotel / Money
honey / I'm counting on you / I was the one / Blue
suede shoes / My baby left me / One-sided love affair /
I'm so glad you're mine / I'm gonna sit right down and
cry over you / Tutti frutti / Lawdy Miss Clawdy / Shake
rattle and roll / I want you I need you I love you / Hound
dog / Don't be cruel.
LP . . . . PL 42101
■ MC . . . . PK 42101
RCA / '78.
LP . . . . RCALP 3025

MC . . . . RCAK 3025
RCA / '81 / BMG.

'56 SESSIONS VOL.2, THE.
Tracks: Anyway you want me / Love me tender / We're gonna move / Poor boy / Let me / Playing for keeps / Love me / Paralysed / How do you think I feel? / How's the world treating you? / When my blue moon turns to gold again / Long tall Sally / Old Shep / Too much / Any place is paradise / Ready Teddy / First in line / Rip it up.
LP. . . . . PL 42102
■ MC . . . . PK 42102
RCA / '79.
LP. . . . . RCALP 3030
MC . . . . RCAK 3030
RCA / '81 / BMG.

1935-1977.
Tracks: Not Advised.
MC . . . . VCA 044
VFM Cassettes / Jan '85 / VFM Children's Entertainment Ltd. / Midland Records / Morley Audio Services.

1968 COMEBACK SPECIAL.
Tracks: Trouble / Guitar man / Lawdy Miss Clawdy / Baby / Heartbreak hotel / Hound dog / All shook up / Can't help falling in love / Jailhouse rock / Don't be cruel (to a heart that's true) / Love me tender / Are you lonesome tonight / Where could I go but to the Lord / Up above my head / I found the light / Saved / That's all right / Tiger man / Trying to get to you / One night with you / Memories / Nothingville / Let yourself go / Big boss man / It hurts me / Little Egypt / If I can dream.
BETA . . . . VVD 082 B
VHS. . . . . VVD 082
Virgin Vision / Jan '86 / Gold & Sons / Terry Blood Dist.
Laser Disc. 74321106626
BMG / Aug '92 / BMG.

20 GOLDEN HITS: ELVIS PRESLEY (VOL. 3).
Tracks: Not Advised.
MC 40165
Astan (USA) / Jun '86.

20 GREATEST HITS: ELVIS PRESLEY (VOL.1).
Tracks: My baby left me / Heartbreak hotel / Blue suede shoes / Hound dog / Love me tender / Got a lot of livin' to do / Teddy bear / Party / All shook up / Old Shep / Don't / Hard headed woman / King Creole / Jailhouse rock / Big hunk o' love, A / I got stung / One night / Fool such as I, A / I need your love tonight / Stuck on you.
■ LP. . . . . INTS 5115
RCA International / '82.
MC . . . . NK 89024
RCA International / '84 / BMG.
■ LP. . . . . NL 89024
RCA International / '84.

20 GREATEST HITS: ELVIS PRESLEY (VOL.2).
Tracks: Fever / It's now or never / Are you lonesome tonight / Wooden heart / Surrender / His latest flame / Wild in the country / There's always me / Rock a hula baby / Can't help falling in love / Good luck charm / She's not you / Return to sender / Devil in disguise / Crying in the chapel / Guitar man / In the ghetto / Suspicious minds / There goes my everything / Don't cry daddy.
■ LP. . . . . INTS 5116
RCA International / '82.
MC . . . . NK 89168
RCA International / '84 / BMG.
■ LP. . . . . NL 89168
RCA International / '84.

32 FILM HITS VOL. 1.
Tracks: Fun in Acapulco / Mexico / Marguerita / Bossa nova baby / Blue Hawaii / Can't help falling in love / Rock a hula baby / Ku-u-i-po / King Creole / Hard headed woman / Trouble / Dixieland rock / Frankie and Johnny / Please don't stop loving me / Easy come, easy go / Sing you children / Tonight's alright for love / Frankfurt special / Wooden heart / G.I. blues / Blue suede shoes / Doin' the best I can / Dog's life / Charro / Roustabout / Little Egypt / Poison ivy league / Girls, girls, girls / Where do you come from / Return to sender / Follow that dream / Angel.
Double LP . . . . NL 89388
MC Set. . . . . NK 89388
RCA(Special Imports Service) / Aug '84 / BMG.
■ CD Set . . . . PD 89388
RCA(Special Imports Service) / Oct '84.

32 FILM HITS VOL. 2.
Tracks: Jailhouse rock / Young and beautiful / Baby I don't care / They remind me too much of you / Beyond the bend / Relax / One broken heart for sale / I'm falling in love tonight / No more / Island of love / Moonlight swim.
Double LP . . . . NL 89550
MC Set. . . . . NK 89550
RCA(Special Imports Service) / Jul '85 / BMG.
■ CD . . . . PD 89550
RCA(Special Imports Service) / Jul '85.

50,000,000 ELVIS FANS CAN'T BE WRONG.
Tracks: Big hunk o' love, A / My wish came true / Fool such as I, A / I need your love tonight / Don't / I beg of you / Santa bring my baby back to me / Party / Paralysed / One night / I got stung / King Creole / Wear my ring around your neck / Doncha' think it's time.
LP. . . . . NL 89429
RCA / Nov '84 / BMG.
CD . . . . ND 89429
RCA / May '90 / BMG.
MC . . . . NK 89429
RCA / Apr '92 / BMG.

50TH ANNIVERSARY.
Tracks: Not Advised.
12" . . . . RCAT 459
RCA International / Jan '85 / BMG.

AIN'T THAT LOVING YOU BABY.
Tracks: Ain't that loving you baby.
■ 7" . . . . RCA 1422
RCA / Oct '64.

AIN'T THAT LOVING YOU BABY.
Tracks: Ain't that loving you baby / Bossa nova baby / Rock a hula (Extra track on 12" version).
12" . . . . PT 49746
7" . . . . PB 49745
RCA / Mar '87 / BMG.

ALL SHOOK UP.
Tracks: All shook up / That's when your heartaches begin.
■ 7" . . . . POP 359
H.M.V. / '57.

ALL SHOOK UP.
Tracks: All shook up / Heartbreak hotel.
7" . . . . RCA 2694
RCA / '77 / BMG.

ALL TIME GREATEST HITS, THE.
Tracks: Heartbreak hotel / Blue suede shoes / Hound dog / Love me tender / Too much / All shook up / Teddy bear / Paralysed / Party / Jailhouse rock / Don't / Wear my ring around your neck / Hard headed woman / King Creole / One night / Fool such as I, A / Big hunk o' love, A / Stuck on you / Girl of my best friend / It's now or never / Are you lonesome tonight? / Wooden heart / Surrender / His latest flame / Can't help falling in love / Good luck charm / She's not you / Return to sender / Devil in disguise / Crying in the chapel / Love letters / If I can dream / In the ghetto / Suspicious minds / Don't cry Daddy / Wonder of you, The / I just can't help believing / American trilogy / Burning love / Always on my mind / My boy / Suspicion / Moody blue / Way down / It's only love.
Double LP . . . . PL 90100
MC Set . . . . PK 90100
RCA / Aug '87 / BMG.
CD . . . . PD 90100
RCA / '88 / BMG.

ALMOST IN LOVE.
Tracks: Not Advised.
■ LP. . . . . INTS 1206
RCA International / Sep '71.

ALOHA FROM HAWAII.
Tracks: What now my love / Fever / Welcome to my world / Suspicious minds / See see rider / Burning love / Hound dog / I'll remember you / Long tall Sally / Whole lotta shakin' goin' on / American trilogy / Big hunk o' love, A / Can't help falling in love / Something / You gave me a mountain / Steamroller blues / My way / Love me / Johnny B. Goode / It's over / Blue suede shoes / I'm so lonesome I could cry / I can't stop loving you.
LP. . . . . DPS 2040
■ MC . . . . PK 5144
RCA / Feb '73.
■ LP. . . . . PL 82642
RCA / Nov '85.
■ CD . . . . PD 82642
RCA / Nov '85.

ALOHA FROM HAWAII.
Tracks: Not Advised.
BETA . . . . VVD 092 B
VHS. . . . . VVD 092
Virgin Vision / Feb '86 / Gold & Sons / Terry Blood Dist.
Laser Disc 74321106616
BMG / Aug '92 / BMG.

ALTERNATIVE ALOHA.
Tracks: Also sprach Zarathustra (Introduction) / See see rider / Burning love / Something / You gave me a mountain / Steamroller blues / My way / It's over / Blue suede shoes / I'm so lonesome I could cry / What now my love / Fever / Welcome to my world / Suspicious minds / I'll remember you / American trilogy / Big hunk o' love, A / Can't help falling in love / Blue Hawaii / Hound dog / Hawaiian wedding song / Ku-u-i-po (Available on Compact Disc only).
CD . . . . PD 86985
LP. . . . . PL 86985
MC . . . . PK 86985
RCA / Aug '88 / BMG.

ALWAYS ON MY MIND.
Tracks: Separate ways / Don't cry daddy / My boy / I miss you / Bitter they are / Solitaire / Hurt / Pieces of my life / It's midnight / I've lost you / Unchained melody / You gave me a mountain / Burning love / Always on my mind.
LP. . . . . PL 85430
RCA / Jul '85 / BMG.
■ MC . . . . PK 85430
RCA / Jul '85.
CD . . . . PD 85430
RCA / '86 / BMG.

ALWAYS ON MY MIND.
Tracks: Always on my mind / Tomorrow night.
12" . . . . PT 49944
■ 7" . . . . PB 49943
RCA / '85.

ALWAYS ON MY MIND.
Tracks: Always on my mind.
■ 7" . . . . RCA 2304
RCA / '72.

ALWAYS ON MY MIND (2).
Tracks: Not Advised.
CD 297 064
MC 497 064
Ariola Express / Jun '92.

ALWAYS ON MY MIND (OLD GOLD).
Tracks: Always on my mind / Burning love.
7" . . . . OG 9744
Old Gold / Jan '88 / Pickwick Records.

AMERICAN TRILOGY.
Tracks: American trilogy / Suspicious minds.
■ 7" . . . . GOLD 506
RCA Golden Grooves / '81.

AMERICAN TRILOGY (OLD GOLD).
Tracks: American trilogy / Until it's time for you to go.
7" . . . . OG 9624
Old Gold / Jun '88 / Pickwick Records.

AMERICAN TRILOGY, AN.
Tracks: American trilogy.
■ 7" . . . . RCA 2229
RCA / Jun '72.

ARE YOU LONESOME TONIGHT.
Tracks: Are you lonesome tonight / Girl of my best friend / Rock a hula baby / There's always me / Wild in the country / Fool such as I, A / Can't help falling in love / Hard headed woman / Don't cry daddy / Blue Hawaii / Wooden heart / Surrender.
LP. . . . . CDS 1207
■ MC . . . . CAM 1207
RCA/Camden / Mar '82.

ARE YOU LONESOME TONIGHT.
Tracks: Are you lonesome tonight / From a jack to a king.
■ 7" . . . . RCA 2699
RCA / '79.
■ 7" . . . . RCA 196
RCA / '82.

ARE YOU LONESOME TONIGHT.
Tracks: Are you lonesome tonight / I gotta know.
■ 7" . . . . RCA 1216
RCA / Jan '61.

ARE YOU LONESOME TONIGHT ('LAUGHING' VERSION).
Tracks: Are you lonesome tonight / Reconsider baby / Runaway / Baby what you want me to do.
7" . . . . PB 49178
RCA / Aug '91 / BMG.
12" . . . . PT 49178
■ CD Single . . . . PD 49178
RCA / Aug '91.

ARE YOU LONESOME TONIGHT (OLD GOLD).
Tracks: Are you lonesome tonight / Wooden heart.
7" . . . . OG 9702
Old Gold / Apr '87 / Pickwick Records.

AT THE WORLD'S FAIR/FUN IN ACAPULCO.
Tracks: Beyond the bend / Relax / Take me to the fair / They remind me too much of you / One broken heart for sale (Film version) / I'm falling in love tonight / Cotton candy land / World of our own, A / How would you like to be / Happy ending / One broken heart for sale / Fun in Acapulco / Vino, dinero y amor / Mexico / El toro / Marguerita / Bullfighter was a lady, The / No room to rhumba in a sports car / I think I'm gonna like it here / Bossa nova baby / You can't say no in Acapulco / Guadalajara.
CD 74321 13431-2
MC 74321 13431-4
RCA / Mar '93 / BMG.

BABY I DON'T CARE.
Tracks: Baby I don't care / True love.
12" . . . . RCAT 332
7" . . . . RCA 332
■ 7" P.Disc . . . . RCAP 332
RCA / Apr '83 / BMG.

BACK IN MEMPHIS.
Tracks: Inherit the wind / This is the story / Stranger in my own home town / Little bit of green, A / And the grass won't pay no mind / Do you know who I am / From a jack to a king / Fair's moving on, The / You'll think of me / Without love (there is nothing).
CD . . . . ND 90599
MC . . . . NK 90599
RCA / Oct '91 / BMG.

BALLADS.
Tracks: Can't help falling in love / In the ghetto / Moody blues / Suspicion / Are you lonesome tonight / Girl of my best friend / Don't / Wooden heart / It's now or never / Wonder of you, The / There goes my everything / Crying in the chapel / My boy / It's only me / Don't cry

daddy / Hawaiian wedding song / Suspicious minds / My way.
MC . . . . **STAC 2264**
Telstar/Ronco / Oct '85 / BMG.
■ LP . . . . **STAR 2264**
Telstar/Ronco / Oct '85.
CD . . . . **TCD 2264**
Telstar/Ronco / '86 / BMG.

BEST OF ELVIS.
Tracks: Not Advised.
LP **130 250**
RCA (Germany) / Apr '84 / BMG.

BEST OF ELVIS, THE.
Tracks: Heartbreak hotel / I don't care if the sun don't shine / Blue moon / Tutti frutti / All shook up / Hound dog / Too much / Anyway you want me / Don't be cruel / Playing for keeps.
■ LP . . . . **DLP 1159**
H.M.V. / '57.

BIG HUNK O LOVE, A.
Tracks: Big hunk o' love, A.
■ 7" . . . . **RCA 1136**
RCA / Jul '59.

BLUE CHRISTMAS.
Tracks: Blue Christmas.
■ 7" . . . . **RCA 1430**
RCA / Dec '64.

BLUE HAWAII (1961 Film Soundtrack).
Tracks: Blue Hawaii / Almost always true / Aloha-oe / No more / Can't help falling in love / Rock a hula baby / Moonlight swim / Ku-u-i-po / Ito eats / Slicin' sand / Hawaiian sunset / Beach boy blues / Island of love / Hawaiian wedding song.
LP . . . . **RD 27238**
RCA / Dec '61 / BMG.
LP . . . . **SF 8145**
RCA / Sep '77 / BMG.
■ MC . . . . **PK 11561**
RCA / Sep '77.
LP . . . . **NL 83683**
■ MC . . . . **NK 83683**
RCA International / '84.
CD . . . . **ND 83683**
RCA / Oct '87 / BMG.

BLUE MOON.
Tracks: Blue moon / I don't care if the sun don't shine.
■ 7" . . . . **POP 272**
H.M.V. / '56.

BLUE MOON (OLD GOLD).
Tracks: Blue moon / I don't care if the sun don't shine.
7" . . . . **OG 9620**
Old Gold / Oct '86 / Pickwick Records.

BLUE RHYTHMS.
Tracks: Trouble / Reconsider baby / Mess of blues, A / Give me the right / Such a night / When it rains it really pours / Trying to get to you / Like a baby / Mean woman blues / Ain't that loving you baby / One night / Little sister / Big boss man / Baby what you want me to do / Stuck on you / Tomorrow night / It feels so right.
LP . . . . **EPC 1000**
MC . . . . **EPK 1000**
Premier (Sony) / '84 / Sony / Pinnacle.

BLUE RHYTHMS (DOUBLE).
Tracks: Trouble / Reconsider baby / Mess of blues, A / Give me the right / Such a night / When it rains it really pours / Trying to get to you / Like a baby / I want to be free / Mean woman blues / Ain't that loving you baby / One night / Little sister / So glad you're mine / Big boss man / I want you with me / Baby what you want me to do / Santa Claus is back in town / Stuck on you / I feel so bad / What'd I say / Tomorrow night / It feels so right / Merry Christmas, baby.
Double LP . . . . **PPD 2001**
MC . . . . **PPK 2001**
Premier (Sony) / Feb '88 / Sony / Pinnacle.

BLUE RIVER.
Tracks: Blue river.
■ 7" . . . . **RCA 1504**
RCA / Dec '66.

BLUE SUEDE SHOES.
Tracks: Blue suede shoes.
MC **40169**
Astan (USA) / Jun '86.

BLUE SUEDE SHOES.
Tracks: Blue suede shoes / Tutti frutti.
7" . . . . **POP 213**
■ 78 rpm **7M 405**
H.M.V. / '56.

BOSSA NOVA BABY.
Tracks: Bossa nova baby / Witchcraft.
■ 7" . . . . **RCA 1374**
RCA / Oct '63.

BURNING LOVE.
Tracks: Burning love.
■ 7" . . . . **RCA 2267**
RCA / Sep '72.

C'MON EVERYBODY.
Tracks: Not Advised.
■ LP . . . . **INTS 1286**
RCA International / Aug '71.

CALIFORNIA HOLIDAY (Film Soundtrack).
Tracks: Stop look and listen / Adam and evil / All that I am / Never say yes / Am I ready / Beach shack / Spinout / Smorgasbord / I'll be back / Tomorrow is a long time / Down in the valley / I'll remember you.
LP . . . . **RD 7820**
RCA / Nov '66 / BMG.
LP . . . . **NL 82560**
RCA / '80 / BMG.
■ LP . . . . **INTS 5038**
RCA International / '80.
■ MC . . . . **INTK 5038**
RCA International / Aug '80.

CAN'T HELP FALLING IN LOVE & OTHER GREAT MOVIE HITS.
Tracks: Can't help falling in love / Rock a hula baby / Follow that dream / What a wonderful life / Easy come, easy go / Rubberneckin' / One broken heart for sale / Girls, girls, girls / G.I. blues / Roustabout / Frankie and Johnny / Charro / I got lucky / Home is where the heart is.
LP . . . . **CDS 1210**
■ MC . . . . **CAM 1210**
RCA/Camden / Apr '83.

CAN'T HELP FALLING IN LOVE (OLD GOLD).
Tracks: Can't help falling in love / Rock a hula baby.
7" . . . . **OG 9754**
Old Gold / Jan '88 / Pickwick Records.

CLAMBAKE (Film Soundtrack).
Tracks: Clambake / Who needs money / House that has everything / Confidence / Hey hey hey / You don't know me / Girl I never loved, The / Guitar man / How can you lose what you never had / Big boss man / Singing trees / Just call me lonesome.
LP . . . . **SF 7917**
RCA / Apr '68 / BMG.
■ LP . . . . **INTS 5040**
RCA International / Oct '80.
LP . . . . **NL 82565**
MC . . . . **NK 82565**
RCA International / '84 / BMG.

CLEAN UP YOUR OWN BACK YARD.
Tracks: Clean up your own backyard.
■ 7" . . . . **RCA 1869**
RCA / Sep '69.

COLLECTION: ELVIS PRESLEY VOL.1.
Tracks: That's alright / Heartbreak hotel / I was the one / Blue suede shoes / My baby left me / Hound dog / Don't be cruel / Peace in the valley / One night / Loving you / I want you I need you I love you / Love me tender / Love me / All shook up / That's when your heartaches begin.
CD . . . . **PD 89248**
RCA / '86 / BMG.

COLLECTION: ELVIS PRESLEY VOL.2.
Tracks: Teddy bear / Party / Jailhouse rock / Don't / Wear my ring around your neck / I got stung / It's now or never / Stuck on you / Girl of my best friend / Mess of blues [illegible] hunk o' love.
CD . . . . **PD 89249**
RCA / '86 / BMG.

COLLECTION: ELVIS PRESLEY VOL.3.
Tracks: Wooden heart / Surrender / Wild in the country / Can't help falling in love / Rock a hula baby / His latest flame / Follow that dream / Good luck charm / She's not you / Return to sender.
CD . . . . **PD 89472**
RCA / Feb '85 / BMG.

COLLECTION: ELVIS PRESLEY VOL.4.
Tracks: Guitar man / US male / If I can dream / In the ghetto / Suspicious minds / Don't cry daddy / Wonder of you, The / American trilogy / Burning love / Always on my mind / It's only love.
CD . . . . **PD 89473**
RCA / Feb '85 / BMG.

COLLECTOR'S GOLD.
Tracks: G.I blues / Pocketful of rainbows / Big boots / Black star / Summer kisses, winter tears / I slipped, I stumbled, I fell / Lonely man / What a wonderful life / Whistling tune, A / Beyond the bend / One broken heart for sale / You're the boss / Roustabout / Girl happy / So close, yet so far / Stop, look and listen / Am I ready / How can you lose what you never had / Like a baby / There's always me / I want you with me / Gently / Give me the right / I met her today / Night rider / Just tell her Jim said hello / Ask me / Memphis, Tennessee / Love me tonight / Witchcraft / Come what may (you are mine) / Love letters / Going home / Blue suede shoes / I got a woman / Heartbreak hotel / Love me tender / Baby, what you want me to do / Runaway / Surrender/Are you lonesome tonight / Rubber neckin' / Memories / Introduction by Elvis Presley / Jailhouse rock/Don't be cruel / Inherit the wind/This is the story / Mystery train / Tiger man / Funny how time slips away / Loving you/Reconsider baby / What I'd say.
CD Set . . . . **PD 90574**
LP Set . . . . **PL 90574**
MC Set . . . . **PK 90574**
RCA / Aug '91 / BMG.

COLLECTOR'S GOLD (EP).
Tracks: Not Advised.
■ EP . . . . **RCX 3**
RCA / Oct '82 / BMG.

COMPLETE BONUS SONGS.
Tracks: I slipped, I stumbled, I fell / Love me tonight / Slowly but surely / Echoes of love / Long lonely highway / You'll be gone / Animal instinct / Wisdom of the ages / Sand castles / Tomorrow is a long time / Down in the alley / I'll remember you / It won't be long / Never ending / Blue river / What now, what next, where to? / Guitar man / Big boss man.
Double LP . . . . **NL 45180**
MC . . . . **NK 45180**
RCA(Special Imports Service) / Aug '84 / BMG.

COMPLETE SINGLES (11 album box set).
Tracks: Not Advised.
LP Set . . . . **RPL 2504 14**
RCA (Japan) / Sep '85 / WRD.

COMPLETE SUN SESSIONS, THE.
Tracks: That's alright mama / Blue moon of Kentucky / Good rockin' tonight / I don't care if the sun don't shine / Milkcow blues boogie / You're a heartbreaker / Baby, let's play house / Im left you're right she's gone / Mystery train / I forgot to remember to forget / I love you because / Blue moon / Tomorrow's night / I'll never let you go / Just because / Trying to get to you / Harbour lights / When it rains, it really pours.
MC Set . . . . **NK 89107**
RCA / Oct '83 / BMG.
■ Double LP . . . . **NL 89107**
RCA / Oct '83.
CD . . . . **PD 86414**
RCA / Jul '87 / BMG.
■ Double LP . . . . **PL 86414**
RCA / Jul '87.
■ MC Set . . . . **PK 86414**
RCA / Jul '87.
DCC **07863564145**
RCA / Jan '93 / BMG.

CONFIDENTIALLY ELVIS.
Tracks: Not Advised.
Double LP . . . . **ARAD 1008**
MC . . . . **ARADC 1008**
Arena / Feb '87.

CRYING IN THE CHAPEL.
Tracks: Crying in the chapel.
■ 7" . . . . **RCA 1455**
RCA / May '65.

CRYING IN THE CHAPEL.
Tracks: Crying in the chapel / I believe.
■ 7" . . . . **RCA 2708**
RCA / '79.

DATE WITH ELVIS, A.
Tracks: Blue moon of Kentucky / Young and beautiful / Baby I don't care / Milk cow blue boogie / Baby let's play house / Good rockin' tonight / Is it so strange / I forgot to remember to forget.
LP . . . . **RD 27128**
RCA / Aug '59 / BMG.
■ LP . . . . **INTS 5032**
RCA International / Oct '80.
LP . . . . **NL 89097**
■ MC . . . . **NK 89097**
RCA / '84.
CD . . . . **ND 90360**
RCA / Sep '89 / BMG.
■ LP . . . . **NL 90360**
RCA / Sep '89.
MC . . . . **NK 90360**
RCA / Apr '92 / BMG.

DEVIL IN DISGUISE.
Tracks: Devil in disguise.
■ 7" . . . . **RCA 1355**
RCA / Jul '63.

DEVIL IN DISGUISE.
Tracks: Devil in disguise / Please don't drag that string around.
■ 7" . . . . **RCA 2707**
RCA / '79.

DIAMOND SERIES: ELVIS PRESLEY.
Tracks: Return to sender / Girls. girls, girls / Because of love / Down by the riverside / When the saints go marching in / Please don't stop loving me / Frankie and Johnny / Girl happy / Puppet on a string / Do not disturb / Do the clam / One broken heart for sale / I'm falling in love tonight / Bossa nova baby / Guadalajara / All that I am / Tomorrow is a long time.
■ CD . . . . **CD 90112**
Diamond Series / Apr '88.

DO THE CLAM.
Tracks: Do the clam / You'll be gone.
■ 7" . . . . **RCA 1443**
RCA / Mar '65.

DON'T.
Tracks: Don't.
■ 7" . . . . **RCA 1043**
RCA / Feb '58.

DON'T (OLD GOLD).
Tracks: Don't / Wear my ring around your neck.
7" . . . . **OG 9752**
Old Gold / Jan '88 / Pickwick Records.

DON'T BE CRUEL.
Tracks: Don't be cruel / Hound dog.
7" . . . . **PB 9265**
RCA / Jun '78 / BMG.

■ DELETED

DON'T BE CRUEL.
Tracks: Don't be cruel / All shook up / Jailhouse rock / I need your love tonight.
■ 7" **74321110777**
RCA / Aug '92.
■ **CD Single** **74321110612**
RCA / Aug '92.
■ **MC Single** **74321110774**
RCA / Aug '92.

DON'T CRY DADDY.
Tracks: Don't cry daddy.
■ 7" . . . . **RCA 1916**
RCA / Feb '70.

DOUBLE DYNAMITE COLLECTION.
Tracks: Old Shep / Fools fall in love / Burning love / Mama / Follow that dream / I'll be there / Flaming star / Tender feeling / Yellow rose of Texas / You'll never walk alone / Easy come easy go / Frankie and Johnny / US male / Big boss man / Charro / Separate ways / Rubberneckin' / It's a matter of time / If you think I don't need you / Peace in the valley.
Double LP . . . . **PDA 057**
MC Set . . . . **PDC 057**
Pickwick / Jan '80 / Pickwick Records.

DOUBLE DYNAMITE VOL.1.
Tracks: Old Shep / Fools fall in love / Burning love / Mama / Follow that dream / I'll be there / Flaming star / Tender feeling / Yellow rose of Texas / You'll never walk alone.
LP . . . . **CDS 1182**
MC . . . . **CAM 494**
RCA/Camden / Jan '80 / BMG / Arabesque Ltd.

DOUBLE DYNAMITE VOL.2.
Tracks: Easy come, easy go / Frankie and Johnny / US male / Big boss man / Charro / Separate ways / Rubberneckin' / It's a matter of time / If you think I don't need you / Peace in the valley.
LP . . . . **CDS 1188**
MC . . . . **CAM 499**
RCA/Camden / Jan '80 / BMG / Arabesque Ltd.

DOUBLE TROUBLE (Film soundtrack).
Tracks: Double trouble / Baby, if you'll give me all your love / Could I fall in love / Long legged girl / City by night / Old McDonald / I love only one girl / There is so much world to see / It won't be long / Never ending / Blue river / What now, what next, where to.
■ **LP** . . . . **SF 7892**
RCA / Sep '67.
LP . . . . **NL 82564**
■ **LP** . . . . **INTS 5039**
RCA International / Oct '80.

EARLY YEARS.
Tracks: Not Advised.
LP . . . . **R&C 1004**
Rock & Country / Oct '88 / Swift.

EASY COME EASY GO.
Tracks: C'mon everybody / Santa Lucia / Guadalajara / Little less conversation, A / Long legged girl with the short dress on.
LP . . . . **CDS 1146**
MC . . . . **CAM 1146**
RCA/Camden / '75 / BMG / Arabesque Ltd.

ELVIS.
Tracks: That's all right / Lawdy Miss Clawdy / Mystery train / Playing for keeps / Poor boy / Money honey / I'm counting on you / My baby left me / I was the one / Shake, rattle and roll / I'm left, you're right / You're a heartbreaker / Tryin' to get to you / Blue suede shoes.
MC . . . . **PK 11529**
RCA / Aug '71 / BMG.
LP . . . . **SF 8378**
RCA / Sep '73 / BMG.
LP . . . . **CDS 1201**
MC . . . . **CAM 1201**
RCA/Camden / Jan '81 / BMG / Arabesque Ltd.
LP **26.21008**
RCA (Germany) / '83 / BMG.

ELVIS (MEDLEY).
Tracks: Elvis (medley) / Blue suede shoes.
■ 7" . . . . **RCA 476**
RCA / Jan '85.

ELVIS - FROM THE HEART (His Greatest Love Songs).
Tracks: Wonder of you, The / I just can't help believin' / Always on my mind / You don't have to say you love me / Until it's time for you to go / Suspicious minds / There goes my everything / Girl of my best friend / It's now or never / Good luck charm / Love letters / Can't help falling in love / Suspicion / She's not you / Are you lonesome tonight? / Wooden heart / Love me tender / Don't / Loving you / (Now and then there's) A fool such as I (Not available on Vinyl format.) / Love me (Not availabe on Vinyl format.) / I want you, I need you, I love you (Not available on Vinyl format.) / It's only love (Not available on Vinyl format.) / Unchained melody (Not available on Vinyl format.).
CD . . . . **PD 90642**
LP . . . . **PL 90642**
MC . . . . **PK 90642**
RCA / Feb '92 / BMG.

ELVIS AARON PRESLEY.
Tracks: Jailhouse rock / Blue Christmas / My way / Follow that dream / Shoppin' around / Heartbreak hotel / Fool such as I / Love me / I got a woman / Such a night / One night / Money honey / Hound dog / Wonder of you / It's still here / See see rider / I'm leavin' / Rags to riches / It's only love / Polk salad Annie / Sweet Caroline / Kentucky rain / My babe.
■ **LP Set** . . . . **ELVIS 25**
RCA / Aug '80.

ELVIS EP COLLECTION NO.2.
Tracks: Not Advised.
■ **EP** . . . . **EP 2**
RCA / Oct '82 / BMG.

ELVIS FOR EVERYONE.
Tracks: Your cheatin' heart / Summer kisses, Winter tears / Finders keepers / In my way / Tomorrow night / Memphis Tennessee / For the millionth and the last time / Forget me never / Sound advise Santa Lucia / Met her today / When it rains it really pours.
LP . . . . **RD 7782**
RCA / Dec '65 / BMG.
LP . . . . **SF 8232**
RCA / Jun '72 / BMG.
LP . . . . **NL 84232**
■ **MC** . . . . **NK 84232**
RCA / '84.

ELVIS FOREVER - 96 HITS.
Tracks: My baby left me / Heartbreak hotel / Blue suede shoes / Hound dog / Love me tender / Got a lot of livin' to do / Teddy bear / All shook up / Don't / Hard headed woman / King Creole / Jailhouse rock / Big hunk o' love, A / I got stung / One night / Stuck on you / Fever / Are you lonesome tonight / Wooden heart / Surrender / Wild in the country / Rock a hula baby / Can't help falling in love / Good luck charm / Return to sender / Crying in the chapel / Guitar man / In the ghetto / Suspicious minds / There goes my everything / Don't be cruel / I want you, I need you, I love you / Too much / Loving you / Treat me nice / I beg of you / Ain't that loving you baby / Wear my ring around your neck / Such a night / Mess of blues, A / I gotta know / Kiss me quick / Little sister / No more / I feel so good / King of the whole wide world / (Such an) easy question / Bossa nova baby / Mexico / Witchcraft / What'd I say / Kissin' cousins / Viva Las Vegas / Ask me / It hurts me / I've lost you / I just can't help believing / Love letters / You don't have to say you love me / Wonder of you, The / Burning love / My way / Blue moon / Money honey / I got a woman / Tutti frutti / Long tall Sally / Blueberry Hill / Mean woman blues / Your cheatin' heart / Dixieland rock / Fool such as I, A / Lover doll / Doncha' think it's time / Make me know it / Fame and fortune / Girl of my best friend / Lonely man / Blue Hawaii / His latest flame / Anything that's part of you / Aloha-oe / Night rider / Suspicion / She's not you / Santa Lucia / (It's a) long lonely highway / Please don't drag that string around / Memphis Tennessee / Little Egypt / Do the clam / Indescribably blue / Gentle on my mind / Any day now.
MC Set . . . . **NK 89930**
RCA / Aug '87 / BMG.
■ **LP Set** . . . . **NL 89830**
RCA / Aug '87.

ELVIS FOREVER VOL.2.
Tracks: Don't be cruel / I want you, I need you, I love you / Too much / Loving you / Treat me nice / I beg of you / Ain't that loving you baby / Wear my ring around your neck / Such a night / Mess of blues, A / I gotta know / Kiss me quick / Little sister / No more (la paloma) / I feel so bad / King of the whole wide world / Easy question / Bossa nova baby / Mexico / Witchcraft / What'd I say / Kissin' cousins / Viva Las Vegas / Ask me / It hurts me / I've lost you / I just can't help believing / Love letters / You don't have to say you love me / Wonder of you, The / Burning love / My way.
Double LP . . . . **CL 42853**
RCA (Germany) / '83 / BMG.

ELVIS FOREVER VOLUME 4.
Tracks: Not Advised.
LP . . . . **NL 89870**
RCA (Germany) / Dec '86 / BMG.

ELVIS IN CONCERT.
Tracks: Elvis fans comment / Opening riff / 2001 / See see rider / That's alright / Are you lonesome tonight / You gave me a mountain / Jailhouse rock / How great thou art / I really don't want to know / Elvis introduces his father / Hurt.
Double LP . . . . **PL 82587**
MC Set . . . . **PK 82587**
RCA / Oct '77 / BMG.
CD **7432114693-2**
MC **7432114693-4**
RCA / Jul '93 / BMG.

ELVIS IN DEMAND.
Tracks: Suspicion / High heel sneakers / Got a lot of livin' to do / Have I told you lately that I love you / Please don't drag that string around / It's only love / Sound of your cry, The / Viva Las Vegas / Do not disturb / Tomorrow is a long time / It's a long lonely highway / Puppet on a string / First time ever I saw your face, The / Summer kisses and winter tears / It hurts me / Let it be me.
LP . . . . **PL 42003**
RCA / Feb '77 / BMG.
■ **MC** . . . . **PK 42003**
RCA / Feb '77.
LP . . . . **RCALP 3018**
MC . . . . **RCAK 3018**
RCA / Sep '81 / BMG.

ELVIS IN GERMANY.
Tracks: Wooden heart / I love only one girl / C'mon everybody / Frankfurt special / Tonights alright for love / Today / Tomorrow and forever / G.I. blues / Tonight is so right for love / Five sleepy heads / Fool / Elvis sails.
LP . . . . **NL 43730**
MC . . . . **NK 43730**
RCA(Special Imports Service) / Aug '84 / BMG.

ELVIS IN HOLLYWOOD.
Tracks: Jailhouse rock / Rock a hula baby / G.I. blues / Kissin' cousins / Wild in the country / King Creole / Blue Hawaii / Fun in Acapulco / Follow that dream / Girls girls girls / Viva Las Vegas / Bossa nova baby / Flaming star / Girl happy / Frankie and Johnny / Roustabout / Spinout / Double trouble / Charro / They remind me too much of you.
LP . . . . **CBR 1014**
MC . . . . **KCBR 1014**
Premier (Sony) / '84 / Sony / Pinnacle.
CD Set **74321 14765-39**
BMG / Aug '93 / BMG.

ELVIS IN HOLLYWOOD.
Tracks: Not Advised.
Laser Disc **74321 13988-62**
VHS **74321 13988-31**
BMG Video / Aug '93 / BMG.

ELVIS IN NASHVILLE 1956-1971.
Tracks: I got a woman / Big hunk o' love, A / Working on the building / Judy / Anything that's part of you / Night rider / Where no one stands alone / Just call me lonesome / Guitar man / Little cabin home on the hill / It's your baby, you rock it / Early mornin' rain / It's still here / I, John.
CD **84682**
RCA (USA) / Sep '88 / RCA (Imports).

ELVIS IN PERSON.
Tracks: Blue suede shoes / Johnny B Goode / All shook up / Are you lonesome tonight / Hound dog / I can't stop loving you / My babe / Mystery train tiger man / Words / In the ghetto / Suspicious minds / Can't help falling in love.
CD . . . . **ND 83892**
MC . . . . **NK 83892**
RCA / Oct '91 / BMG.

ELVIS IS BACK.
Tracks: Make me know it / Fever / Girl of my best friend / I will be home again / Dirty dirty feeling / Thrill of your love, The / Soldier boy / Such a night / It feels so right / Girl next door, The / Like a baby / Reconsider baby.
LP . . . . **RD 27171**
RCA / Jun '60 / BMG.
LP . . . . **SF 5060**
■ **MC** . . . . **PK 11532**
RCA / '79.
■ **LP** . . . . **NL 89013**
RCA / '84.
CD . . . . **ND 89013**
RCA / Feb '89 / BMG.
MC . . . . **NK 89013**
RCA / Apr '92 / BMG.

ELVIS LIVE AT MADISON SQUARE GARDEN.
Tracks: 2001 / That's alright mama / Proud Mary / Never been to Spain / You don't have to say you love me / You've lost that lovin' feeling / Polk salad Annie / Love me / All shook up / Heartbreak hotel / Impossible dream, The / Hound dog / Suspicious minds / For the good times / American trilogy / Funny how time slips away / I can't stop loving you / Can't help falling in love / Why me Lord / How great thou art / Blueberry Hill / Can't stop loving you / Help me / Let me be there / My baby left me / Lawdy, Miss Clawdy / Closing - vamp.
LP . . . . **SF 8296**
MC . . . . **PK 2054**
RCA / '74 / BMG.
CD . . . . **ND 90663**
MC . . . . **NK 90663**
RCA / Apr '92 / BMG.

ELVIS LOVE SONGS.
Tracks: Not Advised.
LP . . . . **NE 1062**
MC . . . . **CE 2062**
K-Tel / Oct '79 / I & B Records / C.M. Distribution / Arabesque Ltd. / Mono Distributors (Jersey) Ltd. / Prism Leisure PLC / PolyGram / Ross Records / Prism Leisure PLC.

ELVIS NBC SPECIAL (TV soundtrack).
Tracks: Trouble / Guitar man / Lawdy Miss Clawdy / Baby what you want me to do / Heartbreak hotel / Hound dog / All shook up / Can't help falling in love / Jailhouse rock / Love me tender / Where could I go but to the Lord / Up above my head / Saved / Blue Christmas / One night / Memories / Nothingville / Big boss man / Little Egypt / If I can dream.
LP . . . . **RD 8011**
RCA / May '69 / BMG.
LP . . . . **PL 42370**
■ **MC** . . . . **PK 42370**
RCA / Sep '78.
■ **LP** . . . . **INTS 5093**
RCA International / Sep '81.
■ **LP** . . . . **NL 83894**
RCA / '84.
CD . . . . **ND 83894**
RCA / Mar '91 / BMG.
MC . . . . **NK 83894**
RCA / Apr '92 / BMG.

P 14

■ DELETED

ELVIS NOW.
Tracks: Help me make it through the night / Miracle of the rosary / Hey Jude / Put your hand in the hand / Until it's time for you to go / We can make the morning / Early mornin' rain / Sylvia / Fools rush in (where angels fear to tread) / I was born ten thousand years ago.
■ **LP** . . . . **SF 8266**
RCA / May '72.
CD **7432114831-2**
MC **7432114831-4**
RCA / Jul '93 / BMG.

ELVIS ON TOUR.
Tracks: Johnny B Goode / Proud Mary / Suspicious minds / Love me tender / Polk salad Annie.
VHS . . . . **SMV 10153**
MGM/UA (Video) / Jan '84 / MGM/UA Video / Gold & Sons / Terry Blood Dist.
VHS . . . . **PES 50153**
Warner Home Video / '91 / WEA / Hollywood Nites / Gold & Sons / Terry Blood Dist.

ELVIS PRESLEY.
Tracks: Blue suede shoes / I love you because / Tutti frutti / I'll never let you go / Money honey / I'm counting on you / I got a woman / One-sided love affair / Just because / Trying to get to you / I'm gonna sit right down and cry over you / Blue moon.
LP **26.21007**
RCA (Germany) / '83 / BMG.
CD . . . . **PD 81254**
LP . . . . **NL 89046**
RCA / Mar '85 / BMG.
CD . . . . **ND 89046**
RCA / Oct '88 / BMG.
CD . . . . **CDCON 117**
Contact (Holland) / Sep '88 / Pinnacle.
MC . . . . **NK 89046**
RCA / Apr '92 / BMG.

ELVIS PRESLEY & JANIS MARTIN (Presley, Elvis & Janis Martin).
Tracks: Not Advised.
LP P.Disc. . . . . **PD 1085**
Picture Disc / Jul '88.

ELVIS PRESLEY (DOUBLE ALBUM).
Tracks: Blue suede shoes / That's alright / Blue moon of Kentucky / Anyway you want me / Mystery train / Long tall Sally / Shake, rattle and roll / Lawdy Miss Clawdy / I don't care if the sun don't shine / Old Shep / Good rockin' tonight / Heartbreak hotel / Separate ways / Are you lonesome tonight / Fool such as I, A / Crying in the chapel / How great thou art / Rip it up / Wonder of you, The / Sweet Caroline / American trilogy.
Double LP . . . . **NL 43054**
RCA / Oct '79 / BMG.

ELVIS PRESLEY - BOX SET.
Tracks: Hound dog / Loving you / All shook up / Heartbreak hotel / Jailhouse rock / Love me / Too much / Don't be cruel / That's when your heartaches begin / Teddy bear / Love me tender / Treat me nice / Anyway you want me (that's how I will be) / I want you, I need you, I love you / I need your love tonight / Don't, wear my ring around your neck / My wish came true / I got stung / One night / Big hunk o' love, A / I beg of you / Fool such as I, A / Don'cha think it's time / It's now or never / Stuck on you / Fame and fortune / I gotta know / Surrender / I feel so bad / Are you lonesome tonight / (Marie's the name) his latest flame / Little sister / Good luck charm / Anything that's part of you / She's not you.
CD Set . . . . **ND 74375**
MC Set . . . . **NK 74375**
RCA / Nov '90 / BMG.
■ **CD Set** . . . . **ND 90573**
RCA / Sep '91.

ELVIS PRESLEY COLLECTION.
Tracks: Peace in the valley / It is no secret / Swing down sweet Chariot / Frankie and Johnny / Guitar man / Big boss man.
Double LP . . . . **PDA 009**
MC Set . . . . **PDC 009**
Pickwick / Jul '76 / Pickwick Records.

ELVIS PRESLEY COLLECTION VOL.2.
Tracks: Separate ways / C'mon everybody / Santa Lucia / Old shep / Little less conversation, A / Long legged girl (with the short dress on).
Double LP . . . . **PDA 042**
MC Set . . . . **PDC 042**
Pickwick / Jun '78 / Pickwick Records.

ELVIS PRESLEY COLLECTION VOL.3.
Tracks: What every woman lives for / Please don't stop me loving you / Change of habit / Come along / Shout it out / Beginners luck / Clean up your own backyard / Rubberneckin' / Edge of reality / Petunia, the gardener's daughter / Hard luck / Have a happy / Flaming star / Wonderful world / All I needed was the rain / Too much monkey business / Tiger man.
Double LP . . . . **PDA 054**
MC Set . . . . **PDC 054**
Pickwick / Apr '79 / Pickwick Records.

ELVIS PRESLEY EP.
Tracks: I just can't help believing / Always on my mind / Separate ways / I've lost you.
■ **EP** . . . . **EP 1**
RCA / Mar '82 / BMG.
MC Single . . . . **RCXK 006**
RCA / May '83 / BMG.

ELVIS PRESLEY FILM CAN.
Tracks: Not Advised.
■ **CD Set** **7863 61835-2**
RCA / Mar '93.

ELVIS PRESLEY IN CONCERT.
Tracks: Not Advised.
VHS . . . . **AVT 1**
Mountain Films / Jan '86 / Gold & Sons.

ELVIS PRESLEY LIVE ON STAGE IN MEMPHIS.
Tracks: See see rider / I got a woman / Love me / Trying to get to you / Long tall Sally (medley) / Flip flop and fly / Jailhouse rock / Hound dog / Why me, Lord / How great Thou art / Blueberry Hill (medley) / Help me / American trilogy / Let me be there / My baby left me / Lawdy Miss Clawdy / Can't help falling in love / Closing vamp.
■ **LP** **APL1 0606**
RCA / Sep '74.

ELVIS PRESLEY SINGS LEIBER & STOLLER.
Tracks: Hound dog / Love me / Loving you / Hot dog / I want to be free / Jailhouse rock / Treat me nice / Baby I don't care / Santa Claus is back in town / Don't trouble / King Creole / Steadfast loyal and true / Dirty dirty feeling / Just tell her Jim said hello / Girls, girls, girls / Bossa nova baby / Little Egypt / Fools fall in love / Saved.
■ **LP** . . . . **INTS 5031**
RCA International / '80.
LP . . . . **NL 89099**
■ **MC** . . . . **NK 89099**
RCA / '84.

ELVIS PRESLEY SUN COLLECTION.
Tracks: That's alright mama / Blue moon of Kentucky / I don't care if the sun don't shine / Good rockin' tonight / Milk cow blue boogie / You're a heartbreaker / I'm left you're right she's gone / Baby let's play house / Mystery train / I forgot to remember to forget / I love you because / Trying to get to you / Blue moon / Just because / I'll never let you go.
LP . . . . **HY 1001**
RCA / Sep '75 / BMG.
LP . . . . **NL 42757**
MC . . . . **NK 42757**
RCA / Mar '79 / BMG.
CD . . . . **ND 89107**
RCA / '88 / BMG.

ELVIS PRESLEY WITH BILL HALEY (Presley, Elvis & Bill Haley).
Tracks: Not Advised.
LP P.Disc. . . . . **PD 1084**
Picture Disc / Jul '88.

ELVIS PRESLEY: INTERVIEW PICTURE DISC.
Tracks: Not Advised.
CD P.Disc . . . . **CBAK 4007**
LP P.Disc. . . . . **BAK 2086**
Baktabak / Apr '88 / Arabesque Ltd.
MC . . . . **MBAK 6024**
Baktabak / Jan '92 / Arabesque Ltd.

ELVIS PRESLEY: INTERVIEW PICTURE DISC.
Tracks: Not Advised.
■ **12" P.Disc** . . . . **ELVIS 1**
Talkies / '88 / Backs Distribution / Mason's Music.

ELVIS PRESLEY: INTERVIEW PICTURE DISC COLLECTION.
Tracks: Not Advised.
■ **7" Set** . . . . **BAKPAK 1008**
Baktabak / Apr '88 / Arabesque Ltd.

ELVIS SAILS.
Tracks: Not Advised.
■ **EP** . . . . **RCX 131**
RCA / '58 / BMG.

ELVIS SINGS HITS FROM HIS MOVIES.
Tracks: Down by the riverside / When the saints go marching in / Guitar man / Frankie and Johnny / How would you like to be big boss man.
LP . . . . **CDS 1110**
MC . . . . **CAM 423**
RCA/Camden / Jan '72 / BMG / Arabesque Ltd.

ELVIS SINGS THE WONDERFUL WORLD OF CHRISTMAS.
Tracks: Oh come all ye faithful / First Noel, The / On a snowy Christmas night / Winter wonderland / Wonderful world of Christmas, The / It won't seem like Christmas (without you) / I'll be home on Christmas day / If I get home on Christmas day / Holly leaves and Christmas trees / Merry Christmas baby / Silver bells.
LP . . . . **PL 42371**
MC . . . . **PK 42371**
RCA / Nov '79 / BMG.
LP . . . . **NL 81936**
RCA / Nov '90 / BMG.
CD . . . . **ND 81936**
■ **MC** . . . . **NK 81936**
RCA / Nov '90.

ELVIS TAPES, THE.
Tracks: Not Advised.
LP . . . . **RED 1**
Redwood / Apr '87 / Pinnacle / A.D.A Distribution.
CD . . . . **CDRD 001**
Ace / Jul '91 / Pinnacle / Hot Shot / Jazz Music / Complete Record Co. Ltd.

ELVIS THE PELVIS (50th anniversary album).
Tracks: Tutti frutti / Money honey / Trying to get to you / Mystery train / Heartbreak hotel / I got a woman / Treat me nice / One-sided love affair / Don't be cruel / Shake, rattle and roll / I want you, I need you, I love you / Good rockin' tonight / Lawdy Miss Clawdy / I'm gonna sit right down and cry over you / I was the one / I want to be free / Ready Teddy / Blue moon of Kentucky / Baby let's play house / Long tall Sally / I'm left your right she's gone / How do you think I feel / I love you because / Blue suede shoes / When my blue moon turns to gold again / Young and beautiful.
Double LP . . . . **NL 89515**
MC Set . . . . **KA 89515**
RCA (Germany) / Nov '85 / BMG.

ELVIS' 40 GREATEST HITS.
Tracks: My baby left me / Heartbreak hotel / Blue suede shoes / Hound dog / Love me tender / Got a lot of livin' to do / Teddy bear / Party / All shook up / Old Shep / Don't / Hard headed woman / King Creole / Jailhouse rock / Big hunk o' love, A / I got stung / One night / Fool such as I, A / I need your love tonight / Stuck on you / Fever / It's now or never / Surrender / Are you lonesome tonight? / Wooden heart / His latest flame / Wild in the country / There's always me / Rock-a-hula-baby / Can't help falling in love / Good luck charm / She's not you / Return to sender / Devil in disguise / In the ghetto / Crying in the chapel / Guitar man / Suspicious minds / There goes my everything / Don't cry Daddy.
■ **Double LP** . . . . **ADEP 12**
Arcade / Jul '75.
Double LP . . . . **PL 42691**
■ **MC** . . . . **PK 42691**
RCA / Feb '79.

ELVIS' CHRISTMAS ALBUM.
Tracks: Santa Claus is back in town / White Christmas / Here comes Santa Claus / I'll be home for Christmas / Blue Christmas / Santa bring my baby back to me / O little town of Bethlehem / Silent night / Peace in the valley / I believe / Take my hand precious Lord / It is no secret.
LP . . . . **INTS 1126**
RCA International / Dec '71 / BMG.
LP . . . . **CDS 1155**
■ **MC** . . . . **CAM 1155**
RCA/Camden / Oct '79.
LP . . . . **NL 89116**
■ **MC** . . . . **NK 89116**
RCA / '84.
■ **LP** . . . . **PL 85486**
RCA / Oct '85.
MC . . . . **CAM 462**
RCA/Camden / '88 / BMG / Arabesque Ltd.
LP . . . . **NL 90300**
RCA / Nov '90 / BMG.
CD . . . . **ND 90300**
■ **MC** . . . . **NK 90300**
RCA / Nov '90.

ELVIS' GOLDEN RECORDS VOL.1 (Reissue).
Tracks: Hound dog / Loving you / All shook up / Heartbreak hotel / Teddy bear / Jailhouse rock / Love me tender / Treat me nice / Anyway you want me / I want you I need you I love you.
LP . . . . **SF 8129**
■ **MC** . . . . **PK 11602**
RCA / '70.
LP . . . . **INTS 5143**
■ **MC** . . . . **INTK 5143**
RCA International / '82.
LP . . . . **NL 81707**
RCA / '84 / BMG.
■ **CD** . . . . **PD 85196**
RCA / '84.
CD . . . . **ND 81707**
RCA / Jun '90 / BMG.
MC . . . . **NK 81707**
RCA / Apr '92 / BMG.

ELVIS' GOLDEN RECORDS VOL.1 (Original issue).
Tracks: Hound dog / I love you because / All shook up / Heartbreak hotel / You're a heartbreaker / Love me / Too much / Don't be cruel / That's when your heartaches begin / I'll never let you go / Love me tender / I forgot to remember to forget / Anyway you want me / I want you, I need you, I love you.
■ **LP** . . . . **RB 16069**
RCA / '58.

ELVIS' GOLDEN RECORDS VOL.2.
Tracks: I need your love tonight / Wear my ring around your neck / My wish came true / I got stung / Loving you / Teddy bear / One night / Hunk o love, A / I beg of you / Fool such as I, A / Doncha think it's time / Jailhouse rock / Treat me nice / Don't.
■ **LP** . . . . **RD 27159**
RCA / Jun '60.
LP . . . . **SF 8151**
■ **MC** . . . . **PK 11531**
RCA / '71.
LP . . . . **INTS 5144**
■ **MC** . . . . **INTK 5144**
RCA International / '82.

ELVIS' GOLDEN RECORDS VOL.3.
Tracks: It's now or never / Stuck on you / Fame and fortune / I gotta know / Surrender / I feel so bad / Are you lonesome tonight / His latest flame / Little sister / Good luck charm / Anything that's part of you / She's not you.
LP	RD 7630
RCA / Apr '64 / BMG.	
LP	SF 7630
RCA / Sep '77 / BMG.	
■ **MC**	PK 11570
RCA / Sep '77.	
LP	INTS 5145
MC	INTK 5145
RCA International / Sep '81 / BMG.	
LP	NL 82765
MC	NK 82765
RCA / '84 / BMG.	
CD	ND 82765
RCA / Oct '90 / BMG.	

ELVIS' GOLDEN RECORDS VOL.4.
Tracks: Love letters / It hurts me / What I'd say / Please don't drag that string around / Indescribably blue / Devil in disguise / Lonely man / Mess of blues, A / Ask me / Ain't that loving you baby / Just tell her Jim said hello / Witchcraft.
LP	SF 7924
■ **MC**	PK 11571
RCA / '79.	
LP	NL 83921
MC	NK 83921
RCA International / Jan '84 / BMG.	
CD	ND 83921
RCA / Nov '90 / BMG.	

ELVIS' GOLDEN RECORDS VOL.5.
Tracks: Suspicious minds / Kentucky rain / In the ghetto / Clean up your own backyard / If I can dream / Burning love / If you talk in your sleep / For the heart / Moody blue / Way down.
LP	PL 84941
■ **MC**	PK 84941
RCA / '85.	
■ **CD**	PD 84941
RCA / '86.	

ELVIS-THE ULTIMATE PERFORMANCE.
Tracks: Also sprach Zarathustra / See see rider / Blue suede shoes / Johnny B. Goode / Are you lonesome tonight / Never been to Spain / You don't have to say you love me / Impossible dream, The / American trilogy / In the ghetto / Suspicious minds / Love me / Burning love / Words / Polk salad Annie / I can't stop loving you / Can't help falling in love.
LP	NE 1141
MC	CE 2141
K-Tel / Nov '81 / I & B Records / C.M. Distribution / Arabesque Ltd. / Mono Distributors (Jersey) Ltd. / Prism Leisure PLC / PolyGram / Ross Records / Prism Leisure PLC.	

ELVIS: A PORTRAIT BY HIS FRIENDS.
Tracks: Not Advised.
VHS	QU 91001
Qube Pictures / '91 / Video Collection.	

ESSENTIAL ELVIS.
Tracks: Teddy bear / Loving you / Mean woman blues / Got a lot of livin' to do / Lonesome cowboy / Jailhouse rock / Treat me nice / Young and beautiful / Don't leave me now / I want to be free / Baby I don't care / Love me tender (With the Jordanaires) / Let me / Poor boy / We're gonna move / Party / Hot dog.
MC	PK 89979
RCA / Dec '86 / BMG.	
■ **LP**	PL 89979
RCA / Dec '86.	
CD	PD 89980
RCA / Jan '87 / BMG.	

ESSENTIAL ELVIS VOL. 2 (Stereo 57).
Tracks: I beg of you / Have I told you lately that I love you / Blueberry Hill / Peace in the valley / Is it so strange / It is no secret / Mean woman blues / That's when your heartaches begin.
CD	PD 90250
LP	PL 90250
MC	PK 90250
RCA / Jan '89 / BMG.	

ESSENTIAL ELVIS VOL.3 (Hits Like Never Before).
Tracks: King Creole / Fool such as I, A / Your cheatin' heart / Dontcha' think it's time / Lover doll / Danny / Crawfish / Ain't that loving you baby / I need your love tonight / I got stung / As long as I have you / Wear my ring around your neck / Big hunk o' love, A / Steadfast, loyal and true / King Creole (instrumental).
CD	PD 90486
RCA / May '90 / BMG.	
■ **LP**	PL 90486
RCA / May '90.	
■ **MC**	PK 90486
RCA / May '90.	

FIFTIES INTERVIEWS, THE.
Tracks: Truth about me, The / Jacksonville, Florida / WMPS, Memphis / Witchita Falls, Texas / LaCrosse, Wisconsin / Little Rock, Arkansas / KLAC-TV, Memphis / New Orleans / New Orleans (2) / St. Petersburg, Florida.
LP	MFLP 074
Magnum Force / Nov '89 / Terry Blood Dist. / Jazz Music / Hot Shot.	

CD	CDMF 074
Magnum Force / Feb '91 / Terry Blood Dist. / Jazz Music / Hot Shot.	

FILM HITS.
Tracks: Not Advised.
LP Set	NL 89797
RCA (Germany) / Nov '85 / BMG.	
■ **CD**	PD 89550
RCA / '88.	

FIRST LIVE RECORDINGS.
Tracks: I wanna play house with you / Maybellene / Tweedle dee / That's alright / Recollections by Frank Page / Hound dog.
LP	PG 89387
MC	PH 89387
RCA / Jul '84.	

FIRST TEN YEARS,THE.
Tracks: Not Advised.
LP	CDS 1213
■ **MC**	CAM 1213
RCA/Camden / Sep '84.	

FIRST YEAR, THE (Presley, Elvis/Bill Black/ Scotty Moore).
Tracks: Bill Collie interview / Good rockin' tonight / Baby let's play house / Blue moon of Kentucky / I got a woman / That's alright mama / Elvis Presley interview / Scotty Moore tells the story of the first year.
LP	SUN 1007
Sun / '83 / Charly / Swift.	

FLAMING STAR.
Tracks: Flaming star / Wonderful night / Night life / All I needed was the rain / Too much monkey business / Yellow rose of Texas / Eyes of Texas, The / She's a machine / Do the vega / Tiger man.
LP	RD 7723
RCA / Sep '65 / BMG.	
LP	INTS 1012
RCA International / Jul '69 / BMG.	
LP	CDS 1185
MC	CAM 490
RCA/Camden / Jan '80 / BMG / Arabesque Ltd.	

FLAMING STAR (EP).
Tracks: Flaming star.
■ **EP**	RCX 7205
RCA / Oct '82 / BMG.	

FLIPHITS.
Tracks: It's now or never / Girl of my best friend / Are you lonesome tonight / Surrender.
MC Single	RCXK 014
RCA / Jul '83 / BMG.	

FOLLOW THAT DREAM (EP).
Tracks: Follow that dream / Angel / What a wonderful life / I'm not the marrying kind.
■ **EP**	RCX 211
RCA / Jun '62.	
■ **EP**	RCX 7196
RCA / Feb '82 / BMG.	

FOOL.
Tracks: Fool.
■ **7"**	RCA 2393
RCA / Aug '73.	

FOOL SUCH AS I, A.
Tracks: Fool such as I, A / Need your love tonight.
■ **7"**	RCA 1113
RCA / Apr '59.	
7"	RCA 2697
RCA / May '77 / BMG.	

FOR LP FANS ONLY.
Tracks: That's all right / Lawdy Miss Clawdy / Mystery train / Playing for keeps / Poor boy / Money honey / I'm counting on you / My baby left me / I was the one / Shake rattle and roll / I'm left, you're right, she's gone / You're a heartbreaker / Tryin' to get to you / Blue suede shoes.
CD	ND 90359
RCA / Sep '89 / BMG.	
■ **LP**	NL 90359
RCA / Sep '89.	
MC	NK 90359
RCA / Apr '92 / BMG.	

FOR THE ASKING.
Tracks: Long lonely highway / Western union / Witchcraft / Love me tonight / What now, what next, where to? / Please don't drag that string around / Blue river / Never ending / Devil in disguise / Finders keepers / Echoes of love / Slowly but surely / It hurts me / Memphis Tennessee / Ask me.
■ **LP**	NL 90513
MC	NK 90513
RCA / Nov '90 / BMG.	
■ **CD**	ND 90513
RCA / Nov '90.	

FOREVER.
Tracks: My baby left me / Heartbreak hotel / I got stung / Hound dog / Teddy bear / Love me tender / Guitar man / In the Ghetto / Suspicious minds / Don't / One night / Stuck on you / Surrender / Wooden heart / All shook up.
MC Set	NK 89004
RCA / Jul '86 / BMG.	
■ **Double LP**	NL 89004
RCA / Jul '86.	

FRANKIE & JOHNNY (Film soundtrack).
Tracks: Frankie and Johnny / Come along / Petunia, the gardner's daughter / Chesay / What every woman lives for / Look out Broadway / Beginners luck / Down by the riverside / When the saints go marching in / Shout it out / Hard luck / Please don't stop loving me.
LP	RD 7793
RCA / Apr '66 / BMG.	
■ **LP**	INTS 5036
RCA International / Oct '80.	
LP	NL 82559
MC	NK 82559
RCA International / Jan '84 / BMG.	

FRANKIE AND JOHNNY.
Tracks: Frankie and Johnny / Please don't stop loving you.
■ **7"**	RCA 1509
RCA / Apr '66.	

FROM ELVIS IN MEMPHIS.
Tracks: Wearin' that loved on look / Only the strong survive / I'll hold you in my heart / Long black limousine / It keeps right on a-hurtin' / I'm moving on / Power of my love / Gentle on my mind / After loving you / True love travels on the gravel road / Any day now / In the ghetto.
■ **LP**	SF 8029
RCA / Aug '69.	
CD	ND 90548
RCA / Mar '91 / BMG.	
LP	NL 90548
RCA / Mar '91.	
■ **MC**	NK 90548
RCA / Apr '92.	

FROM ELVIS PRESLEY BOULEVARD, MEMPHIS, TENNESSEE.
Tracks: Hurt / Never again / Blue eyes crying in the rain / Danny boy / Last farewell, The / For the heart / Bitter they are / Solitaire / Love coming down / I'll never fall in love again.
■ **MC**	PK 11729
RCA / '76.	
LP	RS 1060
RCA / Jun '76 / BMG.	
■ **LP**	PL 89266
RCA / '85 / BMG.	
■ **MC**	PK 89266
RCA / '85.	
CD	7432114691-2
MC	7432114691-4
RCA / Jul '93 / BMG.	

FROM MEMPHIS TO VEGAS.
Tracks: Blue suede shoes (Elvis at the International Hotel, Las Vegas.) / Johnny B. Goode / All shook up / Are you lonesome tonight / Hound dog / I can't stop loving you / Me babe / Mystery train / Tiger man / Words / In the ghetto / Suspicious minds / Can't help falling in love / Elvis back in Memphis / Inherit the wind / This is a story / Stranger in my own home town / Little bit of green, A / And the grass won't pay no mind / Do you know who I am / From a Jack to a king / Fair's moving on / You'll think of me / Without love.
■ **Double LP**	SF 8080/1
RCA / Mar '70 / BMG.	
■ **Double LP**	NL 89068
RCA / Jan '84.	

FUN IN ACAPULCO (FILM) (Film soundtrack).
Tracks: Fun in Acapulco / Vino / Dinero Y amor / Mexico / El toro / Marguerita / Bullfighter was a lady / No room to rhumba in a sports car / I think I'm gonna like it here / Bossa nova baby / You can't say no in Acapulco / Guadalajara / Love me tonight / Slowly but surely.
■ **LP**	RD 7609
RCA / Dec '63.	
LP	PL 42357
LP	NL 89014
■ **MC**	PK 42357
RCA / '79.	
■ **LP**	INTS 5106
RCA International / Sep '81.	

G.I. BLUES (Film soundtrack).
Tracks: Tonight is so right for love / What's she really like? / Frankfurt special / Wooden heart / G.I. blues / Pocketful of rainbows / Shopping around / Big boots / Didja ever? / Blue suede shoes / Doin' the best I can.
LP	RD 27192
RCA / Dec '60 / BMG.	
■ **MC**	PK 5078
RCA / '77.	
LP	SF 5078
RCA / Sep '77 / BMG.	
■ **LP**	INTS 5104
RCA International / Sep '81.	
LP	NL 83735
RCA International / Jan '84.	
CD	ND 83735
RCA / Oct '87 / BMG.	
MC	NK 83735
RCA / Apr '92 / BMG.	

G.I. BLUES (EP) (The alternate takes).
Tracks: Shoppin' around / Big boots / Tonight's all right for love / Frankfurt special.
■ **EP**	RCX 1
RCA / '82.	

■ DELETED

GIRL HAPPY (Film Soundtrack).
Tracks: Girl happy / Spring fever / Fort Lauderdale / Chamber of Commerce / Startin' tonight / Wolf call / Do not disturb / Cross my heart and hope to die / Meanest girl in town / Do the clam / Puppet on a string / I've got to find my baby / You'll be gone.
LP . . . . . **RD 7714**
RCA / May '65 / BMG.
■ **LP** . . . . . **INTS 5034**
RCA International / Oct '80.
LP . . . . . **NL 83338**
MC . . . . . **NK 83338**
RCA International / Nov '84 / BMG.

GIRL OF MY BEST FRIEND.
Tracks: Girl of my best friend / Mess of blues, A.
■ **7"** . . . . . **RCA 2729**
RCA / Sep '76.
■ **7"** . . . . . **GOLD 500**
RCA Golden Grooves / Jul '81.

GIRLS GIRLS GIRLS (Film Soundtrack).
Tracks: Girls, girls, girls / I don't wanna be tied / Where do you come from / I don't want to / We'll be together / Boy like me, a girl like you, A / Earth boy / Return to sender / Because of love / Thanks to the rolling sea / Song of the shrimp / Walls have ears / We're coming in loaded.
■ **LP** . . . . . **RD 7534**
RCA / Jan '63.
LP . . . . . **PL 42354**
■ **MC** . . . . . **PK 42354**
RCA / '79.
■ **LP** . . . . . **INTS 5107**
RCA International / Sep '81.
LP . . . . . **NL 89048**
MC . . . . . **AK 89048**
RCA International / Jan '84 / BMG.
LP . . . . . **CDS 1221**
■ **MC** . . . . . **CAM 1221**
RCA/Camden / '86.

GOLDEN CELEBRATION.
Tracks: Harbour lights / That's all right / Blue moon of Kentucky / I don't care if the sun don't shine / I'm left, you're right, she's gone / I'll never let you go (little darling) / When it rains, it really pours / Shake, rattle and roll / Flip flop and fly / I got a woman / Baby let's play house / Tutti frutti / Blue suede shoes / Heartbreak Hotel / I was the one / Hound dog / I want you I need you, I love you / I want you I need you, I love you (dialogue) / Long tall Sally / Introductions and presentations / Don't be cruel (to a heart's that's true) / Ready Teddy / Love me tender / Love me / Too much / When my blue moon turns to gold again / Peace in the valley / Danny boy / Soldier boy / Fool, The / Earth angel / He's only a prayer away / My heart cries for you / Dark moon / Write to me from Naples / Suppose / Tiger man / Lawdy Miss Clawdy / Baby, what you want me to do? / Are you lonesome tonight / Blue Christmas (Monologue) / One night / Trying to forget you.
LP Set . . . . . **PL 85172**
RCA / Oct '84 / BMG.
■ **MC Set** . . . . . **PK 85172**
RCA / Oct '84.

GOLDEN RECORDS.
Tracks: Hound dog / Loving you / All shook up / Heartbreak hotel / Jailhouse rock / Love me / Toomuch / Don't be cruel / That's when your heartaches begin / (Let me be your) Teddy bear / Love me tender / Treat me nice / Anyway you want me (that's how I will be) / I want you, I need you, I love you.
CD . . . . . **PD 90614**
MC . . . . . **PK 90614**
RCA / Dec '91 / BMG.

GOOD LUCK CHARM.
Tracks: Good luck charm.
■ **7"** . . . . . **RCA 1280**
RCA / May '62.

GOOD LUCK CHARM.
Tracks: Good luck charm / Anything that's part of you.
■ **7"** . . . . . **RCA 2704**
RCA / '79.

GOOD ROCKIN' TONIGHT.
Tracks: Good rockin' tonight.
7" . . . . . **GOLD 534**
RCA Golden Grooves / Oct '81 / BMG.

GOOD ROCKIN' TONIGHT (EP).
Tracks: Good rockin' tonight / Blue moon of Kentucky / Milkcow blues boogie / Just because.
■ **EP** **7EG 8256**
H.M.V. / '57.

GOOD TIMES.
Tracks: Take good care of her / Loving arms / I got a feelin' in my body / If that isn't love / She wears my ring / I got a thing about you baby / My boy / Spanish eyes / Talk about the good times / Good time Charlie's got the blues.
LP **APL1 0475**
RCA / May '74 / BMG.
LP . . . . . **NL 80475**
RCA (Germany) / Dec '86 / BMG.

GRACELAND.
Tracks: Not Advised.
VHS . . . . . **R 1040**
Video Gems / '88.

GREAT PERFORMANCES.
Tracks: My happiness / That's all right / Shake, rattle and roll / Flip flop and fly / Heartbreak hotel / Blue suede shoes / Ready teddy / Don't be cruel / Got a lot of livin' to do / Jailhouse rock / Treat me nice / King Creole / Trouble / Fame and fortune / Return to sender / Always on my mind / American trilogy / If I can dream / Unchained melody / Memories.
CD . . . . . **PD 82227**
LP . . . . . **PL 82227**
MC . . . . . **PK 82227**
RCA / Aug '90 / BMG.

GREAT PERFORMANCES VOL 1 (Centre Stage).
Tracks: Not Advised.
VHS . . . . . **D 610322**
Buena Vista / Oct '90 / Pickwick Records / Sony.

GREAT PERFORMANCES VOL 2 (Man and His Music).
Tracks: Not Advised.
VHS . . . . . **D 610332**
Buena Vista / Oct '90 / Pickwick Records / Sony.

GREATEST HITS: ELVIS PRESLEY.
Tracks: Heartbreak hotel / Jailhouse rock / It's now or never / All shook up / Wooden heart / Are you lonesome tonight?.
MC . . . . . **THPA 1234**
Telstar/Ronco / Nov '87 / BMG.

GREEN GREEN GRASS OF HOME.
Tracks: Green green grass of home / Release me / Solitaire.
7" . . . . . **RCA 405**
RCA / May '84 / BMG.

GUITAR MAN.
Tracks: Guitar man / After loving you / Too much monkey business / Just call me lonesome / Lovin' arms / You asked me to / Clean up your own backyard / She thinks I still care / Faded love / I'm movin' on.
■ **LP** . . . . . **RCALP 5010**
RCA / Mar '81.

GUITAR MAN.
Tracks: Guitar man / Faded love.
■ **7"** . . . . . **RCA 1663**
RCA / Feb '68.
7" . . . . . **RCA 43**
RCA / Feb '81 / BMG.

HARD HEADED WOMAN.
Tracks: Hard headed woman / Don't ask me why.
■ **7"** . . . . . **RCA 1070**
RCA / Jul '58.

HAREM HOLIDAY (Film Soundtrack).
Tracks: Harem holiday / My desert serenade / Go West young man / Mirage / Shake that tambourine / Hey little girl / Golden coins / So close yet so far / Animal instinct / Wisdom of the ages.
LP . . . . . **RD 7767**
RCA / Jan '66 / BMG.
■ **LP** . . . . . **INTS 5035**
RCA International / Oct '80.
LP . . . . . **NL 82558**
MC . . . . . **NK 82558**
RCA International / Jan '84 / BMG.

HARUM SCARUM/GIRL HAPPY.
Tracks: Harum holiday / My desert serenade / Go eat-young man / Mirage / Kismet / Shake that tambourine / Hey little girl / Golden coins / So close, yet so far / Animal instinct / Wisdom of the ages / Girl happy / Spring fever / Fort Lauderdale chamber of commerce / Startin' tonight / Wolf call / Do not disturb / Cross my heart and hopes to die / Meanest girl in town, The / Do the clam / Puppet on a string / I've got to find my baby.
CD **74321 13433-2**
MC **74321 13433-4**
RCA / Mar '93 / BMG.

HE TOUCHED ME.
Tracks: He touched me / I've got confidence / Amazing grace / Seeing is believing / He is my everything / Bosom of Abraham / Evening prayer, An / Lead me, guide me / There is no God but God / Thing called love / I, John / Reach out to Jesus.
■ **LP** . . . . . **SF 8275**
RCA / Aug '72.
CD . . . . . **ND 90661**
MC . . . . . **NK 90661**
RCA / Apr '92 / BMG.

HE WALKS BESIDES ME.
Tracks: He is my everything / Miracle of the rosary / Where did they go Lord? / Somebody bigger than you and I / Evening prayer, An / Impossible dream, The / If I can dream / Padre / Known only to Him / Who am I? / How great Thou art.
LP . . . . . **PL 12772**
■ **MC** . . . . . **PK 12772**
RCA / Apr '78.

HEARTBREAK HOTEL.
Tracks: Heartbreak Hotel / Jailhouse rock / Blue suede shoes / All shook up / Hound dog / King Creole / I got stung / Guitar man / My baby left me / Whole lotta shakin' goin' on / His latest flame / I slipped, I stumbled, I fell.
LP . . . . . **CDS 1204**
■ **MC** . . . . . **CAM 1204**
RCA/Camden / Sep '81.
LP . . . . . **PLP 18**
MC . . . . . **PMC 18**
Platinum (W.Germany) / Oct '85.

HEARTBREAK HOTEL.
Tracks: Heartbreak Hotel.
■ **CD Single** . . . . . **PD 49467**
RCA / Jun '89.

HEARTBREAK HOTEL.
Tracks: Heartbreak Hotel / Hound dog.
■ **7"** . . . . . **RCA 2104**
RCA / Jul '71.

HEARTBREAK HOTEL (Original release).
Tracks: Heartbreak hotel / I was the one.
7" . . . . . **POP 182**
■ **78 rpm** **7M 385**
H.M.V. / '56.

HEARTBREAK HOTEL (EP).
Tracks: Heartbreak hotel / Money honey / I was the one / I forgot to remember to forget.
■ **EP** . . . . . **RCX 7189**
RCA / '82 / BMG.

HEARTBREAK HOTEL (OLD GOLD).
Tracks: Heartbreak hotel / All shook up.
7" . . . . . **OG 9704**
Old Gold / '87 / Pickwick Records.

HIS HAND IN MINE.
Tracks: His hand in mine / I'm gonna walk dem golden stairs / My father's house / Milky white way / Known only to him / I believe / Joshua fit de battle of Jerico / Jesus knows what I need / Swing down sweet chariot / Mansion over the hilltop / If we never meet again / Working on the building.
LP . . . . . **RD 27211**
RCA / May '61 / BMG.
■ **LP** . . . . . **SF 8207**
RCA / '79.
■ **LP** . . . . . **INTS 5105**
RCA International / Aug '81.
LP . . . . . **NL 83935**
MC . . . . . **NK 83935**
RCA International / Jan '84 / BMG.
CD . . . . . **ND 83935**
RCA / Oct '88 / BMG.

HIS LATEST FLAME.
Tracks: His latest flame / Little sister.
■ **7"** . . . . . **RCA 1258**
RCA / '61.
7" . . . . . **RCA 2702**
RCA / '77 / BMG.

HIS LATEST FLAME (OLD GOLD).
Tracks: His latest flame / Girl of my best friend.
7" . . . . . **OG 9622**
Old Gold / Oct '86 / Pickwick Records.

HISTORY OF ROCK AND ROLL.
Tracks: Not Advised.
LP . . . . . **HRL 001**
■ **MC** . . . . . **HRC 001**
RCA / Mar '86.

HITS OF THE 70'S.
Tracks: Wonder of you, The / I'm leaving / Burning love / Always on my mind / I just can't help believing / You don't have to say you love me / There goes my everything / Rags to riches / Until it's time for you to go / I've lost you / Kentucky rain / American trilogy.
LP . . . . . **LPL 17527**
MC . . . . . **LPK 17527**
RCA / Dec '74 / BMG.

HOUND DOG.
Tracks: Not Advised.
MC **40170**
Astan (USA) / Aug '86.

HOUND DOG (Original release).
Tracks: Hound dog / Don't be cruel.
■ **7"** . . . . . **POP 249**
H.M.V. / '56.

HOUND DOG (OLD GOLD).
Tracks: Hound dog / Don't be cruel.
7" . . . . . **OG 9700**
Old Gold / Apr '87 / Pickwick Records.

HOW GREAT THOU ART.
Tracks: How great Thou art / In the garden / Somebody bigger than you and I / Farther along / Stand by me / Without him / So high / Where could I go but to the Lord / By and by / If the Lord wasn't walking by my side / Run on / Where no one stands alone / Crying in the chapel.
■ **LP** . . . . . **SF 7867**
RCA / '67.
LP . . . . . **SF 8206**
RCA / '71 / BMG.
LP . . . . . **NL 83758**
MC . . . . . **NK 83758**
RCA International / '84 / BMG.
CD . . . . . **ND 83758**
RCA / Apr '88 / BMG.

HURT.
Tracks: Hurt / For the heart.
■ **7"** . . . . . **RCA 2674**
RCA / May '76.

I CAN HELP.
Tracks: I can help / Moody blue / If you talk in your sleep / Sweet Angeline / Only the strong survive / Hurt / Promised land / My boy / Green green grass of home / Raised on rock / Fool / Way down / T.R.O.U.B.L.E. / Take good care of her.
LP. . . . . **PL 89287**
RCA / Mar '84 / BMG.
■ **MC** . . . . **PK 89287**
RCA / Mar '84.

I CAN HELP.
Tracks: I can help / Lady loves me.
7" . . . . **RCA 369**
RCA / '83 / BMG.

I GOT A THING ABOUT YOU BABY.
Tracks: I got a thing about you baby.
■ **7"** . . . . **APBO 0196**
RCA / Jul '74.

I GOT A WOMAN.
Tracks: Not Advised.
MC **40172**
Astan (USA) / Aug '86.

I GOT LUCKY.
Tracks: I got lucky / Yoga is as yoga does / Fools fall in love / I need somebody / You gotta stop / Love machine.
LP. . . . . **INTS 1322**
RCA International / Dec '71 / BMG.
LP. . . . . **CDS 1154**
MC . . . . **CAM 496**
RCA/Camden / Nov '75 / BMG / Arabesque Ltd.

I GOT STUNG.
Tracks: I got stung / One night.
7" . . . . **RCA 2696**
RCA / May '77 / BMG.

I JUST CAN'T HELP BELIEVIN'.
Tracks: I just can't help believing.
■ **7"** . . . . **RCA 21578**
RCA / Dec '61.
■ **7"** . . . . **GOLD 510**
RCA Golden Grooves / Jul '81.

I NEED YOU SO.
Tracks: I need you so.
■ **EP.** . . . . **RCX 7200**
RCA / Oct '82 / BMG.

I WANT YOU, I NEED YOU, I LOVE YOU (Original release).
Tracks: I want you, I need you, I love you / My baby left me.
7" . . . . **POP 235**
■ **78 rpm** **7M 424**
H.M.V. / '56.

I WAS THE ONE.
Tracks: I was the one / Baby let's play house / Shake rattle and roll / Flip flop and fly / Don't / Paralyzed / Your cheating heart / Baby i don't care / Don't be cruel / Wear my ring around your neck / My baby left me / Little sister / Heartbreak hotel / Ready teddy / Young and beautiful / Rip it up / Hound dog.
■ **LP.** . . . . **RCALP 3105**
RCA / Aug '83.

I WISH YOU A MERRY CHRISTMAS.
Tracks: O come all ye faithful / First Noel, The / On a snowy Christmas night / Winter wonderland / Wonderful world of Christmas, The / It won't seem like Christmas (without you) / I'll be home on Christmas Day / If I get home on Christmas Day / Holly leaves and Christmas trees / Merry Christmas baby / Silver bells / Santa Claus is back in town / White Christmas / Here comes Santa Claus / I'll be home for Christmas / Blue Christmas / Santa bring my baby back (to me) / O little town of Bethlehem / Silent night / Peace in the valley / I believe / Take my hand, precious Lord / It is no secret.
CD . . . . **ND 89474**
RCA / '87 / BMG.

I'M 10,000 YEARS OLD (Elvis Country).
Tracks: Snowbird / Tomorrow never comes / Little cabin on the hill / Whole lotta shakin' goin' on / Funny how time slips away / I really don't want to know / There goes my everything / It's your baby / Fool, The / Faded love / I washed my hands in muddy water / Make the world go away / I was born ten thousand years ago.
■ **LP.** . . . . **SF 9172**
RCA / Apr '71.
LP. . . . . **INTS 5111**
■ **MC** . . . . **INKT 5111**
RCA International / Sep '81.
LP. . . . . **NL 83956**
MC . . . . **NK 83956**
RCA International / Jan '84 / BMG.
CD **7432114692-2**
MC **7432114692-4**
RCA / Jul '93 / BMG.

I'M LEAVIN'.
Tracks: I'm leaving.
■ **7"** . . . . **RCA 2125**
RCA / Oct '71.

I'M LEFT YOU'RE RIGHT SHE'S GONE.
Tracks: I'm left you're right she's gone.
■ **7"** . . . . **POP 428**
H.M.V. / Jan '58.

I'VE LOST YOU.
Tracks: I've lost you.
■ **7"** . . . . **RCA 1999**
RCA / Nov '70.

IF EVERY DAY WAS LIKE CHRISTMAS.
Tracks: If every day was like Christmas / Blue Christmas.
■ **7"** . . . . **RCA 1557**
RCA / Dec '66.
7" . . . . **GOLD 541**
RCA Golden Grooves / Nov '81 / BMG.

IF I CAN DREAM.
Tracks: If I can dream.
■ **7"** . . . . **RCA 1795**
RCA / Feb '69.

IF YOU TALK IN YOUR SLEEP.
Tracks: If you talk in your sleep / Help me.
■ **7"** . . . . **APBO 0280**
RCA / Jul '74.

IMAGES: ELVIS PRESLEY.
Tracks: That's alright / Blue moon of Kentucky / Good rockin' tonight / I don't care if the sun don't shine / Mystery train / Money honey / My baby left me / Blue suede shoes / All shook up / I'm gonna sit right down and cry over you / Paralysed / Rip it up / I got stung / Big hunk o' love, A / Make me know it / So glad you're mine / It feels so right / Mess of blues, A / Hard luck / Like a baby / Big boss man / Reconsider baby / Steamroller blues / Release me / Fool / Help me make it through the night / I'm leaving / Rags to riches / Do you know who I am / And the grass won't pay no mind.
Double LP . . . . **CR 061**
■ **MC Set** . . . . **CRT 061**
Cambra / Mar '85.

IN HOLLYWOOD.
Tracks: Jailhouse rock / Rock a hula baby / GI blues / Kissin' cousins / Wild in the country / King Creole / Fun in Acapulco / Blue Hawaii / Follow that dream / Viva Las Vegas / Girls girls girls / Bossa nova baby / Flaming star / Girl happy / Frankie and Johnny / Double trouble / Roustabout / Spinout / They remind me too much of you / Charro.
LP. . . . . **PMP 1011**
MC . . . . **PMPK 1011**
Premier (Sony) / Feb '88 / Sony / Pinnacle.

IN PERSON (Presley, Elvis/Scotty Moore/ Bill Black).
Tracks: Not Advised.
LP. . . . . **NR 8973**
Louisiana Hayride / Nov '87.

IN THE BEGINNING (Elvis, Scotty & Bill).
Tracks: Biff Collie interview / There's good rockin' tonight / Baby let's play house / Blue moon of Kentucky / I got a woman / That's alright mama / Elvis Presley interview / Tweedlee dee / Maybellene.
LP. . . . . **KING 1**
Virgin / Nov '79 / EMI.
LP. . . . . **TOP 106**
MC . . . . **KTOP 106**
Topline / Nov '84 / Charly / Swift / Black Sun Records.
CD . . . . **TOP CD 509**
Topline / Apr '87 / Charly / Swift / Black Sun Records.

IN THE GHETTO.
Tracks: In the ghetto.
■ **7"** . . . . **RCA 1831**
RCA / Jun '69.

IN THE GHETTO (OLD GOLD).
Tracks: In the ghetto / Suspicious minds.
7" . . . . **OG 9616**
Old Gold / Oct '86 / Pickwick Records.

INDESCRIBABLY BLUE.
Tracks: Indescribably blue / Fools fall in love.
■ **7"** . . . . **RCA 1565**
RCA / Feb '67.

INSPIRATION.
Tracks: Not Advised.
LP. . . . . **NE 1101**
MC . . . . **CE 2101**
K-Tel / Oct '80 / I & B Records / C.M. Distribution / Arabesque Ltd. / Mono Distributors (Jersey) Ltd. / Prism Leisure PLC / PolyGram / Ross Records / Prism Leisure PLC.

IT FEELS SO RIGHT.
Tracks: Not Advised.
CD . . . . **CD 88003**
World Music (Holland) / '88 / Pinnacle.

IT HAPPENED AT THE WORLD'S FAIR (Film soundtrack).
Tracks: Beyond the bend / Relax / Take me to the fair / They remind me too much of you / One broken heart for sale / I'm falling in love tonight / Cotton candy land / World of our own, A / How would you like to be big boss man / Happy ending.
LP. . . . . **RD 7565**
RCA / May '63 / BMG.
■ **LP.** . . . . **INTS 5033**
RCA International / Oct '80.
LP. . . . . **NL 82568**
MC . . . . **NK 82568**
RCA International / Nov '84 / BMG.

IT WON'T SEEM LIKE CHRISTMAS WITHOUT YOU.
Tracks: It won't seem like Christmas without you / On a snowy Christmas night / If every day was like Christmas / Where no one stands alone / I'll be home on Christmas day / If we never meet again / Wonderful world of Christmas, The / He touched me / Merry Christmas baby / Reach out to Jesus / If I get home on Christmas day / His hand in mine / O come all ye faithful / Holly leaves and Christmas trees / Christmas message from Elvis / Silent night.
MC . . . . **NK 89025**
RCA International / Nov '84 / BMG.
■ **LP.** . . . . **NL 89025**
RCA International / Nov '84.

IT WON'T SEEM LIKE CHRISTMAS WITHOUT YOU.
Tracks: It won't seem like Christmas without you / Merry Christmas baby.
7" . . . . **PB 9464**
RCA / Nov '79 / BMG.
■ **12"** . . . . **PC 9464**
RCA / Nov '79.

IT'S NOW OR NEVER.
Tracks: It's now or never / Surrender / Love me tender / Don't / Stuck on you / She's not you / Teddy bear / Fools fall in love / Crying in the chapel / Have I told you lately that I love you / I need your love tonight / There goes my everything / One broken heart for sale.
LP. . . . . **CDS 1203**
■ **MC** . . . . **CAM 1203**
RCA/Camden / Sep '81.

IT'S NOW OR NEVER.
Tracks: It's now or never / Make me know it.
■ **7"** . . . . **RCA 1207**
RCA / '60.
■ **7"** . . . . **RCA 2698**
RCA / '79.
7" . . . . **PC 60033**
RCA / '83 / BMG.

IT'S NOW OR NEVER (OLD GOLD).
Tracks: It's now or never / Surrender.
7" . . . . **OG 9742**
Old Gold / '88 / Pickwick Records.

IT'S ONLY LOVE.
Tracks: It's only love / Beyond the reef.
■ **7"** . . . . **RCA 4**
RCA / Aug '80.
■ **12"** . . . . **RCAT 4**
RCA / Oct '80.

JAILHOUSE ROCK.
Tracks: Not Advised.
CD **295051**
MC **495051**
Ariola Express / May '92.

JAILHOUSE ROCK (Original release).
Tracks: Jailhouse rock / Treat me nice.
■ **7"** . . . . **RCA 1028**
RCA / '58.

JAILHOUSE ROCK (EP).
Tracks: Jailhouse rock / Young and beautiful / I want to be free / Don't leave me now / Baby I don't care.
■ **EP.** . . . . **RCX 106**
RCA / '58.
■ **EP.** . . . . **RCX 7193**
RCA / '82 / BMG.

JAILHOUSE ROCK (OLD GOLD).
Tracks: Jailhouse rock / Treat me nice.
7" . . . . **OG 9740**
Old Gold / Jan '88 / Pickwick Records.

JAILHOUSE ROCK (SINGLE).
Tracks: Jailhouse rock.
■ **7"** . . . . **RCA 2153**
RCA / Dec '71.
■ **7"** . . . . **PB 2695**
RCA / Sep '77.
■ **7" P.Disc** . . . . **RCAP 1028**
RCA / '83 / BMG.

JAILHOUSE ROCK/LOVE IN LAS VEGAS.
Tracks: Not Advised.
■ **LP.** . . . . **RCALP 9020**
RCA / Apr '83.

JANIS AND ELVIS.
Tracks: Not Advised.
LP. **130253**
RCA (France) / May '85 / Discovery / Silva Screen.

JUST ELVIS.
Tracks: Not Advised.
CD . . . . **ENT CD 212**
Entertainers / Sep '87.

KENTUCKY RAIN.
Tracks: Kentucky rain.
■ **7"** . . . . **RCA 1949**
RCA / May '70.

KID GALAHAD (EP).
Tracks: King of the whole wide world / This is living / Riding the rainbow / Home is where the heart is / I got lucky / Whistling tune.
■ **EP.** . . . . **RCX 7106**

P 18

■ DELETED

RCA / '62 / BMG.
■ EP. . . . . RCX 7197
RCA / '82 / BMG.

KID GALAHAD AND EASY COME EASY GO.
Tracks: Not Advised.
MC . . . . . PK 42791
RCA / '83 / BMG.
LP. . . . . PL 42791
RCA / Apr '83 / BMG.

KID GALAHAD/GIRLS GIRLS GIRLS.
Tracks: King of the whole wide world / This is living / Riding the rainbow / Home is where the heart is / I got lucky / Whistling tune, A / Girls girls girls - girls girls girls / I don't wanna be tied / Where do you come from / I don't want to / We'll be together / Boy like me, a girl like you, A / Return to sender / Because of love / Thanks to the rolling sea / Song of the shrimp / Walls have ears, The / We're coming in loaded / Mama / Plantation rock / Dainty little moonbeams / Girls girls girls.
CD 74321 13430-2
MC 74321 13430-4
RCA / Mar '93 / BMG.

KING.
Tracks: Blue Hawaii / Early morning rain / No more / Relax / So close yet so far / Happy ending.
LP. . . . . CDS 1190
MC . . . . . CAM 500
RCA/Camden / Jan '80 / BMG / Arabesque Ltd.

KING CREOLE (Film soundtrack).
Tracks: King Creole / As long as I have you / Hard headed woman / Trouble / Dixieland rock / Don't ask me why / Lover doll / Crawfish / Young dreams / Steadfast, loyal and true / New Orleans.
LP. . . . . RD 27086
RCA / Nov '58 / BMG.
■ LP. . . . . SF 8231
RCA / '79.
■ LP. . . . . INTS 5013
RCA International / Sep '81.
■ LP. . . . . NL 83733
RCA International / Jan '84.
MC 40173
Astan (USA) / Aug '86.
CD . . . . . ND 83733
RCA / Oct '87 / BMG.
MC . . . . . NK 83733
RCA / Apr '92 / BMG.

KING CREOLE (Original release).
Tracks: King Creole / Dixieland rock.
■ 7". . . . . RCA 1081
RCA / '58.

KING CREOLE (OLD GOLD).
Tracks: King Creole / Hard headed woman.
7". . . . . OG 9750
Old Gold / Jan '88 / Pickwick Records.

KING CREOLE VOL.1 (EP).
Tracks: King Creole / New Orleans / As long as I have you / Lover doll.
■ EP. . . . . RCX 117
RCA / '58 / BMG.
■ EP. . . . . RCX 7194
RCA / '82 / BMG.

KING CREOLE VOL.2 (EP).
Tracks: Not Advised.
■ EP. . . . . RCX 118
RCA / '58 / BMG.
■ EP. . . . . RCX 7201
RCA / '82 / BMG.

KING OF ROCK 'N' ROLL, THE (The Complete 50's Masters).
Tracks: Not Advised.
CD Set . . . . . PD 90689
LP Set . . . . . PL 90689
MC Set . . . . . PK 90689
RCA / Jul '92 / BMG.

KING SPEAKS, THE.
Tracks: Not Advised.
■ LP. . . . . HMR 9005
Hammer / Dec '79.

KING, THE.
Tracks: Not Advised.
CD 15 027
MC 60 969
Laserlight / Aug '91 / TBD / Taylors.

KISS ME QUICK.
Tracks: Kiss me quick.
■ 7". . . . . RCA 1375
RCA / Dec '63.

KISSIN' COUSINS (Film Soundtrack).
Tracks: Kissin' cousins / Smokey mountain boys / Catchin' on fast / Tender feeling / Anyone could fall in love with you / Barefoot ballad / Once is enough / Echoes of love / It's a long lonely highway.
LP. . . . . RD 7645
RCA / Jul '64 / BMG.
LP. . . . . PL 42355
■ MC . . . . . PK 42355
RCA / '79.
■ LP. . . . . INTS 5108
RCA International / Sep '81.
LP. . . . . NL 84115
MC . . . . . NK 84115
RCA International / Nov '84 / BMG.

KISSIN' COUSINS.
Tracks: Kissin' cousins / It hurts me.
■ 7". . . . . RCA 1404
RCA / Jun '64.

LAST FAREWELL, THE.
Tracks: Last farewell, The / It's easy for you.
■ 7". . . . . RCA 459
RCA / Oct '84.

LAWDY MISS CLAWDY.
Tracks: Lawdy Miss Clawdy / Tryin' to get to you.
■ 7". . . . . POP 408
H.M.V. / '57.

LEGEND BEGINS, THE (Elvis live).
Tracks: Not Advised.
LP. . . . . OCN 2031WL
MC . . . . . OCN 2031WK
Ocean (2) / Jul '89.
CD . . . . . OCN 2031WD
Ocean (2) / Jun '89.

LEGEND, THE.
Tracks: Heartbreak hotel / Blue suede shoes / Hound dog / Teddy bear / Jailhouse rock / King Creole / Fool such as I, A / My wish came true / Girl of my best friend / Wooden heart / Rock a hula baby / Return to sender / Devil in disguise / Such a night / Love letters / US male / Rags to riches / It's only love.
LP. . . . . CDS 1212
■ MC . . . . . CAM 1212
RCA/Camden / Nov '83.
CD . . . . . PD 89000
RCA / '84 / BMG.

LEGEND, THE '68-'70.
Tracks: Not Advised.
LP Set . . . . . ELR 4
RCA (Australia) / Apr '86 / WRD.

LEGENDARY ELVIS PRESLEY, THE.
Tracks: Not Advised.
LP. . . . . ENT LP 13040
MC . . . . . ENT MC 13040
Entertainers / Jan '88.

LEGENDARY PERFORMER VOL.1.
Tracks: That's alright / I love you because / Heartbreak hotel / Elvis (excerpt from an interview) / Don't be cruel / Love me / Trying to get to you / Love me tender / Peace in the valley / Elvis (further excerpts from an interview) / Fool such as I, A / Tonight is so right for love / Are you lonesome tonight / Can't help falling in love.
LP. CPL1 0341
MC APK1 0341
RCA / Oct '77 / BMG.

LEGENDARY PERFORMER VOL.2, A.
Tracks: Harbour lights / I want you, I need you, I love you / Blue suede shoes / Interview with Elvis by Jay Thompson (Interview with Elvis backstage following a live performance) / Blue Christmas (With The Jordanaires.) / Jailhouse rock / It's now or never (With The Jordanaires.) / Cane and high starched collar / Presentation of awards to Elvis (Excerpt from press conference, Pearl Harbour, Hawaiii, March 25th 1961.) / Blue Hawaii (With J D Sumner & The Stamps & The Imperials Quartet.) / Such a night (With The Jordanaires.) / Baby what you want me to do / How great thou art / If I can dream.
LP. CPL1 1349
MC . . . . . PK 11717
RCA / Oct '77 / BMG.

LEGENDARY PERFORMER VOL.3, A.
Tracks: Hound dog / Danny / Fame and fortune / Frankfurt special / Britches / Crying in the chapel / Surrender / Guadalajara / It hurts me / Let yourself go / In the ghetto / Let it be me.
■ LP. . . . . PL 13082
RCA / Feb '79.

LEGENDARY PERFORMER VOL.4.
Tracks: Not Advised.
■ LP. . . . . PL 84848
RCA / Nov '83.
■ MC . . . . . PK 84848
RCA / Nov '83.

LONG LEGGED GIRL.
Tracks: Long legged girl with the short dress on.
■ 7". . . . . RCA 1616
RCA / Sep '67.

LOVE IN LAS VEGAS (Film soundtrack).
Tracks: Not Advised.
■ EP. . . . . RCX 7141
RCA / '64 / BMG.
■ EP. . . . . RCX 7206
RCA / Oct '82 / BMG.

LOVE LETTERS.
Tracks: Love letters.
■ 7". . . . . RCA 1526
RCA / Jul '66.

LOVE LETTERS FROM ELVIS.
Tracks: Love letters / When I'm over you / If I were you / Get my mojo working / Heart of Rome / Only believe / This is our dance / Cindy Cindy / I'll never know / It ain't no big thing (but it's growing) / Life.
LP. . . . . SF 8202
RCA / Jul '71 / BMG.
■ LP. . . . . INTS 5081
RCA International / Jun '81.
CD . . . . . ND 89011
MC . . . . . NK 89011
RCA / Jun '88 / BMG.
■ LP. . . . . NL 89011
RCA / Jun '88.

LOVE ME TENDER.
Tracks: Not Advised.
LP. . . . . CL 89518
RCA (Germany) / '85 / BMG.

LOVE ME TENDER (Original release).
Tracks: Love me tender / Anyway you want me.
■ 7". . . . . POP 253
H.M.V. / '56.

LOVE ME TENDER (EP).
Tracks: Love me tender / We're gonna move / Let me / Poor boy.
■ EP. 7EG 8199
H.M.V. / '56.
■ EP. . . . . RCX 7191
RCA / '82 / BMG.

LOVE ME TENDER (OLD GOLD).
Tracks: Love me tender / Teddy bear.
7". . . . . OG 9626
Old Gold / '86 / Pickwick Records.

LOVE ME TENDER (SINGLE).
Tracks: Teddy bear / Love me tender / If I can dream.
12". . . . . ARON T2
■ 7". . . . . ARON 2
RCA / Aug '87.

LOVE SONGS.
Tracks: Not Advised.
CD 15 099
Laserlight / Aug '91 / TBD / Taylors.

LOVE SONGS: ELVIS PRESLEY.
Tracks: Always on my mind / If I'm a fool for lovin' you / Tender feeling / Girl of my best friend / Tonight is so right for love / Fools fall in love / I slipped, I stumbled, I fell / Burning love / I love only one girl / Almost in love / Have I told you lately that I love you / Hawaiian wedding song.
LP. . . . . CDS 1211
■ MC . . . . . CAM 1211
RCA/Camden / Aug '83.

LOVIN' ARMS.
Tracks: Lovin' arms / You asked me to.
7". . . . . RCA 48
RCA / '81 / BMG.

LOVING YOU (Film Soundtrack).
Tracks: Mean woman blues / Teddy bear / Got a lot of livin' to do / Lonesome cowboy / Hot dog / Party / Blueberry Hill / True love / Don't leave me now / Have I told you lately that I love you? / I need you so / Loving you.
■ LP. . . . . RC 24001
RCA / '57.
■ MC . . . . . PK 42358
RCA / '77.
LP. . . . . PL 42358
RCA / Oct '77 / BMG.
■ LP. . . . . INTS 5109
RCA International / Sep '81.
■ LP. . . . . NL 81515
RCA International / Jan '84.
LP. 130 251
RCA (Germany) / May '84 / BMG.
CD . . . . . ND 81515
RCA / Oct '87 / BMG.
MC . . . . . NK 81515
RCA / Apr '92 / BMG.

LOVING YOU (EP) (Re-issue).
Tracks: Not Advised.
■ EP. . . . . RCX 7192
RCA / Feb '82 / BMG.

LOVING YOU (OLD GOLD).
Tracks: Loving you / Paralysed.
7". . . . . OG 9746
Old Gold / Jan '88 / Pickwick Records.

MAGIC MOMENTS.
Tracks: Always on my mind / If I'm a fool for lovin' you / I just can't help believing / Love letters / Kentucky rain / Clean up your own backyard / Hey Jude / Wonder of you, The / Charro / In the ghetto / Your time hasn't come yet, baby / Until it's time for you to go / If I can dream / From a jack to a king / Separate ways / Are you lonesome tonight? / It keeps right on a-hurtin' / It's only love / Any day now / Make the world go away / Jailhouse rock / Teddy bear / Hound dog / Don't be cruel / Suspicious minds / Gentle on my mind / I'll be there if you ever want me / Bridge over troubled water / Edge of reality.
■ MC . . . . . NK 89400
RCA / Jun '84.

MEAN WOMAN BLUES.
Tracks: Mean woman blues / I beg of you / Mean woman blues (dub) (On 12" and CD single only.) / Party (On 12" and CD single only.).

■ 7" . . . . PB 49473
RCA / Jan '89.
■ CD Single . . . . PD 49474
RCA / Jan '89.
■ 12" . . . . PT 49474
RCA / Jan '89.

MEMORIES.
Tracks: Not Advised.
VHS . . . . MA 11054
Vestron Music Video / '87 / Sony / Gold & Sons / Terry Blood Dist.

MEMPHIS ALBUM, THE.
Tracks: Stranger in my own home town / Power of my love / Only the strong survive / Any day now / Suspicious minds / Long black limousine / Wearin' that loved on look / I'll hold you in my heart / After loving you / Rubberneckin' / I'm movin' on / Gentle on my mind / True love travels on a gravel road / It keeps right on a-hurtin' / You'll think of me / Mama liked the roses / Don't cry daddy / In the ghetto / Fair is movin' on, The / Inherit the wind / Kentucky rain / Without love (there is nothing) / Who am I?.
CD . . . . PD 86221
RCA / Jul '87 / BMG.
■ Double LP . . . . PL 86221
RCA / Jul '87.
■ MC Set . . . . PK 86221
RCA / Jul '87.

MESS O BLUES (24 Classic tracks)).
Tracks: Not Advised.
LP . . . . PFP 2000
MC . . . . PFC 2000
Performance / May '89.

MESS OF BLUES, A.
Tracks: Mess of blues, A.
■ 7" . . . . RCA 1194
RCA / Jul '60.

MILLION DOLLAR QUARTET.
Tracks: You belong to my heart / When God dips his love in my heart / Just a little talk with Jesus / Jesus walked that lonesome valley / I shall not be moved / Peace in the valley / Down by the riverside / I'm with a crowd but so alone / Farther along / Bless Jesus (hold my hand) / As we travel along the Jerico road / I just can't make it by myself / Little cabin home on the hill / Summertime is past and gone / I hear a sweet voice calling / Sweetheart you done me wrong / Keeper of the key / Crazy arms / Don't forbid me / Too much monkey business / Brown eyed handsome man / Out of sight, out of mind / Don't be cruel / Paralyzed / There's no place like home / When the saints go marchin' in / Softly and tenderly / Is it so strange / That's when your heartache begins / Rip it up / I'm gonna bid my blues goodbye / That's my desire / End of the road / Slack bottom stomp / You're the only star in my blue heaven / Elvis.
CD . . . . PD 90465
RCA / Mar '93 / BMG.

MILLION SELLERS- 16 NUMBER ONE HITS.
Tracks: Not Advised.
CD . . . . CD 352014
Duchesse (Holland) / Oct '88 / Pinnacle / Taylors.

MOODY BLUE.
Tracks: Unchained melody / If you love me (let me know) / Little darlin' / He'll have to go / Let me be there / Way down / Pledging my love / Moody blue / She thinks I still care.
LP . . . . PL 12428
■ MC . . . . PK 12428
RCA / '77.
LP . . . . RCALP 3021
MC . . . . RCAK 3021
RCA / '81 / BMG.
CD . . . . ND 90252
MC . . . . NK 90252
RCA / '88 / BMG.
■ LP . . . . NL 90252
RCA / '88.

MOODY BLUE.
Tracks: Moody blue / Way down.
■ 7" . . . . GOLD 544
RCA Golden Grooves / May '82.

MOODY BLUE.
Tracks: Moody blue / She thinks I still care.
■ 7" . . . . PB 0857
RCA / '79.

MUSIC AND MEDIA INTERVIEW PICTURE DISC.
Tracks: Not Advised.
LP P.Disc. . . . . ELV 1001
Music & Media / Feb '88.

MY BOY.
Tracks: My boy.
■ 7" . . . . RCA 2458
RCA / Nov '74.

MY BOY (OLD GOLD).
Tracks: My boy / My way.
7" . . . . OG 9756
Old Gold / Jan '88 / Pickwick Records.

MY WAY.
Tracks: My way / America.
■ 7" . . . . PB 1165
RCA / Jun '78.

MYSTERY TRAIN (Original issue).
Tracks: Mystery train / Love me.
■ 7" . . . . POP 295
H.M.V. / '57.

NUMBER ONE HITS.
Tracks: Not Advised.
DCC. 786 3551975
RCA / Dec '92 / BMG.

OLD SHEP.
Tracks: Old Shep.
■ 7" . . . . PB 9334
RCA / Jan '79 / BMG.

ON STAGE (February 1970).
Tracks: See rider blues / Release me (and let me love again) / Sweet Caroline / Runaway / Wonder of you, The / Polk salad Annie / Yesterday / Proud Mary / Walk a mile in my shoes / Let it be me.
■ LP . . . . SF 8128
RCA / Aug '70.
CD . . . . ND 90549
RCA / Mar '91 / BMG.
■ LP . . . . NL 90549
RCA / Mar '91.
MC . . . . NK 90549
RCA / Apr '92 / BMG.

ONE BROKEN HEART FOR SALE.
Tracks: One broken heart for sale / They remind me too much of you.
■ 7" . . . . RCA 1337
RCA / Feb '63.

ONE NIGHT (Original issue).
Tracks: One night / I got stung.
■ 7" . . . . RCA 1100
RCA / Jan '59.

ONE NIGHT WITH YOU.
Tracks: Not Advised.
BETA . . . . VVD 091 B
VHS . . . . VVD 091
Virgin Vision / '86 / Gold & Sons / Terry Blood Dist.
Laser Disc 74321106606
BMG / Aug '92 / BMG.

OUR MEMORIES OF ELVIS.
Tracks: Not Advised.
■ LP . . . . PL 13279
RCA / May '79.

OUR MEMORIES OF ELVIS VOL 2.
Tracks: I got a feelin' in my body / Green green grass of home / For the heart / She wears my ring / I can help / Way down / There's a honky tonk angel / Find out what's happening / Thinking about you / Don't think twice, it's alright.
■ LP . . . . PL 13448
RCA / Feb '80.

PARADISE HAWAIIAN STYLE (Film Soundtrack).
Tracks: Paradise Hawaiian style / Queenie Wamine's papaya / Scratch my back (then I'll scratch yours) / Drums of the islands / Datin' / Dog's life / House of sand / Stop where you are / This is my heaven / Sand castles.
■ LP . . . . RD 7810
RCA / Aug '66 / BMG.
■ LP . . . . INTS 5037
RCA International / Aug '80.
LP . . . . NL 89010
RCA International / Jan '84 / BMG.
MC . . . . NK 89010
RCA International / Jan '84 / BMG.

PARALYSED.
Tracks: Paralysed / When my blue moon turns to gold again.
■ 7" . . . . POP 378
H.M.V. / '57.

PARTY.
Tracks: Party / Got a lot of livin' to do.
■ 7" . . . . RCA 1020
RCA / Oct '57.

PARTY (OLD GOLD).
Tracks: Party / Got a lot of livin' to do.
■ 7" . . . . OG 9618
Old Gold / Oct '86 / Pickwick Records.

PEACE IN THE VALLEY.
Tracks: Peace in the valley / It is no secret / Take my hand precious Lord / I believe.
■ EP . . . . RCX 101
RCA / '57.
■ EP . . . . RCX 7199
RCA / '82 / BMG.

PICTURES OF ELVIS.
Tracks: Return to sender / Roustabout / Little Egypt / Paradise Hawaiian style / Girls, girls, girls / Double trouble / Do the clam / Fun in Acapulco / Bossa nova baby / Clambake / Girl happy / Rock a hula baby.
LP . . . . HY 1023
RCA / Sep '77 / BMG.
LP . . . . INTS 5001

MC . . . . INTK 5001
RCA International / Apr '80 / BMG.

PICTURES OF ELVIS (II).
Tracks: I was the one / Blue suede shoes / Tutti frutti / Blue moon / Lawdy Miss Clawdy / Love me tender / Teddy bear / Loving you / Jailhouse rock / Trying to get to you / Anyway you want me / Just because.
LP P.Disc. . . . . AR 30 002
RCA International / Feb '83 / BMG.

PLEASE DON'T STOP LOVING ME.
Tracks: What every woman lives for / Please don't stop loving me / Change of habit / Come along / Shout it out / Beginners luck / Clean up your own backyard / Rubberneckin' / Edge of reality / Petunia, the gardener's daughter / Hard luck / Have a happy.
LP . . . . CDS 1175
MC . . . . CAM 485
RCA/Camden / Jan '79 / BMG / Arabesque Ltd.

POLK SALAD ANNIE.
Tracks: Polk salad Annie.
■ 7" . . . . RCA 2359
RCA / May '73.

PORTRAIT IN MUSIC (IMPORT).
Tracks: Not Advised.
■ LP . . . . SRS 558
RCA / Feb '70.

POT LUCK WITH ELVIS.
Tracks: Kiss me quick / Just for old time's sake / Gonna get back home some how / Such an easy question / Steppin' out of line / I'm yours / Something blue / Suspicion / I feel I've known you forever / Night rider / Fountain of love / That's someone you never forget.
LP . . . . RD 27265
RCA / Jul '62 / BMG.
■ LP . . . . INTS 5074
RCA International / Jun '81.
LP . . . . NL 89098
MC . . . . NK 89098
RCA International / Jan '84.
CD . . . . ND 89098
RCA / Apr '88 / BMG.

PROMISED LAND.
Tracks: Promised land / There's a honky tonk angel (who will take me) / Help me / Mr. Songman / Love song of the year / It's midnight / Your love's been a long time coming / If you talk in your sleep / Thinking about you / You ask me to.
■ LP APL1 0873
RCA / Feb '75.
CD . . . . ND 90598
MC . . . . NK 90598
RCA / Oct '91 / BMG.

PROMISED LAND.
Tracks: Promised land.
■ 7" . . . . PB 10074
RCA / Jan '75.

RAGS TO RICHES.
Tracks: Rags to riches.
■ 7" . . . . RCA 2084
RCA / May '71.

RAISED ON ROCK.
Tracks: Raised on rock.
■ 7" . . . . RCA 2435
RCA / Nov '73.

RARE ELVIS VOL.1.
Tracks: Early mornin' rain / Hawaiian wedding song / Ku-u-i-po / No more / It's only love / Come what may / I'm yours / First time ever I saw your face, The / Patch it up / Don't cry daddy / High heel sneakers / Lover doll / Doncha' think it's time / Sound of your cry, The / Elvis Presley interview.
LP . . . . PL 89003
RCA / Mar '85 / BMG.
■ MC . . . . PK 89003
RCA / Mar '85.
■ CD . . . . PD 89003
RCA / Jul '86.

RARE ELVIS VOL.2.
Tracks: Datin' / Shopping around / Beyond the reef / Sweet Caroline / Are you lonesome tonight / Shake, rattle and roll / Heartbreak hotel / Flip flop and fly / Long tall Sally / Blue suede shoes / Hound dog.
■ LP . . . . PL 45297
RCA / Nov '83.
MC . . . . PK 89119
RCA / Mar '85 / BMG.
■ LP . . . . PL 89119
RCA / Mar '85.

RARE ELVIS VOL.3.
Tracks: Judy / Little sister / G.I. blues / Viva Las Vegas / What'd I say / Long lonely highway / Life / Almost in love / His latest flame / Good luck charm / Doin' the best I can.
■ LP . . . . PL 89051
■ MC . . . . PK 89051
RCA / Mar '85.

READY TEDDY.
Tracks: Not Advised.
MC 40168
Astan (USA) / Aug '86.

■ DELETED

REAL ELVIS.
Tracks: Not Advised.
■ EP. . . . . RCX 7190
RCA / Feb '82 / BMG.

RECONSIDER BABY.
Tracks: Reconsider baby / Tomorrow night / So glad you're mine / When it rains, it really pours / My baby left me / Ain't that loving you baby / I feel so bad / Down in the alley / High heel sneakers / Stranger in my own home town / Merry Christmas baby.
LP. . . . . PL 85418
■ MC. . . . . PK 85418
RCA / May '85.
■ CD. . . . . PD 85418
RCA / Nov '85.
CD AFL1 5418
RCA / Jan '86 / BMG.

RETURN OF THE ROCKER, THE.
Tracks: Not Advised.
LP. . . . . PL 85600
RCA / Dec '86 / BMG.

RETURN TO SENDER.
Tracks: Return to sender / Have I told you lately that I love you / Roustabout / Hard headed woman / Girls, girls, girls / Whole lotta shakin' goin' on / Girl of my best friend / Do the clam / Once is enough / Steadfast, loyal and true / Slowly but surely / G.I. blues.
LP. . . . . CDS 1200
■ MC. CAM 1200
RCA/Camden / Jan '81.

RETURN TO SENDER.
Tracks: Return to sender / Where do you come from.
■ 7". . . . . RCA 1320
RCA / '62.

RETURN TO SENDER (RE-RELEASE).
Tracks: Return to sender / Where do you come from?.
■ 7". . . . . RCA 2706
RCA / May '77.

RIP IT UP.
Tracks: Rip it up.
■ 7". .POP 305
H.M.V. / Mar '57.

ROCK 'N' ROLL NO. 2.
Tracks: Rip it up / Love me / When my blue moon turns to gold again / Long tall Sally / First in line / Paralysed / So glad you're mine / Old Shep / Ready Teddy / Any place is paradise / How's the world treating you / How do you think I feel.
■ LP. . . . . CLP 1105
H.M.V. / '57.
■ LP. . . . . RD 7528
RCA / '62.
LP. . . . . SF 7528
■ MC. PK 11530
RCA / '79.
LP. . . . . NL 81382
RCA International / Jan '84 / BMG.
■ CD . . . . PD 81382
RCA / '86.
CD . . . . ND 81382
RCA / May '90 / BMG.
MC . . . . NK 81382
RCA / Apr '92 / BMG.

ROCK 'N' ROLL NO.1.
Tracks: Blue suede shoes / I got a woman / I'm counting on you / I'm left you're right she's gone / That's all right mama / Money honey / Mystery train / I'm gonna sit right down and cry over you / One-sided love affair / Lawdy Miss Clawdy / Shake rattle and roll / Trying to get to you.
■ LP. . . . . CLP 1093
H.M.V. / '56.
LP. . . . . SF 8233
■ MC. PK 11620
RCA / '72.
LP. . . . . NL 89125
■ MC. NK 89125
RCA / Jan '84.

ROCK 'N' ROLL REBEL (20 rock 'n' roll originals).
Tracks: Good rockin' tonight / Ready Teddy / Hard headed woman / Shake, rattle and roll / Mystery train / I got a woman / One night / Lawdy Miss Clawdy / King Creole / Jailhouse rock / Dixieland rock / Rip it up / Baby I don't care / I'm left you're right she's gone / Paralysed / Poor boy / Blue moon of Kentucky / I don't care if the sun don't shine / My baby left me / Party.
LP. . . . . NE 1170
MC . . . . CE 2170
K-Tel / Jun '82 / I & B Records / C.M. Distribution / Arabesque Ltd. / Mono Distributors (Jersey) Ltd. / Prism Leisure PLC / PolyGram / Ross Records / Prism Leisure PLC.

ROCK A-HULA BABY.
Tracks: Rock a hula baby / Can't help falling in love.
■ 7". . . . . RCA 1270
RCA / '62.
7". . . . . RCA 2703
RCA / '77 / BMG.

ROCK HITS, THE.
Tracks: Not Advised.
LP. . . . . CDS 1215
■ MC. CAM 1215
RCA/Camden / Apr '86.

ROCKER ELVIS.
Tracks: Blue suede shoes / Tutti frutti / Lawdy Miss Clawdy / I got a woman / Money honey / Jailhouse rock / Ready Teddy / Rip it up / Shake, rattle and roll / Long tall Sally / Hound dog / Baby I don't care.
CD . . . . PD 85182
LP. . . . . PL 85182
■ MC. PK 85182
RCA / Mar '85.

ROMANTIC ELVIS / ROCKIN' ELVIS.
Tracks: Doin' the best I can / You don't know me / Anything that's part of you / It hurts me / Love me tonight / Ask me / I don't want to / World of our own, A / There's always me / I met her today / Indescribably blue / All that I am / Boy like me, a girl like you, A / Starting today I'm yours / Echoes of love / I feel that I've known you forever / Something blue / Mine / Make me know it / Devil in disguise / Finders keepers / One broken heart for sale / I want you with me / Please don't drag that string around / Memphis, Tennessee / Western union / Witchcraft / Return to sender / Long lonely highway / His latest flame / Such a night / I gotta know / Little sister / Shopping around / Judy / I'll be back / US male / I'm coming home / For the millionth and the last time.
Double LP . . . . RCALP 1000
RCA / Aug '82 / BMG.
■ MC Set. . . . . PK 89124
RCA / Jan '84.
■ Double LP . . . . PL 89124
RCA / Jan '84.

ROUSTABOUT (Film Soundtrack).
Tracks: Roustabout / Little Egypt / Poison ivy league / Hard knock / It's a wonderful world / Big love, big heartache / One-track heart / It's carnival time / Carny town / There's a brand new day on the horizon / Wheels on my heels.
LP. . . . . RD 7678
RCA / Jan '65 / BMG.
LP. . . . . PL 42356
■ MC. PK 42356
RCA / '79.
LP. . . . . INTS 5110
RCA International / Sep '81.
LP. . . . . NL 89049
MC . . . . NK 89049
RCA International / Jan '84 / BMG.

SANTA BRING MY BABY BACK (TO ME).
Tracks: Santa bring my baby back to me.
■ 7". . . . . RCA 1025
RCA / Nov '57.

SANTA CLAUS IS BACK IN TOWN.
Tracks: Santa claus is back in town / I believe.
7". . . . . RCA 16
RCA / Nov '80 / BMG.

SEPARATE WAYS.
Tracks: Separate ways / In my way / What now, what next, where to? / Old Shep / I slipped, I stumbled, I fell / It is so strange.
LP. . . . . CDS 1118
MC . . . . CAM 428
RCA/Camden / Jan '73 / BMG / Arabesque Ltd.

SHAKE RATTLE AND ROLL.
Tracks: Shake, rattle and roll.
■ EP. . . . . RCX 7198
RCA / Oct '82 / BMG.

SHE'S NOT YOU.
Tracks: She's not you.
■ 7". . . . . RCA 1303
RCA / Aug '62.

SHE'S NOT YOU.
Tracks: She's not you / Just tell her Jim said hello.
■ 7". . . . . RCA 2705
RCA / '79.

SINGS MORT SHUMAN.
Tracks: Not Advised.
LP. . . . . NL 89504
RCA (Germany) / Jul '85 / BMG.

SINGS WORLD HITS.
Tracks: Not Advised.
LP. . . . . NL 89309
MC . . . . NK 89309
RCA (Germany) / Jan '85 / BMG.

SOMETHING FOR EVERYBODY.
Tracks: There's always me / Give me the right / It's a sin / Sentimental me / Starting today I'm yours / Gently / I'm coming home / In your arms / Put the blame on me / Judy / I want you with me / I slipped, I stumbled, I fell.
LP. . . . . RD 27224
RCA / Nov '61 / BMG.
■ LP. . . . . SF 5106
RCA / '79.
LP. . . . . NL 84116
MC . . . . NK 84116
RCA International / Jan '84 / BMG.
CD . . . . ND 84116
RCA / Nov '90 / BMG.

SOUND OF YOUR CRY.
Tracks: It's only love / Suspicious minds / Angel / What'd I say / Sound of your cry, The / Big hunk o' love, A / Are you lonesome tonight / Steamroller blues / Don't cry daddy / Burning love / You'll never walk alone / Kentucky rain.

■ LP. . . . . RCALP 3060
RCA / '82.

SOUND OF YOUR CRY.
Tracks: Sound of your cry / I'll never know.
7". . . . . .RCA 232
RCA / Jun '82 / BMG.

SPEEDWAY (Film soundtrack).
Tracks: Speedway / There ain't nothing like a song / Your time hasn't come yet, baby / Who are you, who am I? / He's your uncle, not your dad / Let yourself go / Your groovy self / Five sleepy heads / Western Union / Mine / Going home / Suppose.
■ LP. . . . . INTS 5041
RCA International / Oct '80.
LP. . . . . NL 85012
MC . . . . NK 85012
RCA International / Jan '84 / BMG.

SPINOUT.
Tracks: All that I am / Spinout.
■ 7". . . . . RCA 1545
RCA / Oct '66.

STRICTLY ELVIS (EP).
Tracks: Old Shep / Any place is paradise / Paralysed / Is it so strange.
■ EP. .RCX 175
RCA / Feb '60.

STUCK ON YOU.
Tracks: Stuck on you / Anyway you want me.
■ 7". . . . . PB 49595
RCA / Jan '88.
■ 12". PT 49596
RCA / Jan '88.
■ CD Single . . . . PD 49596
RCA / Jun '89.

STUCK ON YOU (Original issue).
Tracks: Stuck on you / Fame and fortune.
■ 7". . . . . RCA 1187
RCA / '60.

SUCH A NIGHT.
Tracks: Such a night.
■ 7". . . . . RCA 1411
RCA / Aug '64.
■ EP. . . . . RCX 7195
RCA / Feb '82 / BMG.

SUN DAYS WITH ELVIS.
Tracks: Not Advised.
VHS. . . . . MMGV 028
MMG Video / '91 / Terry Blood Dist.

SUN YEARS, THE.
Tracks: Not Advised.
■ LP. . . . . SUNLP 1001
Sun / Oct '77.

SURRENDER.
Tracks: Surrender.
■ 7". . . . . RCA 1227
RCA / Mar '61.

SURRENDER.
Tracks: Surrender / Lonely man.
■ 7". . . . . RCA 2701
RCA / '79.

SUSPICION.
Tracks: Suspicion / It's a long lonely highway.
7". . . . . RCA 2768
RCA / Nov '76 / BMG.

SUSPICIOUS MINDS.
Tracks: Suspicious minds / Got a lot of livin' to do / Return to sender / Big hunk o' love, A / In the ghetto / One night / Good luck charm / US male / Party / Fever / Old Shep / Devil in disguise.
LP. . . . . CDS 1206
■ MC. CAM 1206
RCA/Camden / Mar '82.

SUSPICIOUS MINDS.
Tracks: Suspicious minds.
■ 7". . . . . RCA 1900
RCA / '69.

T.R.O.U.B.L.E.
Tracks: T.R.O.U.B.L.E. / Mr. Songman.
■ 7". . . . . RCA 2562
RCA / May '75.

TEDDY BEAR.
Tracks: Teddy bear / Loving you.
■ 7". . . . . RCA 1013
RCA / Jul '57.

TELL ME WHY.
Tracks: Tell me why.
■ 7". . . . . RCA 1489
RCA / Nov '65.

THAT'S ALL RIGHT MAMA.
Tracks: That's alright mama / Harbour lights.
■ 7". .GOLD 520
RCA Golden Grooves / Aug '81.

THAT'S THE WAY IT IS (Film soundtrack).
Tracks: I just can't help believing / Twenty days and twenty nights / How the web was woven / Patch it up / Mary in the morning / You don't have to say you love

me / You've lost that lovin' feeling / I've lost you / Just pretend / Stranger in the crowd / Next step is love, The / Bridge over troubled water.
LP. . . . . SF 8162
RCA / Jan '71 / BMG.
■ MC . . . . PK 11566
RCA / Jan '71.
LP. . . . . NL 84114
MC . . . . NK 84114
RCA International / Jan '84 / BMG.
CD 7432114690-2
MC 7432114690-4
RCA / Jul '93 / BMG.

THERE GOES MY EVERYTHING.
Tracks: There goes my everything.
■ 7" . . . . RCA 2060
RCA / Mar '71.

THIS IS ELVIS.
Tracks: His latest flame / Moody blue / That's alright / Shake, rattle and roll / Flip flop and fly / Heartbreak hotel / Hound dog / Hy Gardner interview excerpts / My baby left me / Merry Christmas, baby / Mean woman blues / Don't be cruel / Teddy bear / Jailhouse rock / Army swearing-in / G.I. blues / Departure for Germany:- press conference excerpt / Home from Germany: press conference excerpt / Too much monkey business / Love me tender / I got a thing about you, baby / I need your love tonight / Blue suede shoes / Viva Las Vegas / Suspicious minds / JC's award to Elvis excerpt / Promised land / Madison Square Gardens press conference excerp / Are you lonesome tonight? / My way / American trilogy / Memories.
LP. . . . . RCALP 5029
RCA / Mar '81 / BMG.
LP. . . . . BL 84031
MC . . . . BK 84031
RCA / '84 / BMG.

THIS IS ELVIS.
Tracks: Not Advised.
VHS. . . . . PES 11173
Warner Home Video / '88 / WEA / Hollywood Nites / Gold & Sons / Terry Blood Dist.

TICKLE ME (Volume 2).
Tracks: Not Advised.
■ EP. . . . . RCX 7174
RCA / '64 / BMG.

TICKLE ME (Volume 1).
Tracks: Not Advised.
■ EP. . . . . RCX 7173
RCA / '64 / BMG.

TODAY.
Tracks: T-R-O-U-B-L-E / And I love you so / Susan when she tried / Woman without love / Shake a hand / Pieces of my life / Fairytale / I can help / Bringing it back / Green green grass of home.
LP. . . . . RS 1011
■ MC . . . . PK 11682
RCA / Jun '75.
CD . . . . ND 90660
MC . . . . NK 90660
RCA / Apr '92 / BMG.

TOO MUCH.
Tracks: Too much / Playing for keeps.
■ 7" . . . . POP 330
H.M.V. / '57.

TOUCH OF GOLD - VOL.1 (EP).
Tracks: Not Advised.
■ EP. . . . . RCX 7202
RCA / '82 / BMG.

TOUCH OF GOLD - VOL.2 (EP).
Tracks: Not Advised.
■ EP. . . . . RCX 7203
RCA / '82 / BMG.

TOUCH OF GOLD - VOL.3 (EP).
Tracks: Not Advised.
■ EP. . . . . RCX 7204
RCA / '82 / BMG.

U.S. MALE.
Tracks: Not Advised.
LP. . . . . CDS 1150
MC . . . . CAM 457
RCA/Camden / Jun '75 / BMG / Arabesque Ltd.

U.S. MALE.
Tracks: U.S. male.
■ 7" . . . . RCA 1688
RCA / '68.

UNTIL IT'S TIME FOR YOU TO GO.
Tracks: Until it's time for you to go.
■ 7" . . . . RCA 2188
RCA / Apr '72.

VIVA LAS VEGAS.
Tracks: Viva Las Vegas / What'd I say.
■ 7" . . . . RCA 1390
RCA / Mar '64.

VIVA LAS VEGAS/ROUSTABOUT.
Tracks: Viva Las Vegas / If you think I don't need you / If you need somebody to lean on / You're the boss (With Ann Margaret) / What I'd say / Do the Vega / C'mon everybody / Lady love me (With Ann Margaret), The / Night life / Today, tomorrow and forever / Yellow rose of Texas/The eyes of Texas, The / Santa Lucia / Roustabout / Little Eygpt / Poison ivy league / Hard knocks / It's a wonderful world / Big love, big heartache / One track heart / It's carnival time / Carmy town / There's a brand new day on the horizon / Wheels on my heels.
CD 74321 13432-2
MC 74321 13432-4
RCA / Mar '93 / BMG.

VOICE OF THE KING (Interviews).
Tracks: Texarkana 1955 / St. Petersburg 1956 / Witchita Falls 1956 / New Orleans 1956 / Memphis 1961 / Houston 1970 / New York 1972.
CD . . . . OCN 2024WD
LP. . . . . OCN 2024WL
MC . . . . OCN 2024WK
Ocean (2) / Apr '89.

VOLUME ONE.
Tracks: Not Advised.
LP. . . . . ENT LP 13011
MC . . . . ENT MC 13011
Entertainers / '88.

VOLUME TWO.
Tracks: Not Advised.
LP. . . . . ENT LP 13019
MC . . . . ENT MC 13019
Entertainers / '88.

WAY DOWN.
Tracks: Way down / Pledging my love.
■ 7" . . . . PB 0998
RCA / Aug '77.

WAY DOWN (OLD GOLD).
Tracks: Way down / Moody blue.
7" . . . . OG 9758
Old Gold / Jan '88 / Pickwick Records.

WEAR MY RING AROUND YOUR NECK.
Tracks: Wear my ring around your neck.
■ 7" . . . . RCA 1058
RCA / May '58.

WELCOME TO MY WORLD.
Tracks: Welcome to my world (With J D Sumner & The Stamps) / Help me make it through the night / Release me / I really don't want to know (With the Imperials Quartet.) / For the good times / Make the world go away / Gentle on my mind / I'm so lonesome I could cry (With J D Sumner & The Stamps) / Your cheatin' heart (With the Jordanaires) / I can't stop loving you.
LP. . . . . PL 12274
RCA / Sep '77 / BMG.
■ MC . . . . PK 12274
RCA / Sep '77.
LP. . . . . RCALP 3020
MC . . . . RCAK 3020
RCA / Sep '81 / BMG.

WHY DON'T YOU PLAY HOUND DOG?.
Tracks: Not Advised.
■ 12" P.Disc . . . . LM 12047
Lost Moment / Oct '90 / RTM / Pinnacle.

WILD IN THE COUNTRY (Original Issue).
Tracks: Wild in the country / I feel so bad.
■ 7" . . . . RCA 1244
RCA / '61.

WILD IN THE COUNTRY (OLD GOLD).
Tracks: Wild in the country / I feel so bad.
7" . . . . OG 9706
Old Gold / Apr '87 / Pickwick Records.

WONDER OF YOU, THE.
Tracks: Wonder of you, The.
■ 7" . . . . RCA 1974
RCA / Jul '70.

WONDER OF YOU, THE (OLD GOLD).
Tracks: Wonder of you, The / If I can dream.
7" . . . . OG 9761
Old Gold / Jan '88 / Pickwick Records.

WONDER OF YOU, THE (REISSUES).
Tracks: Wonder of you, The / Mama liked the roses.
■ 7" . . . . PB 2709
RCA / '77.
■ 7" . . . . RCA 2709
RCA / '79.

WONDERFUL WORLD OF ELVIS.
Tracks: Fools fall in love / Hard luck / What a wonderful life / Santa Lucia / Come along / Old Shep / Yellow rose of Texas / Rubberneckin' / Please don't stop loving me / It's a matter of time / Too much monkey business / I got lucky / Burning love / If you think I don't need you / Wonderful world / Clean up your own backyard / Tender feeling / Home is where the heart is / Little less conversation, A / US male / Let's be friends / Flaming star / Long legged girl with the short dress on / Today, tomorrow and forever.
Double LP . . . . PDA 073
MC Set. . . . . PDC 073
Pickwick / Jan '81 / Pickwick Records.

WOODEN HEART.
Tracks: Wooden heart / Tonight is so right for love.
■ 7" . . . . RCA 1226
RCA / Mar '61.

WOODEN HEART.
Tracks: Wooden heart / Tonight is so right for love.
■ 7" . . . . RCA 2700
RCA / '79.

WORLD WIDE 25 GOLD AWARD HITS - VOL 1.
Tracks: Heartbreak hotel / I was the one / I want you, I need you, I love you / Mess of blues, A / Hound dog / Love me tender / Anyway you want me / Big hunk o' love, A / Playing for keeps / All shook up / That's when your heartaches begin / Loving you / Teddy bear / Jailhouse rock / I got stung / I beg of you / Don't / Wear my ring around your neck / Hard headed woman / Don't be cruel / Too much / Treat me nice / (Now and then there's) A fool such as I / Stuck on you / It's now or never.
■ MC Set. . . . . DPTK 5000
RCA / '79.

WORLD WIDE 25 GOLD AWARD HITS - VOL 2.
Tracks: Are you lonesome tonight / I gotta know / I feel so bad / Surrender / Don't cry daddy / Kentucky rain / Little sister / Can't help falling in love / Rock a hula baby / Anything that's part of you / Good luck charm / She's not you / Return to sender / Where do you come from / Bossa nova baby / Kissin' cousins / Vive Las Vegas / Ain't that loving you baby / Crying in the chapel / In the ghetto / If I can dream / One broken heart for sale / You're the devil in disguise / Wooden heart / Suspicious minds / Excerpts from a press interview.
■ MC Set. . . . . DPTK 5001
RCA / '79.

WORLD WIDE 25 GOLD AWARD HITS - VOL 3.
Tracks: Rip it up / Paralysed / Love me / We're gonna move / Poor boy / Hot dog / New Orleans / Dixieland rock / Crawfish / Don't ask me why / King Creole / One night / His latest flame / They remind me too much of you / Young and beautiful / Fame and fortune / Lonely man / Witchcraft / It hurts me / Puppet on a string / I believe / Any day now / I've lost you / Patch it up / There goes my everything.
■ MC Set. . . . . DPTK 5011
RCA / '79.

WORLD WIDE 25 GOLD AWARD HITS - VOL 4.
Tracks: My baby left me / When my blue moon turns to gold again / Mean woman blues / Lonesome cowboy / Got a lot of livin' to do / Young dreams / Trouble / As long as I have you / Lover doll / Let me / Don'cha think it's time / My wish came true / Wild in the country / (You're so square) Baby I don't care / I want to be free / I need your love tonight / Just tell her Jim said hello / Ask me / Tell me why / Wonder of you, The / Please don't drag that string around / You'll think of me / Next step is love, The / You don't have to say you love me / I really don't want to know.
■ MC . . . . DPTK 5012
RCA / '79.

WORLD WIDE 50 GOLD AWARD HITS - VOL.1.
Tracks: Heartbreak Hotel / I was the one / I want you, I need you, I love you / Don't be cruel / Hound dog / Love me tender / Anyway you want me / Too much / Playing for keeps / All shook up / That's when your heartaches begin / Loving you / Teddy bear / Jailhouse rock / Treat me nice / I beg of you / Don't / Wear my ring around your neck / Hard headed woman / I got stung / (Now and then there's) a fool such as I / Big hunk o love, A / Stuck on you / Mess of blues, A / It's now or never / I gotta know / Are you lonesome tonight / Surrender / I feel so bad / Little sister / Can't help falling in love / Rock a hula baby / Anything that's part of you / Good luck charm / She's not you / Return to sender / Where do you come from? / One broken heart for sale / You're the devil in disguise / Bossa nova baby / Kissin' cousins / Viva Las Vegas / Ain't that loving you baby / Wooden heart / Crying in the chapel / If I can deram / In the ghetto / Suspicious minds / Don't cry daddy / Kentucky rain / Excerpts from a press interview.
■ LP Set . . . . LPM 6401
RCA / Dec '70.

WORLD WIDE 50 GOLD AWARD HITS - VOL.2.
Tracks: Puppet on a string / Witchcraft (With the Jordanaires.) / Trouble / Poor boy / I want to be free / Doncha think it's time / Young dreams / Next step is love, The / You don't have to say you love me / Paralysed / My wish came true (With The Jordanaires.) / When my blue moon turns to gold again / Lonesome cowboy (With The jordanaires.) / My baby left me / It hurts me / I need your love tonight / Tell me why / Please don't drag that string around / Young and beautiful / Hot dog / New orleans (With The Jordanaires.) / We're gonna move / Crawfish / King Creole / I believe / Dixieland rock (With The Jordanaires.) / Wonder of you, The (With The Imperials Quartet.) / They remind me too much of you (With The Mello Men.) / Mean woman blues / Lonely man (With The Jordanaires.) / Any day now / Don't ask me why (With The Imperials Quartet.) / Baby I don't care (With The Jordanaires.) / I've lost you / Let me / Love me / Got a lot of livin' to do / Fame and fortune / Rip it up / There goes my everything (With The Imperials Quartet.) / Lover doll / One night / Just tell her Jim said hello / Ask me (With The Jordanaires.) / Patch it up / As long as I have you (With The Jordanaires.) / You'll think of me / Wild in the country (With The Jordanaires,).

P 22

■ DELETED

LP Set . . . . LPM 6402
RCA / Aug '71 / BMG.

YOU DON'T HAVE TO SAY YOU LOVE ME.
Tracks: You don't have to say you love me.
■ 7" . . . . RCA 2046
RCA / Jan '71.

YOU GOTTA STOP.
Tracks: You gotta stop / Love machine.
■ 7" . . . . RCA 1593
RCA / May '67.

YOU'LL NEVER WALK ALONE.
Tracks: You'll never walk alone / Peace in the valley / I believe / It is no secret / Take my hand precious Lord / Swing low sweet chariot.
LP. . . . . CDS 1088
■ MC . . . . CAM 415
RCA/Camden / '71.

YOU'LL NEVER WALK ALONE.
Tracks: You'll never walk alone.
■ 7" . . . . RCA 1747
RCA / Oct '68.

YOU'RE TIME HASN'T COME YET BABY.
Tracks: You're time hasn't come yet baby.
■ 7" . . . . RCA 1714
RCA / Jul '68.

YOUNG ELVIS (The Early Years).
Tracks: Not Advised.
VHS. . . . . CFV 10342
Channel 5 / Oct '90 / Channel 5 Video / P.R.O. Video / Gold & Sons.
VHS. 0835103
Polygram T.V / Jul '91 / PolyGram.

Preston, Jimmy

JIMMY PRESTON - 1948 TO 1950.
Tracks: Messin' with Preston / Chop Suey Louie / Hucklebuck Daddy / Rock the joint / Early morning blues.
CD . . . . FLYCD 33
Flyright / Apr '91 / Hot Shot / Roots Records / Wellard Dist. / Charly / Swift / Projection.

JIMMY PRESTON 1949-1950.
Tracks: Swingin' in the groove / They call me the champ / I'm lonesome / Hang out tonight / Potato salad / Oh Mr. Possum / Hey everybody / Hey everybody (alternative take) / Early morning blues / Hay ride / Estellina bim bam / Credit blues / Going away.
LP. . . . . KK 806
Krazy Kat / Dec '86 / Hot Shot / C.M. Distribution / Wellard Dist. / Roots Records / Projection / Charly / Jazz Music.

ROCK THE JOINT (Jimmy Preston vol 2).
Tracks: Rock the joint / Drinking woman / Hucklebuck Daddy / Sugar baby / They call me the champ / Let me call you sweetheart / Messin' with Preston / Numbers blues / Chop suey Louie / Home cookin' mama / Hold me baby / Do the bump / They call me the champ (2) / Let's hang out tonight.
LP. . . . . KK 827
Krazy Kat / Apr '88 / Hot Shot / C.M. Distribution / Wellard Dist. / Roots Records / Projection / Charly / Jazz Music.

ROCK THE JOINT (EP).
Tracks: Rock the joint / Do the bump / Hucklebuck daddy / Let's hang out tonight.
■ EP. . . . . KKEP 01
Krazy Kat / Jul '88 / Hot Shot / C.M. Distribution / Wellard Dist. / Roots Records / Projection / Charly / Jazz Music.

Preston, Johnny

CHARMING BILLY.
Tracks: Charming Billy.
■ 7" . . . . AMT 1114
Mercury (EMI) / Dec '60.

COME ROCK WITH ME.
Tracks: Not Advised.
LP. . . . . SR 60609
Treasure / Oct '87 / Jetstar.
LP. . . . . DEMAND 0035
Demand / Oct '87.

CRADLE OF LOVE.
Tracks: Cradle of love.
■ 7" . . . . AMT 1092
Mercury (EMI) / Apr '60.

FEEL SO FINE.
Tracks: Feel so fine / I'm starting to go steady.
■ 7" . . . . AMT 1104
Mercury (EMI) / Aug '60.

HIS TOP HITS.
Tracks: Not Advised.
MC 824
Timeless Treasures / Sep '87 / Terry Blood Dist.

RUNNING BEAR.
Tracks: Running bear.
■ 7" . . . . AMT 1079
Mercury (EMI) / Feb '60.

RUNNING BEAR (CD).
Tracks: Charming Billy / Running bear / Cradle of love / Chief heartbreak / My heart knows / That's all I want / Just little boy blue / Leave my kitten alone / Sitting here crying / I want a rock and roll guitar / Hearts of stone / Do what you did / I played around with my love / Chosen few / Up in the air / Kissin' tree / Four letter word / Feel so fine / She once belonged to me / New baby for christmas / City of tears / I'm startin' to go steady with the blues / Dream / Madre de dios / You'll never walk alone / Danny Boy / Broken heart anonymous.
CD . . . . BCD 15473
Bear Family / '88 / Rollercoaster Records / Swift / Direct Distribution.

RUNNING BEAR (OLD GOLD).
Tracks: Running bear / Cradle of love.
7" . . . . OG 9461
Old Gold / Jan '85 / Pickwick Records.

Price, Malcolm

AND THEN WE ALL GOT UP...
Tracks: Not Advised.
LP. . . . . SFA 017
Sweet Folk & Country / Dec '77 / Wellard Dist.

BOURGEOIS BLUES.
Tracks: Not Advised.
LP. . . . . WF 003
Waterfront / Mar '84 / SRD / Jazz Music / A.D.A Distribution / C.M. Distribution.

IN AN OLD DUTCH HOUSE.
Tracks: Not Advised.
LP. . . . . MU 7437
Stoof / Jan '78 / Roots Records / C.M. Distribution.

Price, Ray

Sadly Ray Price, another of country's all-time most successful artists (No. 6 in the Billboard listings, as published in 1989), never achieved any degree of success on this side of the Atlantic, a great tragedy, as he not only possessed one of the finest voices in the business but was also able to handle a diverse range of material as indicated by almost 40 years of chart success. Nicknamed the Cherokee Cowboy, he was born on January 12, 1926 in Perryville, Texas but raised in Dallas. It was here that he got his initial break on the influential radio show Big D Jamboree, and recorded for the label Small Bullet but quickly moved into the big league on Columbia, achieving his first nationwide hit with *Talk to your heart* . A singer in the raw honky-tonk vein, the decade saw Price putting his inimitable stamp on many subsequent classic songs including *Release me* (1954), *Crazy arms* (1956), *My shoes keep walking back to you* (1957), *City lights* (1958) and *Heartaches by the number* (1959), many of them also achieving success in the pop charts. On stage he was accompanied by the Cherokee Cowboys, an outfit comprising members of the late Hank Williams' Drifting Cowboys. Ray Price was an artist able to foretell change and, with the advent of the smoother Nashville sound in the 60's, he started using strings on his recordings without having any adverse effect on his popularity. *Make the world go away* and *Burning memories* were a couple of the earliest string accompanied recordings and when he tackled Kristofferson's *For the good times* , it went straight to number one in the country and pop charts while the album remained in the US charts for over four years. Since leaving Columbia in 1975, Price has semi-retired, though he continued to record for a succession of labels - and maintained his chart appearances right up to the present date, though not with the force of earlier decades, but Ray Price needn't worry, 110 quality hit singles is a record that puts him in a league of his own. (Tony Byworth)

DIAMONDS IN THE STARS.
Tracks: Diamonds in the stars / Let it rain let her cry / Something to forget you by / It don't hurt me half as bad / Forty and fadin' / When you gave your love to me / She's the right kind of woman / Circle driveway / Getting over you again / I'm still not over you.
■ LP. . . . . YBLP 121
Young Blood / Dec '81.

DIAMONDS IN THE STARS.
Tracks: Diamonds in the stars / Let it rain, let her cry.
■ 7" . . . . YB 121
Young Blood / Nov '81.

ESSENTIAL RAY PRICE 1951-1962.
Tracks: If you're ever lonely darling / Road of no return, The / Talk to your heart / Move on in and stay / I'll be there / Release me / I can't go home like this / You done me wrong / Falling falling falling / Wasted words / Crazy arms / I've got a new heartache / My shoes keep walking back to you / Invitation to the blues / City lights / Heartaches by the number / Same old me, The / One more time / Heart over mind / Pride.
CD 48532
Columbia (USA) / Sep '91 / Columbia (Imports).

HONKY TONK YEARS 1951-53, THE.
Tracks: Not Advised.
LP. . . . . SS 22
Rounder / Dec '88 / Projection / Roots Records / Swift / C.M. Distribution / Topic Records / Jazz Music / Hot Shot / A.D.A Distribution / Direct Distribution.

Pride Of Nashville

COUNTRY SYMPHONY.
Tracks: Country symphony.
7" . . . . TU 102
Thumbs Up / Jan '81.

Pride, Charley

Charley was one of 11 children, born in Sledge, Mississippi - a small town 60 miles south of Memphis. He earned his living picking cotton alongside his family until he was 17 years old. At that time Charley made a bid for what, as a child, had been his first love - baseball. He played in the Negro American League with Detroit and Memphis Red Sox until entering the military during the late 50's. Returning to baseball, he made it to the Major league for a brief period in 1961, playing outfield and pitching for the Los Angeles Angels. Although the career in baseball never fully materialised, his dreams of playing have never died. Charley goes to Spring training with the Texas Rangers every year. Attracted to music (along with baseball), at an early age, Charley learned the songs he heard on his family's radio, which was usually tuned to WSM Radio in Nashville. His attraction to country music grew stronger with age, and he eventually purchased a a Sears' Silvertone guitar and started singing along. Charley likes to downplay his importance in the music world, but his low key, straight forward style speaks for itself. He has not only established himself as an industry leader, but has been instrumental in the careers of country artists Dave and Sugar, Ronnie Milsap, Gary Stewart, Johnny Duncan and Johnny Russell.

20 OF THE BEST: CHARLEY PRIDE.
Tracks: All I have to offer you is me / Wonder could I live there anymore / I can't believe that you stopped loving me / I'd rather love you / I'm just me / It's gonna take a little bit longer / Amazing love / Then who am I / Hope you're feelin' me (like I'm feelin' you) / My eyes can only see as far as you / She's just an old love turned memory / Someone loves you honey / Where do I put her memory / You're my Jamaica / Honky tonk blues / You win again / Never been so loved (in all my life) / You're so good when you're bad / Why baby why / Night games.
CD . . . . ND 89848
RCA / Jul '90 / BMG.
MC . . . . NK 89848
RCA / May '90 / BMG.
■ LP. . . . . NL 89848
RCA / May '90.

AFTER ALL THIS TIME.
Tracks: Even knowin' / Have I got some blues for you / Looking at a sure thing / After all this time / Next to you, I like me / If you still want a fool around / On the other hand / One of these days / Look in your mirror / You took me there.
LP. . . . . RITZLP 0042
MC . . . . RITZLC 042
Ritz / Apr '87 / Pinnacle / Midland Records.
CD . . . . RITZCD 510
MC . . . . RITZC 510
Ritz / '91 / Pinnacle / Midland Records.

AMAZING LOVE.
Tracks: Comin' down with love / If she just helps me (get over you) / I'm only losin' everything I threw away / Footprints in the sands of time / Amazing love / Blue Ridge Mountains turning green / I've just found another reason for loving you / Old photographs / I'm glad it was you / Mr. Joe Henry's happy hand-clappin' open air.
LP. AFL1 0397
■ MC AFK1 0397
RCA / '79.

AMY'S EYES.
Tracks: White house's / Moody woman / Amy's eyes / After me, after you / I made love to you in my mind / Whole lotta love on the line / Nickles and dimes and love / Look who's looking / I wrote the songs that broke her heart / You hold my world together / Right one, The / Plenty good lovin'.
CD . . . . RITZ CD 0057
MC . . . . RITZ LC 0057
Ritz / Nov '90 / Pinnacle / Midland Records.
CD . . . . RITZRCD 525
MC . . . . RITZRC 525
Ritz / Apr '93 / Pinnacle / Midland Records.

AMY'S EYES.
Tracks: Amy's eyes / Whole lotta love on the line.
7" . . . . RITZ 218
Ritz / Dec '90 / Pinnacle / Midland Records.

BEST OF CHARLEY PRIDE.
Tracks: Just between you and me / Does my ring hurt your finger / Kaw-liga / Snakes crawl at night, The / All I have to offer you is me / Easy part's over, The / Day the

world stood still, The / I know one / Gone, on the other hand / Before I met you / Too hard to say I'm sorry / Let the chips fall.
MC . . . . PK 42014
RCA / Sep '77 / BMG.
■ LP. . . . . PL 42014
RCA / Sep '77.

BEST OF CHARLEY PRIDE VOL 2.
Tracks: Place for the lonesome, A / I'd rather love you / Is anybody going to San Antone / Kiss an angel good morning / (In my world) you don't belong / (There's still) someone I can't forget / I'm just me / Let me live / (I'm so) afraid of losing you again / You'll still be the one.
MC . . . . PK 42009
RCA / Jan '77 / BMG.
■ LP. . . . . LSA 3105
RCA / Jan '77.

BEST OF CHARLEY PRIDE VOL 3.
Tracks: I don't deserve a mansion / My eyes can only see as far as you / Happiness of having you, The / Hope you're feelin' me (like I'm feelin' you) / I ain't all bad / Then who am I? / Mississippi cotton picking delta town / Searching for the morning sun / Amazing love / Don't fight the feelings of love / Oklahoma morning.
LP. . . . . LSA 3283
■ MC . . . . MPK 254
RCA / '79.

BEST OF CHARLY PRIDE.
Tracks: Just between you and me / Does my ring hurt your finger / Is anyone going to San Antone / Snakes crawl at night, The / (In my world) you don't belong / Easy part's over, The / I'm just me / I know one / Gone, on the other hand / Before I met you / Too hard to say I'm sorry / Kiss an angel good morning / Place for the lonesome, A / I'd rather love you / Kaw-liga / Let the chips fall / All I have to offer you (is me) / (There's still) someone I can't forget / Day the world stood still, The / Let me live / (I'm so) afraid of losing you again / You'll still be the one.
■ MC Set. . . . . DPTK 5009
RCA / '79.

BURGERS AND FRIES.
Tracks: Burgers and fries / Best in the world / Whose arms are you in tonight / Nothing's prettier than Rose is / Mem'ries / When I stop leaving / I can see the lovin' in your eyes / One on one / Where do I put her memory / You snap your fingers.
■ LP. . . . . PL 12983
RCA / Jan '79.

CHARLEY.
Tracks: Hope you're feelin' me (like I'm feelin' you) / Searching for the morning sun / Hardest part of livin's loving me, The / Now and then / Fools / I ain't all bad / She's as close as I can get to loving you / One mile more / You're the woman behind everything / Lovin' understandin' man.
■ LP. . . . . LSA 3246
RCA / '79.

CHARLEY PRIDE.
Tracks: Not Advised.
VHS. . . . . TVE 1039
Telstar Video / May '92 / BMG.

CHARLEY PRIDE.
Tracks: Mississippi cotton pickin' delta town / Streets of gold / Before the next teardrop falls / Happy street / Pass me by / Then who am I / Mr. Joe Henry's happy hand-clappin' open air rhythm band / Does my ring hurt your finger / Good-hearted woman, A / I'm a lonesome fugitive / Piroque Joe / Best banjo picker / Just between you and me / Folsom Prison blues / Distant drums / Kaw-liga / Act naturally / Amazing love / We could / Able-bodied man / Fifteen years ago / Shoulder to cry on, A / On the southbound / She's too good to be true.
■ MC . . . . DHYK 0002
RCA / '78 / BMG.

CHARLEY PRIDE - LIVE.
Tracks: Whole lot of lovin' / Just between you and me / Anybody going to San Antone / Kiss an angel good morning / All I have to offer you is me / Do what you do well / Does my ring hurt your finger / Love sick blues / I'm gonna love her on the radio / You took me there / Streets of Baltimore / Kaw-liga / Crystal chandeliers / Cottonfields / He'll have to go / I'm gettin' better.
VHS. . . . . V 9095
MSD / Jun '88 / Multiple Sound Distributors / Gold & Sons.
VHS. . . . . RITZV 0006
Ritz / '90 / Pinnacle / Midland Records.

CHARLEY PRIDE COLLECTION.
Tracks: I'd rather love you / Time / Jeannie Norman / Anywhere / When the trains come in / Piroque Joe / Was it all worth losing you / Instant loneliness / This highway leads to glory / Time out for Jesus / Yonder comes a sucker / Able bodied man / What money can't buy / Billy Bayou / Detroit city / Me and Bobby McGee / Act naturally / Banks of the Ohio / That's my way / Last thing on my mind.
Double LP . . . . PDA 058
Pickwick / Apr '79 / Pickwick Records.
MC Set. . . . . PDC 058
Pickwick / Jul '80 / Pickwick Records.

CHARLEY PRIDE GOLDEN COLLECTION, THE.
Tracks: Not Advised.
LP. . . . . NE 1056
K-Tel / Jan '80 / I & B Records / C.M. Distribution / Arabesque Ltd. / Mono Distributors (Jersey) Ltd. / Prism Leisure PLC / PolyGram / Ross Records / Prism Leisure PLC.

CHARLEY PRIDE SINGS HEART SONGS.
Tracks: You'll still be the one / Anywhere (just inside your arms) / I'm beginning to believe my own lies / Kiss an angel good morning / What money can't buy / No one could ever take me from you / Jeannie Norman / Once again / Miracles, music and my wife / Pretty houses for sale.
■ LP. . . . . LSA 3052
RCA / '79.

CHARLEY PRIDE SPECIAL.
Tracks: Able bodied man / Through the years / Is anybody going to San Antone / Thought of losing you / I think I'll take a walk / Things are looking up / Special / Poor boy like me, A / (There's) Nobody home to go home to / This is my year for Mexico.
■ LP. . . . . SF 8171
RCA / Apr '71.
LP. . . . . PL 42013
■ MC . . . . PK 42013
RCA / '79.

CHARLEY SINGS EVERYBODY'S CHOICE.
Tracks: I don't think she's in love anymore / I see the devil in your deep blue eyes / You're so good when you're bad / When she dances / Mountain of love / Oh what a beautiful love song / I haven't loved this way in years / Cup of love / Love is a shadow / I hope (you never cry again).
LP. . . . . RCALP 3075
LP. . . . . PL 84287
MC . . . . RCAK 3075
MC . . . . PK 84287
RCA / Jun '84 / BMG.

CHARLIE PRIDE SONG BOOK.
Tracks: Not Advised.
MC . . . . AM 115
VFM Cassettes / VFM Children's Entertainment Ltd. / Midland Records / Morley Audio Services.

CHRISTMAS IN MY HOMETOWN.
Tracks: Christmas in my home town / Deck the halls with boughs of holly / They stood in silent prayer / Santa and the kids / Silent night / Little drummer boy / Happy Christmas day / First Christmas morn, The / Christmas and love / O holy night.
■ LP. . . . . LSA 3185
RCA / '79.

CLASSICS WITH PRIDE.
Tracks: Most beautiful girl in the world / Always on my mind / You've got to stand for something / After all these years / I don't know why I love you but I do / If tomorrow never comes / Ramblin' rose / You'll never walk alone / Please help me I'm falling / Here in the real world / Walk on by / I love you because / Four in the morning / It's just a matter of time / Ramona / What's another year.
CD . . . . CD 0064
MC . . . . LC 0064
Ritz / Feb '92 / Pinnacle / Midland Records.

COUNTRY CHARLEY PRIDE.
Tracks: Busted / Distant drums / Detroit City / Yonder comes a sucker / Green, green grass of home / That's the chance I'll have to take / Snakes crawl at night, The / Miller's cave / Atlantic coastal line, The / Got leavin' on her mind.
LP. . . . . LSA 3143
■ MC . . . . MPK 183
RCA / '79.

COUNTRY FEELIN'.
Tracks: Which way do we go? / We could / It amazes me / All his children / Streets of gold / I don't see how I can love you anymore / Singin' a song about love / Man I used to be, The / Let my love in / Love put a song in my heart.
LP. AFL1 0534
■ MC AFK1 0534
RCA / '79.

COUNTRY GREATS.
Tracks: Busted / Distant drums / Detroit City / Yonder comes a sucker / Green, green grass of home / That's the chance I'll have to take / Before I met you / Folsom Prison blues / Snakes crawl at night, The / Miller's cave / Atlantic coastal line, The / Got leavin' on her mind.
MC . . . . TCMFP 5816
MFP / Feb '88 / EMI.
■ LP. . . . . MFP 5816
MFP / Feb '88.

COUNTRY STORE: CHARLEY PRIDE.
Tracks: Not Advised.
LP. . . . . CST 24
MC . . . . CSTK 24
Country Store / Aug '86 / BMG.

COUNTRY WAY, THE.
Tracks: Too hard to say I'm sorry / Little folks, The / Crystal chandeliers / Act naturally / Does my ring hurt your finger / Mama don't cry for me / Day the world stood still, The / Gone, on the other hand / You can tell the world / I'll wander back to you / Life turned her that way / I threw away the rose.
LP. . . . . LSA 3145
■ MC . . . . MPK 185
RCA / '79.

CRYSTAL CHANDELIERS.
Tracks: Crystal chandeliers / Honky tonk blues.
■ 7" . . . . PB 9528
RCA / Apr '80.

CRYSTAL CHANDELIERS (OLD GOLD).
Tracks: Crystal chandeliers / Does my ring hurt your finger.
7" . . . . OG 9608
Old Gold / Feb '89 / Pickwick Records.

DIAMOND SERIES: CHARLEY PRIDE.
Tracks: Crystal chandeliers / Act naturally / Does my ring hurt your finger? / Day the world stood still, The / Love turned her that way / Last thing on my mind / Just between you and me / Apartment No.9 / I know one / Happiness of having you, The / My eyes can only see as far as you / Help me make it through the night / She's just an old love turned memory / Rhinestone cowboy / Somebody loves you, honey / Where do I put her memory?.
■ CD . . . . CD 90120
Diamond Series / Apr '88.

DID YOU THINK TO PRAY.
Tracks: Did you think to pray / I'll fly away / Time out for Jesus / Angel band / Jesus, don't give up on me / Let me live / Whispering hope / This highway leads to glory / Church in the wildwood, The / Lord, build me a cabin in glory.
LP. . . . . LSA 3156
■ MC . . . . MPK 188
RCA / '79.

DO WHAT YOU DO, DO WELL.
Tracks: Do what you do do well / If we're just killing time (Let's love it to death).
7" . . . . RITZ 192
Ritz / Oct '88 / Pinnacle / Midland Records.

EASY PART'S OVER, THE.
Tracks: Easy part's over, The / Right to do wrong, The.
7" . . . . RCA 1693
RCA / Nov '79 / BMG.

EVERY HEART SHOULD HAVE ONE.
Tracks: Every heart should have one / Lovin' it up.
7" . . . . RCA 393
RCA / Mar '84 / BMG.

GREATEST HITS.
Tracks: Kaw-liga / I'm so afraid of losing you again / Oklahoma morning / It's going to take a little bit longer / Crystals chandeliers / Does my ring hurt your finger / Too good to be true / I'd rather love you / All I have to offer you is me / I wonder could I live there anymore / Is anybody going to San Antone / I'm just me / Shutters and boards / Happiness of having you, The / My eyes can only see as far as you / Kiss an angel good morning / Let me live in the light of his light / Mississippi cotton picking Delta town / Help me make it through the night / Louisanna man / There goes my everything / Love sick blues / Me and Bobby McGee.
CD . . . . PLATCD 361
MC . . . . PLAC 361
Prism / '91 / Pinnacle / Midland Records.

GREATEST HITS: CHARLEY PRIDE VOL.2.
Tracks: Let a little love come in / Every heart should have one / You're so good when you're bad / Why baby why / Power of love, The / Down on the farm / Night games / I don't think she's in love anymore / Mountain of love / Now and then.
LP. . . . . PL 85426
■ MC . . . . PK 85426
RCA / Jul '85.

HAPPINESS OF HAVING YOU, THE.
Tracks: Happiness of having you, The / I can't keep my hands off you / Everything I am / My eyes can only see as far as you / I've got a woman to lean on / Right back missing you again / Help me make it through the night / Oklahoma morning / Everything she touches turns to love / Signs of love.
■ LP. . . . . LSA 3262
RCA / '79.

HAVE I GOT SOME BLUES FOR YOU.
Tracks: Have I got some blues for you / Even knowin'.
7" . . . . RITZ 175
Ritz / May '87 / Pinnacle / Midland Records.

HELP ME MAKE IT THROUGH THE NIGHT.
Tracks: Help me make it through the night / Crystal chandeliers / Me and Bobby McGee.
■ 7" . . . . RCA 2664
RCA / Apr '76.

HITS OF CHARLEY PRIDE, THE.
Tracks: Happiness of having you, The / Then who am I / Kiss an angel good morning / I ain't all bad / It's gonna take a little bit longer / I'd rather love you / She's too good to be true / Did you think to pray / Mississippi cotton picking delta town / Hope you're feelin' me (like I'm feelin' you) / I'm just me / Amazing love / Don't fight the feelings of love / Shoulder to cry on, A / All his children / We could.
LP. . . . . PL 42178
■ MC . . . . PK 42178
RCA / '79.

HUNGER, THE.
Tracks: Hunger, The / She's just an old love turned memory.

P 24

■ DELETED

■ 7" . . . . PB 9075
RCA / Apr '77.

I DON'T KNOW WHY I LOVE YOU BUT I DO.
Tracks: I don't know why I love you but I do / Ramona.
CD Single . . . . RITZCD 244
Ritz / Oct '92 / Pinnacle / Midland Records.

I'M GONNA LOVE HER ON THE RADIO.
Tracks: I'm gonna love her on the radio / She's soft to touch / Your used to be / Come on in and let me love you / There ain't lovin' / Little piece of Heaven, A / If we're just killing time (Let's love it to death).
CD . . . . RITZCD 108
LP . . . . RITZLP 0048
MC . . . . RITZLC 048
Ritz / Nov '88 / Pinnacle / Midland Records.
CD . . . . RITZCD 511
MC . . . . RITZC 511
Ritz / '91 / Pinnacle / Midland Records.

I'M JUST ME.
Tracks: On the Southbound / (In my world) you don't belong / You never gave up on me / I'd rather love you / Instant loneliness / I'm just me / Place for the lonesome, A / Hello darlin' / You're still the only one I'll ever love / That's my way.
LP . . . . LSA 3050
■ **MC** . . . . MPK 194
RCA / '79.

IN PERSON.
Tracks: Last thing on my mind / Just between you and me / I know one / Lovesick blues / Image of me, The / Kaw-liga / Shutters and boards / Six days on the road / Streets of Baltimore / Crystal chandeliers / Introduction by Po Bowell.
LP . . . . LSA 3100
■ **MC** . . . . PK 42007
RCA / '76.
LP . . . . INTS 5026
LP . . . . NL 80996
MC . . . . INTK 5026
MC . . . . NK 80996
RCA International / Jul '80 / BMG.

JUST PLAIN CHARLEY.
Tracks: Me and Bobby McGee / Good chance of tear fall tonight, A / One time / (I'm so) Afraid of losing you again / Brand new bed of roses, A / That's why I love you so much / If you'd have only taken the time / Gone, gone, gone / Happy Street / I'm a lonesome fugitive / It's all right.
LP . . . . LSA 3146
■ **MC** . . . . MPK 186
RCA / '79.

MAGIC MOMENTS WITH CHARLEY PRIDE.
Tracks: Crystal chandeliers / Just between you and me / All I have to offer you is me / I'm so afraid of losing you again / Is anybody going to San Antone / Wonder could I live there anymore / I can't believe that you've stopped loving me / I'd rather love you / I'm just me / Kiss an angel good morning / Don't fight the feelings of love / Amazing love / Hope you're feelin' me (like I'm feelin' you) / Happiness of having you, The / My eyes can only see as far as you / She's just an old love turned memory / Someone loves you honey / Easy part's over, The / I know one / Kawliga / Does my ring hurt your finger / (there's still) someone I can't forget / Day the world stood still, The / Let the chips fall.
■ **MC** . . . . NK 89621
RCA / May '85.

MAKE MINE COUNTRY.
Tracks: Now I can live again / Word or two to Mary, A / If you should come back today / Guess things happen that way / Before the next teardrop falls / Banks of the Ohio / Wings of a dove / Girl I used to know, A / Lie to me / Why didn't I think of that / Above and beyond / Baby is gone.
LP . . . . LSA 3049
■ **MC** . . . . MPK 181
RCA / '79.
■ **LP** . . . . RD 7966
RCA / Oct '79 / BMG.

NIGHT GAMES.
Tracks: Draw the line / Love on a blue rainy day / Late show, The / Night games / Down in Louisiana / Ev'ry heart should have one / Thanks for wakin' me up this mornin' / Lovin' it up (livin' it down) / Just can't leave that woman alone / I could let her get close to me.
CD . . . . PD 84822
LP . . . . PL 84822
■ **MC** . . . . PK 84822
RCA / Oct '83.

POWER OF LOVE.
Tracks: Not Advised.
LP . . . . PL 85031
■ **MC** . . . . PK 85031
RCA / Aug '84.

POWER OF LOVE.
Tracks: Power of love / Elite, The.
■ 7" . . . . RCA 431
RCA / Jul '84.

PRIDE OF AMERICA.
Tracks: Then who am I / I still can't leave your memory alone / Hard times will be the best times, The / Completely helpless / Mississippi cotton picking delta town / She loves me the way that I love you / Mary go round / That was forever ago / Thorns of life / North wind.
LP . . . . LSA 3202
■ **MC** . . . . MPK 236
RCA / '79.

PRIDE OF COUNTRY MUSIC.
Tracks: In the middle nowhere / Last thing on my mind / Just between you and me / Apartment No.9 / Spell of the freight train / I know one / I'm not the boy I used to be / Good woman's love, A / Silence / Take me home / Touch my heart / Best banjo picker.
LP . . . . LSA 3144
■ **MC** . . . . MPK 184
RCA / '79.

ROLL ON MISSISSIPPI.
Tracks: Roll on, Mississippi, roll on / I used to be that way / Taking the easy way out / She's as good as gone / He can be an angel / Fall back on me / Make it special again / You beat 'em all / Ghost written love letters / You almost slipped my mind.
LP . . . . RCALP 5019
MC . . . . RCAK 5019
RCA / Apr '81 / BMG.

ROLL ON MISSISSIPPI.
Tracks: Roll on Mississippi / Fall back on me.
■ 7" . . . . RCA 49
RCA / Mar '81.

SAMPLE CHARLEY PRIDE.
Tracks: On the Southbound / What money can't buy / Did you think to pray / Louisiana man / Someday you will / Me and Bobby McGee / That's the only way life's good to me / Wings of a dove.
LP . . . . SAS 1005
■ **MC** . . . . MPK 238
RCA / '78 / BMG.

SENSATIONAL CHARLEY PRIDE.
Tracks: Louisiana man / She's still got a hold on you / Let the chips fall / Come on home and sing the blues to Daddy / Never more than I / Let me live / Take care of the little things / Even after everything's she's done / (It's just a matter of) making up my mind / It's the little things / Billy Bayou / We had all the good things going.
LP . . . . PL 42023
■ **MC** . . . . PK 42023
RCA / '79.

SHE'S JUST AN OLD LOVE TURNED MEMORY.
Tracks: She's just an old love turned memory / Rhinestone cowboy / Hunger, The / Whole lotta things to sing about, A / I feel the country callin' me / I'll be leaving alone / We need lovin' / Country music / Rose is for today, The / Get up off your good intentions.
LP . . . . PL 12261
■ **MC** . . . . PK 12261
RCA / May '77.

SOMEONE LOVES YOU HONEY.
Tracks: Someone loves you honey / Georgia keeps pulling on my ring / I love you / Play, guitar, play / Another 'I love you' kind of day / More to me / Days of our lives / Daydreams about night things / Heaven watches over fools like me / Days of sand and shovels, The.
LP . . . . PL 12478
■ **MC** . . . . PK 12478
RCA / Jun '78.

SOMEONE LOVES YOU HONEY.
Tracks: Someone loves you honey / Days of our lives.
■ 7" . . . . PB 1201
RCA / '79.

SONGS OF LOVE BY CHARLEY PRIDE.
Tracks: Too weak to let you go / She's too good to be true / She's that kind / You were all the good in me / Give a lonely heart a home / Good hearted woman / I love you more in memory / My love is deep, my love is wide / (Darlin' think of me) every now and then / I'm building bridges.
■ **LP** . . . . LSA 3155
RCA / '79.

SONGS OF PRIDE.
Tracks: Someday you will / She made me go / Right to do wrong, The / Easy part's over, The / Day you stop loving me, The / I could have saved you the time / One of these days / All the time / My heart is a house / Let me help you work it out / Both of us love you / Top of the world, The.
MC . . . . PK 42015
RCA / Mar '78 / BMG.
■ **LP** . . . . PL 42015
RCA / Mar '78.

SUNDAY MORNING WITH CHARLEY PRIDE.
Tracks: I don't deserve a mansion / Be grateful / He's the man / In Jesus' name I pray / Without mama here / Little Delta church / Next year finally came / Jesus is your saviour child / He took my place / Brush arbour meeting.
■ **LP** . . . . LSA 3267
RCA / '79.

SUNSHINY DAY WITH CHARLEY PRIDE, A.
Tracks: Sunshine day / When the trains come in / You're wanting me to stop loving you / Back to the country roads / Put back my ring on your hand / It's gonna take a little bit longer / Seven years with a wonderful woman / She's helping me get over you / One more year / Nothin' left but leavin' / Is anybody goin' to San Antone / Last thing on my mind, The / Crystal chandeliers / Streets of Baltimore / What money can't buy / Before I met you.
■ **MC** . . . . MPK 171
RCA / '78 / BMG.
■ **LP** . . . . LSA 3122
RCA / Sep '78 / BMG.

SWEET COUNTRY.
Tracks: Along the Mississippi / Happiest song on the jukebox, The / Shelter of your eyes, The / I'm learning to love her / Don't fight the feelings of love / Just to be loved by you / Tennessee girl / Love unending / Pass me by / Shoulder to cry on, A.
LP . . . . LSA 3181
■ **MC** . . . . MPK 214
RCA / '79.

THAT'S MY WAY.
Tracks: Not Advised.
LP . . . . CDS 1166
MC . . . . CAM 1166
RCA/Camden / Mar '85 / BMG / Arabesque Ltd.

THERE'S A LITTLE BIT OF HANK IN ME.
Tracks: There's a little bit of Hank in me / My son calls another man daddy / Moanin' the blues / Mansion on the hill / Mind your own business / I can't help it / Honky tonk blues / I'm so lonesome I could cry / Low down blues / I could never be ashamed of you / Why don't you love me / You win again.
■ **LP** . . . . PL 13548
RCA / Jul '80.

TO ALL MY WONDERFUL FANS FROM ME TO YOU.
Tracks: That's the only way life's good to me / I can't believe that you've stopped loving me / There's still someone I can't forget / Sweet promises / Was it all worth losing you / Fifteen years ago / Wonder could I live there anymore / Piroque Joe / Time (you're not a friend of mine) / Today is that tomorrow.
■ **LP** . . . . LSA 3147
RCA / '79.

VERY BEST OF CHARLEY PRIDE, THE.
Tracks: I'd rather love you / Is anybody going to San Antone / I'm so afraid of losing you again / Kiss an angel good morning / Just between you and me / All I have to offer you is me / Wonder could I live there anymore / I can't believe that you're stopped loving me / I'm just me / Crystal chandeliers / Amazing love / Happiness of having you, The / Easy part's over, The / I know one / Does my ring hurt your finger / For the good times / Kaw-liga / My eyes can only see as far as you / She's just an old love turned memory / Someone loves you honey.
LP . . . . RCALP 5049
■ **MC** . . . . RCAK 5049
RCA / '81.
■ **LP** . . . . PL 89088
RCA / '84.
■ **MC** . . . . PK 89088
RCA / '84.

WHOLE LOT OF LOVIN', A.
Tracks: Whole lot of lovin', A.
7" . . . . RITZ 196
Ritz / Feb '89 / Pinnacle / Midland Records.

WHOLE LOT OF THINGS TO SING ABOUT.
Tracks: Whole lot of things to sing about / Hardest part of living.
■ 7" . . . . RCA 2744
RCA / Oct '76.

YOU TOOK ME THERE.
Tracks: You took me there / One of these days.
7" . . . . RITZ 183
Ritz / Jan '88 / Pinnacle / Midland Records.

YOU'RE MY JAMAICA.
Tracks: What're we doing, doing this again / No relief in sight / Playin' around / Missin' you / You're my Jamaica / Heartbreak mountain / To have and to hold / Let me have a chance to love you / I want you / When the good times outweighed the bad.
MC . . . . PK 13441
RCA / Dec '79 / BMG.
■ **LP** . . . . PL 13441
RCA / Feb '80.

YOU'RE MY JAMAICA.
Tracks: You're my Jamaica / Let me have a chance.
■ 7" . . . . PB 1655
RCA / Oct '79.

YOU'VE GOT TO STAND FOR SOMETHING.
Tracks: You've got to stand for something.
CD Single . . . . RITZCD 253
Ritz / Nov '92 / Pinnacle / Midland Records.

Prine, John

Born 10.10.1946, Maywood, Illinois, and arguably mid America's finest ever singer - songwriter. Served in the US army and walked the beat as a postman. Wrote songs in his spare time, playing the folk club circuit in Chicago where he won a 'open mic' contest. The songs used on this historic occasion being *Sam stoen* , *Hello in there* and *Paradise* - all now hailed as classics. The much recorded *Paradise* (Lynn Anderson had a top 30 hit in 1976) was drawn from his experience as a child, when he'd visit his grandparents down in Muhlenburg County, Kentucky, and was about strip coal mining's desecration of the land. Kris Kristofferson and Steve Goodman (who was to become his close friend and on occasions, his singing partner) were instrumental to him obtaining a recording contract on Atlantic in 1970. Prine's well recieved albums, while not selling in large numbers, were winning him a varied following from folk and country, his astute, wry humour winning through, whatever the subject. Albums include *Diamonds in the rough* , the Memphis Sun recorded *The pink cadillac* , *Storm windows* and *Bruised orange* . *Storm windows* (in 1981) being his last for a major label because Prine had become disenchanted with their line of action. After some thought Prine, and good friend Al Bunetta, came up with the idea of setting up their own label - Oh Boy Records, where, in 1984 *Aimless love* debuted for the trusty songwriter among Prine's snaches of life was *Unwed fathers* . Once again he attracted the attention of the country fraternity - both Gail Davies and Tammy Wynette enjoying chart success. Prine was next to swing towards acoustic music with the album *German afternoons* (1987) based along those lines. Songs of Leon Payne and the Carter Family appear alongside homegrown efforts such as the heavily covered *Speed of the sound of lonliness* (A chart hit for Kim Carnes), whilst Nanci Griffith and Ireland's Susan McCann (among others) have done covers. From his live shows came the 1988 release *John Prine live* , where he's captured telling stories and singing his many fine songs - many as a solo act the intimate surroundings of the Coach House, San Juan, others with Nashville musicians. This album was all the more memorable for the inclusion of *Souvenirs* , a duet with Steve Goodman. In 1989 Prine was found recording with the Nitty Gritty Band, his *Grandpa was a carpenter* gaining inclusion on the band's *Will the circle be unbroken vol.2* on double album. In 1991 his Grammy winning *The missing years* sold in excess of 4000,000 copies, an all-time best - where, like all his Oh Boy product, it gained a UK release on This Way Up. Other projects where his work appears include John Mellencamp's 1992 Mercury film soundtrack *Falling from grace*. Both solo (*All the best*) and, as part of the Buzzin Cousins (1992) *Sweet Suzanne* made the country singles chart - while his live working of *It's a big old goofy world* figures on this way up's *Mountain stage vol.2* . Prine has on more than one occasion shown himself to be the perfect host, presenting channel 4's *The sessions* , a series recorded at Dublin's point depot venue - then a series introducing singer - songwriters. (Maurice Hope)

AIMLESS LOVE.
Tracks: Be my friend / Tonight / Aimless love / Me myself and I / Oldest baby in the world / Slow boat to China / Bottomless lake / Maureen Maureen / Somewhere, someone's falling in love / People putting people down / Unwed fathers / Only love.
CD . . . . **MFCD 856**
Mobile Fidelity Sound Lab(USA).
CD . . . . **OOBR 002CD**
MC . . . . **OOBR 002**
Oh Boy / '85.
LP. . . . . **FIEND 84**
Demon / '87 / Pinnacle.

BRUISED ORANGE.
Tracks: Fish and whistle / There she goes / If you don't want my love / That's the way the world goes round / Bruised orange / Sabu visits the twin cities alone / Aw heck / Crooked piece of time / Iron ore Betty / Hobo song, The.
LP. . . . . **K 53084**
Asylum / Aug '78 / WEA.

DIAMONDS IN THE ROUGH.
Tracks: Everybody / Torch singer, The / Souvenirs / Late John Garfield blues, The / Sour grapes / Billy the bum / Frying pan / Yes I guess they oughta name a drink after you / Take the star out of the window / Great compromise, The / Clocks and spoons / Rocky mountain time / Diamonds in the rough.
LP. . . . . **K 40427**
Atlantic / '74 / WEA.

GERMAN AFTERNOONS.
Tracks: I just want you to dance with me / Love love love / Bad boys / They'll never take her love from me / Paradise / Lulu walls / Speed of the sound of loneliness / Sailin' around / If she were you / Linda goes to Mars.
CD . . . . **FIENDCD 103**
LP. . . . . **FIEND 103**
Demon / Aug '87 / Pinnacle.

HERE SHE GOES.
Tracks: Here she goes / Bruised orange.
■ 7". . . . . **K 13136**
Asylum / Oct '78.

JOHN PRINE LIVE.
Tracks: Come back to us Barbara Lewis / Hare Krishna beauregard / Six o'clock news / Oldest baby in the world / Angel from Montgomery / Grandpa was a carpenter / Blue umbrella / Fish and whistle / Sabru visits the twin cities alone / Living in the future / Illegal smile / Mexican home / Speed of the sound of lonliness / Accident (things could be worse) / Sam Stone / Souvenirs / Aw heck / Donald and Lynda / That's the way the world goes round.
CD . . . . **OBRCD 005**
Double LP . . . . **OBR 005**
MC . . . . **OBRC 005**
Oh Boy / '88.

MISSING YEARS, THE.
Tracks: Picture show / All the best / Sins of Memphisto, The / Everybody wants to feel like you / It's a big goofy world / I want to be with you always / Daddy's like pumpkin / Take a look at my heart / Great run / Way back then / Unlonely / You got cold / Everything is cool / Jesus, the missing years.
CD **512774-2**
MC **512774-4**
This Way Up / '92 / PolyGram.

PINK CADILLAC.
Tracks: Chinatown / Automobile / Killing the blues / No name girl / Saigon / Cold war / Baby let's play house / Down by the side of the road / How lucky / Ubangi stomp.
LP. . . . . **K 52164**
Asylum / Oct '79 / WEA.

SWEET REVENGE.
Tracks: Not Advised.
LP. . . . . **K 40524**
Atlantic / '74 / WEA.

Proffitt, Frank

Traditional singer, guitarist, banjo player and instrument maker Proffitt (1913 - 65) was born in Tennessee but moved as a child to North Carolina. He worked as a tobacco farmer, carpenter and instrument maker. All his life he collected folk songs: he was the original collector of *Tom Dooley*, an international hit in 1958 by the Kingston Trio, based on a true story of the 19th century. Proffitt's recording were available on Folkways and Folk Legacy in the US and on Topic in Britain. (Donald Clarke).

NORTH CAROLINA SONGS AND BALLADS.
Tracks: Not Advised.
LP. **12T 162**
Topic / '81 / Roots Records / Jazz Music / C.M. Distribution / Cadillac Music / Direct Distribution / Swift / Topic Records.

Prophet, Ronnie

Born 26.12.1943, in Calumet, Quebec - Canada. Moved to Nashville in 1969, extremely popular in the UK during the early/mid - 1980s, through his terms as compere/artist at the Wembley Country Music Festival, the Peterborough Festival, live tours and TV appearances - to the extent that he hosted his own special. Prophet's endless jokes and his 'frog' routine and gimmickry/wizardry on guitar won him a large following, and his UK album releases can be found on Westwood Records and RCA. Stateside, his RCA hit singles (1975-1977) were to feature *Sanctuary* , *Shine on* and *It's enough* . Canadian songstress Gloria Anne Carriere is both his partner in life and on stage, and a duet recording has also come from them. Prophet is one of the finest entertainers to tread the boards. (Maurice Hope)

RONNIE PROPHET.
Tracks: Sanctuary / It wouldn't be so bad if it hadn't been so / Shine on / Last night I felt the whole world changing / Big big world / Phone call from Allyson / I want to be touched by you / Feel the magic / It's enough / Day by day (I'm getting over you).
■ LP. . . . . **PL 10164**
RCA / '79.

RONNIE PROPHET.
Tracks: Dont' take her to heart / No holiday in L.A. / If you're up for love / Please don't go / Fire in the feeling / Stealer of hearts / Are you real or am I dreaming / You've got me right where I want me / Breaking up ain't hard to do / For the children.
■ LP. . . . . **NL 71837**
RCA / Aug '88.
■ MC . . . . **NK 71837**
RCA / Aug '88.

RONNIE PROPHET COUNTRY.
Tracks: It ain't easy lovin' me / Misery loves company / Nothing sure look good on you / Who's gonna worry 'bout you now / Tuesday night local / She's an outlaw / Alabama dream girl / Lusty lady / How can anything that feels so good hurt so bad / Hangin' on to what I got.
■ LP. . . . . **PL 40677**
RCA / '79.

Pruett, Jeanne

Born Nora Jean Bowman on 30.01.37 in Pell city, Alabama, and a member of the Grand Ole Opry since 1973. Has made several guest appearances since her debut in 1963. First recordings were with RCA in 1964, albeit a handful of unsucessful tracks. While Jeannie's husband Jack Pruett played lead guitar (for 14 years) with Marty Robbins, she concentrated on songwriting for him and raising a family. Conway Twitty, George Jones, Tammy Wynette and Nat Stuckey, along with Robbins all covered her songs. Jeannie's career took off in 1973, when her first MCA single *Satin sheets* went to number one. After two years of minor hits on Decca, Pruett went on to enjoy a success run with the label until 1978, scoring with *I'm your woman* , *Welcome to the sunshine (Baby Jane)* and *A poor man's woman* . Jeannie then moved on to Mercury (very briefly) and had a spell on IBC - where she enjoyed top ten singles with *Back to back* (1979), *Temporarily yours* and *It's too late* (both 1980). 1981 found her again label hopping to Paid, Audiograph (including the duet, *Love me* - featuring herself and Mary Robbins, who like the writer Pruett, had previously enjoyed chart action with the song) and MSR. (Maurice Hope)

ENCORE.
Tracks: Back to back / Every now and then / Temporarily yours / Star studded nights / Wild side of life / Waitin' for the sun to shine / Ain't we sad today / Love is a fading rose / Love all the leavin' out of you / Please sing satin sheets for me.
■ LP. . . . . **PL 25290**
RCA / Jul '80.

JEANNE PRUETT.
Tracks: Satin sheets / I've been around enough to know / Back to back / Best kept secret in town, The / You're all the man I'll ever need / Let's fall to pieces together / Heart first / I told you so / Rented room.
LP. . . . . **IMCA 39031**
MC . . . . **IMCAC 39031**
MCA / Mar '87 / BMG.

Puckett, Riley

Blind guitar player/vocalist, born George Riley Puckett on 07.05.1894 in Alparetta, Georgia (died on 13.07.1946). Old time musician educated at Macon, Georgia's school for the blind where he learned the banjo. Performed on Atlanta's WSB Radio, and with his partner, Gid Tanner, went to New York to record for Columbia in 1924. the popular duo of pioneering hillbilly musicians were to record *Little Log Cabin In The Lane* and *Rock Our Babies To Sleep* complete with yodel, said to be the first ever from a hillbilly act. In 1926 they made the journey to New York once again - this time collaborating with fiddle - playing Clayton McMichen and banjoist Fate Norris. Despite disbanding in 1931 they re-grouped in 1934 with Gid, his son Gordon, Ted Hawkins and Riley for one final recording session in Dallas. (Maurice Hope)

OLD TIME GREATS VOL. 2.
Tracks: Not Advised.
LP. . . . . **OHCS 174**
Old Homestead (USA) / Oct '87 / Swift.

RED SAILS IN THE SUNSET.
Tracks: Tie me to your apron strings / Margie / Nobody's business / Playmates / When I'm back in Tennessee / Get out and get under the moon / Walkin' my baby back home / Red sails in the sunset / Railroad boomer / South of the border / Oh Johnny, oh Johnny oh / Whistle and blow your blues away / Old fashioned locket / Tuck me to sleep in my old Kentucky home / Where the shy little violets grow / In a little garden.
LP. . . . . **BFX 15280**
Bear Family / Jun '88 / Rollercoaster Records / Swift / Direct Distribution.

Pullins, Leroy

I'M A NUT.
Tracks: I'm a nut / Knee deep.
■ 7". . . . . **HLR 10056**
London-American / Jun '66.

I'M A NUT.
Tracks: I'm a nut / Knee deep / Out in the smokehouse taking a bath / Tatersville auxiliary sewing circle, The / Meter maid / What's his name / I love you drops / Swimming at the bottom of the pool / I done you wrong song / Tickled pink / Okeefenokee / Billy Roy and Jackson Sam / Yellow / S tree towers / World what have I done.
LP. . . . . **BFX 15216**
Bear Family / Mar '86 / Rollercoaster Records / Swift / Direct Distribution.

Pure Prairie League

After the late 1960's ventures by the International Submarine Band with *Safe at home* , the Byrds's *Sweethearts of the rodeo* and the Flying Burrito Bros' *Gilded palace of sin* there was to be a wave of aspiring country rock acts, the Pure Prairie League being one of them, a country - rock group formed in Cincinnati (1971). They recorded a sizeable collection of albums, with the old prospector 'Luke' (created by artist Norman Rockwell) decorating every cover, first with RCA and then Casablanca. Hits were (apart from their 1976 *That'll be the day*) non existant country-wise. Their pop success rate was restricted to *Amie* on RCA and then while operating from the West Coast (now with Casablanca), they charted with *Let me love you tonight* (No. 10), *I'm almost ready* and *Still here in my heart* (1980 - 1981). During this spell, the band's quota included ex-bluegrass musician/country singer Vince Gill, before he left to join Rodney Crowell's Cherry Bombs. (Maurice Hope)

AMIE.
Tracks: Amie.
■ 7" .... RCA 2537
RCA / Mar '75.

BUSTIN' OUT.
Tracks: Jazzman / Angel No. 9 / Leave my heart alone / Early morning riser / Falling in and out of love / Amie / Boulder skies / Angel / Call me, tell me.
■ LP .... SF 8417
RCA / '78 / BMG.

CAN'T HOLD BACK.
Tracks: Can't hold back / I can't believe / Rude rude awakening / White line / Misery train / Restless woman / I'm going away / Jerene / Livin' it alone / Fool fool / Goodbye so long.
■ LP .... PL 13336
RCA / '79.

DANCE.
Tracks: Dance / Help yourself.
■ 7" .... PB 0829
RCA / Feb '77.

DANCE.
Tracks: Dance / In the morning / All the way / Livin' each day at a time / Fade away / Tornado warning / Catfishin' / Help yourself / San Antonio / All the lonesome cowboys.
■ LP .... PL 11924
RCA / Jan '77.

FIRIN' UP.
Tracks: I'm almost ready / Give it up / Too many heartaches in paradise / She's all mine / You're my true love / Let me love you tonight / I can't stop the feelin' / Lifetime of nightmare / I'll be damned / Jenny Lou.

■ LP .... NBLP 7212
Casablanca / Oct '80.

I'M ALMOST READY.
Tracks: I'm almost ready / My true love.
■ 7" .... CAN 229
Casablanca / Oct '80.

IF THE SHOE FITS.
Tracks: That'll be the day / I can only think of you / Sun shone lightly / Long cold winter / Lucille Crawfield / Gimme another chance / Aren't you mine / You are so near to me / Out on the street / Goin' home.
■ LP .... RS 1040
RCA / '78 / BMG.

JUST FLY.
Tracks: Place in the middle / Slim pickin's / Love will grow / You don't have to be alone / Love is falling / Just fly / Lifetime / Working in the coal mine / My young girl / Bad dream.
■ LP .... PL 12590
■ MC .... PK 12590
RCA / '79.

LET ME LOVE YOU TONIGHT.
Tracks: Let me love you tonight / Janni Lou.
■ 7" .... CAN 201
Casablanca / Aug '80.

PURE PRAIRIE COLLECTION.
Tracks: Tears / You're between me / Woman / It's all on me / Early morning riser / Falling in and out of love / Amie / Jazzman / Boulder skies / Angel / Call me, tell me / Two lane highway / Just can't believe it / That'll be the day / Going home.
LP .... INTS 5101
MC .... INTK 5101
RCA International / '81.
MC .... NK 89335
RCA / '86 / BMG.
■ LP .... NL 89335
RCA / '86.

PURE PRAIRIE LEAGUE.
Tracks: Tears / Take it before you go / You're between me / Woman / Doc's tune / Country song / Harmony songs / It's all on me.
■ LP .... SF 8453
RCA / '78 / BMG.

SOMETHING IN THE NIGHT.
Tracks: Don't keep me hangin' / Love me again / Hold on to our hearts / Something in the night / Do you love truly Julie / You're mine tonight / Still right here in my heart / I wanna know your name / Feel that fire / Tell me one more time.
LP .... .6480 016
■ MC .... .7190 016
Casablanca / Jun '81.

STILL RIGHT HERE IN MY HEART.
Tracks: Still right here in my heart / Don't keep me hangin'.
■ 7" .... CAN 1003
Casablanca / Jun '81.

TWO LANE HIGHWAY.
Tracks: Two lane highway / Kentucky moonshine / Runner / Memories / Kansas City Southern / Harvest / Sister's keeper / Just can't believe it / Give us a rise / I'll change your flat tyre / Merle / Pickin' to beat the Devil.
■ LP .... SF 8445
RCA / '78 / BMG.

Putnam String County Band

PUTNAM STRING COUNTY BAND.
Tracks: Not Advised.
LP .... ROUNDER 3003
Rounder / '88 / Projection / Roots Records / Swift / C.M. Distribution / Topic Records / Jazz Music / Hot Shot / A.D.A Distribution / Direct Distribution.

SUNDOWN

MAGNUM MUSIC GROUP
™

presents

THE LEADING COUNTRY MUSIC CATALOGUE

including

JIM REEVES • GRAM PARSONS

FLYING BURRITO BROTHERS

PATSY CLINE

RUSTY & DOUG KERSHAW

RICKY SKAGGS • LOUVIN BROTHERS

and many others

Distributed through:
MMG Distribution 0494 882858
Terry Blood Distribution 0782 566511

Available from all good record stores or by mail order from
Magnum Direct Sales.
Magnum Music Group, Magnum House, High Street,
Lane End, Bucks, HP14 3JG, U.K.
Illustrated catalogue available on request

Q

Queen Ida

Grammy Award winner Queen Ida is one of America's most colourful musical characters. She hails from Louisiana's bayou area and her Bon Temps Zydeco band play an exhilarating mixture of good time dance sounds, sung in a mixture of French and English. Queen Ida, who plays accordion and sings, is the only woman leading a Louisiana zydeco band, and is rapidly gaining an international following with prestigious festival appearances in the USA and Europe and a cameo appearance in the film *Rumble Fish*.

CAUGHT IN THE ACT (QUEEN IDA) (Queen Ida & Her Zydeco Band).
Tracks: Not Advised.
LP . . . . SNTF 951
Sonet / Feb '86 / Swift / C.M. Distribution / Roots Records / Jazz Music / Sonet Records / Cadillac Music / Projection / Wellard Dist. / Hot Shot.
CD . . . . GNPD 2181
LP . . . . GNPS 2181
MC GNP5 2181
GNP Crescendo / '88 / Swift / Silva Screen / Flexitron Ltd.

CELIMENE (Queen Ida & The Bon Temps Zydeco Band).
Tracks: Celimene / Fais deaux deaux.
7" . . . . SON 2261
Sonet / '83 / Swift / C.M. Distribution / Roots Records / Jazz Music / Sonet Records / Cadillac Music / Projection / Wellard Dist. / Hot Shot.

COOKIN' WITH QUEEN IDA.
Tracks: Not Advised.
CD . . . . SNCD 1021
LP . . . . SNTF 1021
Sonet / Nov '89 / Swift / C.M. Distribution / Roots Records / Jazz Music / Sonet Records / Cadillac Music / Projection / Wellard Dist. / Hot Shot.

LIVE IN SAN FRANCISCO (Queen Ida & Her Zydeco Band).
Tracks: Fais deaux deaux / Bad moon rising / Every now and then / La porte / Zydeca taco / Back door / Raywood / Vaporsa / My girl Josephine / Jambalaya.
LP . . . . SNTF 901
Sonet / Oct '83 / Swift / C.M. Distribution / Roots Records / Jazz Music / Sonet Records / Cadillac Music / Projection / Wellard Dist. / Hot Shot.
LP . . . . GNPS 2158
MC GNP5 2158
GNP Crescendo / '88 / Swift / Silva Screen / Flexitron Ltd.

NEW ORLEANS (Queen Ida & The Bon Temps Zydeco Band).
Tracks: Capitaine Gumbo / Mon paradis / La vierge / La Louisiane / Corps solide / Grand basile / Papiers dans mes souliers / Madame Ben / La femme du doight.
LP . . . . SNTF 846
Sonet / Aug '80 / Swift / C.M. Distribution / Roots Records / Jazz Music / Sonet Records / Cadillac Music / Projection / Wellard Dist. / Hot Shot.
LP . . . . GNPS 2131
MC GNP5 2131
GNP Crescendo / '88 / Swift / Silva Screen / Flexitron Ltd.

ON A SATURDAY NIGHT (Queen Ida & The Bon Temps Zydeco Band).
Tracks: Capitaine Gumbo / La Louisiane / Le Mazuka / Grand Basile / P'tit fille o'paradis / Madame Ben / Frisco zydeco / La femme du doight / Vieux Paris / On a Saturday night / Bonjour tristesse / Creole de lake Charles / Celimene / Mal d'amour / Chere duloone / My tu tu / Hey negress / Jolie Blon / Cotton eyed Joe.
LP . . . . GNPS 2172
MC GNP5 2172
GNP Crescendo / '88 / Swift / Silva Screen / Flexitron Ltd.
LP . . . . SNTF 916
Sonet / Jul '88 / Swift / C.M. Distribution / Roots Records / Jazz Music / Sonet Records / Cadillac Music / Projection / Wellard Dist. / Hot Shot.
CD 600256
GNP Crescendo / Jun '91 / Swift / Silva Screen / Flexitron Ltd.

ON TOUR.
Tracks: Capitaine Gumbo / Grand Basile / Mazurka / La Louisiane / P'tit fille o paradis / Madame Ben / Bayou polka / Corps solide / La vierge / La femme du doight / Vieux Paris / C'est la vie.
LP . . . . SNTF 871
Sonet / Jul '88 / Swift / C.M. Distribution / Roots Records / Jazz Music / Sonet Records / Cadillac Music / Projection / Wellard Dist. / Hot Shot.

QUEEN IDA & BON TEMPS BAND ON TOUR (Queen Ida & The Bon Temps Zydeco Band).
Tracks: Not Advised.
CD . . . . GNPD 2147
LP . . . . GNPS 2147
MC GNP5 2147
GNP Crescendo / '88 / Swift / Silva Screen / Flexitron Ltd.

TELL ME PRETTY BABY (Queen Ida & The Bon Temps Zydeco Band).
Tracks: Tell me pretty baby / Laissez le bon temps roulez.
7" . . . . SON 2268
Sonet / Jul '84.

UPTOWN ZYDECO (Queen Ida & The Bon Temps Zydeco Band).
Tracks: Uptown Zydeco / Creole de Lake Charles / Moi mademoiselle / Rosa Majeur / Frisco Zydeco / Lucille Kanai / Moi tit feye o'paradis / Mazurka / On' teres / Tayo Zydeco / Mal d'amour / C'est la vie.
LP . . . . SNTF 884
Sonet / May '82 / Swift / C.M. Distribution / Roots Records / Jazz Music / Sonet Records / Cadillac Music / Projection / Wellard Dist. / Hot Shot.

ZYDECO (Queen Ida & The Bon Temps Zydeco Band).
Tracks: Not Advised.
LP . . . . GNPS 2101
MC GNP5 2101
GNP Crescendo / '88 / Swift / Silva Screen / Flexitron Ltd.

ZYDECO ALA MODE (Queen Ida & The Bon Temps Zydeco Band).
Tracks: Not Advised.
LP . . . . GNPS 2112
MC GNP5 2112
GNP Crescendo / '88 / Swift / Silva Screen / Flexitron Ltd.

Quinn, Brendan

No stranger to the international music scene, Brendan Quinn has appeared regularly in the U.K. as well as touring Canada and the USA. Born in Magherafelt, County Derry, he recorded his first single *Help me make it through the night* while lead singer of the group the Breakaways, before departing to form his own band the Blue Birds. In 1975 he scored a number one record with *Daddy's little girl*. During the 1980's he hosted the BBC series 'Make mine country' while, a decade later, he won one of Irelands most prestigious awards, the EMA's Entertainer of the Year accolade. (Tony Byworth)

BRENDAN QUINN COLLECTION.
Tracks: After sweet memories play born to lose again / I'll bet all my love on you / Lucille / How great thou art / Cowboys ain't supposed to cry / Ruby don't take your love to town / Judy and me / Mother's love's a blessing, A / If the shoe fits / Bandy the rodeo clown / Let me take you in my arms again / Tall you can make it on your own / Rollin' in the aisles / When you and I were young Maggie / Almost persuaded / My wild Irish rose / Daddy's little girl / Before I'm fool enough to give it one more try / Most of all why / I can almost see my home town from here.
LP . . . . BER 018
MC . . . . KBER 018
Emerald / Nov '87 / I & B Records.

CAN'T HOLD BACK THE YEARS.
Tracks: Can't hold back the years.
7" . . . . RITZ 153
Ritz / Aug '86 / Pinnacle / Midland Records.

DADDY'S LITTLE GIRL.
Tracks: Daddy's little girl / Too soon to tell.
7" . . . . MD 1196
Emerald / Jun '77.

HITS OF BRENDAN QUINN.
Tracks: Blanket on the ground / Help me make it through the night / Wedding bells / Four in the morning / Behind closed doors / Find on your finger / You're my best friend / Back home again / Ride me down easy / Backstreet affair / Forever was the name of our sunshine / Ravishing Ruby.
LP . . . . PHL 429
MC . . . . CPHL 429
Homespun (Ireland) / '82 / Homespun Records / Ross Records / Wellard Dist.

HUSTLER.
Tracks: Not Advised.
MC . . . . MBLP 1011
Music Box (Ireland) / '89.

HUSTLER.
Tracks: Mamma she's crazy.
7" . . . . RITZ 168
Ritz / Jan '87 / Pinnacle / Midland Records.

I CAN ALMOST SEE MY HOME TOWN FROM HERE.
Tracks: I can almost see my home town from here / Judy and me.
7" . . . . MD 1203
Emerald / Mar '78.

IRISH HEARTBEAT.
Tracks: Irish heartbeat / Right or wrong.
7" . . . . RITZ 129
Ritz / Jan '86 / Pinnacle / Midland Records.

JUST AN ORDINARY MAN.
Tracks: Not Advised.
LP . . . . RITZLP 0035
MC . . . . RITZLC 0035
Ritz / Nov '86 / Pinnacle / Midland Records.

MELODIES AND MEDLEYS.
Tracks: My lady from Glenfarne / Lovely leitrim / My lovely rose of Clare / My heart skips a beat / Turn out the lights and love me tonight / Some broken hearts never mend / I recall a gypsy woman / Dublin in the rare auld times / Anytipperary town / Among the Wicklow hills / He'll have to go / I won't forget you / I love you because.
CD . . . . RITZRCD 515
MC . . . . RITZRC 515
Ritz / Apr '92 / Pinnacle / Midland Records.

REST YOUR LOVE ON ME.
Tracks: Not Advised.
MC . . . . BTC 302
Ritz / Dec '88 / Pinnacle / Midland Records.

Quinn, Philomena

BEST OF PHILOMENA QUINN (Ireland's country colleen).
Tracks: Wild flowers / Forty shades of green / Last thing on my mind / If we only had old Ireland over here / Behind the footlights / When Irish eyes are smiling / Old country dance / Moonlight in Mayo / My heart cries for you / Too-ra-loo-ra-loo-ra / Where the grass grows the greenest / Mother's Bible.
MC . . . . CPHL 499
Homespun (Ireland) / Jun '88 / Homespun Records / Ross Records / Wellard Dist.

IT'S A COWBOY LOVIN' TONIGHT.
Tracks: I think I'll say goodbye / It's a cowboy lovin' tonight / Jealous heart / Two little orphans / She's got you / Ashes of love / Heaven's just a sin away / Old country dance / Mother's bible / One day at a time / Sing the blues, bluebirds / It's no secret.
LP . . . . GES 5014
Emerald / Feb '79.

IT'S NO SECRET.
Tracks: It's no secret / Old country dance.
7" . . . . MD 1208
Emerald / Jul '78.

ALSO PUBLISHED BY MUSIC MASTER:

MUSIC MASTER

The Official Music Master CD Catalogue, 14th Edition. £14.95
Published October 1993

The 14th Edition of Music Master's best selling CD Catalogue is our most comprehensive listing of recordings released on CD in the UK. This fully revised and updated publication supplies track listings, catalogue numbers, label and distributor details as well as release and deletion dates. It is a must for all CD fans and those who want to find favourite recordings or complete collections. 1,114 pages.

*Lists CD discographies for over 15,000 popular music artists.
*Contains information on over 55,000 CD released recordings.

Labels' and Distributors' Directory 11th Edition

The Who's Who of Labels and Distributors! Fully revised and updated to include full contact details for every UK label and distributor known at the time of going to press. Cross reference sections make it even easier to find out who distributes which label.
£29.95

Tracks Catalogue 4th Edition

Who Recorded Which Track? The Tracks catalogue identifies 750,000 track names, the artists who recorded them and the albums/singles on which they appear. 1480 pages.
£24.95

Directory of Popular Music - compiled and edited by Leslie Lowe

Who wrote that song? This catalogue identifies the composer, publisher and recording artist for over 9,000 of the most popular songs this century. 554 pages.
£14.95

Price Guide for Record Collectors 2nd Edition

This catalogue prices 42,000 collectable LPs, EPs, Singles and Picture Discs. It includes a full colour section of photographs of collectable covers and extensive notes from the editor Nick Hamlyn. 792 pages.
£12.95

To order:

Please send payment (cheques made payable to Music Master) plus postage as follows:
UK: add £1.75,   Europe: add £4.00 per catalogue,   Outside Europe: add £12.00 per catalogue. All books are sent registered delivery in the UK and by Airmail elsewhere.

Music Master, Paulton House, 8 Shepherdess Walk, London, N1 7LB.
Tel: +44-(0)71-490-0049,   Fax: +44-(0)71-253-1308.

R

Rabbitt, Eddie

Eddie Rabbitt a pop/country vocalist and song-writer born in 1941 in Brooklyn. He wrote hits for others including Elvis Presley (*Kentucky Rain* in 1970), Ronnie Milsap (*Pure Love* in 1974); began having his own hits on Elektra 1974-5 including the film song *Every Which Way But Loose*, several country number ones and all pop crossovers; he was the biggest selling country artist in the USA in 1980-2; a WB compilation in 1985 was entirely number one hits. He switched to RCA in 1985 with more contemporary styling, slicker production. (Donald Clarke).

COUNTRY STORE: EDDIE RABBITT.
Tracks: Step by step / I don't know where to start / Early in the morning / You and I / Good night for falling in love / You can't run from love / Someone could lose a heart tonight / You put the beat in my heart / Dim the lights / Rivers / Our love will survive / Years after you / Laughing on the outside / Nothing like falling in love.
CD . . . . CDCST 2
Country Store / '88 / BMG.
■ LP . . . . CST 2
Country Store / '88.
■ MC . . . . CSTK 2
Country Store / '88.

DIM DIM THE LIGHTS.
Tracks: Dim dim the lights / Nobody loves me like my baby.
■ 7" . . . . MER 88
Mercury / Jan '82.

DRINKING MY BABY.
Tracks: Drinking my baby / When I was young.
■ 7" . . . . K 12205
Elektra / Apr '76.

EDDIE RABBITT.
Tracks: I'm a little bit lonesome / I can't help myself / Stop look and listen / Girl on my mind / You make love beautiful / Sure thing / Jewellery store / We can't go on living like this / Is there a country song on the jukebox / She loves me like she means it.
LP . . . . K 52054
Elektra / WEA.

EVERY WHICH WAY BUT LOOSE.
Tracks: Every which way but loose / Under the double eagle.
7" . . . . K 12331
Elektra / Jan '79 / WEA.

GREATEST HITS.
Tracks: I love a rainy night / Drivin' my life away / Step by step / You and I / Suspicions / You put the beat in my heart / Nothing like falling in love / Someone could lose a heart tonight / You can't run from love / Gone too far.
■ LP 8143641
IMS / '84.

HORIZON.
Tracks: I love a rainy night / 747 / Drivin' my life away / Short road to love / Rockin' with my baby / I need to fall in love / What will I write / Pretty lady / Just the way it is.
■ LP Set . . . . K 52225
WEA / '81.

I LOVE A RAINY NIGHT.
Tracks: I love a rainy night / Short road to love.
■ 7" . . . . K 12408
Elektra / Feb '81.

LOVELINE.
Tracks: Pour me another tequila / Gone too far / Love-line / One and only one / Suspicious / So fine / I will never let you go again / Amazing love / It's always like the first time / I don't wanna make love with anyone else.
■ LP . . . . K 52135
Elektra / '77.

RABBIT TRAX.
Tracks: Threw it away / Singing in the subway / This moment / World without love / Gotta have you / Repetitive regret / Both to each other (friends and lovers) / When we make love / Letter from home.
LP . . . . PL 87041
■ MC . . . . PK 87041
RCA / Jun '86.

RADIO ROMANCE.
Tracks: You can't run from love / Years after you / Good night for falling in love / You and I / You got me now / Our love will survive / Stranger in your eyes / Bedroom eyes / Laughing on the outside (crying on the inside) / All my life, all my love.
LP . . . . MERL 13
MC . . . . MERLC 13
Mercury / Mar '83 / PolyGram.

ROCKY MOUNTAIN MUSIC.
Tracks: Do you right tonight / I can't get this ring off my finger / Rocky mountain music / Two dollars in the jukebox / I don't wanna make love with anyone but you / I just got to have you / Tullohoma dancing pizza man / Ain't I something / There's someone she lies to / Could you love a poor boy dolly / Drinkin' my baby (off my mind).
LP . . . . K 52037
Elektra / WEA.

STEP BY STEP.
Tracks: Early in the morning / Bring back the sunshine / Skip-a-beat / Dim dim the lights / Rivers / Step by step / Someone could lose a heart tonight / I don't know where to start / Nobody loves me like my baby / My only wish.
■ LP 6302152
Mercury / Dec '81.
CD 800 046-2
Mercury / '83 / PolyGram.

STEP BY STEP.
Tracks: Step by step / My only wish.
■ 7" . . . . MER 81
Mercury / Sep '81.

SUSPICION.
Tracks: Suspicion / I don't wanna make love (with anyone else).
■ 7" . . . . K 12375
Elektra / '79.

TWO DOLLARS IN THE JUKEBOX.
Tracks: Two dollars in the jukebox / I don't wanna make love with anyone else.
■ 7" . . . . K 12247
Elektra / Mar '77.

YOU AND I (Rabbitt, Eddie & Crystal Gayle).
Tracks: You and I / All my life, all my love.
■ 7" . . . . MER 123
Mercury / Dec '82.

YOU DON'T LOVE ME ANYMORE.
Tracks: You don't love me anymore / Caroline.
■ 7" . . . . K 12319
Elektra / Oct '78.

Rainwater, Marvin

Marvin Rainwater was born Marvin Percy in 1925 in Wichita, Kansas. The country singer/ songwriter took his mother's name when he turned to music and paraded as a full blooded Cherokee in regalia. He won a talent show with own song, *Gonna Find Me A Bluebird*, subsequently a big hit in 1957. He toured the UK in 1971 for the first time in 12 years and found new fans, and made a LP with London-based Country Fever (Albert Lee on guitar). (Donald Clarke).

CLASSIC MARVIN RAINWATER.
Tracks: I gotta go get my baby / Daddy's glad you came home / Albino pink-eyed stallion / Sticks & stones / Tea bag Romeo / Tennessee houn' dog yodel / Dem low down blues / Where do we go from here / Hot & cold / Mr. Blues / Get off the stool / What am I supposed to do / I feel like leaving town (sopmetimes) / Why did you have to go & leave me / Gonna find me a bluebird / 'Cause I'm a dreamer / So you think you've got troubles / Look for me (I'll be waiting for you) / Wayward angel / My brand of blues / My love is real / Lucky star / Majesty of love, The / You my darling you / Whole lotta woman (undubbed version) / Whole lotta woman / That's the way I feel / Baby, don't go / Two fools in love / Because I'm a dreamer / Down in the cellar / Crazy love / Moanin' the blues / Gamblin' man / I dig you baby / Dance me daddy / Nothin' needs nothin' (like I need you) / Need for love (there's always), A / No good runaround / Late for love (don't be) / Last time, The / Can I count on your love / Let me live again / Lonely island / Born to be lonesome / Love me baby (like there's no tomorrow) / That's when I'll stop loving you / Song of new love, A / Halfbreed / Valley of the moon, The / Young girls / Pale faced Indian (lament of the Cherokee), The / Hard luck blues / She's gone / Yesterday's kisses / You're not happy / I can't forget / Boo hoo / Tough top cat / Honky tonk in your heart (There's a) / Hey good lookin' / Do it now / It wasn't enough / That little house / Part time lover / That aching heart / Love's prison / Bad girl / I saw your new love today / My old home town / Branded / Sing the girls a song / Indian burial / Black sheep, The / Troubles my little boy had / Sorrow brings a good man down / I want your heart / Talk to me / Run for your life boy / Old gang's gone / Cold woman / Oklahoma hills / Wedding rings / I love my country / Burning bridges / Black Jack McClain / Heart's hall of fame / Hit & run lover / Korea's mountain northland / Tainted gold / Don't tell my boy (in prison living a lie) / Don't try to change your little woman / Do you want to know / Engineer's song (the boy & the

---

engineer) / Freight train blues / Key, The / Let's go on a picnic / Moment's of love / So long / Teardrops / Wanderer in me, The / What you got, you don't want / Would your mother be proud of you / You can't keep a secret.
CD Set . . . . BCD 15600
Bear Family / Aug '93 / Rollercoaster Records / Swift / Direct Distribution.

ESPECIALLY FOR YOU.
Tracks: Lonesomest guy in town / Darling where are you / Whole lotta woman / Cold woman / Looking good / I dig you baby / Happiness for me / Indian momma / I saw a bluebird / Old rivers / I miss you already / Follow me / Empty pond, The / Oh George / Village blacksmith, The / Sad witch / There's only one of you / Christmas time / Wobbling song / Little flower / Cardboard train / Cinderella / Mr. Snowman / Soft toys / Circus song / What's behind the Moon.
LP . . . . WRS 101
Westwood / '82 / Pinnacle.

HENRYETTA..
Tracks: Henryetta.. / City of angels.
7" . . . . SON 2225
Sonet / Apr '81 / Swift / C.M. Distribution / Roots Records / Jazz Music / Sonet Records / Cadillac Music / Projection / Wellard Dist. / Hot Shot.

I CAN'T FORGET.
Tracks: I can't forget / Boo hoo.
7" . . . . HLU 9947
London-American / '61.

I DIG YOU BABY.
Tracks: I dig you baby / Dance me daddy.
■ 7" . . . . MGM 980
MGM (EMI) / Jun '58.

ROCKIN' ROLLIN'.
Tracks: I dig you baby / Don't be late for love / Whole lotta woman / Get off the stool / Love me baby like there's no tomorrow / Baby don't go / In the valley of the moon / She's gone / Roving gambler / Dance me Daddy / Hard luck blues / Mister blues / So you think you've got troubles / My brand of blues / Moanin the blues / Hot and cold.
LP . . . . BFX 15079
Bear Family / Sep '84 / Rollercoaster Records / Swift / Direct Distribution.

WHOLE LOTTA MARVIN.
Tracks: Mr. Blues / Hot and cold / Tennessee hound dog yodel / I dig you baby.
■ EP . . . . SEP 1001
Southern / Jul '88 / SRD.

WHOLE LOTTA WOMAN.
Tracks: Whole lotta woman.
■ 7" . . . . MGM 974
MGM (EMI) / Mar '58.

WHOLE LOTTA WOMAN (OLD GOLD).
Tracks: Whole lotta woman / It's all in the game.
7" . . . . OG 9446
Old Gold / Jul '84 / Pickwick Records.

WITH A HEART WITH A BEAT.
Tracks: Boo hoo (Original Warwick recording.) / Can't forget (Original Warwick recording.) / Rough top cat (Original Warwick recording.) / That's the way I feel (Previously unissued.) / Last time, The (Previously unissued.) / (There's always) a need for love / Down in the cellar (Previously unissued.) / There's a honky tonk in your heart (Original Warwick recording.) / That's when I'll stop loving you / Two fools in love / Gonna find me a bluebird / Can I count on your love / Because I'm a dreamer / You my darling you / Crazy love (Previously unissued.) / Look for me (I'll be waiting for you).
LP . . . . BFX 15132
Bear Family / Mar '84 / Rollercoaster Records / Swift / Direct Distribution.

Ranch Romance

Lively, modern western swing based, mainly all-girl outfit - it's member's being Jo Miller, Barbara Lamb, Nancy Katz, David Keenan and Nova Karina Devonie. Debut recording *Western dream* (1989), made on their own Ranch Hand label, later issued on Sugar Hill, where they debuted in 1991 with *Blue blazes* (Demon UK). In 1993 Barbara Lamb (fiddle player) released her own album - *Fiddle finale* where she draws upon her colleagues. (Maurice Hope)

BLUE BLAZES.
Tracks: Not Advised.
CD . . . . FIENDCD 709
Demon / Dec '91 / Pinnacle.

BLUE BLAZES.
Tracks: Heartaches / What's wrong with you / Blue blazes / Indeed I do / Arizona moon / Racin' / Burnin' bridges / Buckaroo / Lost heart / Cuttin' a rug / Trouble / Babydoll / Lucky one.
CD . . . . SHCD 3794
MC . . . . SH 3794
Sugarhill(USA) / '91 / Roots Records / Projection / Impetus Records / C.M. Distribution / Jazz Music / Swift / Duncans / A.D.A Distribution.

RANCH ROMANCE.
Tracks: Not Advised.
MC . . . . FIENDCASS 709
Demon / Nov '91 / Pinnacle.

WESTERN DREAM.
Tracks: When the bloom is on the sage / Lovesick blues / Baby's on the town / St. Louis blues / Cowboys and indians / St. James Avenue / Gotta lotta rhythm (In my soul) / Ain't no ash will burn / Why don't you love me (Like you used to) / Birmingham fling / Last one to know, The / Western dream.
CD . . . . SHCD 3799
MC . . . . SH 3799
Sugarhill(USA) / '92 / Roots Records / Projection / Impetus Records / C.M. Distribution / Jazz Music / Swift / Duncans / A.D.A Distribution.

Randells

SING COUNTRY.
Tracks: Not Advised.
MC . . . . ZCFPA 1013
Kingfisher Cassettes / Nov '81.

Raney. Wayne

MORE HOT BOOGIE.
Tracks: Why don't you haul off and love me (one more time) / Gone with the wind this morning / I ain't nothing but a tom cat, kitten / Powerful love / Falling / I want a home in Dixie / I've done sold my soul / Lonesome wind blues / Roosters are crowing, The / Pardon my whiskers / I'd feel like a millionaire / Gonna row my boat / I'm really needin' you / When they let the hammer down / Old fashioned matrimony in mind / No one's crying but me.
■ LP . . . . CR 30263
Charly / Jan '87 / Charly.

REAL HOT BOOGIE.
Tracks: Jack and Jill Boogie / Lost John Boogie / Real hot boogie / Catfish baby / Bootleg boogie / I was there / You better treat your man right / Adam / I had my fingers crossed / If you've got the money I've got the time / Heads or tails I win / Blues at my door / I'm on my way / Undertaking daddy / Real good feeling / Beating around the bush.
■ LP . . . . CR 30247
Charly / Apr '86 / Charly.

SONGS OF THE HILLS.
Tracks: Not Advised.
CD . . . . KCD 588
King / Feb '93 / New Note / Koch International.

Rapone. Al

C'EST LA VIE! (Rapone, Al & The Zydeco Express).
Tracks: Not Advised.
LP . . . . LR 44.012
L&R / '88 / New Note.

LET'S HAVE A ZYDECO PARTY (Rapone, Al & The Zydeco Express).
Tracks: Tit fille / Rosa Majeur / Camden zydeco / Sa mio fait du mal / Pu ils sa / Mazuka / Joe Peter / La vierge / Corps solide / Baby let me ride you home / Tu le ton son ton.
LP . . . . JSP 1092
JSP / Jul '85 / Hot Shot / Swift / Wellard Dist. / A.D.A Distribution / Cadillac Music / Jazz Music.

ZYDECO TO GO (Rapone, Al & The Zydeco Express).
Tracks: Not Advised.
LP . . . . BP 3790
Blind Pig (USA) / '92 / Topic Records / Projection / Swift / C.M. Distribution / Roots Records / Direct Distribution / Impetus Records / Hot Shot.

Rattlesnake Annie

Rattlesnake Annie was born Annie McGowan in 1941 in Paris, Tennessee; she is a country singer and songwriter who has been highly regarded by stars like Merle Haggard and Willie Nelson; David Allen Coe recorded her *Texas lullaby*. She has released an album on Supraphon in Czechoslavakia, as well as two on her own Rattlesnake label; the last called *Country livin*, included a duet with Nelson on Long Black Limousine; it has been picked up and issued on CBS as *Rattlesnake Annie* with some different tracks. The album and single *Callin' your bluff* reached the country charts in the USA. About half the songs on her LP's are her own; she is at last receiving long-overdue wider recognition. (Donald Clarke).

COUNTRY LIVIN'.
Tracks: Not Advised.
■ LP . . . . RATTLE 2020
Rattlesnake (USA) / Apr '86.

LONG BLACK LIMOUSINE.
Tracks: Long black limousine / Goodbye to a river.
■ 7" 6516797
CBS / Jun '88.

RATTLESNAKE ANNIE.
Tracks: Funky country livin' / Sixteen tons / Country music hall of pain / Somewhere south of Macon / Goodbye to a river / Outskirts of town / Callin' your bluff / Long black limousine / Been waitin' that long / Lonesome, on'ry and mean.
■ LP 4500441
CBS / Jul '87.
■ MC 4500444
CBS / Jul '87.

SIXTEEN TONS.
Tracks: Sixteen tons / Somewhere south of Macon.
■ 7" 6513507
CBS / Jan '87.

TENNESSEE WALTZ.
Tracks: Tennessee waltz / Belfast mountains.
■ 7" . . . . CHEW 82
Mint / Aug '83.

Raven. Eddy

Lafayette-born & raised, Edward Garvin Futch (19.8.44), had many musical influences to draw upon with strains of Cajun, pop and rock n roll richly colouring his work. His first break came by way of his regional hit on the Georgia label *Cosmos* in 1962, when working as a D.J. with WHAB Radio. After moving back to Lafayette, Raven toured all around the Gulf coast - part of the time with Edgar & Johnny Winter & the Rockin' Cajun. He moved to Nashville in 1970, and signed to Acuff - Rose as a staff writer. He gained considerable early success through Don Gibson's recordings of his Country green and *Touch of the morning* and Jeannie C. Riley with *Good morning country rain* in 1972. Raven's lengthy, sustained contribution to the world of country music has also seen his material recorded by such acts as Roy Acuff, Moe Bandy, Connie Smith and countless others. While his own chequered recording career has first seen him charting with ABC in 1974 with *The last of the sunshine cowboys*, Raven has over the next ten years, been hopping labels, and with the exception of a single release on Monument in 1979, he improved with every change of label. Dimension Records gave him *Sweet mother Texas*, Elektra the Top Ten hit *She's playing hard to forget*, and RCA saw his *I got Mexico* topping the country charts. Since then Raven reaped rich pickings with *Shine, shine, shine* (1987), *I'm gonna get you* & *Joe knowshow to live*. 1989 once again found Raven changing labels, this time moving to the short-lived MCA/Universal label. His debut album *Temporary sanity* yielding no fewer than four top ten singles, two *In a letter to you* and *Bayou boys* making No.1 that same year, with *Sooner or latter* and *Island* in 1990 makin' up the quartet. Raven, at the moment is between labels, yet such is his durability that this is only temporary lull in what has been both a successful and colourful career. (Maurice Hope)

EDDY RAVEN.
Tracks: Not Advised.
LP 127
La Louisiane / '87 / Swift.

TEMPORARY SANITY.
Tracks: Not Advised.
CD . . . . UVLD 76003
LP . . . . UVL 76003
MC . . . . UVLC 76003
MCA / Jul '89 / BMG.

Rawton. Jimmy

ARIZONA SUNDAY.
Tracks: Not Advised.
LP . . . . WRS 118
Westwood / Jan '78 / Pinnacle.

Ray. Alan

ALAN RAY'S INTERNATIONAL ALBUM.
Tracks: Rollin' in my sweet baby's arms / Crystal chandeliers / Kaw-liga / Green green grass of home / Kansas City / Six days on the road / I wonder where you are tonight / Put another log on the fire / Daydreams about night things / Old dogs, children and watermelon wine.
LP . . . . WRS 137
Westwood / '82 / Pinnacle.

Ray. Bobby

COUNTRY WAY, THE.
Tracks: Not Advised.
LP . . . . BSS 140
Tank / Dec '77.

SOMETHING IN THE AYRE.
Tracks: Not Advised.
LP . . . . BSS 336
Tank / Jun '79.

Raye. Collin

Born in Arkansas, 1960, raised in Texas. Brother Scott and Collin played the local scene in their country-rock band during the 1970's. Moved then to Oregon in 1980 - ending out in Reno, Nevada, at which point Scott pulled out, after a record deal fell through - leaving Collin to work solo. A resident slot ensued in a casino, prior to landing a deal in Nashville in the late 1980's. Raye's debut Epic single, *Love Me* from his album *All I Can* making No. 1. There were heavy radio plays on UK's Radio 2 - which prompted the album to obtain a UK release. Meanwhile Stateside, Raye; one of Nashville's success stories of that year, garnered more hits via the *Every Second* (No. 3) chart topping *In This Life* and top ten singles *Somebody Else's Moon* and *I Want You Bad (And That's Not Good)* . (Maurice Hope)

ALL I CAN BE.
Tracks: All I can be (is a sweet memory) / Every second / Faithful old flame / 'Scuse moi, my heart / Love, me / Blue magic / It couldn't have been so good / Sadly ever after / If I were you.
■ CD 4688852
Epic / Mar '92.
■ MC 4688854
Epic / Mar '92.

IN THIS LIFE.
Tracks: What they don't know / In this life / Big river / Somebody else's Moon / You can't take it with you / That was a river / I want you bad (And that ain't good) / Latter day cowboy / Many a mile / Let it be me.
CD 472314 2
MC 472314 4
Epic / Feb '93 / Sony.

LOVE ME.
Tracks: Love me / Blue magic / Every second (CD single only).
7" 6579127
■ CD Single 6579122
Epic / Mar '92.

Read. Cheese

CAJUN HOUSE PARTY.
Tracks: Not Advised.
LP . . . . ARHOOLIE 5021
Arhoolie (USA) / May '81 / Pinnacle / Cadillac Music / Swift / Projection / Hot Shot / A.D.A Distribution / Jazz Music.
MC . . . . ARHC 5021
Arhoolie (USA) / '88 / Pinnacle / Cadillac Music / Swift / Projection / Hot Shot / A.D.A Distribution / Jazz Music.

Rector. Red

Red Rector was born in 1929 in North Carolina; he is one of country music's top mandolin players, in demand for sessions and on bluegrass circuit. He worked with Johnny & Jack, and such bluegrass outfits as Charlie Monroe's Kentucky Pardners, Bill Clifton, Flatt & Scruggs and played on hundreds of recording sessions. By the early '70s he took centre stage at many a bluegrass or folk festival. (Donald Clarke)

ANOTHER HAPPY DAY (Rector, Red & Bill Clifton).
Tracks: Not Advised.
LP . . . . BD 001
Breakdown / Jan '77.

ARE YOU FROM DIXIE? (Rector, Red & Bill Clifton).
Tracks: Are you from Dixie? / Down in the old cabin home / Spirit of love watches over me, The / Fourteen days in Georgia / Are you my best friend / Dixie cannonball / Keep that wheel a turning / Sugartree stomp / Valley of peace / It takes a long tall brown skin gal to make a preacher.. / Old man's story, The / Ashdown waltz / She has forgotten / On the sea of Galilee / There's no other love for me / Tall pines.
LP . . . . BF 15013
Bear Family / Sep '84 / Rollercoaster Records / Swift / Direct Distribution.

RED RECTOR & FRIENDS.
Tracks: Not Advised.
LP . . . . RS 931
Revonah (USA) / Jun '79.

Red Clay Ramblers

Formed in 1972 playing at Chapel Hill, North Carolina - with Tommy Thompson it's founder/ leader. Pro debut coming in 1975 on the Off Broadway musical *Diamond stud* . Since which time the Ramblers, who's music takes in a broad spectrum covering folk, jazz and country, have recorded albums on Flying Fish and Sugar Hill including the award winning and highly acclaimed soundtrack releases *A lie of the mind* (Sam Shepard's play debuting at New York's Promenade Theatre on 05.12.1985 - starring Geraldine Page) and *Far North* from 1989, another Shepard film sountrack. They've worked closely with Shepard for the last few years - playing/performing on his movie *Silver tongue* and also guested on Michelle Shocked's critically received acoustic/roots album *Arkansas Traveller* in 1992. Members of the multi-instrumental unit over the years being Jim Watson, Mike Carver, Jack Herrick, Bill Hicks, Bland Simpson and Clay Buckner. An early recording featuring them was in 1976 on Innisfree/Green Linnet *Debby McClatchy with the Red Clay Ramblers* - a traditional folk mix with banjoist Debby McClatchy. (Maurice Hope)

CHUCKIN' THE FRIZZ.
Tracks: Not Advised.
LP . . . . **FF 089**
Flying Fish (USA) / Sep '79 / Cadillac Music / Roots Records / Projection / C.M. Distribution / Direct Distribution / Jazz Music / Duncans / A.D.A Distribution.

HARD TIMES.
Tracks: Not Advised.
LP . . . . **FF 246**
Flying Fish (USA) / Mar '89 / Cadillac Music / Roots Records / Projection / C.M. Distribution / Direct Distribution / Jazz Music / Duncans / A.D.A Distribution.

IT AIN'T RIGHT.
Tracks: Not Advised.
LP . . . . **FF 334**
Flying Fish (USA) / Mar '89 / Cadillac Music / Roots Records / Projection / C.M. Distribution / Direct Distribution / Jazz Music / Duncans / A.D.A Distribution.

LIE OF THE MIND, A.
Tracks: Run Sister run / South of the border/In the pines / Honey babe / I love you a thousand ways / Home is where the heart is / Seeing it now / Blue Jay/The gal I left behind / Light years away / Cumberland mountain deer chase / Red rocking chair / Montana underscoring / Killing floor / I can't live without 'em blues / Folding the flag/Hard times.
CD . . . . **SHCD 8501**
Sugarhill(USA) / '86 / Roots Records / Projection / Impetus Records / C.M. Distribution / Jazz Music / Swift / Duncans / A.D.A Distribution.
LP . . . . **SH 8501**
Sugarhill(USA) / Mar '89 / Roots Records / Projection / Impetus Records / C.M. Distribution / Jazz Music / Swift / Duncans / A.D.A Distribution.

MERCHANTS LUNCH.
Tracks: Not Advised.
LP . . . . **FF 055**
Flying Fish (USA) / '88 / Cadillac Music / Roots Records / Projection / C.M. Distribution / Direct Distribution / Jazz Music / Duncans / A.D.A Distribution.

RAMBLER.
Tracks: Cotton-eyed Joe / Cajun Billy / Blue smoke train / Saro-Jane / Annie Oakley / Queen of Skye / Ninety & Nine / Mile long medley / Darlin' say/Pony cart / Hiawatha's lullabye / What does the deep sea say / Ryan's/Jordan reel / Barbeque / One rose/Hot buttered rum / Olkas.
CD . . . . **SHCD 3798**
MC . . . . **SH 3798**
Sugarhill(USA) / '92 / Roots Records / Projection / Impetus Records / C.M. Distribution / Jazz Music / Swift / Duncans / A.D.A Distribution.

STOLEN LOVE.
Tracks: Not Advised.
LP . . . . **FF 009**
Flying Fish (USA) / Mar '89 / Cadillac Music / Roots Records / Projection / C.M. Distribution / Direct Distribution / Jazz Music / Duncans / A.D.A Distribution.

TWISTED LAUREL.
Tracks: Not Advised.
LP . . . . **FF 030**
Flying Fish (USA) / Mar '89 / Cadillac Music / Roots Records / Projection / C.M. Distribution / Direct Distribution / Jazz Music / Duncans / A.D.A Distribution.

Red River

RED RIVER.
Tracks: Broke again / Mercury / Lucky tonight / Fools paradise / Cheap thrills / City doesn't weep, The.
LP . . . . **ROSE 167**
New Rose (1) / Mar '89 / Pinnacle.

TEXAS ADVICE.
Tracks: Ride - ride - ride / Comin' to you live / 8 chrome and wings / Come on over / Dry country blues / Ain't workin' no more / Broke again / Lucky tonight / Cheap thrills / Texas advice / At the roadhouse tonite / I'll drink you're booze / Talkin' to me / Something's gotta give / Goin' down / Mercury / Fools paradise / City doesn't weep, The.
CD . . . . **ROSE 210CD**
New Rose (1) / Aug '90 / Pinnacle.
LP . . . . **ROSE 210**
New Rose (1) / Jul '90 / Pinnacle.

Reed, Jerry

Reed, Jerry was born Jerry Hubbard in Atlanta, Georgia in 1939. As a Nashville session guitarist he became one of the most highly rated in the business; he was already a successful songwriter, having written hits for Brenda Lee and others, with 18 BMI awards for his songs; then he became a vocalist as well, records on RCA including several number one country hits, crossing over to the pop chart as well; his fans only complaint was that they didn't get enough of his guitar playing. His first country hit *Guitar man* was covered by Elvis Presley, who also had a hit with Reed's *U.S. Male*. He was also popular on TV and in films, eg. with Burt Reynolds in Smokey & The Bandit. (Donald Clarke).

20 OF THE BEST: JERRY REED.
Tracks: Guitar man / U.S. male / Georgia sunshine / When you're hot you're hot / Amos Moses / Ko ko Joe / Smell the flowers / Alabama wild man / You took all the rambling out of me / Uptown poker club / Good woman's love, A / Lord Mr. Ford / Crude oil blues / Friend, A / Mind your love / You got a lock on me / Gator / Sweet love feelings / Eastbound and down / Texas bound and flyin'.
LP . . . . **INTS 5117**
MC . . . . **INTK 5117**
RCA International / Jul '82 / BMG.
LP . . . . **NL 89855**
■ **MC** . . . . **NK 89855**
RCA / '87.

ALABAMA WILD MAN.
Tracks: Alabama wild man / Love prints.
■ **LP** . . . . **SF 8006**
RCA / Mar '73 / BMG.

AMOS MOSES.
Tracks: Amos moses / Preacher and the bear.
7" . . . . **RCA 2063**
RCA / '71 / BMG.

HITS OF JERRY REED, THE.
Tracks: Alabama wild man / Mind your love, Lord, Mr. Ford / Smell the flowers / When you're hot, you're hot / You got a lock on me / Boogie woogie rock and roll / Ko ko Joe / You took all the ramblin' out of me / Uptown poker club, The / Good woman's love, A / Telephone, The / Let's sing our song / Crude oil blues, The / Another puff.
LP . . . . **PL 42180**
■ **MC** . . . . **PK 42180**
RCA / '79.

ME AND CHET (Reed, Jerry & Chet Atkins).
Tracks: Jerry's breakdown / Limehouse blues / Liebestraum (Liszt) / Serenade to the summertime / Nashtown Ville / Mystery train / Mad Russian, The / Flying South / Good stuff / All I ever need is you / I saw the light.
■ **LP** . . . . **LSA 3091**
RCA / '75 / BMG.

PLASTIC SADDLE.
Tracks: Plastic saddle / If I promise.
7" . . . . **RCA 1971**
RCA / '70 / BMG.

SHE'S GOT THE GOLDMINE.
Tracks: She's got the goldmine / 44.
■ **7"** . . . . **RCA 273**
RCA / Sep '82.

Reeves, Del

Born Franklin Delano Reeves, 14.07.1933 in Sparta, North Carolina. Debuted on Decca label in 1961 with the top ten single *Be quiet mind* , since which time he's stacked up no fewer than 55 hit singles - including a handful of duets. Had his own radio show when he was 12 and joined the exodus to California during the late 1950s, securing his own TV shows. Moved to Nashville in 1966 - joining the Grand Ole Opry that same year. Had already topped the charts with *Girl on the billboard* (1965) his debut run on United Artists, an association that would see him through until 1978. Other top ten hits during the 1960s include *The belles of the southern bell* , *Women do funny things to me* (both 1965), *Looking at the world through a windshield* , *Good time charlies* (a handle also bestowed on his band) and *Be glad* all 1968. In the 1970s, whilst Reeves solo releases were on the slide (*The Philadelphia fillies* an isolated top 10 success) he has more duet success - to add to the modest entries during the 1960's with Bobby Goldsboro. This time he worked with Penny De Haven (*Landmark tavern* a top ten in 1972) and Billie Jo Spears (*On the rebound* making the top thirty in 1972), with whom he also made the album *By request* . Apart from the songs the multi-instrumentalist recorded himself (many co-written with his wife Ellen Schell Reeves) such acts as Carl Smith, Roy Drusky and Sheb Wooley have drawn on his work. (Maurice Hope)

BABY I LOVE YOU.
Tracks: One life to live / You're not the changing kind / Love love love / Baby I love you / My baby loves to rock and roll / Cool drool / Trot, The / Two teen hearts / He stands real tall / Empty house / As far as I can see / Be quiet mind / Love she offered me / I closed my eyes and saw the light / Only girl I can't forget, The / Once a fool.
LP . . . . **BFX 15269**
Bear Family / Jun '88 / Rollercoaster Records / Swift / Direct Distribution.

Reeves, Jim

Reeves, Jim was born in Galloway, Texas in 1924; he died in a plane crash in 1964. He was the first big country crossover artist, and one of the most popular of all time. He removed the sound of steel guitar and fiddles from his sound and created a pop-country style which scored international hits. He played baseball with the St. Louis Cardinals, but a leg injury stopped his sports career; he became a DJ and newsreader in Texas and soon performed on the Louisiana Hayride. His first hits were on Abbott, scoring a number one country hit with *Mexican Joe*, a number two with *Bimbo*; RCA bought his contract including the Abbott masters; he scored more than 40 top ten hits in the country chart altogether, 25 hits in pop Hot 100. First RCA hit with his own song *Yonder comes a sucker* in 1955; top tens included his own *Am I losing you?* and *Four walls* in 1957 (latter written by Marvin Moore and George Campbell; his biggest pop hit at number two in both country and pop charts); *Billy Bayou, He'll have to go, I guess I'm crazy* were all number ones. After his death he had number one country hits; the hits continued through the 1970's many given new updated backing tracks. Deborah Allen duetted with a Reeves record for top 10 hit *Take me in your arms and hold me* in 1980; Owen Bradley created duets on tape by superstars Reeves and Patsy Cline, who never recorded together when they were alive including top 10 *Have you ever been lonely* in 1981. (Donald Clarke).

12 SONGS FOR CHRISTMAS.
Tracks: Jingle bells / Blue Christmas / Senor Santa Claus / Old Christmas card, An / Merry Christmas polka, The / White Christmas / Silver bells / C-H-R-I-S-T-M-A-S / O little town of Bethlehem / Mary's boy child / O come all ye faithful / Silent night.
LP . . . . **CDS 1160**
■ **MC** . . . . **CAM 463**
RCA/Camden / Oct '79.
LP . . . . **CL 81927**
■ **MC** . . . . **CK 81927**
RCA / '87.
CD . . . . **ND 82758**
■ **MC** . . . . **NK 82758**
RCA / Nov '90.

20 OF THE BEST: JIM REEVES.
Tracks: I won't come in while he's there / Storm, The / I heard a heart break last night / That's when I see the blues / When you're gone / When two worlds collide / Nobody's fool / Angels don't lie / Gypsy feel / Writing on the wall / Missing you / Am I that easy to forget / I'd fight the world / It's nothin' to me / Little ole dime / You're the only good thing that's happened to me / Don't let me cross over / Oh, how I miss you tonight / Take me in your arms and hold me / Have you ever been lonely.
MC . . . . **NK 898 52**
RCA / Mar '86 / BMG.
■ **LP** . . . . **NL 898 52**
RCA / Mar '86.

25 ALL TIME WORLD WIDE FAVOURITES - VOL 1.
Tracks: There's a heartache following me / Danny boy / Yonder comes a sucker / Four walls / Bimbo / Partners / I'm gonna change everything / I know one / Little ole you / Am I losing you / Billy Bayou / Wreck of the number nine, The / Make the world go away / He'll have to go / Stand at your window / It hurts so much / I'm gettin' better / I fall to pieces / Blizzard / Mexican Joe / Anna Marie / This world is not my home / Just out of reach / Letter to my heart, A / Snow flake.
■ **MC** . . . . **DPTK 5002**
RCA / '79.

25 ALL TIME WORLD WIDE FAVOURITES - VOL 2.
Tracks: Welcome to my world / I love you because / I can't stop loving you / You're the only good thing (that's happened) / I won't forget you / Mary's boy child / When two worlds collide / Is it really over / I won't come in while he's there / In the misty moonlight / Fool such as I, A / Angels don't lie / Stranger's just a friend, A / Distant drums / Nobody's fool / That's when I see the blues (in your pretty) / How can I write on paper / When you are gone / But you love me daddy / Oh how I miss you tonight / Not until the next time / Guilty / Storm, The / My cathedral / Adios amigo.
■ **MC** . . . . **DPTK 5003**
RCA / '79.

40 GOLDEN GREATS: JIM REEVES.
Tracks: Not Advised.
■ **Double LP** . . . . **ADEP 16**
Arcade / Sep '75.

50 ALL TIME WORLD FAVOURITES.

Tracks: There's a heartache following me / Mexican Joe / Yonder comes a sucker / Four walls / Bimbo / Partners / I'm gonna change everything / Anna Marie / I know one / Little ole you / Billy Bayou / This world is not my home / He'll have to go / Stand at your window / Am I losing you / I'm gettin' better / I fall to pieces / Blizzard / Just out of reach / Wreck of the number nine, The / Make the world go away / It hurts so much / Letter to my heart, A / Danny boy / Snow flake / Welcome to my world / I love you because / I can't stop loving you / You're the only good thing / I won't forget you / When two worlds collide / Guilty / Is it really over / I won't come in while he's in there / In the misty moonlight / Fool such as I, A / Angels don't lie / Mary's boy child / Distant drums / Nobody's fool / That's when I see the blues / How can I write on paper (what I feel in ..) / When you are gone / But you love me daddy / Oh, how I miss you tonight / Not until the next time / Stranger's just a friend, A / Storm, The / My cathedral / Adios amigo.

■ **LP Set** . . . . **LSP 7403**
RCA / '79.

ABBOTT RECORDINGS, VOL 1.

Tracks: I'll follow you / Where does a broken heart go? / Drinking tequila / Mexican Joe / Give me one more kiss / Shall we gather at the river? / Hillbilly waltz / Butterfly love / It's hard to love just one / Penny candy / Gypsy heart / Red eyed and rowdy / Beatin' on the ding dong / Wilder your heart beats the sweeter you love / Are you the one? / El rancho del Rio / Bimbo.

LP. . . . . **INTS 5222**
MC . . . . **INTK 5222**
RCA International / Aug '82 / BMG.
LP. . . . . **NL 89052**
■ **MC** . . . . **NK 89052**
RCA / '87.

ABBOTT RECORDINGS, VOL 2.

Tracks: Let me remember / How many? / Woman's love / Tahiti / Padre of Old San Antone / My rambling heart / Echo bonita / Each beat of my heart / Then I'll stop loving you / Let me love you just a little / I could cry / Heartbreaking baby / Wagonload of love / You're the sweetest thing / What were you doing last night? / Whispering willow / I'll always love you / Spanish violins / If you love me don't leave me / I'll tell the world I love you.

■ **LP.** . . . . **INTS 5223**
RCA International / Dec '82.
LP. . . . . **NL 89311**
■ **MC** . . . . **NK 89311**
RCA International / '84.

ACCORDING TO MY HEART.

Tracks: Not Advised.

■ **LP.** . . . . **INTS 1013**
RCA International / Jul '69.

ADIOS AMIGO.

Tracks: Adios amigo / Guilty.

■ **7"** . . . . **RCA 1293**
RCA / Jun '62.

ANGEL'S DON'T LIE.

Tracks: Angel's don't lie.

■ **7"** . . . . **RCA 1997**
RCA / Sep '70.

BEST OF JIM REEVES.

Tracks: He'll have to go / Four walls / Guilty / Blue boy / I'm getting better / Blizzard / Am I losing you? / Billy bayou / Anna Marie / Adios amigo / Danny boy.

■ **LP.** . . . . **RD 7666**
RCA / Jan '65.
LP. . . . . **SF 8147**
■ **MC** . . . . **PK 11506**
RCA / '79.
LP. . . . . **NL 83678**
■ **MC** . . . . **NK 83678**
RCA International / Nov '84.

BIMBO.

Tracks: Bimbo / Echo bonita / Penny candy / Mexican Joe / Then I'll stop loving you / Drinking tequila.

LP. . . . . **CDN 1080**
RCA/Camden / '70 / BMG / Arabesque Ltd.

BLIZZARD, THE.

Tracks: Blizzard, The / Danny boy.

■ **7"** . . . . **RCA 1233**
RCA / Nov '68 / BMG.

BUT YOU LOVE ME DADDY.

Tracks: But you love me daddy.

■ **7"** . . . . **RCA 1899**
RCA / Oct '69.

CHRISTMAS COLLECTION.

Tracks: Not Advised.

CD . . . . **ARC 94842**
MC . . . . **ARC 94844**
Arcade / Nov '92 / Sony.

COLLECTION, THE.

Tracks: Memories are made of this / Have you ever been lonely (have you ever been blue) / My happiness / Mexicali rose / Take my hand precious Lord / Charmaine / Distant drums / Good night Irene / I fall to pieces / Mary's little boy child / I love you because / It's only a paper moon / Maria Elena / Have thine own way, Lord / (There'll be bluebirds over) the white cliffs of Dover / You're free to go / Moon river / Auf Wiedersehn, sweetheart.

CD **74321 14229-25**
RCA / Jul '93 / BMG.

COLLECTION: JIM REEVES.

Tracks: From a jack to a king / Fool such as I / White cliffs of Dover, The / I can't stop loving you / Moonlight and roses / That's my desire / You belong to me / Blue skies / Carolina moon / Not until the next time / When two worlds collide / Moon river / Adios amigo / I love you because / Welcome to my world / I won't forget you / There's a heartache following me / It hurts so much / I won't come in while he's there / You're the only good thing that's happened to me / Is it really over / But you love me, daddy / Shifting, whispering sands / Danny boy.

CD . . . . **CCSCD 183**
MC . . . . **CCSMC 183**
Castle Collector Series / Apr '88 / BMG / Pinnacle / Castle Communications.
■ **Double LP** . . . . **CCSLP 183**
Castle Collector Series / Apr '88.

COUNTRY GENTLEMAN.

Tracks: Not Advised.

■ **LP.** . . . . **NE 1088**
K-Tel / Sep '80.

COUNTRY SIDE OF JIM REEVES.

Tracks: Railroad bum / Blue side of lonesome / When two worlds collide / Waiting for a train / My lips are sealed / Yonder comes a sucker.

■ **LP.** . . . . **CDN 5100**
RCA/Camden / Sep '64.
LP. . . . . **CDS 1000**
RCA/Camden / '69 / BMG / Arabesque Ltd.

COUNTRY STORE: JIM REEVES.

Tracks: Not Advised.

LP. . . . . **CST 21**
MC . . . . **CSTK 21**
Country Store / Aug '86 / BMG.

DEAR HEARTS AND GENTLE PEOPLE.

Tracks: Not Advised.

CD . . . . **CDSD 073**
Sundown / Jun '92 / Terry Blood Dist. / Jazz Music / C.M. Distribution.

DIAMOND SERIES: JIM REEVES.

Tracks: Have you ever been lonely? / Just walking in the rain / Welcome to my world / I fall to pieces / White cliffs of Dover, The / Hawaiian wedding song / You are my love / In the misty moonlight / You'll never know / I can't stop loving you / Somewhere along the line / Someday you'll want me to want you / How's the world treating you? / Am I losing you? / Scarlet ribbons.

■ **CD** . . . . **CD 90110**
Diamond Series / Apr '88.

DISTANT DRUMS.

Tracks: Distant drums / I won't forget you / Is it really over? / I missed me / Snowflake / Letter to my heart, A / Losing your love / This is it / Not until the next time / Good morning self / Where does a broken heart go? / Overnight / Gods were angry with me, The.

■ **LP.** . . . . **RD 7814**
RCA / Nov '66.
LP. . . . . **SF 7814**
■ **MC** . . . . **VCS 67119**
RCA / '79.
CD . . . . **ND 89317**
MC . . . . **NK 89317**
RCA / Apr '88 / BMG.
■ **LP.** . . . . **NL 89317**
RCA / Apr '88.

DISTANT DRUMS.

Tracks: Distnat drums / Welcome to my world / There's a heartache following me.

■ **7"** . . . . **RCA 2122**
RCA / '79.

DISTANT DRUMS.

Tracks: Distant drums.

■ **7"** . . . . **RCA 1537**
RCA / Aug '66.

DISTANT DRUMS (OLD GOLD).

Tracks: Distant drums.

7" . . . . **OG 9612**
Old Gold / Oct '86 / Pickwick Records.

DON'T LET ME CROSS OVER.

Tracks: Don't let me cross over / When two worlds collide / I fall to pieces / Take me in your arms and hold me / Oh how I miss you tonight / Guilty / I'm a fool to care / I've enjoyed as much of this as I can stand / Have you ever been lonely / After loving you.

■ **MC** . . . . **PK 13454**
RCA / Apr '80.

FABULOUS JIM REEVES, THE.

Tracks: Welcome to my world / Yonder comes a sucker / According to my heart / Bimbo / Mexican Joe / Am I losing you / One dozen roses / Anna Marie / Golden memories and silver tears / Gypsy feet / Have I told you lately that I love you / Scarlet ribbons / He'll have to go / Blizzard / I fall to pieces / Distant drums / Storm, The / Memories are made of this / Make the world go away / Missing you / Roses are red / Four walls / Hawaiian wedding song / How can I write on paper (what I feel in my heart).

Double LP . . . . **CR 048**
■ **MC Set** . . . . **CRT 048**
Cambra / '83.

FOREVER.

Tracks: Make the world go away / Deep dark water / Welcome to my world / One dozen roses / Hawaiian wedding song / Penny Candy / Four walls / I won't forget you / Wreck of the number nine, The / Missing you / Bimbo / When you are gone / Angels don't lie / According to my heart / Missing angel / Auf wiedersehn sweetheart / Memories are made of this / Guilty / Have I told you lately that I love you / Distant drums / Gypsy feet / Storm, The / Scarlet ribbons / But you love me daddy / He'll have to go / Roses are red / Is it really over / Blizzard / Am I losing you / Mexican Joe / You're the only good thing that's happened to me / Crying in my sleep.

Double LP . . . . **NL 89366**
■ **MC Set** . . . . **NK 89366**
RCA / Jul '86.

FROM THE HEART.

Tracks: Just out of reach / I'd fight the world / I never pass there anymore / After loving you.

■ **LP.** . . . . **RCX 7131**
RCA / May '72 / BMG.

FROM THE HEART VOL.II.

Tracks: It's nothing to me / Mighty everglades, The / Tie that binds, The / Fool's paradise, The.

■ **LP.** . . . . **RCX 7145**
RCA / Jun '70 / BMG.

GENTLEMAN JIM.

Tracks: I'm hurtin' inside / If you were mine / That's a sad affair / Yonder comes a sucker / Jimbo Jenkins / I've lived a lot in my time / Ichabod crane / My lips are sealed / Your old love letters / Waltzing on top of the world / Beyond a shadow of a doubt / Love me a little bit more / According to my heart / Each time you leave / Highway to nowhere / Breeze (blow my baby back to me) / Roly poly / Tweedle o'twill / Have I told you lately that I love you / Oklahoma hills / Pickin' a chicken / I've got just the thing for you / I'm the mother of a honky tonk girl / Am I losing you / Don't tell me / I can't fly / Don't ask me why / Waiting for a train / Look behind you / Four walls / Honey, won't you please come home / Gods were angry with me, The / I know (and you know) / Honey, I won't you please come home / Young hearts / I heard a heart break last night / Image of me, The / Anna Marie / Seabreeze / Blue without my baby / I love you more / Theme of love (I love to say I love you) / Wishful thinking / Two shadows on your window / Everywhere you go (single version) / Teardrops in my heart / Yours / I don't see me in your eyes anymore / I get the blues when it rains / I care no more / Final affair / You belong to me / My happiness / Everywhere you go / Blues in my heart / Need me / That's my desire / He'll have to go / In a mansion stands my love / Billy Bayou / I'd like to be partners / I'm beginning to forget you / If heartache is the fashion / Home after awhile / Overnight blue boy / Charmaine / Mona Lisa / Marie / Goodnight Irene / Linda / Maria Elena / My Mary Ramona / Margie / My Juanita / Sweet Sue / Just you / Snowflake / But you love me daddy / But you love me daddy (2) / Throw another log on the fire / Making believe / 'Til the end of the world / How's the world treating you / Someday (you'll want me to want you) / Just call me lonesome / (Now and then there's) a fool such as I / May the good Lord bless and keep you / Dear hearts and gentle people / Satan can't hold me / Scarlet ribbons / How long has it been / Teach me how to pray / Evening prayer, An / Padre of old San Antone, The / Suppertime / It is no secret / God be with you / Beautiful life / In the garden / Precious memories / Whispering hope / Flowers, The / Sunset, the trees, The.

CD Set . . . . **BCD 15439**
Bear Family / Jun '89 / Rollercoaster Records / Swift / Direct Distribution.

GENTLEMAN JIM.

Tracks: Memories are made of this / Roses are red / After loving you / Waltzing on top of the world / When you are gone / Just out of reach / I love you because / I'd fight the world / One that got away, The / Once upon a time / I never pass there anymore.

■ **LP.** . . . . **RD 7541**
RCA / May '64.
LP. . . . . **SF 7541**
RCA / '74 / BMG.
■ **MC** . . . . **PK 11533**
RCA / '74.

GENTLEMAN JIM REEVES.

Tracks: Not Advised.

VHS. **791.142**
BMG Video / Sep '91 / BMG.

GIRLS I HAVE KNOWN.

Tracks: Marie / Mona Lisa / My Juanita / Charmaine / Margie / Anna Marie / Sweet Sue / Linda / Ramona / Maria Elena / My Mary / Goodnight Irene.

■ **LP.** . . . . **INTS 1256**
RCA International / Aug '71.
■ **LP.** . . . . **NL 89996**
RCA / Jan '87.
■ **MC** . . . . **NK 89996**
RCA / Jan '87.

GOD BE WITH YOU.

Tracks: How long has it been / Teach me how to pray / Padre of Old San Antone / Precious memories / God be with you till we meet again / It is no secret.

■ **LP.** . . . . **RD 7636**
RCA / Aug '64.
LP. . . . . **CDS 1092**
RCA/Camden / '71 / BMG / Arabesque Ltd.

R 4

■ DELETED

GOLDEN RECORDS (IMPORT).
Tracks: Not Advised.
LP. . . . . NL 89340
MC . . . . NK 89340
RCA(Special Imports Service) / Aug '84 / BMG.
LP. . . . . CDS 1145
RCA/Camden / '86 / BMG / Arabesque Ltd.
MC . . . . CAM 449
RCA/Camden / '88 / BMG / Arabesque Ltd.

GOOD 'N' COUNTRY.
Tracks: Don't let me cross over / Talking walls, The / Little ole dime / World you left behind, The / You kept me awake last night / I've enjoyed as much of this as I can stand.
■ LP. . . . . CDN 5114
RCA/Camden / Mar '64.
LP. . . . . CDM 1075
RCA/Camden / '70 / BMG / Arabesque Ltd.

GREATEST HITS: PATSY CLINE & JIM REEVES (see under Cline, Patsy).

GUILTY.
Tracks: Guilty.
■ 7". . . . . RCA 1364
RCA / Oct '63.

HAVE I TOLD YOU LATELY THAT I LOVE YOU.
Tracks: Have I told you lately that I love you? / Waltzing on top of the world / Roly poly / Beyond the shadow of a doubt / Your old love letters / Highway to nowhere.
■ LP. . . . . CDN 5112
RCA/Camden / Apr '65.
LP. . . . . CDM 1049
RCA/Camden / '69 / BMG / Arabesque Ltd.

HE'LL HAVE TO GO.
Tracks: He'll have to go.
■ 7". . . . . RCA 1168
RCA / Mar '60.

HE'LL HAVE TO GO.
Tracks: He'll have to go / I love you more / Wishful thinking / Honey, won't you please come home / I'm beginning to forget you / Billy Bayou / If heartache is the fashion / Partners / Theme of love / I'd like to be / After a while / Home.
■ LP. . . . . RD 27176
RCA / Aug '64.

HIS BEST LOVE SONGS.
Tracks: Not Advised.
■ LP. . . . . CDS 1224
RCA/Camden / Jul '87.
MC . . . . CAM 1224
RCA/Camden / '88 / BMG / Arabesque Ltd.

HITS OF JIM REEVES, THE.
Tracks: Am I that easy to forget / Gypsy feet / Missing you / You belong to me / Nobody's fool / Writing's on the wall, The / I'd fight the world / I love you because / You'll never know / Angels don't lie / That's when I see the blues / When two worlds collide / When you are gone / Why do I love you (melody of love).
LP. . . . . PL 42179
■ MC . . . . PK 42179
RCA / '79.

HOW LONG HAS IT BEEN.
Tracks: How long has it been.
■ 7". . . . . RCA 1445
RCA / May '65.

I HEARD A HEART BREAK LAST NIGHT.
Tracks: I heard a heart break last night.
■ 7". . . . . RCA 1643
RCA / Nov '67.

I KNOW ONE.
Tracks: I know one / I'm gettin' better.
7". . . . . RCA 1197
RCA / '60 / BMG.

I LOVE YOU BECAUSE.
Tracks: When two world's collide / Take me in your arms and hold me / You're free to go / I won't come in while he's there / From a Jack to a king / I love you because / Shifting whispering sands, The / I know one / Fool such as I, A / Someday (you'll want me to want you).
LP. . . . . PL 11224
■ MC . . . . PK 11224
RCA / '79.

I LOVE YOU BECAUSE.
Tracks: I love you because / He'll have to go / Moonlight and roses.
■ 7". . . . . RCA 1385
RCA / Feb '64.
■ 7". . . . . RCA 2092
RCA / Jun '71.
■ 7". . . . . PB 0557
RCA / Mar '77.

I LOVE YOU BECAUSE (OLD GOLD).
Tracks: I love you because / He'll have to go.
7". . . . . OG 9607
Old Gold / Oct '86 / Pickwick Records.

I LOVE YOU MORE (Live).
Tracks: If you were only mine / I love you more / Have I told you lately that I love you / Everywhere you go / Sweet evening breeze / Oklahoma hills where I was born, The / Evening prayer, An / Dear hearts and gentle people / I've lived a lot in my time / If heartaches the fashion / Home / How's the world treating you / I'm beginning to forget you / Rolypoly / Wind up, The / Your old love letters / Till the end of the world / Making believe / Just call me lonesome / Highway to nowhere / Beyond the shadow of a doubt.
CD . . . . DATOM 3
LP. . . . . ATOM 3
MC . . . . CATOM 3
A Touch Of Magic / May '89 / Wellard Dist. / Charly.

I WON'T COME IN WHILE HE'S THERE.
Tracks: I won't come in while he's there.
■ 7". . . . . RCA 1563
RCA / Feb '67.

I WON'T FORGET YOU.
Tracks: I won't forget you.
■ 7". . . . . RCA 1400
RCA / Jun '64.

I'D FIGHT THE WORLD.
Tracks: I'd fight the world / What's in it for me.
■ 7". . . . . APBO 0255
RCA / Apr '74.

I'LL ALWAYS LOVE YOU.
Tracks: I'll always love you / Spell of the Yukon / I'm a fool to care / Streets of Laredo / Wreck of the number nine, The / White cliffs of Dover, The.
LP. . . . . CDS 1163
RCA/Camden / Apr '78 / BMG / Arabesque Ltd.

I'M GETTING BETTER.
Tracks: Am I losing you / I missed me.
■ 7". . . . . RCA 1214
RCA / Oct '69 / BMG.

I'M GONNA CHANGE EVERYTHING.
Tracks: I'm gonna change everything.
■ 7". . . . . RCA 1317
RCA / Nov '62.

INTERNATIONAL JIM REEVES.
Tracks: Auf wiederseh'n sweetheart / Old Kalahari, The / White cliffs of Dover, The / True / I'm crying again / Guilty / Blue Canadian Rockies / Hawaiian wedding song / You are my love / Heartbreak in silhouette / Tahiti / Golden memories and silver tears.
■ LP. . . . . RD 7577
RCA / Aug '64.
■ MC . . . . PK 11536
RCA / '79.

INTIMATE JIM REEVES, THE.
Tracks: Dark moon / Oh, how I miss you tonight / Take me in your arms and hold me / I'm gettin' better / Almost / You're free to go / You're the only good thing / Have I stayed away too long / No one to cry to / I was just walkin' out the door / Room full of roses / We could.
■ LP. . . . . RD 27193
RCA / Aug '64.

IS IT REALLY OVER.
Tracks: Is it really over.
■ 7". . . . . RCA 1488
RCA / Nov '65.

IS THIS ME.
Tracks: Is this me / Missing angel.
■ 7". . . . . RCA 1330
RCA / Dec '65 / BMG.

IT HURTS SO MUCH TO SEE YOU GO.
Tracks: It hurts so much.
■ 7". . . . . RCA 1437
RCA / Feb '65.

IT'S NOTHIN' TO ME.
Tracks: It's nothin' to me / You are my love / Talking walls, The / Little ole you / Trying to forget / World you left behind, The / Crying is my favourite mood / Gypsy feet / Once upon a time / There's that smile again / Deep dark water.
LP. . . . . PL 12309
■ MC . . . . PK 12309
RCA / '79.

JIM REEVES.
Tracks: You're the only good thing / Before I died / Little ole dime / There's a heartache following me / Dark moon / Missing angel / Roses / Talking walls, The / I never pass there anymore / There's a new moon over my shoulder.
LP. . . . . PL 12720
■ MC . . . . PK 12720
RCA / '79.

JIM REEVES AND SOME FRIENDS.
Tracks: Not Advised.
■ LP. . . . . SF 8022
RCA / Aug '69.

JIM REEVES COLLECTION.
Tracks: Have I told you lately that I love you? / Letter to your heart / Your old love letters / I love you because / I'm a fool to care / Welcome to my world.
Double LP . . . . PDA 010
Pickwick / Mar '76 / Pickwick Records.
MC Set. . . . . PDC 010
Pickwick / Dec '79 / Pickwick Records.

JIM REEVES COLLECTION VOL 2.
Tracks: Welcome to my world / Danny boy / Letter to my heart, A / Dear hearts and gentle people / I won't forget you / You're the only good thing.
Double LP . . . . PDA 039
Pickwick / Feb '78 / Pickwick Records.
MC Set. . . . . PDC 039
Pickwick / Jul '80 / Pickwick Records.

JIM REEVES GOLDEN RECORDS.
Tracks: Not Advised.
■ LP. . . . . INTS 1070
RCA International / Aug '71.

JIM REEVES ON STAGE.
Tracks: Mexican Joe / Yonder comes a sucker / Four walls / I missed me / Tennessee waltz / I really don't want to know / He'll have to go / Walking the floor over you / There stands the glass / One by one / Guess things happen that way / I want to be with you always / Wildwood flower / Blizzard / Your old love letters / Am I losing you? / Bimbo / Stand at your window / Danny boy.
■ MC . . . . PK 1383
RCA / '79.

JIM REEVES WAY, THE.
Tracks: Make the world go away / In the misty moonlight / You'll never know / There's that smile again / Bolandse nooientjie / It hurts so much / I can't stop loving you / Nickel piece of candy, A / Where do I go to throw a picture away / Maureen / Ek verlang na jou / Somewhere along the line.
■ LP. . . . . RD 7694
RCA / May '65.
■ MC . . . . VCS 67072
RCA / '79.

JIM REEVES WRITES YOU A RECORD.
Tracks: Not Advised.
■ LP. . . . . SF 8176
RCA / Jul '71.

LEGENDARY PERFORMER, A.
Tracks: Mexican Joe / Yonder comes a sucker / Four walls / Teach me how to pray / He'll have to go / Danny boy / You're slipping away from me / Welcome to my world / Guilty / Roving gambler / I guess I'm crazy / Is it really over / Distant drums.
LP. . . . . RS 1078
■ MC . . . . PK 11751
RCA / '79.

LIVE - THE REAL SOUND OF COUNTRY.
Tracks: Not Advised.
MC . . . . CTP 1002
Submarine / Oct '91 / Charly / Wellard Dist.

LIVE AT THE OPRY.
Tracks: Yonder comes a sucker / Waitin' for a train / Am I losing you / When God dips his love in my heart / According to my heart / Four walls / Mexican Joe / Anna Marie / Blue boy / Softly and tenderly (Jesus is calling) / He'll have to go / Bimbo / I'd like to be / Peace in the valley / Billy bayou / In a mansion stands my love / I'm getting better / (Gimme that) Old time religion / I know one / I missed me.
CD . . . . CMFCD 008
MC . . . . CMFC 008
Country Music Foundation / Jan '93 / Topic Records / Direct Distribution.

LIVE AT THE OPRY.
Tracks: Not Advised.
CD . . . . U 4041
Spectrum (1) / Jun '88 / PolyGram.

MAGIC MOMENTS.
Tracks: He'll have to go / Distant drums / When two worlds collide / I missed me / Blizzard / This is it / Moonlight and roses / You're the only good thing that's happened to me / I love you because / I won't forget you / There's a heartache following me / It hurts so much / Not until the next time / Is it really over? / Snowflake / Guilty / I'd fight the world / Trying to forget / Nobody's fool / Welcome to my world / Four walls / Blue boy / I'm getting better / Am I losing you? / Billy Bayou / Anna Marie / Stand at your window / Adios amigo / Danny boy.
■ MC . . . . NK 89402
RCA / Jun '84.

MEMORIES ARE MADE OF THIS.
Tracks: Not Advised.
MC . . . . CAM 1228
RCA/Camden / Feb '88 / BMG / Arabesque Ltd.

MOONLIGHT AND ROSES.
Tracks: Moonlight and roses / Mexicali rose / Carolina moon / Rosa Rio / Oh what it seemed to be / What's in it for me? / Roses / One dozen roses / Moon river / There's a new Moon over my shoulder / It's only a paper moon / When I lost you.
■ LP. . . . . RD 7639
RCA / Sep '64.
LP. . . . . SF 7639
■ MC . . . . VCS 67037
RCA / '79.
CD . . . . ND 89016
RCA / Apr '88 / BMG.
■ LP. . . . . NL 89016
RCA / Apr '88.

MY CATHEDRAL.
Tracks: Not Advised.
■ LP. . . . . SF 8146
RCA / Dec '70.

MY FRIEND.
Tracks: Not Advised.
■ LP. . . . . SF 8258
RCA / Apr '72.

NOBODY'S FOOL.
Tracks: Nobody's fool.
■ 7". . . . . RCA 1915
RCA / Mar '70.

NOT UNTIL THE NEXT TIME.
Tracks: Not until the next time.
■ 7". . . . . RCA 1446
RCA / Apr '65.

OLD TIGE.
Tracks: Old Tige / Angels don't lie / When two worlds collide / Nobody's fool / What would you do / Read this letter / Writing's on the wall / There's a heartache following me / Wild rose / After loving you / Trying to forget / Seven days.
■ LP. . . . . INTS 5021
RCA International / Aug '80.
LP. . . . . CDS 1216
■ MC . . . . CAM 1216
RCA/Camden / Jul '86.

ON STAGE.
Tracks: Not Advised.
■ LP. . . . . SF 8047
RCA / Nov '69.

PARTNERS.
Tracks: Partners / I'm beginning to forget you.
■ 7". . . . . RCA 1144
RCA / Sep '70 / BMG.

PRETTY BROWN EYES.
Tracks: Pretty brown eyes.
■ 7". . . . . RCA 1672
RCA / Mar '68.

PURE GOLD VOL.1.
Tracks: Four walls / Goodnight Irene / Melody of love / Auf wiederseh'n sweetheart / Hawaiian wedding song / Welcome to my world / From a jack to a king / My happiness / Mona Lisa / You'll never know.
■ LP. . . . . NL 13014
RCA / '79.

REMEMBERING.
Tracks: Distant drums / He'll have to go / I love you because / I won't forget you / Adios amigo / There's a heartache following me / I won't come in while he's here / Have you ever been lonely (have you ever been blue) / Missing you / I can't stop loving you / Fool such as I, A / From a Jack to a King / Nobody's fool / Mona Lisa / Tennessee.
CD . . . . PWKS 4120
MC . . . . PWKMC 4120
Pickwick / Oct '92 / Pickwick Records.

SOMETHING SPECIAL.
Tracks: Guilty / How can I write on paper (what I feel in my heart) / Letter to my heart, A / I'm gettin' better / Wild rose / Stranger's just a friend, A / Blizzard, The / Welcome to my world / Anna Marie / I won't forget you / Stand at your window / I'm gonna change everything / You kept me awake last night / We thank thee.
■ LP. . . . . PK 11579
RCA / '78 / BMG.

SONGS FROM THE HEART.
Tracks: Someday you'll want me to want you / Just call me lonesome / Throw another log on the fire / Fool such as I, A / How's the world treating you? / Dear hearts and gentle people / Till the end of the world / Satan can't help me / May the good Lord bless and keep you / Making believe / Am I losing you? / Scarlet ribbons.
LP. . . . . CDS 1099
■ MC . . . . CAM 1099
RCA/Camden / Jul '84.
MC . . . . CAM 437
RCA/Camden / '88 / BMG / Arabesque Ltd.

SONGS OF LOVE.
Tracks: You'll never know / Blue skies / Oh what it seemed to be / (It's no) sin / Moon river / You belong to me / White cliffs of Dover / That's my desire / Moonlight and roses / Oh how I miss you tonight.
LP. . . . . PL 11037
RCA / Mar '78 / BMG.
■ MC . . . . PK 11037
RCA / Mar '78.

SONGS TO WARM THE HEART.
Tracks: Just call me lonesome / Til the end of the world / How's the world treating you / Satan can't hold me / Am I losing you.
■ LP. . . . . RCX 173
RCA / Nov '71 / BMG.

SONGS TO WARM THE HEART VOL.II.
Tracks: Fool such as I, A / Throw another log on the fire / Scarlet ribbons / Dear hearts and gentle people.
■ LP. . . . . RCX 215
RCA / Dec '71 / BMG.

SONGS TO WARM THE HEART VOL.III.
Tracks: Four walls / Blue boy / Mexican Joe / Someday.
■ LP. . . . . RCX 216
RCA / Dec '72 / BMG.

THERE'S A HEARTACHE FOLLOWING ME.
Tracks: There's a heartache following me.
■ 7". . . . . RCA 1423
RCA / Nov '64.

THERE'S ALWAYS ME.
Tracks: There's always me / Room full of roses / Moon river / All dressed up and lonely / Blue skies / After loving you / Somewhere along the line / Blue side of lonesome / What would you do / I can't stop loving you.
LP. . . . . PL 13827
RCA / Apr '81 / BMG.

THIS WORLD IS NOT MY HOME.
Tracks: This world is not my home.
■ 7". . . . . RCA 1412
RCA / Jul '65.

TOUCH OF SADNESS, A.
Tracks: Where do I go to throw a picture away? / You kept me awake last night / I'm cryin' again / Oh, how I miss you tonight / Lonesome waltz / Your wedding / When you are gone / Missing you / Honey, won't you please come home? / In a mansion stands my love / I'm glad you're better.
LP. . . . . RD 7978
RCA / Oct '72 / BMG.
LP. . . . . SF 7978
RCA / '74 / BMG.
■ MC . . . . PK 11537
RCA / '74.

TOUCH OF VELVET, A.
Tracks: Have you ever been lonely / There's always me / Just walking in the rain / Be honest with me / I fall to pieces / It's no sin / Welcome to my world / Am I that easy to forget / Blue skies / All dressed up and lonely / Wild rose, The / I'm a fool to care.
■ LP. . . . . RD 7521
RCA / Aug '64.
■ LP. . . . . INTS 1089
RCA International / Nov '71.
■ LP. . . . . MFP 5775
MFP / Sep '86.
■ MC . . . . TCMFP 5775
MFP / Sep '86.

TRYING TO FORGET.
Tracks: Trying to forget.
■ 7". . . . . RCA 1611
RCA / Jul '67.

VERY BEST OF JIM REEVES, THE.
Tracks: He'll have to go / Distant drums / When two world's collide / I missed me / Blizzard / This is it / Moonlight and roses / You're the only good thing that's happened to me / I love you because / I won't forget you / There's heartache following me / I hurt so much to see you go / Not until the next time / It is really over / Snowflake / Guilty / I'd fight the world / Trying to forget / Nobody's fool / Welcome to my world.
■ LP. . . . . RCALP 5047
RCA / Aug '81.
■ LP. . . . . NL 89017
RCA / Nov '84.
CD . . . . ND 89017
RCA / Apr '90 / BMG.
MC . . . . NK 89017
RCA / May '90 / BMG.

VERY BEST OF JIM REEVES, VOL. 2, THE.
Tracks: Bimbo / Yonder comes a sucker / My lips are sealed / Four walls / Anna Maria / Billy Bayou / (How can I write on paper) What I feel in my heart / Losing your love / Adios amigo / I'm gonna change everything / Blue side of lonesome / I won't come in while he's there / I heard a heart break last night / That's when I see the blues (in your pretty brown eyes) / Angels don't lie / Missing you / How long has it been / This world is not my home / But you love me daddy / Old tige / Jim Reeves medley, The.
CD . . . . ND 90568
MC . . . . NK 90568
RCA / Aug '91 / BMG.

VERY SPECIAL LOVE SONGS.
Tracks: I love you because / When two worlds collide / Just out of reach / In the misty moonlight / Fool such as I, A / Am I that easy to forget? / He'll have to go / Moonlight & roses / You're the only good thing / I can't stop loving you / Just call me lonesome / Make the world go away.
■ LP. . . . . CBR 1040
Everest (Premier) / Apr '84.
LP. . . . . PMP 1016
MC . . . . PMPK 1016
Premier (Sony) / Feb '88 / Sony / Pinnacle.
LP. . . . . PFP 1010
MC . . . . PFC 1010
Performance / May '89.

WE THANK THEE.
Tracks: We thank thee / Have thine own way / Lord the night watch / I'd rather have Jesus / Take my hand precious Lord / This world is not my home.
■ LP. . . . . RD 7637
RCA / Sep '64.
LP. . . . . CDS 1111
RCA/Camden / '72 / BMG / Arabesque Ltd.

WELCOME TO MY WORLD.
Tracks: Welcome to my world / Adios amigo / I'm a fool to care / Never take no for an answer / I love you because / Old tige / I could cry.
■ LP. . . . . CDS 1152
RCA/Camden / Aug '75.
MC . . . . CAM 461
RCA/Camden / '88 / BMG / Arabesque Ltd.

WELCOME TO MY WORLD.
Tracks: Welcome to my world.
■ 7". . . . . RCA 1342
RCA / Jun '63.

WELCOME TO MY WORLD.
Tracks: Welcome to my world / Roses are red / There's always me / I'm a fool to care.
■ LP. . . . . RCX 7119
RCA / Apr '71 / BMG.

WELCOME TO MY WORLD (OLD GOLD).
Tracks: Welcome to my world.
7". . . . . OG 9649
Old Gold / Nov '86 / Pickwick Records.

WHEN TWO WORLDS COLLIDE.
Tracks: When two worlds collide.
■ 7". . . . . RCA 1830
RCA / Jun '69.

WHEN YOU ARE GONE.
Tracks: When you are gone / How can I write on paper.
■ 7". . . . . RCA 1750
RCA / Aug '65 / BMG.

WHISPERING HOPE.
Tracks: Whispering hope.
■ 7". . . . . RCA 1223
RCA / Mar '61.

YOU BELONG TO ME.
Tracks: You belong to me / Maureen.
■ 7". . . . . RCA 2574
RCA / Apr '75.

YOU'RE FREE TO GO.
Tracks: You're free to go.
■ 7". . . . . RCA 2174
RCA / Feb '72.

YOU'RE THE ONLY GOOD THING.
Tracks: You're the only good thing.
■ 7". . . . . RCA 1261
RCA / Nov '61.

YOUR OLD LOVE LETTERS.
Tracks: Have I told you lately that I love you / Just call me lonesome / How's the world treating you / If heart-aches are the fashion / Home / Dear hearts and gentle people / I'm beginning to forget you / Roly poly / Wind up, The / Sweet evening breeze / Your old love letters / 'Till the end of the world / Making believe / Oklahoma blues, The / Highway to nowhere, The / If you were mine / Everywhere you go / I love you more / I've lived a lot in my time.
CD . . . . GRF 199
MC . . . . MCGRF 199
Tring / Jan '93 / Prism Leisure PLC / Midland Records / Taylors.

YOURS SINCERELY.
Tracks: He'll have to go / Blue yodel No.5 / My Mary / When did you leave heaven / Mexican Joe / Back up and push / Yonder comes a sucker / Wreck of the number nine / Scarlet ribbons / Fool's paradise, The / Billy Bayou / Am I losing you / I grew up / He'll have to go (2nd version).
LP. . . . . RD 7906
RCA / Feb '71 / BMG.

Reid, Lou

WHEN IT RAINS.
Tracks: Ain't it funny / Cry, cry, darlin' / Hand of the higher power, The / You better hold onto your heart / Red, white & blue / Callin' your name / Mom's old picture book / One track man / Absence make the heart grow fonder / First step to heaven, The / Nobody's loves like mine.
CD SH-CD-3788
MC SH-MC-3788
Sugarhill(USA) / '91 / Roots Records / Projection / Impetus Records / C.M. Distribution / Jazz Music / Swift / Duncans / A.D.A Distribution.

Rendall, Ruby

IN PORTRAIT.
Tracks: Just in case you change your mind / Guitar town / Your free to go / Never like this before / South gonna rattle again, The / Blue moon of Kentucky / Girl like Emmylou, A / Evangeline / Two more bottles of wine / Even now / American trilogy.
LP. . . . . AT 013
MC . . . . ATC 013
Attic (USA) / Nov '87 / C.M. Distribution.

NEVER LOOK BACK.
Tracks: Not Advised.
MC . . . . CWGR 095
Ross (1) / '86 / Ross Records / Duncans / Entertainment UK.
LP. . . . . WGR 095

R 6 ■ DELETED

Ross (1) / Aug '86 / Ross Records / Duncans / Entertainment UK.

STRAIGHT FROM THE HEART.
Tracks: Not Advised.
LP . . . . **WGR 079**
MC . . . . **CWGR 079**
Ross (1) / Aug '84 / Ross Records / Duncans / Entertainment UK.

Reno & Smiley

16 GREATEST HITS: RENO & SMILEY.
Tracks: Not Advised.
LP . . . . **SLP 3001**
MC . . . . **GT 53001**
Starday (USA) / Apr '87 / Crusader Marketing Co.
LP . . . . **SD 3001**
Starday (USA) / Mar '88 / Crusader Marketing Co.

20 BLUEGRASS SPECIALS.
Tracks: Not Advised.
LP . . . . **SLP 5025**
MC . . . . **GT 55025**
Starday (USA) / Apr '87 / Crusader Marketing Co.

BEST OF RENO & SMILEY.
Tracks: Not Advised.
LP . . . . **SLP 961**
MC . . . . **GT 5961**
Starday (USA) / Apr '87 / Crusader Marketing Co.

COUNTRY SINGING AND INSTRUMENTALS.
Tracks: Not Advised.
LP . . . . **KLP 776**
MC . . . . **GT 5776**
King (USA) / Apr '87 / Charly.

COUNTRY SONGS.
Tracks: Not Advised.
LP . . . . **KLP 701**
MC . . . . **GT 5701**
King (USA) / Apr '87 / Charly.

GOOD OLD COUNTRY BALLADS.
Tracks: Not Advised.
CD . . . . **KCD 621**
King / Mar '93 / New Note / Koch International.

LAST TIME TOGETHER.
Tracks: Not Advised.
LP . . . . **SLP 485**
MC . . . . **GT 5485**
Starday (USA) / Apr '87 / Crusader Marketing Co.

RENO & SMILEY VOL 2 (83 Collectors edition).
Tracks: Not Advised.
LP . . . . **GT 0111**
Gusto (USA) / Mar '88.

RENO & SMILEY VOL 3 (83 collectors edition).
Tracks: Not Advised.
LP . . . . **GT 0112**
Gusto (USA) / Mar '88.

RENO & SMILEY VOL 4 (83 collectors edition).
Tracks: Not Advised.
LP . . . . **GT 0113**
Gusto (USA) / Mar '88.

SONGS OF YESTERDAY.
Tracks: Not Advised.
LP . . . . **REBEL 1661**
Rebel (1) / '78 / Projection / Backs Distribution.

WORLD'S BEST FIVE STRING BANJO.
Tracks: Not Advised.
LP . . . . **KLP 861**
MC . . . . **GT 5861**
King (USA) / Apr '87 / Charly.

Reno, Don

Don Reno of Reno & Smiley fame was both a banjo player extraordiniare and an accomplished all -round musician being a superb flat -picker (one of the pioneers of the craft, amongst bluegrass musicians) & useful mandolin picker. Reno's three - fingered style of banjo playing, learnt from 'Snuffy Jenkins - from Harris, N.Carolina is equal & more to Earl Scruggs. Reno worked on WSPA, Spartanburg radio when only 13. Played with Arthur "Guitar Boogie" Smith in 1941 (with whom he teamed - up on Smiths *Fuedin' banjoes* , later made famous through Eric Weisburg's soundtrack version *Duelin Banjoes*), Monroe in 1948 - then formed with Arthur Lee ' Red 'Smiley the Smiley - Reno & the Tennessee Cut -Ups a year later, Reno's tenor harmony vocals accompanying Smiley's fluid, warm baritone lead and recording a mix of bluegrass, gospel, mountain music & guitar - based country for Federal & King, their music flooding the country jukeboxes during bluegrass' golden era, the Fifties. Reno is also a fine songwriter, crafting the much sung *I'm using my bible as a road map* - as a comedy unit Smiley - Reno recorded *Jimmy caught the Dickens* billed as Chick & His Hot Rods, the 1961 hit and overspill from their alter-ego stage show. Reno did some work with Benny Martin & Bill Harrell prior to his final recordings on California-based Kaleidoscope label - *Family & friends* (1983/84).(Maurice Hope)

DEAR OLD DIXIE (Reno, Don & Bill Harrell).
Tracks: Dear old Dixie / One morning in May / It's a long, long way from the bottom / Hobo's song / Please keep remembering / At last I'm free / Where would over flowers grow? / B.G. / Chase, The / Wind blew across the wild moor, The / Make believe / Into these hills.
■ **LP** . . . . **CMH 6201**
CMH (USA) / '76.

FAMILY AND FRIENDS.
Tracks: Your love is dying / No longer a sweetheart of mine / Clear skies / Lonesome wind blues / Chokin' the strings / Freight train boogie / Country boy rock 'n' roll / Eastbound freight train / I'm the talk of the town / John Hardy / I want to know / Dixie breakdown.
LP . . . . **F 34**
MC . . . . **C 34**
Kaleidoscope (USA) / '88 / Projection / Ross Records / Roots Records / Swift / C.M. Distribution / Topic Records / Duncans.

FASTEST FIVE STRINGS ALIVE.
Tracks: Not Advised.
LP . . . . **KLP 1065**
MC . . . . **GT 51065**
King (USA) / Apr '87 / Charly.

HOME IN THE MOUNTAINS (Reno, Don & Bill Harrell).
Tracks: Home in the mountain / Miss Elsie's place / Follow the leader / Pretty angel tree, A / If today was tomorrow / Banjo Bill / I want to go back to the mountains / Walking catfish / Once in a while / Booked up in advance / Going back to church with mama.
■ **LP** . . . . **CMH 6210**
CMH (USA) / '76.

VARIETY OF COUNTRY SONGS, A (Reno, Don & Red Smiley).
Tracks: Not Advised.
CD . . . . **KCD 646**
King / Nov '92 / New Note / Koch International.

Restless Heart

Country/rock/pop act formed in 1983, A five piece unit consisting of former sessionmen - often producing a soft, laidback West Coast feel. The original line-up consisted of Larry Stewart (lead vocals), Dave Innis (guitar/keyboards), Greg Jennings (guitar), Paul Gregg (bass) and John Dittrich (drums). They have racked up a formidable run of hit singles, debuting in 1985 on the country charts with *Let the heartache ride* (No. 23) and making the top ten in 1985/86 with the hits *I want everyone to cry* & *(Back to the) Heartbreak kid* . In 1986 they embarked on a run of six chart toppers - spanning the band's 1987 gold selling album *Wheels* . No fewer than four chart topping singles were to hail from Restless Heart - only the second band to register this feat since the Texas band, Alabama. Apart from the chart topping title track, they scored with *Bluest eyes in Texas* , *Why does it have to be* and *I'm still loving you* , following 1986's debut No. 1 *That rock won't roll* . Stewart and company were to score once morewith *Tender lie* (1989) and their hits were to continue on a lesser scale as the 1990s dawned. Top 5 singles *Big dreams in a small town* , *Say what's on your mind* , *Dancy's dream* and *Fast movin' train* all pushed hard. By late 1992 Larry Stewart had leftthe band, striking out as a solo act with RCA. The band are now working as a four - piece and they have recorded the album *Big iron horses* .

BEST OF RESTLESS HEART, THE.
Tracks: You can depend on me / Fast movin' train / Tender lie, A / Bluest eyes in Texas, The / Familiar pain / Wheels / That rock won't roll / Til I loved you / Why does it have to (wrong or right) / I'll still be loving you.
CD . . . . **PD 90608**
MC . . . . **PK 90608**
RCA / Feb '92 / BMG.

BIG IRON HORSES.
Tracks: Mending fences / We got the love / As far as I can tell / When she cries / Meet on the other side / Tell me what you dream / Blame it on love / Born in a high wind / Just in time / Big iron horses.
CD **74321 13899-2**
MC **74321 138999-4**
RCA / Apr '93 / BMG.

FAST MOVIN' TRAIN.
Tracks: Fast movin' train / Dancy's dream / Sweet auburn / I've never been so sure / Long lost friend / Little more coal on the fire, A / When somebody loves you / Lady luck / River of stone (Only on CD.) / Truth hurts, The.
CD . . . . **PD 90456**
MC . . . . **PK 90456**
RCA / Apr '90 / BMG.
■ **LP** . . . . **PL 90456**
RCA / Apr '90.

Revard, Jimmie

OH SWING IT!.
Tracks: Not Advised.
LP . . . . **RAMBLER 108**
Rambler (USA) / Feb '89 / Roots Records / Projection / Swift / Wellard Dist.

Rhodes, Kimmie

Texan - born vocalist, recording typical lively Lone Star material, blending swing, rockabilly and country. popular visitor to the UK, where, apart from two appearances at the Wembley Country Music Festival, she's toured the club scene regularly during the last few years. While unlikely to be a major commercial star, the lively-voiced Rhodes underlines the strength of the Texas scene. Her 1985 album, *Kimmie Rhodes and the Jackalope brothers* on Jackalope records with Bobby Earl Smith and her husband/guitarist and one-time DJ Joe Gracey, gained wide acclaim. Since then, she's had the equally well accepted 1988 Heartland Records album *Man in the Moon* , featuring her own *It'll do* . Rhodes (then still with the now defunct Heartland). In 1989, had *Angels get the blues* , with fellow Texans Joe Ely and Johnny Rodriguez adding vocal harmonies, while Sun legend Jack Clement produced in the Sun studios. (Maurice Hope)

ANGELS GET THE BLUES.
Tracks: Not Advised.
CD . . . . **HLDCD 010**
LP . . . . **HLD 010**
MC . . . . **HLD 010C**
Heartland (1) / Oct '89 / Revolver-APT.

MAN IN THE MOON.
Tracks: Man in the moon, The / Daddy's song / Earth shakin' thing / Just someone I used to know / When you wish upon a star / 1000 musicians / What a love's supposed to be / It'll do / How long.
LP . . . . **HLD 007**
Heartland (1) / Jun '88 / Revolver-APT.

WITH THE JACKALOPE BROS.
Tracks: Not Advised.
CD **HLDCD008**
LP **HLD008**
Heartland (1) / Sep '89 / Revolver-APT.

Rhodes, Roy

COUNTRY HEARTBREAK.
Tracks: I never miss a day missing you / Coward of the county / Today I started loving you again / To daddy / Dream / Crying time / One day at a time / Four in the morning / Walk on by / Answer to everything, The / Almost persuaded.
LP . . . . **BGC 263**
MC . . . . **KBGC 263**
Country House / Jun '81 / Duncans / BGS Productions Ltd.

COUNTRY SIDE OF ROY RHODES.
Tracks: Not Advised.
MC . . . . **CWGR 102**
Ross (1) / Sep '86 / Ross Records / Duncans / Entertainment UK.

Rice Brothers

RICE BROTHERS, THE.
Tracks: Grapes on the vine / This old house / Original unlimited / Teardrops in my eyes / You're drifting away / Don't think twice / Let it ride / Keep the light on Sadie / Soldier's joy / Whisper my name / Life is like a mountain railroad.
CD . . . . **CD 0256**
LP . . . . **ROUNDER 0256**
MC . . . . **ROUNDERC 0256**
Rounder / '89 / Projection / Roots Records / Swift / C.M. Distribution / Topic Records / Jazz Music / Hot Shot / A.D.A Distribution / Direct Distribution.

Rice, Larry

HURRICANES AND DREAMS.
Tracks: Four wheel drive / Deportee / You've got a crazy heart / Starbound heroes (the space shuttle song) / Used to be / Finish line / It's hard to run away (from the storm) / Tabasco / Hurricane Elena / I cried again / Dad's old coat / Move along.
LP . . . . **REB 1646**
MC . . . . **REBMC 1646**
Rebel (1) / '75 / Projection / Backs Distribution.

TIME MACHINE.
Tracks: Not Advised.
LP . . . . **REB 1656**
MC . . . . **REBMC 1656**
Rebel (1) / '75 / Projection / Backs Distribution.

Rice, Tony

Guitarist/singer - songwriter/sessionman born 1951, Danville, Virginia, moving to Los Angeles in 1952., where he formed his first band with brothers Larry and Ronnie. The Rice Brothers, playing L.A. clubs in 1960. Joined "The Bluegrass Alliance" in 1970 as a replacement for Dan Crary - playing alongside Sam Bush, Courtney Johnson and Ebo Walker. A member of J.D. Crowe's The New South from 1971 to 1975, since which time he's played on albums by Emmylou Harris, recorded with Ricky Skaggs, his own Tony Rice Unit, The Bluegrass Album Band, Norman Blake, The Rice Brothers (where in 1989 all four brothers, Larry, Ronnie, Wyatt and Tony got together for the first time - on Rounder 0256) along with a batch of solo albums on King, Rounder and Sugar Hill, making him one of acoustic music's most respected flat - top guitarists. (Maruice Hope)

ACOUSTICS.
Tracks: Not Advised.
LP. . . . . **K 10**
Kaleidoscope (USA) / Oct '88 / Projection / Ross Records / Roots Records / Swift / C.M. Distribution / Topic Records / Duncans.

BACKWATERS (Rice, Tony Unit).
Tracks: Not Advised.
CD . . . . **CD 0167**
LP. . . . . **ROUNDER 0167**
MC . . . . **ROUNDER 0167C**
Rounder / Aug '88 / Projection / Roots Records / Swift / C.M. Distribution / Topic Records / Jazz Music / Hot Shot / A.D.A Distribution / Direct Distribution.

CALIFORNIA AUTUMN.
Tracks: California Autumn / Bullet man / Mr. Poverty / Billy in the law ground / Red haired boy / Good woman's love, A / You don't know my mind / Alone and forsaken / Bugle call rag / Georgia on my mind / Scarborough fair / Beaumont rag.
LP. . . . . **REB 1549**
MC . . . . **REBMC 1549**
Rebel (1) / '75 / Projection / Backs Distribution.
LP. . . . . **SDLP 045**
Sundown / Jun '87 / Terry Blood Dist. / Jazz Music / C.M. Distribution.

CHURCH STREET BLUES.
Tracks: Church Street blues / Cattle in the cane / Streets of London / One more night / Gold rush / Any old time / Orphan Annie / House carpenter / Jerusalem Ridge / Last thing on my mind / Pride of man.
CD . . . . **SHCD 3732**
LP. . . . . **SH 3732**
MC . . . . **ZCSH 3732**
Sugarhill(USA) / '83 / Roots Records / Projection / Impetus Records / C.M. Distribution / Jazz Music / Swift / Duncans / A.D.A Distribution.

COLD ON THE SHOULDER.
Tracks: Cold on the shoulder / Wayfaring stranger / John Hardy / Fare thee well / Bitter green / Muleskinner blues / Song for life / Why don't you tell me so / If you only knew / Likes of me / I think it's gonna rain today.
CD . . . . **CD 0183**
Rounder / Dec '86 / Projection / Roots Records / Swift / C.M. Distribution / Topic Records / Jazz Music / Hot Shot / A.D.A Distribution / Direct Distribution.
LP. . . . . **ROUNDER 0183**
MC . . . . **ROUNDER 0183C**
Rounder / '88 / Projection / Roots Records / Swift / C.M. Distribution / Topic Records / Jazz Music / Hot Shot / A.D.A Distribution / Direct Distribution.

DELVIN (Rice, Tony Unit).
Tracks: Not Advised.
CD . . . . **CD 11531**
Rounder / '88 / Projection / Roots Records / Swift / C.M. Distribution / Topic Records / Jazz Music / Hot Shot / A.D.A Distribution / Direct Distribution.

GUITAR.
Tracks: Not Advised.
LP. . . . . **REB 1582**
MC . . . . **REBMC 1582**
Rebel (1) / '75 / Projection / Backs Distribution.

MANZANITA.
Tracks: Not Advised.
LP. . . . . **ROUNDER 0092**
Rounder / Aug '79 / Projection / Roots Records / Swift / C.M. Distribution / Topic Records / Jazz Music / Hot Shot / A.D.A Distribution / Direct Distribution.
CD . . . . **CD 0092**
MC . . . . **ROUNDER 0092C**
Rounder / '88 / Projection / Roots Records / Swift / C.M. Distribution / Topic Records / Jazz Music / Hot Shot / A.D.A Distribution / Direct Distribution.

MAR WEST (Rice, Tony Unit).
Tracks: Not Advised.
LP. . . . . **ROUNDER 0125**
MC . . . . **ROUNDER 0125C**
Rounder / '88 / Projection / Roots Records / Swift / C.M. Distribution / Topic Records / Jazz Music / Hot Shot / A.D.A Distribution / Direct Distribution.

ME AND MY GUITAR.
Tracks: Not Advised.
CD . . . . **CD 0201**
LP. . . . . **ROUNDER 0201**
MC . . . . **ROUNDER 0201C**
Rounder / Aug '88 / Projection / Roots Records / Swift / C.M. Distribution / Topic Records / Jazz Music / Hot Shot / A.D.A Distribution / Direct Distribution.

NATIVE AMERICAN.
Tracks: Shadows / St. James hospital / Night flyer / Why you been so long / Urge for going / Go my way / Nothin' like a hundred miles / Changes / Brother to the wind / John Wilkes Booth / Summer wages.
CD . . . . **CD 0248**
LP. . . . . **ROUNDER 0248**
MC . . . . **ROUNDER 0248C**
Rounder / Aug '88 / Projection / Roots Records / Swift / C.M. Distribution / Topic Records / Jazz Music / Hot Shot / A.D.A Distribution / Direct Distribution.

NORMAN BLAKE & TONY RICE 2 (see under Blake, Norman).

RICKY SKAGGS & TONY RICE (Rice, Tony & Ricky Skaggs).
Tracks: Not Advised.
LP. . . . . **ROUNDER 0108**
Rounder / Sep '79 / Projection / Roots Records / Swift / C.M. Distribution / Topic Records / Jazz Music / Hot Shot / A.D.A Distribution / Direct Distribution.

STILL INSIDE (Rice, Tony Unit).
Tracks: Not Advised.
LP. . . . . **ROUNDER 0150**
MC . . . . **ROUNDER 0150C**
Rounder / '88 / Projection / Roots Records / Swift / C.M. Distribution / Topic Records / Jazz Music / Hot Shot / A.D.A Distribution / Direct Distribution.

TONY RICE.
Tracks: Not Advised.
CD . . . . **CD 0085**
LP. . . . . **ROUNDER 0085**
MC . . . . **ROUNDER 0085C**
Rounder / '88 / Projection / Roots Records / Swift / C.M. Distribution / Topic Records / Jazz Music / Hot Shot / A.D.A Distribution / Direct Distribution.

Rice, Wyatt

NEW MARKET GAP.
Tracks: Not Advised.
CD . . . . **CDROU 272**
LP. . . . . **ROU 272**
MC . . . . **ROUC 272**
Rounder / Dec '90 / Projection / Roots Records / Swift / C.M. Distribution / Topic Records / Jazz Music / Hot Shot / A.D.A Distribution / Direct Distribution.

Rich, Charlie

Charlie Rich was born in 1932 in Arkansas. He is a country singer with pop crossover success, also called the Silver Fox (his hair turned prematurely white at age 23). A gifted keyboardist, he led a jazz-blues band in the USA; moved back to Arkansas and tried farming, but the pull of music was too strong. He worked as a session player at Sun Records in Memphis, began making his own records in 1958, had a hit with *Lonely Weekends* in 1960; recorded for RCA subsidiary Groove where he made two highly praised LP's in 1963-4; went to Mercury's Smash, had a hit *Mohair Sam* in 1965; recorded for Memphis label 'Hi', then reunited with producer Billy Sherrill, whom he knew from Sun: signed with Epic in Nashville and was groomed by Sherrill in the early days of countrypolitan, an easy listening country style that would appeal to the middle-of-the-road market: *Behind Closed Doors* was his first country number one (number 15 pop, won a Grammy and three CMA awards in 1973 for Best Male Vocalist, Best Single and Best Album. *The Most Beautiful Girl* same year was number one in both country and pop charts. Reached top 10 in UK. Groove tracks were re-issued by RCA and three of them became number one country hits. He slipped in the charts after turning up drunk to present the CMA Awards show in 1975, but soon bounced back with more number ones. He switched to UA in 1978, then Elektra; he has had fewer hits in recent years. (Donald Clarke).

BEHIND CLOSED DOORS.
Tracks: Behind closed doors / If you wouldn't be my lady / You never really wanted me / Sunday kind of woman, A / Peace on you / Most beautiful girl, The / I take it on home / Til I can't take it anymore / We love each other / I'm not going hungry anymore / Nothing in the world (to do with me).
■ **LP.** **65716**
Epic / Mar '74.
■ **MC** . . . . **EPC 4265716**
CBS / '78 / Sony.
LP. . . . . **EPC 32047**
Epic / Aug '87 / Sony.

BEHIND CLOSED DOORS.
Tracks: Behind closed doors.
■ **7"** . . . . **EPC 1539**
Epic / Apr '74.

CHARLIE RICH.
Tracks: Not Advised.
MC Set . . . . **DTO 10044**
Ditto / '88 / Pickwick Records.

CHARLIE RICH (I love country).
Tracks: Big boss man / River stay 'way from my door / Big Jack / Mountain dew / She loved everybody but me / Let me go my merry way / Ol' man river / Grass is always greener, The / Ways of a woman in love, The / Why oh why / Rosanna / Are you still my baby / Behind closed doors / Most beautiful girl, The / Daddy don't walk so fast / My elusive dreams / I love my friend / Sunday kind of woman, A / Papa was a good man / Spanish eyes / Very special love song, A / Rollin' with the flow / Life has it's little up's and downs / Every time you touch me (I get high) / Since I fell for you / On my knees / Somebody wrote that song for me / That's the a cowboy rocks and rolls.
LP. . . . . **NL 89999**
■ **MC** . . . . **NK 89999**
RCA / Jan '87.
LP. . . . . **EPC 54939**
Epic / Mar '87 / Sony.
■ **MC** . . . . **.40 54939**
Epic / Mar '87.

CHARLIE RICH, VOL. 2.
Tracks: Not Advised.
MC Set . . . . **DTO 10092**
Ditto / '91 / Pickwick Records.

COUNTRY STORE: CHARLIE RICH.
Tracks: Behind closed doors / Almost persuaded / Sunday kind of woman, A / We love each other / Very special love song, A / I love my friend / Amazing grace / Most beautiful girl, The / Everytime you touch me I get high / Daddy don't you walk so fast / I take it on home / Sometimes I feel like a motherless child / She / My elusive dreams / Life has its little ups and downs (Only on CD.) / Rollin' with the flow (Only on CD.) / On my knees (Only on CD.) / Woman left lonely, A (Only on CD.).
CD . . . . **CDCST 3**
MC . . . . **CSTK 3**
Country Store / '88 / BMG.
■ **LP.** . . . . **CST 3**
Country Store / '88.

DON'T PUT NO HEADSTONE ON MY GRAVE.
Tracks: Don't put no headstone on my grave (complete session) / Goodbye Mary Ann / Long way from Tennessee / Stop faking your love / Lonely weekends / It's too late / Juanita / Finally find out / Who will the next fool be / My heart cries for you / There's another place I can't go / C.C. rider / Home with me / How's the world treating you / Show me the way back to your heart.
LP. . . . . **Z 2002**
Zu Zazz / Mar '87 / Hot Shot / A.D.A Distribution / C.M. Distribution.

EVEN A FOOL WOULD LET GO.
Tracks: Even a fool would let go / Take me.
■ **7"** . . . . **EPC 5092**
Epic / Mar '77.

FOOL STRIKES AGAIN, THE.
Tracks: Fool strikes again, The / I'd even let you go / Born to love me / Lady / Somewhere there's a love song / She knows just how much to touch me / Life goes on / Standing tall / I love you that way.
LP. . . . . **UAS 30219**
United Artists / Mar '79 / EMI.

FULLY REALISED.
Tracks: Mohair Sam / I can't go on / Dance of love / Field of yellow daisies / I washed my hands in muddy water / Everything I do is wrong / She's a yum yum / It ain't gonna be that way / Just a little bit of you / Moonshine Minnie / Down and out lonely weekends / No home / So long / Best years, The / Party girl / You can have her / Have I stayed away too long / Hawg jaw / Something just came over me / Double dog dare me / Just a little bit of time / Blowin' town / Tears a go-go.
LP. . . . . **.6641 199**
Philips / '80 / PolyGram.

GREATEST HITS: CHARLIE RICH.
Tracks: Most beautiful girl, The / Very special love song, A / Since I fell for you / My elusive dreams / Every time you touch me (I get high) / Behind closed doors / Life has its little ups and downs / All over me / I love my friend / America the beautiful / We love each other.
LP. . . . . **EPC 81478**
■ **MC** . . . . **EPC 4081478**
CBS / Jul '76 / Sony.
■ **MC** . . . . **.40 32568**
Epic / Feb '85.

I'LL SHED NO TEARS.
Tracks: When something is wrong with my baby / Don't tear me down / Hurry up freight train / Pass on by / Can't get right / I'll shed no tears / To fool a fool / Love is after me / Who will the next fool be / You win again / Cold, cold heart / Nobody's lonesome for me / They'll never take her love from me / My heart would know.
LP. . . . . **HIUKLP 418**
Hi! / Jun '88 / Pinnacle / Swift.

I'LL WAKE YOU UP WHEN I GET HOME.
Tracks: I'll wake you up when I get home / Salty dog blues.
■ **7"** . . . . **K 12348**
WEA / '79.

R 8 ■ DELETED

LIFE GOES ON.
Tracks: Life goes on / Standing tall.
■ 7" . . . . UP 608
United Artists / Oct '79.

LONELY WEEKENDS.
Tracks: Not Advised.
■ MC . . . . BRC 2525
Bravo / Feb '80.

LOVE IS AFTER ME.
Tracks: Love is after me.
7" . . . . HLU 10104
London-American / Jan '67.

MOST BEAUTIFUL GIRL IN THE WORLD, THE.
Tracks: Most beautiful girl in the world, The.
■ 7" . . . . CBS 1897
CBS / Feb '74.

MOST BEAUTIFUL GIRL IN THE WORLD, THE (OLD GOLD).
Tracks: Most beautiful girl in the world, The / Behind closed doors.
7" . . . . OG 9186
Old Gold / Jul '82 / Pickwick Records.

MOST BEAUTIFUL GIRL, THE.
Tracks: Behind closed doors / Most beautiful girl, The / Sunday kind of woman, A / Stay / There won't be anymore / Whu oh why / Field of yellow daisies, A / I take it on home / If you wouldn't be my lady / Very special love song, A / Everytime you touch me / We love each other / You never really wanted me / Til I can't take it anymore / I love my friend / Life has it's ups and downs / Since I fell for you / She.
LP. 31653
■ MC 4031653
CBS / '78 / Sony.
CD . . . . PWKS 4168
MC . . . . PWKMC 4168
Pickwick / Sep '93 / Pickwick Records.

MY ELUSIVE DREAMS.
Tracks: Most beautiful girl, The / My elusive dreams / Rolling with the flow / Set me free / July 12th 1939 / I love my friend / Life's little ups and downs / Woman left lonely, A / Very special love song, A / Nice and easy / Raggedy Ann / I take it on home / On my knees / Part of your life / Since I fell for you / Behind closed doors.
LP. PMP 1005
MC . . . . PMPK 1005
Premier (Sony) / Feb '87 / Sony / Pinnacle.

NOBODY BUT YOU.
Tracks: Not Advised.
LP. UAG 30284
United Artists / Mar '80 / EMI.

ONCE A DRIFTER.
Tracks: Once a drifter / Man just don't know what a woman goes through / Angelina / I love my lady / Wonderful night / When it's gone (it's just gone) / Marie / Dream on me / Good time Charlie's got the blues / Are we dreamin' the same dream?.
LP. K 52264
Asylum / Oct '80 / WEA.

ORIGINAL CHARLIE RICH, THE.
Tracks: Whirlwind / Philadelphia baby / Rebound / Big man / Lonely weekends / Everything I do is wrong / Sad news / Red man / Who will the next fool be? / Caught in the middle / Easy money / Midnite blues / Sittin' and thinkin' / I finally found out / There's another place I can't go / I need your love.
■ LP. CR 30112
Charly / Oct '76 / Charly.

ORIGINAL HITS AND MIDNIGHT DEMOS.
Tracks: Whirlwind / Philadelphia baby / Rebound / Big man / Lonely weekends / Everything I do is wrong / School days / Ascap / Gonna be waitin' / Stay / Who will the next fool be / Caught in the middle / It's too late / Just a little bit sweet / Midnight blues / Easy money / Sittin' and thinkin' (2 takes) / I finally found out / I need your love / There's another place I can't go / Little woman friend of mine / Ain't it a shame / Thanks a lot / My baby done left me / There won't be anymore / Juicehead baby / Everyday / Charlie's boogie / You made a hit / Now everybody knows / Baby I need you / Stop thief / Too many tears / Ways of a woman in love, The / Popcorn polly.
■ Double LP . . . . CDX 10
Charly / Dec '85 / Charly.

PICTURES AND PAINTINGS.
Tracks: Pictures and paintings / You don't know me / Don't put no headstone on my grave / Anywhere you are / Somebody broke into my heart / Mood indigo / Every time you touch me (I get high) / Juice head baby / Am I blue / Go ahead and cry / Feel like going home.
CD 7599267302
WEA / Nov '92 / WEA.

PUTTIN' IN OVERTIME AT HOME.
Tracks: Puttin' in overtime at home / Ghost of another man.
■ 7" . . . . UP 36394
United Artists / May '78.

REBOUND.
Tracks: Rebound / Whirlwind / Break up / Philadelphia baby / Big man / Everything I do is wrong / Lonely weekends / You never know about love / School days / There won't be anymore / Juanita / Little woman friend of mine / C.C. rider / Easy money / Gonna be waitin' / There's another place I can't go / Who will the next fool be / Sittin' and thinkin' / Midnight blues / Unchained melody / You finally found out / Stay / My baby done left me / Charlie's boogie.
CD . . . . CDCHARLY 52
Charly / Feb '87 / Charly.

ROLLIN' WITH THE FLOW.
Tracks: Rollin' with the flow / Somebody wrote that song for me / Windsong / That's what love is / Night talk / Beautiful woman / To sing a love song / Love survived / Somewhere in my lifetime / That's the way a cowboy rocks and rolls.
LP. EPC 82229
Epic / Nov '77 / Sony.
■ MC . . . . EPC 4082229
CBS / '78 / Sony.

SHE CALLED ME BABY.
Tracks: She called me baby / Ten dollars and a clean white shirt.
■ 7" . . . . RCA 2532
RCA / Feb '75.

SONGS OF LOVE.
Tracks: Somebody wrote this song for me / That's what love is / Beautiful woman / Night talk / To sing a love song / Love summer / That's the way a cowboy rocks and rolls / Rollin' with the flow / Love survived / Somewhere in my lifetime.
MC . . . . HSC 3025
Hallmark / Feb '80 / Pickwick Records.
■ LP. SHM 3025
Hallmark / Feb '80.

TAKE ME.
Tracks: On my knees / Easy look / Even a fool would let go / Mood indigo / Where do we go from here / Spanish eyes / Take me / Wisdom of a fool / My lady / Road song.
LP. EPC 81841
■ MC . . . . EPC 4081841
CBS / '78 / Sony.

VERY SPECIAL LOVE SONG.
Tracks: Very special love song / I can't even drink it away.
■ 7" . . . . EPC 2259
Epic / Jun '74.

VERY SPECIAL LOVE SONGS.
Tracks: Not Advised.
■ LP. 80031
Epic / Jul '74.

WE LOVE EACH OTHER.
Tracks: We love each other.
■ 7" . . . . EPC 2868
Epic / Feb '75.

WHY DON'T WE GO SOMEWHERE AND LOVE.
Tracks: Why don't we go somewhere and love / Take time to love.
■ 7" . . . . EPC 3894
Epic / Feb '76.

Richards, Digby

BEAUTIFUL TO ME.
Tracks: Beautiful to me / Go for the doctor.
■ 7" . . . . PRIVY 502
Peach River / Sep '81.

CATHY COME HOME.
Tracks: Cathy come home / Typewriter.
■ 7" . . . . BBPR 1
Peach River / Jul '82.

PLAY MOMMA PLAY.
Tracks: Play momma play / Dallas.
■ 7" . . . . PB 5037
RCA / Jun '77.

STUCK BETWEEN THE LIVING AND THE LEAVING.
Tracks: Stuck between the living and the leaving / Falling out of love again.
■ 7" . . . . POSP 227
Polydor / Feb '81.

TIME TO GO TO BED.
Tracks: Time to go to bed / Losing you.
■ 7" . . . . PB 5166
RCA / Nov '79.

WHERE THERE'S SMOKE.
Tracks: Where there's smoke / Falling.
■ 7" . . . . PB 5105
RCA / '79.

WHISKEY SUNDOWN.
Tracks: Samantha / Whiskey sundown / Losing you / Where there's smoke / Suzanne / Play, mama, play / Too long gone / In his songs / Hymn for Rosie / Falling / Louise.
LP. PL 25154
RCA / Jun '78 / BMG.
■ MC . . . . PK 25154
RCA / Jun '78.

WHISKEY SUNDOWN.
Tracks: Whiskey sundown / Too long gone.
■ 7" . . . . PB 5095
RCA / '79.

Riddle, Almelda

BALLADS AND HYMNS FROM THE OZARKS.
Tracks: Not Advised.
LP. ROUNDER 0017
Rounder / '88 / Projection / Roots Records / Swift / C.M. Distribution / Topic Records / Jazz Music / Hot Shot / A.D.A Distribution / Direct Distribution.

MORE BALLADS AND HYMNS FROM THE OZARKS.
Tracks: Not Advised.
LP. ROUNDER 0083
Rounder / '88 / Projection / Roots Records / Swift / C.M. Distribution / Topic Records / Jazz Music / Hot Shot / A.D.A Distribution / Direct Distribution.

Riddle, Leslie

STEP BY STEP.
Tracks: Little school girl / Frisco blues / Broke and weary blues / Hilltop blues / Motherless children / Titanic / I'm out on the ocean a-sailing / I'm working on a building / I know what it means to be lonesome / Red river blues / One kind favor / If you see my saviour / Cannon ball, The / Step by step.
MC . . . . ROU 0299
Rounder / Apr '93 / Projection / Roots Records / Swift / C.M. Distribution / Topic Records / Jazz Music / Hot Shot / A.D.A Distribution / Direct Distribution.
CD . . . . ROU 0299CD
Rounder / May '93 / Projection / Roots Records / Swift / C.M. Distribution / Topic Records / Jazz Music / Hot Shot / A.D.A Distribution / Direct Distribution.

Riders In The Sky

Nashville - based trio comprising of Michigan's Souglas B. Green (ranger Doug) on guitars and vocals, 'Woody Paul' Chrisman on fiddle and vocals and Fred 'Too Slim' Labour on bass and vocals. Hosts of the Tumbleweeds Theatre, an old western movie programme on Nashville Network and regulars on the Grand Ole' Opry. They also brought their fun-loving act (with many songs from the catalogue of the Sons Of The Pioneers including *Tumbling tumbleweeds* and *Cool Water*) to England, playing at the Peterborough and Wembley Country Music Festivals in 1985 and 1987 respectively. The group's zany stage act, deftly blends old time camp-fire songs and cowboy yodels with visual aspects such as rope tricks. It was from the mis-1980s onwards that they garnered most attention as both Rounder and MCA put out their work. (Maurice Hope)

BEST OF THE WEST.
Tracks: Not Advised.
CD . . . . CD 11517
Rounder / '88 / Projection / Roots Records / Swift / C.M. Distribution / Topic Records / Jazz Music / Hot Shot / A.D.A Distribution / Direct Distribution.

BEST OF THE WEST RIDERS AGAIN.
Tracks: Not Advised.
CD . . . . CD 11524
Rounder / '88 / Projection / Roots Records / Swift / C.M. Distribution / Topic Records / Jazz Music / Hot Shot / A.D.A Distribution / Direct Distribution.

COWBOY JUBILEE.
Tracks: Not Advised.
LP. ROUNDER 0147
MC . . . . ROUNDER 0147C
Rounder / '88 / Projection / Roots Records / Swift / C.M. Distribution / Topic Records / Jazz Music / Hot Shot / A.D.A Distribution / Direct Distribution.

LIVE.
Tracks: Cowboy jubilee / Yodel blues, The / When the bloom is on the sage / After you're gone / Cowboy song / Varmit dancing / Hold that critter down / Cielito lindo / Last roundup, The / I grab my saddlehorns and blow / Blue bonnet lady / When the payday rolls around / So long saddle pals.
LP. ROUNDER 0186
MC . . . . ROUNDER 0186C
Rounder / Aug '88 / Projection / Roots Records / Swift / C.M. Distribution / Topic Records / Jazz Music / Hot Shot / A.D.A Distribution / Direct Distribution.

PRAIRIE SERENADE.
Tracks: Not Advised.
LP. ROUNDER 0170
MC . . . . ROUNDER 0170C
Rounder / Aug '88 / Projection / Roots Records / Swift / C.M. Distribution / Topic Records / Jazz Music / Hot Shot / A.D.A Distribution / Direct Distribution.

SADDIE PAIS.
Tracks: Not Advised.
LP. ROUNDER 8011
Rounder / Sep '85 / Projection / Roots Records / Swift / C.M. Distribution / Topic Records / Jazz Music / Hot Shot / A.D.A Distribution / Direct Distribution.

CD . . . . .CD 8011
MC . . . . .ROUNDER 8011C
Rounder / '88 / Projection / Roots Records / Swift / C.M. Distribution / Topic Records / Jazz Music / Hot Shot / A.D.A Distribution / Direct Distribution.

THREE ON THE TRAIL.
Tracks: Not Advised.
LP. . . . . ROUNDER 0102
MC . . . . .ROUNDER 0102C
Rounder / '88 / Projection / Roots Records / Swift / C.M. Distribution / Topic Records / Jazz Music / Hot Shot / A.D.A Distribution / Direct Distribution.

WEEDS AND WATER.
Tracks: Cool water / West Texas cowboy / La cucaracha / Streets of Laredo / Singing a song in the sky / Tumbling tumbleweeds / Pecos bill / That's how the yodel was born / Wasteland / Bound to hit the trail.
LP. . . . . ROUNDER 1038
MC . . . . .ROUNDER 1038C
Rounder / '88 / Projection / Roots Records / Swift / C.M. Distribution / Topic Records / Jazz Music / Hot Shot / A.D.A Distribution / Direct Distribution.

Riley, Billy Lee

Riley, Billy Lee was born around 1933 in Arkansas. The rockabilly singer played guitar, bass, harmonica and drums. First release on Sun *Rock With Me Baby* was recorded by Jack Clement at WMPS Radio in Memphis, Riley's guitar, bass and drums overdubbed, one of the few Sun discs of the era that had so much production in it; it was Clement's entree to Sun as well as Riley's. He never had any big hits despite good looks and powerful rock 'n' roll, but his influence on the Sun sound was great: Lewis played piano on his regional hit *Flying Saucers Rock 'n' Roll* in 1957; his band include the Sun House Band. He added sax to rockabilly (Martin Willis, then Ace Cannon, who both also worked for Bill Black); he also recorded pop, soul and funky country. (Donald Clarke).

BILLY LEE RILEY & THE LITTLE GREEN MEN (Riley, Billy Lee & The Little Green Men).
Tracks: Trouble bound / Rock with me baby / Pearly Lee / Red hot / Flyin' saucers rock and roll / I want you baby / One more time / Baby please don't go / Wouldn't you know / Rock with me honey / No name girl / When a man gets the blues.
LP. . . . . SUNLP 1049
Sun / Jan '90 / Charly / Swift.

BILLY RILEY & THE LITTLE GREEN MEN.
Tracks: Red hot / Dark muddy bottom (Featuring Lightnin' Leon) / Repossession blues (Featuring Lightnin' Leon) / Mud Island / My baby's got love / That's what I want to do / Columbus Stockade blues (Featuring Martin Willis) / San Antonio rock (Featuring Martin Willis) / Beat-nik (Featuring J.M.Van Eaton) / Foggy (Featuring J.M.Van Eaton) / Jump back (Featuring J.M.Van Eaton) / Out-standing (Featuring J.M.Van Eaton) / Something else (Featuring J.M.Van Eaton) / Too much woman for me.
LP. . . . . BFX 15272
Bear Family / Apr '88 / Rollercoaster Records / Swift / Direct Distribution.

BLUE MONDAY.
Tracks: Blue Monday / Good old rock 'n' roll.
■ 7" . . . . SR 706
Rollercoaster / Mar '79.

CLASSIC RECORDINGS 1956-1960.
Tracks: Rock with me baby / Troublebound / Flying saucer rock'n'roll / I want you baby / Red hot / Pearly Lee / Wouldn't you / Baby please don't go / Rockin' on the moon / Is that all to the ball, Mr Hall / Itchy / Thunderbird / Down by the riverside / No name girl / Come back baby / Got the water boiling / Open the door Richard / Dark muddy bottom / Repossession blues / That's what I want to do / Too much woman for me / Flyin' saucer rock'n'roll (version) / I want you (version) / She's my baby / Pearly Lee (unissued) / Red hot (unissued) / That's right / Searchin' / Chatter and college man / Your cash ain't nothin' but trash / Swanee river rock / Betty and Dupree / Let's talk about us / Got the water boiling (unissued) / Saturday night fish fry / Folsom prison blues / Billy's blues / When a man gets the blues / Sweet William / Red hot (version) / Mud Island / My baby's got love.
CD Set . . . . BCD 15444
Bear Family / Jul '90 / Rollercoaster Records / Swift / Direct Distribution.

LEGENDARY SUN PERFORMERS.
Tracks: Red hot / Rock with me baby / Flyin' saucers rock 'n' roll / No name girl / I want you baby / Wouldn't you know / Got the water boiling / Down by the riverside / That's right / Baby please don't go / Open the doors / Richard / Sun goin' down on Frisco / Workin' on the river / Looking for my baby / Pilot town Louisiana.
■ LP. . . . . CR 30131
Charly / '77 / Charly.

RED HOT RILEY (Riley, Billy Lee & The Little Green Men).
Tracks: Not Advised.
■ Double LP . . . . CDX 9
Charly / Oct '85 / Charly.

ROCK WITH ME BABY.
Tracks: Flyin' saucers rock 'n' roll / Swanee river rock / Saturday night fish fry / Come back baby.
CD . . . . CDCHARLY 53
Charly / Jan '87 / Charly.

SUN SOUNDS SPECIAL.
Tracks: Pearly Lee / Swanee river rock / She's my baby / Just one more time / Let's talk about us / Searchin' / Betty and Dupree / Sweet Williams / Troubled bound / Wouldn't you know / Itchy / Nitty gritty / Mississippi / Tallahassee lassie / San Fransico lady / Kay / Old home place.
■ LP. . . . . CR 30151
Charly / Jan '78 / Charly.

Riley, Jeannie C.

Riley, Jeanne C. was born Jeannie Stephenson in Anson, Texas in 1945. She is a country singer who made one of the biggest hits of all time: her debut single of Tom T. Hall's *Harper Valley P.T.A* was number one on both country and pop charts in the USA and a worldwide hit. She was packaged with a sexy image (knee length boots, mini skirts), won a Grammy for Best Female Country Vocal Performance and had more hits on several label; top tens *The Girl Most Likely, There Never Was A Time, Country Girl, Oh Singer, Good Enough To Be Your Wife* all reached the pop charts as well. She also recorded gospel music. (Donald Clarke).

BEST OF JEANNIE C. RILEY.
Tracks: Harper Valley P.T.A. / Girl most likely, The / There never was a time / Back side of Dallas, The / Things go better with love / Country girl / Duty not desire / Satan place / Good enough to be your wife / Oh singer / Darling days / Roses and thorns / I almost called your name / Tell the truth and shame the devil / Light your light / Am I that easy to forget.
■ LP. . . . . CR 30146
Charly / '78 / Charly.

GIRL FROM TEXAS, THE.
Tracks: Price I pay to stay, The / I'll be a woman of the world / How can anything so right be so wrong / No one ever lost more / One slightly used wedding band / You got me singing nursery rhymes / What about them / Heart he kicks around, The / I don't know what I'm doing here / Deaf, dumb and blind / Hey cheatin' man / Faded ribbon / Did you ever / You're for me.
■ LP. . . . . PRCV 110
President / Jun '81.

GIRL MOST LIKELY, THE.
Tracks: Girl most likely, The / My scrapbook.
7" 56756
Polydor / '68 / PolyGram.

HARPER VALLEY PTA.
Tracks: Harper Valley PTA / Yearbooks and yesterdays / Things go better with love / Country girl / Generation gap, The / Back side of Dallas, The / Girl most likely, The / Duty not desire / He made a woman out of me / Help me make it through the night / Macom Georgia ban girl / Will the real Jesus please stand up.
LP. . . . . .TOP 130
MC . . . . .KTOP 130
Topline / May '86 / Charly / Swift / Black Sun Records.

HARPER VALLEY PTA.
Tracks: Harper Valley PTA.
■ 7" 56 148
Polydor / Oct '68.

HERE'S JEANNIE C.
Tracks: Not Advised.
■ CD . . . . CDCOT 105
Cottage / Jun '92.

JEANNIE C.RILEY.
Tracks: Not Advised.
LP. . . . . SPR 8582
MC . . . . SPC 8582
Spot / May '86.

TOTAL WOMAN.
Tracks: Total woman / Love vacation / Shall I sing forever of yesterday / Limousine lovers / Too late for regrets / Gone with the West Texas wind / David play your harp / White as snow / Back to your heart / Return to Harper Vlley.
LP. . . . . SDLP 039
Sundown / '87 / Terry Blood Dist. / Jazz Music / C.M. Distribution.

WHEN LOVE HAS GONE AWAY.
Tracks: When love has gone away / Everyday with you (Is sweeter than the day before) / If you win just one time / Telling lies / I'll sing for you / I take it back / Kiss an angel good morning / If this is love / This is for you / Thou shalt not kill.
LP. 2353 078
MGM (EMI) / '73 / EMI.

Riley, Steve

'TIT GALOP POUR MAMA (Riley, Steve & Mamou Playboys).
Tracks: Not Advised.
CD . . . . ROU 6048CD
MC . . . . ROU 6048C
Rounder / Dec '90 / Projection / Roots Records / Swift / C.M. Distribution / Topic Records / Jazz Music / Hot Shot / A.D.A Distribution / Direct Distribution.

TRACE OF TIME (Riley, Steve & Mamou Playboys).
Tracks: Bayou noir / Mon vieux wagon / Old home waltz / Church point breakdown / Parlez-nous a boire / Lover's waltz / Sur le courtableau / La valse du regret / La Point-au-pic / Corner post, The / Zarico est pas sale.
CD . . . . ROUCD 6053
MC . . . . ROUC 6053
Rounder / Jul '93 / Projection / Roots Records / Swift / C.M. Distribution / Topic Records / Jazz Music / Hot Shot / A.D.A Distribution / Direct Distribution.

Ringer, Jim

ANY OLD WIND THAT BLOWS.
Tracks: Not Advised.
LP. . . . . PHILO 1021
Philo (USA) / May '79 / Roots Records / Projection / Topic Records / Direct Distribution / Ross Records / C.M. Distribution / Impetus Records.

ENDANGERED SPECIES.
Tracks: Roseville fair / Bugler / Wild horses / Wild women / Dusty desert wind / Still got that look / Family tree / Brand new Jole Blon / Linda's out there on her own / Bayou blues / Whiskey and cocaine.
LP. . . . . .FF 242
Flying Fish (USA) / Mar '89 / Cadillac Music / Roots Records / Projection / C.M. Distribution / Direct Distribution / Jazz Music / Duncans / A.D.A Distribution.

GOOD TO GET HOME.
Tracks: Not Advised.
LP. . . . . PHILO 1012
Philo (USA) / May '79 / Roots Records / Projection / Topic Records / Direct Distribution / Ross Records / C.M. Distribution / Impetus Records.

TRAMPS AND HAWKERS.
Tracks: Not Advised.
LP. . . . . PH 1047
Phlox / Oct '88 / Pinnacle.

Rio Grande Band

RIO GRANDE BAND.
Tracks: Not Advised.
LP. . . . . ROUNDER 0105
MC . . . . .ROUNDER 0105C
Rounder / '88 / Projection / Roots Records / Swift / C.M. Distribution / Topic Records / Jazz Music / Hot Shot / A.D.A Distribution / Direct Distribution.

Rio, Bob

TASTE OF COUNTRY, A.
Tracks: Rocky mountain high / Amanda / Old Red / Galveston / Charlie is my name / Spiders and snakes / Wreck of the old '97 / I'd rather love you / Movin' on / Old Shep / You are my best friend / One piece at a time.
LP. . . . . SFA 104
Sweet Folk All / May '81 / Cadillac Music / Projection / C.M. Distribution / Wellard Dist. / Impetus Records.

Ritter, Tex

One of the great singing cowboys, Tex was born Woodward Maurice Ritter in Texas in 1905 and died in Nashville in 1974. He starred on the stage, on radio and in more than 50 films, and began recording in 1934. He was the first country singer to sign with Capitol in 1942. His hits included *High Noon* in 1952: the Oscar-winning theme from the Gary Cooper movie crossed over to the pop chart. Ritter helped to set up the County Music Foundation and Hall of Fame, and was elected to it in 1964. (Donald Clarke).

CAPITOL COLLECTORS SERIES: TEX RITTER.
Tracks: Jingle jangle / I've done the best that I could / New moon over my shoulder / Have I stayed away too long / Wastin' my tears / Jealous heart / We live in two different worlds / You will have to pay (for your yesterday) / Boll weevil / You two-timed me one time too often / Blood on the saddle / Bad brahma bull / Rye whiskey / Green grow the lilacs / Have I told you lately that I love you / When you leave, don't slam the door / Rock and rye / Big rock candy mountain / Deck of cards / High noon / Buffalo dream / I dreamed of a Hillbilly heaven / Just beyond the moon / Americans, The (A Canadian's opinion) / Daddy's last letter.
CD . . . . CZ 419
Capitol / Mar '92 / EMI.
■ MC C4 95036
Capitol / Mar '92.

EVERY DAY IN THE SADDLE.
Tracks: Git along little dogies / Ridin' ole paint, A / Red River valley / High noon / Rounded up in glory / Everyday in the saddle / Deck of cards, The / Blood on the saddle / Old Chisholm trail, The / Border affair, The / Home on the range / Cowboy's prayer, A / Chuckwagon son of a gun / Old glory.

■ LP. . . . . CW 146
Ember / '78 / TKO Records Ltd / President Records.

FRIENDLY VOICE OF TEX RITTER, THE.
Tracks: Not Advised.
LP. . . . . HAT 3114
MC . . . . HATC 3114
Stetson / Sep '89 / Crusader Marketing Co. / Swift / Wellard Dist. / Midland Records / C.M. Distribution.

HIGH NOON.
Tracks: High noon (1) (Movie soundtrack - rare British Capitol recording.) / Boogie woogie cowboy / Pecos Bill / Dallas darling / Eyes of Texas, The / Night Herding song / Pony express / High noon (2) (1st Capitol recording) / He's a cowboy auctioneer / Billy the kid / Texas rangers, The / Cattle call / Goodbye my little cherokee / There's a goldstar in her window / In case you change your mind (Previously unissued.) / I was out of my mind (Previously unissued.) / Dark days in Dallas (Previously unissued.Tribute to J.F.Kennedy).
LP. . . . . BFX 15126
Bear Family / Dec '83 / Rollercoaster Records / Swift / Direct Distribution.
MC 4XL 9296
Capitol (Specials) / Dec '88.
CD . . . . BCD 15634
Bear Family / Feb '92 / Rollercoaster Records / Swift / Direct Distribution.

LADY KILLIN' COWBOY.
Tracks: Sam Hall / Get along little doggies / Thirty three years in prison / Lady killin' cowboy / I'm a do right cowboy / Bill the bar fly / Nobody's darlin' but mine / My brown eyed Texas rose / Take me back to my boots and saddle / Oregon trail, The / Answer to nobody's darling but mine / Melody from the sky, A / Hills of old Wyomin', The / We'll rest at the end of the trail.
LP P.Disc. . . . . BDP 15209
Bear Family / Jul '86 / Rollercoaster Records / Swift / Direct Distribution.

SINGIN' IN THE SADDLE.
Tracks: High wide and handsome / Headin' for the Rio Grande / Out on the lone prairie / Arizona days / My sweet Chiquita / Jailhouse lament / I'm hittin' the trail (for home) / I'm a natural born cowboy / Ride, ride, ride / Ridin' down, the trail of Albuquerque / Sing cowboy sing / Down the Colorado trail / When it's lamplighting time in the valley / Singin' in the saddle / Sundown on the prairie / Ai viva tequila.
LP P.Disc. . . . . BDP 15231
Bear Family / Jul '86 / Rollercoaster Records / Swift / Direct Distribution.

SONGS FROM THE WESTERN SCREEN.
Tracks: Bandit, The / Wichita / I leaned on a man / Brave man / Searchers, The / Last frontier, The / Remember the Alamo / High noon / Marshal's daughter, the / Prairie home / Trooper hook.
LP. . . . . HAT 3041
MC . . . . HATC 3041
Stetson / Jul '87 / Crusader Marketing Co. / Swift / Wellard Dist. / Midland Records / C.M. Distribution.

STREETS OF LAREDO.
Tracks: Blood on the saddle / Barbara Allen / Samuel Hall / Bury me not on the lone prairie / Little Joe the wrangler / When the work's all done this fall / Face on the bar room floor, The / Boll weevil / Billy the kid / Streets of Laredo / Sam Bass / Rye whiskey.
LP. . . . . BDL 1022
Bulldog Records / Jul '82 / President Records / Jazz Music / Wellard Dist. / TKO Records Ltd.
■ MC . . . . BDC 1022
Bulldog Records / Jul '82.
MC . . . . BCD 1022
President / Oct '92 / Grapevine Distribution / Target Records / Jazz Music / Taylors.

TEX RITTER AT HIS VERY BEST.
Tracks: High noon / Billy the Kid / Sam Hall / Cowboy's prayer, A / Ridin' ole paint, A / Home on the range / Rye whiskey / Face on the bar room floor / Sam Bass / Blood on the saddle / Git along little doggies / When the work's all done this fall / Boll weevil / Streets of Laredo / Bury me not on the long prairie / Little Joe the ranger / Rounded up in glory / Chuckwagon son of a gun / Old glory / Old Chisholm trail, The / Border affair, The / Barbara Allen / Red river valley / Deck of cards.
■ MC . . . . ZCE 6005
Ember / '78 / TKO Records Ltd / President Records.

TEX RITTER: COLLECTORS SERIES.
Tracks: Jingle jangle jingle / I've done the best I could / There's a new moon over my shoulder / Have I stayed away too long / I'm wastin' my tears on you / Jealous heart / We live in two different worlds / You will have to pay (for your yesterday) / Boll weevil song / You two timed me one time too often / Blood on the saddle / Bad brahma bull / Rye whiskey / Green grow the lilacs / Have I told you lately that I love you / When you leave, don't slam the door / Rock and rye / Big rock candy mountain / Deck of cards / Daddy's last letter / High Noon (Do not forsake me) / Buffalo dream / I dreamed of a hillbilly heaven / Just beyond the moon / Americans (A Canadians opinion), The.
CD . . . . CDP 795036-2
Capitol (USA) / Sep '92 / Capitol (Imports).

WAYWARD WIND.
Tracks: Wayward wind.
■ 7" . . . . CL 14581
Capitol / Jun '56.

Rivers, Ben Lee

SUNSHINE ON THE SNOW.
Tracks: Jody and the kids / Great mail robbery, The / Behind closed doors / She's in love with a rodeo man / Billy Bayou / Funny how time slips away / Sunshine on the snow / Corner of my life / No hiding place / Make the world go away / Dreaming my dreams with you / Bad guitars players son, The.
LP. . . . . BSS 344
Tank / Sep '79.

Road Runners

C.B. INDEPENDENT.
Tracks: C.B. independent / White line fever.
■ 7" . . . . EMI 5115
EMI / Apr '81.

Robbins, Hargus 'Pig'

CANADIAN SUNSET.
Tracks: Canadian sunset / Roamin' round.
■ 7" . . . . K 12284
Elektra / Apr '78.

PIG IN A POKE.
Tracks: Not Advised.
LP. . . . . K 52071
Elektra / Mar '78 / WEA.

Robbins, Marty

Born 26/9/1925 in Glendale, Arizona, died 8/12/1982 his real name was Martin David Robinson. Marty's early hero Gene Autry, inspired him from an early age to pursue a career as a cowboy singer. He moved to Pheonix playing the local clubs and gained a slot on the Radio Station KPHO. One day a guest for the show failed to show so Marty stepped in. Such was the impact that he was invited to become the resident, having his own show, *Western caravan* (1951). Robbins didn't have long to wait to gain chart recognition, his third single *I'll go it alone* topped Billboard's country charts in 1952. His hits include *Singing the blues A white sport coat (and a pink carnation)*, *The story of my life*, *Just married* and his signature song *El paso* (also No.1 in the pop charts). Over the years Robbins recorded some albums wholly devoted to western themes, *More gunfighter ballads* and *Return of the gunfighter*. Marty's great hit making run carried on through the 60's, with *Don't worrry,Devil woman Ruby Ann* and *Ribbon of darkness* and *Tonight Carmen*. During 1970 Robbins had major heart surgery, and was advised to take it easy. When the old Ryman Auditorium , the home of The Grand Ole Opry since the twenties, closed in 1974, Marty was bestowed with the honour of being the last performer to grace the stage. Marty's epic Mexican tale of *El paso* was to gain even more impetus in 1976, when Marty penned the sequel *El Paso City*, another No.1 hit. (Maurice Hope)

1951-1958.
Tracks: Tomorrow you'll be gone / I wish somebody else loves me / Love me or leave me alone / Cryin' 'cause I love you / I'll go on alone / Pretty words / You're breaking my heart / I can get along / I couldn't keep from crying / Just in time / Crazy little heart / After you leave / Lorelei / Castle in the sky, A / Your hearts turn to break / Why keep wishing / Half way chance with you, A / Sing me something sentimental / At the end of a long lonely day / Blessed Jesus, Should I fall don't let me lay / Kneeland let the lord take your load / Don't make me ashamed / It's a long, long ride / It looks like I'm just in your way / I'm happy 'cause your hurtin' / My isle of golden dreams / Have thine own way lord / God understands / Aloha oe / What made you change your mind / Way of a hopeless love, The / Pain and misery / Juarez / I'm too big to cry / Call me up / It's a pity what money can do / Time goes by / This broken heart of mine / I'll love you 'til the day I die / Don't let me hang around / Pray for me mother of mine / Daddy loves you / That's all right / Gossip / Maybelline / Pretty mama / Mean mama blues / Long gone lonesome blues / I can't quit / Singing the blues / Tennessee toddy / Baby' I need you / Long tall Sally / Mister Teardrop / Respectfully Miss Brooks / You don't owe me a thing / I'll know your gone / How long will it be / Where d'ya go / Most of the time / Same two lips, The / Your heart of blue is showing through / Knee deep in the blues / Little rosewood casket, The / Letter edged in black / Twenty one years / Convict and the rose, The / Bus stop song / Dream the miner's child / Little box of pine in the 7:29, The / Wreck of number nine, The / Sad lover, The / Little shirt that my mother made for me, The / My mother was a lady / When it's lamplighting time in the valley / Wreck of the 12:56, The / It's too late now / I never let you cross my mind / I'll step aside / Bouquet of roses / I'm so lonesome I could cry / Lovesick blues / Moanin' the blues / Rose of ol' Pawnee / I hang my head and cry / Have I told you lately that I love you / All the world is lonely now / You only want me when you're lonely / Crying steel guitar waltz / Beautiful Ohio / Now is the hour / Down where the tradewinds blow / Sweet leilani / Beyond the reef / Constancy / Don't sing aloha when I go / Song of the islands / Moonland / Island echoes / Faded petal from beautiful bouquet, A / When I turned and slowly walked away / Jodie / House with everything but love, A / Nothing but sweet lies / Baby I need you / Kaw liga / Paper / Face / Many tears ago / Address unknown / Waltz of the wind / Hands you're holding now, The / Wedding bells / Shackles and chains / Oh, how I miss you / Footprints in the snow / It's driving me crazy.
CD Set . . . . BCD 15570
Bear Family / Aug '91 / Rollercoaster Records / Swift / Direct Distribution.

ADIOS AMIGO.
Tracks: Adios amigo / Helen.
■ 7" . . . . CBS 5055
CBS / Mar '77.

AFTER MIDNIGHT.
Tracks: I'm in the mood for love / Misty / Looking back / September in the rain / Don't throw me away / Pennies from Heaven / Summertime / It had to be you / All the way / I'm having a ball / If I could cry / On the sunny side of the street.
■ LP. . . . . CBS 32421
CBS / Apr '84.
LP. . . . . SHM 3197
■ MC . . . . HSC 3197
Hallmark / Sep '86.

ALL AROUND COWBOY.
Tracks: All around cowboy / Dreamer, The / Pride and the badge / Restless cattle / When I'm gone / Buenos dias Argentina / Lonely old bunkhouse / San Angelo / Tumbling tumbleweeds / Ballad of a small man.
■ LP. . . . . CBS 83917
CBS / Nov '79.
MC . . . . HSC 3174
Hallmark / Aug '85 / Pickwick Records.
■ LP. . . . . SHM 3174
Hallmark / Aug '85.
CD . . . . PWKS 565
Pickwick / Feb '90 / Pickwick Records.

BEST OF THE MARTY ROBBINS SHOW VOL.1.
Tracks: I could never be ashamed of you / Take these chains from my heart / Singing the blues / Long gone lonesome blues / Lovesick blues / I can't help it / Low and lonely / Tumbling tumbleweeds / Running gun / Chained to a memory / Are you sincere / Tonight Carmen / Big mouthing around / Shoe goes on the other foot tonight, The / Beggin' to you / I can't quit / Take me back to the prairie / El paso / Don't worry / Count me out / Don't go away senor.
VHS. . . . . MFV 0007
Music Farm / Jan '91 / Music Farm Ltd.

BEST OF THE MARTY ROBBINS SHOW VOL.2.
Tracks: Winds go, The / Tell mother I'll be there / Streets of Laredo / Devil woman / Never tie me down / I feel another heartbreak coming on / Old red / El paso / Deep water / Call me up / Ka-lu-a / Time changes everthing / Anytime / Candy kisses / Heart full of love / I'm throwing rice / No one to cry to / Tennessee border / Take me back to Tulsa / Tomorrow's just another day / Sinner's prayer, A.
VHS. . . . . MFV 0008
Music Farm / Jan '91 / Music Farm Ltd.

BIG IRON.
Tracks: Big iron.
■ 7" . . . . H 229
Fontana / May '60.

BIGGEST HITS.
Tracks: Singing the blues / White sports coat / Story of my life / El Paso / You gave me a mountain / Ribbon of darkness / Tonight Carmen / My woman, my woman, my wife / Padre / Devil woman / She's just a drifter / Jenny / My greatest memory / Occasional rose, An / Completely out of love / Teardrops in my heart.
■ LP. . . . . CBS 32301
CBS / Mar '83.
■ MC 40 32301
CBS / Mar '83.

BORDER TOWN AFFAIR.
Tracks: El Paso / Tonight Carmen / Gardenias in her hair / Have I told you lately that I love you / La Paloma / Girl from Spanish town / Maria Elena / Camellia / Bound for old Mexico / Spanish lullaby / In the valley of the Rio Grande / Feleena.
LP. . . . . CBS 31536
Embassy / Aug '87 / Sony.

BY THE TIME I GET TO PHOENIX.
Tracks: By the time I get to Phoenix / Until we meet again / As time goes by / That old feeling / Am I that easy to forget / Love is in the air / To be in love with her / Love is blue / Yesterday / Virginia / You made me love you.
MC . . . . HSC 386
Hallmark / Apr '79 / Pickwick Records.
■ LP. . . . . SHM 989
Hallmark / Apr '79.

COME BACK TO ME.
Tracks: Some memories just won't die / It's not all over / American dream / Here your memory comes again / First song that wasn't the blues / Prayin' for rain / That's all she wrote / Tie your dreams to mine / If her eyes don't get you / Lover lover.
■ LP. . . . . CBS 85794
CBS / Aug '82.

■ DELETED
R 11

COUNTRY STORE: MARTY ROBBINS.
Tracks: Devil woman / Cool water / El Paso / Have I told you lately that I love you / Adios amigo / Big iron / Streets of Laredo / I did what I did for Maria / Maria Elena / By the time I get to Phoenix / Air that I breathe, The / Singing the blues / Ballad of the Alamo / Ruby Ann / Some memories just won't die (Only on CD.) / Honky tonk man (Only on CD.) / El Paso City (Only on CD.) / Yellow roses (Only on CD.).
CD . . . . **CDCST 7**
MC . . . . **CSTK 7**
Country Store / Nov '88 / BMG.
■ **LP** . . . . **CST 7**
Country Store / Nov '88.

COWBOYS, THE (see under Cash, Johnny).

DEVIL WOMAN.
Tracks: Devil woman.
■ **7"** . . . . **AAG 114**
CBS / Sep '62.

DEVIL WOMAN (OLD GOLD).
Tracks: Devil woman / El Paso.
7" . . . . **OG 9866**
Old Gold / Feb '89 / Pickwick Records.

DON'T LET ME TOUCH YOU.
Tracks: Don't let me touch you / There's no more you and me / To get to you / Way I loved you best, The / Try a little tenderness / Return to me / Harbour lights / More than anything I miss you / Tree in the meadow, A / Tomorrow, tomorrow, tomorrow.
LP . . . . **CBS 82429**
CBS / Dec '77 / Sony.

DOUBLE-BARRELLED MARTY ROBBINS, THE.
Tracks: Big irons / Cool water / Billy the kid / Hundred and sixty acre / They're hangin' me tonight / Strawberry roan, The / El paso / In the valley / Street of Laredo / Running gun / Little green valley, The / Utah Carol / San Angelo / Man walks among us tall handsome stranger / Dusty winds / Master's call, The / Fastest gun around, The / Old red / Bend in the river, The / Johnny Fedavo / Abilen rose / Doggone cowboy / Red hill of Utah, The.
Double LP . . . . **CBS 88152**
MC . . . . **.40 88152**
CBS / Aug '75 / Sony.

DRIFTER VOL.1, THE.
Tracks: Cool water / Tumbling tumbleweeds / Running gun / El paso / Bole weevil / Blood on the saddle / Riding ole paint / People's valley / Kathleen / Gal I left behind, The / Billy the kid / When the work's all done this fall / Night time on the desert / Kitty Clyde / Streets of Laredo / Dreamer, The / Virginia / Red river valley / Cattle call / Pecos Bill.
VHS . . . . **MFV 0001**
Music Farm / Jan '91 / Music Farm Ltd.

DRIFTER VOL.2, THE.
Tracks: Take these chains from my heart / Don't worry / An old pal, a real pal / I could never be ashamed of you / Cowboy's dream / Beautiful dreamer / Oh Suzanna / Beyond the reef / Sea and me, The / Night I came ashore, The / My wonderful one / Kohala march / Maui chimes / Bury me not on the lone prairie / Restless cattle / Never tie me down / Bend in the river / When I ride into town / Take me back to the prairie / See the open range / Dusty winds / Comin' round the mountain.
VHS . . . . **MFV 0002**
Music Farm / Jan '91 / Music Farm Ltd.

DRIFTER VOL.3, THE.
Tracks: Long long ago / Mister shorty / Winds go, The / Many tears ago / I hope you learn a lot / Annie Lou / Cottonwood trees / Home on the range / Feleena / Pull mule pull / Roving gambler / Man walks among us / Hand me down my walking cane / No one will ever know / You know how talk gets around / Lobo / Chained to a memory / I couldn't keep from crying / Penny for your thoughts, A / In the valley / Arkansas traveller / Love bells / Sundown.
VHS . . . . **MFV 0003**
Music Farm / Jan '91 / Music Farm Ltd.

DRIFTER VOL.4, THE.
Tracks: Fastest gun around / Yellow rose of Texas / To be in love with her / I feel another heartache coming on / Grandfather's clock / Camptown races / Hawaii's calling me / Blue sands / Drowsy waters / Ka-lu-a / Little grass skirt, The / Hilo march / La paloma / Aloha / Precious jewel / I'll go on alone / Many tears ago / Dream of the miner's child / Count me out / It takes a worried man / I'll be alright tomorrow / Up this hill and down.
VHS . . . . **MFV 0004**
Music Farm / Jan '91 / Music Farm Ltd.

EL PASO.
Tracks: Not Advised.
■ **LP** . . . . **SHM 726**
Hallmark / Jan '71.

EL PASO.
Tracks: El Paso / When I'm gone.
■ **7"** . . . . **CBS 4182**
CBS / Apr '76.

EL PASO.
Tracks: El Paso.
■ **7"** . . . . **H 233**
Fontana / Jan '60.

EVERYTHING I'VE ALWAYS WANTED.
Tracks: Woman in my bed / Completely out of love / There's no wings on my angel / Holding on to you / Gene Autry, my hero / My greatest memory / I'll go on alone / Another cup of coffee / Occasional rose / Crossroads of life.
LP . . . . **CBS 84816**
CBS / Apr '81 / Sony.

FASTEST GUN AROUND, THE.
Tracks: Not Advised.
■ **LP** . . . . **SHM 878**
Hallmark / Nov '75.

GREAT YEARS, THE.
Tracks: Twentieth century drifter / Mother knows best / I heard the bluebirds sing / Way I'm needing you, The / Darling come home / You're an angel disguised as a girl / Georgia blood / Don't you think / I'm wanting to / I couldn't believe it was true / Love needs.
MC . . . . **HSC 3208**
Hallmark / Mar '87 / Pickwick Records.
■ **LP** . . . . **SHM 3208**
Hallmark / Mar '87.

GUNFIGHTER BALLADS.
Tracks: Not Advised.
■ **LP** . . . . **TFL 5063**
Fontana / Aug '60.

HAWAII'S CALLING ME.
Tracks: Lovely Hula hands / Sea and me, The / Night I came to shore, The / Echo island / Kuu ipo Lani (my sweetheart Lani) / Beyond the reef / Hawaiian wedding song / Drowsy waters / Hawaiian bells / My wonderful one / Blue sand / Hawaii's calling me / Ku lu a (love song of kalua) / Drowsy waters (Wailana) / Song of the islands / Don't sing aloha when i go / Crying steel guitar waltz / My isle of golden dreams / Now is the hours (Maori Farewell song) / Sweet leilani / Down where the tradewinds blow / Aloha oe (farewell to thee) / Island echoes / Moonland / Constancy (Ua like no more).
LP . . . . **BFX 15123**
Bear Family / Dec '83 / Rollercoaster Records / Swift / Direct Distribution.
CD . . . . **BCD 15568**
Bear Family / May '91 / Rollercoaster Records / Swift / Direct Distribution.

IN THE WILD WEST PART 1.
Tracks: Cool water / In the valley / Running gun / El Paso / El Paso city / Big iron / Master's call, The / Little green valley / Hundred and sixty acres, A / Billy the kid / Utah Carol / They're hanging me tonight.
LP . . . . **BFX 15145**
Bear Family / Nov '85 / Rollercoaster Records / Swift / Direct Distribution.

IN THE WILD WEST PART 2.
Tracks: Strawberry roan, The (Cover & label erroneously give this track as Utah carol.) / Saddle tramp / She was young and she was pretty / Streets of Laredo / Little Joe / Wrangler, The / I've got no use for women / Billy Venero (Previously unissued.) / This peaceful sod / Five brothers / San Angelo / Song of the bandit / Wind (Previously unissued.) / My love / Ride, cowboy, ride / Red River valley / Prairie fire.
LP . . . . **BFX 15146**
Bear Family / Jul '84 / Rollercoaster Records / Swift / Direct Distribution.

IN THE WILD WEST PART 3.
Tracks: Ballad of the Alamo / Bend in the river, The / Abilene Rose / Dusty winds / Doggone cowboy / Red hills of Utah, The / Tall handsome stranger / Jimmie Martinez / Ghost train / Fastest gun around, The / San Angelo / Old red / Man walks among us.
LP . . . . **BFX 15147**
Bear Family / Nov '85 / Rollercoaster Records / Swift / Direct Distribution.

IN THE WILD WEST PART 4.
Tracks: When the work's all done this fall / Old red / I'm gonna be a cowboy / Rich man, poor man / I've got a woman's love / Small man / Hanging tree, The / Night time on the desert / Yours / Adios mariquita Linda.
LP . . . . **BFX 15183**
Bear Family / Nov '85 / Rollercoaster Records / Swift / Direct Distribution.

IN THE WILD WEST PART 5.
Tracks: Master's call, The / Cowboy in the continental suit, The / Cry stampede / Oh, Virginia / Meet me tonight in Laredo / Take me back to the prairie / Wind goes, The / Never tie me down / Cottonwood tree, The / Mister shorty / Chant of the wanderer, The / Ghost riders in the sky.
LP . . . . **BFX 15213**
Bear Family / Nov '85 / Rollercoaster Records / Swift / Direct Distribution.

JUST ME AND MY GUITAR.
Tracks: Little rosewood casket, The / Letter edged in black / Twenty one years (Previously unissued.) / Convict and the rose, The / Dream of the miner's child / Little box of pine in the 7:29, The (Previously unissued.) / Wreck of the number nine, The (Previously unissued.) / Sad lover, The (Previously unissued.) / Shirt my mother made for me, The (Previously unissued.) / My mother was a lady (Previously unissued.) / When it's lamplighting time in the valley (Previously unissued.) / Wreck of the 1256, The (Previously unissued.) / Just before the battle mother (Previously unissued.) / Long, long ago (Previously unissued.) / Beautiful dreamer (Previously unissued.).
LP . . . . **BFX 15119**
Bear Family / Sep '84 / Rollercoaster Records / Swift / Direct Distribution.

LEGEND.
Tracks: Jumper cable man / Lady, I love you / It's not too hard / Good hearted woman / Air that I breathe, The / My all time high / Honeycombe / Simple little love song / I'm here to get my baby out of jail / Teardrops in my heart.
■ **LP** . . . . **CBS 85308**
CBS / Dec '81.

LIFETIME OF SONG A (1951-1982).
Tracks: Tomorrow you'll be gone / I'll go on alone / That's alright / Knee deep in the blues / Singing the blues / White sports coat / Story of my life / Don't worry / Ruby Ann / Devil woman / El Paso / Big iron / Hanging tree, The / Ribbon of darkness / El Paso city / I walk alone / My woman, my woman, my wife / Among my souvenirs / Return to me / Some memories just won't die.
Double LP . . . . **CBS 22165**
■ **MC** . . . . **.40 22165**
CBS / Feb '84.

LONG LONG AGO.
Tracks: Long long ago / It finally happened / Reach for me / People's valley / When the works all done this fall / I'm gonna be a cowboy / Last night about this time / Address unknown / Lonely old bunkerhouse / Where could I go / (Ghost) Riders in the sky / Baby, talk to me / Night time in the desert / To be in love with her / Wind / Roving gambler, The / Yesterday's roses / This song / Beautiful dreamer / Chant of the wanderer.
LP . . . . **CBS 88649**
■ **MC** . . . . **.40 88649**
CBS / Mar '85.

MAN AND HIS MUSIC, A.
Tracks: Singing the blues / Ribbon of darkness / White sport coat / Devil woman / Big iron / Don't worry 'bout me / Touch me with magic / That's alright mama / Love me / Big boss man / Among my souvenirs / Foggy mountain breakdown / Jambalaya / Chime bells / My woman, my woman, my wife / El paso / Earl's breakdown.
VHS . . . . **MFV 0005**
Music Farm / Jan '91 / Music Farm Ltd.

MARTY ROBBINS (I love country).
Tracks: Some memories just won't die / My woman, my woman, my wife / Good hearted woman / Air that I breathe, The / My elusive dreams / Oh mein papa / She's made of faith / I'm just here to get my baby out of jail / El Paso City / Sometimes when we touch / Return to me / Among my souvenirs / 18 yellow roses / Don't let me touch you / Honky tonk man / Performer, The.
■ **MC** . . . . **.40 54940**
CBS / '87.
LP . . . . **CBS 54940**
CBS / Mar '87 / Sony.

MARTY ROBBINS.
Tracks: Not Advised.
MC Set . . . . **DTO 10046**
Ditto / Jan '83 / Pickwick Records.
MC Set . . . . **DTO 10093**
Ditto / Jan '85 / Pickwick Records.
MC Set . . . . **DTO 10267**
Ditto / '88 / Pickwick Records.

MARTY ROBBINS (2).
Tracks: Not Advised.
■ **LP** . . . . **SHM 662**
Hallmark / Jan '70.
LP . . . . **SPR 8506**
MC . . . . **SPC 8506**
Spot / Feb '83.

MARTY ROBBINS COLLECTION.
Tracks: El Paso / Streets of Laredo / Fastest gun around, The / San Angelo / Cool water / Red river valley.
Double LP . . . . **PDA 018**
Pickwick / Mar '76 / Pickwick Records.
MC Set . . . . **PDC 018**
Pickwick / Dec '79 / Pickwick Records.

MARTY ROBBINS COLLECTION (LOTUS).
Tracks: Not Advised.
■ **LP** . . . . **WH 5009**
Lotus / Feb '79.

MARTY ROBBINS FILES, VOL 1: 1951-1953.
Tracks: Tomorrow you'll be gone / I wish somebody loved me / Love me or leave me alone / Crying cause I love you / I'll go on alone / Pretty words / You're breaking my heart (while you're holding my hand) / I can get along (without you very well) (Previously unissued.) / I couldn't keep you from crying / Just in time (Previously unissued.) / Crazy little heart (Previously unissued.) / After you leave me / Lorelei / Castle in the sky, A / Your heart's turn to break / Why keep wishing (you don't care) (Previously unissued.) / Halfway chance with you, A.
LP . . . . **BFX 15095**
Bear Family / '86 / Rollercoaster Records / Swift / Direct Distribution.

MARTY ROBBINS FILES, VOL 2: 1953-1954.
Tracks: Sing me something sentimental / At the end of a long, lonely day / Blessed Jesus, should I fall don't let me lay / Kneel and let the Lord take your load / Don't make me ashamed / It's a long, long ride / It looks like I'm just in your way (Previously unissued.) / I'm happy 'cause you're hurtin' (Previously unissued.) / My isle of golden dreams / Have Thine own way / God understands / Aloha-oe / What made you change your mind? (Previously unissued.) / Way of a hopeless love (Previously unissued.) / Juarez (previously unissued.) / I'm too big to cry.
LP. . . . . **BFX 15096**
Bear Family / Sep '84 / Rollercoaster Records / Swift / Direct Distribution.

MARTY ROBBINS FILES, VOL 3: 1954-1956.
Tracks: Call me up / It's a pity what money can do / Time goes by / This broken heart of mine / It looks like I'm just in your way / I'll love you 'til the day I die / Don't let me hang around (if you don't care) / Pray for me, mother of mine / Daddy loves you / I'll know you're gone / How long will it be? / Where d'ya go? / Most of the time (Previously unissued.) / Same two lips (Previously unissued.) / Your heart of blue is showing through (Previously unissued.).
LP. . . . . **BFX 15118**
Bear Family / Sep '84 / Rollercoaster Records / Swift / Direct Distribution.

MARTY ROBBINS FILES, VOL 4: 1957-1958.
Tracks: It's too late now (to worry anymore) / I never let you cross my mind / I'll step aside / Bouquet of roses / I'm so lonesome I could cry / Lovesick blues / Moanin' the blues / Rose of ol' Pawnee / I hang my head and cry / Have I told you lately that I love you? / All the world is lonely now / You only want me when you're lonely / Beautiful Ohio (Previously unissued.) / Faded petal from a beautiful bouquet (Previously unissued.) / Then I turned and slowly walked away / Jodie.
LP. . . . . **BFX 15138**
Bear Family / Nov '84 / Rollercoaster Records / Swift / Direct Distribution.

MARTY ROBBINS FILES, VOL 5: 1958/1959/1962.
Tracks: House with everything but love / Nothing but sweet lies / Baby I need you (like you need me) / Kaw-liga / Paper face / Many tears ago (Previously unissued.) / Address unknown / Waltz of the wind / Hands you're holding now, The / Shackles and chains / Oh, how I miss you (since you went away) / Wedding bells / Sweet Cora (Previously unissued.) / Ain't life a crying shame? (Previously unissued.) / Silence and tears (Previously unissued.) / Roving gambler (Previously unissued.).
LP. . . . . **BFX 15139**
Bear Family / Nov '84 / Rollercoaster Records / Swift / Direct Distribution.

MARTY ROBBINS SONG BOOK.
Tracks: Not Advised.
MC . . . . **AM 112**
VFM Cassettes / VFM Children's Entertainment Ltd. / Midland Records / Morley Audio Services.

MARTY ROBBINS VOL.2.
Tracks: Not Advised.
MC Set . . . . **DTO 10286**
Ditto / '88 / Pickwick Records.

MASTER'S CALL, THE.
Tracks: Performer, The / There's power in the blood / Wonderful world of you, The / What God has done / My love / An evening prayer / You gotta climb / Great speckled bird, The / Almost persuaded / Who at my door is standing / Master's call, The / Have thine own way Lord / With his hand on my shoulder / Will the circle be unbroken / When the roll is called up yonder / Little spot in heaven, A.
LP. . . . . **WST 9632**
MC . . . . **WST 9632MC**
Word (1) / '83 / Gamut Distribution.

MUSICAL JOURNEY TO THE CARIBBEAN AND MEXICO.
Tracks: Girl from Spanish Town / Kingston girl / Sweet bird of paradise / Jamaica farewell / Calypso girl / Back to Montego Bay / Girl from Spanish Town (2) / Kingston girl (2) / Woman gets her way, A / Mango song, The / Calypso vacation / Blue sea / Bahama mama / Tahitian boy / Native girl / Girl from Spanish Town (3) / Yours / You belong to my heart / La Borachita / La paloma / Yours (quiereme mucho) (Spanish) / Adios marquita Linda / Amor / Camellia.
CD . . . . **BCD 15571**
Bear Family / May '91 / Rollercoaster Records / Swift / Direct Distribution.

PERFORMER, THE.
Tracks: Please don't play a love song / Confused and lonely / Look what you've done / You're not ready for me yet / Another pack of cigarettes, another glass .. / My elusive dreams / Jenny / Oh, Regina / Touch me with magic / Performer.
LP. . . . . **CBS 83488**
MC . . . . **.40 83488**
CBS / Apr '79 / Sony.

PIECES OF YOUR HEART.
Tracks: Ribbons of darkness / Pieces' of your heart / I'm not ready yet / I feel another heart break coming on / Too far gone / Not so long ago / Ain't I right / My own native land / Girl from Spanish town / Kingston girl / Girl from Spanish town (2) / Never look back.
LP. . . . . **BFX 15212**
Bear Family / Nov '85 / Rollercoaster Records / Swift / Direct Distribution.

ROCKIN ROLLIN' ROBBINS VOL 2 (Ray Conniff recordings).
Tracks: Jeannie and Johnnie (Previously unissued.) / Just married / Stairway of love / Please don't blame me / Grown up tears / Teenage dream / Foolish decision / Once a week date / Story of my life / Sport coat and a pink carnation, A / Ain't I the lucky one / Hanging tree, The / Sittin' in a tree house / She was only seventeen (and he was one year more) / Last time I saw my heart, The / Blues country style, The.
LP. . . . . **BFX 15105**
Bear Family / Sep '84 / Rollercoaster Records / Swift / Direct Distribution.

ROCKIN ROLLIN' ROBBINS VOL.1.
Tracks: Footprints in the snow (Previously unissued) / It's driving me crazy (Previously unissued) / Baby I need you (like you need me)(rock'n'roll version) (Previously unissued) / Mean mama blues / That's alright / Mabellene / Pretty mama / I can't quit (I've gone too far) / Long tall Sally / Singing the blues / Knee deep in the blues / Respectfully Miss Brooks / Mister teardrop / Tennessee Toddy / Pain & misery (Previously unissued) / You don't owe me a thing / Long thing gone lonesome blues.
LP. . . . . **BFX 15045**
Bear Family / Sep '84 / Rollercoaster Records / Swift / Direct Distribution.

ROCKIN' ROLLIN' ROBBINS.
Tracks: That's all right / Maybelline / Pretty mama / Mean mama blues / Tenessee Tody / Singing the blues / Can't quit (i've gone too far), I / Long tall sally / Mister teardrop / Respectfully Miss Brooks / You don't owe me a thing / Baby, I need you (like i need you) / Pain and misery / Footprints in the snow / It's driving me crazy / It's a long, long ride / Call me up (and I'll come calling on you).
CD . . . . **BCD 15566**
Bear Family / May '91 / Rollercoaster Records / Swift / Direct Distribution.

ROCKIN' ROLLIN' ROBBINS VOL.2.
Tracks: White sport coat (and a pink carnation) / Grown up tears / Please don't blame me / Teenage dream / Story of my life, The / Once a week date / Just married / Stairway of love / She was only seventeen (and he was one year . / Sittin' in a tree house / Ain't I the lucky one / Last time I saw my heart, The / Hanging tree, The / Blues country style, The / Jeannie and Johnnie / Foolish decision.
CD . . . . **BCD 15567**
Bear Family / May '91 / Rollercoaster Records / Swift / Direct Distribution.

ROCKIN' ROLLIN' ROBBINS VOL.3.
Tracks: Ruby Ann (chart version) / Sometimes I'm tempted / No signs of loneliness here / While you're dancing / Teenager's Dad / Ruby Ann / Cap and gown (fast) / Last night about this time / I hope you learn a lot / Love can't wait / Cigarettes and coffee / Little rich girl / Hello baby (goodbye baby) / Baby's gone / Cap and gown (slow) / A whole lot easier / She was young and whe was pretty / Cap and gown (New york recording) / Sweet cora / Ain't live a cryin' shame / Silence and tears / You've been so busy baby.
LP. . . . . **BFX 15184**
Bear Family / Nov '85 / Rollercoaster Records / Swift / Direct Distribution.
CD . . . . **BCD 15569**
Bear Family / May '91 / Rollercoaster Records / Swift / Direct Distribution.

RUBY ANN.
Tracks: Ruby Ann.
■ **7"** . . . . **AAG 128**
CBS / Jan '63.

SOME MEMORIES JUST WON'T DIE.
Tracks: Some memories just won't die / Change of heart / What if I said I love you / I'm saving all the good times for you / Devil in a cowboy hat / Angelina / I miss you the most / How to make love to a woman / Baby that's love / Honky tonk man.
■ **LP.** . . . . **CBS 25380**
CBS / Jul '83.
MC . . . . **SPC 8577**
Spot / Apr '86.

SONG OF THE ISLANDS.
Tracks: Song of the Islands / Don't sing Aloha when I go / Beyond the reef / Crying steel guitar waltz / My Isle of Golden Dreams / Now is the hour / Sweet Leilani / Down where the trade wind blows / Constancy (Ua like no a like) / Island echoes / Moonland / Aloha-oe.
LP. . . . . **BFX 15130**
Bear Family / Oct '83 / Rollercoaster Records / Swift / Direct Distribution.

TOUCH ME WITH MAGIC.
Tracks: Touch me with magic / Confused and lonely.
■ **7"** . . . . **CBS 7176**
CBS / Mar '79.

TRY A LITTLE TENDERNESS.
Tracks: Try a little tenderness / To get to you.
■ **7"** . . . . **CBS 6119**
CBS / Feb '78.

TWENTIETH CENTURY DRIFTER.
Tracks: Twentieth century drifter / This much a man / Love me / Don't you think / Crawling on my knees / Walking piece of Heaven / Man and a train,A / Two gun daddy / It takes faith / Life.
LP. . . . . **IMCA 27060**
MCA (Import) / Mar '86 / Pinnacle / Silver Sounds (CD).

WITH LOVE MARTY ROBBINS.
Tracks: She's made of faith / I can't wait until tomorrow / Slipping from me / One man's trash / All I want to do / Sometimes when we touch / I'll go to pieces / Wonderful world of you / Misery in my soul / Oh my papa.
LP. . . . . **CBS 84427**
MC . . . . **.40 84427**
CBS / Aug '80 / Sony.

Roberts, Al Jr.

FROGABILLY.
Tracks: Not Advised.
■ **LP.** . . . . **FROG 002**
Frog / Jan '80.

I WISH I WAS IN LA.
Tracks: I wish I was in LA.
■ **7"** . . . . **REP 1002**
Red Hot / Feb '80.

ROCKABILLY GUITAR MAN.
Tracks: Not Advised.
■ **LP.** . . . . **FROG 001**
Frog / Apr '80.

Roberts, Fiddlin' Doc

KENTUCKY COUNTRY.
Tracks: Not Advised.
LP. . . . . **ROUNDER 1037**
Rounder / '88 / Projection / Roots Records / Swift / C.M. Distribution / Topic Records / Jazz Music / Hot Shot / A.D.A Distribution / Direct Distribution.

Roberts, Kenny

INDIAN LOVE CALL.
Tracks: Not Advised.
LP. . . . . **SLP 336**
MC . . . . **GT 5336**
Starday (USA) / Apr '87 / Crusader Marketing Co.

Robertson, Don

GREATEST THING SINCE SLICED BREAD (Barbour, Tony).
Tracks: Not Advised.
MC Set . . . . **RB 80180**
Recorded Books / May '92 / Bond Street Music / Isis Audio Books.

HAPPY WHISTLER, THE.
Tracks: Happy whistler, The.
■ **7"** . . . . **CL 14575**
Capitol / May '56.

Robertson, Ken

SONGS OF AUSTRALIA.
Tracks: Not Advised.
■ **LP.** . . . . **BF 15026**
Bear Family / '85.

Robins, Butch

FIFTH CHILD, THE.
Tracks: Not Advised.
LP. . . . . **ROUNDER 0130**
Rounder / '88 / Projection / Roots Records / Swift / C.M. Distribution / Topic Records / Jazz Music / Hot Shot / A.D.A Distribution / Direct Distribution.

FORTY YEARS LATE.
Tracks: Not Advised.
LP. . . . . **ROUNDER 0086**
Rounder / '88 / Projection / Roots Records / Swift / C.M. Distribution / Topic Records / Jazz Music / Hot Shot / A.D.A Distribution / Direct Distribution.

FRAGMENTS OF MY IMAGINATION.
Tracks: Not Advised.
LP. . . . . **ROUNDER 0104**
Rounder / May '79 / Projection / Roots Records / Swift / C.M. Distribution / Topic Records / Jazz Music / Hot Shot / A.D.A Distribution / Direct Distribution.

Rock, Dickie

20 GREATEST HITS - DICKIE ROCK.
Tracks: Every step of the way / Yours / Till / I'll hide my teardrops / There's always me / Coward of the county / Angeline / Candy store / Mandy / Just for old times sake / Come back to stay / I left my heart in San Francisco / She believes in me / You're my world / Love me tender / Back home again / You don't have to say you love me / How could you go / I write the songs / Wonder of you, The.
LP. . . . . **DHL 717**

MC . . . . CDHL 717
Homespun (Ireland) / Mar '89 / Homespun Records / Ross Records / Wellard Dist.
CD . . . . DHCD 717
Homespun (Ireland) / May '89 / Homespun Records / Ross Records / Wellard Dist.

BOP.
Tracks: Bop.
7" . . . . CAR 93
I&B / '88 / I & B Records.

DICKIE.
Tracks: Not Advised.
LP. . . . . SOLO 7008
Solo / Jan '76 / Black Sun Records.

DICKIE ROCK IN STYLE.
Tracks: Not Advised.
LP. . . . . SOLO 7011
Solo / Jan '78 / Black Sun Records.

TILL.
Tracks: Not Advised.
LP. . . . . HPE 624
MC . . . . HPC 624
Harp (Ireland) / Jul '80 / C.M. Distribution.

Rockabilly Music

While rock'n'roll was the final result of the fusing of various American genres that included blues, gospel, country, latin and jazz, rockabilly was a Southern variation taken up by the white country singers. Although it became part of the musical map in the mid '50's, there had been several previous instances when country flirted with black music. These were first heard on recordings by the likes of the Allen Brothers, Jimmie Davis, the Delmore Brothers and Arthur 'Guitar Boogie' Smith, representing a period that stretched from the 1920's to the 1940's, with King Records probably being the first label to mix together the two different musical cultures at recording sessions. The Delmore Brothers' *Hillbilly Boogie*, was the first country record to use 'boogie' in the title, embodying a black music form, and quickly led to the other 'boogie' records by artists such as Red Foley, Tennessee Ernie Ford, Moon Mullican and the Maddox Brothers. Of course, it shouldn't be forgotten that several of Hank Williams songs, and the styling that accompanied them, pre-empted rock'n'roll by several years, among them his first record for MGM *Move It On Over*, recorded in May 1947. Nor should it be forgotten that Williams learnt his guitar chords from a black street musician named Teetot. Elvis Presley was the acknowledged leader of the rockabilly movement and the fulfillment of a wish by Sun Records' owner Sam Phillipsto "find a white singer with a negro voice". Once Presley hit then many other country boys threw away their fiddles and banjos, bought guitars and adopted a Presley image in the hope that they, too, would also make it into the bigtime. The majority didn't, just as rockabilly itself was a short-lived movement. But, for a couple of years, during the late 1950's, it created enough attention and commercial success to shake the very foundations of the country music industry and, for a while, threaten its actual survival.(Tony Byworth)

Rockin' Dopsie

Rockin' Dopsie is Alton Jay Rupin, born in Louisiana in 1932; he is a zydeco accordionist, vocalist and bandleader, playing a hot dance music style steeped in R&B. After the New Orleans Jazz and Heritage Festival in 1976 he signed with the Swedish based Sonet label for Europe: he first toured Europe in 1979 with his group the Twisters, his novelty assisting him: with Clifton Chenier and Queen Idahe was among the first in the Louisiana genres to tour there. He guested on the Paul Simon hit LP *Graceland* in 1986; his albums are full of joy and the listener is challenged to keep his toe from tapping. (Donald Clarke).

BIG BAD ZYDECO (Rockin' Dopsie & The Cajun Twisters).
Tracks: Me and my chauffer / Jambalaya / Trouble in mind / Sugar bee / On my way back home / Ma Negresse / Colinda / T'ant na na / Ay-tete fee / Zydeco two step.
■ LP. . . . . SNTF 851
Sonet / Nov '80.
LP. . . . . GNPS 2154
MC GNP5 2154
GNP Crescendo / '88 / Swift / Silva Screen / Flexitron Ltd.

CLIFTON CHENIER AND ROCKIN' DOPSIE (see under Chenier, Clifton).

CROWN PRINCE OF ZYDECO.
Tracks: Back door / Old time Zydeco / I got a woman / Do right tonight / Flip flop and fly / Something on your mind / Make it hot / I'm in the mood baby / Crazy 'bout that married woman / Why you do the things you do / Hey, hey, hey / Zyde-cool.
LP. . . . . SNTF 982
Sonet / Mar '87 / Swift / C.M. Distribution / Roots Records / Jazz Music / Sonet Records / Cadillac Music / Projection / Wellard Dist. / Hot Shot.

DOIN' THE ZYDECO (Rockin' Dopsie & The Twisters).
Tracks: Who's loving you? / Ma negresse / Please come home / Joile blonde / Doin' the zydeco / Jump up / Rock me baby / Josephine / Grand ol mamou / Please don't leave me / Me & my chauffer / Jambalaya / Trouble in mind / Sugar bee / On my way back home / Colinda / T'ant na na / Ay-tete fee / Zydeco two step.
LP. . . . . SNTF 718
Sonet / Jul '77 / Swift / C.M. Distribution / Roots Records / Jazz Music / Sonet Records / Cadillac Music / Projection / Wellard Dist. / Hot Shot.

FRENCH STYLE (Rockin' Dopsie & The Cajun Twisters).
Tracks: Shopick two step / Ti ne / Hound dog / I'm in the mood / Tu connais / Alvina / I passed in front of your door / Flames of hell / Where were you last night / What'd I say.
LP. . . . . SNTF 872
Sonet / Feb '82 / Swift / C.M. Distribution / Roots Records / Jazz Music / Sonet Records / Cadillac Music / Projection / Wellard Dist. / Hot Shot.

GOOD ROCKIN' (Rockin' Dopsie & The Cajun Twisters).
Tracks: Not Advised.
LP. . . . . GNPS 2167
MC GNP5 2167
GNP Crescendo / '88 / Swift / Silva Screen / Flexitron Ltd.
LP. . . . . SNTF 905
Sonet / Jul '88 / Swift / C.M. Distribution / Roots Records / Jazz Music / Sonet Records / Cadillac Music / Projection / Wellard Dist. / Hot Shot.

HOLD ON (Rockin' Dopsie & The Cajun Twisters).
Tracks: Hold on / Baby bye bye / My baby she's gone / Marie / That gets it / Times done gone / Opelousas waltz / You promised me love / Tanya / Tire in the street.
LP. . . . . SNTF 800
Sonet / Sep '79 / Swift / C.M. Distribution / Roots Records / Jazz Music / Sonet Records / Cadillac Music / Projection / Wellard Dist. / Hot Shot.
LP. . . . . GNPS 2156
MC GNP5 2156
GNP Crescendo / '88 / Swift / Silva Screen / Flexitron Ltd.
CD . . . . SNTCD 800
Sonet / Oct '90 / Swift / C.M. Distribution / Roots Records / Jazz Music / Sonet Records / Cadillac Music / Projection / Wellard Dist. / Hot Shot.

MY BABY SHE'S GONE (Rockin' Dopsie & The Twisters).
Tracks: My baby she's gone / Ma negresse / Lucille.
■ 7" . . . . SON 2191
Sonet / Nov '79.

ROCKIN' DOPSIE AND THE TWISTERS (Rockin' Dopsie & The Twisters).
Tracks: Not Advised.
LP. . . . . ROUNDER 6012
MC . . . . ROUNDER 6012C
Rounder / '88 / Projection / Roots Records / Swift / C.M. Distribution / Topic Records / Jazz Music / Hot Shot / A.D.A Distribution / Direct Distribution.

ROCKIN' WITH DUPSEE.
Tracks: Woman I don't want your troubles / Things I used to do, The / Night and day / You told me baby / Ma Negresse / She's my little girl / Rockin' with Dupsee / Don't you want a man like me / Oh negresse / Dupsee shuffle / Don't let the green grass fool you.
LP. . . . . FLY 592
Flyright / Oct '86 / Hot Shot / Roots Records / Wellard Dist. / Charly / Swift / Projection.

SATURDAY NIGHT ZYDECO.
Tracks: Not Advised.
LP. 1025
Maison de Soul(USA) / Jul '88 / Swift.
CD . . . . SNTCD 1003
Sonet / '89 / Swift / C.M. Distribution / Roots Records / Jazz Music / Sonet Records / Cadillac Music / Projection / Wellard Dist. / Hot Shot.
LP. . . . . SNTF 1003
Sonet / Mar '91 / Swift / C.M. Distribution / Roots Records / Jazz Music / Sonet Records / Cadillac Music / Projection / Wellard Dist. / Hot Shot.

ZY-DE-BLUE (Rockin' Dopsie & The Twisters).
Tracks: See see rider / My little girl / Lucille / When I lost my little girl / Cold cold night / Things I used to do, The / It's all right / Worried life blues / This loneliness (about to drive me out of my mind).
LP. . . . . SNTF 761
Sonet / Aug '78 / Swift / C.M. Distribution / Roots Records / Jazz Music / Sonet Records / Cadillac Music / Projection / Wellard Dist. / Hot Shot.

ZY-DE-CO-IN (Rockin' Dopsie & The Cajun Twisters).
Tracks: Ma negresse / Who's loving you tonight / Please come home / Josephine / My little girl / Jump up / Worried life blues / Jolie blonde / Rock me baby / Doin' the zydeco / See see rider / Things I used to do / Please don't leave me / When I lost my little girl.
CD . . . . SNTCD 1035
Sonet / Oct '90 / Swift / C.M. Distribution / Roots Records / Jazz Music / Sonet Records / Cadillac Music / Projection / Wellard Dist. / Hot Shot.

Rockin' Jimmy

BY THE LIGHT OF THE MOON (Rockin' Jimmy & The Brothers Of Night).
Tracks: Stand back / Slow pace / Little Rachel / Crazy / Wind at your back, The / Can't jive enough / Raging storm / Leave my woman alone / Why you doin' what you do / Another chance / Ride it easy / Call on me.
LP. . . . . SNTF 857
Sonet / Mar '81 / Swift / C.M. Distribution / Roots Records / Jazz Music / Sonet Records / Cadillac Music / Projection / Wellard Dist. / Hot Shot.

ROCKIN' ALL NITE (Rockin' Jimmy & The Brothers Of Night).
Tracks: Rockin' all nite / Angel eyes.
7" . . . . SON 2255
Sonet / May '83 / Swift / C.M. Distribution / Roots Records / Jazz Music / Sonet Records / Cadillac Music / Projection / Wellard Dist. / Hot Shot.

ROCKIN' JIMMY AND THE BROTHERS OF THE NIGHT (Rockin' Jimmy & The Brothers Of Night).
Tracks: Rockin' all nite / You got it made / Sugar babe / Beat of my heart / Right on time / Angel eyes / It's a mystery / Mood music / We got love / You got me.
LP. . . . . SNTF 889
Sonet / Jul '88 / Swift / C.M. Distribution / Roots Records / Jazz Music / Sonet Records / Cadillac Music / Projection / Wellard Dist. / Hot Shot.

Rockin' Sidney

BOOGIE BLUES 'N' ZYDECO.
Tracks: Not Advised.
LP. 1008
MC . . . . 1008 TC
Maison de Soul(USA) / Mar '84 / Swift.
LP. . . . . KK 787
Krazy Kat / Jun '85 / Hot Shot / C.M. Distribution / Wellard Dist. / Roots Records / Projection / Charly / Jazz Music.

CREOLA.
Tracks: Not Advised.
LP. 102
MC . . . . 102 TC
ZBC (USA) / '87.

CROWNED PRINCE OF ZYDECO.
Tracks: Not Advised.
LP. 1020
MC . . . . 1020 TC
Maison de Soul(USA) / '87 / Swift.

GIVE ME A GOOD TIME WOMAN.
Tracks: Not Advised.
LP. 1007
Maison de Soul(USA) / Swift.
MC . . . . 1007 TC
Maison de Soul(USA) / '87 / Swift.

HOLIDAY CELEBRATION, A.
Tracks: Party this Christmas / I'm not gonna spend this Christmas alone / It's Christmas / Goin' home for Christmas / Christmas waltz / Christmas celebration / Christmas time is the time / My sweet thing / Christmas without you / Birthday celebration / She's a beautiful bride.
LP. 100
MC . . . . 100 TC
ZBC (USA) / '87.

HOTSTEPPIN.
Tracks: Not Advised.
LP. 101
MC . . . . 101 TC
ZBC (USA) / '87.
LP. . . . . JSP 1119
JSP / Sep '87 / Hot Shot / Swift / Wellard Dist. / A.D.A Distribution / Cadillac Music / Jazz Music.

LIVE WITH THE BLUES.
Tracks: Not Advised.
CD . . . . JSP CD 213
JSP / Mar '88 / Hot Shot / Swift / Wellard Dist. / A.D.A Distribution / Cadillac Music / Jazz Music.

LOUISIANA CREOLE MAN.
Tracks: Louisiana Creole man / Good time.
7" . . . . BH 1013
Baily Hoo (USA) / Dec '82.

MY TOOT TOOT.
Tracks: My toot toot / My zydeco shoes / Joy to the south / Don't be a wallflower (On LP only) / Alligator waltz / Rock and roll me baby (On LP only) / Joe Pete is in the bed / You ain't nothing but fine / If it's good for the gander / Twist to the zydeco / Dance and show off / Let me take you to zydeco / I got the blues for my baby (On LP only) / Louisiana creole man (On LP only) / If I could I would / No good woman (On CD only) / Send me some lovin' / Past bedtime (On CD only) / No good man (On CD only) / You don't have to go (On CD only) / It really is a hurtin' thing (On CD only) / Something's

R 14

■ DELETED

wrong (On CD only) / My little girl (On CD only) / Wasted days & wasted nights (On CD only) / Ya Ya (On CD only) / Jalapeno Lena (On CD only) / Sweet lil' woman (On CD only) / Once is not enough (On CD only) / Cochon de lait (On CD only).
■ LP. . . . . CH 160
Ace / Mar '86.
CD . . . . .CDCH 160
Ace / Jun '93 / Pinnacle / Hot Shot / Jazz Music / Complete Record Co. Ltd.

MY TOOT TOOT.
Tracks: My toot toot.
■ 7" . . . . KID 001
Ace / Oct '85.

MY ZYDECO SHOES (Got the zydeco blues).
Tracks: Not Advised.
LP. 1009
Maison de Soul(USA) / Swift.
MC . . . . 1009 TC
Maison de Soul(USA) / '87 / Swift.

PLAY JOLI BLON FOR ME.
Tracks: Play Joli Blon for me / Go Lucy go.
7" . . . . BH 1017
Bally Hoo (USA) / Nov '82.

SCOOP, THE.
Tracks: Scoop, The / I'm not gonna spend this Christmas alone.
7" . . . . BH 1016
Bally Hoo (USA) / Dec '82.

SHOW ME WHERE IT ITCHES.
Tracks: Show me where it itches / Wet eyes.
7" . . . . BH 1014
Bally Hoo (USA) / Dec '82.

THEY CALL ME ROCKIN'.
Tracks: Not Advised.
LP. . . . . FLY 515
Flyright / Jun '85 / Hot Shot / Roots Records / Wellard Dist. / Charly / Swift / Projection.

Rockingbirds

GOOD DAY FOR YOU IS A GOOD DAY FOR ME, A.
Tracks: Good day for you is a good day for me, A.
12" . . . . HVN 1412
■ **CD Single** . . . . HVN 1412CD
Heavenly / Sep '91 / Sony / RTM / Pinnacle.

GRADUALLY LEARNING.
Tracks: Where I belong / Gradually learning (full version) (On 12"/CD only) / Love has gone and made a mess of me (On CD only) / Gradually learning.
12" . . . . HVN 2112
7" . . . . HVN 21
CD Single . . . . .HVN 21CD
■ **MC Single** . . . . HVN 21MC
Heavenly / Sep '92.

JONATHAN JONATHAN.
Tracks: Jonathan Jonathan / Time drive the truck / Older guys (CD single only).
12" . . . . HVN 1712
7" . . . . HVN 17
■ **CD Single** . . . . .HVN 17CD
Heavenly / Jun '92.

ROCKINGBIRDS.
Tracks: Gradually learning / Further down the line / Standing at the doorstep of love / Jonathan Jonathan / Day my life begins, The / Searching / Restless / Time drives the truck / Halfway to comatose / In tall buildings / Only one flower / Drifting.
CD . . . . HVNCD 2
LP. . . . . HVNLP 2
MC . . . . HVNMC 2
Heavenly / Nov '92 / Sony / RTM / Pinnacle.

ROCKINGBIRDS R US.
Tracks: Gladly / I'm a little less lonely / It won't be long / Harden up your heart.
12" . . . . HVN 03112
CD Single . . . . .HVN 031CD
Heavenly / Jul '93 / Sony / RTM / Pinnacle.

Rockytops

LIFE CAN BE BEAUTIFUL.
Tracks: Virginia / Together again / Love me tonight / Life can be beautiful / She can't read my writing / Bandy the rodeo clown / Fire on the mountain / Amazing grace / Love couldn't be any better / Entertainer, The / Silver wings / Moving on.
LP. . . . . FE 015
Fellside / '83 / Projection / A.D.A Distribution / C.M. Distribution / Direct Distribution / Topic Records.

Rodgers, Jimmie

Jimmie Rodgers was born in Mississippi in 1897; he learned music working on the railroad from workmates and hobos, black and white; he was billed as 'The Singing Brakeman'. He was first recorded in 1927 by Ralph Peer in Bristol, Tennessee, the same day Peer first recorded the Carter Family; by the time he died of TB in a hotel room in New York in 1933 he had become a million-seller at the bottom of the Depression, and this despite the fact that the majority of his fans were poor people. Working in Vaudeville, he regarded himself as an all round entertainer; he may not have been the first to yodel, but he was the first to combine the yodel with 12-bar blues; he was the first to use the steel guitar, then called the Hawaiian guitar and popular in Vaudeville. His mixture of blues, sentimental songs, double-entendre and hard-luck stories defined country music as we know it today. He recorded solo and often with a small band; *In The Jailhouse Now*, *T for Texas* (aka *Blue Yodel No.1*), *Muleskinner Blues*, others have been covered many times. He recorded 13 of the Blue Yodels; *Blue Yodel No.9* made in Hollywood in 1930 has Louis Armstrong in it. He was not a good guitar player; his quirky sense of time caused trouble for others (Louis plays beautifully on *Blue Yodel No.9*, but with unusual caution). Today sales of 110 sides were probably about 12 million by 1950, but were phenomenal for the Depression era. His original talent directly influenced Gene Autry, Ernest Tubb, Lefty Frizzell, Hank Snow and countless others. (Donald Clarke).

20 OF THE BEST: JIMMIE RODGERS.
Tracks: Blue yodel no. 1 (T for Texas) / Soldier's sweetheart, The / Blue yodel no. 9 (Standing on the corner) / Blue yodel no. 2 (My lovin' gal Lucille) / Blue yodel no. 3 / Blue yodel no. 4 (California blues) / Waiting for a train / Blue yodel no. 5 / Blue yodel no. 6 / Hobo Bill's last ride / Anniversary blue yodel (No. 7) / Blue yodel no. 8 (mule skinner blues) / Brakeman's blues, The / T B blues / Blue yodel no. 10 / Blue yodel no. 11 / Blue yodel no. 12 / In the jailhouse now no. 2 / Jimmie Rodgers' last blue yodel.
LP. . . . . NL 89370
MC . . . . NK 89370
RCA / Mar '84 / BMG.

AMERICA'S BLUE YODELER, 1930-1931.
Tracks: Blue yodel No. 8 / Jimmie's mean mama blues / I'm lonesome too / Mystery of number five, The / One rose, The / In the jailhouse now - No. 2 / For the sake of days gone by / Blue yodel No. 9 / T.B. Blues / Travellin' blues / Why there's a tear in my eye / Jimmie the kid / Wonderful city, The / Let me be your side of the track.
CD . . . . CDROU 1060
Rounder / Sep '91 / Projection / Roots Records / Swift / C.M. Distribution / Topic Records / Jazz Music / Hot Shot / A.D.A Distribution / Direct Distribution.

DOWN THE OLD ROAD (1931-32).
Tracks: Looking for a new mama / When the cactus is in bloom / Jimmie Rodgers visits the Carter Family / Carter Family and Jimmie Rodgers in Texas, The / Gambling dot blues / Southern cannon-ball / Roll along, Kentucky moon / What's it my time ain't long / Hobo's meditation / Ninety-nine years blues / Mississippi moon / Down the old road to home.
CD . . . . CDROU 1061
Rounder / Sep '91 / Projection / Roots Records / Swift / C.M. Distribution / Topic Records / Jazz Music / Hot Shot / A.D.A Distribution / Direct Distribution.

EARLY SESSIONS 1928-1929, THE.
Tracks: My little lady / Blue yodel No. 4 / Daddy & home / Lullaby yodel / You and my guitar / Desert blues / Never no mo' blues / Mississippi moon / My Carolina sunshine girl / I'm lonely and blue / Waitin' for a train / My old pal / My old home down in New Orleans / Blue yodel No. 5 / Any old time.
CD . . . . CDROU 1057
Rounder / '90 / Projection / Roots Records / Swift / C.M. Distribution / Topic Records / Jazz Music / Hot Shot / A.D.A Distribution / Direct Distribution.

FAMOUS COUNTRY MUSIC MAKERS.
Tracks: Train whistle blues / Treasures untold / Somewhere down below the Dixon line / Hobo Bill's last ride / Blue yodel no. 5 / My little old home down in New Orleans / High-powered Mama / No hard times / Jimmie's Texas blues / Ben Dewberry's final run / My good gal's gone blues / Down the old road to home / Let me be your sidetrack / Lullaby yodel / Any old time / Mississippi delta blues / Jimmie the Kid (Parts of the life of Rodgers) / Blue yodel no. 12 (Barefoot blues) / Frankie and Johnnie / Miss the Mississippi and you / Blue yodel no. 2 (My lovin' gal Lucille) / Sleep baby sleep / Home call / My old pal / Looking for a new Mama / Memphis yodel / Blue yodel no. 7 (Anniversary) / Mother, queen of my heart / I'm sorry we met / Blue yodel no. 3 (Evening sun yodel) / Tuck away my lonesome blues / Desert blues.
■ LP. . . . . DPS 2021
RCA / '78 / BMG.

FIRST SESSIONS, 1927-1928.
Tracks: Blue yodel / Soldier's sweetheart, The / Ben Dewberry's final run / Sleep, baby sleep / Mother was a lady / Dear old sunny south by the sea / Away out on the mountain / Treasures untold / Blue yodel - No. 11 / Sailor's plea / In the jailhouse now / Memphis yodel / Brakeman's blues, The / Blue yodel - No. 3.
CD . . . . CDROU 1056
Rounder / '90 / Projection / Roots Records / Swift / C.M. Distribution / Topic Records / Jazz Music / Hot Shot / A.D.A Distribution / Direct Distribution.

JIMMIE RODGERS.
Tracks: For the sake of days gone by / Solidiers sweetheart / Gambling barrom blues / Sailor's plea, The / Old love letters / She was happy till she met you / Mississippi river blues / T.B. blues / Sweet mama hurry home or I'll be gone / I'm lonesome too / When the cactus is in bloom / Cowhand's last ride / Yodelling cowboy / Dreaming with tears in my eyes / Roll along, Kentucky moon / I'm free from the chain gang now.
■ LP. . . . . RD 7505
RCA / Aug '69 / BMG.

LAST SESSIONS, 1933.
Tracks: Blue yodel No. 12 / Dreaming with tears in my eyes / Cowhand's last ride, The / I'm free (From the chain gang now) / Yodeling my way back home / Jimmie Rodger's last blue yodel / Yodeling ranger, The / Old pal of my heart / Years ago / Somewhere below the Dixon line / Old love letters / Mississippi delta blues.
CD . . . . CDROU 1063
Rounder / Mar '92 / Projection / Roots Records / Swift / C.M. Distribution / Topic Records / Jazz Music / Hot Shot / A.D.A Distribution / Direct Distribution.

LEGENDARY PERFORMER, A.
Tracks: Sleep, baby, sleep / Blue yodel no. 1 (T for Texas) / In the jailhouse now / Ben Dewberry's final run / You and my old guitar / Whippin' that old TB / TB blues / Mule skinner blues (Blue yodel No. 8) / Old love letters (bring memories of you) / Home call.
LP. . . . . PL 12504
■ MC . . . . PK 12504
RCA / '79.

MY OLD PAL.
Tracks: Blue yodel no.1 (T for Texas) / Away out on the mountain / Frankie and Johnny / Gambling bar room blues / When the cactus is in bloom / Sleep, baby, sleep / My old pal / Daddy and home / My Carolina sunshine girl / Why there's a tear in my eye / We miss him when the evening shadows fall / Never no no' blues / Blue yodel no. 3 / I'm sorry we met / Blue yodel no. 5 / Any old time / Lullaby yodel / Looking for a new mama.
CD . . . . CD AJA 5058
LP. . . . . AJA 5058
MC . . . . ZC AJA 5058
Living Era / Mar '89 / Pinnacle / Koch International.

MY ROUGH AND ROWDY WAYS.
Tracks: Not Advised.
LP. . . . . HAT 3091
MC . . . . HATC 3091
Stetson / Mar '89 / Crusader Marketing Co. / Swift / Wellard Dist. / Midland Records / C.M. Distribution.

NEVER NO MO' BLUES.
Tracks: Never no mo' blues / Daddy and home / Blue yodel no. 4 (California blues) / Waiting for a train / You and my old guitar / Prairie lullaby / Blue yodel no. 6 / Dear old sunny south by the sea / Jimmie's mean mama blues / Pistol packin' papa / Old pal of my heart / My little lady.
LP. . . . . NL 90009
MC . . . . NK 90009
RCA / Jan '87 / BMG.

NO HARD TIMES, 1932.
Tracks: Blue yodel No. 10 / Whippin' that old T.B. / Rock all our babies to sleep / Home call / Mother, the queen of my heart / No hard times / Peach pickin' time in Georgia / Long tall mama blues / Gamblin' bar room blues / I've only loved three women / In the hills of Tennessee / Prairie lullaby / Miss the Mississippi and you / Sweet Mama hurry home.
CD . . . . CDROU 1062
Rounder / Feb '92 / Projection / Roots Records / Swift / C.M. Distribution / Topic Records / Jazz Music / Hot Shot / A.D.A Distribution / Direct Distribution.

ON THE WAY UP, 1929.
Tracks: High powered Mama / Tuck away my lonesome blues / Frankie & Johnny / I'm sorry we met / Train whistle blues / Everybody does it in Hawaii / Jimmy's Texas blues / Home call / Blue yodel No. 6 / Yodeling cowboy / My rough and rowdy ways / Land of my boyhood dreams, The / Whisper you mother's name / I've ranged, I've roamed, I've travelled / Hobo Bill's last ride.
CD . . . . CDROU 1058
Rounder / '91 / Projection / Roots Records / Swift / C.M. Distribution / Topic Records / Jazz Music / Hot Shot / A.D.A Distribution / Direct Distribution.

RIDING HIGH, 1929-1930.
Tracks: Anniversary blue yodel (Blue yodel No. 7) / That's why I'm blue / Mississippi river blues / She was happy till she met you / Blue yodel number eleven / Drunkard's child, A / Nobody knows but me / Moonlight and the skies / Why did you give me your love / Pistol packin' papa / Why should I be lonely / Take me back again / Those gambler's blues / My blue - eyed Jane.
CD . . . . CDROU 1059
Rounder / '91 / Projection / Roots Records / Swift / C.M. Distribution / Topic Records / Jazz Music / Hot Shot / A.D.A Distribution / Direct Distribution.

SINGING BRAKEMAN, THE.
Tracks: Soldier's sweetheart, The / Sleep, baby, sleep / Ben Dewberry's final run / Mother was a lady / Blue yodel / Away out on the mountain / Dear old sunny south by the sea / Treasures untold / Brakeman's blues, The / Sailor's plea, The / In the jailhouse now / Blue yodel No. 2 / Memphis yodel / Blue yodel No. 3 / My old pal / Mississippi moon / My little old home down in New Orleans / You and my old guitar / Daddy and home / My little lady / I'm lonely and blue / Lullaby yodel / Never mo' blues / My Carolina sunshine girl / Blue yodel No. 4 / Waiting for a train / Desert blues / Any old time / Blue yodel No. 5 / High powered mama / I'm sorry we met / Everybody does it in Hawaii / Tuck

away my lonesome blues / Train whistle blues / Jimmie's Texas blues / Frankie and Johnny / Homecall / Whisper your mother's name / Land of my boyhood dreams, The / Blue yodel No. 6 / Yodeling cowboy / My rough and rowdy ways / I've ranged, I've roamed, I've travelled / Hobo Bill's last ride / Mississippi river blues / Nobody knows but me / Anniversary blue yodel / She was happy till she met you / Blue yodel No. 11 / Drunkard's child, A / That's why I'm blue / Why did you give me your love / My blue eyed Jane / Why should I be lonely / Moonlight and skies / Pistol packin' papa / Take me back again / Those gambler's blues / I'm lonesome too / One rose, The / For the sake of days gone by / Jimmie's mean mama blues / Mystery of number five / Blue yodel No. 8 / In the jailhouse now, No. 2 / Blue yodel No. 9 / T.B. blues / Travellin' blues / Jimmie the kid / Why there's a tear in my eye / Wonderful city / Let me be your sidetrack / Jimmie Rodgers visits the Carter Family / Carter Family and Jimmie Rodgers in Texas, The / When the cactus is in bloom / Gambling polka dot blues / Looking for a new mama / What's it? / My good gal's gone / Southern cannonball / Roll along Kentucky moon / Hobo's meditation / My time ain't long / Ninety nine year blues / Down the old road to home / Blue yodel No. 10 / Home call / Mother the queen of my heart / Rock all my babies to sleep / Whippin' that old T.B. / No hard times / Long tall mama blues / Peach picking time down in Georgia / Gambling bar room blues / I've only loved three women / In the hills of Tennessee / Prairie lullaby / Miss the Mississippi and you / Sweet mama hurry home / Blue yodel No. 12 / Dreaming with tears in my eyes / Cowhand's last ride, The / I'm free from the chain gang now / Dream with tears in my eyes / Yodeling my way back home / Jimmie Rodger's last blue yodel / Yodeling ranger, The / Old pal of my heart / Old love letters / Mississippi Delta blues / Somewhere below the Mason Dixon line / Years ago / Singing brakeman, The / Pullman porters, The / In the jailhouse now No. 2 / Mule skinner blues / Mother, the queen of my heart / Never no mo' blues / Blue yodel No. 1.
CD Set . . . . **BCD 15540**
Bear Family / Mar '92 / Rollercoaster Records / Swift / Direct Distribution.

TRAIN WHISTLE BLUES.
Tracks: Jimmie's mean mama blues / Southern Cannonball, The / Jimmie the kid / Travellin' blues / Mystery of number 5, The / Memphis yodel / Blue yodel no. 4 (California blues) / Hobo Bill's last ride / Waiting for a train / Ben Dewberry's final run / My rough and rowdy ways / Blue yodel no. 7 (Anniversary blue yodel) / Brakeman's blues, The / Let me be your side track / Hobo's meditation, The / Train whistle blues.
CD . . . . **CD AJA 5042**
LP . . . . **AJA 5042**
MC . . . . **ZC AJA 5042**
Living Era / Jun '86 / Pinnacle / Koch International.

Rodriguez, Johnny

Johnny Rodriguez started out his country career in 1970 when, through a friendly local Texas ranger (who Rodriguez had come in contact with due to an offence concerning a stolen barbecued goat) he was introduced to Happy Shahan, The Alamo village resort owner putting him to work, singing at Bracketvill's site for the summers of 1970 & 1971. Shahan also became Rodriguez's manager (he was also manager of 70's country singer Dottsy), with the singer moving to Nashville in 1971, and playing in Tom T. Hall's band The Storytellers during 1971 - 1972, before signing for Mercury records in late 1972. Rodriguez born in Sabinal, Texas on 23.5.1951, occasionally colours his songs with Spanish vocals. During the next eight years up to 1980 he was enjoy his most productive period, rarely failing to make Billboard's top ten, chalking up hit after hit from late 1972. Tom T's late brother Hillman's *Pass by me* was the first and it made Billboard's top ten. The following year he achieved three straight number ones with *You always come back* , *Ridin' my thumb to Mexico* and *That's the way loves goes. Amazingly 'heart throb' Johnny repeated the sequence in 1975, reeling off* I just can't get her off my mind , *Just get up and close the door* and *Love put a song in my heart* . As the seventies progressed Rodrigex still kept having hits, with top five/ten numbers *Hillbilly heart* , the Eagles *Desperado* and *If practice makes perfect* in 1977. Moving to Epic in 1979 - where his debut *Down on the rio grande* madae the top ten, Rodriguez teamed up with country lady Charly McClain on *I hate the way you love it* . While the hits continued throughout the eighties, Rodriguez was no longer making the charts upper reaches. Only the 1983 singles *Foolin* and *How could I love her so much* making the top five. Johnny's drug problem plus his easy going approach, had been giving his music a glaring lack of conviction. Only when moving to Capitol in 1987, with his album *Gracies* did he seem to have halted his downward slide. Since which time he's been neglected by the major labels.

COUNTRY CLASSICS FROM..
Tracks: Answer to your letter / Bossier City backyard blues / Easy come easy go / I've never had a thing that ain't been used / I've never loved anyone more / Jealous heart / Leavin' somethin' left to do / Pass me by / Ramblin' man / Release me / Something / You go around.
LP . . . . **.6336 259**
Philips / Feb '79 / PolyGram.

JOHNNY RODRIGUEZ.
Tracks: Down on the Rio Grande / Don't be afraid to say goodbye / When the honeymoon ends / Fools for each other / Driftin' away / Mexico holiday / Paid vacation / Street walker / Hand on my shoulder / I give my life a second look.
■ **LP** . . . . **EPC 83731**
Epic / '79.

LOVE LOOK AT US NOW.
Tracks: Love look at us now / Where did it go.
■ **7"** . . . . **EPC 8769**
Epic / Aug '80.

THROUGH MY EYES.
Tracks: What'll I tell Virginia / One sided love affair / One affair later / Where did it go / I'll go back to her / One, two, three / You've lost that lovin' feeling / Feeling / Whatever gets me through the night / Love, look at us no / Welcome to love.
■ **LP** . . . . **EPC 84196**
Epic / Jun '80.

Rodrique, Gene

BAYOU CAJUN MUSIC OF GENE RODRIQUE, THE.
Tracks: Not Advised.
MC . . . . **6062 TC**
N/A / '87.
LP **6062**
Swallow (USA) / Jun '87 / Swift / Wellard Dist.

Roger, Aldus

KING OF FRENCH ACCORDION.
Tracks: Not Advised.
LP . . . . **.114**
La Louisiane / '87 / Swift.

PLAYS FRENCH MUSIC.
Tracks: Not Advised.
LP . . . . **.107**
MC . . . . **.107 TC**
La Louisiane / '87 / Swift.

PLAYS THE CAJUN FRENCH CLASSICS.
Tracks: Not Advised.
LP . . . . **.122**
La Louisiane / '87 / Swift.

Rogers, Kenny

Kenny Rogers was born 21.8.1938 in Houston, Texas. He has been involved in music of one kind or another ever since high school days, featuring in a school band named The Scolars, followed by work as a bass player with a jazz group, the Bobby Doyle Trio who recorded for Columbia. Kenny's next move was to become a founder member of the Kirkby Stone Four, followed by The New Christy Minstrels. Other members at the time were Mike Settle, Thelma Camach and Terry Williams, who in 1967 formed the pop group The First Edition. From the outset of the venture, Roger's distinctive grainy vocals gained him noted public recognition and to this effect they renamed the band Kenny Rogers & The First Edition. Mickey Newbury's *Just dropped in (to see what condition my condition was in)*, in 1968 on Reprise set the ball rolling, albeit in the pop charts. Country music flavoured material soon followed with *Ruby, don't take your love to town*, and *Ruben James*, making Billboard's country charts in 1969. With the groups popularity beginning to wain as the seventies evolved. Kenny decided to go it alone. Kenny under the supervision of ace producer Larry Butler signed to United Artists, gaining top twenty country recognition with *Love lifted me*, (1975) - the title track of his debut album. What followed in 1976 was possibly Kenny Rogers' best ever country recording, his eponymous titled follow-up featured his top seller *Lucille*, topping the country charts and crossing-over into the pop field. That year, 1977, saw the CMA acclaim it both Single and Song Of The Year. Roger's career now was to start a roll, he signed to RCA for $20 million dollars and his subsequent album sales topped 35 million. During his days with United Artists, Kenny has seen his solo/duet efforts top the country charts on no fewer than 14 occassions. Of the latter his golden partnership with Dottie West was nothing short of remarkable. During the years 1978-1981 they made top-billing with with *Every time two fools collide,All I ever need* and *What are we doin' in love*. The glossy imaged duo became CMA's Duo Of The Year in 1978 and 1979. Kenny also took CMA's Male Vocalist honour on the latter occasion. Kenny's next duet partner was to be the equally uniquely vocalled Kim Carnes, who in 1980 made No.3 on the country charts with *Don't fall in love with a dreamer*. Even Sheena Easton joined Rogers, *We've got tonight* making it in 1983. While Kenny was running up a succession of solo chart toppers, including such monsters as *The gambler* (1978), *The coward of the country* (1979) (both later becoming films starrring Rogers), alongside *Lady, Daytime friends, She believes in me You decorated my life*, and *Love will turn you around*. The new label move of 1983 also saw Kenny strike up another winning duet formula, this time with Dolly Parton. Kenny and Dolly's music was geared very much towards the cross-over market during this period, yet no less successful as *Islands in the stream* (1983) and *Real love* (1985) demonstrated. Slotted between the chart toppers the duo combined for a TV Christmas Special, that gained a multi-national viewing audience. Ronnie Milsap, another RCA stablemate was also to collaborate with the unstoppable Rogers when they partnered on *Make no mistake, she's mine* in 1987.(Maurice Hope)

20 GOLDEN HITS: KENNY ROGERS.
Tracks: Not Advised.
LP . . . . **MA 29284**
Masters (Holland) / Jan '87.
LP **1A 222 929284**
EMI (Holland) / '88.
MC . . . . **MAMC 929284**
Masters (Holland) / '88.

20 GREATEST HITS: KENNY ROGERS.
Tracks: Not Advised.
CD **2630212**
MC **2630214**
Big Country / Sep '89.

25 GREATEST HITS: KENNY ROGERS.
Tracks: Lucille / Lady / Love lifted me / We've got tonight / Scarlet fever / Love or something like it / She believes in me / Ruby don't take your love to town / Don't fall in love with a dreamer / You were a good friend / Gambler, The / Through the years / Daytime friends / You decorated my life / Till I can make it on my own / Reuben James / Coward of the county / I don't need you / Something's burning / Love will turn you around / Abraham, Martin and John / Precious memories / Love is what we make it / Green green grass of home / Desperado / Sweet music man.
■ **CD Set** . . . . **CDS 746 673 8**
Liberty / Apr '87.

ALL MY LIFE.
Tracks: All my life / Farther I go.
7" . . . . **UP 659**
United Artists / Apr '83 / EMI.

ANTHOLOGY - KENNY ROGERS.
Tracks: But I know I love you / Ruby (Don't take your love to town) / Something's burning / Tell it all brother / Lucille / Day time friends,night time lovers / Just dropped in / Gambler, The / She believes in me / You decorated my life / Coward of the county / Don't fall in love with a dreamer / Love the world away / We've got tonight / Buried treasure / This woman / Eyes that see in the dark / What about me / Crazy / Tomb of the unknown love / Make no mistake, she's mine.
CD . . . . **VSOPCD 148**
Double LP . . . . **VSOPLP 148**
MC . . . . **VSOPMC 148**
Connoisseur Collection / Apr '90 / Pinnacle.
CD **911 168**
Double LP **911 144**
MC **911 151**
Connoisseur Collection / Mar '90 / Pinnacle.

AT HIS BEST: KENNY ROGERS.
Tracks: Ruby, don't take your love to town / Me and Bobby McGee / Reuben James.
LP . . . . **FUN 9035**
MC . . . . **FUNC 9035**
Fun (Holland) / Sep '88 / Pinnacle.

BEST OF KENNY ROGERS.
Tracks: Not Advised.
■ **LP** . . . . **BWY 100**
Breakaway / Mar '84.

BEST OF KENNY ROGERS (And the First Edition).
Tracks: Not Advised.
CD . . . . **CTS 55402**
MC . . . . **CTS 45402**
Country Stars / Jan '92.

CHRISTMAS (KENNY ROGERS).
Tracks: Christmas everyday / Kentucky homemade Christmas / Carol of the bells / Kids / Sweet little Jesus boy / Christmas is my favourite time of the year / White Christmas / My favourite things / O' holy night / When a child is born.
LP . . . . **ED 2607201**
■ **MC** . . . . **ED 2607204**
Capitol / Dec '85.
LP . . . . **MFP 5796**
■ **MC** . . . . **TCMFP 5796**
MFP / Sep '87.

CHRISTMAS IN AMERICA.
Tracks: Not Advised.
CD . . . . **.925973 2**
WEA / '89 / WEA.

CHRISTMAS WITHOUT YOU (see under Parton, Dolly).

CLASSICS (Rogers, Kenny & Dottie West).
Tracks: All I ever need is you / Till I can make it on my own / Just the way you are / You needed me / Let it be me / Together again / Midnight flyer / You've lost that lovin' feeling / Let's take the long way round the world / Another somebody done somebody wrong song.

R 16
■ DELETED

■ LP. . . . . UAG 30235
United Artists / '79.
LP. . . . . MFP 5601
■ MC . . . . TCMFP 5601
MFP / Jan '83.
MC 4XLL 9535
Capitol (Specials) / Dec '88.

COLLECTION.
Tracks: Not Advised.
LP. 1A 022 58094
EMI (Holland) / '83.

COLLECTION: KENNY ROGERS.
Tracks: Trying just as hard / Ruby don't take your love to town / Heed the call / We all got to help each other / Ticket to nowhere / Conditions (just dropped in) / She even woke me up to say goodbye / Where does Rosie go / Sunshine / Reuben James / Loser / Church without a name / My Washington woman / Run thru your mind / I just wanna give my love to you / Last few threads of love / Tell it all brother / I'm gonna sing you a sad song Susie / What am I gonna do / Sleep comes easy / After all (I live my life) / For the good times / Lay it down / Me and Bobby McGee / Always leaving always gone / Calico silver / Way it used to be, The / Something's burning / Hurry up love.
■ Double LP . . . . CCSLP 111
Castle Collector Series / Nov '85.
■ MC . . . . CCSMC 111
Castle Collector Series / Nov '85.

COLLECTION: KENNY ROGERS.
Tracks: Not Advised.
CD . . . . SPEC 85001
Spectrum (CD) / Oct '86 / M.S.D.

COUNTRY DOUBLE (Rogers, Kenny & Conway Twitty).
Tracks: Not Advised.
MC Set . . . . M 10164
Spectrum (1) / Jun '88 / PolyGram.

COUNTRY STORE: KENNY ROGERS.
Tracks: Love lifted me / Abraham, Martin and John / Precious moments / I would like to see you again / Runaway girl / World needs a melody, The / You gotta be tired / Home made love / While the feeling's good / Heavenly sunshine / There's an old man in our town.
LP. . . . . CST 34
MC . . . . CSTK 34
Country Store / Apr '87 / BMG.
CD . . . . CDCST 46
MC . . . . CSTK 46
Country Store / Oct '89 / BMG.

COWARD OF THE COUNTY.
Tracks: Coward of the county / I want to make you smile.
7" . . . . BP 427
Liberty / Sep '85 / EMI.

COWARD OF THE COUNTY.
Tracks: Coward of the county.

DAYTIME FRIENDS.
Tracks: Daytime friends.
■ 7" . . . . UP 36289
United Artists / Sep '77.

DAYTIME FRIENDS.
Tracks: Daytime friends / Desperado / Rock and roll man / Living again / I'll just write my music and sing my songs / My world begins and ends with you / Sweet music man / Am I too late / We don't make love anymore / Ghost of another man / Let me sing for you.
■ LP. . . . . UAS 30119
United Artists / '77.

DAYTIME FRIENDS (The very best of Kenny Rogers).
Tracks: Gambler, The / Daytime friends (and nightime lovers) / Lucille / Ruby don't take your love to town / Don't fall in love with a dreamer / Coward of the county / You decorated my life / Reuben James / She believes in me / Long arm of the law / 'Till I make it on my own / Son of Hickory Holler's tramp, The / Sweet music man / Green green grass of home / We've got tonight / Something's burning / Desperado / Lady / Abraham, Martin & John / Everytime two fools collide.
CD . . . . CDEMTV 79
LP. . . . . EMTV 79
MC . . . . TCEMTV 79
EMI / Sep '93 / EMI.

DON'T FALL IN LOVE WITH A DREAMER (Rogers, Kenny with Kim Carnes).
Tracks: Don't fall in love with a dreamer / Goin' to the rock / Golden tanner.
■ 7" . . . . UP 625
United Artists / Jan '81.
7" . . . . EA 208
EMI-America / Oct '85 / EMI.

DUETS.
Tracks: Not Advised.
■ CD . . . . CZ 77
EMI-America / Mar '87 / EMI.

EVERY TIME TWO FOOLS COLLIDE (Rogers, Kenny & Dottie West).
Tracks: Everytime two fools collide / You and me / What's wrong with us today / Beautiful lies / That's the way it could have been / Why don't we go somewhere and love / Baby I'm a want you / Anyone who isn't me tonight / Loving gift, The / We love each other.
■ LP. . . . . UAS 30170
United Artists / Apr '78.

EVERY TIME TWO FOOLS COLLIDE (Rogers, Kenny & Dottie West).
Tracks: Everytime two fools collide / We love each other.
■ 7" . . . . UP 36361
United Artists / Mar '78.

EYES THAT SEE IN THE DARK.
Tracks: This woman / You and I / Buried treasure / Islands in the stream / Living with you / Evening star / Hold me / Midsummer night / I will always love you / Eyes that see in the dark.
■ LP. . . . . RCALP 6088
RCA / Oct '83.
CD . . . . ND 90084
MC . . . . NK 90084
RCA / Oct '87 / BMG.
■ LP. . . . . NL 90084
RCA / Oct '87.

EYES THAT SEE IN THE DARK.
Tracks: Eyes that see in the dark / Buried treasure.
7" . . . . RCA 358
RCA / Sep '83 / BMG.

FABULOUS KENNY ROGERS,THE.
Tracks: Ruby don't take your love to town / Tulsa turnaround / Where does Rosie go / Love woman / Reuben James / I'm gonna sing you a sad song Susie / Me & Bobby McGee / Molly / Something's burning / Elvira / Tell it all brother / King of Oak Street, The / For the good times.
CD . . . . PWK 019
LP. . . . . SHM 3228
MC . . . . HSC 3228
Pickwick / Feb '88 / Pickwick Records.

FOR THE GOOD TIMES (Rogers, Kenny & The First Edition).
Tracks: For the good times / It's gonna be better / Home made lies / Sleep comes easy / But you know I love you / Something's burning / Shine on Ruby mountain / Run thru your mind / My Washington woman / She even woke me up to say goodbye / Elvira / Stranger in my place, A / Hurry up love / Ticket to nowhere / After all I live my life / Me and Bobby McGee / It's raining in my mind / Just dropped in (to see what condition my condition is in) / Shadow in the corner of your mind / Reuben James.
LP. . . . . ARA 1001
MC . . . . ARAC 1001
Arena / Feb '87.
CD . . . . U 4038
Spectrum (1) / Jun '88 / PolyGram.
CD . . . . 30272 AAD
CRC (USA) / Oct '89.

GAMBLER.
Tracks: Gambler, The / Momma's waiting.
■ 7" . . . . UP 36490
United Artists / Feb '79.

GAMBLER, THE.
Tracks: Gambler, The.
7" . . . . BP 425
United Artists / Mar '85 / EMI.

GAMBLER,THE.
Tracks: Gambler, The / I wish that I could hurt that way again / King of Oak Street, The / Making music for money / Hoodooin of Miss Fannie Deberry / She believes in me / Tennessee bottle / Sleep tight, goodnight man / Little more like me / San Francisco Mabel Joy / Morgana Jones.
LP. . . . . UAG 30220
■ MC . . . . TCK 30220
United Artists / Feb '79.

GIDEON.
Tracks: Goin' home to the rock / Gideon Tanner / No good Texas rounder / Don't fall in love with a dreamer / Buckeroos / You were a good friend / Call me up (and I'll come calling on you) / These chains / Somebody help me / One place in the night / Sayin' goodbye.
■ LP. . . . . UAK 30303
United Artists / May '80.

GOLDEN GREATS: KENNY ROGERS (Rogers, Kenny & The First Edition).
Tracks: Ruby, don't take your love to town / Tulsa turn around / Elvira / Reuben James / King of Oak Street, The / Me and Bobby McGee / Just dropped in (to see what condition my condition is in) / For the good times / Something's burning / Tell it all brother / Sunshine / Poem for my little lady / She even woke me up to say goodbye / Heed the call / I believe in music.
LP. . . . . MCM 5018
■ MC . . . . MCMC 5018
MCA / Oct '85.
CD . . . . MCLD 19051
■ MC . . . . MCLC 19051
MCA / Apr '92.

GOODBYE MARIE.
Tracks: Goodbye Marie / These chains.
■ 7" . . . . UP 629
United Artists / Jun '80.

GREATEST HITS: KENNY ROGERS.
Tracks: Gambler, The / Lady / Don't fall in love with a dreamer / Ruby don't take your love to town / She believes in me / Coward of the county / Lucille / You decorated my life / Reuben James / Love the world away / Every time two fools collide / Long arm of the law.
CD . . . . CDP 746 004 2
Liberty / Jan '84 / EMI.

HEART OF THE MATTER.
Tracks: Don't wanna have to worry / You made me feel love / Morning desire / Heart of the matter / Don't look in my eyes / Best of me, The / Tomb of the unknown love / People in love / I can't believe your eyes / Our perfect song.
LP. . . . . PL 87023
■ MC . . . . PK 87023
RCA / Nov '85.
■ CD . . . . PD 87023
RCA / May '86.

I DON'T NEED YOU.
Tracks: I don't need you / Without you in my life.
■ 7" . . . . UP 640
United Artists / Jul '81.

I PREFER THE MOONLIGHT.
Tracks: I prefer the moonlight / Now and forever / We're doin' alright / Make no mistake, she's mine / One more day / She's ready for someone to love her / I don't call him daddy / Factory / We fell in love anyway / You can't say (you don't love me anymore).
CD . . . . PD 86484
■ LP. . . . . PL 86484
RCA / Oct '87.
■ MC . . . . PK 86484
RCA / Oct '87.

ISLANDS IN THE STREAM (Rogers, Kenny & Dolly Parton).
Tracks: Islands in the stream.
■ 7" . . . . RCA 378
RCA / Nov '83.

KENNY.
Tracks: You turn the light on / You decorated my life / She's a mystery / Goodbye Marie / Tulsa turnaround / I want to make you smile / Santiago midnight moonlight / One man's woman / In and out of your heart / Old folks / Coward of the county.
■ MC . . . . TCK 30273
United Artists / Feb '80 / EMI.
■ LP. . . . . UAG 30273
United Artists / Feb '80.

KENNY ROGERS.
Tracks: Laura (what's he got that I ain't got) / I wasn't man enough / Mother country music / Why don't we go somewhere and love / Green green grass of home / Till I get it right / Lucille / Son of Hickory Holler's tramp, The / Lay down beside me / Puttin' in overtime at home / While I play the fiddle.
■ LP. . . . . UAS 30046
United Artists / Jun '77.
■ CD 500 003
Intertape / Jul '87.

KENNY ROGERS.
Tracks: Not Advised.
CD 15342
MC 79342
Laserlight / Nov '92 / TBD / Taylors.

KENNY ROGERS - GREATEST HITS.
Tracks: Not Advised.
CD 2430215
LP. 2230215
MC 2130215
Big Country / May '88.

KENNY ROGERS STORY, THE (20 Golden Greats).
Tracks: Lucille / Lady / Long arm of the law / You decorated my life / Sweet music man / Ruby don't take your love to town / Love or something like it / Through the years / You are so beautiful / Don't fall in love with a dreamer (with Kim Carnes) / Gambler, The / Daytime friends / We've got tonight (With Sheena Easton) / Love lifted me / Coward of the county / Reuben James / Desperado / She believes in me / Something's burning / Blaze of glory.
LP. . . . . EJ 360669 1
LP. . . . . EMTV 39
MC . . . . TC EMTV 39
MC . . . . EJ 360669 4
Liberty / Jul '85 / EMI.
CD . . . . CDEMTV 39
Liberty / Dec '87 / EMI.
DCC. . . . . DCCEMTV 39
Capitol / Jan '93 / EMI.

LADIES AND OUTLAWS.
Tracks: Coward of the county / Lady / Gambler, The / Green green grass of home / Daytime friends / Sail away / I would like to see you again / You are so beautiful / Long arm of the law, The / Don't fall in love with a dreamer / Lucille / Every time two fools collide / Laura / Another somebody done somebody wrong song / She's a mystery to me / All I ever need is you.
LP. . . . . PLAT 4901
MC . . . . PLAC 4901
Platinum Music / Oct '88 / Prism Leisure PLC / Ross Records.

LADY.
Tracks: Lady / Sweet music man.
■ 7" . . . . UP 635
United Artists / Nov '80.

LADY (Rogers, Kenny with Kim Carnes & Dottie West).
Tracks: Lady / Don't fall in love with a dreamer / Lucille / She believes in me / You decorated my life / Coward of the county / Goodbye Marie / Every time two fools collide / Sail away / Gambler, The / Love the world away / Long arm of the law.
■ LP. . . . . LBG 30334
Liberty / Feb '81.
■ MC . . . . TCLBG 30334
Liberty / Jan '81.

LONG ARM OF THE LAW.
Tracks: Long arm of the law / Make me wonder if I ever said goodbye.
■ 7" . . . . UP 650
United Artists / Feb '82.

LONG ARM OF THE LAW.
Tracks: Long arm of the law / You were a good friend.
■ 7" . . . . BP 426
Liberty / Jul '85.

LOVE LIFTED ME.
Tracks: Love lifted me / Abraham, Martin and John / Precious memories / I would like to see you again / Runaway girl / World needs a melody / You gotta be tired / Home-made love / While the feeling's good / Heavenly sunshine / There's an old man in our town.
■ LP. . . . . LBR 1015
United Artists / Nov '80.

LOVE OR SOMETHING LIKE IT.
Tracks: Love or something like it / Starting again.
■ 7" . . . . UP 36419
United Artists / Aug '78.

LOVE OR SOMETHING LIKE IT.
Tracks: Love or something like it / There's a lot of that going around / Buried treasure / Something about your song / Momma's waiting / We could have been the closest of friends / I could be so good for you / Sail away / Even a fool would let go / Highway flyer / Starting again.
■ LP. . . . . UAS 30194
United Artists / '79.

LOVE SONGS: KENNY ROGERS.
Tracks: Always leavin' always alone / What am I gonna do / Girl get a hold of yourself / I found a reason / It's gonna be better / She even woke me up to say goodbye / I just wanna give my love to you / Last few threads of love / Way it used to be, The / I'm gonna sing you a sad song Susie / But you know I love you / Shadow in the corner of your mind / Stranger in my place, A / Sunshine / Once again she's all alone / My Washington woman / Hurry up love / Home made lies / Poem for my little lady.
CD . . . . PWK 070
Pickwick / Jun '89 / Pickwick Records.
MC . . . . HSC 3278
Hallmark / Jun '89 / Pickwick Records.

LOVE SONGS: KENNY ROGERS.
Tracks: Lady / Ruby don't take your love to town / Lucille / She believed in me / Together again / Don't fall in love with a dreamer / You decorated my life / Every time two fools collide / All I ever need is you / You needed me / Why don't we go somewhere and love / Love or somthing like it / Another somebody done somebody wrong song / My world begins and ends with you / You and me / We love each other / You've lost that loving feeling / But you know I love you / Love lifted me / Just the way you are.
CD . . . . CDMFP 5880
MC . . . . TCMFP 5880
MFP / Apr '90 / EMI.

LOVE WILL TURN YOU AROUND.
Tracks: Love will turn you around / Love song / Fighting fire with fire / Maybe you should know / Somewhere between lovers and friends / Take this heart / If you can lie a little bit / I'll take care of you / Fool in me / I want a son.
■ LP. . . . . LBG 30350
Liberty / Sep '82.

LOVE WILL TURN YOU AROUND.
Tracks: Love will turn you around / I want a son.
7" . . . . UP 654
United Artists / Jul '82 / EMI.

LUCILLE.
Tracks: Laura (What's he got that I ain't got) / I wasn't man enough / Mother country music / Why don't we go somewhere and love / Green green grass of home / Till I get it right / Lucille / Son of Hickory Holler's tramp, The / Lay down beside me / Puttin' in overtime at home / While I play the fiddle.
MC . . . . TCMFP 5764
MFP / Aug '86 / EMI.
■ LP. . . . . MFP 5764
MFP / Oct '86.

LUCILLE.
Tracks: Lucille.
7" . . . . UP 36242
United Artists / Apr '77 / EMI.

MORNING DESIRE.
Tracks: Morning desire / People in love.
12" . . . . PT 49926
7" . . . . PB 49925
RCA / Oct '85 / BMG.

ONCE UPON A CHRISTMAS (see under Parton, Dolly).

REAL LOVE (see under Parton, Dolly).

RUBY.
Tracks: Not Advised.
CD . . . . AVC 510
MC . . . . AVM 510
Avid / Dec '92 / ACD Trading Ltd. / BMG.

RUBY DON'T TAKE YOUR LOVE.
Tracks: Not Advised.
CD . . . . CDGFR 027
MC . . . . MCGFR 027
IMD / Jun '92 / BMG.

RUBY DON'T TAKE YOUR LOVE TO TOWN.
Tracks: Ruby don't take your love to town / Lucille.
■ 7" . . . . RS 2089
Reprise / Oct '69.

RUBY DON'T TAKE YOUR LOVE TO TOWN.
Tracks: Ticket to nowhere / Conditions (Just dropped in) / She even woke me up to say goodbye / My Washington woman / Run thru your mind / Sleep comes easy / After all (I live my life) / For the good times / Something's burning / Hurry up. Love / Trying just as hard / Ruby don't take your love to town / Heed the call / we all got to help each other / Poem for my little lady / Where does Rosie go / Sunshine / Ruben James / Loser / Church without a name / Green green grass of home / Sweet music man / Daytime friends.
LP. . . . . SHLP 117
MC . . . . SHTC 117
Castle Showcase / Apr '86 / Arabesque Ltd.
CD . . . . ONN 41
Object Enterprises / May '89 / Gold & Sons / Terry Blood Dist. / Midland Records.

RUBY DON'T TAKE YOUR LOVE TO TOWN.
Tracks: Ruby don't take your love to town / Ruben James / Shine on Ruby mountain / Ticket to nowhere / Conditions (just dropped in) / She even woke me up to say goodbye / My Washington woman / Run thru' your mind / Sleep comes easy / After all (I live my life) / For the good times / Something's burning / Hurry up love / Trying just as hard / Heed the call / We all got to help each other / Poem for my little lady / Where does Rosie go / Sunshine / Loser / Church without a name / Me & Bobby McGee / Always leaving always gone / Calico silver / Way it used to be / Goodtime liberator.
MC Set . . . . TTMC 020
Tring / Jun '92 / Prism Leisure PLC / Midland Records / Taylors.
CD . . . . CDGRF 027
MC . . . . MCGRF 027
Tring / Feb '93 / Prism Leisure PLC / Midland Records / Taylors.

RUBY, DON'T TAKE YOUR LOVE TO TOWN.
Tracks: Ruby, don't take your love to town / Green green grass of home / Sweet music man / Love or something like it / You and me / King of Oak Street, The / Reuben James / Puttin' in overtime at home / Daytime friends / Let it be me / Buried treasure / Son of Hickory Holler's tramp, The / I wasn't man enough (CD only) / Mother country music (CD only) / Lay down beside me (CD only) / Lucille (CD only).
MC . . . . TCMFP 50514
MFP / Apr '81 / EMI.
■ LP. . . . . MFP 50514
MFP / Apr '81.
CD . . . . CDMFP 6001
MFP / Sep '88 / EMI.

RUBY, DON'T TAKE YOUR LOVE TO TOWN.
Tracks: Ruby, don't take your love to town / Girl get a hold of yourself.
■ 7" . . . . K 14009
WEA / '79.
■ 7" . . . . G 45 7
EMI Golden 45's / Mar '84.

RUBY, DON'T TAKE YOUR LOVE TO TOWN.
Tracks: Not Advised.
CD 15 075
MC 79 525
Laserlight / Aug '91 / TBD / Taylors.

SAIL AWAY.
Tracks: Sail away / We could have been the closest of friends.
■ 7" . . . . UP 36470
United Artists / Nov '78.

SHARE YOUR LOVE.
Tracks: Share your love / Blaze of glory / I don't need you / Good life / Makes me wonder if I ever said goodbye / Through the years / So in love with you / Goin' back to Alabama / Without you in my life / Grey beard.
LP. . . . . LBG 30339
■ MC . . . . TC LBG 30339
Liberty / Aug '81.

SHE BELIEVES IN ME.
Tracks: She believes in me / Morgana Jones.
■ 7" . . . . UP 36533
United Artists / Jun '79.

SHINE ON.
Tracks: Something's burning / Just remember you're my sunshine / Tell it all, brother / Ruby don't take your love to town / Stranger in my place / I'm gonna sing you a sad song Susie / She even woke me to say goodbye / Shine on Ruby Mountain / Me and Bobby McGee / Molly / Then I miss you / Sunshine / Someone who cares / Elvira.
■ LP. . . . . K 24037
Reprise / May '80.

SINGLES ALBUM: KENNY ROGERS.
Tracks: Ruby don't take your love to town / Reuben James / But you know I love you / Something's burning / Just dropped in / Lucille / Daytime friends / While the feeling's good / Love lifted me / Today I started loving you again / Love or something like it / Sail away / Gambler, The / She believes in me.
■ LP. . . . . UAK 30263
United Artists / Sep '79.
■ MC . . . . TCK 30263
United Artists / Sep '79.

SO IN LOVE WITH YOU.
Tracks: So in love with you / Share your love with me.
■ 7" . . . . UP 646
United Artists / Oct '81.

SOMETHING INSIDE SO STRONG.
Tracks: Planet Texas / If I knew what I know now / There lies the difference / When you put your heart in it / Maybe / (Something inside) so strong / One night / If I ever fall in love again / Vows go unbroken (always true to you) / Love the way you do.
CD . . . . K 9257922
LP. . . . . K 9257921
MC . . . . K 9257924
WEA / May '89 / WEA.

SOMETHING'S BURNING.
Tracks: Something's burning.
■ 7" . . . . RS 20888
Reprise / Feb '70.

SOMETHING'S BURNING (Rogers, Kenny & The First Edition).
Tracks: Something's burning / Ruby don't take your love to town.
7" . . . . K 14483
Reprise (USA) / May '80 / WEA / Pinnacle.

SOMETHING'S BURNING.
Tracks: For the good times / It's gonna be better / Home made lies / Sleep comes easy / But you know I love you / Something's burning / Shine on ruby mountain / Run thru your mind / My Washington woman / She even woke me to say goodbye / Elvira / Stranger in my place, A / Hyrry up, Love / Ticket to nowhere / After all, I live my life / Me and Bobby McGhee / It's raining in my mind / Conditions (Just dropped in) / Shadow in the corner of your mind / Reuben James.
LP Set . . . . PPD 2004
MC . . . . PPK 2004
Premier (Sony) / '84 / Sony / Pinnacle.

SUNSHINE.
Tracks: Not Advised.
CD 288 07 009
Bellaphon / '86 / New Note.

SWEET MUSIC MAN.
Tracks: Sweet music man / Lying again.
■ 7" . . . . UP 36325
United Artists / Nov '77.

THEY DON'T MAKE 'EM LIKE THEY USED TO.
Tracks: This love we share / If I could hold on to love / You're my love / Time for love, A / They don't make 'em like they used to / Life is good, love is better / Just the thought of losing you / Anything at all / After all this time / Twenty years ago.
■ CD . . . . PD 85633
RCA / Mar '87.
■ LP. . . . . PL 85633
RCA / May '87.
■ MC . . . . PK 85633
RCA / May '87.

THIS WOMAN.
Tracks: This woman / Hold me.
7" . . . . RCA 390
RCA / Jan '84 / BMG.

VERY BEST OF KENNY ROGERS, THE.
Tracks: What I did for love / Ruby don't take your love to town / Don't fall in love with a dreamer / Gambler, The / Daytime friends / Love is strange / She believes in me / Lucille / Lady / Coward of the county / You decorated my life / Love lifted me / Something's burning / Islands in the stream.
CD 7599264572
LP. 7599264571
MC 7599264574
WEA / Nov '90 / WEA.

WE'VE GOT TONIGHT.
Tracks: We've got tonight / Scarlet fever / Farther I go / No dreams / Bad enough / All my life / How long / Love,

love, love / What I learned from loving you / You are so beautiful.
LP. . . . . LBG 30357
■ MC . . . . TC-LBG 30357
Liberty / Mar '83.

WE'VE GOT TONIGHT (see under Easton, Sheena).

WHAT ABOUT ME.
Tracks: Didn't we / Somebody took my love / Crazy / Stranger / Heart to heart / What about me / Night goes on / Dream dancin' / Two hearts one love / I don't want to know.
CD . . . . PD 85043
LP. . . . . PL 85043
■ MC . . . . PK 85043
RCA / Oct '84.

WHAT I DID FOR LOVE.
Tracks: What I did for love.
12" . . . . W 9771T
7" . . . . W 9771
■ CD Single . . . . W 9771CD
WEA / Jul '90 / WEA.

WHEN YOU PUT YOUR HEART IN IT.
Tracks: When you put your heart in it / So little love in the world / Vowels go unbroken, The (Only on 12").
12" . . . . W 7711T
7" . . . . W 7711
WEA / Sep '88 / WEA.

YOU DECORATED MY LIFE.
Tracks: You decorated my life / One man's woman.
■ 7" . . . . UP 606
United Artists / Oct '79.

Rogers, Kenny Jr

YES - NO, MAYBE.
Tracks: Not Advised.
CD . . . . YD 0132
LP. . . . . YL 0132
Cypress / Nov '89 / Sonet Records / Jazz Music / Wellard Dist. / C.M. Distribution.

Rogers, Roy

Roy Rogers was born Leonard Slye in 1912 in Cincinatti, Ohio. He was one of the great singing cowboys of the 1930s-40s, the only real rival of Gene Autry as a Saturday matinee idol, billed as 'The King Of Cowboys'. His father made mandolins and guitars; he grew up on a farm, went to California in 1930, picked peaches and was founder of vocal quintet, The Sons Of The Pioneers. He left in 1939 to go solo, appearing with his palomino horse Trigger (1932-65; now stuffed and mounted at his Californian home). He made about a hundred films, many with Dale Evans (born 1912 in Texas) who had started singing for bandleader Anson Weeks, and married her in 1947. Their late '40s films, often with the Pioneers, with Republic's peculiarly sunsettish colour process, are redolent of nostalgia for millions. They had a popular action TV show 1951-56 on Saturday mornings. (Donald Clarke).

COUNTRY SIDE OF.., THE.
Tracks: Not Advised.
LP. . . . . HAT 3116
MC . . . . HATC 3116
Stetson / Sep '89 / Crusader Marketing Co. / Swift / Wellard Dist. / Midland Records / C.M. Distribution.

GOOD LIFE (Rogers, Roy & Dale Evans).
Tracks: Not Advised.
LP. . . . . SAC 5095
Sacred / Aug '87 / Word Records (UK).

KING OF THE COWBOYS (Rogers, Roy & Sons of the Pioneers).
Tracks: Hawaiian cowboy / Hasta la vista / There'll never be another Pecos Bill / I'm gonna gallop, gallop to gallup, New Mexico / Stampede / With a sweep of my sombrero / Saddle serenade / Make believe cowboy / Horseshoe moon / Church music / Cowboy heaven / Ride, son ride / Don't ever leave me (Previously unissued.) / Buck-eye cowboy / Four legged friend, A.
LP. . . . . BFX 15124
Bear Family / Dec '83 / Rollercoaster Records / Swift / Direct Distribution.

ROLL ON TEXAS MOON.
Tracks: Yellow rose of Texas / Don't fence me in / Gay ranchero, A / Roll on Texas moon / I met a miss in Texas / On the old Spanish trail / May the good Lord take a likin' to ya / San Fernando Valley / I'm a rollin' / Little hula honey / California Rose / Home in Oklahoma / Rock me to sleep in my saddle / Old fashioned cowboy / There's a cloud to the valley of sunshine / Along the Navajo Trail.
LP P.Disc. . . . . BDP 15203
Bear Family / Nov '86 / Rollercoaster Records / Swift / Direct Distribution.

ROY ROGERS & THE SONS OF THE PIONEERS (The Republic Years) (Rogers, Roy & Sons of the Pioneers).
Tracks: Not Advised.
LP. . . . . STV 81212
MC . . . . CTV 81212
Silva Screen / Jan '89 / Silva Screen / Conifer Records / Total / BMG.

SWEET HOUR OF PRAYER (Rogers, Roy & Dale Evans).
Tracks: What a friend / Light of the world is Jesus / Near to the heart of God / Sweet hour of prayer / Where he leads me / Since Jesus came into my heart / In the garden / Old rugged cross, The / Near the cross / I love to tell the story / He is so precious to me / Love lifted me.
LP. . . . . HAT 3088
Stetson / '88 / Crusader Marketing Co. / Swift / Wellard Dist. / Midland Records / C.M. Distribution.
MC . . . . HATC 3088
Stetson / Jan '89 / Crusader Marketing Co. / Swift / Wellard Dist. / Midland Records / C.M. Distribution.

Romaine, Anne

GETTIN' ON COUNTRY.
Tracks: Not Advised.
LP. . . . . ROUNDER 3009
Rounder / '88 / Projection / Roots Records / Swift / C.M. Distribution / Topic Records / Jazz Music / Hot Shot / A.D.A Distribution / Direct Distribution.

TAKE A STAND.
Tracks: Not Advised.
LP. . . . . FF 323
Flying Fish (USA) / Mar '89 / Cadillac Music / Roots Records / Projection / C.M. Distribution / Direct Distribution / Jazz Music / Duncans / A.D.A Distribution.

Ronstadt, Linda

Linda Marie Ronstadt was born in 1946 in Tuscon, Arizona. She made three LPs on Capitol with the Stone Poneys (trio with two guitarists, backing musicians on disc) incl. top 20 hit *Different Drum*; her solo album on Capitol established her as a country rock vocalist with a gorgeous gospel-influenced voice. *Linda Ronstadt* in 1972 included backing by all four original Eagles. She changed labels to Asylum with producer Pete Asher; *Don't Cry Now* '73 made the top 50 LPs without a big hit single; *Heart Like A Wheel* appeared on Capitol, reached number one in 1974 with two big hit singles; *Prisoners In Disguise* and *Hasten Down The Wind*. *Simple Dreams* and *Living In The USA* 1977-78 were number ones; *Mad Love* in 1980 was number three. *Get Closer* in 1982 slipped a bit. Three singles, five LPs were hits in the UK. Her relationship with then Govenor Jerry Brown of California was in the news late '70s. Her appearance on stage in Gilbert and Sullivan's Pirates Of Penzance was praised; she switched to songs by George Gershwin, Irving Berlin, Billy Stayhorn etc. For *What's New*, *Lush Life*, *For Sentimental Reasons* 1983-86, with arrangements by Nelson Riddle; her style was hopelessly wrong for these kinds of songs, but the albums were all hits . She also sang on Philip Glass's LP *Songs From Liquid Days*. In 1987 she joined Dolly Parton and Emmylou Harris in the long-awaited *Trio* album, singing lead on Linda Thompson's beautiful *Telling Me Lies*, she was back where she belonged. (Donald Clarke).

ALISON.
Tracks: Alison / All that you dream.
■ 7" . . . . K 13149
Asylum / May '79.

ALL MY LIFE (Ronstadt, Linda & Aaron Neville).
Tracks: All my life / Shattered.
12" . . . . EKR 105T
7" . . . . EKR 105
■ CD Single . . . . EKR 105CD
Elektra / Feb '90 / WEA.

BACK IN THE USA.
Tracks: Back in the USA / White rhythm and blues.
7" . . . . K 13133
Asylum / '79 / WEA.

BLUE BAYOU.
Tracks: Blue bayou / Maybe I'm right.
■ 7" . . . . K 13106
Asylum / Jan '78.

CANCIONES DE MI PADRE.
Tracks: Por un amor / Los laureles / Hay unos ojos / La cigarra / Tu solo tu / Y andale / Rogaciano el huapanguero / La charreada / Dos arbolitos / Corrido de cannea / La barca de guaymas / La calandria / El sol que tu eres.
CD 960 765-2
Asylum / Dec '87 / WEA.
LP. 960 765-1
■ MC 960 765-4
Asylum / Nov '87.

CRAZY.
Tracks: Crazy / Someone to lay down beside me.
■ 7" . . . . K 13071
Asylum / Feb '77.

CRY LIKE A RAINSTORM, HOWL LIKE THE WIND.
Tracks: Still within the sound of my voice / Cry like a rainstorm / All my life / Don't know much / Adios / Trouble again / I keep it hid / So right, so wrong / Shattered / When something is wrong with my baby / Goodbye my friend.
CD 9608722
LP. . . . . EKT 76
MC . . . . EKT 76C
Elektra / Oct '89 / WEA.

DIFFERENT DRUM.
Tracks: Different drum / It doesn't matter anymore.
■ 7" . . . . CL 15933
Capitol / Jul '77.

DIFFERENT DRUM.
Tracks: Different drum / Rock me on the water / I'll be your baby tonight / Hobo / Stoney end / Long long time / Up to my neck in high muddy water / Some of Shelley's blues / In my reply / Will you love me tomorrow.
LP. . . . . VMP 1010
Capitol / '75 / EMI.

DON'T CRY NOW.
Tracks: I can almost see it / Love has no pride / Silver threads and golden needles / Desperado / Don't cry now / Sail away / Colorado / Fast one / Everybody loves a winner / I believe in you.
LP. . . . . K 43002
Asylum / '74 / WEA.

DON'T KNOW MUCH (Ronstadt, Linda & Aaron Neville).
Tracks: Don't know much.
MC Single . . . . EKR 101C
Elektra / Nov '89 / WEA.
7" . . . . EKR 101
Elektra / Oct '89 / WEA.

EMOTIONAL TRAFFIC.
Tracks: Emotional traffic / Hard enough to show.
■ 7" . . . . BUY 45
Stiff / May '79.

FALLING IN LOVE AGAIN.
Tracks: Falling in love again / Sophisticated lady.
■ 7" . . . . E 9667
Asylum / Jan '85.

FOR SENTIMENTAL REASONS.
Tracks: When you wish upon a star / Bewitched / You go to my head / But not for me / My funny valentine / I get along without you very well / Am I blue / I love you for sentimental reasons / Straighten up and fly right / Little girl blue / Round midnight.
CD 960 474-2
MC 960 474-4
Asylum / Sep '86 / WEA.
■ LP. 960 474-1
Asylum / Sep '86.

GET CLOSER.
Tracks: Get closer / Moon is a harsh mistress, The / I knew you when / Easy for you to say / People gonna talk / Talk to me of Mendocino / I think it's gonna work out fine / Mr. Radio / Lies / Tell him / Sometimes you can't win / My blue tears.
■ LP. 9601851
Asylum / Nov '82.
LP. . . . . E 0185
MC . . . . E 01854
Asylum / Oct '82 / WEA.
CD 9601852
Asylum / Jan '84 / WEA.

GET CLOSER.
Tracks: Get closer / Sometimes you just can't win.
7" 969 948-7
Asylum / Nov '82 / WEA.

GREATEST HITS: LINDA RONSTADT.
Tracks: You're no good / Silver threads and golden / Desperado / Love is a rose / That'll be the day / Long long time / Different drum / When will I be loved? / Love has no pride / Heatwave / It doesn't matter anymore / Tracks of my tears.
LP. . . . . K 53055
MC K4 53055
Asylum / Jan '77 / WEA.
CD 253 055
Asylum / '84 / WEA.

GREATEST HITS: LINDA RONSTADT, VOL 2.
Tracks: It's so easy / I can't let go / Hurt so bad / Blue bayou / How do I make you? / Back in the USA / Ooh baby baby / Poor, poor, pitiful me / Tumbling dice / Just one look / Someone to lay down beside me.
MC K4 52255
Asylum / Nov '80 / WEA.
■ LP. . . . . K 52255
Asylum / Nov '80.
CD 252 255-2
Asylum / '83 / WEA.

HASTEN DOWN THE WIND.
Tracks: Lose again / Tattler / If he's ever near / That'll be the day / Lo siento me vida / Hasten down the wind / Rivers of Babylon / Give one heart / Try me again / Crazy / Down so low / Someone to lay down beside me.
LP. . . . . K 53045
Asylum / Sep '76 / WEA.

CD . . . . K 9606102
WEA / Sep '89 / WEA.

HEART LIKE A WHEEL.
Tracks: You're no good / It doesn't matter anymore / Faithless love / Dark end of the street / Heart like a wheel / When will I be loved / I can't help it (if I'm still in love with you) / Keep me from blowing away / You can close your eyes.
LP. . . . . IC 038 81823
EMI (Germany) / '83.
LP. 3C 054 81823
MC 3C 254 81823
EMI (Italy) / Dec '86.

HOW DO I MAKE YOU.
Tracks: How do I make you / Rambler gambler.
■ 7" . . . . K 12419
Elektra / Feb '80.

HURT SO BAD.
Tracks: Hurt so bad / Justine.
■ 7" . . . . K 12444
Asylum / Jun '80.

I KNEW YOU WHEN.
Tracks: I knew you when / Talk to me of Mendocino.
12" . . . . E 9853T
7" . . . . E 9853
Elektra / Jan '83 / WEA.

IT'S SO EASY.
Tracks: It's so easy / Sorrow lives here.
■ 7" . . . . K 13100
Asylum / Nov '77.

LINDA RONSTADT.
Tracks: Rock me on the water / Crazy arms / I won't be hangin' around / I still miss someone / In my reply / I fall to pieces / Ramblin' round / Birds / Faithful / Rescue me.
■ LP. GO 2013
Capitol Greenlight Series / Jun '81.
LP. . . . . FA 3015
■ MC . . . . TCFA 3015
Fame / May '82.

LINDA RONSTADT & FRIENDS.
Tracks: Not Advised.
LP. 1A 028 81072
EMI (Holland) / Jan '85.

LIVING IN THE USA.
Tracks: Back in the U.S.A. / When I grow too old to dream / Just one look / Alison / White rhythm and blues / All that you dream / Ooh baby baby / Mohammed's radio / Blowing away / Love me tender.
■ LP. . . . . K 53085
Asylum / Oct '78.

LUSH LIFE.
Tracks: When I fall in love / Skylark / It never entered my mind / Mean to me / When your lover has gone / I'm a fool to want you / You took advantage of me / Sophisticated lady / Can't we be friends / My old flame / Falling in love again / Lush life.
LP. 960 387-1
Asylum / Nov '84 / WEA.
■ MC 960 387-4
Asylum / Nov '84.
CD 960 387-2
Asylum / Jun '87 / WEA.

MAD LOVE.
Tracks: Not Advised.
■ LP. . . . . K 52210
Asylum / Mar '80.

MAS CANCIONES.
Tracks: Tata dios / El toro relajo / Mi ranchito / LA mariquita / Gritenme piedras del campo / Siempre haco frio / El crucifijo de piedra / Palomita de ojos negros / Pena de los amores / El camino / El gustito / El sueno.
CD 7559612392
MC 7559612394
WEA / Nov '91 / WEA.

PRISONER IN DISGUISE.
Tracks: Love is a rose / Hey mister, that's me upon the jukebox / Roll um easy / Tracks of my tears / Prisoner in disguise / Heatwave / Many rivers to cross / Sweetest gift, The / You tell me that I'm falling down / I will always love you / Silver blue.
LP. . . . . K 53015
Asylum / '88 / WEA.

RETROSPECTIVE.
Tracks: Not Advised.
Double LP 5C 138 85170
EMI (Holland) / Aug '84.

ROUND MIDNIGHT.
Tracks: Not Advised.

SIMPLE DREAMS.
Tracks: It's so easy / Carmelita / Simple man, simple dreams / Sorrow lives here / I never will marry / Blue bayou / Poor poor pitiful me / Maybe I'm right / Tumbling dice / Old paint.
LP. . . . . K 53065
Asylum / Jan '77 / WEA.
CD 253 065
Asylum / Jan '87 / WEA.

SOMEWHERE OUT THERE (Ronstadt, Linda & Richard Ingram).
Tracks: Somewhere out there (a) / Somewhere out there (b) / Somewhere out there (fievels version) (On Picture disc only.) / Somewhere out there (instrumental) (On Picture disc only.).
12" . . . . MCAS 1172
7" . . . . MCA 1172
■ 7" P.Disc . . . . MCAP 1172
MCA / Jun '87 / BMG.

TELL HIM.
Tracks: Tell him / Mr Radio.
12" . . . . E 9877T
Elektra / Apr '83 / WEA.
7" . . . . E 9877
Elektra / Mar '83 / WEA.

TO KNOW HIM IS TO LOVE HIM (see under Parton, Dolly).

TRACKS OF MY TEARS.
Tracks: Tracks of my tears.
■ 7" . . . . K 13034
Asylum / May '76.

TUMBLING DICE.
Tracks: Tumbling dice / Carmelita.
■ 7" . . . . K 13120
Asylum / Apr '78.

TWO ORIGINALS OF LINDA RONSTADT.
Tracks: I fall to pieces / Crazy arms / I still miss someone.
Double LP . . . . IC 134 52760/61
EMI (Germany) / '83.

WHAT'S NEW.
Tracks: Skylark / Mean to me / My old flame / What's new / Lush life / Love man / Goodbye / For sentimental reasons / Crazy he calls me / When I fall in love.
CD 960 260-2
LP. 9602601
MC 960 260-4
Asylum / Sep '83 / WEA.
CD 960 489-2
MC 960 489-4
Asylum / Nov '86 / WEA.
■ LP. 960 489-1
Asylum / Nov '86.

WHAT'S NEW.
Tracks: What's new / Crazy he calls me.
■ 7" . . . . E 9780
Asylum / Mar '84.

WHAT'S NEW.
Tracks: What's new? / I've a crush on you / Guess I'll hang my tears out to dry / Crazy he calls me / Someone to watch over me / I don't stand a ghost of a chance with you / What'll I do? / Lover man (oh where can you be) / Goodbye.
VHS. . . . . MA 11012
Vestron Music Video / Oct '84 / Sony / Gold & Sons / Terry Blood Dist.

Rooney, Jim

Rhythm guitarist/recording act/producer. Rooney started out as a musician during the folk era of the 1960's in America's northern states, where he was to blend bluegrass, folk and country into his work. Played with such proficient acts banjoist Bill Keith, Joe Val and later Bostonian Peter Rowan. Featured on Waterfront's 1981 live recording *Rowan, Keith and Rooney - Hot Bluegrass* (released 1985), recorded on one of his many trips to the UK. Dates included a number of appearances at Cambridge's Annual Folk Festival and his solo recordings can be found on Italy's Appaloosa label. Rooney's greatest achievements have come via his talents as a producer - furthering the careers of many. Such widely acclaimed acoustic product includes Nanci Griffiths' Philo albums *Once in a very blue moon* , *Last of the true believers* and her 1993 tribute styled MCA release *Other voices, other rooms* , John Prine's *German afternoon* and Iris DeMent's *Infamous angel* . (Maurice Hope)

BRAND NEW TENNESSEE WALTZ.
Tracks: Brand new Tennessee waltz / Be my friend tonight / Amanda / Heaven become a woman / We must believe in magic / Fish and whistle / Dreaming my dreams / Six white horses / Satisfied mind.
LP. . . . . AP 012
Appaloosa / '82 / Roots Records / C.M. Distribution / Wellard Dist. / Projection / Hot Shot / A.D.A Distribution.

COLLECTION: JIM ROONEY & BILL KEITH (see under Keith, Bill).

ONE DAY AT A TIME.
Tracks: Not Advised.
LP. . . . . ROUNDER 3008
Rounder / Oct '88 / Projection / Roots Records / Swift / C.M. Distribution / Topic Records / Jazz Music / Hot Shot / A.D.A Distribution / Direct Distribution.

READY FOR THE TIMES TO GET BETTER.
Tracks: In it for the long run / Only the best / I recall a gypsy woman / Broided orange / Ready for the times to get better / South in New Orleans / Tennessee blues / Interest on the loan / Girl at the end of the hall / No expectations.
LP. . . . . AP 004
Appaloosa / May '81 / Roots Records / C.M. Distribution / Wellard Dist. / Projection / Hot Shot / A.D.A Distribution.

Rose, Judy

GIRL NOBODY KNOWS.
Tracks: Not Advised.
LP. . . . . WRS 127
Westwood / '78 / Pinnacle.

Rose, Pam

PAM ROSE SINGS.
Tracks: Not Advised.
LP. . . . . LKLP 6547
Look / '88 / C.M. Distribution.

Rowan, Peter

Peter Rowan was born in Boston, Massachusetts in 1942. He is a much travelled singer-songwriter and highly accomplished on the guitar, mandolin and mandola. He draws from many influences, making traditional music of the finest order - with celtic flavoured bluegrass and the old timey Bill Monroe (with whom he played out a two year apprenticeship) styled variety just two strings to his bow. Rowan's much acclaimed high soaring vocals, making what he likes to call 'crucial country', places him among the most respected musicians in the business. On the songwriting front, George Strait, Ricky Skaggs and Michael Martin Murphy have all seen success with his carefully crafted creations. While contemporary aces 'New Riders Of The Purple Sage' set the ball rollin' when they picked-up 'Panama Red', with his epic 'Meadow Green' gaining a place for the film *Steel Magnolias* starring Daryl Hannah and Dolly Parton.

ALL ON A RISING DAY.
Tracks: Midnight highway / Last train / Howlin' at the moon / Mr. Time clock / Behind these prison walls of love / Deal with the devil / Undying love / Wheel of fortune, The / All on a rising day / Freedom walkabout / Prayer of a homeless wanderer / John O'Dreams.
CD . . . . SPDCD 1044
■ MC . . . . SPDC 1044
Special Delivery / Sep '91.

AWAKE ME IN THE NEW WORLD.
Tracks: Shaman's vision / Dreams of the sea / Pulcinella sails away / Caribbean woman / Dance with no shoes / Sugar cane / For Gods, for Kings & for gold / Awake me in the new world / All my relations / Remember that I love you / Maria de las Rosas / African banjo / Sailing home dance of Pulcinella.
CD . . . . SH 3807CD
MC . . . . SH 3807C
Sugarhill(USA) / May '93 / Roots Records / Projection / Impetus Records / C.M. Distribution / Jazz Music / Swift / Duncans / A.D.A Distribution.

BACKROADS.
Tracks: Roving gambler / Lone pilgrim / Raglan road (dawning of the day) / Going up on the mountain / Casey's last ride / Old, old house / Hiroshima mon amour / Willow garden / Moonshiner / Thirsty in the rain / Walls of time / Olains of Waterloo.
CD . . . . SHCD 3722
Sugarhill(USA) / '91 / Roots Records / Projection / Impetus Records / C.M. Distribution / Jazz Music / Swift / Duncans / A.D.A Distribution.

DUST BOWL CHILDREN.
Tracks: Dust bowl children / Before the streets were paved / Electric blanket / Little mother / Barefoot country road / Seeds my daddy sowed / Tumbleweed / Dream of a home / Rainmaker.
CD . . . . SHCD 3781
LP. . . . . SH 3781
MC . . . . ZCSH 3781
Sugarhill(USA) / '90 / Roots Records / Projection / Impetus Records / C.M. Distribution / Jazz Music / Swift / Duncans / A.D.A Distribution.

FIRST WHIPPERWILL, THE.
Tracks: I'm on my way back to the old home / I'm just a used to be / I believed in you darling / Sweetheart you done me wrong / When the golden leaves begin to fall / I was left on the street / Goodbye old pal / When you are lonely / First whipperwill, The / Sitting alone in the moonlight / Boat of love / It's mighty dark to travel.
LP. . . . . SH 3749
MC . . . . ZCSH 3749
Sugarhill(USA) / May '86 / Roots Records / Projection / Impetus Records / C.M. Distribution / Jazz Music / Swift / Duncans / A.D.A Distribution.

MEDICINE TRAIL.
Tracks: Riding high in Texas / My foolish pride / River of stone / Revelation / Lying on the line / Medicine trail / Blues come bother me / Dreaming I love you / Maui momma / Prairie lullabye.
LP. . . . . FF 205

Flying Fish (USA) / Mar '89 / Cadillac Music / Roots Records / Projection / C.M. Distribution / Direct Distribution / Jazz Music / Duncans / A.D.A Distribution.

NEW MOON RISING (Rowan, Peter & The Nashville Bluegrass Band).
Tracks: That high lonesome sound / Trail of tears / Memories of you / Moth to a flame, A / I'm gonna love you / One way / New moon rising / Jesus made the wine / Cabin of love / Meadow green.
■ LP. . . . . SPD 1014
Special Delivery / Jul '88.
MC . . . . SPDC 1014
Special Delivery / Oct '88 / Revolver-APT / A.D.A Distribution / Topic Records / Direct Distribution / Jazz Music / C.M. Distribution.
■ CD . . . . SPDCD 1014
Special Delivery / Aug '89.
CD . . . . .SH CD 3762
Sugarhill(USA) / Mar '89 / Roots Records / Projection / Impetus Records / C.M. Distribution / Jazz Music / Swift / Duncans / A.D.A Distribution.

OLD AND IN THE WAY (see under Garcia, Jerry).

PETER ROWAN.
Tracks: Outlaw love / Break my heart again / Woman in love, A / When I was a cowboy / Land of the Navajo / Free Mexican Airforce, The / Panama red / Midnite moonlite / Gypsy King's farewell, The.
LP. . . . . .FF 071
Flying Fish (USA) / May '79 / Cadillac Music / Roots Records / Projection / C.M. Distribution / Direct Distribution / Jazz Music / Duncans / A.D.A Distribution.
LP. . . . . SPD 1005
Special Delivery / Nov '87 / Revolver-APT / A.D.A Distribution / Topic Records / Direct Distribution / Jazz Music / C.M. Distribution.
MC . . . . SPDC 1005
Special Delivery / Oct '88 / Revolver-APT / A.D.A Distribution / Topic Records / Direct Distribution / Jazz Music / C.M. Distribution.
CD . . . . FF 70071
Flying Fish (USA) / '89 / Cadillac Music / Roots Records / Projection / C.M. Distribution / Direct Distribution / Jazz Music / Duncans / A.D.A Distribution.

PETER ROWAN AND RED HOT PICKERS.
Tracks: Hobo song, The / Old old house / Willow garden / Jimmy Brown the Newsboy / Wild Billy Jones / Hiroshima mon amour / Come ye tender hearted / Oh Susanna / Rosalie McFall / Good woman's love. A.
CD . . . . SHCD 3733
LP. . . . . SH 3733
MC . . . . ZCSH 3733
Sugarhill(USA) / Mar '89 / Roots Records / Projection / Impetus Records / C.M. Distribution / Jazz Music / Swift / Duncans / A.D.A Distribution.

PETER ROWAN AND THE WILD STALLIONS (Rowan, Peter & The Wild Stallions).
Tracks: I can't get mellow / Hotter she burns, The / Fool myself again / Baby let's play house / Call it love / Woman in love, A / Cries of love / Refugee / Sheila rendezvous / Primavera dell' amore.

REVELRY.
Tracks: Holly wells of Ireland, The / Maelstrom / Sitting on the top of the world / Rising o' the bones / Lovesick blues / Talkin' bluegrass / Black mountain juice / Mansion on the hill / When I was a cowboy / No place like home.
LP. . . . . WF 012
Waterfront / Mar '84 / SRD / Jazz Music / A.D.A Distribution / C.M. Distribution.

ROWAN, KEITH & ROONEY (Rowan, Peter & Bill Keith/Jim Rooney).
Tracks: Blue Ridge Mountain blues / Riding high in Texas / Outlaw love / Texican badman / Caravan / Midnight moonlight / Sleep with one eye open / Flint hill special / Tennessee blues / Auld lang syne.
LP. . . . . WF 016
Waterfront / Aug '85 / SRD / Jazz Music / A.D.A Distribution / C.M. Distribution.

T FOR TEXAS.
Tracks: T for Texas / Dustbowl children / Dreamed of a home / Before the streets were paved / Harvest is ready, The.
12" . . . . WFT 11
Waterfront / Apr '85 / SRD / Jazz Music / A.D.A Distribution / C.M. Distribution.
MC Single . . . . WFS 011 C
Waterfront / Jun '86 / SRD / Jazz Music / A.D.A Distribution / C.M. Distribution.

TEXICAN BAD MAN.
Tracks: Sweet Melinda / Four corners / Vacant sea, A / I can't help it / Squeeze box man / Texican badman / What of Alicia / While the ocean roars / Awake my love / On the blue horizon.
LP. . . . . AP 010
Appaloosa / Roots Records / C.M. Distribution / Wellard Dist. / Projection / Hot Shot / A.D.A Distribution.

WALLS OF TIME.
Tracks: Roving gambler / Lone pilgrim / Raglan Road / Going up the mountain / Casey's last ride / Moonshiner / Thirsty in the rain / Walls of time / Plains of waterloo.
LP. . . . . SH 3722
MC . . . . ZCSH 3722
Sugarhill(USA) / Oct '88 / Roots Records / Projection / Impetus Records / C.M. Distribution / Jazz Music / Swift / Duncans / A.D.A Distribution.

WILD STALLIONS.
Tracks: Not Advised.
LP. . . . . AP 016
Appaloosa / '88 / Roots Records / C.M. Distribution / Wellard Dist. / Projection / Hot Shot / A.D.A Distribution.

WITH THE RED HOT PICKERS.
Tracks: Not Advised.
LP. . . . . SPIN 108
MC . . . . SPIC 108
Spindrift / Jun '84 / C.M. Distribution / Roots Records / Projection.

Royal, Billy Joe

Born 03.04.1942 in Valdosta, Georgia, raised in Marietta, Georgia. Singer/guitarist/piano/drums. In high school he had his own band, the Corvettes. Debut recording was in 1962. He had a top ten US pop hit with Joe South's *Down in the boondocks* on Columbia, in 1965 (top 40 UK pop entry) the first of three hits penned and produced by South. His first country success came in 1985, when *Burned like a rocket* was a top ten hit. Other successes included *I'll pin a note on your pillow* and *Out of sight, out of mind* in 1987 and 1988 respectively. He had a smaller hit with his 1987 top 30 entry *Members only* , a duet with Donna Fargo. (Maurice Hope)

20 GREATEST HITS.
Tracks: Not Advised.
CD 26 42 052
MC 26 42 054
Point (2) / '92 / Sound Solutions.

DOWN IN THE BOONDOCKS.
Tracks: Not Advised.
CD . . . . .MMCD 5741
MC . . . . .MMMC 4741
Mammoth / Jun '92 / Revolver-APT / Pinnacle.

DOWN IN THE BOONDOCKS.
Tracks: Down in the boondocks.
■ 7" . . . . .CBS 201802
CBS / Oct '65.

HEART'S DESIRE.
Tracks: Heart's desire / Everybody's gotta cry.
■ 7" . . . . .CBS 202087
CBS / '66.

HOW DO I LIKE TO DANCE SLOWLY.
Tracks: How do I like to dance slowly.
■ 7" . . . . MER 36
Mercury / Oct '80.

ROYAL TREATMENT, THE.
Tracks: I'll pin a note on your pillow / Give 'em my number / He'll have to go / Look what you've done to my heart / Let it rain / It's who's in your heart / Out of sight and on my mind / It keeps right on a-hurtin' / She don't cry like she used to / Place for the heartache, A.
CD 790 658-2
LP. . . . . .K 790 658 1
MC . . . . .K 790 658 4
Atlantic / Aug '88 / WEA.

Russell, Calvin

CRACK IN TIME, A.
Tracks: Crack in time, A / Big brother / Nothin' / Behind the eight ball / Automated / North Austin slim / One step ahead / Living at the end of a gun / I should have been home / My way / This is my life / Little stars / Moments / Wagon to stars.
CD . . . . .ROSE 209 CD
LP. . . . . .ROSE 209
New Rose (1) / Jul '90 / Pinnacle.

CRACK IN TIME, A.
Tracks: Crack in time, A.
7" . . . . NEW 137
New Rose (1) / Dec '90 / Pinnacle.

Russell, Johnny

Singer who scored 28 hits between 1971-1987. Nevertheless he remains most famous as the writer of Buck Owens' classic *Act Naturally* also covered by The Beatles on *Help*. A member of The Grand Ole Opry since 1985 he has also toured the U.K. very successfully. His most famous recording was *Rednecks, Whitesocks and Blue Ribbon Beer*.(Tony Byworth).

COUNTRY STORE: JOHNNY RUSSELL.
Tracks: Act naturally / Rednecks, white socks and blue ribbon beer / Making plans / Good hearted woman / Busted / Kaw-liga / Working man blues / Catfish John / All I have to offer you is me / Blue eyes crying in the rain / Luckenbach, Texas / Jambalaya / Today I started loving you again / King of the road.
CD . . . . .CDCST 44
MC . . . . .CSTK 44
Country Store / '88 / BMG.
■ LP. . . . . CST 44
Country Store / '88.

MR. ENTERTAINER.
Tracks: Nobody touches my baby / Our marriage was a failure / Some day I'll sober up / Too late to turn back now / She goes walking through my mind / Over Georgia / She burnt the little roadside tavern down / Finer things in life, The / Queen of my heart / Remembering / Some kind of a woman / Leona / I'm staying / Your fool / This man and woman thing / What a price.
■ LP. . . . . NL 90000
RCA / Jan '87.
■ MC . . . . NK 90000
RCA / Jan '87.

SONG OF THE SOUTH.
Tracks: Song of the south / I'm getting holes in my boots.
■ 7" . . . . MER 68
Mercury / Apr '81.

Russell, Leon

Leon Russel was born in 1941 in Oklahoma: he is a singer, songwriter, pianist, guitarist, bandleader and producer. He formed his first band as a teenager and became one of the busiest session players of his generation, playing on most Phil Spector hits and in studios with everybody from Frank Sinatra to B.B.King. He formed the Asylum Choir in 1968 for two albums, practically stole the show from Joe Cocker on his famous *Mad Dogs And Englishmen* tour, swiping most of Deleaney and Bonnie's band for it; formed Shelter label, later Paradise; recorded with his wife Mary McClearey; helped Eric Clapton with his debut solo album; several of his own albums went top ten in the USA and his credits are as long as your arm, but never achieved the superstar status he seemed to deserve. Maybe it's better that way: he's made a lot of fine music. (Donald Clarke).

AMERICANA.
Tracks: Not Advised.
LP. . . . . K 56534
WEA / '78 / WEA.

ANYTHING CAN HAPPEN.
Tracks: Anything can happen / Black halos / No man's land / Too much monkey business / Angel ways / Life of the party / Stranded on Easy Street / Jezebel / Love slave / Faces of the children.
CD . . . . .CDVUS 50
Virgin America / Apr '92 / EMI.
■ MC . . . . VUSMC 50
Virgin America / Apr '92.

ASYLUM CHOIR.
Tracks: Not Advised.
CD . . . . NEXCD 152
Sequel / Apr '91 / Castle Communications / BMG / Hot Shot.

BEST OF LEON RUSSELL.
Tracks: Shoot out at the plantation / Delta lady / Hummingbird / Song for you / Tightrope / Stranger in a strange land.
■ LP. . . . . ISA 5013
Island / Jan '77.

CARNEY.
Tracks: Not Advised.
CD . . . . NEXCD 147
Sequel / Nov '90 / Castle Communications / BMG / Hot Shot.

COLLECTION: LEON RUSSELL.
Tracks: Not Advised.
CD . . . . CCSCD 313
Castle / Oct '91 / BMG.
■ MC . . . . .CCSMC 313
Castle / Oct '91.

ELVIS AND MARILYN.
Tracks: Elvis and Marilyn / Anita Bryant.
■ 7" . . . . K 17244
Paradise (1) / Oct '78.

HANK WILSONS BACK.
Tracks: Roll in my sweet baby's arms / Window up above, The / I'm so lonesome I could cry / I'll sail my ship alone / She thinks I still care / Six pack to go, A / Jambalaya / Uncle Pen / Battle of New Orleans / Am I that easy to forget ? / Truck drivin' man / Lost highway / Goodnight Irene.
CD . . . . NEXCD 139
Sequel / Oct '90 / Castle Communications / BMG / Hot Shot.

LADY BLUE.
Tracks: Lady blue / Laying right here in heaven.
■ 7" . . . . AMS 7199
A&M / Nov '75.

LEON RUSSELL.
Tracks: Not Advised.
CD . . . . NEXCD 146
Sequel / Nov '90 / Castle Communications / BMG / Hot Shot.

LEON RUSSELL AND THE SHELTER PEOPLE.
Tracks: Stranger in a strange land / Of thee I sing / Hard rains a-gonna fall / Crystal closet queen / Home

sweet Oklahoma / Alcatraz / Ballad of mad dogs and Englishmen, The / It takes a lot to laugh, it takes a train to cry / She smiles like a river / Sweet Emily / Beware of darkness / It's all over now, baby blue / Love minus zero / No limit / She belongs to me.
■ LP. . . . . **AMLS 65003**
A&M / Jul '71.
CD . . . . **NEXCD 137**
Sequel / Oct '90 / Castle Communications / BMG / Hot Shot.

LIVE ALBUM: LEON RUSSELL (Russell, Leon & New Grass Revival).
Tracks: Over the rainbow / I've just seen a face / One more love song / Pilgrim land / Georgia blues / I believe to my soul / Prince of peace / Rollin' in my sweet baby's arms / Stranger in a strange land / I want to be at the meeting / Wild horses / Jambalaya / Caribbean / Jumpin' Jack Flash.
■ LP. . . . . **K 56891**
WEA / Mar '81 / WEA.

MAIN STREET CAFE (Russell, Leon & Edgar Winter).
Tracks: Not Advised.
■ VHS. . . . . **HEN 2163**
Hendring Video / Aug '90.

ONE FOR THE ROAD (see under Nelson, Willie).

STOP ALL THAT JAZZ.
Tracks: Not Advised.
CD . . . . **NEXCD 151**
Sequel / Apr '91 / Castle Communications / BMG / Hot Shot.

TIGHT ROSE.
Tracks: Tight rose / Delta lady.
■ 7". . . . . **WIP 6290**
Island / Feb '77.

WILL O'THE WISP.
Tracks: Not Advised.
CD . . . . **NEXCD 157**
Sequel / Apr '91 / Castle Communications / BMG / Hot Shot.

Russell, Tom

Tom Russell a contemporary singer - songwriter of cult status,a much travelled artist. Through extensive touring Russell's built up a strong following in Europe, notably in Norway - where he's both recorded and had material debut there, all of which has now been made available on Philo and Irish label Round Tower Music (their compilation *Beyond St. Olav's gate 1979 - 1992* featuring many proven songs from Russell utilizing subjects such as old steel towns . *U.S. Steel* , the death of Bill Haley *Haley's comet* , and about a fighting cock in *Gallo Del Cillo*). His songs have been recorded by Johnny Cash (*Veteran's day*) Suzy Bogguss, Nanci Griffith (*Outbound plane* co - penned with Griffith) *Walkin' on the moon* (Janie Frickie and co - writer Katy Moffatt), and *Navajo rug* (with Canadian vetran Ian Tyson). Russell's initial recordings came during his days in West Texas, where he formed a duo with Patricia Hardin and won a folk festival competion with his entry *End of the trail* . His

prize, a $5,000 cheque, had the added bonus of a free trip to New York to collect it from the sponsors. Russell worked for a spell doing various jobs whilst living in New York but got back to playing and recording in the early 80s. *Heart on a sleeve* (1984), on his own Trail Music label, being the first of a string of albums he was to record -with and without the Tom Russell band. His latest Box of visions *gaining it's debut on RTM in early 1993*. *(Maurice Hope)*

BEYOND St. OLAV'S GATE 1979-1992 (Best Of Tom Russell).
Tracks: Not Advised.
CD . . . . **RTMCD 40**
MC . . . . **RTMMC 40**
Round Tower / Apr '93 / Pinnacle / A.D.A Distribution / ACD Trading Ltd. / Topic Records / Direct Distribution / BMG.

BOX OF VISIONS.
Tracks: Not Advised.
CD . . . . **RTMCD 54**
MC . . . . **RTMMC 54**
Round Tower / May '93 / Pinnacle / A.D.A Distribution / ACD Trading Ltd. / Topic Records / Direct Distribution / BMG.

COWBOY REEL.
Tracks: El Liano / Bad half hour, A / Basque, The / Claude Dallas / Navajo rug / Indian cowboy / Gallo del cielo / Rayburn Crane / Sonora's death row / Zane grey / Roanie.
CD . . . . **MRCD 161**
MC . . . . **MR 161**
Munich / '92 / C.M. Distribution / Swift / Cadillac Music / A.D.A Distribution / Hot Shot / Topic Records / Direct Distribution / New Note.

HEART ON A SLEEVE.
Tracks: One and one / Heart on a sleeve / Blinded by the light of love / Touch of grey / Wild hearts / St. Olav's gate / Gallo de cielo / Mandarin oranges / Cropduster / Canadian whiskey / Chinese silver / Bowl of red, A.
CD . . . . **BCD 15243**
Bear Family / Aug '86 / Rollercoaster Records / Swift / Direct Distribution.

HURRICANE SEASON (Russell, Tom Band).
Tracks: Black pearl / Lord of the trains / Beyond the blues / Jack Johnson / Chocolate cigarette / Winnipeg / Evangeline hotel, The / Dollar's worth of gasoline, A / Hurricane season / Haley's comet.
CD . . . . **RTMCD 49**
Round Tower / Jan '93 / Pinnacle / A.D.A Distribution / ACD Trading Ltd. / Topic Records / Direct Distribution / BMG.

POOR MAN'S DREAM (Russell, Tom Band).
Tracks: Blue wing / Heart of the working man / Veteran's day / Walkin' onthe moon / Outbound plane / Bergenfield / Spanish burgundy / Gallo del cielo / La frontera / Navajo rug / Under the gun / White trash song, The.
CD . . . . **PHCD 1139**
MC . . . . **PH 1139**
Philo (USA) / '92 / Roots Records / Projection / Topic Records / Direct Distribution / Ross Records / C.M. Distribution / Impetus Records.

POOR MANS DREAMS.
Tracks: Blue wing / Heart of a working man, The / Veteran's day / Walking on the moon / Outbound plane / Navajo rug / Spanish burgundy / Gallo de Cielo / La Frontera / Under the gun / Bergenfield.
LP. . . . . **RUSS LP 2**
Sonet / Aug '90 / Swift / C.M. Distribution / Roots Records / Jazz Music / Sonet Records / Cadillac Music / Projection / Wellard Dist. / Hot Shot.
CD . . . . **PH 1139CD**
MC . . . . **PH 1139C**
Philo (USA) / '92 / Roots Records / Projection / Topic Records / Direct Distribution / Ross Records / C.M. Distribution / Impetus Records.

ROAD TO BAYAMON (Russell, Tom Band).
Tracks: Home before dark / U.S. Steel / Downtown train / Love makes a fool of the wise / Defination of a fool, The / As the crow flies / Road to Bayamon, The / Alkai / Wise blood / Joshua tree / Mexcal / William Faulkner in Hollywood / Fire.
CD . . . . **PH 1116**
Philo (USA) / '88 / Roots Records / Projection / Topic Records / Direct Distribution / Ross Records / C.M. Distribution / Impetus Records.
LP. . . . . **ROUNDER 1116**
Rounder / '88 / Projection / Roots Records / Swift / C.M. Distribution / Topic Records / Jazz Music / Hot Shot / A.D.A Distribution / Direct Distribution.
MC . . . . **PH 1116C**
Philo (USA) / '88 / Roots Records / Projection / Topic Records / Direct Distribution / Ross Records / C.M. Distribution / Impetus Records.
CD . . . . **PH 1116CD**
Philo (USA) / '89 / Roots Records / Projection / Topic Records / Direct Distribution / Ross Records / C.M. Distribution / Impetus Records.

Ryan, Ron

AH YOU GOT YOUR EARS ON.
Tracks: Ah you got your ears on.
7". . . . . **BUFF 1004**
Buffalo (UK) / Sep '82 / M.I.S.Records.

NASSINGTON FLYER (see under Duffy Brothers).

Rye Whiskey Road Band

I DREAMED OF HIGHWAYS.
Tracks: No use running / I dreamed of highways / My elusive dreams / Help yourself to me / Catfish John / How much time does it take? / I know you've never been this far before / I recall a gypsy woman / Good to be back home again / Millers cave / Loving arms / I'm taking my love to my baby.
LP. . . . . **FHR 072**
Folk Heritage / Jul '82 / Terry Blood Dist.

RUNNING KIND, THE.
Tracks: Running kind, The / When my blue moon turns to gold again / Please Mr., please / Hurt so bad / Some broken hearts never mend / Does Fort Worth ever cross your mind / Sunshine / I've got a couple of more years on you babe / Feelings / Mexican girl / Down and out blues / What have you got planned tonight Diana.
LP. . . . . **FHR 107**
Folk Heritage / Jul '82 / Terry Blood Dist.

■ DELETED

S

Sadler, Sgt. Barry

BALLAD OF THE GREEN BERETS.
Tracks: Ballad of the Green Berets.
■ 7" . . . . RCA 1506
RCA / Mar '66.

SONGS OF OUR FIGHTING MEN.
Tracks: I'm a lucky one / Letter from Vietnam / Badge of courage / Saigon / Salute of the nurses / I'm watching the raindrops fall / Garet trooper / Soldier has come home, The / Lullaby / Trooper's lament / Bamba / Ballad of the Green Berets.
LP . . . . NL 83547
MC . . . . NK 83547
RCA International / Jul '84 / BMG.

Sahm, Doug

Texas singer, songwriter, bandleader Doug Sahm was born 6 November 1942 in San Antonio. His garage band the Sir Douglas Quintet had hits in the 60's including *She's about a mover*. He has moved on to roots music, bringing Tex-Mex, blues, country to his act; after a few years in San Francisco he relocated to Austin, Texas and was influenced in the 'outlaw' movement in country music there. (Donald Clarke).

BACK TO THE'DILLO (Sahm, Doug & Augie Meyers).
Tracks: Same ole story / Don't fight it / I pity the fool / Think / Oh Carol / Crazy arms / Buevo Laredo / Purple haze / Jazzer.
LP . . . . SNTF 890
Sonet / Jul '88 / Swift / C.M. Distribution / Roots Records / Jazz Music / Sonet Records / Cadillac Music / Projection / Wellard Dist. / Hot Shot.

DOUG SAHM & BAND (Sahm, Doug & Band).
Tracks: Is anybody going to San Antone / It's gonna be easy / Your friends / Poison love / Wallflower / Dealer's blues / Faded love / Blues stay away from me / Papa ain't salty / Me and Paul / Don't turn around / I get off.
LP . . . . ED 154
Edsel / Apr '85 / Pinnacle.
CD . . . . EDCD 154
Edsel / Aug '91 / Pinnacle.

DOUG SAHM LIVE.
Tracks: Dynamite woman / Rains came down, The / She's about a mover / Mendocino / San Antone / Papa ain't salty / Things I used to do, The / Mr. Pitiful / I'll go crazy / Next time you see me / Kansas City / Whiter shade of pale, A / Stagger Lee / Let's go, let's go, lets go.
CD . . . . BTCD 971401
Beartracks / Aug '88 / Rollercoaster Records.

FINALLY IN LIGHTS (see under Los Indios Tabajaros).

HELL OF A SPELL.
Tracks: Tunnel vision / Ain't into lettin' you go / All the way to nothing / Hanging on a thread / I'll take care of you / Things I used to do / I don't mind at all / Nothin' but the blues / Hell of a spell / Can't fake it / Next time you see me.
■ LP . . . . CHR 1249
Chrysalis / Jun '80.

JUKE BOX MUSIC.
Tracks: I won't cry / Crazy baby / Hey little girl / Money over love / You're mine tonight / It hurts to love someone / Buzz buzz buzz / She put the hurt on me / I don't believe / Chicken and the bop (Available on CD only) / Goodnight my love (Available on CD only) / My dearest darling / What's your name / Golly gee (Available on CD only) / Talk to me, talk to me.
CD . . . . CDCH 278
LP . . . . CH 278
Ace / Jun '89 / Pinnacle / Hot Shot / Jazz Music / Complete Record Co. Ltd.
MC . . . . ANTC 0008
Antones / Jan '93 / Hot Shot / Topic Records / Direct Distribution.

LIVE IN JAPAN (see under Los Indios Tabajaros).

LIVE: DOUG SAHM.
Tracks: Turn on your lovelight / Stagger Lee / Things I used to do, The / Papa ain't salty / He don't love you like I love you / Next time you see me / Mr. Pitiful / James Brown Medley / Think / Please please please / Night train.
LP . . . . TOP 172
MC . . . . KTOP 172
Topline / Apr '87 / Charly / Swift / Black Sun Records.

SIR DOUG'S RECORDING TRIP (Sahm, Doug & The Sir Douglas Quintet).
Tracks: Are inlaws really outlaws / Sell a song / I'm glad for your sake (but I'm sorry for mine) / Whole lotta peace of mind / You never get too big and you sure don't get too heavy.. / I wanna be your mama again / Mendocino / If you really want me to I'll go / And it didn't even bring me down / Lawd I'm just a country boy in this great big.. / Texas me / Nuevo laredo / Revolutionary ways / Be real / Catch the man on the rise / She's huggin' you, but she's lookin' at me / Keep your soul / Me and my destiny / Wasted days, wasted nights / Gypsy, The / Stoned faces don't lie / Michoacan / Sir Doug's recording trip / Sixty minutes of your love / In the dark / Dynamite woman / Linda Lou / Too many docile minds / You're doin' it too hard / Westside blues again.
Double LP . . . . DED 255
Edsel / Jun '88 / Pinnacle.

SIR DOUGLAS - HIS FIRST RECORDING.
Tracks: Just a moment / Sapphire / Why why why / Whirlaway / Baby tell me / More and more / Slow down / If you ever need me / Crazy Daisy / Can't believe you wanna leave.
■ LP . . . . CR 30188
Charly / Jan '81 / Charly.

SIR DOUGLAS-WAY BACK WHEN HE WAS JUST DOUG SAHM.
Tracks: Not Advised.
LP . . . . LP 8001
Rockhouse / Oct '88 / Charly / C.M. Distribution / Nervous Records.

TEXAS ROAD RUNNER.
Tracks: Not Advised.
LP . . . . BLP 701
Moonshine / May '86 / A.D.A Distribution / Projection / Swift / C.M. Distribution / Impetus Records / Ross Records / Duncans.

TEXAS TORNADO - BEST OF.
Tracks: Not Advised.
CD 8122710322
WEA / Jul '93 / WEA.

Sainte-Marie, Buffy

Singer, guitarist and songwriter Buffy Sainte-Marie was born in Canada in 1941. She was categorised as a folksinger but performed her own material from the beginning. She is part Red Indian and many of her songs reflect a wide-ranging interest in social issues. Six of her albums charted in the USA during the 1960's and most of them are still in print there, testifying to the loyalty of her fans and the lasting quality of her work. The PRT album in Britain is a "Best Of" from her classic Vanguard years. Her best-known song, Universal Soldier, was a hit for Donovan and has been covered many times. (Donald Clarke).

BEST OF BUFFY.
Tracks: Soulful shade of blues / Summer boy / Universal soldier / Better to find out for yourself / Cod'ine / He's a keeper of the fire / Until it's time for you to go / Rolling log blues / God is alive, magic is afoot / Guess who I saw in Paris / Piney wood hills / Now that the buffalo's gone / Take my hand for a while / Ground hog / Circle game / My country 'tis of thy people / You're dying / Many a mile / Cripple creek / I'm gonna be a country girl again / Vampire / Little wheel spin and spin / Winter boy / Los pescadores / Sometimes when I got to thinkin'.
Double LP . . . . VSD 3
Vanguard (Import) / Nov '84.

BEST OF BUFFY SAINTE-MARIE VOL 1.
Tracks: Not Advised.
CD . . . . VMCD 7309
LP . . . . VMLP 5309
MC . . . . VMTC 6309
Start / Mar '89.

BIG ONES GET AWAY, THE.
Tracks: Big ones get away, The / Big ones get away, The (instrumental) (Only on 12" and CD Single.) / I'm going home.
12" . . . . ENYX 650
7" . . . . ENY 650
CD Single . . . . ENYCD 650
MC Single . . . . ENYMC 650
Ensign / Jan '92 / EMI.

COINCIDENCE (AND LIKELY STORIES).
Tracks: Big ones get away, The / Fallen angels / Bad end / Emma Lee / Starwalker / Priests of the Golden Bull / Disinformation / Getting started / I'm going home / Bury my heart at Wounded Knee / Goodnight.
CD . . . . CCD 1920

MC . . . . ZCHEN 23
Ensign / Mar '92 / EMI.
■ LP . . . . CHEN 23
Ensign / Mar '92.

FALLEN ANGELS.
Tracks: Fallen angels / Soldier blue.
12" . . . . ENYX 655
7" . . . . ENY 655
CD Single . . . . ENYCD 655
■ MC Single . . . . ENYMC 655
Ensign / Jun '92.

GOLDEN HOUR OF BUFFY SAINTE-MARIE.
Tracks: Soldier blue (this is my country) / I'm gonna be a country girl again / Universal soldier / Cripple Creek / Now that the buffalo's gone / Many a mile / Soulful shade of blue, A / Little wheel, spin and spin / Suffer the little children / He's a pretty good man if you ask me / No one told me / Circle game, The / Until it's time for you to go / Song to a seagull / Just that kind of man / Guess who I saw in Paris / It's my way / She used to want to be a ballerina / Sweet memories / Carousel, The / Groundhog / Los Pescadores / Take my hand for a while.
LP . . . . GH 852
■ MC . . . . ZCGH 852
Golden Hour / '78 / Midland Records.

I'M GONNA BE A COUNTRY GIRL AGAIN.
Tracks: I'm gonna be a country girl again.
■ 7" . . . . VRS 35143
Vanguard / Mar '72.

IT'S MY WAY.
Tracks: Not Advised.
CD . . . . VMD 79142
Start / Oct '92.

NATIVE NORTH AMERICAN CHILD - AN ODYSSEY.
Tracks: Now that the buffalo's gone / Isketayo Sewow (Cree call) / He's an Indian cowboy in the rodeo / Poppies / It's my way / Moonshot: Soldier Blue / Way, way, way / Piney wood hills, The / My country 'tis of thy people you're dying / Native North American child / Little wheel spin and spin.
■ LP . . . . VSD 79340
Vanguard / '80 / Complete Record Co. Ltd.

SOLDIER BLUE.
Tracks: Soldier blue / I'm gonna be a country girl again.
■ 7" . . . . RCA 2081
RCA / Jul '71.
7" . . . . FBS 17
Flashback / Jan '83.

SOLDIER BLUE (OLD GOLD).
Tracks: Soldier blue / I'm gonna be a country girl again.
7" . . . . OG 9932
Old Gold / Jan '90 / Pickwick Records.

SPOTLIGHT ON BUFFY SAINTE-MARIE.
Tracks: Soldier blue / Universal soldier / My country 'tis of thy people / You're dying / Co'dine / Suffer the little children / She used to wanna be a ballerina / I'm gonna be a country girl again / Little wheel spin and spin / Cripple creek / Many a mile / Ground hog song to a seagull / Smackwater Jack / It's my way / Bells / Sweet September morning / Poppies / Moonshot / Until it's time for you to go / Los Pescadores / Now that the buffalo's gone / Piney wood hills / Song of the French partisan / Take my hand for a while.
Double LP . . . . SPOT 1018
MC Set . . . . ZCSPT 1018
PRT / Oct '81 / BMG.

Sam Brothers 5

LAFAYETTE ZYDECO.
Tracks: Not Advised.
LP . . . . ARHOOLIE 1081
Arhoolie (USA) / May '81 / Pinnacle / Cadillac Music / Swift / Projection / Hot Shot / A.D.A Distribution / Jazz Music.

Sampson, Don Michael

CRIMSON WINDS.
Tracks: Cherokee river / Long black train / Six string healing wheel / Old black guitar case / Fighter / Song in the wind.
CD . . . . R 103 CD
Red Horse / Aug '90 / BMG.

Sayers, Pete

CY-CLONE.
Tracks: Not Advised.
■ LP . . . . DBWLP 1006
Country Roads Records / Nov '81.

WATERMELON SUMMER.
Tracks: Watermelon summer / Raining in my heart / Dark hollow / Rawhide / Through the bottom of the glass / Turn your radio on / Fire on the mountain / Doin' my time / Chariots of fire / All I have to do is dream / Total stranger / Ukelele lady / Radio voices.
■ LP. . . . . XTRA 1168
Xtra / Jan '77.

Schatz, Lesley

BANJO PICKIN' GIRL.
Tracks: Winter it is past, The / Trouble in mind / Cruel sister / Barbara Allen / Little Joe, the wrangler / Zebra dun / Streets of Laredo / Jesse James / Tom Dula / Banjo pickin' girl / Early one morning / Arthur McBride / Jack O'Hazlegreen / Great Silkie / Silver dagger / Rowan tree / White coral bells / Flor del pino / Tumbalalaika / Will the circle be unbroken.
CD . . . . BCD 15729
Bear Family / May '93 / Rollercoaster Records / Swift / Direct Distribution.

BRAVE WOLFE.
Tracks: Red river valley / Gypsy Davy / Oh Susannah / Brave Wolfe / Banks of the Ohio, The / I never will marry / Greensleeves / Greenpeace / I ride an old paint / Shady grove / Rising sun blues / Train that carried my man from town, The / Shortnin' bread / Cripple creek / Mole in the ground / Old Joe Clarke / Nine pound hammer / Turkey in the straw / Sinner man / Careless love / Pretty little horses.
CD . . . . BCD 15735
Bear Family / May '93 / Rollercoaster Records / Swift / Direct Distribution.

COYOTE MOON/ RUN TO THE WIND.
Tracks: It's about time / Alberta blue / Freight train bound / Way she would sing, The / Printed word / Coyote moon / Boppin' at the gamble / Going home / Old tin pot / Les' wish / Alberta waltz / Molly and tenbrooks / To each his own / I'll be on the road again / Run to the wind / Chinese silver / Slow dance / Wind (stay away) / Only sound you'll hear, The / Empty hands.
CD . . . . BCD 15513
Bear Family / May '90 / Rollercoaster Records / Swift / Direct Distribution.

HELLO STRANGER.
Tracks: Hello stranger / Shenendoah / Wayfaring stranger, The / Wayfaring stranger, Thee / Apple blossom time / Beautiful river valley / Sweetest gift, The / Water is wide, The / Somewhere in Tennessee / Froggy went a-courtin' / Farewell to Nova Scotia / Home on the range / Down in the valley / Whiskey in the jar / Girl I left behind, The / Lily of the west, The / Did he mention my name / Spanish is a loving tongue / Cancion de cuna / La source / Brahm's lullaby.
CD . . . . BCD 15725
Bear Family / May '93 / Rollercoaster Records / Swift / Direct Distribution.

WALLS, HEARTS AND HEROES.
Tracks: Walls and borders / Gotta go (Bremen Train) / Dryland / Lonely bird / Back to your arms / Girl gone wild / Old old doll / Take a stand (for the children) / I can hear ya callin' / Foothill's lullaby / My heart stands (at your door) / Gypsy blue / Wastin' the moon / Merlin and the cowboy / I can dance (like Arthur Murray) / New crescent moon / Once a dream / Way o' walkin' / Old Wooley / Christmas wish, A / In the cabin walls / Un Canadien errant.
CD . . . . BCD 15674
Bear Family / Jun '92 / Rollercoaster Records / Swift / Direct Distribution.

Schlitz, Don

GAMBLER.
Tracks: Gambler, The / You can't take it with you.
■ 7" . . . . CL 16031
Capitol / Jan '79.

Schnaufer, David

DULCIMER SESSIONS.
Tracks: If she's gone, let her go / Blackberry blossom / Sandy / Down yonder / Lady Jane / Juley Calhoun / All I have to do is dream / Spaced out & blue / packington's pound/The Almaine / Orphan's picnic / Wait a minute / Santiago's shottis / Spanish Harlem / Wheeling / Ebeneezer/Fly around my pretty little Miss / Colours / Fisher's hornpipe.
CD . . . . SFL 005
SFL Tapes & Discs / Jul '92.

Schneider, John

Born 1954 in Mount Kisco, New York Schneider is best known for his role in the TV series *Dukes of Hazzard*. His singing career has benefitted from his strong singing voice and was also enhanced by his appearances with The Johnny Cash Showband. His first success was a cover of Presley's *It's Now or Never* on Scotti Brothers. He later scored four number ones on MCA. (Maurice Hope).

IN THE DRIVER'S SEAT.
Tracks: In the drivers seat / Let me love you.
■ 7" . . . . A 2231
Scotti Bros (USA) / Apr '82.

IT'S NOW OR NEVER.
Tracks: It's now or never / Stay.
■ 7" . . . . EPCA 1411
Epic / Oct '81.

MEMORY LIKE YOU, A.
Tracks: What's a memory like you (doin' in a love like this) / You're the last thing I needed tonight / Who cares / Somebody's gonna love her / Old rainbow jukebox and you, An / If we can't have forever (let's take tonight) / One more night / He finally made up her mind / One who got away, The / Welcome home.
■ LP. . . . . IMCA 5668
MCA (Import) / Mar '86.
CD . . . . MCAD 5668
MCA / May '87 / BMG.

TAKE THE LONG WAY HOME.
Tracks: At the sound of the tone / Broken promised land / She's ready for someone to love her / Sounds like something I would say / Better class of losers / Gettin'even / Auction, The / This time / Just when / Take the long way home.
LP. . . . . MCF 3348
MCA / Nov '86 / BMG.
■ MC . . . . MCFC 3348
MCA / Nov '86.
CD . . . . MCAD 5789
MCA / Apr '87 / BMG.

WHAT'S A MEMORY LIKE YOU (DOIN' IN A LOVE LIKE THIS).
Tracks: What's a memory like you (doin' in a love like this).
7" . . . . MCA 1156
MCA / Aug '87 / BMG.

YOU AIN'T SEEN THE LAST OF ME.
Tracks: I lost my head last night / So good / When the right one comes along / Angelena / If it was anyone but you / Hillbilly boy with the rock 'n' roll blues / Credit / Gunfighter, The / Redneck is the backbone of America, A / Love, you ain't seen the last of me.
CD . . . . DMCF 3375
LP. . . . . MCF 3375
■ MC . . . . MCFC 3375
MCA / Jun '87.

Schwartz, Tracy

New York born, New Jersey/Vermont-raised fiddler/guitarist. Served two years in Germany before joining the New Lost City Ramblers in 1963 (an old time bluegrass band), featuring founder members Mike Seeger and John Cohen, Schwartz replaced Tom Paley. Shared the stage with Maybelle Carter, Cousin Emmy and Dewey Balfa among others and also helped to form the Strange Creek Singers with Hazel Dickens, Alice Gerrard, Lamar Grier and Mike Seeger. During the 1970's and after the group had disbanded in 1973 (only occasionally reforming for celebration concerts) Schwartz played alongside wife Eloise and son Peter as Tracy's Family Band. He travelled to Louisiana to learn the cajun fiddle, enjoyed a spell working with the late Dewey Balfa and nephew Tony - playing as the Four Bachelors. Both with and without Eloise he has recorded for the Folk Variety and Folkways labels. (Maurice Hope)

HOME AMONG THE HILLS (Schwarz, Tracey & Eloise).
Tracks: Home among the hills / Wild Bill Jones / Wayworn traveller, The / Green valley waltz / Keep my skillet good and greasy / I'll never forsake you / Where the soul of man never dies / Uncle Henry / Meet me tonight in the moonlight / Blind child, The / John Henry / When the bees are in the goldenrod / How beautiful Heaven must be / Fly around my pretty little miss.
LP. . . . . BF 15007
Bear Family / Oct '80 / Rollercoaster Records / Swift / Direct Distribution.

Scoggins, Hoyt

TENNESEE ROCK.
Tracks: Tennessee rock / Why did we fall in love.
■ 7" . . . . NS 53
Ace / Jul '79.

Scots Country Comfort

STILL ROLLIN'.
Tracks: Uncle pen / Time changes everything / Devil went down to Georgia / Rocky top / Lend me your heart / Hank Williams lullabies / Louisiana cajun band / My window faces the south / Big mamou / Me and Paul / Randy Lynn Rag / Makes me wonder / Arcadian rose / Shall we meet.
LP. . . . . WGR 043
Ross (1) / Sep '82 / Ross Records / Duncans / Entertainment UK.
MC . . . . CWGR 043
Ross (1) / Oct '92 / Ross Records / Duncans / Entertainment UK.

Scott, Ellie

LOOK FOR ME.
Tracks: Look for me / Heart over mind / Together again / Dog like that / I wouldn't want to live / In my Tennessee mountain home / Come on Ellie / My grandfather's clock / Almost persuaded / Before I met you / Little green valley / Without knowing.
LP. . . . . BSS 310
Tank / Sep '79.

Scott, Jack

Rock'n'roll singer and songwriter turned country artist Jack Scott was born in 1936, grew up in Detroit listening to country music on the radio. His series of hit singles with a rocker on one side and a ballad on the other began with *Leroy/My True Love* in 1958, his deep voice combined with excellent recorded sound for the period. He had hits on Top Rank and Capitol, veered towards a country sound on the RCA subsidiary Groove in 1963 as the original pure rock'n'roll lost ground in the marketplace. (Donald Clarke).

BURNING BRIDGES.
Tracks: What in the world's come over you / Burning bridges / Oh, little one / Cool water / Patsy / Is there something on your mind / My dream come true / Steps one and two / All I see is blue / Laugh and the world laughs with you / It only happened yesterday / Little feeling called love, A.
MC . . . . JAS C305
Jasmine / Feb '88 / Wellard Dist. / Swift / Swift / Scott Butler Distribution / Jazz Music.
LP. . . . . JAS 305
Jasmine / Jan '88 / Wellard Dist. / Swift / Swift / Scott Butler Distribution / Jazz Music.

BURNING BRIDGES.
Tracks: Burning bridges.
■ 7" . . . . JAR 375
Top Rank (1) / Jun '60.

CAPITOL COLLECTORS SERIES: JACK SCOTT.
Tracks: What in world's come over you / Baby baby / Burning bridges / Oh, little one / True love is blind / It only happened yesterday / Cool water / Patsy / Lonesome Mary / Is there something on your mind / Little feeling (called love), A / Now that I / True true love / My dream come true / Strange desire / Steps 1 & 2 / One of these days / Fancy meeting you / Cry, cry, cry / You only see what you wanna see / I can't hold your letters (in my arms) / Sad story / If only.
■ CD . . . . CZ 381
Capitol / Jan '91.

CLASSIC SCOTT.
Tracks: Greaseball / Baby she's gone / You can bet your bottom dollar / Two timin' woman / I need your love / My true love / Leroy / With your love / Indiana waltz / No one will ever know / I can't help it / I'm dreaming of you / Midgie / Save my soul / Geraldine / Goodbye baby / Way I walk, The / I never felt like this / Bella / Go wild little Sadie / What am I living for / There'll come a time / Baby Marie / Baby, baby / What in the world's come over you / Goo deal Lucille / Oh little one / So used to loving you / Cruel world / Window shopping / Burning bridges / Your cheatin' heart / I can't escape from you / Cold, cold heart / I could never be ashamed of you / They'll never take her love from me / Crazy heart / You win again / Half as much / I'm sorry for you my friend / Take these chains from my heart / My heart would know / May you never be alone / It's my way of loving you / My King / I'm satisfied with you / Am I the one / It only happened yesterday / True love is blind / Fancy meeting you again / Cool water / Take my hand precious Lord / When the Saints go marching in (take 8) / Swing low sweet chariot / Ezekial saw the wheel / Joshua saw the battle of Jericho / Little David play your harp / Roll Jordan roll / Down by the riverside / Old time religion / Gospel train, The / I want to be ready / Just a closer walk with thee / He'll understand & say well done / Lonesome Mary / Patsy / Is there something on your mind / Found a woman / Little feeling (called love), A / Now that I / True true love / One of these days / Strange desire / My dream come true / Steps one & two / Sad story / You only see what you wanna see / I can't hold your letters (on my arms) / Cry cry cry / Grizzly bear / Part where I cried, The / If only (take 8) / Green green valley / Strangers / Laugh & the world laughs with you / Meo myo / All I see is blue / Jingle bell slide / There's trouble brewin' / Thou shalt not steal / I knew you first / I prayed for an angel / Blue skies (movin' in on me) / What a wonderful night out / Wiggle on out / Tall tales / Flakey John / Seperation's now granted / I don't believe in tea leaves / Standing on the outside looking in / Looking for Linda / I hope, I wish, I think / Gone again / Let's learn to live & love again / Don't hush the laughter / This is where I came in / Road keeps winding, The / With your love (stereo) / Indiana waltz (stereo) / No one will ever know (stereo) / I can't help it (stereo) / I'm dreaming of you (stereo) / Midgie (stereo) / Save my soul (stereo) / Geraldine (stereo) / Goodbye baby (stereo) / Way I walk, The (stereo) / If only (take 15) / When the Saints go marching in (take 19) / Go away from here (crying in my beer) / Before the bird flies / Insane / My special angel / I keep changing my mind / Hard luck Joe / Billy Jack / Mary, marry me / Face to the wall / I still love you enough / As you take a walk through my mind / You make it hard not to love you / You're just not gettin'

better / Apple blossom time / Blues stay away from me / Stones / Bo's going to jail / Country witch.
CD Set . . . . BCD 15534
Bear Family / Aug '92 / Rollercoaster Records / Swift / Direct Distribution.

GREASEBALL.
Tracks: Greaseball (Previously unissued) / Lonesome Mary (Previously unissued) / Cryin' in my beer (Previously unissued) / Troubles brewin' (Previously unissued) / True love is blind (Previously unissued) / Precious Lord (Previously unissued) / Baby baby / Good deal Lucille / You can bet your bottom dollar / I'm satisfied with you / Bella / Baby Marie.
LP. . . . . DJLP 2050
Bison Bop / Jun '85 / C.M. Distribution / Swift.
LP. . . . . BB 2050
Buffalo Bop (Germany) / '88.

GRIZZILY BEAR.
Tracks: Two timin' woman / Baby she's gone / You can bet your bottom dollar / Baby baby / Found a woman / Oh little one / Patsy / Cruel world / Good deal Lucille / What in the world's come over you / Burning bridges / It only happened yesterday / Now that I / Steps one and two / Little feeling called love, A / Strange desire / My dream come true / One of these days / Grizzly bear / Cry cry cry / You only see what you wanna see / Part where I cry, The / Strangers / Laugh and the world laughs with you / Meo myo / Sad story / I can't hold your letters / If only / Green green valley / Before the bird flies / May you never be alone / Insance / Face to the wall / You're just getting better / As you take a walk through my mind.
■ **Double LP** . . . . CDX 12
Charly / May '86 / Charly.

I REMEMBER HANK WILLIAMS.
Tracks: Not Advised.
■ **LP.** . . . . BUY 034
Top Rank (1) / May '60.

JACK SCOTT.
Tracks: Baby she's gone / Two timin' woman / What am I living for / Go wild / Little Sadie / There comes a time / I never felt like this / With your love / Leroy / Geraldine / Way I walk, The / Midgie / My true love / Save my soul / Goodbye baby.
LP. . . . . BB 2022
LP P.Disc. . . . . BB 2035
Buffalo Bop (Germany) / '88.

JACK SCOTT (16 TRACKS).
Tracks: Not Advised.
LP. . . . . KK 794
Krazy Kat / Dec '84 / Hot Shot / C.M. Distribution / Wellard Dist. / Roots Records / Projection / Charly / Jazz Music.

LEGENDARY, THE.
Tracks: Not Advised.
LP. . . . . BBR 1003
Mini LP. . . . . BBR 0024
Rockstar (1) / Sep '82 / Swift / C.M. Distribution.

MY TRUE LOVE.
Tracks: My true love.
■ **7"** . . . . HLU 8626
London-American / Oct '58.

ROCKS.
Tracks: Leroy / Geraldine / Way I walk, The / Goodbye baby.

SCOTT ON GROOVE.
Tracks: Flakey John / Jingle bell slide / There's trouble brewin / Tall tales / Wiggle on out / I knew you first / Blue skies (moving in on me) / I prayed for an angel / Separation's now granted / Thou shalt not steal / Road keeps winding, The (Previously unissued) / Let's learn to live and love again / Don't hush the laughter / This is where I came in (Previously unissued) / Looking for Linda / I hope, I think, I wish / Standing on the outside looking in (Previously unissued) / Gone again (Previously unissued) / I don't believe in tealeaves / What a wonderful night out.
LP. . . . . BFX 15005
Bear Family / Sep '84 / Rollercoaster Records / Swift / Direct Distribution.
CD . . . . BCD 15445
Bear Family / '88 / Rollercoaster Records / Swift / Direct Distribution.

SPIRIT MOVES ME, THE.
Tracks: Not Advised.
LP. . . . . RM 348
Top Rank (1) / Nov '87.

WAY I WALK, THE.
Tracks: Leroy / Midgie / Way I walk, The / Goodbye baby / Go wild Little Sadie / Geraldine / Save my soul / Baby she's gone / Two timin' woman / I never felt like this / My true love / I'm dreaming of you / With your love / I can't help it / No one will ever know / Indiana waltz / Baby Marie / Bella / There comes a time / I need your love / You can bet your bottom dollar / What am I living for / There's trouble brewing / Lonesome Mary / Greaseball.
CD . . . . RCCD 3002
Rollercoaster / Aug '90 / Rollercoaster Records / Swift.

WAY I WALK, THE.
Tracks: Way I walk, The.
■ **7"** . . . . HLL 8912
London-American / Sep '59.

WHAT IN THE WORLD'S COME OVER YOU.
Tracks: Not Advised.
■ **LP.** . . . . BUY 024
Top Rank (1) / Sep '60.

WHAT IN THE WORLD'S COME OVER YOU.
Tracks: What in the world's come over you.
■ **7"** . . . . JAR 280
Top Rank (1) / Mar '60.

Scratch Band

SCRATCH BAND FEATURING DANNY FLOWERS.
Tracks: Not Advised.
LP. . . . . MCF 3136
MCA / May '82 / BMG.

Scruggs, Earl

Born Earl Eugene Scruggs in 1924 in Flintvillo, North Carolina. Played with The California Wildcats and The Morris Brothers prior to joining Bill Monroe in 1945. He then left to play with Lester Flatt as Lester & Earl & The Foggy Mountain Boys. In 1950 they moved from Mercury to Columbia while in 1953 they began their own radio show, the obviously sponsored *Martha White Biscuit Time*. In 1955 they joined the Grand Ole Opry with Josh Graves joining on dobro. They gained recognition when the songs *Ballad of Jed Clampett* and *Foggy Mountain Breakdown* were used in the TV show *Beverley Hillbillies* and film *Bonnie and Clyde* respectively. Flatt and Scruggs split in 1969. Scruggs then formed the Earl Scruggs Review scoring top 50 country hits with *Blue Moon of Kentucky* and *I sure use this feeling*. He has since recorded with, amongst others, Tom T.Hall, Ricky Skaggs and The Nitty Gritty Dirt Band.(Maurice Hope).

TOP OF THE WORLD.
Tracks: Sittin' on top of the world / We'll meet again / Sweetheart / Could you love me one more time / Love gone cold / Lindsey / Carolina star / Till the end of the world rolls round / Paradise / Lay me down in Dixie / Rollercoaster.
LP. . . . . CBS 25097
CBS / Mar '83 / Sony.

Sea Train

BEST OF SEA TRAIN & MARBLED MESSENGER,THE.
Tracks: Oh my love / Sally Goodin / Creepin' midnight / I'm willin' / Song of job / Home to you / 13 questions / Marbleheaded messenger / London songs / Gramercy / State of Georgia's mind / Losing all the years / Mississippi moon / How sweet thy song.
LP. . . . . SEE 96
See For Miles / Jun '87 / Pinnacle.

SEA TRAIN.
Tracks: Sea train / Let the duchess know / Pudding street / Portrait of the lady as a young artist / As I lay here losing / Rondo / Sweet creek's suite / Outwear the hills.
CD . . . . ED CD 196
LP. . . . . ED 196
Edsel / Nov '86 / Pinnacle.

Seals, Dan

Born and brought up in Texas, Seals began as something of a child prodigy in the family band. Later formed Southwest F.O.B. with John Ford Coley. His country venture began on the Liberty label where he charted with *Everybody's Dream* and *God Must be a Cowboy*. His first number one was *Meet me in Montana* a duet with Marie Osmond recorded in 1985. He then scored a series of highly successful country singles most notable of which was *Bop* which was awarded the CMA's single of the year in 1986.(Maurice Hope).

ADDICTED.
Tracks: Addicted / Maybe I'm missing you now.
■ **7"** . . . . CL 504
Capitol / Sep '88.

BEST OF DAN SEALS, THE.
Tracks: Three time loser / God must be a cowboy / My baby's got good timing / You still move me / Bop / Everything that glitters (is not gold) / Meet me in Montana / You bring out the wild of me / My old yellow car / I will be there (remix) / One friend.
CD . . . . CDEST 2049
■ **LP.** . . . . EST 2049
Capitol / Nov '87.
■ **MC** . . . . TCEST 2049
Capitol / Nov '87.

BOP.
Tracks: Bop / In San Antone.
7" . . . . EA 214
EMI-America / Apr '86 / EMI.

ON ARRIVAL.
Tracks: Good times / Made for lovin' you / Wood / She flew the coupe / Bordertown / Water under the bridge / Love on arrival / Heart in search of love, A / Lonestar / Game of love.
CD CDC1 91782
■ **MC** C4 91782
Capitol / Apr '90.

ON THE FRONT LINE.
Tracks: On the front line / Three time loser / Fewer threads than these / Gonna be easy now / Guitar man out of control / I will be there / You still move me / While I'm here / I'm still strung out on you / Lullaby.
■ **CD** . . . . CDP 746 352 2
EMI / Jan '87.
LP. . . . . AML 3114
■ **MC** . . . . TCAML 3114
EMI-America / Mar '87.

RAGE ON.
Tracks: Big wheels in the moonlight / They rage on / Five generations of rock county Wilsons / Twenty four hour love / Factory town / Addicted / Heartache just around the bend, A / Maybe I'm missing you now / Fool me once, fool me twice / Long Long Island nights / Those.
CD . . . . CDEST 2070
LP. . . . . EST 2070
■ **MC** . . . . TCEST 2070
Capitol / Oct '88.

SAN ANTONE.
Tracks: Not Advised.
CD . . . . CDP 746 596-2
EMI-America / Apr '87 / EMI.

WON'T BE BLUE ANYMORE.
Tracks: Heading West / I won't be blue anymore / Everything that glitters is not gold / Tobacco Road / Your love / You plant your fields / Still a little bit of love / Meet me in Montana / Bop / So easy to need / City kind of girl.
■ **CD** . . . . CDP 746 559 2
Capitol / Apr '87.

Sebastian, John B

JOHN B SEBASTIAN.
Tracks: Red-eye express / She's a lady / What she thinks about / Magical connection / You're a big boy / Rainbows all over your blues / How have you been / Baby, don't ya get crazy / Room nobody lives in, The / Fa-fana-fa / I had a dream.
CD . . . . EDCD 304
LP. . . . . ED 304
Edsel / Jan '90 / Pinnacle.

Seely, Jeannie

DON'T TOUCH ME.
Tracks: Don't touch me / You tied tin cans to my heart.
■ **7"** . . . . HLU 10052
London-American / Jun '66.

GREATEST HITS: JACK GREENE & JEANNIE SEELY (see under Greene, Jack).

Seldom Scene

Washington - formed (1971) bluegrass aggregation, it's founder members consisting of John Duffy (mandolin/tenor vocals), Mike Auldridge (dobro/vocals), John Starling (guitar/lead vocals) Ben Eldridge (banjo/vocals) and Tom Gray (bass - replaced in 1986 by T. Michael Coleman). Held the Thursday evening resident spot at the Red Fox Inn, Bethesda, Maryland, and then at the Birchmere in Alexandria, Virginia throughout the group's history. The line-up saw them through to 1977, when John Starling took off in pursuit of a solo career (although not before they'd established a winning sound-blending old and new bluegrass elements). Phil Rosenthal, (a singer -songwriter) took Starling's place while they were still with Rebel Records, before moving to Sugar Hill in the early 1980s. Starling returned on Lou Reid's departure in 1992 as lead vocalist. (Maurice Hope)

ACT 3.
Tracks: Chim chim cheree / Little Georgia Rose / Another lonely day / Willie boy / Faded love / Rider / Muddy water / Sing me back home / Hail to the redskins / Don't bother me with white satin / Heaven.
CD . . . . REBCD 1528
LP. . . . . REB 1528
MC . . . . REBMC 1528
Rebel (1) / '75 / Projection / Backs Distribution.

ACT 4.
Tracks: Not Advised.
LP. . . . . SH 3709
MC . . . . ZCSH 3709
Sugarhill(USA) / '80 / Roots Records / Projection / Impetus Records / C.M. Distribution / Jazz Music / Swift / Duncans / A.D.A Distribution.

AFTER MIDNIGHT.
Tracks: Not Advised.
LP. . . . . SH 3721

■ DELETED S 3

MC . . . . ZCSH 3721
Sugarhill(USA) / '88 / Roots Records / Projection / Impetus Records / C.M. Distribution / Jazz Music / Swift / Duncans / A.D.A Distribution.

AT THE SCENE.
Tracks: Girl I know, A / Jamaica say you will / Open up the window, Noah / Winter wind / Heal it / Weary pilgrim, The / It turns inside out / Champion, The / Born of the wind / Peaceful dreams.
LP. . . . . SH 3736
Sugarhill(USA) / Mar '89 / Roots Records / Projection / Impetus Records / C.M. Distribution / Jazz Music / Swift / Duncans / A.D.A Distribution.
CD . . . . SHCD 3726
MC . . . . SHMC 3726
Sugarhill(USA) / '92 / Roots Records / Projection / Impetus Records / C.M. Distribution / Jazz Music / Swift / Duncans / A.D.A Distribution.

BAPTIZING.
Tracks: By the side of the road / Brother John / Dreaming of a little cabin / Fallen leaves / He took your place / Take him in / Hobo on a freight train to heaven / Will you be ready to go home / Were you there / Walk with you again / Gospel medley.
LP. . . . . REB 1573
MC . . . . REBMC 1573
Rebel (1) / '75 / Projection / Backs Distribution.
LP. . . . . SAVE 035
Fundamental / '88 / Plastic Head.

BEST OF SELDOM SCENE, THE.
Tracks: Not Advised.
CD . . . . REBCD 1101
Rebel (1) / '75 / Projection / Backs Distribution.

CHANGE IN SCENERY, A.
Tracks: Breaking new ground / Casting a shadow in the road / Settin' me up / Alabama clay / I'll be a stranger there / West Texas wind / Satan's choir / In despair / What goes on / One way rider.
CD . . . . SHCD 3763
LP. . . . . SH 3763
MC . . . . ZCSH 3763
Sugarhill(USA) / '88 / Roots Records / Projection / Impetus Records / C.M. Distribution / Jazz Music / Swift / Duncans / A.D.A Distribution.

LIVE AT THE CELLAR DOOR.
Tracks: Doing my time / California cottonfield's / Panhandle country / Muddy waters / Rawhide / Baby blue / City of New Orleans / Grandfather's clock / Fields have turned brown, The / Hit parade of love / Will the circle be unbroken / Pickaway / Dark hollow / Small exception of me / If I were a carpenter / Old gray bonnet / C & O canal / Georgia rose / Colorado turnaround / He rode all the way to Texas / White line / Rider.
Double LP . . . . REB 1547/48
MC Set . . . . REBC 1547/48
Rebel (1) / '75 / Projection / Backs Distribution.
CD . . . . CD 1103
Rebel (1) / '85 / Projection / Backs Distribution.

LIVE: CELEBRATION 15TH ANNIVERSARY.
Tracks: Sitting on top of the world / Big train from Memphis / Lorena / Dark as a dungeon / Blue Ridge / Raised by the railroad line / Don't know my mind / Drifting too far from the shore / Those memories of you / Keep me from blowing away / Wheels / Carolyn at the broken wheel inn / If I needed you / Rose of old Kentucky / I couldn't find my walkin' shoes / Workin' on a building / Say you lied / High on a hilltop / Sweetest gift, The / Take me on your life boat.
CD . . . . SHCD 2202
LP. . . . . SH 2202
MC . . . . ZCSH 2202
Sugarhill(USA) / '88 / Roots Records / Projection / Impetus Records / C.M. Distribution / Jazz Music / Swift / Duncans / A.D.A Distribution.

NEW SELDOM SCENE ALBUM, THE.
Tracks: Not Advised.
CD . . . . REBCD 1561
LP. . . . . REB 1561
MC . . . . REBMC 1561
Rebel (1) / '75 / Projection / Backs Distribution.

OLD TRAIN.
Tracks: Not Advised.
CD . . . . REBCD 1536
LP. . . . . REB 1536
MC . . . . REBMC 1536
Rebel (1) / '75 / Projection / Backs Distribution.

SCENE 20 20TH ANNIVERSARY SPECIAL.
Tracks: Intro: Haven't I got the right to love you / Gardens & memories / House of gold / Picture's of life's other side / Satan's jewelled crown / Will you ready to go home / Were you there / Weary pilgrim, The / Leavin' harlan / Take him in / Stompin' at the Savoy / Something in the wind / Muddy water / Open up the window / Breakin' new ground / Old train / Wait a minute / Blue ridge cabin home / Gypsy moon / In the pines / And on bass / Another lonesome day / Have my mercy on my soul / House of the rising sun/Walk don't run / In the midnight hour.
CD SH-CD-2501 02
MC SH-MC-2501-02
Sugarhill(USA) / '92 / Roots Records / Projection / Impetus Records / C.M. Distribution / Jazz Music / Swift / Duncans / A.D.A Distribution.

SCENIC ROOTS.
Tracks: If you ever change your mind / Lost in your memory / Wrath of God, The / Before I met you / Red Georgia Clay / I've cried my last tear / Not in my arms / Highway of heartache / Long black veil / Last call to glory / Distant train / How mountain girls can love.
CD . . . . SHCD 3785
LP. . . . . SH 3785
MC . . . . ZCSH 3785
Sugarhill(USA) / '90 / Roots Records / Projection / Impetus Records / C.M. Distribution / Jazz Music / Swift / Duncans / A.D.A Distribution.

SELDOM SCENE VOL. 1.
Tracks: Not Advised.
LP. . . . . REB 1511
MC . . . . REBMC 1511
Rebel (1) / '75 / Projection / Backs Distribution.

SELDOM SCENE VOL. 2.
Tracks: Not Advised.
LP. . . . . REB 1520
MC . . . . REBMC 1520
Rebel (1) / '75 / Projection / Backs Distribution.

Seratt, Kenny

Born in Manila, Arkansas; raised in Dyess, Arkansas and then California. Traditional country/honky-tonk styled vocalist in the Merle Haggard vein. This isn't surprising, for he was with Haggard for four years after making his comeback in 1972 after a five year lay-off. Seratt an outdoor man, had been ranching and felling timber in Trout Creek, Montana. Previous to which he'd held a slot at the Ramanada in Hermet, California for 11 years. During the 1970's he recorded for MGM, Melodyland, Hitsville and MDJ, with modest hits acquired on them all. His 1980 releases *Saturday in Dallas* (No. 54) and *Until the bitter end* (No. 39) polling the highest. A popular visitor to the UK playing the halls and club circuit, had material released on Drew Taylor's Big R label, including *Give me a title and I'll give you a song* recorded live at the Grapevine Opry in Texas. (Maurice Hope)

DIESEL DEVIL.
Tracks: Diesel devil / Queen of the road.
7" . . . . BRS 06
Big R / Dec '81 / Pinnacle.

GIVE ME A TITLE AND I'LL WRITE YOU A SONG.
Tracks: Give me a title and I'll write you a song / Always chasing rainbows / Hide me / What do you do when it's over / There's just one way / Too many bar rooms / Nothing good in goodbye / That silver haired daddy of mine / Don't put Grandma in a rest home / Jesus makes the sunshine in my life.
LP. . . . . BRA 1005
MC . . . . BRC 1005
Big R / Nov '80 / Pinnacle.

RIDIN' THE BIG A.
Tracks: Ridin' the big A / Queen of the road / It ain't no good to love a truck drivin' man / Diesel devil / I'm truckin' my way to glory / Jody's on the run / I've got a truck / No longer mine / Six days on the road / White blind fever / Snow on the mountain.
LP. . . . . BRA 1007
MC . . . . BRC 1007
Big R / Nov '80 / Pinnacle.

SATURDAY NIGHT IN DALLAS.
Tracks: Saturday night in Dallas / Bitter end, The / Most wanted woman / Sidewalks are grey / Damn good drinking song / Honky tonk nights / We made memories / Never gonna be a country star / Giving up easy / Hung over on love.
LP. . . . . BRA 1002
MC . . . . BRC 1002
Big R / Nov '80 / Pinnacle.

SATURDAY NIGHT IN DALLAS.
Tracks: Saturday night in Dallas / Bitter end.
7" . . . . BRS 02
Big R / Nov '80 / Pinnacle.

Shady Grove Band

MULBERRY MOON.
Tracks: Not Advised.
CD . . . . FF 544CD
LP. . . . . FF 544
MC . . . . FF 544C
Flying Fish (USA) / '92 / Cadillac Music / Roots Records / Projection / C.M. Distribution / Direct Distribution / Jazz Music / Duncans / A.D.A Distribution.

ON THE LINE.
Tracks: Not Advised.
LP. . . . . FF 462
Flying Fish (USA) / Feb '89 / Cadillac Music / Roots Records / Projection / C.M. Distribution / Direct Distribution / Jazz Music / Duncans / A.D.A Distribution.

Shaking Down The Acorns

SHAKING DOWN THE ACORNS.
Tracks: Not Advised.
LP. . . . . ROUNDER 0018
Rounder / '88 / Projection / Roots Records / Swift / C.M. Distribution / Topic Records / Jazz Music / Hot Shot / A.D.A Distribution / Direct Distribution.

Shaver, Billy Joe

Singer - songwriter, born Corsicana, Texas in 1941 raised in Waco, Texas. Best known for his expertise as a songwriter, having written songs for Waylon Jennings (who in 1973 featured no fewer than nine of his songs on his RCA album *Honky tonk heroes*), John Anderson, Bobby Bare (*Ride me down easy*), Johnny Cash (*I've been to Georgia on a fast train , I'm Just an old chunk of coal..*), Doug Kershaw (*Black rose*), Tom T. Hall (*Old five and dimers*), along with hits for George Jones, Jerry Reed, Johnny Rodriguez and Dottie West among a host of others. It was Anderson, with the well covered *I'm just an old chunk of coal* , who gave him his first No. 1. Shaver's own recordings include the Capricorn *When I get my wings* (1976), *Gypsy boy* (1977) and the 1981 Columbia release *I'm just an old chunk of coal* . These are particularly fine examples of his ability. Only twice has he reached the Billboard charts, with the 1970's singles *I've been to Georgia on a fast train* and *You asked me to* (Jennings having a hit with this in 1973). One of the best singer - songwriters to emerge during the fertile 1970s. (Maurice Hope)

HELL RAISERS (I love country) (Shaver, Billy Joe & Johnny Paycheck).
Tracks: I'm just an old chunk of coal / Old five and dimers like me / Fit to kill and going out in style / When the word was thunderbird / AMTRAK (and ain't coming back) / Oklahoma wind / Saturday night / I been to Georgia on a fast train / Take this job and shove it / She's all I got / Drinkin' and drivin' / I'm the only hell (mama ever raised) / Fifteen beers ago / Turnin' off a memory / You better move on / Outlaw's prayer, The.
■ LP. 4504331
CBS / Mar '87.

Shaw, Eddie

IN THE LAND OF THE CROSSROADS.
Tracks: Not Advised.
CD . . . . R 72624CD
MC . . . . R 72624C
Rooster Blues / Feb '93.

KING OF THE ROAD.
Tracks: Not Advised.
LP. . . . . R 7608
Rooster (USA) / Oct '88 / Swift / Cadillac Music.

MOVIN' & GROOVIN' MAN.
Tracks: Highway bound / Blues dues / Blues for tomako / Dunkin' donut woman / Louisiana blues / Movin' and groovin' man / Sad and lonesome / Big leg woman / I've got to tell somebody / My baby and me.
CD . . . . ECD 26028-2
Evidence (USA) / Feb '93 / Harmonia Mundi (UK).

Shaw, Thomas

BORN IN TEXAS.
Tracks: Not Advised.
■ LP. . . . . ADVENT 2801
Advent / May '79.

Shelton, Allen

DARKNESS ON THE DELTA (see under Baker, Kenny).

SHELTON SPECIAL WITH MCREYNOLD.
Tracks: Not Advised.
LP. . . . . ROUNDER 0088
Rounder / Aug '77 / Projection / Roots Records / Swift / C.M. Distribution / Topic Records / Jazz Music / Hot Shot / A.D.A Distribution / Direct Distribution.
MC . . . . ROUNDER 0088C
Rounder / '88 / Projection / Roots Records / Swift / C.M. Distribution / Topic Records / Jazz Music / Hot Shot / A.D.A Distribution / Direct Distribution.

Shepard, Jean

Commencing her musical career as a member of the Melody Ranch Girls while still at school, Oklahoma born Jean Shepard (on November 21, 1933) secured her deal with Capitol Records thanks to the label's big selling act, Hank Thompson, with whom she'd appeared in concert. In 1953 she became one of the very few female artists to secure country chart success (still a male domain at that time, although Kitty Wells was breaking down the walls) - and with a number one record, *A Dear John letter* , on which Ferlin Husky provided the narration. Jean Shepard, who was married to Hawkshaw Hawkins (killed in the plane crash that also took the lives of Patsy Cline, Cowboy Copas and Randy Hughes), scored another 28 hits before departing to United Artists, where she enjoyed a major career revival with *Slippin' away* in 1973. Still a popular attraction on the Grand Ole Opry, Jean Shepard has visited Britain on several occasions. (Tony Byworth)

S 4 ■ DELETED

BEST OF JEAN SHEPARD, THE.
Tracks: Satisfied mind, A / Dear doctor letter, A / Forgive me, John / Other woman, The / Two voices, two shadows, two faces / Root of all evil is a man, The / Beautiful lies / How long does it hurt (When a heart breaks) / I've got to talk to Mary / Don't fall in love with a married man / Under suspicion / I learned it all from you.
LP . . . . ST 1922
Capitol / '63 / EMI.

I'LL DO ANYTHING IT TAKES.
Tracks: At the time / I love / Let me be there / What I had with you / Silver threads and gold needles / I just had you on my mind / I'll do anything it takes (To stay with you) / Would you lay with me (In a field of stone) / I'm not that good at goodbye / He thinks I still care / Love came pouring down.
LP . . . . .SLS 50416
United Artists / '74 / EMI.

I'M A BELIEVER.
Tracks: I'm a believer / It keeps right on a-hurtin' / Another somebody done somebody wrong song / I think I'll wait till tomorrow / Good nights make good mornings / Another neon night / Blanket on the ground / He loves everything he gets his hand on / We had some good times / It doesn't hurt to ask.
LP . . . . MFP 50513
■ MC . . . . .TCMFP 50513
MFP / Apr '81.

LONESOME LOVE.
Tracks: Thief in the night, A / I'll hold you in my heart / Weak and the strong, The / You'd better go / Sweet temptation / I'll never be free / You win again / I hate myself / You're telling me sweet lies again / Memory / You can't break the chains of love / I love you because.
LP . . . . HAT 3072
MC . . . . HATC 3072
Stetson / Aug '88 / Crusader Marketing Co. / Swift / Wellard Dist. / Midland Records / C.M. Distribution.

MERCY AIN'T LOVE GOOD.
Tracks: Mecy / Come on home / Satisfied woman, A / I can't imagine / Name dropper / Ain't love good / Slowly / Sing me an old fashioned song / We're all the way / Wife of a hard working man.
LP . . . . UAS 29974
United Artists / '76 / EMI.

POOR SWEEET BABY.
Tracks: Poor sweet baby / I'm alright / When two fools collide / At the time / Tip of my fingers, The / Slippin, away / It's enough to make a woman lose her mind / Bright lights and country music / City lights / If you can live with it (I can live without it) / Think I'll go somewhere and cry myself to sleep.
LP . . . . UAS 29738
United Artists / '75 / EMI.

SONGS OF A LOVE AFFAIR.
Tracks: Passing love affair, A / Shadows on the wall / Girls in disgrace / Over and over / Hello old broken heart / Mysteries of life, The / Tell me what I want to hear / I'll thank you all my life / Sad singin' and slow ridin' / Did I turn down a better deal / I married you for love / It's hard to tell the married from the free.
LP . . . . HAT 3042
MC . . . . HATC 3042
Stetson / Sep '87 / Crusader Marketing Co. / Swift / Wellard Dist. / Midland Records / C.M. Distribution.

THIS IS JEAN SHEPARD.
Tracks: Not Advised.
LP . . . . HAT 3131
MC . . . . HATC 3131
Stetson / Mar '90 / Crusader Marketing Co. / Swift / Wellard Dist. / Midland Records / C.M. Distribution.

TIPS OF MY FINGERS.
Tracks: Tips of my fingers / Bright lights and country music.
■ 7" . . . . UP 35790
United Artists / Feb '75.

VERY BEST OF JEAN SHEPARD, THE.
Tracks: Slippin' away / Mercy / I'll do anything it takes to stay with you / Ain't love good? / Tip of my fingers, The / Poor sweet baby / Another neon night / Come on phone / Would you lay with me (in a field of stone)? / I'll keeps right on a-hurtin' / At the time / Wife of a hard-working man / Think I'll go somewhere and cry myself to sleep / Namedropper / Let me be there / He loves everything he gets his hands on / Silver threads and golden needles / He thinks I still care / City lights / Bright lights and country music.
LP . . . . LBR 1003
Liberty / Nov '79 / EMI.
■ MC . . . . TCR 1003
Liberty / Nov '79.

Shepard, Ollie

SHEPARD, OLLIE & HIS KENTUCKY BOYS (Shepard, Ollie & His Kentucky Boys).
Tracks: Not Advised.
LP . . . . OT 1210
Old Tramp / Dec '88 / Swift.

Sheppard, T.G.

T.G.Sheppard is a country singer/songwriter with an intimate style that appeals to female fans. He was born William Bowder in Tennessee on 20 July 1944. He recorded for Atlantic as Bryan Stacy in 1962, but had quit performing to do promotional work in Memphis when he couldn't get anyone to record *The Devil In A Bottle*, a song by *Bobby David* that he believed in, so he recorded it himself and had a no.1 country hit in 1975; he's been a star ever since. Among his many hits was *Make My Day*, a duet with actor *Clint Eastwood*. Hits that crossed over to the pop chart include *I Loved Them Every One*.

FINALLY.
Tracks: Only one you / Crazy in the dark / Wasn't it a short forever / All my cloudy days are gone / In another minute / We're walking on thin ice / You're the first to last this song / She's got everything it takes to make me stay / I wish you could have turned my head..
■ LP . . . . K 56978
WEA / Feb '82.

FINALLY.
Tracks: Finally / All my cloudy days are gone.
7" . . . . K 17944
WEA / May '82 / WEA.

I LOVE 'EM ALL.
Tracks: We belong in love tonight / What's forever for / Party time / Silence on the line / Touch me all over again / I loved 'em every one / You waltzed yourself right into my life / Face the night alone / Troubled waters / State of our union, The.
7" . . . . K 56941
Curb / Aug '81 / BMG.

I LOVED 'EM EVERY ONE.
Tracks: I loved 'em every one / I could never dream the way you feel.
7" . . . . K 17792
Curb / Jun '81 / BMG.

MAKE MY DAY (Sheppard, T.G. & Clint Eastwood).
Tracks: Make my day / How lucky we are.
7" . . . . W 9343
WEA / Feb '84 / WEA.

ONLY ONE YOU.
Tracks: Only one you / We belong in love tonight.
7" . . . . K 17923
WEA / Apr '82 / WEA.

PARTY TIME.
Tracks: Party time / You waltzed yourself into my life.
7" . . . . K 17884
Curb / Dec '81 / BMG.

STRONG HEART.
Tracks: What you gonna do about her / Strong heart.
7" 6502747
CBS / Nov '86 / Sony.

Sherman, Ben

CHRISTMAS BELLS.
Tracks: Not Advised.
LP . . . . BSS 317
Tank / Sep '79.

Sherriff, Dave

DON'T TELL ME LIES.
Tracks: Don't tell me lies / Woman's touch.
■ 7" .CEN 383
Dapa / Apr '84.

Shine, Brendan

Reputedly the artist to have most hits in the Irish charts (apart from Cliff Richard and Elvis Presley), Brendan Shine - born in Kielty, County Roscommon - grew up in musical surroundings. He was playing the organ in his local church when he was eleven, and spent some time in his father's band before joining the Kieran Kelly Ceili Band as lead vocalist. He was fronting his own group of musicians when he made his first recording *Treat me daughter kindly* in 1967 and, four years later, scored his first No. 1 with *O'Brien has no place to go* . His most famous song is arguably *Do you want your old lobby washed down* which spent 37 weeks in the Irish charts. (Tony Byworth)

ALL MY ROADS (LEAD BACK TO YOU).
Tracks: All my roads (lead back to you).
■ 7" .PLAY 96
Play / Aug '76.

ALWAYS A WELCOME.
Tracks: Not Advised.
CD . . . . .CDPLAY 1031
MC . . . . CPLAY 1031
Play / Dec '92 / BMG.

AT HOME.
Tracks: Not Advised.
LP . . . . PLAY 1020
Play / Oct '87 / BMG.
■ MC . . . . CPLAY 1020
Play / Dec '92.

BEST OF BRENDAN SHINE.
Tracks: Not Advised.
LP . . . . PLAY 1001
Play / '74 / BMG.

BIDDY FROM GLENROE.
Tracks: Biddy from Glenroe.
7" . . . . PLAY 176
Play / '88 / BMG.

BLUE MISTY EYES.
Tracks: Not Advised.
LP . . . . PLAY 1016
MC . . . . CPLAY 1016
Play / Jun '82 / BMG.

BRENDAN SHINE.
Tracks: Not Advised.
MC . . . . CPLAY 1015
Play / Nov '91 / BMG.

BRENDAN SHINE COLLECTION.
Tracks: Not Advised.
LP . . . . .PLAYTV 1
Play / Nov '83 / BMG.
CD . . . . .CDPLAY 1
Play / Dec '92 / BMG.
■ MC . . . . CPLAYTV 1
Play / Dec '92.

BRENDAN SHINE LIVE AT THE CIRCUS TAVERN.
Tracks: Not Advised.
VHS . . . . BSV 3
Play / Dec '92 / BMG.

BRENDAN SHINE STORY, THE.
Tracks: Not Advised.
MC . . . . CPL 10289
Play / Apr '93 / BMG.

BUNCH OF VIOLETS BLUE.
Tracks: Bunch of violets blue.
7" . . . . PLAY 153
Play / Sep '84 / BMG.

BUNCH OF VIOLETS BLUE (Shine, Brendan & Pat Ely).
Tracks: Bunch of violets blue / Any Tipperary town.
7" . . . . .HIS 19
Homespun (Ireland) / '88 / Homespun Records / Ross Records / Wellard Dist.

CAN'T HOLD BACK THE YEARS.
Tracks: Can't hold back the years.
7" . . . . PLAY 155
Play / '88 / BMG.

CARROTS.
Tracks: Carrots.
7" . . . . PLAY 140
Play / Sep '80 / BMG.

CATCH ME IF YOU CAN.
Tracks: Catch me if you can.
7" . . . . PLAY 135
Play / '88 / BMG.

CATCH ME IF YOU CAN.
Tracks: Not Advised.
LP . . . . PLAY 1015
MC . . . . .CPLALP 1015
Play / Sep '80 / BMG.

CEILI HOUSE.
Tracks: Not Advised.
LP . . . . PLAY 1007 B
MC . . . . CPLAY 1007
Play / '74 / BMG.

CHRISTMAS TIME IN IRELAND.
Tracks: Christmas time in Ireland.
7" . . . . .PLAY 81
Play / Oct '76 / BMG.

COLLECTION :BRENDAN SHINE.
Tracks: Not Advised.

COLLECTION: BRENDAN SHINE.
Tracks: Not Advised.
CD . . . . .CD PLAY TV1
MC . . . . C PLAY TV1
Play / Aug '92 / BMG.

COUNTRY AND IRISH.
Tracks: Not Advised.
LP . . . . PLAY 1011
Play / '88 / BMG.

COUNTY DOWN.
Tracks: County Down / Three pubs in Belmont.
7" . . . . PLAY 149
Play / Aug '83 / BMG.

DO YOU WANT YOUR OLD LOBBY WASHED.
Tracks: Do you want yer old lobby washed down.
7″ . . . . PLAY 122
Play / Sep '79 / BMG.
7″ . . . . PLAY 223
Play / Sep '87 / BMG.

DOOGEENS.
Tracks: Doogeens.
7″ . . . . PLAY 141
Play / May '81 / BMG.

FOUR GREAT TRACKS.
Tracks: Not Advised.
■ EP. PLAYS1
Play / Jul '81 / BMG.

HEY LOUISE.
Tracks: Hey Louise / Got a honey of a deal.
7″ . . . . PLAY 144
Play / Apr '82 / BMG.

I'M SAVAGE FOR BACON & CABBABGE.
Tracks: I'm a savage for bacon & cabbage.
CD Single . . . . CD PLAY 261
MC Single . . . . .C PLAY 261
Play / Aug '92 / BMG.

IRISH SIDE OF BRENDAN SHINE.
Tracks: Ballinasloe fair / Coastline of Mayo / Ou' bally moe / Ballymena hat / Where my Eileen is waiting / If you ever go to Ireland.
LP . . . . HPE 616
Harp (Ireland) / May '80 / C.M. Distribution.

IRISH STARTIME.
Tracks: Not Advised.
LP . . . . .IST 4447
Irish Startime / '78.

LIVE AT BLAZERS.
Tracks: Not Advised.
VHS . . . . BSV 1
Play / Dec '92 / BMG.

LIVE AT THE THATCH.
Tracks: Not Advised.
LP . . . . THATCH 1
MC THATCHC1
Thatch / Aug '87.
CD THATCH1
Play / Aug '92 / BMG.

LONELINESS.
Tracks: Accordion (inst) / These are the sounds I love / My son / Loneliness.
7″ . . . . PLAY 206
Play / Feb '86 / BMG.
12″ . . . . .PLAY 206 T
Play / May '86 / BMG.

MAGIC MOMENTS.
Tracks: Not Advised.
CD . . . . .SMRD 991
LP . . . . SMR 991
MC . . . . .SMRC 991
Stylus / Nov '89.

ME OLD BONESHAKER.
Tracks: Me old boneshaker / Promise and the dream.
7″ . . . . PLAY 146
Play / Nov '82 / BMG.

ME UNCLE MIKE.
Tracks: Me Uncle Mike / Me Mother from County Mayo.
7″ . . . . PLAY 226
Play / Jun '88 / BMG.

MELODY.
Tracks: Melody.
7″ . . . . PLAY 203
Play / Jul '85 / BMG.

MEMORIES.
Tracks: Danny boy / If I were a blackbird / Old bog road / Dublin in the rare oul times / Mountains of Mourne / Banks of my own lovely Lee, The.
LP . . . . .PLAYTV 3
Play / Nov '85 / BMG.
CD . . . . .CDPLAY 3
Play / Dec '92 / BMG.
■ MC . . . . .CPLAYTV 3
Play / Dec '92.

MOONSHINE.
Tracks: Not Advised.
LP . . . . PLAY 1018
Play / Nov '86 / BMG.
MC . . . . CPLAY 1018
Play / Dec '92 / BMG.

MOONSHINE.
Tracks: Moonshine / Girl from Clare, The.
7″ . . . . PLAY 214
Play / Mar '87 / BMG.

MY OLD COUNTRY HOME.
Tracks: Not Advised.
LP . . . . PLAY 1017
Play / '88 / BMG.
MC . . . . CPLAY 1017
Play / Aug '92 / BMG.

MY OLD COUNTRY HOME.
Tracks: My old country home.
7″ . . . . PLAY 147
Play / Jan '83 / BMG.

MY SON.
Tracks: My son / Did you kiss me.
7″ . . . . PLAY 207
Play / Jan '86 / BMG.

NEW ROADS.
Tracks: Not Advised.
LP . . . . PLAY 1012
MC . . . . CPLAY 1012
Play / Oct '76 / BMG.
MC . . . . CPLAY 1030
Play / Dec '92 / BMG.
■ CD . . . . .CDPLAY 1030
Play / Dec '92.

NICE AND EASY.
Tracks: Not Advised.
LP . . . . PLAY 1013
MC . . . . CPLAY 1013
Play / Jan '78 / BMG.

NOW I'M EASY(COCK FARMER).
Tracks: Now I'm easy (cock farmer) / Murphy's widow.
7″ . . . . PLAY 152
Play / May '84 / BMG.

OLD RUGGED CROSS.
Tracks: Old rugged cross, The.
7″ . . . . PLAY 145
Play / Jun '82 / BMG.

PICTURE MY WORLD.
Tracks: Not Advised.

PICTURE OF MY WORLD, A.
Tracks: Not Advised.
LP . . . . PLAY 1022
Play / Dec '88 / BMG.
■ MC . . . . CPLAY 1022
Play / Dec '88.
CD . . . . .CDPLAY 1022
Play / Dec '92 / BMG.

PUB CRAWL.
Tracks: Pub crawl.
7″ . . . . PLAY 143
Play / Nov '81 / BMG.

RINKA.
Tracks: Rinka.
7″ . . . . .PL 258
■ CD Single . . . . PL 258CD
Play / Oct '91 / BMG.

ROBINSON'S BALL.
Tracks: Robinson's ball.
7″ . . . . PLAY 250
Play / Nov '90 / BMG.

SHINE ON.
Tracks: Not Advised.
VHS . . . . BSV 2
Play / Dec '92 / BMG.

SHINE ON 21.
Tracks: Not Advised.
MC . . . . CPLAY 1026
Play / Dec '92 / BMG.
■ CD . . . . .CDPLAY 1026
Play / Dec '92.

SIMPLE LOVE SONGS.
Tracks: Not Advised.
LP . . . . PLAY 1014
Play / '88 / BMG.

THANK GOD FOR KIDS.
Tracks: Thank God for kids.
7″ . . . . PLAY 150
Play / Dec '83 / BMG.

THIS IS BRENDAN SHINE.
Tracks: Not Advised.
LP . . . . PLAY 1009
MC . . . . CPLAY 1009
Play / Nov '76 / BMG.

TIME MARCHES ON.
Tracks: Not Advised.
CD . . . . .CDPLAY 266
Play / Aug '92 / BMG.

VILLAGE WHERE I WENT TO SCHOOL.
Tracks: Village where I went to school / Spuds.
7″ . . . . PLAY 148
Play / May '83 / BMG.

WITH LOVE.
Tracks: Not Advised.
LP . . . . PLAY TV 2
MC . . . . PLAY TCV 2
Play / Sep '84 / BMG.

WITH LOVE BRENDAN SHINE.
Tracks: Not Advised.
MC . . . . CPLAY TV2
Play / Aug '92 / BMG.

YOU'LL NEVER GO BACK.
Tracks: You'll never go back / Biddy from Glenroe.
7″ . . . . PLAY 212
Play / Oct '86 / BMG.

Shucks

HILLBILLY SWING.
Tracks: Gonna romp and stomp / San Antonio rose / Lowdown blues / Kinfolks in Carolina / Honey just allow me one more chance / Rainy night in Georgia / Mystery train / Blues stay away from me / Shotfun boogie / She came from the mountains / Unreal / Heartbreak mountain.
LP . . . . SFA 072
Sweet Folk All / May '81 / Cadillac Music / Projection / C.M. Distribution / Wellard Dist. / Impetus Records.

TWO DAYS TWO TRACKS.
Tracks: My shoes keep walking back to you / Two days two tracks / I'm gonna buy me a jukebox / Wabash cannonball / Mississippi river blues / Blue moon of Kentucky / Tennesse local / You win again / North to Alaska / What do I care / California blues / I won't go huntin' with you Jake.
LP . . . . SFA 052
Sweet Folk All / May '81 / Cadillac Music / Projection / C.M. Distribution / Wellard Dist. / Impetus Records.

Siebel. Paul

LIVE WITH DAVID BROMBERG & GARY WHITE.
Tracks: Lonesome house / Women make a fool out of me / I'm in the jailhouse now / If I could stay / You are my sunshine / I'm so lonesome I could cry / Pinto pony / It's a long way to Nashville / Louise / Honest Sam.
LP . . . . RAG 1006
Rag Baby / Mar '81 / Pinnacle / Roots Records / Charly.

Silvers. Colonel Jim

COLONEL JIM SILVERS.
Tracks: Julie / Cash on the barrelhead / For your own good / I ate the whole damn hog / Call me a cab / Blue night / Crying my heart out over you / Ain't it strange / Last to get the news / Music-making mama / Losing you may be the best thing yet / Scrap of paper and a 20 cent pen.
LP . . . . ABOUT 1009
Rondelet Music / Nov '81 / Pinnacle.

CRYING MY HEART OUT OVER YOU.
Tracks: Crying my heart out over you / Blue night.
7″ . . . . ROUND 1006
Rondelet Music / Oct '81 / Pinnacle.

Silverstein. Shel

Shel Silverstein was born in 1932 in Chicago. For twenty years he was famous for humorous social commentary in the form of cartoons in Playboy and in the Village Voice; he has also published several volumes of delightfully wacky poems and stories for children (with his drawings), and he has written hit songs for Dr Hook, Bobby Bare, Loreatta Lynn and Johnny Cash. Bare and USA country artist Tompall Glaser have recorded entire albums of his songs. *A Boy Named Sue*, recorded by Johnny Cash, a big hit in both the UK and the USA in 1969; the record won two Grammies. (Donald Clarke).

EVERYBODY'S MAKIN' BIG BUT ME.
Tracks: Everybody's makin' big but me / Man who got no sign.
■ 7″ . . . . CBS 2872
CBS / Jan '75.

FREAKING AT THE FREAKERS' BALL.
Tracks: Thumb sucker / I got stoned and I missed it / Sarah, Cynthia, Sylvia Stout would not take the garbage out / Stacy Brown got two / Polly in a pomy / Freakin' at the freakers' ball / All about you / Don't give a dose to the one you love most / Peace proposal, The / Masochistic baby / Liberated lady / Man who got no sign, The.
LP . . . . CBS 31766
MC 40 31766
CBS / Oct '79 / Sony.

GREAT CONCH TRAIN ROBBERY, THE.
Tracks: Not Advised.
LP . . . . FF 211
Flying Fish (USA) / Mar '89 / Cadillac Music / Roots Records / Projection / C.M. Distribution / Direct Distribution / Jazz Music / Duncans / A.D.A Distribution.

Simmons. Gene

CAJUN COUNTRY.
Tracks: Hallelujah I love her so / Something else / You pulled the plug and love went / Five o'clock happy hour / It's so hard to believe / River rat / Why didn't I think of that / Way down yonder in Baton Rouge.
CD . . . . .IMPCD 100.032
Imtrat / Jul '88.

■ DELETED

GOIN' BACK TO MEMPHIS (Simmons, Jumpin' Gene).
Tracks: Goin' back to Memphis / Shape you left me in / Haunted house / Hey, hey little girl / I'm coming down with love / You can have her / Hotel happiness / I'm a ramblin man / Skinny Minnie / Mattie Rea / Folsom Prison blues / Down in the alley / Come on over, put some love on me / Bossy boss / Go on shoes / Keep that meat in the pan.
LP. . . . . **HIUKLP 416**
Hi! / Oct '87 / Pinnacle / Swift.

HAUNTED HOUSE.
Tracks: Catahoula cur dog / You pulled the plug / Five o'clock happy hour / It's so hard to believe / River rat / Haunted house / Wy didn't I think of that / Way down yonder in Baton Rouge / Patchwork quilt / Kings and queens / I'm tired of sharin' Sharon / Next to nothing / I remember loving you / Will the circle be unbroken / 86 more miles to go / In Memphis / J.C. and J.C. / Troubled land over there.
LP. . . . . **MFLP 059**
Magnum Force / Feb '88 / Terry Blood Dist. / Jazz Music / Hot Shot.
CD **100.032**
Magnum Music / '89 / Conifer Records.

I DONE TOLD YOU.
Tracks: I done told you / Drinkin' scotch / Money money money / Juicy fruit / You can't break the chains of love / Crazy woman / Drinkin' wine / I don't love you baby / Pop and mama / Blues at midnight / Down on the border / If I'm not wanted / Guitar boogie / Shake, rattle and roll.
LP. . . . . **SUNLP 1008**
Sun / Feb '88 / Charly / Swift.

LIVE IN THE UK.
Tracks: Hey good lookin' / Hello Josephine / Juicy fruit / I done told you / Blues at midnight / Chains of love / Your true love / I don't love you baby / If I'm not wanted / Shake, rattle and roll / Goin' back to Memphis / Slippin' and slidin' / Bright lights, big city / Haunted house / Drinkin' wine / Pop and Mama.
VHS. . . . . **MMGV 009**
MMG Video / Feb '88 / Terry Blood Dist.

Simpson, Red

20 GREAT TRUCK HITS: RED SIMPSON.
Tracks: Truck drivin' man / Nitro express / Give me 40 acres / Motivatin' man / Big Mack / 6 days on the road / Sleeper, 5 by 2 / Take me home / Tombstone every mile / Born to be a trucker / Diesel smoke, dangerous curves / Truck drivin' fool / Hold on ma'm / Truckin' on down the road / Fur coats and fancy clothes / Country western truck drivin' singer / I'm a truck / Milesaver man / Awful lot to learn about truck drivin' / If the world ran out of diesel.
LP. **7C 062 85895**
EMI (Sweden) / Jan '83.

ROLL, TRUCK, ROLL.
Tracks: Not Advised.
LP. . . . . **HAT 3074**
MC . . . . **HATC 3074**
Stetson / '88 / Crusader Marketing Co. / Swift / Wellard Dist. / Midland Records / C.M. Distribution.

Simpson, Steve

JIVING.
Tracks: Jiving / Battle of New Orleans.
7" . . . . **ROX 024**
Roxon / Oct '81 / Pinnacle.

Siobhan & Pride

SINGING COUNTRY.
Tracks: Daddy Frank / You'll never miss the water / Silver threads and golden needles / If I didn't shed a tear / Sing me an old fashioned song / Give an Irish boy to me / That's a no no / She burned the roadside tavern down / Wait a little longer please Jesus / Things are gonna be alright / What I've got in mind / Down the wrong road again / Once around the dance floor / Three leaf shamrock.
LP. . . . . **HRL 182**
MC . . . . **CHRL 182**
Homespun (Ireland) / Nov '79 / Homespun Records / Ross Records / Wellard Dist.

Sioux

SIOUX.
Tracks: So you say you lost your baby / Here without you / Ooh Las Vegas / Hickory wind / Renaissance fair / In my hour of darkness / Amarillo / Colorado / Feel a whole lot better / God's own singer / Time between.
■ **LP.** . . . . **ANCL 2019**
Anchor (1) / Jan '77.

Sioux, Tammi

ACT NATURALLY.
Tracks: Put your hand in the hand / Crystal chandeliers / Act naturally / Your cheatin' heart / Today I started loving you again / Me and Bobby McGee / Crying time / Okie from Muskogee / Country girl / Is anybody going to San Antone / Honey / Dear God.
LP. . . . . **SFA 037**
Sweet Folk All / May '81 / Cadillac Music / Projection / C.M. Distribution / Wellard Dist. / Impetus Records.

Skaggs, Ricky

Born 18.07.1954. Bushey Creek near Cordell, in Lawrence County, Kentucky. Ricky's music through the years, has been as pure as those clear mountain streams in close proximity to his rural upbringing. Ricky Skaggs, a child prodigy (appeared with Flatt and Scruggs on TV when only 7),brought the traditional values back into the music during the eighties, opening the doors for the current crop of exciting new acts. His exciting updating of bluegrass music in a modern country style thrust the focus back onto the intrumental aspect of country music. Skaggs like a lot more country acts, gained his first audience at the local church gatherings, learning to sing those amazing harmonies. Ricky is a most accomplished musician, from a tender age mastering fiddle, mandolin, banjo and acoustic guitar. While still only 15, he joined Ralph Stanley's Clinch Mountain Boys playing alongside fellow teenager the late Keith Whitley (where they won endless praise and encores) during which time Skaggs and Whitkey recorded two albums together, including on Rebel records *Second generation bluegrass* . Ricky foloowed this with spells working with the Country Gentlemen, J.D. Crowe's New South, featuring most prominently on the latter's Rounder self-titled album of 1975, with Tony Rice and Jerry Douglas who've regularly recorded together through the years. That same year saw Ricky put together the short-lived bluegrass outfit Boone Creek, yet it was together long enough for them to have albums on both Rounder and Sugar Hill (*One way track* the label's very first album release). Skaggs then took on his most exciting challenge so far, joining Emmylou Harris' Hoy Band in 1977, filling the vacancy created when Rodney Crowell left to pursue a solo career. Skaggs at this point in time had already featured on releases by the Seldom Scene, Linda Ronstadt and Emmylou(*Pieces of the sky*). Skaggs stayed with Harris until 1980, when he embarked on what has turned out to be an illustrious venture. Prior to leaving Ricky had greatly influenced Emmylou Harris on her stellar/old time based *Roses in the snow* , Skaggs' own contribution being immeasurable. Ricky's first solo work after leaving Emmylou was *Sweet temptation* (although he'd recorded *That's it* on Rebel in 1975) and was on Sugar Hill, with Emmylou featuring on vocals. Ricky teamed up with fellow accomplished musician/ vocalist Tony Rice on the highly acclaimed old time 1980 *Skaggs and Rice* , this their second offering was steeped in old time traditions - the mould also holding strong on his 1982 Rounder release *Family and friends* . On reflection it wasn't just Willie Nelson who was keeping the recording studios in constant use. Ricky joined the big league in 1981, joining Epic Records. Such modern bluegrass/country as Flatt and Scruggs *Don't get above your raising* and *You see me walkin* were to set the standard during the early/mid-eighties for the supremely talented and influential Skaggs. His first No. 1 came in 1982, when *Crying my heart out over you* was to open the floodgates, a year that also saw him collect CMA's Male Vocalist Of The Year (one of the five categories that he was nominated for) and become the 61st member of the Grand Ole Opry. No less than eight chart toppers came from nine releases, with only *You've got a lover* (1983) breaking the sequence, Hits that included *Heartbroke* , *Highwat Forty blues* , *I don't care* , *Don't cheat in your own town* , *Honey (Open that door)* and *Uncle Pen* his 1984 reworkingof the Monroe standard being the first bluegrass song to top the country charts since Flatt and Scruggs' *The ballad of Jed Clampett* in 1962. Skaggs exciting stage shows were gaining him great acclaim too (anyone who caught his 1985 tour of the UK will readily agree), so it came as no surprise when he won the CMA's coveted Entertainer Of The Year honour that year, while his exciting band took the CMA Intrumental Group Of The Year award. The year also gave Ricky another chart topper with Albert Lee's *Country Boy* followed in 1986 by *Cajun moon* , a feat he wasn't to match for some considerable time. After a thin spell on the recording front, as far as chart recognition goes anyway, his albums *Loves gonna get ya* and *Coming home to stay* saw limited success. Although the former did feature Skagg's hit duet with wife Sharon, *Love can't ever get better than this* - and they were voted by the CMA in 1987 as Vocal Duo Of The Year as a result. Another superb example of their harmony singing can be found on the Seldom Scene's *15th Anniversary celebration* live double album release where they sing Townes Van Zandt's *If I needed you* unaccompanied. His final release on Epic *Kentucky thunder* in 1989 spawned *Lovin' only me* which saw him back topping the singles chart. *My father's son* his 1991 album showed him still to be an excellent all-round talent. Ricky's been involved with many projects, during the latter years - producing Dolly Parton's *White limozeen* amongst them. Others include the integral part he played Dave Grisman's Rounder two-set *Home is where the heart is* (1988) and involvment with the Whites - Sharon White being Ricky's wife since 1981. He was voted Country Act Of The Eighties, by Wally Whyton's Country Club listeners (BBC) in 1990. Skaggs himself presented two series of programmes for BBC's Radio 2, his acclaimed *Hit it boys* impressively retracing the history of country music, it's instrumental theme tune, Skagg's own *Wheel hoss* a country Grammy winner in 1985. Now without a recording contract, there's a feeling that Skaggs, after 24 years in the business, is quite happy to use the break to spend more time with his family, taking stock of the situation - before venturing back in to the recording side of things. (Maurice Hope)

ARTIFICIAL HEART.
Tracks: Artificial heart / Wheel hoss.
7" **650100 7**
Epic / Sep '86 / Sony.

CAJUN MOON.
Tracks: Cajun Moon / Rockin'the boat.
7" . . . . **A 7222**
Epic / May '86 / Sony.

COMIN' HOME TO STAY.
Tracks: I'm tired / Hold what you've got / (Angel on my mind) that's why I'm walking / Home is wherever you are / If you don't believe the bible / San Antonio rose / Lord, she sure is good at lovin' me / Old kind of love / Thanks again / Woman you won't break mine.
■ **CD** **4606922**
Epic / Apr '88.
LP. **4606921**
■ **MC** **4606924**
Epic / Sep '88.

COUNTRY BOY.
Tracks: Wheel hoss / Country boy / Something in my heart / Patiently waiting / Two highways / Rendezvous / Brand new me / Window up / Above / Baby, I'm in love with you / I'm ready to go.
LP. . . . . **EPC 26170**
Epic / Oct '84 / Sony.
■ **MC** **40 26170**
Epic / Oct '84.
■ **CD** . . . . **CD 26170**
Epic / Oct '84.

COUNTRY BOY.
Tracks: Country boy.
7" . . . . **A 6189**
Epic / Jan '86 / Sony.

COUNTRY GENTLEMAN.
Tracks: Not Advised.
CD . . . . **VNP 7319**
LP. . . . . **VNP 5319**
MC . . . . **VNP 6319**
Start / Jun '89.

COUNTRY STORE: RICKY SKAGGS.
Tracks: Don't get above your raising / Crying my heart out over you / Sweet temptation / Heartbroken / You may see me walkin' / Don't let your sweet love die / One way rider / Uncle Pen / I don't care / Wound time can't erase, A / Low and lonely / Don't cheat in your home town / I wouldn't change you if I could / So round, so firm, so fully packed.
MC . . . . **CSTK 37**
Country Store / Apr '87 / BMG.
■ **LP.** . . . . **CST 37**
Country Store / Apr '87.
CD . . . . **CDCST 37**
Country Store / '88 / BMG.

DON'T CHEAT IN OUR HOME TOWN.
Tracks: Don't cheat in your home town / Honey (open that door) / Wound time can't erase, A / Vision of mother, A / Uncle Pen / I'm head over heel in love / Don't step over an old love / She's more to be pitied / Keep a memory / Children go where I send thee.
LP. . . . . **EPC 25654**
Epic / Nov '83 / Sony.
■ **MC** **40 25654**
Epic / Nov '83.

FAMILY AND FRIENDS.
Tracks: Lost and I'll never find the way / Two different worlds / River of memory / Talk about sufferin' / Think of what you've done / Toy heart / Hallelujah I'm ready / Say / Won't you be mine / Won't it be wonderful there / River of Jordan.
LP. . . . . **SDLP 015**
MC . . . . **SDC 015**
Sundown / Feb '85 / Terry Blood Dist. / Jazz Music / C.M. Distribution.
■ **CD** . . . . **CDSD 015**
Sundown / '87.
CD . . . . **CD 0151**
LP. . . . . **ROUNDER 0151**
MC . . . . **ROUNDER 0151C**
Rounder / Aug '88 / Projection / Roots Records / Swift / C.M. Distribution / Topic Records / Jazz Music / Hot Shot / A.D.A Distribution / Direct Distribution.

FAVOURITE COUNTRY SONGS.
Tracks: If that's the way you feel / Sweet temptation / I'll take the blame / Waitin' for the sun to shine / You may see me walkin' / Can't you hear me callin' / Your old love letters / Lost to a stranger / Wound time can't erase, A / Nothing can hurt you.
■ **LP.** . . . . **EPC 26433**

Epic / May '85.
■ MC 40 26433
Epic / May '85.
CD 9825872
Pickwick/Sony Collectors Choice / Jul '91 / Pickwick Records.

GOLDEN MEMORIES.
Tracks: Not Advised.
MC 2630034
Big Country / Sep '89.

HEARTBROKE.
Tracks: Heartbroke / Don't think I'll cry.
7" . . . . .A 3791
Epic / Sep '83 / Sony.

HIGHWAYS AND HEARTACHES.
Tracks: Heartbroke / You've got a lover / Don't think I'll cry / Don't let your sweet love die / Nothing can hurt you / I wouldn't change you if I could / Can't you hear me callin / Highway 40 blues / Let's love the bad times away / One way rider.
LP. . . . . EPC 85715
Epic / Oct '82 / Sony.

HONEY (OPEN THAT DOOR).
Tracks: Honey (open that door) / She's more to be pitied.
7" . . . . .A 4604
Epic / Jul '84 / Sony.

KENTUCKY THUNDER.
Tracks: Hummingbird / Lovin' only me / Fields of home, The / Heartbreak hurricane / Let it be you / Lonesome for you / Kentucky thunder.
CD 4651442
Epic / Jul '89 / Sony.
LP. 4651441
■ MC 4651444
Epic / Jul '89.

LIVE IN LONDON: RICKY SKAGGS.
Tracks: Uncle Pen / Heartbroke / She didn't say why / Cajun moon / Country boy / I've got a new heartache / You make me feel like a man / Rockin' the boat / Honey (open that door) / Don't get above your raising.
LP. . . . . EPC 22618
MC 40 22618
Epic / Jan '86 / Sony.
■ CD . . . . CD 22618
Epic / Jan '86.
LP. . . . . SHM 3252
MC . . . . HSC 3252
Pickwick / Feb '89 / Pickwick Records.
CD . . . . PWKS 4048
Pickwick / Apr '91 / Pickwick Records.

LOVES GONNA GET YA!.
Tracks: Hard row to hoe, A / Love's gonna get you someday / I'm beside myself / I wonder if I care as much / Don't stop gypsy / I won't let you down / Walkin' in Jerusalem / Artificial heart / Love can't ever get better than this / Daddy was a hard working honest man / Raisin' the Dickens / New star shining.
LP. . . . . EPC 57095
■ MC 40 57095
Epic / Nov '86.
■ CD . . . . CD 57095
Epic / May '87.

MY FATHER'S SON.
Tracks: Life's too long (to live like this) / Only daddy that'll walk the line / Same ol' love / You don't count the cost / My father's son / Simple life / Hold on tight (let it go) / You can't take it when you go / Father knows best / Give us a happy home / Somebody's prayin'.
CD 4688212
■ MC 4688214
Epic / Nov '91.

NEW STAR SHINING (Skaggs, Ricky & James Taylor).
Tracks: Walking in Jerusalem / New star shining.
7" 6502507
Epic / Nov '86 / Sony.

PERSONAL CHOICE (I love country).
Tracks: Heartbroke / If that's the way you feel / Sweet temptation / I'll take the blame / Waitin' for the sun to shine / You may see me walkin' / Window up above / Uncle Pen / Highway 40 blues / I don't care / Can't you hear me callin' / Your old love letters / Lost to a stranger / Wound time can't erase, A / Country boy / Love's gonna get you someday.
LP. 4510061
■ MC 4510064
Epic / Mar '88.

RICKY SKAGGS & TONY RICE (see under Baker, Kenny).

SECOND GENERATION BLUEGRASS (Skaggs, Ricky & Keith Whitley).
Tracks: Don't cheat in our home town / Dream of a miner's child / Memories of mother / Poor Monroe / Daybreak in Dixie / All I ever loved was you / My deceitful heart / Son of Hobert / Sea of regret / Those two blue eyes / Wildwood flower / This weary heart you stole away.
LP. . . . . REBEL 1504
Rebel (1) / '75 / Projection / Backs Distribution.
■ LP. . . . . SDLP 043
Sundown / Apr '87.
MC . . . . .SDC 043
Sundown / '89 / Terry Blood Dist. / Jazz Music / C.M. Distribution.

SKAGGS & RICE (Skaggs, Ricky & Tony Rice).
Tracks: Bury me beneath the willow / Mansions for me / There's more pretty girls than one / Memories of mother and dad / Where the soul of man never dies / Talk about sufferin' / Will the roses bloom / Tennessee blues / Old crossroads, The / Have you someone in heaven waiting.
LP. . . . . SDLP 054
Sundown / '87 / Terry Blood Dist. / Jazz Music / C.M. Distribution.
LP. . . . . SH 3711
MC . . . . ZCSH 3711
Sugarhill(USA) / Mar '89 / Roots Records / Projection / Impetus Records / C.M. Distribution / Jazz Music / Swift / Duncans / A.D.A Distribution.

SWEET TEMPTATION.
Tracks: I'll take the blame / Cabin home on the hill / Baby I'm in love with you / I'll stay around / Could you love me one more time / Sweet temptation / Put it off until tomorrow / Baby girl / Forgive me / I know what it means to be lonesome.
LP. . . . . SH 3706
MC . . . . ZCSH 3706
Sugarhill(USA) / Roots Records / Projection / Impetus Records / C.M. Distribution / Jazz Music / Swift / Duncans / A.D.A Distribution.
LP. . . . . RITZLP 0030
MC . . . . RITZLC 0030
Ritz / Apr '85 / Pinnacle / Midland Records.

THAT'S IT.
Tracks: Red apple rag / Darktown strutters' ball / Florida blues / Bubble gum song, The / Whitesburg / Meetn' house branch / Sweet Georgia Town / Hook and line / Southern moon / 21 fiddle salute / That's it / Evergreen shore, The.
LP. . . . . SLP 1550
Rebel (USA) / Feb '85 / Mike's Country Music Room.
CD . . . . .CDSD 040
Sundown / Dec '86 / Terry Blood Dist. / Jazz Music / C.M. Distribution.
LP. . . . . SDLP 040
■ MC . . . . .SDC 040
Sundown / '87.

UNCLE PEN.
Tracks: Uncle Pen / I'm head over heels in love.
■ 7" . . . . .A 4948
Epic / Dec '84.

WAITIN' FOR THE SUN TO SHINE.
Tracks: If that's the way you feel / Don't get above your raising / Your old love letters / Low and lonely / Waitin' for the sun to shine / You may see me walkin' / Crying my heart out over you / Lost to a stranger / I don't care / So round, so firm, so fully packed.
■ LP. . . . . EPC 84986
Epic / Jan '82.

WAITIN' FOR THE SUN TO SHINE.
Tracks: Waitin' for the sun to shine / Uncle Pen / Honey / Highway 40 blues.
■ EP. . . . . .DA 6447
Epic / Sep '85.

Skinner, Jimmy

Kentucky born Jimmy Skinner (1909-79) enjoyed a recording career that stretched over several decades - beginning in 1941 with *Doin' my time* - but had only modest chart success in chart terms. (Out of 10 entries, his most successful were on Mercury in the late 1950's and comprised *I found my girl in the USA*, *What makes a girl wander* and *Dark Hollow*). He was probably more famous as the owner of a retail/mail order store in Cincinatti, the Jimmy Skinner Music Center. (Tony Byworth - August 1993)

ANOTHER SATURDAY NIGHT.
Tracks: Lonesome at your table / Where do we go from here / We've got things in common / Married to a friend / Just ramblin' on / No fault of mine / Hafta do somethin' about it / Another Saturday night / Please don't send Cecil away / Reasons to live / Big city / Walkin' my blues away / Two squares away / Temptation smiles / John Wesley Hardin / I found my girl in the USA.
LP. . . . . BFX 15266
Bear Family / Aug '88 / Rollercoaster Records / Swift / Direct Distribution.

NO.1 IN BLUEGRASS.
Tracks: Not Advised.
LP. . . . . .SLP 988
MC . . . . .GT 5988
Starday (USA) / Apr '87 / Crusader Marketing Co.

SONGS THAT MAKE THE JUKEBOX PLAY.
Tracks: Not Advised.
LP. . . . . HAT 3126
Stetson / '89 / Crusader Marketing Co. / Swift / Wellard Dist. / Midland Records / C.M. Distribution.

Smeck, Roy

PLAYS HAWAIIAN GUITAR ETC.
Tracks: Not Advised.
LP. . . . . .L 1052
Yazoo (USA) / Mar '77 / Roots Records / Projection / Swift / C.M. Distribution / Duncans / Cadillac Music / A.D.A Distribution / Jazz Music.

WIZARD OF THE STRINGS.
Tracks: Not Advised.
LP. 7002
Starry Crown / Dec '88 / Impetus Records / Ross Records / Projection / C.M. Distribution / Duncans.

Smith Sisters

BLUEBIRD.
Tracks: Not Advised.
LP. . . . . .FF 328
Flying Fish (USA) / Mar '89 / Cadillac Music / Roots Records / Projection / C.M. Distribution / Direct Distribution / Jazz Music / Duncans / A.D.A Distribution.

MOCKINGBIRD.
Tracks: Not Advised.
LP. . . . . .FF 370
Flying Fish (USA) / Mar '89 / Cadillac Music / Roots Records / Projection / C.M. Distribution / Direct Distribution / Jazz Music / Duncans / A.D.A Distribution.

ROADRUNNER.
Tracks: Not Advised.
LP. . . . . .FF 496
Flying Fish (USA) / '92 / Cadillac Music / Roots Records / Projection / C.M. Distribution / Direct Distribution / Jazz Music / Duncans / A.D.A Distribution.

Smith, Arthur

Country guitarist, bandleader and composer Smith was born in 1921 in South Carolina and formed the Crackerjacks in 1938. *Guitar Boogie* was a million-selling international hit, recorded for Super-Disc probably in 1946 and picked up by MGM. It was a mystery later because there was no trace of it on any charts at the time, perhaps because it sold slowly for years. A jaunty country instrumental with excellent guitar work, it is often cited as an influence on rock 'n' roll. Smith co-wrote *Beautiful Brown Eyes*, a 1951 American hit for Rosemary Clooney, and composed *Duelling Banjoes*, a No 2 US hit in '72 from the film Deliverance, played by Eric Weissberg and Steve Mandel. He recorded for MGM for years, had his own TV series and also wrote gospel songs. (Donald Clarke)

ARTHUR "GUITAR" SMITH & VOICES (Smith, Arthur "Guitar Boogie").
Tracks: Not Advised.
LP. . . . . HAT 3025
MC . . . . HATC 3025
Stetson / Oct '86 / Crusader Marketing Co. / Swift / Wellard Dist. / Midland Records / C.M. Distribution.

JUMPIN' GUITAR (Smith, Arthur "Guitar Boogie").
Tracks: Not Advised.
LP. . . . . RR 425
Relaxed Rabbit / Oct '88 / Swift.

MISTER GUITAR (Smith, Arthur "Guitar Boogie").
Tracks: Not Advised.
LP. . . . . .SLP 173
MC . . . . .GT 5173
Starday (USA) / Apr '87 / Crusader Marketing Co.

Smith, Bobby

SMOKIN' BLUEGRASS (Smith, Bobby & Boys From Shiloh).
Tracks: Let your love flow / Don't let the smokey mountain smoke / Fifteen miles from Birmingham / Shig-a-dig / Down on the corner / Bluer than midnight / Shiloh march / Packing up and leaving / Fall, The / Jamboree / Gretna Green / Dinner bell.
■ LP. . . . . .CMH 6225
CMH (USA) / '79.

Smith, Carl

Carl Smith was born in 1927 in Tennessee; he was one of the biggest country singers in America, with about 75 hits in 20 years, his top records include *Hey Joe, Loose Talk, Trademark, Satisfaction Guaranteed, There She Goes, You're Free To Go*. He was married to June Carter and is the father of Carlene Carter. (Donald Clarke)

CARL SMITH'S GREATEST HITS: VOL 1.
Tracks: Not Advised.
LP. . . . . .GT 0058
Gusto (USA) / '80.

IT'S TEARDROP TIME.
Tracks: It's teardrop time / This lady loving me.
■ 7" . . . . .DJS 10847
DJM / Mar '78.

OLD LONESOME TIMES 1951-56.
Tracks: Not Advised.
MC . . . . CSS 25

S 8

■ DELETED

Rounder / '88 / Projection / Roots Records / Swift / C.M. Distribution / Topic Records / Jazz Music / Hot Shot / A.D.A Distribution / Direct Distribution.
LP. . . . . SS 25
Rounder / Dec '88 / Projection / Roots Records / Swift / C.M. Distribution / Topic Records / Jazz Music / Hot Shot / A.D.A Distribution / Direct Distribution.

WAY WITH WORDS.
Tracks: Way with words / Drinking champagne.
■ 7". . . . . DJS 10778
DJM / Jul '77.

Smith, Connie

Ohio, West Virginia-raised Smith was born Constance June Meadows on 14.08.1941 in Elkhart, Indiana. The blue-eyed, pure-voiced blonde has, during her twenty year chart career, won over the hearts of many. Whether singing country or gospel (it was in fact for the church and her family that Smith went into semi-retirement during the 1980's) to this day she has few peers. An over-night success, she transformed from housewife to a chart topping country star when Bill Anderson's *Once A Day* (her debut single) gave her a No. 1 country hit in 1964. A rare feat only recently equalled by Trisha Yearwood in 1991 - her *She's In Love With The Boy* doing likewise. Connie's hit singles number almost fifty, and include such top 5 tracks (all coming between 1964-1967) as *Then And Only Then, If I Talk To Him, Ain't Had No Lovin' ,Nobody But A Fool. The Hurtin's All Over, I'll Come Runnin'* and *Cincinnati, Ohio* , all delivered in Smith's sparkling, bouncy style. Smith may not have reached that precious top slot again, yet she wasn't short of viable contenders. In 1971 Don Gibson's *Just One Time* made No. 2, while the likes of early 1970 singles *I Never Stopped Lovin' You* and *Just The Way I Am* gave her top 5 entries. A study of Smith's recordings reveal a noticeable reliance on songwriters Dallas Frazier, AL 'Doodle' Owens and Sanger D. Shafer, who in turn provided her with both hits and album tracks. In 1971 she became a member of the Grand Ole Opry where, apart from church gatherings, she's been noticeable by her absence from the business recently. She starred in the country music films *Las Vegas Hillbillies, Road To Nashville* and *Second Fiddle To A Steel Guitar.* Three times married Connie, a Born Again Christian, has often featured gospel music on her recordings. Most of her later contain the obligatory gospel track, besides the gospel albums themselves. In 1975 she did one of her best-ever albums, *Connie Smith Sings Hank Williams Gospel.* Due to contract wrangles, and her devoting more time to her family and church, the 1980's found her making a few less than convincing attempts to rekindle her career, lightly promoted singles issued on Epic and then with Warner Bros. (Maurice Hope - August 1993)

20 OF THE BEST: CONNIE SMITH.
Tracks: Once a day / Then and only then / I can't remember / If I talk to him / Nobody but a fool / Ain't had no lovin' / Hurtin' all over / I'll come running / Cincinnati, Ohio / Burning a hole in my mind / Baby's back again / Run away, little tears / Ribbon of darkness / You and your sweet love / I never once stopped loving you / Where is my castle? / Just one time / Just for what I am / If it ain't love / Love is the look you're lookin' for.
■ LP. . . . . NL 89523
RCA International / Apr '85.
■ MC . . . . NK 89523
RCA International / Apr '85.

BACK IN BABY'S ARMS.
Tracks: Back in baby's arms / Long black limousine / I can't get used to being lonely / Fool No. 1 / Gone too far / Wedding cake, The / Too many rivers / How great Thou art / Call, The / Now / What would I do without you.
■ LP. . . . . LSA 3129
RCA / '79.

BEST OF CONNIE SMITH, THE.
Tracks: Once a day / I can't remember / Tiny blue transistor radio / I'll come running / I saw a man / If I talk to him / Then and only then / Ain't had no lovin' / Darling, are you ever coming home / Hurtin's all over, The / Cincinnati, Ohio / Nobody but a fool (would love you).
■ LP. . . . . LSA 3055
RCA / '79.

BESTS OF THE SMITH GIRL.
Tracks: Other side of you, The / Hinges on the door / Once a day / Then and only then / It's just my luck / I don't love you anymore / Tiny blue transistor radio / Don't forget (I still love you) / Darling, are you ever coming home / Threshold / I'm ashamed of you / Tell another lie.
LP. . . . . HAT 3089
Stetson / '88 / Crusader Marketing Co. / Swift / Wellard Dist. / Midland Records / C.M. Distribution.
MC . . . . HATC 3089
Stetson / Jan '89 / Crusader Marketing Co. / Swift / Wellard Dist. / Midland Records / C.M. Distribution.

FAMOUS COUNTRY MUSIC MAKERS.
Tracks: Not Advised.

FAMOUS COUNTRY MUSIC MAKERS - CONNIE SMITH.
Tracks: There goes my everything / I love Charley Brown / I don't want your memories / How sweet it is / Sundown of my mind / Dream painter / Love has a mind of its own / If you won't tell / Ain't nothin' shakin' (but the leaves) / It's gonna rain today / Ain't we havin' us a good time / Thank you for loving me / Back in my baby's arms again / Run away little tears / I'm sorry if my love got in your way / Sunshine of my world, The / Today I started loving you again / It's such a pretty world today / Only mama that'll walk the line / It's now or never / Gentle on my mind / Just one time / My heart has a mind of its own / Pas souvent (once a day) / Wait for the light to shine / If God is diead (who's that living in my soul) / Too much to gain to lose / Gathering flowers for the masters bouquet / Amazing grace / That's all this old world needs / Don't let me walk too far from Calvary / Family bible.
■ Double LP . . . . PL 42000
RCA / '79.

GREATEST HITS: CONNIE SMITH VOL 1.
Tracks: Just one time / Hurtin's all over, The / Just for what I am / Once a day / Cincinnati, Ohio / Ribbon of darkness / Where is my castle / I'll come running / Baby's back again / Run away little tears.
■ LP. APL1 0275
RCA / '79.

SO SAD TO WATCH GOOD LOVE GO BAD.
Tracks: So sad to watch good love go bad / Constantly.
■ 7". . . . . CBS 4420
CBS / Aug '76.

WHERE IS MY CASTLE?.
Tracks: Not Advised.
LP. . . . . HAT 3112
MC . . . . HATC 3112
Stetson / Sep '89 / Crusader Marketing Co. / Swift / Wellard Dist. / Midland Records / C.M. Distribution.

Smith, Darden

Texas born singer - songwriter, showing a great aptitude for penning real life situation songs - recording first for his Red Mix label (*Native soil* since released on Watermelon label) and Epic during late eighties, with country, folk and rock music all figuring in his music. Smith, who's from the same environs as such Texan acts as Nanci Griffiths, Lyle Lovett and Robert Earl Keen, enjoyed chart success with his *Little Maggie* and *Day after tomorrow* from the self titled/penned Darden Smith, both very much of the Texas folk - country idiom, underlining his astute songwriting talent, there's such calibre fare as *Two dollar novels* . The nineties found Smith going for a harder, contemporary approach - with albums *Trouble no more* (1990) and the more subtle Columbia release *Little victories* (1993). (Mauric Hope July 1993)

DARDEN SMITH.
Tracks: Two dollar novels / Want you by my side / Love me like a soldier / Little Maggie / Day after tomorrow / God's will / Talk to me / Coldest winter / Place in time / Driving rain.
LP. 4608751
Epic / Nov '88 / Sony.
■ MC 4608754
Epic / Nov '88.

LITTLE VICTORIES.
Tracks: Place in the sun / Loving arms / Little victories / Love left town / Hole in the river / Dream Intro / Dream's a dream / Precious time / Days on end / Levee song / Only one dream.
CD 473603-2
Columbia / Jun '93 / Sony.

NATIVE SOIL.
Tracks: Bus stop bench / Red sky / Little Maggie / Veteran's day / Sticks and stones / Keep an open mind / Wild West show / Painter's song / Two dollar novels / God's will / Clatter and roll.
LP. . . . . RM 001
Redimix / May '89.
CD . . . . WM 1009
Watermelon / Jun '93 / Topic Records.

TROUBLE NO MORE.
Tracks: Midnight train / Frankie and Sue / All the king's horses / 2000 years / Ashes to ashes / Fall apart at the seams / Trouble no more / Long way home / Listen to my own voice / Johnny was a lucky one / Bottom of a deep well.
CD 4671232
LP. 4671231
■ MC 4671234
Epic / Feb '91.

Smith, Margo

One time school teacher, yodeling Smith has enjoyed considerable success since her early days in Dayton, Ohio. Margo, who was born Betty Lou Miller on 9.4.1942, has enjoyed two country number ones with her cross-over flavoured country in 1977 with *Don't break the heart that loves you* and the following year with *It only hurts for a little while* on Warner Brothers, after her initial break through on 20th century. Both were previous pop hits for Connie Francis (1962) and The Ames Brothers (1956) respectively. Margo's other well recieved hits include *Save your kisses for me* , *Still a woman, Little things mean a lot* and in 1979 her version of the old Doris Day hit *If I give my heart to you* (all top ten hits), supplemented with chart making duets with Rex Allen Jr on *Cup of tea* and *While the feelings good* in 1980-1981 on Warner Brothers. Since leaving in 1985, Margo has recorded for AMI, Moon Shine, MCA/Dot, Bermunda D and more recently playback.

BEST OF THE TENNESSEE YODELLER.
Tracks: Way it used to be, The / Take my breath away / Cowboy yodel song / Lovesick blues / Waitin' and Needin' (drives me crazy) / Hand clappin' foot stompin' country / Tenessee yodellers / My weakness / Chime bells / Indian love call / Ridin' high / Wedding bells / I want to be our cowboy sweetheart.
MC . . . . CLC 1838
MCA / Mar '87 / BMG.
■ LP. . . . . MCL 1838
MCA / Mar '87.

LITTLE THINGS MEAN A LOT.
Tracks: Little things mean a lot / Make love the way we used to.
■ 7". . . . . K 17319
WEA / Mar '79.

MARGO SMITH.
Tracks: Don't break my heart that loves you / Still a woman / Love's explosion / If I give my heart to you / It only hurts for a little while / Little things mean a lot / Paper lovin' / Shuffle song / There I said it / Save your kisses for me.
LP. . . . . IMCA 39048
MCA (Import) / '86 / Pinnacle / Silver Sounds (CD).

Smith, Ray

COUNTRY SIDE, THE.
Tracks: It wasn't easy / Thank you love / Lucille / Without you / Oh Danny boy / Light the candles / How's his memory doing today / Walking into your life / One hand on the bottle and one foot in the grave / She's pulling me back again / Kaw-liga.
LP. . . . . CR 30175
Charly / '79 / Charly.

I'M RIGHT BEHIND YOU BABY.
Tracks: Break up / So young / Right behind you baby / Life is the flower / You made a hit / Forever yours / Little girl / Shake around / Why why why / Willing and ready / I want to be free / Sail away / Two pennies and a string / Rockin' bandit.
LP. . . . . SUNLP 1009
Sun / Aug '88 / Charly / Swift.

IT'S GREAT, IT'S RAY SMITH.
Tracks: Not Advised.
LP. 75.002
Judd / Nov '87.

RARE ITEM THE ROCKIN' BANDITS.
Tracks: Not Advised.
LP. . . . . REV 3004
Revival / Oct '88 / EMI.

ROCKIN' IN GERMANY.
Tracks: Not Advised.
LP. . . . . RLP 003
Rundell / Jun '88 / Swift.

ROOM FULL OF ROSES.
Tracks: Room full of roses.
■ 7". . . . . WIX 101
Wix (USA) / Jan '80.

SOUTH SIDE STRUT - A TRIBUTE TO DON EWELL.
Tracks: Not Advised.
LP. . . . . SOS 1162
Stomp Off (USA) / Nov '88 / Jazz Music / Wellard Dist.

Smith, Russell

BOY NEXT DOOR.
Tracks: Not Advised.
LP. 1A 064 24015 1
Capitol (import) / Dec '84 / Pinnacle / EMI.

Smith, Warren

Born 07.02.1933 in Humphrey's County, Mississippi (died 30.01.1980 in Longview, Texas). After serving in the U.S. Airforce in 1950 he set out on a career in music and was discovered by Carl Perkins. Whilst Smith's initial recording came on Sun Records, it wasn't until 1960 that a small, yet sturdy collection of hits materialised on Liberty, both the 1960 single *I don't believe I'll fall in love today* and 1961's *Odds and ends* charting in country's tp ten - a duet with Shirley Collie *Why baby why* also wasn't too far adrift. Smith and his band , the Snearly Ranch Boys, recorded rock 'n' roll and country while with Sun, 1956's *Rock 'n' roll Ruby* backed with *I'd rather be sorry* being his debut. He toured regularly with Perkins, Cash, Orbison and Jerry Lee Lewis as part of Sun's package shows during

■ DELETED

his three year affiliation with Sam Phillips' label. His act in later years was well received in Europe after a lay-off due to a car accident in 1965. (Maurice Hope - August 1993)

CALL OF THE WILD.
Tracks: Cave in / I don't believe I'll fall in love today / After the boy gets the girl / Whole lot of nothin', A / Odds and ends / Call of the wild (unissued) / Old lonesome feeling / Call of the wild / Book of broken hearts / I fall to pieces / Foolin' around / Take good care of her / Pick me up on your way down / Just call me lonesome / Heartbreak Hotel / I still miss someone / Kissing my pillow / I can't stop loving you / Why baby why / Why I'm walking / Five minutes of the latest blues / Put me back together again / Bad news gets around / Hundred and sixty pounds of hurt / That's why I sing in a honky tonk / Big city ways / Blue smoke / Judge and jury / Future x / She likes attention.
CD . . . . **BCD 15495**
Bear Family / Apr '90 / Rollercoaster Records / Swift / Direct Distribution.

CLASSIC SUN RECORDINGS.
Tracks: Rock 'n' roll Ruby / I'd rather be safe than sorry / Black Jack David / Ubangi stomp / Darkest cloud, The / So long I'm gone / Who took my baby / I couldn't take the chance / Miss Froggie / Red Cadillac and a black moustache / Stop the world / I fell in love / Got love if you want it / Old lonesome feeling (incomplete) / Tell me who / Tonight will be the last night / Dear John / Hank Snow medley / Do I love you / Uranium rock / Goodbye Mr. Love / Sweet sweet girl / I like your kind of love / My hanging day.
CD . . . . **BCD 15514**
Bear Family / Apr '92 / Rollercoaster Records / Swift / Direct Distribution.

LAST DETAIL, THE.
Tracks: Red cadillac and a black moustache / Book of broken hearts / That's why I sing in a honky tonk / Heartaches by the number / Blue suede shoes / I don't believe I'll fall in love today / Between the Devil and the deep blue sea / Rock 'n' roll Ruby / Ubangi stomp / Folsom Prison blues / Roll over Beethoven / Movin' on / Golden rocket medley / That's alright mama / Rhumba boogie.
LP . . . . **CRM 2026**
Charly / Dec '81 / Charly.

LEGENDARY SUN PERFORMERS.
Tracks: Red cadillac and a black moustache / Rock 'n' roll Ruby / Ubangi stomp / Miss Froggie / Got love if you want it / So long, I'm gone / Uranium rock / Dear John / Golden rocket / I like your kinda love / Sweet sweet girl / Tonight will be the last night / Who / I'd rather be safe than sorry / Black Jack David / Goodbye Mr. Love.
LP . . . . **CR 30132**
Charly / '77 / Charly.

MEMORIAL ALBUM.
Tracks: Rock 'n' roll Ruby / Roll over Beethoven / Folsom Prison blues / Book of broken hearts / Movin' on / Rhumba boogie / Golden rocket / Ubangi stomp / Blue suede shoes / Between the Devil and the deep blue sea / Red cadillac and a black moustache / That's alright mama.
■ **LP** . . . . **MFM 001**
Magnum Force / Jul '82.

REAL MEMPHIS ROCK & ROLL.
Tracks: Rock 'n' roll Ruby / I'd rather be safe than sorry / Black Jack David / Ubangi stomp / So long I'm gone / Miss froggie / Got love if you want it / I fell in love / Goodbye Mr. Love / Sweet sweet girl / Tell me who / Tonight will be the last night / Darkest cloud, The / Who took my baby / Hank Snow medley / I couldn't take the chance / Dear John / Red cadillac and a black moustache / Stop the world / Do I love you / Uranium rock / I like your kind of love.
Double LP . . . . **CDX 23**
Charly / Apr '88 / Charly.

SO LONG I'M GONE.
Tracks: Rock 'n' roll Ruby / I'd rather be safe than sorry / Black Jack David / Ubangi stomp / Tell me who / Tonight will be the last night / Darkest cloud, The / So long I'm gone / Who took my baby / Miss Froggie / Stop the world / Red cadillac and a black moustache / I got love if you want it / I fell in love / Hank Snow medley / Do I love you / Uranium rock / Goodbye Mr. Love / Sweet sweet girl / Dear John / I couldn't take the chance / I like your kind of love.
CD . . . . **CDCHARLY 94**
Charly / Aug '87 / Charly.

WARREN SMITH.
Tracks: Who took my baby / Rock 'n' roll Ruby / Ubangi stomp / I got love if you want it / Uranium rock / Miss Froggie / Red cadillac and a black moustache / Black Jack David / Do I love you / I like your kinda love / Stop the world I'll jump off / So long I'm gone / Tell me who / Goodbye Mr. Love.
LP . . . . **SUNLP 1048**
Sun / Jan '90 / Charly / Swift.

Smokey Valley Boys

SMOKEY VALLEY BOYS.
Tracks: Not Advised.
LP . . . . **ROUNDER 0029**
Rounder / Jan '77 / Projection / Roots Records / Swift / C.M. Distribution / Topic Records / Jazz Music / Hot Shot / A.D.A Distribution / Direct Distribution.

Snow, Hank

Hank Snow was born Clarence Eugene Snow, 9 May 1914, in Liverpool, Nova Scotia, Canada. One of the biggest post-war country stars, singer, guitarist and songwriter Hank Snow had a record-breaking 45-year association with the same record company, RCA. He ran away to sea from a poverty-stricken background and began singing and playing on Canadian radio as Clarence Snow & His Guitar. RCA signed him in 1934 and within 10 years he was Canada's greatest country star. After several false starts he made the breakthrough in the USA in 1949, with *Marriage Vow*. *I'm Moving On* ('50) was nearly a year on Billboard's country chart, 18 weeks at No 1, and crossed over to pop sales as well. His next 26 hits up to '57 were almost all Top Ten entrants, including *Golden Rocket*, *Rhumba Boogie* and *I Don't Hurt Anymore* at No 1. He made the country charts every year to '79, the year he was elected to the Country Music Hall of Fame. (Donald Clarke)

20 OF THE BEST: HANK SNOW.
Tracks: I'm movin' on / Golden rocket / Rhumba boogie / Music makin' Mama from Memphis / Gold rush is over, The / Lady's man / Gal who invented kissin', The / Fool such as I, A / Spanish fireball / When Mexican Joe met Jole Blon / I don't hurt anymore / Let me go lover / Would you mind / Last ride, The / Miller's cave / Beggar to a king / I've been everywhere / Man who robbed the bank at Santa Fe, The / Ninety miles an hour / Hello love.
■ **LP** . . . . **INTS 5213**
RCA International / Nov '82.
LP . . . . **NL 89422**
MC . . . . **NK 89422**
RCA / Nov '84 / BMG.

AWARD WINNERS.
Tracks: Sunday mornin' comin' down / I threw away the rose / Ribbon of darkness / No one will ever know / Just bidin' my time / Snowbird / (The seashores of) Old Mexico / Me and Bobby McGee / For the good times / Gypsy feet.
■ **LP** . . . . **LSA 3057**
RCA / '79.

BEST OF HANK SNOW.
Tracks: I'm movin' on / Rhumba boogie, The / Let me go, lover / With this ring, I thee wed / Music makin' mama from Memphis / Millers' Cave / I don't hurt anymore / Golden rocket / Bluebird Island / I've been everywhere / (Now and then, there's) a fool such as I / Ninety miles an hour (down a dead end street).
■ **LP** . . . . **LSA 3022**
RCA / '79.

COUNTRY CLASSICS.
Tracks: Not Advised.
LP . . . . **HAT 3084**
Stetson / '88 / Crusader Marketing Co. / Swift / Wellard Dist. / Midland Records / C.M. Distribution.
MC . . . . **HATC 3084**
Stetson / Jan '89 / Crusader Marketing Co. / Swift / Wellard Dist. / Midland Records / C.M. Distribution.

COUNTRY MUSIC HALL OF FAME.
Tracks: Nobody's child / Beggar to a king / Governor's hand / Get on my love train / My Filipino rose / Gloryland march, The / Somewhere someone is waiting for you / Friend / You're wondering why / Blind boy / What more can I say / Tears in the trade winds / He dropped the world in my hands / Poor little Jimmie / Down at the pawnshop / What then / Crashing rolling thunder in my mind / Wild flower / Listen / Who's been here since I've been gone.
LP . . . . **PL 43349**
RCA / Apr '81 / BMG.

DIAMOND SERIES: HANK SNOW.
Tracks: I've been everywhere / When it's Springtime in Alaska / It's a little more like Heaven / Galway Bay / I love you because / (I'd be a) legend in my own time / Return to me / Mansion on the hill / In the misty moonlight / From a jack to a king / She wears my ring / Six days on the road / Waiting for a train / Big wheels / Last ride, The / Ghost trains.
■ **CD** . . . . **CD 90106**
Diamond Series / Apr '88.

FAMOUS COUNTRY MUSIC MAKERS - HANK SNOW.
Tracks: Letter edged in black / Old Shep / Prisoner's prayer, The / Drunkard's child, A / Don't make me go to bed and I'll be good / Convict and the rose, The / Put my little shoes away / Little buddy / There's a little box of pine on the 7.29 / Nobody's child / I'm here to get my baby out of jail / Prisoner's song, The / Colour song, The / Answer to Little Blossom, The / There's a star spangled banner waving / Walking the last mile / Old Rover / Prisoner's dream, The / Put your arms around me / Your little band of gold / Rocking alone in an old rocking chair / Mother I thank you for the Bible you gave / Little Joe.
■ **Double LP** . . . . **DPS 2023**
RCA / '79.

FAMOUS COUNTRY MUSIC MAKERS - HANK SNOW (Volume 2).
Tracks: I'm movin on / I've forgotten you / Honeymoon on a rocketship / In am 18th century drawing room / It's only you (Only you, that I love) / I just telephone upstairs / Jimmie the kid / Why did you give me your love / When Jimmie Rodgers said goodbye / Ben Dewberry's final run / Mystery of number five, The / Golden rocket / How to play the guitar / Let's pretend / No longer a prisoner / On that old Hawaiian shore with you / Silver bells / Goldrush is over, The / First nighters, The / Old spinning wheel, The / Star spangled waltz / Gal who invented kissin', The / I never will marry / Down the trail of aching hearts.
■ **LP** . . . . **DPS 2057**
RCA / '79.

HANK SNOW SINGS YOUR FAVOURITE COUNTRY HITS.
Tracks: In the misty moonlight / Trouble in mind / From a jack to a king / She wears my ring / Mary Ann regrets / White silver sands / Lonesome 7-7203 / Gonna find me a bluebird / Sweet lies / Handcuffed to love / Six days on the road / Bumming around.
■ **LP** . . . . **RD 7741**
RCA / Nov '63 / BMG.

HITS OF HANK SNOW.
Tracks: North to Chicago / Come the morning / Hijack / That's you and me / Merry go round of love / Easy to love / I just wanted to know (how the wind was) / Name of the game was love, The / Late and great love (of my heart), The / Colorado country morning / Vanishing breed / Rome wasn't built in a day / Hello love / Who will answer (Aleluya No. 1).
LP . . . . **PL 42175**
■ **MC** . . . . **PK 42175**
RCA / '79.
LP **2621718**
MC **2421718**
RCA (Germany) / Oct '84 / BMG.

I'VE BEEN EVERYWHERE.
Tracks: I've been everywhere / When it's springtime in Alaska / You're the reason / It's a little more like heaven / Where you are / On that old Hawaiian shore with you / Galway bay / Jamaica farewell / Lili Marlene / In the blue Canadian rockies / Geisha girl / My Filipino rose / Melba from Melbourne.
■ **LP** . . . . **RD 7607**
RCA / Sep '67 / BMG.

JUST KEEP A-MOVIN'.
Tracks: Just keep a-movin' / Music makin' mama from Memphis / Bill is falling due, The / Can't have you blues / Scale to measure love, A / Cryin', prayin', waitin', hopin' / I can't control my heart / Love's game of let's pretend / My Arabian baby / Blue sea blues / Caribbean / Blossoms in the springtime / Chattin' with a chick in Chattanooga / I'm glad I got to see you once again / Cuba rhumba / Owl and I, The.
LP . . . . **DT 33004**
Detour / Dec '83 / Swift / Jazz Music / Pinnacle.

LATE AND GREAT LOVE (OF MY HEART), THE.
Tracks: Late and great love (of my heart), The / Born for you.
■ **7"** . . . . **RCA 1718**
RCA / Mar '63 / BMG.

OLD DOC BROWN AND OTHER NARRATIONS.
Tracks: Old Doc Brown / That pioneer mother of mine / Blind boy / What is a father / Horse's prayer, the / Lazybones / How to play the guitar / Little britches / First nighters, the / Trouble, trouble, trouble / What do I know today.
LP . . . . **HAT 3066**
MC . . . . **HATC 3066**
Stetson / Apr '88 / Crusader Marketing Co. / Swift / Wellard Dist. / Midland Records / C.M. Distribution.

OLD SHEP.
Tracks: Old shep / Last ride, The.
■ **7"** . . . . **RCA 1151**
RCA / Oct '62 / BMG.

RAILROAD MAN.
Tracks: Waiting for a train / Big wheels / Last ride, The / Streamlined canon ball, The / Ghost trains / Pan American / Southbound / 'Way out there / Chattanooga choo choo / Wreck of the number nine, The / Lonesome whistle / Crazy engineer, The.
■ **LP** . . . . **RD 7579**
RCA / Dec '67 / BMG.
LP . . . . **NL 90003**
■ **MC** . . . . **NK 90003**
RCA / Jan '87.

SINGING RANGER VOL. 1 (The Complete Early 50's Hank Snow).
Tracks: I'm movin' on / With this ring / Rhumba boogie / Paving the highway with tears / Golden rocket / Your locket has broken my heart / Unwanted sign upon my heart / (I wish upon) my little golden horseshoe / Confused with the blues / You pass me by / Love entered the iron door / I cried but my tears were too late / One more ride / Hobo Bill's last ride / Wreck of the old '97 / Ben Dewberry's final run / Mystery of number five, The / Engineer's child, The / Law of love, The / Nobody's child / I wonder where you are tonight / Star spangled waltz, The / Blind boy's dog, The / Marriage vow / Only rose, The / Anniversary of my broken heart, The / Music makin' mama from Memphis / Highest bidder, The / Gold rush is over, The / Love's game of let's pretend / Bluebird Island / Down the trail of aching hearts / Lady's man / Fool such as I, A / Why do you punish me / Chattin' with a chick in Chattanooga / Greatest sin, The / Married by the Bible, divorced by the law / There wasn't an organ at our wedding / Zeb

S 10 ■ DELETED

Turney's gal / Golden river / Moanin' / I knew that we'd meet again / Yodeling cowboy / On that old Hawaiian shore with you / On that old Hawaiian shore with you (2) / I'm moving on to glory / Jesus wept / Pray / These things shall pass / He'll understand and say well done / I just telephone upstairs / I'm in love with Jesus / Gal who invented kissin', The / Spanish fire ball / Honeymoon on a rocketship / Between fire and water / Boogie woogie flying cloud, The / I can't control my heart / For now and always / Message from the tradewinds, A / I traded love / Next voice you hear, The / When Mexican Joe met Jole Blon / I went to your wedding / Jimmie the kid / My blue eyed Jane / When Jimmie Rodgers said goodbye / Southern Cannonball, The / Anniversary blue yodel / Why did you give me your love / Mississippi river blues / In daddy's footsteps / Gloryland march, The / Christmas roses / Reindeer boogie, The / Frosty the snowman / Silent night / My mother / Just keep a-movin' / My sweet Conchita / Panamama / Unfaithful / Wabash blues / It's you, only you that I love / Would you mind / In an old Dutch garden / Owl and I, The / I don't hurt anymore / Stolen moments / Hilo march / Act 1, act 2, act 3 / Yellow roses / No longer a prisoner / Sweet Marie / My Arabian baby / Bill is falling duo, The / Blossoms in the springtime / I'm glad I'm on the inside looking out / When it's reveille time in Heaven / My religion's not old-fashioned / Invisible hands / Little children / Alphabet, The / (Angels are lighting) God's little candles / God's little candles.
CD Set . . . . **BCD 15426**
Bear Family / Nov '88 / Rollercoaster Records / Swift / Direct Distribution.

SINGING RANGER VOL. 2.

Tracks: Love's call from the mountain (unissued) / I've forgotten you / That crazy mambo thing / Let me go lover / Old spinning wheel, The / Darktown strutter's ball / Silver bell / Under the double eagle / It's you only you, that I love / Keep your promise, Willie Thomas / Cryin', prayin', waitin', hopin / Someone mentioned your name (unissued) / I'm glad to see you once again / Mainliner (the hawk of the West) / Cuba rhumba / Scale to measure love, A / Blue sea blues / Twelfth Street rag / Rainbow boogie / Vaya condios / Madison madness / Can't have you blues / Dog bone (unissued) / Born to be happy / Golden rocket / Hobo Bill's last ride / Stolen moments / Pray / Nothing but sweet lies (unissued) / Conscience I'm guilty / Hula rock / Two won't care / Party of the second part (unissued) / These hands / Reminiscin' / New Spanish two step / In an 18th century drawing room / La cucaracha / Born to lose (unissued) / I'm movin' in / Sunshine serenade / El rancho grande / Grandfather's clock / Lover's farewell, The / Carnival of Venice / Old Doc Brown / That pioneer mother of mine / Blind boy's prayer, The / Lazy bones / What do I know today / Trouble, trouble, trouble / First nighters, The / How to play the guitar / Little britches / What is father / Horse's prayer, The / Wedding bells / Loose talk / I almost lost my mind / Sing me the song of the islands / Memories are made of this / These tears are not for you / Singing the blues / My life with you / Poison love / Among my souvenirs / Born to lose / It's been so long darling / La paloma / Oh, wonderful world / Chant of the wanderer, The / I really don't want to know (unissued) / Squid jiggin' ground / New blue velvet band, The / Calypso sweetheart / I'm hurtin' all over (unissued) / My memory (unissued) / Party of the second part marriage and divorce / Unfaithful (unissued) / Tangled mind / My arms are a house / Love's call from the mountain / On a Tennessee Saturday night (unissued) / Big wheels / Woman captured me, A / I heard a heart break last night (unissued) / I wish I was the moon / My lucky friend / Whispering rain / I'm hurtin' all over / I'm here to get my baby out of jail / Don't make me go to bed and I'll be good / Convict and the rose, The / There's a little box of pine on the 7.29 / Put my little shoes away / Letter edged in black / Old Shep / Prisoner's prayer / Drunkard's child, A / Little Buddy / Nobody's child / Blue Danube / Waltz, Kitty waltz (unissued) / Brahms lullaby / Sleepy Rio Grande (unissued) / Brahms' lullaby.
CD Set . . . . **BCD 15476**
Bear Family / Jul '90 / Rollercoaster Records / Swift / Direct Distribution.

SINGING RANGER VOL. 3.

Tracks: Casey Jones was his name / Southbound / Streamlined cannonball, The / Lonesome whistle / Waiting for a train / Wreck of the number nine, The / Pan American / Big wheels / Ghost trains / Chatanooga choo choo / Last ride, The / Crazy engineer, The / One more ride / Wreck of the old '97, The / Crazy little train of love / Any old time / Blue yodel £10 / Travelin' blues / Never no' mo' blues / Gambling polka dot blues / You and my old guitar / Roll along Kentucky moon / Moonlight and skies / One Rose, The (that's left in my heart) / Tuck away my lonesome blues / Down the old road to home / I'm sorry we met / Chasin' a rainbow / Doggone that train / Father time and mother love / I heard my heart break last night / Walkin' and talkin' / Rockin' rollin' ocean / Miller's cave / Dreamer's island / Change of the tide, The / I'm movin' on / Golden rocket, The / My mother / I don't hurt anymore / Conscience I'm guilty / I'm asking for a friend / Bluebird Island / (Now and then there's) A fool such as I / Marriage vow / With this ring I thee wed / My Nova Scotia home / Tramp's story, The / Lifetime blues / Maple leaves / Casey's washerwoman boogie / Hawaiian sunset / Man who robbed the bank of Santa Fe, The / Man behind the gun, The / Restless one, The / Call of the wild / (Town of) Laredo / Way out there / Patanio, the pride of the plains / Queen of Draw Poker Town, The / On the rhythm range / Chant of the wanderer / Wayward wind, The / Following the sun all day / Texas plains, The / Teardrops in my heart / Tumbling tumbleweeds / Heartbreak trail / Cool water / Ridin' home / At the rainbow's end / It's a little more like Heaven / I went to your wedding / Just a faded petal from a beautiful bouquet / Blue roses / Human / Breakfast with the blues / Down the trail of achin' hearts / Let me go lover / Tangled mind / Next voice you hear, The / Stolen moments / Gal who invented kissin', The / Gold rush is over, The / Ninety miles an hour (down a dead end street) / My memories of you / Wishing well, The / I stepped over the line / Ninety days / Wedding picture, The / I've cried a mile / Listen / Friend / When today is a long time ago / Black diamond / Ancient history / You're losing your baby / You're the reason / Poor little Jimmie / Beggar to a king / Countdown, The / Down at the pawnshop / I know you / You take the future (and I'll take the past) / Dog bone / If I try hard enough / Poison love / Legend in my time, A / Bury me deep / Fraulein / Mansion on the hill / Send me the pillow that you dream on / On a petal from a faded rose / Return to me / Heart belongs to me, The / I'll go on alone / I care no more / I love you because / Address unknown / Rhumba boogie, The / Music makin' Mama from Memphis / These hands / Letter from Vietnam to mother, A / Born for you / Late and great love of my heart, The / Promised to John / If today were yesterday / For sale / Rose of old Monterey / My adobe hacionda / I never will marry / Mockin' Bird Hill / No letter today / I dreamed of an old love affair / If it's wrong to love you / When my blue moon turns to gold again / Let's pretend / Pair of broken hearts, A / I've been everywhere / Jamaica farewell / Blue Canadian Rockies, The / Geisha girl / When it's Springtime in Alaska / Galway Boy / My Filipino rose / Lili Marlene / Melba from Melbourne / Atlantic coastal line, The / Isle of Sicily / Gypsy and me, The / I ain't been anywhere / Sonny boy / Indian love call / Unchained melody / Beautiful dreamer / My Isle of golden dreams / Brahm's lullaby / Blue tango / Dark moon / Vaya con dios / In an old Dutch garden / By an old Dutch mill / I can't stop loving you / Convict and the rose, The / Limbo rock / Hold me tight / Tammy / Everybody does it in Hawaii / I saw the light / Green leaves of Summer, The / Difficult / Wheels / Tiptoeing / Waltz you saved for me, The / Lay my head beneath the rose / Whispering hope / Wabash blues / Sentimental journey / Am I losing you? / I get the blues when it rains / Sweet Marie / Birth of the blues / White Christmas / Little stranger (in a manger) / Christmas roses / Silent night / C-H-R-I-S-T-M-A-S / Blue Christmas / Reindeer boogie, The / Frosty the snowman / Christmas wants / Rudolph, the red-nosed reindeer / God is my Santa Claus / Long eared Christmas donkey / Face on the ballroom floor, The / Dangerous Dan McGrew / Cremation of Sam McGee / Spell of the Yukon, The / Ballad of blasphemous Bill, The / The ballad of one eyed Mike / Ballad of hard luck Henry, The / My friends / He'll understand and say well done / I saw a man / Rich man am I, A / Jesus wept / I'm movin' on to glory / Gloryland march / Farther along / Invisible hands / Last mile of the way, The / Sweet hour of prayer / These things shall pass / His hands / What then / Lord's way of sayin' goodnight, The / Dear Lord / Remember me / I see Jesus / My religion's not old fashioned / I'm glad I'm on the inside (looking out) / Runt, The / How big is God / Shop worn / Man who is wise, A / This train / I'll go marching into glory / I'd rather be on the inside looking out / Lord it's me again / Lord I do believe / Learnin' a new way of life / Wildflower / Little Joe / Put your arms around me / Color song, The / Your little band of gold / Prisoner's dream, The / Answer to 'Little Blossom', The / There's a star spangled banner waving / Old Rover / Mother I thank you (for the bible you gave) / Prisoner's song, The / Walking the last mile / Rocking alone in an old rocking chair / Lonesome / She wears my ring / White silver sands / Trouble in mind / Mary Ann regrets / Six days on the road / Bumming around / From a Jack to a King / Handcuffed to love / What more can I say / I wish my heart could talk / Hula love / Cry my guitar, cry on / Beyond the reef / To you my sweetheart, aloha when I go / Hawaiian cowboy / My little grass shack in Kealakekua, Hawaii / On the beach in Waikiki / Tradewinds / Pearly shells / On that old Hawaiian shore with you / Now is the hour / Tears in the tradewinds / King's serenade / Whispering tradewinds, The / Spanish fireball / 'Cross the Bravos at Waco / El Paso / Caribbean / Senorita Rosalita / Cuba rhumba / Nuevo laredo / Blue rose of the Rio / Maria Elena / Adios amigo / Among my souvenirs / Miami snow / Springtime in the Rockies / Blossoms in the Springtime / At the first fall of snow / Snowbird / Seasons, The / Roses in the snow / Flying South / January / You're as welcome as the flowers in May / Peach picking time in Georgia / All nite cafe / Tip of my fingers, The / He dropped the world in my hands / Blue blue day / It kinda reminds me of me / All the time / Blue side of lonesome / There goes my everything / Once more you're mine again / Million and one, A / Green green grass of home / Wound time can't erase, A / I just wanted to know how the wind was blowin' / Who will answer / Cure for the blues / That's when the hurtin' sets in / Rome wasn't built in a day / Name of the game was love, The.
CD Set . . . . **BCD 15502**
Bear Family / Jun '92 / Rollercoaster Records / Swift / Direct Distribution.

SONGS OF TRAGEDY.

Tracks: Prisoner's song, The / Colour song, The / Answer to little blossom, The / There's a star spangles banner waving somewhere / Walking the last mile / Old rover / Prisoner's dream, The / Put your arms around me / Your little band of gold / Rockin' alone / Mother I thank you for the Bible you gave / Little Joe.
■ **LP** . . . . **RD 7658**
RCA / Oct '65 / BMG.

THESAURUS TRANSCRIPTIONS, THE.

Tracks: Weary river / Bury me deep / Let's pretend / Address unknown / Golden river / Blue yodel (no. 12) / I'm here to get my baby out of jail / Brand on my heart / With this ring I thee wed / I wonder where you are tonight / Fire on the mountain / Draggin' / Steel guitar rag / Wabash blues / I'm movin' on / Handcuffed to love / Convict & the rose, The / Anniversary blue yodel / Frankie & Johnny / Closed for repairs / End of the world / I wonder if you feel the way I do / Pins & needles / Where romance calls / Streamline cannonball, The / Trouble in mind / Last letter, The / Headin' down the wrong highway / Lonely / Blue eyes crying in the rain / These tears are not for you / Jealous heart / Hawaiian cowboy / I'm thinking tonight of my blue eyes / Whispering hope / It is no secret / Molly darling / I'll remember you, love, in my prayers / Blue dreams / Blow yo' whistle, freight train / Lonely river / I'll never let you go little darling / Texas plains / Born to lose / Too many tears / Travellin' blues / Faded rose, a broken heart, A / Yodeling ranger / Roll along Kentucky moon / Zeb Turner's gal / Sun has gone down on our love, The / I walk alone / Old Shep / Mississippi river blues / Linda Lou / My good gal's gone / Breeze / This cold war with you / I love you Nellie / Beautiful dreamer / 12th Street rag / Bye bye blues / Hilo march / Orange blossom special / Beaumont ride / Just when I needed you / 99 years blues / My blue eyed Jane / Yodeling cowboy / Cannonball, The / It's been so long darling / Lover's farewell, The / You nearly lost your mind / Kentucky waltz / There's a pony standing in his stall / Among my souvenirs / Little old home down in New Orleans / Go on alone, The / Cowhand's last ride, The / I almost lost my mind / Patanio, the pride of the plains / That heart belongs to me / Peach pickin' time in Georgia / Alabama jubilee / Farewell blues / In an old dutch garden / Sally goodin' / Arkansas traveller / Petal from a faded rose, A / It's a sin / Wedding bells / At mail call today / Those blue eyes don't sparkle anymore / Have I stayed away too long / San Antonio rose / Each minute seems a million years / Blue steel blues / Then I turned & walked slowly away / Blue rose of the Rio / My wubba dolly / Tuck away my lonesome blues / Land of my childhood dreams, The / Wreck of the old 97, The / My life with you / One rose that's left in my heart, The / I'm coming home / Song of the saddle / Easter parade / Peter Cottontail / My rough & rowdy ways / Sing me a song of the Islands / Little Joe / White christmas / Blue christmas / Making believe / Any old time / Never no mo' blues / When my blue moon turns to gold again / Katy Hill / Put your arms around me / I was sorta wondering / Over the waves / Do right Daddy blues / As long as I live / Loose talk / Waltz you saved for me, The / Memories are made of this / I really don't want to know / Wayward wind, The / Chant of the wanderer / Put on your old grey bonnet / When you & I were young, Maggie / Sentimental journey / Birth of the blues, The.
CD Set . . . . **BCD 15488**
Bear Family / Feb '91 / Rollercoaster Records / Swift / Direct Distribution.

WHEN TRAGEDY STRUCK.

Tracks: Letter edged in black, The / Old shep / Prisoner's prayer / Drunkard's child / Don't make me go to bed and I'll be good / Convict and the rose, The / Put my little shoes away / Little buddy / There's a little box of pine on the 7.29 / Nobody's child / I'm here to get my baby out of jail.
■ **LP** . . . . **RD 27115**
RCA / Apr '61 / BMG.

WHEN TRAGEDY STRUCK.

Tracks: Drunkard's child, A / Convict and the rose, The / There's a little box of pine on the 7.29 / Nobody's child.
■ **7"** . . . . **RCX 7125**
RCA / Oct '65 / BMG.

YODELLING RANGER, THE 1936-1947.

Tracks: Prisoned cowboy / Lonesome blue yodel / Blue for old Hawaii / We met down in the hills of old Wyoming / My San Antonio Mama / My little swiss maiden / Was there ever a pal like you / Blue velvet band, The / Someday you'll care / I'll ride back to lonesome valley / Bluer than blue / Yodelling back to you / There's a picture on Pinto's bridle / Texas cowboy / On the Mississippi shore / Under Hawaiian skies / She's a rose from the Garden of Prayer / Wanderin' on / Broken wedding ring / You didn't have to tell me / His message home / Answer to 'The Blue Velvet Band' / I'll tell the world that I love you / Polka dot blues / Alphabet song, The / Galveston rose / Broken dreams / Let's pretend / Days are long, I'm weary, The / I traded my saddle for a rifle / When that someone you love, doesn't love you / Rainbow's end, The / We'll never say goodbye, Just say so long / I'm sending you red roses / Goodnight litle buckaroos / When my blue moon turns to gold again / Dream tide / Seal our parting with a kiss / You'll regret those words my darling / You promised to love me to the end of the world / Just across the bridge of gold / There's a pony that's lonely tonight / Old moon of Kentucky / Rose of the Rio / Lonely and heartsick / Your last kiss has broken my heart / When it's over I'll be coming back to you / Mother is praying / Soldier's last letter / Riding along, singing a song / Don't hang around me anymore / Only a rose from my mother's grave / Too many tears / Your little band of gold / Sunny side of the mountains / You broke the chain that held our hearts / My blue river rose / You played love on the strings of my heart / How she could yodel / Headin' home / Dry those tears little girl and don't cry / In memory of you dear old pal / Can't have you blues / Just waiting for you / Just waiting for you (2) / My kalua sweetheart / I'll not forget my mother's prayer / Darling, I'll always love you / Blue ranger / Just a faded petal from a beautiful bouquet / My sweet Texas Bluebonnet Queen / I'm gonna bid my blues goodbye / Down where the dark waters flow / Answer to 'Galveston rose' / Brand on my heart / No golden tomorrow / On that old Hawaiian shore with you / You've broken my heart / Linda Lou / My mother / Drunkard's son, The / Within this broken heart of mine /

My Filipino rose / Night I stole Sammy Morgan's gin, The / My two timin' woman / Wasted love / Broken hearted / You sad kiss goodbye / Somewhere along life's highway / Out on the open range / Little buddy / Journey my baby back home / I knew that we'd meet again / Within this broken heart of mine (Alt) / My two timin' woman (Alt) / Wasted love (Alt) / Life story, Part 1 / Life story, Part 2 / Marriage and divorce / I don't hurt anymore.
CD Set . . . . **BCD 15587**
Rollercoaster / Mar '93 / Rollercoaster Records / Swift.

YOU'RE EASY TO LOVE.
Tracks: You're easy to love / My dreams tell it like it was / Top of the morning / I just want you to know / Follow me / Merry-go-round of love / Colorado country morning / I almost lost my mind / She even woke me up to say goodbye / So good to be back with you.
■ **LP**. **LSA 3234**
RCA / '78 / BMG.

Sokolow, Fred

BLUEGRASS BANJO INVENTIONS.
Tracks: Straw dog / Muddy roads / Dog house blues / Harland stomp / Cotton-eyed Joe / Life's too short / Hell among the yearlings / Sullivan's hornpipe / Bach's two-part invention / Deep elem blues / Demonstration rag / Bonaparte's retreat / Learning to let go of you / Gamelan medley / Windy mountain / Sugar in the gourd / Let me fall.
LP. **SNKF 131**
Kicking Mule / Jan '78 / Roots Records / Swift / Projection / C.M. Distribution / Impetus Records / Ross Records / Duncans.

RAGTIME BANJO BLUEGRASS STYLE.
Tracks: Not Advised.
LP. **KM 212**
Kicking Mule / '92 / Roots Records / Swift / Projection / C.M. Distribution / Impetus Records / Ross Records / Duncans.

Sonnier, Jo El

Born 1946 in Rayne, Louisiana, Sonnier, an accordianist and vocalist recorded for Swallow, Goldband, Mercury and Rounder before his breakthrough signing to RCA in 1987. He had previously worked in Nashville on records by Johnny Cash, Merle Haggard, Hank Williams Jnr. and Eddy Raven. After a short retirement he joined the group Friends with Albert Lee, Garth Hudson and David Lindley. Jo-El's debut RCA LP fused elements of country, blues and rock with cajun and scored a Top 40 hit with the title track *Come on Joe*. He also scored Top Ten hits with *No more one time* and *Tear stained letter*. He also achieved some minor success with tracks off the *Blue Blue Day*LP.(Maurice Hope).

CAJUN LIFE.
Tracks: Cajun life / Tes yeux bleu / Allons a lafayette / Bayou teche / Les flames d'enfer / Lacassine special / Chere Alice / Louisiana blues / Les grande bois / Perrodin two-step.
LP. **SNTF 839**
Sonet / Oct '80 / Swift / C.M. Distribution / Roots Records / Jazz Music / Sonet Records / Cadillac Music / Projection / Wellard Dist. / Hot Shot.
CD . . . . **CD 3049**
LP. **ROUNDER 3049**
MC . . . . **ROUNDER 3049C**
Rounder / Aug '88 / Projection / Roots Records / Swift / C.M. Distribution / Topic Records / Jazz Music / Hot Shot / A.D.A Distribution / Direct Distribution.

COME ON JOE.
Tracks: Baby hold on / Paid the price / So long baby goodbye / No more one more time / Come on Joe / Rainin' in my heart / Louisiana 1927 / Tear stained letter / I've slipped her mind.
MC . . . . **PK 86374**
RCA / May '89 / BMG.
CD . . . . **PD 86374**
■ **LP**. **PL 86374**
RCA / May '89.

HAVE A LITTLE FAITH.
Tracks: Scene of the crime, The / If your heart should ever roll this way again / Ooh ooh ooh / Have a little faith in me / I'll never get over you / Hurt in my heart, The / Solid gold plated fool / Walls / Evangeline special.
CD . . . . **PD 90453**
LP. **PL 90453**
MC . . . . **PK 90453**
RCA / Mar '90 / BMG.

SONNIER, JO-EL.
Tracks: Not Advised.
CD . . . . **CDP 7987612**
MC **C4 98761**
Liberty / Oct '92 / EMI.

Sonnier, Lee

FAIS DO DO BREAKDOWN (Sonnier, Lee & Happy Fats(1940's)).
Tracks: Setre chandelle / Allons dance colinda / Dans les grande meche / Chere Catan / Fais do do breakdown / Dans la platin / Chere eci et cher laba / Along the river / Cankton two step / War widow waltz / La valse de hadocol / Crowley two step / La blues de Cajin / Acadian all star special.
LP. **FLY 609**
Flyright / Nov '86 / Hot Shot / Roots Records / Wellard Dist. / Charly / Swift / Projection.

Sons Of The Pioneers

Close-harmony country-and-western vocal group the Sons of the Pioneers were formed in 1933 by Roy Rogers, Bob Nolan, Tim Spencer and brothers Hugh and Carl Farr. Lloyd Perryman joined, and Roy Rogers left, in the late 30's. They appeared in many films, including *Rhythm on the Range* in 1936 with Bing Crosby, and they recorded for American Columbia and Decca, then RCA from the 1940's, with changing personnel for decades: the Bear Family album has a completely different line-up. (Donald Clarke)

1940.
Tracks: Not Advised.
LP. **JEMF 102**
JEMF (USA) / '88 / Projection.

20 OF THE BEST: SONS OF THE PIONEERS.
Tracks: Riders in the sky / Don't fence me in / Red river valley / Carry me back to the lone prairie / One more ride / Way out there / Song of the bandit / Room full of roses / Ringo twilight on the trail / Cool water / My adobe hacienda / Along the Navajo trail / El Paso / Song of the pioneers / Shifting, whispering sands / Ragtime cowboy Joe / Mystery of his way / Tumbling tumbleweeds / Last round-up, The.
LP. **NL 89525**
■ **MC** . . . . **NK 89525**
RCA / Apr '85.

COWBOY COUNTRY.
Tracks: One more ride / Yaller yaller gold / Graveyard filler of the west / King of the river / All the way (Previously unissued.) / No rodeo dough / Lie low little doggies (The cowboy's prayer) / Little doggies (the cowboy's prayer) / Old pioneer / Bar none ranch, The / Out in pioneer town / Serenade to a coyote (Previously unissued.) / Wagon train.
LP. **BFX 15071**
Bear Family / Sep '84 / Rollercoaster Records / Swift / Direct Distribution.

EDITION 1 (Cool Water 1945/46).
Tracks: Cool water / Timber trail / You'll be sorry when I'm gone / Forgive and forget / Gold star mother with silvery hair / You're getting tired of me / Columbus stockade blues / Cowboy camp meetin' / I wear your memory in my heart / Tumbling tumbleweeds / No one to cry to / Everlasting hills of Oklahoma, The / Grievin' my heart out for you / Out California way / Stars and stripes on Iwo Jima (Isle).
LP. **BFX 15202**
Bear Family / May '87 / Rollercoaster Records / Swift / Direct Distribution.

EDITION 2 (Teardrops In My Heart 1946/47).
Tracks: Teardrops in my heart / Chant of the wanderer, The / Let's pretend / Will there be sagebrush in Heaven? / Penny for your thoughts / Baby doll / Letter marked unclaimed, The / Trees / Cigarettes, whisky and wild, wild women / You don't know what lonesome is / Too high too wide too low / You'll never miss the water / Have I told you lately that I love you / My best to you / Blue prairie / Lead me gently home father.
LP. **BFX 15252**
Bear Family / May '87 / Rollercoaster Records / Swift / Direct Distribution.

EDITION 3 (Hundred And Sixty Acres 1946/47).
Tracks: Hundred and sixty acres, A / Calico apron and gingham gown / Whiffenpoof song, The / Wind / Where are you / Out in pioneer town / Two eyes two lips but no heart / Cowboy country / Power in the blood / Let me share your name / Happy birthday polka / Read the Bible every day / Sea walker, The / Old rugged cross, The / Last round-up, The / Bar-none ranch (in the sky), The.
LP. **BFX 15253**
Bear Family / May '87 / Rollercoaster Records / Swift / Direct Distribution.

EDITION 4 (Riders In The Sky 1947/49).
Tracks: Santa Fe, New Mexico / Down where the Rio flows / I still do / Serenade to a coyote / Red River valley / Riders in the sky / Sentimental, worried and blue / The Missouri is a devil of a woman / My feet take me away / Room full of roses / Let's go west again / Lie low little doggies(The cowboy's prayer) / No rodeo dough / Touch of God's hand / Little grey home in the west / Rounded up in glory.
LP. **BFX 15254**
Bear Family / Dec '87 / Rollercoaster Records / Swift / Direct Distribution.

EDITION 5 (Land Beyond The Sun 1949/50).
Tracks: Land beyond the sun / Wagon's west / Outlaws / Rollin' dust / Song of the wagonmaster / Wind / Love at the country fair / Wedding dolls (from your wedding cake) / Old man atom / I told them about you / Chuckawalla swing / What this country needs / Eagle's heart, The / Baby, I ain't gonna cry no more / Little white cross / Roses.
LP. **BFX 15255**
Bear Family / May '87 / Rollercoaster Records / Swift / Direct Distribution.

EDITION 6 (And Friends 1950/51).
Tracks: Lonesome / Bring your roses to her now / Mexicali rose / San Antonio Rose / Moonlight and roses / Daddy's little cowboy / Baby, I ain't gonna cry no more / America forever / You don't know what lonesome is / Handsome stranger / Grasshopper heart / I still feel the same about you / Wind is a woman, The / Little ol' state of Texas, The.
LP. **BFX 15282**
Bear Family / Dec '87 / Rollercoaster Records / Swift / Direct Distribution.

EDITION 7 (There's a Goldmine In 1951/52).
Tracks: Empty saddles / There's a goldmine in the sky / I still do / Old pioneer / Home on the range / Heartbreak hill / Outlaw / Wind / Diesel smoke x 2 / Waltz of the roses / Ho le o / Almost / Resurrectus / Wondrous word / Lord's prayer, The.
LP. **BFX 15283**
Bear Family / Jun '88 / Rollercoaster Records / Swift / Direct Distribution.

FAVOURITE COWBOY SONGS.
Tracks: Tumbling tumbleweeds / Press along to the big coral / Wind / Bunkhouse bugle boy / Home on the range / La Borachita / Timber trail / Happy cowboy / Cowboy lament / Pajarillo Barrenquero / So long to the Red River Valley / Come and get it / Cool water / Curly Joe from Idaho / Cowboy's dream / Along the Santa Fe trail / Last round-up, The / Far away stomp / Red River Valley / Carry me back to the lone prairie / Sweet Betsy from pike / Slow moving cattle / Texas stomp / Yellow rose of Texas / Everlasting hills of Oklahoma, The.
LP. **HAT 3069**
MC . . . . **HATC 3069**
Stetson / Jun '88 / Crusader Marketing Co. / Swift / Wellard Dist. / Midland Records / C.M. Distribution.

LUCKY U RANCH RADIO.
Tracks: Not Advised.
Double LP . . . . **JEMF 2201**
JEMF (USA) / Mar '85 / Projection.

RADIO TRANSCRIPTIONS VOL.1.
Tracks: 1849 blues / It's a great day / Lord, you made the cowboy happy / Believe me if all those endearing young charms / One more river to cross / Move on, you lazy cattle / That pioneer mother of mine / Sagebush symphony / Tumbleweed trail / Hi filootin' Newton / Yippi yi yippi yo / Yellow rose of Texas / It's a cowboy's life for me / Lazy / Waitin' for the sun to say good.. / Old black mountain trail, The / Mexicali rose / Texas polka / Home again in Wyoming / Song of the San Juan Joaquin.
MC . . . . **CSR 7C**
Outlaw / Dec '87.

RADIO TRANSCRIPTIONS VOL.2.
Tracks: Yodel your troubles away / So long to the Red River Valley / Termite's love song, The / Far away stomp / Slim / I follow the stream / Too high too wide too low / Hi ho little doggies / Rose of ol' Santa Fe / Cattle call rondolet / Westward Ho / Prairie revenge / Santa Fe trail / Jubilation jamboree / Timber trail / Round-up in the sky / Whoopie ti yi yo / Cowboy's serenade, The / Well, well, well / Hard times come again no more.
MC . . . . **CSR 8C**
Outlaw / Dec '87.

RADIO TRANSCRIPTIONS VOL.3.
Tracks: Wagon wheels / Don Juan / Riding down the canyon / Biscuit blues / Cowpoke / Cornflower / Silent trails / Graveyard filler of the west / Song of the bandit / Sky ball paint / West is my soul, The / Cowboy camp meetin' / Following the sun all day / Whispering wind / Trail dreaming / Redwood tree.
MC . . . . **CSR 9C**
Outlaw / Dec '87.

RADIO TRANSCRIPTIONS VOL.4.
Tracks: Pecos Bill / Carry me back to the lone prairie / I follow the stream / Love song of the waterfall / Cherokee strip, The / Cowboy jubilee / Stars of the west / Night falls on the prairie / Lord you made the cowboy happy / Round / Up in the sky / Buffalo / Lillies grow high, The / Too high, too wide, too low / Round up / Time is over / He's ridin' home / Touch of God's hand.
MC . . . . **CSR 10C**
Outlaw / Dec '87.

RIO GRANDE (Orignal soundtrack).
Tracks: I'll take you home again, Kathleen / Cattle call / Erie canal / Yellow stripes / My gal is purple / Down by the glen side / Footstore cavalry.
CD . . . . **VSD 5378**
Colosseum / Aug '93 / Pinnacle.

SONS OF THE PIONEERS.
Tracks: Song of the bandit / At the rainbows end / Hold that critter down / When the golden train comes down / Cajun stomp / You must come in at the door / Devil's great grandson / Cowboy night herd song / Send him home to me / Touch of God's hand.
■ **LP**. **CBS 25015**
CBS / Oct '82.

STANDARD RADIO TRANSCRIPTIONS 1934/35, THE.
Tracks: Swiss yodel / When round-up is over / Hear dem bells / Giddyap Napoleon / Ain't we crazy / Side walk waltz / Bells of Baltimore / White mule of mine /

S 12

■ DELETED

Sweet Betsy from Pike / She came rollin' down the mountain / Grandfather's clock / Little brown jug.
MC . . . . CSR 5C
Outlaw / Dec '87.

STANDARD RADIO TRANSCRIPTIONS 1934/35, VOL.2, THE.
Tracks: Put on your old grey bonnet / Dear old girl / Gospel train / Dese bones gwine to rise again / Lone star trail, The / Little red barn / Hills of old Kentucky / Little Annie Rooney / Jim crack corn / Rufus Rastas Johnson Brown / Jordan am a hard road to travel / Threw it out of the window.
MC . . . . CSR 6C
Outlaw / Dec '87.

WAGON WEST.
Tracks: Forgive and forget / Cool water / Timber trail, The / Stars and stripes on Iwo Jima / You're getting tired of me / Gold star mother with silvery hair / You'll be sorry when I'm gone / I wear your memory in my heart / Cowboy camp meetin' / Tumbling tumbleweeds / Out California way / Grievin' my heart out for you / No one to cry to / Everlasting hills of Oklahoma, The / Chant of the wanderer / Blue prairie / Trees / Letter marked unclaimed, The / Baby doll / Penny for your thoughts, A / Have I told you lately that I love you / Let's pretend / Cigarettes, whiskey and wild women / Teardrops in my heart / My best to you / Will there be sagebrush in heaven / You don't know what lonesome is / You never miss the water to the well / Lead me gently home father / Too high, too wide, too low / Out in pioneertown / Hundred and sixty acres, A / Seawalker, The / Read the bible every day / Last round-up, The / Two eyes, two lips but no heart / Cowboy country / Barnone ranch (in the sky) / Where are you / Calico apron and a gingham gown / Happy birthday polka / Let me share your name / Wind / Whiffenproof song, The / Old rugged cross, The / Power in the blood / Touch of God's hand, The / Rounded up in glory / Santa Fe, New Mexico / Down where the Rio flows / My feet takes me away / Red River valley / Serenade to a coyote / Missouri is a devil of a woman, The / No rodeo dough / Sentimental, worried and blue / Little gray home in the west / I still do / Riders in the sky / Room full of roses / No one here but you / Lie low little doggies (the cowboy's prayer) / Let's go west again / Love at the country fair / Wedding dolls (from your wedding cake) / Outlaws / Roses / Eagle's heart / Land beyond the sun / I told them all about you / Wagons west / Rollin' dust / Song of the wagon master / Chuckawalla swing / Old man atom / What this country needs / Baby, I ain't gonna cry no more / Little white cross / America forever / Daddy's little cowboy / Moonlight and roses (bring mem'ries of you) / Bring your roses to her now / San Antonio rose / Mexican rose / Lonesome / Wondrous word, The / Resurrectus / Waltz of roses / Lord's prayer, The / Heart break hill / Holeo / Diesel smoke / Almost / Empty saddles / There's a goldmine in the sky / Old pioneer / Home on the range / If you would only be mine / Sierra nevada / River of no return, The / Lilies grows high, The / Lonely little.
CD Set . . . . BCD 15640
Bear Family / Aug '93 / Rollercoaster Records / Swift / Direct Distribution.

Sorrels, Rosalie

ALWAYS A LADY.
Tracks: Not Advised.
LP. . . . . PH 1029
Philo (USA) / '88 / Roots Records / Projection / Topic Records / Direct Distribution / Ross Records / C.M. Distribution / Impetus Records.
CD . . . . GLCD 2110
Green Linnet (USA) / May '93 / Roots Records / Projection / C.M. Distribution / W.R.P.M.

BE CAREFUL THERE'S A BABY IN THE HOUSE.
Tracks: Not Advised.
CD . . . . GLCD 2100
MC . . . . CSIF 2100
Green Linnet (UK) / '92 / A.D.A Distribution.

MOMENTS OF HAPPINESS.
Tracks: Not Advised.
LP. . . . . PH 1033
Philo (USA) / '88 / Roots Records / Projection / Topic Records / Direct Distribution / Ross Records / C.M. Distribution / Impetus Records.

THEN CAME THE CHILDREN.
Tracks: Not Advised.
CD . . . . GLCD 2099
MC . . . . CSIF 2099
Green Linnet (UK) / '92 / A.D.A Distribution.

TRAVELIN' LADY RIDES.
Tracks: Not Advised.
CD . . . . GLCD 2109
Green Linnet (USA) / May '93 / Roots Records / Projection / C.M. Distribution / W.R.P.M.

Southern Eagle String..

THAT NASTY SWING (Southern Eagle String Band).
Tracks: Second class hotel / Spinning room blues / N.R.A. blues / Mexican rag / Charles Guiteau / Cole Younger / Do' round my Lindy / There ain't no bugs on me / Bile the cabbage down / Snowdrop / Cotton mill colic / That nasty swing / Willie Moore / Alimony woman / Kansas City blues / Walkin' blues, The.
LP. . . . . BF 15010
Bear Family / Sep '84 / Rollercoaster Records / Swift / Direct Distribution.

Southern Mountain Boys

LOVE SICK AND SORROW (see under Lundy, Ted).

Southern Pacific

They formed in Los Angeles in 1985, consisting of John McFee on guitar and fiddle, Keith Hudson, both of whom previously were in the Doobie Brothers, Stu Cook, formerly with Creedence Clearwater Revival on bass, Kurt Howell on keyboards and on lead vocals Tim Goodman, replaced in the year by David Jenkins who previously sang with Pablo Cruise. During their five years of existence, Warner Brothers' country rock outfit Southern Pacific have enjoyed a good deal of success with 1988 hits *New Shade of Blue*, and *Honey, I Dare You*, gaining placings of No.2 & 5 respectively. Other notable chart entries came in the shape of *Killbilly Hill*, *A Girl Like Emmylou*, and in 1985 *Thing About You*, featuring Emmylou Harris. This appeared on her 1990 *Duets*, album. They also saw moderate chart success in 1990, recording with Carlene Carter. (Maurice Hope)

SOUTHERN PACIFIC.
Tracks: First one to go / Someone's gonna love me tonight / Thing about you / Perfect stranger / Send me somebody to love / Reno bound / Blaster / Luanne / Heroes / Bluebird wine.
CD 9252012
■ LP. 9252011
WEA / Aug '85 / WEA.

ZUMA.
Tracks: Midnight highway / Honey I dare you / New shade of blue / Dream on / Invisible man, The / Wheels on the line / Just hang on / All is lost / Bail out / Trail of tears.
CD 925609 2
LP. 925609 1
■ MC 925609 4
WEA / Jun '88 / WEA.

Sovine, Red

Country singer Sovine was born Woodrow Wilson Sovine in 1918 and died in 1980. He was a popular regular on the Grand Ole Opry for many years before hitting stardom with truck-driving songs, beginning with *Giddyup Go* in '63. *Phantom 309* is the ultimate truck-drivin' ghost story and *Teddy Bear* scored in country, pop and British charts. (Donald Clarke)

16 ALL TIME FAVOURITES.
Tracks: Not Advised.
LP. . . . . SLP 3010
MC . . . . GT 53010
Starday (USA) / Apr '87 / Crusader Marketing Co.

16 GREATEST HITS: RED SOVINE.
Tracks: Not Advised.
LP. . . . . SLP 991
MC . . . . GT 5991
Starday (USA) / Apr '87 / Crusader Marketing Co.
CD . . . . CD 1013
Gusto (USA) / '88.

16 NEW GOSPEL SONGS.
Tracks: Not Advised.
LP. . . . . GT 0013
Gusto (USA) / Mar '88.

BEST OF RED SOVINE.
Tracks: Not Advised.
LP. . . . . SLP 952
MC . . . . GT 5952
Starday (USA) / Apr '87 / Crusader Marketing Co.

CLASSIC NARRATIONS.
Tracks: Not Advised.
LP. . . . . SLP 436
Starday (USA) / Apr '87 / Crusader Marketing Co.

GIDDY UP GO.
Tracks: Giddy up go.
7" . . . . SD 177
Starday (USA) / Sep '81 / Crusader Marketing Co.

GIDDY-UP-GO.
Tracks: Not Advised.
LP. . . . . GT 0073
Gusto (USA) / '80.

LITTLE ROSA.
Tracks: If Jesus came to your house / Are you mine / Hold everything / Why baby why / Outlaw / Best years of my life, The / Little Rosa / I'm so glad / You are mine (blue moon of Kentucky).
LP. . . . . BDL 1028
Bulldog Records / Jul '82 / President Records / Jazz Music / Wellard Dist. / TKO Records Ltd.

ONE AND ONLY, THE.
Tracks: No money in this deal / One is a lonely number / Invitation to the blues / If I could come back / Brand new low / Hold everything / Little Rosa / Why baby why / Color of the blues / Heart of a man, A / Long time to forget / More from habit than desire.
LP. . . . . OFF 9005
Official / '89 / Charly / Cadillac Music / Jazz Music.

PHANTOM 309.
Tracks: Not Advised.
LP. . . . . GT 0072
Gusto (USA) / '80.

SUNDAY WITH SOVINE.
Tracks: Not Advised.
LP. . . . . SLP 427
MC . . . . GT 5427
Starday (USA) / Apr '87 / Crusader Marketing Co.

SUPER COLLECTION - BEST OF RED SOVINE.
Tracks: Not Advised.
Double LP . . . . GTV 111
Gusto (USA) / Mar '88.

TEDDY BEAR.
Tracks: Teddy bear / Daddy.
■ LP. . . . . LSA 3286
RCA / '79.
LP. . . . . GT 0071
Gusto (USA) / '80.
LP. . . . . SD 968X
MC . . . . SDC 968
Starday (USA) / '80 / Crusader Marketing Co.
■ 7" . . . . RCA 80
RCA / May '81.

Spacek, Sissy

Major actress/singer was born Mary Elizabeth Spacek on 25.12.1959 in Quitman, Texas. Gained vast acclaim for her portrayal of Loretta Lynn in the 1980 movie *Coalminer's Daughter* - winning an Academy Award. Also recorded the MCA soundtrack album, where she does songs made famous by Lynn - surprising many with her talent (although she'd previously had some experience recording as Rainbo, on Roulette). Enjoyed a No. 24 hit with the title track and later some modest success on Atlantic during the early 1980's. In 1983 *Lonely but only for you* supplied her with a top 15 single. (Maurice Hope - August 1993)

COAL MINER'S DAUGHTER.
Tracks: Coal miner's daughter / I'm a honky tonk girl.
■ 7" . . . . MCA 674
MCA / Feb '81.

HANGIN' UP MY HEART.
Tracks: Hangin' up my heart / Have I told you lately that I love you / He don't know me / Lonely but only for you / This time I'm gonna beat you to the truck / Honky tonkin' / Old home town / Smooth talkin' daddy / If you could only see me now / If I can just get through tonight.
■ LP. 790 100-1
Atlantic / Nov '83.

Sparks, Larry

BEST OF LARRY SPARKS.
Tracks: Not Advised.
LP. . . . . REBEL 1609
MC . . . . REBEL 1609C
Rebel (1) / '88 / Projection / Backs Distribution.

BLUE SPARKS.
Tracks: Not Advised.
LP. . . . . REBEL 1618
MC . . . . REBEL 1618C
Rebel (1) / '88 / Projection / Backs Distribution.

DARK HALLOW.
Tracks: Not Advised.
LP. . . . . REBEL 1597
Rebel (1) / '88 / Projection / Backs Distribution.

GONNA BE MOVIN'.
Tracks: Not Advised.
LP. . . . . REBEL 1664
MC . . . . REBEL 1664C
Rebel (1) / '88 / Projection / Backs Distribution.

JOHN DEERE TRACTOR.
Tracks: Not Advised.
LP. . . . . REBEL 1588
MC . . . . REBEL 1588C
Rebel (1) / '88 / Projection / Backs Distribution.

LARRY SPARKS SINGS HANK WILLIAMS.
Tracks: No one will ever know / Dixie cannonball / Someday you'll call my name / I'm so lonesome I could cry / Battle of Armegeddon / Waltz of the wind / Singing waterfall / Mind your own business / My heart would know / I saw the light / Mansion on the hill / Blue love.
LP. . . . . CO 759
County (USA) / '89 / Projection / Mike's Country Music Room / Swift.

LONESOME GUITAR (Sparks, Larry & The Lonesome Ramblers).
Tracks: Chittlin' cookin' time in Cheatum County / Faded love / Old spinning wheel, The / Ramblin' guitar / In the garden / Florida blues / Carroll County blues / Time changes everything / Buffalo girls / Farewell blues / Under the double eagle / Low and lonely.
LP . . . . **REBEL 1633**
MC . . . . **REBEL 1633C**
Rebel (1) / '85 / Projection / Backs Distribution.

RAMBLIN' BLUEGRASS (Sparks, Larry & The Lonesome Ramblers).
Tracks: Not Advised.
LP . . . . **GT 0010**
Gusto (USA) / Mar '88.

TESTING TIMES, THE.
Tracks: Not Advised.
LP . . . . **REBEL 1611**
MC . . . . **REBEL 1611C**
Rebel (1) / '88 / Projection / Backs Distribution.

Spears, Billie Jo

A country singer with a bluesy voice and down-home personality, Billie Jo Spears, born in Texas in 1937, is especially popular in Britain. A child prodigy, she appeared on the Louisiana Hayride in 1951 and 1952 and the following year she recorded *Too Old For Toys, Too Young For Boys* on Abbot. She had her first real hit on Capitol in 1968 and her 1975 smash, *Blanket On The Ground*, was a No 1 country hit in America and reached No 6 in the UK pop chart. In recent years she has not had a contract with a major label in the US but all her albums have done well in Britain. (Donald Clarke)

16 COUNTRY FAVOURITES.
Tracks: You're my man / One more chance / Cheatin' kind, The / I'll take a melody / Look what they've done to my song Ma / If it ain't love / Ease the want in me / Dallas / It makes no difference now.
CD . . . . **PWK 069**
Pickwick / Sep '88 / Pickwick Records.
MC . . . . **HSC 3277**
Hallmark / Jun '89 / Pickwick Records.

17 GOLDEN PIECES OF BILLIE JO SPEARS.
Tracks: Look what they've done to my song, Ma / It makes no difference now / He's on the run again / Danny / I'm so lonesome I could cry / Fever / You're my man / Ease the want in me / Dallas / Sunshine / Come on home / Which way are you going / I stayed long enough / I'll never be free / Step child / Souvenirs and Californian memories / It coulda been me.
LP . . . . **BDL 2033**
Bulldog Records / Nov '83 / President Records / Jazz Music / Wellard Dist. / TKO Records Ltd.

57 CHEVROLET.
Tracks: 57 Chevrolet / Last rose of summer.
■ **7"** . . . . **UP 36434**
United Artists / Aug '78.

ANY OLE WIND THAT BLOWS.
Tracks: Any ole wind that blows / Love ain't the question.
■ **7"** . . . . **UP 627**
United Artists / Jun '80.

APOLOGISING ROSE.
Tracks: Apologising Rose.
7" . . . . **RITZ 027**
Ritz / Aug '82 / Pinnacle / Midland Records.

BEST OF BILLIE JO SPEARS.
Tracks: Mr. Walker / It's all over / Blanket on the ground / '57 Chevrolet / Misty blue / Rainy days & stormy nights / What I've got in mind / Never did like whiskey / Standing tall / Your good girl's gonna go bad.
MC Set **4XLL-9282**
Capitol (Specials) / '89.

BILLIE JO SPEARS.
Tracks: Not Advised.
LP . . . . **RITZLP 0016**
MC . . . . **RITZC 0016**
Ritz / Oct '83 / Pinnacle / Midland Records.

BILLIE JO SPEARS EMI COUNTRY MASTERS.
Tracks: I love you because / He's got more love in his little finger / Help me make it through the night / Marty Gray / I'll share my world with you / I stayed long enough / Today I started loving you again / It could a' been me / Snowbird / See the funny little clown / Harper Valley PTA / Blanket on the ground / (I never promised you a) Rose Garden / Stay away from the apple tree / Lay down beside me / Silver wings and golden rings / Livin' in a house full of love / What I've got in mind / Apartment No.9 / On the rebound / Faded love / Never did like whiskey / Your old love letters / I'm not easy / Yours love / If you want me / Heart over mind / Too much is not enough / Mr. Walker it's all over / Lonely hearts club / Tips and tables / Teardrops will kiss the morning dew / True love / I've got to go / Take me to your world / '57 Chevrolet / Stand by your man / Love ain't gonna wait for us / Price I pay to stay, The / Yesterday / I will survive / Livin' our love together / Games people play, The / Sing me an old fashioned song / Rainy days and rainy nights / Standing tall / Misty blue / Your good girl's gonna go bad / For the good times / What the world needs now is love.
CD Set . . . . **CDEM 1481**
MC Set . . . . **TCEM 1481**
EMI / Apr '93 / EMI.

BLANKET ON THE GROUND.
Tracks: Blanket on the ground / I can only judge your future by his past / Then give him back to me / Permanently lonely / Since I fell for you / Come on home / All I want is you / Before your time / I've never loved anyone more.
■ **LP** . . . . **GO 2010**
Liberty / May '81.

BLANKET ON THE GROUND.
Tracks: Blanket on the ground.
7" . . . . **UP 35805**
United Artists / Apr '75 / EMI.

COUNTRY COLLECTION.
Tracks: Not Advised.
CD . . . . **KNCD 13055**
■ **MC** . . . . **KNMC 13055**
Knight / Jul '90.

COUNTRY GIRL.
Tracks: Not Advised.
■ **LP** . . . . **WW 5109**
Warwick / Nov '81.

EVERYTIME I SING A LOVE SONG.
Tracks: Everytime I sing a love song / Don't ever let go of me.
■ **7"** . . . . **UP 36285**
United Artists / Jul '77.

FEVER.
Tracks: Look what they've done to my song, Ma / It makes no difference now / He's on the run again / Danny boy / I'm so lonesome I could cry / Fever / You're my man / Ease the want in me / Dallas / Sunshine.
LP . . . . **CBR 1005**
MC . . . . **KCBR 1005**
Premier (Sony) / May '85 / Sony / Pinnacle.

FOR THE GOOD TIMES.
Tracks: For the good times / I love you because / Games people play / Yours love / What a love I have in you / Your old love letters / Breakaway / Help me make it through the night / True love / I'll share my world with you / Put a little love in your heart / Marty Gray / Today I started loving you again / Snowbird.
LP . . . . **MFP 50515**
■ **MC** . . . . **TCMFP 50515**
MFP / Apr '81.

GREATEST HITS OF BILLE JO SPEARS.
Tracks: Not Advised.
CD . . . . **K 3018-2**
LP . . . . **U 3018-2**
Spectrum (CD) / Jun '89 / M.S.D.

I CAN HEAR KENTUCKY CALLING ME (Spears, Billie Jo & Carrie Duncan).
Tracks: I can hear Kentucky calling me / Million tears.
7" . . . . **RITZ 042**
Ritz / Apr '83 / Pinnacle / Midland Records.

I WILL SURVIVE.
Tracks: I will survive / Angel in your arms / Everyday I have to cry / It should have been easy / I'm good at what I do / Livin' our love together / I think I'll go home / You / Happy ever after / Rainy days and stormy nights.
■ **LP** . . . . **UAG 30249**
United Artists / '79.
■ **7"** . . . . **UP 601**
United Artists / Jul '79.

I'VE GOT TO GO.
Tracks: I've got to go / There's more to a tear.
■ **7"** . . . . **UP 36393**
United Artists / May '78.

IF YOU WANT ME.
Tracks: If you want me / Here comes those lies again.
7" . . . . **UP 36236**
United Artists / Mar '77 / EMI.

IF YOU WANT ME.
Tracks: If you want me / Never did like whiskey / Too far gone / Heartbreak Hotel / Here comes those lies again / I'm not easy / Seeing is believing / Here comes my baby back again / Every word I write / That's what friends are for / No other man.
■ **LP** . . . . **GO 2024**
Liberty / Jun '81.

IT COULD HAVE BEEN ME.
Tracks: He's on the run again / Danny (baby ruby) / Come on home / Which way you gone Billy / You're my man / I'll never be free / Step child / Souvenirs and Californian memories / It coulda been me.
LP . . . . **SHLP 104**
MC . . . . **SHTC 104**
Castle Showcase / Apr '86 / Arabesque Ltd.

LOVE AIN'T GONNA WAIT FOR US.
Tracks: Love ain't gonna wait for us / Say it again.
■ **7"** . . . . **UP 36480**
United Artists / Jan '79.

MAGIC OF BILLIE JO SPEARS, THE.
Tracks: Not Advised.
CD . . . . **TKOCD 002**
MC . . . . **TKOCS 002**
TKO Records / '92 / TKO Records Ltd / President Records.

MIDNIGHT BLUE.
Tracks: Midnight blue / Sweet dreams.
7" . . . . **PS 1004**
Premier (Sony) / Jul '85 / Sony / Pinnacle.
LP . . . . **PMP 1007**
MC . . . . **PMPK 1007**
Premier (Sony) / Feb '87 / Sony / Pinnacle.

MISTY BLUE.
Tracks: Not Advised.
CD **15 476**
MC **79 476**
Laserlight / Nov '92 / TBD / Taylors.

NEVER DID LIKE WHISKY.
Tracks: Never did like whisky / No other man.
■ **7"** . . . . **UP 36218**
United Artists / Feb '77.

ODE TO BILLIE JO.
Tracks: Ode to Billy Joe / Take me to your world / Livin' in a house full of love / Softly and tenderly / Pittsburgh General / Faded love / You and your sweet love / I stayed long enough / I don't wanna play house / Big stick of dynamite / Stand by your man / Tips and tables / Till something better comes along / Get behind me, Satan, and push / When you hurt me (more than I love you) / Apartment No.9 / It coulda been me / Souvenirs and Californian memories / He's got more love in his little finger / Mr. Walker, it's all over.
■ **LP** . . . . **EG 2605281**
Capitol / Apr '85.
■ **MC** . . . . **EG 2605284**
Capitol / Apr '85.

SING ME AN OLD FASHIONED SONG.
Tracks: Sing me an old fashioned song / Let's try to wake it up again.
■ **7"** . . . . **UP 36179**
United Artists / Dec '76.

SINGLES ALBUM: BILLIE JO SPEARS.
Tracks: Not Advised.
■ **LP** . . . . **UAK 30231**
United Artists / '87.

SINGLES: BILLIE JO SPEARS.
Tracks: Blanket on the ground / Silver wings and golden rings / Another somebody done somebody wrong song / What I've got in mind / Sing me an old fashioned song / Every time two fools collide / If you want me / Every time I sing a love song / Misty blue / Never did like whiskey / I've got to go / Lonely hearts club / '57 Chevrolet / Love ain't gonna wait for us.
LP . . . . **UCK 30231**
MC . . . . **TCK 30231**
United Artists / Mar '79 / EMI.
■ **CD** . . . . **CDP 791 240 2**
EMI / Nov '88.

SINGS THE COUNTRY GREATS.
Tracks: 57 Chevrolet / Loving him was easier / Another somebody done somebody wrong..(Hey won't you play) / Till something better comes along / Sing me an old fashioned song / Every time I sing a love song / See the funny little clown / That's what friends are for / Blanket on the ground / Ode to Billy Joe / Misty blue / I don't wanna play house / Hurt / Stand by your man / He's got more love in his little finger / Take me to your world.
LP . . . . **MFP 5784**
MC . . . . **TCMFP 5784**
MFP / Apr '87 / EMI.
CD . . . . **CDMFP 5784**
MFP / May '91 / EMI.

SPECIAL SONGS.
Tracks: What the world needs now is love / Snowbird / Lay down beside me / Broken lady / Everything is beautiful / Heartbreak hotel / Desperado / Your good girl's gonna go bad / I fall to pieces / Rose garden / Bridge over troubled water / Loving him was easier.
■ **LP** . . . . **LBG 30333**
Liberty / Jan '81.

STAND BY YOUR MAN.
Tracks: Not Advised.
CD . . . . **CDCD 1099**
MC . . . . **CDMC 1099**
Charly / Apr '93 / Charly.

SWINGIN.
Tracks: Swingin' / I can hear Kentucky calling me.
7" . . . . **RITZ 046**
Ritz / May '83 / Pinnacle / Midland Records.

TWENTY COUNTRY GREATS.
Tracks: Queen of the silver dollar / Crying time / I'll never love like this again / All I have to do is dream / Tenessee waltz / What I've got in mind / Just the way you are / This ole house / Rocky top / Blue bayou / For the good times / Fire and rain / Crystal chandeliers / It's a heartache / Silver threads and golden needles / Fifty seven Chevrolet / I'm gonna be a country girl again / Here you come again / Blue blue day / Blanket on the ground.
MC . . . . **WW 22010**
Warwick / Nov '86 / Sony / Henry Hadaway Organisation / Multiple Sound Distributors.

UNMISTAKABLY.
Tracks: Every time I close my eyes / One smokey rose / Mutual aquaintance / I got this train to ride / If wishes were wings / We need to walk / Keep me from dreamin' / Star, The / We're over / It won't be long.
CD . . . . **ETCD 194**
Etude / Sep '92 / Total / BMG.

VOICE OF BJS, THE.
Tracks: Not Advised.
LP. . . . . **HAT 3106**
MC . . . . **HATC 3106**
Stetson / Aug '89 / Crusader Marketing Co. / Swift / Wellard Dist. / Midland Records / C.M. Distribution.

WE JUST CAME APART AT THE DREAMS.
Tracks: Can't change my heart / Blowing away / Sweet dreams / Love dies hard / C'est la vie / We just came apart at the dreams / Settin' me up / Too far gone / Ain't no money / Baby on my mind.
LP. . . . . **PREM 101**
MC . . . . **PREMK 101**
Premier (Sony) / May '85 / Sony / Pinnacle.

WHAT I'VE GOT IN MIND.
Tracks: What I've got in mind / Everytime two fools collide.
■ 7" . . . . **BP 428**
United Artists / Sep '85.

WHAT I'VE GOT IN MIND.
Tracks: You could know as much about a stranger / I've never loved anyone more / I can only judge your future by his past / Too much is not enough / Yesterday / What the world needs now is love / I fall to pieces / Blanket on the ground / What I've got in mind / There's more to a tear than meets the eye / Everyday I have to cry / Sweet music man / Husbands and wives / Here come's my baby / Slow movin' outlaw / 57 Chevrolet.
■ LP. . . . . **UAS 29955**
United Artists / Sep '76.
CD . . . . **CDP 791 241 2**
■ CD . . . . **CZ 148**
Liberty / Dec '88.
■ LP. . . . . **EMS 1312**
EMI / Nov '88.
■ MC . . . . **TCEMS 1312**
EMI / Nov '88.

YOUR GOOD GIRL'S GONNA GO BAD.
Tracks: Your good girl's gonna go bad / Heartbreak Hotel.
■ 7" . . . . **UP 636**
United Artists / Nov '80.

Speller, Jenny

RIDING ON A RAINBOW.
Tracks: Riding on a rainbow.
7" . . . . **ROX 015**
Roxon / Apr '81 / Pinnacle.

Spencer, Johnny

ALL MY CLOUDY DAYS ARE GONE.
Tracks: Not Advised.
MC . . . . **IRBC 2004**
Accordion Record Club / '88 / Accordion Record Club.

ONE STRIKE AT A TIME.
Tracks: One strike at a time / Hanging of the monkey.
■ 7" . . . . **PF 3010**
Pastafont / Jun '84.

STRIKE SONG, THE.
Tracks: Strike song, The / Hanging of the monkey.
7" . . . . **PF 3011**
Pastafont / Oct '84 / Pastafont Music.

Spicher, Buddy

AMERICAN SAMPLER.
Tracks: Not Advised.
LP. . . . . **FF 021**
Flying Fish (USA) / Mar '89 / Cadillac Music / Roots Records / Projection / C.M. Distribution / Direct Distribution / Jazz Music / Duncans / A.D.A Distribution.

BUDDIES (Spicher, Buddy & Buddy Emmons).
Tracks: Autumn fling / Little darlin' / Uncle Pen / Magic swing / Watch what happens / Joy spring / Broken down in tiny pieces.
LP. . . . . **SNTF 741**
Sonet / Nov '77 / Swift / C.M. Distribution / Roots Records / Jazz Music / Sonet Records / Cadillac Music / Projection / Wellard Dist. / Hot Shot.
LP. . . . . **FF 041**
Flying Fish (USA) / Mar '89 / Cadillac Music / Roots Records / Projection / C.M. Distribution / Direct Distribution / Jazz Music / Duncans / A.D.A Distribution.

FIDDLE CLASSICS.
Tracks: Not Advised.
LP. . . . . **FF 278**
Flying Fish (USA) / Mar '89 / Cadillac Music / Roots Records / Projection / C.M. Distribution / Direct Distribution / Jazz Music / Duncans / A.D.A Distribution.

ME AND MY HEROES.
Tracks: Not Advised.
LP. . . . . **FF 065**
MC . . . . **FF 065C**
Flying Fish (USA) / '89 / Cadillac Music / Roots Records / Projection / C.M. Distribution / Direct Distribution / Jazz Music / Duncans / A.D.A Distribution.

PLATINUM FIDDLE.
Tracks: Orange blossom special / Black mountain rag / Touch my heart / Norwegian wood / Rocky top / Bobby's rainbow / Twinkle twinkle little star / Haste to the wedding / Eighth of January / Shannon waltz / Fire on the mountain / Snowflake breakdown.
LP. . . . . **PRCV 105**
President / Aug '80 / Grapevine Distribution / Target Records / Jazz Music / Taylors.

Spink, Arthur

COUNTRY BOX.
Tracks: Dixie / Gypsy woman / Three bells / Texas in my heart / Don't it make my brown eyes blue / San Antonio Rose / Sweet surrender / You're the only good thing / There goes my everything / Sittin' alone in an old rockin' chair / Battle hymn of the republic / Island of dreams / Duelling banjos / Last farewell, The.
■ LP. . . . . **GES 1210**
Emerald / Nov '79.

HAPPY ACCORDION.
Tracks: Not Advised.
LP. . . . . **GES 1197**
Accordion Record Club / '84 / Accordion Record Club.

Spittle, Dusty

COUNTRY WORLD OF..
Tracks: Not Advised.
MC . . . . **SPVP 172C**
Viking (New Zealand) / Apr '80 / Harmonia Mundi (UK) / Discovery.

Sprague, Carl T.

Born near Houston, Texas in 1895 and raised in a family of cattlemen, Carl T "Doc" Sprague learned many of his songs at real round up campfires. As a young man Carl used to go on cattle drives with his uncles and their helping cowhands. With such a background, plus a love for music, it was only natural that he became one of the very first to help make the song of the American West popular through the medium of the phonograph record. Carl entered Texas Agricultural and Mechanical College in 1915. After world war I he returned to Texas and stared leading a band. In 1925 backed by a group of student musicians, he put on a 60-minute once-a-week program for the college experimental radio station. During the same summer he packed up his guitar and travelled to Camden, New Jersey to make his first appearance in a recording studio. *When the work's all done this fall*, a touching ballad about a cowpuncher killed in a night stampede, was his first recording and would become his most popular. More than 900,000 copies of the 10-inch 78rpm disc were sold, an unusually large number for that type of record in those days. Once his recording days were over in 1929. Carl T Sprague never aspired to follow music as a profession. But throughout his long life he has enjoyed singing his ballads, most of them with a Western flavour accompanying himself on an antique guitar. Carl died in 1975

CLASSIC COWBOY SONGS.
Tracks: Home on the range / It is no secret / Following the cowtrail / Girl I loved in sunny Tennessee, The / When the work's all done this fall / Kissing / Club meeting, The / Bad companions / Rounded up in glory / Red river valley / Roll on little dogies / Last great roundup, The / Last fierce charge, The / Gambler, The / Boston burglar / Orphan girl, The / Utah Carol / Just break the news to mother / Chicken / Cowman's prayer / Sarah Jane / My Carrie Lee / Zebra dun / Mormon cowboy, The / Cowboy's meditation / Kicking mule, The.
CD . . . . **BCD 15456**
Bear Family / Dec '88 / Rollercoaster Records / Swift / Direct Distribution.

COWBOY SONGS FROM TEXAS.
Tracks: Gold mine in the sky / Boston burglar / Orphan girl, The / Utah Carol / Just break the news to mother / Chicken / When you come to the end of the day / Pal that I love, The / Ole faithful / Cowman's prayer / Sarah Jane / My Carrie Lee / Zebra Dun / Mormon cowboy, The / Cowboy's meditation / Kicking mule, The.
LP. . . . . **BF 15006**
Bear Family / Oct '80 / Rollercoaster Records / Swift / Direct Distribution.

FIRST POPULAR SINGING COWBOY,THE.
Tracks: Home on the range / It is no secret / Following the cowtrail / Girl I loved in sunny Tennessee, The / When the work's all done this fall / Kissing / Club meeting, The / Bad companions / Rounded up in glory / Red river valley / Roll on little dogies / Last round-up, The / Last fierce charge, The / Gambler, The.
LP. . . . . **BF 15002**
Bear Family / Oct '80 / Rollercoaster Records / Swift / Direct Distribution.

Sprouse, Blaine

BLAINE SPROUSE.
Tracks: Not Advised.
LP. . . . . **ROUNDER 0117**
Rounder / '88 / Projection / Roots Records / Swift / C.M. Distribution / Topic Records / Jazz Music / Hot Shot / A.D.A Distribution / Direct Distribution.

BRILLIANCY.
Tracks: Don't let your deal go down / Florida rag / Fireball express / Miss the Mississippi / Brilliancy / Did you ever see the devil, Uncle Joe / Cherokee Maggie / Mist on the moor, The / Tennessee hayride / Paula's waltz / Old Ebenezer.
LP. . . . . **ROUNDER 0209**
Rounder / Aug '85 / Projection / Roots Records / Swift / C.M. Distribution / Topic Records / Jazz Music / Hot Shot / A.D.A Distribution / Direct Distribution.
MC . . . . **ROUNDER 0209C**
Rounder / Aug '88 / Projection / Roots Records / Swift / C.M. Distribution / Topic Records / Jazz Music / Hot Shot / A.D.A Distribution / Direct Distribution.

INDIAN SPRINGS (Sprouse, Blaine & Kenny Baker).
Tracks: Oh demi slippers / Molly darlin' / Owensboro / Avalon / September waltz / Three days in Dublin / Coker creek / K and W waltz / Cottontown breakdown / Indian springs.
CD . . . . **ROUNDER 0259CD**
LP. . . . . **ROUNDER 0259**
MC . . . . **ROUNDER 0259C**
Rounder / '89 / Projection / Roots Records / Swift / C.M. Distribution / Topic Records / Jazz Music / Hot Shot / A.D.A Distribution / Direct Distribution.

SUMMERTIME.
Tracks: Not Advised.
LP. . . . . **ROUNDER 0155**
MC . . . . **ROUNDER 0155C**
Rounder / '88 / Projection / Roots Records / Swift / C.M. Distribution / Topic Records / Jazz Music / Hot Shot / A.D.A Distribution / Direct Distribution.

Stafford, Jim

LITTLE BITS AND PIECES.
Tracks: Little bits and pieces / Banjo Billy.
7" . . . . **A 4235**
CBS / Nov '84 / Sony.

MY GIRL BILL.
Tracks: My girl Bill / L.A. Mamma.
■ 7" **2006 423**
MGM (Polydor) / Jul '74.

SPIDERS AND SNAKES.
Tracks: Spiders and snakes.
■ 7" **2006 374**
MGM (Polydor) / Apr '74.

YOUR BULLDOG DRINKS CHAMPAGNE.
Tracks: Your bulldog drinks champagne / Real good time.
■ 7" **2006485**
MGM (Polydor) / Feb '75.

Staines, Bill

REDBIRD'S WING.
Tracks: Not Advised.
LP. . . . . **PH 1118**
MC . . . . **PH 1118C**
Philo (USA) / '88 / Roots Records / Projection / Topic Records / Direct Distribution / Ross Records / C.M. Distribution / Impetus Records.

RODEO ROSE.
Tracks: Not Advised.
LP. . . . . **PH 1079**
Philo (USA) / '88 / Roots Records / Projection / Topic Records / Direct Distribution / Ross Records / C.M. Distribution / Impetus Records.

WILD WILD HEART.
Tracks: Not Advised.
LP. . . . . **PH 1100**
Philo (USA) / Dec '85 / Roots Records / Projection / Topic Records / Direct Distribution / Ross Records / C.M. Distribution / Impetus Records.
MC . . . . **PH 1100C**
Philo (USA) / '88 / Roots Records / Projection / Topic Records / Direct Distribution / Ross Records / C.M. Distribution / Impetus Records.

Stampley, Joe

Born on 06.06.1943 in Springhill, Louisiana, vocalist Stampley first recorded for Imperial in 1957, then in 1960 joined Chicago's Chess label. His early soulful edged country charted regularly throughout the 1970's and 1980's - following his earlier ventures with his band the Uniques during the late sixties. Made his mark in 1972, when *Soul song* made No. 1, the first of three solo chart toppers - his 1975 trucking single *Roll on big Mama* and the oft recorded Art Neville's *All these things* (1976) repeating the feat. Stampley had originally done the song with his pop unit, the Uniques, but now cut it as a country song. It was also given another airing in 1981 - during his stay with Epic. Stampley's popular run has seen him gain fifty solo hits, studded with top ten affairs - *I'm still loving you, Bring it on home, Red wine and blue memories,If you've got ten minutes* and *Put your clothes back on* a mere sample. In 1979 he had a meeting at London's Hard Rock Cafe that would change his and Moe Bandy's careers - for they were playing the Wembley Country Music Festival, where they came up with the idea of doing some duets together. Stampley's keyboard player, Ansley Fleetwood came up with the belting *Just good ol' boys*. The die had been cast. Moe and Joe during the next six years were to become one of the hottest acts around - garnering six consecutive top ten singles by 1984. The trailblazing, good time, honky-tonking *Just good ol' boys* topped the charts in 1979 and secured them with the CMA's Duo Award in 1980. Other singles from the run were to feature *Holding the bag , Hey Joe (Hey Moe)* and *Where's the dress* (a slick parody of Boy George). Backing up the venture were four albums to go with the deal, all on Columbia - Bandy's label. By the time the embers cooled, both Moe and Joe were to find it difficult to re-establish their respective solo careers - Joe trying out with the Evergreen label. (Maurice Hope - August 1993)

20 GREATEST HITS: JOE STAMPLEY.
Tracks: Not Advised.
LP 20096
MC 40096
Astan (USA) / Nov '84.

GREATEST HITS: JOE STAMPLEY.
Tracks: Roll on big mama / Billy, get me a woman / Whiskey talkin' / What a night / Sheik of Chicago / Dear woman / There she goes again / Everyday I have to cry some / Hey baby / Take me back.
■ **LP** . . . . EPC 83487
Epic / Apr '79.

JOE STAMPLEY.
Tracks: Not Advised.
MC . . . . ZCGAS 709
Audio Fidelity(USA) / Oct '84 / Stage One Records.

SHEIK OF CHICAGO.
Tracks: Sheik of Chicago / Hey baby.
■ **7"** . . . . EPC 7191
Epic / '79.

SOUL SONG.
Tracks: Soul song / Most beautiful girl in the world, The / She's a lady / You make life easy / I can't help myself / If you touch me / Bring it on home (to your woman) / I'm still loving you / How lucky can one man be / Too far gone / I live to love you / Strong comeback / Can you imagine how I feel.
LP . . . . NR 5076
■ **MC** . . . . ZCE 5076
Ember / '80 / TKO Records Ltd / President Records.

TAKE ME HOME TO SOMEWHERE.
Tracks: Take me home to somewhere / Try a little tenderness.
■ **7"** . . . . EMBS 340
Ember / Feb '75.

TAKE ME HOME TO SOMEWHERE.
Tracks: Dallas Alice / Who will I be lovin' now / Backtrackin' / Try a little tenderness / Penny / Night of loving: Take me to somewhere, A / Good things / Unchained melody / Soft as a rose / Hall of famous losers / My Louisiana woman / Weatherman, The.
■ **LP** . . . . NR 5087
Ember / '80 / TKO Records Ltd / President Records.

Stanley Brothers

The Stanley Brothers were Carter Glen Stanley, lead guitar and vocals (1925-66) Ralph Edmund Stanley, banjo and vocals (born 1927). Leading the Clinch Mountain Boys they were the most influential and popular bluegrass group after Carter's death, appearing at bluegrass festivals and recording extensively. Their songs have been covered by John Conlee, Emmylou Harris, Dan Fogelberg and many others. (Donald Clarke)

16 GREATEST HITS: STANLEY BROTHERS.
Tracks: Not Advised.
LP . . . . SLP 3003
MC . . . . GT 53003
Starday (USA) / Apr '87 / Crusader Marketing Co.
LP . . . . SD 3003
Starday (USA) / Mar '88 / Crusader Marketing Co.

1949-52 (Stanley Brothers & The Clinch Mountain Boys).
Tracks: Vision of mother, A / White dove, The / Gathering flowers for the masters bouquet / Angels are singing, The / It's never too late / Have you someone (in Heaven awaiting) / Little glass of wine / Let me be your friend / We'll be sweethearts in Heaven / I love no one but you / Too late to cry / Old home, The / Drunkards hell, The / Fields have turned brown, The / Hey hey hey / Lonesome river, The / I'm a man of constant sorrow / Pretty Polly / Life of sorrow, A / Sweetest love / Wandering boy, The / Let's part the best of friends.
CD . . . . BCD 15564
Bear Family / Apr '92 / Rollercoaster Records / Swift / Direct Distribution.

20 BLUEGRASS ORIGINALS.
Tracks: Not Advised.
LP . . . . SLP 5026
MC . . . . GT 55026
Starday (USA) / Apr '87 / Crusader Marketing Co.

83 COLLECTORS EDITION VOL 1.
Tracks: Not Advised.
LP . . . . GT 0103
Gusto (USA) / Mar '88.

83 COLLECTORS EDITION VOL 2.
Tracks: Not Advised.
LP . . . . GT 0104
Gusto (USA) / Mar '88.

83 COLLECTORS EDITION VOL 3.
Tracks: Not Advised.
LP . . . . GT 0105
Gusto (USA) / Mar '88.

83 COLLECTORS EDITION VOL 4.
Tracks: Not Advised.
LP . . . . GT 0106
Gusto (USA) / Mar '88.

83 COLLECTORS EDITION VOL 5.
Tracks: Not Advised.
LP . . . . GT 0107
Gusto (USA) / Mar '88.

83 COLLECTORS EDITION VOL 6.
Tracks: Not Advised.
LP . . . . GT 0108
Gusto (USA) / Mar '88.

BANJO IN THE HILLS.
Tracks: Not Advised.
LP . . . . KLP 872
MC . . . . GT 5872
King (USA) / Apr '87 / Charly.

BEST OF THE STANLEY BROTHERS.
Tracks: Not Advised.
LP . . . . SLP 953
MC . . . . GT 5953
Starday (USA) / Apr '87 / Crusader Marketing Co.

COUNTRY PICKIN' AND SINGIN'.
Tracks: Not Advised.
LP . . . . HAT 3125
Stetson / '89 / Crusader Marketing Co. / Swift / Wellard Dist. / Midland Records / C.M. Distribution.

FOLK CONCERT.
Tracks: Not Advised.
LP . . . . KLP 834
MC . . . . GT 5834
King (USA) / Apr '87 / Charly.

FOLK SONG FESTIVAL.
Tracks: Not Advised.
LP . . . . SLP 791
MC . . . . GT 5791
Starday (USA) / Apr '87 / Crusader Marketing Co.

HYMNS AND SACRED SONGS.
Tracks: Not Advised.
CD . . . . KCD 645
King / Nov '92 / New Note / Koch International.

LITTLE OLD COUNTRY CHURCH HOUSE, THE.
Tracks: That old country church / Nobody answered me / Shake my mother's hand for me / I heard my mother call my name in prayer / Mother's only sleeping / Shake hands with mother again / Hide in the blood / Give me your hand / Where we'll never grow old / Leaning on the everlasting arms / Angel band / Farther along.
LP . . . . CO 738
County (USA) / Projection / Mike's Country Music Room / Swift.

LONG JOURNEY HOME.
Tracks: Long journey home / Will you miss me / I'll be true to the one I love / No letter in the mail today / Pretty Polly / Wildwood flower / Two more years and I'll be free / Ramshackle shack on the hill / East Virginia blues / Pig in the pen / Your saddle is empty old pal / Nine pound hammer / Cluck old hen / Wild and reckless hobo / Rabbit in a log / Mountain pickin'.
LP . . . . CO 739
County (USA) / Projection / Mike's Country Music Room / Swift.

ON THE RADIO, VOLUME 1.
Tracks: Roll in sweet baby's arms / Few more seasons, A / Love me darlin' just tonight / Black mountain blues / My Lord's gonna set me free / How mountain girls can love / Mississippi sawyer / Orange blossom special / Daniel prayed / Shenandoah waltz / How far to Little Rock / Mother's footsteps guide me on / Pig in a pen / Cripple creek.
LP . . . . CO 780
MC . . . . CO 780MC
County (USA) / Jul '84 / Projection / Mike's Country Music Room / Swift.

ON THE RADIO, VOLUME 2.
Tracks: Uncle Pen / Little glass of wine / Midnight ramble / Heaven / Don't go out tonight / Fire on the mountain / Mother no longer waits at home / He will set your fields on fire / Big Tilda / If we never meet again / Whoa mule.
LP . . . . CO 781
MC . . . . CO 781MC
County (USA) / Jul '84 / Projection / Mike's Country Music Room / Swift.

ON WCYB FARM AND FUNTIME.
Tracks: Not Advised.
LP . . . . REB 855
Rebel (1) / '75 / Projection / Backs Distribution.

RECORDED LIVE VOL. 2.
Tracks: Not Advised.
LP . . . . REB 1495
Rebel (1) / '75 / Projection / Backs Distribution.

SONGS THEY LIKE THE BEST.
Tracks: Not Advised.
LP . . . . KLP 772
MC . . . . GT 5772
King (USA) / Apr '87 / Charly.

STANLEY BROTHERS.
Tracks: Long journey home / Will you miss me / I'll be true to the one that I love / No letter in the mail today / Pretty Polly / Wildwood flower / Two more years and I'll be free / East Virginia blues / Pig in a pen / Your saddle is empty old pal / Nine pound hammer / Cluck old hen / Wild and reckless hobo / Rabbit in a log / Mountain pickin'.
LP . . . . SAVE 040
Fundamental / Feb '88 / Plastic Head.

STANLEY BROTHERS & THE CLINCH MOUNTAIN BOYS (Stanley Brothers & The Clinch Mountain Boys).
Tracks: Not Advised.
LP . . . . KLP 615
MC . . . . GT 5615
King (USA) / Apr '87 / Charly.

STANLEY BROTHERS (REBEL).
Tracks: Not Advised.
LP . . . . REB 1487
MC . . . . REBMC 1487
Rebel (1) / '75 / Projection / Backs Distribution.

STANLEY BROTHERS OF WEST VIRGINIA (Volume 4).
Tracks: Hold to God's unchanging hand / When I lay my burdens down / In Heaven we'll never grow old / Somebody touched me / Lord I'm coming home / Give me the roses while I live / Swing low sweet chariot / Paul and Silas / Gathering flowers for the masters bouquet / Old country church / Will you miss me.
LP . . . . CO 754
MC . . . . CO 754 MC
County (USA) / Projection / Mike's Country Music Room / Swift.

STANLEY BROTHERS SING BLUEGRASS FOR YOU.
Tracks: Not Advised.
LP . . . . OHCS 323
Old Homestead (USA) / Oct '87 / Swift.

STANLEY BROTHERS VOL.1, THE (Columbia Sessions 1949-50).
Tracks: Vision of mother / White dove / Gathering flowers for the master's bouquet / Angels are singing in heaven tonight, The / It's never too late / Have you someone (in heaven waiting).
LP . . . . SS 09
Rounder / Dec '88 / Projection / Roots Records / Swift / C.M. Distribution / Topic Records / Jazz Music / Hot Shot / A.D.A Distribution / Direct Distribution.

STANLEY BROTHERS VOL.2, THE.
Tracks: Old home, The / Drunkard's hell, The / Fields have turned brown, The / Hey hey hey / Lonesome river, The / I'm a man of constant sorrow / Pretty Polly / Life of sorrow, A / Sweetest love, The / Wandering boy, The / Let's part.
LP . . . . SS 10
Rounder / Dec '88 / Projection / Roots Records / Swift / C.M. Distribution / Topic Records / Jazz Music / Hot Shot / A.D.A Distribution / Direct Distribution.

THAT LITTLE OLD COUNTRY.
Tracks: Not Advised.
LP . . . . SAVE 027
Fundamental / Jun '87 / Plastic Head.

TOGETHER FOR THE LAST TIME.
Tracks: Not Advised.
LP . . . . REB 1512
Rebel (1) / '75 / Projection / Backs Distribution.

UNCLOUDY DAY (Volume 3).
Tracks: Not Advised.
LP . . . . CO 753
MC . . . . CO 753 MC
County (USA) / Projection / Mike's Country Music Room / Swift.

Stanley, Ralph

Born February 27, 1927. Banjo player and vocalist. Early recordings taken from daily radio shows on WNVA, Norton, West Virginia and WCYB in Bristol, Tennessee, starting in 1947.

S 16 ■ DELETED

Band members through the years include Darrell 'Pee Wee' Lambert (mandolin and harmony vocals), Curly Sechler (mandolin, later of Flatt-Scruggs Band fame), Art Stamper and George Shuffler (lead guitar). (Maurice Hope)

'LIVE' AT THE OLD PLACE.
Tracks: Not Advised.
LP . . . . REB 1627
MC . . . . REBMC 1627
Rebel (1) / '75 / Projection / Backs Distribution.

CHILD OF A KING.
Tracks: Not Advised.
LP . . . . REB 1616
MC . . . . REBMC 1616
Rebel (1) / '75 / Projection / Backs Distribution.

CLINCH MOUNTAIN GOSPEL.
Tracks: Not Advised.
LP . . . . REB 1571
MC . . . . REBMC 1571
Rebel (1) / '75 / Projection / Backs Distribution.

CRY FROM THE CROSS.
Tracks: Not Advised.
LP . . . . REB 1499
MC . . . . REBMC 1499
Rebel (1) / '75 / Projection / Backs Distribution.

DOWN WHERE THE RIVER BENDS.
Tracks: Not Advised.
LP . . . . REB 1579
MC . . . . REBMC 1579
Rebel (1) / '75 / Projection / Backs Distribution.

HILLS OF HOME.
Tracks: Not Advised.
LP . . . . KLP 1069
MC . . . . GT 51069
King (USA) / Apr '87 / Charly.

I CAN TELL YOU THE TIME.
Tracks: Not Advised.
LP . . . . REB 1637
MC . . . . REBMC 1637
Rebel (1) / '75 / Projection / Backs Distribution.

I WANT TO PREACH GOSPEL.
Tracks: Not Advised.
LP . . . . REB 1522
MC . . . . REBMC 1522
Rebel (1) / '75 / Projection / Backs Distribution.

I WEAR A WHITE ROSE.
Tracks: Not Advised.
LP . . . . REB 1590
MC . . . . REBMC 1590
Rebel (1) / '75 / Projection / Backs Distribution.

I'LL ANSWER THE CALL.
Tracks: Not Advised.
LP . . . . REB 1657
MC . . . . REBMC 1657
Rebel (1) / '75 / Projection / Backs Distribution.

LET ME REST ON A PEACEFUL MOUNTAIN.
Tracks: Not Advised.
LP . . . . REB 1544
MC . . . . REBMC 1544
Rebel (1) / '75 / Projection / Backs Distribution.

LIVE IN JAPAN (Stanley, Ralph & The Clinch Mountain Boys).
Tracks: Not Advised.
Double LP . . . . REB 2202
Rebel (1) / Aug '87 / Projection / Backs Distribution.

LONESOME AND BLUE.
Tracks: Not Advised.
LP . . . . REB 1648
MC . . . . REBMC 1648
Rebel (1) / '75 / Projection / Backs Distribution.

MAN AND HIS MUSIC, A.
Tracks: Not Advised.
LP . . . . REB 1530
MC . . . . REBMC 1530
Rebel (1) / '75 / Projection / Backs Distribution.

MEMORY OF YOUR SMILE, A.
Tracks: Not Advised.
LP . . . . REB 1606
MC . . . . REBMC 1606
Rebel (1) / '75 / Projection / Backs Distribution.

OLD COUNTRY CHURCH.
Tracks: Not Advised.
LP . . . . REB 1508
MC . . . . REBMC 1508
Rebel (1) / '75 / Projection / Backs Distribution.

OLD HOME PLACE.
Tracks: Not Advised.
LP . . . . REB 1562
MC . . . . REBMC 1562
Rebel (1) / '75 / Projection / Backs Distribution.

ON AND ON.
Tracks: Not Advised.
LP . . . . CO 776
MC . . . . CO 776 C
County (USA) / '75 / Projection / Mike's Country Music Room / Swift.

SNOW COVERED MOUND.
Tracks: Not Advised.
LP . . . . REB 1613
MC . . . . REBMC 1613
Rebel (1) / '75 / Projection / Backs Distribution.

SOMETHING OLD, SOMETHING NEW.
Tracks: Not Advised.
LP . . . . REB 1503
Rebel (1) / '75 / Projection / Backs Distribution.

STANLEY SOUND TODAY.
Tracks: Not Advised.
CD . . . . REBCD 1601
LP . . . . REB 1601
Rebel (1) / '75 / Projection / Backs Distribution.

Starcher, Buddy

COUNTRY LOVE SONGS.
Tracks: Beautiful blue-eyed blonde / West Virginia hills, The / Let's / Song of the waterwheel, The / Those brown eyes / I'll still write your name in the sand / Wildwood flower / Foggy mountain top / Too late to worry / My shadow grows tall / We'll be sweethearts when we're old / Midnight special / Todays joy today.
LP . . . . BF 15017
Bear Family / Oct '80 / Rollercoaster Records / Swift / Direct Distribution.

Starling, John

Former army surgeon, founder member of Washington D.C newgrass band Seldom Scene - staying with them from the unit's inception in 1971 til 1977, when he set out on a solo career, recording two albums *Long time gone* and *Waitin' on a southern train*, both on Sugar Hill released 1980/1982 respectively. Worked as music director on Dolly, Linda & Emmylou's 1988 CMA vocal event of the year winning *Trio* album collaboration. It wasn't the first time the Starling family had assisted harris - for Starling's sister, Fayssoux had sung harmony on her mid - 70s albums *Pieces of the sky* and *Elite hotel*. Starling got together with banjoist/singer - songwriter Carl Jackson (c/w Harris & her acoustic band The Nash Ramblers) for the 1991 album *Spring training* - going on to be a much acclaimed 1992 Grammy winner. After an absence of 15 years, Starling has once again taken up his position as Seldom Scene's forceful lead vocalist. He's been involved in their star-studded *15th Anniversary celebration* (dble album), live at the Kennedy Centre in November 1986, both as co-producer & vocalist. After performing on the band's Sugar Hill *Scene 20 – Twentieth anniversary concert* , another live album albeit modest in comparison - this time recorded at the band's regular Thursday night gig at the Birchmere, Alexandria, VA - November 29/30. 1991, where past & present members John Duffey, Ben Eldridge, Mike Auldridge, Lou Reid, Phil Rosenthal, T.Michael Coleman, Tom Gray & Starling plus guest Emmylou Harris (one track only) run through old favourites - released in 1992 (Maurice Hope - July 1993)

LONG TIME GONE.
Tracks: Long time gone / Turned you to stone / Half a man / Jordan / White line / Hobo on a freight train to heaven / Last thing I needed / Brother juke box / Carolyn at the Broken Wheel Inn / He rode all the way to Texas / Drifting too far from the shore / Dark hollow (Only on CD) / Lonesome whistle (Only on CD) / Roads and other reasons (Only on CD) / Sin City (Only on CD).
CD . . . . SHCD 3714
LP . . . . SH 3714
MC . . . . ZCSH 3714
Sugarhill(USA) / '88 / Roots Records / Projection / Impetus Records / C.M. Distribution / Jazz Music / Swift / Duncans / A.D.A Distribution.

WAITIN' ON A SOUTHERN TRAIN.
Tracks: New Delhi freight train / We know better / Carolina star / Other side of life, The / Waitin' on a southern train / Heart trouble / Homestead in my heart / Hey bottle of whisky / Those memories of you / Slow movin' freight train.
LP . . . . SH 3724
MC . . . . ZCSH 3724
Sugarhill(USA) / '88 / Roots Records / Projection / Impetus Records / C.M. Distribution / Jazz Music / Swift / Duncans / A.D.A Distribution.

Starr, Kay

Kay Starr was born in 1922 in Oklahoma; she sang with the bands of Bob Crosby and Charlie Barnet, and was one of the biggest USA pop stars from 1948 on Capitol with her big voice and distinctive vocal colour. *Wheel Of Fortune* was No. 1 for ten weeks in 1952. She was double-tracked for duets with herself, unusual then and particularly effective on *Side By Side*. She switched to RCA and *Rock 'n' Roll Waltz* was No. 1 for six weeks in 1955; then she went back to Capitol. (Donald Clarke)

1947: KAY STARR.
Tracks: Not Advised.
LP . . . . .HUK 214
Hindsight / Jun '86 / Charly.

AM I A TOY OR A TREASURE.
Tracks: Am I a toy or a treasure.
■ 7" . . . . CL 14151
Capitol / Oct '54.

BACK TO THE ROOTS.
Tracks: Not Advised.
LP . . . . GNPS 2090
MC GNP5 2090
GNP Crescendo / '88 / Swift / Silva Screen / Flexitron Ltd.

BLUE STARR.
Tracks: It's a lonesome old town / You're driving me crazy / House is haunted, The / We three / I really don't want to know / Blue Starr / Wedding bells / It's funny to everyone but me / Little white lies / Just like a butterfly (that's caught in the rain) / Blue and sentimental.
LP . . . . NL 90045
■ MC . . . . NK 90045
RCA / Jun '87.

CAPITOL COLLECTORS SERIES: KAY STARR.
Tracks: I'm the lonesomest gal in town / You've got to see mama ev'ry night / You were only fooling (while I was falling in love) / So tired / Bonaparte's retreat / Hoop dee doo / Mississippi / I'll never be free / I waited a little too long / Wheel of fortune / Fool, fool, fool / Kay's lament / Side by side / Comes a-long a-love / When my dream boat comes home / Half a photograph / Allez-vous-en, go away / Changing partners / If you love me (really love me) / Man upstairs, The / Toy or treasure / Lazy river / Foolin' around / Crazy / Rock and roll waltz, The.
CD . . . . CZ 411
Capitol / Mar '91 / EMI.

CHANGING PARTNERS.
Tracks: Changing partners.
■ 7" . . . . CL 14050
Capitol / Mar '54.

COMES A-LONG A-LOVE.
Tracks: Comes a-long a-love.
■ 7" . . . . CL 13808
Capitol / Dec '52.

FABULOUS FAVOURITES.
Tracks: Wheel of fortune / Rock and roll waltz / Side by side / Comes a-long-a-love / Bonapartes retreat / Half a photograph / Mississippi / So tired / I'm the lonesomest gal in town / Hoop dee doo / Allez-vous-en, go away / Foolin' around.
■ LP . . . . MFP 5603
MFP / Jun '83.

IN A BLUE MOOD.
Tracks: After you've gone / Woman likes to be told, A / Maybe you'll be there / I'm waiting for ships that never come in / What will I tell my heart? / Evenin' / He's funny that way / I got the spring fever blues / Don't tell him what happened to me / I got it bad and that ain't good / Everybody's somebody's fool / Until the real thing comes along.
■ MC . . . . EG 2606104
Capitol / Jul '85.
■ LP . . . . EG 2606101
Capitol / Jul '85.

IN THE 40'S.
Tracks: Not Advised.
LP . . . . .HSR 214
Hindsight / '88 / Charly.

JAZZ SINGER.
Tracks: I never knew / My man / Breezin' along with the wind / All by myself / Hard hearted Hannah / Me too / Happy days and lonely nights / I only want a buddy, not a sweetheart / Hummin' to myself / My honey's arms / Sunday / Anything for you.
■ MC . . . . TC CAPS 1867484
Capitol / Sep '83.
■ LP . . . . CAPS 1867481
Capitol / Sep '83.

JUST PLAIN COUNTRY.
Tracks: Pins and needles in my heart / Crazy / Four walls / My last date (with you) / Blues stay away from me / Walk on by / Oh, lonesome me / I can't help it (if I'm still in love with you) / I really don't want to know / Singing the blues / Don't worry.
LP . . . . HAT 3049
MC . . . . HATC 3049
Stetson / Sep '87 / Crusader Marketing Co. / Swift / Wellard Dist. / Midland Records / C.M. Distribution.

KAY STARR COUNTRY.
Tracks: Not Advised.
LP . . . . GNPS 2083
MC GNP5 2083
GNP Crescendo / '88 / Swift / Silva Screen / Flexitron Ltd.

KAY STARR STYLE,THE.
Tracks: Side by side / Someday sweetheart / What can I say after I say I'm sorry.
LP . . . . .PM 1552961
MC . . . . .PM 1552964

Pathe Marconi (France) / Oct '84 / Thames Distributors Ltd.

MOONBEAMS AND STEAMY DREAMS.
Tracks: Not Advised.
CD . . . . STCD 534
Stash (USA) / Oct '91 / Swift / Jazz Music / Jazz Horizons / C.M. Distribution / Cadillac Music / Zodiac Records / A.D.A Distribution / Topic Records / Direct Distribution.

MOVIN'.
Tracks: Not Advised.
■ LP. . . . . T 1254
Capitol / Mar '60.

MOVIN'.
Tracks: On a slow boat to China / I cover the waterfront / Around the world / Sentimental journey / Night train / Riders in the sky / Goin' to Chicago blues / Indiana / Song of the wanderer / Swingin' down the lane / Lazy river / Movin'.
CD . . . . JASCD 307
LP. . . . . JAS 307
MC . . . . JAS C307
Jasmine / Apr '90 / Wellard Dist. / Swift / Swift / Scott Butler Distribution / Jazz Music.

PURE GOLD: KAY STARR.
Tracks: Rock and roll waltz / Rockin' chair / Georgia on my mind / My heart reminds me / Oh, how I miss you tonight / It's a lonesome old town / Dry bones / Fit as a fiddle / You're driving me crazy / Wrap your troubles in dreams / I'll never say "never again" again / Only love me.
LP. . . . . INTS 5090
MC . . . . INTK 5090
RCA International / Jun '81 / BMG.

ROCK AND ROLL WALTZ.
Tracks: Rock and roll waltz.
■ 7" . . . . POP 168
H.M.V. / Feb '56.

ROCK AND ROLL WALTZ (OLD GOLD).
Tracks: Rock and roll waltz / Wheel of fortune.
■ 7" . . . . OG 9724
Old Gold / Apr '87.

SIDE BY SIDE.
Tracks: Side by side.
■ 7" . . . . CL 13871
Capitol / Apr '53.

WHEEL OF FORTUNE AND OTHER HITS.
Tracks: Not Advised.
MC 4XL-9286
Capitol (Specials) / '89.

Statler Brothers

Vocal group from Staunton, Virginia formed in 1955 under the name of The Kingsmen. The group consisted of Lee Dewitt (later replaced by Jimmy Fortune), Philip Balsey, Harold Reid, Virginia Reid and Don Reid. Their debut single *Flowers on the Wall* a Lee Dewitt composition reached the top 5 in both country and pop charts. In the Seventies The Statler Brothers were the most successful vocal group in the country charts. Among their chart topping hits were *Do You Know You Are My Sunshine*, and *The Official Historian Of Shirley Jean Burrell*. They also won the CMA's vocal group of the year award on six consecutive occassions in the 1970's. They also won the Music City News Awards from 1971 to 1982 inclusive. In 1991 they celebrated 21 years on Mercury Records.

ATLANTA BLUE.
Tracks: Atlanta blue / If it makes a difference / Let's just take one night at a time / Angel in her face / Hollywood / One takes the blame / Give it your best / No love lost / One size fits all / My only love.
■ LP. . . . . MERL 40
Mercury / Jul '84.
■ CD 818 652 2
Mercury / Oct '84.

BEST OF STATLER BROTHERS, THE VOL.2.
Tracks: Not Advised.
■ CD 822 524 2
Polygram T.V / '88.

BROTHERS IN SONG.
Tracks: Not Advised.
VHS. . . . . UNKNOWN
Polygram T.V / Sep '86 / PolyGram.

CHRISTMAS PRESENT.
Tracks: Not Advised.
LP. 824 785-1
MC 824 785-4
Mercury (Holland) / Nov '85.

COUNTRY CLASSICS FROM..
Tracks: Baptism of Jesse Taylor / Bed of Rose's / Blackwood Brothers, The / Cowboy buckaroo / Delta dawn / I'll be your baby tonight / Moments to remember / Pictures / Strand, The / Streets of San Francisco, The / Whatever happened to Randolph Scott / When my blue moon turns to gold again.
LP. 6336 263
Philips / Sep '78 / PolyGram.

COUNTRY STORE: STATLER BROTHERS.
Tracks: Bed of roses / Do you remember these / Flowers on the wall / I'll go to my grave loving you / Thank you world / Susan when she tried / Whatever happened to Randolph Scott / Carry me back / Class of 57, The / Pictures / New York city.
MC . . . . CSTK 14
Country Store / '88 / BMG.
■ CD . . . . CDCST 14
Country Store / '88.
■ LP. . . . . CST 14
Country Store / '88.

FLOWERS ON THE WALL.
Tracks: Flowers on the wall.
■ 7" . . . . CBS 201976
CBS / Feb '66.

FOUR FOR THE SHOW.
Tracks: Count on me / You oughta be here with me / We got the memories / I don't dream anymore / Forever / Only you / For cryin' out loud / Will you be there / I believe I'll live for him / More like daddy than me.
LP. . . . . MERH 91
MC . . . . MERHC 91
Mercury / Jun '86 / PolyGram.
■ CD 826 782-2
Mercury / Jun '86.

MAPLE STREET MEMORIES.
Tracks: Our street / Tell me why / Maple Street memories / Deja vu / Am I crazy? / Best I know how, The / I'll be the one / Beyond romance / I lost my heart to you / Jesus showed me so.
■ LP. . . . . MERH 112
Mercury / Jul '87.
CD 832 404-2
Mercury / Sep '87 / PolyGram.
■ MC . . . . MERHC 112
Mercury / Sep '87.

PARDNERS IN RHYME.
Tracks: Hello Mary Lou / Sweeter and sweeter / Memory lane / Remembering you / Too much on my heart / I'm sorry you had to be the one / Her heart of mine / You don't wear blue so well / Autumn leaves / Amazing grace.
CD 824 420-2
LP. . . . . MERH 71
MC . . . . MERHC 71
Mercury / Oct '85 / PolyGram.

TODAY.
Tracks: Oh baby mine (I get so lonely) / Some memories last forever / Promise, The / I'm dyin' a little each day / There is you / Guilty / Elizabeth / Right on the money / I never want to kiss you goodbye / Sweet by and by.
LP. . . . . MERL 25
MC . . . . MERLC 25
Mercury / Jul '83 / PolyGram.

TOO MUCH OF MY HEART.
Tracks: Too much of my heart / Hello Mary Lou.
7" . . . . MER 209
Mercury / Jan '86 / PolyGram.

YEARS AGO.
Tracks: Don't wait on me / Today I went back / In the garden / Chet Atkin's hand / You'll be back / Years ago / Love was all we had / We ain't even started yet / Dad / Memories are made of this.
■ LP. 6337 177
Mercury / Jan '82.

Statman, Andy

FLATBUSH WALTZ.
Tracks: Not Advised.
LP. . . . . ROUNDER 0116
Rounder / '88 / Projection / Roots Records / Swift / C.M. Distribution / Topic Records / Jazz Music / Hot Shot / A.D.A Distribution / Direct Distribution.

NASHVILLE MORNINGS, NEW YORK NIGHTS.
Tracks: Not Advised.
LP. . . . . ROUNDER 0174
MC . . . . ROUNDER 0174C
Rounder / '88 / Projection / Roots Records / Swift / C.M. Distribution / Topic Records / Jazz Music / Hot Shot / A.D.A Distribution / Direct Distribution.

Steady, Freddie

LUCKY 7.
Tracks: Say you'll go / What I got / Night time / Love you tonight / High lonesome country soul / I like whiskey / I hear neon angels sing / You can't judge a book by the cover / I've been framed / Ride through wild country.
LP. . . . . HLD 005
Heartland (1) / Jan '88 / Revolver-APT.

Steagall, Red

Steagall a native of Gainsville, Texas - born on 22.12.1937 started out as a rodeo rider/part-time country singer. Prior to living for a spell in California in the mid-sixties, Red had to overcome polio in his left arm when he was 15. Debuted with Dot records in 1969 and was staff writer for tree and Combine music. Gained first chart entry with Capitol in 1972, *Party dolls and wine* making Billboard's top forty. Red's main (and best) work keenly encompasses western swing/rodeo-western themes. Among those songs most associated with Red we have his biggest hit *Lone star beer and Bob Willis music* (No 11 in 1976) Danny O'Keefe's *Goodtime Charlie's got the blues*, *Truck driving man*, *3 Chord country song* and *Bob's got a swing band in heaven* . This 70-80's Capitol, ABC/Dot, Elektra, Delta and MCA /Dot recording artist - is once again working ranching and working/ breeding quarter horses, playing his music at Rodeo Country fairs, supported by his longtime band The Coleman County Cowboys who feature on his fine 1977 ABC/Dot release *For all our cowboy friends* , an album that stands alongside *Lone star beer and Bob Willis Music* and Capitol's *If you've got the time, I've got the song* as some of this often overlooked and underrated artist's finest work. Steagall is also attributed to having discovered female star act Reba McEntire, when hearing her sing at the National Rodeo finals in 1974. Just when it was thought Steagall's days with a major label were through, Michael Martin Murphy's Warner West came to the rescue, allowing him to put out his 1993 *Born to this land* album, his first album on a major outlet for seven years. Others on Warner Bros Western division are cowboy poet Weddie Mitchell, singer Stoney Edwards and the campfire cowboy outfit Sons Of The San Joaquin. (Maurice Hope - July 1993).

COWBOY FAVOURITES.
Tracks: Horses and wars / When the work's all done this fall / Navajo train / Smokey / Tennessee stud / Red headed stranger / Riding down the canyon / Little Joe the wrangler / Strawberry roan / My heroes have always been cowboys / Bandito gold / Dawson legate / Two pairs of Levis and a pair of Justin boots / Night the Copenhagen saved the day, The / Tight levis and yellow ribbons / Tyin' knots in the devils tails / Willie the wondering gypsy and me / I was born to be a cowboy / Running out of sunsets / One empty cot in the bunkhouse.
Double LP . . . . DELTA 1166
Delta (1) / '85 / Wellard Dist. / Cadillac Music / Zodiac Records.

Stecher, Jody

RASA (Stecher, Jody & Krishna Bhatt).
Tracks: Not Advised.
LP. . . . . CCF 2
Claddagh (Ireland) / Aug '88 / Topic Records / Projection / Impetus Records / Jazz Music / Roots Records / C.M. Distribution / Direct Distribution / I & B Records.

SONG THAT WILL LINGER (Stecher, Jody & Kate Brislin).
Tracks: Not Advised.
LP. . . . . ROUNDER 0274
Rounder / '89 / Projection / Roots Records / Swift / C.M. Distribution / Topic Records / Jazz Music / Hot Shot / A.D.A Distribution / Direct Distribution.

Steele, Jo Ann

COUNTRY GIRL.
Tracks: Loving you, loving me / Bits and pieces / Beginning of goodbye / If I were you babe / Fool in you (ain't foolin' me), The / My want - your fever's going down / I feel the cheater is you / I cry a lot in school / One too many times / Picking up the pieces / I dreamed it was over / Unless you stop hurting me / Love on borrowed time / Children of my mind / I can't keep my hands off you.
LP. . . . . BDL 1053
Bulldog Records / May '84 / President Records / Jazz Music / Wellard Dist. / TKO Records Ltd.

LOVE ON BORROWED TIME.
Tracks: Love on borrowed time / Children of my mind.
7" . . . . BD 12
N/A / May '84.

Stevens, Ray

Ray Stevens was born on 24th January 1941 in Clarkdale, Georgia. He began as a disc jockey at the age of 15, then had a smash novelty hit in the USA *Ahab The Arab* in 1962 but turned out to have more staying power than the usual one-hit wonder: in 1969 he made it back into the USA album chart, in 1970 he first charted in the UK; since then albums and singles have made regular appearances. A popular all-round entertainer. (Donald Clarke).

6 TRACK HITS.
Tracks: Misty / Everything is beautiful / Streak, The / Bridget the midget / Along came Jones / Ahab the Arab.
EP. 7SR 5008
MC 7SC 5008
Scoop 33 / Sep '83.

BESIDE MYSELF.
Tracks: I saw Elvis in a UFO.
CD . . . . MCAD 42303

S 18 ■ DELETED

LP . . . . MCA 42303
MC . . . . MCAC 42303
MCA / Jun '89 / BMG.

BOTH SIDES OF RAY STEVENS.
Tracks: Gitarzan / Moonlight special / Mr. Business man / Bridget the midget / Streak, The / Freddie Feelgood / Misty / Everything is beautiful / Young love / Sunshine / All my trials / Turn your radio on.
LP . . . . GEM 007
■ MC . . . . GEMC 007
Crown / Feb '86.

BRIDGET THE MIDGET.
Tracks: Bridget the midget.
■ 7" . . . . CBS 7070
CBS / Mar '71.

BRIDGET THE MIDGET (OLD GOLD).
Tracks: Bridget the midget / Everything is beautiful.
■ 7" . . . . OG 9036
Old Gold / Jul '82.

DEVIL MAY CARE.
Tracks: Devil may care / Make a few memories.
■ 7" . . . . HLU 10027
London-American / Mar '66.

DON'T LAUGH NOW.
Tracks: Such a night / Written down in my heart / Take that girl away / Always there / Where the sun don't shine / Oh Leo lady / Don't laugh now / This old piano / Country boy country club girl / Why don't we go somewhere and love.
LP . . . . RCALP 3054
RCA / Sep '82 / BMG.

EVERYTHING IS BEAUTIFUL.
Tracks: Not Advised.
■ LP . . . . CBS 64074
CBS / Sep '70.

EVERYTHING IS BEAUTIFUL.
Tracks: Everything is beautiful.
■ 7" . . . . CBS 4953
CBS / May '70.

GET CRAZY WITH ME.
Tracks: Get crazy with me / Dixie hummingbird.
■ 7" . . . . K 16929
WEA / Apr '77.

GREATEST HITS: RAY STEVENS.
Tracks: Streak, The / Shriner's convention / It's me again Margaret / Turn your radio on / Misty / Mississippi Squirrel revival / Gitarzan / Ahab the Arab / Along came Jones / Everything is beautiful.
LP . . . . IMCA 5918
MC . . . . IMCAC 5918
MCA / Apr '87 / BMG.

HE THINKS HE'S RAY STEVENS.
Tracks: Not Advised.
LP . . . . MCF 3265
MCA / Jun '85 / BMG.

HEY THERE.
Tracks: Hey there / You're never goin' to tamper with me.
■ 7" . . . . PB 9525
RCA / May '80.

I NEED YOUR HELP BARRY MANILOW.
Tracks: I need your help Barry Manilow / Daydream romance.
■ 7" . . . . K 17361
WEA / '79.

IN THE MOOD.
Tracks: In the mood / Classical cluck.
■ 7" . . . . K 16875
WEA / Mar '77.

INDIAN LOVE CALL.
Tracks: Indian love call.
■ 7" 6146 205
Janus / Sep '75.

ME.
Tracks: Love will beat your brains out / Mary Lou nights / Special anniversary / Piedmont Park / Me / My Dad / Yolanda / Piece of paradise called Tennessee / Kings and Queens / Game show love.
LP 8127 801
Mercury (USA) / Dec '83 / Pinnacle.

MISSISSIPPI SQUIRREL REVIVAL.
Tracks: Mississippi squirrel revival / Ned Nostril.
12" . . . . MCAT 954
7" . . . . MCA 954
MCA / Apr '85 / BMG.

MISTY.
Tracks: Not Advised.
■ LP 9109 401
Janus / Sep '70.

MISTY.
Tracks: Misty.
■ 7" 6146 204
Janus / Jun '75.

MISTY (OLD GOLD CD SINGLE).
Tracks: Misty / Bridget the midget / Everything is beautiful.

CD Single . . . . OG 6124
Old Gold / Mar '89 / Pickwick Records.

PARTY PEOPLE.
Tracks: Party people / A-B-C.
■ 7" . . . . HLU 10016
London-American / '66.

RAY STEVENS GREATEST HITS COLLECTION, THE.
Tracks: Everything is beautiful / Nashville / Mr. Business man / Little Egypt / Sir thanks a lot / Turn your radio on / Misty / Don't boogie woogie / Gitarzan / Moonlight special / Sunshine / Ahab the arab / Bridget the midget / Isn't it lonely together / Unwind / You've got the music inside / Just so proud to be there / Along came Jones / Streak, The / All my trials / Have a little talk with myself / Sunday morning comin' down / Freddie Feelgood / Lady of Spain.
Double LP . . . . PDA 061
Pickwick / Jul '79 / Pickwick Records.

SHRINER'S CONVENTION.
Tracks: Shriner's convention / Last laugh / Rita's letter / Watch song / Dooright family / Hey there / Put it in your ear / You're never goin' to Tampa with me / Coin machine.
■ LP . . . . PL 13574
RCA / Nov '80.

STREAK, THE.
Tracks: Streak, The.
■ 7" 6146 201
Janus / May '74.

STREAK, THE (OLD GOLD).
Tracks: Streak, The / Misty.
7" . . . . OG 9023
Old Gold / Jul '82 / Pickwick Records.

TURN YOUR RADIO ON.
Tracks: Turn your radio on.
■ 7" . . . . CBS 7634
CBS / Mar '72.

VERY BEST OF RAY STEVENS.
Tracks: Misty / Streak, The / Along came Jones / Ahab the Arab / Bridget the midget / Have a little talk with myself / Everything is beautiful / Turn your radio on / Mr. Business man / Sunday morning coming down / Isn't it lonely together / Gitarzan.
LP . . . . SPR 8554
MC . . . . SPC 8554
Spot / Sep '84.

Stevens, Stu

A sometimes contender for British pop chart success, Nottingham's Stu Stevens was first known to local country fans as 'Willard Pierce', appearing at the 1970 Wembley Festival. A couple of years later he just missed winning 'Opportunity Knocks' by three votes, but secured a recording deal with Youngblood Records - and the following year picked up an American deal with Granite Records, owned by West Coast country music pioneer Cliffie Stone. His version of Marty Robbins' My woman, my woman, my wife received good attention, but it was his 1979 recording The man from Outer Space , released by MCA, that almost put him in the U.K. pop charts. Known affectionately as 'The Voice' by his numerous fans, Stevens tended to move into other music areas during the early 1980's but following the tragic death of his youngest son Steven, has been less active during recent years. (Tony Byworth - August 1993)

ALBERT AND MARY.
Tracks: Albert and Mary / Superman.
7" . . . . YB 831
Young Blood / Jan '84 / Pinnacle.

COMMAND PERFORMANCE.
Tracks: Not Advised.
MC . . . . VCA 108
VFM Cassettes / Jan '85 / VFM Children's Entertainment Ltd. / Midland Records / Morley Audio Services.

COWBOY IN PARIS.
Tracks: Cowboy in Paris.
12" . . . . STUT 001
7" . . . . STU 001
Crazy Viking / Sep '82 / Pinnacle.

DREAM IT BACK.
Tracks: Dream it back / Cherokee mountain.
7" . . . . ASH 021
Ash / May '86 / Ash Records.

EMMA AND I.
Tracks: Mind painter / When I dream / That old brown dog / Loving arms / Emma and I / My woman my wife / Sunday morning coming down / Got my guitar / Room for a boy / Lady lay down / Bridge over troubled water / Hard to be humble / Three kinds of flowers.
LP . . . . EGL 012
Ash / Apr '86 / Ash Records.

EYES OF MY CHILD.
Tracks: Eyes of my child / Sunday comes quickly.
7" . . . . ASH 015
Ash / Nov '82 / Ash Records.

FOREVER.
Tracks: Forever.
7" . . . . CV 004
Crazy Viking / Jul '83 / Pinnacle.

FUNNY FACE.
Tracks: Funny face / Chokin' kind, The / Four strong winds / I don't want to cry / Tree in the meadow, A / Revelation / Mexico City / Good hearted woman / Derby's castle / Love me tender / Colorado / Yours love / Streets I have walked.
MC . . . . ASH 109 C
Ash / Apr '86 / Ash Records.

HELLO PRETTY LADY.
Tracks: Hello pretty lady / Oldest rock 'n' roller.
■ 7" . . . . MCA 563
MCA / Feb '80.

LONER, THE.
Tracks: Lady luck / Riverboat / America you are my woman / Love of the common people / West side of Texas / Miami sunset / Wrap my arms around the world / Rain / Had to run / Every night when I cry myself to sleep.
■ LP . . . . EGL 002
Ash / Apr '86.

MAN AND HIS MUSIC, THE.
Tracks: Rose, The / Dry your eyes / Little boy genius / Three times a lady / Nancy Lee / My heroes have always been cowboys / Always on my mind / Dream it back / Imagine / Suspicious minds / While the feelings good / Girl you love, The.
MC . . . . ASH 020 C
Ash / Apr '86 / Ash Records.

MAN FROM OUTER SPACE.
Tracks: Streets I have walked / Man from outer space.
■ 7" . . . . MCA 417
MCA / Apr '79.
■ 7" . . . . EGL 004
Eagle / '81.
7" . . . . ASH 004
Ash / May '88 / Ash Records.

MAN FROM OUTER SPACE.
Tracks: Not Advised.
■ LP . . . . MCF 3041
MCA / Nov '79.

OLD RUGGED CROSS.
Tracks: Eltigre / I can't keep my hands off you / Winter world away / Red cloud's day / Cowboys and daddies / Biff / Beautiful noise / Lady oh / American trilogy / Old rugged cross, The / Eyes of my child.
LP . . . . ASH C101
Ash / Jul '82 / Ash Records.

REMEMBER ME AT SUNRISE.
Tracks: Remember me at sunrise / Winter world away.
7" . . . . YB 0123
Young Blood / Sep '81 / Pinnacle.

SAD OLD SPANISH GUITAR.
Tracks: Sad old spanish guitar / Square dance.
7" . . . . YB 0084
Young Blood / Aug '84 / Pinnacle.

SONGS THAT MADE STU STEVENS (THE VOICE), THE.
Tracks: I'm from outer space / Hello pretty baby / When I dream / Woman woman my wife / Lion in the winter / Save the last dance for me / Streets of London / One red rose / West side of Texas / Winter world away / If I can't touch her at all / Remember me at sunrise / Looking for a place to sleep / God forsaken land / If I heard you call my name / Hudson bay.
LP . . . . YB LP 123
Young Blood / Jan '81 / Pinnacle.

STU STEVENS.
Tracks: Not Advised.
MC . . . . VCA 092
VFM Cassettes / Jan '85 / VFM Children's Entertainment Ltd. / Midland Records / Morley Audio Services.

TOGETHER AGAIN.
Tracks: Together again / I am .. I said / Lucille / Queen of the silver dollar / What have you got planned tonight Diana / Big house / Legend in my time, A / Broken lady / We had it all / Teach your children / Trying to matter.
■ LP . . . . EGL 001
Ash / Jul '82.

WAY LOVE'S SUPPOSED TO BE, THE.
Tracks: Way love's supposed to be, The / African lady.
7" . . . . RITZ 083
Ritz / Aug '85 / Pinnacle / Midland Records.

WHEN I DREAM.
Tracks: When I dream / Mind painter.
■ 7" . . . . EGL 014
Eagle / Apr '81.

Stevenson, N.A.

BOOGIE WOOGIE COUNTRY GIRL.
Tracks: Boogie woogie country girl.
7" . . . . SP 501
Spade / May '83 / Rollercoaster Records.

Stewart, Gary

Stewart, a hard-core honkytonkin vocalist, with a cutting rock edge, has enjoyed a fluctuating career - recording for RCA (1973 - 1982) and independant labels Red Ash and most recently, the highly successful west coast unit Hightone. Born 28.5.45. in Letcher County, Kentucky, Stewart started out in the rock idiom - recording in 1964 with the Amps on Cory Records. Most success came during the mid - seventies with top ten hits *Drinkin' thing* , *Out of hand* and in 1975, his only No.1 *She's acting single (I'm drinkin' doubles)*, backed up with top twenty chartings *You're not the woman you used to be*, *Your place or mine*, *Ten years of this* and *Whiskey trip* as the 70s progressed. Since then the hits have become more and more infrequent (and less impact obtaining), although he did make some waves during the early eighties when gaining three chart entries with Dean Dillon (*Brotherly love*) . Whilst critical acclaim was high, their albums didn't sell in substantial quantities. (Mauric Hope - July 1993)

20 OF THE BEST: GARY STEWART.
Tracks: Drinkin' thing / Ramblin' man / She's acting single (I'm drinkin' doubles) / Mazelle / Oh, sweet temptations / Quits / Whisky trip / Cactus and the rose / She's got a drink problem / Brotherly love / Out of hand / Flat natural norn good timin' man / In some room above the street / Your place or mine / Ten years of this / Single again / Stone wall (around your heart) / Are we dreamin' the same dream / Let's forget that we're married / She sings amazing grace.
LP. . . . . NL 89372
MC . . . . NK 89372
RCA / Mar '84 / BMG.

GARY.
Tracks: Mazelle / Shady streets / Next thing you know / Everything a good little girl needs / Same man / Blues don't care who's got 'em / I've just seen the rock of ages / Walkaway / Lost highway / One more.
■ LP. . . . . PL 13288
RCA / '79.

OUT OF HAND.
Tracks: Out of hand / Draggin' shackles.
■ 7" . . . . RCA 2510
RCA / Jan '75.

OUT OF HAND.
Tracks: Drinkin' thing / Honky-tonkin' / I see the want to in your eyes / This old heart won't let go / Draggin' shackles / She's actin' single (I'm drinkin' doubles) / Back sliders' wine / Sweet country red / Out of hand / Williamson County.
■ LP. . . . . LSA 3215
RCA / '78 / BMG.

STEPPIN' OUT.
Tracks: Flat natural born good-timin' man / Quits / Trudy / I still can't believe you're gone / Lord, what a woman / Oh, sweet temptation / If you've got the money (I've got the time) / (I can't be) Your backdoor / Hank Western / Easy people / In some room above the street.
■ LP. . . . . LSA 3266
RCA / '78 / BMG.

YOUR PLACE OR MINE.
Tracks: Your place or mine / Rachel / Lea / Drinking again / Blue ribbon blues / Pretend I never happened / I had to get drunk last night / I ain't living long like this / Broken hearted people / Ten years of this.
■ LP. . . . . PL 12199
RCA / '79.

Stewart, John

John Stewart is unclassifiable, a folk/rock/country singer/songwriter who has made 16 albums on seven labels and has a cult following all over the English speaking world. He was born on 5th September 1939 in the USA and was a member of the Kingston Trio 1961-67 (he also wrote *Daydream Believer* for the Monkees) but had started his solo career before that. Evidence of his loyal following is that his albums do not get deleted; *California Bloodlines* (originally 1969) and *The Lonesome Picker Rides Again* (1971) have been underground classics for years. (Donald Clarke).

ARMSTRONG.
Tracks: Armstrong / Lady and the outlaw.
7" . . . . RCA 2422
RCA / '73 / BMG.

BLONDES.
Tracks: Tall blondes / Queen of Hollywood High / Girl down the river / Eyes of sweet Virginia / Judy in G-major / You won't be going home / Jenny was a dream girl / Blonde star / Golden gate / Angeles (the city of angels).
CD . . . . LICD 9.00019
Line / Sep '90 / C.M. Distribution / Grapevine Distribution.

BOMBS AWAY DREAM BABIES.
Tracks: Gold / Lost her in the sun / Runaway fool of love / Somewhere down the line / Midnight wind / Over the hill / Hand your heart to the wind / Spinnin' of the world / Comin' out of nowhere / Heart of the dream.
■ LP. . . . . RSS 6
RSO / '79.

CALIFORNIA BLOODLINES..PLUS.
Tracks: California bloodlines / Razor back woman / She believes in me / Omaha rainbow / Pirates of Stone County Road,The / Shackles and chains / Heart full of woman and a bellyful of Tenness / Willard / Big Joe / Mother country / Lonesome picker / You can't look back / Missouri birds / July, you're a woman / Never goin' back / Friend of Jesus / Marshall wind.
LP. . . . . SEE 87
See For Miles / Mar '87 / Pinnacle.
CD . . . . SEECD 87
See For Miles / May '91 / Pinnacle.

CALIFORNIA BLOODLINES/WILLARD MINUS TWO.
Tracks: California bloodlines / Razor back woman / She believes in me / Omaha rainbow / Pirates of Stone County Road / Shackles and chains / Mother Country / Some lonesome picker / You can't look back / Missouri birds / July, you're a woman / Never goin' back / Big Joe / Julie / Judy angel rain / Belly full of Tennessee / Friend of Jesus / Clack clack / Hero from the war / Back in Pomona / Willard / Golden rollin' belly / All American girl / Oldest living son / Earth rider.
CD . . . . BCD 15468
Bear Family / Jul '89 / Rollercoaster Records / Swift / Direct Distribution.

CANNONS IN THE RAIN/WINGLESS ANGELS.
Tracks: Durango / Chilly winds / Easy money / Anna on a memory / All time woman / Road away / Armstrong / Spirit / Wind dies down / Cannons in the rain / Lady and the outlaw / Hung on your heart / Rose water / Wingless / Angels / Some kind of love / Survivors / Summer child / Josie / Rise stone blind / Mazatlan / Let the big horse run.
CD . . . . BCD 15519
Bear Family / Oct '90 / Rollercoaster Records / Swift / Direct Distribution.

COMPLETE PHOENIX CONCERTS, THE.
Tracks: Wheatfield lady / Kansas rain / You can't look back / Pirates of Stone County Road, The / Runaway fool of love, The / Roll away the stone / July, you're a woman / Last campaign trilogy, The / Oldest living son / Little road and a stone to roll / Kansas / Cody / California bloodlines / Mother country / Cops / Never goin' back / Freeway pleasure / Let the big horse run.
CD . . . . BCD 15518
Bear Family / Feb '91 / Rollercoaster Records / Swift / Direct Distribution.

DAYDREAM BELIEVER.
Tracks: Daydream believer / Just an old love song.
■ 7" . . . . K 17583
WEA / Mar '80.

DREAM BABIES GO HOLLYWOOD.
Tracks: Hollywood dreams / Wind on the river / Wheels of thunder / Monterey / Spirit of the water / Lady of fame / Raven / Love has tied my wings / Nightman / Moonlight rider.
■ LP. . . . . RSD 5007
RSO / May '80.

FIRE IN THE WIND.
Tracks: Fire in the wind / Promise the wind.
■ 7" . . . . .RSO 007
RSO / Apr '78.

FORGOTTEN SONGS OF SOME OLD YESTERDAY.
Tracks: All time woman / Anna on a memory / Armstrong / Cannons in the rain / Road away / Wheatfield lady / You can't look back / July, you're a woman / Let the big horse run / Cody / California bloodlines / Mother country / Hung on the heart / Rodeo Mary.
■ LP. . . . . PL 43155
RCA / Apr '80.

GOLD.
Tracks: Gold / Coming out of nowhere.
■ 7" . . . . RSO 35
RSO / Jun '79.

LONESOME PICKER RIDES AGAIN.
Tracks: Just an old love song / Road shines bright, The / Touch of the sun / Bolinas / Freeway pleasure / Swift lizard / Wolves in the kitchen / Little road and a stone to roll / Daydream believer / Crazy / Wild horse road / All the brave horses.
CD . . . . LECD 9.00948
Line / '90 / C.M. Distribution / Grapevine Distribution.

MEET JOHN STEWART.
Tracks: Mr. Lucky / My heart and I / September affair / Li'l darlin' / Alley cat / Dream acres suite / I'm grinzing.
MC . . . . AC 181
Audicord.

MEMORIES OF JOHN STEWART.
Tracks: My heart and I / Alley cat / Body and soul / Lady is a tramp, The / I got rhythm / It's foolish but it's fun / If I'm lucky / Misty / Showboat selection / Li'l darlin' / Chloe.
MC . . . . AC 167
Audicord.

MIDNIGHT WIND.
Tracks: Midnight wind / Somewhere down the line.
■ 7" . . . . RSO 42
RSO / Sep '79.

NEON BEACH.
Tracks: Not Advised.
CD . . . . LICD 901001
Line / Feb '91 / C.M. Distribution / Grapevine Distribution.

NIGHT MAN.
Tracks: Night man / Love has tied my wings.
■ 7" . . . . RSO 61
RSO / May '80.

ON YOU LIKE THE WIND.
Tracks: On you like the wind / Morning thunder.
■ 7" 2090 274
RSO / Feb '78.

PHOENIX CONCERTS, THE.
Tracks: Not Advised.
LP. . . . . CL 43254
RCA (Germany) / Jul '83 / BMG.

PUNCH THE BIG GUY.
Tracks: Not Advised.
CD . . . . LICD 900762
Line / Feb '91 / C.M. Distribution / Grapevine Distribution.

RUNAWAY FOOL OF LOVE.
Tracks: Runaway fool of love / Heart of the dream.
■ 7" . . . . RSO 51
RSO / Dec '79.

SUNSTORM.
Tracks: Kansas rain / Cheyenne / Bring it on home / Sunstorm / Arkansas breakout / Account of Haley's comet, An / Joe / Light come shine / Lonesome John / Drive again.
CD . . . . .LECD 9.00946
Line / '90 / C.M. Distribution / Grapevine Distribution.

TRANCAS.
Tracks: It ain't the gold / Reasons to rise / Pilots in blue / Chasing down the rain / Till the lights come home / Bringing down the moon / All the lights / Rocky top / American way, The / Chosen, The.
LP. . . . . SSAD 01
Sunstorm / Nov '84 / Greyhound Records / Probe Plus Records / Projection / Roots Records / Charly.
LP. . . . . FEDL 102
MC . . . . CFEDL 102
Sierra / Jul '85.
CD . . . . LICD 9.00059
Line / '90 / C.M. Distribution / Grapevine Distribution.

Stewart, Wynn

CHALLENGE YEARS 1958-1963, THE.
Tracks: Wishful thinking / Heartaches for a dime / Open up my heart / Three cheers for the losers / Rain rain / I sold the farm / Slightly used / Falling for you / I'd rather have America / Yankee go home (Duet with Jan Howard) / Come on (fast take) / Uncle Tom got caught / Never out of my heart / Long black limousine / School bus love affair / She just tears me up / Big big love / Donna on my mind / How the other half lives (Duet with Jan Howard) / With this ring / Another day, another dollar / Wrong company (Duet with Jan Howard) / Judy / We'll never love again / Wall to wall heartaches / I'm not the man I used to be / Couples only / Loversville / Don't look back / I don't feel at home / I done done it / Above and beyond / Come on / Wishful thinking (version 2) / Big city / If you see my baby / Playboy / Girl in white / One more memory / Searching for another you / One way to go / Hungry heart.
Double LP . . . . BFD 15261
Bear Family / Apr '88 / Rollercoaster Records / Swift / Direct Distribution.

SONGS OF WS, THE.
Tracks: Not Advised.
LP. . . . . HAT 3110
MC . . . . HATC 3110
Stetson / Aug '89 / Crusader Marketing Co. / Swift / Wellard Dist. / Midland Records / C.M. Distribution.

Stinit, Dane

In November 1966 Sam Phillips settled into the producer's chair in his new Memphis studio on Madison Avenue and recorded the last session that he would produce for the Sun Record Company. The artist Dane Stinit, a transplated Southerner, a worker from Gary, Indiana, in Phillip's mind was probably the idea of re-creating the Johnny Cash sound of earlier Sun days - and to update this a little - he found his man in Dane Stinit. The second session gave way to let him sound more like himself and featured the cream of the local Memphis pickers from the American studio, led by the incomparable Reggie Young. With his own band Stinit still plays to homesick Southerners on his Indiana circuit, having no thoughts of turning professional. Sam Phillips saw the sessions as a statement about the roots of country music.

ORIGINAL SUN RECORDINGS.
Tracks: Don't knock what you don't understand (take 1) / Always on the go / Don't knock what you don't understand (take 7) / Kilgore jail / Mean eyed cat / Ghost of Mary Lou, The / Flip top flipper / Sweet country girl / Muddy ole river (near Memphis Tennessee) / Heartache catches up with me (take 10) / Windy City / Heartache catches with me (take 15) / Shot out of the saddle / I'm a rounder.
LP . . . . **BFX 15337**
Bear Family / Nov '88 / Rollercoaster Records / Swift / Direct Distribution.

Stone, Cliffie

Born Clifford Snyder, 01.03.1917 in Burbank, California. West coast pioneer/songwriter/singer/bassist/DJ and host of the Hollywood Barn Dance and Lucky Stars during the 1940's. Stone carrying on the musical tradition of his father, banjoist/comedian Herman The Hermit, as bassist with the Anson Weeks and Freddie Slack bands during 1930's, before spells as DJ and Capitol A&R man. He made a handful of albums charting with popular 40's tunes *Silver stars, Purple sage, Eyes of blue, Peepin' through the keyhole* and *When my blue moon turns to gold again* . Stone hosted the daily variety show Dinner Bell Roundup on KXLA in Pasadena - both moving to El Monte, Cal in 1949 and then called the Hometown Jamboree. Discovered Tennessee, Ernie Ford and wrote such hits as *No vacancy, Divorce me C.O.D., New steel guitar rag, Sweet temptation* and *So round, so firm, so fully packed* with Merle Travis. Set up own publishing company, Central Songs (sold to Capitol in 1969) and record label, Granite. Keeping the family's name to the fore is son Curtis, bassist singer-songwriter with Highway 101 - the CMA's Vocal Group Of The Year in 1988/1989, making it a double success that year for the Stones, for Cliffie gained the ultimate honour of induction into the Country Music Hall Of Fame. (Maurice Hope - August 1993)

TRANSCRIPTIONS - 1945-49.
Tracks: Draggin' the bow / Beautiful brown eyes / Mine all mine / Muleskinner blues / Little cabin home on the hill / Blue steel blues / Stuck up blues / Mandolin boogie / Bill Cheatum / Red's boogie / Freight train blues / After you've gone / Flop eared mule / Sugar hill / Cactus set-up / Daughter of Jolie Blon / Steel guitar rag / Free little bird / Honky tonkin' / Lady be good / Sally Goodin / Little rock getaway.
CD . . . . **RFDCD 08**
Country Routes / Oct '91 / Jazz Music / Hot Shot.

Stone, Doug

Vocalist - recording act born Newman, Georgia during the mid - 50s, where, with a couple of friends, he started plying his trade whilst still in his early teens - blending country, folk and rock. Now on Epic, Stone is treading the traditional country path and is one of the finest ballad singers around, . His the first major impact on the charts coming via 1990 top ten hit *I'd Be Better Off In A Pine Box* followed with *In A Different Light* and *These Lips Don't Seem To Know How To Say Goodbye*.Since which time, this no gimicks assisted act (who's road band is cleverly titled the Stone Age Band) has woven together an impressive run of hits, featuring the aptly titled *A Jukebox With A Country Song* (1991) and *Too Busy Being In Love* (1993), both chart topping fare. Other notable high flyers include *Come Out Of The Pain* and *I Thought It Was You* - the title track from which the singles were culled. His onward march continued in 1992 despite him going through a quadruple bypass operation that April. His third album *From The Heart* , as before was found to be a source for hits, with *Winning Labels* and *Made For Lovin' You* both chalking up top 5 slots, lending support to the aforementioned *Too Busy Being In Love*.

FROM THE HEART.
Tracks: Warning labels / Made for lovin' you / Leave me the radio / This empty house / Why didn't I think of that / Ain't your memory got no pride at all / Workin' end of a hoe, The / Too busy being in love / She's got a future in the movies / Left, leaving, goin' or gone.
CD **472131-2**
MC **472131-4**
Epic / Jan '93 / Sony.

I THOUGHT IT WAS YOU.
Tracks: I thought it was you / Jukebox with a country song, A / Feeling never goes away, The / (For every inch I've laughed) I've cried a mile / Remember the ride / Come in out of the rain / Burning down the town / If it was up to me / Right to remain silent, The / They don't make years like they used to.
CD **4688222**
■ **MC** **4688224**
Epic / Nov '91.

Stoneman, Scotty

LIVE IN L.A. (Stoneman, Scotty & Kentucky Colonels).
Tracks: Not Advised.
LP . . . . **SBR 4206**
Sierra Briar (USA) / May '79 / Mike's Country Music Room.

Story, Carl

16 GREATEST HITS: CARL STORY.
Tracks: Not Advised.
LP . . . . **SLP 3004**
MC . . . . **GT 53004**
Starday (USA) / Apr '87 / Crusader Marketing Co.

BLUEGRASS GOSPEL COLLECTION (Story, Carl & His Rambling Mountaineers).
Tracks: Somebody touched me / We shall meet again someday / Fourth man, The / Will you miss me / Million years in glory / Will there be a traffic light / Sweetest gift / Heaven bound train / When the angels carry me home / My loved ones are waiting for me / Shout and shine / Family reunion / Are you afraid to die / You can't believe everything you hear / Angel band / Thank the Lord for everything / Always be kind to mother / Angels rock me to sleep / I'm going home.
LP . . . . **CMH 9005**
■ **MC** . . . . **CMH 9005C**
CMH (USA) / '76.

GOSPEL QUARTET FAVOURITES.
Tracks: Not Advised.
LP . . . . **HAT 3128**
Stetson / '89 / Crusader Marketing Co. / Swift / Wellard Dist. / Midland Records / C.M. Distribution.

GOSPEL REVIVAL.
Tracks: Not Advised.
LP . . . . **SLP 127**
MC . . . . **GT 5127**
Starday (USA) / Apr '87 / Crusader Marketing Co.

Stover, Don

THINGS IN LIFE.
Tracks: Not Advised.
LP . . . . **ROUNDER 0014**
Rounder / '82 / Projection / Roots Records / Swift / C.M. Distribution / Topic Records / Jazz Music / Hot Shot / A.D.A Distribution / Direct Distribution.

WITH THE WHITE OAK MOUNTAIN BOYS.
Tracks: Not Advised.
LP . . . . **ROUNDER 0039**
Rounder / May '77 / Projection / Roots Records / Swift / C.M. Distribution / Topic Records / Jazz Music / Hot Shot / A.D.A Distribution / Direct Distribution.

Strait, George

One of the most consistently successful country music artists of the 1980's he launched his career in 1981 with a top 10 single and ended the decade at the top of the ladder by being named CMA's Entertainer of the Year. Between these two achievements, George Strait was not only acknowledged as one of the finest exponents of pure country music - complete with twin fiddles and steel guitar in his Ace In The Hole band - but also opened up the doorways for a new breed of traditional cowboy entertainers which have included Clint Black and Garth Brooks. Born on May 18, 1952 in Pearsall, Texas, he was the son of a high school teacher and raised on a ranch. Initially a rock 'n' roll fan he became aware of Hank Williams music while learning to play guitar during his stint in the US Army. Although he sang in a military country band, his ambitions lay towards an agricultural career and he later earned a degree from the Southwest Texas State University in San Marcos. He was hooked on country music, however, and he furthered that apprenticeship by playing small bars and clubs throughout Texas. A growing popularity led to him securing a professional manager, Erv Woolsey, a deal with MCA Records and abandoning all thoughts of agriculture (although he now owns a lavish ranch on the outskirts of San Antonio). His first ten years on MCA have seen him achieving around 20 number one hit singles including the classics *Does Fort Worth ever cross your mind, The cowboy rides away, Ocean front property* and *All my ex's live in Texas* - a mass of platinum and gold albums, a stack of awards and phenomenal box office success. If it wasn't enough to end the 1980's in style, he began the new decade even better. He was named the CMA Entertainer for the second year running and broke all existing box office records at the Houston Astrodrome by selling 95,000 tickets in 24 hours. George Strait is also George Bush's favourite singer. In 1991 he added a further dimension to his career with the lead role in the Warner Bros. movie *Pure country*, a project especially created for the entertainer. Besides enjoying a successful run at the American box office, its soundtrack music also provided Strait with his biggest selling album to date. More movies are being considered. (Tony Byworth - August 1993)

ALL MY EX'S LIVE IN TEXAS.
Tracks: All my ex's live in Texas / Nobody in their right mind would've left her / Fool hearted memory (On CD single only).
7" . . . . **MCA 1434**
■ **CD Single** . . . . **DMCAT 1434**
MCA / Jul '90 / BMG.

BLAME IT ON MEXICO.
Tracks: Blame it on Mexico / Friday night fever.
7" . . . . **MCA 774**
MCA / Apr '82 / BMG.

CHAIR.
Tracks: In too deep / Chair.
7" . . . . **MCA 1036**
MCA / Mar '86 / BMG.

CHILL OF AN EARLY FALL.
Tracks: Not Advised.
CD . . . . **MCAD 10204**
LP . . . . **MCA 10204**
■ **MC** . . . . **MCAC 10204**
MCA / Apr '91.

GREAT STRAIT (The Essential Collection).
Tracks: Ocean front property / You're something special to me / Marina Del Ray / Fool hearted memory / Baby's gotten good at goodbye / Does Fort Worth ever cross your mind / Nobody in his right mind would've left her / Deep water / If you're thinking you want a stranger / Let's fall to pieces together / Baby blue / All my ex's live in Texas / Beyond the blue neon / Famous last words of a fool / Chair, The (Only on CD.) / Dance time in Texas (Only on CD.) / Amarillo by morning (Only on CD.).
■ **LP** . . . . **MCG 6082**
MCA / May '90.
CD . . . . **DMCG 6082**
■ **MC** . . . . **MCGC 6082**
MCA / May '90.
CD . . . . **MCLD 19178**
MCA / Mar '93 / BMG.

GREATEST HITS: GEORGE STRAIT.
Tracks: Unwound / Down and out / If you're thinking you want a stranger.. / Fool hearted memory / Marina del ray / Amarillo by morning / Fire I can't put out, A / You look so good in love / Right or wrong / Let's fall to pieces together.
CD . . . . **MCAD 5567**
LP . . . . **IMCA 5567**
■ **MC** . . . . **IMCAC 5567**
MCA / Mar '86.

GREATEST HITS: GEORGE STRAIT VOL 2.
Tracks: Does Fort Worth ever cross your mind / Cowboy rides away, The / Fireman / Chair, The / You're something special to me / Nobody in his right mind would've left her / It ain't cool to be crazy about you / Ocean front property / All my ex's live in Texas / Am I blue.
CD . . . . **DMCF 3400**
LP . . . . **MCF 3400**
■ **MC** . . . . **MCFC 3400**
MCA / Oct '87.

HOLDING MY OWN.
Tracks: You're right I'm wrong / Holding my own / Gone as a girl can get / So much like my dad / Trains make me lonesome / All of me (loves all of you) / Wonderland of love / Faults and all / It's alright with me / Here we go again.
CD . . . . **MCAD 10532**
MC . . . . **MCAC 10532**
MCA / Jun '92 / BMG.

LIVIN' IT UP.
Tracks: Someone had to teach you / Heaven must be wondering where you are / I've come to expect it from you / Lonesome rodeo cowboy / When you're a man on your own / Drinking champagne / We're supposed to do that now and then / She loves me (she don't love me) / Love without end, Amen / Stranger in my arms.
■ **CD** . . . . **DMCG 6115**
MCA / Nov '90.
■ **LP** . . . . **MCG 6115**
MCA / Nov '90.
■ **MC** . . . . **MCGC 6115**
MCA / Nov '90.

LOVE WITHOUT END, AMEN.
Tracks: Love without end, Amen / Drinking champagne.
7" . . . . **MCA 1468**
■ **CD Single** . . . . **DMCAT 1468**
MCA / Jan '91.

NUMBER 7.
Tracks: Deep water / Nobody in his right mind would've left her / Rhythm of the road / I'm never gonna let you go / You still get to me / Stranger things have happened / It ain't cool to be crazy about you / Why'd you go and break my heart? / My old flame is burnin' another honky tonk down / Cow town.
LP . . . . **MCF 3332**
■ **MC** . . . . **MCFC 3332**
MCA / Oct '86.
■ **CD** . . . . **MCAD 5750**
MCA / Feb '87.

OCEAN FRONT PROPERTY.
Tracks: All my ex's live in Texas / Someone's walkin' around upstairs / Am I blue / Ocean front property / Hot burning flames / Without you here / My heart won't wander very far from you / Second chances / You can't buy your way out of the blues / I'm all behind you now.
CD . . . . **MCAD 5913**
MCA / Jul '87 / BMG.
LP . . . . **MCF 3358**
MC . . . . **MCFC 3358**
MCA / Mar '87 / BMG.

SOMEONE HAD TO TEACH YOU.
Tracks: Someone had to teach you.
7" . . . . .MCA 1447
■ CD Single . . . . .DMCAT 1447
MCA / Oct '90 / BMG.

SOMETHING SPECIAL.
Tracks: You're something special to me / Last time the first time / Haven't you heard / In too deep / Blue is not a word / You sure got this ol' redneck feelin blue / Chair, The / Dance time in Texas / Lefty's gone / I've seen that look on me(a thousand times).
LP. . . . . MCF 3306
MC . . . . MCFC 3306
MCA / Mar '86 / BMG.

Strange Creek Singers

STRANGE CREEK SINGERS.
Tracks: Not Advised.
LP. . . . . ARHOOLIE 4004
Arhoolie (USA) / May '81 / Pinnacle / Cadillac Music / Swift / Projection / Hot Shot / A.D.A Distribution / Jazz Music.

Stringbean

SALUTE TO UNCLE DAVE MACON (Stringbean & His Banjo).
Tracks: Not Advised.
LP. . . . . SLP 215
MC . . . . GT 5215
Starday (USA) / Apr '87 / Crusader Marketing Co.

Stringdusters

STRINGDUSTERS, THE.
Tracks: Ten degrees and getting colder / Good time Charlie's got the blues / Streets of Baltimore / Tried so hard / Peaceful easy feeling / Shackles and chains / Woman turn around / Morning / Nashville again / I sure like your smile / Letter to a lady / Early morning rain / Butchie's tune.
LP. . . . . FHR 069
Folk Heritage / Jul '82 / Terry Blood Dist.

Strutt. Nick

LAST TRAIN SOUTH (see under Golbey, Brian).

Stuart. Gene

Longtime entertainer on the Irish scene, Gene Stuart (born in Dungannon, County Tyrone) got his first break as a replacement for singer Larry Cunningham in the Mighty Avons. *Before the next teardrop falls* was the song that put him in the charts, and he followed up with others such as *I'd rather love and lose you* and *Kiss an angel Good Morning*. After the Mighty Avons he formed his own band, the Homesteaders. These days he still delights audiences with his brand of 'Irish'n'Country'. (Tony Byworth - August 1993)

AT HOME.
Tracks: Not Advised.
MC Set . . . . HTC 8015
Not Advised / Dec '88.

DARLIN' THINK OF ME.
Tracks: Not Advised.
LP. . . . . BRL 4067
Release (Ireland) / Nov '76.
LP. . . . . CBRL 4067
Outlet / '88 / Projection / Duncans / C.M. Distribution / Ross Records / Topic Records / Direct Distribution / Midland Records.

FIRST CLASS COUNTRY.
Tracks: Day the blizzard hit our town, The / Picture of your mother / Word or two to Mary / End of everything / I'm not mixed up anymore / My son calls another man daddy / Your old love letters / Down the road I go / Darling think of me / You're no longer a sweetheart of mine / Wreck of the number nine, The / What things money can't buy.
LP. . . . . PHL 413
MC . . . . CPHL 413
Homespun (Ireland) / '82 / Homespun Records / Ross Records / Wellard Dist.

FORTY AND FADING.
Tracks: Forty and fading.
7" . . . . RITZ 136
Ritz / '88 / Pinnacle / Midland Records.

GENE STUART & PRIDESMEN (Stuart, Gene & Pridesmen).
Tracks: Gene Stuart / Shores of Lough Neagh.
■ 7" . . . . FR 1981
Foyle Folk / Feb '80.

GREATEST HITS: GENE STUART.
Tracks: Not Advised.
LP. . . . . HALP 120
Hawk / '76 / C.M. Distribution.

GREATEST HITS: GENE STUART VOL.2.
Tracks: Not Advised.
LP. . . . . SHARP 2
Sharp / Jan '77 / Sharp Records.
MC . . . . SHARP 2 (TC)
Sharp / Mar '77 / Sharp Records.

JUST FOR WHAT I AM.
Tracks: Not Advised.
LP. . . . . BRL 4099
Release (Ireland) / Jun '78.

ME AND THE BOYS.
Tracks: Not Advised.
LP. . . . . DRL 2014
Release (Ireland) / Sep '76.
LP. . . . . RBA 128
Rainbow (Ireland) / '88.

ONCE AGAIN.
Tracks: Not Advised.
LP. . . . . RBA 104
Rainbow (Ireland) / '88.

PRECIOUS MEMORIES.
Tracks: Not Advised.
LP. . . . . BRL 4089
MC . . . . CBRL 4089
Release (Ireland) / Jan '78.

REMEMBER YOU'RE MINE (Stuart, Gene & The Homesteaders).
Tracks: Remember you're mine / Veil of white lace / Foolin' around / Forever and ever / Excuse me I think I've got a heartache / Heartaches by the number / Jealous heart / Careless darling / Leona / Oh lonesome me / Old woman from Wexford / Bold O'Donaghue / Home boy's home / You can't make a heel toe the mark / Out of my mind over you / Where is my Nora.
MC . . . . CHRL 188
Homespun (Ireland) / '88 / Homespun Records / Ross Records / Wellard Dist.

SINCERELY IRISH.
Tracks: Not Advised.
LP. . . . . RBA 134
Rainbow (Ireland) / '88.

TWILIGHT COUNTRY.
Tracks: Not Advised.
LP. . . . . RBA 123
Rainbow (Ireland) / '88.

Stuart. Jerry

ROCKY RUN.
Tracks: Rocky run / Black still waters / Misty mountain / Deliverence will come / Stuart's march / Land of the dead / Shining path, The / Bicycle song / Must I go / Galaxy.
LP. . . . . CO 767
County (USA) / '78 / Projection / Mike's Country Music Room / Swift.

Stuart. Marty

Child bluegrass prodigy and versatile musician, born John Marty Stuart 30.09.1958 in Philadelphia, Mississippi. At 13 played in Lester Flatt's Nashville Grass band whilst still attending high school - proficient on mandolin and guitar. Spent some time touring the gospel circuit with family group the Sullivans - who he later picked-up with again during label changes in 1986. Produced, played on and wrote songs for their acclaimed Country Music Foundation gospel album *A joyful noise* in 1991. After his spell working/recording with Lester Flatt in 1972-1979, came his debut album *Marty, with a little health from my friends* on Ridge Runner (1977). Stuart, married Cindy Cash, then spent six years touring with her father Johnny Cash, in which period he made the Doc Watson/Cash aided *Busy bee cafe* album on Sugar Hill. Also through his association with Cash, he was asked to play on *The class of '55'* reunion sessions, an album featuring Cash, Perkins. Lewis and Orbison, by which time it was felt his apprenticeship had been served. A couple of solo albums for Columbia *Marty Stuart* and *Let there be country* (as with his 1992 *Once upon a time* collection on Californian indie label CMH, it too had been in Storage for some time) met with only limited success. His Columbia release coming from some 1987 recordings, didn't gain an airing until late 1992 - whilst his formative years are really found on the CMH disc. A young Stuart can be found playing mandolin on Flatt's live albums of the seventies on RCA and CMH. Marty's confident approach sees him playing a blend of ebullient country rock, yet retaining his strong traditional roots that take in bluegrass and Cash and Ernest Tubb influences. Reeling off albums *Hillbilly rock, Tempted* and *This one's gonna hurt you* moving purposely into the early 90's, a member of the Grand Ole Opry as from 1992. Listed among his hits to date there's *Hillbilly rock, Cry, cry, cry,* debut No.1 country single *The whiskey ain't working* (with his sometimes touring partner Travis Tritt - they played together on their tongue in cheek 'No hats tour') and *This ones gonna hurt you (For a long time), High on a*

hilltop and *Hey baby* - as a songwriter George Strait and Wynonna Judd have both drawn upon his work. Stuart, apart from his whole - hearted approach to performing underscored with traditional values, doesn't stop at wearing Manuel suits, he's also an avid collector of country memorabilia, owning guitars from the likes of Lester Flatt, Hank Williams, Clarence Whie and Ernest Tubb - he even travels in late Texas Troubadour's old bus. (Maurice Hope - July 1993).

BUSY BEE CAFE.
Tracks: One more ride / Blue railroad train / I don't love nobody / Watson's blues / Busy bee cafe / Down the road / Hey porter / Boogie for Clarence / Get in line brother / Soldier's joy / Long train gone.
LP. . . . . SH 3726
MC . . . . SH 3726C
Sugarhill(USA) / Mar '89 / Roots Records / Projection / Impetus Records / C.M. Distribution / Jazz Music / Swift / Duncans / A.D.A Distribution.

MARTY.
Tracks: Precious memories / Hard hearted / Rawhide / Dock of the bay / Crazy creek blues / Just a little talk with Jesus / Love grown cold / Mystery train / Tiger man / Kansas City / Big boss man / Little help from my friends, A / My Sally Goodin.
LP. 0013
Ridgerunner (USA) / '79 / Mike's Country Music Room / Projection.

Sullivan. Jerry

JOYFUL NOISE, A (Sullivan, Jerry & Tammy).
Tracks: Get up John / He called me baby / I'm working on a building / Soldiers of the cross / Gates of Zion, The / Think about that promise / When Jesus passed by / Brand new church / Gospel plow / What a wonderful saviour he is.
CD . . . . CMFCD 016
MC . . . . CMFC 016
Country Music Foundation / Jan '93 / Topic Records / Direct Distribution.

Summers. Gene

DANCE DANCE DANCE.
Tracks: Not Advised.
■ LP . . . . CRM 2027
Charly / Dec '81 / Charly.

EARLY ROCKING RECORDINGS.
Tracks: School of rock and roll / Floppin' / Nervous / Alabama shake / Loco cat / Turnip greens / Trying to get to you / Straight skirt / Hey, my baby / Gotta lotta that / I'll never be lonely / Twixteen / Suzie Q / Be bop a lula.
LP. . . . . WLP 8826
White Label (Germany) / Dec '86 / Pinnacle / Bear Family Records (Germany) / CSA Tell Tapes.

GENE SUMMERS IN NASHVILLE.
Tracks: Mystery train / I will rock and roll with you / Put your cat clothes on / Blue Monday / Walk on by / Singing the blues / Big river / Tennessee Saturday night / Today I started loving you again / I still miss someone.
■ LP. . . . . MFM 002
Magnum Force / Jul '82.

LIVE IN SCANDINAVIA.
Tracks: Rip it up / Back in the USA / Rockabilly rebel / Almost 12 O'Clock / Rockin' daddy / School of rock'n'-roll / Hoy hoy hoy / Be bop a lula / Let's play house / High school confidential / Boppin' the blues.
LP. . . . . SJLP 841
Sunjay / Feb '89 / CSA Tell Tapes.

TEXAN REBEL ROCK A BOOGIE SHAKE, THE.
Tracks: Not Advised.
■ LP. 33.8011
Jan Records / Jul '81.

Summers. John

COMPROMISE KID.
Tracks: Not Advised.
LP. . . . . LRF 079
Larrikin (Australia) / Mar '89 / Roots Records / Projection / Topic Records / C.M. Distribution / Jazz Music / Ross Records / Duncans / A.D.A Distribution / Direct Distribution.

INDIANA FIDDLER.
Tracks: Not Advised.
LP. . . . . ROUNDER 0194
Rounder / '88 / Projection / Roots Records / Swift / C.M. Distribution / Topic Records / Jazz Music / Hot Shot / A.D.A Distribution / Direct Distribution.

Sumner. J.D

EASY TO LOVE YOU (Sumner, J.D & The Stamps).
Tracks: Easy to love you / Love on / Time is a thief / Glad I don't have a heartache.

■ DELETED

■ 7"........................ BDE 18
Bulldog (USA) / Feb '80.

Sun Records

One of the most famous record labels in pop music history, Sun Records was not only responsible for a music revolution and the creation of rockabilly, but also for the discovery of several of its leading players, with Elvis Presley right at the forefront. Founded by former disc-jockey and promotion man Sam Phillips, Sun was located at 706 Union Street, Memphis - a small recording studio that came into being as the Memphis Recording Service. Initially the service provided custom taping but business developed into recording blues acts for independent record labels like Chess and Modern. It was an understanding of how these independent record companies operated that led Phillips to create Sun Records in February 1952. Also first working with blues artists, Sun made its first moves into the country market in July 1953 by recording the vocal group Ripley Cotton Choppers, with the second release being given over to Bob Price, a Mississippi singer then living in Memphis. At that time Phillips was merely testing the market, but once his deal with Chess was drawing to a conclusion he looked towards country with more commitment. And with a fresh objective, he dreamed about mixing the cultures, in particular finding "a white singer with a negro voice". The dream became reality when Elvis recorded *That's All Right Mama*, (a 1946 song penned by Arthur 'Big Boy' Crudup) and *Blue Moon Of Kentucky*, (Bill Monroe's bluegrass classic) at the Sun studio's on July 5, 1954. Although it created only minor interest at the time, it was the beginning of a roll that was to establish Elvis Presley, Sun Records and a whole new musical movement. (Tony Byworth)

Sun, Joe

Born James J. Paulson in Rochester, Minnesota in 1943. A singer-songwriter incorporated elements of blues and rock 'n' roll into his honky-tonk style country. During the late sixties he had his own band The Branded Man before moving to Nashville in 1972. When that label folded he moved to Elektra making the top 40 with *Holed Up In Some Honky Tonk*, in 1980. He is a popular touring attraction in the U.K.

DARK SIDE OF TOWN (Son, Joe & The Solar System).
Tracks: Dark side of town.
7"........................ SON 2272
Sonet / Oct '84 / Swift / C.M. Distribution / Roots Records / Jazz Music / Sonet Records / Cadillac Music / Projection / Wellard Dist. / Hot Shot.

HANK BOGART STILL LIVES.
Tracks: Hank Bogart still lives / Part of me is missing you, A / Doreen / Slow motion / South of the south being born / Chasing rainbows / Maxine / Gas and food exit off 1-24 / Jimmy 55 / Watermelon time in Georgia / Burning memories / Good loving bad / Ballad of thunder road.
LP........................ DFG 8418
Dixie Frog / Aug '89 / Discovery.

I AIN'T HONKY TONKIN' NO MORE.
Tracks: I ain't honky tonkin' no more / Slow movin' freight train / Stepping out blues / Fraulein / Will the circle be unbroken / Gimme some lovin' / Take the time to tall / Livin' outside of the law / Holed up in some honky tonk / Boys in the back of the bus.
LP........................ K 52327
Elektra / May '82 / WEA.

LIVIN' ON HONKY TONK TIME.
Tracks: Ready for the times to get better / My sweet love ain't around / We're all a bunch of outlaws in our minds / Please pull away from me / Bottom line / I'd better go home (while I still got a home) / Lonesome rainin' city / Bombed, boozed and busted / Alabama rose / Hobo on a freight train / Honky tonkin' / Knockin' on heavens door.
■ LP........................ OV 1755
Ovation / '78 / Gull Records.

OLD FLAMES.
Tracks: Old flames / Blue ribbon blues / I came on business for the king / Born too late / Ozark Mountain lullaby / Midnight train of memories / High and dry / This body that I call my home / That evil child / Long black veil.

■ LP........................ OV 1734
Ovation / Mar '80.

OUT OF YOUR MIND.
Tracks: Out among the stars / Shotgun rider / Out of your mind / I'll find it where I can / Little bit of push / I'd rather go on hurtin' / Mysteries of life / Why you been gone so long / I'm still crazy about you / One timers.
■ LP........................ OV 1743
Ovation / Mar '80.

SHOTGUN RIDER.
Tracks: Shotgun rider / I came on business for the king.
■ 7"........................ OV 1201
Ovation / Apr '80.

SUN NEVER SETS, THE (Sun, Joe & The Solar System).
Tracks: Dark side of town, The / Peel, Arkansas / Light that shines the brightest, The / I don't take much (Ode to teaser) / Next motel, The / Sun never sets, The / Bad for me / No one said it was gonna be easy / Who are they (Somewhere down the line) / Throw me a line / Gimple sing-a-long country song / Everyone in Sweden.
LP........................ SNTF 922
Sonet / Dec '84 / Swift / C.M. Distribution / Roots Records / Jazz Music / Sonet Records / Cadillac Music / Projection / Wellard Dist. / Hot Shot.

TWILIGHT ZONE.
Tracks: Not Advised.
LP........................ DFG 8403
Dixie Frog / Aug '87 / Discovery.

Sundown

ALL ALONE TOGETHER.
Tracks: Rose of Cimarron / Hard hearted / Blue eyes crying in the rain / Carmen / Ride me down easy / Living in the west / Country Joe and Mickey Finn / Till I gain control again / Cotton Jenny / Turn out the light (love me tonight) / Back home again / All alone together.
LP........................ FHR 105
Folk Heritage / Jul '82 / Terry Blood Dist.

HAPPY STATE OF MIND.
Tracks: Not Advised.
LP........................ BSS 142
Tank / Dec '77.

Sundown Playboys

SATURDAY NIGHT CAJUN MUSIC.
Tracks: Not Advised.
LP........................ 6072
MC........................ 6072 TC
Swallow (USA) / Jul '88 / Swift / Wellard Dist.

Sutter, Art

ART OF COUNTRY, THE.
Tracks: Fool such as I / That'll be the day / Only love / You were always on my mind / Evening star / I fall to pieces / Dreams of the everyday housewife / Still / Me and Bobby McGee / Send me the pillow that you dream on / You never can tell / Your cheating heart / Wolverton Mountain / Please help me I'm falling.
LP........................ LIDL 6014
MC........................ LIDC 6014
Lismor / Nov '85 / Duncans / Roots Records / Conifer Records / C.M. Distribution / Ross Records / A.D.A Distribution / Topic Records / Direct Distribution / Lismor Records.

ART OF LOVE.
Tracks: When I fall in love / I love you because / When your old wedding ring was new / I am these goes by / Anniversary waltz / Wedding song, The / Our house / I only have eyes for you / Those endearing young charms / And I love you so / If / Song for you, A / Looking through the eyes of love / Best days of my life.
LP........................ LIDL 6013
MC........................ LIDC 6013
Lismor / Nov '85 / Duncans / Roots Records / Conifer Records / C.M. Distribution / Ross Records / A.D.A Distribution / Topic Records / Direct Distribution / Lismor Records.

Swan, Billy

BILLY SWAN.
Tracks: I can help / You're the one / Ubangi stomp / Vanessa / Just want to taste your wine / Don't be cruel / Blue suede shoes / Swept away / Everything's the same (ain't nothin' changed) / Number one / (You just) Woman-handled my mind / I'm her fool / Overnite thing

(usually) / Shake, rattle and roll / Lover please / Don't kill our love.
■ LP........................ 31674
CBS / '78 / Sony.
■ MC........................ 4031674
CBS / '78 / Sony.

DON'T BE CRUEL.
Tracks: Don't be cruel.
■ 7"........................ MNT 3244
Monument / May '75.

FOUR.
Tracks: Swept away / Playing the game of love / Pardon me / Oliver Swan / Smoky places / Don't kill our love / Not everyone knows / Last call / California song (for Marlu) / Me and my honey.
■ LP........................ MNT 81867
CBS / '78 / Sony.

I CAN HELP.
Tracks: I can help.
■ 7"........................ MNT 2752
Monument / Dec '74.

I'M HER FOOL.
Tracks: I'm her fool / I'd like to work for you.
■ 7"........................ MNT 3057
Monument / Feb '75.

JUST WANT TO TASTE YOUR WINE (Swan, Billy & The Jordanaires).
Tracks: Just want to taste your wine / Love you baby to the bone.
■ 7"........................ MNT 4095
Monument / Apr '76.

SHAKE, RATTLE AND ROLL.
Tracks: Shake, rattle and roll / I've got it for you.
■ 7"........................ MNT 4836
Monument / Jan '77.

YOU'RE OK, I'M OK.
Tracks: You're OK, I'm OK / Never go lookin' again.
■ 7"........................ AMS 7354
A&M / May '78.

Swift Jewel Cowboys

CHUCK WAGON SWING.
Tracks: Chuck wagon swing / My untrue cowgirl / Raggi-in' the rails / Memphis blues / Coney Island washboard / Fan it / Little Willie Green / Memphis oomph / Willie the weeper / Swingin' at the Circle S / Dill pickle rag / Rose room / Bug scuffle / You gotta ho de ho.
LP........................ STR 806
String / '81 / Projection / Roots Records / A.D.A Distribution / C.M. Distribution / Swift / Ross Records / Duncans.

Sylvia

HASTA LA VISTA.
Tracks: Hasta la vista.
■ 7"........................ SON 2005
Sonet / Apr '75.
7"........................ SON 2093
Sonet / Sep '76 / Swift / C.M. Distribution / Roots Records / Jazz Music / Sonet Records / Cadillac Music / Projection / Wellard Dist. / Hot Shot.

SOMEBODY LOVES YOU.
Tracks: Not Advised.
LP........................ SNTF 723
Sonet / Oct '76 / Swift / C.M. Distribution / Roots Records / Jazz Music / Sonet Records / Cadillac Music / Projection / Wellard Dist. / Hot Shot.

WE CAN'T HIDE IT ANY MORE (Sylvia & Chuck Jackson).
Tracks: We can't hide it any more / Bartender.
■ 7"........................ 6146 319
All Platinum / May '77.

Y VIVA ESPANA.
Tracks: Y viva espana.
■ 7"........................ SON 2037
Sonet / Aug '74.

T

Tall, Tom

Amarillo, Texas born singer who appeared on many of the leading live country radio shows during the 1950's (including the Grand Ole Opry, Louisiana Hayride and the Big D. Jamboree), but only achieved one substantial chart record - a duet with Ginny Wright, Are you mine , on Fabor Records. More than quarter of a century later Tom Tall's recordings have received fresh attention via Bear Family. A number of the tracks also featured Ginny Wright as well as other Fabor artists the Creel Sisters and Ruckus Taylor. (Tony Byworth - August 1993)

HOT ROD IS HER NAME.
Tracks: Goldie Jo Mahome / Underway / Give me a chance / If you knew what I know / Please be careful / Are you mine / Out of line / Boom boom boomerang / Will this dream of mine come true / Hot rod is her name / Whose pidgeon are you / Don't you know, don't you know / I want to walk with you / Come with me / Remembering you / You loved another one better than me / Why must I wonder / I gave my heart to two people.
LP . . . . BFX 15189
Bear Family / Feb '86 / Rollercoaster Records / Swift / Direct Distribution.

STACK-A-RECORDS (Tall, Tom & His Tom Cats).
Tracks: Stack-a-records / Mary Jo.
■ 7" . . . . SP 3003
Rockstar (1) / Jan '81.

Talley, James

AMERICAN ORIGINALS.
Tracks: Find somebody and love them / Bury me in New Orleans / Baby she loves a rocker / Whiskey on the side / Are they gonna make us outlaws again / Way to say I love you / New York town / Open all night / Montana song / Ready to please / We're all one family.
LP . . . . BFX 15182
Bear Family / Jun '85 / Rollercoaster Records / Swift / Direct Distribution.
CD . . . . BCD 15244
Bear Family / '86 / Rollercoaster Records / Swift / Direct Distribution.

BLACKJACK CHOIR/ AIN'T IT SOMETHIN'.
Tracks: Bluesman / Alabama summertime / Everybody loves a love song / Magnolia boy / Mississippi river whistle town / Daddy just called it the blues / Up from Georgia / Migrant Jesse Sawyer / You know I've got to love her / When the fiddler packs his case / Ain't it somethin' / Only the best / We keep tryin' / Dixie blues / Not even when it's over / Nine pounds of hashbrowns / Richland, Washington / Middle C mama / Woman troubles / Old time religion / Poets of the West Virginia mines / What will there be for the children.
CD . . . . BCD 15435
Bear Family / Jul '89 / Rollercoaster Records / Swift / Direct Distribution.

GOT NO BREAD/ TRYIN' LIKE THE DEVIL.
Tracks: W.Lee O'Daniel and the Light Crust Dough Boys / Got no bread, no milk, no money / Red river memory / Give him another bottle / Calico gypsy / To get back home / Big battle in the sandy land / No openers needed / Blue eyed Ruth and my Sunday suit / Mehan, Oklahoma / Daddy's song / Take me to the country / Red river reprise / Forty hours / Deep country blues / Give my love to Marie / Are they gonna make us outlaws again / She tries not to cry / Tryin' like the devil / She's the one / Sometimes I think about Suzanne / Nothin' but the blues / You can't ever tell.
CD . . . . BCD 15433
Bear Family / Jul '89 / Rollercoaster Records / Swift / Direct Distribution.

LOVE SONGS AND THE BLUES.
Tracks: Your sweet love / Whatever gets you through your life / I can't surrender / He went back to Texas / Working girl / Little child / Up from Georgia / All because of you / Collection of sorrows, A / Cause I'm in love with you / May your dreams come true.
CD . . . . BCD 15464
Bear Family / Jul '89 / Rollercoaster Records / Swift / Direct Distribution.

ROAD TO TORREON.
Tracks: Maria (on the road to Torreon) / Ramon estevan / H John Tarragon / Demona / La rosa Montana / She was a flower / Rosary, The / Storm, The / Little child of heaven / Anna Maria / I had a love way out West.
CD . . . . BCD 15633
Bear Family / Jun '92 / Rollercoaster Records / Swift / Direct Distribution.

Tanner, Gid

Born James Gideon (Gid) Tanner on 06.06.1885 (died 13.05.1960), fiddle player/chicken farmer from Dacula, Georgia. Made first recordings with the Skillet Lickers on 7 March 1924 - to become Columbia's very first hillbilly band, other pivotal figures of which, were vocalist/ guitarist Riley Puckett and Clayton McMichen (fiddle) before they went seperate ways in 1934. To this day both country and blues acts draw from the Georgia string band's eclectic brand of wild rural old time music, humorous odes and folk ballads. Apart from Columbia, their work has appeared on RCA, Country and Rounder. (Maurice Hope - July 1993).

HEAR THESE NEW SOUTHERN FIDDLE AND GUITAR RECORDS.
Tracks: Not Advised.
LP . . . . ROUNDER 1005
Rounder / Jun '77 / Projection / Roots Records / Swift / C.M. Distribution / Topic Records / Jazz Music / Hot Shot / A.D.A Distribution / Direct Distribution.
CD . . . . ROUNDER 1005C
Rounder / Aug '88 / Projection / Roots Records / Swift / C.M. Distribution / Topic Records / Jazz Music / Hot Shot / A.D.A Distribution / Direct Distribution.

KICKAPOO MEDICINE SHOW (Tanner, Gid & His Skillet Lickers).
Tracks: Nancy rollin' / Farmer's daughter, The / I ain't no better now / Never seen the likes since gettin' upstairs / Arkansas sheik, The / You got to stop drinking shine / You got to stop kickin' my dog around / Cumberland gap / On a buckin' mule / Paddy won't you drink some cider / Don't you hear Jerusalem moan / Prettiest little girl in the county / Kikapoo medicine show parts 1 & 2 / Rake and the rambling boy / New Dixie / Mississippi Sawyer.
LP . . . . ROUNDER 1023
MC . . . . ROUNDER 1023C
Rounder / '88 / Projection / Roots Records / Swift / C.M. Distribution / Topic Records / Jazz Music / Hot Shot / A.D.A Distribution / Direct Distribution.

Tashian, Barry

BARRY AND HOLLY TASHIAN (Tashian, Barry & Holly).
Tracks: Trust in me / Home / Blue eyes / Ramona / Making a change / You're running wild / Party doll / My favourite memory / Poor woman's epitaph / Look both ways / Boy who cried love, The / I can dance.
CD . . . . SDCD 9.00640
Sawdust / '90.

READY FOR LOVE (Tashian, Barry & Holly).
Tracks: Ready for love / Let me see the light / Heaven with you / Heart full of memories / Hearts that break / Highway 86 / Price of pride, The / Diamond, The / Ring of gold / Memories remain, The / If I knew then / This old love.
MC . . . . ROU 0302
Rounder / Apr '93 / Projection / Roots Records / Swift / C.M. Distribution / Topic Records / Jazz Music / Hot Shot / A.D.A Distribution / Direct Distribution.
CD . . . . ROU 0302CD
Rounder / May '93 / Projection / Roots Records / Swift / C.M. Distribution / Topic Records / Jazz Music / Hot Shot / A.D.A Distribution / Direct Distribution.

TRUST IN ME (Tashian, Barry & Holly).
Tracks: Trust in me / Home / Blue eyes / Ramona / Making a change / You're running wild / Party doll / My favourite memory / Poor woman's epitaph / Look both ways / Boy who cried love, The / I can't dance.
LP . . . . RR 302
Request / Oct '89 / Conifer Records / Jazz Music.
CD . . . . CDRR 302
MC . . . . MCRR 302
Request / Mar '92 / Conifer Records / Jazz Music.

Tasty Licks

ANCHORED TO THE SHORE.
Tracks: Not Advised.
LP . . . . ROUNDER 0120
Rounder / '88 / Projection / Roots Records / Swift / C.M. Distribution / Topic Records / Jazz Music / Hot Shot / A.D.A Distribution / Direct Distribution.

TASTY LICKS.
Tracks: Not Advised.
LP . . . . ROUNDER 0106
MC . . . . ROUNDER 0106C
Rounder / '88 / Projection / Roots Records / Swift / C.M. Distribution / Topic Records / Jazz Music / Hot Shot / A.D.A Distribution / Direct Distribution.

Taylor, Chip

Singer - songwriter, born James Wesley Voight, Winchester County, New York in 1940 - brother of actor John Voight. Songwriting credits include the country and pop hit Angel Of The Morning plus Wild Thing and Any Way You Want Me a country hit for Connie Eaton, Melba Montgomery and Juice Newton, who alongside P.P Arnold, Merrilee Rush and Mary Mason gained success on the pop scene. All have helped make it one of the most successful ever compostitions. Country acts who've taken up his work include Bobby Bare, Jim Ed Brown, Waylon Jennings (Sweet Dream Woman) and Floyd Crammer. Taylor's country track record by comparison is modest, although during the 70s he recorded a batch of finely written albums, appearing on Warner Brothers and Columbia. His 1973 debut on his former Last Chance was aglow with clever wit. (Maurice Hope 1993)

LAST CHANCE.
Tracks: (I want) the real thing / Son of a rotten gambler / I read it in a Rolling Stone / (The coal fields of) Shickshinny / I wasn't born in Tennessee / (Likes of) Louise, The / It's still the same / IOU in cash box / Family of one / Clean your own tables / Last chance.
■ LP . . . . K 56036
WEA / '77.

Taylor, Earl

BLUE GRASS TAYLOR MADE.
Tracks: Not Advised.
LP . . . . HAT 3094
MC . . . . HATC 3094
Stetson / Feb '89 / Crusader Marketing Co. / Swift / Wellard Dist. / Midland Records / C.M. Distribution.

Taylor, Eddie

BAD BOY (Charly Blues - Masterworks Vol. 35).
Tracks: Not Advised.
CD . . . . CDBM 35
MC . . . . TCBM 35
Charly / Jan '93 / Charly.

BIG TOWN PLAYBOY.
Tracks: Bad boy / E.T. blues / Ride em on down / Big town playboy / You'll always have a home / Don't knock at my door / Bongo beat / I'm gonna love you / Lookin' for trouble / Find my baby / Stroll out west / Trainfare / Leave this neighbourhood / I'm sittin' here / Do you want me to cry.
LP . . . . CRB 1015
Charly R&B / Mar '81 / Charly.

I FEEL SO BAD.
Tracks: Not Advised.
■ LP . . . . ADVENT 2802
Advent / Apr '79.

MY HEART IS BLEEDING (Taylor, Eddie Blues Band).
Tracks: Not Advised.
LP . . . . LR 42.009
L&R / '88 / New Note.

READY FOR EDDIE (Taylor, Eddie Playboy).
Tracks: I'm a country boy / Seems like a million years / Gamblin' man / After hours / Sloppy drunk / Ready for Eddie / You don't love me / Too late to cry / You'll always have a home / Playboy boogie / My little machine / Cross-cut saw.
■ LP . . . . BEAR 6
Big Bear / May '82.
■ LP . . . . BRP 2032
Big Bear / Oct '86.

RIDE 'EM ON DOWN (see under Reed, Jimmy).

STILL NOT READY FOR EDDIE.
Tracks: Not Advised.
LP . . . . AN 005
Antones / Dec '88 / Hot Shot / Topic Records / Direct Distribution.

Taylor, Tut

FRIAR TUT.
Tracks: Not Advised.
LP . . . . ROUNDER 0011
Rounder / '77 / Projection / Roots Records / Swift / C.M. Distribution / Topic Records / Jazz Music / Hot Shot / A.D.A Distribution / Direct Distribution.

OLD POST OFFICE, THE.
Tracks: Granny Grass's push cart / Old post office, The / Tennessee Dulcimer works / Golden slippers / Pickin' flat / Wayfaring stranger / Monkey wrench / Kentucky long rifle / Alla Lee / Resophonic guitar / Copycat / Bad Blake's blues / Autry's peach orchid / Many anniversaries.
■ LP. . . . . .FF 008
Flying Fish (USA) / '76.

Taylor-Good, Karen

GOOD.
Tracks: Not Advised.
LP. . . . . DFG 8401
Dixie Frog / Nov '88 / Discovery.

Telephone Bill

MANHATTAN DOLL (Telephone Bill & Smooth Operators).
Tracks: Not Advised.
LP. . . . . DID 713
Dingle's / Aug '82 / Roots Records / C.M. Distribution / Projection.

Television

BONANZA (Bonanza Cast).
Tracks: Bonanza / Sourwood mountain / Sky ball paint / Early one morning / Ponderosa / Careless love / Skip to my Lou / In the pines / Happy birthday / My sons, my sons / Hangin' blues, The / Shenendoah / Miss Cindy / Place where I worship / Hark, the Herald Angels sing / Deck the halls / New born King, The / Story: The first Christmas trees / Oh fir tree dear / Christmas is a comin' / O come all ye faithful / Jingle bells / Santa got lost in Texas / Stuck in the chimney / Story: Why we light candles on the Christmas tree / Merry Christmas neighbour / Merry Christmas & goodnight / Intro: Bonanza / Alamo / Pony Express / An ol' tin cup / Endless prairie / Ghost riders in the sky / Ringo / Blue guitar / Sand / Saga of the Ponderosa / Five card stud / Cool water / Devil's grin / Pretty horses / Devil cat / Ol' Chisholm trail, The / Wagon wheels / Frightened town / Shadow of the cactus / Tumbling tumbleweeds / Gold / Whoopee ti yi yo / Search, The / Dig, dig, dig, dig (there's no more water..) / Ol' cyclone / Twilight on the trail / Geronimo / Mule train / I'm a gun / Gunslinger's prayer / Nellie Cole / Home on the range / Virginia town / Place where I worship, The / Pop goes the hammer / End of the track / Nine pound hammer / Bring on the dancin' girls / Oh, what a town / Fourteen men / Destiny / Sixteen tons / Trouble row / Chickasaw mountain / Darling, my darling / Man, The / Ringo (French) / Du sable / Bold soldier, The / Mary Ann / They call the wind Maria / Sylvie / Lily of the west / Water is wide, The / Rake & a ramblin' boy / Quiet girl, A / Shady grove / Alberta / Empty pocket blues / Come all ye fair & tender ladies / Springfield mountain / Roll out, heave that cotton / Battle hymn of the Republic, The / Erie canal, the / Paiute sunrise chant / Charles, steal away / He never said a mumblin'.
CD Set . . . . BCD 15684
Bear Family / May '93 / Rollercoaster Records / Swift / Direct Distribution.

DALLAS - THE MUSIC STORY (T.V. Soundtrack) (Various Artists).
Tracks: I wanna reach out and touch / Makin' up for lost time (the Dallas lovers' song) / Few good men, A / J.R., who do you think you are? / Working man's song (the Ewing/Barnes legacy) / Loneliness in Lucy's eyes (the life Sue Ellen is living) / I'm a survivor / If I knew then what I know now / Dallas, Theme from (Dallas dreams) / Who killed Jock Ewing?.
LP. 925325 1
■ MC 925325 4
WEA / Jul '86 / WEA.

DUKES OF HAZZARD (TV Soundtrack) (Various Artists).
Tracks: Good ol' boys / Laughing all the way to the bank / Duellin' Dukes / General Lee / Flash / Up on Cripple Creek / Cover girl eyes / Keep between them ditches / Ballad of the General Lee / In the driver's seat / Down home, American girl.
LP. . . . . SCT 85593
MC 40 85593
Scotti Bros (USA) / '82 / PolyGram.

YOUR CHEATIN' HEART (Crouch, Dorwood & The Deadwood Playboys).
Tracks: Your cheatin' heart / Tennessee waltz.
■ 7". . . . . RESL 816
BBC / Oct '90.

YOUR CHEATIN' HEART (BBC TV Series) (Various Artists).
Tracks: Not Advised.
CD . . . . .BBCCD 791
MC . . . . .ZCF 791
BBC / Nov '90 / Pinnacle / Bond Street Music.

Terry, Al

AL TERRY & JIM NEWMAN (Terry, Al & Jim Newman).
Tracks: Not Advised.
LP. . . . . FLY 573
Flyright / Jul '86 / Hot Shot / Roots Records / Wellard Dist. / Charly / Swift / Projection.

GOOD DEAL, LUCILLE.
Tracks: Good deal, Lucille (2nd recording) / Roughneck blues / Coconut girl / Bring some rain / Follow me / It's better late than never / Because I'm yours / Am I seeing things / Watch dog / My baby knows / What a fool I was to fall (Previously unissued.) / Last date / What are you to me / Passing the blues around / Your sweet lies / Lesson of love.
LP. . . . . BFX 15107
Bear Family / Nov '84 / Rollercoaster Records / Swift / Direct Distribution.

Texana Dames

TEXANA DAMES.
Tracks: Not Advised.
CD . . . . SNTCD 1026
LP. . . . . SNTF 1026
Sonet / Nov '89 / Swift / C.M. Distribution / Roots Records / Jazz Music / Sonet Records / Cadillac Music / Projection / Wellard Dist. / Hot Shot.

Texas

Tennessee might well be considered the home of country music, with Nashville as its commercial headquarters, but Texas has probably bred far more top country acts. A few of the star names that have emerged from the Lone Star State over the years include: Gene Autry, Vernon Dalhart, Lefty Frizzell, Johnny Horton, Waylon Jennings, George Jones, Roger Miller, Moon Mullican, Willie Nelson, Buck Owens, Ray Price, Jim Reeves, Tex Ritter, Kenny Rogers, George Strait, Hank Thompson, Ernest Tubb and Bob Wills. They're all well known but it's worth considering several of their individual contributions to particular growth areas of Texas music. To start, Gene Autry and Tex Ritter were two of the world's most famous singing cowboys, but this particular genre was purely a development of the Hollywood movie industry. Western swing was a music of the cowboy and owed as much to blues and jazz as it did to country. Texas was its most important breeding ground, a not too surprising fact as the state was a melting pot of different cultures that included Negro, German, Mexican and cajun. Limestone County born Bob Wills was the acknowledged father of western swing, taking the first steps when he formed the Light Crust Doughboys under a sponsorship deal with Birrus, a flour company, which led to radio spots in Fort Worth. (See separate entry for Bob Wills). The 1930's also witnessed a brand of country emerging out of the saloons and taverns, honky-tonk. A new breed of singer was needed to sing a new kind of song within these haunts, where heavy drinking and fighting fitted alongside loud conversation and dancing. The old traditional hillbilly themes of mother, home and church hardly fitted such surroundings, while the venues themselves demanded a change in the sound of the music, louder by means of electrified instruments and a more solid rhythm. Ernest Tubb was the first of the honky-tonk singers, with Ray Price being among the first to claim attention in the post World War II years. Providing a complete contrast, Jim Reeves, who started out as a traditional country singer, developed into one of the smoothest balladeers country music has ever known. In East Texas on the Louisiana border, there's the cajun influence and, in the southwest, the strains of Mexican music has created a hybrid named 'Tex-Mex'. North of San Antonio, in a region that abounds with German town names, they still play the polka at Saturday night dances. And, who knows, out west you might even hear a cowboy song or two. (Tony Byworth)

Texas Lone Star

DESPERADOS WAITING FOR A TRAIN.
Tracks: Good hearted woman / Here I am again / Friend of the devil / Desperados waiting for the train / Fast train / Me & my uncle / Wild horses / In my own way / Bluebirds are singing for you / Luckenbach, Texas / Painted ladies.
■ LP. . . . . BF 15011
Bear Family / '84.
CD . . . . BCD 15692
Bear Family / Aug '92 / Rollercoaster Records / Swift / Direct Distribution.

Texas Tornados

Founded in December 1989, by the rugged, fun-loving Tex-Mex vocalist Freddy Fender, and Mexican accordion legend Flaco Jimeneaz (recording artist/sessionman who has played on albums as diverse as Ry Cooder to Linda Ronstadt, by way of Bob Dylan, Peter Rowan & Bryan Ferry). Spent years recording on minor labels with(*Ay te dejo en san antonio*) album a Grammy winner in 1986) as well as the better known Arhoolie and Rounder labels. 1992 found them debut on a major label - when their guest reprise release *Partner's* emerged. Texas country rock/pop stalwarts Augie Meyers & Doug Sahm (born 6.11.1941, San Antonio, Texas also as Doug Sahm & The Texas Tornados. Spent some time during late 60s in LA, before moving back to Texas in 1969. Mid - seventies recorded for ABC/Dot while his wild rolling rhythms, spiced with Chicano swamp inclinations registering hits with *She's about a mover* & *Mendocino*) Played in San Francisco as The Tex Mex Revue. In 1989 along with Amos Garrett & Gene Taylor under the heading of The Formerly Brothers who like Meyers were one-time members of the Sir Douglas Quintet. Since which time they've toured extensively, recorded three albums *Texas Tornados* , *Zone of our own* , & 1992 recording *Hangin' by a thread* for reprise. (For Freddy Fender see separate bio). (Maurice Hope - July 1993)

TEXAS TORNADOS.
Tracks: Who were you thinking of / (Hey baby) que paso / Laredo rose / Man can cry, A / Soy de San Luis / Adios Mexico / If that's what you're thinking / She never spoke Spanish to me / Dinero / Baby! Heaven sent me you.
CD 7599262512
LP. 7599262511
MC 7599262514
WEA / Aug '90 / WEA.

Thibodeaux, Ambrose

AMBROSE THIBODEAUX.
Tracks: Not Advised.
LP. 112
La Louisiane / '87 / Swift.

AUTHENTIC CAJUN FRENCH MUSIC AND FOLK SONGS.
Tracks: Not Advised.
LP. 143
La Louisiane / '87 / Swift.

MORE AUTHENTIC ACADIAN FRENCH MUSIC.
Tracks: Not Advised.
LP. 119
La Louisiane / '87 / Swift.

THAT FRENCH ACADIAN SOUND.
Tracks: Not Advised.
LP. 133
La Louisiane / '87 / Swift.
MC . . . . .133 TC
N/A / '87.

Thibodeaux, Rufus

CAJUN COUNTRY FIDDLE OF RUFUS THIBODEAUX.
Tracks: Not Advised.
LP. 129
MC . . . . .129 TC
La Louisiane / '87 / Swift.

CAJUN FIDDLE.
Tracks: Not Advised.
LP. 137
La Louisiane / '87 / Swift.

Thomas, B.J.

16 GREATEST HITS.
Tracks: Not Advised.
■ CD . . . . CD 1014
Gusto (USA) / '88.

AMAZING GRACE.
Tracks: Amazing grace / His eye is on the sparrow / Unclouded day, The / In the garden / You'll never walk alone / Old rugged cross, The / Just a closer walk with thee / I believe / Just as I am / Beyond the sunset.
LP. . . . . WST 9611
MC . . . . WC 9611
Word (UK) / May '82 / Word Records (UK) / Sony.

ANOTHER SOMEBODY DONE SOMEBODY WRONG SONG.
Tracks: Another somebody odne somebody wrong song / City boys.
7". . . . . ABC 4043
ABC Records / '75.

B.J.THOMAS.
Tracks: Not Advised.
MC . . . . ZCGAS 723
Audio Fidelity(USA) / Oct '84 / Stage One Records.

BEST OF B.J. THOMAS.
Tracks: Not Advised.
MC 16-14
Creole (Everest-Europa) / Jul '84.

CLOSE TO YOU.
Tracks: Not Advised.
MC . . . . ORC 008
Orchid Music / Feb '82 / Pinnacle.

DON'T WORRY BABY.
Tracks: Don't worry baby / My love.
■ 7". . . . . MCA 313
MCA / Aug '77.

T 2 ■ DELETED

EVERYBODY LOVES A RAIN SONG.
Tracks: Everybody loves a rain song / Dusty roads.
■ 7" . . . . MCA 351
MCA / Feb '78.

MIRACLE.
Tracks: Not Advised.
LP. . . . . MYR 1128
MC . . . . MC 1128
Myrrh / May '82 / Word Records (UK) / Sony.

NEW LOOKS.
Tracks: New looks from an old lover / Wind beneath my wings / I'm saving all the good times for you / You keep the man in me happy (and the child in me alive) / Whatever happened to old-fashioned love? / Rock and roll you're beautiful / Memory machine / I love us / I just sing.
LP. . . . . EPC 25378
MC 40 25378
Epic / Aug '83 / Sony.

RAINDROPS KEEP FALLING ON MY HEAD.
Tracks: Raindrops keep falling on my head.
■ 7" . . . . WN 1
Wand / Feb '70.

WHATEVER HAPPENED TO OLD FASHIONED LOVE.
Tracks: Whatever happened to old fashioned love / I just sing.
■ 7" . . . . EPCA 3244
Epic / Jul '83.

YOU GAVE ME LOVE.
Tracks: Not Advised.
LP. . . . . WRD 3006
MC . . . . TC WRD 3006
Word (UK) / Jun '84 / Word Records (UK) / Sony.

Thomas, Buddy

KITTY PUSS FIDDLER.
Tracks: Not Advised.
LP. . . . . ROUNDER 0032
Rounder / May '77 / Projection / Roots Records / Swift / C.M. Distribution / Topic Records / Jazz Music / Hot Shot / A.D.A Distribution / Direct Distribution.

Thomas, Guthrie

HOBO EAGLE THIEF.
Tracks: Carolyn and Benjamin / Captain Jack / Wake up / Ship of fools / Melisa / Scorn and strife / Gone and come to pass / If you want me to / All the tea in China.
CD . . . . SDCD 9.00915
Sawdust / '90.

Thompson, Hank

Hank Thompson and his Brazos Valley Boys were the most commercially successful Western swing band of the fifties and sixties. Much of their material however, had a more mainstream country approach and could well be called honky tonk. In his late teens, Hank Thompson broadcast as a singer-guitarist over local radio stations, and after wartime service in the navy, returned to Texas and signed to Capitol Records in 1948. He recorded the first country album in stereo.

20 GOLDEN PIECES: HANK THOMPSON.
Tracks: Who left the door to Heaven open? / When my blue moon turns to gold again / Honky tonk angel / I recall a gypsy woman / Mama don't allow / Wait a little longer baby / Loving on a back street / Whatever's left / Fair weather love / Red necks, white socks and blue ribbon beer / Country bumpkin / I've come awful close / Oklahoma hills / Mark of a heel / Humpty Dumpty heart / Green light / Smokey the bear / Squaws along the Yukon / Wild side of life / Next time I fall in love.
MC . . . . BDC 2042
Bulldog Records / Jul '85 / President Records / Jazz Music / Wellard Dist. / TKO Records Ltd.
LP. . . . . BDL 2042
Bulldog Records / May '85 / President Records / Jazz Music / Wellard Dist. / TKO Records Ltd.

AT THE GOLDEN NUGGETT.
Tracks: Not Advised.
LP. . . . . HAT 3076
Stetson / '88 / Crusader Marketing Co. / Swift / Wellard Dist. / Midland Records / C.M. Distribution.
MC . . . . HATC 3076
Stetson / Dec '88 / Crusader Marketing Co. / Swift / Wellard Dist. / Midland Records / C.M. Distribution.

BEST OF THE BEST OF HANK THOMPSON.
Tracks: Not Advised.
LP. . . . . GT 0060
Gusto (USA) / Mar '88.

CAPITOL COLLECTORS SERIES: HANK THOMPSON.
Tracks: Humpty dumpty heart / Whoa, sailor / Wild side of life, The / Waiting in the lobby of your heart / Rub-a-dub-dub / Yesterday's girl / Wake up, Irene / Breakin' the rules / Honky tonk gal / We've gone too far / New green light, The / Breakin' in another heart / Don't take it out on me / Blackboard of my heart / Rockin' in the Congo / Squaws along the Yukon / Six pack to go, A / She's just a whole lot like you / Oklahoma hills / Hangover tavern.
LP. . . . . EMS 1349
■ MC . . . . TCEMS 1349
Capitol / Nov '89.
■ CD . . . . CDP 792 124 2
Capitol / Sep '89.

DANCE RANCH.
Tracks: Not Advised.
LP. . . . . HAT 3027
MC . . . . HATC 3027
Stetson / Oct '86 / Crusader Marketing Co. / Swift / Wellard Dist. / Midland Records / C.M. Distribution.

HANK THOMPSON.
Tracks: Six pack to go / Wild side of life / Oklahoma hills / Breakin' the rules / Blondes with no last name / Walkin' on new grass / Pick pocket / Honky tonk good ole Galls and Hillbilly / Let my heart do the talking for me / Swingin' side of them swingin' doors.
LP. . . . . IMCA 39089
MC . . . . IMCAC 39089
MCA / Mar '87 / BMG.

HANK THOMPSON 1952.
Tracks: Darling what more can I do / Square dab from the country / Brand in my heart / I'm lost without you / Judy / Be my life's companion / Shotgun boogie / Sixty.
LP. . . . . RFD 9003
Country Routes / Oct '90 / Jazz Music / Hot Shot.

HANK THOMPSON COLLECTION, THE.
Tracks: Six pack to go, A / Wild side of life, The / Bubbles in my beer / John Henry / Swing wide your gate of love / San Antonio rose / Most of all / Rovin' gambler / Nine pound hammer / Cocaine blues / Lost John / Total strangers / Wabash cannonball / Shotgun boogie.
CD . . . . KNCD 13059
■ MC . . . . KNMC 13059
Knight / Feb '91.

HANK THOMPSON: COLLECTORS SERIES.
Tracks: (I've got a) Humpty Dumpty Heart / Whoa sailor / Wild side of life, The / Waiting in the lobby of your heart / Rub-a-dub-dub / Yesterday's girl / Wake up, Irene / Breakin' the rules / Honky tonk girl / We've gone too far / New green light, The / Breakin' in another heart / Don't take it out on me / Blackboard of my heart, The / Rockin' in the Congo / Squaws along the Yukon / Six pack to go, A / She's just a whole lot like you / Oklahoma hills / Hangover tavern.
CD . . . . CDP 792124-2
Capitol (USA) / Sep '89 / Capitol (Imports).

HONKY TONK GIRL.
Tracks: Honky tonk gal / Another shot of toddy.
■ 7" . . . . ABC 4180
ABC Records / Jun '77.

IN THE STUDIO, ON THE ROAD.
Tracks: John Henry / Crying in the deep blue sea / You'll be the one / Hang your head in shame / There's no you / Give a little, take a little / Summit ridge drive / Shot gun boogie / September in the rain / Warm red wine / Total stranger / Honky tonk town / Welcome to the fair introduction / Deep in the heart of Texas / My heart is a playground / Charmaine / How many teardrops / New wears off too fast / Rub-a-dub-dub / Beautiful Texas / We will start it all over / River road two step / Texas fight song / I cast a lonesome shadow / Simple Simon / There's a little bit of everything.
LP. . . . . SEE 263
See For Miles / May '89 / Pinnacle.

MOVIN' ON.
Tracks: Who left the door to heaven open / When my blue moon turns to gold again / There's a honky tonk angel (who'll take me back in) / I recall a gypsy woman / Mama don't 'low / Wait a little longer baby / Loving on back streets / Whatever's left / Fair weather love / Red necks, white socks and blue ribbon beer / Country bumpkin.
■ LP. . . . . NR 5085
Ember / '78 / TKO Records Ltd / President Records.

ROCKIN' IN THE CONGO (Thompson, Hank & His Brazos Valley Boys).
Tracks: Rockin' in the Congo / I was the first one.
■ 7" . . . . CR 133
Creole / Jul '76.

SONGS FOR ROUNDERS.
Tracks: Three times seven / I'll be a bachelor till I die / Drunkards blues / Teach 'em how to swim / Dry bread / Cocaine blues / Deep elm / Bummin' around / Little blossom / Roving gambler / Left my gal in the mountains / May I sleep in your barn tonight Mister.
MC . . . . HATC 3052
Stetson / Dec '87 / Crusader Marketing Co. / Swift / Wellard Dist. / Midland Records / C.M. Distribution.
LP. . . . . HAT 3052
Stetson / Oct '87 / Crusader Marketing Co. / Swift / Wellard Dist. / Midland Records / C.M. Distribution.

Thompson, Hayden

BOONEVILLE MISSISSIPPI FLASH.
Tracks: Ah poor little baby / Drivin' me out of my mind / Born to lose / Had a little talk / Don't say that you're sorry / I'm gonna sit right down and cry over you / Eeny meeny miney mo / Hands of time, The / Boy from Tupelo / I wanna get home / Girl named Betty, A / When my blue moon turns to gold again.
■ LP. . . . . CR 30245
Charly / Aug '85.

EARLY DAYS.
Tracks: Brown eyed handsome man / Call me Shorty / It won't be long till the summer / I guess I'd better be moving along / Kansas City / Going steady / Frankie and Johnny / I'll hold you in my heart / Pardon me / Pretending your not wearing my ring / I love country music / Funny how time slips away / I feel the blues coming on / Act like you love me / Pardon me (2) / Queen bee / Keys to my kingdom, The / How I wish / Old Kris Kringle / Mighty big wall.
LP. . . . . SJLP 569
Sunjay / Dec '87 / CSA Tell Tapes.

FAIRLANE ROCK.
Tracks: Love my baby / One broken heart / Blues blues blues / Fairlane rock / One broken heart (take 2) / Love my baby (take 2) / Pretending / Your true love / Kansas City / Four seasons of life, The / This is country / I wanna get home / I guess I'd better be moving along / I need a break / 16.88 / Lonesome for my baby / This old windy city.
LP. . . . . BFX 15263
Bear Family / Apr '88 / Rollercoaster Records / Swift / Direct Distribution.

FUNNY HOW TIME SLIPS AWAY.
Tracks: Frankie and Johnny / Guess I'd better be moving along / Pardon me / Funny how time slips away / How I wish / Keys to my Kingdom, The.
LP. . . . . MFLP 1051
Magnum Force / Apr '87 / Terry Blood Dist. / Jazz Music / Hot Shot.

HERE'S HAYDEN THOMPSON.
Tracks: Not Advised.
LP. . . . . KS 3507
Kapp / Jul '88.

ROCKABILLY GUY 1954-1962.
Tracks: I feel the blues coming on / Act like you love me / Rockabilly gal / Love my baby / One broken heart / Blues blues blues / You are my sunshine / Mama, mama, mama / Call me Shorty / Brown eyed handsome man / I'll hold you in my heart / Kansas City / It won't be long till the summer / Old Kris Kringle / Pardon me / Queen bee / Going steady.
■ LP. . . . . CR 30262
Charly / Nov '86.

ROCKIN' COUNTRY MAN, THE.
Tracks: Ah poor little baby / Drivin' me out of my mind / Born to lose / Had a little talk / Don't say that you're sorry / I'm gonna sit right down and cry over you / Eenie meenie miny mo / Hands of time, The / Boy from Tupelo / I wanna get home / When my blue moon turns to gold again / Girl named Betty, A.
LP. . . . . SJLP 563
Sunjay / Feb '89 / CSA Tell Tapes.

ROCKIN' COUNTRY MAN, THE.
Tracks: Shake, rattle and roll / What'd I say / Blue suede shoes / Kansas City / Matchbox / Love me / Honky tonk / Mean woman blues / Whole lotta shakin' goin' on / Hound dog / Shake, rattle and roll (reprise) / Boppin the blues / Honey don't that's alright mama / Fairlane rock / Stroll, The / Ain't that a shame / Rip it up / Good rockin' tonight / Lucille.
VHS. . . . . MMGV 006
MMG Video / Jun '88 / Terry Blood Dist.

TIME IS NOW, THE.
Tracks: Not Advised.
CD . . . . SPARKCD 13
LP. . . . . SJLP 589
Magnum Force / '89 / Terry Blood Dist. / Jazz Music / Hot Shot.

Thompson, Sue

Born Eva Sue Mckee on 19.07.1926, in Nevada, Missouri, Thompson was raised in San Jose, California and has been singing since a teenager (appearing on KGO - San Francisco's Hometown Hayride TV series, later to work the Opry with red Foley). During this time she was married to entertainer Hank Penney (1953 - 1963). Her initial 'cute' vocals were found singing pop during 1960s, with subsequent hits *Sad Movies* and *Norman* , both on Hickory and top 10 recordings, penned by John D. Loudermilk - as is the case with her later hit *Paper Tiger* . During the 1970s Thompson created herself a healthy country following - scoring with *Big Mable Murphy* (No.50). It was with fellow Hickory act Don Gibson that she enjoyed most chart action - *Good Old Fashioned Country Girl* being one of three top 40 singles credited to them. (Maurice Hope July 1993)

PAPER TIGER.
Tracks: Paper tiger.
■ 7" . . . . HICKORY 1284
Hickory / Jan '65.

SWEET MEMORIES.
Tracks: Stay another day / How I love them old songs / What a woman in love won't do / Candy and roses / Sweet memories / Sad movies / How do you start over / Norman / Find out / Just plain country / Have a good time.

■ DELETED

LP. SDLP 024
Sundown / Sep '85 / Terry Blood Dist. / Jazz Music /
C.M. Distribution.

Thornborough, Julie

I'M YOUR COUNTRY GIRL.
Tracks: Everybody's reachin' / I was raised on country sunshine / Family Bible / I saw the light / Loving him was easier / I'm your country girl / Crying steel guitar waltz / Let me be there / Send me the pillow that you dream on / Louisiana bayou drive / Take me to your world.
LP. . . . . FHR 065
Folk Heritage / Jul '82 / Terry Blood Dist.

Thorpe, TJ

AIN'T NO KINDA STAR (Thorpe, TJ & CB Band).
Tracks: Ain't no kinda star / Part of your heart.
■ 7". INT 594
EMI International / Aug '79.

GIRL.
Tracks: Girl / 5 & 10 cent store.
■ 7". INT 589
EMI International / May '79.

Tillis, Mel

Born in 1932 Tillis has enjoyed over 20 years of chart success. His debut in country music was in 1957. He gained his first hit in Nashville the following year with The Violet and The Rose > released on Columbia. He was absent from the charts from 1959 to 1965 but a move to the Kapp label that year coincided with a change in his fortunes. Tillis wrote some classics including Kenny Rogers' Ruby Don't Take Your Love To Town and Bobby Bare's Detroit City. Mel and his group The Statesiders developed a reputation as an exciting live act. He won the CMA's Entertainer Of The Year Award in 1976 the same year that Good Woman Blues topped the chart. He continued to have hits after joining MCA in 1977 such as Heart Healer and I believe in you. He has recorded with such as Nancy Sinatra and Sherry Bryce having chart success with both. (Maurice Hope).

AIN'T NO CALIFORNIA.
Tracks: Not Advised.
■ LP. MCA 40946
MCA (Import) / Feb '79.

COUNTRY STORE: MEL TILLIS.
Tracks: Ruby don't take your love to town / Heaven everyday / Brand new mister me / Neon rose / Sawmill / Memory maker / Woman in the back of my world / Commercial affection / Arms of a fool, The / I ain't never / I can't stop loving you / Midnight / Best way I know how / Welcome to my world.
CD . . . . CDCST 17
MC . . . . CSTK 17
Country Store / '88 / BMG.
■ LP. CST 17
Country Store / '88.

GREAT MEL, THE.
Tracks: Not Advised.
LP. . . . . GT 0049
Gusto (USA) / Mar '88.

I BELIEVE IN YOU.
Tracks: I believe in you / She don't trust you daddy.
■ 7". MCA 384
MCA / Aug '78.

LONG WAY TO DAYTONA, A.
Tracks: Not Advised.
LP. . . . . E 160016
Elektra / Apr '82 / WEA.

NEW PATCHES.
Tracks: Midnight love / New patches / Slow nights / Almost like you never went away / Faded blue / Texas on a Saturday night / You're as far as I can see (when I close my eyes) / Small change / Bed of roses / He drove her out of his mind.
LP. . . . . MCF 3224
MC . . . . MCFC 3224
MCA / Jun '84 / BMG.

VERY BEST OF MEL TILLIS, THE.
Tracks: Coca cola cowboy / What did I promise her last night / Good woman blues / Ain't no California / I got the hots / Send me down to Tuscon / I believe in you / Heart healer / Charlie's angel / Burning memories.
LP. . . . . IMCA 27070
MCA (Import) / Mar '86 / Pinnacle / Silver Sounds (CD).

Tillis, Pam

Born 24.06.1957 in Plant City, Florida - married to Nashville songwriter / producer Bob Dipiero. Made stage debut at the Grand Ole Opry at the age of 8 with her father Mel Tillis - singing Tom Dooley. Paid her dues playing lounge bars, disco (1981 with Electra), dabbled in the new rock market and sang the Mary Magdalene part

in the Nashville production of Jesus Christ Superstar. Turning to country in 1986, playing Nashville's Opry-styled nightclub revue Twang-Night . Tillis a staff writer with Tree Publishing has seen her songs covered by a host of country acts - Suzy Boggus, Barbara Fairchild, Janie Fricke, Highway 101, Ricky van Shelton and Conway Twitty. The big-voiced singer's own recording saw modest success during the late 1980's, whilst signed to Warner Bros. It was only in 1990 when she moved to Arista that her fortunes were to change - a string of top ten singles ensuing. Notably her 1991 hits Put Yourself In My Place, Don't tell Me What To Do and Maybe It Was Memphis (1992), an impressive opening run from her album Put Yourself In My Shoes. Tillis' position strengthened with her 1992 high selling album Homeward Looking Angel and its top five singles Let Your Pony Run and Shake The Sugar Tree. (Maurice Hope - August 1993)

ANGEL.
Tracks: Not Advised.
CD 7822 18649-2
Arista / Sep '93 / BMG.

HOMEWARD LOOKING ANGEL.
Tracks: How gone is goodbye / Shake the sugar tree / Do you know where your man is / Cleopatra, Queen of denial / Love is only human / Rough and tumble heart / Let that pony run / Fine, fine, very fine love / We've tried everything else / Homeward looking angel.
CD 782218649-2
Arista / Oct '93 / BMG.

Tippin, Aaron

Born 1959 in Travellers Reast, South Carolina in an area known as Dark Corner (the state's north west region). As a teenager he played first with bluegrass; the Dixie Ridge Runners, then when 22 with country unit Tip and the Darby Hill Band. After working at various manual jobs, Tippin moved to Nashville in 1987, where through publisher Charlie Monk he gained a songwriting deal with Acuff - Rose. His RCA debut album You've got to stand for something(1990) earned him much praise for it's straight down the line country approach. Hit singles included the title track You've got to stand for something, adopted by the US troops whilst battling in Iraq - chartwise it made country's top 5. He has strung together a steady supply of hits including You've made a memory out of me alongside a trio from his 1992 Read between the lines album, the top ten fare Wouldn't have it any other way, My blue angel and his 1992 chart topper Ain't nothin' wrong with the radio. (Maurice Hope - August 1993)

YOU'VE GOT TO STAND FOR SOMETHING.
Tracks: In my wildest dreams / I've got a good memory / You've got to stand for something / I wonder how far it is over you / Ain't that a hell of a note / Man that came between us (was me) / She made a memory out of me / Up against you / Sky's got the blues / Many, many, many beers ago.
■ MC . . . . PK 82374
RCA / Jun '91.
■ CD . . . . PD 82374
RCA / Jun '91.
■ LP. PL 82374
RCA / Jun '91.

Tobin, Jim

VERY BEST OF JIM TOBIN.
Tracks: Not Advised.
LP. . . . . CMCSX 2001
CMR/Failte / '88 / I & B Records.

Top Country Sound

IN THE MIDDLE OF NOWHERE.
Tracks: What goes on / Lyin' eyes / Tomorrow never comes / Hey good lookin' / Shutters and boards / Long thin dawn / In the middle of nowhere / Lonesome fugitive / Streets of Baltimore / Louisiana man / Letter edged in black / Steel rail blues.
LP. . . . . FHR 093
Folk Heritage / Jul '82 / Terry Blood Dist.

RIDIN' EASY.
Tracks: If you let me know / Easy loving / Evangeline / In the early morning rain / She thinks I still care / Detroit City / Okie from Muskogee / Waiting for a train / Idol of the band / Spinning wheel / Waiting for a train / Gonna buy me a bluebird.
LP. . . . . FHR 104
MC . . . . CFHR 104
Folk Heritage / Jul '82 / Terry Blood Dist.

Torrance, Bill

BILL TORRANCE SINGS.
Tracks: Heart / To be your man / She thinks I still care / Beyond these walls / When I dream / Fool such as I / Reason to believe / Cotton Jenny / My happiness / Drinkin' them beers / Me and the elephant / I don't want to talk about it.
LP. . . . . KLP 28

Klub / Dec '82 / C.M. Distribution / Ross Records / Duncans / A.D.A Distribution.

CALEDONIA.
Tracks: Caledonia / When you and I were young Maggie.
7". . . . . KLUB 26
Klub / Mar '83 / C.M. Distribution / Ross Records / Duncans / A.D.A Distribution.

INCHLAGGAN.
Tracks: Not Advised.
LP. . . . . TREE 001
MC . . . . TREE 001C
Lapwing / Jun '88 / C.M. Distribution / Duncans / Ross Records / Roots Records / Duncans.

REFLECTION.
Tracks: Not Advised.
LP. . . . . KLP 43
MC . . . . ZCKLP 43
Klub / Apr '84 / C.M. Distribution / Ross Records / Duncans / A.D.A Distribution.

Touchet Brothers

TOUCHET BROTHERS CAJUN MUSIC BAND, THE.
Tracks: Not Advised.
LP. 6055
Swallow (USA) / Swift / Wellard Dist.
MC . . . . 6055 TC
Swallow (USA) / '87 / Swift / Wellard Dist.

Trace, Natchez

BEST OF THE IMMORTAL NATCHEZ TRACE.
Tracks: I'm willin' / Beaucoups of blues / One more night / Jasper and the miners / Lou Marsh / Feelings so low / Night they drove old Dixie down, The / Southbound / She moved through the fair / Bringing Mary home / Pinto pony / Truck driving man / Strutt's strut / You're still on my mind / Are you all alone.
LP. . . . . SFA 048
Sweet Folk All / May '81 / Cadillac Music / Projection / C.M. Distribution / Wellard Dist. / Impetus Records.

Trammell, Bobby Lee

ARKANSAS TWIST.
Tracks: Arkansas twist / Carolyn / Come on baby / It's all your fault / Sally twist (parts 1 & 2) / I tried not to cry / Watch me do the twist / Arkansas stomp / I like it / Bobby Lee needs love / Give me that good lovin' / If you ever get it once / New dance in France.
LP. . . . . BB 2036
Buffalo Bop (Germany) / '88.

BOBBY LEE TRAMMELL.
Tracks: Not Advised.
LP. . . . . BB 2039
Buffalo Bop (Germany) / '88.

TOOLIE FROOLIE.
Tracks: Toolie froolie / Betty Jean / I can't sit still / Skimmy Lou / You make me feel so fine / Come on and love me / Am I satisfying you / Twenty four hours / Whole lotta shakin' goin' on / Little bit of soap, A / Chantilly lace / Love isn't love.
LP. . . . . BBLP 2040
Bison Bop / Jan '85 / C.M. Distribution / Swift.
LP. . . . . BB 2040
Buffalo Bop (Germany) / '88.

Traum, Artie

CAYENNE.
Tracks: Not Advised.
CD . . . . CD 3084
Rounder / Projection / Roots Records / Swift / C.M. Distribution / Topic Records / Jazz Music / Hot Shot / A.D.A Distribution / Direct Distribution.
LP. . . . . ROUNDER 3084
MC . . . . ROUNDER 3084C
Rounder / Aug '88 / Projection / Roots Records / Swift / C.M. Distribution / Topic Records / Jazz Music / Hot Shot / A.D.A Distribution / Direct Distribution.

FROM THE HEART (Traum, Artie & Pat Alger).
Tracks: Not Advised.
LP. . . . . ROUNDER 3039
Rounder / Aug '88 / Projection / Roots Records / Swift / C.M. Distribution / Topic Records / Jazz Music / Hot Shot / A.D.A Distribution / Direct Distribution.

LIFE ON EARTH.
Tracks: Not Advised.
LP. . . . . ROUNDER 3014
Rounder / Jun '77 / Projection / Roots Records / Swift / C.M. Distribution / Topic Records / Jazz Music / Hot Shot / A.D.A Distribution / Direct Distribution.

Traveling Wilburys

END OF THE LINE.
Tracks: End of the line / Congratulations.
12". . . . . W 7637T
7". . . . . W 7637

■ CD Single . . . . W 7637CD
WEA / Feb '89.

HANDLE WITH CARE.
Tracks: Handle with care / Margaruite.
■ CD Single . . . . W 7732CD
WEA / Oct '88 / WEA.
12" . . . . W 7732T
■ 7" . . . . W 7732
WEA / Oct '88.

NOBODYS CHILD.
Tracks: Nobodys child.
12" . . . . W 9773 T
7" . . . . W 9773
■ CD Single . . . . W 9973 CD
WEA / Jun '90 / WEA.

SHE'S MY BABY.
Tracks: She's my baby / New blue moon / Runaway.
7" . . . . W 9523
MC Single . . . . W 9523C
Wilbury / Nov '90 / WEA.
12" . . . . W 9523T
■ CD Single . . . . W 9523CD
Wilbury / Nov '90.

TRAVELING WILBURYS.
Tracks: Handle with care / Dirty world / Rattled / Last night / Not alone anymore / Congratulations / Heading for the light / Margarita / Tweeter and the monkey man / End of the line.
CD 925 796 2
LP . . . . WX 224
MC . . . . WX 224C
Wilbury / Oct '88 / WEA.

TRAVELING WILBURYS VOLUME 3.
Tracks: She's my baby / Inside out / If you belonged to me / Devil's been busy, The / 7 deadly sins / Poor house / Where were you last night? / Cool dry place / New blue moon / You took my breath away / Wilbury twist.
CD 7599263242
MC . . . . WX 384C
Wilbury / Nov '90 / WEA.
■ LP . . . . WX 384
Wilbury / Nov '90.

Travis, Dave

Another longtime artist on the UK scene, North London based Dave Travis has not only narrowed the gap between country and rockabilly with many albums recorded over a quarter of a century, but also lived a double life as a musician and industry executive. He's also highly travelled, visiting many exotic areas of the world and, whilst there, generally getting himself exposure on television or radio. He appeared on Fan Fair's International Show in Nashville in 1980, and has guested on most of the major rock'n'roll festivals in the U.K. during recent years, often in the company of an American celebrity like Carl Perkins, Carl Mann, Eddie Bond or Charlie Feathers. When not gigging, he devotes time to his music publishing and licensing companies, or visiting the USA seeking out rare material for releasing on his Stomper Time record label. Travis would be a fascinating subject for a music industry book. (Tony Byworth - August 1993)

ANGELA JONES.
Tracks: Angela Jones / Alberta.
■ 7" . . . . SRL 1130
Spark (3) / Jul '75.

BANKS OF THE OHIO.
Tracks: Not Advised.
MC . . . . VCA 050
VFM Cassettes / Aug '78 / VFM Children's Entertainment Ltd. / Midland Records / Morley Audio Services.

BLUES AT SUNRISE (With Gerry Lockran & Redd Sullivan).
Tracks: Not Advised.
LP . . . . FID 2165
Fidelity / Jun '70 / Total / BMG.

COUNTRY.
Tracks: Not Advised.
LP . . . . FID 2132
Fidelity / Sep '68 / Total / BMG.

COUNTRY FEVER.
Tracks: Not Advised.
MC . . . . SDC 5059
Silver Dollar / Feb '87.

COUNTRY MUSIC MAN.
Tracks: Not Advised.
MC . . . . SDC 5172
Silver Dollar / Nov '89.

COUNTRY WORLD OF DAVE TRAVIS.
Tracks: Not Advised.
LP . . . . TPRS 103
Teepee / Jun '69.

DAVE TRAVIS.
Tracks: Not Advised.
MC . . . . VCA 037
VFM Cassettes / Dec '77 / VFM Children's Entertainment Ltd. / Midland Records / Morley Audio Services.

DRIVING DOWN THE HIGHWAY.
Tracks: Driving down the highway / Great balls of fire.
■ 7" 56 280
Polydor / Sep '68.

HIGH ON LIFE.
Tracks: High on life / Cycle of life.
■ 7" . . . . SRL 1008
Spark (3) / Apr '73.

HIGH ON LIFE.
Tracks: Big river / Mental revenge / High on life / Tomorrow is a long time / Cycle of life / Go on home / Blue moon of Kentucky / Six days on the road / Swinging doors / I started world war one / Half breed / Your woman may have been here / Tonight I'll be coming back to you / Johnny B. Goode.
■ LP . . . . SRLM 104
Spark (3) / Apr '73.
■ MC . . . . SLB 104
Spark (1) / Apr '73.

LET'S FLAT GET IT.
Tracks: Jukebox cadillac / Tweedle dee dee / Rock it right / Gonna be a fire / Boy meets girl / Shakin' and stompin' / Teen town hop / Hanging on for the blues / Don't that road look rough and rocky / Bip bop boom.
LP . . . . MFLP 061
Magnum Force / Apr '88 / Terry Blood Dist. / Jazz Music / Hot Shot.

LONG BLACK VEIL.
Tracks: Long black veil / Solid gone.
■ 7" . . . . SRL 1138
Spark (3) / Mar '76.

PICKIN' ON THE COUNTRY STRINGS.
Tracks: Not Advised.
■ LP 236 557
Polydor / Jan '69.

ROCKABILLY FEVER.
Tracks: Night train to Memphis / I'm gonna set my foot down / Help me find my baby / Dixiefried / Leroy / Your woman may have been here / Red hot / Put me down / Ooby dooby / I'm changing all those changes / Too much rock 'n' roll music / Since I met you baby / I ain't never / White lightnin' / Buddy's song / I'm on fire.
MC . . . . VCA 048
VFM Cassettes / Mar '78 / VFM Children's Entertainment Ltd. / Midland Records / Morley Audio Services.
■ LP . . . . SRLM 508
Spark (3) / Mar '78.

ROCKABILLY KILLER.
Tracks: Sugaree / Jitterbop baby / My baby's gone / Sugartime / Oklahoma baby / Good rockin' tonight / Everybody's movin' / Bop a Lena / My bucket's got a hole in it / Lightnin' cross the sky / Sarah Lee / All change / Blue levi jeans / Feel like I'm catching / Blues, The / Old country boy.
LP . . . . SDLA 4003
Silver Dollar / Nov '80.
MC . . . . BBR 5010
Big Beat (France) / '81 / C.M. Distribution.
LP . . . . MFLP 013
Magnum Force / '88 / Terry Blood Dist. / Jazz Music / Hot Shot.

SINGS HANK WILLIAMS.
Tracks: Not Advised.
LP 8026
Eros / Apr '68.

SONGS OF REVOLUTION (Travis, Dave & Tolpuddle Martyrs).
Tracks: Not Advised.
■ LP . . . . CHM 628
Hallmark / May '69.

SOUNDS LIKE BUDDY HOLLY.
Tracks: Not Advised.
MC . . . . VCA 040
VFM Cassettes / Oct '77 / VFM Children's Entertainment Ltd. / Midland Records / Morley Audio Services.

Travis, Lane

I'M MOVIN' ON.
Tracks: Not Advised.
LP . . . . BSS 182
Tank / Jun '79.

Travis, Merle

Merle Travis was born in Kentucky in 1917, and died in Oklahoma in 1983. He was a great and influential guitar player as well as a country singer and songwriter. He had hits on Capitol in the late 1940s. when asked to make an album of folk songs, he wrote some. His legendary set of 78s *Folk Songs From the Hills* included *Nine-Pound Hammer*, *I Am A Pilgrim*, *Dark As A Dungeon* and *Sixteen Tons* (the latter one of the biggest hits of all time for *Ernie Ford* in 1955). He co-wrote *Smoke! Smoke! Smoke! (That Cigarette)* with *Tex Williams*, whose recording of it sold over two million in 1947. He was influential in guitar design, allegedly having the first solid-body electric guitar made to his specifications; he sang *Re-enlistment Blues* in the film *From Here To Eternity* in 1953 and made many other films; he made many albums on Capitol and in the 1970s recorded with the *Nitty Gritty Dirt Band* and as a duo with Chet Atkins. (Donald Clarke)

BACK HOME.
Tracks: Nine pound hammer / That's all / John Bolin / Muskrat / Dark as a dungeon / John Henry / Sixteen tons / Possum up a Simmon tree / I am a pilgrim / Over by number nine / Barbara Allen / Lost John.
LP . . . . HAT 3044
MC . . . . HATC 3044
Stetson / Sep '87 / Crusader Marketing Co. / Swift / Wellard Dist. / Midland Records / C.M. Distribution.

CLAYTON MCMICHAN STORY, THE.
Tracks: Not Advised.
Double LP . . . . CMH 9028
MC . . . . CMHC 9028
CMH (USA) / C.M. Distribution / Projection.

COUNTRY GUITAR GIANTS (Travis, Merle & Joe Maphis).
Tracks: Free little bird / Mose Rager blues / Alabama jubilee / Hear dem bells / Eight more miles to Louisville / Little rosewood casket, The / John Henry / Cannonball rag / Beer barrel rag / My adobe hacienda / Lover / Snow deer / Ike Everly's rag / Sweet bunch of daisies / Somebody stole my gal / San Antonio rose / Li'l Liza Jane / Bury me beneath the willow / High noon / Down among the budded roses / Freight train / I wonder where you are tonight / Wildwood flower / Back in the saddle again / Memphis blues / Black mountain rag / Say 'si si' / Columbus stockade blues / Right or wrong smiles / I saw the light.
Double LP . . . . CMH 9017
CMH (USA) / '79 / C.M. Distribution / Projection.

FOLKSONGS OF THE HILLS.
Tracks: Nine pound hammer / That's all / John Bolin / Muskrat / Dark as a dungeon / John Henry / Sixteen tons / Possum up a Simmon tree / I am a pilgrim / Over by number nine / Barbara Allen / Lost John / Black gold / Harlan County boys, The / Pay day comes too slow / Browder explosion, The / Bloody Brethitt County / Here's to the operators, Boys / Miner's wife, The / Courtship of second cousin Claude, The / Miner's strawberries / Paw walked behind us with a cabride lamp / Preacher lane / Dear old Halifax.
CD . . . . BCD 15636
Bear Family / May '93 / Rollercoaster Records / Swift / Direct Distribution.

GREAT SONGS OF THE DELMORE BROTHERS (Travis, Merle & Johnny Bond).
Tracks: Not Advised.
LP . . . . HAT 3107
MC . . . . HATC 3107
Stetson / Aug '89 / Crusader Marketing Co. / Swift / Wellard Dist. / Midland Records / C.M. Distribution.

MERLE TRAVIS.
Tracks: Cincinnati Lou / No vacancy / Divorce me C.O.D. / Missouri / So round, so firm, so fully packed / Sweet temptation / Steel guitar rag / Three times seven / Sixteen tons / Nine pound hammer / I am a pilgrim / Dark as a dungeon / John Henry / Fat gal / Merel's boogie woogie / Crazy boogie / I'm a natural born gamblin' man / I'm sick and tired of you little darlin' / Sioux city Sue / What a shame / Kinfolks in Carolina / Re-Enlistment blues / Wildwood flower / Blues stay away from me / Kentucky means paradise / John Henry Jr / Guitar rag / Way down yonder in New Orleans.
CD . . . . CDP 7 80676
MC . . . . TC-TCEMS 1468
Capitol / Apr '93 / EMI.

MERLE TRAVIS 1944-1946.
Tracks: Nine pound hammer / Cannonball rag / Porky's boogie / Divorce me C.O.D. / Freight train blues / Dapper Dan / Ida / When you and I were young, Maggie / Osage stomp / Kansas City blues.
LP . . . . RFD 9001
Country Routes / Sep '90 / Jazz Music / Hot Shot.

MERLE TRAVIS COMPILATION.
Tracks: Cincinnati Lou / No vacancy / Divorce me C.O.D. / Missouri / So round, So firm, So fully packed / Sweet temptation / Steel guitar rag / Three times seven / Sixteen tons / Nine pound hammer / I am a pilgrim / Dark as a dungeon / John Henry / Fat gal / Merle's boogie woogie / Crazy boogie / I'm a natural born gamblin' man / I'm sick and tired of you little darlin' / Sioux City Sue / What a shame / Kinfolks in Carolina (Featuring Joe Maphis.) / Re-enlistment blues / Wildwood flower (Featuring Hank Thompson.) / Blues stay away from me / Kentucky means paradise / John Henry Jnr / Guitar rag / Way down yonder in New Orleans.
CD . . . . CDEMS 1468
MC . . . . TCEMS 1468
Capitol / Nov '92 / EMI.

MERLE TRAVIS GUITAR, THE.
Tracks: Not Advised.
LP . . . . HAT 3132
MC . . . . HATC 3132
Stetson / Mar '90 / Crusader Marketing Co. / Swift / Wellard Dist. / Midland Records / C.M. Distribution.

ROUGH, ROWDY AND BLUE.
Tracks: Not Advised.
LP . . . . **CMH 6262**
CMH (USA) / '85 / C.M. Distribution / Projection.

TRAVIS.
Tracks: Not Advised.
LP . . . . **HAT 3080**
Stetson / '88 / Crusader Marketing Co. / Swift / Wellard Dist. / Midland Records / C.M. Distribution.
MC . . . . **HATC 3080**
Stetson / Dec '88 / Crusader Marketing Co. / Swift / Wellard Dist. / Midland Records / C.M. Distribution.

TRAVIS PICKIN'.
Tracks: Rose time / There'll be some changes made / Born to lose / Too tight rag / You're nobody 'til somebody loves you / Night sounds / Sugar moon / White heat / Midnight special / World is waiting for the sunrise, The / Sleep / Love letters in the sand / Drifting and dreaming / Sing baby sing.
LP . . . . **CMH 6255**
MC . . . . **CMH 6255C**
CMH (USA) / '82 / C.M. Distribution / Projection.

WALKIN' THE STRINGS.
Tracks: Not Advised.
LP . . . . **PM 1550801**
Pathe Marconi (France) / Jun '84 / Thames Distributors Ltd.

Travis, Randy

Country music's biggest success to emerge from the 80's New country era, multi-award winner Travis (born Randy Bruce Traywick, 4.5.1959 in Marshville, N.Carolina) has deeply engraved his name upon the American country scene. Travis' early grounding was spent singing in a club run in Country City, Charlotte owned by his now wife, Lib Hatcher. Both moved to Nashville in 1981, where Travis worked as dish-washer, short-order cook and singer at the Hatcher-managed Nashville Palace, where he recorded a live show. Hatcher, after many fruitless attempts, got a demo to A&R executive Martha Sharp at Warner Brothers, who upon hearing him live, immediately had Randy Ray sign (1985). Travis' debut single *On the other hand*, made only a modest No.67 (little did he know that within 12 months it would be re-released and sitting at the top of the charts) - a somewhat stronger showing than his effort as Randy Traywick in 1979 with *She's my woman*, on the indie Paula label. Debut album *Storm of life* found Travis' accomplished, strong ballad vocal style showing more class than most can only dream of, and scored with hits *Diggin' up bones* (No.1) , *No place like home* (No.2) and *1982* (No.6). Travis during the following year 1987, went one better reeling off 3 country chart toppers-*Forever and ever, Amen* (from the album *Always and forever*) leading the way. Awards were by now coming at a phenomenal rate 1987 found him voted the CMA's Top Male Vocalist, best album (holding down the No.1 slot for an amazing 38 weeks) and best single *Forever and ever, amen* . By this time Travis, alongside George Strait, was dominating things, when Garth Brooks burst upon the scene. During 1988 Travis swept aside all challengers in the singles charts with *I told you so* , *Honky tonk moon* and *Deeper than the holler* all making the top slot. Subsequent chart-topping singles *Is it still over* and a version of the old Brook Benton hit *It's just a matter of time* and *Hard rock bottom of your heart* have stylishly taken him into the 90s. Country's Mr Cool by this time was allocating more time into the making of videos and writing songs (some while out on the road with Alan Jackson). His special project *Heroes and friends* came out in 1990, featuring such acts as his childhood idol, veteran cowboy singer Roy Rogers backed by many Nashville legendary vocalists, George Jones (*A few ole country boys* charting) Dolly, Tammy, Merle Haggard, and Willie Nelson are all found making solid contributions. Travis strong run of albums (sales had already exceeded 10 million) and singles continued unabated, through 1991 - 1992. *Forever together* gained the No.1 slot (1991), *Better class of losers* (a song he wrote with Alan Jackson which was the subject of a copywrite wrangle) only nudged out by Garth Brook's *What is she doing*. Travis cemented his relationship with his manager Lib Hatcher in May 1991, when they married. *If I didn't have you* also made No.1. in 1993 Travis' appeal is as strong as ever, *Heart look, no hands* earning him another chart topper, backed up with *Old pair of shoes*, from gold-selling *Greatest hits* albums Vol 1 & 2 respectively. During his spare time Travis, a western buff, enjoys nothing better than spending time working with a horse on his ranch as depicted on Warner Music Vision's *Forever and ever* 1992 video release. (Maurice Hope - July 1993).

ALWAYS AND FOREVER.
Tracks: Too gone too long / My house / Good intentions / What'll you do about me? / I won't need you anymore / Forever and ever, Amen / I told you so / Anything / Truth is lyin' next to you, The / Tonight we're gonna tear down the walls.
LP . . . . **K 925568 1**
MC . . . . **K 925568 4**
WEA / May '87 / WEA.
CD **925568 2**
WEA / Aug '88 / WEA.
CD . . . . **WX 107 CD**
LP . . . . **WX 107**
MC . . . . **WX 107 C**
WEA / Aug '90 / WEA.

DEEPER THAN THE HOLLER.
Tracks: Deeper than the holler / I told you so / Diggin' up bones (Track on 12" only) / What'll you do about me (Track on 12" only) / 1982 (Track on CD only) / No place like home (Track on CD only).
12" . . . . **W 7804T**
7" . . . . **W 7804**
■ **CD Single** . . . . **W 7804CD**
WEA / Jul '88 / WEA.

FOREVER AND EVER AMEN.
Tracks: Forever and ever amen / Promises / On the other hand (Avaliable on the CD single format only.).
7" . . . . **W 8384**
■ **CD Single** . . . . **W 8384 CD**
WEA / Apr '88 / WEA.

HEROES AND FRIENDS.
Tracks: Heroes and friends / Do I ever cross your mind / Birth of the blues / All night long / Human race, The / Shopping for dresses / Waiting on the light to change / Few ole country boys, A / Walk your own road / We're strangers again / Smokin' the hive / Come see about me / Happy trails.
CD **7599263102**
LP **7599263101**
MC **7599263104**
WEA / Sep '90 / WEA.

HIGH LONESOME.
Tracks: Let me try / Oh what a time to be me / Heart of hearts / Point of light / Forever together / Better class of losers / I'd surrender all / High lonesome / Allergic to the blues / I'm gonna have a little talk.
CD **759926612**
LP **759926611**
MC **759926614**
WEA / Oct '91 / WEA.

IT'S JUST A MATTER OF TIME.
Tracks: It's just a matter of time.
7" . . . . **W 2726**
WEA / Oct '89 / WEA.

NO HOLDING BACK.
Tracks: Mining for coal / Singing the blues / When your world was turning for me / He walked on water / No stoppin' us now / It's just a matter of time / Card carryin' fool / Somewhere in my broken heart / Hard rock bottom of your heart / Have a nice rest of your life.
CD . . . . **K 925988 2**
LP . . . . **WX 292**
MC . . . . **WX 292 C**
WEA / Sep '89 / WEA.

OLD 8 BY 10.
Tracks: Forever & ever, amen / Honky tonk moon / Deeper than a holler / It's out of my hands / Is it still over? / Written in stone / Blues in black and white / Here in my heart / We ain't out of love yet / Promises.
CD . . . . **WX 162 CD**
CD **9254662**
LP . . . . **WX 162**
MC . . . . **WX 162C**
WEA / Jul '88 / WEA.

ON THE OTHER HAND.
Tracks: Can't stop now / On the other hand.
■ **7"** . . . . **W 8962**
WEA / Jan '87.

STORMS OF LIFE.
Tracks: On the other hand / Storms of life, The / My heart cracked / Diggin up bones / No place like home / 1982 / Send my body / Messin with my mind / Reasons I cheat / There'll always be a honky tonk somewhere.
LP **925435 1**
MC **925435 4**
WEA / Oct '86 / WEA.
CD **925435 2**
WEA / Mar '87 / WEA.

Trio San Antonio

VIVA EL WEST SIDE.
Tracks: Not Advised.
LP . . . . **ARHOOLIE 3004**
Arhoolie (USA) / May '81 / Pinnacle / Cadillac Music / Swift / Projection / Hot Shot / A.D.A Distribution / Jazz Music.

Trischka, Tony

BANJOLAND.
Tracks: Not Advised.
LP . . . . **ROUNDER 0087**
MC . . . . **ROUNDER 0087C**
Rounder / '88 / Projection / Roots Records / Swift / C.M. Distribution / Topic Records / Jazz Music / Hot Shot / A.D.A Distribution / Direct Distribution.

BLUEGRASS LIGHT (BANJO).
Tracks: Not Advised.
LP . . . . **ROUNDER 0048**
Rounder / Aug '77 / Projection / Roots Records / Swift / C.M. Distribution / Topic Records / Jazz Music / Hot Shot / A.D.A Distribution / Direct Distribution.

DUST ON THE NEEDLE.
Tracks: Not Advised.
CD . . . . **CD 11508**
Rounder / '88 / Projection / Roots Records / Swift / C.M. Distribution / Topic Records / Jazz Music / Hot Shot / A.D.A Distribution / Direct Distribution.

HEARTLANDS.
Tracks: Not Advised.
LP . . . . **ROUNDER 0062**
Rounder / Jun '77 / Projection / Roots Records / Swift / C.M. Distribution / Topic Records / Jazz Music / Hot Shot / A.D.A Distribution / Direct Distribution.
MC . . . . **ROUNDER 0062C**
Rounder / '88 / Projection / Roots Records / Swift / C.M. Distribution / Topic Records / Jazz Music / Hot Shot / A.D.A Distribution / Direct Distribution.

HILL COUNTRY.
Tracks: Brandy station / Sunny days / Bloozinee / Crossville breakdown / Hill country / Looking for the light / New York chimes / Strawberry plains / Flat gap / Mississippi sawyer / Stop action.
LP . . . . **ROUNDER 0203**
Rounder / Apr '86 / Projection / Roots Records / Swift / C.M. Distribution / Topic Records / Jazz Music / Hot Shot / A.D.A Distribution / Direct Distribution.
MC . . . . **ROUNDER 0203C**
Rounder / Aug '88 / Projection / Roots Records / Swift / C.M. Distribution / Topic Records / Jazz Music / Hot Shot / A.D.A Distribution / Direct Distribution.

ROBOT PLANE FLIES OVER ARKANSAS, A.
Tracks: Not Advised.
LP . . . . **ROUNDER 0171**
MC . . . . **ROUNDER 0171C**
Rounder / Aug '88 / Projection / Roots Records / Swift / C.M. Distribution / Topic Records / Jazz Music / Hot Shot / A.D.A Distribution / Direct Distribution.

SKYLINE DRIVE.
Tracks: Not Advised.
LP . . . . **FF 388**
MC . . . . **FF 388C**
Flying Fish (USA) / '88 / Cadillac Music / Roots Records / Projection / C.M. Distribution / Direct Distribution / Jazz Music / Duncans / A.D.A Distribution.

SOLO BANJO WORKS (Trischka, Tony & Bela Fleck).
Tracks: Ruben's wah wah / Fourteen / Liberec / Free improvision no.2 / Assunta / Old Joe Clark/June Apple / Max & Gus / Beaumont Rag / Kingfisher's wing / Earl Scrugg's medley: Nashville Skyline/Ground speed/ Shuckin / Jeff Davies medley: Jeff Davies/Fort Monroe/ Danville Days / Yaha yaha / Beatles medley: I feel fine/ Here there & everywhere.. (Includes in medley Eleanor Rigby, I'm a loser, Baby you can drive my car) / Rings of saturn, The / Green Willis/Whiskey before breakfast / Killer bees of caffeine / Oma & Opa / Solaris / Flapperette/Red pepper - Spicy rag / Triplet fever / Bach violin partitain D minor (BWV 1004) / Did you ever meet Gary Owen, Uncle Joe / Middle eastern medley: Improv/ Hilmi Rit/George & Gladys Kaza / Twisted teen / Au lait.
CD . . . . **ROU 0247CD**
MC . . . . **ROU 0247C**
Rounder / Feb '93 / Projection / Roots Records / Swift / C.M. Distribution / Topic Records / Jazz Music / Hot Shot / A.D.A Distribution / Direct Distribution.

STRANDED IN THE MOONLIGHT (Trischka, Tony & Skyline).
Tracks: Not Advised.
LP . . . . **FF 304**
Flying Fish (USA) / Mar '89 / Cadillac Music / Roots Records / Projection / C.M. Distribution / Direct Distribution / Jazz Music / Duncans / A.D.A Distribution.

WORLD TURNING.
Tracks: Not Advised.
CD . . . . **ROU 294CD**
MC . . . . **ROU 294C**
Rounder / Oct '93 / Projection / Roots Records / Swift / C.M. Distribution / Topic Records / Jazz Music / Hot Shot / A.D.A Distribution / Direct Distribution.

Tritt, Travis

TRAVIS TRITT COUNTRY CLUB.
Tracks: Country club / I'm gonna be somebody / Put some drive in your country / Help me hold on / Sign of the times / Son of the new South / If I were a drinker / Road home, The / Drift off to dream / Dixie flyer.
CD **926094-2**
Warner Bros.(USA) / Mar '90 / Warner Bros. (Imports).

Truck Stop

POTZBLITZ.
Tracks: Not Advised.
CD **813 352 2**
Metronome / '88 / Jazz Music.

RODEO.
Tracks: Not Advised.
CD **810 875 2**
Metronome / '88 / Jazz Music.

T 6

■ DELETED

Truesdale, Tommy

C'MON EVERYBODY.
Tracks: Roll over Beethoven / Be bop a lula / Somethin' else / Sunflower / Baby I don't care / I'm ready / C'mon everybody / Lonely blue boy / My kinda life / Sea cruise / Whole lotta woman / Cut across Shorty.
LP. . . . . **NA 116**
Neptune / Nov '79 / Neptune Tapes / A.D.A Distribution.

DON'T BE CRUEL.
Tracks: Not Advised.
LP. . . . . **BGC 294**
Country House / Oct '82 / Duncans / BGS Productions Ltd.

FAREWELL PARTY (Truesdale, Tommy & Sundowners).
Tracks: Farewell party.
7" . . . . **BGC 7S 446**
Country House / Dec '87 / Duncans / BGS Productions Ltd.

OLDER WOMEN (COUNTRY SLOSH).
Tracks: Older women / Amazing grace.
7" . . . . **GBH 7S 472**
August (USA) / Dec '88.

SOMEWHERE BETWEEN.
Tracks: Somewhere between / Blackboard of my heart.
■ 7". . . . . **BGC 7S 381**
Country House / Dec '84.

TOMMY TRUESDALE, SINGS COUNTRY.
Tracks: Not Advised.
LP. . . . . **BGC 401**
Country House / Dec '85 / Duncans / BGS Productions Ltd.
MC . . . . **KBGC 401**
Country House / Jul '88 / Duncans / BGS Productions Ltd.

TREE IN THE MEADOW, A.
Tracks: Not Advised.
MC . . . . **KITV 529**
Scotdisc / Dec '90 / Duncans / Ross Records / Target Records / Conifer Records.

Tubb, Ernest

Tubb (1914-84) was a country singer and guitarist who became one of the all-time kings of country music. He began as a *Jimmie Rodgers* imitator and was given Rodger's guitar by his widow; he became famous as the Texas Troubador after his massive 1942 hit *I'm Walkin' The Floor Over You*. He joined the Grand Ole Opry and became an innovator, taking honky tonk music to that already hallowed institution, a fusion of rough country vocals with the swagger of Western Swing; he was also one of the first to establish the electric guitar in country music. He made over 200 singles and had hits almost every year for decades. (Donald Clarke)

BLUE CHRISTMAS (Tubb, Ernest & His Texas Troubadours).
Tracks: Not Advised.
LP. . . . . **HAT 3020**
MC . . . . **HATC 3020**
Stetson / Oct '86 / Crusader Marketing Co. / Swift / Wellard Dist. / Midland Records / C.M. Distribution.

COUNTRY MUSIC HALL OF FAME.
Tracks: Walking the floor over you / Mean mama blues / Soldier's last letter / Let's say goodbye like we said hello / I'm bitin' my fingernails & thinking of you / Too old to cut the mustard / Hank, it will never be the same without you / Jimmie Rodgers' last thoughts / Thirty days / Hey, Mr. Bluebird / Thoughts of a fool / Thanks a lot / Mr. and Mrs. Used To Be / Pass the booze / Another story, another time, another place / Texas troubadour.
LP. . . . . **CDLM 8078**
Coral / May '79.

DADDY OF EM ALL, THE.
Tracks: Not Advised.
LP. . . . . **HAT 3015**
MC . . . . **HATC 3015**
Stetson / Apr '86 / Crusader Marketing Co. / Swift / Wellard Dist. / Midland Records / C.M. Distribution.

ERNEST TUBB STORY, THE.
Tracks: I'll get along somehow / Slippin' around / Filipino baby / When the world has turned you down / Have you ever been lonely / There's a little bit of everything in Texas / Walking the floor over you / Driftwood on the river / There's nothing more to say / Rainbow at midnight / I'll be glad to take you back / Let's say goodbye like we said hello / Careless darling / I wonder why you said goodbye / Last night I dreamed / Letters have no arms / Though the days were only seven / I love you because / You nearly lose your mind / I'll miss you when you go / It's been so long darling / Tomorrow never comes / Blue christmas.
Double LP **IMCA2 4040**
MCA (Import) / Mar '86 / Pinnacle / Silver Sounds (CD).

FAMILY BIBLE, THE.
Tracks: Not Advised.
LP. . . . . **HAT 3120**
Stetson / '89 / Crusader Marketing Co. / Swift / Wellard Dist. / Midland Records / C.M. Distribution.

FAVOURITES: ERNEST TUBB.
Tracks: Not Advised.
MC . . . . **HATC 3011**
Stetson / Feb '86 / Crusader Marketing Co. / Swift / Wellard Dist. / Midland Records / C.M. Distribution.
LP. . . . . **HAT 3011**
Stetson / Jun '86 / Crusader Marketing Co. / Swift / Wellard Dist. / Midland Records / C.M. Distribution.

GOLDEN FAVOURITES.
Tracks: I'll get along somehow / Slipping around / Filipino baby / Have you ever been lonely / There's a little bit of everything in Texas / Walking the floor over you / Driftwood on the river / There's nothing more to say / Rainbow at midnight / I'll always be glad to take you back / Let's say goodbye like we said hello / When the world has turned you down.
■ LP. . . . . **IMCA 84**
MCA (Import) / Mar '86.

GREATEST HITS: ERNEST TUBB.
Tracks: Walking the floor over you / Rainbow at midnight / Let's say goodbye like we said hello / Another story, another time, another place / Thanks a lot / Half a mind / I'll get along somehow / Waltz across Texas / It's been so long darling / Mr. Juke Box / I wonder why you said goodbye.
■ LP. . . . . **IMCA 16**
MCA (Import) / Mar '86.

HIGH LIVIN'.
Tracks: How long will she keep loving me / Just like the night before / You know how to keep me satisfied / Honey please change your mind / You don't love me yet / Only for me / Who's gonna love me / If it takes forever / She's the greatest kind of woman / Someone to be with me / I'll be back to love you tonight / What about you.
■ LP. . . . . **MAN 5010**
Manhattan Records / Apr '80.

HONKY TONK CLASSICS.
Tracks: Blue eyed Elaine / I ain't going honky tonkin' anymore / Try one more time / You nearly lose your mind / Answer to walking the floor over you / There's gonna be some changes made around here / Filipino baby / That wild and wicked look in your eye / Letters have no arms / You don't have to be a baby to cry / I need attention bad / Jealous loving heart.
MC . . . . **SSC 14**
Rounder / '88 / Projection / Roots Records / Swift / C.M. Distribution / Topic Records / Jazz Music / Hot Shot / A.D.A Distribution / Direct Distribution.
LP. . . . . **SS 14**
Rounder / Dec '88 / Projection / Roots Records / Swift / C.M. Distribution / Topic Records / Jazz Music / Hot Shot / A.D.A Distribution / Direct Distribution.

IMPORTANCE OF BEING ERNEST, THE.
Tracks: I'm a long gone daddy / All those yesterdays / San Antonio rose / That, my darlin', is me / Educated mama / I wonder why I worry over you / Your cheatin' heart / It makes no difference now / Ships that never come in / Don't change your old fashioned sweetheart / It's the age that makes the difference.
LP. . . . . **HAT 3006**
MC . . . . **HATC 3006**
Stetson / Nov '85 / Crusader Marketing Co. / Swift / Wellard Dist. / Midland Records / C.M. Distribution.

LET'S SAY GOODBYE LIKE WE SAY HELLO.
Tracks: You hit the nail right on the head / Two wrongs don't make a right / That wild and wicked look in your eye / Lonely heart knows, A / Don't your face look red / Answer to 'Rainbow at midnight' / Watching my past go by / Woman has wrecked many a good man, A / Headin' down the wrong highway / Let's say goodbye like we said hello / Takin' it easy here / Seaman's blues / How can I forget you / Yesterday's winner is a loser today / I'm with a crowd but so alone / Waiting for a train / Forever is ending today / Have you ever been lonely / Till the end of the world / Daddy, when is mommy coming home / Don't rob another man's castle / I'm biting my fingernails and thinking of you / My Filipino rose / My Tennessee baby / Slippin around / Warm red wine / Driftwood on the river / Tennessee border £2 / Letters have no arms / I'll take a back seat for you / Throw your love my way / Don't be ashamed of your age / Stand by me / Old rugged cross, The / What a friend we have in Jesus / Wonderful city, The / When I take my vacation in heaven / Farther along / I love you because / Give me a little old-fashioned love / Unfaithful one / Hillbilly fever (no.2) / Texas Vs Kentucky / G-I-R-L spells trouble / You don't have to be a baby to cry / Mother, the Queen of my heart / Goodnight Irene / (Remember me) I'm the one who loves you / I need attention bad / I'm lonely and blue / Why did you give me your love? / I'm free from the chain gang now / Why should I be lonely? / Hobo's meditation / Good morning Irene / Love bug itch, The / Don't stay too long / I'm steppin' out of the picture / May the good lord bless and keep you / When it's prayer meetin' time in the hollow / Drunkard's child / Any old time / If you want some lovin' / So long (it's been good to know yuh / Chicken song, The / Strange little girl / Kentucky waltz / Hey la la / Rose of the mountains / Precious little baby / So many times / My mother must have been a girl like you / Somebody's stolen my honey / Heartsick soldier on a heartbreak ridge, A / I'm in love with Molly / Too old to cut the mustard / Missing in action / I will miss you when you go / Fortunes in memories / Dear judge / Don't brush them on me / I love everything you do / Somebody loves you / Don't trifle on your sweetheart / Hank, it will never be the same without you / beyond the sunset / When Jimmie Rodgers said good-bye / Jimmie Rodgers last thoughts / My wasted past / Counterfeit kisses / Honeymoon is over, The / No help wanted £2 / You're a real good friend / Dear John letter, A / Double datin' / It's the mileage that's slowin' us down / Divorce granted / Honky-tonk heart / I'm not looking for an angel / I met a friend / When Jesus calls / Too old to tango / Dr. Ketchum / Love lifted me / White Christmas / Blue Christmas / Christmas Island / C-H-R-I-S-T-M-A-S / We need God for Christmas / Merry Christmas, you all / Blue snowflakes / I'm trimming my Christmas tree with teardrops.
CD Set . . . . **BCD 15498**
Bear Family / Feb '91 / Rollercoaster Records / Swift / Direct Distribution.

MIDNIGHT JAMBOREE.
Tracks: Walking the floor over you / Same thing as me, The / I only meant to borrow / Boy with a future / I hate to see you go / Hands you're holding now, The / Rose city chimes / I'm sorry now / Pass me by / Sweet lips / I want you to know I love you / Shoes / It is no secret.
LP. . . . . **HAT 3032**
MC . . . . **HATC 3032**
Stetson / Apr '87 / Crusader Marketing Co. / Swift / Wellard Dist. / Midland Records / C.M. Distribution.

NASHVILLE 1946 (T. Texas Tyler (NBC 1950)) (Tubb, Ernest & T. Texas Tyler).
Tracks: Not Advised.
CD . . . . **CDMR 1141**
Radiola / Oct '90 / Pinnacle.

YELLOW ROSE OF TEXAS, THE.
Tracks: Till we two are one / Your Mother, your darling, your friend / Baby your mother (Like she babied you) / Jealous loving heart / Two glasses, Joe / Woman's touch, The / Journey's end / Kansas city blues / Lonely Christmas eve / I'll be walking the floor this Christmas / Have you seen my boogie woogie baby / It's a lonely world / I got the blues for Mammy / (I'm gonna make my home) A million miles from here / Yellow rose of Texas, The / Answer phone / Honeymoon is over, The / Thirty days / Doorstep to heaven / Will you be satisfied that way / Steppin' out / If I never have anything else / So doggone lonesome / Old love letters (Bring memories of you) / Jimmy Rodger's last blue yodel / Travelin' blues / You're the only good thing (That's happend to me) / I've got the blues for Mammy / I dreamed of an old love affair / (I know my baby loves me)in her own peculiar way / Mississipp gal / There's no fool like a young fool / I new the moment I lost you / You're breaking my heart / When a soldier knocks and finds nobody home / This troubled mind o'mine / My hillbilly baby / Daisy May / Loving you is my weakness / Treat her right / I want you know (I love you) / Don't forbid me / God's eyes / My treasure / Leave me / Mister love / I always went through / Go home / Hey Mr. Blubird / How do we know / House of glass / Heaven help me / Tangled mind / Home of the blues / I found my girl in the USA / Geisha girl / I wonder why I worry over you / Deep purple blues / Please keep me in mind / I'm a long gone Daddy / Your cheatin' heart / Don't trade your old fashioned sweetheart (For a honky tonk / It makes no difference now / San Antonio rose / I want you to know I love you / That my darlin' is me / I'll get along somehow / Educated Mama / I'm waiting for ships that never come in / Half a mind / Next time / Goodbye sunshine / Hello blues / It's the age that makes the difference / Whay am I living for / Next voice you hear, The / All of those yesterdays / Walkin' the floor over you / When the world has turned you down / I'll always be glad to take you back / It's been so long Darlin' / Careless Darlin' / Though the days were only seven / Last night I dreamed / Slippin' around / I love you because / There's nothing more to say / There's a little bit of everything in Texas / You nearly lose your mind / Blue Christmas / Don't rob another man's castle / What I don't know about her / I cried a tear / Let's say goodbye like we say hello / Driftwood on the river / I wonder why you said goodbye / Tomorrow never comes / Filipino baby / I'd rather be / Letters have no arms / Rainbow at midnight / Have you ever been lonely / I will miss you when you go / Live it up / (I've lost you) So why should I care / Accidently on purpose / Do it now / He'll have to go / Mister blues / Kind of love she gave to me, The / Pick me up on your way down / This ain't the blues (Instrumental) / You win again / I believe I'm entitled to you / Guy named Joe, A / Who will buy the wine / Why I'm walkin' / White silver sands / Am I that easy to forget / Everybody's somebody's fool / Let the little girl dance / Candy kisses / It happend when I really needed you / Wondering / Cold, cold heart / Four walls / Bouquet of roses / Crazy arms / I love you so much it hurts / I walk the line / Little ole band of gold / Wabash connonball / I'm movin' on / Tennessee Saturday night / Signed sealed and delivered / Thoughts of a fool / Girl from Abilene / Same thing as me, The / Christmas is just another day / I hate to see you go / I'm sorry now / What will you tell them / It is no secret / Don't just stand there / Big blue diamonds / I'll just have another cup of coffee.
CD Set . . . . **BCD 15688**
Bear Family / May '93 / Rollercoaster Records / Swift / Direct Distribution.

Tubb, Justin

He was born in 1935 in Texas, the eldest son of Ernest Tubb, who is a fine country artist in his own right. He has written hits for Hawkshaw Hawkins, Jim Reeves and others. His own performance style, derived from his father's honky tonk, which in its day was innovative, but ironically received less radio time in '60-70's. He runs a publishing company and manages Ernest's live radio show from the record shop in Nashville. (Donald Clarke)

JUSTIN TUBB.
Tracks: There's a little bit of everything / Blue eyed Elaine / Walking the floor over you / Just you and me, Daddy / Coronation day / Waltz across Texas / Sing 'blue eyed Elaine' again / I will miss you when you go / Be better to your baby / Thanks, troubadour, thanks.
LP. . . . . **IMCA 39032**
MC . . . . **IMCAC 39032**
MCA / Mar '87 / BMG.

STAR OF THE GRAND OLE OPRY.
Tracks: One for you, one for me / Looking back to see / I'd know you anywhere / Women / How the other half lives / That's alright / Five minutes of the latest blues / How's it feel / One eyed Red / Your side of the story / I've gotta get my baby / If you don't want me.
LP. . . . . **OFF 9004**
Official / '88 / Charly / Cadillac Music / Jazz Music.

Tucker, Marshall

BEST OF THE MARSHALL TUCKER BAND (Tucker, Marshall Band).
Tracks: Can't you see / Fire on the mountain / Another cruel love / Searchin' for a rainbow / Long hard ride / 24 hours at a time / Heard it in a love song / Take the highway / Walkin' the streets alone.
LP. **2429 190**
Capricorn / Sep '79.

FIRE ON THE MOUNTAIN (Tucker, Marshall Band).
Tracks: Not Advised.
CD . . . . **MPG 74018**
Movieplay Gold / May '93 / Target Records.

HEAR IT IN A LOVE SONG (Tucker, Marshall Band).
Tracks: Hear it in a love song / Life is a song.
■ **7"** **208 9045**
Capricorn / Apr '77.

LONG HARD RIDE (Tucker, Marshall Band).
Tracks: Long hard ride / Property line / Am I the kind of man / Walkin' the streets alone / Windy city blues / Holding on to you / You say you love me / You don't live forever.
LP. **2429 140**
Polydor / Jan '79 / PolyGram.

MARSHALL TUCKER BAND, THE (Tucker, Marshall Band).
Tracks: Take the highway / Can't you see / Losing you / Hillbilly band / See you later, I'm gone / Ramblin' / My Jesus told me so / Ab's song.
LP. **2429 114**
Polydor / Mar '77 / PolyGram.

NEW LIFE, A (Tucker, Marshall Band).
Tracks: New life, A / Southern woman / Blue ridge mountain sky / Too stubborn / Another cruel love / You ain't foolin' me / 24 hours at a time / Fly eagle fly.
LP. **2429 101**
Polydor / Feb '78 / PolyGram.

RUNNING LIKE THE WIND (Tucker, Marshall Band).
Tracks: Running like the wind / Last of the singing cowboys / Answer to love, The / Unto these hills / Melody Ann / My best friend / Pass it on.
■ **LP.** . . . . **K 56621**
WEA / Jun '79 / WEA.

SEARCHIN' FOR A RAINBOW (Tucker, Marshall Band).
Tracks: Fire on the mountain / Searchin' for a rainbow / Walkin' and talkin' / Virginia / Bob away my blues / Keeps me from all wrong / Bound and determined / Can't you see.
LP. **2429 129**
Polydor / Sep '77 / PolyGram.

TOGETHER FOREVER (Tucker, Marshall Band).
Tracks: Not Advised.
LP. **2476 139**
Capricorn / Jul '78.

WHERE WE ALL BELONG (Tucker, Marshall Band).
Tracks: This ol' cowboy / Low down ways / In my own way / How can I slow down / Where a country boy belongs / Now she's gone / Try one more time / Ramblin' / 24 hours at a time / Every day / Take the highway.
LP. **2659 042**
Polydor / Jan '76 / PolyGram.

Tucker, Tanya

Texas - born (in Seminols, Texas on 10.10.1958) and Wilcox Arizona - raised, Tucker qualifies as country music's youngest ever veteran - already with twenty one years experience at the top. Tuckers's meteoric rise to fame started in 1972 when still only 13, *Delta dawn* made Billboard's Top Ten singles. Her parents had already by this early stage, been searching relentlessly to obtain a foothold in country music for their young daughter. Apart from singing with older sister in the country Wagoners, she'd already appeared on TV and acted in the Robert Redford film *Jeremiah Johnson*. Billy Sherril, Columbia'a ace producer, found Tanya displaying vocal maturity way beyond her tender years and soon she was to add a sensual/raunchy edge to her already husky tones. Registered her first No.1 in 1973 with *What's your Mama's name* doing the honours. Following in quick succession were 1973/74 No.1 singles *Blood red and goin'n down* and the controversal *Would you lay me (In a field of stone)*, written by ex-con David Allan Coe. Tucker's sixteenth birthday brought about a change of label (MCA), for a $1 million fee, her debut album *Tanya Tucker* brought in producer Snuffy Garrett. Chart success coming in chart toppers *Lizzie and the rainman* and the classic *San Antonio stroll*, both 1975. From then on Tanya's career took on a contemporary pop country edge - with top five hits *I don't believe my heart can stand another you*, *You've got me to hold on to* and No.1 cut *Here's some love* (her next No.1 single coming some 10 years down the line), reflecting the direction her music was taking. Tucker by now was promoting herself as a potential rock act - it was the experimental years, her career stumbling along at times. The mercury plunged dramatically, on release of her *T.N.T.* album - both the country and the desired rock audiences shunning it. Tanya, the Texas Tornado with her tight suits and provocative stances failed to garner even a ripple in the rock field. Almost singulary Ed Bruce's flag-waving *Texas when I die*, kept her career on the rails in 1978. During the early 80's, Tucker struck a stormy personal relationship with Glen Campbell (starred in films *Hard country* and *Georgia Peaches*), recording a few songs together - *Pecos promenade*, *Can I see you tonight* her best chart efforts - til 1986 (after a brief spell with Arista, her recording career was put on hold for three years), when a new chapter evolved. Fresh from a spell of treatment for a cocaine problem at the Betty Ford clinic and now signed to Capitol (Liberty), Tucker was once again a force to be reckoned with - striking gold with No.1 single *Just another love*. In 1987 Tanya teamed - up with Pauls, Davis & Overstreet on *I won't take less than your love*, that went all the way - going one better than her previous effort *Love me like you used to*. Now re-united with producer Jerry Crutchfield, from her MCA days - her career was now very much on a roll (the regular use of video promotion could well be a contributing factor in her upturn in fortunes). 1988 found Tanya retracing some of those country roots, recording Jimmie Rodgers *Daddy & home*, the album's title track *Strong enough to bend*, following *If it don't come easy* to the top. As the 80s/90s merged the bubbling Tanya charted regularly with *Highway robery*, *My arms stay open all night long* (1990), failing by the narrowest margins to gain pole position. Others to follow included Paul Kennerkey- penned rocking country *Walking shoes*, *Don't go out tonight* - a duet with country R & B merchant T.Graham Brown, *It won't be me* and *Down to my last teardrop* (1991), her ultimate reward coming that same year when voted the CMA's Female Vocalist Of The Year. Liberty mean-while, apart from her new material, during a period of 2-3 yrs shipped three Greatest Hits affairs, *Encore* a US only re-recording of her earliest work *Greatest hits* from Capitol & finally Liberty *Hits*, a compilation of her best work from Columbia, MCA & Capitol/Liberty covering her 20 year career and appering in it's original format. Still reeling the hits in, Tuckers recent track record features high flyers *Without you (what do I do with me*, *Two sparrows in a hurricane* (both No.2 hits) and *It's a little too late* alongside *Tell me about it* - her second duet hit with an R & B act, Delbert McClinton filling the part taken from her 1992 gold selling *I can't run from yourself* album on Liberty. (Maurice Hope - July 1993)

BEST OF TANYA TUCKER, THE.
Tracks: Not Advised.
CD **31166**
MCA (USA) / Jun '88 / MCA (Imports).
MC Set. . . . . **GTV 15770**
Gusto (USA) / Mar '88.

CAN'T RUN FROM YOURSELF.
Tracks: It's a little too late / Can't run from yourself / Two sparrows in a hurricane / Don't let my heart be the last to know / Tell me about it / I've learned to live / What do they know / Rainbow rider / Half the moon / Danger ahead.
CD . . . . **CDP 7989872**
MC **C498987**
Liberty / Oct '92 / EMI.

CHANGES.
Tracks: Cry / Shame on the moon / Until you're mine / Baby I'm yours / I don't want you to go / Heartache and a half / Changes / Feel right / Thing called love, A / Too long.
■ **LP.** **204756**
Arista / '83.

COUNTRY STORE: TANYA TUCKER.
Tracks: Delta dawn / Bed of roses / Why me Lord / You are so beautiful / Best of my love / Loving arms / Almost persuaded / I'll be your lady / Blood red and going down / Pass by me / How can I tell him / Let me be there / Jamestown Ferry / Guess I'll have to love him more / Chokin' kind, The (Only on CD) / South is gonna rise again, The (Only on CD) / What if we were running out of love (Only on CD) / I'm so lonesome I could cry (Only on CD).
MC . . . . **CSTK 35**
Country Store / Apr '87 / BMG.
■ **LP.** . . . . **CST 35**
Country Store / Apr '87.
CD . . . . **CDCST 35**
Country Store / '88 / BMG.

DREAM LOVER (Tucker, Tanya & Glen Campbell).
Tracks: Dream lover / Bronco.
■ **7"** . . . . **MCA 675**
MCA / Mar '81.

DREAM LOVERS.
Tracks: Not Advised.
■ **LP.** . . . . **MCF 3109**
MCA / May '81.

GIRLS LIKE ME.
Tracks: One love at a time / I'll come back as another woman / Fool fool heart / Just another love / Girls like me / Somebody to care / It's only over for you / Daddy long legs / You could change my mind / Still hold on.
LP. . . . . **EST 2007**
■ **MC** . . . . **TCEST 2007**
Capitol / Apr '86.

GREATEST HITS: TANYA TUCKER.
Tracks: Daddy and home / Strong enough to bend / Love me like you used to / Just another love / I'll come back as another woman / My arms stay open all night / If it don't come easy / I won't take less than your love / One love at a time / It's only over for you.
LP. **791 814 1**
■ **LP.** **C1 91814**
Capitol / Apr '90.
MC **C4 91814**
■ **MC** **791 814 4**
Capitol / Apr '90.
■ **CD** **CD-C1 91814**
Capitol / Apr '90.

HERE'S SOME LOVE.
Tracks: Here's some love / Round and round / Comin' home alone / Gonna love love anyway / Holding on / You just loved the leavin' out of me / Gospel singer, The / Take me to heaven / Short cut / I use soap.
LP. . . . . **MCF 2772**
MC **2772**
MCA / '76 / BMG.

HITS: TANYA TUCKER.
Tracks: San Antonio stroll / Don't believe my heart can stand another you / Jamestown ferry, The / Here's some love / Would you lay with me (in a field of stone) / Blood red and going down / Pecos promenade / What's your mama's name child / O Texas (when I die) / Just another love / I won't take less than your love / Daddy and home / If it don't come easy / Strong enough to bend / It won't be me / I'll come back as another woman / Love me like you used to / Down to my last teardrop / My arms stay open all night / Walking shoes / Don't go out.
CD . . . . **CDESTU 2169**
MC . . . . **TCESTU 2169**
Liberty / Apr '92 / EMI.

LIZZIE AND THE RAINMAN.
Tracks: Lizzie and the rainman / Travelling salesman.
■ **7"** . . . . **MCA 195**
MCA / Jun '75.

LIZZIE AND THE RAINMAN.
Tracks: Not Advised.
■ **CD** . . . . **CDCOT 108**
Cottage / Jun '92.

LOVE ME LIKE YOU USED TO.
Tracks: If it don't come easy / Love me like you used to / I won't take less than your love / I wonder what he's doing tonight / I'll Tennessee you in / Alien / Temporarily blue / If I didn't love you / Heartbreaker / Hope you find what you're loving for.
CD . . . . **CDEST 2036**
LP. . . . . **EST 2036**
■ **MC** . . . . **TCEST 2036**
Capitol / Aug '87.

LOVER GOODBYE.
Tracks: Lover goodbye / If you feel it.
■ **7"** . . . . **MCA 408**
MCA / Feb '79.

LOVIN' AND LEARNIN'.
Tracks: Franklin county / Depend on you / Ain't that a shame / Leave him alone / You've got me to hold on to / Makin' love don't always make love grow / After the thrill is gone / Don't believe my heart could stand another you / Here we are / My cowboys getting old.
LP. . . . . **MCF 2741**
MC . . . . **MCF 2741MC**
MCA / '76 / BMG.

T 8 ■ DELETED

ONE LOVE AT A TIME.
Tracks: One love at a time / Fool fool heart.
■ 7" ....CL 399
Capitol / Mar '86.

RIDIN' RAINBOWS.
Tracks: Dancing the night away / Love me like you never will again / Wait til Daddy finds out / Let's keep it that way / White rocket / Ridin' rainbows / It's a cowboy lovin' night / It was always you / Knee deep in loving you / Wings.
LP ....MCF 2796
MC 2796
MCA / '77 / BMG.

SAN FRANCISCO.
Tracks: San Francisco / By day by day.
■ 7" .... MCA 552
MCA / Feb '80.

SAVE ME.
Tracks: Save me / Slippin' away.
■ 7" .... MCA 372
MCA / Jul '78.

SHORT CUT.
Tracks: Short cut / Ridin' rainbows.
■ 7" .... MCA 273
MCA / Feb '77.

STRONG ENOUGH TO BEND.
Tracks: You're not alone / Strong enough to bend / As long as I'm dreaming / Lonesome town / Daddy and home / Highway robbery / Lonely at the right time / Playing for keeps / Call on me / Back on my feet.
■ CD ....CDEST 2069
Capitol / Aug '88.
■ MC ....TCEST 2069
Capitol / Aug '88.
■ LP .... EST 2069
Capitol / Aug '88.

TANYA TUCKER.
Tracks: Lizzie and the rainman / Love of a rolling stone / San Antonio rose / I'm no Lisa / King of country music, The / When will you be loved / Serenade we played, The / Son-of-a preacher man / Someday soon / Traveling salesman.
LP ....MCF 2713
MCA / '75 / BMG.

TANYA TUCKER'S GREATEST HITS.
Tracks: Delta dawn / Blood red and goin' down / Jamestown ferry, The / What's your Mama's name / I believe in south gonna rise again / Would you lay with me (in a field of stone) / Love's the answer / Rainy girl / No man's land / Man that turned my Mama on.
LP .... EMB 31180
Embassy / '75 / Sony.
LP 31516
■ MC 4031516
CBS / '78 / Sony.

TENNESSEE WOMAN.
Tracks: Take another run / Shotgun / Your old magic / Don't go out with him / There's a Tennessee woman/ Ben's song / Goodbye baby / It won't be me / As long as there's a heartbeat / Walking shoes / Oh what it did to me.
CD CD-C1 91821
■ MC C4 91821
Capitol / Jun '90.

TNT.
Tracks: Lover goodbye / I'm the singer, you're the song / Not fade away / Angel from Montgomery / Heartbreak Hotel / Brown eyed handsome man / River and the wind / If you feel it / It's nice to be with you.
■ LP ....MCF 3530
MCA / Mar '79.
CD 31152
MCA / Jun '88 / BMG.

TRAVELLING SALESMAN.
Tracks: Travelling salesman / Someday soon.
■ 7" .... MCA 216
MCA / Oct '75.

WHY DON'T WE JUST SLEEP ON IT TO-NIGHT (see under Campbell, Glen).

WOULD YOU LAY WITH ME.
Tracks: Would you lay with me (in a field of stone) / How can I tell him / Let me be there / Bed of roses / Man that turned my Mama on, The / Pass me by / Chokin' kind, The / Teach me the words to your song / I believe the South is gonna rise again / Old Dan Tucker's daughter / No man's land / Why me Lord / Baptism of Jesse Taylor, The / What if we were running out of love / New York city song / If you touch me you've got to love me.
LP 31690
■ MC 4031690
CBS / '78 / Sony.

YOU ARE SO BEAUTIFUL.
Tracks: You are so beautiful / Best of my love, The / There is a place / Can I be your lady / Lovin' arms / You know just what I'd do / Almost persuaded / Spring / Guess I'll have to love him more / I still sing those love songs.
LP 31568
■ MC 4031568
CBS / '77 / Sony.

■ DELETED

BILLY BOY AND MARY LOU (see under Anderson, Bill).

CHEATIN' OVERTIME.
Tracks: Cheatin' overtime / I never had the time.
■ 7" .... MCA 95
MCA / Apr '77.

JERSEY ROCK.
Tracks: Jersey rock / Travellin' boogie / You're my cutie pie / Gone gone gone / Back, back to Baltimore / Tennessee boogie / Chew tobacco rag / Huckleberry boogie / Boogie woogie Lou / Dolly Dimple dance / I got a load / Crazy heart / No more nothing (but getting off your mind) / I'm tying up the blues with a big blue ribbon / I got a lot of things for a lot of nothing / Hard hearted you and chicken hearted you / You're gonna be lonesome someday (Downhearted and blue) / All dressed up / Never been so lonesome / I could lose the blues (if my baby were back).
LP .... BFX 15166
Bear Family / Nov '84 / Rollercoaster Records / Swift / Direct Distribution.

Conway Twitty - born Harold Lloyd Jenkins on September 1, 1933, in Friars Point, Mississippi - was one of the very few artists to enjoy two highly successful careers. First he was one of the biggest sellers of the 1950's rockabilly boom and then moved on to even bigger success in the country music market. The difference between him and other rockers was that he didn't have any prior rhythm'n'blues influences, he grew up listening to the records of Roy Acuff and Ernest Tubb and, during his time in the Army, he formed a country band that he named the Cimarrons. It was after hearing Presley's Mystery Train (1955) that he knew the direction he wanted to follow, though his brief association with Sun Records under the name of Harold Jenkins and his Rockhards did not have a commercial release until 1970). With his name changed to Conway Twitty, he signed to MGM and quickly established himself as the label's rock heavy-weight, selling around 16 million records in five years, the biggest of them being It's only make believe (1958) and Mona Lisa (1960). He also appeared on all the major TV shows and made six movies including Platinum High School and Sex kittens go to college, providing the soundtrack for all of them. In 1966 Twitty made the decision to return to country music, signed with MCA (later to become MCA) and commenced an association that would stretch into the 90's with the hit single, Guess my eyes were bigger than my heart . It wasn't until a couple of years later that he moved into the top 10 with The image of me, with his next single, Next in line going straight to the top, setting a pattern that would see almost 100 chart successes during the following years, with around 40 of them reaching number one, a record unbeaten by any other artist. Significant among this vast array of hits were Hello darlin' (1970), which touched the million mark and put him back in the pop charts, and You've never been this far before (1973), a song that - according to some sections of the industry and media - "set the new standards in dirty lyrics". Unperturbed he included the equally risque (Lying here with) Linda on my mind in a later recording session which, of course, gave him another chart-topper. In the early 1980's he strayed from MCA to have brief associations with Elektra and Warner Bros., one of these successes being a country version of the Pointer Sisters' Slow Hand. He also recorded a series of highly successful duets with Loretta Lynn, an artist with whom he had formed a business partnership, creating the Nashville based booking agency United Talent. Another of the singer's many business ventures was Twitty City, a theme park in Hendersonville (on the outskirts of Nashville) that saw the star living, with his family, on the grounds, a clear indication of Twitty's one hundred percent dedication to his fans. The world of country music was shocked by Conway Twitty's sudden death on June 5, 1993, following a concert appearance in Branson, Missouri. It happened a couple of days before the annual Fan Fair activities were set to commence and, naturally, tributes flowed throughout the week from fans and industry alike. To the country music business he was "the best friend a song ever had". (Tony Byworth - August 1993)

20 CONWAY CLASSICS.
Tracks: Not Advised.
LP ....MCF 3276
■ MC ....MCFC 3276
MCA / Nov '85.

BEAT GOES ON.
Tracks: Not Advised.
■ LP .... CR 30242
Charly / Jul '85 / Charly.

BEST OF CONWAY AND LORETTA (Twitty, Conway & Loretta Lynn).
Tracks: Louisiana woman, Mississippi man / Lead me on / As soon as I hang up the phone / Let me be there / It's only make believe / From seven till ten / Let your love flow / Letter, The / Back home again / Lovin' what your lovin' does to me / Release me / It's true love / Feelings / I can't love you enough / Hey good lookin' / After the fire is gone.
■ LP ....MCL 1823
MCA / May '86.
MC ....MCLC 1823
MCA / Sep '86 / BMG.

BIG TOWN.
Tracks: Ever since you went away / Big town / Blue is the way I feel / Treat me mean, treat me cruel / Road that I walk, The / Don't go too far / Broken heart / Angel's wings / Turn the other cheek / Wonder if you told her / Midnight / You made me what I am / Big train / Sitting in a dim cafe / Let me be the judge / Diggin' / Have I been away too long / Where I stand / Riskin' one.
LP .... SHLP 142
MC .... SHTC 142
Castle Showcase / Sep '86 / Arabesque Ltd.

BIG TRAIN.
Tracks: Not Advised.
LP 20114
MC 40114
Astan (USA) / Nov '84.

BOOGIE BRASS BAND.
Tracks: Boogie brass band / One in a million.
■ 7" .... MCA 389
MCA / Sep '78.

BOOGIE BRASS BAND.
Tracks: Boogie brass band / I've just got to know / She's a woman all the way / Julie / One night honeymoon / Your love had taken me that high / I've been around enough to know / My woman knows / That's all she wrote / You were named the co-respondent.
LP .... MCF 2878
MCA / Apr '79 / BMG.

BORDERLINE.
Tracks: Julia / Lonely town / I want to know you before we make love / Borderline / Not enough love to go 'round / Snake boots / I'm for awhile / Fifteen to forty-three / Everybody needs a hero / That's my job.
CD ....MCAD 5969
LP .... IMCA 5969
MC ....IMCAC 5969
MCA / Jun '87 / BMG.

C'EST SI BON.
Tracks: C'est si bon.
■ 7" .... MGM 1118
MGM (EMI) / Feb '61.

CLASSIC CONWAY.
Tracks: Tight fittin' jeans / I can't believe she gives it all to me / Play guitar play / Grandest lady of them all, The / We had it all / Georgia keeps pulling on my ring / Your love has taken me that high / Over thirty(not over the hill) / I am the dreamer (you are the dream) / Red neckin' love makin' night.
■ LP .... IMCA 1574
MCA (Import) / Mar '86.

CONWAY TWITTY SINGS.
Tracks: Not Advised.
LP .... HAT 3127
Stetson / '89 / Crusader Marketing Co. / Swift / Wellard Dist. / Midland Records / C.M. Distribution.

COUNTRY PARTNERS (see under Lynn, Loretta).

CROSSWINDS.
Tracks: Not Advised.
■ LP ....MCF 3038
MCA / Nov '79.

DON'T TAKE IT AWAY.
Tracks: Don't take it away / Draggin' chains.
7" .... MCA 240
MCA / Nov '89 / BMG.

DYNAMIC DUO (see under Lynn, Loretta).

GREAT CONWAY TWITTY, THE.
Tracks: Not Advised.
LP .... DEMAND 0020
Demand / Oct '87.

GREAT COUNTRY HITS.
Tracks: Not Advised.
LP .... WW 5102
MC .... WW 4 5102
Warwick / Mar '81 / Sony / Henry Hadaway Organisation / Multiple Sound Distributors.
LP ....MCF 3268
MC ....MCFC 3268
MCA / Mar '85 / BMG.

GREATEST HITS: CONWAY TWITTY VOL.1.
Tracks: Hello darlin' / I wonder what she'll think about me leaving / Fifteen years ago / Darling, you know I wouldn't lie to you / That's when she started to stop loving you / To see my angel cry / I can't be without you / Next in line / How much more can she stand / Image of me, The / I love you more today.

■ LP. . . . . IMCA 1473
MCA (Import) / Mar '86.
■ CD 833 729-2
Polydor / Aug '88.

I NEED YOUR LOVIN'.
Tracks: Not Advised.
CD . . . . CDCD 1110
Charly / Jul '93 / Charly.

I SEE THE WANT TO IN YOUR EYES.
Tracks: I see the want to in your eyes / Girl from Tupelo.
■ 7" . . . . MCA 197
MCA / Jun '75.

IS A BLUEBIRD BLUE?.
Tracks: Is a bluebird blue?.
■ 7" . . . . MGM 1082
MGM (EMI) / Jul '60.

IT'S ONLY MAKE BELIEVE.
Tracks: It's only make believe.
■ 7" . . . . MGM 992
MGM (EMI) / Nov '58.

IT'S ONLY MAKE BELIEVE.
Tracks: It's only make believe / Games that daddies play, The / I can't believe she gives it all to me.
■ 7" . . . . MCA 282
MCA / Mar '77.

IT'S ONLY MAKE BELIEVE (OLD GOLD).
Tracks: It's only make believe / Mona Lisa.
7" . . . . OG 9448
Old Gold / Mar '90 / Pickwick Records.

IT'S ONLY MAKE-BELIEVE.
Tracks: Not Advised.
LP. . . . . WW 2044
Warwick / Aug '88 / Sony / Henry Hadaway Organisation / Multiple Sound Distributors.

LET YOUR LOVE FLOW (Twitty, Conway & Loretta Lynn).
Tracks: Let your love flow / Never ending song of love.
■ 7" . . . . MCA 284
MCA / Mar '77.

LIVE AT CASTAWAY LOUNGE 1963.
Tracks: Not Advised.
LP. . . . . DEMAND 0030
Demand / Oct '87.

LOOKING BACK.
Tracks: It's only make believe / Mona Lisa / What am I living for / Hey! Little Lucy / Heavenly / Long black train / Make me know / I viberate / I'd still play the fool / Foggy river / Lonely blue boy / Story of my love, The.
LP. 2354 027
MC 3140 104
Polydor / Jan '78 / PolyGram.

MGM YEARS, THE.
Tracks: Crazy dreams / Give me some love / Need your lovin' kiss / Just in time / Born to sing the blues / Maybe baby / Shake it up / Need your lovin' / Golly gosh oh gee / Doubel talk baby / Why can't I get through to you / It's only make believe / I'll try / When (Will you love me then, as you love me now) / Vibrate (From my head to my feet) / When I'm not with you (I get so lonely) / Don't you know / Story of my love, The / My one and only you / Goin' home / Make you know you're mine / Judge of hearts / First romance / I need you so / Mona Lisa / Sentimental journey / Hallelujah, I love her so / You'll never walk alone / Hey little Lucy (Don'tcha put no lipstick on) / Teasin' / Heavenly / Halfway to heaven / Just because / Cry Janie cry / Blueberry hill / Heartbreak hotel / You win again / Danny boy / Hey Miss Ruby / Restless / She's mine / Beach comber / Easy to fall in love / Rosaleena / My adobe hacienda / Star spangled heaven / A' huggin and A' kissin / Can't we go steady / Lonely blue boy / Sorry / Blue moon / Eternal tears / Foggy river / Platinum high school / Trouble in mind / Pretty eyed baby / Rebound / Hurt in my heart, The / Maybe tomorrow we'll know / Tell me one more time / What am I living for a fallen star / I'd still play the fool / Betty Lou / Knock three times / What a dream / Is a bluebird blue / Whol lotta shakin' goin' on / My heart cries / Sweet Georgia Brown / That's where my lovin' goes / Don't you dare let me down / Send her to me / Flame, The / C'est si bon / Long black train / Blue suede shoes / Great balls of fire / Jailhouse rock / Treat me nice / Handy man / Girl can't help it, The / Shake, rattle and roll / Diana / Splish splash / Reelin' and rockin' / Million teardrops, A / Next kiss (Is the last goodbye), The / Tree in the meadow, A / Above and beyond (The call of love) / I'm a blue, blue mood / Live fast, love hard die young (I Wanna) / Man alone / Donna's dream / Tower of tears / I can hear my heart break / Prisoner of love / Unchained melody / Sweet sorrow / Little bird told me, A / It's driving me wild / Turn around / Walk on by / Portrait of a fool / There is something on your mind / Don't cry no more / Mister Jones / Hang up the phone / Little peice of my heart, A / She knows me like a book / Comfy 'n back / Pledging my love / It's too late / Almost lost my mind / I got a woman / My babe / Let the good times roll / Fever / Boss man / City lights / Faded love / Don't let the stars get in your eyes / Ages and ages ago / I hope I think I wish / Pickup, The / Hound dog / She ain't no angel / Got my mojo working / Lonely boy blue.
LP Set . . . . BFX 15174/9
Bear Family / Nov '85 / Rollercoaster Records / Swift / Direct Distribution.

MONA LISA.
Tracks: Mona Lisa.
■ 7" . . . . MGM 1029
MGM (EMI) / Aug '59.

NEVER ENDING SONG OF LOVE (see under Lynn, Loretta).

REFLECTIONS.
Tracks: It's only make believe / Walk on by / I'm in a blue mood / Fever / Beach comber / Pledging my love / Sentimental journey / Danny boy / My babe / Unchained melody / I almost lost my mind / Going home / You'll never walk alone.
LP. . . . . CN 2091
MC CN4 2091
Contour / Aug '88 / Pickwick Records.

REPLAY ON CONWAY TWITTY.
Tracks: Not Advised.
LP. . . . . FEDB 5014
MC . . . . FEDC 5014
Sierra / Dec '88.

SHAKE IT UP BABY.
Tracks: Born to sing the blues / Golly gosh oh gee / Crazy dreams / Shake it up baby / Maybe baby / Why can't I get through to you / Double-talk baby / I need your lovin' / This road that I walk / I wonder if you told her about me / Midnight / You made me what I am today.
CD . . . . AJKL 1044
LP. . . . . BDL 1044
Bulldog Records / Sep '82 / President Records / Jazz Music / Wellard Dist. / TKO Records Ltd.
LP. 20071
MC 40071
Astan (USA) / Nov '84.

SILVER ANNIVERSARY COLLECTION.
Tracks: Guess my eyes were bigger than my heart / Look into my teardrops / I don't want to be with me / Image of me, The / To see my angel cry / Hello darlin' / I can't see me without you / (Lost her love) On our last date / You've never been this far before / I'm not through loving you yet / Linda on my mind / (I can't believe) she gives it all to me / I've already loved you in my mind / Boogie grass band / Don't take it away / I'd just love to lay you down / Tight fittin' jeans / Slow hand / Rose, The / I don't know a thing about love / Don't call him a cowboy / Desperado love / That's my job / Goodbye time / She's got a single thing in mind.
CD . . . . MCAD 8035
MCA (USA) / Jan '90 / MCA (Imports).

SONGWRITER.
Tracks: Hello darlin' / (Lost her love) on the first date / Baby's gone / You've never been this far before / I'm not through loving you / Linda on my mind / After all the good is gone / Games that daddies play, the / I can't believe she gives it all to me / I've already loved you in my mind.
■ LP. . . . . IMCA 5700
MCA (Import) / Mar '86.

STORY OF MY LOVE.
Tracks: Story of my love.
■ 7" . . . . MGM 1003
MGM (EMI) / Mar '59.

YOU MADE ME WHAT I AM.
Tracks: Treat me mean, treat me cruel / Have I been away too long / You made me what I am / Blue is the way I feel / Where I stand / Ever since you went away / Turn the other cheek / Let me be the judge / This road that I walk / Sitting in a dim cafe.
LP. . . . . ALEB 2306
MC . . . . ZCALB 2306
Allegiance / Apr '84.

YOUR LOVE HAD TAKEN ME THAT HIGH.
Tracks: Your love had taken me that high / Good time Charlie's got the blues.
■ 7" . . . . MCA 414
MCA / Mar '79.

Two Hearts

Late 1980's/early 90's teaming of two of the most popular females on the U.K. country music scene, Tammy Cline and Ginny Brown (Little Ginny) (see separate entries). The joining of forces evolved from their performances together in the West End musical 'Pump Boys and Dinettes'. (Tony Byworth - August 1993)

TWO HEARTS ONE LOVER.
Tracks: Two hearts, one lover / Midnight girl,sunset town / I'll be faithfull to you / Going gone / Mon ami, mon amour / He was onto something / If I could win your love / Friendship / Sister / Turn me loose.
CD . . . . PTCD 005
LP. . . . . PTLP 005
MC . . . . PTLC 005
P.T. Music / Feb '89 / ACD Trading Ltd.

Two's Company

GOLDEN MEMORIES.
Tracks: Not Advised.
■ LP. . . . . KLP 240
K-Tel / '88.

LET'S START ALL OVER AGAIN.
Tracks: Not Advised.
LP. . . . . HPE 642
Harp (Ireland) / Oct '81 / C.M. Distribution.

MADE FOR EACH OTHER.
Tracks: Not Advised.
LP. . . . . BRL 4048
Release (Ireland) / Jan '78.

TWO'S COMPANY.
Tracks: Not Advised.
LP. . . . . TVLP 12
MC . . . . ZCTV 12
Towerbell / Apr '86.

WHEN THE ROSES BLOOM AGAIN.
Tracks: Not Advised.
MC . . . . FACS 018
CMR/Failte / '88 / I & B Records.

YOU'RE MY BEST FRIEND.
Tracks: Not Advised.
LP. . . . . BRL 4074
Release (Ireland) / May '76.

Tyler, T.Texas

Born David Luke Myrick on 20.06.1916 in Mena, Arkansas (died 28.01.1972 in Springfield, Missouri) raised in Texas and educated in Philadelphia. Worked on the Louisiana Hayride in 1942 - before moving to California in 1946. Apart from his composition, the monologue *Deck of cards* (a No. 2 hit in 1948 and also voted Cashbox's country song of the year - later a million seller for Wink Martindale and Tex Ritter - a top ten hit in 1948). Tyler also enjoyed another seven high scoring singles before 1954, all on 4 Star except 1953's Decca recording *Bumming around*. Others from the popular TV host being *Filipino baby*, *Dad gave my dog away*, *Memories of France*, *My bucket's got a hole in it* and *Courtin' in the rain* , material which held him in good stead for three decades. He also figured in the 1949 film *Horsemen of the Sierras*. (Maurice Hope - August 1993)

GREAT TEXAN, THE.
Tracks: Not Advised.
CD . . . . KCD 000689
King / Dec '92 / New Note / Koch International.

T. TEXAS TYLER.
Tracks: Remember me / In my little red book / Filipino baby / Who's to blame / You turned a good man down / Careless love / Texas Tyler / Oklahoma hills / It's been so long darling / T. Texas blues / You nearly lose your mind / I hung my head and cried / Gals don't mean a thing.
LP. . . . . SING 721
Sing / '88 / Charly / Cadillac Music.

T. TEXAS TYLER.
Tracks: Not Advised.
CD . . . . KCD 721
King / Apr '93 / New Note / Koch International.

Tyson, Ian

Born on 25.09.1933, in British Columbia, Canada. A member of the 1960's folk boom duo - Ian and Sylvia. Recorded eight albums for Vanguard, before moving to Columbia by way of MGM and Ampex. Tyson by this time had decided to break away from the folk scene, pursuing country music instead and had already formed his 1970s Great Speckled Bird Band. His debut A&M solo album *Ol' eon* soon joined with his hit *One jump ahead of the devil*. During much of the decade he was to concentrate on TV work, coupled with ranching-out on his 160 acre spread in Longview, Alberta, purchased in 1979 partly from the royalties due to him, after Neil Young's version of *Four strong winds*. During the 1980s Tyson was to record a quartet of albums using the cowboy theme, including *Old corrals and sagebrush*, and his subsequent releases featured Columbia's *Ian Tyson* and his Canadian Stony Plain debut recording *Cowboyography* (1986). At this point the awards and sales began to soar. The album selling a, then all-time, personal best of 50,000 copies and winning many awards from the Canadian music industry. Since this time the popular rancher/singer-songwriter/musician has seen a big upturn in his music, the cowboy theme yielding two more albums, *I outgrew the wagon* and *And sttod there amazed*. *Navajo rug* from the *Cowboyography* album (penned with Tom Russell) gained a cover from the rejuvenated Jerry Jeff Walker - while Suzy Bogguss in 1992 took *Someday soon* to the upper reaches of the country charts, a song previously done by Moe Bandy, Kathy Barnes, Judy Collins and Tanya Tucker. The songwriter's friend Bobby Bare has long been a champion of his work - since enjoying a top five hit in 1964 with *Four strong winds*. Part-time singer/rancher has been a formula which has worked well for Tyson for some considerable time, and found him writing and singing with singer-songwriter Tom Russell, appearing on Russell's Philo album *Cowboy real*. His own

T 10

■ DELETED

1992 release *And stood there amazed* continued his on-going love affair with the West, and was to gain even more Juno awards. He played before millions at the Calgary Winter Olympics, supported by Gordon Lightfoot, who, alongside the likes of Joni Mitchell and Tyson, started his career playing the folkclubs of Toronto. Tyson gained induction into the Canadian Country Hall of Fame in 1989, and subsequently in 1992 Juno likewise bestowed their equivalent honour. (Maurice Hope - August 1993)

COWBOYOGRAPHY.
Tracks: Springtime / Navajo rug / Summer wages / Fifty years ago / Rockies turn rose / Claude Dallas / Own heart's delight / Cowboy pride / Old Cheyenne / Coyote and the cowboy, The.
LP. . . . . SH 1021
MC . . . . ZCSH 1021
Sugarhill(USA) / Mar '89 / Roots Records / Projection / Impetus Records / C.M. Distribution / Jazz Music / Swift / Duncans / A.D.A Distribution.

FOUR STRONG WINDS (Tyson, Ian & Sylvia).
Tracks: Jesus met the woman at the well / Tomorrow is a long time / Katy dear / Poor Lazarus / Four strong winds / Ella Speed / Long lonesome road / V' la l'bon vent / Royal canal / Lady Carlisle / Spanish is a loving tongue / Greenwood side / Every night when the sun goes down / Every time I feel the spirit.
CD . . . . VMD 2149
LP. . . . . VMLP 2149
MC . . . . VMMC 2149
Vanguard / '87 / Complete Record Co. Ltd.

I OUTGREW THE WAGON.
Tracks: Cowboys don't cry / Casey Tibbs / I outgrew the wagon / Arms of Corey Jo / Adelita Rose / Irving Berlin (is 100 years old today) / Since the rain / Wind in the fire, The / Four strong winds / Banks of the musselshell / Steeldust line, The.
CD . . . . SDCD 9.00967
Sawdust / '90.

OLD CORRALS AND SAGEBRUSH & OTHER COWBOY CLASSIC.
Tracks: Gallo de cielo / Alberta's child / Old double diamond, The / Windy Bill / Montana waltz / Whoopie ti yi yo / Leavin' Cheyenne / Old corrals and sagebrush / Old Alberta moon / Night rider's lament / Oklahoma hills / Tom Blasingame / Colorado trial / Hot summer tears / What does she see / Rooke begin to roll / Will James / Murder steer.
CD . . . . BCD 15437
Bear Family / Aug '88 / Rollercoaster Records / Swift / Direct Distribution.

ONE JUMP AHEAD OF THE DEVIL.
Tracks: What does she see / Beverly / Turning thirty / Newtonville waltz / Lone star and coors / One too many / Texas / I miss you / Goodness of Shirley / Freddie Hall / Half a mile to hell.
CD . . . . SPCD 1177
MC . . . . SPMC 1177
Stoney Plain / '92 / Projection / C.M. Distribution.

Tyson. Sylvia

GIPSY CADILLAC.
Tracks: Not Advised.
CD . . . . AMSCCD 102
■ MC . . . . .AMSCMC 102
Silver City / Jun '92.

YOU WERE ON MY MIND.
Tracks: Pepere's mill / Slow moving heart / Rhythm of the road / Walking on the moon / Thrown to the wolves / Night the Chinese restaurant burned down / You were on my mind / Sleep on my mind / Trucker's cafe / River Road / Last call / Le Moulin a Pepere / Blind fiddler's waltz.
CD . . . . SDCD 9.00964
Sawdust / '90.

V

Val, Joe

Born Joe Valiante, in Everett, Massachusettes - 1926 (died 1985), traditional bluegrass mandolin/banjo player/vocalist (judged to be one of the music's finest ever tenor singers). Learnt his trade in and around Boston, an area known for it's folk musicians. Worked with the Charles River Valley Boys, one of the first bands to evolve in the north - featuring Val, Bill Keith and Jim Rooney. Stayed long enough to figure on it's *Beatle Country* album. It was in the company of Keith and Rooney that he recorded the 1960's *Living on a Mountain top* album. While with his own band, the New England Bluegrass Boys (it's original line up reading Herb Applin, Bob French and Bob Tidwell) and keeping with the Monroe tradition, he recorded a string of distinguished albums for Rounder. (Maurice Hope - August 1993)

BOUND TO RIDE (Val, Joe & New England Bluegrass Boys).
Tracks: Not Advised.
LP. . . . . ROUNDER 0109
Rounder / '88 / Projection / Roots Records / Swift / C.M. Distribution / Topic Records / Jazz Music / Hot Shot / A.D.A Distribution / Direct Distribution.

COLD WIND (Val, Joe & New England Bluegrass Boys).
Tracks: Cold wind / Wrong road again / You're running wild / Sea of regret / 'Neath a cold grey tomb of stone / Never again / When the cactus is in bloom / Mother's prayer / Stormy waters / I've been all around this world / Rocking alone in an old rocking chair.
LP. . . . . ROUNDER 0182
MC . . . . .ROUNDER 0182C
Rounder / '88 / Projection / Roots Records / Swift / C.M. Distribution / Topic Records / Jazz Music / Hot Shot / A.D.A Distribution / Direct Distribution.

JOE VAL & THE NEW ENGLAND BLUEGRASS BOYS (Vol. 2) (Val, Joe & New England Bluegrass Boys).
Tracks: Not Advised.
LP. . . . . ROUNDER 0025
Rounder / '88 / Projection / Roots Records / Swift / C.M. Distribution / Topic Records / Jazz Music / Hot Shot / A.D.A Distribution / Direct Distribution.

NOT A WORD FROM HOME (Val, Joe & New England Bluegrass Boys).
Tracks: Not Advised.
LP. . . . . ROUNDER 0082
Rounder / Nov '77 / Projection / Roots Records / Swift / C.M. Distribution / Topic Records / Jazz Music / Hot Shot / A.D.A Distribution / Direct Distribution.

ONE MORNING IN MAY (Val, Joe & New England Bluegrass Boys).
Tracks: Not Advised.
LP. . . . . ROUNDER 0003
Rounder / Oct '77 / Projection / Roots Records / Swift / C.M. Distribution / Topic Records / Jazz Music / Hot Shot / A.D.A Distribution / Direct Distribution.

SPARKLING BROWN EYES (Val, Joe & New England Bluegrass Boys).
Tracks: Not Advised.
LP. . . . . ROUNDER 0152
MC . . . . .ROUNDER 0152C
Rounder / '88 / Projection / Roots Records / Swift / C.M. Distribution / Topic Records / Jazz Music / Hot Shot / A.D.A Distribution / Direct Distribution.

Van Dyke, Leroy

This American singer and guitarist obtained a degree in agriculture before serving with the US Army in Korea. It was while in the Forces that he took up the guitar and started to explore his vocal talents. Upon discharge, however, his special interest in cattle prompted him to begin a career as a livestock auctioneer. In 1956 he hit upon the idea of co-writing and recording *The auctioneer*, a novelty number based on the cry and lifestyle of a member of his profession. The song climbed to no.19 on the US pop chart in early '57. It was also a success on the country and western listings. Van Dyke's next taste of major success did not come until 1961. At the end of that year, he achieved a US no.5 smash with an infectious countrified pop single, *Walk on by*. In early '62, the record reached no.5 in Britain. The song had no connection with a similarly titled number which became a hit for Dionne Warwick). In the US, Van Dyke followed *Walk on by* with *If a woman answers (hang up the phone)*; in the UK, *Big man in a big house* was released. In both cases, only a modest hit

was gained. Subsequently, his warm singing style was confined to the American country charts but even there, he gradually drifted into obscurity. His career was not uplifted by by his movie debut, in 1967's *What am I bid?* (Bob Macdonald)

AUCTIONEER, THE.
Tracks: Auctioneer, The / Pocketbook song / My good mind went bad on me / Honky tonk song / Leather jacket / I fell in love with a pony tail / One heart / Heartbreak cannonball / I'm movin' on / Chicken shack / I fell in love witha pony tail.
■ LP. . . . . CH 99
Ace / Apr '84.

BIG MAN IN A BIG HOUSE.
Tracks: Big man in a big house.
■ 7". . . . . AMT 1173
Mercury (EMI) / Apr '62.

ORIGINAL AUCTIONEER, THE.
Tracks: Auctioneer, The / I fell in love with a pony tail / Leather jacket / I'm movin' on / My good mind (went bad on me) / Heartbreak cannonball / Chicken shack / Poor boy / What this old work needs / Every time I ask my heart / Pocketbook song / Down at the south end of town / Honky tonk song / One heart.
LP. BFX 15270
Bear Family / Mar '88 / Rollercoaster Records / Swift / Direct Distribution.
CD . . . . BCD 15647
Bear Family / Apr '93 / Rollercoaster Records / Swift / Direct Distribution.

WALK ON BY.
Tracks: Walk on by.
■ 7". . . . . AMT 1166
Mercury (EMI) / Jan '62.

WALK ON BY (OLD GOLD).
Tracks: Walk on by / It's four in the morning.
■ 7". . . . . OG 9508
Old Gold / Feb '85.

Van Shelton, Ricky

Born 1952 in Grit, Virginia, he has emerged on the scene relatively recently. He became a member of the Grand Ole Opry in 1988 the same year he won the CMA's Horizon award. Ricky's ability to both pour out undiluted emotion on the big ballads and serve up generous slices of energetic rockabilly gained him the CMA's Male Vocalist Of The Year award in 1989. (Maurice Hope).

LIFE TURNED HER THAT WAY.
Tracks: Life turned her that way / I don't care.
■ 7". 6528317
CBS / Jun '88.

LOVING PROOF.
Tracks: Swimming upstream / I'll leave this world loving you / From a Jack to a King / Let me live with love (& die with you) / Living proof / Hole in my pocket / Picture, The / Somebody's back in town / Don't send me no angels / He's got you.
CD 462622-2
MC 462622-4
Columbia / Jun '93 / Sony.

RVS III.
Tracks: I've cried my last tear for you / Statue of a fool / You would do the same for me / Life's little ups and downs / I'm starting over / Love is burnin' / Not that I care / Oh pretty woman / I meant every word he said / I still love you / Sweet memories.
LP. 4663481
MC 4663484
CBS / Mar '90 / Sony.
■ CD 4663482
CBS / Mar '90.

WILD-EYED DREAM.
Tracks: Ultimately fine / Crime of passion / Life turned her that way / I don't care / Don't we all have the right / Wild-eyed dream / Baby I'm ready / Somebody lied / Crazy over you / Working man blues.
CD 4611202
CBS / Jun '88 / Sony.
■ LP. 4611201
CBS / Jun '88.
■ MC 4611204
CBS / Jun '88.

Van Zandt, Townes

Legendary singer, songwriter and guitarist Van Zandt, from Worth, Texas, is very highly regarded for his ability to enchant an audience.

His best-known work is *Pancho And Lefty*, recorded by Willie Nelson and Emmylou Harris. He made LPs on Poppy and Tomato between 1968 and 1977, but they were not well distributed. At *My Window*, on Sugar Hill in '87, was his first in nine years, accompanied by an acclaimed UK tour. (Donald Clarke)

AT MY WINDOW.
Tracks: Snowin' on Raton / Blue wind blew / At my window / For the sake of the song / Ain't leaving your love / Buckskin stallion blues / Little sundance / Still lookin' for you / Gone gone blues / Catfish song, The.
LP. HLD 003
Heartland (1) / Nov '87 / Revolver-APT.
CD . . . . HLDCD 003
Heartland (1) / '88 / Revolver-APT.
LP. SH 1020
Sugarhill(USA) / Oct '88 / Roots Records / Projection / Impetus Records / C.M. Distribution / Jazz Music / Swift / Duncans / A.D.A Distribution.
CD . . . . EDCD 351
Edsel / Jun '92 / Pinnacle.

DELTA MOMMA BLUES.
Tracks: FFV / Delta momma blues / Only him or me / Turnstyled, junkpiled / Tower song / Come tomorrow / Brand new companion / Rake / Nothin'.
LP. TOM 7013
Tomato (USA) / Mar '79 / Revolver-APT.
■ CD . . . . CDCHARLY 110
Charly / Apr '88 / Charly.
LP. LIK 25
MC . . . . TCLIK 25
Decal / Apr '88 / Charly / Swift.

FIRST ALBUM.
Tracks: For the sake of the song / Tecumseh valley / Many a fine lady / Quick silver daydreams of Maria / Waitin' around to die / I'll be there in the morning / Sad Cinderella / Velvet voices, The / Talkin' karate blues / All your young servants / Sixteen summers, fifteen falls.
CD 598 1091 29
Tomato (USA) / Aug '93 / Revolver-APT.

FLYIN' SHOES.
Tracks: Loretta / No place to fall / Flyin' shoes / Who do you love / When she don't need me / Dollar bill blues / Rex's blues / Pueblo waltz / Brother flower / Snake song.
CD . . . . CDCHARLY 193
Charly / Jul '89 / Charly.
LP. LIK 59
MC . . . . TCLIK 59
Decal / Jul '89 / Charly / Swift.

FOR THE SAKE OF THE SONG.
Tracks: Not Advised.
LP. PYS 40001
Poppy / Aug '90.

HIGH LOW AND IN BETWEEN.
Tracks: Two hands / You are not needed now / Greensboro woman / Highway kind / Standin' / No deal / To live is to fly / When he offers his hand / Mr. Gold and Mr. Mud / Blue Ridge mountains / High low and in between.
■ LP. . . . . TOM 7012
Tomato (USA) / Mar '79.
■ CD . . . . CDCHARLY 151
Charly / Nov '88 / Charly.
LP. LIK 50
MC . . . . TCLIK 50
Decal / Nov '88 / Charly / Swift.

LATE, GREAT TOWNES VAN ZANDT, THE.
Tracks: No lonesome tune / Sad Cinderella / German mustard / Don't let the sunshine fool ya' / Honky tonkin' / Snow don't fall / Fraulein / Pancho and Lefty / If I needed you / Silver ships of Andilar / Heavenly houseboat blues.
■ LP. . . . . TOM 7001
Tomato (USA) / Mar '79.
LP. ED 293
Edsel / Aug '88 / Pinnacle.
■ CD . . . . CDCHARLY 145
Charly / Oct '88 / Charly.
LP. LIK 49
MC . . . . TCLIK 49
Decal / Oct '88 / Charly / Swift.

LIVE AND OBSCURE.
Tracks: Dollar bill blues / Many a fine lady / Pueblo waltz / Talking Thunderbird blues / Loretta / Snake Mountain blues / Waitin' around to die / Tecumseh Valley / Pancho and Lefty / You are not needed now.
LP. HLD 004
Heartland (1) / Oct '87 / Revolver-APT.
CD . . . . HLDCD 004
Heartland (1) / Apr '88 / Revolver-APT.

LIVE AT THE OLD QUARTER, HOUSTON, TEXAS.
Tracks: Announcement / Pancho and Lefty / Mr Mudd and Mr Gold / Don't you take it too bad / Tow girls / Fraternity blue / If I needed you / Brand new companion / White freightliner blues / To live is to fly / She came and she touched me / Talking thunderbird blues / Rex's blues / Nine pound hammer / For the sake of the song / No place to fall / Loretta / Kathleen / Tower song / Waiting 'round to die / Tecumseh valley / Lungs / Only him or me.
CD . . . . **CDCHARLY 183**
Double LP . . . . **LIKD 57**
MC Set . . . . **TCLIKD 57**
Decal / Oct '89 / Charly / Swift.

NASHVILLE SESSIONS, THE.
Tracks: At my window / Rex's blues / No place to fall / Buckskin stallion / White freight liner / Snake song, The / Loretta / Two girls / Spider song, The / When she don't need me / Pueblo waltz / Upon my soul.
CD **598 1079 29**
Tomato (USA) / Aug '93 / Revolver-APT.

OUR MOTHER THE MOUNTAIN.
Tracks: Be here to love me / Kathleen / She came and she touched me / Like a summer Thursday / Our mother the mountain / Second lovers song / St. John the gambler / Tecumseh valley / Snake mountain blues / My proud mountains / Why she's acting this way.
■ **CD** . . . . **CDCHARLY 104**
Charly / Jan '88 / Charly.
LP . . . . **LIK 17**
MC . . . . **TCLIK 17**
Decal / Jan '88 / Charly / Swift.

PANCHO & LEFTY (Live & Obscure).
Tracks: Dollar bill blues / Many a fine lady / Nothin' / Pueblo waltz / Talking thunderbird blues / Rex's blues / White freightliner blues / Loretta / Snake Mountain blues / Waitin' round to die / Tecumseh Valley / Pancho and Lefty / You are not needed now.
CD . . . . **EDCD 344**
Demon / Jan '92 / Pinnacle.

RAIN ON A CONGO DRUM.
Tracks: Mr. Mudd and Mr. Gold / If I needed you / Buckskin stallion blues / Short haired woman blues / Ain't leavin' your love / Pancho and Lefty / Dollar bill blues / Fraulein / Shrimp song, The / Blaze's blues / No place to fall / To live is to fly / Lungs / Nothin' / Tecumseh Valley / Dead flowers / White freightliner blues / Catfish song, The.
LP . . . . **EXLP 02**
Exile / Oct '91 / RTM / Pinnacle.
CD **2695752**
MC **2695754**
Silenz / Jun '92 / Terry Blood Dist.

TOWNES VAN ZANDT.
Tracks: For the sake of the song / Columbine / Waiting around to die / Don't take it too bad / Colorado girl / Lungs / I'll be here in the morning / Fare thee well, Miss Carousel / (Quick silver day dreams of) Maria / None but the rain.
CD . . . . **CDCHARLY 119**
LP . . . . **LIK 32**
MC . . . . **TCLIK 32**
Decal / Jun '88 / Charly / Swift.

TOWNES/LIVE IN THE LATIN QUARTER.
Tracks: Not Advised.
MC . . . . **TCAD 21**
Charly / Dec '90 / Charly.

Vanwarmer, Randy

Singer - songwriter/ guitarist, born Randall Van Wormer, 30.03.1955 Indian Hills, Colorado - moved to Cornwall, England in 1967 before returning to the States in 1979, at which time his Bearsville recording *Just When I needed You* was riding high on both sides of the Atlantic (US No. 4) in the respective pop charts. Turned his attention to country in 1980s and had modest single success of the 16th Avenue label. His subsequent album *Every now And Then* gaining sound acclaim. On the songwriting front, his songs have been covered by Michael Johnson / *Will Whisper your Name*, the Oak Ridge Boys *Bridges and Walls* both 1988 top ten hits Charley Pride, Johnny Rodriguez and Conway Twitty, augmented by such pop acts as Laura Brannigan, Millie Jackson and Pat Boone. (Mauric Hope July 1993)

EVERY NOW AND THEN.
Tracks: Stories, trophies and memories / Ain't nothin' coming / Every now and then / You were the one / Tomorrow would be better / She's the reason / Appaloosa night / Beautiful rose / Just when I needed you most / Love is a cross you bear / Safe harbour / I never got over you.
CD . . . . **ETCD 190**
Etude / Apr '90 / Total / BMG.
■ **MC** . . . . **ETCAS 190**
Etude / Apr '90.

HANGING ON TO HEAVEN.
Tracks: Hanging on to heaven.
7" . . . . **AAA 116**
Avatar / Dec '81 / C.M. Distribution.

JUST WHEN I NEEDED YOU MOST.
Tracks: Just when I needed you most / Your light.
7" . . . . **WIP 6516**
Island / Jul '81 / PolyGram.

JUST WHEN I NEEDED YOU MOST.
Tracks: Just when I needed you most / You were the one.
■ **7"** . . . . **ET 5**
Etude / Feb '90.

JUST WHEN I NEEDED YOU MOST (OLD GOLD).
Tracks: Just when I needed you most / I saw the light.
7" . . . . **OG 9800**
Old Gold / Oct '88 / Pickwick Records.

SUZI FOUND A WEAPON.
Tracks: Suzi found a weapon / I guess it never hurts to hurt sometimes.
7" . . . . **AAA 118**
Avatar / Feb '82 / C.M. Distribution.

TERRAFORM.
Tracks: Whatever you decide / I discovered love / All we have is tonight / I'm gonna prove it / Doesn't matter anymore / Down like a rock / Terraform / Falling free / I've got a ticket / 21st century / Farther along.
■ **LP** . . . . **ILPS 9618**
Island / Jun '80.

WARMER.
Tracks: Losing out on love / Just when I needed you most / Your light / Gotta get out of here / Convincing lies / Call me / Forever loving you / I could sing / Deeper and deeper / One who loves you.
■ **LP** . . . . **ILPS 9586**
Island / Oct '79.

WHATEVER YOU DECIDE.
Tracks: Whatever you decide / Losing out on love.
■ **7"** . . . . **WIP 6611**
Island / May '80.

Vega Brothers

INTO SOMETHING GOOD.
Tracks: Not Advised.
■ **LP** . . . . **IMCA 5686**
MCA (Import) / Mar '86.

Vincent, Gene

Seminal 50's rock 'n' roller Gene Vincent was born Eugene Vincent Craddock in Norfolk, Virginia, in 1935, and died in 1971. He broke a leg in the US Navy and subsequently wore a brace. *Be-Bop-A-Lula* featured in the film *The Girl Can't Help It* was his biggest hit and, like Buddy Holly and Eddie Cochran, he was more popular in the UK than America during his lifetime. His haircut and demeanour inspired British Teds more than any other single figure. His band, the Blue Caps, split up in 1958. He didn't get on with his record label and he emigrated to Britain in 1959, when Jack Good helped him become rock 'n' roll's biggest live draw. The car crash that killed Cochran injured his leg again in 1960. He returned to America in '65, recorded some country music and became a parody of himself. He drank too much and died of ulcers. (Donald Clarke)

2 ORIGINALS OF GENE VINCENT.
Tracks: Not Advised.
Double LP **2C 134 82076/7**
EMI (France) / '83 / EMI.

20 ROCK'N'ROLL HITS: GENE VINCENT.
Tracks: Not Advised.
LP . . . . **IC 064 85997**
EMI (Germany) / '83.

ABC OF ROCK.
Tracks: Not Advised.
LP P.Disc. . . . . **AR 30076**
Exclusive Picture Discs / Nov '87.

AIN'T THAT TOO MUCH.
Tracks: Ain't that too much / Bird doggin' / Love is a bird / Lonely street / Hurtin' for you baby / Poor man's prison / Born to be a rolling stone / Hi lili hi lo / I'm a lonesome fugitive / I've got my eyes on you.
LP . . . . **CBR 1006**
MC . . . . **KCBR 1006**
Premier (Sony) / '84 / Sony / Pinnacle.

BABY BLUE.
Tracks: Story of the rockers / Pickin poppies / Be bop a lula / Pistol packin mama / Say mama / Rocky road blues / Baby blue / Whole lotta shakin' goin' on / Day the world turned blue, The / Story of the rockers (instrumental).
LP . . . . **SHLP 122**
MC . . . . **SHTC 122**
Castle Showcase / Apr '86 / Arabesque Ltd.

BE-BOP-A-LULA.
Tracks: Not Advised.
MC . . . . **ENT MC 13060**
Entertainers / Mar '92.
CD . . . . **CDCD 1102**
Charly / Jul '93 / Charly.

BE-BOP-A-LULA.
Tracks: Be bop a lula.
■ **7"** . . . . **CL 14599**
Capitol / Jul '56.
7" **2C 008 81170**
EMI (France) / Apr '83 / EMI.
■ **7"** **G45 8**
EMI Golden 45's / Mar '84.

BEST OF GENE VINCENT AND HIS BLUE CAPS, THE.
Tracks: Race with the devil / Be bop a lula / Woman love / I sure miss you / Crazy legs / Gonna back up baby / Who slapped John / Important words / Rollin' Danny / In my dreams / Baby blue / Git it / Somebody help me / Summertime / Beautiful brown eyes / Say Mama.
■ **MC** . . . . **EG 2607604**
Capitol / Oct '85.
■ **LP** . . . . **EG 2607601**
Capitol / Oct '85.
CD . . . . **CZ 114**
Capitol / Jul '88 / EMI.
LP . . . . **ATAK 151**
MC . . . . **TCATAK 151**
Capitol / '89 / EMI.

BIRD DOGGIN'.
Tracks: I've got my eyes on you / Ain't that too much / Bird doggin' / Love is a bird / Lonely street / Hurtin' for you baby / Poor man's prison / Born to be a rolling stone / Hi lili hi lo / I'm a lonesome fugitive.
LP . . . . **BDL 3001**
Bulldog Records / Aug '82 / President Records / Jazz Music / Wellard Dist. / TKO Records Ltd.
MC . . . . **AJLK 3001**
N/A / Nov '82.

BIRD DOGGIN'.
Tracks: Bird doggin' / Ain't that too much.
7" . . . . **HLH 10079**
London-American / '66.

BLUE JEAN BOP.
Tracks: Not Advised.
LP **2C 064 82077**
EMI (France) / '83 / EMI.

BLUE JEAN BOP.
Tracks: Blue jean bop.
■ **7"** . . . . **CL 14637**
Capitol / Oct '56.

BOP THEY COULDN'T STOP, THE.
Tracks: Rockin robin / In the pines / Be bop a lula / Rainbow at midnight / Black letter / White lightning / Sexy ways / Ruby baby / Lotta lovin / Circle never broken / No.9 (Lonesome whistle) / Scarlet ribbons.
LP . . . . **MFLP 007**
MC . . . . **MFC 007**
Magnum Force / Jul '82 / Terry Blood Dist. / Jazz Music / Hot Shot.

BORN TO BE A ROLLING STONE.
Tracks: Born to be a rolling stone / Hi lili hi lo / Bird doggin' / Love is a bird / Ain't that too much / Am I that easy to forget / Hurtin' for you baby / I'm a lonesome fugitive / Poor man's prison / Words and music / I've got my eyes on you / Lonely street.
MC . . . . **KTOP 122**
Topline / Jan '85 / Charly / Swift / Black Sun Records.
LP . . . . **TOP 122**
Topline / Apr '87 / Charly / Swift / Black Sun Records.
CD . . . . **TOP CD 506**
Topline / Jan '87 / Charly / Swift / Black Sun Records.
LP . . . . **MA 11101183**
Masters (Holland) / '88.
MC . . . . **MAMC 01183**
Masters (Holland) / Dec '88.

CAPITOL YEARS, THE (BOX SET).
Tracks: Not Advised.
■ **LP Set** . . . . **BOX 108**
Charly / '87 / Charly.

CRAZY BEAT.
Tracks: Not Advised.
LP **2C 064 85037**
Capitol (import) / '83 / Pinnacle / EMI.

CRAZY TIMES.
Tracks: Not Advised.
■ **LP** . . . . **T 1342**
Capitol / Jul '60.
LP **1432**
Capitol / Oct '87 / EMI.

CRUISIN' WITH GENE VINCENT (Vincent, Gene & The Bluecaps).
Tracks: Not Advised.
LP . . . . **RSRLP 1007**
Rockstar (1) / Mar '85 / Swift / C.M. Distribution.

DRESSED IN BLACK.
Tracks: Be bop a lula / Say mama / Pistol packin' mama / Whole lotta shakin' goin' on / Good golly Miss Molly / Rocky road blues / Last word in lonesome, The / Pretty girls / Blue jean bop / Baby blue / I'm movin' on.
LP . . . . **MFLP 016**
Magnum Force / Nov '82 / Terry Blood Dist. / Jazz Music / Hot Shot.

EDDIE COCHRANE & GENE VINCENT (Vincent, Gene & Eddie Cochran).
Tracks: Not Advised.
LP P.Disc. . . . . .PM 2600440
Pathe Marconi (France) / Jun '84 / Thames Distributors Ltd.

EP COLLECTION, THE: GENE VINCENT.
Tracks: Race with the devil / Crazy legs / Hold me, hug me, rock me / Wayward wind / Somebody help me / Five feet of lovin' / Peace of mind / Look what you gone and done to me / Summertime / Keep it a secret / Rocky road blues / Dance to the bop / Baby blue / Dance in the street / Lovely Loretta / Important words / Gone gone gone / She she little Sheila / Weeping willow / Crazy beat / I'm gonna catch me a rat / If you want my lovin'.
CD . . . . SEECD 253
LP . . . . SEE 253
MC . . . . SEEK 253
See For Miles / May '89 / Pinnacle.

FOR THE COLLECTORS ONLY.
Tracks: Why don't we get ourselves together? / No. 9 (lonesome whistle) / Pistol packin' mama / Good golly Miss Molly / Be bop a lula / Speech message from Gene to English fans 1967 / Say mama / Rocky road blues / Baby blue / Maybellene / Whole lotta shakin' goin' on / Dance to the bop.
LP . . . . MFM 020
Magnum Force / Jun '84 / Terry Blood Dist. / Jazz Music / Hot Shot.

FROM L.A. TO 'FRISCO.
Tracks: Interviews / Sunshine / Lonesome whistle / Maybellene / Whole lotta shakin' goin' on / Woman love / Be bop a lula / Rainday sunshine / Green grass / Mister love / Roll over Beethoven.
LP . . . . MFLP 1023
Magnum Force / Nov '83 / Terry Blood Dist. / Jazz Music / Hot Shot.

GENE SINGS VINCENT, '56.
Tracks: Race with the devil / Be bop a lula / Jezebel / Who slapped John? / Jumps giggles and shouts / Blue jean bop / You told a fib / Teenage partner / Catman / Hold me, hug me, rock me / Cruisin' / Important words.
LP 2C 068 86309
Capitol (import) / '83 / Pinnacle / EMI.

GENE SINGS VINCENT, '57-'59.
Tracks: Time will bring you everything / True to you / Baby blue / Yes, I love you, baby / Teenage partner / Night is so lonely, The / In love again / Be bop boogie boy / Important words / My baby don't know / Vincent blues / Pretty pearly / Darlene / Greenback dollar.
LP 2C 068 86310
Capitol (import) / '83 / Pinnacle / EMI.

GENE VINCENT.
Tracks: Say mama / Blue jean bop / Wild cat / Right here on earth / Who slapped John / Walkin home from school / Five feet of lovin / She-she little Sheila / Be bop a lula / Jump back / Dance in the street / Pistol packin mama / Crazy beat / High blood pressure / Five days, five days / Bi bickey bi bo boo.
LP . . . . MFP 41 5749 1
■ MC . . . . MFP 41 5749 4
MFP / Apr '86.
■ MC . . . . TC MFP 5749
MFP / Sep '88.

GENE VINCENT AND THE BLUE CAPS.
Tracks: Not Advised.
LP 2C 064 82076
EMI (France) / '83 / EMI.

GENE VINCENT CD BOX SET (Complete Capitol & Columbia recordings 1956-64).
Tracks: Not Advised.
CD Set . . . . CDGV 1
EMI / Aug '90 / EMI.

GENE VINCENT RECORD DATE, A.
Tracks: Not Advised.
LP 2C 066 80038
EMI (France) / '83 / EMI.

GENE VINCENT ROCKS AND THE BLUE CAPS ROLL.
Tracks: Not Advised.
LP 2C 064 82075
EMI (France) / '83 / EMI.

GENE VINCENT SINGLES ALBUM, THE.
Tracks: Blue jean bop / Lotta lovin' / Race with the devil / Pistol packin' Mama / Baby blue / Wild cat / I'm goin' home / Woman love / Rocky road blues / Dance to the bop / Say mama / Crazy legs / My heart / Well I knocked him (bim bam) / She little Sheila / Rollin' Danny / Over the rainbow / Git it / Bi bickey bi bo boo / Be bop a lula.
■ MC . . . . TCEST 26223
Capitol / Apr '80.
■ LP . . . . .EST 26223
Capitol / May '81.

GENE VINCENT'S GREATEST.
Tracks: Be bop a lula / Race with the devil / Gonna back up baby / Who slapped John / Blue jean bop / Bop street / Jump back / Honey / Bi bickey bi bo boo / Lotta lovin' / Dance to the bop / Dance in the street / Rocky road blues / Say mama / Anna Annabelle / She she little Sheila / Wild cat.

■ LP. . . . . CAPTS 1001
Capitol / Feb '77.
LP. . . . . FA 3017
■ MC . . . . TCFA 3017
Fame / May '82.

GENE VINCENT'S TOP SIXTEEN.
Tracks: Not Advised.
LP. . . . . PM 1562474
Pathe Marconi (France) / '88 / Thames Distributors Ltd.

GREATEST HITS VOL 2: GENE VINCENT.
Tracks: Cruisin' / Baby blue / Crazy legs / Git it / Jumps, giggles and shouts / Hold me, hug me, rock me / Night is so lonely / Right here on earth / Pistol packin' mama / Brand new beat / Red blue jeans and a pony tail / Five feet of lovin' / I got a baby / Blues stay away from me / Woman love / Unchained melody.
■ LP. . . . . CAPS 1028
Capitol / '79.

HIS 30 ORIGINAL HITS.
Tracks: Not Advised.
CD . . . . .ENT CD 260
Entertainers / Mar '92.

I'M BACK AND I'M PROUD.
Tracks: Rockin robin / In the pines / Be bop a lula / Rainbow at midnight / Black letter / White lightning / Sexy ways / Ruby baby / Lotta lovin / Circle never broken / I heard that lonesome whistle blow / Scarlet ribbons.
CD . . . . CDNTF 001
Nightflite / Aug '87.
CD . . . . REP 4205-WP
Repertoire (Germany) / Aug '91 / Pinnacle.

I'M GOING HOME.
Tracks: I'm going home.
■ 7" . . . . CL 15215
Capitol / Aug '61.

IMPORTANT WORKS (Previously unissued recordings & studio chatter).
Tracks: Maybelline / You're the one for me / High blood pressure / Lonesome boy / Rip it up / I might have known / Beautiful brown eyes / Important words / Crazy beat / I'm gonna catch me a rat / It's been nice / That's the trouble with love / Good lovin' / Mr. Loneliness / Teardrops / If you want my lovin' / Spaceship to Mars.
LP. . . . . RSRLP 1020
Rockstar (1) / Nov '89 / Swift / C.M. Distribution.

INTO THE SEVENTIES.
Tracks: Sunshine / I need woman's love / 500 miles from home / Slow time's coming / Listen to the music / If only you could see me today / Million shades of blue, The / Tush hog / How I love them old songs / High on life / North Carolina line / There is something on your mind / Day the world turned blue, The / Boppin' the blues / Looking back / Oh lonesome me / Woman in black, The / Danse colinda (Available on CD only) / Geese (Available on CD only) / You can make it if you try (Available on CD only) / Our souls (Available on CD only).
LP. . . . . SEE 233
See For Miles / Jul '88 / Pinnacle.
CD . . . . SEECD 233
See For Miles / Sep '88 / Pinnacle.

LAST SESSION, THE (1.10.71).
Tracks: Sa mama / Be-bop-a-lula / Roll over Beethoven / Distant drums.
12" . . . . SFNT 001
Night Tracks / Jul '87 / Grapevine Distribution.

LONESOME FUGITIVE.
Tracks: Ain't that too much / Bird doggin' / Love is a bird / Lonely street / Hurtin' for you baby / Poor man's prison / Born to be a rolling stone / Hi lili hi lo / I'm a lonesome fugitive / I've got my eyes on you / Words and music / Am I that easy to forget.
LP. MFM 027
Magnum Force / '88 / Terry Blood Dist. / Jazz Music / Hot Shot.

MEMORIAL ALBUM.
Tracks: Be bop a lula / Race with the devil / Say mama / Frankie and Johnnie / Ready Teddy / Double talkin' baby / Dance in the street / Catman / Bop street / Flea brain / Maybellene / I got a baby / Somebody help me / I love you / Blue jean bop / Jump back / True to you / Woman love / Rollin' Danny / It's no lie / My baby don't know / Baby blue / Red blue jeans & a pony tail / I can't help it / Lovely Loretta / Over the rainbow / Lotta lovin' / 5 feet of lovin'.
Double LP 2C 156 81001/2
EMI (France) / '83 / EMI.

MY HEART.
Tracks: My heart.
■ 7" . . . . CL 15115
Capitol / Mar '60.

ON TOUR (see under Cochran, Eddie).

PISTOL PACKIN' MAMA.
Tracks: Pistol packin' mama.
■ 7" . . . . CL 15136
Capitol / Jun '60.

PRIVATE DETECTIVE.
Tracks: Private detective / You are my sunshine.
7" . . . . DB 7343
Columbia (EMI) / '64 / EMI.

RACE WITH THE DEVIL.
Tracks: Race with the devil.
■ 7" . . . . CL 14628
Capitol / Oct '56.

RAINY DAY SUNSHINE.
Tracks: Rainy day sunshine / Miss the love.
■ EP. . . . . MFEP 003
Magnum Force / Jan '81 / Terry Blood Dist. / Jazz Music / Hot Shot.

REBEL HEART.
Tracks: Not Advised.
CD . . . . .CDMF 087
Magnum / Nov '92 / Hot Shot / Swift / Cadillac Music / Arabesque Ltd. / Roots Records.

ROCK 'N' ROLL HEROES (see under Cochran, Eddie).

ROCK 'N' ROLL LEGENDS.
Tracks: Not Advised.
LP Set 2C 154 85071/4
EMI (France) / '83 / EMI.

ROCK ON WITH GENE VINCENT.
Tracks: Say Mama / Be bop a lula / Rip it up / Flea brain / Ready Teddy / Maybellene.
■ LP. . . . . MFP 50463
■ MC . . . . TCMFP 50463
MFP / Feb '80.

ROLL OVER BEETHOVEN.
Tracks: Roll over Beethoven.
7" . . . . BEEB 001
Beeb / '74.

SAY MAMA.
Tracks: Say mama / Lotta lovin' / Race with the devil.
■ 7" . . . . CL 15906
Capitol / Feb '77.

SHAKIN' UP A STORM (Vincent, Gene & The Shouts).
Tracks: Hey hey hey / Lavender blue / Private detective / Shimmy shammy shingle / Someday you'll want me to want you / Another Saturday night / Slippin' and slidin' / Long tall Sally / Send me some lovin' / Love love love / Good golly Miss Molly / Baby blue / Suzie Q / You are my sunshine.
LP. 3C 054 82021
EMI (Italy) / '83.
LP. . . . . EMS 1050491
MC . . . . TCEMS 1050491
EMI / Jun '83 / EMI.
LP. . . . . PM 1550821
Pathe Marconi (France) / Jun '84 / Thames Distributors Ltd.

SHE SHE LITTLE SHEILA.
Tracks: She she little Sheila / Say mama / Dance to the bop.
■ 7" . . . . CL 15202
Capitol / Jun '61.
■ 7" . . . . .CL 203
Capitol / Jun '61.

SINGS SONGS FROM HOT ROD GANG.
Tracks: Not Advised.
LP. . . . . DEMAND 0045
Demand / Oct '87.

SOUNDS LIKE GENE VINCENT.
Tracks: Not Advised.
LP. 2C 066 82074
EMI (France) / '83 / EMI.

STAR - '56-'58.
Tracks: Not Advised.
LP Set . . . . PM 1551953
Pathe Marconi (France) / Jun '85 / Thames Distributors Ltd.

THEIR FINEST YEARS 1956 & 1958 (see under Cochran, Eddie).

TWIST CRAZY TIMES.
Tracks: Not Advised.
LP. 2C 064 82073
EMI (France) / '83 / EMI.

WILD CAT.
Tracks: Wild cat.
■ 7" . . . . CL 15099
Capitol / Jan '60.

Vincent, Rhonda

DREAM COME TRUE, A.
Tracks: Not Advised.
LP. . . . . REBEL 1682
MC . . . . .REBELMC 1682
Rebel (1) / '90 / Projection / Backs Distribution.

NEW DREAMS AND SUNSHINE.
Tracks: Not Advised.
LP. . . . . REBEL 1665
MC . . . . .REBELMC 1665
Rebel (1) / '88 / Projection / Backs Distribution.

Vipers Skiffle Group

Important contributors to the short-lived skiffle movement of the mid 1950's, achieving chart status with *Don't you rock me daddy-o*, *Cumberland Gap* and *Streamline train*. Original group member Wally Whyton subsequently created Ollie Beak and other puppet friends prior to commencing a longterm BBC Radio 2 career presenting country music shows on a weekly basis. In 1992 he celebrated his 25th anniversary as a broadcaster. Other Vipers members included future Shadows Hank Marvin and Bruce Welch. (Tony Byworth - August 1993)

CUMBERLAND GAP.
Tracks: Cumberland gap.
■ 7" . . . . .R 4289
Parlophone / Mar '57.

DON'T YOU ROCK ME DADDY-O.
Tracks: Don't you rock me daddy-o.
■ 7" . . . . .R 4261
Parlophone / Jan '57.

STREAMLINE TRAIN.
Tracks: Streamline train.
■ 7" . . . . .R 4308
Parlophone / May '57.

VIPERS SKIFFLE GROUP (Coffee bar session).
Tracks: Gloryland / John B. sails / Wanderin / I saw the light / Precious memories / I know the Lord laid his hands on me / This land is your land / If I had a hammer / Easy rider / Cumberland gap / Hey Liley Liley o / Don't you rock me daddy-o / It takes a worried man / Maggie Mae / 10,000 years ago / Streamline train / Pick a bale of cotton / Ain't you glad / Darlin'.
LP . . . . ROLL 2011
Rollercoaster / May '86 / Rollercoaster Records / Swift.

W

Wade, Norman

REAL COUNTRY.
Tracks: Not Advised.
LP. . . . . JIN 9021
Jin / Swift.

Wagoneers

I CONFESS
Tracks: I confess / I can't stay.
12" . . . . AMY 461
■ 7" . . . . AM 461
A&M / Oct '88.

I WANNA KNOW HER AGAIN.
Tracks: I wanna know her again.
12" . . . . AMY 454
■ 7" . . . . AM 454
A&M / '88.
■ CD Single . . . . AMCD 454
A&M / '88.

STOUT AND HIGH.
Tracks: I confess / Help me to get over you / So many mistakes / Please don't think I'm guilty / Stout and high / I wanna know her again / It'll take some time / Lie and say you love me / Every step of the way / Hell town / All nite.
CD . . . . CDA 5200
LP. . . . . AMA 5200
■ MC . . . . AMC 5200
A&M / Oct '88.

Wagoner, Porter

Born in Missouri around 1930, Porter Wagoner signed with RCA and had Top Ten USA country hits in the mid-50's. His syndicated TV show in the 60's became the most popular of its kind. His stream of hits included *Misery Loves Company* in '62 his first No 1 followed by *Sorrow On The Rocks, Green Green Grass Of Home,Skid Row Joe, The Cold Hard Facts Of Life, The Carroll County Accident* and *Big Wind*, all Top Five in the 60's. His touring act was among the most popular, with his band the Wagonmasters and vocalist Norma Jean, replaced in the late 60's by Dolly Parton. Wagoner and Parton had eight Top Ten duet hits between 1967 and 1971 and carried on through the 70's. Both were also good writers. Their *Say Forever You'll Be Mine* in '75 was Parton's Song, *Is Forever Longer Than Always?* the following year, was his and he had a solo hit with her *Carolina Moonshine*. Wagoner was also Parton's producer. She began to feel constrained and their parting in the late 70's was acrimonious. He performed honky tonk, bluegrass and other styles, but always remained within the country genre. (Donald Clarke)

20 OF THE BEST: PORTER WAGONER.
Tracks: Satisfied mind, A / Your old love letters / Carroll County accident / Eat drink and be merry / I'll go down swinging / Company's coming / Big wind / Cold dark winter / Skid Row Joe / What would you do if Jesus came to your house / Green green grass of home / Everything I've always wanted / I just came to smell the flowers / Misery loves company / Old slew foot / What ain't to be just might happen / I've enjoyed as much of this as I can stand / When Lea Jane sang / Sorrow on the rocks / Cold hard facts of life, The.
■ LP. . . . . INTS 5197
RCA International / Jul '82.
LP. . . . . NL 89094
■ MC . . . . NK 89094
RCA International / '84.

BEST OF PORTER WAGONER.
Tracks: Cold hard facts of life / Big wind / Little boy's prayer / I couldn't wait forever / Men with broken hearts / Ol' slew foot / Carroll County accident / The / You gotta have a licence / When you're hot you're hot / Banks of the Ohio / Pastor's absent on vacation.
LP. . . . . LSA 3006
RCA / '74 / BMG.

BEST OF PORTER WAGONER AND DOLLY PARTON, THE (see under Parton, Dolly).

BLUEGRASS STORY, THE.
Tracks: Not Advised.
LP. . . . . HAT 3113
MC . . . . HATC 3113
Stetson / Sep '89 / Crusader Marketing Co. / Swift / Wellard Dist. / Midland Records / C.M. Distribution.

COUNTRY MEMORIES.
Tracks: Not Advised.
MC . . . . GM 0215

K-Tel Goldmasters / Aug '84 / C.M. Distribution / Arabesque Ltd. / Ross Records / PolyGram.

HITS OF DOLLY PARTON & PORTER WAGONER (Wagoner, Porter & Dolly Parton).
Tracks: Better move it on home / Just someone I used to know / If teardrops were pennies / Tomorrow is forever / We found it / Yours, love / Burning the midnight oil / Please don't stop loving me / Daddy was an old time preacher man / Say forever you'll be mine / Right combination, The / Lost forever in your kiss / Together always / How can I (help you forgive me).
LP. . . . . PL 42193
MC . . . . PK 42193
RCA / Oct '77 / BMG.

HITS OF PORTER WAGONER.
Tracks: Not Advised.
LP. . . . . PL 42182
MC . . . . PK 42182
RCA / Jun '78 / BMG.

JUST THE TWO OF US (see under Parton, Dolly).

LOVE SHINE.
Tracks: Not Advised.
LP. 20115
MC 40115
Astan (USA) / Nov '84.

MAKING PLANS (see under Parton, Dolly).

PORTER WAGONER.
Tracks: One more time / Love paid it all / Sugar foot rag / For a good time call Naomi / Louisiana Saturday night / Same way you came in, The / Sorrow on the rocks / What a memory we'd make / Satan wore satin / Uncle Pen.
MC . . . . ZCGAS 710
Audio Fidelity(USA) / Oct '84 / Stage One Records.
LP. . . . . IMCA 39053
MCA (Import) / Mar '86 / Pinnacle / Silver Sounds (CD).

PORTER WAGONER COLLECTION.
Tracks: Green, green grass of home / Ole slew foot / Skid Row Joe / I thought I heard you call my name / Katy did / Carroll County accident / I've enjoyed as much of this as I can stand / Pick me up on your way down / Trouble in amen corner / I'm so lonesome I could cry / He stopped loving her today / If you're gonna do me wrong (do it right) / Cold hard facts of life, The / Old love letters / Satisfied mind, A / Rose, The / Crying my heart out over you / Have I told you lately that I love you? / Misery loves company / Is anybody going to San Antone?.
Double LP . . . . PPD 2005
MC . . . . PPK 2005
Premier (Sony) / Sony / Pinnacle.

SATISFIED MIND.
Tracks: Satisfied mind, A / I like girls / Company's coming / Midnight / I guess I'm crazy / Living in the past / My bonfire / Ivory tower / Born to lose / That's it / I'm stepping out tonight / Tricks of the trade.
LP. . . . . HAT 3064
MC . . . . HATC 3064
Stetson / Apr '88 / Crusader Marketing Co. / Swift / Wellard Dist. / Midland Records / C.M. Distribution.

THIN MAN FROM WEST PLAINS.
Tracks: Settin' the woods on fire / Headin' for a weddin' / Lovin' letters / I can't live with you (I can't live without you) / Bringing home the bacon / An angel made of ice / Takin' chances / All roads lead to love / That's it / Beggar for your love, A / Trademark / Don't play that song / Flame of love, The / Dig that crazy moon / Trinidad / Bad news travels fast / Get out of here / My bonfire / Town crier / Love at first sight / Be glad you ain't me / Our shivaree / Company's comin' / Tricks of the trade / Satisfied mind, A / Good time was had by all, A / Hey, maw / How quick / I like girls / Itchin' for my baby / Eat, drink and be merry / I'm stepping out tonight / Let's squiggle / Living in the past / What would you do (if Jesus came to your house) / How can you refuse him now / Tryin' to forget the blues / Uncle pen / How I've tried / I've known you from somewhere / Seeing her only reminded me of you / Midnight / I guess I'm crazy / Born to lose / Ivory tower / I should be with you / Would you be satisfied / I'm day dreamin' tonight / I'll pretend / Who will he be / Good mornin', neighbor / My brand of blues / Thinking of you / I thought I heard you call my name / Turn it over in your mind / Pay day / Big wheels / Wound time can't erase, A / As long as I'm dreaming / Your love / Doll face / I don't want this memory / Burning bridges / Five O'clock in the morning / Heaven's just a prayer away / Tomorrow we'll retire / Just before dawn / Dear lonesome / Tell her lies and feed her candy / Haven't you heard / Don't ever leave me / Who'll buy the wine / Me and Fred and Joe and Bill / Out of sight out of mind / I thought of God / I'm gonna sing / Our song of love / Battle of little big horn, The / Luannie Brown / Your kind of people / Girl who didn't

need love, The / Legend of the big steeple / Wakin' up the crowd / An old log cabin for sale / Falling again / Old Jess / Your old love letters / Heartbreak affair / Everything she touches get the blues / I cried again / My name is mud / Sugarfoot rag / I thought I heard you calling my name / One way ticket to the blues / Take good care of her / I went out of my way / Tennessee border / I gotta find someone (who loves like I do) / Misery loves company / Cryin' loud / I wonder where you are tonight / Frosty the snowman / Cold dark waters / Ain't it awful / Wasted years / Private little world / I've enjoyed as much of this as I can stand / Blue house painted white.
LP. . . . . HAT 3099
MC . . . . HATC 3099
Stetson / Mar '89 / Crusader Marketing Co. / Swift / Wellard Dist. / Midland Records / C.M. Distribution.
CD Set . . . . BCD 15499
Bear Family / May '93 / Rollercoaster Records / Swift / Direct Distribution.

TODAY.
Tracks: I'm gonna feed you now / Ole slewfoot / I'm gonna act right / Tennessee Saturday night / High country / Banks of the Ohio / I couldn't care less / I guess I'm crazy / Old love letters / All I need.
■ LP. . . . . PL 13210
RCA / '79.

Wakefield, Frank

FRANK WAKEFIELD & GOOD OL' BOYS (Wakefield, Frank & Good Ol' Boys).
Tracks: Bluegrass band No. 1 / Blue and lonesome / T for Texas / Cattle in the cane / Musician's waltz / Hobo song, The / Sally Ann / I though I heard you calling my name / Train I ride, The / David, David / New musician's waltz / Greek, The.
LP. . . . . FF 049
Flying Fish (USA) / Mar '89 / Cadillac Music / Roots Records / Projection / C.M. Distribution / Direct Distribution / Jazz Music / Duncans / A.D.A. Distribution.

FRANK WAKEFIELD WITH COUNTRY COOKING.
Tracks: Not Advised.
LP. . . . . ROUNDER 0007
Rounder / '88 / Projection / Roots Records / Swift / C.M. Distribution / Topic Records / Jazz Music / Hot Shot / A.D.A. Distribution / Direct Distribution.

Wakely, Jimmy

Country-and-western/pop singer Jimmy Wakely (1915-82) was a major star of the late 40's and the 50's. The Jimmy Wakely Trio, with Johnny Bond and Scotty Harrell, were on Gene Autrey's radio show and Wakely appeared himself in more than 50 cowboy films. By the late 40's he was a big-name recording artist and his band included Spade Cooley, Cliffie Stone, Merle Travis and Wesley Tuttle. He recorded for US Decca then switched to Capitol. His biggest success was one of several duets with Margaret Whiting, *Slippin' Around* was a huge hit on both country and pop charts. The song, by Floyd Tillman, was one of the first "cheatin' songs" as country music began realistically to deal with the subject of adultery. Wakely had a network radio show until 1960, remained popular in the clubs and was still recording on his own Shasta label in the mid-70's. (Donald Clarke)

SANTA FE TRAIL.
Tracks: Along the Santa Fe trail / Take me back to my boots and saddle / There's a goldmine in the sky / Red river valley / Blue shadows on the trail / Call of the canyon, The / We'll rest at the end of the trail / Sierra Nevada / It's a lonely trail tonight / Carry me back to the lone prairie / True love (is a sacred thing).
LP. . . . . HAT 3012
MC . . . . HATC 3012
Stetson / Apr '86 / Crusader Marketing Co. / Swift / Wellard Dist. / Midland Records / C.M. Distribution.

Waldman, Wendy

LETTERS HOME.
Tracks: Not Advised.
CD . . . . YD 0102
LP. . . . . YL 0102
Cypress / Nov '88 / Sonet Records / Jazz Music / Wellard Dist. / C.M. Distribution.

Walk The West

WALK THE WEST.
Tracks: Living at night / Backside / Too much of a good thing / Precious time / Lonely boy / Sheriff of love /

■ DELETED

W 1

Think it over / Solitary man / Calvary Hill / Do you wanna dance.
MC . . . . .TCEST 2021
Capitol / Feb '87 / EMI.
■ LP. . . . . EST 2021
Capitol / Feb '87.

Walker, Billy

Born on 04.01.1929 in Ralls, Texas, gained initial acceptance as The Masked Singer, later affectionately taged the Tall Texan. Walker is a big favourite in the UK, due considerably to his 1980's appearance at the Wembley Country Music festival, taking up the mantle previously held by Marty Robbins - singing old western ballads. Like Robbins he too could work an audience with his showmanship. Walker's career has been one of the most enduring with over sixty hits, along with three modest duet entries with Barbara Fairchild in 1980. At only 15, Walker had his own radio show on KICA Clovis, New Mexico - before spells on Dallas' Big D Jamboree in 1949 (as the Masked Singer). During the Fifties he was to enjoy a spell on the Louisiana Hayride and the Ozark Jubilee, by which time he had two hits on Columbia. Additions to 1954's *Thank you for calling* were slow, *Charlie's shoes* his first and only chart topper (1962) shored - up with mid 60s top 5 affairs *Willie the weeper*, *Cross the brazos at waco*, *A million to one* and *Bear with me a little longer*. Walker, a member of the Grand Ole Opry performing in the traditional mould, was also to reap harvest with 1970's ballads *She goes walking through my mind*,*I'm gonna keep on lovin' you* and *Sing me a love song to my baby* (all on MGM). Labels that have proved resting places for him have included Momument, RCA, Casino, MRC, Scorpio, Caprice and his own Tall Texan outlet - from which Ireland's Hawk label issued *Wild Texas Rose* (1987). (Maurice Hope July 1993)

BEST OF THE BEST OF BILLY WALKER.
Tracks: Not Advised.
LP. . . . . GT 0040
Gusto (USA) / Mar '88.

BILLY WALKER.
Tracks: Charlie's shoes / Funny how time slips away / Cross the Brazos at Waco / Singing those lovesick blues again / Coffee brown eyes / I won't ever let you down / Stop hiding your heart / Am I blue / I'm gonna love you / Someone left the light on.
LP. . . . . .IMCA 39090
MC . . . . .IMCAC 39090
MCA / Mar '87 / BMG.

FOR MY FRIENDS.
Tracks: Singing those lovesick blues again / Jesse / He sang the songs about El Paso / Charlie's shoes / Touch of my woman / Don't ever leave me in Texas / Instead of giving up (I'm giving in) / Love boat / Cross the Brazos at Waco / Anything your heart desires / Cool in the daylight (fire in the dark) / Funny how time slips away.
LP. . . . . BDL 3004
Bulldog Records / Aug '87 / President Records / Jazz Music / Wellard Dist. / TKO Records Ltd.

PRECIOUS MEMORIES.
Tracks: Not Advised.
LP. . . . . .WST 9664
MC . . . . .WC 9664
Word (UK) / Sep '85 / Word Records (UK) / Sony.

Walker, Billy Jr.

BILLY WALKER JR.
Tracks: Under the stars / 5th of July / Ballerina dance / Marotta / Hot steel / China girl / Night rider / Add two / Perfect love / Water bells.
CD . . . . .GEFD 24469
MC . . . . .GEFC 24469
Geffen / Mar '92 / BMG.

HOUSE, THE.
Tracks: Midnight romance / Flower song / Creation / Peace and harmony / Defeated creek / Lost in Mexico / Raindrops on the roof / Moonlight on the water / Enchanted forest / Children play, The.
CD . . . . MCAD 42041
LP. . . . . .IMCA 42041
MC . . . . .IMCAC 42041
MCA / Mar '88 / BMG.

WALK, THE.
Tracks: Walk, The / Hourglass / Dream on / Mystery man / Street dancing / Illusions / Free flight / Fields of stone / Crystal speak to me / Breezes.
CD . . . . .GEFD 24315
MC . . . . .GEFC 24315
Geffen / May '91 / BMG.

Walker, Charlie

Born 11.11.1926 on a farm in Copeville, Collin County, Texas - one time disc jockey, including a spell for the Armed Forces Network during world War II. Walker had already sampled performing himself, playing in Bill Boyd's Cowboy Ramblers in 1943. It wasn't until 1956 that Walker, a highly - rated DJ, MC sports broadcaster gained a record release. His single *Only you, only you* making the top ten, followed two years later when *Pick me up on your way down* (No.2) provided him with an all-time high. Opry member since 1967, Walker would never again recapture such success, his honky tonk style found him scoring on Epic, RCA and Capitol, decorating the scene with hits *Wild as a wildcat*, *Don't squeeze my sharmon* and *Will you buy the wine* by 1974. (Maurice Hope - July 1993)

CHARLIE WALKER.
Tracks: Pick me up on your way down / Mean woman with green eyes / One step away / If I were you I'd fall in love with me / I was doin' her wrong / Don't squeeze my sharmon / Right or wrong / I'm gonna get together with your.. / That ol' Texas two step / Does Fort Worth ever cross your mind.
LP. . . . . .IMCA 39078
MC . . . . .IMCAC 39078
MCA / Mar '87 / BMG.

WHO WILL BUY THE WINE (see under Reeves, Jack).

Walker, Jerry Jeff

Jerry Jeff Walker, born Paul Crosby on 16.3.1942, was raised in his native upstate New York - taking his name from the label on a beer bottle. It was in his adopted state of Texas, that he gained recognition as one of it's most revered contemporary country singer-songwriters, slongside Guy Clark & Townes Van Zandt. His first recordings were 1966, with the group Circus Maximus, quickly followed with solo releases *Drifting way of life* (Vanguard), and three on the Atco label, including his *Mr. Bojangles* album, Walkers's cover of the title track making only minor placings in the US pop charts in 1986. This later became a Top Ten charter for the Nitty Gritty Dirt Band in 1970. Jerry Jeff, backed by his Lost Gonzo Band, saw his solo career gain impetus in the Seventies with a string of notable, finely-crafted albums on MCA. With releases *Jerry Jeff Walker*, *Walker's collectables*, *It's a good night for singing*, the live album *Viva terlingua* (recorded out in Luckenbach, Texas on a mobile recording unit) and *A man must carry on* Jerry Jeff earned himself a strong Texas following (along with his free wheeling stage performances). Walker's music lost that sharp innovative feel as the Seventies came to a close, with rock and jazz-edged albums on MCA and Elektra proving disappointing. Since his seemingly barren spell, Walker has re-emerged on the Tried & True label, turning out worthy releases *Gypsy song man* and *Live at Gruene Hall* - the 1989 release featuring JJW's much requested latter-day minor hit *Man with the big hat* - penned by Steve Fromholz. Even as the Eighties were ebbing, Walker's music was still very much held in high esteem. *Navajo rug* in 1991 found JJ welding his own material with that from Fromholz, Guy Clark & Bill Staines . Walker's driving 1970's style returned for much of *Hill country rain*, his 1992 offering, where *Curly and Lil* & *Hill country rain* originally on his 1972 Jerry Jeff Walker release (possibly his finest era) gain new covers. A man who's played toured the UK a few occasions (playing both the Wembley Country & Cambridge folk festivals) in the past ten years and still revered both sides of the Atlantic. (Maurice Hope - July 1993)

CONTRARY TO ORDINARY.
Tracks: Tryin' to hold up the sail with you / Saturday night special / Suckin' a big bottle of gin / What are you doing / Till I gain control again / Contrary to ordinary / We were kinda crazy then / Deeper than love / I spent all my money on lovin' you / Carry me away.
LP. . . . . MCF 2851
MCA / '78 / BMG.

DRIFTIN' WAY OF LIFE.
Tracks: Driftin' way of life / Morning song to Sally / Shell game / Ramblin' scramblin' / No roots in ramblin' / Old road / North Cumberland blues / Let it ride / Fading lady / Gertrude / Dust on my boots.
CD . . . . VMD 73124
Vanguard / Complete Record Co. Ltd.

GYPSY SONGMAN.
Tracks: Gypsy songman / David and me / Mr. Bojangles / Hands on the wheel / Ramblin' hearts / Then came the children / She knows her daddy sings / Long afternoons / Borderline / Driftin' way of life / Hard livin' / Railroad lady / Jaded lover / Rain just falls / Night riders lament / We were kind of crazy then / Cadillac cowboy / Pass it on / Charlie Dunn / Hill country rain.
CD . . . . SDCD 900 419
TM (Temple Music) / Jan '89.
CD . . . . RCD 20071
MC . . . . RACS 0071
Rykodisc / May '92 / Revolver-APT.

HILL COUNTRY RAIN.
Tracks: Not Advised.
CD . . . . RCD 10241
MC . . . . TTCS 9241
Rykodisc / Jun '92 / Revolver-APT.

IT'S A GOOD NIGHT FOR SINGIN'.
Tracks: Lookin' for the heart of a Saturday night / Standin' at the big motel / Couldn't do nothing right / Won't you give me one more chance / Head full of nothin' / Old five and dimers like me / Very short time / Some day I'll get out of these bars / Stoney / Dear John letter lounge / Leroy / It's a good night for singing.
LP. . . . . MCG 3522
MCA / '76 / BMG.

JERRY JEFF WALKER.
Tracks: Eastern Avenue river / Railway blues / Lone wolf / Bad news / Boogie mama / I'm not strange / Her good lovin' grace / Comfort and crazy / Follow / Banks of old Bandera.
■ LP. . . . . K 52106
Elektra / Mar '79.

LEAVIN' TEXAS.
Tracks: Leavin' Texas / Ro-deo-deo cowboy.
■ 7" . . . . MCA 340
MCA / Jan '78.

LIVE AT GRUENE HALL.
Tracks: Lovin' makes livin' worthwhile / Pickup truck song / Long, long, time / I feel like Hank Williams tonight / Man with the big hat / Quiet faith of man / Little bird / Woman in Texas / Rodeo wind / Trashy wind.
CD . . . . RCD 10123
MC . . . . RACS 0123
Rykodisc / May '92 / Revolver-APT.

NAVAJO RUG.
Tracks: Navajo rug / Just to celebrate / Blue mood / Lucky man / Detour / I'm all through throwing good love after bad / Rockin' on the river / Nolan Ryan (a hero to us all) / Flowers in the snow / If I'd loved you then.
CD . . . . RCD 10175
MC . . . . TTCS 9175
Rykodisc / Jul '91 / Revolver-APT.

Wallace, Jerry

YOU'RE SINGING OUR LOVE SONG TO SOMEBODY ELSE.
Tracks: You're singing our love song to somebody else.
■ 7" . . . . HLH 9110
London-American / Jun '60.

Walsh, Sean

COUNTRY AND IRISH.
Tracks: Not Advised.
MC . . . . .GTDC 103
GTD / '89 / A.D.A Distribution.

HAYMAKER, THE.
Tracks: Not Advised.
MC . . . . .HAYC 001
GTD / '89 / A.D.A Distribution.

WILL THE CIRCLE BE UNBROKEN.
Tracks: Not Advised.
MC . . . . .GTDC 008
GTD / '89 / A.D.A Distribution.

Walters, Hank

PROGRESS.
Tracks: Not Advised.
LP. . . . . ROXLP 003
Rox / Dec '79 / Rox Records.

Wangford, Hank

Born Samuel Hutt on 15.10.1940, he became a London - based gynaecologist. After living in the States for awhile he returned to England and met, through his surgery, Gram Parsons in 1970. Took an eclectic interest in country music, its origins and roots in general. Hank (his music business handle) has built himself up a healthy club following, both through his own rough-hewn vocal efforts,his entertaining band and via his TV programmes on Channel 4 *A - Z of Country and Western* and *Big, big country* which at times reflect his offbeat appearance. Album releases have been on Rue, Cowpie, WEA and Hawk who put out Hank Wangford and the Lost Cowboys live album *Hard shoulder to cry on*. (Maurice Hope - August 1993)

COWBOYS STAY ON LONGER (Wangford, Hank Band).
Tracks: Not Advised.
CD . . . . .CDSD 070
Magnum / '89 / Hot Shot / Swift / Cadillac Music / Arabesque Ltd. / Roots Records.

COWBOYS STAY ON LONGER (Wangford, Hank Band).
Tracks: Cowboys stay on longer.
12" . . . . HONKY TX 12
Honky / Mar '87.

HANK WANGFORD.
Tracks: Not Advised.
LP. . . . . .COW 1
Cow Pie / May '85 / Cow Pie Records.

W 2 ■ DELETED

HANK WANGFORD BUMPER PACK, THE.
Tracks: Not Advised.
MC . . . . **CCP 1**
Cow Pie / Dec '84 / Cow Pie Records.

HANK WANGFORD CHRISTMAS EP, THE.
Tracks: Not Advised.
■ **EP** . . . . **CCP 2**
Cow Pie / Dec '84 / Cow Pie Records.

HARD SHOULDER TO CRY ON (Wangford, Hank & The Lost Cowboys).
Tracks: Dim lights / You're still on my mind / Jealousy / My lips want to stay (but my heart wants to go) / Birmingham hotel / Stormy horizons / My baby's gone / Gonna paint this town / Jalisco / What happens / Get rhythm / Prisoner song, The / Lay down my old guitar / I'm coming home / End of the road.
CD . . . . **HANKCD 001**
MC . . . . **HANKC 001**
Sincere Sounds / Mar '93 / Pinnacle.

LIVE: HANK WANGFORD.
Tracks: Not Advised.
LP . . . . **COW 2**
Cow Pie / May '82 / Cow Pie Records.

RIDERS IN THE SKY.
Tracks: Riders in the sky / Pain in my wrist.
12" . . . . **CB 411-12**
■ **7"** . . . . **CB 411**
Charisma / Nov '83.

RODEO RADIO.
Tracks: Not Advised.
LP . . . . **SITU 16**
■ **MC** . . . . **SITC 16**
Situation 2 / Sep '85.

ROOTIN' TOOTIN' SANTA CLAUS (Wangford, Hank Band).
Tracks: Rootin' tootin' Santa Claus / White Christmas / Mama won't be home for Christmas.
7" . . . . **PIE 005**
Cow Pie / Nov '82 / Cow Pie Records.

STORMY WEATHER.
Tracks: Not Advised.
CD . . . . **RUECD 004**
LP . . . . **RUE 004**
■ **MC** . . . . **RUEMC 004**
New Routes / Sep '90.

WILD THING.
Tracks: Wild thing / All I want.
7" . . . . **PIE 001**
Cow Pie / Jun '80 / Cow Pie Records.

Ward, Fields

BURY ME NOT ON THE PRAIRIE.
Tracks: Not Advised.
LP . . . . **ROUNDER 0036**
Rounder / '88 / Projection / Roots Records / Swift / C.M. Distribution / Topic Records / Jazz Music / Hot Shot / A.D.A Distribution / Direct Distribution.

Wariner, Steve

Born 25-12-1954 in Noblesvile, Indiana - singer/songwriter guitarist who served his apprenticeship playing back-up for such luminaries as Dottie West (1971 - 1974), Bob Luman and his idol, Chet Atkins, who got him a recording deal with RCA in 1977 (although it wasn't until 1980 that Wariner's promise came to fruition). His single *Your memory* made country's top ten slot, with *All roads leads to you* in 1981 making No.1. Wariner is a fine all - round performer and writer/guitarist and singer, his ballads rendering him no fewer than another seven chart topping singles during the 1980's. *Some fools never learn, You can dream on me, Life's highway, Small town girl, The weekend* and *Lynda* all coming during a two year (1985 - 1987) spell on his new label), MCA. Before he closed his account with MCA he was to score another three chart toppers with *Where did I go wrong, I got dreams* and *The domino theory*. In 1990, amazingly he found himself without a label and his next stop was the fledgling label Arista - his debut 1991 album *I'm ready* selling a million copies. On the singles front, his remake of Bill Anderson's *Tips of my fingers* made No.1. whilst his part on Mark O'Connor's *Restless* (Carl Perkins oldie) mustn't be left out. Wariner, Vince Gill and Ricky Skaggs gave sterling support as the New Nashville Cats on what was voted by the CMA in 1991 as 'Vocal event of the year'.

DRIVE.
Tracks: Drive / If I didn't love you / One believer / It won't be over you / (You could always) come back / Drivin' and cryin' / Same mistake again, The / Missing you / Married to a memory / Sails.
CD **7822 18721-2**
Arista / Oct '93 / BMG.

I GOT DREAMS.
Tracks: Not Advised.
CD . . . . **MCAD 42272**
LP . . . . **MCA 42272**
MC . . . . **MCAC 42272**
MCA / Jun '89 / BMG.

IT'S A CRAZY WORLD.
Tracks: Small town girl / Lynda / If I could make a livin' (out of lovin' you) / There's always a first time / Why do heroes die so young / When it rains / It's a crazy world / Hey alarm clock / Weekend, The / Fast break.
CD . . . . **MCAD 5926**
LP . . . . **MCF 3363**
■ **MC** . . . . **MCFC 3363**
MCA / Apr '87.

LAREDO.
Tracks: Not Advised.
CD . . . . **MCAD 42335**
MCA / May '90 / BMG.

WEEKEND, THE.
Tracks: Weekend, The / Why do heroes die so young?.
7" . . . . **MCA 1204**
MCA / Oct '87 / BMG.

Warren, Johnny

JUST PLAYIN' IN THE RAIN.
Tracks: Indian creek / Tom and Jerry / 50 year ago waltz / Limerock / Tea kettle hornpipe / Saint Anne's reel / Just playin' in the rain / Frank Ryan's hornpipe / Hiram's hornpipe / What a friend we have in Jesus / Daley's reel / Black eyed Susan Brown.
LP . . . . **REBEL 1614**
MC . . . . **REBELMC 1614**
Rebel (1) / '83 / Projection / Backs Distribution.

Warren, Paul

Born Hickman County, Tennessee 1917. Died Jan 12th 1977. Paul worked for almost 23 years with Lester Flatt, starting back in 1954 with Flatt and Earl Scruggs, during which time he made appearances numbering into the thousands - on stage, radio and TV. Paul's first professional work was with Johnny and Jack/The Kitty Wells Show, 1938-1953.

AMERICA'S GREATEST BREAKDOWN FIDDLER (Warren, Paul & Lester Flatt & Nashville Grass).
Tracks: Durham's reel / Indian creek / Katy Hill / 8th of January / Twinkle little star / Pretty Polly Ann / Denver belle / Listen to the mockingbird / Stony fork / Liberty / Leather britches / Sally Johnson / Dusty Miller / Hop light ladies / New five cents / Grey eagle / Sally Goodin' / Tennessee wagoner / Hoedown in Hickman county / Black eyed Susan Brown.
LP . . . . **CMH 6237**
■ **MC** . . . . **CMHC 6237**
CMH (USA) / '79.

Watkins, Geraint

GERAINT WATKINS AND DOMINATORS (Watkins, Geraint & Dominators).
Tracks: Blue moon of Kentucky / Cakewalk into town / Casting my spell / Deep in the heart of Texas / Don't you just know it / Grow, too old / I got to find my baby / If walls could talk / In the night / Man smart, woman smarter / My baby left me / Nobody / Paralysed.
■ **LP** **9102033**
Vertigo / '79.

I'M A FOOL TO CARE.
Tracks: I'm a fool to care.
7" . . . . **BEEB 028**
Beeb / Sep '81.

NOBODY (Watkins, Geraint & Dominators).
Tracks: Nobody / My babe left me.
■ **7"** **6059224**
Vertigo / Apr '79.

Watson Family

TRADITION.
Tracks: Not Advised.
LP . . . . **ROUNDER 0129**
Rounder / Jan '87 / Projection / Roots Records / Swift / C.M. Distribution / Topic Records / Jazz Music / Hot Shot / A.D.A Distribution / Direct Distribution.

WATSON FAMILY TRADITION THE.
Tracks: Georgie / Fish in the mill pond / Children's songs / I heard my mother weeping / Reuben's train / Biscuits / Tucker's barn / Give the fiddler a dram / Am I born to die / Marthy, won't you have some good old cider / Roving on a winter's night, A / Arnold's tune / Pretty saro / Early early in the spring / Little Maggie / Bill Banks / Rambling hobo / One morning in may / Faithful soldier, The / Omie wise / Jimmy Sutton.
LP **12TS 336**
Topic / Jan '81 / Roots Records / Jazz Music / C.M. Distribution / Cadillac Music / Direct Distribution / Swift / Topic Records.

Watson, Doc

Blind from birth, Doc Watson became one of the best flat-picking guitarists in traditional music. Born in Deep Gap, North Carolina, in 1923, he started playing in 1954 in a band for local dances and other functions. He was discovered when Folkways came to town to record his neighbour, Clarence "Tom" Ashley. He recorded for Vanguard in the mid-60s. His son, Merle, joined him: born in 1949, Merle, who soon became almost as good, was killed in a tractor accident in 1985. *Then And Now and Two Days In November*, on the Poppy label, won Grammies in '73 and '74. Doc and Merle played on the Nitty Gritty Dirt Band's *Will The Circle Be Unbroken?* His latest albums are on Sugar Hill and Flying Fish. (Donald Clarke)

BALLADS FROM DEEP (Watson, Doc & Merle).
Tracks: Roll in my sweet baby's arms / Wreck, The / Cuckoo, The / My rough and rowdy ways / Gambler's yodel.
CD . . . . **VMD 6576**
MC . . . . **VMMC 6576**
Vanguard / Mar '90 / Complete Record Co. Ltd.

DOWN SOUTH.
Tracks: Solid gone / Bright sunny south / Slidin' delta / Coal miner's blues / Hesitation blues / What a friend we have in Jesus / Fifteen cents / Twin sisters / Hobo, The / Cotton eyed Joe / Hello stranger / Down south.
CD . . . . **SHCD 3742**
LP . . . . **SH 3742**
MC . . . . **ZCSH 3742**
Sugarhill(USA) / Mar '85 / Roots Records / Projection / Impetus Records / C.M. Distribution / Jazz Music / Swift / Duncans / A.D.A Distribution.

ESSENTIAL DOC WATSON VOL.1.
Tracks: Tom Dooley / Alberta / Froggie went a courtin' / Beaumont rag / St. James hospital / Muskrat / Down in the valley to pray / Blue railroad train / Rising sun blues / Shady grove / My rough and rowdy ways / Train that carried my girl from town, The.
CD . . . . **VMCD 7308**
LP . . . . **VMLP 7308**
MC . . . . **VMMC 7308**
Vanguard / Oct '89 / Complete Record Co. Ltd.

ESSENTIAL DOC WATSON, THE.
Tracks: Tom Dooley / Alberta / Froggie went a courtin' / Beaumont rag / St. James hospital / Down in the valley to pray / Blue railroad train / Rising sun blues / Shady grove / My rough and rowdy ways / Train that carried my girl from town, The / Black mountain rag / I was a stranger / Blue Ridge Mountain blues / Country blues / Ground hog / Little orphan girl / Blackberry blossom / Goin' down the road feeling bad / Rambling hobo / Little Omie Wise / Handsome Molly / White house blues / I want to love him more / Way downtown.
Double LP . . . . **VSD 45/46**
Vanguard / Jan '74 / Complete Record Co. Ltd.

FOLK AND COUNTRY LEGEND,A (Watson, Doc & Merle).
Tracks: Not Advised.
LP . . . . **LR 44.008**
L&R / '82 / New Note.

GUITAR ALBUM, THE (Watson, Doc & Merle).
Tracks: Sheeps in the meadow / Stoney fork / Talking to Casey / Liza / Lady be good / Black pine waltz / Guitar polka / Going to Chicago blues / Black mountain rag / Cotton row / John Henry / Worried blues / Twinkle twinkle / Take me out to the ballgame / Gonna lay down my old guitar.
■ **LP** . . . . **FF 301**
Flying Fish (USA) / Dec '88.
CD . . . . **FF 301CD**
MC . . . . **FF 301C**
Flying Fish (USA) / Jul '92 / Cadillac Music / Roots Records / Projection / C.M. Distribution / Direct Distribution / Jazz Music / Duncans / A.D.A Distribution.

IN THE PINES.
Tracks: Doc's guitar / In the pines / Mama blues / Sally Goodin / Am I born to die / What would you give in exchange for your soul / Tom Dooley / Little stream of whiskey / Worried blues / Doc's talking blues / Liza Jane / Midnight on the stormy deep.
LP . . . . **SDLP 1012**
Sundown / Nov '84 / Terry Blood Dist. / Jazz Music / C.M. Distribution.
MC . . . . **SDC 1012**
Sundown / Aug '85 / Terry Blood Dist. / Jazz Music / C.M. Distribution.

MY DEAR SOUTHERN HOME.
Tracks: My dear old southern home / Ship that never returned, The / Your lone journey / My friend Jim / No telephone in heaven / Dream of the miner's child / Wreck of old number nine / Grandfather's clock / Don't say goodbye if you say you love me / Sleep baby sleep / Signal light / That silver haired Daddy of mine / Life is like a river.
CD . . . . **SHCD 3795**
MC . . . . **SHMC 3795**
Sugarhill(USA) / '91 / Roots Records / Projection / Impetus Records / C.M. Distribution / Jazz Music / Swift / Duncans / A.D.A Distribution.

OLD TIMEY CONCERT.
Tracks: New river train / What does the deep sea say / Sunny Tennessee / Walkin' in Jerusalem / Sittin' on top of the world / Pretty little pink / My home's across the Blue Ridge Mountains / Slewfoot / Little orphan girl /

Long journey home / Rank stranger / Crawdad / Fire on the mountain / Eastbound train / On the old banks of the old Tennessee / Mountain dew / Corina, Corina / Footprints in the snow / I saw a man a the close of day / Cacklin' hen, The / Wanted man / Way downtown / Will the circle be unbroken.
CD Set . . . . **VCD 107/8**
Vanguard / Dec '92 / Complete Record Co. Ltd.

ON PRAYING GROUND.
Tracks: You must come in at the door / Precious Lord / On praying ground / I'll live on / Gathering buds / Beautiful golden somewhere / We'll work 'till Jesus comes / Ninety and nine, The / Farther along / Christmas lullaby / Did Christ o'er sinners weep / Uncloudy day.
CD . . . . **SHCD 3779**
LP . . . . **SH 3779**
MC . . . . **ZCSH 3779**
Sugarhill(USA) / '90 / Roots Records / Projection / Impetus Records / C.M. Distribution / Jazz Music / Swift / Duncans / A.D.A Distribution.

OUT IN THE COUNTRY.
Tracks: Not Advised.
LP . . . . **MA 24983**
Masters (Holland) / '88.

PICKIN' THE BLUES (Watson, Doc & Merle Watson).
Tracks: Mississipppi heavy water blues / Sittin' hear pickin' the blues / Stormy weather / Windy and warm / St. Louis blues / Jailhouse blues / Freight train blues / Hobo Bill's last ride / Carroll county blues / Blue ridge mountain blues / I'm a stranger here / Honey babe blues.
■ **LP** . . . . **FF 352**
Flying Fish (USA) / Jan '86.
CD . . . . **FF 352CD**
MC . . . . **FF 352C**
Flying Fish (USA) / Jul '92 / Cadillac Music / Roots Records / Projection / C.M. Distribution / Direct Distribution / Jazz Music / Duncans / A.D.A Distribution.

PORTRAIT: DOC WATSON.
Tracks: I'm worried now / Nobody knows but me / Leaving London / Stay in the middle of the road / Risin' sun blues / George Gudger's overalls / Tucker's barn / Storms on the ocean / Prayer bells of Heaven / Tough luck man / My blue eyed Jane.
LP . . . . **SH 3759**
MC . . . . **ZCSH 3759**
Sugarhill(USA) / Oct '88 / Roots Records / Projection / Impetus Records / C.M. Distribution / Jazz Music / Swift / Duncans / A.D.A Distribution.

RED ROCKING CHAIR (Watson, Doc & Merle).
Tracks: Sadie / Fisher's hornpipe / Devil's dream / Along the road / Smoke, smoke, smoke / Below freezing / California blues / John Hurt / Mole in the ground / Any old time / Red rocking chair / How long blues / Down yonder.
■ **LP** . . . . **FF 252**
Flying Fish (USA) / Dec '88.
CD . . . . **FF 252CD**
MC . . . . **FF 252C**
Flying Fish (USA) / Jul '92 / Cadillac Music / Roots Records / Projection / C.M. Distribution / Direct Distribution / Jazz Music / Duncans / A.D.A Distribution.

REMEMBERING MERLE (Watson, Doc & Merle).
Tracks: Not Advised.
■ **CD** . . . . **DFG 8427 CD**
Dixie Frog / Jul '92.

RIDIN' THE MIDNIGHT TRAIN.
Tracks: I'm going back to the old home / Greenville high trestle / Highway of sorrow / Fill my way with love / We'll meet again sweetheart / Ridin' that midnight train / Stone's rag / Ramshackle shack / Midnight on the stormy deep / Blue baby eyes / What does the deep sea say / Let the church roll on / Sweet heaven when I die.
CD . . . . **SHCD 3752**
LP . . . . **SH 3752**
MC . . . . **ZCSH 3752**
Sugarhill(USA) / Dec '88 / Roots Records / Projection / Impetus Records / C.M. Distribution / Jazz Music / Swift / Duncans / A.D.A Distribution.

SONGS FOR LITTLE PICKERS.
Tracks: Talkin' guitar / Mole in the ground / Mama blues / Foggy went a courtin' / Shady grove / Riddle song, The / Sing song kitty / John Henry / Sally Goodin / Crawdad song / Grass grew all around, The / Liza Jane / Tennessee stud, The.
CD . . . . **SHCD 3786**
LP . . . . **SH 3786**
MC . . . . **ZCSH 3786**
Sugarhill(USA) / '90 / Roots Records / Projection / Impetus Records / C.M. Distribution / Jazz Music / Swift / Duncans / A.D.A Distribution.

TREASURES UNTOLD (Watson, Doc & Family).
Tracks: Intro / Lights in the valley / Beaumont rag / I heard my mother weeping / Billy in the low ground / Omie wise / Rueben's train / Hick's farewell / Ramblin' hobo / White house blues / Jimmy Sutton / The old buck ram / I want him to love me more / Grandfather's clock / Chinese breakdown / Handsome Molly / Beaumont rag (2) / Farewell blues / Lonesome road blues / Footprints in the snow.
CD . . . . **VCD 77001**
MC . . . . **V 77001**
Vanguard / '91 / Complete Record Co. Ltd.

Watson, Gene

Watson a dyed-in-the-wool country act and possessor of one of the music's finest singing voices, was born on 11.10.1943 in Palestine, Texas and raised in Paris, Texas. Ironically, he enjoyed his most productive period during what was viewed as traditional-based country music's undermined years (the 1970's) and beyond. Gene started out at 13, fronting Gene Watson and the Other Four and in 1967 he became the resident at Houston's Dynasty Club, during his time there he recorded singles for various local labels, including the 1975 minor placing *Bad Water* on Resco. Other material being on Tonka and Wide World, who were later to release the album *Gene Watson* . His longtime manager/producer Russ Reeder guided his career to fruition and beyond. From his Capitol debut single *Love in the hot afternoon* the affable Texan was to consistently find the higher reaches of the Billboard Country Singles chart during the following ten years. Amongst Watson's early successes there was to be the 1975 - 1977 top five cuts *Where love begins* and *Paper Rosie*, a song that alongside 1979's top singles *Farewell party* and *Pick the wildwood flower* were to become very much Watson's stock identity songs. Watson's strong run on Capitol was to run through to 1980 - producing the top 5 hits *Should I go home (or should I go crazy)* and his clever titled *Nothin' sure looked good on you.* His late 1970's albums *Paper Rosie*, *Reflections* and *No one will ever know*, and his successful UK tour of 1979 did much to endear him to country fans over here. His subsequent move to MCA in 1981 brought about little change in his music - the hits were also to keep rolling in with *Fourteen carat mind* of that year supplying him with his first No. 1 single. Watson went back on the road with the Farewell Party Band, working as hard as ever and chimed in with more of those hits, featuring *This dream's on me* in 1982. Also of note were *You're out doing what I'm here doing without* and *Drinkin' my way back home* two of four top ten singles during 1983 - 1984. After a year with MCA/Curb where he scored with yet another sad bar-room drinking song *Got no reason for going home*, he was once again on the move. Epic, who he stayed with for two years may have only garnered the only top 5 hit *Memories to burn* but his albums were as strong as ever - producing quality material such as *Carmen*, which couldn't, for some strange reason, even make the top 30. Warner Brothers, his home during 1988 - 1992, may not have seen much chart action, though Watson's debut strike *Don't waste it on the blues* made the top 5. With the introduction during the 90's of so much young, marketable talent, the drag-racing loving Watson, in 1993, found himself without a major label. (Maurice Hope - July 1993)

GREATEST HITS: GENE WATSON.
Tracks: Between this time and next time / Maybe I should have been listening / Fourteen carat mind / Speak softly (you're talking to my heart) / This dream's on me / What she don't know won't hurt her / You're out doing what I'm here doing without / Sometimes I get lucky and forget / Drinkin' my way back home / Forever again.
LP . . . . **IMCA 5572**
MCA (Import) / Mar '86 / Pinnacle / Silver Sounds (CD).
CD **31128**
MCA (USA) / Jun '88 / MCA (Imports).

HEARTACHES LOVE AND STUFF.
Tracks: Not Advised.
LP . . . . **MCF 3256**
MCA / Feb '85 / BMG.

LITTLE BY LITTLE.
Tracks: Little by little / My memories of you / Chesapeake bay, The / Leavin's been comin' for a long, long time / Ballad of Richard Lindsey, The / Forever again / With any luck at all / Growing apart / She has no memory of me / Drinkin' my way back home.
LP . . . . **MCF 3213**
MC . . . . **MCFC 3213**
MCA / Apr '84 / BMG.

LOVE IN THE HOT AFTERNOON.
Tracks: Not Advised.
MC **4XL 9048**
Capitol (Specials) / Dec '88.

OLD LOVE NEVER DIES.
Tracks: Old love never dies / Girl I used to run around with, The / Roads and other reasons / Till Melinda comes round / Speak softly (you're talking to my heart) / Nothing about her reminds me of you / Fourteen carat mind / Lonely me / Sun never comes up again, The / Missing you just started hittin' home.
LP . . . . **IMCA 27066**
MCA (Import) / Mar '86 / Pinnacle / Silver Sounds (CD).

REFLECTIONS.
Tracks: One sided conversations / Take off them shoes / Farewell party / Let's give it up or get it on / For the memories / I wonder how it is in Colorado / Pick the wildwood flower / I know what it's like in her arms / Mama sold roses / I don't know how to tell her.
■ **LP** . . . . **EST 11805**
Capitol / '79.

SOMETIMES I GET LUCKY.
Tracks: Speak well of me / Sometimes I get lucky and forget / She sure makes leaving look easy / You waltzed yourself right into my life / You put out an old flame last night / You're just another beer drinkin' song / Thinkin' 'bout leaving / If I were you I'd fall in love with me.
LP . . . . **IMCA 5384**
MCA (Import) / Mar '86 / Pinnacle / Silver Sounds (CD).

TEXAS SATURDAY NIGHT.
Tracks: Texas Saturday night / Got no reason now for going home / You waltzed yourself right into my life / My memories of you / If I were you I'd fall in love with me / You're just another beer drinkin' song / One hell of a heartache / You sure make cheatin' seem easy / I'm tellin' me a lie / Drinkin' my way back home.
■ **LP** . . . . **IMCA 5670**
MCA (Import) / Mar '86.

THIS DREAM'S ON ME.
Tracks: This dream's on me / Fighting fire with fire / Baby me baby / Full time fool / This torch that I carry for you / What she don't know won't hurt her / From cotton to satin / You sure make cheatin' seem easy / Last thing I planned to do today was cheat, The / Somethin' 'bout bein' gone.
■ **LP** . . . . **IMCA 885**
MCA (Import) / Mar '86.

Watson, Jim

MEETING IN THE AIR (Watson, Jim/Craver/Thompson).
Tracks: Anchored in love / While the band is playing Dixie / Stern old bachelor / Winding stream, The / School house on the hill, The / Wayworn traveller / Meeting in the air / I ain't gonna work tomorrow / One little word / Dixie darling / Lulu walls / Are you tired of me my darling / Give me the roses / When the roses bloom in Dixieland.
LP . . . . **FF 219**
Flying Fish (USA) / Mar '89 / Cadillac Music / Roots Records / Projection / C.M. Distribution / Direct Distribution / Jazz Music / Duncans / A.D.A Distribution.

Weissberg, Eric

This American multi instrumentalist was an important session musician during the Sixties and Seventies. Amongst his most successful credits were records by Judy Collins, Jim Croce, Bob Dylan, Billy Joel and Melanie; he also played with a host of lesser talents, and released occasional discs in his own right. His range of instruments included banjo, bass guitar, harp, kazoo, mandolin, and violin. It was as a banjo player that Weissberg suddenly stepped into the limelight in 1973. In collaboration with his long-time musical friend Steve Mandell, he recorded an old tune called *Duelling banjos* for inclusion in John Boorman and James Dickey's movie *Deliverance*. The instrumental single, arranged and produced by Weissberg, reached No.2 on the US charts in '73, and climbed to No.17 in the UK. It was a delightfully unusual hit single; but its success story was complicated by a copyright dispute. The label of Weissberg & Mandell's disc claimed that the tune was traditional, but guitarist Arthur Smith (also composer of the 1959 Virtues/Bert Weedon hit *Guitar boogie shuffle*) contested that he had written and recorded it in 1955 under the title *Feuding banjos*. Smith ended up as the winner. After the success of *Duelling banjos*, Weissberg & Mandell formed a short-lived group called Deliverance. Weissberg then resumed his session career. His musical base was always New York. (Bob MacDonald)

DUELLING BANJOS.
Tracks: Duelling banjos / End of a dream.
■ **7"** . . . . **K 16223**
Automatic / Nov '79.

DUELLING BANJOS (OLD GOLD).
Tracks: Duelling banjos / Deliverence, Theme from / Reuben's train.
7" . . . . **OG 9574**
Old Gold / Mar '86 / Pickwick Records.

YAKETY YAK (Weissberg, Eric & Deliverance).
Tracks: Yakety yak / Meadow muffins.
■ **7"** . . . . **EPC 3186**
Epic / Apr '75.

Weller, Freddy

Progressive pop/country act, born on 09.09.1947 in Atlanta, Georgia. He worked on the Atlanta Jubilee alongside such acts as Jerry Reed, Ray Stevens and Joe South (later bassist with his band). Prior to his country ventures, Weller saw success with rock act Paul Revere and The Raiders in 1967, whilst as a songwriter he teamed - up with Tommy Roe, providing Roe's big hit *Dizzy*. In 1969 he made the country charts with *Games people play* (No.2) and *These are not my people* (No.5). Others to figure amongst his impressive hit tally with Columbia are *Promised land* (a remake of Chuck Berry's hit), *Indian lake* and *Another night of love*, a run that took him to 1980. The last release of note to feature this Vegas - styled rocker is the 1988 Appoloosa album White *Wheels* recorded live at Nashville's Cannary. (Maurice Hope - July 1993).

BACK ON THE STREET.
Tracks: Midnight driver / Right in the prime of her love / Shootin' from the heart / Trying to get around to 'em all / If you knew how much I wanted you / Back on the street / Time machine / Intensive care / You believed in a dreamer / Midlife crisis / One dream at a time / Atlanta.
LP . . . . **BDL 3003**
Bulldog Records / Aug '87 / President Records / Jazz Music / Wellard Dist. / TKO Records Ltd.

Wells, Kitty

Queen of country music in the 50's and 60's, Kitty Wells was born Muriel Deason in Nashville in 1918. She married Johnny Wright, of the popular duo Johnnie & Jack, and he suggested her name change, from a Carter Family song *I'm A'Goin' To Marry Kitty Wells*. She raised a family, appeared on the *Grand Ole Opry*, recorded for RCA and switched to Decca (now MCA). Her first Decca record was her first hit and the first No 1 for a woman artist since the Billboard country charts began: *It Wasn't God Who Made Honky Tonk Angels* was an answer song (to Hank Thompson's *Wild Side Of Life*). *I Don't Want Your Money, I Want Your Times* was also an answer, this time to Lefty Frizzell's *If You've Got The Money I've Got The Time*. Her sincerity and choice of good songs led to more than 50 country hits in the 50's and 60's 25 in the Top Ten with more than 450 singles and 40 albums released by 1973. Other big hits in the 50's were *Makin' Believe* (covered by Emmylou Harris in '77) and *Searching* and two-sided hit such as *Repenting/I'm Counting On You* and *She's No Angel/I Can't Stop Loving You*. Heartbreak USA was a No 1 hit in '61. She was part of the Johnnie & Jack show until Jack's death ended that successful duo; the Johnny Wright-Kitty Wells Family Show was syndicated on TV; their son Bobby also had hits in the 60's. The Golden Years (1949-57), on the German-based Bear Family label, is a five-disc boxed set including the early RCA tracks and all her biggest hits from Decca/MCA, with a bonus EP, totalling nearly 100 selections. (Donald Clarke)

COUNTRY HIT PARADE.
Tracks: Not Advised.
LP . . . . **HAT 3037**
MC . . . . **HATC 3037**
Stetson / Apr '87 / Crusader Marketing Co. / Swift / Wellard Dist. / Midland Records / C.M. Distribution.

COUNTRY MUSIC HALL OF FAME.
Tracks: Not Advised.
■ **LP** . . . . **CDL 8504**
MCA / May '80.

GOLDEN YEARS 1949-57, THE.
Tracks: Death at the bar / Love or hate / Gathering flowers for the master's bouquet / Don't wait until the last minute to pray / How far is heaven / My mother / Make up your mind / I'll be all smiles tonight / It wasn't God who made honky tonk angels / I don't want your money, I want your time / Searching for a soldier's grave / I'm too lonely to smile / Things I might have been, The / I heard the jukebox playing / Wedding ring ago, A / Divided by two / Crying steel guitar waltz / Paying for that back street affair / Icicles hanging from your heart / I don't claim to be an angel / Honky tonk waltz / Life they live in songs, The / You said you could do without me / Whose shoulder will you cry on / Hey Joe / My cold cold heart is melted now / I'll love you til the day I die / I've kissed you my last time / You're not easy to forget / Satisfied, so satisfied / One by one / I'm a stranger in my home / I gave my wedding dress away / Cheatin's a sin / Release me / After dark / (Don't hang around) he's married to me / Thou shalt not steal / Lonely side of town / I hope my divorce is never granted / I'm in love with you / As long as you live / No one but you / Make believe / I'd rather stay home / I was wrong / There's poison in your heart / Goodbye Mr. Brown / Searching / Dust on the bible / Beside you / I'm counting on you / They can't take your love / I'm tired of pretending / Oh so many years / One week later / When I'm with you / Can you find it in your heart / Repenting / I guess I'll go on dreaming / Each day / Pace that kiss, The / Change of heart, A / Stubborn heart / Standing room only / Mansion on the hill / Your wild life's gonna get you down / Right or wrong / Winner of your heart, The / Dancing with a stranger / Three ways (to love you) / She's no angel / Broken marriage vows / What about you / Sweeter than the flowers / You can't conceal a broken heart / Just when I needed you most / Lonely street / That's me without you / Cheated out of love / Waltz of the angels, The / May you never be alone / If teardrops were pennies / Touch and go heart / My used to be darling / I'll always be your fraulein / Love me to pieces / What I believe dear (is all up to you) / I can't stop loving you / Slowly dying.
LP Set . . . . **BFX 15239/6**
Bear Family / Dec '87 / Rollercoaster Records / Swift / Direct Distribution.

GOLDEN YEARS, THE.
Tracks: Not Advised.
LP . . . . **SS 13**
MC . . . . **SSC 13**
Rounder / Dec '88 / Projection / Roots Records / Swift / C.M. Distribution / Topic Records / Jazz Music / Hot Shot / A.D.A Distribution / Direct Distribution.

GREATEST HITS: KITTY WELLS.
Tracks: Not Advised.
MC . . . . **GM 0211**
K-Tel Goldmasters / Aug '84 / C.M. Distribution / Arabesque Ltd. / Ross Records / PolyGram.

GREATEST HITS:KITTY WELLS.
Tracks: It wasn't God who made honky tonk angels / This white circle / Mommy for a day / Release me / I gave my wedding dress away / Amigo's guitar / Heartbreak USA / I'll repossess my heart / Password / Searching (for someone like you) / Making believe.
■ **LP** . . . . **IMCA 121**
MCA (Import) / Mar '86.

KITTY WELLS STORY, THE.
Tracks: It wasn't God who made honky tonk angels / I heard the jukebox playing / Wedding ring ago, A / Paying for that back street affair / I don't claim to be an angel / Whose shoulder will you cry on / I gave my wedding dress away / Release me / After dark / Lonely side of town / Making believe / Searching (for someone like you) / Repenting / Your wild life's gonna get you down / Three ways to love you / She's no angel / Touch and go heart / Jealousy / I can't help wondering / Mommy for a day / Amigo's guitar / All the time / Other cheek The / Left to right.
Double LP **IMCA2 4031**
MCA (Import) / Mar '86 / Pinnacle / Silver Sounds (CD).

KITTY'S CHOICE.
Tracks: Not Advised.
LP . . . . **HAT 3018**
MC . . . . **HATC 3018**
Stetson / Sep '86 / Crusader Marketing Co. / Swift / Wellard Dist. / Midland Records / C.M. Distribution.

MAKIN' BELIEVE.
Tracks: Not Advised.
LP . . . . **N 23006**
MC **43006**
Colorado / Dec '85.

ORIGINAL QUEEN OF COUNTRY MUSIC, THE.
Tracks: Thou shalt not steal / I don't claim to be an angel / After dark / One by one / Making believe / Poison in your heart / I've kissed you my last time / On the lonely side of town / You and me.
LP . . . . **BDL 1025**
MC . . . . **BDC 1025**
Bulldog Records / Jul '82 / President Records / Jazz Music / Wellard Dist. / TKO Records Ltd.

QUEEN OF COUNTRY MUSIC (1949-58), THE.
Tracks: Death at the bar / Love or hate / Gathering flowers for the master's bouquet / Don't wait til the last minute to pray / How far is heaven / My mother / Make up your mind / I'll be all smiles (tonight) / I'm too lonely to smile / Things I might've been, The / I heard the jukebox playing / Wedding ring ago, A / Divided by two / Crying steel guitar waltz / Paying for that backstreet affair / Icicles hanging from your heart / I don't claim to be an angel / Honky tonk waltz / Life they live in songs, The / You said you could do without me / Whose shoulder will you cry on / Hey Joe / My cold cold heart is melting now / I'll love you till the day I die / I've kissed you my last time / I'm a stranger in my home / I gave my wedding dress away / Cheatin's a sin / You're not easy to forget / Satisfied, so satisfied / One by one / Release me / After dark / (Don't hang around) he's married to me / Thou shalt not steal / Lonely side of town / I hope my divorce is never granted / I'm in love with you / Make believe / You & me / As long as I live / No one but you / Makin' believe / I'd rather stay home / I was wrong / There's poison in your heart / Goodbye Mr. Brown / Mother hold me tight / Searching (For someone else) / Dust on the bible / Beside you / I'm counting on you / They can't take your love / I'm tired of pretending / Oh so many years / One week later / When I'm with you / Can I find it in your heart / Repenting / I guess I'll go on dreaming / Each day / Pace that kills, The / Change of heart, A / Stubborn heart / Standing room only / Mansion on the hill, A / Your wild life's gonna get you down / Right or wrong / Winner of your heart, The / Dancing with a stranger / Three ways (to love you) / She's no angel / Broken marriage vows / What about you / Sweeter than the flowers / You can't conceal a broken heart / Just when I needed you / Lonely street / That's me without you / Cheated out of love / Waltz of the angel, The / May you never be alone / If teardrops were pennies / Touch & go heart / My used-to-be darling / (I'll always be your) Fraulein / Love me to pieces / What I believe dear (is all up to you) / I can't stop loving you / Slowly dying / I can't help wondering / He's lost his love for me / Jealousy / Mommy for a day / Hands you're holding now, The / Let me help you forget / All the time / (I've got my) one way ticket to the sky / I heard my saviour call / I dreamed I searched heaven for you / Great speckled bird, The / Matthew 24 / I need the prayers / My loved ones are waiting for me / Lord I'm coming home / He will set your fields on fire / Lonesome valley / We buried her beneath the willows.
CD . . . . **BCD 15638**
Bear Family / Jul '93 / Rollercoaster Records / Swift / Direct Distribution.

SONGS MADE FAMOUS BY JIM REEVES.
Tracks: Four walls / Billy Bayou / Is it really over? / I'm gonna change everything / I won't forget you / She'll have to go / Welcome to my world / Bimbo / Am I losing you? / According to my heart / Guilty / This is it.
LP . . . . **HAT 3009**
MC . . . . **HATC 3009**
Stetson / Jun '86 / Crusader Marketing Co. / Swift / Wellard Dist. / Midland Records / C.M. Distribution.

Wells, Tracy

BEST OF TRACY WELLS.
Tracks: Not Advised.
LP . . . . **HRL 145**
Homespun (Ireland) / May '88 / Homespun Records / Ross Records / Wellard Dist.

BEST OF TRACY WELLS VOL 2
Tracks: Honey / Dear John, a letter / Delta Dawn / One day at a time / I fall to pieces / Letter to heaven / Country sunshine / Cry, cry again / No charge / Come my little son / I love you Jesus / Making believe / Little boy soldier / Family bible.
LP . . . . **HRL 165**
MC . . . . **CHRL 165**
Homespun (Ireland) / May '88 / Homespun Records / Ross Records / Wellard Dist.

COUNTRY ROADS.
Tracks: Not Advised.
LP . . . . **STOL 125**
Outlet / '75 / Projection / Duncans / C.M. Distribution / Ross Records / Topic Records / Direct Distribution / Midland Records.
LP . . . . **CTV 125**
Homespun (Ireland) / '89 / Homespun Records / Ross Records / Wellard Dist.

COUNTRY SUNSHINE.
Tracks: Not Advised.
LP . . . . **HRL 124**
MC . . . . **CHRL 124**
Homespun (Ireland) / Jan '77 / Homespun Records / Ross Records / Wellard Dist.

GIVE DADDY BACK TO ME.
Tracks: Not Advised.
LP . . . . **HRL 108**
Homespun (Ireland) / Jan '76 / Homespun Records / Ross Records / Wellard Dist.

JUST BECAUSE I'M A WOMAN.
Tracks: Back home again / Queen of the silver dollar / Burning bridges / Rodeo cowboy / All for the love of sunshine / Further along / Harper Valley P.T.A. / To know him is to love him / Rollin' in the sunshine / Just because I'm a woman / Ribbon of darkness / Wedding.
LP . . . . **PHL 421**
MC . . . . **CPHL 421**
Homespun (Ireland) / '82 / Homespun Records / Ross Records / Wellard Dist.

MAY THE GOOD LORD BLESS AND KEEP YOU.
Tracks: Not Advised.
LP . . . . **HRL 157**
Homespun (Ireland) / May '88 / Homespun Records / Ross Records / Wellard Dist.

OTHER SIDE OF THE MORNING.
Tracks: Other side of the morning / Would you lay with me (in a field of stone) / I'll get over you / Goodbye clothes / Teddy bear's last ride / Bunch of thyme / One night of cheatin' / No man's land / Fool number one / Partner nobody chose, The / Behind the footlights / Never ending love affair.
MC . . . . **CWGR 037**
Ross (1) / Oct '92 / Ross Records / Duncans / Entertainment UK.

THROUGH THE EYES OF A CHILD.
Tracks: Not Advised.
LP . . . . **HRL 139**
MC . . . . **CHRL 139**
Homespun (Ireland) / May '88 / Homespun Records / Ross Records / Wellard Dist.

West, Dodie

GOING OUT OF MY HEAD.
Tracks: Goin' out of my head.
■ **7"** . . . . **F 12046**
Decca / Jan '65.

West, Dottie

Dottie West was born Dorothy Marie Marsh on October 11, 1932 in McMinville, Tennessee. Good looks and solid professional skills won her success in several areas. She is the oldest of ten children, earned a degree in music; her first country hits were on RCA from 1963. As a songwriter she wrote *Is This Me?* for a Jim Reeves hit in 1963; her top 10 hit with her own *Here Comes My Baby* was covered by Perry

Como and won her a Grammy. She had duet hits with Reeves and made an album with him. *Country Girl* was a 1968 hit turned into an award-winning Coca-Cola TV advert in 1970 that showed her tending a garden which turned out to be atop a sky-scraper; *Country Sunshine* in 1973 became another Coke advert and reached top 50 of the pop chart. She toured Europe, became popular in the UK; had duet hits with Kenny Rogers including album *Every Time Two Fools Collide* in 1981, a number one country album which also reached the pop chart; their duet single *What Are We Doin' In Love* went top 15 pop. She was still having country chart singles on Permian in the mid 80's. Dottie West died on September 4, 1991, as the result of an auto accident that occurred en route to the Grand Ole Opry where she was making one of her regular appearances. She was the mother of Shelly West, an artist who enjoyed a couple of dozen chart successes in the early 1980's. (Tony Byworth - August 1993)

20 OF THE BEST: DOTTIE WEST.
Tracks: Let me off at the corner / Love is no excuse / Gettin' married has made us strangers / Would you hold it against me / Mommy, can I still call him daddy ? / There's a story (goin' round) / Paper mansions / Forever yours / Rings of gold / Last time I saw him / Here come's my baby / Before the ring on your finger turns green / What's come over my baby ? / Like a fool / Sweet memories / Country girl / Reno / Slowly / House of love / Country sunshine.
LP . . . . **NL 89851**
■ **MC** . . . . **NK 89851**
RCA / Mar '86.

BEST OF DOTTIE WEST, THE.
Tracks: Here comes my baby / Careless hands / Once you were mine / Country girl / Six weeks every summer / Forever yours / Paper mansions / If you go away / Would you hold it against me / Reno.
■ **LP** . . . . **LSA 3152**
RCA / '79.

CLASSICS (see under Rogers, Kenny).

COME SEE ME AND COME LONELY.
Tracks: Come see me and come lonely / Even if you were Jesse James.
■ **7"** . . . . **UP 36396**
United Artists / May '78.

EVERY TIME TWO FOOLS COLLIDE (see under Rogers, Kenny).

I FALL TO PIECES.
Tracks: Not Advised.
LP . . . . **GT 0085**
Gusto (USA) / Mar '88.

LESSON IN LEAVIN'.
Tracks: Lesson in leavin', A / Love's so easy for two.
■ **7"** . . . . **UP 621**
United Artists / May '80.

SPECIAL DELIVERY.
Tracks: Not Advised.
■ **LP** . . . . **UAG 30290**
United Artists / Feb '80.

WHAT ARE WE DOING IN LOVE.
Tracks: What are we doing in love / Choosin' means losin'.
■ **7"** . . . . **UP 639**
United Artists / May '81.

West, Gordie

Canadian raised singer, brought up on a farm north of Calgary in Alberta was born in Skipton, Yorkshire. Played the local Canadian circuit, turning professional in 1974. One of a number of Canadian acts who gained UK exposure during the late 1970's/ early 1980's via regular tours and recordings on the Westwood label, its roster including singer-songwriter Dallas Harms, Ronnie Prophet and fiddle player Shoji Tabuchi. (Maurice Hope - August 1993)

ALBERTA BOUND.
Tracks: Alberta bound / Strawberry roan, The / Sweet music man / Blue Canadian Rockies / Canadian Pacific / That's my pa / Alberta skyline / Loser making good, A / Boot rockies / Rose of San Antone.
LP . . . . **WRS 138**
Westwood / '82 / Pinnacle.

GORDIE WEST.
Tracks: Not Advised.
LP . . . . **CBS 32343**
CBS / Jul '83 / Sony.
CD **833 433-2**
Polydor / May '88 / PolyGram.

West, Hedy

BALLADS.
Tracks: Love Henry / Beaulampkin / Down in Adairsville / Unquiet grave, The / Lucy Wan / Sheffield apprentice, The / Foggy dew, The / George Collins / Texas rangers / Cruel mother / Little Sadie / Girl I left in Danville.
LP **12T 163**
Topic / '81 / Roots Records / Jazz Music / C.M. Distribution / Cadillac Music / Direct Distribution / Swift / Topic Records.

GETTING FOLK OUT OF THE COUNTRY (West, Hedy & Bill Clifton).
Tracks: Free little bird / Maid on the shore / Little Sadie / Pity me all day / Whitehouse blues / Mary of the wild moor / Blow ye gentle winds / Curly headed baby / S.A.V.E.D. / Picture's from life's other side / Angel band / Instrumental / Mississippi sawyer.
LP . . . . **BF 15008**
Bear Family / Sep '84 / Rollercoaster Records / Swift / Direct Distribution.

LOVE, HELL AND BISCUITS.
Tracks: Shady grove / Erin's green shore / Molly Bawn / Single girl / Whores lament, The / Devil perceived / When I lay my burden down / Pans of biscuits / How can a poor man stand such times and live / Little lump of coal / Green rolling hills of West Virginia / Come all ye Lewiston factory girls / Babies in the mill / Red river valley / Rio Jarama / Roll on weary river, roll on.
LP . . . . **BF 15003**
Bear Family / Sep '84 / Rollercoaster Records / Swift / Direct Distribution.

OLD TIMES AND HARD TIMES.
Tracks: Wife wrapt in weather's skin, The / Fair Rosamund / Barbara Allen / Old Joe Clark / Coal miner's child, The / Gamblin' man / Brother Euphus / Polly / Davison wilder blues, The / Rich Irish lady, The / Shut up in the mines at coal creek / Wife of Usher's well, The / Lament for Barney Graham.
LP **12T 117**
Topic / '81 / Roots Records / Jazz Music / C.M. Distribution / Cadillac Music / Direct Distribution / Swift / Topic Records.

PRETTY SARO.
Tracks: House carpenter / Pretty Saro / Old smokey / Blow ye gentle winds / My soul's full of glory / Promised land / Over there / Little matty groves / Rake and the rambling boy / Joe Bowers / Whistle daughter whistle / I'm an old bachelor / Johnny sands / My good old man / Frankie silvers / Lee Tharin's bar room.
LP **12T 146**
Topic / '81 / Roots Records / Jazz Music / C.M. Distribution / Cadillac Music / Direct Distribution / Swift / Topic Records.

West, Speedy

Steel guitarist, born in Missouri in 1924. Worked for many years out of California, an invaluable session musician - he also featured on Cliffie Stone's 1950's Hometown Jamboree radio broadcasts. Recorded for Capitol during the 1960's, alongside two albums with guitarist Jimmy Bryant. Bear Family releases have renewed interest in his dexterous work. (Maurice Hope - August 1993)

GUITAR SPECTACULAR.
Tracks: Not Advised.
LP . . . . **HAT 3093**
MC . . . . **HATC 3093**
Stetson / Feb '89 / Crusader Marketing Co. / Swift / Wellard Dist. / Midland Records / C.M. Distribution.

STEEL GUITAR.
Tracks: Speedin' west / Railroadin' / West of Samoa / Caffeine patrol / Our paradise / Flippin' the lid / This ain't the blues / Stainless steel / Steelin' moonlight / Truck driver's ride / Sunset / Steel strike.
LP . . . . **HAT 3045**
MC . . . . **HATC 3045**
Stetson / Sep '87 / Crusader Marketing Co. / Swift / Wellard Dist. / Midland Records / C.M. Distribution.

STEEL GUITAR FROM OUTER SPACE.
Tracks: Steel guitar rag / Hub cap roll / Roadside rag / Crackerjack / Skiddle dee boo / Bustin' through / Yankee clover / Shuffleboard rag / Sand canyon swing / Shawnee trot / On the Alamo / Water baby blues / Space man in orbit / Sunset at Waikiki / Lazy summer evening / Totem pole dance / Afternoon of a swan / Speedy's special / Double or nothing / Slow and easy / Reflections from the moon / Tulsa twist / Rippling waters / Wild and woolly west.
LP . . . . **SEE 249**
See For Miles / Feb '89 / Pinnacle.

TWO GUITARS COUNTRY STYLE (see under Bryant, Jimmy).

Western Swing

Western swing is a country music genre influenced by jazz and often employing a large band,at its most popular from the mid-1930's to the early 1950's when economics forced artists to reduce costs and as a result put an end to the big bands; the style, however, is still influential today. Bob Wills was the most important artist in Western Swing, enormously popular all over the Southwest from the early 1930's. He grew up picking cotton in a family of accomplished fiddlers and was exposed to the music of both blacks and whites, this informal grounding in many genres of music was reflected both in his own playing which transcended category and in his band, which often resembled the typical swing band of the era, even playing some of the same tunes as Benny Goodman's sextet. Wills first exposure to a mass audience came on radio with the Light Crust Doughboys, who were named after striking a sponsorship deal with a flour mill. Wills later wrote *San Antonio Rose* which was successfully covered by Bing Crosby amongst others. Hank Penny, Milton Brown and his Musical Brownies, Cliff Brunner and his Texas Wanderers were amongst other popular acts along with Spade Cooley, who filled the dancehalls during World War II. Hank Thompson in the 50's and Buck Owens in the 60's were also obviously inluenced by Western Swing but its emergence as a musical force was wrecked by the same misfortunes that put an end to to the Big Bands, entertainment tax, closure of ballrooms during the war as a result of petrol rationing (later because of competition from television) and the econonmics of the road meant that it became impossible to keep a big band together permanently. The legacy of the music is probably most obvious in the recording studio, many sidemen can swing with the best jazzers. But perhaps the best known and musically closest descendant of Wills and the Western Swing style is the band Asleep at the Wheel who were formed in the late 60's and coincided with the emergence of the country rock movement in the early 70's, bringing them critical acclaim and a little success, which even if it did not match that of their country rock contemporaries (the Eagles, Flying Burrito Brothers etc.) has carried the legacy of Western Swing into successive decades and generations of country fans. (Merle Lynne - August 1993)

Western, Johnny

Living up to his name, Minesota born Johnny Western moved into singing after deejaying in Northfield but, through his association with Gene Autry, the music was put to one side in favour of acting which stretched over 37 western movies. Creating *The ballad of Paladin* for the TV series 'Have gun will travel', led onto a recording deal with Columbia. Although he's never had any chart success, he's continued to record spasmodically over the years for outlets such as Phillips, Hep and House of Country, and remained closely associated with the country scene via people like Waylon Jennings, Johnny Cash and George Strait. (Tony Byworth - August 1993)

GUNFIGHT AT OK CORRAL.
Tracks: Ghost riders in the sky / Gunfight at the OK corral / Gunfighter, The / Don't take your guns to town / Ringo / Hangin' tree, The / Cross the Brazos at Waco / Johnny Yuma, the rebel / Bonanza / Ballad of Paladin / Rawhide / Searchers, The / High noon / Song of the bandit / Hannah Lee / Lillies grow high, The / Ballad of Boot Hill / Cheyenne / Wyatt Earp / Bat Masterson.
CD . . . . **BCD 15429**
Bear Family / Jun '89 / Rollercoaster Records / Swift / Direct Distribution.

GUNFIGHTER.
Tracks: Ballad of Paladin / Guns of Rio Muerto, The / Lonely man / Rollin' dust / Hannah Lee / Long tall shadow, The / Nineteen men / Searchers, The / Gunfighter, The / Geronimo / Echo of your voice, The / Ten years / Uh huh (Previously unissued.) / Stranger drive away (Previously unissued.) / All by my lonesome (Previously unissued.) / Time has run out on me (Previously unissued.).
LP . . . . **BFX 15081**
Bear Family / Sep '84 / Rollercoaster Records / Swift / Direct Distribution.

HEROES AND COWBOYS.
Tracks: Ballad of the paladin, The / Guns of the Rio Muerto (& Richard Boone), The / Gunfighter, The / Geronimo / Lonely man, The / Hannah Lee (high are the gallows) / Streets of Laredo / Cowpoke / Lillies grow high, The / Cottonwood tree / Rollin' dust / Searchers, The / Nineteen men / Long tall shadow, The / Last round up, The / Streets of old dodge city, The / Mr.Rodeo cowboy / Singin' man, The / Big battle, The / Forty shades of green / Violet and a rose / Give me more, more, more (of your kisses) / Let old mother nature have her way / Little buffalo Bill / Love me, love me, love me / Honey, how sweet can you be / Echo of your voice / Ten years / Uh huh! / Delia's gone / Time has run out on me / Willowgreen / Don't cry little girl / Darling Corey / Stranger, drive away / I love you more / All by my lonesome / Just for the record / Kathy come home / Only the lonely / Light the fuse / Tender years / Turn around and look at me / Sincerely your friend / Ruby, don't take your love to town / Used to / I'll try hard to forget you if I can / Whoever finds this, I love you / Last time I saw phoenix, The / Hustler, The / You wouldn't know love / Arizona morning / Stay a little longer, stay all night (theme) / Lonely street / You weren't ashamed to kiss me last night / John Henry / Remember me / Wayward wind, The / Gotta travel on / Ghostriders in the sky / I still miss someone / I take a country girl for mine (Texas Bill strength) / I walk the line / Ballad of paladin, The / Guns of Rio Muerto, The.
CD Set . . . . **BCD 15552**
Bear Family / May '93 / Rollercoaster Records / Swift / Direct Distribution.

W 6
■ DELETED

JOHNNY WESTERN.
Tracks: Not Advised.
■ **LP.** . . . . **BFX 15070**
Bear Family / '84.

Wheater, Paul

Wheater, his music largely influenced by the late Jim Reeves came to fame in 1992, when his work found favour with the BBC's radio 2 network. He made an appearance on Anne Robinson's popular Saturday morning show, and hired the prestigious London Palladium on 21 June, 1992 at the cost of 10,000 to do a concert. (Maurice Hope - July 1993)

DING DONG (HAPPY CHRISTMAS).
Tracks: Ding dong (Happy Christmas) / You're all I want for Christmas.
7" . . . . **LCY 101A**
Paul Wheater / Dec '90 / Pinnacle / Pinnacle / TBD.

PAUL WHEATER PLAYS THE PALLADIUM.
Tracks: Not Advised.
MC . . . . **LCYC 110**
Paul Wheater / Dec '92 / Pinnacle / Pinnacle / TBD.

SOUVENIRS.
Tracks: Not Advised.
CD . . . . **LCYCD 109**
MC . . . . **LCYC 109**
Paul Wheater / Jul '92 / Pinnacle / Pinnacle / TBD.

TWENTY GOOD YEARS.
Tracks: Not Advised.
CD . . . . **CLCD 01**
MC . . . . **CLMC 01**
Rio Digital / Feb '91 / Grapevine Distribution.

Wheeler, Billy Edd

Billy Ed Wheeler has covered a great deal of ground since his childhood days in the coal mining camps of Whitesville, West Virginia, where he was born on 9.12.1932 he studied at Berea college, gaining a Bachelor's Degree in English, then onto Yale university to do playwriting at their school of drama (he has a number of summer play productions to his credit). He is an avid gatherer of folk ballads, many of them obtained on his trips into the rural environs of the south, in a way not unlike that of A.P.Carter some years previous. Wheeler has written such material as *Rev Mr. Black*, a 1963 hit for both the Kingston Trio and for Johnny Cash in 1982 (who, along with wife June Carter, had a big hit with Wheeler's *Jackson* in 1962), both records being superseded by *Coward of the county* , which Kenny Rogers' didn't just take to the top of Billboard's county charts in 1979, but also had a massive crossover success. (Rogers starred in the subsequent film version). Folk singer, turned country tunesmith/playwright Billy Edd's hit came in 1964 with the humrous *The little brown shack out back* on Knapp, followed by lesser successes on the United Artists, RCA, Radio Cinema and NSD - his subsequent albums including such delights as *Fried chicken and a country tune, The interstate is comin' through my outhouse* alongside his *Woman's talkin' liberation blues.* Wheeler's 1979 album *Wild Mountain Flowers* on Flying Fish shows him dividing his ingeneous poetic prowess with a simple love of rural life, aided with quality pickers, the late steel guitarist Pete Drake among them.

WILD MOUNTAIN FLOWERS.
Tracks: Coal tattoo / Gypsies drink whisky / Flowers / Lullaby to dad / Coming of the roads, The / Rev. Mr Black, The / High flyin' bird / All American boy / Whistling in the rain / Picker's prayer, A.
LP. . . . . **FF 085**
Flying Fish (USA) / Mar '89 / Cadillac Music / Roots Records / Projection / C.M. Distribution / Direct Distribution / Jazz Music / Duncans / A.D.A Distribution.

Wheeler, Cheryl

ACES.
Tracks: Aces / Estate sale / Hard line to draw (Not on 7".).
7" . . . . **CL 591**
■ **CD Single** . . . . **CDCL 591**
Capitol Nashville / Oct '90.

CIRCLES AND ARROWS.
Tracks: I know this town / Hard line to draw / Aces / Estate sale / Don't wanna / Northern girl / Soon as I find my voice / Miss you more than I'm mad / Moonlight and roses / When you're gone / Arrow.
■ **CD** . . . . **CDP 792 063 2**
Capitol / Sep '90.

Wheeler, Onie

Harmonica player/vocalist born Onie Daniel Wheeler on 10.1.1921, in Silkeston, Missouri (died 26.05.1984 while singing on stage at the Grand Ole Opry). Debuted as recording act on Agna covering *Shackles and chains* with Betty Jean Crowe. Toured with Elvis in 1955 (sharing the same manager, Bob Neal). Also toured with Johnny Cash, Jerry Lee Lewis & Carl Perkins in 1957 - recording for Sun, and one time member of Roy Acuff's Smokey Mountain Boys. As a solo act he recorded for Royal America and Columbia's Okeh label, blending hillbilly bop, spiritual and comedy with most songs being his own creations. His sole chart success came in 1973, when *John's been shuckin' my corn* made No.53 on the country charts. His daughter, Karen Wheeler is also a singer-songwriter, having recorded for chart and RCA during the 1970s. (Maurice Hope - August 1993)

JOHN'S BEEN SHUCKIN' MY CORN.
Tracks: John's been shuckin' my corn / Shuckin' my way to the hall of fame / Run em off / Onie's bop / Might as well hang my britches up / Mother prays loud in her sleep / I saw Mother with God last night / Mother rang the dinner bell / There's heaven to gain, hell to lose / Go home.
■ **LP.** . . . . **IB 1001**
I&B.

ONIE'S BOP.
Tracks: Jump right out of this jukebox / Tell em off / I wanna hold my baby / Onie's bop / Booger gonna getcha, A / Going back to the city / Long gone / Steppin' out / I'll love you for a lifetime / Beggar for your love, A / Walkin' shoes / That's all / Cut it out / That's what I like / She wiggled and giggled / I'm satisfied with my dreams / No, i don't guess i will / Would you like to wear a crown / Saw mother with god last night, I / My home is not a home at all / Little mama / Hazel / Closing time / Tried and tried, I / I'll swear you don't love me / Love me like you used to do / When we all fet there / Mother prays loud in her sleep / Million years in glory. A / Run 'em off / Bonaparte's retreat.
CD . . . . **BCD 15542**
Bear Family / May '91 / Rollercoaster Records / Swift / Direct Distribution.

Whelan, Cliff

Burma born singer/guitarist, moved to England in 1966. Started out as a country singer the following year working the clubs as a solo act. His debut album *Welcome to my world* on Sweet Folk and Country in 1977 is among his handful of recordings. (Maurice Hope - August 1993)

COUNTRY BOY.
Tracks: Country boy / Where in this world / When your love was mine / Bridle hanging on the wall / My special angel / My cathedral / Fools rush in / How important can it be? / I'll bet you my heart I love you / Rainbow in my daddy's eyes / Billy Bayou / What God made mothers for.
LP. . . . . **SFA 101**
Sweet Folk All / May '81 / Cadillac Music / Projection / C.M. Distribution / Wellard Dist. / Impetus Records.

HEAVEN TOGETHER.
Tracks: Unchained melody / They'll never know / Danny boy / Old spinning wheel / Bless you / She wears my ring / I love you more / Trees / Wishful thinking / Heaven together / Railroad bum / It is no secret.
LP. . . . . **SFA 081**
Sweet Folk All / May '81 / Cadillac Music / Projection / C.M. Distribution / Wellard Dist. / Impetus Records.

WELCOME TO MY WORLD.
Tracks: When you are gone / Welcome to my world / Rose Marie / Virginia / He'll have to go / Legend in my time, A / Yo ho valley / Be nobody's darling but mine / Worthless without you / You're the only good thing / Cup of joy / Kathleen.
LP. . . . . **SFA 061**
Sweet Folk All / May '81 / Cadillac Music / Projection / C.M. Distribution / Wellard Dist. / Impetus Records.

Whisnant, Johnnie

JOHNNIE WHISNANT.
Tracks: Not Advised.
LP. . . . . **ROUNDER 0038**
Rounder / '88 / Projection / Roots Records / Swift / C.M. Distribution / Topic Records / Jazz Music / Hot Shot / A.D.A Distribution / Direct Distribution.

White Brothers

LIVE IN SWEDEN (White Brothers & The New Kentucky Colonels).
Tracks: Not Advised.
LP. . . . . **ROUNDER 0073**
Rounder / '88 / Projection / Roots Records / Swift / C.M. Distribution / Topic Records / Jazz Music / Hot Shot / A.D.A Distribution / Direct Distribution.

White, Buck

BUCK WHITE/DOWNHOME FOLKS.
Tracks: Not Advised.
LP. . . . . **SAVE 033**
Fundamental / Oct '87 / Plastic Head.

DARKNESS ON THE DELTA (see under Baker, Kenny).

MORE PRETTY GIRLS THAN ONE.
Tracks: Not Advised.
LP. . . . . **SH 3710**
Sugarhill(USA) / Mar '89 / Roots Records / Projection / Impetus Records / C.M. Distribution / Jazz Music / Swift / Duncans / A.D.A Distribution.

White, Howard

NASHVILLE SIDEMAN WITH FRIENDS.
Tracks: Jealous heart / Blue eyes crying in the rain / Roly poly / Deep water / Rose of old pawnee / San Antonio rose / Faded love / Midnight / Columbus stockade blues / Before I met you / Steel guitar dowve / Ensonata / Rosette / Steel guitar swallow.
CD . . . . **BCD 15575**
Bear Family / Apr '92 / Rollercoaster Records / Swift / Direct Distribution.

WESTERN SWING & STEEL INSTRUMENTALS.
Tracks: Jealous heart / Blue eyes crying in the rain / Roly poly / Deep water / Rose of old pawnee / San Antonio rose / Faded love / Midnight / Columbus stokade blues / Before I met you / Steel guitar dove / Ensonata / Rosette / Steel guitar swallow.
CD . . . . **BCD 15575**
Bear Family / Apr '93 / Rollercoaster Records / Swift / Direct Distribution.

Whites

The Whites originally started out as the Down Home Folks in 1971 with County records, consisting of the Buck White (piano, mandolin and guitar), his wife Patty, (who soon retired) and daughters Sharon (guitar) and Cheryl (bass). Buck, during his younger days, had played piano with a number of western swing bands in the Whitchita Falls region and was also a sessionman during the 1950's. He played on Slim Willet's 1952 best seller *Don't let the stars get in your eyes*, a chart topper on Four Star. Prior to recording for Nashville's majors, The Whites had material out on Ridge Runner, Sugar Hill and a live release in Japan 1979 on Japan PA 6349. The Whites, with Sharon and Cheryl on vocals produced a blend of harmony - lined blugrass/country (something Emmylou Harris put to use in 1979, when she had them play support to her on the Blue Kentucky Girl tour) that saw them become a much admired group of the eighties. In 1983 they gained nomination in CMA's Group Of The Year category - the following year they joined the Grand Ole Opry. Sharon later Married Ricky Skaggs, who also produced all but one of their latter - day albums. Skaggs and wife Sharon had a top ten hit in 1987 with *Love can't ever get better than this* for his Epic label. The Whites music on the major labels consists of releases on Wea Curb, MCA Curb and their debut only single for Capitol. Enjoying singles chart success between 1981 and 1987 - headed by top ten efforts *You put the blue in me, Hangin' around* (both Elektra 1982), *I wonder who's holdin' my baby tonight* and *Give me back that old time feeling* (both Warner Brothers 1983). *Pins and needles* 1984 on Curb was their last top ten rates single, although such numbers as *Hometown gossip* and *If it ain't love* among others made useful chart placings during the later 1980's. Last album can be found on the Word gospel label - *Doing it by the book (1988).*

FOREVER YOU.
Tracks: Forever you / Pins and needles / Mama don't you know your little girl / (Our own) Jole' Blon / Ring of clover / Move it on over / Blue baby now / I didn't come here to cry / I just started living today / Living in the name of love.
LP. . . . . **IMCA 5490**
MCA (Import) / Mar '86 / Pinnacle / Silver Sounds (CD).

GREATEST HITS: WHITES.
Tracks: You put the blue in me / Hangin' around / Give me back that old familiar feeling / It ain't love (let's leave it alone) / I wonder who's holding my baby tonight / Love won't wait / Pins and needles / Forever you / When the new wears off our love / Home town gossip.
MC . . . . **IMCAC 5717**
MCA / Apr '87 / BMG.
■ **LP.** . . . . **IMCA 5717**
MCA / Apr '87.

PINS AND NEEDLES.
Tracks: Pins and needles / Move it on over.
■ **7"** . . . . **MCA 917**
MCA / Oct '84.

POOR FOLKS PLEASURE.
Tracks: Cowboy lives forever, The / Home / Jealous heart / Virginia's real / Southland / Poor folks pleasure / Another lonesome morning / By the fireside with baby / House of gold / Mexican holiday.
LP. . . . . **SDLP 052**
MC . . . . **SDC 052**
Sundown / Aug '87 / Terry Blood Dist. / Jazz Music / C.M. Distribution.

WHOLE NEW WORLD.
Tracks: If it ain't love (Let's leave it alone) / I don't have the heart to care (Just as long as you love me) / Whole new world / Angel band / Hometown gossip / I don't want to get over you / No one has to tell me (What love is) / Daddy's hands / Down in Louisiana.
LP . . . . **MCF 3283**
MC . . . . **MCF 3283MC**
MCA / '85 / BMG.

Whitley, Keith

Born 1955 in Sandy Hook, Kentucky, died 1989. Whitley's early bluegrass upbringing saw him performing with Buddy Starcher on a Charleston radio station while still only eight years old. He had his own band called the East Kentucky Mountain Boys from 1968 to the 70's. After a spell playing alongside Ricky Skaggs he joined Ralph Stanley's Clinch Mountain Boys. In 1983 he moved to Nashville, signing to RCA the following year. In 1984 he released the honky tonk styled LP entitled *A Hard Act To Follow* which showed the influence of his hero Lefty Frizzell. His 1986 LP *LA To Miami* yielded three country top ten hits. His 1988 album *Don't Close Your Eyes* consolidated this success with the title track also providing his first number 1 single. This feat was repeated by both *When You Say Nothing At All* and *I'm No Stranger To The Rain*. More hits followed until his untimely death in 1989 which was brought about by his alcohol problem. (Maurice Hope).

DON'T CLOSE YOUR EYES.
Tracks: Flying colours / It's all coming back to me now / Lucky dog / Don't close your eyes / Birmingham turnaround / Some old side road / Would these arms be in your way / I'm no stranger to the rain / I never go around mirrors / When you say nothing at all / Day in the life of a fool, A / Honky tonk heart.
CD . . . . **PD 90313**
RCA / Apr '89 / BMG.
■ **LP** . . . . **PL 90313**
RCA / Apr '89.
■ **MC** . . . . **PK 90313**
RCA / Apr '89.

SUNDOWN (see under Skaggs, Ricky).

Whitman, Jim

CUTTIN' LOOSE (Whitman, Jim & Texas).
Tracks: Not Advised.
LP . . . . **LLR 5**
Lady London / Sep '84 / M.I.S.Records.

GREEN FIELDS OF IRELAND.
Tracks: Green fields of Ireland / My lovely Lagan River / Up in the Paltry Mountains / Just a blind Irish boy / My heart is in Connemara / Today you say you are leaving / Kiss the Blarney Stone / In Annalee / River Bann flows on forever / Girl from Carlow Town / Pride of County Down / Take me back to Ireland.
LP . . . . **PFL 3015**
■ **MC** . . . . **PFT 3015**
Pastafont / Jun '87.

STOLEN KISS, A.
Tracks: Stolen kiss, A.
7" . . . . **PF 3016**
Priority / Jan '87 / BMG.

Whitman, Slim

This American singer, born Otis Dewey Whitman Jr in Florida, worked as a shipfitter and served in the US. Navy before turning professional at the age of 24 (1948). By this time, he was also a skilled baseball player. He began to make headway in the country-and-western market, and achieved his major breakthrough in 1951 with the international success of *Indian love call*. This 1924 song, from the musical *Rose Marie*, was a perfect vehicle for Whitman's distinctive vocal talents: it showed off his rich texture, his clarity of tone and his yodelling capabilities. A stream of US country hits followed. Whitman's biggest claim to fame in Britain was his staggering 1955 success with the title song from *Rose Marie* (written in the year of the singer's birth - 1924). This infuriatingly catchy ballad was No.1 in the UK for 11 consecutive weeks. Thirty years later, this feat still stood as the all time longest uninterrupted reign at the top of the British charts. The UK success of *Rose Marie* caused Whitman to become the first C&W star to tour Britain on his own. The genre was largely unknown in the UK at that time, and there is no doubt that he played a leading role in bringing country music to the attention of British ears. However, it is arguable that Whitman was ultimately detrimental to its long-term acceptance - UK listeners were given a stereotyped image of country & western, being led to believe that cowboy ballads and sentimental love numbers were its be-all and end-all.From the mid-Fifties onwards, Whitman never entered the Top 40 of the American pop charts, but continued to score heavily on the C&W listings. In Britain, the pop hits continued for a short while - *Serenade* reached No.8 in '56 - but after the Top 10 success of 1957's *I'll take you home again, Kathleen*, Whitman's name fell off the UK lists. Suddenly in 1974, Whitman made a return to pop stardom with *Happy anniversary*. This cloying single was in his traditional romantic style, and reached No.14 on the British chart. The song soon became a standard, with Whitman's disc becoming a perennial gift item between spouses and enjoying frequent plays on radio request shows. It's UK popularity made United Artists Records realise that despite a 17 year dearth of pop hits, the singer was still a marketable commodity. They compiled *The very best of Slim Whitman*, and, inspired by recently successful TV campaigns mounted for Jim Reeves and Perry Como LP collections, they launched a major blitz of television ads. This heavy promotion pushed the album to No.1 in Britain for six weeks in 1976. The idea was milked for all it was worth - the TV-advertised *Red river valley* LP was released a year later, and logged four weeks atop the UK LP listing; mere months later, *Home on the range* gave the yodelling yank a No.2 album. Although Whitman had a solid reputation in Nashville, the scale of his British recognition certainly outweighed his importance in the UK country market. Most of the UK housewives who bought his TV-marketed LPs had probably never heard of the genre's greatest artists, such as Merle Haggard, Waylon Jennings and George Jones. Nonetheless, it should be noted that, in addition to his LP chart success, Whitman's name was bandied about during the mid-Seventies for another reason - Queen, Wings and John Travolta and Olivia Newton John all enjoyed running British No.1 singles and threatened to challenge the record set by Whitman's 1955 chart topper. But all three acts stopped at nine weeks - the 11-week *Rose Marie* remained the champ. (Bob MacDonald)

20 GREATEST LOVE SONGS.
Tracks: I love you because / It's all in the game / Love letters in the sand / Fool such as I / Please help me I'm falling / Tammy / I'll never find another you / Unchained melody / Very precious love / Don't let the stars get in your eyes / Only you / Together / More than yesterday / Just lovin' you / Loveliest night of the year / My heart cries for you / Guess who / My happiness / Silver threads among the gold / Stranger on the shore.
■ **LP** . . . . **MFP 50516**
MFP / Jun '81.

ALL KINDS OF EVERYTHING.
Tracks: Not Advised.
■ **MC** . . . . **TCIDL 20**
Ideal / Jun '81.

ANGELINE.
Tracks: Cry baby heart / But she loves me / Tryin' to outrun the wind / Angeline / Blue memories / Dreamin' / Scarlet ribbons / Blue bayou / Place in the sun / Four walls.
■ **LP** . . . . **EPC 25901**
Epic / May '84.

BEST OF SLIM WHITMAN.
Tracks: Not Advised.
LP **1A 022 58098**
MC **1A 222 58098**
EMI (Holland) / '83.

BIRMINGHAM JAIL AND OTHER COUNTRY ARTISTS.
Tracks: Birmingham jail / Wabash waltz / Let's go to church / I'm casting my lasso towards the sky / Tears can never drown the flame (that's in my heart) / I'll never pass this way again.
MC . . . . **CAM 433**
RCA/Camden / '69 / BMG / Arabesque Ltd.
LP . . . . **CDM 1018**
RCA/Camden / Apr '86 / BMG / Arabesque Ltd.

BLUE BAYOU.
Tracks: Blue bayou / Blue memories.
■ **7"** . . . . **A 4303**
Epic / Mar '84.

CAN'T HELP FALLING IN LOVE WITH YOU.
Tracks: Can't help falling in love / Open up your heart.
7" . . . . **BP 408**
Liberty / Jan '82 / EMI.

CHRISTMAS ALBUM, THE.
Tracks: Not Advised.
LP . . . . **ED 2607341**
■ **MC** . . . . **ED 2607344**
Capitol / Nov '85.

COLLECTION: SLIM WHITMAN.
Tracks: Not Advised.
CD . . . . **KNCD 13053**
■ **MC** . . . . **KNMC 13053**
Knight / Apr '90.

COLLECTION: SLIM WHITMAN.
Tracks: Rose Marie / My blue heaven / Bouquet of roses / Lorena / How could I not love you / Take me in your arms and hold me / When my dreamboat comes home / I'd trade all of my tomorrows (for just one day) / White silver sands / Nobody's darlin' but mine / Indian love call / I'm walking behind you / I'd climb the highest mountain / Tell me / Ride away (with a song in my heart) / Little green valley / Born to lose / At mail call today / In the valley of the moon / Blue eyes crying in the rain / Marie Elena / Home (when shadows fall) / Song of the waterwheel, The / Ages and ages ago / Each night at nine / Smoke signals / Brahms' lullaby / I'll never stop loving you / Never / Forty shades of green / Among my souvenirs / Careless love / I dreamed of an old love affair / Travellin' man / From heaven to heartache / Forever / I really don't want to know / I'll hold you in my heart / Silver threads among the gold / Happy anniversary.
CD Set . . . . **CDEMS 1326**
Liberty / Apr '89 / EMI.
■ **Double LP** . . . . **EM 1326**
Liberty / Apr '89.
■ **MC Set** . . . . **TCEM 1326**
Liberty / Apr '89.

COUNTRY CLASSICS.
Tracks: Most beautiful girl in the world, The / Send me the pillow that you dream on / My elusive dreams / Don't be angry / Candy kisses / Lovesick blues / I love you a thousand ways / Blue eyes crying in the rain / Just call me lonesome / I forgot more than you'll ever know / There goes my everything / Satisfied mind, A / Faded love / From a jack to a king / Little bitty tear, A / I'll sail my ship alone / Think I'll go somewhere and cry myself to sleep / Walk through this world with me / She thinks I still care / I fall to pieces.
■ **LP** . . . . **ED 2606821**
Liberty / Aug '85.
■ **MC** . . . . **ED 2606824**
Liberty / Aug '85.

COUNTRY CLASSICS BY SLIM.
Tracks: Not Advised.
MC **4XLL 8315**
Capitol (Specials) / Dec '88.

COUNTRY STYLE.
Tracks: Rhinestone cowboy / Red river valley / Tumbling tumbleweeds / Kentucky waltz / Home on the range / I can't stop loving you / Cattle call / Rose Marie / Riders in the sky / From a jack to a king / Broken wings / Paper roses / It keeps right on a-hurtin' / Wayward wind / Top of the world / Cool water.
MC . . . . **TCMFP 5688**
MFP / Jan '85 / EMI.
■ **LP** . . . . **MFP 41 5688 1**
MFP / Jan '85.
CD . . . . **CDMFP 6035**
MFP / Nov '88 / EMI.

FAVOURITES.
Tracks: Beautiful dreamer / I went to your wedding / Marjie / I remember you / Carolina moon / Oh my darling (I love you) / Just an echo in the valley / If I had my life to live over / Silver haired daddy of mine / Ghost riders in the sky / Edelweiss / Take good care of her / Secret love / Can't help falling in love / When you wore a tulip / You are my sunshine / Rose Marie / Mr. Songman / Goodbye little darlin' goodbye / Where did yesterday go?.
■ **LP** . . . . **EMS 1281**
EMI / Nov '87.
■ **MC** . . . . **TCEMS 1281**
EMI / Nov '87.
LP . . . . **HAT 3135**
MC . . . . **HATC 3135**
Stetson / Mar '90 / Crusader Marketing Co. / Swift / Wellard Dist. / Midland Records / C.M. Distribution.

FOUR WALLS.
Tracks: Four walls / Trying to outrun the wind.
7" . . . . **A 4695**
Epic / Sep '84 / Sony.

GHOST RIDERS IN THE SKY.
Tracks: Ghost riders in the sky / Carolina moon / All kinds of everything / Girl of my dreams / Margie / Perfect day / Calypso / You are my sunshine / Puff, the magic dragon / Tears stained my pillow / When it's harvest time sweet Angeline / Goodbye little darlin' goodbye.
■ **LP** . . . . **UATV 30202**
United Artists / Jan '79.

GHOST RIDERS IN THE SKY.
Tracks: Ghost riders in the sky / Carolina moon.
■ **7"** . . . . **UP 36491**
United Artists / Feb '79.

GOLDEN COUNTRY HITS.
Tracks: Not Advised.
MC **4XLL 8348**
Capitol (Specials) / Dec '88.

GREATEST HITS: SLIM WHITMAN.
Tracks: Indian love call / Keep it a secret / Northwind / Secret love / Rose Marie / Cattle call / I'm a fool / China doll / Tumbling tumbleweeds / I'll take you home again Kathleen / More than yesterday / Twelfth of never / Rainbows are back in style / Shutters and boards / Guess who / Something beautiful / Happy anniversary.
■ **LP** . . . . **LBR 2600531**
Liberty / Apr '84.
■ **MC** . . . . **TCLBR 2600534**
Liberty / Apr '84.

HAPPY ANNIVERSARY.
Tracks: Not Advised.
■ **LP** . . . . **UAS 29670**
United Artists / Dec '74.

HAPPY ANNIVERSARY.
Tracks: Happy anniversary / Indian love call.
■ **7"** **G45 14**
EMI Golden 45's / Mar '84.

W 8 ■ DELETED

HAPPY ANNIVERSARY.
Tracks: Happy anniversary / Indian love call.
7" .... UP 35728
United Artists / '74 / EMI.

HAPPY ANNIVERSARY (OLD GOLD).
Tracks: Happy anniversary.
■ 7" .... OG 9716
Old Gold / Apr '87.

HOME ON THE RANGE.
Tracks: Not Advised.
■ LP .... UATV 30102
United Artists / Oct '77.

HONEYMOON FEELING.
Tracks: Honeymoon feeling / Foolish question.
■ 7" .... UP 35775
United Artists / Jan '75.

I'LL TAKE YOU HOME AGAIN, KATHLEEN.
Tracks: Not Advised.
LP .... SHM 959
■ MC .... HSC 334
Hallmark / Apr '78.

I'LL TAKE YOU HOME AGAIN, KATHLEEN.
Tracks: I'll take you home again Kathleen.
■ 7" .... HLP 8403
London-American / Apr '57.

I'M A FOOL.
Tracks: I'm a fool.
■ 7" .... HLU 8252
London-American / Apr '56.

INDIAN LOVE CALL.
Tracks: Indian love call / China doll.
■ 7" .... HL 1149
London-American / Jul '55.

IRISH SONGS, THE SLIM WHITMAN WAY.
Tracks: Not Advised.
LP .... LBS 83019
EMI (Ireland) / '88 / EMI (Ireland) Records / Roots Records / C.M. Distribution.

LOVE SONGS OF THE WATERFALL.
Tracks: Not Advised.
LP .... SLS 50153
Sunset (Liberty) / '70 / EMI.
MC .... TCS 50153
Sunset (Liberty) / '81 / EMI.

MR SONGMAN.
Tracks: Destiny / Can't help falling in love / Open up your heart / Flowers / My melody of love / Mr. Songman / I went to your wedding / Tonight is the night (we fell in love) / Oh my darling (I love you).
LP .... LBG 30343
■ MC .... TCLBG 30343
Liberty / Feb '82.

RED RIVER VALLEY.
Tracks: Rhinestone cowboy / Mr.Ting-a-ling / Too young / Let me call you sweetheart / Small world / Somewhere my love / Una paloma blanca / Red river valley / My elusive dreams / Cara mia / When the moon comes over the mountain / Now is the hour.
■ LP .... UAS 29993
United Artists / Jan '77.

ROSE MARIE.
Tracks: Rose Marie / I'll take you home again Kathleen.
■ 7" .... HL 8061
London-American / Jul '55.

ROSE MARIE (OLD GOLD).
Tracks: Rose Marie.
■ 7" .... OG 9712
Old Gold / May '87.

SERENADE.
Tracks: Serenade.
■ 7" .... HLU 8287
London-American / Jun '56.

SLIM WHITMAN.
Tracks: Rose Marie / I wanna go to heaven / Where did yesterday go / Aura Lee / I remember you / Lavender blue / Girl of my dreams / Secret love / You are my sunshine / Margie / Nearer my love to you / When you wore a tulip / Till we meet again / Sands of time / Since you went away / All kinds of everything / Ghost riders in the sky / Take good care of her / Edelweiss / Just an echo in the valley / Goodbye little darlin' goodbye / When it's harvest time sweet Angeline / Calypso / Carolina moon / My buddy / When / Tears stained my pillow / Puff the magic dragon / Where do I go from here / That silver haired daddy of mine.
■ MC Set .... CRT 019
Cambra / '83.

SLIM WHITMAN (2).
Tracks: Rose Marie / Virginia / When I'm gone you'll soon forget / Valley of tears / Careless hands / Gonna find me a bluebird / Mockingbird Hill / My blue heaven / From a jack to a queen / Tears on my pillow / Roses are red my love / I can't stop loving you / Love song of the waterfall / Please help me I'm falling / Silver threads among the gold / Ramblin' rose.
LP .... SHM 3089
■ MC .... HSC 3089
Hallmark / Feb '82.

SLIM WHITMAN SONG BOOK.
Tracks: Not Advised.
MC .... AM 51
MC .... AM 116
VFM Cassettes / '88 / VFM Children's Entertainment Ltd. / Midland Records / Morley Audio Services.

SLIM WHITMAN STORY, THE.
Tracks: Not Advised.
LP Set .... ALBUM 24
MC Set .... CASSETTE 24
World Records / Dec '81 / EMI.

SLIM WHITMAN VOL. 1.
Tracks: I'm casting my lasso towards the sky / Indian love call / Love songs of the waterfall / Rose Marie / I leave the Milky Way / Tumbling tumbleweeds / Danny boy / You have my heart / I must have been blind / Lord help me be as thou / China doll / When it's springtime in the Rockies / Love knot in my lariat / Riding the range for Jesus / Poor little Angeline / Cryin' for the moon / Serenade / Many times / I'll take you home again Kathleen / First one to find the rainbow, The / Secret love / Stairway to heaven / I'm a fool / Heartbreak hill / Too late now / My wild Irish rose / You're the only one / Just call me lonesome / Annie Laurie / Bells that broke my heart, The / Sweeter than the flowers / Happy Street / Eileen / When I grow too old to dream / Tomorrow never comes / I wanna go to heaven / Blue Canadian Rockies / Yesterday's roses / I climbed the mountain / I'll see you when / Stranger on the shore / What's this world a-comin' to / Rockin' alone (In an old rockin' chair) / Little drops of silver / Another tomorrow / Twelfth of never, The / It's a small world / Mr. Ting-a-Ling (Steel guitar man) / It's a sin to tell a lie / As you walk through my mind / Happy Anniversary.
CD Set .... CDEM 1482
MC Set .... TCEM 1482
EMI / Mar '93 / EMI.

SLIM WHITMAN'S 20 GREATEST LOVE SONGS.
Tracks: Please help me, I'm falling / Loveliest night of the year / Fool such as I, A.
■ LP .... UAG 30270
United Artists / Dec '79.

SONG I LOVE TO SING.
Tracks: When / Secret love / Since you went away / I could only dream / Last farewell, The / I remember you / Rose Marie / Where do i go from here / Silver haired daddy of mine, The / Beautiful dreamer.
LP .... UAG 30322
United Artists / '82 / EMI.
LP .... CBS 32774
MC 40 32774
CBS / Apr '86 / Sony.

THAT SILVER HAIRED DADDY OF MINE.
Tracks: That silver haired daddy of mine / If I could only dream.
■ 7" .... BP 377
Liberty / Oct '80.

TILL WE MEET AGAIN.
Tracks: I wanna go to heaven / Just an echo in the valley / White cliffs of Dover, The / Lavender blue / When you wore a tulip / Where did yesterday go / Edelweiss / My buddy / Nights of splendour / Nearer my love to you / Aura Lee / Take good care of her / Sands of time / Till we meet again.
LP .... UAG 30297
MC .... TCK 30297
United Artists / Apr '80 / EMI.

TUMBLING TUMBLEWEEDS.
Tracks: Tumbling tumbleweeds.
■ 7" .... HLU 8230
London-American / Mar '56.

UNA PALOMA BLANCA.
Tracks: Una paloma blanca / Somewhere my love.
■ 7" .... UP 36220
United Artists / Feb '77.

VERY BEST OF SLIM WHITMAN, THE.
Tracks: Rose Marie / Cool water / I'll take you home again, Kathleen / I remember you / Secret love / Snowbird / Ramblin' rose / Love song of the waterfall / Old spinning wheel / It's a sin to tell a lie / Happy anniversary / Twelfth of never / Serenade / Roses are red / China doll / Walking in the sunshine / When you were sweet sixteen / Honeymoon feelin' / Have I told you lately that I love you / Indian love call.
■ LP .... UAS 29898
United Artists / Jan '76.
■ MC .... TCK 29898
United Artists / Jan '76.

WHEN.
Tracks: When / Till we meet again.
■ 7" .... BP 394
Liberty / May '81.

WHEN YOU WERE SWEET SIXTEEN.
Tracks: When you were sweet sixteen / How could I not love you.
■ 7" .... UP 36017
United Artists / Oct '75.

YODELLING.
Tracks: Not Advised.
MC 4XLL 9278
Capitol (Specials) / Dec '88.

Whitstein Brothers

Colfax, Louisiana-born Brothers Robert (guitar/lead vocals) and Charles (madolin/guitar/vocals)were born at the end of World War II. Both parents were musically inclined, singing in churches, whilst at home on their family farm the brothers would listen to the old timey harmony singing of Ira and Charlie Louvin, the Delmores and the Blue Sky Boys. They had some work touring with the Grand Ole Opry in 1964, alongside Faron Young, Porter Wagoner amongst others. Since coming into contact with Ken Irwin at Rounder (through a demo tape made for Tillman Franks, manager of David Houston and handed to him by Jesse Reynolds), they got to playing festivals (Europe and Cambridge Folk Festival included) on a broader scale - impressing many with their traditional releases. Their third album, 1988's *Old Time Duets* is an exemplary demonstration of the craft. They've toured the UK twice in 1988 and 1990, when Charlie Louvin stood in for Robert, when other commitmentes wouldn't allow him the time. (Maurice Hope July 1993)

OLD TIME DUETS.
Tracks: Mansion on the hill / We parted by the riverside / There's an open door waiting / Sinner you'd better get ready / We met in the saddle / I'm troubled / That silver haired daddy / Seven year blues / Weary lonesome blues / Somewhere in Tennessee / Maple on the hill / If I could hear my mother pray again / Pitfall / Beautiful lost river valley.
CD .... ROUNDERCD 0264
LP .... ROUNDER 0264
MC .... ROUNDERC 0264
Rounder / '89 / Projection / Roots Records / Swift / C.M. Distribution / Topic Records / Jazz Music / Hot Shot / A.D.A Distribution / Direct Distribution.

ROSE OF MY HEART.
Tracks: Rose of my heart / Highway headin' South / Kentucky / My curly headed baby / Weary days / Weary blues from waiting / Arkansas / Bridge over troubled water / Eighth wonder of the world / Scared of the blues / Where the old river flows / Smokey mountain memories.
LP .... ROUNDER 0206
Rounder / Apr '85 / Projection / Roots Records / Swift / C.M. Distribution / Topic Records / Jazz Music / Hot Shot / A.D.A Distribution / Direct Distribution.
MC .... ROUNDER 0206C
Rounder / Aug '88 / Projection / Roots Records / Swift / C.M. Distribution / Topic Records / Jazz Music / Hot Shot / A.D.A Distribution / Direct Distribution.

TROUBLE AIN'T NOTHING BUT THE BLUES.
Tracks: Showboat gambler / What about you / Freight train boogie / When I found you / High cost of living / Everglades, The / Looks like rain today / Trouble in mind / I don't believe you've met my baby / Ozark Mountain lullaby / My baby came back / My Texas girl.
LP .... ROUNDER 0229
MC .... ROUNDER 0229C
Rounder / Aug '88 / Projection / Roots Records / Swift / C.M. Distribution / Topic Records / Jazz Music / Hot Shot / A.D.A Distribution / Direct Distribution.

Wier, Rusty

KUMBAK BAR & GRILL.
Tracks: Kum-bak bar & grill / Cheryl Doreen / Daytime drinkin' / Wonderful tonight / I kept thinkin' about you / Other side of the hill / Close your eyes / Alibi lies / All my give a damn is gone / Lone star lady.
LP .... SDLP 057
MC .... SDC 057
Sundown / Jan '88 / Terry Blood Dist. / Jazz Music / C.M. Distribution.

Wilburn Brothers

Doyle Wilburn, born Virgil Doyle Wilburn on 07.071.932 (died 16.10.1982) and Teddy Wilburn, born Thurman Theodore Wilburn died on 30.11.1931 (both in Hardy, Missouri). As far back as 1937 you could find five skinny Wilburn kids singing for nickels on the street corners of Thayer, Missouri. Doyle and Teddy made their debut on Grand Old Opry in 1941 as part of The Wilburn Family Group and appeared on the Louisiana Hayride from 1948-1951 they left in 1951, to do a stint in the US Army. 1953 Saw them back singing as a duo, touring with Faron Young and Webb Pierce. Joining the Opry in 1954, showed shrewd business acumen when they opened their own publishing company, Sure Fire Music in 1957. By 1960 they'd also set up Wil-Hem talent agency. Apart from their own Decca recordings, their popular live shows and TV series (starting 1963) they have been very much instrumental in helping to bring both Loretta Lynn (who also recorded for Decca) and Patty Loveless up through the ranks. The Wilburn's music is a blend of old and new and they have had a career which has held firm from 1955. Additional 1950's successes include two hit duets with Ernest Tubb *Mister love* and *Hey Mr Bluebird*. As a duo they ran up a hefty tally of hits, from such 1950's fare as *Go away with me, Somebody's back in town* and *Which one is to blame* to the memorable early 1960's *Trouble's back in town* (Cashbox's Country Record of 1962) and *Roll muddy river* giving them a winning run to take them through the decade before the hits dried up. (Maurice Hope - July 1993).

CITY LIMITS.
Tracks: Not Advised.
LP . . . . HAT 3061
MC . . . . HATC 3061
Stetson / '88 / Crusader Marketing Co. / Swift / Wellard Dist. / Midland Records / C.M. Distribution.

COUNTRY GOLD.
Tracks: I don't care / When I stop dreaming / I don't love you anymore / Crazy arms / I dreamed of an old love affair / Wonder why you said goodbye / I wonder where you are tonight / Before I'm over you / I can stand it / World of forgotten people / I guess I'm crazy / Don't let me cross over.
LP . . . . HAT 3007
MC . . . . HATC 3007
Stetson / Nov '85 / Crusader Marketing Co. / Swift / Wellard Dist. / Midland Records / C.M. Distribution.

TEDDY AND DOYLE.
Tracks: Not Advised.
LP . . . . HAT 3035
MC . . . . HATC 3035
Stetson / Apr '87 / Crusader Marketing Co. / Swift / Wellard Dist. / Midland Records / C.M. Distribution.

WILBURN BROTHERS SHOW, THE.
Tracks: Not Advised.
LP . . . . HAT 3017
MC . . . . HATC 3017
Stetson / Sep '86 / Crusader Marketing Co. / Swift / Wellard Dist. / Midland Records / C.M. Distribution.

WONDERFUL WILBURN BROTHERS.
Tracks: Not Advised.
CD . . . . .KCD 746
King / Nov '92 / New Note / Koch International.

Wild Canyon

'TWAS A LONG TIME AGO.
Tracks: 'Twas a long time ago / Rodeo rider, The / Good old days will not return, The / Poor boy jamboree / You shouldn't do it / Golden ages (are they gone) / Buffalo skip / Blanket on the ground / Vacation time / Bob Wills is still the king / Jim Bridger / Door is always open, The / Taker, The / Folsom Prison blues.
■ LP . . . . BFX 15131
Bear Family / '87.

18 GUITAR TRACKS.
Tracks: Enchanted canyon / Raunchy / Teen scene / Trambone / Strollin' / Mexican lady / Corn pickin' / My memories / We were born with the music of rock / Dobro / Buffalo skip / Sunny river / Skip along / Poor boy jamboree / Flamingo shuffle / Snail pace / Take me back home / Blue steel blues.
CD . . . . BCD 15538
Bear Family / Nov '90 / Rollercoaster Records / Swift / Direct Distribution.

LIKE A POKER GAME.
Tracks: Where are you / I dreamed I was a cowboy / It's just like a poker game / Everything I do / Things we say are true / I'll be here with you / Step up / Blue steel blues / Come on with me / Okie from Muskogee / Mexican lady.
LP . . . . BFX 15290
Bear Family / Nov '87 / Rollercoaster Records / Swift / Direct Distribution.

NEW WRAPPING.
Tracks: Teen scene / Entertainer, The / Canyon hop / Dobro / My memories / New wrapping medley / Enchanted canyon 86 / Skip along / Flamingo shuffle / What is happiness / Country gentleman / Sail place.
LP . . . . BFX 15251
Bear Family / Nov '86 / Rollercoaster Records / Swift / Direct Distribution.

THIS WORLD OF OURS.
Tracks: Cinder track, The / Great adventure / This world of ours / Imprisoned, but wasn't guilty / Why must we wait so long? / Nur wur / Walking in the sunshine / Good-hearted woman / Laura / Mamas don't let your babies grow up to be cowboys / What about you? / She thinks I still care.
LP . . . . BFX 15197
Bear Family / Nov '85 / Rollercoaster Records / Swift / Direct Distribution.

Wilkin, Marijohn

ONE DAY AT A TIME.
Tracks: One day at a time / So much to thank you for / Behold the man / Let your light so shine / God is love / Here I am / Living sermon for thee, A / Back in the fold / Living tree, The / Where I'm going / Give it away / Speak louder / Our little old home town / Let the spirit work in silence / Scars in the hands of Jesus, The / Reach up and touch God's hand / You still the troubled waters / Follow the Jesus sign / It's a brand new world / I have returned.
LP . . . . TWE 6005
MC . . . . TC TWE 6005
Word 20 / May '82 / Sony.

Williams, Audrey

From anyone's earliest memories of Audrey Williams, she was not content to be rural and poor. Audrey always wanted to be somebody. Born on February 28th, 1928 in the red clay farm country near Brundidge, Alabama, she dreamed of romance, pretty clothes and the exciting life of an actress or a singing star. A childhood playmate remembers Audrey gathering her friends together on the back of her daddy's old pick-up truck and pretending it was their stage. She talked of singing one day from the stage of the Grand Ole Opry. A tall thin, hard-living country singer from Montgomery named Hank Williams was like the answer to her prayers. Audrey's voice was raw country. In the early years of their marriage, she played stand-up bass and sang back-up for Hank's band. She recorded her first sides for Decca in the spring of 1950, backed by Hank Williams and the Drifting Cowboys. Further sessions were also accompanied by the Drifting Cowboys, and the final session found her with the famous bunch of the Nashville session musicians.

RAMBLIN' GAL.
Tracks: What put the pep in Grandma / I like that kind / My tight wad daddy / Model "T" love / Don't be too quick to judge / How can you refuse him now / Honky tonkin' / I forgot more than you'll ever know / Slowly you taught me / Help me understand / Ramblin' gal / To my pal - Bosephus.
LP . . . . BFX 15346
Bear Family / Nov '88 / Rollercoaster Records / Swift / Direct Distribution.

Williams, Diana

This American singer is known solely for her minor hit single, *Teddy Bear's Last Ride*. In 1976 Red Sovine, a veteran country singer, released a sickly narrative single called Teddy Bear, which told the tale of a young disabled kid whose life was suddenly made happier by a troupe of truckers taking him for a spin in their vehicles. A million record buyers were also taken for a ride: *Teddy Bear* went gold in the States, reaching No.1 on the country chart and No 40 on the pop list. Two of the song's writers, Billy Joe Burnette and Dale Royal, quickly penned an equally "sincere" sequel, *Teddy Bear's Last Ride*. Diana Williams recorded it but could only manage a No.66 placing on the Billboard Hot Hundred. In 1981, a year after Sovine's death, *Teddy Bear* suddenly became a UK smash, speeding to No 4 on the chart. Inevitably, the Williams record was also dug out from the vaults but it peaked at No 54. (Bob MacDonald)

TEDDY BEAR'S LAST RIDE.
Tracks: Teddy bear's last ride / If you cared enough to cry.
■ 7" . . . . .CL 207
Capitol / Jun '81.

Williams, Dicky

COME BACK PUSSY.
Tracks: Come back pussy / Same motel, The.
7" 89 514
CMC / Feb '90 / Backs Distribution / Ichiban Records (UK).

I WANNA KNOW WHY.
Tracks: I wanna know why / Laughin' and grinnin'.
7" 90 603
CMC / Apr '90 / Backs Distribution / Ichiban Records (UK).

I WANT YOU FOR BREAKFAST.
Tracks: Weekend playboy / You hurt the wrong man / I've been loving you too long / Letter from a soldier / Need your love / Lost my woman to a woman / Good used man / I'm in love with two women / I want you for breakfast / Let me love you before we make love / Don't give your love to anyone but me / Little closer, A.
CD . . . . ICH 1115CD
LP . . . . ICH 1115
MC . . . . ICH 1115MC
Ichiban / Aug '91 / RTM / Pinnacle.

IN YOUR FACE.
Tracks: Same motel, The / I didn't do nothin' / Come back pussy / Laughin' and grinnin' / I wanna know why / Ugly men / Fat girls / Do you know (where your woman is tonight) / Bad luck and hard times.
CD . . . . CMCCD 4012
LP . . . . CMC 4012
MC . . . . CMCMC 4012
CMC / Oct '89 / Backs Distribution / Ichiban Records (UK).

Williams, Don

Singer-songwriter and guitarist, the true 'Gentle Giant' of country music, who's enjoyed a twenty year career at the top of his profession. Enjoying a universal appeal, his affable, easy and laid-back style holding a special place in the

hearts of his many UK devotees. Born in Floydada, Texas on 27.05.1939. Williams, who had a folk background, turned professional in 1957 and moved to Corpus Christi, where he formed Pozo-Seco (a folk/pop group who had fleeting appearances on Billboards top 100) in 1964 with Susan Taylor and Lofton Cline. Williams, with his trademark denim jacket and stetson, embarked on a solo career in 1971 after moving to Nashville in 1967. Working as a staff writer for Jack Clements (Jack Music) he was soon back in the recording studio, doing what was to become his trademark laid-back country style for the Clements JMI label. Allen Reynolds was the producer of Don Williams *Volume 1, 2* and *3* which provided a winning blend of material from Bob McDill and Williams himself. *We should be together* gave Don his first top five success (1974), and in the same year his Dot debut single *I wouldn't want to live if you didn't love me* went all the way. During the next ten years he was to truly capitalise, embarking on a run of 27 singles all securing top ten placings. Williams popularity in the UK since 1975 (making the Wembley Country Music Festival almost his own) has seen few parallels. He enjoyed chart success with *I recall a gypsy woman* and the song which was to become synonymous with him *You're my best friend*. Sellout tours and healthy album sales have been the order of the day ever since. Stateside he's had great success through recording the songs of Bob McDill - *(Turn out the light and)* *Love me tonight* (1975), *Say it again* (1976), *It must be love* (1979), *Good ole boys like me* (1980) and the wry *If Hollywood don't need you* (1983) all going to No. 1 Such was the wealth of prospective single material available to ABC/ Dot and MCA that choosing what not to release would be the most difficult task. Wayland Holyfield another ace songwriter, apart from supplying *You're my best friend*, gave the smooth-voiced singer such top singles as *Til' the rivers all run dry* (1976) and *Some broken hearts never mend* (1977). Williams has written such hit songs as *Lay down beside me* and his albums have crowded the country charts on both sides of the Atlantic. The top selling *Harmony* was supported with the likes of *I'm just a country boy* and *Expressions* (besides some top selling TV advertised compilations making great inroads into the UK pop charts), featuring sideman Danny Flowers' *Tulsa time*, a 1978 No. 1. Later, through his admiration of Don's music, rock act Eric Clapton was to also record it. 1978 also saw Williams voted CMA's Male Vocalist of the year, while 1980 brought him into contact with songwriter Roger Cook (*I believe in you*), backing it with *Love is on a roll* (with John Prine) a 1983 chart topper. *Stay young* (No. 1) from Gallagher and Lyle continuing the British connection and 1986 saw him signing to Capitol. Admittedly some of the sheen had by now begun to leave him, Williams a private family man, who shunned the glamour, was spending more time at home - a ranch near Ashland City, Tennessee. With the emergence of the New Country set, who were obtaining most of the promotional/marketing attention, Williams' hits slowed down, although he was still active chartwise with *Heartbeat in the darkness* (1986) another No. 1 supplemented with a healthy collection of top ten hits during his three year sojourn at Capitol. Next stop was RCA Records (1989 - 1992), long enough to make three fine albums, his *True love* album finding him once again reaping success with another Bob McDill song, *Lord have mercy on a country boy*. During 1992 Don released *Currents*, where African musicians the Bhundu Boys appear on one track. Prior to this, in 1981, he'd duetted with Emmylou Harris and their version of Townes Van Zandt's *If I needed you* soaring to No. 3. Highlights from his spring UK tour (where Mickey Newbury played as support) in 1993 were recorded for a live album. He has two film credits to his name - 20th Century Fox's *WW and the Dixie Dance Kings* (with Jerry Reed) and Universal's 1980 film *Smokey and the Bandit 2*, featuring Burt Reynolds and Reed. (Maurice Hope - August 1993)

6 TRACK HITS: DON WILLIAMS.
Tracks: Ruby Tuesday / There's always something there to remind me.
EP 7SR 5055
MC 7SC 5055
Scoop 33 / Oct '84.

AMANDA.
Tracks: Amanda.
■ 7" . . . . ABE 12014
ABC Records / Feb '77.

AS LONG AS I HAVE YOU.
Tracks: Learn to let it go / One good well / Cryin' eyes / I've been loved by the best / Broken heartland / Just as long as I have you / Why get up / Maybe that's all it takes / We're all the way / Flowers won't grow (in the gardens of stone) / If you love me, won't you love me like you love me.
■ CD . . . . PD 90393
RCA / Oct '89.
■ LP . . . . PL 90393
RCA / Oct '89.
■ MC . . . . PK 90393
RCA / Oct '89.

■ DELETED

CD . . . . ND 90597
MC . . . . NK 90597
RCA / Apr '92 / BMG.

BROKEN HEART NEVER MENDS, A.
Tracks: I recall a gypsy woman / Fairweather friends / It must be love / Falling again / Such a lovely lady / Especially you / Some broken hearts never mend / Oh misery / You're the only one / Standin' in a sea of teardrops / Nobody but you / You've got a hold on me / You're my best friend / Years from now / (Turn out the lights) and love me tonight / Loving you for so long now / I'll need someone to hold me when I cry / Now and then / Slowly but surely / Fly away / Down the road I go / If I needed you / I'll take your love anytime / Don't stop loving me now.
Double LP . . . . VSOPLP 115
MC . . . . VSOPMC 115
Connoisseur Collection / Nov '88 / Pinnacle.
■ CD . . . . VSOPCD 115
Connoisseur Collection / Apr '90.

CAFE CAROLINA.
Tracks: Only game in town, The / Walkin' a broken heart / Maggie's dream / That's the thing about love / Leaving / Beautiful woman / True blue hearts / I'll never need another you / It's time for love / I'll be faithful to you.
LP. . . . . MCF 3225
MCA / May '84 / BMG.

COUNTRY BOY.
Tracks: Not Advised.
■ LP. . . . . ABCL 5233
ABC Records / Oct '77.

COUNTRY COLLECTION.
Tracks: I believe in you / Listen to the radio / (Turn out the light and) love me tonight / I'm just a country boy / Amanda / Say it again / If Hollywood don't need you / Love me over again / You're my best friend / Some broken hearts never mend / Only love / Down the road I go / Don't you believe / Miracles / Fairweather friends / I recall a gypsy woman.
LP. . . . . ADEH 403
MC . . . . ADEHC 403
Arcade / '82 / Sony.

COUNTRY GREATS.
Tracks: You're my best friend / We should be together / I believe in you / Miracles / It must be love / That's the thing about love / If I needed you / Fairweather friends / Tulsa time / Lay down beside me / Story of my life / Steal my heart away / Come early morning / Down the road I go.
MC . . . . TCMFP 5805
MFP / Oct '87 / EMI.
■ LP. . . . . MFP 5805
MFP / Oct '87.

COUNTRY SUPERSTARS (see under Bare, Bobby).

CUP OF TEA, A.
Tracks: Cup of tea, A / In the morning.
■ 7" . . . . ABC 4162
ABC Records / Feb '77.

CURRENTS.
Tracks: Only water (shining in the air) / Too much love / That song about the river / Catfish bates / Back on the street again / So far, so good / Gettin' back together tonight / In the family / Standing knee deep in a river (dying of thirst) / Lone star state of mind / Old trail, The / It's who you love.
CD . . . . PD 90645
MC . . . . PK 90645
RCA / Mar '92 / BMG.

DON WILLIAMS VOL.1.
Tracks: Gypsy woman / Amanda / Shelter of my arms.
LP. . . . . MCL 1628
■ MC . . . . MCLC 1628
ABC Records / Aug '81.

DON WILLIAMS VOL.2.
Tracks: I wish I was in Nashville / Your sweet love / She's in love with a rodeo man / Atta way to go / We should be together / Loving you so long now / Miller's cave / Oh misery / I don't think about her no more / Down the road I go.
■ LP. . . . . MCL 1541
MCA / Feb '82.

ESPECIALLY FOR YOU.
Tracks: Fairweather friends / I don't want to love you / Years from now / Lord, I hope this day is good / Especially you / If I need you / Now and then / Smooth talking baby / I've got you to thank for that / Miracles.
■ LP. . . . . MCF 3114
MCA / Aug '81.

ESPECIALLY FOR YOU.
Tracks: Especially for you.
7" . . . . MCA 735
MCA / Jul '81 / BMG.

EXPRESSIONS.
Tracks: Not Advised.
LP. . . . . ABCL 5253
MC . . . . CAB 5253
ABC Records / Sep '78.

EXPRESSIONS/PORTRAIT.
Tracks: I would like to see you again / You've got a hold on me / Tears of the lonely / All I'm missing is you / Tulsa time / Lay down beside me / Give it to me / Not a chance / It must be love / When I'm with you / It only rains on me / We've never tried it with each other / We're all the way / Circle driveway / You get to me / Steal my heart away / Love's endless war / Woman you should be in movies / Love me over again / Good ole boys like me.
■ MC Set . . . . MCA 2 104
MCA (Twinpax Cassettes) / Apr '82.

FALLING AGAIN.
Tracks: Falling again / I keep putting off getting over you.
■ 7" . . . . MCA 678
MCA / Mar '81.

GOLDEN GREATS: DON WILLIAMS.
Tracks: Amanda / Come early morning / We should be together / I wouldn't want to live if you didn't love me / I'm just a country boy / Tulsa time / Turn out the lights (love me tonight) / Till the rivers all run dry / I recall a gypsy woman / You're my best friend / I believe in you / Years from now / Story of my life / Stay young / Love is on a roll / Listen to the radio.
LP. . . . . MCM 5016
MCA / Dec '90 / BMG.
■ MC . . . . MCMC 5016
MCA / Dec '90.
■ CD . . . . DMCM 5016
MCA / Sep '91.

GREATEST HITS: DON WILLIAMS, VOL.1.
Tracks: Amanda / Come early morning / Shelter of your eyes, The / What a way to go / She's in love with a rodeo man / Down the road I go / I wouldn't want to live if you didn't love me / We should be together / Ties that bind, The / Ghost story / Don't you believe? / I recall a gypsy woman.
■ LP. . . . . ABCL 5147
ABC Records / Jul '76.
LP. . . . . MCL 1761
■ MC . . . . MCLC 1761
ABC Records / May '83.
LP. . . . . SHM 3193
MC . . . . HSC 3193
Hallmark / Sep '86 / Pickwick Records.
CD . . . . PWKS 503
Pickwick / Jan '89 / Pickwick Records.

HARMONY.
Tracks: Till the rivers all run dry / You keep coming 'round / Don't you think it's time / I don't want the money / Where the Arkansas river leaves Oklahoma / Say it again / Maybe I just don't know / Magic carpet / Time / Ramblin' (instrumental) / She never knew me.
LP. . . . . MCL 1801
■ MC . . . . MCLC 1801
MCA / Feb '86.

HARMONY/VISIONS.
Tracks: Till the rivers all run dry / You keep coming round / Don't you think it's time? / I don't want the money / Where the Arkansas river leaves Oklahoma / Say it again / Maybe I just don't know / Magic carpet / Time / Ramblin' / She never knew me / Time on my hands / I'll forgive but I'll not forget / I'm getting good at missing you / Some broken hearts never mend / Falling in love again / We can sing / I'll need someone to hold me (when I cry) / Expert at everything / Cup of tea, A / In the morning / Missing you, missing me.
■ MC Set . . . . MCA 2 112
MCA (Twinpax Cassettes) / Oct '83.

HEARTBEAT IN THE DARKNESS.
Tracks: Light in your eyes / Heartbeat in the darkness.
■ 7" . . . . CL 412
Capitol / Jun '86.

I BELIEVE IN YOU.
Tracks: Falling again / Good to see you / I want you back again / Simple song / I believe in you / Ain't it amazing? / Just enough love (for one woman) / I keep putting off getting over you / Rainy nights and memories / Slowly but surely.
MC . . . . MCFC 3077
MCA / Aug '80 / BMG.
■ LP. . . . . MCF 3077
MCA / Aug '80.

I BELIEVE IN YOU.
Tracks: I believe in you / Simple song.
■ 7" . . . . MCA 631
MCA / Aug '80.

I RECALL A GYPSY WOMAN.
Tracks: I recall a gypsy woman / Amanda.
■ 7" . . . . ABC 4098
ABC Records / Jun '76.
■ 7" . . . . MCA 711
MCA / Aug '80.

I RECALL A GYPSY WOMAN (OLD GOLD).
Tracks: I recall a gypsy woman / You're my best friend.
7" . . . . OG 9320
Old Gold / Apr '83 / Pickwick Records.

I WOULDN'T BE A MAN.
Tracks: I wouldn't be a man / Easy touch.
12" 12CL 496
■ 7" . . . . CL 496
Capitol / May '88.

I'VE GOT A WINNER IN YOU.
Tracks: I've got a winner in you / Fly away.
■ 7" . . . . ABC 4208
ABC Records / Apr '78.

IMAGES: DON WILLIAMS.
Tracks: Not Advised.
■ LP. . . . . NE 1033
K-Tel / Aug '78.

IN MY LIFE.
Tracks: Where do we go from here / Strawberry fields forever / Something / Apartment No.9 / Ruby Tuesday / Always something there / Follow me back to Louisville / On her way to be a woman / Take my hand for a while / Long walk from childhood / In my life.
LP. 20016
MC 40016
Astan (USA) / Nov '84.
LP. . . . . SHLP 120
MC . . . . SHTC 120
Castle Showcase / Apr '86 / Arabesque Ltd.

IT MUST BE LOVE.
Tracks: It must be love / Not a chance.
■ 7" . . . . MCA 530
MCA / Oct '79.

IT'S GOTTA BE MAGIC.
Tracks: It's gotta be magic / I would like to see you again / Lay down beside me / Tears of the lonely / You've got a hold on me / Fallin' in love again / I need someone to hold me (when I cry) / Turn out the light and love me tonight / Lovin' understandin' man / Fly away / Your sweet love / Tempted / No use running / Oh misery / Sweet fever / Missing you, missing me.
CD . . . . PWKS 535
MC . . . . HSC 3283
Pickwick / Feb '90 / Pickwick Records.

LISTEN TO THE RADIO.
Tracks: Not Advised.
■ LP. . . . . MCF 3135
MCA / Apr '82.

LISTEN TO THE RADIO.
Tracks: Listen to the radio / Only love.
7" . . . . MCA 771
MCA / Mar '82 / BMG.

LOVE IS ON A ROLL.
Tracks: Love is on a roll.
7" . . . . MCA 811
■ 7" P.Disc . . . . MCAP 811
MCA / Mar '83.

LOVE ME OVER AGAIN.
Tracks: Love me over again / Circle driveway.
■ 7" . . . . MCA 551
MCA / Jan '80.

LOVE STORIES.
Tracks: I believe in you / Listen to the radio / Good to see you / Love's endless war / Yellow moon / Fool, fool heart / Falling again / Years from now / I'm still looking for you / Story of my life / You get to me / Stay young / Now and then / Love is on a roll / Miracles / Ain't it amazing / Especially you / Only love.
LP. . . . . NE 1252
MC . . . . CE 2252
K-Tel / Sep '83 / I & B Records / C.M. Distribution / Arabesque Ltd. / Mono Distributors (Jersey) Ltd. / Prism Leisure PLC / PolyGram / Ross Records / Prism Leisure PLC.

LOVE'S ENDLESS WAR.
Tracks: Love's endless war / We're all the way.
■ 7" . . . . MCA 581
MCA / Apr '80.

LOVERS AND BEST FRIENDS.
Tracks: You're my best friend / Story of my life / Pressure makes diamonds / Love me tonight / You get to me / Love me over again / I would't want to live if you didn't love me / Ain't it amazing / Love is on a roll / I'll need someone to hold me when I cry / We're all the way / I'll be faithful to you.
LP. . . . . MCF 3357
MCA / Mar '87 / BMG.
■ MC . . . . MCFC 3357
MCA / Mar '87.

NEW HORIZONS.
Tracks: Not Advised.
■ LP. . . . . NE 1048
K-Tel / Sep '79.

NEW MOVES.
Tracks: Heartbeat in the darkness / I'll never love this way again / Shot full of love / We got love / Send her roses / Senorita / Light in your eyes / It's about time / Then it's love / We've got a good fire goin'.
■ LP. . . . . EST 2004
Capitol / Mar '86.
■ MC . . . . TCEST 2004
Capitol / Mar '86.

ONLY LOVE.
Tracks: Only love / Listen to the radio.
7" . . . . MCA 783
MCA / Jun '82 / BMG.

SENORITA.
Tracks: Senorita.
■ 7" . . . . CL 442
Capitol / Feb '87.

SOME BROKEN HEARTS.
Tracks: Stay young / You're my best friend / I'm just a country boy / Listen to the radio / All I'm missing is you / Some broken hearts never mend / I believe in you / Turn out the lights (love me tonight) / Tulsa time / Years from now / Say it again / 'Till the rivers all run dry / Amanda / I wouldn't want to live if you didn't love me / We should be together / Come early morning.
LP. . . . . PLAT 301
MC . . . . PLAC 301
Platinum Music / Apr '88 / Prism Leisure PLC / Ross Records.
CD . . . . PLATCD 301
Prism / Oct '92 / Pinnacle / Midland Records.

STAY YOUNG.
Tracks: Stay young.
■ 7" . . . . MCA 820
MCA / Jun '83.

STORY OF MY LIFE.
Tracks: Story of my life / I'm still looking for you.
■ 7" . . . . MCA 838
MCA / Oct '83.

THAT'S THE THING ABOUT LOVE.
Tracks: That's the thing about love / I'm still looking for you.
7" . . . . MCA 888
MCA / Apr '84 / BMG.

TRACES.
Tracks: Desperately / Easy touch / Come from the heart / Running out of reasons to run / I wouldn't be a man / Looking back / Till I can't take it anymore / Another place, another time / Old Coyote town / You love me through it all.
CD . . . . CDEST 2048
Capitol / Nov '87 / EMI.
■ CD . . . . CDP 748 034 2
Capitol / Nov '87.
■ LP. . . . . EST 2048
Capitol / Nov '87.
■ MC . . . . TCEST 2048
Capitol / Nov '87.

TRUE LOVE.
Tracks: True love / Lord have mercy on a country boy / Darlin' that's what your love does to me / Come a little closer / Just 'cause I'm in love with you / Back in my younger days / Donald and June / Diamonds to dust / Jamaica farewell / Lovin' you is like comin' home.
CD . . . . PD 90538
RCA / Nov '90 / BMG.
■ LP. . . . . PL 90538
RCA / Nov '90.
■ MC . . . . PK 90538
RCA / Nov '90.

TULSA TIME.
Tracks: Tulsa time / Not a chance.
■ 7" . . . . ABC 4231
ABC Records / Sep '78.

VERY BEST OF DON WILLIAMS.
Tracks: You're my best friend / Lay down beside me / Till the rivers all run dry / Ghost story / Good ole boys like me / Love me over again / It must be love / Amanda / Tulsa time / Shelter of your eyes, The / She's in love with a Rodeo man / I believe in you / Time on my hands / Turn down the lights / Some broken hearts never mend / I recall a gypsy woman.
CD . . . . DMGC 4014
MC . . . . MCGC 4014
MCA / Nov '80 / BMG.
■ LP. . . . . MCG 4014
MCA / Nov '80.

VERY BEST OF DON WILLIAMS, VOL 2.
Tracks: Listen to the radio / Miracles / I wouldn't want to live without your love / She never knew me / Story of my life / I'm just a country boy / I've got a winner in you / Falling again / Love is on a roll / I hope this day is good / Rake and ramblin' man / Mistakes / Say it again / Nobody but you / If Hollywood don't need you.
LP. . . . . MCF 3203
MC . . . . MCFC 3203
MCA / Feb '84 / BMG.

VISIONS.
Tracks: Not Advised.
■ LP. . . . . ABCL 5200
ABC Records / Feb '77.

WALKING A BROKEN HEART.
Tracks: Walking a broken heart / True blue heart.
7" . . . . MCA 945
MCA / Mar '85 / BMG.

WE'VE GOT A GOOD FIRE GOING.
Tracks: Shot full of love / We've got a good fire going.
■ 7" . . . . CL 392
Capitol / Feb '86.

WHERE DO WE GO FROM HERE.
Tracks: Where do we go from here? / Just an ordinary day / Apartment No.9 / Ruby Tuesday / Always something there / Follow me back to Louisville / On her way to be a woman / Take my hand for a while / Long walk from childhood / In my life.
LP. . . . . SDLP 1004
Sundown / Nov '83 / Terry Blood Dist. / Jazz Music / C.M. Distribution.

YEARS FROM NOW.
Tracks: Years from now / Maybe I just don't know.
7" . . . . MCA 743
MCA / Oct '81 / BMG.

YELLOW MOON.
Tracks: Not Advised.
■ LP. . . . . MCF 3159
MCA / Apr '83.

YOU'RE MY BEST FRIEND.
Tracks: You're my best friend / Help yourselves to each other / I don't wanna let go / Sweet fever / Someone like you / Love me tonight / Where are you? / You're the only one / Reason to be / Tempted.
■ LP. . . . . ABCD 5127
ABC Records / Aug '78.
LP. . . . . MCL 1768
■ MC . . . . MCLC 1768
ABC Records / May '83.

YOU'RE MY BEST FRIEND.
Tracks: You're my best friend.
■ 7" . . . . ABC 4144
ABC Records / Oct '76.

YOU'RE MY BEST FRIEND.
Tracks: Not Advised.
LP. . . . . SHM 3222
MC . . . . HSC 3222
Hallmark / Oct '87 / Pickwick Records.
CD . . . . PWKS 438
Pickwick / Sep '89 / Pickwick Records.

YOU'RE MY BEST FRIEND, VOLS I & 2.
Tracks: You're my best friend / Help yourselves to each other / I don't wanna let go / Sweet fever / Someone like you / Love me tonight / Where are you? / You're the only one / Reason to be / I wish I was in Nashville / Your sweet dream / She's in love with a rodeo man / What a way to go / We should be together / Loving you so long now / Oh misery / Miller's cave / I don't think about her no more / Down the road I go.
MC Set . . . . MCA 2 116
MCA (Twinpax Cassettes) / Sep '84.

Williams, Hank

Hank Williams was born in Alabama in 1923, he died on New Year's Day 1953 in the back seat of a chauffered Cadillac. He is undoubtedly the biggest star in the history of country music. People around the world still sing his songs, perhaps not even knowing who wrote them, so great is the appeal of his unforgettable tunes and simple, rhyming lyrics. He was practically illiterate and never read anything but comic books, but was one of the greatest folk-poets of all time, his sincerity and concern for the lives of everyday people the very epitome of country music. He wrote happy songs and funny songs, but his aching ballads of heartbreak and infidelity were his greatest hits. He also recorded sentimental monologues such as *Luke The Drifter*. He led an excellent small band called the Drifting Cowboys, and insisted that they play on his records, which was unusual then. He was influenced by a black street singer called Tee-Tot (real name: Rufe Payne). He started a band while still in school, sang on the radio in Montgomery, Alabama at the age of 13, but served a hard apprenticeship in honky tonks ('blood buckets') all over the Southeast. He took his songs to Acuff-Rose in Nashville, where Fred Rose recognised his genius and subsequently helped him to polish many a lyric; his first big hit in 1949 was *Lovesick Blues*, ironically not his own song, but older than he was. He suffered back pain all his life, and probably had an undiagnosed case of spina bifida (he was born at home into an utterly poverty-stricken family). He was addicted to pain pills and became an alcoholic at an early age. His long-suffering, strong-willed mother didn't help, and neither did his wife, Audrey who wanted to be a country star too, but couldn't sing very well. Some of his happiest and some of his saddest songs came out of his stormy marriage. He was such a big star that the Grand Ole Opry had to have him, despite his honky tonk style (which the Opry didn't really like) and despite his reputation for unreliability, which got so bad the Opry had to let him go; Audrey divorced him and his heart gave up the struggle. he wrote about 125 songs and the records will never stop selling. (Donald Clarke).

16 GREATEST HITS: HANK WILLIAMS.
Tracks: Not Advised.
CD . . . . CD 43
Bescol / '87.

16 ORIGINAL HITS: HANK WILLIAMS.
Tracks: Not Advised.
MC . . . . MC 1625
Timeless Treasures / Sep '87 / Terry Blood Dist.

BEYOND THE SUNSET.
Tracks: Not Advised.
LP. 831 574-1
Polydor / Jan '88 / PolyGram.

COLLECTOR'S HANK WILLIAMS, VOL. 1, THE.
Tracks: Nobody's lonesome for me / Crazy heart / Funeral, The / We live in two different worlds / When you're tired of breaking other hearts / Wait for the light to shine / Singing waterfall / Lost on the river / I won't be home no more / Weary blues from waitin' / Blue love / Pale horse and his rider, The / No no Joe / Faded love and winter roses / There's no room in my heart / Last night I dreamed of heaven.
LP. 2353 118
MC 3110 230
Polydor / Jan '77 / PolyGram.

COLLECTORS NO. 4.
Tracks: I'm a long gone daddy / Message to my mother / Beyond the sunset / Jesus remembered me / With tears in my eyes / If you'll be a baby to me / Teardrops on a rose / No not now / I don't care / Fool about you / When God comes and gathers His jewels / Please don't let me love you / Help me understand / I ain't got nothin' but time / Home in heaven / Wearin' out your walkin' shoes.
■ LP. 2391 519
Polydor / Aug '81.

COUNTRY STORE: HANK WILLIAMS.
Tracks: Lovesick blues / You're gonna change / I just don't like this kind of livin' / Moanin' the blues / Howlin' at the moon / I'll never get out of this world alive / Lost highway / Mind your own business / My bucket's got a hole in it / Why don't you leave me / Cold cold heart / I can't help it / Baby we're really in love / Jambalaya.
CD . . . . CDCST 50
MC . . . . CSTK 50
Country Store / '88 / BMG.
■ LP. . . . . CST 50
Country Store / '88.

ESSENTIAL HANK WILLIAMS, THE.
Tracks: My bucket's got a hole in it / Honky tonk blues / May you never be alone / Lovesick blues / Kaw-liga / I'm so lonesome I could cry / Move it on over / Ramblin' man / Honky tonkin' / Long gone lonesome blues / Howlin' at the moon.
LP. 2354 004
MC 3140 117
Polydor / Jan '78 / PolyGram.

FIRST RECORDINGS, THE.
Tracks: Not Advised.
MC . . . . CMFC 007
Country Music Foundation / Jan '93 / Topic Records / Direct Distribution.

GRAFFITI COLLECTION.
Tracks: Not Advised.
CD . . . . GRCD 14
MC . . . . GRMC 14
Graffiti Collection / Aug '90 / Terry Blood Dist.

GREAT HITS OF HANK WILLIAMS SNR.
Tracks: Hey good lookin' / Lovesick blues / My son calls another man daddy / You win again / Take these chains from my heart / Your cheatin' heart / Jambalaya / I'm so lonesome I could cry / Settin' the woods on fire / Kaw-liga / My bucket's got a hole in it / Cold, cold heart.
LP. . . . . CN 2076
MC CN4 2076
Contour / Aug '85 / Pickwick Records.
CD . . . . PWK 114
Pickwick / Jun '89 / Pickwick Records.

GREATEST HITS 1.
Tracks: Not Advised.
MC 65001
Grand Canyon / May '88.
■ LP. 35001
Grand Canyon / May '88.

GREATEST HITS 2.
Tracks: Not Advised.
LP. 35002
MC 65002
Grand Canyon / May '88.

HANK WILLIAMS & THE DRIFTING COWBOYS (Williams, Hank & The Drifting Cowboys).
Tracks: Jambalaya / Hey porter / Half as much / If I were a carpenter / Cold cold heart / Howlin' at the moon / Then you can tell me goodbye / Dear John / Your cheatin' heart / Raining in my heart / Window shopping / After you / Ain't that a shame / Endless sleep / Mule skinner blues / I'm so lonesome I could cry.
LP. . . . . CW 202
MC . . . . JAM 202
Jambalaya / Feb '87 / Charly.

HANK WILLIAMS 40 GREATEST HITS.
Tracks: Baby, we're really in love / Cold cold heart / Crazy heart / Dear John / Half as much / Hey, good lookin' / Honky tonk blues / Howlin' at the moon / I can't help it / I just don't like this kind of living / I saw the light / I won't be home no more / I'll never get out of this world alive / I'm so lonesome I could cry / I'm sorry for you my friend / Jambalaya / Kaw-liga / Lonesome whistle / Long gone lonesome blues / Lost highway / Lovesick blues / Mansion on the hill / Mind your own business / Moanin' the blues / Move it on over / My bucket's got a hole in it / My son calls another man daddy / Nobody's lonesome for me / Ramblin' man / Settin' the woods on fire / Take these chains from my

W 12

■ DELETED

heart / They'll never take her love from me / Weary blues / Wedding bells / Why don't you love me / Why should we try anymore / Window shopping / You win again / Your cheatin' heart / You're gonna change.
Double LP 2683 071
■ **MC Set** 3271 302
MGM (Polydor) / Jan '78.
■ **CD Set** 8212332
Polydor / Mar '89.

HANK WILLIAMS COLLECTION (20 Golden Greats).
Tracks: I'm so lonesome I could cry / Honky tonk blues / Your cheatin' heart / Lovesick blues / Half as much / Hey good lookin' / Lost highway / Move it on over / Kaw-liga / Jambalaya / Take these chains from my heart / I'll never get out of this world alive / I'm sorry for you my friend / Cold cold heart / My bucket's got a hole in it / Long gone lonesome blues / Ramblin' man / I heard that lonesome whistle blow / Howlin' at the moon / My son calls another man daddy.
LP . . . . DVLP 2081
MC . . . . DVMC 2081
Deja Vu / Jan '87 / Jazz Music / Music Collection International.

HANK WILLIAMS GREATEST HITS VOL.1.
Tracks: Your cheatin' heart / Move it on over / I'm so lonesome, I could cry / Honky tonk blues / Ramblin' man / Honky tonky / There'll be no teardrops tonight / Mind your own business / My bucket's got a hole in it / Long gone lonesome blues.
LP 2482 505
■ **MC** 3192 631
MGM (Polydor) / Jun '81.

HANK WILLIAMS GREATEST HITS VOL.2.
Tracks: Jambalaya / Wedding bells / Hey, good lookin' / Window shopping / Settin' the woods on fire / I can't help it / Howlin' at the moon / (I heard that) lonesome whistle / Half as much / Why don't you love / You win again / May you never be alone / Baby, we're really in love / Take these chains from my heart / Blues come around, The / Lost highway.
MC 3110 049
Polydor / Sep '78 / PolyGram.
■ **LP** 2482506
MGM (Polydor) / Jul '81.

HANK WILLIAMS GREATEST HITS VOL.3.
Tracks: I can't get you off my mind / My love for you / Ready to go home / No one will ever know / Let's turn back the years / I've been down that road before / House of gold / I'm satisfied with you / Rootie tootie / Be careful of stones that you throw / Angel of death / My heart would know / I wish I had a nickel / Just waitin' / I can't escape from you.
■ **LP** 419
Polydor / Sep '80.

HANK WILLIAMS MEMORIAL ALBUM.
Tracks: Calling you / Cool water / Never again / First year blues / Dixie cannonball / Old home, The / Battle of Armageddon / Roly poly / I've just told mama goodbye / Devils train / Dear brother / Wearin' out your walkin' shoes / Mother is gone / Sundown and sorrow / Six more miles / I'm free at last / Fool about you / Low down blues / Wealth won't save your soul / Picture from life's other side, A / Swing wide your gate of love / If you'll be a baby / You're gonna change / Tramp on the street / Jesus died for me / Why should we try anymore / It just don't matter now / When the book of life is read.
LP 2683 016
Polydor / Jan '77 / PolyGram.

HANK WILLIAMS ON STAGE, VOL.1.
Tracks: Happy rovin' cowboy / Wedding bells / Lovesick blues / I'll have a new body / Lost highway / Joe Clark / Where the soul of man never dies / I'm a long gone daddy / I'm tellin' you / Bill Cheatam / When God comes and gathers his jewels / Blues come around, The / I wanna live and love always / You're gonna change / Settin' the woods on fire / (There's a) bluebird on your windowsill / Fiddle tune / I saw the light / Tramp on the street, The / Help me understand / Fingers on fire.
LP 2683 046
Polydor / Jul '79 / PolyGram.

HEY GOOD LOOKIN' (Dec 1950-July 1951).
Tracks: Not Advised.
Double LP 831 634-1
Polydor / Jan '88 / PolyGram.
CD 8316342
Polydor / Jan '93 / PolyGram.

HOME IN HEAVEN.
Tracks: Home in heaven / In my dreams / I'm going home / Mother is gone.
7" . . . . .EP 548
Arhoolie (USA) / Mar '83 / Pinnacle / Cadillac Music / Swift / Projection / Hot Shot / A.D.A Distribution / Jazz Music.

I AIN'T GOT NOTHIN' BUT TIME.
Tracks: You're gonna change / My son calls another man daddy / First year blues / Are you building a temple in heaven / No one will ever know / I'm so lonesome I could cry / House without love / When the book of life is read / You better keep it in your mind / Fool about you / Wedding bells / I've just told mama goodbye / If you'll be a baby to me / House of gold / We're getting close to the grave each day / Thy burdens are greater than mine / I just don't like this kind of living / My bucket's got a hole in it / Waltz of the wind / How can you refuse him now.
Double LP 825 548-1
Polydor / Jan '88 / PolyGram.
■ **CD** 825 548-2
Polydor / Mar '90.

I WON'T BE HOME NO MORE (Vol. 8 June - December 1952).
Tracks: Not Advised.
Double LP 833 752-1
Polydor / Dec '87 / PolyGram.

I'M SO LONESOME I COULD CRY.
Tracks: Not Advised.
LP 825557 1
Polydor / Jan '87 / PolyGram.
CD 825 557 2
Polydor / Jul '90 / PolyGram.

JUST ME AND MY GUITAR.
Tracks: Not Advised.
MC . . . . .CMFC 006
Country Music Foundation / Jan '93 / Topic Records / Direct Distribution.

LET'S TURN BACK THE YEARS (Vol.7 July 1951 - June 1952).
Tracks: Not Advised.
Double LP 833 749-1
Polydor / Dec '87 / PolyGram.
CD 8337492
Polydor / Jan '93 / PolyGram.

LIVE AT THE GRAND OLE OPRY.
Tracks: Moanin' the blues / Nobody's lonesome for me / I just don't like this kind of living / Why don't you love me / They'll never take her love from me / Lovesick blues / Long gone lonesome blues / Cold cold heart / Dear John / Hey, good lookin' / You're gonna change.
LP 2353 128
MC 3110 370
Polydor / Sep '77 / PolyGram.
LP . . . . .MG 15019
MGM (Polydor) / Oct '86.

LONG GONE LONESOME BLUES (August 1949 - December 1950).
Tracks: Not Advised.
Double LP 831 633-1
Polydor / Dec '87 / PolyGram.
CD 8316332
Polydor / Jan '93 / PolyGram.

LOST HIGHWAY (December 1948 - March 1949).
Tracks: There'll be no teardrops tonight / Lost on the river / I heard my mother praying for me / California zephyr / Teardrop on a rose, A / Honky tonk blues / Mind your own business / I'm free at last / Wait for the light to shine / No, not now / Lost highway / May you never be alone / Dixie cannonball / Blue love in my heart / Angel of death / Jesus remembered me / Dear brother / Singing waterfall / I'm going home / Sundown and sorrow / Alabama waltz.
Double LP 825 554-1
MC 825 554-4
MGM (Polydor) / Jul '86.
CD 825554-2
Polydor / Jan '88 / PolyGram.

LOVESICK BLUES.
Tracks: Not Advised.
LP 825 551 1
Polydor / Oct '86 / PolyGram.
■ **CD** 825 551 2
Polydor / Mar '90.

MORE RARE RADIO PROGRAMMES VOL.1.
Tracks: Not Advised.
MC . . . . .JAM 201
Jambalaya / May '86 / Charly.

ON THE AIR.
Tracks: Not Advised.
LP 825531 1
MGM (Polydor) / Oct '86.
LP 827 531-1
Polydor / Jan '88 / PolyGram.

ORIGINAL SINGLES COLLECTION..PLUS, THE.
Tracks: I'm not coming home anymore / Never again (will I knock on your door) / Calling you / Wealth won't save your soul / When God comes and gathers his jewels / My love for you (has turned to hate) / I don't care (if tomorrow never comes) / Pan American / Honky tonkin' / (Last night) I heard you crying in your sleep / Move it on over / On the banks of the old Pontchartrain / Fly trouble / My sweet love ain't around / Rootie tootie / Honky tonkin' (2) / I'll be a bachelor 'til I die / I'm a long gone daddy / Blues come around, The / Six more miles (to the graveyard) / I saw the light / Mansion on the hill / I can't get you off my mind / Lovesick blues / Wedding bells / I've just told my mama goodbye / Mind your own business / There'll be no teardrops / Lost highway / You're gonna change (or I'm gonna leave) / I'm so lonesome I could cry / My bucket's got a hole in it / May you never be alone / I just don't like this kind of living / Long gone lonesome blues / My son calls another man Daddy / Why don't you love me / House without love, A / Why should we try anymore / They'll never take her love from me / Moanin' the blues / Nobody's lonesome for me / Cold, cold heart / Dear John / I can't help it (if I'm sill in love with you) / Howlin' at the moon / My heart would know / Hey good lookin' / (I heard that) lonesome whistle / Crazy heart / I'd still want you / Baby, we're really in love / I'm sorry for you my friend / Honky tonk blues / Half as much / Let's turn back the years / Jambalaya (on the bayou) / Window shopping / Settin' the woods on fire / You win again / I'll never get out of this world alive / I could never be ashamed of you / Kaw-liga / Your cheatin' heart / I won't be home no more / Take these chains from my heart / Please make up your mind / Ramblin' man / House of gold / With tears in my eyes / Alone and forsaken / Fool about you / I'm free at last / Someday you'll call my name / I can't escape from you / Something got a hold of you / Weary blues from waitin' / I ain't got nothin' but time / Angel of death / There's no room in my heart for the blues / At the first fall of snow / Log train, The / All the love I ever had / There's a tear in my beer.
CD Set 847 194 2
MC Set 847 194 4
Polydor / Mar '91 / PolyGram.

RADIO SHOWS.
Tracks: Not Advised.
LP . . . . ATOM 6
A Touch Of Magic / Sep '89 / Wellard Dist. / Charly.

RARE DEMOS: FIRST TO LAST.
Tracks: Won't you sometimes think of me / Why should I cry / Calling you / You break your own heart / Pan American / Mother is gone / I watched my dreamworld crumble like clay / In my dreams you still belong to me / Wealth won't save your soul / I told a lie to my heart / Singing waterfall / I'm goin' home / Jambalaya / Heaven holds all my treasures / You better keep it on your mind / Lost on the river / Your cheatin' heart / House of gold, A / Honky tonk blues / Help me understand / 'Neath a cold grey tomb of stone / There's nothing as sweet as my baby / Fool about you / Log train, The.
CD . . . . .CMFCD 067
MC . . . . .CMFC 067
Country Music Foundation / Jan '93 / Topic Records / Direct Distribution.

RARE RADIO BROADCASTS 1949.
Tracks: Not Advised.
LP . . . . CW 201
Jambalaya / Jul '85 / Charly.

RARE TAKES AND RADIO CUTS.
Tracks: Not Advised.
LP 823 695-1
Polydor / Jan '88 / PolyGram.

VERY BEST OF HANK WILLIAMS.
Tracks: Not Advised.
LP . . . . .ADAH 446
MC . . . . .ADAHC 446
Arcade Music Gala / Apr '86.

VERY BEST OF HANK WILLIAMS VOL.1, THE.
Tracks: Lovesick blues / Crazy heart / I'm sorry for you my friend / Wedding bells / Window shopping / Honky tonk blues / I heard that lonesome whistle blow / Half as much / Jambalaya / Dear John / Prodigal son / I saw the light / I won't be home no more / There's room in my heart (for the blues) / We live in two different worlds / Long gone lonesome blues.
LP . . . . .CN 2084
MC CN4 2084
Contour / Mar '87 / Pickwick Records.
CD . . . . .PWK 138
Pickwick / Jun '90 / Pickwick Records.

Williams, Hank Jr.

Hank Williams Jr. was born in 1949 in Shreveport, Louisiana, where his famous father was a regular on the Louisiana Hayride. His father nicknamed him Bocephus. During high school he excelled in sports and became a health fanatic. He toured with his mother Audrey in her Caravan of Stars show in the early '60s, signed a contract with MGM and was moulded by the elder statesman of Nashville as a second Hank Williams.He sang Hank's songs for the soundtrack of the biopic *Your Cheatin' Heart* in 1965 and crossed to the pop chart with *Long Gone Blues* in 1964. He began writing his own songs and scored minor hits, but the public demanded endless replays of Hank Sr.'s songs. His own first country number one was *All For The Love Of The Sunshine* in 1970. He broke from the Nashville elite in 1974, moved to Alabama and began work on a sound of his own. He made the album *Hank Williams Jr. And Friends* with country-rock musicians including Charlie Daniels, Toy Caldwell of the Marshall Tucker Band and Chuck Leavall (ex-Allman Brothers), just before its release he literally fell down a mountain on a hunting trip, suffered appalling head injuries, and was almost two years on the mend. He switched to Warner Brothers and slowly climbed to the top, demonstrating talent of his own. His number one hits between 1980-1983 included *Women I've Never Had* , *Old Habits*, *Texas Woman*, *All My Rowdy Friends*, *A Country Boy Can Survive*, *Honky Tonkin'* '83; he once had eight million albums in the Billboard charts at once. He duetted with Ray Charles on *Two Old Cats Like Us* in 1985, and had the solo hit *Are You Sure Hank Done It This Way* in 1986, among others. The album *Hank Live* in 1987 sold half a million copies without a single to help it; after selling 13 million albums he was finally named Entertainer of the Year by the CMA in 1987, and said 'This is the one old

Bocephus has been looking for'. (Donald Clarke).

AIN'T MISBEHAVIN'.
Tracks: I've been around.
■ **7"** . . . . **W 8794**
WEA / Apr '86.

ALL MY ROWDY FRIENDS ARE COMING OVER TONIGHT.
Tracks: All my rowdy friends are coming over tonight / Video blues.
7" . . . . **W 9184**
Curb / Feb '86 / BMG.

ARE YOU SURE HANK DONE IT THIS WAY.
Tracks: Family tradition / Kaw-liga / Whisky bent and hell bound / Are you sure Hank done it this way / Women I've never had / Old habits / Dixie on my mind / If you don't like Hank Williams / Move it on over / Texas women / All my rowdy friends are coming over tonight / Heaven ain't a lot like Dixie / Country boy can survive, A / Honky tonkin' / Leave them boys alone / Man of steel.
■ **LP** **2405181**
WEA / Jan '85.
■ **MC** **2405184**
WEA / Mar '86.

BEST OF HANK WILLIAMS JR. VOL 3.
Tracks: Not Advised.
CD **K925 834 2**
■ **MC** **K925 834 4**
WEA / Jun '89 / WEA.
■ **LP** **K925 834 1**
WEA / Jun '89.

COUNTRY STORE: HANK WILLIAMS JR.
Tracks: Long gone lonesome blues / Standing in the shadows / Cajun baby / Rainin' in my heart / Send me the pillow that you dream on / Ain't that a shame / Losing you / Wolverton Mountain / Walk on by / Ring of fire / It's all over but the crying / I'd rather be gone / All for the love of sunshine / I walk the line.
CD . . . . **CDCST 20**
MC . . . . **CSTK 20**
Country Store / Nov '88 / BMG.
■ **LP** . . . . **CST 20**
Country Store / Nov '88.

FIVE-O.
Tracks: I'm for love / I really like girls / Nashville scene, The / Ain't misbehavin' / Something to believe in / Lawyers, guns and money / This ain't Dallas / I've been around / New Orleans / Outlaws reward.
LP **925267 1**
■ **MC** **925267 4**
WEA / Jul '86.

GREATEST HITS VOL.3.
Tracks: I'm for love / This ain't Dallas / Ain't misbehavin' / Country state of mind / Mind your own business / My name is bocephus (Live version) / Born to boogie / Young country / Heaven can't be found / Finders keepers / There's a tear in my beer.
LP **925 834-1**
MC **9250834-4**
Warner Bros. / '89 / WEA.

GREATEST HITS: HANK WILLIAMS JNR.
Tracks: Not Advised.
■ **CD** **9601932**
Elektra / '84.

HANK WILLIAMS JNR. FEATURING HANK WILLIAMS SNR.
Tracks: Jambalaya / Your cheatin' heart / Ain't that a shame.
LP . . . . **CN 2092**
MC **CN4 2092**
Contour / Aug '88 / Pickwick Records.

HANK WILLIAMS JR. AND FRIENDS.
Tracks: Losing you / On Susan's floor / I really did / Can't you see / Montana song / Clovis, New Mexico / Jukebox / Living proof.
LP **2353 124**
MC **3110 361**
Polydor / Sep '77 / PolyGram.

HIGH NOTES.
Tracks: Heaven ain't a lot like Dixie / Whisky on ice / High and pressurized / I can't change my tune / South's gonna rattle again, The / Ain't makin' no headlines (here without you) / I've been down / If you wanna get to heaven / Norwegian wood / Honky tonkin'.
LP . . . . **K 52384**
Asylum / Jun '82 / WEA.

WILD STREAK.
Tracks: Wild streak / If the south woulda won / What you don't know (Won't hurt you) / You're gonna be a sorry man / Love M.D / Early in the morning and late at night / I'm just a man / Social call / You brought me down to earth.
CD **925725 2**
LP **925725 1**
■ **MC** **925725 4**
Curb / Sep '88.

Williams, Lawton

LIGHTNING JONES.
Tracks: Blue grass skirt / Foreign love / I'll still love you / Casino on the hill / Train of thought / If you're waiting on me / Don't burn the bridge behind you / Rhinelander waltz / Moon Joe / Lightning Jones / Carpetbaggers / Squawlein / Stay on the ball / Mama pinch a penny / Everything's OK on the L.B.J.(parts 1 & 2).
LP . . . . **BFX 15178**
Bear Family / Nov '85 / Rollercoaster Records / Swift / Direct Distribution.

Williams, Leona

Born Leona Helton on 07.01.1943 in Vienna, Missouri Williams - now married to sessionman Dave Kirby, father of Paul lead singer/songwriter with The Cactus Brothers. Williams, one-time member of Merle Haggard's and The Strangers, toured with him during 1970s and later became his wife (1978 -1983). Recorded the 1983 Mercury duet album *Heart To Heart*, culled from which was their top ten hit single *The Bull And The Beaver*. Leona's own solo career meanwhile has never reached such heights, yet her downhome honky tonk style of music has been well admired. Apart from singing back-up for Haggard, she's toured as part of the Loretta Lynn show (with her first songwriting husband Ron Williams. As well as having singles on Hickory, Elektra and Mercury, she's recorded albums for MCA Tally (*San Quentin's First Lady* recorded live in 1976 before it's prison inmates) and Hickory - released in the UK on DJM label and concept compilation titled *A Woman Walked Away* . Williams songs have also made it onto albums by Tammy Wynette and Loretta Lynn. (Maurice Hope July 1993)

GOOD NIGHTS MAKE GOOD MORNINGS.
Tracks: Good nights make good mornings / Yes Mam.
■ **7"** . . . . **MCA 422**
MCA / May '79.

HEART TO HEART (see under Haggard, Merle).

LEONA WILLIAMS AND HER DIXIE BAND (Williams, Leona & Her Dixie Band).
Tracks: Not Advised.
LP . . . . **FB 303**
Fountain / Apr '79 / Charly / Wellard Dist. / Swift / Cadillac Music.

WOMAN WALKED AWAY, A.
Tracks: Happy anniversary baby / Woman's man, A / Broadminded / I narrowed this triangle (Down to two) / This ain't a home no more / Anything goes (Til everything's gone) / Ten minutes till heartaches / They'll never take his love from me / When I stop dreaming / I'm not supposed to love you anymore / I spent a week there last night / He's just you made all over / Gentleman on your mind. A / Yes Ma'm (He found me in a honky tonk).
LP . . . . **DJM 22060**
DJM / '77 / PolyGram.

Williams, Lucinda

This singer songwriter was born in 1953 in Louisiana. Her music contains a number of influences reflecting the many places in which she has lived in the U.S.A. Prior to her Califonia recorded Rough Trade album *Lucinda Williams* , she had done two for the Folkways label. The 1979 country/blues *Ramblin' on my mind* (Mississippi) release and her Houston recorded *Happy woman blues* released 1980. Williams' career after years playing the blues, folk and contemporary club circuit looks set to blossom. Her debut on Chameleon/Elektra *Sweet old world* proving to be an eclectic serving of strong story-ballads gathering acclaim both sides of the Atlantic. She toured the UK in early 1993, playing support to Mary-Chapin Carpenter. (Maurice Hope - July 1993).

HAPPY WOMAN BLUES.
Tracks: Lafayette / I lost it / Maria / Happy woman blues / King of hearts / Rolling along / One night stand / Howlin' at midnight / Hard road / Louisiana man / Sharp cutting wings (song to a poet).
CD . . . . **MRCD 149**
Munich / '90 / C.M. Distribution / Swift / Cadillac Music / A.D.A Distribution / Hot Shot / Topic Records / Direct Distribution / New Note.
CD . . . . **NETCD 12**
Network (Rounder) / '90 / Sony.

I JUST WANTED TO SEE YOU.
Tracks: I just wanted to see you so bad / Something about what happens when we talk / Sundays / Changed the locks.
12" . . . . **RTT 224**
7" . . . . **RT 224**
Rough Trade / Apr '89 / Pinnacle.

LUCINDA WILLIAMS.
Tracks: I just wanted to see you so bad / Big red sun blues / Night's too long, The / Like a rose / Changed the locks / Passionate kisses / Crescent city / Price to pay / Abandoned / Am I too blue / Side of the road / I asked for water.
CD . . . . **ROUGHCD 130**
Rough Trade / Jan '89 / Pinnacle.
LP . . . . **ROUGH 130**
■ **MC** . . . . **ROUGHC 130**
Rough Trade / Jan '89.

PASSIONATE KISSES.
Tracks: Passionate kisses / Side of the road / Nothin' in ramblin' (12" only) / Disgusted (12" only).
12" **RTT232**
Rough Trade / Aug '89 / Pinnacle.
7" . . . . **RT 232**
■ **CD Single** . . . . **RT 232CD**
Rough Trade / Aug '89.

SWEET OLD WORLD.
Tracks: Not Advised.
CD **3705613512**
MC **3705613514**
WEA / Jan '93 / WEA.

Williams, Robin

ALL BROKEN HEARTS ARE THE SAME (Williams, Robin & Linda).
Tracks: Rollin' & ramblin' (the death of Hank Williams / All broken hearts are the same / Baby rocked her dolly / Leaving this land / Annie / Riding on the Santa Fe / Pan handle wind / Pine country / Stone wall country / Across the blue mountains / After the flood.
LP . . . . **SH 1022**
Sugarhill(USA) / Mar '89 / Roots Records / Projection / Impetus Records / C.M. Distribution / Jazz Music / Swift / Duncans / A.D.A Distribution.

CLOSE AS WE CAN GET (Williams, Robin & Linda).
Tracks: Not Advised.
LP . . . . **FF 327**
Flying Fish (USA) / Mar '89 / Cadillac Music / Roots Records / Projection / C.M. Distribution / Direct Distribution / Jazz Music / Duncans / A.D.A Distribution.

CLOSE AS WE CAN GET/9 TILL MIDNIGHT (Williams, Robin & Linda).
Tracks: Not Advised.
CD . . . . **FF 359CD**
MC . . . . **FF 359C**
Flying Fish (USA) / May '93 / Cadillac Music / Roots Records / Projection / C.M. Distribution / Direct Distribution / Jazz Music / Duncans / A.D.A Distribution.

NINE 'TIL MIDNIGHT (Williams, Robin & Linda).
Tracks: Not Advised.
LP . . . . **FF 359**
Flying Fish (USA) / Mar '89 / Cadillac Music / Roots Records / Projection / C.M. Distribution / Direct Distribution / Jazz Music / Duncans / A.D.A Distribution.

REALITY..WHAT A CONCEPT.
Tracks: Nicky Lenin / Pop goes the weasel / Touch of Fairfax / Kindergarten of the stars / Reverend Earnest Angry / Shakespeare / Thank you Boyce / Roots people / Hollywood casting session / Come inside my mind / Grandpa Funk.
■ **LP** . . . . **CALH 2053**
Casablanca / Oct '79.
LP . . . . **NBLP 7162**
Casablanca (Import) / Apr '82 / Pinnacle.

RHYTHM OF LOVE, THE (Williams, Robin & Linda).
Tracks: Rhythm of love, The / When I hear that whistle blow / House of gold / I'll remember your love in my prayers / Gone to the West / Hired gun / They all faded away / Six o'clock news / Hill county song / Devil is a mighty wind, The / Poor wayfaring stranger / You done me wrong.
CD . . . . **SHCD 1027**
LP . . . . **SH 1027**
MC . . . . **ZCSH 1027**
Sugarhill(USA) / '90 / Roots Records / Projection / Impetus Records / C.M. Distribution / Jazz Music / Swift / Duncans / A.D.A Distribution.

Williams, Tex

Tex Williams (1917-85) was a singing cowboy who began as a one-man band on local radio at thirteen, playing banjo, harmonica and singing. He joined the Spade Colley band in 1946 and sang on its huge hit *Shame on you*. He formed his own 12-piece Western Caravan and recorded for Capitol *The Rose Of The Alamo* which is said to have sold 250,000 copies, but his record of the Tex Ritter/Merle Travis song *Smoke! Smoke! Smoke! (That Cigarette)* was a number one pop hit in 1947 which was Capitol's first million-seller. More hits the same year included *Don't Telephone, Don't Telegraph, Tell A Woman*. *Bluebird On Your Windowsill* was a number 12 country hit in 1949. His band remained a popular act, appearing with stars like Dinah Shore and Jo Stafford. He returned to the USA country charts in the 60s and early '70s with *The Night Miss Nancy Ann's Hotel For Single Girls Burned Down*. He appeared in scores of Western films between 1935-55 with Ritter, Buster Crabbe and Charles Starrett.

W 14

■ DELETED

Smoke! Smoke! Smoke! on Capitol in 1960 (reissued on Stetson) included a remake of the big hit, but its production was typical of the period, with too much brass. (Donald Clarke).

14 ALL TIME COUNTRY HITS (Williams, Texas T.).
Tracks: Not Advised.
LP . . . . . **HRL 115**
Homespun (Ireland) / Feb '78 / Homespun Records / Ross Records / Wellard Dist.
MC . . . . . **CHRL 115**
Homespun (Ireland) / '88 / Homespun Records / Ross Records / Wellard Dist.

IN LAS VEGAS, LIVE.
Tracks: My window faces the south / Tomorrow's just another day to cry / Wild card / Dusty skies / Time changes everything / You can't break my heart / Downtown poker club / With men who know tobacco death / Ten years / Cowboy's prayer / Nine pound hammer / I'd trade all of my tomorrows / Little Dollie.
■ **LP** . . . . . **SLS 50429**
Sunset (Liberty) / '79.

SMOKE, SMOKE, SMOKE.
Tracks: Smoke, smoke, smoke / Start even / One-eyed Sam / Leaf of love, The / Shame on you / That's what I like about the west / Shot gun boogie / Castle of my dreams / Reno / Who me / He'll have to go / Ballad of thunder road, The.
LP . . . . . **HAT 3047**
MC . . . . . **HATC 3047**
Stetson / Sep '87 / Crusader Marketing Co. / Swift / Wellard Dist. / Midland Records / C.M. Distribution.

TEX WILLIAMS IN LAS VEGAS.
Tracks: Not Advised.
LP . . . . . **HAT 3105**
MC . . . . . **HATC 3105**
Stetson / Aug '89 / Crusader Marketing Co. / Swift / Wellard Dist. / Midland Records / C.M. Distribution.

Williams, Vern

BEAUTIFUL BOUQUET, A (see under Maddox, Rose).

BLUEGRASS FROM GOLD COUNTRY (Vern Williams Band).
Tracks: Not Advised.
LP . . . . . **ROUNDER 0131**
MC . . . . . **ROUNDER 0131C**
Rounder / '88 / Projection / Roots Records / Swift / C.M. Distribution / Topic Records / Jazz Music / Hot Shot / A.D.A Distribution / Direct Distribution.

ROSE MADDOX & VERN WILLIAMS BAND (see under Maddox, Rose).

Williamson, Ann

ANNE WILLIAMSON.
Tracks: Precious memories / It is no secret / Lord is my shepherd, The / Tell me the old, old story / Safe in the arms of Jesus / By cool Siloam's shady rill / O perfect love / Why me Lord / Abide with me / One day at a time / In the garden / Morning has broken / Whispering hope / O love that will not let me go / Count your blessings / How great thou art.
VHS . . . . . **TVE 1040**
Telstar Video / Nov '91 / BMG.

BLUE BABY BLUE.
Tracks: Don't it make my brown eyes blue / I fall to pieces / Like strangers / Seeing is believing / Four in the morning / She's got you / Blue baby blue / I'll get over you / (Why me) why me Lord / Cold, cold heart / Forsaking all the rest / Heaven's just a sin away.
LP . . . . . **JULEP 22**
MC . . . . . **KJULEP 22**
Mint / Oct '81 / RTM / Pinnacle.

BLUE BABY BLUE.
Tracks: Blue baby blue / When you and I were young Maggie.
■ **7"** . . . . . **CHEW 81**
Mint / Apr '83.

BLUE EYES CRYING IN THE RAIN.
Tracks: Blue eyes crying in the rain / She's got you.
■ **7"** . . . . . **CHEW 113**
Mint / Jul '87.

COUNT YOUR BLESSINGS.
Tracks: Morning has broken / By cool Siloam's shady rill / O love that wilt not let me go / Safe in the arms of Jesus / Mine eyes have seen the glory / How sweet the name of Jesus sounds / All things bright and beautiful / Whispering hope / When I survey the wondrous cross / O perfect love / All people that on Earth do dwell / Count your blessings / I need thee every hour / In the sweet bye and bye.
CD . . . . . **ERTVCD 2**
LP . . . . . **ERTV 2**
MC . . . . . **ERTVC 2**
Emerald / Nov '87 / I & B Records.

COUNTRY EVERGREENS.
Tracks: I can't stop loving you / Send me the pillow that you dream on / How great thou art / Invisible tears / Bonaparte's retreat / Bargain store / Tennessee waltz / When you and I were young Maggie / Your cheatin' heart / I can't help / Dear John a letter.
LP . . . . . **GES 5016**
MC . . . . . **KGEC 5016**
Emerald / Oct '81 / I & B Records.

FAMILY BIBLE, THE.
Tracks: Family bible, The / Hey Lord it's me.
■ **7"** . . . . . **CHEW 115**
Mint / Nov '87.

LIKE STRANGERS (see under Daniels, Roly).

MORE EVERGREENS.
Tracks: Ramblin' rose / Release me / Amazing Grace / Answers on a postcard please / True love / Heartaches by the number / Blueberry Hill / I'm not that lonely yet / Blue eyes crying in the rain / Old rugged cross, The / Tie a yellow ribbon / Always / You'll never walk alone / Married by the Bible.
LP . . . . . **GES 1235**
MO . . . . . **KGEC 1235**
Emerald / Sep '87 / I & B Records.

PAL OF MY CRADLE DAYS.
Tracks: Pal of my cradle days.
■ **7"** . . . . . **CHEW 77**
Mint / Dec '82.

PRECIOUS MEMORIES.
Tracks: Precious memories / In the garden / Abide with me / Rock of ages / Just a closer walk with thee / What a friend we have in Jesus / When the roll is called up yonder / It is no secret / Tell me the old, old story / Nearer my God to thee / One day at a time / Lord's my shepherd, The / Old time religion / Shall we gather at the river?.
LP . . . . . **ERTV 1**
MC . . . . . **ERTVC 1**
Emerald / Apr '86 / I & B Records.

RAMBLIN' ROSE.
Tracks: Ramblin' Rose / Snowbird.
■ **7"** . . . . . **CHEW 109**
Mint / Nov '87.

TINY BUBBLES.
Tracks: Just out of reach / Heart of my heart / You don't have to tell me / Tiny bubbles / Nightingale sang in Berkley Square / Rose coloured glasses / Among my souvenirs / Crying time / Softly softly / Baby blue / Let bygones be bygones / Behind the footlights.
LP . . . . . **GES 1225**
MC . . . . . **KGEC 1225**
Emerald / Nov '83 / I & B Records.

TINY BUBBLES.
Tracks: Tiny bubbles / Why me Lord.
■ **7"** . . . . . **CHEW 85**
Mint / Oct '83.

WHEN YOU AND I WERE YOUNG MAGGIE.
Tracks: When you and I were young Maggie / Forsaking all the rest.
■ **7"** . . . . . **CHEW 72**
Mint / Oct '82.
■ **7"** . . . . . **MD 1222**
Emerald / May '86.

Willing, Foy

FOY WILLING & THE RIDERS OF THE PURPLE SAGE.
Tracks: Holiday for the blues / Little white house (with you inside) / Twilight on the trail / Ragtime Cowboy blues / Blue shadows on the trail / Across the valley from the Alamo / Prairie echoes / Nobody's lost on the lonesome trail / Hang your head in shame / Trail to Mexico / Cool water / When the white roses bloom down in red river valley.
MC . . . . . **CSR 4C**
Outlaw / Dec '87.

Willis Brothers

BEST OF THE WILLIS BROTHERS.
Tracks: Not Advised.
LP . . . . . **SLP 960**
MC . . . . . **GT 5960**
Starday (USA) / Apr '87 / Crusader Marketing Co.

Wills, Billy Jack

BILLY JACK WILLS & HIS WESTERN SWING BAND (Wills, Billy Jack & His Western Swing Band).
Tracks: Not Advised.
LP . . . . . **WESTERN 2002**
Western (USA) / Feb '89.

CRAZY MAN CRAZY (Wills, Billy Jack & His Western Swing Band).
Tracks: Not Advised.
LP . . . . . **WESTERN 2004**
Western (USA) / Feb '85.

Wills, Bob

Bob Wills was born on a farm in Texas in 1905, he died in 1975 in Fort Worth. He worked in cotton fields alongside blacks and other poor whites, learning music from both. He came from a family of fiddlers and became a bandleader on Texas radio, leading the original edition of Light Crust Doughboys (sponsored by a flour mill) in 1931 with Milton Brown, who later became a prominent bandleader in the genre until killed in a car crash in 1936. Wills replaced Brown with vocalist Tommy Duncan; he quarrelled with Wilbert Lee 'Pappy' O'Daniel, president of Burrus Mills and a future governor of Texas, and left the Doughboys, taking most of them with him; by 1935 he was playing packed dance halls six nights a week and began recording for Brunswick. The sessions produced by Art Satherley (born in Bristol, England; he also produced the classic records of Roy Acuff, Gene Autry, Blind Lemon Jefferson, and others). Wills called his band the Texas Playboys, with such stars as Duncan, Herman Arnspiger on guitar, Jesse Ashlock on second fiddle, brother Johnnie Lee Wills on bass and Leon McAuliffe on steel guitar . Wills' music was called Western Swing; it included ragtime and blues as well as traditional frontier fiddle styles. It called for a large band with horns and drums, unusual then in country music, and was directly influenced by jazz. He was enormously popular all over the Southwest and the classic records are still unique today, *San Antonio Rose* was a million-seller in 1941, covered by Bing Crosby. He made about 250 sides for what became CBS labels (albums are available in CBS USA's Historical series). Tiffany Music recorded 16" transcription discs in 1945-47 for sale to radio stations, totalling 220 selections, the whole breadth and versatility of Wills' repertoire at its peak. He recorded for MGM in the late '40s-early '50s, then Decca (now MCA) in the mid-'50s, when the heyday of Western Swing was over, it was no longer economically possible to keep a big band on the road. In the '60s-'70s there were albums on Liberty and United Artists, some of the last ones tribute albums with Merle Haggard and others *The Best Damn Fiddler In The World)*. At the end Wills could no longer play following a stroke, but was still the undisputed king of Western Swing. Johnnie Lee Wills has albums *Tulsa Swing* on Rounder, *Reunion* on Flying Fish. (Donald Clarke).

BEST OF BOB WILLS.
Tracks: San Antonio rose / Eight'r from decatur / Deep in the heart of Texas / Silver bells / Across the valley from the Alamo / Cimarron / South of the border / Milk cow blues / My adobe hacienda / Southwestern waltz / Big ball in cowtown, A.
LP . . . . . **IMCA 153**
MCA (Import) / Mar '86 / Pinnacle / Silver Sounds (CD).

BEST OF BOB WILLS VOL. 1 & 2.
Tracks: San Antonio rose / Eight'r from decatur / Deep in the heart of Texas / Silver bells / Across the valley from the Alamo / South of the border (down Mexico way) / Milk cow blues / My adobe hacienda / Southwestern waltz / Four or five times / Time changes everything / Texas double eagle / You're the only star in my blue heaven / Song of the wanderer / Pan handle rag / My Mary / Beaumont rag / Whose heart are you breaking now / Brown skin gal / Cimarron.
Double LP **IMCA2 4092**
MCA (Import) / Mar '86 / Pinnacle / Silver Sounds (CD).

BEST OF THE TIFFANYS (Wills, Bob & His Texas Playboys).
Tracks: Roly poly / Bring it down to my house / Faded love / Stay a little longer / Take me back to Tulsa / Steel guitar rag / Maiden's prayer / Cotton eyed Joe / Corina, Corina / San Antonio rose / Time changes everything / Right or wrong / Cherokee maiden / Ida red.
CD . . . . . **EDCD 322**
LP . . . . . **ED 322**
MC . . . . . **EDC 322**
Edsel / '90 / Pinnacle.

BOB WILLS & HIS TEXAS PLAYBOYS (Wills, Bob & His Texas Playboys).
Tracks: Talking 'bout you / Panhandle rag / Across the alley from the Alamo / Running bear / Milk cow blues / Slow poke / San Antonio rose / Faded love / Four or five times / Brown skin gal / Kansas City / Wills breakdown / Riders in the sky / Lone star rag / Orange blossom special / Big beaver.
■ **LP** . . . . . **CR 30223**
Charly / '88 / Charly.

BOB WILLS ANTHOLOGY (Wills, Bob & His Texas Playboys).
Tracks: New Osage stomp / Maiden's prayer / Steelguitar rag / Blue yodel no. 1 / Silver bell / That's what I like 'bout the South / Waltz you saved for me, The / Corrine Corrina / Time changes everything / Big beaver / Take me back to Tulsa / San Antonio rose / I knew the moment I lost you / Twin guitar special / Roly poly / Brain cloudy blues.
LP **31611**
■ **MC** **4031611**
Embassy / Dec '77 / Sony.

FIDDLE.
Tracks: Not Advised.
MC . . . . **CMFC 010**
Country Music Foundation / Jan '93 / Topic Records / Direct Distribution.

FROM THE HEART OF TEXAS (Wills, Bob & His Texas Playboys).
Tracks: Deep in the heart of Texas / You're the only star in my blue heaven / What's Fort Worth / Big ball in Cowtown, A / Pinto beans / Where do I go from here / My Adobe hacienda / Kansas City / Gone Indian (instrumental) / Guess I'll move on down the line / If no news is good news / I just can't take it anymore.
LP . . . . **HAT 3058**
MC . . . . **HATC 3058**
Stetson / '88 / Crusader Marketing Co. / Swift / Wellard Dist. / Midland Records / C.M. Distribution.

GOLDEN ERA, THE (Wills, Bob & His Texas Playboys).
Tracks: Not Advised.
Double LP . . . . **C 240149**
Not Advised / Jan '88.

GREATEST HITS OF TEXAS,THE (Wills, Bob & His Texas Playboys).
Tracks: Not Advised.
LP . . . . **RNDF 284**
Rhino (USA) / Feb '85 / WEA.

KXLA RADIO BROADCASTS - JANUARY 1943.
Tracks: In the mood / Jambalaya / Crippled turkey / Dusty skies back in Texas / Yearning / Silver bells / Faded love.
LP . . . . **RFD 9004**
Country Routes / Feb '91 / Jazz Music / Hot Shot.

LONGHORN RECORDINGS, THE.
Tracks: Sooner or later / Buffalo twist / All night long / You can't break a heart / If he's movin in / Let's get it over and done with / Big tater in the sandy land / Mayflower waltz / Billy in the lowground / Beaumont rag / Faded love / Dian waltz / Done gone / Put your little foot / Bob's first fiddle tune / Bob's schottische / Gone indian / No disappointments in heaven / Will's junction / You'll never walk out of my heart / Betty's waltz / San antonio rose.
CD . . . . **BCD 15689**
Bear Family / Aug '93 / Rollercoaster Records / Swift / Direct Distribution.

MCKINNEY SISTERS, THE (Wills, Bob & His Texas Playboys).
Tracks: Betcha my heart / I'm crying my heart out / All by myself / It's all over now / Jealous hearted me / Don't sweetheart me / Miss you / I want my Mama / You're only in my arms / It's a good day / I dreamed of an old love affair / Echoes from the hills / Haiwiian war chant / When day is done / Put your arms around me / Will there be any yodeling in heaven / Feudin' and fightin' / Tumbling tumbleweeds / To you sweet aloha / Blue skies / There's a silver spoon on the golden gate / Pal of my lonely hour.
CD **K-6002**
MC **C-6002**
Kaleidoscope / '90 / A.D.A Distribution / Discovery.

MORE RARE PRESTO TRANSCRIPTIONS.
Tracks: Bob Wills talks to Allen Franklyn / In the mood / Sugar moon / Elmer's tune / My life's been a pleasure / Texas home / Dipsy doodle / Just a little lovin' / Sunrise serenade / Cherokee maiden / Osage stomp / You're the sweetest rose in Texas / Don't let your deal go down / Molly darling / Yearning (just for you) / Those gone and left me blues / Little star of heaven.
MC . . . . **CSR 2C**
Outlaw / Dec '87.

PAPA'S JUMPIN'.
Tracks: Silver lake blues / Little cowboy lullaby / Closed for repairs / Dog house blues / Bubbles in my beer / 'Neath Hawaiin palms / Papa's jumpin' / Don't be ashamed of your age / Blackout blues / Spanish fandango / I want to be near you / Sally Goodin / She's gone / I had a little mule / Go home with the girls in the mornin' / Still the water runs deepest / Cotton pitch blues / Nothin' but the best for my baby / Blues for Dixie / Cross my heart I love you / Keeper of my heart / I have somebody else / Thorn in my heart / Playboy charms / Hop, skip and jump over Texas / Texas drummer boy / I married the rose of San Antone / Ida Red likes the boogie / Warm red wine / I ain't got nobody / Boot Hill rag / Nothing but trouble / Anything / Bob Wills square dance (Parts 1-4) / King without a queen / Hold your tears / When it's Christmas on the range / Santa's on his way / Mean woman with green eyes / My little rock candy baby / Jolie Blonde likes the boogie / Pastime blues / Faded love / Awake but dreamin' / I betcha my heart I love you / I laugh when I think how I cried over you / I'll be lucky someday / I didn't realise / Rock a bye baby blues / I'm dotting each "i" with a teardrop / End of the line / 'Tater pie / Little girl, little girl / I'm tired of living this lie / Pitney Jane / Twinkle star / Brown skin gal / Sitting on top of the world / Silver bells / Last goodbye / Just to be loved / Send me a red rose / Hubbin' it / I can't stand this loneliness / You always keep me in hot water / 'Cause I'm in love / Three miles south of cash in Arkansas / I'm all alone / Three little kittens / Won't be back tonight / Charlie changed his mind / I'm only a friend / Steamboat stomp / I want to be wanted / Snatchin' and grabbin' / Real hot needle, A / Trouble, trouble blues (take 1) / Trouble, trouble blues / Broken heart for a souvenir, A / As I sit broken hearted / Bottle baby boogie / I want to go to Mexico / I'm human same as you / I hit the jackpot (when I won you) / Maiden's prayer / Fallen angel / She's a quarter house type of gal / B. Bowman hop / Doin' the bunny hop / St. Louis blues / So long, I'll see you later / Cadillac in model "A" / Waltzing in old San Antone / I've got a new road under my wheels / Texas blues / Live for you.
LP Set . . . . **BFX 15179/6**
Bear Family / May '85 / Rollercoaster Records / Swift / Direct Distribution.

RARE PRESTO TRANSCRIPTION, THE.
Tracks: Tennessee Saturday night / Draggin' the bow twin guitar special / Will you miss me when I'm gone / Bob Wills boogie / No wonder / Tierney's boogie / Sitting on top of the world / C jam blues / San Antonio rose / There'll be some changes made / C Schottische / Judy / Tumbling tumbleweeds / Sally Johnson / Blues for Dixie / Blue flame.
MC . . . . **CSR 1C**
Outlaw / Dec '87.

SAN ANTONIO ROSE AND OTHER HITS (Wills, Bob & His Texas Playboys).
Tracks: Not Advised.
MC **4XLL 9193**
Capitol (Specials) / Dec '88.

TIFFANY TRANSCRIPTIONS VOL.1 (Wills, Bob & His Texas Playboys).
Tracks: Nancy Jane / Mission to Moscow / Dinah / Lone star rag / Cotton patch blues / Sweet Jennie Lee / I hear you talking / Girl I left behind me, The / Straighten up and fly right / Little Betty Brown / Nobody's sweetheart now / Blackout blues / What's the matter with the mill / Jumpin' at the woodside.
CD . . . . **K 16**
LP . . . . **F 16**
MC . . . . **C 16**
Kaleidoscope (USA) / '82 / Projection / Ross Records / Roots Records / Swift / C.M. Distribution / Topic Records / Duncans.
CD . . . . **EDCD 321**
LP . . . . **ED 321**
Edsel / Jun '90 / Pinnacle.

TIFFANY TRANSCRIPTIONS VOL.2 (Wills, Bob & His Texas Playboys).
Tracks: Not Advised.
CD . . . . **K 19**
LP . . . . **F 19**
MC . . . . **C 19**
Kaleidoscope (USA) / Jul '87 / Projection / Ross Records / Roots Records / Swift / C.M. Distribution / Topic Records / Duncans.

TIFFANY TRANSCRIPTIONS VOL.3 (Basin street blues) (Wills, Bob & His Texas Playboys).
Tracks: Basin Street blues / I'm a ding dong daddy / Crazy rhythm / Milk cow blues / Please don't talk about me when I'm gone / Four or five times / Frankie Jean / It's your red wagon / Good man is hard to find, A / You just take her / Barnard blues / Baby won't you come home / Take the A train.
CD . . . . **K 20**
LP . . . . **F 20**
MC . . . . **C 20**
Kaleidoscope (USA) / Jul '87 / Projection / Ross Records / Roots Records / Swift / C.M. Distribution / Topic Records / Duncans.
CD . . . . **EDCD 323**
LP . . . . **ED 323**
MC . . . . **EDC 323**
Edsel / '89 / Pinnacle.

TIFFANY TRANSCRIPTIONS VOL.4 (Wills, Bob & His Texas Playboys).
Tracks: Texas Playboy theme / You're from Texas / Beaumont rag / Lum and Abner special / Texarkana baby / Little Joe the wrangler / New Spanish two-step / Texas plains / Home in San Antone / Blue Bonnet Lane / Across the alley from the Alamo / Along the Navajo trail / Spanish fandango / My brown eyed Texas rose / Red river valley / Texas Playboy theme (closing).
LP . . . . **F 21**
MC . . . . **C 21**
Edsel / Jul '87 / Pinnacle.
CD . . . . **EDCD 324**
LP . . . . **ED 324**
MC . . . . **EDC 324**
Edsel / Aug '90 / Pinnacle.

TIFFANY TRANSCRIPTIONS VOL.5 (Wills, Bob & His Texas Playboys).
Tracks: My window faces South / Swing blues / I had someone else before I had you / Smooth one, A / Don't cry baby / Three guitar special / China town / Fat boy rag / Lazy river / Sweet Georgia Brown / At the woodchoppers ball / Sweet kind of love / If it's wrong to love you.
LP . . . . **F 25**
MC . . . . **C 25**
Kaleidoscope (USA) / Jul '87 / Projection / Ross Records / Roots Records / Swift / C.M. Distribution / Topic Records / Duncans.
CD . . . . **EDCD 325**
LP . . . . **ED 325**
MC . . . . **EDC 325**
Edsel / Sep '90 / Pinnacle.

TIFFANY TRANSCRIPTIONS VOL.6 (Sally Goodin') (Wills, Bob & His Texas Playboys).
Tracks: Oklahoma hills / Sally Goodin / I had a little mule / Playboy chimes / Never no more hard time blues / I'll get mine bye and bye / Jesse polka / Oh Monah / Smith's reel / I'm putting all my eggs in one basket / Oklahoma rag / Dev'lish Mary / It's my lazy day / Sally Goodin (inst).
CD . . . . **K 27**
LP . . . . **F 27**
MC . . . . **C 27**
Kaleidoscope (USA) / Dec '87 / Projection / Ross Records / Roots Records / Swift / C.M. Distribution / Topic Records / Duncans.
CD . . . . **EDCD 326**
LP . . . . **ED 326**
MC . . . . **EDC 326**
Edsel / Sep '90 / Pinnacle.

TIFFANY TRANSCRIPTIONS VOL.7 (Wills, Bob & His Texas Playboys).
Tracks: Keep knockin' (but you can't come in) / Honeysuckle Rose / Worried mind / Okie boogie / C-Jam blues / I can't go on this way / Sweet moments / My gal Sal / I'm gonna be boss from now on / Lonesome hearted blues / Joe's place / Sugar blues / Too long / Tea for two.
CD . . . . **K 29**
LP . . . . **F 29**
MC . . . . **C 29**
Kaleidoscope (USA) / Oct '88 / Projection / Ross Records / Roots Records / Swift / C.M. Distribution / Topic Records / Duncans.
CD . . . . **EDCD 327**
LP . . . . **ED 327**
MC . . . . **EDC 327**
Edsel / Sep '90 / Pinnacle.

TIFFANY TRANSCRIPTIONS VOL.8 (More Of The Best) (Wills, Bob & His Texas Playboys).
Tracks: Miss Molly / Ten years / Blues for Dixie / Twinkle twinkle little star / Sun bonnet Sue / Sitting on top of the world / Big beaver / There's gonna be a party for the old folks / South / Trouble in mind / Little Liza Jane / Sioux City Sue / My confessions / Get along home Cindy.
CD . . . . **K 32**
LP . . . . **F 32**
MC . . . . **C 32**
Kaleidoscope (USA) / '88 / Projection / Ross Records / Roots Records / Swift / C.M. Distribution / Topic Records / Duncans.
CD . . . . **EDCD 328**
LP . . . . **ED 328**
MC . . . . **EDC 328**
Edsel / Sep '90 / Pinnacle.

TIFFANY TRANSCRIPTIONS VOL.9.
Tracks: Texas playboy rag / My life's been a pleasure / Elmer's tune / G.I wish / Milk cow blues / Shame on you / 12th street rag / In the mood / You don't care what happens / St Louis blues (part one) / St Louis blues (part two) / What is this thing called love / Sentimental journey / Black home in Indiana.
CD . . . . **EDCD 329**
LP . . . . **ED 329**
MC . . . . **EDC 329**
Edsel / Sep '91 / Pinnacle.

TIME CHANGES EVERYTHING.
Tracks: Not Advised.
LP . . . . **HAT 3024**
MC . . . . **HATC 3024**
Stetson / Oct '86 / Crusader Marketing Co. / Swift / Wellard Dist. / Midland Records / C.M. Distribution.

VERY BEST OF BOB WILLS & THE TEXAS PLAYBOYS,THE.
Tracks: San Antonio rose / Bubbles in my beer / Stay a little longer / Keeper of my heart / Deep water / Hang your head in shame / Roly poly / Trouble in mind / Heart to heart talk / Time changes everything / Right or wrong / Blue for Dixie / Cindy / Image of me, The / Mississippi river blues / Convict and the rose / Ida Red likes the boogie / Take me back to Tulsa.
MC . . . . **TC SLS 2600434**
Liberty / Apr '84 / EMI.
■ **LP** . . . . **SLS 2600 431**
Liberty / Apr '84.

Wills, Johnny Lee

OPERATORS' SPECIALS.
Tracks: Swing me / Milk cow blues / She's sweet / Blue man / Rockin' rollin' mama / Ramblers stomp / Nickel in the kitty / Panhandle shuffle / Big ball's in cowtown, A / Too long / Jive and smile / Mean old sixty-five blues / Woodchip blues / Sometimes / It's a long way to Tipperary.
LP . . . . **STR 807**
Topic / Aug '79 / Roots Records / Jazz Music / C.M. Distribution / Cadillac Music / Direct Distribution / Swift / Topic Records.

REUNION.
Tracks: Not Advised.
LP . . . . **FF 069**
Flying Fish (USA) / May '79 / Cadillac Music / Roots Records / Projection / C.M. Distribution / Direct Distribution / Jazz Music / Duncans / A.D.A Distribution.

W 16 ■ DELETED

ROMPIN', STOMPIN', SINGIN', SWINGIN' (Wills, Johnny Lee & His Boys).
Tracks: She took / Hat check baby / There are just two I's in Dixie / Thingamajig / Let me be / Two timin' / Bees in my bonnet / Oo oooh daddy / Ten little bluebirds in my lapel / Blackberry boogie / Honey in the horn / A-l-b-u-q-u-e-r-q-u-e / Sold out doc / Two step side step.
LP. . . . . BFX 15103
Bear Family / Sep '84 / Rollercoaster Records / Swift / Direct Distribution.

TULSA SWING.
Tracks: Not Advised.
LP. . . . . ROUNDER 1027
Rounder / Aug '88 / Projection / Roots Records / Swift / C.M. Distribution / Topic Records / Jazz Music / Hot Shot / A.D.A Distribution / Direct Distribution.

Wills, Luke

HIGH VOLTAGE GAL.
Tracks: Shut up and drink your beer / Never turn your back to a woman / Louisiana blues / Bob Wills two-step / Corn fed Arkanasas gal / Is it true what they say / Gotta get to Oklahoma city / Long train blues / I'm a married man / Uncle Tom Wills Schottische / High voltage gal / Texas special, The / Oklahoma blues / Si si senorita / Cain's stomp / Honky tonkin' Sal / Nickel in the jukebox, A / Woman was the cause of it all, A / Fly in the ointment / High voltage gal (2).
LP. . . . . BFX 15333
Bear Family / Jun '88 / Rollercoaster Records / Swift / Direct Distribution.

Wilson, Justin

C'EST SI BON.
Tracks: Not Advised.
LP. 11017
MC . . . . 11017 TC
Great Southern (USA) / '87 / Swift.

CAJUN CHRISTMAS, A.
Tracks: Santa Claus done brought himself to town / When Christmas angels sing / All I want for Christmas is my two front teeth / Randolph the rouge nosed reindeer.
LP. 5010
MC . . . . 5010 TC
Kom-a-Day (USA) / '87 / Swift.

CHRISTMAS STORIES.
Tracks: Night before Christmas, The / Santa Claus and the mouse / Year without a Santa Claus, The / Little engine that could, The.
LP. 5014
MC . . . . 5014 TC
Kom-a-Day (USA) / '87 / Swift.

FOR TRUE.
Tracks: Not Advised.
LP. 5015
MC . . . . 5015 TC
Kom-a-Day (USA) / '87 / Swift.

GOIN' FISHIN'.
Tracks: Not Advised.
LP. 11015
MC . . . . 11015 TC
Great Southern (USA) / '87 / Swift.

HUNT DEM DUCK AND SHOOT.
Tracks: Not Advised.
LP. 11014
MC . . . . 11014 TC
Great Southern (USA) / '87 / Swift.

HUNTING.
Tracks: Not Advised.
LP. 5007
MC . . . . 5007 TC
Kom-a-Day (USA) / '87 / Swift.

IN ORBIT.
Tracks: Not Advised.
LP. 5013
MC . . . . 5013 TC
Kom-a-Day (USA) / '87 / Swift.

INTOXICATED TALES.
Tracks: Not Advised.
LP. 5009
Kom-a-Day (USA) / Swift.
MC . . . . 5009 TC
Kom-a-Day (USA) / '87 / Swift.

KEEP IT CLEAN.
Tracks: Not Advised.
LP. 5011
MC . . . . 5011 TC
Kom-a-Day (USA) / '87 / Swift.

LET THE GOOD TIMES ROLL.
Tracks: Not Advised.
LP. 11016
MC . . . . 11016 TC
Great Southern (USA) / '87 / Swift.

OLD FAVORITES.
Tracks: Not Advised.
LP. 11013
MC . . . . 11013 TC
Great Southern (USA) / '87 / Swift.

OLD MASTER STORY TELLER, THE.
Tracks: Not Advised.
LP. 5008
MC . . . . 5008 TC
Kom-a-Day (USA) / '87 / Swift.

PASS A GOOD TIME.
Tracks: Not Advised.
LP. 5006
MC . . . . 5006 TC
Kom-a-Day (USA) / '87 / Swift.

SPORT, THE.
Tracks: Not Advised.
LP. 5012
MC . . . . 5012 TC
Kom-a-Day (USA) / '87 / Swift.

Wilson, Tug

COUNTRY MUSIC LOVIN' KINDA GUY.
Tracks: Not Advised.
LP. . . . . WGR 024
MC . . . . CWGR 024
Ross (1) / May '82 / Ross Records / Duncans / Entertainment UK.

NASHVILLE HALL OF FAME.
Tracks: Not Advised.
MC . . . . KBGC 221
Country House / '79 / Duncans / BGS Productions Ltd.

Winston Brothers

TRUCKER SONGS.
Tracks: Not Advised.
CD 100 001
Bridge (MCS Bridge) / '86 / Pinnacle.

TRUCKER SONGS VOL.2.
Tracks: Not Advised.
CD 100 025 2
Bridge (MCS Bridge) / Oct '86 / Pinnacle.

Wiseman, Mac

Mac Wiseman is a bluegrass guitarist and singer, born in 1925 in Virginia. He worked with Lester Flatt and Earl Scruggs, then Bill Monroe, then went solo. Not only a fine guitarist but one of the half-dozen best singers in bluegrass. He was country music A&R man for Dot records, had his own radio show Mac's Music Shop and ran annual bluegrass festival in Renfro Valley, Kentucky. (Donald Clarke).

BLUEGRASS FAVOURITES.
Tracks: Not Advised.
LP. . . . . HAT 3039
MC . . . . HATC 3039
Stetson / Jul '87 / Crusader Marketing Co. / Swift / Wellard Dist. / Midland Records / C.M. Distribution.

CLAYTON MCMICHAN STORY, THE (see under Travis, Merle).

CONCERT FAVOURITES.
Tracks: Not Advised.
LP. . . . . HAT 3100
MC . . . . HATC 3100
Stetson / Mar '89 / Crusader Marketing Co. / Swift / Wellard Dist. / Midland Records / C.M. Distribution.

COUNTRY MUSIC MEMORIES.
Tracks: They'll never take her love from me / I'll sail my ship alone / Don't be angry / Green light / All for the love of a girl / My baby's gone / I wonder where you are tonight / I love you a thousand ways / Flesh and blood / Me and Bobby McGee / Mother, the queen of my heart.
LP. . . . . CMH 6202
■ MC . . . . CMHC 6202
CMH (USA) / '76.
LP. . . . . CMLF 1022
Checkmate / Oct '77.

EARLY DOT RECORDINGS VOL 1.
Tracks: Love letters in the sand / I'm a stranger / Dreams of mother and home / Going to see my baby / When the roses bloom again / Little white church, The / I wonder how the old folks are at home / Little home in Tennessee / Dreaming of a little cabin / Let me borrow your heart / Rainbow in the valley / By the side of the road.
LP. . . . . CCS 108
MC . . . . CCS 108MC
County (USA) / '85 / Projection / Mike's Country Music Room / Swift.

EARLY DOT RECORDINGS VOL 2.
Tracks: Not Advised.
LP. . . . . CCS 109
MC . . . . CCS 109MC
County (USA) / '85 / Projection / Mike's Country Music Room / Swift.

ESSENTIAL BLUEGRASS ALBUM, THE (see under Osbourne Brothers).

GOLDEN CLASSICS: MAC WISEMAN.
Tracks: Not Advised.
LP. . . . . GT 0047
Gusto (USA) / Oct '79.

GRASSROOTS TO BLUEGRASS.
Tracks: Don't let your deal go down / Train 45 / Little rosewood casket, The / Poor Ellen Smith / Kentucky / Salty dog blues / Dust on the bible / It's mighty dark to travel / Old camp meeting time / Streamlined cannonball / Red rocking chair / Doin' my time / I'm just here to get my baby out of jail / Wait for the light to shine / Lonely mound of clay / Short life of trouble / Crying heart blues / Don't give your heart to a rambler / I'm using my bible as a road map / How mountain girls can love / Sailor of the deep blue sea / Light at the river.
CD . . . . CMHCD 9041
CMH (USA) / '90 / C.M. Distribution / Projection.

MAC WISEMAN STORY, THE.
Tracks: Love letters in the sand / Little blossom / I've got no use for women / Dark hollow / Wreck of old 97, The / Ballad of the Lawson family, The / May I sleep in your barn tonight, Mister / Bringing Mary home / Girl in the blue velvet band / I'll be all smiles tonight / I wonder how the old folks are at home / Jimmie Brown, the newsboy / Little box of pine in the 7:29, The / These hands / Baggage coach ahead, The / I still write your name in the sand / Six more miles / 'Tis sweet to be remembered / Dreaming of a little cabin.
Double LP . . . . CMH 9001
MC . . . . CMHC 9001
CMH (USA) / '76 / C.M. Distribution / Projection.

SHENANDOAH VALLEY MEMORIES.
Tracks: Not Advised.
LP. . . . . CGS 8510
Canaan / Aug '77 / Word Records (UK) / Sony.

SINGS GORDON LIGHTFOOT.
Tracks: Did she mention my name? / Cotton Jenny / Rainy day people / Summertime dream / For lovin' me / Steel rail blues / Ribbon of darkness / House you live in, The / Early morning rain / Old Dan's records / Sundown.
LP. . . . . CMH 6211
■ MC . . . . CMHC 6211
CMH (USA) / '77.

SONGS THAT MADE THE JUKEBOX PLAY.
Tracks: Not Advised.
Double LP . . . . CMH 9021
MC . . . . CMHC 9021
CMH (USA) / C.M. Distribution / Projection.

TEENAGE HANGOUT.
Tracks: Teenage hangout / Step it up & go / Sundown / I hear you knockin' / Meanest blues in the world, The / Hey, Mr. Blues man / One mint julep / I'm waiting for the ships that never come in / Fool, The / I like this kind of music / Now that you have me / Talk of the town / Glad rags / I'm eatin' high on a hog / I want someone / Camptown races / I'll still write your name in the sand / Promise of things to come / Thinkin' about you / Because we are young / Be good baby / 'Tis sweet to be remembered / Running bear / Ballad of Davy Crockett, The / Tom Dooley / Sixteen tons / El Paso / Old lamplighter, The / Three bells, The / I'm movin' on.
CD . . . . BCD 15694
Bear Family / Jul '93 / Rollercoaster Records / Swift / Direct Distribution.

Withers, Tex

Born Alan Frank Withers, died on 29.12.1986 aged 53. The diminutive singer's able showmanship won over the hearts of many around the UK country clubs during the 60's and 70's prior to his retirement in 1979. He held the resident slot at Wimbledon's Tennessee Centre, when not on the road and played Wembley's Country Music Festival in 1972, sharing the stage with America's finest. Troubled with spinal problems during his early life, Withers went on to gain 1971's Top Country and Western Singer award. Made recordings on Avenue, RCA (receiving a silver disc in 1972 for his album *Tex Withers sings country style* for sales in excess of 136,000 copies), Shannon and Topspin. (Maurice Hope - August 1993)

BLUE RIBBON COUNTRY.
Tracks: Wreck of the old '97 / I can't stop loving you / Billy bayou / Jambalaya / For the good times / They don't understand / Heartaches by the number / Help me make it through the night / Okie from Muskogee / Crazy arms / Burn some bridges / Me and Bobby Magee.
MC . . . . CHRL 206
Homespun (Ireland) / May '84 / Homespun Records / Ross Records / Wellard Dist.

TRUCK DRIVING MAN.
Tracks: Not Advised.
MC . . . . VCA 005
VFM Cassettes / Jan '85 / VFM Children's Entertainment Ltd. / Midland Records / Morley Audio Services.

Wolf, Kate

Born January 27, 1942 - died December 10, 1986. Born Kathryn Louise Allen, San Francisco, Kate made her name as a pure voiced singer-songwriter during the 70's and early

80's. Performing most regularly throughout America's west, especially in Sonoma County (her adopted home). Later encompassing Philadelphia and Texas, much loved Kate won many admirers during an all too-short career. With her warm personality, this communicator captured many a heart, before succumbing to Leukaemia. (Maurice Hope)

AN EVENING IN AUSTIN.
Tracks: Eyes of a painter / Green eyes / Picture puzzle / Brother warrior / Carolina pines / Crying shame / Love still remains / Like a river / Give yourself to love / Pacheco - the redtail hawk / These times we're living in / Let's get together / Friend of mine / One more song.
VHS . . . . **MFV 0006**
Music Farm / Jan '91 / Music Farm Ltd.

BACKROADS (Wolf, Kate & Wildwood Flower).
Tracks: Lately / Emma Rose / Sitting on the porch / Redtail hawk, The / Telluride / Goodbye babe / It ain't in the wine / Tequila and me / Legend in his time / Riding in the country / Oklahoma going home / Back roads.
LP . . . . **F 6**
MC . . . . **C 6**
Kaleidoscope (USA) / Oct '88 / Projection / Ross Records / Roots Records / Swift / C.M. Distribution / Topic Records / Duncans.
CD . . . . **K 6**
Kaleidoscope (USA) / Apr '90 / Projection / Ross Records / Roots Records / Swift / C.M. Distribution / Topic Records / Duncans.

CLOSE TO YOU.
Tracks: Across the great divide / Legget serenade / Like a river / Unfinished life / Friend of mine / Love still remains / Eyes of a painter / Here in California / Stone in the water / Close to you.
LP . . . . **F 15**
MC . . . . **C 15**
Kaleidoscope (USA) / Oct '88 / Projection / Ross Records / Roots Records / Swift / C.M. Distribution / Topic Records / Duncans.
CD . . . . **K 15**
Kaleidoscope (USA) / Jan '90 / Projection / Ross Records / Roots Records / Swift / C.M. Distribution / Topic Records / Duncans.

EVENING IN AUSTIN, AN.
Tracks: Eyes of a painter / Green eyes / Carolina pines / Give yourself to love / Let's get together / Friend of mine.
CD . . . . **K 36**
MC . . . . **C 36**
Kaleidoscope (USA) / Mar '90 / Projection / Ross Records / Roots Records / Swift / C.M. Distribution / Topic Records / Duncans.

GIVE YOURSELF TO LOVE.
Tracks: Give yourself to love / Desert wind / Peaceful easy feeling / Ballad of Weaverville, The / Green eyes / You're not standing like you used to / Hobo, The / Hurry home / Some kind of love / Who knows were time goes / Cornflower blue / Picture puzzle / Far off shore / Agent orange / These times we're living in / Sweet companion / Medicine trail / Pacheco / Redtail hawk / Friend of mine.
LP . . . . **F 3000**
MC . . . . **C 3000**
Kaleidoscope (USA) / Oct '88 / Projection / Ross Records / Roots Records / Swift / C.M. Distribution / Topic Records / Duncans.
CD . . . . **K 3000**
Kaleidoscope (USA) / Jan '90 / Projection / Ross Records / Roots Records / Swift / C.M. Distribution / Topic Records / Duncans.

GOLD IN CALIFORNIA.
Tracks: Full time woman / She rises like a dolphin / Like a river / Telluride / Muddy roads / Across the great divide / Lilac and the apple, The / Unfinished life / Early morning melody / Safe at anchor / Redtail hawk, The / Sun is burning, The / Brother warrior / Two way waltz / Eyes of a painter / Emma Rose / Here in California / Poet's heart / Carolina pines / Trumpet vines, The.
LP . . . . **F 3001**
MC . . . . **C 3001**
Kaleidoscope (USA) / Oct '88 / Projection / Ross Records / Roots Records / Swift / C.M. Distribution / Topic Records / Duncans.
CD . . . . **K 3001**
Kaleidoscope (USA) / Jan '90 / Projection / Ross Records / Roots Records / Swift / C.M. Distribution / Topic Records / Duncans.

LINES ON THE PAPER (Wolf, Kate & Wildwood Flower).
Tracks: I don't know why / Lines on paper / You're not standing like you used to / Picture puzzle / Heart, The / Trumpet vine, The / I never knew my father / Amazed to find / Everybody's looking for the same thing / Lilac and the apple, The / Midnight on the water / Lay me down easy.
LP . . . . **F 7**
MC . . . . **C 7**
Kaleidoscope (USA) / Oct '88 / Projection / Ross Records / Roots Records / Swift / C.M. Distribution / Topic Records / Duncans.
CD . . . . **K 7**
Kaleidoscope (USA) / Apr '90 / Projection / Ross Records / Roots Records / Swift / C.M. Distribution / Topic Records / Duncans.

POET'S HEART.
Tracks: Poet's heart / In China or a woman's heart / Slender thread / Brother warrior / Crying shame / Muddy roads / Carolina pines / All he ever saw was you / See here, she said.
LP . . . . **F 24**
MC . . . . **C 24**
Kaleidoscope (USA) / Oct '88 / Projection / Ross Records / Roots Records / Swift / C.M. Distribution / Topic Records / Duncans.
CD . . . . **K 24**
Kaleidoscope (USA) / Jan '90 / Projection / Ross Records / Roots Records / Swift / C.M. Distribution / Topic Records / Duncans.

SAFE AT ANCHOR.
Tracks: Safe at anchor / Early morning melody / Sweet love / She rises like a dolphin / Great love of my life / Shining / September song / Seashore mountain lady / Looking back at you / Two way waltz.
LP . . . . **F 11**
MC . . . . **C 11**
Kaleidoscope (USA) / Oct '88 / Projection / Ross Records / Roots Records / Swift / C.M. Distribution / Topic Records / Duncans.
CD . . . . **K 11**
Kaleidoscope (USA) / Jan '90 / Projection / Ross Records / Roots Records / Swift / C.M. Distribution / Topic Records / Duncans.

WIND BLOWS WILD.
Tracks: Old Jerome / Statues made of clay / Monday in the mountains / Streets of Calgary / Give yourself to love / Wind blows wild, The / Clearing in the forest.
CD . . . . **K 30**
LP . . . . **F 30**
MC . . . . **C 30**
Kaleidoscope (USA) / '88 / Projection / Ross Records / Roots Records / Swift / C.M. Distribution / Topic Records / Duncans.

Wood, Smokey

HOUSTON HIPSTER,THE.
Tracks: Not Advised.
LP . . . . **RAMBLER 107**
Rambler (USA) / Feb '89 / Roots Records / Projection / Swift / Wellard Dist.

Wood, Windy

WEST TEXAS SWING.
Tracks: Let's be sure we know / Somewhere in San Antone / Sugar moon / Texas bluebonnet swing / Don't keep it a secret / Ten years / Right or wrong / Rosetta / If no news is good news / Heart to heart talk / When my dreamboat comes home / Orange blossom special.
LP . . . . **SDLP 036**
MC . . . . **SDC 036**
Sundown / Nov '86 / Terry Blood Dist. / Jazz Music / C.M. Distribution.

Wooley, Sheb

Wooley, Sheb was born in 1921 in Oklahoma. The country singer, songwriter and actor recorded for Bullet in Nashville and guested on radio shows. He landed a radio show in Fort Worth, Texas advertising Calument Baking Powder in 1946, singing, writing the adverts and creating character the Chief from the company's logo. Wooley moved to the West Coast in the late'40s and studied acting. He signed with MGM and began writing parodies of hits. *When Mexican Joe Met Jolie Blon* was a hit for Hank Snow in 1953. He played in more than 40 films, best known role in High Noon in 1952 as the baddie trying to gun down Gary Cooper While working on the set of Giant, he wrote *Are You Satisfied?*, and had a minor hit in 1955. He wrote and recorded the novelty *The Purple People Eater*, a number one USA pop hit for six weeks in 1958. *That's My Pa*, in 1962 made the pop chart but was a number one country hit. Sheb Wooley had sporadic hits in that chart for the rest of the decade. He also acted in TV shows including Rawhide with Clint Eastwood for five years. As Ben Colder he made LPs and singles of parodies such as *Detroit City No.2*, *Almost Persuaded No.2*, *Harper Valley P.T.A. (Later That Same Day)*. Wooley was named comic of the year by the CMA in 1968. Seen on every major country TV show, Sheb Wooley was still entertaining in the '80s. (Donald Clarke)

BLUE GUITAR.
Tracks: Blue guitar / Natchez landing.
7" . . . . **MGM 1263**
MGM (EMI) / '64 / EMI.

BLUE GUITAR.
Tracks: Whatcha gonna do / It takes a heap of livin' / Humdinger / Boogie woogie waltz / Don't stop kissing me tonight / Hillbilly mambo / Texas tango / Panama Pete / Blue guitar / Changing your name (Now you're) / Fool about you / Listening to your footsteps / Knew I had lost / I'll return the letters / Love at first sight / Aircastle.
LP . . . . **BFX 15175**
Bear Family / Nov '85 / Rollercoaster Records / Swift / Direct Distribution.

COUNTRY BOOGIE, WILD & WOOLEY (1948-1955).
Tracks: Love is a fever / Tom / Boogie woogie Tom Cat, The / Mule boogie / Country kisses / Hoot owl boogie / I go outa my mind / I flipped / Back room boogie / Over the barrel / White lightning / Down in the toolies / 38 25 35 / You're the cat's meow / Love is just another merry go round / Wha' happen to my baby / Rover scoot over.
LP . . . . **BFX 15099**
Bear Family / Jul '84 / Rollercoaster Records / Swift / Direct Distribution.

PURPLE PEOPLE EATER.
Tracks: Purple people eater.
■ **7"** . . . . **MGM 981**
MGM (EMI) / Jun '58.

Work, Jimmy

CRAZY MOON.
Tracks: Don't play with my heart / If I should lose you / Crazy moon / I'm lonesome for someone / Little popcorn man / How can I love you / Puttin' on the dog / Out of my mind / Smokey mountain moon / Bluegrass ticklin' my feet / Please don't let me love you / Surrounded by water and bars / Who's been here since I've been gone / I would send roses (but they cost too much).
LP . . . . **BFX 15267**
Bear Family / Mar '88 / Rollercoaster Records / Swift / Direct Distribution.

MAKING BELIEVE.
Tracks: That's the way it's gonna be / Rock Island line / Puttin' on the dog / When she said you all / Digging my own grave / Don't give me a reason to wonder why / Blind heart(1) / You've got a heart like a merry-go-round / That cold, cold look in your eyes / Hands away from my heart / That's the way the juke box plays / There's only one you / Making believe / Blind heart(2) / Let 'em talk / Just like downtown / My old stomping ground / Don't knock just come on in / Those Kentucky bluegrass hills / You're gone, I won't forget / Rainy, rainy blues / Hear that steamboat whistle blow / Tennessee border / Your jealous heart is broken now / Bluegrass is tickling my feet / Please don't let me love you / I would send you roses (but they cost too much) / Surrounded by water & bars / Smokey mountain moon / Who's been here since I been gone / Mr. & Mrs. Cloud / Hospitality / Pickup truck / Do your honky tonkin' at home / Southern fried chicken / Let's live a little / If I should lose you / Don't play with my heart / I'm lonesome for someone / Puttin' on the dog (Tom cattin' around) / Crazy moon / Little popcorn man / How can I love you (when you're not around) / Out of my mind / That's what make the jukebox play / Don't knock, just come in / Blind heart / That cold, cold look in your eye / Let me be alone / I never thought I'd have the blues / I dreamed last night.
LP . . . . **BFX 15177**
Bear Family / Mar '86 / Rollercoaster Records / Swift / Direct Distribution.
CD . . . . **BCD 15651**
Bear Family / Aug '93 / Rollercoaster Records / Swift / Direct Distribution.

Workman, Nimrod

MOTHER JONES' WILL.
Tracks: Not Advised.
LP . . . . **ROUNDER 0076**
Rounder / '88 / Projection / Roots Records / Swift / C.M. Distribution / Topic Records / Jazz Music / Hot Shot / A.D.A Distribution / Direct Distribution.

Wright, B.J.

J.R.
Tracks: J.R. / Memory bound.
■ **7"** . . . . **SS 3001**
Stateside / Jun '80.

Wright, Bobby

CAROLINE'S FOOTSTEPS.
Tracks: Caroline's footsteps / I'm coming down lonely.
■ **7"** . . . . **UP 36428**
United Artists / Aug '78.

Wright, Ginny

WHIRLWIND THE FABOR RECORDINGS VOLUME 1.
Tracks: Lonesome seagull / I'm in heaven / Wonderful world / I love you / My chihuahua dog / Indian moon / Your eyes feasted upon her / Where were you / I want you yes / I saw Esau (kissing Mary Lou) / Whirlwind / I could still tell you more / Turn around my darling / I've got somebody new / Please leave my darlin' alone / How to get married.
LP . . . . **BFX 15188**
Bear Family / Mar '86 / Rollercoaster Records / Swift / Direct Distribution.

Wright, Michelle

Michelle Wright is one of a rare breed - a Canadian country music artist making it big in the USA. Growing up in Merlin, Ontario,a small Canadian farming community just 45 minutes from Detroit, she heard plenty of rhythm'n'blues and Motown on the radio, but her preference lay with country. She began touring and playing clubs right after high school, and by 1988 had secured a contract with Savannah Records. A year or so later she made her UK concert debut at the Peterborough Festival. It was Michelle's record success, the mass of awards that kept coming her way from the CCMA (Canadian Country Music Association) and that distinctive husky voice that made her the third artist to be signed to Arista records when it opened its country division in Nashville in 1991. Two years later - with a couple of American albums, *Michelle Wright* and *Now and then*, and hits like *Talk it like a man* and *He would be sixteen* to her credit - she walked away with the Academy of Country Music's 'Best New Female Vocalist' award, further ensuring her growing stature in the U.S. market. (Tony Byworth - August 1993)

DO RIGHT BY ME.
Tracks: Not Advised.
CD . . . . **SVCD 9206**
LP . . . . **SVLP 9206**
MC . . . . **SVMC 9406**
Savannah / Feb '89 / Sony / ACD Trading Ltd.

HE WOULD BE SIXTEEN.
Tracks: He would be sixteen.
7" **7432114105-7**
CD Single **7432114105-2**
■ **MC Single** **7432114105-4**
RCA / Apr '93.

NOW & THEN.
Tracks: Take it like a man / If I'm ever over you / Now and then / One time around / He would be 16 / Change, The / Don't start with me / Guitar talk / Fastest healing heart / Little more comfortable, A / All you wanna do / New kind of love / Like a hurricane / As far as lonely goes.
CD **74321 14543-2**
MC **74321 14543-4**
Arista / Oct '93 / BMG.

NOW AND THEN.
Tracks: Take it like a man / If I'm ever over you / Now and then / One time around / He would be sixteen / Change, The / Don't start with me / Guitar talk / Fastest healing wounded heart / Little more comfortable, A / All you really wanna do / New kind of love / Like a hurricane / As far as lonely goes.
CD **7432114543-2**
MC **7432114543-4**
Arista / May '93 / BMG.

Wright, Peggy Sue

DYNAMITE COUNTRY.
Tracks: Not Advised.
LP . . . . **SKYL 7004**
Meteor / Jun '78 / Terry Blood Dist. / Jazz Music.

GENTLY HOLD ME.
Tracks: Not Advised.
LP . . . . **BRA 1003**
MC . . . . **BRC 1003**
Big R / Nov '80 / Pinnacle.

Wright, Ruby

BIMBO.
Tracks: Bimbo.
■ **7"** . . . . **R 3816**
Parlophone / Apr '54.

THREE STARS.
Tracks: Three stars.
■ **7"** . . . . **R 4556**
Parlophone / May '59.

Wynette, Tammy

Born Wynette Pugh in Mississippi, singer, pianist, guitarist and songwriter Tammy Wynette is one of the most successful women in the history of country music. Her early career was in hairdressing and beauty but she later moved to Nashville with her three children of a teenage marriage. After building her reputation in local clubs while working as a song-plugger by day, she secured a recording deal with Epic Records in the mid-60's. Her first single *Apartment No 9*, was a rapid success on the American country charts and was followed by a bigger hit *Your good girls gonna go bad*. During the late 60's and early 70's she was never very far from the top of country listings, thanks to her string of tear-jerking singles and albums. In 1968 Wynette married fellow country star George Jones and they enjoyed many duet successes. Her biggest solo smash *Stand by your man* came in that year. It cruised to No.1 on the billboard C & W chart and was her only song to cross over to the US Top Forty pop list. Produced and written by long standing studio colleague Billy Sherrill, this record summed up her style: emotional vocals encassed in lavish string arrangements, with lyrics emphasising her conservative moral values on the subjects of marriage, family life and heart-break. Much of her material was written by Sherrill with Glenn Sutton and Wynette was herself an occasional contributor. *Stand by your man* and *D.I.V.O.R.C.E.* were the records that made her really famous - the package was sickly but effective - and with her *Greatest hits* album she became the first woman country singer to sell a million copies. Suddenly in 1975, *Stand by your man* went to No.1 in the British pop chart. She had previously been unknown in the UK and this unexpected smash quickly led to the arrival of two concurrent chart LPs. However, in the same year she divorced Jones amid wide publicity and *Stand by your man* was rapidly making her a laughing stock. when *D.I.-V.O.R.C.E.* made the UK No.12 in late '75 it inspired a hilarious parody version by Scots comedian Billy Connolly which reached No.1. The following year saw J.J. Barrie gaining a sickly British No.1 with another Wynette-associated song, *No charge*. *Twenty country classics* took Wynette into the Top Three of the UK album chart in 1978, the year she married George Richey, who became her producer. In the 80's she was no longer an important force on the American country charts or the British pop lists, but she remained a high earner with numerous cabaret, concert and television appearances. A biographical TV movie, Stand by your man was made in 1981. She returned to the charts with pop/dance hipsters KLF on the novelty offering *Justified And Ancient*.

20 COUNTRY CLASSICS.
Tracks: Not Advised.
■ **LP** . . . . **PR 5040**
CBS / Dec '77.

25TH ANNIVERSARY COLLECTION.
Tracks: Another chance / Apartment 9 / I don't wanna play house / Your good girl's gonna go bad / I still believe in fairytales / D.I.V.O.R.C.E. / Singing my song / Changes / 'Til I can make it on my own / Rocky top / Let's call it a day today / Heart over mind / Instrumental medley / Stand by your man.
VHS . . . . **TVE 1035**
Telstar/Ronco / Oct '91 / BMG.

ALIVE AND WELL.
Tracks: I'll be thinking of you / Alive and well / Copy to come.
7" **6504397**
Epic / Feb '87 / Sony.

ANNIVERSARY: 20 YEARS OF HITS.
Tracks: I don't wanna play house / D.I.V.O.R.C.E. / Stand by your man / Singing my song / Run, woman, run / We sure can love each other / Good loving (makes it right) / Bedtime story / Till I get it right / Kids say the darndest things / Another lonely song / We're gonna hold on (with George Jones.) / Woman to woman / Till I can make it on my own / Golden ring (with George Jones.) / You and me / One of a kind / Two storey house (with George Jones.) / Alive and well / Apartment No.9 / Your good girl's gonna go bad.
■ **LP** **4503931**
Epic / Apr '87.
CD **4503932**
MC **4503934**
Epic / Mar '91 / Sony.

ANOTHER LONELY SONG.
Tracks: Another lonely song / Crying steel guitar / What my thoughts do all the time / Stayin' home woman / Satin sheets / Homecoming / Help me make it through the night / Keep me in mind / Oh, how I miss him / With child / One final stand.
■ **LP** . . . . **EPC 80024**
CBS / '78 / Sony.

BEST OF TAMMY WYNETTE.
Tracks: Stand by your man / Lonely street / D.I.-V.O.R.C.E. / Gentle on my mind / Take me to your world / Almost persuaded / Your good girl's gonna go bad / Apartment No.9 / Hey good lookin' / I don't wanna play house / My arms stay open late / There goes my everything.
■ **LP** . . . . **EPC 63578**
Epic / May '75.
LP . . . . **CBS 32015**
MC **40 32015**
CBS / Mar '81 / Sony.
CD . . . . **CD 32015**
CBS / Jun '91 / Sony.

BEST OF TAMMY WYNETTE VOL 2.
Tracks: You and me / Let's get together (one last time) / Womanhood / I still believe in fairytales / One of a kind / Till I can make it on my own / This time I almost made it / Southern California / I'd like to see Jesus / Dear daughters.
■ **LP** . . . . **EPC 83214**
Epic / '79.

BIGGEST HITS.
Tracks: I don't wanna play house / Take me to your world / D.I.V.O.R.C.E. / Stand by your man / Ways to love a man, The / When he loves me (he loves me all the way) / Run woman run / Bedtime story / My man / Till I get it right / Kids say the darndest things / Till I can make it on my own / You and me / Starting over / Cowboys don't shoot straight / Crying in the rain.
LP . . . . **EPC 32302**
Epic / Mar '83 / Sony.

CHRISTMAS WITH TAMMY.
Tracks: Silent night, holy night / O little town of Bethlehem / It came upon a midnight clear / Joy to the world / Away in a manger / Gentle shepherd / Blue Christmas / Merry Christmas (We must be having one) / White Christmas / One happy Christmas / Lonely Christmas call / Let's put Christ back into Christmas.
LP . . . . **EPC 69214**
■ **MC** . . . . **EPC 4069214**
CBS / '78 / Sony.
■ **LP** **4604631**
Epic / Dec '87.
■ **MC** **4604634**
Epic / Dec '87.

CLASSIC COLLECTION.
Tracks: Stand by your man / You and me / I don't wanna play house / Golden ring / No charge / Apartment No.9 / Gentle on my mind / Womanhood / Your good girl's gonna go bad / Almost persuaded / Ode to Billy Joe / Southern California / Let's get together (one last time) / Crying in the chapel / Yesterday / Help me make it through the night / D.I.V.O.R.C.E. / There goes my everything / Cheatin' is / My elusive dreams / One of a kind / Sweet music man / Bedtime story / Roll in my sweet baby's arms / Till I can make it on my own / Honey (I miss you) / Woman to woman / Near you / Please come to Boston / I'd like to see Jesus on the midnight special / Kids say the darndest things / My man (understands).
Double LP . . . . **EPC 22136**
Epic / May '82 / Sony.
■ **MC Set** **40 22136**
Epic / May '82.

COUNTRY GIRL MEETS COUNTRY BOY.
Tracks: Not Advised.
■ **LP** . . . . **PR 5039**
Warwick / Feb '78.

COUNTRY STARS (Wynette, Tammy & George Jones).
Tracks: No show jones / Race is on, The / Bartender blues / I always get lucky with you / She's my rock / Chicken reel instr, / He stopped loving her today / Who's gonna fill their shoes / One I loved back then, The / Welcome to my world / Another chance / You good girl's gonna go bad / D.I.V.O.R.C.E. / Singing my song / 'Til I can make it on my own / Womanhood / Fairy tales / When the grass grows over me / Amazing grace / I'll fly away / Will the circle be unbroken / I saw the light / Stand by your man / Cryin' in the rain.
CD . . . . **PLATCD 351**
MC . . . . **PLAC 351**
Platinum Music / May '91 / Prism Leisure PLC / Ross Records.

COUNTRY STARS LIVE (Wynette, Tammy & George Jones).
Tracks: No show Jones / Race on, The / Bartender blues / Always get lucky with you / She's my rock / Chicken reel / He stopped loving her today / Who's gonna fill their shoes / One I loved back then, The / Welcome to my world / Another chance / Your good girl's gonna go bad / D.I.V.O.R.C.E. / Singing my song / Til I can make it on my own / Woman hood / Fairy tales / When the grass grows over me / Amazing grace / I'll fly away / Will the circle be unbroken / I saw the light / Stand by your man / Cryin' in the rain.
VHS . . . . **PLATV 351**
Platinum Music / Mar '90 / Prism Leisure PLC / Ross Records.

COUNTRY STORE: TAMMY WYNETTE.
Tracks: Heaven's just a sin away / You needed me / Only the strong survive / Yesterday / Take me to your world / My elusive dreams / I don't wanna play house / Stand by your man / Starting over / Crying in the rain / Help me make it through the night / There goes my everything / Gentle on my mind / It's just a matter of time / Unwed fathers (Only on CD.) / If I could only win your love (Only on CD.) / Bottle, The (Only on CD.) / Cowboys don't shoot straight (Only on CD.).
CD . . . . **CDCST 1**
MC . . . . **CSTK 1**
Country Store / '88 / BMG.
■ **LP** . . . . **CST 1**
Country Store / '88.

COUNTRY STORE: TAMMY WYNETTE AND GEORGE JONES (see under Jones, George).

COUNTRY SUPERSTAR - TAMMY WYNETTE.
Tracks: Not Advised.
MC Set . . . . **DTO 10306**
Ditto / '89 / Pickwick Records.

COUNTRY WORLD OF TAMMY WYNETTE.
Tracks: Ode to Billy Joe / There goes my everything / Cry / Hey good lookin' / Gentle on my mind / This time I almost made it / Old reliable / (When he loves me) he loves me all the way / Dear daughter / Bring my baby back to me / Take me to your world / Honey / He was there (when I needed you) / Slighly used woman, A / Let's get together (one last time) / Starting over / Easy come, easy go / Only the strong survive / Yesterday / Crying in the rain.
MC Set . . . . **DTO 10083**
Ditto / Aug '84 / Pickwick Records.
MC Set . . . . **DTOL 10083**
Ditto / Feb '90 / Pickwick Records.

■ DELETED W 19

COWBOYS DON'T SHOOT STRAIGHT.
Tracks: Cowboys don't shoot straight / You brought me back.
7" . . . . EPC A 1211
Epic / May '81 / Sony.

CRYING IN THE RAIN.
Tracks: Crying in the rain / Bring back my baby.
7" . . . . EPCA 1719
Epic / Nov '81 / Sony.

D.I.V.O.R.C.E.
Tracks: D.I.V.O.R.C.E. / Send me no roses / Please come to Boston / Just as soon as I get over loving you / Don't touch me / Almost persuaded / Your good girl's gonna go bad / I wound easy / I'm not mine to give / Walk through this world with me / Jackson ain't a very big town / Apartment No.9.
■ MC 4031676
CBS / '78 / Sony.
■ LP. . . . . CBS 31676
CBS / Nov '79.

D.I.V.O.R.C.E.
Tracks: D.I.V.O.R.C.E.
■ 7" . . . . EPC 3361
Epic / Jun '75.

EVEN THE STRONG GET LONELY.
Tracks: Unwed fathers / I'm so afaid that I'd live through it / Slightly used woman / Only the strong survive / With a friend like you / Still in the ring / Midnight love / Overdue / Darlin' take care of yourself / Even the strong get lonely.
■ LP. . . . . EPC 25585
Epic / Sep '83.

FIRST LADY OF COUNTRY.
Tracks: You and me / Every now and then / You hurt the love right out of me / Hawaiian wedding song / Little things / Jesus send a song / One of these days / When love was all we had / Dixieland / Funny face.
LP. . . . . SPR 8509
MC . . . . SPC 8509
Spot / Feb '83.

FIRST LADY OF COUNTRY (PICKWICK).
Tracks: Stand by your man / There goes my everything / Gentle on my mind / Honey / Almost persuaded / I can still believe in you / Your good girl's gonna go bad / Ode to Billy Joe / No charge / If we never love again / Crying in the chapel / Cry / Heaven's just a sin away / D.I.V.O.R.C.E.
LP. . . . . SHM 3182
MC . . . . HSC 3182
Hallmark / Sep '85 / Pickwick Records.
CD . . . . PWKS 4047
Pickwick / Apr '91 / Pickwick Records.

FIRST LADY OF COUNTRY MUSIC.
Tracks: Not Advised.
VHS. . . . . PLATV 307
Prism Video / Feb '91 / Terry Blood Dist. / Gold & Sons / Prism Leisure PLC.

GOLDEN RING (see under Jones, George).

GREATEST HITS.
Tracks: I don't wanna play house / Take me to your world / D.I.V.O.R.C.E. / Stand by your man / Ways to love a man, The / When he loves me / Run woman run / Bedtime story / My man / Till I get it right / Kids / Til I can make it on my own / You and me / Starting over / Cowboys don't shoot straight / Crying in the rain.
MC 9021224
Pickwick / Jul '92 / Pickwick Records.

GREATEST HITS: TAMMY WYNETTE.
Tracks: I don't wanna play house / D.I.V.O.R.C.E / Kids / Cowboys don't shoot straight / Starting over / Run woman run / Take me to your world / Ways to love a man, The / Till I can make it on my own / Crying in the rain / Bedtime story.
CD 902122
Pickwick / Aug '89 / Pickwick Records.

GREATEST HITS: TAMMY WYNETTE AND GEORGE JONES (see under Jones, George).

HEART OVER MIND.
Tracks: Let's call it a day today / I'm turning you loose / Suddenly single / What goes with blue / Just for a minute there / Half the way home / I'm falling heart over mind / Where's the fire / If you were the friend / One stone at a time.
■ LP. 4673551
Epic / Oct '90.
CD 4673552
■ MC 4673554
Epic / Oct '90.

HIGHER GROUND.
Tracks: Your love / Tempted / Some things will never change / Beneath a painted sky / I wasn't meant to live my life alone / Higher ground / Talkin' to myself again / Slow burning fire, A / There's no heart so strong / All through throwing good love after bad.
LP. 4511481
MC 4511484
Epic / Sep '87 / Sony.
■ CD 4511482
Epic / Sep '87.

I CAN STILL BELIEVE IN YOU.
Tracks: I can still believe in you / Loving you, I do.
■ 7" . . . . EPC 5376
Epic / Jun '77.

I DON'T WANNA PLAY HOUSE.
Tracks: I don't wanna play house.
■ 7" . . . . EPC 4091
Epic / Jun '76.

I LOVE COUNTRY.
Tracks: Womanhood / Two storey house / Crying in the rain / Bring my baby back to me / He was there when I needed you / Cheatin' is / Heaven's just a sin away / Cowboys don't shoot straight / Sometimes when we touch (With Mark Gray) / Funny face / You need me / Sweet music man / Pair of old sneakers, A / Dear daughters / Easy come, easy go / I'd like to see Jesus (on the midnight special).
LP. . . . . EPC 54943
Epic / Mar '87 / Sony.
■ MC 40 54943
Epic / Mar '87.

IN LOVE.
Tracks: Just in case / Easy come easy go / You can be replaced / If I could only win your love / World's most broken heart / Where some good love has been / Till I can make it on my own / Love is something good for everybody / He's just an old love turned memory.
LP. . . . . SHM 3026
■ MC . . . . HSC 3026
Hallmark / Feb '80.

IT SURE IS GOOD (Wynette, Tammy & George Jones).
Tracks: Ceremony, The / Up and at 'em / We're gonna hold on / Back home again in Indiana / Too marvellous for words / (We're not) the jet set / We loved it away / Mean to me / God's gonna getcha (for that) / Sweet Georgia Brown / I'm confessin' / Golden ring / Neenah / Near you / Southern California / I cover the waterfront / Pair of old sneakers, A / Two storey house / We could / Crying time / Did you ever / When I stop dreaming / After the fire is gone / It sure was good.
LP. . . . . PMP 1006
MC . . . . PMPK 1006
Premier (Sony) / Feb '87 / Sony / Pinnacle.

JUST TAMMY.
Tracks: They call it making love / We'll talk about it later / Somewhere / Mania / Your little girl fell / I'm not ready yet / No one else in the world / You don't know the half of it / I L-O-V-E Y-O-U / You never cross my mind / Let me be me.
LP. . . . . EPC 83695
Epic / Jul '79 / Sony.
■ MC 40 83695
Epic / Jul '79.

KING AND QUEEN OF COUNTRY MUSIC (Wynette, Tammy & George Jones).
Tracks: I'll be there / If you don't somebody else will / Even the bad times are good / I've seen better days / Keep the change / Tattle tale eyes / Did you ever / Golden ring / Cryin' time / Near you.
■ LP. . . . . SHM 3024
Hallmark / Feb '80.

LET'S GET TOGETHER.
Tracks: Let's get together (one more time) / If we never love again / Loving you, I do / It's gonna take a long, long time / You could be coming to me / Your sweet lies (turned down my sheets again) / Cheatin' is / I can love you / No one can take his place / I can still believe in you.
LP. . . . . EPC 82026
■ MC . . . . EPC 4082026
Embassy / '78 / Sony.

LET'S GET TOGETHER ONE LAST TIME.
Tracks: Let's get together (one last time) / Hardly a day goes by.
■ 7" . . . . EPC 7230
Epic / Apr '79.

LIAR'S ROSES.
Tracks: Liar's roses.
■ 7" 6547767
Epic / Apr '89.

LIVE IN NASHVILLE.
Tracks: Another chance / Apartment no. 9 / I don't wanna play house / You're good girls gonna go bad / I still believe in fairytales / D.I.V.O.R.C.E / Singing my song / Changes / 'Till I can make it on my own / Rocky top / Let's call it a day today / Heart over mind / Instrumental medley (Duelling banjo's etc.) / Stand by your man.
VHS. . . . . TVE 1035
Telstar Video / '91 / BMG.

MY ELUSIVE DREAMS (Wynette, Tammy & George Jones).
Tracks: My elusive dreams / Near you.
■ 7" . . . . EPC 8300
Epic / Mar '80.

NEXT TO YOU.
Tracks: Next to you / I'm so afraid of losing you again / You left memories layin' (all over the place) / When a girl becomes a wife / If you let him drive you crazy (he will) / Note, The / Thank the cowboy for the ride / I almost forgot / We called it everything but quits / Liar's roses.
LP. 4650281
MC 4650284
Epic / Apr '89 / Sony.
■ CD 4650282
Epic / Apr '89.

NO CHARGE.
Tracks: No charge / Yesterday / There goes my everything / I believe / Honey / Crying in the chapel / Ode to Billy Joe / Legend of Bonny & Clyde / Cry / It is no secret (what God can do) / Kiss away / Don't come home a-drinkin'.
LP. 31532
■ MC 4031532
CBS / '78 / Sony.

ONE OF A KIND.
Tracks: One of a kind / That's the way it could've been / Love survived / That's just the way I am / Sweet music man / What I had with you / I'm not that good at goodbye / Heaven's just a sin away / I'll be your bridge (just lay me down) / Dear daughters.
LP. . . . . EPC 82453
■ MC . . . . EPC 4082453
CBS / '78 / Sony.

ONLY LONELY SOMETIMES.
Tracks: He was there (when I needed you) / I'll be thinking of you / Never knew / Come with me / You needed me / Starting over / Out of the spotlight / Only the names have been changed / When you love me / Ozark Mountain lullaby.
■ LP. . . . . EPC 84343
Epic / Aug '80.
MC . . . . SPC 8578
Spot / Apr '86.

QUEEN OF COUNTRY.
Tracks: D.I.V.O.R.C.E. / Don't touch me / Almost persuaded / (You make me want to be) a mother / Another lonely song / Kid's say the darndest things / Love's the answer / Send me no roses / Apartment No.9 / Woman to woman / Bedtime story / Stand by your man / Your good girl's gonna go bad / Wound easy (but I heal fast) / I'm not mine to give / Walk through this world with me / Jackson ain't a very big town / Just as soon as I get over you / Good lovin' (makes it right) / Reach out your hand / My man understands / Please come to me / 'Til I get it right / There goes that old steel guitar / Help me make it through the night.
MC Set. . . . . DTOL 10043
Ditto / Feb '90 / Pickwick Records.

QUEEN OF COUNTRY.
Tracks: Not Advised.
LP. . . . . SSP 3073
■ MC . . . . SSC 3073
Pickwick / Sep '80.

SOFT TOUCH.
Tracks: Old reliable / She can't take my love off the bed / Being gone / What's it like to be a woman / I'll still be loving you this much / Another chance / If I didn't have a heart / You still get to me in my dreams / Sometimes I'm a little girl / Dancing your memory away.
■ LP. . . . . EPC 85727
Epic / Jul '82.

SOMETIMES WHEN WE TOUCH.
Tracks: Sometimes when we touch / You can lead a heart to love (but you can't make it fall) / Breaking away / Everytime you touch her / Between twenty-nine and danger / It's only over for you / Party of the first part, The / It's hard to be the dreamer (When I used to be the dream) / If it ain't love / He talks to me.
■ LP. . . . . EPC 26403
Epic / May '85.
■ MC 40 26403
Epic / May '85.

SOMETIMES WHEN WE TOUCH (Wynette, Tammy & Mark Gray).
Tracks: Sometimes when we touch / Even the strong get lonely.
■ 7" . . . . A 6326
Epic / Jun '85.

STAND BY YOUR MAN.
Tracks: You make me want to be a mother / Another lonely song / Kids say the darndest things / Love's the answer / Woman to woman / Bedside story / Stand by your man / Good lovin' / Reach out your hand / Please come to Boston / Till I get it right / My man (understands) / There goes that old steel guitar / Help me make it through the night.
■ LP. . . . . EPC 69141
Epic / Jun '75.
■ MC . . . . EPC 4069141
CBS / '78 / Sony.
■ LP. . . . . CBS 32772
CBS / Mar '86.
■ MC 40 32772
Epic / Mar '86.

STAND BY YOUR MAN.
Tracks: Stand by your man / I'll be thinking of you / I'm falling heart over mind (Only available on CD single).
7" 6569537
CD Single 6569532
■ MC Single 6569534
Epic / Jun '91.

STAND BY YOUR MAN.
Tracks: Stand by your man.
■ 7" . . . . **EPC 7137**
Epic / Apr '75.

STAND BY YOUR MAN (OLD GOLD).
Tracks: Stand by your man / D.I.V.O.R.C.E.
7" . . . . **OG 9313**
Old Gold / Feb '89 / Pickwick Records.

SWEET MUSIC MAN.
Tracks: Sweet music man / That's the way it could have been.
■ 7" . . . . **EPC 6092**
Epic / Feb '78.

TAMMY WYNETTE.
Tracks: I'll see him through / Love me, love me / It's just a matter of time / Cold lonely feeling / Divorce sale, The / When he loves me (he loves me all the way) / He thinks I love him / Our last night together / Lighter shade of blue, A / Lonely days (and nights more lonely) / You make my skies turn blue.
LP 31487
■ MC 403148/
CBS / '78 / Sony.

TAMMY WYNETTE IN CONCERT.
Tracks: Not Advised.
VHS . . . . **MA 11061**
Vestron Music Video / '87 / Sony / Gold & Sons / Terry Blood Dist.

TEARS OF FIRE, THE 25TH ANNIVERSARY COLLECTION.
Tracks: You can steal me / Apartment £9 / She didn't color daddy / Your good girl's gonna go bad / Walk through this world with me / My elusive dreams (Featuring David Houston.) / I don't wanna play house / take me to your world / D-I-V-O-R-C-E / Sweet dreams / Lonely street / I believe / He / Stand by your man / You'll never walk alone / Great thou art / Singing my song / Too far gone / Ways to love a man, The / I'll see him through / Kids (Say the darndest things) / He loves me all the way / We sure can love each other / Deepening snow, The / Good lovin' (Makes it right) / Bedtime story / 'Til I get it right / My man understands / We're gonna hold on (Featuring George Jones.) / (We're not) The jet set (Featuring George Jones.) / Another lonely

song / I don't think about him no more / No charge / Woman to woman / This time I almost made it / Near you (Featuring George Jones.) / I still believe in fairytales / 'Til I can make it on my own / Golden ring (Featuring George Jones.) / Did you ever (Featuring George Jones.) / You and me / Let's get together (One last time) / One of a kind / Southern California (Featuring George Jones.) / Dear daughters / They call it making love / Two story house (Featuring George Jones.) / Cowboys don't shoot straight (Like they used to) / Crying in the rain / Another chance / You still get to me in my dreams / Unwed fathers (I'm not) A candle in the wind / Sometimes when we touch (Featuring Mark Grey.) / Between twenty-nine and danger / Alive and well / Talkin' to myself again (Featuring The O'Kanes.) / I wasn't meant to live my life alone (Featuring Vince Gill.) / Beneath painted sky (Featuring Emmylou Harris.) / Your love (Featuring Ricky Skaggs.) / Higher ground (Featuring Larry, Steve & Rudy Gatlin.) / Liar's roses / We're strangers again (Duet with Randy Travis.) / Suddenly single / It could've been so good / Justified and ancient (Featuring The KLF.) / Precious memories (Featuring The Masters Five.).
CD Set 472894 2
MC Set 472894 4
Epic / Jan '93 / Sony.

TIL I CAN MAKE IT ON MY OWN.
Tracks: Til I can make it on my own / Just in case / He's just an old love turned memory / World's most broken heart, The / If I could only win your love / Heart, The / You can be replaced / Love is something good for everybody / Where some good love has been / Easy come, easy go.
LP . . . . **EPC 81182**
■ MC . . . . **EPC 4081182**
Embassy / '78 / Sony.

TOGETHER AGAIN (see under Jones, George).

WOMAN TO WOMAN.
Tracks: Your good girl's gonna go bad / Singing my song / Ways to love a man, The / I'll see him through / He loves me all the way / Run woman run / We sure love each other / Good lovin' / Bedtime story / My man / Till I get it right / Kids say the darndest things /

Another lonely song / Woman to woman / Till I can make it on my own / You and me.
LP . . . . **PMP 1001**
MC . . . . **PMPK 1001**
Premier (Sony) / Feb '87 / Sony / Pinnacle.

WOMANHOOD.
Tracks: Womanhood / Fifty words or less.
■ 7" . . . . **EPC 6505**
Epic / Aug '78.

WOMANHOOD.
Tracks: Womanhood / That's what friends are for / You oughta her the song / What's a couple more / One song I could never write, The / I'd like to see Jesus (on the midnight special) / Memories / Standing tall / Love doesn't always come (on the night it's needed) / 50 words or less.
LP . . . . **EPC 82972**
■ MC . . . . **EPC 4082972**
CBS / '78 / Sony.

YOU AND ME.
Tracks: You and me / Every now and then / Funny face / Hawaiian wedding song / Little things / Jesus, send a song / One of these days / You hurt the love right out of me / When love was all we had / Dixieland (you will never die).
LP . . . . **EPC 81569**
■ MC . . . . **EPC 4081569**
Embassy / '78 / Sony.

YOU BROUGHT ME BACK.
Tracks: Cowboys don't shoot straight / Crying in the rain / Bring back my baby to me / You brought me back / Goodnight cowboy goodnight / Easy street / I don't think I see me in your eyes anymore / Best there is / Easy come easy go / He's rolling over and over.
■ LP . . . . **EPC 84987**
Epic / Aug '81.

YOUR LOVE.
Tracks: Your love / I wasn't meant to live my life alone.
■ 7" 6515377
Epic / Apr '88.

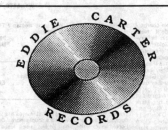
Future Titles from Music Master MUSIC MASTER

The Official Music Master Jazz Catalogue, 2nd Edition. £14.95 Published January 1994

The second edition of this highly acclaimed catalogue includes new and expanded entries for many historical and contemporary Jazz and Blues artists. All Biographies have been fully updated. 1000 pages (approximately).

To order:

Please send payment (cheques made payable to Music Master) plus postage as follows:
UK: add £1.75,   Europe: add £4.00 per catalogue,   Outside Europe: add £12.00 per catalogue. All books are sent registered delivery in the UK and by Airmail elsewhere.

Music Master, Paulton House, 8 Shepherdess Walk, London, N1 7LB.
Tel: +44-(0)71-490-0049,   Fax: +44-(0)71-253-1308.

Y

Yates, Lori

CAN'T STOP THE GIRL.
Tracks: Promises promises / Scene of the crime / Time after time / Heaven's waiting / How much does it take / Can't stop the girl / Blue side of town / Lonesome desire / Lover's jamboree / Heart in a suitcase.
LP. **4632881**
■ **MC** **4632884**
CBS / Jun '89.

Yearwood, Trisha

Trisha Yearwood's breakthrough is the end product of a determined, step-by-step climb up the music business ladder. She grew up on a farm in Monticello, Georgia, and had been singing for as long as she can remember, first taking inspiration from Elvis Presley records before absorbing many other formats that ranged from country artists of her parent's record collection and southern rock on the radio to high school musicals and choral groups. She arrived in Nashville in 1985, secured a music business degree at Belmont College and got her foot in the industry door by landing a job with MTM Records. Gradually she began singing demos, then background vocals on master sessions. With the support of producer Garth Fundis (best known for his work with Don Williams, Keith Whitley and New Grass Revival), she played a showcase and secured a deal with MCA Records. Her first public appearances were on tour with Garth Brooks (no better way than start at the top!) and her debut single, *She's in love with the boy*, went straight to number one in August 1991. Since she's continued to enjoy high chart placings with singles such as *The woman before me* and *Walkaway Joe* , while her first two albums, *Trisha Yearwood* and *Hearts in armour*, have both sold over one million copies each. Definately a big name for the 1990s. (Tony Byworth - August 1993)

HEARTS IN ARMOUR.
Tracks: Wrong side of Memphis / Nearest distance shore / You say you will / Walkaway joe / Woman walk the line / Oh lonesome you / Down on my knees / For reasons I've forgotten / You don't have to move that mountain / Hearts in armor.
CD . . . . **MCD 10641**
MC . . . . **MCC 10641**
MCA / Sep '92 / BMG.
DCC. . . . . **MCAX 10641**
MCA / Apr '93 / BMG.

TRISHA YEARWOOD.
Tracks: Not Advised.
CD . . . . **MCAD 10297**
MC . . . . **MCAC 10297**
MCA / Nov '91 / BMG.
■ **LP.** . . . . **MCA 10297**
MCA / Nov '91.

WALK AWAY JOE.
Tracks: Walk away Joe.
7" . . . . **MCS 1742**
CD Single . . . . **MCSTD 1742**
■ **MC Single** . . . . **MCSC 1742**
MCA / Mar '93.

Yelvington, Malcolm

GONNA HAVE MYSELF A BALL.
Tracks: Drinkin' wine spo-dee-o-dee / Just rolling along / Yakety yak / Blues in the bottom of my shoes / Gal named Jo, A / It's me baby / Rockin' with my baby / Gonna have myself a ball / Goodbye Marie / First and last love / Mr. Blues / Did I ask you to stay / Trumpet / Ocean / Let the moon say goodnight.
LP. . . . . **SUN 1010**
Sun / Aug '88 / Charly / Swift.

Yoakam, Dwight

Born, 23.10.56 in Pikesville, Kentucky. Dwight Yoakam's direct approach to country music, along with his forthright opinions on the music have gained him much attention. Yoakam's honky tonk style, decorated with influences of the Bakersfield sound have made his music very popular. He paid his dues playing out on the west coast, where he now lives (L.A.), and had his first work out on the Oak label. Yoakam's early heroes include such acts a Roy Orbison, Johnny Cash, Hank Williams, Johnny Horton (it was a cover of Horton's *Honky tonk man* in 1986 that first brought Dwight to the public's attention). Making country's top five, on reprise (Warner Brothers). Yoakam's potent songwriting (often drawing on his childhood upbringing in the coal mining rural environs of Kentucky), along with some tasty remakes of honky tonk standards has proved to be a winning formula for the denim-clad country act. The title track from Yoakam's debut album *Guitars, cadillacs, ect* , also made country's top 5 singles slot. Hard on it's heels and in rapid succession were three slightly lesser singles *Little sister* (a hit for Elvis in 1961), *Little ways* and *Please, please baby*. While in 1988 he was again found dusting down another oldie, Lefty Fizzell's *Always late, with your kisses.Streets of Bakersfield* his debut No.1, found him working with his longtime hero Buck Owens. It's success was responsible for prompting Owens, to venture out of retirement and to start recording/performing again. Yoakam meanwhile was chalking up another chart topper, with the strong *I sang Dixie*, both coming from his album *Buenas noches from a lonely room*. From that moment his singles successes were to become somewhat stifled, although his own *I got you* made the top 5 slot (1989). With his career toned down somewhat all around, his output of new material went down to a trickle - after the initial burst. For in 1989 the label put out a compilation release, *Lookin' for a hit* (featuring two new tracks *Sin city* and *Long white limousine*). Late 1990 brought about *If there was a way*, with Top 10 singles coming in the way of *You're the one* and *It only hurts when I cry* - whilst *Turn it on, turn it up, turn me loose*, stalled outside the region. His music was now showing more rock elements, it seemed his career was very much at the crossroads/experimental juncture. Although intertwined with it all, Yoakam's music was appearing in excellent light on other releases, e.g. John Mellancamp's *Falling from grace* soundtrack piece, where he donates *Common day man*, Whilst on Flaco Jimenez's major label debut release *Partners*, Yoakam does the business with the accordion wizard on Warren Zevon's *Carmelita*. *Suspicious minds* a chart entry in 1992, also gained a wider audience and figured on his *La croix d'amour* album, where he runs the full gamut, featuring remakes of Van Morrison's *Here comes the night* , his tribute to the Grateful Dead *Truckin* & *Let's work together* - as well as inclusions of previously released tracks. Yoakam appeared on Sony's *Honeymoon in Vegas* soundtrack album, where other coutnry acts like Vince Gill and Trisha Yearwood appear covering Elvis hits alongside rock acts like Billy Joel, Bono & John Mellencamp. Yoakam in 1993, through the release of *This time* was once again making himself known to the country audience - *Ain't that lonely yet* saw him make a welcome return to country's Top 5 singles (No.2) whilst the album likewise registered a high rating, although this was nothing new, for his albums have always been consistant sellers. (Maurice Hope - July 1993)

1,000 MILES FROM NOWHERE.
Tracks: 1,000 Miles from nowhere / Ain't that lonely yet.
7" . . . . **W 0193**
CD Single . . . . **W 0193CD**
MC Single . . . . **W 0193C**
Reprise / Jul '93 / WEA.

BUENOS NOCHES FROM A LONELY ROOM.
Tracks: I got you / One more name / What I don't know / Home of the blues / Buenos noches from a lonely room / She wore red dresses / I hear you knocking / I sang Dixie / Streets of Bakersfield / Floyd county / Send me the pillow that you dream on / Hold onto God.
■ **MC** . . . . **WX 193C**
WEA / Aug '88 / WEA.
■ **LP.** . . . . **WX 193**
WEA / Aug '88.
CD . . . . **.925749-2**
Reprise / Jan '89 / WEA.

GUITARS, CADILLACS.
Tracks: Ring of fire / Guitars, cadillacs.
■ **7"** . . . . **W 8528**
WEA / Nov '86.

GUITARS, CADILLACS ETC.ETC.
Tracks: Honky tonk man / It won't hurt / I'll be gone / South of Cincinnati / Bury me / Guitars, cadillacs / 20 years / Ring of fire / Miner's prayer / Heartaches by the number.
MC . . . . **.925372 4**
Reprise (USA) / Apr '86 / WEA / Pinnacle.
■ **LP.** . . . . **.925372 1**
Reprise (USA) / Apr '86.
CD . . . . **.925372 2**
Reprise (USA) / Jan '87 / WEA / Pinnacle.

HILLBILLY DELUXE.
Tracks: Little ways / Smoke along the track / Johnson's love / Please, please baby / Readin', rightin', RT.23 / Always late with your kisses / 1,000 miles / Throughout all times / Little sister / This drinking will kill me.
LP. . . . . **.925567 1**
MC . . . . **WX 106C**
Reprise / Jun '87 / WEA.
■ **CD** . . . . **.925567 2**
Reprise / Jun '87.

HONKY TONK MAN.
Tracks: Honky tonk man / Miner's prayer / I'll be gone (12" single only).
12" . . . . **W 8793T**
■ **7"** . . . . **W 8793**
WEA / Jul '86.

IF THERE WAS A WAY.
Tracks: Distance between you and me, The / Heart that you own, The / Takes a lot to rock you / Nothing's changed here / Sad, sad music / Since I started drinkin' again / If there was a way / Turn it on, turn it up, turn me loose / It only hurts when I cry / Send a message to my heart / I don't need it done / You're the one.
CD **7599263342**
■ **LP.** . . . . **WX 392**
WEA / Nov '90 / WEA.
■ **MC** . . . . **WX 392C**
WEA / Nov '90.

JUST LOOKIN' FOR A HIT.
Tracks: Long white cadillac / Little ways / Honky tonk man / I got you / Little sister / I sang Dixie / Guitars & cadillacs / Sin City / Please, please baby / Streets of Bakersfield.
CD . . . . **K 925989 2**
■ **LP.** . . . . **WX 310**
WEA / Sep '89 / WEA.
■ **MC** . . . . **WX 310 C**
WEA / Sep '89.

LA CROIX D'AMOUR.
Tracks: Things we said today / Truckin' / If there was a way / Hey little girl / What I don't know / Here comes the night / Dangerous man / Let's work together / Doin' what I did / Takes a lot to rock you / Suspicious minds / Long white cadillac.
CD **9362451362**
MC **9362451364**
Reprise / Nov '92 / WEA.

LITTLE SISTER.
Tracks: Little sister / This drinking will kill me / Honky tonk man (live) (on 12" only.) / Cadillacs (live) (Extra track on 12" only).
12" . . . . **W 8432T**
■ **7"** . . . . **W 8432**
WEA / May '87.

STREETS OF BAKERSFIELD (Yoakam, Dwight & Buck Owens).
Tracks: Streets of Bakersfield / One more name / Honky tonk man (live) (Only on 12") / Guitars, cadillacs (Only on 12").
12" . . . . **W 7964T**
7" . . . . **W 7964**
Reprise / Sep '88 / WEA.

THIS TIME.
Tracks: Pocket of a clown / Thousand miles from nowhere, A / Home for sale / This time / Two doors down / Ain't that lonely yet / King of fools / Fast of you / Try not to look so pretty / Wild ride / Lonesome roads.
CD . . . . **.936245241-2**
MC . . . . **.936245241-4**
Reprise / Apr '93 / WEA.

Yonco, Frank

OLD GREYHOUND (Yonco, Frank & The Everglades).
Tracks: Not Advised.
LP. . . . . **SFA 091**
Sweet Folk All / May '81 / Cadillac Music / Projection / C.M. Distribution / Wellard Dist. / Impetus Records.

Young, Faron

This American country singer, born in Louisiana in 1932, built his career via two conventional country and western outlets - the *Louisiana Hayride radio show* and Nashville's *Grand Ole Opry*. His upward climb was interrupted by the draft but, after a few struggles, he established himself as an unadventurous but in demand entertainer, with such country chart hits as 1959's *Country Girl*. In 1961 he scored his only Top 40 hit on the US pop charts - *Hello Walls* reached No. 12 on the Billboard Hot 100, and gave an early success to it's composer, Willie Nelson. By the end of the Sixties, Young had chalked up dozens of Top 10 singles on the American country charts, thanks to his smooth vocal delivery and his forays into television and

■ **DELETED**

cinema. 1972 brought the singer his only British pop hit, a middle-of-the-road ballad entitled *It's Four In The Morning*, which reached No.3 and logged an impressive total of 23 weeks on the charts. The album of the same name hit the UK Top 30. By this time, he was publisher of *Music City News*, Nashville's country paper, and was one of the genre's elder statesmen. (Bob Macdonald)

CAPITOL COUNTRY CLASSICS.
Tracks: Live fast, love hard / Going steady / If you ain't lovin' / All right / It's a great life / I've got five dollars and it's Saturday night / Sweet dreams / I miss you already / Alone with you / Country girl / Riverboat / Your 'old used to be / Hello walls / Backtrack / Three days / Comeback.
■ LP. . . . . **CAPS 1036**
Capitol / Apr '80.

CAPITOL YEARS, THE: FARON YOUNG.
Tracks: If you ain't lovin' (you ain't livin') / I've got five dollars & it's Saturday night / Place for girls like you, A / I can't tell my heart / In the chapel in the moonlight / If that's the fashion / Forgive me, Dear / Just married / Baby my heart / What's the use to love you / That's what I do for you / I'm gonna tell Santa Claus on you / You're the angel on my christmas tree / I hardly knew it was you / That's what it's like to be lonesome / You're right (but I wish you were wrong) / Down Lover's Lane alone / So I'm in love with you / Goin' steady / Just out of reach / I can't wait (for the sun to go down) / Have I waited too long / Tattle tale tears / What can I do with my sorrow / Good Lord must have sent you, The / I knew you when / Saving my tears for tomorrow / Foolish pride / Live fast, love hard, die young / Go back, you fool / All right / For the love of a woman like you / It's a great life / Better things than these / Turn her down / You're still mine / Sweet dreams / Until I met you / I'm gonna live some before I die / Candy kisses / Have I told you lately that I love you / I'll be satisfied with love / I can't help it / Your cheatin' heart / I'll be yours / Sweethearts or strangers / Shame on you / Worried mind / I miss you already / I'm a poor boy / You call everybody darlin' / You are my sunshine / Moonlight mountain / Anything your heart desires / Vacation's over / Shrine of St. Cecilia / Love has finally come my way / Face of love / That's the way it's gotta be / We're talking it over / I made a fool of myself / I'll be all right / You old used to be / Out of my heart / Every time I'm kissing you / Alone with you / That's the way I feel / I hate myself / Last night at the party / Long time ago, A / Hey good lookin' / Tennessee waltz / Let old Mother Nature have her way / Making believe / Almost / Mom & Dad's waltz / Don't let the stars get in your eyes / Bouquet of roses / Slowly / Bimbo / Chattinooga shoeshine boy / I don't hurt anymore / I'll go on alone / Honey stop / Locket, The / Snowball / When it rains it pours / Rosalie (is gonna get married) / I can't dance / Once in a while / Riverboat / Country girl / Face to the wall / There's not any like you left / Forget the past / World so full of love, A / Hello walls / Is she all you thought she'd be / Congratulations / Three days / Safely in love again / Down by the river / Part where I cry, The / I hear you talkin' / Big shoes / Believing it yourself / Comeback, The / Overlonely & underkissed / Things to remember / I fall to pieces / Moment isn't very long, A / Moments to remember / Lifetime isn't long enough, A / I can't find the time / Trail of tears / I let it slip away / Let's pretend we're lovers again / Backtrack / How can I forget you / I'll fly away / Mansion over the hilltop / He was there / How long has it been / Beautiful garden of prayer / My home sweet home / Suppertime / May the good Lord bless & keep you / What can he do / He knows just what I need / When I've learned enough to live / Now I belong to Jesus / I won't have to cross Jordan alone / Travelling on / My wonderful Lord / I know who holds tomorrow / Where could I go but to the Lord / God bless God / Don't take your love from me / If I had you / Stay as sweet as you are / My darling, my darling / Who wouldn't love you / I can't believe you're in love with me / Object of my affection, The / It all depends on you / Thank you for a lovely evening / Everything I have is yours / Nearness of you, The / Sweet & lovely.
CD Set . . . . **BCD 15493**
Bear Family / Mar '92 / Rollercoaster Records / Swift / Direct Distribution.

FOUR IN THE MORNING.
Tracks: It's four in the morning / If you ain't lovin' (you ain't livin') / All right / Three days / Sweet dreams / Going steady / Hello walls / Backtrack / Wine me up / Your times comin' / I miss you already / This little girl of mine / Four in the morning / Seasons come, seasons go / Alone with you / Heartache for a keepsake, A / If you ain't lovin' / Apartment £ 9 / Live fast, love hard & die young / Your cheatin' heart / Satisfied mind / As far as I'm concerned / Is it really over / Chapel in the moonlight / Some of those memories / There goes my everything / Crying time / Swingin' doors / Tiger by the tail / Here comes my baby back again / Once a day / Sweet thang / I could never be ashamed of you / Are you sincere / Memphis.
LP. . . . . **TOP 144**
MC . . . . **KTOP 144**
Topline / Sep '86 / Charly / Swift / Black Sun Records.
CD . . . . **CDGRF 073**
Tring / Feb '93 / Prism Leisure PLC / Midland Records / Taylors.

IT'S FOUR IN THE MORNING.
Tracks: Not Advised.
■ LP. **6338 095**
Mercury / Oct '72.

IT'S FOUR IN THE MORNING.
Tracks: It's four in the morning.
■ 7" **6052 140**
Mercury / Jul '72.

SHERIFF, THE.
Tracks: Hello walls / I'll be there / I fall to pieces / Once a day / Your cheatin' heart / I can't help it / Life is a picture / Is she all you thought she would be / Hey Mr. Bluebird.
LP. . . . . **ALEB 2305**
MC . . . . **ZCALB 2305**
Allegiance / Apr '84.

SWEETHEARTS OR STRANGERS.
Tracks: Not Advised.
LP. . . . . **HAT 3026**
MC . . . . **HATC 3026**
Stetson / Oct '86 / Crusader Marketing Co. / Swift / Wellard Dist. / Midland Records / C.M. Distribution.

TALK ABOUT HITS.
Tracks: Don't let the stars get in your eyes / I'll go on alone / Almost / Mom and Dad's waltz / I don't hurt anymore / Chattanooga shoeshine boy / Hey good lookin' / Bouquet of roses / Slowly / Tennessee waltz / Making believe / Bimbo.
LP. . . . . **HAT 3046**
MC . . . . **HATC 3046**
Stetson / Sep '87 / Crusader Marketing Co. / Swift / Wellard Dist. / Midland Records / C.M. Distribution.

THIS IS FARON YOUNG.
Tracks: Not Advised.
LP. . . . . **HAT 3092**
MC . . . . **HATC 3092**
Stetson / Feb '89 / Crusader Marketing Co. / Swift / Wellard Dist. / Midland Records / C.M. Distribution.

TOP COUNTRY FRIEND.
Tracks: Hello walls / You're still mine / Three days / Alone with you / Country girl / Riverboat / Congratulations / Back track / Face to the wall / If you ain't lovin' (you ain't livin').
LP. . . . . **BDL 1030**
Bulldog Records / Jul '82 / President Records / Jazz Music / Wellard Dist. / TKO Records Ltd.

WINNING YOU SURE MADE A LOSER OUT OF ME.
Tracks: Winning you sure made a loser out of me / Old songs.
7" . . . . **MCA 412**
MCA / '79 / BMG.

Young, Steve

Singer songwriter/guitarist born 12.7.1942 in Noonan, Georgia gained himself a cult following this side of the Atlantic - his regular visits to the UK, playing the smaller, intimate venues and supplying a wealth of country/blues. Early albums of note include his *Rock, Salt & Nails* on A & M in 1969, although he had previously done some shortlived recordings & an album with Stone Country. Best known though, are his RCA albums during the Seventies. Among his own compositions are *Seven Bridges Road* (hit for the Eagles), *Montgomery In The Rain,Lonesome, On'ry* and *Mean* - brought to a greater audience's attention due to covers by David Allan Coe & Waylon Jennings respectively) and his trademark song *Renegade Picker*. Label moves have included spells with Rounder and Watermelon (*Solo Live*) - whilst Rounder's releases featured their share of oft used standards, some duplicated. (Maurice Hope July 1993)

HONKY TONK MAN.
Tracks: Not Advised.
LP. . . . . **ROUNDER 3087**
MC . . . . **ROUNDER 3087C**
Rounder / Aug '88 / Projection / Roots Records / Swift / C.M. Distribution / Topic Records / Jazz Music / Hot Shot / A.D.A Distribution / Direct Distribution.

LONG TIME RIDER.
Tracks: Not Advised.
LP. . . . . **VD 105**
Voodoo / Sep '90 / ACD Trading Ltd.

LOOK HOMEWARD ANGEL.
Tracks: Not Advised.
LP. . . . . **MILL 5031**
Mill (USA) / Sep '86.

NO PLACE TO FALL.
Tracks: No place to fall / Montgomery in the rain / Dreamer / Always loving you / Drift away / Seven Bridges road / I closed my heart's door / Don't think twice, it's alright / I can't sleep / I got the same old blues.
MC . . . . **PK 12510**
RCA / May '78 / BMG.
■ LP. . . . . **PL 12510**
RCA / May '78.

OLD MEMORIES.
Tracks: Renegade picker / Lonesome on'ry & mean / Old memories / Always loving you / Don't think twice, it's all right / Seven Bridges Road / Light of my life / Dreamer / All her lovers want to be the hero / Montgomery in the rain.
■ LP. . . . . **CRLP 1002**
Country Roads Records / Nov '81.

RENEGADE PICKER.
Tracks: Renegade picker / I can't be myself / Old memories / It's not supposed to be that way / Tobacco Road / Light of my life / Lonesome, on'ry and mean / All her lovers want to be the hero / Broken hearted people / Sweet thing / Home sweet home.
■ LP. . . . . **PL 11759**
RCA / Jan '77.

ROCK, SALT & NAILS.
Tracks: That's how strong my love is / Rock, salt & nails / I'm a one woman man / Coyote / Gonna find me a bluebird / Love in my time / Seven bridges road / Kenny's song / Holler in the swamp / Hoboin' / My sweet love ain't around.
LP. . . . . **ED 193**
Edsel / Oct '86 / Pinnacle.
CD . . . . **EDCD 193**
Edsel / Feb '91 / Pinnacle.

SEVEN BRIDGES ROAD.
Tracks: Seven bridges road / Montgomery in the rain / Ragtime blue guitar / Long way to Hollywood / Down in the flood / Ballad of William Sycamore / My Oklahoma / Wild goose / Days of 49 / Lonesome, on'ry and mean.
LP. . . . . **SNTF 870**
Sonet / Oct '81 / Swift / C.M. Distribution / Roots Records / Jazz Music / Sonet Records / Cadillac Music / Projection / Wellard Dist. / Hot Shot.
LP. . . . . **ROUNDER 3058**
MC . . . . **ROUNDER 3058C**
Rounder / Aug '88 / Projection / Roots Records / Swift / C.M. Distribution / Topic Records / Jazz Music / Hot Shot / A.D.A Distribution / Direct Distribution.

SOLO LIVE.
Tracks: Not Advised.
CD . . . . **WM 1004**
Watermelon / Jun '93 / Topic Records.

SOLO/LIVE.
Tracks: Not Advised.
CD . . . . **FIENDCD 701**
Demon / Jul '91 / Pinnacle.

TO SATISFY YOU.
Tracks: Think it over / To satisfy you / Top of the world / No expectations / Contender, The / Corina, Corina / All your stories / Wild world / They call it love / River and the swan, The.
LP. . . . . **ROUNDER 3057**
MC . . . . **ROUNDER 3057C**
Rounder / '88 / Projection / Roots Records / Swift / C.M. Distribution / Topic Records / Jazz Music / Hot Shot / A.D.A Distribution / Direct Distribution.
CD . . . . **SDCD 9.00143**
Sawdust / '90.

Z

Zydeco

Zydeco is a black American musical genre. Indigenous to southwest Louisiana and West Texas, it is the equivalent of white Cajun and often very similar to it. 'La La' (La Musique Creole) was a dance music created from cajun, old French, Afro-American and Afro-Caribbean idioms from the mid-19th century onwards. In modern times urban and country blues crept in, making zydeco. Its influence appearing in the work of Leadbelly and Lightnin' Hopkins. The term is believed to come from a creolised pronounciation of les haricots, from the one step *Les haricots Sont Pas Sales* ('the snap beans aren't salted') Zydeco is characterised by syncopated, driving rhythms; the piano accordion replaced Cajun's diatonic instrument and the saxophone tended to substitute the fiddle. One of the best saxophonists in this genre is John Hart in Rockin' Dopsie. In zydeco, Rub or washboard (or frittoir, which worn like a metal vest) adds a percussive element, as it did in skiffle. Amplification and rhythm sections of drums and electric bass have further coloured the music. (Donald Clarke)

Y 2 ■ DELETED

COMPILATIONS

NUMERICAL

6 TRACK HITS: COUNTRY.
Tracks: Not Advised.
EP. **7SR 5041**
MC **7SC 5041**
Scoop 33 / Jun '84.

10 YEARS COLLECTOR RECORDS.
Tracks: Eager boy: *Lonesome Drifter* / Teardrop valley: *Lonesome Drifter* / Wait a little baby: *Roby, Jimmy* / Be boppin' baby: *Roby, Jimmy* / Walking and strolling: *Wayne, Billy* / I love my baby: *Wayne, Billy* / Bad, bad boy: *Lollar, Bobby* / Servant of love (take 1): *Van Bros* / Spin the bottle, 1955: *Joy, Benny* / Piano man: *Redell, Teddy* / Why worry: *Crain, Jimmy* / It's the way you are: *Mask, James* / Too old to rock 'n' roll: *Taylor, Carmol* / Parking in the dark: *Dean, Charles* / Itchy: *Dean, Charles* / Train whistle boogie: *Dean, Charles.*
LP. . . . . **WLP 8816**
White Label (Germany) / '88 / Pinnacle / Bear Family Records (Germany) / CSA Tell Tapes.

14 COUNTRY FAVOURITES.
Tracks: Not Advised.
MC . . . . **KGEC 5012**
Emerald / '78 / I & B Records.
■ **LP.** . . . . **GES 5012**
Emerald / '78.

14 GREAT TRUCK HITS.
Tracks: Movin' on: *Haggard, Merle* / From a jack to a king: *Miller, Ned* / Six days on the road: *Dudley, Dave* / Born to be a trucker: *Simpson, Red* / Trucker's paradise: *Reeves, Del* / Tombstone every mile: *Curless, Dick.*
LP. **022-58173**
MC **222-58173**
MFP (Holland) / '86 / Pinnacle.

16 BLUEGRASS HITS.
Tracks: Not Advised.
LP. . . . . **SLP 3015**
MC . . . . **GT 53015**
Starday (USA) / Apr '87 / Crusader Marketing Co.

16 NUMBER ONE COUNTRY HITS VOL.1.
Tracks: Boy named Sue, A: *Cash, Johnny* / Most beautiful girl, The: *Rich, Charlie* / Rose garden: *Anderson, Lynn* / When it's Springtime in Alaska: *Horton, Johnny* / Grand tour, The: *Jones, George* / I can help: *Swann, Billy* / Teddy bear song: *Fairchild, Barbara* / Big bad John: *Dean, Jimmy* / Stand by your man: *Wynette, Tammy* / Ballad of Jed Clampett: *Flat, Lester, Earl Scruggs & The Foggy Mountain Boys* / El Paso: *Robbins, Marty* / Baby, baby (I know you're a lady): *Houston, David* / For the good times: *Price, Ray* / Golden ring: *Jones, George & Tammy Wynette* / Thinkin' of a rendezvous: *Duncan, Johnny* / Blue eyes crying in the rain: *Nelson, Willie.*
LP. . . . . **CBS 31456**
CBS / '87 / Sony.

16 NUMBER ONE COUNTRY HITS VOL.2.
Tracks: D.I.V.O.R.C.E. / Crazy arms / El Paso City / Saginaw Michigan / Just good ol' boys / Almost persuaded / All the gold in California / Take this job and shove it / One piece at a time / Rolling with the flow / Games people play / Door / What a man my man is / Candy kisses / North to Alaska / If you've got the money, I've got the time.
LP. . . . . **CBS 31805**
MC **40 31805**
CBS / Mar '80 / Sony.

16 REBEL SONGS VOL.1.
Tracks: Not Advised.
MC . . . . **DOCB 7030**
Dolphin (Ireland) / Dec '88 / C.M. Distribution / I & B Records / Midland Records.

16 REBEL SONGS VOL.2.
Tracks: Not Advised.
MC . . . . **DOCB 7031**
Dolphin (Ireland) / Dec '88 / C.M. Distribution / I & B Records / Midland Records.

16 REQUESTED BALLADS OF IRELAND.
Tracks: Not Advised.
■ **LP.** . . . . **HRL 178**
Homespun (Ireland) / Jun '80.

16 SONGS OF ROMANCE.
Tracks: Not Advised.
LP. . . . . **SPC 399**
Ritz / '88 / Pinnacle / Midland Records.
MC . . . . **RITZSC 399**
Ritz / Dec '88 / Pinnacle / Midland Records.

16 SUPER IRISH HITS.
Tracks: When you were sweet sixteen: *Woods, Pat* / Pal of my cradle days: *Breen, Ann* / Home town on the Foyle: *Coll, Brian* / Bunch of thyme: *Mitchell, Mark* / Cottage by the Lee: *Cunningham, Larry* / Galway shawl: *O'Brien, Dermot* / Cliffs of Dooneen: *Margo* / Four country roads: *Watt, John* / Green fields of France: *Woods, Pat* / Old flames: *Bell, Crawford* / Rare ould times: *Woods, Pat* / Old cross of Arboe: *Begley, Philomena* / Bunch of violets blue: *Shine, Brendan* / Among the Wicklow hills: *Ely, Pat* / Three leaf shamrock: *Kerr, John* / One day at a time: *Leon.*
LP. . . . . **PHL 455**
MC . . . . **CPHL 455**
Homespun (Ireland) / Dec '82 / Homespun Records / Ross Records / Wellard Dist.

16 TRUCK DRIVER GREATS.
Tracks: Not Advised.
LP. . . . . **SLP 3024**
MC . . . . **GT 53024**
Starday (USA) / Apr '87 / Crusader Marketing Co.

20 BLUEGRASS INSTRUMENTALS.
Tracks: Not Advised.
LP. . . . . **SLP 5027**
MC . . . . **GT 55027**
Starday (USA) / Apr '87 / Crusader Marketing Co.

20 BLUEGRASS ORIGINAL HYMNS.
Tracks: Not Advised.
LP. . . . . **SLP 5030**
MC . . . . **GT 55030**
Starday (USA) / Apr '87 / Crusader Marketing Co.

20 BLUEGRASS ORIGINALS.
Tracks: Not Advised.
LP. . . . . **SLP 5028**
MC . . . . **GT 55028**
Starday (USA) / Apr '87 / Crusader Marketing Co.
CD . . . . **CD 1039**
Gusto (USA) / '88.

20 BLUEGRASS ORIGINALS VOL.2.
Tracks: Not Advised.
LP. . . . . **SLP 5029**
MC . . . . **GT 55029**
Starday (USA) / Apr '87 / Crusader Marketing Co.

20 CLASSIC COUNTRY TRACKS.
Tracks: Let's think about living / You comb her hair / Have I stayed away too long / Building heartaches / Rueben's train / Wings of a dove / I've got to be somebody / Gambler's guitar / Snowbird / Mental revenge / Sticks and stones / Follow me back to Louisville / Sally was a good old girl / So sad / Love hurts / Honky tonk angels / Those other boys / My kingdom for a car.
LP. . . . . **SMT 003**
Starburst / Jan '85 / Terry Blood Dist. / Jazz Music.
MC . . . . **SMTC 003**
Starburst / '87 / Terry Blood Dist. / Jazz Music.

20 CLASSIC ROCK 'N' ROLL TRACKS.
Tracks: Be bop a lula / Forty days / Rumble / Sheila / Monkey's uncle / Good rockin' tonight / Tutti frutti / Down at the in den / We did it in '54 / Reelin' and rockin' / Memphis earthquake / All the way to the USA / Wrapped up in rockabilly / Lucille / Rockabilly baby / Maybelline / Blue suede shoes / Say mama / That's alright mama / Disciple in blue suede shoes.
LP. . . . . **MTB 001**
Meteor / Apr '85 / Terry Blood Dist. / Jazz Music.
LP. . . . . **SMT 001**
Starburst / Jan '85 / Terry Blood Dist. / Jazz Music.

20 COUNTRY CLASSICS.
Tracks: Just someone I used to know: *Wagoner, Porter & Dolly Parton* / When you're hot you're hot: *Redd, Jerry* / Would you hold it against me?: *West, Dottie* / Angels don't lie: *Reeves, Jim* / Then you can tell me goodbye: *Arnold, Eddy* / Please help me, I'm falling: *Locklin, Hank* / Cold hard facts of life, The: *Wagoner, Porter* / I never once stopped loving you: *Smith, Connie* / Brown eyed handsome man: *Jennings, Waylon* / Lonesome number one: *Gibson, Don* / Five hundred miles: *Bare, Bobby* / Coat of many colours: *Parton, Dolly* / Amos Moses: *Reed, Jerry* / Big wind: *Wagoner, Porter* / End of the world: *Davis, Skeeter* / Taker, The: *Jennings, Waylon* / Mule skinner blues: *Parton, Dolly* / I won't come in while he's there: *Reeves, Jim* / Better move it on home: *Wagoner, Porter & Dolly Parton* / Country hall of fame: *Locklin, Hank.*
LP. . . . . **CBR 1022**
MC . . . . **KCBR 1022**
Premier (Sony) / Jan '84 / Sony / Pinnacle.

20 COUNTRY GREATS.
Tracks: Not Advised.
LP. . . . . **PLE 7018**
MC . . . . **PLC 7018**
Pickwick / Jan '78 / Pickwick Records.

20 COUNTRY GREATS.
Tracks: Not Advised.
LP. . . . . **WW 2010**
MC . . . . **WW 20104**
Warwick Reflections / Jun '86 / Sony.

20 COUNTRY LOVE SONGS.
Tracks: It's only make believe: *Campbell, Glen* / When I dream: *Gayle, Crystal* / There'll be no teardrops tonight: *Nelson, Willie* / July, you're a woman: *Stewart, John* / Come to me: *Newton, Juice* / Summer wind: *Newton, Wayne* / Will you love me tomorrow?: *Ronstadt, Linda* / You're the reason I'm living: *Darin, Bobby* / Misty blue: *Spears, Billie Jo* / For the good times: *Ford, Tennessee Ernie* / Sharing the night together: *Dr. Hook* / Let it be me: *Campbell, Glen & Bobbie Gentry* / I'll take you home again, Kathleen: *Whitman, Slim* / Stand by your man: *Jackson, Wanda* / It doesn't matter anymore: *Anka, Paul* / Give me your word: *Ford, Tennessee Ernie* / Everything a man could ever need: *Campbell, Glen* / Think I'll go somewhere and cry myself to sleep: *Shepard, Jean* / Minute you're gone, The: *James, Sonny* / We must believe in magic: *Gayle, Crystal* / Don't it make my brown eyes blue: *Gayle, Crystal.*
LP. . . . . **MFP 5722**
LP. . . . . **MFP 41 5722 1**
MC . . . . **MFP 41 5722 4**
MC . . . . **TCMFP 5722**
MFP / Sep '85 / EMI.
CD . . . . **CDMFP 6036**
CD . . . . **CDB 790 684 2**
MFP / Oct '87 / EMI.

20 GOLDEN COUNTRY SONGS (Teenage Rebels).
Tracks: Not Advised.
CD **26 41 992**
MC **26 41 994**
Point (2) / '92 / Sound Solutions.

20 GOLDEN HITS: COUNTRY SUPERSTARS.
Tracks: Not Advised.
CD . . . . **SPEC 85012**
Spectrum (CD) / Dec '88 / M.S.D.

20 GOLDEN PIECES: COUNTRY CHARTS.
Tracks: I walk the line: *Cash, Johnny* / Poor man's riches: *Barnes, Benny* / Girl most likely, The: *Riley, Jeannie C.* / Am I that easy to forget: *Belew, Carl* / King of the road: *Miller, Roger* / A-11: *Paycheck, Johnny* / Roll truck roll: *Simpson, Red* / Give my love to Rose: *Cash, Johnny* / Deck of cards: *Tyler, T.Texas* / Auctioneer, The: *Van Dyke, Leroy* / Six days on the road: *Dudley, Dave* / Slippin' around: *Tillman, Floyd* / Window up above: *Jones, George* / Blue suede shoes: *Perkins, Carl* / All for the love of a girl: *Horton, Johnny* / Fancy pants: *Cramer, Floyd* / Big river: *Cash, Johnny* / Little green apples: *Miller, Roger* / Sally let your bangs hang down: *Maddox Bros.* / Don't let the stars get in your eyes: *Willet, Slim.*
LP. . . . . **BDL 2015**
Bulldog Records / '80 / President Records / Jazz Music / Wellard Dist. / TKO Records Ltd.

20 GOLDEN PIECES: COUNTRY HITS.
Tracks: Heartaches by the number: *Jones, George* / I love you so much it hurts: *Lewis, Jerry Lee* / Thanks a lot: *Cash, Johnny* / Born to ramble: *Locklin, Hank* / Dang me: *Miller, Roger* / In a cotton candy world: *Wallace, Jerry* / Remember me: *Tyler, T.Texas* / I can't help it (if I'm still in love with you: *Tillman, Frank singers* / Pickin' sweethearts: *Dean, Jimmy* / Folsom Prison blues: *Cash, Johnny* / Wishful thinking: *Stewart, Wynn* / No help wanted: *Carlisles* / Domino: *Orbison, Roy* / 42 in Chicago: *Kilgore, Merle* / Cotton patch, The: *Riley, Jeannie C.* / Born to sing the blues: *Twitty, Conway* / Release me: *Wallace, Jerry* / Down the street to 301: *Cash, Johnny* / With pen in hand: *Miller, Roger* / C.C. rider.
LP. . . . . **BDL 2014**
Bulldog Records / Jan '80 / President Records / Jazz Music / Wellard Dist. / TKO Records Ltd.

20 GOLDEN PIECES: COUNTRY MUSIC.
Tracks: Stop the world: *Cline, Patsy* / I heard the jukebox playing: *Young, Faron* / Rock Island line: *Cash, Johnny* / Doin' my time: *Flatt, Lester & Earl Scruggs* / Honey: *Miller, Roger* / Heartbreak, Tennessee: *Paycheck, Johnny* / Your cheatin' heart: *Tillman, Frank singers* / Misty blue: *Smith, Jerry* / Letter you promised to write, The: *Husky, Ferlin* / You're the nearest thing to Heaven: *Cash, Johnny* / Shutters and boards: *Wallace, Jerry* / Crazy dreams: *Twitty, Conway* / Walk right in: *Campbell, Glen* / Box of memories: *Riley, Jeannie C.* / My heart cries for you: *Rich, Charlie* / Train of love: *Cash, Johnny* / I love you because: *Jones, George* / Miss Brown: *Houston, David* / I wish I could fall in love again: *Howard, Jan* / Oh lonesome me: *Dudley, Dave.*
LP. . . . . **BDL 2017**
Bulldog Records / Jan '80 / President Records / Jazz Music / Wellard Dist. / TKO Records Ltd.

20 GOLDEN PIECES: COUNTRY NOSTALGIA.
Tracks: Do wacka do: *Miller, Roger* / He made a woman out of me: *Riley, Jeannie C.* / Careless love: *Tyler, T.Texas* / There she goes: *Wallace, Jerry* / Everybody's trying to be my baby: *Perkins, Carl* / I heard that lonesome whistle blow: *Cash, Johnny* / High geared daddy: *Pierce, Webb* / Bouquet in Heaven: *Flatt, Lester & Earl Scruggs* / Little Miss Heartache: *Belew, Carl* / I'm a free man now: *Young, Faron* / Will the circle be unbroken?: *Lewis, Jerry Lee* / Cold, cold heart: *Jones, George* / Get rhythm: *Cash, Johnny* / Crazy over you: *Locklin, Hank* / Done rovin': *Horton, Johnny* / Man with the golden gun, The: *Campbell, Glen* / In case of the blues: *Cline, Patsy* / Dear heart: *Miller, Roger* / Seven lonely days: *Dudley, Dave* / There you go: *Cash, Johnny*.
LP . . . . **BDL 2016**
Bulldog Records / Jan '80 / President Records / Jazz Music / Wellard Dist. / TKO Records Ltd.

20 GOLDEN PIECES: VINTAGE ROCK 'N' ROLL.
Tracks: House of blue lights: *Slack, Freddie & Ella Mae Morse* / Bonnie B: *Lewis, Jerry Lee* / Ooby dooby: *Orbison, Roy* / Rock rockola: *Moore, Merrill E.* / Stranded in the jungle: *Cadets* / Voo vee ah vee: *Platters* / Well now dig this: *Jodimars* / Heartbreak Hotel: *Jones, George* / Hole in my heart: *Berry, Richard & The Pharoahs* / Esquerita: *Berry, Richard & The Pharoahs* / Louie Louie: *Berry, Richard & The Pharoahs* / Good golly: *Otis, Johnny* / Rock house: *Orbison, Roy & Teen Kings* / Rock rock rock: *Berry, Richard & The Pharoahs* / Down the line: *Lewis, Jerry Lee* / Rockin' the joint: *Esquerita* / Do you wanna rock?: *Cadets* / Rock everywhere: *Teen Queens* / Dixie fried: *Perkins, Carl* / Poppin' Johnny: *Miller, Frankie* / Guitar shuffle: *Fulson, Lowell*.
LP . . . . **BDL 2018**
MC . . . . **AJKL 2018**
Bulldog Records / Mar '81 / President Records / Jazz Music / Wellard Dist. / TKO Records Ltd.

20 GREAT COUNTRY RECORDINGS OF THE 50'S & 60'S.
Tracks: Man with the blues: *Nelson, Willie* / I shot Sam: *Ward, Margie* / If you see my baby: *Burns, Sonny* / Much to much: *Louisiana Lannis* / Family bible: *Gray, Claude* / Never been so weary: *Jones, George* / Cup of loneliness: *Jones, George* / Crawling back to you: *Dollar, Johnny* / Lights are on, The: *Busby, Jim* / Me and my baby: *Noack, Eddie* / Living high and wide: *Barber, Glen* / I'm a real gone Jesse (I'm hot to trot): *Tabor, Gene* / Poor man's riches: *Morris, Fitz* / Poor little heart: *Morris, Fitz* / Dead lost: *Jones, Neal* / What a way to live: *Nelson, Willie* / When I came thru town: *Mathis, Johnny* / Careless words: *Carson, Joe* / I dare you to love me: *Faulkner, Dessie* / Stranger shake hands with a fool: *Carter, Bill*.
LP . . . . **DROP 1004**
MC . . . . **CROP 1004**
Cascade / Jun '83 / Pinnacle / Hot Shot / Jazz Music.

20 GREAT COUNTRY RECORDINGS OF THE 50'S & 60'S VOL.2.
Tracks: Texas honky tonk: *Baker, Clay* / Diesel smoke: *Barnes, Benny* / Time lock: *Barnes, Benny* / Tender age: *Dee & Patty* / Would you be waiting (for my ship to come in): *Davis, Link* / Pappy Daily's breakdown: *Allen, Ward* / Shackled: *Sadie & Bobby* / Must I leave it there: *Burns, Sonny* / Guy you used to be, The: *Cornish, Joyce* / Big town baby: *Adams, Don* / Night life: *Nelson, Willie* / Thunder and lightning: *Nelson, Willie* / Cotton: *Bowman, Cecil* / Go home letter: *Barber, Glen* / Love's gonna live here: *Jones, George* / There goes my heart: *Drake, Charles* / Storm has just begun, The: *Nelson, Willie* / Wanderin' Oakie: *Noack, Eddie* / No memories: *Dollar, Johnny* / Race is on, The: *Jones, George*.
LP . . . . **DROP 1011**
Cascade / Apr '85 / Pinnacle / Hot Shot / Jazz Music.
MC . . . . **CROP 1011**
Cascade / May '85 / Pinnacle / Hot Shot / Jazz Music.

20 GREAT ROCKABILLY HITS OF THE 50'S.
Tracks: Pink cadillac: *Todd, Johnny* / My baby left me: *Rogers, Rock* / Everybody's movin': *Glenn, Glen* / Let's get it on: *Almond, Hershel* / *Al Good & his Band* / Red hot rockin' blues: *James, Jesse* / Baby doll: *Dale, Jimmie* / Snake eyed Mama: *Cole, Don* / I'm gonna rock with my baby tonight: *McIntyre, Chester* / Move baby move: *Urban, Al* / Prettiest girl at the dance: *Wyatt, Gene* / All the time: *La Beef, Sleepy* / Spin the bottle: *Joy, Benny* / Jitterbop baby: *Harris, Hal* / Be boppin Daddy: *Cole, Les & The Echoes* / Rockin Daddy: *Fisher, Sonny* / Rock it: *Jones, George* / Circle rock: *Matchbox* / Blue jeans: *Glenn, Glen* / I walk the line: *Barnes, Benny*.
LP . . . . **DROP 1003**
MC . . . . **CROP 1003**
Cascade / Nov '82 / Pinnacle / Hot Shot / Jazz Music.

20 GREAT ROCKABILLY HITS OF THE 50'S VOL.2.
Tracks: I'm through: *La Beef, Sleepy* / I'm a hobo: *Reeves, Danny* / Gee whiz: *Dee & Patty* / Rock candy rock: *Crawford, Fred* / Raw deal: *Thompson, Junior* / It's Saturday night: *Mack, Billy* / Shadow my baby: *Barber, Glen* / That ain't it: *Rogers, Rock* / My big fat baby: *Hall, Sonny & The Echoes* / I don't know when: *Harris, Hal* / Hollywood party: *Busch, Dick* / If I had a woman: *Glenn, Glen* / Rockin' and rollin': *Fisher, Sonny* / Little bit more, A: *La Beef, Sleepy* / True affection: *Johnson, Blind Willie* / Rock, roll and rhythm: *McGinnis, Wayne* / Tongue tied Jill: *Feathers, Charlie* / Pink cadillac: *Todd, Johnny* / Strange kinda feeling: *Dugosh, Eddy & The Ah-Ha Playboys* / Maybe little baby: *Jones, George*.
LP . . . . **DROP 1009**
MC . . . . **CROP 1009**
Cascade / Sep '84 / Pinnacle / Hot Shot / Jazz Music.

20 OF THE BEST COUNTRY DUETS.
Tracks: Not Advised.
LP . . . . **NL 89521**
■ **MC** . . . . **NK 89521**
RCA International / Apr '85.

20 ORIGINAL COUNTRY GREATS.
Tracks: Southern nights: *Campbell, Glen* / Wichita lineman: *Campbell, Glen* / Don't it make my brown eyes blue: *Gayle, Crystal* / Talking in your sleep: *Gayle, Crystal* / When you're in love with a beautiful woman: *Dr. Hook* / Sexy eyes: *Dr. Hook* / Ode to Billy Joe: *Gentry, Bobbie* / I'll never fall in love again: *Gentry, Bobbie* / Blanket on the ground: *Spears, Billie Jo* / Sing me an old fashioned song: *Spears, Billie Jo* / Lucille: *Rogers, Kenny* / Coward of the county: *Rogers, Kenny* / Snowbird: *Murray, Anne* / You needed me: *Murray, Anne* / Games people play: *South, Joe* / Hello walls: *Nelson, Willie* / There'll be no teardrops tonight: *Nelson, Willie* / It keeps right on a-hurtin': *Shepard, Jean* / Angel of the morning: *Newton, Juice* / July, you're a woman: *Stewart, John*.
CD . . . . **CDB 793 807 2**
CD . . . . **CDMFP 6084**
MFP / Jun '90 / EMI.

20 ORIGINALS FROM THE COUNTRY & WESTERN HALL OF.
Tracks: Not Advised.
LP . . . . **PLE 7006**
MC . . . . **PLC 7006**
Pickwick Limited Edition / '78 / Clyde Factors.

20 STAR STUDDED COUNTRY HITS.
Tracks: Not Advised.
LP . . . . **PLE 7003**
MC . . . . **PLC 7003**
Pickwick Limited Edition / '78 / Clyde Factors.

20 TRACKS OF COUNTRY HITS VOL.1.
Tracks: Sing another song: *Grant, Manson* / Send me the pillow: *Devine, Mike* / Arcadian rose: *Scots Country Comfort* / I love the sound of a whistle: *Wilson, Tug* / Other side of the morning: *Wells, Tracy* / Devil went down to Georgia, The: *Scots Country Comfort* / Pride goes before a fall: *Kerr, Moira* / They won't let you rock 'n' roll: *Devine, Mike* / Goodbye clothes: *Wells, Tracy* / Shutters and boards: *Grant, Manson* / One night of cheatin': *Wells, Tracy* / Some broken hearts never mind: *Wilson, Tug* / Rocky top: *Scots Country Comfort* / Key's in the mailbox, The: *Grant, Manson* / Wings of a dove: *Devine, Mike* / Wrap your arms around the world: *Grant, Manson* / Wabash cannonball, The: *Wilson, Tug* / My window faces South: *Scots Country Comfort* / Filipino rose: *Devine, Mike* / Alone with you: *Sutherland, Mackie*.
MC . . . . **CWGR 051**
Ross (1) / Aug '83 / Ross Records / Duncans / Entertainment UK.

20 TRACKS OF COUNTRY HITS VOL.2.
Tracks: Partner nobody chose, The: *Wells, Tracy* / Arms full of empty: *Grant, Manson* / I'll never forget yesterday: *Kerr, Moira* / Lend me your heart: *Scots Country Comfort* / Just call my name out loud: *Wilson, Tug* / Long stemmed Rosie: *Devine, Mike* / Tiger by the tail: *Wilson, Tug* / No man's land: *Wells, Tracy* / I'm a lonesome fugitive: *Devine, Mike* / Dancing right across my memory: *Grant, Manson* / Louisiana cajun band: *Scots Country Comfort* / Would you lay with me: *Wells, Tracy* / Kingdom I call home, A: *Holliday, Jim* / Message from Daddy: *Wilson, Tug* / Before the next teardrop falls: *Grant, Manson* / Time changes everything: *Scots Country Comfort* / I overlooked an orchid: *Grant, Manson* / It keeps right on a' hurtin': *Wilson, Tug* / Say goodbye to your daddy: *Kerr, Moira* / 57 Chevrolet: *Grant, Manson*.
MC . . . . **CWGR 052**
Ross (1) / Aug '83 / Ross Records / Duncans / Entertainment UK.

20 TRACKS OF COUNTRY HITS VOL.3.
Tracks: Linda on my mind: *Holliday, Jim* / Don't you ever fall in love with me: *Kerr, Moira* / Follow me: *Devine, Mike* / Time changes everything: *Scots Country Comfort* / Behind the footlights: *Wells, Tracy* / Streets of Baltimore: *Wilson, Tug* / Heaven's just a sin away: *Grant, Manson* / I'll fly away: *Grant, Manson* / I saw the light: *Grant, Manson* / Makes me wonder: *Scots Country Comfort* / Country music lovin' kinda guy: *Wilson, Tug* / Your old standby: *Sutherland, Mackie* / I'll get over you: *Wells, Tracy* / Cowboys ain't supposed to cry: *Wilson, Tug* / Bunch of thyme: *Wells, Tracy* / I believe in marriage: *Grant, Manson* / Baby is gone: *Devine, Mike* / Never ending love affair: *Wells, Tracy* / Randy Lynn rag: *Scots Country Comfort* / Someone is looking for someone like you: *Grant, Manson* / Fighting side of me, The: *Wilson, Tug* / Wine in the cellar: *Grant, Manson*.
MC . . . . **CWGR 053**
Ross (1) / Aug '83 / Ross Records / Duncans / Entertainment UK.

24 ORIGINAL NUMBER ONE COUNTRY HITS.
Tracks: Jolene / 9,999,999 tears / (I'd be a) legend in my own time / Lord, Mr Ford / She's acting single (I'm drinking doubles) / I'm a ramblin' man / Door is always open, The / Out of hand / Marie Laveau / Are you sure Hank done it this way / She called me baby.
LP . . . . **NL 89175**
MC . . . . **NK 89175**
RCA(Special Imports Service) / Aug '84 / BMG.

25 COUNTRY BALLADS.
Tracks: Not Advised.
MC . . . . **ZCWW 17072**
Westwood / Apr '76 / Pinnacle.

25 COUNTRY BALLADS VOL.2.
Tracks: Not Advised.
MC . . . . **ZCWW 17075**
Westwood / '78 / Pinnacle.

25 COUNTRY STORIES.
Tracks: Not Advised.
MC . . . . **ZCWW 17071**
Westwood / Apr '76 / Pinnacle.

25 YEARS OF TOP TEN COUNTRY HITS.
Tracks: Cryin' heart blues: *Johnnie & Jack* / Silver and gold: *King, Pee Wee* / (How much is that) Hound dog in the window: *Homer & Jethro* / This ole house: *Hamblen, Stuart* / In the Jailhouse now, no. 2: *Rodgers, Jimmie (1)* / Trouble in mind: *Arnold, Eddy* / Geisha girl: *Locklin, Hank* / Blue blue day: *Gibson, Don* / Scarlet ribbons: *Browns* / Miller's cave: *Snow, Hank* / When two worlds collide: *Miller, Roger* / Hello out there: *Belew, Carl* / Is this me: *Reeves, Jim* / Once a day: *Smith, Connie* / Yakety axe: *Atkins, Chet* / Stand beside me: *Dean, Jimmy* / Break my mind: *Hamilton, George IV* / Only Daddy that'll walk the line: *Jennings, Waylon* / Lincoln Park Inn, The: *Bare, Bobby* / Sherriff of Boone County, The: *Price, Kenny* / When you're hot, you're hot: *Reed, Jerry* / What ain't to be, just might happen: *Wagoner, Porter* / Rednecks, white socks and blue ribbon beer: *Russell, Johnny* / Please don't tell me how the story ends: *Milsap, Ronnie* / Bargain store: *Parton, Dolly*.
■ **LP** . . . . **DPMK 1034**
RCA / '78 / BMG.

32 GOLDEN COUNTRY HITS - VOL.1.
Tracks: Not Advised.
Double LP . . . . **NL 43886(2)**
MC Set . . . . **NK 43886(2)**
RCA (Germany) / Jan '85 / BMG.

32 GOLDEN COUNTRY HITS - VOL.2.
Tracks: Not Advised.
Double LP . . . . **NL 43887(2)**
MC Set . . . . **NK 43887(2)**
RCA (Germany) / Jan '85 / BMG.

40 COUNTRY CLASSICS.
Tracks: Not Advised.
Double LP . . . . **PLD 8011**
MC Set . . . . **PLDC 8011**
Pickwick / Sep '79 / Pickwick Records.

40 COUNTRY MASTERPIECES.
Tracks: Not Advised.
Double LP . . . . **PLD 8002**
MC Set . . . . **PLDC 8002**
Pickwick / Sep '79 / Pickwick Records.

40 GOLDEN COUNTRY HITS - VOL.2.
Tracks: Not Advised.
LP **DS6 28532**
MC **CS4 28532**
Teldec (1) / Jun '81 / Pinnacle / C.M. Distribution / Swift.

40 MILES OF BAD ROAD.
Tracks: Not Advised.
LP . . . . **GT 0057**
Gusto (USA) / Apr '88.

40 SMASH HITS COUNTRY STYLE.
Tracks: Not Advised.
Double LP . . . . **MFP 1006**
■ **MC Set** . . . . **TCMFP 1006**
MFP / Aug '80.
MC . . . . **TC DL 1006**
MFP / '88 / EMI.

50 ALL TIME COUNTRY HITS.
Tracks: Not Advised.
Double LP **50DA 300**
MC Set **50DA 4300**
Pickwick / May '77 / Pickwick Records.

50 COUNTRY CLASSICS.
Tracks: Not Advised.
MC Set . . . . **DBXC 001**
Dolphin (Ireland) / Jun '88 / C.M. Distribution / I & B Records / Midland Records.

50 COUNTRY FAVOURITES.
Tracks: Not Advised.
MC Set . . . . **MFP 411 509 5**
MC Set . . . . **TR 1509**
Trio / Oct '83 / EMI.

50 GREAT NASHVILLE HITS.
Tracks: Not Advised.
Double LP . . . . **RML 103**
MC Set . . . . **RML 4 C 103**
Ronco / Nov '83.

50 MORE COUNTRY FAVOURITES.
Tracks: Folsom Prison blues: *Cash, Johnny* / Treat me mean, treat me cruel: *Twitty, Conway* / I'm building

heartaches: *Nelson, Willie* / I'm blue again: *Cline, Patsy* / Time has made a change in me: *Oak Ridge Boys* / Love's gonna live here: *Jennings, Waylon* / Daddy sang bass: *Perkins, Carl* / Promises and hearts: *Jackson, Stonewall* / I fall to pieces: *Young, Faron* / Lost and I'll never find the way: *Skaggs, Ricky* / Where do we go from here?: *Williams, Don* / Little jewels: *Parsons, Gene* / All that's keeping me alive: *Fargo, Donna* / Livin' in the sunshine of your love: *Pillow, Ray* / Baby I want to love you: *Fender, Freddy* / That's all it took: *Parsons, Gram & Emmylou Harris* / Blue is the way I feel: *Twitty, Conway* / Will you remember mine?: *Nelson, Willie* / Girl I used to know, A: *Jones, George* / Just out of reach: *Cline, Patsy* / Take my hand for a while: *Williams, Don* / Sticks and stones: *Fargo, Donna* / Home is where you're happy: *Nelson, Willie* / Wild and windy night: *Little Sister* / You made me what I am: *Twitty, Conway* / Say, won't you be mine?: *Skaggs, Ricky* / Hey porter: *Cash, Johnny* / Release me: *Parton, Dolly* / World's worst loser: *Jones, George* / Your cheatin' heart: *Young, Faron* / I've loved and lost again: *Cline, Patsy* / What am I living for?: *Perkins, Carl* / Forgive and forget: *Cunningham, Tom* / We're together again: *Pillow, Ray* / I don't need to know that right now: *Paycheck, Johnny* / Two different worlds: *Skaggs, Ricky* / I can't help it: *Cash, Johnny* / And so will you, my love: *Nelson, Willie* / Where I stand: *Twitty, Conway* / It wasn't God who made honky tonk angels: *Parton, Dolly* / Lighthouse bar: *Blackwater Band* / Silver wings: *Fender, Freddy* / Love hurts: *Parsons, Gram & Emmylou Harris* / Tonight, ain't gonna fight again: *Little Sister* / It's so easy: *Jennings, Waylon* / Is there something on your mind?: *Nelson, Willie* / Sugartime: *Cash, Johnny* / I can't change overnight: *Jones, George* / You still want to go: *Henderson, Kelvin* / You'll never walk alone: *Oak Ridge Boys*.
■ **MC Set** . . . . **T 1569**
Trio / Sep '86.

50 YEARS OF COUNTRY MUSIC - VOL.1.
Tracks: Not Advised.
LP . . . . **CDS 1179**
MC . . . . **CAM 491**
RCA/Camden / Feb '80 / BMG / Arabesque Ltd.

50'S: ROCKABILLY FEVER, THE.
Tracks: I guess it's meant that way: *Cupp, Pat* / Long gone daddy: *Cupp, Pat* / Don't do me no wrong: *Cupp, Pat* / Everybody's movin': *Glenn, Glen* / If I had me a woman: *Glenn, Glen* / I don't know when: *Harris, Hal* / True affection: *Johnson, Byron* / Be boppin' daddy: *Cole, Les & The Echoes* / Rock little baby: *Cole, Les & The Echoes* / My big fat baby: *Hall, Sonny & The Echoes* / Rock my warriors rock: *Jackson, Joe* / Snake eyed mama: *Cole, Don* / Nuthin' but a nuthin': *Stewart, Jimmy & his Nighthawks* / Wild wild party: *Feathers, Charlie* / Pink cadillac: *Todd, Johnny* / Slipping and sliding: *Davis, Link* / All the time: *La Beef, Sleepy* / Go home letter: *Barber, Glen* / Boppin' wigwam Willie: *Scott, Ray* / I can't find the doorknob: *Jimmy & Johnny* / Jitterbop baby (Available on CD only): *Harris, Hal* / Little bit more, A (Available on CD only): *La Beef, Sleepy*.
CD . . . . **CDCH 218**
Ace / Jul '87 / Pinnacle / Hot Shot / Jazz Music / Complete Record Co. Ltd.
MC . . . . **CHC 218**
Ace / Jun '87 / Pinnacle / Hot Shot / Jazz Music / Complete Record Co. Ltd.
■ **LP** . . . . **CHA 218**
Ace / Jun '87.

70'S COUNTRY.
Tracks: Country boy (you got your feet in L.A.): *Campbell, Glen* / Country Willie: *Nelson, Willie* / Today I sarted loving you again: *Haggard, Merle* / Everytime two fools collide: *Rogers, Kenny & Dottie West* / Have a dream on me: *McDaniel, Mel* / He thinks I still care: *Murray, Anne* / She believes in me: *Rogers, Kenny* / Misty blue: *Spears, Billie Jo* / Mama's don't let your babies grow up to be cowboys: *Bruce, Ed* / I cheated on a good woman's love: *Craddock, Billy Crash* / Just a matter of time: *James, Sonny* / I'm not Lisa: *Colter, Jessi* / Lover's question, A: *Reeves, Del* / I could almost say goodbye: *Harden, Arlene* / I'm leaving it up to you: *Mosby, Johnny & Jonie* / Hank and Lefty raised my country soul: *Edwards, Stoney* / Lay back in the arms of someone (CD only.): *Newton, Juice* / Angel of the morning (CD only.): *Montgomery, Melba* / Another lonely night (CD only.): *Shepard, Jean* / Mr Bojangles (CD only.): *Nitty Gritty Dirt Band*.
CD . . . . **CDB 792 768 2**
CD . . . . **CDMFP 6079**
MC . . . . **TCMFP 5876**
MFP / Oct '89 / EMI.
■ **LP** . . . . **MFP 5876**
MFP / Oct '89.

100 COUNTRY CLASSICS.
Tracks: Reuben James: *Rogers, Kenny* / I believe: *Laine, Frankie* / You'll always have someone: *Nelson, Willie* / Wasted days and wasted nights: *Fender, Freddy* / Burning memories: *Jennings, Waylon* / Daddy: *Fargo, Donna* / Your tender years: *Jones, George* / Come on in: *Cline, Patsy* / Take these chains from my heart: *Drusky, Roy* / Slippin' away: *Fairchild, Barbara* / Shine on Ruby Mountain: *Rogers, Kenny* / Ol' blue: *Jackson, Stonewall* / Ragged but right: *Jones, George* / Sticks and stones: *Fargo, Donna* / High noon: *Laine, Frankie* / Last letter, The: *Drusky, Roy* / Wild side of life, The: *Fender, Freddy* / Should I go home: *Jackson, Stonewall* / Dream baby: *Jennings, Waylon* / Crazy love: *Fairchild, Barbara* / Cry not for me: *Cline, Patsy* / Ruby don't take your love to town: *Rogers, Kenny* / Luckinback Texas: *Drusky, Roy* / Wishful thinking: *Fargo, Donna* / Money: *Jennings, Waylon* / Singin' the blues: *Mitchell, Guy* / Hello walls: *Drusky, Roy* / I've lost at love again: *Cline, Patsy* / Mule train: *Laine, Frankie* / Kaw-liga: *Mandrell, Barbara* / Wedding bells: *Jones, George* / Four in the morning: *Young, Faron* / Blue eyes cryin' in the rain: *Drusky, Roy* / Sally was a good old girl: *Jennings, Waylon* / It wasn't God who made honky tonk angels: *Parton, Dolly* / Touch me: *Nelson, Willie* / Release me: *Mandrell, Barbara* / Heartaches by the number: *Mitchell, Guy* / Shake 'em up roll 'em: *Jackson, Stonewall* / Sunshine: *Rogers, Kenny* / Things have gone to pieces: *Jones, George* / 9,999,999 Tears: *Bailey, Razzy* / I let my mind wander: *Nelson, Willie* / Crying: *Jennings, Waylon* / Honky tonk merry-go-round: *Cline, Patsy* / Ticket to nowhere: *Rogers, Kenny* / Keep off the grass: *Jackson, Stonewall* / Daddy sang bass: *Perkins, Carl* / Ghost, The: *Nelson, Willie* / If you ain't lovin': *Young, Faron* / Kentucky means paradise: *Mandrell, Barbara* / Stop, look and listen: *Cline, Patsy* / I can't escape from you: *Jones, George* / Making believe: *Wells, Kitty* / Honk tonk angels: *Parton, Dolly* / Abilene: *Jennings, Waylon* / Ruby Tuesday: *Williams, Don* / Elvira: *Rogers, Kenny* / Maybellene: *Robbins, Marty* / If you ain't lovin' (2): *Young, Faron* / Dream baby (2): *Jennings, Waylon* / Good rockin' tonight: *Lewis, Jerry Lee* / Little blossom: *Parton, Dolly* / From a Jack to a King: *Miller, Ned* / I can't find the time: *Nelson, Willie* / Love's gonna live here: *Jennings, Waylon* / Jambalaya: *Jones, George* / Where do we go from here: *Williams, Don* / Homemade lies: *Rogers, Kenny* / Turn the cards slowly: *Cline, Patsy* / Things to talk about: *Jackson, Stonewall* / Your song: *Lee, Johnny* / I didn't sleep a wink: *Nelson, Willie* / Cold cold heart: *Jones, George* / Town without pity: *Pitney, Gene* / Send me the pillow you dream on: *Locklin, Hank* / Six days on the road: *Dudley, Dave* / I never promised you a rose garden: *Anderson, Lynn* / Rawhide: *Laine, Frankie* / Walkin' after midnight: *Cline, Patsy* / Rhythm & booze: *Owens, Buck* / Wings of a dove: *Husky, Ferlin* / Always leaving, always gone: *Rogers, Kenny* / Rambling rose: *Lee, Johnny* / I feel sorry for him: *Nelson, Willie* / In care of the blues: *Cline, Patsy* / Have I stayed away too long: *Ritter, Tex* / I'll repossess my heart: *Wells, Kitty* / Waterloo: *Jackson, Stonewall* / Last day in the mines: *Dudley, Dave* / Moonlight gambler: *Laine, Frankie* / This old house: *Perkins, Carl* / Candy store: *Lee, Johnny* / Don't think twice: *Jennings, Waylon* / I can't get enough of you: *Jackson, Stonewall* / The heart you break may be your own: *Cline, Patsy* / Hey good lookin': *Cash, Johnny* / Open pit mine: *Jones, George* / If I don't understand: *Nelson, Willie* / Please don't let that woman get me: *Jones, George*.
CD Set . . . . **TFP 003**
MC Set . . . . **MCTFP 003**
Tring / '88 / Prism Leisure PLC / Midland Records / Taylors.

A

AAAAHHHH ROCKABILLY.
Tracks: Track down baby: *James, Tom* / Hey baby: *James, Tom* / Rock and roll baby: *Round Up Boys* / Let's jive it: *Ebert, Lee* / Tom cat boogie: *Ebert, Lee* / Weird session: *Stephens, Steve* / Blues for Oklahoma: *Bozman, Virgil* / Please be mine: *Kid Rock* / Don't knock it: *Dickerson, Dub* / T.N.T.: *Rikki & The Rikatones* / Part time hero: *Poovey, Joe* / Sie Simon shuffle: *Owen, Jim* / I've got the right key baby: *Nettles, Norman*.
LP . . . . **WLP 8821**
White Label (Germany) / '87 / Pinnacle / Bear Family Records (Germany) / CSA Tell Tapes.

ALABAMA: BLACK COUNTRY DANCE BANDS 1924-49.
Tracks: Not Advised.
CD . . . . **DOCD 5166**
Document / May '93 / Revolver-APT / Hot Shot / Jazz Music / SRD.

ALL AROUND BLUEGRASS.
Tracks: On the southbound / Chalk up another one / Blue moon of Kentucky / You can't go in the red playing bluegrass / Carolina breakdown / Have you come to say goodbye / It's only a phonograph record / I'll go steppin' too / Windy mountain / Save it, save it / Cuttin the grass / Corn cob blues / Kentucky ridgerunner / Bringin' in the Georgia mail / I won't be hanging around / Nashville grass breakdown / Kentucky / Special / When it's peach pickin' time in Georgia / Williams Lake stampede.
■ **LP** . . . . **INTS 5188**
RCA International / Sep '82.
LP . . . . **NL 89139**
■ **MC** . . . . **NK 89139**
RCA International / May '84.

ALL ROUND COWBOYS.
Tracks: Lorne Green / Cool water / Reno / Jesse James / Old Doc Brown / My adobe hacienda / That palomino pal of mine / Gunslinger's prayer / Rancho Grande / Fools Paradise, A / Cattle call / Last gunfighter ballad, The / Hang the key on the bunkhouse door / Marshal of Silver City, The / When the work's all done this fall / She's in love with a rodeo man / Pinto pal, A / Strawberry roan, The / Streets of Laredo / Bandit, The.
LP . . . . **NL 89416**
■ **MC** . . . . **NK 89416**
RCA International / Oct '84.

ALL STAR COUNTRY DUETS.
Tracks: Not Advised.
MC Set . . . . **DTO 10223**
Ditto / '88 / Pickwick Records.

ALL STAR COUNTRY MUSIC FAIR.
Tracks: Not Advised.
VHS . . . . **RVT 20451**
RCA/Columbia (video) / May '87 / BMG / Gold & Sons / Terry Blood Dist. / Sony.

ALL STAR COUNTRY ROUND UP.
Tracks: Oh lonesome me / Geisha girl / Six days on the road / What am I worth / Things go better with love / Mississippi woman / Jambalaya / Pick me up on your way down / DJ for a day / Night life / Flyin' south / Yes Mr. Peters / Sixteen tons / Folsom Prison blues.
LP . . . . **SPR 8515**
MC . . . . **SPC 8515**
Spot / Feb '83.

ALL THAT COUNTRY.
Tracks: Not Advised.
CD . . . . **LECD 418**
MC . . . . **LEMC 418**
Wisepack / Nov '92 / Terry Blood Dist.

ALL TIME COUNTRY & WESTERN HITS.
Tracks: Not Advised.
CD . . . . **KCD 000710**
King / Dec '92 / New Note / Koch International.

ALL TIME COUNTRY AND WESTERN.
Tracks: Kentucky waltz: *Copas, Cowboy* / I'll sail my ship alone: *Mullican, Moon* / Tennessee tango: *York Brothers* / Signed, sealed and delivered: *Copas, Cowboy* / Tennessee wig-walk: *Lou, Bonnie* / Old rattler: *Grandpa Jones* / Tennessee waltz: *Copas, Cowboy* / Blues stay away from me: *Delmore Brothers* / New Jole Blon: *Mullican, Moon* / Filipino baby: *Copas, Cowboy* / I'm the talk of the town: *Smiley, Red* / Why don't you haul off and love me: *Raney, Wayne*.
LP . . . . **SING 537**
Sing / '88 / Charly / Cadillac Music.

ALL TIME COUNTRY HITS.
Tracks: Not Advised.
Double LP **80010**
MC Set **850101/2**
Black Tulip / May '88.

ALL-TIME COUNTRY AND WESTERN HITS.
Tracks: Not Advised.
CD . . . . **KCD 537**
King / Nov '92 / New Note / Koch International.

APARTMENT NO 9 AND OTHER COUNTRY LOVE SONGS.
Tracks: Not Advised.
CD . . . . **PRCD 201**
President / Jan '88 / Grapevine Distribution / Target Records / Jazz Music / Taylors.

APPALACHIA THE OLD TRADITIONS (Blue Ridge Mountain Music).
Tracks: Not Advised.
LP . . . . **LP 002**
Home Made Music / '85 / Duncans / Ross Records / Projection / C.M. Distribution / Impetus Records.
CD . . . . **CD 002**
Home Made Music / Oct '88 / Duncans / Ross Records / Projection / C.M. Distribution / Impetus Records.

B

BANDERA ROCKABILLIES.
Tracks: Not Advised.
LP . . . . **JSP 1005**
JSP / Jan '82 / Hot Shot / Swift / Wellard Dist. / A.D.A Distribution / Cadillac Music / Jazz Music.

BANJO IN THE HILLS.
Tracks: Not Advised.
LP . . . . **SLP 104**
MC . . . . **GT 5104**
Starday (USA) / Apr '87 / Crusader Marketing Co.

BEST OF 80'S COUNTRY.
Tracks: Stranger in my house: *Milsap, Ronnie* / John Deere tractor: *Judds* / From where I stand: *Collins, Judy* / Read all about it: *Sylvia* / Stand on it: *McDaniel, Mel* / Out goin' cattin': *Brown, Sawyer* / Jagged edge of a

broken heart: *Davies, Gail* / Out on the front line: *Seals, Dan* / Feels so right: *Alabama* / Then it's love: *Williams, Don* / Memphis roots: *Bruce, Ed* / You're still new to me: *Osmond, Marie* / I tell it like it used to be: *Brown, T. Graham* / Letter from home: *Rabbitt, Eddie* / Turn me loose: *Gill, Vince* / Just another love: *Tucker, Tanya.*
■ LP. . . . . **MFP 5788**
MFP / Mar '87.
■ MC . . . . **TC-MFP 5788**
MFP / Mar '87.

BEST OF 90'S COUNTRY.
Tracks: If tomorrow never comes: *Brooks, Garth* / Shotgun: *Tucker, Tanya* / Never ending song of love: *Gayle, Crystal* / On a good night: *Campbell, Glen* / I'm a survivor: *Dalton, Lacy J* / My side of the story: *Bogguss, Suzy* / Race is on, The: *Brown, Sawyer* / On the bayou: *Wild Rose* / Moonshadow Road: *Brown, T. Graham* / Other side of love, The: *Davies, Gail* / Do you know where your man is: *Mandrell, Barbara* / Good times: *Seals, Dan* / Everything: *Chapman, Cee Cee* / What would you do about you (if you were me): *Osmond, Marie* / Country girl heart: *Gatlin, Larry & The Gatlin Brothers* / Tear it up: *Harms, Jonie.*
CD . . . . **CDMFP 5912**
MC . . . . **TCMFP 5912**
MFP / Apr '91 / EMI.

BEST OF ACE ROCKABILLY.
Tracks: Rockin' daddy: *Fisher, Sonny* / Everybody's movin': *Glenn, Glen* / I can't find the doorknob: *Jimmy & Johnny* / My big fat baby: *Hall, Sonny & The Echoes* / How come it: *Jones, Thumper* / Trucker from Tennessee: *Davis, Link* / Little bit more, A: *La Beef, Sleepy* / Jitterbop baby: *Harris, Hal* / Let's get on with it: *Almond, Hershel* / One cup of coffee: *Glenn, Glen* / I'm a hobo: *Reeves, Danny* / Rock it: *Jones, George* / Sneaky Pete: *Fisher, Sonny* / I'm through: *La Beef, Sleepy.*
LP. . . . . **CH 45**
Ace / Dec '81 / Pinnacle / Hot Shot / Jazz Music / Complete Record Co. Ltd.

BEST OF BRITISH COUNTRY.
Tracks: Not Advised.
LP. . . . . **SDLA 4001**
Silver Dollar / Mar '79.

BEST OF BRITISH ROCKABILLIES.
Tracks: Not Advised.
■ LP. . . . . **CRM 2002**
Charly / Feb '79 / Charly.

BEST OF BRITISH ROCKABILLY.
Tracks: Not Advised.
LP. . . . . **SNTF 787**
Sonet / Jan '79 / Swift / C.M. Distribution / Roots Records / Jazz Music / Sonet Records / Cadillac Music / Projection / Wellard Dist. / Hot Shot.

BEST OF C & W VOL 1.
Tracks: Not Advised.
CD **75304**
BMG / Nov '92 / BMG.

BEST OF C & W VOL 2.
Tracks: Not Advised.
CD **75305**
BMG / Nov '92 / BMG.

BEST OF CANADIAN COUNTRY, THE.
Tracks: Not Advised.
CD . . . . **SVCD 9510**
Savannah / Feb '89 / Sony / ACD Trading Ltd.

BEST OF CHESS, CHECKER, CADET ROCKABILLIES.
Tracks: Tall dark handsome man / Suzy Q / Cool off baby / True love / Sweet talk / Save it / Why did you leave me? / Just go wild over rock 'n' roll / Roses are blooming / Pardon Mr. Gordon / Sugaree / Jet tone boogie / Rock yea / Go go go / Vacation's over / Are you with me / All night long / Nothing's shaking / Love me / Look out Mabel.
■ LP. . . . . **CXMP 2054**
Chess (PRT) / '84.

BEST OF CHURCH STREET STATION LIVE VOL 1.
Tracks: D.I.V.O.R.C.E.: *Wynette, Tammy* / I just keep singing my song: *Wynette, Tammy* / Hello walls: *Young, Faron* / Crazy: *West, Dottie* / I fall to pieces: *West, Dottie* / Sweet dreams: *West, Dottie* / Behind closed doors: *Rich, Charlie* / Mama don't let your sons grow up to be cowboys: *Bruce, Ed* / This land is your land: *Allen, Rex Snr & Rex Allen Jnr* / Duellin' banjos: *Devol, Skip* / Night they drove old Dixie down: *Tucker, Tanya* / Texas when I die: *Tucker, Tanya* / Satisfied mind: *Wagoner, Porter* / Before the next teardrop falls: *Fender, Freddy* / Wasted days and wasted nights: *Fender, Freddy* / He stopped loving her today: *Jones, George* / Love in the hot afternoon: *Watson, Gene* / Detroit city: *Tillis, Mel* / He ain't heavy, he's my brothet: *Watson, Gene* / Nobody: *Sylvia* / Red necks, white socks and cold beer: *Russell, Johnny* / Act naturally: *Russell, Johnny* / Baptism of Jessie Taylor, The: *Russell, Johnny* / Cheatin' situation: *Bandy, Moe* / Wabash Cannonball: *Boxcar Willie* / Big bad John: *Dean, Jimmy* / Tequila Sheila: *Bare, Bobby* / Once a day: *Smith, Connie* / Rose garden: *Anderson, Lynn* / Today I started loving you again: *Haggard, Merle* / Fighting side of me, The: *Haggard, Merle.*
VHS. . . . . **PLATV 359**
Prism Video / Mar '91 / Terry Blood Dist. / Gold & Sons / Prism Leisure PLC.

BEST OF CHURCH STREET STATION LIVE VOL 2.
Tracks: Delta dawn: *Tucker, Tanya* / Mr. Bojangles: *Nitty Gritty Dirt Band* / Heart of the country: *Mattea, Kathy* / If I said you had a beautiful body: *Bellamy Brothers* / Mexico rose: *Fender, Freddy* / Secret love: *Fender, Freddy* / North of the border: *Rodriguez, Johnny* / Whose gonna fill their shoes: *Jones, George* / Danger of stranger: *Parton, Stella* / Lonely days, lonely nights: *Loveless, Patty* / Door is always open, The: *Dave & Sugar* / Two faces have I: *Christie, Lou* / Great balls of fire: *Lewis, Jerry Lee* / Who do you know in California: *Raven, Eddy* / Midnight heaven: *Bailey, Razzy* / Just another day in paradise: *Higgins, Bertie* / Carmen: *Watson, Gene* / Chains of gold: *Sweethearts Of The Rodeo* / Auctioneer, The: *Van Dyke, Leroy* / I like beer: *Hall, Tom T.* / Love don't care: *Conley, Earl Thomas* / Please Mr. Please: *Morgan, Lorrie* / God bless America: *Greenwood, Lee* / Harper Valley P.T.A.: *Riley, Jeannie C.* / Okie from Muskogee: *Haggard, Merle.*
VHS. . . . . **PLATV 360**
Prism Video / '91 / Terry Blood Dist. / Gold & Sons / Prism Leisure PLC.

BEST OF CHURCH STREET STATION, VOL. 1 (Country Stars - Live).
Tracks: D.I.V.O.R.C.E: *Wynette, Tammy* / Four in the morning: *Young, Faron* / Behind closed doors: *Rich, Charlie* / Mamma don't let your babies grow up to be cowboys: *Bruce, Ed* / This land is your land: *Allen, Rex Snr & Rex Allen Jnr* / Duellin' banjoes: *Devol, Skip* / Texas when I die: *Tucker, Tanya* / Before the next teardrop falls: *Fender, Freddy* / He stopped loving her today: *Jones, George* / Love in the hot afternoon: *Watson, Gene* / Detroit city: *Tillis, Mel* / He ain't heavy he's my brother: *Osmond Brothers* / Cheating situation: *Bandy, Moe* / Wabash canonball: *Boxcar Willie* / Big bad John: *Dean, Jimmy* / Teddy bear: *Fairchild, Barbara* / Tequila sunrise: *Bare, Bobby.*
CD . . . . **PLATCD 359**
MC . . . . **PLAC 359**
Prism / '91 / Pinnacle / Midland Records.

BEST OF COUNTRY & WESTERN.
Tracks: Not Advised.
CD Set **441727-2**
Pilz / Oct '92 / BMG.

BEST OF COUNTRY (MFP LABEL).
Tracks: Dukes of Hazzard: *Jennings, Waylon* / Jolene: *Parton, Dolly* / Forty hour week (for a livin'): *Alabama* / Why not me: *Judds* / Here come's my baby: *West, Dottie* / Kiss an angel good morning: *Pride, Charley* / Gonna get along without you now: *Davis, Skeeter* / Canadian Pacific: *Hamilton, George IV* / I've always been crazy: *Jennings, Waylon* / Here you come again: *Parton, Dolly* / Love in the first degree: *Alabama* / Would you hold it against me: *West, Dottie* / Just between you and me: *Pride, Charley* / Night life: *Nelson, Willie* / I'm a lover (not a fighter): *Davis, Skeeter* / Rose and a baby Ruth, A: *Hamilton, George IV* / Always on my mind: *Presley, Elvis* / Most beautiful girl, The: *Rich, Charlie* / Rose garden: *Anderson, Lynn* / Lay down beside me: *Williams, Don* / Stand by your man: *Wynette, Tammy* / I can help: *Swann, Billy* / Wind beneath my wings: *Greenwood, Lee* / Let your love flow: *Bellamy Brothers* / Two doors down: *Parton, Dolly* / There's no getting over me: *Milsap, Ronnie* / It's only make believe: *Twitty, Conway* / Thing called love, A: *Cash, Johnny* / Luckenbach, Texas: *Jennings, Waylon* / Funny face: *Fargo, Donna* / Georgia on my mind: *Nelson, Willie.*
MC . . . . **TCMFP 5843**
MFP / Nov '88 / EMI.
■ LP. . . . . **MFP 5843**
MFP / Nov '88.

BEST OF COUNTRY (TRAX LABEL).
Tracks: Not Advised.
CD . . . . **TRXCD 5001**
MC . . . . **TRXMC 501**
Trax / Aug '88 / BMG.
■ LP. . . . . **TRX 501**
Trax / Aug '88.

BEST OF COUNTRY 1.
Tracks: Not Advised.
LP. . . . . **NL 89176**
MC . . . . **NK 89176**
RCA / Oct '84 / BMG.

BEST OF COUNTRY 2.
Tracks: Not Advised.
LP. **26.21182**
MC **24.21182**
RCA / Oct '84 / BMG.

BEST OF COUNTRY 3.
Tracks: Not Advised.
LP. **26.21187**
MC **24.21187**
RCA / Oct '84 / BMG.

BEST OF COUNTRY AND IRISH, THE.
Tracks: Not Advised.
CD . . . . **KCD 255**
MC . . . . **KMC 255**
K-Tel (Ireland) / Feb '93 / I & B Records / Ross Records / Prism Leisure PLC.

BEST OF COUNTRY AND WEST, VOL 2.
Tracks: Only Daddy that'll walk the line: *Jennings, Waylon* / Little bit later on down the line, A: *Bare, Bobby* / Home away from home: *Belew, Carl* / Reno: *West, Dottie* / Let the chips fall: *Pride, Charley* / God help you woman: *Glaser, Jim* / Johnny one time: *Nelson, Willie* / It's a long, long way to Georgia: *Gibson, Don* / Jack and Jill: *Brown, Jim Ed* / Warm and tender love: *Campbell, Archie & Lorene Mann* / Run away little tears: *Smith, Connie* / Rememberin: *Reed, Jerry* / Thing called love, A: *Dean, Jimmy* / Instinct for survival: *Davis, Skeeter* / Who will answer: *Snow, Hank* / Woman hungry: *Wagoner, Porter.*
■ LP. . . . . **RD 7991**
RCA / Oct '65 / BMG.

BEST OF COUNTRY AND WEST, VOL.1.
Tracks: Detroit city: *Pride, Charley* / Last thing on my mind, The: *Wagoner, Porter & Dolly Parton* / Learnin' a new way of life: *Snow, Hank* / In my baby's arms again: *Smith, Connie* / Walk on out of my mind: *Jennings, Waylon* / Steel rail blues: *Hamilton, George IV* / Heaven help the working girl: *Jean, Norma* / I'm going back to Louisiana: *Tubb, Justin* / Home away from home: *Belew, Carl* / You're driving me out of my mind: *Jean, Norma* / Piney wood hills, The: *Bare, Bobby* / By the time I get to Phoenix: *Cramer, Floyd* / That's the way I talk: *Oxford, Vernon* / Childhood places: *West, Dottie* / Cajun stripper, The: *Brown, Jim Ed* / Green, green grass of home: *Wagoner, Porter.*
■ LP. . . . . **RD 7939**
RCA / Dec '63 / BMG.

BEST OF COUNTRY AND WESTERN 4.
Tracks: Distant drums / Rose garden / All I ever need is you / Taker, The / Just for what I am / Never ending song of love / Four strong winds / Morning / Snowbird / One tin soldier / Thing called love, A / I'm movin' on.
LP. **26.21189**
MC **24.21589**
RCA / Aug '84 / BMG.

BEST OF COUNTRY AND WESTERN, THE.
Tracks: San Quentin / Let it go / Stand by your man / Together again / Blue moon / All the gold in California / Mr D.J. / Thing called love, A / Tie a yellow ribbon / Divorce / I recall a gypsy woman / Is it really over / Blanket on the ground / Sunday morning coming down / Coward of the county / Ruby.
CD . . . . **BSP 227**
BS Production / Oct '91.

BEST OF COUNTRY GOSPEL.
Tracks: Not Advised.
LP. . . . . **HRL 179**
MC . . . . **CHRL 179**
Homespun (Ireland) / '88 / Homespun Records / Ross Records / Wellard Dist.

BEST OF COUNTRY IRISH.
Tracks: Not Advised.
■ LP. . . . . **KLP 255**
K-Tel / '88.

BEST OF COUNTRY MUSIC.
Tracks: Not Advised.
LP. . . . . **FUN 9020**
Fun / '88 / Pinnacle / Roots Records / C.M. Distribution.
MC . . . . **FUNC 9020**
Fun / Dec '88 / Pinnacle / Roots Records / C.M. Distribution.

BEST OF COUNTRY VOL.1, THE.
Tracks: Not Advised.
CD . . . . **CTS 5420**
Crusader / Mar '89.

BEST OF COUNTRY VOL.2, THE.
Tracks: Not Advised.
CD . . . . **CTS 5421**
Crusader / Mar '89.

BEST OF COUNTRY VOL.3, THE.
Tracks: Not Advised.
CD . . . . **CTS 5422**
Crusader / Mar '89.

BEST OF COUNTRY VOL.4, THE.
Tracks: Not Advised.
CD . . . . **CTS 5423**
Crusader / Mar '89.

BEST OF DIXIE RECORDS, VOL 3.
Tracks: Three little wishes / Dizzy: *Peters, Pete* / Rockin' in my sweet baby's arms: *Peters, Pete* / Red Rover: *Bragg, Doug* / Pretty little thing: *Bragg, Doug* / Lovin' on my mind: *Bragg, Doug* / Gotta keep it swinging: *Skelton, Eddie* / Curly: *Skelton, Eddie* / Love you too much: *Skelton, Eddie* / Rebel's retreat: *Skelton, Eddie* / Handful of love: *Keefer, Lyle* / Blues hanging around: *Kelley, C..*
LP. . . . . **MILLION 3**
Million (Holland) / Jul '84.

BEST OF DIXIE RECORDS, VOL 4.
Tracks: Feel so good: *Carroll, Bill* / Who shot Sam?: *Jones, George Thumper* / This little girl of mine: *Half Brothers* / Way you want it, The: *Meers, Arvil* / Little things you do, The / Never again: *Clayton, Johnny* / Don't tease me: *Pat & Dee* / Little dog blues: *Price, Mel* / Lonesome tavern blues: *Benson, Eddy.*
LP. . . . . **MILLION 4**
Million (Holland) / Jul '84.

BEST OF DIXIE RECORDS, VOL 5.
Tracks: I like to go: *McDaniel, Floyd* / Meanest blues: *Thomas, Jake* / Poor boy blues: *Thomas, Jake* / Concussion: *Holidays* / Big, big man: *Brockman, Danny* / Easy does it: *Couch, Orville* / She told a lie: *Mishoe, Watson* / Teen lover: *Reynolds, Eddy* / What's gonna do now?: *Williams Brothers* / My baby don't want me no more: *Ridings, Jim* / You're gonna pay: *Ridings, Jim* / Ali Baba: *Williams Brothers*.
LP . . . . **MILLION 5**
Million (Holland) / Jul '84.

BEST OF DIXIE RECORDS, VOL 6.
Tracks: Queen from Bowling Green: *Buchanan, Art* / Wonder why: *Buchanan, Art* / It must be me: *Ontario, Art* / Just look, don't touch, she's mine: *Johnson, Dee* / Crazy legs: *Gallegher, Jay* / Steady: *Gallegher, Jay* / Piano polka: *Bailey, M. & D.* / Blue guitar stomp: *Hammock, Ken* / Rock and roll: *White, J.R.* / Weekend boogie: *Croock, Tom* / I'm your guy: *Johnson, Dee* / Brady and Dunky: *Hanna, Jack*.
LP . . . . **MILLION 6**
Million (Holland) / Jul '84.

BEST OF DIXIE RECORDS, VOL 7.
Tracks: Not Advised.
LP . . . . **MILLION 7**
Million (Holland) / '88.

BEST OF SUN ROCKABILLY VOL 1.
Tracks: Ten cats down / Jump right out of this jukebox / Gonna romp and stomp / Domino: *Orbison, Roy* / Rakin' and scrapin' / Slow down / Red cadillac and a black moustache / Break up / Greenback dollar / Red headed woman / Flyin' saucers rock 'n' roll / Crawdad hole: *Earls, Jack* / Love my baby / Red hot / We wanna boogie / Come on little mama / Right behind you baby / Ubangi stomp / Let's bop / Rabbit action / Put your cat clothes on / Rocking with my baby.
LP . . . . **CR 30123**
Charly / Charly.
CD . . . . **CDSUN 16**
Sun / Apr '86 / Charly / Swift.

BEST OF SUN ROCKABILLY VOL 2.
Tracks: Got love if you want it: *Smith, Warren* / That don't move me: *Perkins, Carl* / Itchy: *Burgess, Sonny* / Drinkin' wine: *Simmons, Gene* / How come you do me: *Thompson, Junior* / Gimme some lovin': *Jenkins, Harold* / Johnny Valentine: *Anderson, Andy* / Baby please don't go: *Riley, Billy Lee* / Sentimental fool: *Pittman, Barbara* / Rebound: *Rich, Charlie* / Miss Froggie: *Smith, Warren* / Rock around the town: *Beard, Dean* / Wild one: *Lewis, Jerry Lee* / My baby don't rock: *McDaniel, Luke* / Find my baby for me: *Burgess, Sonny* / My gal Mary Ann: *Earls, Jack* / Me and my rhythm guitar: *Powers, Johnny* / All night rock: *Honeycutt, Glenn* / Your loving man: *Taylor, Vernon* / Madman 1: *Wages, Jimmy* / Fairlane rock: *Thompson, Hayden* / I need your loving kiss: *Jenkins, Harold* / Perkins wiggle: *Perkins, Carl* / Ain't got a thing: *Burgess, Sonny*.
LP . . . . **CR 30124**
Charly / Charly.
CD . . . . **CDCHARLY 36**
Charly / Nov '86 / Charly.

BEST OF THE BIG COUNTRY (20 Hit Singles From The Country Charts).
Tracks: It couldn't have been any better: *Duncan, Johnny* / Wrap your love all around your man: *Anderson, Lynn* / I don't know why (I just do): *Robbins, Marty* / For all the right reasons: *Fairchild, Barbara* / Home, sweet home: *White, L.E. & Lola Jean Dillon* / She just loved the cheatin' out of me: *Bandy, Moe* / Baby boy: *Place, Mary Kay* / Statues without hearts: *Gatlin, Larry* / You are so beautiful: *Tucker, Tanya* / In the jailhouse now: *James, Sonny* / Rollin' with the flow: *Rich, Charlie* / You and me: *Wynette, Tammy* / Everyday I have to cry some: *Stampley, Joe* / I'm sorry for you, my friend: *Bandy, Moe* / Slide off your satin sheets: *Paycheck, Johnny* / Willie, Waylon and me: *Coe, David Allan* / What're you doing tonight: *Frickie, Janie* / Adios amigo: *Robbins, Marty* / I don't wanna cry: *Gatlin, Larry* / Near you: *Jones, George & Tammy Wynette*.
LP Set . . . . **CBS 88299**
■ **MC** **4088299**
CBS / Sep '78 / Sony.

BEST OF THE TRUCK DRIVER SONGS.
Tracks: Not Advised.
LP . . . . **SLP 454**
MC . . . . **GT 5454**
Starday (USA) / Apr '87 / Crusader Marketing Co.

BIG COUNTRY 50'S VOL.1.
Tracks: Not Advised.
CD . . . . **TRXCD 5007**
LP . . . . **TRX 507**
■ **MC** . . . . **TRXC 507**
Trax / Dec '89.

BIG COUNTRY 50'S VOL.2.
Tracks: I forgot to remember to forget: *Presley, Elvis* / Sixteen tons: *Ford, Tennessee Ernie* / There stands the glass: *Pierce, Webb* / I want to be with you: *Frizzell, Lefty* / My special angel: *Helms, Bobby* / Story of my life: *Robbins, Marty* / It wasn't God who made honky tonk angels: *Wells, Kitty* / I'm movin' on: *Snow, Hank* / Young love: *James, Sonny* / Billy Bayou: *Reeves, Jim* / Blue blue day: *Gibson, Don* / Cattle call: *Arnold, Eddy* / In the jailhouse now: *Pierce, Webb* / Loose talk: *Smith, Carl* / Slow poke: *King, Pee Wee* / Singing the blues: *Robbins, Marty* / Whole lotta shakin' goin' on: *Lewis, Jerry Lee* / Guess things happen that way: *Cash, Johnny* / Wake up little Susie: *Everly Brothers* / Bird dog: *Everly Brothers*.
CD . . . . **TRXCD 5008**
LP . . . . **TRX 508**
■ **MC** . . . . **TRXC 508**
Trax / Feb '89.

BIG COUNTRY 60'S VOL.1.
Tracks: Distant drums: *Reeves, Jim* / I love you more today: *Twitty, Conway* / Please help me: *Locklin, Hank* / Ode to Billy Joe: *Gentry, Bobbie* / Act naturally: *Owens, Buck* / Once a day / Mama sang a song: *Anderson, Bill* / Crazy arms: *Price, Ray* / Ballad of Jed Clampett: *Flatt & Scruggs* / Harper Valley PTA: *Riley, Jeannie C.* / Love's gonna live here: *Owens, Buck* / Ribbons of darkness: *Robbins, Marty* / Wings of love: *Husky, Ferlin* / Misery loves company: *Wagoner, Porter* / Wichita lineman: *Campbell, Glen* / Ring of fire: *Cash, Johnny* / I don't wanna play house: *Wynette, Tammy* / Baby baby: *Houston, David* / Make the world go away: *Arnold, Eddy* / There goes my everything: *Greene, Jack*.
CD . . . . **TRXCD 5009**
LP . . . . **TRX 509**
■ **MC** . . . . **TRXC 509**
Trax / Feb '89.

BIG COUNTRY 60'S VOL.2.
Tracks: Folsom prison blues: *Cash, Johnny* / She's got you: *Cline, Patsy* / Big bad John: *Dean, Jimmy* / Running bear: *Jones, Sonny* / I don't care: *Owens, Buck* / All I have to offer you is me: *Pride, Charley* / With one exception: *Houston, David* / Walk on by: *Van Dyke, Leroy* / Next in line: *Twitty, Conway* / Galveston: *Campbell, Glen* / I guess I'm crazy: *Reeves, Jim* / What's he doin'..: *Arnold, Eddy* / All the time: *Greene, Jack* / Honey: *Goldsboro, Bobby* / Devil woman: *Robbins, Marty* / Stand by your man: *Wynette, Tammy* / City lights: *Price, Ray* / Still: *Anderson, Bill* / I've been everywhere: *Snow, Hank* / I've a tiger by the tail: *Owens, Buck*.
CD . . . . **TRXCD 5010**
LP . . . . **TRX 510**
■ **MC** . . . . **TRXC 510**
Trax / Apr '89.

BIG COUNTRY 60'S VOL.3.
Tracks: You're the one: *James, Sammy* / Almost persuaded: *Houston, David* / Girl on the billboard: *Reeves, Del* / Saginaw Michigan: *Frizzell, Lefty* / Together again: *Owens, Buck* / Throw it away: *Anderson, Bill* / It's such a pretty world today: *Stewart, Wynn* / Heartbreak USA: *Wells, Kitty* / This is it: *Reeves, Jim* / Daddy sang bass: *Cash, Johnny* / Turn the world around: *Arnold, Eddy* / Abliene: *Hamilton, George IV* / BJ the DJ: *Jackson, Stonewall* / Begging to you: *Robbins, Marty* / Laura: *Ashley, Leo* / Woman of the world: *Lynn, Loretta* / North to Alaska: *Horton, Johnny* / D.I.-V.O.R.C.E.: *Wynette, Tammy* / I fall to pieces: *Jackson, Wanda* / Tall dark stranger: *Owens, Buck*.
CD . . . . **TRXCD 5011**
LP . . . . **TRX 511**
■ **MC** . . . . **TRXC 511**
Trax / Feb '89.

BIG COUNTRY CLASSICS VOL.1.
Tracks: Not Advised.
CD . . . . **TRXCD 5002**
LP . . . . **TRX 502**
■ **MC** . . . . **TRXMC 502**
Trax / Aug '88.

BIG COUNTRY CLASSICS VOL.2.
Tracks: Not Advised.
CD . . . . **TRXCD 5003**
LP . . . . **TRX 503**
■ **MC** . . . . **TRXMC 503**
Trax / Aug '88.

BIG COUNTRY CLASSICS VOL.3.
Tracks: Moody blue: *Presley, Elvis* / Till I can make it on my own: *Wynette, Tammy* / Chantilly lace: *Lewis, Jerry Lee* / Jolene: *Parton, Dolly* / Year that Clayton Delaney died, The: *Hall, Tom T.* / You're my best friend: *Williams, Don* / Georgia on my mind: *Nelson, Willie* / Let your love flow: *Bellamy Brothers* / You've never been this far: *Lynn, Loretta* / Near you: *Bare, Bobby* / It couldn't: *Duncan, Johnny* / Shoulder to cry on: *Pride, Charley* / Luckenbach, Texas: *Jennings, Waylon*.
CD . . . . **TRXCD 5004**
LP . . . . **TRX 504**
■ **MC** . . . . **TRXMC 504**
Trax / Aug '88.

BIG COUNTRY CLASSICS VOL.4.
Tracks: Two doors down: *Parton, Dolly* / Amanda: *Jennings, Waylon* / Way down: *Presley, Elvis* / Somebody, somewhere: *Lynn, Loretta* / Faster horses: *Milsap, Ronnie* / All for the love of sunshine: *Williams, Don* / Convoy: *McCall, C.W.* / If I said you had a beautiful body: *Bellamy Brothers* / Say it again: *Rich, Charlie* / Mamas don't let your babies grow up to be cowboys: *Jennings, Waylon & Willie Nelson* / Amazing love: *Pride, Charley* / Among my souvenirs: *Robbins, Marty* / Touch the hand: *Twitty, Conway*.
CD . . . . **TRXCD 5005**
LP . . . . **TRX 505**
■ **MC** . . . . **TRXMC 505**
Trax / Aug '88.

BIG COUNTRY CLASSICS VOL.5.
Tracks: I'm just a country boy: *Williams, Don* / Old dogs, children and watermelon wine: *Hall, Tom T.* / Lady lay down: *Conlee, John* / Do you know you: *Statler Brothers* / You and me: *Wynette, Tammy* / Don't all the girls get prettier: *Gilley, Mickey* / Heaven's just a sin away: *Kendalls* / Funny face: *Fargo, Donna* / Out of my head and back in my bed: *Lynn, Loretta* / Only one love in my life: *Milsap, Ronnie* / Would you lay with me (in a field of stone): *Rich, Charlie* / There must be more to love than this: *Lewis, Jerry Lee* / I can help: *Swann, Billy* / All the gold in California: *Gatlin, Larry*.
CD . . . . **TRXCD 5006**
Trax / Aug '88 / BMG.
LP . . . . **TRX 506**
■ **MC** . . . . **TRXMC 506**
Trax / Aug '88.

BIG COUNTRY COLLECTION.
Tracks: Not Advised.
Double LP . . . . **CR 068**
■ **MC Set** . . . . **CRT 068**
Cambra / Feb '85.

BLUEBERRY HILL - 40 COUNTRY & LIVERPOOL FAVOURITES.
Tracks: Not Advised.
CD . . . . **SOW 505**
MC . . . . **SOW 105**
Soundsrite / Jun '93 / TBD.

BLUEGRASS ALBUM.
Tracks: Blue ridge cabin home / We can't be darlings anymore / Molly and tenbrooks / I believe in you darling / Model church / On my way back to the old home / Gonna settle down / Toy heart / Pain in my heart / Chalk up another one / River of death.
LP . . . . **ROUNDER 0140**
MC . . . . **ROUNDER 0140C**
Rounder / '88 / Projection / Roots Records / Swift / C.M. Distribution / Topic Records / Jazz Music / Hot Shot / A.D.A Distribution / Direct Distribution.

BLUEGRASS ALBUM VOL. 2.
Tracks: Not Advised.
LP . . . . **ROUNDER 0164**
MC . . . . **ROUNDER 0164C**
Rounder / Aug '88 / Projection / Roots Records / Swift / C.M. Distribution / Topic Records / Jazz Music / Hot Shot / A.D.A Distribution / Direct Distribution.

BLUEGRASS ALBUM VOL. 3.
Tracks: Not Advised.
LP . . . . **ROUNDER 0180**
MC . . . . **ROUNDER 0180C**
Rounder / '88 / Projection / Roots Records / Swift / C.M. Distribution / Topic Records / Jazz Music / Hot Shot / A.D.A Distribution / Direct Distribution.

BLUEGRASS ALBUM VOL. 4.
Tracks: Age / Cheyenne / Cora is gone / Old home town, The / Talk it all over with him / Head over heels / Nobody loves me / When you are lonely / I might take you back again / Lonesome wind blues.
LP . . . . **ROUNDER 0210**
Rounder / Dec '85 / Projection / Roots Records / Swift / C.M. Distribution / Topic Records / Jazz Music / Hot Shot / A.D.A Distribution / Direct Distribution.
MC . . . . **ROUNDER 0210C**
Rounder / Aug '88 / Projection / Roots Records / Swift / C.M. Distribution / Topic Records / Jazz Music / Hot Shot / A.D.A Distribution / Direct Distribution.

BLUEGRASS ALBUM VOL. 5 (Sweet Sunny South).
Tracks: Rock hearts / Big black train / Thinking about you / Out in the cold war / On the old Kentucky shore / Preaching, praying, singing / Someone took my place with you / Foggy mountain rock / My home's across the Blue Ridge Mountains / Along about daybreak / Sweet sunny South.
CD . . . . **ROUNDER 0240CD**
LP . . . . **ROUNDER 0240**
MC . . . . **ROUNDER 0240C**
Rounder / '89 / Projection / Roots Records / Swift / C.M. Distribution / Topic Records / Jazz Music / Hot Shot / A.D.A Distribution / Direct Distribution.

BLUEGRASS COMPACT DISC.
Tracks: Not Advised.
CD . . . . **CD 11502**
Rounder / '88 / Projection / Roots Records / Swift / C.M. Distribution / Topic Records / Jazz Music / Hot Shot / A.D.A Distribution / Direct Distribution.

BLUEGRASS HALL OF FAME.
Tracks: Not Advised.
LP . . . . **SLP 181**
MC . . . . **GT 5181**
Starday (USA) / Apr '87 / Crusader Marketing Co.

BLUEGRASS: THE WORLD'S GREATEST SHOW.
Tracks: Not Advised.
CD . . . . **SH CD 2201**
LP . . . . **SH 2201**
MC . . . . **ZCSH 2201**
Sugarhill(USA) / Mar '89 / Roots Records / Projection / Impetus Records / C.M. Distribution / Jazz Music / Swift / Duncans / A.D.A Distribution.

BOB MOONEY AND 'REM RECORDS'.
Tracks: Not Advised.
LP . . . . **WLP 8948**
White Label (Germany) / '88 / Pinnacle / Bear Family Records (Germany) / CSA Tell Tapes.

■ DELETED

BOPPIN' HILLBILLY VOL. 1.
Tracks: Not Advised.
LP. . . . . WLP 2801
White Label (Germany) / Aug '88 / Pinnacle / Bear Family Records (Germany) / CSA Tell Tapes.

BOPPIN' HILLBILLY VOL. 2.
Tracks: Not Advised.
LP. . . . . WLP 2802
White Label (Germany) / Jan '89 / Pinnacle / Bear Family Records (Germany) / CSA Tell Tapes.

BOPPIN' HILLBILLY VOL. 3.
Tracks: Not Advised.
LP. . . . . WLP 2803
White Label (Germany) / Mar '89 / Pinnacle / Bear Family Records (Germany) / CSA Tell Tapes.

BOPPIN' HILLBILLY VOL. 4.
Tracks: Not Advised.
LP. . . . . WLP 2804
White Label (Germany) / '88 / Pinnacle / Bear Family Records (Germany) / CSA Tell Tapes.

BOPPIN' HILLBILLY VOL. 5.
Tracks: Not Advised.
LP. . . . . WLP 2805
White Label (Germany) / Apr '89 / Pinnacle / Bear Family Records (Germany) / CSA Tell Tapes.

BOPPIN' HILLBILLY VOL. 6.
Tracks: Not Advised.
LP. . . . . WLP 2806
White Label (Germany) / Apr '89 / Pinnacle / Bear Family Records (Germany) / CSA Tell Tapes.

BOPPIN' HILLBILLY VOL. 7.
Tracks: Not Advised.
LP. . . . . WLP 2807
White Label (Germany) / '88 / Pinnacle / Bear Family Records (Germany) / CSA Tell Tapes.

BOPPIN' HILLBILLY VOL. 8.
Tracks: Not Advised.
LP. . . . . WLP 2808
White Label (Germany) / '88 / Pinnacle / Bear Family Records (Germany) / CSA Tell Tapes.

BOPPIN' HILLBILLY VOL. 9.
Tracks: Not Advised.
LP. . . . . WLP 2809
White Label (Germany) / '88 / Pinnacle / Bear Family Records (Germany) / CSA Tell Tapes.

BOPPIN' HILLBILLY VOL. 10.
Tracks: Not Advised.
LP. . . . . WLP 2810
White Label (Germany) / '88 / Pinnacle / Bear Family Records (Germany) / CSA Tell Tapes.

BOPPIN' HILLBILLY VOL. 11.
Tracks: Nursery rhyme blues: *Miller Bros.* / When the band played: *Noack, Eddie* / Your big beaver: *Jones, Paul & Jimmie Short* / Down the road: *Whitney, Don* / Cherokee rose: *Scott, Tommy* / Super market day: *Key, Jimmy* / Slick chick boogie: *Maston's Music Makers* / Juke box baby: *Ward, Reggie* / Clean town blues: *Leaders, Benny* / Hey Miss Fannie: *Leaders, Benny* / Flour, lard, coffee, sugar: *Lucky White* / Freeport blues: *Woytek, Lester* / Spanish fireball: *Hendon, R.D.* / Cotton pickin' boogie: *Bryant, Doc* / Highball boogie: *Prine, Richard* / K Bar blues: *Adams, Dub* / Old jalopy bounce: *Alexander, Murl.*
LP. . . . . WLP 2811
White Label (Germany) / '88 / Pinnacle / Bear Family Records (Germany) / CSA Tell Tapes.

BOPPIN' HILLBILLY VOL. 12.
Tracks: You've got to give me what's mine: *Bruner, Cliff* / Out of business: *Bruner, Cliff* / Guitar shuffle: *Frontiersmen* / Honky tonk hop: *Frontiersmen* / Man in the moon, The: *Carl, Utah* / Silver sage stomp: *Manning, Bob* / Love made a wreck out of me: *Red River Dave* / Nacogdoches county line: *Torok, Mitchell* / Fisherman blues: *Ham, Claudie* / Who flung that 'mater: *Jordan, Troy* / Jelly roll blues: *Thompson, Cotton* / Crying my heart out over you: *Armstrong, Gene* / Tennessee Avenue: *Phelps, Helen* / Look what love has done to me: *Wilcox, Coye* / Backin' up: *Johnson, Mark* / Juvenile love: *Colbert, Tiny* / Love me baby: *Willet, Slim* / Blues won't bother me: *Crabbe, Gene.*
LP. . . . . WLP 2812
White Label (Germany) / '88 / Pinnacle / Bear Family Records (Germany) / CSA Tell Tapes.

BOPPIN' ROCK'N'ROLL.
Tracks: Not Advised.
LP. . . . . WLP 8941
White Label (Germany) / Mar '89 / Pinnacle / Bear Family Records (Germany) / CSA Tell Tapes.

BOPPIN' TONIGHT.
Tracks: Let's go boppin' tonight: *Ferrier, Al* / Honey baby: *Forrier, Al* / No no baby: *Ferrier, Al* / What is that thing called love: *Ferrier, Al* / My baby done gone away: *Ferrier, Al* / Couple in the car: *Earl, Little Billy* / Who's baby are you: *Earl, Little Billy* / Go dan tucker: *Earl, Little Billy* / I never had the blues: *Earl, Little Billy* / Honey baby o: *Earl, Little Billy* / Freight train: *Hart, Larry* / Oh Nellie: *Hart, Larry* / I'm just a mender: *Hart, Larry* / Coffins have no pockets: *Hart, Larry* / Come on baby: *Hart, Larry* / Flashiest classiest: *Hart, Larry* / Never run out of love: *Hart, Larry* / Hold me baby: *Bill & Carroll* / Bluff city rock: *Bill & Carroll* / Bop stop rock: *Victorian, Ray* / Oh baby: *Jano, Johnny* / Mabel's gone: *Jano, Johnny* / High voltage: *Jano, Johnny* / Castro rock: *Chevalier, Jay.*
CD . . . . CDCHD 442
Ace / Feb '93 / Pinnacle / Hot Shot / Jazz Music / Complete Record Co. Ltd.

BRISTOL SESSIONS, THE.
Tracks: Skip to ma Lou: *Dunford, Uncle Eck* / O Molly dear: *Shelton, B.F.* / Walking in the way of Jesus: *Shelton, B.F.* / Newmarket wreck, The: *Barker, J.W.* / Soldier's sweetheart, The: *West Virginia Coon Hunters* / Greasy string: *West Virginia Coon Hunters* / Are you washed in the blood: *Stoneman, Ernest V.* / Henry Whitter's fox chase: *Whitter, Henry* / Bury me beneath the weeping willow: *Carter Family* / Jealous sweetheart, The: *Johnson Brothers* / Will they ring the golden bells: *Karnes, Alfred G.* / Sandy river belle: *Dad Blackard's Moonshiners* / Sleep: *Rodgers, Jimmie (1)* / Johnny Goodwin: *Bull Mountain Moonshiners* / I'm redeemed: *Alcoa Quartet* / Little log cabin by the sea: *Carter Family* / Old time corn shuckin': *Blue Ridge Corn Shuckers* / I want to go where Jesus is: *Phipps, Ernest* / Midnight on the stormy deep: *Stoneman, Ernest; Irma Frost & Erk Dunford* / Wandering boy, The: *Carter Family* / To the work: *Karnes, Alfred G.* / Blackeyed Susie: *Nestor, J.P.* / Passing Policeman, A: *Johnson Brothers* / Tell mother I will meet her: *Stoneman, Ernest V.* / Single girl, married girl: *Carter Family* / Potlicker blues: *Watson, El* / Longest train I ever saw, The: *Tenneva Ramblers* / Resurrection, The: *Stoneman, Ernest V.* / Storms are on the ocean, The: *Carter Family* / Wreck of the Virginian, The: *Reed, Blind Alfred* / Billy Grimes, the Rover: *Shellor family* / Standing on promises: *Tennessee mountaineers* / Mountaineer's courtship, The: *Stoneman, Ernest; Irma Frost & Erk Dunford* / Poor orphan child, The: *Carter Family* / I am bound for the promised land: *Karnes, Alfred G.*.
CD Set . . . . CMFCD 011
MC Set . . . . CMFC 011
Country Music Foundation / Jan '93 / Topic Records / Direct Distribution.

BUFFALO BOP 35.
Tracks: Not Advised.
LP. . . . . BBLP 2045
Bison Bop / Jul '85 / C.M. Distribution / Swift.

BUFFALO BOP 37.
Tracks: Not Advised.
LP. . . . . BBLP 2047
Bison Bop / Jul '85 / C.M. Distribution / Swift.

BUFFALO BOP 38.
Tracks: Not Advised.
LP. . . . . BBLP 2048
Bison Bop / Jul '85 / C.M. Distribution / Swift.

BUFFALO BOP 39.
Tracks: Not Advised.
LP. . . . . BBLP 2051
Buffalo Bop (Germany) / Jan '86.

BUFFALO BOP 40.
Tracks: Not Advised.
LP. . . . . BBLP 2052
Buffalo Bop (Germany) / Jan '86.

BUFFALO BOP 41.
Tracks: Not Advised.
LP. . . . . BBLP 2053
Buffalo Bop (Germany) / Jan '86.

BUSY ROCK & ROLL.
Tracks: Not Advised.
LP. . . . . WLP 8927
White Label (Germany) / Apr '88 / Pinnacle / Bear Family Records (Germany) / CSA Tell Tapes.

C

CAJUN & CREOLE MUSIC.
Tracks: Not Advised.
MC . . . . T 110
Topic / Apr '93 / Roots Records / Jazz Music / C.M. Distribution / Cadillac Music / Direct Distribution / Swift / Topic Records.

CAJUN COUNTRY MUSIC.
Tracks: La branche de mon murier: *Stutes, Jay* / Mariez-vous donc jamais: *Stutes, Jay* / Bayou pom pom: *Bonsall, Joe* / Pauvre hobo: *Bonsall, Joe* / Petite ou la grosse: *Bonsall, Joe* / Pardon pour ca qu j'aifait: *Bonsall, Joe* / J'ai fait mon idee: *Bergeron, Shirley & Alphee* / Attrape ma corde et mes eperons: *Bergeron, Shirley & Alphee* / Quel etoile: *Bergeron, Shirley & Alphee* / Perrodin two step (instrumental): *Bergeron, Shirley & Alphee* / Allons a lake Charles: *Bertrand, Robertt* / S'en aller dedans lake Charles: *Bertrand, Roberrt* / Demain, moi je va m'marier: *Stutes, Jay.*
LP. . . . . GCL 125
Goldband / Jan '90 / Charly / Swift.

CAJUN DANCE HALL SPECIAL.
Tracks: Not Advised.
CD . . . . ROU 11570CD
MC . . . . ROU 11570C
Rounder / Feb '93 / Projection / Roots Records / Swift / C.M. Distribution / Topic Records / Jazz Music / Hot Shot / A.D.A Distribution / Direct Distribution.

CAJUN ROCK'N'ROLL.
Tracks: Good morning blues: *Stutes, Jay* / Sugar bee: *Stutes, Jay* / Drunkard's dreams: *Stutes, Jay* / Sweet thing: *Stutes, Jay* / Midnight blues (come back little girl): *Stutes, Jay* / Telephone Port Arthur: *Stutes, Jay* / Hound dog baby: *Leblanc, Shorty* / Linda Lee: *Bonsall, Joe* / Poor ole Kawliga: *Stutes, Jay* / Belle promesse que t'as cassee: *Bonsall, Joe* / Sha catin: *Bonsall, Joe* / I'm leavin' you: *Bonsall, Joe* / Playmates: *Stutes, Jay* / Comin' home: *Stutes, Jay.*
LP. . . . . GCL 124
Goldband / Jan '90 / Charly / Swift.

CALIFORNIA COUNTRY CLASSIX.
Tracks: Hands / There goes that song again / Friend of a friend of mine / Whispering grass / Whoa mule whoa / Pancho / Tears / Jamestown Ferry / You mean all the world to me / Fallen star / Jambalaya / Gimme that Western swing.
■ **LP. . . . . ITW 2**
I.T.W. / Oct '83.

CALIFORNIA ROCKABILLIES.
Tracks: Don't you love me: *Glenn, Glen* / Blue suede shoes: *Glenn, Glen* / Jailhouse rock: *Glenn, Glen* / I'm gonna sit right down and cry over you: *Glenn, Glen* / Mystery train: *Brooks, Tommy* / Be bop a lula: *Brooks, Tommy* / Hound dog: *Brooks, Tommy* / Breathtaking baby: *Brooks, Tommy* / I wish I knew: *Brooks, Tommy* / Love me tender: *Brooks, Tommy* / Lonely town: *Brooks, Tommy* / Dixie: *Cochran, Eddie & Gary Lambert* / Boogie woogie breakdown: *Cochran, Eddie & Gary Lambert* / Gary's tune: *Cochran, Eddie & Gary Lambert* / Beginning of the end: *Lambert, Gary* / I'll never stop loving you: *Lambert, Gary* / Wait wait: *Lambert, Gary.*
LP. . . . . SJLP 582
Sunjay / Nov '89 / CSA Tell Tapes.

CAPITOL COUNTRY CRUISIN'.
Tracks: Not Advised.
LP. . . . . EST 24451
Capitol / '78 / EMI.

CAPITOL COUNTRY GEMS.
Tracks: Long black limousine / Loving him was easier / San Antonio rose / Radiator man from Wasco / Good hearted woman / I got a new field to plough / Jambalaya / Take me home country roads / Stand by your man / Just a strand from a yellow curl / Sad situation / Wabash cannonball / Lay some happiness on me / To hear the family sing.
LP. . . . . MFP 50550
MC . . . . TCMFP 50550
MFP / '82 / EMI.

CAPITOL COUNTRY KICKS.
Tracks: Not Advised.
■ **LP. . . . . CAPS 1005**
Capitol / '77.

CAPITOL COUNTRY MUSIC CLASSICS - 1940'S.
Tracks: Jingle jangle: *Ritter, Tex* / Texas blues: *Willing, Foy* / I'm wastin' my tears on you: *Ritter, Tex* / Oklahoma hills: *Guthrie, Jack* / With tears in my eyes: *Tuttle, Wesley* / Divorce me C.O.D.: *Travis, Merle* / So round, so firm: *Travis, Merle* / Oakie boogie: *Guthrie, Jack* / Silver stars, purple sage, eyes of blue: *Stone, Cliffie* / Smoke smoke smoke (that cigarette): *Williams, Tex* / Humpty dumpty heart: *Thompson, Hank* / Peepin' through the keyhole: *Stone, Cliffie* / Rye whiskey: *Ritter, Tex* / Cigareets, whusky and wild, wild women: *Ingle, Red & The Natural Seven* / Cocaine blues: *Hogsed, Roy* / One has my name (the other has my heart): *Wakely, Jimmy* / Dear Oakie: *Rivers, Jack* / Life gits tee-jus, don't it: *Williams, Tex* / Candy kisses: *Kirk, Eddie & The String Band* / Tennessee border: *Ford, Tennessee Ernie* / Gamblin' polka dot blues: *Duncan, Tommy* / Slippin' around: *Whiting, Margaret & Jimmy Wakely* / Whoa sailor: *Thompson, Hank* / Give me a hundred reasons: *Jones, Ann* / I love you because: *Payne, Leon* / Mule train: *Ford, Tennessee Ernie.*
CD . . . . CDEMS 1412
Capitol / Jun '91 / EMI.
■ **MC . . . . TCEMS 1412**
Capitol / Jun '91.

CAPITOL COUNTRY MUSIC CLASSICS - 1950'S.
Tracks: Broken down merry-go-round: *Whiting, Margaret & Jimmy Wakely* / I'll never be free: *Ford, Tennessee Ernie & Kay Starr* / Shot gun boogie, The: *Ford, Tennessee Ernie* / Hot rod race: *Dolan, Jimmy* / Mockin' Bird Hill: *Paul, Les & Mary Ford* / Wild side of life, The: *Thompson, Hank & His Brazos Valley Boys* / High noon: *Ritter, Tex* / Don't let the stars get in your eyes: *McDonald, Skeets* / Goin' steady: *Young, Faron* / That's me without you: *James, Sonny* / Dear John letter, A: *Shepard, Jean & Ferlin Husky* / Forgive me, John: *Shepard, Jean & Ferlin Husky* / Wake up, Irene: *Thompson, Hank* / Release me: *Heap, Jimmy & The Melody Mastg* / You

better not do that: *Collins, Tommy* / Watcha gonna do now: *Collins, Tommy* / Satisfied mind, A: *Shepard, Jean* / When I stop dreamin': *Louvin Brothers* / Sixteen tons: *Ford, Tennessee Ernie* / Waltz of the angels: *Stewart, Wynn* / I gotta know: *Jackson, Wanda* / I don't believe you've met my baby: *Louvin Brothers* / Young love: *James, Sonny* / Gone: *Husky, Ferlin* / Alone with you: *Young, Faron* / Country music is here to stay: *Husky, Ferlin.*
CD . . . . **CDEMS 1413**
Capitol / Jul '91 / EMI.
■ **MC** . . . . **TCEMS 1413**
Capitol / Jul '91.

CAPITOL COUNTRY MUSIC CLASSICS - 1960'S.
Tracks: Six pack to go, A: *Thompson, Hank* / He'll have to stay: *Black, Jeanne* / Wings of a dove: *Husky, Ferlin* / Hello walls: *Young, Faron* / Right or wrong: *Jackson, Wanda* / In the middle of a heartache: *Jackson, Wanda* / I dreamed of a hillbilly heaven: *Ritter, Tex* / Sing a little song of heartache: *Maddox, Rose* / Must you throw dirt in my face: *Louvin Brothers* / Tips of my fingers, The: *Clark, Roy* / Second fiddle (to an old guitar): *Shepard, Jean* / I don't love you anymore: *Louvin, Charlie* / Just between the two of us: *Owens, Bonnie & Merle Haggard* / You're the only world I know: *James, Sonny & the Southern Gentleman* / Born to be with you: *James, Sonny & the Southern Gentleman* / (My friends are gonna be) Strangers: *Haggard, Merle* / Tombstone every mile, A: *Curless, Dick* / Queen of the house: *Miller, Jody* / Hicktown: *Tennessee Ernie Ford* / Yodel, sweet Molly: *Louvin, Ira* / I'll take the dog: *Shepard, Jean & Ray Pillow* / Burning bridges: *Campbell, Glen* / Gentle on my mind: *Campbell, Glen* / It's such a pretty world today: *Stewart, Wynn* / Just hold my hand: *Mosby, Johnny & Jonie* / Mr Walker, it's all over: *Spears, Billie Jo* / Okie from Muskogee: *Haggard, Merle & the Strangers.*
CD . . . . **CDEMS 1422**
Capitol / Aug '91 / EMI.
■ **MC** . . . . **TCEMS 1422**
Capitol / Aug '91.

CAPITOL COUNTRY MUSIC CLASSICS - 1970'S.
Tracks: Fightin' side of me, The: *Haggard, Merle & the Strangers* / Cherokee maiden: *Haggard, Merle & the Strangers* / All I have to do is dream: *Campbell, Glen & Bobbie Gentry* / Big wheel cannonball: *Curless, Dick* / Snowbird: *Murray, Anne* / Something to brag about: *Louvin, Charlie & Melba Montgomery* / Empty arms: *James, Sonny* / I'm a truck: *Simpson, Red* / She's my rock: *Edwards, Stoney* / Comin' after Jinny: *Ritter, Tex* / Fiddle man, The: *Stegall, Red* / Bonparte's retreat: *Campbell, Glen* / Rhinestone cowboy: *Campbell, Glen* / Get on my love train: *La Costa* / I'm not Lisa: *Colter, Jessi* / What's happened to blue eyes: *Colter, Jessi* / Hurt: *Connie Cato* / Letter that Johnny Walker read, The: *Asleep At The Wheel* / Miles and miles of Texas: *Asleep At The Wheel* / Couple more years, A: *Dr. Hook* / Bluest heartache of the year: *Dale, Kenny* / Paper Rosie: *Watson, Gene* / Gambling polka dot blues: *Texas Playboys* / I cheated on a good woman's love: *Craddock, Billy Crash* / Gambler, The: *Schitz, Don* / Ain't life hell: *Cochran, Hank & Willie Nelson.*
CD . . . . **CDEMS 1423**
Capitol / Aug '91 / EMI.
■ **MC** . . . . **TCEMS 1423**
Capitol / Aug '91.

CAPITOL COUNTRY MUSIC CLASSICS - 1980'S.
Tracks: Nothing sure looked good on you: *Watson, Gene* / Something 'bout you baby I like: *Campbell, Glen & Rita Coolidge* / Could I have this dance: *Murray, Anne* / (You say you're) a real cowboy: *Craddock, Billy Crash* / Louisiana Saturday night: *McDaniel, Mel* / Sweetest thing (I've ever know): *Newton, Juice* / Step that step: *Brown, Sawyer* / Meet me in Montana: *Osmond, Marie & Dan Seals* / I tell it like it used to be: *Brown, T. Graham* / Darlene: *Brown, T. Graham* / Heartbeat in the darkness: *Williams, Don* / Old coyote town: *Williams, Don* / Just another love: *Tucker, Tanya* / I don't want to set the world on fire: *Bogguss, Suzy* / Unconditional love: *New Grass Revival* / I won't take less than your love: *Tucker, Tanya/Paul Davis & Paul Overstreet* / I didn't (every chance I had): *Rodriguez, Johnny* / New never wore off my sweet baby, The: *Dilon, Dean* / Addicted: *Seals, Dan* / I wish I could fall in love today: *Mandrell, Barbara* / Much too young (to feel this damn old): *Brooks, Garth* / If tomorrow never comes: *Brooks, Garth.*
CD . . . . **CDEMS 1424**
Capitol / Aug '91 / EMI.
■ **MC** . . . . **TCEMS 1424**
Capitol / Aug '91.

CAPITOL COUNTRY MUSIC CLASSICS - HILLBILLY.
Tracks: Yearning, burning heart: *Farmer Boys* / Wabash cannonball: *Acuff, Roy & His Smokey Mountain Boys* / Honky tonk girl: *Thompson, Hank* / Put my little shoes away: *Lee, Rose & Joe Maphis & Blue Ridge Mountain Boys* / There's a new moon over my shoulder: *Ritter, Tex* / In the jailhouse now: *Duncan, Tommy* / Philadelphia lawyer: *Maddox, Rose* / Prisoner's song, The: *Brown, Hylo & The Timberliners* / Knoxville girl: *Louvin Brothers* / When my blue moon turns to gold again: *Stone, Cliffie* / Satisfied: *Carson, Martha* / Hank's song: *Husky, Ferlin* / Deck of cards: *Tyler, T.Texas* / Corrine Corrina: *Travis, Merle & Joe Maphis* / Great speckled bird, The: *Acuff, Roy & His Smokey Mountain Boys* / Detour: *Tuttle, Wesley* / I'm brandin' my darlin' with my heart: *Guthrie, Jack* / Rollin' in my sweet baby's arms: *Maddox, Rose* / San Antonio rose: *Thompson, Hank* / Will the circle be unbroken: *Blue Sky Boys* / Hillbilly hula: *Carmen, Jenks 'Tex'* / Pistol packin' Mama: *Dexter, Al* / Sixteen tons: *Travis, Merle* / Cash on the barrelhead: *Louvin Brothers* / Freight train: *Wiseman, Mac* / Flowers on the sunny side: *Lee, Rose & Joe Maphis & Blue Ridge Mountain Boys.*
CD . . . . **CDEMS 1455**
MC . . . . **TCEMS 1455**
EMI / Jun '92 / EMI.

CAPITOL COUNTRY MUSIC CLASSICS - ROCKABILLY.
Tracks: You're there: *McDonald, Skeets* / Maybellene: *Sands, Tommy* / Rock your baby: *Jackson, Wanda* / Barrelhouse Bessie: *Moore, Merrill E.* / Woman love: *Vincent, Gene* / Mr. Whizz: *Reed, Jerry* / Flash crash and thunder: *Farmer Boys* / Cincinnati Lou: *Travis, Merle* / Hoping that you're hoping: *Louvin Brothers* / Don't push me too far: *McDonald, Skeets* / Honey bop: *Jackson, Wanda* / I ain't gettin' rid of you: *Sands, Tommy & The Sharks* / Snatchin' and grabbin': *Moore, Merrill E.* / Crazy legs: *Vincent, Gene* / You're gonna have to bawl, that's all: *Parks, Ray* / Guitar rag: *Travis, Merle & Joe Maphis* / If you want it, you got it: *Rivers, Johnny* / Don't laugh: *Louvin Brothers* / Kentucky means paradise: *Green River Boys* / Turn my picture upside down: *Travis, Merle* / Gonna back up baby: *Vincent, Gene* / I'm stuck: *Reed, Jerry* / Blue ribbon baby: *Sands, Tommy & The Raiders* / Gone and left me blues: *McDonald, Skeets* / Hot dog, that mad him mad: *Jackson, Wanda* / Buttermilk baby: *Moore, Merrill E.* / Be bop a lula: *Vincent, Gene.*
CD . . . . **CDEMS 1456**
MC . . . . **TCEMS 1456**
EMI / Jun '92 / EMI.

CAPITOL COUNTRY VOL.1 (Too hot to handle).
Tracks: I believe in lovin' em / Merle's boogie woogie / Butane blues / Automatic mama / Too hot to handle / Okeefenokee / If you ain't lovin' (you ain't livin') / Playin' dominoes & shootin' dice / Smokey mountain boogie / Lost John boogie / I get the blues when it rains / Double up & catch up / My Tennessee talkin' doll / Done gone crazy / I'm a poor boy / Humpty dumpty boogie.
LP . . . . **CR 30255**
Charly / Jan '87 / Charly.

CAPITOL COUNTRY VOL.2 (Oakie Boogie).
Tracks: Freight train boogie / My gal Gertie / I'm gettin' rid of you / Alone with you / Wait a little younger / I've got five dollars and its Saturday night / Red hen boogie / Stand up sit down shut your mouth / You're there / When I found you / I've had enough / Go ahead on / Country junction / Hambone / Fatback Louisiana USA.
LP . . . . **CR 30256**
■ **MC** . . . . **TCCR 30256**
Charly / Jun '86 / Charly.

CAPITOL ROCKABILLY ORIGINALS.
Tracks: Not Advised.
■ **LP** . . . . **CAPS 1009**
Capitol / Sep '77.

CAT TALK (Best of Imperial Rockabilly).
Tracks: Make with the lovin': *Herrold, Dennis* / Cat talk: *Williams, Lew* / Warm love: *Burnette, Brothers* / Oh la baby: *Perkins, Laura Lee* / Rockin' by myself: *Gowans, Sammy* / Everybody's got a baby but me: *Miller, Warren* / Please give me something: *Allen, Bill* / All night long: *Luman, Bob* / So long good luck and goodbye: *Rogers, Weldon* / Gone ape man: *Williams, Lew* / Buddy: *Dee, Jackie* / Hey baby: *Lawrence, Bill* / Red hot: *Luman, Bob* / Hip hip baby: *Herrold, Dennis* / Sweet baby doll: *Burnett, Johnny* / If you can't rock me: *Strikes* / Something I said: *Williams, Lew* / Bop bop ba doo bop: *Williams, Lew* / Rockin' baby: *Henslee, Gene* / Chew tobacco rag No. 2: *Briggs, Billy* / Rockin': *Strikes* / Dirty dog: *Banks, Dick* / Centipede: *Williams, Lew* / Hip shakin' baby: *Brown, Roy* / Play my boogie (CD only.): *Mack, Billy* / Let's go baby (CD only.): *Eldridge, Billy* / Don't wait up (CD only.): *Perkins, Laura Lee* / Baby I'm sorry (CD only.): *Strikes* / It's late (CD only.): *Burnette, Dorsey* / Everybody needs a little lovin' (CD only.): *Kilgore, Merle.*
MC . . . . **TCGO 2020**
Liberty / Sep '89 / EMI.
■ **LP** . . . . **GO 2020**
Liberty / Sep '89.
■ **CD** . . . . **CZ 225**
Liberty / Sep '89.

CAVALCADE OF COUNTRY.
Tracks: Not Advised.
CD . . . . **HAWCD 173**
MC . . . . **HAWMC 173**
Hawk / Dec '91 / C.M. Distribution.

CBS ROCKABILLY VOL. 1.
Tracks: Hoy hoy: *Collins Kids* / Big fool: *Self, Ronnie* / Beautiful baby: *Lord, Bobby* / Sixteen tons of rock 'n' roll: *Murphy, Jimmy* / Long tall Sally: *Robbins, Marty* / Bo bo: *Walker, Wayne* / Dig boy dig: *Hart, Freddie* / Go away houndog: *Johnson, Cliff* / Woman I need, The: *Horton, Johnny* / Let 'er roll: *King, Sid* / Did we have a party: *Brown, Billy* / Ain't I'm a dog: *Self, Ronnie* / Tennessee toddy: *Robbins, Marty* / Beetle bug bop: *Collins Kids* / Rockin' with red: *Dickens, Jimmy* / Everybody's rockin' but me: *Lord, Bobby* / Granpaw's a cat: *Murphy, Jimmy* / When my baby left me: *King, Sid* / Booger gonna getcha, A: *Wheeler, Onie* / I'm coming home: *Horton, Johnny.*
MC **40 82401**
CBS / '77 / Sony.
LP . . . . **CBS 82401**
CBS / '79 / Sony.

CBS ROCKABILLY VOL. 2.
Tracks: Not Advised.
LP . . . . **CBS 82993**
CBS / '78 / Sony.

CBS ROCKABILLY VOL. 3.
Tracks: That's all she wrote / Romp stompin' boogie / Flip out / It's a great big day / Sugar diet / Purr, Kitty purr / Teenage wedding / Honky tonk man / Black land blues / Bump, The / Boogie blues / I like it / Petrified / Hurricane.
LP . . . . **CBS 83911**
■ **MC** **40 83911**
CBS / Nov '79.

CHESS ROCKABILLIES.
Tracks: Man: *Sisco, Bobby* / Suzie Q: *Hawkins, Dale* / Cool off baby: *Barrix, Billy* / True love: *Diamond, Larry* / Sweet talk: *York, Rusty* / Save it: *Robbins, Mel* / Why did you leave me. *Josie, Lou* / Just go wild over rock 'n' roll: *Artist Unknown* / Roses are blooming: *Silvatones* / Sugaree: *York, Rusty* / Jet tone boogie: *Tones, Jet* / Rock yea: *Saint, Del the devils* / Go go go: *Sisco, Bobby* / Vacation's over: *Josie, Lou* / Are you with me: *Robbins, Mel* / All night long: *Fuller, Johnny* / Love me: *Lee, Jimmy* / Look out Mabel: *Crockett, G.L.*
LP . . . . **DET 204**
Chess (Charly) / '87 / Charly.
CD . . . . **VGCD 670 076**
Vogue / Oct '88 / BMG.

CHESS, CHECKER, CADET ROCKABILLIES.
Tracks: Not Advised.
■ **LP** **9124213**
Chess (PRT) / Apr '78.

CHICKEN ROCK.
Tracks: Not Advised.
LP . . . . **EAGLE 301**
Eagle (West Germany) / Jan '82 / C.M. Distribution.

CHICKEN ROCK VOL.3.
Tracks: Not Advised.
LP . . . . **EAGLE 306**
Eagle (West Germany) / Jan '82 / C.M. Distribution.

CHICKEN ROCK VOL.4.
Tracks: Not Advised.
LP . . . . **EAGLE 307**
Eagle (West Germany) / Jan '82 / C.M. Distribution.

CHRISTMAS COUNTRY.
Tracks: Please come home for Christmas: *Lee, Johnny* / Little drummer boy: *Williams, Hank* / Silver bells: *Tompall & The Glaser Brothers* / Blue Christmas: *Raven, Eddy* / Christmas song, The: *Curtis, Fonny* / Silent night: *Sun, Joe* / Rudolph the red nosed reindeer: *Tillis, Mel & Nancy Sinatra* / O holy night: *Cornelius, Helen* / White Christmas: *Tillis, Mel.*
LP . . . . **K 52326**
Planet / Nov '81 / Grapevine Distribution.

CLASSIC COUNTRY DUETS.
Tracks: Not Advised.
■ **LP** . . . . **IMCA 5599**
MCA (Import) / Mar '86.

CLASSIC COUNTRY ROCK.
Tracks: Last gunfighter ballad, The / Montgomery in the rain / Such a waste of love / Dreamer / If you could touch her at all / I ain't living long like this / Broken hearted people / Renegade picker / L.A. freeway / Desperados waiting for the train / Luckenbach, Texas / Your place or mine.
LP . . . . **INTS 5027**
MC . . . . **INTK 5027**
RCA International / Jul '80 / BMG.

CLASSIC COUNTRY VOL.9.
Tracks: Not Advised.
CD . . . . **PLSCD 509**
MC . . . . **PLSMC 509**
Pulse / Jan '92 / BMG.

CLASSIC IRISH COUNTRY.
Tracks: Summertime in Ireland: *O'Donnell, Daniel* / Blanket on the ground: *Begley, Philomena* / Rose of my heart: *Flavin, Mick* / Close all the honky tonks: *McCann, Susan* / I'm going to hire a wino: *Dallas, T.R.* / Old rugged cross, The: *Irish Mist* / Red river valley: *Foster & Allen* / Back in love by Monday: *Lynam, Ray* / She's got you: *Duff, Mary* / Thank God I'm a country boy: *Hogan, John* / Heartaches by the number: *Cunningham, Larry* / One day at a time: *Gloria* / Hills around Clonmell, The: *Coll, Brian* / Simply divine: *Begley, Philomena & Ray Lynam.*
CD . . . . **KNCD 14004**
LP . . . . **KNLP 14004**
MC . . . . **KNMC 14004**
Irish Collection / Apr '89 / BMG.

CLASSIC ROCKABILLY.
Tracks: Not Advised.
CD . . . . **OCN 2035WD**
LP . . . . **OCN 2035WL**
MC . . . . **OCN 2035WK**
Ocean (2) / Jun '89.

CLASSIC SONGS (I love country).
Tracks: Please help me, I'm falling: *Frickie, Janie* / Jambalaya: *Bandy, Moe* / Goodnight Irene: *Bare, Bobby* / Tumbling tumbleweeds: *Robbins, Marty* / I'm just here to get my baby out of jail: *Robbins, Marty* / Sweet temptation: *Skaggs, Ricky* / Mom and Dad's waltz: *Nelson, Willie* / Roll in my sweet baby's arms: *Paycheck, Johnny* / Tennessee waltz: *Dalton, Lacy J.*
■ LP. 4504301
CBS / Mar '87.
■ MC 4504304
CBS / Mar '87.

CLASSIC SONGS II (I love country).
Tracks: To all the girls I've loved before: *Haggard, Merle* / He'll have to go: *Goldsboro, Bobby* / Crying in the rain: *Gayle, Crystal* / Blue bayou: *Whitman, Slim* / Wound time can't erase, A: *Bandy, Moe* / Some days are diamonds: *Bare, Bobby* / Snowbird: *Anderson, Lynn* / If I said you had a beautiful body would you hold it ..: *Duncan, Johnny* / Gambler, The: *Cash, Johnny* / Funny face: *Wynette, Tammy* / Window up above: *Gilley, Mickey* / Almost persuaded: *Jones, George* / Stand by your man: *Coe, David Allan* / Mr. Bojangles: *Paycheck, Johnny* / Big river: *Cash, Rosanne with Bobby Bare.*
LP. 4510031
■ MC 4510034
CBS / Mar '88.

CONVOY TRUCK 1.
Tracks: Not Advised.
MC . . . . VCA 619
VFM Cassettes / '88 / VFM Children's Entertainment Ltd. / Midland Records / Morley Audio Services.

COOL BABY COOL.
Tracks: Not Advised.
LP. . . . . EAGLE 310
Eagle (West Germany) / '82 / C.M. Distribution.

COTTON CHOPPER COUNTRY.
Tracks: Not Advised.
LP. . . . . REDITA 126
Redita (Holland) / Oct '88 / Swift.

COUNTRY & WESTERN BONANZA.
Tracks: Don't go near the Indians: *Allen, Rex* / Mule skinner blues: *Draper, Rusty* / When two worlds collide: *Draper, Rusty* / Abilene: *Drusky, Roy* / Detroit City: *Drusky, Roy* / El paso: *Drusky, Roy* / Ballad of 40 dollars: *Dudley, Dave* / Don't fence me in: *Dudley, Dave* / Don't let the stars get in your eyes: *Dudley, Dave* / Oh lonesome me: *Dudley, Dave* / Heartaches by the number: *Van Dyke, Leroy* / Take good care of her: *Van Dyke, Leroy* / Walk on by: *Van Dyke, Leroy* / My cabin in Caroline: *Flatt & Scruggs* / Roll in my sweet baby's arms: *Flatt & Scruggs* / Seasons of my heart: *Jones, George* / I'm a lonesome fugitive: *Lewis, Jerry Lee* / North to Alaska: *Lewis, Jerry Lee* / Walk right on: *Lewis, Jerry Lee* / Jackson: *Lewis, Jerry Lee & Linda Gail Lewis* / Ballad of waterhole 3: *Miller, Roger* / In the summertime: *Miller, Roger* / Walking in the sunshine: *Miller, Roger* / I found my girl in the USA: *Skinner, Jimmy* / Gentle on my mind: *Young, Faron* / High noon: *Young, Faron* / I can't stop loving you: *Young, Faron* / Streets of Laredo, The: *Young, Faron.*
LP. 6640 007
Philips / Apr '76 / PolyGram.

COUNTRY & WESTERN FESTIVAL.
Tracks: Not Advised.
CD Set 441708-2
Pilz / Oct '92 / BMG.

COUNTRY & WESTERN FESTIVAL VOL. 1.
Tracks: Not Advised.
MC . . . . SUCCESS 2027
Success (1) / Oct '85.

COUNTRY & WESTERN FESTIVAL VOL. 2.
Tracks: Not Advised.
MC . . . . SUCCESS 2028
Success (1) / Oct '85.

COUNTRY & WESTERN FESTIVAL VOL. 3.
Tracks: Not Advised.
MC . . . . SUCCESS 2029
Success (1) / Oct '85.

COUNTRY & WESTERN HITS.
Tracks: Ring of fire / High noon / Fugitive / Oh lonesome me / Take good care of her / King of the road / Ruby / 16 tons / Jackson / My cabin in Carolina / I can't stop loving you / Kansas City.
LP. 818 284 1
IMS / Aug '84 / PolyGram.

COUNTRY & WESTERN HITS 1 (1950-1959).
Tracks: Not Advised.
■ CD . . . . DELTA 11021
Delta (1) / '86.

COUNTRY & WESTERN HITS 2 (1960-1969).
Tracks: Not Advised.
■ CD . . . . DELTA 11022
Delta (1) / Feb '86.

COUNTRY & WESTERN HITS 3 (1970-1979).
Tracks: Not Advised.
■ CD . . . . DELTA 11023
Delta (1) / '86.

COUNTRY & WESTERN HYMNAL, NO.2.
Tracks: Cleanse me / Amazing grace / Surely goodness and mercy / I'll fly away / In the valley / He restoreth my soul / Oh how I love Jesus / Whispering hope / Old rugged cross, The / Love lifted me / Beyond the sunset / Now I belong to Jesus / Heaven came down and glory filled my soul / No one understands like Jesus / Pass me not / Brighten the corner where you are / Somebody bigger than you and I / Whisper a prayer / Higher ground / No, never alone / Where could I go.
LP. . . . . PC 849
Pilgrim.

COUNTRY & WESTERN MUSIC.
Tracks: Not Advised.
■ CD 11013
Delta (1) / '86.

COUNTRY & WESTERN MUSIC FESTIVAL.
Tracks: Not Advised.
■ CD 11072
Delta (1) / '86.

COUNTRY 'N' IRISH.
Tracks: Forty shades of green / Gentle mother / My wild Irish Rose / Two little orphans / I'll take you home again Kathleen / Rose is a rose, A / I'll get over you / Wonderin' what to do / Mother's love's a blessing, A / How are things in Gloccamorra? / Rose of Tralee, The / She's got you / That silver haired daddy of mine / Sunset years of life, The / Nobody's child / Irish way to love, The.
MC . . . . 4 HOM 006
Homeland / Mar '88 / Midland Records / Music Collection International.
CD . . . . 2 HOM 006
Homeland / Sep '88 / Midland Records / Music Collection International.

COUNTRY AND WESTERN.
Tracks: Not Advised.
■ LP. 668061
IMS / Aug '82.
LP. . . . . SM 3856
MC . . . . MC 3856
Joker (USA) / '88 / C.M. Distribution / Jazz Horizons / Jazz Music.

COUNTRY AND WESTERN.
Tracks: Not Advised.
CD Set . . . . OX 0007
Music Collection International / Dec '87 / Terry Blood Dist. / Jazz Music.

COUNTRY AND WESTERN GOSPEL HYMNAL VOL. 4.
Tracks: Not Advised.
MC . . . . ZL C 03599
Word (UK) / Nov '89 / Word Records (UK) / Sony.

COUNTRY BONANZA.
Tracks: Not Advised.
CD . . . . LECD 417
MC . . . . LEMC 417
Wisepack / Nov '92 / Terry Blood Dist.

COUNTRY BOYS.
Tracks: Country boy: *Campbell, Glen* / Amazing grace: *Campbell, Glen* / Reuben James: *Rogers, Kenny* / Son on Hickory Hollers tramp, The: *Rogers, Kenny* / Crazy: *Nelson, Willie* / Night life: *Nelson, Willie* / Rose Marie: *Whitman, Slim* / Red River valley: *Whitman, Slim* / Folsom Prison blues: *Haggard, Merle* / San Antonio rose: *Haggard, Merle* / Desperately: *Williams, Don* / Another place another time: *Williams, Don* / I heard you crying in your sleep: *Jones, George* / I get lonely in a hurry: *Jones, George* / Jambalaya: *Nitty Gritty Dirt Band* / Sweet dreams: *Young, Faron* / Baby's got her blues jeans on (CD only): *McDaniel, Mel* / I just had you on my mind (CD only): *Craddock, Billy Crash* / I've got a tiger by the tail (CD only): *Owens, Buck* / Wings of a dove (CD only): *Husky, Ferlin.*
CD . . . . CDMFP 5910
MC . . . . TCMFP 5910
MFP / May '91 / EMI.

COUNTRY BREAKERS.
Tracks: Not Advised.
CD . . . . 30202 AAD
CRC (USA) / Oct '89.

COUNTRY CHARTBUSTER, VOL. 2.
Tracks: Not Advised.
LP. . . . . SHM 3189
MC . . . . HSC 3189
Hallmark / Jul '86 / Pickwick Records.
CD . . . . PWK 026
Pickwick / Jul '90 / Pickwick Records.

COUNTRY CHRISTMAS.
Tracks: White Christmas / Little drummer boy / Angels we have heard on high / Cowboy's prayer / Rockin' around the Christmas tree / Happy Birthday, Jesus (A child's prayer) / Jingle bells / Merry Christmas to you from me / Rudolph the red nosed reindeer / Away in a manger / Silent night / When you're 21 / Christmas is for kids / Jingle bell rock / Christmas as I knew it / FirstNoel, The.
LP. . . . . CBS 31605
Embassy / Nov '77 / Sony.

COUNTRY CLASSICS.
Tracks: Diggy liggy lo: *Newman, Jimmy C.* / Harper Valley PTA: *Riley, Jeannie C.* / Please help me, I'm falling: *Locklin, Hank* / Auctioneer, The: *Van Dyke, Leroy* / Me and ole CB: *Dudley, Dave* / Honky tonk song: *Pierce, Webb* / What a way to live: *Nelson, Willie* / Angel of the morning: *Remington, Rita* / Rockin' cajun: *Thibodeaux, Rufus* / Big river: *Cash, Johnny* / Why you been gone so long: *Coe, David Allan* / Big boss man: *La Beef, Sleepy* / Just..
LP. . . . . TOP 134
MC . . . . KTOP 134
Topline / '86 / Charly / Swift / Black Sun Records.

COUNTRY CLASSICS.
Tracks: Kentucky means paradise: *Mandrell, Barbara* / Stop look & listen: *Cline, Patsy* / I can't escape from you: *Jones, George* / Making believe: *Wells, Kitty* / Honky tonk angels: *Parton, Dolly* / Abilene: *Jennings, Waylon* / Good rockin' tonight: *Lewis, Jerry Lee* / Little blossom: *Parton, Dolly* / From a jack to a king: *Miller, Ned* / I can't find the time: *Nelson, Willie* / Love's gonna live here: *Jennings, Waylon* / Jambalaya: *Jones, George* / Homemade lies: *Rogers, Kenny* / Turn the cards slowly: *Cline, Patsy* / Things to talk about: *Jackson, Stonewall* / Your song: *Lee, Johnny* / I didn't sleep a wink: *Nelson, Willie* / Cold cold heart: *Jones, George* / Town without pity: *Pitney, Gene* / Send me the pillow you dream on: *Locklin, Hank* / Six days on the road: *Dudley, Dave* / Rose garden: *Anderson, Lynn* / Rawhide: *Laine, Frankie* / Walkin' after midnight: *Cline, Patsy* / Rhythm & booze: *Owens, Buck* / Wings of a dove: *Husky, Ferlin* / Always leaving, always gone: *Rogers, Kenny* / Rambling roses: *Lee, Johnny* / I feel sorry for him: *Nelson, Willie* / In care of the blues: *Cline, Patsy* / Have I stayed away too long: *Ritter, Tex* / I'll repossess my heart: *Wells, Kitty* / Waterloo: *Jackson, Stonewall* / Last day in the mines: *Dudley, Dave* / Moonlight gambler: *Laine, Frankie* / Old house, The: *Perkins, Carl* / Candy store: *Lee, Johnny* / Don't think twice: *Jennings, Waylon* / I can't get enough of you: *Jackson, Stonewall* / Heart you break may be your own, The: *Cline, Patsy* / Hey good lookin': *Cash, Johnny* / Open pit mine: *Jones, George* / If I don't understand: *Nelson, Willie* / Please don't let that woman get me: *Jones, George* / Ruby Tuesday: *Williams, Don* / Elvira: *Rogers, Kenny* / If you ain't lovin': *Young, Faron* / Dream baby: *Jennings, Waylon* / Maybellene: *Robbins, Marty.*
MC Set . . . . TTMC 014
Tring / Jun '92 / Prism Leisure PLC / Midland Records / Taylors.

COUNTRY CLASSICS.
Tracks: Just.. / 500 miles away from home / When you're hot you're hot / Would you hold it.. / Angels don't lie / Then you can tell me goodbye / Please help me, I'm falling / Cold hard facts of love, The / I never once stopped loving you / Brown eyed handsome man / Country hall of fame / Lonesome number one / Coat of many colours / Amos Moses / Big wing / End of the world / Taker, The / Mule skinner blues / I won't come in while he's there / Better..
LP. . . . . PMP 1014
MC . . . . PMPK 1014
Premier (Sony) / Feb '88 / Sony / Pinnacle.

COUNTRY CLASSICS.
Tracks: Not Advised.
LP. . . . . NE 1214
MC . . . . CE 2214
K-Tel / Jun '83 / I & B Records / C.M. Distribution / Arabesque Ltd. / Mono Distributors (Jersey) Ltd. / Prism Leisure PLC / PolyGram / Ross Records / Prism Leisure PLC.
CD . . . . ONCD 5140
K-Tel / Aug '87 / I & B Records / C.M. Distribution / Arabesque Ltd. / Mono Distributors (Jersey) Ltd. / Prism Leisure PLC / PolyGram / Ross Records / Prism Leisure PLC.
LP. . . . . NE 1369
MC . . . . CE 2369
K-Tel / Oct '87 / I & B Records / C.M. Distribution / Arabesque Ltd. / Mono Distributors (Jersey) Ltd. / Prism Leisure PLC / PolyGram / Ross Records / Prism Leisure PLC.

COUNTRY CLASSICS (3 LP SET).
Tracks: Not Advised.
LP Set . . . . STAR 2001
MC Set . . . . STAC 2001
Telstar/Ronco / Nov '84 / BMG.

COUNTRY CLASSICS 60'S.
Tracks: Not Advised.
■ CD . . . . CDP 797 541 2
EMI / Jun '90.

COUNTRY CLASSICS VOL 1.
Tracks: Not Advised.
MC . . . . CIN 1
Homespun (Ireland) / May '88 / Homespun Records / Ross Records / Wellard Dist.

COUNTRY CLASSICS VOL 2.
Tracks: Not Advised.
MC . . . . CIN 2
Homespun (Ireland) / May '88 / Homespun Records / Ross Records / Wellard Dist.

COUNTRY CLASSICS VOL 3.
Tracks: Not Advised.
MC . . . . CIN 3

Homespun (Ireland) / May '88 / Homespun Records / Ross Records / Wellard Dist.

COUNTRY CLASSICS VOL 4.
Tracks: Not Advised.
MC . . . . **CIN 4**
Homespun (Ireland) / May '88 / Homespun Records / Ross Records / Wellard Dist.

COUNTRY CLASSICS VOL 5.
Tracks: Not Advised.
MC . . . . **CIN 5**
Homespun (Ireland) / May '88 / Homespun Records / Ross Records / Wellard Dist.

COUNTRY CLASSICS VOL 6.
Tracks: Not Advised.
MC . . . . **CIN 6**
Homespun (Ireland) / May '88 / Homespun Records / Ross Records / Wellard Dist.

COUNTRY CLASSICS VOL 7.
Tracks: Not Advised.
MC . . . . **CIN 7**
Homespun (Ireland) / May '88 / Homespun Records / Ross Records / Wellard Dist.

COUNTRY CLASSICS VOL 8.
Tracks: Not Advised.
MC . . . . **CIN 8**
Homespun (Ireland) / May '88 / Homespun Records / Ross Records / Wellard Dist.

COUNTRY CLASSICS VOL 9.
Tracks: Not Advised.
MC . . . . **CIN 9**
Homespun (Ireland) / May '88 / Homespun Records / Ross Records / Wellard Dist.

COUNTRY CLASSICS VOL 10.
Tracks: One day at a time / Married by the Bible / When God comes and gathers his jewels / Why me Lord? / Dear God / Little country church / Farmer and the Lord / Picture from life's other side / Old rugged cross / On the wings of a dove.
MC . . . . **CIN 10**
Homespun (Ireland) / May '88 / Homespun Records / Ross Records / Wellard Dist.

COUNTRY CLASSICS VOL 11.
Tracks: Not Advised.
MC . . . . **CIN 11**
Homespun (Ireland) / May '88 / Homespun Records / Ross Records / Wellard Dist.

COUNTRY CLASSICS VOL 12.
Tracks: Not Advised.
MC . . . . **CIN 12**
Homespun (Ireland) / May '88 / Homespun Records / Ross Records / Wellard Dist.

COUNTRY CLASSICS VOL 13.
Tracks: Not Advised.
MC . . . . **CIN 13**
Homespun (Ireland) / May '88 / Homespun Records / Ross Records / Wellard Dist.

COUNTRY CLASSICS VOL 14.
Tracks: Not Advised.
MC . . . . **CIN 14**
Homespun (Ireland) / May '88 / Homespun Records / Ross Records / Wellard Dist.

COUNTRY CLASSICS VOL 15.
Tracks: Not Advised.
MC . . . . **CIN 15**
Homespun (Ireland) / May '88 / Homespun Records / Ross Records / Wellard Dist.

COUNTRY CLASSICS VOL 16.
Tracks: Not Advised.
MC . . . . **CIN 16**
Homespun (Ireland) / May '88 / Homespun Records / Ross Records / Wellard Dist.

COUNTRY CLASSICS VOL 17.
Tracks: Not Advised.
MC . . . . **CIN 17**
Homespun (Ireland) / May '88 / Homespun Records / Ross Records / Wellard Dist.

COUNTRY CLASSICS VOL 18.
Tracks: Not Advised.
MC . . . . **CIN 18**
Homespun (Ireland) / May '88 / Homespun Records / Ross Records / Wellard Dist.

COUNTRY CLASSICS VOL 19.
Tracks: Not Advised.
MC . . . . **CIN 19**
Homespun (Ireland) / May '88 / Homespun Records / Ross Records / Wellard Dist.

COUNTRY CLASSICS VOL 25.
Tracks: Not Advised.
MC . . . . **CWIN 106**
Homespun (Ireland) / May '88 / Homespun Records / Ross Records / Wellard Dist.

COUNTRY CLASSICS VOL.1.
Tracks: Heartbreaker: *Parton, Dolly* / Dukes Of Hazzard: *Jennings, Waylon* / Bargain store: *Parton, Dolly* / Shadows of my mind: *Everette, Leon* / Delta dawn: *West, Dottie* / You made a believer out of me: *Bare, Bobby* / Foggy mountain breakdown: *Hall, Tom T.* / Touch your woman: *Parton, Dolly* / We had it all: *Jennings, Waylon* / Shelter of your eyes, The: *Bare, Bobby & Jeanne* / I know one: *Reeves, Jim* / If you can touch her at all: *Nelson, Willie* / Devil went down to Georgia: *Reed, Jimmy* / Tennessee river: *Alabama*.
CD . . . . **PLS CD 501**
MC . . . . **PLS MC 501**
Pulse / Aug '89 / BMG.
■ **LP** . . . . **PLS LP 501**
Pulse / Aug '89.

COUNTRY CLASSICS VOL.2.
Tracks: Old flames (can't hold a candle to you): *Parton, Dolly* / You win again: *Pride, Charley* / Cowboys and daddies: *Bare, Bobby* / Put it off until tomorrow: *Davis, Skeeter* / Giving up easy: *Everette, Leon* / It was love while it lasted: *West, Dottie* / Mr. Bojangles: *Hall, Tom T.* / Cowgirl and the dandy: *Parton, Dolly* / Lord, Mr. Ford: *Reed, Jerry* / Back on my mind again: *Milsap, Ronnie* / Sweet memories: *Nelson, Willie* / Night games: *Stevens, Ray* / Hollywood: *Alabama* / Singing the blues: *Gibson, Don*.
CD . . . . **PLS CD 502**
MC . . . . **PLS MC 502**
Pulse / Aug '89 / BMG.
■ **LP** . . . . **PLS LP 502**
Pulse / Aug '89.

COUNTRY CLASSICS VOL.3.
Tracks: But you know I love you: *Parton, Dolly* / When you're hot you're hot: *Reed, Jerry* / It's not supposed to be that way: *Everette, Leon* / Bigger they are, harder they fall: *West, Dottie* / True life country music: *Bailey, Razzy* / Cowboys and clowns: *Milsap, Ronnie* / Honky tonk blues: *Pride, Charley* / You're the one that taught me to swing: *Parton, Dolly* / Legend in my own time, A: *Milsap, Ronnie* / You ought to hear me cry: *Nelson, Willie* / Why lady why: *Alabama* / Mama's don't let your babies grow up to be cowboys: *Jennings, Waylon* / Burgers and fries: *Pride, Charley* / She's a little bit country: *Hamilton, George IV*.
CD . . . . **PLSCD 503**
MC . . . . **PLS MC 503**
Pulse / Aug '89 / BMG.
■ **LP** . . . . **PLS LP 503**
Pulse / Aug '89.

COUNTRY CLASSICS VOL.4.
Tracks: Two doors down: *Parton, Dolly* / Detroit City: *Pride, Charley* / Tonight she's gonna love me: *Bailey, Razzy* / Queen of the silver dollar: *Dave & Sugar* / Only one love in my life: *Milsap, Ronnie* / Guitar man: *Reed, Jerry* / Sweet music man: *Jennings, Waylon* / Life's like poetry: *Parton, Dolly* / Early morning rain: *Hamilton, George IV* / Take your love: *Stevens, Ray* / Good-hearted woman: *Nelson, Willie* / I'm your country girl: *West, Dottie* / From a jack to a king: *Reeves, Jim* / Ride the train: *Alabama*.
CD . . . . **PLS CD 504**
MC . . . . **PLS MC 504**
Pulse / Aug '89 / BMG.
■ **LP** . . . . **PLS LP 504**
Pulse / Aug '89.

COUNTRY CLASSICS VOL.5.
Tracks: He'll have to go: *Reeves, Jim* / End of the world: *Davis, Skeeter* / Rhiannon: *Jennings, Waylon* / Oh lonesome me: *Gibson, Don* / Canadian Pacific: *Hamilton, George IV* / Crystal chandeliers: *Pride, Charley* / Jolene: *Parton, Dolly* / Ruby don't take your love to town: *Jennings, Waylon* / Make the world go away: *Arnold, Eddy* / I'm movin' on: *Snow, Hank* / 500 miles away from home: *Bare, Bobby* / Last date: *Cramer, Floyd* / Ringo: *Greene, Lorne* / Spanish eyes: *Snow, Hank*.
CD . . . . **PLS CD 505**
MC . . . . **PLS MC 505**
Pulse / Aug '88 / BMG.
■ **LP** . . . . **PLS LP 505**
Pulse / Aug '88.

COUNTRY CLASSICS VOL.6.
Tracks: Green green grass of home: *Waggoner, Porter* / Once a day: *Smith, Connie* / Pure love: *Milsap, Ronnie* / Fire and rain: *Nelson, Willie* / You don't bring me flowers: *Brown, Jim Ed & Helen Cornelius* / Would you hold it against me: *West, Dottie* / My Tennessee mountain home: *Parton, Dolly* / Gentle on my mind: *Hartford, John* / I fall to pieces: *Nesmith, Michael* / Let's go all the way: *Norma Jean* / Funny, familiar, forgotten feelings: *Newbury, Mickey* / Tennessee waltz: *King, Pee Wee* / Wabash cannonball: *Davis, Danny* / Orange blossom special: *Monroe, Bill*.
CD . . . . **PLS CD 506**
MC . . . . **PLS MC 506**
Pulse / Aug '88 / BMG.
■ **LP** . . . . **PLS LP 506**
Pulse / Aug '88.

COUNTRY CLASSICS VOL.7.
Tracks: Do I ever cross your mind: *Atkins, Chet & Dolly Parton* / Invisible tears: *Bare, Bobby & Skeeter Davis* / Am I that easy to forget: *Davis, Skeeter* / Lonesome number one: *Gibson, Don* / Send me the pillow (that you dream on): *Locklin, Hank* / One in a row: *Nelson, Willie* / Hurtin's all over, The: *Smith, Connie* / Just the two of us: *Wagoner, Porter & Dolly Parton* / Healing hands of time: *Colter, Jessi* / Your cheating heart: *Davis, Skeeter* / Make up your mind: *Wells, Kitty* / Don't throw it all away: *Dave & Sugar* / Together again: *Bare, Bobby & Skeeter Davis* / Young love: *James, Sonny*.
CD . . . . **PLS CD 507**
MC . . . . **PLS MC 507**
Pulse / Aug '89 / BMG.
■ **LP** . . . . **PLS LP 507**
Pulse / Aug '89.

COUNTRY CLASSICS VOL.8.
Tracks: I can't stop loving you: *Reeves, Jim* / Take me home country roads: *Davis, Skeeter* / From here to there to you: *Locklin, Hank* / Take these chains from my heart: *Gibson, Don* / Abilene: *Hamilton, George IV* / Me and Bobby McGee: *Pride, Charley* / Coat of many colours: *Parton, Dolly* / Amanda: *Jennings, Waylon* / Witchita lineman: *Arnold, Eddy* / I don't hurt anymore: *Snow, Hank* / Son of Hickory Holler's tramp, The: *Bare, Bobby* / San Antonio rose: *Cramer, Floyd* / My elusive dreams: *Davis, Skeeter* / Have I told you lately that I love you: *Nelson, Willie*.
CD . . . . **PLS CD 508**
MC . . . . **PLS MC 508**
Pulse / Aug '88 / BMG.
■ **LP** . . . . **PLS LP 508**
Pulse / Aug '88.

COUNTRY COLLECTION (1).
Tracks: Not Advised.
CD . . . . **U 4033**
Opectrum (1) / Jun '88 / PolyGram.

COUNTRY COLLECTION (2).
Tracks: Not Advised.
CD Set . . . . **OXO 18**
Object Enterprises / Oct '88 / Gold & Sons / Terry Blood Dist. / Midland Records.

COUNTRY COLLECTION (3).
Tracks: Not Advised.
LP . . . . **MA 11587**
MC . . . . **MAMC 911587**
Masters (Holland) / '88.

COUNTRY COLLECTION (5).
Tracks: Not Advised.
CD Set . . . . **BOXD 5**
MC Set . . . . **BOXC 5**
Pickwick / Feb '90 / Pickwick Records.

COUNTRY COLLECTION VOL 1.
Tracks: Not Advised.
VHS . . . . **VC 9998**
Video Collection / '88 / Gold & Sons / Video Collection / Terry Blood Dist.

COUNTRY COLLECTION VOL 4.
Tracks: Stand by your man: *Wynette, Tammy* / She thinks I still care: *Jones, George* / I still sing the old songs: *Tucker, Tanya* / From cotton to satin: *Paycheck, Johnny* / Everyday I have to cry some: *Stampley, Joe* / February snow: *Bare, Bobby* / Love is just a game: *Gatlin, Larry* / Tall handsome stranger: *Robbins, Marty* / What're you doing tonight: *Frickie, Janie* / I don't know why (I just do): *Robbins, Marty* / In the jailhouse now: *Cash, Johnny* / Red red wine: *Duncan, Johnny*.
CD . . . . **PWK 091**
LP . . . . **SHM 3260**
MC . . . . **HSC 3260**
Pickwick / Feb '89 / Pickwick Records.

COUNTRY COLLECTION VOL.1.
Tracks: Folsom Prison blues: *Cash, Johnny* / Hey porter: *Cash, Johnny* / Blue is the way I feel: *Twitty, Conway* / You make me what I am today: *Twitty, Conway* / Home is where you're happy: *Nelson, Willie* / I'm building heartaches: *Nelson, Willie* / I've loved and lost again: *Cline, Patsy* / Just out of reach: *Cline, Patsy* / Hello walls: *Young, Faron* / I can't help it: *Young, Faron* / Where do we go from here: *Williams, Don* / Take my hand for a while: *Williams, Don* / World's worst loser: *Jones, George* / I can't change overnight: *Jones, George* / I don't need to know that right now: *Paycheck, Johnny* / Georgia in a jug: *Paycheck, Johnny* / Release me: *Parton, Dolly* / It wasn't God who made honky tonk angels: *Parton, Dolly* / How do I hide from a memory: *Pillow, Ray* / We're together again: *Pillow, Ray*.
CD . . . . **OS 0004**
Music Collection International / Aug '87 / Terry Blood Dist. / Jazz Music.

COUNTRY COLLECTION VOL.2.
Tracks: It's four in the morning: *Young, Faron* / Harper Valley PTA: *Riley, Jeannie C.* / Luckenbach, Texas: *Russell, Johnny* / Blue eyes crying in the rain: *Russell, Johnny* / Take this job and shove it: *Paycheck, Johnny* / No charge: *Montgomery, Melba* / From a jack to a king: *Miller, Ned* / Please help me, I'm falling: *Locklin, Hank* / Wolverton mountain: *King, Claude* / I love you because: *Jackson, Stonewall* / Big bad John: *Dean, Jimmy* / Rose garden: *Anderson, Lynn* / Everything is beautiful: *Felts, Narvel* / Good hearted woman: *Russell, Johnny*.
CD . . . . **PWKS 568**
Pickwick / Aug '87 / Pickwick Records.
LP . . . . **SHM 3227**
MC . . . . **HSC 3227**
Hallmark / '88 / Pickwick Records.

COUNTRY COLLECTION VOL.3.
Tracks: Blue eyes crying in the rain / Country girl: *Anderson, Lynn* / I forgot more than you'll ever know / Mississippi / Barstool Mountain / Come a little bit closer / Kiss it all goodbye / Almost persuaded / Man in black: *Cash, Johnny*.
LP . . . . **SHM 3231**
Hallmark / '88 / Pickwick Records.
MC . . . . **HSC 3231**
Hallmark / Feb '88 / Pickwick Records.

CD . . . . PWKS 569
Pickwick / '89 / Pickwick Records.

COUNTRY COLLECTIONS.
Tracks: Not Advised.
■ LP. . . . . NB 118
Neptune / Dec '80.
MC . . . . NC 118
Neptune / Nov '80 / Neptune Tapes / A.D.A Distribution.

COUNTRY COMES ALIVE.
Tracks: Not Advised.
VHS. . . . . RVT 11014
RCA/Columbia (video) / '88 / BMG / Gold & Sons / Terry Blood Dist. / Sony.

COUNTRY COMMENT.
Tracks: Hello, I'm Johnny Credit (ain't never had no cash): *Credit, Johnny* / If I could sing a country song (exactly like George Jones): *O'Gwynne, James* / Good Lord giveth and Uncle Sam taketh away: *Pierce, Webb* / Before the next teardrop falls: *Martell, Linda* / Baby, you're habit forming: *Adams, Rusty* / Blue moon of Kentucky: *Ellis, Jimmy* / I'm ragged but right: *La Beef, Sleepy* / Stormy Monday blues: *La Beef, Sleepy* / Harper Valley PTA: *Riley, Jeannie C.* / School bus: *Cutrer, Tommy* / Hippy from Mississippi: *Adams, Rusty* / She hates to be alone: *Russell, Ryan* / Uncle Boogie Red and Byrdie Nelle: *Allen, Rex Jnr.* / Cajun interstate: *Bernard, Rod* / Night they drove old Dixie down, The: *Bluegrass Alliance*.
■ LP. . . . . CR 30118
Charly / Mar '77 / Charly.

COUNTRY COMPILATION NO. 1.
Tracks: Not Advised.
LP. . . . . SM 4002
Joker (USA) / '88 / C.M. Distribution / Jazz Horizons / Jazz Music.

COUNTRY COMPILATION NO. 2.
Tracks: Not Advised.
LP. . . . . SM 4003
Joker (USA) / '88 / C.M. Distribution / Jazz Horizons / Jazz Music.

COUNTRY COOKING.
Tracks: Not Advised.
CD . . . . CD 11551
LP. . . . . ROUNDER 0006
Rounder / '88 / Projection / Roots Records / Swift / C.M. Distribution / Topic Records / Jazz Music / Hot Shot / A.D.A Distribution / Direct Distribution.

COUNTRY CROSSOVER.
Tracks: It's only make believe: *Twitty, Conway* / As usual: *Young, Faron* / Pretend: *Smith, Margo* / Little things mean a lot: *Kendalls* / Love me tender: *Haggard, Merle* / You don't have to say you love me: *Tucker, Tanya* / Crying: *Thomas, B.J.* / Crazy: *Lynn, Loretta* / Everlasting love: *Hamilton, George IV* / Tear fell, A: *Craddock, Billy Crash* / True love: *Cline, Patsy*.
CD . . . . PWKS 570
MC . . . . HSC 3298
Pickwick / Feb '90 / Pickwick Records.

COUNTRY CRYIN'.
Tracks: It's a crying shame: *Mandrell, Barbara* / As usual: *Young, Faron* / Think I'll go somewhere and cry myself to sleep: *Craddock, Billy Crash* / We had it all: *Twitty, Conway* / Too far: *Gayle, Crystal* / Who broke your heart?: *Thomas, B.J.* / Tears of the lonely: *Williams, Don* / I've cried the blue right out of my eyes: *Gayle, Crystal* / Last thing she said, The: *Bruce, Ed* / You only broke my heart: *Lee, Brenda* / Morning after baby let me down: *Tillis, Mel* / If only I'd known it was the last time: *Young, Faron* / Tear fell, A: *Craddock, Billy Crash* / Sometime, somewhere, somehow: *Mandrell, Barbara* / I'm getting good at missing you: *Williams, Don* / I'll be seeing you: *Tillis, Mel* / Broken trust: *Lee, Brenda* / Burning memories: *Jennings, Waylon* / Just out of reach: *Thomas, B.J.* / Broken down in tiny pieces: *Craddock, Billy Crash* / Some broken hearts never mend: *Williams, Don* / Years: *Mandrell, Barbara*.
■ MC Set. . . . . CRT 038
Cambra / Aug '83.

COUNTRY DANCES.
Tracks: Not Advised.
LP. . . . . UD 301447
Unidisc (France) / May '85 / Pinnacle / Greyhound Records.

COUNTRY DOUBLE.
Tracks: Not Advised.
MC Set. . . . . WW 6052
Warwick / Oct '87 / Sony / Henry Hadaway Organisation / Multiple Sound Distributors.

COUNTRY DUETS.
Tracks: Not Advised.
LP. . . . . SPR 8559
MC . . . . SPC 8559
Spot / Mar '85.

COUNTRY DUETS.
Tracks: Vision of mother, A / Candy man / Sometimes when we touch / Rock and roll shoes / It's a dirty job / Golden ring / Get a little dirt on your hands / No memories hangin' around / All the soft places to fall / On my knees / It's only make believe / Where's the dress / There ain't no country music on this juke box / Making believe.
■ LP. . . . . CBS 54947
CBS / Sep '86.
■ MC 40 54947
CBS / Sep '86.

COUNTRY DUETS CLASSICS 1935-1955.
Tracks: Not Advised.
LP. . . . . OT 126
Old Timey (USA) / '88 / Projection.

COUNTRY FARE.
Tracks: Not Advised.
MC Set. . . . . WW 6028
Warwick / Nov '87 / Sony / Henry Hadaway Organisation / Multiple Sound Distributors.
CD . . . . U 4012
Spectrum (1) / Jun '88 / PolyGram.

COUNTRY FAVOURITES (I can't stop loving you).
Tracks: I fall to pieces: *Jackson, Wanda* / Big bad John: *Dean, Jimmy* / Rose garden: *Anderson, Lynn* / Green green grass of home: *Wagoner, Porter* / Top of the world: *Anderson, Lynn* / Please help me, I'm falling: *Locklin, Hank* / Crazy: *Jackson, Wanda* / It's four in the morning: *Young, Faron*.
CD . . . . OCN 2018WD
LP. . . . . OCN 2018WL
MC . . . . OCN 2018WK
Ocean (2) / Apr '89.

COUNTRY FESTIVAL.
Tracks: Not Advised.
LP. 1A 022 58070
MC 1A 222 58070
EMI (Holland) / '88.
CD . . . . U 4047
Spectrum (1) / Jun '88 / PolyGram.

COUNTRY FIDDLERS.
Tracks: Not Advised.
LP. . . . . RL 316
Roots (Germany) / Oct '88 / Swift / C.M. Distribution.

COUNTRY FOR LOVERS.
Tracks: Not Advised.
CD . . . . DCD 5277
Kenwest Records / Nov '92.

COUNTRY FRIENDS (I love country).
Tracks: Yesterday's wine: *Haggard, Merle & George Jones* / Slow movin' outlaw: *Nelson, Willie & Lacy J Dalton* / Chet's country: *Atkins, Chet & Albert Coleman's Atlanta Pops* / I still hold her body (but I think I've lost her mind): *Jones, George/Dennis & Ray 'Dr. Hook'* / You can lead a heart to love (but you can't make it fall): *Wynette, Tammy & Oakridge Boys* / Country side: *Bandy, Moe & Becky Hobbs* / Big river: *Jennings, Waylon, Willie Nelson,Johnny Cash,K. Kristofferson* / Ridin' high: *Frickie, Janie & Merle Haggard* / This bottle (in my hand): *Coe, David Allan & George Jones* / Beer drinkin' christian: *Dalton, Lacy J & Bobby Bare* / Don't sing me no songs about Texas: *Bandy, Moe & Merle Haggard* / Mamas don't let your babies grow up to be cowboys: *Gilley, Mickey & Johnny Lee* / Indian Summer: *Gatlin, Larry/Gatlin Bros. Band/Roy Orbison/ Barry Gibb* / Friendship: *Charles, Ray & Ricky Skaggs*.
■ LP. 4504261
CBS / Mar '87.
■ MC 4504264
CBS / Mar '87.

COUNTRY FRIENDS OF PAT & ROGER JOHNS VOL.3.
Tracks: Not Advised.
■ LP. . . . . FER 013
Future Earth / May '83.

COUNTRY GALA.
Tracks: Not Advised.
CD 01436061
LP. 01436022
MC 01436041
Arcade / May '90 / Sony.

COUNTRY GEMS.
Tracks: Honey come back: *Campbell, Glen* / Cry me a river: *Gayle, Crystal* / Daytime friends: *Rogers, Kenny* / Wayward wind: *Ritter, Tex* / Raindrops keep falling on my head: *Gentry, Bobbie* / Deulin banjos: *Jackson, Carl* / Race is on, The: *Jones, George* / Angel of the morning: *Newton, Juice* / Life gits tee-jus don't it: *Wiliams, Tex* / Tumbling tumbleweeds: *Husky, Ferlin* / Lesson in leavin', A: *West, Dottie* / Sing me an old fashioned song: *Spears, Billie Jo* / Hello walls: *Nelson, Willie* / Country girl: *Young, Faron* / Home on the range: *Whitman, Slim* / Destiny: *Murray, Anne* / I got a new field to plough: *McDonald, Skeets* / Take me home country roads: *Newton-John, Olivia* / Loving him was easier: *Carter, Anita* / Jambalaya: *Axton, Hoyt* / Stand by your man: *Jackson, Wanda* / Mercy: *Shepard, Jean* / Mule train (CD only): *Ford, Tennessee Ernie* / Young love (CD only): *James, Sonny*.
MC . . . . HR 8172
Hour Of Pleasure / Mar '89 / EMI.
CD . . . . CC 243
CD . . . . CDB 792 186 2
Compacts For Pleasure / Sep '89 / EMI.

COUNTRY GIANTS.
Tracks: Not Advised.
MC Set. . . . . DTO 10313
Ditto / '89 / Pickwick Records.

COUNTRY GIANTS.
Tracks: So close I can taste it / Smoke, smoke, smoke / Darktown poker club / Decks of cards / Wild card / Night Miss Nancy Ann's hotel, The / How long will she keep loving me / Just like the night before / You know how to keep me satisfied / Honey please change your mind / You don't love me yet / Only for me.
LP. . . . . MAN 5032
Manhattan Records / Apr '81 / EMI.

COUNTRY GIANTS COLLECTION VOL.2.
Tracks: Not Advised.
Double LP . . . . PDA 041
Pickwick / Feb '78 / Pickwick Records.

COUNTRY GIANTS USA.
Tracks: Not Advised.
■ LP. . . . . SHM 3028
Hallmark / Feb '80.

COUNTRY GIANTS VOL 8.
Tracks: Not Advised.
■ MC . . . . CAM 480
RCA/Camden / '76.
■ LP. . . . . CDS 1169
RCA/Camden / '79.

COUNTRY GIANTS VOL.1.
Tracks: Reuben James: *Rogers, Kenny* / Honky tonk angels: *Rogers, Kenny* / Sweet dreams: *Young, Faron* / Then you'll know: *Young, Faron* / I'm so lonesome I could cry: *Spears, Billie Jo* / I can't find the time: *Nelson, Willie* / Ruby, don't take your love to town: *Rogers, Kenny* / Things to talk about: *Jackson, Stonewall* / Talk about me: *Paycheck, Johnny* / I didn't sleep a wink: *Nelson, Willie* / From a Jack to a King: *Miller, Ned* / White lightning: *Jennings, Waylon* / Look what they've done to my song: *Spears, Billie Jo* / Makin' believe: *Parton, Dolly* / Home is where you're happy: *Nelson, Willie* / Wings of a dove: *Husky, Ferlin* / Shine on Ruby mountain: *Rogers, Kenny* / Sticks & stones: *Fargo, Donna* / Rose Garden: *Anderson, Lynn* / Turn the cards slowly: *Cline, Patsy* / Ramblin' rose: *Lee, Johnny* / Country girl: *Young, Faron* / Dear heart: *Miller, Roger* / Heart you break may be your own, The: *Cline, Patsy* / Little green apples: *Miller, Roger*.
CD . . . . CDGFR 003
MC . . . . MCGFR 003
Tring / Jun '92 / Prism Leisure PLC / Midland Records / Taylors.

COUNTRY GIANTS VOL.2.
Tracks: Is there something on your mind: *Nelson, Willie* / Rhythm 'n' booze: *Owens, Buck* / Candy store: *Lee, Johnny* / Stop, look & listen: *Cline, Patsy* / Four in the morning: *Young, Faron* / Hello walls: *Young, Faron* / Wishful thinking: *Fargo, Donna* / Reuben James: *Rogers, Kenny* / Both sides now: *Murray, Anne* / Billy Jack Washburn: *Paycheck, Johnny* / Shelter of my arms: *Nelson, Willie* / This old house: *Perkins, Carl* / Then you'll know: *Cline, Patsy* / Letter to heaven: *Parton, Dolly* / Ol' blue: *Jackson, Stonewall* / Sally was a good old girl: *Jennings, Waylon* / Honky tonk merry go round: *Laine, Frankie* / Moonlight gambler: *Laine, Frankie* / Wine me up: *Young, Faron* / Send me the pillow that you dream on: *Locklin, Hank* / Building heartaches: *Nelson, Willie* / Ease the want in me: *Spears, Billie Jo* / Sad & lonely days: *Dudley, Dave* / Heartaches by the number: *Mitchell, Guy* / Blue is the way I feel: *Twitty, Conway*.
CD . . . . CDGFR 004
MC . . . . MCGFR 004
Tring / Jun '92 / Prism Leisure PLC / Midland Records / Taylors.

COUNTRY GIANTS VOL.3.
Tracks: Not Advised.
Double LP . . . . PDA 059
Pickwick / Jul '79 / Pickwick Records.

COUNTRY GIRLS.
Tracks: Not Advised.
LP. . . . . LBR 1030
MC . . . . TCB 1030
Liberty / Mar '80 / EMI.

COUNTRY GIRLS (2).
Tracks: Wrong road again: *Gayle, Crystal* / Somebody loves you: *Gayle, Crystal* / What I've got in mind: *Spears, Billie Jo* / '57 Chevrolet: *Spears, Billie Jo* / Daddy and home: *Tucker, Tanya* / Strong enough to bend: *Tucker, Tanya* / All I have to do is dream: *Newton, Juice* / Sweetest thing (I've ever known), The: *Newton, Juice* / I wish that I could fall in love today: *Mandrell, Barbara* / It all came true: *Mandrell, Barbara* / Pinkertons flowers, The: *Montgomery, Melba* / Hey Mr. Dream Maker: *West, Dottie* / Still crazy after all these years: *Dalton, Lacy J* / Reuben James: *Jackson, Wanda* / Mississippi delta: *Gentry, Bobbie* / Under the sun: *Bogguss, Suzy* / Slippin' away (CD only): *Shepard, Jean* / Coat of many colours (CD only): *Peppers, Nancy* / It's morning (and I still love you) (CD only): *Colter, Jessi* / Simple little words (CD only): *Lane, Cristy*.
CD . . . . CDMFP 5911
MC . . . . TCMFP 5911
MFP / Apr '91 / EMI.

COUNTRY GIRLS (SPECTRUM CD LABEL).
Tracks: Not Advised.
CD . . . . U 4069
Spectrum (CD) / Jun '88 / M.S.D.

COUNTRY GIRLS 1926-29.
Tracks: Kitchen blues: *Miller, Lillian* / Harbour blues: *Miller, Lillian* / You just can't keep a good woman down: *Miller, Lillian* / Butcher shop blues: *Miller, Lillian* / Dead drunk blues: *Miller, Lillian* / Doggone my good luck soul: *Hudson, Hattie* / Black hand blues: *Hudson, Hattie* / No easy rider blues: *Perkins, Gertrude* / Gold daddy blues: *Perkins, Gertrude* / 12 pound daddy: *Dickson, Pearl* / Little Rock blues: *Dickson, Pearl* / He's coming soon: *Henton, Laura* / Heavenly sunshine: *Henton, Laura* / Lord you've sure been good to me: *Henton, Laura* / I can tell the world about this: *Henton, Laura* / Pretty good room in my Father's kingdom: *Henton, Laura* / Lord I just can't keep from crying: *Henton, Laura* / Sometimes: *Henton, Laura* / Carbolic acid blues: *Cadillac, Bobbie.*
LP . . . . **MSE 216**
Matchbox / Apr '84 / Roots Records / C.M. Distribution / Projection.

COUNTRY GIRLS AND BOYS.
Tracks: One piece at a time: *Cash, Johnny* / Take this job and shove it: *Paycheck, Johnny* / I'll leave the bottle on the bar: *Paycheck, Johnny* / If drinkin' don't kill me (her memory will): *Jones, George* / Honky tonk merry go round: *Bandy, Moe* / Loving arms: *Duncan, Johnny & Janie Fricke* / Other side of me, The: *Gayle, Crystal* / True love ways: *Gilley, Mickey* / Roland the rodeo and Gertrude: *Dr. Hook* / Tumbling tumbleweeds: *Robbins, Marty* / Baby it's you: *Frickie, Janie* / Gambler, The: *Bare, Bobby* / Right in the wrong direction: *Jones, George & Tammy Wynette* / Would you lay with me (in a field of stone)?: *Tucker, Tanya* / You needed me: *Wynette, Tammy* / Silence of the mornin': *Gatlin, Larry* / San Antonio rose: *Nelson, Willie & Ray Price* / Hard times: *Dalton, Lacy J* / Lonely heart cafe: *Anderson, Lynn* / Just one look: *Carter, Lynda.*
MC Set . . . . **DTO 10136**
Ditto / '88 / Pickwick Records.

COUNTRY GIRLS, COUNTRY HITS.
Tracks: Mississippi / Lonely hearts club / River road.
LP . . . . **HRL 167**
MC . . . . **CHRL 167**
Homespun (Ireland) / May '88 / Homespun Records / Ross Records / Wellard Dist.

COUNTRY GOLD.
Tracks: Tie a yellow ribbon: *Carver, Johnny* / Turn your radio on: *Davis, Skeeter* / Tennessee birdwalk: *Jack & Misty* / Let's think about living: *Luman, Bob* / From a jack to a king: *Miller, Ned* / Gonna find me a bluebird: *Rainwater, Marvin* / Wild side of life: *Thompson, Hank* / Heartbreak USA: *Wells, Kitty* / Tears: *Williams, Don* / Harper Valley PTA: *Riley, Jeannie C.* / Old rugged cross, The: *Philips, Bill* / Please help me, I'm falling: *Locklin, Hank* / Nashville: *Huston, David* / Three hearts in a tangle: *Drusky, Roy* / Amazing grace: *Warner, Mack* / Help me make it through the night: *Smith, Sammi* / Four in the morning: *Young, Faron* / Put your hand in the hand: *Posey, Sandy* / Girl on the billboard: *Reeves, Del* / Wings of a dove: *Husky, Ferlin* / Send me the pillow that you dream on: *Locklin, Hank* / Peace in the valley: *Price, Kenny* / Where do I go from here?: *Williams, Don & Susan Taylor* / Ruby, don't take your love to town: *Darrell, Johnny* / My elusive dreams: *Huston, David* / In the middle of a heartache: *Jackson, Wanda* / Wolverton mountain: *King, Claude* / Ruby Tuesday: *Williams, Don.*
■ **MC Set** . . . . **CRT 021**
Cambra / '83.

COUNTRY GOLD.
Tracks: Not Advised.
LP . . . . **EGS 4 5001**
MC . . . . **EC EGS 4 5001**
Effects Gold / Nov '80 / Ronco Records.

COUNTRY GOLD (HALLMARK).
Tracks: Jambalaya: *Lewis, Jerry Lee* / Everybody's trying to be my baby: *Perkins, Carl* / I love you because: *Cash, Johnny* / Cold cold heart: *Pittman, Barbara* / Honeycomb: *Van Dyke, Leroy* / Wayward wind: *Dudley, Dave* / I hope I don't talk in my sleep: *Pillow, Ray* / Before the next teardrop falls: *Riley, Jeannie C.* / Crazy arms: *Lewis, Jerry Lee* / Unchained melody: *Rich, Charlie* / Blue eyes crying in the rain: *Walker, Charlie* / Oh lonesome me: *Drusky, Roy* / Matchbox: *Perkins, Carl* / Ride me down easy: *Coe, David Allan* / Help me make it through the night: *Riley, Jeannie C.* / Jeanie with the light brown hair: *Rich, Charlie* / Rainy day blues: *Nelson, Willie.*
CD . . . . **PWK 063**
Pickwick / '89 / Pickwick Records.
MC . . . . **HSC 3276**
Hallmark / Jun '89 / Pickwick Records.

COUNTRY GOLD - 30 ALL TIME COUNTRY & WESTERN HIT.
Tracks: I'm so lonesome I could cry / So fine / I need a thing called love / Back home again / Can't you see / Blue train / I'm gonna feed them now / Who's been here since I've been gone / When I stop leaving / Look who I'm cheating on tonight / I can't believe that's it all over / Loving arms / Shadows of my mind / It don't hurt to dream / If I keep on going crazy / Fair and tender ladies / Let's take the long way round the world / If you gotta make a fool of somebody / Hurtin's all over, The / Then you can tell me goodbye / Whisky trip / On the road again / That's the way love should be / Far far away / Light of a clear blue morning / I'm a trucker / Shine on / It should have been easy / True life country music / Loving you / Soldier of fortune.
LP . . . . **NL 89500**
MC . . . . **NK 89500**
RCA (Germany) / Nov '85 / BMG.

COUNTRY GOLD VOL.III.
Tracks: Not Advised.
LP . . . . **CDS 1119**
MC . . . . **CAM 1119**
RCA/Camden / Mar '85 / BMG / Arabesque Ltd.

COUNTRY GOLD VOL.IV.
Tracks: Not Advised.
LP . . . . **CDS 1127**
MC . . . . **CAM 1127**
RCA/Camden / Mar '85 / BMG / Arabesque Ltd.

COUNTRY GOSPEL.
Tracks: Family bible: *Wells, Tracy* / Farther along: *Wells, Tracy* / Life's railway to Heaven: *Wells, Tracy* / I love you Jesus: *Wells, Tracy* / Wait a little longer, Dear Jesus: *Greer, John* / Dust on the bible: *Greer, John* / Kneel down and pray: *Greer, John* / One day at a time: *Leon* / Pastors on vacation: *McFarland, Billy* / When God comes and gathers his jewels: *Countrymen* / Old rugged cross: *Goodacre, Tony.*
LP . . . . **HRL 163**
MC . . . . **CHRL 163**
Homespun (Ireland) / Jan '79 / Homespun Records / Ross Records / Wellard Dist.
CD . . . . **CD 1021**
Gusto (USA) / '88.

COUNTRY GOSPEL GUITAR CLASSICS.
Tracks: Not Advised.
LP . . . . **WSE 115**
Wolf / Apr '85 / Jazz Music / Swift / Hot Shot.

COUNTRY GREATS.
Tracks: Not Advised.
CD . . . . **PWK 044**
Pickwick / Dec '87 / Pickwick Records.

COUNTRY GREATS 76.
Tracks: Not Advised.
MC . . . . **VCA 014**
VFM Cassettes / Jan '85 / VFM Children's Entertainment Ltd. / Midland Records / Morley Audio Services.

COUNTRY GREATS AT WEMBLEY.
Tracks: Della and the dealer: *Axton, Hoyt* / Wild bull rider: *Axton, Hoyt* / Devil woman: *Robbins, Marty* / Lord you gave me a mountain: *Robbins, Marty* / El Paso: *Robbins, Marty* / 57 Chevrolet: *Spears, Billie Jo* / Lonely hearts club: *Spears, Billie Jo* / Misty blue: *Spears, Billie Jo* / Blanket on the ground: *Spears, Billie Jo* / Evangelina: *Axton, Hoyt* / If I said you had a beautiful body: *Bellamy Brothers* / Let your love flow: *Bellamy Brothers* / Big boss man: *Rich, Charlie* / Most beautiful girl, The: *Rich, Charlie* / Behind closed doors: *Rich, Charlie.*
VHS . . . . **BBCV 4046**
BBC Video / '87 / Sony / Gold & Sons / Terry Blood Dist.

COUNTRY GREATS USA.
Tracks: Not Advised.
■ **MC** . . . . **HSC 3028**
Hallmark / Apr '80.

COUNTRY HARVEST.
Tracks: Fools rush in: *Nelson, Rick* / Little bitty tear, A: *Ives, Burl* / Easy: *Oak Ridge Boys* / Love me tender: *Haggard, Merle* / San Antonio rose: *Cline, Patsy* / Satin sheets: *Pruett, Jeannie* / Sleeping single in a double bed: *Mandrell, Barbara* / One step at a time: *Lee, Brenda* / Your cheatin' heart: *Lynn, Loretta* / Oh lonesome me: *Anderson, Bill* / Ruby, don't take your love to town: *Tillis, Mel* / Games that daddies play, The: *Twitty, Conway.*
LP . . . . **SSP 3082**
MC . . . . **SSC 3082**
Pickwick / Sep '80 / Pickwick Records.

COUNTRY HARVEST 16 GOLDEN COUNTRY HITS.
Tracks: Behind closed doors: *Rich, Charlie* / Big City: *Haggard, Merle* / Gambler, The: *Bare, Bobby* / Just started livin' today: *Jones, George & Tammy Wynette* / Take this job and shove it: *Paycheck, Johnny* / Till I gain control again: *Nelson, Willie & Waylon Jennings* / Key Largo: *Higgins, Bertie* / Stand by your man: *Wynette, Tammy* / Thing called love, A: *Cash, Johnny* / Very special love song, A: *Mandrell, Barbara* / Rose garden: *Anderson, Lynn* / He stopped loving her today: *Jones, George* / Sleeping with your memory: *Frickie, Janie* / Delta dawn: *Tucker, Tanya* / If you ever change your mind: *Gayle, Crystal* / El Paso: *Robbins, Marty.*
LP . . . . **WW 2008**
MC . . . . **WW 20084**
Warwick Reflections / Jun '86 / Sony.

COUNTRY HEROES LIVE.
Tracks: Wine me up: *Young, Faron* / This little girl of mine: *Young, Faron* / Going steady: *Young, Faron* / Hello walls: *Young, Faron* / Four in the morning: *Young, Faron* / I like beer: *Hall, Tom T.* / Ravishing Ruby: *Hall, Tom T.* / Year Clayton Delaney died, The: *Hall, Tom T.* / Old dogs, children and watermelon wine, The: *Hall, Tom T.* / Walk on by: *Van Dyke, Leroy* / Auctioneer, The: *Van Dyke, Leroy* / Got no reason now for going home: *Russell, Johnny* / Crystal chandeliers: *Russell, Johnny* / Bill Bailey: *Dean, Jimmy* / Big bad John: *Dean, Jimmy* / Ole slewfoot: *Wagoner, Porter* / I thought I heard you calling my name: *Wagoner, Porter* / Sugaefoot rag: *Wagoner, Porter* / Louisiana Saturday night: *Wagoner, Porter* / Satisfied mind: *Wagoner, Porter* / Y'all come: *Wagoner, Porter.*
VHS . . . . **PLATV 355**
Platinum Music / Mar '90 / Prism Leisure PLC / Ross Records.

COUNTRY HEROES LIVE.
Tracks: Not Advised.
CD **15 402**
MC **79 402**
Laserlight / Aug '91 / TBD / Taylors.

COUNTRY HIGHWAY.
Tracks: Not Advised.
CD . . . . **LECD 416**
MC . . . . **LEMC 416**
Wisepack / Nov '92 / Terry Blood Dist.

COUNTRY HITS.
Tracks: Not Advised.
■ **MC** . . . . **NK 89625**
RCA / May '85.

COUNTRY HITS VOL.1.
Tracks: Dear me: *Morgan, Lorrie* / Don't close your eyes: *Whitley, Keith* / Better man, A: *Black, Clint* / Mama he's crazy: *Judds* / I can't turn the tide: *Baillie & the Boys* / Bluest eyes in Texas: *Restless Heart* / I'm no stranger to the rain: *Whitley, Keith* / Killin' time: *Black, Clint* / Out of your shoes: *Morgan, Lorrie* / I'll always come back: *Oslin, K.T.* / Woman in love, A: *Milsap, Ronnie* / All of the fun: *Overstreet, Paul.*
■ **VHS** **790 386**
BMG Video / Sep '90.

COUNTRY HITS, VOL. 1.
Tracks: Heartbreaker: *Parton, Dolly* / Dukes of Hazzard: *Jennings, Waylon* / Bargain store: *Parton, Dolly* / Shadows of my mind: *Everette, Leon* / Delta dawn: *West, Dottie* / You made a believer out of me: *Bare, Bobby* / Crystal chandeliers: *Pride, Charley* / Touch your woman: *Parton, Dolly* / We had it all: *Jennings, Waylon* / Shelter of your eyes, The: *Bare, Bobby & Jeanne* / I know one: *Reeves, Jim* / If you can touch her at all: *Nelson, Willie* / Pure love: *Milsap, Ronnie* / Pretend: *Stevens, Ray* / Seeker, The: *Parton, Dolly* / Tennessee River: *Alabama* / My heroes have always been cowboys: *Jennings, Waylon* / Making believe: *Davis, Skeeter* / Devil went down to Georgia, The: *Reed, Jerry* / Is anybody going to San Antone?: *Pride, Charley* / Dreaming my dreams with you: *Jennings, Waylon* / My eyes can only see you: *Parton, Dolly* / Door is always open, The: *Dave & Sugar* / You don't bring me flowers: *Brown, Jim Ed & Helen Cornelius.*
Double LP . . . . **CR 030**
■ **MC Set** . . . . **CRT 030**
Cambra / Aug '83.

COUNTRY HITS, VOL. 2.
Tracks: Dreaming my dreams with you: *Jennings, Waylon* / I know one: *Reeves, Jim* / Bargain store: *Parton, Dolly* / Shadows of my mind: *Everette, Leon* / Delta dawn: *West, Dottie* / You make a believer out of me: *Bare, Bobby* / Pretend: *Stevens, Ray* / Seeker, The: *Parton, Dolly* / Tennessee River: *Alabama* / Making believe: *Davis, Skeeter* / My eyes can only see you: *Parton, Dolly* / Crystal chandeliers: *Pride, Charley* / Touch your woman: *Parton, Dolly* / We had it all: *Jennings, Waylon* / Shelter of your eyes, The: *Bare, Bobby & Jeanne* / If you can touch her at all: *Nelson, Willie* / Pure love: *Milsap, Ronnie* / Dukes of Hazzard: *Jennings, Waylon* / Devil went down to Georgia, The: *Reed, Jerry* / Is anybody going to San Antone? / Heartbreaker: *Parton, Dolly* / My heroes have always been cowboys: *Jennings, Waylon* / Door is always open, The: *Dave & Sugar* / You don't bring me flowers: *Brown, Jim Ed & Helen Cornelius.*
Double LP . . . . **CR 045**
■ **MC Set** . . . . **CRT 045**
Cambra / '83.

COUNTRY JUKEBOX.
Tracks: Not Advised.
CD . . . . **WSP 27603**
Warner Super Savers (USA) / Jun '88 / Silver Sounds (CD).

COUNTRY JUKEBOX HITS.
Tracks: Not Advised.
CD Set . . . . **DCD 5061**
Disky Communications Ltd / Jul '89 / Swift / Terry Blood Dist.
Double LP **DLP2061**
MC Set **DMC4061**
Not Advised / Jul '89.

COUNTRY JUNCTION.
Tracks: Country junction: *Ford, Tennessee Ernie* / Goin' steady: *Young, Faron* / Satisfied mind, A: *Shepard, Jean* / My home town: *Husky, Ferlin* / High noon: *Ritter, Tex* / There my future goes: *Thompson, Hank* / Smoke smoke smoke (that cigarette): *Williams, Tex* / I don't hurt anymore: *Ford, Tennessee Ernie* / Cold, cold heart: *Jackson, Wanda* / Ain't it funny what a fool will do: *Jones, George* / What's bad for you is good for me: *Montgomery, Melba* / I'm wasting my tears on you: *Ritter, Tex* / You're calling me sweetheart again: *Shepard, Jean* / Sixteen tons: *Ford, Tennessee Ernie* / Sioux city Sue: *Husky, Ferlin* / That's what I like about the West: *Williams, Tex* / Sweet dreams: *Young, Faron* / Streets of Laredo: *Ritter, Tex* / Tears on my pillow: *Ford, Tennessee Ernie* / Left my gal in the mountains: *Thompson, Hank* / Forget the past: *Young, Faron* / Wild side of life: *Thompson, Hank* / Funny how time slips

away: *Ford, Tennessee Ernie* / My wedding ring: *Shepard, Jean* / Billy the kid: *Ritter, Tex* / My home in San Antone: *Husky, Ferlin* / Shot gun boogie: *Williams, Tex* / Silver threads and golden needles: *Jackson, Wanda* / There'll be no teardrops tonight: *Ford, Tennessee Ernie* / I can still see him in your eyes: *Mack, Billy* / You'd better go: *Shepard, Jean* / If I could keep you off my mind: *Mathis, Johnny* / (We must have been) out of our minds: *Jones, George & Melba Montgomery* / Alabama Jubilee: *Husky, Ferlin* / Don't let the stars get in your eyes: *McDonald, Skeets* / Mule train: *Ford, Tennessee Ernie* / I've got five dolars and it's Saturday night: *Young, Faron* / Crying steel guitar: *Shepard, Jean* / Don't walk away: *Husky, Ferlin* / Rye whisky: *Ritter, Tex*.
CD Set . . . . **CDDL 1215**
MC Set . . . . **TCDL 1215**
MFP / Nov '91 / EMI.

COUNTRY LADIES (I love country).
Tracks: Little bit of rain, A: *Prentice, Suzanne* / Tell me a lie: *Frickie, Janie* / If you ever change your mind: *Gayle, Crystal* / Livin' in these troubled times: *Gayle, Crystal* / Sea of heartbreak: *Anderson, Lynn* / Hillbilly girl with the blues: *Dalton, Lacy J* / Everybody makes mistakes: *Dalton, Lacy J* / I'm not losin' any sleep: *Blanch, Jewel* / Laying it on the line: *Riggir, Patsy* / Radio heart: *McClain, Charly* / I don't know why you don't want me: *Cash, Rosanne* / Mississippi: *Fairchild, Barbara* / Would you lay with me (in a field of stone): *Tucker, Tanya*.
MC **40 54942**
CBS / Mar '87 / Sony.
■ **LP** . . . . **CBS 54942**
CBS / Mar '87.

COUNTRY LADIES LIVE.
Tracks: Not Advised.
CD **15 404**
MC **79 404**
Laserlight / Aug '91 / TBD / Taylors.

COUNTRY LADIES LIVE.
Tracks: Rocky top / Leavin's for unbeliever's / What are we doin' in love / Patsy Cline medley / I'm only in it for the love / Because I love you, that's why / Did we have to come this far to say goodbye / Right or wrong / Once a day / Rocky top (2) / Tip of my fingers / Y'all come / Teddy bear song / Even cowgirls get the blues / Cry / Rose garden / I've never loved anyone more / Where's the fire.
VHS . . . . **PLATV 352**
Platinum Music / Mar '90 / Prism Leisure PLC / Ross Records.

COUNTRY LEGENDS.
Tracks: Not Advised.
LP . . . . **RTL 2050**
Ronco / Oct '80.

COUNTRY LIVING.
Tracks: It's only make believe / It's four in the morning / Teddy bear song / Heartbreak USA / Carroll County accident, The / My last date with you / Wild side of life / Once a day / Don't break the heart that loves you / Mr. Walker it's all over / Harper Valley PTA / Girl on the billboard / DJ for a day / Oh lonesome me / No charge / From a jack to a king / Deck of cards / Bridge washed out, The / Please help me, I'm falling / Rose garden.
CD . . . . **CRXCX 15**
LP . . . . **CRX 15**
MC . . . . **CRXC 15**
Creole / Feb '93 / Terry Blood Dist.

COUNTRY LOVE.
Tracks: Not Advised.
CD . . . . **TRXCD 512**
LP . . . . **TRX 512**
■ **MC** . . . . **TRXC 512**
Trax / Feb '89.

COUNTRY LOVE.
Tracks: Not Advised.
CD . . . . **TCD 2654**
LP . . . . **STAR 2654**
MC . . . . **STAC 2654**
Telstar/Ronco / Feb '93 / BMG.

COUNTRY LOVE.
Tracks: Not Advised.
LP . . . . **NE 1068**
K-Tel / Jan '80 / I & B Records / C.M. Distribution / Arabesque Ltd. / Mono Distributors (Jersey) Ltd. / Prism Leisure PLC / PolyGram / Ross Records / Prism Leisure PLC.

COUNTRY LOVE (1).
Tracks: Not Advised.
CD . . . . **MCLD 19175**
MCA / Oct '92 / BMG.

COUNTRY LOVE (2).
Tracks: Not Advised.
■ **CD** . . . . **DMCDM 7005**
MCA / Feb '90.
■ **Double LP** . . . . **MCMD 7005**
MCA / Feb '90.
■ **MC Set** . . . . **MCMDC 7005**
MCA / Feb '90.

COUNTRY LOVE AND COUNTRY HEARTACHE.
Tracks: Not Advised.
MC Set . . . . **DTO 10237**
Ditto / May '86 / Pickwick Records.

COUNTRY LOVE SONGS.
Tracks: Just to satisfy you: *Jennings, Waylon* / Can't forget about you: *Alabama* / I'll hold you: *Arnold, Eddy* / From here to there to you: *Locklin, Hank* / You are: *Bare, Bobby* / Help me make it through the night: *Nelson, Willie*.
CD . . . . **DRIVE 3012**
In-Market / Dec '87.
MC . . . . **CAM 1227**
RCA/Camden / Feb '88 / BMG / Arabesque Ltd.

COUNTRY LOVE/COUNTRY STYLE.
Tracks: Not Advised.
CD . . . . **LECD 419**
MC . . . . **LEMC 419**
Wisepack / Nov '92 / Terry Blood Dist.

COUNTRY LOVIN', VOL. 1.
Tracks: If loving you is wrong I don't want to be right: *Mandrell, Barbara* / It's not love (but it's not bad): *Robbins, Marty* / You don't have to say you love me: *Tucker, Tanya* / Easy to love: *Kendalls* / Never loved a woman like you: *Hamilton, George IV* / Love me over again: *Williams, Don* / I can't stop loving you: *Twitty, Conway* / Rest your love on me: *Twitty, Conway* / I'm still loving you: *Stampley, Joe* / Tell me that you love me: *Gibbs, Terri* / When you fall in love: *Bruce, Ed* / Sea of love: *Thomas, B.J.* / Loving you so long now: *Williams, Don* / Everybody loves a rain song: *Thomas, B.J.* / Love me tender: *Haggard, Merle* / Goodbye love: *Lee, Brenda* / True love: *Cline, Patsy* / Wasted love: *Gibbs, Terri*.
■ **MC Set** . . . . **CRT 039**
Cambra / Aug '83.

COUNTRY LOVIN', VOL. 2.
Tracks: Hurtin's all over, The / Just the two of us: *Wagoner, Porter & Dolly Parton* / Fire and rain: *Davis, Skeeter* / Healing hands of time: *Coulter, Jessie* / Make up your mind: *Wells, Kitty* / San Antonio rose: *King, Pee Wee* / Do I ever cross your mind?: *Atkins, Chet & Dolly Parton* / Invisible tears: *Bare, Bobby & Skeeter Davis* / Together again: *Bare, Bobby & Skeeter Davis* / Queen of the silver dollar: *Dave & Sugar* / Don't throw it all away: *Dave & Sugar* / Am I that easy to forget?: *Davis, Skeeter* / Lonesome number one: *Gibson, Don* / There's a story going round: *Gibson, Don & Dottie West* / Shelter of your eyes, The: *Bare, Bobby* / Send me the pillow that you dream on: *Locklin, Hank* / Sweet memories: *Nelson, Willie* / In the ghetto: *Parton, Dolly* / Four strong winds: *Bare, Bobby* / Young love: *James, Sonny* / Early morning rain: *Hamilton, George IV* / End of the world: *Davis, Skeeter* / Careless hands: *West, Dottie* / Green green grass of home: *Hamilton, George IV*.
Double LP . . . . **CR 043**
■ **MC Set** . . . . **CRT 043**
Cambra / May '85.

COUNTRY MOODS.
Tracks: When you're in love with a beautiful woman: *Dr. Hook* / Let your love flow: *Bellamy Brothers* / Ruby don't take your love to town: *Rogers, Kenny* / Good year for the roses: *Costello, Elvis & The Attractions* / Jolene: *Parton, Dolly* / Wichita lineman: *Campbell, Glen* / Don't it make my brown eyes blue: *Gayle, Crystal* / Thing called love, A: *Cash, Johnny* / Ode to Billie Joe: *Gentry, Bobbie* / We're all alone: *Coolidge, Rita* / Blue bayou: *Ronstadt, Linda* / Horse with no name, A: *America* / Crazy: *Cline, Patsy* / Help me make it through the night: *Kristofferson, Kris* / Behind closed doors: *Rich, Charlie* / D.I.V.O.R.C.E.: *Wynette, Tammy* / You're my best friend: *Williams, Don* / It's four in the morning: *Young, Faron* / Here, there and everywhere: *Harris, Emmylou* / Me and Bobby McGee: *Nelson, Willie* / Angel of the morning: *Newton, Juice* / Harper Valley P.T.A.: *Riley, Jeannie C.* / King of the road: *Miller, Roger*.
CD **515 299 2**
LP **515 299 1**
MC **515 299 4**
Polygram T.V / Apr '92 / PolyGram.

COUNTRY MUSIC (South & West).
Tracks: There'll come a time: *Blue Sky Boys* / Wanna be a cowboy's sweetheart: *Montana, Patsy & The Prairie Ramblers* / Rescue from moose river gold mine, The: *Carter, Wilf* / Railroad boomer: *Acuff, Roy & His Smokey Mountain Boys* / Born to lose: *Daffan, Ted & The Texans* / It won't be long: *Choates, Harry* / Chant of the wanderer, The: *Sons Of The Pioneers* / Dark as a dungeon: *Travis, Merle* / Cotton-eyed Joe / Georgia wildcat breakdown: *McMichen, Clayton & His Georgia Wildcats* / Blue yodel no. 11: *Rodgers, Jimmie & Billy Burke* / Sweet fern: *Carter Family* / Dreaming with tears in my eyes / Gospel ship: *Carter Family* / Fais pas ca: *Hackberry Ramblers* / Last round-up, The: *Autry, Gene* / Forgotten soldier boy: *Monroe Brothers* / Ida, sweet as apple cider: *Brown, Milton & The Brownies*.
LP . . . . **NW 287**
New World (USA) / Aug '86 / Pinnacle.

COUNTRY MUSIC.
Tracks: Not Advised.
VHS . . . . **E 1305**
Excalibur (video) / Jun '90.

COUNTRY MUSIC - A NEW TRADITION.
Tracks: I ain't living long like this / Give a little love / Don't be cruel / My baby thinks he's a train / No memories hangin' round / This is the way we make a broken heart / Memphis in the meantime / Blue suede shoes / You ain't woman enough to make my man / Chill factor / We never touch at all / Blue moon of Kentucky.
VHS . . . . **MMGV 022**
MMG Video / Feb '91 / Terry Blood Dist.

COUNTRY MUSIC COUNTRY STYLE.
Tracks: Not Advised.
MC . . . . **AIM 13**
AIM (2) / Feb '83 / Topic Records / Direct Distribution.

COUNTRY MUSIC EMBERS.
Tracks: I saw your face in the moon / Making believe / Excuse me / Keep on the sunny side / I'll make it all up to you / Crying heart blues / Blue bonnets o'er the border / Forever yours / I'll take the chance / You are my sunshine / Hidin' out / Are you from Dixie? / Korea's mountain Northland / Beyond the sunset / Corina, Corina / Prison grey / Heartbreak USA / I'll sail my ship alone / Last date / I saw the light / Mental cruelty / Tattooed lady / It's your world / We need a lot more of Jesus / Window up above / Medley / Au revoir / Charlie's shoes / Wound time can't erase / Your old love letters / Red River Valley / Setting my tears to music / Big big day tomorrow / Back in the race / People / Mama's hungry eyes / Comin' after Jenny / Country girl / I took a memory to lunch / It's a little more like Heaven.
■ **Double LP** . . . . **EMBD 2004**
Ember / '79.

COUNTRY MUSIC EXPRESS VOL.1.
Tracks: Not Advised.
Double LP . . . . **SUCCESS 2038X**
MC Set . . . . **SUCCESS 2038**
Success (1) / Oct '85.

COUNTRY MUSIC FESTIVAL - VOL 2.
Tracks: Distant drums: *Reeves, Jim* / (Never promised you) A rose garden: *West, Dottie* / All I ever need is you: *Reed, Jerry & Chet Atkins* / Taker, The: *Jennings, Waylon* / Just for what I am: *Smith, Connie* / Never ending song of love: *Lee, Dickey* / Four strong winds: *Bare, Bobby* / Morning: *Brown, Jim Ed* / Snowbird: *Davis, Danny* / One tin soldier: *Davis, Skeeter* / Thing called love, A: *Reed, Jerry* / I'm movin' on: *Snow, Hank*.
■ **LP** . . . . **MPK 173**
RCA / '79.

COUNTRY MUSIC FESTIVALS (Wembley Highlights).
Tracks: Not Advised.
MC Set . . . . **DTO 10080**
Ditto / Mar '84 / Pickwick Records.
CD . . . . **PWK 049**
Pickwick / Jan '88 / Pickwick Records.

COUNTRY MUSIC HITS, VOL.1.
Tracks: Green green grass of home / King of the road: *Miller, Roger* / Together again: *Drusky, Roy* / Anymore: *Brewer, Teresa* / Mule train: *Laine, Frankie* / Please help me, I'm falling: *Draper, Rusty* / Gentle on my mind: *Young, Faron* / We know it's over: *Dudley, Dave & O'Donnal, Karen* / Take me home country roads: *Statler Brothers* / Pass me by: *Rodriguez, Johnny* / Singing the blues: *Jones, George* / Easier: *Miller, Roger* / Year that Clayton Delaney died, The: *Hall, Tom T.* / Yes Mr. Peters: *Drusky, Roy & Priscilla Mitchell*.
LP **6463 179**
MC **7145 179**
Mercury (Import) / Jun '83.

COUNTRY MUSIC HOOTENANNY.
Tracks: Opening and introduction / Y'all come: *Henson, Cousin Herb* / Down to the river: *Maddox, Rose* / Your Mother's prayer: *Cagle, Buddy* / Green corn: *Kentucky Colonels* / Blue Ridge Mountain blues: *Bond, Johnny* / Paper of pins: *Lee Maphis, Joe & Rose* / I got mine: *Collins, Tommy* / You took her off my hands: *Campbell, Glen* / Foggy mountain top: *Shepard, Jean* / Silver bells: *Nichols, Roy* / Midnight special: *Travis, Merle* / Comedy routine, A: *Clark, Roy* / Alabama jubilee: *Clark, Roy* / God be with you: *Henson, Cousin Herb* / Hurry back: *Henson, Cousin Herb*.
LP . . . . **SEE 254**
See For Miles / May '89 / Pinnacle.

COUNTRY MUSIC IN THE MODERN ERA.
Tracks: Bouquet of roses: *Arnold, Eddy* / Never no more blues: *Frizzell, Lefty* / Much too young to die: *Price, Ray* / Squid jiggin' ground: *Snow, Hank* / There's poison in your heart: *Wells, Kitty* / Try me one more time: *Tubb, Ernest* / Love letters in the sand: *Cline, Patsy* / Jean's song: *Atkins, Chet* / Mystery train / Little ole you: *Reeves, Jim* / Jimmy Martinez: *Robbins, Marty* / I'm a honky tonk girl: *Lynn, Loretta* / Lorena: *Cash, Johnny* / Don't let her know: *Owens, Buck* / All I love is you: *Miller, Roger* / Sing a sad song: *Haggard, Merle* / Coat of many colours: *Parton, Dolly* / Help me make it through the night: *Kristofferson, Kris*.
LP . . . . **NW 207**
New World (USA) / Aug '86 / Pinnacle.

COUNTRY MUSIC LEGENDS.
Tracks: Not Advised.
MC . . . . **ORC 020**
Orchid Music / Feb '82 / Pinnacle.

■ DELETED

COUNTRY MUSIC ORIGINALS, VOL 1.
Tracks: Silver bells: *Ripley Cotton Choppers* / Blues waltz: *Ripley Cotton Choppers* / Boogie blues: *Peterson, Earl* / In the dark: *Peterson, Earl* / Troublesome waters: *Seratt, Howard* / I must be saved: *Seratt, Howard* / Fallen angel: *Gunter, Hardrock* / Gonna dance all night: *Gunter, Hardrock* / Now she cares no more for me: *Poindexter, Doug* / My kind of carryin' on: *Poindexter, Doug* / Great medical menagerist, The: *Harmonica Frank* / Rockin' chair daddy: *Harmonica Frank* / Just rolling along: *Yelvington, Malcolm* / Drinkin' wine spo-dee-o-dee / Movie Magg: *Perkins, Carl* / Turn around: *Perkins, Carl* / Lonely sweetheart: *Taylor, Bill* / Split personality: *Taylor, Billy & Smokey Joe* / Don't believe: *Rhodes, Slim* / Uncertain love: *Rhodes, Slim* / I've been deceived: *Feathers, Charlie* / Peepin' eyes: *Feathers, Charlie* / Gotta let you go: *Louis, Joe Hill* / Boogie in the park: *Louis, Joe Hill* / Drivin' slow: *London, Johnny* / Flat tire: *London, Johnny* / Got my application baby: *Jackson, Handy* / Trouble will bring you down: *Jackson, Handy* / We all gotta go sometime: *Louis, Joe Hill* / She may be yours but she comes to see me sometimes: *Louis, Joe Hill* / Seems like a million years: *Nix, Willie* / Baker shop boogie: *Nix, Willie* / Easy: *Jimmy & Walter* / Before long: *Jimmy & Walter* / Bear cat: *Thomas, Rufus* / Walking in the rain: *Thomas, Rufus* / Heaven or fire: *Brooks, Dusty* / Lonesome old jail: *Hunt, D.A.* / Greyhound blues: *Hunt, D.A.* / Call me anything but call me: *Big Memphis Marainey* / Baby no no: *Big Memphis Marainey* / Take a little chance: *Deberry, Jimmy* / Time has made a change: *Deberry, Jimmy*.
CD . . . . **CDSUN 2**
Sun / Oct '87 / Charly / Swift.

COUNTRY MUSIC ORIGINALS, VOL 2.
Tracks: Someday you will pay: *Miller Sisters* / You didn't think I would: *Miller Sisters* / There's no right way to do me wrong: *Miller Sisters* / You can tell me: *Miller Sisters* / Hey Porter: *Cash, Johnny* / Cry cry cry: *Cash, Johnny* / Folsom Prison blues: *Cash, Johnny* / So doggon' lonesome: *Cash, Johnny* / Let the juke box keep on playing: *Perkins, Carl* / Gone gone gone: *Perkins, Carl* / Sure to fall: *Perkins, Carl* / Tennessee: *Perkins, Carl* / House of sin, The: *Rhodes, Slim* / Are you ashamed of me: *Rhodes, Slim* / Bad girl: *Rhodes, Slim* / Gonna romp and stomp: *Rhodes, Slim* / How long: *Wimberly, Maggie Sue* / Daydreams come true: *Wimberly, Maggie Sue* / Defrost your heart: *Feathers, Charlie* / Wedding gown of white: *Feathers, Charlie* / No more: *Haggett, Jimmy* / They call our love a sin: *Haggett, Jimmy* / I'd rather be safe than sorry: *Smith, Warren* / Rock 'n' roll ruby: *Smith, Warren*.
CD . . . . **CDSUN 5**
Sun / Apr '88 / Charly / Swift.

COUNTRY MUSIC ORIGINALS, VOL 3.
Tracks: Slow down: *Earls, Jack* / Fool for lovin' you, A: *Earls, Jack* / Get rhythm: *Cash, Johnny* / I walk the line: *Cash, Johnny* / There you go: *Cash, Johnny* / Next in line: *Cash, Johnny* / Home of the blues: *Cash, Johnny* / Give my love to Rose: *Cash, Johnny* / Fiddle bop: *Rhythm Rockers* / Jukebox help me find my baby: *Rhythm Rockers* / Dixie fried: *Perkins, Carl* / I'm sorry I'm not sorry: *Perkins, Carl* / Ten cats down: *Miller Sisters* / Finders keepers: *Miller Sisters* / Feeling low: *Chaffin, Ernie* / Lonesome for my baby: *Chaffin, Ernie* / I'm lonesome: *Chaffin, Ernie* / Laughin' and jokin': *Chaffin, Ernie* / Easy to love: *Self, Mack* / Everyday: *Self, Mack*.
CD . . . . **CDSUN 8**
Sun / Aug '88 / Charly / Swift.

COUNTRY MUSIC ORIGINALS, VOL 4.
Tracks: Big river: *Cash, Johnny* / Guess things happen that way: *Cash, Johnny* / Ways of a woman in love, The: *Cash, Johnny* / Thanks a lot: *Cash, Johnny* / I forgot to remember to forget: *Cash, Johnny* / Ballad of a teenage queen: *Cash, Johnny* / Come in stranger: *Cash, Johnny* / It's just about time: *Cash, Johnny* / Luther played the boogie: *Cash, Johnny* / Katy too: *Cash, Johnny* / Ten years: *Clement, Jack* / Your lover boy: *Clement, Jack* / Wrong: *Clement, Jack* / Black haired man: *Clement, Jack* / Born to lose: *Chaffin, Ernie* / Don't ever leave me: *Chaffin, Ernie* / My love for you: *Chaffin, Ernie* / Miracle of you: *Chaffin, Ernie* / Sweet sweet girl: *Smith, Warren* / Goodbye Mr. Love: *Smith, Warren* / Jump right outa this: *Wheeler, Onie* / Tell 'em off: *Wheeler, Onie*.
CD . . . . **CDSUN 11**
Sun / May '89 / Charly / Swift.

COUNTRY MUSIC ORIGINALS, VOL 5.
Tracks: You tell me: *Cash, Johnny* / Goodbye little darling: *Cash, Johnny* / Straight A's in love: *Cash, Johnny* / I love you because: *Cash, Johnny* / Story of a broken heart, The: *Cash, Johnny* / Down the street to 301: *Cash, Johnny* / Mean eyed cat: *Cash, Johnny* / Port of lonely hearts: *Cash, Johnny* / Oh lonesome me: *Cash, Johnny* / Life goes on: *Cash, Johnny* / Sugartime: *Cash, Johnny* / My treasure: *Cash, Johnny* / Blue train: *Cash, Johnny* / Born to lose: *Cash, Johnny* / Belshazar: *Cash, Johnny* / Wide open road: *Cash, Johnny* / Willie Brown: *Self, Mack* / Mad at you: *Self, Mack* / Guess I'd better go: *Strength, Texas Bill* / Senorita: *Strength, Texas Bill* / Miss Brown: *Houston, David* / Sherry's lips: *Houston, David* / Always on the go: *Stinit, Dane* / Don't knock what you don't understand: *Stinit, Dane* / Sweet country girl: *Stinit, Dane* / That muddy ole river: *Stinit, Dane*.
CD . . . . **CDSUN 13**
Sun / Jan '90 / Charly / Swift.

COUNTRY MUSIC PEOPLE, VOL. 2.
Tracks: Sunny side of the mountain / Montgomery in the rain / Little rock getaway / Jolie blonde / Old cane press / Waiting for a train / Somewhere my love / Cocaine blues / San Antonio blues / Lost in a world / Some old day / Milwaukee blues / It's over / Bottle baby boogie / McKinley's blues / Rocky top.
LP . . . . **SNTF 797**
Sonet / Oct '79 / Swift / C.M. Distribution / Roots Records / Jazz Music / Sonet Records / Cadillac Music / Projection / Wellard Dist. / Hot Shot.

COUNTRY MUSIC SAMPLER.
Tracks: Never been to Spain / Country roads / Dream a little dream / Sunday morning / Hobo Bill / North to Alaska / Sidewalks of Chicago / Hawaiian wedding song / Battle of New Orleans / Orange blossom special / Me and Bobby McGee.
LP . . . . **SFA 050**
Sweet Folk All / May '81 / Cadillac Music / Projection / C.M. Distribution / Wellard Dist. / Impetus Records.

COUNTRY MUSIC STANDARDS, VOL.2.
Tracks: Not Advised.
MC . . . . **BBM 114**
Bibi (Budget Cassettes) / Jan '82.

COUNTRY MUSIC STORY.
Tracks: Not Advised.
MC . . . . **VCA 087**
VFM Cassettes / VFM Children's Entertainment Ltd. / Midland Records / Morley Audio Services.

COUNTRY MUSIC VIDEO MAGAZINE VOL. 3.
Tracks: Not Advised.
■ **VHS** **791 095**
BMG Video / Jul '91.

COUNTRY MUSIC VOL.1.
Tracks: Not Advised.
■ **VHS** **790 453**
BMG Video / Oct '90.

COUNTRY MUSIC VOL.2.
Tracks: Not Advised.
■ **VHS** **790 498**
BMG Video / Jan '91.

COUNTRY MUSIC VOL.3.
Tracks: Not Advised.
VHS **791096**
BMG Video / May '91 / BMG.

COUNTRY MUSIC, VOL.2.
Tracks: Not Advised.
MC . . . . **VCA 003**
VFM Cassettes / Apr '79 / VFM Children's Entertainment Ltd. / Midland Records / Morley Audio Services.

COUNTRY MUSIC,VOL.4 (Take Me Home Country Roads).
Tracks: Not Advised.
MC . . . . **VCA 007**
VFM Cassettes / Jan '85 / VFM Children's Entertainment Ltd. / Midland Records / Morley Audio Services.

COUNTRY MUSIC: CAT'N AROUND.
Tracks: Not Advised.
CD . . . . **KKCD 07**
Krazy Kat / Feb '93 / Hot Shot / C.M. Distribution / Wellard Dist. / Roots Records / Projection / Charly / Jazz Music.

COUNTRY NEGRO JAM SESSIONS.
Tracks: Not Advised.
LP . . . . **ARHOOLIE 2018**
Arhoolie (USA) / May '81 / Pinnacle / Cadillac Music / Swift / Projection / Hot Shot / A.D.A Distribution / Jazz Music.
CD . . . . **ARHCD 372**
Arhoolie (USA) / Jun '93 / Pinnacle / Cadillac Music / Swift / Projection / Hot Shot / A.D.A Distribution / Jazz Music.

COUNTRY NO.1'S VOL 1.
Tracks: Not Advised.
CD Set . . . . **CD 74334**
MC Set . . . . **CK 74334**
RCA / May '90 / BMG.
■ **Double LP** . . . . **CL 74334**
RCA / May '90.

COUNTRY NO.1'S VOL 2.
Tracks: Not Advised.
MC Set . . . . **CK 74335**
RCA / Oct '90 / BMG.
CD Set . . . . **CD 74335**
■ **Double LP** . . . . **CL 74335**
RCA / Oct '90.

COUNTRY NO.1'S VOL 1.
Tracks: Jambalaya / Fraulein / He'll have to go / El pase / Three bells, The / Please help me, I'm falling / Make the world go away / She called me baby / Walk on by / I fall to pieces / Big bad John / My elusive dreams / Still / Ring of fire / King of the road / Stand by your man.
CD . . . . **OG 3508**
LP . . . . **OG 1508**
MC . . . . **OG 2508**
Old Gold / Mar '89 / Pickwick Records.

COUNTRY NO.1'S VOL 2.
Tracks: Is it really over / There goes my everything / Almost persuaded / Harper Valley PTA / D.I.V.O.R.C.E. / Bridge washed out, The / Oh lonesome me / North to Alaska / Boy named Sue, A / All I have to offer you is me / Next in line / Coal miner's daughter / Rose garden / When you're hot you're hot / It's four in the morning / Year that Clayton Delaney died, The.
CD . . . . **OG 3509**
LP . . . . **OG 1509**
MC . . . . **OG 2509**
Old Gold / Mar '89 / Pickwick Records.

COUNTRY NO.1'S VOL 3.
Tracks: Then you can tell me goodbye: *Arnold, Eddy* / Distant drums: *Reeves, Jim* / Folsom Prison blues: *Cash, Johnny* / Hello darlin': *Twitty, Conway* / Happiest girl in the whole USA: *Fargo, Donna* / Chantilly Lace: *Lewis, Jerry Lee* / Is anybody going to San Antone: *Pride, Charley* / Good hearted woman: *Waylon & Willie* / Behind closed doors: *Rich, Charlie* / Satin sheets: *Pruett, Jeannie* / Teddy bear song: *Fairchild, Barbara* / Eleven roses: *Williams, Hank Jr.* / Keep me in mind: *Anderson, Lynn* / I will always love you: *Parton, Dolly* / Convoy: *McCall, C.W.* / Before the next teardrop falls: *Fender, Freddy*.
CD . . . . **OG 3510**
LP . . . . **OG 1510**
MC . . . . **OG 2510**
Old Gold / Mar '89 / Pickwick Records.

COUNTRY NO.1'S VOL 4.
Tracks: Jolene: *Parton, Dolly* / I can help: *Swan, Billy* / (I'd be a) legend in my own time: *Milsap, Ronnie* / Would you lay with me (in a field of stone)?: *Tucker, Tanya* / Hello love: *Snow, Hank* / Wasted days and wasted nights: *Fender, Freddy* / Are you sure Hank done it this way: *Jennings, Waylon* / One piece at a time: *Cash, Johnny* / You're my best friend: *Williams, Don* / Blue eyes crying in the rain: *Nelson, Willie* / She's got you: *Lynn, Loretta* / You've never been this far before: *Twitty, Conway* / We're gonna hold on: *Jones, George & Tammy Wynette* / Abilene: *Hamilton, George IV* / For the good times: *Price, Ray* / I'll be leaving alone: *Pride, Charley*.
CD . . . . **OG 3511**
LP . . . . **OG 1511**
MC . . . . **OG 2511**
Old Gold / Mar '89 / Pickwick Records.

COUNTRY OVATIONS.
Tracks: Not Advised.
CD . . . . **CDCH 390**
MC . . . . **C 390**
SPI Milan (France) / Feb '91 / Silva Screen / PolyGram.

COUNTRY PEOPLE, VOL.2 (Live at the British Country Music Festival).
Tracks: Not Advised.
MC . . . . **BBM 138**
Bibi (Budget Cassettes) / Jan '83.

COUNTRY PIE (Session Artists).
Tracks: Not Advised.
MC . . . . **AM 11**
AIM (2) / Feb '83 / Topic Records / Direct Distribution.

COUNTRY PORTRAITS.
Tracks: Not Advised.
LP . . . . **WW 5057**
Warwick / Jan '79 / Sony / Henry Hadaway Organisation / Multiple Sound Distributors.
MC **1A 220 1583374**
EMI (Holland) / '88.

COUNTRY RAINBOW.
Tracks: Not Advised.
LP Set . . . . **WW 1001**
MC . . . . **WW 10014**
Warwick / Nov '85 / Sony / Henry Hadaway Organisation / Multiple Sound Distributors.

COUNTRY ROCK.
Tracks: Long train runnin': *Doobie Brothers* / Let your love flow: *Bellamy Brothers* / That'll be the day: *Ronstadt, Linda* / Tulsa time: *Williams, Don* / You're only lonely: *Souther, J.D.* / Cover of the Rolling Stone / Weight, The: *Band* / More than a feeling: *Boston* / Bad moon rising: *Creedence Clearwater Revival* / Rocky mountain way: *Walsh, Joe* / Going up the country: *Canned Heat* / Feeling single seeing double: *Harris, Emmylou* / American girl: *McGuinn, Roger* / Hotel ritz: *Axton, Hoyt* / Rose of Cimarron: *Poco* / Sweet home Alabama: *Lynyrd Skynyrd* / Dixie chicken: *Little Feat*.
LP . . . . **WW 5120**
MC . . . . **WW 4 5120**
Warwick / Sep '82 / Sony / Henry Hadaway Organisation / Multiple Sound Distributors.

COUNTRY ROCK SIDES.
Tracks: Your lovin' man: *Taylor, Vernon* / This kind of love: *Taylor, Vernon* / Please be mine (come to me): *Pendarvis, Tracy* / Tonight will be the last night: *Smith, Warren* / So young: *Smith, Ray* / Forever yours: *Smith, Ray* / Me and my rhythm guitar: *Powers, Johnny* / Waiting for you: *Powers, Johnny* / Huh huh oh yeah: *Pendarvis, Tracy* / Love love memory: *Self, Mack* / Dear John: *Smith, Warren* / I'm movin on - golden rocket: *Smith, Warren* / Mystery train: *Taylor, Vernon* / Eight wheel: *Bruce, Edwin*.
LP . . . . **SUN 1031**
Sun / May '85 / Charly / Swift.

COUNTRY ROCKERS LIVE.
Tracks: Motor runnin': *Lewis, Jerry Lee* / Somewhere over the rainbow: *Lewis, Jerry Lee* / Rock 'n' roll medley: *Lewis, Jerry Lee* / Great balls of fire: *Lewis, Jerry Lee* / Rockin' my life away: *Lewis, Jerry Lee* / Whole lotta shakin' goin' on: *Lewis, Jerry Lee* / Mr. Tambourine man: *McGuinn, Roger* / Mr. Spaceman: *McGuinn, Roger* / Turn turn turn: *McGuinn, Roger* / Tiffany queen: *McGuinn, Roger* / So you want to be a rock 'n' roll star: *McGuinn, Roger* / High horse: *Nitty Gritty Dirt Band* / Home again in my heart: *Nitty Gritty Dirt Band* / Long hard ride: *Nitty Gritty Dirt Band* / Partners, brothers, friends: *Nitty Gritty Dirt Band* / Cadillac ranch: *Nitty Gritty Dirt Band* / Dance little Jean: *Nitty Gritty Dirt Band* / Mr. Bojangles: *Nitty Gritty Dirt Band*.
VHS . . . . **PLATV 354**
Platinum Music / Mar '90 / Prism Leisure PLC / Ross Records.

COUNTRY ROCKERS LIVE.
Tracks: Not Advised.
CD **15 403**
MC **79 403**
Laserlight / Aug '91 / TBD / Taylors.

COUNTRY ROCKERS, VOL.1.
Tracks: Not Advised.
LP . . . . **TH 275**
Teenage Heaven / Nov '87.

COUNTRY ROCKERS, VOL.2.
Tracks: Not Advised.
LP . . . . **TH 376**
Teenage Heaven / Nov '87.

COUNTRY ROCKERS, VOL.3.
Tracks: Not Advised.
LP . . . . **TH 576**
Teenage Heaven / Nov '87.

COUNTRY ROCKERS, VOL.4.
Tracks: Not Advised.
LP . . . . **TH 676**
Teenage Heaven / Nov '87.

COUNTRY ROCKERS, VOL.5.
Tracks: Not Advised.
LP . . . . **TH 583**
Teenage Heaven / Nov '87.

COUNTRY ROUND UP.
Tracks: Not Advised.
MC . . . . **AM 64**
VFM Cassettes / VFM Children's Entertainment Ltd. / Midland Records / Morley Audio Services.

COUNTRY ROUND UP VOL.1.
Tracks: Reuben James: *Rogers, Kenny* / I believe: *Laine, Frankie* / You'll always have someone: *Nelson, Willie* / Wasted days & wasted nights: *Fender, Freddy* / Burning memories: *Jennings, Waylon* / Daddy: *Fargo, Donna* / Your tender years: *Jones, George* / Come on in: *Cline, Patsy* / Take these chains from my heart: *Drusky, Roy* / Slippin' away: *Fairchild, Barbara* / Shine on ruby mountain: *Rogers, Kenny* / Ol' blue: *Jackson, Stonewall* / Ragged but right: *Jones, George* / Sticks & stones: *Fargo, Donna* / High noon: *Laine, Frankie* / Last letter, The: *Drusky, Roy* / Wild side of life: *Fender, Freddy* / Should I go home: *Jackson, Stonewall* / Dream baby: *Jennings, Waylon* / Crazy love: *Fairchild, Barbara* / Cry not for me: *Cline, Patsy* / Ruby don't take your love to town: *Rogers, Kenny* / Luckinback Texas: *Drusky, Roy* / Wishful thinking: *Fargo, Donna* / Money: *Jennings, Waylon* / Singin' the blues: *Mitchell, Guy* / Hello walls: *Drusky, Roy* / I've lost at love again: *Cline, Patsy* / Mule train: *Laine, Frankie* / Kaw-liga: *Mandrell, Barbara* / Wedding bells: *Jones, George* / Four in the morning: *Young, Faron* / Blue eyes cryin' in the rain: *Drusky, Roy* / Sally was a good old girl: *Jennings, Waylon* / It wasn't God who made honky tonk angels: *Parton, Dolly* / Touch me: *Nelson, Willie* / Release me: *Mandrell, Barbara* / Heartaches by the number: *Mitchell, Guy* / Shake 'em up roll 'em: *Jackson, Stonewall* / Sunshine: *Rogers, Kenny* / Things have gone to pieces: *Jones, George* / 9,999,999 tears: *Bailey, Razzy* / I let my mind wander: *Nelson, Willie* / Crying: *Jennings, Waylon* / Honky tonk merry go round: *Cline, Patsy* / Ticket to nowhere: *Rogers, Kenny* / Keep off the grass: *Jackson, Stonewall* / Daddy sang bass: *Perkins, Carl* / Ghost, The: *Nelson, Willie* / If you ain't lovin: *Young, Faron*.
MC Set . . . . **TTMC 013**
Tring / Jun '92 / Prism Leisure PLC / Midland Records / Taylors.

COUNTRY ROUND UP VOL.2.
Tracks: Not Advised.
MC . . . . **TTMC 0014**
IMD / Jun '92 / BMG.

COUNTRY ROUND-UP.
Tracks: Not Advised.
MC Set . . . . **M 10144**
Spectrum (1) / Jun '88 / PolyGram.

COUNTRY ROUND-UP.
Tracks: Not Advised.
MC Set . . . . **DTO 10025**
Ditto / Jul '82 / Pickwick Records.

COUNTRY ROUNDUP, VOL.2.
Tracks: Not Advised.
MC . . . . **AIM 20**
AIM (2) / Feb '83 / Topic Records / Direct Distribution.

COUNTRY SCENE.
Tracks: Galveston: *Campbell, Glen* / Don't it make my brown eyes blue: *Gayle, Crystal* / Little bit more, A: *Dr. Hook* / It doesn't matter anymore: *Ronstadt, Linda* / Hey won't you play another somebody done somebody wrong song: *Shepard, Jean* / I don't want to put a hold on you: *Flint, Bernie* / Snowbird: *Murray, Anne* / Gambler, The: *Schlitz, Don* / Ode to Billy Joe: *Gentry, Bobbie* / Blanket on the ground: *Spears, Billie Jo* / You needed me: *Murray, Anne* / If not you: *Dr. Hook* / When will I be loved: *Ronstadt, Linda* / I love you because: *Spears, Billie Jo* / Talking in your sleep: *Gayle, Crystal* / Me and my guitar: *Jennings, Frank Syndicate* / I'll never fall in love again: *Gentry, Bobbie* / Games people play: *South, Joe* / I'm a believer (in a whole lot of lovin'): *Shepard, Jean* / Rhinestone cowboy: *Campbell, Glen*.
MC . . . . **TCMFP 5571**
MFP / Aug '82 / EMI.
■ **LP** . . . . **MFP 5571**
MFP / Aug '82.

COUNTRY SHOWCASE.
Tracks: Not Advised.
MC Set . . . . **DTO 10138**
Ditto / '88 / Pickwick Records.
MC Set . . . . **DTO 10314**
Ditto / '89 / Pickwick Records.

COUNTRY SMASH HITS, VOL. 1.
Tracks: Not Advised.
CD **100 008**
Bridge (MCS Bridge) / '86 / Pinnacle.

COUNTRY SMASH HITS, VOL.2.
Tracks: Not Advised.
CD **100 012**
Bridge (MCS Bridge) / '86 / Pinnacle.

COUNTRY SPECIAL.
Tracks: Queen of hearts: *Locklin, Hank* / Big big day tomorrow: *Clark, Sanford* / People: *Conway, Lee* / Let the teardrops fall: *Cline, Patsy* / Country girl: *Young, Faron* / When love is gone: *Bare, Bobby* / Red haired boy: *Country Deputies* / Fingerprints: *Cline, Patsy* / There goes my love: *Owens, Buck* / I took a memory to lunch: *Bare, Bobby* / You're wasting your time girl: *Jordanaires* / That's the way I feel: *Jones, George*.
LP . . . . **BDL 1006**
Bulldog Records / Jul '82 / President Records / Jazz Music / Wellard Dist. / TKO Records Ltd.

COUNTRY SPECIAL, VOL.1.
Tracks: Blanket on the ground: *Quinn, Brendan* / Me and Bobby McGee: *Morris, Mick* / I fall to pieces: *Little Lynda* / When my blue moon turns to gold again: *Coll, Brian* / Family Bible: *Lynam, Ray* / River road: *Leon* / Blue eyes crying in the rain: *Ely, Pat* / Devil woman: *Hamilton, Joe E.* / 500 miles from home: *Dunphy, Tom* / Drunken driver: *McFarland, Billy*.
MC . . . . **CWIN 101**
Homespun (Ireland) / Feb '83 / Homespun Records / Ross Records / Wellard Dist.

COUNTRY SPECIAL, VOL.2.
Tracks: Four in the morning: *Quinn, Brendan* / Little ole wine drinker me: *Mitchell, Mark* / Red necks, white socks and blue ribbon beer: *Ely, Pat* / Don't read the letter I wrote you: *Chucknees, Margo* / Mother went a walkin: *McFarland, Billy* / Lucille: *Morris, Mike* / Heaven's just a sin away: *Leon* / Happy anniversary: *Tony & Ventures* / She's mine: *Coll, Brian* / Ghost of Jim Bob Wilson: *Colm & Sundowners*.
MC . . . . **CWIN 102**
Homespun (Ireland) / Feb '83 / Homespun Records / Ross Records / Wellard Dist.

COUNTRY SPECIAL, VOL.3.
Tracks: Turn out the light (love me tonight): *Glenn, John* / Lonely hearts club: *Margo* / That's what makes the jukebox play: *Kid Wayne* / Blackboard of my heart: *Williams, Texas T.* / Behind closed doors: *Brendan Quinn* / Wild side of life: *Williams, Texas T.* / San Antonio rose: *Margo* / Some broken hearts never mend: *Colm & Sundowners* / Little country town in Ireland: *Devlin, Sheila* / Deck of cards: *McFarland, Billy*.
MC . . . . **CWIN 103**
Homespun (Ireland) / Feb '83 / Homespun Records / Ross Records / Wellard Dist.

COUNTRY SPIRITUALS.
Tracks: Not Advised.
LP . . . . **SLP 135**
Storyville / Jan '88 / Jazz Music / Wellard Dist. / C.M. Distribution.

COUNTRY STARDUST.
Tracks: Not Advised.
Double LP **6686 038**
MC Set **7523 038**
Mercury (USA) / Nov '81 / Pinnacle.

COUNTRY STARS (CAMBRA).
Tracks: Not Advised.
Double LP . . . . **CR 040**
■ **MC Set** . . . . **CRT 040**
Cambra / Aug '85.

COUNTRY STARS (PICKWICK).
Tracks: I recall a gypsy woman: *Williams, Don* / Always: *Cline, Patsy* / I'm knee deep in loving you: *Tucker, Tanya* / Most beautiful girl, The: *Stampley, Joe* / Sweet dreams: *Lynn, Loretta* / Burning memories: *Jennings, Waylon* / Remember me - I'm the one who loves you: *Haggard, Merle* / Forever young: *Hamilton, George IV* / I believe you: *Mandrell, Barbara* / I'm wanting you: *Robbins, Marty* / Too far: *Gayle, Crystal* / Dream on: *Oak Ridge Boys* / We had it all: *Twitty, Conway*.
CD . . . . **PWK 098**
Pickwick / Feb '89 / Pickwick Records.

COUNTRY STARS AND HITS.
Tracks: Not Advised.
■ **CD** **19417**
Delta (1) / May '87.

COUNTRY STARS OF THE 80'S - LIVE.
Tracks: Not Advised.
CD **15 405**
MC **79 405**
Laserlight / Aug '91 / TBD / Taylors.

COUNTRY STARS OF THE 80'S VOL. 1.
Tracks: Memories to burn: *Watson, Gene* / You're out doin': *Watson, Gene* / Drinkin' my wat back home: *Watson, Gene* / Carmen: *Watson, Gene* / Farewell party: *Watson, Gene* / If I said you had a beautiful body: *Bellamy Brothers* / Redneck girl: *Bellamy Brothers* / Sugar daddy: *Bellamy Brothers* / Let your love flow: *Bellamy Brothers* / San Antonio stroll: *Tucker, Tanya* / Night they drove old Dixie down, The: *Tucker, Tanya* / Texas when I die: *Tucker, Tanya* / Pecos promenade: *Tucker, Tanya* / What's your mama's name: *Tucker, Tanya* / Baby I'm yours: *Tucker, Tanya* / You are so beautiful / Delta dawn: *Tucker, Tanya*.
VHS . . . . **PLATV 356**
Platinum Music / Mar '90 / Prism Leisure PLC / Ross Records.

COUNTRY STARS OF THE 80'S VOL. 2.
Tracks: Hobo heaven: *Boxcar Willie* / Hank Williams medley: *Boxcar Willie* / White freight liner blues: *Bare, Bobby* / 1960's hits medley: *Bare, Bobby* / Tequila Sheila: *Bare, Bobby* / Maria Laveau: *Bare, Bobby* / Whiskey river: *Fender, Freddy* / Mexican rose: *Fender, Freddy* / Secret love: *Fender, Freddy* / Jambalaya: *Fender, Freddy* / Rains came, The: *Fender, Freddy* / Before the next teardrop falls: *Fender, Freddy* / Wasted days and wasted nights: *Fender, Freddy* / How could I love her so much: *Rodriguez, Johnny* / North of the border: *Rodriguez, Johnny* / Love me with all your heart: *Rodriguez, Johnny* / We're over: *Rodriguez, Johnny*.
VHS . . . . **PLATV 357**
Platinum Music / Mar '90 / Prism Leisure PLC / Ross Records.

COUNTRY STARTIME, VOLUMES 1 AND 2.
Tracks: Not Advised.
Double LP . . . . **CMCSB 003**
CMR/Failte / '88 / I & B Records.

COUNTRY STARTRACKS.
Tracks: Love is a rose: *Ronstadt, Linda* / Mockingbird Hill: *Fargo, Donna* / Coat of many colours: *Harris, Emmylou* / Diggy uggy lo: *Kershaw, Doug* / Chokin' king, The: *Gosdin, Vern* / Sweet dreams: *Robbins, Hargus 'Pig'* / Why me: *Montgomery, Melba* / Heartaches by the number: *Smith, Margo* / Sure thing: *Rabbitt, Eddie* / Streets of Laredo: *Allen, Rex Jnr.* / Danger of a stranger, The: *Parton, Stella* / Ruby, don't take your love to town: *Rogers, Kenny & The First Edition* / I can't stop loving you: *Smith, Sammi* / Black mountain rag: *Dillards & Byron Berline* / Here, there and everywhere: *Harris, Emmylou* / My Tennessee mountain home: *Muldaur, Maria* / I really had a ball last night: *Taylor, Carmol* / Our old mansion: *Owens, Buck* / Brand new Tennessee waltz: *Winchester, Jesse* / Texas tornado: *Owens, Buck*.
■ **LP** **K4 58040**
WEA / '77.

COUNTRY STORYTELLERS (I Love Country).
Tracks: Poncho and lefty: *Haggard, Merle & Willie Nelson* / Let him roll: *Bare, Bobby* / He stopped loving her today: *Jones, George* / 16th Avenue: *Dalton, Lacy J* / Weevils in the flour: *Bushwackers* / Engineers don't wave from trains anymore, The: *Scruggs, Earl & Tom T Hall* / Baron, The: *Cash, Johnny* / Seven Spanish Angels: *Charles, Ray & Willie Nelson* / She used to sing on Sunday: *Gatlin, Larry & The Gatlin Brothers* / Country Comfort: *Scruggs, Earl* / Music man: *Blanch, Arthur* / Ride, The: *Coe, David Allan* / El Paso City: *Robbins, Marty* / Red headed stranger: *Nelson, Willie*.
LP . . . . **CBS 54951**
■ **MC** **40 54951**
CBS / Mar '87.

COUNTRY SUNRISE.
Tracks: I saw the light: *Price, Ray* / One day at a time: *Bryant, Anita* / Using things and loving people: *Thomas, B.J.* / Since Jesus came into my heart: *Ives, Burl* / What a friend we have in Jesus / Walk with me the rest of the way: *Payne, Jimmy* / Breaker breaker a sweet Jesus: *Thrasher Brothers* / This little light of mine: *Davis, Jimmie* / Sweetest song, The: *Boone, Pat* / Last Sunday, The: *Cathedrals* / You got the power: *Mills, Walt* / Heavens gonna be a blast: *Jackson, Wanda* / Our little old home town: *Florida Boys* / He is everything: *Clark, Roy* / Jesus is coming very soon: *Bagwell, Wendy & The Sunliters* / I like the old time way: *Ford, Tennessee*

Ernie / I didn't stop dancing: *Wilkin, Marijohn* / I heard my mother call my name in prayer: *Wiseman, Mac* / I'll fly away: *Rogers, Roy & Dale Evans* / This old house: *Hambin, Stuart.*
LP . . . . **TWE 6007**
MC . . . . **TC TWE 6007**
Word 20 / May '85 / Sony.

COUNTRY SUNRISE.
Tracks: Not Advised.
MC Set . . . . **DTO 10137**
Ditto / '88 / Pickwick Records.

COUNTRY SUNRISE & COUNTRY SUNSET.
Tracks: I love a rainy night: *Rabbitt, Eddie* / Blue bayou: *Ronstadt, Linda* / There ain't no good chain gang: *Jennings, Waylon & Johnny Cash* / Applejack: *Parton, Dolly* / I'm so lonesome I could cry: *Boxcar Willie* / Girls, women, and ladies: *Bruce, Ed* / Enough of each other: *Frickie, Janie* / Kaw-liga: *Williams, Hank Jr.* / Dear John: *Shepard, Jean* / Something's burning: *Rogers, Kenny* / Boxer, The: *Harris, Emmylou* / Somewhere over the rainbow: *Lewis, Jerry Lee* / Any which way you can: *Campbell, Glen* / What the world needs now is love: *Spears, Billie Jo* / You light up my life: *Drusky, Roy* / Sometimes when we touch: *Robbins, Marty* / True love ways: *Gilley, Mickey* / He's out of my life: *Mandrell, Barbara* / Good old boys: *Prophet, Ronnie* / Help yourself to me: *Gatlin, Larry* / Mamas don't let your babies grow up to be cowboys: *Nelson, Willie* / She never knew me: *Williams, Don* / Miss the Mississippi: *Gayle, Crystal* / Mr. Bojangles / He'll have to go: *Reeves, Jim* / Sweet dreams: *Cline, Patsy* / Lay lady lay: *Drake, Pete* / I wouldn't want to live: *Powers, Earl* / Dallas: *Ely, Joe* / Do I have to draw a picture? / Last time, The: *Bare, Bobby* / Maybellene: *Jones, George & Johnny Paycheck* / Drivin' my life away: *Rabbitt, Eddie* / Coal miner's daughter: *Lynn, Loretta* / Abilene: *Hamilton, George IV* / Teddy bear: *Kilgore, Merle* / I washed my hands in muddy waters: *Jackson, S.* / Your cheatin' heart: *Williams, Hank* / Faded love: *Kennedy, Blair* / Blue blue day: *Gibson, Don.*
Double LP . . . . **RTL 2059 A/B**
MC Set . . . . **4CRTL 2059 A/B**
Ronco / Sep '81.

COUNTRY SUPERSESSION, THE.
Tracks: With the one who loves you / Scarlet revisited / Face from the past / All I can do is sing / Big city / In my time / New York city / Time will make it right / Place in the country, A / Maybe Monday / Country boy / Man / Demolition zone.
LP . . . . **SDLP 059**
Sundown / Jun '88 / Terry Blood Dist. / Jazz Music / C.M. Distribution.

COUNTRY SUPERSTARS (20 Golden hits).
Tracks: Not Advised.
LP . . . . **MA 261285**
Masters (Holland) / '88.
MC . . . . **MAMC 9261285**
Masters (Holland) / Dec '88.

COUNTRY SUPERSTARS, VOLS. 1 & 2.
Tracks: Gentle on my mind: *Snow, Hank* / Taker, The: *Jennings, Waylon* / Special: *Flatt, Lester & Mac Wiseman* / Misery loves company: *Prophet, Ronnie* / I never promised you a rose garden: *West, Dottie* / Early morning rain: *Hamilton, George IV* / Am I that easy to forget?: *Gibson, Don* / Paper roses: *Smith, Connie* / Oh what a woman: *Reed, Jerry* / Release me: *Locklin, Hank* / Cold hard facts of life: *Wagoner, Porter* / I'm getting better: *Reeves, Jim* / Need in me, The: *Baker, Carroll* / It's four in the morning: *Arnold, Eddy* / Four walls: *Gibson, Don* / Scarlet ribbons: *Brown, Jim Ed* / West Texas highway: *Hamilton, George IV* / Ruby, don't take your love to town: *Jennings, Waylon* / I'm a lover not a fighter: *Davis, Skeeter* / Honey: *Snow, Hank* / Send me the pillow that you dream on: *Locklin, Hank* / Four strong winds: *Bare, Bobby* / Guilty: *Reeves, Jim* / I'm so lonesome I could cry: *Davis, Skeeter.*
Double LP . . . . **SSD 8034 A/B**
MC Set . . . . **SSC 8034 A/B**
Pickwick / Mar '85 / Pickwick Records.

COUNTRY TRAIL.
Tracks: Not Advised.
MC Set . . . . **DTO 10056**
Ditto / Apr '83 / Pickwick Records.

COUNTRY TRUCK FESTIVAL VOL.1.
Tracks: Not Advised.
MC . . . . **SUCCESS 2030**
Success (1) / Oct '86.

COUNTRY TRUCK FESTIVAL VOL.2.
Tracks: Not Advised.
MC . . . . **SUCCESS 2031**
Success (1) / Oct '85.

COUNTRY VOL.2.
Tracks: Not Advised.
VHS . . . . **TVE 1054**
Telstar/Ronco / Jun '93 / BMG.

COUNTRY WAY, THE.
Tracks: Too hard to say I'm sorry / Little folks, The / Crystal chandeliers / Act naturally / Does my ring hurt your finger / Mama don't cry for me / Day the world stood still, The / Gone, on the other hand / You can tell the world / I'll wander back to you / Life turned her that way / I threw away the rose.
■ **LP** . . . . **NL 89997**
RCA / Jan '87.
■ **MC** . . . . **NK 89997**
RCA / Jan '87.

COUNTRY'S GREATEST HITS.
Tracks: Lucille: *Rogers, Kenny* / Stand by your man: *Wynette, Tammy* / By the time I get to Phoenix: *Campbell, Glen* / Ode to Billy Joe: *Gentry, Bobbie* / Always on my mind: *Nelson, Willie* / Honey: *Goldsboro, Bobby* / Rose garden: *Anderson, Lynn* / Boy named Sue, A: *Cash, Johnny* / Don't it make my brown eyes blue / Funny how time slips away: *Nelson, Willie* / Games people play / Jolene: *Parton, Dolly* / Take me home country roads: *Denver, John* / Bobby McGee: *Kristofferson, Kris* / Oh lonesome me: *Gibson, Don* / Long long time: *Rondstadt, Linda* / Dukes of Hazzard (theme from): *Jennings, Waylon* / He'll have to go: *Reeves, Jim* / Snowbird: *Murray, Anne* / Behind closed doors: *Rich, Charlie* / I believe in you: *Williams, Don* / Blanket on the ground: *Spears, Billie Jo.*
MC . . . . **CGHC 1**
Island / Nov '85 / PolyGram.
■ **LP** . . . . **CGH 1**
Island / Nov '85.

COUNTRY'S GREATEST HITS.
Tracks: I walk the line: *Cash, Johnny* / Stand by your man: *Wynette, Tammy* / Okie form Muskogie: *Haggard, Merle* / You're my best friend: *Williams, Don* / Lucille: *Rogers, Kenny* / It's four in the morning: *Young, Faron* / Harper Valley P.T.A.: *Riley, Jeannie C.* / Most beautiful girl, The: *Rich, Charlie* / Don't it make my brown eyes blue: *Gayle, Crystal* / Blue skies: *Nelson, Willie* / Blanket on the ground: *Spears, Billie Jo* / Rose Marie: *Whitman, Slim* / Coalminer's daughter: *Lynn, Loretta* / Devil woman: *Robbins, Marty.*
VHS . . . . **TVE 1020**
Telstar Video / Mar '91 / BMG.

COUNTRY'S GREATEST HITS.
Tracks: Not Advised.
DCC . . . . **DCC 8055**
MiniDisc . . . . **MDISC 805**
Disky Communications Ltd / Apr '93 / Swift / Terry Blood Dist.

COUNTRY'S GREATEST HITS.
Tracks: Lucille / By the time I get to Phoenix / Always on my mind / Rose garden / Don't it make my brown eyes blue / Games people play / Behind closed doors / Coat of many colours / I ain't living long like this / Rose Marie / Devil woman / Stand by your man / Ode to Billy Joe / Honey / Boy named Sue, A / Funny how time slips by / He'll have to go / Blanket on the ground / On lonesome me / Rhinestone cowboy / We love each other / Mason Dixon line.
■ **LP** . . . . **STAR 2433**
Telstar/Ronco / Sep '90.
■ **CD** . . . . **TCD 2433**
Telstar/Ronco / Sep '90.
■ **MC** . . . . **STAC 2433**
Telstar/Ronco / Sep '90.

COWBOY SONGS.
Tracks: Not Advised.
■ **MC** **4510094**
CBS / '88.

COWBOYS.
Tracks: Mama's don't let your babies grow up to be cowboy / All around cowboy / Jo and the cowboy / Bull rider / Cosmic cowboy / Sweetwater Texas / Don't take your guns to town / Texas lullaby / Cowboys ain't supposed to cry / Gambler, The.
■ **LP** . . . . **CBS 84693**
CBS / May '81.

COWBOYS AND TRUCKS RIDING HARD.
Tracks: Not Advised.
LP . . . . **GT 0082**
Gusto (USA) / Mar '88.

COZY LABEL, THE.
Tracks: Hot guitars: *Anderson, Keith* / I need a hit: *Anderson, Keith* / She's gone: *Vandergift Bros.* / Sittin' here a' cryin': *Vandergift Bros.* / Ambridge boogie: *Brooks, Dale* / I can read between the lines: *Lambert, Bruce* / Let's rock: *Watson, Johnny* / I'm not crazy: *Watson, Johnny* / Mexican rock: *Lewis, Dorse* / Hot rod boogie: *Lewis, Dorse* / Baby I don't mind: *Jones, E. & V. Dickerson* / Rosie: *Lester, Butch* / One little teardrop too late: *Plain Slim* / Popcorn boogie: *Hank The Cowhand* / She's a hum-dinger: *Hank The Cowhand* / Fan it and cool it: *Hank The Cowhand.*
LP . . . . **WLP 8823**
White Label (Germany) / '87 / Pinnacle / Bear Family Records (Germany) / CSA Tell Tapes.

CRAZY ALLIGATOR.
Tracks: Crazy alligator: *Russ, Irvin* / My imagination: *Russ, Irvin* / Speed limit: *Twisters* / Countdown 1, 2, 3: *Twisters* / Bandstand rocket: *Twisters* / Kat walk: *Twisters* / One way ticket: *Lumpkin, Bobby* / Your conscience: *Lumpkin, Bobby* / That Jim: *Beers, Mackey* / Lorilee: *Beers, Mackey* / Crying over you: *Dale, Larry* / Wombie zombie: *Taylor, Billy* / I'm long gone: *Belew, Carl* / Gertrude: *Neal, Meredith* / Lookie, lookie, lookie: *Grand, K.C..*
LP . . . . **WLP 8877**
White Label (Germany) / Feb '85 / Pinnacle / Bear Family Records (Germany) / CSA Tell Tapes.

CREAM OF COUNTRY.
Tracks: Not Advised.
LP . . . . **BRA 1015**
Big R / Nov '81 / Pinnacle.

CUCA RECORDS STORY, VOL 1.
Tracks: I'm movin' on: *Hiorns, Dick* / Frankie's rock: *Tremain, Willie Thunderbirds* / Midnight express: *Tremain, Willie Thunderbirds* / You didn't listen: *Kennedy, Dave* / Rotation: *Six Shooters* / Don't you just know it?: *Six Shooters* / Weary blues: *Don & The Dominoes* / Just let me be: *Don & The Dominoes* / Rockin' Abe: *Tranes, Nigh* / Miami road: *Phillipson, Larry Lee* / If you are a coward: *Phillipson, Larry Lee* / Say mama: *Rock-a-Fellas* / Reaction: *Rock-a-Fellas* / Peenin' and hidin': *Kennedy, Dave* / Rocker: *Montereys* / Rockin' fool: *Montereys.*
LP . . . . **WLP 8847**
White Label (Germany) / Jul '87 / Pinnacle / Bear Family Records (Germany) / CSA Tell Tapes.

CUCA RECORDS STORY, VOL 2.
Tracks: Like now: *Squires, Bud* / Spin out: *Squires, Bud* / Orbit rock: *Orbits* / Molly and ten brooks: *Sun, Jimmy* / Wasted: *Zakins* / Trackin': *Zakins* / Jitterbug Joe: *Nighthawks* / Hawk, The: *Nighthawks* / That ain't so: *Sperry, Steve* / What's all this?: *Mattice, Bob* / Safari: *Mattice, Bob* / Kaw-liga: *Mattice, Bob* / I'm wondering now: *Phillipson, Larry Lee* / Muleskinner: *Kannon, Ray* / This way out: *Furys* / St. Louis blues: *Furys.*
LP . . . . **WLP 8848**
White Label (Germany) / Jul '87 / Pinnacle / Bear Family Records (Germany) / CSA Tell Tapes.

CUCA RECORDS STORY, VOL 3.
Tracks: Little Boy Blue: *Blihovde, Marv* / Bye bye baby: *Blihovde, Marv* / White lightning: *Blihovde, Marv* / Nobody's darlin' but mine: *Blihovde, Marv* / Sweet little wife: *Blihovde, Marv* / Sensation: *Blihovde, Marv* / Ramblin' on: *Vigilantes* / Badger, The: *Vigilantes* / Cherokee song: *Miller, Dick* / I might have known: *Teen Kings* / Told ya, little baby: *Teen Tones* / Borderline: *Teen Tones* / St. Louis: *Smith, Bobby* / Sitting on top of the world: *Hodge, Bobby* / Sidewinder, The: *Vibratones* / White lightnin' effect: *Lavenders* / War party: *Catalinas* / Rocky road blues: *Muleskinners* / Sands of Arabia: *Teen Tones.*
LP . . . . **WLP 8849**
White Label (Germany) / Jul '87 / Pinnacle / Bear Family Records (Germany) / CSA Tell Tapes.

D

DISCOVER NEW COUNTRY.
Tracks: Not Advised.
Double LP . . . . **DNC 1**
MC . . . . **DNCK 1**
Starblend / Jul '86.

DON'T YOU STEP ON MY BLUE SUEDE SHOES (Sun's Greatest Hits).
Tracks: Whole lotta shakin' goin' on: *Lewis, Jerry Lee* / Great balls of fire: *Lewis, Jerry Lee* / High school confidential: *Lewis, Jerry Lee* / Matchbox: *Perkins, Carl* / Blue suede shoes: *Perkins, Carl* / Honey don't: *Perkins, Carl* / I walk the line: *Cash, Johnny* / Folsom Prison blues: *Cash, Johnny* / Whirlwind: *Rich, Charlie* / Rebound: *Rich, Charlie* / We wanna boogie: *Burgess, Sonny* / Red hot: *Riley, Billy Lee* / Mona Lisa: *Mann, Carl* / After the hop: *Pinkney, Bill* / Miss Froggie: *Smith, Warren.*
LP . . . . **CR 30119**
MC . . . . **CFK 1003**
Sun / Jul '81 / Charly / Swift.

DUELLING BANJOS (20 Country and Western Bluegrass Hits).
Tracks: Duelling banjos / Eighth of January / Farewell blues / Pony Express / Mountain dew / Old Joe Clark / Little Maggie / Buffalo girls / Rawhide / Earl's breakdown / Reuben's train / Fire on the mountain / Hard ain't it hard / Movin' on / Foot tappin' / Riding the waves / End of a dream / Eight more miles to Louisville / Shuckin' the corn / You're looking at country.
MC . . . . **AIM 120**
AIM (2) / Sep '83 / Topic Records / Direct Distribution.
MC . . . . **AM 120**
VFM Cassettes / '87 / VFM Children's Entertainment Ltd. / Midland Records / Morley Audio Services.
LP . . . . **PLAT 02**
MC . . . . **PLAC 02**
Platinum Music / Dec '88 / Prism Leisure PLC / Ross Records.

E

EARLY DAYS OF BLUEGRASS 2.
Tracks: Not Advised.
LP . . . . **ROUNDER 1014**
Rounder / '88 / Projection / Roots Records / Swift / C.M. Distribution / Topic Records / Jazz Music / Hot Shot / A.D.A Distribution / Direct Distribution.

EARLY DAYS OF BLUEGRASS 3.
Tracks: Not Advised.
LP . . . . **ROUNDER 1015**
Rounder / '88 / Projection / Roots Records / Swift / C.M. Distribution / Topic Records / Jazz Music / Hot Shot / A.D.A Distribution / Direct Distribution.

EARLY DAYS OF BLUEGRASS 4.
Tracks: Not Advised.
LP . . . . **ROUNDER 1016**
Rounder / '88 / Projection / Roots Records / Swift / C.M. Distribution / Topic Records / Jazz Music / Hot Shot / A.D.A Distribution / Direct Distribution.

EARLY DAYS OF BLUEGRASS 5.
Tracks: Not Advised.
LP . . . . **ROUNDER 1017**
Rounder / '88 / Projection / Roots Records / Swift / C.M. Distribution / Topic Records / Jazz Music / Hot Shot / A.D.A Distribution / Direct Distribution.

EARLY DAYS OF BLUEGRASS 6.
Tracks: Not Advised.
LP . . . . **ROUNDER 1018**
Rounder / '88 / Projection / Roots Records / Swift / C.M. Distribution / Topic Records / Jazz Music / Hot Shot / A.D.A Distribution / Direct Distribution.

EARLY DAYS OF BLUEGRASS 7.
Tracks: Not Advised.
LP . . . . **ROUNDER 1019**
Rounder / '88 / Projection / Roots Records / Swift / C.M. Distribution / Topic Records / Jazz Music / Hot Shot / A.D.A Distribution / Direct Distribution.

EARLY DAYS OF BLUEGRASS 8.
Tracks: Not Advised.
LP . . . . **ROUNDER 1020**
Rounder / '88 / Projection / Roots Records / Swift / C.M. Distribution / Topic Records / Jazz Music / Hot Shot / A.D.A Distribution / Direct Distribution.

EARLY DAYS OF BLUEGRASS 9.
Tracks: Not Advised.
LP . . . . **ROUNDER 1022**
Rounder / '88 / Projection / Roots Records / Swift / C.M. Distribution / Topic Records / Jazz Music / Hot Shot / A.D.A Distribution / Direct Distribution.

EARLY ROCKIN' IN ARKANSAS.
Tracks: Not Advised.
LP . . . . **WLP 8947**
White Label (Germany) / '88 / Pinnacle / Bear Family Records (Germany) / CSA Tell Tapes.

EAST VIRGINIA: NEW SOUNDS, NEW SEASONS.
Tracks: Not Advised.
LP . . . . **ROUNDER 0114**
Rounder / '88 / Projection / Roots Records / Swift / C.M. Distribution / Topic Records / Jazz Music / Hot Shot / A.D.A Distribution / Direct Distribution.

EAST VIRGINIA: PATHWAYS OF TRADITION.
Tracks: Not Advised.
LP . . . . **ROUNDER 0134**
Rounder / '88 / Projection / Roots Records / Swift / C.M. Distribution / Topic Records / Jazz Music / Hot Shot / A.D.A Distribution / Direct Distribution.

EASYRIDING: COUNTRY & WESTERN.
Tracks: Jambalaya: *Lewis, Jerry Lee* / Detroit City: *Drusky, Roy* / King of the road: *Miller, Roger* / Six days on the road: *Dudley, Dave* / Battle of New Orleans: *Drusky, Roy* / You can have her: *Rich, Charlie* / Ring of fire: *Drusky, Roy* / Rawhide: *Young, Faron* / Jackson: *Lewis, Jerry Lee & Linda Gail Lewis* / Green, green grass of home: *Miller, Roger* / Mule-skinner blues: *Draper, Rusty* / Shutters and boards: *Wallace, Jerry* / More and more: *Draper, Rusty* / Save the last dance for me: *Young, Faron* / North to Alaska: *Lewis, Jerry Lee* / Don't let the stars get in your eyes: *Dudley, Dave* / I washed my face in the morning dew / Let's do what's right even if it's wrong: *Drusky, Roy & Priscilla Mitchell* / Chug a lug: *Miller, Roger* / Sweet thang: *Lewis, Jerry Lee & Linda Gail Lewis* / Truck drivin' son of a gun: *Dudley, Dave* / Foggy mountain breakdown: *Flatt, Lester & Earl Scruggs*.
■ **LP** . . . . **KNLP 11004**
Easyriding / Jul '88.
■ **MC** . . . . **KNMC 11004**
Easyriding / Jul '88.

EASYRIDING: ROCK 'N' ROLL KINGS.
Tracks: Great balls of fire: *Lewis, Jerry Lee* / Let the four winds blow: *Domino, Fats* / Donna: *Wilde, Marty* / Let the good times roll: *Jordan, Louis* / Hucklebuck, The: *Bell, Freddy & The Bellboys* / Long tall Sally: *Lewis, Jerry Lee* / Rock & roll: *Prysock, Red* / I'm on fire: *Lewis, Jerry Lee* / Caldonia: *Jordan, Louis* / Whole lotta shakin' goin' on / What'd I say: *Lewis, Jerry Lee* / Handclappin': *Prysock, Red* / Blueberry Hill: *Domino, Fats* / Good golly Miss Molly: *Lewis, Jerry Lee* / Please don't leave me: *Domino, Fats* / Landy Miss Clandy / Breathless: *Lewis, Jerry Lee* / Giddy up a ding dong: *Bell, Freddy & The Bellboys* / Jambalaya: *Domino, Fats* / Hound dog: *Bell, Freddy & The Bellboys* / Corina Corina: *Lewis, Jerry Lee* / Lawdy Miss Clawdy: *Prysock, Red*.
■ **LP** . . . . **KNLP 11002**
Easyriding / Jul '88.
■ **MC** . . . . **KNMC 11002**
Easyriding / Jul '88.

EL PRIMITIVO (American Rock'n'Roll & Rockabilly).
Tracks: Save it: *Robbins, Mel* / Oh yeah: *Jeffrey, Wally* / I wanna dance all night: *Wiley, Chuck* / It's love: *Wiley, Chuck* / Bandstand: *Nash, Cliff* / Times is tough: *Wiley, Chuck* / Are you with me: *Robbins, Mel* / I wanna shake it: *Hobock, Curtis* / I love you dearly: *Hurt, Jimmy & the Del Rio's* / Thump!, The: *Embers* / Baby moon: *Smith, Herbie* / Best dressed beggar in town: *Turner, Buck* / Door to door: *Wiley, Chuck* / Uh oh: *Imps* / I walked all night: *Embers* / Explosion: *Nash, Cliff* / Out of gas: *Howard, Chuck* / Tell me baby: *Nash, Cliff* / Why worry about me: *Wiley, Chuck* / That'll get it: *Imps* / No time for sister: *Nash, Cliff* / I love you so much: *Wiley, Chuck* / Jenny Lou: *Nash, Cliff*.
CD . . . . **CDCHD 473**
Ace / Aug '93 / Pinnacle / Hot Shot / Jazz Music / Complete Record Co. Ltd.

ELVIS PRESLEY'S AMERICA.
Tracks: Not Advised.
VHS . . . . **MMGV 029**
MMG Video / '91 / Terry Blood Dist.

ENCHANTING WORLD OF COUNTRY MUSIC.
Tracks: Not Advised.
MC . . . . **AIM 73**
AIM (2) / Feb '83 / Topic Records / Direct Distribution.

ENGLISH COUNTRY SIDE, THE.
Tracks: You all come / Find out what's happening / Love's gonna live here / I love you drops / I washed my face in the morning dew / Goin' home / Great snow man, The / Blue is my only room / Release me / Sweet dreams / Six days on the road.
■ **LP** . . . . **RD 7918**
RCA / Oct '64 / BMG.

ESSENTIAL COUNTRY.
Tracks: Not Advised.
■ **LP** . . . . **KNLP 15004**
Replay / May '89.
CD . . . . **KNCD 15004**
■ **MC** . . . . **KNMC 15004**
Replay / May '89.

F

FEDERAL ROCKABILLIES.
Tracks: Not Advised.
LP . . . . **BID 8041**
Bellaphon / Jul '88 / New Note.

FEEL LIKE ROCKIN'.
Tracks: Rockin' love: *Mann, Carl* / Some enchanted evening: *Mann, Carl* / Take these chains from my heart: *Mann, Carl* / Hey baby doll: *Bush, Eddie* / No more cryin' the blues: *Alton & Jimmy* / Tied to your apron string: *Hoback, Curtis* / I fell in love: *Cooke, Ken* / Walkin' with my best friend: *Hoback, Curtis* / Apron strings: *Hoback, Curtis* / Crazy baby: *Cooke, Ken* / I feel in love: *Cook, Ken* / Lordy hoody: *Blake, Tommy* / Feel like rockin': *Parchman, Kenny* / Tennessee zip: *Parchman, Kenny* / Love crazy baby: *Parchman, Kenny* / You call everybody darlin': *Parchman, Kenny* / Treat me right: *Parchman, Kenny*.
LP . . . . **SUN 1038**
Sun / Mar '87 / Charly / Swift.

FEELIN' COUNTRY: VOL 1.
Tracks: Daddy sang bass / Just out of reach / Some other time / You made me a fool / Where love used to live / Help me make it through the night / White lightning / Double dare / He really must have loved you / Let the teardrops fall / Sunday morning coming down / Moment isn't very long, A / You win again / Tennessee waltz / It's four in the morning / Living in a house full of love.
LP . . . . **CBR 1026**
MC . . . . **KCBR 1026**
Premier (Sony) / Jun '85 / Sony / Pinnacle.

FEELIN' COUNTRY: VOL 2.
Tracks: Walk through this world with me / Ease the want in me / Cold, cold heart / There goes my everything / Last thing on my mind / Enough to make a grown man cry / Have I been coming too long? / Hey good lookin' / All the time / You make me what I am today / I can't help it (if I'm still in love with you) / It could have been / Moment isn't very long, A / Good year for the roses, A.
LP . . . . **CBR 1043**
MC . . . . **KCBR 1043**
Premier (Sony) / Jun '85 / Sony / Pinnacle.

FERNWOOD ROCKABILLIES VOL.1.
Tracks: Not Advised.
LP . . . . **REDITA 118**
Redita (Holland) / Oct '88 / Swift.

FERNWOOD ROCKABILLIES VOL.2.
Tracks: Not Advised.
LP . . . . **REDITA 119**
Redita (Holland) / Oct '88 / Swift.

FIDDLE & BANJO BLUEGRASS.
Tracks: Low down Billy / Talkin' fiddlin' blues / Ole Joe Clark / Party time / Fire in the mountain / Billy low ground / 8th of January / Baby Sue / Runnin' wild / Banjo pickin' time / Orange blossom hoedown / Cacklin' hen, The / Feeling bad / Wildwood flower / Weepin' willow / Mockingbird, The / String time / Honeysuckle / Lonesome road.
LP . . . . **ARN 33717**
MC . . . . **ARN 433717**
Arion / Aug '83 / Discovery.

FIDDLE TUNES FOR BANJO.
Tracks: Not Advised.
LP . . . . **ROUNDER 0124**
MC . . . . **ROUNDER 0124C**
Rounder / '88 / Projection / Roots Records / Swift / C.M. Distribution / Topic Records / Jazz Music / Hot Shot / A.D.A Distribution / Direct Distribution.

FIDDLE TUNES VOL.2.
Tracks: Not Advised.
LP . . . . **ROUNDER 0058**
Rounder / '88 / Projection / Roots Records / Swift / C.M. Distribution / Topic Records / Jazz Music / Hot Shot / A.D.A Distribution / Direct Distribution.

FIRST LADIES OF COUNTRY.
Tracks: Don't it make my brown eyes blue: *Gayle, Crystal* / Snowbird: *Anderson, Lynn* / Ode to Billy Joe: *Wynette, Tammy* / Dumb blonde: *Parton, Dolly* / Delta dawn: *Tucker, Tanya* / 57 chevrolet: *Spears, Billie Jo* / No charge: *Wynette, Tammy* / It's only make believe: *Anderson, Lynn* / Fuel to the flame: *Parton, Dolly* / Stand by your man: *Wynette, Tammy* / Blanket on the ground: *Spears, Billie Jo* / Divorce: *Wynette, Tammy* / Wrong road again: *Gayle, Crystal* / Honey come back: *Anderson, Lynn* / You are so beautiful: *Tucker, Tanya* / Your ole handy man: *Parton, Dolly* / Little bit more, A: *Anderson, Lynn* / Let me be there: *Tucker, Tanya* / Rose garden: *Anderson, Lynn*.
■ **LP** **10018**
CBS / May '80.
MC **40 32235**
CBS / '84 / Sony.
■ **LP** **32235**
CBS / '84.
CD . . . . **CD 32235**
Columbia / Mar '91 / Sony.

FIRST LADIES OF COUNTRY MUSIC.
Tracks: Snowbird: *Murray, Anne* / Different drum: *Ronstadt, Linda* / Hand that rocks the cradle, The: *Colter, Jessi* / Simple little words: *Various original artists* / Coat of many colours: *Peppers, Nancy* / Reuben James: *Jackson, Wanda* / Pinkerton's flowers, The: *Montgomery, Melba* / Someday soon: *Gayle, Crystal* / 57 chevrolet: *Spears, Billie Jo* / Get on my love train: *La Costa* / Ode to Billy Joe: *Gentry, Bobbie* / Queen of the house: *Miller, Jody* / Delta dawn: *Reddy, Helen* / Lesson in leavin', A: *West, Dottie* / Mercy: *Shepard, Jean* / Angel of the morning: *Newton, Juice*.
■ **LP** . . . . **MFP 41 5687-1**
MFP / Sep '84.

FIRST LADIES OF COUNTRY MUSIC.
Tracks: Not Advised.
MC . . . . **AM 67**
VFM Cassettes / '88 / VFM Children's Entertainment Ltd. / Midland Records / Morley Audio Services.

FIRST LADIES OF COUNTRY, VOL.II.
Tracks: But love me / Other side of me, The / Your good girl's gonna go bad / Would you lay with me (in a field of stone) / Takin' it easy / Blue side, The / When I fall in love / My elusive dreams / Loving arms / Wrap your love all around your man / Half the way / Womanhood / Best of my love / Enough of each other / Hard times / Angel in your arms / Miss the Mississippi and you / Pass me by / Help me make it through the night / Sea of heartbreak.
■ **LP** . . . . **CBS 85442**
CBS / Jan '82.

FOUR STAR COUNTRY.
Tracks: Not Advised.
LP . . . . **NE 1278**
MC . . . . **CE 2278**
K-Tel / Aug '85 / I & B Records / C.M. Distribution / Arabesque Ltd. / Mono Distributors (Jersey) Ltd. / Prism Leisure PLC / PolyGram / Ross Records / Prism Leisure PLC.

FRIENDS AGAIN.
Tracks: I recall a gypsy woman: *Williams, Don* / Jolene: *Parton, Dolly* / Right time of the night: *Warnes, Jennifer* / I'll never fall in love again: *Gentry, Bobbie* / Gentle on my mind: *Campbell, Glen* / Why have you left the one you left me for?: *Gayle, Crystal* / Sexy eyes / It doesn't matter anymore: *Ronstadt, Linda* / Desperado: *Spears, Billie Jo* / Lady: *Rogers, Kenny* / Coat of many colours: *Parton, Dolly* / Stay young: *Williams, Don* / Rhinestone cowboy: *Campbell, Glen* / Talking in your sleep: *Gayle, Crystal* / Little bit more, A / When will I be loved?: *Ronstadt, Linda* / Your good girl's gonna go bad: *Spears, Billie Jo* / All I have to do is dream: *Campbell, Glen & Bobbie Gentry*.
LP . . . . **LPIMP 8**
MC . . . . **TCIMP 8**
Impression / Nov '84 / Pinnacle.

G

GENTLEMEN OF C & W.
Tracks: Not Advised.
CD . . . . **ENT CD 211**
Entertainers / Sep '87.

GEORGIA MUSIC.
Tracks: Not Advised.
LP . . . . **WLP 8936**
White Label (Germany) / Nov '88 / Pinnacle / Bear Family Records (Germany) / CSA Tell Tapes.

GET HOT OR GO HOME (Vintage RCA Rockabillies 1956-59).
Tracks: Duck tail: *Clay, Joe* / Sixteen chicks: *Clay, Joe* / Doggone it: *Clay, Joe* / Goodbye goodbye: *Clay, Joe* / Slipping out & sneaking in: *Clay, Joe* / Get on the right track: *Clay, Joe* / You look that good to me: *Clay, Joe* / Cracker Jack: *Clay, Joe* / Did you mean Jelly Bean (what you said cabbage head): *Clay, Joe* / Ooh-eee: *Cartey, Ric* / Heart throb: *Cartey, Ric* / I wancha to know: *Cartey, Ric* / Mellow down easy: *Cartey, Ric* / My babe: *Cartey, Ric* / Two tone shoes: *Homer & Jethro* / Catty Town: *King, Pee Wee* / Sugar sweet: *Houston, David* / Honky tonk mind (woman I need): *Blake, Tommy & the rhythm rebels* / All night long: *Blake, Tommy & the rhythm rebels* / Now stop: *Carson, Martha* / Love me to pieces: *Martin, Janis* / Two long years: *Martin, Janis* / All right baby: *Martin, Janis* / Chicken house: *Rich, Dave* / Teen Billy Baby: *Sprouts* / Don't bug me baby: *Allen, Milt* / Rainbow Doll: *Dell, Jimmy* / It ain't right: *Terry, Gordon* / Let's get goin': *Morgan Twins* / Almost eighteen: *Orbison, Roy* / Little boy blue: *Johnson, Hoyt*.
CD . . . . **CMFCD 014**
MC Set . . . . **CMFC 014**
Country Music Foundation / Jan '93 / Topic Records / Direct Distribution.

GET WEAVING - THE CAJUN/ZYDECO COLLECTION.
Tracks: Not Advised.
CD . . . . **GWD 02CD**
Weaving Records / Aug '93 / ACD Trading Ltd. / A.D.A Distribution.

GET WITH THE BEAT - THE MAR-VEL' MASTERS (A Lost Decade of American Rock & Roll).
Tracks: Get with the beat: *Nix, Billy* / Honky tonkin' rhythm: *Sisco, Bobby* / Come on let's go: *Dallis, Chuck* / Jump baby jump: *Carter, Harry* / My friend: *Dallis, Chuck* / Seven lonely days: *Carter, Ginny* / Out of the picture: *Bradshaw, Jack* / I'm settin' you free: *Allen, Harold & J T Watts* / I need some lovin': *Allen, Harold* / Heartsick and blue: *Wall, Rem* / Count down: *Smith, Lorenzo* / Hot lips baby: *Duncan, Herbie* / Ha ha hey hey: *Kimbrough, Mel* / Would it matter at all: *Gatlin, Jim* / Boogie woogie baby of mine: *Burton, Bob* / I don't want you: *Carter, Harry* / Basil Smith stomp: *Smith, Basil* / Way you're treating me, The: *Gatlin, Jim* / Forty acres of my heart: *Burton, Bob* / Panhandle rag: *Durbin, Ronnie* / A-sleepin' at the foot: *Ashford, Shorty* / Let me love you: *Hall, Billy* / Ronnie's boogie: *Durbin, Ronnie* / Tired of rocking: *Burton, Bob* / Itchy feet: *Jennings, Rex* / Sweet Lucy: *Ashford, Shorty*.
CD . . . . **RCD 20126**
MC . . . . **DOCS 9126**
Rykodisc / Feb '93 / Revolver-APT.

GIRLS ARE ROCKIN', THE.
Tracks: Big midnight special: *Armstrong, Joan & The Shakers* / Rock, baby, rock: *Tennant, Barbara* / He's my man: *Gunter, Launa* / Big Daddy Rabbit: *Bennett, Barbara* / Ballin' keen: *Lee, Sandy* / Jackpot: *Fredericks, Dolores* / Baby doll: *Wells, Ardis* / Real gone: *Acorn Sisters* / You treat me like a baby: *Lovett, Glenda* / Let's trade a little: *Bryant, Audrey* / Needle in a haystack: *West, Penny* / Leaving you this time: *Roy, Thelma* / Hey good lookin': *Rogers, Betty* / Jukebox on the moon: *Millay, Ginny* / Lover man: *Sherman, Nancy* / Baby oh honey: *Emerson, Jeannie* / What for?: *Dolly & The Deans*.
LP . . . . **WLP 8919**
White Label (Germany) / Aug '87 / Pinnacle / Bear Family Records (Germany) / CSA Tell Tapes.

GOD LOVES COUNTRY MUSIC.
Tracks: God loves country music / O Lord I thank you / Servant of all / If we walk in the light / Draw me nearer / Freely, freely / Psalm 5 / From the rising of the sun / Come let us worship and bow down / Create in me a clean heart / Christian life, The.
LP . . . . **MM 0080**
MC . . . . **TC MM 0080**
Maranatha / May '82 / Word Records (UK) / Sony.

GOING WEST.
Tracks: Folsom Prison blues: *Cash, Johnny* / Just another rhinestone: *Drum, Don* / Country comes west: *Henderson, Kelvin* / Hey little cowboy: *Meister, Gary* / Run boy run: *Country Cats* / Yours and mine: *Turner, Mary Lou* / Get the bird flyin': *Campbell, Glen* / Takin' it easy: *Henderson, Kelvin* / Rock Island line: *Cash, Johnny* / Boy from Indiana, The: *Kahlenberg Company* / Don't turn around: *Dickey, Bob* / It's alright: *Sinatra, Frank*.
LP . . . . **Q 90033**
MC . . . . **MQ 990033**
Polygram (Import) / May '83 / Pinnacle.

GOLDBAND ROCKABILLY.
Tracks: Not Advised.
LP . . . . **R&C 1015**
Rock & Country / Oct '88 / Swift.

GOLDEN AGE, VOL. 1, THE.
Tracks: Can the circle be unbroken (bye bye): *Carter Family* / Great speckled bird: *Acuff, Roy & His Crazy Tennesseans* / After the sunrise: *Chuck Wagon Gang* / You are my sunshine: *Autry, Gene* / I want to be a cowboy's sweetheart: *Montana, Patsy & The Prairie Ramblers* / Pistol packin' mama: *Dexter, Al & His Troopers* / Back in the saddle again: *Autry, Gene* / New San Antonia Rose: *Wills, Bob & His Texas Playboys* / It makes no difference now: *Autry, Gene* / Take me back to Tulsa: *Wills, Bob & His Texas Playboys* / Don't let that man get you down: *Ruby, Texas* / Shame on you: *Cooley, Spade* / Born to lose: *Daffan, Ted & The Texans* / When my blue moon turns to gold again: *Walker Wiley & Gene Sullivan* / Wreck on the highway: *Acuff, Roy & His Smokey Mountain Boys* / When God comes and gathers his Jewels: *O'Day, Molly & The Cumberland Mountain Folks* / I saw the light: *Acuff, Roy & His Smokey Mountain Boys* / Are you walking and a-talking for the Lord: *Lee, Wilma & Stoney Cooper* / Molly and Tenbrooks (The race horse song): *Munroe, Bill & His Bluegrass Boys* / Poor Ellen Smith: *O'Day, Molly & The Cumberland Mountain Folks* / Wabash Cannonball: *Acuff, Roy & His Smokey Mountain Boys* / Blue moon of Kentucky: *Munroe, Bill & His Bluegrass Boys* / Fields have turned brown, The: *Stanley Brothers & The Clinch Mountain Boys* / Don't get above your raisin': *Flatt, Lester & Earl Scruggs*.
CD **4681192**
MC **4681194**
Columbia / Nov '91 / Sony.

GOLDEN COUNTRY.
Tracks: Stand by your man: *Wynette, Tammy* / Daddy won't be home anymore: *Parton, Dolly* / Love is just a game: *Gatlin, Larry* / Blue skies: *Nelson, Willie* / Cowboys ain't supposed to cry: *Bandy, Moe* / Me and Bobby McGhee / Delta dawn: *Tucker, Tanya* / Very special love song, A: *Rich, Charlie* / Colorado cool aid: *Paycheck, Johnny* / Little bit more, A: *Anderson, Lynn* / Maria Elena: *Robbins, Mary* / It ain't me babe: *Cash, Johnny*.
MC . . . . **HSC 3058**
Hallmark / Apr '81 / Pickwick Records.
■ **LP** . . . . **SHM 3058**
Hallmark / Apr '81.

GOLDEN COUNTRY HITS.
Tracks: Not Advised.
MC Set **850121/2**
Black Tulip / May '88.

GOLDEN COUNTRY HITS.
Tracks: My shoes keep walking back to you: *Price, Ray* / Jambalaya: *Walker, Billy* / Fraulein: *Helms, Bobby* / Loose talk: *Hart, Freddie* / Greener pastures: *Jackson, Stonewall* / Fireball mail: *Flatt & Scruggs* / Have I told you lately that I love you: *Dickens, Little Jimmy* / Heart over mind: *Tillis, Mel* / Honky tonkitis: *Butler, Carl* / Long black veil: *Frizzell, Lefty*.
■ **LP** . . . . **HM 517**
Hallmark / Jan '65.

GOOD OLE MEMPHIS COUNTRY.
Tracks: Feeling low: *Chaffin, Ernie* / Laughin' and jokin': *Chaffin, Ernie* / Destiny: *King, Cast* / Baby doll: *King, Cast* / Round and round: *King, Cast* / Please believe me: *King, Cast* / When you stop lovin' me: *King, Cast* / Easy to love: *Self, Mack* / Down on the border: *Simmons, Gene* / Goin' crazy: *Self, Mack* / Poor boy: *Holt, O.C.* / This train: *Holt, O.C.* / Pink wedding gown: *Holt, O.C.* / Satisfied with me: *King, Cast*.
LP . . . . **SUN 1016**
Sun / Sep '88 / Charly / Swift.

GOTTA ROCK ME DADDY.
Tracks: Little Willy: *Deram, Richie* / Girl and a hot rod: *Deram, Richie* / She's gone, gone, gone: *Davis, Dale* / Gotta rock me daddy: *Davis, Dale* / Shady lady: *Shades* / I'm not moving: *Wheatley, Paul* / Rockin' the blues: *Griffith, Peggy* / It looks like a dead end to me: *Van Winkle, Arnold* / Woke up this morning: *Spivey, Kenny* / Waitin' in line: *Rutledge, Bobby* / Go slow, fatso: *Rutledge, Bobby* / Think it over, baby: *Cleary, Eddie* / Crawdad song: *Haney, Bill* / Richmond, Chicago, Mexico and home: *Miller, Sonny* / Sweet lies: *Chapparrals*.
LP . . . . **WLP 8862**
White Label (Germany) / '87 / Pinnacle / Bear Family Records (Germany) / CSA Tell Tapes.

GRAND COUNTRY TOUR.
Tracks: Grand country tour / City of New Orleans / Detroit City / Mississippi / Canadian sunset / Colorado cool aid / Dixie on my mind / El Paso / Dallas / Georgia on my mind / Cincinnati / Abilene / Banks of the Ohio / Nashville / Wolverton Mountain / America the beautiful.
■ **LP** . . . . **CBS 31764**
CBS / Dec '79.

GREAT AMERICAN COUNTRY HITS.
MC . . . . **AM 31**
VFM Cassettes / VFM Children's Entertainment Ltd. / Midland Records / Morley Audio Services.

GREAT COUNTRY FESTIVAL.
LP **6600 003**
Mercury / Mar '81 / PolyGram.

GREAT COUNTRY HITS.
Double LP **80019**
MC Set **850191/2**
Black Tulip / May '88.

GREAT COUNTRY HITS OF THE 70'S.
MC . . . . **VCA 018**
VFM Cassettes / May '79 / VFM Children's Entertainment Ltd. / Midland Records / Morley Audio Services.

GREAT COUNTRY MUSIC SHOW.
Double LP . . . . **RTD 2083**
MC Set **4CRTD 2083**
Ronco / Nov '82.

GREAT LABELS OF THE SOUTH - TREPUR & RIDGECREST.
Tracks: Elvis in the army: *Wasden, Jaybee* / De castrow: *Wasden, Jaybee* / Let's rock: *Howard, Rusty* / I'm gonna do you like you are doing me: *Howard, Rusty* / Milkman blues: *Joyce, Chuck* / Bounce baby bounce: *Lofton, Fuzzy* / I've been down this road: *Wydemon, Jimmie* / Vulcan song, The: *Wydemon, Jimmie* / Don't cry little darling: *Carpenter Bros.* / Day I heard you say goodbye, The: *Worley, David* / I'm being haunted: *Melson, Lee 'Red'* / Rockin' through the tunnel of love: *Melson, Lee 'Red'* / Mean ole bartender blues: *Melson, Lee 'Red'* / Carmen Sue rock: *Melson, Lee 'Red'*.
LP . . . . **WLP 8834**
White Label (Germany) / '87 / Pinnacle / Bear Family Records (Germany) / CSA Tell Tapes.

GREAT SONGS OF THE AMERICAN TRUCK DRIVERS.
Tracks: Six days on the road: *Dudley, Dave* / Truck drivin' son of a gun: *Dudley, Dave* / Highways / Truck driver's prayer: *Dudley, Dave* / Going to Memphis: *Perkins, Carl* / Truck driver's waltz: *Dudley, Dave* / Sunday morning coming down: *Kennedy, Jerry* / Convoy: *McCall, C.W.* / Truck drivin' man: *Dudley, Dave* / King of the road: *Miller, Roger* / Just a few miles more: *Dudley, Dave* / Sugerland USA: *Dudley, Dave* / I'm movin' on: *Dudley, Dave* / Take me home country roads: *Statler Brothers*.
LP **6498 214**
MC **7133 214**
Mercury (USA) / Mar '83 / Pinnacle.

GREATEST COUNTRY DUETS.
Tracks: Reasons to quit / Thinkin' of a rendezvous / It's only make believe / It's a dirty job / C.C. Waterback / Whiter shade of pale.
LP . . . . **EPC 25933**
MC **40 25933**
Epic / Mar '84 / Sony.

H

HE'LL HAVE TO GO.
Tracks: Not Advised.
CD . . . . **YDG 74610**
MC . . . . **YDG 45744**
Yesterday's Gold / Feb '93 / Target Records / Midland Records / Taylors.

■ DELETED

HI-TONE POPPA.
Tracks: Hot rod shotgun boogie: *Franks, Tillman* / Walking the dog: *Grimsley, Tex* / Teardrops: *Grimsley, Tex* / Beer and pinballs: *King, Claude* / 51 beers: *King, Claude* / You're just imagination: *Young, Faron* / Have I waited too long: *Young, Faron* / Hi-tone poppa: *Franks, Tillman* / Heard the juke box playing: *Faron Young & Tillman Franks* / Million mistakes, A: *King, Claude* / Why should I: *King, Claude* / Court of justice: *Wilburn, Teddy* / Call me sweetheart: *Wilburn, Teddy* / I'm a free man now: *Faron Young & Tillman Franks.*
LP. . . . . **KK 830**
Krazy Kat / Apr '88 / Hot Shot / C.M. Distribution / Wellard Dist. / Roots Records / Projection / Charly / Jazz Music.

HICKORY COUNTRY.
Tracks: You win again / How I love them old songs / Blue eyes crying in the rain / Goin' out of my head.
■ **EP.** . . . . **SDEP 001**
Sundown / '87 / Terry Blood Dist. / Jazz Music / C.M. Distribution.

HICKORY ROCKABILLY.
Tracks: Hey Mae / Hey you there / I ain't gonna waste my time / I've got a brand new baby.
■ **EP.** . . . . **MFEP 011**
Magnum Force / Jan '87 / Terry Blood Dist. / Jazz Music / Hot Shot.

HILL BILLY HOUN' DAWGS AND HONKY TONK ANGELS.
Tracks: Not Advised.
LP. . . . . **DT 33008**
Detour / Jan '90 / Swift / Jazz Music / Pinnacle.

HILLBILLIES ON SPEED.
Tracks: Not Advised.
LP. . . . . **REDITA 116**
Redita (Holland) / Oct '88 / Swift.

HILLBILLY BOOGIE.
Tracks: Not Advised.
LP. . . . . **WH 2812**
White Label (Germany) / Dec '88 / Pinnacle / Bear Family Records (Germany) / CSA Tell Tapes.

HILLBILLY BOOGIE & ROCK A BILLY.
Tracks: Not Advised.
LP. . . . . **RR 2009**
Esoldun / Oct '87 / New Note.

HILLBILLY BOP-MEMPHIS STYLE.
Tracks: Not Advised.
LP. . . . . **M 5000**
Meteor / '88 / Terry Blood Dist. / Jazz Music.

HILLBILLY HOP.
Tracks: Courtin' in the rain / Flirting with you / Skinny Minnie / 8 more miles to Louisville / Mississippi / Texas vs. Alaska / Steel guitar rag / Four aces and a queen / Lie Detector / My heart, my heart / Kiss me like crazy / Crawdad song / All alone / Happy go lucky / 40th and plum.
LP. . . . . **CR 30251**
Charly / Jul '86 / Charly.

HILLBILLY ROCK (Canadian rockabilly).
Tracks: Not Advised.
LP. . . . . **REDITA 127**
Redita (Holland) / Oct '88 / Swift.

HILLBILLY ROCK 'N' ROLL.
Tracks: Not Advised.
LP. . . . . **WLP 8939**
White Label (Germany) / Dec '88 / Pinnacle / Bear Family Records (Germany) / CSA Tell Tapes.

HILLBILLY STOMP.
Tracks: Blue moon on the bayou: *Le Blance, Red* / Marrita: *Le Blance, Red* / Memory in my heart: *Le Blance, Red* / I love that woman (right or wrong): *Le Blance, Red* / Freed my silly heart: *Le Blance, Red* / You're laughing at me: *Le Blance, Red* / Wanna go steady: *Hutto, Bill & His Playboys* / Boogie woogie tout le temps: *Martin, Frenchie* / Mable's done gone: *Noble, Jerry* / Yesterday we were married: *Ferrier, Al* / I'll never do any wrong: *Ferrier, Al.*
LP. . . . . **GCL 108**
Goldband / Jan '90 / Charly / Swift.

HILLBILLY SWEETHEART.
Tracks: Not Advised.
LP. . . . . **REDITA 128**
Redita (Holland) / Oct '88 / Swift.

HILLS AND HOME (Thirty years of bluegrass).
Tracks: Why did you wonder?: *Monroe, Bill* / Blue ridge cabin home: *Flat, Lester, Earl Scruggs & The Foggy Mountain Boys* / Daniel prayed: *Stanley Brothers* / Love please come home: *Reno, Don & Red Smiley* / You'd better wake up: *Wiseman, Mac* / Your old standby: *Eanes, Jim* / Twenty one years: *Lonesome Pine Fiddlers* / Springhill disaster: *Clifton, Bill* / Old age: *Woolum, Dave* / Blackberry blossom: *Baker, Billy* / Hold what you've got: *Martin, Jimmy* / Diesel trains: *Jim & Jesse* / Pathway of teardrops / Hills and home: *Country Gentlemen* / Raise a ruckus tonight: *Lonesome River Boys* / Fox on the run: *Emerson & Waldron* / Body and soul: *New Grass Revival* / Dill pickle rag: *Bluegrass All Stars.*
LP. . . . . **NW 225**
New World (USA) / Dec '86 / Pinnacle.

HISTORY OF COUNTRY MUSIC, THE: THE 1940S VOL. 1.
Tracks: Bouqet of roses: *Arnold, Eddy* / When it's lamplighting time in the valley: *Ritter, Tex* / Guitar polka: *Dexter, Al* / Smoke on the water: *Foley, Red* / I'm biting my fingernails & thinking of you: *Dexter, Al* / At mail call today: *Autry, Gene* / Detour: *Willing, Foy* / Prodigal son, The: *Acuff, Roy* / Lovesick blues: *Williams, Hank* / No letter today: *Daffan, Ted & The Texans* / Each night at nine: *Tillman, Floyd* / I'll hold you in my heart: *Arnold, Eddy* / I want to be a cowboy's sweetheart: *Allen, Rosalie* / Soldier's last letter: *Tubb, Ernest* / Shame on you: *Cooley, Spade* / Pistol packin' mama: *Dexter, Al* / New Spanish two step: *Willis, Bob & his Texas Playboys* / Riders in the sky: *Monroe, Vaughn* / New San Antonio rose: *Willis, Bob & his Texas Playboys* / It's been so long, darling: *Tubb, Ernest* / Waltz of the wind: *Acuff, Roy* / It's a sin: *Arnold, Eddy* / Cool water: *Sons Of The Pioneers* / They took the stars out of heaven: *Tillman, Floyd* / New Jole blonde: *Foley, Red* / There's a new moon over my shoulder: *Javis, Jimmie* / Someday you'll want me to want you: *Britt, Elton* / Candy kisses: *Morgan, George* / I'll forgive you but I can't forget: *Acuff, Roy* / Sugar moon: *Willis, Bob & his Texas Playboys* / Rainbow at midnight: *Tubb, Ernest* / Deep in the heart of Texas: *Autry, Gene* / Wedding bells: *Williams, Hank* / Tennessee saturday night: *Foley, Red* / Don't rob another man's castle: *Arnold, Eddy* / Pistol packin' mama (2): *Crosby, Bing.*
CD Set . . . . **KNEWCD 715**
MC Set . . . . **KNEWMC 715**
Disky Communications Ltd / Mar '93 / Swift / Terry Blood Dist.

HISTORY OF COUNTRY MUSIC, THE: THE 1950S VOL. 1.
Tracks: Crazy arms: *Price, Ray* / Rhumba boogie: *Snow, Hank* / Let old mother nature have her way: *Smith, Carl* / Jambalaya (On the bayou): *Williams, Hank* / Always late (With your kisses): *Frizzell, Lefty* / Gambler's guitar: *Draper, Rusty* / Chattanooga shoe shine boy: *Foley, Red* / I take the chance: *Browns* / In the jailhouse now: *Pierce, Webb* / Cattle call, The: *Arnold, Eddy* / White lightning: *Jones, George* / It wasn't god who made honky tonk angels: *Wells, Kitty* / Slow poke: *King, Pee Wee* / Mexican Joe: *Reeves, Jim* / So many times: *Acuff, Roy* / Singing the blues: *Robbins, Marty* / Golden rocket: *Snow, Hank* / Blue suede shoes: *Perkins, Carl* / Story of my life, The: *Robbins, Marty* / I let the stars get in my eyes: *Hill, Goldie* / Let me go lover: *Snow, Hank* / Four walls: *Reeves, Jim* / I wanna play house with you: *Arnold, Eddy* / (When you feel like you're in love) Don't just stand there: *Smith, Carl* / I want to be with you always: *Frizzell, Lefty* / Birmingham bounce: *Foley, Red* / I forgot more than you'll ever know: *Davis Sisters* / There you go: *Cash, Johnny* / Hey Sheriff: *Rusty & Doug* / Your cheatin' heart: *Williams, Hank* / When it's springtime in Alaska (It's forty below): *Horton, Johnny* / City light: *Price, Ray* / Why baby why: *Pierce, Webb & Red Sovine* / Blue blue day: *Gibson, Don* / I walk the line: *Cash, Johnny* / One by one: *Wells, Kitty & Red Foley.*
CD Set . . . . **KNEWCD 717**
MC Set . . . . **KNEWMC 717**
Disky Communications Ltd / Mar '93 / Swift / Terry Blood Dist.

HISTORY OF COUNTRY MUSIC, THE: THE 1960S VOL. 1.
Tracks: Not Advised.
CD Set . . . . **KNEWCD 719**
MC . . . . **KNEWMC 719**
Disky Communications Ltd / Mar '93 / Swift / Terry Blood Dist.

HISTORY OF COUNTRY MUSIC, THE: THE 1970S VOL. 1.
Tracks: Kiss an angel good morning: *Pride, Charley* / Hello darlin': *Twitty, Conway* / I ain't never: *Tillis, Mel* / Happiest girl in the whole USA, The: *Fargo, Donna* / All for the love of sunshine: *Williams, Hank Jr.* / Chantilly lace: *Lewis, Jerry Lee* / Country bumpkin: *Smith, Carl* / Wasted nights and wasted days: *Fender, Freddy* / Riding my thumb to Mexico: *Rodriguez, Johnny* / Year that Clayton Delaney died, The: *Hall, Tom T.* / Only one love in my life: *Milsap, Ronnie* / On my knees: *Rich, Charlie & Janie Frickie* / Luckenbach (Back to the basics of love): *Jennings, Waylon* / Lizzie and the rainman: *Tucker, Tanya* / She never knew me: *Williams, Don* / (Hey won't you play) Another somebody done something wrong s: *Thomas, B.J.* / Georgia on my mind: *Nelson, Willie* / Here you come again: *Parton, Dolly* / Rose garden: *Anderson, Lynn* / (Old dogs, children and) Watermelon wine: *Hall, Tom T.* / Linda on my mind: *Twitty, Conway* / There must be more to love than this: *Lewis, Jerry Lee* / Most beautiful girls, The: *Rich, Charlie* / Coca cola cowboy: *Tillis, Mel* / Teddy bear song, The: *Fairchild, Barbara* / I'm a ramblin' man: *Jennings, Waylon* / Eleven roses: *Williams, Hank Jr.* / Rub it in: *Craddock, Billy Crash* / Golden tears: *Dave & Sugar* / You're my best friend: *Williams, Don* / Sunday morning coming down: *Cash, Johnny* / El paso city: *Robbins, Marty* / Coal miner's daughter: *Lynn, Loretta* / Blue eyes crying in the rain: *Nelson, Willie* / You can't be a beacon (If your lights don't shine): *Fargo, Donna* / Secret love: *Fender, Freddy.*
CD Set . . . . **KNEWCD 721**
MC Set . . . . **KNEWMC 721**
Disky Communications Ltd / Mar '93 / Swift / Terry Blood Dist.

HISTORY OF COUNTRY MUSIC, THE: THE 1980S VOL. 1.
Tracks: 9 to 5: *Parton, Dolly* / City of New Orleans: *Nelson, Willie* / Love in the first degree: *Alabama* / Theme from the dukes of hazzard (Good ol' boys): *Jennings, Waylon* / Thank god for the radio: *Kendalls* / My heart: *Milsap, Ronnie* / She got the goldmine (I got the shaft): *Reed, Jerry* / True love ways: *Gilley, Mickey* / Seven year ache: *Cash, Rosanne* / I believe in you: *Williams, Don* / Give me wings: *Johnson, Michael* / You look so good in love: *Strait, George* / He's back and I'm blue: *Desert Rose Band* / Goin' gone: *Mattea, Kathy* / Whatever happend to old fashioned love: *Thomas, B.J.* / Fire I can't put out, A: *Strait, George* / I wouldn't change you if I could: *Skaggs, Ricky* / Can't stop my heart from loving you: *O'Kanes* / Have mercy: *Judds* / Lost in the fifties tonight (In the still of the night): *Milsap, Ronnie* / My heroes have always been cowboys: *Nelson, Willie* / Somebody lied: *Shelton, Ricky Van* / Cajun moon: *Skaggs, Ricky* / He stopped loving her today: *Jones, George* / Bobbie Sue: *Oak Ridge Boys* / Fourteen carat mind: *Watson, Gene* / Never been so loved (In all my life): *Pride, Charley* / Older women: *McDowell, Ronnie* / Drifter: *Sylvia* / Wanderer: *Rabbitt, Eddie* / I'll still be loving you: *Restless Heart* / I think I'll just stay here and drink: *Haggard, Merle* / Radio heart: *McClain, Charly* / Common man: *Conlee, John* / Take me down: *Alabama* / Elizabeth: *Statler Brothers.*
CD Set . . . . **KNEWCD 723**
MC Set . . . . **KNEWMC 723**
Disky Communications Ltd / Mar '93 / Swift / Terry Blood Dist.

HOLLYWOOD HILLBILLIES.
Tracks: I'll take a long long time: *McDonald, Skeets* / Long time ago, A: *Young, Faron* / Gambler's love: *Maddox, Rose* / Lost John: *Thompson, Hank* / Forgive me: *James, Sonny* / My last chance with you: *Collins, Tommy* / Too busy cryin' the blues: *Reed, Jerry* / Cincinnati Lou: *Travis, Merle* / Dragging the river: *Husky, Ferlin* / I know my baby cares: *Luman, Bob* / Black cat: *Collins, Tommy* / Fallen angel: *McDonald, Skeets* / That's the way I feel: *Young, Faron* / Rockin' in the congo: *Thompson, Hank* / Looking back: *Husky, Ferlin* / You've turned into stranger: *Jackson, Wanda* / You've got that touch: *James, Sonny* / Bessie baby: *Reed, Jerry* / Move it on over: *Maddox, Rose* / Try me: *Luman, Bob.*
LP. . . . . **SEE 98**
See For Miles / Jul '87 / Pinnacle.

HOLLYWOOD ROCK'N'ROLL (12 Rare Rockabilly Tracks).
Tracks: Blue jeans: *Glenn, Glen* / Everybody's movin': *Glenn, Glen* / Would you: *Rock 'n' Roll* / Goofin' around: *Glenn, Glen* / I'm glad my baby's gone away: *Glenn, Glen* / One cup of coffee: *Glenn, Glen* / Don't push: *Deal, Don* / Topsy turvy: *Zeppa, Ben Joe* / Great shakin' fever: *Burnette, Dorsey* / Ezactly: *Busch, Dick* / Hollywood party: *Busch, Dick* / He will come back to me: *Leslie, Alis.*
LP. . . . . **CH 1**
Ace / '79 / Pinnacle / Hot Shot / Jazz Music / Complete Record Co. Ltd.
CD . . . . **CDCHM 1**
Ace / Oct '89 / Pinnacle / Hot Shot / Jazz Music / Complete Record Co. Ltd.

HOME MADE EARLY ROCK & ROLL.
Tracks: Foggy river: *Holder, Jimmy* / Don't you be still: *Dixieland Drifters* / Rock away: *Sexton, Orden* / Just rockin': *Cooper, Glen* / These blues are driving me mad: *Cooper, Glen* / Scalping party: *Tornados* / 707: *Tornados* / I'm gonna let you go: *Rector, Hank* / Concussion: *Holydays* / Pearl River: *Holydays* / Well, come on: *Kingsmill, Steve* / Cool, cool baby: *Smith, Bobby* / Cotton pickin': *Freeze, Sonny* / Bop a little: *Riley, Pat* / Walkin' and talkin': *Moore, Lucky.*
LP. . . . . **WLP 8867**
White Label (Germany) / Mar '84 / Pinnacle / Bear Family Records (Germany) / CSA Tell Tapes.

HOMESPUN COUNTRY SHOWTIME.
Tracks: It's hard to be humble / Teddy bear / Hey good lookin' / When it's Springtime in the Rockies / Be careful of stones that you throw / I have a dream / Kingdom I call home / I dreamed about mama last night: *Derry, Pat* / Heart you break will be your own, The: *Breen, Ann* / Angeline would you like to dance again: *Bell, Crawford* / Roses for mama: *Greer, John* / Jimmy quit the drinking: *Fitzpatrick, Gene* / You need me: *Leon* / Little Rosa: *McFarland, Billy* / Back home again: *Hamilton, J.E.* / Kentucky in the morning: *Derry, Pat.*
MC . . . . **CPHL 439**
Homespun (Ireland) / '82 / Homespun Records / Ross Records / Wellard Dist.

HOMESPUN'S COUNTRY HALL OF FAME.
Tracks: Harper Valley PTA / China doll / Truck drivin' woman / Church courtroom and then goodbye / Door is always open, The / Mississippi / Blue eyes crying in the rain / Lucille / Little isle of green / Union mare and confederate grey / Jeannie Norman / Silver threads and golden needles / My son calls another man daddy / What's wrong with the way that we're doing it now / Once a day / Sunny side of the mountain / Back home again / I'll settle for old Ireland.

■ DELETED

LP. . . . . PHL 427
MC . . . . CPHL 427
Homespun (Ireland) / '82 / Homespun Records / Ross Records / Wellard Dist.

HONKY TONK HEROES, VOL. 2.

Tracks: Brain cloudy blues: *Wills, Bob & His Texas Playboys* / Slipping around: *Tillman, Floyd* / This cold war with you: *Tillman, Floyd* / (Remember me) I'm the one who loves you: *Hamblen, Stuart* / I love you so much it hurts: *Tillman, Floyd* / Room full of roses: *Morgan, George* / I overlooked an orchid: *Smith, Carl* / Country boy: *Dickens, Little Jimmy* / Let old mother nature have her way: *Smith, Carl* / Sleepin' at the foot of the bed, A: *Dickens, Little Jimmy* / If you've got the money, I've got the time: *Frizzell, Lefty* / I love you a thousand ways: *Frizzell, Lefty* / I couldn't keep from crying: *Robbins, Marty* / Always late (with your kisses): *Frizzell, Lefty* / Hey Joe: *Smith, Carl* / Honky tonk man: *Horton, Johnny* / Crazy arms: *Price, Ray* / Knee deep in the blues: *Robbins, Marty* / Invitation to the blues: *Price, Ray* / Pick me up on your way down: *Walker, Charlie* / Heartaches by the number: *Price, Ray* / Why I'm walkin'. *Jackson, Stonewall* / Who will buy the wine: *Walker, Charlie* / Honky tonkin: *Butler, Carl* / Heart over mind: *Price, Ray* / Don't let me cross over: *Butler, Carl*.
CD 4681202
MC 4681204
Columbia / Nov '91 / Sony.

HONKY TONKIN'.

Tracks: Not Advised.
LP. . . . . PL 13422
RCA / Feb '80 / BMG.

HOOKED ON COUNTRY.

Tracks: Not Advised.
CD . . . . NCD 3459
LP. . . . . NE 1459
MC . . . . CE 2459
K-Tel / Apr '90 / I & B Records / C.M. Distribution / Arabesque Ltd. / Mono Distributors (Jersey) Ltd. / Prism Leisure PLC / PolyGram / Ross Records / Prism Leisure PLC.

HOP FLOP AND FLY.

Tracks: Go ahead baby / Uh babe / High high high / Treat me right / Love crazy / My baby don't rock / Greenback dollar / You call everybody darlin' / Look at that moon / Get it off your mind / Stop the world, I'll jump off / Juicy fruit / Money money money / All night rock.
LP. . . . . SUN 1025
Sun / May '85 / Charly / Swift.

HOP SKIP AND JUMP.

Tracks: Hop skip and jump: *Roberts, Bobby* / R'n'roll Santa: *Farr, L. Joe* / Fifty megatons: *Russell, Sonny* / Nicotine: *Chaplain, Paul* / Shortnin' bread: *Chaplain, Paul* / I don't need no more / Pretty baby rock: *Myers, J. & T. Regan* / I ain't gonna be around: *Therien, Joe Jnr.* / Rock'n chair rock: *Cavalier, Johnny* / Knock off the rock: *Cavalier, Johnny* / Motorcycle Mike: *Day, Davey* / Run here honey: *Johnson, Glenn* / Rockin little mama: *Pasett, Tony* / Roll over Beethoven: *Paige, Joey*.
LP. . . . . RR 2007
Esoldun / Dec '86 / New Note.

HOT AS I AM.

Tracks: Not Advised.
LP. . . . . RAMBLER 105
Rambler (USA) / Feb '82 / Roots Records / Projection / Swift / Wellard Dist.

HOT SOUTHERN BOPPERS.

Tracks: Chains of love: *Summons, Gene* / Bop bop baby: *Moore, Wade & Dick Penner* / Don't need your lovin' baby: *Penner, Dick* / Take me to that place: *Earls, Jack* / My gal Mary Ann: *Earls, Jack* / She's my baby: *Riley, Billy Lee* / Come on little mama: *Harris, Ray* / Trying to get to you: *Orbison, Roy* / Take and give: *Rhodes, Slim* / She's gone away: *Barton, Ernie* / Do what I do: *Rhodes, Slim* / Red cadillac and a black moustache: *Smith, Warren* / Eight wheel: *Bruce, Edwin* / Rock boppin' baby: *Bruce, Edwin*.
LP. . . . . SUN 1024
Sun / Jan '86 / Charly / Swift.

I

I LOVE COUNTRY (Golden oldies).

Tracks: Not Advised.
■ LP. 4510011
CBS / '88.

I LOVE COUNTRY (Cowboy songs).

Tracks: Not Advised.
■ LP. 4510091
CBS / '88.

I'M A HILLBILLY YANKEE DOODLE BOY.

Tracks: I'm a hillbilly yankee doodle boy: *Lewis, Texas Jim* / Smoke on the water: *Tuttle, Wesley* / Mother's prayer: *Tuttle, Wesley & Travis Merle* / Cannon song, The: *Rodgers, Slim* / Soldiers last letter: *Colorado Hillbillies* / I'm comin' home to you: *Rodgers, Slim* / I'd like to give my dog to Uncle Sam: *Waters, Ozzie* / Gold star in her window: *Colorado Hillbillies* / Rodeo down in Tokyo: *Waters, Ozzie* / Tommy gun boogie: *Rodgers, Slim* / Hillbilly soldier Joe: *Johnson Sisters* / If it's gonna help win the way: *Hoosier Hot Shots*.
MC . . . . K 1004
Killroy / Jul '88.

I'M A TRUCK (The Very Best of US Truck-driver Songs).

Tracks: Not Advised.
CD 15 059
MC 79 593
Laserlight / Aug '91 / TBD / Taylors.

IF IT AIN'T A HIT I'LL EAT MY..BABY.

Tracks: Not Advised.
LP. . . . . Z 2009
Zu Zazz / '88 / Hot Shot / A.D.A Distribution / C.M. Distribution.

IMPERIAL ROCKABILLIES, VOL 1.

Tracks: Not Advised.
LP. 2C 068 83098
Pathe Marconi (France) / '88 / Thames Distributors Ltd.

IMPERIAL ROCKABILLIES, VOL 2.

Tracks: Sweet baby doll / Oh la baby / Kiss me sweet / Rockin' / Abracadabra / Ernie / Loretta / Rockin' baby / I don't want to cry over you / Hey baby / Hip hip baby / Kiss me baby / All night long / Baby, I'm sorry / Cat talk / Ride Jesse ride / Be my love tonight / Dig'n and datin' / Lies / Willa Mae.
LP. . . . . UAS 30173
United Artists / May '79 / EMI.
LP. 2C 068 83097
Pathe Marconi (France) / '88 / Thames Distributors Ltd.

IMPERIAL ROCKABILLIES, VOL 3.

Tracks: Loverboy: *Lewis, Wally* / It's late: *Burnette, Dorsey* / I only came here to dance: *Venet, Nick* / Love in bebop time: *Venet, Nick* / Long black hearse: *Greaves, Cliff* / Gone ape man: *Williams, Lew* / Something I said: *Luman, Bob* / Make up your mind, baby: *Luman, Bob* / My poor heart: *Strikes* / Buddy: *Dee, Jackie* / Chew tobacco rag: *Briggs, Billy* / Number two: *Banks, Dick* / Dirty dog: *Banks, Dick* / Get off my back: *Blue, Jay* / Speed crazy: *Slavin, Slick* / Only teenagers allowed: *Walker, Jackie*.
LP. . . . . UAG 30312
United Artists / Aug '80 / EMI.
LP. 2C 068 83096
Pathe Marconi (France) / '88 / Thames Distributors Ltd.

IMPRESSIONS OF DON WILLIAMS (Various Session Musicians).

Tracks: Not Advised.
MC . . . . AIM 65
AIM (2) / Feb '83 / Topic Records / Direct Distribution.

IN CONCERT WITH HOST CHARLEY PRIDE.

Tracks: Kaw-liga: *Pride, Charley* / Mississippi cotton picking delta town: *Pride, Charley* / Louisiana man: *Pride, Charley* / Jolene: *Parton, Dolly* / Love is like a butterfly: *Parton, Dolly* / Girl who waits on tables: *Milsap, Ronnie* / Slippin' and slidin' (medley): *Milsap, Ronnie* / Kiss an angel good morning: *Pride, Charley* / Chaplin in new shoes: *Atkins, Chet* / Entertainer, The: *Atkins, Chet* / Rollin' in my sweet baby's arms: *Milsap, Ronnie & Dolly Parton* / Let's sing our song: *Reed, Jerry* / Thing called love: *Reed, Jerry* / Lord, Mr Ford: *Reed, Jerry* / Coat of many colours: *Parton, Dolly* / Bargain store: *Parton, Dolly* / Out of hand: *Stewart, Gary* / Colonel Bogey: *Reed, Jerry & Chet Atkins* / For the good times: *Pride, Charley* / John Henry: *Atkins, Chet & Jerry Reed*.
■ Double LP . . . . DPS 2064
RCA / '79.

INSTRUMENTAL COUNTRY, VOL II.

Tracks: Not Advised.
■ LP. . . . . CBS 31861
CBS / Nov '80.

INTERNATIONAL FESTIVAL OF COUNTRY MUSIC, AN.

Tracks: Keep on the sunny side: *Hamilton, George IV* / Healing hands of time: *Colter, Jessi* / Leaning on your love: *Ryles, John Wesley* / Honky tonk heart: *Walker, Charlie* / Blue is my lonely room: *Hillsiders* / Blue, blue day: *Gibson, Don* / Permanent kind of lovin': *Glaser, Jim* / Best guitar picker: *Atonemans* / Nobody's child: *Snow, Hank* / Mouth to mouth resuscitation: *Hartford, John* / I can't get enough of you, baby: *Baker, Carroll* / Night coach out of Dallas: *Withers, Tex* / Mowing the lawn: *Brown, Jim Ed & Vernon Oxford* / At least part of the way: *Gems* / Make up your mind: *Wells, Kitty* / Travelling minstrel man: *Payne, Jimmy* / Last letter, The: *Smith, Connie* / Someone else's arms: *Houston, David* / Little Rosa: *Red Sovine* / Rocky top: *West, Dottie* / Dreaming country: *Young Johnny Four* / Morning after baby let me down: *Mercey Brothers* / You can't go in the red playing bluegrass: *Wiseman, Mac* / I'm the mail she's waiting for: *Owens, George* / Organized noise: *Newbury, Mickey* / In the good old days: *Parton, Dolly* / Where you been so long: *Hall, David* / It's my time: *Loudermilk, John D.* / As a matter of fact: *Pruett, Jeanne* / Gardenia waltz, The: *Waylors & Johnny Gimble* / Colour of the blues: *Davis, Skeeter* / Orange blossom: *Monroe, Bill & His Blue Grass Boys*.
■ Double LP . . . . PL 42407
RCA / '79.

INTERNATIONAL FESTIVAL OF COUNTRY MUSIC, FRUTIGEN (recorded live, May 1987).

Tracks: I'm goin', I'm leaving: *Hollow, Traver* / Lonesome, on'ry and mean: *Young, Steven & Tom Russell Band* / Mezcal: *Russell, Tom* / Alkali: *Russell, Tom* / Walking after midnight: *Moffatt, Katy & Tom Russell Band* / First taste of Texas: *Bruce, Ed* / Man who turned my mama on, The: *Bruce, Ed* / Summer wages: *Tyson, Ian & Andrew Hardin* / Someday soon: *Tyson, Ian & Andrew Hardin* / Navajo rug: *Russell, Tom* / Edge of a heartbreak: *Moeller, Dee* / Where is the magic: *Moeller, Dee* / Mamas don't let your babies grow up to be cowboys: *Bruce, Ed*.
CD . . . . BCD 15466
Bear Family / Jun '89 / Rollercoaster Records / Swift / Direct Distribution.

IRELAND'S COUNTRY & WESTERN CARNIVAL VOL 1.

Tracks: Country roads / Little rose / There goes my everything.
LP. . . . . HRL 103
MC . . . . CHRL 103
Homespun (Ireland) / May '88 / Homespun Records / Ross Records / Wellard Dist.

IRELAND'S COUNTRY & WESTERN CARNIVAL VOL 2.

Tracks: Old Shep / Your cheatin' heart / It keeps right on a-hurtin'.
LP. . . . . HRL 111
Homespun (Ireland) / Jul '76 / Homespun Records / Ross Records / Wellard Dist.
MC . . . . CHRL 111
Homespun (Ireland) / '82 / Homespun Records / Ross Records / Wellard Dist.

IRELAND'S COUNTRY & WESTERN CARNIVAL VOL 3.

Tracks: 21 years / I can't stop loving you.
LP. . . . . HRL 121
Homespun (Ireland) / May '88 / Homespun Records / Ross Records / Wellard Dist.

IRELAND'S COUNTRY FESTIVAL.

Tracks: Someday you'll call my name / Sing me back home / Shenandoah.
LP. . . . . HRL 146
Homespun (Ireland) / May '88 / Homespun Records / Ross Records / Wellard Dist.

IRELAND'S COUNTRY GIRLS.

Tracks: Any Tipperary town: *Margo* / Where the river Shannon flows: *McCann, Susan* / Bunch of violets blue: *Breen, Ann* / Three leaf shamrock: *Margo* / Moonlight in Mayo: *Quinn, Philomena* / Travellin' people: *McCann, Susan* / West of the old river shannon: *Margo* / Boys from County Armagh: *Margo* / Love is teasin': *Breen, Ann* / Forty shades of green: *Quinn, Philomena* / Boys from County Mayo: *Margo* / Gentle mother: *Breen, Ann* / If we only had old Ireland over here: *Quinn, Philomena* / Isle of Innisfree: *McCann, Susan*.
MC . . . . CPHL 501
Homespun (Ireland) / '88 / Homespun Records / Ross Records / Wellard Dist.

IRELAND'S COUNTRY QUEENS (Ann Breen, Leon, Margo, Philomena Begley).

Tracks: Who's sorry now / Lonely hearts club / You never were mine / Mississippi / Will you love me tomorrow / Never again will I knock on your door / Teddy bear / Hello darlin' / One day at a time / Old arboe / Family bible / River road.
LP. . . . . PHL 456
MC . . . . CPHL 456
Homespun (Ireland) / Dec '82 / Homespun Records / Ross Records / Wellard Dist.

IRISH COUNTRY FLAVOUR.

Tracks: Old log cabin: *Big Tom & The Mainliners* / Blue Kentucky girl: *Durkin, Kathy* / Love's gonna live here: *Flavin, Mick* / We'll sweep out: *Cassidy, Noel* / Five little fingers: *McBride, Frankie* / He'll have to go: *Allen, Tony* / Hanging tree, The: *Coll, Brian* / New moon over my shoulder: *Flynn, Joe* / I love you because: *Foster & Allen* / Sea of heartbreak: *Coll, Brian* / My thanks to you: *Flynn, Joe* / Devil woman: *O'Brien, Paddy* / I fall to pieces: *McCann, Susan* / Tenessee waltz: *Morrissey, Louise* / Food on the table: *Cassidy, Noel* / I heard the bluebirds sing: *Flavin, Mick*.
LP. . . . . HM 054
Harmac (Ireland) / Mar '90 / I & B Records / Prism Leisure PLC.

IRISH COUNTRY VOL.1.

Tracks: Not Advised.
MC . . . . FACS 009
CMR/Failte / Dec '88 / I & B Records.

■ DELETED

J

JIN ROCKABILLY.
Tracks: Not Advised.
LP . . . . **R&C 1016**
Rock & Country / Oct '88 / Swift.

JUKE BOX COUNTRY.
Tracks: Not Advised.
CD Set . . . . **WMCD 5603**
Kwest / Dec '92 / Terry Blood Dist.

K

KEEP ON TRUCKING.
Tracks: Let's truck together: *Price, Kenny* / Roll on truckers: *Newton, Juice & Silver Spur* / Truck driving man: *Fell, Terry* / Little diesel driving devil: *Bowman, Dan* / Caffeine, nicotine and benzedrine: *Stuckey, Nat* / White line fever: *Brewer, Bud* / Peterbilt: *Knight, Carl* / I'm a truck: *Russel, Johnny* / Somebody stole my rig: *Silverstein, Shel* / Six days on the road: *Snow, Hank* / Long thin dawn: *Hamilton, George IV* / Roll big wheels roll: *Oxford, Vernon* / Truckers paradise: *Nicholls, Nev* / Truck driving woman: *Jean, Norma* / Truck driver truck driver: *Bare, Bobby* / Mama was a truck driver queen: *Brewer, Bud* / Diesel cowboy: *McAuley, Ray & Wild Country* / Ten miles from home: *McKenna, Fred* / One more dusty road: *Hawkes, Chip.*
■ **LP** . . . . **INTS 5076**
RCA International / Jun '81.
LP . . . . **NL 89023**
■ **MC** . . . . **NK 89023**
RCA International / Oct '84.

KENTUCKY ROCK-A-BILLY.
Tracks: Be bop battlin' ball: *Gaines, Eddie* / Man alive: *Pate, Gus* / Kick off: *Pate, Gus* / Wild side of life: *Rothering, Dewey* / Long black shiny car: *Page, Mike* / Baby you done flubbed your dub with me: *Tag & Effie* / Rock 'n' roll on a Saturday night: *Bell, Dwain* / I'm gonna ride: *Bell, Dwain* / Hula hoop boogie: *Orr, J.D.* / Come to me baby: *Oller, Shady* / You sure look good to me: *Oller, Shady* / Wildfire: *Herman, Norman* / Don't play around with my heart: *Piper, Jimmy.*
LP . . . . **WLP 8802**
White Label (Germany) / Feb '87 / Pinnacle / Bear Family Records (Germany) / CSA Tell Tapes.

KINDA COUNTRY.
Tracks: Not Advised.
CD . . . . **MATCD 221**
MC . . . . **MATMC 221**
Castle / Dec '92 / BMG.

KINDA COUNTRY VOL.1.
Tracks: Not Advised.
Double LP . . . . **CR 064**
MC Set . . . . **CRT 064**
Cambra / '88.

KINDA COUNTRY VOL.2.
Tracks: Not Advised.
CD . . . . **MATCD 265**
MC . . . . **MATMC 265**
Castle / Apr '93 / BMG.

KING OF THE ROAD.
Tracks: King of the road: *Miller, Roger* / Most beautiful girl, The: *Rich, Charlie* / Devil woman: *Robbins, Marty* / I can help Billy Swan: *Bare, Bobby* / Don't take your guns to town: *Cash, Johnny* / Heroes: *Cash, Johnny & Waylon Jennings* / Whiter shade of pale, A: *Nelson, Willie* / Help me make it through the night: *Kristofferson, Kris* / Oh pretty woman: *Orbison, Roy* / I'll see you in my dreams: *Atkins, Chet* / Good year for the roses, A: *Jones, George* / Highwayman: *Jennings, Waylon & Friends* / Eagle wayon, The: *Jennings, Waylon* / Devil went down to Georgia, The: *Daniels, Charlie* / Under the gun: *Kristofferson, Kris.*
MC **4680944**
CBS / '91 / Sony.

KING/FEDERAL ROCKABILLIES (14 Hits).
Tracks: Not Advised.
CD . . . . **CD 1041**
Gusto (USA) / '88.

LP . . . . **K 5016**
King (USA) / Mar '88 / Charly.

KINGS OF COUNTRY.
Tracks: Not Advised.
CD **6 6450152**
BMG / Dec '92 / BMG.
MC **6 6450154**
BMG / Nov '92 / BMG.

KINGS OF COUNTRY.
Tracks: Reuben James: *Rogers, Kenny* / Sweet dreams: *Young, Faron* / I can't find the time: *Nelson, Willie* / Things to talk about: *Jackson, Stonewall* / Ruby don't take your love to town: *Rogers, Kenny* / Talk about me: *Paycheck, Johnny* / From a jack to a king: *Miller, Ned* / I didn't sleep a wink: *Nelson, Willie* / White lightning: *Jennings, Waylon* / Wings of a dove: *Husky, Ferlin* / Ramblin' rose: *Lee, Johnny* / Country girl: *Young, Faron* / Home is where you're happy: *Nelson, Willie* / Dear heart: *Miller, Roger* / Shine on ruby mountain: *Rogers, Kenny* / Rhythm & booze: *Owens, Buck* / Four in the morning: *Young, Faron* / Is there something on your mind: *Nelson, Willie* / Hello walls: *Young, Faron* / Candy store: *Lee, Johnny* / For the good times: *Rogers, Kenny* / Billy Jack Washburn: *Paycheck, Johnny* / Ol' blue: *Jackson, Stonewall* / Shelter of my arms: *Nelson, Willie* / This old house: *Perkins, Carl* / Something's burning: *Rogers, Kenny* / Sally was a good old girl: *Jennings, Waylon* / Moonlight gambler: *Laine, Frankie* / Wine me up: *Young, Faron* / Send me the pillow you dream on: *Locklin, Hank* / Building heartaches: *Nelson, Willie* / Sad and lonely days: *Dudley, Dave* / Heartaches by the number: *Mitchell, Guy* / Blue is the way I feel: *Twitty, Conway.*
MC Set . . . . **TTMC 047**
Tring / Jun '92 / Prism Leisure PLC / Midland Records / Taylors.

KINGS OF COUNTRY AND WESTERN.
Tracks: Not Advised.
CD **290 13 006**
Bellaphon / Jan '86 / New Note.
CD **100 013**
Bridge (MCS Bridge) / Jan '86 / Pinnacle.

KINGS OF COUNTRY LIVE.
Tracks: Not Advised.
CD . . . . **JHD 009**
MC . . . . **MCJHD 009**
IMD / Jun '92 / BMG.

KINGS OF MEMPHIS TOWN.
Tracks: Not Advised.
LP . . . . **RL 333**
Roots (Germany) / Oct '88 / Swift / C.M. Distribution.

KINGS OF ROCKABILLY.
Tracks: Not Advised.
MC Set . . . . **DTO 10236**
Ditto / May '86 / Pickwick Records.

KINGS OF ROCKABILLY VOL 1.
Tracks: Not Advised.
■ **LP** **10CH 18**
Chiswick Records / Jun '80.

KINGS OF ROCKABILLY VOL 2.
Tracks: Not Advised.
■ **LP** **10CH 19**
Chiswick Records / Jun '80.

KINGS OF THE ROAD.
Tracks: King of the road: *Miller, Roger* / Most beautiful girl, The: *Rich, Charlie* / Devil woman: *Robbins, Marty* / I can help: *Swan, Billy* / Gambler, The: *Bare, Bobby* / Don't take your guns to town: *Cash, Johnny* / Heroes: *Cash, Johnny & Waylon Jennings* / Whiter shade of pale, A: *Nelson, Willie* / Help me make it through the night: *Kristofferson, Kris* / Oh pretty woman: *Orbison, Roy* / I'll see you in my dreams: *Atkins, Chet & Mark Knopfler* / Good year for the roses, A: *Jones, George* / Highwayman: *Jennings, Waylon, Willie Nelson,Johnny Cash,K. Kristofferson* / Eagle, The: *Jennings, Waylon* / Devil went down to Georgia, The: *Daniels, Charlie Band* / Under the gun: *Nelson, Willie/Kris Kristofferson/Dolly Parton.*
CD **4680942**
Columbia / Mar '91 / Sony.
■ **MC** **4680844**
Columbia / Mar '91.

L

L.A. ROCKABILLY.
Tracks: Not Advised.
LP . . . . **LP 8707**
Rockhouse / Jan '88 / Charly / C.M. Distribution / Nervous Records.

LEGEND OF JESSE JAMES.
Tracks: Ride of the redlegs / Quantrill's querillas / Six gun shooting / Have you heard the news: / Heaven ain't ready for you yet / Help him Jesus / Old clay county, The / Riding with Jesse James / Hunt them down / Wish we were back in Missouri / Northfield the plan / Northfield the disaster / High walls / Death of me / Plot, The / One more shot.
■ **Double LP** . . . . **AMLK 63718**
A&M / Nov '80.
■ **MC Set** . . . . **CKM 63718**
A&M / Nov '80.

LEGENDARY COUNTRY & WESTERN HITS.
Tracks: Gentle on my mind: *Young, Faron* / Me and Bobby McGee: *Statler Brothers* / Sweet dreams: *McEntire, Reba* / Mama don't let your babies grow up to be cowboys: *White, Tony Joe* / Touble in mind: *Lewis, Jerry Lee* / Rock Island line: *Donegan, Lonnie* / Week in a country jail, A / Green green grass of home: *Miller, Roger* / Early morning rain: *Lewis, Jerry Lee* / Street of Laredo, The: *Young, Faron* / Country boy: *Wolf, Micky* / That's the way a cowboy rocks and rolls: *Ward, Jacky* / Cold cold heart: *Jones, George* / Sixteen tons: *Dudley, Dave* / Sunday morning coming down: *Kennedy, Jerry* / Country roads: *Donegan, Lonnie.*
MC **818 229 4**
Mercury (Germany) / Apr '85 / Pinnacle.

LEGENDARY SUN SOUND, THE.
Tracks: Not Advised.
CD Set . . . . **CDBOX 255**
LP Set . . . . **BOX 255**
■ **MC Set** . . . . **TCBOX 255**
Charly / Nov '89 / Charly.

LET'S FLAT GET IT.
Tracks: Let's flat get it / Billy boy / Baby lets play house / Such a night / Once with you / Shape I'm in, The / Can'tcha see / Little ole you / I'd rather be lucky / Pretty blue jean baby / Mama mama / When I'm alone with you / You've got me lyin' / Satisfaction guaranteed / Where did you stay last night / Talk about my baby.
■ **LP** . . . . **CR 30253**
Charly / Jul '88 / Charly.

LET'S ROCK TONIGHT.
Tracks: Let's rock tonight: *Grubbs, Jimmy* / Six foot down: *Ski, Gene* / Fool about you: *Darren, Danny* / Bitter feelings: *Phillipson, Larry* / Venus rock: *Rollettes* / Shake bop: *Garland, Dickie* / Ce'ny: *Jerry & The Silvertones* / Mystery train: *Waleen, Johnny* / Take my everything: *Cay, Phil* / You shake me: *Lane, Bobby* / Blacksmith rock: *Short, Bill* / Here we go again: *Short, Bill* / Budd's bounce: *Clarke, Gene* / Never: *Jones, Sweetie* / Dark eyes: *Chessmen* / Oh baby: *Jackson, Bobby.*
LP . . . . **WLP 8843**
White Label (Germany) / '87 / Pinnacle / Bear Family Records (Germany) / CSA Tell Tapes.

LIBRARY OF CONGRESS BANJO COLLECTION, VOL. 1 (1937-1946).
Tracks: Not Advised.
LP . . . . **ROUNDER 0237**
Rounder / '88 / Projection / Roots Records / Swift / C.M. Distribution / Topic Records / Jazz Music / Hot Shot / A.D.A Distribution / Direct Distribution.
MC . . . . **ROUNDER 0237C**
Rounder / Aug '88 / Projection / Roots Records / Swift / C.M. Distribution / Topic Records / Jazz Music / Hot Shot / A.D.A Distribution / Direct Distribution.

LITTLE JUMP JOINT.
Tracks: I get the blues when it rains: *Payne, Jimmy & Dick Barton* / Whatcha gonna say?: *Miller, Rich* / Hep, 2, 3, 4: *Manis, Georgie* / Hang up my rock 'n' roll shoes: *Oldham, Ronnie* / Good good lovin': *Bissett, Jim* / Please come back: *Starfires* / Rocky bop: *Starfires* / Hold me tight tonight: *Starfires* / Jungle boogie: *Starfires* / Blonde headed woman: *Lee, Harold* / Little jump joint: *McKinnon, Harold* / You don't love me, baby: *McKinnon, Harold* / Krunchy: *Boy, Donnie* / Flippin' over you: *Pearson, Ronnie* / Wigwam Willie: *Phillips, Carl* / Salty dog blues: *Phillips, Carl.*
LP . . . . **WLP 8909**
White Label (Germany) / Oct '86 / Pinnacle / Bear Family Records (Germany) / CSA Tell Tapes.

LOTS OF ROCKIN'.
Tracks: Just for tonight: *Trent, Tommy* / Spider, The: *Lee, Eddie* / Everybody rock: *Lee, Eddie* / Show boat boogie: *Winkler, Al* / High steppin' woman: *Hardin, Jim* / Lowdown feeling: *Blair, Retus* / Scroungy man: *Aldrich, Charlie* / Don't move me more no: *Cavallo, Jimmy* / Lot of shakin', lot of jivin': *Piano Red* / Key jammer: *Piano Red* / Rockin' down Mexico way: *Clingman, Loy* / Don't stop the rockin': *Richmond, Pat* / Tommy: *Richmond, Pat* / Can't I have you tonight?: *Deltones* / Beatnik: *Royal Jokers* / Vibrations: *Royal Jokers.*
LP . . . . **WLP 8871**
White Label (Germany) / Jan '85 / Pinnacle / Bear Family Records (Germany) / CSA Tell Tapes.

LOVE COUNTRY.
Tracks: Almost persuaded: *Rich, Charlie* / There goes my everything: *Wynette, Tammy* / Woman in my..: *Robbins, Marty* / Right time of the night: *Anderson, Lynn* / Thing called love, A: *Cash, Johnny* / Love's a hurting thing: *Robbins, Marty* / Loving arms: *Tucker, Tanya* / Satisfied man, A: *Rich, Charlie* / We loved it away: *Jones, George & Tammy Wynette* / Very special love song, The: *Mandrell, Barbara* / Let it be me: *Tucker,*

Tanya / Your sweet lies: *Wynette, Tammy* / I'd run a mile to you: *Anderson, Lynn* / I lost her to a Dallas cowboy: *Bandy, Moe* / My elusive dreams: *Rich, Charlie* / Honey come back: *Anderson, Lynn* / Another lonely song: *Wynette, Tammy* / If I were a carpenter: *Cash, Johnny* / Satisfied: *Mandrell, Barbara* / Near you.
MC Set .... **DTO 10264**
Ditto / '88 / Pickwick Records.
MC Set .... **DTOL 10264**
Ditto / Feb '90 / Pickwick Records.

LOVE SONGS (I love country).
Tracks: Takin' it easy: *Dalton, Lacy J* / Love can't ever get better than this: *Skaggs, Ricky* / Natural high: *Haggard, Merle & Janie Fricke* / Let it be me / You are so beautiful: *Tucker, Tanya* / Shine on shine all your sweet love on me: *Jones, George* / Always have always will: *Frickie, Janie* / My woman my woman my wife: *Robbins, Marty* / Behind closed doors: *Rich, Charlie* / You needed me: *Wynette, Tammy* / Nothing but your love matters: *Gatlin, Larry & The Gatlin Brothers Band* / You never gave up on me: *Gayle, Crystal* / True love ways: *Gilley, Mickey* / I love how you love me: *Anderson, Lynn* / If I were a carpenter: *Cash, Johnny & June Carter* / Sunrise: *Atkins, Chet.*
LP **4510101**
■ **MC** **4510104**
Epic / Mar '88.

LUCKEY LABEL, THE.
Tracks: Look what I found: *Hubbard, Orangie* / Is she sore?: *Hubbard, Orangie* / Missed the workhouse: *Watkins, Bill* / I got troubles: *Watkins, Bill* / Creepin' and crawlin': *Browning, Bill Zekie* / I'll pay you back: *Browning, Bill Zekie* / Spinning wheel rock: *Browning, Bill Zekie* / Bad case of the blues: *Browning, Bill Zekie* / If it's lovin' that you want: *Martin, Billy* / Love is just that way: *Brady, Pal* / When you're gone: *Brady, Pal* / Rock old sputnik: *Young, Nelson* / Charlie Brown's mule: *Young, Nelson* / Jealous dreams: *Grove, Bobby* / Black train: *Dale, Larry & Rudy Thacker.*
LP .... **WLP 8857**
White Label (Germany) / '87 / Pinnacle / Bear Family Records (Germany) / CSA Tell Tapes.

M

MARVEL-MASTERS VOL 1.
Tracks: Not Advised.
LP .... **COWBOY CARL 100**
Cowboy Carl / Apr '79 / Mike's Country Music Room.

MASTER OF COUNTRY.
Tracks: Not Advised.
LP .... **MFP 41 5690 1**
■ **MC** .... **MFP 41 5690 4**
MFP / Jan '85.

ME & OL' C.B. TRUK 3.
Tracks: Not Advised.
MC .... **VCA 621**
VFM Cassettes / VFM Children's Entertainment Ltd. / Midland Records / Morley Audio Services.

MEMPHIS HONKY TONK HILLBILLY.
Tracks: Not Advised.
LP .... **CH 168**
Ace / Jun '86 / Pinnacle / Hot Shot / Jazz Music / Complete Record Co. Ltd.

MEMPHIS LABEL STORY, THE.
Tracks: Rockin' at the Y: *Ingle, Thomas* / Wild wild party: *Feathers, Charlie* / Prom, The: *Roundabouts* / I couldn't make..: *Arnold, Lloyd* / Sugaree: *Arnold, Lloyd* / I've waited too long: *Christian, Jody* / Tomorrow I'll..: *Boyd, Eddie* / Go go go: *Longhairs* / Rockin' boppin' teenager: *Shaw, Jim* / Love don't..: *Feathers, Charlie* / What's the matter: *Shaw, Jim* / Hey rena: *Maupin, Ramon* / Today and tomorrow: *Feathers, Charlie* / I'll cry today: *Ingle, Thomas* / Next to me: *Arnold, Lloyd* / Night surfing: *Rebel Rousers.*
LP .... **CHAD 197**
Ace / Mar '87 / Pinnacle / Hot Shot / Jazz Music / Complete Record Co. Ltd.

MEMPHIS ROCKABILLY.
Tracks: Jukebox mama / Got the blues from waiting / Boppin' wigwam Willie / Here comes that train / Joints really jumping, The / Got you on my mind / How can I go / Lowdown feeling / Standing in your window / Eenie meenie minie mo / Boo be ah be / Baby don't you know me any more / Short skirts / I'm asking but I'm not getting / Goodbye she's gone / Slowly dying.
■ **LP** .... **CH 167**
Ace / Mar '86.
■ **LP** .... **SJLP 568**
Sunjay / Oct '87.

MEMPHIS ROCKABILLY VOL 2.
Tracks: Rockin' at the Y / Wild wild party / Tomorrow I'll be gone / Hey Rena / Night surfing / Make my dreams come true / What's the matter with my heart / Tennessee twist / Zombie walks, The / Let's make the party sweet / Prom, The / Rockin' boppin' teenager / I'll cry today / Tomorrow we'll know / Go go go.
LP .... **SJLP 578**
Sunjay / '88 / CSA Tell Tapes.

MEMPHIS SATURDAY NIGHT.
Tracks: Not Advised.
LP .... **Z 2005**
Zu Zazz / '88 / Hot Shot / A.D.A Distribution / C.M. Distribution.

MEMPHIS-ROCK'N'ROLL CAPITAL OF THE WORLD.
Tracks: Let's talk about us / Strength of love / Rockin' guitars / Diamond of my heart / Rock bottom boogie / Doin' it live / Memphis Tennessee / Wash my hands in a muddy stream / My rock & roll daddy / Witchapoo / Big fat mama / My bonny / Walkin' Charlie / My friends call me shorty / Don't be angry.
LP .... **WLP 8914**
White Label (Germany) / Feb '87 / Pinnacle / Bear Family Records (Germany) / CSA Tell Tapes.

MEMPHIS-ROCK'N'ROLL CAPITAL OF THE WORLD VOL.4.
Tracks: Rockin' at the Y: *Ingle, Thomas* / Bright lights and wild, wild women: *Shaw, Jim* / Boogie beat: *Shaw, Jim* / Rockin' boppin' teenager: *Shaw, Jim* / Wishing on a star: *Shaw, Jim* / Today and tomorrow: *Feathers, Charlie* / Sweet girl of mine: *Nelson, Doyle* / Rising mercury: *Sabres, Les* / Prom, The: *Runabouts* / When I get the blues: *Runabouts* / Tennessee twist: *Arnold, Lloyd* / Sugaree: *Arnold, Lloyd* / Go go go: *Arnold, Lloyd* / Night surfing: *Rebel Rousers* / You don't know what to do: *Rebel Rousers* / Run don't walk: *Davis, Bobby.*
LP .... **WLP 8916**
White Label (Germany) / May '87 / Pinnacle / Bear Family Records (Germany) / CSA Tell Tapes.

MEMPHIS-ROCK'N'ROLL CAPITAL OF THE WORLD VOL.5.
Tracks: Dudley do rite: *Evans, Jimmy* / Messy Bessy: *Evans, Jimmy* / Pink cadillac: *Evans, Jimmy* / J & E twist: *Evans, Jimmy* / Call me Mr Lonesome: *Evans, Jimmy* / Kassavubu boogie: *Skylarks* / Drop it: *Skylarks* / Look coming yonder: *Hogan, Joel* / Go on and say goodbye: *Hogan, Joel* / Spinning top: *Graves, Glenn* / Quicksand love: *Skipper, Macy* / Who put the squeeze on Eloise?: *Skipper, Macy* / Midnight train: *Rocco, Tommy* / Battle of Earl K. Long: *Barton, Bart* / Ain't I a mess?: *Barton, Bart* / Walk with me: *Barton, Bart* / Man with the heart of gold: *Barton, Bart.*
LP .... **WLP 8918**
White Label (Germany) / May '87 / Pinnacle / Bear Family Records (Germany) / CSA Tell Tapes.

MEMPHIS-ROCK'N'ROLL CAPITAL OF THE WORLD VOL.6.
Tracks: It's all your fault: *Smith, Jerry Lee* / Girl can't help it, The: *Smith, Jerry Lee* / Cocklebur: *Fuller, Tiny* / I am a pilgrim: *Fuller, Tiny* / Running wild: *Starks, Blackie* / What's on your mind?: *Smith, Shelby* / Since my baby said goodbye: *Smith, Shelby* / You have this and more: *Moore, Ronnie* / Firefly: *Wammack, Travis* / Honky tonk ways: *Turney, Carvis* / Jimmy the kid: *Stone, Doug* / Memphis yodel blues: *Stone, Doug* / She moved to Kansas City: *Stone, Doug* / Pick me up on your way down: *Stone, Doug* / Boll Weevil Junction: *Blankenship, Sonny.*
LP .... **WLP 8920**
White Label (Germany) / '87 / Pinnacle / Bear Family Records (Germany) / CSA Tell Tapes.

MERCURY NEW ORLEANS SESSIONS, THE (1950).
Tracks: Hey now baby: *Byrd, Roy* / Bald head: *Byrd, Roy* / Her mind is gone: *Byrd, Roy* / Oh well: *Byrd, Roy* / Hadacol bounce: *Byrd, Roy* / Longhair stomp: *Byrd, Roy* / Been foolin' around: *Byrd, Roy* / Between the night and day: *Byrd, Roy* / Byrd's blues: *Byrd, Roy* / Her mind is gone (2): *Byrd, Roy* / Hadacol bounce (2): *Byrd, Roy* / Between the night and day (2): *Byrd, Roy* / Longhair stomp (2): *Byrd, Roy* / Miss lollipop's confession: *Mondy, Alma* / Love troubles: *Mondy, Alma* / Still my angel child: *Mondy, Alma* / Baby get wise: *Mondy, Alma* / Just as soon as I get home: *Mondy, Alma* / No stuff for me: *Mondy, Alma* / Street walkin' daddy: *Mondy, Alma* / Job for a jockey, A: *Mondy, Alma* / Miss lollipop's confession (2): *Mondy, Alma* / Love troubles (2): *Mondy, Alma* / Just as soon as I get home (2): *Mondy, Alma* / Mercury boogie: *Craven, Dwight* / New way of lising: *Craven, Dwight* / She won't leave no more: *Gaines, Little Joe* / Snuff dipper: *Gaines, Little Joe* / I walk in my sleep: *Johnson, Theard* / Lost love: *Johnson, Theard* / Boogies the thing: *Miller, George* / Bat Lee swing: *Miller, George* / Bat Lee swing (2): *Miller, George.*
Double LP .... **BFD 15308**
Bear Family / Apr '89 / Rollercoaster Records / Swift / Direct Distribution.

MERCURY ROCKABILLIES.
Tracks: Flip flop mama / Boppin Bonnie / You nearly lose your mind / You're my big baby now / That's my reward / Mean mistreatin' baby / Burning the wind / You're the one that done it / Slip slip slippin' in / Baby, baby, baby, what'm I gonna do / Born to sing the blues / Lonesome train / Wild wild mind / Crazy blues / Draggin' / Sittin' on top of the world.
■ **LP** **6463 084**
Mercury / Apr '81.

METEOR ROCKABILLIES.
Tracks: Mama's little baby: *Thompson, Junior* / Raw deal: *Thompson, Junior* / Tongue tied Jill: *Feathers, Charlie* / Get with it: *Feathers, Charlie* / Rock, roll and rhythm: *McGinnis, Wayne* / Lonesome rhythm blues: *McGinnis, Wayne* / Don't shoot me baby (I'm not ready to die): *Bowen, Bill* / Have myself a ball: *Bowen, Bill* / All messed up: *Hooper, Jess* / Sleepy time blues: *Hooper, Jess* / Latch on to your baby: *Lamberth, Jimmy* / Bop baby bop: *Suggs, Brad* / Charcoal suit: *Suggs, Brad* / Can't steal my way around: *Burcham, Barney* / Much too young for love: *Burcham, Barney* / Curfew: *Carl, Steve & The Jags* / 18 year old blues: *Carl, Steve & The Jags* / Gonna shut you off baby: *Haggett, Jimmy* / Women: *Smith, Lendon & the Jesters* / Brother, that's all: *Hadley, Red* / Real gone baby: *Velvetones* / Gal named Joe, A: *Sales, Mac* / Yakety yak: *Mac & Jake* / Don't worry 'bout nothin': *Dixon, Mason.*
CD .... **CDCHM 484**
Ace / Jul '93 / Pinnacle / Hot Shot / Jazz Music / Complete Record Co. Ltd.

MGM ROCKABILLY COLLECTION (Original Artists).
Tracks: Rockin' rollin' stone: *Starr, Andy* / I want a go South: *Starr, Andy* / She's a going jessie: *Starr, Andy* / Old Deacon Jones: *Starr, Andy* / Mr Blues: *Rainwater, Marvin* / Rock 'n' roll fever: *Campbell, Cecil & His Tennessee Ramblers* / Give me a woman: *Starr, Andy* / Round and round: *Starr, Andy* / No room for your kind: *Starr, Andy* / One more time: *Starr, Andy* / Stutterin' papa: *Griffin, Buck* / Watchin' the 7.10 roll by: *Griffin, Buck* / Bow my back: *Griffin, Buck* / My brand of blues: *Rainwater, Marvin* / Dixieland rock: *Campbell, Cecil & His Tennessee Ramblers* / My square dancin' mama (She done learned to rock 'n' roll): *Gallion, Bob* / Rockin' and rollin' with granmaw: *Robison, Carson* / Old bee tree: *Griffin, Buck* / Jessie Lee: *Griffin, Buck.*
MC **3110 394**
MGM (Polydor) / '77.
LP **2315 394**
MGM (Polydor) / Oct '77.

MGM ROCKABILLY COLLECTION VOL.2.
Tracks: Not Advised.
■ **LP** **2354147**
MGM (Polydor) / Jul '81.

MGM ROCKABILLY KINGS.
Tracks: Not Advised.
■ **LP** .... **MID 1001**
MGM (Polydor) / Sep '81.

MIAMI ROCKABILLY, VOL 1.
Tracks: Not Advised.
LP **1001**
AFS / Jul '88 / Swift.

MIAMI ROCKABILLY, VOL 2.
Tracks: Not Advised.
LP **1002**
AFS / Jul '88 / Swift.

MIAMI ROCKABILLY, VOL 3.
Tracks: Not Advised.
LP **1003**
AFS / Jul '88 / Swift.

MINNESOTA ROCKABILLY ROCK, VOL 1.
Tracks: Record hop: *Scott, Tom* / I dig: *Don & Jer* / Rock the blues away: *Jack & The Knights* / Mean mama blues: *Ray, Ronnie* / Vulture, The: *Ray, Ronnie* / Sally Jol: *Thaxter, Jim* / Cyclone: *Thaxter, Jim* / Three bad habits: *Fritz, Hal* / Goin' out on you: *Fritz, Hal* / Switchblade: *Thompson, Ron* / Queen bee: *Harmony Twins* / Barnyard rock 'n' roll: *Harmony Twins* / Moonlight rock: *Carson, Chuck* / Downbeat rock: *Randall, Eddie.*
LP .... **WLP 8852**
White Label (Germany) / Feb '85 / Pinnacle / Bear Family Records (Germany) / CSA Tell Tapes.

MINNESOTA ROCKABILLY ROCK, VOL 2.
Tracks: My little Sue: *Lee, Terry & The Poorboys* / Driftin': *Lee, Terry & The Poorboys* / Dream night: *Houle Brothers* / Homicide: *Lee, Myron* / Mary's swinging lamb: *Lee, Myron* / Aw c'mon baby: *Lee, Myron* / Watch your step: *Galaxies* / Minus one blast off: *Sonics* / Marlene: *Sonics* / Wild party: *Vilados* / Bloodshot: *String Kings* / Bash, The: *String Kings* / Hush hush little baby: *Dennis, Bob & Denny* / Guitar boogie: *Walsh, Andy* / Flyin' high: *Thundermen.*
LP .... **WLP 8853**
White Label (Germany) / Feb '85 / Pinnacle / Bear Family Records (Germany) / CSA Tell Tapes.

MINNESOTA ROCKABILLY ROCK, VOL 3.
Tracks: Diggin' that rock 'n' roll: *Stinton Brothers* / Lightning strikes: *D.J. & The Cats* / What's up, Doug?: *Inn Truders* / Never been blue: *Urness, Harvey* / Ad lib: *Danny & The Galaxies* / If you want to be my baby: *Danny & The Galaxies* / Oh yeah: *Blue Kats* / Volcano: *Carvairs* / Come back baby: *Carroll, Evens* / Living doll: *Eddy, Jim* / Wrong kinda lovin': *Tucker, Les* / Flip, The: *Arlington, Sue* / Lost love: *Torrells* / Blue black hair: *Jades* / Surfin' cow: *Jades.*
LP .... **WLP 8854**
White Label (Germany) / Feb '85 / Pinnacle / Bear Family Records (Germany) / CSA Tell Tapes.

MINNESOTA ROCKABILLY ROCK, VOL 4.
Tracks: Baby, baby: *Waggoner, Mike & The Bops* / Basher number five: *Waggoner, Mike & The Bops* / Hey mama: *Waggoner, Mike & The Bops* / Good rockin'

tonight: *Waggoner, Mike & The Bops* / Coming up: *Waggoner, Mike & The Bops* / Guitar man: *Waggoner, Mike & The Bops* / Bye bye Johnny: *Waggoner, Mike & The Bops* / Three little pigs, The: *Waggoner, Mike & The Bops* / Work with me, Annie: *Waggoner, Mike & The Bops* / Scramble: *Barkdall, Eddie* / Wailin' wailin' party: *Barkdall, Eddie* / I still love her: *Buchwitz, Junior* / Revel rock: *Buchwitz, Junior.*
LP. . . . . **WLP 8855**
White Label (Germany) / Feb '85 / Pinnacle / Bear Family Records (Germany) / CSA Tell Tapes.

MINNESOTA ROCKABILLY ROCK, VOL 5.
Tracks: Hurry: *Robbins, Robbie* / Easy rhythm: *Glenrays* / Haunted by reception: *Glenrays* / That's alright mama: *James, Deviny* / Ivy League baby: *Garcia, Augie* / Be my guest: *Garcia, Augie* / Hi ho Silver: *Garcia, Augie* / Goin' to Chicago: *Garcia, Augie* / Lili Marlene: *Jades* / Little girl: *Leonard, Ben* / Congo bongo: *Leonard, Ben* / Buggin' the boogie: *Delricos* / Voodoo: *Delricos* / Rockin' the blues: *Flames* / Arabian caravan: *Flames* / Minor chaos: *Treasures* / Black rock: *Five Spots* / Mr. Fortune: *Five Spots.*
LP. . . . . **WLP 8878**
White Label (Germany) / '87 / Pinnacle / Bear Family Records (Germany) / CSA Tell Tapes.

MISTER ROCK 'N' ROLL.
Tracks: Matchbox: *Netherton, Fred* / You are the one: *Volk, Dennis* / I hear thunder: *Ballenger, Paul* / Annie Mae: *Dewitt, Bobby* / Rockin' the blues: *Bowman, Leon & Jerry Parker & His Buddies* / Baby tonight: *Harmony Brothers* / Saturday night bop: *Harmony Brothers* / You'll come running back to me: *Collier, Ralph* / Long lost John: *Owens, Kenny* / My queen and me: *Lenny & The Star Chiefs* / Ruby baby: *Boni, Johnny* / Train rock: *Boni, Johnny* / Mister rock 'n' roll: *Star Combo* / Love flame: *Kilgore Brothers & Howard Vokes* / Hot rod race: *Williams, Bob.*
LP. . . . . **WLP 8859**
White Label (Germany) / '87 / Pinnacle / Bear Family Records (Germany) / CSA Tell Tapes.

MODERN COUNTRY SOUND, THE.
Tracks: You took all the rambling out of me: *Reed, Jerry* / Back home again: *Denver, John* / I saw the light: *Buck, Gary* / You know who: *Bare, Bobby* / Claim on me: *Hamilton, George IV* / Gentle on my mind: *Hartford, John* / Mississippi woman: *Lane, Red* / Paradise: *Everly Brothers* / North Carolina: *Frazier, Dallas* / City of New Orleans: *Mercy Brothers* / Why have you gone so long: *Colter, Jessi* / Let's all help the cowboy: *Colter, Jessi* / Delta dawn: *West, Dottie* / Rambling man: *Stewart, Gary* / Funny, familiar, forgotten feelings: *Gibson, Don* / Bloody Mary morning: *Nelson, Willie* / Sweet memories: *Newbury, Mickey* / Jamestown ferry, The: *Russell, Johnny* / Darling raise the shade: *Wilson, Norro* / Night they drove old Dixie down, The: *Davis, Skeeter* / I use the soap: *Lee, Dickey* / Winonah: *Nesmith, Michael* / Where you been so long: *Hall, David* / Goodtime Charlie's got the blues: *Stuckey, Nat* / It's all on me: *Pure Prairie League.*
■ **LP.** . . . . **DHYK 0006**
RCA / '78 / BMG.

MONTH'S BEST FROM THE COUNTRY AND WEST.
Tracks: Once a day: *Smith, Connie* / Four strong winds: *Bare, Bobby* / I thank my lucky stars: *Arnold, Eddy* / Truck driving man: *Hamilton, George IV.*
■ **LP.** . . . . **RCX 7159**
RCA / Jan '65 / BMG.

MORE HOME MADE EARLY ROCK & ROLL.
Tracks: She's mine: *Adkins, Hasil 'Haze'* / Chicken walk: *Adkins, Hasil 'Haze'* / Hunch, The: *Adkins, Hasil 'Haze'* / Have mercy: *Hobock, Curtis* / Whole town's talking, The: *Hobock, Curtis* / I can't stay mad at you: *Friar, Hugh* / Hey, hey, don't tease me: *Ratliff, Bo* / I just learned to rock: *King, Jack* / Two ruby lips: *King, Jack* / Ooh yeah baby: *Tyler, Kip* / Jungle hop: *Tyler, Kip* / Don't try to get away: *Trowbridge, Cliff* / Man, what a party: *Walton & The Silver Lake Boys* / Cheretta rock: *Jasper, Bob* / Hillbilly hop: *Prevette, Colin.*
LP. . . . . **WLP 8868**
White Label (Germany) / Mar '84 / Pinnacle / Bear Family Records (Germany) / CSA Tell Tapes.

MORE PENNSYLVANIA BOPPERS.
Tracks: You fit me like a glove: *Sizemore, Gordon & Rex Roat* / Anything: *Sizemore, Gordon & Rex Roat* / 3 0 3: *Foley, Nick* / If you stayed: *Neat, Bill* / Squirmin' at the Sherman: *Anthony, Chuck* / Hydrogen, nitrogen, potassium: *Hall, Jim* / You found a new love: *Patrick, Sue* / Impact, The: *Impacts* / Light my rockets: *Alan, Neil* / Send me to the moon: *Alan, Neil* / Pizza pizza pizza pie: *Alan, Neil* / Eager lips: *Huckaby, Gary & Joyce Duval* / Fat mama: *Sharpe, Buddy* / White house rock: *Sharpe, Buddy* / Tommy Teen: *Colin & Jerry* / Little bit of lovin': *Pcono Playboys* / Wild stallion: *Wilson, Billy.*
LP. . . . . **WLP 8910**
White Label (Germany) / Oct '86 / Pinnacle / Bear Family Records (Germany) / CSA Tell Tapes.

MORE PRIMITIVE SOUND.
Tracks: You are my sunshine: *Woodard, Jerry* / You don't love me: *Woodard, Jerry* / Downbeat: *Woodard, Jerry* / Mean woman blues: *Woodard, Jerry* / Six long weeks: *Woodard, Jerry* / Our love & romance: *Woodard, Jerry* / Who's gonna rock my baby (1 & 2): *Woodard, Jerry* / Midnight train: *Newman, Wayne* / Rita Juanita: *Newman, Wayne* / Eeny meeny miney mo: *Davis, Jim* / Free ride: *Davis, Rebel & Big Hoe* / Big Daddy rock: *Watts, Hunter* / Whirlin' twerlin' rock: *Duncan, Bill* / Rosalie: *Lett, Roy* / Big fat papa: *Boyer, Tommy & Carl & Bill.*
LP. . . . . **WLP 8833**
White Label (Germany) / '87 / Pinnacle / Bear Family Records (Germany) / CSA Tell Tapes.

MORE RARE ROCKIN' GIRLS.
Tracks: I'm not gonna do it anymore: *Hunt Sisters* / You're not doin' me right: *Darlene, Donna* / Move over, tall woman: *Hubbard, Doris M.* / Long sideburns: *Barry, Boelean* / Chilli dippin' baby: *Poynter, Joyce* / Record hop dream: *Mae, Lonnie* / Babysitter's blues: *Paul, Bunny* / Gonna spend my time: *Myers, Orella* / Give a little, take a little: *Myers, Orella* / Ask Lucille: *Myers, Orella* / Rock 'n' roll thunderbird: *Burt Sisters* / Yeah baby: *Smith, Betty* / Two timin' woman: *Lee, Bella* / Going to hold my baby: *Wheeler, Karen* / Wait till I'm sixteen: *Wheeler, Karen* / Red thunderbird: *Howard, Lynn* / I wanna be free: *Harlene, Evelyn* / Rockin' the blues: *Griffith, Peggy* / Stagger Lee: *Johnson, Kay* / If again: *Neal, Abbie.*
LP. . . . . **WLP 8899**
White Label (Germany) / Feb '87 / Pinnacle / Bear Family Records (Germany) / CSA Tell Tapes.

MORE REAL ROCKABILLY AND COUNTRY.
Tracks: Long gone lonesome blues: *Champion, Hollis* / Big beat, The: *Champion, Hollis* / Sundown boogie: *Clour, Deral & Charly Drake* / Poor me: *McRill, Chandos* / Teddle, The: *McRill, Chandos* / Money lovin' woman: *McRill, Chandos* / Flat foot Sam: *Scoggins, Johnny* / Learning how to live: *Draper, Joseph June* / When you kissed me: *McPeak, Henry.*
LP. . . . . **WLP 8819**
White Label (Germany) / '88 / Pinnacle / Bear Family Records (Germany) / CSA Tell Tapes.

MORE SUNDOWN ROCKERS.
Tracks: I was a fool: *Cook, Ken* / Why do I love you?: *Alton & Jimmy* / I just don't know: *Alton & Jimmy* / Don't you know: *Parchman, Kenny* / Treat me right: *Parchman, Kenny* / Problem child: *Cook, Ken* / I'll wait forever: *Honeycutt, Glenn* / Heartbreak's girl: *Ballman, Wanda* / Ain't got a worry on my mind: *Ballman, Wanda* / Hey Mr. Blues: *Woods, James* / Somehow we'll find a way: *Fakes, Roger* / Gonna give a party: *Woods, James* / Lock you in my heart: *Woods, James* / Be wise don't cry: *Honeycutt, Glenn.*
LP. . . . . **SUN 1036**
Sun / Oct '88 / Charly / Swift.

MORE TENNESSEE ROCKIN'.
Tracks: I ain't gonna do it no more: *Pritchett, Dubb* / Five o'clock hop: *Pritchett, Dubb* / I don't know how to cook: *Pritchett, Dubb* / Bill's special: *Lyle, Bill* / Get off my toe: *Blakley, Cliff* / I'm not going steady anymore: *Blakley, Cliff* / High steppin': *Blakley, Cliff* / Want to be with you: *Blakley, Cliff* / Linda Lu: *Ford, Bubba* / Wiggling blonde: *Ford, Bubba* / Tiger: *Allen, Little Joe* / Nancy: *Tedder, Randy* / Good gosh gal: *Beasly, Phil* / Bedlam: *Sounds* / Ain't got a nickel: *Lowe, Max.*
LP. . . . . **WLP 8840**
White Label (Germany) / Sep '87 / Pinnacle / Bear Family Records (Germany) / CSA Tell Tapes.

MORE WILD ROCKIN'.
Tracks: Don't be that way: *Lawson, Bobby* / If you want my love: *Lawson, Bobby* / Petty blue: *Alexander, Charles* / Unknown riders: *DeWayne, Dick* / Witchcraft: *DeWayne, Dick* / Short stuff: *Jenkins, Gene* / Janet: *Martin, Jerry* / If you're gonna shake it: *Carter, Bobby* / Weird: *Vidone, Bob* / Ain't that a dilly: *Grisham, Marlon* / Sugarfoot: *Grisham, Marlon* / Wiggle: *Chearlanders* / Saturday night: *Stephens, Big Will* / She left me crying: *Harris, Dinky* / Pig pen boogie: *Bowers, Chuck* / You tore your playhouse down: *Sanders, Rabon.*
LP. . . . . **WLP 8858**
White Label (Germany) / '87 / Pinnacle / Bear Family Records (Germany) / CSA Tell Tapes.

MUSIC ON THE MOVE (20 COUNTRY GREATS).
Tracks: Not Advised.
MC . . . . **INTK 9001**
RCA International / Jun '81 / BMG.

N

NASHVILLE COUNTRY CLUB VOL. 1.
Tracks: Not Advised.
CD **288 07 006**
Bellaphon / '88 / New Note.

NASHVILLE COUNTRY ROCK, VOL 3: STEPPIN' OUT TONI.
Tracks: Not Advised.
LP. . . . . **REDITA 121**
Redita (Holland) / Jun '85 / Swift.

NASHVILLE COUNTRY ROCK, VOL 4: CRAZY ABOUT THE B.
Tracks: Not Advised.
LP. . . . . **REDITA 122**
Redita (Holland) / Jun '85 / Swift.

NASHVILLE DREAM.
Tracks: Not Advised.
CD Set . . . . **QTVCD 014**
LP Set . . . . **QTV 014**
MC Set . . . . **QTVC 014**
Quality / Oct '92 / Pinnacle.

NASHVILLE JUMPS.
Tracks: Not Advised.
LP. . . . . **KK 783**
Krazy Kat / May '84 / Hot Shot / C.M. Distribution / Wellard Dist. / Roots Records / Projection / Charly / Jazz Music.

NASHVILLE SOUND, VOL. 4.
Tracks: I still miss someone: *Cash, Johnny* / Singing the blues: *Robbins, Marty* / Charlie's shoes: *Walker, Billy* / Devil woman: *Robbins, Marty* / Ring of fire: *Cash, Johnny* / Jackson: *Cash, Johnny & June Carter* / Wound time can't erase, A: *Jackson, Stonewall* / I can't seem to say goodbye: *Hawkins, Hawkshaw* / I think I know: *Worth, Marion* / Funny how time slips away: *Walker, Billy* / Night life: *Price, Ray* / Almost persuaded: *Houston, David* / My elusive dreams: *Houston, David & Tammy Wynette* / Behind closed doors: *Rich, Charlie* / Most beautiful girl, The: *Rich, Charlie* / She's all I got: *Paycheck, Johnny* / Picture of me (without you), A: *Jones, George* / Midngiht oil, The: *Mandrell, Barbara* / Grand tour, The: *Jones, George* / I never promised you a rose garden: *Anderson, Lynn* / For the good times: *Price, Ray* / Would you lay with me (in a field of stone): *Tucker, Tanya.*
CD **4681222**
MC **4681224**
Columbia / Nov '91 / Sony.

NASHVILLE STARS IN DEUTSCHLAND.
Tracks: Not Advised.
■ **LP.** . . . . **BFX 15040**
Bear Family / '88.

NASHVILLE TODAY VOL. 1.
Tracks: Not Advised.
■ **LP.** . . . . **PL 43475**
RCA / Jun '81.

NASHVILLE TODAY VOL. 2.
Tracks: Not Advised.
■ **LP.** . . . . **PL 43284**
RCA / Aug '80.

NASHVILLE WEST.
Tracks: Nashville west / Mental revenge / I wanna live / Sweet Suzanna / Green green grass of home / Love of the common people / Tuff and stringy / Washed my hands in muddy water / Ode to Billy Joe / Louisiana rain / Send me back home / Memphis / By the time I get to Phoenix.
LP. . . . . **SRS 8701**
Sierra Briar (USA) / Jan '79 / Mike's Country Music Room.
LP. . . . . **SDLP 1011**
Sundown / Jun '84 / Terry Blood Dist. / Jazz Music / C.M. Distribution.

NASHVILLE'S FINEST HOUR.
Tracks: Not Advised.
■ **LP.** . . . . **PL 43207**
RCA / Jul '80.

NEW COUNTRY GIRLS LIVE.
Tracks: Not Advised.
CD **15 406**
MC **79 406**
Laserlight / Aug '91 / TBD / Taylors.

NEW COUNTRY GIRLS LIVE.
Tracks: Ball and chain: *Mattea, Kathy* / Street talk: *Mattea, Kathy* / Someone is falling in love: *Mattea, Kathy* / Put yourself in my place: *Mattea, Kathy & John Thompson* / Heart of the country: *Mattea, Kathy* / Chains of gold: *Sweethearts Of The Rodeo* / Hey doll baby: *Sweethearts Of The Rodeo* / Stuck on you: *Morgan, Lorrie* / Please Mr.Please: *Morgan, Lorrie* / Love is fair: *Morgan, Lorrie* / You're gettin' to me again: *Morgan, Lorrie* / It's what you don't do: *Loveless, Patty* / Lonely days, lonely nights: *Loveless, Patty* / Dixie man: *Forester Sisters* / Just in case: *Forester Sisters* / I fell in love again last night: *Forester Sisters* / Night they drove old Dxiie down, The: *Tucker, Tanya* / Texas when I die: *Tucker, Tanya.*
VHS. . . . . **PLATV 353**
Platinum Music / Mar '90 / Prism Leisure PLC / Ross Records.

NEW NASHVILLE COUNTRY MUSIC.
Tracks: Not Advised.
MC Set . . . . **DFG 8410**
Dixie Frog / Nov '88 / Discovery.

NEW STARS FROM THE HEARTLAND.
Tracks: Shameless: *Brooks, Garth* / Down at the twist & shout: *Carpenter, Mary-Chapin* / Here's a quarter (call someone who cares): *Tritt, Travis* / She's in love with the boy: *Yearwood, Trisha* / Don't rock the jukebox: *Jackson, Alan* / We both walk: *Morgan, Lorrie* / Forever together: *Travis, Randy* / Young love (strong love):

Judds / Put yourself in my shoes: *Black, Clint* / Walk on faith: *Reid, Mike (2)* / For my broken heart: *McEntire, Reba* / Restless: *O'Connor, Mark & New Nashville Cats* / Bing bang boom: *Highway 101* / You know me better than that: *Strait, George* / Pocket full of gold: *Gill, Vince* / Down to my last teardrop: *Tucker, Tanya* / Jukebox with a country song, A: *Stone, Doug* / Someday soon: *Bogguss, Suzy* / Life's too long: *Skaggs, Ricky* / You don't count the cost: *Dean, Billy*.

CD . . . . **CDESTU 2172**
MC . . . . **TCESTU 2172**
EMI / Apr '92 / EMI.
■ **LP** . . . . **ESTU 2172**
EMI / Apr '92.

NEW TRADITION. VOL. 5, A.

Tracks: Daddy sang bass: *Cash, Johnny* / I'll be your baby tonight: *Dylan, Bob* / Hickory wind: *Byrds* / When I stop dreaming: *Jim & Jesse* / Pickin' up the pieces: *Poco* / Can't you hear me calling: *Pedersen, Herb* / Uncle Pen / Blue eyes crying in the rain: *Nelson, Willie* / Miss the mississippi and you: *Gayle, Crystal* / Faded love: *Nelson, Willie & Ray Price* / Big city: *Haggard, Merle* / Choo choo ch'boogie: *Asleep At The Wheel* / Houston (means I'm one day closer to you): *Gatlin, Larry & The Gatlin Brothers* / El Paso city: *Robbins, Marty* / Ride, The: *Coe, David Allan* / Hank Williams, you wrote my life: *Bandy, Moe* / There's a song on the jukebox: *Wills, David* / He stopped loving her today: *Jones, George* / Life turned her that way: *Shelton, Ricky Van* / Oh darlin': *O'Kanes* / I couldn't leave you if I tried: *Crowell, Rodney* / So sad (to watch good love go bad): *Sweethearts Of The Rodeo* / Seven year ache: *Cash, Rosanne*.

CD **4681232**
MC **4681234**
Columbia / Nov '91 / Sony.

NO.1 COUNTRY - 80'S COUNTRY.

Tracks: Rockin' with the rhythm of the rain: *Judds* / Do ya': *Oslin, K.T.* / Strong heart: *Sheppard, T.G.* / Crying my heart out over you: *Skaggs, Ricky* / Houston means I'm one day closer to you: *Gatlin, Larry* / Can't stop my heart from loving you: *O'Kanes* / Love in the first degree: *Alabama* / Seven year ache: *Cash, Rosanne* / Once in a blue moon: *Conley, Earl Thomas* / Somebody lied: *Van Shelton, Ricky* / It'll be me: *Exile* / Got my heart set on you: *Conlee, John* / My only love: *Statler Brothers* / True love ways: *Gilley, Mickey*.

■ **LP** . . . . **KNLP 13005**
Country Collection / Feb '89.
CD . . . . **KNCD 13005**
■ **MC** . . . . **KNMC 13005**
Country Collection / Feb '89.

NO.1 COUNTRY - COUNTRY BALLADEERS (14 country no.1's).

Tracks: Coward of the county: *Rogers, Kenny* / El Paso: *Robbins, Marty* / Don't take your guns: *Cash, Johnny* / Wichita lineman: *Campbell, Glen* / Golden ring: *Jones, George & Tammy Wynette* / When it's Springtime in [illegible] the DJ: *Jackson, Stonewall* / What's your mama's name: *Tucker, Tanya* / She thinks I still care: *Jones, George* / Girl on the billboard: *Reeves, Del* / Running bear: *James, Sonny* / Saginaw, Michigan: *Frizzell, Lefty*.

■ **LP** . . . . **KNLP 13010**
Country Collection / Sep '89.
CD . . . . **KNCD 13010**
■ **MC** . . . . **KNMC 13010**
Country Collection / Sep '89.

NO.1 COUNTRY - COUNTRY BOYS.

Tracks: One piece at a time: *Cash, Johnny* / Me and Bobby McGee: *Lewis, Jerry Lee* / Living in the promised land: *Nelson, Willie* / I cheated me right out of you: *Bandy, Moe* / Country boy: *Skaggs, Ricky* / Faster horses: *Hall, Tom T.* / Lucille (you won't do your Daddie's will): *Jennings, Waylon* / Why baby why: *Pride, Charley* / Natural high: *Haggard, Merle* / I always get lucky with you: *Jones, George* / Lost in the fifties tonight: *Milsap, Ronnie* / Love don't care (whose heart it breaks): *Conley, Earl Thomas* / Lonely nights: *Gilley, Mickey* / My woman my woman my wife: *Robbins, Marty*.

■ **LP** . . . . **KNLP 13003**
Country Collection / Feb '89.
CD . . . . **KNCD 13003**
■ **MC** . . . . **KNMC 13003**
Country Collection / Feb '89.

NO.1 COUNTRY - COUNTRY CLASSICS.

Tracks: Walk on by: *Van Dyke, Leroy* / Stand by your man: *Wynette, Tammy* / Tender years: *Jones, George* / For the good times: *Price, Ray* / Eleven roses: *Williams, Hank Jr.* / Year that Clayton Delaney died, The: *Hall, Tom T.* / I ain't never: *Tillis, Mel* / Big bad John: *Dean, Jimmy* / King of the road: *Miller, Roger* / North to Alaska: *Horton, Johnny* / Rose garden: *Anderson, Lynn* / Sunday morning coming down: *Cash, Johnny* / It's four in the morning: *Young, Faron* / There must be more to love than this: *Lewis, Jerry Lee* / Almost persuaded: *Houston, David* / Devil woman: *Robbins, Marty*.

■ **LP** . . . . **KNLP 13006**
Country Collection / Feb '89.
CD . . . . **KNCD 13006**
■ **MC** . . . . **KNMC 13006**
Country Collection / Feb '89.

NO.1 COUNTRY - COUNTRY DUETS.

Tracks: Near you: *Jones, George & Tammy Wynette* / Poncho and Lefty: *Nelson, Willie & Merle Haggard* / Why not me?: *Judds* / Both to each other (friends and lovers): *Rabbitt, Eddie & Juice Newton* / On my knees: *Rich, Charlie & Janie Frickie* / I don't want to have to marry you: *Brown, Jim Ed & Helen Cornelius* / Just good ol' boys: *Bandy, Moe & Joe Stampley* / Mamas don't let your babies grow up to be cowboys: *Jennings, Waylon & Willie Nelson* / Please don't stop loving me: *Wagoner, Porter & Dolly Parton* / My elusive dreams: *Houston, David & Tammy Wynette* / Paradise tonight: *McLain, C. & M.Gilley* / Tear time: *Dave & Sugar* / Yes Mr. Peters: *Drusky, Roy & Priscilla Mitchell* / Yesterdays wine: *Haggard, Merle & George Jones*.

■ **LP** . . . . **KNLP 13004**
Country Collection / Feb '89.
CD . . . . **KNCD 13004**
■ **MC** . . . . **KNMC 13004**
Country Collection / Feb '89.

NO.1 COUNTRY - COUNTRY GIANTS (14 country no.1's).

Tracks: Guess I'm crazy: *Reeves, Jim* / Lucille: *Rogers, Kenny* / Flesh and blood: *Cash, Johnny* / Ruby Ann: *Robbins, Marty* / Sixteen tons: *Ford, Tennessee Ernie* / This time: *Jennings, Waylon* / Southern nights: *Campbell, Glen* / Blue eyes crying in the rain: *Nelson, Willie* / I've been everywhere: *Snow, Hank* / She's just an old love..: *Pride, Charley* / She's actin' single: *Stewart, Gary* / You've got the touch: *Alabama* / Am I losing you: *Milsap, Ronnie* / Grand tour, The: *Jones, George*.

■ **LP** . . . . **KNLP 13008**
Country Collection / Sep '89.
CD . . . . **KNCD 13008**
■ **MC** . . . . **KNMC 13008**
Country Collection / Sep '89.

NO.1 COUNTRY - COUNTRY GIRLS.

Tracks: Think about love: *Parton, Dolly* / It's like we never said goodbye: *Gayle, Crystal* / Never be you: *Cash, Rosanne* / What a man my man is: *Fairchild, Barbara* / Drifter: *Sylvia* / You and me: *Wynette, Tammy* / Have mercy: *Judds* / Hurt: *Newton, Juice* / Always have, always will: *Frickie, Janie* / Who's cheating who: *McClain, Charly* / Would you lay with me (in a field of stone): *Tucker, Tanya* / Once a day: *Smith, Connie* / You're the first time I've thought about: *McIntyre, Reba*.

LP . . . . **KNLP 13002**
Country Collection / Feb '89 / BMG.
CD . . . . **KNCD 13002**
■ **MC** . . . . **KNMC 13002**
Country Collection / Feb '89

NO.1 COUNTRY - COUNTRY GOLD (14 country no.1's).

Tracks: Most beautiful girl in the town: *Rich, Charlie* / Boy named Sue, A: *Cash, Johnny* / I can help: *Swan, Billy* / Battle of New Orleans: *Horton, Johnny* / When you're hot, you're hot: *Reed, Jerry* / Wild side of life, The: *Thompson, Hank* / Cattle call: *Arnold, Eddy* / Crazy arms: *Price, Ray* / Great balls of fire: *Lewis, Jerry Lee* / Waterloo: *Jackson, Stonewall* / White sports coat, A: *Robbins, Marty* / Mexican Joe: *Reeves, Jim* / Shotgun boogie: *Ford, Tennessee Ernie* / Harper valley PTA: *Riley, Jeannie C.*

■ **LP** . . . . **KNLP 13012**
Country Collection / Sep '89.
CD . . . . **KNCD 13012**
■ **MC** . . . . **KNMC 13012**
Country Collection / Sep '89.

NO.1 COUNTRY - COUNTRY LADIES.

Tracks: Old flames: *Parton, Dolly* / Talking in your sleep: *Gayle, Crystal* / Keep me in mind: *Anderson, Lynn* / My baby thinks he's a train: *Cash, Rosanne* / Nobody: *Sylvia* / Blood red and going down: *Tucker, Tanya* / Maybe your baby's got the blues: *Judds* / Ways to love a man: *Wynette, Tammy* / Radio heart: *McClain, Charly* / You make me want to make: *Newton, Juice* / He's a heartache: *Frickie, Janie* / I'm not Lisa: *Colter, Jessi* / If you ever change your mind: *Gayle, Crystal* / One day at a time: *Lane, Cristy*.

■ **LP** . . . . **KNLP 13009**
Country Collection / Sep '89.
CD . . . . **KNCD 13009**
■ **MC** . . . . **KNMC 13009**
Country Collection / Sep '89.

NO.1 COUNTRY - COUNTRY LEGENDS (14 country no.1's).

Tracks: Ring of fire: *Cash, Johnny* / Blue side of lonesome: *Reeves, Jim* / Door, The: *Jones, George* / Hello walls: *Young, Faron* / (I'm a) ramblin' man: *Jennings, Waylon* / Hello love: *Snow, Hank* / Ribbon of darkness: *Robbins, Marty* / Blanket on the ground: *Spears, Billie Jo* / Too many lovers: *Gayle, Crystal* / You're my man: *Anderson, Lynn* / Take me to your world: *Wynette, Tammy* / It ain't easy bein' easy: *Frickie, Janie* / Every time two hearts collide: *Rogers, Kenny & Dottie West* / You're the only one: *Parton, Dolly*.

■ **LP** . . . . **KNLP 13011**
Country Collection / Sep '89.
CD . . . . **KNCD 13011**
■ **MC** . . . . **KNMC 13011**
Country Collection / Sep '89.

NO.1 COUNTRY - COUNTRY LOVE.

Tracks: Always on my mind: *Nelson, Willie* / Cry myself to sleep: *Judds* / When we make love: *Alabama* / I'm a stand by my woman man: *Milsap, Ronnie* / Till I make it on my own: *Wynette, Tammy* / I love: *Hall, Tom T.* / Very special love song, A: *Rich, Charlie* / Luckenbach, Texas: *Jennings, Waylon* / Would you like to take another chance on me: *Lewis, Jerry Lee* / That's the way love goes: *Haggard, Merle* / Way we make a broken heart, The: *Cash, Rosanne* / Love put a song in my heart: *Rodriguez, Johnny* / I don't want to be a memory: *Exile* / I will always love you: *Parton, Dolly*.

■ **LP** . . . . **KNLP 13001**
Country Collection / Feb '89.
CD . . . . **KNCD 13001**
■ **MC** . . . . **KNMC 13001**
Country Collection / Feb '89.

NO.1 COUNTRY - COUNTRY NIGHTS (14 country no.1's).

Tracks: Tonight, Carmen: *Robbins, Marty* / Night games: *Pride, Charley* / What goes on when the sun goes down: *Milsap, Ronnie* / City lights: *Price, Ray* / She can put her shoes under my bed: *Duncan, J* / First thing ev'ry morning: *Dean, Jimmy* / Georgia on my mind: *Nelson, Willie* / (There's a) fire in the night: *Alabama* / Stand by me: *Gilley, Mickey* / She called me baby: *Rich, Charlie* / Moon is still over me: *Johnson, M* / Woke up in love: *Exile* / Twinkle twinkle lucky star: *Haggard, M.* / Bedtime story: *Wynette, Tammy*.

■ **LP** . . . . **KNLP 13007**
Country Collection / Sep '89.
CD . . . . **KNCD 13007**
■ **MC** . . . . **KNMC 13007**
Country Collection / Sep '89.

NUMBER ONE IN THE COUNTRY.

Tracks: Abilene: *Hamilton, George IV* / Misery loves company: *Hamilton, George IV* / Once a day: *Smith, Connie* / Marie Laveau: *Bare, Bobby* / Blue, blue day: *Gibson, Don* / Thank God I'm a country boy: *Denver, John* / Cattle call: *Arnold, Eddy* / This time: *Jennings, Waylon* / Three bells: *Browns* / Ringo: *Greene, Lorne* / She's actin' single (I'm drinkin' doubles): *Stewart, Gary* / I will always love you: *Parton, Dolly* / I forgot more than you'll ever know: *Davis Sisters* / Lord, Mr. Ford: *Reed, Jerry* / She called me baby: *Rich, Charlie* / Please don't stop loving me: *Wagoner, Porter & Dolly Parton* / Slow poke: *King, Pee Wee* / Please help me, I'm falling: *Locklin, Hank* / I guess I'm crazy: *Reeves, Jim* / Hello love: *Snow, Hank* / End of the world, The: *Davis, Skeeter* / Please don't tell me how the story ends: *Milsap, Ronnie* / Ballad of the Green Berets, The: *Sadler, Barry* / It's gonna take a little bit longer: *Pride, Charley*.

■ **LP** . . . . **DHYK 0001**
RCA / '78 / BMG.

O

OFF THE RECORD..COUNTRY CLASSICS.

Tracks: Not Advised.

Double LP . . . . **FEDD 1009**
MC Set . . . . **CFEDD 1009**
Sierra / Aug '87.

OKEH WESTERN SWING.

Tracks: Hesitation blues: *Bernard, Al & Goofus Five* / Lovesick blues: *Miller, Emmett & Georgia Crackers* / Sadie Green: *Newman, Roy & his boys* / Give me my money: *Blue Ridge Playboys* / Range riders stomp: *Range riders* / There'll be some changes made: *O'Daniel, W. Lee & His Hillbilly boys* / Fort Worth stomp: *Crystal Springs Ramblers* / Get with it: *Willia, Bob & his Texas boys* / Who walks in when I walk out? / Too busy / Play boy stomp / Ozzlin' daddy blues / Pray for the lights to go out / Girl I left behind me, The / Hot as I am: *Sadie tramps* / One more river to cross: *Sons Of The Pioneers* / Knocky knocky: *Light Crust Doughboys* / Zeke Terney's stomp: *Hi-Neighbour boys* / Chill tonic: *Penny, Hank & His Radio Cowboys* / When I put on my long white robe: *Swift* / I love your fruit: *Sweet Violet Boys* / Bass man jive: *Stockard, Ocie & his Wanderers* / Reno Street blues: *Hi-Flyers* / Panhandle shuffle: *Sons of the West* / Gulf Coast special: *Hofner, Adolf & his orchestra* / Brown bottle blues: *Harbert, Slim & His boys* / Three way boogie: *Cooley, Spade & Tex Williams* / Take it away, Leon: *McAuliffe, Leon & his Western swing band*.

Double LP . . . . **EPC 22124**
MC **40 22124**
Epic / '84 / Sony.

OLE TENNESSEE COUNTRY.

Tracks: Feeling low / Laughin' and jokin' / Round and round / My destiny / Baby doll / Believe me / When you stop lovin' me / Easy to love / Down on the border / Goin' crazy / Poor boy / This train / Pink wedding gown / Satisfied with me.

LP . . . . **SUN 1032**
Sun / '86 / Charly / Swift.

ON STAGE AT THE GRAND OLE OPRY.

Tracks: Little Ida Red / South of the border (down Mexico way) / Well maybe / Bye bye love / Rest of the way / Last heartbreak / Old rugged cross, The / Lovesick blues / Our paths crossed again / On and on and on / Where were you / Blue grass part one (twist) / Please keep me in mind / Acorn Hill breakdown.

LP . . . . **HAT 3010**
MC . . . . **HATC 3010**

Stetson / Jun '86 / Crusader Marketing Co. / Swift / Wellard Dist. / Midland Records / C.M. Distribution.

OPRY TIME IN TENNESSEE.
LP . . . . **SLP 177**
MC . . . . **GT 5177**
Starday (USA) / Apr '87 / Crusader Marketing Co.

ORIGINAL ROCKABILLY COLLECTION.
Tracks: Long black train: *Twitty, Conway* / My brand of blues: *Rainwater, Marvin* / Rockin' rollin' stone: *Starr, Andy* / One more time: *Starr, Andy* / Round and round: *Starr, Andy* / Stutterin' papa: *Griffin, Buck* / Rockin' chair: *Campbell, Cecil* / Rock and roll fever: *Campbell, Cecil* / My square dancin' mama: *Gallion, Bob* / Rock doll: *Early, Bernie* / Rollin' the boogie: *Hyman, Dick* / Rockin' and rollin' with grandmaw: *Robinson, Carson* / Latch on: *Hargrave, Ron* / Midnight line: *Riley, Bob* / I ain't studyin' you, baby: *Gibson, Don* / Who shot Willie?: *Smith, Arthur.*
LP **2486 257**
MC **3186 092**
MGM (Polydor) / Oct '83.

OTHER SIDE OF NASHVILLE.
BETA . . . . **UMB 10351**
VHS . . . . **UMV 10351**
MGM (Polydor) / Sep '86.
VHS . . . . **CFM 02542**
Channel 5 / Jul '90 / Channel 5 Video / P.R.O. Video / Gold & Sons.

OUTLAWS.
CD . . . . **PD 81321**
RCA / Sep '85 / BMG.

P

PENNSYLVANIA ROCKS.
Tracks: Come in world: *Ellis, Don & The Royal Dukes* / Half of me: *Ellis, Don & The Royal Dukes* / Navajo: *Ellis, Don & The Royal Dukes* / Blue fire: *Ellis, Don & The Royal Dukes* / Party doll: *Ellis, Don & The Royal Dukes* / Big Daddy: *Rays, Del* / Radar: *Rays, Del* / Duke, The: *Rays, Del* / Slim little Annie: *Genos* / Hey hot rod: *Herman, Hermy* / Eight days a week: *Herman, Hermy* / Rock all night with me: *Tacker, Dick* / Jet: *Royal Rockers* / My bird dog: *Denver Bill & His Ranch Hands* / Susie or Mary Lou: *Barr, Chuck & The Rockabillies* / Come on back: *Barr, Chuck & The Rockabillies.*
LP . . . . **WLP 8897**
White Label (Germany) / '87 / Pinnacle / Bear Family Records (Germany) / CSA Tell Tapes.

PIKE RECORDINGS.
Tracks: Shake bop: *Garland, Dickie* / Breakin': *Thomas, Freddie* / Like thunder: *Thomas, Freddie* / Ring round your neck: *Hollister, Bobby* / Keep a knockin': *Sessions, Little Ronnie* / I got a lot on my conscience: *Sessions, Little Ronnie* / What a man: *Flowers, Cancie* / Karate: *Rialtos* / Monkey bite: *Hendrix, Al* / Rhonda Lee: *Hendrix, Al* / Toolin' around: *Hendrix, Al* / Jumping Johnny: *Hendrix, Al* / Go, daddy, go rock: *Hendrix, Al* / Bingo's bongo bingo party: *Baby Bugs* / Sheep: *Dee, Tommy & Gene Moles.*
LP . . . . **WLP 8888**
White Label (Germany) / '87 / Pinnacle / Bear Family Records (Germany) / CSA Tell Tapes.

PRIMITIVE SOUND.
Tracks: Only cowgirl in town: *Barr, Glen & Roger Harrison* / I'm in no position: *Barr, Glen & Roger Harrison* / Country rock 'n' roll: *Harrison, Roger* / How I love you: *Speck, Darrell* / Take me back: *Speck, Darrell* / Lies, lies, lies: *Bullock, Norman* / Moanin' the blues: *Bullock, Norman* / My ramblin's over: *Johnson, Dan* / Just over a girl: *Renfro Bros.* / Ever ready: *Renfro Bros.* / Lover man: *Cox, Jerry* / Rock & roll daddy O: *Castle, Joey* / Look coming yonder: *Scott, Ray* / Tennessee shake: *Scott, Ray* / He's a headed South: *Hopper, Evelyn.*
LP . . . . **WLP 8830**
White Label (Germany) / '87 / Pinnacle / Bear Family Records (Germany) / CSA Tell Tapes.

Q

QUEENS OF COUNTRY.
Tracks: Honky tonk angels: *Parton, Dolly* / Then you'll know: *Cline, Patsy* / I'm so lonesome I could cry: *Spears, Billie Jo* / Slippin' away: *Fairchild, Barbara* / I'll repossess my heart: *Wells, Kitty* / Walkin' after midnight: *Cline, Patsy* / Sticks & stones: *Fargo, Donna* / Makin' believe: *Parton, Dolly* / Look what they've done to my song: *Spears, Billie Jo* / I never promised you a rose garden: *Anderson, Lynn* / Turn the cards slowly: *Cline, Patsy* / Crazy love: *Fairchild, Barbara* / Your good girl's gonna go bad: *Wynette, Tammy* / Daddy: *Fargo, Donna* / Danger of a stranger, The: *Parton, Stella* / Release me: *Mandrell, Barbara* / Heart you break may be your own, The: *Cline, Patsy* / Stop look & listen: *Cline, Patsy* / Letter to heaven: *Parton, Dolly* / Wishful thinking: *Fargo, Donna* / Both sides now: *Murray, Anne* / Ease the want in me: *Spears, Billie Jo* / D.I.V.O.R.C.E.: *Wynette, Tammy* / Kentucky means paradise: *Mandrell, Barbara* / Little blossom: *Parton, Dolly* / Singing my song: *Wynette, Tammy* / Cry: *Anderson, Lynn* / Honky tonk merry go round: *Cline, Patsy* / Night they drove old Dixie down, The: *Tucker, Tanya* / Kaw-liga: *Mandrell, Barbara* / Texas when I die: *Tucker, Tanya* / I loved and lost again: *Cline, Patsy.*
MC Set . . . . **TTMC 048**
Tring / Jun '92 / Prism Leisure PLC / Midland Records / Taylors.

QUEENS OF COUNTRY MUSIC.
Tracks: Just out of reach: *Cline, Patsy* / You belong to me: *Page, Patti* / Am I that easy to forget: *Riley, Jeannie C.* / Walking after midnight: *Cline, Patsy* / Stop the world: *Cline, Patsy* / I can see an angel: *Cline, Patsy* / Why don't you believe me: *Page, Patti* / Mockin' Bird Hill: *Page, Patti* / Tennessee waltz: *Page, Patti* / Gentle on my mind: *Page, Patti* / Things go better with love: *Riley, Jeannie C.* / Help me make it through the night: *Riley, Jeannie C.* / Before the next teardrop falls: *Riley, Jeannie C.* / Roses and thorns: *Riley, Jeannie C.* / Harper Valley PTA: *Riley, Jeannie C..*
CD . . . . **PWK 030**
Pickwick / '88 / Pickwick Records.
MC . . . . **HSC 3274**
Hallmark / Jun '89 / Pickwick Records.

R

RABBIT ACTION.
Tracks: Blue suede shoes / Rhythm called rock and roll / Honey don't / Rabbit action / Everybody's trying to be my baby / How come you do me / Rock-me-baby / Dixie fried / Cat clothes / You can't make love to somebody / Cat clothes (version 2) / That don't move me / Honey don't (2).
LP . . . . **SUN 1018**
Sun / Apr '85 / Charly / Swift.

RADIO GOLD.
Tracks: Promised land, The: *Allan, Johnnie* / La bamba: *Valens, Ritchie* / When the boys happy (the girl's happy too): *Four Pennies* / Wake up little Susie: *Everly Brothers* / Wanderer, The: *Dion* / My true love: *Jive Five* / Dizzy Miss Lizzy: *Williams, Larry* / Mr. Sandman: *Chordettes* / I fought the law: *Fuller, Bobby Four* / Hushabye: *Mystics* / Hello, this is Joannie: *Evans, Paul* / Will you love me tomorrow: *Shirelles* / Where or when: *Dion & The Belmonts* / Venus: *Avalon, Frankie* / Sixteen candles: *Crests* / When will I be loved: *Everly Brothers* / One fine day: *Chiffons* / Rockin' robin: *Day, Bobby* / Twist and shout: *Isley Brothers* / Little bit of soap, A: *Jarmels* / I'll come running back to you: *Cooke, Sam* / Earth angel: *Penguins* / Runaround Sue: *Dion* / Since I don't have you: *Skyliners* / Good golly, Miss Molly: *Little Richard* / Poetry in motion: *Tillotson, Johnny* / Denise: *Randy & The Rainbows* / Tell it like it is: *Neville, Aaron* / Sweet dreams: *McLain, Tommy* / Goodnight my love: *Belvin, Jesse.*
CD . . . . **CDCHD 347**
Ace / Feb '92 / Pinnacle / Hot Shot / Jazz Music / Complete Record Co. Ltd.

RARE COLLECTION OF ROCK.
Tracks: Goshamody whatabody: *Goza, Glen* / Little girl: *Lara, Sammy* / Silly Sally: *Lara, Sammy* / So lonely: *Sunday, Salty* / Hard hat: *Worley, Jim* / I'm a long-gone daddy: *Wright, Rebel* / Eeny meeny miney mo: *Javis, Jimmie* / El Diablo: *Lofton, Ronny* / Tell me: *Ronnie & The Regals* / Baggy Maggie: *Levoy, Henry* / Pretty baby: *Angel, Johnny* / Boogie man: *Angel, Johnny* / Top string boogie: *Jackson, Marvin* / Amazon dance: *Dean, Bobby* / Path of regrets: *Ross, Jack* / Little bull and buttercup: *Homer, Chris.*
LP . . . . **WLP 8894**
White Label (Germany) / '87 / Pinnacle / Bear Family Records (Germany) / CSA Tell Tapes.

RARE ROCK-A-BILLY BOPPIN'.
Tracks: Not Advised.
LP . . . . **RR 2023**
Esoldun / Jan '88 / New Note.

RARE ROCKABILLY VOL.1.
Tracks: Cast iron arm: *Wilson, Peanuts* / Be bop baby: *Inman, Autrey* / Sweet love on my mind: *Jimmy & Johnny* / Hot rock: *Carroll, Johnny* / Rock 'n' roll Ruby: *Carroll, Johnny* / Wild wild women: *Carroll, Johnny* / Trying to get to you: *Carroll, Johnny* / Alligator come across: *Duff, Arlie* / Crazy baby: *Maltais, Gene* / Barking up the wrong tree: *Woody, Don* / Make like a rock and roll: *Woody, Don* / Morse code: *Woody, Don* / Bird dog: *Woody, Don* / Ruby pearl: *Cochran, Jackie Lee* / Teenage boogie: *Pierce, Webb* / Whole lotta shakin' goin' on: *Hall, Roy* / Diggin' the boogie: *Hall, Roy* / Offbeat boogie: *Hall, Roy* / Shakin' the blues: *Young, Donny* / Three alley cats.
■ **MC** . . . . **MCLC 1755**
MCA / '83.
■ **LP** . . . . **MCL 1755**
MCA / '83.

RARE ROCKABILLY VOL.2.
Tracks: Mama don't you think I know: *Cochran, Jackie Lee & Jimmy Pruett* / Ten little women: *Noland, Terry* / Cool it baby: *Fontaine, Eddie* / Shake baby shake: *Raney, Wayne* / Here comes the night: *Guitar, Billy* / All by myself: *Hall, Roy* / See you later alligator: *Hall, Roy* / Behave, be quiet, or be gone: *Hall, Roy* / Flip flop and fly: *Ball, Johnny* / Rock it on down to my house: *Tubb, Justin* / Tennessee rock'n'roll: *Helms, Bobby* / Crazy crazy lovin': *Carroll, Johnny* / Corina Corina: *Carroll, Johnny* / Wee Willy Brown: *Graham, Lou* / Crazy chicken: *Gallagher, James* / Is that all to the ball, Mr Hall?: *Riley, Billy Lee* / She wanna rock: *Derksen, Arnie* / Don't go baby: *Coker, Al* / Hypnotised: *Noland, Terry.*
■ **LP** . . . . **MCL 1756**
MCA / '83.
■ **MC** . . . . **MCLC 1756**
MCA / Nov '86.

RARE ROCKABILLY VOL.3.
Tracks: Lorraine: *Covell, Buddy* / It would be a doggone lie: *Inman, Autrey* / Everybody's trying to be my baby: *York Brothers* / Moon's rock: *Mullican, Moon* / Teenage love is a misery: *Kennedy, Jerry* / Don't stop me now: *Hall, Roy* / Move on: *Hall, Roy* / You gotta move: *Smith, Chester* / Juke joint Johnny: *Sovine, Red* / Way out there: *Chuck & Bill* / Cheat on me baby: *Rockin' Saints* / I wanna bop: *Harlan, Billy* / Schoolhouse rock: *Harlan, Billy* / Knock knock rattle: *Allen, Rex* / Crazy little guitar man: *Foley, Red* / Pan American boogie: *Glosson, Lonnie* / Sputnik: *Engler, Jerry* / Baby's gone: *Claud, Vernon* / Hey Ruby: *Osbourne, Arthur* / Let's go downtown: *Therien, Joe Jnr..*
■ **LP** . . . . **MCL 1757**
MCA / '83.
■ **MC** . . . . **MCLC 1757**
MCA / Nov '86.

RARE ROCKABILLY VOL.4.
Tracks: Tennessee Toddy: *Grey, Billy & His Western Okies* / Baby don't leave me: *Five Charles Brothers* / Uncle John's bongos: *Johnnie & Jack* / Jenny Lee: *Mullican, Moon* / One and only: *Fontaine, Eddie* / Rockabilly boogie: *Therien, Joe Jnr & His Rockets* / Come back to me: *Therien, Joe Jnr & His Rockets* / Touch of loving: *Sykes, Bobby* / Crazy bullfrog: *Pruitt, Lewis* / You've got me where I wanna be: *Walker, Wayne* / Rock around the world: *Reeves, Glenn* / Rock a boogie Lou: *Reeves, Glenn* / Got a lot of rhythm in my soul: *Cline, Patsy* / Be my bride: *Phillips, Charlie* / Show me how: *Hackett, Veline* / You played on my piano: *Gunter, Hardrock* / California blues: *Pierce, Webb* / Falling in love: *Warner, Mack* / It hurts the one who loves you: *Doggett, Ray* / All nite boogie: *Sosebee, Tommy.*
■ **LP** . . . . **MCF 3035**
MCA / Nov '79.
■ **LP** . . . . **MCL 1758**
MCA / '83.
■ **MC** . . . . **MCLC 1758**
MCA / Nov '86.

RARE ROCKING GIRLS.
Tracks: Gotta rock: *Carter Kids* / Satellite: *Aguirre, J.* / Boy watcher: *Parker, Pat* / Everybody's trying to be my baby: *Stevens, Rosie* / Wrong yo yo: *Stevens, Rosie* / Crazy little heart: *Holly, Brenda* / Squeeze box rock: *Browning Sisters* / Dallas chiggers: *Martin, Mamie* / Never gonna let you go: *Wells, Karen* / Rockin' in the nursery: *Starr, Sally* / Eeny meeny miney mo: *Herren, Joyce* / I'm a bop: *Parr, Lona* / Walking papers: *Anderson, Dot* / Jealous hearted woman: *Anderson, Dot* / What for?: *Dolly & The Deans* / Someone to love: *Kelley, Jean.*
LP . . . . **WLP 8885**
White Label (Germany) / Jul '87 / Pinnacle / Bear Family Records (Germany) / CSA Tell Tapes.

RAREST ROCKABILLY & HILLBILLY BOOGIE.
Tracks: Nothin' but a nuthin': *Stewart, Jimmy* / Darlin': *Dale, Jimmie* / Baby doll: *Dale, Jimmie* / Pretending is a game: *Jeffers, Sleepy & The Davis Twins* / Don't sweep that dirt on me: *Shaw, Buddy* / My baby left me: *Rogers, Rock* / Little dog blues: *Price, Mel* / Henpecked daddy: *Johnson, Ralph & The Hillbilly Show Boys* / Um boy, you're my baby: *Johnson, Bill & The Dabblers* / Stoney mountain boogie: *Stoney Mountain Playboys* / My blackbirds are bluebirds now: *Jeffers, Sleepy & The Davis Twins* / No more: *Shaw, Buddy* / Big black cat: *Hendon, R.D. & The Western Jamboree Cowboys* / It's Saturday night: *Mack, Billy.*
LP . . . . **CH 44**
Ace / Feb '82 / Pinnacle / Hot Shot / Jazz Music / Complete Record Co. Ltd.

■ DELETED

RAREST ROCKABILLY & HILLBILLY BOOGIE/BEST OF ACE ROCKABILLY.
Tracks: Nothin' but a nuthin': *Stewart, Jimmy & his Nighthawks* / Darlin': *Dale, Jimmie* / Baby doll: *Dale, Jimmie* / Pretending is a game: *Jeffers, Sleepy & The Davis Twins* / My blackbirds are bluebirds now: *Jeffers, Sleepy & The Davis Twins* / Don't sweep that dirt on me: *Shaw, Buddy* / No more: *Shaw, Buddy* / My baby left me: *Rogers, Rock* / Little dog blues: *Price, Mel* / Henpecked daddy: *Johnson, Ralph & The Hillbilly Show Boys* / Umm boy you're my baby: *Johnson, Bill & The Dabblers* / Stoney mountain boogie: *Stoney Mountain Playboys* / Big black cat: *Hendon, R.D.* / It's a Saturday night: *Mack, Billy* / Rockin' daddy: *Fisher, Sonny* / Everybody's movin': *Glenn, Glen* / One cup of coffee: *Glenn, Glen* / I can't find the doorknob: *Jimmy & Johnny* / My big fat baby: *Hall, Sonny & The Echoes* / How come it: *Jones, Thumper* / Trucker from Tennessee: *Davis, Link* / Little bit more: *La Beef, Sleepy* / I'm through: *La Beef, Sleepy* / Jitterbop baby: *Harris, Hal* / Let's get it on: *Almond, Hershel* / I'm a hobo: *Reeves, Danny* / Rook it on: *Jones, George* / Sneaky Pete: *Fisher, Sonny.*
CD . . . . CDCHD 311
Ace / Jul '91 / Pinnacle / Hot Shot / Jazz Music / Complete Record Co. Ltd.

RARIN' ROCKABILLIES.
Tracks: Not Advised.
■ LP. RARIN' 666
Rarin' / Apr '79.

RAUNCHY ROCKABILLY (Sun Sounds Special).
Tracks: How come you do me: *Thompson, Junior* / Jukebox help me find my baby: *Rhythm Rockers* / Truckin' down the avenue: *Burgess, Sonny* / Daddy blues: *Burgess, Sonny* / Listen to me: *Baugh, Smokey Joe* / Your lovin' man: *Taylor, Vernon* / Blues blues blues: *Thompson, Hayden* / Fairlane rock: *Thompson, Hayden* / Willing and ready: *Smith, Ray* / Shake around: *Smith, Ray* / Baby that's good: *Bruce, Edwin* / Miss Pearl: *Wages, Jimmy* / Fine little baby: *Penner, Dick* / I'll change my ways: *Stewart, Danny* / Never did I: *Hosea, Don* / John Henry: *Hosea, Don.*
■ LP. CR 30147
Charly / '78 / Charly.

REAL FINE PRIMITIVE ORIGINALS.
Tracks: Not Advised.
LP. WLP 8931
White Label (Germany) / Jun '88 / Pinnacle / Bear Family Records (Germany) / CSA Tell Tapes.

REAL ROCKIN' NOW.
Tracks: Girl named Sue, A: *Tolleson, Tommy* / Cindy: *Fay, Johnny* / Rock 'n' roll rover: *King, Jesse Lee* / Nervous wreck: *King, Jesse Lee* / Cuddles: *Butterball, Maximilian* / One little kiss: *Newsome, Chubby* / So ,long, baby: *Newsome, Chubby* / Barracuda: *Fausz, Gary L.* / Walking the blues: *Beacg, Ray* / Shame: *Brown, Johnny* / Angel eyes: *Warr, Doug* / Guitar boogie: *Faulkner, G. & D.* / Tom cat: *Gaggard, J.C.* / I want you now: *Gaggard, J.C.* / Honey doll: *Gaggard, J.C.* / I will ask, I will plead: *Gaggard, J.C..*
LP. WLP 8881
White Label (Germany) / Feb '85 / Pinnacle / Bear Family Records (Germany) / CSA Tell Tapes.

REAL SOUND OF COUNTRY, THE.
Tracks: Not Advised.
MC . . . . CONE 2
One For The Road / Aug '89 / Jazz Music / Wellard Dist.

RED HOT ROCKABILLIES.
Tracks: My pink cadillac / Watch your mouth / Judy / Rave on / Swingin' baby doll / I wanna rock / Drinkin' wine spo dee o dee / Piano Nellie / Party party / Ding dong daddy / She's sumpin' else / Sugar / Can't you see / Walkin' 'n' talkin' / Bop a dee / Rockin' country style / Baby please don't go / Rockin' redwing.
■ LP. K 58344
WEA / Dec '81.

RED HOT ROCKABILLY.
Tracks: Hip shakin' mama / Bip bop boom / Look out Mabel / Grits / Sunglasses after dark / Okies in the pokie / Hot dog / Made in the shade / Down on the farm / Fool, The / Oakie boogie / Blue swingin' mama.
LP. MFLP 030
Magnum Force / Feb '85 / Terry Blood Dist. / Jazz Music / Hot Shot.
CD . . . . CDMF 030
Magnum Force / Jul '90 / Terry Blood Dist. / Jazz Music / Hot Shot.

RED HOT ROCKABILLY VOL 2.
Tracks: 49 women / One way ticket / Jackson dog / Satellite hop / Roll over Beethoven / You don't mean to make me cry / Clickety clack / Go go heart / Rock on Mabel / Puppy love / Tore up / Move over Rover.
LP. MFLP 043
Magnum Force / Jul '87 / Terry Blood Dist. / Jazz Music / Hot Shot.

RED HOT ROCKABILLY VOL 3.
Tracks: Jitterbuggin' baby / No.9 train / Dig that crazy driver / You bet I do / Oh little girl / Long tall Sally / That'll get it / No doubt about it / Live your life with care / Fool about you / Elvis stole my gal / Lonely heart.
LP. MFLP 055
Magnum Force / Sep '87 / Terry Blood Dist. / Jazz Music / Hot Shot.

RED HOT ROCKABILLY VOL 5.
Tracks: Bop hop jamboree / Wondering if you still care / Train's done gone, The / I just don't love you anymore / Last time, The / Spanish rock and rolla / Surge / No one but you / Midnight train / How can I go / Rainbow love / Standing in your window / Hello Memphis / Big Johnny blues / Just behind your smile / Two timing lover.
LP. MFLP 060
Magnum Force / Mar '88 / Terry Blood Dist. / Jazz Music / Hot Shot.

RED HOT ROCKABILLY VOL 6 (Memphis).
Tracks: Boo be ah be / My life's desire / That's the reason I'm leaving town today / Look coming yonder / Guess I'll cry instead / Blues got to me, The / Go on and say goodbye / I'm leavin' this town / Lowdown feeling / Just skip it / Got you on my mind / Three long years / Walk with me / What's in store for me / J & E twist / Ain't I'm a mess.
LP. MFLP 062
Magnum Force / Jun '88 / Terry Blood Dist. / Jazz Music / Hot Shot.

RED HOT ROCKABILLY VOL 7.
Tracks: Rock 'n' roll on a Saturday night / Rock a socka hop / Grandma rock 'n' roll / Servant of love / Knocking on the backside / Walking and a' strolling / Black Cadillac / D.J. blues, The / Don't cry little darling / Linda Lou / Teenage lover / So help me gal / Snake eyed woman / Depression blues / Quick sand love / Nicotine.
CD . . . . CDMF 069
LP. MFLP 069
Magnum Force / Aug '89 / Terry Blood Dist. / Jazz Music / Hot Shot.

RED HOT ROCKABILLY VOL 8.
Tracks: 49 women / That'llget it / Lonely heart / Clickety clack / Satellite hop / Dig that crazy driver / My baby's still rockin' / Crawdad hole / Go go heart / You bet I do / It hurts the one who loves you / Puppy love / No doubt about it / Rollover Beethoven / No. 9 train / Rock on Mabel / Long tall Sally / Jitterbuggin' baby / One way ticket / Elvis stole my gal / Fool about you / You don't mean to make me cry / Tore up / Jackson dog / Move over Rover.
CD . . . . CDMF 082
Magnum Force / Feb '92 / Terry Blood Dist. / Jazz Music / Hot Shot.

RED HOT VICTOR (20 American country chart hits).
Tracks: If you can touch her at all: *Nelson, Willie* / Here in love: *Dottsy* / May the force be with you always: *Hall, Tom T.* / You know what: *Reed, Jerry & Seidina* / Quits: *Stewart, Gary* / Love is a word: *Lee, Dickey* / Leona: *Russell, Johnny* / It should have been easy: *Dottsy* / It ain't easy lovin' me: *Prophet, Ronnie* / Born believer: *Brown, Jim Ed & Helen Cornelius* / Eastbound and down: *Reed, Jerry* / Baby me, baby: *Miller, Roger* / If it ain't love by now: *Brown, Jim Ed & Helen Cornelius* / Lean on Jesus: *Craft, Paul* / (After sweet memories) play born to lose again: *Dottsy* / Ten years of this: *Stewart, Gary* / I'm a memory: *Nelson, Willie* / Two doors down: *Lehr, Zella* / Virginia, how far will you go?: *Lee, Dickey* / I wished I loved somebody else: *Hall, Tom T..*
LP. PL 42528
■ MC . . . . PK 42528
RCA / '79.

REED RECORDINGS.
Tracks: You hit the nail on the head: *Perry, Bill* / Go fly a kite: *Perry, Bill* / Thunder: *Starliners* / Static: *Starliners* / Go, cat, go: *Bowman, Leon* / Rockin' the blues: *Bowman, Leon* / Black widow spider: *Bowman, Leon* / Panama City blues: *Larry & The Loafers* / Teenage bop: *Quinn, Botie* / Barbara Allen: *Smith, Eddie Arnold* / Mason Dixon: *Smith, Eddie Arnold* / Queen of my heartaches: *Smith, Eddie Arnold* / I want my baby back: *Smith, Eddie Arnold* / Somebody else is taking my place: *Smith, Eddie Arnold* / Same thing: *Mizzell, Bobby* / Heart and soul: *Mizzell, Bobby* / Atomic fallout: *Mizzell, Bobby & J. Woodward* / Seven times Heaven: *Ballenger, Paul.*
LP. WLP 8872
White Label (Germany) / '87 / Pinnacle / Bear Family Records (Germany) / CSA Tell Tapes.

REMEMBER THESE.
Tracks: Not Advised.
LP. SOLP 1009
MC . . . . SOCAS 1009
Sonus / Mar '84.

REQUESTED BALLADS OF IRELAND VOL 1.
Tracks: Kelly's, The / Mary from Dungloe / Butcher boy.
LP. TOL 123
Homespun (Ireland) / May '88 / Homespun Records / Ross Records / Wellard Dist.

REQUESTED BALLADS OF IRELAND VOL 3.
Tracks: Give an Irish girl to me / Real old mountain dew / I'll remember you love in my prayers.
MC . . . . GC 004
Outlet / '88 / Projection / Duncans / C.M. Distribution / Ross Records / Topic Records / Direct Distribution / Midland Records.
LP. G 004
Homespun (Ireland) / May '88 / Homespun Records / Ross Records / Wellard Dist.

RETURN OF ROCKAPHILLY.
Tracks: Sixteen cats: *Wellington, Rusty* / Rock with me baby: *Coleman, Ray* / Rockin' jamboree: *Raye, Michael & Judy Shaye* / Wee willy waterdilly: *Keefer Sisters* / Jukebox cannonball: *Rogers, Jesse* / Go man go get gone: *Zario, Rex* / Rockin' in the nursery: *Starr, Sally* / I gotta go: *Rex, Al* / Jumpin' Jackie: *Lee, Jacky* / Buzz buzz buzz: *Satellites* / Philadelphia baby: *Hatcher, Ray* / Bitter tears: *Tanner Bros* / Bulldoggin' the steel: *Nastos, Nick* / I ain't a movin' on no more: *Wellington, Rusty* / Jump, jump honey: *Wellington, Rusty* / Rock chicken rock: *Coleman, Ray* / ABC rock: *Starr, Sally* / I'm rockin': *Coleman, Ray* / Toodle oo bamboo: *Coleman, Ray.*
■ LP. ROLL 2004
Rollercoaster / Sep '84.

RITZ RADIO FAVOURITES (VOLUME 1 - COUNTRY).
Tracks: Not Advised.
LP. RITZSP 411
MC . . . . RITZSC 411
Ritz / Nov '85 / Pinnacle / Midland Records.

ROADHOUSE ROCK.
Tracks: Elaine: *Hall, Sam* / Roadhouse rock: *Hanyel, Arbis* / Cross-eyed Susie wakeup: *Bob & Vic* / Funky: *Wallace, Vince* / Let's take a chance: *Dawson, Jimmie* / Froggie went a-courtin': *Dawson, Jimmie* / I'm in love with you and my honda: *Mighty Four* / Satellite baby: *Stanley, Skip* / Stella got a fella: *Fireflies* / Party date: *Canida, Carl* / Rock that rhythm: *Whisnant, Ray* / Gals don't mean a thing: *Whisnant, Ray* / How much do you miss me: *Montgomery, Harold* / Glynns hop: *Bittle, Walker* / Go go Gertrude: *Dodge, Percy* / Don't touch me: *Cupit, Earl* / Baby don't knock: *Mike & Jim* / Dungaree cutie: *Mike & Jim.*
LP. WLP 8937
White Label (Germany) / '88 / Pinnacle / Bear Family Records (Germany) / CSA Tell Tapes.

ROCK & RHYTHM.
Tracks: I got it made: *Lott, Alton* / I can't stand it: *Rogers, Buck* / Forbidden love: *Donelly, Jimmy* / Look out: *Bird, Bobby* / Tootsie: *Truck, James* / Every time I see you: *Lee, Harry* / Call the law: *White, Danny* / Education fool: *White, Danny* / Rock & roll bells: *Seacrest, Eddie* / I'm winning now (take 1): *Harris, Ray* / Love me: *Ray, Danny* / Just you and me: *Millet, Lou* / Baby it's love: *Angels, Johnny* / Atlanta, Georgia: *Hobb, Bobby.*
LP. WLP 8801
White Label (Germany) / Jul '79 / Pinnacle / Bear Family Records (Germany) / CSA Tell Tapes.

ROCK & ROCKABILLY AGAIN.
Tracks: Sun would never shine, The: *Johnson, Brownie* / Ray's theme: *Awalt, Ray* / Rowdy: *Awalt, Ray* / My woman: *Witter, Jimmy* / Aaaaaaaahh: *Witter, Jimmy* / Joint bank account: *Lancaster, Bill* / Tapping that thing: *Shagnasty, Boliver* / Bumble boogie: *Fraley, Dale* / Date at eight, A: *King, Ray* / Silence baby: *Kriss, Bobby* / Judy Judy: *Chancellers* / Hey bop bop: *Phantom* / Rock & roll rock: *Kelly, Roy* / You shake me: *Wayne, Jimmy.*
LP. WLP 8822
White Label (Germany) / '87 / Pinnacle / Bear Family Records (Germany) / CSA Tell Tapes.

ROCK 'N' ROLL -- LET'S GO.
Tracks: Let's go: *Manning, Chuck* / Live it up: *Martin & The Sundowners* / Pretty woman blues: *Moore, Lattie* / Jukebox Johnny: *Moore, Lattie* / No doze blues: *Leonard, Sonny* / Wow, wow: *Love, Tommy* / Mister Blues: *Kross, Jack* / Billy Boy hop: *Sounds* / Street walkin': *Sounds* / I wanna rock now: *Blockbusters* / Rock all night: *Blockbusters* / Baby, baby, baby: *Wesley, Chuck* / Be my baby: *Orrell, David* / You're the one: *Orrell, David* / Chattanooga drummer man: *Flying Tornados* / Paper moon: *Robinson, Jerry.*
LP. WLP 8922
White Label (Germany) / Oct '87 / Pinnacle / Bear Family Records (Germany) / CSA Tell Tapes.

ROCK 'N' ROLL CANNIBALS.
Tracks: Rock 'n' roll cannibals: *Coffee, Red & B.Jones* / Jungle hop: *Tyler, Kip* / Come on: *Stewart, Wynn* / Uncle Tom got caught: *Stewart, Wynn* / School bus love affair: *Stewart, Wynn* / Nancy: *Barker Bros.* / Cute: *Coburn, Kimball* / My little girl: *Coburn, Kimball* / Boo be ah be: *Coburn, Kimball* / Down on the farm: *Downing, Big Al & The Poe Kats* / Oh babe!: *Downing, Big Al & The Poe Kats* / Wail man wail: *Coffee, Red & B.Jones* / Nothing but tough: *Tyler, Kip* / Ooh yeah baby: *Tyler, Kip* / She got eyes: *Tyler, Kip* / Shadow street: *Tyler, Kip* / Hello Mr. Dee-Jay: *Tyler, Kip* / Make her love me: *Barker Bros..*
LP. BFX 15233
Bear Family / Sep '87 / Rollercoaster Records / Swift / Direct Distribution.

ROCK 'N' ROLL CLASSICS.
Tracks: Great balls of fire: *Lewis, Jerry Lee* / Ooby dooby: *Orbison, Roy* / Rockin' pneumonia/Woogie flu: *Smith, Huey "Piano"* / Good golly Miss Molly: *Little Richard* / Rock'n'roll music: *Berry, Chuck* / Jungle rock: *Mitzell, Hank* / Breathless: *Lewis, Jerry Lee* / Maybelline: *Berry, Chuck* / Bo Diddley: *Diddley, Bo* / Suzie Q: *Hawkins, Dale* / Boppin' the blues: *Perkins, Carl* / Raunchy: *Justis, Bill* / Flying saucers rock'n'roll: *Riley, Billy Lee* / Whole lotta shakin' goin' on: *Lewis, Jerry Lee.*
■ LP. KNLP 15001
Replay / May '89.

■ CD . . . . KNCD 15001
Replay / May '89.
■ MC . . . . KNMC 15001
Replay / May '89.

ROCK 'N' ROLL ORIGINALS CD EP.
Tracks: Ooby dooby: *Orbison, Roy* / Jungle rock: *Mizell, Hank* / Flyin' saucers rock 'n' roll: *Riley, Billy Lee* / Red cadillac and a black moustache: *Smith, Warren.*
■ **CD Single** . . . . CDS 8
Charly / Feb '89 / Charly.

ROCK 'N' ROLL ORIGINALS VOL. 1 (Sun CD Collection).
Tracks: Right or wrong: *Cunningham, Buddy* / Why do I cry: *Cunningham, Buddy* / Signifying monkey, The: *Smokey Joe* / Blue suede shoes: *Perkins, Carl* / Honey don't: *Perkins, Carl* / Ooby dooby: *Orbison, Roy* / Go go go: *Orbison, Roy* / Boppin' the blues: *Perkins, Carl* / All mama's children: *Perkins, Carl* / Trouble bound: *Riley, Billy Lee* / Rock with me baby: *Riley, Billy Lee* / Welcome to the club: *Chapel, Jean* / I won't be rockin' tonight: *Chapel, Jean* / Rockin' with my baby: *Yelvington, Malcolm* / It's me baby: *Yelvington, Malcolm* / Red headed woman: *Burgess, Sonny* / We wanna boogie: *Burgess, Sonny* / Ubangi stomp: *Smith, Warren* / Black jack David: *Smith, Warren* / You're my baby: *Orbison, Roy* / Rock house: *Orbison, Roy.*
CD . . . . CDSUN 3
Sun / Feb '88 / Charly / Swift.

ROCK 'N' ROLL ORIGINALS VOL. 2.
Tracks: Love crazy baby: *Parchman, Kenny* / I feel like rockin': *Parchman, Kenny* / No matter who's to blame: *Pittman, Barbara* / I need a man: *Pittman, Barbara* / Come on little mama: *Harris, Ray* / Where'd you stay last night: *Harris, Ray* / Take and give: *Rhodes, Slim* / Do what I do: *Rhodes, Slim* / Crazy arms: *Lewis, Jerry Lee* / End of the road: *Lewis, Jerry Lee* / It'll be me: *Lewis, Jerry Lee* / Whole lotta shakin' goin' on: *Lewis, Jerry Lee* / Flyin' saucers rock 'n' roll: *Riley, Billy Lee* / I want you baby: *Riley, Billy Lee* / Restless: *Burgess, Sonny* / Ain't got a thing: *Burgess, Sonny* / I'll be around: *Honeycutt, Glenn* / I'll wait forever: *Honeycutt, Glenn* / Sweet and easy to love: *Orbison, Roy* / Devil doll: *Orbison, Roy* / Matchbox: *Perkins, Carl* / Your true love: *Perkins, Carl.*
CD . . . . CDSUN 6
Sun / Apr '88 / Charly / Swift.

ROCK 'N' ROLL ORIGINALS VOL. 3.
Tracks: Miss Froggie: *Smith, Warren* / So long I'm gone: *Smith, Warren* / Bob bob baby: *Wade & Dick* / Don't need your lovin' baby: *Wade & Dick* / Please don't cry over me: *Williams, Jimmy* / That depends on you: *Williams, Jimmy* / Foolish heart: *Harris, Ray* / Greenback dollar: *Harris, Ray* / That's right: *Perkins, Carl* / Forever yours: *Perkins, Carl* / Rock boppin' baby: *Bruce, Edwin* / More than yesterday: *Bruce, Edwin* / Red hot: *Riley, Billy Lee* / Pearly Lee: *Riley, Billy Lee* / Flatfoot Sam: *Blake, Tommy* / Lordy hoody: *Blake, Tommy* / Love my baby: *Thompson, Hayden* / One broken heart: *Thompson, Hayden* / Two young fools in love: *Pittman, Barbara* / I'm getting better all the time: *Pittman, Barbara* / Midnight man: *Justis, Bill* / Raunchy: *Justis, Bill.*
CD . . . . CDSUN 9
Sun / Jul '88 / Charly / Swift.

ROCK 'N' ROLL ORIGINALS VOL. 4.
Tracks: That's the way I love: *Carroll, Johnny* / I'll wait: *Carroll, Johnny* / Memories never grow old: *Lee, Dickey* / Good lovin': *Lee, Dickey* / You win again: *Lewis, Jerry Lee* / Great balls of fire: *Lewis, Jerry Lee* / Cindy Lou: *Penner, Dick* / Your honey love: *Penner, Dick* / I like love: *Orbison, Roy* / Chicken hearted: *Orbison, Roy* / Sweet misery: *Burgess, Sonny* / My buckets got a hole in it: *Burgess, Sonny* / I got love if you want it: *Smith, Warren* / I fell in love: *Smith, Warren* / Glad all over: *Perkins, Carl* / Lend me your comb: *Perkins, Carl* / Treat me right: *Thomas, Cliff* / I'm on my way home: *Thomas, Cliff* / Down the line: *Lewis, Jerry Lee* / Breathless: *Lewis, Jerry Lee* / Wouldn't you know: *Riley, Billy Lee* / Baby wouldn't you know: *Riley, Billy Lee.*
CD . . . . .CDSUN 12
Sun / Nov '89 / Charly / Swift.

ROCK 'N' ROLL ORIGINALS VOL. 5.
Tracks: College man: *Justis, Bill* / Stranger, The: *Justis, Bill* / Wild rice: *Justis, Bill* / Scroungie: *Justis, Bill* / Point of view: *Powers, Wayne* / My love song: *Powers, Wayne* / I think of you: *Grayzell, Rudy* / Judy: *Grayzell, Rudy* / Sweet woman: *Bruce, Edwin* / Part of my life: *Bruce, Edwin* / Love is a stranger: *Sunrays* / Lonely hours, The: *Sunrays* / Memories of you: *Priesman, Magel* / I feel so blue: *Priesman, Magel* / High school confidential: *Lewis, Jerry Lee* / Fools like me: *Lewis, Jerry Lee* / Dreamy nights: *Lee, Dickey* / Fool, fool, fool: *Lee, Dickey* / So young: *Smith, Ray* / Right behind you baby: *Smith, Ray* / Drinkin' wine: *Simmons, Gene* / I done told you: *Simmons, Gene* / Sweetie pie: *Blake, Tommy* / I dig you baby: *Blake, Tommy.*
CD . . . . .CDSUN 14
Sun / Jan '90 / Charly / Swift.

ROCK 'N' ROLL ORIGINALS VOL. 6.
Tracks: Not Advised.
CD . . . . .CDSUN 15
Sun / Apr '90 / Charly / Swift.

ROCK BOP BOOGIE.
Tracks: Hula baby / Sentimental fool / Ten cats down / Rakin' and scrapin' / I need your lovin' kiss / When you're gone / She's a woman / Paul Rivere / I'm sorry I'm not sorry / It's me baby / Rock and roll with my baby / Signifying monkey, The / Listen to me.
LP. . . . . SUN 1021
Sun / Apr '85 / Charly / Swift.

ROCK FROM ARKANSAS.
Tracks: Please, please baby: *Brown, Bobby* / Bobby's blues: *Brown, Bobby* / Down at big Mary's house: *Brown, Bobby* / I get the blues when it rains: *Brown, Bobby* / Black Cadillac: *Green, Joyce* / Saddle rag: *Redell, Teddy* / Country girl: *Moore, Johnny* / Frog man hop: *Owens, K.* / Come back baby: *Owens, K.* / Knocking on the backside: *Duniven, Bill* / Black river bay: *Smith, Earl* / Little more lovin': *Comer, Chuck.*
LP. . . . . WLP 8818
White Label (Germany) / Apr '87 / Pinnacle / Bear Family Records (Germany) / CSA Tell Tapes.

ROCK FROM EAST TO WEST.
Tracks: Flea circus: *Baxter, Bobo* / She wore pink pedal pushers: *Circo, Re & Row* / Dangerous redhead: *Raines, Jerry* / Crawdad song: *Harrod, Chuck* / Don't you go chicken: *Preston, Rudy* / Four-tyred car: *Preston, Rudy* / Alone with a memory: *Scott, Tommy* / School's out: *James, Bill* / Juke joint honey: *Gosnell, Leo* / Shake it over sputnik: *Hogan, Billy* / That's love: *Wendell & The Dreamers* / Rockabilly boogie: *Rockabilly Three* / Hey doll baby: *Patey Brothers* / Jeannie: *Patey Brothers.*
LP. . . . . WLP 8846
White Label (Germany) / '87 / Pinnacle / Bear Family Records (Germany) / CSA Tell Tapes.

ROCK FROM RARE LITTLE LABELS.
Tracks: That's alright: *Hines, Ronnie* / I got a woman: *Hines, Ronnie* / Green stamps: *Flynn, Freddie* / Hazel: *Flynn, Freddie* / Big Chief Buffalo Nickel: *Ross, Macey* / Black Jack: *Werley, Coy* / Bubblegum boogie: *McBride, Jim/Curly Rash/South Texas Playboys* / Speedway rock: *Woodard, Jerry* / Gamblin' man: *Starvin' Marvin* / Party line: *May, Haskell* / Tears: *England, Hank* / Space needle: *Starfires* / Ginger: *Parker, Wayne* / PM rock: *Ginsburg, Arnie & The Three D's* / Arnie's theme: *Ginsburg, Arnie & The Three D's.*
LP. . . . . WLP 8898
White Label (Germany) / '87 / Pinnacle / Bear Family Records (Germany) / CSA Tell Tapes.

ROCK FROM THE OTHER SIDE, VOL 1.
Tracks: Four city rock: *Lewis, Peter* / Money honey: *Lewis, Peter* / D.J. blues, The: *Hewitt, Red* / Gravediggers' rock: *Scott, Clyde* / Bluebird: *Scott, Clyde* / Able Mabel: *Davis, Bobby* / Tallahassee lassie: *Davis, Bobby* / I'm in love: *Tucker, Clynllan Lowe/Tornadoes* / Carol: *Tucker, Clynllan Lowe/Tornadoes* / Cool 'n' crazy: *Maxman, Ron* / Moo cow boogie: *Callaher, Vince & Will Jess* / Gone but not forgotten: *Riggir, Jack* / Pretty baby: *Riggir, Jack* / Hippy hippy shake: *Howell, Eddie & Ben Tawhiti.*
LP. . . . . DS 9211
Down South Records / '87 / Bear Family Records (Germany).

ROCK FROM THE OTHER SIDE, VOL 2.
Tracks: Girl in the teddy bear coat: *Hewitt, Red* / Is a bluebird blue?: *Hewitt, Red* / Tennessee waltz: *Hewitt, Red* / Betty Lou's got a new pair of shoes: *Hewitt, Red* / Don't you leave me: *Two Davies* / Big girl: *Paris, Bob Combo* / Bar X boogie: *Zito* / Just because: *Zito* / Spaceman: *Zito* / All I can do is cry: *Zito* / Teenage beat: *Jess, Will* / Mean woman blues: *Sundin, Ronnie* / Moo cow boogie blues: *Sundin, Ronnie* / Way I walk, The: *Sundin, Ronnie* / Be bop a Lula: *Fisher, Ivor* / Hot rod Lincoln: *Butler, Eddie.*
LP. . . . . DS 9212
Down South Records / '87 / Bear Family Records (Germany).

ROCK FROM THE OTHER SIDE, VOL 3.
Tracks: Everlovin' honey bee: *Bryant, Bix* / Let's have a party: *Bryant, Bix* / Judy: *Lincoln & The Lawmen* / Cool it, baby: *Lincoln & The Lawmen* / Lotta lovin': *Richard & The R'Jays* / Nature boy: *Raiders* / Nightmare: *Raiders* / Cloudburst: *Wades, Laurie* / Cincinnati fireball: *Benton, Marv* / Nervous breakdown: *Benton, Marv* / Love bug blues: *Buckley, Colin* / My baby calls: *Buckley, Colin* / Board boogie: *Aztecs & Billy Thorpe* / Shakin' in the Shaky Isle: *Maori Troubadours* / Meet me in the alley, Sally: *Thunderbirds/Billy O'Rourke/Billy Owens* / Warrant for arrest: *Thunderbirds/Billy O'Rourke/Billy Owens.*
LP. . . . . DS 9213
Down South Records / '87 / Bear Family Records (Germany).

ROCK FROM THE OTHER SIDE, VOL 4.
Tracks: Mama rock: *Brown, Johnny Scat* / Cross my heart: *Arthur, Malcolm & The Knights* / Saturday night: *Blue Jays* / Hound dog: *Welch, Les* / Rumble: *Popcorn* / Great balls of fire: *Miller, Bob* / Geronimo: *Convairs* / Jukebox hop: *Wayne, Dale* / Tallahassee lassie: *Harmony Flames* / Reet petite: *McLean, Peter* / My bucket's got a hole in it: *Trailblazers* / Prettiest baby: *Wicker, Grade* / Go man go: *Thomas, Bob.*
LP. . . . . DS 9215
Down South Records / '87 / Bear Family Records (Germany).

ROCK, BABY, ROCK.
Tracks: Snake-eyed woman: *Sundowners* / Sundown stomp: *Sundowners* / Ubangi stomp: *Sundowners* / Savage: *Bernicoat, Alan* / Trip to the Orient: *Bernicoat, Alan* / Screamin' Mimi: *Roy, Ricky* / My baby's gone: *Ranado, Chuck* / Studio blues: *Highlights* / Rag roof roadster: *Foster, Jim* / Rock and roll daddy o: *Castle, Joey* / Baby I don't care: *Gregg, O. David* / Picture yourself: *Gregg, O. David* / Rock, baby, rock: *Milo Choir* / Go, girl, go: *Powers, Jet* / Teena: *Carney, Sandy* / She's a fine cat: *Darrow, Neil* / I'm a wile ol' cat: *Mitchell, Thomas.*
LP. . . . . WLP 8890
White Label (Germany) / '87 / Pinnacle / Bear Family Records (Germany) / CSA Tell Tapes.

ROCK-A-BILLY BLUES.
Tracks: Blues at midnight: *Simmons, Gene* / Hey Slim: *Earls, Jack* / Bottle to the baby: *Feathers, Charlie* / Drinkin' scotch: *Simmons, Gene* / Pop and mama: *Simmons, Gene* / You can't make love to somebody: *Perkins, Carl* / Crawdad hole: *Earls, Jack* / They can't keep me from you: *Earls, Jack* / Fool for loving you: *Earls, Jack* / Hey Jim: *Earls, Jack* / Uh babe: *McDaniel, Luke* / Go ahead baby: *McDaniel, Luke* / Slow down: *Earls, Jack* / Sign on the dotted line: *Earls, Jack.*
LP. . . . . SUN 1019
Sun / May '86 / Charly / Swift.

ROCK-A-BILLY LEGENDS.
Tracks: Not Advised.
MC . . . . AIM 108
AIM (2) / Sep '83 / Topic Records / Direct Distribution.

ROCK-A-BILLY TIME (Best of Linn & Kliff).
Tracks: Jitterbuggin' baby: *Ray, David* / Lonesome baby blues: *Ray, David* / Lonesome feeling: *Ray, David* / Swinging boogie: *Smith, D. Ray* / Gone baby gone: *Smith, D. Ray* / Tell me why: *Starr, Frank "Andy"* / Disc jockey fever: *Chuck A Lucks* / Guitar smoke: *Brinkley, Jay* / Rough tough man: *Curtis, Don* / Rockin' hall: *McClarey, Butch* / Knees shakin': *Terry, Don* / Dog fight: *Jokers* / Meadowlark boogie: *Griffin, Buck* / It don't make no never mind: *Griffin, Buck* / Let's elope baby: *Griffin, Buck* / Bawlin' and squallin': *Griffin, Buck.*
LP. . . . . WLP 8827
White Label (Germany) / Apr '87 / Pinnacle / Bear Family Records (Germany) / CSA Tell Tapes.

ROCKABILLY & COUNTRY.
Tracks: Have you heard the gossip: *Charlie Brown* / Mean mean mama: *Charlie Brown* / My hungry heart: *Charlie Brown* / Boogie woogie mama: *Charlie Brown* / Pickin': *Charlie Brown* / Don't put the blame on me: *Charlie Brown* / Milkcow blues boogie: *Charlie Brown* / Hound dog: *Banks, Mack* / Be Boppin' daddy: *Banks, Mack* / They don't come in droves like me: *Banks, Mack* / Mack's boogie: *Banks, Mack* / You're so dumb: *Banks, Mack* / They raided the joint: *Banks, Mack.*
LP. . . . . WLP 8804
White Label (Germany) / '88 / Pinnacle / Bear Family Records (Germany) / CSA Tell Tapes.

ROCKABILLY BASH.
Tracks: Not Advised.
LP. . . . . BOPL 100
Boplacious / Jun '85 / Swift.

ROCKABILLY BOP VOL.1.
Tracks: Look kat: *Sherrell, Bill* / Little jewels: *Heap, Jimmy* / Hard hearted girl: *Davis, Cliff* / Rocky road blues: *Davis, Cliff* / Flat top box: *Jackson, Tommy* / Got rockin' on my mind: *Griffin, Curley* / Got the best of me: *Bowser, Donny* / Hey Mr. Porter: *Pruitt, Ralph* / Rocket on the moon: *Caves, John Wesley* / Curfew cop: *Cole, Sonny* / Robinson Crusoe bop: *Cole, Sonny* / Hey doll baby: *Kelly, Pat* / Cloud 13: *Kelly, Pat* / Rockin' Rochester: *Tempests.*
LP. . . . . RR 2002
Esoldun / Dec '86 / New Note.

ROCKABILLY BOP VOL.2.
Tracks: Alley cat: *Brown, Walter* / Jelly roll rock: *Brown, Walter* / Teenage ball: *Deitzel, Elroy* / Night club r'n'roll: *Parsons, Gene* / Come to your Tommy now: *Clark, Leonard* / Dig me a crazy record: *Senns, Charles* / Gee whiz Liz: *Senns, Charles* / Saturday night party: *Perkins, Reggie* / Pretty Kitty: *Perkins, Reggie* / Big Sandy: *Roberts, Bobby* / Rattle shakin' mama: *McGonnigle, Mel* / That big old moon: *Burke, Buddy* / Rockin' with r'n'b: *Haig, Ronnie* / Calypso boogie: *Hager, Don.*
LP. . . . . RR 2003
Esoldun / Dec '86 / New Note.

ROCKABILLY BOP VOL.3.
Tracks: Cat all night: *Finn, Lee* / It's night: *Finn, Lee* / Jukebox Johnny: *Moore, Lattie* / Pretty woman blues: *Moore, Lattie* / How about me?: *Johnson, Jimmy* / Cat daddy: *Johnson, Jimmy* / 21 carpenters: *Roberts, Marty* / Let's all go wild: *Pullen, Whitey* / Drinkin' wine: *Pullen, Whitey* / Walk me back home: *Pullen, Whitey* / Moonshine liquor: *Pullen, Whitey* / Tuscaloosa Lucy: *Pullen, Whitey* / Tight slacks: *Pullen, Whitey* / I dreamed I was Elvis: *Cole, Sonny.*
LP. . . . . RR 2006
Esoldun / Dec '86 / New Note.

ROCKABILLY BOPPIN'.
Tracks: Rock 'n' roll fever: *Ray, Gene* / I'm going to Hollywood: *Ray, Gene* / Too old to rock 'n' roll: *Sloan, Chucklin' Chuck* / You gotta show me: *Lane, Ralph* / Bartender's blues: *Buskirk, Kenny* / Get with it: *Buskirk, Kenny* / Thermostat baby: *Dorn, Dick* / My screamin' screamin' Mimi: *Campi, Ray* / Waddle, The: *Slades* / I'll give you all my love: *Berry, Ron* / Tell me, baby: *Smith, Billy* / Rock a long time: *Ratcliff, Bozo* / Let me in: *Ratcliff, Bozo* / I wanna go steady with you: *Armstrong, Dick* / At the high school dance: *Taylor, R. Dean.*
LP. . . . . WLP 8842
White Label (Germany) / Jul '87 / Pinnacle / Bear Family Records (Germany) / CSA Tell Tapes.

ROCKABILLY CLASSICS VOL. 1.

Tracks: Not Advised.
LP. . . . . **MCA 25088**
MCA / Nov '87 / BMG.

ROCKABILLY CRAZY.

Tracks: Not Advised.
■ **LP.** . . . . **CFM 506**
Charly / Feb '82.

ROCKABILLY FROM TENNESSEE VOL.1.

Tracks: Dreamer boy: *Hardin, Bobby* / I'm loving you baby: *Hardin, Bobby* / Sweet, sweet dreams: *Hardin, Bobby* / Gettin' better: *Hardin, Bobby* / My old lonesome love: *Rickman, Joe* / Lonely heart: *Rickman, Joe* / Puppy love: *Snyder, Tony* / Jackson dog: *Brinkley, Larry* / Move over Rover: *Brinkley, Larry* / I hate to leave you: *Brinkley, Larry* / All night long: *Brinkley, Larry* / Tornado: *Brinkley, Larry* / Pins and needles: *Stevenson, N.A.* / Boogie woogie country girl: *Stevenson, N.A.*.
LP. . . . . **WLP 8806**
White Label (Germany) / Jul '79 / Pinnacle / Bear Family Records (Germany) / CSA Tell Tapes.

ROCKABILLY FROM TENNESSEE VOL.2.

Tracks: Swing it, little Katy: *Owens, Clyde* / Last bouquet, The: *Owens, Clyde* / Rocket city rock: *Hillis, Clayton* / Don't you know I love you: *Hillis, Clayton* / Hoochie coochie man: *Long, Curtis* / After all: *Long, Curtis* / Mystic Madonna: *Jay Dee's* / Old red devil: *Champion, Hollis* / Little rock: *Four Sons* / Good times in Memphis: *Delmore, Alton* / What's going on: *Moore, Marvin* / Jumpin' the boogie: *Moore, Marvin* / I'm on this rocket: *Moore, Marvin*.
LP. . . . . **WLP 8808**
White Label (Germany) / Jul '79 / Pinnacle / Bear Family Records (Germany) / CSA Tell Tapes.

ROCKABILLY GREATEST HITS.

Tracks: Not Advised.
LP. **20004**
MC **40004**
Astan (USA) / Nov '84.

ROCKABILLY HEROES.

Tracks: Not Advised.
LP. . . . . **RLP 005**
Rundell / Oct '88 / Swift.

ROCKABILLY INFLUENCE 1950-60.

Tracks: Not Advised.
LP. . . . . **CGB 1008**
Capitol / Dec '81 / EMI.

ROCKABILLY JAMBOREE.

Tracks: Not Advised.
■ **LP.** . . . . **CFM 505**
Charly / Sep '81.

ROCKABILLY JAMBOREE.

Tracks: Not Advised.
VHS. . . . . **RVC 001**
ReVision / Aug '92 / RTM / Pinnacle.

ROCKABILLY PARTY.

Tracks: Jitterbop baby / Rock little baby / Looking / Little rock rock / Be boppin' daddy / By big fat baby / Trucker from Tennessee / That ain't it / I don't know when / One of these days.
■ **LP.** . . . . **CH 17**
Ace / Jul '79.

ROCKABILLY PSYCHOSIS.

Tracks: Surfin' bird: *Trashmen* / Psycho: *Sonics* / Crusher, The: *Novas* / Paralysed: *Legendary Stardust Cowboy* / She said: *Adkins, Hasil 'Haze'* / My daddy is a vampire: *Meteors* / Radioactive kid: *Meteors* / Dateless nites: *Falco, Tav's Panther Burns* / Jack on fire: *Gun Club* / Folsom prison blues: *Geezers* / Catman: *Stingrays* / Just love me: *Guana Batz* / Love me (Not available on CD): *Phantom* / Red headed woman: *Dickinson, Jimmy & the Cramps* / Scream! (Available on CD only): *Nielsen, Ralph & The Chancellors* / Hidden charms (Available on CD only): *Wray, Link* / Run chicken run (Available on CD only): *Milkshakes*.
■ **LP.** . . . . **WIK 18**
Big Beat / Jun '84.
MC . . . . **WIKC 18**
Big Beat / Jan '85 / Pinnacle / Hot Shot / Jazz Music.
CD . . . . **CDWIK 18**
Big Beat / Oct '89 / Pinnacle / Hot Shot / Jazz Music.

ROCKABILLY REBELS (CAMBRA RELEASE).

Tracks: Going home: *Burgess, Sonny* / Yakety yak: *Vevington, Malcolm* / Tootsie: *McVoy, Carl* / Cadillac man: *Jester* / Rockin' Daddy: *Bond, Eddie* / I've been deceived: *Feathers, Charlie* / Dear John: *Smith, Warren* / Rock with me baby: *Riley, Billy Lee* / Drinking wine: *Simons, Gene* / Pink pedal pushers: *Perkins, Carl* / Caldonia: *Perkins, Carl* / Flyin' saucers rock 'n' roll: *Riley, Billy Lee* / Hillbilly music: *Lewis, Jerry Lee* / Teddy jive / Jungle rock: *Mizell, Hank* / Sadie's back in town: *Burgess, Sonny* / Domino: *Orbison, Roy* / Ten cats down: *Miller Sisters* / Red cadillac and a black moustache: *Smith, Warren* / Milkshake mademoiselle: *Lewis, Jerry Lee* / Let's bop: *Earls, Jack* / Love my baby: *Thompson, Hayden*.
Double LP . . . . **CR 104**
■ **MC Set** . . . . **CRT 104**
Cambra / Apr '85.

ROCKABILLY REBELS (HALLMARK RELEASE).

Tracks: Girl in red: *Stevens, Shakin' & Sunsets* / Heavenly: *Showaddywaddy* / Buzz buzz a diddle it: *Matchbox* / Come on let's go: *Sharpe, Rocky & The Replays* / James Dean: *Jets (2)* / Crazy little teddy girl: *Crazy Cavan & The Rhythm Rockers* / If I ain't home: *Rock Island Line* / When I see my baby: *Sneekers* / Jungle rock: *Stevens, Shakin' & Sunsets* / King of the jive: *Showaddywaddy* / Rockabilly rebel: *Matchbox* / Shout, shout: *Sharpe, Rocky & The Replays* / Rockabilly baby: *Jets (2)* / Put a light in the window: *Crazy Cavan & The Rhythm Rockers* / Barking up the wrong tree: *Rock Island Line* / Good good rockin': *Sneekers*.
LP. . . . . **SHM 3147**
■ **MC** . . . . **HSC 3147**
Hallmark / Jul '84.

ROCKABILLY SHAKEOUT - NUMBER 1.

Tracks: Shadow my baby: *Barber, Glen* / Atom bomb: *Barber, Glen* / I don't know when: *Harris, Hal* / My little baby: *Jimmy & Johnny* / True affection: *Johnson, Byron* / Slipping and sliding: *Davis, Link* / Hey hey little boy blue: *Lindsay, Merle* / Gee whiz: *Dee & Patty* / All the time: *La Beef, Sleepy* / Spin the bottle: *Joy, Benny* / Chicken bop: *Truitt Forse* / My big fat baby: *Hall, Sonny & The Echoes* / Cat's just got back in town: *Mack, Billy* / Tennessee rock: *Scoggins, Hoyt* / Uranium fever: *Gaddis, Ruddy* / Prettiest girl at the dance: *Wyatt, Gene*.
MC . . . . **CHC 191**
Ace / Nov '86 / Pinnacle / Hot Shot / Jazz Music / Complete Record Co. Ltd.
■ **LP.** . . . . **CH 191**
Ace / Nov '86.
CD . . . . **CDCH 191**
Ace / Feb '92 / Pinnacle / Hot Shot / Jazz Music / Complete Record Co. Ltd.

ROCKABILLY STARS VOL.1.

Tracks: Not Advised.
■ **LP.** . . . . **EPC 12165**
Epic / Jun '82.

ROCKABILLY STARS VOL.2.

Tracks: Not Advised.
■ **Double LP** . . . . **EPC 22116**
Epic / Jun '82.

ROCKABILLY STARS VOL.3.

Tracks: Not Advised.
■ **Double LP** . . . . **EPC 22100**
CBS / Oct '82.

ROCKABILLY TUNES.

Tracks: I was a fool: *Orbison, Roy* / Rockabilly gal: *Thompson, Hayden* / Johnny Valentine: *Anderson, Andy* / Tough tough tough: *Anderson, Andy* / Love dumb baby: *Harris, Ray* / Heart breakin' love: *Wages, Jimmy* / Take me: *Wages, Jimmy* / Thinkin' I am tonight of blue eyes: *Carter* / Don't come crying: *Ruick, Tommy* / Prisoner of the blues: *Ruick, Tommy* / Let 'em know: *Ruick, Tommy* / Lonely river: *Felts, Narvel* / Foolish thoughts / Lonesome feeling.
LP. . . . . **SUN 1026**
Sun / Apr '85 / Charly / Swift.

ROCKABILLY WORLD.

Tracks: Bug boat song, The: *Mac, Johnny* / Go, cats, go: *Rhodes, Texas Red* / Boogie rock: *Ringhiser & Rhythm Drifters* / Uranium miner's boogie: *Walker, Riley* / Shakedown: *Thomas, Bill* / Sputnik story, The: *Thomas, Bill* / Steel guitar rag: *McCann, Dennis* / Hadacol boogie: *Sims, Babe* / Permit blues: *Davis, Link* / Airliner: *Davis, Link* / Dance, baby, dance: *Crum, Tom* / Lonesome guitar: *Garland, Bill* / Guitar blues: *Garland, Bill* / I stubbed my toe: *Walker, Bryan* / Trick or treat: *Walker, Bryan* / Annie Mae: *Dewitt, Bobby*.
LP. . . . . **WLP 8908**
White Label (Germany) / Oct '86 / Pinnacle / Bear Family Records (Germany) / CSA Tell Tapes.

ROCKAPHILLY - PHILADELPHIA ROCK 'N' ROLL.

Tracks: Sky rock - jukebox rock 'n' roll: *Coleman, Ray* / Everybody's rockin' tonight: *Coleman, Ray* / You look like something that the cat drug in: *Moss, Bill* / Rockabilly hop: *Moss, Bill* / Ducktail: *Wellington, Rusty* / Rockin' the blues: *Wellington, Rusty* / Rock 'n' roll Ruby: *Wellington, Rusty* / It should have been me: *Kingsmen* / Hot to trott: *Highliters* / Four alarm boogie: *Collett, Jimmy* / Beetlebug boogie: *Collett, Jimmy* / Rock around the clock (Original version): *Dae, Sonny & His Knights* / Jump cats jump: *Rogers, Jesse* / Hydrogen bomb: *Rex, Al* / Buck fever boogie: *Herdman, Curly* / Chuck's boogie: *Hess, Chuck*.
LP. . . . . **ROLL 2001**
Rollercoaster / Sep '84 / Rollercoaster Records / Swift.

ROCKAROLLA AHILLABILLY WING DING DO (Red hot rockabilly 1955-62).

Tracks: Not Advised.
LP. . . . . **SIN ALLEY 2**
Sin Alley / Oct '87 / Swift.

ROCKIN' IN LOUISIANA VOL. 3.

Tracks: End of the hunt: *Darnell, Bozo* / I shouldn't [illegible] *Mike* / Late at night: *Perrywell, Charles* / Mama, mama, mama: *Hobbs, Louis* / Honey don't you listen: *Wayne, Roy* / Any way you do: *Wayne, Roy* / Allons rock 'n' roll: *Walker, Lawrence* / Martin's special: *Martin & The Rockers* / My Suzie Q: *Segura, Allen* / Barefoot rock: *Raines, Jerry* / Sha Marie: *Kerry, Marvin* / One boy, one girl: *Evans, Dean* / Geraldine: *Casanova & The Chants*.
LP. . . . . **WLP 8893**
White Label (Germany) / Jul '87 / Pinnacle / Bear Family Records (Germany) / CSA Tell Tapes.

ROCKIN' IN THE 50'S.

Tracks: Been away too long: *Blihovde, Marv* / Nobody's darlin' but you: *Blihovde, Marv* / Sweet little wife: *Blihovde, Marv* / Pickles: *Blihovde, Marv* / Cigarette and coffee blues: *Blihovde, Marv* / Teenage partner: *Hanson, Ronnie* / I got a baby: *Roubik, Jack* / Live it up: *Roubik, Jack* / Shake a leg: *Hodges, Sonny* / Date with you, A: *Hodges, Sonny* / Big dog, little dog: *Hodges, Sonny* / That's alright: *Faile, Tommy* / Little girl: *Ramistella, Johnny* / Two by two: *Ramistella, Johnny* / Party party: *T.J.'s*.
LP. . . . . **WLP 8839**
White Label (Germany) / Sep '87 / Pinnacle / Bear Family Records (Germany) / CSA Tell Tapes.

ROCKIN' ORIGINAL ARTISTS.

Tracks: Sweet love on my mind: *Burnette, Johnny* / Honey hush: *Burnette, Johnny* / Drinkin' wine: *Burnette, Johnny* / Dum dum: *Lee, Brenda* / Sweet nothin's: *Lee, Brenda* / Jambalaya: *Lee, Brenda* / Razz dazzle: *Haley, Bill & The Comets* / See you later alligator: *Haley, Bill & The Comets* / Rip it up: *Haley, Bill & The Comets* / Maybe baby: *Holly, Buddy* / Rave on: *Holly, Buddy* / Peggy Sue got married: *Holly, Buddy* / I fought the law: *Crickets* / Rockin' pneumonia: *Crickets*.
■ **LP.** . . . . **MFP 50466**
MFP / Apr '80.

ROCKIN' PEG.

Tracks: You're just that kind: *Jones, Little Montie* / Rockin' Peg: *Redd, Johnny* / Early one morning: *Gillen, Jack* / Wrapped in green, made for ten: *Ferguson, Bobby* / I've been seasick: *Meadows, Bill* / Moonshine: *Garrison, Red* / You're gonna reap what you sow: *Strong, Ray* / That cat: *Brown, Tommy* / Wicked: *Rudy & Vince* / Nite beat: *Edwards, Slim* / Jerico rock: *Mysterians* / Screamin' and dyin': *Blass, Charles* / Judy's clown: *Lee, Dennis* / Raw deal: *Dickens, Doug* / Hep cat baby: *Criss, Gene* / Please don't say goodbye: *Criss, Gene*.
LP. . . . . **WLP 8950**
White Label (Germany) / Nov '89 / Pinnacle / Bear Family Records (Germany) / CSA Tell Tapes.

ROCKIN' ROLLIN' COUNTRY STYLE.

Tracks: Drivin': *Vickery, Mack* / Foolproof: *Vickery, Mack* / Have you ever been lonely: *Vickery, Mack* / My one desire: *Williams, Jimmy* / All I want is you: *Williams, Jimmy* / Walkin' shoes: *Wheeler, Onie* / That's all: *Wheeler, Onie* / Tell 'em off: *Wheeler, Onie* / Jump right out of this jukebox: *Wheeler, Onie* / Bonaparts retreat (instr.): *Wheeler, Onie* / Trumpet: *Yelvington, Malcolm* / First and last love: *Yelvington, Malcolm* / Mr.Blues: *Yelvington, Malcolm* / What I tell my heart: *McDaniel, Luke* / Don't come crying: *Ruick, Tommy*.
LP. . . . . **SUN LP 1030**
Sun / Feb '90 / Charly / Swift.

ROCKIN' ROLLIN' HIGH SCHOOL VOL.1.

Tracks: Pig Latin song: *Luman, Bob* / Shopping centre: *Lord, Bobby* / Barbara: *Melson, Joe* / Shook up: *Melson, Joe* / What should I do: *Jensen, Kris* / There came a tear: *Folger, Dan* / Tell her for me: *Folger, Dan* / Girl in the night: *Folger, Dan* / Mary is my little lamb: *Folger, Dan* / Love is all I'm asking for: *Mitchell, Sinx 'Earl Sinx'* / Ring around my Rosie (Previously unissued): *Mitchell, Sinx 'Earl Sinx'* / Return to Thunder road: *Mitchell, Sinx 'Earl Sinx'* / Run Opic run: *Dinning, Mark* / Should we do it: *Dinning, Mark* / Last rose, The: *Dinning, Mark* / I love to dance with Annie: *Ashworth, Ernest*.
■ **LP.** . . . . **BFX 15064**
Bear Family / '86.

ROCKIN' ROLLIN' HIGH SCHOOL VOL.2.

Tracks: Not Advised.
■ **LP.** . . . . **BFX 15065**
Bear Family / '85.

ROCKIN' ROLLIN' HIGH SCHOOL VOL.3.

Tracks: Rock 'n' roll that hula hoop (Available on 12" only): *LeGarde Twins* / Little brother: *Lane Brothers* / Somebody sweet: *Lane Brothers* / Boppin' in a sack: *Lane Brothers* / Goodbye she's gone: *Sprouts* / Every little once in a while: *Sprouts* / Shake me up again: *Sprouts* / Luscious lovin' Lucy: *Sprouts* / I'll never tell (Previously unissued.): *Orbison, Roy* / Young love (original version): *Cartey, Ric* / Crying goodbye (Previously unissued.): *Cartey, Ric* / Hey little ducky (Previously unissued.): *James, Sonny* / Apache (Previously unissued.): *James, Sonny* / Stand in (Previously unissued.): *Robertson, Doc* / Edge of town, The (Previously unissued.): *Clement, Jack* / Whole lotta lookin' all over this world (Previously unissued.): *Clement, Jack*.
LP. . . . . **BFX 15111**
Bear Family / Sep '84 / Rollercoaster Records / Swift / Direct Distribution.

ROCKIN' ROLLIN' HIGH SCHOOL VOL.4.

Tracks: Teeny weeny: *Dell, Jimmy* / Cool it, baby: *Dell, Jimmy* / Message, The: *Dell, Jimmy* / It's simply grand: *Allen, Milt* / Love a, love a lover: *Allen, Milt* / Just look, don't touch, she's mine: *Allen, Milt* / Half loved (1st recording) (Previously unissued.): *Allen, Milt* / Love twister: *Denson, Lee* / It took too long (Previously unissued.): *Denson, Lee* / Heart of a fool: *Denson, Lee* / Pied piper: *Denson, Lee* / Let me tell you about love: *Cartey, Ric* / Born to love one woman: *Cartey, Ric* / Heart throb: *Cartey, Ric*.

■ LP. . . . . BFX 15112
Bear Family / Sep '84.

ROCKIN' ROLLIN' HIGH SCHOOL VOL.5.
Tracks: Red sweater: *Rich, Dave* / School blues: *Rich, Dave* / Sunshine in my heart: *Rich, Dave* / Dream boat: *Inman, Autrey* / Hard way, The: *Inman, Autrey* / Teenage wonderland: *Pruitt, Tommy* / Remember the night: *Fagan, Tom* / You look good to me: *Clay, Joe* / Doggone it: *Clay, Joe* / Goodbye goodbye: *Clay, Joe* / Slipping out and sneaking in: *Clay, Joe* / Keep a lovin' me baby: *Endsley, Melvin* / I like your kind of love: *Endsley, Melvin* / I got a feeling: *Endsley, Melvin* / I ain't gettin' nowhere with you: *Endsley, Melvin.*
■ LP. . . . . BFX 15113
Bear Family / Sep '84.

ROCKIN' ROLLIN' HIGH SCHOOL VOL.6.
Tracks: Jamboree: *Allen, Milt* / Youthful lover (Previously unissued.): *Allen, Milt* / One love too many (Previously unissued.): *Allen, Milt* / Land of tomorrow (Previously unissued.): *Allen, Milt* / Lovin' at night: *Salvo, Sammy* / My perfect love: *Salvo, Sammy* / Oh Julie: *Salvo, Sammy* / Julie doesn't love me anymore: *Salvo, Sammy* / Wake up little Susie: *Lane Brothers* / Uh uh honey: *Lane Brothers* / Ding dang danglin': *Lane Brothers* / Lips of wine: *Lane Brothers* / Come a little bit closer baby: *Castle, Joey* / Shake hands with a fool (Previously unissued.): *Castle, Joey* / Please love me (Previously unissued.): *Castle, Joey.*
■ LP. . . . . BFX 15114
Bear Family / Sep '84.

ROCKIN' ROLLIN' HIGH SCHOOL VOL.7.
Tracks: Man in the moon is a lady, The: *Robinson, Floyd* / Ooba ooba ooba: *Burton, Dave* / Rock 'n' roll Ruby: *Burton, Dave* / Oh baby (Previously unissued.): *Dell, Jimmy* / Nite rock: *Nite Rockers* / Dear Tommy: *Teeners (Teen Queens)* / King of rock 'n' roll (Previously unissued.): *Teeners (Teen Queens)* / Ring around the rock (Previously unissued.): *Teeners (Teen Queens)* / Oh, oh baby (Previously unissued.): *Dell, Jimmy* / Chicken hearted (Previously unissued.): *Dell, Jimmy* / Left right here (Previously unissued.): *Dell, Jimmy* / Me and big mouth (Previously unissued.): *Dell, Jimmy* / Tuggin' on my heart strings: *Rich, Dave* / Burn on love fire: *Rich, Dave* / I believe in love (Previously unissued.): *Robinson, Floyd* / Back in school again: *Robinson, Floyd.*
■ LP. . . . . BFX 15115
Bear Family / Sep '84.

ROCKING DESS & POOR BOY MASTERS.
Tracks: Rock & roll joys: *Bowshier, Little Donnie* / I thought I heard you call my name: *Baker, Rob 'Boy'* / Impact: *Ramblin' Rebels* / Lost safari, The: *Ramblin' Rebels* / Grandma rock 'n' roll: *Sisco, Gene* / Turning the tables: *Sisco, Gene* / Mind your own business: *White, Evelyn* / Servant of love: *Van Bros* / Sweet Marie: *Van Bros* / Uncle Jim Riggs will: *Van Bros* / Wake me: *Witcher, Norman* / Somebody's been rocking my boat: *Witcher, Norman* / Doing things: *Richmond Boys.*
LP. . . . . WLP 8811
White Label (Germany) / '88 / Pinnacle / Bear Family Records (Germany) / CSA Tell Tapes.

ROCKING RUFUS.
Tracks: Rocking Rufus: *Mauphin, Ramon* / What's the use?: *Mauphin, Ramon* / 'Cause I love you: *Allen, Little Joe* / When mom and pop started to rock: *Briggs, Gail & Steve* / Red lips: *Mondo* / Everybody needs somebody: *Mondo* / She's a square: *St. Germaine, Ray* / Hound dog guitar: *D'Valiant, Ronnie* / Iggy Joe: *Ward, Willie* / Meanest blues: *Thomas, Jake* / Iftic: *Emcees* / Born to ramble: *Loren, Keith* / Row boy: *O'Mary, Slim* / Sink or swim: *O'Mary, Slim* / I cried: *Purdy, Steve* / Walking in my sleep: *Dean, Jerry* / Not for love or money: *Hodge, Gary.*
LP. . . . . WLP 8856
White Label (Germany) / '87 / Pinnacle / Bear Family Records (Germany) / CSA Tell Tapes.

ROOTS OF ROCK VOL.4 (Cotton City Country).
Tracks: Defrost your heart: *Feathers, Charlie* / My kind of carrying on: *Poindexter, Doug* / I'd be a millionaire: *Hadley, Red* / How long: *Wimberly, Maggie Sue* / Uh babo: *McDaniel, Luke* / Chains of love: *Miller Sisters* / Trouble bound: *Riley, Billy Lee* / Sweethearts or strangers: *Perkins, Carl* / It all depends: *Lewis, Jerry Lee* / Feelin' low: *Chaffin, Ernie* / Easy to love: *Self, Mack* / Blue days and sleepless nights: *Smith, Warren* / Come in stranger: *Cash, Johnny* / Black haired man: *Clement, Jack* / Thanks a lot: *Newman, Jeanne* / Sweet country girl: *Stinit, Dane.*
■ LP. . . . . CR 30104
Charly / Jan '77 / Charly.

S

SANCTIFIED COUNTRY GIRLS 1927-31.
Tracks: Not Advised.
LP. . . . . WSE 119
Wolf / Oct '86 / Jazz Music / Swift / Hot Shot.

SATURDAY NIGHT AT THE GRAND OLE OPRY.
Tracks: Bitter creek / Must it be me / Words come easy / Thinking about you / Livin' on love / I like mountain music / How can I believe / Flowing water and shifting sands / Lovin' in vain / Love problem / Which one will it be / Fiddlers dream.
LP. . . . . HAT 3059
MC . . . . HATC 3059
Stetson / Jun '88 / Crusader Marketing Co. / Swift / Wellard Dist. / Midland Records / C.M. Distribution.

SEND ME THE PILLOW YOU DREAM ON.
Tracks: Send me the pillow you dream on: *Locklin, Hank* / Reuben James: *Rogers, Kenny* / I feel sorry for him: *Nelson, Willie* / Come on in: *Cline, Patsy* / Hey good lookin': *Cash, Johnny* / You'll always have someone: *Nelson, Willie* / 6 days on the road: *Dudley, Dave* / Always leaving always gone: *Rogers, Kenny* / Burning memories: *Jennings, Waylon* / Walkin' after midnight: *Cline, Patsy* / Singin' the blues: *Mitchell, Guy* / Take these chains from my heart: *Drusky, Roy* / Mule train: *Laine, Frankie* / Don't think twice: *Jennings, Waylon* / If I don't understand: *Nelson, Willie* / Ramblin' rose: *Lee, Johnny* / Rose garden: *Anderson, Lynn* / Heart you break could be your own, The: *Cline, Patsy* / Ticket to nowhere: *Rogers, Kenny* / Release me: *Mandrell, Barbara* / I can't find the time: *Nelson, Willie* / Waterloo: *Jackson, Stonewall* / Last letter, The: *Drusky, Roy* / Wild side of life: *Fender, Freddy* / Sunshine: *Rogers, Kenny.*
CD . . . . CDGRF 120
MC . . . . MCGRF 120
Tring / Feb '93 / Prism Leisure PLC / Midland Records / Taylors.

SHAKE AROUND.
Tracks: Rockin' bandit: *Smith, Ray* / Judy: *Grayzell, Rudy* / Shake around: *Blake, Tommy* / You better believe it: *Blake, Tommy* / That's the way I feel: *Pritchett, Jimmy* / Don't you worry: *Watson, Sid* / With your love, with your kiss: *Powers, Johnny* / Dear John: *Smith, Warren* / Sweet sweet girl: *Smith, Warren* / Sweet woman: *Bruce, Edwin* / I dig you baby: *Blake, Tommy* / Sweetie pie: *Blake, Tommy* / Be mine, all mine: *Powers, Johnny* / Doll baby: *Bruce, Edwin* / I'm evil: *Powers, Johnny.*
LP. . . . . SUN 1029
Sun / May '85 / Charly / Swift.

SILVER HEART COUNTRY, VOL 1.
Tracks: Not Advised.
LP. . . . . DEAGLE 1
MC . . . . DEAGLE 1C
Silver Heart / Sep '88 / Silver Heart Records.

SIZZLING COUNTRY INSTRUMENTALS.
Tracks: Not Advised.
LP. . . . . SPR 8560
MC . . . . SPC 8560
Spot / Mar '85.

SOLID GOLD COUNTRY.
Tracks: Your cheatin heart: *Arnold, Eddy* / Green green grass of home: *Bare, Bobby* / Wayward wind: *Browns* / Ruby don't take your love to town: *Jennings, Waylon* / I love you because: *Snow, Hank* / Roses are red: *Reeves, Jim* / Take these chains from my heart: *Gibson, Don* / I walk the line: *Davis, Skeeter* / Release me: *Hamilton, George IV* / Everything is beautiful: *Hamilton, George IV* / Rose garden: *West, Dottie* / Silver threads and golden needles: *Davis, Skeeter* / Behind closed doors: *Milsap, Ronnie* / Paper roses: *Smith, Connie* / It wasn't God who made honky tonk angels: *Norma Jean* / Gonna find me a bluebird: *Davis, Skeeter & Porter Wagoner* / Love sick blues: *Milsap, Ronnie* / I can't stop loving you: *Locklin, Hank* / Banks of the Ohio: *Wagoner, Porter* / Act naturally: *Pride, Charley.*
MC . . . . INTK 9011
RCA International / Jun '82 / BMG.

SON OF REDNECK.
Tracks: Not Advised.
CD . . . . MCAD 10367
■ MC . . . . MCAC 10367
MCA / Aug '91.
■ CD . . . . MCLD 19041
MCA / Apr '92.
■ MC . . . . MCLC 19041
MCA / Apr '92.

SONGBIRDS.
Tracks: I've never been to me: *Charlene* / Hurtin's all over, The: *Smith, Connie* / There goes my everything: *Wynette, Tammy* / I've cried the blue right out of my eyes: *Gayle, Crystal* / Songbirds: *Brown, Polly* / Delta dawn: *Tucker, Tanya* / Other side of me, The: *Gayle, Crystal* / Rose garden: *Anderson, Lynn* / Help me make it through the night: *Smith, Sammi* / Diamonds and rust: *Baez, Joan* / Single girl: *Posey, Sandy* / Just the way I am: *Parton, Dolly* / Misty blue: *Burgess, Wilma* / We're all alone: *Coolidge, Rita* / Will you love me tomorrow?: *Ronstadt, Linda* / Blanket on the ground: *Spears, Billie Jo* / Harper Valley PTA: *Riley, Jeannie C.* / True love: *Cline, Patsy* / End of the world: *Davis, Skeeter* / There's a party going on: *Miller, Jody* / I love how you love me / Don't it make my brown eyes blue?: *Gayle, Crystal* / Take me to your world: *Wynette, Tammy* / Put your hand in the hand: *Posey, Sandy* / For all the right reasons: *Fairchild, Barbara* / What're you doing tonight?: *Frickie, Janie* / Careless hands: *West, Dottie* / Lonely comin' down: *Parton, Dolly.*
Double LP . . . . STD 3
MC Set . . . . STDK 3
Solitaire / '83 / BMG.

SONGS OF FAITH (I love country).
Tracks: Jesus was a carpenter: *Cash, Johnny* / Amazing grace / Steps: *Gatlin, Larry & The Gatlin Brothers Band* / Far side of Jordan: *Carter Family* / Silent night holy night: *Thomas, B.J.* / Just a closer walk with thee: *James, Sonny* / Preacher said "Jesus said": *Cash, Johnny with Billy Graham* / Where the soul never dies: *Oak Ridge Boys* / Why me Lord: *Jones, George* / What a friend we have in Jesus: *Jackson, Stonewall* / Leaning on the everlasting arms: *Dean, Jimmy* / Children go where I send thee: *Skaggs, Ricky* / Lonesome valley: *Scruggs, Earl with Tom T.Hall* / When the roll is called up yonder: *Robbins, Marty* / How great thou art: *Statler Brothers* / Trouble maker.
LP. 4510051
■ MC 4510054
CBS / Mar '88.

SONGS OF HARLAN HOWARD, THE.
Tracks: Blizzard: *Reeves, Jim* / She's a little bit country: *Hamilton, George IV* / Deepening snow, The: *Smith, Connie* / She called me baby: *Loudermilk, John D.* / I've got a tiger by the tail: *Jean, Norma* / Yours love: *Nelson, Willie* / Chokin' kind, The: *Davis, Skeeter* / Streets of Baltimore: *Bare, Bobby* / Thing called sadness, A: *Gibson, Don* / Too many rivers: *Colter, Jessi* / Watermelon time in Georgia: *Oxford, Vernon* / Heartaches by the number: *Cramer, Floyd* / Lonely people: *Arnold, Eddy* / It's raining all over the world: *Locklin, Hank* / Mary Ann regrets: *Snow, Hank* / Old podner: *Harlan, Howard.*
■ LP. . . . . PL 42012
RCA / '79.

SONGS OF LOVE, COUNTRY STYLE.
Tracks: Not Advised.
LP. . . . . MCTV 7
MC . . . . MCTVC 7
ABC Records / Mar '82.

SOUND OF SUN, THE.
Tracks: Bear cat: *Thomas, Rufus* / Just walkin' in the rain: *Prisonaires* / Feeling good: *Parker, Junior & the Blue Flames* / Drinkin' wine spo-dee-o-dee: *Yelvington, Malcolm* / Boogie disease: *Dr. Isiah Ross* / Red hot: *Emerson, Billy 'The Kid'* / Blue suede shoes: *Perkins, Carl* / Rock 'n' roll ruby: *Smith, Warren* / I walk the line: *Cash, Johnny* / Ooby dooby: *Orbison, Roy & Teen Kings* / Red headed woman: *Burgess, Sonny* / Flyin' saucers rock 'n' roll: *Riley, Billy Lee & The Little Green Men* / Whole lotta shakin' goin' on: *Lewis, Jerry Lee* / Raunchy: *Justis, Bill & His Orchestra* / Pretend: *Mann, Carl* / Lonely weekends: *Rich, Charlie* / Tiger man: *Thomas, Rufus* / Mystery train: *Little Junior's Blue Flames* / Boppin' the blues: *Perkins, Carl* / Come on little mama: *Harris, Ray* / Great balls of fire: *Lewis, Jerry Lee* / Right behind you baby: *Smith, Ray.*
CD . . . . CDSAM 103
LP. . . . . SAM 3
MC . . . . TCSAM 3
Sun / Jul '88 / Charly / Swift.

SOUTHERN NIGHTS (The very best of country).
Tracks: Southern nights: *Campbell, Glen* / Somebody loves you: *Gayle, Crystal* / When you're in love with a beautiful woman: *Dr. Hook* / It keeps right on a-hurtin': *Shepard, Jean* / Angel of the morning: *Newton, Juice* / Six days on the road: *Dudley, Dave* / Sing me an old fashioned song: *Spears, Billie Jo* / Daydream believer: *Murray, Anne* / Hello walls: *Nelson, Willie* / I fall to pieces: *Ronstadt, Linda* / Raindrops keep falling on my head: *Gentry, Bobbie* / Better love next time: *Dr. Hook* / Break my mind: *Murray, Anne* / I'll be your baby tonight: *Ronstadt, Linda* / Route 66: *Asleep At The Wheel* / All I have to do is dream: *Gentry, Bobbie & Glen Campbell* / Why have you left the one you left me for: *Gayle, Crystal* / Honey come back: *Campbell, Glen* / He loves everything he gets his hands on: *Shepard, Jean* / What I've got in mind: *Spears, Billie Jo.*
LP. . . . . MFP 41 5671 1
■ MC . . . . MFP 41 5671 4
MFP / Sep '84.

SOUTHERN NIGHTS.
Tracks: Southern nights: *Campbell, Glen* / Let your love flow: *Bellamy Brothers* / Blue bayou: *Ronstadt, Linda* / Coward of the county: *Rogers, Kenny* / Wind beneath my wings, The: *Greenwood, Lee* / I will always love you: *Parton, Dolly* / Feels so right: *Alabama* / Help me make it through the night: *Kristofferson, Kris* / I love a rainy day: *Rabbitt, Eddie* / I just fall in love again: *Murray, Anne* / I'd be a legend in my time: *Milsap, Ronnie* / All my ex's live in Texas: *Strait, George* / Together again: *Harris, Emmylou* / You're my best friend: *Williams, Don* / Hurt: *Newton, Juice* / Ain't misbehavin': *Williams, Hank Jr.* / Streets of Bakersfield: *Yoakam, Dwight & Buck Owens* / Talking in your sleep: *Gayle, Crystal* / Country boy: *Skaggs, Ricky* / Dukes of Hazzard, Theme from: *Jennings, Waylon* / Way we make a broken heart, The: *Cash, Rosanne* / Yesterday's wine: *Jones, George & Merle Haggard* / Hold me: *Oslin, K.T.* / Cry myself to sleep: *Judds* / Delta dawn: *Reddy, Helen* / Forever and ever, Amen: *Travis, Randy* / Always on my mind: *Nelson, Willie* / Another somebody done somebody wrong song: *Thomas, B.J.*
LP. . . . . KTVLP 1
Knight / Apr '91 / Castle Communications / BMG.

CD . . . . KTVCD 1
■ MC . . . . KTVMC 1
Knight / Apr '91.

SOUTHERN ROCKIN'.
Tracks: You'll never change me: *Allen, Lonnie* / Verbena: *Smith, Lanier* / Can't stand to be alone: *Guy, Dewey* / Rock a while: *Guy, Dewey* / Have a tear on me: *Wilson, Jim* / I'm the wrong one: *Hunt, Kenneth* / Teenage tease: *Hunt, Kenneth* / Packing my dud: *Marvin, Eddie* / Tutti frutti: *Shaul, Lawrence* / Hey little mama: *Shaul, Lawrence* / Loco choo choo: *Miller Bros.* / G.I. Blues: *Knull, Roger* / Country boy shuffle: *Sewell, Homer Lee* / I want my baby back: *Dixon, Mason.*
LP . . . . WLP 8835
White Label (Germany) / Sep '88 / Pinnacle / Bear Family Records (Germany) / CSA Tell Tapes.

SPADE ROCKABILLY.
Tracks: Not Advised.
LP . . . . R&C 1007
Rock & Country / Oct '88 / Swift.

STAR SPANGLED COUNTRY: THE HITS OF '84.
Tracks: Don't cheat in your home town: *Skaggs, Ricky* / Candy man: *Gilley, Mickey & Charly McClain* / Double shot: *Stampley, Joe* / You made a wanted man of me: *McDowell, Ronnie* / Someday when things are good: *Haggard, Merle* / Left side of the bed: *Gray, Mark* / Let's stop talkin' about it: *Frickie, Janie* / Woke up in love: *Exile* / You've really got a hold on me: *Gilley, Mickey* / Sentimental ol' you: *McClain, Charly* / Two car garage: *Thomas, B.J.* / That's the way love goes: *Haggard, Merle* / We didn't see a thing: *Charles, Ray & George Jones* / Honey: *Skaggs, Ricky* / I dream of women like you: *McDowell, Ronnie* / Without a song: *Nelson, Willie.*
LP . . . . EPC 26090
MC 40 26090
Epic / Aug '84 / Sony.

STARDAY DIXIE ROCKABILLIES.
Tracks: Not Advised.
LP . . . . K 5017
King (USA) / Mar '88 / Charly.

STARDAY DIXIE ROCKABILLIES - VOL.2.
Tracks: Not Advised.
LP . . . . GD 5031
Gusto (USA) / Oct '79.

STARS OF THE COUNTRY.
Tracks: If you could read my mind: *Riley, Jeannie C.* / Crazy dreams: *Twitty, Conway* / Tumbling tumbleweeds: *Newman, Jimmy C.* / It's too late: *Orbison, Roy* / I forgot to remember to forget: *Lewis, Jerry Lee* / Hey good lookin': *Cash, Johnny* / Tennessee waltz: *Page, Patti* / You love me, don't you?: *Locklin, Hank* / King of the road: *Dudley, Dave* / Yellow rose of Texas: *Newman, Jimmy C.* / Sail away: *Lewis, Jerry Lee & Charlie Rich* / Goodnight, Irene: *Cash, Johnny* / Gentle on my mind: *Page, Patti* / Say you'll stay until tomorrow: *Drusky, Roy* / Truck drivin' son of a gun: *Dudley, Dave* / Sweethearts or strangers?: *Perkins, Carl* / Devil doll: *Orbison, Roy* / Little ole wine drinker me: *Walker, Charlie* / Welcome home: *Drusky, Roy* / Games people play: *Riley, Jeannie C.* / I heard that lonesome whistle blow: *Cash, Johnny* / Give me some love: *Twitty, Conway* / Walk on by: *Van Dyke, Leroy* / Together again: *O'Gwynn, James.*
MC Set . . . . DTO 10060
Ditto / Sep '83 / Pickwick Records.

STARS OF THE GRAND OLE OPRY.
Tracks: Not Advised.
LP . . . . SPR 8561
MC . . . . SPC 8561
Spot / Mar '85.

STARS OF THE GRAND OLE OPRY.
Tracks: Railroadin' and gamblin' / San Antonio rose / Orange blossom special / Jealous hearted me / Anytime / Father's table grace / I'm my own grandpa / Yakety axe / I don't hurt anymore / I'm thinking tonight of my blue eyes / Down yonder / Satisfied / Ashes of love / Old blue / How far is heaven / Four walls / Carroll country accident, The / I can't stop loving you / Trouble in the Amen corner / End of the world / Early morning rain / Send me the pillow you dream on / Young love / Morning / Three bells, The / Country girl / Four strong winds / Ribbon of darkness / Mule skinner blues (Blue yodel No. 8) / Just a little after heartaches.
■ **LP Set** CPL2 0466
RCA / '79.

STARS OF THE GRAND OLE OPRY.
Tracks: I'm moving on: *Snow, Hank* / Here comes by baby: *West, Dottie* / Satisfied mind, A: *Wagoner, Porter* / I forgot more than you'll ever know: *Davis, Skeeter* / Cockfight, The: *Campbell, Archie & Lorene Mann* / I'll keep my skillet good and greasy: *Macon, Uncle Dave* / How far is heaven: *Wells, Kitty* / Abilene: *Hamilton, George IV* / How to catch a man: *Pearl, Minnie* / Please help me, I'm falling: *Locklin, Hank* / He'll have to go: *Reeves, Jim* / Once a day: *Smith, Connie* / Walk softly: *Wade, Ray* / Keep on the sunnyside: *Carter Family* / Young love: *James, Sonny* / Road hog: *Loudermilk, John D.* / Letter edged in black, The: *Kincaid, Bradley* / Chet Atkins, make me a star: *Bowman, Dan* / Old rattler: *Grandpa Jones* / Detroit city: *Bare, Bobby* / Oh lonesome me: *Gibson, Don* / Scarlet ribbons: *Browns* / Bown's ferry blues: *Delmore Brothers* / Battle of New Orleans, The: *Driftwood, Jimmie* / Poison love: *Johnnie & Jack* / Party's over, The: *Nelson, Willie* / Orange blossom special: *Monroe, Bill* / Ten thousand tomorrows: *Payne, Leon* / Birmingham jail: *Whitman, Slim* / Down yonder: *Wood, Del* / Country gentlemen: *Atkins, Chet* / Hey little star: *Miller, Roger* / Let's go all the way: *Jean, Norma* / I'm my own Grandpa: *Lonzo & Oscar* / Satisfied: *Carson, Martha* / Take a letter, Miss Gray: *Tubb, Justin* / Yakety sax: *Randolph, Boots* / Sourwood mountain: *Stoneman, Ernest V.* / Back up and push: *Willis Brothers* / Tennessee waltz: *King, Pee Wee.*
■ **LP Set** . . . . RD 7921-2
RCA / Dec '79 / BMG.

STOMPIN' AT THE HONKY TONK (Western swing in Houston 1936-1941).
Tracks: Not Advised.
LP . . . . STR 805
String / '81 / Projection / Roots Records / A.D.A Distribution / C.M. Distribution / Swift / Ross Records / Duncans.

SUN BOX, THE.
Tracks: Rocket 88 (with the Delta Cats): *Brenston, Jackie* / T-Model Boogie: *Gordon, Roscoe* / Howlin' for my baby: *Howlin' Wolf* / Mr. Highwayman: *Howlin' Wolf* / Treat me mean and evil: *Louis, Joe Hill* / Tiger man: *Louis, Joe Hill* / Prison bound blues: *Nix, Willie* / My baby left me: *Hill, Raymond* / Sweet home Chicago: *Williams, Albert* / Easy: *Jimmy & Walter* / Bear cat: *Thomas, Rufus* / Just walking in the rain: *Prisonaires* / Feeling good: *Parker, Junior & the Blue Flames* / Mystery train: *Little Junior's Blue Flames* / Cotton crop blues: *Cotton, James* / Boogie disease: *Dr. Isiah Ross* / When it rain it really pours: *Emerson, Billy 'The Kid'* / So long baby goodbye: *Lewis, Sammy & Willie Johnson* / Rockin' chair daddy: *Harmonica Frank* / My kind of carryin' on: *Poindexter, Doug & The Starlite Wranglers* / Cry cry cry: *Cash, Johnny* / Let the juke box keep on playing: *Perkins, Carl* / Defrost your heart: *Feathers, Charlie* / Rock 'n' roll Ruby: *Smith, Warren* / Slow down: *Earls, Jack & The Jimbos* / It's me baby: *Yelvington, Malcolm* / Feeling low: *Chaffin, Ernie* / Folsom prison blues: *Cash, Johnny & The Tennessee Two* / I walk the line: *Cash, Johnny & The Tennessee Two* / Home of the blues: *Cash, Johnny & The Tennessee Two* / Ballad of a teenage queen: *Cash, Johnny & The Tennessee Two* / Way of a woman in love, The: *Cash, Johnny & The Tennessee Two* / Boppin' the blues: *Perkins, Carl* / Dixie fried: *Perkins, Carl* / Breathless: *Lewis, Jerry Lee* / Come on little mama: *Harris, Ray* / Flyin' saucers rock 'n' roll: *Riley, Billy Lee & The Little Green Men* / Ain't got a thing: *Burgess, Sonny* / Put your cat clothes on: *Perkins, Carl* / Rock baby rock it: *Carroll, Johnny* / Love me baby: *Thompson, Hayden* / Milkshake mademoiselle: *Lewis, Jerry Lee* / Red cadillac and a black moustache: *Smith, Warren* / Blue suede shoes: *Perkins, Carl* / Ooby dooby: *Orbison, Roy & Teen Kings* / Whole lot of shakin' going on: *Lewis, Jerry Lee* / So long I'm gone: *Smith, Warren* / Raunchy: *Justis, Bill & His Orchestra* / Great balls of fire: *Lewis, Jerry Lee* / Guess things happen that way: *Cash, Johnny & The Tennessee Two* / Mona Lisa: *Mann, Carl* / Lonely weekends: *Rich, Charlie.*
LP Set . . . . SUN BOX 100
Sun / '82 / Charly / Swift.

SUN COUNTRY BOX (11 record set).
Tracks: Not Advised.
■ **LP Set** . . . . BFX 15211/11
Bear Family / Nov '86.

SUN INTO THE SIXTIES.
Tracks: Not Advised.
LP Set . . . . SUN BOX 109
Sun / Feb '89 / Charly / Swift.

SUN RECORDS - THE ROCKING YEARS.
Tracks: Not Advised.
LP Set . . . . SUN BOX 106
Sun / '87 / Charly / Swift.

SUN STORY VOLUME 1 ('Sunrise').
Tracks: Not Advised.
CD . . . . CDINS 5039
Instant (2) / Dec '90 / Charly.

SUN STORY VOLUME 2 (Rockabilly Rhythm).
Tracks: Not Advised.
CD . . . . CDINS 5040
Instant (2) / Dec '90 / Charly.

SUN'S GOLD HITS.
Tracks: Whole lotta shakin' goin' on: *Lewis, Jerry Lee* / You win again: *Lewis, Jerry Lee* / Breathless: *Lewis, Jerry Lee* / I walk the line: *Cash, Johnny* / Guess things happen that way: *Cash, Johnny* / Blue suede shoes: *Perkins, Carl* / Boppin' the blues: *Perkins, Carl* / Mona Lisa: *Mann, Carl* / I'm coming home: *Mann, Carl* / Lonely weekends: *Rich, Charlie* / Stay: *Rich, Charlie* / Raunchy: *Justis, Bill.*
LP . . . . CRM 2010
Sun / Feb '81 / Charly / Swift.

SUN'S GREATEST HITS.
Tracks: Not Advised.
LP . . . . RNDF 256
Rhino (USA) / Feb '85 / WEA.

SUNSET SPECIAL.
Tracks: Your honey love: *Penner, Dick* / Willing and ready: *Smith, Ray* / Judy: *Grayzell, Rudy* / Shake around: *Smith, Ray* / You made a hit: *Smith, Ray* / Behind you baby: *Smith, Ray* / Why why why: *Smith, Ray* / Show me: *Bond, Eddie* / Broke my guitar: *Bond, Eddie* / Break up: *Smith, Ray* / This old heart of mine: *Bond, Eddie* / Christine: *Hall, Roy* / Sweet love on my mind: *Hall, Roy* / I lost my baby: *Hall, Roy.*
LP . . . . SUN 1035
Sun / Jan '86 / Charly / Swift.

SUPER COUNTRY VOL.1.
Tracks: You're my best friend / Just out of reach / Picture of your mother / Coat of many colours / Waiting for a train / Don't let me cross over / Stand by me Jesus / Hello blues and down the road I go / Philadelphia lawyer / Hello darlin'.
MC . . . . CWIN 104
Homespun (Ireland) / Feb '83 / Homespun Records / Ross Records / Wellard Dist.

SUPER COUNTRY VOL.2.
Tracks: Hard to be humble / Harper Valley PTA / Four strong winds / Tennessee waltz / Help me make it through the night / Gypsy Joe and me / What things money can't buy / Church, a courtroom and then goodbye, A / Pinto the wonder horse is dead / Mama say a prayer.
MC . . . . CWIN 105
Homespun (Ireland) / Feb '83 / Homespun Records / Ross Records / Wellard Dist.

SWALLOW RECORDS LOUISIANA CAJUN SPECIAL VOL.1.
Tracks: Hee haw breakdown: *Cormier, Nolan & the LA Aces* / Saturday night special: *Cormier, Lesa & The Sundown Playboys* / Pine grove blues: *Abshire, Nathan* / Cajun ramblers special: *Derouen, Wallace & The Cajun Ramblers* / Oh Lucille: *Richard, Belton* / Cajun stripper: *Richard, Belton* / Opelousas two step: *Walker, Lawrence* / Back door: *Badeaux & The Louisiana Aces* / Louisiana Aces special: *Badeaux & The Louisiana Aces* / Eunice two step: *Barzas, Maurice & The Mamau Playboys* / Hippy ti yo: *Bonsall, Joe* / Triangle club special: *Prejean, Leeman* / I am so lonely: *Hebert, Adam* / Lacassine special: *Balfa Brothers* / Don't shake my tree: *Pitre, Austin.*
LP . . . . CH 141
Ace / Dec '88 / Pinnacle / Hot Shot / Jazz Music / Complete Record Co. Ltd.

SWALLOW RECORDS LOUISIANA CAJUN SPECIAL VOL.2.
Tracks: Choupique two step: *Abshire, Nathan* / Cypress inn special: *Cormier, Lionel* / Chinaball blues: *Pitre, Austin* / Cameron two step: *Barro* / Calcasieu rambler's special: *Broussard, August* / Waltz of regret: *Matte, Doris* / Little cajun boy: *Leger, Bobby* / Zydeco cha cha: *Mouzas & Lignos* / Mamou hot step: *Mamou Playboys* / Every night when it's dark: *Hebert, Adam* / La valse de grand bois: *Balfa Brothers* / Cankton two step: *Prejean, Leeman* / She didn't know I was married: *Menard, D.L* / Family waltz: *Menard, Phil & Don Guillory* / Two steps de vieux temps: *Rambling Aces* / One step de duson: *Cormier, Louis.*
LP . . . . CH 166
Ace / '86 / Pinnacle / Hot Shot / Jazz Music / Complete Record Co. Ltd.
CD . . . . CDCH 368
LP . . . . CH 368
Ace / Mar '92 / Pinnacle / Hot Shot / Jazz Music / Complete Record Co. Ltd.

SWEET DREAMS (20 country ballads).
Tracks: Cry myself to sleep: *Judds* / Thing called love, A: *Cash, Johnny* / Stand by your man: *Wynette, Tammy* / I won't forget you: *Reeves, Jim* / Lay lady lay: *Byrds* / Rose garden: *Anderson, Lynn* / It's four in the morning: *Young, Faron* / Kiss an angel good morning: *Pride, Charley* / End of the world: *Davis, Skeeter* / Always on my mind: *Nelson, Willie* / Help me make it through the night: *Kristofferson, Kris* / In dreams: *Orbison, Roy* / You and I: *Rabbitt, Eddie & Crystal Gayle* / Amanda: *Jennings, Waylon* / Delta dawn: *Tucker, Tanya* / Crystal chandeliers: *Hamilton, George IV* / I've been loving you: *Mandrell, Barbara* / Little green apples: *Miller, Roger* / Coat of many colours: *Parton, Dolly* / Lonesome number one: *Gibson, Don.*
CD . . . . STDCD 29
Solitaire / Mar '90 / BMG.
MC . . . . STDMC 29
Masterpiece / Mar '90 / BMG.

SWITCHED ON COUNTRY.
Tracks: Not Advised.
MC Set . . . . TTMC 086
Tring / Mar '93 / Prism Leisure PLC / Midland Records / Taylors.

SWITCHED ON COUNTRY: THE RANCH HANDS.
Tracks: Not Advised.
CD . . . . GRF 214
MC . . . . MCGRF 214
Tring / Mar '93 / Prism Leisure PLC / Midland Records / Taylors.

T

TANK TOWN BOOGIE.
Tracks: Tank town boogie (Take 1 & 3): *Harral, Hank* / She's gone: *Harral, Hank* / Dream band boogie: *Harral, Hank* / Oklahoma land: *Harral, Hank* / D.J. blues, The: *Harral, Hank* / Dilly dally doodle: *Harral, Hank* / Summit ridge drive: *Nix, Hoyle* / Without you: *Haggett, Jimmy* / That's the way it goes: *Daly, Durwood* / Little Rome: *Alexander, Max & Hank Harral* / Rock, rock everybody rock: *Alexander, Max & Hank Harral* / Casanova: *Tate, Jack* / Blue tomorrow: *New, Roy* / I've lost again: *Ball, Ace* / You can't stop me from dreaming: *Dolly, Andy* / Hey ba ba re bop: *Dolly, Andy* / Boogie walk: *Dolly, Andy* / Gotta have you: *Dolly, Andy* / Rollin' rhythm: *Dolly, Andy* / Oodabegga wow: *Dolly, Andy* / Stockade rock: *Dolly, Andy* / Honky tonk queen: *Hankins, Bobby* / Wild side of life: *Thurn, Ike & Andy Doll* / If I had me a woman: *Vale, Blacky* / Star of love: *Vale, Blacky* / Tattle tale: *Dane, Jimmy* / Please have mercy: *Dane, Jimmy* / Honky tonkin' baby: *Smith, Bob* / Meet me in the barnyard: *Cay, Phil* / Mutha: *Bing, Jim.*
LP . . . . **WLP 8831**
White Label (Germany) / Sep '87 / Pinnacle / Bear Family Records (Germany) / CSA Tell Tapes.

TENNESSEE ROCKIN'.
Tracks: Oh love: *Wade, Don* / Bust head gin: *Wade, Don* / Gone gone gone: *Wade, Don* / Forever yours: *Wade, Don* / Loving on my mind: *Barnes, David* / Corina Corina: *Lipford, Preston* / I'll sail my ship alone: *Lipford, Preston* / Midnight piano rock: *Lipford, Preston* / Flip flop and fly: *Lipford, Preston* / High school love: *Allen, Ronnie* / River of love: *Allen, Ronnie* / Juvenile delinquent: *Allen, Ronnie* / This love of yours: *Allen, Ronnie.*
LP . . . . **WLP 8820**
White Label (Germany) / '87 / Pinnacle / Bear Family Records (Germany) / CSA Tell Tapes.

TEX ARKANA LOUISIANA COUNTRY 1927-32.
Tracks: Not Advised.
LP . . . . **L 1004**
Yazoo (USA) / Dec '88 / Roots Records / Projection / Swift / C.M. Distribution / Duncans / Cadillac Music / A.D.A Distribution / Jazz Music.

TEXAS & LOUISIANNA COUNTRY.
Tracks: Not Advised.
LP . . . . **RL 335**
Roots (Germany) / Oct '88 / Swift / C.M. Distribution.

TEXAS COUNTRY BLUES 1948-52.
Tracks: Not Advised.
LP . . . . **KK 7434**
Krazy Kat / Dec '86 / Hot Shot / C.M. Distribution / Wellard Dist. / Roots Records / Projection / Charly / Jazz Music.

TEXAS COUNTRY MUSIC VOL.1.
Tracks: Not Advised.
LP . . . . **RL 312**
Roots (Germany) / Oct '88 / Swift / C.M. Distribution.

TEXAS COUNTRY MUSIC VOL.2.
Tracks: Not Advised.
LP . . . . **RL 315**
Roots (Germany) / Oct '88 / Swift / C.M. Distribution.

TEXAS COUNTRY MUSIC VOL.3.
Tracks: Not Advised.
LP . . . . **RL 327**
Roots (Germany) / Oct '88 / Swift / C.M. Distribution.

TEXAS COUNTRY ROAD SHOW.
Tracks: Not Advised.
■ **LP** . . . . **BFX 15035**
Bear Family / '85.

TEXAS HILLBILLY BOOGIE.
Tracks: Not Advised.
LP . . . . **RR 2018**
Esoldun / Sep '87 / New Note.

TEXAS ROCKABILLY.
Tracks: Love come back to me: *Patton, Jimmy* / Let me slide: *Patton, Jimmy* / I'm not skukin: *Patton, Jimmy* / Oakies in the pokie: *Patton, Jimmy* / High class feelin: *Finn, Lee* / Pour me a glass of wine: *Finn, Lee* / Sleep rock'n'roll baby: *Wayne, Alvis* / Swing bop boogie: *Wayne, Alvis* / I gottum: *Wayne, Alvis* / Lay your head on my shoulder: *Wayne, Alvis* / Don't mean maybe, baby: *Wayne, Alvis* / Oklahoma blues: *Chapman, Gene* / Don't come cryin': *Chapman, Gene.*
LP . . . . **RR 2001**
Esoldun / Dec '87 / New Note.

TEXAS ROCKABILLY VOL. 2.
Tracks: Not Advised.
LP . . . . **RR 2012**
Esoldun / Oct '87 / New Note.

THAT'LL FLAT GIT IT VOL. 1 (RCA Rockabillies).
Tracks: Sixteen chicks: *Clay, Joe* / Born to love one woman: *Cartey, Ric* / Sugar sweet: *Houston, David* / New shoes: *Denson, Lee* / Little boy blue: *Johnson, Hoyt* / Drugstore rock 'n' roll: *Martin, Janis* / Rosie let's get cozy: *Rich, Dave* / Catty town: *Glasser, Dick* / Star light, star bright: *Castle, Nan* / TV hop: *Morgan Twins* / Honky tonk mind: *Blake, Tommy* / Teen billy baby: *Sprouts* / Don't bug me baby: *Allen, Milt* / Now stop: *Carson, Martha* / Milkcow blues: *Rodgers, Jimmie (1)* / Duck tail: *Clay, Joe* / Heart throb: *Cartey, Ric* / One and only: *Houston, David* / I've got a dollar: *Dell, Jimmy* / Lovin' honey (2): *Morris, Gene* / Barefoot baby: *Martin, Janis* / Rock-a-bye-baby: *Bonn, Skeeter* / That ain't nothing but right: *Castle, Joey* / Mary Nell: *Inman, Autrey* / Hey jibbo: *Wood, Art* / All night long: *Blake, Tommy* / Full grown cat: *McCoys* / Just thought I'd set you straight: *Harris, Ted* / Oooh-wee: *Cartey, Ric* / Dee, Frankie: *Dee, Frankie* / Lovin' honey (1): *Morris, Gene.*
CD Set . . . . **BCD 15622**
Bear Family / May '93 / Rollercoaster Records / Swift / Direct Distribution.

THAT'LL FLAT GIT IT VOL. 2 (Decca Rockabillies).
Tracks: Hot rock wild: *Carroll, Johnny* / Wild women - crazy: *Carroll, Johnny* / Crazy lovin': *Carroll, Johnny* / Tryin' to get you: *Carroll, Johnny* / Corrine, Corrina: *Carroll, Johnny* / Rock 'n' Roll Ruby: *Carroll, Johnny* / Flip, flop and fry: *Carroll, Johnny* / Baby don't leave me: *Five Chavis Brothers* / Way out there: *Chuck & Bill* / Ruby Pearl: *Cochran, Jackie Lee* / Mamy don't you think I know: *Cochran, Jackie Lee* / Lorraine: *Covelle, Buddy* / Cool it baby: *Fontaine, Eddie* / Whole lotta shakin' goin' on: *Hall, Roy* / Off beat boogie: *Hall, Roy* / See you later alligator: *Hall, Roy* / Three alley cats: *Hall, Roy* / Diggin' the boogie: *Hall, Roy* / I wanna bop: *Harlan, Billy* / I would be a doggone lie: *Harlan, Billy* / Be bop baby: *Harlan, Billy* / Sweet love on my mind: *Jimmy & Johnny* / Teenage love is misery: *Kennedy, Jerry* / Crazy baby: *Maltais, Gene* / Ten little women: *Noland, Terry* / Teenage boogie: *Pierce, Webb* / Cast iron arms: *Wilson, Peanuts* / You're barking up the wrong tree: *Woody, Don* / Make like a rock and roll: *Woody, Don.*
CD . . . . **BCD 15623**
Bear Family / Jun '92 / Rollercoaster Records / Swift / Direct Distribution.

THAT'LL FLAT GIT IT VOL. 3 (Capitol Rockabillies).
Tracks: You oughta see Grandma rock: *McDonald, Skeets* / Heart breakin' Mama: *McDonald, Skeets* / My little baby: *Maddox, Rose* / Sebbin' come elebbin: *Heap, Jimmy* / Go ahead on: *Heap, Jimmy* / Try me: *Luman, Bob* / Cash on the barrelhead: *Louvin Brothers* / Red hen hop: *Louvin Brothers* / Worryin' kind, The: *Sands, Tommy* / Playin' the field: *Sands, Tommy* / My gal Gertie: *Dickerson, Dub* / When I found you: *Reed, Jerry* / I've had enough: *Reed, Jerry* / Mr. Big feet: *Charlie Bop Trio* / Cool down Mame: *Farmer Boys* / My baby done left me: *Farmer Boys* / Party kiss: *Fallin, Johnny* / Party line: *Fallin, Johnny* / There's gonna be a ball: *Grayzell, Rudy* / Bop cat bop: *Crum, Simon* / Jeopardy: *Shepard, Jean* / He's my baby: *Shepard, Jean* / Alone with you: *Young, Faron* / I can't dance: *Young, Faron* / Black cat: *Collins, Tommy* / I chickened out: *Loran, Kenny* / Slow down brother: *Huskey, Ferlin* / I went rockin': *Norris, Bobby* / You mostest girl: *Trammell, Bobby Lee.*
MC . . . . **BCD 15624**
Bear Family / Jun '92 / Rollercoaster Records / Swift / Direct Distribution.

THAT'S SAWDUST COUNTRY VOLUME 1.
Tracks: Not Advised.
CD . . . . **SDCD 9.00711**
Sawdust / '90.

THEY ARE ALL ROCKIN' KATS.
Tracks: Not Advised.
LP . . . . **WLP 8934**
White Label (Germany) / Nov '88 / Pinnacle / Bear Family Records (Germany) / CSA Tell Tapes.

THIRTY YEARS OF BLUEGRASS.
Tracks: Not Advised.
Double LP . . . . **GTV 101**
Gusto (USA) / Mar '88.

THIS IS COUNTRY MUSIC.
Tracks: End of the world: *Davis, Skeeter* / Fantasy: *Alabama* / Abilene: *Hamilton, George IV* / Too many rivers: *Colter, Jessi* / 500 miles away from home: *Bare, Bobby* / Dukes of Hazzard: *Jennings, Waylon* / She called me baby: *Rich, Charlie* / Nobody's child: *Snow, Hank* / Sea of heartbreak: *Gibson, Don* / (I'd be a) legend in my own time: *Milsap, Ronnie* / Guitar man: *Reed, Jerry* / Once a day: *Smith, Connie* / He'll have to go: *Reeves, Jim* / Send me the pillow that you dream on: *Locklin, Hank* / Here you come again: *Parton, Dolly* / Kiss an angel good morning: *Pride, Charley.*
■ **LP** . . . . **MFP 5786**
MFP / Apr '87.
■ **MC** . . . . **TCMFP 5786**
MFP / Apr '87.

THIS IS COUNTRY MUSIC (2).
Tracks: Eyes big as Dallas: *Stewart, Wynn* / Down on the farm: *Stewart, Wynn* / Could I talk you into lovin' me again / Wild one: *Reno, Jack* / Blue roses: *Reno, Jack* / Divorce suit: *Phillips, Bill* / Goldie is an oldie: *Carlisle, Bill* / Too old to cut the mustard: *Carlisle, Bill* / Country music lovin' cowboy: *Pillow, Ray* / Justin Tubb: *Pillow, Ray* / Red necks, white socks and blue ribbon beer: *Pillow, Ray* / Warm, warm love: *Louvin, Charlie* / Store up love: *Louvin, Charlie* / Pull the covers over me: *Collins, Tommy* / Hello hag: *Collins, Tommy* / Hogtown: *Curless, Dick* / Iceman, The: *Curless, Dick.*
■ **LP** . . . . **BFX 15020**
Bear Family / Oct '80.

THOUGHTS OF COUNTRY.
Tracks: Stand beside me: *O'Donnell, Daniel* / Almost persuaded: *Kirwan, Dominic* / Jennifer Johnson and me: *Flavin, Mick* / Dear God: *Duff, Mary* / Four in the morning: *Pride, Charley* / Way old friends do, The: *Begley, Philomena* / Back in love by Monday: *Lynam, Ray* / Still got a crush on you: *Hogan, John* / Daisy chain: *Begley, Philomena & Mick Flavin* / Apologising roses: *Spears, Billie Jo* / Queen of the Silver Dollar: *Begley, Philomena* / Travellin' light: *Flavin, Mick* / Amy's eyes: *Pride, Charley* / Forever and ever Amen: *Duff, Mary* / Just between you and me: *Begley, Philomena & Mick Flavin* / I'm no stranger to the rain: *Curtis, Sonny* / Take good care of her: *O'Donnell, Daniel* / Don't fight the feeling: *Hogan, John* / Sweethearts in heaven: *Margo* / Sea of heartbreak: *Kirwan, Dominic.*
CD . . . . **RITZRCD 518**
MC . . . . **RITZRC 518**
Ritz / May '92 / Pinnacle / Midland Records.

THOUGHTS OF IRELAND.
Tracks: Summertime in Ireland: *O'Donnell, Daniel* / Isle of Innisfree: *Foster & Allen* / Beautiful meath: *Duff, Mary* / Golden dreams: *Kirwan, Dominic* / Shanagolden: *Margo* / Home to Donegal: *Flavin, Mick* / Red is the rose: *Begley, Philomena* / Spancil Hill: *Duff, Mary* / If we only had old Ireland over here: *McCaffrey, Frank* / Carrickfergus: *Quinn, Brendan* / Girl from Wexford town, The: *Flavin, Mick* / Bunch of thyme: *Foster & Allen* / Galway Bay: *Begley, Philomena* / Give an Irish girl to me: *Nerney, Declan* / Noreen Bawn: *Kirwan, Dominic* / Moonlight in Mayo: *McCaffrey, Frank* / Lady from Glenfarne: *Quinn, Brendan* / Rose of Allendale: *Morrissey, Louise* / Forty miles to Donegal: *Margo* / Sing an old Irish song: *O'Donnell, Daniel.*
CD . . . . **RITZRCD 519**
MC . . . . **RITZRC 519**
Ritz / May '92 / Pinnacle / Midland Records.

THOUGHTS OF YESTERDAY.
Tracks: I need you: *O'Donnell, Daniel* / Do what you do do well: *Pride, Charley* / Crazy: *Duff, Mary* / More than I can say: *Curtis, Sonny* / Maggie: *Foster & Allen* / Before the next teardrop falls: *Kirwan, Dominic* / Pal of my cradle days: *Gloria* / Seven lonely days: *Spears, Billie Jo* / Sentimental old you: *Begley, Philomena* / More than yesterday: *McCaffrey, Frank* / Roses are red: *O'Donnell, Daniel* / China doll: *Hogan, John* / Say you'll stay until tomorrow: *Kirwan, Dominic* / After all these years: *Foster & Allen* / Ramblin' rose: *Pride, Charley* / Little things mean a lot: *Dana* / It's our anniversary: *McCaffrey, Frank* / Yellow roses: *Duff, Mary* / He stopped loving her today: *Lynam, Ray* / Old flames: *Begley, Philomena.*
CD . . . . **RITZRCD 520**
MC . . . . **RITZRC 520**
Ritz / Apr '92 / Pinnacle / Midland Records.

THREE COUNTRY GENTLEMEN.
Tracks: Ivory tower: *Locklin, Hank* / Followed closely by my teardrops: *Locklin, Hank* / Sweet temptation: *Locklin, Hank* / It keeps right on a-hurtin': *Locklin, Hank* / Laredo: *Snow, Hank* / Call of the wild: *Snow, Hank* / Black diamond: *Snow, Hank* / I went to your wedding: *Snow, Hank* / False true lover: *Wagoner, Porter* / They listened while you said goodbye: *Wagoner, Porter* / Keeper of the key: *Wagoner, Porter* / Eat, drink and be merry: *Wagoner, Porter.*
LP . . . . **SF 7590**
RCA / Dec '69 / BMG.

THREE TIMES A LADY - LADIES OF COUNTRY.
Tracks: Not Advised.
CD . . . . **KNCD 15016**
Knight / Sep '91 / Castle Communications / BMG.
■ **MC** . . . . **KNMC 15016**
Knight / Sep '91.

TODAY'S COUNTRY CLASSICS.
Tracks: Cowboy rides away, The: *Strait, George* / How blue: *McEntire, Reba* / Make my life with you: *Oak Ridge Boys* / Knock on wood: *Baily, Razzy* / Mississippi squirrel revival: *Stevens, Ray* / Country girls: *Schneider, John* / Sweet country music: *Atlanta* / What I didn't do: *Wariner, Steve* / Happy birthday dear heartache: *Mandrell, Barbara* / God bless the U.S.A: *Greenwood, Lee.*
LP . . . . **IMCA 390 29**
MCA (Import) / Mar '86 / Pinnacle / Silver Sounds (CD).

TOGETHER AGAIN (14 country duets).
Tracks: Something to brag about: *Louvin, Charlie & Melba Montgomery* / Together again: *Rogers, Kenny & Dottie West* / What's in your heart: *Jones, George & Melba Montgomery* / Heart to heart talk: *Campbell, Glen & Bobbie Gentry* / Let your love flow: *Reeves, Del & Billie Jo Spears* / Something 'bout you baby I like: *Campbell, Glen & Rita Coolidge* / We've got tonight:

■ DELETED

Rogers, Kenny & Sheena Easton / Love story (you and me): *Campbell, Glen & Anne Murray* / Don't fall in love with a dreamer: *Rogers, Kenny & Kim Carnes* / Willingly: *Nelson, Willie & Shirley Collie* / Forgive me John: *Shepard, Jean & Ferlin Husky* / Why don't we just sleep on it tonight: *Campbell, Glen & Tanya Tucker* / Vaya con dios: *Paul, Les & Mary Ford* / I'll take the dog: *Shepard, Jean & Ray Pillow*.
MC . . . . **TCMFP 5771**
MFP / Apr '87 / EMI.
■ LP . . . . **MFP 5771**
MFP / Apr '87.

TOMBSTONE AFTER DARK.
Tracks: Honky tonk masquerade (£): *Shepard, Jean & Ray Pillow* / Gypsy rider: *Clark, Gene & Carla Olsen* / Hey good lookin': *Sledge, Percy* / Shady was a lady from Louisville: *Alexander, Larry 'Jinx'* / Fools fall in love: *Hancock, Butch* / Further: *Halley, David* / My baby don't dance to nothing but Ernest Tubb: *Brown, Junior* / Where I grew up: *Durham, Bobby* / West Texas waltz: *Hancock, Butch* / Dallas (£): *Hancock, Butch* / Me and Billy the Kid: *Fly, Joe* / Border radio: *Alvin, Dave* / Big beaver: *Asleep At The Wheel*.
CD . . . . **FIENDCD 713**
Demon / Apr '92 / Pinnacle.

TOP COUNTRY HITS.
Tracks: Not Advised.
MC . . . . **AM 36**
VFM Cassettes / VFM Children's Entertainment Ltd. / Midland Records / Morley Audio Services.

TOP COUNTRY SOUND IN CONCERT.
Tracks: Rollin' in my sweet baby's arms / Crystal chandeliers / If I said you had a beautiful body / From here to there to you / Blue eyed girl of Berlin / American trilogy / Scarlet ribbons / Fishing for fish / This song is just for you / Do what you do do well / Folsom Prison blues / Ghost riders in the sky.
LP . . . . **FHR 115**
Folk Heritage / Jul '82 / Terry Blood Dist.

TOP COUNTRY STARS.
Tracks: Not Advised.
CD **15 214**
MC **79 088**
Laserlight / Aug '91 / TBD / Taylors.

TOUCH MORE CLASS, A.
Tracks: All that love went to waste: *Bennett, Tony* / End of a love affair: *Bennett, Tony* / Sing: *Doonican, Val* / Tie a yellow ribbon round the old oak tree: *Doonican, Val* / For all we know: *Gillies, Stuart* / There goes my heart: *Gillies, Stuart* / Little boat: *Laine, Cleo* / American patrol: *Lawrence, Syd Orchestra* / Nearness of you, The: *Lawrence, Syd Orchestra* / Minuet: *Loussuer, Jacques Trio* / Someone to watch over me: *Maughan, Susan* / If you go away: *Mouskouri, Nana* / Mayday: *Mouskouri, Nana* / Closer: *Peters & Lee* / Send in the clowns: *Peters & Lee* / My only fascination: *Roussos, Demis* / My reason: *Roussos, Demis* / New love: *Solomon, Diane* / Look of love, The: *Springfield, Dusty* / Yesterday when I was young: *Springfield, Dusty* / Ghost of a chance: *Torme, Mel* / Embraceable you: *Vaughan, Sarah* / Me I never knew, The: *Walker, Scott* / Will you still be mine: *Walker, Scott* / They didn't believe me: *Washington, Dinah* / Hey love: *Williams, Danny* / Moon river: *Williams, Danny*.
LP Set **6612 056**
Philips / Jul '78 / PolyGram.

TRADITIONAL COUNTRY FAVOURITES.
Tracks: Not Advised.
MC . . . . **AM 114**
VFM Cassettes / VFM Children's Entertainment Ltd. / Midland Records / Morley Audio Services.

TRAILBLAZERS.
Tracks: We're gonna go fishin' / Ride me down easy / I walk the line / Help me make it through the night / Pool shark / Cry cry darlin' / Blue moon of Kentucky / New Jole Blon / Sittin' and thinkin' / Swinging doors / Hey good lookin' / If the whole world stopped loving / My shoes keep walking back to you / Send me the pillow that you dream on.
LP . . . . **SPR 8525**
MC . . . . **SPC 8525**
Spot / Feb '83.

TRIBUTE TO ELVIS.
Tracks: Not Advised.
MC . . . . **AIM 45**
AIM (2) / Feb '83 / Topic Records / Direct Distribution.

TRIBUTE TO HANK WILLIAMS.
Tracks: Honky tonkin': *Nitty Gritty Dirt Band* / Half as much: *Campbell, Glen* / Hey good looking: *Young, Faron* / I don't like this kind of living: *Jones, George* / Your cheatin' heart: *Miller, Jody* / Mansion on the hill, A: *Whitman, Slim* / I can't help it (If I'm still in love with you): *Watson, Gene* / Jambalaya (On the Bayou): *Jackson, Wanda* / There'll be no teardrops tonight: *Nelson, Willie* / Lovesick blues: *James, Sonny* / House of gold: *Jones, George & Melba Montgomery* / May you never be alone: *Ford, Tennessee Ernie* / Nobody's lonesome for me: *Hawkins, Ronnie* / Move it on over: *Maddock, Rose* / I could never be ashamed of you: *Jones, George* / I saw the light: *Nitty Gritty Dirt Band & Roy Acuff* / I'm so lonesome I could cry: *Campbell, Glen* / Kaw-liga: *Ifield, Frank* / You win again: *Jackson, Wanda* / There's a tear in my beer: *Lister, Big Bill* / Why should we try anymore: *Huskey, Ferlin* / I'll never get out of this world alive: *Asleep At The Wheel*.
CD . . . . **CDEMS 1473**
EMI / Feb '93 / EMI.
MC . . . . **TCEMS 1473**
Capitol / Mar '93 / EMI.

TRIBUTE TO HANK WILLIAMS, A.
Tracks: Lonesome whistle: *Snow, Hank* / Hey, good lookin': *Brown, Jim Ed* / Lovesick blues: *Milsap, Ronnie* / Wedding bells: *Oxford, Vernon* / Take these chains from my heart: *West, Dottie* / Why don't you love me: *Davis, Danny* / May you never be alone: *Locklin, Hank* / Jambalaya: *Family Brown* / House of gold: *Wagoner, Porter* / Alone and forsaken: *Atkins, Chet* / Half as much: *Arnold, Eddy* / Pan American: *Rivers, Hank* / Mansion on the hill: *Browns* / I'm so lonesome I could cry: *Lee, Dickey* / Kaw-liga: *Living Strings* / Your cheatin' heart: *Davis, Skeeter* / There'll be no teardrops tonight: *Locklin, Hank* / I'm gonna sing: *Monroe, Charlie* / I can't help it (if I'm still in love with you: *Pridesmen* / Tramp on the street, The: *Jean, Norma* / I saw the light: *Buck, Gary* / They'll never take her love from me: *Gibson, Don* / I've been down that road before: *Wagoner, Porter* / Honky tonkin': *Brown, Jim Ed* / Picture from life's other side: *Wagoner, Porter* / Cold, cold heart: *Nashville string band* / Settin' the woods on fire: *Gibson, Don* / You win again: *Cramer, Floyd* / Crazy heart: *Sons Of The Pioneers* / Hank Williams will live forever: *Johnnie & Jack*.
■ Double LP . . . . **PL 42281**
RCA / '79.

TRIBUTE TO KENNY ROGERS.
Tracks: Not Advised.
MC . . . . **AIM 42**
AIM (2) / Feb '83 / Topic Records / Direct Distribution.

TRUCK DRIVER SONGS.
Tracks: Not Advised.
LP . . . . **KLP 866**
MC . . . . **GT 5866**
King (USA) / Apr '87 / Charly.

TRUCKER SONGS 2.
Tracks: Not Advised.
CD **100 025**
Bridge (MCS Bridge) / '86 / Pinnacle.

TRUCKIN' ON.
Tracks: Not Advised.
LP . . . . **GT 0054**
Gusto (USA) / Mar '88.

TRUCKING U.S.A.
Tracks: Not Advised.
MC . . . . **AIM 61**
AIM (2) / Feb '83 / Topic Records / Direct Distribution.

TRUCKING U.S.A. VOL.2.
Tracks: Not Advised.
MC . . . . **AM 65**
VFM Cassettes / VFM Children's Entertainment Ltd. / Midland Records / Morley Audio Services.

TRUCKING VOL. 2.
Tracks: Not Advised.
MC . . . . **AM 111**
VFM Cassettes / VFM Children's Entertainment Ltd. / Midland Records / Morley Audio Services.

TRUCKS TRAINS & AIRPLANES.
Tracks: Not Advised.
LP . . . . **GT 0081**
Gusto (USA) / Mar '88.

TWENTY COUNTRY GREATS.
Tracks: Not Advised.
CD . . . . **U 4032**
Spectrum (1) / Jun '88 / PolyGram.

TWENTY ORIGINAL COUNTRY GREATS.
Tracks: Southern nights: *Campbell, Glen* / Wichita lineman: *Campbell, Glen* / Don't it make my brown eyes blue?: *Gayle, Crystal* / Talking in your sleep: *Gayle, Crystal* / When you're in love with a beautiful woman: *Dr. Hook* / Sexy eyes: *Dr. Hook* / Ode to Billy Joe: *Gentry, Bobbie* / I'll never fall in love again: *Gentry, Bobbie* / Blanket on the ground: *Spears, Billie Jo* / Sing me an old fashioned song: *Spears, Billie Jo* / Lucille: *Rogers, Kenny* / Coward of the county: *Rogers, Kenny* / Snowbird: *Murray, Anne* / You needed me: *Murray, Anne* / I fall to pieces: *Ronstadt, Linda* / Hello walls / There'll be no teardrops tonight / It keeps right on a-hurtin': *Shepard, Jean* / Angel of the morning: *Newton, Juice* / July, you're a woman: *Stewart, John*.
■ CD . . . . **CDMFP 6008**
MFP / Oct '87.

TWENTY TRACKS OF COUNTRY HITS VOL 4.
Tracks: 1460 Elder Street: *Grant, Manson* / Rose garden: *Karen* / Walk tall: *Rhodes, Roy* / Green rolling hills: *Rendall, Ruby* / Some broken hearts never mend: *Wilson, Tug* / Teddy Bear's last ride: *Wells, Tracy* / I wish I was 18 again: *Cannon, Noel* / Rocky top: *Devine, Mike* / Sweet little miss blue eyes: *Mackie* / Don't let me cross over: *Grant, Manson* / Always on my mind: *Rendall, Ruby* / Fiddler Joe: *Mackie* / Snowbird: *Karen* / Banks of the Ohio: *Rhodes, Roy* / Ashes of love: *Mackie* / Part of me, A: *Devine, Mike* / Never look back: *Rendall, Ruby* / Acadian rose: *Mackie* / Keeping up appearances: *Karen* / Never ending song of love: *Rhodes, Roy*.
MC . . . . **CWGR 125**
Ross (1) / Jul '89 / Ross Records / Duncans / Entertainment UK.

TWENTY TRACKS OF COUNTRY HITS VOL 5.
Tracks: Ruby red wine: *Rendall, Ruby* / Waltz across Texas: *Grant, Manson* / Blanket on the ground: *Karen* / Little ole wine drinker me: *Rhodes, Roy* / He stopped loving her today: *Mackie* / Down River Road: *Wilson, Tug* / Fool number one: *Wells, Tracy* / Colorado cool aid: *Cannon, Noel* / In the middle of nowhere: *Devine, Mike* / Blue blue day: *Rhodes, Roy* / Silver threads and golden needles: *Rendall, Ruby* / Union mare and confederate grey: *Grant, Manson & James Smith* / Apartment No.9: *Karen* / Wedding bells: *Rhodes, Roy* / Ruby don't take your love to town: *Mackie* / Me and Bobby McGee: *Wilson, Tug* / Bright city lights: *Rendall, Ruby* / Arizona whiz, The: *Cannon, Noel* / Pick me up (on your way down): *Grant, Manson* / Good hearted woman: *Karen*.
MC . . . . **CWGR 126**
Ross (1) / Jul '89 / Ross Records / Duncans / Entertainment UK.

TWENTY TRACKS OF COUNTRY HITS VOL 6.
Tracks: Bring back the waltzes: *Grant, Manson* / Bright lights and country music: *Karen* / Try a little kindness: *Rhodes, Roy* / Honey: *Mackie* / Time goes by: *Rendall, Ruby* / Wedding bells: *Devine, Mike* / From here to there to you: *Rhodes, Roy* / Slow healing heart: *Mackie* / Heartaches by the number: *Karen* / Phantom 309: *Cannon, Noel* / Mansion on the hill: *Grant, Manson* / Ring around the rosie: *Karen* / I'm gonna be a country boy again: *Rhodes, Roy* / Amanda: *Mackie* / Let me be there: *Rendall, Ruby* / Tonight the bottle let me down: *Wilson, Tug* / Never been this far before: *Wells, Tracy* / Born for loving you: *Devine, Mike* / Stone cold heart: *Mackie* / Home town gossip: *Rendall, Ruby*.
MC . . . . **CWGR 127**
Ross (1) / Jul '89 / Ross Records / Duncans / Entertainment UK.

U

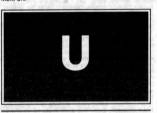

UK NEW COUNTRY VOL.1.
Tracks: Not Advised.
LP . . . . **BGE LP 1002**
MC . . . . **BGE C 1002**
Barge / Sep '86 / Jay-Cee Music.

ULTIMATE CAJUN COLLECTION.
Tracks: J'aime grand gueydan: *Allan, Johnnie* / Colinda: *Raven, Eddy* / Jole Blon: *Thibodeaux, Rufus* / Grand Texas: *Roger, Aldus* / Gabriel: *Broussard, Alex* / Cajun two step: *Forester, Blackie* / Le sud de la Louisianne: *Bruce, Vin* / Allons a lafayette: *Thibodeaux, Rufus* / Pine grove blues: *Abshire, Nathan* / Creole stomp: *Roger, Aldus* / Tout son amour: *Foret, L.J.* / Pauvre hobo: *Thibodeaux, Rufus* / Married life: *Cormier, Louis* / La Lou special: *Broussard, Pee-Wee* / Tous les deux pour la meme: *Forester, Blackie* / Crawfish festival time: *Raven, Eddy* / Mon tit baille: *Newman, Jimmy C.* / Chere Alice: *Richard, Zachary* / One scotch, one bourbon, one beer: *Roger, Aldus* / Tee Maurice: *Guidry, Doc* / Mamou two-step: *Walker, Lawrence* / la valse de amite: *Thibodeaux, Rufus* / Comment ca se fait: *Newman, Jimmy C.* / I'm Cajan cool: *Storm, Warren* / Evangeline: *Dusenberry Family* / La maison a deux portes: *Storm, Warren* / La valse de KLFY: *Doucet, Michael* / Fais do do: *Thibodeaux, Rufus* / La valse d'anniversaire: *Forester, Blackie* / Le two-step de l'acadien: *Abshire, Nathan* / Grand mamou: *Thibodeaux, Rufus* / Chemin des coeurs casser: *Foret, L.J.* / Le nouveau two-step: *Richard, Zachary* / One more chance: *Roger, Aldus* / Dans la Louisianne: *Bruce, Vin* / Alligator Bayou: *Raven, Eddy* / Lake Arthur stomp: *Thibodeaux, Rufus* / Ma belle Evangeline: *Allan, Johnnie* / Le two-step de choupique: *Abshire, Nathan* / Bayou Sam: *Forester, Blackie* / Elle n'est pas la plus belle: *Foret, L.J.* / Tu es la mienne pour toujours: *West, Clint* / La valse de Quebec: *Thibodeaux, Rufus* / Lafayette two-step: *Roger, Aldus* / Le blues Francais: *Abshire, Nathan* / Cotton fields: *Forester, Blackie*.
CD . . . . **DCD 5254**
Disky Communications Ltd / Aug '92 / Swift / Terry Blood Dist.

ULTIMATE COUNTRY COLLECTION.
Tracks: Most beautiful girl in the world, The: *Rich, Charlie* / I recall a gypsy woman: *Williams, Don* / I fall to pieces: *Cline, Patsy* / Crystal chandeliers: *Pride, Charley* / Stand by your man: *Wynette, Tammy* / Walk on by: *Van Dyke, Leroy* / Before the next teardrop falls: *Fender, Freddy* / Poor boy blues: *Atkins, Chet & Mark Knopfler* / Blanket on the ground: *Spears, Billie Jo* / Make the world go away: *Arnold, Eddy* / He'll have to go: *Reeves, Jim* / He stopped loving her today: *Jones, George* / Ring of fire: *Cash, Johnny* / Rose garden: *Anderson, Lynn* / I couldn't leave you if I tried: *Crowell, Rodney* / Lucille: *Rogers, Kenny* / (I'd be) A legend in

my time: *Milsap, Ronnie* / Rhinestone cowboy: *Campbell, Glen* / I'm movin' on: *Snow, Hank* / Feel so right: *Alabama* / Always on my mind: *Nelson, Willie* / Please help me, I'm falling: *Locklin, Hank* / For the good times: *Price, Ray* / Coal miner's daughter: *Lynn, Loretta* / Oh lonesome me: *Gibson, Don* / Hillbilly girl with the blues: *Dalton, Lacy J* / Abilene: *Hamilton, George IV* / It's four in the morning: *Young, Faron* / Loving her was easier (than anything I'll ever do again): *Kristofferson, Kris* / Baby don't get hooked on me: *Davis, Mac* / Lone star state of mind: *Griffith, Nanci* / If I said you had a beautiful body: *Bellamy Brothers* / Here you come again: *Parton, Dolly* / Theme from The Dukes of Hazzard (Good ol' boys): *Jennings, Waylon* / Down at the twist and shout: *Carpenter, Mary-Chapin* / El Paso: *Robbins, Marty* / Don't close your eyes: *Whitley, Keith* / Wind beneath my wings, The: *Greenwood, Lee* / Talking in your sleep: *Gayle, Crystal* / Don't rock the jukebox: *Jackson, Alan*.
CD . . . . **MOODCD 26**
Double LP . . . . **MOOD 26**
MC Set . . . . **MOODC 26**
Columbia / Oct '92 / Sony.

ULTIMATE SUN COUNTRY COLLECTION (56 legendary original sun recordings).
Tracks: Hey porter: *Cash, Johnny* / Cold cold heart: *Lewis, Jerry Lee* / (Tell me) who: *Smith, Warren* / Turn around: *Perkins, Carl* / Uncertain love: *Rhodes, Slim* / Daisy bread boogie: *Steele, Gene* / Feelin' low: *Chaffin, Ernie* / Chains of love: *Miller Sisters* / My kind of carryin' on: *Poindexter, Doug* / Show me: *Bond, Eddie* / Blues in the bottom of my shoes (way down blues): *Yelvington, Malcolm* / When you stop loving me: *King, Cast* / Easy to love: *Self, Mack* / Home of the blues: *Cash, Johnny* / Let the jukebox keep on playing: *Perkins, Carl* / Tonight will be the last night: *Smith, Warren* / Will the circle be unbroken: *Lewis, Jerry Lee* / Standing in your window: *Bond, Eddie* / Down on the border: *Simmons, Gene* / How long: *Wimberly, Maggie Sue* / Heartbreakin' love: *Wages, Jimmy* / I'm bluer than anyone can be: *Mann, Carl* / Muddy ole river: *Stinit, Dane* / Tragedy: *Wayne, Thomas* / You're the nearest thing to heaven: *Cash, Johnny* / This old heart of mine: *Bond, Eddie* / That black haired man: *Clement, Jack* / Who will the next fool be: *Rich, Charlie* / Wayward wind, The: *Mann, Carl* / Bummin' around: *Feathers, Charlie* / In the dark: *Peterson, Earl* / Just rolling along: *Yelvington, Malcolm* / Fool for loving you, A: *Earls, Jack* / Jump right out of the jukebox: *Wheeler, Onie* / I'd rather be safe than sorry: *Smith, Warren* / Someday you will pay: *Miller Sisters* / That's what I tell my heart: *McDaniel, Luke* / Country boy: *Cash, Johnny* / Sure to fall: *Perkins, Carl* / Jumbalaya: *Lewis, Jerry Lee* / Take & give: *Rhodes, Slim* / We're getting closer to being apart: *Feathers, Charlie* / Tell 'em off: *Wheeler, Onie* / Everyday: *Self, Mack* / I'm lonesome: *Chaffin, Ernie* / When I dream: *Earls, Jack* / Nothing to lose but my heart: *Peterson, Earl* / I've been deceived: *Feathers, Charlie* / Day I found you, The: *Bond, Eddie* / 10 years: *Clement, Jack* / Sittin' & thinkin': *Rich, Charlie* / Goodbye Mr.Love: *Smith, Warren* / If I could change you: *Mann, Carl* / Who's gonna shoe your pretty little feet: *Anthony, Rayburn* / I know what it means: *Lewis, Jerry Lee* / Tennessee: *Perkins, Carl*.
CD . . . . **DCD 5201**
Disky Communications Ltd / Aug '91 / Swift / Terry Blood Dist.

UP COUNTRY.
Tracks: Not Advised.
MC . . . . **DY 05**
Dynamic (Cassettes) / Sep '81.

UP COUNTRY.
Tracks: Not Advised.
CD . . . . **SOV 014CD**
MC . . . . **SOV 014TC**
Sovereign Music / Jan '93 / Terry Blood Dist. / ACD Trading Ltd. / Taylors.

US COUNTRY CHARTS 1950-1959.
Tracks: Not Advised.
LP . . . . **.812793 1**
Mercury (Germany) / Apr '85 / Pinnacle.

US COUNTRY CHARTS 1960-1969.
Tracks: Not Advised.
LP . . . . **.812794 1**
Mercury (Germany) / Apr '85 / Pinnacle.

V

VERY BEST OF IRISH COUNTRY.
Tracks: Not Advised.
LP . . . . **FALP 009**
CMR/Failte / '88 / I & B Records.

VERY BEST OF IRISH COUNTRY, VOLUME 2.
Tracks: Not Advised.
MC . . . . **FACS 014**
CMR/Failte / '88 / I & B Records.

VERY BEST OF SUN ROCK 'N' ROLL.
Tracks: Whole lotta shakin' going on: *Lewis, Jerry Lee* / Ain't got a thing: *Burgess, Sonny* / Boppin' the blues: *Perkins, Carl* / Devil doll: *Orbison, Roy* / Red hot: *Riley, Billy Lee* / Got love if you want it: *Smith, Warren* / All night rock: *Honeycutt, Glenn* / Love my baby: *Thompson, Hayden* / Flatfoot Sam: *Blake, Tommy* / Love crazy baby: *Parchman, Kenny* / Put your cat clothes on: *Perkins, Carl* / Baby please don't go: *Riley, Billy Lee* / Wild one (real wild child): *Lewis, Jerry Lee* / Domino: *Orbison, Roy* / My bucket's got a hole in it: *Burgess, Sonny* / Blue suede shoes: *Perkins, Carl* / Come on little mama: *Harris, Ray* / Ubangi stomp: *Smith, Warren* / Break up: *Smith, Ray* / Mad man: *Wages, Jimmy* / We wanna boogie: *Burgess, Sonny* / That don't move me: *Perkins, Carl*.
CD . . . . **MCCD 024**
MC . . . . **.MCTC 024**
Music Club / May '91 / Gold & Sons / Terry Blood Dist. / Video Collection.

VICTOR ROCK'N'ROLLERS.
Tracks: Duck tail / Drugstore rock'n'roll / Blue suede shoes / Hip couple / Mary Nell / That ain't nothing but right / Ooh wee / Teen Billy baby / TV hop / Sixteen chicks / Sugar sweet / New shoes / Crackerjack / Get on the right track / Rosie let's get cozy / Lovin' honey / Will you Willyum / It's called rock and roll / I've got a dollar / Don't bug me baby.
■ LP . . . . **PL 42809**
RCA / '79.

VINTAGE COUNTRY (I love country).
Tracks: Back in the saddle again: *Autry, Gene* / I love you a thousand years: *Frizzell, Lefty* / Strawberry roan, The: *Robbins, Marty* / Foggy mountain breakdown: *Flatt, Lester & Earl Scruggs* / When it's Springtime in Alaska: *Horton, Johnny* / Deep water: *Smith, Carl* / Rawhide: *Laine, Frankie* / Folsom Prison blues: *Cash, Johnny* / Big iron: *Robbins, Marty* / All for the love of a girl: *Horton, Johnny* / Wabash cannonball: *Carter, Mother Maybelle* / Big river: *Cash, Johnny* / High noon: *Laine, Frankie* / Mom and dad's waltz: *Frizzell, Lefty* / Goodnight Irene: *Autry, Gene* / Pride: *Price, Ray*.
LP . . . . **CBS 54949**
CBS / Mar '87 / Sony.
■ MC . . . . **.40 54949**
CBS / Mar '87.

VIRGINIA ROCK-A-BILLY & COUNTRY.
Tracks: I ain't gonna rock tonight: *Saul, Hender* / Hard right to my heart: *Saul, Hender* / Where have you been all night: *Martin Bros* / That was yesterday: *Martin Bros* / Rock & roll baby: *Spangler, Randy* / My Spanish senorita: *Spangler, Randy* / Rock run blues: *Leon & Carlos* / Rock everybody: *Leon & Carlos* / Bip bop boom: *Mullins, Moon & Mickey Hawks* / Rock & roll rhythm: *Mullins, Moon & Mickey Hawks* / Reel it and roll it: *Mullins, Moon & Mickey Hawks* / One step away: *Saul, Hender & Billy Foley*.
LP . . . . **WLP 8807**
White Label (Germany) / Sep '87 / Pinnacle / Bear Family Records (Germany) / CSA Tell Tapes.

W

WAY OUT WEST (Songs Of The Singing Cowboys).
Tracks: Not Advised.
MC . . . . **CMOIR 506**
Memoir / Nov '89 / BMG / Jazz Music.
■ LP . . . . **MOIR 506**
Memoir / Nov '89.

WESTERN SWING.
Tracks: Not Advised.
MC . . . . **C 214**
Arhoolie (USA) / '88 / Pinnacle / Cadillac Music / Swift / Projection / Hot Shot / A.D.A Distribution / Jazz Music.

WESTERN SWING ON THE AIR 1948-61.
Tracks: Not Advised.
CD . . . . **RFCD 07**
Country Routes / Oct '91 / Jazz Music / Hot Shot.

WESTERN SWING VOL.1.
Tracks: Not Advised.
LP . . . . **OT 105**
Old Timey (USA) / '88 / Projection.

WESTERN SWING VOL.2.
Tracks: Not Advised.
LP . . . . **OT 116**
Old Timey (USA) / Jan '76 / Projection.

WESTERN SWING VOL.3.
Tracks: Not Advised.
LP . . . . **OT 117**
Old Timey (USA) / '88 / Projection.

WHEN I WAS A COWBOY: SONGS OF COWBOY LIFE.
Tracks: Not Advised.
LP **45008**
Morning Star / Sep '84 / Roots Records / Projection / Swift / C.M. Distribution / Ross Records / Duncans.

WHITE MANSIONS (A tale from the American Civil War 1861-65).
Tracks: Story to tell / Dixie, hold on / Join around the flag / White trash / Last dance and the Kentucky racehorse, The / Southern boys / Union mare and confederate grey / No one would believe a summer could be so cold / Southland's bleeding, The / Bring up the twelve pounders / They laid waste to our land / Praise the lord / King has called me home, The / Bad man / Dixie now your done.
■ MC . . . . **CXM 64691**
A&M / May '78.
■ Double LP . . . . **AMLX 64691**
A&M / May '78.
CD . . . . **CDA 6491**
A&M / Jun '89 / PolyGram.

WILD ROCKIN'.
Tracks: My rockin' baby: *Watson, Gene* / Interplanetary rock: *Watson, Gene* / Life's valley: *Watson, Gene* / Drummer boy rock: *Watson, Gene* / Don't be cruel: *Watson, Gene* / School day: *Watson, Gene* / Whole lotta shakin' goin' on: *Watson, Gene* / Tick tock: *Calloway, Bob* / What's the matter with you: *Calloway, Bob* / Bonfire: *Piper, Jimmy* / Love me, love me: *Piper, Jimmy* / Summertime rock: *Rodney & The Blazers* / Oriental nightmare: *Rodney & The Blazers* / Warpaint: *Rodney & The Blazers*.
LP . . . . **WLP 8829**
White Label (Germany) / '87 / Pinnacle / Bear Family Records (Germany) / CSA Tell Tapes.

WONDERFUL WORLD OF COUNTRY.
Tracks: Not Advised.
LP . . . . **SPR 8562**
MC . . . . **SPC 8562**
Spot / Mar '85.

WONDERFUL WORLD OF COUNTRY MUSIC.
Tracks: Not Advised.
LP . . . . **CDS 1180**
MC . . . . **.CAM 1180**
RCA/Camden / Feb '80 / BMG / Arabesque Ltd.

Y

YODELLING CRAZY.
Tracks: Yodelling song, The: *Ifield, Frank & The Backroom Boys* / Drovin': *Dusty, Slim & Anne Kirkpatrick* / Night rider's lament: *Bogguss, Suzy* / Night guard: *Rogers, Roy* / Erzherzog: *Unknown artist/s* / September's sweet child: *Horsburgh, Wayne* / New muleskinner blues: *McLean, Don* / Mei vater is a appenzeller: *Scholl, Thomas* / Mockingbird yodel: *Schneider, Mary* / Second fiddle (to an old guitar): *Shepard, Jean* / There's a rainbow in every teardrop: *Whitman, Slim* / Swiss maid: *Ifield, Frank* / Looking for a girl who can yodel: *Payne, George* / Chimebells: *Whitman, Slim* / Betcha my heart I love you: *Jackson, Wanda* / Lonely goatherd: *Ronalde, Ronnie* / Runaway train, The: *Hawthorne, Jim* / Yodelling craze, The: *Ifield, Frank* / Sioux City Sue: *Travis, Merle* / Satisfied mind: *Murray, Chick* / Le patre des montagnes (the shepherd's yodel): *Andreany* / Honeymoon yodel: *Torrani, Harry* / I'm a happy go lucky cowhand: *Dawson, Smoky* / Cuckoo in the wood: *Reverelli, Minna* / Big rock candy mountain: *Morton, Tex* / Lily Lucy Lane: *Hillbillies*.
CD . . . . **CDEMS 1439**
EMI / Feb '92 / EMI.

YOUR CHEATIN' HEART.
Tracks: Not Advised.
CD . . . . **YDG 74630**
MC . . . . **YDG 45753**
Yesterday's Gold / Feb '93 / Target Records / Midland Records / Taylors.

YUCCA ROCKABILLY.
Tracks: Not Advised.
LP . . . . **R&C 1010**
Rock & Country / Oct '88 / Swift.

YUKKA RECORDS & OTHER THINGS.

Tracks: Green gator: *Sims, Al* / You giggle too much: *Sims, Al* / Here comes that train: *Sims, Al* / If you've got a lot of dough: *Sims, Al* / Taylor's rock: *Taylor, Bob* / Sky diver: *Cooper, Steve* / Your lovin' get's the best of me: *Vine, Steve* / Boo boo bear: *Vine, Steve* / Jungle bunny: *Bell, Jerry* / Bacardi: *Bell, Jerry* / Pretty baby: *Bell, Jerry* / China doll: *Smith, Dappa* / Rockin' with Joe: *Renaults* / March to eternity: *Renaults* / You're my baby: *Nighthawks* / Jim's jive: *Bright, Jerry*.
LP. . . . . WLP 8836

White Label (Germany) / '87 / Pinnacle / Bear Family Records (Germany) / CSA Tell Tapes.

ALSO PUBLISHED BY MUSIC MASTER:

MUSIC MASTER

The Official Music Master CD Catalogue, 14th Edition. £14.95
Published October 1993

The 14th Edition of Music Master's best selling CD Catalogue is our most comprehensive listing of recordings released on CD in the UK. This fully revised and updated publication supplies track listings, catalogue numbers, label and distributor details as well as release and deletion dates. It is a must for all CD fans and those who want to find favourite recordings or complete collections. 1,114 pages.

*Lists CD discographies for over 15,000 popular music artists.
*Contains information on over 55,000 CD released recordings.

Labels' and Distributors' Directory 11th Edition

The Who's Who of Labels and Distributors! Fully revised and updated to include full contact details for every UK label and distributor known at the time of going to press. Cross reference sections make it even easier to find out who distributes which label.
£29.95

Tracks Catalogue 4th Edition

Who Recorded Which Track? The Tracks catalogue identifies 750,000 track names, the artists who recorded them and the albums/singles on which they appear. 1480 pages.
£24.95

Directory of Popular Music - compiled and edited by Leslie Lowe

Who wrote that song? This catalogue identifies the composer, publisher and recording artist for over 9,000 of the most popular songs this century. 554 pages.
£14.95

Price Guide for Record Collectors 2nd Edition

This catalogue prices 42,000 collectable LPs, EPs, Singles and Picture Discs. It includes a full colour section of photographs of collectable covers and extensive notes from the editor Nick Hamlyn. 792 pages.
£12.95

To order:

Please send payment (cheques made payable to Music Master) plus postage as follows:
UK: add £1.75, Europe: add £4.00 per catalogue, Outside Europe: add £12.00 per catalogue. All books are sent registered delivery in the UK and by Airmail elsewhere.

Music Master, Paulton House, 8 Shepherdess Walk, London, N1 7LB.
Tel: +44-(0)71-490-0049, Fax: +44-(0)71-253-1308.

THE
BRITISH
COUNTRY MUSIC
ASSOCIATION

Has been keeping its members fully informed of all that's happening on the British and American scene for the past 25 years.

We organise regular trips to the USA for members, present our own annual awards to the top British country performers and publish regular newsletter packed with news of clubs, concerts, festivals and tours plus a comprehensive listing of the latest album releases and much more.

For a FREE copy of our latest newsletter
send SAE to:

BMCA (MM)
PO Box 240, Harrow
Middlesex HA3 7PH

USEFUL ADDRESSES

FAN CLUBS

Benny Berry International Fan Club
Contact: Heather McCann
91 Derryhale Road, Portadown, Co Armagh, N Ireland, BT62 3SR

Bill Conlon Fan Club
Contact: K Cahill
3 Arun Court, Riverdene, Basingstoke, Hants, RG21 2BP

Billy McFarland Fan Club
Contact: Kitty Colins
Rathflesk, Rathmolyon, Enfield, Co Meath, Ireland

Campbells Country Fan Club
Contact: Mrs Vera A White
70 Cannon Leys, Galleywood, Chelmsford, Essex, CM2 8PD
Tel: 0245 76455

Fever International Fan Club
Contact: Mrs Ann Humm
8 Todd Close, St James Place, Aylesbury, Bucks, HP21 8EN
Tel: 0296 84386

Friends of Dave Lee-Field
Contact: Sandy
Bodawel, Washway Road, Penny Hill, Holbeach, Lincs, PE12 8BT
Tel: 0406 25484

Gerry Ford Fan Club
Contact: Joan Ford
13 Winton Park, Edinburgh, Scotland, EH10 7EX
Tel: 031 445 1687

Gordie West Fan Club
Contact: Trevor Rhodes
39 Woodkirk Gardens, Dewsbury, W Yorks, WF12 7HT
Tel: 0924 476248

Haley Sisters Fan Club
Contact: Lynne Richards
10 Caradoc View, Hanwood, Shrewsbury, SY5 8NB
Tel: 0743 860012 **Fax:** 0743 244877

Hege V Fan Club
Contact: Sue Marshall
3 Hamilton Drive, Edinburgh, Scotland, EH15 1NP
Tel: 031 669 4572

Hollywood Cowboys Fan Club
Contact: R C Johnson
44 Church Road, Walsoken, Wisbech, Cambs, PE13 3RA

Jim Ryder Fan Club
Contact: Josie Roberts
2 Celyn Avenue, Connah's Quay, Deeside, Clwyd, CH5 4SZ
Tel: 0244 813009

John C King Fan Club
Contact: Catherine Laidlaw
68 Firthview Drive, Inverness, IV3 6QE
Tel: 0463 222729

Keith Manifold Fan Club
Contact: Alice Manifold
Trenton House, 30 Bank Road, Matlock, Derby, DE4 3NF
Tel: 0629 584363

Lazy Daisy Fan Club
Contact: Joan McNeill
6 Rufford Place, Milnsbridge, Huddersfield, HD3 4RN
Tel: 0484 643551

LeGarde Twins International Fan Club UK
Contact: Yvonne Turner
8 Westfield Way, Ruislip, Middx, HA4 6HN
Tel: 0895 673726

Lemon Grass Fan Club
Contact: Olwen Mitchell
176 Wigton Road, Carlisle, Cumbria, CA2 6JW
Tel: 0228 21191

Manson Grant & The Dynamos Fan Club
Contact: Heather Sutherland
Achnaclyth, Roadside, Tanneach, Wick, Caithness, KW1 5SF

Mervyn J Futter Fan Club
Contact: Lin Chilvers
6 Thorpeland Close, Runcton Holme, King's Lynn, Norfolk, PE33 0AG
Tel: 0553 810438

Sarah Jory International Fan Club
Contact: Pam Walsh
23 Boyne Road, Budleigh Salterton, Devon, EX9 6SE
Tel: 0395 446217

Slim Whitman Appreciation Society of Great Britain
Contact: Yvonne Evans
'Wychita', 1 Blakeney Grove, Nailsea, Bristol, Avon, BS19 2RG

Spill The Beans Fan Club
Contact: Iris Leach
61 Woodhouse Road, Wheatley, Doncaster, DN2 4DG
Tel: 0302 328060

Steve Scott & Rio Fan Club
Contact: Janet Dyer
School House, Church Lane, Doddinghurst, Brentwood, Essex, CM15 0NJ
Tel: 0277 823105

Stu Page Fan Club
Contact: Jackie Nelmes
25 Blenheim Drive, Yate, Bristol, Avon, BS17 5DD
Tel: 0454 319103

Texas Gun Fan Club
Contact: Catherine Laidlaw
68 Firthview Drive, Inverness, Scotland
Tel: 0463 222729

Tony Goodacre Fan Club
Contact: Brian Hayes
11 Baytree Road, Clayton le Woods, Chorley, Lancs, PR6 7JW

Wes Cardy Fan Club
Contact: Janet Barker
East View, Gardiners Lane North, Crays Hill, Billericay, Essex, CM11 2XE
Tel: 0268 521717

West Virginia Fan Club
Contact: Yvonne
62 Bankside, Banbury, Oxon, OX16 9SN

Yvonne Lawley Fan Club
77 Abbey Fields, Telford, Shropshire, TF3 2AT
Tel: 0952 592522

INFORMATION

UK Country Line
Rosslyn House, Rosslyn Avenue, Shoreham by Sea, W Sussex, BN43 6WJ
Tel: 0891 800633

1

MAGAZINES

BCM Yearbook

Contact: Tony Byworth
PO Box 240, Harrow, Middx, HA3 7PH
Tel: 0273 559750 Fax: 0484 657055

BCMA Bulletin

Contact: Jim Marshall
3 Chester Terrace, Brighton, Sussex, BN1 6GB
Tel: 0273 559750 Fax: 0484 657055

Bluegrass Unlimited

Box 111, Broad Run, Virginia 22014-9850, USA

British Bluegrass News

10 Bishops Wood, Woking, Surrey, GU21 3QA

British Country Music News

Contact: Mick Green
Pebble View Publishing Ltd, 8 Pebble View Walk, Hopton-on-sea, Norfolk, NR31 9SG
Tel: 0502 732040 Fax: 0502 731800

Brum Country

Contact: John Meier
61 Tinkers Farm Road, Northfield, Birmingham, B31 1RN
Tel: 021 476 9979

Cajun Users Manual

Contact: Chris Hall
PO Box 94, Derby, Derby, DE22 1XA
Tel: 0332 32336 / 204090
Fax: 0332 32336

Country Dance Lines

Contact: Michael Hunt
Drawer 139, Woodacre, California 94973, USA

Country Matters

Contact: John Nelmes
25 Blenheim Drive, Yate, Bristol, Avon, BS17 5DD
Tel: 0454 319103

Country Music & Dance In Scotland

Contact: Brigitte Lyell
119 Cambusdoon Place, Kilwinning
Tel: 0294 52094

Country Music Gazette

Contact: Derek Burns
24 Highfield Grove, Allerton Bywater, W Yorks, WF10 2EL
Tel: 0977 556568 Fax: 0977 558137

Country Music People

Contact: Craig Baguley
225a Lewisham Way, London, SE4 1UY
Tel: 081 692 1106 Fax: 081 469 3091

Country Music Round-up

Contact: John Emptage
PO Box 111, Waltham, Grimsby, DN37 0YN
Tel: 0522 750150 / 0472 821707
Fax: 0472 821808

Folk Roots

Contact: Iain Anderson
PO Box 337, London, N4 1TW
Tel: 081 340 9651 Fax: 081 348 5626

International Country Music News

Pebble View Publishing Ltd, 8 Pebble View Walk, Hopton on Sea, Norfolk, NR31 9SG
Tel: 0502 732040 Fax: 0502 731800

Lonesome No More!

Contact: Adam Sanderson
112c Agar Grove, London, NW1 9TY
Tel: 071 485 2547

North Country Music

Contact: Dr. A Souter
455 Alfreton Road, Nottingham, Notts, NG7 5LX
Tel: 0602 422615 Fax: 0602 422359

Southern Country

Contact: Sue McCarthy
72 Clare Gardens, Petersfield, Hants, GU31 4EU
Tel: 0730 263753 Fax: 0703 333134

Stage & Television Today

Carson & Comerford Ltd, Stage House, 47 Bermondsey Street, London Bridge, London, SE1 3XT
Tel: 071 403 1818 Fax: 071 403 1418

Western Dancer, The (BWDA)

Contact: John & Janette Sandham
British Western Dance Association, 71 Sylvancroft, Ingol, Preston, Lancs, PR2 7BN
Tel: 0772 734324

ORGANISATIONS

British Bluegrass Music Association

10 Bishops Wood, Woking, Surrey, GU21 3QA

British Country Music Association

Contact: Tony Byworth
PO Box 240, Harrow, Middx, HA3 7PH
Tel: 0273 559750 Fax: 0484 657055

British Country Music Club

PO Box 76, Footscray, Sidcup, Kent, DA14 5AS

British Western Dance Association

Contact: John & Jannette Sandham
71 Sylvancroft, Ingol, Preston, PR2 7BN
Tel: 0772 734324

Country Music Association

Contact: Martin Satterthwaite
Suite 3, 52 Haymarket, London, SW1Y 4RP
Tel: 071 930 2445 Fax: 071 930 2446

Country Music Association of Ireland

Contact: Roger Ryan
Nashville, 4 Silverdale Road, Ballinlough, Cork, Ireland
Tel: 010-353-21-294412

English Folk Dance & Song Society

Cecil Sharp House, 2 Regents Park Road, London, W1N 7AY
Tel: 071 486 2206

European Teachers Association (Country & Western Dance)

Contact: John & Jannette Sandham
71 Sylvancroft, Ingol, Preston, Lancs, PR2 7BN
Tel: 0772 734324

Guild of International Songwriters & Composers

12 Trewartha Road, Praa Sands, Penzance, Cornwall, TR20 9ST
Tel: 0736 762826 Fax: 0736 763328

Incorporated Society of Musicians

10 Stratford Place, London, W1N 9AE
Tel: 071 629 4413 Fax: 071 408 1538

International Bluegrass Music Association

326 St Elizabeth Street, Owensboro, Kentucky 42301, USA
Tel: 0101 502 684 9025

Jersey Country Music Association

Contact: Chas Larbalestier
Arbalette, Les Landes, St John, Jersey, Channel Islands

Mechanical Copyright Protection Society
Elgar House, 41 Streatham High Road,
London, SW16 1ER
Tel: 081 769 4400 Fax: 081 769 8792

Music Publishers Association Ltd
3rd Floor, Strandgate, 18 - 20 York
Buildings, London, WC2N 8JU
Tel: 071 839 7779 Fax: 071 839 7776

Musicians Union
60 - 62 Clapham Road, London,
SW9 0JJ
Tel: 071 582 5566 Fax: 071 582 9805

Performing Rights Society Ltd
29 - 33 Berners Street, London,
W1P 4AA
Tel: 071 580 5544 Fax: 071 631 4138

Swamp Agency
50 Stroud Green Road, London,
N4 3EF
Tel: 071 263 6403 Fax: 071 281 5671

RECORD COMPANIES

A & M Records
136/140 New Kings Road, London,
SW6 4LZ
Tel: 071 736 3311 Fax: 071 731 4606

Ace Records
48 - 50 Steele Road, London,
NW10 7AS
Tel: 081 453 1311 Fax: 081 961 8725

Alligator Records
78 Stanley Gardens, London, W3 7SN
Tel: 081 746 1234 Fax: 081 740 9899

American Activities
29a St Michaels Road, Headingley,
Leeds, Yorks, LS6 3BG
Tel: 0532 742106 Fax: 0532 786291

Ammi
177 High Street, London, W1M 9IA
Tel: 081 961 3889 Fax: 081 961 4620

Arcade Records UK Ltd
58 Queen Anne Street, London,
W1M 9LA
Tel: 071 935 2887 Fax: 071 224 6073

Arista
Cavendish House, 423 New Kings
Road, London, SW6 4RN
Tel: 071 973 8040 Fax: 071 371 9324

Arrival Records
39 Leyton Road, Harpenden, Herts,
A15 2JB
Tel: 0582 715098 Fax: 0582 715098

ASV (Academy Sound & Vision)
The ASV Group, 179 - 181 North End
Road, London, W19 9NL
Tel: 071 381 8747 Fax: 081 385 2653

Awareness Records
6 Vernon Avenue, London, SW20
Tel: 081 543 1537 Fax: 081 545 0272

BBC Records
Woodlands, 80 Wood Lane, London,
W12 0TT
Tel: 081 576 2000 Fax: 081 576 2977

Bear Family Records (Germany)
Eduard Grunow Strasse 12, 2800
Bremen, Germany,
Tel: 010 49479 41399
Fax: 010 49479 41574

Bearcat Records
50 Stroud Green Road, London,
N4 3EF
Tel: 071 263 6403 Fax: 071 281 5671

BGS Records
Newtown Street, Kilsyth, Glasgow,
Strathclyde, G65 0JX
Tel: 0236 821081 Fax: 0236 825683

BMG Records
Bedford House, 69 - 79 Fulham High
Street, London, SW6 3JW
Tel: 071 973 0011 Fax: 071 973 0332

BSW Records
Contact: Frank Wilson
PO Box 2297, Universal City, Texas
78148, USA
Tel: 0101 512 653 3989

Bulldog Records
Exmouth House, 11 Pine Street,
London, EC1R 0JH
Tel: 071 837 5020 Fax: 071 837 4795

Capitol Records
20 Manchester Square, London,
W1A 1ES
Tel: 071 486 4488 Fax: 071 465 0753

Castle Communications
29 Barwell Business Park,
Leatherhead Road, Chessington,
Surrey, KT9 2NY
Tel: 081 974 1021 Fax: 081 974 2674

Celtic Music
2 High Street, Starbeck, Harrogate, N
Yorks, HG2 7HY
Tel: 0423 888955 Fax: 0432 885761

Charly Records
155 - 166 Ilderton Road, London,
SE15 1NT
Tel: 071 639 8603 Fax: 071 639 2532

Chrysalis Records
The Chrysalis Building, Bramley Road,
London, W10 6SP
Tel: 071 221 2213 Fax: 071 221 6455

Columbia Records
17/19 Soho Square, London, W1V 6HE
Tel: 071 734 8181 Fax: 071 287 9959

Comstock
10603 N Hayden Road, Suite 114,
Scottdale, Arizona, USA, AZ 85260
Tel: 0101 602 951 3115
Fax: 0101 602 951 3074

Conifer Records
Horton Road, West Drayton, Middx,
UB7 8JL
Tel: 0895 447707 Fax: 0895 420713

Connoisseur Collection
2 - 3 Fitzroy Mews, London, W1P 5DQ
Tel: 071 383 7773 Fax: 071 383 7224

Cooking Vinyl
PO Box 1845, London, W10 4BT
Tel: 081 960 6000 Fax: 081 960 1120

Cottage Records
Flat 7, 133 Deptford High Street,
London, SE8 4NS
Tel: 081 692 3767 Fax: 081 692 3503

Demon Records
Canal House, Stars Estate, Transport
Avenue, Brentford, Middx, TW8 9HF
Tel: 081 847 2481 Fax: 081 568 8223

Detour Records
PO Box 72, Northwood, Middx,
HA6 2PW
Tel: 0895 623020

Dragon Records
5 Church Street, Aylesbury, Bucks,
HP20 2QP
Tel: 0296 415333 Fax: 0296 397092

EMI Records (UK) Ltd
20 Manchester Square, London,
W1A 1ES
Tel: 071 486 4488 Fax: 071 465 0770

Epic Records
17 - 19 Soho Square, London,
W1V 6HA
Tel: 071 734 8181 Fax: 071 287 8854

Etude Records
2 Wych Elms, Park Street, St Albans,
Herts, AL2 2AS
Tel: 0727 872611

Fellside Records
15 Banklands, Workington, Cumbria,
CA14 3EW
Tel: 0900 61556 Fax: 0900 61556

Garden Isle Records
45 Brook Road, Shanklin, Isle of Wight,
PO37 7LD
Tel: 0983 866601

Grapevine
Unit 32, Third Floor, Camden Lock
Place, London, NW1 8AF
Tel: 071 267 7770 Fax: 071 284 2112

Grasmere Records
62 Pont Street Mews, London,
SW1X 0EF
Tel: 071 584 9765 Fax: 071 823 7100

Greentrax Records
3 Morven Street, Edinburgh, Scotland,
EH14 7LG
Tel: 031 339 4567 Fax: 031 339 8575

Hannibal Records
Unit 3, Linen House, 253 Kilburn Lane,
London, W10 4BQ
Tel: 081 964 3031 Fax: 081 964 2989

Harbourtown Records
PO Box 25, Ulverston, Cumbria, LA12 7UN
Tel: 0229 580776 Fax: 0229 580577

Harmac Records
67 Amiens Street, Dublin 1, Eire
Tel: 010 3531 366599
Fax: 010 3531 366997

Hawk Records
123 - 137 York Street, Belfast,
N Ireland, BT15 1AB
Tel: 0232 325225 Fax: 0232 439069

Hazel Records
Dublin Road, Monasterevin,
Co Kildare, Ireland
Tel: 045 25373 Fax: 045 25810

I & B Records
2a Wrentham Avenue, London,
NW10 3HA

Tel: 081 960 9169/9160
Fax: 081 968 7332

Icebreaker Records
Emyvale, Monaghan, Ireland
Tel: 010 353 4787309
Fax: 010 353 4787311

Island Records
22 St Peter's Square, London,
W6 9NW
Tel: 081 745 1511 Fax: 081 748 1998

Jennie Records
21 Cutler Court, Schomberg, Ontario,
Canada
Tel: 010 416 939 7900

Kenwest Records
Connaught House, 112 - 120 High
Road, Loughton, Essex, IG10 4HJ
Tel: 081 508 3723 Fax: 081 508 0432

Lake Records
15 Banklands, Workington, Cumbria,
CA14 3EW
Tel: 0900 61556 Fax: 0900 61556

Lismor Recordings
27 - 29 Carnoustie Place, Glasgow,
Strathclyde, G5 8PH
Tel: 041 420 1881 Fax: 041 420 1892

London Records
PO Box 1422, Chancellors House,
Chancellors Road, London,
W6 9SG
Tel: 081 741 1234 Fax: 071 741 2600

Magnum Music Group
Magnum House, High Street, Lane
End, High Wycombe, Bucks,
HP14 3JG
Tel: 0494 882858 Fax: 0494 882631

MCA
139 Piccadilly, London, W1V 0AX
Tel: 071 957 8600 Fax: 071 957 8560

Memoir Records
PO Box 66, Pinner, Middx, HA5 2SA
Tel: 081 866 4865 Fax: 081 866 7804

Minidoka Records
27 Windsor Road, Wraysbury, Staines,
Middx, TW19 5DE
Tel: 078448 2681 Fax: 078448 2203

Mosrite
PO Box 40013, Nashville, Tennessee
37204, USA

Music Farm
225a Lewisham Way, London,
SE4 1UY
Tel: 081 691 2523 Fax: 081 469 3091

Music For Pleasure
1/3 Uxbridge Road, Hayes, Middx,
UB4 0SY
Tel: 081 561 8722 Fax: 081 569 2163

Nashville Collection
Gemma House, 43a Old Woking Road,
West Byfleet, Surrey, KT14 6LG
Tel: 0932 351925 Fax: 0932 336431

New Music
'Meredale', Reach Lane, near Leighton
Buzzard, Beds, LU7 0AL
Tel: 052 5237700

Nimbus Records
Wyastone Leys, Monmouth, Gwent,
NP5 3SR
Tel: 0600 890682 Fax: 0600 890779

Old Gold Records
The Waterfront, Elstree, Herts,
WD6 3EE
Tel: 081 207 6207 Fax: 081 207 5759

Oval Records
326 Brixton Road, London, SW9 7AA
Tel: 071 326 4907

Pastafont
Richland House, Hambledon Hill,
Epsom, Surrey, KT18 7BZ
Tel: 0372 722202 Fax: 0372 742327

Phonogram
Chancellors House, 72 Chancellors
Road, London, W6 9QB
Tel: 081 741 1212 Fax: 081 741 4901

Pickwick
Pickwick House, The Waterfront,
Elstree Road, Elstree, Herts, WD6 3BS
Tel: 081 207 6207 Fax: 081 207 5789

Play Records
266 King Street, London, W6 0SP
Tel: 081 563 0585/6 Fax: 081 741 7644

Polydor
PO Box 1421, 1 Sussex Place,
Hammersmith, London, W6 9XT
Tel: 081 846 8090 Fax: 081 741 4901

Polygram UK Ltd
PO Box 1420, 1 Sussex Place,
Hammersmith, London, W6 9XS
Tel: 081 846 8515 Fax: 081 741 4901

4

President Records
Exmouth House, 11 Pine Street, London, EC1R 0JH
Tel: 071 837 5020 **Fax:** 071 837 4795

Prism Leisure
Unit 1, Baird Road, Enfield, Middx, EN1 1SJ
Tel: 081 804 8100 **Fax:** 081 805 8001

PT Records
27 Windsor Road, Wraysbury, Staines, Middx, TW19 5DE
Tel: 078448 2681 **Fax:** 078448 2203

Ragged But Right
225a Lewisham Way, London, SE4 1UY
Tel: 081 691 2523 **Fax:** 081 469 3091

Range
7 Garrick Street, London, WC2 4PF
Tel: 071 240 1628 **Fax:** 071 497 9242

RCA
Bedford House, 69/79 Fulham High Street, London, SW6 3JW
Tel: 071 973 0011 **Fax:** 071 371 9298

Reader's Digest
Berkeley Square House, Berkeley Square, London, W1X 6AB
Tel: 071 629 8144 **Fax:** 071 499 9751

Ritz Records
1 Grangeway, London, NW6 2BW
Tel: 071 328 9599 **Fax:** 071 624 4471

Riviera Records
The Powder Keg, Chelsey Hill, Wick, Bristol, Avon, BS15 5NE
Tel: 0272 374140 **Fax:** 0272 571500

Road Goes On Forever
9d Park Road, London, N8 8TE
Tel: 081 340 4158 **Fax:** 081 340 4158

Roadside Records
1 Miller Av, Wick, Scotland, KW1 4DF
Tel: 0955 3369

Rollercoaster
Rock House, London Road, St Mary's, Chalford, Glos, GL6 8PU
Tel: 0453 886252 **Fax:** 0453 885361

Round Tower Music
78 Stanley Gardens, London, W3 7SN
Tel: 081 746 1234 **Fax:** 081 740 9899

Run River Records
Westhill House, 10 Leechwell Street, Totnes, Devon, TQ9 5SY
Tel: 0803 867026 **Fax:** 0803 868394

Rykodisc
Unit 3, Linen House, 253 Kilburn Lane, London, W10 4BQ
Tel: 081 964 3031 **Fax:** 081 964 2989

See For Miles
Unit 10, Littleton House, Littleton Road, Ashford, Middx, TW15 1UU
Tel: 0784 247176 **Fax:** 0784 241168

Shanachie
23 Warple Way, London, W3 0RX
Tel: 081 749 0785 **Fax:** 081 749 2207

Silver Heart
Riverside, Cropredy Bridge, Cropredy, Oxon, OX17 1PQ
Tel: 0295 758545 **Fax:** 0295 750116

Sonet Records
78 Stanley Gardens, London, W3 7SN
Tel: 081 746 1234 **Fax:** 081 740 9899

Sony/CBS
17/19 Soho Square, London, W1V 6HE
Tel: 071 734 8181 **Fax:** 071 734 0979

Special Delivery
50 Stroud Green Road, London, N4 3EF
Tel: 071 263 6403 **Fax:** 071 281 5671

Start Records
Unit 20a, Canada House, Blackburn Road, London, NW6 1RZ
Tel: 071 625 7113 **Fax:** 071 624 3258

Stox
'Stocks Cottage', 411 Cronton Road, Cronton Village, Widnes, Cheshire, WA8 9QF
Tel: 051 424 4725

Sylvantone
17 Allerton Grange Way, Leeds, Yorks, LS17 6LP
Tel: 0532 687788

Tara Records
8 Anne's Lane, Dublin 2, Eire
Tel: 010 3531 776921

Telstar
Prospect Studios, Barnes High Street, London, SW13 9LE
Tel: 081 878 7888 **Fax:** 081 878 7886

Temple Records
Shillinghill, Temple, Midlothian, EH23 4SH
Tel: 0875 30328 **Fax:** 0875 30392

Topic
50 Stroud Green Road, London, N4 3EF
Tel: 071 263 6403 / 1240
Fax: 071 281 5671

Trax Records
First Floor, 121/123 Camden High Street, London, NW1 7JR
Tel: 071 482 6368 **Fax:** 071 267 9279

Universal Athena
PO Box 1264, Peoria, Illinois 61604, USA
Tel: 010 309 673 5755

Virgin Records
Kensal House, 553/559 Harrow Road, London, W10 4RH
Tel: 081 968 6688 **Fax:** 081 968 6533

Warner Brothers
83 Baker Street, London, W1M 1AJ
Tel: 071 486 1414 **Fax:** 071 935 3837

Waterfront Records
19 Mount Pleasant, Crewkerne, Somerset, TA18 7AH
Tel: 0460 74551 **Fax:** 0460 77444

WEA
The Warner Building, 28a Kensington Church Street, London, W8 4EP
Tel: 071 937 8844 **Fax:** 071 938 3901

Widetrax Records
'Flock House', 37 Main Street, Colinsburgh, Leven, Fife, Scotland, KY9 1LR
Tel: 0334 334525 **Fax:** 0334 334525

Word UK
9 Holdom Avenue, Milton Keynes, Bucks, MK1 1QU
Tel: 0908 648440 **Fax:** 0908 648592

RECORD DEALERS

A & R Booksearch
Contact: Robert Ronald
High Close, Winnick Cross, Lanreath, Nr Looe, Cornwall, PL13 2PF
Tel: 0503 220246 **Fax:** 0503 220965

Buds Music Store
184 High Street, Penge, SE20 7QB
Tel: 081 676 8801 **Fax:** 0689 850637

Buygone Music
Contact: John Goldman
30 Radcliffe Road, West Bridgford,
Nottingham, Notts, NG2 5HH
Tel: 0602 813905 **Fax:** 0602 818034

CD Express
Contact: Nigel Daly
42-48 The Market, Pontefract Lane,
Leeds LS9 OQP
Tel: 0532 351 865 **Fax:** 0532 484 666

Country Music Store, The
Milroy House, Sayers Lane, Tenterden,
Kent, TN30 6BW
Tel: 0580 763936 **Fax:** 0580 764579

Double 'L' Music
121 Pershore Road, Popley,
Basingstoke, Hants, RG24 9BG
Tel: 0256 53359

Eddie Carter Records
Contact: Eddie Carter
Cross Country, Chapel Lane, High
Broadgate, Tydd St Giles, Wisbech,
Cambs, PE13 5LT
Tel: 0945 870993

Goff Greenwood Records
PO Box 20, Bradford, Yorks, BD1 1DR

J & J Records
Oakridge, Chootersway, Berkhamstead,
Herts

Jan Jerrold's Bluegrass Record Service
10 Bishops Wood, Goldsworth Park,
Woking, Surrey, GU31 3QA

Just Country
Contact: Philip Thomas
439 Clock Face Road, St Helens,
Merseyside, WA9 4QL
Tel: 0744 812376 **Fax:** 0744 812376

Newmarket Tapes
Contact: Mrs D Morris
New Market, Aberdeen, Scotland,
AB1 2PA
Tel: 0224 571433 **Fax:** 0224 571433

Peggy's Irish Shop
Contact: Peggy
87 High Street, Wealdstone, Harrow,
Middx, HA3 5DL
Tel: 081 861 1267

Projection Record Distribution
Contact: David Hatfield
19 Mount Pleasant, Crewkerne,
Somerset, TA18 7AH
Tel: 0460 74551 **Fax:** 0460 77444

Record Corner
Contact: 27 Bedford Hill, Balham,
SW12 9EX
Tel: 081 673 1066 **Fax:** 081 675 6665

Record Savings
Contact: Chris Stuart
3 White Lion Walk, Banbury, Oxon,
OX16 8UD
Tel: 0295 267378 **Fax:** 0295 269631

Ryan's Country
Contact: Peter Ryan
35 Hall Street, Penycae, near
Wrexham, Clwyd, LL14 2RU
Tel: 0978 841075 **Fax:** 0978 841075

Swamp
Contact: Chris Hall
PO Box 94, Derby, Derby, DE22 1XA
Tel: 0332 32336 **Fax:** 0332 32336

Topic Records
Contact: Miles Evans
50 Stroud Green Road, Finsbury Park,
London, N4 3EF
Tel: 071 263 6403 **Fax:** 071 281 5671

Track Records
19 Castlegate, Coppergate Centre,
York, Yorks, YO1 1RN
Tel: 0904 629022 **Fax:** 0904 610637

WOMAD Shop, The
Contact: Dave Longly
3 The George Shopping Centre,
Crewkerne, Somerset, TA18 7JW
Tel: 0460 77444 **Fax:** 0460 77444

Future Titles from Music Master — MUSIC MASTER

**The Official Music Master Jazz Catalogue, 2nd Edition. £14.95
Published January 1994**

The second edition of this highly acclaimed catalogue includes new and expanded entries for many historical and contemporary Jazz and Blues artists. All Biographies have been fully updated. 1000 pages (approximately).

To order:

Please send payment (cheques made payable to Music Master) plus postage as follows:
UK: add £1.75, Europe: add £4.00 per catalogue, Outside Europe: add £12.00 per catalogue. All books are sent registered delivery in the UK and by Airmail elsewhere.

Music Master, Paulton House, 8 Shepherdess Walk, London, N1 7LB.
Tel: +44-(0)71-490-0049, Fax: +44-(0)71-253-1308.